# Proceedings

## OF THE 28TH ANNUAL PROJECT MANAGEMENT INSTITUTE 1997 SEMINARS & SYMPOSIUM

Presented by the World's Leading Project Management Association

PMI
PROJECT MANAGEMENT INSTITUTE®

**Library of Congress Cataloging-in-Publication Data**

Project Management Institute. Seminar/Symposium (28th : 1997 :
Chicago, Ill.)
Project management : the next century : proceedings of the 28th
annual Project Management Institute Seminars & Symposium, Chicago,
Il, September 26-October 2, 1997.
p. cm.
Includes index
ISBN: 1-880410-33-8 (pbk)
1. Industrial project management--Congresses. I. Title.
T56.8.P778 1997
658.4'04--dc21 97-33556
CIP

Published by:

Project Management Institute
130 South State Rd.
Upper Darby, PA 19082
Phone: 610-734-3330
Web Site: www.pmi.org



*Production Team:*

James S. Pennypacker, Publisher/Editor-in-Chief
Bobby R. Hensley, Proceedings Manager
Dewey L. Messer, Managing Editor
Mark S. Parker, Editor, Production Coordinator
Toni D. Knott, Editor
Jeannette M. Cabanis, Editor
Sandy D. Jenkins, Editor
Lisa M. Fisher, Editor
Allison S. Boone, Graphic Designer
Michelle T. Owen, Graphic Designer

# Table of Contents

To the PMI Membership:

As we stand poised on the brink of a new millennium, many futurists believe that we are also on the brink of an economic change more dramatic than the industrial revolution. Whether we talk of the "Post-Modern Era", the "Information-Age", or the "Third Wave", we sense that the world will be a very different place in the next century.

Our symposium theme is, Project Management: The Next Century. In choosing this theme, the '97 project team wanted to give the institute the opportunity to reflect on both past successes and the future. Approximately 100 years ago, the city of Chicago hosted the world's fair, A Century of Progress. Such events allow the participants to take time out from the hectic pursuit of their day-to-day activities to examine the larger currents of human progress. This is what we wanted to do, in the same city, over one hundred years later.

Project management as a discipline has come a long way in one hundred years. In 1897 the Gantt chart was still 20 years away (in 1917 by Henry Gantt), most of the technologies that we take for granted today were not yet developed, and the industrial revolution had yet to have a significant impact on the economy, society or the organization of business. Henry Ford had not yet conceived the idea of the moving assembly line, Frederick Taylor had not yet developed the principles of scientific management, and Maslow's hierarchy-of-needs theory, so diligently studied by those taking the PMP exam, was over 50 years in the future.

The question we posed to PMI authors was: What will the next 100 years hold for project management? Authors were asked to cast their sights well into the next century to envision how the project manager of the future will approach the ever increasing task of managing complex, interdisciplinary efforts.

The response was tremendous. I am pleased to report that we have been successful in attracting authors who will add greatly to the understanding of project management principles and practices. Each of the tracks has been successful in both developing a technical program that will be of interest to participants and of achieving a focus on the future. I believe the *Proceedings* that follow represent the finest of what PMI represents. The collective effort put forth by authors, track chairs, SIG chairs and all of the other volunteers will stand as a testament to the quality of the Institute.

On behalf of the PMI '97 technical program team I would also like to extend special thanks to Bobby Hensley, Proceedings Manager and Technical Program Coordinator for PMI. Without his diligence and professional competence, as well as his quiet fortitude in dealing with the myriad of issues and unexpected contingencies that surface on any project of this size, these *Proceedings* and the '97 Symposium Technical Program would not be what I believe them to be: The best yet.

It has been an honor for me to serve PMI in this capacity and it will be with some sadness that I view the completed product. But, the future ever beckons, and I am sure that PMI will continue to exceed expectations. I look forward to watching that future unfold.

Sincerely,

David L. Overbye

David L. Overbye
Director of Curriculum, Keller Graduate School of Management
PMI '97 Technical Program Chair
Chicago, Illinois

# PMI 1997 Board of Directors

# PMI 1997 Specific Interest Groups

**SIG Council Co-Chairs**
Ms. Becky Winston
1020 Stevens Drive
Idaho Falls, ID 83401
(208) 526-1165
Fax: (208) 526-6802
e-mail: rzw@inel.gov

Mr. Paul Nelson, PMP
476 Chase Street
Sonoma, CA 95476
(707) 938-2417
Fax: (707) 938-2417
e-mail: tbgisbig@aol.com

**SIG Board Representative**
Ms. Julie M. Wilson, ACS, PMP
P.O. Box 8054
Newport Beach, CA 92658
(714) 650-4526
Fax: (714) 646-9932
e-mail: jmwilson@ix.netcom.com

**Aerospace & Defense (3/96) $10.00**
Mr. Fred Ayer, PMP
8427 Briar Creek Drive
Annandale, VA 22003
703-805-4611/ 2215(fax)
e-mail: ayerf@dsmc.dsm.mil

**Automotive ( 3/95) $15.00**
Mr. William E. Skimin
Integrated Management Systems, Inc
3135 S. State Road, Suite 104
P.O. Box 2777
Ann Arbor, MI 48106
313-996-0500 / 0266 (fax)
e-mail: billinhw@aol.com

**Design - Procurement - Construction (10/95) $15.00**
Mr. Mark O. Mathieson, PMP
Sverdrup Civil, Inc.
Project Office for WWTP Expansion
5607 West Jensen Road
Fresno, CA 93706-9458
209-498-1764 / 2500 fax
e-mail: mathiemo@sverdrup.com

**Environmental Management (10/94) $15.00**
Mr. Tom Vanderheiden, PMP
Project Mgmt. & Control Consultants, Inc.
P.O. Box 4093
1451 E. Northcrest Drive
Highlands Ranch, CO 80126
303-791-3121/ 9036 (fax)
74277.2605@compuserve.com

**Financial Services (3/95) $10.00**
Mr. Scott Mairs, PMP
Citicorp
4 Campus Circle
Westlake, TX 76262
817-491-7464 / 7783 fax
e-mail: scott.mairs@citicorp.com

**Government (3/96) $5.00**
Mr. David Blackburn
4435 Bevington Lane, Apt. B
Indianapolis, IN 46240
317-637-0085
Fax: 317-877-3400
e-mail: davidc@pmadvisors.com

**Information Management & Movement ( 3/95) $15.00**
Ms. Angel Barlow, PMP
AT&T Global Bus. Communications
832 Los Positos Dr.
Milpitas, CA 95035-4515
916-389-8664
Fax: 602-604-2937
e-mail: abarlow@lucent.com

Mr. Wade Stone, PMP
Project Manager
Lucent Technologies
1964 Canta Lomas
El Cajon, CA 92019
619-588-9380 / 9551 (fax)
e-mail: wstone@lucent.com

**Information Systems (3/95) $15.00**
Mr..Kumar Bhagavatheswaran, PMP -- Co-Chair
Beekay Systems International
7200 Bollinger Road, #702
San Jose, CA 95129-2744
408-252-8441/ 8442 fax
e-mail: kumarb@compuserve.com

Mr. Michael Haig, PMP Co-Chair
10 Silkwood Crescent
North York, ON M2J 1G9
CANADA
416-498-5270 / 0100 (fax)
e-mail:mhaig@ibm.net

**Manufacturing(7/96) $10.00**
Mr. Bill Moylan, PMP
Plan Tech, Inc.
22000 Springbrook , Suite 201
Farmington Hills, MI 48336
810-615-0333, x. 22 (0292 fax)
e-mail: bill@ltu.edu

Ms. Diana Day, PMP
Lord Corp.
Mechanical Product Division
2000 W. Grandview
P.O. Box 10038
Erie, PA 16514-0038
814-868-5424, x. 6558
Fax: 814-864-8813
e-mail: diana_day@lord.com

**New Product Development (10/96) $10.00**
Mr. Greg Githens, PMP
Maxicomm Project Services
2429 South Main Street
Findaly, OH 45840
Phone/fax: 419-424-1164
Greg_Githens@compuserve.com

**Pharmaceutical (3/95) $20.00**
Mr. Kimm Galbraith
ViroPharma, Inc.
76 Great Valley Parkway
Malvern, PA 19355
610-651-0200, x. 3127
Fax: 610-651-0588
e-mail: kgalbraith@viropharma.org

**Service & Outsourcing (6/97) $15.00**
Mr. Max B. Smith, PMP
Digital Equipment Corp
8750 Niblick Drive
Alpharetta, GA 30202
770-343-1343
Fax: 770-343-6859
e-mail: smithmax@mail.dec.com

**Utility Industry ( 10/95) $10.00**
Mr. Don Pedersen, PMP
Northern States Power Co.
414 Nicollet Mall
RSQ 8
Minneapolis, MN 55401
612-330-6570
Fax: 612-337-2042
donald.e.pedersen@nspco.com

**Utility cont.**
Mr. Ren Phillips, PMP
Carolina Power and Light Company
3822 Pebble Road
Florence, SC 29501
803-857-5364
Fax: 803-857-1864
e-mail: ren.phillips@cplc.com

**Women in PM (3/95) $10.00**
Ms. Janis Sherick, Co-Chair
PO Box 1625-3710
Idaho Falls, ID 83415
208-526-5469
Fax: 208-526-5142
e-mail: nis@inel.gov

Ms. Mary-Elizabeth Diab, Co-Chair
6457 W. Bell Road #3118
Glendale, AZ 85308
602-921-0809 / 8253 (fax)
e-mail: diabme@megasyschem.com

## *Potential SIGs*

**Diversity - $10.00**
Mr. Todd F. Brown
1701 S. Mays
Ste. J177
Round Rock, TX 78664
512-246-8633
Fax: 512-728-5931
ren.phillips@cplc.com

**Education - $15.00**
Mr. Robert Ware, Co-Chair
NegEntropy, Inc.
2670 April Dawn Way
Gambrills, MD 21054
410-519-3120
Fax: 410-519-3120
e-mail: robware@tmn.com

Ms. April J. O'Koren, Co-Chair
Project Masters, Inc.
2404 Fairway Oaks Court
Hampstead, MD 21074
410-239-1997
Fax: 410-374-1608
e-mail: aokoren@erols.com

**Oil, Gas, Petrochemical - $10.00**
Mr. Charles Waligura, PMP
Chief Engineer
Bechtel Corp.
P.O. Box 2166
Houston, TX 77252-2166
713-235-2193
Fax:713-235-3422
E-mail:cwaligur@bechtel.com

**Quality in Project Management $5.00**
Ms. Bobbye Underwood
BellSouth
4488 Gingerwood Lane
Stone Mountain, GA 30083
404.529.0675
Fax: 404.688.5982
E-mail:
bobbye.s.underwood@bridge.bellsouth.com

CONTACT LISTING -
Rev. August 21, 1997

## PMI 97 Project Team

**Beth Partleton, PMP**
**Project Manager**
Miller Brewing Company

**Dave Blackburn**
**Deputy Project Manager**
Project Management Advisors

**David Overbye, PMP**
**Technical Program Chairman**
Keller Graduate School

**Jim Bieser**
Johnson Controls

**Jan Wells**
Allegiance Healthcare

**Gerri Martin, PMP**
Software Analysis Corporation

**Jane Holum**
CUNA Mutual Group

**Jim Neslson, PMP**
Lucent Technologies

**Tom Walsh, PMP**
G.F.S.C., Inc.

**Jerry Dassler**
Foth & Van Dyke

**Vicki Schmieding**
CUNA Mutual Group

**Margaret Sanders**
Chicago Public Schools

**Barbara Marino**
Integrated Project Management Co.

**Jeanine Para**
Software Analysis Corporation

## PMI Staff Team Members

**Liz Ely**
Manager, Meetings and Conventions

**Mary Bushong**
Meeting and Exhibits Coordinator

**Bobby Hensley**
Proceedings Manager & Technical Program Coordinator

## PMI Staff Contributors

**Allison Boone**
Graphic Designer
**David Bruhin**
Marketing Manager
**Rich Cavallero**
Web Master
**Dorothy Hamilton**
Executive Assistant
**Maria Kelly**
Education Administrator
**Toni Knott**
Editor
**Liz Magnotta**
Finance Manager
**Lisa McCann**
Manager, Information
**Dewey Messer**
Managing Editor
**Michelle Triggs Owen**
Graphic Designer
**Mark Parker**
Editor, Production Coordinator
**Jim Pennypacker**
Publisher/Editor-in-Chief
**Kathleen Schietroma, PMP**
Manager, Education
**Christian Shea**
Marketing Assistant

**Central Services Staff**

# Technical Program Track Chairs

| | |
|---|---|
| Automotive/Manufacturing | Dale Jordan, General Motors |
| Defense/Aerospace | Quentin Fleming, Primavera<br>Brian Gegan, KPMG Pete Marwick |
| Design-Procurement-Construction | David Scott, Applied Integration Mgt. |
| Education/Training | Lowell Dye, Project Mentors |
| Environmental Management | Daniel McGrath, Battelle Pantex |
| Financial Services | Rodger Clawson, State of Oregon |
| Future of Project Management | Jim McBride |
| Global Project Management | Alaa Zeitoun,<br>International Institute for Learning |
| Government | David Blackburn<br>Project Management Advisors, Inc. |
| Information Management & Movement | Lynn Holley, AT&T |
| Information Systems | Ida Harding<br>Lisa Holly |
| New Product Development | Kim Johnson, 3M Corporation |
| Oil, Gas & Petrochemical | Ray Piper, Union Carbide |
| Pharmaceutical / Biotechnology Healthcare | Ruth Hill, Center Corps Inc. |
| PMBOK Functions | Bill Leban<br>Keller Graduate School of Management |
| Utilities | Noel Hutson, Portland Chapter<br>John Duggan, COMED |

# PMI '97 Corporate Sponsors

**PMI and the PMI '97 Team wish to thank the following companies for their support:**

ABT Corporation

Boston University

IBM

Keller Graduate School of Management

NCR

Primavera

# Technical Program Paper Index

## Automotive / Manufacturing Track



## Defense Aerospace Track

## Design-Procurement-Construction Track

## Education & Training Track

## Environmental Management Track



## Financial Services Track

## Future of Project Management Track

## Global Project Management Track

## Government Track



## Information Management and Movement Track

## Information Systems Track

## New Product Development Track

## Oil, Gas & Petrochemical Track



## Pharmaceutical / Biotechnology / Healthcare Track



## PMBOK Functions Track

## Utilities Track



## PMI 1997 Student Paper Award Winner

# PMI '97 Technical Program Author Index

# Automotive/ Manufacturing

# Developing & Documenting Your Company's Program Management Process

Rose Russett, General Motors Powertrain Group

## Why Develop and Document a Program Management Process Model?

Imagine this scenario. You have just been appointed to a position to implement "program management" within your company. "Great! This is just what my company needs!" you say to yourself. You begin this endeavor by talking to various managers within your company to get their thoughts and support, and you soon realize that everyone has a different vision and understanding of what "implementing program management" really means.

Stating your organization's commitment to using program management may be quite easy to accomplish but actually putting it into a common language that can be understood by the entire organization and implemented in a common format can be significantly more complicated than it appears on the surface.

What you need is a documented program management process model to explain how program management will work within your organization. This process model needs to be effective, efficient, and adaptable.

- It is effective because it:
- Clearly reflects management's direction
- Is easily communicated
- Provides for templates and checklists
- Clarifies terminology specific to your company.

It provides efficiency because it:

- Reduces variation from program to program by using a single common process
- Provides for a common program management training tool.

The model is also adaptable because it

- Can be used as a common process for the management of all programs within the entire company
- Has the flexibility to change as continuous improvements are made.

The objective of this paper is to explain:

***1. "How" to create and document your program management process model, which includes:***

- How to identify the key stakeholders and get their buy in
- How to set up a process documentation workshop
- What tools to use to document the process so it is easily understood by all stakeholders
- How to implement the process once the documentation is complete
- How to use the process model document for training and communication

***2. "What" to include in your program management process model, such as:***

- Program scope, or charter
- Program manager and team appointments
- Program team member roles, responsibilities, and reporting relationships
- Program review process at key milestones
- Program timing plan development and critical path management
- Part level detail tracking
- Transition planning
- Documentation of lessons learned.

It is important to note that this process does not replace the product development process in any way. It merely explains specifically how project management will be utilized to achieve program objectives. Many companies have a very well defined process of designing, building, testing, and marketing their products, but may not have a clearly defined methodology of how to manage this activity from start to finish.

## How Should the Program Management Process Model Document Be Organized?

In order to explain how to start the documentation process, it will be helpful to explain what the end result will look like. You must have a format for the documentation developed before gathering the stakeholders together to actually write the process. Although the specific template that General Motors Powertrain Group (GMPTG) used to document its process is copyrighted, you can create a template for your own organization that contains the same information displayed in an organized, logical, and easy-to-read format. You can create these templates in your standard word processing or presentation software. The key is to start with the highest level of detail and work down to the lowest level of detail. This will allow the users of this process model to access only the appropriate level of detail needed for their specific job. The project sponsor may only want a description of the high-level process steps to understand the big picture, while the program manager may want all of the detail needed to execute the process. Another key to remember is to keep the process document simple and in a logical flow of steps. Summarizing information in a one-page document can be worth more in terms of understanding than many pages of detail. Since this process is documented in levels that build upon one another, the amount of detail should not become too overwhelming for the various users.

The process document should be organized in the following ascending order of detail:

1. A one-page description of the purpose of the process and its measurements
2. A list of the major process steps, usually between one and ten
3. A list of tasks for each major process step, usually between two and ten
4. Roles and responsibilities for each of the tasks in the process
5. Detailed statements of work for each task that explains how it will be accomplished
6. Templates and checklists for each task as appropriate.

The *first* level of detail should be documented on one page and contain the following information:

1. The **name of the process**, such as "program management process."
2. The **name of the process owner**, usually the manager or key executive who has the responsibility and accountability for the implementation of projects, such as "Jane Doe, Director, Engineering."
3. The **business purpose of the process**, which is what the process is to accomplish and why it exists. This should be a brief statement such as: "Provide a disciplined process to integrate cross-functional planning and execution of product programs in order to effectively manage company resources and accomplish program deliverables with measurable performance."
4. The **customers of the process**, which includes internal and external customers.
5. The **starting point of the process**, such as issuance of a program charter or signing of a contract with a customer. This clearly defines the event that starts this process.
6. The **ending point of the process**, such as completing the program performance review or program closure document. This clearly defines the event that signifies completion of the program.
7. The **measurements** of efficiency, effectiveness, and adaptability, which can include meeting customer deliverables, meeting budget and cost targets, schedule, reducing rework, and so on. List what to measure as opposed to specific program targets.

This one-page document allows all members of the organization to have clear expectations of the project and the steps that will be taken to ensure successful completion. It helps to eliminate any potential misunderstanding of how projects will be run, by whom, the duration of the project, and how it will be measured.

The *second* level of detail should identify the major process steps that must be completed from beginning to end of the process. This should be at a high level, listing up to ten overall process steps. Further detail will be included in the next levels. The steps are names of actions and should start with a verb, such as "appoint program manager" or "develop program plans."

The *third* level further breaks down the major steps into more detailed tasks. Be sure to number each step and each task within each major step. This level will provide sufficient detail for most stakeholders to understand the program management process.

The *fourth* level of detail is a roles and responsibilities matrix for each task in the process. This provides further clarification of who is responsible for completing each task.

The *fifth* level of detail should be a complete statement of work for each task. This is a one-page document for each task that lists the task number, name, owner, duration, description, deliverables, customer for deliverables, inputs, outputs, resources, and methodology. This level of documentation is quite detailed and would be written after agreement of the major process steps and tasks. This information would be used mostly by the Program Manager and program office support.

The *sixth* level of detail should include common templates, checklists, and forms that will be used as the document demonstrating completion of that task. For example, if the step indicates "develop a communication plan," a template can be created to identify the exact form of the communication plan. This will eliminate the need for each team to execute the process step by creating its own communication plan format, which will take more time and increase variation between all programs. Develop templates for each task as appropriate to improve program management efficiency.

In summary, the documentation of this process will allow the program teams to focus on **execution** of their program deliverables and not the **development** of systems, processes, forms, and templates that are needed to manage the program. This will simplify the program management process for all stakeholders and greatly reduce variation between programs.

**Exhibit 1.** Process Steps

Program Management Process Development & Documentation Steps

**STEP 1: Prepare for Workshop**

- 1.1 Determine the right participants
- 1.2 Set the schedule
- 1.3 Book conference room/facility
- 1.4 Notify participants
- 1.5 Procure all necessary materials for workshop
- 1.6 Establish roles for workshop facilitators and participants
- 1.7 Establish a "draft version" of model as a starting point
- ➔ Participant List
- ➔ Meeting schedules
- ➔ Materials & supplies on hand

**STEP 2: Conduct Workshop**

- 2.1 Set up conference room/facility
- 2.2 Create open atmosphere to enhance participation
- 2.3 Explain roles & responsibilities of everyone in the workshop and how draft model will be used as a starting point for discussion
- 2.4 Document changes per participant input
- 2.5 Confirm next meeting date/time/location
- 2.6 Conduct additional meetings following the same process as the initial workshop until all issues are resolved
- 2.7 Explain how feedback will be provided to participants and any expectations for individual review
- 2.8 Communicate results of meeting to participants and their bosses to acknowledge their contributions
- ➔ Intial Program Management Process Model

**STEP 3: Complete all Documentation and Gain Approvals**

- 3.1 Complete all documentation
- 3.2 Schedule and conduct final review meeting with participants
- 3.3 Develop implementation plan of how program management process model will be distributed and explained to all members of organization
- 3.4 Schedule and conduct staff review for fianl approval of process model and implementation plan
- ➔ Final Program Management Process Model
- ➔ Implementation Plan

**STEP 4: Publish Process Model**

- 4.1 Print process model guidebooks
- 4.2 Print wall charts as needed
- 4.3 Distribute materials to organization per implementation plan
- ➔ Published guidebooks and wall charts of Program Management Process Model
- ➔ Execution of implementation plan

## How to Document Your Program Management Process

Now that you have a vision of what this process model should contain, plans can be made to conduct a workshop with the key stakeholders to actually complete the documentation. Who are these "key stakeholders?" Include in your list of workshop participants current program managers, program support personnel, and functional managers who are actively involved in programs. If you are just starting to organize in a project structure and program managers are not yet in place, you may need to solicit assistance from members of your organization that have a strong interest in program management and its implementation, regardless of their current functions. The greatest success can be achieved by utilizing those individuals within the organization who will have the most impact on program execution. In addition, it would be helpful to have an executive champion kick off this workshop, lending support and organizational commitment to the effort.

The following exhibit details the program management process development and documentation steps, summarized as:

1. Prepare for the process documentation workshop(s)
2. Conduct the workshop(s)
3. Complete all documentation and gain approvals
4. Publish process model

## What to Include in Your Program Management Process Model

The purpose of the process model is to provide answers to the most frequently asked questions on how programs will be managed and to give clear direction to those responsible for program management. Recognize that it probably will not answer every possible question, since there are many exceptions that can arise for each program. Most programs by nature are unique and unlike any other your company has done. The objective of the process model is to provide guidelines that can be applied in general terms for all programs. Exceptions can be dealt with on an individual basis and updates to the process model made if the issue should apply to all programs. Try not to make the detail too cumbersome because the success and usefulness of the model will be greatly diminished. Some general guidelines to follow include:

- Document what your organization currently does, enhancing it with sound program management practices, but do not try to create elaborate new processes and systems that may not gain acceptance.
- Don't use acronyms because they can lead to misunderstanding.
- Incorporate lessons learned from previous programs into model.

Here are some questions that your process model should provide answers for:

- How will the project be initiated? Will a charter or statement of scope be issued to the team?
- How and when will the program manager be appointed? How will the program team be named?

- What are the roles, responsibilities, and reporting relationships of the program manager, line managers, and executive sponsor(s) with regard to programs?
- How will the skill levels of program team members be assessed and how and when will training be conducted?
- What is the communication plan that will be used throughout the program?
- How will program team members be evaluated and measured?
- What is the program review process?
- How will critical path timing plans be developed and used?
- What program reports will be generated, how frequently, and to whom?
- What is the change management process that will be used?
- How will program risks be managed?
- Will plans be developed for every part number within the final assembled product and how will they be tracked throughout the program?
- How will programs transition from the program team to the production organization?
- How will program team members transition to another position once the program is complete?
- How will program lessons learned be documented and used on future programs?
- What is the program archive process?

This is by no means an exhaustive list but should be used as thought starters. The next decision you must make is how to best organize the process model for ease of understanding and use. GMPTG constructed its process model by phase and further subdivided each phase into three categories—organization issues, timing issues, and content issues. Here is an outline of how its process model is organized:

### Planning Phase

#### *Organization*

1. Receive program charter (scope)
2. Assign program manager, program administrator, and leadership team
3. Create plan to transition from advanced engineering to launch center
4. Define program team roles and responsibilities
5. Establish program archive process
6. Identify communication process and meeting schedules
7. Identify team training needs
8. Conduct initial kick-off meeting
9. Identify resource requirements for next phase
10. Complete planning phase gate review

#### *Timing*

1. Receive program charter
2. Develop and evaluate initial master program timing
3. Develop initial functional timing plans
4. Integrate and analyze timing plans and set program baseline
5. Develop program timing reports

#### *Content*

1. Receive program charter
2. Gather additional requirements and translate program charter into contract requirements
3. Identify program content
4. Evaluate program risks
5. Document initial program contract
6. Initialize program tracking system

### Execution Phase

#### *Organization*

1. Execute resource plan and communication process
2. Update training needs assessment and conduct training
3. Develop and implement transition plan from program team to production organization
4. Prepare and execute milestone gate reviews and program close down review

#### *Timing*

1. Update existing timing plans
2. Develop additional functional timing plans
3. Integrate and analyze timing plans and set functional timing plan baselines
4. Publish program timing reports

#### *Content*

1. Update technical specifications
2. Update program content
3. Update program risks
4. Update program contract
5. Update program tracking system

There are many ways to organize your data. You should refer to *A Guide to the Project Management Body of Knowledge* for further discussion on the program management processes but should try to customize and simplify the steps to meet your organization's needs.

## How to Implement Your Program Management Process Model

It must be stated that the act of documenting your process does not automatically ensure that it will be implemented. An implementation plan should be developed that includes:

- How the process model will be distributed (important for adherence to QS-9000)
- How training will be developed
- Who will receive training
- Which team or teams will be targeted as the "pilot" implementation
- How will lessons learned get captured and updated in the process model.

## Summary and Conclusions

It is certainly easy to proclaim the use of "program management" at any company, but what does that really mean to an organization that is comprised of individuals from a variety of backgrounds, knowledge, and experiences? It means a potential for confusion, misunderstanding, and variation!! Developing and documenting how you will **manage** programs will help reduce those effects. Having key members of the organization involved in the process documentation efforts not only produces the actual process model, but it also trains and educates all of the workshop members and establishes ownership and "buy-in" for the process at the same time. Once complete, it can be used as an effective training and communication tool for the entire organization. Although the effort involved in development and documentation is great, the benefits realized for the organization can be very significant and measurable in terms of successful program execution and can become a key factor for acquiring future business.

# A Model for Project Management Acceptance

Richard E. Ryder PMP, Plan Tech, Inc.

Project management is not used unless it is accepted. This embarrassingly obvious statement hides a central problem for our profession: how to achieve that acceptance. We refer to "cultural" barriers and lagging skill levels and a multitude of other topics when discussing the issue. There are lists of excellent practical advice: how it worked elsewhere; how it takes three to five years; how when the government commands, they obey. Believers gather trade to trade knowing war stories about converting the non-believers. In the end, our attempts to get the problem in hand are similar to picking up a wet tomato seed from a smooth surface. We all seem to agree on one thing: this is still a difficult problem.

When we talk about this issue I believe an element is missing, namely a good model. This paper will explain one example of a model intended to focus on the problem of acceptance. We use models to help us think and predict; most are in our heads rather than on paper. In project management work, generally, we take the next step and spend a lot of time creating an explicit model of a project. We believe in the value of exposing our team's assumptions about the project for discussion and critique. Our critical path method techniques break down, however, when attempting to analyze something composed of complicated, iterative feedback loops. Yet that is the nature of the cultural change phenomena behind the acceptance of project management. So, as a profession, we tend to value formal models to help with decision-making and deep thinking on complex topics. All we need is a good modeling method for this particular topic.

## A Tool for the Job

Something that fits the bill, a product of operations research thinking, was invented around the same time as the critical path method—1956—principally by Professor Jay W. Forrester at MIT's School of Industrial Management. At the time it was called industrial dynamics. Forrester grew up on a Nebraska cattle farm, then moved through electrical engineering, servomechanism development, and the management of several technical organizations. At one point he was even a project manager for one of the first digital computers, optimistically named the Whirlwind I. This was the ideal experience mix to develop someone with a driving need to ponder and explain how the world works. We now call it systems thinking. After inventing magnetic core memory for computers he turned his considerable attention to the behaviors of industries, companies and, well, almost everything else. He first called it industrial dynamics because it was applied to management and industrial problems. He saw these complex phenomena as interactive components that are knitted into systems and behave in non-intuitive ways. As the thinking became more generalized and the technique was applied on a wide range of issues, it was renamed system dynamics. This did little for it's popularity despite its use to predict riveting events like the end of the world and the spread of plagues.

Though not the usual topic for dinner table conversation, nearly everything on or around the dinner table can be described with system dynamics: the cooling of food; the metabolism of the beings present; the supporting food chain; family relationships; their financial affairs; the learning behaviors of growing children; and the growth patterns of the community, just to name a few. "Systems thinking looks at the connections between parts rather than treating them in isolation; studying the whole to understand the parts" (O'-Connor 1996).

Proponents of system dynamics sometimes sound like proponents of project management; that is to say, zealots who challenge the world to throw them a problem their tool cannot comprehend and smash it to bits. Indeed, system dynamics is pretty universal since everything is, after all, part of a system. System dynamics can, and has, been applied to the behaviors of projects. A research project is the example topic in the book *Introduction to System Dynamics Modeling with DYNAMO* by George Richardson and Alexander Pugh. System dynamics was also behind the scenes in the March 1994 *Project Management Journal* article by Kenneth Cooper provocatively titled "The $2000 Hour: How Managers Influence Project Performance Through the Rework Cycle."

At the heart of system dynamics is the creation of a model to help think about the system in question. This tool can be applied to understanding that tough nut we are always trying to crack: getting people to accept project management so it can grow in a self-sustaining manner. The following sections describe the components of such a model.

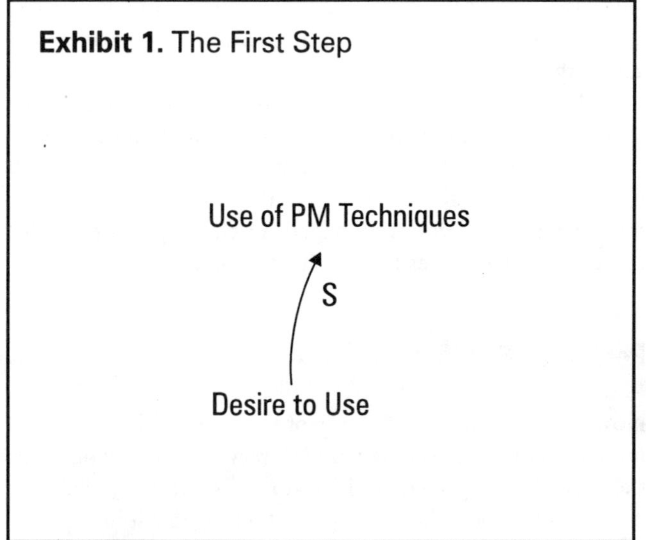


**Exhibit 1.** The First Step

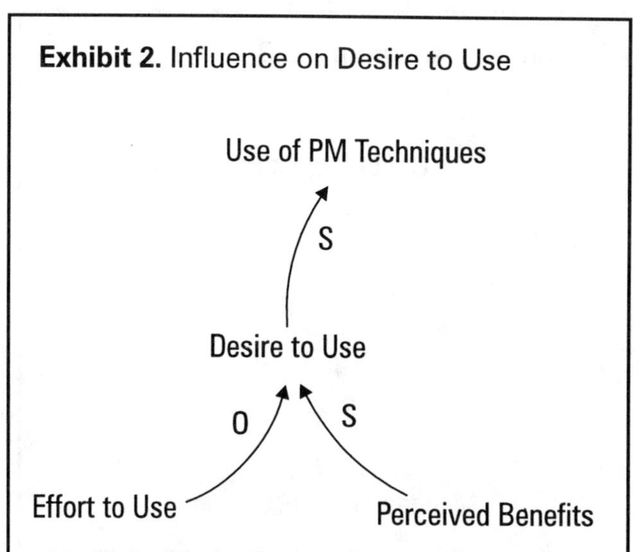


**Exhibit 2.** Influence on Desire to Use

## The Model

System dynamics advises one to state the central problem that the model is meant to address. Here it is: how to increase the use of project management tools and techniques. The assumption here is that if the observable behaviors in using the tools and techniques exist, then many other good things are happening as well. These items do not exist alone, however. Effort is required to apply them, projects are needed as objects of their focus, and larger economic benefits must support them. System dynamics advises one to draw a boundary around the problem—a bit of scope management if you will—since everything can seem to relate to everything else, and it is easy to spin off into oblivion. Our boundary will circle the most immediate influences on a given person, the smallest behavioral unit in which we are interested. Perhaps if we understand how individuals behave in these circumstances we can get some idea of how the group will. This modeling technique begins with describing a chain of cause and effect.

The first relationship of cause and effect is simple: for project management to be used, the individual must *desire* to use it. It is helpful to view these things as if they were levels of water in tanks. When the level of the "desire to use" tank increases, then the level in the "use of project management techniques" tanks will increase as well. This is a positive causal relationship in that they move in the same direction. In "causal loop" diagramming method it looks like Exhibit 1. The "S" on the arrow stands for "same direction" and indicates that if **desire to use** increases, then the **use of project management techniques** will also. This is also true for a decrease.

Our problem is easy to solve now: all we have to do is increase the level of **desire to use.** What are the influences on

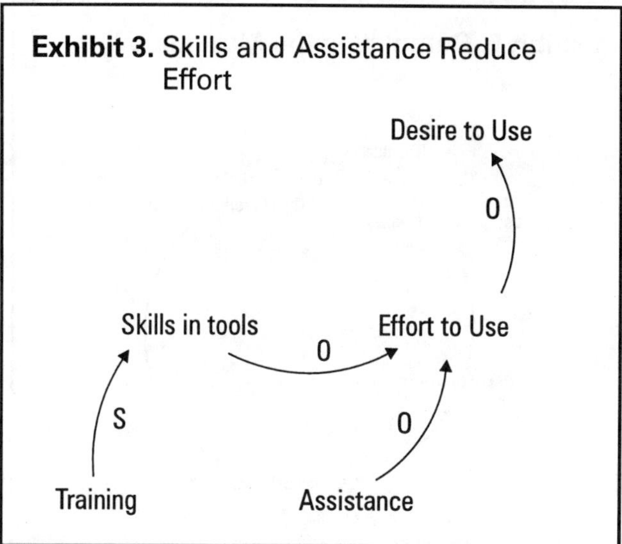


**Exhibit 3.** Skills and Assistance Reduce Effort

this? Here are two: the **level of effort** required to use the techniques, and the **perceived benefits** the individual has from project management use. This is just cost versus benefit, with the cost being expressed in terms of effort. The benefits are only real from the individual's point of view, hence the emphasis on perception. Adding these two items to our model gives Exhibit 2.

More **effort to use** will *decrease* **desire to use**, hence the "O" on the arrow, which indicates an opposite movement. More **perceived benefits** will likely *increase* the **desire to use**; therefore, we indicate this positive correlation again with an "S" on the arrow. This suggests we just have to figure how to *decrease* the effort and *increase* the perception of benefits.

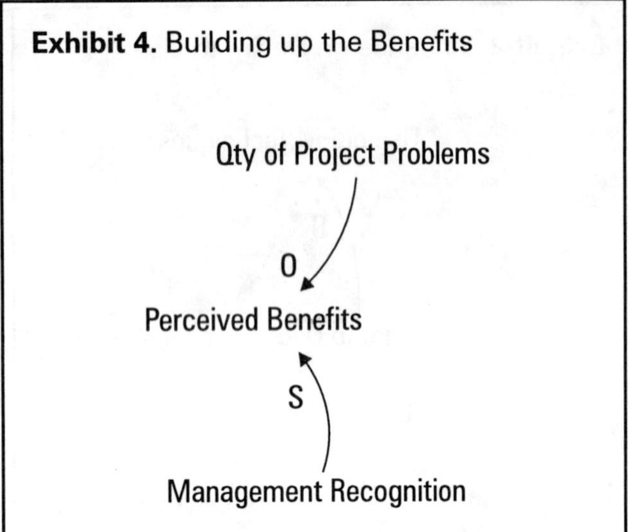


**Exhibit 4.** Building up the Benefits

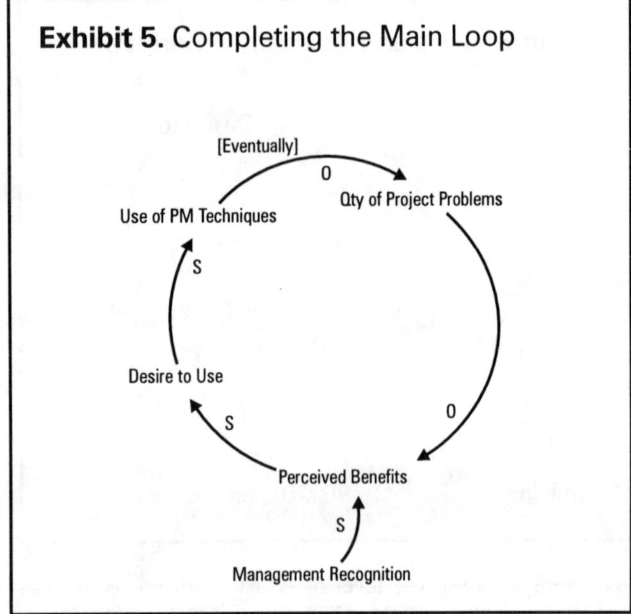


**Exhibit 5.** Completing the Main Loop

## Effort to Use

Next let's examine the influences on **effort to use.** Common sense confirmed by personal experience would lead us to believe that someone *more* skilled in the tools and techniques of project management will experience lower **effort to use** than someone *less* skilled. Despite the wonderful and intuitive user interface presented to us by the great minds in Redmond, Washington, there is still a knack for using project management software. Despite the best efforts of Henry Gantt and Project Management Institute, there is still a skill level required to extract meaning from the information the tools provide. Another way to reduce **effort to use** is to provide **assistance** in the use of the tools. This could range from coaching to direct operation of the tools. In our growing diagram this looks like Exhibit 3.

Skills, in turn, can be influenced positively by **project management training; therefore, we'll** add that as an influence at the bottom of the diagram in Exhibit 3. The signs on the arrows again reflect the movement of the levels on each end of the arrow: More **project management training** causes more (+) **skills** which causes less (-) **effort to use.**

## Perceived Benefits

Now go down the benefits side of the model. What are the influences on **perceived benefits?** A very large one would be the reduction of **project problems**; that is, after all, what attracts most of us to the use of project management in the first place. This is an inverse causal relationship, so we diagram it with a minus sign: *fewer project problems* would cause *more* **perceived benefits.** In a corporate structure another influence would be **management recognition** for the individual's use of project management tools: more recognition and plus marks on the report card would yield more benefits for most people because that usually leads to unspecified good things down the road. More of one leads to more of the other, so it is a positive relationship and calls for an "S" on the connection. This is shown in Exhibit 4.

## What Goes Around Comes Around - Completing the Loops

Now we can complete a "causal loop" that will help to increase **desire to use project management.** Loops are a big part of system dynamics modeling because they describe a feedback process which might ultimately become self reinforcing. Here is a description of the loop: **desire to use** *increases* **use of project management techniques,** which in turn *eventually decreases* the **quantity of project problems,** which *increases* the level of **perceived benefits,** which *increases* **desire to use project management.** This loop is shown in Exhibit 5.

In a similar way we can complete the loop that reduces the cost side influence on the individual's desire to use project management. The **use of project management tools and techniques** will *eventually increase* the *skills* in using those tools and techniques which will in turn *decrease* the **effort to use** them, which will be less of a drag on **desire to use.** The full diagram looks like Exhibit 6.

## So What?

Now that we have a model of the system we need to use it to tell us something useful. Our goal is to increase the use of project management, which is a dynamic phenomenon. To get some insight we need to put the model in motion conceptually and watch what happens.

The kicker in our system is in the word "eventually" that we used to described the impact of **use of project management tools and techniques** on *both* **skills** and the **quantity of project problems.** This is a **delay** phenomenon that plagues many systems, particularly the ones that involve difficult problems. In fact, delay is often what makes such problems difficult to understand in the first place since cause and effect are widely separated in time. In this case the proof of effectiveness, which will sustain and grow the **desire to use**, doesn't necessarily happen right away. The **skills** will take a while to develop, and the **quantity of project problems** will take a while to shrink. Project management devotees will span this delay with belief in the cause and effect link between project management practices and better projects. They also have the skills that make it "easy" to use the tools. As we all know, many people new to project management tend to doubt that relationship until it has been proven to their own satisfaction. In the beginning they do not, in fact, believe it to be so. After all, isn't a little skepticism healthy? The model suggests that we need to do something to overcome the delay. This is not a situation where wishful thinking will work.

One course of action is to look at the *other* influence on the level of **perceived benefits,** namely **management recognition.** Unlike the number of **project problems,** which take time to reduce, **management recognition** can be applied *without delay*. This validates part of the model in that it jibes with a recognized reality of project management implementation: there is no substitute for high level management support. Project sponsors and other executives who appear indifferent to project management will not see it grow. Someone who matters must provide the reward for immediate use. The model further suggests that demanding immediately better projects, or conversely fewer project problems, without addressing the delay will not lead to success. The answer, at least for the benefits side, lies in the low-cost, high leverage move of increasing **management recognition** for the mere *use* of project management tools and techniques.

Now lets look at the other influence on **effort to use** to see what the model suggests. Again we must contend with a delay between use and the development of skills that reduces the effort to a sustainable level. Training is a must, of course, and it will boost skill. There are delays in it as well, however, and it is difficult to train during the throws of an intense project or with the continuing pressures of a string of multiple projects. **Assistance** is an attractive and fast acting alternative that can help reduce the **effort.**

**Exhibit 6.** A Model for Project Management Acceptance

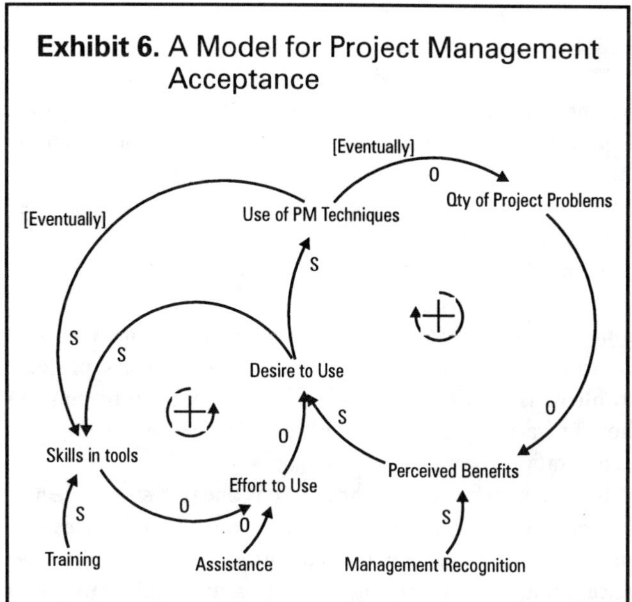


One lesson from system dynamics is that all solutions also cause problems, and here is the problem with **assistance.** It has to do with the *learning* effect from expending the effort to apply the project management tools and techniques. Some of that learning is about the nature of project problems and how and why to reduce them in number. This suggests it is wise to apply assistance with care or it will be the classic Band-Aid quick fix that delays the growth of project management **use** because it delays learning. System dynamic literature is full of stories about the folly of the quick fix.

## Next Steps

Forrester and subsequent practitioners didn't stop with the diagram (called a causal loop diagram). They applied mathematics and computer software that allow these models to be set in motion. Above we have merely speculated on how the parts interact. Simulation offers a means to confirm or deny those speculations. The problem, of course, is what to put into the equations. Level of desire and perceived benefits, for example, are hard to put a number on. How long should the delay be? Is it a function of project size or can a few months usually show a benefit. What about when people attribute the improvements to factors other than project management because they don't know what the term means?

Difficult, of course, is not impossible: just look at the variety of computer games based on simulation these days. Nevertheless, we can get plenty of value without full simulation by using the model as a thinking tool. After all, we just need to decide what is a good course of action, not prove the point beyond the shadow of a doubt.

The model can be used to communicate with members of the implementation team. It is simple enough to be easily explained, but valid enough to focus discussion. A conversation about why it is so important to reinforce tool use with short term rewards can be quickly illustrated with this model. The limits of assistance are also easy to show. If the various levels in the model are useful entities, then some excellent discussion could ensue on just how to measure their overall direction. For example, there may be several ways to measure **desire to use**, and putting a number on the **quantity of project problems** is always a good idea. The model can become a thought starter and a framework for ideas for use by the implementation team.

It can also produce insights. Here is one that struck me after drawing out the model. The three outside influences on the system are **management recognition, training**, and **assistance.** Training and assistance can be easily bought, but their impact is on the *weaker* influence on **desire to use**: all they do is reduce **effort to use.** As an upper-level manager, however, it would be easy to believe you had done the best thing possible to encourage implementation in your organization after such a purchase. The model suggests that a better course of action is to *also* increase the positive influences on **desire to use,** rather than just reduce the negative ones. So the course of action that is as close as the nearest phone is also the fastest and the cheapest! This is, of course, management recognition for the use of project management tools and techniques. Now I may have believed this before, but now I know why, and I can explain it with conviction.

The model also prompted me to think about the problems of over-reliance on assistance. I have noticed that the people who operate the tools—press the keys, so to speak—generally have the greatest appreciation for the principles involved with project management. While commendable, if those people provide administrative support, and the same appreciation doesn't exist in the project manager, there is still a problem. Ironically, the person who needs the knowledge and understanding the most is "too busy" to develop it. As a substitute, more is spent on assistance for tool use, with no noticeable effect on desire to use project management tools and techniques. The model shows a reason why: the improvement is to the *wrong* loop. The **quantity of project problems** is on the *other* side of the model, and remains virtually unscathed.

It would be easy to dismiss the model as an elaborate description of the obvious if it weren't for the fact that we see so many people ignore what it says. Perhaps it should be more complex, but with complexity comes loss of comprehension and credibility. Adding to it should generate thought-provoking discussions, which, after all, is why it was made. The premise of system dynamics is that the behavior of a system is a product of it's structure, which is how the components influence one another. The method presents us with both the challenge and the method of looking beyond the obvious, such as personalities and events, to see patterns; and further still to see the structures which are the true root cause of the system's behavior.

## Conclusion

This paper has demonstrated the application of system dynamics, a forty-year-old method, to the human behavior problems associated with initiating and sustaining the use of project management tools and techniques. The model reveals that the three most immediate influences on an individual's desire to use project management tools and techniques are management recognition, training, and assistance. Of the three, management recognition for the use of project management, rather than the results of the project, are likely to have the greatest impact. Putting together a system dynamics model to show a diagram of the causal relationships brings about the same benefits we often see when building a work breakdown structure or project model—putting it on paper lets others see what we are thinking and discuss it more effectively.

### References


Forrester, Jay W. 1961. *Industrial Dynamics.* Cambridge, MA: The MIT Press.

———.. 1975. *The Collected Papers of Jay W. Forrester.* Cambridge, MA: The MIT Press.

Roberts, Nancy. 1983. *Introduction to Computer Simulation, A System Dynamics Modeling Approach.* Reading, MA: Addison-Wesley.

Richardson, George P., and Alexander L. Pugh. 1981. *Introduction to System Dynamics Modeling with DYNAMO.* Cambridge, MA: The MIT Press.

Cooper, Kenneth G. 1994. The $2000 HOUR: How Managers Influence Project Performance Through the Rework Cycle. *Project Management Journal.* XXV: Number 1. (March).

*Help System Tutorial for The Ventana Simulation Environment—Vensim PLE Version 1.62-11.* 1996. Ventana Systems, Inc.

O'Conner, Joseph. 1996. *Thinking Past the Obvious.* Available from http://www.radix.net/~crbnblu/assoc/oconnor/chapt1.htm; INTERNET.

# Who Needs a Project Sponsor? You Do…

Bruce J. Kay, PMP, EDS, Project Management Consulting

## Introduction

This paper will review the importance of a project sponsor in modern project management within the automotive vehicle development process. In particular, we'll review:

- What Is the Vehicle Development Process;
- What Is a Project Sponsor;
- Why the Project Sponsor Is Crucial in the Current Vehicle Development Process Environment;
- An Evaluation Model for Project Sponsors;
- Steps to Support Your Project Sponsor.

## What Is the Vehicle Development Process?

The vehicle development process consists of all the functions required to develop a vehicle from concept to production. On a ground-up or clean sheet type program, all functions within the process are called upon to contribute to the development and ultimate production of a brand new vehicle. Some of the organizations include: drafting, analysis, development, a variety of build organizations, product and manufacture engineering, validation, a large number of ancillary support organizations, an array of first and second tier suppliers, and, ultimately the manufacturing plant(s). The actual number of organizations involved is well into the hundreds.

## What Is a Project Sponsor?

The project sponsor plays a "godfather " role for the program. The sponsor provides guidance and leadership for the project manager as well as for line managers. He watches over the project, nurtures it during the initiation phase, strengthens the project during development, protects it during execution, and reaps the benefit when it terminates and goes into production. As "godfather," his knowledge and authority are used wisely to benefit the entire organization. He helps to ensure that "project participants are focused on and committed to a common purpose and vision of success" (Currey 1995, 8).

The project sponsor typically provides guidance in:

- Object setting

**Exhibit 1.** Support Structure for Successful Projects (Kerzner 1991)

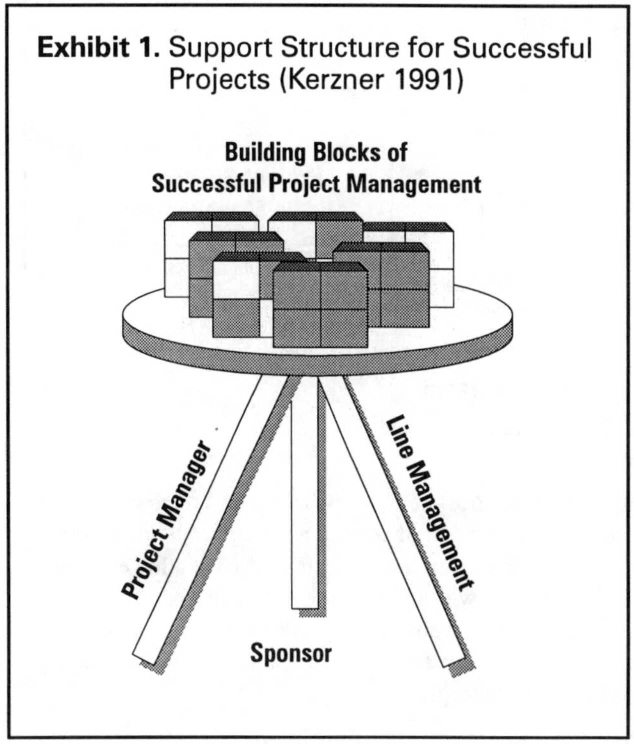


- Policy setting
- Up-front planning
- Monitoring execution
- Project organization
- Master plan development
- Key staffing
- Conflict resolution

The project organization can be viewed as a three-legged stool. Project manager, line management, and the executive sponsor all provide support to the project. Each leg of the organization provides a different means of support. Without one leg the stool becomes unstable. Exhibit 1 provides an illustration of this triad. A sponsor must balance the needs of the line functions and the project with the requirements of the organization, maintaining a balancing act, and managing trade-offs within the entire organization (Kerzner et al. 1995).

The actual location of the project sponsor within the organization is significant. Generally, projects with a multitude of resources, a large amount of integration between functional lines, the potential for disruptive conflicts, or a large

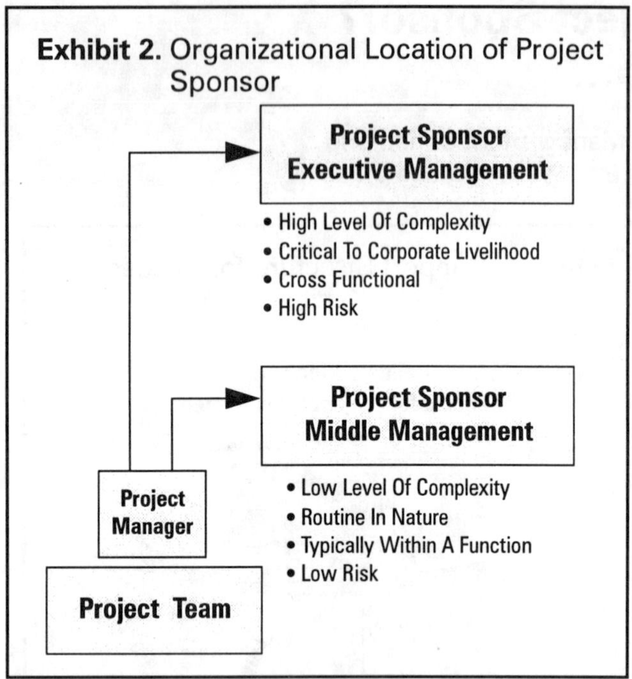

**Exhibit 2.** Organizational Location of Project Sponsor

amount of business at stake will require an executive level project sponsor. Span of control must cover all line functions involved in the program. Projects that have a lower level of priority, remain within functional lines, and have clearly defined goals that pertain to all parties within the project will require sponsorship from middle management. Exhibit 2 illustrates this concept.

### How Is a Project Sponsor Appointed?

Within the vehicle development process sponsorship can be attained through a number of methods. Often a project sponsor is named by the same committee that selected the project. For large projects, such as a vehicle development project, the sponsor most likely will be a member of the executive committee that approved the project. If an executive sponsor is too busy, an acting sponsor may be designated. Acting sponsors must carry the full authority of the appointing executive. In order to be effective, the acting sponsor must communicate and exercise his authority early in the program.

The worst case situation occurs when no sponsor is selected. This may occur because the project make-up does not appear to warrant a sponsor or the organization is early in the development of its project management practices. Organizations that are early in the application of project management techniques are typically characterized by:

- "Arts and charts" mentality;
- Project management software is perceived as equal to the full application of project management techniques;
- Project management is viewed as clerical work—not necessary for core business;
- Project management equals "timing ";
- The corporate culture is reactive in nature.

It is important to understand the difference between operating in a mature or immature project management organization. Not receiving a sponsor because the project does not appear to warrant it versus not receiving a sponsor because the organization does not demonstrate mature project management practices is critical to your evaluation of your sponsorship situation.

### Sponsor Relationship

There are two types of sponsor relationships—formal and informal. Formal relationships are clearly defined through organization structure and policy. Informal relationships are normally born from the project manager's need for management support. An experienced project manager will identify and lobby the correct executive to become a sponsor. Sponsors that are informally selected usually are key stakeholders in the project.

## Why the Project Sponsor Is Crucial in the Current Vehicle Development Process Environment

### Current Environment

The automotive vehicle development process has become a war zone where market share is won by the company who can define the customer's need, develop a product to meet that need, then get the product to market before the competition. Time to market has become the competitive weapon. To increase their competitive advantage, the Big Three have initiated a number of efforts to compress the vehicle development process to make the process lean and more timely. Car and truck programs that once took seventy-two months to complete are now required to finish in under forty months. Overseas competition strives for a thirty to twenty-four month development process (Womack et al. 1990). In the automotive industry, those companies that can consistently define the customer needs and quickly get the right product to market will have the competitive advantage necessary to dominate in the 21st century.

This rush to reduce time to market has moved the war zone from the market place into the vehicle development process within each automotive company. Battles are taking place between individual process owners over process scope, requirements, hand-offs, quality, and schedule. As vehicle programs continue to be compressed, line functions must strive to satisfy program requirements of time, cost, and quality. Line functions will often streamline their processes to the detriment of their downstream customers. This intense internal pressure to be the fastest kid in the organization can lead to an internal cannibalization where individual functions streamline their processes while sub-optimizing the overall process.

Two key issues compound the complexity of the vehicle development process: the size of the vehicle development process and the immaturity of project management techniques within the automotive industry.

The sheer size of the vehicle development process inhibits an organized change from current state to future competitive state. Consequently, change within the process is painfully slow and difficult to control. Established traditional processes change and evolve while programs are under way. Issues abound over the difference between time-tested traditional processes and radical unproven new processes. Functional groups who benefit from process changes adapt while non-benefactors passively resist. Communicating process change is also extremely complex given the number of functions and geographic disbursement of the organizations involved. During this *internal revolution,* schedule, scope, and cost of the program are based on the radical unproven new processes that *will be implemented concurrently* during the program's execution phase.

While there are islands of mature project management practices within the automotive industry, generally throughout the industry there appears to be a general lack of acceptance of modern project management practices. Programs are developed and executed using simple milestone charts with no ability to forecast or track progress. Cost, scope, and schedule are treated as independent aspects of the program.

### Why A Sponsor?

Large complex programs consisting of many projects and hundreds of sub-projects, covering hundreds of different functions, launched using evolving processes under extreme time pressure, require executive guidance from start to finish. A properly trained sponsor will provide the management support required to insure program success. Numerous studies have identified lack of upper management support as reasons for project failures (Gioia 1996; Black 1997). Sponsorship clearly identifies what executive to look to for support and what her involvement will be.

## An Evaluation Model For Project Sponsors

How do you know if you have the right sponsor? What are the fundamental traits of the right sponsor? In order to analyze the characteristics of a successful sponsor a simple scale was developed. This scale is loosely based on the work of Pinto, Smalley & Kerzner, and Currey (Pinto et al. 1992; Smalley et al. 1992; Currey March 1995).

### Project Sponsor Critical Traits

At the simplest level the critical traits of a project sponsor can be broken down into two characteristics - *-authority* and *knowledge*. While not perfect this simple breakdown provides a means of assessing sponsorship support.

#### *1.) Formal / Informal Authority*

Is the sponsor at an appropriate level within the organization to make conflict resolution decisions across all functional lines within the project? This person needs to possess organizational authority equal to, or greater than, the scope of the influence of the project. Informal authority is attained through recognized experience and/or relationships within the organization. Experience may support a "technical-expert" type of informal authority. A sponsor's ability to develop and maintain an informal network of influential executive stakeholders would be another type of informal authority.

#### *2.) Business Knowledge / Project Management Understanding*

The depth of understanding the sponsor has regarding how the business is run is the basis for business knowledge. Does the sponsor have the width and breadth of experience to understand the inner workings of the business? Project management experience is based on the depth of understanding the sponsor has regarding project management methodologies. Has he been a sponsor before? Does he understand the role of a sponsor? Is he part of the immature project organization? Does his leadership demonstrate mature project management techniques? Is he leading by example, demonstrating and requesting sound project management practices (Currey 1995)?

These fundamental characteristics can be calibrated to score an individual sponsor's traits, identifying areas of strength and weakness.

### Measurement

#### *Formal / Informal Authority*

1) Has responsibility for line functions affected by the project.
   0 - 25 - 50 - 75 - 100
2) Has recognized technical expertise to understand line functions affected by the project.
   0 - 25 - 50 - 75 - 100
3) Has strong informal network of management support to direct line functions affected by the project.
   0 - 25 - 50 - 75 - 100
4) Demonstrates a willingness to resolve conflict when appropriate.
   0 - 25 - 50 - 75 - 100

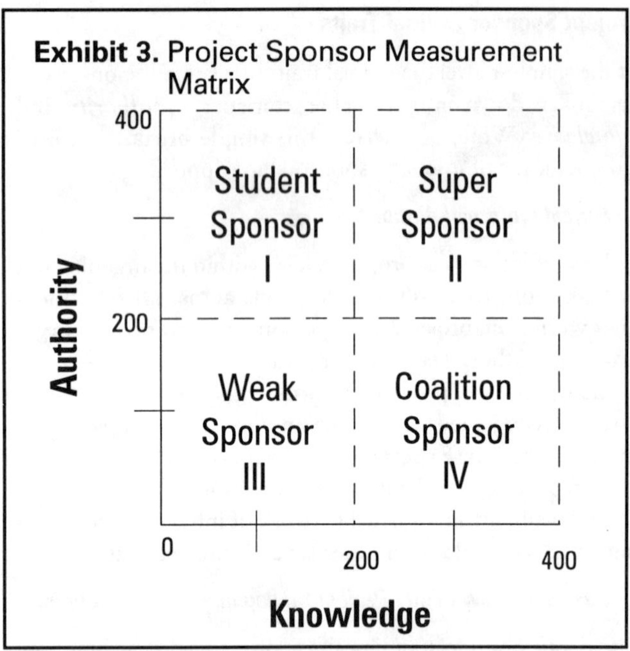


***Business Knowledge and Project Management Understanding***

1) Understands how business is conducted.
   0 - 25 - 50 - 75 - 100
2) Understands the requirements of a sponsor.
   0 - 25 - 50 - 75 - 100
3) Understands the key elements and importance of project management methodologies (PMBOK Guide).
   0 - 25 - 50 - 75 - 100
4) Demonstrates a willingness to make decisions using project management methods.
   0 - 25 - 50 - 75 - 100

## Scoring

To quantify your sponsor's characteristics, score each question using your experience with the sponsor. Total each section. Using the Sponsor Evaluation Graph (Exhibit 3) plot the point using Formal / Informal Authority for the vertical axis and Business & Project Management Knowledge for the horizontal axis.

## Sponsor Matrix Explanation

The graph can be broken into quadrants to facilitate grouping and explanation.

***Quadrant I - Student Sponsor***

This sponsor has the authority to get the job done. His weakness may lie in understanding project management methodologies or the details of everyday working business. Given the right teaching approach this sponsor could deliver significant benefits to the program and the organization.

***Quadrant II - Super Sponsor***

The ideal sponsor falls within this quadrant. He has the authority to get the job done and the knowledge to fully support the project manager. Most likely this sponsor was at one time a project manager.

***Quadrant III - Weak Sponsor***

Sponsors that fall in this quadrant have abundant opportunities for growth. This sponsor lacks authority and business knowledge to get the job done. This score may also represent the lack of a sponsor.

***Quadrant IV - Coalition Sponsor***

This sponsor has the business and project management knowledge but lacks the authority within the organization. He is in need of the organizational support garnered through a coalition of project stakeholders.

## Steps To Support Your Project Sponsor

Now that the sponsor can be scored, the next step is to determine the requirements to enhance your sponsor's position on the evaluation graph. In looking at the specific points used in scoring, we can now address how to facilitate the sponsor's growth. Please refer to the **Measurement** section above as reference. **Exhibit 4** illustrates this concept.

## Formal / Informal Authority—Developing Sponsor Authority

Organizational authority, the Y axis, is determined by the location and span of control of the sponsor. Following are some suggestions to support your sponsor's authority within the vehicle development process.

***1. Responsibility For Line Functions Affected By Project***

If the sponsor does not have the span of control necessary to effectively influence the program, build a stakeholder coalition. The process for building a stakeholder coalition can be summarized by a few key points:

**Select Stakeholders**

- Identify significant stakeholders for the project.
- From this pool of stakeholders, identify those executives who will support the project and who carry adequate cross functional authority.

**Build A Coalition Of Stakeholders**

- Develop a common set of stakeholder's goals and objectives (these must align with the project).
- Facilitate sponsor stakeholder project reviews.
- Work one-on-one meetings focusing on the stakeholder's needs within the project.

**Maintain The Coalition For The Duration Of The Program**

- Apprise stakeholders of pertinent critical issues
- Provide regular stakeholder status reviews

#### *2. Recognized Technical Expertise To Understand Line Functions Affected By Project*

A sponsor's technical expertise will affect project success. This form of expertise is particularly important when the sponsor lacks positional authority. Relying solely on technical authority will most likely not produce successful results. This sponsor should look for alignment with a key stakeholder to solidify cross-functional support.

#### *3. Strong Informal Network Of Management Support To Direct Line Functions Affected By Project*

An informal network of management support is a fundamental building block for program success. Sponsors with positional authority may not focus on this effort—this situation is analogous to the general and his troops. Even though the troops take commands from the general, informal support and commitment from the troops will deliver superior results. Informal networks are best developed and leveraged through stakeholder coalitions.

#### *4. Demonstrates A Willingness To Resolve Conflict When Appropriate*

A demonstrated ability to resolve conflict in a timely manner is critical to project success. Oftentimes a sponsor's inability to act is based on unmet information requirements. Some suggestions:

- Let the truth speak to power—provide accurate and timely information;
- Present information in such a way as to force decision-making;
- Coach the sponsor and stakeholders on possible solutions;
- Develop and maintain a sense of urgency.

## Business and Project Management Knowledge—Increasing Your Sponsor's Knowledge Base

Formal classroom training or, most likely, informal training will be the primary agent to move your sponsor along on the knowledge—X axis. Following are some suggestions to support your sponsor's growth.

### Knowledge:

#### *1. Understands How The Business Is Conducted*

With the sponsor, walk through the high-level process model for the project. Develop a common understanding of the project and the processes that support it. Identify the areas with high occurrence of poor performance to plan.

**Exhibit 4.** Project Sponsor Enhancement

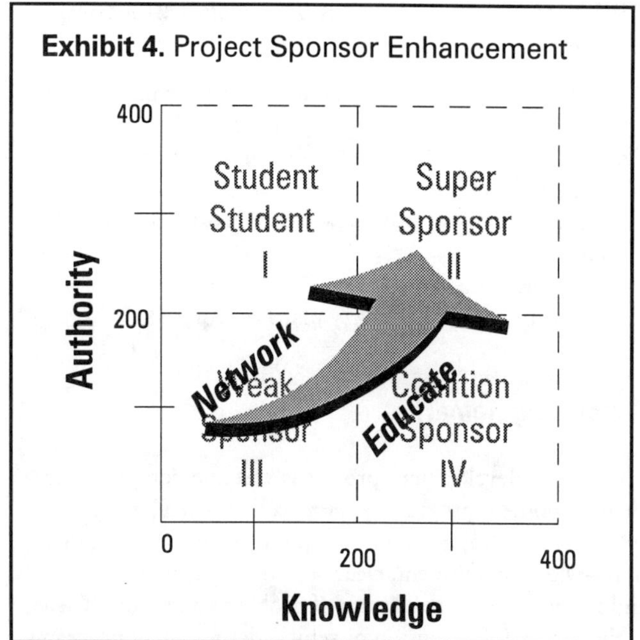


#### *2. Understands The Requirements Of A Sponsor*

Develop a sponsorship agreement, clarifying the sponsor's role and specific responsibilities (Currey 1995). Sponsorship agreement should cover:

- Conflict resolution process;
- Information requirements for project status;
- Visible support at meetings;
- Time and format of formal communications to the organization;
- His role in focusing the organization on a common purpose and vision of the project.

#### *3. Understands Key Elements Of Project Management Methodologies*

Establish an informal training program tailored for the sponsor. Utilize the *Guide to the Project Management_Body_of Knowledge* as a basis. Focus initial discussion on issues that will provide immediate payoff such as scope, risk, communications, and schedule. If the time constraints of the sponsor do not permit for a period of training, provide training during the execution of the program. Take every opportunity to educate on the fundamentals while the program is going through execution.

Prepare your sponsor for significant reviews. Involve him in the preparation for the reviews with particular focus on decisions to be made. Provide crib sheets with questions and issues for use during project reviews.

#### *4. Willingness To Make Decisions Using Project Management Methods*

Develop a simple project criteria checklist for project decisions. The sponsor could run through the checklist for each significant decision. The checklist should contain:

- Date for follow-up;
- Impact analysis to program—scope, cost, schedule, risk, and so on.
- Functions impacted;
- Review of detailed recovery plans as required.

## Concluding Remarks

The vehicle development process is vast and complex. Vehicle development programs *require* executive leadership to insure success. Proper sponsorship will help drive organization—wide commitment, clear objectives, adequate resources and funding, quick resolution of problems and more. Clearly the successful execution of vehicle development programs will be enhanced by well trained, knowledgeable project sponsors.

### References


Black, Ken. 1996. "Causes of Project Failure: A Survey of Professional Engineers." *PM Network* (November).

Currey, Jane. 1995. "Project Sponsorship." *PM Network* (March).

———. 1995. "Management Support: If it Looks Like A Duck . ." *PM Network* (October).

Gioia, John. 1996. "Twelve Reasons Why Programs Fail." *PM Network* (November).

Kerzner, Harold, and Jo Ellyn Berk-Kerzner. 1995. *White Paper. Planning for Project Management: The Next 20 Years.*

Pinto, Jeffery K., and Dennis P. Slevin. 1992. *Project Implementation Profile.*

Project Management Standards Committee. 1996. *A Guide To The Project Management Body of Knowledge (PMBOK Guide)*. Project Management Institute.

Smalley, Lionel., and Harold Kerzner. 1993. *White Paper. Project Sponsorship.*

Womack, James P., Daniel T. Jones, and Daniel Roos. 1990. *The Machine That Changed The World.* NY: Rawson Associates.

# Supplier Selection and Partnering Alignment: A Prerequisite for Project Management Success for the Year 2000

Steven Pascale PMP
Steve Sanders Ph.D.

## Introduction

The great industrial revolution created the need for project managers, although it would be many years before the label evolved. At the birth of manufacturing, project managers structured and organized manufacturing and supply processes to optimize speed to market and control costs and quality. The job is much the same today, with one major difference. Supply originally meant raw materials; today it means components. Complete, in-house production is dead. Although the news did not come to the manufacturing world with the drama or immediacy of a crier's call, project managers now know that there is a new crown prince in supply: component outsourcing with partners.

Component outsourcing may have simplified the manufacturing process, but it has created a new and equally important duty. If a project manager is to successfully optimize speed to market and exert control over quality and costs, that manager must grapple with the choice of supplier partners. Indeed, this requirement may be the most critical aspect of a modern project manager's duties. This paper will review the issues in managing the supplier relationship and outline a model of the partnering process.

## Suppliers and Product Development

Outsourcing is nothing new to the manufacturing world. The reliance on outside suppliers really began in this country in the fifties and sixties. At that time, major companies began replacing non-essential service departments with outside suppliers and contractors. Today manufacturing focus means learning how not to make things—how not to make the parts that divert a company from cultivating its skill, parts its suppliers could make more efficiently (Venkatesan 1992). Cleaning services replaced the janitor staff, then food service specialists took over the company cafeteria. Before long, companies began to realize that if services could be farmed out to specialists, so, too, could the manufacture of components. Soon, every company was buying at least some parts from outside sources. Today, there are very few products entirely manufactured by a single company. Indeed in some areas, notably the computer industry, nearly all components are provided by outside suppliers.

The principal advantage of outsourcing is very simple: it can be less expensive. Additional production departments, manufacturing facilities, and warehouses all translate into more overhead for a company. That overhead is invariably passed along to consumers as a higher price for the product. As profit margins have grown increasingly thin, companies began looking for ways to save money. Enter the supplier. The supplier eliminates a company's need for expensive departments and facilities. Supplier effectiveness is crucial to the survival of the business, explains Mel Friedman, vice-president of corporate supplier management, for the company has traditionally fought shy of a heavy manufacturing involvement: consequently, it is unusually dependent upon externally sourced components (Grotzinger 1994). As a specialist, the supplier also has more experience in doing what it does and is more likely to use state-of-the-art technology and fabrication techniques than an in-house, minor, corporate department. The upshot is that buyers are realizing that their success relies heavily on the performance of their supply base, and they are taking the necessary steps to ensure that suppliers make the grade (Minahan 1992). In short, the advantage to using a component supplier is that it can provide goods faster, better, and cheaper than can an in-house departments.

Another advantage of using outside suppliers is that they bring additional resources to a project. In addition to technical expertise, a supplier often has better access to tools and information of value to a project than the company itself. Working with a supplier in a partnership role can produce synergistic results: ideas may emerge that the project team would not have considered on its own. Further, by accepting responsibility for a part of a product or project, the supplier also accepts a portion of the project risk. Spreading out the risk both improves the project schedule and helps lower project costs for the primary manufacturer. Indeed a supplier may even help reduce overall project risk in some instances.

The advantages to outsourcing goods and services are considerable, and in many fields it is essential to rely on suppliers for certain services or product components. However, using suppliers also involves risk. Any number of problems with the supplier can seriously affect the quality of a product, or the project schedule in product development. A late-arriving order, defective goods, or poor communication between the supplier and the project team each can have a direct and significant impact on a project schedule.

With the *performance management* of a project tied more closely than ever to the performance of suppliers, a company's success has come to depend on the effectiveness of its suppliers. The supplier has become a crucial link in a company's attempt to serve its customers. Therein lies the risk. How much risk a supplier introduces depends upon the quality of its service. A good supplier partner, who delivers high quality products on time, with prompt support service as necessary, may actually reduce risk. Its service can keep a project on track and may even help move it ahead of schedule. On the other hand, a supplier whose service is poor, or whose products are late or defective, adds risk to the project. A poor supplier partner will inevitably delay a product development project and endanger it to the point of late release, or even worse, cause a project to be canceled entirely.

## Evaluation Framework: The Missing Link

With nothing less than a project's success riding on the performance of suppliers, the selection of those suppliers is critical. Procurement represents by far the largest cost of our production; sixty percent to 70 percent of our sales value is in the material-component costs as opposed to labor, overhead, and distribution (Wood 1993). In industries with short time-cycles, procurement is the single greatest challenge a business faces. As important as supplier selection is, one would assume that purchasing specialists and project managers have a detailed system for selecting the best suppliers for a project. Unfortunately, this is not necessarily the case. Some companies do have data-based methods for selecting suppliers, but experience has shown that many do not. Most often a supplier is chosen based on a single factor, i.e., cost. It may be that the choice is made because the project team *liked* the supplier representatives. Worse, the selection could be based on personal friendships or common educational backgrounds. Tossing a coin to choose a supplier partner is no less valid than such selection techniques.

Making the best possible supplier decision requires more than educated guesses or collegiate friendships: it requires an empirical method of evaluation. Over the past few years, project managers have come to realize the benefits of evaluating suppliers. A survey of large manufacturers conducted by *Purchasing* magazine found that 59 percent of those queried had some sort of supplier evaluation program in place. The primary reason given for those evaluations is the desire *to improve supplier quality*. By rating supplier performance, companies can identify the strengths and weaknesses of various partners and help those partners improve on weaknesses. The motivation for rating and ranking suppliers is simple: a better supplier means a better product and the forging of a mutually beneficial, long-term partner relationship.

We propose that evaluation can not only help improve supplier performance, but it can also help a company select the best supplier for a project. To be meaningful, any supplier evaluation process must be both empirical and objective. Objectivity of the measurement is critically important. If the success of a project depends upon a supplier, confidence that one has made the appropriate decision is imperative. Distinguishing between a supplier who is *somewhat favorable* versus *more favorable* is a difficult and unnecessary burden. The task becomes even more difficult if a number of factors are under evaluation. A clear, numerical measurement system is the easiest, most objective way to compare a group of potential vendors.

A potential supplier evaluation process must be able to evaluate both suppliers with whom a company has a history and *new* suppliers that have never been used. In the computer industry there are only a few suppliers of the most critical components: disk drives, processor chips, and so on. Consequently, every manufacturer has worked with nearly every supplier. In other fields there are dozens of suppliers for any given component. Any evaluation method must be able to accommodate both old and new suppliers, and, when necessary, compare them to each other.

Supply chains in technology manufacturing are subject to tremendous variability. Not only is there variance among potential costs of components but time availability will vary. In some cases, availability of components themselves will vary. How successful the execution of a project will be is dependent upon how well the variability and risk is managed and communicated. The key to managing variability is measurement. To be useful, a supplier evaluation methodology must be able to measure and to account for the variability in the supply process among potential partners.

## The Supplier Fidelity Model

The supplier fidelity model is based on the premise that using empirical data in a systematic way will consistently lead to the best choice of supplier for a project. *Best* means the supplier most suited to the needs of the project and who adds the least in terms of time, cost, and risk. This model contrasts suppliers objectively across a variety of factors and is able to evaluate both old and new vendors. It also is able to quantify the variability involved in dealing with a particular vendor. Ultimately, the supplier fidelity model makes it possible to identify the single supplier best suited for a given project.

The supplier fidelity model operates in three phases. In the first phase, the criteria for evaluating potential suppliers are determined by ranking with respect to importance. These criteria are then weighted based on monetary terms relative to the total cost of the product. The second phase involves the actual evaluation of vendors. Each vendor is evaluated on each criteria. A statistical analysis of the data employs an empirical rule and identifies vendors with one sigma above the mean. The suppliers with the highest scores are pushed up the list. In the final phase, an overall project analysis is performed.

## The Criteria

A project manager working in product development cannot afford to lose valuable planning time to conduct detailed research on every potential supplier partner for every component. In some industries, there could be a tremendous number of alternatives. The first phase of the supplier fidelity model is a preparation to reduce the list of potential partners down to a few *finalists*. It is very difficult to judge suppliers without a means of evaluation; consequently, this first phase is the construction of the test. The idea is to establish those criteria that are most important to the project in the order of their importance.

Ultimately a supplier evaluation is concerned with the bottom line; however, to be meaningful, the process must consider more factors than cost and on-time delivery. When selecting measurement criteria, one must be sure to determine those things that are most important to the project. Frequently, on-time delivery and prices are not the most important factors.

To identify actual selection criteria, we polled one hundred purchasing specialists involved in product development at a large computer manufacturer. The top (ten) factors purchasers identified are listed in Table 1 in the order in which they were determined to be most valuable. It should be noted that these criteria may be the most important for the computer industry, but they may not be applicable to other industries or projects.

As Table 1 illustrates, time to market ranks number one in the computer industry, but component cost is fourth on the list. Functionality and quality are considered to be more important than cost.

Once the criteria have been established and ranked, they must also be weighted. The purpose of an initial evaluation is to determine the true cost of doing business with a vendor. A plastic injection computer cabinet supplier's price may be less than that of a competitor's, but for a computer manufacturer the true cost of doing business is actually higher if one out of every ten of the cabinets is found to be defective. Similarly, one factor may be clearly more important than others, but many of the factors may be of relatively equal value. To accurately calculate the cost of doing business with a potential supplier partner, each of the criteria must be assigned a weight or value.

## Evaluate the Potential Suppliers

The second phase of the supplier fidelity model is the initial evaluation of suppliers using statistical analysis like ANOVA or time series analysis. This process is an attempt to pick the three or four vendors who provide the best options for the project. Each vendor is assessed on each of the criteria. Statistical examination identifies those venders that are substantially above the mean performance level of the group as a whole. These are the vendors who are the best candidates for consideration.

## The Project Analysis

The final phase of the supplier fidelity model involves a project analysis. A computer model consisting of a project plan with logical sequences and interrelationships among activities is established and programmed into a robust project management software system in order to perform the analysis. Once all tradeoffs are closely scrutinized, risk analysis software is used to compare the time and cost variability produced by the most qualified vendors identified in the second phase. The results demonstrate how a potential supplier's estimated performance will affect the overall project schedule and budget.

## Partnering and Alignment Problems with the Traditional Approach

Relationships between manufacturers and suppliers in the computer industry have traditionally been adversarial. In an adversarial paradigm, each party is pitted against the other, the mind set being that one party has to lose in order for the other to win. When the organizations involved think in this manner, communication breaks down, which in turn leads to an ill-defined scope of work and poor project performance. In an adversarial environment, the parties involved do not enter into the extended dialogue that is necessary to collaboratively develop objectives that everyone supports and strives to achieve. As a result, much time, money, and effort is wasted *fixing things* that could have been *done right* the first time and in trying to work through inadequate or non-existent channels of communication.

**Table 1.** The Top Ten Criteria for Evaluating Suppliers to the Computer Industry.

| | |
|---|---|
| **1. Time to market:** | **How fast can the order be available for the production crews?** |
| **2. Functionality:** | **How much better is this component than one offered by the competition?** |
| **3. Quality:** | **Is the component well-made and reliable?** |
| **4. Cost:** | **How much does the supplier charge for the component?** |
| **5. Past on-time service:** | **How well has the supplier met deadlines in the past?** |
| **6. Trade-name:** | **What is the reputation, in the public mind, of the supplier's products?** |
| **7. Supplier discount schedule:** | **How much cheaper will the component's price get over time?** |
| **8. Availability/flexibility:** | **How well will the vendor supply what the company needs when it is needed?** |
| **9. Past purchase service:** | **How well has the supplier provided technical support when it was needed in the past?** |
| **10. Other factors:** | **Supplier's financial soundness, management stability, production capacity, resources, etc.** |

## The Purpose of Partnering

A relatively new form of relationship known as partnering has the potential to bring relief to organizations suffering from the ravages of an adversarial environment. Partnering provides a new, harmonious environment, in which the parties involved can interact effectively and free of obstacles. The objective of the partnering process is to design for each project an effective problem finding/problem-solving management team composed of personnel from both parties, thus creating a single culture with one set of goals and objectives for the project (Moore, Mosley, Stagle 1992). In the new environment multiple sourcing is not always possible or desirable, and competition is often non-existent or less than effective (DeRose 1989). In a partnering environment, the focus is on the relationship or the project. There is a fundamental belief that everyone can win from the success of the project: one party's gain does not preclude the chances of the other organization benefiting. The methodology of the partnering process provides for the project to be successful and for all parties involved to gain from the beginning. Two necessary inputs that make partnering more successful than the typical relationship are the setting of aligned objectives and the development of the scope by both manufacturer and supplier. Supply-chain visioning is an effective approach to forging functional integration, for pushing innovative thinking, and for linking operations to strategy (Copacino 1994).

The term *aligned objective* refers to an objective that is common to all pertinent parties. The process through which an aligned objective is developed involves the creation of individual lists of objectives by each organization. These separate lists are then compiled and modified by the project team as a whole until mutually acceptable goals are identified. The identified goals are the success criteria for the project: if they are achieved, the project will have been a success for all parties. Each of the organizations in the partnering relationship is committed to the project objectives because they helped create them. This commitment can extend downward to the individual employee, who *buys in* to the project success criteria because he or she can associate them with personal gain.

It is important to remember, however, that ultimate success is directly proportional to how thoroughly the alignment process has been conducted. Without the basic belief that everyone can win, and that aligned objectives are achievable and worth the effort and time to develop, attempts at aligning objectives will never be successful. The various team members must have an attitude of "win/win or no deal" (Covey); that is, they believe so strongly in everyone experiencing some degree of success that they will either reach a mutually agreeable set of objectives or make no transaction at all.

It is important that a project's scope be developed by all parties. The needs of the manufacturer must be incorporated into the design. Again, cost and time are important factors in the supplier fidelity model. The supplier contributes through his knowledge of systems development and implementation. He knows what can be accomplished in terms of supply and the most efficient way of achieving the objectives. Suppliers can provide information on materials, equipment specifications, and quality. The compilation of all this knowledge means that the needs of the manufacturer are satisfied. Implementation runs more smoothly than it would have otherwise because the manufacturer's needs have been designed properly beforehand in a way that can be easily constructed. The supplier is committed to the project and is more efficient because he is using the methods that he specified.

## Examples of Partnering

The traditional approach to supplying services is basically an arm's length relationship in an adversarial environment. The supplier and the manufacturer behave as separate entities, only interacting where absolutely necessary. Communication and the sharing of knowledge is limited. Because of this, the scope is often not as well defined as it could be, and the project suffers as a result. When problems arise, disputes escalate rapidly, primarily because each party believes that the other is acting against its interests.

### Approved Supplier

The *approved supplier* approach is the least advanced form of partnering. It requires minimum investment in the relationship by the organizations involved, but the benefits achieved are also limited. Suppliers are approved for a particular project with no promise of future work. The group of approved suppliers still compete for the award of the bid, but each has already been determined by the manufacturer to meet a given set of criteria. These criteria, as described earlier, include factors like time, cost, financial stability, reputation for quality, brand names, service agreements, and warranties. The establishment and communication of project objectives is the manufacturer's major concern. Having an approved supplier helps to ensure that these objectives are met, because the supplier is already in tune with the company's culture and needs and knows what the company expects.

### Preferred Supplier

The *preferred supplier* model represents another step along the partnering continuum. It is a more comprehensive form of partnering than having an approved supplier; it requires greater investment and consequently the returns to both parties are increased. A preferred supplier provides single-source services as work is available. Preferred suppliers are not included in initial planning, which is one potential advantage that is lost. Using preferred suppliers requires more investment on the company's part, since the bidding process is foregone, but the benefits should outweigh the cost. One benefit is that lessons learned can be applied to the relationship for continuous improvement, since the partners are working together on a continuous basis. Because of this, the company is getting a better product and is experiencing cost, schedule, and other savings.

### Strategic Alliance

*Strategic alliance* is the most advanced, or complete, form of partnering. In a strategic alliance, the manufacturer and supplier form a team that becomes a separate entity from the originating organizations. Some alliances even hire outside the parent organizations to overcome ingrained mind-sets and eliminate ties to old practices. The strategic alliance team *owns* the project from start to finish and sometimes helps to make strategic business decisions. The team is involved in the conceptual stage and carries the project through to its completion and operation. The investment required is tremendous on both sides, but the rewards have been shown to well justify the costs. In order to have a successful strategic alliance, the traditional adversarial paradigm must be changed. Complete trust and a belief that one party's gain does not exclude the other party's gain are essential.

### Investment Versus Benefit

The four classifications of partnering relationships outlined above differ in the amount of investment required and the benefits received. It should be noted that the term "investment," as well as applying to monetary expenditure, also refers to expenditures of time and even the risk associated with trusting the other organization. A manufacturer's organization must evaluate its needs and determine whether the benefits of a particular type of relationship warrant the costs. If a company has only a single project, it may not be interested in an advanced form of partnering. It may determine that the rewards are not that great, except in special instances. The traditional approach or an approved supplier model might be sufficient.

If, on the other hand, the company has a need for multiple projects and has a driving goal such as cutting costs or schedule, it is well worthwhile to consider a strategic alliance. The main point is that the type of relationship must be tailored to suit the needs of the organization, and the alliance model should not be selected simply because it is *the latest thing*.

## Partnering Benefits

The first benefit of partnering is that it is focused on meeting the needs of the company. Critics of partnering may doubt the practicality of partnering, but it is, in fact, a very pragmatic, goal-oriented approach. The partnering environment stimulates new ideas and facilitates the conceptualization and communication of the manufacturer's objectives. Since the sole purpose of the relationship is to enhance the ability to meet these objectives, the parties are already committed to finding the best solution to a given problem. The company has help and input in developing its goals, and the supplier has time to align. The supplier knows how it can help the company and has a chance to communicate how the company can help him.

A partnering relationship allows for the development of synergistic solutions based on "win/win" objectives. Synergy is the concept that two organizations working together will accomplish more than the total of what they would accomplish working separately. The fact that many partnered projects have experienced a greater degree of success and demonstrated a greater ability to meet established objectives confirms the concept of synergy. By developing objectives that all parties support, because all parties win, the relationship reduces the adversarial culture and relationships so common with the traditional approach. The aligned objectives integrate the appropriate risk-sharing with innovative incentive schemes to produce a culture in which all parties pull in the same direction to make the project successful. If the project is successful, all parties are successful. "Win/win" objectives provide a reward for all parties involved. Both parties will have gained from the common objective of meeting and beating the schedule. This kind of system goes against the traditional adversarial belief that one party's gain has to be the other party's loss.

Unwillingness of an organization to share proprietary information has been shown to be a barrier to the achievement of maximum project success. If the supplier does not have a complete understanding of the manufacturer's circumstances and needs, how can it help the company to achieve the best solution? When information is shared, trust is enhanced, and both organizations have a complete picture of the situation and the information they need to establish and meet objectives. The parties are then capable of tailoring the project process to an understood situation.

In the adversarial environment, the organizations involved will treat risk like a "hot potato," each trying to pass it on to someone else, regardless of whether or not that entity is in a position to control it. A major advantage of a partnering relationship is that risk is allocated appropriately. Controlling risk increases the opportunity for both parties to gain. Instead of trying to pass the risk to someone else, as is the case in traditional risk management, the risk is assigned to the party most able to control it. Some risks may be managed mutually. Another advantage of partnering regarding risks is the partnering paradigm itself. The focus is on meeting objectives, not on collecting from the other party for wrongs incurred, so when something goes wrong (and it does from time to time), there is an attitude of, "Let's deal with this together and try to get the project back on track" rather than, "Tough luck, I'm going to make you pay for that!" The obvious result of these benefits is improved project performance. Partnered projects have experienced reduced cost and schedule, improved quality, and greater pay back to manufacturers and suppliers alike, all within an environment that puts the fun back into work. The results achieved depends on the commitment of the project team, as demonstrated by the resources allocated to making the relationship successful.

## The Partnering Process

The objectives and phases of the partnering process are summarized in the partnering process model displayed in Exhibit 1. The model identifies five key phases.The manufacturer's *internal alignment*, shown in Phase 1, incorporates the concept that the company must first determine its strategic goals and objectives and then evaluate partnering to determine if it is the best vehicle for achieving those goals. Too many companies have jumped into partnering because it seemed to be the thing to do, without first analyzing where the company was going and how partnering would help it to get there. The company also needs to conduct internal alignment and training prior to seeking a partner.

In Phase 2, *partner selection*, the manufacturer conducts a formal process to select the appropriate partner. This process centers around developing a list of selection criteria, circulating requests for proposals based on the criteria to potential partners and analysis of the responses. It is paramount

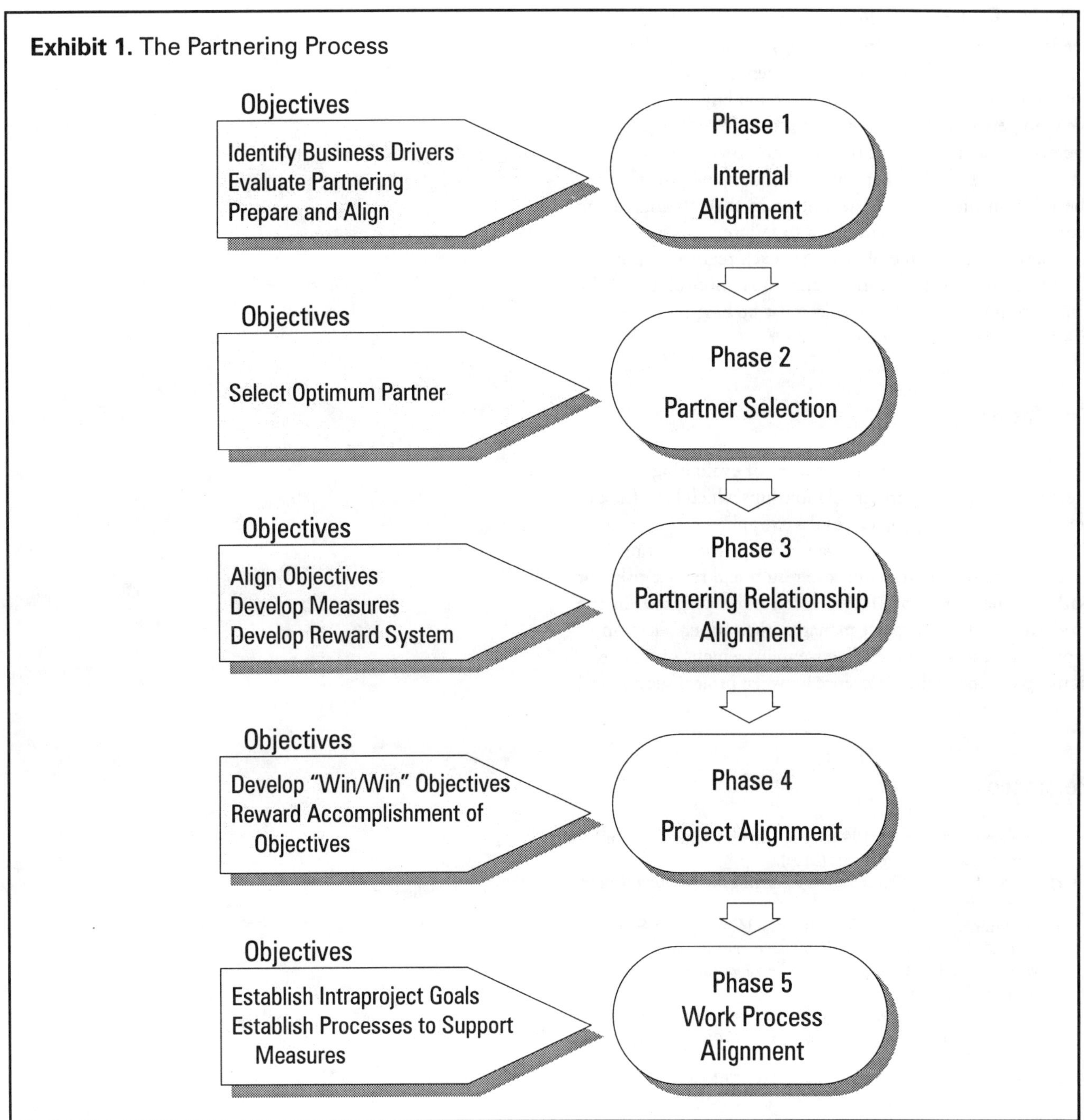


that the selection criteria support the strategic goals established in Phase 1.

Phase 3, the *partnering relationship alignment*, centers around the involved parties integrating company specific objectives into mutually beneficial objectives that allow all the companies involved to succeed. Developing trust through information sharing, proper risk allocation, and establishing personal relationships is key if the participants are to rise above the traditional adversarial relationship and aspire to developing "win/win" solutions.

The *project alignment phase*, Phase 4, consists of developing the project specific objectives and activities necessary for producing single project success. Phase 3 determines how the relationship would operate at the strategic level; Phase 4 addresses how the relationship will be implemented on individual projects.

Finally, *work process alignment* incorporates the activities needed to obtain buy-in from all organizational levels within a project. One of the major reasons identified for partnering failure was the lack of understanding and buy-in by the people who performed the day-to-day work. Even if upper management strongly endorses the idea and provides all the needed resources, if the workers either do not know how to make the relationship work or do not want the relationship to work, the relationship is doomed to failure.

A key point to remember is that each relationship is different. Each step shown in the model is important, but the application to each relationship must be based on the relationship's objectives and environment.

## Conclusion

This paper has reviewed the process of evaluating and implementing supplier partner relationships which have the potential to improve project results. Supplier choice can be based on objective, empirical evaluation. Partner relationships that have the potential to improve results and reduce risks for both supplier and manufacturer can be established. In the modern world of a project manager, the proper selection of supplier partners and the effective management of that relationship can mean the difference between project success and failure.

## Reference


1) Copacino, William C. 1994. "The Ultimate Supply Chain Vision. "*Traffic Management* (May).
2) DeRose L. 1989. "Purchasing's Changing Negotiating Roles." *Purchasing World.*
3) Grotzinger S.J. 1994. "Electronics Heading for Sunshine State." *Purchasing & Supply Management* (Oct.).
4) Minahan T. 1992. "Big Buyers Keep Eye on Supplier." *Purchasing* (Jan 16).
5) Moore C., D. Mosley, and M. Stagle. "Partnering: Guidelines for Win-Win Project Management." *Project Management Journal* (March).
6) Vekatesan R. 1992. "Strategic to Make or Not to Make Outsourcing." *Harvard Business Review* (Nov- Dec).
7) Wood L. 1993. "Dell Computers Tries to Get Back on Track." *Electronic Business Buyer* (Oct.).

# Commitment Management—Moving from Organizational to Commitment Hierarchical

M. Dale Jordan, GM Truck Group
Thomas Nepa, PMP, EDS Project Management Consulting

## Introduction

A consistent theme in today's competitive automotive environment is the pressing need for the program team to compress complex product development cycles. As a result, project and program management methodologies have gained increased recognition. Recently, a process called commitment management (CM) is providing a foundation to broaden into other project management (PM) knowledge areas. Commitment management is being used to focus the matrix organization and all its associated issues to a "network of commitments" directed to vehicle programs.

Commitment management is simply the effective integration of project management principles with the General Motors Four Phase Vehicle Development Process (4ΦVDP). It is fundamentally based upon negotiated program deliverables emphasizing accountability and boundaries to which all constituents commit. The commitments are the instruments by which the organization can clarify and propagate communications about decisions.

Commitments are organizationally dependent, and as corporations move to matrix organizational structures, the need for a process that focuses the matrix to the program is necessary. Therefore, a matrix organization is highly dependent on successfully working through commitment management. Each functional group contributing to the program must realize that it can no longer exist as a lone entity, "a silo." Reliance upon others for input is crucial. Thus, commitment management becomes the process for integration and communication of a vehicle program.

## Commitment Management is Highly Dependent Upon a Sound Product Development Process.

The 4ΦVDP for General Motors has evolved over the last ten years. It has its foundation in the principles of systems engineering and project management. It was created by documenting the exiting processes for the development of a vehicle using the "tribal knowledge" of the organization and then dividing the process into four phases. The first phase emphasis is on planning before execution begins.

In this first phase, the vehicle development process ensures that all functional areas plan their respective parts of the vehicle program, thus negating the need to "plan on the fly" as the program is executed. As the organizational structure moved from a hierarchical to a matrix organizational structure, the program team need for commitment management became even more important in order to maintain a coherent environment for the vehicle program. The key was the need for a common understanding of the program scope by all of the functional groups through some type of communication process.

## A Process Implementation Case Study

### Background

Program teams currently are implementing the process in support of a future new vehicle program. It is "happening" at the tactical level between the matrix team members and the functional groups/partners. The commitment management process described within this case study focuses on "schedule imperatives" (critical path timing).

### Purpose and Objectives

The purpose of implementing the commitment management process in support of the scheduling imperatives is to insure accountability to the baselined program critical path timing plan. Program timing is based on work as defined within 4ΦVDP. A committed timing plan is one of the primary ways of managing 4ΦVDP performance. The commitment management process objectives as they relate to scheduling imperatives include:

- Gain commitment to work activities/deliverables within a matrix organization (commitments both horizontally and vertically).
- Provide both a framework and a "pull" mechanism for detailed planning within the functional organizations.
- Facilitate early detection and resolution of timing and deliverable roadblocks.
- Assure cross-functional agreement of the critical path "hand-offs" (integration points).



PROJECT MANAGEMENT INSTITUTE 28th Annual Seminars & Symposium
Chicago, Illinois: Papers Presented September 29 to October 1, 1997

**Exhibit 1.** "Commitment Management Process Model (Heckel 1995)"

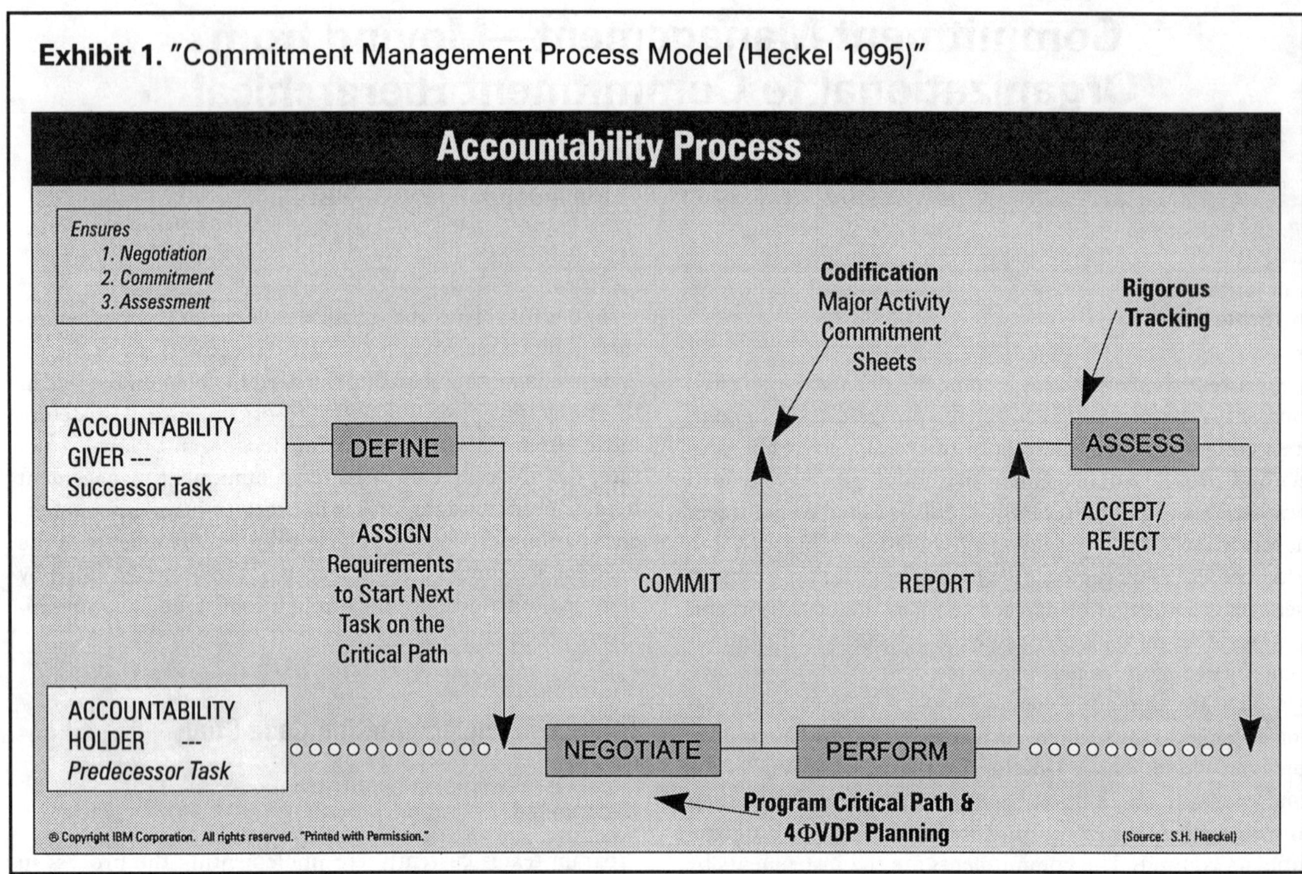


- Baseline a program critical path plan ready for "execution."

## Process Implementation

The commitment management process consists of four stages *define, negotiate, perform*, and *assess*. The process begins with pre-"*defined*" targets. These targets will require commitments that are derived through *"negotiations."* Commitment *"performance"* will be reported through completion. The deliverables will be *"assessed"* and either accepted or rejected. (See Exhibit 1—"Commitment Management Process Model")

## Stage #1 Define

The "define" stage is when the initial timing imperative targets are provided. The targets are program critical path activities with standard lead times. The activities and lead times are based on "common templates," differentiated based on program cost and complexity. The templates are reflective of the organization's common processes, best practices, and improvement efficiencies. They are documented/supported through actual process examples and/or specific enabler requirements.

Given the "assignor role" at the program level (tactical) are the matrix team members, also recognized as the "accountability giver(s)." The targets are further understood and managed through the functional organizations and various team structures. They are regarded as the "accountability holder(s)." A functional representative performs detailed planning activities on behalf of his or her functional organization. Ultimately, this provides a functional plan supporting the program timing plan.

## Stage #2 Negotiate

The practice of negotiating rather than assigning targets is the "cornerstone" of the commitment management process. The negotiation starts with pre-defined targets. If a commitment is not obtainable the downstream customer is requested to specify minimum requirements, trade-offs, and related risk. Multiple iterations of this process can ensue until an agreement is reached with equitably shared risk.

The goal of a successful negotiation is two-fold: get the deliverable owner to commit while identifying "risk" in the accomplishment of her deliverable.

Risk is a natural consequence of the negotiation. Initial imperative targets from the "define" stage reflected improved efficiencies and best practices. As a result, risk trade-offs become part of the negotiation. Risk items are identified both functionally and cross-functionally. These risk items are researched and evaluated in terms of the probability of occurring and potential consequence. Some risks will require immediate mitigation prior to contract signing, and the balance are monitored and managed throughout the life of the program.

The actual negotiations are facilitated through numerous small meetings between the commitment requester and performer. This involves offers and counter-offers resulting in an initial set of commitments with all parties understanding the impacts of the deliverables. The aggregates of all commitments are reviewed in a large formalized workshop setting. Prior to baselining, all commitment "stakeholders" have the opportunity to review program hand offs and understand the impact to their committed deliverables. The output of these meetings and workshops are made available to all program constituents and submitted as a baseline program timing plan for contract signing.

Negotiating is most rigorous at inception of each commitment. However, commitments, once made, should be renegotiated based on unforeseen circumstances. For example, if the organization is able to implement a process improvement to achieve shorter deliverable lead times, this would necessitate re-negotiating the commitment and downstream customer commitments. This is possible, since once all of the commitments are linked, understanding of relationships between commitments are available to understand impacts in changing deliverables.

An essential tool in facilitating these negotiations is the use of a templated document referred to as the "commitment detail sheet." The template content is completed based on negotiations addressing program specifics. All significant commitment dialog is defined, negotiated, performed, and assessed based on this document. Each individual commitment detail sheet includes the following:

- Functional ownership and responsibility
- Outcomes (including range of likely performance, e.g., duration's)
- Work scope
- Assumptions
- Risk/barriers and enablers
- Required inputs (measurable through conditions of satisfaction)
- Deliverables (measurable through conditions of satisfaction).

The deliverable commitments are highly integrated due to a continuous focus on "hand-offs" (deliverables and inputs). Hand-offs are clearly defined and documented through detailed evaluation criteria ("conditions of satisfaction") to which both the performer and requester agree. After several iterations, the final hand-offs are agreed upon and committed to in a formal program planning workshop. Initially, the hand-offs addressed are critical path-based. A natural progression continues on to non-critical path items with potential to be critical.

Without negotiation, the true understanding of expectations and commitment to a pre-defined set of deliverables is missing. Otherwise, deliverable owners will interpret what they thought was requested and/or expected. Often they assume somebody else will monitor the delivery of their required inputs to start their work activity. However, when the first late input is received, "all bets are off," which results in greater emphasis put on "why" they will be late versus "what" is an acceptable alternative. It is imperative at the onset of the process that deliverable owners understand that an avenue to renegotiate exists.

The underlining philosophy of the commitment management process is that before a commitment is meaningful to the performer, he must be confident that the "conditions of satisfaction" can be met. If there is uncertainty, mutually acceptable ranges of performance should be negotiated and documented between the requester and performer. Both should strive to have agreed deliverables and specifications of those deliverables. This is in support of the management axiom, "If you cannot measure it, you cannot manage it." In addition, management must make known the consequences of not meeting the commitments.

### Stage #3 Performance

Performance is measured to a set of deliverables committed to at contract signing. They are measured and monitored by the accountability givers (matrix members). Performance evaluation is based on the committed deliverables and whether or not the conditions of satisfaction have been met. Emphasis is put on early detection and recovering before a critical event occurs that is at risk. When unanticipated conditions require that a given commitment be renegotiated, all inter-dependent commitments are known and can be immediately examined for impact and renegotiated if necessary.

The deliverable commitments are at the macro level, which can be insufficient to evaluate or manage progress in a timely fashion. This results in utilizing further detailed planning (on deliverables of high risk), supplied by the functional groups. Performance is reviewed at a minimum of two-week intervals with an outlook of approximately six months (rolling wave approach). All deliverables' hand-offs will be reviewed on an exception basis. Program schedule performance is rolled-up to a common high-level business process that links all imperative commitments (e.g., cost, schedule, quality). It is a strategic tool to measure performance on all programs in the portfolio.

To make the reviews more successful, it must be encouraged to provide advanced warning of commitments in jeopardy. Furthermore, there should not be any fear of punishment for surfacing these advanced warnings. It offers an opportunity to renegotiate. This will verify that a system exists that rewards early warning but will result in consequences if the warning is at the last minute or after it has already happened.

### Stage #4 Assessment

The assessment should be straight forward. It is based on the evaluating deliverables (includes all hand-offs, inputs, and outputs) as defined within the "conditions of satisfaction." Deliverable outcomes are either accepted or rejected. Assignors cannot reject the deliverable if the "conditions of satisfaction" agreed upon were met. At the program level, the assessment process is performed at each macro-level milestone. If rejected, an action plan resolution process is enacted. Paramount to this assessment is a constant evaluation of any risk to the ultimate program deliverable. The commitment management process is applicable both at the individual commitment level and the sum of all commitments for a program. This assessment of the program during and when finished will provide valuable lessons learned to others coming down the road.

## Benefits of Commitment Management in a Matrix Organization.

In both a hierarchical and a matrix organization, the work is done in "silos." The difference is that in a hierarchical structure each program has its own individual functional group/partners, while in a matrix structure a single functional partner provides for multiple programs. While in a hierarchical organizational structure, there may be multiple degrees of competency in each of the multiple duplicate functional groups.

In a matrix, there is potential for increased competency in a single functional partner serving multiple programs. In addition, there are opportunities to reduce structural cost. This comes from the reduction in work force as a result of restructuring the work force. This may or may not be in the core competency depending on requirements of certain skill sets. But assuredly it comes from the decrease in the support infrastructure required by multiple duplicate functional partners in a hierarchical structure.

"Commitment hierarchy" replaces the traditional "organizational hierarchy" present in a non-matrix. The direction and focus to the organization comes from commitments and not management direction. "Commitment hierarchy" is required in a matrix organization to provide accountability of the functional partners to the program team. Commitment management provides this by focusing on communication and integration of the process. These processes are required to avert the functional partners from remaining in their "silos." Without these processes, each silo acts as an independent entity not concerned with upstream or downstream activities. This results in suboptimizing their functional requirements, and, in turn, making it impossible to perform tradeoffs in the program. Thus, commitment management brings to the program the integration (cross functional) and communication (scope) processes that enable the program to deliver the product by the requirements defined in the program targets.

This is accomplished by defining the functional partner's deliverables and how they interact. All partners are responsible for their detailed plan containing the required input and the desired outputs. To accomplish this, all partners meet together to understand each of their respective deliverables and how they interact with each other. Consensus of deliverables and inputs at the integration points in the plan is the secret of commitment management. One partner's deliverable is another partner's downstream input.

By coming to a common agreement on the deliverables and the inputs and their quality in the program plan, each partner understands what is expected to meet the program targets. To solidify the plan, commitment management requires that a formal documented commitment be made by each partner, one that is mutually agreed upon by the program team and the partners. This seals the ownership in the program by the functional partners. In the past, this has been handled casually. Commitment management removes ambiguity and misunderstandings between partners and clarifies the expectations of the program.

## Who Is the Boss?

In a hierarchical organization, everyone knows who the "boss" is. She is the person who owns the scope of the program and the resources to accomplish the end result. The lines of communication are up and down (one dimensional, up and down within the chain of command). Integration is attained through co-location. In a matrix, there is an additional degree of freedom (left and right or back to the functional group). In the developing matrix organization, the worker is still thinking "up and down" because he or she desires to be part of a program that has an identified product. The functional groups in a matrix do not offer this personal fulfillment. Commitment management provides the functional partner's link to the program. Commitment management creates the link between the partners and the program team through hierarchical commitments, thus identifying what the functional partners must do to make the program a success.

Commitment management also offers a process for the program manager—"the Boss of the Program"— to engage the functional partners who may be trying to pull back into their "silo." Defining deliverables by the program to the partners provides the scope management and integration of the program.

Being dependent on others for upstream deliverables is not comfortable for functional partners. This discomfort is the "trust factor." By depending on others, they feel that they are increasing their risk of being able to provide a deliverable. They are aware of the risk within their respective processes, and an additional risk from an unknown entity is frightening.

Commitment management offers all partners a way to identify where they fit into the program plan and assess the risks introduced by their partners. This can be captured by the term "interdependency." With clear understanding of the plan by the functional partners and all of the risks involved, it is the responsibility of the program team not to "shoot the messenger" when an issue arises. The anticipated result is that the functional partners will come forward, pulling the "Andon cord" immediately upon discovery of a problem. At GM, we say that "red is good." This term comes from the way colors are used to portray status of activities in a plan. "Green" means no problems exist now and in the future. "Red" means that there is a problem. "Red" is a call to the program team to include all partners to rally in support of solving the problem. "Red is good" because it exposes problems and yields solutions and progress. Hiding problems is "bad."

The program manager must put into place a reward system to complement the commitment management process. It must reward performance and attainment of the requirements of the functional partners. It must also contain consequences for non-performance to the program requirements. But it should be benevolent when external and unforeseen events change the context of the program. The program must identify "wins" by the team and celebrate them as a team that includes the functional partners.

## Requirements of Commitment Management

The concept of rolling down requirements to the contributing functional partners is the essence of the commitment management process. Although this paper focuses on the tactical level (the program), it can be utilized from the strategic, through the tactical, and down to the operational levels. It is the responsibility of a target setter to provide the attainable allocated requirements. Realism is ensured by benchmarking within the corporation as well as the competition. A strategic outcome assignor provides requirements and process templates to the program. In turn, the program allocates the requirements to the partners and orchestrates the processes. It then becomes the responsibility of the partners to determine what it will take to meet the allocated targets and proposed necessary tradeoffs.

Traditionally, the functional partners roll up requirements which are contrary to the roll down process being proposed in commitment management. The functional partners are naturally uncomfortable with this process due to their nature to be "risk averse." Roll down is uncomfortable for the partners, but it is necessary to create and manage tension to achieve aggressive business objectives. It is not the intention to prescribe the partner's processes, but focus on the deliverables. Commitment management helps relieve these anxieties. Each functional partner is given the opportunity to define issues, risks, and proposed tradeoffs that they have identified. The integration issues are identified, since this process is reviewed in an open forum with all functional partners present and the program team facilitating. For each issue, a risk assessment is required, which provides better understanding of the issues.

There are two types of issues that arise out of the process. The first surfaces the issues missing from the plan. The second type of issue is a possible future path to take the plan amiss. One resolution for this is to anticipate it happening and have a solution ready before it occurs while another resolution may be to take a different tactic and circumvent the occurrence. This alerts the partners to always be in the proactive mode and not just moving along executing to the program plan waiting for "fires to fight."

To meet the program plan, commitment management encourages the partners to create supportive plans. There is a tendency for functional partners not to create their own individual plans but to expect all of their requirements to be contained in the program plan. Commitment management makes it very clear that detailed plans are necessary to help meet the allocated requirements.

## Commitment Management Tool Kit

In order to obtain commitment to targets, it may be necessary for users of the process to utilize additional processes that complement commitment management, such as "sensitivity analysis." Since we always strive to improve, the program team will drive optimistic targets to get to market faster, at less cost, and with the best quality. On the other hand, the functional partners have the opposite point of view. Since they are risk averse, they are prone to be more pessimistic.

This dilemma drives the need to do sensitivity analysis to the plan. This entails evaluating each deliverable for the extremes in performance to targets. By doing this, we can identify those requirements that have the greatest possible variance and potential impact to the program. Knowing these areas up front in the planning process will identify those deliverables that pose the greatest risk. We can graphically show this with a "Tornado Diagram" (See Exhibit. 2) The name is

**Exhibit 2.** "Tornado Diagram"

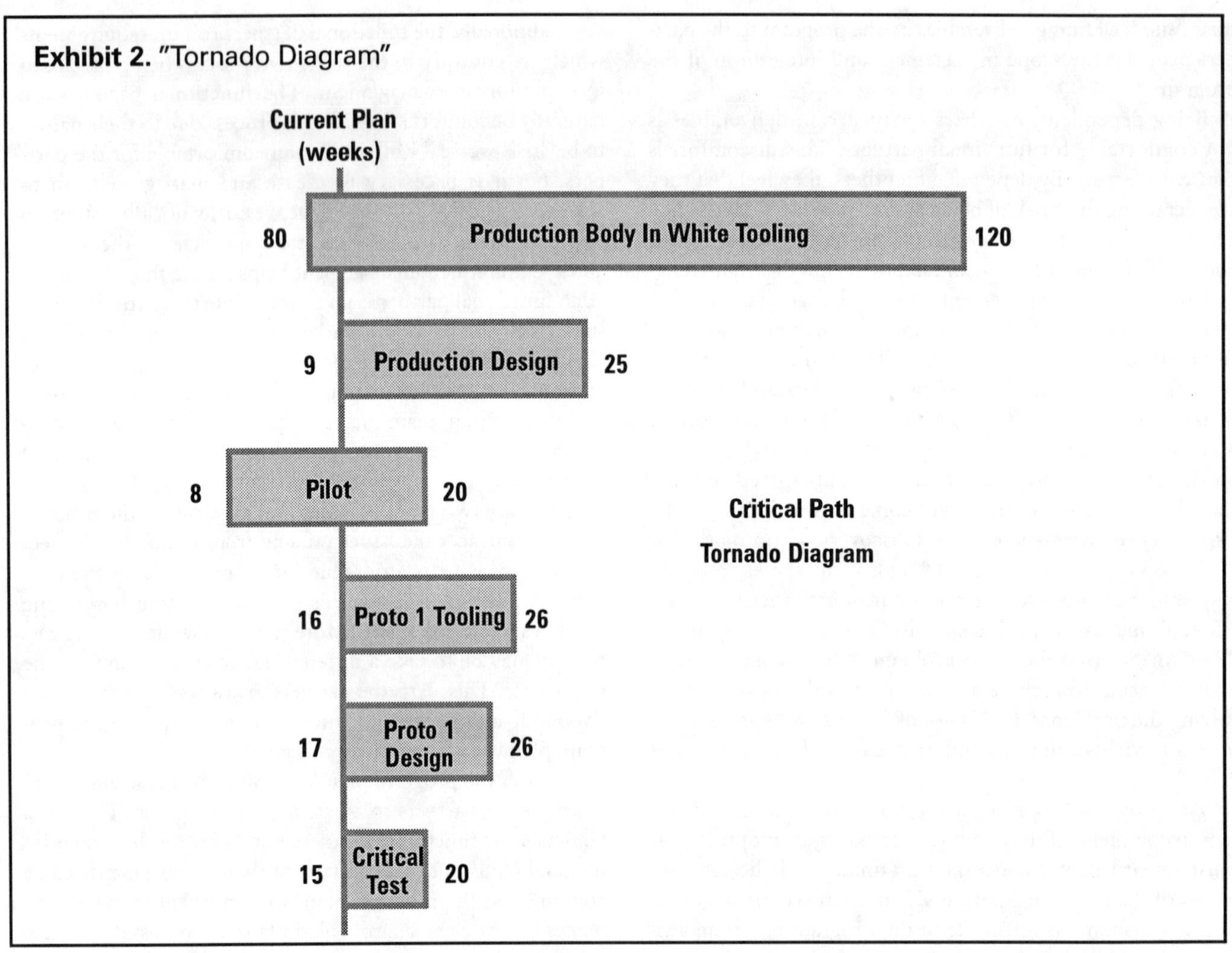


derived from its shape. The areas of greatest risk are positioned at the top and descending in variance. This seems to be a simple process but after the analysis, individuals are sometimes surprised at the insights that they obtain. Experience has shown that the areas of greatest variance are those where there is not an established process or where a plan has not been developed.

This drives the program and the functional partners to either develop or improve their processes or create a more robust plan. This seems to be an obvious solution in the world of project management. But in an immature project management environment consisting of milestone spreadsheets and "arts and charts," this is a revelation.

As program teams use commitment management on additional programs after its initial introduction, learnings will provide improvements to the process. This results in the functional partners becoming more comfortable with "signing up" for commitments. They will also begin to improve their processes and create more adequate plans to support the program plan. They will recognize the advantage of identifying risk up front.

## Extension of Commitment Management to Other Areas

As previously stated, the commitment management process can be utilized at all levels of the organizational structure (strategic, tactical, and operational). The example that was used in this paper was at a tactical level. It rolled down to the functional partners at the operational level. Because value was perceived in commitment management, it was adopted by the functional partners and utilized to roll down requirements into their respective functional organization.

The use of the commitment management process at the strategic level is the next step. Based upon the program commitments to the corporation, the total portfolio can better be assessed and balanced.

Once the commitment management process is in place from the strategic to the operational level, the executive board can review the entire portfolio with a higher confidence level in the validity of the information. Caution should be noted when doing this. Since the view is at such a high level, decisions should not be made for an individual program. The focus should be on enabling processes and resource requirements. This review should be for systemic problems with processes to execute the portfolio. Detailed program reviews should be conducted on an individual basis.

Commitment management is a powerful tool for the integration and communication of the program plan. The use of commitment management will drive the organization to higher levels of the project management discipline. The attainability is dependent on two major factors in the organization:

- Recognizing project management as a core competency.
- Utilization of project management and commitment management at all levels of the organization.

## Summary

Achieving today's aggressive business objectives will be challenging. Organizations are working to improve their product development process throughput while meeting cost and quality objectives. The commitment management process is one of the enablers in meeting these challenges.

Organizations are evolving to project/program (matrix) oriented organizations from a hierarchical program structure. Consequently, a "commitment hierarchy" is required in a matrix organization to provide accountability of the functional partners to the program. Doing without it results in optimizing functional objectives, therefore making it impossible to accomplish trade-offs for the benefit of the program. Traditionally, the functional partners roll up requirements which is contrary to the commitment management roll down process.

The commitment management process focuses on defining the functional partner deliverables to the program and how they interact with other partners. This helps to remove ambiguity and misunderstandings between functional partners and clarifies the expectations of the program. It also encourages the partners to provide detailed plans in support of the program commitments.

The practice of negotiating rather than assigning targets and agreeing on integration points are the secrets to the commitment management process. The commitment management process can be utilized at all levels within the organization—strategic, tactical, and operational. The ongoing benefits of the commitment management process are only beginning to be realized.

## Endnotes


Haeckel, S.H. 1995. "Adaptive Enterprise Design: The Sense-and-Respond Model," *Planning Review* (May-June).

Haeckel, S.H. 1996. "Commitment Management." *ABI White Paper* (February).

# Deliverables Management: Managing Project Complexity

Elliot Chocron, Integrated Management Systems, Inc.
John C. Krolicki, Integrated Management Systems, Inc.

## Introduction

In recent years a number of environmental and competitive pressures have resulted in corporate organizations that are increasingly complex and dynamic. These pressures have caused many corporations and project management professionals to question the appropriateness of the critical path method model for all project phases. Although a detailed discussion of these factors is beyond the scope of this paper, they can be generalized as follows:

- **The increasingly rapid change in technology**: As new product manufacturing methods have come into use, product development processes have also been revised. Less familiar processes can result in poor time, cost, and risk estimates where no historical data are available. Consequently, *there is considerable risk of significant variation and uncertainty along many paths in the traditional critical path method network.*
- **The globalization of both markets and manufacturing operations**: In this environment *the need to focus less on how to do work at a detailed level and more on how to manage interactions among various groups becomes paramount.* Lack of attention to cross-functional and/or other organizational interactions can create situations that additional resources cannot adequately address.
- **Greater competitive pressures for project compression**: Manufacturers, particularly in the automotive industry, have responded to an increasingly demanding customer with faster product turnover. *This creates tremendous pressure to reduce project lead times.*

In this environment an organization is typically charged with a broad scope of work involving many functional units, and automotive manufacturing projects have evolved to reflect these changes. No longer content to throw the project "over the wall," managers are requiring integration of planning and execution between all functional areas. Although each functional area has its own internal goals and planning needs, it is also either directly or indirectly dependent on other groups. Any large project planning model must comprehend these dependencies.

## The Softly Constrained Network Model

Developing a planning approach that successfully models these dependencies must begin by recognizing that large, cross-functional projects are often *softly constrained.* Simply put, the softly constrained project cannot be easily modeled using traditional critical path method techniques without a very high degree of maintenance, if at all. Manufacturing activities can typically start without the desired finished-to-start relationship by assuming a higher degree of risk. Because the project, and by extension the model, is softly constrained, it requires that managers balance timing and quality risks(decisions whose outcomes will greatly impact the project network model. A product designer can deliver a high-quality late design, or he can adjust the quality and deliver it on time by either cutting back the information contained in the design or by making certain assumptions. The question for the project manager is: Which is more important, timeliness or quality? Although awareness of critical path method's limitations for addressing this question has to some extent always been present and is lately receiving greater attention, project managers and planners often continue applying the same techniques that worked reasonably well on small, well-defined, and self-contained projects to large and dynamic cross-functional projects. For those large and complex projects, in particular, the project manager must constantly make decisions that balance risk along multiple paths to best ensure project success. How can a timing plan allow for and support such decisions? Additionally, how can a planning approach drive the kind of organizational "openness" needed to support such a decision-making process?

## A New Approach

The deliverables management (DM) approach shifts the focus from managing the detail in each functional area schedule to managing the relationships between the various functional areas to produce a stable and cohesive master plan. Although each functional area still has a need to manage its own day-to-day work, developing a fully integrated project plan requires a different approach. The deliverables management approach differs from the traditional critical path method approach in certain fundamental ways:



PROJECT MANAGEMENT INSTITUTE 28th Annual Seminars & Symposium
Chicago, Illinois: Papers Presented September 29 to October 1, 1997

- **Network Logic Complexity:** Traditional critical path method networks typically model all relationships in the network logic. Critical path method does not deal well with softly constrained project models and therefore attempts to fully resolve all activity relationships (hard-constraints). Because many of these relationships are truly "soft," the resulting network is highly complex and requires a high degree of maintenance. By contrast, deliverables management models soft-constraints(typically functional schedule relationships(in a project database, thereby greatly simplifying the network logic and its maintenance.
- **Effect of Changes:** Changes made to a traditional critical path method network model typically flow through to the end of the project, creating significant plan instability. Because(as stated above(many relationships are truly soft, these 'flow-throughs' often result in project changes that are incorrect. The deliverables management approach breaks up a plan precisely where relationships are soft. In doing so it limits the effect of changes downstream until the true impact can be evaluated, thereby preserving confidence in the plan.
- **Ability to Isolate Impacts:** Because traditional critical path method networks are both complex and unstable, the true impact of changes are often difficult to isolate. The deliverables management approach, by contrast, relies on managing key functional interfaces or hand-offs. By focusing on these key hand-offs, impacts to downstream functional schedules are easily isolated and highly visible.

## Implementing the Deliverables Management Approach

Establishing the deliverables management approach involves three key steps: breaking the larger plan down into manageable functional plans, identifying interfaces among functional areas, and, finally, tracking and managing the interfaces or deliverables.

The complex, cross-functional nature of automotive projects requires that a project be broken down into manageable segments. Typically these segments are based on areas of functional responsibility and the deliverables management approach splits the plan along these functional lines. Each group is responsible for its own plan and may develop its schedules within the context of traditional project management practices. The focus, though, is on the interactions between the functional groups. Therefore, data consistency need only be maintained at pre-defined hand-off points or deliverables.

After a plan has been split into functional schedules, the deliverable interfaces between the various plans must be defined. Often, simply dividing a plan into its functional components clarifies the interdependencies between the functional groups. For this reason, the first two steps are often performed simultaneously. A deliverable represents a "hand-off" where the product of one functional group's work is needed and used by another group. It may consist of either information or a physical object(a specification, a design, a part, a tool, or any other entity required for one group to proceed based on the work of another. Furthermore, the information or object to be handed-off will be available on a certain date and required on a certain date. The definition of a deliverable must also include a detailed description of the contents and quality of the information or object to be delivered. This description must be agreed to by both the producer and the user of the deliverable. *A simple conceptualization of a deliverable, therefore, is of two dates representing its availability and requirement and a description of the object or information.*

In the deliverables management approach, the availabilities and requirements are defined by their roles in the process and not by their means of generation. Instead of referring to "late finish" or "baseline date," deliverables management defines a deliverable requirement as "the delivery date needed to minimize risk in the receiving functional schedule." This date is strictly controlled by the group receiving the deliverable. Similarly, a deliverable availability is "the deliverable date that minimizes risk to the deliverable quality."

Since the deliverables management process focuses on the interfaces between the functional groups, any number of means may be used within the group to maintain the availability and required dates of those interfaces. Within each functional schedule, different project management tools may be used. Each group may also use different tools over the project's life cycle, as different levels of clarity and detail become available. Early in the plan's life cycle, a manager may use a critical path method schedule based on summary activities with estimated durations. As the plan becomes more clearly defined, he may switch to a more detailed critical path method schedule with best/worse/average case activity duration risk management, S-curve formulas for activity completion estimation, or shop-floor quotes written on the back of an envelope. The manager of a given functional schedule is responsible for the veracity of the deliverable dates, and none of the other functional schedules needs to be planned by the same methods. Ideally, the manager of one functional area isn't concerned with how an upstream manager tracks his timing; he is only concerned with the timeliness and quality of the expected deliverables.

Similarly, the means of producing requirement dates is owned by the manager of the functional schedule that uses the deliverable. A variety of methods may be used to determine when the receiving group can accept a deliverable

**Exhibit 1.** Traditional CPM Network Model (fragment)

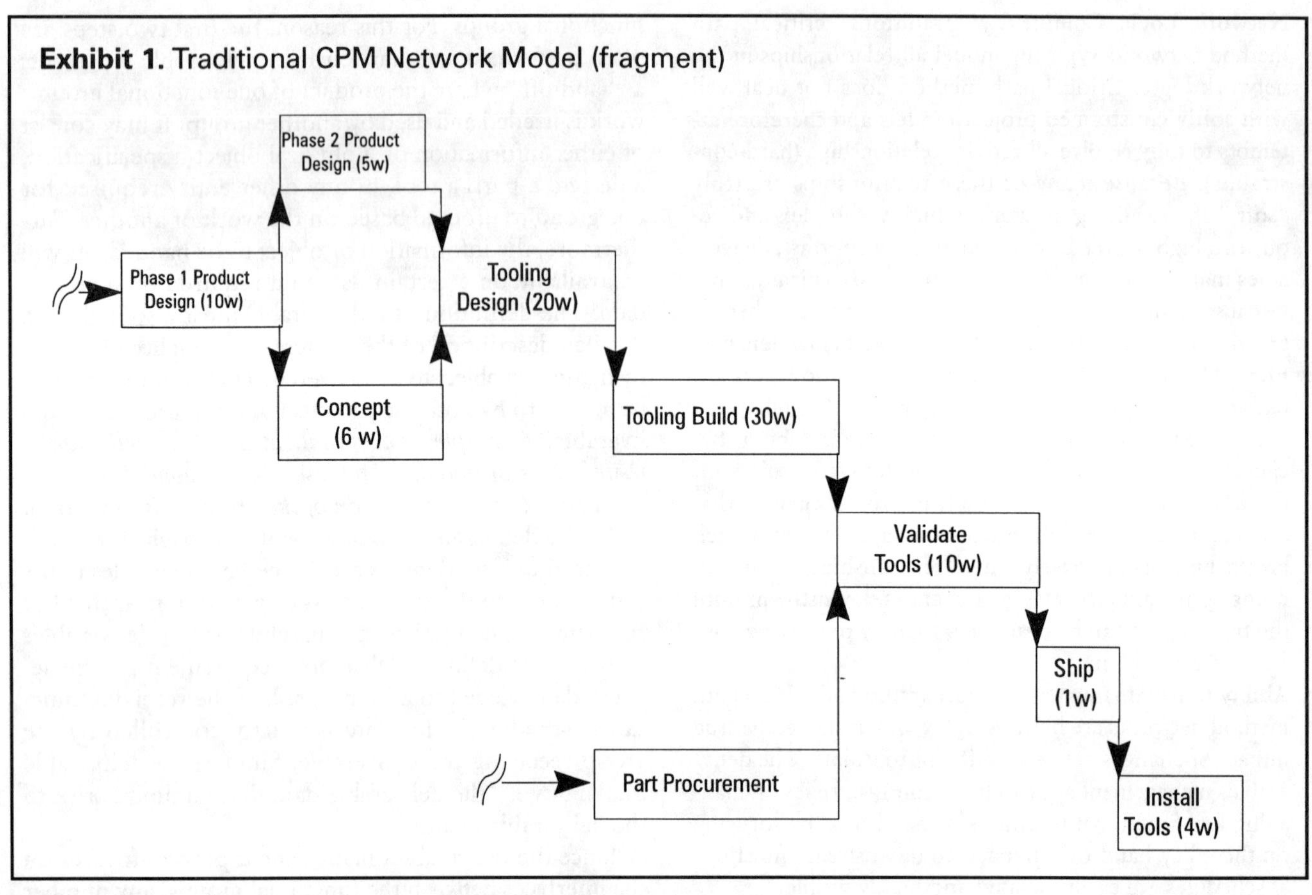


with minimal risk to its schedule. Because deliverable requirement dates are not strictly tied to critical path method calculated dates, there is a tremendous flexibility inherent in the deliverables management approach for setting requirements. Requirements may be based on forward-pass dates or tied to the availability of other high priority deliverables, or they may even represent a date not reflected anywhere in the critical path method schedule (e.g., the relationship is too soft to model and must be hand-maintained).

As noted earlier, deliverables management is especially useful for managing "soft" constraints between functional schedules. A downstream functional manager needs to plan around the availability of a deliverable produced by an upstream group. Using a rigid constraint between the upstream and downstream events over-sensitizes the downstream schedule to every variation in the upstream schedule, resulting in a "whipsawing" effect. The schedule loses stability, usefulness, and credibility. One possible alternative is to use a schedule baseline date but that forces the downstream manager to plan to a snapshot of a schedule that may grow meaningless with time. Using a deliverable availability defined as the minimal risk availability allows the downstream manager to build a meaningful schedule with risk shared between functional groups.

## The Process in Action

Once everything is in place deliverables management can be used to track a program. Consider the example of the fictional ABC Automotive Company—a manufacturer with a new product. ABC has put together a project schedule and the plan includes product design activities and assembly tool development activities, as well as part procurement activities. (Although ABC does the design and engineering work, part fabrication is outsourced for both production and pre-production.) A simplified view of the network (or part of it) appears in Exhibit 1.

This example represents only a portion of the total network. ABC has actually put together a 10,000+ activity network representing each design schedule, summarized part procurement schedules from the vendors, tooling schedules, and plant activities. Additionally, this plan represents an idealized view of what the product development process should entail, and does not recognize, upfront, any potential trade-offs that may come to play during execution of the plan.

**Exhibit 2.** Deliverables Management Network Model (fragment)

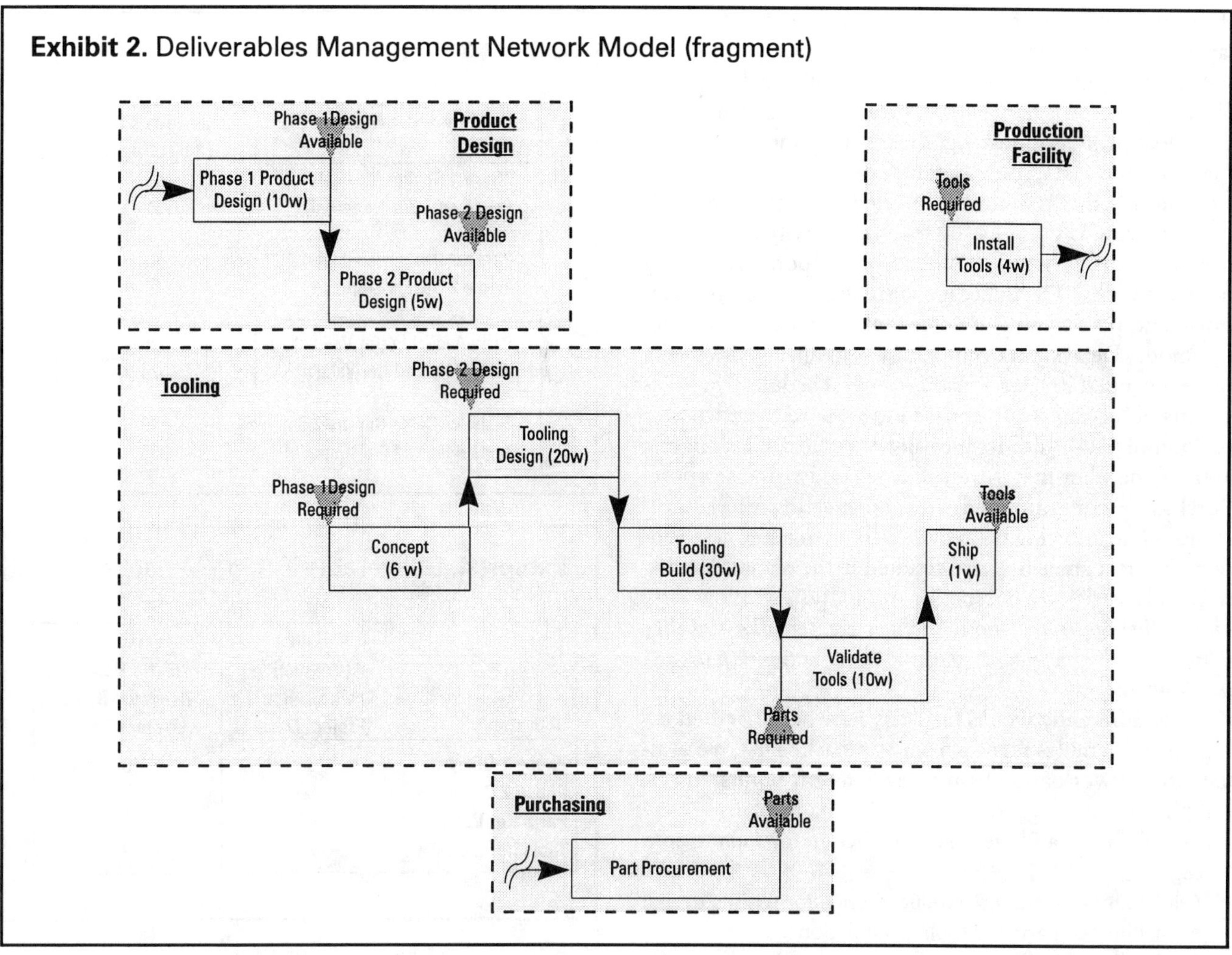


Once the initial plan has been approved, ABC begins tracking against the baseline critical path. After several updates, "Phase 2 Product Design" has been delayed five weeks due to the late addition of new product requirements from the marketing division. These changes have increased the activity duration from five weeks to ten weeks. Although "Phase 2 Product Design" was not on the original critical path (denoted by bold boxes in Exhibit 1), it has delayed the schedule end date by four weeks and has resulted in a revised critical path.

Ideally, the tooling manager prefers to begin work with a "Phase 2 Product Design," but, beginning with the phase 1, product design can be acceptable under certain conditions. The difference between the phases is that the phase 1 design is not as mature or stable as the phase 2 design, where usually some test results have validated the product engineering work. In our example, the tooling manager elects to accept the risk of a less mature product design rather than deliver late tooling. He made this decision by also considering the impact to the plan downstream of him—the plant could not risk missing an upcoming plant downtime window for tool installation. Missing that window by even a few days could result in a project delay of four months (coinciding with the next available window). The network is reworked to show that tooling designs may begin with a "Phase 1 Product Design," so long as "Phase 1 Product Design" is available at approximately the halfway point. Although the network changes were extensive(requiring modifications to hundreds of activities representing the approximately 400 tools in the functional schedule(the tooling manager expects the changes will help recover the lost time from product design.

Unfortunately, something else has happened while the tooling manager was evaluating his options. Because the forecasted delay in the product design caused a similar delay in some key critical path activities—including tooling validation—purchasing has now gained four weeks of float. In reaction, the part procurement activity has been delayed by four weeks to take advantage of a low cost vendor's availability in that time frame. The end result is that the tooling manager can recover only one week of the delay due to other changes in the schedule. Because tool installation is now projected to miss the available down-time window, the program is now delayed by four months. Only lost production or significant overtime can recoup this lost time and at considerable cost.

Although this is an oversimplified example, it does illustrate a few key points. By focusing heavily on the critical path, it is easy to lose sight of other potentially risky network paths. The schedule is subject to wide fluctuations, and participants are constantly forced into a reactive mode. Delays can occur in downstream activities only to be recouped in later versions of the schedule. These incidents of "crying wolf" can lead to reduced confidence in the overall plan. Additionally, any reduction of risk in one area of the plan may result in increased risk elsewhere. Purchasing congratulated itself on meeting its requirements while reducing costs by switching to a low cost vendor. Unfortunately, this also resulted in the plant incurring tremendous risk by missing its installation window. *Any alternative approach should deliver greater plan stability while providing a means to evaluate all network paths simultaneously.*

How differently would the delay have been handled using the deliverables management approach? First, we evaluate the network and identify key hand-off points. In this sample, we see that there are four key hand-offs:

- Availability of a Phase 1 Product Design for tooling concept
- Availability of a Phase 2 Product Design for tooling design
- Availability of parts for tooling validation
- Availability of tools for installation at the plant

With these hand-offs in mind, we redraw the network model as shown in Exhibit 2. Note that we now have four separate functional schedules (denoted by a broken-line box) representing different functional groups: product design, tooling, purchasing, and the production facility. Although each functional schedule may have an internal critical path, the overall critical path is not maintained in the logic.

In this example, although we have identified four hand-offs there are, in fact, eight dates (denoted by triangles in Exhibit 2.) For a true hand-off to exist, there must be both an available date and a requirement date, representing a producer and a receiver of data or some physical object. The requirement represents the date the downstream schedule needs the deliverable in order to minimize risk to its process. In our example, risk is minimal when tooling design begins with a Phase 2 Product Design. Finally, the deliverables must be available when the downstream schedule intends to use them (usually the forward-pass, or early start, date). The deliverables in our example might appear as follows

**Exhibit 3.** Network Deliverables

| Deliverable Description | Deliverable Date (Project Days) |
|---|---|
| Phase 1 Design Available | 50 |
| Phase 1 Design Required | 51 |
| Phase 2 Design Available | 70 |
| Phase 2 Design Required | 76 |
| Parts Available (for Valid'n) | 325 |
| Parts Required (for Valid'n) | 326 |
| Tools Available (for Install'n) | 380 |
| Tools Required (for Install'n) | 383 |

**Exhibit 4.** Deliverable Timing Variance

| Deliverable | Variance (Original) Avail. vs. Req'd (Project Days) | Variance (After Delay) Avail. vs. Req'd (Project Days) |
|---|---|---|
| Phase 1 Design | 0 | 0 |
| Phase 2 Design | 5 | -20 |
| Parts (for Valid'n) | 0 | 0 |
| Tools (for Install'n) | 2 | 2 |

Requirements in this example are not set based on the backward pass (late-finish) dates. Often, requirement dates represent forward-pass ( early start) dates, although they also may be negotiated to minimize overall risk by sharing available float. In the latter case, dependence on critical path method is even further reduced. In our example, the "tools required" date—the date the plant wants the tools in order to begin installation—represents a negotiated date. The tools will not be considered late unless they delay installation by more than two days; in other words, the tools may be delivered up to two days into the start of the plant downtime and still permit installation to complete on time.

When Phase 2 Product Design is delayed, the remaining schedules are not automatically delayed forcing everyone into a reactive mode. Instead, the tooling manager's schedule alone is impacted. He evaluates the delay, implements a recovery plan, and the overall plan remains stable.

One might comment that purchasing, in the above example, would not have seen the tooling schedule delay until all the issues had been resolved and therefore would not have reacted prematurely. Unfortunately, in the real world this typically means that the true plan status is not revealed until the tools are loaded on the truck for delivery, whether early, on time, or late. Furthermore, product design may take a similar approach and not publicize *its* schedules until it is simply too late for the tooling manager to initiate any meaningful recovery plan. Using the deliverables management approach, when a deliverable is late to its requirement, all of the players are alerted to a potential problem. Although downstream functional areas can begin to internally evaluate the potential impact, no changes are made in downstream functional schedules until recovery plans have been considered.

## Conclusion

The deliverables management approach to managing projects combines traditional critical path method scheduling techniques with a relational database concept for modeling functional interfaces. Although the database infrastructure for such a planning approach has not been addressed in this paper, the techniques involved are common.

The deliverables management approach changes the focus of plan management from "why did the project date slip?" to "who is potentially in trouble and needs help?" Perhaps the greatest benefit of applying the deliverables management approach is that by focusing closely on functional interfaces, an organization is forced to identify and carefully define up-front any critical hand-off points across all project paths. A simple look at the differences between a deliverable's available date and its required date allows the project manager to quickly scan all paths in the project model. By closely monitoring deliverables, an organization can more effectively manage the project outcome by applying resources and recovery plans where they are most needed, regardless of their relationship to the *critical path*. The end result is a well-understood and stable plan that focuses the organization on the truly high risk areas.

### Additional Reading


Skimin, William E. 1993. *Working Around CPM: Planning and Managing Complex Projects.* Proceedings of the 1993 Project Management Institute Annual Seminar/Symposium.

Skimin, William E.. and Elliot Chocron. 1997. *The Mythical Critical Path:Managing for Project Failure with CPM.* Proceedings, 1997 PMI Annual Seminar/Symposium.

# Project Management In The Manufacturing Environment

Stephen P. Gress, PMP — Consulting Manager, Management Technologies, Inc.

Most manufacturing organizations have a well-defined structure and well-established, capable, and robust manufacturing processes to produce goods for their customers. The business functions of these manufacturing organizations (accounting, human resources, marketing, engineering, material control, production, and so on) are designed to measure and support these manufacturing processes. The maintenance function, as well, is focused on supporting the manufacturing processes in keeping the plant's equipment running and making goods. However, there are also many maintenance activities that interfere with the operation of the plant's facilities but are necessary to continue supporting the plant's capable and robust manufacturing processes.

Some of these maintenance activities include major machine repairs, equipment upgrades and modifications, new equipment installations, facility rearranges, process improvements, facility decommissions, and new product launches. All manufacturing organizations perform these activities at one time or another and some quite often. However, these activities carried out by the maintenance forces are usually assigned at the last minute, with little time for preparation or planning, and delegated to the foremen or supervisors to "get it done however they need to" with little oversight or performance tracking. This might work out all right if we have enough resources available to do the work.

Unfortunately, we don't always have the people available to do these maintenance activities, or, if they are available, they are usually assigned to supporting production demands. Once we free the maintenance forces to do the work, all too often we don't have materials on site or the right equipment to do the job. We then waste valuable time scrambling to acquire all of the materials and the right equipment only to find out we don't have a budget allocated to do the work in the first place. Why don't we apply the same sense of discipline and structure to our maintenance activities as we do to our manufacturing activities?

## What Is Project Management?

Project management provides us the tools and techniques to apply the discipline and structure needed to complete our projects successfully. First, let's define what a project is. A project is a temporary endeavor undertaken to create a unique product or service (PMBOK Guide 1996). Projects within a manufacturing environment share many common characteristics, some of which are: they have a defined duration, a preset budget, involve people with different skills, compete for the same limited resources that are needed for production, and they produce unique results. From this definition all of the maintenance activities mentioned earlier can be defined as projects; they have a beginning and end, a budget, many different resource requirements, and they have a predetermined objective. Resources are usually the largest constraining factor in our manufacturing plants; therefore, it is imperative that we maximize their utilization. These resource requirements can be referred to as the 4M's: money, manpower, machines, and materials.

Since these activities can be considered as projects we can apply modern project management principles and techniques to our maintenance projects to complete them successfully. Successful projects are projects that are completed on time, within budget, and to the specified quality levels, and they satisfy the customer. The modern definition of project management is the application of knowledge, skills, tools, and techniques to project activities in order to meet or exceed stakeholder needs and expectations from a project (PMBOK Guide 1996). The manufacturing organization is the project stakeholder whose needs and expectations we are trying to meet or exceed.

Project management enables the manufacturing organization to better manage their time, resource utilization, budget, and quality parameters for all of their maintenance projects.

## Developing a Project Management Process

Even though each maintenance project requires different skills and resources and produces a unique result, we can plan, execute, and control our many maintenance projects by applying modern project management principles and techniques in a consistent and repeatable method. This means that if we perform project management in a consistent and repeatable manner, we can define a process for it. Project management, when considered as a manufacturing support process, enables the manufacturer to consistently implement and complete their projects successfully.

A typical project management process has approximately twelve steps. We begin by defining the scope of our project (1) and then validate it against our organizational objectives (2). Once we determine it is aligned with our objectives, we need to assign a champion (3) to guide the project through to completion and assign a project team (4) to plan and implement the project. The team then develops a plan with the 4M requirements (5) to satisfy the project objectives and validates the plan with subject matter experts (6). Once we agree on a plan, we have to balance the 4M's of the project against the accumulated resource needs of all of the other projects (7) since we are constrained by the 4M's. We can then schedule and acquire our resource needs (8) in a more disciplined and structured manner. When the scheduled time arrives to implement our project, we conduct a kick-off meeting (9) to brief all of the project participants on the project scope and plan and clarify any last minute issues and questions. We now have a well-defined plan of action and all of our resource requirements scheduled to implement the project successfully (10). As the project is under way, we must track and monitor our progress (11) to measure our performance and take corrective actions when needed and for continuous improvement. Upon completion of the project, we conduct a project close-out meeting (12) to verify we completed our project scope, document lessons learned, close the budget, and reassign the project team to other projects.

Depending on the size and complexity of the manufacturing organization and the number of projects they undertake, they might combine some of the above steps or break down the steps in further detail. Regardless, these are the basic process steps that any manufacturing organization should include in its project management process. Let's take a closer look at this process.

## Defining and Validating the Scope of the Project Work (Steps 1 & 2)

The first step, in order to complete your projects successfully, is to document the scope of the project before you begin so that every participant has the same understanding of the project's objectives. It is also important to validate and get consensus from the organization that the scope will meet its needs and expectations. This is no simple matter but is necessary to get proper management support and sponsorship. This documented scope will also serve as the basis for all future decisions regarding the project and guard against scope creep. Scope creep can ruin a project by having other members of the organization throw in additional work once the project is under way "since the skilled tradesmen were there anyway" or "as long as the equipment is down." This is a sure-fire way to blow your budget and distract the project participants from the project's original objectives.

**Exhibit 1.** The 4M's

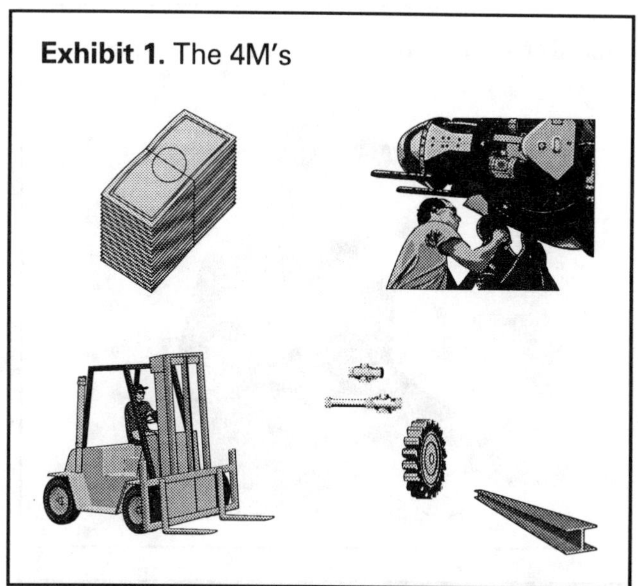

## Assigning the Champion and Team (Steps 3 & 4)

Next, we have to assign a project champion who has some familiarity with the project's scope and can coordinate the appropriate resources (4M's) to successfully complete the project. The project champion's first objective should be to assemble a project team. It is important to get the skilled tradesmen involved in the project management process, and the best way to do this is to have the people that do the work plan the work. Though it is impractical to have all tradesmen participate in the planning of all projects, and it is not necessary, we should have a representative from each of the major trades as a member of the project team. Depending on the organization, this might be a permanent team that plans all of the organization's projects, or the members might rotate with each project.

Either way, this will take a considerable amount of effort in training the maintenance forces in project management principles and techniques, but once they develop these skills, their work on the floor usually improves as well.

This is because they have thought through the entire project with other skilled tradesmen, developed a plan of action, exchanged ideas for improvement, and achieved a sense of ownership and commitment to get the project done on time and within budget.

## Developing a Plan with the 4M's (Steps 5 & 6)

The project champion and project team should review the project scope document and all supporting documentation—such as engineering drawings and prints, open work orders and maintenance records, allocated budgets, replacement parts lists, and operating procedures—to put together a logical plan of activities and 4M requirements. The team then

**Exhibit 2.** Document the Scope

**Exhibit 3.** Assign Project Champion

should conduct a site visit to determine if there will be any interferences or special equipment needs and how to minimize the disturbance to the production process. With this information, the team can decompose the project into successive levels of detail using a work breakdown structure format until they reach the task level. At the task level the activities should have a duration, resource assignment, and cost associated with each task. The next step is to take these tasks and sequence them into a logical order of progression by assigning dependencies between tasks, either mandatory or discretionary, and imposing any timing constraints on the project. Once the plan is put together, again, we must validate that the plan fulfills the objectives of the scope and satisfies the expectations of the organization. This is best done by having the project champion and any subject matter experts review the plan for completeness. By determining the tasks required

**Exhibit 4.** Develop a Plan of the 4M's

to complete a project, how long it will take to do each task, who will do each task, and the order in which they must occur, we have put together a comprehensive plan to complete our project successfully.

### Scheduling the 4M's (Steps 7 & 8)

Using one of the many project management software packages available on the market today, the project team can easily input a project plan with activities, logical dependencies, resource assignments, and constraints into a computer. This software will calculate a critical path method (CPM) schedule for the project and determine the start and finish dates for all of the project activities as well as generate a variety of reports to review the project tasks, resource needs, and costs. Before we can commit to this project schedule, though, we need to compare it against the other projects the manufacturing organization is planning to do as well. A project schedule might look good to one manager, but there might also be three other managers planning on doing their projects at the same time with the same resources. We have to balance the resource requirements of all maintenance projects against the resources available within the entire manufacturing organization. Once we have balanced the competing resource demands of the various projects and reached agreement on when the projects will be done—so as to minimize interferences with production demands—we can schedule our manpower, allocate money, and order materials and machines to arrive when needed.

### Kicking off and Implementing the Project (Steps 9 & 10)

Before we actually perform any work, the project champion needs to bring all of the project participants together to review the scope of the project, its objectives, and the plan for implementation in a kick-off meeting. Since it is impractical to involve everybody in the planning process, this is the time

**Exhibit 5.** Balancing the 4M's

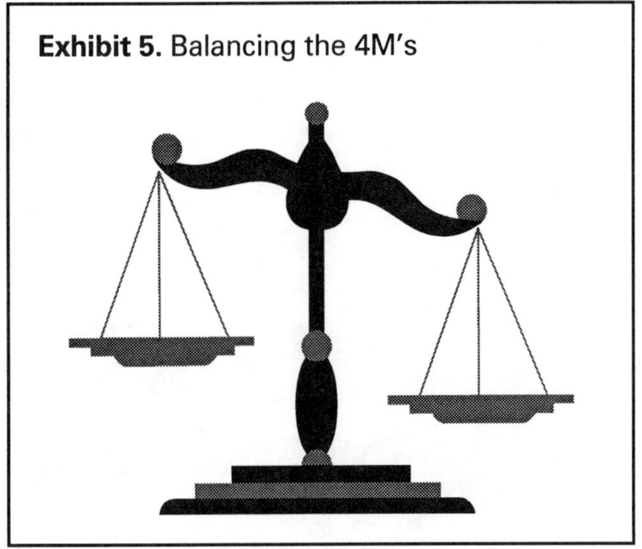

**Exhibit 6.** Kick Off Meetings

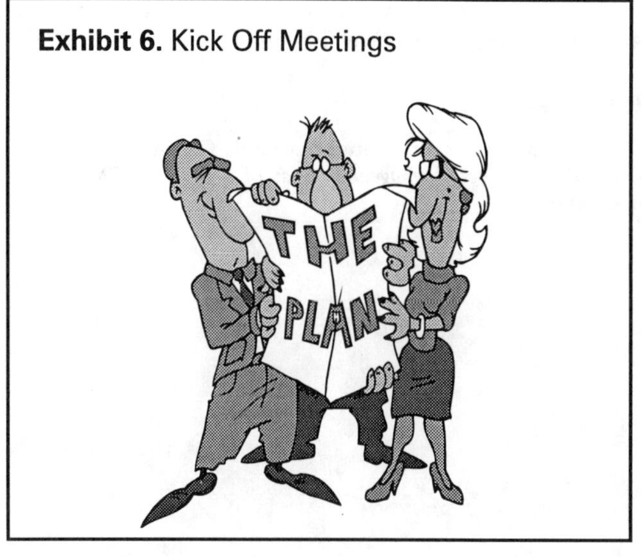


to brief all of the tradesmen and engineers on what the objectives of the project are, the plan of action to accomplish them, and the manpower assignments for each task. It also provides a final review and validation of the plan and will prevent a lot of duplication of effort and rework when everybody knows the entire scope of the project, not just their assignment for the day. Now we are ready to go out and implement our maintenance project.

### Monitoring and Closing out the Project (Steps 11 & 12)

As we are implementing our project, it is also important to track our progress. This will provide valuable feedback in improving future project plan development. More importantly, though, it will allow us to measure how we are performing to our plan, if we are ahead of or behind schedule, and the impact on the project completion date and budget. This is called earned value analysis and is an important tool in keeping the project on track. We can now develop corrective actions to get the project back on schedule and within budget prior to the scheduled completion date. This beats finding out I'm only 80 percent done with my project, I'm already over budget, and I was supposed to be done last week!

When the project is done, and before everybody walks away (or runs away, depending on how the project turns out), the project participants should have a close-out meeting. All of the project documentation is organized and brought to this meeting to review whether the project's objectives were satisfied and how we performed to schedule and budget. This also allows the project champion to capture lessons learned that can be applied to future projects because, if the project went well, he will inevitably be assigned to another project. This brings formal closure to the project and allows the participants to be assigned to the next project.

**Exhibit 7.** Monitoring Performance

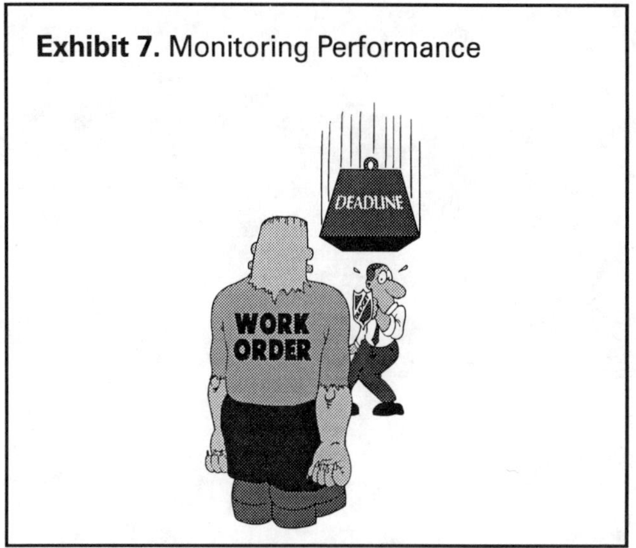


## Why Implement a Project Management Process?

Maintenance forces do a considerable amount of project work and by implementing a standard project management process the manufacturing organization can make better use of their 4M's. A project management process also enables the maintenance organization to better support the manufacturing processes by minimizing the impact of necessary project work on production.

Since very few manufacturing organizations in today's competitive manufacturing environment have unlimited manpower, machines, materials, and money to keep their manufacturing processes running, they have to do as much as possible with what they currently have or less. The application of project management in the manufacturing plant enables the organization to maximize its return on the investment in 4M's and be competitive well into the future.

## References

Project Management Institute Standards Committee. 1996. *A Guide to the Project Management Body of Knowledge*. PMI Communications.

# Critical Path Management in a Part Number World

Matthew J. Steigerwald, Integrated Management Systems, Inc.

## Overview

A new model vehicle development program is a large undertaking. The scope of the project and the number of interfaces among the stakeholders make it one of the most complicated endeavors regularly undertaken by American industry. The project management activity to support this effort takes many forms. Program planning establishes the overall benchmarks. System planners work with the product development teams to manage interface areas. Functional planners support the engineering organizations—die engineering, prototype, dimensional management, chassis and powertrain engineering. At the component level, timing plans are constructed to plan and track the development of the thousands of parts that make up the vehicle.

The detail component and tool planning must be able to support the needs of program and system planning efforts. Part status information can be summarized according to part characteristics to provide views across many vehicle subsystems and for the entire vehicle. However, to ensure that they are comprehensive, these summaries must be based on detailed information that captures the entire program scope.

Scope management is an essential concern of any project. In the automotive industry scope management at its most elemental level boils down to definition and maintenance of the parts list. This responsibility is officially assigned to the specifications and release group, in support of the procurement activity. However, other parts of the engineering community have a need for this information in the performance of daily activities; thus, groups tracking design, cost, mass, and tooling frequently maintain parts lists of their own. Similarly, the component timing activity requires an accurate parts list.

In support of the early phases of the program planning activity—which includes long lead part planning—associating the component plans to part numbers is not necessary. At this stage, plans are developed based on generic part content. As the program matures, however, the ability to report at a detail level becomes more important. Program management requires status information at the part number level as critical program benchmarks approach. The component planning activity must be able to manage part level status information in order to fully serve the needs of its customers.

While a critical path schedule is a flexible and effective method of planning and tracking the part development process, the owners of part deliverables typically track status in table format. Detailed databases are developed to track activities such as part design and release, prototype part procurement, and production part approval. These systems may track intermediate events that support the final part deliverable, but the events are typically not linked with critical path constraints. This type of system is less adept at planning functions than a critical path approach, but it is well suited for tracking large numbers of detail events. By incorporating the parts list into the critical path planning system, component planning can establish an interface to the information in these databases.

## The Production Parts Database

Developing and maintaining the production parts database is a complex endeavor. At the big three automotive manufacturers the activity is assigned to a specific department. At General Motors it is the responsibility of the specification group; at Ford it is the timing release and materials control department; at Chrysler the function is performed by operations and releasing. Large corporate databases have been developed to hold this information. General Motors uses a database known as PDS (Product Description System); Ford's system is called WERS (Worldwide Engineering Release System); at Chrysler it is PDB (Parts Database).

The production parts database contains many related tables designed to track various part characteristics, many that are not of interest to the scheduling activity. For example, engineering change information will not be useful if parts schedules are not tracked to this level of detail. The first step in constructing an effective interface is to develop a set of queries that will extract information from the production system. The queries must extract all the relevant information without overwhelming the recipient with the sheer volume of data that can be found in the production system.

Two types of part information in the production parts database are of primary interest: general part data and part usage data. General part information captures data about the part that is true for all of its usages. Part number, generic part name, and overall design responsibility are examples of general part information. Part usage information describes a part



PROJECT MANAGEMENT INSTITUTE 28th Annual Seminars & Symposium
Chicago, Illinois: Papers Presented September 29 to October 1, 1997

**Exhibit 1.** Interfacing to the Production Parts Database

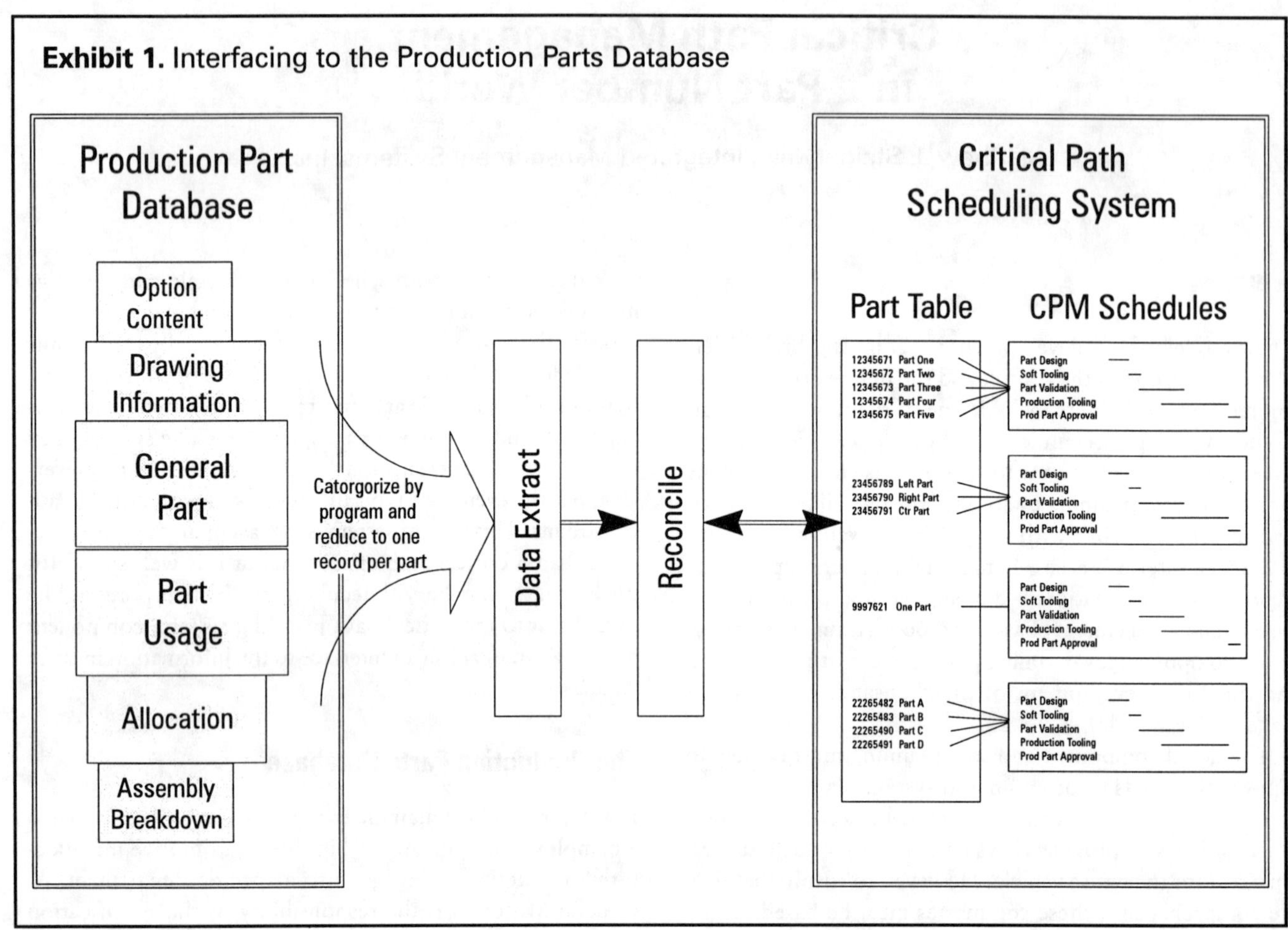


as it applies to a specific model and to a specific usage on that vehicle. Much of the interesting information about a part is related to its usages: the part name specific to its usage, the model years that a part is used, the models that it is used on, the first model year that a part is used, product development team, and release engineer.

In order to make the production part data useful to the planning activity, the data extract must perform two key functions. It must first be able to assign parts to the vehicle programs as defined in the critical path method scheduling system. A part may be used on several programs, and with the growing focus on flexible manufacturing and part commonization, this is ever more prevalent. While the vehicle program(s) that a part belongs to is a key piece of information, it is not specifically captured in the production database. The application of a part to its programs must be derived from information such as model year, carline, and marketing division.

Secondly, the data extract must reduce the part data to one record per part number. What may seem simple intuitively—a single line item for each part number—can require involved queries to achieve. A part can have many usages, both on different vehicles and different applications on the same vehicle. A part might be used on the two door and the four door versions of the same car. A part such as a fastener or a bracket can be used in multiple areas of the vehicle, serving different functions. These situations create multiple part usage records. To the engineering community, however, the part is a single entity. The extraction queries will need to perform some elaborate functions to retain all the key information from the many usages while presenting the part as a single record. Establishing an effective process to extract data from the production parts database accomplishes the first step in implementing an interface to the critical path scheduling system (see Exhibit 1).

The data extract from the production parts database provides the basis for an electronic interface to the critical path method scheduling system. In doing so it can also serve other uses. Extracting this information and making it accessible to the engineering community in a consistent format adds value. Much redundant effort is spent by the various functional groups maintaining their own parts lists. Moreover, greater visibility will improve the quality of the data in the production database. Data consistency will also be enhanced as standard naming conventions for part names and style codes are made available. Making the information available electronically further increases its value.

## Tracking Part Data in the Critical Path Scheduling System

Before we can consider coordinating part content in the critical path scheduling system with the production parts database, the scheduling system must contain part numbers. A separate table to store part information, as depicted in Exhibit 1, is advised. This table will capture data, such as part number, part name, and release responsibility, from the production system. It may also contain fields not found in the production system, such as the manufacturing process, whether the part is considered long lead, and whether a detailed schedule is required.

An electronic interface to the production parts database requires a process for reconciling content. The definition of part content is an evolutionary process. Shifts in program direction, analysis of test results, and cost and manufacturing initiatives can cause parts to be added or deleted from a program. In other situations, a part may receive a new part number as part of the engineering change control process although ideally both systems would share a stable common key, allowing for more efficient reconciliation. These situations make it necessary to institute a process to keep the part table in the critical path method scheduling system up to date with the production part content.

As shown in Exhibit 1, the reconciliation process receives data from both the production database and the critical path method system. The process itself occurs outside the two systems. A typical reconciliation process queries the production database every two weeks. The data is extracted and formatted as outlined above, and then compared both to the part data from the scheduling system and to the previous extract. For part numbers that exist in both systems, reports that highlight discrepancies in part demographic information are generated. The reconciliation process also produces reports for parts that exist in one system but not the other. Similarly, the extracted data is compared to the previous extract from the production database; reports will show changes to part information as well as added and deleted parts. Once the data has been reconciled, the part information in the critical path method system can be refreshed.

With the part content incorporated into the critical path scheduling system, parts can be linked to the critical path method schedules. In general, component and tool schedules represent the timing for more than one part number. As shown in Exhibit 1, a single schedule can be related to the group of part numbers it represents. In this manner, timing can be associated to the program part content without unduly burdening the component scheduling activity.

Once the critical path activities have been linked to the part content, the scheduling system can associate milestone dates from the networks to the parts. Alternatively, key deliverable data from other systems can be incorporated into the scheduling system and used to drive the activity networks.

Incorporating the part content into the scheduling system through an interface to the production parts database ensures that the component planning is based on a solid scope foundation. Furthermore, it provides the opportunity to establish interfaces with other part-based systems.

## Interfacing with Part Status Systems

Many groups within the engineering organization track status information at a part number level. The critical path method scheduling system interfaces with these systems at three critical points: the design schedule, prototype procurement, and production parts readiness. Each of these systems is in turn fed with part information from the production parts database. In many situations they are adjuncts of the production parts database. While an effective interface to the production database will greatly reduce the task of reconciling part content with these systems, it will not eliminate it altogether.

### Design Schedule

Perhaps the most important interface to the component schedules is the design schedule. A comprehensive process for scheduling the design activity is a key success factor for a vehicle development program. Management of this activity through an integrated schedule is essential. A thorough effort to establish design release requirements, obtain forecasts of estimated completions, enact recovery plans where necessary, and monitor progress to schedule is a primary focus of project management in the automotive industry. The design schedule enables component and tool planning to proceed based on the receipt of a verifiable deliverable.

The development of detail designs is the first activity that produces a measurable deliverable at a part number level. As such, the design schedule serves as an important source of confirmation of the part content from the production database. The design schedule is also the official source for design release dates. During the early planning phases, design releases are projected using estimated design durations and critical path techniques. Once a design schedule is available, the scheduled dates are used to kick off the downstream tooling and procurement activities. Information that would affect a promised release date should be fed back through the design schedule process.

The critical path component schedules also provide information back to the design schedule. Design release requirement dates are developed using a backward pass from part availability requirements, incorporating tooling and procurement lead times. Using a critical path system provides the necessary flexibility to model the various activities and relationships that may be required for different parts. Based on this late schedule date and some knowledge of what the design activity can achieve, a part release requirement date can be negotiated. This requirement may reserve some of the float for the manufacturing activity.

An effective component and tool scheduling system will leverage the data in the design schedule. To reenter these dates into the component schedules would be time consuming and prone to clerical error. The preferred solution is an electronic interface. The design schedule release dates can be matched to the part content in the scheduling system. The corresponding part release milestones in the activity networks can be updated via the link to the part table.

### Prototype Procurement

Prototype or experimental vehicle and subsystem builds are major events in the vehicle development cycle. While more and more emphasis and engineering resources are being placed on computer-aided analytical tools, physical builds still represent the best opportunity to develop and confirm vehicle, subsystem, and part designs. Unlike analytical models, it takes parts to build a physical property. As elsewhere in the automotive industry, where there are parts, there is a system to track them.

Part availability is a major factor in determining readiness for the build. For build events that are months or years in the future, critical path networks provide the best means of tracking part status. After the prototype procurement group has begun tracking its activity in the procurement system, however, this data becomes the master source of part status information. Since the purchasing group works directly with the part suppliers, and is ultimately responsible for providing the parts to the build, their dates take precedence over the critical path method forecasts. However, every effort should be made to resolve discrepancies between the two tracking systems.

Leveraging the procurement system also provides the opportunity to monitor part procurement at a more detailed level. Critical path networks typically track a tooling activity that ends with a part availability milestone. The detail tasks that occur over the part procurement duration do not lend themselves to critical path networking. However, some key deliverables are tracked in the procurement system. Events such as purchase request issued, purchase order issued, and part available in warehouse are also key indicators of part readiness. This information can be extracted from the procurement system and used to monitor the progress of the detail events supporting the part delivery. Making the information more readily available to engineering improves its reliability and highlights areas of concern before they become genuine problems.

### Production Parts Readiness

The primary focus of the production parts readiness organization is to ensure that production approved parts are available for the start of production. The component and tooling schedules are similarly focused. If a design intent part is not available for a prototype build, work around plans are developed. But if a dimensionally correct part from a capable production tool is not available for Pilot or Job One, serious countermeasures are in order. The need for accurate status information at a part number level is most urgent when management reviews readiness for the production build.

Production part status is tracked in the production parts readiness database. This database is typically an electronic offshoot of the production parts database. Much of the complexity in the production database is driven by the requirement to support parts readiness and the downstream production scheduling activity. Processing the information from the parts readiness database involves similar challenges to those presented by the production part database. The parts must be assigned to their respective vehicle programs. Also a part may be sourced to more than one supplier, requiring processing to reduce the data to one record per part number.

The longer lead times of production tools allow greater opportunity to balance the information in the production readiness database with the component schedules. Typically, the production readiness group starts at square one. They contact the parts suppliers to obtain status information with no reference to the component plans that have been developed and maintained since the early phases of the program. With the production part content integrated into the critical path scheduling system, the planning activity can provide part status forecasts to initiate the readiness database in a format that can be easily used.

Once the parts readiness organization has taken responsibility for tracking production part status, component scheduling should defer to it. The existence of two competing sets of parts status information within the organization is an untenable situation. The scheduling group may choose to incorporate the parts readiness data into the critical path method system for reporting purposes and to retain a historical record. Great care should be taken to ensure that the data is consistent between the two.

### Managing Multiple Interfaces

As we have seen, extracting data from the production systems allows the project management activity greater access to part

**Exhibit 2.** Managing Multiple Interfaces

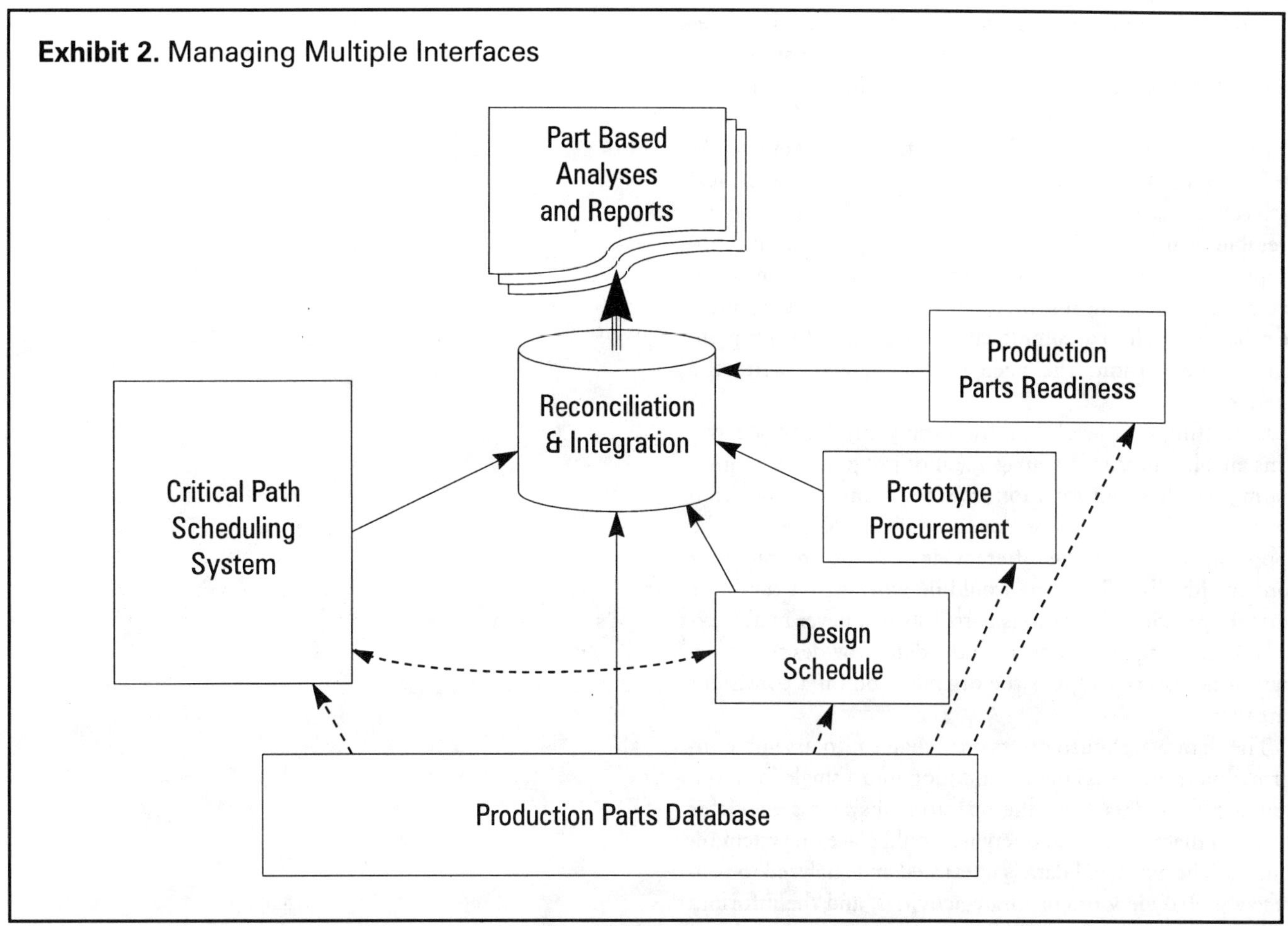


level content and status information. Part status information from the owners of the various detail part deliverables can be compared and integrated with the critical path component plans. To provide a more complete view of the program, part level information from these various sources can be collected and integrated in a central repository. This data will by its nature be static and must be refreshed on a regular basis from the source databases. This approach, known as data warehousing, is a powerful technique for integrating and managing information across a corporation.

The data warehouse receives inputs from many sources of part information, as shown in Exhibit 2. Frequently, there are interfaces that occur outside this process, such as the one shown between the critical path method scheduling system and the design schedule. These interfaces are important and serve to improve the quality of the incoming data. They should not, however, be confused with the enterprise level integration that takes place in the data warehouse.

Before part data can be integrated, it must be reconciled. Data extraction routines are required to provide a consistent flow of data from the various sources. The data is extracted from the source tables on a regular basis and presented in a format ready for integration. Next, we will need a process to establish the part content upon which demographic and status information from the source databases will be compiled.

Different systems produce different part lists because the diverse sources consider parts differently. The production parts database, for example, is designed to track all engineering intent content. Once a part has been replaced by an improved or less costly design, it is no longer considered engineering content. The part may, however, still be scheduled. Plant operations will consider the part number valid until stocks have been depleted and replaced with the new part. Part tracking databases focus on those parts for which that organization is responsible. Parts acquired from an outside supplier and parts produced by the automaker are often the responsibility of different groups. No one list can provide an overall assessment of the part content The first and most important task in managing these multiple interfaces is to construct a definitive list of the part scope.

The data warehouse must also determine the appropriate source for each part data element. All of the systems will contain information describing the part. It is most appropriate to recognize the production parts database as the authoritative source for demographic information. However, certain demographic fields of interest to a specific group may be candidates for integration; for example, whether a part is considered long lead or high risk.

Part status is also tracked in more than one database. As we have seen, the part deliverables forecasted in the critical path schedules also appear in the detail databases of the deliverable owners. At different stages of the program, it is appropriate to look to one system or the other as the most reliable source of status information. The data processing must be robust enough to accommodate these shifts in the program time frame without the need to completely rewrite the queries.

Collecting part level data from the many corporate systems enables improved management of program scope. Integrating part level information from the many groups within the organization responsible for part deliverables presents the opportunity to assess the different views of the program part content. Ideally, all groups would be working on the same parts. In practice, the various parts lists will never match exactly. Extracting and reconciling the data provides the information necessary to focus the organization on a consistent part scope.

The data warehouse offers a mechanism to assemble information from across the organization into a single location. Removing the data from the operational systems alleviates the drain that widespread querying would place on system resources. The extracted data is integrated and analyzed to produce a global view of corporate activities, and the information is made widely available in a consistent format. Information is the grease that allows the wheels of modern industry to turn efficiently. Data warehousing offers an integrative solution to corporate information management needs.

# Panel Discussion: "PM and QS9000 - A Match Made in Heaven?"

Mr. Nial Finn, Director of Corporate/Operations Quality, Steelcase, Inc.
Mr. Doug Reith, Director, Magna Interior Systems
Mr. Tim Sennett, Director of Program management, Inalfa Roof Systems

## Description

Come with the AutoSIG, Manufacturing SIG, and New Product Development SIG as we journey through the wonderful world of corporate process mapping - ***QS/ISO 9000 style!*** In this panel discussion you will hear three veterans talk about their experiences in the development and implementation of program management systems that comply with QS and ISO9000 standards. The panelists are from three very prominent companies all located in Michigan, supplying their products to the world.

Look for this session to show you three different methods of project management system definition. You will learn the trials and eventually the successes that were experienced in their efforts to become certified to their respective standard. You will also see a good overview of the structure of the operational procedures and work instructions that guide their employees in their day-to-day project management activities. At the end of each presentation you will be encouraged to not only ask any questions you may have but to also relate your personal experiences in QS/ISO definition.

# Periodic Prototyping and Project Management

Richard E. Ryder, PMP. Plan Tech, Inc.
Parviz Daneshgari, Phd. University of Michigan, Flint

This paper will present a method to build a bridge in both terminology and concept between two disciplines: project management and engineering development. It will also describe how project management can be sharply focused on the essence of developing a new product. Ironically, this method is based on an underlying principle we have used all our lives: scheduled learning.

Let's start by describing how we experience scheduled learning every day. Consider the following occurrences: a high school play, the preparation of a sports team, catching a plane to the coast (or anywhere else, for that matter). At first glance (or maybe even sixth or seventh) they all seem vastly different with little to offer either engineering or project management. Of course, the results *are* quite different: no one would confuse catching the plane with catching a pass or the props on a stage to the props on an aircraft. They are all the same, however, in some very basic ways that have to do with how we structure our time and how we learn. They also suggest ways to better manage engineering development projects.

## Learning Everyday

When a high school student lands a part in the "big play," the first cast meeting provides two key pieces of information: the date of opening night and the rehearsal schedule. Between then and opening night the budding thespian must commit to memory a massive amount of information needed to portray a character on stage. This is propelled and encouraged by the rehearsals. All total, this is a *learning* experience, and moreover, it is learning according to a schedule.

We would be astounded if a sports team were instantly excellent. A universally accepted notion is that sports requires practice, and excellence in sports requires massive amounts of practice. At the first team meeting each player receives two key pieces of information: the date of the first game and the practice schedule. It is during practice sessions that sports teams *learn* how to perform in ways that will increase their chances for victory. This learning, once again, happens according to a schedule.

One must stretch a bit to see significant learning taking place during a late dash to the airport. Besides the mentally stimulating time and distance calculations (which are thrown off by traffic), there doesn't appear to be much there. If, however, we find ourselves panting before a large window, watching "our" airplane back out of the gate (sans us!) the question on our mind is: *When* is the next flight? We don't ask *if* there is another, we know it is *already* scheduled. The airline didn't wait for us—as expected—but, despite our failure, we *did* hurry up. At some point before flight time we altered our behavior by focusing all our energy and attention on the task of getting to the airport as fast as possible. But a closer look reveals there *is learning* going on. Not many people miss two flights in a row. The next time, they leave for the airport sooner, get ready faster, or take a shortcut. It doesn't take long before we learn how to avoid the unpleasantness of watching that plane lift off without us.

The preceding examples describe behavior being altered for the purpose of learning in obedience to a schedule. They all have periodic events and they are fault tolerant. When we miss one we can catch up on the next. If our thespian neglects to memorize lines before the first rehearsal the chances are good that the resulting embarrassment will motivate extra effort to be better the next time. The athlete might miss a practice, but choice words from the coach will motivate attendance the next time. The traveler can catch the next plane after some apologetic phone calls. The systems which surround these events are tolerant to human foibles in that missing one event isn't a disaster, but it is unpleasant enough to motivate us to do better the next time. Our actions are structured by the schedule, and by performing those actions, often in spite of ourselves, we learn and strive to change future behavior.

## Engineering Learning

Engineering development is a team or organizational learning process. The development phase is where the engineering organization learns about a design's ability to perform as intended. If it is done well, the term "design freeze" can have real meaning. To keep the learning cost low we use surrogates for both the real product and the real world. These are called prototypes and tests.

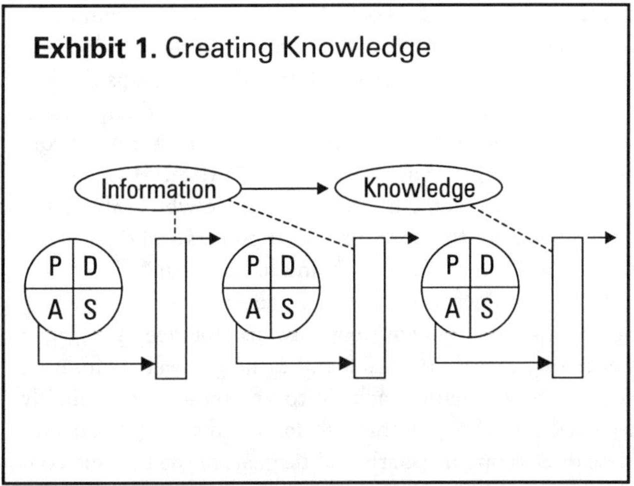


**Exhibit 1.** Creating Knowledge

In the book *Product Development Performance,* Clark and Fujimoto describe a design-build-test cycle as the basic pattern of engineering development (Clark and Fujimoto 1990). In each cycle something new is learned as the design steadily improves. Nothing provides the "Ah ha!" learning experience quite as efficiently as testing a prototype. But not *any prototype* will do; it must have specific qualities that reflect the "real" product. Not *any test* will do; it must reflect "real" conditions to yield the right information. And not *any time* will do either; the point of the exercise is learning, and it must happen early in the development process. A miss on any one of these three points seriously degrades the effectiveness of the learning from the design-build-test cycle. The first two points are well understood by engineers and nearly everyone else, but less obvious is the critical importance of time. The information from the test must be available within a critical window of opportunity. If it happens late, it is called "fixing," which is a vastly inferior method of learning. Later still and the learning might also involve the consumer and be termed a recall. In all cases where it happens too late, it is called "expensive".

The cyclical nature of learning was observed back in the thirties by Shewhart as a "learning loop." Popularized by Demming and the quality movement, we know it as: plan, do, study, act (PDSA drawn on a circle). Learning is the path to improving quality, but the cycle also applies in engineering development. *Planning* is the stage where a hypothesis of what will work is proposed; d*oing* is testing that hypothesis by building and testing a prototype; s*tudying* is evaluating the results; and a*cting* is deciding if and how to revise the design for the next iteration. String them together and you put structure into the learning process: (Exhibit 1.) At each stage, information is accumulated. If this information is accumulated early enough it becomes knowledge built into the product.

## Managing Engineering Learning

This looping nature of engineering development is frustrating to project managers who must contend with the immutable arrow of time. This is one reason project managers and engineers frequently do not communicate well. The voice of the project manager asks: "When will it be done?" The voice of the engineer responds: "When it works!" with an inflection that says: "the longer I talk to you the longer it takes, so put THAT in your Gantt chart, and recalculate!" As a result we see engineering development activities scheduled somewhat loosely with long overlapping tasks for "design" and "prototype testing." Attempts to add more detail raise engineering hackles and prompt accusations of "micro-management." Faced with this, project managers frequently resign themselves to coping with late design releases and schedule twisting engineering changes. It has been said that the sense of urgency decreases the farther upstream you are from production. It has also been said that engineers are never done—they just run out of time.

Engineering thought tends not to concern itself with schedules. We suspect it is because of the nature of complex problem solving where the next step depends on the result of the current one. This dilemma defeats predictability. At any rate, technical issues grab the spotlight in most engineering development meetings, and the schedules produced for project management are clearly of secondary importance.

Development engineers do want good tests, however. The information generated by the test is their immediate work product, and it is frustrating to see their "baby" fail to measure up because of preparation error. For a test to be good many things have to come together at the same time, and it doesn't happen by accident. To a person in the street, and maybe even some executives, a test sounds like a short-term affair. The actual running of the test, however, is just one small part—a tremendous amount of preparation that can take several months is required. With little effort, all the activity needed to accomplish a test fits the classic definition of a project: a temporary endeavor, uniqueness...the whole shot. Consequently, we have an excellent application for project management tools and techniques.

## Periodic Prototyping

One rehearsal or practice is a learning experience to be sure, but several strung together are needed before opening night or the first game. We expect to test several prototypes as well. The timing of those tests is critical. Wheelwright and Clark apply the term "periodic prototyping" to a specific method of scheduling and learning from prototype testing in the book, *Revolutionizing Product Development*. They make a persuasive case for the method and expand on many aspects including applicability (platform type products), managerial involvement (highly recommended), and uses for prototypes in general (more than will fit in this paper). They also mention the possibility of using prototypes to help in "establishing, pacing, and monitoring the development schedule" (Wheelwright and Clark 1992, 274). This is difficult to do if the application of project management techniques to engineering development projects doesn't address the communication barriers between the management structure and the engineering development work.

Periodic prototyping involves setting a schedule for a series of relatively short duration learning loops early in the development process. The earliest learning objectives focus on components and sub-systems, which helps to keep the learning loop duration short, followed by learning loops for the full system. These prototype build and test schedules are set as far in advance as possible, and every attempt is made to adhere to them.

## What to Do

To go beyond mere attempts to meet the schedule requires full participation of everyone and, theoretically, this should be possible. A remarkable congruence exists between engineering goals and project management goals. An engineer wants good tests, and the project manager wants them to happen on schedule. Good tests mean the learning objectives are met, but this requires advanced planning and preparation. That is exactly what is celebrated by project management. As with our everyday examples, it is learning according to a schedule. Project management tools become useful and powerful means to an end instead of the symbols of onerous control.

The way to do it is to make each prototype cycle/learning loop a sub-project. Then make the deliverables of the sub-project, as built into the work breakdown structure, the *learning objectives* for that loop. Determining the learning objectives requires that many questions be asked. They may not be easy to answer, and perhaps that is the point. The better the questions can be answered, however, the greater the chance the tests will yield the needed information. These are essentially engineering-based technical questions that often go to the heart of what is needed to advance the development of the product.

Another consideration is the timing of the learning loops, which must be set to allow proper preparation and evaluation of the results. A balance must be struck between the learning loops and the development time allowed. This sets the pace of engineering development.

Instead of long-term or high-level milestones, which are difficult to relate to everyday work, the planning focus is on relevant and meaningful goals. Instead of sterile corporate issues, which really don't help engineers do their work (and are not particularly interesting to them), these plans are woven from more personal concerns about product details, technology, and nuts and bolts. These plans are not faxed over from the "program management" office. Most significantly, they are created by the only people who really know enough to do so: the development engineers and their teammates. The plans are thorough and have "teeth."

Now what does this achieve? In general it encourages the engineering development people to become deeply engaged in planning. This is no small feat. Learning objectives for each test, and consequently each prototype build, are explicitly discussed and thought through far in advance of test day. These discussions also clarify subtle goals of the product concepts when there is still time to achieve them.

That's good for planning, but during execution additional subtle yet significant benefits also appear. Behavior is altered in many small ways that have a big impact on the value of the engineering development learning and yield significant benefits for project management. Remember how we focused our thinking and made difficult choices when dashing to the airport? Imagine that happening hundreds of times a week during engineering development. Important tests proceed; marginal ones are discarded; choices are made. If engineers indeed are never really done and just run out of time, this method recognizes that tendency and copes with it through enlightened self-interest and working level schedule ownership. The system gently urges people and events forward. The principle of scheduled learning, as we stated, is time tested.

The main benefits of periodic prototyping are:

- Engineers have a reason to learn about project management tools and techniques.
- Greater predictability of test facility resource requirements.
- A predictable cadence imparted to the engineering activities.
- Convincing reasons to be on time early in the program.
- More accessible feedback about the status of the product development.
- Insight into the system capacity of the product development organization.
- Faster learning for improvement of the process for repeated product development.
- Learning happens on demand—when it is needed to be applied.

In the long run, the last two items on this list are potentially the most powerful from the standpoint of achieving a strategic, competitive advantage. Learning is good, but learning faster and more effectively than your competitor is better.

## Applicability

Wheelwright and Clark caution that periodic prototyping works best for specific circumstances, which they call platform projects (Wheelwright and Clark 1992, 279). But they are essentially reporting on what they observed in their study; for that reason alone this can't be the final word on the subject. The use of this method as a means to focus the common interests of project management and engineering thinking may have much broader application where learning is a key component to project performance.

Something very much along the lines of periodic prototyping is described in the book, *Microsoft Secrets*. The technique, called "daily builds," requires code under development to be "checked in" precisely at 2 A.M. every day. A software engineering manager is quoted as saying: "Doing daily builds is just like the most painful thing in the world. But it is the greatest thing in the world, because you get instant feedback." He adds "You always take a snapshot every day; it doesn't matter what happens...everybody just gets to know the rhythm and feels that there's control of the project" (Cusumano and Selby 1995). Quick and effective feedback, of course, is a key requirement for learning, but the statement also speaks to the beneficial psychological factors that accompany the technique.

Many project management practitioners recognize the characteristics of engineering thought processes that run counter to project goals but tend to wish for more enlightened individuals or bigger sticks to enforce schedule compliance. Both approaches have exceedingly slim chances for long-term success. Perfect people do not exist so the odds are against finding a fully enlightened team. Even if one existed, new members would soon dilute the mix. The motivational ability of external force, as we all know, is limited in time and effectiveness. The answer lies in setting up a structure that motivates the desired behaviors through common goals, and multiple small nudges in the right direction.

We frequently talk about the need for buy-in and schedule ownership; this is a method to take positive steps in that direction. It applies wherever learning objectives are the necessary steps toward project success. If we think about it, this condition may exist right under our noses in many projects. To see it only takes the right point of view.

## Conclusion

Periodic prototyping combined with learning concepts and project management tools offer competitive advantages to companies that seize them. The power comes from achieving a congruence between the goals of individuals engaged in engineering development and the goals of project managers. It forms a bridge between two disciplines that historically have not communicated well by applying the principle of scheduled learning.

### References


Clark, Kim B., and Takahiro Fujimoto. 1991. *Product Development Performance.* Boston, MS: Harvard Business School Press.

Wheelwright, Steven C., and Kim B. Clark. 1992. *Revolutionizing Product Development.* NY: The Free Press.

Cusumano, Michael A. and Richard W. Selby. 1995. *Microsoft Secrets.* NY: The Free Press.

# Can the Automotive Industry Survive in the Next Century Without Project Management ?

Ramakrishnan Krishnan, B.E.(ME), M.S. (ME), M.B.A., Ford Motor Company

## Introduction

Management as a discipline is 100 years old. Project management as a discipline is about fifty years old . The first major applications include the Navy's Polaris missile project and E.I. Dupont De Nemours' engineering projects. The automotive industries have been embracing project management methodology for nearly thirty years, particularly in the product development arena. Any successful implementations have been perhaps in the past five to ten years. While the project management field itself is evolving and growing aided by the efforts of the Project Management Institute, the product development arena is undergoing "massive surgery" commonly known as reengineering. The product development process has been largely a creative process analogous to the tool and die makers of 100 years ago. The major premise of the "massive surgery" is to have a defined product development process that incorporates a controlled technology deployment. This is paramount to achieving the goals: Faster time-to-market, lowest cost production, enhanced quality, customer satisfaction, and employee pride.

Now comes the crucial issue. Project management, by definition, is to plan, design, and execute a well-defined project. Should it wait until the product development process is defined ?

The author proposes to discuss how project management can play an important role in the current wave of product development reengineering taking place in the industry. It is also the opinion of the author that if the automotive industry is to survive in the next century, it needs to position itself to have a well-defined project management system in place. Conversely, the project management profession, including the project management processes and tools, needs to be flexible, nimble, and adaptive to be value-added.

## The Evolution Of Organizations

### Transition from "Management" to "Leadership"

"Organizations are turning upside down and flattening. The models for our organizations are rooted in the traditions of the church and military, where an authoritative leader commands respect, decides on courses, and directs action through a rigid and mechanistic departmental command structure. These models have defined tasks and boundaries to work within. But this is changing. Organizations are increasingly becoming customer-driven. The old command structures are being broken down and replaced with new corporate goals and strategies that require teamwork and empowered people for their achievement" (Goldsbury 1997).

The transition in the automotive product development world would be from *management of achieving deliverables* in the past to a *leadership in developing and managing processes that would result in achieving the deliverables*. Lack of such a leadership is bound to lead to failure, which can be likened to a saying passed down from the Tuhoe people, who are part of the indigenous Maori people of New Zealand: *E mua kai kai* (Those who journey at the front get time to eat well), *e muri kai huare* (while those at the rear must survive on their own saliva) (Boznak 1996).

Corporate leadership is a challenging task in the wake of current global impact. "Tomorrow's successful corporate leadership must simultaneously integrate, manage, and control their multiple and diverse projects— projects that are vital to their continued corporate success. Sorting out the winners from the losers is vital to achieving long-term corporate success" (Boznak 1996).

Mass communications, including CNN and World Wide Web have contributed enormously to the enhancement of people's awareness. A practical application of self-empowerment is to synergize people energies and intelligence. Detroit, the auto capital of the world, perhaps ought to pay attention to Rick Lepley, senior vice president, Mitsubishi (United States): "Unlike Detroit, there is no caste system here. Our people don't think about which executives they work for, just which project they are working on" (Fleming and Koppelman 1997).

### Evolution Of Product Development—"Craftsmanship" to "Factory Approach"

Automotive product development is evolving from the arts and crafts of the past to a set of tools and techniques that are proven and available in a bookshelf for future use.

"A century ago new product development centered on the individual 'craftsman' approach. One person did everything

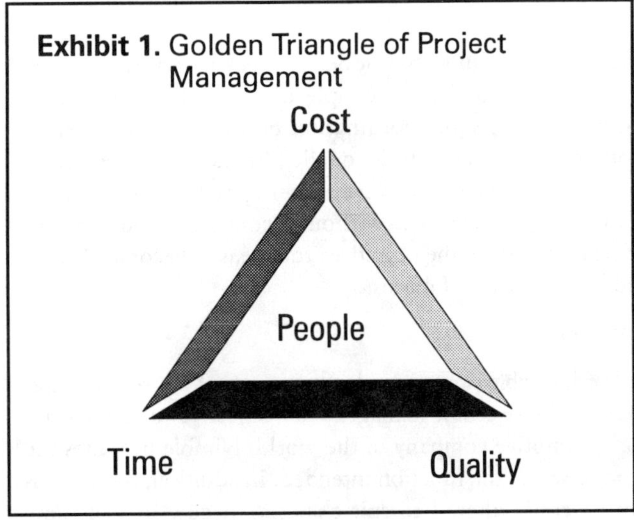

**Exhibit 1.** Golden Triangle of Project Management

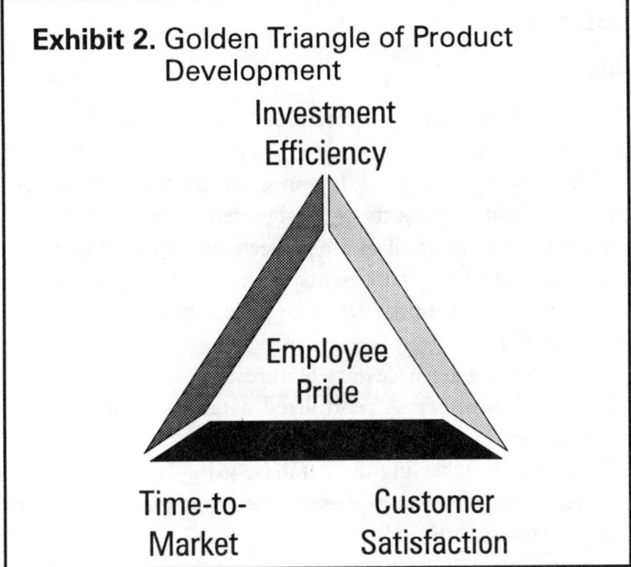

**Exhibit 2.** Golden Triangle of Product Development

needed to produce a new article. It was a simple time and the products were of the highest quality. People took personal pride in their work, in what they did."

"Then industrial products became more complex. Out of necessity, new product developments evolved into the efforts of multiple, highly specialized functions, working toward a common objective of producing a new item." 3

"Empirically, the results with the use of integrated project development teams provided companies with three clear benefits: (1) shortened new product development cycle, (2) reduced overall new product development costs, and (3) produced a higher quality product at first release. No wonder the concept has received wide acceptance among the corporate community" (Fleming and Koppelman 1997).

In a factory, one would choose the best machine for each component, then the machines could be laid out so as to maximize the output. The factory workers would operate the machines.

Analogously, in the product development world, the aim is to have the best process (i.e., process to manage a program or process to set vehicle targets and cascade them to components' targets) developed and defined. Then the processes would be organized to achieve the maximum throughput—cars, trucks, and parts. The engineers are responsible for executing the various processes.

## Lessons Learned

The following are some of the key lessons learned based upon experiences in implementing a disciplined project management as an integral part of automotive product development. In addition to personal experiences at Ford, the author has drawn ideas from attending seminars (i.e., PMI annual conference in Boston, October 1996) and reviewing published literature (i.e. *PM Network*).

### Need

The need to have an organized way of implementing product programs has been felt in the automotive industry for many years. The organized way is the project management discipline, the 9 major areas of project management as described in *A Guide to the Project Management Body of Knowledge.* Exhibit 1 shows the golden triangle of project management. People, project time, project cost, and project quality are four of the nine major areas of project management. Exhibit 2 shows the golden triangle of product development. Self-empowered people, time-to-market, investment efficiency, and customer satisfaction are four of the major objectives of product development. It is obvious how closely the two arenas are linked. Consequently, the need for tools that would skillfully employ the methodology has been well documented.

### Acceptance

There are many ways to measure how well the project management discipline is accepted in the automotive industry.

- Users (both providers and customers of the project management services) base
- Software products
- Number of projects *formally* implementing the methods
- Increased impact of the PMI Auto SIG (special interest group) and AIAG (automotive industry action group)
- Number of training programs
- Organizational structure; i.e., a core group of project management professionals

### Implementation

Implementation successes need to be measured carefully. If program objectives are not met, would project management be considered a failure? This is a frequently asked question, and there is no easy or obvious answer. It is possible to have a well-executed project management process and yet have the supported product/program not meet the expected objectives. The reasons may be varied and could include poor marketing forecast, incorrect strategic direction, insufficient headcount or funding, unmanageable data structure, and unclear goals and objectives. This is where senior management intervention is needed: to provide continued support for the project management effort in the face of seemingly contradictory experiences.

### Training

Training programs need to be tailored to the targeted audiences, monitored continuously, and updated periodically to suit participants' needs. Certification is effective in determining whether the trainee has really assimilated the learning materials. It is not sufficient to say that a participant has attended a session.

## Future Directions

Since teaching project management in 1973 at the University of Minnesota Graduate School of Business, the author has had an extensive application experience mostly at Ford Motor Company in the product development function and the supporting functions. The following are some of the recommended directions for the future:

### Trust

"Trust—it's the key ingredient in any relationship, be it family or business" (EDS 1996). Sheilagh Whittaker, president of EDS Canada, is a mother of six children, ages 3 to 29. Whittaker sees many parallels between leading an effective work team and running a family. "It has a great deal to do with trust," she says. "You have to trust people to develop their own sense of responsibility and pride, just like in a family."

### Learning

Learning is the end result of any training program—an understanding of the information, including the tools. As a practical matter, learning is very effective when delivered in small "chewable bites." This leads to the concept of "just-in-time" learning. To enhance this further, certification would be useful.

### Integration

The PMBOK Guide has added project integration as the ninth module in the last couple of years. The integration module is to ensure coordination between the other eight modules: scope, cost, time, quality, human resources, communication, risk, and procurement. In practice, such an integration plays a key role. Without a consistent and constant effort to integrate, the objectives could easily become obscure and lead to project failures.

### Flexibility

At Ford, nimble process leadership is one of the seven strategies to achieve senior management's objective to be the leading automotive company in the world. Nimble indicates the process serves the function intended. In addition, the process can be easily altered to suit changing needs. In that same sense, the project management process needs to be nimble to be effective.

### Tools

Life cycle of tools will be determined by their usefulness as perceived by users.

"There is a paradigm shift going on, from the management of individual projects, by designated project managers, to the management of all of the projects in the enterprise, by varied interests and participants. Software toolmakers are scrambling to create products that reflect this new reality" (Levine 1997).

The following are necessary features:

- Central Repository: A centralized database of project information
- WEB-based: Accessing the database using Internet
- E-Mail: Notification of events and other project-related information via E-mail

## Conclusions

Let's reexamine the question, "Can the automotive industry survive in the next century without project management?". Of course not. But a more important and perhaps more practical question is: "How can the project management profession position itself to effectively support the product development process in the automotive industry?" Some of the recommended directions for the future by the author are: just-in-time learning, WEB-based tools, implementation success metrics, and professional development.

## Acknowledgments

Several team members have contributed to the development of the ideas expressed in this paper. The author wishes to express special thanks to Graham Lockett and Art Hyde of the product development system department of Ford Motor Company.

## References

Boznak, Rudolph G. 1996. "Management of Projects: A Giant Step Beyond Project Management." *PM Network* (January): 27.

EDS. 1996. *Annual Report:* Back Page.

Fleming, Quentin W., and Joel M. Koppelman. 1997. "Integrated Project Development Teams: Another FAD or a Permanent Change." *Project Management Journal* (March): 4.

Goldsbury, Peter. 1997. "Will We Become Dinosaurs of an Enabled Age?" *PM Network* (February): 43.

Levine, Harvey A. 1997. "Keeping Up With the Users—Shifting Needs Foster New PM Software Categories." *PM Network*, (April): 17.

PROJECT MANAGEMENT: THE NEXT CENTURY

PROJECT MANAGEMENT INSTITUTE CHICAGO 1997

# Defense/ Aerospace

# Earned Value Management: What Is The Government's Role?

Wayne F. Abba, U.S. Department of Defense

## Introduction

"And then there were three."

That Business headline in the The Washington Post on July 4, 1997, led a report on Lockheed Martin's plan to acquire Northrop Grumman. If the deal goes through—and given the pace of similar acquisitions, that seems likely—it will leave the aerospace industry with three major defense contractors: Boeing, Lockheed Martin and Raytheon.

This rapid transformation of an industry, as about a dozen contractors became four (and likely three), can be traced to a dinner now referred to as "the last supper." In 1993, then-Deputy Secretary of Defense William Perry urged defense industry executives to combine into fewer, larger companies because shrinking Department of Defense (DoD) budgets would endanger at least half the contractors represented at the dinner that night.

The military procurement budget plummeted 67 percent from its height in 1985, forcing layoffs and plant closings at a pace rarely seen—perhaps unprecedented—in modern U.S. corporate history. But as larger, dominant companies emerge, concerns inevitably arise about the effects of their consolidation on competition and government oversight. If the government finds itself less able to rely on market forces to obtain efficient performance on defense projects, how can its project managers succeed while prudently expending precious public resources? Recent observers have noted "The market has sounded the warning bell for the DoD, and it is up to program managers to heed the call. The late 1990s and the early 21st Century will mark a difficult and expensive procurement era (Ciccotello, Green and Lynch 1997)."

Fortunately for DoD project managers, acquisition reform has kept pace with the dramatic changes in DoD budgets and in the defense industrial base. Management concepts developed over many years for large, complex defense programs will serve managers and taxpayers well in the challenging new business environment. Those concepts are teamwork, planning, and integrated project management. They are reflected in DoD acquisition guidance as Integrated Product Teams (IPT), Integrated Baseline Reviews (IBR) and Earned Value Management (EVM).

The DoD management concepts are enjoying widespread acceptance in other industries and in other countries. In addition, the Office of Management and Budget is adopting them for application government-wide. With several years of experience in applying these concepts and with many examples of successful project management as a result, DoD continues to lead in the development of universally-recognized project management techniques.

## Teamwork

The introduction of IPTs in DoD Directive 5000.1 has served to reinvigorate the interdisciplinary nature of project management organizations and explicitly recognizes the need for closer cooperation with industry.

*The IPT is composed of representatives from all appropriate functional disciplines working together with a Team Leader to build successful and balanced programs, identify and resolve issues, and make sound and timely recommendations to facilitate decision-making. There are three types of IPTs: Overarching IPTs focus on strategic guidance, program assessment, and issue resolution. Working Level IPTs identify and resolve program issues, determine program status, and seek opportunities for acquisition reform. Program IPTs focus on program execution, and may include representatives from both government, and after contract award, industry* (DoD 1996).

The three IPT types comprise a continuum from the contract execution level through the senior levels of DoD acquisition management. By streamlining communications and reporting, IPTs have reduced dramatically the burdens previously borne by project managers and by acquisition staff at all levels. But more important in the new business management context, IPTs provide a means for customers and suppliers to work together far more effectively than in the past.

The IPT is more than just an organizational concept. Although it is not unlike the typical project management team, it is more effective through increased *empowerment*, defined by DoD as encompassing both government people and our vendors. The DoD acquisition regulations do not reduce responsibility, but seek to balance responsibility with authority. Prudent risk acceptance and management therefore is essential to the reformed DoD acquisition process—and of course to IPTs.

## Planning

The really nice thing about not planning is that failure comes as a complete surprise and is not preceded by long periods of worry and depression! (MPI)

That poor planning contributes to project failure is beyond conjecture. After DoD recognized that inadequate planning was a major reason for the relative ineffectiveness of earned value management as implemented under the provisions of Cost/Schedule Control Systems Criteria (C/SCSC or CS2), it introduced the IBR as a major initiative to address the problem. The IBR was conceived in 1994 with two objectives: To improve the use of contractor cost performance data by contractor and government program managers and to reduce the number of government reviews of contractor management systems.

Not only have those objectives been met, the IBR was cited by the General Accounting Office as "One of the more successful initiatives to date ... By involving the program manager directly in this review, the process highlights the merits of using earned value to track progress. It has also reduced the number of CS2 compliance reviews. For example, CS2 reviews have decreased from 56 in 1993 to 5 in 1995 while the number of IBRs have increased from 3 in 1993 to 29 in 1995. The program managers that we surveyed strongly supported the IBR as a valuable management tool. (GAO 1997)"

Program managers support the IBR because it provides them a robust planning process they can use as appropriate for individual projects. Set up deliberately as a counterpoint to the traditional "one size fits all" C/SCSC implementation approach, DoD IBR policy required simply that within six months of contract award, the program manager and his or her technical staff (usually IPTs) would review contractor plans to achieve contract objectives in terms of work scope, schedule and resources—with emphasis on integration of the plans and identification of risk.

## Integrated Project Management

The "glue" that ties together the three elements of any project—scope, schedule and resources—is earned value management. When resources are a concern, earned value is not just the best way to achieve effective integration of project performance management, it is the only way. That assertion is supported by U.S. companies with experience both in defense and commercial projects. This growing acceptance contributed to a decision by the Executive Office of the President, Office of Management and Budget (OMB) to extend the earned value concept to capital asset acquisition government-wide beginning with the Fiscal Year 1998 budget. OMB issued with the FY 1998 budget documents an introduction to the principles it will use to improve the effectiveness of Federal investments in capital assets, including the following definition:

*Earned value refers to a performance-based management system for establishing baseline cost, schedule and performance goals for a capital project and measuring progress against the goals. Earned value is described in OMB Circular A-11, Part 3, "Planning, Budgeting and Acquisition of Fixed Assets" (July 1996), Appendix 300C* (GPO 1998).

Earned value has come a long way since its introduction as defense policy in 1967. Its acceptance transcends national boundaries as other governments increasingly discover that it can work for them and for their industry just as it has in the United States. In June 1997, the Swedish Defence Materiel Administration announced a strategic decision to implement earned value management as an element of acquisition reform. Also in 1997, New Zealand joined with Australia, Canada, Sweden and the United States in the International Performance Management Council, a voluntary forum dedicated to improved management of defense projects. The United Kingdom also is expected to join soon.

There are by now too many examples of integrated project management in DoD using the proven concepts of IPT, IBR and EVM to address all of them in a short paper. Readers are encouraged to visit the DoD Earned Value web site at http://www.acq.osd.mil/pm to learn more—or to contribute their own stories. However, one example serves to illustrate how effective these fundamental management and acquisition reform principles can be in this "difficult and expensive procurement era."

The U.S. Army Patriot Advanced Capability-3 (PAC-3) program is a block upgrade to the Patriot Air Defense Missile System. The prime contractor for the missile and its command and launch system is Lockheed Martin Vought Systems in Grand Prairie, Texas. Raytheon, Inc., in Bedford, Massachusetts, is the missile segment integration contractor. The Army Product Manager is located in Huntsville, Alabama.

The PAC-3 program established six IPTs early on. Three were responsible for products (missile, seeker and command and launch systems) while three were responsible for key processes (performance and simulation, test and evaluation, and production). The teams created the organizational foundation for baselining project performance. Immediately following the preliminary design review, an IBR was conducted. Technical knowledge gained during the design review prepared participants to review the contractors' detailed work package planning (scope, schedule and resources) during the IBR (O'Reilly, Brown 1997).

(At this point, someone will no doubt be thinking "Hold on—this must be an expensive process." Well, yes—or then again, maybe not. The thing to remember is that the extent of detailed planning must be commensurate with expected risk. And while it is extremely difficult to reckon the cost vs. benefit of effective management, it is all too easy to tote up the billions of dollars that have been wasted as the result of ineffective management. In fact, using these integrated techniques, some DoD programs are beating their cost, schedule and performance goals. The bottom line is that effective planning and management probably *saves* money.)

Lessons learned on the PAC-3 program include these:

- IPT members need education in non-engineering disciplines, coupled with the temperament to work in teams
- IPT skills in EVM, technical performance measurement, and critical path analysis are essential
- A robustly supported IBR is essential
- Pure technical reviews are obsolete
- IPTs must control all the project, technical and functional elements needed for the product or process
- Asking IPTs to forecast earned value performance for a prescribed future period (PAC-3 used 90 days) encourages proactive management in realistic time periods (O'Reilly, Brown 1997).

By way of comparison, the IBR process is much shorter than the traditional C/SCSC review process, yet adds more value to project management by involving the right team members at the right time. There are no guidelines for the length or team composition for an IBR, as each program must be free to decide what will work best in its unique circumstances and management philosophy. For example, some project managers prefer to work with the contractor on IPTs as elements of the performance management baseline are established, rather than conduct a review after the fact.

## Government's Role

The success of DoD project management improvements, coupled with industry's increasing acceptance, led in 1996 to issuance by industry of "Industry Standard Guidelines for Earned Value Management Systems." The DoD responded by accepting those guidelines to replace the C/SCSC requirements which had been in place for some thirty years. The EVMS guidelines are equivalent to C/SCSC (a tribute to those who originally developed the principles in the 1960s), but their ownership has shifted to industry. In due course, the industry guidelines probably will evolve into industry or international standards.

For DoD, industry ownership means that DoD-unique EVMS requirements will fade into history. For now, DoD regulations mirror the industry guidelines. To the extent that industry puts in place integrated project management systems that meet a test of public trust, DoD can respond by reducing—and potentially canceling—its requirements. There is a danger that the increasing worldwide acceptance of similar management principles will lead to proliferation of standards, regulations, or guidelines. Because it no longer wishes to issue unique regulations, DoD must stay abreast of those developments, adjust its guidance accordingly, and encourage development of a universally accepted set of management principles to the greatest possible extent. To that end, DoD representatives take part in the activities of voluntary standards-setting bodies, both domestic and international, and in related activities sponsored by professional associations including the Project Management Institute, the Performance Management Association, and the National Contract Management Association.

One of the most promising of those activities is the American Project Management Forum, intended to provide a means for dialogue between project management professionals in the public and private sectors. From humble beginnings, the Forum has grown to include more than a dozen Federal agencies. Another promising offshoot of its activities is a global management standards forum, with PMI again cast in a leading role. This group seeks to identify not the differences among various national standards and regulations, but those things we have in common. By seeking common ground, we discover that there are more similarities than differences, while the differences tend to recede in importance.

## Summary

The observers quoted in the introduction to this paper concluded their article by outlining three possible approaches to how a program manager might use defense market information to good advantage: Change the industry structure, improve cost visibility, and/or change the contracting environment, perhaps by shifting more to cost-type contracting. The first approach is clearly not in the cards in the short term; on the contrary, defense industry has shaken itself out quite thoroughly and appears likely to enter a steady state for the foreseeable future. The second holds much promise, offering more cost insight to offset the loss of market power in a downsized industry. And DoD has the means in place to do just that—the organizational concept (IPTs) that encourage us to work more closely with industry, the planning process (IBRs) that empower our IPTs, and integrated cost, schedule and technical performance management using earned value as the integrating tool. The third approach also holds promise in the face of declining competition and equally is supported by our management concepts.

Thus the DoD, its industrial base, and the federal government at large approach the new millennium with effective management tools that have been honed over decades of experience. As always, our greatest challenge is to teach our managers how to wield those tools effectively. The combined efforts of government, industry, professional associations, and academia are up to the challenge.

## References


Ciccotello, Conrad, Steve Green and Tim Lynch. 1997. Consolidation and Value in the U.S. Defense Industry. *Program Manager.* July-August.

Department of Defense. 1996. Directive Nr. 5000.1. Defense Acquisition. Part E.2.f. March 15.

Micro Planning International Pty Ltd. Used with permission.

General Accounting Office. 1997. Report GAO/NSIAD-97-108. Major Acquisitions: Significant Changes Underway in DoD's Earned Value Management Process. May. pp. 14-15.

Government Printing Office. 1998. Budget of the United States Government. Principles of Budgeting for Capital Asset Acquisitions. Fiscal Year 1998. p. 10.

O'Reilly, Patrick J., and Kenneth N. Brown. 1997. A PM's Perspective on Cost Control: The Army-Industry PAC-3 Experience. *Army RD&A.* January-February.

# In Search of Excellence: Leadership Lessons from DoD's Best PMs

Dr. Owen C. Gadeken, Defense Systems Management College

## Introduction

The traditional view of project management has emphasized both the technical and management expertise required of project managers. However, there is an emerging view in the project management community that while technical and management expertise are important, the primary role of project managers in the future will be to provide a leadership focus on their projects. This is becoming even more clear as current project managers are forced to cope simultaneously with reorganizations, downsizing, the environment, new technology, and global competition.

Many project managers fail to recognize the shifting role demands over their careers. This gradual role evolution toward leadership is depicted in Exhibit 1. The shifts between the dashed lines from technical to managerial and then to leadership are actually quite dramatic and call for significant new skills development. The underlying question to be addressed in this paper is what are the specific leadership skills required of project managers.

The nature of the leadership challenge facing defense project managers has been extensively researched by the Defense Systems Management College (DSMC). This paper summarizes the results of four separate research studies (Cullen 1990, Gadeken 1991, Best 1991, McVeigh 1994) to determine the competencies of top performing defense project managers. These studies were based on the premise that the best way to find out what it takes to be a good project manager is to analyze a current group of outstanding project managers and identify what they do that makes them so effective. The four research studies involved both surveys and in-depth interviews of a broad cross-section of project managers.

The top performing project managers were found to possess a unique set of managerial and leadership competencies and to employ them more frequently and in more situations than other project managers in their organizations. This paper discusses the research findings and resulting issues involved in selecting and developing top performing project managers for the future.

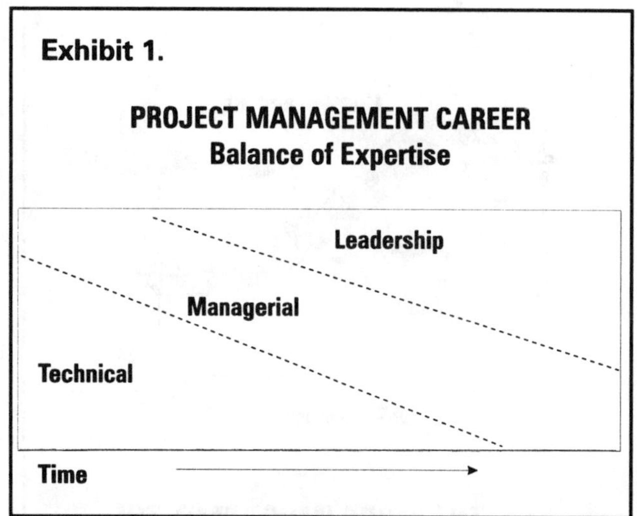


## The Competency Approach

What are competencies? Any job can be considered from two perspectives: tasks and competencies. Tasks are characteristic of the job itself. Tasks usually are defined as the minimum or threshold requirements for effective performance. By contrast, competencies are characteristics of the person. They describe what the person brings to the job that allows him or her to do the job in an outstanding way. Competencies may include motives, traits, aptitudes, knowledge, or skills. For any given job, competencies are what superior performers do more often and more completely to achieve superior results.

A systematic approach to job analysis should consider both tasks and personal competencies (See Exhibit 2. Note: Exhibits 2 and 4 are provided courtesy of Cambria Consulting in Boston, MA.). The inclusion of the competency dimensions pushes beyond the minimum job requirements to what makes for superior performance.

DSMC selected the competency-based approach rather than traditional methods like task analysis and expert panels because of the complexity and variety of project manager jobs in the defense acquisition process. The more complex the job, the more important it is to study what each project manager brings to the job that results in outstanding performance.

As an example, consider the difference between a capable pilot and a fighter ace. The basic skills of flying

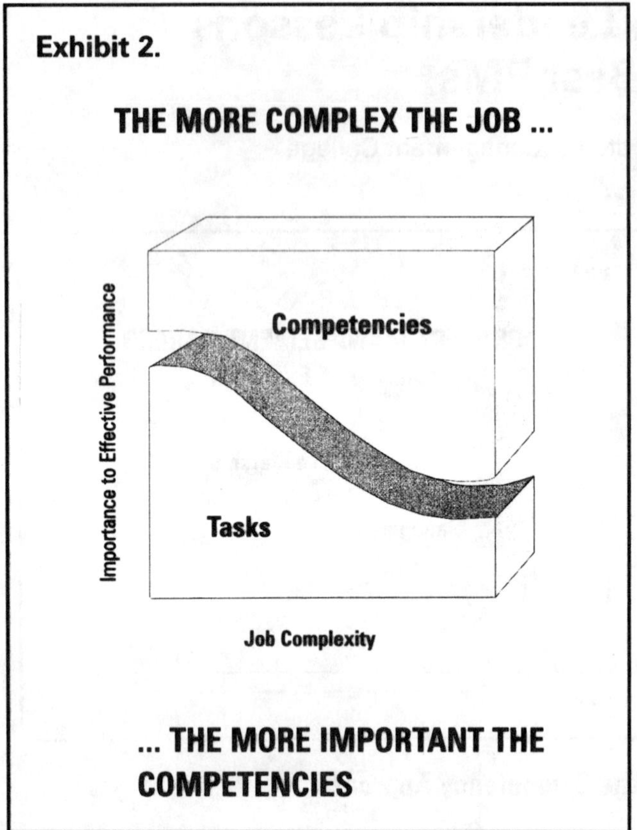

Exhibit 2.

could be considered of moderate complexity on the Exhibit 2 diagram and are probably amenable to a task-analysis approach. On the other hand, a fighter ace or "top-gun" pilot would be difficult to characterize based on tasks alone. This is especially true if you were interested in what differentiates the ace from the other capable pilots in the squadron. This is where competency analysis is of most value. Clearly, a project manager's job is on the right of the complexity scale in Exhibit 2 along with the fighter ace and, therefore, is also most appropriate for competency analysis.

Using critical incident interviews and detailed follow-up surveys, the job competency research process gets beneath espoused theories about what it takes to do a job, to what the best performers actually do. Past studies have shown that job experts are often wrong in their assumptions about what it takes to do a job well (Klemp 1982).

Even the top performers themselves are often unaware ("unconsciously competent") of what they do that makes them so effective. An interesting example which illustrates this point can be found in the August 1988 issue of Training magazine (Gilbert 1988). Two researchers interviewed the late college football coach Paul "Bear" Bryant at the University of Alabama and asked what he did that made him such a great coach. Instead of immediately writing up the findings from their interview notes, the researchers stayed on for several days and actually observed coach Bryant in practice sessions and during games. What they found was that coach Bryant didn't actually do most of the things he alluded to in the interviews. They discovered other "new" behaviors such as detailed observation of player performance and immediate feedback which really accounted for coach Bryant's success. As the article states, "exemplary performers differ very little from average ones, but that the differences are enormously valuable."

The research process has several benefits. It distinguishes the competencies of outstanding project managers from their contemporaries. The research focuses on the critical few competencies that make the most difference in job performance. The competencies are defined in terms of observable job-related behavior rather than abstract concepts. The resulting job competency model serves as an excellent communication tool and training model to move organizations toward their goal of creating a cadre of top flight project managers.

## Project Manager Competencies

With the 1990 DSMC research study as a model, the subsequent research studies found a common set of leadership competencies with some variation in rank order. The DSMC study of United Kingdom (UK) defense project managers (Gadeken 1991) validated these same competencies, with UK project managers favoring more of the analytical rather than interpersonal skills. Several underlying themes emerged from the set of competencies found in the research. These themes are listed in Exhibit 3 and discussed below along with selected quotes from the project managers interviews.

Top ranked project managers are first and foremost mission focused and results oriented. They take personal ownership of their projects in a manner almost approaching the quest of a medieval knight going off to the crusades. They model their personal commitment with such dedication and enthusiasm that it permeates their project team, external customers, and support organizations. In the words of one Army project manager:

*"I felt frustrated. But at the same time I feel like it is such good thing we are doing for the Army that it is worth all the frustration and hard work and whatever else we need to do to make it successful."*

Outstanding project managers are both systematic and innovative thinkers. They understand the complex and rapidly changing environment in which they must work. Further, they are able to see through this complexity to provide a structure for sound decision making as well as a point of departure for more innovative solution options.

In the words of Admiral Carlisle Trost, a former Chief of Naval Operations:

*"Figuring out what is going on in a complex world is the heart of leadership. Otherwise leaders are defeated by events they do not understand."*

The best project managers interpret events from a big picture (mission) perspective with an eye toward future consequences of immediate decisions.

*"We were heading to a point where, although it was years away from happening, things would start to diverge. But action needed to be taken right then and there, so that...we would have enough canisters to go around and support the missile base. That was the driving factor in what I was doing."*

The best project managers are masters of working with and through others. They focus their efforts on finding the best people for their project team and then let them handle the myriad of decisions and details that epitomize even the most basic projects.

*"The first thing you do is get the right people. My contractors have made an observation. They told me I don't have many people here but the ones I've got are terrific. And, that's exactly the way they were picked."*

Effective project managers do not try to do everything themselves. They typically focus on a few strategically important areas, leaving the mass of administrative and technical matters to subordinates. This is most clearly illustrated in the DSMC research interviews (Cullen 1990) which focused on critical incidents selected by the project managers. Of the 285 critical incidents, over half were concentrated in just four functional areas: contracting (62), personnel management (42), test and evaluation (31), and acquisition strategy (i.e., project planning) (26).

While outstanding project managers craft effective project teams, they also spend considerable time networking with external customers and support organizations. The number of external stakeholders who can potentially impact a project is huge. Thus, the project managers must determine who the key players are and what is important to them. Since project managers have no formal power over these external stakeholders, they must rely on their ability to cultivate relationships and use influence strategies to achieve their objectives. To reverse a potentially devastating budget cut, this Army project manager knew who to involve, at what point and why:

*"I finally recognized that I needed heavy hitters with more influence and authority than I had, so I set up a meeting with the program executive office, the head of procurement, my staff, an attorney advisor, and the Army's contract policy expert. In other words, I had to go in there and literally stack the deck in terms of influence and independent representatives who would vouch for what I had said."*

**Exhibit 3.**

## THE BEST PROJECT MANAGERS

- Are strongly committed to their mission
- Have a long term and big picture perspective
- Are both systematic and innovative thinkers
- Find and empower the best people for their project team
- Are selective in their involvement in project issues
- Focus heavily on external stakeholders
- Thrive on relationships and influence
- Proactively gather information and insist on results

Finally, the best project managers constantly probe for information and push for results as illustrated in the following quotes:

*"At this meeting, I asked the contractor what they knew about the subcontractor status. You know, where precisely are they? What are their plans to do this? With each answer, I would just ask one question, I would just ask one question deeper than that. When they started to stutter, I knew they were in trouble because I shouldn't be able to go that one level deeper and ask a question they can't answer."*

*"Everything you do [as a project manager] has got to be focused on results, results, results."*

An interesting finding from the DSMC study (Cullen 1990) emerged from the comparison of importance rankings of the competencies by project managers with ranking from other project management professionals (functional managers from different specialty areas such as contracting, budgeting, engineering, and logistics). The functional managers considered technical expertise, attention to detail, and creativity (defined as developing novel technical solutions) as far more important than did project managers.

On the other hand, project managers rated sense of ownership/mission, political awareness, and strategic influence much higher than functional managers. An underlying issue emerges from the difference in competency requirements for project managers and functional specialists: the transition from functional specialist to project manager may be conceptually quite difficult. A review of the literature (Gadeken 1986) supports this conclusion, especially for scientists and engineers who currently make up the bulk of defense project managers.

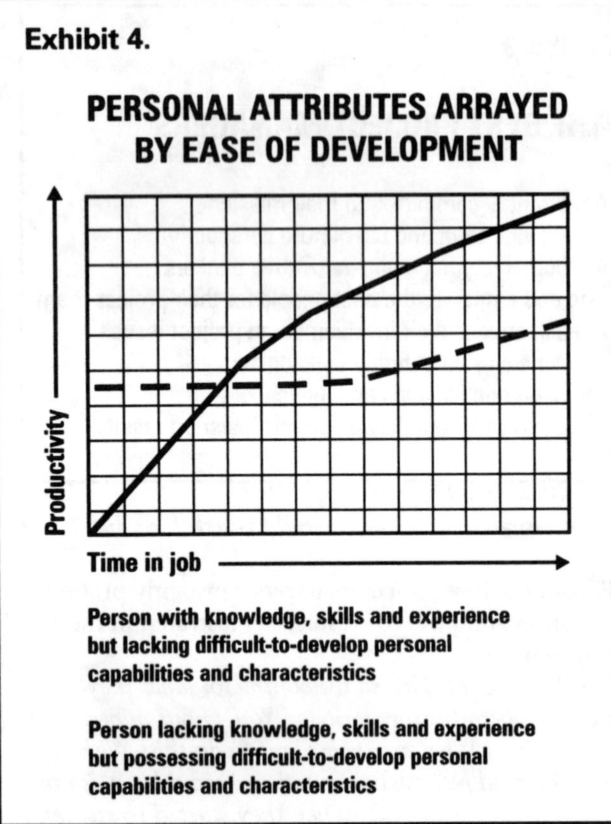


## Project Manager Selection

Selection of US defense project managers is currently conducted by special panels in the military services. Although future potential is considered, most of the evaluation is of necessity based on the candidates' performance in their prior jobs. Project manager candidates are given in-depth training (3 courses totaling 20 weeks as a minimum) covering project management functional disciplines. The assumption here is that these project managers have already acquired the necessary leadership and management competencies through their prior work and supervisory experience. This assumption appears to be flawed based on the conclusion made earlier in this paper that there are several unique project manager competencies not normally developed by more junior project management professionals.

An alternate selection approach would be to use the current selection process based on knowledge and experience but then train the project manager candidates in the critical leadership and management competencies. While this approach appears attractive, it ignores basic limitations of the training process. Specialized knowledge can easily be imparted in a training environment even under time constraints (a few days). However, leadership and management competencies are by their nature complex and are generally developed only with time and experience perhaps over an entire career.

Thus, the preferred alternative for project manager selection is to assess which candidates have or can more readily develop the critical leadership and management competencies. Training can then be provided or tailored in project management functional disciplines (knowledge areas) to augment the candidates' prior knowledge and experience base. This training is much more likely to succeed than a training program to develop critical leadership and management competencies in candidates lacking such skills.

A project manager selection process focused on the critical leadership competencies should have a multiplier effect on project results over time as illustrated in Exhibit 4. Although candidates possessing the critical personal competencies (but lacking experience) may start off as less productive, they will rapidly overtake their less competent but more experienced counterparts in the organization. The main question then becomes how to assess which candidates have or can more readily develop the critical project management competencies.

## Competency Assessment

Assessing project manager candidates' ability to perform critical management and leadership skills is a difficult proposition. This is due in part to the fact that many of these competencies were not required to a great degree in candidates' prior jobs. However, assessment techniques have emerged in recent years which are quite useful. Tailored survey assessment instruments can be created and given to candidates' prior supervisors, peers, and subordinates asking for their assessment of the candidates' past performance and future potential in each of the project manager competency areas. This "360 degree feedback" (from above, at the same level, and below in the organization) has rapidly gained momentum in both US public and private sector organizations. Several commercially-developed multi-rater instruments are now available. Most feature computer scoring, automated feedback (report) generation, and even tailoring of items to fit the individuals and organization using the instruments.

Another useful method is the critical incident interview process used in DSMC's competency research (Cullen 1990). Here, the project manager candidate is asked to recount several significant prior job situations of their own choosing. In each situation, the interviewer listens and probes for detail seeking to identify which competencies the candidate has used (and not used) in the past. Such discussions often cut through generic statements of capability and accomplishment by the candidates to what they actually did in real-life situations.

Experiential exercises and behavioral simulations are ideally suited to assess leadership and management competencies. These exercises vary from short role-playing scenarios requiring minimal preparation to more elaborate behavioral simulations with several participants, each provided with a detailed in-basket of background information. Project manager candidates can be put into these realistic situations and asked to respond, not by stating what they would do in the situations, but by actually doing it. Participants then step aside and become students of their own behavior through follow-up discussions including feedback from trainers and other participants. Assessment instruments and behavioral checklists can also be used to augment the personal feedback provided. Clearly, no project manager career development model is complete without a credible competency assessment process.

## Competency Development

Even with effective assessment and selection processes, further improvement of critical project manager skills is desirable for all project manager candidates, even the most competent. Efforts to achieve this improvement should be directed both on the job and in the series of professional training opportunities which may be available or sponsored by the organization. Several self-development and training methodologies exist which can be adapted for this purpose.

Case studies have proven effective in addressing project manager competencies when imbedded in established training programs. Case studies based on past projects can bring the real world dimension to the classroom and provide additional focus on project manager unique skill requirements. Several such real work cases have been developed by DSMC and are now used in the curriculum.

Experiential exercises can add the behavioral dimension to the classroom environment. Here, understanding is only the first step in mastering the complex set of project manager competencies. In his book "The Competent Manager," (Boyatzis 1982) noted management researcher Dr. Richard Boyatzis states:

*"Too often training programs attempt to teach the fundamentals using lectures, readings, case discussions, films, and dynamic speakers to transfer knowledge to course participants. Unfortunately, it is usually not the lack of knowledge, but the inability to use knowledge that limits effective managerial behavior."*

To focus on this application of knowledge, DSMC uses several experiential exercises in its project management courses. They range from short team building exercises to the elaborate Mouse Trap Car which covers the entire project life cycle with student work groups acting as project team. These simulations offer project manager candidates the opportunity to integrate their specialized knowledge along with the complex management and leadership skills necessary to be effective in the real world project management environment (Gadeken 1989, 1994).

## Conclusions

The role of the project manager has and will continue to be the corner stone of the effective project management. As this paper has shown, project managers require a unique set of competencies focused extensively on managerial and leadership skills. However, considerable planning and attention must be applied now to ensure that future project managers will have these prerequisite skills. This includes carefully structuring processes for selection, assessment and development of project managers with the "right stuff" for the complex global environment of the future.

### References


Best, G.D. and Kobylarz, K.L. 1991. *Establishing a Department of Defense Program Management Body of Knowledge (Masters Thesis).* Wright-Patterson Air Force Base, OH: Air Force Institute of Technology.

Boyatzis, R.E. 1982. *The Complete Manager: A Model for Effective Performance.* New York: Wiley-Interscience: 4.

Cullen, B.J. and Gadeken, O.C. 1990. *A Competency Model of Program Managers in the DoD Acquisition Process.* Fort Belvoir, VA: Defense Systems Management College.

Gadeken, O.C. 1989. DSMC Simulations (Games that Teach Engineers and Scientists How to Manage). *Program Manager* (May-June): 29-39.

Gadeken, O.C. 1994. Developing Project Leadership Skills Using Behavioral Simulations. *Proceedings.* Upper Darby, PA: Project Management Institute.

Gadeken, O.C. 1991. *Competencies of Project Managers in the MOD Procurement Executive.* Shrivenham, England: Royal Military College of Science.

Gadeken, O.C. 1986. Why Engineers and Scientists Often Fail as Managers (and What to Do About It). *Program Manager* (January-February): 37-45.

Gilbert, T.F. and M.B. 1988. The Science of Winning. *Training* (August): 33-40.

Klemp, G.O. 1982. Job Competency Assessment: Defining Attributes of the Top Performer. *Pig and the Python and Other Tales.* American Society for Training and Development, Research Series No.8.

McVeigh, B.J. 1994. *Army Program Managers: A Competency Perspective (Masters Thesis).* Monterey, CA: Naval Postgraduate School.

# Life On *VentureStar™*: The Use of Integrated Product Teams to Perform Concurrent Engineering on a 21st Century Space Program

Clinton A. Jullens, Lockheed Martin Skunk Works

## Introduction

Imagine stepping into a new program at your company and feeling like a new hire because you recognize only a dozen or so of the several hundred workers. This was my first reaction when I came to work on *VentureStar™*, the highly publicized new space program. With few exceptions, most team based programs at the Skunk WorksTM typically involve the company's own work force or perhaps a joint venture with one or two other organizations. *VentureStar™*, however, is quite different. The program is organized into large Integrated Product Teams (IPTs) each involving over a dozen organizations from many different levels and niches in the aerospace industry. Right from the start, I knew this was going to be an interesting program. In this article, I'll describe to you what life is like on *VentureStar™*, starting with a brief description of the program and the role of the Skunk Works™, followed by a discussion on the program's use of IPTs. Afterwards, I'll discuss some of the challenges and opportunities, and offer a few important considerations for other programs.

## The Program

Space access is presently very limited. It can cost on the order of $10,000 a pound and take several years of waiting to place hardware into space using existing launch vehicles like the Space Shuttle. Most of the cost and time is due to the refurbishment or replacement of components consumed during flight. In addition, integrating these vehicles with payload and support facilities is operationally complex, further increasing cost and time. Even with its ability to fly repeatedly, the Space Shuttle is a costly, high maintenance vehicle. Expendable Launch Vehicles (ELV), such as Atlas and Titan class rockets, have similar constraints because they are multi-stage systems that "expend" their very expensive rocket stages in the process of reaching space.

Fortunately, the limitations of space access can be overcome. A launch vehicle that can reuse its components to reduce per launch requirements and decrease turnaround time can significantly reduce its operational costs and increase its availability. A vehicle that fits this description is termed Reusable Launch Vehicle (RLV).

RLV is important to United States space operations. Confronted with escalating maintenance costs and the aging airframe of the Space Shuttle, NASA is in need of an affordable method of accessing space for projects such as the Space Station. RLV is the most cost effective means of providing space access. RLV is also a means of recapturing the leadership position that the United States has lost in the commercial launch market. Presently, only the United States is capable of developing RLV.

Despite the need, many in industry realize that in order to make RLV a commercial reality, its development cost and risk must be kept low and confidence in its viability must be high. Once the cost and complexity of accessing space is reduced with an operational RLV, the launch service market could actually expand appreciably.

*VentureStar™*, is Lockheed Martin's version of RLV with a complete low cost space launch service targeted at the launch service market (Exhibit 1). The concept is based on a reusable Single Stage To Orbit (SSTO) vehicle with a low Gross Lift-Off-Weight (GLOW), a key to low cost RLV development. The vehicle is complemented by a fully integrated launch service that includes mission planning and launch site / payload integration. Lockheed Martin anticipates that *VentureStar™* can place hardware into space at a cost of around $1000 a pound with a two day turnaround.

In July 1996, NASA signed with Lockheed Martin a Cooperative Agreement to build and fly the X-33 Advanced Technology Demonstrator and to conduct RLV risk reduction and development. The four year Cooperative Agreement is an intensive program intended to prove the concept and generate decision criteria data before proceeding with the next stage of RLV development. The program covers the whole infrastructure including the launch and landing sites, vehicle development, operational support and business plans. The culmination of the program is in 1999 with the flight testing of the X-33, a scaled down prototype of the RLV, and completion of ground technology development on the full-scale engine and composite liquid oxygen tank.

The program's organization consists of a teaming arrangement of industry and Government (Exhibit 2). Each member

**Exhibit 1.** *VentureStar*TM Operational Concept and Market

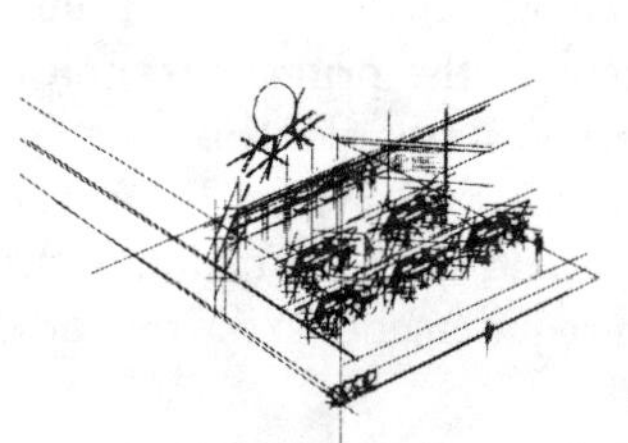

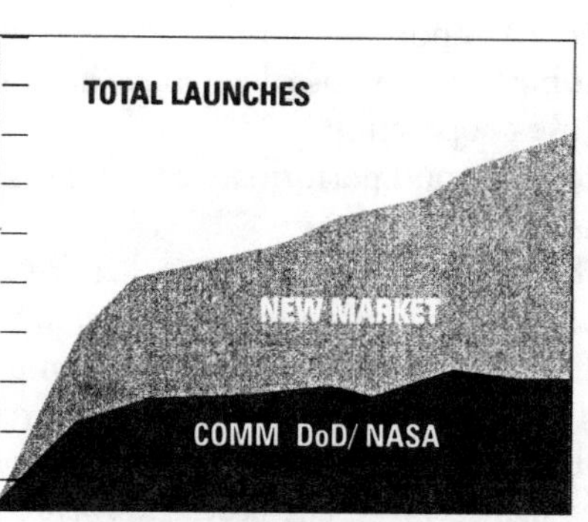


**Single Operations Control Center (OCC)**
- Mission Planning
- Ground Operations
- Launch Operations
- Mission Operations

**24 Hour Vehicle Processing**
- Payload Carrier Removal
- Vehicle Maintenance
- Vehicle Servicing
- Payload Carrier Installation

**24 Hour Launch Operations**
- Vehicle Rotation
- Propellant Loading
- Station Crew Ingress
  On-Site Crew Accommodations
- Vertical Launch

**Horizontal Landing**
- Towed to pad within 1 hr

**Exhibit 2.** *VentureStar*TM Team Members and Major Subcontractors

| LOCKHEED MARTIN | NASA | AEROJET |
|---|---|---|
| ASTRONAUTICS | AMES | ALLIANT TECHSYSTEMS |
| CONTROL SYSTEMS | DRYDEN | ALLIED SIGNAL AEROSPACE |
| ENGINEERING SCIENCES | HEADQUARTERS | BOEING, ROCKETDYNE DIV. |
| INFORMATION SYSTEMS | JPL | ROHR |
| MANNED SPACE SYSTEMS | JOHNSON | SVERDRUP |
| MISSILE SYSTEMS | KENNEDY | THIOKOL |
| SANDERS | LANGLEY | UNITED SPACE ALLIANCE |
| SKUNK WORKS | MARSHALL | USAF |
| TECHNICAL OPERATIONS | STENNIS | EDWARDS AFB |
| | LEWIS | MALSTROM AFB |
| | | MICHAEL AAF |
| | | BICYCLE LAKE |
| | | PHILLIPS LAB |
| | | WRIGHT LAB |

brings to the team unique and essential experience in key technical, marketing, operational and financial areas. Examples are Rocketdyne's development of the linear aerospike engine or Sverdrup's design of launch complexes. Various procurement mechanisms, such as Cooperative Agreements and Task Agreements with NASA, Strategic Alliances with industry, and Intercompany Work Transfers with other Lockheed Martin companies provide program control.

## The Skunk Works™ Heritage- Need For Speed

The Skunk Works™ experience with rapid development of prototype aircraft made it an appropriate choice as the prime integrator of the team. Kelly Johnson, the founder of the Skunk Works™, operated from 14 basic principles, including the following which are particularly suited to concurrent engineering:

- The Program Manager has complete control of all program aspects.
- Company and Customer project offices must be small but strong.

- A small team of motivated and experienced personnel achieves superior results.
- Minimize the number of reports, but thoroughly record important work.
- Company and customer must have mutual trust and close cooperation.
- Reward good performance rather than number of personnel supervised.

The Skunk Works$^{TM}$ teaming concepts evolved from a critical skills assessment of many programs. The skill mix was implemented to fit with the short term prototype development and limited production specialty aircraft. Kelly utilized small, dedicated work teams with open communications between management, engineering, procurement, manufacturing and flight test. Key individuals with a high degree of experience and commitment were given substantial responsibility for coordinating all aspects of major tasks. This resulted in the ability to run efforts in parallel with minimum risks and in the use of informal integrated teams where mutual trust and commitment often substituted for documentation and rigid procedures. The application of Kelly's principles have helped the Skunk Works$^{TM}$ earn a reputation for producing sophisticated aircraft in a short time span and with a low development cost. In recent years, these principles have been applied to programs with formal IPTs, such as on the YF-22 fighter program and the Joint Strike Fighter (JSF) program. The scope of *VentureStar*$^{TM}$ falls well within the dimensions of these programs.

## The Structure

The concept of Integrated Product Teams is certainly not new, but its interpretation and application varies. As author Morgan Swink puts it, "there is no single correct vision of concurrent engineering" (Swink 1996). The organizational approach on *VentureStar*$^{TM}$ is based on a need to develop and validate the commercial viability of the technical and operation concepts in a very short time frame. The ambitious schedule and wide spread involvement of the program requires that efforts be conducted in parallel among several distinct organizations, and in many cases without complete information. The *VentureStar*$^{TM}$ teaming arrangement allows team members to participate in the whole product acquisition function, from engineering development and procurement, to testing, manufacturing and operations. This allows for tasks to be performed simultaneously even though the effort may be physically conducted across the country by personnel in different companies.

An inherent benefit to this arrangement is the availability of multiple resources and optimum usage of individual company strengths. Procurement of parts by one member for use by other team members is a perfect example of this benefit. Use of a common test facility or materials and processes department is another example. The overall program is not limited by the capability of a single organization.

At the program level there are three system level teams, the RLV System Team, the X-33 System Team, and the Enterprise Development Team (Exhibit 3). The first two teams, RLV System and X-33 System, are the primary technical workhorses. The majority of technical risk reduction and development tasks are contained in the X-33 System Team. The third team, Enterprise Development, serves to maintain the program focus and flows down requirements to the two other teams.

All three teams are founded on a set of decision criteria. The criteria are derived from the Program Plan which identifies high risk in four primary areas: business, technical, marketing and operations. Each team's objective is to reduce these high risk areas to acceptable levels for the next stage of RLV development.

Beneath each system level team are several major IPTs supported by many sub-IPTs and ad hoc "tiger" teams. Individual responsibilities are derived from the Statement of Work (SOW), requirements allocation, and detailed schedules. The IPTs are accountable through periodic status reviews and a set of preestablished metrics. Within each IPT are documents such as cooperative agreements and intercompany work transfers that authorize personnel from different organizations to work together.

The IPTs are staffed with appropriate personnel from all the required disciplines and functions, irrespective of company affiliation. This includes having the program customer, NASA, participate as a team member at all levels of the organization from the high level program teams to smaller sub-IPTs. In many instances, companies that normally assume suppliers roles, such as Allied Signal Aerospace (ASA), function as full team members with substantial integration responsibility. The overall effect of this arrangement establishes mutual trust and cooperation, and aids in the Skunk WorksTM effort to document only essential data.

A key application of the IPTs and a fundamental premise of the Skunk Works$^{TM}$ is to have the same individuals that define the tasks also execute the tasks. To facilitate communications, experienced personnel with established relationships are used. As these teams complete their tasks they are carried over intact to work on the next effort; thereby, maintaining the knowledge base and reducing learning curve inefficiencies.

All team members have a core group of personnel physically collocated. Communication and design work are greatly enhanced by collocation. Furthermore, documentation and correspondence are minimized. However, there are many instances where utilizing specialties or unique resources located

**Exhibit 3.** *VentureStar*TM Integrated Product Team Organization (Lockheed Martin, 1996)

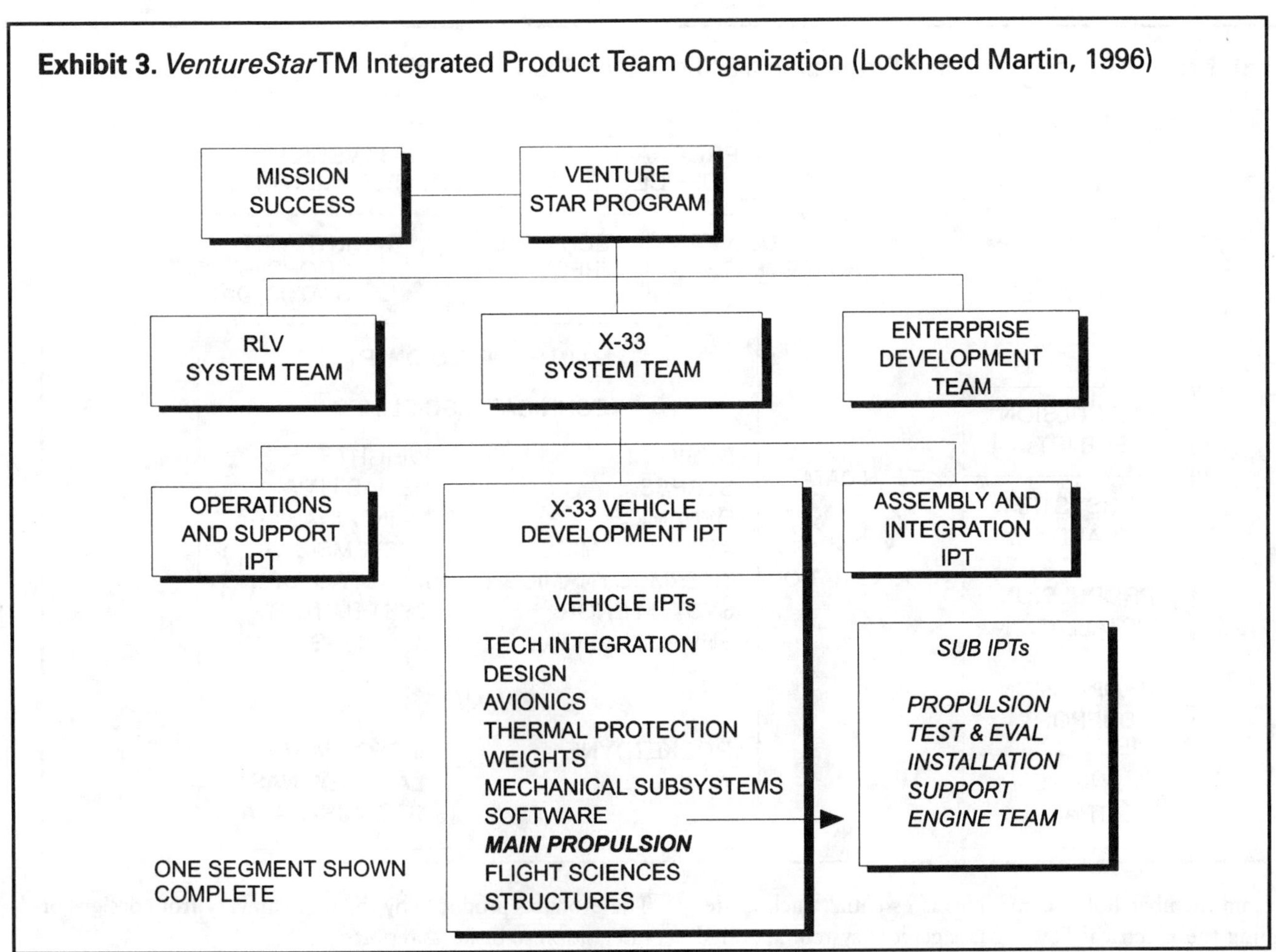


**Exhibit 4.** Selected Behicle and Ground Operations IPT Responsibility for Program Activities on th X-33 System Team (Lockheed Martin, 1997)

| IPT PROGRAM ACTIVITY | IPT RESPONSIBILITY |
|---|---|
| Design Baseline | Product Design |
| Configuration Control | IPT Impacts & Approval |
| Baseline & Changes | Product Baseline & Changes |
| Technical Performance Measures (TPMs) | Compute, Evaluate, Project TPMs |
| Trade Studies | Product Trades |
| Budget & Cost Control | IPT Budgets Allocation, Management, Reporting |
| Schedule | IPT Schedules (Includes Margin Management) |
| Risk Management | Risk Identification, Monitoring, Mitigation |
| Interfaces | Product Interfaces |
| Performance Effectiveness | Product Performance & Operation |
| Reliability | Product Reliability |
| Acceptance & Qualification | Product |
| Production | Product Production |
| Logistics | Product Logistics |
| Subcontracts & Procurement | Subcontract Management |

**Exhibit 5.** IPT Process—Main Propulsion IPT (Lockheed Martin, 1996)

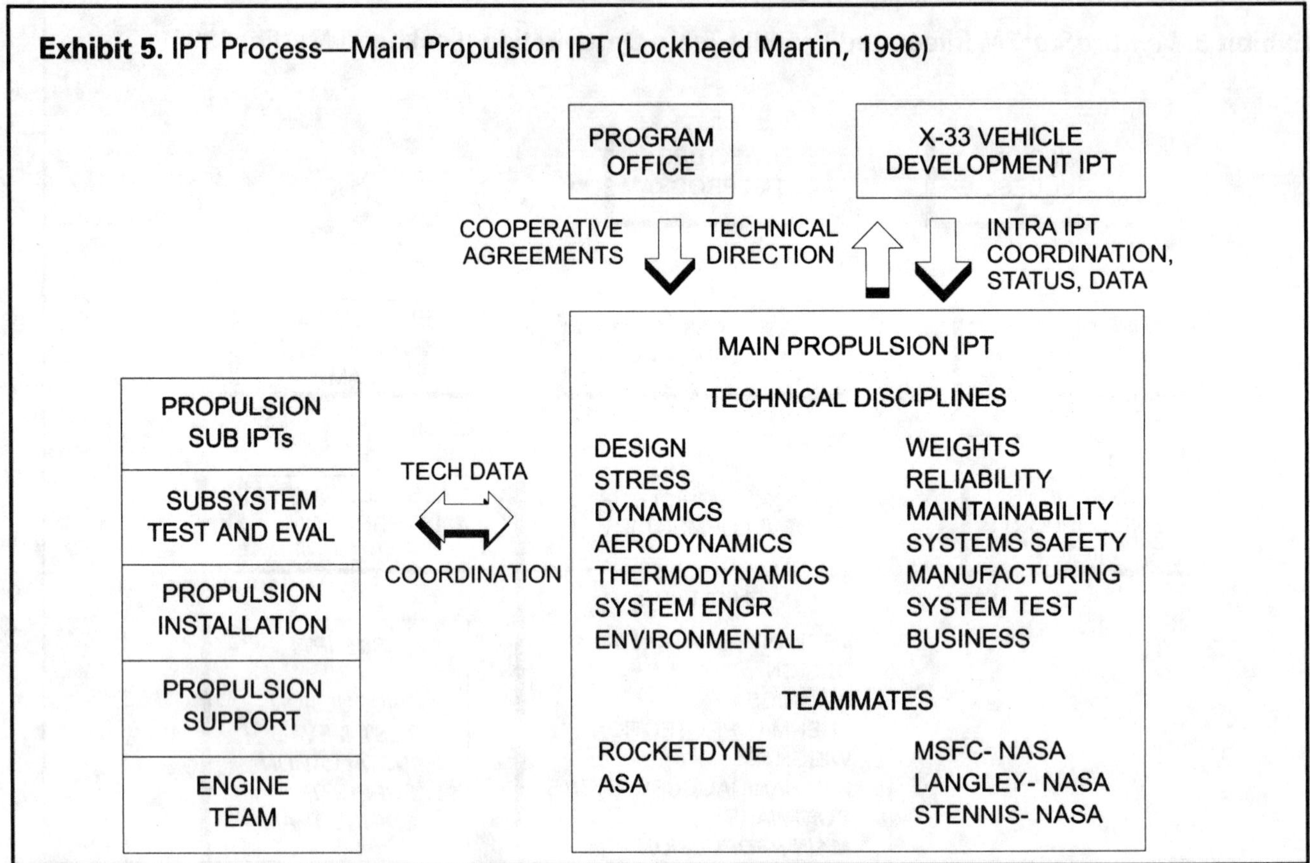


at team member home companies is essential, such as designing the Electrical Power Management system at Allied Signal Aerospace in Canada. In such instances, Interface Control Documents (ICDs) and functional specifications are used in combination with on site system engineers, networked computers, and regular face to face working group meetings. In this sense, "Virtual" IPTs are created.

An entire program communications network has been set-up that allows remote sites to access information and communicate within the program. The program makes intensive use of the Internet, e-mail and FTP in a combination of secured and unsecured modes. All forms of documentation are exchanged ranging from uncontrolled informal messages to tightly controlled deliverable CAD drawings and documents. This capability also aids in conducting parallel tasks at various locations.

## The Process

The IPT structure is used throughout the program. In addition to vehicle development, this structure is also used in the development of the launch control center, launch and landing facilities, operations, marketing and business planning. The products produced by the IPTs can vary from designs or integration to business reports.

Following the Skunk Works™ philosophy, product development is accomplished in the smallest forum possible. An IPT has full responsibility and authority for the implementation of any change that affects its own product. Exhibit 4 illustrates a few examples of IPT responsibility as defined in the System Engineering Management Plan (SEMP) for the X-33 System Team. If the change affects other IPTs or program level cost and schedule, the IPT summarizes the impact and presents it to a small but formal review board consisting of high level IPT leads, who have the authority to approve major configuration changes provided it does not affect program cost or schedule. Changes that affect cost and schedule are presented to the program manager for approval.

Within each IPT, the team retains authority to govern all performance, schedule and cost aspects of its product (Exhibit 5). IPTs at the same level freely exchange data and define requirements. The higher level teams (i.e., Ground Operations, Vehicle Development, etc.) govern integration and coordination of the lower level IPTs beneath them. Program management supports the teams with resources, business agreements, and overall guidance. Numerous contract specialists and other administrative personnel also support the IPT.

The IPT also performs the function of measuring and reporting their own progress. Metrics for measuring progress of each IPT are derived from the decision criteria. Depending on the risk and definition of the criteria, the performance measurement used can involve technical performance, design to cost, life cycle cost, schedule, demonstrations, or analysis. These measurements are reported frequently (weekly) at the lower level IPTs and less frequently (monthly) at the higher levels. Cost and schedule are tracked through an automated reporting system, 'COSTRACK', on a weekly basis. Use of small detailed work packages and short term progress payments help to make deviations visible for a quick response.

Systems Engineering assists with the definition, development, production and operation of the IPT and the integration of all of their products. The SEMP facilitates the work flow between IPT and other organizations by defining a set of activities and simple operating procedures, such as the review board. Systems Engineering also bridges the gap between program level activities and IPT activities. However, the ultimate responsibility for implementing the system engineering process rests with the IPT.

## The Challenges And Opportunities

Despite the program's complexity and size, *VentureStar™* IPT challenges are similar to those on other concurrent engineering programs. There are numerous case studies in the literature (see suggested reading list) suggesting that cultural work differences and geographically dispersed team members are among the most fundamental of challenges. Cultural work differences on *VentureStar™* go a step beyond the functional company disciplines (i.e., engineering, manufacturing, etc.). In fact, it is actually a combination of disciplines from many different companies, where similar groups, say engineering in two different companies, or dissimilar groups, such as engineering in one company and manufacturing in another, must work together. In addition, there are other cultures brought about by the pool of numerous new hires at each company. Many of these new hires are recent college graduates or former employees of other companies who bring with them a variety of unique cultural differences. Establishing good working relationships early on helps reduce the difficulties associated with cultural work differences.

Team member dispersion is the other challenging situation. Dispersed teams or "Virtual" IPTs as they are sometimes called, tend to limit responsiveness to changing requirements and configuration. Distance is also a source of misunderstanding since the communication tools used (i.e., written correspondences, telecons, etc.) remove visual references like facial expressions, which can communicate subtle information. There is a heavy reliance on the network tools, such as e-mail and shared files to overcome this problem, but in situations filled with uncertainties and hard decisions, it is vital to have a cohesive team in one location.

The same two challenges mentioned above, cultural work differences and dispersed team members, are also sources of opportunity. If harnessed properly, conflicts and disagreements stemming from culture work differences can lead to a better design. They stimulate creativity and surface potential problems. As the authors of the book *Team Handbook* (Scholtes 1996, 7-2) point out, conflict can also prevent "groupthink," an unchallenged consensus that can lead to bad or less than optimal decisions.

Dispersed teams can also be beneficial. As mentioned earlier, multi-company involvement opened up a plethora of specialized resources on the program. In their article, "Virtual and Real Organizations: Optimal Pairing," Yeack and Sayles (Yeack 1996, 29) see virtual organizations (IPTs in this case) as being an advantageous way of economically using expertise. Also available are numerous test facilities, knowledge databases, and informational leads. The key here is to know when face to face interaction is necessary.

## Considerations

A program like *VentureStar™* is certainly an exciting learning experience for everyone involved. As a team member you are involved in more than just building another aircraft or subcomponent. You are actually part of a whole new infrastructure and potential new segment of the industry. Yet, despite the satisfaction of being part of the big picture, it's the participation in the sub-IPTs that is the most exciting. It is here where the dynamics of evolving requirements and continuous change challenges the effectiveness of team work and where all the scenarios of contemporary IPTs are played out.

The following are some important considerations for others contemplating IPTs on similar programs and are particularly applicable to lower level teams:

### 1. Keep teams small but effective.

Teams should have the minimum number of members representing the key areas of a team's product. It is not necessary to include a member from every discipline. Teams should be aware of the total picture but stay focused on their product.

### 2. Select team leaders that are experienced and people-oriented.

A team leader should function primarily as a facilitator and strive for team based decision making, but also know when unilateral decision making is necessary. The team leader should continuously make the team function properly by providing direction, resolving conflicts, helping individual members meet their needs and communicating effectively both within and outside the team. The team leader should be experienced enough to help individual members, but avoid doing the work himself.

### 3. Collocate team members whenever possible.

Tasks with well defined parameters and stable requirements can be performed by physically separate team members using control documents. Resolving ambiguous or evolving tasks is best done through collocation. When this is not feasible, either due to budget or distance, communicate with team members frequently making maximum use of routine telecons and network tools. Conduct face to face working group meetings as necessary.

### 4. Bring down the work cultural barriers as quick as possible.

Work out differences as quickly as possible before they manifest. Develop operating procedures for teams and have teams monitor the implementation of their own procedures. Know when replacing a team member is necessary.

### 5. Support teams with adequate resources.

Inadequate resources can cause rework and distract a team. Resources should be timely and adequate. This includes manpower, materials, computer resources, budgets, office services, and facilities.

### 6. Train team members.

Make effective use of a team by training the members. Train team members to take ownership of the team's product and the responsibility of being a team member. Train team leaders on key IPT leadership skills such as facilitating and communicating. If possible, train leaders in technical areas where they lack experience.

## Conclusion

*VentureStar*™ is an exciting program that offers technical and organizational challenges. It will broaden our knowledge of space technology and give us insight into the large scale use of concurrent engineering and integrated product teams involving multiple organizations.

The Skunk Works™ is playing an important role. As prime integrator, the company must implement a teaming arrangement that will broaden the application of its principles. The company's strategy is to flow decision making down to the lowest level practical using empowered IPTs.

Challenges on the program are very similar to those on other IPT programs. Cultural work differences and dispersed team members are two of the most common challenges. Cultural differences can impede information sharing and dilute team benefits. Dispersed team members can slow team responsiveness and create miscommunication. These challenges, if handled properly, can be turned to opportunities that could improve innovation, identify quality problems and tap into larger resources.

There are several important considerations to be made for other programs. Among them are using small effective teams, selecting appropriate leaders, collocating team members, bringing down cultural barriers, providing adequate resources and training team members. These considerations apply to all levels of IPTs, but are particularly beneficial to lower level IPTs.


### Acknowledgement

Special thanks to Jim Mellady, Hal Arbogast, Tony Iles, Gary Wendt, Jerry Rising, Bob Baumgartner, and Todd Paulos for their help in preparing this article.


### References And Suggested Reading


1992. Creating Teamwork In Engineering. *Machine Design* 6 (March) 99(8).

Filipczak, B. 1996. Concurrent Engineering: A Team By Any Other Name? *Training* 8 (August): 54(6).

Kerzner, H. 1995. *Project Management, A Systems Approach to Planning, Scheduling, and Controlling*. New York. Van Nostrand Reinhold

Rich, B. and Janos, L. 1994. *Skunk Works*. NY: Little, Brown and Company.

Scholtes, P.; Joiner, B.; and Streibel, B. 1996. *The Team Handbook, Second Edition*. WI: Joiner Associates Inc.

Swink, M.; Sandvig, C.; Mabert, V. Adding "Zip" To Product Development: Concurrent Engineering Methods and Tools. *Business Horizons* 2 (March): 41(9).

Tippett, D. and Peters, J. 1995. Team Building and Project Management: How Are We Doing? *Project Management Journal* 4 (December): 29-37.

Yeack, W. and Sayles, L. 1996. Virtual and Real Organizations: Optimal Pairing. *PM Network* 8 (August): 29-32.

# Managing Risk

Bill Shepherd, PMP, Decision Dynamics Inc.

## Identify Risk

### Ignorance isn't bliss

Managing risk is a central aspect of program or project management. In the life-cycle of a project, things will happen that are completely beyond the ability of the program manager to control or predict. This is why every project needs a strong risk management program. Cost, schedule, performance—or all three—will suffer unless there is a proactive process in place to actively seek out these uncertainties and manage them. Differences in scope, availability of resources, management structure and even individual skill levels will influence how best to implement risk management within a given project. Tools or techniques that worked for one project or organization may need to be tailored to work well for another, but the general concepts and principles are the same..

As a project moves from concept through completion, the uncertain future is replaced with 20/20 hindsight. In the beginning, there are things you know, things you know you don't know (but need to find out), and things you don't know you don't know. The items in this last group—the surprises you don't even see coming—are the most dangerous since you can't develop mitigation plans for them. A structured process should be put in place early to actively seek out these problems and change them from "unknown-unknowns" into at least "known-unknowns" as soon as possible. There are several practical approaches to this that can be tailored to meet the needs of any project.

### Open Communication

Never shoot a messenger. If you do, you soon stop getting messages and then you are in the dark. The free flow of accurate information is essential and a good program manager will encourage open communication up, down, and across the organization. Every member of the team has to feel free to identify a risk or potential problem. There are enough "unknowns" to uncover, don't permit an environment that encourages people to withhold bad news from you or each other.

When operating in an Integrated Product Team environment, include the functional organizations in this information flow. The functional organizations are the "technical conscience" for their particular core competencies and you should welcome their input on potential problems. The facts are what they are; it's people's perceptions that vary. Get problems out on the table and deal with them openly and professionally, using all the resources that are available. The functional organization can provide additional resources to assist if they are needed.

The organizational structure of the risk management program, and how it relates to day to day technical and management decision making needs to be clearly defined and communicated to everyone on the program. This is especially true in a large development program that uses multifunctional teams. The teams will be composed of people who come from different organizations, often in different geographic locations, from different functional backgrounds and even organizational culture. They have to share a common understanding of the risk management process.

Open communication does not mean undisciplined communication. (Freedom of speech is a right, not an obligation.) Too much communication will make you data rich and information poor. Modern tools such as the internet and Email can be a powerful aid to program management, but use them carefully. If everybody "info's the boss" on every Email they send, the boss will get overloaded; there is only a finite amount of useful conscious time in the day. Also, this abrogates the responsibility, accountability and authority of second and third tier team leaders who should be making sure this information gets into the hands of people who need to know. The goal should be to highlight important information and make it rapidly available throughout the organization to people who need to know or can help solve the problem. Everybody can't know everything. Create an organizational structure, procedures and climate that encourages people to use their judgment in this "filter and highlight" process so that important issues aren't obscured by trivial ones and get the attention they merit. Back that up with a way for *anyone* on the project to get information to the boss if they feel strongly that something is being missed.

### "Graybeards"

In this era of down sizing and consolidation in the defense industry, the probability that many people in the program office have worked on more than a few major development programs is usually quite small. There just aren't that many programs around. No matter what project you are working on, you probably know the person who had the job before you or who did something similar. They may have been successful and been promoted way above you, they may have moved on to other areas of work, they may have retired, or



PROJECT MANAGEMENT INSTITUTE 28th Annual Seminars & Symposium
Chicago, Illinois: Papers Presented September 29 to October 1, 1997

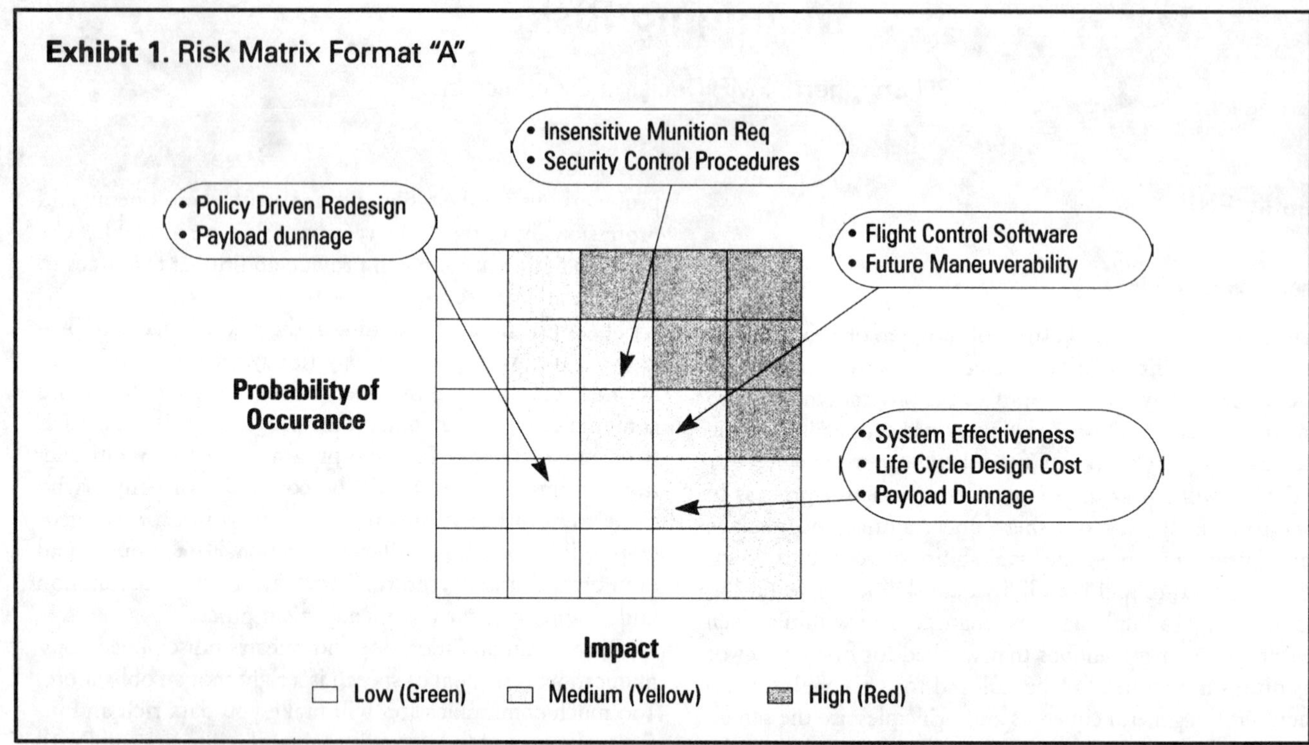


**Exhibit 1.** Risk Matrix Format "A"

they may have failed for a variety of reasons. Regardless of where they are, these people represent a pool of talent and experience that can give you valuable insight. A gathering of these experts is an excellent forum for discussing program status, identifying foreseen challenges, and soliciting input from these assembled experts. The "graybeards" will give you ideas for handling problems you know about and point out others you haven't thought of yet.

### Independent Assessment Teams

An independent group that is familiar with the program, but not directly responsible for running it on a day to day basis, can provide the Program Manager with a valuable perspective on program risks while there is still time to react or mitigate them. By standing apart from the action, they have a broader perspective and can see problems that the team doesn't see yet. Chartered by senior management as an independent group with free rein to go anywhere, talk to anyone, sit in on any meeting, and ask any question, their task is to look ahead of the project to identify problems that are "lead time away". In essence, they are the scouts riding ahead of the wagon train to find the deserts, tainted water holes and blind canyons that lay ahead while there is still time to stock up the provisions or change course.

For Program Independent Assessment (PIA) teams to be effective, they must not just be—they must also be perceived to be—a neutral party by all concerned. Senior management must set the proper climate by not overreacting to PIA reports. If done properly, the project team will view PIA as a helpful way to communicate important concerns to upper management. PIA reports should result in management help only if it's needed, and delivered in a way that allows the team to do their job. Done improperly, the PIA will be viewed as just another team of inspectors looking for faults to report and as a source of non-value added work. This will make people defensive and reluctant to be completely open with them.

### Define risk categories

Everyone on the team has to share a common understanding of how to characterize risk. It is difficult to compare the impact of failing to achieve a performance threshold with the impact of a schedule slip or cost overrun. While it is true that one may cause the other, it is helpful to keep the root cause of the risk in mind when developing mitigation plans.

One approach, which is used by the F/A-18 program, is to create a matrix similar to Exhibit 1. The team periodically reviews the risks to place them into the appropriate category. Another approach is to define bands of Low, Medium, and High impact in terms of cost, schedule, and performance, and assign a score or normalized cost based on that assessment. That value is plotted with the associated probability as shown in Exhibit 2. (The numbers in the chart refer to the risk number in the database.)

For briefing purposes, Exhibit 1 is generally easier for people to understand, although the distinction between a "red"

**Exhibit 2.** Risk Matrix Format "B"

Probability of Occurance
HI
MED
LOW
7
26
23
29
30
12
31
27
18
3
25
LOW
MED
HI
Normalized Cost of Risk


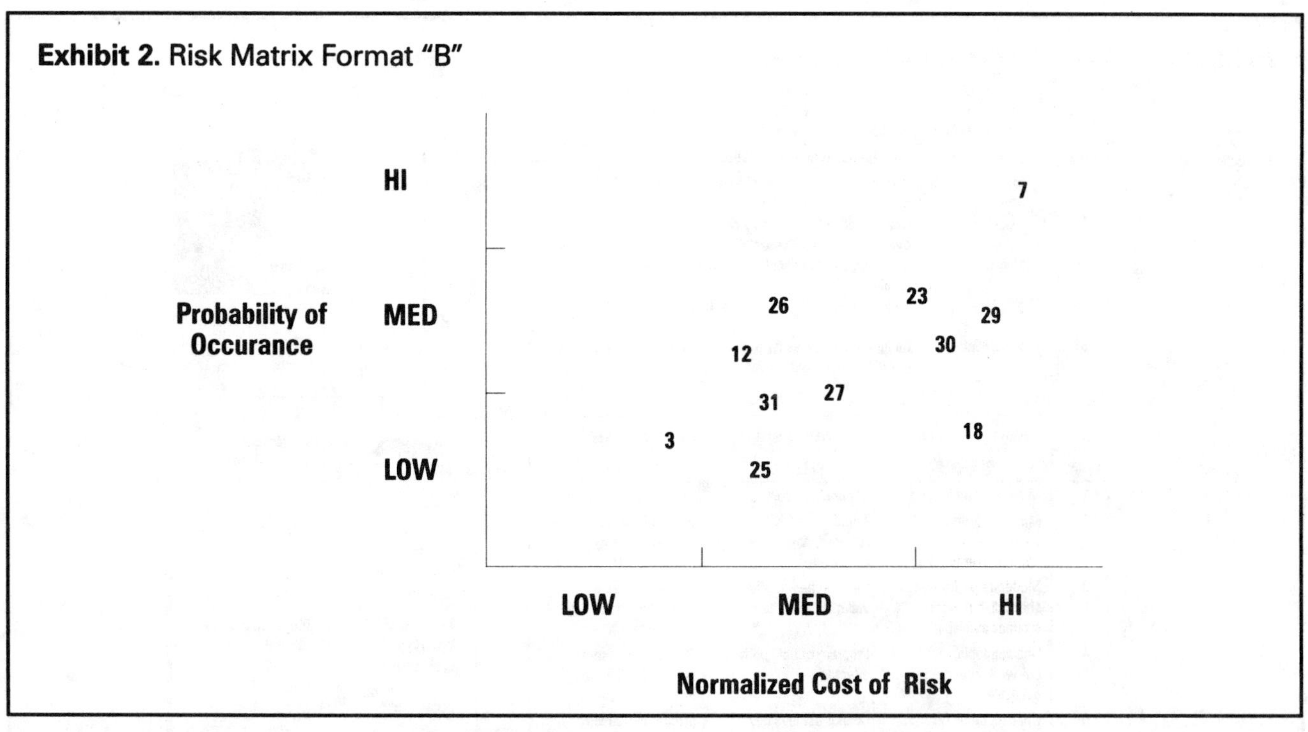

**Exhibit 3.** F/A-18 Risk Management Process

**Risk**: An undesirable situation or circumstance which has both a probability of occurring and a potential consequence to program success; risks are normally associated with uncertainties
**Risk Management**: An organized, systematic decision-making process that efficiently identifies risks, assesses or analyzes risks, and effectively reduces or eliminates risks to achieving program goals

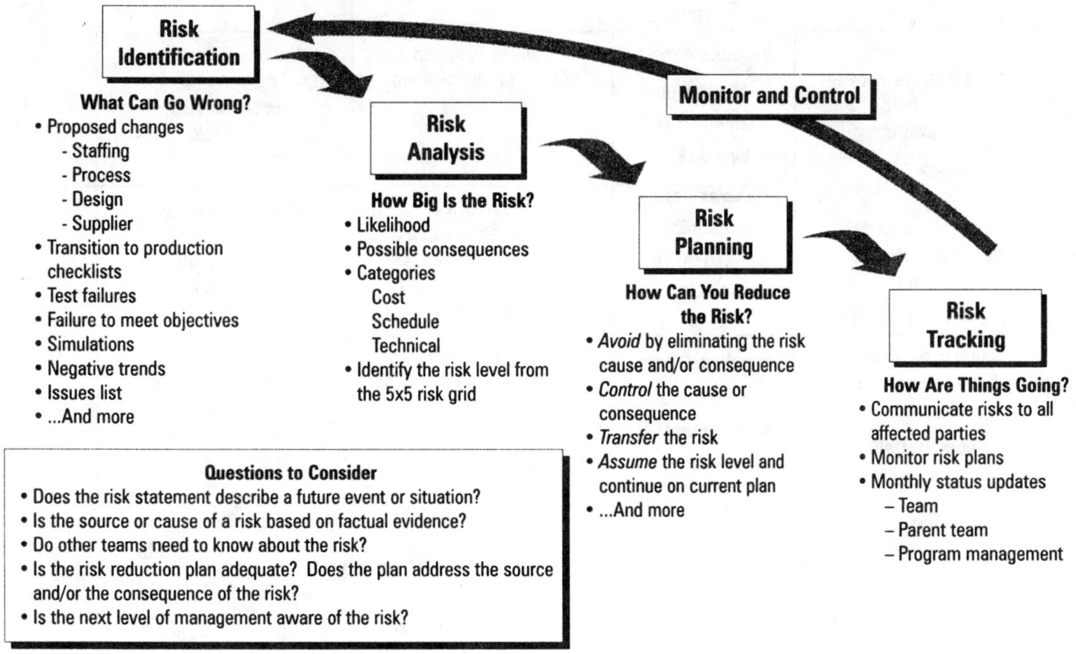

Risk Identification
What Can Go Wrong?
• Proposed changes
- Staffing
- Process
- Design
- Supplier
• Transition to production checklists
• Test failures
• Failure to meet objectives
• Simulations
• Negative trends
• Issues list
• ...And more
Risk Analysis
How Big Is the Risk?
• Likelihood
• Possible consequences
• Categories
Cost
Schedule
Technical
• Identify the risk level from the 5x5 risk grid
Risk Planning
How Can You Reduce the Risk?
• Avoid by eliminating the risk cause and/or consequence
• Control the cause or consequence
• Transfer the risk
• Assume the risk level and continue on current plan
• ...And more
Risk Tracking
How Are Things Going?
• Communicate risks to all affected parties
• Monitor risk plans
• Monthly status updates
– Team
– Parent team
– Program management
Monitor and Control
Questions to Consider
• Does the risk statement describe a future event or situation?
• Is the source or cause of a risk based on factual evidence?
• Do other teams need to know about the risk?
• Is the risk reduction plan adequate? Does the plan address the source and/or the consequence of the risk?
• Is the next level of management aware of the risk?

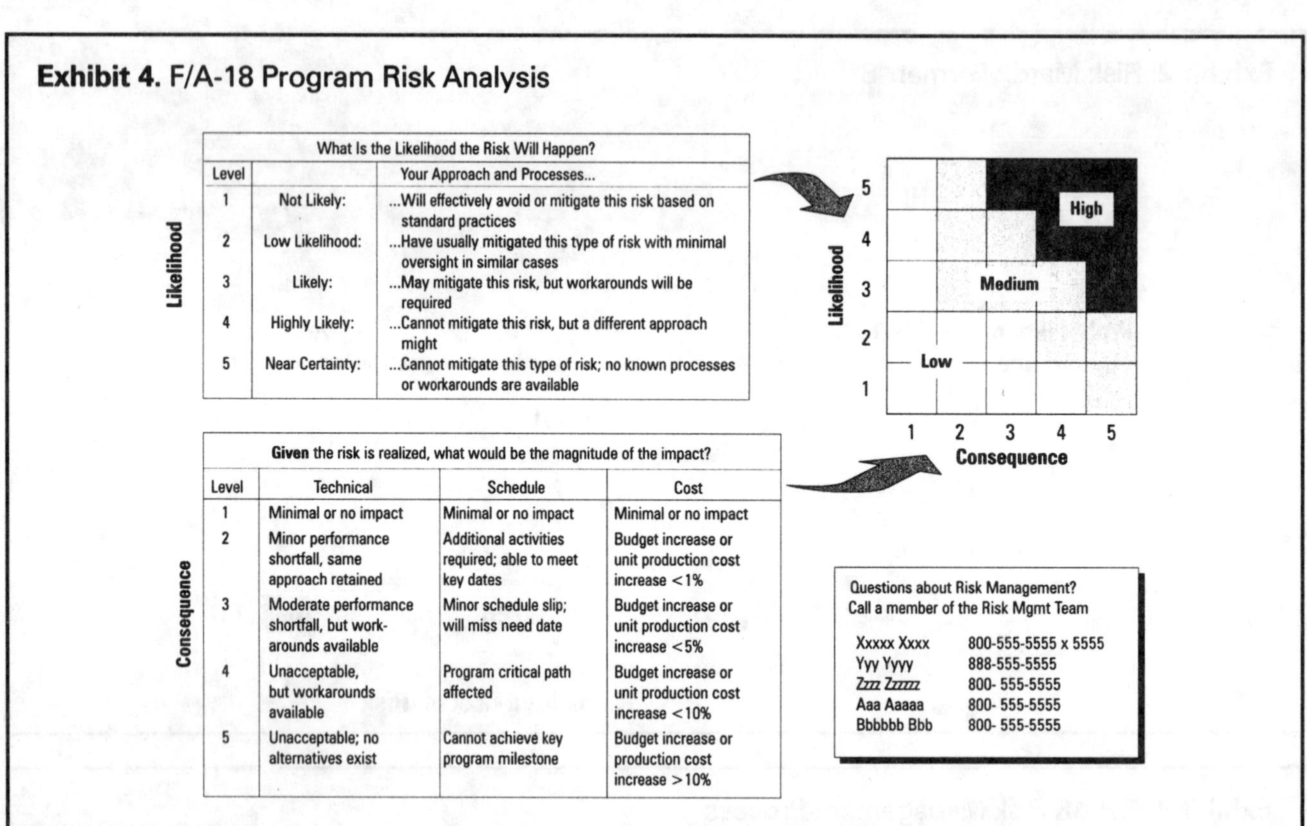

**Exhibit 4.** F/A-18 Program Risk Analysis

Likelihood

| What Is the Likelihood the Risk Will Happen? | | |
|---|---|---|
| Level | | Your Approach and Processes... |
| 1 | Not Likely: | ...Will effectively avoid or mitigate this risk based on standard practices |
| 2 | Low Likelihood: | ...Have usually mitigated this type of risk with minimal oversight in similar cases |
| 3 | Likely: | ...May mitigate this risk, but workarounds will be required |
| 4 | Highly Likely: | ...Cannot mitigate this risk, but a different approach might |
| 5 | Near Certainty: | ...Cannot mitigate this type of risk; no known processes or workarounds are available |



Consequence

| **Given** the risk is realized, what would be the magnitude of the impact? | | | |
|---|---|---|---|
| Level | Technical | Schedule | Cost |
| 1 | Minimal or no impact | Minimal or no impact | Minimal or no impact |
| 2 | Minor performance shortfall, same approach retained | Additional activities required; able to meet key dates | Budget increase or unit production cost increase <1% |
| 3 | Moderate performance shortfall, but workarounds available | Minor schedule slip; will miss need date | Budget increase or unit production cost increase <5% |
| 4 | Unacceptable, but workarounds available | Program critical path affected | Budget increase or unit production cost increase <10% |
| 5 | Unacceptable; no alternatives exist | Cannot achieve key program milestone | Budget increase or production cost increase >10% |

Questions about Risk Management?
Call a member of the Risk Mgmt Team

| | |
|---|---|
| Xxxxx Xxxx | 800-555-5555 x 5555 |
| Yyy Yyyy | 888-555-5555 |
| Zzzz Zzzzzz | 800- 555-5555 |
| Aaa Aaaaa | 800- 555-5555 |
| Bbbbbb Bbb | 800- 555-5555 |

**Exhibit 5.** Cost of Consequences

| | COST | COST | SCHEDULE | PERFORMANCE | Normalized COST |
|---|---|---|---|---|---|
| HI | Requires assets above PMA or above-threshold reprogramming cost>$4M | Requires Assets exceeding Component LCC by> $15% | Causes Program breach or slip > 4 mo. | Causes failure to meet spec/ requirement threshold | $4M or Greater |
| MED | PMA may have assets to cover risk, but Contractor/LFA do not. $100k> cost > $4m | Requires Assets exceeding Component LCC by >$5M% < $15% | Slides DAES milestone to within 2 months of breach, or schedule slip over 1 month | Causes failure to meet objective, but meets spec/ requirement threshold | $100K-$4M |
| LOW | Contractor or LFA have resources to absorb cost < 100K | Requires Assets exceeding Component LCC by <$5% | Slides less than 4 weeks | Meets both threshold and objective spec/ requirement, but performance is degraded | $100K or Less |

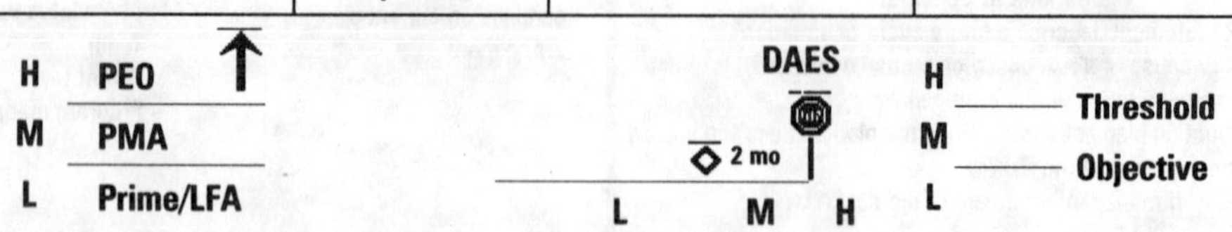

H PEO
M PMA
L Prime/LFA

DAES
2 mo
L M H

H Threshold
M Objective
L

and a "yellow" will tend to generate more discussion than it merits. Exhibits 3 and 4 are the risk templates that were used by the F/A-18 program. They were printed on both sides of a 5x8 card, laminated and passed out to the program team. Each sub-team used these templates or a derivative of them to characterize risk likelihood and consequence. This ensured everyone was using the same definitions and procedures.

Exhibit 5 shows a template for defining normalized cost. Providing definitions of cost, schedule and performance at each level will help create impact assessments that show the relative importance of risks across the program. This will allow upper management to focus attention and resources in the right areas. It's important to remember that the absolute value of these estimates are not as important as their relative value.

### Rough estimates based on Delphi techniques

A lot of useful conscious time can be wasted trying to get what amounts to a Rough Order of Magnitude estimate carried to two decimal places. It's often better to seek consensus on what constitutes the "reasonable range" and use an estimate within it.

In decision theory, when both courses of action have the same expected value, you are at the point of indifference. When your point of indifference lies outside the reasonable range, then all estimates support the same course of action and further debate is moot. When the point of indifference lies within the reasonable range—that is, the preferred course of action would be different depending on which side of the range is correct—then it may be worth refining the estimate.

The easiest way to do this is to ask several experts independently for an assessment. If there is general agreement, then you have your answer. If not, the estimators at the extremes can be asked to explain their reasoning to the rest of the group and then poll them again. The estimates will probably tend to merge. If not, and the potential impact is high, then more analysis is justified.

### Is better information worth the cost of obtaining it?

Before initiating analyses or asking for budgetary or detail cost estimates, ask yourself if you already have enough information to make the decision. Cost estimates take time (and money) to develop with accuracy. Consider the reasonable range of the cost estimate and ask yourself if the appropriate course of action is the same for all values in it. If so, the point of indifference is outside the reasonable range of the estimate and you have all the information you need. If your decision would change, compare the expected value of the risk assuming each cost were correct. The difference is the most you should be willing to pay for this information, since this represents the expected value of perfect information. (For a more complete discussion, see Baird, 1989). If the expected value of perfect information does not exceed the cost of obtaining it, you could be wasting time and money, unless there are other reasons for requesting the analysis.

Don't be a victim of analysis paralysis. If you see a truck coming and you're standing in the middle of the road, you can analyze it's speed to see when you would have to start moving, you can get the maintenance history on the truck to see if the brakes are in good condition, you can try to get a psychological profile on the driver to see if he's likely to swerve... or you can walk to the side of the road and get on with managing the program.

## Describe Risk

### There is a chance that....

What—precisely—is the event that concerns you? How will you know that the event has occurred? Are you concerned about something that might happen, or about something that might NOT happen? If the event occurs, is there only one possible outcome, or are there several?

A careful statement of the risk will help focus the team on the real problem. A risk statement that does not accurately describe the risk will lead to confusion, debate, and wasted effort.

### ...and that chance is neither 0 nor 1.

People sometime state risks in terms of events that have either already occurred or are certain to occur. Risk implies uncertainty, and uncertainty means the probability of occurrence is neither 0 nor 1. If the event has already occurred, or will certainly occur, then you do not have a risk, you have a situation that needs to be managed. It may be a crisis, but it is not a risk.

### Crisis Management

Which brings up crisis management. A crisis is an "unknown-unknown" that has occurred and suddenly needs to be managed. By not foreseeing it, we've lost the ability to be proactive and must now react. Later, with the benefit of 20/20 hindsight, we may discover ways that we might have seen it coming, and it is worthwhile to conduct such a post to learn and improve our ability to deal with risks. In the meantime, the program manager has to keep things moving and must do so quickly.

We tend to think of crisis management in negative terms, but crisis management is a very real skill that has unique characteristics and deserves a place in our management tool kit. In the course of a major program, no one can foresee everything. A crisis will almost certainly occur and we need to be ready to handle it.

**Exhibit 6.** Risk Summary Sheet

| Risk # | Title | Pevt | Consequence | Pcon | C con | EV con | EV risk |
|---|---|---|---|---|---|---|---|
| 3 | Policy driven redesign | 0.9 | | | | $4.40 | $3.96 |
| | | | Minor redesign | 0.7 | $2.00 | $1.40 | |
| | | | Waiver Approved | 0.2 | $0.00 | $0.00 | |
| | | | Major redesign and retrofit | 0.1 | $30.00 | $3.00 | |
| 7 | Development Costs | | | | | | |
| 12 | Security control Procedures | | | | | | |
| 18 | Payload Dunnage | | | | | | |
| 23 | Key control measures | | | | | | |
| 25 | Material performance issue | | | | | | |
| 26 | Flight control software | | | | | | |
| 27 | Insensitive Munitions | | | | | | |
| 29 | Future maneuverability | | | | | | |
| 30 | System Effectiveness | | | | | | |
| 31 | Life Cycle Design-To Cost | | | | | | |
| | | | | | | Total Program Risk | $3.96 |

Focus on these to mitigate risk

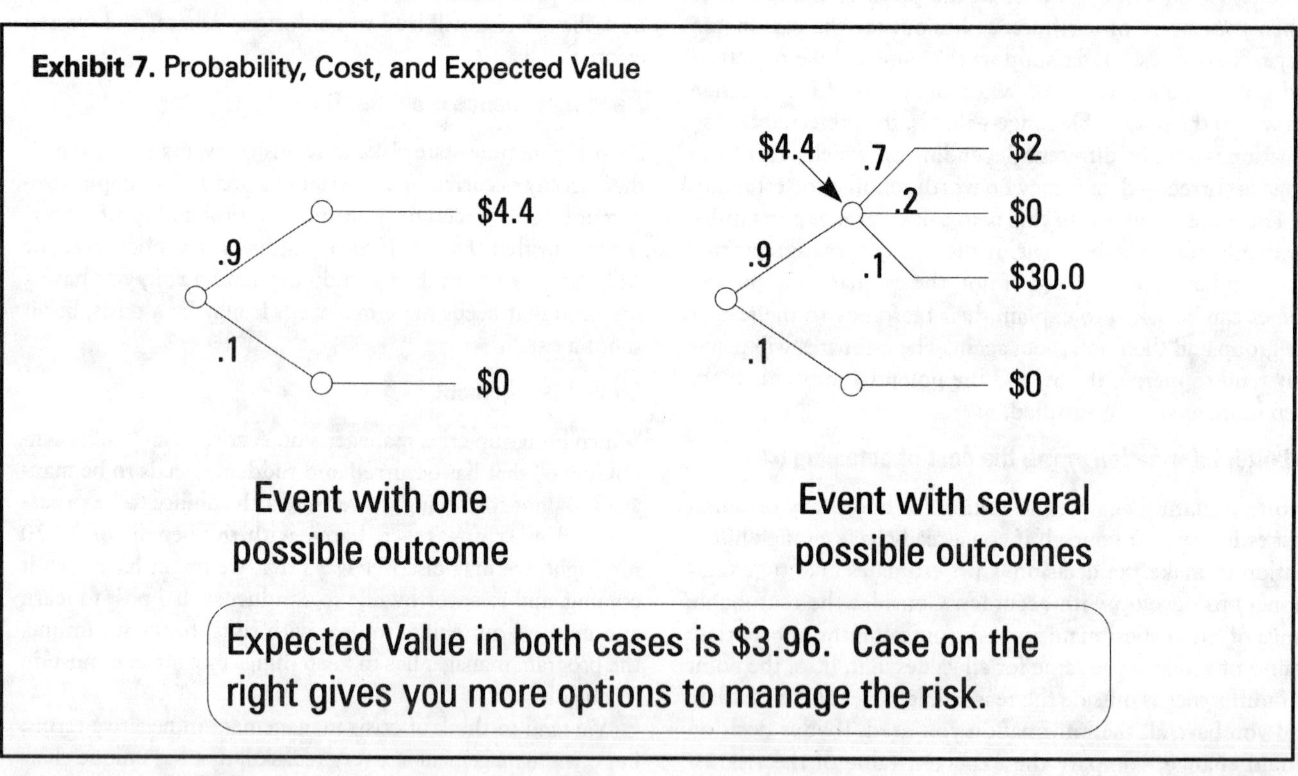


The best way to manage a crisis is for the program manager to have four things in place ahead of time:

- Rapid communication capability with a clear path for communicating critical news
- Points of contact established in key support organizations, even those that don't normally support the program

- Key personnel who are both knowledgeable and trained in communication techniques
- Established credibility with upper management and—if appropriate—trade press and other news media

When you have these things in place, you can rapidly obtain and communicate accurate information that will establish your credibility and command of the situation, and allow you to get out ahead of the crisis and manage the situation properly.

If you do not have these things in place, you won't be able to create any of them quickly after the event has occurred and you'll be in for a very difficult time. You may not get information as rapidly as the journalists and will be perceived as uninformed and not in control of the situation. Program members untrained in media relations may speculate and wind up being quoted as an "authoritative source" with partial or even wrong information that then has to be corrected. In both cases you find yourself fighting not only the crisis itself, but negative press as well, having to explain things that were never true in the first place.

In today's world, we have 24 hour news delivered nearly instantaneously from around the globe in 20 second sound bites that have to be understandable to the public. If you don't understand what that means or the needs of the journalists, you'll be ineffective in communicating the situation facing your program and how you are dealing with it. Nothing sinister is going on, you just need to help the journalists do their job so you can do yours. Professional media training for key management personnel or anyone likely to be interviewed is essential. If you contrast the results of Three Mile Island (1979) and the Tylenol Crisis (1982) in the book "Crisis Management", you'll see the difference. (Fink 1986)

#### More than one thing may result from a risk event occurring.

Sometimes a risk event only has one possible outcome; sometimes there are several. Exhibit 6 shows a risk summary sheet with one risk expanded to show the possible outcomes. The particular risk was that a pending policy change might require a change in the design. If the policy change occurs, a minor redesign might suffice, a major redesign and retrofit could be required, or a waiver might be granted. It's much like a decision tree except that the first branch is the probability of the risk event, not a decision. Exhibit 7 shows the decision tree analogy both for the case when the risk is considered to have only one outcome and when it is considered to have three. When there are multiple possible outcomes, they should be identified such that the list is collectively exhaustive, mutually exclusive, and the probabilities of occurrence sum to 1.0. Exhibits 6 and 7 also show pretty clearly where you can have the most impact on reducing expected value. Clearly, it was in the interest of the program to highlight the costs of major redesign to policy makers (which turned out to affect more than just the program in question) and seek to improve the chances of either obtaining a waiver or ensuring that a minor redesign would suffice.

### Manage the Risk

The risk event, its probability of occurrence and overall impact have been determined. Now what? How do you develop mitigation strategies to reduce the risk? Focus on the factors that you can alter that will have the most impact on expected value. While "expected value" is not the "value you expect", it's what keeps the lights on in Las Vegas and keeps people buying lottery tickets. Focus on the probabilities and impacts that have the most pay off, if you can affect them. Understand that if a particular risk event and outcome occur, their probability is now 1.0 (it's happened), and the expected value won't be the cost you see.

#### Always have an alternative that works.

ALWAYS have an option you can execute. It may not be the one you want or even one that meets requirements, but stopping the program dead in its tracks while everyone asks "Now what?" is absolutely unacceptable. Leaders have to lead, and that means thinking ahead. Don't force the program to wait on an option to become available that you should have developed months ago.

#### Increase the probability of more acceptable outcomes.

If there is more than one possible outcome of a risk event, then look for ways to increase the probability of more favorable outcomes to occur (load the dice in your favor). For instance, if a certain characteristic is desired but the requirement is waiverable, lay the groundwork for getting the waiver approved while completing the design work. If there is reluctance in approving the waiver, it's best to find that out while there is still time to redirect additional resources to solving the design problem.

Most problems can be solved with enough time and money. If you have enough time, it then becomes a question of how much money is the requirement worth before it will be waived or reduced? This is the heart of the "Cost as an Independent Variable" (CAIV) discussion currently going on within DoD. If you wait until the test of the design has failed, then you present a Hobson's choice to the waiver authority. Do they waive the requirement and approve what they consider to be a deficient design, or do they force the program to pursue an improved design while the program is at it's highest cost rate? The resource sponsor may not be willing or able to afford the latter choice, so the waiver becomes almost forced, although be prepared for lots of acrimony and

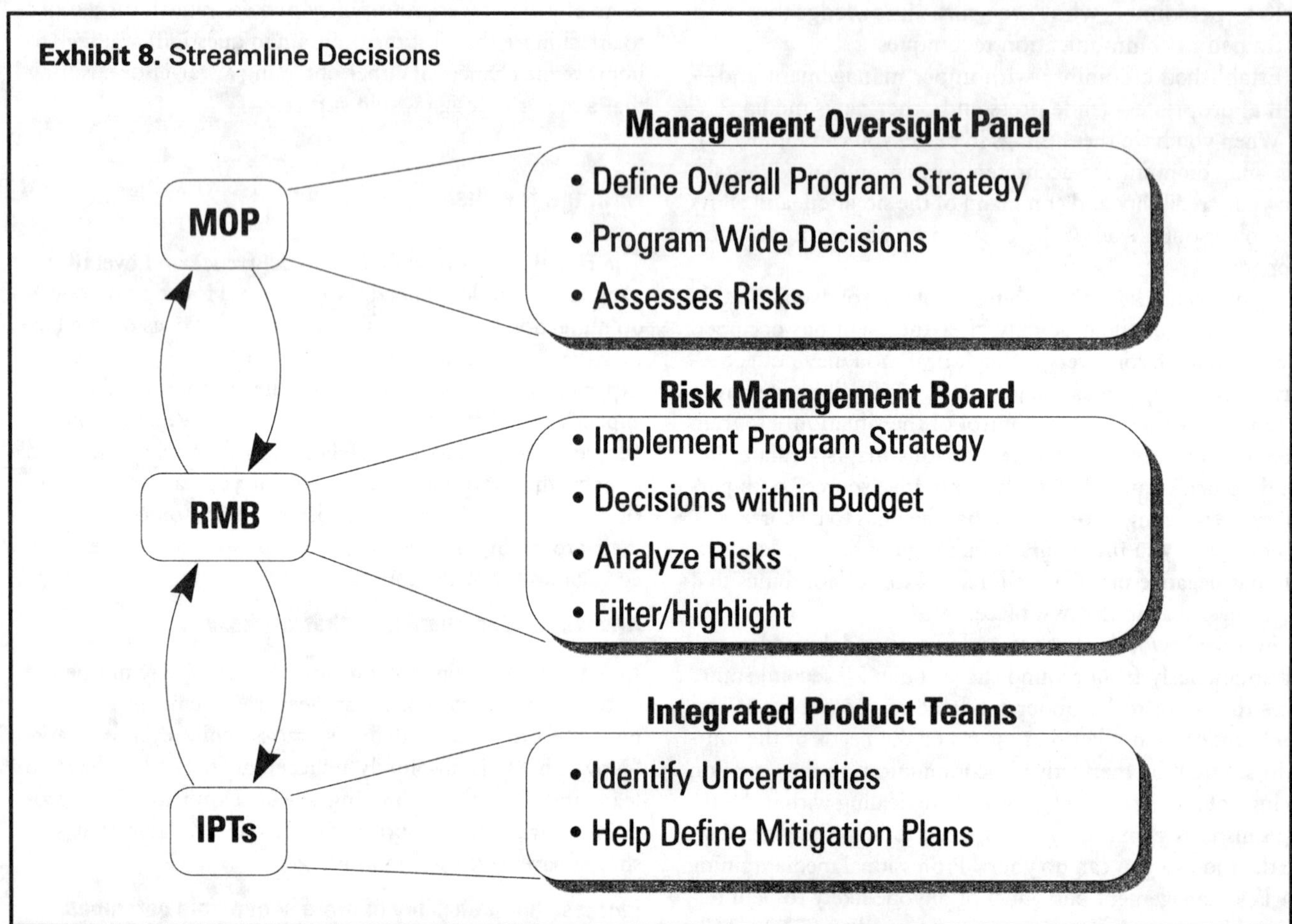


debate. It's seldom a good plan to try to force the hand of policy makers or even policy implementors.

A much more responsible approach is to keep the waiver authority involved and aware of design progress so they can participate in the tradeoffs between cost and performance. If they feel like their hand is being forced by not having a realistic alternative, they can look for many avenues to stall or delay the program. If they have had an input to the decision-making process all along, they will be much more inclined to grant the waiver and support the decision. People support what they help create.

**Reduce the impact of less desirable outcomes.**

If a particular path through the decision tree is too costly and you can't reduce the probability of the outcome occurring, it may be possible to reduce its cost. Are there ways to make the "major redesign" (in the above example) less expensive? Are entirely different concepts worth exploring that consider the life cycle impact of the redesign and foreseeable parts obsolescence? By focusing on where the leverage is, you can identify the payoff points for out-of-the- box thinking.

**Decrease the probability of the risk event.**

Look for ways to decrease the probability that the risk event will occur in the first place. It may be possible to reduce the probability of the risk event occurring at all. In the particular example, identifying the costs of the major redesign and highlighting the issue to other programs who had not yet had to deal with it, made it clear that the issue had dimensions that hadn't been clearly voiced before.

**Parallel paths, lead time, decision points, and action plans.**

One way to keep your options open is to maintain a parallel development path as long as you can afford the cost. At some point however, cost will exceed your ability to keep both developments going and you will have to commit to one or the other. Lay out the path that leads to the future risk event. Create an action plan that describes any parallel developments options, the studies and analysis that are to be completed, when they are due, and what decisions they will support. Have the wheels in motion well in advance and review the status of the analyses to be sure they will meet your expectations for thoroughness and consider all the options you think are important. For major risks being tracked, have a chart that shows the overall plan, when key events and decisions are expected, and review progress periodically with the extended team. If the risk event occurs, the team should have a clear plan in place to keep moving forward.

### Have a clear management path for resolving issues

There should be a clear, unambiguous, and streamlined path for elevating decisions to the proper level and recording decisions that are made. Don't let the team wait on decisions when they are required, but also make sure that decision makers will have the necessary information at the appropriate time in order to make the decision. Make sure decisions that are made are recorded and communicated to the team. Exhibit 8 shows the process used by the Joint Standoff Weapon program for this decision flow.

### Risk can be opportunity

A final thought to consider is that not all uncertainty is bad. Encourage people to look for possibilities and opportunities that, if they can be capitalized upon, would benefit the program. Identify them, target them, and look for ways to increase their chance of occurring.

## Conclusion

We manage risk is so we can responsibly manage the resources with which we have been entrusted to achieve our program goals. Just quantifying risk probability and impact is only an initial step in managing it. By identifying all possible outcomes of a risk event, it becomes clearer how to go about actually managing risk: stack the deck in favor of an outcome that's acceptable (increase the probability of low cost outcomes), reduce the cost of unattractive outcomes, or reduce the probability that the risk event ever occurs at all. Clarify and streamline the decision making process so the proper people have the information needed to support decisions at the proper time, and clearly communicate the results to the team.

### References

Fink, Stephan. 1986. *Crisis Management.* American Management Association

Baird, Bruce F. 1989. *Managerial Decisions Under Uncertainty.* New York: John Wiley & Sons.

# The Future of Project Management of Large International Projects—A Short Study of an International Space Station Research Facility.

Bruce D. Yost, Lockheed-Martin Engineering and Sciences Company
Laura Lewis, Lockheed-Martin Engineering and Sciences Company

## Introduction

The trend in the implementation of large, complex, high cost projects through international collaboration is on the rise. Old political alliances have changed and national economies are becoming more and more globally linked. The present era of budget deficit reduction, the reluctance to assume high levels of risk, and the general global economy has lead a number of nations, including the United States, to realize they can no longer afford unilateral sponsorship of multi-billion dollar projects. Additional political considerations which advocate international participation may also be a factor, such as improved balances of trade or modernization of specific technologies or industries.

For a number of years, a group of nations has been cooperating on a scale rarely seen in peacetime to develop and construct the International Space Station (ISS) in low Earth orbit. The ISS will require the successful integration of a number of large space and ground elements provided by the United States, Russia, Europe, Japan and Canada. The space elements must safely support human habitation and provide a laboratory environment suitable for space-based research. The associated challenges of the ISS for project managers, and for project management approaches are considerable. This paper provides a short case study of one of the major research facility systems in development for the ISS with multi-national involvement - the 2.5 meter Centrifuge.

## The International Space Station

When initially conceptualized, the ISS (formerly known as Space Station Freedom) was predominately a United States platform that provided some opportunities for international collaboration. When Congress began to question the cost of building and operating a Space Station, increasing international involvement and cost-sharing was recognized as an essential mechanism for maintaining the project's viability. Success of the ISS is now dependent upon the contributions of a number of international partners. In exchange for involvement with the ISS, each partner is presented with both opportunities and costs. Opportunities are presented in the ability of investigators from each of the partner's countries to utilize the unique laboratory facilities of the ISS. Cost will be incurred by each partner to build and launch the element that they are contributing to the ISS, as well as to support the general operations of the ISS itself. Some of these costs will be incurred within the respective countries that each agency represents, some, like those associated with general operations, will be paid to NASA.

The ISS, as currently planned at completion, will have a number of modules built by the United States and international space agencies that are linked together (See Exhibit 1). First to be deployed are Service Modules provided by Russia, followed by the United States Laboratory Module (Lab). Immediately after the United States Lab, Japan plans to launch its Japanese Experiment Module (JEM) and associated external platform. ISS external structures will also have to be assembled to generate power from solar arrays, and to deploy thermal radiators to manage waste heat that will be generated on-board. Next will come the United States provided Habitation Module (Hab), or crew living quarters, and then the Japanese provided Centrifuge Accommodations Module (CAM), dedicated to housing a major life sciences research facility, the 2.5 meter Centrifuge Facility. Assembly phase will be completed with the attachment of the European laboratory module. Canada will also provide some key elements of the ISS, notably the external manipulator robot. Within each module will be International Standard Payload Racks (ISPRs) which house the scientific equipment used on the ISS. The ISS Program manages the interfaces between each of the modules, down to the ISPR level. "Users" (sponsoring research agencies) are responsible for integrating their research equipment into the ISPRs, themselves.

Once assembly of the ISS is complete, continual research operations will begin. It is expected that the material sciences and life sciences will provide the bulk of the research on ISS. This research may lead to the discovery of new materials, alloys, and space-aged pharmaceuticals, and will certainly result in an increased understanding of biological processes here on Earth.

**Exhibit 1.** International Space Station

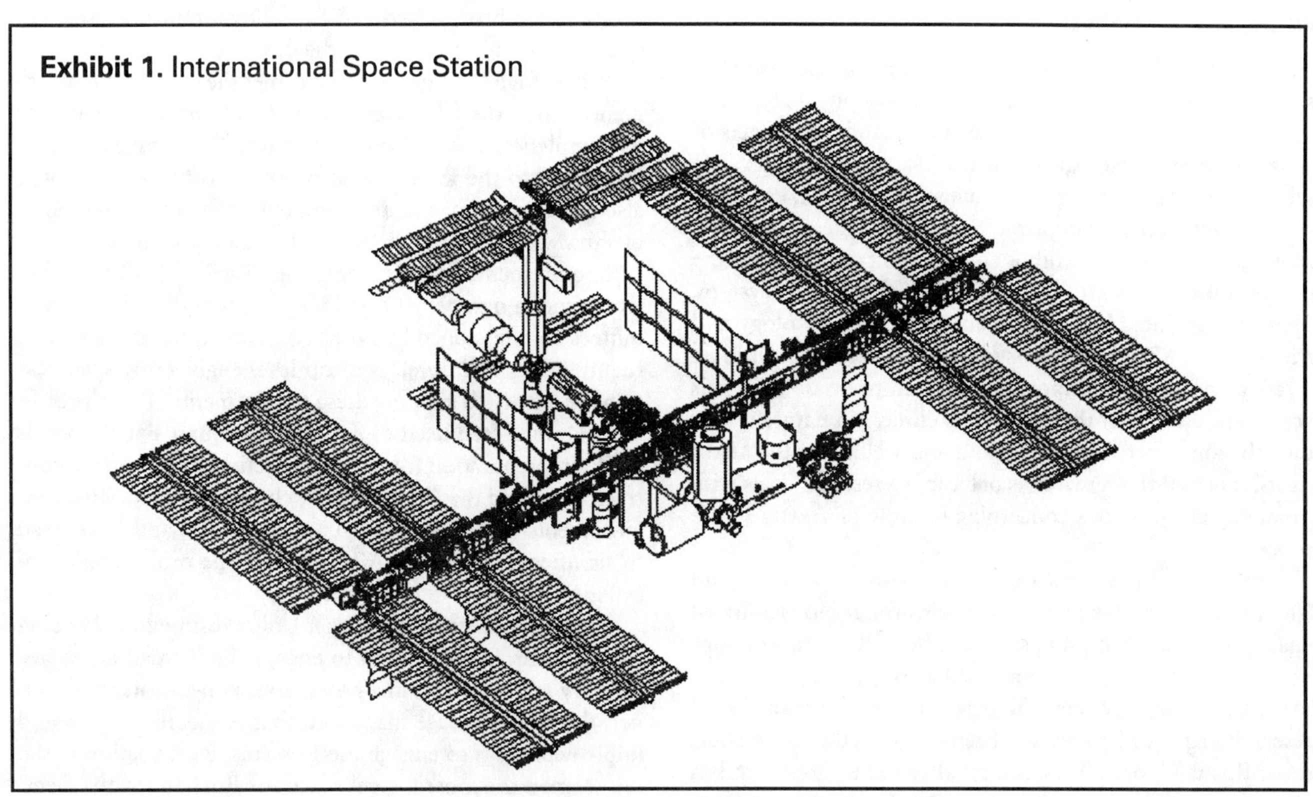

**Exhibit 2.** Centrifuge Accommodations Module (CAM)

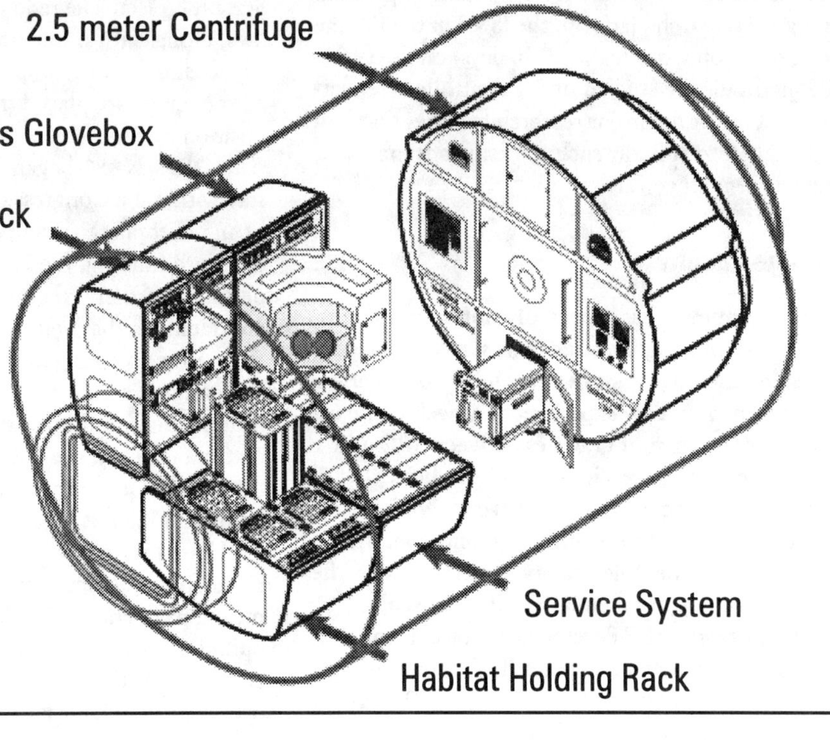

2.5 meter Centrifuge

Life Sciences Glovebox

Habitat Holding Rack

Service System

Habitat Holding Rack

## NASA Life Sciences

Ever since the United States has been sending astronauts to space, NASA has maintained a Life Sciences office chartered to monitor crew member's health and to study the effects of weightlessness on biological systems. The goals of NASA's life sciences program are to enable human exploration, use space as a research tool, and improve the quality of life of on Earth. Maintenance of crew health is an important challenge for the exploration and eventual colonization of the solar system. However, as noted by the Committee on Space Biology and Medicine (1987), the field of space life sciences is still in its infancy and there is important research to be done in this area. While some of the research is clinical in nature and is directly concerned with the health and welfare of the astronauts, much of the research is of basic interest and deals with fundamental questions concerning the role of gravity in life processes.

The NASA Ames Research Center (ARC), in Mountain View, California, has been tasked with the responsibility of enabling the conduct of basic research. ARC primarily supports research using non-human subjects such as plants, animals, and cellular systems. To date, most of the space-based research managed by ARC has been flown on the Space Shuttle or Russian biosatellites. A limited amount of research has also been conducted on the Russian Space Station Mir, presently in orbit. These research opportunities have been invaluable in forming a knowledge base on the acute effects of space flight ($^2$ 18 days duration) on living systems, but NASA and the space research community is now poised to proceed to the next logical research platform, the ISS. On the ISS the effects of long duration space flight (> 30 days) on living systems will be methodically studied under controlled, repeatable conditions. One of the major research facilities that will be on-board the ISS to support such scientific advancement is the 2.5 meter Centrifuge Facility.

## The Centrifuge Facility

The scientific community has repeatedly noted that an important tool for conducting life sciences research in space is a large diameter centrifuge with the capability to provide a one-g control for microgravity experiments, as well as the capability to explore a range of gravities between $10^{-5}$ and 1 gravity (Committee on Space Biology and Medicine 1987. Task Group on Life Sciences 1988). To this end, NASA headquarters directed the ARC to plan, design and construct a large (2.5 m diameter) variable-gravity centrifuge with the ability to house a variety of potential experiment subjects.

To conduct this work, ARC developed a project team, designated as an Integrated Product Team (IPT), composed of NASA civil servants and contractor staff. The IPT was responsible for brokering the scientific requirements of the research community, managing the design and development of the Centrifuge Facility such that it met the scientific requirements within the ISS Program constraints, and ensuring that its completion was timed such that the Centrifuge could be integrated to the ISS at the appropriate time. The IPT was also responsible for the development of the associated habitats that would eventually be used on the Centrifuge.

Requirements for the Centrifuge Facility (CF) were derived from a number of scientific panels and advisory committees commissioned by NASA. ARC analyzed the scientific requirements and developed top-level engineering specifications necessary to support these requirements. These specifications were then used to develop a Request For Proposals (RFP) in preparation for a 1996 selection of an outside contractor to build the CF. However, changes in the political environments within the United States, Russia, and Japan lead to significant changes in ARC's role in the project, and cancellation of the CF procurement.

Earlier this decade, the Soviet Union disintegrated ending the cold war. In an attempt to engage the Russian aerospace industry and academia in a productive, non-threatening manner, the White House mandated that NASA investigate and implement ways to engage the Russians. Participation in the ISS seemed the most logical place for Russian involvement. However, the incorporation of the Russians required a significant redesign of both the ISS and the attending project management structures. These activities resulted in delaying the "First Element Launch", or the official start of the Space Station Project. The redesign activities and accompanying delays, along with other problems, resulted in cost overruns. The cost overruns, coupled with a Congressionally mandated spending cap, placed the ISS program in a very precarious position.

In 1996 NASA began to explore a number of options to stay within the Congressional spending limits. Finally, as part of an offset plan to retain current year funding at the expense of future funding, the ISS Program decided to ask the international partners to construct certain research instruments and facilities that were to have been built by NASA. In exchange for accepting the cost for developing these items now, the partners would receive a "credit" to be applied towards future launch and operations costs.

Concurrently, the political climate in Japan was such that the Japanese government was expressing great reluctance participate in ISS if it required them to make actual payments to the United States government. Therefore, the National Space Development Agency of Japan (NASDA) saw benefit in minimizing payments to the United States by accepting the cost of building at least one of the research facilities and its associated module Ð the funds for which would be spent within their own country. Thus they agreed to pay for the development of the Centrifuge Facility and the Centrifuge Accommodations Module (CAM). NASDA will coordinate with the ISS Program in Houston, Texas, for the construction of the CF and CAM.

Throughout all of these changes, ARC has still remained accountable to the scientific community for ensuring their research requirements can be met. In addition, they have maintained management of the development of the habitats that will eventually be used to house specimens on the Centrifuge.

## New Requirements for Project Management

Although the conditions leading to the changes in the CF project may be fairly unique, the major challenges now being faced are common to all projects. These include, but are certainly not limited to, understanding and managing project requirements, defining and managing interfaces, and implementing project controls. While the fundamentals of managing a successful project still apply in a global arena, new insights and techniques for implementing projects across geographical and cultural "boundaries" will be required. This is especially true in a project such as the CF where the responsibility for requirements management, hardware development, and project controls have been relegated to three distinctly separate and geographically distant organizations which all have different project objectives: ARC is striving to maintain accountability to the scientific community; NASDA is seeking relief from payment to the United States for their participation in ISS; and the ISS Program is trying to contain current costs within mandated limits.

In light of such challenges, the strategy to achieve project success should include the development of an effective project team with a common project vision (Cleland 1997; Thoms 1997). The following is a simple example of how employing such a strategy can affect the success of the CF project.

Cultural differences, such as language barriers between the the United States and Japan, increase the risk of confusion and misunderstanding of project requirements. This could lead to increased costs to either or both of the agencies. These cultural differences could be further compounded by organizational and/or nationalistic biases. These are biases that may come into play when one organization develops a design approach that satisfies an overall project requirement, yet does so in such a way that it meets the individual organization's objectives at the expense of the other organization. For example, the scientific requirement of one of the habitats being built for the CF is that it accommodate a variety of aquatic species. The technological and cost differences between developing and integrating habitats to accommodate fresh water versus marine species is vast. ARC, which is responsible for the development of the habitats, is currently planning to house fresh water species. However, NASDA which is responsible for building the CF structure, has already developed a marine habitat for the Space Shuttle that it would like to also fly on the ISS. The way the CF Project is now structured, neither ARC or NASDA has control over how the other agency decides to implement these requirements. Therefore, the agencies must rely on a common project vision, and a cohesive project team motivated to achieve project success in order to overcome this potential hurdle.

While the value of a project strategy that includes a common vision and cohesive team may be easy to recognize, project managers are just now beginning to address how to implement such a strategy over geographical distances where team members may never actually meet face-to-face (Adams and Adams 1997). Fortunately, both NASA and NASDA are fairly savvy regarding the use of several of the key communications tools required to employ these strategies. Even still, employing these tools Ð which include the use of inter- and intranets, teleconferencing, and videoconferencing Ð on a regular basis may require a new level of commitment to project communications than either of the agencies has previously experienced.

## Conclusion

The new CF project, with the responsibility for requirements management, hardware development, and project controls relegated to three distinctly separate and geographically distant organizations, has become a classic example of a virtual project. The associated issues and challenges of managing such a project are compounded by cultural differences and the fact that each of the organizations has different, potentially conflicting project objectives. In a situation such as this, developing a shared project goal or vision, and establishing an effective and productive project team may be the greatest challenges of all. Yet overcoming these two challenges would likely have the greatest impact on the success of the project.

### References


Committee on Space Biology and Medicine, Space Science Board, Commission on Physical Sciences, Mathematics, and Resources. 1987. A Strategy for Space Biology and Medical Science for the 1980s and 1990s. National Research Council.

Task Group on Life Sciences, Space Science Board, Commission on Physical Sciences, Mathematics and Resources. 1988. Space Science in the Twenty-First Century: Imperatives for the Decades 1995 to 2015. National Research Council.

Cleland, David I. 1997. Team Building: the New Strategic Weapon. *PM Network* 1 (January): 29-30.

Thoms, Peg. 1997. Creating a Shared Vision With a Project Team. *PM Network* 1 (January): 33-35.

Adams, John R. and Adams, Laura L. 1997. The Virtual Project: Managing Tomorrow's Team Today. *PM Network* 1 (January): 37-41.

# Project Management in a Federal Government Privatization and Closure Environment

Brian J. Gegan, Manager, KPMG Peat Marwick LLP
Gonzalo I. Vergara, Major, United States Air Force

## Introduction

On July 13, 1995, President Clinton accepted the recommendations of the 1995 Defense Base Closure and Realignment Commission (Commission) to close or realign 132 military installations in the United States. Representing the final round under Public Law 101-510, the 1995 Commission proposal recommended additional base closures to those previously identified during the 1988, 1991 and 1993 rounds. Included in the 1995 Base Realignment and Closure (BRAC 95) list was the recommendation to close McClellan Air Force Base and the Sacramento Air Logistics Center (SM-ALC) located in Sacramento, CA. Functioning as one of the Air Force's five major aircraft depots, McClellan AFB provides employment to over 13,000 civilian and military personnel, contributes over $2.2 billion to the local economy and serves as Northern California's largest employer. By accepting the BRAC 95 recommendations, President Clinton signed into law the requirement that McClellan AFB transition all workloads, functions and programs to other DoD locations, disestablish a variety of base organizations, and formally close this major, industrial installation by July 13, 2001. When viewed in the context of project management, the closure and re-use of McClellan AFB represents a major five-year effort that will challenge the project management skills, practices and processes of all affected government and commercial stakeholders. This paper will discuss the project management challenges and initiatives undertaken in the closure, transition and re-use of McClellan AFB.

## The Ramifications of Planning for a Major, High-Visibility Base Closure

The previous BRAC rounds of 1988, 1991, and 1993 resulted in the closure of more than seventy major and almost 200 smaller bases. After unsuccessfully attempting to avert the closure of McClellan AFB, the city and county of Sacramento were distressed by the potential loss of jobs and the consequent "ripple effects" on the local economy. This was especially threatening because California was slow to emerge from the latest economic recession and had witnessed a dramatic downturn in the aerospace industry, a critical element of the state's economy. Citing "excess capacity" at McClellan AFB and the other four Air Force depots, the 1995 Commission recommended formal closure of McClellan AFB as the only available option to significantly improve utilization at the remaining depots and reduce DoD operating costs. When President Clinton accepted the 1995 Commission's recommendations, the following requirements were imposed:

- Disestablish the Sacramento Defense Distribution Depot
- Move the common-use ground-communication electronics to Tobeyhanna Army Depot in Letterkenney, PA
- Retain the McClellan Nuclear Radiation Center and make it available for dual-use and/or research or close it as appropriate
- Consolidate the remaining workloads to other DoD depots or to private sector commercial activities as determined by the Defense Depot Maintenance Council (DDMC)
- Move the required equipment and personnel to the appropriate receiving locations
- Close McClellan Air Force Base including the Sacramento Air Logistics Center (SM-ALC)

Congress concurred with President Clinton's acceptance of the Commission's recommendation to close McClellan AFB, therefore, BRAC 95 requirements became law with a completion date of July 13, 2001.

Concurrent with the acceptance of the BRAC 95 recommendations, President Clinton announced a willingness to consider the "Privatization in Place" of the workloads at McClellan and a sister depot at Kelly AFB in San Antonio, TX. Privatization, achieved through a "Public-Private Competition," would allow private industry to compete for the opportunity to win government contracts to perform the remaining workloads. These contracts represent major business opportunities and are potentially worth several hundred million dollars on an annual basis. The Public-Private Competition at McClellan would allow for private industry to compete with another public depot, and if successful, use the existing facilities, equipment and workforce to perform the work. If the public depot won, the workload, equipment, and some of the personnel would move to the winning depot. Vigorously criticized by government unions and members of Congress that represent districts that host other depots, the Clinton Administration has steadfastly supported "Public-Private Competition." Regardless of the outcome of these efforts, McClellan AFB will close and the majority of base organizations and federal tenants will be disestablished or re-located to other installations.

The implementation of BRAC 95 directly affects the interests of many stakeholders and presents a tremendous challenge from the standpoint of project management. In addition to the military/civilian leadership and workforce at McClellan AFB, which number over 13,000 personnel, major stakeholders include the parent Air Force Materiel Command, the Air Force Base Closure Agency (AFBCA), the Sacramento County Department of Military Base Conversion acting as the Local Redevelopment Authority (LRA), and a host of directorate and tenant organizations that are required to plan and execute literally thousands of activities to implement the BRAC 95 requirements.

The Air Force and the rest of DoD possess extensive experience in the closure of military bases, however, the size and scale of McClellan AFB present unique challenges and obstacles. Over 150 command and tenant organizations must be closed or disestablished and over fifty programs and functions must be re-located to gaining sites. During this massive closure and transition process, equipment repair and overhaul must continue with minimal impact experienced by Air Force squadrons and other customer organizations. To further complicate matters, all of this must be accomplished within the context of the Public-Private Competition which has introduced an additional set of uncertainties and risks that must be carefully managed.

## Translation of a Base Closure and Re-use Strategy into Effective Project Management Implementation

In many respects, McClellan AFB possesses all of the facilities, roads and infrastructure of a city. McClellan AFB represents the last major DoD installation in Sacramento and Northern California. Originally established as the Sacramento Air Depot in 1936, McClellan AFB grew over the years to become one of DoD's largest aeronautical and communications-electronics repair depots in the U.S. In addition to providing program management, logistics and materiel support to a variety of combat aircraft such as the A-10, F-15, F-16, F/B/E-111, F-117 and F-22, McClellan AFB supports the Space Shuttle program and a host of radar systems, missile-tracking and communications-electronics programs for other armed services. This major, industrial, depot maintenance and materiel management support installation:

- Serves as a high-tech industrial center with advanced capabilities in composites, microelectronics, electro-optics, software, hydraulics/pneudraulics, manufacturing and environmental technologies
- Employs over 13,000 military and civilian personnel
- Supports over 80,000 dependents in the Sacramento area
- Operates over 740 facilities (11,502,767 square feet) including medical, dental and commissary/exchange as well as over 673 housing units
- Includes over 3,752 acres of real property, 10,600 feet of runways, and 43 miles of paved roads at the main base and related government properties
- Serves as the location for a host of tenant organizations including the Defense Logistics Agency (DLA), Defense Information Services Agency (DISA), the Defense Finance and Accounting Service (DFAS) and the Coast Guard Air Station
- Contains unique facilities such as a "state of the art" casting facility and the McClellan Nuclear Radiation Center - the world's largest neutron radiography facility dedicated to aircraft component inspection and corrosion measurement
- Serves as Northern California's largest employer and contributes over $2.2 billion to the local economy on an annual basis

From a management perspective, the scope and scale of the efforts to close McClellan AFB are daunting. The transition and closure of McClellan AFB exhibit the classic elements of a major project, including:

- The requirement to carefully plan, implement, and track thousands of dependent activities and tasks
- The need to guide and coordinate a large number of functional organizations and programs that possess multiple reporting structures
- A constrained end date, mandated by law, of July 13, 2001
- Limited resources (BRAC funding, personnel, material transportation and movement capacities, contractor support, etc.)
- High visibility at the local, regional, and national levels
- Multiple stakeholders with both complimentary and competing economic and political interests, agendas and timetables.

In reality, closure will involve a myriad of efforts, tasks and sub-projects throughout the installation. Over 150 organizations will need to be disestablished and closed. More than fifty programs will be relocated to other DoD sites and federal government locations. Major contract solicitation and evaluation efforts must be completed under the mandate to conduct the Public-Private Competition. A major driver for all transition efforts is the disposition and conveyance of real property to the LRA. Transition, in turn, is contingent upon the completion of National Environmental Protection Act (NEPA) and California Environmental Quality Act (CEQA) requirements including joint programmatic Environmental Impact Statement/ Environmental Impact Report (EIS/EIR) activities. From a human resources standpoint, the existing workforce must be prepared for the closure of McClellan AFB and this preparation involves a variety of transition assistance, referral and placement programs and efforts. The complexity and volume of closure tasks will pose major challenges to executive leadership at the base.

## Development of an Enterprise Project Control System (EPCS) and Organizational Infrastructure

Recognizing that effective project management requires appropriate processes and infrastructure, the EPCS was developed according to the following tenets:

- Manage by facts
- Capture the known, then proceed to the unknown
- Integrate and synchronize operations
- Centralize control and decentralize execution
- Incorporate continuous improvement

The senior leadership at McClellan AFB determined that an effective project control strategy requires an integrated approach emphasizing: incremental data capture and analysis; organizational development to incorporate data growth and complexity, integration and synchronization of activities (dependencies among activities and schedules), innovative and creative approaches to solving complex problems.

The newly created Closure and Privatization Directorate (which is now the Closure and Competition Directorate) was tasked as the executive agency for McClellan's closure, transition and re-use efforts. The Directorate was a "prime mover" of the efforts to establish a coherent project control system. In addition to identifying the goals and objectives to meet BRAC 95 requirements, the Directorate understood the need to develop project management skills and organizational capabilities.

First, an Integrated Process Team (IPT) was established to spearhead project control efforts. The IPT, which represented a cross-section of the functional organizations at McClellan, defined the purpose of the EPCS:

- Conceptualize, develop, and establish the necessary project control architecture to support and execute the mission of public-private competition and closure
- Develop and establish schedules, define dependencies, report progress and/or deficiencies;
- Manage progress
- Propose corrective actions
- Provide executive management with appropriate analysis and advice to facilitate the closure and competition process

The IPT formalized itself into the Enterprise Project Control Working Group (EPCWG), and was charged with developing, establishing, and directing the project control efforts at McClellan AFB. Membership in the EPCWG consisted of actual Project Officers (POs). Hand-picked by their respective organizations, POs were empowered to actually direct activities and develop baseline closure schedules for their organizations and programs. These are the people with the power to make actual decisions at the lowest possible level.

The EPCWG membership consists of a Project Control Director (PCD), a Database Manager (DBM), a Requirements Manager (RM), Project Officers (PO), and outside consultants. The EPCWG meets on a weekly basis to assess schedules, coordinate efforts, identify problems and develop alternative solutions, develop policy and provide guidance, and exchange information so that all schedules and efforts are synchronized and integrated into the overall master schedule. The enterprise schedules provide a ready reference for a host of planning and implementation efforts, and serve as the foundation for the monthly Program Management Reviews (PMR) that are presented to the Sacramento Air Logistics Center Commander and his senior staff.

The PCWG developed an Enterprise Process Description Document (EPDD) to formally document processes, methodologies, and guidance. The EPDD documents critical planning and implementation considerations such as roles and responsibilities, sub-project/master-project architecture and relationships, activity classifications and dependencies, and consistent processes for schedule development, integration, maintenance and analysis. The success of these efforts is evidenced by the number of McClellan organizations that have emulated this approach to planning and control.

Second, the heart of the EPCS is the project management software, Primavera Project Planner (P3). After an evaluation of various project management software applications, P3 was selected due to its extensive data collection, integration, and reporting capabilities. The software can integrate up to 100,000 activities and an unlimited number of interlocking sub-projects. This capability was essential because of the numerous activities which need to be tracked and the variety of detailed schedules to be populated and analyzed. Currently, the Closure and Competition Directorate is developing the capability to track over 300 schedules with upwards of 50,000 activities. The software resides on a centralized network with security links established to prevent accidental or intentional interference of data by persons other than the Schedule Owners or the respective Project Officers. Formal project management and software training was developed from in-house resources and provided to POs and senior leadership.

Third, the EPCWG determined that risk analysis was a key component in the measurement and evaluation of what schedule slippage actually means in terms of time lost, and to quantify the "domino effect" for the whole schedule. The EPCWG acquired the Monte Carlo Risk Analysis software from Primavera Systems, Inc. Working in conjunction with P3, the EPCWG used Monte Carlo risk simulations to project completion dates, resource consumption, and alternative solutions through statistical analysis of project outcomes. This capability provided the EPCWG ample opportunities to proceed beyond Critical Path Method Analysis (CPM), to identify major risk events, and their resultant impacts on the various schedules. By identifying risk events in advance, the EPCWG developed contingency plans and provided proactive recommendations to senior management. As a result of this capability, we are able to predict and rationally deal with potential problems. The EPCWG's commitment to fact-based management combined with a quality initiative that is committed to continuous improvement in data management and process efficiency has made this project management system a viable model for others to follow.

## Quality Management Practices Are Applied to the Enterprise Project Control System (EPCS)

It was recognized early in the effort that the EPCS and the supporting infrastructure needed to be responsive to the needs of McClellan AFB leadership. With this in mind, the "Customer and Integrator Concept" was applied to ensure that the performance of the EPCS was optimized. "EPCS Customers" represent the various project teams, organizations, programs and representatives of management that needed project management information to effectively implement BRAC 95 requirements. "EPCS Integrators" are the organizations and individuals that were tasked to ensure that the EPCS met the needs of the Customers. The EPCWG, the Project Control Director, the Data Base Manager and CL served as "Integrators" and provided the guidance, direction and maintenance to operate the EPCS.

To successfully meet the needs of the Customers, a Quality Management Program (QMP) was implemented. Consisting of a Customer Satisfaction Questionnaire (CSQ) and an Operational Indicators Evaluation (OIE), the QMP was designed to provide objective feedback on performance to both the Integrators and the customers. The CSQ used five indicators to measure Customer satisfaction with the EPCS. Organizational Development, Software Functionality and Utility, Hardware Utility, Project Management Training, and Overall EPCS Performance were formally measured through surveys that were provided to Customers on a quarterly basis. Objective numerical results were tabulated and combined with subjective comments to identify desired improvements and modifications to EPCS processes and practices.

The Operational Indicators Evaluation (OIE) consists of three specific indicators that enable the Data Base Manager to evaluate the project management practices of the various Project Officers. The Schedule Development, Maintenance and Analysis indicator measurement provides insight on the application of schedule development concepts and principles as well as problem identification and resolution. Schedule availability and data file integrity are also measured to determine how effective the Project Officers are in organizing, accessing and protecting schedule data. Because teamwork is the foundation of the EPCS, attendance, participation, and responsiveness are also measured to ensure that Project Officers are working closely with EPCS Integrators.

The CSQ routinely identified deficiencies, particularly in the area of training, that enabled the Project Control Director to enhance EPCS performance. Because Customers were queried on a periodic basis, the CSQ also tended to encourage involvement and ownership of the EPCS - essential ingredients of success. The OIE provided direct feedback on the actual practices and working knowledge of the various Project Officers in an objective, non-threatening fashion. Like any effective quality program, involvement, consistency and cooperation yielded significant benefits and served to improve all areas of EPCS performance.

## The Challenging Reality Of Large-Scale, Project Management Implementation In A Base Closure Environment

Projects that involve developing new software applications, building new skyscrapers or airports, or winning an election signify achievement and realization of goals and objections. These types of projects, although tremendously complex and formidable, upon completion signify a successful transition to a desired state or status. The closure of a major installation, like McClellan AFB, is not greeted with the same sense of optimism or fanfare. Instead, the completion of this project signifies the end of careers for many people that have never worked outside of the government environment. The closure and transition of McClellan AFB involve significant

Exhibit 1.

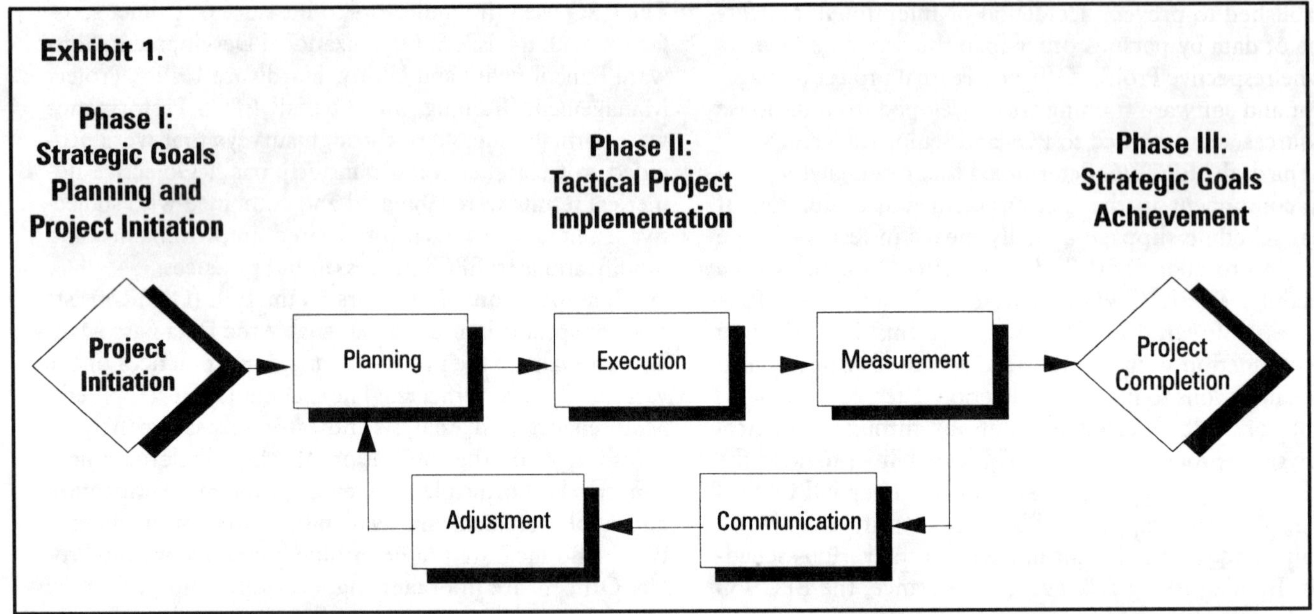


organizational, process, and technology related challenges and obstacles.

From an organizational perspective, senior leadership is confronted by a host of organizational issues. The large number of command and tenant organizations, numbering well into the hundreds, must somehow find a means to effectively plan, direct, coordinate, and track the accomplishment of thousands of activities. Consistent with other depot organizations, McClellan AFB has excelled in performing functional operations but is challenged in its ability to carry out massive projects that affect the entire base. The sheer volume and diversity of organizations, programs and functions generate a huge number of "reporting paths" to a multitude of internal and external customers and stakeholders. Responsible for the completion of BRAC 95 requirements, senior leadership at SM-ALC conducted a number of high-level strategic planning sessions that culminated in the establishment of the Closure and Competition Directorate (CL). Subject to the "growing pains" of any new organization, CL has been challenged to perform a role that had previously never been done before at McClellan AFB, namely plan, coordinate, and implement a major base closure while simultaneously facilitating highly visible transition, re-use, and privatization initiatives.

Just as people are essential for successful project completion, the psychological effects on the workforce play a major role in this particular project. For the management and workforce of McClellan AFB, the BRAC 95 decision represented the "beginning of the end" of a proud tradition of service to the country. Some personnel are experiencing the doubt, denial, frustration, and anger that accompanies any perceived threat to one's security. The anxieties of knowing that one's career will be terminated and the lingering uncertainty regarding the Public-Private Competition directly affect the attitude and performance of all employees at McClellan AFB. The mandatory Reductions in Force (RIF), early retirements, relocation's to other federal sites, and other consequences of the closure process dramatically affect the personal and professional lives of the employees that serve this depot. One McClellan employee compared the effort to close McClellan AFB to the painful ordeal of having to plan the burial of a much loved, family member.

Although the closure and transition process of this installation is a major project in and of itself, success is dependent upon a process-oriented approach to managing work. As shown by Exhibit 1, the management of these efforts really depends upon a consistently applied process of planning, execution, measurement, communication of results and adjustment of efforts. To afford executive leadership with the greatest likelihood of completing BRAC 95 requirements on schedule and within budget, this process-based approach must prevail over the chaos of conducting normal, every day functional work. The success of this approach is, in turn, dependent upon a fundamental knowledge and understanding of project management ideas, concepts, and practices. For those individuals that can effectively manage major organizational change and "thrive on chaos," they stand a much greater chance of successfully managing this project and will avoid the "act-react" loop that characterizes poorly executed efforts. The ability to successfully apply effective, process-oriented management represents a major challenge for executive leadership.

The other major obstacle to managing this project involves the appropriate use of "enabling technology." Just as there is no substitute for knowledge and experience in working with any tool, the ability to understand and employ available technology enhance the probability of project success. CL understood early in the effort that more was required than just enterprise project management software, networks, computers and plotters. CL, after designating the Project Control Director and EPCWG conducted an informal skills and knowledge assessment to determine the ability of personnel to effectively apply project management concepts while maximizing the use of available technology. After carefully analyzing the results of this assessment, the EPCWG embarked upon an aggressive training effort to enhance project management skills and knowledge. A variety of formal and informal training efforts were initiated to not only train individuals to develop and maintain schedules, but also to prepare organizations and programs for the detail-oriented planning, coordination, and tracking of necessary activities. One of the greatest challenges encountered was to manage the expectations of project management stakeholders. Like any functional organization trying to scale the "project management learning curve," this requires time and patience, which are sometimes precious commodities.

The EPCWG effectively employed many of the concepts contained within the Project Management Institute's *A Guide to Project Management Body of Knowledge*. The concepts and practices regarding project time management, communication, risk management, and project integration were germane to the efforts of the EPCWG. The greatest challenge that faced the PCWG was how to "jump start" the various organizations and programs and help them to implement the necessary processes while employing valid concepts and project management practices. Even the most progressive organizations require some time to adapt to change and the effort to implement enterprise project management required months of meetings, presentations, and training sessions. For many individuals that were experiencing stress related to BRAC-95 requirements, enterprise project management was challenging to learn and apply.

## Accomplishments to Date

In spite of the significant challenges and obstacles facing the leadership and workforce of McClellan AFB, significant progress has been made since the establishment of the EPCS 15 months ago. Major accomplishments include the following:

- The EPCWG is fully functional and it's organizational structure, roles, and responsibilities have remained intact even though McClellan AFB is experiencing fundamental change
- The project management software and schedule development, maintenance and analysis processes are fully established and enable many organizations, programs and functions to build inter-locking schedules
- The P3 Project Database Architecture is fully developed and schedules are being developed and maintained
- McClellan AFB personnel are rapidly developing project management skills and abilities as evidenced by the large number of personnel, over 125 to date, that have received software and basic project management training
- Measurement tools and probabilistic forecasting processes have been established and are available to the various project teams to actively perform schedule risk simulation
- Senior leadership has realized a "return on investment" and has firmly advocated that organizations, programs and functions integrate their planning and scheduling efforts within the EPCS
- The capability exists to integrate cost and resource information into the schedules at an appropriate point in the future

Even though the bulk of the project management work remains to be accomplished, significant progress has been made. When the size, scope and scale of the efforts are taken into consideration, McClellan AFB has taken on a tremendously complex and involved task and has provided tangible results in a short 15 month period. A large number of organizations and programs are applying project management practices to plan, coordinate and track their efforts. As the project management skills, knowledge and capabilities grow, McClellan AFB is maximizing the opportunities to meet BRAC 95 requirements and implement a successful closure, transition and re-use.

# Project Management, Configuration Management and Systems Engineering: What's Needed Most For The Next Century?

Carl C. Lang, The Boeing Company
J. Michael Stratton, PMP, The Boeing Company

## Introduction

As the 20th Century draws to a close we are seeing a growth explosion of activity and interest in Project Management (PM), Configuration Management (CM), and Systems Engineering (SE). These disciplines are a must for any successful project in the Defense and Aerospace industry. But what represents the most effective balance of these disciplines? Most importantly, can we as project managers survive in The Next Century without one or more of these disciplines and still meet our project's goals?

Upon some evaluation of each of the three disciplines, it becomes clear that each brings with it several elements which serve as tools for managing a successful project; that is, project management in the purest sense. Experts closely aligned with these specific disciplines often impart such enthusiasm over their respective subjects that the message received by non-experts is often one of: *"Gee, it looks like if I can only get some good (fill in the next words with your choice of: PM, CM or SE) in place on my project, things will go very smoothly and our project will succeed."* The question we will answer in this paper is: "What is really needed from these three disciplines for the project manager in The Next Century?"

This paper will examine the fundamental key tools of PM, CM, and SE on their own merit and "net out" those activities within each discipline which are shared by one or more of the other two disciplines. An attempt will be made to "place" each of the shared tools into a primary role in only one of the three disciplines. Those elements that are truly unique characteristics of a particular discipline are then identified. Finally, a brief discussion of the role and value of each element in effectively managing and executing a project will be presented. The paper will show that although it is somewhat useful to understand the relationship of PM, CM and SE as whole disciplines, the key to managing successful projects in The Next Century lies in understanding the relationship of the shared and unique core elements of each discipline and the most efficient and effective way to integrate these elements together to manage our projects.

## PM, CM and SE Spawn Societies and Organizations that Don't Integrate

Project Management, CM and SE are three essential disciplines for effectively managing a project. We acknowledge that these are not the only three disciplines present on the battlefront of project management. There are other disciplines in the arsenal of the project manager as he/she heads into The Next Century. However, we will focus on the recognized disciplines of PM, CM and SE in this paper for we believe they represent the highest leverage areas for sound, overall project management. Further, we believe they constitute the disciplines requiring the most significant outlay of energy in order to successfully manage projects in The Next Century.

The disciplines of PM, CM and SE are so important that there are numerous professional societies established around them. These societies include the Project Management Institute (PMI), the International Council on Systems Engineering (INCOSE), and the Association for Configuration & Data Management (ACDM). Each of these disciplines offer key ingredients which prove valuable in managing projects, but which often overlap with those provided by the other two disciplines. These project "solutions" include varying methodologies, procedures, mandates, policies, rules, handbooks, guides (such as A Guide to the Project Management Body Of Knowledge, or PMBOK) and biases. Interest and growth in these kinds of societies has translated into the creation of similarly-aligned, discrete organizations within many of our enterprises (companies, governments, etc).

The fascinating result is that each of these discipline-aligned organizations confront our projects with their own potentially competing and conflicting packaged approaches to our project needs. While each of these broader approaches have certain strengths, by themselves they typically do not fully satisfy the needs of the project manager. In addition, due to overlapping elements, these approaches are difficult to integrate into a single complete project approach.

It appears that, in a genuine quest for increased knowledge and more comprehensive solutions to industry demands, each of these disciplines have essentially been expanding their

**Exhibit 1.** Significant Elements Matrix

## Significant Elements Matrix

(Typical Excerpt From Matrix; Characterizations Abbreviated)

| Tools | CM | PM | SE | Characterization |
|---|---|---|---|---|
| Audits | X | X | X | Includes modifiers of: Configuration , Configuration Management, Quality, Change Package., Physical and Functional Configuration. Any assessment to determine conformance to documentation and plans. |
| Baselining | X | X | X | Record of the original plan of activity related to tasks and deliverables of the project. Includes As-Sold, Customer-Approved, As-Planned, As-Released, As-Built, As-Modified, As-Maintained, Schedule, Performance, Cost, Configuration and Product baselines. |
| Benefit/Cost Analysis | | X | X | Also called Trade Study, Cost Analysis and Risk Analysis. Evaluating the costs and benefits of various project alternatives and determine return on investment. |
| Certificate Of Conformance | X | | | Documentation assuring conformance of an item to its design documents. |
| Change Control System | X | X | X | System by which changes are evaluated for inclusion based on the established scope of the project. Also includes coordinating and managing the changes on the project and revising schedules, staffing, costs, risk plans and quality impact. |
| Communication Management Plan | | X | | Documentation of creation, distribution and storing of information related to the project. Includes plans for how and when to communicate project activities to project team members, project stakeholders, news media and the public. |
| Configuration Documents | X | | | Documents that define the requirements, design, build/production and verification for a configuration item. Also called Specifications, Schematics and Layouts. |
| Configuration Item Documentation | X | | | Includes all the necessary functional and physical characteristics of a configuration item including interfaces, changes, deviations and waivers. |
| Configuration Management Plan | X | | | Documentation setting out the organization and procedures for the configuration management of a specific product or project. |
| Contractual Agreements | | X | X | A mutually binding agreement for products or services in trade for something of value. Agreements are entered into for such items on a project as insurance, services & other items to avoid or mitigate risks or threats. Also referred to as risk transfer. |
| Corrective Action | X | X | X | Anything done to bring expected future project performance into line with the project plan. Also referred to any action requiring Intervention Resources. |
| Cost Management Plan | | X | X | Describes how cost variances will be managed and how costs will be estimated and collected. A subsidiary element of the project plan. |

respective subject areas by annexing and developing subject areas outside of their scope of expertise. These are often in areas where another discipline has previously demonstrated leadership. The inevitable outcome of this "disciplinary capitalism" is the creation of friction within our projects and the enterprise as a whole, thus making it more difficult to achieve our project goals.

This friction causes project managers to expend significant energy continually seeking ways to reconcile these constraints in order to select the best elements from each discipline and effectively navigate to successful completion of their projects. However, many project mangers may be unaware that the fire fighting they engage in is often due to the friction created by this non-integrated relationship within their enterprises. In fact, the custodians of these disciplines within the enterprise would likely take the view that they are not competing with other disciplines. Rather, they believe they are aware of their boundaries and interfaces with the other disciplines.

However, in reality the boundaries usually overlap in several areas, especially in larger or more mature enterprises. In newer or smaller enterprises this general case may not apply directly. There are nevertheless hidden constraints which may exist in these smaller or newer enterprises. For example, the smaller or newer enterprise may have defaulted to a single discipline, or bent, for *all* of their generic project management needs and hence, may be ignorant of better methods offered by other disciplines. The smaller or newer enterprise project managers are now suffering the same fate as their counterparts in the larger or mature enterprises—that of being an unwitting victim of "disciplinary capitalism."

## Traditional Roles Of PM, CM and SE In Managing Projects—A Brief Look

"Project management is the application of knowledge, skills, tools, and techniques to project activities in order to meet or exceed stakeholder needs and expectations from a project. Meeting or exceeding stakeholder needs and expectations invariably involves balancing competing demands among:

- Scope, time, cost, and quality
- Stakeholders with differing needs and expectations
- Identified requirements (needs) and unidentified requirements (expectations)" (PMBOK 1996, 6).

Configuration Management "is a management discipline that applies technical and administrative direction to the development, production and support life cycle of a configuration item. This discipline is applicable to hardware, software,

**Exhibit 2.** Critical Elements and Depth of Disciplines

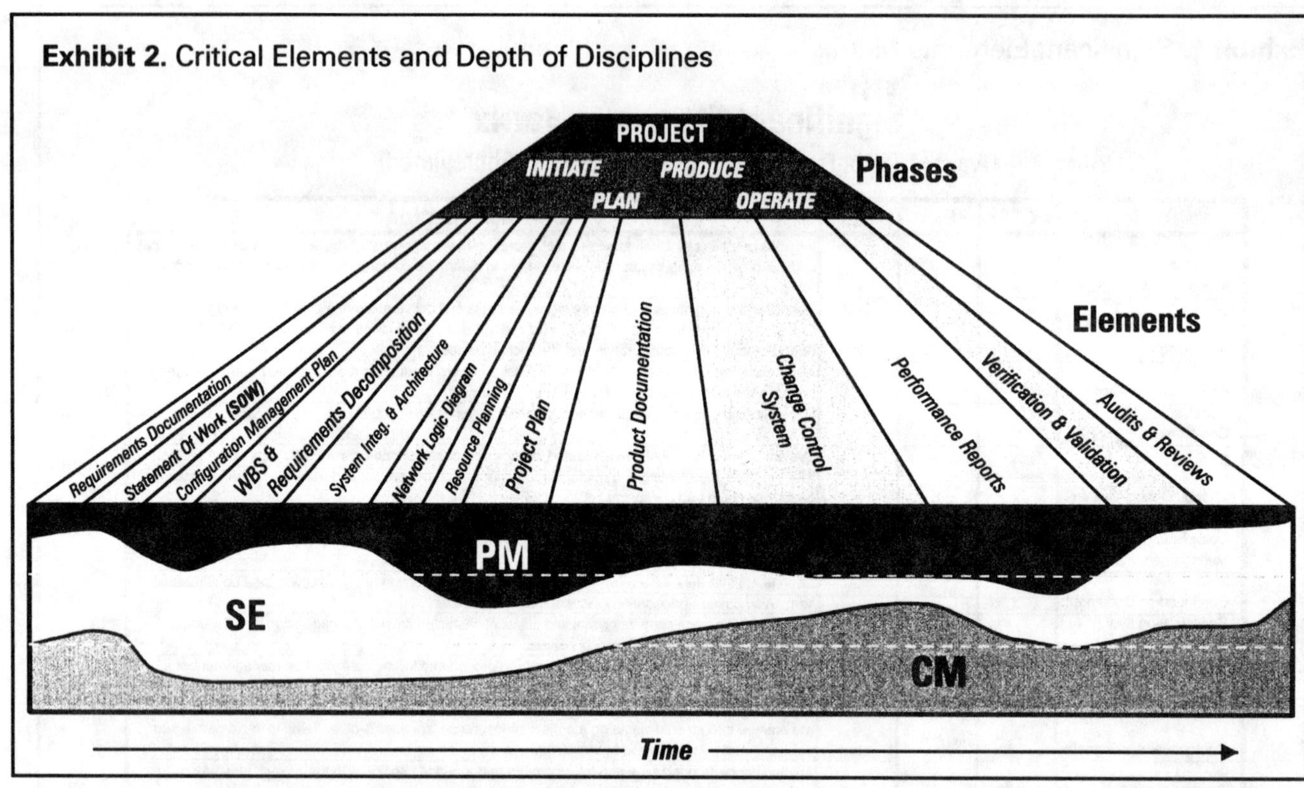


processed materials, services and related technical documentation. CM is an integral part of life-cycle management" (ISO 10007 1995). The standard goes on to say that: "The main objective of CM is to document and provide full visibility of the product's present configuration and on the status of achievement of its physical and functional requirements. Another objective is that everyone working on the project at any time in its life cycle uses correct and accurate documentation" (ISO 10007 1995). The Institute of Configuration Management states that CM "is the process of managing products and processes through the management of documents, records and data" (ICM 1985-1996).

Systems Engineering is "the discipline of developing systems products or processes based on a total systems perspective and utilizing a systems engineering approach. It focuses on defining customer needs and required functionality early in the development cycle, documenting requirements, then proceeding with design synthesis and system validation while considering the complete problem" (INCOSE 1996).

Systems Engineering focuses heavily on detailing all forms of requirements of the system. The discipline relies heavily on a structured approach to then further decompose the overall system requirements into successively lower and lower-level system and component requirements which include detailed specifications. System interfaces between components at all levels are meticulously understood and documented, thus insuring that even the lowest levels of components, if built as described, will eventually integrate into a complete, testable system that meets the top-level requirements.

## Major Elements Of SE, CM and PM

All three disciplines bring a plethora of elements for use by project managers. Amazingly, many of the elements used by the disciplines are the quite similar, though they may be called by slightly different names. We assembled a list of major elements from each of the three disciplines. The list compares how each respective discipline characterizes each major element, if applicable. Upon study of the various elements we discovered that in many cases, similar elements were referred to by different names depending on which discipline was involved. Often, in these cases, one discipline appeared to clearly have a more complete understanding of the element involved, and more robust methods supporting it. However, each discipline also had its unique elements which appeared to have no overlap or complement in the other two disciplines.

## What's Really Needed To Manage Projects In The Next Century?

What we as project managers need in The Next Century need is a tool kit with the essential elements necessary to effectively manage a project in the purest sense. A mechanic builds his/her tool kit from the best tools available to do the job. The tools selected are rarely of the same brand; rather his/her tool kit likely contains the best tools available from a variety of manufacturers. Similarly, the project manager must build his/her tool kit by shopping in the marketplace of ideas for the best tools to do the job regardless of the source. The project manager's search is for the strongest elements to satisfy the need regardless of the associated discipline. These essential elements must be merged with a generic process flow into a fully integrated solution set of the true best practices in industry; taking the very best elements each discipline has to offer.

So, let's look at some essential elements required to effectively manage a project in The Next Century. Please refer to the exhibit entitled "Essential Elements & Depth of Disciplines" which depicts when various essential elements are typically used during the phases of a project—Initiate, Plan, Produce and Operate. These elements come from each of the disciplines, SE, CM and PM.

The front of the "Critical Elements & Depth of Disciplines" exhibit shows SE, PM and CM in relation to time. The vertical height of each band at a given point in time represents the relative focus of that discipline on the project based on our assessment of the body of knowledge each discipline brings to the elements above. This graphic illustrates our assertion that each of the disciplines bring essential elements and expertise for working through a project from its inception to its conclusion. Each discipline offers a greater depth of expertise in certain elements involved in dealing with a particular phase of a project. We have tried to illustrate this complement graphically in this exhibit.

As noted earlier, each of the disciplines appear to include a number of elements. These elements, when carefully examined and compared with the elements of the other disciplines, reveal that although the names may be different, the elements are often striving to fulfill similar needs, but present different and often competing approaches.

We will now briefly look at sixteen elements we deem essential for the project manager in The Next Century. We assert that these elements, when integrated together into an overall approach, represent a foundation of the most critical elements in any overall project management process. Included in each description is our assessment of the general discipline which provides the best approach for satisfying the particular element. The elements are presented in order of first appearance in the life cycle of a project.

## 16 Critical Elements:

1. Requirements Documentation. SE has the most depth in the use of this element in terms of extracting requirements, however CM plays a substantial role in the control and documentation of these requirements. With this element the project manager gathers requirements and documents them in a "clear, concise and valid" manner (ICM 1985-1996). The requirements include those from the customer, applicable laws, regulations, ordinances and contractual requirements. The requirements form the basis for the project. Each of the disciplines emphasize the necessity of gathering sound requirements for the project. These will be later used in the verification that the deliverables of the project are correct.
2. Statement Of Work (SOW). SE has the most depth in the use of this element. This is a generic term used to describe the collection of deliverables, constraints, objectives, goals, expectations, evaluation criteria and other key elements of the project. In some of the disciplines this term also applies to the descriptions levied on each product or service involved in the project. When used on the individual products or services of the project, this SOW is used for procurement, including production or purchase, of the item or service (PMBOK 1996).
3. Configuration Management Plan. CM has the most depth in the use of this element. This CM Plan refers to the collection of documentation setting out the organization and procedures for the configuration management of a specific product, service or project (ISO 10007 1995, 2). This information is foundational for the successful control of changes which inevitably occur on a project.
4. Work Breakdown Structure (WBS). PM has the most depth in the use of this element. This is a deliverable-oriented grouping of project elements that organizes and defines the total scope of the project (PMBOK 1996, 171). The top of the WBS usually contains the deliverables of the project with the subordinate elements being the physical components followed by the activities required to complete the deliverable. This term is used by each of the disciplines, but may be used in different ways. Similar names sometimes used are: Organizational Breakdown Structures (OBS), Product Breakdown Structures (PBS) and Resource Breakdown Structures (RBS). The WBS is one of the critical foundations of a project. The WBS is used by a number of other elements and in a number of the process steps in the Generic Project Management Process. The WBS is often used as a framework for requirements decomposition.

5. Requirements Decomposition. SE has the most depth in the use of this element. It involves successively breaking down higher-level requirements into lower level (configuration item) requirements and specifications. Another name used for this element is Product Analysis (PMBOK 1996, 51). Requirements decomposition is often guided by the WBS.
6. System Integration and Architecture. SE has the most depth in the use of this element. This is a core element of the systems engineering process that iterates with requirements decomposition activity to effectively architect the framework for the system. This effort is accomplished according to a structured process that insures an optimized system solution is achieved where all segments, prime items and lowest-level configuration items integrate together to meet all system requirements.
7. Network Logic Diagram. PM has the most depth in the use of this element  This diagram has its foundations in the traditional PM discipline. This element is a graphical format which shows the tasks or activities required to implement the project in their logical sequence. This element is critical in performing the tasks and activities of the project in the best order. When resources, constraints and time duration estimates have been applied then this diagram becomes time-based. It then is able to be used to develop the schedule and identify the critical path for the project (PMBOK, 1996).
8. Resource Planning.. PM has the most depth in the use of this element. This element is used to place various tasks or activities in the proper time-frames based on resource availability. The resource can be either human or machine. This is a critical step in developing realistic project schedules. (PMBOK 1996)
9. Project Plan. PM has the most depth in the use of this element. This PM-discipline element is the key document containing all the subsidiary plans, such as scope, risk, SOW, procurement, etc., including performance baselines, especially for cost and schedule elements. It is often a "living" document from which the project is managed as changes are required. (PMBOK 1996)
10. Product Documentation. CM has the most depth in the use of this element. This element comprises the documentation which describes the project's products. This takes the form of drawings, plans, technical documents, end-item specifications, etc. It is generally from these documents that the deliverables of the project are procured, produced and inspected for conformity.
11. Change Control System. CM has the most depth in the use of this element. This element comprises the system by which changes against configuration-controlled products and documentation are evaluated for inclusion in the project based on the established scope. It also includes coordinating and managing the changes on the project and revising schedules, staffing, costs, risk plans and quality impact. (ICM 1985-1996; *PMBOK Guide* 1996, 44)
12. Performance Reports. PM has the most depth in the use of this element. This generic name refers to all the reports produced, on-line or hard-copy, which provide information on the project's performance to support decision making. This monitoring of the project looks for trends and causes of anomalies. From this information corrective action is pursued.
13. Verification. CM has the most depth in the use of this element. "Verification is proof of compliance with specification performance requirements. Verification may be determined by test, analysis, inspection, or demonstration" (Forsberg, Mooz and Cotterman 1996). This element is heavily dependent on documented, "clear, concise and valid" requirements at many levels (ICM 1985-1996).
14. Validation. SE has the most depth in the use of this element. "Validation is the process of providing evidence that a system meets the needs of the User" (Forsberg, Mooz and Cotterman 1996).
15. Audits. CM has the most depth in the use of this element. Each of the three disciplines refers to the use of a variety of audits. An audit is basically any detailed and specific assessment used to determine conformance to specific documentation and plans. It includes such modifiers as: Configuration, Configuration Management, Quality, Change Package, Physical and Functional Configuration. The use of the element in its many flavors is required to assure the project is fulfilling its mission and objectives. (ISO 10007 1995; ICM 1985-1996; PMBOK 1996; Forsberg, Mooz and Cotterman 1996)
16. Reviews. SE has the most depth in the use of this element. Each of the three disciplines refers to the use of a variety of reviews. A review is used to determine in a general fashion conformance to documents and plans. It includes such modifiers as: Preliminary Design, Critical Design, Technical, Design, Project, Performance, Status, Budget, System Concept, System Design, System Requirements, Qualification, Architecture Design, Acceptance, Test Readiness & Rate Readiness. (ISO 10007 1995; ICM 1985-1996; PMBOK 1996; Forsberg, Mooz and Cotterman 1996)

## Working Together In The Next Century—An Action Plan

After viewing the list of 16 critical elements and our assessment of the respective disciplines that demonstrate the most depth in each element, are we implying that all project managers must become experts in SE, CM and PM? Absolutely not! That would be a very tall requirement for any individual to fulfill, and a quite unnecessary one. So how do we apply the knowledge and experience of each of these three disciplines in their strongest elements in order to manage our projects? We think that the answer lies in completing the following action plan. We all must:

- Learn to let go of some of the long-held labels and conflicting claims of "ownership" by these disciplines of the shared elements.
- Realize that if we choose to "align" primarily with the approaches of a specific discipline we still need elements from each of the other two disciplines in order to survive and excel in The Next Century.
- Question the value of maintaining separate definitions and understandings of these core elements and yield to a single agreed-to primary ownership role fulfilled by the discipline which possesses the greatest demonstrated leadership and expertise with that element. We need to then reference the element *and* the custodian discipline to which we can all turn for education, assistance and guidance. We can then all agree to the prime custodian's definition of the element. The definitions and reference information can then be reproduced in texts of the other disciplines for completeness, but recognizing the authority for evolutionary change rests with the primary custodial discipline.
- Realize that the key to managing successful projects in The Next Century lies in understanding the relationship of the shared and unique core elements of each discipline and the most efficient and effective way to integrate these elements into our tool kit in order to manage our projects.
- Challenge ourselves to work toward the fulfillment of this action plan in The Next Century. Challenge our thinking—let's think progressively toward *working together as disciplines in The Next Century*. We alone do not have all the answers to the questions facing us. However, we can all work together to pull out the right tools and the expertise from the appropriate disciplines to create the best tool kit which we can all possess and use as project managers in The Next Century.

## Conclusion

To summarize:

We must have in integrated tool kit to successfully manage projects in The Next Century. This tool kit must contain at least the 16 critical elements described to manage a project; this being project management in the purest sense of the term. These elements cannot be working against each other, existing with competing definitions and supporting methods in our professional societies and organizations if we are to be truly effective in our project endeavors. Otherwise, we will reap the consequences of "disciplinary capitalism:" friction, confusion and difficulty in managing our projects.

We must challenge ourselves to adopt at least the described 16 critical elements needed to manage our projects without regard to their affiliation with a particular discipline. We can buy single tools from the broader marketplace of ideas, and we don't have to buy our whole set of tools from one discipline just to obtain our needed tools. We simply need the best integrated tool kit to do the job regardless of brands.

We must migrate toward a relationship among the professional societies of SE, CM and PM where each serves as the sole-source custodian of definitions and understanding for an agreed-to sub-set of the critical elements. The definitions and understanding of the elements must then be referenced in the writings of the other disciplines and must change if and when the custodian discipline changes them. Over time, these behaviors will re-translate into our organizations and enterprises. This surely will represent an easier way to "live" for all of us and will result in less of an overall maintenance burden for our organizations, and each single discipline.

Finally: Why wait? We urge you to start now and implement this action plan on your own projects and in your own organizations. Let's all challenge our thinking and the notion that one discipline has *the* answer to all of our needs. Let's think progressively, *working together* to eliminate "disciplinary capitalism", and rather "capitalize" on the demonstrated strengths of each respective discipline in this *and* The Next Century.

### References


Project Management Institute. 1996. *A Guide To The Project Management Body Of Knowledge*. Upper Darby, PA: Project Management Institute

International Organization For Standardization (ISO). 1994-04-01. *ISO 8402:1994(E/F/R) Quality management and quality assurance — Vocabulary. Second edition.*: International Organization For Standardization (ISO).

International Organization For Standardization (ISO). 1995-04-15. *ISO 10007:1995(E) Quality management — Guidelines for configuration management. First edition.*: International Organization For Standardization (ISO).

International Organization For Standardization (ISO). 1994-12-15. *ISO 10303-1:1994(E) Industrial automation systems and integration — Product data representation and exchange — Part 1: Overview and fundamental principles. First edition.*: International Organization For Standardization (ISO).

International Organization For Standardization (ISO). 1994-12-15. *ISO 10303-41:1994(E) Industrial automation systems and integration — Product data representation and exchange — Part 41: Integrated generic resources: Fundamentals of product description and support. First edition.*: International Organization For Standardization (ISO).

International Organization For Standardization (ISO). 1994-12-15. *ISO 10303-44:1994(E) Industrial automation systems and integration — Product data representation and exchange — Part 44: Integrated generic resources: Product structure configuration. First edition.*: International Organization For Standardization (ISO).

Marca, David A., McGowan, Clement L., Ross, Douglas T. 1988. SADT: Structured Analysis and Design Technique. : McGraw-Hill, Inc.

Turner, Rodney J. 1993. *Handbook of Project-based Management: Improving the Processes for Achieving Strategic Objectives.* Maidenhead, Berkshire, England: McGraw-Hil Book Company Europe.

Lewis, James P. 1991. *Project Planning, Scheduling & Control: A Hands-On Guide to Bringing Projects In On Time and On Budget.* Chicago, IL: Probus Publishing Company.

Institute of Configuration Management. 1985-1996. *Configuration Management II.* Scottsdale, AZ: The Institute of Configuration Management, Inc.

International Council on Systems Engineering. 1996. *What Is Systems Engineering?*. International Council on Systems Engineering: Available: http://www.incose.org/whatis.html, (Last Modified: January 5, 1997.)

Forsberg, Kevin, Ph.D., Mooz, Harold; and Cotterman, Howard. 1996. *Visualize Project Management.* New York, NY: Professional, Reference and Trade Group, John Wiley & Sons, Inc.

"Special Report: PepsiCo." 1996. Corporate Information: Environmental Commitment. 28 Apr. 1997. Available: http://www.pepsico.com/web_pages/environment.html

DeFoe, J. C. 1993. *An Identification of Pragmatic Principles - Final Report. INCOSE: SE Practice Working Group, Subgroup on Pragmatic Principles.*: International Council on Systems Engineering. Available:
http://www.incose.org/workgrps/practice/pragprin.html#AppxA

Electronic Industries Association. 1994. *EIA/IS-632 Systems Engineering.*: Electronics Industries Association. Available: http://www.eia.org/scripts/search/query...%5Bd%5D&HTML-QueryForm=%2Feng%2Findex.htm

# NASA Project Management and Preparing for the New Millenium: A Study Into the Critical Factors Facing People in Projects and Identifying Best Practices for Future Success

Dr. Edward J. Hoffman, NASA
MS. Janice Moore, NASA
Mr. Lawrence Suda, Management Worlds, Inc.

## Introduction

For the better part of four decades NASA achieved some of the greatest feats of the 20'th century and experienced some of the worse public disasters. Throughout this entire period, NASA relied upon project management as a core organizational competency. The tools and techniques of effective project management were considered vital to organizational effectiveness.

As NASA prepares to enter a new century it is critical to understand the changing environmental factors which impact projects. This paper's focus is on the findings of a major organizational assessment into the key issues impacting people in projects and recommended best practices for project management.

The paper starts with a background into the factors driving major change at NASA and how an understanding of this turbulent environment led to the decision to conduct an agency-wide study into project management. The study focused on two primary objectives, first, to identify the fundamental issues which are increasing the complexity of managing projects; second, to search for and identify best practices in project management which are used in both public and private sector organizations.

In conducting this research, a large sample of the NASA project management community were involved in offering their views. In addition, the views of experts external to NASA were also incorporated into this work. A discussion of the approach used to conduct the study is covered. In addition, specific findings are offered regarding the critical issues facing project managers. Issues such as full cost management, professional development and certification, maintaining quality in a time of downsizing and the demands for managing projects in a better, faster, cheaper mode are some of the issues discussed.

Equally interesting are the identified best practices for how projects can be managed effectively in this time of great change. A look at what some of the most successful innovative projects are doing offers insight into the critical competencies as we enter a new century.

The paper concludes with specific insight into how NASA is preparing its workforce for future projects. The paper also presents insights covering the critical competencies for NASA project managers, strategies for managing fast track projects and approaches to establishing an organization-wide corporate knowledge support system through the use of available technology.

## Background

The National Aeronautics & Space Administration is one of the most visible and prestigious organizations in the world. For decades multitudes of people read books and articles, watched major movie and television productions, and visited Air and Space museums all associated with the work of NASA. During it's entire history, the science and technological feats were largely accomplished within the rigorous framework of a disciplined project management methodology. Indeed, it is hard to think of NASA without quickly thinking of programs and projects. The use of project management to further the accomplishment of national goals was a part of the organization since its inception.

Project management during most of those years was represented by a relatively stable set of environmental characteristics. It was during the last ten years that the discipline witnessed significant change within NASA, and more so over the last five years that the change has been most dramatic.

To understand the present it is necessary to have an understanding of the past. In the case of project management at NASA this is no exception. The history of project management indicates that NASA project management was a relatively stable discipline during the first three decades of the organization's existence. In fact, from approximately 1958 through 1986, one can paint a fairly clear image. If Charles Dickens captured a character called the *Ghost of Project*

*Management Past* a broad brush depiction would focus on several key attributes:

1. Large, Expensive Programs
2. Primacy of Technical Accomplishment
3. Subservience of Cost and Schedule
4. Project Management Methodology
5. Project Manager As All Powerful Being
6. NASA Control Over Design, Development And Operations
7. Risk Elimination Strategy
8. Almost Unquestioned Public Support.

While the ghost would clearly carry other attributes, the seven characteristics do a just job of that seemingly long, bygone era. In specific terms, the NASA of the late fifties and through the mid-80's was reflected by several features. The programs which characterized this period were large, massive efforts. They required major resources, money and human energy. The ultimate judge of a project manager's success was simple - if the technical objectives were met than all else was forgiven, and you were considered a success. It is nonsensical to suggest that cost and schedule were completely ignored or considered with minimal thought. However, in a world where tradeoffs must always be made, it was clear that cost and schedule always took a back seat to technical achievement.

During this period one would also see the structured and rigorous use of the project management method. This is not saying that the method was conducted in a consistent and disciplined manner. However, the essentials of the project management method were used at NASA. The project management approach was further supported by a strong project manager who often had total control of major decisions that impacted a project. The project manager was clearly King. (To describe a project manager as a King is clearly politically incorrect today, however, during the era we are describing there were virtually no Queens in power).

The other key attribute of this era was the control NASA had over projects. Industry involvement was always vital to NASA projects (today about 90% of the NASA budget goes directly to industry). In the past, NASA strongly controlled all aspects of project management. The notion of empowered partnerships was not known during this time period. Similarly, the concept of risk management was practiced at NASA with the single objective being to do whatever was necessary to eliminate risk.

The final primary attribute of this era was the clear public support of NASA. While there were always criticisms of any effort, NASA was blessed with the support of public opinion and powerful political allies. These factors were about to undergo a transformation leading to the modern changes underway.

## The New Realities

A paradigm change would be triggered by a major event that is understood in one word - Challenger. The Challenger explosion altered NASA in an infinite array of angles. Pertaining to project management, Challenger lead to a greater scrutiny of how NASA was developing future people in project management. In addition more effort was placed on making safety the number one value for future Shuttle missions. As a result of this tragedy, the management of projects was forever altered, starting with a major emphasis on improving the competencies of people in project management through a broad-based training and development initiative - the Program Project Management Initiative (PPMI).

After the Challenger, project management endured significant change. During this present era the project manager would still be a powerful leader, however, there were increased checks on power with extended emphasis on safety and limiting risk. Shortly after Challenger many other external shifts occurred in the geopolitical, economic and social environment order of the world which also became key drivers for the mandatory changes at NASA. The geopolitical world changed with the end of the cold war, the world economy became more global and suddenly the rest of the world was catching-up to NASA's preeminence in space technology. New political realities in American and throughout the world also presented formidable challenges to NASA. The threat of drastic budget cuts, rapidly advancing technology and shifts in public opinion were also factors contributing to the need for change. It was no longer business as usual. Additionally, one of the most significant changes to occur was the appointment of Daniel Goldin as administrator in 1992. The new administrator immediately began promoting major reforms within NASA, with strategic and project management becoming the cornerstones and the leading areas for improvement.

The catalyst for much of the change would stem from the strategic decision to place a greater emphasis on "better, faster, cheaper" projects. The thinking behind this approach was to stretch the shrinking budget dollars by finding more innovative ways to reduce costs. It is within this context that over the past few years increasing efforts are exploring new ways of doing business and identifying best practices.

## Methodology

In light of the need to find and communicate new ways for improving work processes, this study was conducted to identify key issues and best practices. The data for this effort was derived from practicing project managers and other leading experts, who could candidly provide input into some of the trends and approaches that they have found most useful in their daily work environments.

The study was designed to be a mixture of focal group discussions and individual, one on one interviews. Interview protocols and questions were developed as established guides for the practicing members of the project management community to identify and discuss their best practices and new ways of doing business. These discussions provided a plethora of material reflecting a wide range of thoughts on how to better manage and improve work processes. The best practices were uncovered in the focus group meetings and later validated by those practicing managers who directly experienced or in some capacity was responsible for that practice.

## Findings

The interviews and group discussions identified a wide variety of approaches for improving project management. What became apparent very early in the study was the fact that we were dealing with different models and time perspectives of NASA. Those managers working on past-present projects the discussions centered on those practices that worked well in the past that NASA needed to keep and disseminate and continue building skills in those areas. These included past practices like having a good WBS, writing good requirements, using good control metrics. The other group of managers interviewed working on future related projects to NASA discussed the new ways as doing business. The practices discussed in these interviews centered on areas believed to be more of what the NASA would be like in the future and these were clustered under a separate heading of emerging practices. The interviews revealed the following clusters of areas for best practices and emerging practices:

## Business Management Systems

One of the areas that received the greatest attention was in the area of business management systems. This refers to a broad category of approaches outlining ways to improve the costing, procurement and acquisition functions. In many of the interviews specific and common tools were described (e.g. earned value, performance-based contracting and full cost management). The point made in many of these interviews was that there needs to be a dedication to simply making effective use of existing methodologies as opposed to trying to avoid them. In addition, in business management there needs to be more emphasis on enhancing analytic competency and simultaneously streamlining unnecessary reviews and protocol. Several other examples of best practices obtained in the interviews were:

Earned Value Management System
NASA's Life Cycle Development Methodology
Information Management Technology
Risk Management System
ISO 9000 Certification
Annual Assessment of Projects
Full Cost and IFMP System
Different Contract Mechanisms
NASA Strategic Plan and Center Strategic Plans
Lead Center MIS.

## Tools and Techniques

The foundation for fundamental improvement is creating the competency and awareness for practitioners to use the best techniques and tools. There is a need for education and benchmarking into new ways of doing business. Many individuals cited the need to have time to share learnings with colleagues in other organizations. The benefit of attending conferences was cited as one of the ways in which skills can be brought back and applied. The use of internet-based communication forums also provide a way to cross-communicate instantly and establish active learning communities. It was also stated by several practicing managers that the proper leadership and culture needed to exist in order for the tools to work well. Several examples of the tools and techniques mentioned by the project managers and experts were:

- Lessons Learned Data Base
- TechTracks
- E-Log
- Workable WBS
- Preliminary Hazard Analysis
- Lead Center MIS
- Scenario Based Planning
- Control Metrics
- Parametric Estimating Technique
- Use of Rapid Prototyping
- Video Conferencing
- Electronic Status Reporting
- CAD/CAM
- CAN/NRA
- Electronic Meetings
- Write Good Minimum Requirements
- Minimize/No Changes to Requirements
- Electronic Meeting System.

## Organization Culture

All organizations find ways in which to be successful. Over time, these successful behaviors take the form of a rigid procedures for what is the right way. While these behaviors can provide clear guidance and efficient thought as to action, they can also become great barriers to innovation. In the interviews the single factor which received the most attention was the need to promote an environment which fostered creative approaches and a freedom to try new strategies. Other examples cultural practices mentioned were:

- Cross Functional Integration
- Up-Front Agreements
- Up-Front Planning
- Use of Partnering and Co-location of Partners
- Fewer Reviews
- More Insight and Less Oversight
- Individual and Team Rewards
- Rewards and Not Punishment For Risk Finders
- Push Decision-making to Lowest Levels
- Badgeless Community
- Orlando's Principle Based Management Style
- Developing Team and Partner Trust
- Use of Concurrent Engineering
- Operate Like a Business
- Alliances with International Space Agencies
- Let People Do Their Jobs
- Use of Wide Personal Network.

## Policies and Structure

Many respondents indicated that time was required to review organizational policies and structure. Many of the innovative project managers said that they were able to be more innovative because they did not have to deal with the typical structures that normally take place. Examples referred to the need to lighten the rein on excessive reviews and documentation, as well as the use of controls which limit or slow down the ability to respond quickly. Policies that increase tailoring and work responsibility to the working level were viewed as critical to improved performance. Several other examples found in the interviews were:

- Blanket Travel Orders
- Life Cycle Development Model
- Credit Card Purchases
- Liberal Interpretation of FAR
- Documenting Lessons Learned
- Lead Center Concept
- Cooperative Agreements.

## Teaming

While a potentially over discussed area, the effective utilization of teams was a central finding. Time and other resources must be made available which allow teaming arrangements to form and develop. The use of integrated product teams was one example used to promote the philosophy of bringing together the team early with an emphasis on joint objectives and common purpose. The need for finding effective strategies for supporting virtual teams was another area of opportunity. More examples of other practices cited were:

- Using Integrated Product Teams
- Co-locating a Project Team
- Knowing How To Manage Partnerships
- Consensus Building
- Calling Time-outs
- Periodic Updates to Team Members
- Team Responsible For Project Success
- Leading A Team - Enlightened Leadership
- Using 'Skunkworks' when feasible
- User As A Team Member.

## Emerging Practices

Within the context of this study there were many technologies referred to which were on the cutting edge of performance enhancement. The use of computer-aided tools represents one area where significant opportunities exist to improve team performance. The ability to effectively integrate these emerging practices into the day to day management of a team remains a significant challenge. In addition, it is critical to constantly maintain the search for emerging practices which can improve performance. Examples cited by those working with innovative approaches to projects were:

- Team X
- Single Process Initiative
- Front Load Funding Profile
- Driving Towards Customer Focus Environment
- Cost Sharing With Partners
- Partnerships With Industry
- Co-existence of Competition and Cooperation
- Fast Track
- On-line Collaborative Design Efforts
- Simulation Based Design
- Virtual Simulation Center
- Reduction In Rigidity Of Life Cycle
- Tie Award Fee To On-orbit Performance
- Reduction Of Documentation Requirements
- Use Of Commercial Off-The-Shelf Technology
- Bruce Holmes 4th Generation Research
- Tools for Project & Financial Analysis
- Design To Cost; Design To Schedule
- Management Of Reviews.

## Conclusions

A central finding of this study is that best practices throughout NASA. It is vital that there remains an openness to searching out and trying out new ways of doing business. It is also important tailor a practice to the specific need and situation. A best practice in one area, can become an annoying burden in another environment.

There were recurring themes throughout study focusing on how successful project management in today's constrained world of "Better, Faster, Cheaper" requires an experienced project manager with the ability to manage to the plan. There is little, if any time, for major changes in requirements or to the established plan during project execution in this new era for space mission science and spacecraft development. Managers need to clearly understand the Life-Cycle Development model used by NASA and how to use this model to create a comprehensive project plan.

Team structure and teamwork are essential for success. Teamwork now means working with cross-functional integrated disciplines and the eliminating the stovepipes approaches of the past. A variety of disciplines must work together well and be able to understand and receive cross-training in other disciplines in order to shorten the project cycle time. Good teamwork provides the framework to achieve schedule compression and to identify and eliminate problems early on in the project. Team leadership and team management go hand in hand and it is vital for the project manager to be well balanced and competent in both areas in order to be successful.

In the "Better, Faster, Cheaper management era, there is little time for incorrect starts or mid-course redirection. Since there is little time to recover, trust becomes a very important factor to manage properly. For trust to exist among team members, the right people must be chosen for the team, whether in-house or contractor personnel, and provided the proper working climate for empowered decision-making. This requires that goals, roles, responsibilities and working procedures be clearly articulated and that the necessary and appropriate management tools be made available for the tasks at hand. Working closely with procurement, safety, contractor and customer personnel early on and frequently are absolute requirements for success.

Risks must be identified early and risk mitigation planned, along with a system that allows the team to implement risk management. Insight into team and contractor work is preferred and whenever needed oversight must be as least disruptive as possible. For this reason, documentation and reviews should only be used to help the project team actively manage the project. Higher level reviews should accommodate the project team by allowing those required reviews to fit the project team's plans and to present status reports from the project team's management tools and metrics.

Both management and technical innovations must be encouraged, as cost and schedule drive the design. This does not mean that science and engineering needs to take a back seat, but management must recognize early what good enough is and use better as a design margin. Simplicity and industry standard designs plus off-the-shelf technology should be used whenever possible. Design-to-Cost and Design-to-Schedule need to be emphasized and taught as a way as part of the new ways of doing business.

The entire team must look for opportunities to perform activities in parallel and to help each team member identify new opportunities and find ways to start work as early in the process as possible. Value-added work must be identified for each functional area, while minimizing non-value added work and disruptive activities. Concurrent teamwork is now a way of life and must be fully understood by all team members. More than ever before, good communication of information is essential and can provide significant benefits in time and cost savings.

The ideas uncovered in this study also provide a clear call for establishing approaches for identifying and communicating best practices so that just-in-time learning can take place. There is a need to provide just in time learning through training and education. Most significantly, there is need for a genuine desire on the part of all to innovate and constantly look for ways to improve.

# Project Management on the Space Shuttle Program: Modifying the Space Shuttle

By Rick Goltz, Project Engineer - United Space Alliance

## Introduction

America's Space Shuttle program encompasses hundreds of projects ranging from the creation of a new business form to the construction of a new Space Shuttle. One of the most tightly controlled processes in the entire program is the implementation of modifications on the shuttle fleet. In fact, this procedure is so tightly controlled that NASA's project management system for implementing the modifications requires no single, central project manager. Instead, each step is performed by people who require exacting input and output processes before their jobs can completed.

A Space Shuttle may be modified for a number of reasons; A new mission requirement may drive a change in configuration, a problem may dictate corrective action, or a change may simply make launch processing faster and cheaper. One of the primary concerns to the Shuttle Program Office is safety of flight. The Shuttle is too valuable of a national asset to risk loss or damage, not to mention the potential loss of life should an accident occur. Another primary goal is, of course, the successful completion of each mission. The physical configuration of the Shuttle is of paramount concern to both of these requirements. Should the Shuttle be assembled incorrectly, or a payload improperly installed, either goal could be jeopardized.

It should be noted that modifications to the Space Shuttle are relatively small projects when compared to other industrial undertakings. Projects may be as small as upgrading a single bolt to a stronger material, or as large as upgrading the original cockpit avionics to modern "glass cockpit" standards. Either way, modifications to the Space Shuttle are significantly smaller projects than, for instance, construction of a new airport or chemical refinery.

## NASA's Contractors

Previous to October 1996, NASA utilized two contractors for its Shuttle program. Rockwell International Space Transportation and Systems Division in Downey, California, who originally built the Shuttles under another contract, was responsible for all design and manufacturing of Space Shuttle components. Lockheed Martin Space Operations Company at Kennedy Space Center (KSC), Florida was responsible for processing, launching and landing recovery of the Space Shuttle. In 1996, NASA decided it would rather deal with a single contractor for all Shuttle design, manufacturing and processing tasks. This contract came to be known as the Space Flight Operations Contract (SFOC). As is usually the case with any large government aerospace contract, all of the big aerospace corporations entered the competition. It quickly became obvious that Rockwell International and Lockheed Martin Space Operations Company would enjoy a distinct advantage over other competitors if they joined forces. Thus, United Space Alliance (USA) was developed as a 50/50 joint venture between Rockwell International and Lockheed Martin. In October 1996, the SFOC contract was awarded to USA. Due to technical, financial, and human resource benefits complexities, USA actually employed Rockwell International as a subcontractor to its overall SFOC contract. Late in 1996, the Boeing Company purchased Rockwell International Space Transportation and Systems Division and renamed the company Boeing North American (BNA), who is now Lockheed Martin's partner and subcontractor in USA.

After all the renaming, re-contracting and subcontracting, virtually nothing has changed in the day-to-day activities and relationships of the various players. BNA still performs all design and manufacturing tasks and USA (ex-Lockheed) still performs all launch and landing activities. Even NASA still interfaces with the original contractors as they have in the past. Only the money trail has changed. USA is currently working on the seamless integration of the marriage, but for the purposes of being clear and uncomplicated, the remainder of this paper will deal with USA and BNA as distinctly separate and unrelated contractors since that is essentially the case for now.

Boeing North American's contract includes a myriad of tasks, one of which is supporting modifications to the Shuttle fleet. This task includes the design and manufacture of new components as well as generation of the required installation drawings. The portion of their contract that deals with supporting modifications is a cost reimbursable - fixed profit contract. NASA will pay BNA for the actual cost of the design and manufacturing plus 9 percent profit. If costs overrun, NASA may decide to pay the extra cost, reduce the scope, or cancel the modification entirely. In any case, BNA will only receive 9 percent of the original bid as profit. This removes any incentive for cost overruns from the contractor.

Modifications are treated on a case by case basis with each modification bid, tracked, and paid for individually.

United Space Alliance (USA) is the contractor responsible for processing, launching and recovering the Space Shuttle at Kennedy Space Center (KSC) and remote landing sites. USA's contract with NASA is a cost plus incentive fee contract where NASA has direct control over all facilities and headcount. The contract is essentially for a "standing army" level of effort contract that includes Shuttle processing as well as implementation of modifications. Contractor profits are a direct percentage of payroll plus incentives for outstanding support. During the implementation phase, modification costs are not tracked on an individual basis, rather, modifications are considered to be part of normal Shuttle processing.

## Approving a New Modification

When a modification to the Space Shuttle is required, the agency sponsoring the change presents the desired modification to the NASA Orbiter Configuration Control Board (CCB). The CCB is a technical and cost control board consisting of engineering specialists from each of the Shuttle subsystems as well as the Board Chairman who controls the Shuttle modification budget. The CCB will assess the technical merits and risks of the modification under consideration and if the modification is deemed mandatory, or at least desirable, the CCB Chairman will request Boeing North American (BNA) to develop a cost estimate for the modification. The cost estimate will be generated by considering the usual resource and material costs and must include the design and manufacture of any required new components, as well as the generation of the installation drawings. Depending on the technical complexity of the modification at hand, NASA may be closely involved with development of the modification strategy or, in the case of relatively benign modifications, BNA may be left to design the modification as they see fit. In either case, after the design strategy has been decided upon, BNA will submit a cost estimate to the CCB. The CCB Chairman may accept the initial estimate or pursue any of the options available to him to reduce the cost and/or the scope of the modification to bring the cost in-line. In addition to the technical feasibility and cost assessments, USA Shuttle Flow Management at Kennedy Space Center is consulted to determine if the modification can be implemented during the desired window of opportunity and if the required resources will be available.

Once the CCB has accepted the technical merit, cost, and implementation window for the modification, the request is forwarded to the Program Requirements Control Board (PRCB) for final approval. The PRCB consists of each of the various program level element representatives such as Orbiter (the Space Shuttle Orbiter CCB Chairman), External Tank (the ET CCB Chairman), Solid Rocket Booster (the SRB CCB Chairman), Main Engines (the SSME CCB Chairman), flight software and flight crew representatives. The sponsor presents the desired modification and answers questions on a nation-wide tele-conference with dozens of listeners and technical experts on-line. The PRCB Chairman will typically ask questions to ensure all of the required risk assessment considerations have been addressed before he will allow the modification to proceed. A consensus decision is made to approve or disapprove the new modification with significant emphasis placed on Shuttle Program compatibility (i.e. does the modification support a specific payload or mission requirement?) and technical merit. In addition, the PRCB will consider which of the Shuttles will receive the modification and when it will be implemented. The PRCB will issue a document called a PRCB Directive, which is the official approval for the modification.

## Scope Management

Upon PRCB approval, NASA is essentially finished handling the modification. Responsibility for design and manufacturing is handed over to BNA. The modification is entered into a specialized database called the Mission Requirements Control System (MRCS) for tracking purposes along with the literally hundreds of other modifications that are "on the books" at any given time. All participants will use this database to track requirement approval status, implementation effectivity and parts and work status. This will become the primary Scope Management tool since it will dictate and limit the work to be performed.

Program level scope change requests must be processed back through the PCRB. Examples of program scope changes are a change in which Shuttle(s) will receive the modification or when it will be implemented. Requests to change the detailed scope (design changes) must be processed back through the design agency.

## The Design Process

The modification is assigned to a BNA Project Engineer (PE) who is responsible for ensuring that all design and manufacturing functions are completed in time to support the implementation as dictated by the PRCB. BNA Planning schedules the design and manufacturing tasks utilizing project management software to ensure the required products are available to support the modification implementation at KSC. The BNA schedule is limited to BNA tasks and does not include the actual installation of the modification. That task will be left to USA planning at KSC.

The Design Engineers will have already determined the basic design strategy in order to develop the estimated cost of the design and manufacturing. New design drawings may be required and existing drawings may require revision. The format and content of these drawings are strictly controlled by the BNA/NASA Drawing Requirements Manual to ensure the required level of Quality Control and Configuration Management when manufacturing and installing components. As the design drawings are completed, they enter an approval process where the Stress Analysis, Quality Control, Manufacturing and Configuration Management Groups must approve each drawing. Each of the drawing changes is entered into the MRCS database as a detailed list of the work to be performed.

## The Component Manufacturing Process

BNA manufactures (or subcontracts) all of the hardware required to support the modification per NASA approved quality guidelines, which dictate the quality standards and procedures for inspection and certification of flight hardware. Components must be manufactured exactly as designed and, of course, must pass Quality Control inspections. Parts that are found to be out of tolerance are either brought into tolerance or their condition is documented. Design Engineers will review any out-of-tolerance condition and either recommend scrapping the part, modifying the part to make it usable, or using the part "as-is". Either of the last two recommendations requires approval by a Material Review Board (MRB). New components that perform any active function (valves, transducers, electronics, motors, etc.) must pass a rigorous flight certification process. In fact, this process is so rigorous that designers will go to great lengths to utilize components that have been previously certified.

## The Modification Implementation Process

In parallel with the BNA's design and manufacturing efforts, a USA PE is assigned responsibility for implementing the change into the Shuttle(s) at KSC. Upon release of the Design and Manufacturing products, the USA PE coordinates with the appropriate Systems Engineer(s) for generation of the work instructions. The Systems Engineer will interpret the drawings and referenced specifications and generate detailed work instructions called a Work Authorization Document (WAD). Technicians will use the WAD to implement the required changes. The WAD must be based upon the approved design drawings and specifications and conform to NASA requirements for Quality and Configuration Management control. Each and every component and process requirement called out on the modification drawings must be provided for in the work instructions. In fact, the Systems Engineer has only three choices on how he may implement the drawing requirements. He must either: 1) Implement the change exactly as the drawings require, or 2) get the design drawings changed and then implement the change exactly as the updated drawings require, or 3) face a Material Review Board and explain why options 1 & 2 are not feasible. The Configuration Management Group will review the scope management database to determine the approved drawings and then compare the WAD to the drawings to verify each part is installed and each process is performed.

The USA PE will have to coordinate with Systems Engineering and the Shop to ensure that the WAD is released to the floor in time to support the desired implementation window. Any problems that might jeopardize the implementation are the responsibility of the USA Project Engineer. Typical problems include; MRCS (the scope management database) errors, late drawing releases, parts availability, drawing errors and incomplete WADs.

The work is scheduled for implementation by the Flow Planning Organization. Project Management software is utilized to generate a Gantt chart that reflects all of the tasks that are required to process a Shuttle for a mission. The modifications are simply entered as single line items in the overall schedule. Tasks are sequenced and durations are estimated based on the experience of shop personnel and Flow Management. Surprisingly, tasks are not resource loaded in the computer and no computerized resource pools are utilized. This is probably best attributed to the "old school" of planning that is still present in KSC culture.

KSC scheduling meetings are held daily for each Shuttle. The scheduling meetings are chaired by Flow Management and are attended by the Systems Engineers, Shop Supervisors and Facility and Planning Representatives. Every task currently in progress and in the immediate future is discussed. Typical concerns for discussion are current work status, resource, parts and WAD availability as well as any problems that may occur. Problems that cause an impact to the schedule are assessed on a real time basis by the Flow Manager and rescheduled as necessary. Mandatory modifications in support of the next Shuttle mission cannot be deferred to a later Shuttle flow. The modification must either be implemented, or the Shuttle Program Office must be notified that their mission schedule is in jeopardy (this has never happened due to a modification project).

The actual implementation of the modification is undoubtedly the most straightforward and simplest phase in the entire process. Technicians simply follow and perform the detailed work instructions. Technicians must be certified to perform each required task and every action is closely scrutinized by Quality Control personnel to ensure the work is performed exactly per the instructions. If for some reason the WAD cannot be implemented as written, the SE will be notified and a WAD revision must be generated. The revision must endure the same review and approval process as the original WAD.

## Project Closure

Upon completion of the modification, the WAD is "closed" and is returned to the Configuration Management group for a second review to: 1) ensure that no requirements were missed during the first review, and 2) verify that the WAD was not illegally changed since the first review. WADs may be "reopened" and hardware removed and replaced as a result of this post-modification WAD reviews, however, these are rare events. Upon successful review of the closed WAD, Configuration Management will "buy" the requirements in the MRCS modification database. The "buy-off" of these requirements is then reported back to NASA, thus closing the loop for the modification.

## Conclusion

NASA's Space Shuttle modification implementation process utilizes many of the recognized Project Management processes except that there is no single, central Project Manager. All of the required PM checks and balances are in place, but a strict Project Management "process" replaces the Project Manager. This method was developed over many years, dating back to the Apollo program era, and is so complex and tightly controlled that it would be too cumbersome on virtually any other program. However, in the case of the Shuttle program where thousands of requirements are routinely processed over governmental, corporate and geographic boundaries, the "controlled process" form of Project Management works well.

# Earned Value, Clear and Simple

Tammo T. Wilkens, Los Angeles County Metropolitan Transportation Authority

## Introduction

The term "Earned Value" is gaining in popularity around project management circles as if it is some wonderful new concept to be embraced. Yet, it has been in use since the 1960s when the Department of Defense adopted it as a standard method of measuring project performance. The concept was actually developed as early as the 1800s when it became desirable to measure performance on the factory floor. Today, it is both embraced and shunned, often in response to prior experience or stories told "in the hallway." The opponents will generally cite the cost and effort to make it work, and the limited benefit derived from its implementation. The proponents will cite the cost savings to the project overall, the improved analysis, communication and control derived from its implementation. No doubt, the two camps have vastly different experiences to formulate their perceptions.

This paper will explore the three major questions regarding this topic: What, Why and How? The purpose is to allay any fears the reader might have about applying this useful project management tool and to point the way to making it work. It is expected that the reader will gain a thorough understanding of the concept as well as a recipe for implementing Earned Value on his/her project.

## What Is Earned Value?

When we speak of Earned Value, we generally are speaking of a methodology. While Earned Value is just one element of this methodology, it is the key element. The simplest way to think of Earned Value is to equate it with physical progress. As the name implies, it is something that is gained through some effort. In project management, this value is earned as activities are completed

Consequently, Earned Value is also a measure of progress. As we shall see later, there is a direct relationship between Earned Value and per cent complete. The attributes of Earned Value are threefold. First, it is a uniform unit of measure for total project progress or for any sub-element of the project. Second, it is a consistent method for analysis of project progress and performance. Third, it is a basis for cost performance analysis of a project.

If set up properly, Earned Value provides a uniform unit of measure for reporting progress of a project. The traditional units that are used include workhours and dollars. For labor intensive efforts, workhours are often considered adequate In such instances, the financial details of the remaining project cost are controlled by the accounting system. These costs include subcontractors, overheads and other direct costs. When the entire project cost is to be controlled from the project control system, then it is more effective to use dollars as the unit of measure for Earned Value. Since each labor hour has a price, dollars can be used to control labor as well. However, when using dollars, additional factors enter into the performance evaluation. This includes salary rate differences, escalation, overhead adjustments and differences, for example. Consider the effect if the plan calls for Tom, Dick and Harriet to do the work, but the actual work is performed by Lucy, Bill and Mary, who have different salaries. The dollar measure will include the effect of the salaries. For project financial control, this is good information. However, for project performance control, this information muddies up the waters.

Earned Value also is a consistent method for analysis of project performance. Suppose you ask the bricklayers and the carpenters how they're doing. You are likely to get different answers, influenced not only by how they are actually doing, but also by how they calculate their plan and their progress. As we shall see below in the discussion of "How," using Earned Value establishes a particular method for determining what the plan to date is and what the progress actually achieved is.

Earned Value provides the basis for cost performance analysis. If you want to know what's happening to the cost of your project BEFORE it is completed, you need to know what the planned cost at any time was and also what the cost of the completed work is. Referring to Exhibit 1, should this project manager be happy or concerned? It seems that the actual costs are considerably below the planned cost. This appears to be good news. However, unless you look at the planned cost of the completed work, you don't really know if this is good news or not. That is exactly the missing information that Earned Value provides.

In order to understand Earned Value thoroughly, we must become familiar with all the elements of the Earned Value method. Exhibit 2 provides an overview of these elements. While many people shy away from the acronyms used to label the elements, they quite accurately describe the elements. The project management practitioner should be familiar with the "alphabet soup." In this paper, we will use both the formal acronyms and more familiar terms to describe the elements.

The BCWS is the Budgeted Cost of Work Scheduled. Quite literally, it represents the budgets of the activities that are planned or scheduled to be completed. In the discussion of how to apply Earned Value, we shall see how this is developed and why the BCWS curve has the traditional S-curve shape.

The ACWP is the Actual Cost of Work Performed. Again, quite literally, it represents the actual cost charged against the activities that were completed. Later we shall see how we deal with activities that are in progress but not yet completed.

The BCWP is the Budgeted Cost of Work Performed. This is the traditional Earned Value that we speak of. It represents the planned or schedule cost of the activities that are completed. The distinction between the BCWS and the BCWP is that the former represents the budget of the activities that were planed to becompleted and the latter represents the budget of the activities that actually were completed.

These are the three major components of Earned Value. At any point in time, we have the planned work, the actual work and the cost of the actual work. This allows us to make the full analysis of our project progress and performance. Some of the other, related terms shown in Exhibit 2, include the Budget At Completion (BAC), the Estimate At Completion (EAC), the Schedule Variance (SV) and the Cost Variance (CV). We will learn more about these in the discussion on how to apply Earned Value.

## Why Use Earned Value?

Before we consider the mechanics of Earned Value, let us examine the reasons for using it. After all, it does cost something to put it into operation. And, to do it right, it requires some effort on the part of the project team. If we review the discussion above on what Earned Value is, we have the main reasons for using it. Recall that Earned Value is a uniform unit of measure, a consistent methodology and a basis for cost performance analysis.

You might ask "What's so great about a uniform unit of measure?" Suppose that you are the project manager of a software development project. You're part way through your project and you wonder how things are. First, you want to know what per cent complete the project is. At a summary level, let's say that the project includes conceptual design, program specification, coding, documentation, user manual production, and debugging. Further, let's say that conceptual design and program specification are complete, coding and documentation are in process, manual production and debugging haven't started yet. So, how complete is the project? We've completed two out of six parts and are in process with two more. Does that mean we are 50 percent complete? Maybe, but, we don't know. What is each part worth? Does writing one line of program specification equal one line of code and they, in turn, equal one line in the documentation? How is one to equate the various parts?

Now suppose we determine that conceptual design is expected to take 200 wokhours, program specification writing 300 hours, coding 600 hours, documentation 100 hours, user manual 400 hours and debugging 500 hours. These labor "budgets" can easily be used as a weighting factor in establishing the worth of the various parts. That is exactly what Earned Value does. Since conceptual design and spec writing are done, we have "earned" 500 hours of value. For the in-process activities, we need to decide how we will earn the value. More on earning rules later. For now let's just say we are one quarter done with the coding and 10 percent with the documentation. We could then claim 150 hours for the coding and 10 hours for the documentation. The total earnings are then 660 hours. So, how complete is the project? Using Earned Value methodology, we would determine that the project is 31.4 percent complete (660 earned hours divided by 2100 hours of total project budget). Earned Value has allowed us to combine the progress of vastly different work efforts. The same thing works with any kind of project. Earned Value lets us combine cubic yards of concrete with square feet of forms, tons of rebar, feet of pipe, feet of conduit and cabling, etc. If we're in the banking business, Earned Value allows us to combine product development with market research, systems design, marketing and product introduction. In Hollywood, we can combine writing the screenplay with scouting for locations, set production, filming, editing, and marketing. By now you probably get the idea that Earned Value can be employed whenever your project involves defined tasks.

So much for a uniform unit of measure. What does consistent methodology do for me? Remember the bricklayers and carpenters? If you ask the carpenters how they are doing, you might get an answer such as: "We're doing fine, we've already used half the lumber you sent us at the beginning of the project. We'll have the rest used up by next week." The bricklayer might say: "We're doing great. Ninety per cent of the budgeted labor hours are spent, therefore we're 90 percent complete." Both parties might be correct, but what can you as the project manager do with that information? You can pass it along, but chances are that your management is not interested in the nitty gritty details, they want summary information. Using Earned Value, the bricklayers and the carpenters would measure the total quantities of bricks and lumber installed and compare that against the budgeted quantities to determine the per cent complete. Similarly, they would compare the installed quantities against the quantities planned to be installed up this point in time to determine if they are ahead or behind schedule. You can see that Earned Value has provided a method that both the bricklayers and the carpenters can use to report progress.

Now let us consider the third reason. Using Earned Value enhances the cost performance analysis of a project. Traditional cost analysis centers around the actual cost of the work that was completed. Therefor, much progress has been done to collect the actual costs through the time charge and accounting systems that exist on practically all projects. What Earned Value brings to the process is a measure of the amount of work that has been done in a unit of measure that is consistent and comparable with costs. In other words, it allows us to compare "apples and apples" by using the same unit of measure for physical progress as for cost. Now we can more meaningfully assess whether the costs spent to date in Exhibit 1 are higher or lower than was planned.

## How Do We Use Earned Value?

At this point we come to the practical part of actually seeing how Earned Value is applied on any project. There are 5 steps in setting up the Earned Value system on a project, and 4 steps in using it. These steps are described generically but they are the same for all projects. Each of these steps will be discussed in detail. To set up the Earned Value system:

1. Establish the Work Breakdown Structure (WBS) to divide the project into manageable portions.
2. Identify the activities to be scheduled that represent the entire project.
3. Allocate the costs to be expended on each activity.
4. Schedule the activities over time.
5. Tabulate, plot and analyze the data to confirm that the plan is acceptable.

To use the information generated by the Earned Value calculations:

6. Update the schedule by reporting activity progress.
7. Enter the actual costs on the activities.
8. ·Execute the Earned Value calculations, print and plot the reports and charts.

Analyze the data and write the performance narrative.

### Step 1: Establish the WBS

The WBS is the roadmap for analyzing the project progress and performance. It provides a multi-level structure for analyzing the project at varying degrees of detail. A properly defined WBS also provides that each element of the structure at each level is the responsibility of an individual who has management authority over that element and all the elements that roll up into that element. Furthermore, the WBS must contain the full scope of the project. Otherwise, the information generated will not represent the total project. The WBS is generally a hierarchical structure in which each lower level element rolls into one and only one element at the level above it. The bottom level of the WBS should be the activities of the project. Exhibit 3 illustrates this. The key here is that each element has a responsible individual identified with it and each element represents a part of the project that someone or more people are interested in monitoring.

While this personal responsibility might bring to mind an Organizational Breakdown Structure (OBS), the WBS should not be confused with an OBS. Either structure can function as the framework for analyzing the project performance. However, an OBS is generally employed in a matrix organization where the functional management of the organization wants to analyze the performance of their functional unit on the project. The WBS is organized along the component lines of the project. For example, the project team member who is responsible for the Fan Assembly in Exhibit 3, has components (cost accounts and activities) in several engineering disciplines within the OBS. On the other hand, the Mechanical Design Manager in the OBS is interested in all the mechanical elements of all project components.

### Step 2: Identify The Activities

The second step is to identify the activities of the project. The WBS provides the framework for identifying the project components. As illustrated in Exhibit 3, each activity should be assigned to one element in the WBS. The completion of this step will produce the project schedule of activities, typically in a CPM network.

### Step 3: Allocate The Costs

The third step is to identify and allocate the costs to be expended for each activity. Since an activity represents a finite effort within the project, it has a duration of time and it requires the expenditure of some resources. The practitioner needs to decide whether to use labor resources only, such as work hours, or to use dollars and load all project costs into the schedule. The allocation of resources (costs) requires a choice of the degree of detail with which one will allocate the resources. These options include linear spread across the duration of the activity or use of a curve to approximate the expected expenditure during the activity's execution. These curves have an unlimited variety of shapes, the most common ones being symmetrical bell shape, front loaded triangle, back loaded triangle, equal triangle, lump sum at the beginning or end of the activity. However, detailed discussion of the application of resource curves is beyond the scope of this paper.

### Step 4: Schedule The Activities

The fourth step is to calculate the schedule of the activities. This step generally provides the spread of the resources over the entire time duration of the project. It generates the traditional S-curve of the project plan or baseline, also called the BCWS Curve.

### Step 5: Tabulate, Plot and Analyze

The final step is to tabulate and plot the information that was loaded and then to analyze this information. The purpose is to assure that the allocation of resources is properly planned. This includes analysis of individual resources to see if the maximum requirement during any time period is available. It also includes review of cash flows, if dollars are entered, to see if the financing plan for the project supports the schedule. Third, it provides a review to see that all project resources and costs that are budgeted are entered into the program. Of course, correction of any anomalies discovered during this step is implied to be a part of this step. Exhibit 4 represents a very simple illustration of this process. It also illustrates with this very simple example, that the result is the traditional S-curve.

Once these five steps are completed, the project team will have the basis for conducting periodic analysis of the project progress and performance. That process is explained in the next four steps.

### Step 6: Update the Schedule

The first step in the periodic process is to update the schedule with the period progress. This is generally done whether Earned Value is used or not. The project schedule activities are reported as started, completed or with a remaining duration, as appropriate. The per cent complete of unfinished activities should also be reported. Here is where the practitioner should avoid subjectivity. For physical work it may be easy to determine the per cent complete. If 1000 cubic yards of concrete are planned to be poured and 300 yards have been done to date, then the activity is 30 percent complete. For efforts that are not so easily measured, special earning rules might have to be employed. Full discussion of earning rules is also beyond the scope of this paper. Two examples are presented to illustrate the point. One common rule is to report per cent complete according to completed milestones within the activity. For example, if the activity is the creation of a design drawing, progress might be reported as follows: 10 percent when the preliminary research and background study are completed, 20 percent when the drawing draft is completed and passed on to drafting, 40 percent when the first draft is printed, 50 percent when the first draft is reviewed, 60 percent when the second draft is completed, 75 percent when the client review is completed, 90 percent when the final draft is completed and 100 percent when the drawing is issued for construction. The key in defining this kind of rule is that each "milestone" is discrete, and its achievement is easily recognized by such evidence as transmittal memos.

A second common rule that is quite effective when the project has several thousand activities is to use the 50-50 rule. In this rule, each activity is considered 50 percent complete when its start date is reported and it is 100 percent complete when the activity finish date is reported. Reporting progress provides the basis for the Earned Value calculations

### Step 7: Enter The Actual Costs

The second step in the periodic process is to enter the actual costs into the schedule. This information comes from the time sheets and invoices to the project. Whether the data is entered manually or electronically is a matter of choice, depending on the degree of integration between the company's financial accounting system and the project control systems. In any case, it is necessary to determine which costs are to be allocated to which activity. By proper integration of the financial and project accounting systems, this process is facilitated to the point of total automation. However, human analysis of the actual data is recommended to assure that improper data doesn't inadvertently enter the system.

### Step 8: Calculate, Print And Plot

The next step in the periodic process is to calculate the Earned Value and to print reports and plot charts for analysis. The Earned Value is simply the per cent complete of an activity times its budget. This provides the key value in the Earned Value process. Other calculations include the schedule and cost variances, performance indices, estimates at completion and per cent complete of the upper elements of the WBS. Referring to Exhibit 2 will aid in understanding the following calculation discussion.

Schedule Variance (SV) is the Earned Value minus the planned budget for the completed work (BCWP-BCWS.

Cost Variance (CV) is the Earned Value minus the actual cost (BCWP-ACWP.

Performance indices are merely ratio expressions of the SV and CV. The Schedule Performance Index (SPI) is the Earned Value divided by the planned value (BCWP/BCWS).

The Cost Performance Index (CPI) is the Earned Value divided by the actual cost (BCWP/ACWP).

The Estimate At Completion (EAC) is a number of great interest each update cycle. It indicates where the project cost is heading. Calculating a new EAC is one of the great benefits of Earned Value. However, the actual formula to use for this calculation is a matter of much discussion. For the purpose of this paper, we will look at the basic impact of cost performance on the EAC. The intent is to show that Earned Value is a key forecasting tool for managing a project. Referring to Exhibit 5, let us assume a project is having some trouble meeting its cost goals. At the data date, the actual cost is greater than the planned cost for the completed work (ACWP > BCWP). If performance continues at the same trend, we can easily see that at completion the actual cost (EAC) far exceeds

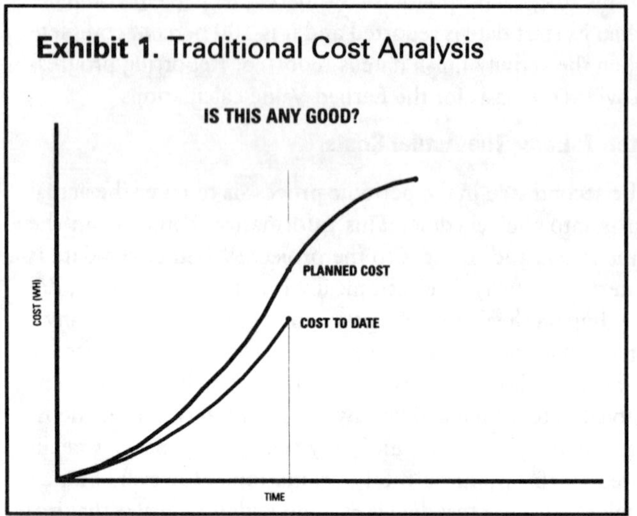


**Exhibit 1.** Traditional Cost Analysis

the budget (BAC). The simplest formula for arriving at the EAC at the time of the data date is:

$$EAC = \frac{(BAC - BCWP)}{CPI} + ACWP$$

This formula determines the unfinished or unearned work (BAC –BCWP) and divides it by the CPI. To that is added the sunk cost, or the cost of the completed work (ACWP). From this we can see that poor cost performance. a CPI less than 1, would result in an EAC that is greater than the BAC. More complex formulas are used which factor the CPI to give it more or less influence on the EAC.

One more calculation is noteworthy since it is specifically made possible by the use of Earned Value. That is the per cent complete at the upper levels of the WBS. While progress is typically recorded at the activity level of detail (the bottom of the WBS), those responsible for the project at higher levels of the WBS want to know the same kind of information as the "activity managers." The process involves rolling up the data through the WBS. Budgets and actual costs are easy to roll up; simply add the values of the lower elements to get the value of the parent element. However, how does one roll up per cent complete? The answer is, of course, Earned Value. Since Earned Value is directly related to per cent complete, one can simply add the Earned Value of the lower elements to get the value of the parent element. Then, one can use this information at the upper levels to back calculate the per cent complete of the upper elements. Just as Earned Value equals the BAC times the per cent complete at the lower levels, so does per cent complete equal BAC divided by Earned Value for any element in the WBS.

### Step 9: Analyze and Report

The final step in the Earned Value process is to analyze the data and the report the result of that analysis. The scope of this paper does not allow detailed discussion of the analysis process. However, from the above, the reader can recognize the significance of the various calculations discussed above. How he or she interprets that information is left to his or her common sense.

## Conclusion

With the above presentation, we have explored the What, Why and How of Earned Value. We have seen that Earned Value is a tool for improving the performance analysis of a project, by: providing a uniform unit of measure for project progress, enforcing a consistent method for analysis and providing a basis for cost performance analysis of the project. The reason for using Earned Value is tied closely to what Earned Value is. The process of implementing Earned Value is organized into five steps and the process of periodic analysis consists of four additional steps. While the manipulation of the vast amount of data that is involved may seem daunting, the use of available computer tools designed for the purpose, make the implementation a relatively simple "cookbook" procedure. If the reader takes one thing away from this paper, it should be that Earned Value simply represents the budgeted value of the completed work and is directly related to the per cent complete of the activity or WBS element under consideration.

**Exhibit 2.** Earned Value Elements

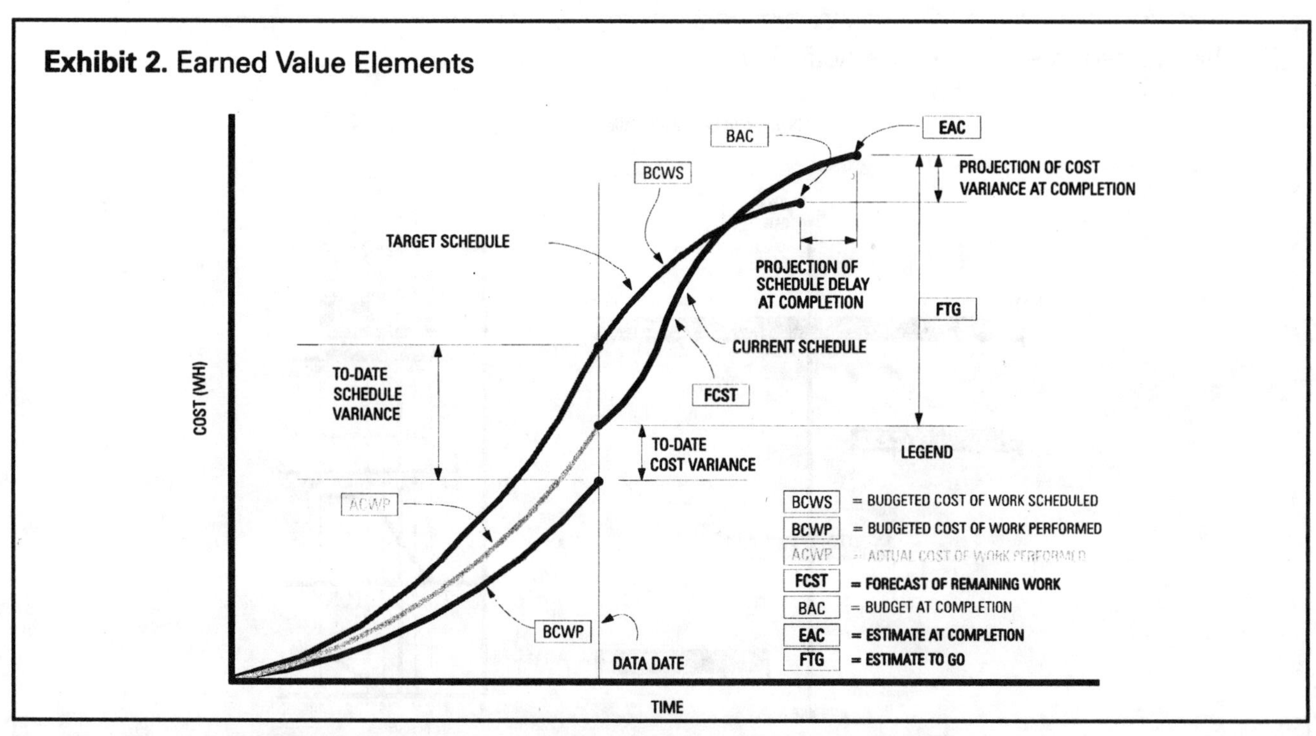


**Exhibit 3.** Work Breakdown Structure

Contract Work Breakdown Structure

Contract

Engine
Training

Fan
Compressor
Turbine

Fan Assembly
Full Fan Rig
Minor Fan Rig
Dual Spool Compressor

Case Assy
Rotor Assy
Stator Assy

Functional Organization Breakdown Structure

Company
Testing
Engineering
Mfg.
Design
Docum.

Mech Design
Analyt. Design
Draft/ Check

Cost Account
Cost Account
Cost
Cost Account
Cost Account
Cost Account

Activities

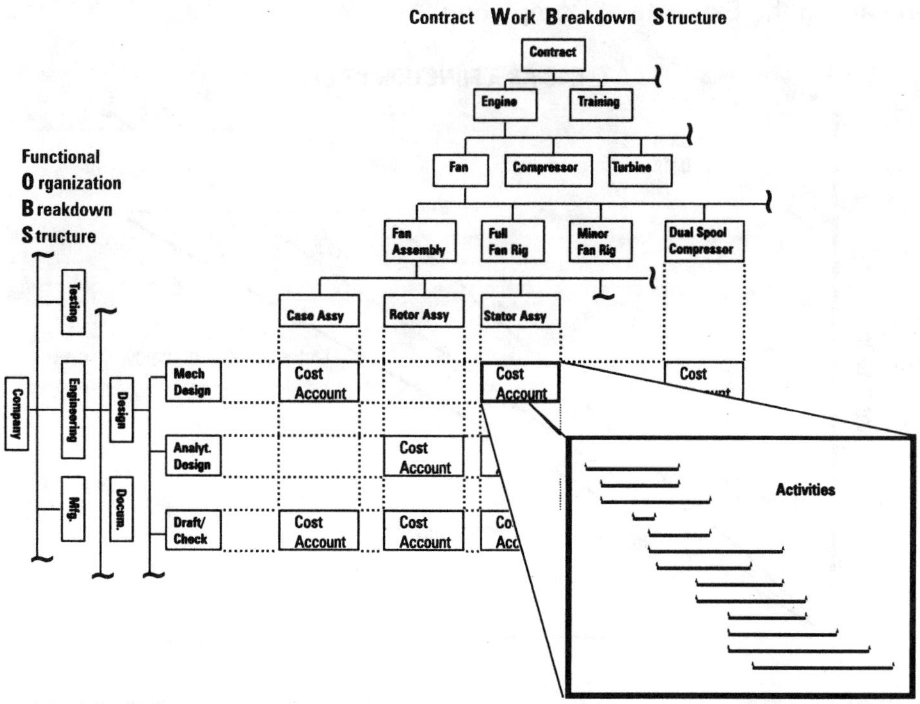

**Exhibit 4.** Resource Loading the Activities

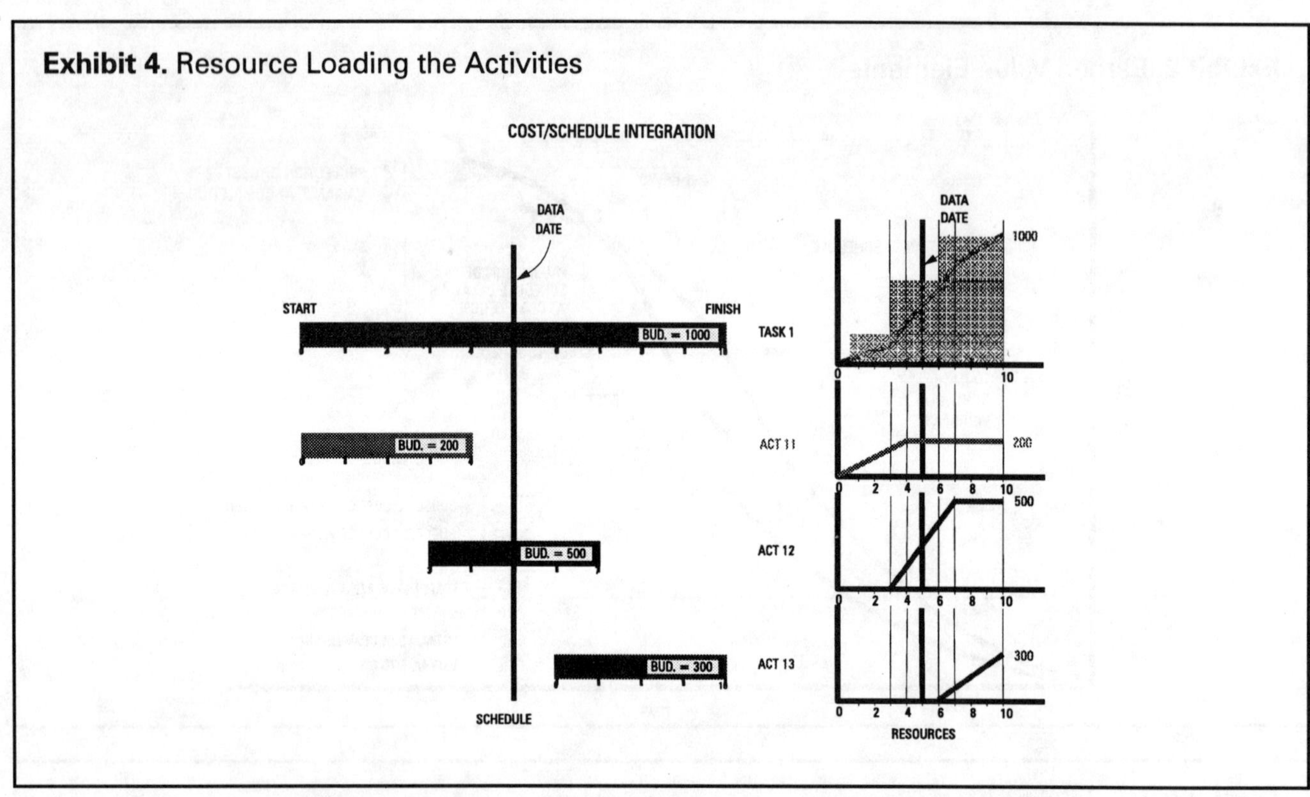


**Exhibit 5.** Forecasting the Estimate at Completion

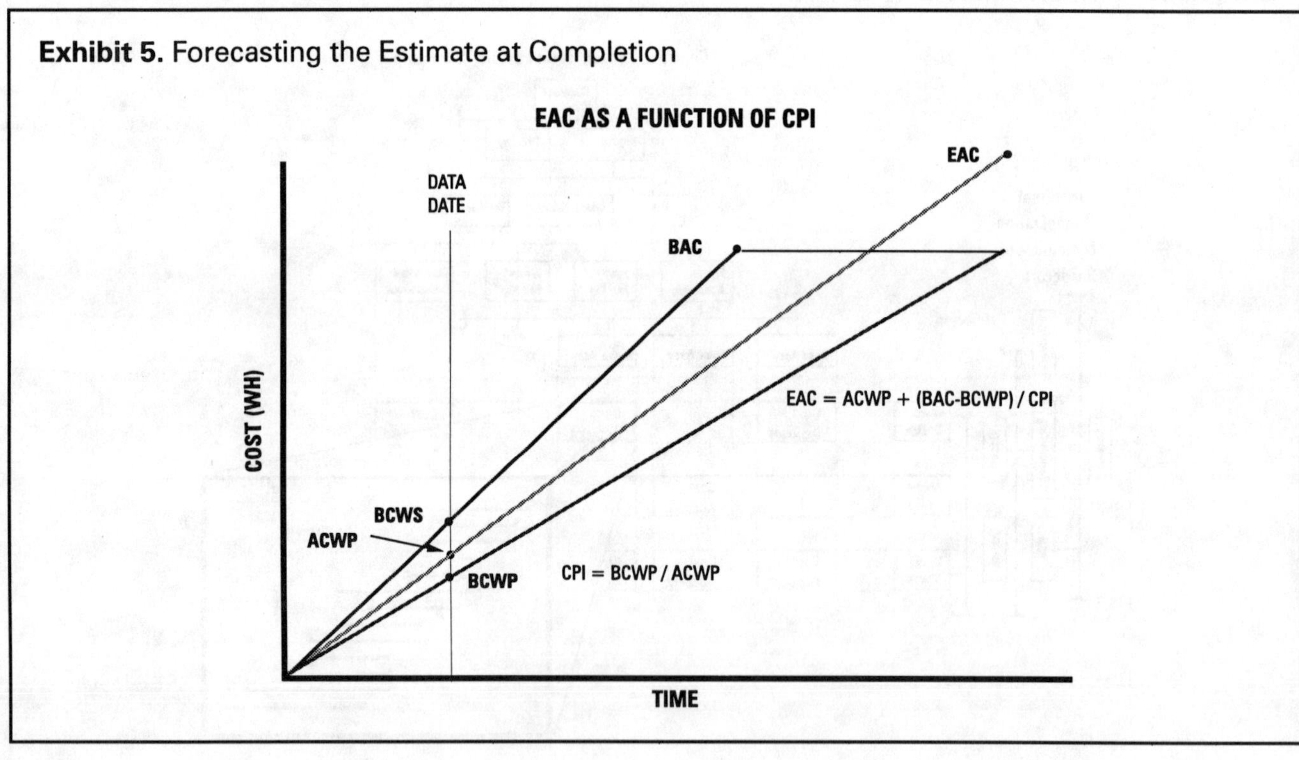

# Earned Value Supports Enterprise-Wide Project Management

Michael J. Barlow, ACS, Project Management
Major Thomas A. Klingelhoets, USAF, ILS Reengineering Program, Arnold AFB.

Earned value is a proven methodology for measuring cost and schedule performance on large projects with interdependent tasks. The methodology is well documented by many authors such as Quentin Fleming, Joel Koppelman, and Zeev Barr. Earned value's use has grown beyond this to paying its way in many industries in the 1990s (Singletary 1996). Levi Strauss' Albuquerque plant is a prime example of this (Hatfield 1996). This paper documents a cost effective application of the earned value methodology to multiple, "small" projects at the Arnold Engineering and Development Center (AEDC). AEDC is an Air Force-managed and contractor-operated ground flight test and evaluation center located in southern Middle Tennessee. AEDC's customer base includes DoD, other government agencies, and private industry.

## Project Management at Arnold Engineering Development Center

ACS, the Support Contractor at AEDC, is responsible for approximately 150 projects each year. The projects range in size from $50,000 to over $1 million totaling over $20 million. Project durations range from months to years. They vary technically from simple office modifications to large utility system repairs/modifications and include environmental projects. Projects are executed in a typical life cycle strongly tied to the fiscal year (FY) budgeting process. Normally, projects are planned and designed in one year and executed the next.

Project management is centralized operating in a matrix organizational structure. Project managers are responsible for project management and construction inspection of multiple projects. Projects are either designed by ACS or an A/E and are executed by ACS , an outside contractor, or a combination of the two.

## Changing Business Environment

Over the last several years the business environment within DoD has changed, in part driven by budget decreases. Besides the direct budget pressure, there is extensive restructuring of government test and evaluation facilities, more competition, and an increased reliance on commercial customers. The organizational structure and management system result in multiple entities competing for the same resources. AEDC embraced the Air Force Total Quality Initiative demanding management based on good metrics describing the health of key processes. These pressures helped highlight the need for a broader application of project management in the early 1990s. The project managers are the "who" and the project management body of knowledge provided the "how". The key is deciding which tools to use and how to optimize their use.

## Decision to Adopt Earned Value Management System

Initially project managers were quessing at the status of their projects. Budget variances and gross percent complete assessments were being made. Milestone and/or Gnatt charts were updated in an attempt to reflect schedule performance. The quality of the information was inconsistent and was being articulated in a myriad of different ways. There was no easy means to roll up or peel back the data. On top of this, there was often not a good plan (time-phased budget) for projects, certainly not at the program level. The bottom line was that AEDC didn't know the real status of projects until they were complete. Given the current business environment, this was simply not acceptable.

Earned value had been used at AEDC on large programs but had never been used on the smaller projects. However, some of the literature suggested that earned value was being successfully applied to construction, information services, and manufacturing. Earned value is simple to understand, it provides a common language regardless of project type, and can be peeled back and rolled up as required for reporting and analysis. Earned value appeared to answer all the immediate problems relative to cost and schedule reporting. This set the stage to press with earned value. There were many obstacles to overcome including the lack of understanding of earned value by many functional and project managers and by the workforce in general. This resulted in misconceptions such as earned value was too expensive, that it was too complex to learn, and that it doesn't apply to small projects.

**Exhibit 1.** Performance Trend Charts

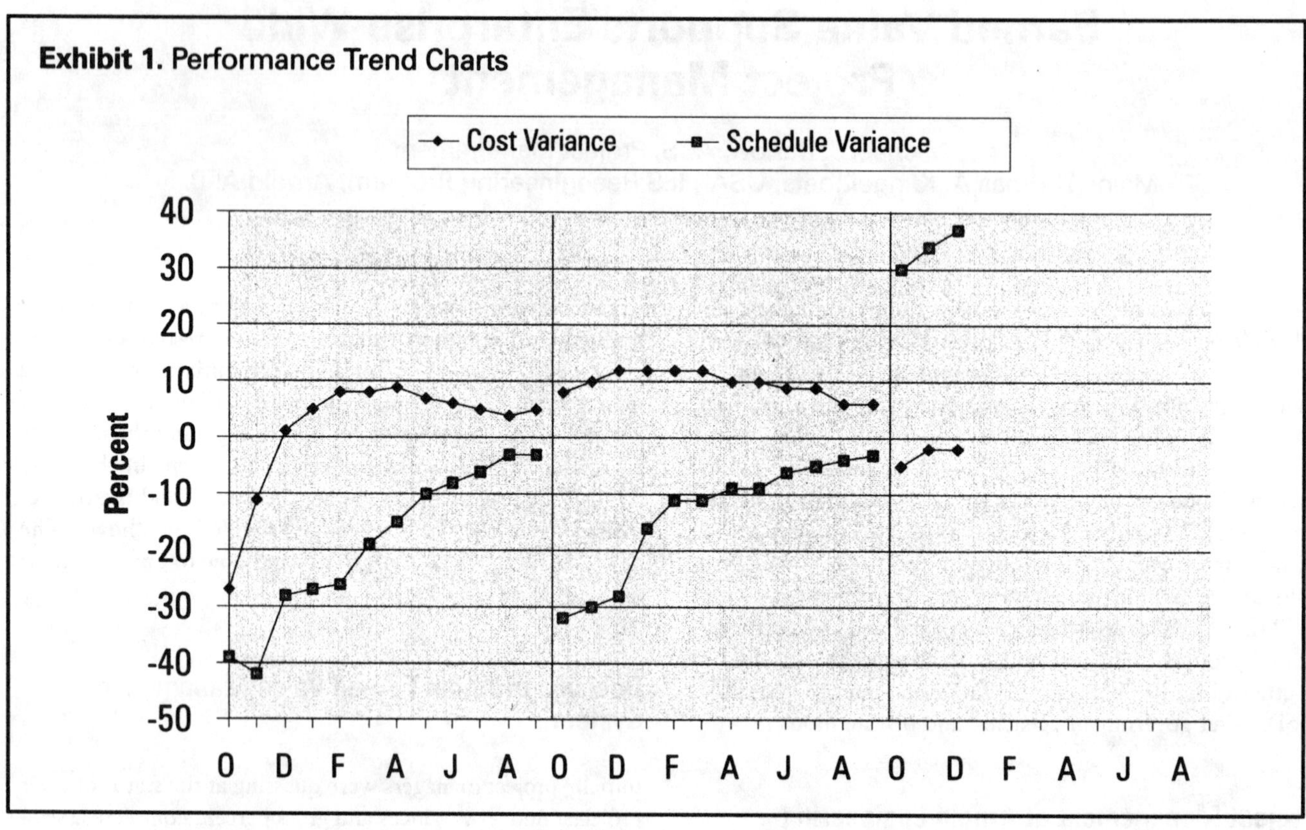


It was decided that a earned value management system would be implemented. There was now a nucleus of people who understood it and believed in it. After all, "what management tool is out there to replace it?" ( Hatfield, 1996) The trick was to optimize the application of this tool and sell it to the naysayers.

## Application of Earned Value

During the last quarter of FY94 a very rudimentary earned value system was implemented. Gross assessments of percent complete were provided by the project managers. This percent complete was applied to the BAC to produce a BCWP for each project which was in turn summed to the program level. The BCWS, BCWP, and ACWP were expressed in units of man-hours. Man-hours were the largest resource and of interest to the broadest range of people.

Project managers and management were learning the concepts of earned value and the associated language, despite the questionable data. The act of exploring the variances led to the identification of performance problems as well as problems with the earned value and work management systems. It forced the development of an integrated program plan driving the planning of individual projects.

Schedule variance was the first problem to surface; cause unknown. A team was formed and identified the causes as poor planning, scheduling, adherence to the schedule, and performance (resource availability), and changes in work scope and inaccurate earned value assessments. Corrective actions were taken but it was obvious that project management had a lot of work and learning to do. Individual projects had to be planned better and an integrated schedule had to be developed and adhered to by the functional managers. Resource availability must be considered and a better assessment of earned value must be made at the individual project level. A baseline management process had to be put in place to deal with scope changes including the cancellation and addition of entire projects.

### FY95

It was obvious that earned value had potential but needed a strong sponsor and time to mature. A new general manager, trained and experienced in project management and earned value, became the sponsor. The monthly project status reviews became earned value centered. The functional managers, and the customer were exposed to, and trained on, earned value during these reviews. The general manager put pressure on project management to improve and adhere to the master plan. A consultant was brought in to review the

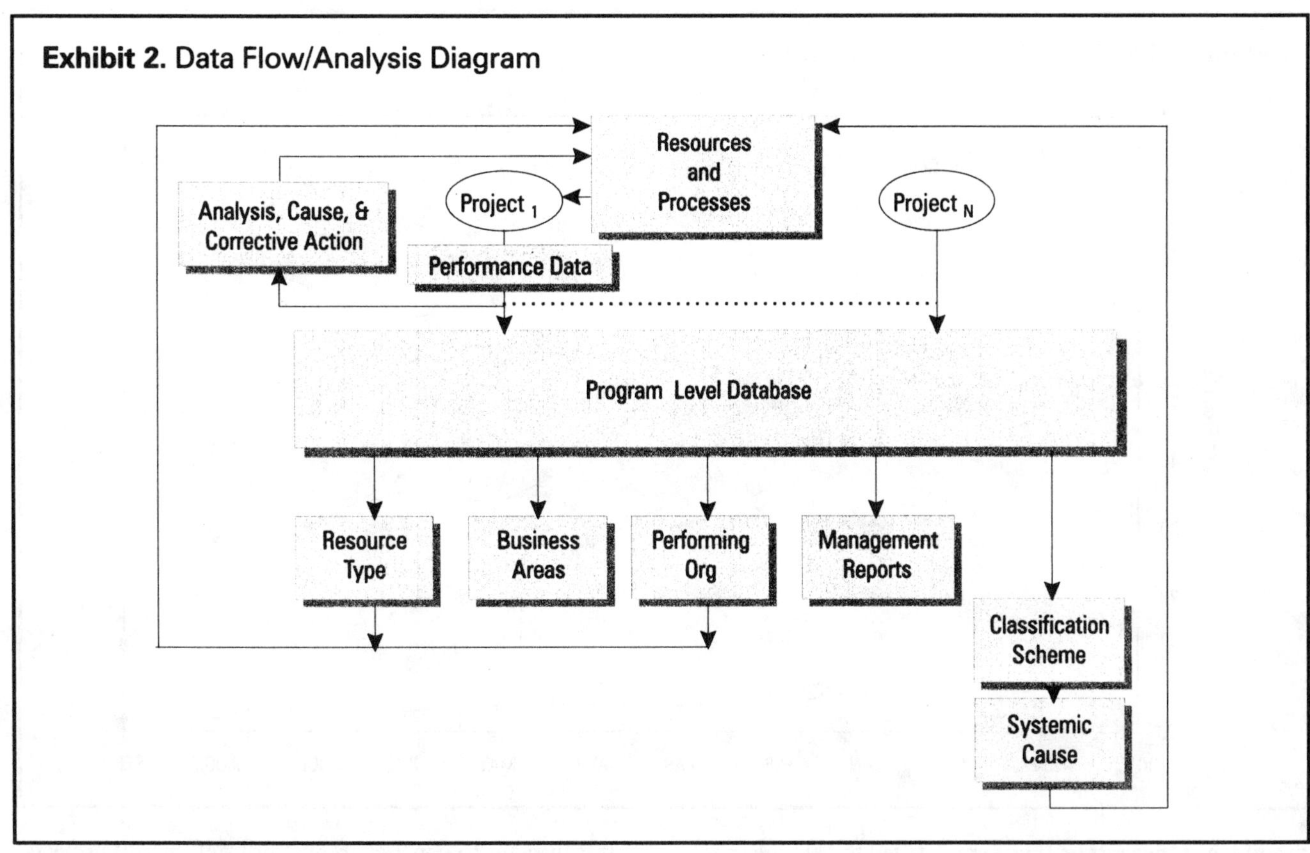


**Exhibit 2.** Data Flow/Analysis Diagram

performance measurement system and to provide recommendations for improvement.

The performance measurement baseline for FY95 included materials and non-craft man-hours (design, project management, etc.). Emphasis was increased on planning. Therefore, FY95 started with a better baseline and increased expectations for solid performance against that baseline. The optimism was unfortunately short lived. Both cost and schedule performance were unfavorable during the first months of the FY (see Exhibit 1). Schedule again was the biggest concern. The majority of the planning was done under the assumption that the designs needed to support execution would be complete at the beginning of the FY. This assumption, born of poor communication and the lack of a truly integrated project delivery process, proved to be wrong. Designs had to be complete before detailed planning could be accomplished and materials ordered. Materials had to be delivered before craft man-hours could be utilized. The result was unfavorable schedule variance. Critical designs were accelerated. Long lead time materials were ordered prior to completion of designs where possible. Temporary craft resources were brought on board during the last half of the FY to accomplish the projects. Designers, project managers and the planner/estimators were collocated to facilitate communications. Another discovery was that our projects weren't clearly defined. System engineering discipline was applied to the design process to facilitate requirements definition.

The picture painted by earned value drove actions resulting in recovery. FY95 ended with a favorable five percent cost variance and an unfavorable four percent schedule variance. Much of the "final" schedule variance resulted from denied outage requests, late subcontractors and other factors outside of project management's control. At the end of the FY, the unfavorable schedule variance should equal the work that did not get done (carryover) and for which must be budgeted for the following FY. The budget variance at the end of the FY must be the sum of the negative of schedule variance and the cost variance. FY95 carryover was approximately 50 percent of what it had been in previous years. Again, earned value, even in its crudest form was driving the appropriate actions. The key players were learning earned value, a performance measurement system was being developed, and converts were being gained along the way. Beginning in FY96 earned value became a contractual requirement for projects.

## FY96

The baseline for FY96 was developed utilizing detailed planning with earned value in mind. Project management focused on the integrated schedule development incorporating lessons learned. Resource management, in particular, resource

**Exhibit 3.** FY96 SV Cause Trend Analysis

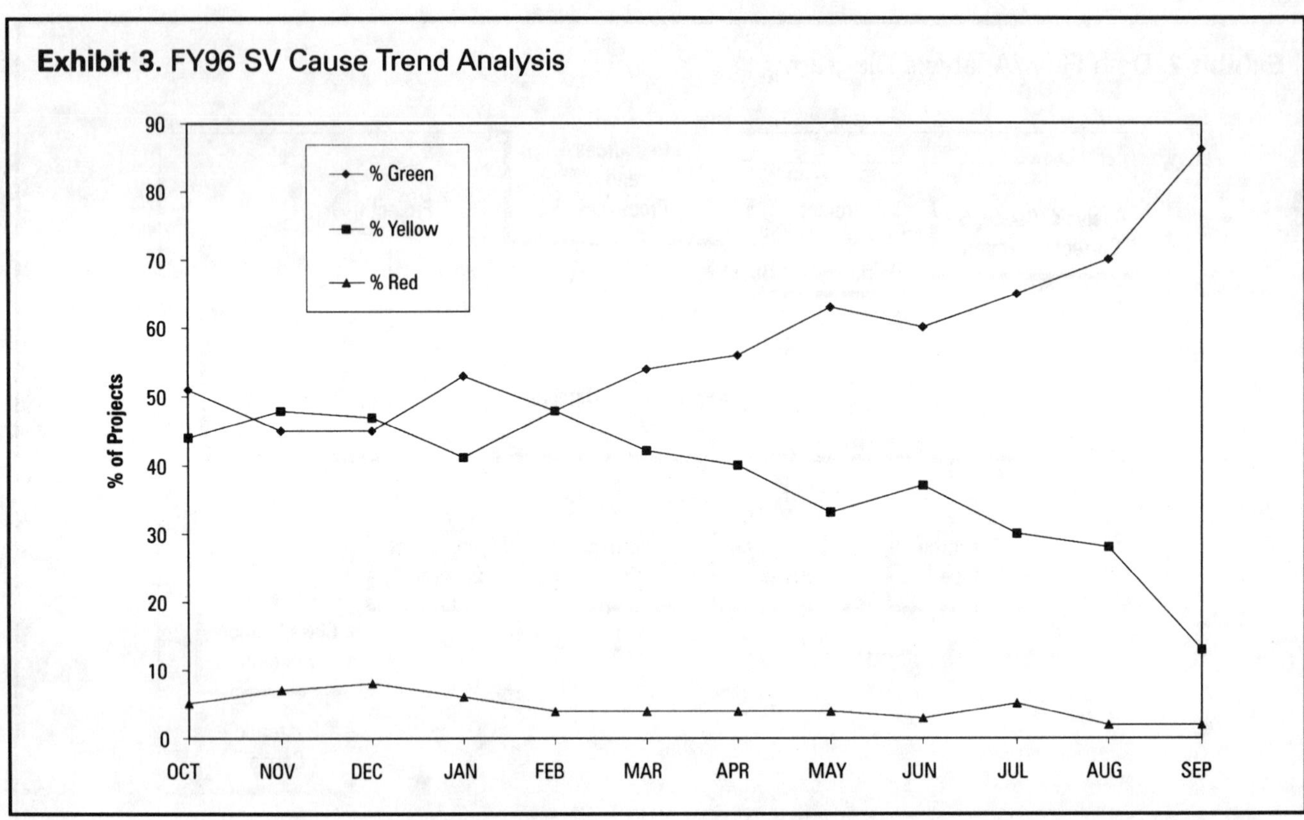


smoothing at the craft level was emphasized to help the functional managers staff the project workload. When resource management is done smartly, efficiencies increase and improved cost performance is obtained. Increased emphasis was placed on functional management agreement to the baseline. The greatest area of import was design engineering. The reporting done in FY95 painted a solid picture and set the stage for communications between project management and the workers.

FY96 is considered to be the first year that a credible, though non-C/SCSC-compliant, earned value system was in place. It is worth while to explore in a little more detail how the data was used (see Exhibit 2). In FY96 project managers provided monthly performance (C/SSR) reports at a fairly detailed level (15-20 activities per project) for each project. The BCWS came from the baseline which was built from the project level. The baseline changed only as a result of contract modifications or project change agreements approved by the client. The ACWP came from the management information system used across the Center. The BCWP came from the project manager based on collaboration with the doers and a selected earned value assessment technique. C/SSR reports gave project managers the data needed to manage their projects. The data was stored in an Access database facilitating roll up to the program level and various peel backs or sorts.

It is difficult to concisely report or brief on 100 projects. The roll up or program level data is ideal for reporting overall cost and schedule status to executive management, but can mask problems. Therefore, a variance classification scheme was established pinpointing problem projects. Projects with a cost or schedule variance less then 10 percent unfavorable and/or a variance less than $1,000 were classified as "green." Projects with a cost or schedule variance between 10 and 15 percent unfavorable were classified as "yellow." Projects with a cost or schedule variance worse than an unfavorable 15 percent or a variance worse than $20,000 were classified as "red." The above thresholds applied to cumulative data at the individual project level (see Exhibit 3). Each of the "red" projects were specifically addressed during project status reviews. The cause, corrective action(s), and impact(s) were discussed. "Yellow" projects were not specifically addressed at the project status review but were reviewed off line with the respective project manager. This scheme supported program-level reporting but still clearly put accountability on the project manager. Project managers were sometimes invited to review their project personally with executive management if corrective actions were not being taken or didn't seem to work. [Insert Exhibit 3. FY96 Variance Classification Chart]

Projects share the same resources, particularly design engineers and craft. In addition, these same resources were used to accomplish other nonproject work. The same procurement offices were used to procure materials and subcontracts for all projects. To facilitate correction of these systemic causes, the schedule variance causes of all "yellow" and "red" projects were classified into several high-level causes; manpower availability, materials, outside contracts, requirements definition, outage, and other. A Pareto chart was produced by systemic cause indicating the schedule variances (in dollars) associated with each cause. If manpower availability was a key cause, the data could be peeled back to determine what resource(s) and organization(s) were involved. That functional manager could then be advised of the problem and actions taken to provide the needed resources.

FY96 performance trends paint an interesting picture (see Exhibit 4). Designs were done but funding delays and other causes were driving the variance. Craft resources were being diverted to other types of work and materials were not ordered. A marked improvement occurred in January and February as materials were finally ordered. The schedule variance held constant for a few months as material was delivered. However, craft availability was still an issue and functional management used overtime and reassigned craft from other types of work. Temporary personnel were brought in during the last four months of the FY and the schedule variance steadily improved. The cost variance suffered somewhat due to overtime charges and inefficiencies associated with temporary personnel.

FY96 was the year that the importance of resource management was recognized. A resource management organization was set up to integrate project workload requirements with the other workload requirements and make sure the right resources were available at the right time to do the work. Therefore, earned value was used to drive better planning and integrated scheduling.

Earned value analysis offered new and better tools to determine estimates at complete. These tools along with engineering estimates and others were used to produce estimates at complete at the resource, project and program levels. Given the barriers (real or contrived) at the end of the FY, funds management becomes very important. Accurate estimates at completion made as early as possible allows the optimum utilization of funds. In mid-FY96 a favorable at EAC variance was determined. These funds were used to execute other important activities and to buy some FY97 project materials in advance.

Certainly, early FY 96 performance was better than that experienced in FY95. However, schedule variance was still the problem (see Exhibit 1). This time more detailed performance data was available allowing peel back to better isolate the causes of the unfavorable schedule variance. As a result, FY96 ended with an unfavorable three percent schedule variance and a favorable six percent cost variance. This was an improvement over FY95. The earned value system was used by project mangers to manage their projects and to report to executive management involving them in corrective actions (systemic causes ) were required. Project managers were becoming more comfortable with earned value analysis. Functional managers and the client were recognizing earned value as the performance measurement tool of choice in project management and were discussing the possibilities of applying it elsewhere at the Center. The earned value system itself was being improved and refined.

### FY97

It was clearly understood that a performance measurement system without a good baseline is meaningless. A good baseline is realistic, integrated, built with earned value in mind, agreed to by the functional organizations, and approved by the client. The baseline for FY97 would for the first time include outside contracts. Also the reporting system must be able to shred by Business Area. Instead of all projects being funded from the same source, each project was funded by a Business Area within the Center. Each Business Area must be treated as a separate client and performance reports generated and briefed accordingly. Again, earned value allowed us to respond to this changing business requirement.

The plan for FY97 was much improved over previous years. However, the first three months again reflected a schedule problem (See Exhibit 1). The peel back capability allowed sorting by resource type; labor, material and outside contracts. This revealed the our schedule problem was in the outside contracts area. There were two problems. First, the contracts were not being awarded due to a funds availability issue and second, our earned value system was not optimum. Outside contracts were baselined, earned, and accounted for as a milestone. The BCWS, BCWP, and ACWP were all tied 100 percent to the contract award milestone. This is obviously not the best approach, but was the short term compromise. Even so, the problem was identified and efforts taken to obtain the funds as soon as possible. Performance was analyzed excluding outside contracts indicating improvement in cost and schedule performance. For the first three months of FY97 both cost and schedule variances were favorable. A significant improvement over FY96. A much more integrated and realistic plan was in place and functional organizations were in step with the plan.

## Benefit/Cost of Earned Value

In terms of dollars the cost to implement this tailored and non-C/SCSC-compliant earned value system is nominal. The project managers would have been required to plan and report status/progress regardless of the tool used. There was some resources spent to train and develop databases/systems

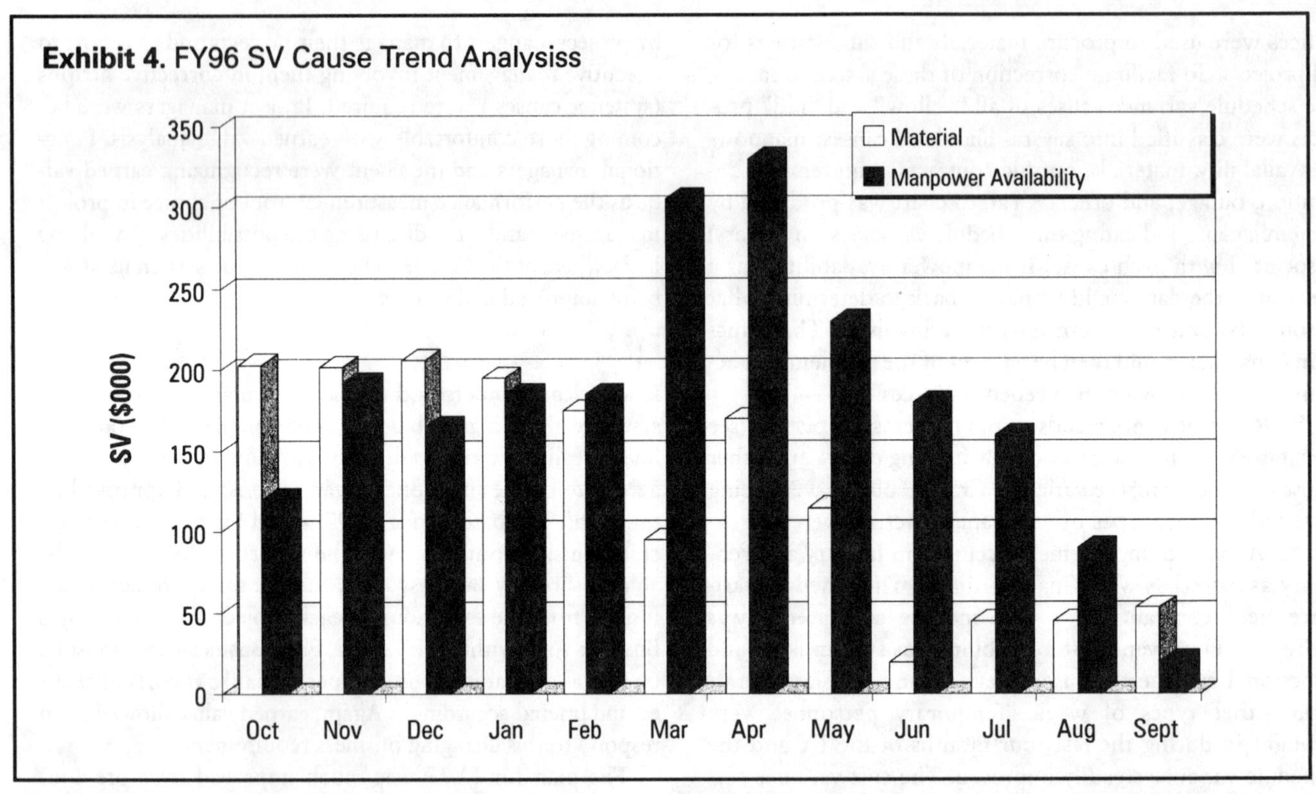


to deal with earned value. It is estimated that these initial investments cost $75,000 above "normal" control costs. On an annual basis it is estimated that earned value cost around $50,000 above "normal" control cost. This puts the annual cost at around 0.25 percent of total program costs. Along with this minimal financial investment people had to be willing to learn and accept a new tool.

Given this minimal investment, the results are significant. The benefits experienced are much like those described by many authors and what AEDC expected to gain. Project managers and executive management now know the answer to the question, "How are we doing?" The status can be articulated via a common, easily understood language regardless of size or type of project. Perhaps more fundamentally, earned value was used to drive, in a top-down manner, adequate planning at the individual project level and highlighted the needed for resource management at the appropriate, higher level. Earned value supported development and empowerment of project managers and gave a way to highlight systemic problems. The project managers were clearly held accountable. The information provided facilitated sound management decisions particularly in the areas of resource and funds management. It forced better contract/change management. Even when poor baseline management resulted in the reporting of variances that weren't performance problems these variances were used as drivers to improve the earned value system. Perhaps the most important outcome is a satisfied customer. The customer, rightfully so, believes that a solid control system is in place that is used at the lowest level but also can be used to readily convey status at the highest level.

## Future

Certainly, improvements need to be made in the earned value system. Better, more detailed planning needs to take place at the project level. The whole art of developing the work breakdown structure for these small projects needs to be refined. It is currently too functionally oriented. Baseline management needs to be improved with better procedures in place. Often baseline management is confused with contract management. The two must be separated. The earned value assessment itself needs to be improved. Particularly, materials and contracts need to be looked at closely in terms of how they are planned, earned, and accounted for to improve the quality of performance data. The estimating system needs to be more consistent and supported by standards or even best practices for doing various tasks. This will result in a baseline built on should cost as opposed to a conservative estimate based largely on past practices. This is the mechanism required to truly drive cost down. Fleming offers some advise in this area (Fleming 1992). The rules used in the earned value system need to be continually reviewed. Things like variance thresholds at different levels and phases of projects and at different points in the FY needed to be looked at closely. Much of this will come from experience.

Finally, earned value is and will be applied to other areas of the contract. Beginning in FY97 it is being applied in the Information Services area where much of the workload has many of the characteristics of mini projects; defined scope/objective and time and budget constraints. It is hopeful that positive results will come from this effort. Recurring maintenance of facilities and equipment is another area that is being looked at closely in terms of earned value application.

## Summary

Using earned value to manage multiple small projects within the context of a contract where projects are just a part of the overall effort has been a challenge. Applying earned value appropriately was the key. The systems in place really weren't designed with project management or earned value in mind. Most information and experience with earned value has centered around a single large program with systems and organizations in place explicitly to support project management and earned value. In spite of the struggle, it has been discovered that earned value can be effectively applied in this manner. This approach is not always possible, but in this case it was and might be possible in similar applications in other organizations. An incremental and evolutionary application of the tool can work with executive management understanding, support, and patience. You can reap rewards by applying an "imperfect" or non-C/SCSC-compliant earned value system across the enterprise. By Kerzner's definition, project management is not mature but is improving. Part of the whole journey in project management has been to develop project managers and the project management system.

### References


Barr, Zeer. 1996. Earned Value Analysis: A Case Study. *PM Network* 10 (December): 33-37.

Fleming, Quentin W. 1992. *Cost/Schedule Control Systems Criteria: The Management Guide to C/CSCSC.* Chicago, ILL: Probus Publishing Company.

Fleming, Quentin W., and Koppelman, Joel M. 1996b. The Earned Value Body of Knowledge. *PM Network* 10 (May): 11-15.

Hatfield, Michael A. 1996. The Case for Earned Value. *PM Network* 10 (December): 25,27.

Kerzner, Harold. 1995. Project Management: *A Systems Approach to Planning, Scheduling, and Controlling.* New York, NY: Van Nostrand Reinhold.

Singletary, Nancy. 1996. What's the Value of Earned Value? *PM Network* 10 (December): 28, 30.

Westney, Richard E. 1992. *Computerized Management of Multiple Small Projects.* New York, NY: Marcel Dekker.

# Major Challenges in the Implementation of Concurrent Engineering

Gerard P. O'Keefe, P.E., Resolution Management Consultants Inc.

## Introduction

The Department of Defense has implemented major changes in its defense acquisition policies. These changes are geared toward reducing the cost and time to complete large defense projects. Some of these changes have already been introduced in the procurement of military aircraft, and the Navy has introduced these changes on the procurement of its new LPD-17 class vessels. The significant features of these changes are: (1) the replacement of MIL-SPECs with commercial specifications; (2) a transition from paper-intensive acquisition and logistic processes to a highly automated and integrated mode of operation; (3) the replacement of detailed specifications with performance specifications; and, (4) the implementation of the concepts of Concurrent Engineering. Numerous technical papers have been written, in a broad general sense, on the anticipated impact of these changes. This paper will examine a specific element of these changes, Concurrent Engineering, and the potential difficulties that must be managed in order to achieve success.

## Concurrent Engineering Definition

Concurrent Engineering has been defined by the Concurrent Engineering Research Center (CERC) in the following manner: "Concurrent Engineering is a systematic approach to the integrated development of a product and its related process. This approach emphasizes responsiveness to customer expectations and embodies team values of cooperation, trust and sharing. This is done in such a manner that decision making proceeds with large intervals of parallel working by all its life cycles perspectives, and synchronized by comparatively brief exchanges to produce consensus."

An integral part of the Concurrent Engineering (CE) concept—also referred to as Integrated Product and Process Development (IPPD)—is the establishment of Integrated Product Teams (IPT). Decision making by the IPTs requires that all parties must provide input in order to reach team consensus. Within the engineering process, this means taking into account the needs of the supplier, fabricator and constructor, as well as the user/operator before and during design. IPPD/Concurrent Engineering exists for the life of the program.

**Exhibit 1.** Concurrent Engineering Benefits

| | |
|---|---|
| Development Time | 30% to 70% Reduction |
| Engineering Changes | 65% to 90% Reduction |
| Time to Market | 20% to 90% Reduction |
| Overall Quality | 200% to 600% Improvement |
| White Collar Productivity | 20% to 110% Improvement |
| Dollar Sales | 5% to 50% Improvement |
| Return on Assets | 20% to 120% Improvement |
| Source: Institute for Defense Analysis | |

CE is a philosophy not a technology. The main objective of CE is to shorten the time from order to delivery of a new product, at the lowest cost and highest quality. According to Dr. Ralph Wood of CERC: "All functions work as a team in parallel, plan early, validate often and maintain oversight of product life cycle decisions within their control." In other words, CE is systems engineering performed by "cross-functional teams."

## Why Use Concurrent Engineering

In CE, also known as Simultaneous Engineering, Concurrent Product Design and Integrated Product Development, it is the approach that is important, not the name. CE is not new. The approach has been used by many companies world wide for some time. To successfully compete in the global commercial shipbuilding market, U.S. shipbuilders must change their approach to enable them to produce a high quality, competitively priced ship in the shortest possible time. The goal of CE is to produce products that meet given functional and quality requirements while optimizing cost and schedule parameters. CE recognizes that most of the cost of a product is decided early in the design stage and that the cost of making changes increases proportionally as the product progresses through the development cycle. Various benefits to be delivered from the implementation of CE is reflected in Exhibit 1.

**Exhibit 2.** Teamwork

| TEAM PARAMETERS | CE TEAM | TASK TEAM | TIGER TEAM |
|---|---|---|---|
| Objective | Product delivery | Task Completion | Problem solving and proposals |
| Orientation | Design for life cycles (proactive) | Ensure task requirements met (reactive) | Solve the problem (reactive) |
| Responsibility | Deliver product to realistic specifications at low cost in minimum time | Complete task within budget and on time | Recommend and implement solutions |
| Authority | At team level | Functional managers and designers | Team leader |
| Leadership Function | Facilitate, coordinate, spokesperson | Coordinate | Coordinate, direct |
| Duration | Product development from proposal to disposal | Short term for each task and then disband | Short term, for time to solve problems |
| Structure | Cross functional teams | Single function teams working on single function task | Cross functional teams solving a specific problem |
| Source: Concurrent Engineering Research Center | | | |

## Critical Use of Concurrent Engineering

The critical elements for CE can be recognized as being the same as some of the requirements for Total Quality Management (TQM). This overlap is not surprising as many of the goals of TQM are essential parts of the technological and cultural change necessary for CE to be successfully implemented. There must be enabling technologies such as systems and tools for:

- The sharing of information
- Communicating
- Coordinating
- Capturing design history (configuration control)
- Integrating computer tools and databases.

Another critical element is the ability to capture and document current product characteristics, processes and company organization (structure and policies). What and how things are done today and what and how they should be done in the immediate future are important questions that should be asked.

The findings of CERC is that the implementation of CE can deliver a 20% improvement at the first attempt and up to 50% as the approach becomes the normal way of doing business. However, an organization must change to successfully adopt a CE approach. Typical changes require moving from:

- Department focus to customer focus
- Directed individual or group to coached team
- Individual interests to team interests
- Autocratic management to leadership with empowered followers
- Dictated decisions to consensus decisions.

Three aspects must be controlled by management, namely: (1) management practices, (2) organizational culture, and (3) technology/systems.

Management must adopt and emphasize attention to customer needs and quality improvement. Additionally, team building with cooperation, communication and collaboration must be initiated along with employee participation and supplier interfaces/participation. If a shipyard is serious about using CE, it must become committed to continual performance evaluation and improvement process.

## Teams

A major characteristic of CE is the use of cross-functional teams integrating the concurrent development of product and process design. In fact, there is no CE if there are no cross-functional teams. The cross-functional team is a central concept of CE. Teamwork occurs when individuals in a group or organization behave in a cooperative manner with all other individuals for the benefit of the group or organization as a whole. Teamwork does not require teams. A generalized summary of three types of teams is shown in Exhibit 2.

## Cross-Functional Teams

The CE process requires real time, interactive, integrated and unconstrained input from many traditional functional specialists from the start to the finish of the product design. The members must be willing to share their knowledge and discuss their design decisions and accept the consensus of the team over their own preference. Management must give the team the time it takes to reach consensus decisions and show continuous support for the approach. The major problem with cross-functional teams is breaking the control of the functional managers over the team members. This can only be done by full participation of the functional managers in the change process and their direct involvement in designing their new role.

## Team Training

It is essential that a team be given training in how to operate as a team. Training should be given on team skills such as communication, emphasizing listening skills, group decision making, conflict resolution as well as specific CE skills. In addition, the team members should be given clear direction on how the team fits into the existing organization structure and whether changes are planned. It has been found to be beneficial to include the CE steering committee, team sponsors and functional managers with the team when they are learning how they are to operate. This provides involvement of all affected parties resulting in a wide basis for decisions on required changes to existing practices. This joint involvement should ensure that ownership of the approach and a completely aligned organization are achieved.

## Major Challenges

The motivating force driving the implementation of these changes is to shorten the time from order to delivery of a new product at a lower cost and higher quality. Some non-defense industries have already started down this path and some of the findings are:

- Most of the product cost is decided early in the design stage and the cost to make changes increases geometrically as the product progress through the developmental cycle.
- Engineering, procurement and production should not be performed sequentially but in parallel.
- Early decision making will require new considerations in risk allocation and reward evaluations.
- A reliable Cost and Schedule Control System(C/SCS) is required and the information must be shared with all the parties in the project.
- There must be a willingness to empower IPT team members with decision making capabilities.

For the U.S. Naval Shipbuilding industry, the implementation of CE will require radical changes by all the players. This will require a tremendous culture change and there will be significant challenges in contract reform.

Numerous articles have been written in the last couple of years that have addressed the issues, challenges and the need for CE. At the Society of Naval Architects and Marine Engineers 1996 Ship Production Symposium Mr. Robert Keane (Director of Ship Systems, NAVSEA Carderock) and Captain (retired) Barry Tibbitts (John J. McMullen Associates) presented a paper titled "A Revolution in Warship Design: Navy-Industry Integrated Product Teams." The authors strongly support the concepts of Integrated Product and Process Development (IPPD). With regard to the Integrated Product Teams (IPT), the authors state:

*"IPT are formed to ensure that these different voices of the customer are heard early enough in the process to influence design decisions. . . . a team approach is needed. Teams of engineers—not lawyers. Among the details which need to be worked out are defining the relationships between the NAVSEA engineers, Program Manager, and the local SUPSHIP office, as well as the different departments within the shipyard."*

One of the major changes in the new acquisition reforms, is that the responsibility for the detailed design will shift from Naval Sea Systems Command (NAVSEA) Code 03 to the shipbuilder. This transition will not be easy, and will require a cooperative working relationship between the parties. The IPT representatives need to respect one anothers individual contract responsibilities and obligations and seek collective solutions to the obstacles encountered.

In an article in the Winter 1997 edition of the Procurement Lawyer, Volume 32 Number 2, titled "The New Environment of IPPDs and IPTs", Lt. Col., Wycliffe S.G. Furcron, Associate General Counsel (Acquisition and Logistics) Office of General Counsel, Department of Defense wrote:

*"To avoid confusion, the roles and responsibilities of each of the parties to this government/contractor team must be spelled out in advance. . .Government personnel, other than the contracting officer, cannot change the requirements stated in the Request for Proposal (or after award, in the contract)."*

IPT's greatest strengths, and greatest weaknesses, arise out of the same things: cooperation and empowerment. With

**Exhibit 3.** Concurrent Engineering Implementation (Concurrent Engineering Research Center)

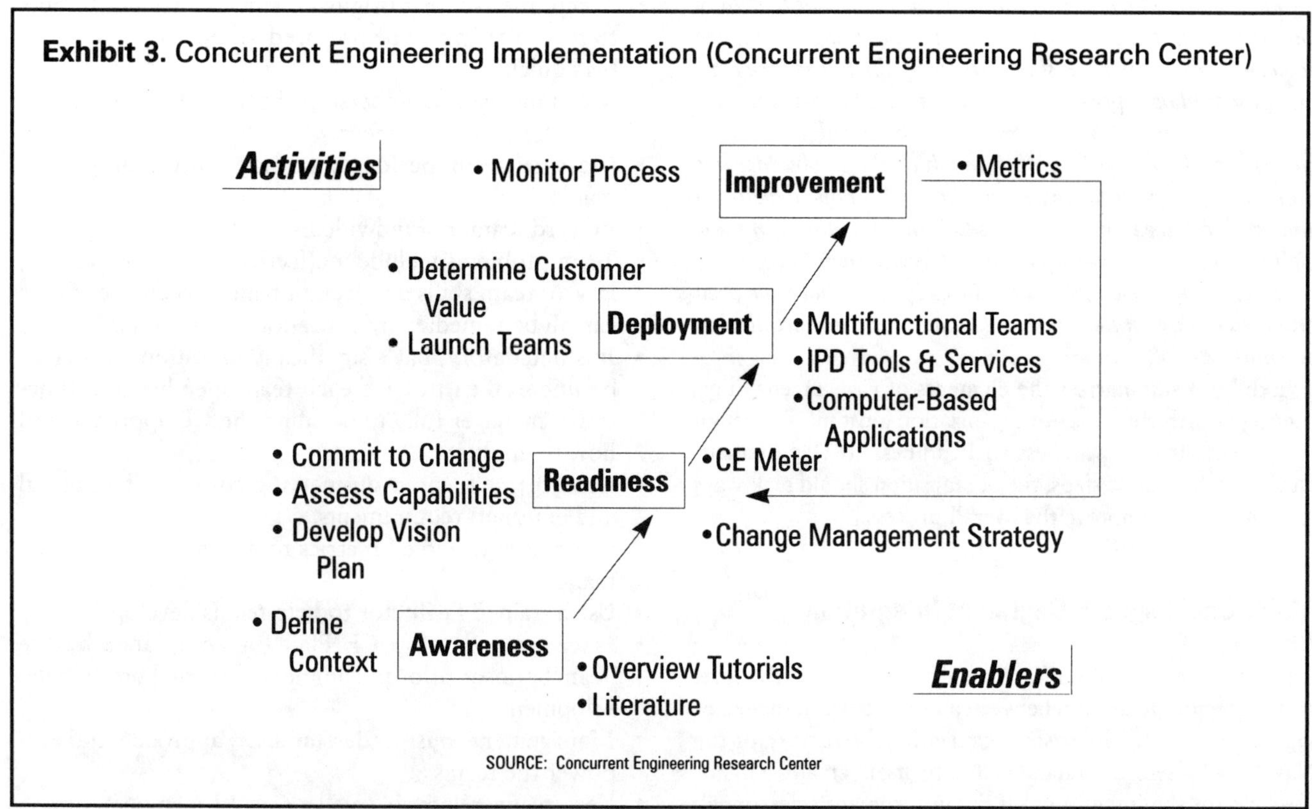


SOURCE: Concurrent Engineering Research Center

empowerment comes responsibility. Because of the unique aspects of government contracting, special rules have developed about who has authority to create obligations on behalf of the government. Only a warranted contracting officer has actual authority to obligate the government, and even that person's authority may be limited. In the context of IPTs, contractors will deal with many government personnel, some of whom may have apparent authority to obligate the government. But apparent authority is insufficient to create an obligation on behalf of the government, even in the context for IPT.

Secretary of Defense, William Perry, has described empowerment this way:

*"The purpose of the IPT is to assist the parties in understanding the contract requirement, facilitate timely issue resolution, and to allow the government to gain early insight into the contractor's performance. It must be clear to the contractor that the IPT guidance will not change the contract requirements. Any perceived change to those requirements must be addressed to the PCO for resolution and potential contractual resolution."*

In an article titled "Concurrent Engineering in Ship Design" published by the Society of Naval Architects and Marine Engineers at the 1996 Ship Production Conference, Dag Runar Elvekrok, University of Trondheim, Norway sates:

*"The concepts and ideas of concurrent engineering are to effectively treat all the different elements influencing the product and the product development processes in community. The intention is to establish an environment for better decision and solutions early in the design phase."*

*"To successfully achieve concurrent engineering a concurrent engineering environment must be introduced. A concurrent engineering environment provides that the different conditions for concurrent engineering are arranged, systematized and controlled. The conditions are dependent on each other and sub-optimizations must be avoided. The purpose of the concurrent engineering environment is to keep the different processes and conditions in balance to achieve a successful optimization."*

Captain Maurice Gauthier, LPD-17 Program Manager states in a supplement to Maritime Reporter and Engineering News, Marine Technology International,

*"Navy and industry Integrated Product and Process Development (IPPD) team will exist for the life of the LPD-17 class and future derivatives. Unlike most shipbuilding programs, this Navy-industry team will be established at the prime contractor's site, not in Washington, D.C., so that real-time, continuous process streamlining can be achieved. The full service contractor will be capable of procuring, or if necessary, leading the development of selected sensors, weapons, and other digital systems under the direction of the Navy*

*through the IPPD team. It is through this team that the Navy will ensure that technical obligations, including safety, are achieved. Procurement of ship systems by the full service contractor would be superior to current practice, because the contractor team would have more expert knowledge of all requirements than in an approach in which the shipbuilder has no systems integration team members who have developed and produced weapons, sensors, satellites and other complex, high-technology systems. Also, the integrator may be the same contractor who develops and produces systems that have been provided as government furnished equipment for installation on ships."*

Exhibit 3 summarizes the elements of Concurrent Engineering implementation. An organization must move through the process from Awareness to Readiness to Deployment. During each of these steps, the organization should seek ways to continuously improve the overall process.

## Major Challenges & Degree of Integration

There are fundamental differences of opinion as to the level and degree of integration between all the parties in the teaming arrangement. The basic organizational structure of the Naval Sea System Command in and by itself, creates a major obstacle for the integration of the government's personnel. The next obstacle is merging the government, shipbuilder and vendors into a cohesive group. The key to this success will be 1) a recognition of the need to release centralized control of function and technical matters; 2) the willingness to empower the personnel in order that they will be effective team players and 3) implement continual education training programs as is the practice with successful Total Quality Management (TQM) programs.

In the shipbuilding industry, CE is not the future; it has arrived. The players need to get up to speed if they want to participate. To overcome the challenge related to the degree of integration between the parties in the IPT's, the following steps must be taken:

- Clearly define how teams fit into the organization.
- Tell the team why change in approach is being made.
- Use your best people on the early teams to increase probability of success.
- Make sure team members realize that team success is their number 1 priority.
- Give the team adequate training in necessary skills.
- Set broad overall goals.
- Make sure functional managers are cared for during the transition period.
- Train functional managers along with the team.
- Let the team decide how it will operate.
- Give the team time to develop into a team.
- Accept the fact that original members may not be able to form a team and be prepared to replace some members quickly.
- Maintain team membership through the duration of the product development.
- Measure team performance not individual performance.
- Reward team, not individuals.
- Team problems include ineffective team management, lack of team skills and lack of team experience. These can all be remedied by education and training.
- It is mandatory that a significant educational program be undertaken to have each team member and functional manager fully understand the CE approach and how to apply it.
- Keep teams focused on meeting customer's (internal and external) requirements.
- Use mutually agreed metrics to monitor team performance.
- Use a trained facilitator to help teams develop.
- Have team develop CE Plan for acceptance by the Team Sponsor prior to commencing actual product development.
- Management must understand CE approach and empower the teams.
- Keep teams relatively small—6 to 12 members.
- Make sure that entire team understand that all members must accept product ownership.

## Proprietary Information

The basic concern of shipbuilders is the ability to safeguard proprietary information and data. The basic reason given for this concern is, that the information and data could be obtained by the competition and thereby pose a business threat to the shipbuilder. This issue has been discussed by the government and industry in various formal and informal forums with little, if any, progress over the years. The end result has been that the information and data provided on the normal shipbuilding contract is of such a summary nature, it provides extremely limited value as a management tool.

The success of CE will be dependent upon a major change in the prevailing attitude of the shipbuilder to provide the detailed information and data for proper decision making by the IPT's. Additionally, the successful implementation of DOD 5000.2R, which sets forth the Cost Schedule and Performance reports for new acquisition programs, will depend very heavily on the willingness of the shipbuilder and government to share information and data, yet safeguard that which is proprietary. This problem is further exacerbated by the unwillingness of companies to share new and innovative engineering and production systems (which were privately funded) with the government and competitors. Programs such as those sponsored by MARITECH, wherein companies and the government have become partners financially in the development of new and innovative solutions to problems facing the industry, has been somewhat of a break-through and hopefully the participating companies will share the results with industry.

## Integrated Data Environment (IDE)

Significant gaps exist in the ability to implement an Integrated Data Environment (IDE) to achieve an effective interchange of information and data in an electronic form. Captain Gauthier in the previously mentioned article goes on to further state:

*"The LPD-17 Navy-industry program team will implement an Integrated Product Data Environment which will electronically link remote sites into program relational data bases; three dimensional product models; management, technical, production and logistics information; performance models and simulations; and operational, training and maintenance information. The Integrated Product Data Environment will be the common medium of communications and the repository of expert knowledge throughout the life of the LPD-17 class."*

A successful Concurrent Engineering design process includes the following IDE Components:

- An automated link among design engineering, manufacturing, and the logistics processes and functions in order to facilitate the transfer of technical information.
- Databases of product definition, configuration, and logistics data that are shared among the various disciplines.
- Software tools that support the integration of computer-aided engineering analysis tools with the computer-aided design function. This implies the existence of component part libraries, materials characteristics databases, and component performance characteristics databases.
- The capability to distinguish between various categories of design data (working, submitted, approved) and to provide data traceability throughout various design iterations.
- The ability to restrict access to design data by unauthorized personnel, while providing remote access to data by the customer.
- The capability to develop a comprehensive product model of the ship component system.
- The capability to manage and rapidly communicate design and configuration changes.

The central problem to be addressed is not hardware, but software. Computer software support for CE has basic elements such as (1) Integrating tools and services; (2) Capturing corporate history; (3) Sharing information; (4) Coordination of the team; and (5) Co-locating people and programs

## Partnering and Total Quality Management

The elements of IPPD are not technical but cultural. Most of the government and industry players are not experienced in this "team culture" concept, because it is contrary to the manner in which prior business relationships have been conducted.

The government has had a form of TQM implemented in its various commands, but has never graduated to the middle or upper levels of TQM. The concept of Partnering was introduced in the government by the U. S. Army Corps of Engineers in the 1980's.

The elements of successful Partnering are:

- The parties share a common set of goals.
- Each party's expectations are clearly stated, up front, and provide the basis for working together.
- Partners' actions are consistent and predictable. Trust is earned when one's actions are consistent with one's words. We must "walk the talk."
- Each partner must be willing to make a real commitment to participate in the partnership.
- Responsibility is recognized and the consequences of our choices are accepted. Partners are accountable to each other and should agree up front on measures for mutual accountability.
- Partners have the courage to forthrightly confront and resolve conflict.
- Partners understand and respect each other's responsibilities, authority, expectations and boundaries, as well as any honest differences between them.
- The partnership is more than the sum of the individual partners. The relationship is more powerful than any of the partners working alone because it is based on the collective resources of the partners.
- Partners expect excellence from each other and give excellence in return.

Although it has many advantages, Partnering is not always a valid alternative. The specific situation and the mutual work history of the parties will be a major influence on the ability of the parties to establish a Partnering arrangement.

## Summary

Management must adopt and emphasize attention to customer needs, as well as quality improvement. Team building must be a cooperative effort with good communication and collaborations on the decisions of the team. Just like TQM, CE requires employee participation and supplier interface in order to be successful. It requires the improvement of every aspect of an organization's life, from empowerment of the individual to growth of the company as a whole, by integrating all of its suppliers, internal processes, and its customers' needs.

The major challenges addressed in this paper need to be carefully analyzed by all the players in the CE process and they must demonstrate a willingness to seek solutions that are workable and make good business sense.

# Uss Gonzalez (Ddg 66) Reconstruction

Waldemar H. Koscinski - Department of the Navy

## Introduction

On January 7, 1997, USS Gonzalez (DDG 66), the US Navy's most modern and sophisticated warship, arrived into Bath Iron Works (BIW) in Portland, ME to commence a large reconstruction effort. Gonzalez arrived with damage to her sonar dome, Main Reduction Gears (MRGs), drive train and propellers. This paper will examine all aspects of the Reconstruction Availability planning and execution conducted by both the US Navy and BIW to bring this billion dollar warfighting vessel back to life.

## USS Gonzalez (DDG 66) History/Characteristics

Delivered to the US Navy on July 26, 1996, Gonzalez is the ninth USS Arleigh Burke (DDG 51) Class Destroyer to be built by BIW. The ship is equipped to operate in a high-density, multi-threat environment as an integral member of an aircraft carrier battle group. Gonzalez' Aegis Weapon System is the most sophisticated in the world, characterized by the SPY-1D phased array radar and Vertical Launch System. Powered by four General Electric (GE) LM2500 Gas Turbine Engines capable of providing 100,000 shaft horsepower and coupled to two controllable pitch propellers (CPPs), Gonzalez has a top speed in excess of 30 knots (see Exhibit 1).

**Exhibit 1.** Overview of USS Arleigh Burke (Dug 51) Class Ship Characteristicw. Note Location of AN/SAS-53 Hull-mounted Sonar at Forward End of Ship.

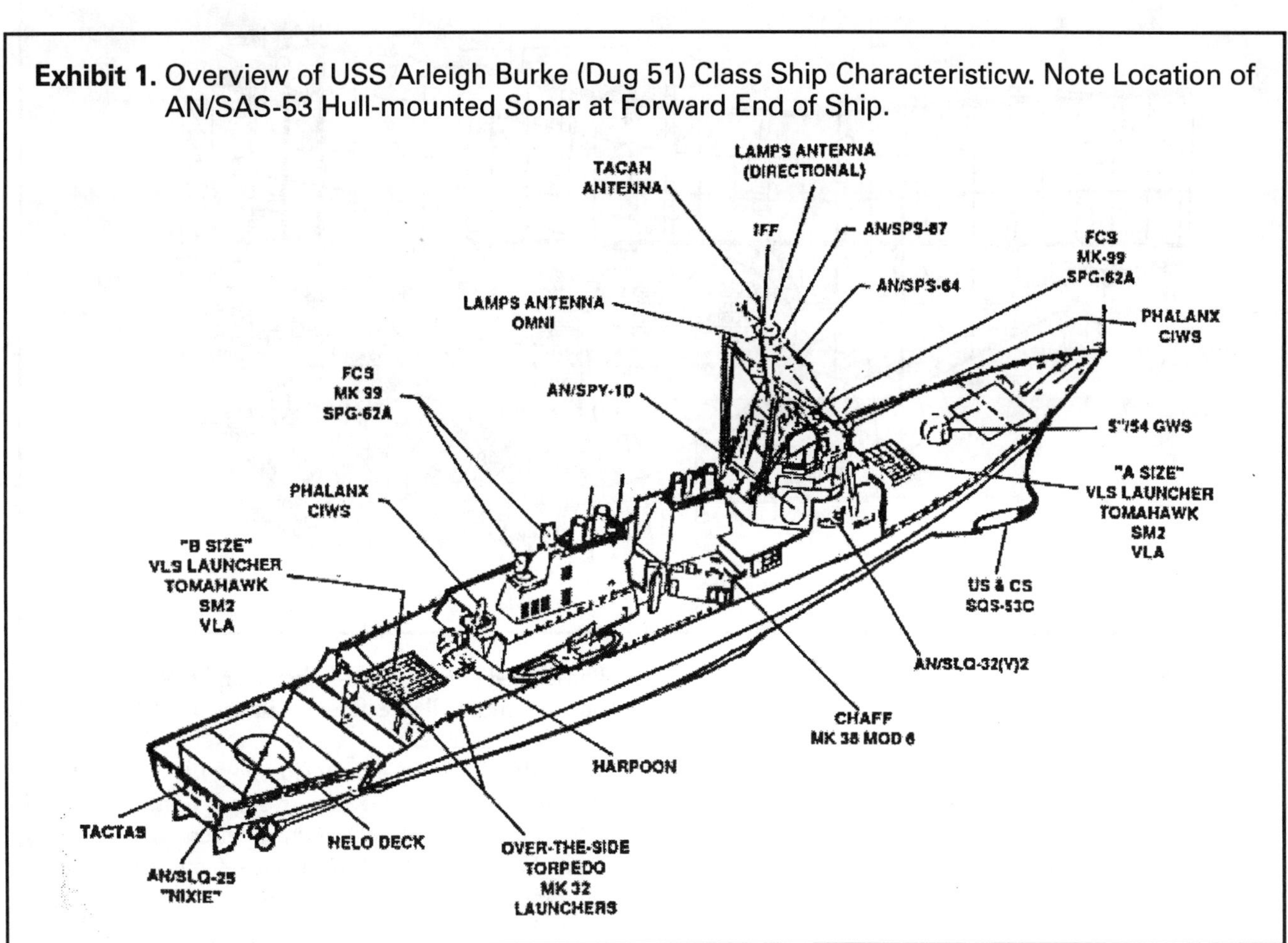

**Exhibit 2.** Overall USS Gonzalez (DDG 66) Reconstruction Availability Schedule

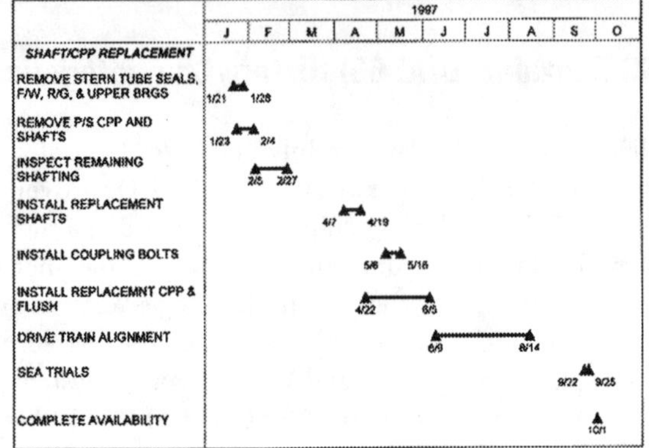


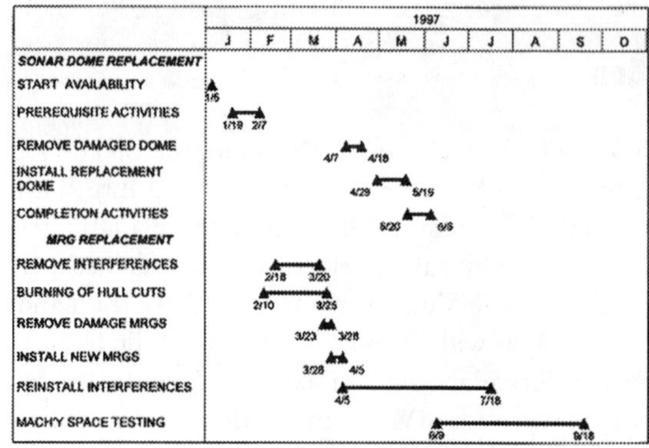

**Exhibit 3.** Damaged Areas of Gonzalez' Sonar Done (Shown as Crosshatched Section

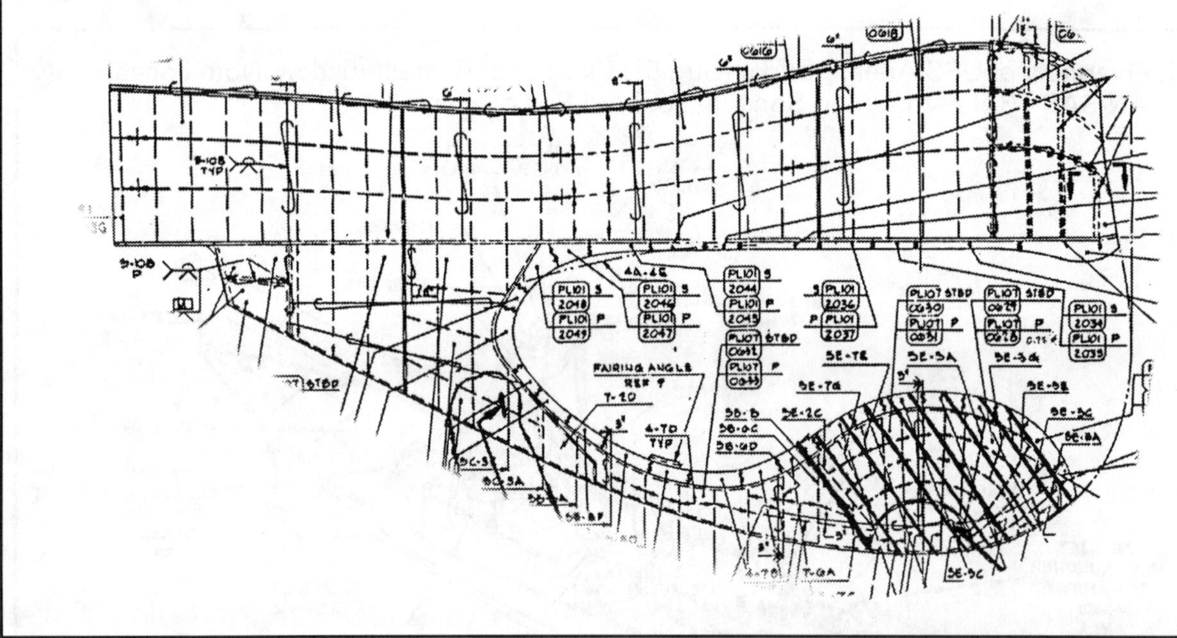

## Overall Schedule

The Reconstruction Availability was characterized by four distinct phases:

- Phase I—*Damage Assessment*—Initial Dry-docking to conduct all inspections, remove shafts, hubs and propellers and make preparations for sonar dome replacement (Jan-Feb '97);
- Phase II—*Preparations*—In between Dry-docking periods to remove all interferences in way of MRG removal path (Feb-Mar '97);
- Phase III—*Replacement Of Components*—Second Dry-docking to replace MRGs and sonar dome and install replacement shafts, hubs and propellers (Mar-Jun '97);
- Phase IV—*Alignment And Testing*—Conduct drive train alignment, post-reconstruction testing and sea trials (Jun '97-Oct '97).

**Exhibit 4.** Photograph of BIW Rigging the Dome Using the Barge and Cradle Support Assembly

**Exhibit.** Layout of Barge and Sonar Dome

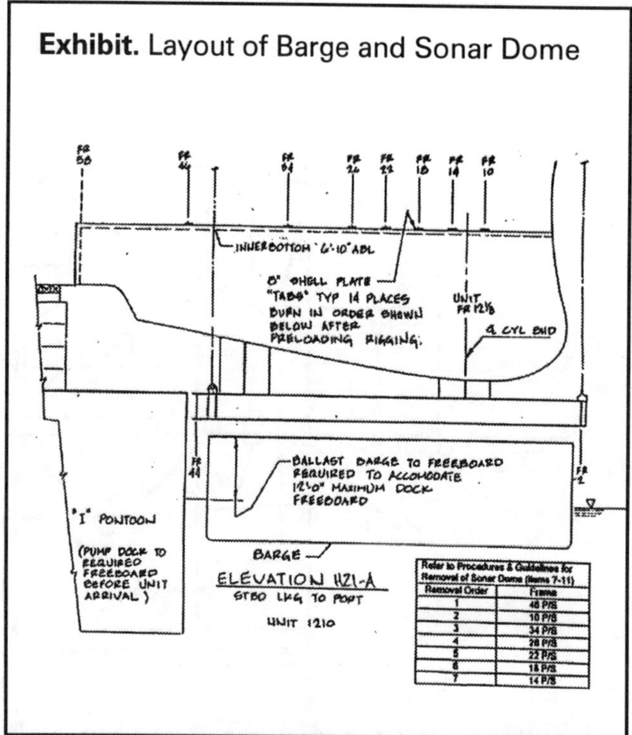


| Removal Order | Frame |
|---|---|
| 1 | 48 P/S |
| 2 | 10 P/S |
| 3 | 34 P/S |
| 4 | 28 P/S |
| 5 | 22 P/S |
| 6 | 18 P/S |
| 7 | 14 P/S |

While clearly the highest priority was placed on returning Gonzalez to the Fleet as quickly as possible, BIW's availability schedule also balanced accomplishing and testing all shipboard repairs with production manning requirements in their new construction program.

With the overall framework in place, BIW planners and engineers and US Navy personnel set out to develop the repair plan for each of the three major damaged ship components. Due to the extremely short time-frame prior to the availability and the evolving, dynamic and complex nature of the damage, planning for all repair efforts was extremely short-fused. Some planning was accomplished using analyses results conducted by component technical representatives prior to the availability. However, virtually all repair scope development, job sequencing and material identification was accomplished concurrently with the execution of the work. The resulting schedule by major repair activity is provided as Exhibit 2.

## Sonar Dome Replacement

### Introduction

The AN/SQS-53 Hull-Mounted Sonar System (see Exhibit 1) is one component of the most advanced anti-submarine warfare system in the world today. The sensitive acoustic transducers within the AN/SQS-53 Sonar Dome provide long range search, detection, classification and tracking of enemy submarines.

Gonzalez arrived in Portland with severe damage to her sonar dome banjo, rubber window, cylindrical bulkhead and several areas of plating aft of the rubber window (see Exhibit 3). Early in the availability, it was determined that replacing the entire sonar dome module vice repairing damaged areas was the most cost-effective and least schedule impacting course of action to take. This was possible, in part, because BIW "borrowed" a partially completed dome unit from their new construction program deferring to a later time the fabrication of a replacement sonar dome. This strategy thereby decoupled the material procurement and production efforts associated with dome fabrication from the severe time constraints of the reconstruction availability..

### Replacement of the Sonar Dome

BIW replaced Gonzalez' Sonar Dome using a barge and cradle support assembly (see Exhibit 4). Prerequisite key activities prior to removing the dome included:

- cleaning and gas freeing the voids and tanks around the dome
- installation of eight lifting and handling pads on the sideshell
- removal of approximately 576 sonar dome transducers.

All of these activities were accomplished during Gonzalez' first dry-docking period. During Gonzalez' second dry-docking period, removal of Gonzalez' old dome commenced when BIW floated a ballasted barge underneath the ship and attached the cradle support assembly to the old dome. This part of the process was possible due to the unique way that BIW drydocks Navy ships allowing the sonar dome to overhang the water. BIW then flame cut the dome loose just

**Exhibit 6.** Layout of USS Arleigh Burke (DDG 51) Class Propulsion System

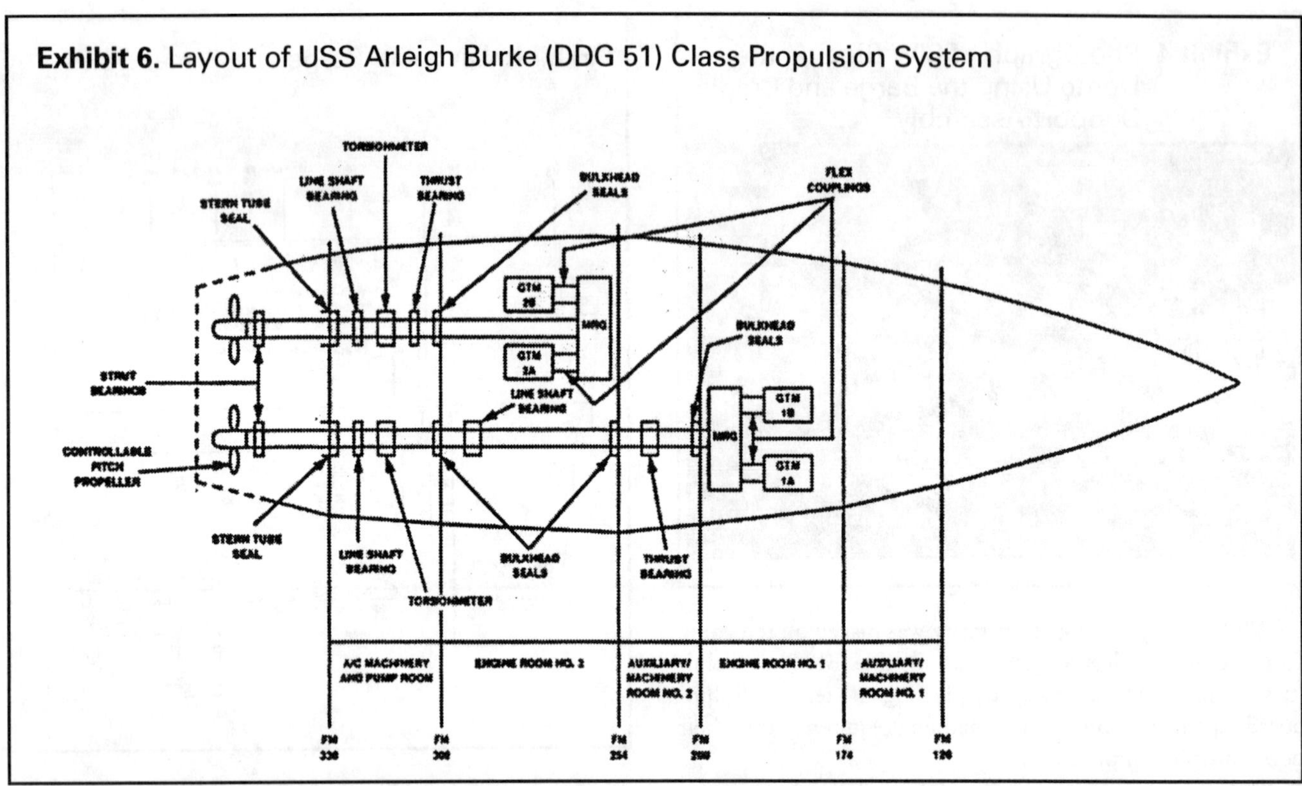


above the airlock (6ft-10in platform) and aft of the sonar dome cable trunk leaving shell plate tabs at pre-determined lengths and locations to support the unit (see Exhibit 5). After the final cuts were made, BIW lowered the cradle (now bearing the full weight of the dome) onto the barge.

Installation of the new dome was a complex effort of the dome using the barge and cradle Herculean proportions yet requiring surgical precision. BIW floated the barge holding the new 119 Long Ton (LT) Sonar Dome/cradle support assembly underneath the ship and aligned it with the ship's centerline. Using chainfalls and the afore-mentioned lifting pads, BIW riggers hoisted the dome to within six inches of the ship to allow BIW electricians to pull the approximately eighty sonar dome cables into the ship. BIW riggers and welders then aligned and tack-welded into place (using exterior welded strongbacks) the new sonar dome still largely supported by the cradle rigged to the ship. After initial alignment, a massive four week internal and external welding effort took place, complicated by periodic verification that the new sonar dome remained in alignment with the ship. Meanwhile, inside the dome, BIW electricians were busy connecting the sonar dome cables to the sending and receiving units and tradesmen from virtually all crafts were installing support systems, such as the pressurization system.

As the welding of the dome unit neared completion, BIW removed the cradle assembly, thus transferring sonar dome support to the ship. In the end, some clad welding was required to reach the required precise (within one-thousandth of one inch) fairness tolerances. Upon completion of the installation, BIW flooded the new sonar dome and conducted a forty-eight hour soak test to once again verify structural integrity and water-tightness of the sonar dome cables and transducers. Removal of the lifting pads and painting of the sideshell brought to a close this five month, 18,000 man-hour evolution.

## Mrg Replacement

### Introduction

Exhibit 6 is a layout of the Arleigh Burke Class Propulsion Plant system. As a component of this system, the primary function of the MRG is to reduce the rotating speeds of the gas turbines from 3,586 revolutions per minute (rpm) to a speed suitable for turning the ship's propellers (168 rpm). The MRGs are laid out such that the forward MRG in Main Engine Room (MER) #1 serves the starboard propeller shaft, while the aft MRG in MER#2 serves the port shaft. The MRGs are double reduction locked train type with hardened and ground gears designed to transmit 51,500 horsepower continuously from two gas turbines to a propeller shaft. Magnetic particle inspections of the gear teeth conducted by General Electric revealed extensive cracking of the bull gear teeth approximately two millimeters deep. This necessitated the replacement of both of Gonzalez' MRGs.

BIW conducted MRG replacement in four phases:

- Removal of shipboard interferences and flame cutting of athwartship hull access cuts
- Replacement of the MRGs using outboard barges and a lateral rigging path
- Closure of hull access cuts, interference re-installation and testing of all affected systems
- MRG-to-Gas Turbine and MRG-to-shaft in-water alignment and post-installation MRG testing.

### Interference Removal/Burning of Hull Access Cuts

After extensive study, BIW determined that replacing the MRGs laterally vice vertically through the ship's bottom would be the most efficient and least disruptive approach to undertake. This conclusion was based on the following:

- projected vertical clearance requirements to rig the MRGs if dropped and moved out from under the hull
- projected substantial overhead structural stiffening to hang the MRGs
- untried rigging methods; and, most importantly
- the desire to save the structural integrity of the MRG foundation and its connections to the hull.

Nonetheless, removing the MRGs laterally required a tremendous amount of ship's structure, piping, cabling and ventilation ducting to be removed from the ten foot lateral rigging path. These interferences, summarized in Exhibit 7, affect virtually all Arleigh Burke Class hull, machinery and electrical support systems.

To accommodate the shear size of both MRGs, BIW flame cut hull access cuts each measuring 19 feet wide by 22 feet high. As part of each access cut, BIW removed all structure, equipment and piping that was attached to the sideshell. As a result, each access cut weighed approximately 22 LT. Exhibit 8 is a photograph of the starboard side hull cut.

### Replacement of MRGs

MRG replacement was accomplished by using a barge and rail system and laterally translating the 120,000 pound MRGs. See Exhibit 9 for an overview. Only the MRGs themselves were removed—the sub-bases and shock isolators were reused to facilitate MRG alignment..

With internal interferences removed and hull access cuts burned, BIW initiated MRG replacement by floating a barge (containing the replacement MRG) outboard of each access cut. Using a one and one-half LT A-Frame assembly and a shipyard gantry, BIW riggers removed the 22 LT access cuts and transferred them onto the dry-dock deck. Next, BIW riggers and shipfitters laid portable six foot transition rails between the barges and the existing MRGs upon which the MRGs would be transferred. The existing damaged MRGs, now moved away from the gas turbines, were jacked sixteen inches into the air allowing. BIW riggers to place high capacity rollers underneath them. The MRGs were then set on the rails and rolled off the ship and onto the barge. By using the rail system installed on the barge BIW riggers then translated

**Exhibit 7.** Summary of Interferences Removed

**Significant Interferences Removed:**

- 94,800 linear feet (lf) of cabling
- 4,300 lf of piping
- 200 lf of ventilation ducting
- 100 square feet of deck plating
- 15 overhead lights
- Two major structural stanchions

**Significant Equipment Removed:**

- Lube Oil Storage Tank
- CPP Duplex Strainer
- CPP Sump Tank
- Lube Oil Storage and Conditioning Assembly
- Various Electrical Panels and Controllers

**Significant Systems Impacted:**

- 60 Hz/400 Hz Power Distribution
- Numerous Firefighting Systems
- Data Multiplex/Machinery Control System
- Steering System
- Firemain System
- Machinery Space Communications

**Exhibit 8.** Photograph of the Starboard Side Hullcut Removed and Translated Onto the Barge

**Exhibit 9.** Overview of the MRG Replacement Barge and Rail System (Port Side Plan View)

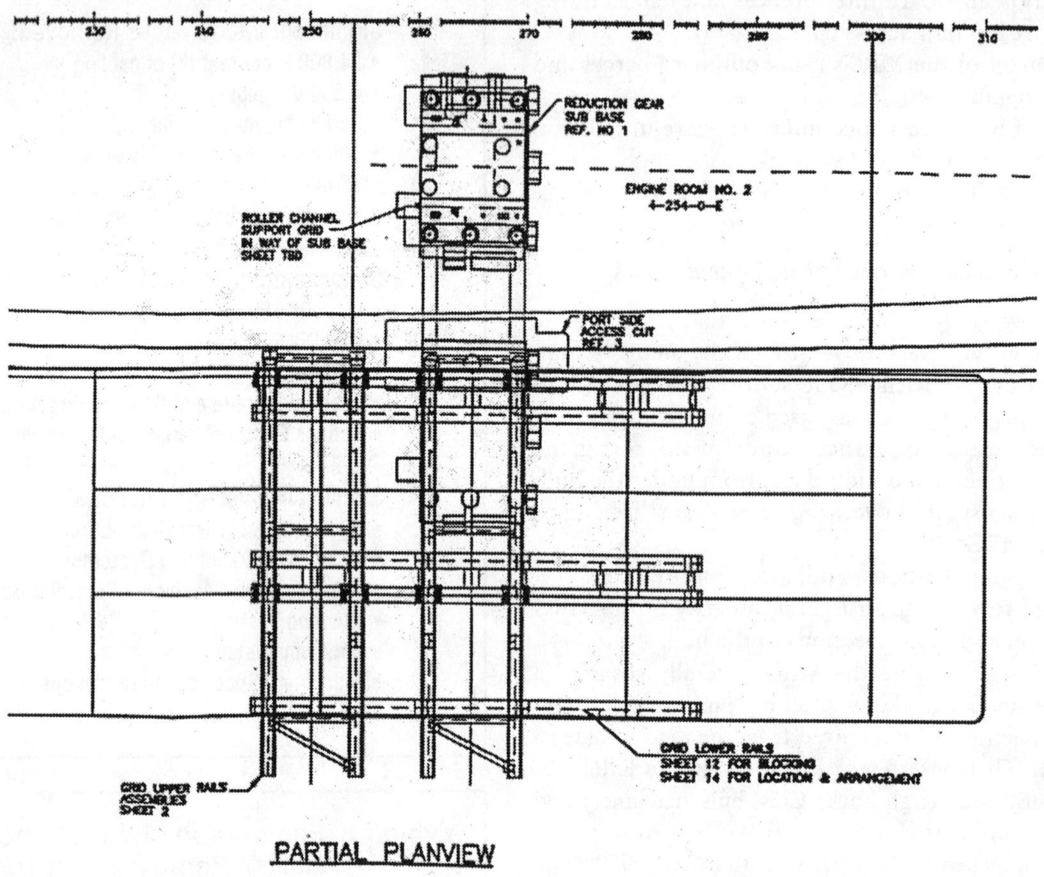

PARTIAL PLANVIEW

**Exhibit 10.** Photograph of Damaged and Replacement MRGS on the Barge (Starboard Side)

the damaged MRGs to one side of the barge and positioned the replacement units into place in front of the access openings, ready to be installed. See Exhibit 10 for MRG orientation overview on the barge.

Like the sonar dome installation, installation of the replacement MRGs was essentially a mirror image of the removal process of the old MRGs. Both MRGs were translated laterally into each engine room using chainfall and the aforementioned transition rails and high capacity rollers. Once set on the existing sub-base and shock isolators, this 15,500 man-hour job was completed when the sub-base jack screws were tightened snugly to the MRG gear casing bottom flange. Accomplished within two weeks, hundreds of BIW engineers, planners and craftsmen, many working around-the-clock, successfully brought to closure this nautical, rarely accomplished "open heart surgery".

**Exhibit 11.** Layout of USS Arleigh Burke (DDG 51) Class CPP System

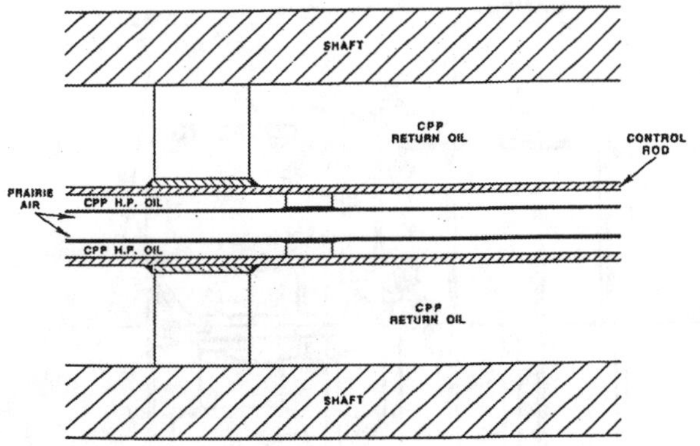

SHAFT
CPP RETURN OIL
CONTROL ROD
PRAIRIE AIR
CPP H.P. OIL
CPP H.P. OIL
CPP RETURN OIL
SHAFT

**Exhibit 12.** Photograph of Replacement Stern Tube and Tail Shafts on the Rail Assemblies

### Interference Reinstallation & System Testing

Interference reinstallation and system testing was accomplished jointly between BIW and Gonzalez ship's force. The shipyard was responsible for putting the ship back together. This effort included welding back structural interferences, reinstalling and hydrostatically testing all disturbed piping and re-installing all electrical interferences and accomplishing cable hook-up. Successful cable hook-up was verified by test signal transmission through the cables and impedance/ground fault testing.

With the shipboard systems intact, Gonzalez ship's force then operationally tested all machinery space equipment, regardless of whether or not it was impacted by the MRG replacement. This all encompassing effort started with providing support systems to the equipment, such as air conditioning and chilled water and gradually built up to bringing out of lay-up and operationally testing Gonzalez' major equipment such as gas turbines and gas turbine generators. Along the way, various US Navy training groups assisted ship's force with equipment operational training and engineering space drills. This monumental five month effort culminated with Gonzalez' successful completion of the US Navy's most stringent and comprehensive machinery space readiness examination—the Engineering Plant Light-Off Assessment.

## Shaft/Cpp Replacement

### Introduction

The Arleigh Burke Class of ships has two independent shafting systems. The starboard shaft, driven from MER#1 is 240 feet long, while the port shaft, starting in MER#2, is 178 feet long. The purpose of the propulsion shafting is to transmit the torque generated by the gas turbines from the MRGs to the CPPs. Simultaneously, the shaft acts in the propeller control system, providing CPP system oil and prairie air through tubes in the shaft, allowing for pitch position change of the seventeen foot diameter blades (see Exhibit 11).

Gonzalez arrived in Portland with four missing and six damaged blades and a CPP/shaft system contaminated with seawater. Due to the material condition of the propeller hubs, it was not considered possible to restore the CPP to any kind of working order. As a result, the entire CPP system, including the valve rod and prairie tubes in the shaft required replacement. Furthermore, when put on a lathe, the two aftmost sections of port and starboard shaft tubing (aft of the stern tube seal in Exhibit 6)—the stern tube and tail shafts (52 and 54 feet in length, respectively) were found to be bent ten times beyond allowable limits and had excessively cocked flange faces. As a result, all four pieces of shafting required to be repaired. However, due to time constraints, it was decided to replace the four damaged shafts with spare shafts and defer to a later date the repair and refurbishment of the damaged shafts.

### CPP/Shaft Replacement

Like the Sonar Dome and MRG replacements, the replacement of GONZALEZ' port and starboard stern tube and tail shafts (total weight approximately 72 LT) required a diverse mixture of both brute-force rigging strength and surgical precision. Prior to removing the CPP and shafts, BIW drained the CPP oil from both shafts and removed port and starboard stern tube seals and all fairwaters, rope guards and upper bearings. Then, using a system of lifting pads welded to the

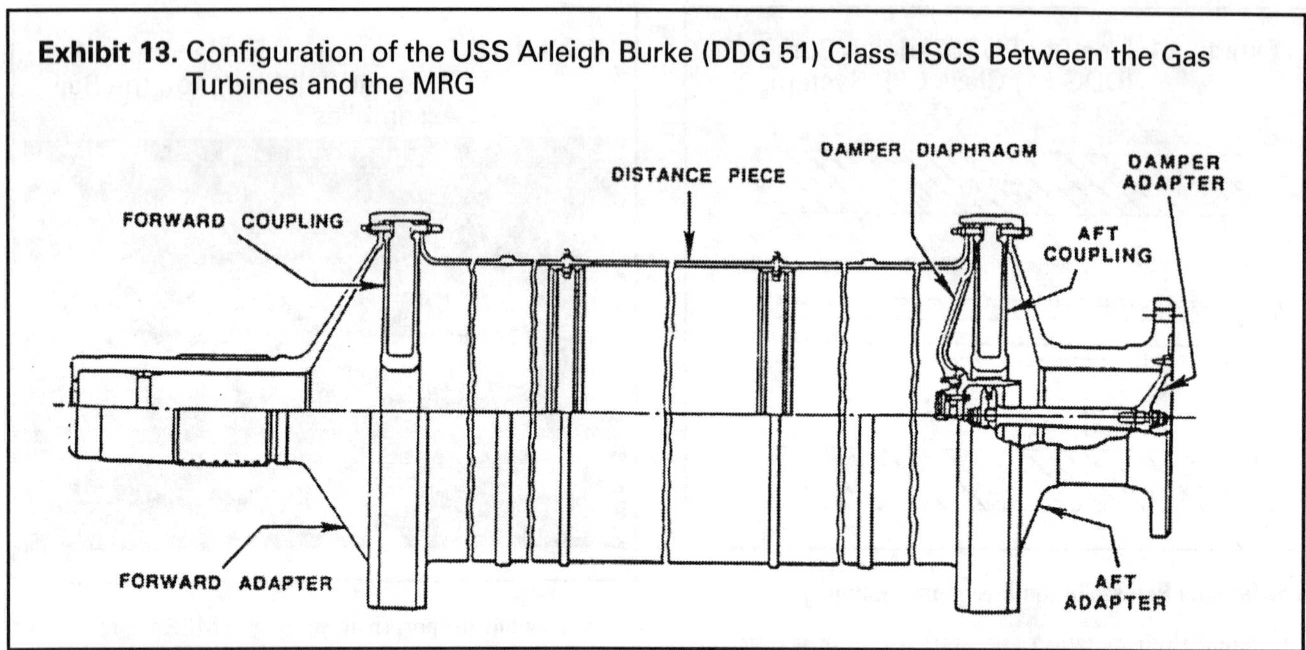


**Exhibit 13.** Configuration of the USS Arleigh Burke (DDG 51) Class HSCS Between the Gas Turbines and the MRG

ship's hull, chain falls and 120 foot long portable rails, BIW riggers and mechanics removed Gonzalez' port and starboard CPP and stern and tail shafts. BIW then conducted an optical alignment and took run-out readings on the shaft pieces forward of the stern tube and verified them to be corrosion-free and in alignment. Finally, so as to accommodate the MRG replacement, the shaft sections not replaced were rigged away from the MRGs approximately three feet.

Prior to installing the replacement CPP and shaft, BIW verified the main strut alignment and machined bearings that would align the strut to the replacement shaft. BIW riggers then re-installed the existing port and starboard line shafts and thrust and strut bearings Next, using the afore-mentioned lifting pad/chainfall/rail assemblies, BIW riggers installed the replacement stern tube and tail shafts (see Exhibit 12). What followed was the coupling of the existing line shafts to the MRGs and replacement stern tube/tail shaft assemblies. This process required that each of the 48 flange bolt holes (initially undersized) be reamed out to within. .001 inch tolerance to accept the replacement tapered (initially oversized) coupling bolts, which, in parallel, were machined to fit. All this work had to be accomplished within the confines of the Shaft Alley using portable boring and reaming equipment. BIW approached this coupling process in two phases—forward port/aft starboard first followed by forward starboard/aft port. Each flange connection demanded that three to four of twelve bolts be replaced at a time, all the while rotating the shaft to ensure complete peripheral and facial alignment and bolt/hole contact.

Once all coupling bolts were installed, BIW machinists installed all components of the CPP system, including hubs and blades. Following that, BIW re-installed underwater rope guards and fairwaters. And finally, BIW accomplished a two week flush of the CPP system to ensure that all industrial contaminants were removed and that the system was watertight. Completion of the flush brought to closure this three month, 34,000 man-hour evolution.

**Exhibit 14.** Configuration of the USS Arleigh Burde (DDG 51) Class MRG Support Isolators and Shock Snubbers (AFT Port Sid MRG)

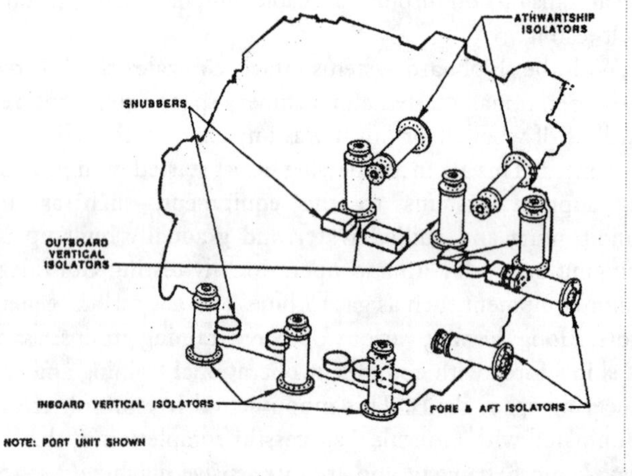

## Drive Train Alignment

A critical evolution associated with the MRG/CPP/shafting replacement was the alignment of the drive train. With the ship water-borne and MRGs and shafting replaced, BIW accomplished the drive train alignment in two phases: MRGs-to-Gas Turbines and MRGs-to-shafting.

The MRGs-to-Gas Turbines alignment centered around the alignment of the four high speed coupling shafts (HSCS), which allow for radial deflections between the two units during operation. The HSCS consists of a forward adapter which mates with each of the four gas turbines, two flexible couplings, a distance piece and an aft adapter which mates with the MRG (two per set) (see Exhibit 13). The objective of this phase of the drive train alignment was to ensure that each of the HSCSs were longitudinally deflected enough (measured as an 'H' (gas turbine end) or 'J' (MRG end) dimension) provide for proper flexibility and even loading between the MRG and gas turbines and allow for thermal expansion.

The MRGs-to-shafting phase of the drive train alignment was centered around alignment of the MRGs support isolators and shock snubbers (see Exhibit 14). The ten isolators, bolted to the MRG casing and ship's foundation, provide support in all planes for the MRGs while the snubbers provide for vertical restraint of the MRGs. The objective of the isolator alignment was to shim and/or machine, as required, the isolators to provide for even MRG loading on each of the isolators. The objective of the snubber alignment was to machine the snubber assembly, using shipboard measurements and mathematical calculations, to ensure to provide for adequate vertical restraint of the MRGs due to shock loading.

## Conclusions

As of this writing, the restoration of USS Gonzalez (DDG 66) is virtually complete, with but one significant hurdle remaining—sea trial operational testing of the MRGs and sonar dome. However, based on the track record established to date, this too will be accomplished successfully. And with sea trials and, hence, the reconstruction availability completed, USS Gonzalez (DDG 66), will once again be poised and positioned to go "beyond the call" in defense of freedom. And the men and women of the US Navy and, particularly, BIW can proudly look upon their heroic efforts of the past nine months with the knowledge that Gonzalez has been reborn into a powerful instrument of peace.

# If This is a Team, How Come We Never Practice?

Karl W. Croswhite, PMP
Program Planning & Control Manager, Boeing Defense & Space Group

American industry is enthusiastically adopting the concept of integrated, cross functional product teams. In this paper we will discuss how industry has arrived at the need to execute projects in a team environment. We will look at the major reasons that projects fail and why the establishment of teams does not eliminate these failures. We will examine the effect of organizational structure on the efficacy of teams and we will look at the role that Project Management should play in correcting these deficiencies.

## Are We Really On Teams?

We all know the value of teamwork. Our leaders constantly encourage us to work together. The worst possible reputation a person can have is that they are not a team player. But how valid is this analogy? How many of you are on a team? When was the last time your team held a practice? Do you have a play book that describes the processes that you will follow to achieve success? Does it describe the roles and responsibilities of the players on the team. Who is your coach? Do you have all of the necessary players on your team? If you were responsible to organize a practice for your team what sort of activities would you include? Let's see if we can find the answers we need, assemble our team, and practice in a manner which will enable us to win.

## Groundrules and Assumptions

For ease and clarity of discussion, let us make the following assumptions:

- The terms Project Management, Project, and Program are as defined in the *Project Management Body of Knowledge*.
- The enterprises we are discussing have multiple product divisions, each of which is executing multiple programs.
- The enterprises we are discussing generate their revenue through the successful execution of projects.
- The enterprises we are discussing wish to operate in a team environment.
- Our ultimate goal is to create an environment which will foster team success.

## Why do Projects Fail?

Since the game we are playing is the accomplishment of projects, we need to understand what causes teams to lose. There have been numerous studies done on this subject. Most of our companies do some form of post proposal or post project analysis. We have produced volumes and volumes of "lessons learned" and the findings are remarkably similar. Projects fail for the following reasons:

- Lack of planning
- Lack of executive management support
- Incomplete requirements
- Changing requirements
- Lack of user (customer) involvement
- Inadequate resources

It is important to note that projects are not failing due to inadequate technical expertise. They are not failing due to inadequate tools or systems. They are failing due to bad management. They are failing because we let them fail

## Why Teams ?

To understand how we can establish the necessary environment for successful teams we must first answer two basic questions.

1. What is the reason for moving to a team approach?
2. What is the primary purpose or function of a team?

To answer the first question we have to examine the environment from which the team concept emerged.

Most of our companies were originally structured as functional hierarchies. All of the thinking was done at the top and direction flowed down through functional chains of command to people actually performing tasks that contributed to the production of a product or service. Project management existed only as the byproduct of the general management of the business. As the business grew, a need developed to focus attention upon specific product lines or market segments individually, thus creating product divisions within the overall enterprise. These divisions adopted an organizational structure that mirrored that of the existing enterprise with each of the functions reporting in a dedicated "hard line" relationship to the division manager, thereby adding a layer of overhead functions and costs. They constitute a complete enterprise within the enterprise. Again, project management exists only as the sum of the management of the functional departments.

As these product divisions developed multiple customers and contracts, the same need developed to be able to focus attention on each of them individually and the same evolution was repeated. People performing a specific type of task report to a functional manager who reports to the project manager. This time the result is what is defined as a "projectized" organization structure. Unfortunately, it also has the effect of adding another layer of overhead costs and organizational burden. The project manager reports to the division manager who reports to the president of the company, each of whom maintains a staff to execute the overhead tasks at their level in the enterprise. The resulting organization is shown in Exhibit 1.

Unfortunately, some of us are still functioning in this structure. I say unfortunately, but many will say that there is nothing unfortunate about it. Many companies have been very successful having followed this evolutionary pattern, have been in existence a long time, and have provided a very good return to their stockholders. I can't argue that. But I can argue that even though a company may have a long history of successful projects, producing high quality products, this traditional approach to working projects has inherent inefficiencies built into it which will not be affordable in the coming century. It forces our experts to communicate in series and generally by paper. This is a slow process that limits, and even precludes, interaction between functional organizations. As a result, many mistakes are made which necessitate costly rework. This approach also tends to compartmentalize activities, making processes more resistant to change and organizations less sympathetic to the needs of other organizations.

To remain competitive, we have to find a way to satisfy our customers' requirements while minimizing our costs and reducing our product cycle times. This is where the concept of teams comes in. Integrated, cross-functional product teams are seen as a means to reduce project flow and costs, and improve communication. The assertion is that project flow times can be reduced because decisions that were once made sequentially can now be made concurrently. Furthermore, these decisions are based upon a life cycle perspective which should minimize the number and degree of changes during the project. Overall project cost should be reduced as a result of fewer and less drastic design and engineering changes, better coordination with manufacturing, and so forth. Finally, by removing most of the physical barriers that have stifled communication in the past, there should be freer and more open discussion between all represented functions. There is also a significant reduction in overhead costs *if* the overall organizational structure of the enterprise is reengineered to fit the team approach to the execution of projects. Figure 2.

## What is the Function of the Team?

Now that we understand why we are pursuing the team approach, we need to answer the second question. What is the primary purpose or function of the team?

The purpose of the team is to execute all of the tasks necessary to produce the product for which it is responsible. That is to say that the team must develop specifications, design, develop, test, produce, and deliver the product which satisfies the customers' requirements. There is nothing new or unique here. This same statement is just as accurate when applied to a project operating in a projectized functional organization or in a strict functional hierarchy. So, what is unique about a team?

*The unique aspect of the team is that it also has the responsibility for planning and managing its work and processes.* The team is responsible for defining the scope of its work, defining the tasks required to execute that scope, scheduling the execution of those tasks, assigning budget to those tasks, assessing and planning the mitigation of risk, and then monitoring and reporting their progress. In other words, the team has responsibility for scope management, time management, cost management, quality management, risk management, procurement management, communications management, and, to some degree, human resources management. The team is responsible for project management.

## Why Teams Do Not Perform Successfully

A few years ago, a national survey of innovative work practices was done by Paul Osterman, an economist at MIT. He found that more than half of the companies surveyed were using teams – and that approximately forty per cent of those companies reported having more than half of the organization working in teams. (Osterman, 1994). The effect of teaming, if you read the literature aimed at the managerial audience, would indicate that the results are excellent: teams outperform individuals, and self-directed teams perform best of all.

But the results are really not that clear. Research on team performance shows that teams usually *do not* perform as well as the sum of their members' individual efforts. It seems that there is really no empirical data that teams are more efficient. In fact, when interacting teams are compared to "nominal" groups (i.e. groups that never meet, whose output is constructed by combining the separate contributions of those who would have been team members), nominal groups actually perform better. This is illustrated Ivan Steiner's equation AP=PP-PL. That is, the *actual* productivity of a group equals its' *potential* productivity (what the team is theoretically capable of, given the resources brought by the members) minus what he calls *process losses* such as coordination and motivational problems (Steiner, 1972).

We have seen the reasons that projects fail. We have seen the reasoning behind the implementation of project teams and the unique responsibility that teams have. We know that teams, for the most part, do not execute projects successfully. Why?

The reason that teams do not overcome these failure modes is that they are not structured to do so. Or maybe I should say that the structure in which the team exists does not enable them to do so.

## The Effect of Organizational Structure on Teams

"Different people in the same structure tend to produce qualitatively similar results. When there are problems, or performance fails to live up to what is intended, it is easy to find someone or something to blame. *But, more often than we realize, systems cause their own crises, not external forces or individuals' mistakes." (Senge, 1990)*

As we can see from our earlier description of the company, division, and project structure, the only thing that is really changed in the team environment is the way in which functional organizations interact. The team may be able to execute some series of processes more rapidly by increasing the concurrency of tasks, but the processes haven't really changed and the team has not added the catalyst that is required for success. Since we have not really changed the overall structure in which the team operates, it should not be surprising that our results are unchanged. Refer once again to Exhibit 2. Notice that all of the functions are represented and report to the team leader. From what function is the team leader?

In some implementations, it is intended that the leadership role is transferred from function to function as the project progresses. At the outset, the team would be led by a Systems Engineer, since the most immediate product would be requirements and specifications. The leadership role would then pass to a Design Engineer, since the next major product would be drawings. From here, leadership would pass to Manufacturing Engineering, etc. From the perspective of the traditional functional hierarchy this may seem like a significant improvement, but there is a problem with this idea.

This approach actually perpetuates one of the paradigms we are trying to eliminate: functional stove pipes! Systems Engineering leads until the requirements and specifications are complete and then hands off to Design. "Good luck!" Design hands off to Manufacturing, "Here are the drawings, sorry they're late. You can make it up can't you? What's the matter, aren't you a team player?" This is the same old toss-it-over-the-fence attitude that has been hurting us for years; the nagging groin injury of project performance.

In regard to our sports analogy this approach never fits at all. Can you imagine a football team where the guards, tackles, running backs, etc. took turns calling plays? The fact of the matter is that even the quarterback doesn't fulfill this function any more. A new, de facto, position has been created for this purpose: the offensive coordinator. If this was a design team, and Engineering was in charge, that would make sense. If it was a production team, and Manufacturing was in charge, that would make sense. If it was a subcontracts management team, and Procurement was in charge, that would make sense. But an integrated product team is none of those things. It is *all* of those things with the additional unique task of project management. In fact, project management is the only function of the team that remains constant throughout the life cycle of the project. We need to create an offensive coordinator for our team, whose role is to lead the integration of the functions of the other players. I would suggest that it would be logical for this leader to come from a Project Management functional organization. Why is this not the case?

## Cultural and Political Influences on Structure

Each of our companies has its own corporate culture and that culture reflects how we view ourselves as a company. We may be an engineering company, a manufacturing company, an accounting firm, or a service company, but each of us identifies with some technical specialty or core competency. When the company was founded, that specialty was the key to success or failure. Those companies which succeeded and grew quite logically promoted those who were responsible for that success. As a result, those companies are today dominated by managers from those specialties. This isn't to say that there is no executive management representing other functions, but I would feel safe in saying that 80 per cent or more of the CEOs, product division managers, program managers, project managers, and team leaders are from the functional specialty with which the company is identified. Even if we could overcome this cultural imperative, what would be the source of project management players?

## Required Structural Changes

In most of our companies there is no project management organization. Some of us have a small group of individuals somewhere addressing project management processes and tools, but this is usually a group contained within some other functional organization (probably IT) distanced from the arena of day-to-day project execution. More typically, scope management gets handled by a contracts organization, Time management is done by some sort of planning/scheduling organization, cost is done by some form of estimating/accounting group, etc. These functions are usually included in the category of "support organizations" and are not part of the core team. What is required to create teams that can avoid project failures is a reengineering of our basic organizational structure.

Since our assumptions say that we want to create an environment which will foster team success, let us look at our existing structure to see what does or does not contribute to team success. We could approach this from either perspective, but let's go from the top down.

Let's go back to figure 1. At the corporate level, is there anything that is not required for the success of the team? I suppose some items could be debated. However, most of the staff functions illustrated here are necessary for the successful functioning of the enterprise and there would be no teams if there was no enterprise. As for the functional organizations, I suppose you could argue that functionals are only necessary where they exist on teams. I would suggest that this argument does not hold up. The functional organization at the highest level exists to provide members to the teams and to provide the processes, tools, and training required by the team members to perform their task.

So, do we leave the top level organization structure as is? I don't think so. There needs to be one functional organization added.

## The Missing Link

To complete the foundation for our new structure we need to create one new organization: Project Management. To create this new function we will combine pieces of several already existing functions. From contracts we'll take that portion of the effort that pertains to defining and controlling scope. We will leave those aspects of the effort that pertain to the legalities of contracting. From finance we will take those things which pertain to budgeting and cost control at the team/project/program level and leave those things which relate to overhead, taxes, payroll, and financial accounting in general. From planning we will take all aspects of planning at the team/project/program level and leave those things which pertain to planning at the strategic level. From operations (procurement) we will take subcontract management.

Finally, from all functional organizations we will take those people who aspire to a career in project management. This is in addition to all of the people who perform the tasks listed above. If an engineer (planner, buyer, cost analyst, etc.) is selected for, and agrees to accept, an assignment as a team leader, s/he would be transferred (hard line) to the project management organization. From that point forward their performance would be measured on how well they performed the function of project manager (at whatever level) and not on their original technical specialty.

So, what do we do at the product division level in our restructured organization? This may be the most difficult question to answer. I would argue that there is really no unique, value added function at this level. I would then argue that, in an enterprise of any magnitude, this level is necessary if only to provide for a reasonable span of control in the management structure. For the time being I would say that the decision to remove or retain a division level organizational structure is dependent upon the size of the overall enterprise. If we do decide to retain it, it will be structured differently from the organization shown in figure 1. Rather than having a division manager who reports to the president, there will be a division project manager who reports to the vice president of project management at the company level. Since all of the program/project managers report to this position, this is the means by which we will accomplish the vertical integration of the project management processes.

Since our program level structure already has a project manager there is nothing we need to change here.

As previously discussed, the only change we need to make at the team level is that the team leader is now a hard line member of the project management functional organization. The rest of the team members report in a matrix structure: hard line to their functional manager and soft line to the team leader. The resulting organization structure is referred to as a "strong matrix organization" and is illustrated in figure 3. This matrixed team organization is what will enable us to accomplish the horizontal integration of processes necessary to release the potential productivity of the team.

## What About Practice?

Now that we have reengineered our organizational structure to enable the teams to perform their primary function, what else do we have to do to maximize their performance?

Well, I would suggest that the first thing is to make sure that the priorities of the entire organization (enterprise) are in alignment. If this were a professional sports team it would be clearly recognized that the number one priority is for the team to win games. All revenue generated in the organization is predicated upon a winning team. I see no difference in our business teams. All of the revenue of the enterprise is generated through the successful execution of projects (contracts). Therefore the entire enterprise needs to be aligned to provide maximum support to the team. The demand for support

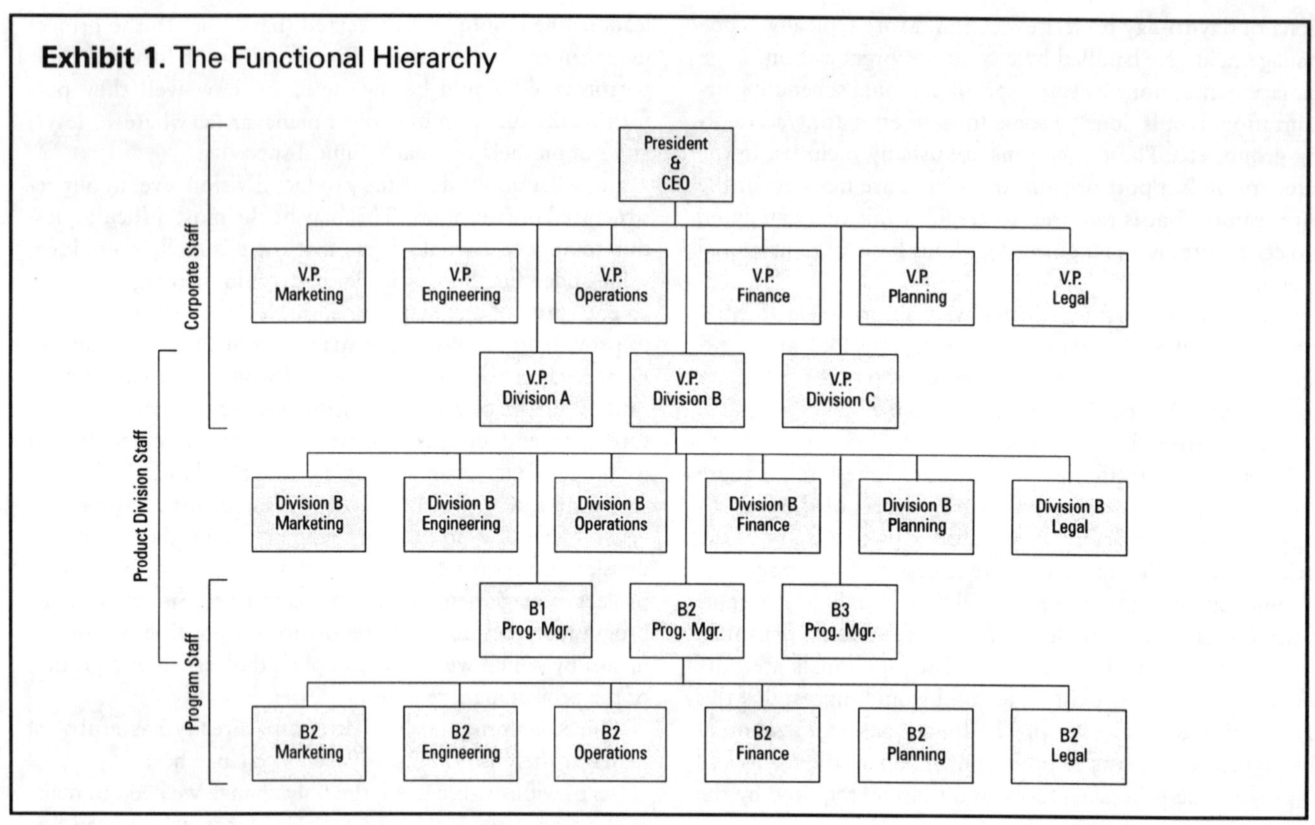

**Exhibit 1.** The Functional Hierarchy

should be from the bottom up, not, as is so often the case, from the top down.

Just as there are many members of a sports team who never take the field, there are many members of our enterprises who will not be on our teams. In sports we have the general manager, the coaching staff, the trainers, equipment managers, etc. The function of this off-field staff is to create and maintain the necessary environment for the on-field team to perform successfully. In business we have the company president and corporate staff, the functional managers, the training staff, etc. Is it unreasonable to believe that the function of the "off-field" team in a business enterprise is to create and maintain the necessary environment for the team to perform successfully? If this is *not* their prime function, what is?

As with professional sports teams, our business teams should be formed far in advance of the game. Even in an all star game the team is brought together to practice for some time before they are expected to perform. Doesn't it seem strange that our teams usually aren't formed until the last possible instant before the game and, in some instances, aren't even completed until the game is in progress. I wonder how many coaches would wait until fourth down before they hired a punter?

Recent research has identified three times in the life of a team when members are likely to be especially open to coaching interventions: the beginning, when a group is just forming; the midpoint, when the group is halfway through the work; and the end, when a piece of work has been finished (Hackman, 1996).

Professional teams conduct preseason training camps. Wouldn't it be a good idea for us to have a pre-project training session? This would provide the opportunity to finalize the composition of the team. It would also provide the environment in which the team could study the play book, clarify the expectations for each player and, participate in developmental exercises to perfect timing and execution.

Like athletic teams, business teams need to learn continually from their actions and to adjust them on an ongoing basis. As a sports team has scrimmages, the business team has dry runs. As a sports team reviews game films, the business team should conduct weekly reviews of team performance. The business team's review of its performance against cost, schedule, and technical goals fulfills the same need as the sports team's review of its statistics. Finally, the sports team's daily practice is, or should be, mirrored in the business team's meetings. Do not make the mistake of thinking that team meetings are the game. The game consists of all of the effort outside of the meeting. Upon completion of the project, the team needs to conduct a post mortem to identify those areas that can be improved to increase the chances of success on the next project.

**Exhibit 2.** Integrated Product Team

**Exhibit 3.** The Strong Matrix Organization

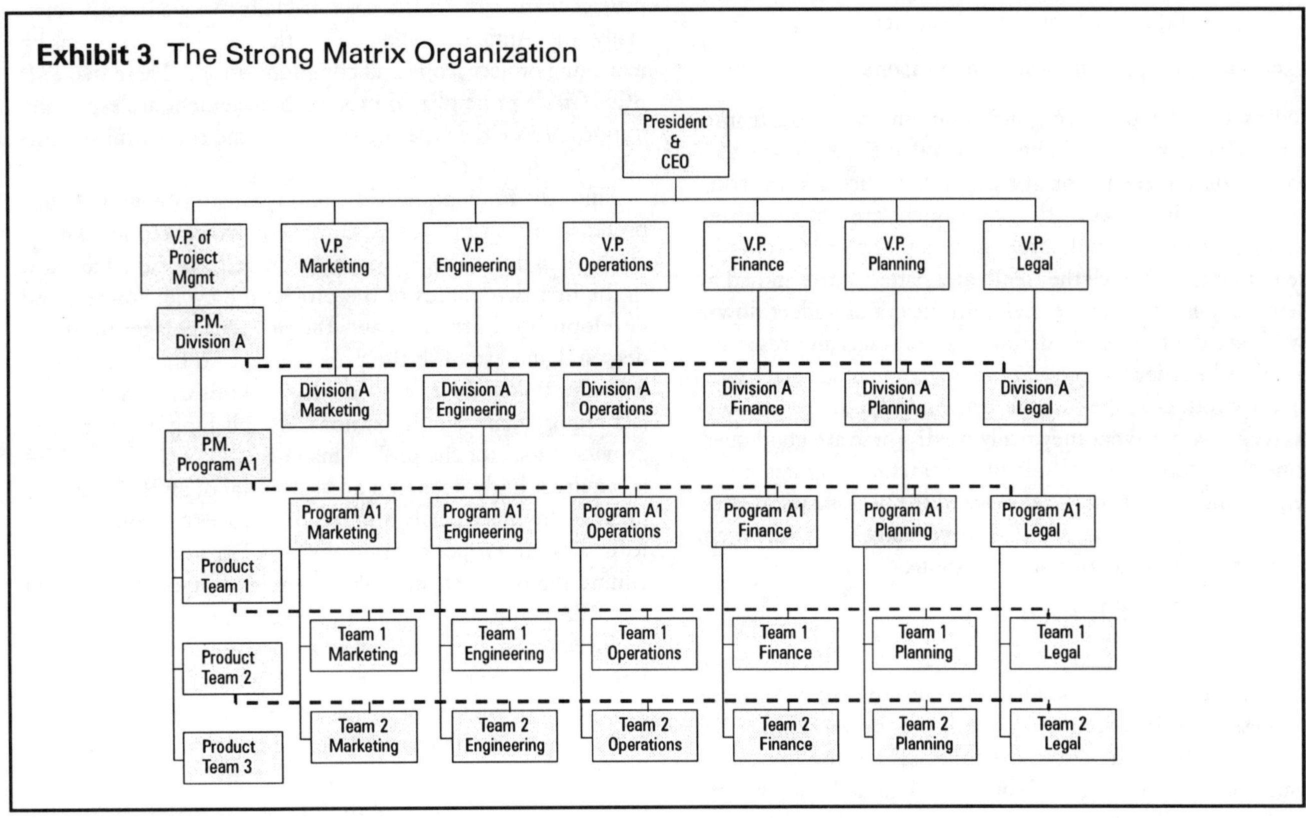


## One Last Thing

While the sports team may not have a one hundred per cent correlation to the business team, it seems clear that we can make substantial improvements by holding more closely to this analogy. By establishing an organization focused on maximizing team performance, staying in training, and never missing an opportunity to practice, we can be a winning team.

Now, if I could just figure out where to get a three piece spandex suit, Nike wingtips, and a one ounce composite briefcase……

# REA's and Claims Against the U.S. Government

David A. Maynard, ITT
Wilbur L. Armstrong, Systems Engineering Internationall, Inc.

## Background

Contractor's claims against the government are as old as the government itself. During the American Revolution, Nathaniel Green, the Quartermaster General wrote: "Business in the civil departments of any army, is like making dictionaries; if any errors are committed, there is the severest criticism and blame; but the merit of the performance passes off with little notice an no honor." Green also noted: "A charge against a quartermaster-general is most like the cry of a mad dog in England. Every one joins in the cry, and lends their assistance to pelt him to death." In the days of the revolution, most claims centered on the supply of food and uniforms. Today they are vastly more complex.

### Disputes often happen—for many reasons

Contractual disputes are quite common and range from a simple Request for Equitable Adjustment (REA) to the ultimate dispute mechanism, the claim. Statistics are not compiled and claims against the government are not submitted through a single appeals process. It is unfortunate statistics are not available, since the trends and patterns determined by their analysis could prove useful. In the era of budget downsizing, are contractors underbidding contracts and resorting to claims in order to recover? Are government agencies writing the contract scope to match the budget, but then allow it to creep towards what they really need? These are good questions that statistical analysis of contractual disputes could help us understand. In the absence of the necessary statistics, empirical data indicates a high percentage of government contracts result in a contractual dispute.

### Request for Equitable Adjustment

In the course of a contract, invoices are routinely presented under the contract terms. Occasionally, the contractor finds it necessary to invoice for items outside contract terms. If a request is submitted "under the contract" but for a price adjustment, it is defined as a Request for Equitable Adjustment (REA). The REA requests a price adjustment in writing and is submitted based on a theory supporting the adjustment. Theories may include, but are not limited to, constructive changes, breach of contract, government errors, or government mistakes.

### Claim

The contracting officer may reject an REA. If this is the case, a claim asserting the contractors right to payment is the next option. Unlike the REA, claims are submitted outside the terms of the contract. Detailed written descriptions of the events leading to the claim and the associated costs are the key elements.

## Intent of the Paper

"Prevention is the best medicine" is tried and true advice for project managers. In the case of claims this advice is especially true. Anticipate and control the possibility of claims by managing project scope and communications. These two *PMBOK Guide* principles of project management are especially important in either the prevention or the successful submittal of a claim or REA.

Since the foundation of a claim is an adjustment or interpretation of contract terms, control of project scope is key to establishing this basis. Project scope is defined and established in the first two phases of the project life cycle; concept and development. In these phases the project manager must understand and establish the project scope so that team members and stakeholders are thoroughly familiar with the project requirements and limitations. Establishing the scope will provide a tool for the project manager to know when a REA is required. Early detection and submittal of an REA can also prevent the more costly and tedious process of submitting a formal claim. Proper documentation of project scope will facilitate the contract officer's understanding of the basis for any REA and lead to a prompt determination.

Effective management of project communication is also important in prevention or successful submittal of claims. The project manager must be aware of the team's activities and proactively manage the scope and implementation of the project. Key to accomplishing this requirement is effective project communication. Both internal and external communications effect the project manager's success.

Internally, the project manager should establish a "control room" where all project communications take place. This room is the focal point of the project and the only place where meetings and project discussions are allowed. It includes charts, graphs, metrics and lists that communicate the discussions and decisions to all project members. If used effectively, this method can prevent project members from deviating from project scope outside the project manager's control and knowledge. It will also document the reasons, work performed and authorizations acquired for use in the REA.

Externally, the project manager should establish a single point of contact for communication with the customer on contractual or statement of work issues. Require that all communication external to the project is routed through this contract manager (perhaps this is also the project manager) so that it can be established if an out of scope requirement is requested. Remember that out of scope requirements can be implied or explicit. This is an effective method for the project manager to defend against unauthorized changes to scope.

## Contractor's Claims

The Federal Acquisition Regulations (FAR) defines a claim as: "... a written demand or written assertion by one of the contracting parties seeking, as a matter of right, the payment of money in a sum certain, the adjustment or interpretation of contract terms, or other relief arising under or relating to the contract." Historically, several different "theories of recovery" have been successfully utilized and are recognized within the body of law governing claims by contractors against the government. Documented below are the most common of those theories.

### Work performed outside the "scope of work" of the contract

Often a contractor will assert that work the government is demanding for a particular contract is "beyond the scope of work" of that contract. Unfortunately, defining the "Scope of work" can be quite difficult. In general, the scope of work can be defined as the work both parties had in mind at the time the contract was negotiated. For example, if the contractor was awarded a contract to modify an existing device, already in the government's inventory, correcting deficiencies in the original device could be considered out of scope. Expansive interpretations of the work to be performed after contract award would normally be considered beyond the current scope of work. Although the government has the right to require additional work to be performed, a "scope fight" should be avoided!

### Government imposed changes

Most changes to the contractor's intended effort are caused by the government's ability to change the work. The Federal Acquisition Regulations (FAR) grants the government's contracting officers the power to change the contracted work at any time—as long as a written order is given. But, changes to the contract are not always handled via documented change orders. A "constructive change" to the contract is caused by either oral or circumstantial actions alter the contract, and without written change orders.

In the case of a change order to the contract, the causes of the contractor's increased scope and costs are not disputed. With constructive changes, the contractor may prepare a Request for Equitable Adjustment (REA) to provide compensation for the additional work. When the contractor has decided upon the preparation of an REA, they have the duty to provide adequate notice to the government of its intention to seek an equitable adjustment.

At all times, while the contract is not breached, the Contractor retains the "duty to proceed with changed work." Both the FAR and the Contracts Dispute Acts (CDA) require the contractor to proceed. The tempting path of simple refusal to accept additional work may result in the government's default termination of the contract. Clearly, for the contractor, keeping the contract "whole" (not refusing the work) and preparing a claim is the preferred approach.

## Commonly Used Recovery Theories

The recovery of any costs by the contractor must be based upon entitlements. There must be a reason the contractor is entitled to recover costs from the government. Briefly described below are several commonly used and well-supported theories. Perhaps the most important facet of developing an REA is the establishment of a "casual connection" between the event and the stated costs. The connection must be "clear and convincing" between the cause and calculated effect.
Defective or impossible specifications

A contractor may recover costs based upon the theory that the government's specifications were defective. This is possible because, when the government prepares a specification, there is an implied warranty that the specification, if followed, will produce an item that is fit for its intended purpose.

There are two principal types of specifications in government contracting—design and performance specifications. While design specifications describe exact details of the desired item, a performance specification describes the desired item's performance. Both may be mixed and combined when used in a single contract.

A defective design specification may cause the contractor to build an item incorrectly. If the contractor incurs costs related to redesign, rework or remanufacture of the item, the theory of defective specifications may be used as the basis to recover these costs.

Defective performance specifications may be simply impossible (or impracticable) to achieve. The government may earnestly want the performance specified, they may have considered the requirements for years, the contractor may have accepted the work, but it still may be impossible!

### Government's Superior Knowledge

If the government knew (or should have known) that the contractor was unknowledgeable about a critical portion of the contract, a recovery claim can also be made. For example, if a contractor were bidding on a contract for a different product than they have traditionally and undocumented requirements are known by contractors already participating in that product area, the government had the duty to identify these undocumented requirements. To not inform the contractor of the unwritten knowledge may dramatically increase their costs of performance.

### Termination for Convenience

The government may terminate a contract when it "is in the government's interest" to do so. If a contractor receives a convenience termination, costs incurred before the termination are recoverable. Additionally, the contractor may also recover a reasonable profit for the work completed. No profit will be recoverable for work not done.

### Schedule Delay

Each party, government and contractor, are responsible for any schedule delays they may cause. The government has three vehicles for contract delay: Stop Work Orders, Suspension of Work, Delay of Work. These FAR clauses permit the contractor to recover costs associated with these delays. The Contractor may face termination if the delay cannot be shown to be "beyond the control and without the fault of negligence" of the contractor. It is important that each time an excusable delay is recognized, the contractor inform the government by written notice requesting the delay, as soon as practical.

### Schedule Acceleration

After a schedule has been properly modified for excusable delays, the government may wish to accelerate the completion of the contract in advance of the calculated completion date. If the government directs the contractor, in writing, of an acceleration order, costs associated with the acceleration are clearly recoverable. It is important to note that a voluntary acceleration in schedule by the contractor does not entitle the contractor for recovery.

### Schedule Disruptions

The government is (of course) permitted to monitor progress, request status updates and verify that the stated requirements of the specification are being met. But, the government also has the duty not to disrupt or hinder the contractor's performance. Types of schedule disruption can include failure to cooperate, unnecessary additional paperwork and repeated and unnecessary inspections.

### Proprietary Data

If the contractor believes the government has wrongfully used a contractor's proprietary data, there are several theories for recovery. The contractor may appeal to the Boards of Contract Appeals. Protest may be filed with the General Accounting Office (GAO). Or, the contractor may sue in Federal Court. However, a contractor may claim recovery for the abuse of data developed at private expense. If it were developed at government expense, the contractor has no rights to the data.

### Inspection and Acceptance

Costs associated with additional, unnecessary or over-zealous government inspection of the contractor's work which force a higher level of quality than specified in the contract may be recoverable. The government is generally limited to the acceptance criteria specified within the contract. Once the goods or services are found to meet the contractual requirements, the government must issue an acceptance certificate.

## Contractor's Claim Cost Estimation

The objective of estimating the claim costs is to arrive at an equitable settlement for the contractor's additional expenses. A detailed examination must be made of the claim's cost estimates to insure they are reasonable, can be allocated, adhere to the terms of the contract, and are according to Cost Accounting Standards (CAS) board.

In a claim made by the contractor, the effort of proving the various entitlements lies with the contractor. It is important that each point made in the Contractor's documentation be based upon actual cost records or realistic estimates of these costs. The requested adjustments must be directly and firmly tied to the stated theories listed above.

### Impact, Delay or Disruption Costs

This type of claim seeks recovery of additional costs the contractor incurred in the development or delivery of the final work product. Essentially, a fair recovery should seek enough funds to replace expenditures of the contractor, caused by the delay only. In other words, the recovery sought is equal to the extra costs incurred by not performing the work at another time. Critical to the support of schedule related claims are historically accurate and detailed project schedules.

### Idle labor and equipment

Equipment or labor may be idled by a delayed start in any particular activity. If it can be shown that delay, acceleration or disruption of the contract schedule (by the government) created costly idle periods in labor or equipment they may be a part of the recovery. While it is doubtful the contractor will have direct evidence of these impacts, there are well-accepted methods of estimating the effects of the schedule perturbation on the rest of the contractor's business. Again, the constant and continual use of detailed project plans will be a great help in establishing the damages caused by government-caused delayed event starts.

### Escalation

If delays by the government have caused escalation in the rates or prices that a contractor had anticipated, these increases may be recoverable.

### Unabsorbed Overhead

Each contractor's rate structure is calculated by the anticipated direct and indirect costs. Indirect costs are those that are impractical to individually track and account for, but are rather put into a pool and charged out to each contract depending upon a measurement of the direct effort involved. These "overhead" pools may be compensated via a claim for idle facilities, work stoppages or inability to use labor effectively due to government fault. By its very nature overhead costs are difficult, or impossible to track with precision. For that reason, the Eichleay formula has been generally accepted.

Along with the use of the Eichleay formula, the following must be established:

- The government caused delay extended the contract period.
- The delay caused a suspension of work that could not be performed.
- The contractor's overhead costs continued during the suspension period.
- It was not reasonable to reduce overhead costs reducing the work force (lay-offs) or cutbacks.
- The unabsorbed overhead could not be absorbed by new work during the same period.
- An additional burden (mark up) on the direct costs will not sufficiently compensate the contractor for the unabsorbed overhead.

### Profit

While there are particular cases where profit may not be recovered, generally it is limited to the percentage of profit the contractor originally bid into the contract. Additional profit, above what was originally anticipated and negotiated may not be claimed.

### Costs of Preparing Claims

If the contractor's entitlement to relief is clear and the claim has arisen during the performance of the contract (not after the completion of the contract), and the claim aids in the future performance of the contract, recovery of professional fees related to the preparation of claims may be recoverable. However, generally the FAR states the costs of attorneys and other professionals are not allowable when they occur in the "prosecution of claims against the government." Sound confusing? It is!

## Claim Planning

### Outsourcing

For larger claims, outsourcing the preparation makes a great deal of sense. The collection of data and substantiation of recovery theories takes a great deal of time, patience and skill. The contractor should think of the claim preparation as another proposal. Costs will be expended to prepare the claim, but monies may well be recovered.

Outsourcing the preparation of a claim reduces the impacts to the contract project team (who are required and by FAR to continue to perform) while insuring a certifiable cost estimate. A number of well-qualified firms exist just for the purpose of helping the contractor through the claim process.

### Document the History

There are no substitutes for a well-documented and detailed contract history. The disciplines all program managers should insure during the normal course of contract performance become critical during claim preparation. Project schedules, contract letters, cost estimates, cost accounting records, customer meeting minutes all become vital to the preparation of a defensible claim.

At the outset of the claim preparation process, a brief history of the contract pointing out the faults that are attributable to the government is essential. The history should read easily and convincingly, and at each point must be supported by documented facts. The facts must be supported by indexed and filed documents.

### Interview the Project Team

Each person that participated in the contract should be interviewed, notes taken and compared to the documented history. Often, these interviews bring to light additional facts that may support or invalidate a theory of recovery. The recollections of the contract team must be consistent with the positions being taken in the claim. Depositions and affidavits may be required from some members of the project team.

### Gather & Copy Documents

All evidence related to the claim should be gathered as soon as possible. Project memos, meeting minutes, organization charts, accounting records, trip reports, notes taken in a meeting, all can form valid evidence and should be collected. Often this becomes a large task and a very large compilation of paper. One technique is to devote an area to the collection and filing of documents important to the claim position.

### Accounting & Legal Assistance

Many just claims have been rejected simply because of poor accounting or legal advice. Remember that the costs detailed in the claim must be certified by the contractor—hire an accountant familiar in government accounting and claim to insure the costing model is accurate and thorough. While the costs of accounting and legal assistance may not be recoverable, they are a very good investment.

### Experts in the field

Often, outside experts can give qualified opinions that are extremely helpful in developing the claim. Or, experts can be used to validate a strong position taken by within the claim. Points or positions that may appear weak in a draft claim are potential areas for soliciting outside expert opinions.

## Writing the Claim

Creating the actual claim documentation itself is a critical area. The claim documentation must be clearly worded, self-contained and explicitly point out the governments errors and the resultant difficulty and costs. This one document will receive a great deal of scrutiny and it must "hold together." While there is no single method for documenting the claim, the thoughts detailed below should be strongly considered.

### Background Information

The narrative must include a background section with enough information that someone totally unfamiliar with the contract or the claim can understand what is at issue. It should be written to an uninformed, but intelligent reader. It is very risky to assume the persons reading the claim will have intimate technical or programmatic knowledge of the contract.

### Causation / Entitlements

This is the heart of the claim. A direct connection must be made between an action or inaction by the government and the resulting increase in contract costs. The majority of the effort in preparing the claim documentation should be spent in insuring that causation is proven.

It is in the creation of an iron-tight causation that claims often fail. Often, when the contractor cannot prove causation to its own satisfaction, the claim is dropped. A valuable practice in the preparation of the causation is to appoint a member of the Project team to be the "devil's advocate." Their task is to question and ask for proof of areas of interest.

### Explanation of Costs

Along with spreadsheets prepared to illustrate the claimed impact to the contractor, separate worksheets demonstrating the Eichleay method (if used) should be prepared. Additionally, any detailed calculation should be supported by independent worksheets. If additional, lengthy financial backup is required, it should be considered for inclusion in an appendix to the claim so as not to distract from its "readability."

Perhaps as important as the numbers is the accompanying narrative that explains the calculations, the source for any estimates, the source and location of historical numbers. The narrative should walk the reader through the calculations in a logical step-wise fashion. Again, the narrative should not assume the reader to be familiar with the in-depth details of the contract or the dispute.

### Legal Precedent

In building a claim, it's often helpful to cite legal precedents. Wherever a citation will help strengthen the contractor's claim, it should be included.

### Cost Certification

The costs identified in claims against the government in excess of $50,000 must be certified. By certification, the Office of Federal Procurement means: "...the claim is made in good faith, that the supporting data are accurate and complete to the best of the contractor's knowledge and belief, that the amount requested accurately reflects the contract adjustment for which the contractor believes the government is liable, and that the certifier is duly authorized to certify the claim on behalf of the contractor."

## Guidance for the Project Manager

### Recognize a potential claim as early as possible

Early recognition of a potential claim is the best tactic a project manager has at his disposal. Management of project scope and communication is a good method for early detection. When detected early, the project manager and the contracting officer have time to resolve the issue and correct the problem prior to its evolution into a full-scale dispute. If this fails, and a dispute results, the early detection allows thorough documentation and capture of cost to be used in claim preparation.

### Avoid emotional involvement

Emotional involvement is counterproductive for the project manager and the entire project team. Honesty, accuracy and objectivity are the key elements required for preparing a claim. If the project manager sets the example in this regard, the resulting atmosphere will only serve to enhance the project team's performance. Claim submittal will not relieve the project from the objectives it has to accomplish. During the entire process, the team must remain focused on the goals they need to make the project successful. When an individual member of the team becomes emotionally involved, isolate them from the claim process if necessary to refocus their attention where it is needed.

### The best claims are supported by the best project level documents

A claim is a written document and is only as good as its backup material. Make sure that project documentation is accurate, up-to-date, organized, and protected. Without project documentation, the claim may prove unsupportable. Control rooms will aid in the documentation of project events and progress. Instill a discipline in the project team, especially team leaders, to protect and organize documentation that is used in the course of the project.

### Duty to Proceed!

Do not stop performing. Contract performance requirements are not suspended with the submission of a claim. Since claims can take years to resolve, the project life could be extended indefinitely if it did not proceed during claims. Also, if the project stops, valuable resources could be lost preventing the project from ultimate success.

## Summary

As long as there are government contracts, there will be claims made by contractors against the government. The practice is as old as the government itself. Contractual disputes range from a Request for Equitable Adjustment (REA) to claims. While an REA is a request for a price adjustment "under the contract," a claim is essentially a suit against the government.

Many of these situations are unfriendly, detract from the essential work at hand and could / should be avoided if at all possible. Advice for the contractor's project manager includes keeping detailed and accurate cost accounting records, establishing and maintaining project records (minutes, plans, control rooms etc) and constant awareness of potential scope growth. The best position for the contractor in either an REA or claim situation is to have well documented plans, costs as well as documented theories that have caused cost increases to occur.

The Bottom Line:

- Contractor's program managers should make every possible effort to recognize a potential REA or Claim situation as early as possible and strive to avoid it!
- Failing the possibility of avoidance, the project manager should remember the words of an attorney, whom both authors have worked with on numerous occasions: "The party with the best documentation wins."

### References

1. Excavation-Construction, Inc., ENG BAC No. 3858, 82-1 BCA ¶ 15,770 at 78,071, reaffirmed 83-1 BCA ¶ 16,293 and 83-1 BCA ¶ 16,338.

2. 41 U.S.C. § 605

TUTE
CHICAGO 1997
PROJECT
MANAGEMENT:
THE NEXT
CENTURY
Design/
Procurement/
Construction

# Managing Decision-Making in a Dynamic Environment

Alexander Laufer, University of Maryland at College Park
Hugh Woodward, The Procter & Gamble Company

## Introduction

Businesses today must operate in a highly dynamic world, characterized by accelerated speed, and uncertainty. In recent years speed has become essential to business to such an extent that many authorities argue that speed is the single most significant basis for competitive advantage in the years ahead. Some of the reasons why speed has become a competitive requirement are: a) dramatic increase in global competition, b) accelerated pace of technological development, and c) both market share and profit margins are increased by being first to the market (Peters 1989).

Uncertainty has been shown to be one of the major factors that influence project performance and determine its ultimate success. This situation is the result of the significant transformation that industry and business have undergone in the past few decades. The unprecedented growth of uncertainty in recent years has resulted from increasing demands for project speed, greater environmental awareness and the resulting greater community impact on decisions that affect quality of life. In short, uncertainty simply reflects the complexities of today's world (Howell et. al. 1993, Mitroff 1988, Turner and Cochrance 1993).

The decision-making process, which has been always the central pillar of the team's effort to construct, maintain, and follow a viable project plan, becomes even more crucial in this dynamic environment.

During the early stages of a project, the frequency and importance of decision-making are very high. Later, the beginning of each new subsequent phase (e.g., definition, execution, close-out) is marked by an additional wave of important decision-making. This paper focuses on the project manager's role in *managing* the process of making these important decisions (as opposed to *making* these decisions) in an ever-present climate of uncertainty (Laufer 1996).

We will present a simple but powerful tool, employed by successful project managers, for managing the decision-making process under these difficult conditions. Following a detailed example and the procedure for using the tool, the benefits of using the tool for managing uncertainty will be discussed.

## Decision Matrix

Decision-making at the beginning of each major phase of the project, can be viewed as a production process for decisions. In manufacturing, production managers ensure that all the elements of production mesh at the right time to deliver a quality finished product. They ensure that the appropriate raw materials are available, that the process is suitable, and that the finished product is acceptable and available when the customer needs it. This is achieved by managing and scheduling the individual elements of production while never losing sight of the end result.

Successful project managers assume a similar role for decision-making during the early stages of each major project phase. They must ensure that decision are made on time, which require that both the information and participants, are identified and available when needed. They also ensure that there is a consensus on the decision-making process and that the decision itself is known to all because it is communicated broadly and on time.

To manage decision-making, successful project managers employ the decision matrix, a simple yet powerful planning, monitoring, and communication tool. It is a one or at the most, two page document in the form of a table, which displays the critical elements required to manage the process. The matrix formalizes the decision-making process so that people know when and how to input.

Employment of this tool is based on two central premises.

1. Most major decisions on a given project require significant interdisciplinary input and involvement.
2. It is possible, and often desirable, to separate the decision definition from decision making. Frequently, the team responsible for defining the decisions will not be the team responsible for making those decisions.

Exhibit 1 presents an example of a decision matrix used in a modification project to improve the production performance of certain large, similar (but not identical) machines in three plants. One of the tasks was to conduct a series of experiments that would demonstrate the validity of the modification scheme. It was expected that once that scope had been successfully demonstrated, each plant would reapply identical scope. This decision matrix was drawn up by members of the project team, led by Ms. Smith, the project manager. The following story, is her description of determine outage timing, the first decision item in the table.

## Determine Outage Timing

The first column in the table, is a description of the decision required. In this case, we needed to determine the timing for the construction outage of the first machine. This decision is a lot narrower in focus than the first draft of the decision, which attempted to determine timing for all the machines. After struggling to complete the matrix we limited our focus to this smaller decision, which greatly simplified collecting the information required to make the decision.

We had two options for the outages, which are identified in column 2. Use of the iterative process had eliminated several other options and narrowed the decision down to these two dates.

The third column provides the rationale for addressing the decision now. Clarifying the reason(s) for making a decision helps determine the timing and priority. We knew that continuity of key staff was critical for the project; another potential issue was getting machine time for upcoming initiative projects that would need the same machine. Highlighting these two issues, in particular, helped rally the decision-makers to make the decision by the required time.

The fourth column highlights the criteria that are important for making the decision. To decide outage timing, we were driven by two conflicting needs. The project was necessary if we were to meet ongoing production needs. On the other hand, assuming our traditional engineering approach, complying with these needs might delay the demonstration of the technology because it would not be completed in time to allow an orderly application at the other plants. By identifying these as the key bases for our decision, along with the staffing issue mentioned earlier, we focused our energy on understanding the risks and limitations of each option as it related to those needs. Our final decision was to modify the engineering approach, taking manageable risks in some areas to meet production timing.

Column 5 lists those who will be involved in making the decision, who will be responsible for leading the process, whose agreement will be needed, and who has the data and should participate. The plan project leader (Ms. Rose) led the effort to resolve this issue. She had the most data regarding staffing and specific plant production needs and the greatest access to the affected people in the plant. This highlights an important point—the responsibility for leading a decision does not rest solely with the project manager. Rather, those with the data and knowledge may be the most appropriate persons to work the process to conclusion.

Timing (column 6) is a critical element, since one of the project manager's key roles is to ensure a timely decision. The timing for this decision related directly back to the project schedule that indicated we needed to begin engineering definition four months in advance of the outage.

Finally, the comments column is often used to describe preparatory tasks that must be accomplished prior to making the decision. We used this matrix to follow up on the status of all those activities. This particular comment, concerning plant input on available resources, highlights information we felt was critical to making the decision

## Decision Matrix Procedure

The following essential steps, comprise the procedure for using the decision matrix tool to manage decision-making.

1. The project manager is responsible for initiating, developing, reviewing, updating, and communicating the matrix. In particular, he/she leads the review discussion of the matrix at all project meetings.
2. The team, led by the project manager, rather quickly prepares the first draft of the Decision Matrix. The team refers to it as a tentative plan that is continuously modified. Its accuracy improves as the team learns the project situation first-hand, collects more information, and starts making decisions.
3. The matrix is a dynamic document. Periodically—weekly or monthly, depending on project pace—the project manager and his/her team delete implemented decisions and add new ones, add details to the near-term decisions, and ensure that the imminent decisions are on track. Once decisions are completed, the selected choices are recorded. Maintaining the record of accepted decisions, ensures that they are not reopened unless justified by new significant data.
4. The matrix typically contains 5-15 short-term decision items for the coming 1-3 months. A few additional important mid-term decision items for the following 3-6 months are also presented but without detailed information.
5. The success of the decision matrix is due largely to its simplicity, clarity, and brevity. One should never allow a decision matrix document to be longer than two pages.
6. In the Participants column, the (A) role is specified only when the decision-making team requires an explicit approval (Approve: "the person who must sign off or veto a decision before it is implemented"). The (R) role is always specified (Responsible: "the person

who takes .the initiative for the particular decision item, and is accountable if nothing happens in the decision item"). More specific roles (e. g., Consult: "must be consulted before the decision is made"), may be assigned later by the decision-making team.

In successful teams, there is an attempt to make most decisions by consensus. Group consensus is often thought to be synonymous with unanimity. It is not. In a consensus, the group arrives at "substantial" agreement. Consensus decisions are based on a process where *all* participants contribute thoughts and express their feelings about an issue. The selected option, which is rarely everyone's first choice, nevertheless has each person's understanding and support (the hallmark of a team player). The atmosphere of "keep on moving," which dominates the deliberations of these teams and the "smallest team" rule they typically adopt (the smallest team necessary for a quality decision), help to ensure a fast consensus decision. Under extreme time pressure, however, decisions are often made by the project manager alone or by a very small subset of the team.

## Major Benefits of the Decision Matrix

Project managers who use the decision matrix tool enjoy the following major benefits:

- It provides the necessary conditions for decision *quality* by separating decision definition from decision-making. This separation facilitates problem isolation, explicit identification of assumptions, strategic thinking, efficient involvement of multiple stakeholders, early information collection and generation of alternatives, the addressing of interconnected decisions, and improved communication.
- It helps the project manager *reduce uncertainty*. By constantly looking several months ahead for short-term and mid-term decisions, the tool helps identify the missing information which can still be collected at this early stage without delaying the decision. Skillful project managers will actually use the matrix to find the right balance between collecting more information and making timely decisions (Butler 1991).
- It instills the required *sense of urgency*, right from the beginning and throughout project life. This tool in today's projects, where time for contemplation and deliberation is limited, helps the team maintain a rapid decision-making process.
- It ensures that decisions are prioritized. This process helps the team decide which, and in what *order*, decisions require attention; as well as when decisions should be made and how much time should be devoted to each. It also helps in identifying those decisions that one team can ignore because another team is responsible for making them.
- It serves as a useful "to-do" list of high *priority* items for the project manager and his/her team. It ensures that the team first focuses on making timely decisions early in the life of the project. Other demands will have to compete for whatever time is available after decisions are addressed. It also ensures that early in the project, decisions rather than project tasks (similar to those presented in the project schedule) will receive most of the team's limited available time.
- It helps to determine the best decision *timing* in another related way. Due to the minimal level of detail presented in the decision matrix, the team can easily see the trees as well as the forest. The decision matrix helps ensure that decision timing is neither premature nor too late.
- It helps clarify the decision-making *roles*, inside and outside the project team.
- It is communicated to other related parties as well (upper management, customer, functional managers), motivating everyone to contribute and *align* to the process during the early formative stages.

## Summary

In the command-and-control hierarchical model of the past, decision processes were clear to everyone. In today's chaotic world, where temporary organizational structures—projects—are the norm and project managers operate in an environment clouded with uncertainty, systematic and explicit management of decision-making is a must. The decision matrix provides a simple yet powerful means for managing decision-making because it 1) instills the required sense of urgency while providing the necessary conditions for decision quality, and 2) helps clarify the decision-making roles, aligns all the parties, determines the best decision timing and ensures that decisions are prioritized, and 3) reduces uncertainty. It is this last area that the decision matrix makes a crucial contribution to project teams operating in our turbulent era.

### References

Butler, R., 1991, *Designing Organizations: Decision-Making Perspective,* Routledge, London.

Howell, G., Laufer, A., and Ballard, G., 1993, "Uncertainty and Project Objectives," *The Project Appraisal,* 8, 37-43.

**Exhibit 1.** Decision Matrix

| Decision | Options | Why Critical | Basis for Decision | Participants | Timing | Comments |
|---|---|---|---|---|---|---|
| Determine outage timing | • March-April, 1995<br>• May - June, 1995 | • Need to develop staffing plans<br>• Integration with other initiatives | • Staffing to support<br>• Production needs<br>• Maximize reapplication of demonstration | Rose (R)<br>Smith (A)<br>Janis<br>Miles | 11/15/94 | Awaiting plant input on available resources |
| Select machines for demonstration | • Machines A & C<br>• Machines E & F | Need to charter technical and start-up teams | • Speed of demonstration<br>• Plant disruption<br>• Machine readiness<br>• Technical complexity | Smith (R)<br>Kraft<br>Harding<br>Bennis<br>Hillman<br>Miles<br>Torbert | 12/15/95 | Assuming product reliability can be maintained or improved with any option |
| Determine long-delivery equipment* | • Wrapper<br>• Log saw | Need to order by 2/95 | • Project schedule<br>• Project risk<br>• Standardization | Smith (R)<br>Harding<br>Miles<br>Oldham<br>Thomas<br>Welch | 1/95 | Need to expedite the revised estimate |
| Future Decisions<br>• Procurement strategy<br>• Determine maintenance criteria | | | | | | |

10/5/94 * Change since last meeting R -- Responsible A -- Approve

Laufer, A., 1996, Simultaneous Management: Managing Projects in a Dynamic Environment, *AMACOM*, American Management Association, New York.

Mitroff, I.I., 1988, *Break-Away Thinking,* Wiley, New York .

Peters, T., 1989, "Drucker, Ohmae, Porter & Peters," Special Report No. 1202, *The Economist,* p. 70.

Turner, J. R., and Cochrance, R. A., 1993, "Goals-and-methods matrix: coping with projects with ill defined goals and/or methods of achieving them," *International Journal of Project Management,* 11 93-102

# Bridge to New Beginnings

Jhan Schmitz, New Airport Projects Coordination Office, Hong Kong

*"The qualities of the people of a city are so often revealed by the things they choose to build around them. There could be no better symbol of the boldness, the vision, and the energy of the people of Hong Kong than the Tsing Ma Bridge."* From a speech by Baroness Thatcher at the completion ceremony for the Lantau Link, 27 April 1997.

## Introduction

The Lantau Link represents the centerpiece of the new 34-kilometer transport corridor constructed as part of Hong Kong's $20-billion airport core program (ACP). The opening of the Lantau Link in mid-1997 coincides with the transition to new beginnings in Hong Kong, including the transfer of sovereignty from Britain to the Peoples Republic of China (PRC), and the start of a new era in project management building on the success of the ACP.

The Hong Kong Special Administrative Region of the PRC encompasses a land area of 1,092 square kilometers, with developed lands constituting less than 100 square kilometers. The region includes 235 islands, of which Lantau Island is the largest, significantly exceeding Hong Kong Island in size. While the urban centers of Hong Kong Island, Kowloon and the New Territories have a population of approximately 6.3 million, Lantau Island has recently had a population of only 20,000 residents, due primarily to the fact that access has been limited to sea ferry services. A region-wide infrastructure development strategy approved by Hong Kong government in 1989 focused the direction of future development to Lantau Island. This strategy called for construction of a new international airport at Chek Lap Kok off the north coast of Lantau Island, a new town to house 260,000 residents adjacent to the new airport, and a transport corridor connecting the urban and commercial areas of Hong Kong with the new airport. The key element of this transport corridor is a fixed link of bridges and viaducts allowing expressway and rail access to Lantau Island.

The Lantau Link is one of the projects of the Hong Kong Airport Core Programme (ACP), which represents the "core" scope of the original development strategy. The magnitude and complexity of the ACP have been unprecedented in Hong Kong. Indeed, the ACP is one of the most extensive transportation/infrastructure developments undertaken in the late 20th century. The ACP (see Exhibit 1) comprises 10 inter-related projects (over 200 total contracts) being performed by four separate sponsors. Each of these projects alone, including the Lantau Link, represented a large and complex development, which had to be managed individually and in concert to meet the prime objective of completion within time, budget and political constraints.

The Lantau Link consists of the Tsing Ma suspension bridge crossing the Ma Wan Channel between Tsing Yi and Ma Wan Islands; multi-span viaducts crossing Ma Wan Island; and the Kap Shui Mun cable-stayed bridge crossing the Kap Shui Mun Channel between Ma Wan and Lantau Islands. The bridges and viaducts of the Lantau Link each include six lanes for expressway traffic on an open upper deck structure, and two rail tracks together with two emergency road lanes on a sheltered lower deck arrangement. The Tsing Ma Bridge is the world's longest and largest suspension bridge carrying both vehicular and railway traffic. It is larger than San Francisco's Golden Gate Bridge, and is second in length only to the Humber Bridge in Britain.

The Lantau Link project was completed on time and well below budget. Construction of the Lantau Link bridges started in May 1992, with a 60-month completion schedule. With completion of the Lantau Link in April 1997 and commencement of traffic operations in May 1997, this completion schedule was successfully achieved. The original total budget for the project was $2.19 billion versus the current forecast at completion of $1.71 billion, reflecting substantial cost savings.

This paper reviews the history and physical parameters of the Lantau Link project, focusing on the Tsing Ma Bridge, and discusses the project management methods introduced in Hong Kong for the ACP as applied to the project, highlighting the management of changes and claims.

## History

The conceptual beginnings of the Lantau Link date back to at least the early 1970s. From studies undertaken in the period 1973-1975, it was concluded that Chek Lap Kok potentially offered the best site for a new airport and would be compatible with other developments proposed for Lantau Island. In 1976, a Lantau Bridge Steering Committee was formed to investigate a transport link to Lantau Island and the proposed new airport. A number of methods of providing the link, including bridges, bored tunnels, and immersed

**Exhibit 1.** Hong Kong Airport Core Programme (ACP) Projects

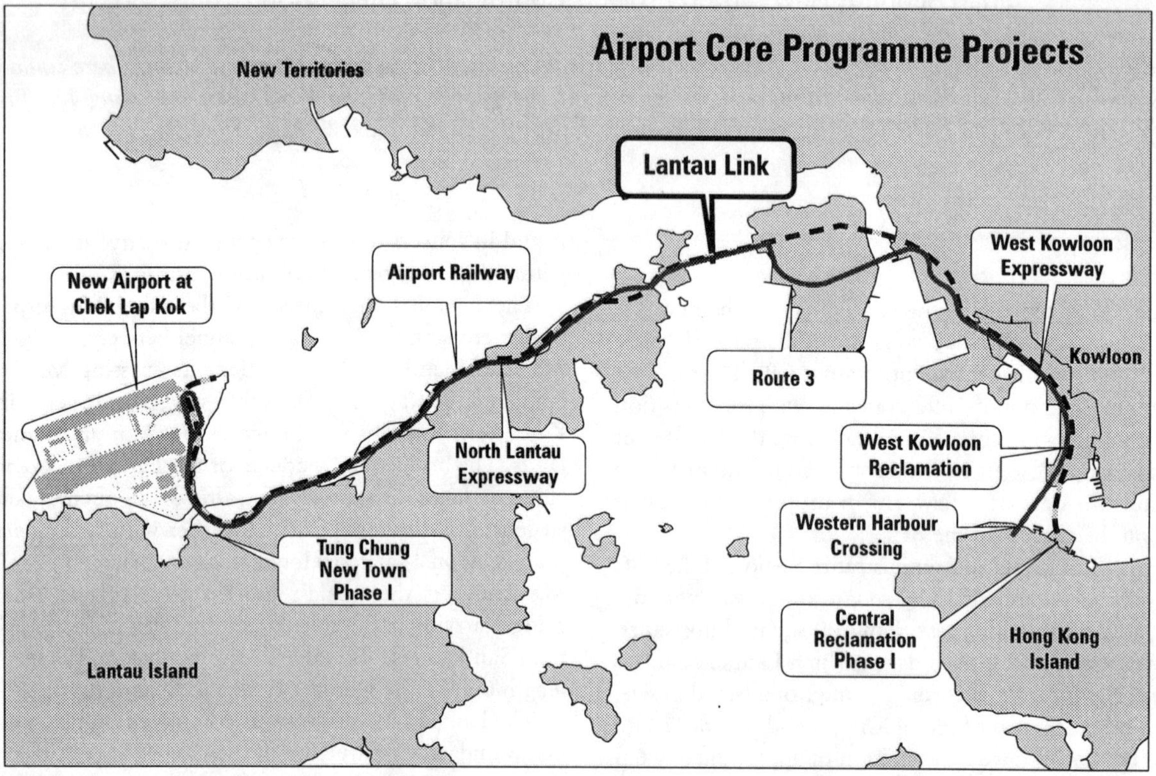

tube tunnels were reviewed. Based on extensive site investigations, it was concluded that suspension and/or cable-stayed bridge construction was the best solution to satisfy various design and operational requirements at an acceptable economic cost.

On the basis of these studies, the government appointed consultants in 1977 to undertake a feasibility study for a bridge-based link. Following feasibility approval in 1978, a pilot airport concept study was undertaken in 1979-1980 to prepare a preliminary master plan, construction schedule and project cost estimate. An initial airport master plan was developed starting in 1981 in parallel with studies encompassing selected infrastructure, including preliminary design of the Lantau Link bridges. However, in 1983, at the point where commitment was necessary for work to proceed, the project was put on hold due to recessionary economic conditions in Hong Kong.

The project planning cycle did not resume until commencement of the Port and Airport Development Strategy (PADS) study sponsored by Hong Kong Government in 1987. PADS, which was approved in 1989, formally called for development of a new airport at Chek Lap Kok as well as a five-fold expansion of Hong Kong's container port, already the world's busiest, with extensive transport infrastructure including the Lantau Link to connect the new port facilities and airport with urban and industrial areas. Throughout the PADS study period, consultations proceeded between the British, Chinese, and PRC governments on issues related to the scope and financing of the proposed undertaking. Agreement was ultimately reached in September 1991, and a Memorandum of Understanding was signed by the governments allowing the ACP to proceed.

The Lantau Link portion of the ACP baseline plan as developed and implemented consisted of 14 contract packages, including the Tsing Ma Bridge and Kap Shui Mun Bridge; rail movement joints and track-form bearings contracts for the bridges; earthworks and expressway interchange works; electrical and mechanical, traffic surveillance and control, toll collection, and lighting systems contracts; and administration building and toll plaza contracts.

Final design of the Tsing Ma Bridge was carried out by consultants to Hong Kong government on a fast-track basis starting in August 1990, and pre-qualification submissions for the Tsing Ma Bridge construction contract were solicited in November 1990. Tenders were invited in July 1991, and bid proposals were received in December 1991. The Tsing

**Exhibit 2.** Lantau Link—Tsing Ma Bridge Features

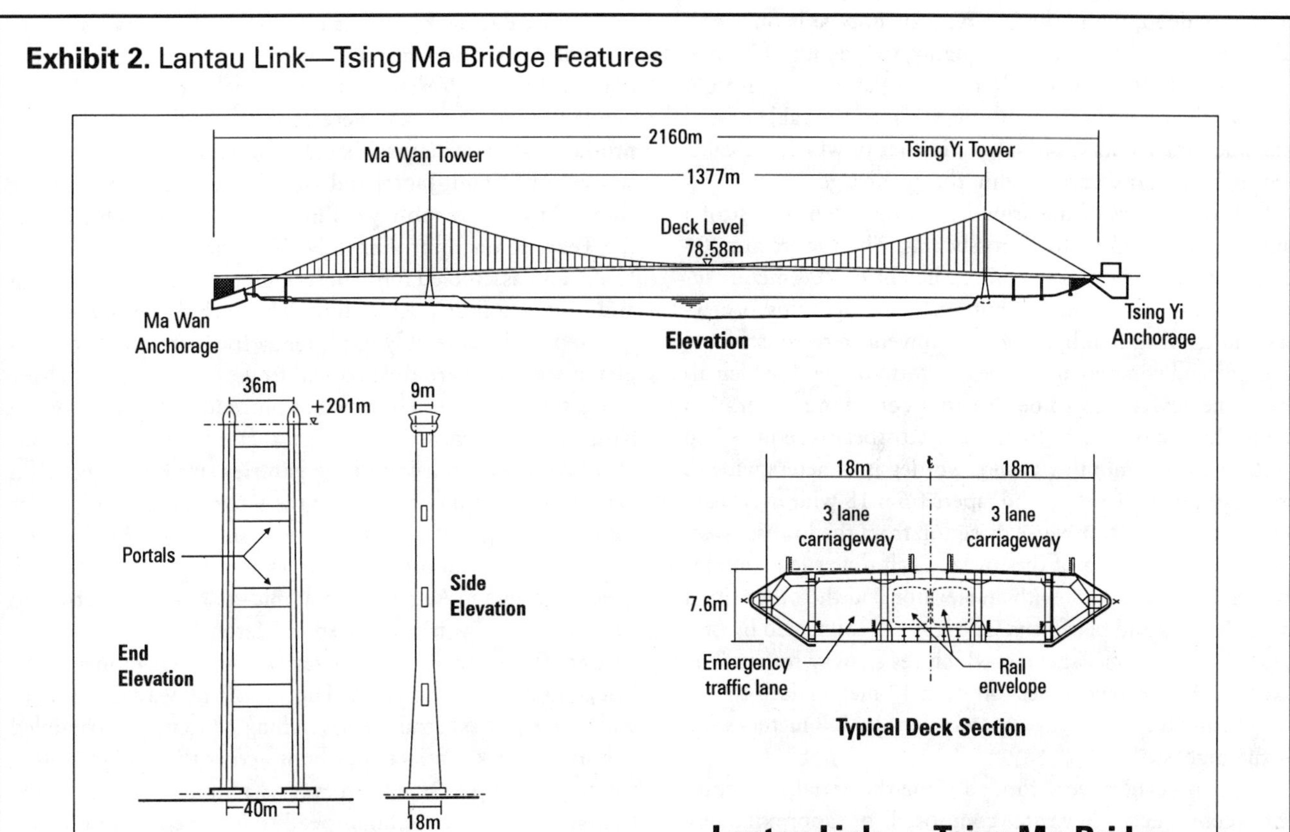


Ma Bridge contract was awarded on 18 May 1992, with contractor site operations commencing the following week. In that the Lantau Link was to provide access to Lantau Island and support operation of the new airport, originally targeted to open by 30 June 1997, the 60-month contract duration was considered a primary critical path for the ACP. While airport opening was subsequently delayed, the 30 June 1997 target remained fixed for the ACP transport corridor. In addition to the tight schedule, the fixed-price contract award value for the Tsing Ma Bridge exceeded the original baseline budget, requiring an initial allocation from contingency. These concerns mandated close co-ordination and strict adherence to the program/project controls set forth for the ACP.

## Physical Parameters

The Tsing Ma Bridge is a double-deck, road-rail suspension bridge with a main span of 1,377 meters and a total length of 2,160 meters. It spans the Ma Wan Channel between the islands of Tsing Yi and Ma Wan, which provides the main navigation channel for ocean-going ships between Hong Kong's Western Harbor and the Pearl River estuary and ports upstream. Exhibit 2 displays major features of the bridge.

The Tsing Ma Bridge was designed in accordance with Hong Kong Transport Department standards for urban expressways and Civil Engineering structural design standards, which had to be modified as necessary to reflect specific roadway, railway and wind loading criteria for the suspension bridge and its unique location. Modified specifications included criteria for coexistent lane loading on the upper and bottom decks as well as local wind speed design criteria. Tropical storms and typhoons often sweep the Ma Wan Channel, and the Tsing Ma Bridge was designed to operate with maximum wind speed gusts of 160 to 180 kilometers per hour. Other criteria included protection against the impact forces resulting from the collision of ships.

The principal foundations of the bridge are the massive gravity anchorages for the cables, and the tower piers. The two anchorages are massive concrete structures, which are integral with the deck abutments, resisting safely a maximum pull of 50,000 tons from each of the two suspension cables. Each anchorage is in the shape of a concrete box cast into an excavation in rock. The Tsing Yi the anchorage is largely below ground in a 290,000 cubic meter rock excavation some

50 meters deep, while the Ma Wan anchorage is only partially buried due to better rock quality, to a depth of 20 meters. At the front of each anchorage is a slanted wall at right angles to the cable direction, through which the cable passes. Each anchorage contains a splay chamber in which the cable is spread out and secured within the anchorage.

The two towers of the Tsing Ma Bridge each consist of a pair of legs, joined by four crossbeams. The towers are 201 meters high, rising to a maximum height of 206 meters inclusive of the tower saddles, but excluding lightning protectors and navigational lighting. The towers were constructed of reinforced concrete using the slip form method, which allowed the tower legs to be cast in a continuous operation lasting three months; casting of the crossbeams required an additional three months. Each tower leg is 6 meters wide in the longitudinal direction and tapers from 18 wide at its base to 9 meters in the transverse direction from the lowest crossbeam level to the top of the tower. Each tower leg contains two vertical shafts; one with an elevator and the other fitted out with stairs and platforms. The legs are connected by prestressed concrete crossbeams, which resist sway forces. The crossbeams vary in cross-section from 12 meters deep by 4.2 meters wide for lowest, to 7 meters deep by 2.8 meters wide for the highest.

The main cables were formed using the aerial wire spinning technique. They are composed of approximately 160,000 kilometers of parallel 5.38-millimeter galvanized steel wires. Each of the two main cables has an overall diameter of approximately 1.1 meters, containing over 35,000 individual wires, and weighs over 13,000 tons. The spinning operation was completed during a 9-month period, between July 1994 and April 1995. After the cables had been spun, they were compacted with hydraulic rams and strapped in place with steel cable bands. At each band location, suspender cables were then installed to receive the suspended deck sections. The suspender cables consist of 76-millimeter-diameter wire wrapped over grooves in the cable bands clamped onto the main cables. After passing through guides, the suspender cables were attached to the deck using cast steel sockets. There are four suspender cables at each of the 190 cable band locations.

Saddles are required to support each of the main cables wherever they change direction. In addition to saddles at the top of each main tower leg (four total) which take the load from the main cables bending over them, a pair of saddles was required in each anchorage, where the cable changes direction and splays into 97 strands for attachment to the anchorage wall. The largest saddles are the main tower saddles, measuring 13 meters long by 4 meters wide and 6 meters deep, and weighing 500 tons.

The Tsing Ma Bridge deck must be stable at typhoon-speed winds, requiring both high strength and a low drag factor. The bridge deck sections use double-deck box construction with truss stiffening, and aerodynamically designed ventilation slots and V-shaped stainless steel sheathing. The suspended deck sections were constructed of high-grade pre-fabricated structural steel components from supply sources in Britain, Japan and Dubai. The components were shipped to an assembly yard in Shatian, China which is on the Pearl River approximately 80 kilometers from Hong Kong, and assembled into 44 deck units each 36 meters long and weighing nearly 1,000 tons. The deck sections were fully fitted in the assembly yard, ready for erection. The completed sections were then barged to the project site in Hong Kong, two at a time. The erection procedure was to moor the barge directly beneath the bridge, then lift the deck sections into final position using lifting gantries straddling the main bridge cables, and finally attach the sections to the suspender cables running vertically from the main cables. Bolting and welding were then used to connect adjoining deck sections. Erection began in August 1995 at mid-span, working towards the towers, and was completed in March 1996.

The Tsing Ma Bridge carries two rail tracks inside the bridge lower deck structure. The airport railway trains, consisting of eight-axle train sets weighing 17 tons, are scheduled to run at 135 kilometers per hour across the bridge, with a frequency of up to one train every 3 minutes. To reduce the noise emitted by these high-speed trains, the rail base-plates are padded, and supporting beams are seated on rubber bearings. A necessary feature of any bridge is its expansion joints. Braking or acceleration forces result in one end of the bridge moving in relation to the other, and changes in temperature cause the bridge to expand and contract. To adjust for these movements, rail movement joints, the largest of their kind in the world, were installed on the Tsing Ma Bridge which can accommodate a movement of 1.1 meters either side of its mean position (total movement range of 2.2 meters).

## Program/Project Organization

Overall program management of the ACP, including the Lantau Link, was under the auspices of the New Airport Projects Coordination Office, an integrated team of project managers from Bechtel and Hong Kong Government. The project sponsor for the Lantau Link project, encompassing all 14 contracts within the project area including the Tsing Ma Bridge, was the Hong Kong Government (Highways Department). The Highways Department established a project office dedicated to the Lantau Link project, and assigned a project manager and project technical and administrative staff. The project office also included site staff from the Engineer (Mott MacDonald Hong Kong Ltd.) and construction management consultant (Sir William Halcrow and Partners Ltd.).

The contractor for the Tsing Ma Bridge was the Anglo Japanese Construction Joint Venture, consisting of Trafalgar House (Asia) Ltd. (now part of the Kvaerner Group of Norway), Costain Civil Engineering Ltd., and Mitsui and Company Ltd. The primary subcontractor for the superstructure works, which represented approximately 60 percent of the total works, was a joint venture consisting of Cleveland Structural Engineering Ltd. and Mitsui Engineering and Shipbuilding Company Ltd. The work force on the Tsing Ma Bridge totalled approximately 1,800 workers at the peak of construction in 1994. They included workers from Hong Kong and China, as well as Australia, Britain, Japan, Nepal, New Zealand, the Philippines and the United States.

## Project Management Approach—Contract Management and Claims Resolution

As described by the author in previous Project Management Institute and International Project Management Association Proceedings, a comprehensive integrated program/project control approach and system were devised and implemented for the ACP. Key elements of this approach included advanced contract and contingency management methods.

Regardless of the form of contract, a construction contract will seldom be completed exactly as it was envisaged when bid. This applies to ACP construction contracts, especially in view of their complex nature and tight design/construction schedules and interfaces, requiring enhanced visibility and control. The decision to use a fixed-price form of contract rather than the existing standard quantity re-measurement model, and to significantly revise the existing general conditions of contract for the ACP was made at an early stage, in 1990-1991. The primary objectives in revising the general conditions were to strengthen the government's contractual position in a multi-project program context; ensure contractor participation in the overall integrated project control system; encourage early identification and resolution of conflicts, changes and claims; and provide government with additional powers to mitigate delays, including the ordering of acceleration.

In line with Hong Kong government's commitment to complete and open the ACP transport corridor prior to 30 June 1997 within budget and a minimum of contingent liability, it was ACP policy that the events giving rise to claims, and claims notifications, were to be addressed as early as possible so as to identify those that might be valid and report them to NAPCO, which monitored their likely cost and schedule impact on the overall ACP. In the case of project delays, this allowed alternative actions to be considered promptly. The philosophy of claims settlement for ACP projects was that protracted delays in settling claims are not acceptable, may have a schedule impact on the subject contract or interfacing contracts, and should be avoided or resolved by a proactive approach. To this end, claims were to be discussed regularly between the Engineer and the contractor, and the contractor was encouraged to submit his claims as early as possible in accordance with his obligations under the contract. Where a claim was deemed likely to become a dispute, and where the progress of dispute resolution might impact achievement of schedule target dates or have significant adverse consequences to the ACP, or early settlement was for whatever reasons commercially desirable, then alternative approaches to resolution were to be considered.

Specific procedures were established to deal with the evaluation, assessment, and settlement of claims, and to create an integrated claims monitoring system to ensure that current information would be available to the project sponsor and the program manager (NAPCO).

These procedures require that, upon receipt of a contractor's notice of claim, an initial evaluation be made by the Engineer to establish the best estimate of the cost and schedule implications from the available information. Claims, which are deemed by the Engineer to have no entitlement on the part of the contractor, are rejected and returned. However, such claims continue to be classified as active until withdrawn by the contractor, or until further justification is put forward which satisfies the Engineer that the claim is valid. The claim estimate is revised, as further details become available. It is the responsibility of the contractor to submit full and substantiated details of the claim to permit a decision to be taken on the merits of the claim. If the contractor fails to notify within a specified period of time, usually 28 calendar days, his claim may become invalid, via the "time barring" provisions of the contract. If the event spawning the claim is continuing or the contractor is otherwise justifiably unable to supply details, "time barring" may be waived, as long as the contractor re-notifies the claim at specific intervals.

To assist in the assessment of more difficult claims, provision was made for the establishment of claims advisory panels covering government ACP contracts. Such panels are normally convened in circumstances where an unsettled claim adversely impacts project cost and/or schedule, where there is an accumulation of unsettled claims, and/or when circumstances are such that an extra-contractual commercial settlement may be possible. The panel is chaired by an officer from the project office, and includes representatives from the project sponsor, the Engineer and NAPCO. The claims advisory panel sets and agrees settlement strategy and financial limits to be adopted in discussions with the contractor, subject to approval by the government's finance branch.

While settlement of claims is normally made in accordance with the conditions of contract, there are occasions where it is in the best interests of all parties to "wrap up" claims by way of extra-contractual commercial settlements. This pragmatic approach has been actively encouraged for the ACP, in that it helps speed up the claims settlement process and achieves management benefits. The objective of such negotiations is to achieve identifiable cost or schedule benefits even if what is given in return exceeds the project sponsor's strict contractual interpretation. The primary benefits accruing to government include, of course, an early resolution of claims, often a group of individual claims wrapped into the settlement package, certainty of contingent liability, and staff and legal cost savings.

If after the full assessment has been made there is no agreement forthcoming from the contractor, under the terms of the contract, a final decision will be issued to the contractor. After reaching a final decision should there still be a disagreement between the parties, then either party, contractor or project sponsor, can elect to take the claim to dispute. All government ACP contracts have a three-level dispute resolution procedure - mediation, adjudication, and arbitration. In mediation, which is a mandatory step for dispute resolution, the parties attempt to reach an agreement with the mediator's assistance. If no agreement is reached, the next step, if requested by one of the parties, is adjudication. Adjudication is binding on all parties until the end of the construction period, following issuance of a certificate of substantial completion. If any of the parties still disagree with the adjudication, the matter may be referred to arbitration on completion of construction for final resolution. The ruling of the arbitrator is binding on all parties.

## Claims and Contingency Experience

On the Tsing Ma Bridge contract, the contractor notified more than 370 claims, primarily related to substructure and superstructure. As at June 1997, over 250 of these claims had been resolved or rejected. Several unresolved claims resulted in disputes, and the contractor lodged a total of 15 disputes during the contract period. To date, 10 of these disputes have been resolved before the mediation stage, and an additional three have been resolved through mediation. Two major disputes remain, of which one, involving the tower saddles, is likely to be included in an extra-contractual commercial settlement. The one remaining contentious dispute relates to the concrete mix design specification for the bridge towers, which the contractor alleged was impossible to meet. While the Engineer subsequently accepted a modified mix design, interim delays resulted from the contractor's protracted attempts to meet the original specification. The contractor claimed for additional costs incurred to recover schedule. This claim has proceeded through both mediation and adjudication, and the contractor has requested arbitration.

The original total budget for the Lantau Link project was $2.19 billion versus the current forecast at completion of $1.71 billion (inclusive of all actual and pending claims and changes), reflecting cost savings of some $480 million and a budget reduction of over 20 percent. These cost savings are net of substantial tender price savings due to a very competitive construction market, alternative design proposal savings and excess contingencies, as well as additional costs related to design development, end-user requirements and variations and claims settlements. The total project forecast at completion of $1.71 billion includes $1.52 billion for construction, with the remainder related to lands resumption (right of way), design, site supervision and other cost items. The construction expenditure grew by a net 6.7 percent overall for the Lantau Link from original construction contract award values, well within contingency provisions.

In the specific case of the Tsing Ma Bridge contact, the forecast at completion is in the range of $959 million versus the original 1992 baseline budget of $1.02 billion (inclusive of allocated contingencies). The contract was tendered at $916 million, and claims, variations and other changes over the contract duration, including both executed changes and assessed values for unresolved changes and claims (some of which are deductive in nature), therefore total some $43 million, resulting in the forecast at completion of $959 million, or a 4.7 percent cost growth from the original value

## Conclusion

The massive and complex Lantau Link project was completed successfully on a tight schedule with a mandatory delivery date, with substantial cost savings and contingent liability well below original risk expectations. Successful project execution has been the result of dedicated efforts on the part of the project team, and the implementation of advanced project management methods, particularly streamlined contract and claims management. The methods so successfully adopted for the ACP are now being deployed for the overall public works program in Hong Kong, and applied to new mega-project endeavors, as Hong Kong moves into a new era of development - and project management.

### References


Chow, C.K. 1991. *Engineering Development in Hong Kong*, Hong Kong Engineer, pages 40-41. July 1991.

Hong Kong Government Information Services Department. 1991. *Hong Kong's Port and Airport Development Strategy*. Hong Kong Government. October 1991.

Structural Engineering International. 1995. Tsing Ma Bridge, Hong Kong. SEI Volume 5, Number 3, pages 138-140. August 1995.

Schmitz, Jhan. 1995. *Communicating Constraints: Schedule Baseline and Recovery Measures on the Hong Kong Airport Projects.*

# Construction Project Preplanning Delays

Dr. Janet K. Yates, San Jose University, CA.
Dr. Adel K. Eskander, P.E., U.S. General Services Administration.

## Introduction

This research is a continuation of an ongoing research project that is summarized in several articles written by Dr. Janet K. Yates et al (Yates, and Rahbar 1990, D3.1-3.9; Yates and Rahbar 1991; Yates, Rahbar, and Spencer 1991; Yates 1992; Yates 1993; Yates and Aoude 1995a; Yates and Aoude 1995b; Yates and Aoude 1995c, 495-593; Yates and Audi 1996a, Yates and Audi 1996b). During 1991-1992, "A Knowledge Engineering System for Inquiry-Feedback Project Management" was developed to address the deficiencies of existing control systems and the Project Management Knowledge Engineering System (PMKES) was later developed to model the construction environment functions, with technical variables dealing with schedule and cost control. This study resulted in the establishment of a specific list of technical causes of construction delays, indicators of delays, and delay reduction measures (Yantes and Rahbar 1991; Yates and Audi 1996).

As a result of the original study a second phase called the Delay Analysis System (DAS), in 1994 the DAS was renamed the Construction Delay Analysis System (CDAS), this phase was performed to gather data on delays related to specific parameters such as type of project, type of firm, type of contract, contract value, and project location. The research addressed construction delays, and a computer system that helps predict and reduce delays and their effects was developed.

The CDAS research provides knowledge databases on construction delays based on knowledge obtained from construction professionals locally and internationally. The data collected and created during these studies was utilized to develop the knowledge bases used in the computer program called the Project Management Perception (PMP).

The CDAS and the PMP as developed did not include the early project stages such as: preplanning, planning, scope development, budget, etc., therefore, an additional research was conducted that addressed these phases which allows full coverage of the entire life cycle of a project from project inception to project completion.

The primary objectives of project management are to deliver a completed project within budget, on schedule, and with the level of quality (workmanship and materials) expected by the owner. In order to achieve these objectives the project team must reduce, or eliminate, those factors that increase the cost of a project and the duration.

There are two major areas that can be tracked when managing a project, one is success factors and the other is delay factors. Success factors are subjective in nature depending on who is evaluating the project and at what stages these evaluations are made. Delay factors are objective and they can be assessed in terms of cost and time. Project delays are not predictable, and as a result project progress is impeded. Each delay contains certain risk factors, and depending on the importance of the activity being delayed and the amount of risk involved, the delay factors can be prioritized.

The longer it takes to develop a project, the more expensive it becomes due to the cost of the project team, cost of money, loss of profit or income, inflation, scope changes, loss of interest income, cost of construction acceleration, and cost of construction extras due to design omissions as a result of insufficient design time.

The intent of this Total Project Management Delay Analysis Method (TPM-DAM) research project was to provide a guideline for project planning and development and recommendations on how to correct, or avoid, project development delays.

## Project Life Cycle

The following ten major phases describes the life cycle of a constructed facility, and the various phases during project delivery, such as preplanning, planning, budgeting, scheduling, procurement, design, and construction. These ten major phases in a project are:

| | |
|---|---|
| Phase 1: | Identify the need. This is usually done by the staff of the owner or a contract Architect/Engineer |
| Phase 2: | Field survey and site condition assessment |
| Phase 3: | Scope development and budget development |
| Phase 4: | Economic, financial, and risk analysis |
| Phase 5: | A/E and Construction Management (CM) procurement and predesign survey phase |
| Phase 6: | Design phase |
| Phase 7: | Construction phase |
| Phase 8: | Start up, construction contract close out, commissioning, and delivery to owner phase |
| Phase 9: | Operation and maintenance phase |

Phase 10: Demolition

For most Capital Projects (CP) the project development process is slow, the efforts at this stage are not organized, and the resources are not committed, whereby, most of the efforts are contingent on availability of funds, and allocation of staff. This commitment of funds and staff usually is a low priority, since other projects are already on the way to design or construction and they require more time and involvement. As a result, the project development process is done in an extended time period.

## Problem Statement

Currently, project planning and development processes vary between similar types of projects. In reviewing existing government policies, results of previous research, and standard industry practice, it was determined that very few of the existing project control systems can be used during the early stages of project development, and they do not identify the possible reasons for delays at these stages of the project life cycle. Currently, there is no complete project management system that addresses all of the project phases, nor that addresses and analyzes project development related delays, their impacts, and the methods to reduce delays and improve the overall project delivery time.

A preliminary investigation of federal and local government processes demonstrated that there is a need to research these early project phases with respect to the types of delays encountered before construction commences. Currently, there is no project planning and development standard system, method, or procedure that is followed by either the public or private sector. For project planning and development stages, owners must rely on their own experience from prior projects, or use the experience of consultants in developing projects. As a result, the information about delays is not distributed or published for use by industry professionals.

## Purpose Of Research

For this research project an investigation and evaluation of current industry practices related to the project preplanning phase was undertaken in order to develop a guideline for the Total Project Management (TPM) and a Delay Analysis Method (DAM) that, if followed, could reduce the time and cost incurred due to delays. As a result of the research, the Total Project Management Delay Analysis Method (TPM-DAM) was developed with assistance from members of the construction industry and other knowledge acquisition systems. The various methods currently being used were investigated and a methodology was developed that will assist owners, and other construction personnel, in creating more cost effective projects.

The purpose of the Delay Analysis Method (DAM) research was to investigate construction project scope, budget, quality, cost, original schedule, and actual schedule in an effort to establish common preplanning delay factors that can be used as a guide and standard reference when developing new projects. Another purpose of this research was to develop and establish a set of recommendations associated with each established delay factor through the results of a survey and interviews with industry professionals. Systematic solutions were developed that address the various parts of the early phase of the project such as preplanning, planning, and scope development.

## Definitions

To insure the understanding of the issues surrounding the project development and construction planning and development, the following definitions are provided:

### *Preplanning*

In order to understand the TPM-DAM model it is important to understand what is meant by preplanning. Preplanning is the process of identifying the needs of an owner (client) and the extent of the project scope and budget. It is the collection of sufficient information and details to allow owners to decide whether to proceed with a commitment for funding and resources to develop the next phase of the project and start design.

### *Planning*

Planning is the strategies required to develop the various project phases and how to accomplish them. There are various project phases where extensive planning is required, such as the project development phase, design phase, procurement phases, and the construction phase. In the project development phase a project plan is developed that shows project variables such as schedule, team members, cost, and so on.

### *Project Control Systems*

Project control systems contains procedures for project scheduling such as Critical Path Method (CPM), Precedence Diagramming Method (PDM), Program Evaluation and Technique (PERT), and Linear Scheduling Method (LSM). These systems identify and flag project problems and delays as they occur, but they do not analyze or recommend solutions to problems.

### *Total Project Management (TPM)*

The TPM system is the method that provides monitoring of the different project cycles and phases. It is the method of coordinating people, time, cost, scope, and quality. The TPM relies on a logical flow diagram that provides guidelines for the various project phases including preplanning, planning, scope development, and so on.

### *Delay Analysis Method (DAM)*

The DAM is a knowledge system that contains databases that list possible delay factors that are common to construction projects. It includes recommendations provided by industry professionals on how to avoid delays, or provide corrective measures, to reduce the impact of delays on project delivery.

## Project Preplanning And Planning

According to a recent research project conducted by the Construction Industry Institute (CII 1994, 11, 21) entitled "Pre-Project Planning: Beginning a Project the Right Way" there are two issues of concern to the professionals who participated in this research from the construction industry. These issues are:

- There is no one standard method that currently exists and that is commonly used by the industry for total project management.
- There is a need to develop a total project management guideline (CII 1994, 11, 21).

Donnelly and Cooney argue the significance of proper project planning in minimizing delays, they stated that planning should include issues beyond traditional engineering design, right-of-way clearing, construction cost estimating, and scheduling. Their research suggests the adoption of a phased approach that includes a feasibility study, preliminary engineering, environmental permitting, permit tracking, final design and construction (Donnelley and Cooney 1994).

In the area of total project management, the development of a standard methodology, that would quantify existing information, would be beneficial to the construction industry as it would assist with the planning and development of projects and the analysis of time delays relating to planning processes. There are three major variables involved in total project management time, cost, and resources which makes it difficult to standardize. Also, many owners and professionals deal with project development one step at a time, therefore, it is hard to coordinate all three areas.

The issue of developing a control schedule for project development and planning was addressed by Deng Guishi in "The Interaction Method in Intelligent Decision Support Systems (IDSS) for Project Planning and Scheduling" when he stated that "Classical project planning and scheduling have been successful for project management and control. However, multi-objective attribute has not been involved in them because project planning and schedule issues are ill-structured problems, so it is hard to build up synthetic mathematics models dealing with parameters of time, resources, and cost" (Guishi 1993, 9-14).

## Delay Analysis Method (DAM)

Since there is no recognized standardized total project management procedure, there is also no standardized Delay Analysis Method (DAM) for project planning and development. It should be noted that project development can take several years before construction starts and this planning time involves resources, costs, several iterations, and changes. In most major projects the planning process involves legal, institutional, political, environmental, and funding issues all of which are time consuming (Goodman 1994).

The longer it takes to develop a project the more costly it becomes. It is difficult to examine the actual cost a developer incurs in the process of developing a project because of the number of parties involved in this process and they do not fill out time cards, therefore, the time they spend on project development is not accounted for as part of the total project cost. These individuals usually are decision makers and policy makers that earn high salaries. The decision makers salaries and other levels of engineers and architects base salaries are established based on the United States Civil Service Grades and various professional engineering and architectural societies salaries surveys (ASCE 1997).

Another side of project development is the cost of money such as financing and taxes. The longer it takes to initiate construction the more costly the development period becomes. Inflation rates are also considered another costly factor (Courtland and Halperin 1983, 5, 91,120, 121).

The current industry trends are to practice project development through management by exception which involves the identification and isolation of critical, or conflicting, information related to a particular situation, which are urgently related to the proper persons for their consideration, decision and action (Barrie and Paulson 1984, 171).

According to Kerzner, in order to improve the project development process management by objective should be considered and evaluated. Management by objective is a systems approach for aligning project goals with the goals of other subunits of an organization, and project goals with individuals goals (Kerzner 1984, 345). Management by objective helps set performance objectives at the beginning of projects, aids in the development of action plans, and insures accountability for results at the end of the project (Yates 1992).

## Phases Of The Research

### *Phase One*

The first phase of the research was to investigate existing research similar to this topic and evaluate the scope of this research project to determine whether any changes in direction, or a modification to the goals and objectives, needed to be made. Also initial nonstructured interviews were conducted with selected construction professionals to evaluate the validity of researching delays in the project development phase.

### *Phase Two*

The second phase of the research was to establish four different hypothesis in order to determine the research parameters and boundaries. These hypothesis were distributed to the research committee for review and evaluation and after comments and revisions were made a final set of hypothesis was established.

### *Phase Three*

The third phase of the research was the compilation of a list of construction professionals and owners, and the preparation of a questionnaire that was used to investigate current project planning and development processes and its consistency, determine whether a standardized TPM-DAM would satisfy current industry needs, investigate the difference between public and private sectors in planing and developing projects, and evaluate the cost percentage of direct and indirect cost of the preplanning phase in comparison to the total project cost.

### *Phase Four*

The fourth phase was to distribute the questionnaire, collect the results, and catalog them. Statistical tests were used to analyze and summarize the questionnaire results, and test the hypotheses using results obtained from the questionnaire.

### *Phase Five*

The fifth phase was a series of structured telephone interviews that were conducted with selected project executives and owners to quantify their knowledge on how they deal with project development obstacles and delays. These interviews were designed to obtain information regarding the proposed standardized TPM logic diagram, the possible project development delay factors that can be foreseen, or forecasted, and the list of corresponding corrective actions that were collected from the survey results.

### *Phase Six*

The sixth phase was the development of the TPM-DAM by using the results obtained from the questionnaires and the interviews to establish the final TPM logic diagram and the project preplanning delay factors. A set of recommendations were established to accommodate each identified delay factor.

## Research Results

The survey respondent were 64 percent from private companies and 36 percent from public agencies. The survey contained forty-five questions that addressed various construction project preplanning problems and measures. The survey results showed that the perspective of construction industry professionals of the Capital Construction Project (CCP) are consistent and indicated that CCP budget exceeds $2,000,000 in construction cost. There was inconsistencies between members of the public and private sectors regarding project preplanning durations, where the private sector requires 6-12 months and the public sector requires 3-5 years. The results also showed that both private and public sectors are collectively agreeing to a need for a standardized Total Project Management Delay Analysis Method (TPM-DAM), which can help improve and control current industry project preplanning processes, and it can help reduce delays.

The survey questions evaluated direct and indirect cost for the project preplanning phase in both private and public sectors. The results showed that the private sectors spends approximately 1-2 percent and the public sector spends approximately 2-3 percent of the total construction cost on project preplanning direct costs, and both public and private sectors spend approximately 3-5 percent of the total construction cost on project indirect costs. The results also showed that the private sector spends approximately 4-5 percent of the total project cost on project preplanning, whereas the public sector spends approximately 6-7 percent.

## Conclusions

Leaders in the U.S. political, construction, and research sectors are in support of improving the initial planning and development processes for projects. The current administration has encouraged the members of the construction industry to immediately initiate efforts to refine and improve project delivery time, and also to develop innovative methods and techniques which are essential components for U.S. economic prosperity and well-being.

Several researchers, writers, and industry leaders have indicated that current industry project planning and development processes are in need of improvement to provide a better understanding of the total process. The ability to control costs and reduce project delays are easier to accomplish during the planning process where the cost for changes are minimal compared to the cost for changes during the construction phase.

A standardized TPM-DAM model, or guideline, does not exist in the construction industry, but each corporation and organization have their Owen models for performing TPM-DAM, and these individual models, or guidelines, have their strengths and weaknesses. Building owners and developers use their experience on prior projects to develop new projects, but this experience and knowledge is limited to those individuals. Obstacles and delay factors are known only to those individuals in each particular organization and this information is neither distributed, nor shared. Therefore, errors and project planning delays continue to occur on various projects in different organizations and they continue to increase the total project time and cost.

## Recommendations

The participants of the survey are all in agreement with respect to the industry's need for a systematic approach to deal with predictive project preplanning delays. Several solutions and suggestions on preventing common known delays were provided. The following are a few examples of these preplanning delays and some of the corrective measures that were recommended by professionals from the construction industry:

### Delay Factor

- Constant changes in the project requirements

### Recommended Corrective Measures

- Reset objectives
- Set change process
- Establish limits to restrict changes
- Provide good communication and coordination with client and urge them to clearly define scope
- Freeze scope early
- Require the team to define scope and requirements
- Require the owner to define scope, schedule and budget
- Stress total schedule
- Clearly inform client of the cost of changes in time and money
- Expedite approvals and design completion
- Provide single point of contact, track changes and charge the project account for the cost of changes
- Stop work until project requirements are clearly defined
- Formalize the process with required steps to follow
- Make changes as quickly as possible
- Have early project reviews with all parties involved
- Develop scope at the beginning of the planning process, then provide thorough reviews with project participants, and document changes
- Limit the amount of people having input

### Delay Factor

- Lack of communication between various divisions

### Recommended Corrective Measures

- Schedule routine meetings
- Have the project manager act as a catalyst
- Team empowerment
- Develop and implement electronic mail system
- Define deadlines and stay on the schedule
- Provide management staff meetings with all departments as necessary
- Provide more thorough initial reviews
- Require sign offs
- Use questionnaires that are complete and distribute to all players
- Require the project manager to have routine visits to clients
- Develop and implement aggressive communication plan and procedure with one page memo
- Establish a chain of command and assign tasks and milestones

### Delay Factor

- Developing multiple projects at the same time causes delays to projects with less importance and other projects take precedence.

### Recommended Corrective Measures

- Prioritize project list
- Schedule resource requirements and requests
- Adjust resources
- Provide overtime hours for back-logged projects
- Project manager to direct team leaders and oversee study, schedule, and budget
- Life cycle reporting on project to headquarters
- Establish company/agency priorities
- Contract out
- Increase resource management
- Increase program reviews
- Ask for updates on priorities, and provide update memos on budget and schedule to all team members and CFO's
- Fight for your project
- Assign a project manager to each project
- Communication with clients should include time and budget

#### Delay Factors

- Slow decision making process

#### Recommended Corrective Measures

- Stream line and reduce the review process
- Make a project schedule and hold everyone to it
- People think preplanning is not important, therefore project managers should demand cooperation
- Revise schedule to reflect progress
- Document delays, and the individuals responsible for them
- Target decision makers
- Make decisions for decision makers
- Communicate decision needs early on
- Put decision needs as milestones on the schedule
- Empower employees to make decisions
- Assign one person to expedite this process

#### Delay Factor

- Assigning the project to the wrong person

#### Recommended Corrective Measures

- Measure customer complaints
- Reassign a more qualified person
- Allow more involvement by senior management
- Hire from the outside
- Allow project management to review the persons resume
- Ask for qualified assistance for the project manager
- Reassess project managers performance at the project management meetings
- Require management to make proper selection
- Assign persons with similar project experience to the current project
- Review credentials at the beginning of the project
- Provide on the job training
- Provide pre-project training in a team approach, use senior manager as mentors

## References


American Society of Civil Engineers (ASCE). 1997. *Salary Survey.*

Barrie D. and B. Paulson. 1984. *Professional Construction Management.* New York: McGraw Hill, Inc.

Collier Courtland A., P.E. and Don A. Halperin, F.A.I.G. 1983. *Construction Funding, Where The Money Comes From.* New York: John Wiley & Son.

Construction Industry Institute (CII). 1994. *Per-Project Planning: Beginning A Project the Right Way*, Publication 39-1, pp. 11 and 21.

Donnelly, G. and D. Cooney 1994. "Proper Project Planning Helps Minimize Overruns and Delays", *Pipeline & Gas Journal.*, (February) Vol. 221, pp. 43-52.

Goodman Alvin S. 1994. *Analysis of Public Works*, under development.

Guishi D. 1993. "The Interaction Methods in IDSS for Project Planning and Scheduling" *Proceeding of Institute of Electrical Engineering and Electronics.* International Conference, Le Touquet, France. Piscataway, NJ: IEEE.

Kerzner, H. 1984. *A Systems Approach to Planning Scheduling, and Controlling.* New York: Van Nostrand Reinhold.

Yates, J. and F. Rahbar. 1990. Executive Summary Status Report. *Transactions.* St. Louis: American Association of Cost Engineers. D3.1 - D3.9.

Yates, J. and F. Rahbar. And Spencer. 1991. A Knowledge Engineering System for Inquiry Feedback Project Management. *ASCE Construction Congress II Proceedings.* Boston: ASCE. April.

Yates, J. and F. Rahbar. 1991. Project Management Knowledge Engineering Systems. *American Association of Cost Engineers Journal*, Vol. 33, No. 7, 15-23.

Yates, J. 1992. A Computerized Inquiry Feedback Knowledge Engineering System. *Transactions of the American Association of Cost Engineers (AACE) Annual Conference.* Orlando: AACE. Vol. 2, R1.1-R1.7.

Yates Janet K., 1993. Construction Decision Support System for Delay Analysis—DAS. *Journal of Construction Engineering and Management, ASCE*, Vol. 119, No. 2, pp. 226-244.

Yates, J. and H. Aoude. 1995a. Construction Delay Analysis System, *Transactions of the 39th International Association of Cost Engineers (IACE) Annual Conference.* St. Louis: IACE. C&C.9.1 - C&C.9.4.

Yates, J. and H. Aoude. 1995b. Construction Delay Information Management Communication System, *Project Management Institute (PMI) 26th Annual International Seminar/Symposium*, New Orleans. Upper Darby, PA: PMI. October. pp. 495 - 503.

Yates, J. and H. Aoude. October 1995c. Construction Delay Analysis System Computer Program, *Proceedings of the American Society of Civil Engineers (ASCE) Construction Congress '95.* San Diego: ASCE 495-503.

Yates, J. and J. Audi. 1996. Project Management Perception (PMP) Program, *Journal of the Project Management Institute.* Upper Darby, PA: PMI. Submitted for publication. July.

Yates, J. and J. Audi. 1996. Development of the Project Management Perception (PMP) Program. American Association of Cost Engineers International. *Cost Engineering Journal.* Submitted for publication. July.


This paper reflects the opinion of the authors and not those of the United States Government or the General Services Administration.

# Project Budgets, Friend or Foe?

John Homer BMW Constructors, Inc.

## Introduction

In far too many projects, the core concept of a budget is poorly understood and implemented. Budgets become bogey men instead of management tools. In this paper the author will endeavor to identify some fundamental concepts about budgets and highlight some steps toward making budgets an effective tool of project management. While the concepts of budget are applicable to areas of the project other than cost, the discussion will initially be restricted to discussion of cost budgets.

The Gospel of Luke identifies the fundamental issue of budgets in projects: "For which of you, intending to build a tower, sitteth not down first and counteth the cost, whether he have sufficient to finish it?" Luke 14:28

No project manager I know would admit to undertaking the construction of a tower (or any other project) without counting first, but, having counted the cost, what do we have?

The American Heritage Dictionary gives three different senses of the core concept of a budget.

- First, "an itemized summary of probable expenditures and income over a given period," what the *PMBOK Guide* would term an estimate.
- Second, "The total sum of money allocated for a particular purpose or time period," an outcome measure for addressing the question did we meet the budget or not.
- Third, "A systematic plan for meeting expenses in a given period," what we might term a performance plan, one element of which would be cost based.

The problems with a project budget often arise out of failure to deal with the distinctions between the concepts behind these definitions. In some circumstances the term "budget" may apply on a project to any of these concepts. However, the concepts are not interchangeable.

The first step in making a budget serve as a tool is understanding what it *should* be, and what it *should not* be. This may be very different than what it *is*, and what it *is not*, project-specific dogmas we will only touch here.

### What It Should Be Is Summarized As:

The identification of the probable project cost, cast in sufficient detail and divisions to allow for informed management decisions. The budget should help managers see the performance tradeoffs on the project and facilitate meaningful tracking of performance across the project's timeline.

### What It Should Not Be Is Summarized As:

A fundamental metric of the project, independent from the other measures of scope, results, or performance.

## How is a Budget Arrived At?

The first budget safety violation is often made with the educated guess. Someone SWAGs, "We should be able to do this for $X." A budget set by such a method has a zero probability of being right (which makes it about as accurate as some other common methods.) This SWAG method remains the technique of choice for many.

Once pronounced, this SWAG figure usually takes on a life of its own and probably becomes the chief metric of the project. If the budget is arrived at on this basis, the rest of my comments are pointless, as rationality can not hope to counter the attractiveness of irrationality. We will proceed on the assumption that our projects avoid this first trap by placing appropriate qualifiers on the first budget numbers.

## Project Definition and the Budget

Let us assume the existence of a project with identified results sought, necessary scope to accomplish those results, and performance targets. Given those elements of project definition, we can begin to make predictions of cost. That is, we can perform an estimate. This estimate is a budget in the first sense of the definitions above.

In doing the estimate, each element of the project is identified in cost terms based on the history we have for performance of similar things. Judgments are applied to adjust for variation between what we want to do and the reference history definition. Where specific history is missing, judgments are also applied to stretch knowledge of non-similar things to this situation. Further adjustments are applied in an attempt to account for differences in geography or economic conditions, where such changed conditions might impact the value of the history in making this prediction. Finally, the estimator, being rational, assesses the variation expected as a result of the quality of the sources of information and cost extrapolation methods used.

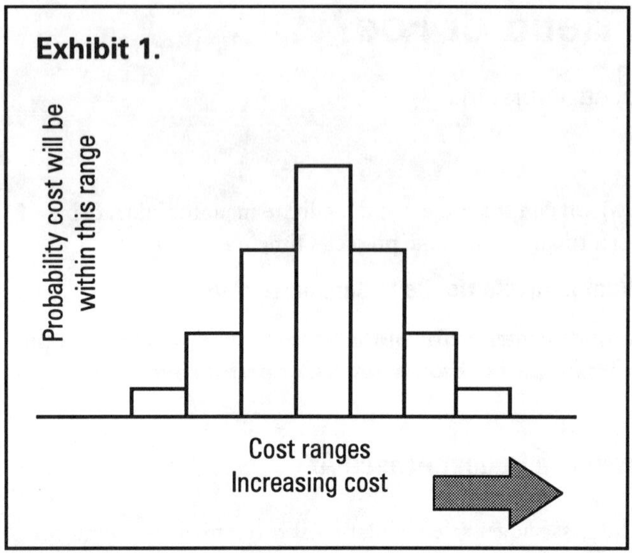


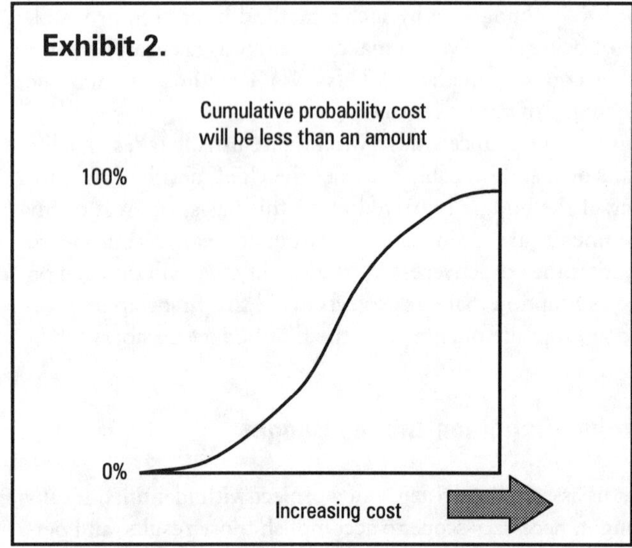


The summary result is a series of estimates for the project's cost elements, each a sum of many individual cost judgments, with each judgment impacted by many sources of variation. Those variations arise from the nature of the individual cost judgments and are related to their source.

For each cost judgment, we can draw a probable cost distribution based on the knowns and unknowns. Such a figure might appear as Exhibit 1, the discreet probability of cost falling in each of a set of ranges, or as Exhibit 2, the cumulative probability of final cost being less than or equal to some value.

The shape and spread of these distributions depends on the sources of variation. For our purposes, we might classify each cost judgment as to the quality of its source support in a 4-way distribution.

Class 1: Wal-Mart pricing. Knowable cost, competitively driven, exhibiting low variation.

Class 2: Auto dealer pricing. Cost in a knowable range but varying within that range based on bargaining power.

Class 3: Custom software pricing. Pricing based on absorbing the cost of the efficiency, and inefficiency, with which the element is executed. This may be very difficult to predict accurately. Typically, it exhibits great variation. Estimates of this type are continually impacted by changing requirements.

Class 4: Junkyard pricing. Wide variation in pricing, with no underlying floor, uncertainty in determining other coupled cost elements.

Each cost element into which we classify our cost judgments is likely to be a composite of judgments in two or more of these categories. We will assume that, by the brilliance of our analysis, we can draw composite probability curves for each cost element derived from the variation curves for the individual judgments. The methodology of combining these specific curves into larger composite curves for larger cost elements is beyond the scope of this effort. The principles involved are well known and can be likened to the use of PERT calculations in a schedule. Monte Carlo simulations have also been used successfully to assist in understanding the variation to be expected in project outcomes.

The sum total of these cost elements is run out on the tape to arrive at "the budget." In conventional project practice, the second major budget safety hazard may appear at this point. If the budget is made up of a series of elements, each with its own probable variation profile based on cost judgments from several different variation profiles, it is irrational to assume that the budget can now meaningfully take on a single value. Of course, many project teams will so assign a value.

It is equally irrational to assume that any budget number set at this point, set low enough to gain project authorization, can serve as a practical maximum for the project. That this often happens is the third budget safety hazard: the hazard that the budget itself takes on an importance greater than the project definition it helps describe. The word budget used in this sense is an example of the second definition. It now describes all the money available for the project.

The budget concept is now beset by three possible debilitating forces (Exhibit 3): the SWAG, the assignment of a single value as having mystical meaning, and the adoption of an arbitrary value as a maximum. By this process, the usefulness of the budget may be defeated before we ever deal with any practical use the budget might have as a management tool.

The distinction between the last two of these points should be clear. Both reflect a tendency to set a single value as representing the budget. That single number is often used to represent either concept without distinction, but the difference between them can be very important. Hazard two deals with the lack of acknowledgment of the expected impact of variation on the budget over time. Hazard three deals with the arbitrary selection of any number as a maximum.

Brian Joiner deals with this issue when he comments that selection of a median point in the distribution of cost probabilities would suggest that one-half of all projects should exceed that budget and one-half complete under the budget. That this is not reflected in the statistics of project management suggests tampering with the system. Such tampering is not automatically bad, but, it does suggest a common lack of understanding of the expectation built into setting the budget number. (Joiner 1993, 169)

Further, there is an asymmetrical pain threshold associated with deviation from the budget that suggests less than ideal management understanding of the whole concept of variation. (Exhibit 4)

If we have tripped on any or all of the budget safety hazards, we now have a budget that looks a lot like the definition above of what the budget should not be: An overriding metric for the project. If this is the case, the budget is unlikely to ever emerge from the primordial soup as a useful tool. Instead, it is likely to be a central focus of witch-hunts through the duration of the project.

To proceed to consideration of the budget's use as a tool, let us assume that we have avoided all of the hazards given. We have a rationally derived budget for each element, a budget that takes into consideration likely variation in the cost outcome based on common cause sources of variation. This budget reflects the probable cost of planned performance of the scope necessary for achieving project results.

For simplification, we will assume expression of this budget as a single number. However, we will operate in the knowledge that every person working with the budget recognizes it as a statement of probabilities, not a "guaranteed maximum." Further, we will acknowledge that the only sense in which this budget number represents a maximum is at some level of agreed probability.

**Exhibit 3.**

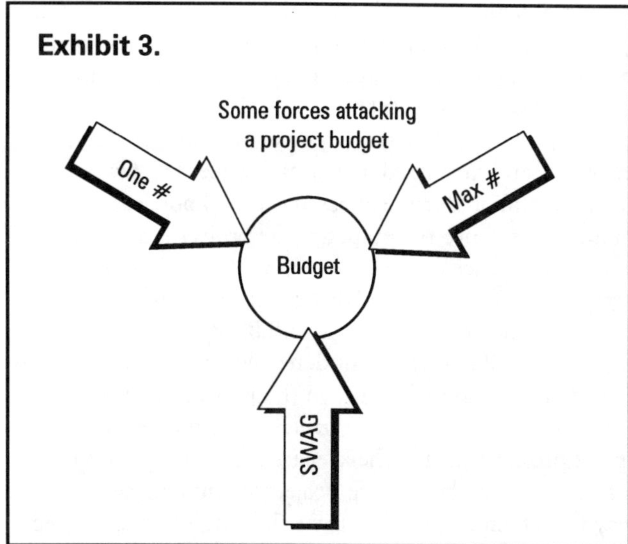


**Exhibit 4.**

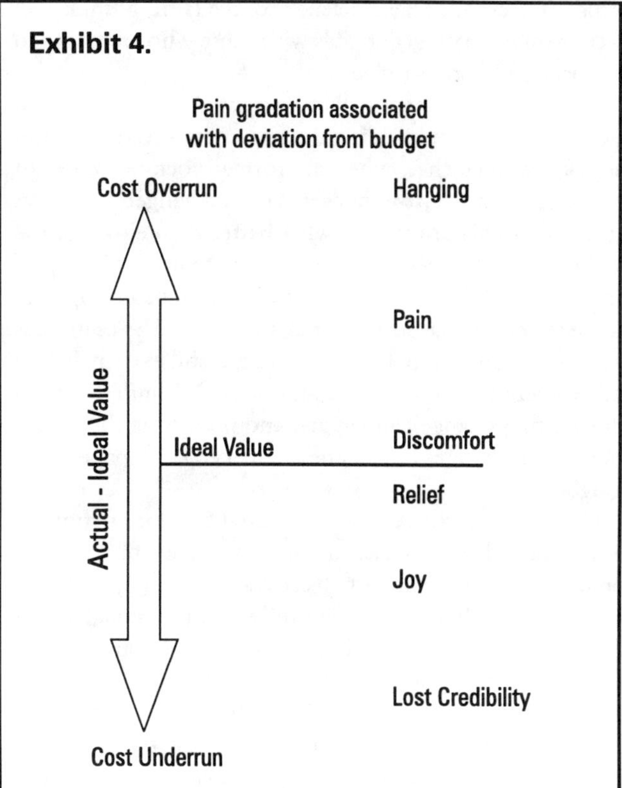


## So What Do We Do With the Budget?

Once formulated, there are four distinct ways in which we might use the budget:

- As a weapon of project self destruction.
- As a cost prediction at the moment of its adoption, never to be changed.
- As a cost prediction to be modified by recognition of changes after they occur.
- As a cost prediction for the project from now until the completion.

How does the budget get used as a weapon? The use of the budget as a weapon of project destruction will hopefully be reserved for projects whose budget process tripped over hazards one to three. If the budget represents a remote best guess, it will provide little help to formulating current plans and strategies. If it is presented as a single fixed total, or worse yet as fixed components totaling a single number, the budget is not helpful in any discussion of project adaptation to current realities. If the budget is defended as a maximum cost point, it is about as helpful as sign on a Bosnian road warning of land mines. It restates the obvious without offering any help on obtaining safety. Under any of these conditions, the budget will become more of a weapon against project purposes than a useful tool.

Of slightly less destructive power is a budget arrived at reasonably and then fixed in time and space. The first budget is a base-defining document based on our knowledge at that point in time. Since the output of the project is a unique accomplishment, we can speculate that change is going to be part of the project. Any tool that arbitrarily prevents change, or failing to prevent it, denies it, will be of limited use to the project team. By adoption of defensive mechanisms which prevent recognition of change in the project, the keepers of the budget render themselves irrelevant to the decisions facing the project leaders. The keepers of the budget are likely to feel increasingly like the project discussion has moved away from them. Naturally, they will be deferred to as keepers of some holy grail, but their involvement will be more formal than useful. Their "defender of the faith" attitude will place them increasingly at odds with those who are trying to accomplish the project objectives.

A slight improvement will be associated with recognition of change to the budget after the fact. With this mechanism we acknowledge that, when the formal documentation of change is complete, the budget will be changed to reflect those facts. This use is somewhat better than either of the two above, as the keepers of the budget are now at least performing a useful function. They can be assigned to operate the mechanisms that formally track changes. The usefulness of this function as a tool for the project is still extremely limited. Generally, it constitutes a poor compromise between denying that change can happen and predicting the consequences of change, but it does help keep the paperwork straight.

The final alternative revolves around the third definition above: the budget as an element of a "systematic plan" for accomplishment of the project objectives. This concept suggests the budget as a living document reflecting the probable cost of the current plan for reaching the project objectives.

As the current plan, it is useful in evaluating alternatives identified when inevitable change occurs. If the priorities are clearly known, and the elements of cost clearly identified, then the current budget may help. Managers can use it in evaluating those decisions, driven by change, that are a critical part of the project and its success. In such a case, the keepers of the budget may even be invited to meetings talking about the real work of meeting the project objectives.

Purists may suggest that the concept of current budget is dangerous in that implies a constantly changing budget. Better, they say, to hold to the original budget and measure the deviations than to allow slippage.

To illustrate differences with this approach, let's turn to the project schedule for an example. First, some basic schedule principles:

- The project schedules represents the time budget of the project.
- There is at most one controlling schedule operating on a project.
- The only important schedule is the one that represents the plan to get from the current situation to the planned end date.

The first statement is probably obvious. All budgets represent the project plan in a dimension. The total project plan is the plan for the use of all resources to achieve the objectives. Cost and Time are two of those resource measures, so budgets are appropriate for both. We normally call the time budget a schedule.

The second point will be asserted without lengthy defense. The author has long argued that the existence of the a schedule is a binary condition. There is one controlling schedule, or there is none. If there is one, it is that schedule that guides consideration of alternatives and decisions. If there is none, then the project is inherently out of control. Subsidiary schedules are allowed as long as they recognize the primacy of the controlling schedule.

The controlling schedule can not be the original one for the project. Conditions have changed. At best, that schedule will yield a target end date for the project. That target is no more "the project schedule" than the first guess of cost is "the budget." The only meaningful time-based plan is that sequence of actions and activities whose accomplishment will move the project from where it is now to completion. It is that plan that reflects what needs to be done and when to accomplish this transformation. To contend the "original schedule" remains the controlling schedule suggests either:

- Project participants will receive great motivation and encouragement from being told that their goal is accomplishing certain actions retroactively.
- We are better off pronouncing high-sounding goals and leaving the details to chance.

Neither prospect is enchanting. Both are at significant variance with the framework of project understanding the schedule helps form. We must therefore conclude that, distasteful as it might at first seem, the only important schedule is one based on the reality of the current project experience.

Among the subsidiary schedules for the project, it may be useful to contrast the current schedule with the original schedule, or any intermediate schedule, by way of recording variance. However, if the project is in control, that control is based on the current schedule.

Likewise, the cost budget is a useful controlling tool only if it offers a reflection of the in-force plan to move from now to completion. Comparison with subsidiary cost documents may be useful, but attempting to monitor current actions against outdated plans is not. Reduction in variation between the current cost expectation and the original budget may be cause for celebration, but its accomplishment should not drive ill-considered compromise in the project objectives.

## Summary

Budgets are a key part of successful project management. Successful use of budgets as a project tool must rest on a shared understanding of what the budget means and how it is used. This understanding must be codified in the budget rule set for the project. Project managers must avoid or defuse the emotional baggage often associated with budgets if they are to focus management attention on the objectives of the project. They can expect to frequently have to return to the shared understanding of the use of budgets. Taking this step can avoid having the project objectives compromised by misuse of the budget tool as a weapon.

Budgets as arbitrary targets, or mistakenly used as fixed metrics of project success, ignore the realities of the project process. Useful budgets are arrived at by allowing reasoned consideration of sources of variance, and they must reflect a tolerance for variance in the project performance measured by the budget.

Budgets assist the project management team most when they are living documents reflective of the plan to get from the current condition to the project completion. As such, they can illuminate decisions and tradeoffs and assist the project in its evolution.

### References

Joiner, Brian. 1993. *Fourth Generation Management*. New York: McGraw-Hill

Johnson, H. Thomas and Robert S. Kaplan. 1991. *Relevance Lost: The Rise and Fall of Management Accounting*. Boston: Harvard Business School Press.

# Design-Build—Will it be the Delivery Method of Choice for the 21st Century?

Charles J. (Chuck) Williams, PE; PMP

## Introduction

I'm pleased to talk with you today about one of the most important trends of our time; the growth and impact of the Design Build method of project delivery. As project managers, who are, or will be, involved in this delivery method, it will challenge your skills, stretch your capabilities and provide the most comprehensive experience in project management of your careers.

## Overview

The Design-Build delivery method has gained significant acceptance in the last decade and promises to gain even more popularity as we move into the 21st Century. In the private sector, Design-Build has been utilized for some time. There have been numerous benefits demonstrated in utilizing this delivery method, and there have been some failed experiences. The federal government has recently modified it's approach by permitting use of the Design-Build delivery by government agencies under specific guidelines.

However, Design-Build continues to be controversial and many owners, engineers, architects and contractors have significant doubts and discomforts about the process. To what extent will it be the delivery method of choice in the 21st Century ? What really are the benefits of utilizing this delivery method over the traditional Design-Build method, and what steps should owners take to achieve them. What are the major constraints and threats for Design-Build to be successful on individual projects and, for the longer term, how can they be overcome ?

## Background

By way of background, Design-Build project delivery commonly means that the single point of responsibility for both design and construction of a project is one entity with the prime contract with the client (owner). The Design-Build contractor is both the engineer and builder of record, guaranteeing both in terms of performance and workmanship. The Design-Build contract can have various provisions for performance, price and schedule, and some may have operations and/or maintenance responsibilities subsequent to commissioning of the project. It's purported that the pyramids of Egypt and the great churches of medieval Europe were essentially established through the Design-Build method. The Code of Hammurabi made the master builders responsible for both design and construction in 1800 B.C. One recent General Services Administration report concluded that, "Design Build is applicable to all types of projects, regardless of size or complexity, as long as the project's requirements are relatively known and stable". Some owners have concluded that the more complex the project, the more important it is to consider for the Design Build delivery approach.

In the last decade, Design-Build work by United States contractors has more than tripled. Worldwide use has accelerated. The public sector, while previously not employing Design-Build, has recently seen several small projects and some very large projects, each over $100 million in value, be awarded through the Design-Build delivery method. Congress enacted the 1966 Federal Acquisition Reform Act to permit two-phase selection for Design-Build projects and, on March 3, 1997, Design-Build rules took effect for implementing those provisions The use of Design-Build in both public and private sectors has increased over 200 percent since 1986 to over $50 billion per year. It is perceived that, based on a Commerce Department study, by the year 2000, approximately 50 percent of all construction value in the United States will be executed through Design-Build delivery.

## Benefits of Design-Build

First, let's examine potential benefits of the Design-Build delivery method, and determine how these might be realized:

### Shorter overall project duration through integrated engineering, procurement and construction activities:

Some studies indicate schedule savings can be between 10-30 percent, depending on the type and size of Project. Federal agency experience indicates anywhere from 18 percent on DOD ( Non Appropriated Funds) Projects to 28 percent on those by Veterans Affairs. From personal experience, I've seen savings up to 25 percent when the owner becomes a full partner with the Design-Builder and assists in expediting the permitting and regulatory review process.

To capture this savings, which is a large contribution to the costs savings we'll talk about next, many interfaces between the Design-Builder and other parties must be managed proactively and controlled. Interfaces with the owner and regulatory agencies include permitting, design reviews, submittals, scope changes, payments, acceptance of work, and disputes. Interfaces with resources utilized by the Design-Builder include procurements, subcontractors, labor unions, equipment suppliers, and professional services. Since the Design-Build delivery method is new to many of these participants, such as owner's staffs, permitting agencies, and many trade subcontractors, Some of these participants are not quick to recognize and meet different responsibilities, and they are not comfortable with this different approach.

**Lower project cost as a result of the shorter project duration and cost efficiencies achieved through integrating design, procurement and construction activities.**

This savings is real and there are big dollars at stake, and another advantage to the owner is that a firm price can be established before the start of detailed design. Studies of various projects indicate cost savings up to 15 percent, compared to the traditional design-bid-build method. I can personally tell you that on some Projects, it can be much more. On a current ozone plant project in Milwaukee, in which I'm involved in , costs are expected to be almost 30 percent less than what was first estimated. The key to achieving this savings is in giving the Design -Builder substantial opportunity for innovation, and integrating the activities of design, procurement and construction, while maintaining the significant requirements of the Project. Basically, give the Design-Builder opportunity to save time and money, within the confines of what is truly required.

**Lower risk exposure for the owner through having a single point responsibility for design and construction, and less claims between several parties.**

Disputes and claims are reduced through Design-Build. Studies of various projects indicate that claims frequency have been reduced by 50 percent through the use of Design-Build delivery. There is less finger pointing and closer coordination in the Design-Build method. Disputes are resolved earlier and more frequently because the participants have usually built up a closer and more cooperative, partnering relationship through the design development and procurement stage of the project. The two parties usually have more to gain by resolving their disputes than by creating more differences.

**Less change orders through having the design-build contractor have responsibility for both design and construction.**

One of the most appealing benefits for the owner of Design-Build is that the owner won't hear from the contractor that he wants to get an change order since the engineer had errors and omissions in his design, or hear from the engineer that some of this problem is a normal standard of care, and nobody is perfect which is true. The Design-Builder is singularly responsible for the finished product, and make it work according to the approved requirements.

However, there is another source of changes in Design-Build that must be managed effectively; that is the infamous scope creep caused by the many stakeholders of the project. Those stakeholders, the regulators, plant operators, owner staff, politicians and, sometimes,the owner's engineer, now don't have the luxury of the getting all those bells and whistles added during the detail design period, and the Design-Builder typically will not include them. Scope control is always a challenge to your project management skills, whether as owner or Design-Builder.

**Less surprises for the owner through having the cost and schedule established in advance of starting the detail design.**

This benefit is inherent in the Design-Build method but is contingent upon the owner and Design-Builder having a early and clear understanding of the basic Project requirements Within the normal expectations that some changes may occur due to unforeseen and uncontrollable conditions, major surprises are minimized.

**Lower owner costs for administering fewer contracts and coordinating fewer parties.**

The owner's and design-builder's efforts can be better focused on the factors affecting Project success, and less on maximizing the paperwork between all parties. The nature of the Design-Build delivery method promotes better understanding and communication between the owner and the design-builder. In addition, most Design-Build contracts provide for a "workshop" environment to mutually conduct design and submittal reviews and resolve related issues, so that elapsed time is minimized. This cooperative effort reduces multiple transmittals of data between the parties.

In addition, the owner will normally assist the design-builder by promoting a receptive attitude by the permitting and regulatory agencies. Since the design-builder is technically knowledgeable about the project, he is typically more effective than the average contractor in working with these agencies and meeting their needs.

**Improved quality and warranty service since the constructor is also the designer, and has capability to address the technical aspects of the work.**

It's always advisable to have your builder be technically responsible and knowledgeable about what he's building. It's important for the owner to assure that the designer element of the design-builder is fully involved in the Design-Build process, not just preparing a design and "throwing it over the fence". In this respect, it is most advisable for the owner that both the design and construction elements of any Design-Build team participate in the bonding and guarantees embodied in the prime contract.

Warranty issues are more likely resolved in light of the technical aspects involved , not just the minimum work required for a quick fix. It's most important to Design-Build firms that they maintain their reputation for technical excellence and reliability, since that is their best marketing tool for future work, especially if "qualifications based" selection is employed.

**Improved constructability and overall project implementation, since the contractor is intimately involved during the early design of the work.**

The process of design, procurement and construction is more fluid and integrated in design-build. There is significant involvement of the construction staff during the design development, and detailed procurement planning in the earliest phases of the project. This early planning and involvement by procurement and construction staff make the project implementation more coordinated and predictable. The project is designed and planned to be built, and the means and methods to do that are determined, for the most part, early during the design phase. This situation promotes early and mutual buy-in and understanding by both owner and design-builder staff, who are tasked to execute the project.

**More flexibility in issuing changes, including the additional work, because the technical capability of the designer is integrated with the construction delivery.**

Various changes desired by the owner, or other changed conditions encountered in progress of the work, can be concurrently evaluated in light of both technical and constructability issues involved. This saves time and provides a more flexible environment to modify changes to maintain budget and schedule objectives.

## Constraints and Threats to Design Build

However, there are numerous threats and constraints to Design / Build, and these may stand in it's way of becoming " all it can be". Let's discuss some of these and examine their significance and potential impact.

**Numerous state and local legal restrictions currently exist that prevent utilizing the design-build delivery method.**

Design-Build is still not legal in several states, and many States that allow Design-Build still have numerous hurdles to planning and executing a Design-Build project. While this is changing as we speak, it will remain a slow process that complex legislation often invites. The Design-Build Institute of America, which was recently established to promote the use of Design-Build and be an industry repository of "best practices", has assisted the federal government and several states to develop the necessary legislation to make the legal and regulatory changes that are necessary.

**Difficulty for the owner to overcome organizational and political resistance to change.**

Let's face it; we're all resistant to change. Organizations which have been structured and utilized to function in a certain way for a long time will not dramatically change overnight, or over several years, unless there is a strong motivation for such change. These organizations can feel threatened by this change, especially when they must modify their behavior to work in a different way. Industry participants such as engineers, suppliers, and contractors, who have formed their companies to meet a specific marketplace are not naturally quick to embrace a dramatic change in that marketplace. These companies are not thrilled by the challenge of forming new alliances, developing new capabilities, and taking on new risks that are not clearly understood. In addition, they are not happy seeing new competitors who may have deeper and broader experience in Design-Build, and both the financial and technical capabilities to take on greater risk.

**Inability of governmental entities to prequalify design/build firms to limit the project quality and performance risk.**

It's essential that owners use a qualified firm to be their Design-Builder. This can be achieved in the Private Sector through selective negotiation; only utilizing firms you know are qualified. In the Public Sector, owners can use a two step procurement process to establish a short list of firms that are fully qualified and experienced to execute the Project. It's the fear of successful Design-Build firms that owners will not use extreme care in selecting the Design-Builder and have bad experiences, thus damaging the successful track record needed to encourage further use of Design-Build delivery. It is true that, in the Design-Build delivery method, the owner has more of the eggs in one basket, and that basket must be carefully selected.

### Difficulty in determining what the owner really wants without completing the design.

It's true that many private sector owners and most public sector owner's have used or abused the luxury of the design development process to determine their needs. As one owner asked, "How will I know what I'll get until it's totally designed?" This is a real obstacle for many owners. How do I really define the significant aspects of what I want, without significantly decreasing the potential for innovation and cost reduction ? The answer is, "everyone's approach will be different" and experience will help significantly. Beyond the key technical performance aspects of the project, some things that are important to one owner will not be so important to another. Perhaps, trying Design-Build on a smaller project will provide each owner with some experience. However, projects still need to be of a significant size to attract the more experienced firms. It would not be advisable to have two firms, who have not ever done Design-Build delivery, team up to try a new thing.

### Real or perceived conflict of interest with the contractor also being the designer

Many people schooled all their professional lives on the premise that all contractors must be forced to meet the plans and specifications, will not ever accept that the Design-Builder can be trusted to inspect his own work. However, the major engineer-construct firms with strong technical capabilities, and many regional engineering and construction firms have made their reputation in providing client service and standing behind their work.

If clients feel or have the need to have the assistance of an independent firm, they should engage one with experience in the Design-Build method. That firm can assist them in developing a request for qualifications and evaluate Design-Build firms, and preparing a request for proposals/bids, incorporating the basic project technical requirements.

### Limited established industry standards or history for contracting under this method.

There are established methods and significant history in the industry and in each organization relative to design-bid-build, but little with respect to Design-Build. However, that is changing quickly due to the significant experience that Design-Build is gaining in the marketplace. With the increased interest in design-build, many industry organizations have issued standard templates for Design-Build contracting; these include the AIA, EJCDC, AGC and, for international projects, the FIDIC organization. In addition, The Design Build Institue of America (DBIA) has the beginnings of a Manual of Standard Practice and plans to issue a template for Design Build contracting later this year. Also, most experienced Design-Builders have tried and true contracting documents that may be a starting point for review and negotiation.

### Lack of experience and expertise within owner organizations to administer and manage this delivery method, while supporting a "fast track" project schedule.

It's true that Design-Build project delivery assigns new responsibilities to the contracting parties, and many owner organizations are not prepared to operate differently than they have under the design-bid-build approach. For example, since the Design-Builder is the engineer of record, he has some latitude to make changes in the design as long as it still meets project requirements as outlined in the prime contract. Many owners want total control over all those changes, and the right to impose their own standards on all designs that the Design-Builder may develop. This will defeat the purpose of the Design-Build approach.

In addition, it's difficult for many owner organizations to redirect their staff efforts toward supporting the Design-Builder's need for expedited directions and decisions. The design-bid-build approachwhich assigns as much risk as possible to the contractor, is not a recipe for success in Design-Build. Design-Build must have close cooperation, a supportive environment, and a risk sharing approach between the owner and the Design-Builder.

### The lack of experience of many of the firms attempting to compete in the design-build marketplace, either ndividually or in joint ventures and alliances, and the significance of those firms taking on of new and increased risks.

Yes, there are many firms our there with varying levels of experience and capabilities, and it's important to only select those that can perform effectively. There is also limited performance records of Design-Build entities, especially those with "first time" teaming partners. In joint ventures and other alliances, it's important to see clear leadership and full participation by all parties, including bonding and participation in the project design and construction planning process. It's also significant if such ventures have a seemless project organization, whereby the project team integrates staff from both the engineer and the constructor.

### Obstruction by "single service" entities and some industry organizations.

Not everyone sees opportunity in the Design-Build method of project delivery; many only see a threat to their traditional markets and clients. Unless a firm self performs many of the Design-Build services, especially those activities that control the critical path to achieve an optimum schedule, it may not find a way to compete and participate successfully. It certainly will not be positioned to control it's risk. The firm may not be financially able to take on the added risk of being a "bonded player", thus reducing itself to a sub-consultant without significant management participation in overall execution of the project.

## Conclusion

While the proven benefits of Design-Build are extremely desirable, there remain several significant threats and constraints to Design-Build being the delivery method of choice. These include technical, legal, commercial, organizational, and institutional issues that must be "worked through" as time goes on. There are real anxieties in owner organizations, industry firms, political and regulatory bodies that the Design-Build method is " all it's cracked up to be". Some may argue," since we still have significant problems to execute a project even after all design details are known, how can we "raise the bar" of complexity by also dealing with design issues on top of that". Or another common point; " we're not ready to give up total control of the design or having the engineer be our advocate in the construction process".

Can, and will, the Design-Build delivery method be the choice for the 21st Century ? My answer to both parts of that question is yes. I believe that continued successes over the next few years will support this contention. If fact, there is evidence to demonstrate that in some industries, and to some extent in the public sector, the change is already well underway. In the public sector, many state and local governments are following the federal initiative to experiment with Design-Build. Each day, there are more examples of successes. Before year end, the Detroit plans on having over $500 million in water/wastewater contracts awarded under the Design-Build delivery method. Memphis, Pensacola, Seattle, and Milwaukee are all successfully executing projects through the Design-Build method. Private owners in manufacturing, pharmaceuticals, food processing, high tech, etc. have constructed numerous facilities, worth billions of dollars through Design-Build. These owners have seen that the Design-Build delivery method gives opportunity for innovation in design, procurement and construction to provide mutual benefits, while maintaining design excellence and good craftsmanship. Since there are continued challenges , each project will still require the dedication, commitment and hard work of all parties to be successful.

In conclusion, the benefits of Design-Build are there to be achieved for the stout of heart, and the owners willing to "get out of the box" to grasp them. Anything new has risks, but each day there are more tools and more assistance available to make the first or next experience a successful one. The key will be to continue successful projects. While there are bound to be some failures, due to a variety of reasons, owners, design-builders, engineers, contractors, permitting and regulatory agencies, political organizations, and industry groups, need to work together to reap the benefits of Design-Build for the ultimate customer, you and me, the taxpayer and consumer.

# The *Qualidex* System—Measuring Project Performance

Bryan McConachy, P.Eng, PMP, PMI Fellow, Bramcon, Vancouver, B.C., Canada
Randy Bourne, P.Eng, PMP, BC Hydro, Burnaby, B.C., Canada

## Background

Quality management is nothing new to the design and construction industry. It has always had quality assurance and quality control (QA/QC) programs that involved the inspection of completed works and pre-qualification of vendors. The quality movement of the 1980's, with its focus on prevention and broad perspective of the entire organization, promoted Total Quality Management (TQM) as a new business philosophy. While it may have worked for some industry sectors, the widespread use of TQM created confusion of what role quality management has in the design and construction industry. Before that dilemma was resolved, the industry was further confused by various ISO certifications and their relation, if any, to TQM.

We determined that the people in the industry needed a visual model or graphical representation to enhance or maybe even initiate understanding of how all the elements of quality management, including ISO 9000, fit together. While understanding is a necessary condition to establishing a quality management program, it is not sufficient. Our pragmatic industry is unwilling to embark on a potentially costly program based on faith that the benefits experienced by the manufacturing and services sectors will be realized in their unique environment. On the basis that one can only manage what one can measure, any system that was going to be accepted by the industry had to provide a cost-effective method of measuring performance and identifying specific areas requiring improvement. Training and coaching had to be targeted on problem areas rather than applied over the entire organization.

## The *Qualidex* Approach

The *Qualidex* model, first presented in Exhibit 1, separates the multitude aspects of TQM into two distinct categories—conventional or contemporary quality. Conventional quality is the industry's traditional quality management programs; it involves meeting specifications, schedule and budget by utilizing a series of processes with appropriate QA/QC measures. Conventional quality has a technical orientation and seeks increasing control of things to reduce variation and conform to requirements. ISO 9000, the internationally recognized QA standard, is a conventional quality process.

Because it is relatively new, the other dimension of quality is called Contemporary quality. As the approach to quality changed from catching variations after the fact to preventing variations before they occur, the focus of the quality movement shifted to involving people in improving their work processes to achieve better performance (conventional quality). In contrast to conventional quality, Contemporary quality has a psychological orientation and seeks to increase the competence and motivation of people. Contemporary quality can be considered as a measure of corporate culture or organizational effectiveness. It initially focuses on team competence to perform the required tasks and subsequently on team commitment to excellence through continuous improvement.

Although the "total" in TQM is considering the contemporary aspects as well as the conventional, the objective of any quality management program is improvement of conventional quality—the contemporary quality is only the means to that end.

The *Qualidex* model presents its two-dimensional results on a simple x-y plot. conventional quality, measured on a 0-100 scale, is plotted on the x-axis while contemporary quality, also measured on a 0-100 scale, is plotted on the y-axis. The intersection of the two ratings is called the *Qualidex* rating and the co-ordinates are expressed as "xx/yy". Exhibit 1 shows our *Qualidex* ratings for 13 projects. The *Qualidex* concept not only facilitates understanding of TQM and ISO 9000 but also proposes that there is a relationship between the two dimensions, i.e. the greater the involvement and commitment of the team to the project goals (Contemporary quality), the greater the likelihood of meeting project requirements of specifications, schedule and budget (Conventional quality).

## The *Qualidex* for BC Hydro

B.C. Hydro, a government-owned utility, generates about 80 percent of the electricity in the province of British Columbia from a predominantly hydroelectric system with nameplate capacity of about 10,300MW (1000 MW thermal). About 1.4 million customers are connected by over 70,000 kilometers of transmission and distribution lines. The utility spends about $450 million annually on capital projects to upgrade, reinforce and extend the existing electrical system.

**Exhibit 1.** The *Qualidex* Concept

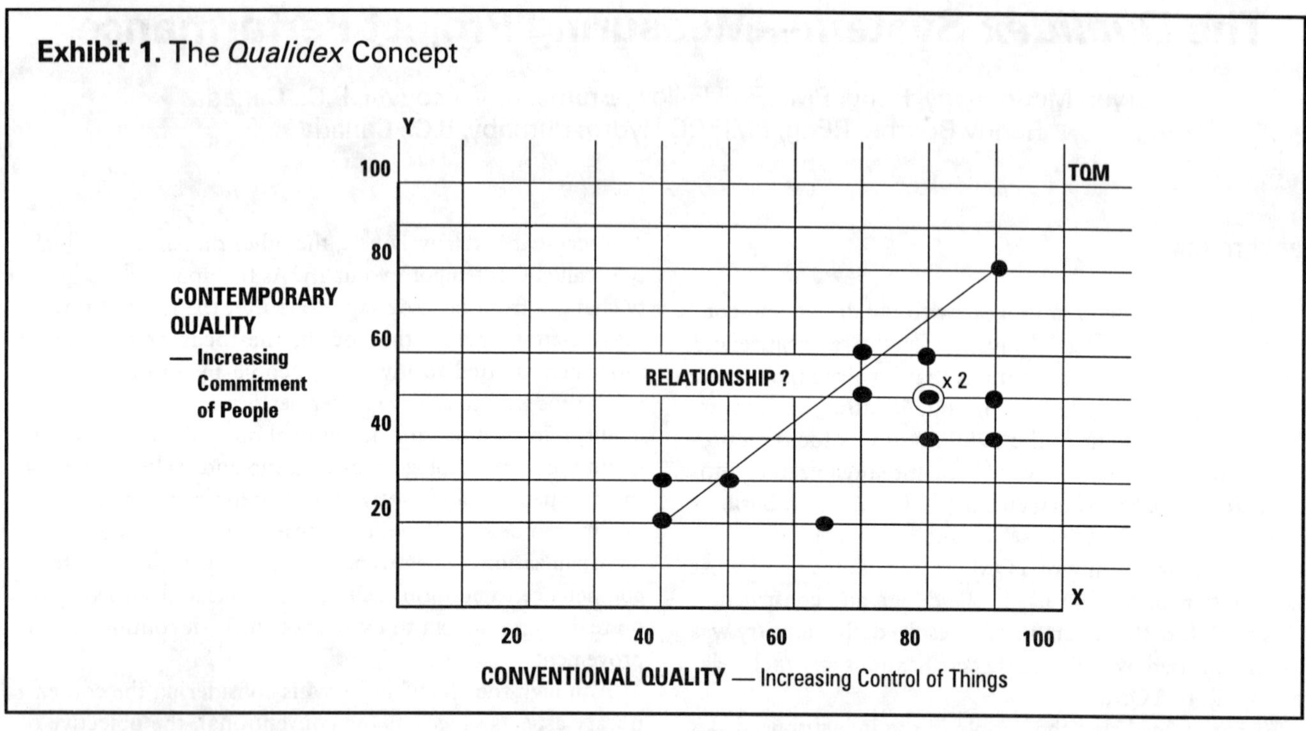


The power supply business unit is responsible for the supply of electricity. The Project Services Department (PSD) in B.C. Hydro's Power Supply Group is responsible for supplying project management, project support and environmental coordination. PSD sponsored the development of a *Qualidex* to identify areas requiring improvement in order that scarce training resources could be allocated in an optimum way. In order to develop the specific surveys for both the conventional and contemporary aspects for each of the three areas within PSD, a representative of each area was assigned to work with the consultant.

## Survey Development

### Conventional Quality (Controlling Things)

The starting point for the conventional quality survey was the life cycle diagram from the Project Management Policies as presented at Project Management Institute Seminar/Symposium 1995 in New Orleans ( 2). While the corporation's Project Management Policies dictate that the project phases be identification, definition and implementation, this breakdown did not lend itself to measuring the quality control aspects as there were relatively few QC practices in place (or contemplated) in either the identification or definition phases but there are many in the Implementation phase. In fact, the QC for the detail design portion of implementation was quite different from the construction portion. The result was that for the survey, the two early phases (identification and definition) were combined and the detail design portion of Implementation was treated as a separate phase from the construction portion of Implementation.

The detailed rating survey developed by the participants used the following components:

*Performance of Tasks*: The Pareto Principle was used to select the significant few from the trivial many. The critical project tasks are generally in sequence as they occur during the project life cycle.

*QA/QC*: For each task that is selected and rated, the quality control measure for that task is identified and rated as is the quality assurance procedure for the QC activity. Quality Control, which is the practice of checking the performance of the tasks against the established standards or customer expectations, involves action by a team member or a person to whom a team member reports. Quality Assurance refers to the documented procedures that set out how work processes are conducted and identifies the standards or expectations to be used for QC. Once established, QA is a passive component of the process. For formal certifications like ISO 9000, the documentation and processes are audited to confirm compliance.

Following are some examples of typical task performance, quality control practices and quality assurance procedures:

***Task Performance***

Identify customer requirements
Recruit project team

Establish design/construction controls
Monitor design/construction progress

#### QC Practices

Confirm competent staff
Concept/design reviews
Organized records

#### QA Procedures

Internal documentation
Internal audit
ISO 9000 certification

### Contemporary Quality (Motivating People)

We developed a detailed rating survey for Contemporary quality to suit PSD. There was some latitude permitted for selecting the items in the survey but, in order to facilitate benchmarking with other organizations, we were constrained to stay within the long list of items provided in Exhibit 1. The selected items are listed in a hierarchy with earlier items generally being prerequisites for later items. There are two groups of items—"Training for Competence" followed by "Motivation to Achieve Excellence". These groups are separated by a decision node—"Senior and Middle Management Commitment"—which is intended to ensure that the team is not wasting its time on a program to achieve excellence that management will not support.

The rationale for the division between the training and motivation is that there is no benefit to motivating the incompetent (inadequately trained) to strive for excellence. If they do not know how to adequately perform their assigned tasks, they require training and only when the competence has been obtained should the program enter the motivation phase. Similarly, once the team members have reached an acceptable level of competence in performing their tasks, there is limited value in continuing to provide further training for that task. Unlike Conventional quality, which has a different survey for each of the three groups, there was a single Contemporary quality survey for all members of the department.

## Survey Results

Completing the surveys followed these steps:

*Step 1*—Each member of the department was asked to complete the Conventional quality survey for their specific group. This first pass asked how well they thought their group currently performed the listed tasks, how well the current quality control practices are applied and how effective are the current quality assurance procedures.

*Step 2*—Each member of the department was asked to complete the current activities column of the Contemporary quality survey. The survey is the same for all members of the department. Numerical scores were preferred (increments of 5 adequate) but the survey form is set up to subjectively solicit opinions in 4 broad categories—nothing significant, some, extensive or very extensive activities.

*Step 3*—For the first part of this step, management was asked to set the Conventional goal for a reasonable period of time. For PSD, the program goal was set at a conventional ***Qualidex*** rating of 75 percent in 3 years (October 1999). For the second part, the participants were asked how to best attain that goal. To facilitate timely completion of the survey, the scoring sheet shows default scores required to make the 75 percent target in each item. If they did not think that all items should score the same, they could change the default scores but where they increased one item by an amount, they should have decreased another by the same amount to keep the total the same.

*Step 4*—Establishing the requirements for Contemporary quality is the most significant step in the process and the most unique element of ***Qualidex***. It asks the members of the Department what has to change in the organization structure/environment before management's desired goal for Conventional quality can be achieved. The theory is that improvements in Conventional ratings will come when the team gets to the Contemporary stage of continuous improvement. The items preceding that stage are the prerequisites to improvement.

## Summary Level Results

The ***Qualidex*** chart on Exhibit 2 shows the complete picture of the department's current status and goals. The histograms show the survey results for each item as well as several roll-ups of survey items. The summary levels for the current and ultimate goal are plotted on the ***Qualidex*** (x-y graph) along with two interim targets to show our path to the goal. These are not just arbitrary points—they translate back to specific items (tasks, QC/QA, training, motivation) that need to be improved by specific amounts to achieve the goal. The current ***Qualidex*** rating for PSD is 65/37—that is 65 percent of maximum Conventional and 37 percent of maximum Contemporary. The PQI goal as determined by the department members is 77/58 by 1999. For the conventional goal where default scores were provided for the management selected total of 75 percent, some participants increased the score on some items without an offsetting decrease. These higher scores increased the conventional quality goal to 77 percent.

**Exhibit 2.**

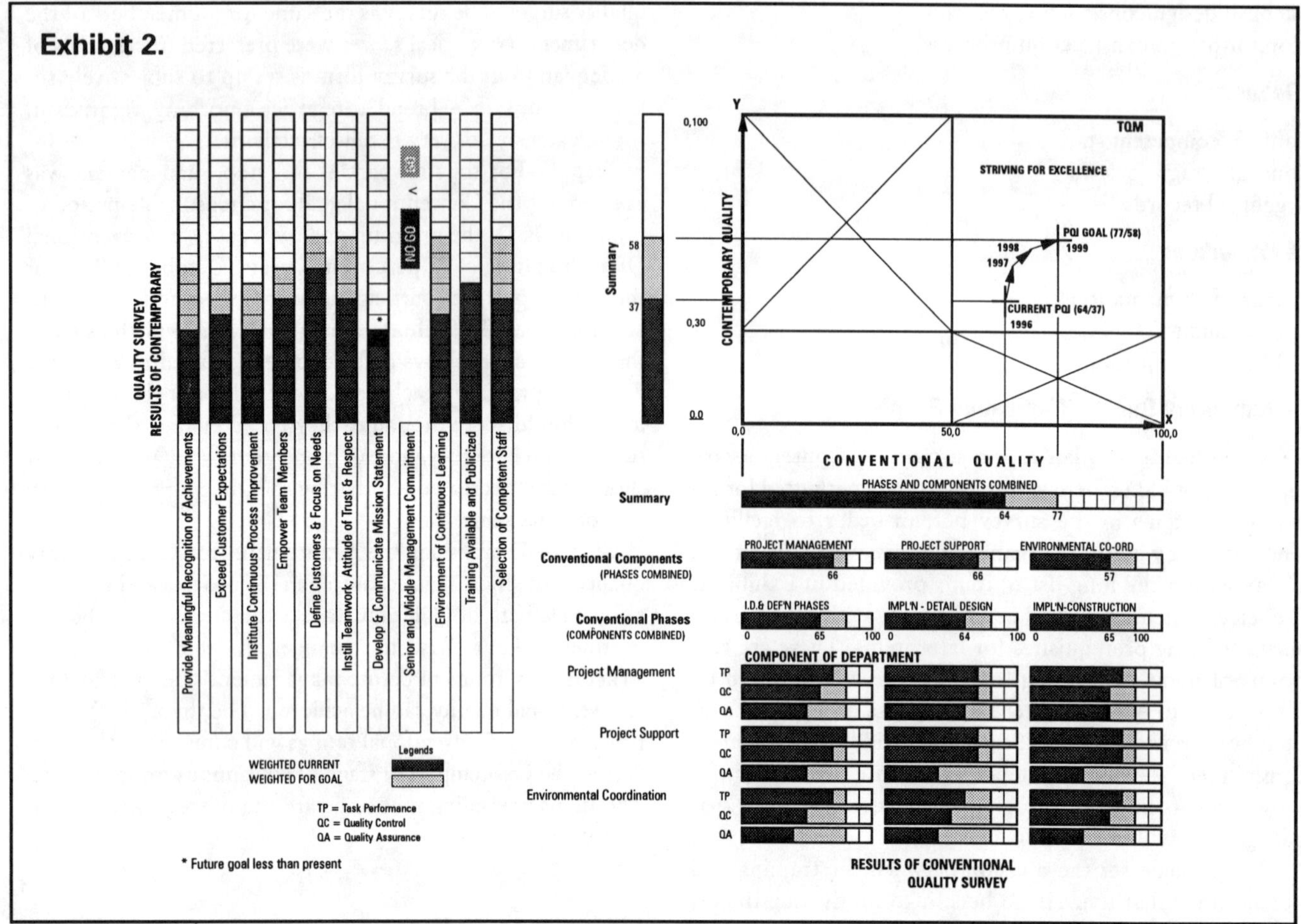


## Outcome

The survey recommended a three year program to achieve the program goal and provided the following recommendations for action in the first year.

With respect to Contemporary quality, which applies to all members of the department, the recommendations were:

1. Drop the development of a mission statement—The objective of collectively developing a mission statement was to "develop and communicate goals and values". This requirement remains and generally, the collective development of a mission statement is still considered a valuable team-building exercise. However, in this case, the department rated the future requirement lower than the current score.
2. Management commits to the program—Management commitment had the highest gap between current rating and rating required to achieve the results. PSD management should demonstrate their commitment to excellence.
3. Address negative reaction to "Selection by Competency"—Due to reductions and re-organizations, PSD are currently required to use what staff is available. This conflicts with one of the values set out by the department members but since PSD management is unable to change that corporate requirement in the short term, the issue should be set up as a future goal when the corporate environment changes.
4. Enhance the Environment of Continuous Learning—PSD management should determine if a reduction of the training budgets is the source of the large gap between current rating and rating required to achieve the results. If so, seek local low cost programs until budgets are re-established or determine other alternatives within the available funds.
5. Nurture "Teamwork, Trust and Respect"—As a minimum, establish several groups that have this critical aspect involved. For example, use a team of project managers and project support to implement several improvement programs.
6. Provide training in "Continuous Improvement"—The group does not appear to appreciate the role of continuous improvement. Assign one of the project

managers to develop a training session for presentation to the department.

With respect to Conventional quality, which is specific to the three groups in the department, the recommendations were:

1. Organized Records—This item scored low with all three groups. If the ISO 9000 program does not catch this item, PSD should set up a task force with one representative from each group to confirm the concern and to determine resolution.
2. Competent Staff—This item showed up as a weakness in the quality control sections of both project management and project support. We believe this reflects the same concern (3. Above) about having to work with available personnel regardless of their capability.
3. Quality Assurance—The cross surveys indicated that project managers and environmental coordinators understood the role of QA but project support personnel did not. If the forthcoming ISO 9000 program does not already incorporate training in the basics of QA/QC, PSD should consider their own program. This would not be a high priority item.
4. Risk Analysis—This project management issue consistently received a low rating (1/3). As described in 5 Above, set up a program and hopefully get benefits of both team building and performance enhancement.
5. Customer Acceptance—This unique project management issue had widely dispersed ratings. This item is not always included in the project procedures that may be why so many do not recognize the need. PSD to review their project procedures and, if appropriate, draft a new procedure to capture this item.
6. Feedback to Design—This is another item unique to project management where the rating was widely dispersed. PSD should review their project procedures and, if appropriate, draft a new procedure to capture this item.
7. In-house Reviews—This Environmental Coordination issue was rated low. PSD should review their project procedures and, if appropriate, draft a new procedure to capture this item.
8. Agency Feedback—This Environmental Coordination issue is rated less than 50 percent currently and in excess of 90 percent as a future requirement. PSD to confirm the deficiency, then ask the environmental coordinators to develop options to resolve.

## ISO 9000—Certification

Concurrent with the ***Qualidex*** survey, Power Supply embarked on obtaining ISO 9000 certification for the engineering and project management functions. The ***Qualidex*** survey results indicated a considerable amount of confusion about ISO 9000 and QA/QC concepts in general. In addition, the survey indicated a number of process deficiencies (for example, Organized Records) and it is anticipated that documenting our process in relation to these items will greatly reduce the current confusion. The ISO documentation has been in place since October 1996 and already has added clarity and consistency to our processes. At the time of publication of this paper, PSD was embarking upon an auditing program with regard to ISO 9000 and results should be available for presentation at the PMI seminar/symposium.

Since the ISO 9000 program is also being introduced to PSD, the action plan for year 1 was limited to producing two training modules—one in continuous improvement (project management) and the other in risk assessment.

## Future Developments

The ***Qualidex*** survey is scheduled to be repeated with the PSD in October 1997. Substantial improvements in conventional items are expected both as a result of the PSD action plan and the groups' steps towards ISO 9000 certification. The next step to be considered would be to survey PSD's internal customers and incorporate their ratings into the system.

Bramcon continues to work with other groups interested in improvement programs but we are finding that anything associated with "Quality" is passé. Business has moved on to other potential processes. The director of quality at one major corporation who has encouraged development of the ***Qualidex*** system prefers the labels "Performance Measurement" for our Conventional quality and "Organizational Effectiveness," for our Contemporary quality. Our next step may be a new name for the same concept.

Bramcon is working with a university to conduct a large survey that would confirm the proposed relationship between Conventional and Contemporary quality.

### Exhibits

1. McConachy, B.R. 1996. Concurrent Management of Total Cost and Total Quality. *Proceedings of the Annual Meeting of American Association of Cost Engineers.*.

2. Bourne, D.R., McConachy, B.R. and M.K. Strachan. 1995. One Size Conducts All?—PM Policies for an Electric Utility. *Proceedings.* Upper Darby, PA: Project Management Institute. pp. 728-735.

# Innovative Project Management Techniques on Central Artery (CA/T) Design Contract

Dr. John Audi, Edwards and Kelcey, Inc.
Kevin Maloney, PE and John Giudici, PE, Edwards and Kelcey, Inc.

## Introduction

The future of project management in the 21st Century will be defined by how the principles enlisted in the *Guide to the Project Management Body Of Knowledge* (PMI 1996) are integrated with continuous technological advancements in the computer science and engineering disciplines. The utilization of increasingly powerful computer processors for extensive data manipulation and analysis, and the efficiency in which scanners, and e-mail usage have evolved, are all keys in assuring that pertinent information during decision processes are properly communicated, thus contributing to the success of projects.

In charge of providing project management services as the Section Design Consultant (SDC) of one of the design contracts of the highly complex Central Artery project calls for innovative managerial measures. A $12 million design contract performed by a team comprising of eleven firms, and heavily dependent on constant coordination with entities, public agencies, and four adjacent design contracts, requires the implementation of a dynamic program that will assure information processing and decision making in a timely fashion.

Document control, an integral part of this managerial effort, consists of an integrated Microsoft Access database with multiple tables for recording, managing, and tracking all correspondence. All incoming documents are scanned and linked to a respective log table of the database, providing instant access for sought after information. Additional tables were developed for managing client furnished information and updates throughout the design process in accordance with the work scope of all eleven design firms. Add-on commercial and customized programs to Microsoft Access have enabled managers with minimum computer knowledge to query for and locate requested information with unparalleled ease.

An Action List table was developed within Microsoft Access listing all tasks that need to be performed as deemed critical on a weekly basis and all requests that arise on a daily basis. This list is prioritized by assigning responsibility, a desired action date, and a status for each task which is updated on a weekly basis. This action list serves as a historical database forming a traceable link between tasks and decisions, allowing managers to review those decisions made under similar circumstances, thus assuring more informed decisions in the future.

The use of e-mail between the client, and our firm, and between our firm and eight of the eleven other design firms has been significant in terms of assuring timely flow of information. Notices and reminders of key milestones, and meetings, and the transmittal as file attachments of meeting minutes, monthly update reports, invoices, and CADD drawings have helped streamline the flow of information among team members. Significant cost savings have been realized as a result of the diminished need for couriers, and data entry personnel.

Project time management is being performed with the use of Primavera where the progress of over 600 activities are updated on a monthly basis allowing for subsequent risk analyses to be conducted. Schedule and cost performance indices for each firm are analyzed on a monthly basis as part of an overall project control procedure. These aforementioned automated managerial tools assure that quality control on this project is achieved with high caliber

## Project Background

Edwards and Kelcey, Inc. (EK), engaged in a joint venture with Weidlinger Associates, is in charge of providing project management services as the Section Design Consultant (SDC) of the D018A Central Artery (CA/T) section design contract. This complex design contract consists of three distinct construction contracts comprising of a tunnel rehabilitation, an air intake structure, and an emergency response station. The $12 million, eighteen month duration, design contract is being performed by a team of eleven firms, two of which represent Edwards and Kelcey branch offices, all providing various discipline services including civil, traffic, structures, architecture, electrical, mechanical, geotechnical, survey, corrosion control, landscape, urban design, construction staging, and construction traffic management. Exhibit 1 summarizes the D018A team structure.

The location of the three construction contracts, which are scheduled to be completed by the year 2005, within the overall scope of the entire $10 billion central artery design contract, stipulates constant coordination with four other adjacent design contracts. This coordination is needed to avoid interface problems, and assure that civil alignment and construction staging requirements are addressed in a timely fashion so that appropriate changes for any of the affected contracts are incorporated accordingly. Moreover, mechanical, electrical and IPCS requirements of the D018A contract are dependent on the designs of two of the adjacent contracts.

Conforming to central artery design, drafting, and control standards established by Bechtel/Parsons Brinckerhoff (B/PB), the CA/T construction manager, adhering to the requirements of public agencies such as the Department of Public Safety, the Boston Fire Department, the Boston Water and Sewer Commission, and the City of Boston, justifying actions to the Massachusetts Highway Department (MHD) and the Federal Highway Administration (FHWA), and satisfying the demands of the community and future development plans, are all issues that need to be continuously dealt with throughout the design process.

## Project Communications Management

### Document Control

Recognizing the aforementioned project demands, Edwards and Kelcey, had to adopt and implement a dynamic managerial program to assure information processing and decision making in a timely fashion. This was critical in lieu of the active role Edwards and Kelcey needs to assume during construction, especially when factoring in the potential for changes in the roles and responsibilities of project managers during the eight year course of job.

Document control, an integral part of this program consists of an integrated Microsoft Access database with multiple tables for recording, managing, and tracking all correspondence, transmittals, faxes, and e-mails from and to B/PB, and from and to all other eleven firms. All incoming documents are scanned and linked to a respective log table of the database, providing instant access for sought after information. An English Wizard add on has enabled project managers with minimum computer knowledge to query for and locate requested information with ease. The add on program allows project managers to search for documents by simply typing requests in plain English text. Exhibit 2 shows a sample input and output process result.

With all documents electronically linked to the database, project managers can simply double click the "Electronic Link" field to view the desired documents.

Additional tables were developed for managing B/PB furnished information relating to CA/T design standards updates and adjacent contracts design progress updates so as to assess and evaluate interface, time, and cost implications from all D018A team members.

**Exhibit 1.** DO18A Team Structure

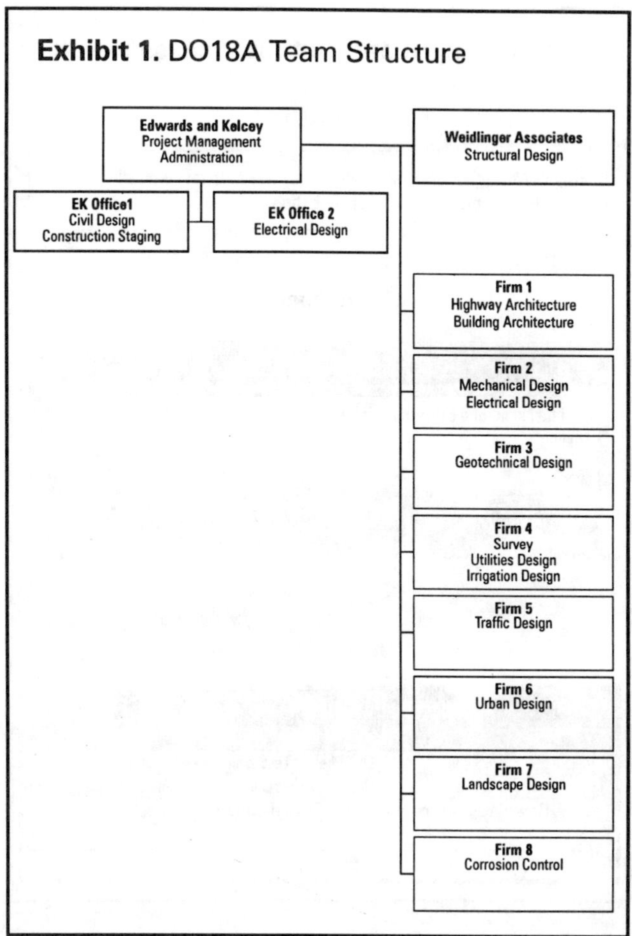


### Action List

An Action List table was developed within Microsoft Access listing all tasks that need to be performed as deemed critical on a weekly basis and all requests that arise on a continuous basis. This list is prioritized by assigning responsibility, a desired action date, and a status for each task which is updated on a weekly basis. Bi-weekly meetings held at B/PB offices attended by project managers representing the joint venture team, bi-weekly meetings held at Edwards and Kelcey offices attended by representatives from firms comprising the D018A team, and weekly internal EK staff meetings constitute the forums for which information is added to the action list. This action list serves as a historical database forming a traceable link between tasks and decisions, allowing managers to review those decisions made under similar circumstances, thus assuring more informed decisions in the future. Exhibit 3 shows a sample structure of the Action List.

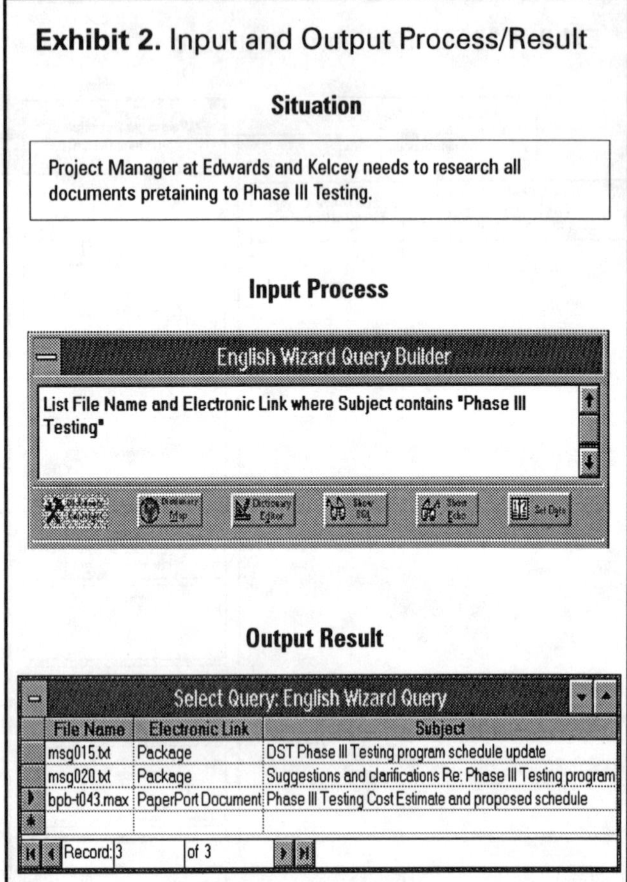
Situation
Project Manager at Edwards and Kelcey needs to research all documents pretaining to Phase III Testing.
Input Process
English Wizard Query Builder
List File Name and Electronic Link where Subject contains "Phase III Testing"
Output Result
Select Query: English Wizard Query
Record: 3 of 3

| File Name | Electronic Link | Subject |
|---|---|---|
| msg015.txt | Package | DST Phase III Testing program schedule update |
| msg020.txt | Package | Suggestions and clarifications Re: Phase III Testing program |
| bpb-t043.max | PaperPort Document | Phase III Testing Cost Estimate and proposed schedule |

**Exhibit 2.** Input and Output Process/Result

## E-Mail and Internet Access

The use of e-mail between the client, and our firm, and between our firm and eight of the eleven other design firms has been significant in terms of assuring timely flow of information. Notices and reminders of key milestones, and meetings, and the transmittal as file attachments of meeting minutes, monthly update reports, invoices, and CADD drawings have helped streamline the flow of information among team members. The ability to quickly obtain electronic files from various team members, has streamlined the process of incorporating needed changes prior to submittal milestones. Significant cost savings have been realized as a result of the diminished need for couriers, and data entry personnel.

Access to the Internet at EK has been extremely useful in supporting the development of a cost estimate and bid item specifications for the various disciplines of the D018A project. Information regarding manufacturer material specifications, labor productivity, and equipment sizes is extracted and compiled from various contractor, and engineering organization internet sites. This tool has provided EK engineers with a quick and effective tool for supporting team member designers evaluate various material selections, for the development of a cost effective design.

## Project Time and Cost Management

A critical success factor in scheduling is good planning with due allowance to communicating schedule results to the different parties involved. Communication between responsible parties of the D018A team is essential to cost and schedule conflict resolution.

Recognizing the importance of meeting project objectives within the framework of schedule and budget resources, EK has developed and implemented a comprehensive project control system based upon realistic goals to measure the actual status of this project against planned objectives and goals. Consequently corrective management measures are taken when warranted. This control system includes:

1. A baseline CPM network schedule of over 600 activities developed in Primavera.
2. A monthly procurement schedule depicting actual progress compared with scheduled progress.
3. Monthly cost reports comparing expenditures against budget estimates.

The baseline schedule depicts how the various milestone dates are being met and highlights the interaction that is to be performed by the various technical disciplines.

The procurement schedule allows for the early recognition of potential milestone contract slippage. Schedule and cost performance indices for each firm are analyzed on a monthly basis as part of an overall project control procedure. Remedial actions or plans are initiated and implemented when deemed necessary.

Monitoring monthly expenditures against predefined budget estimates is essential for assuring the on-budget completion of this design project. Integrated spreadsheet forms have been created to monitor the expenditures of all D018A firms against their monthly work progress.

Utilizing a real time centralized accounting system at EK - BST Project Management System, project mangers can instantaneously inquire or report on project charges by branch office, discipline, employee, or accounting period range, and check on the status of invoice payments. This flexibility allows project managers to evaluate and assess the productivity of D018A employees from all EK offices on a weekly basis with relative ease.

## Project Quality Management

A project quality control program was established for the D018A project and agreed upon by all team members. In assuring that all team members adhere to the QC program, a database in Microsoft Access was needed to track compliance. Tables were developed to manage responses of design and drafting related concerns, to assure proper implementation of changes, and to monitor overall contract conformity of all disciplines.

With the complexity of this project, the utilization of this database assures that quality control for this design contract is neither overlooked nor undermined. Within a matter of seconds the status of outstanding issues can be brought to the attention of team members thus assuring timely response actions.

**Exhibit 3.** Action List Structure

| Field Name | Data Type |
|---|---|
| EK Action | Text |
| Responsible EK Employee | Text |
| Date Listed | Date/Time |
| Status | Text |
| Comments | Text |
| Follow up Action | Text |
| Follow Up Action Status | Text |
| Desired Action Date | Date/Time |

## Conclusion

This paper discussed innovative project management techniques utilized on the D018A Central Artery Design Contract. The aforementioned automated managerial tools have streamlined the process of information processing and decision making by reexamining the philosophy of project management and the principles listed in the *Guide to the Project Management Body of Knowledge* (PMI 1996).

### References

Harris, Larry. 1997. *English Wizard User's Guide.* Littleton, MA: Linguistic Technology Corp.

Project Management Institute (PMI) Standards Committee. 1996. *A Guide to the Project Management Body of Knowledge*. Upper Darby, PA: Project Management Institute

# Alignment of Cross Functional Teams During Pre-Project Planning

Andrew F. Griffith, Ph.D., P.E., Independent Project Analysis, Inc., Reston, Virginia
G. Edward Gibson, Jr., Ph.D., P.E., Dept. of Civil Engineering, The University of Texas at Austin

## Introduction

As the project management profession enters the 21st Century, project teams will face increased pressure from business trends like re-engineering, downsizing, outsourcing, and globilization. In this environment of changing organizational structures, the human factor aspects of developing a team will present continued challenges to project management practitioners. Project teams are typically comprised of individuals representing a wide variety of project stakeholder groups. In order to have a successful project, these individuals must clearly define and work toward a common set of project objectives. Although the need for project teams to have a common set of project objectives is well documented, research has identified the existence of misalignment between project team members representing different stakeholder groups. This condition of misalignment results in poor communications and may negatively affect the chances of having a successful project. *A Guide to the Project Management Body of Knowledge (PMBOK Guide)* (PMI 1996) discusses team alignment as a part of leadership within general management skills and is not specifically identified as an aspect of the project management process. However, project teams encounter unique problems regarding alignment because, by design, they are staffed with individuals from different stakeholder groups with conflicting objectives and priorities for the same project. What are the most effective ways available to improve team alignment and what effect does team alignment have on project outcomes? These questions were addressed by a research investigation into alignment of capital facility project teams. The results of this investigation, the implication for the *PMBOK Guide*, and recommendations for project management professionals are discussed in this article.

## Alignment

### Background

The research presented in this paper was sponsored by the Construction Industry Institute (CII) at The University of Texas at Austin and was conducted by a team of industry representatives and academicians. The research team began with the objective of investigating project teams and front-end planning of capital facility projects. The research effort started with a detailed literature review of published information regarding teams, project management, and organizational behavior.

The key organizational unit in project management is the group or team. Groups have existed throughout history and are the subject of many books and research articles (Ross 1989, Katzenbach & Smith 1993, Cartwright & Zander 1968, Parker 1993, Tjosvold 1986, and Napier & Gershenfeld 1983). Groups can be defined as systems within systems, complete with external and internal dependencies and constraints. Groups are everywhere. They are the primary means of socialization in families, in schools, clubs, and sport teams. In the business world, groups are currently experiencing a resurgence. When an organization takes the initiative to assemble a gathering of people from different functional areas, that organization has not necessarily formed a true team or group. According to Ross (1989), for a collection of people to form a group, the individuals would have to exhibit at least five interdependent characteristics to be considered a true group. These five characteristics are:

1. They have open lines of communication
2. They have common goals and know it
3. They have structure
4. They experience pressure to conform
5. They take unitary actions

Throughout the literature review conducted for this research, the concept that groups "need to have common goals and know it" is a recurring theme. Parker (1993) advises managers of cross-functional teams to insist on a clear set of team goals and a plan to achieve those goals. Katzenbach and Smith (1993) define a team as a "small number of people with complementary skills who are committed to a common purpose, performance goals, and approach for which they hold themselves mutually accountable." Cartwright and Zander (1968) assert that setting common goals is an essential aspect of the motivational process in managing groups. Tjosvold (1986) devotes one entire chapter to the topic of developing cooperative goals. The importance of having common goals for teams is also found in project management literature.

Pinto and Kharabanda (1995) specifically note that clearly defined goals are one essential element of the definition of a project. Kerzner (1995) specifies that a project must have a clearly defined objective or goal. Although much has been written about the importance of developing common team objectives, the references cited do not provide any empirical evidence regarding the most effective methods used to establish those goals or the effect that clearly defined goals have on the results of team efforts.

Goal setting, or the idea of assigning employees a specific amount of work to be accomplished based on a task, a quota, a performance standard, an objective, or a deadline, dates back more than 70 years to Frederick Taylor and scientific management. According to Locke and Latham (1985), goals affect performance by means of three major mechanisms. First, goals help to focus a person's attention on goal-relevant factors rather than alternative activities. Second, goal setting helps to regulate a person's energy expenditure. Finally, "hard" goals that are accepted increase a person's persistence. Research studies into goal setting have provided a great deal of support for the theory. One literature review noted that over a 15 year time-span there were more than 110 goal setting experiments conducted in both laboratory and organizational settings. Of those 110 experiments, 90 percent found that goal setting increased performance significantly (Locke, Shaw, Saari, & Latham 1981).

As part of a previous research project into pre-project planning of capital facility projects, in-depth telephone interviews were conducted with the project participants of sixty-two projects concerning their perceptions of project success and pre-project planning effort. The qualitative results of these surveys were analyzed and categorized according to three response groups: business managers, project managers, and operations managers (Gibson, Tortora, & Wilson 1994). The respondents were asked an open-ended question that was used to determine the perceptions of the project representatives about the relative importance of project goals. The results showed a considerable disagreement between the groups of project representatives concerning the importance of different project goals. The project managers were most concerned with the execution phase of the project and the project turnover. The operations managers were most concerned with the downstream results of the planning and execution phase of the project. In addition, operations managers were very concerned with having more input into project planning, especially in the area of technology evaluation. The business managers appeared to be more concerned with the overall project from a "macro" level rather than how well it was executed or operates. This overall difference in success emphasis may contribute to disagreement among project representatives over project goals and objectives and can lead to breakdowns during the pre-project planning of capital facilities.

This disagreement of project goals and the resulting communication breakdowns is an example of misalignment of project participants. Alignment, as a concept, is not an easy one to describe and its effect on projects is even less understood. However, based on the research results described above, alignment and its relationship to project goal setting is an important issue that deserves further study.

## PMI on Alignment

The *PMBOK Guide* (1996) devotes an entire chapter to Project Human Resource Management. This chapter is divided into three major sections, Organizational Planning, Staff Acquisition, and Team Development. The final section, Team Development, only addresses team alignment through an indirect reference. The section covering tools and techniques for team development references general management skills. General management skills are discussed in more detail in Chapter Two of the *PMBOK Guide*. In Chapter Two, there is one brief sentence that discusses alignment as a part of leadership. In this section, alignment is described as "Communicating the vision by words and deeds to all those whose cooperation may be needed to achieve the vision."

In project management, proper goal setting and alignment of the cross-functional team behind those goals is a critical aspect of team development. However, this issue is only indirectly addressed by the current version of the *PMBOK Guide*. Because project teams are typically comprised of individuals from different functional groups with different priorities and objectives for the project, the project manager needs to pay a great deal of attention to proper alignment. Without a clear set of project objectives and commitment by the entire team to those objectives, a project team is likely to experience individual team members making project decisions that are in direct conflict. But what is alignment, what are the factors that affect the team's level of alignment, and what effect does team alignment have on project success?

## Alignment in the Project Environment

As with any concept, a clear and specific definition is required so that the discussion can begin from a common starting point. The following definition of alignment provides that framework:

Alignment—The dictionary defines alignment as: The condition of being in satisfactory adjustment or having the parts in proper relative position. In the context of capital projects, alignment may be defined more specifically as: The condition where appropriate project participants are

**Exhibit 1.** Graphical Representation Of Alignment

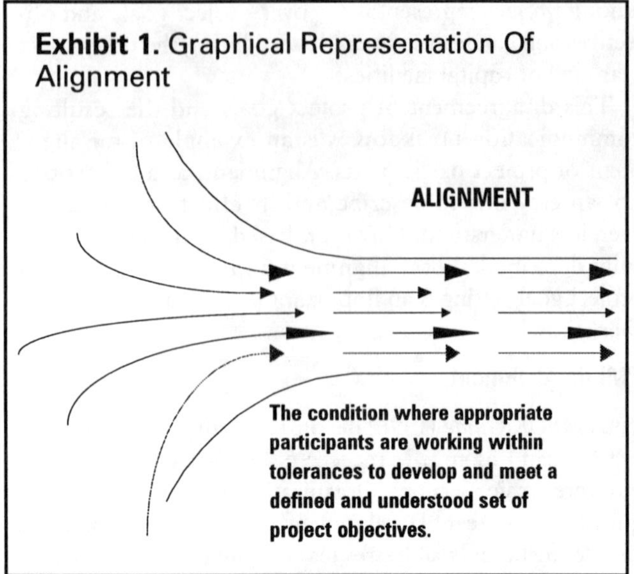
ALIGNMENT
The condition where appropriate participants are working within tolerances to develop and meet a defined and understood set of project objectives.

working within acceptable tolerances to develop and meet a uniformly defined and understood set of project objectives. These project objectives must meet business requirements and the overall corporate strategy. They are formed in the early stages of project development and have a critical impact on the success of the project delivery process (Griffith & Gibson 1995).

Whenever a project team is formed of people from different functional groups, each team member brings with him/her the values and goals of the specific functional group to which they belong. These individual values and goals often conflict with the values and goals of the other team members and also may conflict with the organization's overall project goals. Aligning the team involves developing superordinate objectives for all team members and gaining the commitment to work toward those goals. This concept is graphically presented in Exhibit 1 by the arrows bending to "align" in the same direction.

Alignment involves adjusting individual priorities and objectives and becoming committed to an overall set of project goals. Without individual commitment, there is no alignment. It is not enough to simply tell the team what are the project objectives. At the end of the alignment process, each member is focused on the same set of project objectives. Note that each individual arrow in the figure is still unique with different experiences and specialties. Alignment does not imply eliminating differences but simply focusing the different team members on the same objective.

Issues that effect alignment during pre-project planning can be divided into five different categories. These five categories of alignment issues are centered around topics commonly addressed in the project environment. They include:

- Company Culture which is described as the attitudes, values, behavior, and environment of the company and the pre-project planning team.
- Execution Processes which are project systems, processes, and procedures.
- Information which is described as data elements used to define the scope of the project.
- Project Management Tools which include software programs, checklists, and aide-memoirs which are typically used to develop and manage projects.
- Barriers which are obstacles to creating and maintaining alignment.

## Research

### Hypothesis

The research discussed in this paper focuses on the early planning phase of capital facility projects. It is during this early project phase when significant project decisions are made by the project team. The project scope definition developed during the pre-project planning phase has a tremendous effect on the final project cost and schedule as well as the project functional features at completion. Additional information regarding pre-project planning and its relationship with project success can be found in Gibson Kaczmarowski, & Lore (1993) and Gibson & Hamilton (1994).

The primary purpose of this study was to build on previous research concerning goal setting, pre-project planning, and team alignment by developing and testing a path analytic framework that includes antecedents that appear to effect the development of clear and accepted project goals and the subsequent performance outcomes. Many factors may influence alignment within a project team such as technical skill, reward structure, interpersonal skill, organizational structure, cultural norms, and corporate strategy. This study examined the effects of five categories of antecedents on project team alignment: execution processes, tools, information, barriers, and organizational culture. Exhibit 2 illustrates a three-stage path analytic model showing the factors involved in a project which influence team alignment. In the *PMBOK Guide*, this initial phase of the project life-cycle is covered in Project Scope Management.

### Methodology

The research team used brainstorming techniques to develop an exhaustive list of issues that could possibly have an effect on team alignment during pre-project planning. This list of

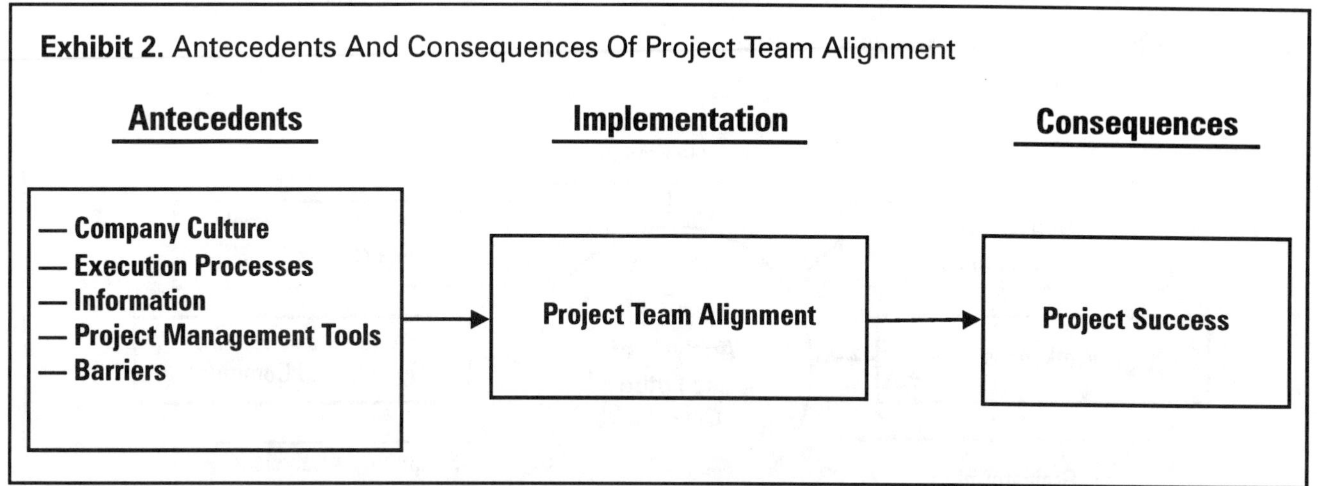

**Exhibit 2.** Antecedents And Consequences Of Project Team Alignment

sixty-six items was then used as a starting point for the data collection phase of the research. The list of possible alignment factors were first divided into the five categories of alignment factors shown in the above causal path model. A three-stage research approach was used to investigate alignment of project teams during pre-project planning. The research approach provided the research team with extensive information related to alignment during pre-project planning.

The first stage of the research involved workshops with industry experts where participants were asked to complete a written survey and to participate in round-table discussions regarding alignment during pre-project planning.

The second stage of the research involved actual industrial capital facility projects. Mail surveys and telephone interviews were used to collect data regarding alignment during pre-project planning and project outcomes from 20 industrial construction projects.

The last stage of the research effort involved three extensive personal interviews with executives from two owner organizations and one contractor organization. These "Best Practice" interviews provided information regarding current best practices and future trends regarding team alignment during pre-project planning.

Each of the three phases of data collection and analyses utilized different samples and different techniques. The results from each phase were also different to some degree. The next logical question is: How do you combine these results into a single list of significant alignment issues? There is no natural weighting system that can be used in an statistical equation that will produce a ranked list of significant issues. Each data collection phase has its own advantages and disadvantages and produced its own set of results. For this analysis, a combination of quantitative and qualitative techniques were used to combine the results from each phase of the research. Recent developments in the evaluation profession have led to an increase in the use of multiple methods, including combinations of qualitative and quantitative data (Patton 1990). In this analysis, the results of various quantitative techniques are combined using qualitative techniques.

Various analysis techniques were used as inputs into the qualitative analysis. Brainstorming sessions were used to identify the possible factors that could effect team alignment. Workshops with industry experts were used to provide an initial ranking of those possible factors and ensure that the research was on the right track. ANOVA statistical analysis, bivariate statistical analysis, and path analysis techniques were used to evaluate the correlation within the data collected from sample projects. Frequency analysis techniques were used to evaluate transcripts from both the open-ended comments from the telephone interviews and the best practice interviews. All of these techniques provided the input into the comprehensive qualitative analysis used to arrive at the basic research conclusions and recommendations. Exhibit 3 is a graphical representation of this process.

## Results

The research described in this paper was initiated with two primary objectives which are graphically represented by the causal diagram in Exhibit 2:

1. To identify factors that significantly effect project team alignment during pre-project planning
2. To identify the relationship that exists between project team alignment and project success

Data were collected from twenty completed capital facility projects representing thirteen different owner organizations and $2.2 billion in authorized cost. Expert input from over 100 individuals who participated in the initial brainstorming sessions, workshops, telephone interviews, and best practice interviews were also incorporated into

**Exhibit 3.** Qualitative Data Analysis Process

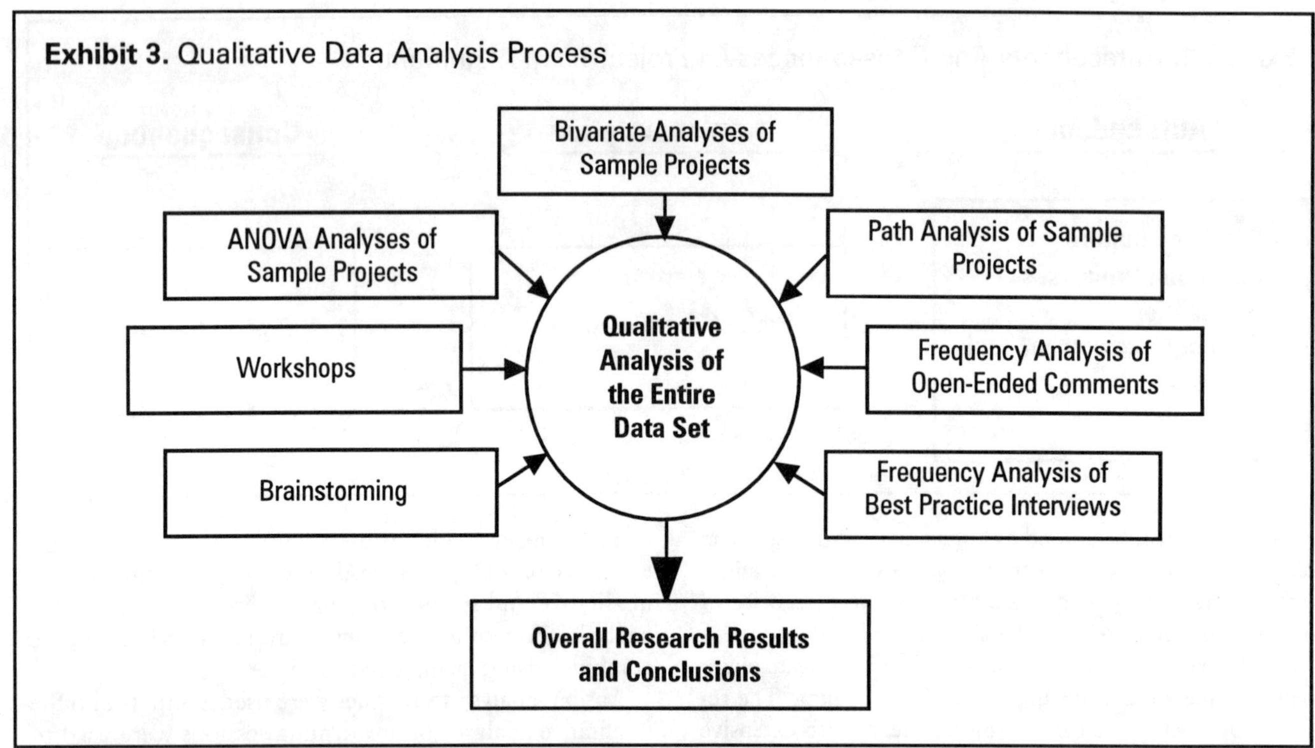


the data analysis. The data collected from this effort supported the hypothesized relationship presented in Exhibit 2. Each of the five categories of alignment factors demonstrated a significant effect on team alignment during the early planning phase of capital facility projects. Execution processes, project management tools, information available to the project team, and organizational culture all showed a positive correlation with the level of team alignment. The category of barriers to alignment demonstrated a negative correlation.

The data also supported the second stage of the causal relationship presented in the hypothesis. The level of team alignment during pre-project planning demonstrated a significant and positive correlation with the ultimate success of the project. Project success was measured by an index comprised of four quantifiable project performance measurements: budget performance as compared to the authorized budget, schedule performance as compared to the authorized schedule, production capacity as compared the designed capacity planned at the time of authorization, and plant utilization as compared to the planned utilization at the time of authorization. Projects that exhibited a higher level of team alignment during the pre-project planning phase also performed better in the four elements of the success index (Griffith & Gibson 1997).

## Conclusions and Recommendations

### Research Conclusions

The research effort and the analysis of the data collected arrived at four primary conclusions that relate to team alignment during pre-project planning and the *PMBOK Guide*:

1. The alignment of team members during pre-project planning of capital facilities has a significant and positive effect on overall project success.
2. There are specific factors that project teams can address that can have a significant and positive effect on team alignment.
3. Although the research focused on pre-project planning, alignment is also important during the entire life of the project.
4. The *PMBOK Guide* should place more emphasis on team alignment. The section on Team Development in Chapter Nine should include a discussion concerning alignment and the factors that affect team alignment. This focus on alignment should also emphasis the need for teams to be aligned with the overall project business needs as discussed in Project Scope Management. Team members need to be aligned with one another and with the business objectives of the project.

## Recommendations for Project Management Professionals

In addition to the general conclusions of this research, the analysis of the data collected identified ten specific recommendations for project teams wishing to improve the level of alignment within their teams. These issues demonstrated the strongest effect on project team alignment in both the statistical analysis of the sample projects and the open-ended comments from both the telephone and the best practice interviews. Project leaders initiating the planning phase of complex capital facility projects should actively address the following recommendations in order to improve the level of alignment within the project planning team.

Many recommendations can be made based on the findings and conclusions of this research. Project teams initiating pre-project planning or scope definition should consider the importance of alignment and its effect on the ultimate success of the project. Specifically, project teams should (Griffith & Gibson 1997):

- Staff the pre-project team with representatives from all appropriate stakeholder groups. Include representatives from operations, construction, business management, and other groups with a significant stake in the project's success.
- Foster and develop leadership on the project team. Pre-project planning teams need strong leadership to guide them through the process, otherwise the project is likely to languish and never develop a clear set of project objectives.
- Clearly define and communicate the priorities between the project cost, schedule, and required features.
- Develop an environment of open communications between team members and with individuals outside the team.
- Ensure that project team meetings are both timely and productive.
- Develop a team culture that fosters trust, honesty, and shared values among the team members.
- Establish and follow a structured pre-project planning process that includes sufficient funding, schedule, and scope to meet its objectives.
- Establish a reward and recognition system that promotes the overall project objectives. This system should include contracting strategies with outside contractors and suppliers.
- Initiate and maintain a formal team building program to help develop the environment of a true team.
- Use the available planning tools to solicit the input from the entire team during pre-project planning. Involve the entire team in the use of these tools to gain buy-in and commitment to the project objectives. Examples of tools cited in the research include scheduling techniques, risk analysis, cost control, budgeting and estimates, and checklists.
- Frequently monitor the progress achieved on each of the above issues and take appropriate corrective actions when needed.

### References


Cartwright, D. & Zander, A. 1968. *Group Dynamics: Research and Theory.* New York: Harper & Row, Publishers.

Gibson, G.E., & Hamilton, M.R. 1994. *Analysis of Pre-Project Planning Effort and Success Variables for Capital Facility Projects, - Source Document #105.* Austin, Texas: Construction Industry Institute, The University of Texas at Austin.

Gibson, G.E., Kaczmarowski, J.H., & Lore, H.E. 1993. *Modeling Pre-Project Planning for the Construction of Capital Facilities - Source Document #94.* Austin, Texas: Construction Industry Institute, The University of Texas at Austin.

Gibson, G.E., Tortora, A.L., & Wilson, C.T. 1994. *Perceptions of Project Representatives Concerning Project Success and Pre-Project Planning Effort - Source Document #102.* Austin, Texas: Construction Industry Institute, The University of Texas at Austin.

Griffith, A.F., & Gibson, G.E. 1997. *Alignment During Pre-Project Planning of Capital Facilities - Research Report 113-12.* Austin, Texas: Construction Industry Institute, The University of Texas at Austin.

Griffith, A.F., & Gibson, G.E. 1995. Project communication and alignment during pre-project planning. In *1995 Proceedings: Project Management Institute Annual Conference:* 76-83. Upper Darby, Pennsylvania: Project Management Institute.

Katzenbach, J.R., & Smith, D.K. 1993. *The Wisdom of Teams: Creating the High-Performance Organization.* Boston: Harvard Business School Press.

Kerzner, H. 1995. *Project Management: A Systems Approach to Planning, Scheduling, and Control.* New York, New York: Van Nostrand Reinhold.

Locke, E.A., & Latham, G.P. 1985. *Goal Setting for Individuals, Groups, and Organizations.* Chicago, Illinois: Science Research Associates.

Locke, E.A., Shaw, K.N., Saari, L.M., & Latham, G.P. 1981. *Goal setting and task performance: 1969-1980.* Psychological Bulletin, 90: 125-152.

Napier, R.W., & Gershenfeld, M.K. 1983. *Making Groups Work: A Guide for Group Leaders.* Boston: Houghton Mifflin Company.

Parker, G.M. 1994. *Cross-Functional Teams: Working with Allies, Enemies, and Other Strangers.* San Francisco: Jossey-Bass Publishers.

Patton, M.Q. 1990. *Qualitative Evaluation and Research Methods.* London: Sage Publications.

Pinto, J.K., & Kharabanda, O.P. 1995. *Successful Project Managers.* New York: Van Nostrand Reinhold.

*A Guide to the Project Management Body of Knowledge (PMBOK Guide).* 1996. Upper Darby, PA: Project Management Institute.

Ross, R.S. 1989. *Small Groups in Organizational Settings.* Englewood Cliffs, New Jersey: Prentice Hall.

Tjosvold, D. 1986. *Working Together to Get Things Done.* Lexington, Massachusetts: Lexington Books.

# Understanding Risk in Construction Contracts

Francis Hartman, The University of Calgary, Canada,
Zainul Khan, The University of Calgary, Canada
George Jergeas, The University of Calgary, Canada

In the construction industry, the contract documents are more than just evidence of an agreement between the contracting parties. The contract is a codification of the private law which governs the relationship between the parties to it. It defines the responsibilities, spells out the conditions of its operation, defines the rights of the parties in relation to each other and grants the remedies to a party if the other one breaches its obligations. It is also an agreement to allocate risk between the parties involved in the building process. Risk arises out of the obligations assumed by the parties to each other under the contract and from common law. In the absence of contractual provisions, terms may be implied in certain circumstances by law, or liability may be imposed in tort. Beyond liability to each other, the parties may also be exposed to risk from third party designers, supervisors, suppliers and ultimate users of the construction project. Therefore, it is crucial for all parties to understand contractual requirements fully prior to entering into the construction agreement and to be prepared to fulfill those provisions during the performance of the project. Just as ignorance of the law is no excuse in a criminal or quasi criminal matter, ignorance of contract provisions is no excuse in civil law. And to ignore them is to do so at one's peril. In some cases, valuable rights may be waived by ignorance or inadvertence. In other cases, obligations overlooked or ignored could be much more costly to undertake at a later point in time.

This paper explains why it is crucial for project managers and all parties to understand fully and manage within contractual requirements and how to minimize real risk exposure. The paper begins with a brief discussion of some of the objectives of the parties to a construction contract and how risk should be allocated on a construction project. In this paper, we will then review areas of risk in construction contracts and in some instances review recent judicial decisions which highlight the practical effect of some of the risk assigning clauses. Additionally, we will review a few court decisions in order to test the viability of the doctrine of fundamental breach and its specific application to these clauses. The paper closes by addressing some of the means to help understand and minimize risk exposure in a construction contract.

## Parties' Objectives

Normally, the objectives of the parties to a construction contract include:

- Certainty of obligations of each party and the avoidance of ambiguities and such definiteness of understanding as to preclude ultimate controversy. Certainty allows for the best price and allows construction to proceed in an orderly and harmonious atmosphere, minimizing surprises and hostility which frequently lead to litigation.
- A mechanism for the speedy and equitable resolution of issues which may arise during construction in order to assist contracting parties to work together in a productive relationship.
- Assignment of risk: A properly drafted contract will be clear not only with respect to those contractual duties which the parties are respectively assuming, but also with respect to those duties which the parties have agreed not to assume.
- A precise definition of the scope of the work and responsibility assumed by each party.

This stated, these objectives for clarity are often not met for many reasons. Sometimes these reasons are unavoidable.

## Areas of Risk

The ground rules for allocating risk in the construction industry begin with the construction contract. The importance of the contract cannot be overemphasized. After a project is awarded, the interpretation of the contract terms and interpretation of risk allocation between the owner, engineer, and contractor can vary considerably. Thus, the source of a costly dispute was latent within the contract clauses (Hartman, Snelgrove 1996). This conclusion is consistent with Thompson and Perry's (1992):

"The parties to a contract are also frequently at odds over the interpretation of risk allocation in the contract and the responsibility for managing risks (or carrying the consequences of the risk)... The result has been the rapid growth in the "claims industry," contract arbitration and litigation, in building and civil engineering in the United Kingdom, United States, and some commonwealth countries."

Areas of risk to be considered in the preparation of contractual documents include:

- Responsibility for design
- Responsibility for quality control
- Responsibility for performance of the work after completion and turnover
- Unexpected or changed site conditions
- Changes in quantities of work
- Weather and other natural causes
- The causes and effects of delay
- Supply, delivery and price of equipment and material to be incorporated in the work
- Labour problems (availability and quality)
- Work changes and the decisions to be made by the consultant in interpreting the responsibility of parties under the contract
- Site availability
- Interference from other contractors involved in the construction process
- Government and regulatory intervention
- Environmental hazards
- Extra work
- Insolvency
- Inadequate construction methods or equipment.

## Understanding and Minimizing Risk

The importance of careful risk allocation has been recognized in various reports (Hartman 1993; ACEC and AGCA 1990; NPCW 1990; CII 1986). Reports analyzing risk allocation in the construction industry and the underlying causes of disputes conducted in Australia, Canada, and the United States suggest that a major reason for what some might say is the dramatic increase in construction disputes lies not with the quality of the design or the performance by the contractor but rather with the failure of the actual wording to describe clearly and precisely the respective roles, responsibilities and rights of the parties. In other words, it is the quality of the contract documentation itself and not the quality of the design or the contractor's performance that is the root of the problem.

Disproportionate allocation of risk, even in the most detailed and carefully drafted agreements, may lead to acrimony and an adversarial relationship during the performance of the work. In return, this may lead to litigation involving claims in breach of contract, tort or fraud as attempts are made to adjust responsibility. In such events, owners may end up paying twice. First, by increased price and second, by the cost of litigation and possibly the payment of claims.

In considering the allocation of risk on a construction project, the following questions should be taken into consideration:

- Who has control of the task or area giving rise to the risk?
- Who is receiving the benefit and is the risk assumed proportionate to the benefit received by the responsible party?
- Who is receiving the residual or long-term benefit when considering the allocation of ongoing risk?
- Which party is most capable of dealing with, insuring against or minimizing the assumed risk?
- Which party customarily assumes the risk in the industry or trade?
- Who has the required expertise between the respective parties?

## Expressly Defining the Work in the Contract

The most obvious means to allocate risk arising during construction is through specific and express terms of the contract governing the relationship between the participants. The effectiveness of specific contractual risk allocation will depend on how well the intention of the parties is expressed. A court will be able to give effect only to the intention of the parties which it is able to interpret from the language used in the contract. In case of doubt or ambiguity, the rule of "contra proferentem" will normally apply and the contract will be strictly construed against the party attempting to enforce the provision in question (Marston 1996). Generally, a court will not refer to evidence beyond the language of the contract itself to vary or alter the clear and unambiguous meaning of a written contract, no matter how harsh the provision is (Graham 1985; Green 1994). In Olin Corporation v. Aluminum Corporation, 5 F3d 10 (2nd Circuit 1993), the court stated that "this is a seemingly harsh result for a company that must pay for the cleanup of contamination that it apparently did not cause. However, we are unwilling to ignore the broad inclusive language of the agreements freely entered into by two sophisticated parties. Parties should be able to rely on the terms of an agreement arrived at after arduous negotiations."

Therefore, by using clear and unambiguous language to express the intentions of the parties, risk can be allocated to various participants in the construction process by properly defining the scope of each parties' responsibility. As a consequence, many construction contracts employ exculpatory clauses to specifically allocate certain risk. Such clauses are intended to limit or exclude an owner and/or his representatives liability in contract and often also in tort for costs or expenses incurred by a contractor. Typically, these clauses will include a declaration that the bidder is entirely satisfied with every condition affecting the work to be performed and that the submission of the tender shall be conclusive evidence that the bidder has made such an investigation. They will usually be accompanied by disclaimers as to the accuracy of information provided by the owner and/or his representative. Many courts will enforce the clause in question as a matter of law (McClain 1995, Hunter 1989; Olin 1993). Below are some examples of exculpatory clauses with explanations following in some cases:

1."*The bidder is not entitled to rely on any data or information included in the bid documents as to the job site or subsurface conditions or test results indicating the suitability or quantity or otherwise of the job site or subsurface material for backfilling or other uses in carrying out the construction of the work.*"

Can you imagine fifteen bidders drilling a site for core samples to figure out how much to include in their bids in order to meet this requirement ? Extensive below-grade investigations are not cheap and much duplication is implied. How many owners would give permission for all those bidders to access the site with their drilling/sampling rigs ? This clause prevents the contractor from claiming relief in case of encountering differing soil/site conditions to those supplied by the owner.

2. "*The contractor shall not have any claim for compensation for damages against the owner for any stoppage or delay in the work from any cause whatsoever.*"

This provision is intended to prevent the contractor from claiming monetary and time extension compensation from the owner for delays caused by whatever event, including acts or omissions of the owner or of its agent.

3. "*Any representation in the tender documents were furnished merely for the general information of the bidder and were not in any way warranted or guaranteed by or on behalf of the owner or the owner's consultants or its employees, and neither the owner or its consultants or its employees shall be liable for any representations, negligent, or otherwise contained in the documents.*"

This clause requires the contractor to find out what is missing from the general conditions and specifications. Some will argue that this clause means the contractor is required to bring forth its own architectural and engineering or other design, working drawings and specification-writing talents, essentially duplicating all the work an owner has already paid for. And it should be done by every bidder.

4. "*The owner is entitled to alter required quantities of material without waiving any condition of the contract, it being always understood that the contractor would be paid the agreed unit price.*"

If quantities are significantly reduced, the contractor loses its right to recover the associated overhead, profit and other costs it incurs that are not quantity dependent but must be built into unit rates in order to be recovered.

In reviewing and understanding these types of contract clauses, it is important to remember that while most of these clauses are not beneficial to the contractor's or subcontractor's interests and should be removed from the construction agreement whenever possible, as a practical manner, the general contractor, and more likely the subcontractor, may not be able to negotiate the removal of these clauses from the contract documents. Thus, the goal is to recognize the potentially onerous clauses, to understand the situations or conditions under which these clauses may apply, to avoid those circumstances whenever possible, and where avoidance is not possible, to manage the risks presented by such clauses.

## Fundamental Breach

The doctrine of fundamental breach, until recently, was one of the most powerful devices involved in common law for dealing with "unconscionable" contracts and to limit the effect of exculpatory clauses. The origin of the doctrine of fundamental breach can be traced to a judgment of Lord Denning in the Karsales (Harrow) Ltd. v. Wallis case (Karsales 1956), where it was held that the doctrine was a "rule of law" that operated to defeat any exculpatory clauses, regardless of the intention of the clear and express language used. The approach of Lord Denning was widely embraced by United States, English and Canadian courts (Canadian 1966) and prevailed until the decision of the House of Lords in the Suisse Atlantique v. N.V. Rotterdamsche case (Atlantique 1967). In that case, the House of Lords significantly restricted the application of the doctrine and held that the effect of a fundamental breach on the applicability of an exculpatory clause was a matter of contractual interpretation only. If the parties clearly intended to waive liability in the event of a fundamental breach and occupied positions of equal bargaining power, the exculpatory provisions would apply. In other words, a fundamental breach did not automatically negate an exculpatory clause. The question of "equal bargaining power" however, remains an interesting one in the context of construction contracts.

## Types of Contracts

Under the common law parties have the right to choose their contract terms and conditions; thus there is no prescribed format for a construction contract. There are, however, certain general types or categories of contractual arrangement and contract formats that are being used in the industry. The form of contract entered into generally reflect the risk each party is prepared to bear in relation to the work performed and unforeseen circumstances which may arise. Construction contracts are typically categorized based on the form of payment and broken down into three basic types: stipulated price, unit price and cost plus contracts. Each has distinct differences and produces very important effects on project performance. For example, the main risk inherent to contractor in a stipulated price arrangement is that, absent any "extras", the stipulated price is all that he is entitled to. Should he encounter severe problem in the performance of his work he is, prima facie, not entitled to claim his extra expenses from the owner.

The degree of success in project performance is normally measured in terms of three variables: cost, schedule and technical performance. Selecting the optimal contract type and making the necessary project-specific modifications requires sensitivity and awareness to the impact of these decisions. The owner's goal can best be achieved by selecting the contract type that will most effectively motivate the contractor to the desired end.

## Recommendations

An awareness of good contracting practices is the best available loss prevention or control technique for construction claims. The contractual process entails the potential for negotiating a reasonable balance of rights, responsibilities and risk acceptable to each party. It thus provides the opportunity to structure your own legal liabilities. It is simply poor business practice not to utilize the process intelligently, in order to understand risk and to minimize involvement with construction claims and litigation.

There is no magic formula to eliminate all risk associated with construction contracts. The following simple tips are offered randomly to owners, contractors, project manages and drafters to maximize protection and minimize risk in construction contracts:

### Know the risk of the contract.

It has been argued that contractors often avoid identifying the risks associated with a particular construction project when the tender is being prepared, particularly in economic times when the need for work is greatest (McKim 1992). Typically, contractors will be better placed to bid properly if they check out details, take time to study all the available drawings, specifications and reference materials carefully, and carry out a site visit or site investigation. They should also assess their own expertise to carry out the required work, read and obtain legal advice on the obligations arising out of the contract documents, to identify any associated risks and decide rationally how to bid on the job.

### Know your contract

Recent cases seen by the authors include the following two. In the first, there was a contractor who thought he had signed a stipulated price contract but in fact, had signed a unit rate contract and did not realize until he filed a claim on completion of the work. The second was an owner who could no longer afford to proceed with his project when an exculpatory clause required by the lending bank added $10 million to his previous quote of $90 million. There are two parts to knowing your contract. First, it must be read carefully and understand properly. Second, the implications in specific contract clauses need to be fully understood (and agreed) by both parties. The courts in the United States, Canada and the United Kingdom have recently shown very little sympathy to the contracting parties who have chosen to make claims and assert rights without any regard for the specific terms of their contracts.

### Communicate! Communicate! Communicate!

Most contracts define how communications under the contracts is to be carried out. Pay close attention to these requirements. Effective communication and good records are not something to be encouraged just to be ready for claims and lawsuits. Effective communication is key to good working relationships. One of the questions we encourage all parties to a contract to ask is "are you sure you mean the same thing that I understand with this clause?" The way to ask is not directly, as often the answer is yes, but by asking- usually only for the key risk-assigning clauses- "who carries the risk?" Scoring +5 if the risk is entirely with the owner and -5 if it is all with the contractor (0 means risk is shared equally) reduces this to a number. If numbers do not match, you can be sure that the two parties do not agree on what that clause means! Such clauses are worth talking about!

On the basis that few people deliberately make mistakes, rework - be it design or construction - is likely to be a symptom of miscommunication. Watch for this symptom and make sure no further rework is likely to emerge. In particular, this is important if you have:
new or innovative technology;
people who have not worked together before; and
cross-functional or inter-disciplinary teams.

### Keep it together

Avoid the duplication of information in drawings and specifications. This tends to lead to errors. It is easy to make a change in one place and forget it somewhere else. Remember that most people read drawings not specifications on site, but it is the specifications that normally govern over drawings. Put key field construction information on drawings, not in the specifications. Keep similar information together in the same or adjacent sections.

### Ask for clarification

If something is unclear, it usually pays to get clarification from the owner or its representative. One good reason for this is that it is usually better to price the right item. Another reason is that, as a contractor, you do not want the competition to make a mistake that will get them the project instead of you. Transfer the responsibility for information or clarification back to the owner.

### Consider the impact of recent court cases on your contract documents

Make any amendments or changes to react constructively to them. Keeping current with court cases may be tedious. The easiest way is to subscribe to Law Letters, Law Reports or rely on your own lawyer to keep you abreast.

### Consider your contracting strategy

From an owner's point of view, this means balancing such issues as are summarized below:

- *Trust v. Cost*: An inverse relationship (within limits) has been demonstrated between cost and trust (CII 1988). The higher the trust level, the lower the cost. Most contract forms engender mistrust from the outset.
- *Risk sharing*: Develop a formula (as has been done successfully in the North Sea and elsewhere) to share risk and rewards with the contractor. Done right, this helps keep stakeholders aligned on key issues such as life cycle costs, completion schedules and safety.
- *Consider fast-tracking v. the real cost of doing so*: This is little understood. Clear cost/benefit profiles are being developed at The University of Calgary to help owners and contractors understand and evaluate fast tracking to determine the correct amount to use.
- *Pick the best form of contract* (Stipulated price, unit rate or cost plus) as well the scope (design, construct, design/build, EPC, BOT, BOOT etc.) and the way it is packaged (single prime contract, phased packages, multiple prime contracts, project management, construction management etc.). Each of the above decisions involve multiple trade-offs in terms of how the work will be done and who may be eligible to do it. Other factors in these decisions include:
  1. risk apportionment
  2. cost v. time v. quality
  3. trust levels
  4. opportunities for value engineering and constructability to be implemented
  5. project team effectiveness v. certainty of outcome.

The above are just few of the most important factors in avoiding disputes. Although most of the decisions rest with the owner, contractors should be able to interpret the intent of the owner from these decisions, and then govern itself accordingly.

- We encourage owners to take a hard look at their real needs and determine if their current contract provisions respond fairly and reasonably to these needs. Then we encourage them to consider the interests and needs of the contractor and to determine if the current contract provisions respond to those needs in a reasonable fashion without necessarily compromizing the owner's requirements. We have seen , with the exception of few enlightened owners, very few contracts in the Canadian construction industry which demonstrate a balanced approach to the allocation of risk. These contracts reflect the economic power exercised by the owner and require the contractor to accept harsh provisions. The owners should realize that no prudent contractor will accept a risk without charging an appropriate premium to cover such risk. After all is said and done, money apparently paid by the contractor or supplier ultimately comes from their only source of revenues - their clients, the owner.

## Conclusions

The rights and responsibilities of the parties will generally be determined with reference to the Contract Documents. The Contract Documents will normally incorporate exculpatory provisions exempting or limiting the Owner's liability. Unambiguous exculpatory provisions will be enforced to deny claims against the Owner in Contract and in negligence.

Given the evolving state of law that appears to be heading back to reliance on contractual relationships between the parties, it is important that all parties in the construction contract pay close attention to the contractual matrix and the methods by which risks and liabilities are allocated. Contracting parties must ensure that they have entered into an effective and appropriate contract. There is significant benefit to be achieved in understanding risk and managing it within contractual requirements. Proper contract strategy and subsequent document drafting is, and remains, the parties' primary risk management tool. Understanding and applying the contract is the parties' second most important tool.

### References

Hartman, Francis and Snelgrove, Patrick. 1996. Risk Allocation in Lump Sum Contracts- Concepts of Latent Dispute. *Journal of Construction Engineering and Management (September)*, Vol. 122 (3): 291-296.

American Consulting Engineers Council and Associated General Contractors of America. 1990. Owners Guide to Saving Money by Risk Allocation. Washington: 6.

Atlantique v. N.V. Rotterdamsche. 1967. *A.C.* 1: 361.

Canadian Dominion Leasing Corporation Ltd. v. Suburban Superdrug Ltd. 1966. *Dominion Law Reports* 56 (2d): 43.

Construction Industry Institute (CII). 1986. Impacts of Various Construction Contract Types and Clauses on Project Performance. *CII.* Publication (July) #5-1:10.

*CII.* 1988. Risk Allocation & Cost Effectiveness. A Report to the CII, 5-3.

Graham Construction and Engineering (1985) Ltd. v. Alberta. 1990. *Construction Law Reports* 37:125-151.

Green Construction Co. v. Kansas Power and Light Co. 1994. *Civil Engineering* (March): 27.

Hartman, Francis. 1993. Construction Dispute Reduction through an Improved Contracting Process in the Canadian Context. *Ph.D. Thesis.* Loughborough University of Technology, UK.

Hunter Engineering Co. v. Syncrude Canada Ltd. 1989. *Supreme Court Reports* 1: 426-523.

Karsales Ltd. v. Wallis. 1956. *W.L.R.* 1: 936.

Marston, D.L. 1996. *Law for Professional Engineers.* McGraw-Hill Ryerson Limited, 3rd edition.

McClain, Inc. v. Arlington County. 1995. *Civil Engineering* (September): 38.

McKim R.A. 1992. Systematic Risk Management Approach for Construction Projects. *J. of Constr. Engrg. & Mgmt.*, 118(2): 414-415.

National Public Works Conference and National Building and Construction Council Report. 1990. *No Dispute: Strategies for Improvements in the Australian Building and Construction Industry.* Pirie Printers Sales. Australia: 8.

Olin Corporation v. Consolidated Aluminum Corporation. 1993. 5 F3d 10 (2nd circuit).

Thompson, P.A. and Perry, J.G. 1992. *Engineering Construction Risks.* Thomas Telford Services Ltd., UK.

# It's Not Time, Cost, or Quality That Ensures Project Success: Learn Project Fundamentals and Core Project Processes Which are Keys to Project Success

Lee A. Peters, M.S.C.E., P.E., Peters & Co.
John L. Homer, M.S.C.E., P.E., BMW Constructors

Can you stop one hundred dollars from being spent on one project activity? Can you ensure project success by spending one million dollars over the budget? Can you reduce the time of one task by two hours by reducing the duration? Can you produce results ten times faster by adding ten times the resources? Does testing for quality of materials guarantee that the result will meet the expected life cycle?

Control means having the power to change - to turn down, to turn off. We do not control time, cost, nor quality! They are simply yard sticks, metrics, for measuring where we are in the project. Yardsticks that are frequently bogus. They are often either self created or needlessly imposed. Few are objective. They are project metrics without any knobs for control! Time, cost, and quality are also traps - projects that are on time, on budget, with the expected quality can be abysmal failures. Projects that miss all three, are at times, roaring successes.

What should a project manager concentrate on? Continuing on a theme beginning at the 1996 Project Management Institute Seminar/Symposium in Boston, the authors believe the fundamental activities forming foundation of project success are found in the triangle of results, scope, and performance.

Energy, effort, and management skills should be focused on defining the result with embedded, specified, and implied expectations. A project that does not meet expectations—all expectations—is not successful. Expectation management becomes a key focus of the project leadership.

Defining the scope is paramount to determining the size of the budget, the required effort, the technology, the risk, the time. Scope is what the project is and what the project is not—the boundaries. Scope can creep—ask any custom home buyer.

Finally, performance—accomplishing work and producing deliverable intermediate results—is what time, cost, and quality attempt to measure and then compare to the plan. Performance is what the project manager influences by changing methods, adding resources, locating information, focusing management, and improving materials. The yardsticks are only as good as the plan - change the plan and project progress changes.

Measuring performance tells the rate of change and if the rate is changing. Progress only tells how much is complete. The remaining scope divided by the performance rate will provide the time to complete. The rate change can predict early or late completion.

The project scope dictates required work, time, and cost. Expected results define the required quality. Performance is the completion of that work. If a project leader is going to influence cost, time, or quality, methods must be examined. Methods are where materials, tools, equipment, and information meet people and management. (Exhibits 2 and 3) Methods drive cost and time. (Exhibit 4)

We realized that this is where planning meets methods. Planning is a crucial process in project management. Yet we find over and over again entire organizations which are action prone. They learn by doing. Planning reduces execution time by a power of six. Why, then, is this a corporate disability? Planning gets to the details of the methods, the interface of people, tools, and materials. Methods dictate effort and durations. Scheduling assembles durations of all operations together for a total project duration. How many schedules are not based on planned methods? The planned method dictates costs. Costs are assembled into budgets. How many budgets are not based on planned methods?

Planning (preparation) and Evaluating (measuring) are core processes. Executing (doing) is the third core project process. (Exhibit 6) The model demonstrates dependancies between the fundamental activities and the core processes. These relationships drive the efficiency (doing things right), effectiveness (doing the right things), and efficacy (doing right things right at the right time) of the project. (Exhibit 7)

Results, Scope, and Performance each have a unique repetitive cycle of planning, executing, and evaluating as the project moves through the project process. This means that each fundamental will be in different part of the cycle from the other two throughout the project. This illustrates the dynamic nature of projects, e.g., analyzing risk never stops.

Control only occurs when result, scope, and performance are carefully planned, thoughtfully executed, and methodically evaluated.

Exhibit 1.

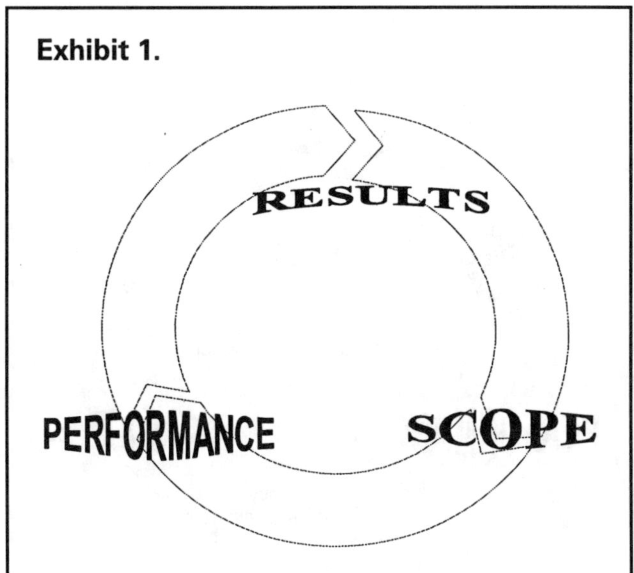


Exhibit 2.

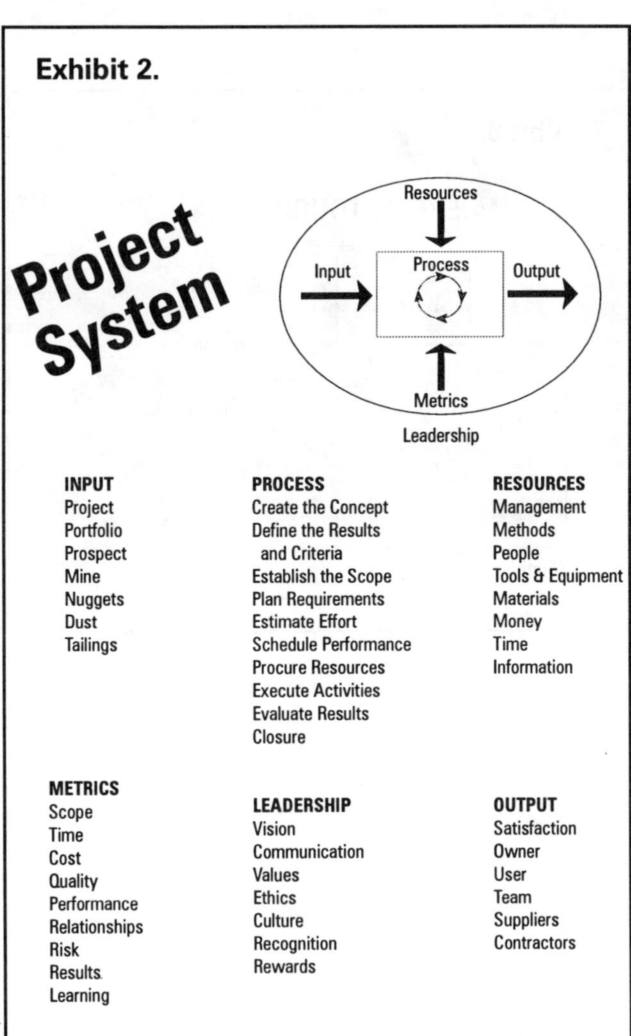


Exhibit 3.

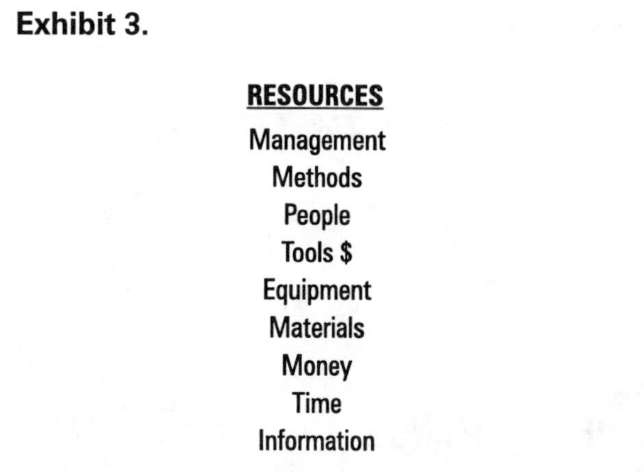

RESOURCES
Management
Methods
People
Tools $
Equipment
Materials
Money
Time
Information


Exhibit 4.

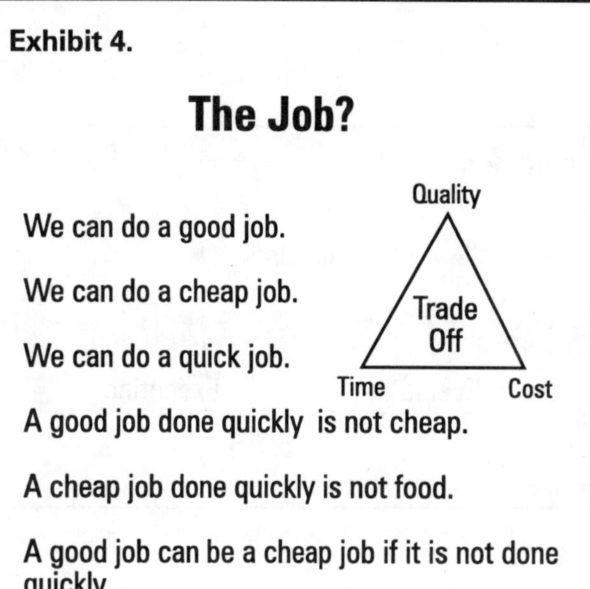

The Job?
We can do a good job.
We can do a cheap job.
We can do a quick job.
Quality
Trade Off
Time
Cost
A good job done quickly is not cheap.
A cheap job done quickly is not food.
A good job can be a cheap job if it is not done quickly.

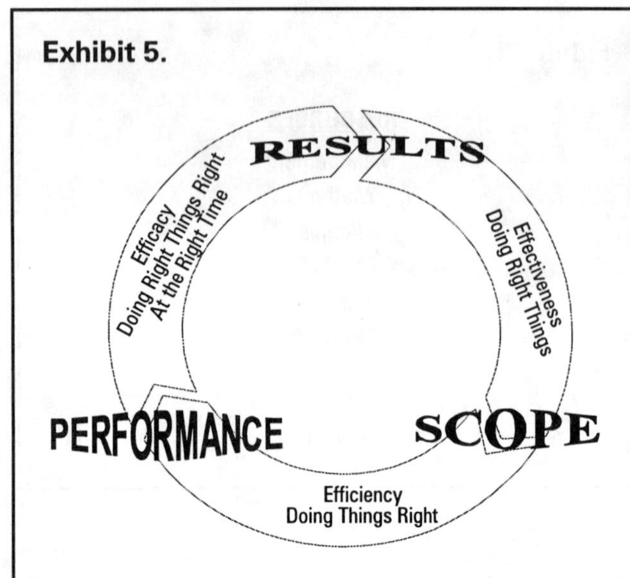


Exhibit 5.

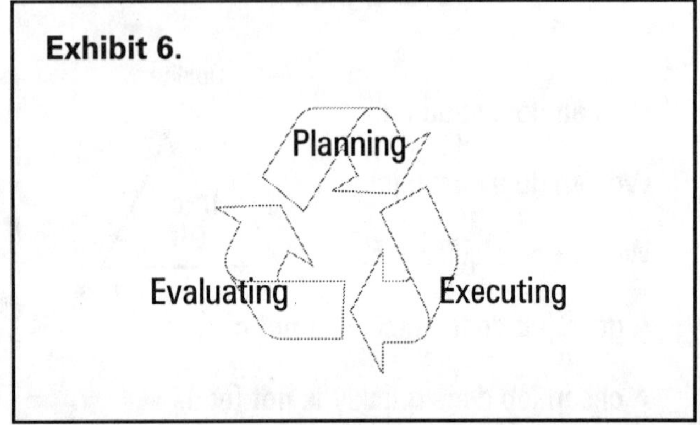


Exhibit 6.

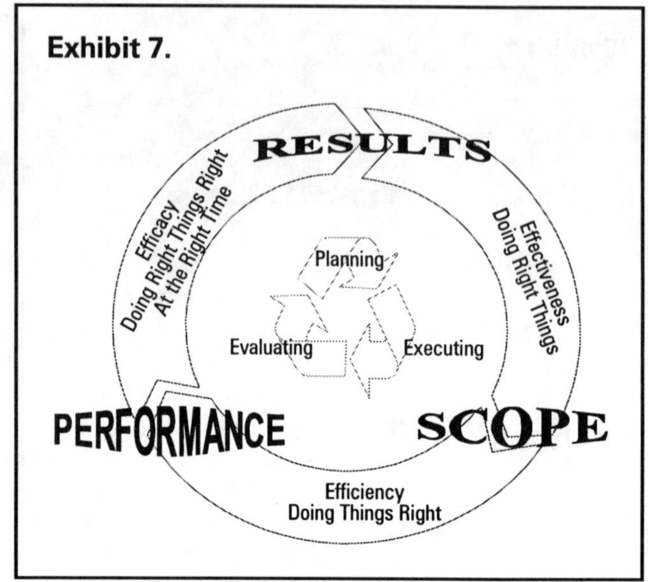


Exhibit 7.

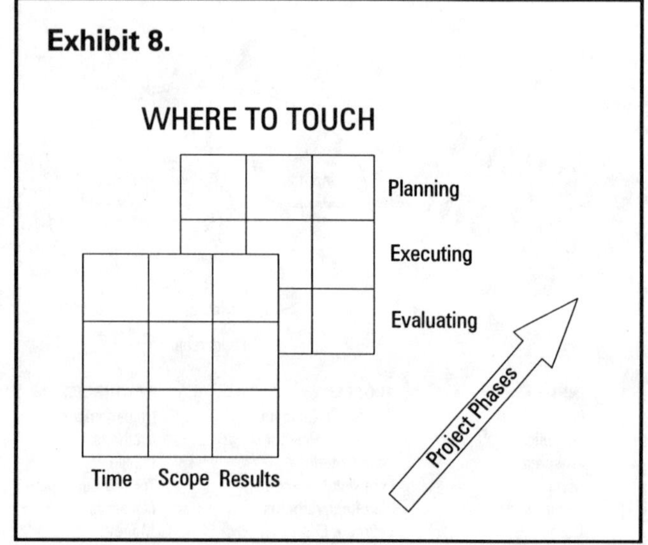


Exhibit 8.

# The 21st Century Competitive Edge: Effective Alliances

Joseph A. Lukas, PE PMP, Eastman Kodak Company

## Introduction

As we head into the next century, companies will face even tougher competition in the global marketplace. Companies will continue to reduce or eliminate internal staff groups, with the resultant need to contract for more services.

Many large manufacturing companies used to have internal capital organizations capable of designing and building capital assets needed by the business. However, competitive pressures have caused many companies to greatly reduce (or even eliminate) their capital organization. This means companies have to rely on contract suppliers of engineering, construction, and even project management to get new capital assets installed. Frequently the relationship between the company and suppliers has consisted of arms' length haggling over the price. However, many companies are now recognizing the importance of customer-supplier alliances, which can result in dramatic improvement in cost, quality, and schedule. As we move into the 21st Century, the use of alliances will become even more important for manufacturing companies, but very few really know how to make an alliance work.

This paper will discuss the use of an alliance relationship at Eastman Kodak in Rochester, New York for site infrastructure capital projects such as office renovations, labs, buildings, parking lots, and light manufacturing areas. Over the years, the Kodak capital community lost many people to retirement programs and internal company transfers. The remaining resources are now primarily utilized on high technology projects such as film sensitizing and finishing facilities. This resulted in a need to find external contractors to handle site capital projects.

In 1995, two engineering and design firms, plus two construction and project management firms were selected to support Kodak's site capital program. This paper will discuss the selection criteria and process used to pick the site alliance partners, along with the many steps taken to ensure success of the alliance as we head into the 21st Century.

## Background

Eastman Kodak is a multi-billion dollar, worldwide company that manufactures film, photographic paper, chemicals, copiers, health imaging products, and digital imaging equipment. Kodak Park is the biggest part of Kodak in terms of people and area, and is one of the largest manufacturing sites in the world. The plant is about 7-1/2 miles long, and has over 200 buildings. Kodak Park is a "city within a city" with support facilities such as power plants, waste disposal, railroad, bus system, fire department and security.

The Capital and Maintenance Organization (C&MO) is responsible for providing new capital assets, and includes Engineering & Project Management (E&PMD), Construction & Fabrication Shops, and Maintenance & Manufacturing Engineering. The C&MO provides capital support for Kodak Park and other US and International plant sites. The capital workload averages several hundred million dollars a year and is growing rapidly. The workload greatly exceeds the internal capital resources, hence contracting is used on many capital projects.

To focus the limited internal resources on proprietary and confidential processes, a participation strategy has been developed for Kodak's internal customer segments. These segments are Site, Utilities, Chemicals, Roll Coating, Film, Paper, Finishing, and International. The intent is to focus internal capital resources on the proprietary silver halide and chemicals work, with contracting used for most of the remaining work. For Site (offices, labs, warehouses, parking lots, buildings, light manufacturing) and Utilities projects, the intent is to do the strategic front end of projects, then contract the remaining engineering and construction work. For the other segments, the intent is to do more of the front end of projects, keep the proprietary and confidential work internal, and contract the remaining work. This paper will focus on the Site projects business.

A Capital Contracting Office (CCO) was established early in 1995 to facilitate contracting of capital projects in accordance with the C&MO participation strategy. The Contract Office is responsible for the contracting process, procedures, documentation, and preferred suppliers' selection. Before the Contract Office was established, selection of contractors was not managed. This resulted in a large number of companies being used for engineering, construction management, and construction. It seemed every Kodak engineer had their favorite contractor, and it was common to see multiple engineering firms utilized on a single project. This obviously is not the most efficient method to accomplish projects due to the number of interfaces and potential confusion over work boundaries. In addition, using a large number of contractors created more work within Kodak, such as teaching contractors our project process and design standards, contacts for permits, and plant safety rules.

## Selection Process

In mid 1995 the Contract Office decided to form an alliance to handle Kodak's site projects. An alliance is a long term contractual relationship between the owner and contractors that aims to provide business benefits to both parties through improved efficiency. The objective was to establish preferred supplier relationships for site and building projects with a select group of high quality service providers that demonstrate the ability to work in a partnership to achieve cost effective delivery of projects to Kodak. The scope of the alliance was selection of two architectural & engineering (A/E) firms and two construction management (CM) companies.

The process used for selection of the alliance partners consisted of the following steps:

1. *Prepare site contracting strategy document*—this document was prepared to gain internal agreement on the scope, strategy and objectives for contracting site projects.
2. *Conduct overview meeting*—a general meeting with all prospective companies was held to explain the proposed Site Alliance, the selection process and sequence of events.
3. *Submit qualifications*—each prospective company submitted a proposal responding to Kodak's request for qualifications.
4. *Evaluate proposals for further discussion*—all proposals were reviewed, and the top five A/E and CM firms were invited in for further discussions.
5. *Conduct interviews*—detailed discussions were held to gather all needed information to enable evaluation based on the selection criteria.
6. *Select alliance partners*—final evaluation was done based on the interviews and scoring of the selection criteria.

Specific criteria were developed for evaluation and selection of the two A/E and CM firms. Every item was assigned a relative weight, then scored for each company. This allowed a total score to be calculated for each company, with the top two representing the best selections. The criteria used for the selection process was:

1. *Financial stability*—dollar volume of projects in progress and completed in the last year, any current litigation, Dun and Bradstreet rating, bond rating for CM firms
2. *Overall experience*—portfolio of projects over the last two years
3. *Experience with Kodak project process*—relevant projects done using Kodak's project process
4. *Core competencies*—depth of local internal personnel supporting core competencies of company
5. *Contractual structure*—proposed charge rates, reimbursables, contract types
6. *Health, Safety and Environmental (HSE) history*
7. *Use of minority businesses*
8. *AutoCAD capability and compatibility*—for the A/E firms

The entire selection process was completed by late October 1995, and was done by a team of eight Kodak people representing the Contract Office, engineering supervision, and project managers involved in site projects.

## Meetings and Training

The goal was to get the Site Alliance up and running smoothly and quickly. Each contractor appointed a relationship manager to handle all alliance business with Kodak. Site Alliance meetings were held twice a month, and included the relationship managers, representatives from the Capital Contracting Office, and the Kodak Site Segment Manager. Agenda items for the meetings include a status review of active projects, workload levels, proposed policies and procedures review, discussion of any issues or concerns, and measures review for the Site Alliance performance. These meetings were extremely useful in developing teamwork and promoting communications among the four alliance partners and Kodak. The Site Alliance meetings are still held, but the frequency is now once per month since the alliance is well into implementation and there are fewer issues to discuss.

Soon after formation of the Site Alliance, a special four hours training session on the Kodak project process was conducted. The expectation is that Kodak capital customers should see no difference in project approach when contractors are used instead of Kodak personnel. All key contractor personnel with potential involvement in Kodak projects attended the four hour class. The project phases were reviewed in detail, which are preproject analysis, requirements, project definition, project execution, and commissioning. The class covered in detail the work and deliverables needed in each project phase. The Site Alliance partners have also been included in some other training events designed specifically for C&MO personnel, such as HSE training. This ensures Kodak's alliance partners have the same knowledge and understanding as Kodak personnel in doing capital projects.

Recently implemented is a monthly lunch meeting of Kodak's site project managers and the alliance relationship managers. This provides another opportunity for sharing of issues, discussion of projects, and review of proposed policies and procedures. Other team building events have been held to help strengthen the Site Alliance. A year after the alliance formation, a half day workshop was held with key personnel from Kodak and the four alliance companies. The agenda included discussion of what was going well and what items needed attention and improvement. Informal events such as golf outings and parties have also been used to help build the teamwork among the companies.

## Procedures

One of the key issues was ensuring use of common procedures by all four contractors. A site procedures' manual was established early in the alliance to provide a common understanding on project standards and policies. The procedures manual covered standard forms for use on Kodak site projects, key contacts within Kodak, and policies and guidelines. The alliance partners and Kodak jointly developed many of the procedures and forms in the manual.

One example of a standard procedure is the success matrix used on each project, which defines the criteria for project success based on negotiations between the project team and the client sponsor for the project. During the definition phase of the project the success matrix is developed. Specific pinpoints with relative weights are determined under each of the four major categories of cost, schedule, quality and functionality. Each pinpoint is scored at project completion based on actual results versus the project plan. A score of seven means the project plan goal was met, a score of ten means a stretch goal was achieved, and any score below seven implies the project plan was missed. For example, the cost performance pinpoint for a budget of $1 million would score a seven if the final project cost was $1 million. A score of ten is achieved by completing the project below $900k, and under seven for final costs over $1 million. Multiplying each pinpoint score by the relative weight provides a measure of project success based on the client's criteria, with a total score of 700 considered meeting goal. Exhibit 1 is an example of a project success matrix for the installation of a shredder.

Another example of a standard procedure is a client sponsor survey used on all projects. This survey establishes the overall level of satisfaction of the client with the project, looking at teamwork, functional performance, cost, schedule and project process. This provides an opportunity to capture best practices on a project, along with improvement opportunities.

## Quality Leadership Process

To ensure continuous improvement in the Site Alliance, Kodak's Quality Leadership Process was used. This is a systematic and pervasive approach to constantly improving the quality of services from suppliers. The relationship manager from each alliance partner, along with key Kodak personnel, attended a two day workshop on the quality leadership process. By the end of the workshop, the team established measures for each key result area, defined as product & technology leadership, service & support leadership, quality, delivery and cycle time performance, and total cost management. These measures demonstrate how well the Site Alliance is doing.

## Fee Computation

Projects done by the Site Alliance use the cost plus incentive fee contract method. It is important to recognize that alliance partners are in business to make money. For the Site Alliance, the fee is visible since all profit normally built into the charge rates is removed, and becomes a bottom line addition to the estimate. Competitive bidding is not typically used for the site A/E and CM work. Ensuring best value for Kodak is achieved by monitoring various measures such as percentage A/E and CM costs, benchmark data, and value improving cost saving ideas driven by the Site Alliance.

A fee computation worksheet is used on each project to determine the profit.. Five project factors are scored one to ten (with the highest), and can be assigned relative weights. The project factors are:

1. *Project process experience*—refers to contractor individuals experience with Kodak's project process, customer area, construction practices, etc.
2. *Level of risk & difficulty*—refers to aggressiveness of cost and schedule, site conditions, project environment, and project complexity
3. *Project value adding potential*—refers to the ability and opportunities to add value by reducing cost and schedule below market value
4. *Level of technology*—refers to the amount of technology associated with the project, with low being offices and roads, and high being light manufacturing such as clean rooms
5. *Percent A/E and CM*—costs for A/E and CM as a percentage of the total project budget

A total score is calculated by scoring each project factor, multiplying by the relative weight, then adding the total. This total weighted score relates to an equivalent profit percentage for the project, and when multiplied by the project budget yields a base fee for the project. This fee is modified at the project completion based on the success matrix score. The fee is multiplied by the success matrix score divided by 700 to determine the final incentive fee. If a project reaches all stretch goals, and achieves a perfect score of 1,000, the alliance partner would receive 1.43 times (1000/700) the base profit. The key is both the A/E and CM works off the same project matrix, so this helps drive cooperation between companies to ensure a successful project outcome. Exhibit 2 is a sample fee computation sheet for the construction management work on a project to install a shredder.

## Alliance Status

The Site Alliance has been in place for over one-and-a-half-years, and has been very successful. Major highlights include:

- *Introduction of market driven best practices*—Kodak established many materials and construction standards over the years, and the Site Alliance has been effective in introducing cost savings' materials and construction techniques for site projects.
- *Teamwork*—there is excellent teamwork between the Site Alliance partners. Even though they compete in the marketplace, within Kodak they consistently work as a team.
- *Project process*—the Site Alliance partners are doing a good job at using Kodak's project process.
- *Customer focus*—all alliance partners work to ensure customer satisfaction on projects

Even though the Site Alliance has been very successful, there are areas of difficulties. The major concerns are:

- *Design tools*—compatibility of design systems is an issue, especially when Kodak and the A/E firm are using different versions of a software package.
- *Challenging Customers*—an opportunity for the alliance partners is to challenge requests from customers that add little value to the project. Our alliance partners are reminded to act as though they are major stockholders in Kodak, and to challenge scope items that do not add value.
- *Perceptions*—there are some Kodak engineers that believe contractors cannot be as good as Kodak, and go out of their way to criticize contractors' work. This is slowly changing as the reality that contracting is not going away sinks in, and by our site contractors providing quality projects.

## Conclusion

The Site Alliance established by Kodak has been effective in accomplishing site projects at Kodak Park. The keys to making the site alliance effective include:
focused objectives

- strong in-house engineering organization (even though minimal staff)
- strong owner focus on a project process, and training of contractors in the process
- orientation to allow contractors to do their role professionally with minimal oversight
- use of effective measurement systems to monitor the health of the alliance

As Kodak heads into the next century, the Site Alliance will be vital to Kodak as the limited internal resources will be focused on proprietary and confidential projects.

## **Exhibit 1.** Sample Project Success Matrix

**Project Title:** **Install Shredder**

**Building:** 352
**SER #:** CXA875

| Pinpoints | 1 | 3 | 5 | GOAL 7 | 8 | 9 | 10 | Weight | Score |
|---|---|---|---|---|---|---|---|---|---|
| **1. Cost Performance - capital + expense** | | | | | | | | **25%** | |
| 1.1 Project Cost | >$548 | $548< | $528< | $498 | $473 | $448 | $398 | | |
| Cost Perform Index | >1.10 | 1.1 | 1.05 | 1.0 | 0.95 | 0.9 | 0.8 | 10% | 80 |
| 2.1 Cost Savings | | none | 1 savings | 4% | 6% | 8% | 10% | 5% | 35 |
| 1.3 General Requirements | >10% | 10% | 9.50% | 9% | 8% | 7% | 6% | 5% | 40 |
| 1.4 Engrg. % | 19% | 18% | 17% | 15% | 14% | 13% | 12% | 5% | 35 |
| **2. Schedule Performance** | | | | | | | | **20%** | |
| 2.1 Project Schedule | 11/10/97 | 11/3/97 | 10/27/97 | 10/20/97 | 10/13/97 | 10/6/97 | 9/29/97 | | |
| Sch Perform Index | 1.07 | 1.04 | 1.02 | 1 | 0.98 | 0.95 | 0.93 | 10% | 80 |
| 2.2 Punchlist Done | 12/1/97 | | | 11/1/97 | | | 10/20/97 | 5% | 35 |
| 2.3 Commissioning | | 3 weeks | 2 weeks | 1 week | 4 days | 3 days | 2 days | 3% | 27 |
| 4. FEL/FDP Audit | 5.5 | | | 5 | | | 4.25 | 2% | 14 |
| **3. Quality** | | | | | | | | **20%** | |
| 3.1 Customer Survey | 1 | 2 | 3 | 4 | 5 | 6 | 7 | 5% | 45 |
| 3.2 HSE Measure | > 0 LTI | | | 0 LTI | 1 Audit >90% | 2 Audits >90% | 3 Audits >90% | 5% | 50 |
| 3.3 Project Quality | | | | QA/QC Plan | 1 Audit okay | 2 Audits okay | 3 Audits okay | 5% | 50 |
| 3.4 Project Process | 1 point | 3 points | 5 points | 7 points | 8 points | 9 points | 10 points | 5% | 50 |
| **4. Functionality** | | | | | | | | **35%** | |
| 4.1 Noise measurement | >82 db | | | 82 db | | | 80 db< | 5% | 35 |
| 4.2 Run Rate | | 4k lbs./hr. | | 5k lbs./hr. | | | 6k lbs./hr. | 10% | 100 |
| 4.3 Streams handled | | | | all but one | | | all | 10% | 100 |
| 4.4 Operator Rating | 1 | 3 | 5 | 7 | 8 | 9 | 10 | 10% | 90 |
| | | | | | | | | **Total Score** | **866** |

**NOTES:**

1.3 General Requirements based on $46.9k budget (measure is actual gen'l req'ts divided by final total project cost
1.4 Engineering % is based on $85.4k budget (measure is actual SB costs divided by final total project cost)
2.1 Gate 1 date is 12/19/96, so project duration is 43 weeks total (Gate 1 to completion of commissioning)
3.2 Rating of 7 is based on 0 LTI and having the HSE plan posted on the jobsite. Audits use the HSE inspection form.
3.3 Audits done by the Kodak QA group.
3.4 Project process points are 3 for project launch meeting, 2 for PHRAS done, 2 for physical progressing used, 2 for change log, and 1 for closed project files submitted.
4.2 Sustained rate over 10 hrs. test for different streams
4.3 Streams handled during start-up successfully (split rolls, stalks, noodles)
4.4 Operator rating on operability based on score of 1-10 (10 = best)

| MATRIX APPROVALS: | | SIGNATURES: | DATE: |
|---|---|---|---|
| FAMT LEADER: | Dom Mancini | | |
| SPONSOR: | Mike Alt | | |
| PROJ MGR/CM: | Bill Goodrich | | |
| ENGINEERING MANAGER: | Rick Marczewski | | |
| CUSTOMER REP: | Fred Demmans | | |
| PROJECT ADVISOR: | Joe Lukas | | |

**Exhibit 2.**

## Sample Construction Management Fee Computation *WORKSHEET*

**Project Title:** **Install Shredder, Building 351** **Date:** **May 13, 1997**

**CM Firm:** **LeChase Construction**

### Project Evaluation

| ***Project Factor*** | ***Score*** 1–10 | | | Score | Wgt. | Wgt Scr. |
|---|---|---|---|---|---|---|
| Project Process Experience | Learning | Practicing | Mastering | 4 | 0.15 | 0.60 |
| Level of Difficulty | Low | Medium | High | 3 | 0.15 | 0.45 |
| Project Value-Add Potential | Low | Medium | High | 9 | 0.35 | 3.15 |
| Project Risk | Low | Medium | High | 4 | 0.25 | 1.00 |
| % Gen. Cond. Labor | 5.0% and Above | 4.9% - 4.5% | 4.5% and Below | 2 | 0.1 | 0.10 |
| | | | | | 1.00 | 5.30 **Total** |

| GC Labor $ | | Proj. Budget w/Exclusions | | % GC Labor |
|---|---|---|---|---|
| $37,200 | div | $380k | = | 9.80% |

**Note:** Gen'l Conditions % based on site projects, not really applicable to Chem projects

### Fee Computation

Project Budget $$ :

**Up to $1.5M :** Total Weighted Score = ***Fee Factor*** (ie: 4.5 = 4.5% of Project Budget)

| Fee Factor | | Proj. Budget w/Exclusions | | Budget Fee |
|---|---|---|---|---|
| 5.30% | x | $380,000 | = | $20,000 |

**Above $1.5M :** Negotiated

| | |
|---|---|
| Project Process Experience | Refers to individuals experience with project processes and Kodak Park construction practices. |
| Level of Difficulty | Refers to project degree of difficulty (complexity, site conditions, project environment). |
| Project Value-Add Potential | Refers to ability and opportunities to add value by reducing cost/schedule below market value. |
| Project Risk | Refers to aggressiveness of cost/schedule, functionality based on realistic targets. |
| General Conditions Labor | Total labor component as a percentage of Project Budget w/Exclusions. |

### Approvals:

*Kodak Project Leader* Date

*CM Representative* Date

*Capital Contracting Office* Date

**Revision A on 5/13/97:** changed from total project budget to Const costs only & modified value add factor

| Notes: | **Total $** | $380 |
|---|---|---|
| | Construction Directs | $310 |
| | Gen'l Conditions | $47 |
| | Commission | $1 |
| | Class S | $4 |
| | Cont. @ 5% | $18 |

Final Fee Calculation (CPPF *only* )

| Budget Fee | PSM/700 | Fee Paid |
|---|---|---|
| $20,000 | x 866/700 | = $24,700 |

# Facility Planning: The Solution for Effective Project Execution

Lawrence K. Stern AIA, People Places LLC

In today's dynamic business environment, organizations are changing at a rapid pace, creating unrelenting pressure for facility resources to keep up. As a result, the scope of new facility projects is subject to continual change while schedules become compressed and budgets tighten. Furthermore, the growing business application of project management methodology has created a more sophisticated customer who is becoming increasingly aware of the need to control projects, even during the early phases. To meet these new business conditions, the planning and execution of facility projects demands a fresh perspective.

Not only do the customers need their facility projects sooner, cheaper and better, they demand that the facility development process becomes as well-organized, efficient, and flexible as their other business processes. However, the planning and delivery of most facility projects today is often still premised on management systems developed when business relationships were less dynamic and facility resources were less tied to an organization's business objectives.

To meet the needs of a changing business world, this paper argues that a business-driven planning process is a critical step in the facility development process. An effective facility planning process translates the end user's business objectives into the project's facility requirements, thus creating facilities that are adaptable and fully supportive of core business goals and priorities. Further, by establishing the methodology on the Project Management Institute's *A Guide to the Project Management Body of Knowledge* (*PMBOK Guide*), the process goes far beyond the traditional programming emphasis on scope and identifies a much wider range of client requirements and expectations. The process creates mutual understanding, realistic expectations, and a shared vision among the development team. Thus, the likelihood is increased for both a successful project and a satisfied customer.

## Facility Planning Includes Both Resource and Project Planning

Similar to other business planning functions, facility planning identifies solutions to both present and anticipated problems through a systematic process of analysis and evaluation. A range of facility issues can be investigated and are subdivided into two hierarchical levels: 1) strategic issues—determining the optimal allocation of resources to achieve business goals and 2) tactical issues—translating strategic decisions into specific project actions.

As conceptualized by this author, strategic facility issues can be further subdivided into two Resource Planning categories: a) Workplace Effectiveness—the optimal effectiveness of workplace environments and b) Real Estate Utilization—the optimal utilization of the total real estate portfolio. The physical workplace can make a significant contribution to the overall performance of an organization, and should therefore be continually evaluated to ensure its optimal support of strategy, people, process and technology. Similarly, real estate assets are a vital resource which need to be periodically evaluated to ensure their adaptability to changing markets, organizational structures, and business conditions.

When the need for a specific project (or a program of actions) is identified during Resource Planning, the planning then becomes tactical. The focus shifts to a facility solution (whether new construction or a major modification to existing facilities) which satisfies a distinct business need. This Project Planning phase has two major elements: a) Project Feasibility—prioritizing needs and defining the proposed project by identifying a wide range of project attributes and b) Implementation Planning—identifying the most appropriate delivery method, development team, and project control systems to execute the proposed project.

These planning activities all share similar processes. Each studies alternative scenarios to arrive at the optimal business solution. Each is an integrative business planning process, requiring the coordination of multiple inputs. And they are all business-driven, with a greater focus on satisfying the business requirements instead of determining the design solution. Consequently, these processes yield valuable benefits to the customer—increasing profitability, enhancing worker productivity, and improving facility utilization. Finally, by establishing the processes on rigorous project management methodologies, business objectives are clarified, organizational consensus is facilitated, and risk is minimized.

## A Changing Business World Provides Opportunities for New Planning Models

Until recently, most corporate organizations changed slowly and incrementally. Their facilities reflected this rather static and bureaucratic structure. But as the rate of change accelerates, all business components are becoming transformed—impacting reporting structures, work processes, personnel policies, and technological tools. In this new era, facilities become a vital asset by enabling new organizational models, facilitating new ways of work, and enhancing new communication methods.

This business transformation will impact the planning of facility projects in numerous ways. Perhaps the most important being the need to plan adaptable facilities which support the rapidly changing organization. Whereas a simple programming effort might have been satisfactory before, the new workplace requires an integrated planning approach which identifies a broad range of requirements supporting worker performance both now and in the future. Because of the increasing complexity of how work gets done, facility planning needs to investigate a wider range of issues than simply facility design: organizational effectiveness, workflow, and information technology. When these four are integrated together into a total system, a solution is created which supports the business need for flexibility.

Furthermore, dynamic business conditions necessitate a facility development process which provides the customer with both a rigorous organizing framework to integrate these multiple elements and a flexible structure to accept unanticipated events. The solution is the use of consistent project management processes from early planing through project execution. Therefore, one of the primary goals of an effective facility planning process is to initiate the appropriate management processes and control systems which will guide the subsequent project execution.

## The Planning Process Should Focus on the Business Need

As this paper presents, a fresh approach to project planning is needed to meet the new requirements of an increasingly sophisticated and demanding business world. Historically, when a new facility was proposed it was relatively easy to determine the facility requirements. The planning team simply had to gather space needs information, replicate the existing working relationships, and create the design solution.

However, the business community is beginning to insist that their facilities support, enable, and make a significant contribution to their changing organization. Interpretation of economic concepts, industry trends, and the business' goals and initiatives are all going to become a necessary part of the planning process. Only with a full understanding of the richness of this information, will solutions be provided that truly support business objectives.

Of particular concern is the need to develop facility strategies which contribute to the organization's effectiveness—enhancing productivity, optimizing efficiency, increasing employee motivation, and improving organizational adaptability. To do so requires a common basis of understanding between the customer and the other members of the planning team. The team needs to investigate the dynamic interaction between the organization and its physical space, evaluating the options, and selecting the best approach which will optimize organizational performance. The vehicle to accomplish this is a business-focused planning process which bridges the traditional gap between the recognition of the business need and the design of its facility solution.

The proposed process, as diagrammed in Exhibit 1, begins with an investigation of the business problem as a Resource Planning issue—how to allocate and align facility resources to meet the business need. The first step in solving the problem requires analyzing how the workplace and its location can most effectively support the other vital assets of the enterprise—strategy, people, processes and technology. Some key questions to be addressed by this phase might then include:

- Strategy—How does a proposed merger, or a restructuring affect facilities and their location?
- People—How can innovation and employees satisfaction be enhanced by workplace design.?
- Process—How can facility resources support re-engineering or new work processes?
- Technology—How do new network and software products impact people location and work setting design?

Once the problem is understood and defined, it can be solved as a Project Planning issue—identifying the project's major attributes and then determining how it should best be executed (corresponding to the Project Feasibility and Implementation Planning subphases). Key questions include:

- Scope—How can facility adaptability support changing business conditions?
- Time—What are the important milestone dates, necessitated by the business need.?
- Cost—What is the total project cost model and cash flow projections to meet the business plan?
- Risk—How can the project criteria be managed to minimize risk and the business exposure?

**Exhibit 1.** Bridging the Planning Gap

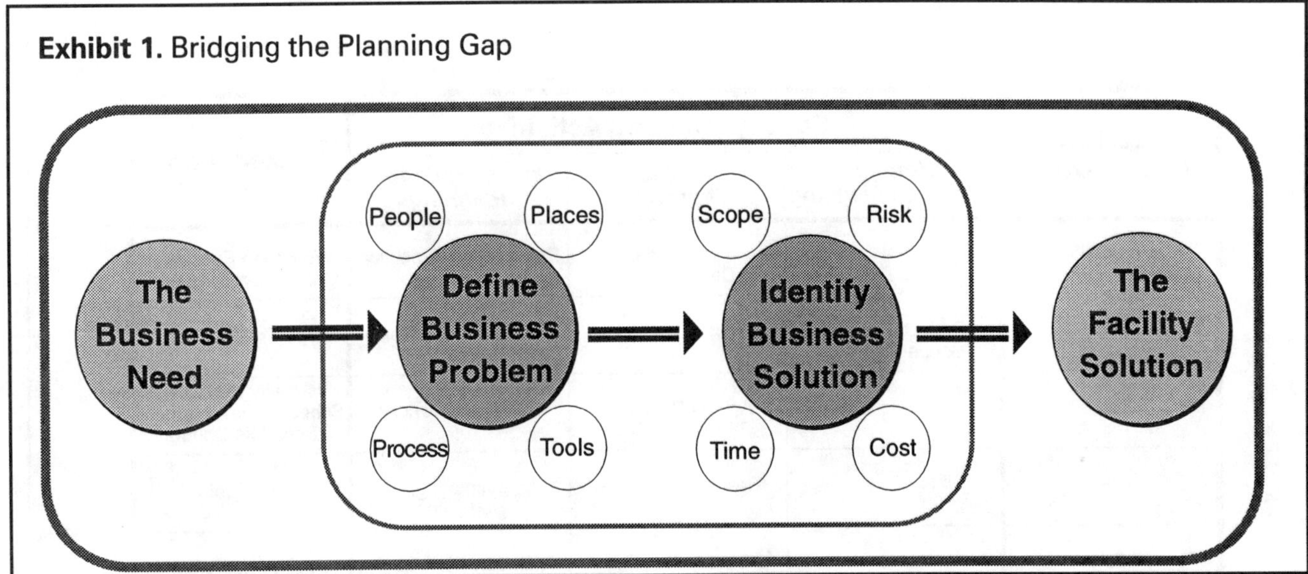


## The Planning Solution is a Comprehensive Process

Creating an effective planning process requires integrating a number of functional services which have traditionally been the responsibility of separate professions: business requirements have been provided by management consultants through their strategic, marketing and organizational consulting; site selection and due diligence by the real estate industry; project scope definition by design professionals through their programming/pre-design services; timing and cost analysis by the construction industry; perhaps limited risk assessment by an insurance company; and project communications would probably fall between the cracks. In the old way of doing business, these services would be separately procured by the owner, seldom coordinated, and rarely integrated into a total system.

In the future, dynamic business conditions and increasing customer sophistication will demand a better coordinated and more expeditious facility planning process to ensure that business objectives are directly linked to the project solution. Assuming that the primary objective of the process is to determine the customer's facility requirements and expectations, in summary the attributes of a successful planning effort then become:

- Cross-Functional Integration—a comprehensive process requires the coordination of numerous planning inputs from a broad range of functional groups
- Business Perspective—the key planning participants require in-depth business understanding as well as technical facility knowledge.
- Planning Competency—team members require analysis and evaluation skills to select the most appropriate facility attributes from competing alternatives. (Traditionally, the planning effort has been seen simplistically as a forward extension of the implementation process, resulting in focusing too quickly on the final solution without giving adequate consideration to other options.)
- Project Management Processes—an organized process should be used to identify the full range of owner expectations and requirements during the planning phase and provide the framework for the subsequent execution.
- Planning Leadership—the right person, possessing the above skills, should be designated to guide and monitor the process.

## Project Management Processes Provides a Framework for the Planning Process

As the business community increasingly embraces comprehensive project management processes in the initiation, definition, and planning phases of their core business projects, the same approach will be insisted upon for their facility projects. The customers will realize the value of instituting project management methodologies and control systems during the early facility planning phase, rather than waiting for the execution phase. They will understand that a well-defined facility planning process provides an opportunity to create a seamless linkage between the business planning processes which precede it and the project execution which follows it, thus enhancing the ability of the owner's requirements and expectations to be fully translated into the final facility solution.

**Exhibit 2.** Categorization of PMBOK Activities

| PMBOK Focus Areas | Facility Planning Activities | | | Project Execution Activities |
|---|---|---|---|---|
| | *Strategic Resource Planning* | *Project Feasibility* | *Implementation Planning* | |
| Integration | | Project Plan Development | Project Plan Execution | Work Plan Execution Change Order Control |
| Scope | Project Initiation Scope Planning | Scope Definition | Scope Verification | Scope Change Control |
| Time | | Activity Definition | Activity Sequencing | Activity Duration Schedule Development Schedule Control |
| Cost | | Resource Planning | Estimating, Budgeting | Cost Control |
| Quality | | Quality Planning | Quality Planning | Quality Assurance & Control |
| Human Resources | | Organizational Planning | Staff Acquisition | Team Development |
| Communication | | Communications Planning | Information Distribution | Performance Reporting, Closure |
| Risk | | Risk Identification & Quantification | Risk Response Development | Risk Response Control |
| Procurement | | | Procurement & Solicitation Planning, Source Selection | Contract Administration, Close-out |

Unfortunately, the current way of doing business is not structured to meet this challenge. The construction industry most often utilizes project management processes; however, this application has been limited generally to the project execution phase (i.e. design and construction). Those responsible for early project planning, usually either the customerÕs in-house facility staff or design consultants providing pre-design services, have failed to utilize project management practices. Furthermore, the pervasive lack of vertical integration often results in a lack of continuity between the planning and execution phases.

By introducing project management systems in the early planning phase, there is now an opportunity to create consistency and continuity throughout the development process. The Project Management Institute's "A Guide to the Project Management Body of Knowledge" (PMBOK) can become the organizing framework to ensure that stakeholder interests are satisfied during both the planning and execution phases. The table in Exhibit 2 categorizes all *PMBOK Guide* activities and identifies the ones which should be considered during facility planning prior to the design and construction of the project. The table further categorizes the tasks according to the appropriate planning phase in which that activity should occur.

The *PMBOK Guide* can be used as a framework to broaden the range of issues which are typically investigated during the planning phase. Consequently, a more comprehensive set of owner requirements can be identified early in the project, resulting in a more complete definition of the project attributes. By following PMBOK activity sequencing, planning can proceed in an orderly manner, ensuring that the following project attributes are properly addressed:

- Project Charter—the owner's goals, the project objectives, and the scope of work
- Project Management Processes—the risk management plan, the organization plan, and the milestone schedule
- Project Controls Systems—value engineering, constructability, cost and schedule management, quality management, and information management

By engaging in this comprehensive planning process, the development team develops a more in-depth understanding of the business requirements, the business solution and the resulting facility requirements. The objective, systematic process aligns expectations between the end-user and the fa-

**Exhibit 3.** Project Life Cycle

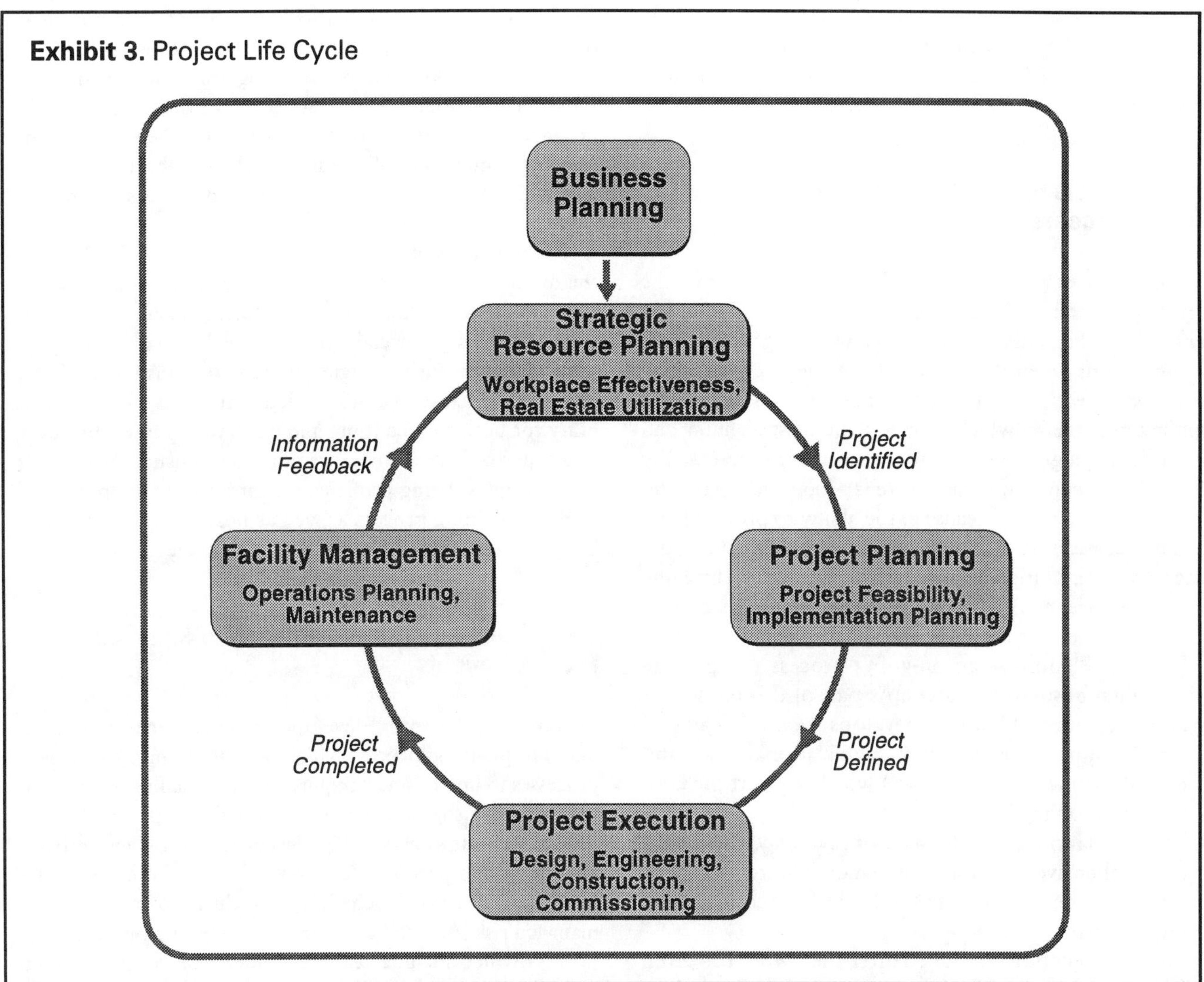


cility development team, builds team consensus, minimizes risk and uncertainty, and creates a facility benefiting a wide range of stakeholders. By doing so the process results in a facility solution that is optimally designed, delivered when needed, within affordable budget targets, and consistent with the team's risk tolerance.

## Facility Planning Managers Require a Broad Range of Skills

The leadership and management of this process necessitates a broader set of skills than has traditionally been required. Because of the integrated systems approach, the planning manager requires a wide range of competencies in addition to traditional project management skills: business / financial perspective, design understanding, and technical / construction knowledge. Overlaid over these capabilities is the capacity to act as an independent, facility planner offering objective analysis and evaluation. The ability to guide and monitor the process takes priority over executing the product.

In the last few years, different professional groups have begun to position themselves to lead the planning effort. Unfortunately, no particular group yet exhibits the broad range of attributes required for the job. Most do not really understand the business world of their clients—the general economic trends, business concepts, industry dynamics, or company initiatives. Very few are grounded in comprehensive project management skills, and fewer yet belong to the Project Management Institute. Management consultants know the most about business, but have the least design or technical knowledge. Design professionals who have the greatest design sensibilities, are traditionally weak in cost and timing controls. Construction professionals, who know the most about project management, know the least about business planning and design. Real estate professionals who are well-informed about making major capital transactions, generally do not have adequate consulting and planning skills. The challenge for the educational system is to create professionals with a new set of multi-discipline skills.

## The Life-Cycle of Facility Development is a Circular Process

The project life-cycle has been traditionally viewed from the narrow perspective of the design and construction industry, being seen as beginning with design and ending with project close-out. But when it is viewed from the end-user / customer's perspective, a broader picture emerges. It becomes a continuum of phases which begin with business planning and continues through the on-going management of the facility after initial occupancy. In fact, there is a loop back to the Resource Planning phase because of the ability to provide feedback and assessment of facility usage for future planning decisions (i.e. modifications to space standards, building systems criteria, etc.). Therefore, the major phases of a facility project can be shown as a circular diagram in Exhibit 3:

- Business Planning—an on-going process to optimize and align business resources. As part of this phase, Facility Resource Planning develops facility strategies which support business and organizational goals and identifies new projects (tactics) which support the continually evolving business need.
- Project Planning—as discussed previously, this phase comprehensively defines the owner requirements and identifies the appropriate method of executing those requirements.
- Project Execution—initiated after the owner has given final project approval, this phase includes all subphases from design through commissioning.
- Facility Management—initiated upon project completion, this phase includes ongoing operations, facility maintenance, minor renovations, and generally adapting the facility to constantly changing needs.

The life-cycle process has implications for project staffing. If the cycle of facility actions can be categorized into three broad types—planning, execution, and management, then there are implications for assigning roles and responsibilities to these tasks. As discussed previously, planning staff require special aptitudes and skills. Similarly, those responsible for execution and management require a separate set of skills.

For the end-user, its internal staff should ideally reflect the different "core competencies" of each type of facility action. This may be achievable for large facility staffs, but in instances where size limit such specialization, a staffing analysis will be required. The staff could become generalists in all three functions with the specialized assistance of outside expertise as needed, or specialists in one or two functions and outsourcing the other(s). Because Facility Management is ongoing and is responsible for providing timely information for subsequent Resource Planning decisions, these tasks should probably remain in-house. Contrarily, because Project Planning is the most specialized and usually the shortest in duration, this function could be outsourced to outside consultants.

For the design and construction industry, recognition of the different competencies required by planning and execution actions will result in enhanced performance by the project team. This is especially true for the designation of a project manager with single source responsibility. It is conceivable that such a project manager could take responsibility for both the planning and execution phases, however this super-project manager requires an unusual set of skills and aptitudes: being proficient at formulating an integrated systems planning process as well as possessing the technical know-how of implementing the facility project.

## Good Planning Processes Result in Significant Project Benefits

In summary, the entire development team benefits from an up-front planning process which uses program management processes to link business requirements to the final project solution. The customer obtains a facility that supports its business goals and priorities. The design and construction firms benefit from a predictable process derived from a well defined scope, a realistic schedule, an inclusive cost model, and managed risk. And all benefit from a comprehensive planning process which includes early consideration of quality controls, human resource allocation, and team communications.

The customer specifically benefits from a business-driven process which evaluates alternatives and identifies those requirements from which optimum project value is derived and organizational effectiveness is enhanced. The customer also obtains benefits from a planning process which evaluates execution options subsequent to defining the attributes of feasible project; by first defining the projects requirements, the owner is then able to select the most appropriate delivery method, team members, and project control systems to realize the project's goal and objectives.

Participants of the facility development team, accustomed to functioning in the traditional implementation mode may question the need for this type of planning approach. Many might say that a such detailed planning process can become too belabored, cumbersome, and therefore not worth the effort. These skeptics should consider the following cost ratios for a typical office facility. Various studies have shown that 95% of the operating cost of a facility is actually for the peo-

# Risk Management of Joint Venture Construction Projects of Foreign Cooperation in Russia

Artem Aleshin, Institute for Project Management and Business Informatics IPMI, University of Bremen, Germany
Dr. Dr. HC. Sebastian Dworatschek, Director of IPMI, University of Bremen, Germany

## Business Risks During the Transition Period in Russia

At the present time in Russia the process of transition from central planned to market economy. This process initiated a great number of projects, many of which were joint ventures with foreign corporations. Expert's estimate in the next 15-20 years there will be about 56,000 interrelated projects (Vining 1994). At the same time this transient process predetermined a high degree of riskiness of their successful implementation.

In condition of transient period the spectrum of risk events affected the projects has become significant greater. The extent of its effect and the probability of its onset increases. In practice of Russian projects implementation there is no distinct and clear concept about what risk events may, namely, affect projects, what their probabilistic characteristics are, and what degree of their negative impact is. Different Russian and foreign participants of the investment process do not possess full and reliable enough information about Russian projects market from the point of view of project implementation riskiness. Therefore many projects investedly specified due to risk events impact are failure (Poszniakov, Aleshin, 1994).

Greater riskiness of project implementation in Russia limits the obvious interest in them. It restrains the investment activity. It defines the actuality of the problem of risk management of joint venture projects of foreign cooperation under Russian conditions. It is obvious that the solution of this problem in the area of Project Management has become one of the most important tasks for successful cooperation between Russia and the World Society in the 21st century.

For efficient risk management applicable under Russian conditions it is necessary to receive replies to the following questions:

- what types of risk events arise during the project implementation?
- in what way do risk events affect the project? what are their probabilistic characteristics and the degree of negative impact?
- what risk events are the most dangerous ones?
- in what way can the degree of negative consequences of risk events be minimized?
- what preventive mechanisms must be fitted?

The present article is mostly devoted to the problem of risk management in the joint venture construction projects of foreign cooperation in Russia.

## Russian-German Cooperation

One may make manifest and assess the risk events on the basis of analysis and research of particular project implemented in Russia today. It is obvious that the completed projects are the most suitable ones for it, as on their basis one may trace and assess impact of risks on the project detailed enough. Carrying out the analysis of the completed project we have exactly known the end of the project if it is a success or a failure.

The information received on the basis of such an approach to the risk analysis cannot be applied to the risk management in the projects analyzed since these projects have been completely accomplished. However, this information may be used effectively in the process of development and implementation of future projects. The efficiency of its use in many cases depends on the fact how close the project in which this information is used by its characteristics and content on which this historical result was received.

The present article is based on the results of the research carried out on the basis of the International Dwelling Construction Program for the Soviet troops withdrawn from Germany. This research was implemented in the frames of cooperation between Institute for Project Management and Business Informatics (Bremen University), the Russian Association of Project Management and the Russian Federation Ministry of Defense.

The Dwelling Program was one of the results of significant changes in politics which occurred in Europe in 1989-1990. These events were as follows: the distraction of the Berlin Wall, reunion of the West and East parts of Germany, withdrawal of the Soviet troops from Germany.

The program was financed by the FRG Government. The program cost made up 8.35 billion DM, the implementation



PROJECT MANAGEMENT INSTITUTE 28th Annual Seminars & Symposium
Chicago, Illinois: Papers Presented September 29 to October 1, 1997

period was from 1990 to 1996. The customer of this construction Program is the RF Ministry of Defense. As a result there were built more than 45 thousand apartments of the total space more than 2.5 million square meters instead of previously planned 36 thousand apartments of total space of 2 million square meters. The Program was implemented on the vast territories.

The construction of the dwelling houses was carried out in the form of military settlements on the 44 construction sites, located on the territory of Russia, Belorussia and the Ukraine. 190 companies from 28 countries of the world took part in this Program.

Although this Program was considered to be successful and reached the goals put, in the process of realization it was subject to impact of significant number of external and internal risk events.

In the research carried out by the authors 16 settlements (projects) are studied. They were chosen from the point of view of interest to the research. The construction of these settlements was accomplished by different contractual companies in various parts of Russia. In this case the advantage was given to those finished settlements where Contractors were German companies.

This research included three steps (Exhibit 1):

- risk events identification;
- risk events classification;
- risk events assessment.

As a result there were revealed risk events having arisen during the Program implementation. There were carried out their classification and assessment. There was also developed a technology of revelation and analysis of risk events applicable to the conditions of large projects and programs accomplishment in Russian conditions.

## Risk Events Identification

Applicable to the given research the purpose of the risk identification consisted of the establishment of the list of those risk events which really having appeared in the process of realization of the projects.

At the step of identification the collection and primary processing of large volume of initial data are carried out. Its main result is a set of risk events; they are further classified and assessed. So, risk identification actually creates the information base for further steps of the analysis. How well and qualitatively the risk identification is made, as much the following steps may be possible qualitatively to accomplish. (Avots, Dworatschek 1990; Franke 1991)

It is known when the risk identification carried out it is important to define the choice of information sources. The composition of the sources used is defined in each particular case separately and it depends on what stage of the realization the analyzed project is. As a result of the analysis the Dwelling Program there defined the following main sources for risk identification:

1. project documentation
2. project participants
3. events occurred in the frames of the program

Documentation used in the frames of this research included three principle groups:

- *planned documentation* (e.g. program manual, prequalification of the contractor documentation, tender and contract documentation, );
- *current documentation* (e.g. project diary, correspondence among project members, monthly report on project realization);
- *resultant documentation* (e.g. claims of the contractor, resultant reports)

The customer, contractors and other projects participants were also involved in this research. As the research was carried out in the program central office in Moscow it made possible to draw the projects participants in the process of the whole research.

For risk events identification and registration there developed a standardized data card. This data card includes the following data: full name of the project and a contractor, name of the risk event and its ordinal number, WBS element code where risk event occurred, stage at ffect connections is carried out along the hierarchical system. According to the hierarchical system at the beginning the classified set of objects according to certain chosen characteristic is divided into types. Then each type according to the predetermined characteristic is divided into classes. Then in the same way each class is divided into groups and groups are split into more smaller subgroups and so on. So the scheme of the hierarchical system of classification can be seen in the form of a tree. The top of this tree is the classified sets of objects and the process of classification is a multistepped one.

Different characteristics can be used to break down risk events into types, types into classes and so on. These characteristics are accomplished in the process of the detailed analysis of risk events at each step of the classification. In this case a characteristic is believed to be a cause of risk event appearance. Only those risk events enter into one type, class or group which have one and the same cause of their occurrence correspondingly.

At the first step of classifying the risk events set showed: all revealed risk events can be divided into internal risk events and external ones. Internal risk events are initiated inside the project. External risk events are originated by the project environment respectively (Exhibit 2).

At the second step the classification was carried out separately inside of each type. For example, the analysis of the set

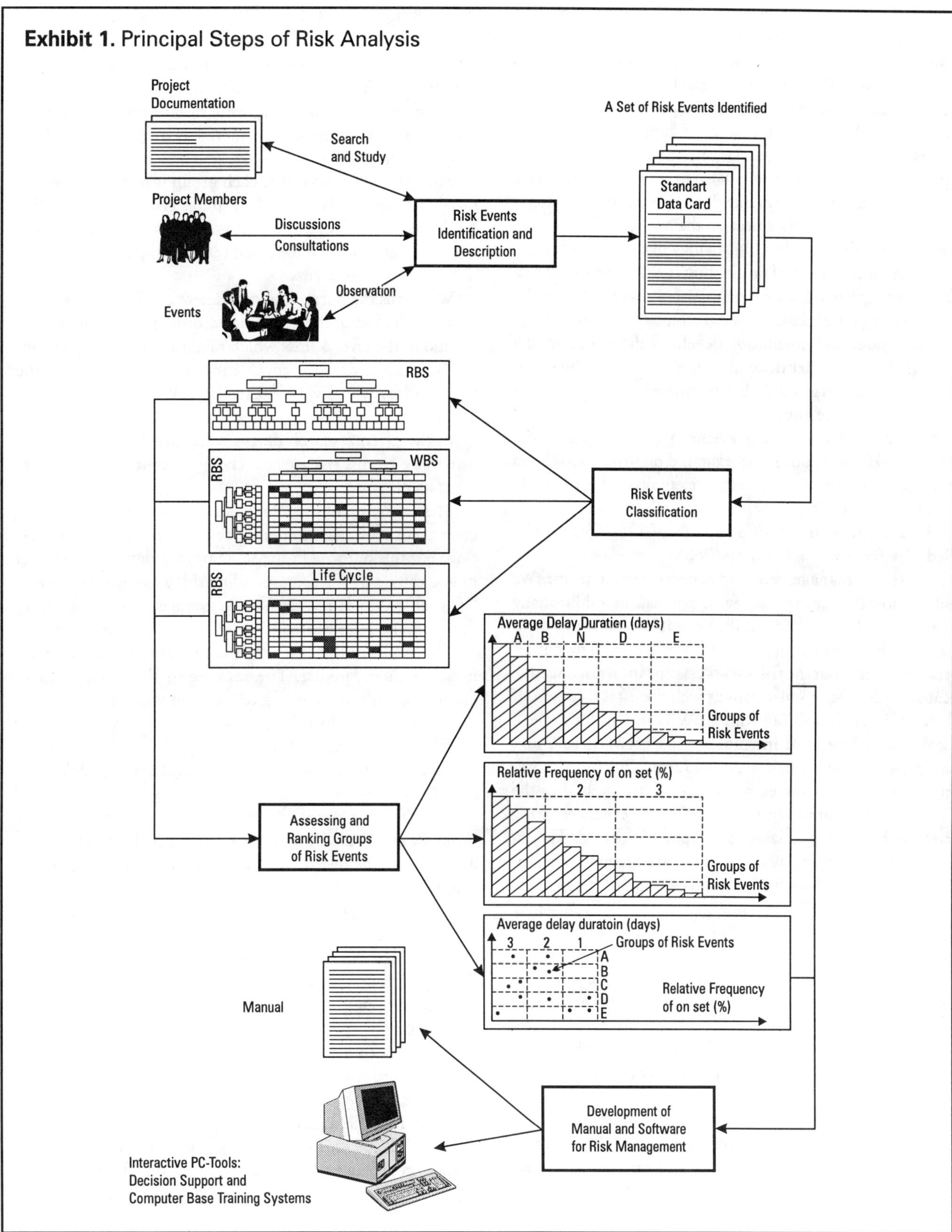


**Exhibit 1.** Principal Steps of Risk Analysis

of internal risk events showed that each risk event originated due to certain causes. Generally, these causes are the actions of project participants. So, for example, some risk events were the result of the Customer's mistakes, admitted by him when the tender documentation developed. Other risk events were originated by nonperformance of duties by the Engineer in charge due to the contract. Depending on the cause there approached the onset of the risk event, the set of identified internal and external risk events decomposed into classes.

At the third step of classification the analysis of risk events takes place inside each class. By analogy of the previous steps depending on the cause of originating the risk events are distributed into groups. So, for example, as a result of the analysis of the risk events class, that is, customer's mistakes on the phase of tender documentation development was formed a group, that is, in Tender documentation absence of full list of overhead and underground objects situated on the construction sites and on the approaches to them. Each group of risk events represents a set of risk events, attributed to it in the process of classification. As an example of a risk event is on the construction site there found a telephone cable or trees.

Thus, in the result of the classification there received a risk tree. By analogy with the WBS and the OBS this tree may be called *Risk Breakdown Structure (RBS)*.

For the risk management two aspects are important. We need to know the cause of risk event origination. Additionally we ask: when this risk event has been built into the project and with what element of the WBS it is connected. The consequence is to carry out the risk events classification not only due to cause-and-effect connections as well the establishment of risk events interconnections with the WBS and the life cycle.

For establishment of interconnection between RBS and WBS there was developed a special form. This form represents a matrix. The elements of the WBS are located in the columns of the matrix. In the lines the risk events entering corresponding groups, classes and types are located. The interconnection between WBS and RBS are mapped onto intersection of corresponding lines and columns of the matrix..

In reality, one and the same group of risk events may equally appear on different WBS elements. However the size of loss is greater in case of its onset on the object elements located on the external construction sites. Then one may consider it to be more characteristic to the external object elements.

The interconnection between the RBS and the life cycle is established similarly as it is established between the RBS and the WBS.

The results received in the process of classification allow the groups of risk events onset by the concentration of attention on certain the WBS elements and on certain project phases and stages to be avoided.

## Assessing and Ranking Groups of Risk Events

As a result of risk events classification there was found that risk events related to one classification group had general cause of their formation and were homogeneous. Then the risk event onset might be considered as manifestation of the whole group to which this risk event was related. Here, the number of risk events inside each group is nonfinite, but the number of groups risk events is finite. Proceeding from this on the basis of risk events hit into one group one might assess the whole group. So in the given research there were assessed the groups of risk events.

What was the purpose of assessment of group risk events? It lied in the fact of their ranking according to probability onset and in the level of loss which might form under their onset. The initial data for conduction of assessment were the levels of loss which were caused by risk events coming into one group.

In the given research delays were considered to be loss caused by groups risk events. The main characteristic of delay is its duration.

The collection of the initial data for the conduction of the assessment took place in the process of risk events identification. For this purpose in the standardized data card the level of loss caused by the corresponding risk event was registered. For each group of risk events the average value of the delay duration and relative frequency of its onset were defined.

The results of the estimation of the groups risk events are used for their ranking. The ranking of the groups of risk events takes place according to the following items:

- average delay duration;
- relative frequency of onset;
- both relative frequency of onset and average delay duration.

As a result of ranking on average delay duration the groups were divided into 5 ranks: A,B,C,D,E. When ranked according to the relative frequency of onset they were ranked into three ranks: 1,2,3.

The ranking of groups risk events according to average duration and relative frequency of onset together is the fullest one. In this case, average delay duration along ranks A,B,C,D,E is presented along the vertical axis. Along the horizontal axis relative frequencies of risk events onset according to ranks 1, 2, 3 are presented. Each group of risk events corresponds to a point with abscissa equal to frequency of onset and ordinate equal to average delay duration. Points are distributed among squares which represent the combination of ranks 1,2,3, and A,B,C,D,E (Exhibit 1).

Thus, all the set of groups risk events was distributed together according to average delay duration and the frequency of the onset and it is presented by squares. And also the groups risk events of different classes and types come into

**Exhibit 2.** The Steps of Risk Events Classification

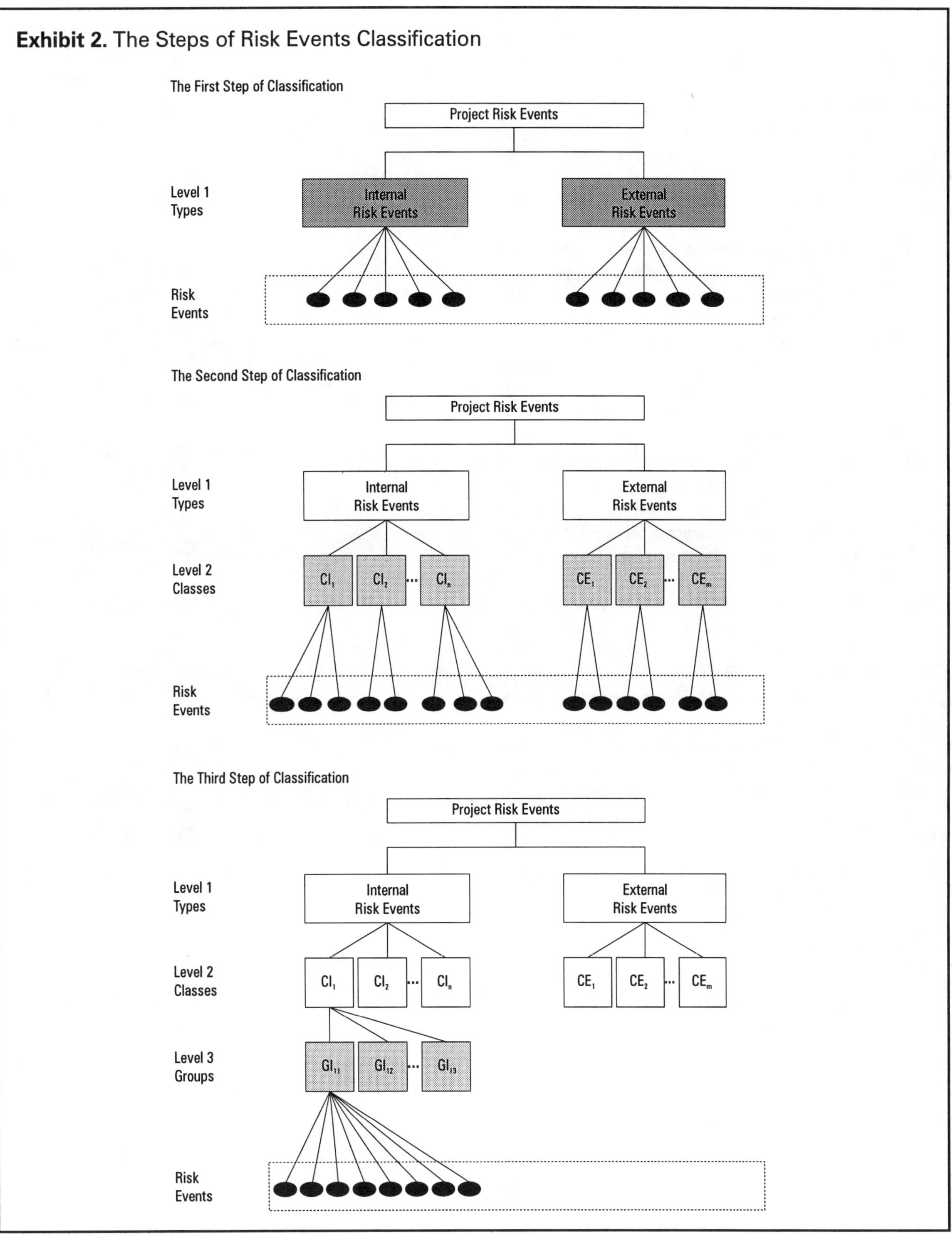

one and the same square, that is, they have different reason for their appearance. Further the received results in the course of assessment were discussed by the Program participants.

The results of the carried out empirical study, are identification, classification and assessment of risk events. They allow corresponding conclusions for each group to be made. These conclusions concern the following points:

1. Quantitative assessment of the group. (What is the frequency of onset? What is the delay duration?)
2. The cause of group originating. (Who caused this group of risk events? What made this group to appear?)
3. The interaction of the group with the life cycle of the project. (At what stage of the project is the group built? At what stage it is revealed ?)
4. The interaction of the group with the WBS. (For what object elements is the group mostly characterized? Is it for external elements, or internal elements either for the whole project?).
5. The dependency of the quantitative characteristics of the group on the location of the construction site. (Does the frequency of the group appearance and the average delay duration depend on the location in which the construction is carried out? City or countryside?).
6. The recommendations on reduction of probability of the group originating and possible negative consequences in case of its onset (What should be done to avoid the risk or to reduce it?).

On the basis of the results received out of the research study a training course on risk management in building projects, will be developed., and implemented in Russia. The training course will be accomplished in the form of the manual and decision support and computer base training system.

## References

Avots, Ivars and Dworatschek, Sebastian (Eds.). 1990. *The state of the art in project risk management* INTERNET International Expert Seminar in connection with the PMI/INTERNET Joint Symposium Atlanta USA 10/1989, Zurich

Babenko, A. Vasiliev Vladimir. 1995. *Practical manual on contractual tenders organization in the Russian Federation.,* Building Ministry.

Franke, Armin. 199. *Risikobewußtes projekt-controlling.* Ph.D. Dissertation at IPMI, University of Bremen

Poszniakov, Vjacheslav. Aleshin, Artem. 1994. The features of CIS countries management and exchange of experience. Proceedings of the 12th INTERNET World Congress, Vol. 1: 502-506

Schnorrenberg, Uwe. 1990. *Expertensystem-werkzeug zur risikoanalyse im projektmanagement.* Ph.D. Dissertation at IPMI, University of Bremen.

Vining, Robert. 1994. Project management and the dynamics of change in Russia. Proceedings of the 12th INTERNET World Congress, Vol. 1: 262-268

# Sydney 2000 Olympic Games: A Project Management Perspective

David Eager, University of Technology, Sydney


## Summary

The Sydney 2000 Olympic Games is a large scale and very complex project involving a diverse range of activities and large numbers of people. Given the nature and vast scale of this project sound and exemplary project management techniques and principles are essential for its success. The strict time constraints set for the project increase the difficulties of managing cost and quality. The project will be regarded as successful if it is finished to time, on budget and to the required quality. Good quality means meeting the needs specified by the organizer, to the standard and specification laid down, with a predictable degree of reliability and uniformity, at a price consistent with the organizerÕs budget and to the satisfaction of the end users. This review discusses issues that need to be addressed to make this project a success.


## Introduction

The Sydney 2000 Olympic Games will be held between Friday September 15 and Sunday October 1 2000 in Sydney's spring.

Sydney, competing against bids from four other cities, was awarded the right to host the Games of the 26th modern Olympiad after a vote by the members of the International Olympic Committee in Monte Carlo in September 1993.

The bid was prepared by Sydney Olympics Bid Limited which drew on funds from the private and public sectors and worked in close cooperation with the Australian Olympic Committee. It enjoyed broad public support with 90 percent of the people across Australia supporting the bid. More than 100,000 volunteers offered their services. The bid was centered on the theme *Share the Spirit* and called on the people of Sydney to join in the excitement of the bid, and invited the world to come and share the spirit of Sydney at the Olympic Games in the year 2000. The bid also included a comprehensive set of environmental guidelines recognizing the principle of ecologically sustainable development. The guidelines promote energy conservation, water conservation, waste avoidance and minimization, protection of air, water, and soil from pollution, and protection of significant natural and cultural environments.

## Some Significant Features

The New South Wales Government underwrites the Games and is responsible for the provision of new permanent venues and facilities needed for the Games. It also provides support services particularly in the areas of transport, security and health care. The construction of new sporting facilities and refurbishment of existing facilities for the Games is being undertaken by the State Government's Olympic Coordination Authority, namely: Sydney Organizing Committee for the Olympic Games (SOCOG).

Staging of the 2000 Games is the responsibility of SOCOG which was established in November 1993 by legislation in the New South Wales Parliament.

The Sydney Para-Olympic Organizing Committee will stage the Para-Olympic Games following the Olympic Games and will draw extensively on SOCOG expertise in their Games organization.

Sydney's Olympic plan is based on a commitment to provide the right conditions for athletes to perform at their optimum level. For the first time in Olympic history, all athletes will live together in one village, and many will be within walking distance of the venues for their events.

Except for some football preliminaries, all Olympic events are planned to be held in metropolitan Sydney in venues within 30 minutes travel from the Olympic Village. No training facility will be more than 45 minutes away from the village. The focus is mainly on two Olympic zones, namely: the Sydney Olympic Park, situated at Homebush Bay about 14 km west of the Sydney city center; and the Sydney Harbor zone, located near the Sydney city center and accessible by road, rail and ferry from Sydney Olympic Park.

A series of test events in the years preceding the Olympic Games is planned with the aim of trailing the Olympic venues, training the technical officials and volunteers who will help conduct the events at the Olympic Games and selectively trailing arrangements for accreditation, transport, security, broadcasting, media and other services.

## Infrastructure—Preparation Work For The Games

A significant number of Sydney's Olympic venues already exist. Most of the remaining facilities required for the Games will be constructed as part of the redevelopment program being undertaken at Homebush Bay.

Key elements of the Homebush Bay area include the construction of new sporting facilities, establishment of a new showground and major exhibition center, development of residential and retail areas and the establishment of a commercial center for high technology industries. A main press center and the Olympic village with accommodation for 10,000 athletes and team officials also comes under the umbrella of the Olympic Park.

Recently completed major transport projects such as Sydney Harbor Tunnel, M4 and M5 Motorways and Glebe Island bridge, together with the major projects currently in progress such as City West Development, Ultimo-Pyrmont light rail system, Airport City Link and the railway loop line to link the Olympic Park with the Sydney rail network's main western rail line will ensure that an effective transport system will be available for the Olympic Games.

Telecommunications infrastructure such as Integrated Services Digital Network (ISDN), Intelligent Networks (IN) and Cellular Mobile Telephone Service (CMTS), together with Broadband ISDN (B-ISDN) currently being established are considered sufficient to successfully service the international and domestic demand of the Games.

During Sydney's bid a campaign to register volunteers was conducted by the St George Bank which attracted more than 100,000 people. Sydney will require 35,000 people from all walks of life to form a volunteer workforce essential for the smooth running of the Games.

Revenue for the Games is expected primarily from television rights fees, sponsorships, coin marketing royalties, licensing fees and ticket sales.

It is estimated that during the period 1994-2004 the Olympics could add A$7.3 billion to Australia's Gross Domestic Product, create 150,000 full and part-time jobs and bring an extra 1.3 million visitors to Australia. In order to safeguard sponsorship fees and sponsors and licensees benefits from ambush marketing the New South Wales Government has legislated the Sydney 2000 Games (Indicia and Images) Protection Bill 1996.

## Definition of the Project

The objective of the Sydney Olympic Games Program is to stage the year 2000 Olympic Games at specified locations in Sydney. Although the New South Wales Government is underwriting the project activities, there is no clearly defined client for the program. There are many stakeholders and customers, including the citizens of New South Wales, the New South Wales Government, the Australian people, the International Olympic Organization, the international community as a whole, the athletes and Australian and international business communities. The scope of the project comprises organizing all the Games and ceremonies, putting in place technology and resources required to stage the Games, public relations and fundraising. Criteria for the success of the project include trouble-free performance of the Games, the level of public enthusiasm and enjoyment generated by the activities and resultant sustained economic activity generated within New South Wales and Australia and continued interest in Olympic Games for the future.

SOCOG was appointed as the project managers by legislation. In addition to SOCOG there are other organizations that directly contribute to the success of the Games. International Olympic Committee, Australian Olympic Committee, Sydney City Council, and Olympic Coordination Authority (New South Wales Government) have been made party to the Host City Contract. Olympic Coordination Authority is responsible for all the infrastructure projects almost all of which are not being built specifically for the Olympic Games. These projects are either already under way or are being reprogrammed to accommodate the Games. Completion of these projects on time is vital to the success of the Olympic Games. The general rule-of-thumb used by the Government has been to relocate infrastructure projects initially external to the Games under the Games umbrella.

The infrastructure construction is the responsibility of the government and is overseen by the Olympic Coordination Authority. To make matters more complicated, the scope of work of SOCOG is restricted to organization of the events. The Games budget in nominal terms is $ A1.847 billion ($US 1.4 billion). There is an explicit need to control the cost of all its activities very carefully. Any major cost overruns will alienate the public and will have adverse effects on the success of the Games.

The project can be broken in to the following major areas of work (as a work breakdown structure):

- Events
- Venues and facilities including accommodation
- Transport
- Media facilities and coordination
- Telecommunications
- Security arrangements
- Medical care
- Human resources including volunteers
- Cultural Olympiad
- Pre-Games training;
- Information technology projects
- Opening and Closing ceremonies
- Public relations
- Financing
- Test Games and trial events

- Sponsorship management and control of ambush marketing.

Each of these items could be treated as a project in its own right. Further, an enormous co-ordination effort will be required to ensure these, and therefore the entire Games project is delivered on time.

## Critical Project Dimensions

Time is the most critical dimension of the Sydney 2000 Olympic Games project. As the project must be completed and ready for staging the Olympic Games on the stipulated dates, any shortcomings in the time dimension will have to be offset by sacrificing the other two dimensions, namely: cost and quality. However, performance on all three dimensions is vital for the success of the project.

## Time Dimension

Sydney is fortunate in having sufficient infrastructure capacity either existing or under construction to cater for an event of this magnitude. It is anticipated that the infrastructure projects under construction will be completed well in advance of the commencement of the Olympic Games. Any delays in the completion dates could be accommodated without much difficulty. The criticality of the time dimension applies mainly to other activities and timing of individual activities such as events, opening and closing ceremonies and so on. To ensure that the time dimension is achieved, the Sydney Organizing Committee for the Olympic Games has adopted strategies such as: holding frequent coordination meetings with the organizations and parties responsible for delivering the required items; setting target dates well in advance of the main event; designing test events; and trailing events as milestones for the critical items.

For the construction projects, estimation of the time dimension should be relatively straight forward. Expertise is available within the construction industry to produce reasonable estimates. Critical path methods (CPM), precedence block diagrams and program evaluation and review are employed to control the uncertainties in the time dimension. Proper plans must be prepared for these construction activities. All persons who may be affected by these programs should have an opportunity to comment on the plan. Instruments should be put in place to monitor the progress against the program continually. The program should include enough leeway or float to allow minor problems to be accommodated without causing major changes to the timing of the overall program. Elements which are expected to have most impact on the program must be identified and defined as early as possible, and an adequate series of milestones must be established to allow monitoring of the progress of the program.

At this early stage of the program or the project life cycle the time required to complete tasks for particular events introduces uncertainties. These uncertainties are related to the nature of the tasks involved. Some non-construction projects such as developing the software program for monitoring the Games progress and establishing the Games data base, and for dissemination of the information to general public have larger uncertainties inherent in the system. Some new technologies may have to be developed to adapt to the advances in the way the information is distributed to the public and media. For example, the Atlanta 1996 Olympic Games had a dedicated Internet facility to give the public access to Games information. Since Internet technologies are changing very rapidly and the way information is given out to the public may also change in line with advances in technology. It is difficult to predict what these advances may involve until much closer to the actual event. However, a comprehensive information technology strategic plan is essential to safe guard against these rapid changes. It has been said that one internet year is equivalent to seven earth years, hence the three years that lie ahead for Sydney 2000 Olympic is equivalent to twenty one years of Internet development, quite a daunting time scale to anticipate. But anticipating and facing this is nevertheless necessary.

Certain other programs such as cultural events and the opening and closing ceremony performances are based on inspirations. The time dimension of inspirations is quite difficult to anticipate. Allowing sufficient time for inspirations to prosper, whilst necessary, will severely restrict the possible lead times on these programs. Time, Cost and Quality dimensions on these kinds of activities are tightly interrelated. Sufficient safeguards need to be incorporated so that persons involved do not get carried away and ego conflicts are avoided. Several alternative proposals may have to be developed beyond the conceptual stage to select the best. Such an exercise could add to the overall cost of these activities and compromises may need to be negotiated.

Activities that have several unknowns, by their very nature, need to be planned towards the later stage of the project life cycle. The time dimension becomes extremely critical for these activities.

## Cost Dimension

The cost estimates of the construction projects are not reflected in the Games budget as the infrastructure projects are undertaken outside the Games project.

Sydney's Games budget is based on conservative assumptions and estimates of Games receipts and payments. Receipts are mainly from television rights and international and local participation (SOCOG, 1996). The financial planning process included:

- Consultations with both national and international experts in the fields relevant to both receipts and payments.
- Consultations with the Barcelona Organizing Committee, the International Olympic Committee and the Australian Olympic Committee.
- Review and analysis of results and budgets from previous Games and bid candidature.
- Independent analysis of construction costs by quantity surveyors Rider Hunt.
- Independent review of the estimates by auditors Price Waterhouse.

SOCOG has stated (SOCOG, 1996) that the NSW Audit Office has conducted a detailed review of the Games Budget, concluding that " the bid estimates have been developed following the due process, the assumptions were considered sound, the procedures adopted for developing the estimates were rigorous, and the processes used to develop the estimates were appropriate for the purpose."

SOCOG has also advised that the factors influencing the process included (SOCOG, 1996):

- Bipartisan support for the Games, both at Federal and State Government levels;
- The support of trade unions, minimizing the risk of construction disputes;
- Australia's low level of inflation; and
- Process undertaken by Sydney to implement procedures for accommodation price control, particularly in relation to hotel tariffs.

The NSW Audit Office cost estimates appear to have been produced using appropriate methodologies. However, even though the cost estimates were prepared using appropriate methodologies it is necessary to develop strict cost control mechanisms in order to keep the overall project costs to the minimum. It is worth noting that the major portion of the Games budget is for the events and ceremonies and the nature of these programs is such that there are considerable uncertainties inherent in these items. Further, the time and cost dimensions of these events are tightly interrelated. Consequently, any slippage in timing of the programming, training and testing of these activities could lead to large cost escalations.

Due to the predicted rapid change in technology it is highly likely that there will be variations in requirements or design. As a general rule, it is undesirable to allow too many such changes, since they are a major source of cost escalation in any project and especially in projects such as this. Some variations may be to a cost advantage but this is the exception rather than the norm.

Economic and social factors will also play a major part in cost escalation in the Games Budget. Currently, the Games project enjoys overwhelming public support, thus minimising the risk of labour strikes and other legal conflicts. However, if not managed properly the tide could turn leading to spiralling cost escalations. For example, SOCOG is negotiating with the hotel industry to ensure stable room rates for the period in time surrounding the Games.

Cost escalations would lead to disillusionment amongst the public and would diminish the public appeal of the Games thus affecting public support and a vital source of volunteer Games staff. Any cost overrun will have to be met by the taxpayer, as the New South Wales Government has underwritten the Host City Contract. This could also become a major political issue. Maintaining the costs within budget is vital to the Games success.

## Quality Dimension

This is the most difficult dimension of the project to define. The quality is three fold.

- Good quality vs high quality
- Fit for purpose
- Conforming to the customer requirement.

As part of the Host City Contract the International Olympic Committee has specified certain quality requirements for the Sydney 2000 Olympic Games. The New South Wales Government has specified certain environmental guidelines that all Olympic ventures should follow. Within the public mind there is also a concept of the level of quality and excellence the Olympic Games should achieve. The SOCOG itself will set their own quality standards mainly in performing its duties. Sponsors will demand a certain quality standard. Some of these standards are currently only at the conceptual stage. As the project progresses through its life cycle these standards need to emerge. Each program component will have its own definition of quality and standards.

One of the major areas a quality which should not be under estimated nor forgotten is the aspect of security. Responsibility for management of Olympic Games security lies with the Olympic Security Planning and Implementation Group (OSPIG). It would appear that there is a significant weakness in the security planning process in that it lacks co-ordinated project control. Rather than being developed as a strategic program, activities are being undertaken as disparate tactical operations. This has occurred because *Olympic Security* is being used to expand existing programs rather than being managed as a separate program. The focus has been on integrating existing activities to provide security for the Games, rather than on developing an effective Games security plan and then integrating existing programs where practical.

Generally, wherever there is public involvement in large projects it is generally not sufficient to have good quality or fit for purpose quality. The public demands very high quality standards. The quality of the Game events is likely to be judged by the absence of delays and clock-work precision with which the public expect events to proceed. In the case of transport, quality is judged by lack of traffic jams and hold-ups. The quality of security will be judged by perceived public safety and lack of incidents such as terrorism.

In construction projects quality can be clearly defined, for example, as fit for purpose or conforming to strict environmental guidelines. In projects such as the Games there are difficulties in defining quality, particularly in the early stages of the development cycle. For example, quality of performances and ceremonies might be measured by how spectacular they are, how precisely orchestrated and how much they appeal to majority audiences. Qualitative criteria such as these are not easy to quantify or to monitor in early stages of the development cycle.

Adoption of total quality management techniques in these programs could improve the quality of the delivered Olympic Games. The essential ingredients of a total quality management system are: quality of the product as the ultimate goal; quality management process; quality assurance systems and attitude.

Where clear specifications and well defined standards are difficult to formulate, engaging experienced personnel and experts may be particularly desirable. The product (eg. events or performances) should be thoroughly tested prior to the Games allowing ample time to make necessary modifications at least cost.

A good management process is vital to the delivery of a high quality product. It is necessary to establish milestones and set procedures for the management process to achieve quality.

As mentioned above, cost and quality are closely related. Quality comes at a price. This applies particularly to a project like the Olympic Games where completion on time is critical and the cost of failure is extremely high for any of the items included in the project.

Only through a closely controlled quality management processes and early identification of the possibility of failure can the success of the program be ensured. Several safeguards have been put in place both by the International Olympic Committee and the New South Wales Government to ensure the delivery of the Games is to an acceptable quality.

## Conclusions

The Sydney 2000 Olympic Games is a venture that requires considerable use of project management techniques and skills to make it a success. The large scale and very nature of the event requires good time management and the control of all three project dimensions, namely: time, cost and quality.

All three dimensions of the project are interrelated and careful monitoring is needed at every stage of the project life cycle. The estimates of the initial bid were prepared carefully and thoroughly with adequate checks and safeguards. During the bid stage and subsequent stages there was no leeway for varying the time dimension. This restriction, however, applies only to the delivery of the overall project. If the program is broken down to manageable items of work, the time dimension becomes something that can be manipulated. Careful programming and identifying proper milestones can improve the time management of the project.

The quality of the Games project is vital for its success and the project requires careful orchestration. Quality control can be achieved using proven project management delivery techniques. Some activities of the Games have a very high correlation of time and quality. Such events should be identified early in the planning process and test methods developed. Quality is hard to impose on events such as performances which involve subjective qualitative judgements. However, excellence can still be achieved with proper planning and commitment of the personnel involved.

The cost aspect of the project is closely interrelated to the time and quality aspects. In the Olympic Games project if a compromise has to be made, the cost aspect will be the first dimension that will be sacrificed.

Good communications are vital to the success of the project and to effective control of all three dimensions. Trial Games and test programs will serve to control all three dimensions and should be treated seriously. The planned trials in the coming years will be an excellent opportunity to monitor, control or correct any deficiencies in the project.

### References


Badiru AB and P.S. Pulat. 1994. *Comprehensive Project Management: Integrating Optimisation Models, Management Principles and Computers.* Prentice Hall. 1994.

Birner W, Geddes M and C. Hastings. 1994. *Project Leadership.* Aldershot, UK: Gower Publishing.

Burke R. 1994. *Project Management: Planning and Control.* John Wiley & Sons.

Davison I. 1994 *Project Procedures Handbook.* Hypertext Publishing.

Eager D.M. 1996 *Project Management 49002 Notes.* Graduate School of Engineering, UTS Printing Services,

Nicholas J.M; 1990. *Managing Business and Engineering Projects—Concepts and Implementation.* Prentice-Hall.

Meredith J.R and S. J. Mantel. 1995. *Project Management: A Managerial Approach.* John Wiley & Sons.

Sydney Organising Committee of the Olympic Games (SOCOG). 1996. Fact Sheets. September.

Turner RJ. 1993. *The Handbook of Project-Based Management.* McGraw-Hill.

# A Key To Success of Global Project Operations

Tsuneyoshi Oguri, JGC Corporation

## Introduction

The success of construction projects worth hundreds of millions of dollars will increasingly depend on shorter project schedules, improved quality and optimized utilization of worldwide project resources under stringent project budget limitations, which will demand faster and higher quality communications, concurrent work execution and unified information bases.

Managing project information, especially design engineering information, is an essential element in advancing global project operations. As we move from a paper-centric environment to a digital one, rapid retrieval and easy access to stored information and data in a consistent and structured way becomes crucial to success.

JGC Corporation, one of Japan's leading engineering and construction (EC) companies, has developed its own electronic Document Management System (EDMS) and has applied it to a major-sized Liquefied Natural Gas (LNG) plant project in Qatar.

The intent of this paper is to describe the necessity of global project operations in the EC industry, the key to success of global project operations, an overview of JGC EDMS, and key issues and characteristics of the system, and to discuss how the system contributes to project management objectives.

## Current Issues Facing E/C Companies

Currently, EC companies face the following issues:
Professional services costs are high.

- There exists mega competition among Japanese ECs, Western ECs, and others emerging in the international marketplace.
- Lump-sum contract capabilities are required by which contractors can take manageable risks and demonstrate self-motivated, efficient project execution leading to shorter project schedules, while meeting contractual quality requirements.
- Multiple-location engineering capabilities are required.
- Worldwide materials sourcing capabilities are required.
- Ability to form cross-cultural project teams with industry colleagues is required.
- Organized build-up of knowledge and key data is essential for effective ongoing planning and operations.
- Clients demand shorter project schedules from the standpoint of life-cycle costs.
- Clients demand electronic project information exchange from the standpoint of plant life-cycle support.

To cope with such issues, the major EC companies have been establishing global project operations environments over the past ten years.

## Global Engineering

Global engineering is to carry out the engineering operations concurrently among offices worldwide by means of international telecommunications networks. It allows project people to transfer project data seamlessly from one office to the other, regardless of geography or time zone.

The word engineering, in this context, means a series of activities to reach the final objectives of the project in optimum manner, using given, limited human and non-human resources.

Typically, engineering advances concurrently within given time constraints. Therefore, engineers on projects must always proceed with the work, taking into account the influence of their work on others.

Traditionally, engineering work in EC companies was carried out in a centralized manner. However, from the standpoint of reduced total installed costs and cycle time, global engineering operation is needed, including diversification of project operation centers.

The primary benefit of global engineering is to utilize optimal resources worldwide in a timely fashion and to adapt to the unique circumstances of each project.

To establish a global engineering environment effectively and efficiently, the following are essential elements for success:

### 1. Efficient project management information system based on the work package concept

Global engineering operations at diversified operation centers require an efficient project management system, so that the project manager and engineering manager are able to monitor the current status of the work and areas of concern by remote access from project directorate offices. In this situation, the work package concept based on a work breakdown structure (WBS) technique is an effective communication tool to track the status of the project.

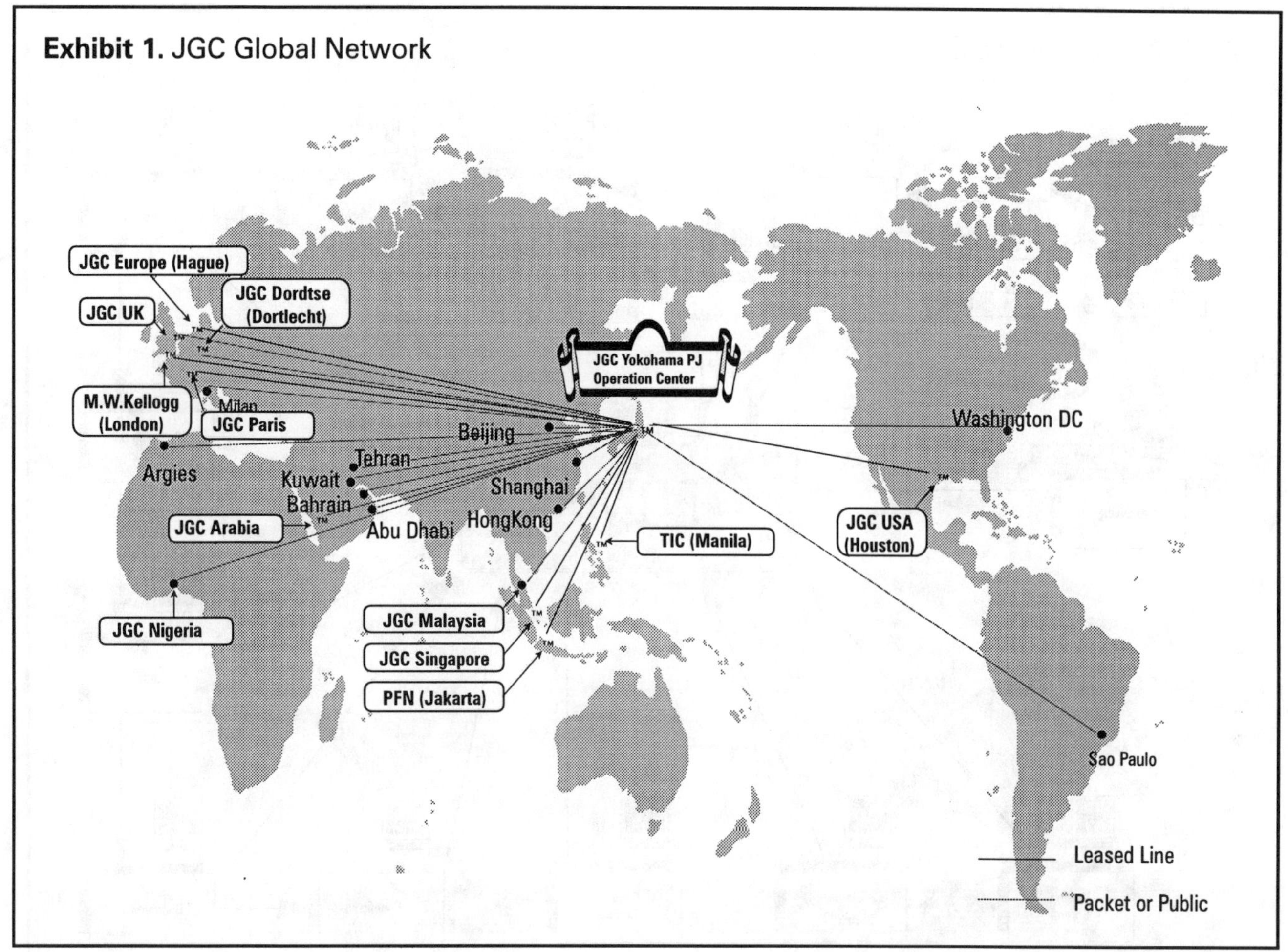


**Exhibit 1.** JGC Global Network

### 2. Global information network which electronically links major company offices worldwide

A high speed communications network infrastructure which connects all the major project operation centers, client offices, and construction sites is required to establish global engineering operation.

The network should support voice, facsimile, electronic mail, electronic file transfer, video conferencing, and database access under a client/server computing environment.

In recent years, the telecommunications network technology has advanced rapidly, and a variety of wide bandwidth circuits, such as conventional leased lines, fiber optic lines, satellite links, ISDN digital dial-up lines, and the internet can be selected.

### 3. Accessibility to a common database

Concurrent engineering and around-the-clock work operations which are the key to the global engineering, can only be performed by enabling access to a common engineering and document database. Once some engineering work package has been completed at one office, then the information related to that work package must be available to the engineers or parties concerned at the same and other offices.

The major related tools for engineering work in the process industry are:

- Electronic document management system (EDMS),
- STEP based engineering database

STEP is an international standard for exchanging product model data, undertaken by the International Organization for Standardization (ISO). STEP is ISO 10303 (Product Data Representation and Exchange) The objectives of STEP are:

- Exchange of information between engineering applications
- Long-term archiving of product information
- Implementation of shared product databases

JGC Corporation embarked on building a global engineering office network in 1991.

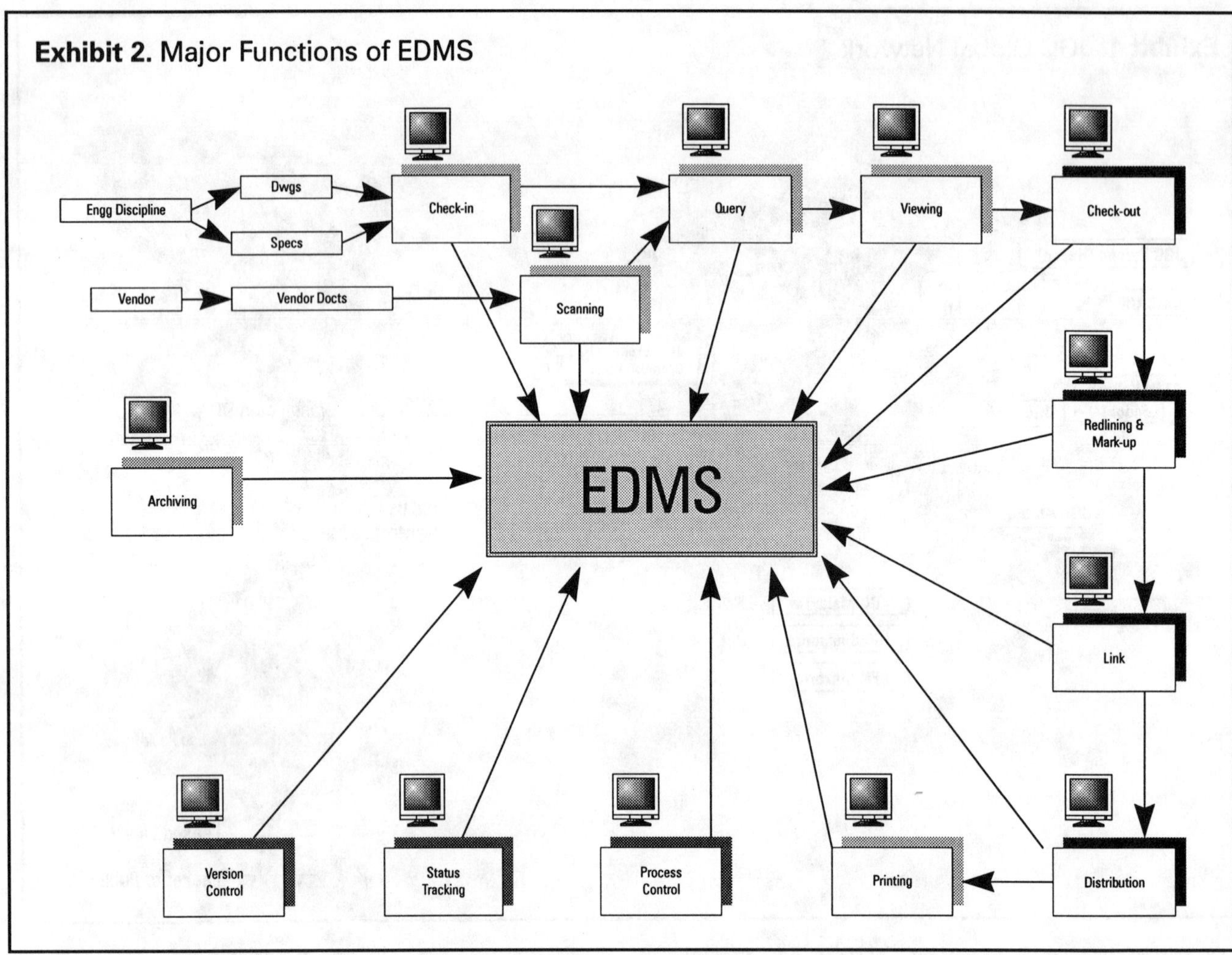


The project management information system (PMIS), labeled as "JGC-PMS" which is based on the work package concept, was commissioned in 1980, and the international telecommunications network which connects JGC's major overseas offices has been constructed in an step by step manner. To gear up for multi-location engineering capabilities, an EDMS, one of the major challenges for an effective global engineering office network, has just been implemented.

Exhibit-1 shows JGC's current international telecommunication network.

## What is EDMS ?

The electronic document management system provides a structure in which all types of document information used for design, procurement, and construction for a project are stored, managed, and controlled. Typically, EDMS is used to work with digital files and database records. These may include design specifications, CAD drawings, data sheets, calculation sheets, vender prints, engineering correspondence, project plans, construction photographs, and others.

Any information needed throughout a plant life-cycle can be managed by EDMS, making correct data accessible to project participants. The document development process can be managed by EDMS, as well as the documents themselves.

Use of EDMS ensures that users always get and share the most current engineering information.

The functionality of EDMS falls into the following four categories:

### Electronic Vault Management

Electronic vault management provides secure storage and retrieval of document information, check-in and check-out functions, security and access control, meta-data management, and establishment document inter-relationships.

Electronic vault management is the core function of EDMS.

**Exhibit 3.** JGC-EDMS Functional Flow Diagram (1/2)

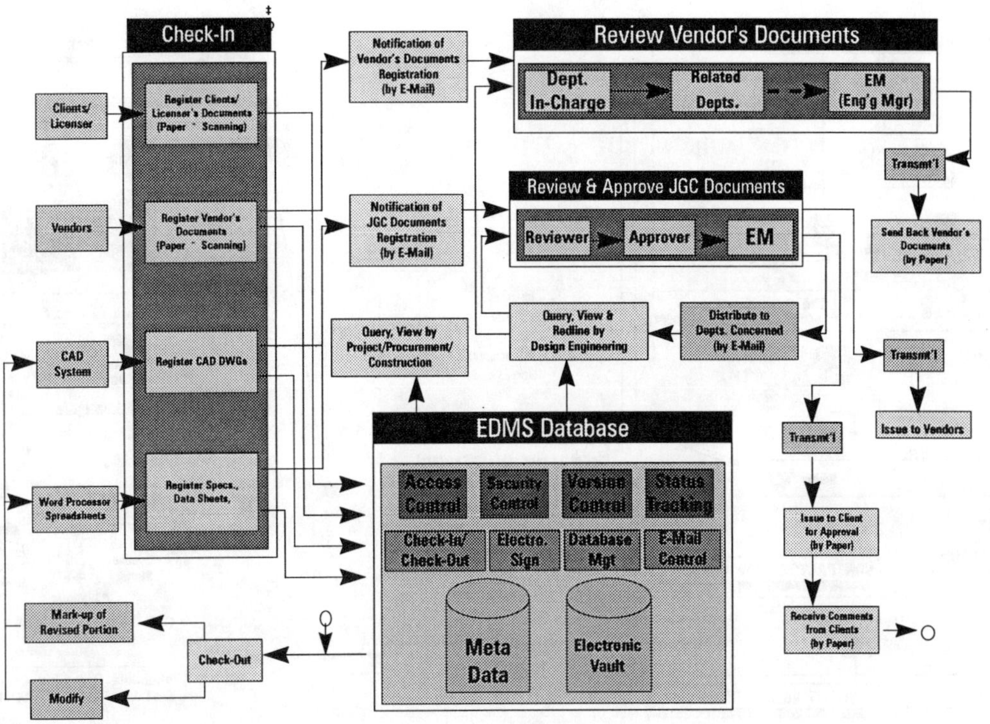

Check-In
Clients/ Licenser
Register Clients/ Licenser's Documents (Paper ~ Scanning)
Vendors
Register Vendor's Documents (Paper ~ Scanning)
CAD System
Register CAD DWGs
Word Processor Spreadsheets
Register Specs., Data Sheets,
Notification of Vendor's Documents Registration (by E-Mail)
Review Vendor's Documents
Dept. In-Charge
Related Depts.
EM (Eng'g Mgr)
Transmt'l
Send Back Vendor's Documents (by Paper)
Notification of JGC Documents Registration (by E-Mail)
Review & Approve JGC Documents
Reviewer
Approver
EM
Query, View by Project/Procurement/ Construction
Query, View & Redline by Design Engineering
Distribute to Depts. Concerned (by E-Mail)
Transmt'l
Issue to Vendors
EDMS Database
Access Control
Security Control
Version Control
Status Tracking
Check-In/ Check-Out
Electro. Sign
Database Mgt
E-Mail Control
Meta Data
Electronic Vault
Transmt'l
Issue to Client for Approval (by Paper)
Receive Comments from Clients (by Paper)
Mark-up of Revised Portion
Check-Out
Modify

**Exhibit 4.** JGC-EDMS Functional Flow Diagram (2/2)

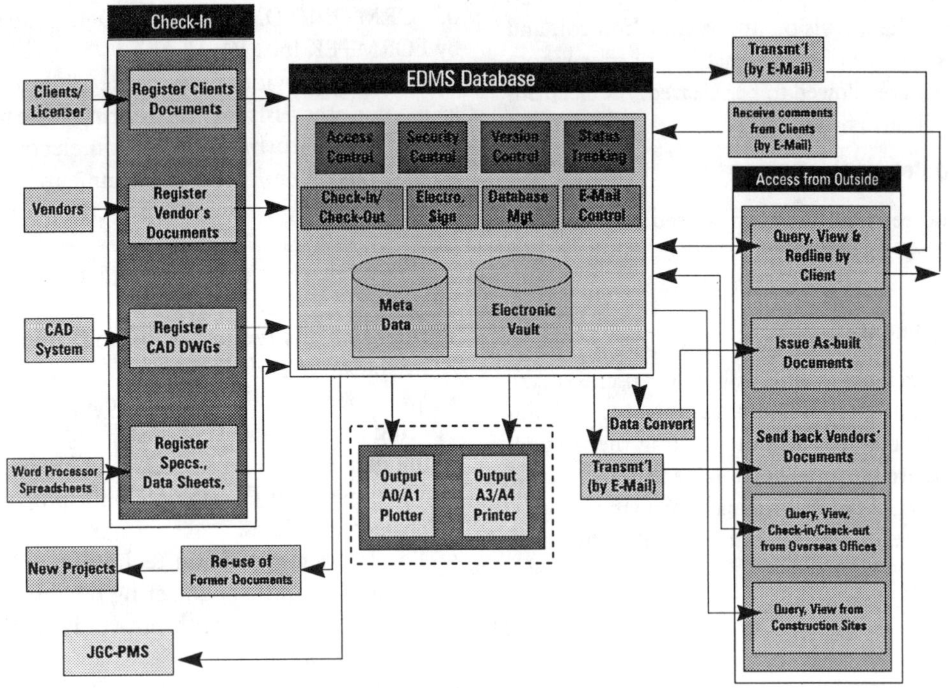

Check-In
Clients/ Licenser
Register Clients Documents
Vendors
Register Vendor's Documents
CAD System
Register CAD DWGs
Word Processor Spreadsheets
Register Specs., Data Sheets,
EDMS Database
Access Control
Security Control
Version Control
Status Tracking
Check-In/ Check-Out
Electro. Sign
Database Mgt
E-Mail Control
Meta Data
Electronic Vault
Transmt'l (by E-Mail)
Receive comments from Clients (by E-Mail)
Access from Outside
Query, View & Redline by Client
Issue As-built Documents
Send back Vendors' Documents
Query, View, Check-in/Check-out from Overseas Offices
Query, View from Construction Sites
Data Convert
Transmt'l (by E-Mail)
Output A0/A1 Plotter
Output A3/A4 Printer
New Projects
Re-use of Former Documents
JGC-PMS

**Exhibit 5.** Network Configuration for Ras Laffan LNG Project

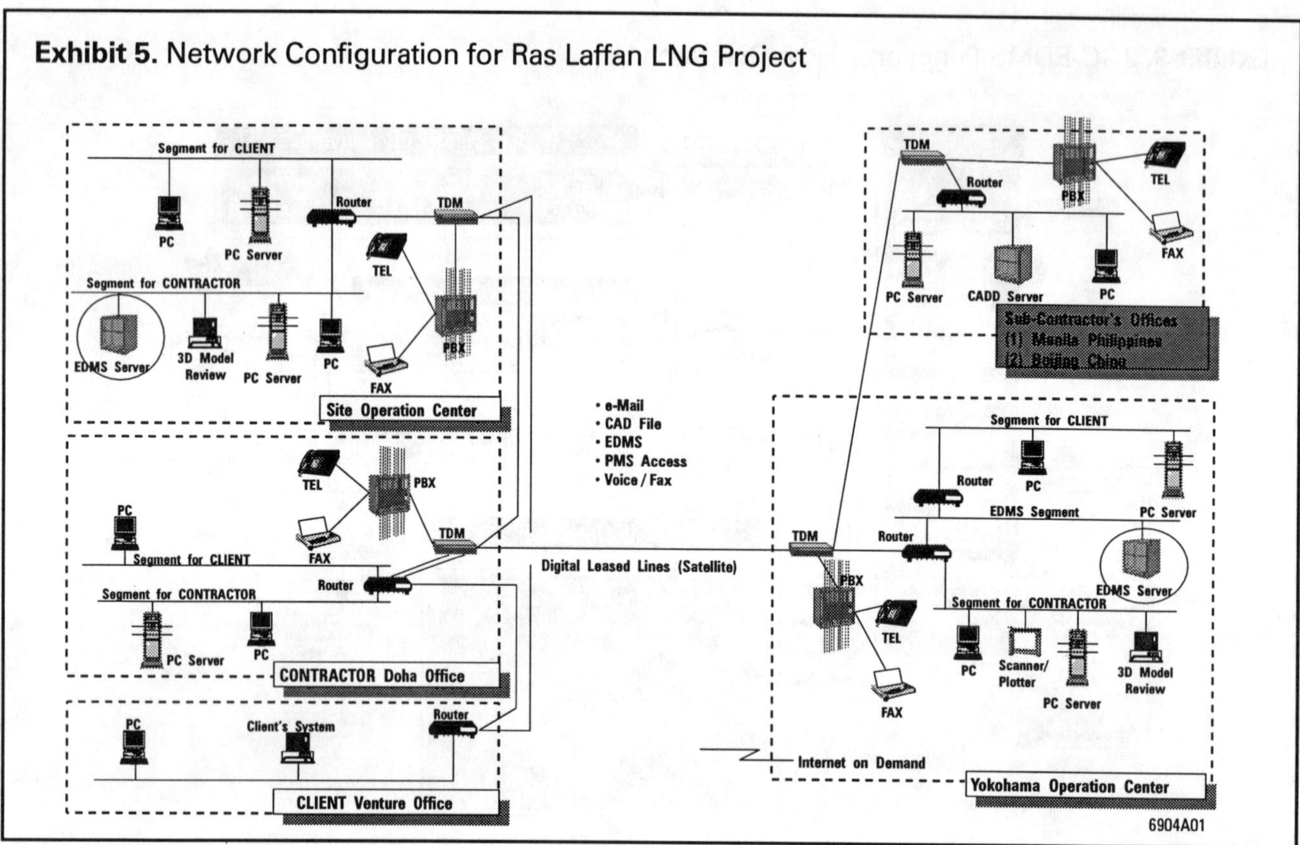


### Workflow and Process Management

Workflow and process management defines and controls the process of review and approval of documents, that is, who approves what and when, revision and version control, and the workflow or sequence of events that must occur before modified documents are allowed to be released. An electronic sign-off function is also included.

### Classification and Retrieval

A classification and retrieval function is used to search for documents. In EDMS, classification schemes can be maintained in the form of hierarchical structures.

### Annotation Management

An annotation management function allows the user to make comments, annotations, redlines, and markups for communicating change information without affecting the original object. Annotations are separately maintained from the original, ensuring full integrity of the original information object.

Exhibit-2 illustrates the major functions of EDMS.

## J-DOME Project

J-DOME is JGC's EDMS, which is based on a customization of FORMTEK/TDM (Technical Data Manager), developed by FORMTEK Inc., PA, USA.

J-DOME provides easy-to-use applications, and serves as a computer assisted engineering information management system, storing information electronically in a heterogeneous, client/server environment.

In 1994, JGC started pre-study on implementing EDMS.

The primary reasons for targeting at EDMS were as follows.

- Major clients request us to implement EDMS in their Invitation to Bid (ITB).
- We expect that EDMS will be a powerful tool for lowering total engineering costs, and improving engineering quality.
- We expect that EDMS will contribute toward reducing project schedules.
- The latest information technology allows us to electronically handle engineering documents easily.

Through the six-month pre-study work, the following results were obtained:

Confirmation of the project scope of EDMS development

Client and internal user needs
Modeling of the document data and document handling process
Definition of the required functionality
Restating the requirements using ranked objectives
Slate of technologies that would meet the objectives

Exhibit-3 and 4 shows JGC EDMS functional flow diagram.

The pre-study work team reported the results of the study to the JGC information technology steering committee, and discussions were held within the committee. Although some members of the committee were concerned over the effectiveness of EDMS and employees' resistance to the change from paper based work processes to digital work processes, the committee finally decided to proceed with the EDMS implementation.

The expected benefits of EDMS at that time were:

- Enhance engineering quality by using latest document information
- Collaborate with clients by sharing electronic document database
- Shorten document query time
- Shorten document distribution time
- Reduce printing and courier services costs

In November 1995, an EDMS implementation project team called "J-DOME", which stands for JGC Document Management Environment was kicked off.

In the original plan, we estimated the required duration of system development to be at least one year.

However, due to the pressing need to use EDMS on a newly awarded major-sized construction project, which will be described latter in this paper, the J-DOME project team was forced to accelerate the implementation schedule.

By effective use of our project management system, the development work, including software selection, system customization, integration with legacy systems, was carried out in eight months, which was three months ahead of the original schedule.

The key features of J-DOME are as follows:

- Seamless interface with JGC's in-house project management information system (JGC-PMS)
- Easy-to-use batch check-in module for large batches of documents such as vendor prints
- Access from bilingual (English/Japanese) platforms

## Application Case of J-DOME

In August 1996, J-DOME was released to a major-sized Liquefied Natural Gas (LNG) plant project in Qatar, as a first user for the system.

1. The outline of the project is as follows:
2. Project: Ras Laffan LNG project
3. Client: Ras Laffan LNG Company
4. Plant: Liquefied Natural Gas (LNG) Plant
5. Construction site: Ras Laffan, Qatar
6. Project schedule: March 1996 - April 1999
7. Contractor: JGC/M.W Kellogg joint venture
8. Scope: Project management, engineering, procurement, construction, start-up assistance
9. Engineering documents: 660,000 sheets

The main reasons why we adopted the J-DOME system into the project are as follows:

- The client and JGC wished to prove the viability of EDMS as an efficient engineering tool of new era on a large scale project.
- The client requested the contractor to submit all the as-built documents and drawings electronically.
- Since there are many stakeholders in this project, the use of a common database will be effective for close communication among parties concerned.

The joint venture home office is located in JGC's Yokohama office, and in this office, 60 client resident engineers and over 150 joint venture engineers are accessing the J-DOME server. The system enables users to search, retrieve, and print any project document or drawing and make comments on, or annotate the documents by redlining.

In March 1997, the joint venture started J-DOME operation at the construction site in Qatar using a replica server set up at site. The document database on the replica server is updated and maintained through a dedicated line between the joint venture home office and the site.

Exhibit-5 shows the network configuration for Ras Laffan LNG project.

Since the application of EDMS in this project has just been started, JGC's EDMS experience is still limited, but to date, the following results have been obtained in this project:

- Document printing and mailing costs are being saved, especially at the construction site.
- Document distribution time is shorter.
- Document query time is reduced.
- Employees' information literacy is improved.

This project is the first step towards enterprise-wide electronic document management.

## Benefits of EDMS from the Standpoint of Project Management

Through the application of EDMS in the global engineering environment, the following benefits from the standpoint of project management are expected.

### Scope management

According to the *PMBOK Guide*, project scope management is the process required to ensure that the project includes all the work required to complete the project successfully.

In the course of the scope planning, scope definition for the project is carried out using a work breakdown structure (WBS) technique. The WBS is a deliverable-oriented grouping of project elements that organizes and defines the total scope of the project. In engineering and construction projects, engineering documents are the key deliverables of the work. EDMS, by which inter-relationships among engineering documents and the relationships between documents and drawings and engineering work packages can be defined, serves as an effective scope management tool.

### Time management

The primary objectives of project time management are to ensure timely completion of the project and evaluate the influence of changes that have occurred on the overall project schedule in the course of the project.

Electronic document management contributes to such objectives of project time management by allowing the project users to access any project information at any time within seconds, and also to obtain the current document information which includes all changes that have occurred.

### Quality management

Using EDMS, the user can always access the latest version of engineering documents and drawings and recognize the relationship among documents, which is useful information where changes occur. Accordingly, EDMS will contribute to enhanced engineering quality management.

### Communication management

Project communication management is one of the key areas of project management. According to the *PMBOK Guide,* communication management provides the critical links among people, ideas, and information that are necessary for project success. In order to accomplish effective communication management, it is very important to apply an adequate information retrieval system. In this regard, EDMS is a powerful tool for information retrieval under the global project operating environment.

## Conclusion

The EDMS greatly enhances the speed and quality of communications among the project participants within the project organization. EDMS also enables the project participants to rapidly perform many interactions within a short period of time to arrive at the optimum solution.

It should be recognized that the barrier to implementing EDMS is not the technology, but the work process changes that result and individuals' resistance to change. No longer can an engineer just be a process specialist or a piping layout specialist.

In a global engineering environment, it is not necessary to have all of the information in proprietary systems, but rather through telecommunications networks, to access the information wherever it is created and maintained.

The ability to utilize and interact with all of these sources of information in a timely fashion is the key to successfully completing plant construction projects.

# Project Management Approach in Japan and Advanced Information Technology to Construction Projects for the Future

Hiromitsu Sakamoto, PMP, Makoto Hoshino, Tetsuya Sekiya, PMP,
Toru Ide, Construction Management Group, Takenaka Corporation, Tokyo, Japan

## Introduction

Japan is now one of the largest construction markets in the world. Total construction investment of the fiscal year 1995 was about US $699 billion ($1=\115), and it was about 16.6 percent of GDP (Gross Domestic Product) of the same year. There are about 552,000 construction firms in the industry and seven Japanese contractors were ranked among the world's ten largest contractors in 1995. Many Japanese contractors are very active in the international construction market. Not only in the Asian region, these firms are also active in construction markets of the United States and Europe. Most large-size general contractors in Japan have in-house architects and engineers and perform design-build type works. Large-size general contractors also have in-house research and development centers and heavily invest in research and development activities. Japanese general contractors' research and development activities highly contributed to the success of the manufacturing industry in Japan by bringing technologies such as superclean rooms and antivibration technology. These have been essential for many areas of the electronics industry where Japanese manufactures lead the world market. Shorter construction schedules and intensive quality control efforts by general contractors enabled many manufactures to bring quality products to the market within the targeted time.

Historically architecture in Japan was made of wood. This was true until the end of Edo Period, which continued nearly 300 years under the Tokugawa shogunate, ending in 1868 with increasing pressure from many foreign countries that demanded more openness. Modernization of Japan began in 1868, and Japan rapidly industrialized itself as a nation. Western architecture and building technology greatly contributed to modernize Japan, and the Meiji government invited many western architects and building engineers to Japan. Architects and building engineers from the United States helped the Meiji government to build a number of western-style government offices, public buildings, schools and many other types of buildings. It was the beginning of the modern Japanese construction industry, and the integration of historical Japanese architecture and modern western technology began. Again after World War II, new concepts of quality control known as Statistical Quality Control were introduced to Japan by Dr. Edward Deming, and this concept evolved into TQM (Total Quality Management). As Western construction technology contributed to modernize Japanese construction technology in the Meiji Period, the concept of TQM greatly contributed to improve the quality of construction from the 1970s.

The Japanese construction industry has had major influences from the United States twice in its history. Japan rapidly grew, and it is one of the industrially advanced nations. However, it has been pointed out that there are several differences in the project management approach between the United States and Japan. Nationality, history, culture and business customs are different for both countries. But even though such project management environments vary between two countries, the goal of the project management effort is universal. The Japanese construction industry is again being significantly influenced from the United States by new technology. It is information technology. The world of the Internet has grown so fast, and the flow of information is huge in volume. Decision making processes need to be continuously improved to meet the rapidly changing environment, and the project management function is at the heart of the construction process. Newly developed information technology has been applied to the construction process in Japan, and the Internet is one of the key technologies to drastically improve the construction management process to bring the clients to the next level of customer satisfaction.

## Project Management Characteristics in Japan

The most important project management functions for construction projects in Japan is control of cost, schedule and quality. One of the world's finest building quality standards has been established with precise schedules and cost control by many quality-minded general contractors that developed during the rapid economic growth period in Japan. Once a project is initiated, the magnitude of the project is unknown at that time, but owners are reassured by the commitment of reliable general contractors closely working for them.

**Exhibit 1.** Design-Build Process

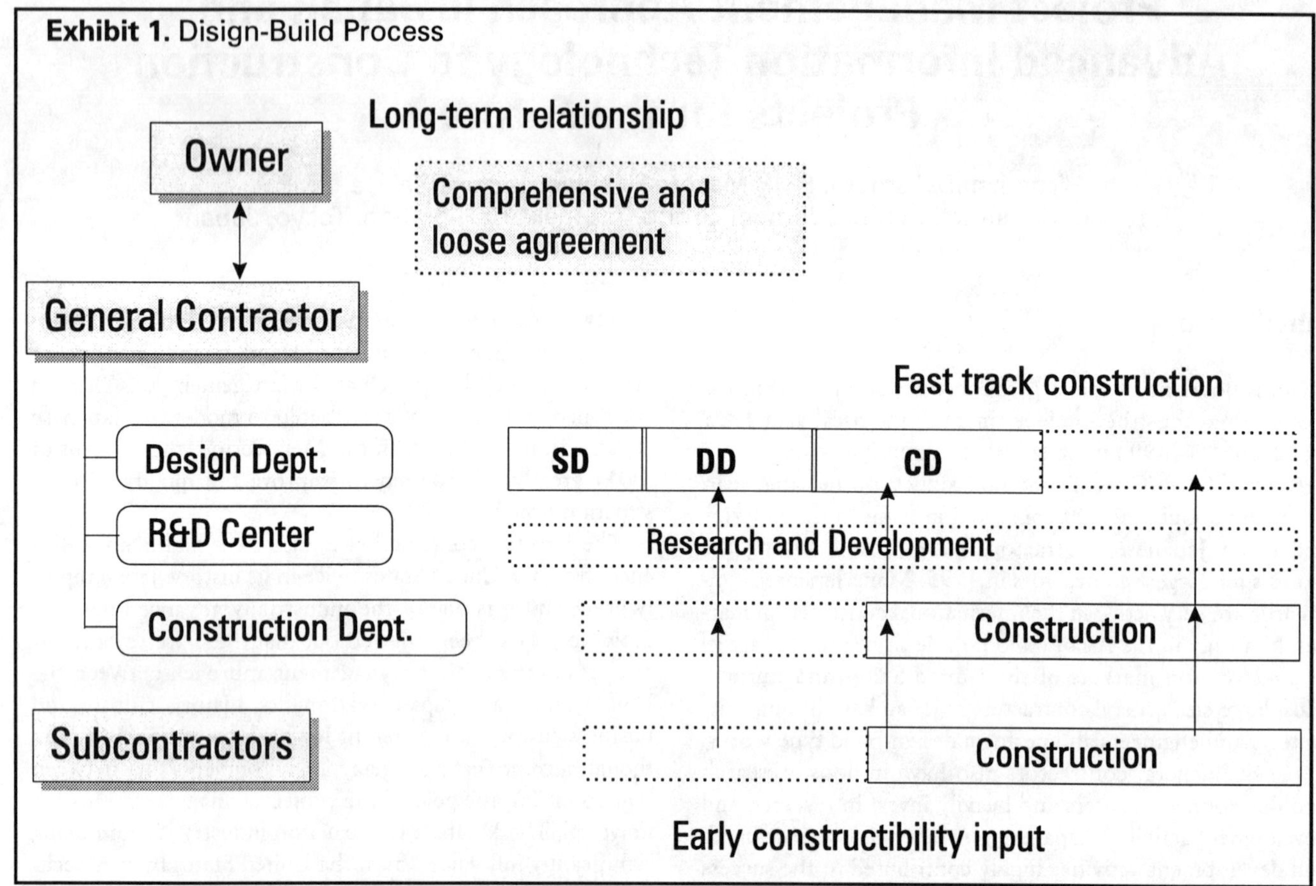


Project management efforts in Japan will mainly focus on the final products of the construction process, the buildings themselves. During the design phase, detailed construction planning is studied, and potential problems that may cause serious results in the future will be solved by intensive coordination between the design team and the construction team. The construction manager who is responsible for the project will have very intensive coordination with various departments such as the design department, technical department and estimation department to bring the best solution to the project.

Another role of the project management function in Japan is how to balance quality and cost with relation to the total construction schedule. There are many changes that have major cost impact, and VE studies to reduce costs and detailed schedule studies to eliminate negative schedule impact are very important. Otherwise general contractors would lose credibility with clients.

## Management Process in Design-build Projects

The design-build approach is one of the most preferred project approaches by private sector owners, and it is also the approach that Japan's leading general contractors integrate into their total capability. Advantages of the design-build process are:

### 1. Early Constructibility Input

Early constructibility input from not only in-house construction section but also subcontractors during the design phase.

### 2. Comprehensive and loose agreements

There are comprehensive and loose agreements between owners and general contractors as well as between general contractors and subcontractors. Such an environment eliminates unnecessary effort and time to prepare bid documents and carry out negotiation.

### 3. In-house design department and research and development center

In-house design departments accumulate experience with construction projects in the past, and lessons learned from each project including problems during the construction phase will be reflected in the future projects. Necessary technology development will be worked out by an in-house research and development center simultaneously through the design and construction phase.

#### 4. Small Involvement by the owner

Design-build is an approach possible only for the projects where the owner and the general contractor trust each other. From the planning stage to maintenance stage, general contractors take full responsibility to successfully execute all the phases of a project. Thus, the owner's involvement is minimized.

#### 5. Partnering Process

Every day activities of the design-build process constitute a partnering process in Japan. Everyone involved in the project will share the same goals, and that is only possible through close communication and coordination carried out with numerous activities such as morning meetings, morning exercises, tool box meetings, safety patrols, daily coordination meetings and sometimes barbecue parties held with all of the projects participants including hundreds of trade workers.

On design-build projects, the above advantages are maximized, and a lot of concurrent activities and interactive information exchange are made by in-house architects and construction engineers. Since design-build includes constructibility input through the design phase and fast-track construction phase, it is considered that the system is compatible with the construction management approach in the United States. For several decades the Japanese construction industry has been improving the unique way of construction approach driven by large-scale general contractors in the different business customs and cultures from western countries. Long-term relationships with private sector companies allow general contractors to put large amounts of investment into research and development. This also creates an environment in which owners and contractors have high motivation toward research and development for mutual interest. Therefore, large-scale contractors compete to provide various types of services from the early stages of a project, sometimes even before a project exists.

In Japan, even for a $100 million project, the project will be started under a very loose agreement based on a long-term relationship between the private owner and general contractor. Lump-sum price agreed at the beginning of the project without any detailed contract documents works as a GMP, and on-going changes by the owner are balanced through VE carried out by the general contractor. Heavy risks are taken by general contractors but that is also the incentive for general contractors to win the trust of the owner and keep a long-term relationship with them.

### Latest Trend of Project Approach and Construction Management in Japan

The Japanese economy has been so slow and the business environment is becoming more competitive than ever before. A new competition to survive in the construction industry has just began. Private and public sectors owners are looking for alternative delivery method that can suit the goal of individual projects. General contractors are restructuring the total production system of design-construction process for more productive, cost-effective and customer-oriented direction.

Many new approaches and ongoing trials including the following are now practiced and underway industrywide:

#### 1. Construction Management

Recently in Japan, construction management has been one of the very hot topics and industry-wide studies have been carried out on a variety of occasions. Even though traditional methods (design-bid-build) and the design-build method remain as the major project approaches in Japan, there is a growing need for the construction management approach in both the public sector and private sector. Background for needs of the construction management approach include:

- Owners look for access to more clear project information.
- Owners look for a more competitive approach.
- Owners look for tighter project controls.

#### 2. Project Management

Until very recently in Japan, soft services including project management services were not well recognized, and they were considered as part of specialty services (i.e., design or construction services). However, the need for pure project management services is increasing because today's complex project environment requires a separate PM function, and the importance of the PM function is becoming understood industrywide.

#### 3. Value Engineering

The value engineering approach developed in the United States has recently been applied to many public work projects in Japan.

#### 4. Project Benchmarking

Some of Japan's leading multinational companies are looking into their procurement approach and using benchmarking methods to find the best practice to procure for construction projects.

**Exhibit 2.** Information Management Platform

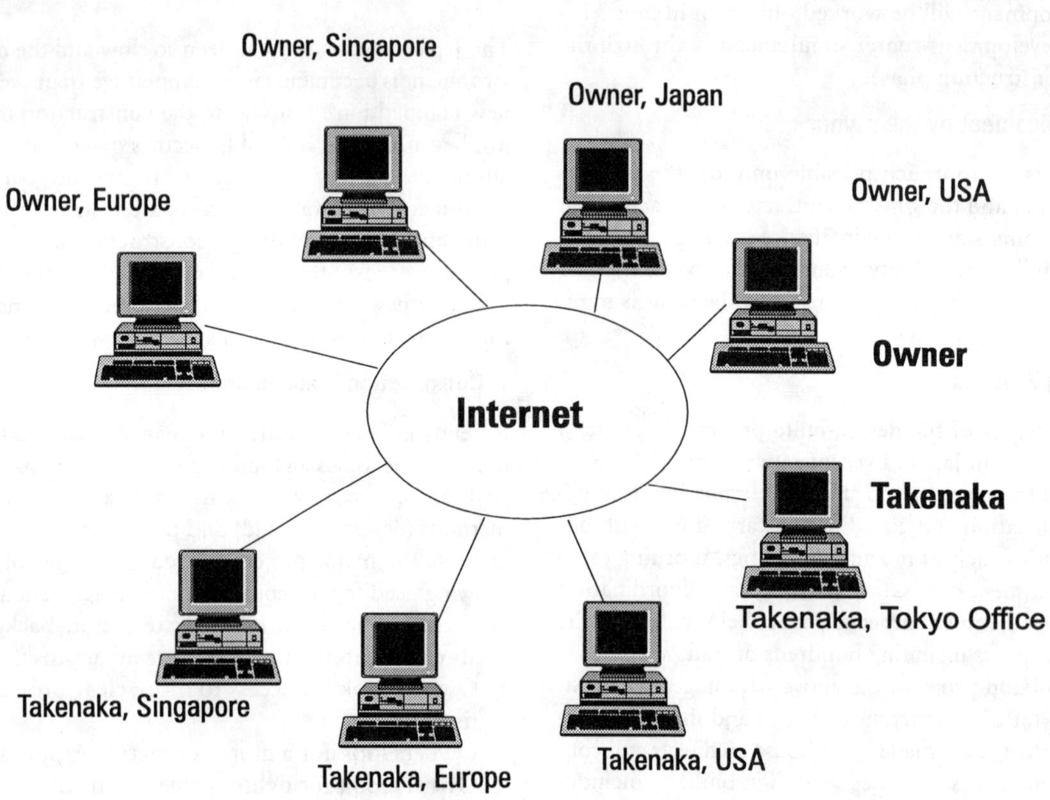

Owner, Singapore

Owner, Japan

Owner, Europe

Owner, USA

**Owner**

**Internet**

**Takenaka**

Takenaka, Tokyo Office

Takenaka, Singapore

Takenaka, USA

Takenaka, Europe

**Exhibit 3.** Project Web Site

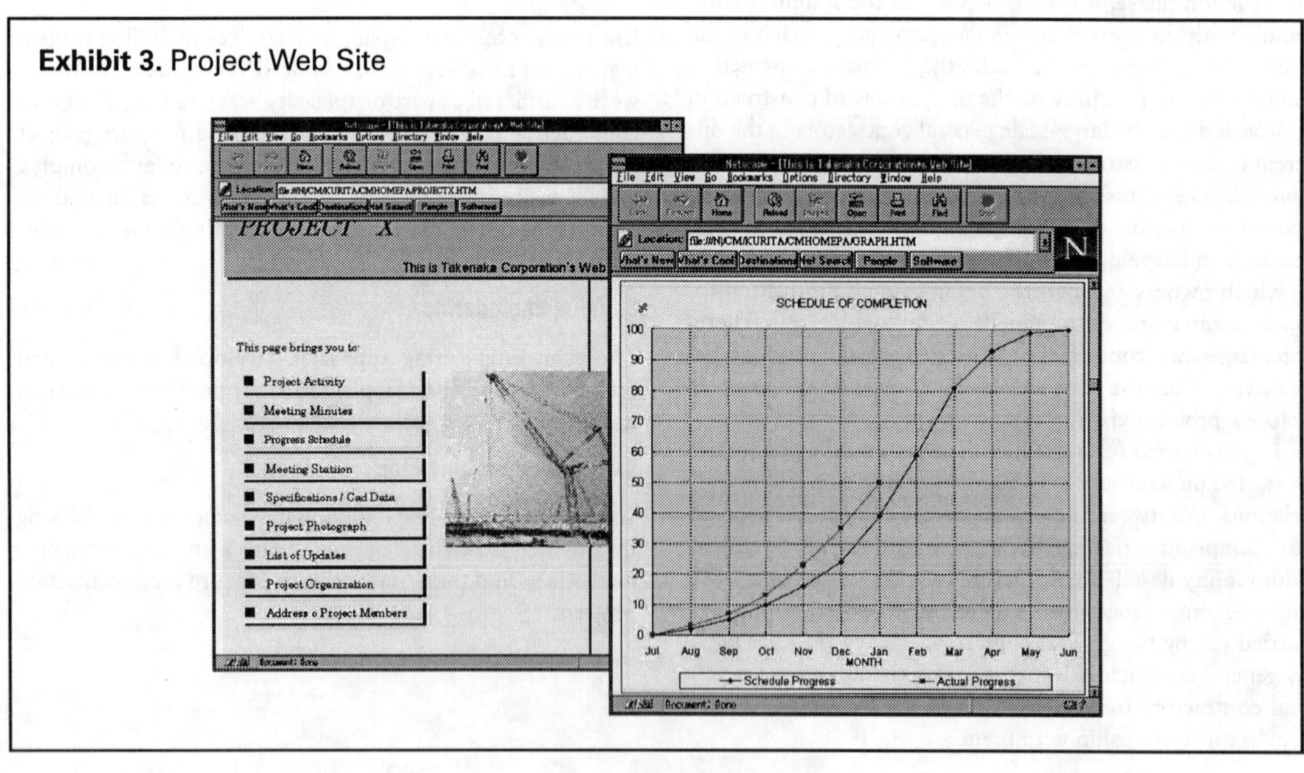

## Advanced Information Technology With Recent Construction Projects

Information technology has drastically advanced during the past few years, and what was a kind of dream several years ago has now become reality. Not many people knew of the word "Internet" five years ago, but it is now a standard business word everywhere. As everyone has experienced during daily business life, the world of the Internet has grown so rapidly and the flow of information is now so fast and huge in volume. Advanced information technology is applied to the construction process by many leading consultants and contractors to improve the total productivity and quality, and it is the key to successfully execute today's complex projects in various countries.

Takenaka Corporation developed the technology that enables every participant of a project, even in distant locations, to work together by using the Internet as an information management platform. Our project Web site on the Internet is only accessible by designated project participants who have an ID and password, and all project-related information is handled in a very easy way; just click it. On this project Web site, not only can you see the progress report, photographs, CAD data or minutes of meetings for the project, but you will also be able to make a timely decision on the virtual conference room where all project information is available. You will know what kind of problems need to be solved for the project to smoothly progress.

Another dream will come true soon. Once you develop 3D CAD drawings, an automatic estimation system will give you the total project cost instantaneously, and the cost impact from the change of design, material or dimensions will be reflected at the same time. All the project information will be shown on the project Web site, and video conferences will be held on the same PC that you access to the project Web site. Real time video and photographs of the construction site will be available through the project Web site, and on-site assistance will be made by project engineers even the engineer travels overseas. As-built drawings and maintenance manuals will be supplied in the shape of a compact disc when a project is complete, and the history of all the changes made during the course of the project can be traced. The construction industry has entered into a new era, and what was just a dream several years ago is becoming a reality.

# Strategic Planning for Computer Integrated Construction

Youngsoo Jung, Ssangyong Engineering and Construction Co., Ltd.
G. Edward Gibson, Jr., The University of Texas at Austin

## Introduction

Information systems (IS) are widely recognized as being an enabler not only for effective project management, but also for better engineering and construction automation. In addition, dramatic advances in information technology in recent years have motivated the construction industry to explore better methods of utilization of innovative information systems, so as to improve its productivity. As a comprehensive concept, in order to maximize the utilization of information technologies, computer integrated construction (CIC) has recently evolved to mean handling separate applications effectively. However, CIC is a broad and strategic concept. Complicating CIC solutions are the dynamics of technology development and business requirements. It is challenging, therefore, to design systems that are based on the available technology, resources, needs, and benefits. Although this situation calls for an effective IS planning process for implementing the CIC concept, no planning methodology currently exists for the construction industry to handle this daunting task that is coupled with limited resources and conflicting needs.

In order to help with this problem, a strategic planning process for the CIC implementation is proposed, and a real-world case study investigating overall corporate requirements by using the methodology is presented in this paper. A comprehensive framework is introduced to discuss the concerns and functions of information systems over the project life-cycle. The entire planning process condenses these complex issues into a simplistic portfolio providing clear insight for CIC planning requirements.

Information is a key resource for effective project management, and the role of information systems has changed to a great extent as those are deeply interrelated with business processes beyond merely supporting of specific transactions. Designing information systems in these days does mean configuring a firm's business processes and strategies. Rapidly changing information technology in the next century will complicate the role tremendously. In this context, this paper will stress the importance of IS planning and its impact on project management for the construction industry. The CIC planning methodology also will be mapped onto the framework of *A Guide to the Project Management Body of Knowledge (PMBOK Guide)* (PMI 1996).

## Background

The general role of information systems has, to a great extent, changed in organizations. The traditional role of information systems had been to support business functions by replacing labor intensive transactions. However, as information systems have proliferated and become deeply interrelated with business processes, the role of information systems has expanded further to support or even shape corporate strategy (Bakos and Treacy 1986; Henderson and Venkatraman 1993). Therefore, at the present time, information is a key corporate resource, and designing an information system means configuring a firm's business processes and strategies. For example, Hammer (1990) defines IT as the most critical enabler for reengineering, and Henderson and Venkatraman (1993) explain how IT can achieve a strategic fit for an organization by proposing their four strategic alignment models.

Being a crucial corporate resource, information systems constitute a very large and complex structure and are costly. A survey by Bacon (1992) reveals that the average IS expenses for the overall industry in the United States was 2.7 percent of annual revenue. This situation makes the information systems an area needing effective control. Due to the rapidly changing characteristics of information systems, in terms of scale, complexity, and technologies, managing all of the aspects of a firm's information systems by in-house staff is becoming more difficult. In order to sustain effective information systems, various professional experts in specific domains are essential. For these reasons, Parker and Case (1993) argue that "downsizing" and "outsourcing" are the key information resource management (IRM) issues of the decade. It would appear, therefore, that it is more important for the construction industry to have IS *planning* capability than it is to have more IS implementation or maintenance skills.

Even though the information systems in the construction industry are not as advanced as that in other industry sectors (Tucker et al. 1994; Nam and Tatum 1992a), the issue of IRM are serious enough for management to be concerned. In recent years, dramatic advances in information technology has also motivated the construction industry to look for better ways to utilize information systems. Many effective and efficient ways of using computers for almost every sector in the construction engineering and project management (CEPM) area have been developed. Some of these are successfully implemented while

**Exhibit 1.** CIC Framework

| Variable | PMBOK (1996)* | Element |
|---|---|---|
| Project Life-Cycle | Initial Phase | Planning |
| | Intermediate Phases | Design<br>Procurement<br>Construction<br>Maintenance and Operation |
| | Final Phase | Disposal |
| Business Functions | 4.0 Project Integration Management | |
| | 5.0 Project Scope Management | Sales<br>Planning |
| | 6.0 Project Time Management | Scheduling |
| | 7.0 Project Cost Management | Estimating<br>Cost Control |
| | 8.0 Project Quality Management | Quality Management |
| | 9.0 Project Human Resource Management | Human Resource Management |
| | 10.0 Project Communications Management | General Administration |
| | 11.0 Project Risk Management | |
| | 12.0 Project Procurement Management | Contracting<br>Materials Management |
| | | Design<br>Safety Management<br>Finance/Accounting<br>R&D |
| IS Concern | | Corporate Strategy<br>Management<br>Computer Systems<br>Information Technology (IT) |

* 'Generic Life Cycle' and 'Nine Areas of Project Management Knowledge' defined in PMBOK.

some have not been widely adopted yet. Nevertheless, most claim that they have a significant impact on managing construction projects.

With all the potential that information systems and the CIC concept have to offer, there has been no logical, regimented effort to investigate a methodology for IS planning in the construction industry. This lack of effort makes it difficult for the industry (especially on a firm level) to decide how to implement information technologies, how far to develop, how to prioritize them, and so forth. In order to address this problem, a recent research (Jung 97) developed an IS planning methodology for the construction industry. Some parts of the research are briefly included in this paper.

## Computer Integrated Construction (CIC)

The concept of CIC is mainly derived from that of computer integrated manufacturing (Sanvido and Medeiros 1990). As Scheer (1991) defines, "...computer integrated manufacturing (CIM) refers to the integrated information processing requirement for the technical and operational tasks of an industrial enterprise. The operational tasks can be referred to as the production planning and control system." Researchers in the construction industry interpret CIC by emphasizing the nature of construction project management, while adapting basic CIM concepts. This nature notably includes the project life-cycle and fragmented participants for subjects of discussion. As the CIC concept has been dispersed, IS research efforts in the industry are often forced to pursue CIC, and the terms CIC and IS have become synonymous. However, without a commonly conceived CIC concept, a great deal of CIC research efforts has focused on technical systems for a group of particular business functions. The concept of CIC should be broad and abstract, as it is not a specific system. In order to better understand the characteristics and requirements of information systems in the industry, CIC is defined in this paper as the *integration of corporate strategy, management, computer systems, and information technology throughout the project's entire life-cycle and across different business functions*.

This definition, with strongly emphasized managerial issues, helps make CIC much more viable than it is when only dealing with technical matters. The broad definition of CIC in this paper forms a conceptual framework with three variables: project life-cycle, business functions, and IS concern. The project life-cycle variable is fundamentally a time variable and represents the linear characteristics of construction projects. Phases of the project life-cycle usually involve many construction business functions and organizations. The business function variable depicts the business processes of the industry. The IS concern variable contains internal and external business environment issues (corporate strategy, management, computer systems, and IT) as the considerations for CIC planning. Variables and elements for this CIC framework are summarized in Exhibit 1, and elements of the variables are compared with "generic life cycle" and "nine areas of project management knowledge" defined by *PMBOK Guide* (PMI 1996). This comparison also indicates how *PMBOK Guide* (PMI 1996) information can be expanded further so as to incorporate the distinct characteristics of the construction industry, especially for the purpose of information systems planning (Jung 1997). Exhibit 1 was developed by incorporating literature review, corporate concerns through a case-study, and guidance from researchers in construction engineering and project management area.

## Issues for CIC Planning

As discussed in the definition of CIC, this paper addresses four major areas of IS concern for strategic CIC planning: corporate strategy, management, computer systems, and IT. These four areas encompass a variety of IS assessment issues, as the planning of CIC necessitates corporate-wide efforts. Complicating CIC solutions are the dynamics of technology development and business requirements.

### Corporate Strategy

Corporate strategy at the highest level of an organization directs information systems, as well as all other activities. The strategic significance of information systems has been asserted by many authors, and Bakos and Treacy (1986) propose three perspectives on the strategic impact of information systems: internal strategy, competitive strategy, and business portfolio strategy. Impact from the strategic uses are also found in the construction industry. For example, project information management systems can be an IS for internal strategy. Shimizu's SMART system (Miyatake and Kangari 1993) or Bechtel's 3D CAD system (Laborde and Sanvido 1994) may be understood as information systems for competitive impact. Using an information system for business portfolio strategy is very rare, but a possible scenario for its use is in a project that constructs and manages a huge residential complex equipped with highly sophisticated communications devices through which a variety of value added services is provided. This scenario shows how the construction industry competes with the communications or entertainment industry. Considering the immaturity of information systems in construction and successful precedence in other industries (Henderson and Venkatraman 1993; Clemons and Row 1991; Gray 1994), opportunities for strategic uses of information systems in construction seem promising. "Corporate strategy" as an IS concern observes how information systems can support these opportunities for an organization.

### Management

Management needs to be integrated with CIC in many ways. First, CIC implementation without management support will not succeed. Davenport and Short (1990) emphasize the importance of visible commitment from senior management during IT driven process redesign. In addition, since business processes cut across different organization functions causing resistance, they regard maintaining management commitment as the most difficult task. Second, new management skills can enhance business performance. For example, researchers (Rasdorf and Abudayyeh 1991; Rowings 1991) suggest that an integrated cost and schedule control system utilizing a combined breakdown system can reduce the inefficiency and limitations of current project control systems. Third, Adams and Campbell (1990) point out the lack of managerial skills in project managers' who are promoted from the technical fields with no training or education in managerial function. Managerial skills can be greatly enhanced by using systematic information systems that provide guidance for right managerial processes. Finally, designing new information systems makes it possible to change business procedures. Business reengineering is a good example (Hammer 1990). Thus, the "management" issues are concerned with how information systems can attain management commitment, enhance business performance, and change business processes.

### Computer Systems

The major technical component of CIC planning and implementation is the integration between computer systems. Due to the advances of database management systems (DBMS), communications systems, and the application systems of the construction business functions, physical integration between any computer systems is viable. However, difficulties involve such issues as common standards, business processes, and project management skills (Gibson and Bell 1992). Integration of computer systems can occur along with the project life cycle and different business functions (two variables in the proposed framework) at the same time. An effort to combine design and construction systems shows how systems integration improves construction performance (Reinschmidt et al. 1991). In their research and implementation, they utilized a relational database management system (DB2), a three dimensional CAD system (CATIA), and a telephone based communications system (T1) to integrate design, engineering and construction. This integrated system is used in constructability review, planning, construction management, and progress reporting. The results reveal an improved design, engineering and construction process, enhanced communications and coordination between all parties, and, moreover, a permanent asset for improved operation and maintenance of the constructed facility (Reinschmidt et al. 1991). The "computer systems" of IS concern

**Exhibit 2.** Portfolio Analysis for CIC Planning

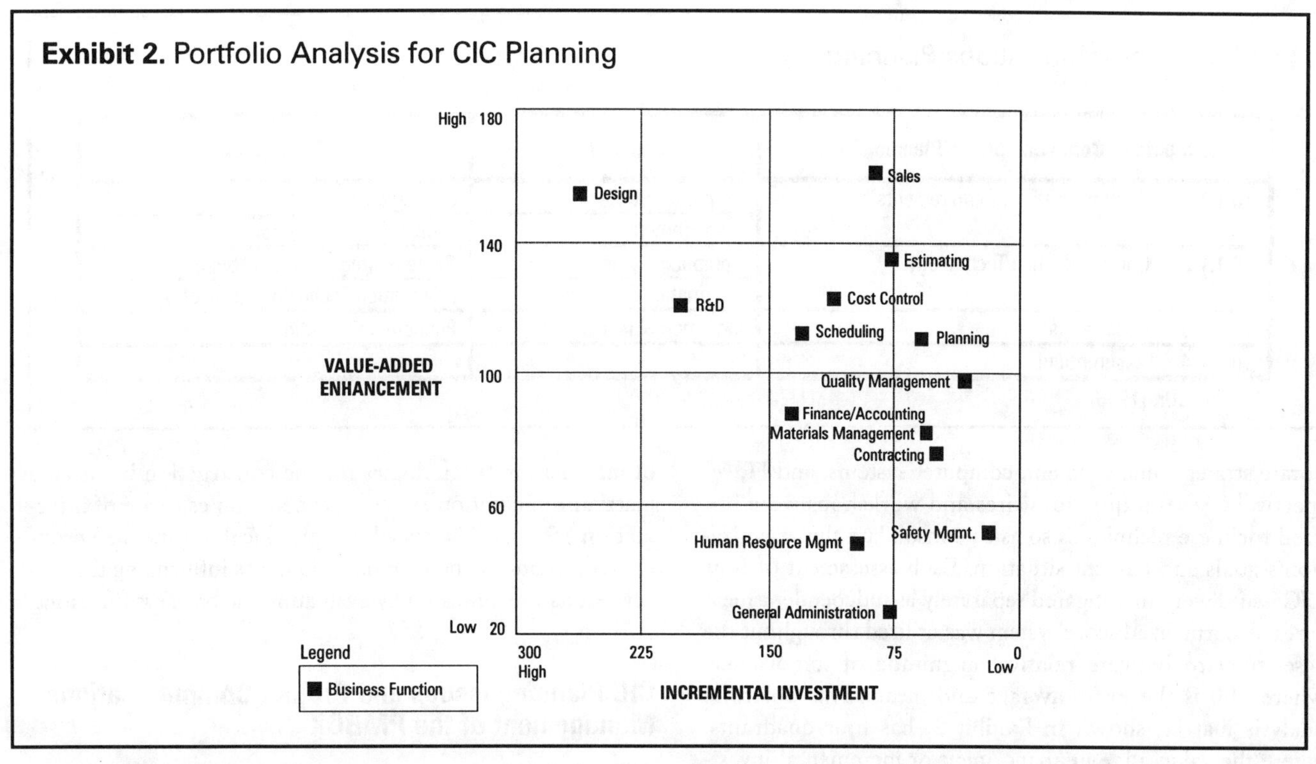


deals with the issues of systems integration between computer applications in construction in terms of data sharing, communications, and system configurations.

### Information Technology (IT)

Integrating technology with information systems deals not only with IT, but with construction technology as well. However, note that IT is still playing an important role in almost all advanced construction technologies. As enabling information technologies, object oriented programming (OOP), knowledge based systems (KBS), database management systems (DBMS), 3D CAD systems, dynamic simulation, and communications systems are required for CIC (Miyatake and Kangari 1993; Teicholz and Fischer 1994). From an economic, technical, and social viewpoint, prefabrication and robotics are increasingly feasible. Research by Greer et al. (1996) supports the importance of IT applications in controlling automated construction equipment, such as a large scale manipulator and an automated pavement crack sealer that are developed by the University of Texas. While pursuing such advanced technology, the construction industry still relies heavily on traditional technology. One of the findings of Nam and Tatum's research (1992b), surveying construction innovations, shows that the major technical ideas used for innovation in the construction industry are already-known technologies. Integrating information systems with this improvement is also fundamental. In this sense, "IT" in the framework deals with the creation of business opportunities or improvement of construction processes that can be attained by utilizing information technologies.

## Portfolio Analysis for CIC Planning and a Case Study

Corporate strategy, management, computer systems, and information technology were discussed in the previous sections as four issues of CIC planning. Each issue can be used to examine the effectiveness of information systems and identify promising areas. Though separate measurement can provide indications for decision-making in IS planning, the overall IS planning process on a company level requires a process which incorporates all relevant considerations. In order to facilitate this process, based on the CIC framework, a portfolio analysis for CIC planning is developed by mapping the "value-added enhancement" versus "incremental investment" of information systems for each business function (Jung 97).

The case-study company is a large construction firm that is also currently providing limited engineering services but is planning to diversify its capability. The case-study took approximately six weeks to analyze four major issues of CIC planning. Seventy-nine people participated in the case-study generating 108 responses. Techniques to measure the four areas of IS concern were developed. These include strategic fit analysis, critical success factor analysis, integration effectiveness analysis, and IT assessment for the IS concerns of cor-

**Exhibit 3.** Communications Planning

| 10.1.1 Inputs to Communications Planning* | Planning Issue | Description |
|---|---|---|
| 10.1.1.1 Communications Requirements | Corporate Strategy | Strategic Fit |
| | Management | Critical Success Factors |
| 10.1.1.2 Communication Technology | Computer Systems | System Integration Effectiveness |
| | Information Technology | Information Technology Impact |
| 10.1.1.3 Constraints | Incremental Investment | Economic Evaluation |
| 10.1.1.4 Assumptions | | |

* PMBOK (1996).

porate strategy, management, computer systems, and IT, respectively. Several questionnaires and workshops were utilized for these techniques so as to consolidate the organization's goals and current situation. Each assessment of four CIC issues were investigated separately as independent measures. A normalized score system was utilized throughout the case-study to indicate relative magnitude of importance, where 100 is the exact average and mean. This portfolio analysis matrix, shown in Exhibit 2, has four quadrants, where the value-added enhancement or incremental investment is high or low, respectively, containing high-high, high-low, low-low, and low-high, clockwise (Jung 97).

Exhibit 2 shows this portfolio analysis of a case-study. In order to investigate value-added improvement of each business function, in terms of the consolidated business requirements and technical improvement, an index for value-added enhancement from planned information systems is formulated. Business requirements (issues of "corporate strategy" and "management") are totaled by using weights that are identified in an expert workshop. This value-added improvement is then multiplied by integration leverage factor (issues of "computer systems") and IT leverage factor (issues of "IT"). When resources are limited, the business functions in upper-right (high-low) quadrant should have a higher priority in developing the new information systems.

The case-study survey has identified the functions of "sales" and "estimating" as being the most promising areas for new IS development for the company because of low investment and high value-added. It is noteworthy that the IS needs for sales function has the highest emphasis while the literature in construction has not addressed this issue. Though design and R&D are also emphasized as being critical areas of improvement for the company's future, continuous and steady investment is recommended. Evaluations of each business function has effectively illustrated the IS requirements. Factors influencing the results have also been clearly revealed. Deliverables of this method also included prioritized strategies, prioritized critical success factors, a list of information technologies for the construction industry, a matrix of integration effectiveness, and an estimate of information systems. The social, geographical, business-environmental, technical and economical factors influencing the survey results was validated by evaluating the business functions.

## CIC Planning Issues and Project Communications Management of the PMBOK

Portfolio analysis examines *four CIC issues as planning requirements* and *incremental investment as a planning constraint*. These items are not limited to issues for the construction industry only, and can be generalized with communications planning from the *PMBOK Guide* (PMI 1996). In other words, "corporate strategy" and "management" should be considered as *communication requirements* (10.1.1.1), "computer systems" and "IT" as *communication technology* (10.1.1.2), and "incremental investment" as a *constraint* (10.1.1.3). These relationships are summarized in Exhibit 3, and the authors recommend that the Project Management Institute consider including these items in the *PMBOK Guide* (PMI 1996).

## Conclusions

The concept of CIC defined in this paper provides critical issues for strategic CIC planning. The proposed framework broadly encompasses all the components of information systems and deals with details of systems at the same time. Managerial issues such as corporate strategy and project management are strongly stressed in the framework, representing the characteristics of the industry. The rationale behind the emphasis here is that the perspective of the information systems is no longer confined within the physical concept of computer-based applications, but extensively expands its interrelationship with the overall strategic management of an organization. The CIC framework has also identified the "issues for information systems planning," "phases of project life-cycle," and "areas of business functions" that would be considered as a standard ramification of *PMBOK Guide* (PMI 1996) standards.

Portfolio analysis for CIC provides an effective planning process while employing a broad range of aspects. This methodology is developed in order to facilitate in-house identification of IS requirements both for large or small companies in the construction industry. The case-study proves that the methodology is effective and provides a worthy point of departure for subsequent planning efforts. Company-specific requirements of information systems can be effectively analyzed by implementing this methodology. It is also inferred that managerial issues help make CIC much more viable.

## Acknowledgment

This research was partially supported by Science & Technology Policy Institute of Korea under Grant No. EG-05-03-06.

## References

Adams, J.R. and Campbell, B.W. 1990. *Roles and Responsibilities of the Project Manager.* Upper Darby, Pennsylvania: Project Management Institute.

Bacon, C. J. 1992. The Use of Decision Criteria in Selecting Information Systems/Technology Investment. *MIS Quarterly*, 16(3): 335-353.

Bakos, J.Y. and Treacy M.E. 1986. Information Technology and Corporate Strategy: A Research Perspective. *MIS Quarterly*, 10(2): 107-119.

Clemons, E.K. and Row, M.C. 1991. Sustaining IT Advantage: The Role of Structural Differences. *MIS Quarterly*, 15(3): 275-292.

Davenport, T.M. and Short, J.E. 1990. The New Industrial Engineering: Information Technology and Business Process Redesign. *Sloan Management Review*, 31(4): 11-27.

Gibson, G. E. and Bell, L.C. 1992. Integrated Data-Base Systems. *Journal of Construction Engineering and Management*, 118(1): 50-59.

Gray, D.A. 1994. Under Fire: Lessons from the Front. *OR/MS Today*, (October): 18-23.

Greer, R.L., Haas, C.T., Gibson, G.E., Traver, A.E., and Tucker, R.L. 1996. Advances in Control Systems for Construction Manipulator. *Proceedings of the 13th International Symposium on Automation and Robotics in Construction (ISARC)*, Tokyo, Japan: 615-624.

Hammer, M. 1990. Reengineering Work: Don't Automate, Obliterate. *Harvard Business Review*, (July-August): 104-112.

Henderson, J.C. and Venkatraman, N. 1993. Strategic Alignment: Leveraging Information Technology for Transforming Organizations. *IBM Systems Journal*, 32(1): 4-16.

Jung. Y. 1997. Information Systems Planning Methodology for the Construction Industry. Ph.D. Dissertation, The University of Texas at Austin, Austin, Texas.

Laborde, M. and Sanvido, V. 1994. Introducing New Process Technologies into Construction Companies. *Journal of Construction Engineering and Management*, 120(3): 488-508.

Miyatake, Y. and Kangari, R. 1993. Experiencing Computer Integrated Construction. *Journal of Construction Engineering and Management*, 119(2): 307-322.

Nam, C.H. and Tatum, C.B. 1992a. Noncontractual Methods of Integration on Construction Projects. *Journal of Construction Engineering and Management*, 118(2): 385-398.

Nam, C.H. and Tatum, C.B. 1992b. Strategies for Technology Push: Lessons From Construction Innovations. *Journal of Construction Engineering and Management*, 118(3): 507-524.

Parker, C. and Case, T. 1993. *Management Information Systems*, 2nd Ed., Watsonville, California: McGraw-Hill.

Project Management Institute (PMI). 1996. *A Guide to Project Management Body of Knowledge (PMBOK Guide).* Upper Darby, PA: PMI.

Rasdorf, W.J. and Abudayyeh, O.Y. 1991. Cost- and Schedule-Control Integration: Issues and Needs. *Journal of Construction Engineering and Management*, 117(3): 486-502.

Reinschmidt, K.F., Griffis, F.H., and Bronner, P.L. 1991. Integration of Engineering, Design, and Construction. *Journal of Construction Engineering and Management*, 117(4): 756-772.

Rowings, J.E. 1991. Project-Controls Systems Opportunities. *Journal of Construction Engineering and Management*, 117(4): 691-697.

Sanvido V. E. and Medeiros D. J. 1990. Applying Computer-Integrated Manufacturing Concepts to Construction. *Journal of Construction Engineering and Management*, 116(2): 365-379.

Scheer, A. 1991. *CIM : Towards the Factory of the Future*, 2nd Ed. Berlin, Germany: Springer-Verlag.

Teicholz, P. and Fischer, M. 1994. Strategy for Computer Integrated Construction Technology. *Journal of Construction Engineering and Management*, 120(1): 117-131.

Tucker, R.L., O'Connor, J.T., Gatton, T.M., Gibson, G.E., Haas, C.T., and Hudson, D.N. (1994). The Impact of Computer Technology on Construction's Future. *Microcomputers in Civil Engineering Journal*, 9(1): 3-11.

# Education/ Training

# How to Get the Most from Your Project Management Training

Dr. Owen C. Gadeken, Defense Systems Management College

## Introduction

Our global work environment is rapidly changing and with this change has come the shift from functionally based to project-based organizations using cross-functional teams. Coupled with these organizational changes is the advent of new technologies and work processes that are redefining the nature of projects, management, and team-based work. A striking example is the portable project management career model; i.e., changing companies and careers as you change projects. One of the central tenants of workplace change is the growing need for project management skills at all levels in the organization. Thus, there has been an exponential rise in demand (and soon, supply) of project management training. This paper examines the project management training challenge from two perspectives—the project management organization (the training provider) and the individuals being trained (the training receivers).

## Training Providers

### Needs Assessment

The first question to ask before any project management training is conducted is "Why are we doing this training?; i.e., "What is the need?" Having traced this question in several organizations where I was used as an outside trainer, I was often surprised and even amused by the answers I received: "Our vice president (management council, director, boss, and so on) told us to do it." "The training department thought it would be a good idea." "Joe saw this at a conference last year and convinced the company to sponsor it." "We needed something right away and this course was available at a reasonable price."

Needless to say, these are all the wrong reasons to conduct training. Since project management training is both time consuming and expensive, it should not be undertaken unless a clear business case for it can be established. In other words, such training should have a return on investment. The first key point is that training should be based on specific needs of the organization. Although there are many self-appointed "experts" on what training an organization needs, the best way to determine training needs is to use a more comprehensive and rigorous needs assessment process. This could include surveys and focus groups of potential participants as well as expert panels of project managers and senior management. There are good references that treat this topic more fully (Rossett 1987, Zemke 1987).

### Benchmark Top Performers

Most project management training addresses basic skill needs of the workforce. This can be a formidable task for both new hires or experienced employees whose organization is converting to management by projects. However, this training generally falls far short of meeting the real needs of an organization, which include how to create new products and services, how to stay competitive in the marketplace, and how to continuously improve key work processes, i.e., do things better, faster, and cheaper. In project management terms, this translates into how to create project managers (and project teams) who are "top performers," i.e., who perform at or hopefully well above the competition.

There are two key points embodied in the concept of top performance. The first is the obvious implication of knowledge and skills that are well above the minimum or basic skills found in most training programs. The second key is the process used to set or describe the criteria for top performance. While there are many approaches that can be used to define performance criteria for project managers, my personal experience and research suggest that by far the most superior method is to derive the criteria by benchmarking (analyzing) a set of top performers (or top project teams) in your own organization. Surveys, critical incident interviews, and focus groups of current project managers can all be used to gather performance data. The most critical part of this process is the designation of the top performers to use in the study. To do this requires the organization to articulate what constitutes top performance in its company or industry. This can be a very useful exercise in its own right. Study findings often add new insights into how to improve not only project management training but also the processes and results achieved by the project management function within the organization.

### Make Versus Buy Decisions

Organizations wishing to initiate or expand their project management training are faced with the dilemma of whether



PROJECT MANAGEMENT INSTITUTE 28th Annual Seminars & Symposium
Chicago, Illinois: Papers Presented September 29 to October 1, 1997

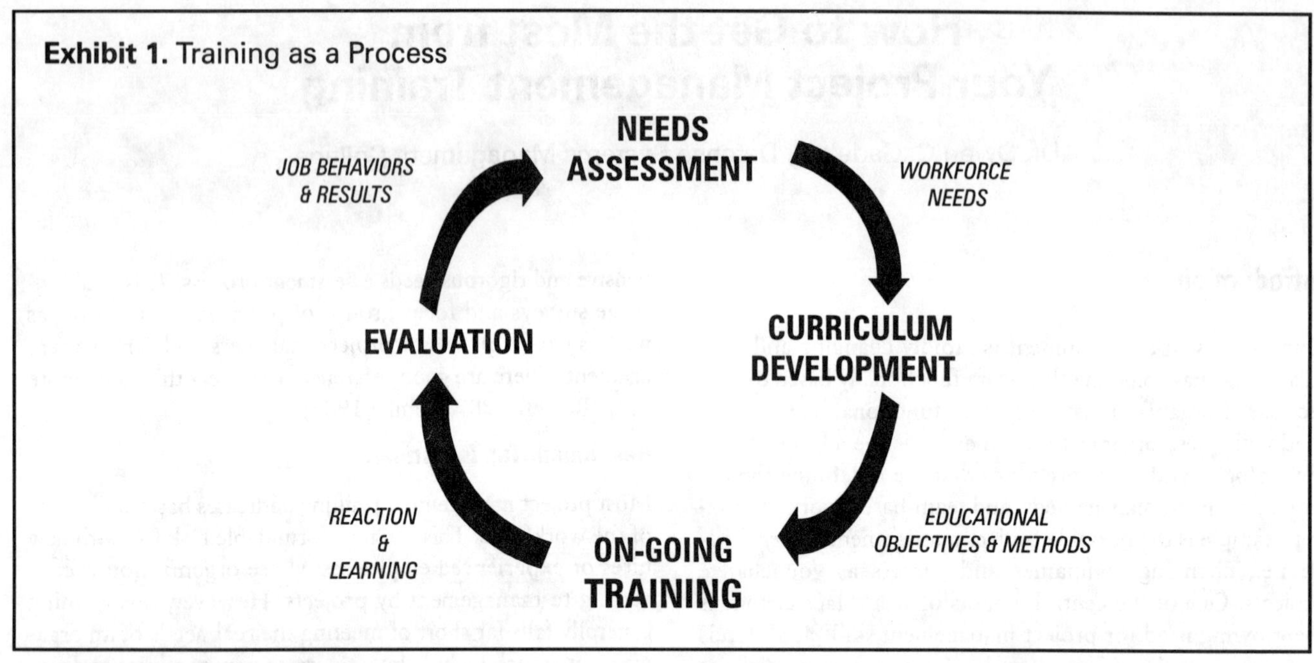

Exhibit 1. Training as a Process

to develop and deliver the training themselves or buy training from outside vendors. There is no easy answer to this question since several factors must be considered. Among the most important are the existing expertise in project management and training delivery within the organization, the specific training needs (remember the needs assessment topic discussed above), the general availability and cost of such training from vendors, the career development and training culture in the organization (are outside trainers the norm or the exception?), and the desires of the project management workforce as well as its top management.

There is no one best solution to the make or buy dilemma. In fact, there is a whole spectrum of possible solutions that range from contracting out all training development and delivery to the opposite extreme of designing and conducting all project management training in-house. In between are combinations of in-house and vendor support such as buying-off-the-shelf courses and then tailoring them for in-house delivery. Another option is having a vendor design the training and then conduct a train-the-trainer session to prepare in-house staff to deliver the course. A typical solution that I see frequently is for organizations with limited training resources to buy or send their project managers to outside basic project management courses but design and conduct advanced training (benchmarked on top performers as described above) in-house. The decision to keep advanced project management training in-house is due to the unique subject matter, and the organization's desire to retain it for its competitive advantage.

### Learner Versus Teacher-Centered

When it comes to how the actual training itself is conducted, a considerable body of literature has been amassed over the last twenty five years under the general topic of "adult learning." One of the leading proponents of this body of knowledge and also one of the most prolific authors has been Malcolm Knowles, now a professor emeritus at the University of North Carolina (Knowles 1973, 1975). While there are many principles embodied in adult learning theory, probably the most central idea is the need for learner-centered training versus teacher-centered training. An easy but oversimplified illustration of this difference is the subject matter expert conducting a one-way lecture versus the highly skilled facilitator allowing his or her students to work on an independent team project and present it in class. This distinction is particularly applicable to job-related training since most of the workforce has prior experience and motivation to succeed. Lectures from professional trainers or outside experts often fail to bridge the gap between project management theory and practical techniques that can be immediately applied back on the job. My experience with most project management training is that it can be markedly improved by using more learner-centered (adult learning) methods and applications.

### Evaluate Results

Evaluation is usually an afterthought in most project management training programs. If there is any evaluation at all, it is usually a quick survey completed as participants are ready to walk out the door at the end of the training. While an end-of-course survey is certainly better than gathering no data, it does have significant limitations. The best way to highlight these limitations is to use the framework for evaluating management training developed by Donald Kirkpatrick, Professor Emeritus from the University of Wisconsin. The Kirkpatrick Model contains four levels of evaluation: (1) Reaction: how well the participants liked the program, (2) Learning: did the participants learn what the program had intended to teach, (3) Behavior: do the participants carry this learning back to the job and use it, and (4) Results: what are the organizational impacts of the training in terms of the "bottom line," i.e., sales, profits, new products, lower employee turnover, or other financially-related measures (Kirkpatrick 1994).

Past research has shown that of those organizations evaluating their training (many do not), over 90 percent do not go beyond Kirkpatrick's Level 1. The implications of this are rather striking. Without more data there is no way to assess whether the training has any significant job-related impact at all. Another way of stating this conclusion is that without evaluation, most organizations conduct their project management training on "faith" with no proof that it does any good (or harm) to the workforce. I hope you agree that lack of evaluation is a critical issue that must be addressed in any project management training program.

To summarize this section on training providers and highlight the beneficial aspects of evaluation, please refer to the training process model I have included as Exhibit 1. This process model has four main steps that are highly interdependent: needs assessment, curriculum development, training, and evaluation. Evaluation conducted during and just after the training can be quite useful in updating and improving an on-going training program. But evaluation should also be conducted after participants return to the workplace to determine what parts of the training "stuck" and its impacts on the job. The best evaluation planning can only be done as the curriculum is being developed; otherwise you may wind up with a curriculum which cannot be evaluated after the fact.

## Training Receivers

### Take Ownership

Switching perspectives to those who will receive the project management training, the first principle for project managers in training is to take personal ownership of their training plan. This is important regardless of whether the training is fulfilled entirely from within the organization or is provided from outside sources. In the current work environment of shifting project priorities and portable careers, each of us must act as our own "personnel officer." This may be a difficult move for many of us who joined our organizations expecting to stay for an entire career. We also expected the organization to take care of our career development needs. These assumptions are simply not valid in today's turbulent times.

### Set Goals

With the pace of change in today's work environment, we are constantly confronted with new concepts, technology, and management practices. To keep up with this pace of change requires a strong commitment to continuous learning. This is the personal equivalent of the concept of continuous improvement embodied in the quality movement. Steven Covey (1989) talks about maintaining balance between productive output (job performance) and personal development (which Covey refers to as "sharpening the saw").

To insure that job demands do not continually overshadow professional development, I recommend you treat professional development as you would one of your important work projects. It has been said that we spend more time each year planning our family vacation than we do planning our career. So to give career planning its proper emphasis, I recommend that you set specific short- and long-term goals for your professional development. This would include both formal training courses as well as self-development activities. One of my goals is to get at least forty hours of formal training (courses and conferences) each year. With the current pace of change, I believe that doubling or tripling this figure may be more realistic. But the key point is that specific goals and topics are needed to insure that both you and the organization will honor your commitment to continually improve and not be overcome by events of the moment.

### Seek Nontraditional Opportunities

While it is tempting to assume that your organization will provide or allow you to take the project management training you need to stay current, this often is not the case. Organizations usually put the priority on meeting their near term business objectives thinking (or hoping) that the future will take care of itself. This often means that the training offered in the organization will be less than you need in terms of topics covered and currency, both to do your current job and especially to prepare for the future. So the solution is again to take personal responsibility for your training and design your own set of developmental activities. The wider your search field and array of external resources, the better your options and resulting training plan will be. While you can pursue many of the activities on your own, others will require top management and financial support from your organization. With a personal plan of action, you will be more prepared to sell the elements of your training plan to your organization, even the more nontraditional ones.

**Exhibit 2.** Career Development Resources

**CAREER DEVELOPMENT RESOURCES**

- **Your Network**
- **Your Agency**
- **Training Centers**
- **Industry Associations**
- **Professional Associations**
- **Internet**
- **Libraries**
- **Academia**
- **Government Agencies**
- **Consultants & Vendors**

I strongly advocate "out of the ordinary" development strategies and training opportunities. As one example of how I have benefited from nontraditional training, I was able to set up an overseas development assignment for seven months as a visiting faculty member at a military college in the United Kingdom (UK). This opportunity was not part of my organization's career development program. In fact, I created it myself from scratch. Faculty members in my organization are allowed (but not encouraged) to take developmental or career broadening assignments after they have been with the organization at least five years. The normal assignment is to work in a Pentagon staff office or a Navy project team in the Washington area, and this is what I was offered when I initially requested a developmental assignment. However, with the nontraditional view in mind, I decided to test the system by proposing an assignment of my own choosing.

Looking ahead in my career field of defense project management, I saw the increasing trend toward international collaborative projects with our European allies. So I did some research on overseas organizations where I could explore this issue firsthand. Our college had just concluded a cooperative agreement with two other defense management colleges in Europe, so I factored this into my planning by proposing one of these colleges as my work assignment. To sweeten the pot, I offered to do a personal research project during the trip which would compare United States and United Kingdom defense project managers. I was interested in this topic, and this would give me official endorsement to pursue it in face-to-face interviews with top United Kingdom defense project managers. Although I have not always been successful in my entrepreneurial development activities, I readily got approval for this one and it has proved to be the high point of my career development to date.

### Build Your Network

When it comes to planning and participating in career development, nothing succeeds as well as developing an on-going network of personal contacts and support organizations. I have repeatedly found many new ideas and training sources I have received from casual conversations with colleagues and vendors, even outside the workplace. Exhibit 2 gives a partial listing of useful sources of project management career development information. Many of the newer ideas will not have filtered down through the traditional training pipelines. Other nontraditional training opportunities are "diamonds in the rough" that most people would not recognize as potentially valuable learning experiences (until you come along).

Since I am in the training business, my personal strategy is to frequently ask people, even new acquaintances, what training and development they have found to be valuable. Even if I get only one new idea a month, this process is still valuable as a simple benchmarking exercise to see what's in the marketplace and how well it is being received. Besides, I enjoy talking about professional development with others in the project management field.

### Get Feedback

For the same reasons that project management training should be evaluated to insure that it meets the needs of the organization, project managers should insure that they get feedback from their own training, even the nontraditional parts. Since most project management training is not evaluated, this again puts the responsibility on the individual to set up an evaluation process or even to assess themselves. Using the Kirkpatrick model as a template, the most viable and obtainable feedback for project managers is Level III, on-the-job behavior.

Evaluation methods for on-the-job behavior include self-assessment, candid feedback from peers, project-related feedback, and automated feedback instruments. The later category of instruments has become quite popular in both public and private sector organizations in conjunction with the move to team-based management cultures. This "360-degree" feedback process compares standard input data on each manager received from self, peers, subordinates, and supervisors. Both strengths and weaknesses are identified as well as how perceptions differ from various groups.

## Summary

In this paper, we have examined project management training from both the provider and customer perspectives. While separate topic areas were discussed for each, in reality the two perspectives compliment and reinforce each other. Both providers and receivers want the best project management training for themselves and for their organization.

The topics offered in this paper were chosen from the author's personal experience. There are many other aspects of project management training which should also be considered. It should be clear even from the overview presented in this paper that there is much more to training than developing and delivering courses. What goes on before and after training is usually just as important as the training itself. The whole area of project management training is ripe for reengineering and innovation. I am convinced we are on the brink of major innovations in entrepreneurship, technology insertion, and customer service. What an exciting time to be training project managers!

## References


1. Rossett, A. 1987. *Training Needs Assessment*. Englewood Cliffs, NJ: Educational Technology Publications.
2. Zemke, R., and T. Kramlinger. 1987. *Figuring Things Out: A Trainer's Guide to Needs and Task Analysis*. Reading, MA.: Addison Wesley Publishing.
3. Knowles, M. 1973. *The Adult Learner: A Neglected Species*. Chicago, IL: Follett Publishing.
4. Knowles, M. 1975. *Self-directed Learning*. Reading, MA: Addison-Wesley Publishing.
5. Kirkpatrick, D. 1994. *Evaluating Training Programs: The Four Levels*. San Francisco, CA: Berrett-Koehler Publishers.
6. Covey, S. 1989. *The 7 habits of Highly Effective People*. New York, NY: Simon & Shuster.

# Performance Improvement in a Project Environment: A Survey Analysis

Shmuel Ellis, School of Business Administration, Tel Aviv University
Shlomo Globerson, School of Business Administration, Tel Aviv University
Robert Parsons, College of Business Administration, Northeastern University

## Introduction

The last decade has been characterized by a growing interest in organizational learning. In today's hyper-competitive environment, where organizations are struggling for survival, knowledge has emerged as one of the most important determinants of a firm's competitive advantage (Cohen & Levinthal 1990; Benet and O'Brien 1994; Wishart, Elam and Robey 1996). In response, managers are making a concerted effort to turn their organizations into learning organizations (Senge 1990). A learning organization is one that improves its actions through better knowledge and understanding (Fiole and Lyles 1985) or, in other words, is an organization "skilled at creating, acquiring, and transferring knowledge, and at modifying its behavior to reflect the new knowledge and skill (Garvin, 1993, p. 80).

An organization's knowledge is embodied in its standard operating procedures, routines, common perceptions of past events, common goals, shared assumptions or cause maps, architecture, and strategic orientations or behaviors (March and Simon 1958; Levitt and March 1988; Hall 1984). These expressions of knowledge guide future organizational actions but are based on interpretations of the past (Levitt and March 1988). Organizations revise their behavior in response to feedback about outcomes. Feedback is gained either by trial and error experimentation or by organizational search for new data.

In the present research the focus is on the issue of learning in project organizations. The concept of organizational learning is not new to scholars of industrial engineering. It was formulated as early as 1936, by Wright, and termed the learning curve. This well-known concept relates performance (i.e., direct labor hours, percentage of defects, and cost per repetition) on a specific task to the number of repetitions of that task. In more general terms, the learning curve literature examines the relationship between changes in organizational experience and changes in performance. Learning curves focus on improved performance through repetition as contrasted with learning from the experience of others. Evidence for interest in learning curves is exhibited by the large number of empirical works published (see, for example, Yelle 1979; Dutton and Thomas 1982; Globerson et al. 1988).

Learning curve researchers have mainly been interested in exploring the mathematical relations between experience and performance. However, recent literature on organizational learning concentrates on the process of learning; that is, on the way knowledge is attained, changed, diffused, and retained in the organization (Cyert and March 1963; Argyris and Schon 1978; Duncan and Weiss 1976; Hedberg 1981; Levitt and March 1988; Walsh and Ungson 1990; Nonaka 1994). It has been argued that a better understanding of learning processes would enable managers to improve their organizational effectiveness. In general, the learning process consists of three main phases:

### Information Gathering

In this phase individuals play the main role. They function as idea generators (Nonaka 1994) and as organizational sensors (Allen 1977; Argyris and Schon 1978; Tushman 1977) who gather and elaborate information during their day-to-day activities. They acquire knowledge and disseminate it among the organization's members (Huber 1991; Nonaka 1994), and also serve as experts who facilitate and affect the process of initial data interpretation (Ellis and Kruglanski 1992).

### Information Elaboration

Walsh and Ungson (1990) and Daft and Weik (1984) argued that (a) an organization is an interpretation system, i.e., a network of shared meanings that is activated during everyday social interactions, and (b) that organizational knowledge is the product of this kind of activity. Nonaka (1994) suggested that all kinds of knowledge, beliefs, mental models, or concrete know-how, crafts or skills, and data bases, are converted into codified knowledge (records, formal decisions) via socialization or interactions. The codified knowledge is then elaborated through sorting, adding, re-categorizing, and re-contextualizing. All this leads to the creation of new organizational knowledge that is internalized or learned by the organization's members.

### Retention and Retrieval

If organizations act like information systems, some sort of memory should be incorporated (Daft and Weik 1984). The distribution of their memory, its accuracy, and the conditions under which it is treated are crucial determinants of organizational effectiveness. Organizational knowledge is stored in various retention facilities, like organizational culture, various transformations, structures, workplace ecology, external archives, and, of course, the memories of individuals (Walsh and Ungson 1990). The way this knowledge has been created, its accessibility, and the ability to retrieve it and apply it to individual and organizational decisions or to use it as input for the creation of further knowledge are the best indicators of how the organizational memory is being managed.

The fact that projects are typically non-repetitive one-time operations that do not repeat themselves makes the project organization a unique learning entity. However, similar processes may be identified in different projects. Within-project similarity occurs when an identical component repeats within a project; for example, the construction of a pipeline that consists of repeated modules, such as pump stations, and similar pipe segments. A classic example of within-project similarity is a batch project: it produces a batch of identical items. Examples are a project to supply ten transformers or to renovate five planes.

Between-projects similarity can also be found. It results from identical modules in different projects. For example, the installation of two identical large scale transformers in two different projects. The knowledge acquired by installing the first transformer is used in the installation of the second. Even when products are totally different, a resemblance in certain basic processes exist. An example is configuration management. The objective of configuration management is to make sure that every design, or design change, is properly coordinated with all relevant parties(see Shtub et al. 1994). Configuration management principles apply to all projects, regardless of their nature, so experience is gained as a function of the number of completed projects.

The similarities within and between projects demonstrate that knowledge may be imbedded in any project that might be relevant to other projects undertaken by the organization. Establishing organizational procedures across project teams is difficult, however, because of the diversity of the projects, the organizational structure, and the independence of project teams. Clearly it is easier to coordinate organizational learning within a single project team than among several teams. Therefore, in contrast to other kinds of organizations, management of project organizations needs to place considerably more emphasis on developing organizational procedures that facilitate learning. If the similarity between projects is high, managerial emphasis should be placed on developing organizational knowledge that will be easily accessible to team members. When projects are diverse, the emphasis should be placed on the development of formal and informal communication channels among members and information systems that will assist members in identifying the preferred sources of information.

**Exhibit 1.** Distribution of Participants According to Organizational Structure

| Structure | Frequency | Percent |
|---|---|---|
| Functional | 39 | 9.8 |
| Weak matrix | 83 | 21.0 |
| Matrix | 139 | 35.1 |
| Strong matrix | 76 | 19.2 |
| Project | 52 | 13.1 |
| Unknown | 7 | 1.8 |
| Total | 396 | 100.0 |

The aim of the present study was (1) to demonstrate to managers how a diagnostic tool can be used to better understand how project organizations learn. The questionnaire captures the actual and the desired pattern of the organizational learning process across a wide variety of project environments, exploring what these organizations do (or aspire to do) in order to manage the learning process. Another aim (2) was to diagnose and compare the learning profile of organizations in the United States that function in project environments. Under the auspices of the study , 398 United States project managers from different industries, working under different organizational structures, completed an organizational learning mechanisms diagnostic questionnaire.

## Research Methods

### Sample

A questionnaire was distributed to about four thousand project managers, listed as members in the Project Management Institute. Three-hundred-and-ninety-eight properly completed questionnaires were returned. Respondents provided information about industry type and the structure of their organization. The distribution of participants according to their organizations' structure is presented in Exhibit 1.
Matrix was the most frequently reported organizational structure. The form encountered least frequently was the functional form.

### Organizational Learning Diagnostic Tool

The organizational learning mechanisms questionnaire utilized in the study was previously developed and applied by Ellis and Globerson (Ellis and Globerson 1995; Globerson

**Exhibit 2.** Distance from the Desired Intensity for Items with the Hightest Actual Intensity

| ITEM | SCORE | DISTANCE |
|---|---|---|
| Formal and regular meetings are maintained | 3.71 | .26 |
| Informal professional discussions are common | 3.55 | .09 |
| Individuals do not hesitate to ask for assistance | 3.55 | .55 |
| Supplier-customer information support | 3.51 | .54 |
| Updating and coordination meetings are held | 3.47 | .49 |
| Employees share information with one another | 3.46 | .60 |
| A new product joint venture is common | 3.35 | .28 |
| A new business joint venture is common | 3.35 | .28 |
| Mobility of employees among units exists | 3.31 | .43 |
| Archives for retrieval of information are available | 3.31 | .51 |

and Ellis 1995). The questionnaire was designed to assess the extent to which the responding organizations utilized learning activities in the project management process. The questionnaire consisted of forty-eight items, each of which was evaluated for actual and the desired intensity of use in the organization. Respondents were provided with forty-eight descriptive scenarios and asked to indicate the extent to which the scenario existed in their organization and its importance on a five point Likert scale. The forty-eight scenarios explored the various organizational learning activities—information gathering and analysis, information diffusion, and knowledge maintenance and retrieval. An example of a descriptive scenario for each category is provided below:

***Information Gathering and Analysis:***

There are on-going investigative procedures for checking causes for mishaps and failures.

***Information Diffusion:***

Information is continually provided about the fields of expertise of various individuals within the organization.

***Information Maintenance and Retrieval:***

Information is indexed by categories for easy retrieval.

Finally, in order to assess the factorial validity of the questionnaire, a factor analysis was performed. Principal component factor solutions utilizing varimax rotation were obtained for all scales. Factor analysis performed on the forty-eight items yielded five factors: formal learning procedures, information diffusion, employees' training, information gathering, and information maintenance.

## Findings

The aim of the study was to characterize project organizations according to their organizational learning mechanisms profile. As already noted, each item was rated twice, once for actual intensity of use and once for the desired intensity. To evaluate the discrepancy between observed and desired use of the various learning mechanisms, the difference between the actual and desired ratings was computed . Exhibit 2 presents the ten items that obtained the highest actual score and their distance and direction from the desired intensity.

The item, "formal and regular meetings are maintained," received the highest actual score. That is, of all the items specified in the questionnaire, this one is used most intensively in all organizations. For desired intensity, project managers assigned this item an even higher score (the difference is +0.26). In other words, they considered that it should be used even more intensively. The greatest discrepancy was found for the item, " employees share information with one another." That is, project managers wished to establish an environment that would encourage stronger interaction among company members. All the distances in Exhibit 3, as well as in the exhibits that follow, are positive. That is, participants perceived a lack of intensity for all the items listed in the exhibits.

The items with the highest desired intensity and their discrepancies from actual intensity are presented in Exhibit 3.

Interestingly, a large portion of the items listed in Exhibit 3 relate to the need for strong personal contact with other colleagues within the company.

The items with the greatest discrepancy between the perception of actual intensity and the desired intensity were identified and are presented in Exhibit 4.

From Exhibit 4 it is possible to identify those items with the greatest perceived need for action. Regarding the first item, two interpretations are possible: either managers think

**Exhibit 3.** Score of the Items with the Highest Desired Intensity (i.e. perceived as the most important) and Their Discrepancy from Actual Intensity

| ITEM | SCORE | DISTANCE |
|---|---|---|
| Individuals do not hesitate to ask for assistance | 4.10 | .55 |
| Employees share information with one another | 4.06 | .60 |
| Formal and regular meetings are maintained | 3.96 | .26 |
| Updating and coordination meetings are held | 3.95 | .49 |
| It is simple to retrieve information | 3.88 | 1.04 |
| Failures are routinely investigated with procedures | 3.87 | .77 |
| Funds are assigned for individual prof. development | 3.84 | .61 |
| It is simple to transfer info. within the organization | 3.83 | .76 |
| Archives for retrieval of information are available | 3.83 | .51 |
| Knowledgeable employees are nourished and used | 3.82 | .55 |

**Exhibit 4.** Items with the Greatest Discrepancy Between the Perception of Actual Intensity and Desired Intensity

| ITEM | DISTANCE |
|---|---|
| There are on going investigative procedures for analyzing successes | 1.13 |
| A new employee receives a document summarizing the previous work | 1.11 |
| Proper analysis of professional and business information is performed | 1.06 |
| It is simple to retrieve information | 1.04 |
| There is overlap time for departing and arriving managers | 1.02 |
| There is a procedure for job rotation | .99 |
| Bonuses are given for successful teamwork | .99 |
| Information is indexed by categories for easy retrieval | .96 |
| Each assignment has up-to-date procedures on file | .92 |
| Significant resources (time, money, personnel) are allocated for learning | .89 |

that much can be gained by analyzing successes, or they believe that successes receive insufficient attention in comparison to failures. The second interpretation seems likely since managers claim that an effective bonus scheme is lacking.

Since the questionnaire included items reflecting different organizational learning mechanisms, a factor analysis was used to identify various groups. The analysis revealed five factors, as presented in Exhibit 5. The exhibit presents the gaps between actual and desired use of organizational learning mechanisms for each of the five factors yielded by the factor analysis.

Exhibit 5 is interpreted as follows. In general, participants in the study expressed a need for more learning-related activities, as expressed in the "difference" column. The largest discrepancy was found to be in the application of formal learning procedures, where the difference between the actual and the desired score was 21 percent. Included among the thirteen items that were assigned to the formal learning procedures group were:

- Each project has up-to-date-procedures on file.
- Every manager receives a summary of the previous manager's work.
- There is overlap time for departing and arriving managers.

Given a symmetrical pattern of disagreement over the range from one to five on any item, the average score would be equal to 3.00. A total disagreement means that subjects will use the whole scale from one to five, with a high variation as expressed by an indicator such as the standard deviation. Since the standard deviation expresses variation, a smaller value indicates a higher level of agreement. An alternative way of viewing dispersion is to use the ratio of the standard deviation to the mean. This measure is called the coefficient of variation and has the advantage of being unit independent. This facilitates comparison of **relative dispersion when variables are of different magnitude or expressed in different units of measurement.** Analysis of the level of agreement on the different items revealed significant differences among them, as described in Exhibit 6.

**Exhibit 5.** Gaps Between Actual and Desired Use of Learning Mechanisms for Each of the Five Identified Factors

| FACTOR | DIFF. |
|---|---|
| Formal learning procedures | .21 |
| Information distribution | .14 |
| Employees' training | .14 |
| Information collection | .16 |
| Information conservation | .00 |

Exhibit 6 may be interpreted as follows. The item, "coordination meetings," obtained the lowest value. Therefore, there is the highest agreement among all the respondents with regard to its desired value. The opposite may be said about "encouraging champions." That is, there is little agreement concerning its importance.

## Conclusions

The questionnaire enabled the capture of the actual and the desired pattern of the organizational learning processes within a large sample of project managers. Analysis of the questionnaire items revealed that project managers desire a stronger intensity of all aspects of organizational learning with more emphasis on the following dimensions: analysis of successful projects, documentation when changing staff, information storage and retrieval systems, analysis of business and professional information, and overlap when managers are changed. The next evolutionary step for companies is to improve their abilities to share knowledge via different mechanisms such as more structured and unstructured meetings; "yellow pages" listing the expertise of individuals within the organization and among organizations, and so on. Use of a medium such as the Internet will facilitate the learning process.

**Exhibit 6.** Items with the Lowest and Highest Coefficient of Variation

| ITEM | Coeff. Of Var. |
|---|---|
| Coordination meetings | .26 |
| Group training | .28 |
| Failure investigation procedures | .28 |
| Informal meetings | .30 |
| Report is written after task completion | .44 |
| Summary of previous work | .47 |
| Overlap time in replacing managers | .48 |
| Use of think tanks | .56 |
| Collection of business information | .56 |
| Encouraging Champions | .72 |

### References


Adler, P., and K. Clark. 1991. "Behind the Learning Curve: A Sketch of the Learning Process." *Management Science* 37: 267–281.

Allen, T.J. 1977. *Managing the Flow of Technology: Technology Transfer and the Dissemination of Technological Information within R&D Organizations*. Cambridge: MIT Press.

Argyris, C., and D. Schon. 1978. *Organizational Learning*. Reading, Massachusetts: Addison Wesley.

Belhaoui, A. 1986. *The Learning Curve*. Westport, Connecticut: Quorum Books.

Bennet, K.J., and M.J. O'Brien. 1994. "The Building Blocks of the Learning Organization." *Training* (June): 41–49.

Cyert, R., and J. March. 1963. *A Behavioral Theory of the Firm*. Englewood Cliffs, New Jersey: Prentice-Hall.

Cohen, W.M., and D.A. Levinthal. 1990. "Absorptive Capacity: A New Perspective on Learning and Innovation." *Administrative Science Quarterly* 35: 128–142.

Daft, R. L., and K.E. Weik. 1984. "Toward a Model of Organizations as Interpretation Systems." *Academy of Management Review* 9: 284–295.

Duncan, R., and A. Weiss. 1976. "Organizational Learning: Implications for Organizational Design. In *Research in Organizational Behavior* (75–123). Greenwich, Connecticut: JAI Press.

Dutton, J., and A. Thomas. 1982. "Treating Progress Functions as a Managerial Opportunity." *Academy of Management Review* 9: 235–247.

Ellis, S., and A.W. Kruglanski. 1992. "Self as Epistemic Authority: Effects on Experiential and Instructional Learning." *Social Cognition* 10: 357–375.

Fiole, C. M., and M.A. Lyles. 1985. "Organizational Learning." *Academy of Management Review* 10: 803–813.

Globerson, S, and J. Riggs. 1988. "The Effects of Imposed Learning Curves on Performance Improvement." *IIE Trasactions* 20: 317–324.

Garvin, D. 1993. "Building a Learning Organization." *Harvard Business Review* (July–August): 78–91.

Hedberg, B. 1981. "How do Organizations Learn and Unlearn?" In *Handbook of Organizational Design* (8–27). London: Oxford UP.

Hall, R.I. 1984. "The Natural Logic of Management Policy Making: Its Implication for the Survival of an Organization." *Management Science* 30: 905–927.

Hancock, W., and F. Bayha. 1992. "The Learning Curve." In *Handbook of Industrial Engineering*. John Wiley.

Hofmann , D., R. Jacobs, and S. Gerras. 1992. "Mapping Individual Performance Over Time." *Journal of Applied Psychology* 77: 185–195.

Huber, G.P. 1991. "Organizational Learning: The Contributing Processes and the Literatures." *Organization Science* 2: 88–115.

Levitt, B., and G. March. 1988. "Organizational Learning." *Annual Review of Sociology* 14: 319–340.

Nonaka, I. 1994. "A Theory of Organizational Knowledge Creation." *Organization Science* 5: 14–37.

Senge, M. 1990. *The Fifth Discipline: The Art and Practice of the Learning Organization*. Doubleday.

Shtub, A., J. Bard, and S. Globerson. 1994. *Project Management: Engineering, Technology and Implementation*. Prentice-Hall.

Tushman, M.L. 1977. "Special Boundary Roles in the Innovation Process." *Administrative Science Quarterly* 22: 587–605.

Walsh, P., and R. Ungson. 1990. "Organizational Memory." *Academy of Management Review* 26: 57–91.

Wishart, N.A., J.J. Elam, and D. Robey. 1996. "Redrawing the Portrait of a Learning Organization: Inside Knight-Ridder, Inc." *Academy of Management Executive* 10(1): 7–20.

Wheelwright, S., and K. Clark. 1992. "Creating Project Plans to Focus Product Development." *Harvard Business Review* (March–April): 70–82.

Wright, T. 1936. "Factors Affecting the Cost of Airplanes." *Journal of Aeronautical Sciences* 3: 122–128.

Yelle, L. E. 1979. "The Learning Curve: Historical Review and Comprehensive Survey." *Decision Sciences* 10: 302–328.

# Developing Documentation and Training for Information Systems Under Development

Gary Neights, RWD Technologies
Marc Sattler, RWD Technologies

## Importance of Documentation and Training

Information system (IS) development projects, especially for enterprise-wide resource planning (ERP) systems, pose implementation and post-implementation challenges that are partially met by solid documentation and training (either electronic or paper). Users must be able to use a new system on day one to avoid startup problems. Users need to understand how to run the business using the new system to maximize profits over the long run. Completing system testing and bringing it on-line may be the technical developers' view of project success, but a better definition of project success is "users can run the business better using the new system than by using alternative choices." As shown in Exhibit 1, training and documentation play a central role in how quickly and effectively users can utilize the features of a new system to run the business.

Actual performance attained by users, rather than technical features of the system, should impact an information system project as follows:

- Early in the project life-cycle, before systems have been selected, the selection process and/or design should place a priority on the ease of use. User training required to maximize actual system performance should be determined and budgeted.
- For projects under way, the project manager should budget the proper level of user performance support. For a difficult-to-use system, this can mean appropriating funds to expend effort to improve interfaces and user information and decrease funds to develop technical functions.

The rest of this paper will assume that a system has been selected and will focus on issues and risks that the project manager can influence with documentation and training. It will present how documentation and training development methodologies are linked to information system development methodologies. This paper is focused on how documentation and training content is developed; the presentation of content could be any combination of media (for example: paper, classroom, on-line help, intranet, computer-based terminal, video, satellite transmission, and so on.)

## How Users View Project Outputs

Users of a system have a different view of the system than technical developers. Rather than viewing the system based on its technical features, users tend to view the system based on how easily the system lets them perform their jobs. As shown in Exhibit 2, they may view the success of an information system development project based only on the exposure they receive: their training, the system interface and features, the new business processes they must execute, and the on-going user support provided, such as documentation and help desk support. The project manager and development teams need to understand that, like the iceberg shown in Figure 2, only a small part of the entire project effort is seen. Many aspects are hidden from view.

During project execution, project management holds together all the pieces to ensure that the project stays afloat. Quality assurance (QA) processes help ensure that systems and measures are in place to keep the project on target. Quality assurance includes facilitating the ongoing involvement of the organization and users to ensure that the project outputs through all project phases are still meeting the needs of the organization. A key goal in nearly every information systems project is to develop a technically sound system that will cause project sponsors to declare the system a success. Equally important is that the users declare the system a success based on how they view the system and are able to use it over time.

## Components of a Typical Information System Documentation and Training Program

Documentation and training for an information system are often developed together and used in concert with one another to increase user performance. However, they serve different purposes. Documentation enables users to access information they need on the job. The experienced user will generally know what information she is looking for; efficient access to information at the time of need is her primary success criteria. The new user requires training. Initial training prior to going live is designed to teach people how business



PROJECT MANAGEMENT INSTITUTE 28th Annual Seminars & Symposium
Chicago, Illinois: Papers Presented September 29 to October 1, 1997

**Exhibit 1.** Project Success Is Determined by System Use

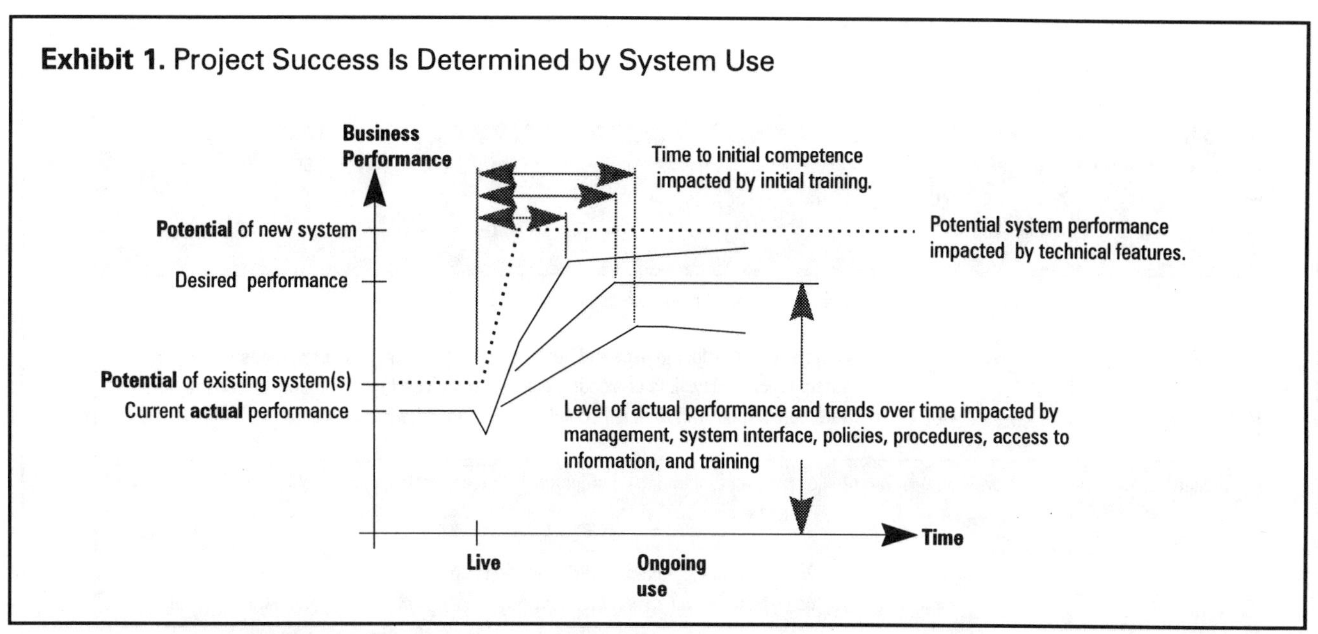


**Exhibit 2.** User Perspective of Completed Project

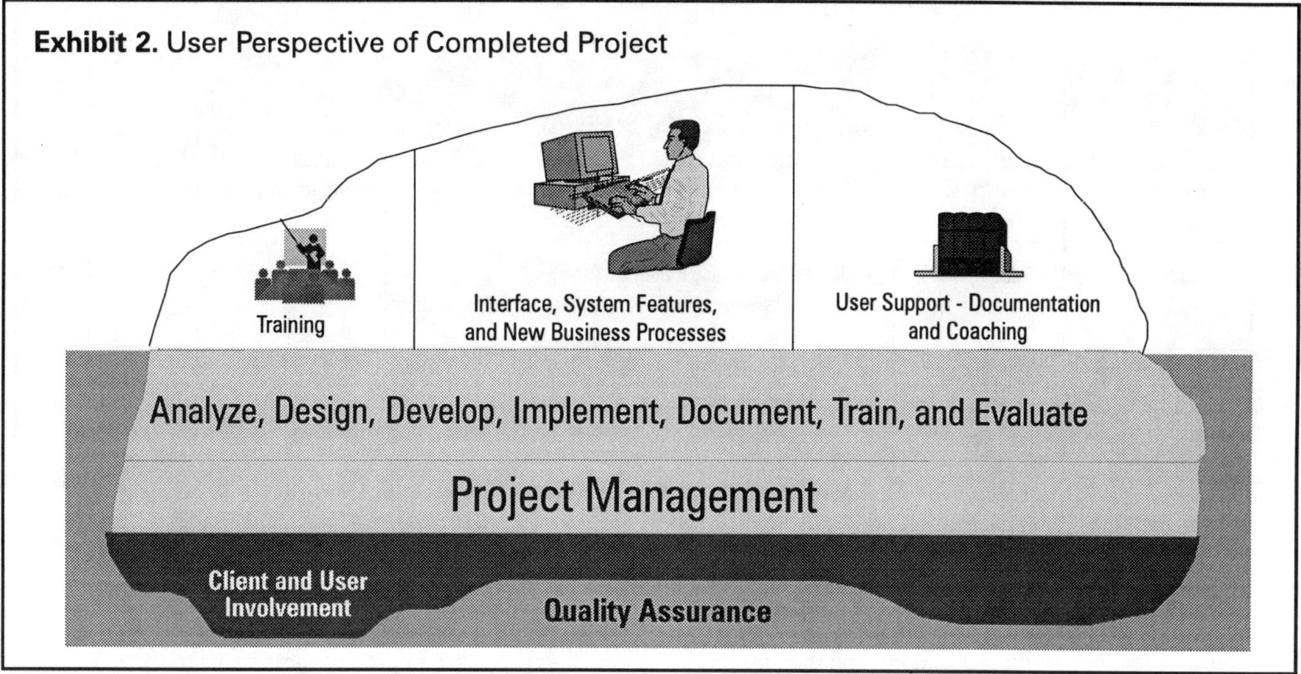


processes have changed, new terminology, system tasks, and non-system tasks. Post-live training focuses on teaching people new skills as they are ready to learn them. A primary objective of training should be to teach people to effectively use the documentation system. This enables them to teach themselves new skills on the job over time.

Some basic components of an integrated documentation and training system include:

- Policies and procedures
- Business process descriptions and flowcharts
- Work instructions and job aids
- System exercises
- Certification processes

Policies and procedures present new authorities and decision points, as well as how to handle new information requirements. For example, a new customer service system may give customer service representatives the ability to immediately assess credit risk of customers, whereas in the past approval from the supervisor or credit department was necessary. Closely linked to policies and procedures are business

**Exhibit 3.** Development Phases

| Project Phases: Typical Information System | Project Phases: Documentation and Training | Documentation and Training Outputs |
|---|---|---|
| | Plan | • Preliminary project plan with assumptions |
| Analysis | Analyze | • Analysis report including user and business requirements, business process/user matrix, system functionality, lists of existing policies and procedures, and project constraints<br>• Draft project plan with options, schedules, and budget estimates |
| Design | Design | • Media and structure of chosen documentation and training approach<br>– Paper, on-line, CBT, video<br>– Classroom, OJT, distance learning<br>– Document management and distribution approach<br>• Graphic (1-page) summarizing business processes, system functions, organizations, and users<br>• Initial outlines and objectives<br>• Recommendations to system integrators<br>• Final project plan |
| | Prototype | • Prototype(s), standard(s), template(s), and development tools |
| Development | Develop and review | • Technically accurate policies, procedures, flowcharts, work instructions, job aids, and training reference materials |
| Testing | Pilot | • User tested training materials<br>• Comments incorporated into training and documentation |
| Implementation | Deliver | • Employees prepared for system going live<br>• Updates to documentation and training<br>• Materials placed in document management and distribution system |
| Post-Implementation | Evaluate | • Measures of user performance of business and system tasks<br>• Enhancements to system, documentation, and training |

process descriptions and flowcharts that clearly present new processes, process flows, tasks interactions, and their business case. Work instructions present step-by-step instructions to perform job duties. Work instructions often include system transactions and non-system tasks (new systems often result in changes to off-line activities). Job aids can be thought of as information that a person may wish to post near his work station for easy access, such as lists of commonly used codes or decision matrices. System exercises allow people to practice new tasks on the system being implemented in a structured fashion. Certification processes allow knowledge and skills to be evaluated before a person uses the system. Training materials based on new job roles and responsibilities provide an overriding structure to present these items to the new users.

Incorporating these documentation and training components into your information program will help mitigate the following risks:

- **Users' concerns impact their ability to use the system.** A major concern to employees and managers is that the new system will change their role in the organization. While communication and change management programs are generally needed on major system implementations, the documentation and training program also needs to address these areas. Employees and managers both need to understand the rationale for the new system and the impact it will have on their jobs. If the system will bring increased efficiency to the organization, and this efficiency is going to fuel future growth or reduce cost cutting, incorporating this information into training can help ensure that people are willing to use the system to its potential.

- **Users cannot use the system.** People may not understand the new system and how to use it. This may lead to a fear that the system is too complex or will cause a decrease in efficiency. This fear is usually validated when the system goes live. As shown in Figure 1, the learning curve on any new system will show an initial decrease in work efficiencies. However, with proper training, work efficiency should rapidly increase because users can exploit the capabilities of the system; errors will be minimized. Additionally, the documentation and training developed for the initial go-live can support training of new employees over the system's life-cycle.

## Integration of System Development Tasks with Documentation and Training Development Tasks

At the highest level, documentation and training development involves determining requirements, gathering data from system experts, writing materials, reviewing materials for technical accuracy and usability, distributing the materials, and maintaining them over the life-cycle of the system. Performing these activities efficiently for a custom information system requires that the documentation and training sub-project personnel be able to effectively interface with business managers, technical developers, and users to gather information efficiently. Just as the information system development effort requires a structured methodology to ensure the timely, on-budget development of a high quality system, the documentation and training effort should also follow a similar process to ensure that its outputs meet the needs of users over the life-cycle of the system. Exhibit 3 shows the overlap between the phases of a typical information system project with the phases of the associated documentation and training effort.

When beginning the development, review the present documentation to determine what information is useful and what should be reworked. Most companies already have many effective practices in place and the development, documentation, and training of a new system should not delete good practices. The worthwhile documentation in place may be found by talking to subject matter experts, managers, and accomplished users. Also, some people in the organization may have created useful tools to help them perform their jobs. All of this information should be assessed and incorporated into the documentation and training under development. Also, some of this material may contain valuable information, but it is presented in a confusing manner. This information should be reworked and incorporated in a different format. Very little existing documentation is useless. Analyzing all possible materials can help generate ideas on even better methods to document the new process.

**Exhibit 4.** Role and Respnsibility Matrix

| | | | Output | | | | | Role | | | | | | | | |
|---|---|---|---|---|---|---|---|---|---|---|---|---|---|---|---|---|
| Task Number | | | Business Process Graphic | Policy | Procedures | Flowchart | Work Instructions | Job Aids | Doc&Tmg PM | Business Manager | InfoSys PM | Doc&Tmg Developer | Doc&Tmg Editor | InfoSys Developer | InfoSys User |
| DR- | 1 | Finalize business process graphic | | | | | | | ● | ✓ | ✖ | | | | |
| DR- | 2 | Refine business processes lists | | | | | | | | ❑ | ❑ | ● | | | |
| DR- | 3 | Clarify roles and responsilities | | | | | | | | ❑ | ❑ | ● | | | |
| DR- | 4 | List activities and tasks | | | | | | | | ✖ | ✖ | ● | | ❑ | |
| DR- | 3 | Develop detailed objectives | | | | | | | | | ✓ | ● | ✖ | ❑ | |
| DR- | 4 | Develop detailed outlines | | | | | | | ✖ | ✓ | ✖ | ● | ✖ | ✖ | ✖ |
| DR- | 5 | Draft materials | | | | | | | | | | ● | ✓ | ❑ | ❑ |
| DR- | 6 | Review technically | | | | | | | | | ✓ | | | ● | ✖ |
| DR- | 7 | Review usability | | | | | | | ✖ | ✓ | | | | ✖ | ● |
| DR- | 8 | Finalize | | | | | | | ✖ | ✓ | | ● | ✖ | | |

Documentation and training development should occur concurrently with system development tasks. This is important for a number of reasons:

- Input from the training and documentation team that reduces project costs or increases the value of the system can be incorporated. For example, a difficult-to-use interface or process may require significant training. The user performance support analysis may identify this and suggest value-adding interface or process changes that can reduce life-cycle training requirements.
- Most businesses desire to bring systems on-line as soon as possible. Waiting until the system is nearly completed to develop documentation and training entails the risk that training does not occur before going live or that going live is delayed.
- Documentation and training development can be used to increase team communications. Inherent in many projects are functional stovepipes of knowledge. A properly designed documentation and training program and development process will teach the entire development team subjects that fall outside of their functional area.

To illustrate the last point, on a recent project a training diagram that showed all the business processes from sales to production to accounts receivable and accounting was developed. A maintenance process designer asked for a copy so he could understand what was happening outside his area and to help him explain his maintenance reengineering efforts to people inside and outside the project.

The use of process diagrams provides the entire organization with a visual representation of how everyone's part in the overall process affects other areas of the system. Some projects have an "over-the-wall" syndrome, and the people within one area of the development process believe that when they send information to the next group of people, their part is done. However, they may not realize how their work impacts other areas. By documenting and training everyone in an overview of the entire system, each group's understanding of how its efforts affect other areas can be improved.

Once a group knows and understands the job functions of other areas (even at a high level), the communication between the groups becomes more effective and efficient. When both people involved in a conversation have an understanding of the other person's perspective, each will be able to comprehend what the other person is saying. Also, if there is any conflict, having a single process diagram can help resolve the conflict.

Properly defined roles and responsibilities will help ensure that everyone involved in the project knows what they have to do and will enhance team communications. Defining roles and responsibilities also prevents multiple people from working on the same task while no one is working on other important tasks. Exhibit 4 illustrates one method to present the roles and responsibilities to develop documentation and training. This matrix focuses on the develop and review phase of a project. Each section of the matrix is highlighted by a separate box and presents:

- Who is responsible for completing the task - ●
- Who must provide information to complete task - ❑
- Who must review deliverables - ✖
- Who must approve the output from the task - ✔

In addition to process graphics, another way of enhancing team communications while developing documentation and training is to have people in one functional area serve as reviewers for other functional areas. For example, a sales process design expert could perform as *user* reviewer for the production documentation and training. Production process experts would still have to perform *technical* reviews.

## Watchouts

Some obstacles that often cause project organizations not to provide proper documentation and training include:

- **The need for training is not seen until near the end of the project.** Early in a project, people often focus on developing the most technically advanced system possible. The team understands how the system will work and does not see the need for training. Once team members involve the end users, they realize that the system may not be as user-friendly as they originally thought. However, if the project is far into the system life-cycle, the creation of documentation and training may be too late to capture the required information in time for the go-live date. Once the system goes live without the necessary documentation and training, a good system may get a bad reputation because the end users do not know how to use the functionality built into the system.
- **Budget cuts remove funding for documentation/training.** If the project costs more than the original budget, or the project team believes that added functionality is required to properly use the system, the money to complete the project has to come from somewhere. Many times the extra funds come from the documentation and training budget. This causes the final documentation and training to be either minimal or non-existent.
- **Experts who know the business process and system are over-tasked with implementation.** When creating documentation and training, the developer of the material must talk to experts to determine what to include in this material; however, since the experts on the system are busy developing the product, they may not have the time to talk to the developer of the training and documentation. Another possibility is that the system experts are called upon to create the training and documentation.
- **Implementors perform the startup training.** When implementors are tasked to perform startup training they must be aided by training experts who can help them develop materials and assist them during training delivery. People who develop information systems are not necessarily the best people to document the system and lead the training effort. Often these system development experts are not training experts. Since they understand all the intricacies of the project, they may not include items that they believe are "simple" when, actually, these simple items are difficult to comprehend for someone who does not know the system. Finally, since this is only one of their many duties, the creation of supporting materials is given a low priority.
- **System documentation used for training could present a problem.** Some projects plan on leveraging system documentation as source material for user documentation and training. For this to work, the system documentation must be kept current by system developers or system documentors throughout the project. Typically implementors maintain system documentation early in the project. Once they become comfortable with the system, they stop documenting their work in the system. This requires user documentors to identify

**Exhibit 5.** Total Cost to Achieve Desired Performance Determines ROI

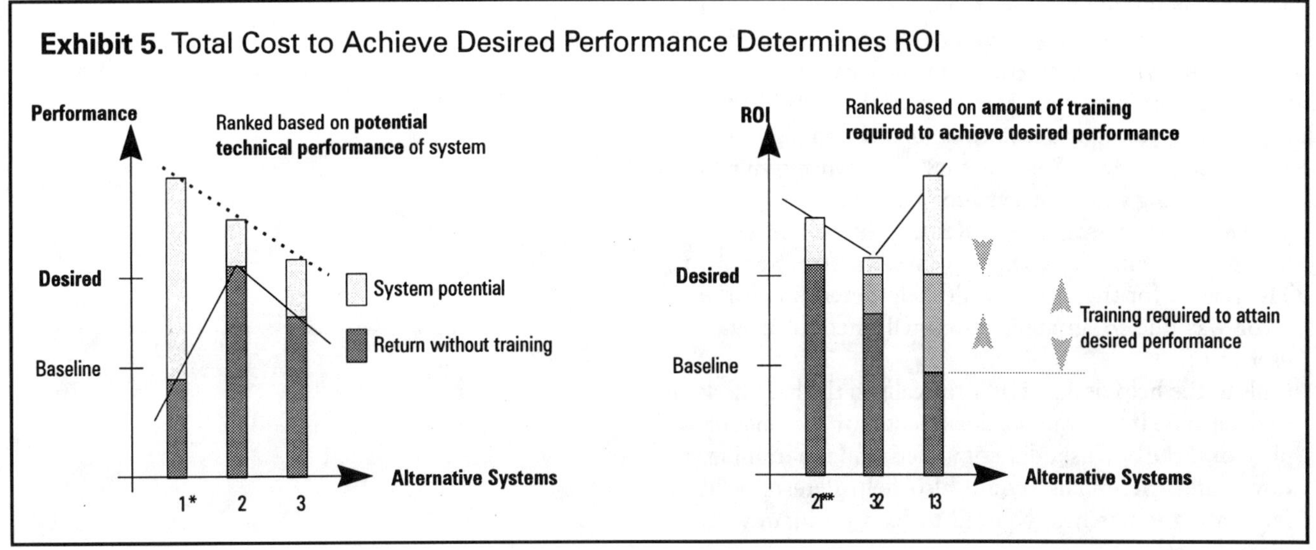


all the gaps between the system and the system documentation. This can lead to an unexpected scope increase.

- **A hasty training decision was made.** When the company realizes that the training and documentation is inadequate for the system they may decide to bring in a training consultant. However, since it is late in the development, one of two things may occur:
  1. The trainers may not be the correct type of consultant for the system. The consultant may not understand the company's business processes or the system's interactions with other systems. The consultant may not have the time to determine the best type(s) of training interventions.
  2. Since the consultant was contracted late in the project, she may require significant time to understand all the processes that have already occurred during the development. She may ask questions that have already been thought out or may ask a question that requires significant effort to answer without adding value to the final product.

When any of these situations occurs, the project schedule may slip due to delays in the development of material. The project manager will have to contend with scope creep to resolve new issues, cost increases to use additional resources to develop the materials, quality issues when trying to complete the documentation and training within an aggressive schedule, and schedule slippage to allow more time to develop the required training and documentation.

## Conclusion

When developing the budget for a system implementation, all costs associated with the system must be included. These include development, documentation, training, implementation, hardware upgrades, overhead, and ancillary costs. Once developed, these costs will determine the return on investment. Positive returns from the system are possible once users are effective and efficient with the system.

If a highly technical system is difficult to use and causes the end user to require a year to properly use the system and the embedded functionality, the return on investment may not begin until a year after implementation. What this means in training terms is that *time to competency determines the timing of returns.* Return also depends on performance levels over time. Users need to be able to use system features to meet business goals; if users cannot use the system, performance will be lower. In training terms, *increased levels of user performance lead to increased returns.* Figure 1 illustrates these points.

Exhibit 5 shows that the other factor in the return on investment equation is the total investment (system costs plus training costs) required to reach a given level of performance. System 1 is has the most technical potential (features, throughput, cycle times, and so on) but requires a large amount of training and user support to reach desired performance levels. System 2 exceeds desired performance both in terms of technical potential and usability without training. While system 3's technical potential is the lowest, it requires less training to meet desired user performance objectives than the technically superior System 1. To determine which system provides the greatest return on invstment, you need to calculate the total cost of the system including training development and delivery to reach a given level of performance.

Monitoring the performance of users on the new system can provide feedback on the system's effectiveness. Performance metrics will help determine the benefits of effective training and documentation. Metrics may also help identify changes in the system or documentation and training to improve user performance. Some metrics to use when trying to assess the training and documentation include:

- System error messages logs. Review the system error logs to determine how and why system errors occur. The reason for the error should help determine if the error was due to an application malfunction or end-user error.
- Calls to the help desk. Review the calls to the help desk to determine if the training documentation was incomplete or if the end user did not understand the training. Reviewing these calls should also help determine if there are any patches required to fix a problem with the application.

Finally, the cost of maintaining and distributing materials over the system's life-cycle must be included in the overall project budget analysis. Developing paper-based materials may seem like the lowest cost solution until revision control and distribution costs over time are tallied. Focusing on life-cycle documentation and training costs, rather than initial development costs, may cause organizations to gravitate towards electronic document management and distribution.

# Learning Project Management Lessons from Games

John Homer BMW Constructors, Inc

Successful project management is about the integration of parts and pieces of work and process to create a unique outcome. Whether the project is as simple as a doghouse or as complex as the Boeing 777, every project shares aspects that are totally unique, aspects that constitute adaptation of what we have done before, and repetition of past behaviors. When we overemphasize the unique nature of the outcome, we put an artificial barrier in the way of learning how to manage projects better.

Observing successful behavior in games can help us highlight specific elements of project behavior that can bring improvement in our management process. To this end, the author will portray some basic project management lessons and highlight examples of how we can improve our performance by emulating learning from games.

In a 1996 *Project Management Journal* paper, the author reported on the use of simulations in training project management personnel. The specific simulations reported in that paper continue to be used to help focus project managers on an understanding of their behaviors as a precursor to improved project performance. In one company 120 people have participated in these simulation exercises. One comment is fairly typical of the reported experience: "I know it's a stupid little game, but that exercise engaged me more thoroughly than any formal project management exercise I have every participated in. From that engagement has come improved understanding."

In their book *Strategic Thinking,* Avinash Dixit and Barry Nalebuff define game theory as "the science of strategic thinking." (Dixit and Nalebuff 1991, ix). Project managers need to apply strategic thinking to their projects. Unfortunately, the length of the time cycle in projects tends to be so long that we ignore cycles of repetition as a strategic method to improve our project performance. What is often lacking is a sense of scale: recognition of those elements of the project that are repetitive and can be improved by concentrated attention. Games from our social environment can provide such lessons to the careful observer. Because of the short time cycle, gaming provides an excellent opportunity for drawing lessons to improve strategic thinking.

Most games introduce enough elements of random variation that each playing can be regarded as having a unique outcome. Yet, in the compressed cycle of a game, it is much easier to recognize elements of repetition and to draw lessons from those elements. Gamers will adopt some strategies that are common from one playing to another in much the same way that project managers in even roughly similar projects will adopt similar strategies based on their experiences.

What is obvious in games, but often overlooked in projects, is that the ability to adapt strategies to the situation is a developing art. Few of us played chess as well the first time we tried it as we did the tenth time. In games we can regard this as an intentional strategy. Repetition helps us develop our skills. We call this "experience" and use it to help us make better decisions and pick better strategies. In a project, that learning opportunity is often overlooked.

The specific lessons to be highlighted are:

- Every project has a human element.
- Projects need a clear mission.
- Planning ahead helps eliminate dead-ends.
- Improved performance over time is an element of planning.
- Risk comes with entry to the game.
- Keeping score is not without a price.
- Start well and stay the course.

## Projects and the Human Element

In my industry, project leaders tend to be drawn from a technical environment. In common with technically trained people everywhere, they tend to look at issues as the solution to technical problems. When we underestimate the human element, we sub-optimize our project performance. I loved the way Dr. Robert Ballard put it in his keynote address at PMI '96: "In my experience, the vast majority of project problems are people problems." (Ballard 1996)

In his report on the design and marketing of the Boeing 777, Karl Sabbagh comments that in the 777 project, "Each member of this top management team appeared to have a respect for the special skills of the others, and a willingness to accept judgments he might not wholeheartedly agree with." (Sabbagh 1996, 36) One might suggest that this element of human dimension had more to do with the ultimate success of the project than all the computers used.

For a game example, consider the chess rematch between Gary Kasparov and Deep Blue. Steven Levy observes, "As the match unfolded, the psychological component became as prominent as any human-to-human contest." (Levy 1997, 72)

Observe players in any game. Ultimately the fun, or lack thereof, has little to do with the fall of the cards. It has to do with the behavior of the players when faced with the fall of the cards.

Our projects will be more successful when we have compatible teams and invest in building the sense of teamwork. We may root for Deep Blue, but every successful project must allow for the human failings of individuals a lot less logical than Gary Kasparov.

## Projects and a Clear Mission.

Any project must have a shared sense of mission among the team members. Success will come to project teams that are unified in that mission. A team wandering through the days without that unity of shared understanding becomes a lost team. Projects run by lost teams are rarely successful.

Consider the popular perception of some major projects shared through the published project reports:

- Tracy Kidder reporting on the design of an Eclipse Computer. (Kidder 1995)
- Karl Sabbagh on the Boeing 777. (Sabagh 1996)
- Paul Carroll on the battle between Microsoft and IBM Windows 3.0 vs OS/2. (Carroll 1993)

In each case, a successful outcome was foreshadowed by a clarity of vision shared across the project team.

In most any board or computer game, the objective of the game is simple, clear, and measurable. When it has been accomplished, everyone will know. A classic example from a computer game is the mission of Billy in the game Commander Keen: "to save the world." No one sits down at the joystick for this game and believes that he is literally saving the world, but the clarity of that simple vision propels many to spend considerable time making the attempt.

When undertaking any project, take some time to enlist your team and clarify the mission. If the mission is fuzzy for any team member, his contribution will be less than it should be.

## Planning Ahead

Any project involves a balance between planning and action. Overplanning can lead to inaction. Overemphasis on action can lead to arrival in blind alleys that are avoidable through good planning. Sabbagh quotes Tom Gaffney of Boeing as saying, on the door design for the 767 "we found there were 13,341 changes . . . according to our assessment, sixty-four million dollars was spent in changing the design of the doors."(Sabbagh 1996, 90) Planning will not eliminate lost motion from changes, but Gaffney was extremely encouraged to see "a ninety-five percent reduction in the number of errors we were expected to have." (Sabbagh 1996, 91)

In using the simulation series ProjectManTM, the author has observed dozens of teams. The preponderant behavior is one of under-planning. The team gets so excited about getting under way that they fail to look ahead.

Typically a team will:

- Set a broad mission but fail to flesh it out with a realistic plan.
- Mistake action for progress, leading to blind alleys.
- Once having set a course of action, stick to it without adequate consideration of needed changes in thinking.

Far less frequently we see teams get so bound up in process that they fail to take effective action.

Each of these problems has its parallel in project work. Each can be addressed through effective planning, but teaching planning is much more complex than teaching the use of scheduling software.

Again, I think that we can highlight paths around some of these tendencies by observing the play of games and what works well.

As stated earlier, the objective of games is rarely at issue, but the identification of means can be critical.

In the computer game TETRIS, odd shaped blocks fall from the top of the screen to build a structure from the bottom of the screen. As complete rows are filled, they disappear from the screen. Thus, successful play eliminates these problem rows by filling them. Successful players do this by developing a vision of what they are building and a plan for accomplishment. They are constantly looking for a missing element to place in a particular place in the structure. Since they have a constantly updated plan for play, these players can benefit by optional information about what is coming next.

Unsuccessful players tend to play on a totally reactive basis, considering each piece as it falls and trying to deal with it. Since they have no future-oriented vision, they can rarely benefit from all the information that is available. Often they will even turn off the option of displaying advance notice of the next falling piece.

In the solitaire-like game Freecell, the objective is to restack the cards in suite order. The rules are somewhat complex, but four central points apply to planning.

- You will never see the end from the beginning. The further you can see ahead the better your chances of success, but only in the end game will you truly see the end as accomplishable.
- While you can't see the end, the further you look ahead the more likely success is to come.
- When you fail to accomplish the end goal you can start again. However if you do again what you did before,

**Exhibit 1.** A Reversi Solution

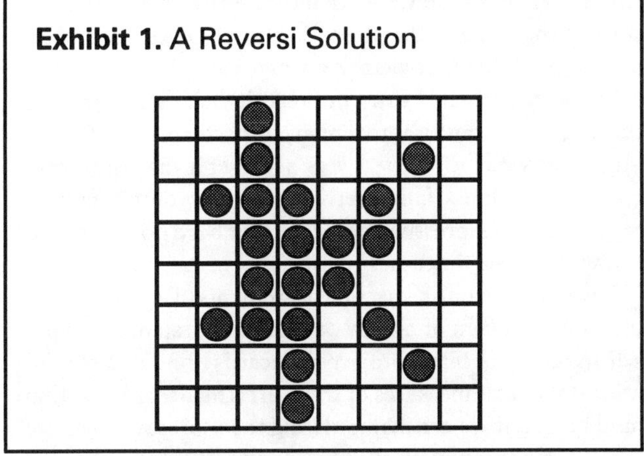

you will obtain the same result. A restart following failure, without a modified strategy, will yield another failure.

- Some obvious, early moves are a trap. Action for the sake of action leads to gridlock. Action must be in pursuit of an effective plan.

Project management is very similar. Successful project teams look ahead and integrate information about what is coming into the current vision of the project. That vision evolves, and their means of addressing it evolves as well. Lessons are learned and applied to future action. Early actions are not undertaken for the sake of action, but only as they fit the accomplishment plan.

Unsuccessful project teams get bogged down in reaction and fail to integrate the knowledge of what is coming into a plan in order to reach the objective. They repeat the same bankrupt strategies, irrationally hoping for a different result. They undertake easy action that is often fruitless and then let that action direct their future course.

Successful project planning is a team sport. It is hard work that must start with a clear vision of the plan objective. As in a game, it is much more than a projection of future events. It must include effective feedback elements to aid in modifying the plan to meet changes in the project.

## Plan for Improved Performance

What if a toddler decided that walking was overrated the second, twentieth, or two hundredth time he fell? Clearly, the state of human locomotion would quickly decline.

In Commander Keen we enter a first game totally unaware of the hazards. Most first-time players will hardly get off the initial screen before expending their energy or losing their final life. To quit at this point, as many do, misses the real opportunity to learn and grow.

Project teams face the paradox that improvement requires investment, but investment is only paid back over time. Since projects have a finite life, the project team usually is very suspicious of the amount of investment that can be justified on the project. As a result, a team often becomes trapped in an ineffective process for want of investing time and effort in improvement. We need to take a lesson from Commander Keen. The greatest fun comes from improving our skill and dealing with the tougher problems ahead, not from ducking the problems as being beyond our ability. In our project-performing organizations, we should identify specific learning opportunities we hope to develop. Some opportunities should address accomplishing the project, and some others should address improvement that may only come to fruition in the next project.

In the Windows 3.0 version of Reversi, there exists an apparent bug in the program that can cause the computer to be trapped in one of several patterns of total loss. The action is repeatable so that the game can become just a series of simple repetitions of defeat for the computer. Given the objective of the game, each of these outcomes is near optimum for the human player. Exhibit 1 shows the board for one such pattern. An interesting observation of many players is that, even knowing this bug exists, the players will continue to play the game trying different strategies, not so much to find a more optimum solution as to avoid the idea that the game is not challenging. Players see no fun in routinely beating the computer by fixed moves, so they improvise. In so doing, they win some and lose some games but they will not generally improve on the optimum solution already known.

These players emulate those project teams who lose sight of the objective and ban routine processes as unworthy of the project environment. Routine application of procedure will not guarantee a project's successful outcome, but it will allow project management to concentrate its creativity and problem solving on those issues that need them, rather than on endlessly trying new approaches to previously solved problems.

Improvement requires experimentation and change, but experimentation requires application of a theory more specific than random play. Random play in the absence of a theory of improvement is wasted motion.

As in games, the opportunity exists in projects for learning by controlled experiment and by extracting from experience lessons for future use. The best lessons learned will be drawn from the details of behavior and will include successes and failures. Effective lessons learned are about sharing our successes and failures (something fun to watch with children playing Commander Keen), not about trumpeting our successes and ignoring our failures, a common behavior on projects.

## Dealing with Risk

In the game Minesweeper, the player starts with a field that contains mines. Any first move might blow him up, but there can be no success without a move. The first few moves will likely reveal little about the overall situation. Each move has the potential to advance our knowledge about the game screen, but several moves are necessary before we can form any picture of future actions. While the first few moves are essentially random, holding to a random action strategy will kill us.

Early in the game, after these first few moves, we may have many more possible no-risk moves than we can process quickly, so we develop a strategy and proceed. Our continued success will eliminate many risks. Late in the game we are likely to encounter situations again where we cannot know the outcome of a particular move. Yet we must proceed. A careful execution of strategy and a little luck can lead to record performance.

There are some "unk-unks," unknown-unknowns, in any project. We can never entirely eliminate them. Some beginning moves may appear fairly random. Yet, random performance strategies will ultimately kill the project. Unlike a game where we usually start again at small cost, our projects must proceed from the present, not the beginning. Still, we can do a number of things to reduce the risk. We can gather knowledge and disseminate it effectively to the team members. We can use our radar to look ahead and avoid controlled flight into terrain. We can judge potential courses of action against the known risk involved, sometimes choosing a course for its limited downside risk as for its upside potential. The key to effectively dealing with risk is knowledge and communication.

## Keeping Score

Few significant projects are undertaken without some concept of a success scorecard; to do so would be futile. Unfortunately, the scoring system often lacks clarity, and we find ourselves manipulating the scorecard more earnestly than planning our performance.

In the game Freecell, the primary scoring metric is first attempt wins. Any set of cards solved on the first attempt is a victory. Any set of cards ending in a defeat the first time is a loss. Moral victory is obtained by subsequent attempts on failed sets. After the first time they can't ever be victories, but they only count as a single loss.

Moral victories can result in improved methods, increased player skill, and satisfaction at challenges met. They still don't count as victories on the scorecard.

Scoring trends in this game, as in most games, are subject to statistical analysis. When is a run of victories or losses significant? When do the statistics indicate that a fundamental change in the game or the player's ability has occurred? Certainly not with the first victory or loss.

One observer found a run in Freecell data that seemed to indicate a significant improvement in performance. On investigation, what it showed was a player's discovery of a means to abandon a failed set without recording a failure. This created an impressive scorecard that bore no relation to the way the game outcomes really happened.

How good are our project measurements? Do they reflect our accomplishment or merely our manipulation of the scorecard? In review of many project scorecards I find that manipulating dominates measures of true performance. My caution would be that if we are manipulating the scorecard, then we can't possibly learn much about underlying performance.

In identifying project measures we ought to recognize variation and the possibility of tampering. When the rule set is established, we ought to make it meaningful or quit wasting money on the measurement process.

## Start Well and Stay the Course

In the 100-meter dash, world class performance requires a good start off the blocks. It is that simple. The difference between the fastest and the slowest runner in a high profile event is so small that any one of many individual failings can defeat any runner. A bad start is one such failing. Every one of the fundamental points of performance must be world class to assure a world class performance.

So it is in projects. There are many individual events that can lead to project failure. Quality performance in many areas is required for success. Yet, ultimately good performance in all of them is not enough to guarantee victory.

Still, we can't expect a great outcome with a poor beginning. Building the team, setting the vision, planning the project, targeting improved performance, and keeping score are all important. When the starter's gun goes off, every team member has to be pulling for the success of the team.

Our project teams, as much as any game-playing team, must improve individual and team abilities and focus on the scorecard. I think that careful observation of games and game players can help us to victory in our project games.

## References


Sabbagh, Karl. 1996. *Twenty-First Century Jet*. New York, NY: Scribner.

Dixit, Avinash, and Barry Nalebuff. 1991. *Thinking Strategically*. New York, NY: W.W. Norton.

Carroll, Paul. 1993. *Big Blues: The Unmaking of IBM*. New York, NY: Crown Publishers.

Levy, Steven. 1997. "Big Blue's Hand of God." *Newsweek* (May 19): 72.

Ballard, Robert. 1996. Keynote address. PMI '96 .

Kidder, Tracy. 1995. *Soul of a New Machine*. New York, NY: Avon.

# Project Management Can Help Business Education To Prepare For The Challenges Of The Next Century— Business Schools Should Practice What They Teach

Andras Nemeslaki, Ph.D., International Management Center

## Introduction

After the breakdown of the Berlin Wall several business schools diversified into the Central Eastern European region. During the first years of the economic transition they exclusively based their operation, strategic alliances, and partnerships on generous grants pouring into the region. Recently, pressures have begun to increase to transfer these educational enterprises into self-sustaining ventures: grants are dying, competition is increasing, and local businesses are developing and starting to act like real customers. The era of educational technology push seems to have come to an end. Only those business schools that are able to compete under the new rule will survive into the next phase of economical development. Complexity of scope, rapidly evolving and changing teaching materials, and cycle time pressures on program delivery are some of the critical factors to determine these new rules.

As a senior administrator at one of these business schools—namely the International Management Center (IMC) in Hungary—I would like to argue for the usefulness of project management to address these challenges. International Management Center has been operating as a project-based organization since its inception in 1989. We manage funds and educational programs and coordinate resources between continents; even our master of business affairs programs have to be organized on a project basis because of the nature of our constituencies.

I believe if we look into the Central Eastern European management school models, we can draw conclusions even for established North American institutions. Central Eastern European schools can serve as prototypes or test grounds for the next century's learning environment. In this paper I illustrate the application of two major project management tools: stakeholder management and resource planning.

### The Business School Model Represented by the International Management Center

International Management Center was founded with a mission of promoting market-oriented management knowledge and skills mainly for Hungary but also for the region. As do several similar management schools in the region, International Management Center has an academic program (master of business affairs) and an executive development program scheme. As a foundation governed by a board of trustees, International Management Center's operation depends both on tuition revenues and grants received. Since 1996 International Management Center has entered into a strategic alliance with Case Western Reserve University (CWRU) to deliver an accredited master in business affairs degree; this has been the first major step to transfer International Management Center's graduate education to a truly market-driven program. The delivery of this joint venture took less then a year from the idea to the launching of the first cohort joint Case Western Reserve University-International Management Center students.

## Stakeholder Management to Determine Scope of the Learning Process

In order to describe International Management Center's master of business affairs program, I use a stakeholder map, described in Exhibit 1. The stakeholder map contains the key constituencies and their major influences on the master of business affairs program in the unique circumstances of Hungary or Central Eastern Europe. First I describe them, then briefly analyze the dynamics between the different stakeholders to illustrate how we determine program scope using the map. I will close the section with some recommendations for other business schools.

### Stakeholders

In the case of the International Management Center the following stakeholders are identified:

- Donors who provide core funding either in the form of cash, asset, or personnel.
- Employers who hire graduates after the completion of their studies or during their studies for internships.
- Alumni or the growing number of graduates who possess an international master of business affair degree.
- Competition, which are the different kinds of organizations delivering master of business affair programs.

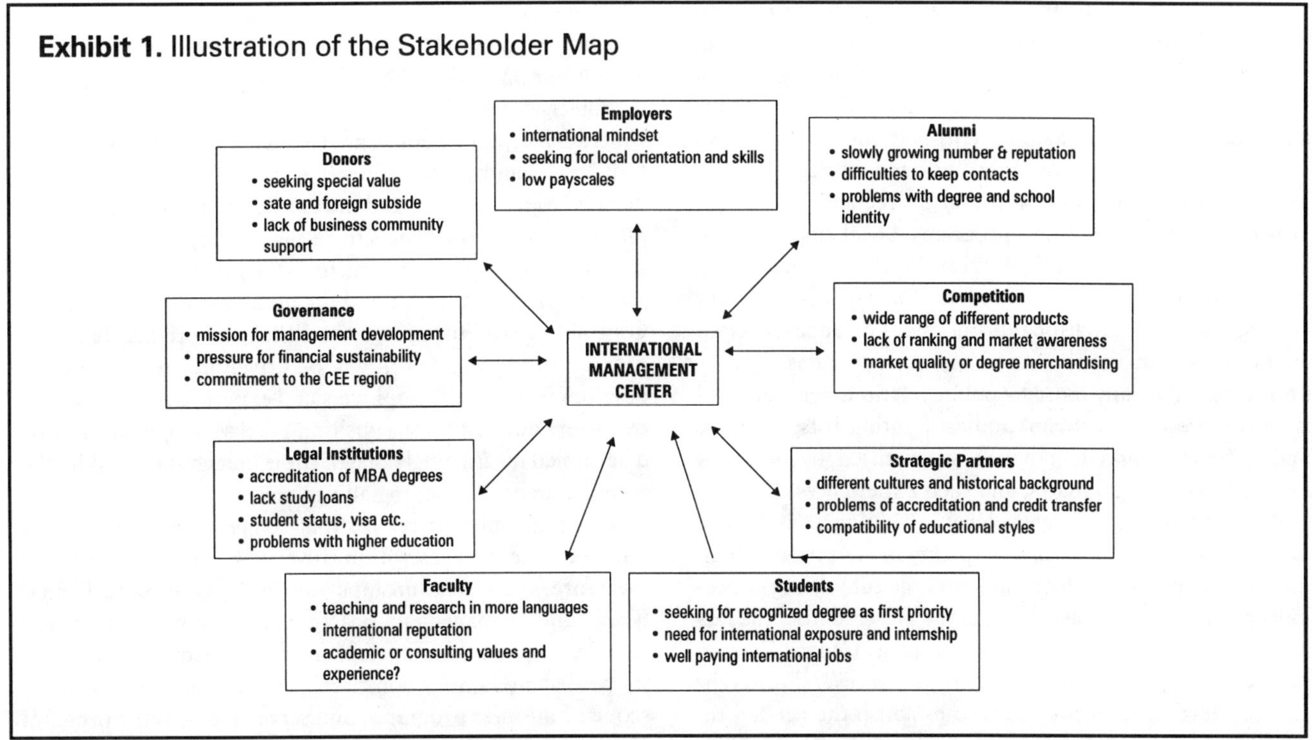


**Exhibit 1.** Illustration of the Stakeholder Map

- Strategic partners who provide assistance in granting degrees, enhancing curriculum, and administration of program delivery.
- Students, full or part time, who enroll in the program.
- Faculty, consisting of local Hungarian and visiting, mainly North American business school faculty.
- Legal institutions, such as accrediting ministries and the surrounding higher education.
- Governing body of the school, which is a board of trustees in International Management Center's case.

## Stakeholder Analysis

During the early nineties the key constituencies were the donors and strategic partner schools of Central Eastern European institutions. The region has had a major hunger for all kinds of knowledge in management, and at the same time there has been little awareness both of the specific demand and the qualitative differences in supply of management programs. In this situation some quickly reacting United States and West European business schools deployed management programs using stable government funding (USIAD, Know-How Fund). I have to say that it was almost the only way because other stakeholders could not seriously influence the business educational scope. Local employers were ignorant of what masters of business affairs graduates can bring to them; students did not know exactly what to expect from the curriculum that is presented to them; alumni simply did not exist; and, most importantly, faculty had to be imported because of the lack of qualified Central Eastern European faculty to teach these courses.

By the mid-nineties the management education market became saturated with all kinds of master of business affairs programs: full and part time, distance educational, American and British, university-affiliated, imported, and several non-degree programs. The demand from the students and employers only had focused on the type degree that has been awarded upon completion of these programs. Competition was degree-driven although everybody preached market acceptance, but public relations and promotions only emphasized the diploma's type and country of origin as a critical marketing tool. Legal institutions—mainly the educational ministries—have played a great role in influencing the "degree market" by regulating accreditation and protecting academic quality with administrative tools. This again was a natural reaction to providing guidance for student and employers to orient themselves among the diversified supply.

Since the mid-nineties several forces have been changing the International Management Center's scope or strategy formulation. Looking at the stakeholder map, the most pressing issue is on the donor side; stable government funding drastically drops, and at the same time, the governing Board of Trustees is pushing for a higher and higher earned revenue donation financial ratio. Over nine years of existence the International Management Center has changed this ration from 80/20 to 40/60 percent, basically making more money from tuition then from gifts.

Parallel with the financial pressure, dynamics of constituencies have changed on the market as well. Hungary receives the highest direct foreign investment in the region, and this resulted in the appearance of several multi- national corporations (MNC). Multinational corporations have started to create real market pressure for business schools; consequently placement, internships, and market recognition are increasing pressure on business programs. Local employers require international thinking with local expertise from graduating students. The production of this mix is the major challenge in all international programs. The appearance of alumni is also a major impact in business programs. Quality is not determined any more by public relations materials and using the Western partners' domestic rating lists; all these kinds of promotional activities are verified by word of mouth, success of graduates, and their experiences.

Whatever happens between legal institutions, employers, alumni, students, or governance, quality of education will ultimately be determined by faculty and the supporting educational partners. In the early nineties the pressure from the faculty side was in training and development. Central Eastern European professors have been enrolled in several different kinds of development programs to establish the needed resource pool for teaching and consulting. From the mid-nineties on, development research has started to become the key issue. The reason is that basic finance, marketing, operations management, and other disciplines are delivered by hundreds of smaller and bigger educational firms. Differentiation in the market will happen only through added value to these basics that, on the other hand, can only be done through the creation of new knowledge relevant to the Central Eastern European region. The International Management Center tries to form its educational partnership also according to this philosophy. With Case Western Reserve University, we moved away from the "grant based" cooperation and lifted that to the level of professional strategic alliance. Financially, both institutions cover certain expenses of the joint program in order to achieve their strategic objectives: Case Western to strengthen its international focus and International Management Center to strengthen its academic quality.

### Recommendation for Stakeholder Analysis

There are several ways that business schools can use stakeholder analysis to enhance their educational programs. Cleland describes the major steps of stakeholder analysis in an industrial setting, and similar frameworks can be applied for education as well (Cleland 1988). Based on my experience at International Management Center and from observing our past and present partner schools' strategies, I have found the logic of stakeholder analysis extremely useful.

There are several constituencies of the educational process and finding the balance between them is very important. Stakeholder analysis draws the attention of the complexity that business school management is facing. Top schools in the United States, for instance, are following the "employer" and "student" bandwagon. They are shortening programs, reducing academic rigor, and increasing the importance of the placement function. Seems to be that the Ivy League is going one direction, but will it leave its faculty behind? What about the influence of research and the academic environment? In Central Eastern Europe it is not difficult to predict that competition in the longer run will be driven much more by the development of local employers and expertise than by degree exporters and temporary visiting faculty. Scope will not be determined by any single one of these units but instead by the complex dynamics among all of them.

It is important to realize that scope changes are determined by the changes within the stakeholder relationships; therefore, these relationships have to be continuously analyzed, and management has to react according to those changes. Stakeholder management can help determine the proper balance among constituencies, determine the winning scope of business programs, and serve as a basis for program plans. Case Western Reserve University's master of business affairs program innovations are perfect illustrations of the systematic application of stakeholder inputs to determine high value program scope (Boyatzis et. al. 1995).

## Planning and Resource Loading Using Project Scheduler 6

As International Management Center moved from the grant-based operation to the more profit-oriented operation, the efficient use of its resources became very important. The key resources—as well as important stakeholders—are our faculty. Ultimate quality is determined by faculty, undoubtedly the most expensive commodity in the educational process.

International schools, like International Management Center, work generally with four different types of resources:

#### *Full -Time Faculty:*

These are professionals in specified functional areas of business administration. Beyond teaching they are involved in research, consulting, and service activities.

#### *Visiting Faculty:*

These are temporary appointments, usually for a specific assignment. Beyond the regular honorarium they are provided housing and travel. In International Management Center's case, we differentiate between two separate kinds of individuals: faculty from the partner school, Case Western Reserve University, and faculty from other universities.

**Exhibit 2.** Illustration of Resource Planning with ProjectScheduler 6.0

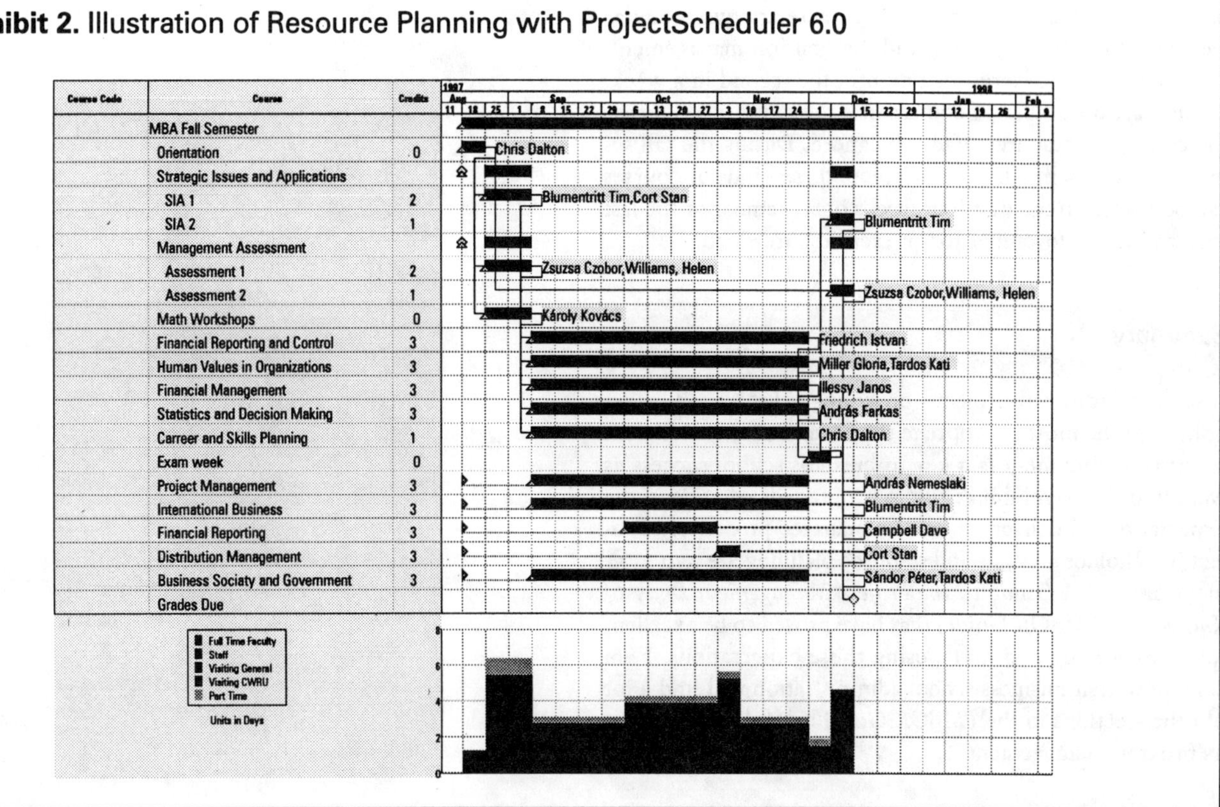


### *Staff:*

Some classes are conducted by staff who do not hold an academic appointment, but their skills and experience are suitable for particular topics. This is how we solve carrier development, communication, and presentation skills.

### *Part-Time Faculty:*

These are local individuals, contracted for a temporary period similar to visiting. They do not require housing and transportation, though.

The decision on the mix of these faculty resources is driven by several factors in any given time period. Very often these factors are conflicting, so to select the appropriate portfolio is the same kind of balancing activity as with stakeholder management. International Management Center applies the balance of the following criteria: international expertise, sufficient familiarity with the Central Eastern European region, and desire to create knowledge, costs, and capability for institutional building.

Some schools in the region work exclusively with foreign visiting faculty. These are the "virtual business schools" or universities that provide superior international expertise, high flexibility, and manageable cost structure. The sacrifice they make is in institutional building and the lack of organizational memory. This kind of set up seems only appropriate in modularity-based programs. Some schools, on the other hand, work exclusively with locals, permanent and part-time faculty. We have found this to be true in undergraduate programs where international exposure, research, and flexibility are not that relevant. The first type of institutions manage their faculty by coordination and objectives (teach one particular course or other deliverables) because they are scattered around the globe. The other types manage them with control and workload definition (number of hours to teach in a given period). International Management Center strategically seeks a healthy balance among costs, institutional building, flexibility, and international expertise.

In Exhibit 2, I illustrate one typical semester workload. We are using Project Scheduler to plan semester course and workloads.

The "critical path" is meaningless in this constellation, although it shows that with some courses there is a float to collect grades. (All courses connect to "grades due" closing milestone.) We use the effort base resource allocation because this way we can keep course-elapsed time and actual teaching hours separate. Exhibit 2 shows the resource mix where full-time faculty carries the significant load, and others are "uploaded" to represent a healthy professional diversification.

This technique is the only one to plan and control alternative course deliveries. In Exhibit 2 there are two modular electives: financial reporting and distribution management. The first one is delivered in a month, the second in a week. If there are a number of courses like these, it is crucial that the composite resource load is balanced. During the fall semester of our schedule, for instance, these kinds of courses can be loaded to the first four weeks of September or the last four weeks of November for an even resource load.

## Summary

Just as in industrial projects, providing value for all stakeholders in the most appropriate time span and most efficient resource deployment is a key to business school success as well. In order to minimize risk in program development, the expectations of delivery should be managed proactively. Project stakeholder analysis and resource planning are two tools mentioned in *A Guide to the Project Management Body of Knowledge (PMBOK Guide)* that have proved to be excellent for summarizing and juxtaposing those expectations. I am convinced that business school administration will find a lot of other sections in the *PMBOK Guide* helpful in improving its program management.

### References

Boyatzis, Richard E, S. Scott Cowen, and David E. Kolband Associates. 1995. *Innovation in Professional Education*. Jossey-Bass Publishers.

Cleland, David I. 1988. Project Stakeholder Management. *Project Management Handbook*. Van Nostrand Reinhold: 275-301.

# Crashing the Critical Path of Training: Using Alternative Training Delivery Strategies to Reduce Classroom Learning

Joan Knutson, Project Mentors

As companies continue to downsize, right-size and reengineer, the demands placed on project managers require a greater investment of time than ever before. Project customers and stakeholders want to be sure that the selected project manager has the necessary knowledge and experience to complete the project and meet the triple constraint. How do you provide comprehensive training for the project manager of this era? Compounding the issue of an era where project managers are investing more time are the issues of distance where more and more companies are not only nationally dispersed but also globally dispersed.

How do you train people across distances, or multiple people in multiple locations with different schedules and time-frames? How do you do this and still provide a *team* approach as opposed to a lecture approach? And more importantly, how do you maintain the benefits of classroom training when restricted by logistics and time?

This paper will outline and discuss Bellcore and Project Mentors' initial processes, decision-making, and implementation of using an alternative training delivery as means to reduce classroom learning. We will then visit the new technology available for alternative learning, often referred to as distance learning.

## The Bellcore Experience

In 1994 Bellcore and Project Mentors had joined together to develop and offer comprehensive project management training that consisted of a twenty-one-day core curriculum spread over a one-year period.

The training program had two goals:

- Train project managers to better manage time, schedule, resources, cost, and quality requirements
- Prepare project managers to successfully complete the project manager professional exam.

Approximately sixty project managers completed the training. When the managers took the project manager professional exam, 89 percent of those individuals passed. The training was considered a success in preparing the project managers, but the demands on their time was increasing and attendance at class began to decline. Attendance also suffered due to the financial pressures for project managers to reduce their non-billable hours—thus students were not scheduled to attend the training program.

A study was conducted by interviewing the project managers on the program quality. It was discovered that the project managers felt that even though they learned a lot and were well prepared for the exam, much of the information was very theoretical and did not allow for a lot of practical application. Project managers also felt that some of the programs overlapped.

From this data Bellcore developed a project plan objective:

- Identify the key learning experiences needed
- Determine which ones were classroom-based and which could be learned in other ways
- Develop the training
- Revise the curriculum accordingly
- Implement in a phased approach
- Evaluate the effectiveness of the training.

### Lessons Learned:

As a result of Bellcore's data gathering, the company made the following decisions:

- Project planning, scheduling, and risk tools could be taught via multimedia, self-paced courses. Some classroom follow-up would be necessary to ensure that project managers saw the value of applying these tools in the workplace.
- "Soft skills," those interpersonal skills that are critical to project success (e.g., conflict resolution, teaming, communication) would continue to be taught in a classroom-based environment.
- The application of what was learned would be covered using a computer-based simulation during a three- day classroom session.
- Review for the Project Management Institute exam would be expanded to a four-day class with one-half day coverage of each area from *A Guide to the Project Management Body of Knowledge (PMBOK Guide)*.

It became apparent that the training program needed to change its delivery format to reduce classroom learning. In 1996 Bellcore undertook a complete training redesign by consolidating course material and creating a multi-media independent study computer-based training (CBT) CD-ROM program.

The computer-based training was labeled *Tools & Techniques of Project Management* and focused on the how-to's of project management based on Project Mentors' ten-step project management process. The learning is facilitated by interactive exercises that allows the user to test his comprehension of the presented material. At the end of each module there are test exercises, which are tallied and can be printed out or copied to a disk. The user name and identification number are automatically written to the test result record.

A computer simulation course that Project Mentors developed was also incorporated into the new training program. The simulation course compressed a twenty-six week project into a computer simulation class, which is designed to be highly experiential. Participants were divided into groups of three to four, and each team acted as the project leader for a separate, although similar, project. Several months of experience were condensed into a few days as participants immersed themselves into a realistic, dynamic project.

These decisions resulted in a reduction of nine classroom days, thus totaling twelve classroom days. Additionally, the program length was compressed to six months. The new curriculum path integrated the multimedia programs with traditional classroom sessions resulting in a comprehensive program that met the needs of project managers whose demanding schedules required less time spent in training.

As a result of these efforts of implementing the current technology, over two hundred project managers completed training. One hundred took the Project Management Institute exam and are continuing to maintain our 89 percent pass rate.

## Current Trends in Distance Learning

As the technology that affects the effective management of projects grows and expands to heights difficult to see, let alone reach, so does the technology applicable to the training environment. We find ourselves now at a training industry cusp that is bringing us leaps and bounds forward in terms of:

- How to train people across distances,
- How to train multiple people in multiple locations,
- How to provide distance training using a team approach versus a lecture approach,
- How to provide training to people with different schedules and time frames.

Having the ability to address all of the above gives us a unique opportunity and edge when changing the very fluid creature called the project manager. The project manager is often separated from her team members, often by miles and borders. The project manager works on her own schedule in her own world. The project manager probably prefers to feel like she's working alone while working as part of a group.

All of the following possibilities address alternatives to the preferred and standard stand-up training course in ways to train the unique creature known as "project manager." All of this technology is fairly new as it is applied to training and is evolving even as I speak. The key is FLEXIBILITY. We now have much greater flexibility in reaching project managers with the training that they need. The "I have no time to learn" whine will no longer hold water. The various approaches to consider are as follows.

## Computer-Based Training and Multimedia

Computer-based training is still an effective tool for dealing with the topic at hand because it is an attainable technology that can be made available to a multitude of users. In regards to the technology we are going to discuss, computer-based terminals are a useful transition for those companies or training departments who are not ready for the technology to still train via an alternative to the classroom. The Bellcore experience combined classroom with multimedia programs to reach time-restrained project managers faced with *A Guide to the Project Management Body of Knowledge (PMBOK Guide)* examination.

This option is even more in reach for training departments because there are multimedia tools now that allow "non-programmers" to develop a multimedia training session. A course developer could (with some basic computer experience) design a course that could easily be transformed into a CD-ROM product or coded with HTML (web language) and put on the company's intranet or web site. These tools offer more options to enhance the classroom learning experience with ease, which could eliminate quite a bit of the typical development time of a computer-based terminal product.

## Internet and Corporate Intranet

The evolution of the Internet technology is incredibly challenging to keep up with. What started in the seventies as a government tool for communication exploded in the nineties into businesses and homes across the world. The technology is impressive, and corporations are using it to form their own private Internets for the use of their employees and customers; hence, the intranet is born. There are no set subscribers to Internet/intranet technology; just about every industry can flourish with the Internet, as can training.

Classroom training is extended to the desktop with the use of multimedia computer-based terminal products. And now, real time video and sound can be used on the Internet, which extends the traditional use of the CD-ROM computer-based terminal to the Internet and corporate intranets. Infrastructure issues—mostly slow lines—still complicate the use of the Internet for live video and sound. As we mentioned, CD-ROM-based computer-based terminal units will still be in high demand, especially while we are waiting for the next technological upgrade that addresses the issue of slow communication lines.

With the rise in programming technology and languages like JAVA, interactive training sites are predominate on the Internet and corporate intranets. Computer-based simulations, traditionally used in a classroom setting, can be set on a corporate intranet to reinforce the application that was learned in the classroom.

Skill assessment, skill development planning, and training schedules are other areas that could be available on the Internet/intranet. One could take a test and have their results e-mailed back to them and also filed in a general employment file so both parties, employer and employee, could track skill levels. For example, if project managers were preparing for the *PMBOK Guide* exam, they could review, take practice tests, and track their preparedness for the exam.

## Teleconferencing

Current technology around teleconferencing is far more "real" than what "real" was—time delays in sound and video, annoying tracks on the video, and uncomfortable huddling around a tiny camera and phone. Real time remote interactively today includes multi-media presentations, the shared whiteboards for brainstorming, and view interactive keypads with built-in microphones.

Teleconferencing is by far the most useful technology when faced with distance issues. With the current options in teleconferencing you can still use the favored classroom techniques to conduct training of multiple people in multiple locations. The option is available to use shared whiteboards that are so conducive to training in capturing the team experience. It is also a very useful tool for teams who are forced to work together on a project but are miles and miles apart.

## Conclusion

We are in an interesting era when companies are faced with various reengineering issues. Technology is changing fast and offers every day new solutions to the growing demands of the nineties business culture. The technology is there and more flexible than ever. The time is now for trainers to embrace the options and make their training more effective and flexible.

# Managing Your Instructional Design Project

Laurie K. Bosley, PMP, Solbourne

Many well-managed projects often list training as an activity on the work breakdown structure (WBS). Some even go so far as to make training a work package. However, the development and implementation of training is seldom treated as the project that it truly is.

Recall the definition of project: "a temporary endeavor undertaken to create a unique product or service (*PMBOK Guide* 1996, 167)." A new training program fits this definition perfectly. I have seen experienced project managers assigned to training development scoff at the idea of planning, scheduling, budgeting, and tracking a training project's performance. "It's training, not a REAL project," they say. Do we agree that project management is used to ensure that the customer receives the most effective and efficient product? Then by applying project management techniques to the development of training, we can ensure that the trainees receive the most effective and efficient training.

## The Instructional Design Model

There are a variety of instructional systems design (ISD) models used systematically to manage training program development as a project. While most contain the same basic elements, I will refer to the one designed by Walter Dick and Lou Carey (Dick and Carey 1990).

Dick and Carey's instructional design model has nine basic stages that occur in sequence. They are:

1. Identify instructional goal(s)
2. Conduct instructional analysis
3. Identify entry behaviors and characteristics
4. Write performance objectives
5. Develop criterion-referenced test items
6. Develop instructional strategy
7. Develop and select instructional materials
8. Design and conduct formative evaluation
9. Design and conduct summated evaluation.

A tenth stage, revise instruction, occurs throughout the design process. Project management identifies five processes to be used in the management of most projects (*PMBOK Guide* 1996, 30-34). The ten steps of instructional systems design fit hand-in-hand with the five processes used to manage a project.

### Identify Instructional Goal

The instructional goal is based upon a thorough needs assessment and should identify what the learner is expected to be able to do at the end of the instruction; this is the initiation phase of the project. The goal should also be related to a particular performance problem. In addition, instruction must be the most efficient means of achieving the desired results. If instruction is not the most efficient means of achieving the results, other interventions should be examined and undertaken if necessary.

Once the instructional goal is identified, you must decide whether or not to develop training to meet this goal. A feasibility analysis is one method of making this decision. If it's going to take four months to develop the training and the process being trained on is going to change in the fifth month, the cost of development may not be warranted. If the needed instruction can be acquired from an outside source, you might decide to purchase, rather than develop, the instruction. Students must also be available to "test drive" the materials for clarity and to assist with any revisions that may be necessary.

These initial steps of identifying the instructional goal (project scope) and making detailed time and cost estimates constitutes the majority of the planning phase of project management. Another part of the planning process includes confirming both the availability of resources and any assumptions that were made during the planning process. These items are documented in a project plan. In training, this project plan is sometimes called a design document or a training development and administrative guide.

### Conducting Instructional Analysis

Instructional analysis will verify the scope that was previously identified and agreed to. The process determines not only what the student needs to know but what they **already** know. Instructional analysis is a two-part process of goal analysis and subordinate skills analysis. Goal analysis requires the designer to classify the goal statement according to the kind of learning that will occur, and describe what actions constitute correct goal performance. Subordinate skills analysis requires identification of all skills that must be learned in order to reach the goal.

Instructional goals fall under one of five learning domains: verbal information, intellectual skills, cognitive strategies, attitudes, and motor skills (Gagne and Driscoll 1988). Verbal information is often referred to as declarative knowledge. If the goal requires the listing of information, where no problem solving must take place, it is in the verbal information domain. Rote memorization is another example of verbal information. Intellectual skills involve problem-solving tasks. Balancing a checkbook requires problem-solving and therefore falls into the intellectual domain. Cognitive strategies are the strategies that a person uses in obtaining information. The strategies that a person learns for converting word problems to mathematical form are cognitive strategies. The fourth domain, attitudes, includes goals that require the learner to make behavioral choices or act a certain way in a given situation. The fifth and final domain, motor skills, includes those skills that require using muscles to accomplish a task like operating a piece of equipment.

Once the domain of the goal has been determined, the steps necessary to complete that goal must be listed. Developing a flow chart is an effective means to determine what steps are necessary (Exhibit 1). Instructional designers must be very careful to list each step required. The outcome of the instructional analysis is used throughout the remainder of the design process, so steps that are missed in the analysis phase are not included in the instruction.

Subordinate skills analysis requires the instructional designer to list the skills necessary to complete each of the steps identified during the goal analysis. The identification of subordinate skills involves identifying the individual tasks necessary to complete an activity. Different learning domains result in very different subordinate skills diagrams.

Instructional analysis is very similar to task identification when scheduling a project. The goal analysis identifies the tasks needed to meet the instructional goal. The subordinate skills analysis identifies the sub-tasks that need to be accomplished as part of the overall task. This is also the first step in the execution process-information gathering.

**Exhibit 1.** Chart of Goal and Subordinate Skills Analysis

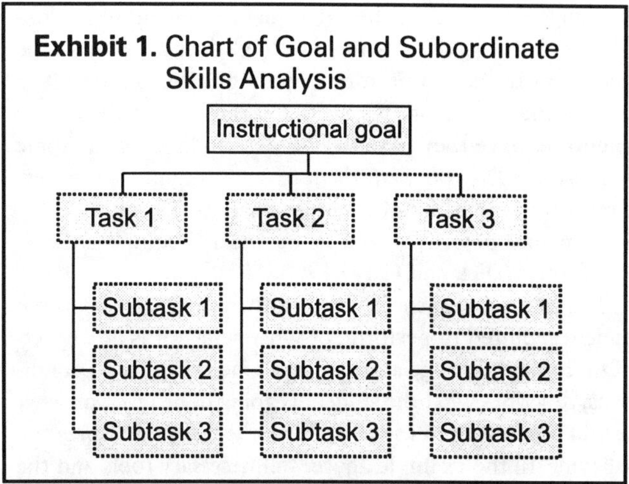


## Identify Entry Behaviors and Characteristics

This step is often overlooked by the customer (and sometimes, by the designer) and results in a dangerous assumption about the target audience. To assume they "know this" or "can do that" can be fatal to a training program's ultimate success. Well-designed training programs often fail because of just such assumptions, some as seemingly safe as "They can read." A thorough study of the target audience should be completed, not only to determine what skills they already have, but more importantly to identify what skills they do not have but need at an entry level.

The previously completed subordinate skills analysis is the starting point for the identification of what the anticipated audience does or does not know. A certain point in each "leg" of the flowchart would be identified as entry level skills or knowledge and anything above that line would be included in the instruction. Anything below the line would represent entry level skills and knowledge. In Exhibit 1, all "Subtask 3" items would be considered entry level skills and knowledge. For those members of the audience who do not already have the entry level skills and knowledge, a methodology for them to achieve the desired level should be identified before they begin training.

If you have performance prerequisites for the intended training, such as three years' experience managing five to twenty-five people, you should be able to make some accurate assumptions based on this prerequisite, such as the audience has basic management and leadership skills. I still prescribe caution in such blanket statements. Basic management and leadership may have entirely different meanings in different organizations. Also, many new management and leadership techniques are developed each decade. There may be a particular new technique that your company or customer would like to see utilized and that should be addressed in the training. It may be that current managers do not possess this skill at equivalent levels. The second step in the execution process, identification of entry level skills and knowledge, is imperative for the success of the instructional design project.

## Writing Performance Objectives

A performance objective is a statement of the task you want the student to be able to perform upon completion of the training. The key word in this area is **performance**. An example of a performance objective would be "Upon completion of this module, the student will correctly change a tire in fifteen minutes or less, given all the necessary tools and the car's user manual." Vague objectives need to be analyzed to determine the "what" that is the important element of the training. An objective such as "Students will understand how to change a tire," lacks the performance element of a properly worded objective. "Understanding" does not require the student or trainee to perform anything and it is difficult to test for understanding. What do you want the student to be able to do once they have the "understanding" of the topic in question? Do you want them to act a certain way or perform a certain task? Robert Mager has set the standard for performance objectives, and that standard requires a three-part format (Dick and Carey 1990, 103).

The first component is the performance. What task is the student required to perform, or what behavior is he expected to display? Change a tire. The second component, conditions, describes what the student is going to be given or what he will be allowed to use to perform the task and display the behavior. In the example above, "all necessary tools and the car's user manual" are the conditions. The final component is the criteria. It describes to what level of expertise the student will perform. Must it be 100 percent correct, or will displaying eight of ten traits constitute mastery? How many times must the correct behavior be displayed? Does one time demonstrate mastery, or must the student be presented with five completely different scenarios and demonstrate the stated level of mastery in all five instances? In the tire changing example, the criteria are "correctly and within fifteen minutes." The student must meet both of these criteria to demonstrate mastery of the objective.

All too often performance objectives are written with the criteria assumed to be "correct." The problem with this assumption is that not all tasks and behaviors have one correct answer or response. If the objective is being written for an attitudinal goal, this is particularly true. For an attitudinal goal's objective to be written correctly, the objective must clearly state the conditions present, including specifics about the scenario the students are expected to deal with.

Writing performance objectives is a necessary step in the execution of an instructional design project. How else will you determine if the training program is a success?

## Developing Criterion-Referenced Test Items

Tests. The word alone is enough to strike fear in the hearts of students and instructors alike! One reason for this fear is that test historically meant paper and pencil, multiple-choice or fill-in-the-blank, pass or fail test. Not only were you locked in a room for an hour or so to complete the test, but you had no idea what the test was going to cover. Instructional systems design relates test items directly back to the objectives for the module being tested and reduces the unpredictability of test taking. Test items should be objective rather than subjective and systematically developed rather than randomly chosen.

A criterion-referenced test is based on the performance objectives written for the instructional goal. Any criterion-referenced test should directly relate to the objective it is being designed for. If the objective states that they will be able to perform a certain task, then the test should have them perform that task. It is pretty difficult to demonstrate mastery of a psychomotor skill using paper and pencil! The test for the tire changing objective should have the student actually change a tire.

Tests can be useful in several ways: (1) to ensure that the student has learned the material (post-test), (2) to ensure the student meets the entry level skills and knowledge or behavior (pretest) and (3) to ensure the student is able to perform each of the subordinate skills (embedded test), often known as practice or review items. All test items must be written in such a way that they measure the effectiveness of the training. If the training is not effective in teaching what it is designed to teach, why are time and money being spent attending? Quality assurance instruments are designed to measure how well a non-instructional design project meets the objectives. The same is true for an instructional design project.

The objectives determine what the student is supposed to be able to do after completion of the training. The test measures whether or not they can do it. Not only do tests measure the ability of the student to perform the task, but also measures the effectiveness of the product—the training itself.

## Developing an Instructional Strategy

Once you have determined what the student needs to be able to do after completing the training, you must determine how you are going to get the necessary information delivered for mastery of the objectives. An instructional strategy has five major components: pre-instructional activities, information presentation, student participation, testing, and follow-through activities.

Pre-instructional activities start with motivation, informing the student of the objectives and determining the prerequisite skills. A wide variety of motivational techniques can be utilized, but care must be taken to find ones that will work with your given audience. Informing the students of the objectives is a way to focus them on the task at hand. By informing the student of any prerequisite skills, the student has an anchor to base the upcoming instruction on. A pre-test for or a brief description of prerequisite skills can be used to recall existing knowledge for use during the current instruction.

The second major component is information presentation. Often this component is the only requirement for training thought about by the customer. "I want to tell them this, this, and this." All information presented should be directly related to the goal and the individual objectives. Information presentation deals not only with developing the overhead transparencies and study guide for the student but also with the order in which the information will be presented, what objectives will be grouped together, and what examples will be used to demonstrate the material.

The third component, student participation, identifies not only what activities the student does during the course of the instruction, but also what thought-provoking questions the instructor will ask to start discussions about the topic being taught. It is one of the most powerful tools the instructional designer has available. Practice and feedback are used by both the instructor and the students. The instructor uses the results of the practice session to measure how effective the instruction is, and the student uses the feedback to measure how close she is to achieving the objectives. At the end of each module, the tasks associated with each objective for that module should be practiced. Feedback from the instructor is necessary to inform the student whether the particular task was done correctly and also to keep the student motivated. Many people still believe that "Practice makes perfect." This is not true. Practice makes **permanent.** Incorrect practice will result in incorrect habits. Having to break a deeply imbedded habit is much more difficult than correcting the process after one or two incorrect practices. The use of regular and consistent practice and feedback will keep incorrect practices from becoming habits.

Testing is the fourth component of developing an instructional strategy. At this stage the test items have already been developed, so the instructional designer needs to decide when and how the tests will be administered. Will a pretest be used? If so, when will it be administered, and exactly what skills will it cover? How and when will the post-test be administered? Will embedded test items be used? These decisions are needed to ensure that the instructor utilizes the tests appropriately.

The final component, follow-through activities, is based on the results of the post-test. If students do not perform adequately on the post-test, remediation training or enrichment activities may be needed to ensure that the students meet the objectives. In the case of instructor-led training, detailed plans for these activities are not made until the formative evaluation process is almost complete, and there is a clearly identified need for these items. For self-paced instruction, these activities should be planned and incorporated early in the development process.

The development of the instructional strategy is another part of the project management execution process. The product being developed is a training program, and the strategy for presenting the training program is an integral part of the program.

### Develop and Select Instructional Materials

The first step in developing instructional materials is to review what is currently available. Some objectives will have an abundance of readily available materials while others will have little or no material available for them. If there are materials available, those materials need to be reviewed to ensure that all the components, from motivational techniques to follow-through activities, are present. If they are not available in the existing materials, they will need to be developed to ensure that the overall materials meet the instructional goal.

The next step is to determine what media will be used and how the instruction will be conveyed. Will the instruction be computer-based? Will it be instructor-led? Video tape? Trying to "force-fit" instruction using the newest fad results in the objectives and the presentation being poorly matched. If the objective deals with the student being able to ride a horse, it is difficult for the student to meet the objective when the only "animal" they have available is a mouse!

Once the media are determined, the actual instructional package needs to be developed. A package usually contains a student manual that can be used as a reference guide after the class is over. Instructional materials containing the information the student will use to meet the objective need to be developed, or existing materials need to be incorporated. Instructional materials can contain transparencies, film strips, posters, and any other materials the instructor will use to teach the class. An instructor's manual is also part of the instructional package. The instructor's manual should include an overview of the materials to be presented and how the information is incorporated in the overall sequence of instruction. The instructor's manual should also include how and when the instructional materials should be used—the instructor's directions.

You have now determined what the objectives of the training are, how the material is going to be presented to the students, and what materials are going to be provided. You have completed the project management execution process and are ready to check the product for accuracy and completeness.

### Design and Conduct Formative Evaluation

Formative evaluation is the testing of the instructional materials as they are being developed. The first step is to have several learners review the materials individually with the designer and give their reaction to them. The learners should be chosen from various ability and knowledge levels rather than using all experts in the field. Subject matter experts should also review the materials for accuracy and currency. These individual reviews should include any tests to be given during instruction. This type of review will identify mechanical problems that may exist, such as typographical errors, incorrect content, mislabeled graphs, missing pages, and omission of materials.

The second step is to have a small group of "students" review the material independently. The learners utilized for the small group evaluation should be as representative of the target population as possible. This will serve as a review of changes made as a result of the previous evaluation and identify any remaining problems with the materials. In-depth debriefings should be used to get overall impressions of the program.

The final step is a field trial. Many instructors will conduct a "pilot" or field test of the instruction to evaluate the materials for relevancy and ease of use. This is actually the third step in formative evaluation rather than the only step. A group is selected and all materials, including tests, are utilized in a form that as closely as possible resembles the intended use. In the previous steps of formative evaluation, the instructional designer was actively involved with the review process. If the instruction is to be presented by an instructor, then the instructor, not the designer, should conduct the field trial. The group of "students" should be representative of the target audience and should be thoroughly debriefed after completing the instruction.

The testing of the instruction is part of the project management controlling process. Performance information is collected and studied. This performance information is used to determine what revisions to the instructional materials, if any, are needed.

## Revise Instruction

Revision of instruction occurs throughout the development process. As you review materials, you will make revisions based on both accuracy of content and flow of the material. If the material does not flow properly, comprehension will be reduced. Additionally, the data you receive from the formative evaluation is utilized to revise instructional materials.

Revision of instruction based on all aspects of the formative evaluation should be conducted. It should review all phases of the instructional design process. Any problems with the original instructional analysis or the identification of entry level behaviors and characteristics should be addressed. Any changes made, regardless of the phase they affect, will affect all materials developed, so a check must be made to ensure the program's validity and consistency.

Performance on each individual test item should be related back to the objective it is evaluating. If a particular item is being missed by the majority of the population, one of two things may be occurring. Either the evaluation item itself is written poorly, or the materials designed for that objective are not thorough or clear enough to aid the student in meeting the objective. The actual cause should be determined and the evaluation item or the materials rewritten to remedy the situation.

A variety of information can be obtained from examining the data from the formative evaluations. Pay particular attention to those items based on identified entry level skills and knowledge. Was the assumption pertaining to what the students would know prior to beginning the course accurate or not? You may need to revisit those assumptions and modify the materials based on your findings.

One thing to remember during the revision of the materials is that each step of the instructional systems design process builds on the previous step. If you make changes to anything completed in the fourth stage, writing performance objectives, all steps that follow that will have to be carefully reviewed for potential impact.

The revision to instruction, or quality control, is also part of the project management controlling process. Unsatisfactory performance is identified and changes are made to the material or presentation to remedy the problem.

## Design and Conduct Summative Evaluation

The final stage of instructional systems design is summative evaluation. Summative evaluation should be used not only to decide whether to maintain materials or instruction that you design but also to decide whether to adopt any materials or instruction from an outside source that are recommended for use. There are two phases of summative evaluation: expert judgment and field trial. Formative evaluation is conducted by the development team, while summative evaluation is done by an external evaluator.

The expert judgment phase involves analyzing the "match" between the organization's needs, characteristics of the target population, and the materials under consideration. The materials should be reviewed for accuracy and completeness, adequacy of design, and the utility of the materials. If the product undergoing evaluation was purchased from an outside source, you may also want to gather information from organizations currently using the product.

If you are reviewing several products to determine which one best fits the needs of the organization, the expert judgment phase will typically "weed out" several candidates for use. Products that have incorrect information or that do not match the organization's needs or the needs of the target audience need not go through a field trial as they should have already been discarded. The field trial phase involves the same type of activities for purchased materials as for "in-house" developed materials. The collection of data from the field trial should be carefully planned and implemented and thoroughly analyzed.

Summative evaluation is one of the final steps in the project management control process. All internal reviews were previously completed. Summative evaluation may be done by the customer to ensure that the product meets the specifications for the project.

## Project Management and Instructional Design

The systematic approach to instructional design is almost identical to the systematic approach to managing a project. The processes (initiating, planning, executing, controlling, and closing) are all completed if the instructional design project is to be a success. Schedules, budgets, and documentation should be completed as they would be for any other project. You never know; you may design more instruction in the future, and the documentation you develop here can help save time and effort on your next instructional design project!

### References


Dick, Walter, and Lou Carey. 1990. *The Systematic Design of Instruction*. Harper Collins Publishers.

Gagné, Robert M. 1987. *Instructional Technology: Foundations.* Hillsdale, NJ: Lawrence Erlbaum Associates, Publishers.

Gagné, Robert M., and Marcy P. Driscoll. 1988. *Essentials of Learning for Instruction.* Englewood Cliffs, NJ: Prentice-Hall.

Greer, Michael. 1992. *ID Project Management: Tools & Techniques for Instructional Designers and Developers*. Educational Technology Publications.

Greer, Michael. 1996. *The Project Manager's Partner*. Amherst, MA: HRD Press.

Project Management Institute Standards Committee 1996. *A Guide to the Project Management Body of Knowledge (PMBOK Guide)*. Upper Darby, PA: Project Management Institute.

# Keeping the Platform Alive: Project Management Training in the 21st Century

Carl L. Pritchard, PMP Director of Distance Learning, ESI International

Training project managers (PM) is challenging under the best circumstances. Project managers have limited available time for training. In many cases, they hold training organizations circumspect, as they doubt any training can supplement or supplant the training that occurs in the real-world workplace. As we enter a new decade, training organizations are looking for new and challenging ways to keep training engaging, informative, and profitable for their customers. Concurrently, project and program management support organizations are looking for training that is limited in scope, yet virtually unlimited in impact.

## Distance Learning

### Distance Learning—The Answer?

Many organizations are looking to distance learning as the panacea in this time of trouble. There is little to lose. Distance learning can often be done asynchronously, allowing project managers to train themselves on their next plane flight, train trip, or in their hotel rooms. Under many distance learning models, optimization is achieved. Project managers don't have to interfere with their busy work schedules to garner the training they report that they need. The organization is able to take full advantage of the PM's billable hours, while the project manager is able to expand her understanding of the field.

There's only one problem with that model. It won't work. If project managers are extremely over-committed, the first thing they may be tempted to do is to cut the training experience short. Few of the models include sufficient checkpoints for regular assessment of the student's progress as that tends to dilute the asynchronous training model. On the other side of the fence, those programs which require extensive synchronous exposure to the instructor can reduce the efficacy sought in distance learning models. Because students must participate in regularly scheduled sessions, they are not able to take advantage of training as *their* schedules and connections allow.

### Distance Learning—What Was the Question?'

The key problem here is that many distance learning models forget the critical element of learning objectives. What do we want the students to learn, and equally important, how do we expect them to learn it? Judging by history, marketing research, and a review of project management literature including textbooks, the *PMNet,* and proceedings from past Project Management Institute (PMI) symposia, PM competencies are one of the (if not *the*) watchwords for project management training today. If competencies are what organizations and project managers hope to improve, is distance learning the appropriate approach? Fortunately for progressive and traditional training organizations, the answer is yes—and no.

Reflecting back on the classic study of program management competencies conducted by the Defense Systems Management College (DSMC) in the eighties, project managers needed to excel in four critical competency areas: leadership, achievement, problem-solving, and political awareness. Within these sets, there are subset descriptions of individual competency areas that need to be addressed. Since that study was released, numerous related studies have been conducted and developed within a variety of corporate cultures. While the results have changed from one organization to the next, the balance of competencies (and the general descriptions thereof) have not changed radically. While there's no major shift in the competencies, there has been a major shift in the environment in which those competencies must evolve. Technology has escalated expectations on a variety of fronts, including communications and problem-solving. Inasmuch as even written communication has become virtually instantaneous, customers expect more and more expeditious responses.

In David Frame's *Managing Projects in Organizations,* (Frame 1995), he cites a project management war story relating to Imhotep's construction of the pyramid of Zoser. He discusses pyramid construction process and some of the challenges associated with the massive construction effort. As an extension of that line of thinking, while the expectations for Imhotep's tomb were high, Imhotep had an edge over the modern project manager. Imhotep could delay communication by days or weeks by blaming a recent sandstorm. The customer didn't expect instantaneous response. Similarly, even if a message was received, the duration of the project gave Imhotep the opportunity to develop a lot of pyramid "vaporware" (that which is claimed as complete but is still in design) by virtue of the huge spans of time required for progress. A thirty-year project affords many more of those luxuries than a twenty-week effort.

The competencies, as well as most of the other aspects of project management, continue to exist, but they do so in accelerated form. The question for training in project management has evolved. It now requires delivery of the same level of competency improvements, but in a more efficacious approach.

## Platform Training—The Logical Alternative?

In dozens of training programs around the world, I have lectured students on both the fundamentals and the complexities of project management. Interestingly, I often marvel at how some elements of the lecture have remained unchanged from class to class, from audience to audience. There are components which are effectively static both in their delivery and in their content. As with any presenter, I have caught myself in the awkward moment when I happen to repeat the same war story twice to the same audience. It is during those humbling moments when I wish there were a more effective delivery method.

In conversations with my peers, leadership instructor Barry Smith has often remarked that he truly enjoys the facilitative moments of the classroom experience most. It is not the lecture that inspires him, it is instead the opportunity to spend time one-on-one with the students and the student groups. Other PM instructors whom I respect (Jimmie West and Connie Emerson, to name two) also cite the facilitative moments as the most positive that the classroom has to offer.

In a 1996 PMI symposium paper ( Warren and MacIsaac 1996 ), the authors cite the need to keep training vital and real-world on an ongoing basis. They stress the need for training, which is concurrent with the project management experience in the field. They say that's where the successes will occur.

All of these individuals point to the same key elements. Students need to have a vital, real, personal, shared, interactive experience. That doesn't come out of a computer. However, the shared, interactive experience makes far greater sense when all of the participants share a baseline of knowledge. To get to that point, instructors lecture, review, and guide students to a common level of understanding. This means re-reviewing material, which is old hat to the project management professional (PMP), while (from a different perspective) racing through material that is fresh and new to a novice PM. Branding, separating, and categorizing students is not the answer. In approach after approach with various clients, we have tried to drive organizations to recognize that project management competencies are difficult to assess, even under the best of circumstances. A veteran PM with twenty-five years in the field may still know little or nothing about some of the advances in project management software. A fresh-faced novice may grasp the software with ease but be totally confused about the need for traceability within requirements. The young and the old, the newbie and the vet, all need each other. They need to understand project management through a fresh set of eyes, and often they only meet those eyes across a table in a project management classroom.

## So Which One?

Yes! Distance learning is the key. So is the classroom. The hybrid experience will be the key in the 21st century classroom. Without an emphasis on various media and various pedagogy, project management trainers can anticipate a decline in business. Few customers will seek training provided exclusively through the classroom. Few will seek a complete distance perspective. As customers are challenged by their efforts to deal with that dichotomous perspective, training organizations must be prepared to nurture the customer through the process.

One of the most popularly discussed distance learning experiences to date is the University of Phoenix model. This model is notable for its incorporation of an on-line classroom experience with conventional on-line training. While this is an outstanding start for the next decade, it cannot remain the model. Analyses of students who have taken in excess of five project management training courses in the classroom shows that they find interaction with their peers to be among the greatest assets of the experience. While that can be accomplished *in absentia* to a degree in distance formats (via chat rooms and on-line forums), it cannot be completely replicated.

As we revel in the new century, we can expect training organizations time and again to tout their ability to "Go the distance . . . " and "provide classroom training without the classroom." The trick will be to find the trainer, trainers, or training organizations who ultimately provide a hybrid that matches (and can exceed) the customer organization's goals for time commitments, training objectives, and overall customer satisfaction.

## Who is that Trainer?

Good platform trainers are hard to find. Quality platform trainers who respect other delivery methods are even harder to find. Many perceive distance learning as a threat to their environment. They have for years. I have heard instructors over the past ten years argue that the only *true* education occurs in the classroom. The ubiquity of the Internet is proving (to a limited degree) that such an assertion is a fallacy. There is information available through other media. In many cases, the quality of that delivery is quite good. For many classrooms, it is the multimedia experience, not the facilitator, that makes the difference. In some measure, that *will* be the measure in the years ahead.

The platform trainer who is going to succeed in project management training into the next century will have to be adaptable to all the delivery methods available. Historically, distance learning has meant little more than video, workbooks, and correspondence. With the speed of communication and diversity of delivery now available, the successful project manager will have to be multimedia-conscious and literate. To deny the effectiveness of other media is to be usurped by them. Instead, effective instructors will focus on what I call my CADRE model:

- Cooperation
- Availability
- Delivery
- Relevance
- Edutainment Value

I named it CADRE by virtue of what the word means—*A nucleus of trained personnel around which a larger organization can be built and trained.* Most organizations enter into training relationships or develop training departments in project management in hopes of building a cadre. Based on customer requests and student feedback, instructors who will succeed as the training dynamic changes will be those who recognize each element of the model, and show it on the platform.

## Cooperation

Cooperation goes far deeper than simply working with the customer. It involves working with the *customers,* toward a common goal or purpose. That goal or purpose must be supported by the trainer, and there must be evidence of that in the classroom. The best evidence will not be simple rote memorization of the customer's principles and precepts. Instead, it will be the provision of "best practice" information as it can be applied in the customer environment.

Cooperation does not imply that the trainer should accede to all of the customer's wishes. In fact, customers who do not understand project management training will sometimes suggest pedagogy, which is counter-productive and potentially demoralizing. A classic example came several years ago when a customer went to one of my peer's training organizations and demanded project management training at a variety of levels for introductory PMs, intermediate PMs, and advanced PMs. No project manager wished to be labeled a novice. Only a handful pursued the introductory track. As a result, when the intermediate course began, many of the more seasoned project managers were caught in the awkward position of being educationally behind the newer PMs in the organization and were forced to slow down the class to ensure that they understood the concepts. As one might imagine, a great deal of quality learning time was lost.

The trainers who will succeed are those who will acknowledge that students have something to learn (and often *more* to contribute) at the introductory level and all levels. No level of project management training should lack sufficient challenge. It should all be constructed to ensure that if there is a room full of seasoned managers, they can hone their skills on the whetstone of the classroom. If PM training is properly presented, even a twenty-five-year veteran can identify new lessons learned and applications understood in a quality classroom environment.

In dealing with parent organizations, however, cooperation will also mean acknowledging their need to modify delivery methodologies from past models. Customer organizations rarely want a training package without at least *some* customization. The challenge for the trainer is to know his delivery capabilities without taking on an adventure in vaporware. The allure of hybrid delivery is to be able to promise a great deal without developing deliverables in advance. The terror of the hybrids is the demand that the training be brought on-line (on disk, on video, over satellite) immediately. Cooperation includes an intense level of honesty with the customer. Customers would rather hear alternative approaches than cope with veiled promises on an alternative approach as "in beta" and "just around the corner."

## Availability

The Internet, cyberspace, teleconferencing, and videoconferencing give the impression that virtually anything can be accomplished in real time. Customers may believe that there should be little or no delay between the original request and delivery of the product or service. Nowhere is this more true than for platform training. Customers often determine they want training only after extensive internal discussion and argument. When they finally determine training is appropriate for their project management organization, they want it fast. Interestingly, they expect training materials development to be quicker than their decision to move ahead. The trainer or training organization who succeeds in the decades ahead will have clear availability and an understanding that clients who cannot see significant progress quickly will seek out other trainers.

This does not mean that the "lone ranger" consultant is in jeopardy. If anything, this enhances her value. Having solo trainers with the capacity to back up major training organizations will likely become a more prevalent business trend. However, the solo trainers who succeed will be those who have the flexibility and the subject matter expertise to step in and perform admirably on extremely short notice. One solution will be to establish these relationships in advance with training organizations. Although it is not yet common practice, anticipate that customers will request that their back-up consultant(s) or specific internal trainers receive authorization to train the materials in the event that the training provider cannot meet the requested schedule. Since this will be limited to a one- or two-trainer scenario, it will preclude the contractually difficult "train-the-trainer" arrangement and will still allow the customer enhanced flexibility.

## Delivery

As a component of that flexibility, delivery must be integrated. Instructors who attempt to teach their materials in a vacuum will invariably disappoint their customers. As the classroom incorporates more and more diverse components, instructors must be familiar with all of them. In the early days of facilitated learning, all Socrates needed was a willing group of students and their minds. Over the years, different components have been added to the mix. Workbooks, textbooks, software, videos, overheads, and a wealth of other tools are all part of the presentation. The instructor who teaches in this environment must know all of the instructional materials, and know them intimately. Students expect the instructor to know what was said in the on-line experience just as they know what's said in a textbook. As hybrid instructional environments become more commonplace, students will expect the instructor to be familiar with all of the components of the hybrid. In other words, the instructor should reinforce the video, which reinforces the textbook, which reinforces what's said on-line, which reinforces the teaching objective. Any breaks in that chain are noticeable and detrimental.

This means that instructors will have to do more homework. Instructors who have subject matter expertise will not get by on that expertise alone. They'll be expected to have perspective on what has been said in all of the other elements of the instructional environment.

In addition, their delivery approach will be expected to be consistent. In the publishing industries, there is what's known as "trade dress." That's the look or feel that a particular publishing house, catalog, magazine, or advertisement always has. Think of *Time* magazine. The familiar red border identifies it as *Time*. If the word "Time" in the next issue appeared in white print in a blue box in the upper-left-hand corner of the magazine, it might be mistaken for *U.S. News*. It's noteworthy that *Time*'s Internet sites (http://www.timemag.com.au) also have the same familiar look and feel. You get what you expect.

In delivery, the art comes in knowing and understanding all of the components and presenting the material in the same fashion. If the videos are bright and lively and the instructor is grim, there can be a serious disconnect between the way the materials are perceived and the way the instructor is perceived. It no longer comes across as a training "package." Instead, it may now be perceived as a series of distinct components with different messages. This can occur even if the messages are identical. Image counts on the platform. It will become progressively more vital to ensure that your trade dress matches the expectations of the customer.

## Relevance

No matter the quality of the materials or the instructor, and no matter how well they are integrated with each other, they will be rendered completely ineffective if they are not relevant to the student. Strangely enough, relevance is largely a function of presentation, not content. In a fundamental project management course, many providers offer insights on tools used for project selection. Return on nvestment (ROI) is not, frankly, something many project managers are interested in. Most would rather busy themselves with the end product or the project plan that will get them there. "I don't get to participate in project selection," they will argue. "I really don't need to know this stuff."

The critical issue here is not to argue about course design and a broader understanding of the issue at hand. What *is* critical is to make the issue relevant to the participant. If the organization in which he works does not use ROI, all is not lost. Did the customer use ROI? Is ROI under consideration as a project measure? Is there a chance that he may someday work for another organization? Might *that* organization use ROI? Could he run into the issue on the project management professional certification exam? The participant should find out where and how it *could* become critical in his life. Only then can effective instruction begin. By targeting an issue relative to a group's or an individual's needs, it becomes possible to draw them in to subject matter they might otherwise dismiss (and which could ultimately prove invaluable).

Critical to this process is that the trainer has ensured that all of the materials do, realistically, have the potential to be relevant. While the graphical evaluation review technique (GERT) is a fabulous item for project management professionals to discuss in their free time, it is generally not highly relevant to the project manager doing work in the field. The more esoteric (and unrealistic) an element of subject matter is, the more likely it is to turn off a customer or an end-user.

## Edutainment

To keep the customers (all of them, from the purchasing organization to the student) engaged and excited about the possibilities of the training, it becomes vital to show enthusiasm about the product, the organization, and project management. The most effective instructors will attest to this by virtue of their evaluation forms and "smile sheets" at the end of a class.

*The instructor took dry material and made it come to life! I didn't think anyone could make network diagramming fun. Look out, here comes another Backward Pass!*

Comments like these do not stem from the workbooks, the textbooks, the course materials, or any on-line experience. The challenge is to embrace the materials with sufficient commitment to ensure that students know there are advantages to using the materials and there are ways these materials can make a project (and their lives) easier.

Edutainment may be a "pop" term, but it is not a "pop" approach to training. It does *not* dilute the value or the interest of the content. It is a quality approach to education that keeps the students participating and fully engaged. Think of the activities you enjoy most. Even the most obsessive couch potato will acknowledge that the reason watching television is enjoyable is that the participants become a part of it. Talk to those who love TV, and they will tell you that they allow themselves to "soak in" the story. Talk to those who love sports, and they enjoy being part of the action. The classroom can offer no less. In fact, the Socratic classroom started this process over 2,400 years ago. Rather than idle participants, the students were encouraged to challenge ideas through their arguments. Socrates had followers and disciples (Plato among them). You don't win that kind of loyalty and support if you are remarkably boring. The Socratic classroom of 400 B.C. had to have a reasonably lively atmosphere.

Today, we think it novel and experiential to bring activity into the classroom. It's old hat. But it is *great* old hat. The practice that has been renamed and repackaged for the twenty-first century is Socrates in new clothing—he's in a suit, and he's carrying a laptop.

How can you bring the classroom to life? How do you implement edutainment? Look to the most successful models in all media. John Cleese trains on video with humor. John Naismith captures audiences with intellect and a willingness to share it. Robert Schuller holds an audience with passion for his message. Laura Schlessinger communicates with brutal honesty. Tom Peters communicates with eternal optimism. Can these individuals bring a room to life? Can they communicate well? Can they persuade on a message? Can they make their message memorable? The answer is yes. There will be a name or two in that list that may raise a few hackles with a few individuals. Why? Because they are experts in their craft and they have opinions. The average PMI meeting provides ample evidence of how even a topic as seemingly antiseptic as project management can drive strong opinions. There are schools of thought. The task-oriented versus the product-oriented WBS. The resource-driven schedule versus the date-driven schedule. Arguments can extend for hours. The effective instructor will take a lesson from those listed above, recognizing the merits of the various arguments, but acknowledging one as being best practice. That does not mean the other practices are inappropriate or are not more utilitarian in a given environment, but it does give a sense that there are, indeed, best practices. Failure to stake a claim on what are best practices eliminates any argument that project management itself can be a best practice.

The tools to bring these components to life manifest themselves according to the strengths of the instructor. Among the most effective tools are:

- Humor
- Depth of insight
- Passion
- Openness
- Optimism

These tools operate effectively when they are tied closely to the four other components of the CADRE model. Noticeably absent are the qualities of enlightenment, understanding, and empathy, to name but a few. Those elements (which are invaluable in the training environment) become the by-products of quality education.

## Will I make it in the next century?

The more instructors do to apply themselves within the models established here, the more opportunities they have to succeed. It is not a function of pure dynamism or charisma. It is a function of hard work and research. Passion does not require Dale Carnegie classes. It requires a commitment to fundamental concepts and a belief in the validity of those concepts. Humor can just as readily spring from a deadpan expression as from a jovial presenter. Depth of insight is not inborn. It is nurtured and developed over a long period of time through research, discussion, and an open mind. Openness requires an understanding of personal limitations, as well as capabilities, and a willingness to express them and listen to others. Optimism in PM training is a function of the belief that there is inherent value in the work we do. By wedding these components to the model cited above instructors will flourish and will continue to flourish on the platform.

Platform training is not going by the wayside just by virtue of new media and new approaches. If anything, the demands on platform instructors will continue to evolve into more and more of a specialty. Those who know how to maneuver within this environment, as outlined within the CADRE model,will have the edge in preparing for, delivering, and evaluating training.

## Book

Frame, J. Davidson. 1995. *Managing Projects in Organizations*. San Francisco, CA. Jossey-Bass.

## Paper

Warren, Peter J., and Steven J. MacIsaac. 1996. "Concurrent Project Management Training." *PMI Symposium Papers*. Boston, MA.: Project Management Institute.

# The Class of 2010: Project Management in Adult Education

Michael J. Seiden, MS,Western International University, Phoenix, AZ
Donna M. Stout, MAED, Western International University, Phoenix, AZ
Kenneth G. Bobis, Information Systems, Western International University, Phoenix, AZ; Application Development FHMB, AlliedSignal Aerospace, MS&S Business Systems, Phoenix, AZ

## Introduction

A revolution is occurring in adult higher education. Driven by such issues as corporate downsizing, rapid technology advances, and competition for jobs, working adults are returning to school in large numbers. This new breed of student differs from the traditional college student in that today's student typically has a demanding job and is often married with a family. While she feels that further education is necessary for her professional development and future employment, she views education as a means to an end and is, in large part, an opportunist. Often it is the type of program that attracts a prospective student to a school and not necessarily the content of the program. Since they must maintain the delicate balance between work, home, and school, today's students demand alternative delivery methods to those practiced in the past. Evening and Saturday classes are a must. Independent studies and flexible schedules are preferred.

Due to this increased business opportunity, "for-profit" educational institutions, such as Western International University (WIU), are providing a "customer-focused" approach that is resulting in a market-share shift away from traditional degree-granting institutions. This success is due, in large part, to the ability of these companies to move quickly to establish alternate course delivery methods. Due to competition, successful organizations have become truly customer-focused as practiced for years in the manufacturing sector. No longer can an institution have a "take-it-or-leave-it" attitude towards professionals who are paying substantial tuition and demanding comparable educational value in return.

Distance learning is one genre of alternative delivery methods. The ability to educate students no matter where they are located in the world is attractive to education companies for whom tuition is the primary source of income and increased shareholder equity is a must. This trend will continue well into the twenty-first century assisted by advances in technology, which make knowledge of personal computers and the Internet basic requirements for entry into the workforce. Educators are thereby being challenged to develop a "virtual classroom" which will help bring education to the student anytime, anywhere.

This paper focuses on the demands of this new educational arena and specifically the issues involved in a project to develop a virtual classroom environment. It references a pilot project conducted by Western International University in which a class was presented to students on its London, England, campus by a faculty member located in Phoenix, Arizona, utilizing the Internet as the primary means of communication. The project manager responsible for this project was faced with several challenges that had to be addressed to ensure success.

## The Changing Face of Education

Among the critical issues faced by higher education are accountability, quality of programs and services, economic viability and responsiveness, flexible course delivery, and curriculum relevancy. These schools are experiencing evolutionary change from the traditional vertically integrated "industrial age" campus model to a networked "information age" virtual model. Literally, the brick and mortal walls are being replaced by information highways providing customers/students in higher education with virtual access to services on a global scale.

Dr. John Sperling, president and CEO of the Apollo Group Inc. (Apollo), the parent company of WIU, states, "It is only by transforming education from something accomplished prior to entering the workforce to a life-long process that America can regain its competitive position in the global economy." (Sperling 1989). These concerns are confirmed by the Wingspread Group, leaders in higher education and industry, in its 1993 report, "America Imperative: Higher Expectations for Higher Education." This report addresses the concern for the future of education in this way: "A disturbing and dangerous mismatch exists between what American society needs of higher education and what it is receiving. The imperative for the 21st century is that society must hold higher education to much higher expectations or risk national decline." Dr. Carol

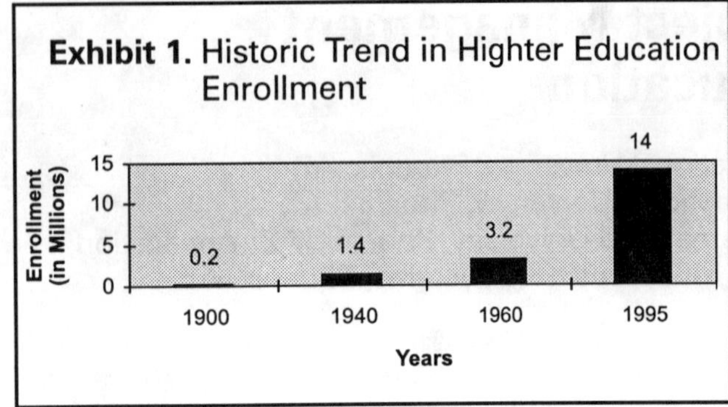


Twigg maintains changes in higher education occur in response to two kinds of external factors: "society's expectations of what constitutes a college education (what students 'need to know' ) and the delivery mechanisms or technologies available to serve those expectations." (Twigg 1997). Dr. Twigg also believes that the changing needs of business are reflected in workplace trends such as life-long learning, knowledge explosions, new skills and competencies, telecommuting, home-based businesses, and increasing emphasis on improved productivity.

## Movement Towards Adult Education

Over the years, the size and structure of higher education has changed dramatically. Exhibit 1 shows the steadily increasing numbers of students enrolled in degree-granting institutions.

It is generally acknowledged that each person in today's workforce will need thirty credit hours of instruction over each seven-year period in order to stay current and employable. This means that at any one time, one seventh of the workforce, or twenty million workers, will be involved in some type of organized education. Some of these individuals may be degree-seeking students while others will only be refreshing existing skills. Since this thirty-credit hour figure is probably underestimated (4.3 hours/year), this challenge is very attraction to higher education companies while perhaps overwhelming to traditional degree-granting institutions. As a matter of fact, many major United States corporations advocate forty hours of annual training for each employee. Add to this basic demand the need for existing workers to obtain formal degrees, and the demand on the system increases.

## The Apollo Group, Inc., and Western International University (WIU) Model

The Apollo Group, Inc., the parent company of the University of Phoenix, Western International University, and the Institute for Professional Development has 55,000 currently enrolled students. It offers degrees in business, management, and other professions to working adults in twenty-nine states, Puerto Rico, and England, along with its online campus. Last fall, *Forbes* magazine ranked it number three among the two hundred best small companies in America (Larson 1997).

The teaching/learning model of the Apollo Group, Inc., provides working adults, both domestic and international, with affordable, accessible, flexible, and continuous higher education and training. The Apollo philosophy focuses on: practitioner faculty (working professionals in the field); a competency-based curriculum delivered in a compressed format (an emphasis on learning, not just classroom contact hours); flexible course scheduling; accessible locations; and multi-delivery modes. Classes consist of working professionals averaging 35 years of age, with the average class size only fifteen students. Courses are provided at centralized locations, on-site at major corporations, and through multi-technology delivery options. These include traditional classroom, directed study, independent study, distance learning (online), and experiential learning..

Western International University is accredited by the North Central Association (NCA) to offer courses and degree programs leading to the associate's degree, bachelor in arts and science degrees, and master's degrees in business. These programs are offered at the main campus in Phoenix, Arizona, and teaching sites in Arizona and London, England. Western International University utilizes the Apollo teaching/learning model with an international emphasis throughout the curriculum and degree programs.

## Education for Profit

The major operational elements of the Apollo system are the governing board, administration, staff, faculty, and students. The academic governance addresses curriculum, academic affairs, and faculty involvement in the university. This system is unique in its dual approach of operations management and academic governance.

Apollo and WIU are for-profit, education systems in which the board defines policies and business strategies, the administration develops operational procedures that the staff carries through, and the governance oversees the quality and integrity of the programs being delivered, with all parties participating with students/customers in creating the dynamics of the learning process. As adult learners, the students have an active role in the education process during their course work through sharing and applying knowledge and expertise, actively participating in groups/activities, and by providing feedback to faculty and administrative services on the quality of instruction, curriculum, facilities, and services.

## Education on a Global Scale

The development of technologies and the explosive growth of these networks provide opportunities for educational programs to be available to students globally by moving toward combining technological capabilities with educational needs. Western International University's mission is to infuse an international perspective and the use of technology throughout the content of all degree programs. This approach uniquely positions it to take advantage of the opportunity to provide higher education to student/customers worldwide.

## Project Management in Education

There are a number of distinct differences between the traditional educational environment and the adult-oriented, non-traditional educational environment which can significantly impact the management of projects. Western International University management experiences these differences as a for-profit, private university, which provides educational programs primarily to working adults.

## Contrasting Styles of Education

The contrast between traditional education and the WIU model of education will focus on several elements: educational schedules, facilities, faculty, curriculum, and organizational structure.

In the traditional university, education is presented in terms or semesters, generally sixteen weeks in length with a nearly three-month break over the summer months. At the start of a semester, registration is completed, course assignments are made, materials and books are distributed, and faculty and students are established in the courses. In non-traditional universities, courses can start as frequently as every month throughout the year. At WIU, in order to allow students to complete their degree requirements in a compressed timeframe, there is no summer break. Administrative activities, such as registration and faculty scheduling, are ongoing processes with little time between sessions to analyze, organize, and restructure events. Therefore, while in a traditional institution, concentration on project components may take place during some of the "dead" administrative time between the start and end of semesters, in a non-traditional institution the project is always competing for time with a never-ending array of administrative tasks.

Non-traditional universities have, in many cases, brought the education to the students, rather than requiring students to come to the education. Traditional universities are rapidly adopting this approach, as well. Courses are offered at a number of sites—auxiliary campuses, corporate training centers, office buildings, hospitals, military bases, and hotels. Projects must incorporate this multiplicity of locations and sites in planning the delivery of the educational product. This often increases the complexity of the project and the need for coordination by removing the known deployment environment. In many cases, networked communication is required to insure that there is adequate opportunity for input and communication from various personnel at the dispersed sites.

Traditional and non-traditional universities alike are continuing to evolve systems for distance education. Current trends indicate that, as our population ages and the workplace becomes more complex, more and more students are requesting to participate in the education process without leaving home and/or the workplace. Distance education delivery systems that utilize the Internet and other forms of information technology increase the complexity of projects and require that those who develop the projects possess a sufficient level of knowledge of information technology and the capability to use that knowledge. The unpredictable and unreliable nature of the privately administered Internet results in a critical project component whose reliability is beyond the control of the project team.

There are often substantial differences between faculty at traditional and non-traditional institutions. Faculty at traditional institutions are employed full-time by the institution, have offices and, in most cases, tenure. They have specific schedules for their various work-related activities: teaching, advising, academic governance, and curriculum development. While traditional institutions also utilize adjunct faculty, non-traditional institutions make much more extensive use of adjunct faculty. In many cases, these adjunct faculty have full-time positions outside of the institution. They teach on a course-by-course basis, often have no on-campus offices, and their stake in the university is often limited. Since faculty are key constituents in any project involving the institution's educational product, it is important that project managers motivate these educators and secure the support of these part-time employees. The project risk assessment usually contains several substantial aspects that result from this highly leveraged use of adjunct faculty. In addition, it is more difficult to communicate with adjunct faculty than with full-time faculty. Media such as electronic mail, video conferencing, and the Internet have become essential in maintaining effective communications.

Curriculum is often taken for granted in the educational environment. However, in "education for profit" it is the essence of the educational product. In today's rapidly changing environment, curriculum—especially in technology-related fields—must be kept current, and it must be effectively distributed to faculty and students. With respect to achieving currency and a common understanding , it is important, once again, to communicate with faculty, which tends to be somewhat more difficult in a non-traditional environment. However, since most of the non-traditional faculty are working in their professional areas, they can bring a high level of current knowledge to the curriculum development process. Distribution of curriculum is an essential element. Since many non-traditional students seldom, if ever, actually visit the main campus, the means must be developed to insure that they receive course syllabi, textbooks, and materials. Projects associated with non-traditional delivery systems must include components of such delivery systems.

While the organizational structures of most traditional universities have served their institutions reasonably well over the years, these organizations tend to be bureaucratic, with many different constituencies. It often takes a long time to reach consensus on major issues and come to a decision. It is also often difficult to remove a non-productive member of the project team due to tenure or other academic protection. Many non-traditional institutions, on the other hand, are organized utilizing the for-profit business model, focusing on customer service and separating the administrative and academic functions, so that decisions can be made in a more timely manner. Once decisions are made, they can be communicated and enforced more directly.

## A Project Management Approach for Adult Education

Traditionally, educational institutions have been comprised of disparate departments and disciplines that did not necessarily consider a team approach necessary for individual success. Infusion of business principles to the educational setting will have a major cultural impact on organizations who never had to adhere to a rigid schedule of project deliverables.

As a result of the unique aspects of adult, non-traditional education, a project management approach has been selected that effectively fits this model. The first step in this approach is to develop the project in the same manner as one would in any well-managed organization. This includes the development of a small, but effective, project team; planning the project in a well-structured manner; and use of information technology to develop, monitor, and revise the project plan and implement an effective communications environment that will insure that all affected parties are part of that communications environment.

Students, faculty, administrators, and university management are all deeply involved in the project. The project plan is developed by forming a small team with representation from each of these constituencies and developing a plan that meets their requirements. The team is led by a faculty member who has experience in project management, information technology, and teaching non-traditional students. A project management software tool (Microsoft *Project*) is used for defining and managing all projects within the university. The project time line is developed and the milestones selected in order to provide small, achievable results that indicate progress and maintain an atmosphere of enthusiasm and confidence in the approach and execution.

The approach to projects has been that small projects are better than large projects (large projects can be broken down into smaller projects). The smaller projects can produce results in short time frames. These results can be extended and built in a step-by-step process, adding complexity and a broader perspective over time. Larger projects can threaten the enthusiasm of the employees and the commitment of management when results are not readily apparent.

For-profit education companies are becoming national and global organizations in an effort to provide a steady history of expansion and value for the investor. This leads to a wide range of issues due to the distance involved between central and local administrators. Among these are policies and procedures that are set by local certification boards that are active throughout the world.

## The Virtual Classroom Project

The virtual classroom project has two goals. The first is to provide the ability for students throughout the southwestern United States to take part in a class from their individual home or work locations. The second is to provide the ability to use faculty members located in the United States to teach classes in the United Kingdom, Europe, and Asia. Due to WIU's charter to provide education on a global scale, the traditions and sensitivities of the world community had to be taken under consideration when planning the virtual classroom. For example, in the United Kingdom a course centers around the in-class lecture, often with no textbook available to the student. This puts substantial pressure and additional responsibility on the faculty member to cover the material completely enough to provide the student with all that is needed for full comprehension. This presents a different requirement from many existing distance learning programs that employ bulletin boards, audio tapes, video tapes, e-mail, chat groups, and reading assignments to meet the course objectives. The virtual classroom is designed to provide the student with the same traditional classroom experience without requiring collocation with the instructor. While this has been done before by traditional universities—by means of satellite television and cable television networks such as the Mind Extension University—the WIU current approach is inherently different. The virtual classroom project was designed to provide these same benefits utilizing common Internet technology. Its goal is to produce the same learning results with the only cost being that of an Internet connection.

The virtual classroom project included a pilot project in which an undergraduate BASIC programming class was presented to students on WIU's London campus by a faculty member located in Phoenix, Arizona. All evaluations received from this pilot indicated high student/instructor satisfaction with the quality of course content, the use of technology in real time interactions and feedback during the learning process, and requests for further course offerings utilizing "virtual" delivery modalities. These positive results were encouraging even though some of the original technology (namely real-time voice) was somewhat uneven in its performance.

The classroom environment was created through the use of Microsoft's *NetMeeting* software. *NetMeeting* provides all of the capabilities of a traditional classroom including real-time video, shared personal computer software applications, whiteboarding, chat, and real-time voice.

The real-time video, while at four frames/second is substantially slower than television at thirty frames/ second, does provide the students with a visual connection to their instructor. Using the shared PC software applications, the instructor can develop the lecture in Microsoft's *Powerpoint* and make it available to the students for downloading and printing before class. This enhances the learning process by making the class notes available to the student before class. They can, therefore, concentrate on the lecture and not on taking comprehensive notes. *NetMeeting's* whiteboarding feature mimics the traditional use of a blackboard. It is a bit more advanced because multiple whiteboards can be maintained and randomly referred to throughout the lecture. Additionally, the instructor can prepare an example on a whiteboard and store it for future reference. Moreoever, multiple pen colors can be used on a single whiteboard to highlight key concepts. The Chat capability is just like that used in many bulletin board systems. However, due to its text-only nature, it should probably only be used during system setup and debugging sessions. While full-duplex voice is possible with *NetMeeting,* it is still too immature to use as a practical means of communication, resulting in fragmented or partial speech. However, this is only a temporary situation. As the speed of personal computers increase past the 200Mhz level and 56,000 BPS modems become commonplace, products such as *NetMeeting* will be able to sustain speech in an acceptable manner. In the interim, a standard speaker phone was used at both the central and remote locations. This solution highlights the value of using new technology to gain valuable experience though some of its aspects may need improvement.

## The Virtual Classroom Project and the Project Management Body of Knowledge (PMBOK)

Several aspects of the virtual classroom project presented project management challenges. Among these are: project scope management, communications management, human resource management, risk management, and procurement management.

### Project Scope Management

While the project's owners and sponsors are internal to WIU, its requirements are being dictated by external forces: the students. Since the students are not a part of the university and are ever-changing, gathering their requirements poses a unique problem. One of the primary issues is that they are not under any obligation to provide feedback on the results of the project. If their needs are not met by WIU, they may just go elsewhere without explaining their actions. As such, the business owners of the project may never fully know if the needs of the student population were met. Suggestions for gathering project requirements include: focus groups, end-of-course surveys, onsite industry sessions, surveys, canvassing, prototypes, and a pilot project.

### Communications Management

Time zone and cultural differences had to be considered for the proper conduct of the virtual classroom. Practitioner faculty are generally employed in demanding jobs during the day, yet find time to present the 6–10 p.m. class sessions. For classes offered to students in the southwestern United States this is not a major issue. However, if a 6 p.m. course is to be presented in the United Kingdom by United States-based faculty, the instructor would have to be free from 10 a.m.—2 p.m. (Phoenix time) to conduct the course. If the class time in the United Kingdom is shifted to noon, the United States-based faculty would have to awake in enough time to begin the lecture at 4 a.m. (Phoenix time). Not many employers would be so understanding as to allow such absences on a recurring basis.

Administration of examinations is different in the virtual classroom. Tests must either be interactive in nature or structured as "take home" examinations. Moreover, if the identity of the student is not verified by some failsafe method, a "stand-in" could complete the examination causing a distrust that the results are reflective of the actual student's work. A simple solution is to require a proctored examination at a mutually conducive location, but this diminishes the virtual nature of the project. In the pilot project, the exam was proctored in London by local WIU staff.

### Human Resource Management

Project deadlines are generally extended in traditional academia. If a project is delayed due to an ineffective worker, it is usually hard to replace that worker with another due to tenure and the inefficiencies of the organization. Moreover, time zone differences put a large responsibility on faculty members to either arise early (4 a.m. (MST)) for a noon class in the United Kingdom or schedule into their normal work day, as was previously mentioned. Faculty members who agree to partake in the classes generally are truly examples of educators who sacrifice their own comforts due to their passion for learning.

### Procurement Management

Import restrictions often prevent products from being purchased in the U.S. and drop-shipped to the United Kingdom. During the pilot project, orders for two products were placed with the domestic representatives of companies with European distribution channels, but were never processed properly to be shipped to London.

### Risk Management

The risk involved in the virtual classroom is substantial due to the relative immaturity of the hardware and software tools currently available and the privately administered nature of the Internet. Before a larger roll-out is conducted, a substantial risk assessment must be performed that anticipates problems and provides fallback capabilities to maintain a class session in the event of hardware or software failure.

## Conclusion

All indications show that the need to bring education to the students by means of distance learning will continue to be a requirement of the adult education market for the foreseeable future. Schools that experiment with this emerging technology stand to gain a competitive edge on traditional institutions that cannot move as quickly to respond to changing market conditions and technologies. However, such projects are not without their risks and provide unique challenges to project management in the educational community.

### References

Larson, J. 1997. *Apollo Group rockets to 10h place.* The Arizona Republic ( May 18).

Sperling, J. G. 1989. *Against All Odds.* Phoenix, AZ: Apollo Press.

Twigg, C. A. 1997. *Meeting Tomorrow's Learning Needs.* Speech presented at NCA Annual Conference in Chicago, Ill.

# A New Model for Training Project Managers

Aaron J. Shenhar, Stevens Institute of Technology
Brian Nofzinger, Harmon AutoGlass

## Introduction

As many newly appointed, young project managers discover, they get very little training upon becoming managers. Having excelled previously in technical or functional roles, they assume project management responsibility without much preparation either from the organization or from their side. Furthermore, the little training that is offered is typically focused on the details of how to make a specific package work or the use of scheduling and other tools. For the most part, project managers are left alone to figure out how to manage the myriad issues of getting the project done: project buy-in, establishing scope, leading people, and creating the right vision.

This paper suggests moving beyond the tool-based project management training. Its premise is that project management is more than just a practice or application of tools. Effective project management requires the right "state of mind," or attitude and style, and to become an effective project manager one needs to develop this attitude and select the right style that will be congruent with the project environment and the manager's personality. This article is based on extensive studies in recent years, which involved more than 250 projects, and it provides a framework and a new model for project management understanding and training.

To develop this new model for training and learning, this paper integrates several frameworks (including our own) that were developed in recent years for a better understanding of project management. The integrative framework for learning includes the mindset, the skill-set, the learning strategies, and continuous improvement. To augment project management learning and training, organizations and individuals may follow the steps suggested in this model to develop coherent and effective competencies in project management.

## Developing the Attitude and Mindset I: Using Frameworks for Understanding Project Management

In order to understand more about the discipline of project management, we first present several frameworks that will be helpful in understanding and conceptualizing project management. Each framework defines the concepts of project management from a different perspective.

### The Skillset Framework of A Project Manager

The following framework was developed by Paul Dinsmore (1984). It assumes that a strong managerial slant is needed to carry out the tasks of project management. It then identifies the necessary skills for project management, as listed below:

**Leadership Skills**: clear direction and leadership; technical problem solving; setting goals and objectives; ability to foster teamwork; delegating; sound decision-making

**Technical Expertise**: understanding the technologies relevant to the project; understanding the applications, markets, and customer requirements; managing technology; assessing risks and trade-offs; predicting technology trends; assisting in problem solving; communicating effectively with technical team members and on technical topics

**Human Skills**: team building; motivating team members; managing conflict; communication; creating a positive project environment; involving senior management

**Administrative Skills**: project planning; resource negotiations; securing commitments; creating measurable milestones; establishing operating procedures; maintaining reporting and review systems; managing project controls; effective use of management tools and techniques; effective resource planning

**Organizational Skills**: ability to navigate in the organization; building multi-functional work teams; working effectively with senior management; understanding organizational interfaces; setting up an effective project organization

**Entrepreneurial Skills**: general management perspective; managing a project as a business; meeting profit objectives; developing new and follow-on business.

The skill-set framework should help managers and organizations develop awareness of what is needed in their personal and organizational development programs. It could help identify areas of strengths and weaknesses and develop a strategy to compensate and overcome these weaknesses.

### The Adaptive Project Management Approach

This framework is focused on differences among projects, assuming that all projects cannot be completed while using the same techniques. Furthermore, to increase project effectiveness, managers must identify their project type and adapt their style, processes, tools, and people to the specific project type. To help in identifying the proper style we suggest using the framework developed by Shenhar (1997). According to this framework, projects can be classified according to four levels of technological uncertainty and three levels of system scope or complexity.

The adaptive management approach should help managers and organizations determine among various types of projects what is the right approach to each project. It may help in selecting the proper project manager and the team members and in determining the planning, the systems, and the tools used.

### The Simultaneous Management Approach

This framework, which was conceived by Alexander Laufer (1997), assumes that project management requires the continuous balancing of contending demands, simultaneously responding to contradicting forces. It consists of nine principles that are organized into three areas: planning, leadership and integration, and systems, as follows.

**Planning**: systematic and integrative planning, making timely and stable decisions, and isolation and absorption

Leadership and Integration: inward and outward leadership, early downstream involvement, and multi-disciplinary teams

Systems: intensive communication, simple procedures, and systematic monitoring.

The simultaneous management approach should help project managers realize that project management is a multifaceted activity. It has many contradictory demands, and, unlike technical contributors, as project managers they must be involved with a myriad of contending demands.

### The Project Management Body of Knowledge

Created by the Project Management Institute, this framework maps project management into nine knowledge areas and into thirty-seven processes that are to be conducted across these areas. The knowledge areas include: integration management, scope management, time management, cost management, quality management, human resources management, communications management, risk management, and procurement management.

The project management body of knowledge may help project managers capture and integrate the intricacies of project management and perform the needed functions along the different processes of the knowledge areas.

### Keys to Success as a Project Manager

In his book, *Managing Projects in Organizations* (1987), Davidson Frame identifies five basic principles for making projects succeed. The value of this framework is that it provides project managers with a mindset to carry out their management functions. The principles are: be conscious of what you are doing; invest in the front-end spade work; anticipate problems; go beneath the surface illusions; be flexible.

The perspective of the framework is that with the hectic role that a project manager plays, it is often hard to step back and look at the big picture. By using this framework project managers could develop the right mindset and awareness to critical things that are often overlooked.

### The Cumulative Use of Frameworks

These four frameworks point strongly to the conclusion that new project managers must develop leadership, mindset, attitude, style, communication, and interpersonal skills in order to be successful in project management. The overall education and development of project managers should include exposure and training in the different frameworks before one moves to the tools and applications.

## Developing the Attitude and Mindset II: Building Your Personal Set of Skills and Mindset

Project management is not a science and not a technical activity. It is, to a large extent, a personal trip, and different people have to travel it via different routes. There is no one best way to approach it and do the travel. One needs to learn to "think like a manager" but to develop his or her own style and awareness. Project managers must understand and diagnose situations and adjust their style and process to the situation and task.

This section identifies several personal mindsets that will help project managers develop their own style with greater depth and speed.

### Maintaining a Personal Vision and a Value System

The ideal situation is that new project managers (as with any profession) are motivated by their own personal and professional aspirations to be a part of the profession and to raise their skill levels. Project management is about leading people, and a prerequisite for leading people is having a personal vision and sense of direction. Project managers should also be cognoscente of and sensitive to their value systems (Frame 1987) while establishing and maintaining the personal vision, a set of values, and creative tension.

Project managers that have this kind of mindset may find that they are less frustrated with their occasional failures and able to learn better from them because they will view them as a part of a struggle that will take place over time. They will also be seen as more credible, which will increase their influence and leadership abilities.

### Re-Assess and Develop Basic Skills

The basic traits that make up a good project manager may be substantially different than the traits that make a good technical staff worker. When making the transition from technical work to project management, it is essential to evaluate basic work and style characteristics and begin tuning them towards a career in project management.

Robert Block's book, *The Politics of Projects* (1983), recommends assessing your capabilities on common skill-sets. Stress the fundamentals of communication and management styles, and perform self evaluation. Tune interactions towards strengths or towards building new capabilities. Look for opportunities to improve or update skills (examples below). Maintain a mindset towards improvement. It is often necessary to leave your "comfort zone" in order to improve your skills.

### Understanding Personal Styles

"There is nothing so unequal as the equal treatment of unequals." People are different and inconsistent. There are as many different approaches to life and work as there are people. For a project manager to be effective, he or she will need to be able to work with many different people with many different styles and ability levels.

One of the most popular tools for assessing personality types is the Myers Briggs Type Indicator (MBTI) based on the work of Carl Jung. The MBTI measures four categories of behavior. Each category is measured on a continuum between two temperament variables. This leads to sixteen different personality types, depending upon one's leanings in each of the categories. The four dimensions are: Extrovert(E)—Introvert(I), Sensing(S)—Intuition(N), Thinking(T)—Feeling(F), and Judging(J)—Perceiving(P).

The Myers Briggs Type Indicator is designed to indicate how people will behave. As such, the test is normally used more as a tool for understanding others and for team building, than as a forecast of a person's ability to perform in any given role.

### Maintain a Systemic View

Complexity within an organization can be characterized into one of two types: detail and dynamic (Senge 1990). Managing detail complexity is a matter of identifying and managing many different variables. Examples would include managing inventory reorder points in an inventory system, or writing instructions to assemble a machine. However, managing dynamic complexity would involve identifying cause and effect relationships that are subtle or separated by time or organizational structure.

Project management is clearly a problem of dynamic complexity. As such, project managers will need to look deeply to understand the cause and effect relationships that exist and operate within an organization. These may be separated organizationally or by time from the events that the project manager has direct control over. However, looking for solutions to problems with dynamic complexity will allow the project manager to create solutions that are of the greatest management leverage.

### Develop Your Leadership Style

The project manager has a responsibility to provide leadership throughout the project to all individuals associated with or reliant on the project. The relationships will most likely be different for every project, and the project manager will need to be adaptive.

Project managers must develop a variety of leadership styles that permit them to respond appropriately to the challenges of their individual projects and the issues that they face. Some decisions will be more authoritative in nature, while others will be delegated or highly participate. The choice of style is based on the situation that is faced.

### Develop Problem Solving Skills

A key skill for project managers is the ability to solve problems. The following is a generic template for solving problems of most any kind (Block 1983): define the problem, assess the environment, identify goals, assess your own capabilities, develop solutions, and test and refine the solutions.

### Develop Communication Skills

No single skill-set is more important than the ability to communicate well. This will include all levels within the organization and all types of communication. Improving communication skills will improve the ability to perform all of the other skill-sets effectively. Interpersonal and communication skills normally require a higher investment for improvement and each individual will have different needs with regard to improving communications, and each organization will have different requirements.

## The Learning Strategies in Project Management

Developing understanding through frameworks and skill-sets can be performed in many ways. Yet, each project manager will obviously have his or her own preferences as to how to pursue the process of learning project management. They will also have their own development needs that must be assessed. However, the following basic learning strategies will very likely be included in every project manager's development to one extent or another. It is important to understand what can be expected from these learning strategies and to understand how they can impact the learning process for project managers.

### Self Reading and Coursework

Project managers can increase their understanding of the project management skill-sets through readings and coursework. These methods can introduce a project manager to the basic theory of the skill-sets and many different thoughts as to how to apply or implement them. They can also provide ideas and approaches that wouldn't be considered otherwise by the project manager or the project participants.

It is important, however, to understand the limitations of this learning strategy. Most readings and coursework will not be oriented specifically to the local project environment and appropriately address its specific constraints. Also, the understanding that comes from this type of learning will most likely not be as deep as learning that comes from experience.

### Personal Experience

In most cases, knowledge of how to run projects is not acquired through a systematic process. The literature and our interviews point consistently to experiential learning as the backbone learning strategy for project managers. Project managers learn to carry out projects successfully by working on them and "learning the ropes." Project managers can maximize the benefits of experiential learning by:

**Learning from Failure** : Making a point to learn from failures; visualize them as opportunities and as a natural part of the learning experience and development process.

**Complementing with Other Learning Strategies:** Complement experiential learning with the other learning strategies (reading, coaching) in order to understand what other options might be (or have been) available.

**Sharing Experiences:** Sharing experiences with other project managers and listening to the experiences of other project managers.

**Reflection:** Look back on experiences and try to understand what was done right and what was done wrong.

**Iterations:** Repetition will provide opportunities to learn by performing tasks over and over again.

### Mentoring and Coaching

Mentoring with supervisors and managers with more experience and insight is a key development strategy for project managers. This can help project managers because these strategies allow the project manager to see and benefit from the perspectives of other experienced managers.

Although this is true, there is sometimes very little precedent in an organization for mentoring or coaching to occur. Also, it would appear that the depth of learning from this method depends greatly on the trust and rapport that can be developed with the mentor or coach.

## Continuous Improvement: The Process of Constant Learning in Project Management

The process of learning project management is highly experiential and will vary greatly due to the individual needs of the project manager and the project environment. However, it is a never-ending process and it goes on throughout the entire career of the project manager. The following provides a framework for the experiential process of continuous learning in project management. It is a combination of the "Deming Cycle" and Peter "Limits to Growth" system archetype and creative rension concepts.

### The Deming Cycle

**Plan:** The first step in the process is establishing a goal or personal vision. The goal for a project manager might be: "To excel at project management in the information systems industry". Next, you must assess and understand current capabilities and knowledge levels. Then plan: "What do I need to learn in order to improve my methods on this project task?". The end result of this stage of the cycle is to identify the actions that will be taken on the project or on a specific project task.

**Do:** Since learning project management is usually experiential, in this part of the cycle the actions identified in the plan stage will be tested in actual project work.

**Study:** Study the outcome and evaluate whether the action was a good one. If it was not, another plan to carry out the project activity will have to be tested the next time.

**Act:** Did the plan work? Our possible actions are: implement the change; try another method; abandon the change. Basically, we decide whether the change or approach that we tested was a good one. If it is, of course, we will use this approach again. Note that the current base of knowledge is always enhanced by these learning activities, whether they are successfully implemented or not.

### Limits to Growth

Growth in project management will not be without struggle and setbacks. There are always some negative forces that keep us from realizing our personal vision or efforts to grow as a project manager. These forces will counteract our continuous improvement cycle and work to slow our growth. These forces could be environmental factors or personal habits that limit our ability to succeed. An example would be a project manager whose success at previous projects has won him or her the opportunity to manage a rather large project. However, this hypothetical person begins to sense discomfort in large groups, which inhibits them from calling large meetings or assembling the project group for important communications.

Addressing such limitations openly and frankly will remove a barrier to future growth for the project manager and will improve performance on the project at hand.

## Conclusion

This paper has studied the topic of project management using frameworks existing in literature and interviews with practicing project managers. Clearly, project management is not learned through a systematic process and project managers are seldom groomed, mentored, or otherwise prepared to perform their duties. Rather, project management is learned experientially in a hit and miss fashion that is mostly driven by the project manager. Most organizational training is still focused on low leverage concepts and techniques while neglecting high-leverage concepts like the human, organizational, or interpersonal aspects of project management.

The framework developed in this paper may help project managers and organizations see the project management learning experience in a more systematic way. It provides the frameworks to deal with this question rigorously and comprehensively. The framework has the following components: donceptual frameworks to understand project management, developing a personal mindset, strategies for learning project management, and continuous improvement in project management.

The framework can be used to guide project managers in their efforts to learn the profession. It does so by targeting the necessary skill-sets for project management, identifying relevant learning strategies, proposing a process for learning, and suggesting some mindsets that can enhance the learning process.

### References


Block, Robert. 1983. *The Politics of Projects.*

Dinsmore, Paul C. 1984. *Human Factors in Project Management.*

Dunton, Peter. 1996. "Project Management Skills—A Training Strategy." *Project Manager Today* (May).

Evans, James R., and William M. Lindsay. 1993. *The Management and Control of Quality*, 2nd Edition. p. 245.

Frame, J. Davidson, 1987. *Managing Projects in Organizations.*

Gluckson, Fred, and Lockwood Lyon. 1994. *MIS Manager's Appraisal Guide.*

Kezsbom, Deborah S., Donald L. Schilling, and Katherine A. Edward. 1989. *Dynamic Project Management: A Practical Guide for Managers and Engineers.*

Laufer, Alexander. 1997. "Simultaneous Management." AMACOM

The Project Management Institute. 1987. *The Project Management Body of Knowledge (PMBOK).*

Reiss, Geoff. 1992. *Project Management Demystified: Today's Tools and Techniques.*

Senge, Peter M. 1990. *The Fifth Discipline.*

Shenhar, Aaron J. 1997. "From Theory to Practice: Toward a Typology of Project Management Styles." *IEEE Transactions on Engineering Management* (forthcoming).

Smith, Hyrum W. 1994. *The 10 Natural Laws of Successful Time and Life Management.*

# Training Project Managers Through In-House Programs

Lúcio José Diniz , LD & M Consultores Associados

## Introduction

Training project managers is an important task that is being more and more considered and applied in different industries. Even in the project-oriented companies, the need to establish a common structure and logic to be used in different projects has been considered as a way to improve entrepreneurial efficiency.

Project management training may be conducted through open programs or in-house programs. In open programs the information is presented in a generic way, and participants must decide after the training sessions what concepts, methodologies, and tools discussed to use and when. In open programs it is possible to train participants with different backgrounds, needs, and companies. Open programs may be applied to specific companies if a generic approach is used in the conduction of the training sessions.

In-house project management training programs are specific and tailored to each company. The training sessions are conducted as part of a whole program of entrepreneurial development. Such programs may have various groups of project managers that are trained to understand and apply project management knowledge and principles in a specific entrepreneurial environment. In order to be effective, in-house training programs must be conducted and managed, from concept to implementation, as specific projects. Therefore, the concepts, methodologies, and tools of professional project management must be applied to these training projects.

The purpose of this paper is to discuss the importance and implementation of in-house project management training programs, designed and developed to be applied in specific entrepreneurial environments. These programs must consider the company's business, culture, and specific needs of the target population. The main feature of these training programs is that the contents and methodology of the training sessions are defined and developed based on real needs of participants.

An approach to the project life cycle will be first considered. Considerations to be made during the conceptual phase (proposal preparation) will be discussed, and a model to be used in the development phase will be presented. Post-training necessary actions will be considered as important elements to assure the use of the training on a daily basis.

## The Project Life Cycle

A training project, to be effective, must be understood and conducted in a specific context with the objectives and results of the project clear to the client and participants. Especially in in-house programs, it is necessary to consider that the training sessions are only part of a whole project and not the project itself.

It is possible to repeat the same information related to the project management body of knowledge to different groups of project managers of any company in the world and be "successful" in the process of transmitting concepts, methodologies, and tools to all of them. It does not mean that this information will be used in an effective way by the participants after the training sessions are over. There are some aspects that must be taken into consideration before and after the training sessions.

Using the life cycle concept may help to understand the specific considerations to be made in relation to the training project. Exhibit 1 presents the phases of a PM training project that we have used as a reference from concept to implementation in different companies.

The conceptual phase (1) starts with the first contact with the client and finishes when the contract is signed. Experience has shown that this phase is one of the most important and also one that takes most of the time required when considering in-house training programs. The development phase (2) involves the understanding of the clients' reality and participants' needs in terms of concepts, methodology, and tools. During this phase specific cases and examples according to the participants' needs will be developed. This phase finishes with the preparation of the material to be used in the training sessions. The execution phase (3) corresponds to the training sessions and must occur in a smooth way if the previous phases are conducted appropriately. At the end of these sessions the participants should be motivated to use and feel comfortable using the information presented. The conclusion phase (4) is the one in which the change in behavior should occur. It is a mistake to assume that well-conducted training

Exhibit 1. In-House Training Project Life Cycle

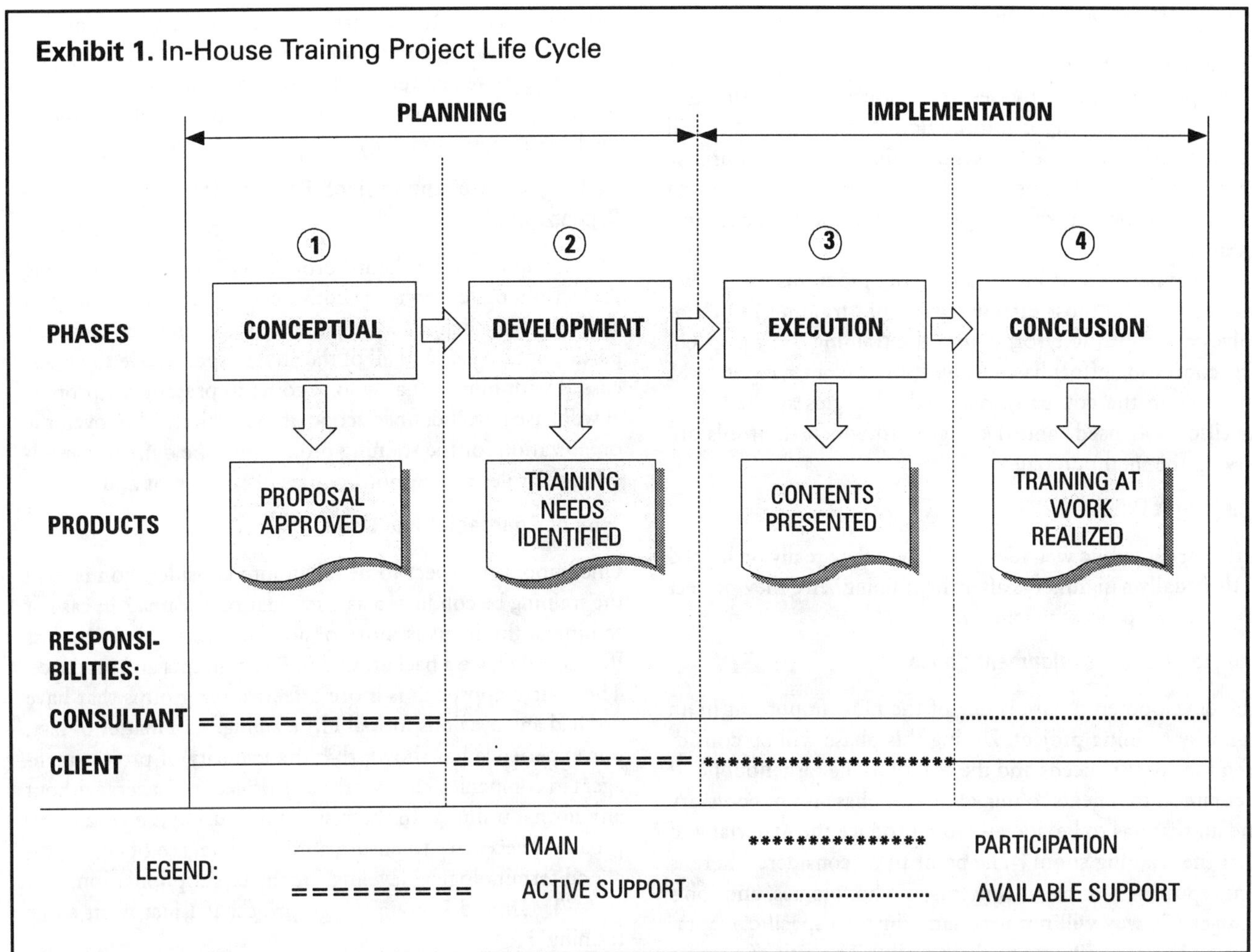


sessions will necessarily lead to the effective use of the information made available during the training period. A set of activities and environmental conditions must be considered during this phase in order to justify all of the effort and investment made. These conditions must be clear and understood by the clients' training project manager in the very beginning during the conceptual phase.

Specific aspects related to the life cycle of a training project will be considered as follows.

## Considerations During Proposal Preparation

Proposal preparation is part of the conceptual phase of an inhouse PM training project. It is natural that the clients' project manager for the training project give emphasis in the contents and training sessions themselves more than on environmental conditions that surround the whole process.

Experience has shown that before presenting a written proposal, it is important to make sure that some aspects related to the project are clear to the clients' project manager. The proposal then will be just a formal presentation of the aspects already discussed and understood . Some of these aspects are:

### Context of the Training Project

It is necessary that the professionals responsible for the consulting and training project be aware of the context in which the specific project is conducted. Training only to satisfy a training demand may not be effective and sooner or later will imply additional considerations. So, why not take those considerations in the first place?

How is the training project perceived by the clients' project manager and participants? Are there other actions been considered and taken to facilitate the use of the training? How will the information , concepts, methodology, and tools be used after the training sessions are over?

### Training IN x Training FOR

The difference between training IN and training FOR relies in the post-training activities. If the focus of the training is only the transferring of information ("training IN") it will not be as effective if the focus is on training for some purpose ("training FOR"). In this case, the participants will be using the information and knowledge applied to specific needs in a given reality.

Our experience in in-house training programs has shown that one of the most effective ways of "training FOR" involves a consulting effort before the training itself is given. The consulting effort has the objective of identifying the PM practices in the company, the methodologies applied , the specific tools used, and the degree to which the tools are serving the methodologies.

### The Target Public

Is the target public well identified? Will they really be helped in their daily assignments after the training? Are they project managers or process managers?

### The Need of a Development Phase

The development phase is one of the most important in an in-house training project. During this phase will be considered the specific needs and the reality of the target public. It is common for clients to think that this phase is not necessary and all that has to be done is "to reproduce the material and start the training soon!" The point to be considered here is that repeating a series of concepts, methodologies, and tools in a generic way will not necessarily imply a specific adaptation by the participants to their reality. The risk of using a generic approach is that there will always be someone to say that "My reality is different and it does not apply!"

In the conceptual phase of an in-house training project ,it is a must to discuss the need of a development phase and that it will always be necessary even though the contents of the training sessions may be defined in a generic format.

### The Conclusion Phase: " What Am I Going to Do on Monday"?

One of the first natural questions that occur to anyone in the beginning of a training session is: "How will this information be used in a real situation"? "Will I be able to use it if I think it makes sense"?

"What will be the interaction with my peers"? "Will they have the same training and information"? After all, will the basic environmental conditions be present for the use of the information?

During the discussions that precede the proposal preparation these questions must be considered, and the degree of participation of the consultant during the conclusion phase of the project has to be clarified as part of scope definition. In any situation, the person responsible for the training sessions must have answers to the questions above. These questions should be discussed as part of the methodology used in the beginning sessions .

### Defining the Training Project: Project Manager and Organization

The definition of the clients' project manager for the training project is a basic step to be considered during the conceptual phase. The clients' PM must understand and represent the participants' needs and all of the above aspects have to be discussed with him so that who is going to present the proposal will have a well-defined scope of the project. Moreover, the organization for the training project must be defined considering the roles and responsibilities of consultant and client.

### Type of Approach to be Used

One important aspect to be taken into consideration is: will the training be conducted as a seminar or a course? In case of seminars, the focus is more of actualization of participants that already have a background in PM concepts and practices. The course approach is more effective for groups that have not had any previous formal PM training. As a matter of fact, our experience has shown that the majority of project managers in companies have worked as project managers without any formal training. In these situations, using the course approach is necessary to ensure a minimal degree of conceptual and terminological leveling for the target population.

"Why should I buy a whole project if I just want some training"?

Clients may question undertaking and paying for a "whole project" while they expect only the training sessions themselves. Our understanding and experience reveals that the development of a training project tailored to the clients´ needs is what justifies a real in-house program. It is the role of the consultant in the conceptual phase to clarify to the clients' project manager for the training project that the training sessions in in-house training programs should be a natural consequence of the participants' needs identified during the development phase. If the training sessions are conducted based on real needs, the effort, time, and cost of the previous phases will turn into compatible return during the conclusion phase.

### The Basic Contents—An Appendix:

The proposal must contain a basic reference of the contents to be discussed during the sessions. These contents will naturally be revised during the development phase as a function of the training needs of participants. The basic contents shall constitute an appendix of the proposal.

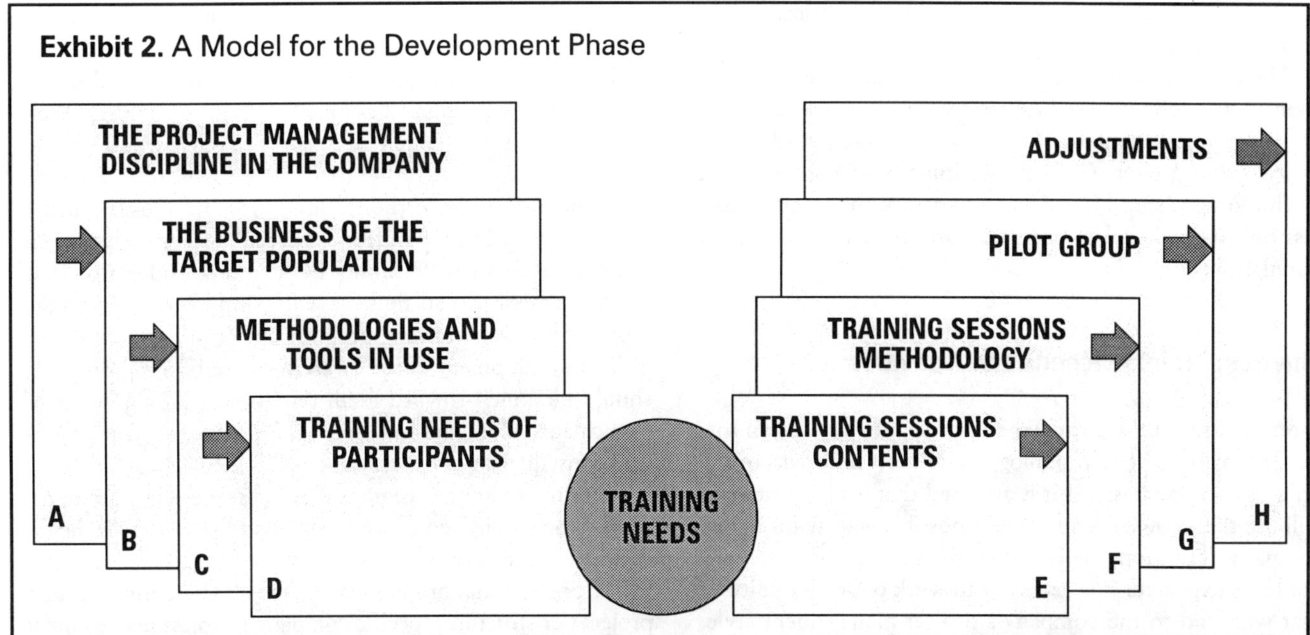


**Exhibit 2.** A Model for the Development Phase

## A Model for the Development Phase

In-house training programs are more effective when conducted through the "training for" approach. Based on the clients' needs, within the real spirit of the project management discipline, a model to be used during the development phase is shown in Exhibit 2.

The model considers two phases: Phase 1 involves the steps necessary to identify the clients' needs, while Phase 2 consists in establishing the contents and methodology based on the needs identified.

The following steps shall be considered in Phase 1:

### The Project Management Discipline in the Company

In this step , the general understanding and status of the project management discipline must be evaluated. The company's philosophy and the origin of strategic projects should be assessed. The main point to be understood is if the company has specific politics and procedures that make project management an entrepreneurial practice that is not a function of specific and personal beliefs, knowledge, and initiatives.

### The Business of the Target Population

To be able to identify specific project management training needs, it is necessary to know and understand, in the first place, the reality of the participants in the training sessions. This is done through interviews with a sample population. The following aspects should be considered:

1. The business of the functional areas: clients and products
2. Nature and size of projects conducted in the functional areas
3. Project management and process management
4. Main processes conducted by the functional areas
5. The business of participants: clients and products
6. The practice of professional project management.

### Methodologies and Tools in Use

Taking into consideration the business of the participants, the nature and size of the projects conducted by the target population, and the degree of process management as a recurring activity of participants, this step involves the identification and analysis of the project management methodologies and tools in use in order to verify if they are appropriate to the reality of participants.

### The Training Needs of Participants

The final step of Phase 1 considers the identification of training needs of participants based on:

1. The business of the functional areas
2. The business of participants
3. Basic conditions to the practice of project management
4. Project management methods and tools in use
5. Modern project management methods and tools
6. Compatibility of methodology and tools in use with the nature of the projects.

The training needs of participants are the basis necessary for the development of phase 2. Once these needs are diagnosed, they should be validated with the sample population and with the client's project manager. The steps E through H of phase 2 indicated in Exhibit 2 are a natural consequence of the needs identified in step D.

The training sessions contents (step E) and methodology (step F) are defined based on the training needs and profile of the target population. These definitions are tested with a "pilot group" (step G) and adjustments in contents and methodology (step H) are made to assure that the training sessions are tailored to the needs and reality of the target population.

## The Post-Training Needs and Activities

After the training sessions, the participants have the information in terms of methodologies and tools necessary to use on a day-to-day basis. If it is assumed that each participant will use the knowledge in the best possible way, without any company definition, the return on the investment made may not be as expected. It is necessary to work out the conditions that will lead to the company's project management style. These aspects have to be considered in the conclusion phase of the training project and may be conducted as a project itself. The final objective is to have an entrepreneurial methodology for the practice of professional project management.

Among the post-training actions is the establishment of a typology of projects defining the categories of projects in the company. This classification is based on criteria like the nature of the project , technology, level of investment, duration, cost, and areas of the company involved.

With the types of project defined, it is possible to establish specific company procedures to be used for each type of project. These procedures involve project management methodology and tools to be applied according to the typology of projects.

One important aspect is the definition and use of project management software as a tool. The identification, definition, and use of the same software with a degree of reports standardization helps the communication process and the implementation of project management.

A training at work program is necessary to consolidate the concepts and practice of professional project management in the company and is one of the most important post-formal training actions to be implemented.

## Conclusions

This paper analyzed the main aspects to be considered in the life cycle of an in-house project management training program. Effective in-house training programs must be defined and developed to present the necessary information and not the available information related to professional project management.

The use of the project life cycle concept applied to in-house training programs has been used and demonstrated to be an important element of success in such training programs.

Scope definition of the training program must be made during proposal preparation and the difference between "training IN" versus "training FOR" is a consideration that consultants and clients must have in mind when defining the scope of in-house training programs.

The development phase of an in-house training program should be aimed toward identifying real training needs of participants. Contents and methodology to be used are a natural consequence of the training needs identified.

After the training sessions are over, there are important aspects to be considered and implemented to assure that the individual knowledge will be used as a company's methodology for professional project management. The definition of a project tier structure, specific company's project management procedures, and a training at work program are basic for the application of the knowledge in a practical and professional way.

# Project Management Needs to Address Training

David M. Gallegos, Robbins-Gioia, Inc.

## Introduction

With the benefit of several years' experience in both Training Development and Project Management; I have seen several parallels within both worlds. Also, I have had the benefit of learning the technical development process that attaches to both. In both worlds extensive research has been accumulated on how one goes about developing training interventions, and also how one should go about the process of launching, controlling, and delivering a Project undertaking. Given the strict adherence to professionalism in each arena, there are still striking and logical similarities between them.

This comes as no surprise to me. What is surprising, is that in spite of the professed professional stance of both, why we still labor to create training episodes which are glaringly devoid of professional project management techniques, and why project management remains a stranger to the training world.

Management by projects is rapidly becoming the leading business practice in small and large companies alike. Everything from product development to a marketing launch is managed like a professional project which means that you deliver what is expected, when it is due. In today's incredibly competitive environment there is little room for error. Ensuring success means managing expectations, mitigating risk, controlling quality and managing change. This can only be achieved through careful planning, execution, and control. The training project is not exempt from this regimen. It is surprising that among costly undertakings, the training project has not been held to this demanding and precise accountability.

Frequently, we view training as a commodity, or as a treatment to address some specific symptoms. When viewed from a technical perspective, as a planned effort to deliver certain specific functionality, we see that it really is a Project, with several defined sets of Activities, Processes, and Deliverables that parallel the formal Project Management portfolio. In both areas: the ability to follow a discipline; the ability to articulate and highlight the process; and the ability to demonstrate success, results, and consistency; are important criteria.

Theodore B. Kinni offered this observation in *Industry Week*, November 21, 1994; "...Success depends on continuous life-long learning. Employee training and education must become a strategic priority for small businesses. The question is how this priority can be pursued effectively, and cost-efficiently..."

## Training Paradigms/Project Paradigms

Within the realm of Human Resources Development, I had occasion to examine several models, that would purport to build successful training and education programs. (ISD, the Critical Events Model), etc. Again, to my knowledge, none of these models have ever been used to guide the development of any other type of project. I am not so naive as to believe that my experience is unique; that somewhere, someone else has not had the same questions or puzzlement that I have, which is, Why don't we make use of basic successful project management techniques to build more effective training systems?

Trainers and developers will readily recognize the Instructional System Design (ISD) framework. The phases feed logically into one another as training is created and implemented. ISD is represented by several graphic variations in Exhibit 1 and 2.

The fact that there are several models to follow offers us the flexibility to pick and choose among them. We can tailor one to allow a more precise fit to the application area.

The Project Life Cycle Model (Robbins-Gioia, 1991) is a very useful and practical template on which to build and control any project. It has been used successfully in a variety of environments. To my knowledge, however, it has never been used to govern the development of an Educational Project/System.

## Needs Analyses/Functional Requirements

Probably the first and most obvious question to ask is, "Is training really needed?" Many managers and organizations in general default that question to the conclusion that training is, in fact, needed. While training, like chicken soup, generally "couldn't hurt," it may not be the most effective remedy to what is probably a performance problem. In their excellent book, *Analyzing Performance Problems,* Mager and Pipe set forth a more practical process to be applied in determining root causes of performance issues. Their diagram

**Exhibit 1.** The ISD Model

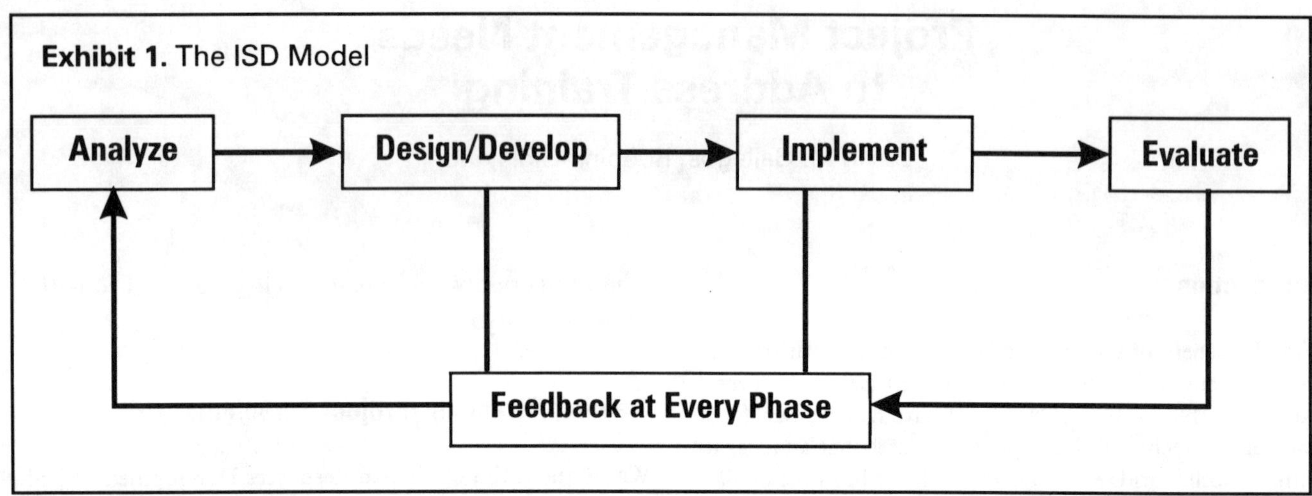


**Exhibit 2.** The Critical Events Model (Nadler, 1982)

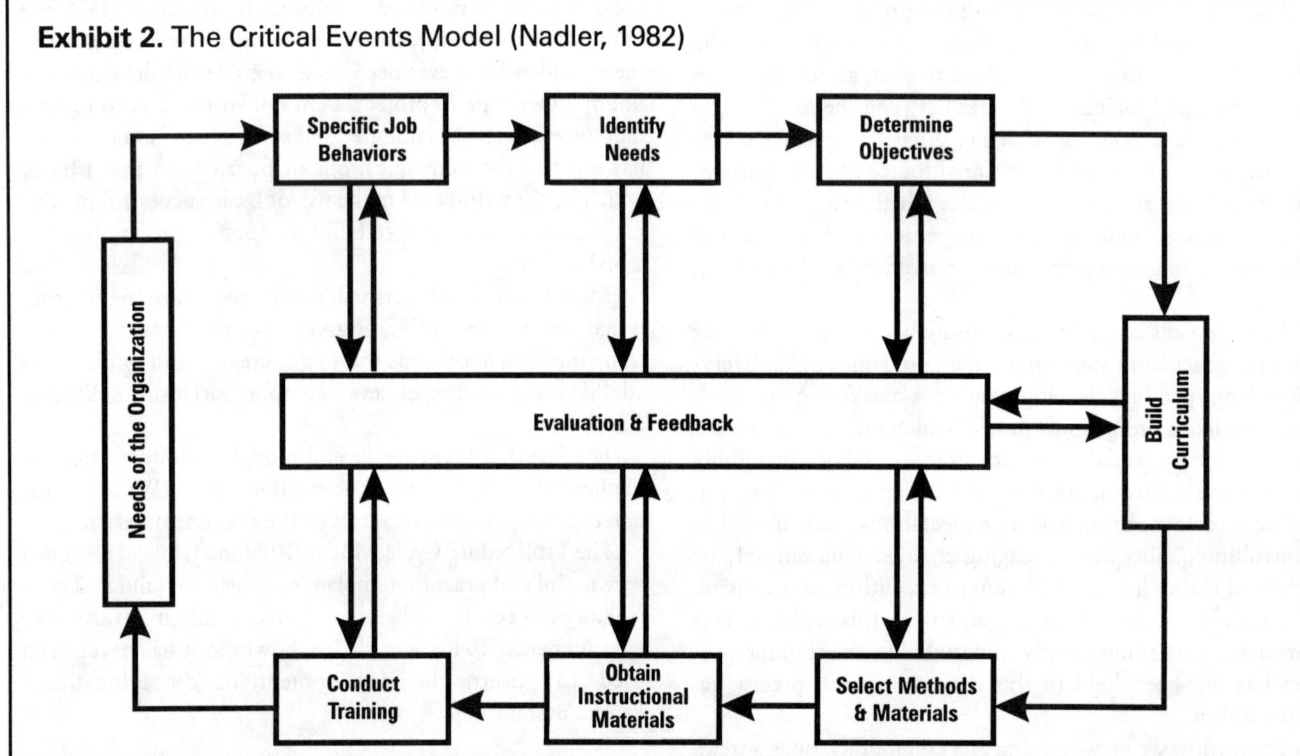


appears here as a suggested process to uncover actual problems and to avoid treating *symptoms* of problems.

Good training doctrine demands that we perform an analysis of training (performance) needs as prelude to course development, no matter how sure we may be of what training is required. Similarly, project management doctrine insists that, very early, we determine the functional requirements to be served by any project that we undertake. The reasons for these preliminary steps are steeped in reason and logic. They constitute the essentials of what either system or product is to deliver. In the normal project development effort, this includes extensive participation by the client/user. The specific form and methodology of making these determinations will vary with preferred style and method. What is important, is that they are done. It can, and should be, no less for the training venture. Without these essential precursors, a project/training program is doomed to either failure, or, at best, coincidental, partial success.

Foregoing this analysis in favor of embarking on a training solution is a wider practice than one might think. The cardinal sin in project management is to have a solution identified, then go searching for a problem to which to apply it.

**Exhibit 3.** Life Cycle Project Management Model, Robbins-Gioia, 1991

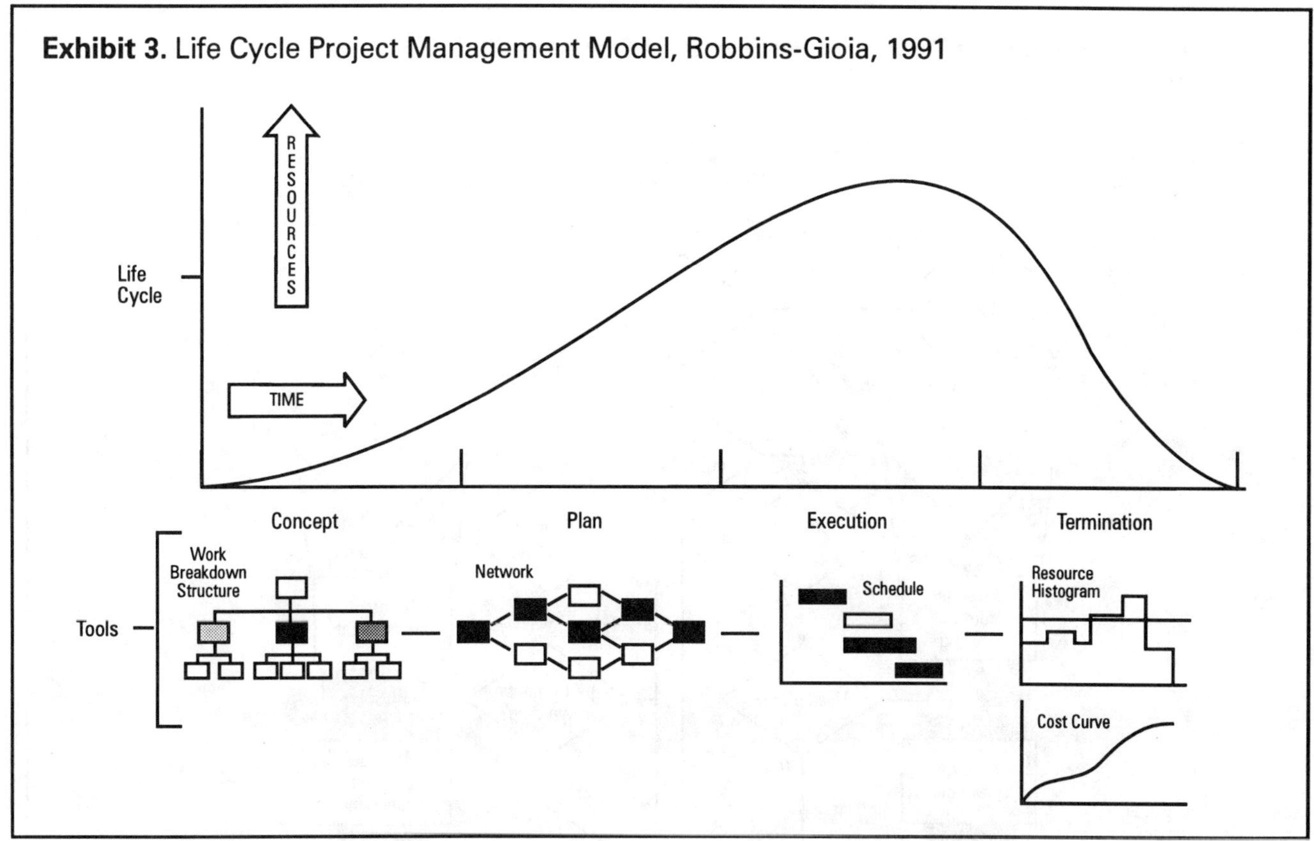


Training, particularly the readily-available type, is frequently applied in this manner. An "interested" party makes a cursory observation that performance could be improved with some training. Without the benefit of analysis of what problems/situations could be improved by this application, the effort is already under way. In this moment of opportunity, training is supposed to make a major contribution and result in a sizable improvement. Expectations are falsely raised, only to be cruelly dashed, and in the process, training becomes the culprit.

This issue is amplified by the observation of Joe Harless in the *Training and Development Journal* for January, 1996, where he ventures that "Many trainees now realize that instruction should be and can be avoided because analysis often shows that non-training interventions are required. . . . It isn't just a behavior change that management wants—it's an improvement in the output. . . . "

Even if training is identified as the appropriate treatment, there are effective ways to administer it. In a recent article appearing in a national publication, Dean Spitzer enumerated his "nine causes of training failure . . . " They are listed here with my own amplification:

1. **Resources not focused.** This could be interpreted as not knowing which resources are necessary, or where a particular expertise is best applied.
2. **Real objectives were not clear.** Essentially, the trainer did not determine the functional requirements to be met by the training system, which is an early, critical priority in project management.
3. **Training does not cause (result in) performance improvement.** Trainers have recently realized that they are not in the lecturing, demonstrating, or testing business; they are in the *performance improvement* business.
4. **Training is aimed at symptoms.** Again, the trainer did not take the necessary time, and perform the necessary analyses, to determine the true cause(s) of performance deficiencies.
5. **Critical non-training factors are ignored.** Experienced project managers will tell you that it's not usually the *technical* issues that create major problems, but frequently it's *supportability* or non-programmatic areas that cause difficulties. For example, developing a highly sophisticated computer simulation program without the ability to maintain or modify it.
6. **Management support is lacking.** There are various and several junctures in the project's life cycle when milestones are arrived upon which need management concurrence and approval before the project proceeds. While management may profess support, and

**Exhibit 4.** Mager and Pip's *Analyzing Performance Problems* Flowchart

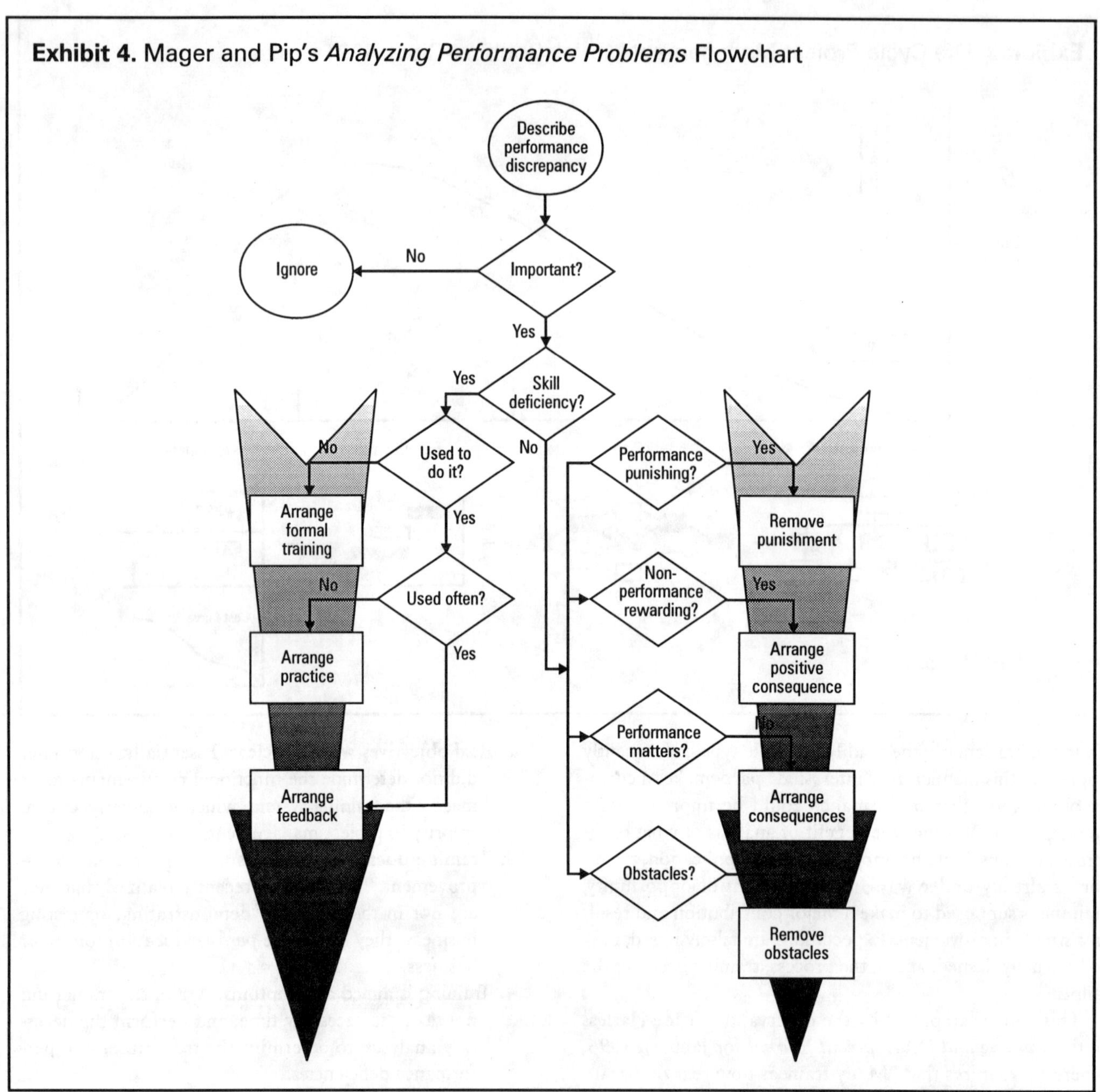


even involvement, life cycle project orchestration accommodates (and occasionally prods) their participation.

7. **Central role of the supervisor is not recognized.** Any system must be tailored to the target organization. Users may take on new roles. It is important that any system identify and assign such new functions to individuals within the organization. If supervisors are to continue as such, any training project must make clear their function and involvement in that system.

8. **Trainers are poorly chosen.** This probably alludes to their lack of project management skills, or it could relate directly to their lack of instructional skills. In the former case, it makes a strong argument for the theme of this paper. In the latter, it should have been a specification made from an assessment of resources necessary to enable the system to succeed.

9. **Little or no preparation or follow-up.** Project management techniques place a high priority and importance on start-up tasks, generally of the planning and organizing variety. Similarly, no successful project is ever

merely curtailed or ended. There are numerous transitional or turn-over tasks that are identified for attention; some will occur after formal conclusion.

## Training Plans and Project Baselines

There comes a point in the project's early stages when development effort commences. The arrival at this point is not strictly mandated, but it is a commonly held conclusion that planning has proceeded sufficiently to begin measuring work efforts. It is at this juncture that the project plan is said to be "baselined." By one definition, the baseline plan is "the completed and approved project plan that is currently being used to assess progress and success in meeting the business objectives of the project. . . . " (David Weill 1995). There is a natural tendency on the part of the project entity to resist this commitment. It's easier to continue in a planning/monitoring mode for as long as possible prior to establishing a baseline. The danger here is that, in the absence of anything to compare against, the current level of performance is "according to plan." A comparison of current status versus baseline is an assessment of where we actually are in a project, compared to where we had *planned* to be. This is the only way to determine whether or not the project is on time and on budget, or at some other point. In a business context, this is a matter of dollars and sense. There may well be justifiable reasons for variances from plan, but baselining the plan provides a common denominator for evaluating progress. Training projects have long been exempt from this hard and fast, impersonal evaluation because of the promise they hold, the expectation of benefit, and the belief that training is a "good investment" on its own merits.

The project developer is also well-served by the baseline. Part of the baseline concept is the development of functional uses/purposes to be satisfied by the training project. By establishing the functional baseline, the user/client has also committed to a set of functionality which the training project is to deliver. Estimates of time, resources, and budget to build the system have been based upon this defined functionality. Changes in scope, performance, or technical elegance become changes to this baseline, if approved, and are the basis of any re-estimating of time and other resources required to accommodate these changes.

## Curriculum Development and Work Breakdown Structures

The value of training development models and paradigms is that they help us to anticipate, plan, and provide for the work that is to be done. This project fragmenting, or work decomposition effort has the value of exhaustively describing and detailing the work to be done. This practice is commonly referred to as "work breakdown." and the resulting decomposed graphic is termed the "work breakdown structure." This serves to define every product, service, or process to be developed in the system. Conversely, anything not included in the work breakdown structure (WBS) is **not** a part of the system to be built.

The decomposing progresses to a very detailed, discrete description of work to be accomplished. At a level which allows assignment of discrete pieces of the system to be built, we terminate the process and define the results as work elements, or work packages. These packages become the "building blocks" of the training project. Most training development models take great care in outlining the *processes*, but few of the **tools**, necessary to develop a successful training system. The work breakdown structure is a necessary and essential tool in the project's development. It goes to the cardinal principal of successful project development: **defining** the work to be done.

Many projects, training projects included, fall prey to defaulting the work **breakdown** process to a work *assignment* process. In this instance, work is not defined, but general responsibilities for development of pieces of the project are assigned to "logical" elements of the organization. Here is where problems begin, because then the project organization begins work on *assumptions* when more specific information could be available.

The typical scenario that ensues without work breakdown is: confusion over status, differences over responsibility, and wasted or redundant effort. One group that I was consulting with described their project status meetings as "chaotic." It turned out that they had never accomplished or attempted a work breakdown process. When this was pointed out, they wondered aloud if they should return to that juncture and accomplish that step. My answer was, "unless you want your meetings to continue to be chaotic!"

## Cost Estimating and Work Breakdown Structures

The processes of estimating and budgeting are important steps in the training project. Work decomposition greatly assists and enhances the completeness and accuracy of these two essential processes. Arguments like, "we won't know the cost of development until we do it . . . " are vacuous and specious.

In any business context, the value of a product or component is always compared against the benefit or capability that it provides. Work breakdown also allows us to calculate the cost, or costs, of any individual component or family of components in the project. In addition to allowing us greater visibility of the internal costs of any component, it also serves as an indicator of where functionality, or pieces of the project, can deliberately be curtailed if costs are a factor. In this way, the project manager is served as well as the client, because then the areas of omission can be made clearly and specifically, and thereby preclude any expectation of full (original) functionality, only at a cheaper cost.

## Training Module Development and Logic Diagrams (Networks)

Work breakdown processes further allow the logical sequencing of included tasks. It also reveals dependencies among tasks, and identifies which development paths are independent of others. This concurrent opportunity allows us to make greater use of resources, to concentrate resources where they will do the most good, and, potentially, to shorten the overall development time.

You won't know where the skeletons are until you open the closets! Detailing the tasks in the projects will also highlight areas of potential risk. Knowing where critical junctures are will allow us to insure against their occurrence, or at least make provision for their happening and allow us to practice damage control.

The seemingly rhetorical question may be asked: "How does a project get to be a year late?" The answer, both humorous and accurate, is "one day at a time!" When the project is decomposed to finite tasks, and sequenced over a time schedule, tracking progress is simplified and objective.

## Project Team Composition and Training and Development Resources

What core competencies are required—when? This is presaged for us by Alan Radding, in his work, "A Future for Training Managers." Radding ventures that "IS curriculum is evolving—including instruction in management and interpersonal skills . . . " Radding goes on to say that this training includes: finding appropriate instructors; scheduling and coordinating sessions; supervising administrative functions, such as billing; and taking on additional functions such as budgeting, and controlling . . . " If these sound vaguely like project management functions I believe the similarities are purely intentional, and highly appropriate.

Managers are naturally territorial over their personnel. While projects may universally be held to be a valuable and necessary development, stakeholders are normally reluctant to have their "ox gored." The work breakdown and task execution network tools help to identify, limit, and lessen the impact on organizational resources being taken from normal activities, and committed to project work. While these steps are not a precise science, it is still a far cry from being committed "for the duration."

As a profession, training has its share of specialists and engineers. Knowing when and where to apply expertise is, potentially, as valuable as the expertise itself. It greatly aids a project to make efficient use of scarce resources. It is usually not possible to have these specialists on call, awaiting the moment wherein they can apply their expertise. Even if this were a budgetary possibility, the extended "wait-times" would be de-motivating and unproductive. Better that "star performers" come in "on cue" to deliver their lines. The play then becomes a "hit."

## Progress Reviews

On the occasions of the technical review, which is a cardinal practice in systems development, not only is progress evaluated but critical assessment on the wisdom of *continuing* the project is determined. The theory here is that if the project is not going to be capable of delivering the functionality desired, then perhaps it should be curtailed. These reviews can be likened to Kirkpatrick's levels of evaluation: student evaluations, performance evaluations, measures of improvement, and benefits to the organization. Each one is progressive, and allows successful attainment of the next.

## Leadership and Specialists

In a recent article in *Computer World*, January 22, 1996, Leslie Goff ventured that "Project Management skills are becoming must-have commodities for top information systems professionals . . . " It is not a giant step to apply that recommendation to the training world. Certainly, training systems impart information as part of their deliverable. This advice, then, would be equally applicable to the training project manager.

Successful training project managers must be strong advocates of the practice. Experience, as always, helps. The successful training project manager may or may not be an experienced trainer. However, he or she must know how to use the experienced trainer's expertise. In training projects, as in any other successful project, the elegance of the design is not the driving factor. It is the ability to see the value delivered, as compared to the costs, that enables the project design to be successful, and not merely expensive.

The successful training project manager must be politically "aware." Project managers need to have "political savvy" in order to be successful. They need to discover how things work in the served organization, and who can get things done. In many cases they must have the ability to function without specific authority. In this, they rely heavily on influence, leadership, and the practice of empowerment. Political skills are not unsavory, under-the-table, or nefarious. They are a skill set that frequently is the only one the manager can use to achieve the desired results. People know and expect this. Attempting to successfully manage a problem while neglecting the politics of the situation is, frankly, naive.

## Conclusion

The practices of technical management, configuration management, and risk management are present in any training system development, yet the professional practitioner does not give adequate attention to these areas. Training should not try to tell the client what (training) they need. The systems developer doesn't tell the client what the organization needs; rather he elicits from the client what is needed, then designs a system to satisfy these articulated needs. Training projects need to be more business-oriented. Successful project management satisfies business objectives. John Hendrickson offered this observation in the *Training and Development Journal* for February 1989, "Successful trainers target business needs . . . and understand the **job context** of learning objectives . . . ." (emphasis added).

Building on Kirkpatrick's fourth level of evaluation, Jack Phillips reported in the *Training and Development Journal* for January 1996 that training made the following differences:

- The Coca-Cola Bottling Company realized a 1447 percent return on investment (ROI), and established a ratio of benefits to cost of 15:1.
- A health maintenance organization (HMO) enrolled 20,700 new members, experienced a 1270 percent ROI, and established a benefits to cost ratio of 13.7:1.
- Litton Avionics improved employee productivity by 30 percent, reduced scrap by 50 percent, and realized a 700 percent ROI.

In the same issue, Pat McGlagan offers that, "HR Systems Designers and developers. Their role involves designing and preparing HR systems for implementation so that HR systems and actions . . . have a maximum impact on organizational performance . . . " (emphasis added).

To have maximum impact, systems and projects need to be planned, controlled, and measured. Training certainly is not exempt from these concerns.

### References


Chalofsky, Neal and Carnie Ives Lincoln. 1983. *Up the HRD Ladder.* Addison-Wesley Publishing Company.

Galagan, Patricia A. 1997. "Strategic Planning is Back." *Training and Development Journal* (April): 32–37.

Gill, Stephen J. 1995. "Paradigm Shift from the Business of Training—to the Business of Learning." *Training and Development Journal* (May): 26.

Goff, Leslie. 1996. *Computer World* (January 22): 77.

Harless, Joe. 1996. "The Search for Best Practices." *Training and Development Journal* (January): 52–53.

Hendrickson, John. 1989. "Getting Close to Business." *Training and Development Journal*(February): 68–70.

Holton & Bailey. 1995. "Top-to-Bottom Curriculum Re-design." *Training and Development Journal* (March).

Kinni, Theodore B. 1994. *Industry Week* (November 21): 55–56.

Kirkpatrick, Donald. 1994. *The Four Levels of Evaluation.* San Francisco: Berrett-Koehler.

Mager, Robert F., and Peter Pipe. 1984. *Analyzing Performance Problems.* Second Edition, Pittman Learning, Inc.

McGlagan, Pat. 1996. "The Search for Best Practices." *Training and Development Journal* (January): 64.

McIntosh, Stephen S. "The Virtual Training Organization." *Training and Development Journal* (May): 47.

Nadler, Leonard. 1984. *The Handbook of Human Resource Development.* John Wiley & Sons.

Nilson, Carolyn. 1996. *Training & Development Yearbook 1996/1997.* Prentice-Hall.

Phillips, Jack J. "The Search for Best Practices." *Training and Development Journal* (February): 42–49.

Radding, Alan. 1989. "A Future for Training Managers?" *COMPUTERWORLD* (November 20): 117.

Robbins-Gioia, Inc. 1991. "Life Cycle Project Management."

Spitzer, Dean. 1986. *TRAINING* (June): 37–39.

Weill, David E. 1995. Nutshell Productions Ltd..

Zenger, John H. "Great Ideas Revisited." *Training and Development Journal* (January): 48–51.

# Using Coaching to Rapidly Develop Project Managers in Consensus Cultures

Colin Huddy, CLEAR Communications Ltd, NZ

## The Situation

A major impact of the deregulation of telecommunications in New Zealand was the recognition of a shortage of competent project managers. For years the services and products offered were controlled by the incumbent monopoly, and people had become used to receiving products and services that suited this environment. The demand for improvement had been well and truly suppressed, and it had reached the situation where they were happy in the belief that you do not miss what you have never had.

Following deregulation of telecommunications the start up companies immediately began to differentiate themselves, and they did this by offering new products and services. The first offering began an immediate rush to take up the new facilities, and this created a demand for more advanced products and services. At this point there grew within the newer companies—and it must be said within the incumbent monopoly—an even greater corresponding demand for infrastructure and support systems capable of ensuring the continuity of supply. The project managers capable of delivering these were few and far between or missing entirely and so whilst sales and marketing groups had no difficulty selling, the customers had great difficulty getting reliable service. The demand for experienced project managers far outstripped the supply.

Fortunately the average standard of education was quite high, and there was a relatively large group of educated project managers with the basic knowledge of project management techniques. However, they lacked the experience gained from the successful completion of large complex projects. A further complication was the fact that there was a small core of experienced project managers who were not New Zealanders and who were overloaded with projects. The result of this overloading was that the experienced project managers were so busy putting out fires that they did not have sufficient time to devote to prevention in the form of developing local project managers. They were seen to be keeping the knowledge to themselves, and the barrier between locals and outsiders was getting higher .The development of additional project managers became a critical path item and had to be solved if progress was to be continued.

## The Challenge

The challenge was to develop project managers, have it seen that it was not an imposition from outside, and create an environment in which inexperienced managers could seek assistance without seeming to be admitting incompetence.

New Zealand is an egalitarian culture where consensus is the preferred decision-making technique. The people are proud of their "Kiwi Ingenuity" approach and do not easily accept outside ideas and influences. "Not invented here is grounds for rejection." They tend to disparage individual success and will attack individuals who appear to separate themselves from the group. It is called the "tall poppy" syndrome. To be successful is admired only if it is seen that the person is still in touch with the ordinary person.

The challenge was to find an acceptable process that would rapidly develop the inexperienced project managers and at the same time avoid the costly and unsatisfactory approach of having them learn by their mistakes. We had to avoid the school of hard knocks.

## The Solution—Project Coaching

In this sport mad society the role of the coach and the coach's authority is well understood. Further there is universal acceptance that the best way to improve performance is to get a good coach. There is no disgrace in asking a coach for assistance, and in fact people who do not ask the coach are seen to be foolishly independent. A final point in the company's favor was that a good coach can simultaneously develop the whole team.

Thus in a company with many educated but inexperienced project managers, with a culture of team working with consensus decision-making, it became obvious that the best use of the experienced project managers was not as project managers but as project coaches.

Thus project coaching or project mentoring was chosen as the process most suitable for ensuring both the project success and the rapid development of project management skills.

## Two Truths and a Picture

1. The best player does not always make the best coach.
2. Consulting is not coaching.

The first step on the path to success was the selection of the people most suited to the role of coaching. They had to have the characteristics of team leaders. Some successful project managers display the characteristics of a dictator, and some achieve great success by driving through every obstruction. Unfortunately this type of project manager does not easily fit into the role of coach. It was recognised that we had to first develop coaches before we could develop project managers.

A consultant group was engaged to provide advice and to draw up a profile of project manager suitable for development into coach. An important aspect was not to seek a profile of the ideal coach but to focus on the profile of a project manager who would make a successful coach. There is much information concerning the various characteristics of successful project managers but very little about the characteristics of successful project manager coaches. By working with various project managers, and more importantly various project team members, they were able to develop a comprehensive selection procedure that was initially tested on a few selected groups and after refinement finally used for profiling potential project manager coaches. The final profile has proved to be quite successful and has established several very successful coaches measured by the results of project managers who worked with them.

The fact that some of the very successful project managers did not make the cut, so to speak, was an issue that had to be resolved with some sensitivity. They rightly saw themselves as star performers and felt that their techniques would be right for others. This was not the case, and, as our consultant pointed out, techniques have to be adapted to suit the personality and communications style of each individual. The final analysis saw the rejection of some of the star players; i.e., project managers with very good records of success. A communications plan was developed and by using the coach and star player analogy we were able, in most cases, to ensure that this was a reasonably painless process. Thus we were able to select the most appropriate people and at the same time not alienate other essential experts.

The second was to teach the techniques of coaching. This was not left to chance, and expert trainers and developers were engaged. These trainers made sure that the coaches knew the differences between providing information, expertise, and advice as a player and as a coach. Most importantly they were taught the difference between acting as a coach and acting as a consultant. Technical consultants (with apologies to all consultants) tend to come into an organisation and deliver the required system and al l of its components in an efficient manner. They do not as a general rule add to the total knowledge of the organisation. It was essential that the coaches saw and were committed to the need for transfer of expertise and that at the end of the exercise, they would leave in place expert project managers who had gained extensive knowledge because they had been associated with the experts. By instituting a system of performance measurement based on how well the "student manager" developed, we were able to ensure satisfactory knowledge transfer.

**Exhibit 1.**

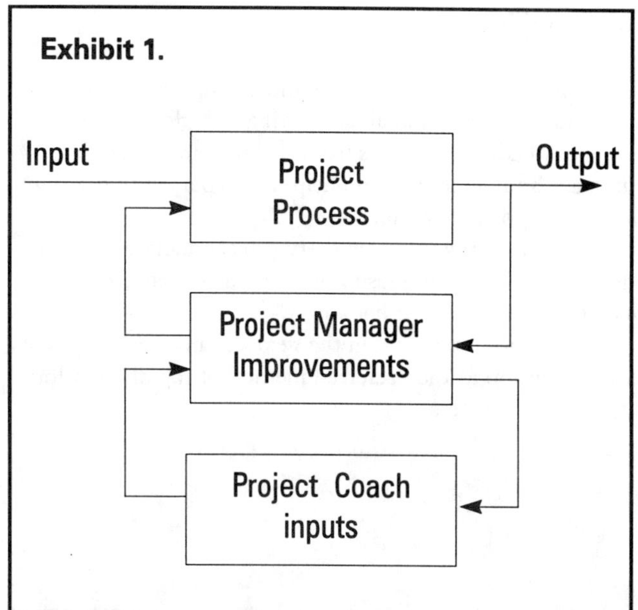


The third step was the development of the model shown in Exhibit 1.

This model helped to ensure that all participants understood the relationships and what their roles were to be. The project manager is clearly responsible for processing information and creating actions based on the results. The coach is responsible for three main items:

1. Ensuring that the project manager is getting the best possible information
2. Providing guidance and so on to ensure it is processed correctly
3. Helping the project manager analyze options
4. Helping the project manager implement the resultant decisions.

The model emphasises that the role of the coach is not to help the project manager to do the work but to provide guidance. Specifically, the coach is separated from the actual project management and deals with the project manager only.

## The Benefits

Coaching is not about making world champions out of everybody. It is not even about making a single champion. It is about taking a person's natural ability and by advice, guidance, and demonstration helping the person to become the best he possibility can.

Imagine a company in which every project manager is well educated in the techniques of project management and is operating at the peak of her ability.

There is no doubt that in the next century coaching will further develop as the preferred method of rapidly developing project managers.

# Project Management Training at USAA—A Curricula for the Next Century

Colleen Andreoli, USAA

## About the Company

USAA, founded in 1922, is a worldwide insurance and diversified financial services association headquartered in San Antonio, Texas. It has over 16,500 employees worldwide, is made up of seventy-nine subsidiaries and affiliates and owns and manages over $34 billion in assets. USAA members insure one another and share in any profits realized. Its 2.7 million members are primarily present and former military officers and their dependents. It is the nation's fifth largest insurer of private automobiles and fourth largest homeowners' insurer. In addition, USAA currently has more than $65.1 billion of life insurance in force, and ranks as the nation's thirty-seventh largest life insurance company. USAA's Investment Management Company offers a diverse family of twenty-nine no-load mutual funds, and it ranks thirty-second of 366 companies in assets under management.

## Project Management at USAA—A Three Year Summary

Rapidly changing and increasingly complex technology combined with the business demand for quicker solutions revitalized an interest in project management. USAA's information systems (IS) recognized the need for project management to be a formalized discipline throughout the organization with consistent training, methodologies, and tools to ensure that projects are on schedule, within budget, and meet expectations.

In February 1994, USAA formed a working group composed of managers from IS and Information Technology Training (I/TT) staff to formulate a project management curricula. The first offering of the curricula was piloted in November 1994, for IS employees. In 1996, the program was expanded to include all business areas. To date, 104 students have graduated from the formal curriculum. The number of 1997 graduates is estimated at ninety-six. Other significant training events in 1996 included the launch of an awareness level training program for project team members and functional managers, and a series of two-day executive seminars for senior management. Of note in 1997 are efforts toward utilizing in-house expertise to provide project management training instead of outsourcing.

To promote the benefit of networking with their peers, graduates from the curriculum established a USAA PM forum which meets quarterly. Guest speakers from within the organization give presentations on topics relevant to project management. There are plans to expand the program to include an electronic forum through the USAA intranet.

Also during 1994, several USAA employees participated in the founding of a Project Management Institute (PMI) chapter in San Antonio. The chapter currently has two hundred plus members, the majority of whom are from USAA. Four of the six officers for 1997 are USAA employees. In 1995, ten USAA employees attended the annual PMI Seminar/Symposium. In 1996, twenty-two attended. Also in 1996, USAA became a corporate member of PMI.

In July of 1995, USAA approved the Project Management Professional (PMP) as a recognized designation, eligible for reimbursement of expenses related to its achievement. Employees achieving the PMP are honored at the employee recognition breakfast, and may include the designation after their names on any company correspondence or business cards. In December 1995, fifteen USAA employees sat for the exam in pursuit of their PMP certification. During 1996, ninety employees sat for the exam, including eighteen executives and our chief information officer (CIO). To date, we have nineteen PMP's and thirty-eight others who have passed the test and are awaiting approval of their points.

Today, the job title of project manager is used only informally at USAA. However, a committee is at work exploring competencies required and an appropriate compensation plan.

This year a project was begun to "institutionalize" project management, to include developing a common set of tools and processes (to be accessed through the USAA intranet), defining and supporting standardized program control, creating an in-house mentoring capability (consultants have been used to date), and creating a data repository to store current and historical project data.

## The Project Management Training Program Background

In February 1994, a ten-member working group was formed consisting of representatives at the management level from

**Exhibit 1.** Project Management Curriculum–Information Technology Track 2

**Core Modules**

| | |
|---|---|
| Building Effective Teams 8hrs | Risk Management 24hrs |
| Planning, Scheduling and Cost 38hrs | USAA's Acquisition Process 8hrs |
| Implementation and Control 32hrs | Project Leadership Workshop 38hrs |

**I/T Track 2 Modules**

| |
|---|
| The Complete Project Manager ™ 16hrs |
| Managing Information Technology Projects 24hrs |

**Practitioner Electives**

| |
|---|
| Project Management Software Tool 16hrs |
| PMP Exam Review Course 40hrs |

**Soft Skill Electives**

| | | |
|---|---|---|
| Winning Support From Others 4hrs | Coaching for Performance 4hrs | Resolving Team Conflicts 4hrs |
| Communicating One on One 8hrs | Building a Foundation of Trust 4hrs | Helping Your Team Reach Consensus 4hrs |
| Building Collaborative Relationships 4hrs | Giving a Briefing 8hrs | Resolving Team Conflicts 4hrs |
| Facilitation for Leaders 8hrs | Leadership Training 8hrs | Making the Most of Team Differences 4hrs |
| Effective Writing 4hrs | Outcome Thinking 8hrs | Negotiation 8hrs |

Information Systems and one Information Technology Training representative. Over a period of several months, a thorough needs analysis was conducted. The working group received presentations from senior managers who offered advice on the most important qualities of a project manager. The working group also was briefed by project managers who had led both successful and unsuccessful projects during their careers. They provided input as to what kinds of training would have been helpful to them. These became the foundation for the content of the curricula.

## Evolution of Content and Structure

Initially, three levels of training for Project Management were defined based on work experience. Pilots for each level were conducted using IS project managers. An additional pilot was added by request for the business community. At the conclusion of the pilots, student feedback was analyzed and the curriculum was restructured accordingly. Key discoveries were:

- All students needed the same core project management skills training. Because the "as-is" culture had only practiced project management by heroics, even experienced project managers were unfamiliar with project management as a formal discipline.
- By eliminating redundancy, the curriculum could be condensed from eleven months to six or eight months depending on electives selected.
- Combining IS and business partners together in class promoted better communication and understanding between the two communities.
- Some business partners needed a less in-depth curriculum as they only managed projects occasionally or part time.
- Excellence in content and delivery was essential. Evaluation forms were completed and analyzed for each

class. Only the best of breed classes and vendor providers were retained.
- The price of success is that the demand will exceed the supply. Three course directors are required to administer the program today. Competition for entry in the program is keen.
- Two key forms of support for graduates from the curriculum were needed: one-on-one mentoring and awareness level training for project team members and functional managers.

## Curriculum Organization Today

The curriculum is organized by a set of common core classes, track-related modules, and electives (see Exhibit 1). The core classes cover the essential technical and leadership skills related to project management. Track modules cover other areas of specialization such as managing information technology projects, program management, or additional leadership training. Electives include topics such as business process reengineering courses, project management software tool training, a variety of soft skill modules, or review of the Project Management Body of Knowledge for those pursuing the PMP designation.

To accommodate their workload, students attend class three to four days of each month. This approach has proved less of a burden on both the organization and the students. A policy statement is signed by both the student and her manager to confirm their understanding of and commitment to the program. Most of the core modules include an exam. Students are required to maintain a running grade average of 80 percent or better. All required classes must be completed for a student to achieve graduate status.

## Student Selection

Entry into the curriculum is by nomination. Approximately two months prior to the start of a curriculum, a call for candidates is issued to senior management. The number of students in each offering is apportioned on a percentage basis across the organization for a total of twenty-four students per offering.

To kick off each curriculum offering, a welcome party is hosted with the executive sponsor as the guest speaker. At the conclusion of the curriculum, a graduation ceremony is held. Each student is awarded by executive management a certificate honoring his completion of the curriculum and a plaque containing the Project Manager's Professional Code of Ethics. Managers of the students are expected to attend both functions.

## Student Placement

All students are required to complete the core modules. Beyond the core are Tracks 1, 2, and 3.

- Track 1 is intended for individuals who have little or no prior project management experience, or experience leading or managing others.
- Track 2 is designed for individuals who have prior project management experience and wish to increase their knowledge in project management as a formal discipline. Track 2 then divides into either the information technology track or the business partner track.
- The audience for Track 3 is individuals already in line management positions who also manage (a.) projects and/or (b.) other project managers or (c.) programs.

Placement in the various tracks is based on several criteria: current position in the organization, experience level determined from a written resume and personal interview, input from the candidate's manager, a leadership assessment device, and a skill gap analysis test.

## Leadership Assessment

To determine soft skill training requirements and track placement, students and their managers both complete the leadership assessment. Students will assess themselves; managers will assess their respective students. Results should be reviewed together and, as needed, an appropriate set of soft skill classes selected to improve the student's leadership skills.

## Skills Gap Analysis Test

This vendor-provided test is administered at the start and conclusion of each curriculum for benchmarking purposes. Individual scores are held in confidence. Managers are provided with roll-up averages for the entire group. The questions closely follow the eight areas of the PMI Body of Knowledge. The test's purpose is two-fold:

- to gauge student placement
- to measure the student's overall progress.

Perfect scores are not expected; rather, an acceptable range and progress within that range is what is desired. We typically see a twenty to twenty-five point improvement in student scores.

## Mentoring Program

To support the graduates from the curriculum or others who needed project management advice and guidance, consultants were engaged to provide this service. The long-term plan is to develop this ability within our own organization.

## Awareness Level Series

Also in support of the graduates from the curriculum, three-day classes are offered periodically for project team members and functional managers who provide resources to projects or who manage project managers.

## Executive Seminars

A series of two-day executive seminars were offered to educate those in senior management about the discipline of project management.

## Conclusion

Critical success factors for our evolution in project management have been the combination of both an avid grassroots movement and strong executive sponsorship. Dual sponsorship was initially provided at the vice president level. The 1996 arrival of a new CIO well-versed in and a strong proponent of project management jettisoned USAA's progress. USAA regularly appears in the top ten of The Best U.S. Companies to Work For. The corporate culture has a long history of supporting employee development and encouraging a learning environment.

Other lessons learned from our three-year experience include:

- Be aware that you are introducing change into the existing corporate culture and manage it accordingly.
- Communicate, communicate, communicate in many different forms, as often as you can.
- Pick your battles wisely and don't expect overnight results.
- Adopt a spirit of continuous improvement. Listen to your customer and faithfully and personally address her concerns.
- Just training the project managers will not be enough. Expect to support the graduates in multiple ways. You must convince them that they can make a difference.
- Sincerely believe that you can make a difference. The rest will follow.

# Simulation/Gaming, An Effective Tool for Project Management

Shigehisa Tsuchiya, Ph.D., Professor, Chiba Institute of Technology
Researcher, The University of Tokyo, Visiting Professor, The University of Michigan

The purpose of this paper is to present a middle range theory on effectiveness of simulation/gaming for the management of a loosely coupled, flat organization using my model of double-loop learning. In the new organization, best suited for coping with the fast changing and ambiguous environment, project teams play predominant roles.

## Reengineered Organization

One of the most important purposes, or the results, of business reengineering is to produce a flatter organization, which is ad hoc, loosely coupled, and flat, whereas the traditional structure is permanent, tightly coupled, and hierarchical. It has become increasingly apparent that the traditional organization style designed to thrive on mass production, stability, and growth cannot be fixed to succeed in the current world where customers, competition, and change demand flexibility and quick response. In the reengineered structure, work is organized around process, and process teams replace the old departmental structure (Hammer and Champy 1993, 66).

The new organization relies heavily on project teams, process teams with shorter life spans, to cope with the frequent and drastic environmental changes. Teams, of one person or several, performing process-oriented work are inevitably self-directing. Within the boundaries of their obligations to the organization—agreed upon deadlines, productivity goals, quality standards, and so on—they decide how and when work is going to be done. Empowerment is an unavoidable consequence of reengineered processes; process cannot be reengineered without empowering process workers (Hammer and Champy, 71).

By flattening its structure and loosening its couplings, an organization can (1) promote entrepreneurship and innovation from the bottom by retaining more mutations and novel solutions, and (2) improve sensitivity to the environmental changes by having many sensing elements in the organization. A loosely coupled, flat organization can adapt to a considerably wider range of changes in the environment, and also can "know" its environment better.

However, empowering the individual subsystems (or teams) when there is a relatively low level of alignment worsens the chaos and makes managing the organization even more difficult. In organizations, the energies of individual subsystems may work at cross purposes. If we drew a picture of the organization as a collection of subsystems with different degree of ability headed in different directions in their lives, the picture might look something like exhibit 1. The fundamental characteristic of the relatively unaligned organization is wasted energy. Individual subsystems may work extraordinary hard, but their efforts do not efficiently translate to organization effort. By contrast, when an organization becomes more aligned, a commonality of direction energies and individuals' energies harmonize. Resonance or synergy develops.

**Exhibit 1.** Alignment

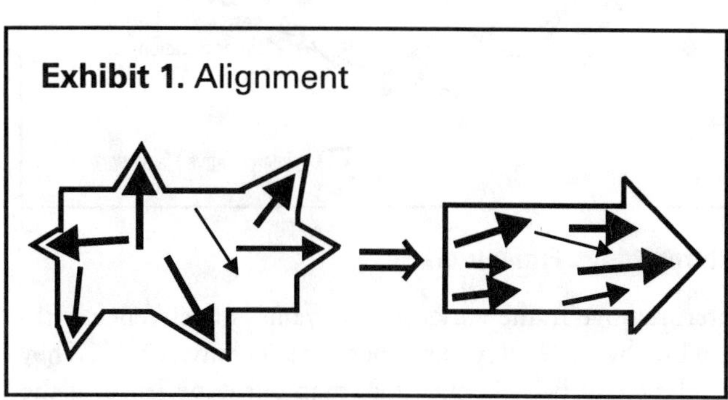

Successful management of a loosely coupled, flat organization, therefore, requires realizing coexistence of firm central direction and maximum individual autonomy. In their book *In search of Excellence*, Peters and Waterman point out that simultaneous loose-tight properties, the last of their "eight basics" of excellent management practice, is mostly a summary point. They claim that organizations which live by the loose-tight principle do this literally through "faith"—through value systems.

## Commensurability

The shared value system, or commensurability, of interpretative framework in this paper realizes coexistence of firm central direction and maximum individual autonomy, which is indispensable for a loosely coupled, flat organization where project teams play crucial roles.

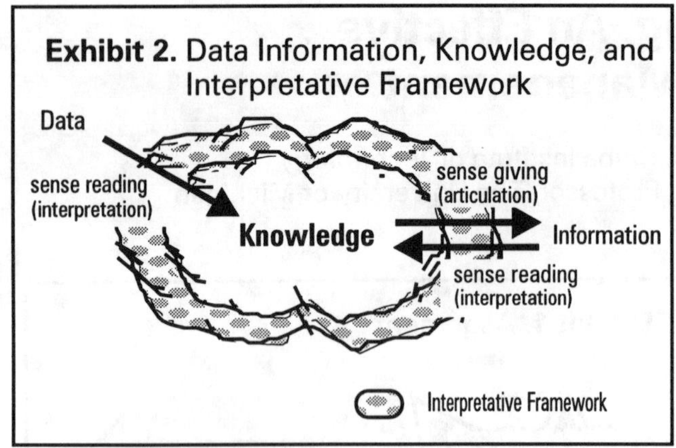


**Exhibit 2.** Data Information, Knowledge, and Interpretative Framework

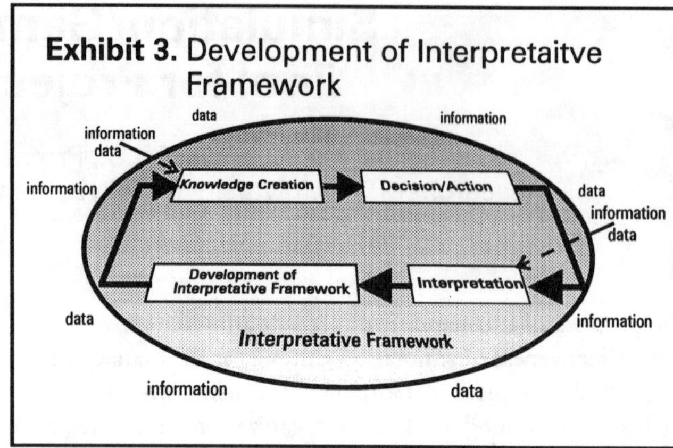


**Exhibit 3.** Development of Interpretaitve Framework

## Interpretative Framework

Interpretative frameworks are the frames of reference within which we interpret our experience (Polanyi 1958). They are the cognitive schemata that map our experience of the world, identifying both its relevant aspects and how we are to understand them.

All knowledge is either tacit or rooted in tacit knowledge and can only be expressed and transferred indirectly by means of metaphor or language in a broad sense. Michael Polanyi classified human knowledge into two categories: explicit knowledge and tacit knowledge (1966). Explicit knowledge refers to knowledge that can be expressed in words, pictures, or other articulate devices. Tacit knowledge, which includes intuition, is knowledge that can hardly be expressed in any kind of language. While tacit knowledge can be possessed by itself, explicit knowledge must rely on being tacitly understood and applied. Therefore, all knowledge is fundamentally tacit.

It is important to make clear distinctions among the terms knowledge, information, and data, although they are often used interchangeably (Tsuchiya 1994). Information is knowledge expressed by means of metaphors. Information carries its sender's knowledge articulated through his interpretative framework. To become knowledge of its receiver, however, the information needs to be interpreted through the framework of the receiver. Each person has her own framework, which functions in similar manner to a filter. When the sender's framework is quite different from the receiver's, the receiver seldom acquires the knowledge that the sender intended to transfer (see exhibit 2).

## Development of Framework

Organizations as well as individuals develop their interpretative frameworks through learning by experience, or through making sense of the outcomes of their decisions and actions. They form and implement decisions and actions based on their knowledge. And the creation of knowledge is regulated by their frameworks, because their frameworks distort, exaggerate, minimize, or even ignore any information or data. It is difficult to accept and incorporate new information or data if it conflicts with the governing framework. Thus, the four stages— knowledge creation, decision and action, interpretation, and development of framework—are interconnected through a feedback loop, as shown in exhibit 3. Since this loop tends to reinforce the existing interpretative framework, the framework for interpreting experience is generally resistant to change (Tsuchiya 1996a, 105).

## Commensurability

Commensurability is that aspect of Kuhn's doctrine that deals with the cognitive compatibility of concepts, problems, facts, and assertions. It is a kind of common denominator of interpretative frameworks (Murakami 1992, 134). The chief consequence of incommensurability—or, if one takes a different stand, its chief cause—is the impossibility of translating from the language of one conceptual framework into the language of another framework (Pearce 1987, 3). Communication breakdown regularly characterizes discourse between participants in incommensurable point of view (Kuhn 1970, 232).

Organizational knowledge creation is not possible if the interpretative frameworks of the organization and its members are incommensurable. The first reason is that new knowledge is not likely to be accepted when it conflicts greatly with the governing framework. If new knowledge raises issues beyond those included in the framework, involves new environmental factors, or specifies radically different kinds of action-outcome relationships, its acceptance will require major changes in the framework. The second reason is that the same data or information can be interpreted differently in the organization. Incommensurability prevents the organization and its members from sharing knowledge, which is the most important condition to create organizational knowledge.

The original source of organizational knowledge is the tacit knowledge of its individual members. However, organizational knowledge is not a mere gathering of individual

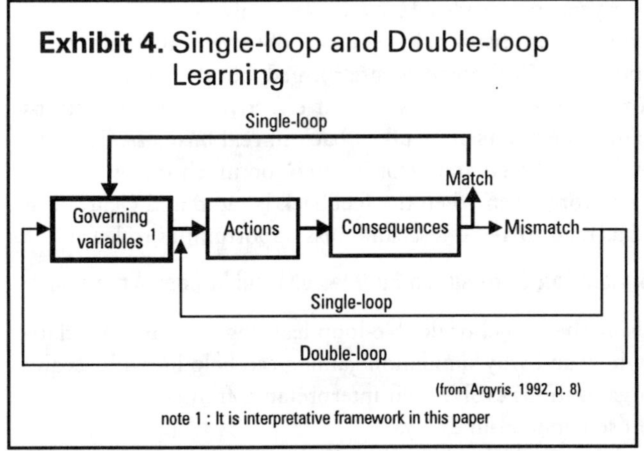

**Exhibit 4.** Single-loop and Double-loop Learning

knowledge. To become organizational knowledge, individual knowledge has to be shared and legitimated among the decision-makers of the organization (Tsuchiya 1994).

To improve commensurability, the organization has to reform the governing interpretative frameworks. The organization and its members have to learn new frame-works. It is what Argyris and Schön called double-loop learning (1978, 18–20).

## Model of Double-Loop Learning

### Single-Loop and Double-Loop Learning

Learning is defined as occurring under two conditions. First, learning occurs when there is a match between its design for action and the actuality or outcome. Second, learning occurs when a mismatch between intentions and outcomes is identified and corrected; that is, a mismatch is turned into a match. Single-loop learning occurs when matches are created, or mismatches are corrected by changing actions. Double-loop learning occurs when mismatches are corrected by first examining and altering the governing interpretative framework, or the culture (values and beliefs), and then the actions (exhibit 4). Single-loop learning leads to the development of some rudimentary associations of behavior and outcomes, but these usually are of short duration and impact only part of actions. Results from double-loop learning change culture and have long-term effects and impacts on the individual or the organization.

Double-loop learning, however, is extremely difficult because interpretative frameworks are resistant to change. Individuals and organizations develop their interpretative frameworks by interpreting, or making sense of, the outcomes of their decisions and actions. They learn from experience, but learning is problematic because history offers only meager samples of experience. In addition, these interpretations of experience depend on the frames within which events are comprehended (Daft and Weick 1984). We assume that individuals and organizations modify their understandings in a way that is intended to be adaptive. They are, however, operating under conditions in which (a) what happened is not immediately obvious, (b) why it happened is obscure, and (c) whether what happened is good is unclear (March and Olsen 1975).

Since what has happened is not always obvious, and the causality of events is difficult to untangle, outcomes can be interpreted in various ways. Individuals and organizations seldom acknowledge mismatch between intentions and outcomes, which can only be corrected by altering governing interpretative frameworks. They often seem to be able to reinterpret their objectives or the outcomes in such a way as to make themselves successful even when the shortfall seems quite large. Even when they admit mismatch, they try to develop stories in support of interpretations that sustain governing frameworks. Therefore, learning is almost always single-loop, which reinforces the governing interpretative framework.

### Model of Double-Loop Learning

New knowledge is not likely accepted if it conflicts greatly with the paradigm held by the organizational members. The cognitive limits suggested by March and Simon (1958 ), which affect decision-making, also affect this acceptance, which is essentially a decision itself. Even given evidence of the validity of new knowledge in terms of organizational criteria, individuals will be limited in their ability to make major changes in how they view the organization or its environment. If new knowledge raises issues beyond those included in the paradigm, involves new environmental or organizational factors, or specifies radically different kinds of action-outcome relationships, its acceptance will require such changes. Thus, new knowledge will be accepted only if it is consistent with the existing paradigm within the organization.

Since these paradigms are frameworks which simplify reality, they will be imperfect in that they will not include potentially relevant factors. Performance gaps may occur, which cannot be resolved within the paradigm, because they in fact reflect such factors. Given this paradigmatic nature of organizational learning, such performance gaps will be analogous to what Kuhn (1962) calls anomalies.

If the number of anomalies of this kind remains relatively small, this will not cause a major problem within the organization. If, however, the number of anomalies becomes great, their existence will begin to undermine the belief of organizational members in the validity of organizational knowledge. These anomalies will indicate that the knowledge on which action within the organization is based is inadequate. Under these conditions, non-paradigmatic knowledge will become increasingly acceptable. Indeed, there may occur a "paradigm revolution," to borrow Kuhn's (1970) term (Duncan and Weiss 1979, 95).

To make double-loop learning, therefore, organizations have to cut the loop in Exhibit 3. All decisions and actions are based on knowledge, which include intuition. The interpretations of experience depend on the governing interpretative framework. Therefore, the only possible way to cut the loop is by creating new knowledge free from the limitations of the governing framework. Based on the new knowledge, the organization can make new decisions and actions, and evolve its interpretative framework by interpreting the outcomes.

## A New Role Of Simulation/Gaming

Simulation/gaming is an effective tool for double-loop learning. Simulation/gaming can promote a shared image of the complex system and help participants create a common framework for understanding the issue. Simulation is an attempt to abstract and reproduce the central features of a complex system for the purpose of understanding, experimenting with, and predicting the behavior of the system (Miller and Duke 1975). For the purpose of this paper, simulation/gaming is taken as a general category, which may contain elements of games and/or role play.

### Dilemma of Learning from Experience

Human beings and organizations learn from experience and learn best through firsthand experience (March, et al. 1991). We learn to walk, ride a bicycle, drive an automobile, and play the piano by trial and error; we act, observe the consequences of our action, and adjust (Senge 1990). Taking in information is only distantly related to real learning. ( It would be nonsensical to say, "I just read a great book about bicycle riding—I've now learned that.")

However, "learning by doing" only works so long as the feedback from our actions is rapid and unambiguous. In the real world, there exist many factors that lead to the "dilemma of learning from experience."

We each have a "learning horizon," a breadth of vision in time and space within which we assess the consequences of our actions. When our actions have consequences beyond our learning horizon, it becomes impossible to learn from direct experience.

Herein lies the core learning dilemma that confronts organizations: we learn best from experience but we never directly experience the consequences of many of our most important decisions. The most critical decisions made in organizations have system-wide consequences that stretch over years or decades. History offers only meager samples of experience. Historical events are observed, and inferences about historical processes are formed, but the paucity of historical events conspires against effective learning. Actions cannot be reversed or taken back in real business. The risk and cost of trial and error is often too much for us to take. Therefore, even when the feedback is rapid and clear, most of us tend to avoid tests and miss opportunities to learn.

### Simulation/Gaming, an Enabler of Double Loop-Learning

Using the model of double-loop learning, we can now clarify how and why simulation/gaming can help individuals and organizations evolve their interpretative frameworks and improve commensurability.

First of all, simulation/gaming compresses time and space so that we can learn from experience even when the consequences of our decisions and actions are in the future and in distant parts of the organization. Secondly, it can be employed to expand the range of experiences that make sense to participants. In the simulated world, the participants have an opportunity to make a variety of decisions and actions which are quite unlikely in the real world, and to interpret their outcomes. Although they are 'lesser' experiences (Greenblat 1989), they are far less costly in time and money, and can be made available to far more people. The third reason is that simulation/gaming may give opportunities to share experience in an experimental setting. By sharing experience and interpreting its outcomes, the participants can convey holistic thought and share knowledge which would otherwise not be possible, and increase commensurability of their frameworks.

In addition, computerized simulation can make unique contributions—it can evolve the mode of interpretative frameworks. New knowledge is not likely to be accepted if it conflicts greatly with the governing framework. Nevertheless, computerized simulation can create metaphors which penetrate through incommensurable frameworks, convey sender's knowledge to the receiver, and create new knowledge. The new knowledge created free from the limitations of the governing interpretative framework triggers double-loop learning and the framework evolves.

The reasons are as follows:

1. Such metaphors can easily be shared on computer networks. Sharing metaphors (or information) is an essential precondition for sharing knowledge although it is not the sufficient condition.
2. People tend to regard the metaphors created through computerized simulation as objective. Objective ideas transfer very easily and rapidly throughout a culture and between cultures on an explicit and outward basis (Prosser 1978).

3. Computerized simulations give legitimacy to the metaphors and the knowledge behind them. Legitimacy makes it easy for people to accept metaphors representing knowledge. Legitimacy is established by showing that the knowledge accomplishes appropriate objectives or by showing that it was made in appropriate ways. The first demonstration is often difficult because it is hard to show the linkage. Thus, legitimacy often depends on the appropriateness of the process as it does on the outcomes (March and Olsen 1986). Computerized simulation provides appropriateness of the process and gives legitimacy to the metaphors and knowledge.

## Conclusion

To cope with today's fast changing, ambiguous environment, organizations need to change their structures from traditional permanent, tightly coupled, and hierarchical to ad hoc, loosely coupled, and flat. In the new organizational structure, work is done mainly by process teams, which include project teams. To manage such an organization successfully, we have to achieve coexistence of firm central direction and maximum individual autonomy, which commensurability alone can realize. Simulation/gaming can improve commensurability and realize simultaneous loose-tight properties through facilitating double-loop learning, which is extremely difficult because frameworks for interpreting experience are generally resistant to change. Computerized simulation can make a unique contribution: its outcomes can be accepted even by non-participating people with incommensurable frameworks. When accepted, the outcomes create new knowledge free from the limitations of the governing framework and trigger its evolution.

### References


Argyris, C., and D.A. Schön. 1978. *Organizational Learning: A Theory of Action Perspective*. Reading, MA: Addison-Wesley.

Daft, R.L., and K.E. Weick. 1984. "Toward a Model of Organizations as Interpretation Systems." *Academy of Management Review* 9: 2, 284–295.

Duncan, R., and A. Weiss. 1979. "Organizational Learning: Implications for Organizational Design." In *Research in Organizational Behavior*, Vol. 1, JAI Press, 75–123.

Greenblat, C.S. 1989. "Extending the Range of Experience." In *Communication and Simulation: From Two Fields to One Theme*. Clevedon, UK: Multilingual Matters, 269–283.

Hammer, M., and J. Champy. 1993. *Reengineering the Corporation: A Manifesto for Business Revolution*. New York: HarperCollins.

Kuhn, T.S. 1962. *The Structure of Scientific Revolutions*. Chicago: University of Chicago Press.

———. 1970. "Reflections on my Critics." In *Criticism and the Growth of Knowledge*. New York, NY: Cambridge University Press, 231–278.

March, J.G. and J.P. Olsen. 1975. "The Uncertainty of the Past: Organizational Learning under Ambiguity." *European Journal of Political Research* 3: 147–171.

———. 1986. "Garbage Can Models of Decision Making in Organizations." In *Ambiguity and Command*. Marsfield, MA: Pitman Publishing, 11–35.

March, J.G., and H.A. Simon. 1958. *Organizations*. New York, NY: John Wiley.

March, J.G., S. Sproull, and M. Tamuz. 1991. "Learning from Samples of One or Fewer. *Organization Science* 2: 1, 1–13.

Miller, R.I., and R.D. Duke. 1975. "Gaming: A Methodological Experiment." *Gaming-Simulation: Rationale, Design, and Applications*. Thousand Oaks, CA: Sage Publications, 362–372.

Murakami, Y. 1992. *Hankoten no keizaigaku* (Japanese). Tokyo: Chuo Koron sha.

Pearce, D. 1987. *Roads to Commensurability*. Holland: D. Reidel Publishing.

Polanyi, M. 1958. *Personal Knowledge*. London: Routledge & Kegan Paul.

———. 1966. *The Tacit Dimension*. London: Routledge & Kegan Paul.

Prosser, M.P. 1978. *The Cultural Dialogue: An Introduction to Intercultural Communication*. Boston: Houghton Mifflin.

Senge, P.M. 1990. *The Fifth Discipline: The Art and Practice of the Learning Organization*. Century Business.

Tsuchiya, S. 1994. "A study of Corporate Knowledge." IIIA, *Proceedings of International Symposium on the Management of Industrial and Corporate Knowledge 94*, 105–111.

———. 1996a. "A New Role for Computerized Simulation in Social Science: Summary Thoughts on a Case Study." *Simulation & Gaming: An International Journal* 27: 1, 103–109.

———. 1996b. "New Challenge to Japanese Corporations in Organizational Knowledge Creation. In *Knowledge Management: Organization Competence and Methodology*. Würsburg: Ergon Verlag, 207–212.

# The Pros and Cons of Solo and Co-Presentations

Noel Hutson, PMP

## Introduction and Overview

Human communications is the heart of human behavior, and it enables human individuals and persons to be individuated and integrated, whether they are acting or accepting. When there is no communication, poor communication, or failure in communication, there is isolation, islanding, project, and human failure.

To stick together during good times and bad times is the pro-active behavior of persons integrated by good two-way communications. Reactive people disintegrate under inevitable human conflicts, because the communication channels are non-existent and conflict is never resolved by reactive methods. A prerequisite for the pro-active problem solving approach is good two-way communications.

The ability to communicate successfully is a skill that can be learned, practiced, and honed, provided one understands the purpose and the method of human communications.

## The Purpose of Human Communications

The purpose of human communications is to act or accept together.

When a group of individuals act together as a team there is synergy, motivation, focusing on a common purpose, and successful two-way inter-communications between members of the team, which makes acting and accepting together possible.

When a group of individuals are in conflict, or when negative events occur during the project, those who are trained in good communications know how to solve conflict. By respecting individuals and focusing on the problem solving approach, good can be brought out of the negative event that threatened to stop the project. The event that threatens to sever communication channels and halt the project can be turned into good, by accepting it, together, as a team, through good communications and pro-active conflict management.

## The Method of Human Communications

The building blocks of human communications are transmitter, message, encoding, channel, decoding, and receiver.

### Message

For successful communications, a person should first have a clear message, an idea, or thought that is rooted in rich emotion and psychic energy of a well individuated person.

### Transmitter

The individual or person transmitting the message is called the transmitter. In order to successfully communicate, the transmitter should be as individuated as she can be, and, if possible, time the communications when the person receiving the message is most individuated. The transmitter should know the theory of the fundamentals of good communications and have experience in practicing these skills. The transmitter should know the power of words, tone of voice, and body language.

The trust and credibility are primarily transmitted or received by three communicating power components, namely, WORDS, TONE OF VOICE, and BODY LANGUAGE.

The communicating power of these components is:

| | | |
|---|---|---|
| • Verbal Channel | WORDS | 7% |
| • Vocal Channel | TONE OF VOICE | 38% |
| • Visual Channel | BODY LANGUAGE | 55% |

### Encoding

Depending on the channel used, the message is then encoded per accepted evolution of human communications. If the audible channel is chosen, the message is coded in speech, directly as in one-to-one communications or indirectly as on the telephone. If the visual channel is chosen the message is converted into script or body language.

### Channel

The average person has five senses and hence there are five channels of communications: audible, visual, touch, smell, and taste.

#### *How We Learn*

| | |
|---|---|
| Taste | 1% |
| Touch | 1 1/2% |

Smell 3 1/2%
Hearing 11%
Sight 83%

### *What We Retain*

10% of what we READ
20% of what we HEAR
30 % of what we SEE
50% of what we SEE and HEAR
70% of what we HEAR and TELL
90% of what we TELL and DEMONSTRATE

The superiority of the visual channel can be seen during transmission and reception. However, good presenters know the superiority of using as many channels as possible to reinforce their message.

### De-Coding

Decoding is the process by which the receiver interprets the received coded message for content, assimilation, and understanding by the psyche. In active communications, the decoded message is retransmitted to the transmitter for verification of the transmitter's original intention.

### Receiver

The receiver is the person receiving the coded message, who in turn decodes the message and acts or accepts together with the transmitter. For successful communications, the receiver should be as individuated as possible and trained in the fundamentals and be experienced in the practice of these communication skills.

## The Attributes of a Good Presentation

There are three parts to a good presentation: the introduction and overview, the body of the presentation, and the summary and conclusion. In the introduction, the presenter tells the audience what he is going to tell them; in the body of the presentation, the presenter tells it to them; and in the conclusion the presenter tells them what he told them.

### Introduction and Overview

After the introduction of the presenter by the moderator, the presenter should at the very outset state the purpose of his presentation in clear language, with a good tone of voice and with a body language that complements her message. The presenter's credibility and trust as a speaker will be judged by the audience's perception of the presenter's body language before they begin to listen to the inner meaning of the presenter's words and tone of voice. Audience eye contact is vital.

### Body of Presentation

The presenter or presenters should begin the body of the presentation by gradually stressing the key points of it, until they have won the trust and acceptance by the audience. When they have brought the audience to the point of listening, they should share their inner convictions and beliefs for the main point or points of their message. The audience hears with their ears but listens with their minds. The success of their presentation will be measured by the sharing of their gifts of illumination and by the sparks of fire they are able to generate in the minds of the audience, with which their listeners are motivated to act or accept together, the human task of transfiguration of matter into spirit.

### Summary and Conclusion

One of the strokes of genius of a good presenter is his ability to recapitulate his presentation in a few words, sentences, a key phrase or quote that summarizes his presentation, and end with an outstanding conclusion that leaves the audience wanting more.

## The Attributes of a Good Audience

Modern audiences at international presentations are composed of world experts in their respective fields. With their global experience of the world's countries, they are able to transcend country, culture, language, religion, caste, color, gender, age, business position, and disability. They are open to holistic thinking. They are usually good communicators and hence good listeners and they listen as a team, not to the details but to the message as a whole. They also offer pin-drop silence that is a clue to inner listening to the speaker's message. They are also listening in relation to their personal ability to think and believe and hence can be a challenge to the international speaker.

## Solo Presentations

Solo presenters are special persons with leadership skills. They usually have two or more of the three requisites of being a good presenter:

1. **Be a good person.** Good solo presenters have developed themselves into being a good person. They have progressed themselves through the four stages of individuation: I, Thou, We, and God.
2. **Be a good speaker.** Good solo presenters are not only born speakers, but they have trained themselves in the art of communications and practiced their speaking

skills to the point of possessing the ability to effectively deliver their message.

3. **Have a good message.** Solo presenters believe in the eternal value of their message that has universal value and truth, and they are under a commitment to share their vision with others.

### Advantages

1. Solo presenters enjoy being in total control of their presentations, from beginning to end, and this keeps the audience attention and involvement heightened, providing a most enjoyable experience.
2. Solo presenters who are gifted individuals do the audience a favor by communicating their vision and unique experience, first hand, to the audience.
3. Solo presenters are good persons, good speakers with a good message, and their genius and talents in these three areas enable them to contribute to the emotional, psychological, and growth needs of the audience.
4. A solo presenter is totally responsible for the organization, layout, flow, and cohesiveness of the presentation, which makes it easy for the audience listening pleasure.

### Disadvanages

1. If a solo presenter is weak in one or more areas of being a good person, a good speaker, and having a good message, she will lose her audience, and there will be no contribution, growth, or message transfer.
2. A solo presenter can sometimes use the audience for his ego needs rather than serving the audience needs.
3. If something happens to the solo presenter before or during the presentation—if the solo presenter has not prepared himself, planned his presentation, and practiced the presentation—the presentation could become a failure and a displeasure to the audience.
4. If the presenter is not good at his art, he might intimidate the audience sooner, and there is no strategy for a recovery plan.

## Co-Presentations

Sometimes a topic or theme may be too deep and broad that it may be too much for a solo presenter. It becomes necessary to distribute the responsibility to specialists and have a team of two or more presenters with a head panelist, moderator, or lead presenter.

### Advantages

1. If something happens to one of the presenters, the other presenter or presenters can carry the whole presentation, without disruption to the audience. This is especially helpful when there are last minute emergency changes in presenters' schedules. Each speaker backs up the other in content, message, and failure of one of the presenters.
2. When a certain presenter is performing, the other presenter or presenters can observe audience reaction and feedback to the presenter, making any corrections if necessary.
3. The audience enjoys the variety of multiple speakers, a change of style, and a change in perspective of the presentation theme.
4. The weakness of one of the presenters is compensated by the strengths of the other presenters.
5. When there is team work, there is synergy, and impossible goals are attained that are not possible by the sum total of the individual presenters.
6. With co-presenters there is more opportunity to team together, for ebb and flow of information and education.
7. With the different styles of co-presenters there is more potential for blending of the presentation into a completely cohesive whole that is complementary and educational.
8. There is less work for each person and hence each person can do a better job at presenting.

### Disadvantages

1. Costs more due to increased number of presenters.
2. If presenters are not trained in teamwork, co-presentations can be confusing, with multiple perspectives or visions of the message, for the audience, which defeats the purpose of communications.
3. Because of friendship, co-presenters can make the mistake of relating to each other, rather than together serve the audience. Jokes, entertainment, ego needs, and so on could deflect the energy normally reserved to focus on a clear message and share it with the audience.
4. There is more work up front, in the way of planning, coordination, presentation draft review by the team, and editing by the moderator, rehearsals, and dress rehearsal.
5. If not cohesive, the presentation could be annoying to the audience.

## Increasing the Knowledge Level through Team-Work

Communications helps ideas and thoughts from one psyche to be transferred to another. The presenter and the audience working as a team enable this knowledge transfer that is unique, enlightening, and enriching. The unique talents, expertise, and knowledge of one or more persons is shared by others for the edification of the whole group. Individualism, which leads to isolation, islanding and vegetating, gives place to community through the bonds of professional friendships and acceptance, through unity and togetherness.

## Summary and Conclusions

We have defined the purpose of human communications as acting or accepting together. Solo and co-presentations are the means of the attaining the purpose of human communications. The choice of solo or co-presentations should be based on which method will best help the presenter and audience attain the purpose or end of human communications.

A successful presentation can be a rare experience for the presenter or presenters and the audience. The super-human delight of being part of a successful presentation, whether as presenter or audience, can linger in our minds for years to come.

When the human purpose of life dawns on a well developed humanity of integrated persons, when the noosphere has found its eyes, a tremendous and fantastic future awaits our species that is globalized, universalized, and integrated through successful communications as we act and accept together the same and common purpose; namely, the transfiguration of matter into spirit.

# Using a PMBOK Approach to Starting a Successful Student Chapter

Ed O'Connor, PMP - Bausch & Lomb, Inc.

Following the Project Management Institute '94 Symposium in Vancouver we began exploring the potential for a student chapter of the Project Management Institute in the Rochester, New York, area. Rochester Institute of Technology (R.I.T.) and Nazareth College of Rochester currently offer courses in project management as part of their graduate business programs; other colleges are showing interest as well.

With some initial market testing consisting of interviews with business college students, faculty, and staff it was determined that there was a need for a student chapter in the area. Students have a strong desire to network with project management professionals in the immediate area. Also attractive to adult learners is the project management professional certification program as an add-on to their credentials. With local firms down-sizing, this additional credential can prove to be valuable in maintaining a job or providing a competitive advantage during the job search process.

## Project Initiation

To start the process of chapter formation a presentation to Rochester Institute of Technology's College of Business senior staff was developed with support from Charles Koster, an adjunct faculty member teaching project management at the institute. The dean of the College of Business and department chair agreed with the proposal and assigned a faculty advisor and administrative assistant to support the new chapter.

As a result of this presentation made in August, 1995, a bulletin was sent to one thousand graduate students announcing the formation of a student chapter. In October, 1995, the first meeting was held explaining the financial benefits associated with student membership. These are shown in Figure 1.

## Project Planning

Students attending this first meeting showed great interest, and officers were immediately elected to serve for the 1995–96 school year term. Most of the new members were part-time students pursuing graduate studies. All were adult learners and most were currently employed in the Rochester area. Project Management Institute regulations stipulate that to be recognized by the Project Management Institute as student members, they need to be full-time matriculated students. This problem was overcome by obtaining financial support from the local project management institute chapter for reduced fees for local seminars and luncheon meetings, plus an agreement to partially subsidize students who pursue project management professional certification. Therefore, part-time students were provided the same benefits as full-time students, except for the personal copies of the *Project Management Journal* and *PM Network* magazine. It is important to note that this initial "seed money" from the Rochester PMI Chapter was critical to attracting new student members and to the overall successful start-up of the student chapter. Student officers then focused on recruiting new members with special emphasis on attracting the minimum number of full-time students required by the Project Management Institute for receiving the new chapter charter.

A "resolution of support" from the Rochester PMI Chapter was signed by the officers and submitted to Project Management Institute's executive offices. Students then began to develop a constitution and by-laws. These documents were approved by both the Rochester PMI Chapter and the student chapter and submitted to the Project Management Institute in mid-1996. The required minimum number of full-time students was reached during the summer of 1996.

### Program Implementation

During the first year in the life of the chapter five excellent programs for student members were held:

#### *"Project Planning in the Classroom Environment"*

This presentation by a local project management professional focused on the application of project management planning tools for student projects.

#### *"What Does Project Management Institute Mean to Me?"*

Three local project management professionals led a panel discussion describing to students how project management and involvement with Project Management Institute has helped their careers.

**Exhibit 1.**

| | Full-Time Member Cost | Student Cost | Student Savings |
|---|---|---|---|
| **Dues** | $115 | $35 | $80 |
| Annual PMI Symposium | 570 | 125 | 445 |
| Annual Local PMI Conference | 125 | 25 | 100 |
| Monthly PMI Rochester Chapter Meetings (10/years) | 100 | 50 | 50 |
| *PmNETwork & PM Journal* | Included ($40/year annual) | Included ($40/year annual) | |
| Monthly Newsletter (Local) | Free | Free | |
| Networking Opportunities with Professionals | Free | Free | |

***"Project Management Certification"***

The Rochester PMI Chapter certification officer reviewed the certification process, including the exam preparatory course offered by the local chapter, and some examples of exam questions.

***"Team Building"***

One of the adjunct professors presented an interactive session on the importance of working together in teams and the value of team decisions versus individual decisions.

***"Health Systems Project Management"***

A project management professional from Johnson & Johnson profiled the process utilized by that company for blood analyzer equipment development. This presentation was videotaped for distance-learning students.

Students also participated for the first time in the Rochester PMI conference held in May 1996.

Objectives for the chapter's second year of operation continued to focus on increasing student membership through exciting and dynamic educational programs on project management. Student chapter officers voted to have one excellent student-chapter-sponsored program per quarter to ensure high quality results. This proved to be very effective with excellent attendance.

The first major program during the second year was jointly sponsored by the student chapter and the local Project Management Institute chapter. In November 1996 the first annual PMP/Student Recognition Night was held with the goal of bringing together student members and project management professionals for networking opportunities. A team of project management students from one of the local colleges offering project management as part of its curriculum presented *A Guide to the Project Management Body of Knowledge* analysis of a recent three-story expansion of the lodge at Woodcliff Resort, the site of the PMP/Student Recognition event. Nine project teams from local colleges competed for the honor of participating in this special event. The winning team was selected by project management faculty members and local Project Management Institute board officers. Over eighty students and project management professionals attended this successful free event that included in excess of $1,000 in door prizes. A major software training firm, ExecuTrain, provided a product display and a door prize for one free course in Microsoft Project. Funding was provided for this event by the Rochester PMI Capter using

**Exhibit 2.** PMI Student Chapter—
Student Benefits

- ✓ Membership in the top professional organization for project managers
- ✓ Subsidized dues - $35 versus $115
- ✓ Reduced costs to PMI meetings & symposiums
- ✓ Networking opportunities with local PMI executives & project managers.
- ✓ Opportunity to serve as local officers of student chapter.
- ✓ Specific Interest Group networking opportunities.

**Exhibit 3.** PMI Student Chapter—Benefits to (College)

- ❑ Vehicle to promote & recruit future students.
- ❑ Attract industry support.
- ❑ Gain competitive advantage.
- ❑ Close affiliation with PMI - 390 members locally.
- ❑ Positive recognition in PMI publications.

proceeds from the local spring Project Management Institute conference.

Quarterly programs continued and included a jointly sponsored conference on team-building and conflict resolution. The co-sponsor was the student chapter of ASQC. This proved to be very helpful in planning and executing the program with the added benefit of attracting ASQC student chapter members.

A conference on the use of project management computer tools, including Primavera and Microsoft Project, was presented on campus in a day-long forum complete with door prizes from the software vendors.

## Strategy for Continued Growth

Our growth strategy for the chapter includes expanding student membership within the Rochester Institute of Technology, as well as actively recruiting students from other area colleges and universities that have an interest in the field of project management. To date, students from Nazareth College of Rochester and State University of New York at Brockport have joined the student chapter with Rochester Institute of Technology students. Supporters continue to look for ways to link students with project management professionals (PMP's) to expand students' understanding of the real world environment. This includes facilitating the job search process for students as part of their involvement in the Project Management Institute.

The Rochester student chapter is the fifth student chapter chartered by the Project Management Institute and the first time that the chapter consists of students from more than one college in a community. The PMP/Student Recognition Night was the first ever for the Project Management Institute directed at promoting interest in project management professional certification, recognizing project management professionals for their achievement, and providing a forum for networking.

## Factors for Success

1. Start with colleges that currently teach project management as part of their curriculum. If no college teaches project management, sell the college on the merits of offering a course initially, followed by a master's degree in project management. Prepare a slide presentation similar to Table II.
2. Gain support early-on from the local Project Management Institute chapter, a college or university dean, and faculty member.
3. Utilize the resources of the Project Management Institute's chapter coordinator at the executive office. Templates for a chapter constitution and by-laws, plus publicity materials, are available free of charge to help launch a new chapter.
4. Sell financial benefits of joining the student chapter using a straight-forward message.
5. Develop effective networking opportunities for students, such as an evening event designed to link students and project management professionals.
6. Provide seed money from the local Project Management Institute chapter to subsidize student participation in Project Management Institute seminars and the project management professional certification exam. During the first two years of operation, three students received their project management professional certification.
7. Get students involved with the local Project Management Institute chapter (e.g., program committee, special interest groups, and so on). Encourage students to take the initiative to sell other students on membership in the Project Management Institute student chapter.
8. Support the student chapter with its plans for quarterly workshops or conferences. Let students take charge, but be there for guidance as needed.

9. Contact other chapters that have experience in developing student chapters and learn from them what works and what does not work.

## Lessons Learned

Do not limit your message to just one college within a university or to one university for that matter. Approach all colleges in the area that already offer project management as part of their curriculum. Our approach was to focus just on the College of Business at Rochester Institute of Technology. Approaching other schools simultaneously no doubt would have helped the chapter grow faster.

Do not underestimate the membership turnover due to graduation. Keep student members involved with the chapter even after graduation if possible. Encourage them to join the local Project Management Institute chapter and continue their support in obtaining new members, participating in student-sponsored programs, and making presentations to faculty and students on the benefits of student chapter membership.

Edward A. O'Connor is currently a project manager for Bausch & Lomb, Inc., in Rochester, New York. He is a project management professional, president of the Rochester PMI Chapter, and is on the adjunct faculty of Rochester Institute of Technology teaching project management as part of that institute's master of business affairs program.

For further information you may contact the author at EAOCONNOR@aol.com or call Colleen Dougherty at Project Management Institute's executive office.

**Exhibit 4.** PMI Student Chapter—the Next Step?

- Obtain list of all potential student members.
- Develop faculty awareness of chapter.
- Provide in-class presentations re: chapter activities.
- Assign administrative contact for "on campus" publicity of programs.

**Exhibit 5.** PMI Student Chapter—How Organized?

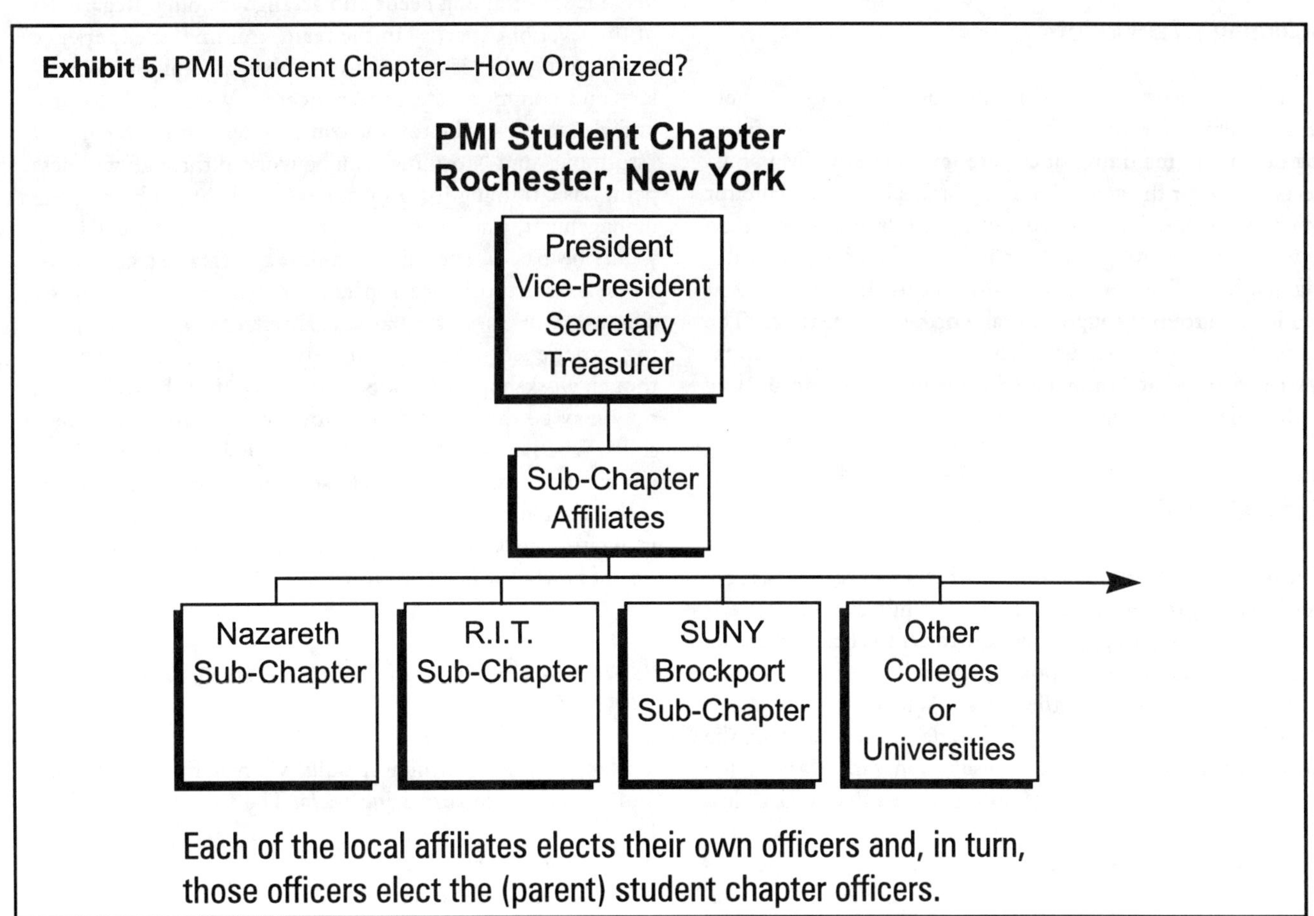


Each of the local affiliates elects their own officers and, in turn, those officers elect the (parent) student chapter officers.

# Project Management's Role with Facilitators

Roger L. Erickson, W. J Schafer Associates, Inc.

Facilitator skills are essential in the increased power-sharing project environments that project managers find today. Not only must the project manager (PM) know how to utilize the talents of a dedicated facilitator person, but the project manager must practice facilitation techniques to fully utilize the talents on the project. A facilitator that is focused on the team processes can be a high value person on a diverse multi-discipline project, if working in concert with the project manager. The project manager needs to understand the focus, methods, and vocabulary of the facilitator. Further, the project manager must schedule time and budget for dedicated facilitation activities. Keeping a balance of cost and pay-back will depend on experience of both the project manager and facilitator.

## Selecting a Facilitator

There is no recognized certification for facilitators. However, there are numerous training courses and applicable training up to and including doctorate-level material. Many aspects fall under the general heading of facilitator. A facilitator can be someone that has had a one-week training course on how to run a meeting software and may do a fine job of doing just that. There are Myers-Briggs certified analysts that can lead a group through several worthwhile exercises. The advice to a project manager that would like to use a facilitator is: select a facilitator based on prior success in dealing with similar situations.

## Facilitator's Focus

The focus of a facilitator is the inter-human processes that occur in the course of doing a project. While everyone else is head down trying to figure out how to get the best widget designed, the facilitator is looking around to see if all inputs have been considered in the design. When everyone else is wrestling with complex technical trade-off in a meeting, the facilitator is taking notes for consultation with Mary or Joe on how they can make their points more effectively in less time.

Without the knowledge of the project manager's priorities and the support of the project manager, the facilitator's actions may result in dilution of the team focus rather than support. The facilitator should support the project manager by attending to the processes that enhance the chances of successfully achieving the project manager's goals and objectives. The project manager must understand and support what the facilitator is doing by keeping him in the information loop. Aside from direct involvement in activities, the facilitator needs to act as a coach to transfer facilitation techniques to the team members. The facilitator's goal is to work herself out of a job.

## Training

Although the facilitator may do some training, more often he may identify training needs and arrange training. Regardless of the level of expertise in the team, training or experience working together is needed to establish a common vocabulary and common reference concepts. With the help of a knowledgeable facilitator, the common team growth pains of "storming" and "norming" can be worked through with less pain. Basic training for project personnel should be meeting management, time management, and facilitation skills. Beyond the basics, specialized training for target groups or workshops that produce a specific project product may be facilitated. Workshops are particularly effective in quickly gaining experience in the use of new tools and methods. Although workshops may take some days out of the work area, they may be the quickest way for a project to acquire new skills. Whether or not a workshop should be taken in a group environment with peers, supervisors, or subordinates is a topic that should be discussed with the workshop facilitator. The facilitator needs to follow up on early training to assure practice of newly learned behavior.

## What Benefits Can a Facilitator Bring to the Project?

The application of facilitator skills will benefit in many areas and sometimes in surprising ways. The following is a short list:

- Common terminology
- Break old bad habits

- Establish expectations of all players
- Reduce meeting time
- Increase quality of decisions
- Defuse potential destructive conflicts
- Enhanced exchange of ideas

**Common terminology** is not only a challenge to multi-lingual teams, but it is common when outsiders interface with people from a discipline that has used common words in very specific meanings. An astute facilitator would detect this non-agreement and call for a clarification of terms.

The **breaking of old bad habits** can be done if focus and peer pressure is brought to bear on the undesired habit. The recognition of a group or individual norm is the first step followed by an expressed desire to change the norm. Now the question is: how does a facilitator make this happen? First the facilitator observes that there may be an undesirable activity or lack of activity that needs correction, then the appropriate tool(s) are used to establish expectations. The methods result in more accurate communications and visioning between the people to bring a positive response. It may be top-down, bottom-up, interpersonal, or cross-organization communication. An example is a group that had a well established habit of showing up late for meetings. When this group norm was pointed out, discussion covered excuses such as: "Everyone else does it"; "The boss pulls us into ad hoc meetings just before scheduled meetings"; and so on. When the boss was presented with the group desire to establish a new norm of being on time to meetings, he asked to be informed if he was holding up another meeting. Then he (the boss) could make a decision as to whether his meeting should hold up "real work." The norm took large steps in the correct direction over the following weeks, saving the program hundreds of labor hours a month. Sometimes it is not so easy. Facilitation workshops of a few days spread over weeks or months can identify root causes and provide a good habit practice to establish the desired behavior. As an extreme remedy to a bad group habit, a member or members may have to be replaced.

**Establishing the expectations** of all players goes with breaking old bad habits. If the expectation is that "everyone else is going to do something," the peer pressure is to do the same, be it beneficial or not. Further, establishing expectations provides a guide for future actions. In multi-disciplinary groups it will accelerate understanding to know the position (agenda, priorities, and so on) of the participants.

Everyone complains about **meetings** that are too long and not effective. There are two parts to the answer: preparation and discipline. If the correct people come to the meeting and know what is to be done and stick to the agenda, it will be a productive meeting.

OK, how do you prepare for a meeting? Establish a doable agenda. A common failing is to put too much on the agenda and/or try to accomplish additional items off the agenda because "the right people" are present. The targets of opportunity are attractive, but don't let them distract from the main agenda. If the agenda starts looking too long or involves sub-groups, create another meeting; two good short meetings are better than a long ineffective one. Once the agenda is set, only invite those to the meeting that need to participate. Resist the temptation to invite people that only need to be notified of the results. When the people are invited, give them an agenda and advise what they need to bring along. Check back with the invited to assure enough attendance to accomplish the agenda. Don't be afraid to reschedule; stuff happens.

Another area of preparation that often throws a meeting on the rocks is the facilities: the presence or absence of telephones (this one works both ways); a room too small or lacking the needed items; lack of lunch planning, if the meeting is to go through lunch—added benefit and better post-lunch attendance will result from feeding them; and outlets for laptops, projectors, flip charts, white boards, and so on. All need to be considered.

Communications have been discussed, but focus is needed on this most important area. Pre-meeting, in meeting, and post-meeting communications each need effort.

Pre-meeting information to the invited is critical for them to prepare; getting information back from them is essential to the meeting manager in preparing. This also affords a lobbying opportunity for both and prevents minor side issues from popping up in the meeting.

During the meeting opportunities abound for lack of, missed, misdirected, and misunderstood communications and general mayhem regarding communications. Things that can go off track, will. With a facilitator to focus on the interpersonal communications, it shouldn't go off track as far and should get back on track quicker. Establishing and maintaining the appropriate attitudes and focus will provide good groundwork for dealing with contentious issues. Facilitating the input from someone who may have an input but is not taking the opportunity to speak or summarizing for another in a filibuster can add significantly to the value of the meeting. Maintaining side notes for the meeting chairman to assure all points on the agenda are covered and providing closure on completed points will move the meeting along and assure coverage of the planned items. Items that need reminders on side notes might include: a welcome, introductions, agenda review for adds and deletes, any ground rules (breaks, speaking time limits), logistics (bathrooms, lunch), action items, summary of meeting, and thank you(s).

Post-meeting communications in the form of minutes and consolidated action item lists will assure that the intentions of a good meeting are followed through. A project manager knows that this is important and wants to do it; the problem is time. The facilitator with a focus on process can support the project manager from meeting planning to wrap-up.

The facilitator can increase the **quality of decisions** in four areas. In the fact collecting and situation analysis stage, the facilitator can introduce appropriate tools to capture ideas and foster synergistic exchanges that will assure the best input in a given amount of time. Summarization of the situation and options so that an informed decision can be made is the second area. In the third area, guiding the group toward the best decision process will depend a lot on the project manager's management style, but also it will depend on the issue and how it is to be implemented. In the fourth area, implementation is the test of a good decision. The decision process can expedite the implementation or cause barriers to implementation that may not be overcome. If the players are understanding of their personal consequences of a decision in terms of things to be done and benefits, they will be able to move forward quickly. This can happen before the decision is made through discussion balancing the various decision options against implementation effort. Conversely, if the players are simply told of a decision and have to reconcile their personal situation without visibility of the total consequence of a decision, it may be difficult to implement in their work group. There is more on decision-making in the section on coaching.)

The facilitator can be very effective in **defusing potentially destructive conflicts** that may otherwise occur. By consulting with people on both sides of a contentious issue, common ground can be identified and focus drawn to the win-win aspects, thereby making compromise or accommodation possible on the other aspects of the issue. Without the facilitator's recognition of a potential conflict and active involvement to redirect the defensive/aggressive energies, much time and progress on the project could be lost.

The topic of **enhanced exchange of ideas** was touched on above in decision making but it goes further than the group process. In a synergistic exercise, a personal realization or dawning is not uncommon, and what an energizer that can be! That energy will spill over into other work areas and is a reward in itself. The facilitator will interject a measure of formality to assure value added participation and provide feedback to encourage and focus the discussion.

## Facilitator Roles and Tools

The facilitator's tool box needs to have several tools for any particular type problem. The tool selection will depend on the consequences (+/_), amount of time available, size of group, and the role that the facilitator is fulfilling. Facilitator roles discussed here are consulting, diagnosing, and coaching.

## Consulting

The consulting role for a facilitator allows her the latitude to get involved in most aspects of the project. The consulting role is an active involvement in groups to facilitate them in moving forward toward their goals (sometimes, defining the goal!). By having a facilitator on the project team that is focused on the processes, the project manager can spend time on the product-focused issues and enjoy a higher level of assurance that basics and facilitating issues are not forgotten. Items such as potential (or real) conflict and team building are the purview of the facilitator.

When a diverse group—each individual having his own agenda and priorities—is brought together on a single focus (design and build a product), **conflict** can be expected. Conflict is not necessarily a bad thing. However, the aim needs to be task-focused, synergistic, and positive, not destructive or divisive. Through respect for the other opinions and goals, the area of conflict can be defined and a resolution found that can be accepted by all. In those instances where there is potential conflict but no possible resolution, or not relevant to the task, conflict avoidance techniques are in order. Quite a bit of literature has been written about "win-win or no-deal." Win-win or no-deal is a good development in negotiating position and can result in a good implementation; however, it will take time.

The facilitator will be a good source of ideas for **team-building** activities. Within the constraints of budget and time there are various activities that can be done to enhance the team's working relationships. A convenient method of team building is a brown bag lunch with a topic. Suggested topics focused on team building may be: decision-making, attendance, communications, coaching, roles and responsibilities, growth, accountabilities, problem solving, honesty, risk taking, conflict resolution, renewal, listening/feedback, or confidentiality. A facilitation workshop can be a time-efficient way to gain an appreciation of facilitation skills and associated vocabulary by all on the team. Much of the learning of facilitation skills are behavior modifications that are best learned in a "doing" environment, such as a workshop. At the other end of the spectrum may be a week in the woods with Outward Bound. The benefits that will come from a positive understanding of the other team members' situations and working methods will go a long way in establishing mutual confidence. How a team capitalizes on personal communications will determine to a large extent the level of project success.

## Diagnosing

Diagnosing may easily be the largest and most important part of the facilitator's day. The facilitator may initiate change based on her interpretations of comments and actions and/or in-actions. It is during the diagnosis that the project manager and facilitator need to compare notes on observations and talk through the consequences of any actions. What are the costs and pay-backs to engaging in a particular change? It may be that the action should be carried out by the project manager.

In a work session the facilitator is constantly evaluating the group with questions such as: Is there a general understanding? Are there conflicting personal agendas? Is additional Information really needed? Can the group move to a decision? How can this session arrive at a better decision quicker? Some of the tools that the facilitator uses in the observations are: observing, listening, analyzing communication patterns, analyzing messages, and reviewing progress against plans.

## Coaching

Real time guidance by the facilitator can move a group to an action plan quickly and with a better quality decision by introducing tools and facilitating the group action. A good example is what I call the "decision road." The stages passed through on the way to a decision are: situation analysis, idea generation, clarification, consensus building, decision-making, and implementation. Often in group action, individuals will bore in on a particular stage without considering the earlier or later stages; yet they are ready to make a decision.

In this **situation analysis** of a issue, it may be labeled a problem, an opportunity, or simply a condition to be monitored. What are the forces to do anything? What are the options for our action? Who is in control? What other events may affect the situation? Will this situation be overcome by other events that will render it or any actions moot? What is the point in time a decision must be made? Who should be involved in the decision? The outcome of this stage may be a resolve to do nothing, monitor the situation, or move towards a decision of some action.

The **idea generation** stage may be to collect ideas on the above questions that need expansion and answers to the questions. There are a number of tools that a facilitator can use in this stage such as: plain old brain storming, normal group technique (plain old brain storming written down), or innovation transfer (application of lessons learned from similar situations). The output of this stage is a large collection of ideas that may or may not be terribly relevant to the situation.

The **clarification** stage will define some pattern to the ideas and develop priorities of where to focus energies. Pareto diagrams, fishbone diagrams, interpretive structural modeling, and a problem statement are all tools that may be appropriate for bringing clarity to the mess of information. In the course of working through these tools, the team members are learning. The learning experience can be taxing but also rewarding. Recognition of the new-found information is an important function of the process that allows people to change their position on a subject. However, it is important to NOT have people constantly reevaluating their position during the process. Too much time and energy would be wasted in explaining the incremental position moves (or non-moves) that may happen. The output of this stage is clarity of options and priorities.

The basis for **consensus building** is an understanding of the various positions people hold relative to the decision at hand. (We will omit personal power exercises.) Negotiation is an important aspect of this stage but certainly not unique to this stage. An interesting example of driving to consensus can be seen in the old movie (check it out at your nearest video store) *Twelve Angry Men*. In the jury room they first did an open vote to see if there was anything to talk about, then they took a secret vote to protect against reprisals. In between votes, various methods of persuasion were used. Every aspiring facilitator should see the movie.

Often the decision is not merely "yes" or "no." When multiple options are available with several major forces and several time factors, the consensus can easily jump to the decision. If the focus can be held to getting consensus on the options, forces, and factors, the decision will happen with much less rancor. Force-field diagram, Gantt charts, and win-win discussions are helpful tools. The output of this stage may be the decision, or it may be an agreement as to what to decide and how to decide it.

How are **decisions** to be made on the team? Collaborative exchange of ideas and facts with a consensus decision or, at the other extreme, present ideas and facts to the team leader for a decision? Or, select a decision process between the extremes based on the issue at hand? How is the process changed to suit a special issue? The facilitator can guide the team through the steps to rationally come to a effective decision process for that team, thereby keeping the team productive. General guidelines need to be established in the project plan, but coaching by the facilitator and support by the project manager in this most important area will be helpful, if not essential, for smooth team functioning.

The decision manager method is a particularly effective way of moving to a decision with a multi-disciplinary team that traditionally is slow to make a decision. The first step is to classify each player as either decision-maker, input, or notified, and assign one person as the decision manager (good job for the facilitator). The decision manager will not make the decision but is responsible for getting the best decision made on time. As decision manager, he is responsible for getting consensus on who should vote on the decision

(decision-maker), who should provide input, and who should be notified of actions. The decision manager makes sure that information from the input providers is distributed to the decision-makers. The decision-makers are prepared by the decision manager for the method of decision-making (recommendation to a single decision-maker, straight vote, weighted ballot, selection grid, and so on). After the decision, the team decision is presented to the notified with appropriate support information.

The **implementation** is the test of a decision. If the correct people have been on the decision road, the implementation considerations have been balanced against the various options and time constraints. The players know what needs to be done and how their actions will affect the other players. Essential to a successful implementation is maintaining communications and adhering to the spirit of the decision. In any complex decision there will be latitude of execution. If considerations and what-ifs are aired as part of the decision process the implementation difficulties will be worked out in a timely fashion.

## When Can the Facilitator Go Away?

As stated earlier, the facilitator's goal is to work herself out of a job. A good indicator is when the group is working effectively with all members participating fully in their roles and are well into the "performance" team stage. Another important indicator is when various members have taken on the functions of the facilitator. At that point the facilitator can back away and let the group function on it own.

## When Should the Facilitator Come Back?

Even though the facilitator may have done a great job in coaching the team to self sufficiency, outside help may be needed from time to time. The team may get "stuck" and ask for help on the use of tools or need new tools for a new problem, or, an outside view of an issue may be needed. Aside from the requested help, the project manager and/or facilitator may monitor the progress of the team and if non-productive conflict starts or if effectiveness or productivity starts to slide, the facilitator can revisit the team to help them get back on track.

## Summary

Power-sharing project environments require collaborative skill sets that may not be part of the project manager's tool kit. Not only must the project manager (PM) know how to utilize the talents of a dedicated facilitator, but the project manager must practice facilitation techniques to fully utilize the project talents. A process-focused facilitator that understands and supports the project manager's priorities can be a high value person on a multi-discipline project. The project manager needs to understand the focus, methods, and vocabulary of the facilitator. Further, the project manager must schedule time and budget for dedicated facilitation activities. Keeping a balance of cost and pay back will depend on the experience of both the project manager and facilitator.

TUTE
CHICAGO 1997
PROJECT MANAGEMENT: THE NEXT CENTURY
Environmental Management

# Integration of Project Management and Systems Engineering: Tools for a Total Cycle Environmental Management System

Paul B. Blacker, Lockheed Martin Idaho Technologies Company
Rebecca Winston, Lockheed Martin Idaho Technologies Company

An expedited environmental management process has been developed at the Idaho National Engineering and Environmental Laboratory (INEEL). This process is one result of the Lockheed Martin commitment to the U.S. Department of Energy to incorporate proven systems engineering practices with project management and program controls practices at the INEEL.

Lockheed Martin uses a graded approach of its management, operations, and systems activities to tailor the level of control to the needs of the individual projects. The Lockheed Martin definition of systems engineering is:

"Systems Engineering is a proven discipline that defines and manages program requirements, controls risk, ensures program efficiency, supports informed decision making, and verifies that products and services meet customer needs."

## The Need for An Expedited Environmental Management Process

Environmental cleanups cost too much, take too long, and the project information usually is not properly integrated. Project costs and times are often underestimated because of a failure to define requirements and to complete rigorous planning actions. An EPA official recently succinctly described the problem by saying that many cleanup projects are initially underestimated by a factor of three to five times.

Additionally, another major cause of cost overruns is the lack of rigorous management controls during cleanup work. With several hundred activities starting and ending at various times during a multiyear project, managers lose control and make mistakes. Our process reduces cost by controlling the planning and execution.

The protection of human health and the environment is one of the important activities of our time. To achieve that objective, society has dedicated billions of dollars a year for environmental cleanups. The development of new and innovative cleanup technologies is a major part of our national environmental effort.

We are convinced, however, that as important as new technologies are, the most important developments that will reduce the cost and time and improve the quality of cleanups are *management* tools—used in conjunction with new technologies.

## How the System Was Developed

The development of this unique process was accomplished as a result of the following.

- Lessons learned from successes and failures on one of the Nation's largest Superfund cleanup project,
- Project management tools implemented, such as those promulgated by the Project Management Institute,
- Program Controls adopted by the DOE and contractors, and
- The Systems Engineering tools developed by.

The U.S. Department of Energy's (DOE) Idaho National Engineering Lab is one of the Nation's largest Superfund sites. It is composed of hundreds of different contaminated sites contaminated with hazardous and toxic, radioactive, and mixed wastes. The extent of contamination, the need to protect public health and the environment, and the high visibility of the Department of Energy waste problem has provided fertile ground for the development of better, faster, and cheaper ways to clean up contaminated sites. The large size of the contamination problem and the large number of environmental professionals and concerned agencies generated new insights into how environmental cleanup projects can be managed better and more effectively.

Secondly, the Department of Energy, as have other federal agencies, has been strong proponents of project management concepts, such as earned value. These project management tools have been an integral part of the management of projects and has been an integral element of management activities required by DOE and its contractors.

Third, Program Controls, such as DOE orders and other requirements are specifically designed for operation within the unique requirements of the Department of Energy complex.

Lockheed Martin has strongly promoted the benefits of systems engineering and, in compliance with its management contract at the INEEL, has instituted systems engineering program at the INEEL. Subsequently, the DOE has decided that the systems engineering process will be extended throughout the entire DOE Complex. The INEEL, as a result, has been designated as the DOE's lead laboratory for systems engineering.

We have witnessed the problem of the slavish incorporation of the above disciplines without tailoring the tools to the unique needs of environmental cleanup projects. To overcome such problems, we adopted an approach of a streamlined incorporation of the required tools in a fashion that best met the unusual needs of the project team members. Instead of overlaying either project management and/or systems engineering systems, we intentionally asked the question "What does the environmental project management team need to successfully manage a cleanup." Based upon the answers to those requirements, we developed this expedited system to meet the unique needs of environmental managers.

## What the System Is

This process is a total-cycle environmental management system. An extensive series of analyses of twenty environmental cleanup projects was conducted to identify the needs and requirements for successful cleanups. The expedited cleanup process was then developed to provide the project management team with a product that has the following features:

- Complete incorporation of the EPA cleanup requirements into a repeatable, measurable process,
- Combination of project management and systems engineering processes for total control of planning, execution, and closure of projects,
- Integration of requirements with computer software and hardware to accelerate performance and improve accuracy, and
- Placement of this system into the hands of the highly trained environmental professional.

## What the System Does

The system is designed to provide the management team with those tools that reduce error and enhance efficient project planning and execution. Analysis of many environmental projects identified outputs that we refer to as products that provide the team with needed information for informed management decisions. The process provides managers the following products:

- A *template* ensuring inclusion of all the essential regulatory components of the cleanup process,
- A *roadmap* showing the relationships, precedent and successor activities of the entire cleanup process,
- A *planning tool* for initial baseline, intensive top-down and bottom up strategy, resource and schedule,
- A *regulatory negotiation tool* for acquiring cooperation of regulatory personnel by showing mastery of the entire project,
- A *management control process* seamlessly operating from initial planning through execution, closure, and delisting,
- A *value-added analysis* tool determining the value received from each activity,
- A *strategic, tactical planning and "what-if" analysis* tool for fine-tuning each project,
- A *business negotiation tool* to be used with contractors to ensure compliance to good business practices,
- An *audible, verifiable record* of the decision making process used during the project,
- A *metric system* that applies measures of performance and quality to all elements of the process and yields accurately measured and quantified information,
- A *quality assurance, audit, and independent evaluation tool*,
- An *education, training, and testing tool*,
- A *change control tool*,
- A *cost-benefit analysis tool*,
- A *risk analysis tool*,
- A *quality control mechanism* for acquiring information, lessons-learned, and measurements,
- An *electronic communication platform* for rapid, accurate and "real-time" project communication.

## An Overview of Key Components of the Process

The remainder of the presentation illustrates examples of our process. The first graphic is an overview of the entire process. It gives an integrated view of how the project management and systems engineering components work together. Following a review of the overview, the following graphic examples of each of the following constituents of the process will be presented.

- Identification of project requirements,
- Validation of requirements,
- Definition of products that meet those requirements,
- Definition of scope and quality of each product,
- Determination of the activities necessary to complete each product,
- Verification that requirements have been satisfied and products are complete,
- Integration of management controls (such as earned value, etc.).

This overview and brief description of each of the components has shown how the components, when used together, provide the project team with integrated set of tools for improving the efficiency and reliability of environmental cleanup operations.

# Two Keys to Future Success: Formal and Informal Partnering

Richard D. May, ABB Environmental Services, Inc.
Harry Y. Doo, Southern Division, Naval Facilities Engineering Command

In the past several years the word "partnering" has conjured up traumatic images among federal and state agencies, as well as government contractors. The feeling has been that this is perhaps an experiment that should have gone the way of the dinosaur. A feeling that what is involved is holding hands and singing "Kum-ba-yah," or that perhaps, in partnering, an agency or entity may have to give up its predominance and be placed in a compromised position. This is especially the case in dealing among federal government agencies and state and federal environmental regulating agencies. On the contrary, this is a case study of the absolute, unqualified success of not one, but two very different kinds of partnering. The first being formal facilitated partnering among once adversarial agencies, the second being informal, self-directed partnering among the Navy and five of its environmental contractors.

## Formal Partnering

Working relationships between the Navy, the U.S. Environmental Protection Agency, and the State of Florida had become so adversarial that disputes over environmental cleanup were being addressed only through formal legal channels, often with implied fines and penalties. The cleanup process had ground to a halt with more resources being used to respond to formal allegations. The Navy and the EPA were receiving increasing pressure from headquarters to make better progress on environmental cleanup. In February 1993, representatives of Naval Facilities Engineering Command, Southern Division (SDIV) and the Environmental Protection Agency, Region 4 (EPA) agreed that the present situation would cause both agencies to fail in their missions and that a détente was needed between the agencies. Each organization had been exposed to Total Quality Management (TQM) and teaming within their own organizations and agreed that a facilitated meeting would be the first step. They agreed on a common goal, 'provide a team approach to accomplish our common CERCLA goals.'

The first facilitated meeting among management representatives of the Navy, the EPA and the State of Florida was held in March 1993. The focus of the first meeting was on team building and brainstorming training. The group developed the expectations for the sessions and established a set of ground rules to use for their meetings. Brainstorming generated a list of forty-eight items considered obstacles to a successful program. These were grouped into eight categories: policy issues; threat of dispute or litigation; risk taking; lack of teaming (rice bowls); lack of strategy or overall plan; distrust between agencies; internal Navy issues; timeliness. During their second meeting the group developed goals for the team and a Partnering Charter was signed by the participants. The charter is a commitment by the individual agencies to a common goal, mission, vision and objectives. This team (which started as the Environmental Restoration Partnership) has come to be known as the Environmental Restoration Management Alliance (ERMA).

Once the management of each of the agencies had pledged support, the partnering process could now be expanded to include the Navy's investigation contractors and exported to the working level of the programs, the project teams. Project teams are designated as Tier I teams, the management partnering team has been designated as Tier II. The Navy, on behalf of Tier II, contracted with two outside consultants to provide meeting facilitation and team building training to Tier II and the Tier I teams. Tier I teams are comprised of from five to eight members, from the various agencies, each being a stakeholder in the cleanup success at Navy and Marine Corps facilities. Typically, the EPA Remedial Project Manager (RPM); the State Regulatory Agency RPM, the Navy RPM (of Naval Facilities Engineering Command); a facility representative (usually from the Environmental Coordinator's office); the project managers from the Navy's contractors (investigation and remediation contractors); and the Base Realignment and Closure (BRAC) Environmental Coordinator (BEC) for closing bases.

During the development of the Tier II team, four major elements were defined that would lead to the success of this partnering process, both at the management level, and at the project team level: Management Level Commitment; Facilitated Communication; Empowerment; and Training. Management Level Commitment began with the development of the charter and the mission and continued with management briefing from the three agencies at the Tier I team-building workshops. Facilitated Communication uses outside consultants to demonstrate the effectiveness and importance of assertiveness, trust, facilitated communication techniques, and the use of the Myers-Briggs Type Indicator. Empowerment of the project teams involves demonstrated management support and definition of "acceptable risk" by each agency's member on the team. Training, both in workshop form and ongoing for individual teams, teaches effective meeting methodologies, problem solving techniques, and the definition and use of group leadership styles and skills (situational or shared leadership).

The first Partnering Workshop, to train newly formed Tier I teams, was held in December 1993. This was the first opportunity to bring project team members together and for management to define the partnering concept and process to the teams. Since that first training workshop, six more workshops have been held as Tier I Teams in Florida and the other EPA Region 4 partnering states of North Carolina, South Carolina and Kentucky have been initiated and chartered to become high performing teams. In July 1994, the partnership was expanded to include the Marine Corps. In July 1996, partnering was launched in EPA Region 5 to include installations in Illinois, Indiana and Minnesota. In EPA Region 5, partnering includes the Army, the Air Force and the Department of the Interior. In South Carolina, partnering has been expanded to include the Army and the Air Force. Many members of the project teams had never met one another, they had been kept apart, some just by chance and some by the old 'rice bowl' paradigms. An initial focus in the workshops is to demonstrate the four stages of team development to the teams in order that they may perceive the end result of the partnering or team building process. These four stages are:

- Forming —The stage when the team members are first brought together, either voluntarily or involuntarily.
- Storming—The stage when impatience with the lack of progress occurs.
- Norming—The stage when team members begin contributing and helping one another out.
- Performing—The stage when the mature team understands its strengths and weaknesses. Members are satisfied with the teams progress.

Some Tier I Teams have progressed toward becoming "high performing teams" and have been recognized and rewarded by the Tier II management team. These teams have developed a working atmosphere that is informal and relaxed, without obvious tension among participants. Their team discussions are well focused and everyone participates. The task at hand is fully understood and accepted be all team members. Members listen to each other and allow all opposing opinions to be heard before testing for consensus. Conflict is part of the process, it is not avoided simply to move forward. Decisions are reached by consensus of the team, not by majority rule. There are no personal attacks allowed, any criticism is open, frank and constructive. Team members are free to express their feelings and ideas on the problem at hand. Each member (being from different agencies) is willing to identify his or her own agency constraints when attacking an issue. When actions are taken, clear assignments are made and carried out. The leader does not dominate, nor do any other members. Leadership is rotated on a by meeting/by issue basis. In order to become more effective teams, the Tier I teams and the Tier II team have actively worked to understand and improve their teams' performance in the "Ten Ingredients for a Successful Team":

- Clarity of team goals ,
- An improvement plan,
- Clearly defined team member roles,
- Clear communication among team members,
- Beneficial team behaviors,
- A well-defined decision process,
- Balanced participation by all members,
- Established team ground rules,
- Awareness of the group process, and
- Use of the scientific process.

There are currently seventeen Tier I project teams, covering seven states. Each has developed its own team goals, ground rules, team norms, and roles and responsibilities. While each team may approach and solve problems in different ways, owing to its makeup, this type of formal partnering has been a enormous success for each of the stakeholders, leading to (as the teams refer to it) "better, cheaper, faster" site cleanups. In one case the team's effort helped their installation achieve the Department of Defense's annual award for environmental cleanup. When asked, teams identified increased trust, better communications, a team identity, camaraderie and situational leadership as some of the benefits of participating in the facilitated partnering process. The real benefits have come as a result of reduced levels of effort by stakeholders and reduced project life cycle durations, resulting in lower costs to the Navy, Marine Corps and ultimately the taxpayer.

Examples of some of the cost and schedule reducing team achievements are:

- Simultaneous review of decision documents by approving agencies instead of passing documents for comment in series.
- Buy-in of the scope of data collection requirements prior to mobilization in the field, instead of identification of data gaps once field data has been collected and incorporated into reports.
- Buy-in of work plan methodology and investigation rationale prior to field mobilization.
- By-pass of the feasibility study phase in favor of an expedited Proposed Plan and Record of Decision for quick removal of contaminated soil.

- Elimination of "preliminary draft" and "draft final" documents.
- Cost avoidance of over $200,000 by producing "master" Contamination Assessment Reports (CARs) for four base "areas" as opposed to two hundred individual CARs for each tank in the Tank Management Program.
- Avoidance of a dredging work stoppage and $30,000 in potential fines.
- Within a period of four years, at one National Priority List installation, Records of Decision for thirteen of thirty-three sites have been signed.
- Reduction of Action Levels for pesticides resulting in $300,000 in avoided soil removal costs.
- Avoidance of $90,000 in disposal costs of Investigative Derived Waste by defining acceptable pretreatment criteria allowing discharge into the local wastewater treatment system.

This successful partnering endeavor has demonstrated an average 50% reduction in project cycle times and has documented twenty-three million dollars in cost avoidance to date.

## Informal Partnering

As the formal partnering process was beginning, concurrent team building activities, an informal partnering process, had begun between technical representatives of Southern Division, Naval Facilities Engineering Command (SDIV) and ABB Environmental Services, one of the Navy's environmental investigation and design contractors. This teaming arrangement was developed to address generic, programmatic technical issues facing the program. The team was named the Quality Improvement Forum (QIF). It allowed for the surfacing and resolution of technical problems faced by as many as sixteen diverse project teams. It provided a platform for senior technical scientists and engineers from the Navy and ABB seek the most efficient and cost effective solutions to issues faced by many teams in the program and promulgate these solutions.

In May 1995, the QIF was restructured and expanded to included all five of the Navy's Installation Restoration Program contractors, program management representatives and contracts representatives. By including all five contractors, actual competitors in the marketplace, the Navy was able to address regional and national issues. It allows the Navy to take advantage of the best technical expertise each organization has to offer. It also provided a common ground for programmatic processes. As issues are discovered, they are defined and prioritized for resolution. This forum also allows for the rapid dissemination of Navy and DoD policy information to the contractors and program teams. The QIF members created and committed to their own charter: "The QIF provides a formal mechanism for exchange, development, and communication of process improvements that expedites cost-effective environmental restoration." With the charter came the following list of expectations:

- Provide a mechanism to promote and implement new ideas,
- Demonstrate cost effectiveness,
- Make processes more efficient,
- Foster consistency throughout the Navy CLEAN/RAC Program,
- Operate in a results-oriented manner,
- Communicate resolutions to each member organization uniformly, unambiguously, and with one voice, and
- Have all levels within member organizations endorse and support implementation of QIF objectives.

This team also established it's own ground rules to define the way they will interact with one another: be professional and courteous; no side conversations; obtain consensus on issue resolution; start on time; keep on track; don't beat a dead horse; maintain confidentiality; and others. All team members diligently, but cordially, enforce the ground rules when they are in danger of being broken. The Core Team business practices have been identified and documented. These define much of the meeting and team performance mechanics the QIF will use on an ongoing basis: meeting mechanics, meeting duration; attire; time limits; communications. The QIF meets formally every quarter, and communicates as needed via e-mail, phone conference and fax. Quarterly meetings are generally one and a half to two days, with the agenda being published in advance, based on progress at and since the previous meeting. Responsibility for "hosting" the meeting revolves among the contractor representatives. "Hosting" involves arrangements for the meeting facilities, sleeping room arrangements for travelers, and publishing the schedule and agenda.

When the team reformed in May 1995, they brainstormed a list of issues that were germane to process improvements in the Navy's Installation Restoration Program. There were thirty-five major issues with some minor issues that were considered as subcomponents of the major ones. Each issue was prioritized as high, medium, low priority or a "quick fix," meaning it was an issue with which minimal effort could be solved and completed. In order to address the high priority issues, Focus Groups have been created to resolve the issues and bring the solutions back to the QIF for validation and dissemination among all member organizations. Focus Groups are assigned a Core Team Link, a Focus Group Leader and the Core Team members assign Focus Group members from their organizations based on the subject and expertise needed. There are three phases to problem resolution by a Focus Group: Initial Phase, which includes formulation of the problem statement by the group, identification of group goals and expected deliverables, a plan of action and identifying the team membership; Intermediate Phase, which includes providing a written status to the core team link prior to the next meeting of the core team, the schedule for problem resolution, and any problems encountered; and the Completion Phase, which includes restatement of the problem and resolution in writing, and a recommendation for deployment of the resolution or guidance. Focus Groups have returned solutions or recommendations to the Core Team, which in-turn have been passed on as guidance or for management approval on several of the original thirty-five issues:

- Site closure documentation
- Performance criteria packages (design packages),
- Analytical laboratory approval,
- Use of innovative technologies,
- Risk based cleanup criteria,
- Monitoring well installation criteria,
- Data quality objectives,
- Electronic communications among team organizations,
- Retention of records,
- Investigative derived waste guidance, and
- Technical report writing and formatting guidance.

One focus group of note is the CLEAN/RAC Interface Focus Group. This team is comprised of the program managers from each of the of the five contractors, the five Administrative Contracting Officers (ACO) and the five Contracting Officer's Technical Representatives. These members represent the core policy implementation group for the Navy's Installation Restoration Program. At their first meeting, they defined eleven activities that would enhance and streamline the working relationships among and between the Comprehensive Longterm Environmental Action Navy (CLEAN) contractors and the Remedial Action Contractors (RAC):

- Preparation of a Responsibility Assignment Matrix (RAM) guide,
- Definition of design guidelines,
- Preparation of guide specifications for CLEAN/RAC work,
- Preparation of an operations and maintenance instruction,
- Train Navy RPMs on the RAC manual,
- Provide RAC manual to the CLEAN and RAC contractors,
- Educate teams on CLEAN/ROICC oversight responsibilities,
- Program teams visit project teams,
- Navy ownership of processes,
- More guidance and oversight from Navy, and
- Define scope of closure reports.

A major team achievement was the development of the Responsibility Assignment Matrix (RAM) guide. Southern Division's environmental program managers were challenged to develop processes that would capitalize on the resources of the contractors and enhance the smooth transition from the CLEAN contractor to the RAC contractor. Teaming became the apparent mode of operation that brought the contractors together to develop common goals. The RAM is a product of this teaming. The RAM is a document that is collectively and collaboratively developed by all parties in a teaming environment. Its purpose is to provide a global scenario of a specific remedial tasking that requires multiple actions from all parties involved. The interaction among team members will enhance the maximum utilization of the teams' corporate knowledge. The RAM also provides the parameters to develop a statement of work that will be submitted to the respective contractor for contractual support. The RAM is a dynamic management tool that can also serve as a vehicle to encourage open and honest communication among project team members.

The success of the QIF in streamlining processes, solving problems and using common terminologies has come from the same attributes that make formal partnering successful: productive communications; trust; effective meeting mechanics; and management support of the stakeholders.

In an era when customers and stakeholders are demanding that we "do more, with less," these two forms of partnering have proven to be beneficial from not only a cost standpoint, but also from a time standpoint. The cost and time spent by stakeholders in forming high performing teams, with their "forming, storming, norming and performing" phases is rewarded many times over by the benefits realized as a result of the teams reaching consensus on win-win solutions.

# Cost Risk Analysis: Applications for Environmental Restoration Project Management

W. David Featherman, Project Performance Corporation
Todd A. Walsh, Project Performance Corporation

## Introduction

The use of risk analysis techniques to evaluate decision alternatives during conceptual project planning has become standard practice within high-technology industries over the past decade. Owners, designers, and constructors have embraced quantitative methods of risk and decision analysis to aid in assessing the prospect of returns on capital investments, selecting design safety criteria, and evaluating the likelihood of winning competitively bid contracts. More recently, risk analysis has begun to play an important role in environmental restoration. In project settings wrought with both technical and regulatory uncertainty, quantitative risk analysis techniques have been used to forecast the cumulative effects of project cost growth and schedule slip, as well as to develop contingency factors for baseline cost and schedule estimates. One relatively new extension of these applications is the use of cost risk analysis as a management tool during project execution. Through the combined efforts of project owners, designers, and constructors, quantitative risk analysis methods have been used to identify the potential cost impacts of design and construction uncertainties and to mitigate the impacts of those uncertainties through the proactive implementation of sound contingency plans.

The U.S. Department of Energy (DOE) recently funded a study to assist its project managers in establishing a formalized methodology for conducting quantitative cost risk analyses. The study focused on implementing quantitative risk modeling techniques at DOE field sites engaged in environmental restoration efforts. Using a combination of risk and uncertainty analysis concepts developed through prior research and project experience, the authors were able to facilitate real-time evaluations of potential cost growth and to support the formulation of contingency plans to counter such growth in its early stages during a project. Specifically, the study used cost risk analysis procedures to achieve the following goals:

- Provide a basis for determining contingency and establishing levels of confidence in baseline cost estimates,
- Focus project management efforts on uncertainties having the greatest potential cost impacts, and
- Establish a means of communicating the potential impacts of project uncertainties to DOE and contractor personnel, state and federal regulators, and various stakeholders.

These analysis procedures were applied to environmental restoration projects at two DOE field sites employing substantially different cleanup strategies. This paper summarizes the results of those case studies and offers general recommendations for using cost risk analysis as a tool for environmental restoration project management.

## Methodology

The cost risk analysis for each case study was performed by a core project team comprised of both DOE and contractor project managers, one or more project engineers, a cost estimator, and the authors serving as facilitators for the risk modeling process. The methodology used by the project team to perform the cost risk analyses included five major steps:

- Identification of project uncertainties,
- Assessment of their probabilities of occurrence,
- Quantification of their potential cost impacts,
- Analysis of total project cost risk, and
- Development of recommendations for focusing project management efforts.

Each of these steps is described in general terms below, with project specific details being provided in the results section of this paper.

### Identification of Project Uncertainties

The project team first focused on identifying both technical and programmatic uncertainties having the potential to impact total project cost. Technical uncertainties arise from elements found within the project design or implementation plan such as waste volumes, remediation technologies, disposal methods, etc. Such elements are under the direct control of the project manager but often produce some deviation from the baseline cost estimate. In contrast, programmatic uncertainties include items such as changing regulations, fiscal year funding, and site prioritization strategy—elements beyond the specific scope of the project but having significant influence over its execution. The project team engaged in brainstorming sessions to develop a comprehensive list of



PROJECT MANAGEMENT INSTITUTE 28th Annual Seminars & Symposium
Chicago, Illinois: Papers Presented September 29 to October 1, 1997

**Exhibit 1.** Example Influence Diagram

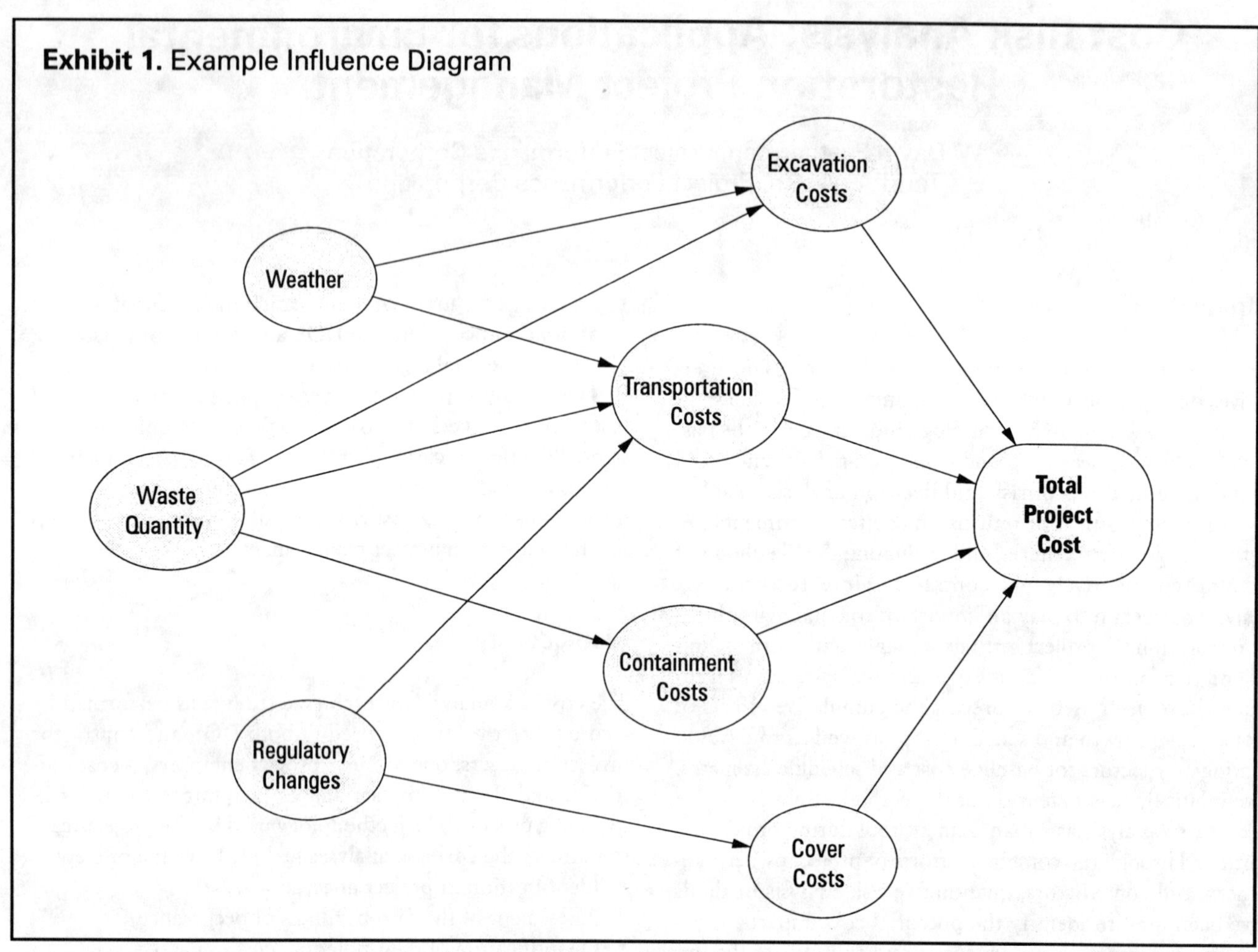


uncertainties that could impact the cost of completing the environmental restoration work. This step involved extensive participation by project managers, as they generally possessed expertise in all relevant areas of work at their sites.

The team then qualitatively defined the uncertainties in terms of their expected conditions (commonly referred to by cost estimators as assumptions) and their potential deviations. This qualitative assessment was used as the basis for determining relationships between uncertainties as well as for assessing probabilities of occurrence (Step 2) and quantifying potential cost impacts (Step 3). Finally, the relationships among project uncertainties and major project cost elements were captured in the form of an influence diagram. Influence diagrams are alternate representations of probability trees formed using chance nodes to represent uncertain project conditions and costs. The chance nodes are linked by arrows to depict the influences that technical and programmatic uncertainties have on each other and on particular project cost elements. For illustrative purposes, an example influence diagram for a hypothetical mill tailings remediation project is provided in Exhibit 1.

### Assessment of Probabilities of Occurrence

Each of the uncertainties identified in Step 1 was further defined using three unique states to represent a "better than expected" outcome, an "as expected" outcome, and a "worse than expected" outcome. For example, uncertain waste volumes for a soil remediation project could be defined using three states such as "less than 75% of estimated volume," "75% to 110% of estimated volume," and "greater than 110% of estimated volume." Each state of uncertainty was then assigned a probability of occurrence based on the expert judgments of project managers and project engineers, with the sum of the probabilities within each chance node equaling exactly 1.0 (i.e., a 100% probability of experiencing one of the three outcomes). In cases where interdependency existed among project uncertainties, the team had to assess conditional probabilities based on the precedent relationships.

### Quantification of Potential Cost Impacts

The authors then facilitated a range estimating exercise with the project cost estimator to develop best and worst

**Exhibit 2.** Mound Plant Ou–4 Influence Diagram

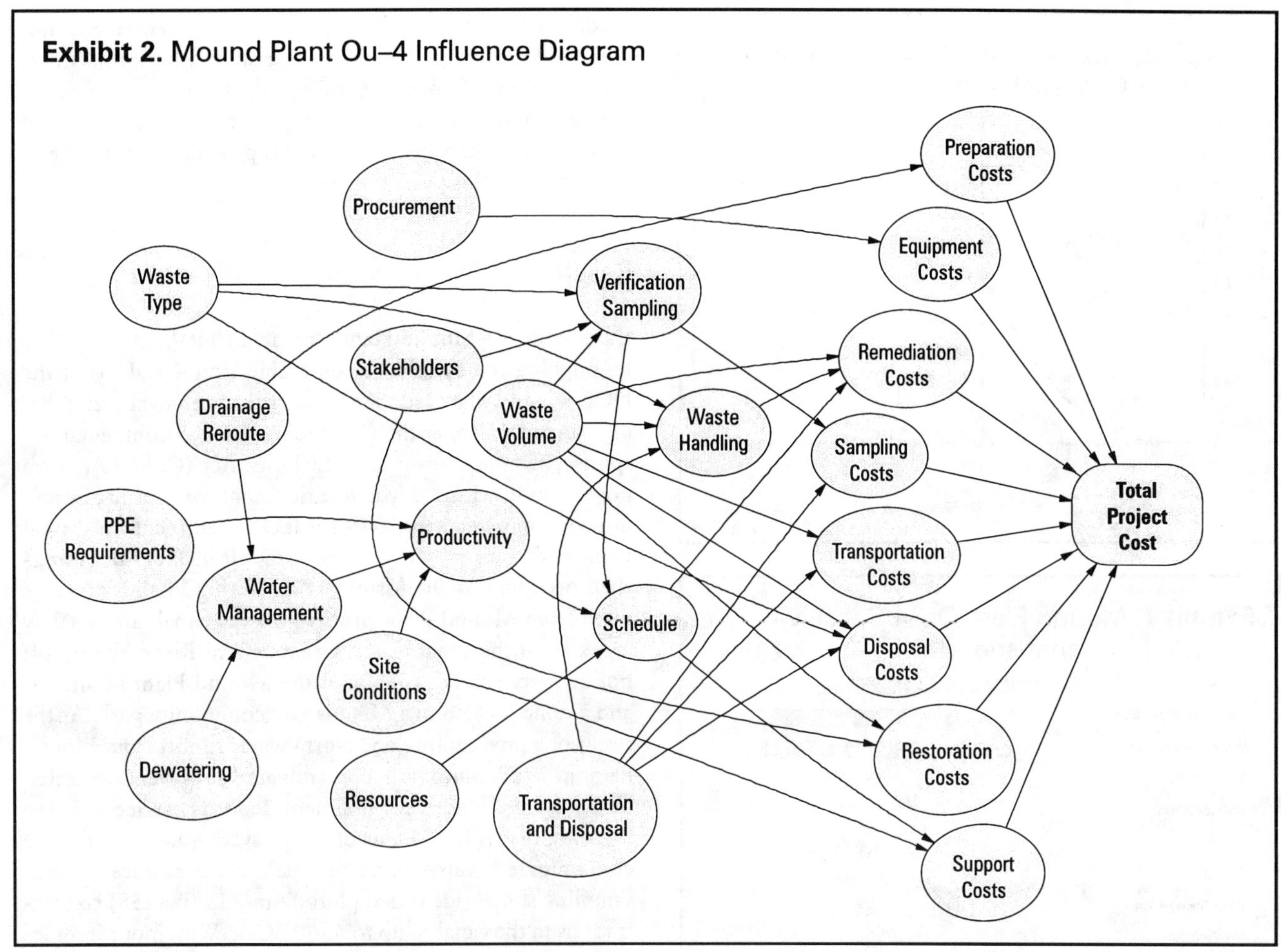


case estimates for selected line items from the major cost elements in the project baseline. Line items included in the range estimating exercise generally were chosen using Pareto's rule, which suggests that eighty percent of the total project cost is contained in only twenty percent of its components. Ranges were developed to reflect the potential impacts of project uncertainties as defined in Step 1. A Monte Carlo simulation of the line item ranges provided a set of summary probability distributions for the major project cost elements represented in the influence diagram. From these summary distributions, the tenth, fiftieth, and ninetieth percentiles were used to define three states of uncertainty within each major project cost element representing an optimistic cost, a most likely cost, and a pessimistic cost, respectively.

### Analysis of Total Project Cost Risk

For each major project cost element represented in the influence diagram, the cost estimator and project manager were asked to assess probabilities of experiencing the three states of uncertainty defined within its chance node, i.e., of incurring the optimistic, most likely, and pessimistic cost for that project element. This required the iterative assessment of conditional probabilities for various scenarios presented by the technical and programmatic uncertainties influencing each cost element. For example, in the influence diagram shown in Exhibit 1, Excavation Costs are influenced by both Weather and Waste Quantity. It is reasonable to assume that if Weather is "as expected" and Waste Quantity is "better than expected" during execution of the project, then Excavation Costs are more likely to approach their optimistic value than if both Weather and Waste Quantity are "worse than expected." Such evaluations were thus required for all combinations of uncertain conditions influencing each major project cost element. In cases where the project manager and cost estimator assessed different probability combinations, consensus was reached by discussing their underlying assumptions and resolving any technical discrepancies. Finally, the quantified influence diagram model was run to determine the expected value for the total project cost as well as the range of total costs that could be expected as a result of the identified uncertainties. This information was then used to determine a level of confidence in the existing baseline cost

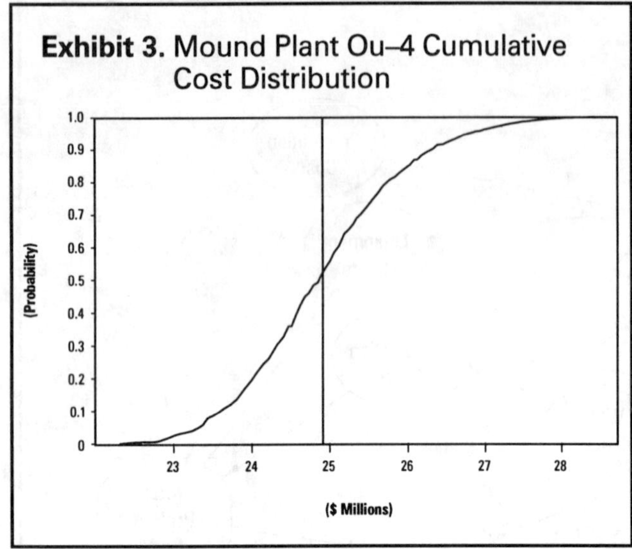


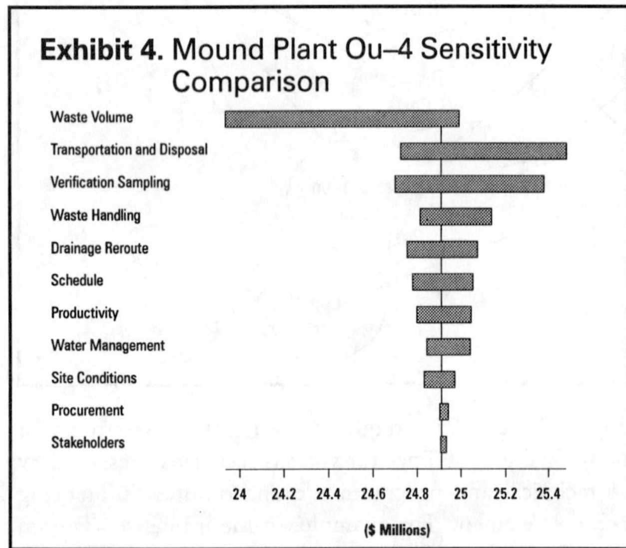


estimate as well as to evaluate the adequacy of the contingency funds available to counter the effects of project risk predicted by the influence diagram model.

### Development of Recommendations for Focusing Project Management Efforts

Based on the results of the cost risk model, the project team determined the appropriate contingency needed to achieve the desired level of confidence in the baseline cost estimate. The team also developed recommendations for how to manage and mitigate the potential impacts of technical and programmatic uncertainties during project execution. These recommendations were focused on the uncertainties most likely to impact project costs as determined by a sensitivity analysis performed on the influence diagram model. In addition, the project team used the outputs from the influence diagram model to communicate both the range of potential cost impacts and the likely sources of cost risk to other project personnel, site regulators, and stakeholders from the surrounding community. A more detailed, project-specific account of theses project management efforts is provided in the following section of this paper.

## Results

Case Study 1—Mound Plant Operable Unit 4
he ongoing remediation of Operable Unit 4 (OU-4) at the DOE Mound Plant is a non-time critical removal action being conducted under the Comprehensive Environmental Response, Compensation, and Liability Act (CERCLA) for a portion of the disused Miami-Erie Canal containing plutonium contaminated soils. OU-4 is located adjacent to Mound Plant in the city of Miamisburg, Ohio. It includes the watershed occupied by the former Miami-Erie Canal, a drainage ditch from Mound Plant property to the canal, an overflow creek from the canal to the Great Miami River, the runoff hollow between the canal and the Mound Plant boundary, and a pond located in a Miamisburg community park. As the result of a pipe rupture and storm water runoff from Mound Plant in 1969, plutonium contaminated soils were deposited in the canal. Subsequent sediment deposits carried into the canal by the Mound Plant drainage system have buried the contaminated soils several feet below the surface. Recent sampling studies identified plutonium-238 (Pu-238) concentrations in the canal of up to 4560 pCi/g. With input from local stakeholders including the U.S. Environmental Protection Agency (EPA), the city of Miamisburg, and public interest groups, DOE has concluded that the goal of the removal action is to excavate all Pu-238 contaminated soils and sediments at concentrations exceeding 75 pCi/g.

The OU-4 removal action is being performed by the prime contractor at Mound Plant, EG&G Mound Applied Technologies (MAT). To provide DOE with a defensible cost estimate and to demonstrate their ability to manage project uncertainties in the field, EG&G MAT opted to conduct a cost risk analysis. The following objectives for the cost risk analysis were identified by the OU-4 project manager:

- Verify the chosen remediation strategy could be implemented in a cost effective manner,
- Determine the potential impacts of project uncertainties on the baseline cost estimate, and
- Identify risky project activities that should be closely monitored during the removal action.

The project team developed the influence diagram shown in Exhibit 2 to describe the relationships among project uncertainties and project costs for the OU-4 project.

**Exhibit 5.** WSSRAP Influence Diagram

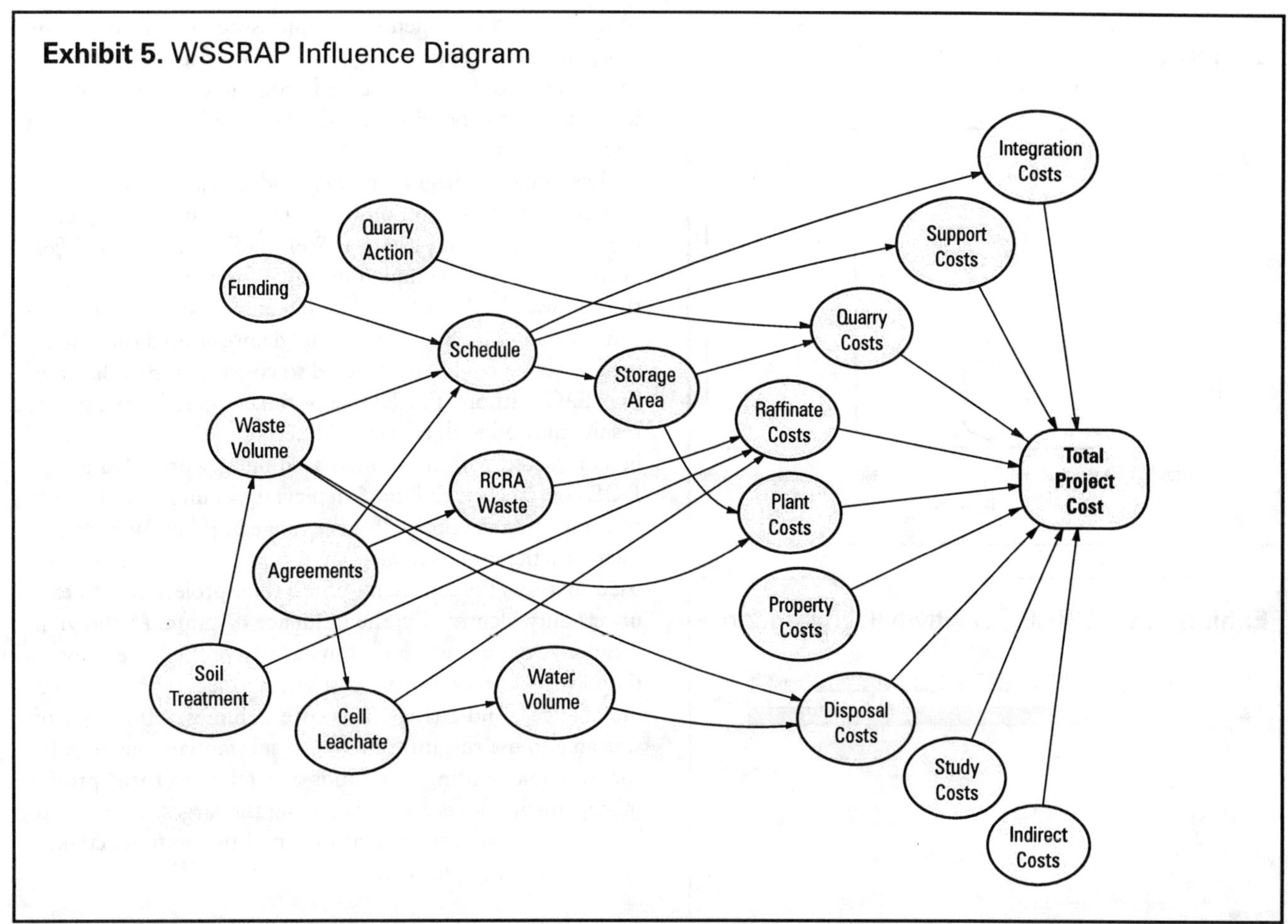


Quantitative analysis of the influence diagram model provided an expected value of nearly $25 million for the total project cost. The model also produced a distribution of potential project costs ranging from $22 million to $28 million, offering only a 20% probability of completing the project within the $24 million baseline cost estimate (see Exhibit 3). In addition, the model predicted the total project cost was most likely to increase due to additional waste volume, changes in transportation and disposal requirements, and increased verification sampling (see Exhibit 4). EG&G MAT was able to use this information to minimize its exposure to cost risk by refining and improving the project design and by developing specific field procedures for monitoring the performance of high-risk variables. This allowed the contractor to focus its limited resources on managing items having the largest potential to increase the final cost of the removal action.

## Case Study 2—Weldon Spring Site Remedial Action Project

The Weldon Spring Site Remedial Action Project (WSSRAP) near St. Louis, Missouri is being performed under the DOE Environmental Management program. The project consists of a two hundred and seventeen-acre chemical plant and a nine-acre limestone quarry located four miles south of the main site. The Weldon Spring Site has a complex history of production processes. Between 1941 and 1944, the Department of the Army operated the Weldon Spring Ordnance Works at the site, producing dinitrotoluene (DNT) and trinitrotoluene (TNT) during World War II. In 1955, two hundred and five acres of the former ordnance works were transferred to the U.S. Atomic Energy Commission (AEC) for construction of the Weldon Spring Uranium Feed Materials Plant, now called the Weldon Spring Chemical Plant. From 1957 until 1966, the feed materials plant processed uranium ore and a small amount of thorium. Wastes generated during these operations were stored in four settling basins called the raffinate pits. The AEC also used the quarry and raffinate pits to dispose of uranium and radium contaminated building rubble and soils from the demolition of a uranium ore processing facility in St. Louis. The prime contractor for the remedial action project, MK-Ferguson, is now implementing a phased cleanup approach encompassing several interim response actions and four separate operable units:

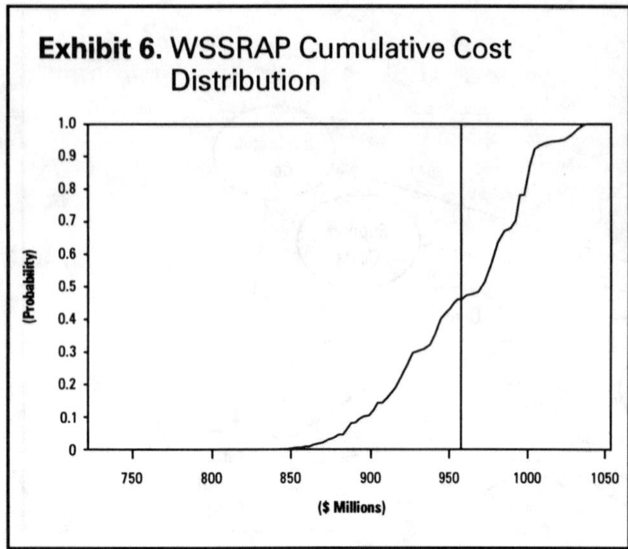


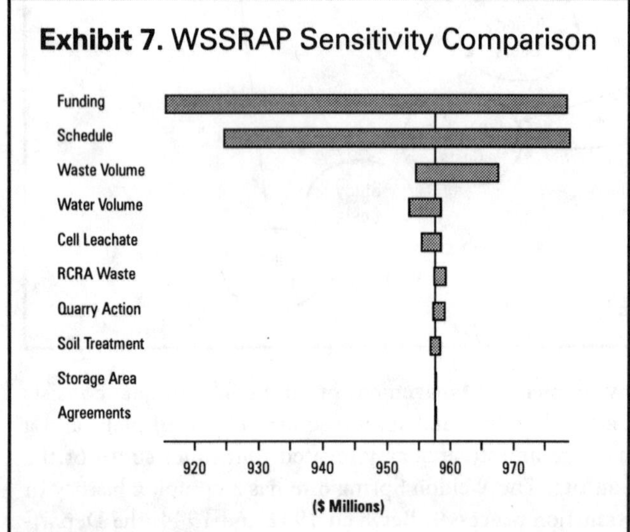


- The chemical plant area,
- Quarry bulk wastes,
- Quarry residual wastes, and
- Site groundwater.

Decontamination and decommissioning of all buildings in the chemical plant area and removal of the quarry bulk wastes had already been completed at the time the cost risk analysis was conducted. The analysis therefore was limited to the remaining response actions in the chemical plant area and the remediation of quarry residual wastes and site groundwater. The primary objective of the WSSRAP cost risk analysis was to identify and quantify the potential impacts of site-wide uncertainties, i.e., conditions capable of affecting multiple response actions or operable units rather than isolated risks that could be managed within a specific project. To accomplish this objective, the project team first defined nine major cost elements encompassing all the remaining work at the Weldon Spring Site. These cost elements were then related to the technical and programmatic uncertainties identified by the project team through the influence diagram depicted in Exhibit 5.

The influence diagram model produced a cost distribution ranging from $840 million to $1.029 billion for completing the remedial action project at Weldon Spring Site. MK-Ferguson's estimate at completion (EAC) for all work planned at the site was $838 million, supplemented by a DOE contingency of $149 million. The model demonstrated that the remedial action could be expected to cost more than the baseline EAC without the DOE contingency. In contrast, the results showed with nearly 70% certainty that project could be completed within the increased budget provided by the DOE contingency. Exhibit 6 depicts the cumulative certainty of completing the project for the range of potential costs predicted by the influence diagram model. The model also was used to assess the sensitivity of the total project cost to each uncertainty identified in the influence diagram. As shown in Exhibit 7, the uncertainties found to have the largest potential to vary the total project cost were project funding, schedule changes, and changes in waste volumes. MK-Ferguson was able to use this information to substantiate the need for the available contingency funds as well as to focus project management efforts on areas having the largest potential to impact the final cost of environmental restoration activities at the Weldon Spring Site.

## Conclusions

Cost risk analysis techniques, specifically the use of Monte Carlo simulation and influence diagram modeling, can be used not only to develop contingency factors for project cost estimates but also as a tool for managing the uncertain conditions, quantities, and events most likely to impact the ultimate cost of a project. At two DOE environmental restoration sites, these methods were used as a basis for improving project design and developing focused monitoring and contingency plans to mitigate the effects of risk during project execution. Furthermore, the successful application of cost risk analysis at these sites has produced the following general recommendations:

Cost risk analysis is most effective when performed by a team consisting of the project manager, the lead project engineer, a cost estimator, and a modeling expert.

To fully account for the potential impacts of project cost risk, an influence diagram model should include both technical and programmatic uncertainties.

Modeling is only the first step in managing project cost risk—analysis must be followed by detailed monitoring and contingency planning to minimize cost growth during field operations.

By implementing a team approach to cost risk analysis, project managers can better position themselves to identify the sources of uncertainty in their projects, to understand the relationships among numerous project uncertainties, to predict the potential range of total project costs, and to implement effective management plans to mitigate the impacts of project cost risk.

## References


Diekmann, James E., W. David Featherman, A. Rhett, Keith R. Molenaar, and Maria Y. Rodriguez-Guy. 1996. "Project cost risk analysis using influence diagrams." *Project Management Journal*. 28:23–30.

Featherman, W. David, James E. Diekmann, and Stephen W. Meador. 1994. Applying influence diagrams to environmental restoration projects for improved project risk management. *Proceedings of the Second Annual EM Cost Management Conference*. San Francisco, CA.

Morgan, M. Granger, and Max Henrion. 1990. *Uncertainty: A guide to dealing with uncertainty in quantitative risk and policy analysis*. New York: Cambridge University Press.

Schuyler, John R. 1996. *Decision analysis in projects*. Upper Darby, PA: Project Management Institute.

# Design/Build of Complex Environmental Restoration Projects Though Client Service: A Case Profile

John David Harrison, PMP, REM, CCM, Metcalf & Eddy, Inc.
Daniel J. Levy, PG, CHMM, Metcalf & Eddy, Inc.
Shannon Rives, Metcalf & Eddy, Inc.
Richard Kaminska, Metcalf & Eddy, Inc.

## Introduction

Client service is essential for the success of complex design/build projects in the 21st Century. The client service approach allows risk management by both the owner and contractor while expediting the project schedule and without sacrificing project quality. This paper profiles one such environmental restoration project in which a client service program was successfully implemented by Metcalf & Eddy, Inc. with the Dade County Aviation Department (DCAD).

DCAD operates and maintains the Miami International Airport (MIA). MIA handles over fourteen hundred flights per day, employs thirty-two hundred workers, and introduces roughly $12 billion per year into the South Florida economy. Presently, MIA is undergoing a major facilities and construction expansion estimated at $2.5 billion and is working with Metropolitan Dade Department of Environmental Resources Management (DERM) to investigate and remediate environmentally impacted areas stemming from past operations.

One such impacted area was located at the former Eastern Airlines Main Base Hangar 22. In this area, environmental assessments identified jet fuel and VarsolSM (petroleum naphtha) in both soil and shallow groundwater. The plumes covered an area of approximately fourteen acres, most of which was situated under the 18" concrete tarmac inside and in front of this active hangar. Expansion activities required a fast-track schedule for environmental restoration of this area. Completion of this project was on time, under budget, and met the technical requirements for remediation of the site.

## The Client's Challenge

Challenges facing DCAD for this project were numerous. Three primary challenges for DCAD were: (1) meet the environmental restoration requirements of DERM and obtain permit approvals from eight agencies or departments in a timely manner; (2) meet the requirements of the master schedule for the $2.5 billion expansion, specifically, to release the site to a new tenant by December 26, 1994, and (3) complete the project cost effectively and within budget.

DCAD selected M&E to be the design/build contractor for this project to help them meet their challenges. M&E received the notice to proceed on September 12, 1994 with the understanding that the project must be completed by December 25, 1994. This allowed thirteen weeks for M&E to take the project from conceptual design through implementation of this six+ million dollar project because a new tenant agreement became effective on December 26, 1994.

## Remedy

To meet the challenges that DCAD set for M&E, M&E in conjunction with DCAD developed a project plan that would meet the following goals: (1) communicate during the design and construction phases both openly and frequent to ensure that the client's needs were being met and to keep the client fully informed of the project status; (2) design the project in accordance with Federal Aviation Administration (FAA), DCAD, DERM, and Dade County Building and Zoning Department (B&Z) requirements, while maintaining good common sense constructability; (3) schedule and coordinate construction activities to ensure that the construction phase would not interfere with the day-to-day MIA operations while still meeting the required completion date; and (4) organize the project management team into a cohesive group.

## Project Meetings and Design Reviews

Key project/progress meetings were held at the 90% design completion milestone and the 100% design completion/construction mobilization milestone. The attendees consisted of key staff members of the DCAD organizations and key M&E project personnel. The meetings were used to communicate major milestone accomplishments while at the same time planning for the next phase of the project. These meeting were key to having everyone participate as a team member. The acting DCAD Assistant Director for Environmental Engineering stated,

"We wish to congratulate you and your staff for the meeting of October 17th. We found your presentation well documented and to the point. Also, we find your mobilization of resources to produce 90% drawings and implementation schedule for a job of this magnitude, in such a short time, truly remarkable."

Weekly construction progress meetings were started one week before mobilization was to start and continued for the duration of the project. Representatives of concerned parties were kept informed of upcoming reviews and inspections, project milestones, changed conditions, and key decisions. This type of close communication from the very beginning allowed DCAD and M&E to obtain expedited approval of the Maintenance of Traffic Plan for construction vehicles, implement tasks off-hours to accommodate tenant and air traffic constraints, and secure a series of concurrent inspections and reviews that permitted uninterrupted construction progress at the site.

Design documents and construction drawings were submitted to eight departments associated with MIA operations. These departments were: Airside Operations (includes Technical Support Division, Access Control Division, and Ramp Control Division); Dade Aviation Consultants; DCAD; the DCAD-affiliated consulting firm, Howard, Needles, Tammen, and Bergdoff; Midfield Fire Station; Landside Operations; Maintenance Division; and Properties Division. Due to the varied concerns and responsibilities of these departments and the potential for parallel and sequential review processes that result in iterations and resubmittals that could adversely impact the project, M&E and DCAD emphasized from the onset of the project a partnership approach involving key representatives among airport officials, regulatory officials, tenants, vendors, and subcontractors.

## Planning and Design

Integration of the design criteria, state of the art remediation technology, and constructability was accomplished by obtaining current remediation construction drawing details and updating them with the newest specifications, Technical Advisory Team reviews by technology leaders within M&E, constructability reviews at the sixty and ninety percent designs, concurrent project cost estimating after completion of the 60% design, and review and comment on the drawings by MIA, DERM and B&Z. Of these five items, the review and comments by MIA were the key to customer service.

The Notice to Proceed was received on September 12, 1994. Remediation Action Plan (RAP) documents were evaluated and 90% construction drawings submitted for DCAD's review on October 21, 1994. M&E mobilized November 14, 1994 and began construction of Phase I. In an action typical of the close cooperation that characterized interaction with permitting agencies throughout the project, DERM and B&Z provided a careful "dry run" review of the 90% drawings to identify issues that could affect final permitting. This "dry run" review allowed mobilization to the site four to six weeks sooner than would have occurred if the "dry run" review had not taken place.

## System Description

The integrated remediation system was a combination groundwater and vapor extraction treatment system with over six miles of pipe under active tarmac. The remedy utilized cost-effective remediation technologies as well as free product removal methodologies to enhance the system performance. The groundwater remediation system consisted of eight vertical extraction wells (including five dual groundwater/vapor extraction wells) and nine hundred feet of horizontal extraction wells. Groundwater was extracted and delivered to an oil/water separator and a forty-two-foot high, seven-foot diameter air stripper tower. Free floating product encountered in the system influent is removed by the oil/water separator and collected in a separate holding tank. Treated water is discharged to a four hundred-foot-long recharge gallery.

The soil remedial system consisted of three thousand feet of screened piping to extract soil vapor from the subsurface. The soil vapor extraction (SVE) wells include eight, two hundred-foot horizontal wells, three vertical wells, five dual groundwater/vapor extraction wells, and six "passive" wells that allow air flow into the subsurface. Soil gas is delivered to four thermal treatment units. Each thermal unit is equipped with sensors to automatically shut down the SVE blower if soil gas concentrations entering the thermal units exceed 65% of the lower explosive limit (LEL). When soil gas concentrations entering the thermal units are insufficient to maintain combustion at required temperatures, propane is fed into the thermal units as a supplemental fuel. A total of eight heat sensors have been installed to monitor temperatures external to the thermal units, due to the internal soil gas incineration temperature of 1,300 to 1,500 degrees Fahrenheit (F) and the proximity of the treatment compound to parked aircraft. Recorded temperatures at the top of the vent stack are 1,100 to 1,200 degrees F. At the fence line approximately twenty feet from the top of the vent stack, temperatures fall nearly to the level of ambient temperature.

**Exhibit 1.** Hangar 22 Remediation Project During Construction

## Construction

The professional trust and cooperation that had developed between M&E, DCAD and regulatory agencies allowed M&E to mobilize to the site one week before building and zoning permits were issued. Construction started on November 11, 1994 for Phase I of the project, which included most trenching, pipe placement, backfill, compaction, and resurfacing (see Figure 1). Work was performed twenty-four hours/day (two twelve-hour shifts), seven days/week for three weeks. Construction schedules were maintained through severe storm events, including Tropical Storm Gordon that raised the water table to the point where alternative construction techniques were required to proceed with trench work. Once it became clear that the schedule would be met, site work was reduced to one twelve-hour shift per day to control overtime expenditures. To augment construction staff for the large, short-duration project, M&E obtained subcontractor services' commitments from twelve other firms, including participation by minority-owned businesses in excess of $1 million.

To perform work in the high security, airside operations area (the FAA has assigned MIA the most stringent possible security rating—"X"), M&E obtained security training and monitored the distribution and use of security badges as required for the approximately two hundred and fifty individuals involved in onsite work. M&E provided to Access Control officials a list of personnel and vehicles, along with the times of entry and exit from the site. During the Summit of the Americas Presidents' Conference in Miami (December, 1994), M&E coordinated on a special basis with the Access Control Division and the Metro-Dade Police Department to prevent a shutdown or curtailment of construction operations.

M&E also communicated closely with the Technical Support Division and Ramp Control Division on such issues as repainting the "Fuchsia Line," that establishes a boundary for the outer extremes of aircraft parking areas, after the completion of trenching and repaving, adjusting site boundaries to provide increased space for aircraft parking, activating floodlights and barricade lights for nighttime construction (all lighting, markers, and structures met FAA lighting, marking, and height restrictions, respectively), providing scrubber trucks and water trucks to clean up dirt and dust and prevent potential foreign object damage (FOD) to aircraft, and posting a twenty-four-hour security guard during trenching operations beneath the security fence separating airside from landside.

All site work was performed in strict accordance with airport security regulations and a site-specific Health & Safety Plan, and was monitored by a full-time Health & Safety Officer. Preshift safety meetings were held each day to inform workers of issues, progress, and concerns. Organic Vapor Analyzers with Flame Ionization Detectors and Combustible Gas meters were used to monitor breathing zones during trench work and other tasks where potential exposures could occur. Hearing protection was used against noise from jets and heavy machinery, and communication tools ranged from hand signals during routine trench work, to radio transmitters with headsets and microphones during the installation of portions of the treatment compound when detailed, clear, and immediate communication was of critical importance. All site activities were conducted without any lost-time worker injuries.

Phase I was completed December 23, 1994 to allow the new tenant for Hangar 22 to occupy the property beginning December 26, 1994. Aircraft as shown in Exhibit 1 were parked on top of the new construction within twenty-four hours of completion. Phase II, which included treatment train installation, system startup, and the completion of "asbuilt" drawings, was completed by March 24, 1995. Both Phase I and Phase II were completed on schedule, under budget, and in accordance with the Consent Agreement.

## Project Organization

The reason for the successful completion of this project was the way in which the project management team was organized to communicate and work with the client. The project management team was organized to assure effective communications with MIA, allowing M&E to understand the needs of MIA and respond quickly. Project communications flow was managed to allow the proper DCAD and M&E resources to

**Exhibit 2.** Project Communications/ Organization Chart

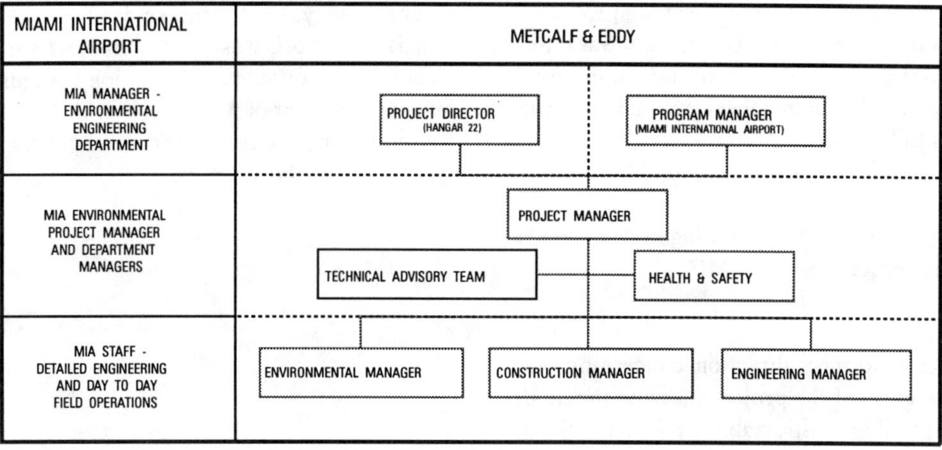


**Exhibit 3.** Hangar 22 Remediation System and Two Other Design/Build Projects Completed After Hangar 22

focus on the key manageable issues at hand while allowing upper management to become involved in a timely manner when required. The three levels of communication between MIA and M&E project personnel are indicated in Exhibit 2.

Organization of the project management team was critical due to the numerous client departments and local government agencies. Key M&E team members and their client service duties were as follows:

### *Program Manager*

Provide specific project direction concerning how project execution would affect other projects at MIA.

### *Project Director*

Provide specific senior project direction concerning engineering and construction of the project ensuring timely design peer reviews as well as constructability reviews of the design by M&E's construction experts.

### *Project Manager*

Single point of contact for client concerning project engineering, permitting, and financial management. Primary client contact during upfront planning, design, permitting, and operations and maintenance.

### *Construction Manager*

Single point of contact for client for day-to-day operations during construction.

Organization of the project management team and the proactive management style of the team were the key factors for making this a win/win project for the client and M&E.

## Conclusion

Successful completion of this design/build environmental restoration project was the result of an effective client service program that developed a partnering attitude between the stakeholders. This program allowed the design team to work in conjunction with the construction team, client, and regulators to design and construct a remediation system that would meet both the technical requirements and the rigorous schedule demands imposed by this project. This program also provided resolutions to the numerous obstacles encountered, such as delays from Tropical Storm Gordon, limited site access, FAA restrictions, airside access requirements, and airport permitting, to be implemented without exceeding the budget or delaying the completion schedule. The only measure of true client service is receiving additional projects after the completion of the current project. Exhibit 3 identifies the Hangar 22 project and two other design/build projects that were awarded to M&E upon completion of Hangar 22.

Client service provides synergy and is essential for successful completion of complex design/build projects in the 21st Century. The successful completion through client service of these types of complex design/build remediation projects is why M&E was rated Number 1 for remediation services by Environmental Technology, August, 1996. M&E's mission statement of providing world class solutions, local focus, and cost effective results illustrates the essence of client service in the 21st Century.

# Panel Discussion: Environmental Management

Moderator: Mr. Tom Vanderheiden

This interactive panel will investigative what has been done in the past and identify who is making the greatest strides towards the changing of their culture. The panel will be instructive on what a modern and fully integrated project management system should include. Discussion will include benchmarking measures on various government sponsored environmental projects, where they are, and what their plans are for future continued improvements. The discussions will be specific to environmental projects and will compare planned development by government agencies to the commercial side of the industry and how they are managing environmental projects.

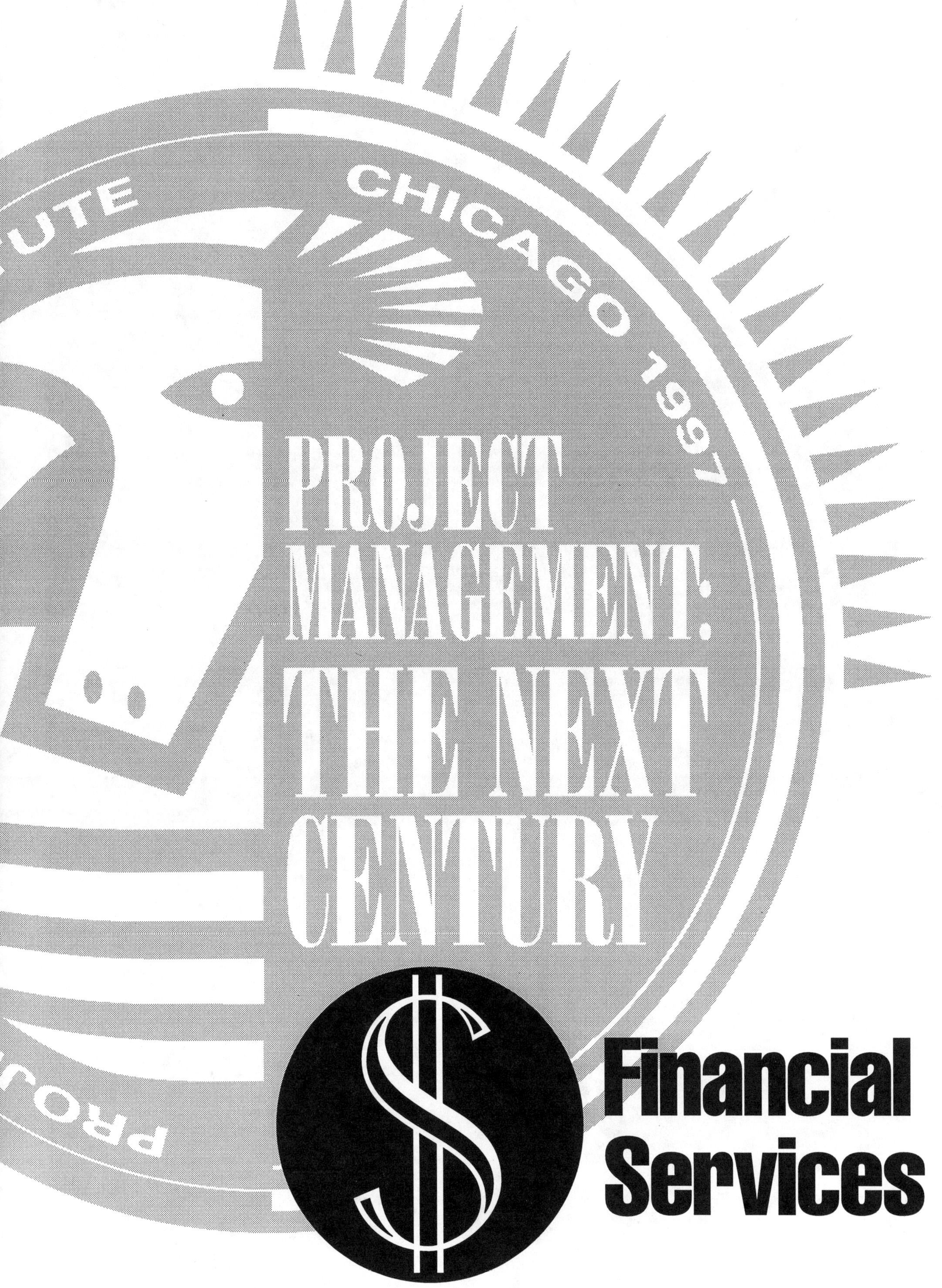


# Financial Services

# A Trio of Project Managers Creates a Successful Project

Rodger Clawson, PMP, State of Oregon Controllers Division

How can one person have and maintain the project, functional, and technical knowledge required to successfully complete projects in today's rapid changing environment? Previously, a person in either the technical or functional area is given the job of project manager. In my opinion, the skills to complete a successful project is not necessarily learned as a database analyst or an accountant. One approach would take a competent functional person, give them a two-day project management course and anoint them project leader. This anointment after two days has not produced many successful projects. Since the technology piece is a critical success factor, another approach makes a technical person the project leader. This approach also leaves room for improvement in project success. There is little correlation between producing great COBOL code and leading a project.

Yet another approach is to have the project leader be a project management professional. This paper discusses an approach to managing Information Technology (IT) projects using a collegial approach blending the project management talent with the IT expertise and functional knowledge. Our project office was formed with three individuals from the three separate disciplines. The three people are in constant communication with each other and use a shared style of management. The functional person in the project office is a CPA with twenty-five years of experience in the accounting profession. The IT person in the project office has thirty years developing computer-based systems. A Project Management Professional (PMP #1245) served as the project person to round out the project office. This unusual approach to project management has proved successful on this project. This approach was chosen after the two previous project directors left the project.

This paper will describe the organizational structure, the communications, and the characteristic that made the concept work. To set the stage for the project I will first describe the scope, cost, time and quality characteristics of the Statewide Financial Management System (SFMS). See Exhibit 1.

## Scope

The scope of this project is to install one common accounting system in one hundred state agencies for the State Controllers Division in the State of Oregon. The software is an off-the-shelf software package from KPMG Peat Marwick LLP with modifications made specifically for the State of Oregon. This same software is installed in fifteen states. The project is divided into manageable pieces. Each agency implementation is considered and managed as a separate project with a separate plan and project leader.

## Cost

The cost of the SFMS project is budgeted at $23.8 million. Costs measured include vendor services, state salaries and state services. Vendor services included the following factors: (1) Software acquisition and installation costs, (2) Vendor support costs for the initial installation, and (3) Vendor costs for assistance with agency implementation. State costs include the following: (4) Salaries for implementation assistance, (5) Computer time and technical support provided by state I/T resources, and (6) Central training instructors and materials. (7) Consultants hired to provide an overall master plan and Quality Assurance during the project were also included.

Costs not included in the calculations include: agency installation time, agency interface design and testing, volunteer agency testing time, and agency training time. Each agency required from one to three thousand hours of staff time to

**Figure 1.**

SFMS Project

- Statewide Financial Management System Implementation Project
  - Scope - Implement standardized accounting and purchasing functionality in 100 state agencies
  - Cost - $23.8 Million ($238,000 per agency)
  - Time - Implementation complete 12/97
  - Quality - software & installation



PROJECT MANAGEMENT INSTITUTE 28th Annual Seminars & Symposium
Chicago, Illinois: Papers Presented September 29 to October 1, 1997

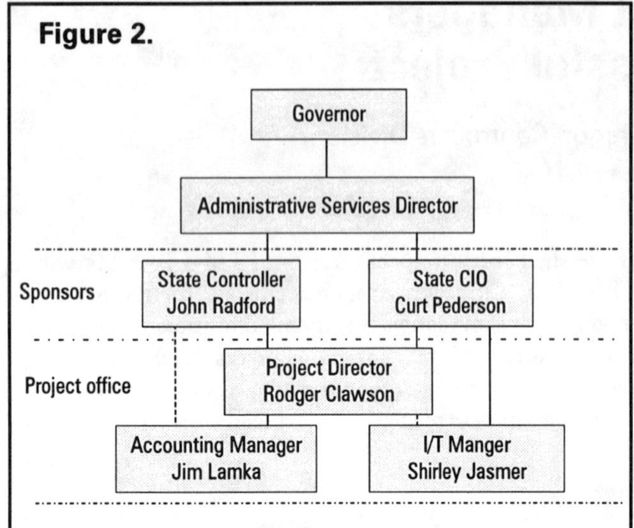


define parameters and adapt to the accounting system. Some agencies required interfaces to move accounting transactions from a program specific application to the accounting system. While no records were kept of these costs, some agencies spent as much as three person-years on the interfaces. When the software was originally installed, agencies volunteered to send staff to conduct the acceptance testing. Again, this was not tracked, but it could be estimated at four person-years. Part of each agency implementation is training for the agency. While in a small agency this training could be only two weeks, in some large agencies this involved hundreds of persons and many trainers. Since the state had no common time reporting system, it is not cost effective to attempt to track costs at the agency level.

## Time

This project is scheduled to end in December of 1997. While the concept was initiated in 1989 the master plan was prepared in 1991. The contract with KPMG was signed in August 1993, and the first group of agencies implemented in March 1995. The last group of agencies will be installed in the fall of 1997.

## Quality

We planned quality into the project in two basic approaches. The base software was acceptance tested prior to implementing the first agencies. While this process took longer than originally expected, the quality of the software was enhanced. The other quality approach centered around each agency conversion. We used checklists and reconciliation prior to implementing each agency. While the checklists ensured the agency was ready to operate the system after conversion, the reconciliation ensured the agency's books balanced when they started to use the accounting system. These two basic approaches maintained a good level of quality throughout the project.

## Organization

The organization set-up for the collegial project office required some nontraditional approaches. The nontraditional thinking started at the project sponsor level. While on a typical project there would be one sponsor, this project has cosponsors. One cosponsor is the Chief Information Officer (CIO) for the State of Oregon. The other cosponsor is the State Controller. These two individuals report to the director of the Department of Administrative Services (DAS) who reports to the Governor. This cosponsor arrangement brought together the State Controller who had the passion for the project and the CIO who had the technical capacity to make it happen. This is shown in Exhibit 2.

Building on the cosponsor concept, the trio of project managers includes a functional manager, a technical IT manager and a project director. The functional manager was moved from his position as a key manager in the controllers office. While he is currently assigned full-time to the project, he will continue in the State Controller's Division after completion of the project. He brings to the project both institutional and functional knowledge and since he has been in the Controllers Division for ten years, he has historical perspective and knows the political landscape. Being a CPA gives him credibility in resolving the accounting issues that arise during the project. Prior to being assigned to the project, he reported directly to State Controller. Currently, he maintains a dotted line relationship with the Controller and a reporting relationship with the project director. All the central support Agency Implementation Analysts (AIA's) report to him.

The technical manager has a dotted line reporting relationship with the project director and a direct reporting relationship to the CIO. While most of the people required for the project report to her, she has a direct line to other IT resources through the CIO. Her years of experience and knowledge of technical resources throughout the state are instrumental to the project success. She is a respected IT professional who spends most but not all of her time on this project.

The project director reports directly to the two cosponsors. Yes, this works. Performance appraisals are done by two people and there is open communication among the three (or five) of us. The project director brings the central leadership and project focus to the collegial team. The contractor related issues are handled directly by the project director. Exhibit 3 depicts staff reporting.

As each agency prepares to convert to the central system, they appoint an Agency Project Manager (APM). This person has dotted line responsibility to the project director. The typical APM also has accounting and IT staff working on the project. While the APM reports to and is related to the project director, the agency IT staff relates to the IT part of the project. The accounting staff have a relationship with and work directly with the functional part of the project office. See Exhibit 4.

## Communications

Since this project was organized in a nontraditional manner, a unique approach was required for project communications. The most important piece to making a collegial project office work is constant communication. In this case, we used one extremely old method and one new method. The old method consisted of placing the project director and the functional manager in the same office. This is called the "project office," "ready room," "war room," or "delivery room" depending on how the project is going. This room contains the individual agency produced plans, white boards for tracking critical items, and, of course, the contracts. This office is where impromptu meetings are held, if needed. The new technique included a direct video from the project director's desk to the IT manager's desk. This means that there could be three of us in the office at any one time. When I look to the right I see the IT professional member of the project team. When I look to the left I see (in the same room) the accounting professional on the project. Although we may be working on different aspects of the project, we can hear the other people work. While this took some getting used to, we would not have it any other way now.

The technology used for the computer connection includes a high-speed communications line and peripheral computer equipment. We have a leased ISDN line connecting the two offices. The project director and the IT managers' computers have a video camera and microphone that operate at all times. We purchased the VTEL Personal Collaborator from US WEST (for information contact Kimberly Tyson at 303/299-1862). The additional equipment for each computer was less than $3,000 and the telephone connections cost less than $75 each month.

## Human Resources

Using the collegial style project office with open communication called for some specific characteristics for the three

**Figure 3.**

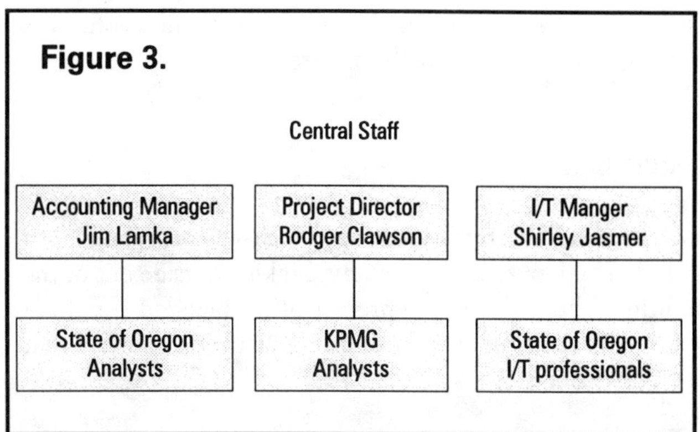


**Figure 4.**

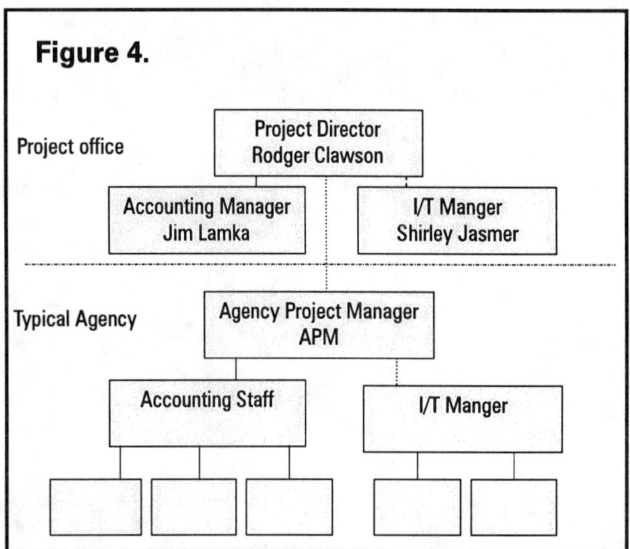


people in the project office including, trust, openness, and knowledge. While the three people in the project office are in direct communication, we do not attend all meetings as a team. Since there is a close bond and sharing of information, any one person can speak for the project. This is the real open office. Individuals using this approach need the ability to be completely candid, willing to share all aspects of their lives. Any call from home is immediately shared with the other members of the project office. Since there are no secrets, this approach requires a high level of openness. As the team was formed, knowledge in the represented area was assumed. In order for this approach to work, individual team members credentials in accounting, data processing or project management are critical. Each individual must be a recognized expert in their respective area.

The trust and openness did not just happen; we worked hard to build it. The project bond was first formed between the project director and the functional accounting manager. After this bond was cemented, the IT manager was incorporated into the team. We started with face-to-face meetings in alternating locations. After these meetings we started a pilot using the VTEL equipment. The pilot was so successful it is now a permanent tool for this project.

## Conclusion

Look beyond the traditional approach when organizing a project. Think outside the box. By thinking outside out of the traditional box, the SFMS project office blended the three skill sets needed for success in a collegial project office that functions effectively.

# The Application of Chaos Theory in Financial Services

Richard Watson

*Life is a bifurcating chaotic attractor, then you die.*
User's Guide to the New Edge

## Prelude

The growing application of nonlinear, complex models to describe the behavior of financial markets raises the likelihood that project managers in the financial services industry will be asked to implement information systems that make use of them. A basic understanding of the concepts and tools currently used to apply such models will greatly increase the chances of success of such a project. This paper will attempt to:

- Identify the basic concepts of chaos theory,
- Outline the business problems to that chaos theory can be applied,
- Introduce some of the tools available to apply chaos theory in financial services,
- Discuss the challenges they present to project managers expected to use them, and
- Identify resources to gain more knowledge on this topic.

## Chaos Theory_

Chaos theory, more formally known as complexity theory, is essentially a branch of mathematics pioneered in the early parts of the 20th century by Russian and French mathematicians. While mathematics can be a fascinating topic in its own right, its usefulness depends on its ability to produce models that accurately describe interesting real world processes. Many interesting processes are dynamic, nonlinear, and contain feedback. These attributes create the conditions for chaotic behavior, and the need for chaotic models to describe the systems that exhibit them.

Chaotic systems are characterized by several distinct features, including turbulence, bifurcation, self-similarity, and extreme dependence on initial conditions. Most people know turbulence when they see it. Behavior such as the billowing of clouds and the spray of water from a hose are in a common experience. Financial market traders see it in the price movements of liquid securities. Turbulence is fascinating to watch because one can see patterns develop and change, but can't really guess what will happen next.

To bifurcate is to split. When a particular process within a system bifurcates, any measure tracking it becomes unpredictable. Chaotic systems exhibit phase transitions between bifurcation and periodic or linear behavior when the energy in the system varies. In the water hose example, when the water pressure is low, the outflow can be described with simple equations, and one can guess fairly accurately where the water will land. As the water pressure increases, the system goes through a phase transition, and the water starts to spray (i.e., one flow bifurcates into many). In liquid financial markets, volume provides the energy that leads to a spray of price volatility over time.

Self-similarity refers to scale independence. One well-known example of scale independence is the Mandelbrot set, which belongs to the class of mathematical structures called fractals or Julia sets. Examination of the Mandelbrot set reveals the same patterns recurring at vastly different scales of observation. In financial markets, the scale of observation is time, and similar patterns are evident in price fluctuations over hours, weeks, and years.

Extreme dependence on initial conditions says that the long-term behavior chaotic systems can never be predicted, because even if a model of the system is perfect (a big if), the initial conditions cannot be measured with enough precision. Any error in measurement will be amplified by feedback within the system, to the point that the error term is larger than the computable terms in the model. In high-energy systems, the error term can dominate very quickly. This hypothesis, borne out by much experimental study and theoretical exploration, has profound implications for building models to predict prices in financial markets.

The holy grail of financial markets—the perfect prediction machine—cannot exist, because of the extreme dependence on initial conditions of chaotic systems. This does not preclude, however, the possibility that trading systems can be devised that operate profitably in a wide range of markets. If anything, the recent contributions of complexity theory to the discipline of portfolio management have generated new avenues of pursuit for such systems.

The notion of a predictive trading system is alluring. If a system could be constructed that inputs all relevant information pertaining to the future price of a security, processes it

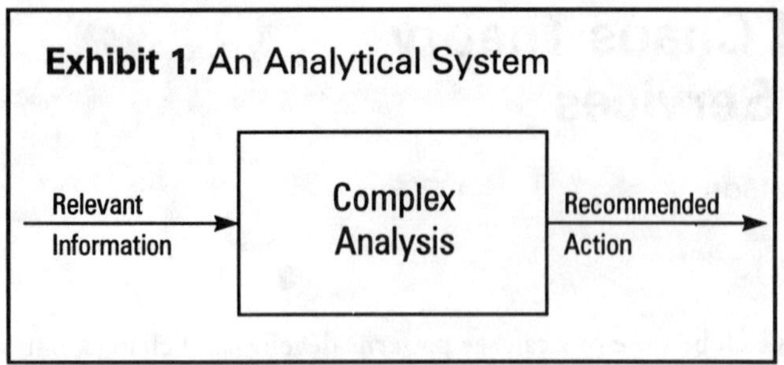

**Exhibit 1.** An Analytical System

through an accurate model of price behavior, and outputs an estimate of the future price, large profits would be possible, even if the system was correct only some of the time. The phenomenal success of financiers such as Warren Buffet and George Soros suggests to some people that not only may such a system be possible, but that one may actually exist already. Chaos theory offers attractive avenues of pursuit of this goal because it provides many useful insights into the characteristics of an accurate model of price behavior.

## Chaos Theory in Financial Services

Accurate models of real systems are useful because they help people to solve problems. Most of the examples above relate to the security selection problem—the question of which specific securities should be held in a portfolio in order to achieve specific investment objectives. The systems being modeled in this case are the financial markets in which the securities trade. Empirical evidence in the price fluctuations of financial markets suggests that such systems are chaotic, so a model based on chaos theory might be more accurate than a linear model. Furthermore, complex behavior is evident in many other processes that make up the financial services industry, which suggests that chaos theory might apply to a wide range of problems. Another area that has attracted much interest in building accurate models besides security selection is that of credit risk and fraud.

Financial institutions make thousands of decisions on a daily basis that extend credit to their customers. Whether the decision is to syndicate a bond, issue a loan, or underwrite an insurance policy, the creditworthiness of the customer has substantial bearing on the form and price of the provider's delivery of financial service. In making these decisions, financial institutions collect and analyze large amounts of information to assess counterparty credit risk and determine whether and how to do business. This problem profile shares many similarities with the security selection problem, and can also be modeled with chaos theory.

Since the assessment of information is so fundamental to the delivery of financial services, the appropriate vehicle for implementing chaotic models is, of course, information technology. Exhibit 1 diagrams an analytical system. Chaos theory comes into play in the complex analysis performed as an internal function of the system. This type of functionality will increasingly appear in the requirements for information systems in the financial services industry. Project managers will likely be asked to process each trade, loan, and property, then deliver results to decision makers in a high-volume, real-time environment, with a high degree of data integrity. This is a new requirement, because it involves a complex analysis function in the middle of the data processing. Most business processes today rely on a human component to perform complex analysis. In the future, this function will increasingly be performed within the information system itself.

## Modern Portfolio Theory

Analysis of the financial markets has traditionally been based on Modern Portfolio Theory (MPT). Two major components of MPT are the Capital Asset Pricing Model (CAPM) and the Efficient Market Hypothesis (EMH). CAPM provides a model that relates risk and return, in which riskier investments provide higher returns to compensate investors for holding risk. It also provides a theoretical basis for portfolio diversification, a common practice for both private and professional portfolio managers. CAPM demonstrates that portfolio diversification delivers better returns relative to risk.

The Efficient Market Hypothesis asserts that all information relevant to the price of a security is incorporated in its price. New information is reflected in security prices as soon as it is discovered, which leads to random fluctuations in prices (the proverbial random walk), because each piece of new information could be positive or negative. Different versions of EMH define what constitutes relevant information, which lead to different styles of information analysis.

Vast amounts of research have investigated the extent to which financial markets are efficient, and convincing evidence has been presented on both sides of the question. On one hand, MPT is intellectually appealing and empirically testable. Market prices do fluctuate as new information becomes available, as seen in market responses to, for example, corporate earnings reports and actions by the Federal Reserve. On the other hand, MPT fails to account for the apparent "mob psychology" of markets, which leads to bubbles and crashes. Also, many anomalies have been identified in the price history of financial markets, particularly the heavily studied U.S. equity market, such as the January effect, the small-cap effect, and so forth.

Complexity theory is emerging more as a supplement to MPT, rather than an alternative to it. To the extent that markets are efficient, MPT provides a reasonable approximation of price behavior. Complexity theory steps in to explain what happens when markets undergo a phase transition (such as a market crash). While MPT has the advantage of ease of implementation, in that the normal-distribution assumptions behind it are much easier to calculate, chaos theory provides advantages that may at times be worth the extra effort. Of course, one never knows when the effort will be worth it, so those with much to gain are likely to expend the effort more readily. In practical terms, the question is not whether each model is right or wrong, but which model to use at what time.

## Building on Chaos Theory

As mentioned earlier, the most immediate and practical use of chaos theory in financial services is the construction of analytical information systems. Computers have been used to assist with mathematical analysis for decades. In many fields, the most common computer analyses are statistical in nature. In statistical analysis, one postulates a set of the mathematical equations to describe the system, then runs regression analysis on the known inputs and outputs of the system to estimate the coefficients of each term in the equations. One can easily buy software libraries and utilities to perform different kinds of statistical analysis.

Chaos theory extends the discipline of rigorous analysis to problems that render statistical analysis ineffective. This can occur when the equations are unknown, are too large to calculate, or insufficient data exists on the inputs and outputs of the system. The commercial market for tools to perform complexity analysis is still maturing. The most widely used tool today is a neural network, which can be augmented with technologies such as fuzzy logic and genetic algorithms.

A neural network is a collection of nodes that process inputs and outputs, as shown in Exhibit 2. Each node receives one or more inputs, performs some transfer function, and generates typically only one output. That output can then be passed as input to another node. The nodes can be arranged in any number of configurations, but the boundaries of the network (its overall inputs and outputs) need to map to the boundaries of the real system being modeled.

The usefulness of neural networks comes from the ability of each node, and hence the overall network, to determine its own transfer function. Nodes in the network determine their transfer function through training. A neural network is trained by applying sets of inputs for which the desired output is known, and giving it feedback on the accuracy of its output. The network then adjusts its internal functions to converge on the desired output. Once the network responds satisfactorily to the training data, it needs to be tested on new data from the same real system. If it performs well on the test data, it can be expected to behave similarly when processing live data from the system it models.

**Exhibit 2.** A Neural Network

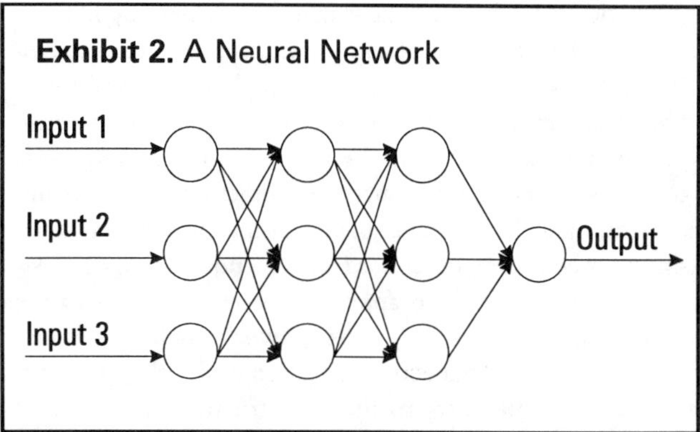


Neural networks are a viable technology for problems that involve the analysis of many data inputs, where the inputs have high degrees of correlation between them, or the functions that relate the inputs to the outputs are not known. Research has shown that neural networks can yield better results than regression analysis in such cases, even if the system is not chaotic. Project managers should consider the use of neural network technology when confronted with such a problem.

The relative newness of neural networks creates several practical problems in the implementation of systems that use them. During construction, a project team must address a number of basic architecture questions before a working system emerges. In implementation, the inability of a neural network to describe why a given set of inputs results in the specific output can be vexing to the users of the system.

The architecture of the network includes the number of nodes, the density of interconnections, the form of the internal transfer function of each node, and the rules for adjusting the function in response to feedback. No deterministic formula exists to advise a project team on the proper architecture of a neural network. No one architecture works best for all problems. Some basic guidelines can be found, both in the research literature and in the materials that come with most commercial tools, but in most cases the project team is left with a trial-and-error approach to answer these design questions.

A poorly designed or improperly trained network is fairly evident. A bad neural network performs well with training data, but fails to give good results for test or live data. For this reason, neural networks should be thoroughly tested, and the training data should fully represent the production environment. When a network trains well but tests poorly, it is possible that the architecture is not suitable for the problem at hand, or the network simply needs more training. Again, guidelines are available, but it is left to the project team to analyze the situation and choose a course of action.

Genetic algorithms augment neural networks by helping determine the transfer function for each node. Genetic algorithms borrow from evolution theory, in that successful transfer functions are retained for further use, and unsuccessful algorithms are removed from the population. Simple genetic algorithms merely cull the successful functions from the unsuccessful ones. More complex algorithms provide a mechanism to "breed" new functions from the population of existing ones. One could also apply a genetic algorithm to the arrangement of nodes within the network, by letting nodes create and destroy connections between each other. However, it is inadvisable to try to alter the structure of nodes and the transfer functions within the nodes at the same time.

The business context in which neural networks operate often begs the question of why the network has generated a specific output in response to its inputs. In the security selection problem, a network may give buy or sell recommendations on a single security. Few active portfolio managers will accept such recommendations on blind faith, especially if they come from a computer. The need for explanations in this case is acute, and would most likely be among the requirements of any security selection system. It is possible to examine the transfer functions of each node in the network, but since the network is highly interconnected, these functions do not abstract well to the vocabulary of the problem domain. One possible answer to the explanation problem is to augment the neural network with fuzzy logic.

Fuzzy logic is a formal treatment of the commonsense approach most people take in describing complex situations. If an equity analyst was asked to explain a buy recommendation, she might say "this company is highly profitable, it has a low price-to-earnings ratio, and the growth prospects of its industry are good." These are all fuzzy statements. They express relative, comparative attributes of the security, but provide no absolute, definitive truths about it. Fuzzy logic treats relative truths in a manner similar to probability theory, in that it assigns a truth value between zero and one to each statement. It also provides a framework for the mathematical treatment of relative truths in the context of an analytical model.

One approach to applying fuzzy logic to the explanation problem of neural networks is to borrow from the field of expert systems. As in expert systems, the first step would be to define a set of rules that apply to the problem. However, rather than simply firing the rules in a yes/no fashion as in a traditional expert system, a neural network could assign a relative truth values to each rule to provide an explanation. A small neural network could be constructed for each rule, with the same inputs as the overall network, but with output set as the truth value of one rule. Of course, in order to get textual explanations, the wording of the rules would have to map in some way to the truth values. One would then have a set of networks, all of which process the same inputs. One network would provide the overall recommendation, and the others would process the rules provided by an expert to give some explanation of the recommendation. The key to ensuring that the networks work together would be to train them on the same data.

The commercialization of fuzzy logic to date has focused primarily on hardware components for embedded controllers. General purpose fuzzy logic software components are not widely available today, but several neural network vendors have begun to incorporate this technology in their products. A project team could use one of these products, follow the strategy outlined above, or pursue a hardware-based alternative to incorporate fuzzy logic within an analytical system.

## Managing Chaos Projects

The challenges that chaos theory and neural networks present to project managers are considerable. Among them are the maturity of the technology, the availability of experienced engineers and analysts, and the high pressure demands of the financial services industry. Taken together, these challenges indicate that such projects will require rigorous application of the PMI Project Management Body of Knowledge to maximize the chances of success.

As new technology gains acceptance, it typically appears first in unstructured, experimental, research-oriented projects. It then moves into more clearly defined, managed, and planned projects. Chaos theory and neural networks are currently going through this transition. In the past, chaos theory has been applied by "rocket scientists," who earned advanced degrees in mathematics or physics, then came to Wall Street to cash in on their pioneering efforts. Most early applications were the result of the long, sustained efforts of gifted individuals. In the future, chaos theory will be seen as a powerful yet accessible set of concepts applicable to a variety of business objectives. Projects will be initiated specifically to achieve the potential demonstrated by earlier efforts, and project managers will be assigned to deliver working information systems in specific time frames for definable cost.

Projects will be performed by integrated teams of experts from varying knowledge domains. These teams will need mathematics, computer science, and financial services expertise. Initially, individuals with wide experience in implementing advanced analytical applications will be rare. Developing and retaining such expertise is already a high priority for many firms in the industry. Most importantly, project managers will need a certain degree of knowledge in all of these areas, in order to properly plan and coordinate the activities of team members with such diverse backgrounds.

The business sponsors of the type of project described above are likely to have intense focus on the money-making objectives of such projects, and have little time to contemplate the mathematical concepts involved. Project managers will be continually challenged to create realistic expectations of project cost, schedule, and functional deliverables. Additionally, the quality standards for any information system entrusted with a firm's financial assets are extremely high, second only to the standards for systems that sustain human life. All of these fundamental dimensions of project performance are strained by new technology.

The combination of limited expertise, complex new technology, and demanding project objectives creates a project environment fraught with risk. Identifying, prioritizing, and mitigating risks that would prevent the project from delivering will occupy a great deal of effort and attention. Admittedly, these issues are always part of the job description for project managers. However, the combined effect of all these difficulties simultaneously suggests that such a project will require something more than a nine-to-five level of commitment from the entire project team.

If one follows the traditional line of thinking, increased risk should be accompanied with greater rewards. In this case, the rewards are likely to be both financial and professional. The potential impact of a good application of chaos theory on the financial condition of any organization able to do it provides the resources to handsomely compensate those who participate in the effort. Furthermore, the knowledge that successful information systems in financial services add liquidity to financial markets and enhance the robustness of the global economy can create significant intrinsic job satisfaction.

## A Few Final Words

The purpose of this paper has been to raise the level of awareness of chaos theory among project managers in the financial services industry. Chaos theory has attracted much interest from an academic research perspective and as a tool to apply to real business problems. As the track record of successful applications of chaos theory grows, so too will interest in all sectors of the industry. Those who stay abreast of developments in this field will be better positioned to carry themselves and their firms forward through the uncertainty of tomorrow's financial services industry. The references below are an excellent starting point for those interested in expanding their knowledge in this field further. The author can be reached by e-mail at rwatson@world.std.com.

## References


Babcock, Bruce. 1997. *Chaos Theory and Market Reality*. http://www.rd_trading.com/articles.html (May).

Barber, John C. 1997. *Chaos Theory as a Framework for Studying Financial Markets.* http://www.falconasset.com/html/research.html (May).

Bodie, Zvi, Alex Kane and Alan Marcus. 1989. *Investments*. Irwin. Boston.

Brealey, Richard and Stewart Myers. 1988. *Principles of Corporate Finance*. McGraw-Hill, New York.

Chorofas, Dimitris N. 1994. *Chaos Theory in the Financial Markets*. Probus, Chicago.

Freedman, Roy, Robert Klien and Jess Lederman ed. 1995. *Artificial intelligence in the Capital Markets*. Irwin, Chicago.

Gleick, James. 1987. *Chaos—Making a New Science*. Viking Press, New York.

Kosko, Bart. 1993. *Fuzzy Thinking—The New Science of Fuzzy Logic*. Hyperion, New York.

LeBaron, Blake. 1997. Working Papers. http://www.econ.wisc.edu/~blebaron/research.htmld/index.html. (March).

London Business School Neuroforecasting Club. 1997. http://www.cs.ucl.ac.uk/intelligent_systems/neuro.htm. (May).

Merz, Kevin and Joseph Rosen. 1997. *The Handbook of Investment Technology*. Irwin, Chicago.

Peters, Edgar. 1991. *Chaos and Order in the Capital Markets*. Wiley and Sons, New York.

Rucker, Rudy, R.U. Sirius and Queen Mu. 1992. *Mondo 2000: A User's Guide to the New Edge*. Harper Collins, New York.

Santa Fe Institute. 1997. http://www.santafe.edu (Jan.).

Trippi, Robert and Efriam Turban, ed. 1993. *Neural Networks in Finance and Investing*. Probus, Chicago.

Trippi, Robert and Jae Lee. 1992. *State of the Art Portfolio Selection*. Probus, Chicago.

Vaga, Tonis. 1994. *Profiting from Chaos*. McGraw Hill, New York.

# The Copernicus Project: Reinventing An Information Services Business

Donald J. Miller, Ph.D., Experian Information Solutions, Inc.

## Introduction

In early 1992, TRW's Information Services Division began formulating plans to reinvent its core consumer credit reporting business. That decision, involving many tens of millions of dollars and several years of effort, was necessary to position its commercial information services businesses for expansion into broader market areas and secure a leading edge position in the industry.

This project, known internally as Copernicus, formally began in June of 1992. By early 1994, the project was in trouble. It had routinely missed deadlines, had no clearly defined plan, and had lost much of its management support and sponsorship. Overall success appeared unlikely, and the project was in jeopardy of being canceled. Copernicus appeared headed for the fate that befalls the majority of large-scale information technology (IT) projects(to end in failure or otherwise fade away without completing its intended objectives.

In mid-1994, after several attempts by management to put the project back on a clear footing, the decision was made to bring in a new management team. The view was that the basic design of the underlying information systems was acceptable, but a new approach to project management was needed to put Copernicus back on track.

This paper reviews the implementation of project management tools and techniques used, starting in July 1994, to put the Copernicus project on a renewed footing that eventually led to its successful conclusion on June 15, 1996.

## Project Scope

One of the first steps taken in the turn-around process was to clearly define the project scope. At a very top level, the project scope consisted of the four areas: The *Consumer Credit Services System (CCSS), Associate Systems, Business Implementation, and Database Cutover.*

1. The *Consumer Credit Services System (CCSS)* was a new system that would entirely replace the outdated legacy credit reporting system. The work on CCSS consisted of new software and hardware as well as an entirely new approach to the database structure.
2. *Associate Systems* scope involved modifying a series of Associate Systems to interact with and transfer data between themselves and CCSS. In all, more than a dozen Associate Systems were involved. Most of these systems, already existing at the time CCSS began and were performing a variety of business functions such as (a) different input channels used to put data to file, (b) interactions with specialized product lines, and (c) back-end systems such as billing, customer service, and monitoring system security. All of these systems needed to read, write or read/write data between themselves and CCSS, and the new database structure of CCSS dictated changes to these Associate Systems. Some systems, most notably the Consumer Assistance System, required enough modification that an entirely new Associate System was designed and implemented as part of Copernicus.
3. Copernicus was not simply the design and implementation of new IT systems, but its scope also included *Business Implementation*(training and documentation for the business operations; training the sales force to effectively promote the new features and functions of CCSS; preparation of an overall marketing communications plan introducing our new system to the industry; and a set of detailed customer proofs and other analyses for release to selected key customers convincing them of the new system's viability prior to the cutover date.
4. The final area of project scope was *Database Cutover.* The data stored in the legacy database was in good shape and represented a significant asset to be preserved for the new system. The key issue revolved around the need for the data to be transformed from its flat-file legacy format into the new relational database structure of CCSS. This, in itself, was a massive undertaking involving writing specialized software code used *one-time only* for conversion; rehearsing the actual cutover numerous times, first with subscale and then full-size databases; and then eventually implementing the final production database at system cutover.



PROJECT MANAGEMENT INSTITUTE 28th Annual Seminars & Symposium
Chicago, Illinois: Papers Presented September 29 to October 1, 1997

## Project Schedule

When the project began in June of 1992, it was planned for completion in eighteen months. Clearly, by July of 1994 it was nowhere close to completion but the imperative remained to "complete Copernicus as soon as possible." However, two other factors needed consideration:

- First, we could not shortchange quality in any way that would jeopardize our current business or that of our customers. The consumer credit industry, a government regulated business, requires strict adherence to provisions of the Fair Credit Reporting Act (FCRA) and other rulings by federal and state entities. Also, our customers relied on our systems and information to perform their own risk analyses and make critical business operations decisions. And since our industry is very competitive and offers several capable suppliers of consumer credit information, any perception by our customers, whether real or imagined, of a deficiency in our system could significantly impact this core line-of-business.
- Second, all things being equal, it was more advantageous to implement a massive new system like CCSS in the first half of a calendar year. This would give our customers and ourselves time to adapt to any new system issues well before the end of summer and prior to the back-to-school season and then the fall and winter holiday events that drive up the seasonal demand for consumer credit reports.

Therefore, the overall schedule criteria became "as soon as possible without any compromise on quality." By late Summer 1994, we had targeted the first half of 1996 for Copernicus implementation. By the Fall our detailed, bottoms-up planning and scheduling had led to a target implementation date of Saturday, March 30, 1996. Due to various operational considerations, implementation had to take place "early" on a Saturday morning, meaning that even a one-day schedule slip would delay the implementation date by a full week (to the following Saturday).

## Project Planning and Tracking

One of the new methodologies introduced as part of the Copernicus turnaround was rigorous project planning and tracking. Prior to July 1994, the project had relied on a simple Gantt chart approach with three- to six-month long activity bars that generally represented a top-down "hoped for" schedule rather than activity duration estimates based on more substantial methods.

This approach was replaced with a system that first divided the entire project scope into approximately eighty work packages. Work packages were defined by a four-tier work breakdown structure (WBS) that was organized around project deliverable end-items rather than existing company departments or functions.

Cross functional teams were then assembled with responsibility for successfully completing their individual work package deliverables. These cross functional teams were also responsible for producing a network schedule that included all the activities deemed necessary for their work package. In general, a work package would consist of about two hundred individual activities, all with predecessor and successor activities to define the network.

Dependencies between different work packages were made by specific linkages between individual activities found in two or more work packages. The result was an overall network of more than 2,000 activities with durations estimated for each activity and a person's name associated with every activity. That person had bottom-line responsibility for (1) estimating the activity's duration and (2) completing the required work within the estimated duration and with the required scope and quality. This bottom-up detailed planning led to the March 30, 1996 predicted cutover date.

The schedule network was so large that practicality dictated the plan could only be updated every two weeks. Therefore, on a two-week basis all active, or soon to be active, work packages were statused, problems identified, work-arounds proposed or implemented, remaining activity durations revised, and the entire network's critical path was recalculated. The result was a new prediction every two weeks about the cutover date(however, this was expressed in terms of being behind or ahead of the March 30, 1996 target date. In other words, the cutover date was expressed in terms of having *positive* (being ahead) or *negative* (being behind) slack versus the target date. For almost the entire course of the project, *the target date did not change.* Nonetheless, it was not unusual to have several weeks positive or negative slack each time we updated the schedule network. The status of positive or negative slack (typically only ± plus or minus several weeks) was openly communicated to the entire project team of more than four hundred people in addition to management and other interested internal parties.

## Project Target Date is Revised

By early 1996 about eight weeks of negative slack had built up and almost all reasonable approaches for winning back schedule slips had been exhausted. It was now necessary to revise the target date. Our now well-established planning and scheduling techniques were used to establish a new, more valid (based on then-current information) schedule baseline. A newly-predicted target date of June 15, 1996 was fixed, and this indeed became the eventual, and successful cutover date for the project.

Even though the project took ten weeks longer than originally planned, because of our very effective network schedule, we could predict that schedule slip well in advance and have confidence that everything within reason had been done to work around the schedule slip. The schedule was like a map telling us when we were off course and how best to get back on. *It became a problem solving tool and not just a management communications tool.*

In spite of the schedule slip, we did complete the labor portion of the system development and implementation within less than 1% of the $64.6 million budget established as part of the Fall 1996 baseline. Admittedly, there may have been some luck in that number given how big the project was(at the peak, we had more than four hundred people working directly on the project. We were not so lucky on the hardware side where we overran the $27 million budget baseline by 32%, due primarily to a significant underestimation in the system performance requirements based on the original design.

## Project Organization

Steps were also taken to improve upon the project organization, primarily in three areas:

- First, many people were assigned to the project on a part-time basis without any reduction in their "normal job duties." This practice was revised so that people were assigned to the project full-time and relieved of their previous nonproject duties. This was further reinforced by using collocation for most of the project teams as well as assigning the project manager responsibility for each individual's annual performance reviews, raises, bonuses, etc.
- Second, cross-functional teams were organized so that all the functions and skills needed to deliver results on any one work package were contained within the same team. For example, a particular new software product would have a team made up of software designers and developers, technical testers, marketing product managers to define the product requirements, business operations people for further quality assurance testing, and documentation and training people to provide new product support. In general practice, it was the marketing product manager or operations manager needing the new product who was put in charge of the work package and had bottom-line responsibility for delivering what was needed.
- Finally, some new functions not previously used in this part of our business were added to the project. The best example, perhaps, is the formal systems integration and test (I&T) approach. This function was used to integrate all the individual software products at the work package level into a coherent process to test that system both in a functional and performance sense as well as test and verify all the system interfaces.

## Change Management Process

A project as complex and far reaching as Copernicus cannot expect to have all requirements well understood at the onset but must rather accommodate, in a controlled fashion, the inevitable and beneficial change in requirements, understanding, priorities, etc. I say beneficial because it is important to continuously improve the objectives of the project as new information is obtained or revealed during the course of the work. On the other hand, open-ended and continuously changing requirements and understandings will require that a project be forever trying to catch up to a moving target and never get completed.

Therefore a formal, multi-tiered change management process was implemented. First a Software Change Board (SCB) was established to document, review and approve software changes. This included routine changes needed for software as a result of testing other changes to bring software into compliance with already understood requirements and performance-related changes. The senior software development manager was chairman of the SCB with *51% of the vote* to approve any changes at this level. More important, it was the SCB's responsibility to forward more complex or far reaching changes to the Change Management Board (CMB).

The CMB initially met every two weeks, but as the project progressed weekly meetings were implemented. Indeed in the final months of the project as the deadline for implementation approached, the CMB met almost every day to handle last minute changes. The CMB was widely attended with technical, operations and marketing groups all participating. However, I appointed the senior marketing manager to chair the CMB with *51% of the vote.* This accomplished two things:

- First, it eliminated most finger pointing between the marketing people who were specifying the products, and the technical people who were designing and building them. Marketing product managers were full-fledged members of the CMB and their voices were fully heard. Indeed, at the end of the day, the final responsibility for determining "what" we did was in the hands of marketing, since the senior marketing manager was responsible for all final decisions. This left the technical resources to focus on the "how" to accomplish the needed changes. Also, almost all change decisions were done with an estimate of the cost and schedule impact caused by the change. In this way, the overall business impact and tradeoffs could be taken into account.

- Second, by having one person with *51% of the vote*, the CMB quickly moved from a debating committee to a decision-making function. The result was a quick convergence on necessary decisions. In some cases, decisions had to be referred back for additional study before making a final determination, but eventually a decision was reached. In other cases, decisions needed to be reversed or further compromises made when additional information on market or technical limitations came to light. But the CMB, with practice over time, became a nimble and reasonably wise decision-making team. Without it, we would never have converged on a final, agreed-to set of requirements to define the detailed scope of what was being built, tested and implemented.

In all cases, either at the SCB or CMB level, the change management process was supported by a relatively simple one-page sheet that defined the needed change, background, issues, impact, etc. This was kept in a single electronic database that could be accessed by all who needed it(tracked, sorted, and prioritized, etc., to support the world of the SCB, CMB, and other project teams.

## Final Outcome

As mentioned above, Copernicus was successfully implemented on Saturday, June 15, 1996. The external marketing name used for the new CCSS system is File One™. The system was implemented without any material technical or operational issues, either with us or with our customers. There have been the usual collection of bugs and other fixes that have been implemented as part of system maintenance, but all in all, the system has been a tremendous business and technical success.

And especially on the business side, there is even more to come. In its first year of operation, File One™ can boast the implementation of four new releases providing new functions, products and data elements to its customers. This significantly shorter product development cycle and time-to-market performance has been due largely to two factors:

1. The flexibility of the more modern and up-to-date software and database design embodied in the new system, and
2. The utilization of project management techniques and training now fully evident in all ongoing projects.

# Why NOW is the Right Time for YOU to Start a Grassroots Project Management Movement Within Your Company!

Scott Mairs, PMP, Citicorp N.A.

## Introduction

This paper will address the process of increasing awareness and institutionalizing project management in a large global bank through grassroots actions and why NOW is the right time to start!

Today's global economy and complex markets are driving financial services organizations into an increased focus on process, quality, and technology. For the last two decades, large 'legacy' mainframe systems provided the consistent and secure delivery mechanisms necessary to support local and regional businesses. However, the world's economy has changed—the pace is quicker, and the number of global businesses is increasing at an exponential rate. In the past, there were only a few truly global companies such as Coca-Cola, Hershey's, and PepsiCo. Today there are literally thousands.

With only a handful of such companies, it was manageable (although very taxing) to manually deliver the type of customer service these customers needed. It is no longer possible. The complexity of financial products, the number of global customers, and the rapid change in the world's economy have driven financial institutions (and all other large corporations) into more sophisticated technology, faster cycle times, increased systems integration, and more intelligent customer and management information systems.

This paper will look into the following issues:

- How to begin a grassroots movement in your financial services company to: "Create an innovation pipeline within [your company] that will learn, discuss, promote, and teach the latest project management techniques in order to increase both internal and external customer satisfaction by completing projects on time, within budget, and according to specifications."
- Quantify those results over time and present those results within your organization to gain the upper management support and achieve the desired results.
- Why the time is NOW to begin such a movement, if you haven't already done so.
- How project management can enable the business, operations, and technology to meet this increasing demand.
- How PMI can play an important role in selling project management to your upper management.

## How To Begin

First, it is very important to treat this grassroots project just as you would any other major business or technology project. If you demonstrate the benefits of project management during this initiative, it will be easy to convince senior management of potential benefits in other areas. To take a closer look at the individual components, we will use the nine PMBOK knowledge areas:

### Scope

The scope of this project is important to set from the beginning. It is critical not to take on too much, too soon. Our founding group held a kick-off meeting to address the mission, goals, and objectives. The next step was to use brainstorming to identify all of the activities that would move us into the direction that we established. The resulting action items were put into a spreadsheet and distributed to each member to prioritize. The top ten action items were shared with the group. Finally, first-level estimates were completed and teams were assigned to each action item.

### Time

The time required to successfully complete the project is closely related to the benefits received. However, the membership can see faster benefits by working closely with a senior management champion. Similar to any large project, it is essential to identify the key stakeholders and identify a sponsor for the project. The champion or sponsor can help your team get the necessary visibility and occasional financial support to accelerate the schedule. In our case, one of the breaks came with an opportunity to present the benefits of project management at the Global Quality Network (GQN) monthly meeting. This presentation generated a great deal of interest in project management and allowed us to reach areas where we did not have any members. Many of the GQN members are now active participants on our e-mail distribution list.

### Cost

The cost/benefit ratio for creating a grassroots project management initiative is extremely high. However, it is hard to quantify. The higher the process maturity of the organization, the easier it will be to accurately measure the benefit. In most cases, organizations without mature project management will have low process maturity. One of the most recognized process maturity measurements is the Software Engineering Institute's Capability Maturity Model. Level 2 is referred to as Defined, and some texts refer to this level as Project Management. While it is difficult to measure at lower maturity levels, the benefit can still clearly be seen. For the minimal cost of newsletter publications, occasional conference calls, and use of the corporate e-mail system, project managers across the organization can save time and money through sharing best practices and reusing document templates.

### Quality

Due to the diversity in this group, it is essential to produce quality deliverables. To address this concern, several senior members in our group were consulted on each publication and presentation that was released. This group acted as an informal steering committee for the membership. The result was higher quality deliverables and a more professional presentation.

### Human Resource

While the human resources department did not play a major role in our group, the leadership team worked diligently to ensure that all human resources and other corporate policies where followed. Informally, human resource management played a major role in the success of this group. Occasionally, the project management forum faced criticism from other process-oriented groups, who where worried about competition, and management who was not supportive of process-oriented activities. Careful conflict management reduced these concerns.

### Communications

Due to the global aspect of our group (members from Dallas to Singapore), typical face-to-face meetings were impossible. Therefore, we used three communication medians. The first was conference calls; however, it was ineffective because of the time difference and cost of international calls. The second communications tool was a quarterly newsletter to report on current issues, tool reviews, project best practices, and many related topics. This method worked well, but the information was only delivered quarterly. The third, and most effective tool, was e-mail. A distribution list was established and maintained to allow nearly instantaneous communication between our members.

### Risk

A risk assessment was conducted after the initial action items and teams were assigned. Again, brainstorming was used to identify the risk elements, and each risk was finally assigned a criticality. One of the greatest risks identified was that each member would go back to their daily job, and none of the action items would be completed. In order to mitigate that risk, a president and vice president were elected to track the progress of each action item. These officers would also be the voice of the group throughout the company.

### Procurement

One recent development was the creation of a Contract Management Office to use the corporate buying power and reduce the overhead and risk associated with hundreds of outstanding contracts for consultants. This establishment was not a direct result of the project management initiative, however the *PMBOK Guide* was used in creating the policies and procedures of this new organization. The project management forum distributed the *PMBOK Guide* across several areas of the bank. Many of our corporate standards and policies now reference the *PMBOK Guide*.

### Integration

Integrating with other process initiatives such as the Software Engineering Process Group (SEPG) and the GQN provided a great boost to the project management momentum. Initially, these organizations did not see the additional benefit a focus on project management could bring to their own initiatives, but once it was clear that each group could coexist and would clearly benefit from the others' success, cross functional teams were established. Additionally, each process-oriented group now includes at least one representative from each of the other groups.

## Selling the Results

Track your progress! Initially, this may include a list of monthly or quarterly newsletters, conference calls, membership information, and action items. But, as these action items are completed, your list might include the following: distribution of PMI materials, establishment of a project management library, review of products, and repository of project plans, test plans, risk assessments, etc.

Another strong selling point is to track your members' individual and team successes. For instance, several of our members were involved in creating project offices in their local area, others were promoted to head major projects or programs, and still others were involved in writing corporate standards and procedures. Each of these accomplishments adds to the credibility of the initiative.

## Why Now is the Right Time

Never before has there been a greater focus on project management. The 1996 PMI membership grew 46% to over twenty-five thousand members, the Financial Services SIG has grown over 300% in twelve months, and business publications such as *The Wall Street Journal* and *CIO Magazine* continually run articles that talk about the benefits of project management. Most major Sunday papers anywhere in the country list job openings for project managers or managers with strong project management skills.

The financial services industry is more complex and facing faster changes than any other time in history. They have more global customers, and those customers have higher expectations. In the seventies and early eighties, only a few global customers existed. Handling these customers' financial services was manually intensive and expensive, but it was manageable due to the small volume. During the last decade, well over one thousand such customers have emerged, and the banking industry is unable to manually handle the volume.

The consumer side of the banking industry has seen similar growth. Only twenty years ago, individual investors had only a handful of investment options. Today, there are literally thousands, from domestic commodities to emerging market securitization. The result has been a strong focus on global systems, regional processing centers, and common data models. It is impossible to manage this magnitude of change and integration under the older business models.

The increased pressure for integrated processes and systems, the high level of complexity, and the increased cycle-time has forced financial and other companies in the service industry to find a solution. Part of that solution is project management. The pressure is building, and as a result, senior management is looking for solutions to increase productivity, decrease overhead, and introduce these new systems and products on time, within budget, and according to specifications.

## Project Management As An Enabler

The Project Management Institute defines project management as, "The application of knowledge, skills, tools, and techniques to project activities in order to meet or exceed stakeholder needs and expectations from a project."

Today's business environment includes increasing emphasis on time-to-market, integration of technologies, global competitiveness, and reduced costs. The overall objective is to do more with less and, to deliver on these initiatives, senior executives are drawing in the reins. They must eliminate the slack that might cause their wagon to steer off course.

Projects operate under the 'quadruple constraint' of time, cost, scope and quality (customer satisfaction). Disciplined project management provides a focal point for effective communications, coordination and control; a plan to assess progress; an emphasis on time and cost performance; and the framework for methods, processes, monitoring, and change control. These results enable business leaders to make better and faster decisions.

## How PMI Can Assist You with the Corporate Initiative

PMI has prepared a great deal of material on the Institute that can be used when promoting project management in your company. On several occasions, the PMI Corporate Membership Marketing Slides where used in our presentations to senior management. The PowerPoint slides are available from the Executive Office free of charge, and their content is regularly updated to reflect membership growth rates and the latest PMI achievements.

Other great tools for building momentum is distributing the *PMBOK Guide*, PMI Membership Packets, and PMP certification information. The *PMBOK Guide* is a well-written document that compiles the findings of thousands of project managers from around the world. Early into our initiative, we purchased copies of the *PMBOK Guide* for all senior and project managers at our technology center. When the next version of the Engineering Standards and Procedures was released, several references to the *PMBOK Guide* began to appear. The facility has just recently been assessed at a CMM Level 2 development center, and the scheduled to move to Level 3 in first quarter 1998. Other PMI publications, such as the *PM Network*, *Project Management Journal*, numerous books, and newly-released software can be purchased at a member discount. These works will provide a solid foundation for a corporate project management library. We started as a 'Special Collection' within our Technical Reference Center, and we have grown over time.

Anther great tool for instilling project management into your corporation is the PMI Corporate Membership Program. This program provides a discount to all employees for the Annual Seminar/Symposium, PMP certification application and testing, and PMI publications. Additionally, the corporation receives recognition in PMI publications and discounts on advertising. In May of 1997, PMI's Corporate Membership program has grown worldwide to one hundred and nine members with three thousand one hundred and eight individual members with corporate representation in New Zealand, Australia, Saudi Arabia, Japan, United Arab Emirates, Canada, and the United States.

The PMI local chapters and specific industry groups—a network of over twenty-eight thousand members—can provide the support and information about best practices that will enable you to demonstrate immediate bottom line results. PMI also provides professional products and services at discounted member prices, and you can use these tools to market the benefits of project management to senior managers. Finally, PMI's professional staff will answer any additional project management questions, and if they cannot directly address your situation, they can provide an industry contact to assist you.

## Conclusion

Large financial institutions can no longer do 'project management by accident.' The global economy is forcing large corporations to focus on professional project management. This environment provides a great opportunity to begin a grassroots project management initiative within your corporation, and the Project Management Institute can facilitate this change. Many organizations are trying to reinvent the wheel, but the basic elements of managing projects are universal to all project types, regardless of industry application. By applying proven project management disciplines and continuous networking, the individual, department, and entire corporation can greatly benefit from YOU starting a grassroots project management initiative NOW!

### References


Duncan, William R. 1996. *A Guide to the Project Management Body of Knowledge*. Upper Darby, PA: Project Management Institute.

Paulk, Mark C. 1993. *Capability Maturity Model for Software, Version 1.1*. Pittsburgh, PE: Software Engineering Institute.

*Project Management Institute Corporate Presentation*. Upper Darby, PA. Project Management Institute.

# Emerging Career Patterns for Project Managers in Financial Services

Itzhak Wirth, Ph.D., Department of Management, St. John's University
Vipul K. Bansal, Department of Economics and Finance, St. John's University

## Introduction

The objective of this paper is to introduce an outline of the financial engineer's work profile, qualification requirements and likely career pattern. This would be interesting for financial service professionals seeking new avenues for their career advancement and for project management professionals in search of innovative project management applications.

## Context

Financial engineering is an autonomous professional discipline employed by financial institutions for the formulation, development, and implementation of new financial products. Along with a tremendous growth in the rate of new financial product development over the past decade, there has been a significant increase in the employment of financial engineers. The financial engineer is a project manager in charge of the new financial product development process throughout the entire concept-to-market life cycle. Previous publications described in some detail the new financial product development process (Pinchot 1985); the organization structure and team composition involved (Stallworthy, Kharbanda 1987), and the role played by the financial engineer/project manager within this context (Scheuing, Johnson 1989).

The growing variety of financial products, the increasing need for new products, and the resulting shortening of product life cycles generated an awareness in financial institution with respect to effective management of the financial product development process itself and managers qualifications. A growing number of financial institutions are placing the financial product development function close to top management in their organizational hierarchies. New product or product derivatives creators occupy "trading desks" or are members of a "derivatives group," "structured product group," "financial engineering group," or "global risk management department."

## Methodology

A mail questionnaire was administered during June 1996 in a population of financial engineering professionals, members of the International Association of Financial Engineering (IAFE). The results of this survey reflect three aspects of the financial engineering profession as follows:

First, approximate percentage breakdown of the financial engineer's work-time among specialty areas, such as, financial accounting, legal aspects, mathematics, statistics, and others.

Second, skills profile prerequisites and areas of expertise needed to qualify for the financial engineering practice, including leadership, teamwork, communications, as well as computer skills, statistics, finance, law, and others.

Third, employment history and emerging career patterns in the financial engineering profession. The results of this pilot study are based upon thirty questionnaire responses.

## The Financial Engineer's Work Profile

Like project managers in other industry sectors, the financial engineer's work profile would be task-specific and product-focused. The financial product is most frequently an algorithm reflecting the relationships among a set of independent variables. For example, residential mortgage loan repayment is dependent upon the relationships among interest rate, fee, duration, and number of periods, risk and other factors.

Throughout a new financial product development process, the financial engineer/project manager must communicate with outside consultants, regulatory agencies, and foreign institutions, in addition to in-house specialists, committees, and superiors. This work diversity is reflected by the study results introduced in Exhibit 1. At the core of the financial engineer's work profile is finance, employing 26% of his total work-time, followed by modeling skills (16%) and by computer skills (12%). The remaining specialty areas, statistics, economics, legal aspects, mathematics, accounting, taxation, calculus (employing 9% or less of total work-time) can be categorized as supportive specialty areas. Additional supportive specialty areas were suggested by survey respondents

**Exhibit 1.** The Financial Engineer's Work Profile

| Specialty Area | Sample Size | Percentage Work Time Commitment | Z-Score | Rank Order |
|---|---|---|---|---|
| Finance | 30 | 26 | 2.46 | 1 |
| Modeling Skills | 30 | 16 | 0.92 | 2 |
| Computer Skills | 30 | 12 | 0.31 | 3 |
| Statistics | 30 | 9 | -0.15 | 4 |
| Economics | 30 | 9 | -0.15 | 4 |
| Legal Aspects | 30 | 8 | -0.31 | 5 |
| Mathematics | 30 | 7 | -0.46 | 6 |
| Accounting | 30 | 7 | -0.46 | 6 |
| Taxation | 30 | 6 | -0.62 | 7 |
| Calculus | 30 | 1 | -1.39 | 8 |
| Mean | | 10 | | |
| Standard Deviation | | 6.50 | | |
| Variable | | 42.25 | | |

including management (0.8%), communications (0.5%), meetings (0.3%), and planning/marketing (0.7%).

## The Financial Engineer's Skills Needs

Financial engineering professionals' responses produced a wide range of skills needs expectations with respect to new entrants into the profession. This is reflected in Exhibit 2, where responses to the question "what will you be looking for in an assistant that you hire?" and "what skills are needed?" is presented. The sample variance observed is 812.25, substantially higher than the 42.25 variance obtained with respect to the specialty areas sample and the work profile demonstrated in Exhibit 1. Leading the skill-needs, as shown in Exhibit 2, is computer skills need (supported by 87% of the respondents) and finance (80%). A second half of skills-needs is then broadly defined to include statistics, mathematics, teamwork, communications, accounting, calculus, leadership and law (supported by 13% to 67% of the survey respondents). Salesmanship, administration and negotiations skills-needs achieved only minor support (surprisingly), 7%, 7% and 3% respectively. Survey respondents including trading experience (3%), economics (3%), and research ability (3%) suggested additional skills-needs.

## The Financial Engineer's Career Patterns

The results introduced above (see Exhibit 1 & 2) are reaffirmed by the presentation in Exhibit 3. Seventeen respondents had outlined their personal careers and job contents, and in Exhibit 3 their occupation are introduced in an emergent two-phase career pattern. The results in Exhibit 3 show nineteen exclusive occupations reported in phase I, leading to fifteen different, presumably more demanding, occupations in phase II of the financial engineering career line. Years of employment in phase I, immediately preceding position change and promotion into phase II, are recorded within Exhibit 3, ranging from two to thirteen years, averaging 5.4 years. As well, employment year's to-date within phase II positions is indicated.

Visibly, these results demonstrate much diversity offered in the financial engineering profession and only modest trend towards uniformity when moving away from phase I and into phase II of the profession's career line.

**Exhibit 2.** The Financial Engineer's Skills Needs

| Specialty Area | Sample Size | Percentage Expressed Skill-Need | Z-Score | Rank Order |
|---|---|---|---|---|
| Computer | 30 | 87 | 1.65 | 1 |
| Finance | 30 | 80 | 1.40 | 2 |
| Statistics | 30 | 67 | 0.95 | 3 |
| Mathematics | 30 | 60 | 0.70 | 4 |
| Team work | 30 | 57 | 0.60 | 5 |
| Communications | 30 | 57 | 0.60 | 5 |
| Accounting | 30 | 40 | 0.00 | 6 |
| Calculus | 30 | 20 | -0.70 | 7 |
| Leadership | 30 | 20 | -0.70 | 7 |
| Law | 30 | 13 | -0.95 | 8 |
| Salesmanship | 30 | 7 | -1.16 | 9 |
| Administration | 30 | 7 | -1.16 | 9 |
| Negotiations | 30 | 3 | -1.30 | 10 |
| Mean | | 10 | | |
| Standard Deviation | | 6.50 | | |
| Variable | | 42.25 | | |

## Conclusions

The survey results produced the following hypotheses:

- H1: The financial engineer's optimal work profile includes at the core finance, modeling and computer employment, surrounded by supportive specialty areas such as statistics, economics, legal aspects, mathematics, accounting, taxation, calculus and others.
- H2: The financial engineer's optimal skills needs are diverse and include finance and computer skills along with statistics, mathematics, team work, communications, accounting, calculus, leadership, law and others.
- H3: Career patterns in financial engineering are highly diverse and demonstrate a modest trend towards uniformity at later career phases.

## Further Research

A more extensive sample survey should unveil further refined career patterns and career phases. As well, more definitive work profiles and skills-needs will enable educators develop effective training programs for students considering careers in financial engineering.

### References

Bansal, V.K. and J.F. Marshall. 1992. *The complete guide to financial innovation*. New York: Institute of Finance (a Simon & Schuster Company).

Bansal, V.K., A. Tucker, A. Herbst and J.F. Marshall. 1992. Hedging quantity risk with macro swaps and macro options. *Journal of Applied Corporate Finance*. 4:103–108.

Bansal, V.K., M.E. Ellisand and J.F. Marshall. 1992. The pricing of short-dated & forward interest rate swaps. *Financial Analyst Journal*.

**Exhibit 3.** The Financial Engineer's Sareer Pattern (Sample Size 17)

| Phase I | Intersection of Phase I and II | Phase II |
|---|---|---|
| Mergers & acquisitions (2 years)<br>Project financing (2 years)<br>Quantitative analysis (3 years)<br>Credit analysis (3 years)<br>Internal financial analysis (2 years)<br>Desk trading ( 3 years)<br>Corporate finance and banking (8 years)<br>Computer programming ( 5 years)<br>Commercial banking ( 5 years)<br>Proprietary trading ( 10 years)<br>Investment banking ( 13 years)<br>Engineering (5 years)<br>General ledger supervision (2 years)<br>Portfolio management ( 2 years)<br>Foreign exchange (2 years)<br>Non-profit organization research (2 years)<br>Trading futures & options on treasury bonds (5 years) | Trading futures (5 years)<br>Mathematical modeling (8 years) | International corporate treasury (7 years)<br>Exotic trade design ( 2 years)<br>Capital market regulatory policy development and enforcement (6 years)<br>Derivatives valuation and risk management (2 years)<br>Structured financing ( 5 years)<br>Risk management (4 years)<br>Assets backed securities (3 years)<br>Bond market risk surveillance (credit and market risk) (5 years)<br>Corporate swaps marketing (3 years)<br>Operational/administration management (4 years)<br>Financial engineering management (6 years)<br>Currency risk management (10 years) |
| Phase I<br>MEAN 5.4 years<br>RANGE 2 to 13 years<br>Number of occupations 19 | Intersection of Phase I and II | Phase II<br>MEAN 5 years<br>RANGE 2 to 10 years<br>Number of occupations 15 |


Booz, Allen & Hamilton. 1982. *New products management for the 1990s*. New York: Booz, Allen & Hamilton.

Bugie, Frederick D. 1981. *New products development strategies*. New York: AMACOM

Finnerty, J.D. 1988. Financial engineering in corporate finance: An overview. *Financial management*.

Larsen, E.W. and D.H. Gobeli. 1985. "Project management structures: Is there a common language." *Project Management Journal*.

Lynn, Gary. 1988. *From concept to market*. New York: Wiley.

Martin, Don. 1993. *Team work*. New York: Dutton Books, The Penguin Group.

Scheuing, E.E. and E.M. Johnson. 1989. New product development and management in financial institutions. *International Journal of Financial Management.* 7:2.

Stallworthy, E.A. and O.P. Kharbanda. 1987. The project manager in the 1990's. *International Journal of Operations and Production Management*, 7:5.

Pinchot, Gifford III. 1985. *Intrapreneuring.* New York: Harper & Row.

Wirth, I. 1989. *The project manager's profile: field data and analysis.* Project Management Institute and International Project Management Association (PMI/IPMA) Joint Seminar/Symposium Proceedings, Atlanta, Georgia, USA October 7–11.

Wirth, I. 1995. *Expanding the scope of project management: Financial engineering and financial product development.* Prosjekt, Ledelse, Oslo, Norway. February, 13–15.

Wirth, I., K.T. Liaw and E.E. Scheuing. 1995. "Project management in financial engineering." *Project Management Journal.* 26:16–24.

UTE
CHICAGO 1997
PROJECT
MANAGEMENT:
THE NEXT
CENTURY
ROJ
PM
The Future
Of Project
Management

# PM's Role With Integrated Product Teams

Roger L. Erickson, W. J Schafer Associates, Inc.

The project manager (PM) faces new challenges and opportunities when working with Integrated Product Teams (IPTs). A well-functioning IPT organization can tap the creative energies at all levels of an organization to help the project move efficiently forward with the best decisions and implementations of those decisions. If early and continued guidance is not provided to the IPTs, it is the PM who will be driven by multiple groups to a less than optimal outcome. This paper will detail the proactive things the PM can do to enhance his or her program's chances of success.

## What Is and Is Not an IPT?

There are many in-practice variations on the IPT concept. This paper will focus on large programs that have a number of major products and large-scale integrations. The four earmarks of an IPT are: (1) a product focused (2) multidisciplinary group that (3) has a charter and (4) team plan. An IPT is not a renamed unfocused group without direction or authority to function. With the advent of the IPT buzzword, many managers have renamed existing meeting groups, that were ineffectual, to IPTs on the news that IPTs really get work done. Simply renaming does not an IPT make!.

There is no magic number for the correct number of IPTs on a program. How many IPTs there should be on a program is guided by a number of factors, with the focus on the product(s) to be produced by the IPTs. A starting list of factors may include expertise, location of members, interfaces (technical and human), and PM style. Efficiency and opportunity are lost if IPTs are allowed to form on their own without an architecture to assure program coverage without gaps and major overlaps.

Exhibit 1 depicts a sample project organization that has 15 IPTs, with three layers of integrating IPTs and the supporting functional organizations. The integrating IPTs are made up of members from the included IPTs. The meeting time requirements alone that this number of IPTs would impose could be excessive without some structure and formality.

## Why Use IPTs?

On complex, long-duration projects utilizing current technology the amount of detail that can cause failure on a project is

**Exhibit 1.** IPT Organization Example

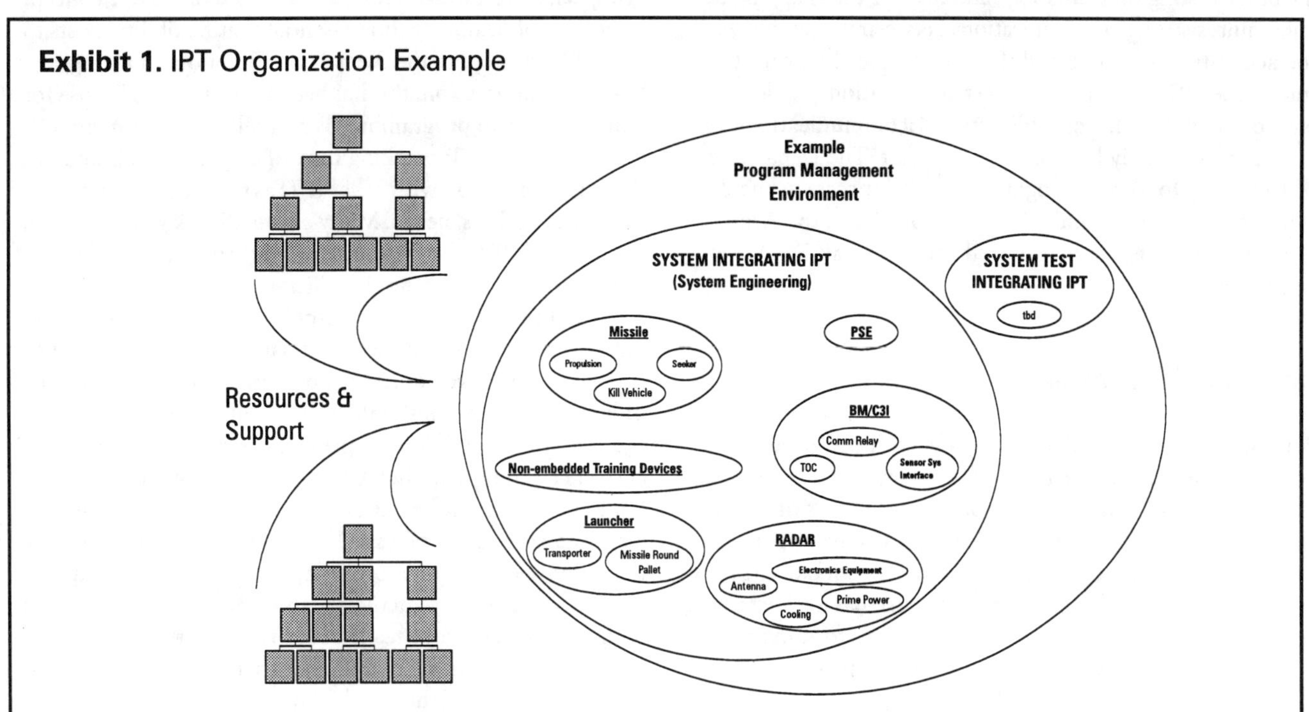

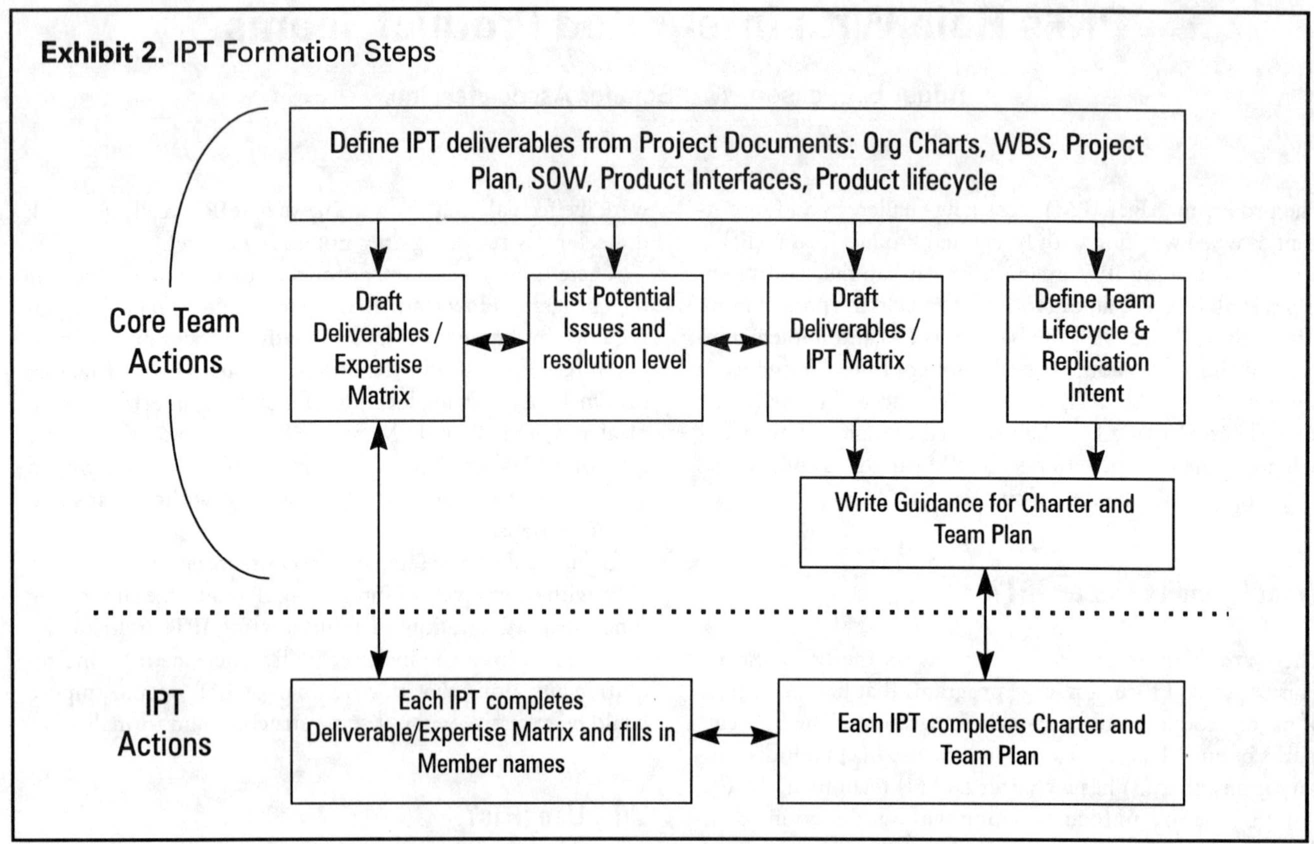


**Exhibit 2.** IPT Formation Steps

well beyond the core project management team's span of control. To maintain coordination of the interfaces, include the best thinking on technology and manage the changing detail requires strong communications between the people with the accurate knowledge and those that keep the project on track. The IPT concept of project organization provides the environment for the multidirectional communications required to accurately handle that detail fast. The Department of Defense (DoD) has recognized the IPT success in the private sector and has mandated the use of IPTs in the Acquisition Reform initiative that started roll-out to all DoD agencies in 1995.

## How Are IPTs Formed?

The interest to form IPTs has spawned a proliferation of groups labeled IPT with a range of formality and effectiveness. Formality ranges from single issue ad hoc groups of self-appointed teams to chartered, product-focused teams performing in concert under the sponsorship and direction of the project manager. Effectiveness, in practice, also has a wide range, from discouraged, fragmented groups to performing teams working in concert with other teams and the project office.

Many of the existing IPTs today are groups that were formed under different methodologies or sprang up as a result of a special interest. A double-edged sword of the IPT concept is the idea of *flexibility*. It is essential that flexibility exists to fit the IPT concept to the special considerations of a program. However, on occasion, this has been interpreted as license for nonalignment to program needs and self-empowerment. Often the result is IPTs working toward disparate goals and not sharing information with other IPTs as there is little appreciation for the others' needs. Many existing work groups should not be titled 'IPT' for they are not *Integrated* nor *Product-focused* and may, in fact, not be a *Team*.

In contrast, if a top-down architecture is provided to lay out the IPT responsibilities and relationships, clarity of IPT roles can be achieved quickly and maintained throughout the program. A core team should be made up of the project manager and other high-level representatives of the user group, customer group, supplier group(s) and other major stakeholder groups as may be available at the inception of the project. The core team (not an IPT) should be the architects of the number of IPTs on a program and their relationships. In Exhibit 2 the focus of activities above the dotted line is this architecture. The core team needs to write the guidance to the forming IPTs in such a manner that the guidance can be modified in accordance with the actual member expertise

**Exhibit 3.** Responsibility Matrix

## IPT RESPONSIBILITY MATRIX

| TEAM ==> <br> RESPONSIBILITY | IPT #1 | IPT #2 | IPT #3 | .... | IPT #n |
|---|---|---|---|---|---|
| WBS Level 4 Product A | x | | | | |
| WBS Level 4 Product B | | x | | | |
| WBS Level 4 Product C | | | x | | |
| : | | | | | |
| : | | | | | |
| WBS Level 4 Product n | | | | | x |
| Develop Expertise/ member matrix | x | | | | |
| Maintain Expertise/ member matrix | x | x | x | | x |
| Develop decision making process | x | x | x | | x |
| Develop Training plan | | | x | | |
| Maintain Training plan | x | x | x | | x |
| Maintain IPT man-loaded schedule | x | x | x | | x |
| Develop Orientation procedure | x | x | x | | x |
| Develop Tools list | | | | | x |
| Maintain Tools list | x | x | x | | x |

and the working relationships they have with other teams, suppliers and customers. Below the dotted line, the IPTs with the expertise of its members will bring the detail knowledge of the products and processes to provide verification of the architecture and further rationalize the assignment of tasks between the IPTs. The process of verifying the architecture and rationalizing the assignment of tasks will generate conversation and negotiation among the IPTs and the PM staff. The remainder of this paper will explain the detail of Exhibit 2 and associated considerations.

## IPT Deliverables or Responsibilities

The deliverables or responsibilities of an IPT can be identified by review of source documents such as the Statement of Work (SOW), Work Breakdown Structure (WBS), project schedule, project and product interfaces, stakeholder organization charts and product lifecycle description. Each of these items needs to be examined for deliverables and potential issues as the SOW and associated WBS may not address all phases of the lifecycle. The other items will give hints as to the amount of and type of issues that may surface to confound the project's best efforts. As an example, if a project has many organizations involved it will require more attention to communications and review processes than if only one organization is involved.

**Exhibit 4.** Expertise Matrix

## EXPERTISE/ DELIVERABLE MATRIX

| Expertise | | WBS Level 4 Missle | WBS Level 4 Launcher | WBS Level 4 RADAR | WBS Level 4 BM/C3I |
|---|---|---|---|---|---|
| | Effort to start | Now | in 1 month | in 3 months | in 3 months |
| | When due | 10 months | 8 months | one year | one year |
| Fabrication | | x | x | x | x |
| Facilitator | | x | x | x | x |
| Logistics | | x | | x | x |
| Procurement | | x | | | |
| Quality Assurance | | x | x | | |
| Safety | | x | | | x |
| Sys Management | | | | x | x |
| System Design | | | x | x | x |
| Test and Validation | | | | x | x |
| User Functional Area 1 | | x | x | x | x |
| User Functional Area 2 | | | x | x | |
| User Functional Area 3 | | | x | x | x |

**Exhibit 5.** IPT Lifecycle

## EXPERTISE/ DELIVERABLE MATRIX

| Expertise | | WBS Level 4 Missle | WBS Level 4 Launcher | WBS Level 4 RADAR | WBS Level 4 BM/C3I |
|---|---|---|---|---|---|
| | Effort to start | Now | in 1 month | in 3 months | in 3 months |
| | When due | 10 months | 8 months | one year | one year |
| Fabrication | | x | x | x | x |
| Facilitator | | x | x | x | x |
| Logistics | | x | | x | x |
| Procurement | | x | | | |
| Quality Assurance | | x | x | | |
| Safety | | x | | | x |
| Sys Management | | | | x | x |
| System Design | | | x | x | x |
| Test and Validation | | | | x | x |
| User Functional Area 1 | | x | x | x | x |
| User Functional Area 2 | | | x | x | |
| User Functional Area 3 | | | x | x | x |

## Potential Issues

Again, in the review of the source documents, thought should be given to the potential issues that may surface in the effort. In defining the potential issues, thought should be given to delegation of authority and what resources the IPT would need to effectively deal with the issue. There can be no reluctance to assign authority to carry out the assigned responsibilities. If there is any reluctance to grant authority, assign the responsibility to a higher level.

The Responsibility Matrix, Exhibit 3, is a device to help determine the number of IPTs and make a high-level assignment of responsibilities. The matrix is built by first listing in the left column the project products, followed by a brainstormed list of time-consuming issues that may surface, and followed by a list of maintenance items for the IPTs. Once the responsibilities and deliverables are listed in the left-hand column, than thought can be given to logical assignment to IPTs. First consideration should be given to the product focus of a team. If a non-product deliverable is needed by several IPTs, than it should be assigned to one IPT for development in consultation with the other concerned IPTs. This is only a first grouping. Once the major items are captured in the left column, the items can be grouped into IPTs by putting 'X's in the columns to the right. Once the teams are formed with real people and their respective talents, establishing the Team Plans will illuminate trade-offs between teams and efficiency gains. You can expect considerable discussion and additional side notes to rationalize the grouping of work.

## Expertise and People

When the subject of *expertise* and *people* on an IPT is considered, it is inseparable from the consideration of how long the team is to last and what the need is for expanding the team's capability. Such as, what is the need to replicate the team? If the team is expected to be the genesis of several other teams and also carry on the original tasks, than additional people will be needed, perhaps as understudies.

The highest efficiency team, in the short duration, is made up of the fewest number of people with all the needed expertise. However, efficiency of that small team is seriously hurt if one of the members cannot participate. In the long-duration team, consideration must be given to other duties and attrition.

The expertise needed and when it is needed on the team is driven by the deliverables. Planning back from when the deliverables are due and build up of the deliverable will determine when the expertise is needed. Generally, plan to include the expertise on the team before productive output from that expertise is needed.

The Expertise/Deliverable Matrix, Exhibit 4, is a useful tool that can serve as an organizing tool, a reference for the IPTs and a checklist for ongoing planning. It is initially drafted by the core team in conjunction with the Deliverables/IPT matrix as a view of the type of skills needed to accomplish the deliverables. In the initial draft it only has 'x's to show the need for an expertise. Once the planning has matured somewhat, estimates of time can replace the 'x's. When the IPTs are formed and the detailed task descriptions are complete, the initial time estimates can be replaced by people's names and better time estimates. The matrix serves as a guide in negotiating for people on the teams. Once the teams are formed, the matrix serves as a reference to find a skill if an IPT needs short-term help.

## Team Membership Over Time

The IPT will have a changing makeup over the lifecycle of the product, Exhibit 5. The IPT members will take on different roles in the same IPT, gain new skills and/or may move to another IPT as needs change. Mentors and trainers can diminish their activity as new skills are acquired within the group. Leadership, informal as well as formal, will change as the project moves forward and the team develops. These realities need to be considered by the PM and core team in setting the expectations of the IPT and putting tools in place to train new members as they come on the team. Consideration must be given to the life of the project; depending on whether the project is short and highly intensive (normal) or long-term and personnel changes are expected. In the short-term project, highly experienced, multidisciplined people will minimize learning, communications and overhead effort of the team, which will enhance the chances of success. However, this may not be affordable and it may be beneficial to have redundant members to give training, fill in during vacation, in the case of attrition or for team replication. If little turnover is expected, and the members all know the processes, a minimal set of common training is needed and "short-cut" group rules can be established. For the long-term IPT, a chronology of team decisions and orientation training will be helpful for new members joining the team.

To keep the team vital, new ideas need to be explored and established methods challenged. Normal attrition provides an opportunity that must be made the most of by having a plan of what expertise or viewpoints are needed on the team. Also, if someone is lost from the team, their expertise should be questioned as presently needed or not. As people have no contribution to be made to the team in the foreseeable future, they need to be gracefully released from the team.

Sometimes we have the luxury of picking a team. Most of the time we have the team defined by circumstances or availability.

Regardless, it is helpful to know how far off ideal the team is so that compensating activities can be executed. A team that is short on a particular expertise can be augmented by a temporary expert or additional training. A team that is loaded with additional members can take on additional tasks.

## Team Training

Regardless of the level of expertise in the team, training or experience working together is needed to establish a common vocabulary and common reference concepts. Basic skills training that should be common to all:

- Facilitator
- Time management
- Meeting management.

The basic skills training may vary depending on the project or the general IPT membership but should include as a minimum: facilitator, time management, and meeting management. Another training effort that pays big dividends is a standard orientation procedure. This procedure should include a checklist to assure that new members meet the various people that they will need to work with to be successful at their job. The checklist should also include review of training and scheduling of needed training. Another high-value orientation step is a brief by someone in upper management that welcomes the newcomer and gives them a 'big picture' view of how their job will contribute to the mission. If a team is to be working on a new product or with new technology, New Skills training will be beneficial for a quick start and good foundation. If there is not a formal class, the New Skills training may take the form of briefings by an outside group. Or, one or two team members may research the area and provide a training session to the rest of the team.

## Communications

Up-front consideration of how the team will get information and communicate with their suppliers and customers will minimize the inevitable cross communications that will occur in new relationships. An example: In a multiteam situation, an outside proponent will shop around the various teams for a desired answer, not the official or consensus answer. A general knowledge of who is responsible for what and how information should pass can minimize this problem. Misinterpretations can be expected in the early days of a team, extra effort needs to be expended by the PM in the early days to minimize the consequences.

## Charter and Team Plan

The Charter and Team Plan need to be considered together. Together these two documents form the basis for team empowerment. The bounds of team activity are set and the relationships to other teams are explained. The sources and methods for obtaining resources are outlined. With these two documents in hand, there should be no confusion about what goals the team is pursuing and what resources are available. The charter and team plan attack the common causes of team failure. Unclear goals and lack of management support are eliminated by a charter. The team plan addresses the problem of changing objectives and who should be doing what.

The charter can take several forms. In some organizations it is as brief as a one-line Mission Statement and in other organizations it can take on the function of Project Plan. One should be aware of the general nature of the term *charter* when talking with other groups. The format of the charter should follow the guidance as set down by the PM office. A uniform format will make the team charter much easier to be read by others that may be comparing the charters of the various teams. The charter's content is the information that is not going to change much in the full lifecycle. It sets the basic direction and tone of the team. The writing style of the charter can be bullets or narrative; however, the following points should be covered: Title, Introduction, References/Guidance, Background, Purpose/Goals, Period of Performance, Budget, Responsible Agent, Team Responsibilities, and Team Products.

The Team Plan is a collection of detailed plans and status statements. It supports and amplifies the Integrated Project Master Plan (IMP). Much of the content of the Team Plan are items that are written early in the formation of the team and get put in someone's desk drawer. The plan serves as a concise directory for anyone that needs a current understanding of what the team is doing, has done and should do. Further, it details who is on the team and what resources the team can call on to be successful. The Team Plan is a dynamic document that is updated on an as-needed basis to keep it current. One of the first items that is published in the Team Plan is the Charter. The Team Plan, like the Charter, is approved and signed off by the PM. If modifications to the original Charter are made, they should be included in an annotation page following the Charter in the Team Plan. The following points should be covered: Charter, Communications Plan, Expertise/Member Matrix, Authority, Decision Making, Training Plan, Team man-loaded Schedule, Orientation Procedure, Tools List, and Demobilization Plan.

## Summary

The IPT concept, although flexible, needs the attention of the PM both early on to set the architecture and throughout the life of the IPT. Team failure is more common than team success. The difference is leadership in establishing clear goals and guidance. As conditions and forces change, all the IPTs on a project need to be aware of the change and have leadership as to how to respond. The PM needs to be involved in the IPT to assure that the IPT members are aware of their level of empowerment and support the IPT decisions. IPTs are a new way of doing business, a better way to tap the creative energies at all levels of an organization to help the project move efficiently forward with the best decisions and implementations of those decisions.

# Trends and Improvements: Looking Beyond Modern Project Management

Francis Hartman, PhD, PEng, The University of Calgary, Alberta, Canada

## Introduction

Over the past few years, we have been collecting the best practices of different industries using both formal and informal methods. Some interesting trends emerge pointing the way towards where the profession of project management is heading. By understanding the underlying causes and drivers for change, we can rationally predict where these changes will lead us.

The impact of key technologies, available information, and societal influences on projects and their success are presented in this paper. These changes will be profound, powerful, and far-reaching. Just three of these include the following.

Technology and engineering knowledge will continue to double every three to five years and may go faster yet. Even the largest companies will not be able to retain the required expertise for their core businesses in-house. This will lead to more outsourcing and more on-going training, as well as a growth in the use of alliances, even with traditional competitors. In turn, this will increase the number of projects and change how we manage them.

Telecommunications will merge fully with computer technology, leading to new approaches and attitudes towards information, its security, and value. This will have a powerful impact on the management of projects as access to, and the use of, new technologies will be diverse within each significant project. This will extend project management to include technology bridging challenges.

The gap between the rich and the poor, technology "haves" and "have-nots" will continue to grow, changing both business relationships and viability, as well as the social environment in which we work, doubtless making it more volatile than before.

What these changes mean to the successful project manager and to the skill set we will need to develop or modify is identified and explained. Examples of how some multinational project-oriented corporations have started to prepare for future change is used to illustrate the evolutionary process required to prepare for the projects of the next century.

## Background

We are all aware of change. There is so much of it today that it becomes difficult to see where it is all leading us. This paper, like all that venture into predicting the future, is speculative. The studies and reviews that led to this paper were driven by the search for best practices in project management. This search, in turn, led to development of SMART Project Management. SMART is a project management approach that takes advantage of many existing best practices and a few innovations that help to make these practices work well together. The resulting process has led to step changes in performance with up to 25 percent improvements in cost and schedule performance while improving quality. These improvements are based on documented results of field trials in industry.

Unfortunately, the results of field trials implementing SMART project management were on individual projects and, although successful, were not sustainable beyond the project. They were, however, repeatable. The issue of sustainability of high performance project teams and effective project delivery methods was then studied. The overarching issues that emerged were linked to two elements. The first element was the working environment, and the second was the rate at which this environment was changing. Addressing a static work environment is relatively simple and is being addressed through the use of the project management maturity model (PM3).

The project management maturity model identifies five performance levels for project delivery. To move from one level to the next, all elements of the lower level must be in place. This ensures that the development of project management skills is based on a solid foundation. This structured approach to the development of project management skills is expected to help organizations improve performance for project delivery in a sustainable way.

Addressing the changing and evolutionary nature of the work environment was—and remains—a bigger challenge. A number of large-impact elements were sought, not as exclusive elements that will impact on future project management, but as ones that will significantly change the way we think of projects in general, and their management in particular. Three significant changes were identified, and are examined below.

## The Three Big Changes

### 1. Burgeoning Technology

We are seeing the amount of technology available to us doubling every three to five years, depending on to whom you are talking. This is phenomenal growth that affects the way we do business and the way we live. Yesterday's luxuries are rapidly becoming today's necessities. The capacity to handle the increase in technology options, or even to stay current in any specific area, is decreasing inversely to growth. Regardless of our business, technology changes impinge on us.

There are three ways in which we can handle this. We could double the number of people involved in our business every three or so years. Nobody can afford to do this, as they would price themselves out of the market. We could double the intelligence of our employees each three to five years. There is no evidence of that happening. Or we could do something else. There is a growing body of evidence that we are doing the latter! Here are some of the things we are doing in businesses today.

- We downsize (or right-size!) and after a year or so we are back with the same headcount we had before.
- We "focus on core business."
- We redefine this core business on a regular basis, making it more focused each time.
- Work that a few scant years ago was "core" to our business is now being outsourced (such as payroll, recruiting and personnel services, and IT services) or is being done through alliance-based groups (such as manufacturing, R&D, marketing, and sales).
- Small cottage-industry businesses are recognized as leaders in specific technologies or other forms of expertise and are used as parts of larger teams, where previously such teams were all in-house.
- Competitors are sharing information and resources in areas that were previously considered too sensitive for this to happen.

All of these "emerging" practices are symptomatic of the need to capture the expertise we need to sustain our business. This expertise is now broader and deeper than it ever was—a direct result of explosive technological growth.

Alliances and outsourcing will be the way of surviving in business in the future, as this is the only way in which mutually dependent businesses will be able to carve out a niche in which they can survive. This, however will bring its own suite of challenges. Not least of these will be the need for team members on the inter corporate projects to speak the same language. They will also need to develop their own culture and ways of doing business that will likely be independent of the culture of any of the participating organizations. The process of building these teams will be increasingly difficult and inefficient as their complexity and the number of participating businesses continues to grow. One important issue in this is the need for a common language.

The primary—and arguably the only—source of failure in projects is a breakdown in communication. As we move towards larger teams with more specialized team members, so the challenges we face in effective communication will grow. Consider the concept of an implicit specification. This is the detailed requirements for a particular element in a project. Some elements will be universally understood (such as drywall, a two-ohm resistor, or Times Roman font). Other elements will have a broader range of meanings, depending on experience, position, role in the project, and more (such as acceptable working tolerances, a user-friendly interface, or an obscure typeface). In the former examples, the implicit specification is relatively clear, in the latter it is not. As the amount of new technology increases, so the potential for poor implicit specifications increases, with potential communications breakdowns as a result. Recently one software company struggled with the word "function," which meant different things to virtually everyone on a particular project team, varying from a subroutine call to a specific type of code, the work that a particular user does, and more. Thus technology will impact on our ability to communicate as we develop language to catch up with innovation.

Language also varies between team members, and cultures. Whoever controls language usually controls the project. It becomes important, as a result, to create a unique culture for each project so that the dominant corporate or departmental culture does not become the culture of the project. If this should happen, then all the project team members from other parts of the organization will be placed at a disadvantage as they try to learn the game rules and norms of the dominant and imported culture. The resulting imbalance will likely lead to friction and other problems.

Interestingly, as technology has grown, companies and nations have worked hard to develop standards for specific technologies. Examples abound in computer languages, data transmission protocols, process technologies, telecommunications, and more. As we move towards increased collaboration between disparate companies and individuals, the need for standards in business management of technology will likely become a necessity. The reason for this is simple. As we are forced into more and increasingly frequent interactions or collaborations between partners, so we will need to attack inefficiencies. One obvious area is the need to become productive quickly. Standards in management practices will help to reduce learning curves, will overcome some cultural barriers, and will reduce the amount of rework that is the result of miscommunication.

### 2. Enhanced Telecommunications

Arguably this is a subset of the previous item. However its impact is so large that it deserves to be considered separately. Telecommunications are merging with other technologies, so that telephone, fax, E-mail, cellular phones, the Internet, computers, and television will become essentially the same to the end user in the next few years. As this happens, a hierarchy of users will emerge. The richest will have access to the best, while others will only be able to afford lesser subsets of these technologies. Access to technologies will dictate the degree to which we can compete in some industries, and eventually in any business.

Technology "haves" will develop and fight to retain advantages over "have-nots." If human history is likely to repeat itself, we will likely see trade barriers develop through the use of technology and language. This trend—if it occurs—will create significant communication challenges as organizations with different levels of communication technology try to do business together. The spotty use of electronic data interchange (EDI) today is perhaps symptomatic of the start of this trend.

One of the new challenges that has already emerged as a result of the use of better telecommunications is the one of getting virtual teams to work effectively. With project teams spread over the face of the earth, we still find a real need for face-to-face communication. The most sophisticated teams struggle with time zones, language, cultural differences, and more. Without the opportunity to work with real people and interact with them so we can learn about each other and what we really mean when we try to communicate, we tend to find that conflict is more likely to occur. Companies that have tried to work entirely with technology for communication across long distances have typically reverted to at least occasional travel to maintain human contact.

Information sharing through today's technology is orders of magnitude easier than it was before. This has a flip side too: illegal or accidental sharing of the wrong information is also much easier. This in turn will increasingly raise issues of who owns intellectual property. Already a significant barrier to business opportunities, intellectual property issues will continue to be complicated as proprietary information is shared more between businesses.

### 3. Societal Shifts

Technology haves and have-nots are just one aspect of the next decade's business environment. Already we have seen a shift: most home computer systems are more up-to-date than the ones that the owners use at work. In some communities, it is the exception to find a home without a computer (and in some households, several computers), while in neighboring areas the converse will be true. Individuals may well hold the technological clout that some organizations cannot afford to maintain in the future. Alternatively, technology distribution in organizations will become more diverse as fewer people will be kept current with the latest and best in technology. These few people will likely be chosen for strategic advantages, perhaps based on their role or their need for technology in order to be effective, as well as other factors.

Thus, within communities as well as within businesses, there will be a growing rift between those who have access to technology and those who do not. The people with access to the latest and best in technology will have significant competitive and informational advantages over those who do not. This will contribute to the already visible and growing gap between the wealthy and the poor.

Just as when we entered the industrial revolution we saw new social classes emerge and we saw significant social unrest, so we may well see similar changes as we step into the knowledge era. Large parts of our society are being disenfranchised by the changes that are taking place today. Old standards that dictate social standing based on wealth, position, and how you earn a living will need to change. As project managers, we have an increasingly important role to play in addressing the societal issues that our projects create. These may have to do with job creation or with breaking others' bread bowls. As project managers, however, we have limited control over the larger impact issues such as this. We need to bring our clients along with us. . . .

## Corporate Responses

We have already discussed the three responses possible in corporations and seen that the only viable option is already under way. Many project managers on large or interdisciplinary projects are already struggling with cultural, social, and conflicting business issues. They will typically find that communication has become more than just a mechanistic process. And these issues are currently not really addressed well. As one example, team building is only part of the solution to effective communication. Which raises the question of why we seem to need team building more now, when we did not seem to need it in the same way ten years ago?

Where is all this leading? Corporate responses have been mixed in response to the changes that are taking place. They include the following elements:

- increased use of alliances and other longer-term business relationships
- increased use of risk-sharing processes in contracts
- more collaboration with the competition
- more outsourcing of non-"core" businesses
- increasingly focused and narrow definitions of what core business is all about

- greater use of external expertise in core business
- role shifts into two main categories: specialist producer and integrator
- more collaboration on the development of technology standards.

All of these changes point towards blurring of corporate entities, just as we are seeing technologies blurring. The interaction between companies or legal entities will become much more complex to accommodate project needs within the core competencies of the businesses involved. Key individuals or small businesses with niche technologies or expertise may well carry dominant roles in projects involving multinationals. Some standards in management become an obvious need in this new work environment.

## Future Trends

Technology growth will not slow or stop. It will accelerate. So the changes already discussed will happen quickly. Or the world will take another twist on this projection. Risk will undoubtedly increase either way. As a result, alliances and other shared risk, resource, expertise, and technology relationships will need to evolve and develop. The roles of specific players in the project will likely change as a result.

Previously we saw three or four clear roles, splitting the project vertically: client, designer (engineer, architect, other), constructor, and operator. Now we are seeing horizontal splits as well, as companies reconfigure themselves as producers, integrators, distributors, marketing, and sales and possibly other splits of the traditional business package.

Exchange of people between organizations will also be likely in the future. Already we see the use of a "hired gun" for project manager as well as other key team members on projects. It is likely that new joint venture companies will be formed to act as employers or brokers for employees who are then shared between the different organizations.

Speculation on where businesses will go could continue forever and will likely be wrong. The above points are based on what companies are already doing today. To be competitive tomorrow, we cannot afford to wait for then to develop the project management skills needed. That work needs to start today.

## Starting to Solve Tomorrow's Problems

The first thing that becomes obvious is that we will need stronger and more universally acceptable standards for project management skills and expertise. These skills and the required expertise will likely go beyond *A Guide to the Project Management Body of Knowledge (PMBOK Guide)* as we know it today.

SMART project management, the product of three years of research into best practices in several industries and testing of ideas on live projects, is a start on this process. What needs to be challenged is whether it is the right start. And where it needs to go next in its evolution, to prepare for tomorrow's needs. Already SMART project management has demonstrated significant savings to its users. And its users—so far—have been experienced and skilled project managers and their teams.

Interestingly, though, despite significant savings in both cost and time, as well as discernible improvements in quality reported by participating companies in the use of SMART, it seems to be a non-sustainable process. The problem is that teams revert to old practices as soon as they can. The problem has been diagnosed. Without a solid foundation of good project management practices as promoted by PMI, there can be no sustainable enhancement in project performance.

To address the need for a structured growth of project management skills, the project management maturity model was developed. This model has five levels. The first one is where everyone starts. The second is where you would be if you were a PMP and your employer or client allowed you to do everything you know to be needed for effective project delivery. At level three, predictable project outcomes are a symptom of achievement. Level four gives you performance at about 25 percent to 30 percent better in all aspects than equivalent projects benchmarked at level 1. The fifth level is for those who can consistently outperform those at level four through controlled and managed continuous improvement. The model is currently being refined and will be tested and published by the author.

## Conclusions

We need to start acting now to address future changes—at least the ones that we can reasonably predict. We can influence the future. Let us do so by constructively improving project management and its value to business. This is bigger than any single organization, association, or institution. It is a project in itself that will require careful planning to be implemented effectively. Developing some global standards for project management in the next century will achieve the following.

- We will speak the same language and thus will reduce communication problems
- Learning curves for new teams will be significantly reduced
- Errors and rework will be reduced or eliminated

- Process improvements will be shared and thus will be easier to implement and will do the most good.

The bottom line is that SOMEONE will do this work. And the participants will benefit from the results, gaining competitive edges through faster and more effective delivery of projects and the related products to market.

## References


Construction Industry Institute. 1989. "Partnering: Meeting the Challenges of the Future" Partnering Taskforce Interim Report, A Special CII Publication, Texas (August).

———. 1991. *In Search of Partnering Excellence."* Special Publication 17-1, Texas (July).

Hartman, F.T. 1995. "A Case Study of the application of Self-Managing Project Team Principles" *Proceedings of Project Management Institute (PMI) 26th Annual Symposium.* New Orleans: 290–298.

———. 1997. "S.M.A.R.T. Project Management" Construction and Engineering Leadership Conference, Calgary (May).

Hartman, F.T., and Ilincuta, A. 1997. "The 'Mad House' Concept." Software Engineering Institute Conference on Risk Management, Virginia Beach. In Press.

# Utilization of Advanced Computing Techniques in Project Management

Hashem Al-Tabtabai, Civil Engineering Department, Kuwait University

## Introduction

The rapid growth and technological advancement in computer industry in recent years have produced powerful hardware and software systems capable of performing tasks which were previously considered complex and time consuming. This growth has accelerated the evolution of a set of advanced tools and techniques that made the decision-making process faster than ever. Accurate and quick decision-making within the limits of time and budget constraints is very significant in a project management environment. This paper examines two tools in artificial intelligence computing domain and demonstrates how these systems can be effectively utilized for project management functions. The first computing technique is artificial neural networks (ANN), which are a class of modeling tools inspired by the workings of biological neural systems. These networks are trained to learn the relation between a set of input patterns to an output pattern. Knowledge is effectively learned and stored by the network during training. Once the training has been completed, it is anticipated that the neural network will be able to generate the required output for problems not considered during training. The second computing technique is genetic algorithm (GA) which is a computerized search method based on the ideas of genetics and natural selection. This adaptive search technique, which has powerful non-linear processing capabilities, can be used for solving multi-dimensional optimization problems in project management.

The paper describes how ANN and GA can be applied in the field of project management by describing two case studies. The first case study involves the application of ANN in forecasting construction project completion, in which an ANN system is developed to predict the variances in schedules by observing the values of a set of variables affecting the project schedules. The second case study involves the application of the GA to find the optimum manpower levels that need to be maintained by a construction firm involved in multiple projects. The paper concludes by discussing the lessons learned from the application of ANN and GA techniques in project control and manpower optimization problems, and shows the potential of these tools to other project management applications.

## Artificial Neural Networks

Artificial neural networks (ANN) are becoming widely implemented in construction with the main objective of assisting project personnel in decision-making. Artificial neural networks are a class of modeling tools inspired by the workings of biological neural systems (Caudill 1989). ANN have advantages over expert systems that include self-learning, self-organization, and parallel processing, and they are well-suited for problems involving matching input patterns to a set of output patterns where deep reasoning is not required. ANN are composed of neurons or processing elements (PE) and connections, which are organized in layers: an *input layer, middle or hidden layer(s),* and *output layer*, as illustrated inExhibit 1. The signals entering the input layer flow to the output layer through the middle layer(s), with the input signals detailing the problem to be solved and the output signals representing the network's solution to that problem. The connections between the neurons are associated with numerical values called *connection weights* which determine the influence of one neuron on another. The connection weights modify the output signal on each of the connection paths making some connections stronger and others weaker. The neurons in the input layer receive their activation from the environment, while the activation levels of neurons in the middle and output layers are computed as a function of the activation levels of the neurons feeding into them. Typically, this involves the summation of all incoming signals (along with a bias associated with the middle layer neuron) followed by the application of a non-linear function termed as the *transfer function.*

A training process is involved in the design of ANN, in which the connection weights are learned by the network as training examples are presented repeatedly. In this process, the connection weights are modified continuously until the error between the desired output and the actual output is minimized. Knowledge is effectively learned and stored by the weights on the connections between the neurons. Once training has been completed, it is anticipated that the neural network will be able to generate the required output for example problems not considered during training.

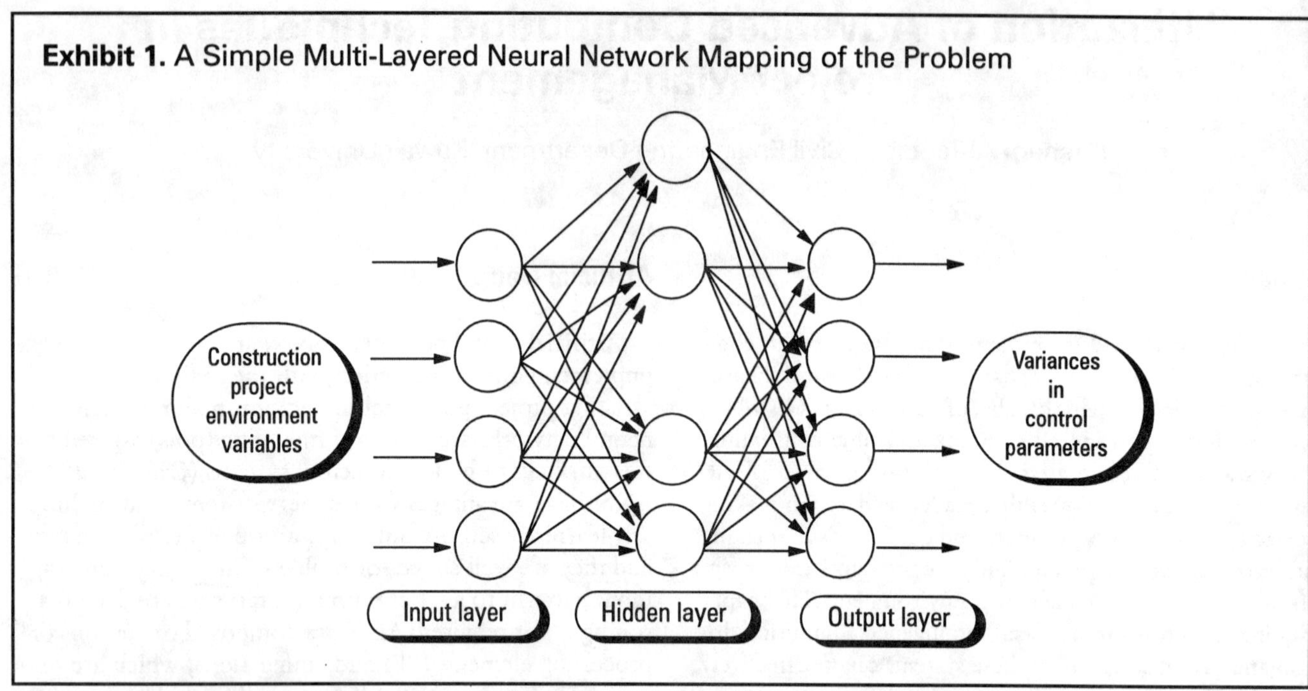

**Exhibit 1.** A Simple Multi-Layered Neural Network Mapping of the Problem

The number of hidden layer(s) and the number of hidden neurons in the hidden layers, provide the power of internal representation in capturing the non-linear relationship between the input and output vectors. Hence, a larger number of hidden layers and hidden neurons provides the potential for developing a more effective network. However, the addition of more hidden neurons increases the number of undetermined parameters (weights and biases) associated with the network. A large number of training examples is then needed to solve these parameters and to get a good approximation of the problem domain. When too few training examples are provided, the network will try to memorize, resulting in poor generalization.

An application area of ANN to project management domains, specifically forecasting construction project, is presented in this section. This application area illustrates how ANN can be applied on observations made from the project environment. The process of forecasting the completion of construction projects is an expert-based process practiced by a project manager, in which a project manager relies on his own intuition and expertise to deal with ill-structured problems. The subjective and intuitive nature of expert decision-making can utilize the non-linear modeling capability of ANN' approach and their ability to learn from noisy and incomplete data.

## An Example of Applying ANN: The Development of Schedule Forecasting Model

The prediction of a completion date of any construction project involves the identification of factors that influence the performance of various categories of work, such as concrete work, masonry work, site work, and so on. For efficient management and control of these categories, construction projects are normally divided into many manageable units, termed work packages (WPs). Completion date estimates for WPs, which are made during the planning phase, are based on the experience and knowledge of the estimator and published information from historical cost data banks and standards. During control phase, project managers measure and monitor the performance of these estimates. Variables that affect project control parameters (variations in schedule, cost, quantity, and so on) are identified, and their status are determined. An expert in project control can make an intuitive judgment, without the necessity of deep reasoning, about the expected influence of these variables on the project's future performance. A systêmatic pattern of these judgments can be coded and represented using neural network-based tools, in which a trained neural network model can be developed that mimics the decision process of the expert.

The study focuses on forecasting the expected schedule variance, which can be quantified as the variation between the budgeted cost of work performed and the budgeted cost of work scheduled. Variables, or attributes that influence the forecast of expected schedule variance for a construction project, are identified for this case study based on personal interviews with project experts. These experts have more than twenty years of experience in the Kuwait construction industry. These variables, listed below, are selected as the input pattern for the schedule forecasting experiment.

1. Performance of the contractor/consultant's management in terms of efficiency and experience in planning and control, and the decision-making ability to cope with technical problems.
2. Cash flow situation.
3. Material and equipment availability and procurement difficulties.
4. Labor productivity and availability.
5. Weather and environment influences: such as change in temperature, rainfall, rise in ground water levels, remote sites, poor access, and so on).
6. Unexpected degree of job difficulty.
7. Percentage of work completed.
8. Schedule variance trend.

Case profiles, totaled seventy-five case profiles with random values for each of the input variables, were provided to the same experts to ascertain their decisions. Each case represents a unique situation of a project. The experts exercised their judgments, i.e., forecasting the expected change of schedule variance at project completion as compared to the current schedule variance level., by responding on a scaled answer, ranging from one to nine. The value of one corresponds to a forecast of 100 percent increase in SV from the current schedule variance level, while the value of nine corresponds to a forecast of 100 percent decrease in schedule variance from the current level. . The judgments of each expert on these case profiles were further given as feedback to other participants for modification and revision of judgments. The revised judgments were averaged to reach a smoothed output, which form the output vector for this ANN model. Moreover, each of the case profile's values with the extracted output values were coded to generate a set of training data. The total number of possible cases is effectively infinite since the input variables are inherently continuous. The fact that the authors chose to limit the actual values of each input to a finite set does not alter this point. As far as the neural network is concerned, it is fitting a continuous function to the training data. The number of training points that are needed to develop an accurate continuous function model depends on other factors, most notably: the complexity of the solution surface being modeled (i.e., how many hills and valleys it contains); the stochastic content of the data (i.e., one needs enough training points to prevent bias due to random fluctuations); and the number of input variables.

## Neural Network Design

Certain parameters were adopted in the design of the neural network schedule forecasting model. They include the following:

1. A continuous mapping function network has been adopted in this example, since the values of the output variable (schedule variance) and the input variables are continuous.
2. A back propagation algorithm training technique is adopted. This algorithm is the most widely used for continuous function mapping, is simple to code, and has been shown to perform well in modeling non-linear functions. Back propagation algorithm training develops the input to output mapping by minimizing a sum squared error cost function measured over a set of training examples.
3. Another important network design variable is the learning rate coefficient (h) which represents the degree by which the weights are changed when two neurons are excited. Each time a pattern is presented to the network, the weights leading to a neuron are modified slightly during learning in the direction required to produce a smaller error at the outputs the next time the same pattern is presented. The value of (h) ranges between 0.0 and 1.0, where a value closer to one indicates significant modification in weight while a value close to zero indicates little modification. A small learning rate of 0.15 was arbitrarily chosen for the current problem since larger learning rates have often been found to lead to oscillations in weight changes resulting in a never ending learning process.

## Implementation, Training, and Validation of Results

The generated input-output data pairs (seventy-five cases) were each divided into a training set and a test set. The test set was derived from the data set by selecting 10 to 20 percent of data pairs randomly. A neural network development software entitled Neuroshell$^{TM}$ was employed to train and develop the neural network model. Eight input neurons and one output neuron with fourteen hidden neurons constitute the neural network arrangement for the schedule control module. The training of a neural network is stopped when the error falls below a user-specified level, or when the user-defined number of training iterations has been reached. In this case, twenty thousand iterations were planned for the final training process, as this was found adequate in a series of test runs. Training took thirty minutes and the least average error of the network, which was accumulated over all the training sample cases, reached 0.0000054.

A comparison between the actual output (expert judgment) and the ANN generated output for the training set

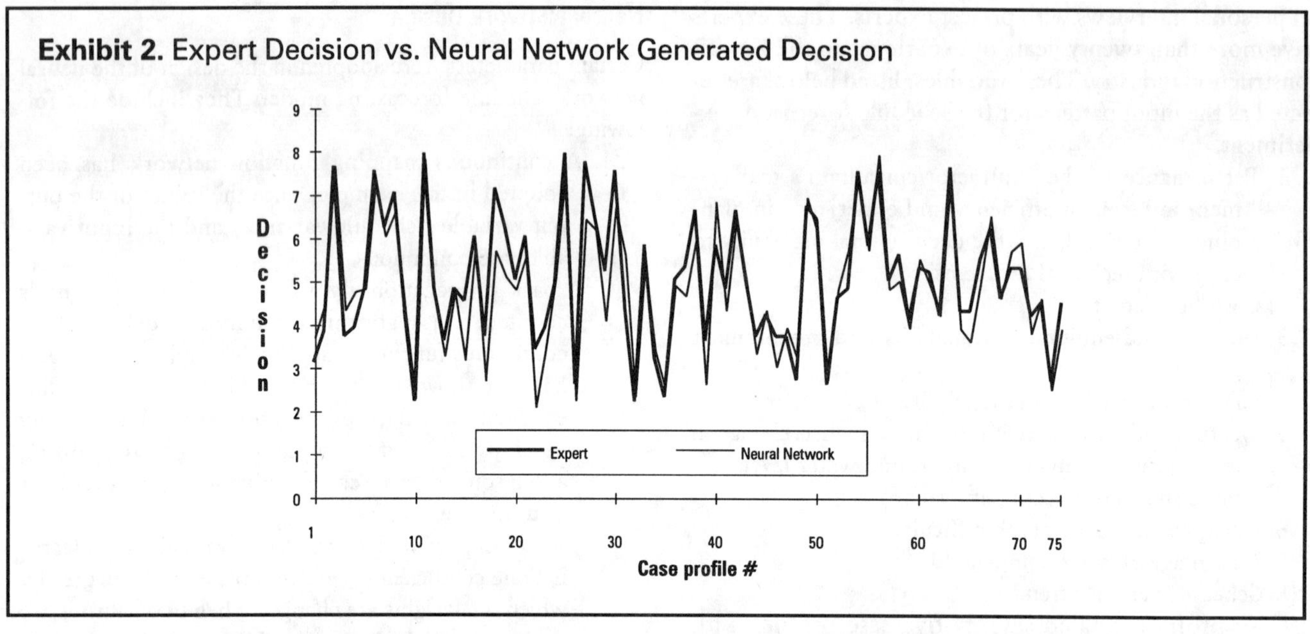


is made. The mean square error for the neural network model when applied to the test cases was found to be 0.481, and the percentage of average operational error for the test cases was found to be only 3.86 percent. These statistics show the ability of the network to predict schedule variance values with moderate to high precision. Exhibit 2 plots the expert judgment (solid line) and the predicted values by the neural network (thin line) for the complete data set of the SV-Module.

## Genetic Algorithms

Genetic algorithms (GAs) are computerized search methods based on the ideas of genetics and natural selection (Holland 1975). GAs use random techniques and exploit information from past experience to evolve solutions to real-world problems. GAs have proved themselves as robust heuristic search techniques that are capable of rapid identification of optimal design options, whilst avoiding convergence on local optima (see Austin 1990 for more details). Even though GAs are not guaranteed to find a global optimum solution within finite time, they are generally proved to be valuable in finding near optimal solutions to problems that were previously considered too large or complicated and within a reasonable amount of time. Their powerful non-linear processing capabilities can be used in solving multi-dimensional optimization problems, which has discrete variables and discontinuous functions. The application area of GAs is rapidly growing in the fields of machine learning and non-linear optimization.

### How Do Genetic Algorithms Work

GAs mimic natural selection and biological evolution to achieve their capabilities. Their operation characteristics are typically analogous to the evolution theory. GAs work with a *population* of individuals representing possible solutions to a given problem. Each candidate solution (individual) is represented as a string of bits (a set of binary/character strings), which is analogous to chromosomes and genes in the evolution theory. GAs then assign a fitness score to each individual based on the quality of the solution it represents. As different individuals compete for resources in the environment, those individuals with high fitness scores are more likely to survive and propagate their genetic material, and consequently are used to reproduce better solutions. Therefore, new populations are continuously evolved over *generations*. During the evolution process, i.e., progressing from one generation to another, the quality of the population increases, converging to an optimal (or near optimal) solution.

The concepts and procedures of genetic algorithms are based on schema theorem, which views the solution space of an optimization problem as a group of distinct hyperplanes (Holland 1975). Each hyperplane contains a population of numerous solutions. The quality of a hyperplane corresponds to the average quality of all solutions that lie in that hyperplane. Good solutions are given a high chance or an exponentially increasing number of opportunities or trails in successive generations. The number of solutions that are effectively being processed in each generation is of the order n3, where "n" is the population size. Every problem to be solved by a GA is represented by an *objective function*, which provides a measure of performance with respect to a particular set of parameters, which will be transformed into an allocation of reproductive opportunities. Objective function is generally used to map individual bit strings into a positive number which is called the individual's fitness. Probability that an individual in the current population is propagated to the future generation is proportional to its fitness. Survival-of-the-fittest method adopted by a GA selects new strings from the old population randomly, but is biased by their fitness. During a GA evolution process, the best characteristics of both the parents are combined to generate a new and better set of solutions. This is accomplished through three main reproduction operators of GA, namely: (a) *selection*, (b) *crossover*, and (c) *mutation*.

*Selection:* In this process, individuals (solutions) are selected from the population for recombination to generate new offspring. The objective of selection process is to give exponentially increasing trials to the fittest individuals, consequently less fit individuals are eradicated and higher quality individuals are selected for reproduction.

*Crossover:* Crossover is a reproduction process by which the bit-strings of two fit parent individuals (solutions) combine to produce two child individuals. Single point crossover is usually performed by swapping the fragments between two parents at a random point along the bit-string.

*Mutation:* GA applies mutation as another reproductive operator which provides a theoretical guarantee that no bit value is ever permanently fixed in all strings. During mutation, a portion of the new individuals will be flipped, to generate a new bit. Mutation introduces random modifications, and thereby induces a random walk through the search space. Mutation is a critical GA operator to maintain diversity within the population by allowing the entry of new members into the population and thus avoid being trapped at good but non-optimal solutions.

## GA Application in Project Management

To illustrate the optimization capabilities of GA, the problem of determining optimum levels of multiple labor trades to be maintained by a medium sized construction firm is presented in this section. Multi-project resource allocation is an important area that has not received enough attention from researchers. Literature on resources allocation have tended to be written with the overriding assumption that projects managed are single projects. However, the simultaneous management of multiple projects is a common situation for medium to large construction firms which are involved in different projects. Therefore, optimal resources allocation among multiple projects was selected as the application area of GA.

Any decision on the optimum number of labor required to be hired by a construction company for allocating to various projects depends mainly on the following factors as identified from interviews with experts in construction field:

1. The level of labor demand for present projects undertaken by the construction company,
2. The level of labor demand for new projects expected to be undertaken by the construction company,
3. Priority given by the management to each of the projects, and
4. The rate of overtime cost for each of the trades.

The objective of the problem is to minimize the deviation of the labor allocation against the requirement based on the wage rate and overtime cost.

### Example

Arabian Builders & Developers Co. (ABD), a firm involved in building construction, is required to hire the following class of labor for its future construction operations: (1) surveyor (2) mason (3) concreter, (4) plasterer, (5) steel fixer, (6) carpenter, and (7) unskilled labor. Any decision on the optimum number of manpower required to be hired by the company mainly depends on the level of manpower-demand for the present and future projects undertaken by ABD, hiring/firing costs, and overtime cost. The main projects constructed by ABD in the next twelve months are identified as P1, P2, P3, P4, and P5. The monthly labor requirement for each trade and for each project is initially developed from the baseline plan of these five projects. This estimate is considered as the labor required by ABD to carry out the work for the next twelve-month scheduling period. Exhibit 3 provides the manpower requirements for all the trade in the next twelve-month period for projects P1, P2, P3, P4, and P5.

Operational constraints with which ABD has to comply are mainly two, as follows:

1. Due to the inadequacy of site facilities, the total number of workers, at project sites P1 and P3, should not exceed 100; while the project sites P2 and P4 cannot accommodate more than 125 workers at any instance of time.
2. As mandated by local work authorities, the maximum number of workers that ABD can hire for each labor trade is eighty, except for unskilled labor.

In addition to these operational constraints, priority factors set by the management, which have an influence on the labor allocation, are also considered for each of the projects. Project P3 is given the highest priority while P5 has the least. It can be observed that any number of similar constraints can be conveniently incorporated in a GA implementation.

**Exhibit 3.** Manpower Requirement for Next 12 Months for Each $P_j$ (No. in Man-Months)

| Trade | Labor Requirement (Man-Months) | | | | | | | | | | | |
|---|---|---|---|---|---|---|---|---|---|---|---|---|
| | Months | | | | | | | | | | | |
| | 1 | 2 | 3 | 4 | 5 | 6 | 7 | 8 | 9 | 10 | 11 | 12 |
| Surveyor-P1 | 10 | 11 | 11 | - | - | - | - | - | - | - | - | - |
| Surveyor-P2 | - | 11 | 10 | 8 | - | - | - | - | - | - | - | - |
| Surveyor-P3 | - | - | 15 | 15 | 10 | - | - | - | - | - | - | - |
| Surveyor-P4 | - | - | 13 | 12 | 10 | - | - | - | - | - | - | - |
| Surveyor-P5 | - | - | 12 | 10 | 9 | - | - | - | - | - | - | - |
| Mason-P1 | 20 | 21 | 22 | 24 | 25 | 25 | 25 | 23 | 20 | - | - | - |
| Mason-P2 | - | 10 | 10 | 10 | 13 | 12 | 12 | 13 | 12 | 10 | - | - |
| Mason-P3 | - | - | 8 | 9 | 9 | 10 | 10 | 9 | 9 | 8 | 8 | 6 |
| Mason-P4 | - | - | 15 | 10 | 14 | 16 | 16 | 13 | 16 | 17 | 15 | 13 |
| Mason-P5 | - | - | - | - | - | 14 | 17 | 17 | 17 | 15 | 14 | 14 |
| Concreter-P1 | 10 | 11 | 11 | 11 | 13 | 12 | 11 | 11 | 10 | - | - | - |
| Concreter-P2 | - | 15 | 15 | 17 | 17 | 18 | 17 | 15 | 15 | 15 | - | - |
| Concreter-P3 | - | - | - | 10 | 10 | 10 | 13 | 15 | 13 | 10 | 9 | 9 |
| Concreter-P4 | - | - | - | 11 | 11 | 12 | 15 | 15 | 15 | 15 | 15 | 10 |
| Concreter-P5 | - | - | - | 13 | 14 | 15 | 15 | 16 | 17 | 16 | 16 | 15 |
| PlastererP1 | 10 | 11 | 12 | 15 | 15 | 15 | 14 | 13 | 11 | - | - | - |
| PlastererP2 | - | - | 15 | 16 | 16 | 17 | 18 | 18 | 17 | 16 | - | - |
| PlastererP3 | - | - | - | 7 | 9 | 10 | 10 | 9 | 9 | 10 | 10 | 10 |
| PlastererP4 | - | - | - | 8 | 8 | 10 | 12 | 12 | 10 | 9 | 9 | 8 |
| PlastererP5 | - | - | - | 9 | 12 | 13 | 14 | 14 | 13 | 13 | 13 | 11 |
| Stl. Fixr.-P1 | - | - | 5 | 6 | 6 | 6 | 6 | 6 | 6 | - | - | - |
| Stl. Fixr.-P2 | - | - | - | 13 | 15 | 15 | 15 | 14 | 14 | 13 | - | - |
| Stl. Fixr.-P3 | - | - | - | - | 7 | 7 | 8 | 8 | 8 | 8 | 7 | - |
| Stl. Fixr.-P4 | - | - | - | - | 10 | 10 | 11 | 12 | 12 | 12 | 12 | - |
| Stl. Fixr.-P5 | - | - | - | - | - | 7 | 8 | 8 | 8 | 8 | 8 | 8 |
| Carpenter-P1 | - | 7 | 7 | 9 | 9 | 8 | 8 | 7 | 7 | 7 | - | - |
| Carpenter-P2 | - | - | 15 | 15 | 15 | 14 | 13 | 14 | 14 | 13 | - | - |
| Carpenter-P3 | - | - | - | 7 | 7 | 8 | 8 | 9 | 9 | 9 | 8 | 8 |
| Carpenter-P4 | - | - | - | 16 | 18 | 18 | 18 | 19 | 19 | 17 | 17 | 16 |
| Carpenter-P5 | - | - | - | - | - | 10 | 10 | 10 | 9 | 10 | 9 | 9 |
| Unskild Lbr.P1 | 20 | 20 | 20 | 22 | 22 | 23 | 23 | 20 | 20 | 20 | - | - |
| Unskild Lbr.P2 | - | 30 | 30 | 33 | 33 | 33 | 33 | 30 | 30 | 30 | - | - |
| Unskild Lbr.P3 | - | - | 25 | 25 | 25 | 27 | 27 | 30 | 27 | 27 | 25 | - |
| Unskild Lbr.P4 | - | - | - | 25 | 28 | 30 | 30 | 30 | 30 | 28 | 28 | 25 |
| Unskild Lbr.P5 | - | - | - | 20 | 22 | 22 | 25 | 25 | 25 | 22 | 20 | 20 |

GeneHunter™, a GA software from Ward Systems Group, Inc., was used for the GA implementation. GeneHunter™ allows the user to run an optimization problem from an Excel™ spreadsheet. The user is required to enter the relevant data into the spreadsheet and specify the problem-solving parameters in a dialog screen provided in

**Exhibit 4.** Manpower Allocation for Next 12 Months for Project-$P_j$ (No. in Man-Months)

| Trade | Labor Allocation (Man-Months) Months | | | | | | | | | | | |
|---|---|---|---|---|---|---|---|---|---|---|---|---|
| | 1 | 2 | 3 | 4 | 5 | 6 | 7 | 8 | 9 | 10 | 11 | 12 |
| Surveyor-P1 | 11 | 11 | 11 | - | - | - | - | - | - | - | - | - |
| Surveyor-P2 | - | 11 | 11 | 11 | - | - | - | - | - | - | - | - |
| Surveyor-P3 | - | - | 14 | 14 | 14 | - | - | - | - | - | - | - |
| Surveyor-P4 | - | - | 11 | 11 | 11 | - | - | - | - | - | - | - |
| Surveyor-P5 | - | - | 12 | 12 | 12 | - | - | - | - | - | - | - |
| Mason-P1 | 23 | 23 | 23 | 23 | 23 | 23 | 23 | 23 | 23 | - | - | - |
| Mason-P2 | - | 13 | 13 | 13 | 13 | 13 | 13 | 13 | 13 | 13 | - | - |
| Mason-P3 | - | - | 9 | 9 | 9 | 9 | 9 | 9 | 9 | 9 | 9 | 9 |
| Mason-P4 | - | - | 14 | 14 | 14 | 14 | 14 | 14 | 14 | 14 | 14 | 14 |
| Mason-P5 | - | - | - | - | - | 17 | 17 | 17 | 17 | 17 | 17 | 17 |
| Concreter-P1 | 11 | 11 | 11 | 11 | 11 | 11 | 11 | 11 | 11 | - | - | - |
| Concreter-P2 | - | 15 | 15 | 15 | 15 | 15 | 15 | 15 | 15 | 15 | - | - |
| Concreter-P3 | - | - | - | 10 | 10 | 10 | 10 | 10 | 10 | 10 | 10 | 10 |
| Concreter-P4 | - | - | - | 15 | 15 | 15 | 15 | 15 | 15 | 15 | 15 | 15 |
| Concreter-P5 | - | - | - | 15 | 15 | 15 | 15 | 15 | 15 | 15 | 15 | 15 |
| Plasterer-P1 | 11 | 11 | 11 | 11 | 11 | 11 | 11 | 11 | 11 | - | - | - |
| Plasterer-P2 | - | - | 18 | 18 | 18 | 18 | 18 | 18 | 18 | 18 | - | - |
| Plasterer-P3 | - | - | - | 10 | 10 | 10 | 10 | 10 | 10 | 10 | 10 | 10 |
| Plasterer-P4 | - | - | - | 8 | 8 | 8 | 8 | 8 | 8 | 8 | 8 | 8 |
| Plasterer-P5 | - | - | - | 11 | 11 | 11 | 11 | 11 | 11 | 11 | 11 | 11 |
| Stl. Fixr.-P1 | - | - | 6 | 6 | 6 | 6 | 6 | 6 | 6 | - | - | - |
| Stl. Fixr.-P2 | - | - | - | 14 | 14 | 14 | 14 | 14 | 14 | 14 | - | - |
| Stl. Fixr.-P3 | - | - | - | - | 8 | 8 | 8 | 8 | 8 | 8 | 8 | - |
| Stl. Fixr.-P4 | - | - | - | - | 12 | 12 | 12 | 12 | 12 | 12 | 12 | - |
| Stl. Fixr.-P5 | - | - | - | - | - | 8 | 8 | 8 | 8 | 8 | 8 | 8 |
| Carpenter-P1 | - | 9 | 9 | 9 | 9 | 9 | 9 | 9 | 9 | 9 | - | - |
| Carpenter-P2 | - | - | 15 | 15 | 15 | 15 | 15 | 15 | 15 | 15 | - | - |
| Carpenter-P3 | - | - | - | 9 | 9 | 9 | 9 | 9 | 9 | 9 | 9 | 9 |
| Carpenter-P4 | - | - | - | 19 | 19 | 19 | 19 | 19 | 19 | 19 | 19 | 19 |
| Carpenter-P5 | - | - | - | - | - | 10 | 10 | 10 | 10 | 10 | 10 | 10 |
| Unskild Lbr.-P1 | 21 | 21 | 21 | 21 | 21 | 21 | 21 | 21 | 21 | 21 | - | - |
| Unskild Lbr.-P2 | - | 30 | 30 | 30 | 30 | 30 | 30 | 30 | 30 | 30 | - | - |
| Unskild Lbr.-P3 | - | - | 26 | 26 | 26 | 26 | 26 | 26 | 26 | 26 | 26 | - |
| Unskild Lbr.-P4 | - | - | - | 30 | 30 | 30 | 30 | 30 | 30 | 30 | 30 | 30 |
| Unskild Lbr.-P5 | - | - | - | 25 | 25 | 25 | 25 | 25 | 25 | 25 | 25 | 25 |

the program. The dialogue screen enables us to identify the cells in the spreadsheet that are involved in solving the problem The constrains that need to be met by the solution can also be conveniently represented by the program. Once the fitness function is entered to one of the cells in the spreadsheet, then the location of this cell can be linked to GeneHunter™ which will be used by the program to measure the success of each evolution. The fitness function cell is designed as an aggregation of the absolute deviations of the required manpower (known from baseline plan) from the allocated manpower (adjustable cells) biased by the labor wage rate (known from the labor wage rate standards), priority of the project (as decided by the top management), and constrained by the operational constraints (as mentioned above).

GeneHunter™ adjusts a set of cells in the spreadsheet referred as the "adjustable cells," which hold the optimum manpower values that need to be hired by the company. The values in the adjustable cells are related to the fitness function cell. GA starts with a set of solutions (initially parameters are randomly set throughout the search space), which are not necessarily desirable, and proceeds to continuously evolve into better solutions during each generation. A population of 100 individual solutions is considered during each evolution. From the initial population, the worst are discarded, and the best solutions are bred with each other by crossover, thus creating a new population. The probability of crossover used for the problem was 0.9 ($P^c$=0.9). A one-point crossover was used for the problem. Occasionally a gene will be altered to produce a mutation. The probability of mutation adopted for the current problem was 0.1 ( $P^m$=0.1). Fitness of the current population is determined and the above steps are repeated on the current population until the subsequent adaptation creates a very robust solution. The whole process continues through many generations, with the best genes being handed down to future generations, and continues until the best solution is good enough as the required solution.

The work-force levels computed using the GA iteration is shown in Exhibit 4, which gives the man-months of labor to be hired for each of the projects for each of the trades to minimize losses due to slack and idle time. These levels shall be taken as a guideline to decide the number of labors to be hired by the company based on the conditions and constraints set by the problem. The slack during any month shall be taken care of by employing overtime staff. The GA implementation can be further refined by incorporating the provision of overtime and other similar constraints, which is under investigation by the authors.

## Concluding Remarks

The subjective and intuitive nature of expert decision-making and the inability of these experts to accurately justify the basis of their own decisions, makes the process of modeling the decision-making process of experts a complex task. Advanced computing techniques that include artificial neural networks and genetic algorithms represent a solution to this issue and can be widely applied in construction domain for modeling and representing various decision tasks. The nonlinear modeling capability combined with the ability to learn from noisy and incomplete data makes the ANN a powerful and efficient choice in representing various domains of the dynamic construction environment. ANN can be effectively used to overcome the procedural complexity involved in the decision modeling.

On the other hand, a typical optimization problem faced by construction project managers is presented and the GA technique is utilized to solve the presented problem. The availability of commercial software systems like GeneHunter™ with its integration capabilities to popular spreadsheet like Excel™ helps the project managers to conveniently adopt GA technique to many optimization problems faced within a typical construction office as demonstrated in this paper. The strength of GA is that it does not search much of the possible solution, but only a fraction of it, to evolve the optimal solution. Further the project managers only need to know preliminary understanding of how a GA works, unlike the traditional methods where good knowledge of the technique is absolutely necessary to utilize them for solving the problems.

### References

Austin, S. 1990. "An Introduction to Genetic Algorithm." *AI Expert* (March): 48–53.

Caudill, M. 1989. "Neural Networks Primer." *AI Expert* 1X: 2 (Feb.): 61–67.

Holland, J. 1975. *Adaptation in Natural and Artificial Systems.* Ann Arbor: The University of Michigan Press.

# Project Management Competence for the Next Century

Lynn Crawford, Director of Program, Project Management, University of Technology, Sydney

## Introduction

As we move into the twenty-first century, project management, as the management of change, is emerging as the primary management paradigm for the future. Already, a project management approach is being adopted in organizations outside such traditional project-based industries of engineering, construction, and defense procurement (Stewart 1995). At the same time there is a growing recognition that the nature of projects and, therefore, project management is changing. Projects are becoming increasingly complex and multi-disciplinary with recognition of a wider range of stakeholders than in the past. As the distinctions between disciplines become blurred, discipline-based approaches to project management such as those followed in engineering and construction do not always provide the recipe for success.

Organizations are looking for new and more reliable guideposts than they have had in the past to help them identify and develop project personnel who are able to meet these challenges as they approach the next century. There is growing interest in project management competence arising from:

- a need for project personnel with the competence to manage different types of projects in rapidly changing project environments
- an increasing demand for competent project personnel as project management is adopted by organizations outside traditional areas, and more and more business activities are defined as projects
- a need for more effective ways of selecting project personnel and of recognizing and developing project management competence.

In response to these demands on industry and on the project management profession, the Australian government and industry are funding a major project management competency research project, which is being undertaken in collaboration with the University of Technology, Sydney, the Australian Institute of Project Management, and industry partners. The Project Management Institute (PMI), the International Project Management Association (IPMA), the Association for Project Management (APM), and international industry partners have been invited to join the project as international partners.

Aims of the project are:

- to identify competency profiles of effective project personnel for a range of application areas and project environments
- to design and validate a model for assessment and development of project management competence.

This paper describes the project management competence research project, the progress achieved to date, and the contribution that the research outcomes will make to project management in the next century.

## Background

In May 1996 the University of Technology, Sydney (UTS), and the Australian Graduate School of Engineering Innovation (AGSEI), in partnership with the Australian Institute of Project Management (AIPM) and other industry partners, lodged a collaborative grant application with the Australian Research Council, Australia's peak research funding body. The application was successful, and the project commenced in February 1997. A senior research officer was appointed in April 1997.

The title of the research project is *Developmental Assessment of Project Management Competence.* The purpose of the project is: *to develop profiles of underlying knowledge, attitudes, and behaviors which lead to high performance in a range of project management roles and to provide a framework for both attribute and performance-based competency assessment and development, job desig,n and selection of project personnel for improved project performance.*

The success of the grant application can be seen as recognition, by a national government, of the importance of project management, and, as such, is a significant achievement for the project management profession internationally.

The initial research funding covered the conduct of the research project in Australia. The researchers and industry partners recognized the contribution the project could make in establishing a sound research base for development of global project management standards, if conducted internationally. To facilitate this, project management professional organizations and corporations, worldwide, were invited to participate in the project. Response was extremely positive, and arrangements have now been made to collect data on project

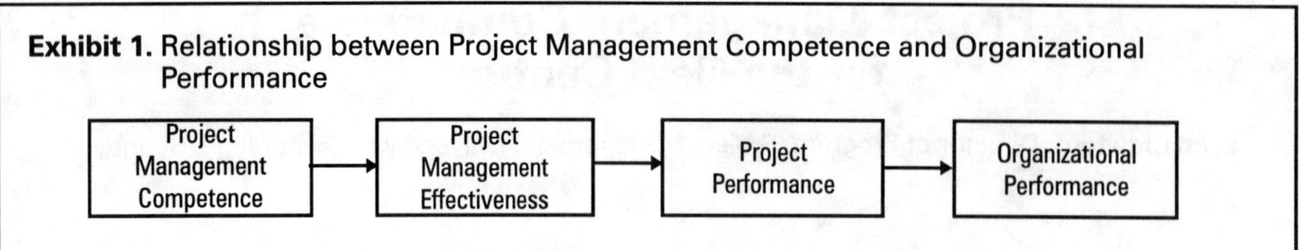

**Exhibit 1.** Relationship between Project Management Competence and Organizational Performance

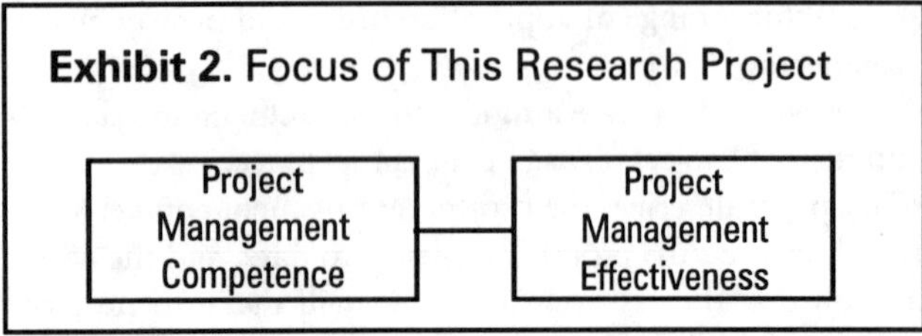

**Exhibit 2.** Focus of This Research Project

personnel in Australia, the United States, Canada, the European Union, Asia, South Africa, and Latin America.

## Project Management Competence

Professional organizations (AIPM (sponsor) 1996; PMI 1996; APM 1993) and various commercial organizations (i.e., Digital, Texas Instruments, Natwest) have attempted to identify the skills, knowledge, and behaviors that they believe a competent project manager should possess. Writers and researchers (Thamhain and Wilemon 1977; Posner 1987; Gadeken and Cullen 1990; Gadeken 1991; Price 1994; Pettersen 1991; McVeigh 1995) have endeavored to identify aspects of competence that are characteristic of effective or high performing project managers.

Interest in project management competence stems from the very reasonable and widely held assumption that if people who manage and work on projects are competent, they will perform effectively and that this will lead to successful projects and successful organizations (Karpin 1995; Beer, Eisenstat et al. 1990; Smith, Carson et al. 1984).

The concern of this research project is the relationship between project management competence and project management effectiveness as a basis for developing competency profiles of effective project personnel in a range of project environments.

To investigate this relationship it is necessary to establish measures of both project management competence and project management effectiveness.

Competence is a term which is widely used but which has come to mean different things to different people. It is generally accepted, however, as encompassing knowledge, skills, attitudes, and behaviors that are causally elated to superior job performance (Boyatzis 1982). This understanding of competence has been described as attribute-based inference of competence (Heywood et al. 1992). To this can be added what is referred to as a performance-based approach to competence, which assumes that competence can be inferred from demonstrated performance at pre-defined acceptable standards in the workplace (Gonczi et al. 1993). The performance-based approach is the basis for what has become known as the competency standards movement that underpins the National Vocational Qualifications in the United Kingdom and the Australian Competency Standards Framework.

Australia's Competency Standards for Project Management were developed over a three-year period, from 1993 to 1996, in association with industry, under the sponsorship of the Australian Institute of Project Management and with funds provided by both government and industry. They are endorsed by the Australian government as part of what is now known as the Australian Qualifications Framework. As the first government-endorsed performance-based competency standards for project management, the Australian National Competency Standards for Project Management (1996) may be considered as a de facto international standard for what project managers are expected to be able to do.

PMI's *A Guide to the Project Management Body of Knowledge (PMBOK Guide)*(1996) can be considered as a de facto international standard for what project personnel can be expected to *know.*

For the purposes of the research project being described here, instruments have been developed to provide measures of project management competence, which encompass both attribute and performance-based approaches. This has been further broken down into a framework of input, process, and output competencies (Finn 1993), where competence is considered as a combination of:

This understanding of the dimensions of competence has been translated into the following integrated model of project management competence:

Based on this model, the following instruments have been developed:

**Exhibit 3.** Dimensions of Competence

| | | |
|---|---|---|
| ***Knowledge*** (qualifications) + ***Skills*** (ability to do a task) | **Input Competencies:** | the knowledge and understanding, skills and abilities that a person brings to a job |
| + | + | |
| ***Core Personality Characteristics*** (Motives + Traits + Self-Concept) | **Process Competencies:** | the core personality characteristics underlying a persons capability to do a job |
| + | + | |
| ***Demonstrable performance*** in accordance with occupational / professional / organizational Competency Standards. | **Output Competencies:** | the ability to perform the activities within an occupational area to the levels of performance expected in employment |

**Exhibit 4.** An Integrated Model of Project Management Competence

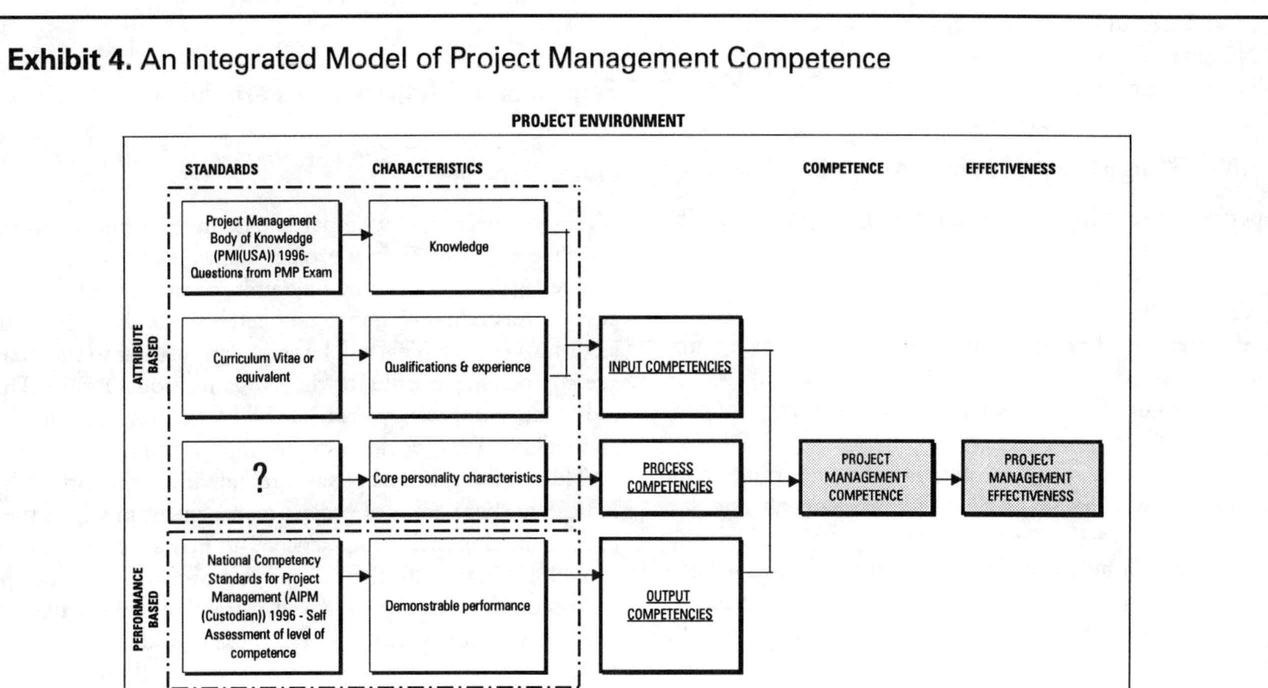


## 1. Project Management Competence

### *1.1 Project Management Knowledge:*

A test, using PMI's *PMBOK Guide* as the knowledge standard. The test is based on PMI's project management professional (PMP) exam and is intended to identify the extent of a person's knowledge of formal project management processes and terminology.

### *1.2 Qualifications and Experience:*

A questionnaire, based on the qualifications and experience questionnaire used by PMI as part of qualification for the PMP award. Sections on non-project management experience and service have been added.

### *1.3 Personality Tests:*

Two personality tests will be used to identify core personality characteristics, which can be causally related to effective project management performance. The two tests to be used are:

- 16 PF: a personality questionnaire that measures sixteen primary aspects of adult personality .
- Caliper Profile: initially known as the Multiple Personal Inventory (MPI), is an instrument which has been specifically developed to predict successful performance in a number of job roles (Greenberg and Greenberg 1980).

#### *1.4 Performance-Based Competence:*

Self assessment against Australian National Competency Standards for Project Management.

### 2. Project Environment:

A questionnaire, which establishes the nature of the project environment in which the person normally operates, including such factors as:

- Job title
- Project size and duration
- Number of projects
- Project complexity
- Application area (industry).

### 3. Project Management Effectiveness:

Supervisor and self rating on a number of dimensions including:

- Value to the client
- Value to the organization
- Effectiveness of relationship with peers in achieving project goals
- Ability to inspire and encourage the performance of others
- Frequency with which the person completes projects on time, within budget, and achieving project goals
- Use of recognized project management methodologies
- A number of behavioral characteristics which have been validated as causally related to superior performance.

Instruments which have been developed for this project (Items 1.1, 1.2, 1.3, 1.4, 2, and 3) have been tested in pilot studies conducted in Australia, the United States, the United Kingdom, and South Africa, and modifications have been made in response to this feedback. The full process, which takes eight hours, including the two personality tests, has also been piloted, in both the United States and Australia. The data collection process is conducted as three hours of prework, followed by a half-day workshop conducted in a location to suit the participating organizations.

## Sample

Organizations are asked to nominate a minimum of five and a maximum of twenty project personnel according to the industry/application area indicated in Exhibit 5. The minimum of five is intended to allow smaller organizations or project management functions in larger organizations to contribute to the project. The upper limit of twenty is to ensure that one organization does not dominate the sample in a particular project industry/application area category. Multi-functional organizations will be offered the opportunity for participation of separate sample groups from distinctly different parts of their organizations, which would fall into different project industry/application areas.

Arrangements have been made to collect data from project personnel in Australia, the United States, Canada, the European Union, South Africa, Latin America, and Asia. The intended minimum sample, per country, is as follows:

## Feedback and Benefits for Participants

### Project Personnel

All project personnel who participate in the project will receive a copy of their own project management competency profile, against each of the nine units of the *PMBOK Guide* and the Australian National Competency Standards for Project Management. This will be shown in relation to the average competency profile for their organizational group. The individual competency profiles will be entirely confidential and will NOT be provided to the employing organization.

This feedback will be of value to individual participants by indicating those areas of project management in which they need to develop their competence. This may suggest that they should negotiate with their employing organizations for opportunities for experience as well as training in particular aspects of project management. For those considering applying for certification or registration under the PMP program, the Australian National Competency Standards for Project Management, or other national schemes, the feedback will give them an indication of how successful they are likely to be and whether they may need more experience or training before applying.

### Participating Organizations

Participating organizations will receive the average competency profile for their set of project personnel. As the project data builds, they will receive bulletins that indicate their organizational average competency profile in relation to the:

- Average competency profile for the whole sample
- Average competency profile for each country sample

**Exhibit 5.** Proposed Sample Composition Per Country

| Industry Sector / Application Area | No of organizations | No of personnel |
|---|---|---|
| **Aerospace & Defense** | 2 to 4 | 30 |
| **Construction, mining, petroleum** | 2 to 4 | 30 |
| **Financial services, banking, insurance** (incl. management consulting) | 2 to 4 | 30 |
| **Government** (n.e.c.) | 2 to 4 | 30 |
| **Information Systems and Management** (including IT and telecommunications) | 2 to 4 | 30 |
| **Manufacturing** (incl. automotive, pharmaceutical, & new product development) | 2 to 4 | 30 |
| **Utilities** (inc. transportation and environmental management) | 2 to 4 | 30 |
| **TOTAL** | **14 to 28** | **210** |

- Average competency profile for their industry sector/application area.

The average competency profile for each organization will be confidential to that organization and will not be released to other organizations other than as part of the averages for the whole sample, each country, and each industry sector/application area.

This information will be particularly useful to organizations in:

- Benchmarking the competence of their project personnel
- Benchmarking their organizational project management competence by identifying any project management practices which are not generally followed within the organization
- Providing guidance for project management training and development of project management systems.

The feedback information from the research will assist organizations and individuals in preparing for the next century.

## Data Analysis and Dissemination of Results

Multivariate data analysis will be used to test a number of hypotheses, the key being that statistically significant profiles of input, process, and output competencies can be developed that differentiate the most effective from the least effective project personnel across application areas and project environments.

Results will be disseminated to the research partners and participating organizations in bulletins issued at three to six month intervals commencing in late 1997. These will continue to be issued for the duration of the project, which is funded until the end of 1999. Results will be made available to participating project management professional organizations (AIPM, PMI, IPMA, APM) and through these organizations to their members.

## Use for Research Results

Proposed deliverables from this research project are:

1. Competency profiles of effective project personnel in a range of project environments
2. Performance appraisal process for project management personnel
3. Assessment centers for project management personnel
4. Job design for effective project performance.

It is envisaged that the results of this research will provide assistance:

5. To project management professional associations in developing and maintaining the currency of registration/certification of individuals and in accreditation of project management education and training courses
6. To organizations in assessing and enhancing their project management systems and competence of their project personnel
7. To individuals in providing guidance for self development.

It will also provide a basis for review of both the PMI's *PMBOK Guide* and the Australian National Competency Standards for Project Management to ensure that they correctly reflect what effective project managers need to know and do.

An important aspect of the project is that it will provide research-based guidance as to those core personality characteristics that can be demonstrated to relate to effective project performance in a range of project environments.

## Project Management Competence for the Next Century

With funding carrying it through to February 2000, this research project is perfectly timed to assist the project management profession in preparing for the next century. With the support of project management professional organizations and industry, worldwide, it is well placed to make a significant contribution to the development of project management standards that will meet the needs of the global project management community of the twenty-first century.

### References


AIPM (Sponsor). 1996. *National Competency Standards for Project Management*. Sydney, Australian Institute of Project Management.

APM (UK). 1993. *Project Management Body of Knowledge*. High Wycombe, Bucks, Association for Project Management (APM).

Beer, M. R., R. Eisenstat, et al. 1990. *The Critical Path to Corporate Renewal*. Boston: Harvard Business School Press.

Boyatzis, R. E. 1982. *The Competent Manager: a Model for Effective Performance*. New York: John Wiley and Sons.

Cattell, R. B., H. W. Eber, et al. 1970. *Handbook for the 16PF*. Illinois: IPAT.

Finn, R. 1993. *A Synthesis of Current Research on Management Competencies*. Henley-on-Thames: Henley Management College.

Gadeken, O. C. 1991. *Competencies of Project Managers in the MOD Procurement Executive*. Shrivenham: Royal Military College of Science.

Gadeken, O. C., and B. J. Cullen. 1990. *A Competency Model of Program Managers in the DOD Acquisition Process*. Defense Systems Management College.

Gonczi, A., P. Hager, et al. 1993. *The Development of Competency-Based Assessment Strategies for the Professions*. Canberra: Australian Government Publishing Service.

Greenberg, H. M., and J. Greenberg. 1980. "Job Matching for Better Sales Performance." *Harvard Business Review* 58(5, September–October): 128–133.

Heywood, L., A. Gonczi, et al. 1992. *A Guide to Development of Competency Standards for Professions*. Canberra: Australian Government Publishing Service.

Karpin, D. C. 1995. *Enterprising Nation: Renewing Australia's Managers to Meet the Challenges of the Asia-Pacific Century*. Canberra: Australian Government Publishing Service (AGPS).

McVeigh, C. B. J. 1995. "The Right Stuff—Revisited: A Competency Perspective of Army Program Managers." *Program Manager*(January–February): 30–34.

Pettersen, N. 1991. "Selecting Project Managers: An Integrated List of Predictors. *Project Management Journal* XXII(2): 21–25.

PMI. 1996. *A Guide to the Project Management Body of Knowledge (PMBOK Guide)*. Upper Darby, PA: Project Management Institute.

Posner, B. Z. 1987. "What it Takes to Be a Good Project Manager. *Project Management Journal*(March): 51–54.

Price, J. E. 1994. *A Study of the Leadership and Managerial Competencies Used by Effective Project Managers*. 12th INTERNET (IPMA) World Congress on Project Management, Oslo, Norway, IPMA.

Smith, J. E., K. P. Carson, et al. 1984. "Leadership: It Can Make a Difference. *Academy of Management Journal* 27: 765–76.

Stewart, T. A. 1995. "The Corporate Jungle Spawns a New Species: The Project Manager." *Fortune* 132(1, July 10): 179–180.

Thamhain, H. J., and D. Wilemon. 1977. "Leadership Effectiveness in Program Management." *Project Management Quarterly*(June): 25–31.

# Leveraging Project Resources: Tools for the Next Century

Robert C. Newbold, Creative Technology Labs, LLC

## Introduction

We are all aware that virtually every business sector has become more and more competitive in recent years. There is cutthroat competition both at home and abroad, and the need for improvement embraces virtually every aspect of business. The popularity of downsizing, right-sizing, and reengineering attests to the need for change. There can be no question that this need will grow even stronger in the next century. We need more than one-time fixes; there is a clear need for processes for ongoing improvement, processes that can enable major leaps in performance.

This paper explores such a process, which is derived from an improvement methodology called "theory of constraints" (TOC). TOC consists of a number of common-sense tools and processes. These tools allow us to focus efforts on those few areas, called "constraints," which restrict our ability to improve. These constraints are the leverage points towards which successful improvement efforts must be directed.

The TOC concepts are well-established in manufacturing; see for example (Noreen, Smith and Mackey 1995). Application of TOC to project management is relatively new, but initial results are very promising. Completion times have been dramatically shrunk for defense R&D contracts, aircraft repair, new product development, and various types of construction.

## The Goal

What is a process for ongoing improvement? Intuitively it sounds like a useful idea, but we need to be very clear about what we want. A "process" is a systematic series of actions. "Ongoing" means the process can be repeated over and over. We want a process that we can use more than once; otherwise we'll have to spend all our time looking for the next bandage and hoping that it works.

What is an improvement? In order to know this, we first need to understand the goal of the organization we're talking about. For what reason was it created? We could define the goal of the United States military to be "defense readiness." It needs to be as prepared as possible to protect U.S. interests, primarily (let's say) as a response to aggression. The goal of a school district might be to educate children who can live up to their potentials to contribute to society. The goal of a public company is better bottom-line results, now and in the future. People invest in it in order to make money.

**Exhibit 1.** fundamental Measurements

| Type of Organization | Throughput | Operating Expense |
|---|---|---|
| U. S. military | "Defense units" | Federal tax dollars |
| School district | "Potential achieved" | Local tax dollars |
| Public company | Money made (through sales) | Expenses |

In determining an organization's performance there are two important, fundamental measurements: what goes into the company to allow it to produce, and what it produces. Since we are measuring over time, these measurements must be rates. The rate of input is called "operating expense"; the rate of output is called "throughput" (Goldratt 1992, 60–61). Some examples are found in Exhibit 1.

It is not easy to measure throughput of not-for-profit organizations precisely. However, many counter-productive actions and attitudes can be avoided just by a broad understanding of the organization's throughput, by asking: "What are people supposed to be achieving?" We will simplify the discussion by confining ourselves to organizations whose goal is to make money, now and in the future.

In for-profit organizations, "throughput" is the rate at which the organization generates money through sales. Usually the costs that directly depend on an individual product (also known as truly variable costs), such as raw materials and contractor prices, are subtracted from sales in order to get a value for throughput (Goldratt 1990, 19–20). Operating expense is the rate at which money is spent generating throughput. The standard bottom-line measurement "net profit" can be defined as throughput minus operating expense (Goldratt 1990, 32).

In addition to net profit, there is another common bottom-line measurement: return on assets. Return on assets is net profit, divided by total asset value. Goldratt (1990, 23) concentrates on inventory rather than assets in this calculation, probably because of the importance of physical inventory in manufacturing. Typically the effect of increasing assets is difficult to assess. On the one hand, more capital is tied up, and on the other hand, those assets represent value that the company could (through sales) turn into cash. For purposes of this discussion we'll assume that reduction of assets is not a major avenue for improvement.

We're now in a position to be much more precise about the meaning of "improvement." We want throughput to go

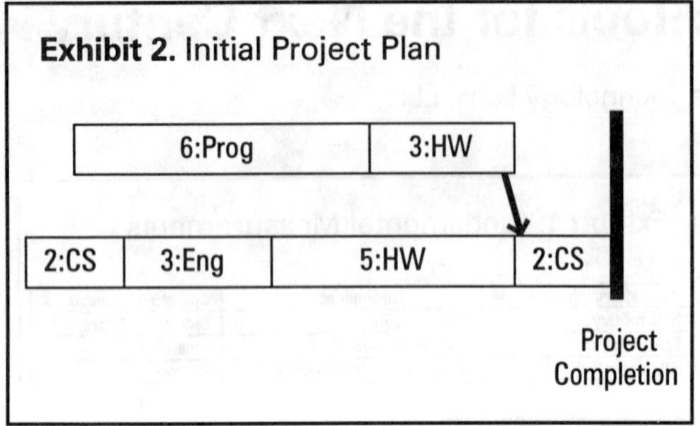


**Exhibit 2.** Initial Project Plan

up and operating expense to go down. To make operating expense go down, we can reduce head count, if necessary, by laying people off. This avenue has a lower limit for improvement. To make throughput go up, we can sell more, or sell at higher prices; the potential here is unlimited. Whether we choose the limited or unlimited direction, we must leverage our resources to improve. We must find those key areas that are most important to focus improvement efforts. There are several ways to do this.

## Leverage Points

Let's look at a hypothetical company that sells projects to develop custom hardware. This company has no problem with sales; the demand will meet the supply for the foreseeable future. Furthermore, the times and resources required to complete each project are very similar. The generic flow is shown in Exhibit 2.

Each rectangle represents a task. The horizontal lengths of the rectangles are proportional to the expected task durations. Inside each rectangle is printed the number of weeks the task is expected to take and the type of person doing the work. The required resources are a customer services representative (CS), an engineer (Eng), a hardware technician (HW), and a computer programmer (Prog). Each rectangle that immediately follows another is dependent on the prior task. The arrow between 3:HW and 2:CS also represents a dependency. This means that both 3:HW and 5:HW must finish before the last 2:CS can start. The vertical bar to the right represents project completion.

How many of these projects could be completed in a year, assuming that the organization has one person of each type, and that each person has fifty productive weeks in a year? We can at least answer this theoretically by noting that the hardware technician is going to be the most busy. Since eight weeks of her time are required for each project, about six projects can be completed per year. How can the company produce more? There are a few choices:

- Make sure the technician is focused on her work, and that she has as few distractions as possible. Every minute she is productive translates to more projects completed. Every project completed increases the bottom line.
- Make sure that everyone else produces in order to keep her busy. The programmer or engineer can't take a vacation unless there is sufficient work to keep the technician busy in the meantime.
- Hire another technician.

In fact, we have just gone through the following five-step improvement process, derived from Goldratt (1990, 59–62):

1. **Identify the system's leverage points.** We noted that lack of hardware technician's time prevented us from making more projects, and, hence, more money.
2. **Exploit the leverage points.** That is, squeeze as much as possible from the technician. This might be as simple as freeing the technician from distractions or communicating her importance.
3. **Subordinate everything else to the above decisions.** Make sure everyone else is working to keep the "leverage point" busy. It only makes sense for others to produce enough to keep the technician busy, and no more. It only makes sense for the sales people to sell as much as the technician can produce.
4. **Elevate the leverage points.** That is, spend money to eliminate them. An example might be hiring another technician. What happens if a new technician is hired? How many projects could be completed in a year? Assuming the new technician comes up to speed quickly, the new leverage point will in software department. At six weeks per project, we now expect to be able to produce about eight projects per year. Further improvement focused on the technician will be, at best, useless. This suggests a fifth step:
5. **Go back to step 1; don't let inertia become a constraint.**

It looks simple and logical. Why aren't we doing it? Here we address two key reasons: local performance measurements and uncertainty. Local performance measurements are formal and informal means used to evaluate individuals. Uncertainty is embodied in Murphy's Law: if anything can go wrong, it will. The one thing we can be sure of regarding our project schedules is that they will never be followed precisely.

## Local Performance Measurements

How can local performance measurements hurt the application of the five-step process? Let's use the company in Exhibit 2. What "improvements" would typical management look for? They would probably note that several people aren't working all the time. In fact, the customer service rep. is spending half his time on coffee breaks. Maybe the engineer and programmer could help with customer service. With the purchase of an automated phone system, the customer service person could be let go, and money would be saved. The bottom line has improved, and, therefore, the company seems better off.

The reality is that the "keep busy" mentality is a measurement. The message is "work or be laid off." It may not even be a formal measurement, but chances are everyone knows about it. If they don't, they will learn very quickly after the first layoff. What is the response to this measurement? One must keep busy. There are then two choices for someone who has insufficient work to do: slow down, or accept more work.

Slowing down is a manifestation of Parkinson's Law (Parkinson 1957, 2): the work expands to fill the time available for its completion. People become less productive. People procrastinate.

Accepting more work sounds promising. On the other hand, if people besides the technician continue to accept enough work to keep busy, uncompleted work will build up in the system. For a discussion of some of the results of this buildup of work, including increased lead times and reduced quality, see Goldratt and Fox (1986, 32–53). For now, it's sufficient to note that excess work adds to the overall confusion. The more papers on your desk, the less likely you are to find the ones you need. The combination of Parkinson's Law and the buildup of uncompleted work means that management can't really predict when tasks will be done, or how much time is available to do more. It therefore becomes very difficult to predict how long a given project, or even a given task, will take.

There's another local performance measurement that causes problems: the necessity of keeping individual commitment dates. When people commit to finishing a task by a certain date, they are likely to be held to this date. At first this seems both sensible and inevitable. But consider what typically happens in order that people can make their personal commitments. Suppose someone has a task that should take, on average, five weeks of work. If they estimate five weeks, they'll be late at least half the time, even if no other tasks come up. That is unacceptable. In order to have a good chance of finishing on time, they'll probably estimate at least ten. They'll provide for the worst case. Of course, they're only busy half the time, so they'll have to take some other actions— either slow down or accept more work.

Now consider how these local measurements affect the bidding process. The project bid must be competitive. Time to complete is usually a significant factor. In order to be competitive, task times are often factored down, sometimes arbitrarily. In the process project performance criteria may be compromised as well. The chances of completing on time, and the chances of satisfying the customer, suffer.

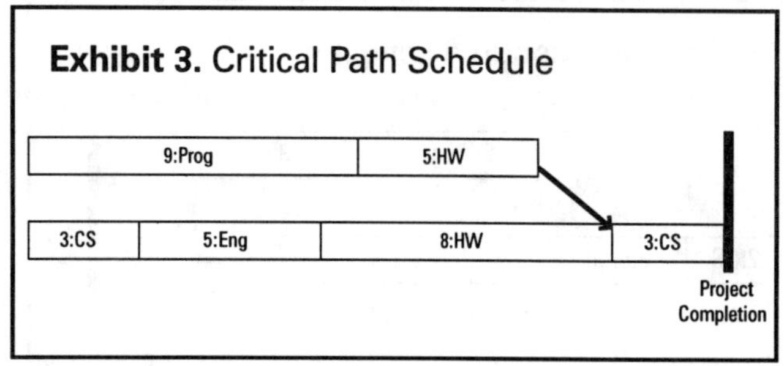


**Exhibit 3.** Critical Path Schedule

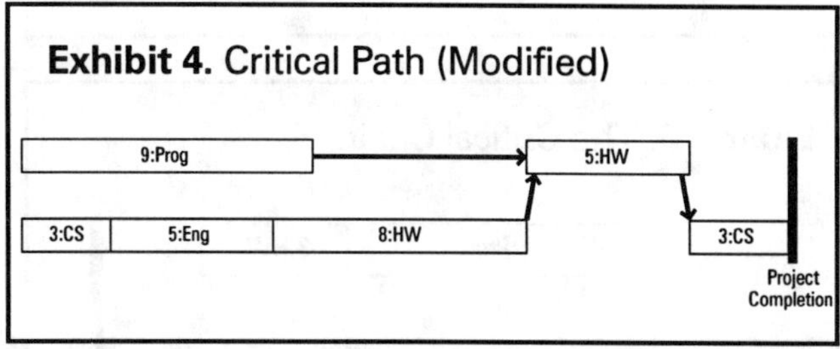


**Exhibit 4.** Critical Path (Modified)

Let's look at how this affects project schedules. A possible critical path schedule for the project in Exhibit 2 is shown in Exhibit 3.

The tasks with bold borders are on the critical path. Note that the individual tasks have been padded to protect their completion times. Some of that padding may have been reduced to make a competitive bid. The overall project duration is nineteen weeks. The task durations, and hence the project completion date, are rather arbitrary.

An astute project manager might note that there is a conflict for the hardware technician's time. They might decide to resolve the conflict by creating an artificial dependency between the two technicians' tasks, as shown in Exhibit 4.

This plan is probably more realistic. But now the project duration is twenty-four weeks, which is twice the duration of the critical path in Exhibit 2. Furthermore, the last task has only one week of protection; this may still be insufficient to protect the project due date from problems.

This scheduling approach also raises many questions. Suppose everyone gave estimated average completion times for tasks. Suppose we're not worried about keeping everyone busy. It seems that at this point we're more exposed than ever to the effects of Murphy's Law. How can we protect project completion dates against inevitable fluctuations? If we want to implement the five-step improvement process, if we want to establish some predictability, we will need a new approach to project planning. We need a technique that provides significantly more protection to the project commitment dates, without adding more slack time than traditional methods.

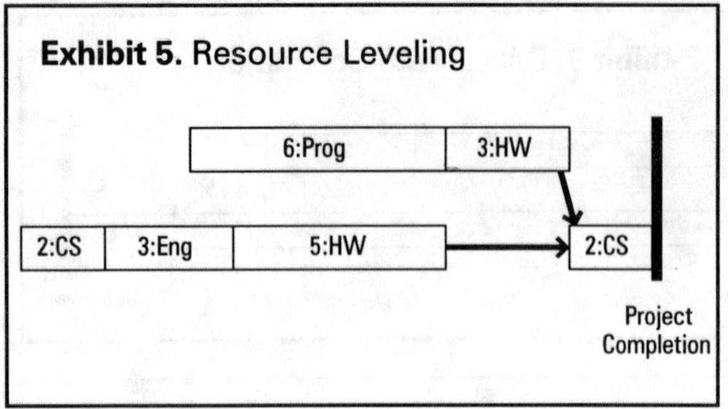


**Exhibit 5.** Resource Leveling

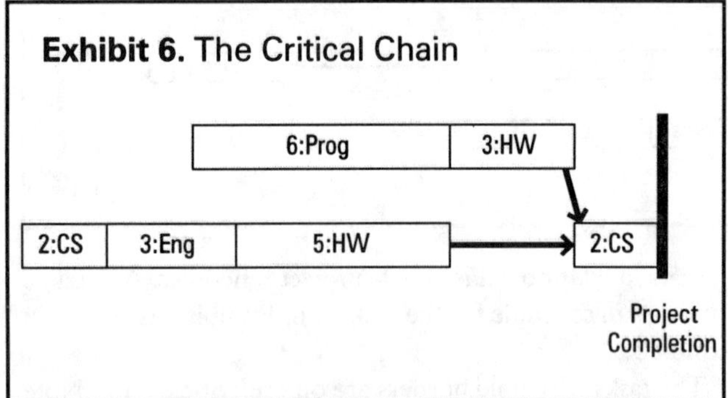


**Exhibit 6.** The Critical Chain

## The Critical Chain: Breaking Murphy's Law

Our new technique is called "critical chain" scheduling and is discussed in Goldratt (1997) and Pittman (1994). We start with the initial project layout, Exhibit 2, and completely ignore uncertainty. Exhibit 2 is not really a feasible schedule because it has two tasks contending for the hardware technician's time. As our first scheduling step, let's resolve the resource contention.

This schedule would be perfect if there were no uncertainty. So next we need to protect against the uncertainty. We need to protect the commitment date because the commitment date is directly tied to throughput. In order to protect it, we must decide which tasks are responsible for the current project duration. If delayed, those tasks would make the project longer. Those tasks should therefore be considered most important. They should be protected. That set of tasks is called the "critical chain." The critical chain tasks are shown with bold outlines in Exhibit 6.

It's easy to see that a delay of any of the bold tasks would delay the project. Note that this is different from the traditional critical path in two ways: resource contention is taken into account, and tasks are placed at their late start times. Because of the resource contention, the critical chain, unlike the critical path, can hop from one path to another.

Having identified the key tasks, how can we best protect the customer? We are dealing with a fixed number of resources, so the only feasible way of adding protection is by adding time. Traditionally we protect the schedule by padding individual tasks or "spreading the slack" throughout the schedule. Using the critical chain approach we don't protect individual tasks; we protect the project completion. We do this by means of lumps of protection, scheduled blocks of time, called buffers. The buffers look like slack and feel like slack, but they are not slack. They are necessary components of the schedule.

We need to identify the key places to put these buffers. First, since the critical chain determines the project duration, we need to protect the critical chain itself. If work is not ready for the critical chain tasks to start, the critical chain will be delayed, thus likely delaying project completion. This means we must have some protection every time a non-critical chain task feeds the critical chain. This type of protection is called a "feeding buffer."

With the feeding buffer we have protected the critical chain from fluctuations. We haven't yet protected the commitment date from fluctuations on the critical chain. This is done by means of a "project buffer" placed after the last-scheduled task. Exhibit 7 shows the fully buffered schedule.

The feeding buffer protects the critical chain task 3:HW from uncertainty in the task 6:Prog. The project completion date is also protected by a project buffer of five weeks. This means that every task has at least five weeks of protection. By specifying average task durations and by removing the necessity to keep everyone busy, we have drastically reduced the need for people to take on multiple tasks to keep busy. This, in turn, helps reduce the normal chaos associated with fighting fires across multiple projects. If you compare this schedule with Exhibit 4, you'll see that while the overall project duration is seven weeks shorter, we have actually gained significantly in reliability by pooling our slack into buffers.

Imagine for a moment that the critical chain tasks in Exhibit 7 are parts of an automobile and that the uncertainty causes them to vibrate unpredictably. The buffers act as shock absorbers, so that the vibrations don't affect the passenger, who also happens to be the customer. If we think about Exhibit 7 in this context, we'll realize that the vibrations go both ways, left and right. Some tasks complete early; some complete late.

The critical chain approach helps projects to complete more quickly by encouraging tasks to start early. Typically, opportunities for starting tasks early are lost or ignored, because people don't know which are high priority tasks and therefore need to be started early. When things go well, these "positive" schedule disruptions can't accumulate. Frequent rescheduling ensures that late tasks or "negative" disruptions do accumulate, because they must be taken into account in the revised schedules. If we know which tasks are most important, i.e., the critical chain tasks, we know which tasks we would like to start early. Furthermore, the buffers allow this to happen. Suppose in Exhibit 7 the task 5:HW completes in four weeks. Unless 6:Prog is very late, the feeding buffer ensures that 3:HW can start a week early, thus speeding project along.

There is a useful refinement that can be added to the schedule. Consider what will happen if the engineer is working on another project before the 3:Eng task starts, and other work is delayed. That delay can delay the entire critical chain of this project and potentially use up some of the project buffer. To avoid that, we can schedule a "wake-up call" (also known as a "resource buffer") some time before resources are due to start their critical chain tasks. The resources are told in advance when they will be needed to perform these key tasks. This lets them know that they need to be ready for high-priority work and adds further reliability to the critical chain schedule.

In creating a critical chain schedule, we have in fact carried out the five-step improvement process. We identified the leverage point by resolving resource contention and identifying the critical chain. We will exploit the leverage point by focusing on critical chain tasks. We have allowed everyone else to subordinate to the leverage point by inserting buffers. We know how to elevate the leverage point or "crash the project" if we so desire; we can increase the resources available to work on critical chain tasks. Of course, this may create a new critical chain, so we must then go back to step 1.

An important question remains. If we don't worry about late tasks, how do we monitor project status? The answer is simple: we monitor how much of the buffers have been used up compared with how much work remains on the path feeding it. For example, suppose delays have pushed completion of the final project task into the project buffer, so that only 30 percent of the buffer remains. If the project is 90 percent complete, we're probably in good shape. If it's only 50 percent complete, there may be a serious problem.

## Conclusions

We can expect a number of benefits from the critical chain process for individual projects. Completion dates are more reliable due to the addition of buffers to the schedules. Project times-to-complete are reduced by pooling the slack into buffers. Costs typically go down as lead times go down. Lower lead times also minimize the opportunity for customers to change specifications, which is a common cause of uncertainty in projects. Because people are not rigidly held to task start and finish times, they can feel comfortable taking the time to address quality problems without fear of missing their completion dates. This reduces rework, a common and severe problem with defects discovered late in a project (Boehm 1983, 40) and helps ensure a higher-quality result.

**Exhibit 7.** The Buffered Schedulr

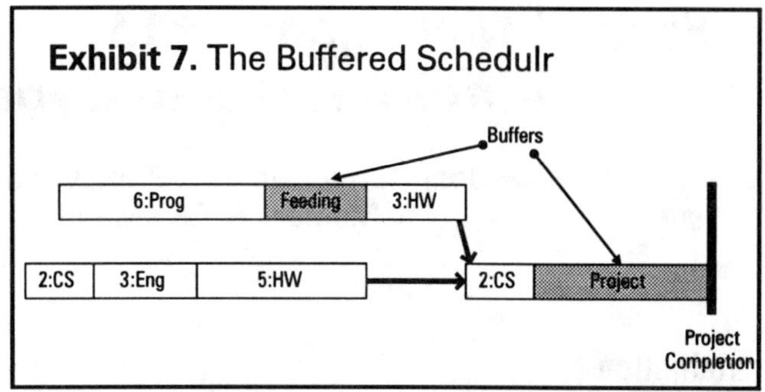


In a multiple-project environment, there are additional benefits. If people are not measured by how busy they are or by precisely when their tasks complete, the incentive to slow down or accept multiple tasks is reduced. They are then free to follow an important rule: when you have work, finish it as quickly as possible. It is then much easier to estimate resource availability. It becomes possible to identify "constraint" resources that are leverage points for the organization to produce more projects; it even becomes possible to select such resources as strategic leverage points around which the business can be managed.

The TOC improvement tools come with a warning: there is no single individual who can implement these concepts. In an individual project, the entire project team needs to understand what is needed. In a company, the entire organization must be involved. A successful implementation requires going from a cost-oriented approach that requires attention everywhere, to a throughput-oriented approach in which everyone must work together and focus on key leverage points.

### References

Boehm, Barry W. 1981. *Software Engineering Economics*. Englewood Cliffs, NJ: Prentice Hall.

Goldratt, Eliyahu M. 1990. *The Haystack Syndrome*. Croton-on-Hudson, NY: North River Press.

———. 1992. *The Goal*. Second Revised Edition. Croton-on-Hudson, NY: North River Press.

———. 1997. *Critical Chain*. Great Barrington, MA: North River Press.

Goldratt, Eliyahu M., and Robert E. Fox. 1986. *The Race*. Croton-on-Hudson, NY: North River Press.

Noreen, Eric, Debra Smith, and James Mackey. 1995. *The Theory of Constraints and Its Implications for Management Accounting*. Great Barrington, MA: North River Press.

Pittman, Paul Howard. 1994. *Project Management: A More Effective Methodology for the Planning and Control of Projects*. Ann Arbor, MI: University Microfilms International.

# Project Management for the Twenty-First Century: The Internet-Based Cybernetic Project Team

John Tuman, Jr., P.E., PMP, Management Technologies Group, Inc.
Pat McMackin, P.E., Management Technologies Group, Inc.

## Introduction

About every thirty to fifty years the business environment undergoes a sharp transformation. New technologies, new skills, and new values combine to significantly change the world we work in. We are at the pivotal point of just such a major transformation. The twenty-first century is upon us, and project management will be a major force in shaping the new corporate environment.

## Objectives

This paper will discuss how project management will use technology, teams, and the Internet to fashion a real-time collaborative work environment to significantly enhance our ability to manage complex undertakings. Much of the material presented in this paper is derived from ongoing work related to development of a twenty-first century project management process and philosophy. The goal of the paper is to stimulate thinking and foster new ways of applying project management concepts to the changing business environment.

## Project Management for the Twenty-First Century

### The Challenge

The future is difficult to predict, but business globalization, corporate downsizing, reengineering, partnering, and accelerated use of information technology are converging to give us a fair idea of the business environment ahead. Certainly the environment will be volatile, with organizational structures and business alliances changing frequently in response to opportunities and economic conditions in different parts of the world. Multinational project teams will be common as business becomes more globalized. In addition, managing by projects will emerge as a necessary way of handling an ever-increasing portfolio of time-sensitive critical business initiatives. The Internet will emerge as the technology to enable corporations to orchestrate a dynamic business environment, overcoming traditional barriers of time, distance, complexity, and diversity of participants. And it's probably safe to say that project management will play a significant role in corporate success in the global marketplace. To be viable in this arena, project management must forge a new process and a new philosophy that can meet the challenges of the twenty-first century. In the highly complex, competitive, global environment of the twenty-first century, project management systems must provide more powerful mechanisms for ensuring that agreed-upon goals and commitments are accomplished as planned—no excuses, no exceptions.

## Developing A No Excuses Project Management Philosophy

### Pragmatic Considerations

The ability of the project manager to monitor events, detect problems early, and initiate timely corrective action depends entirely on the information system that supports the project. In spite of vast sums spent on computers, software, networks, and support personnel, most organizations still do not have an information system that can do the job, and the problem is compounded on projects that involve many outside organizations, each with its own information system. At best, the project manager gets project-level status reports, but rarely has access to the detail needed to detect *emerging* problems early. A typical example is that of one of our recent client projects, as follows.

The project required installation of a new 69 kV to 13.8 kV substation and feeder lines at a major United States oil refinery. Transformers for the project were manufactured at the supplier's plant in Mexico. As the transformer delivery date approached, the project manager was advised that the plant was having problems meeting its schedule. Corrective action involved a trip to Mexico, overtime effort at the plant, and special handling and shipping of the transformers to the site. Examination of the shop's detailed fabrication and production schedule indicated that the problem had been in the making months before it surfaced at the project reporting level.

This situation is not unusual. Project managers are rarely in a position to drill into their vendors' or contractors' information systems to see how work at the sub-task level is progressing. Yet this is only part of the limitations in current project management systems. Project management information systems are designed to *inform* the project manager of conditions as measured against some criteria, and to *enable* the project manager to take corrective action. The systems do not force anyone to do anything—the systems are passive, and it is up to the user to decide what to do and when to do it. If the project manager is under pressure, overworked, and handling a mass of details, the information may be available but not acted on for dozens of good reasons. Project management information systems must do more than just present facts arranged in a way that informs or advises. In the twenty-first century these systems must embody a collaborative, cybernetic project management process.

### Cybernetics and Project Management

Wiener defined cybernetics as "the science of control and communication, in the animal and the machine" (1948). The word cybernetics is from the Greek for "steersman," and seems a very appropriate term to associate with project management. The concept of communication (i.e., feedback) and control has been applied to machines since the earliest days of the Industrial Revolution. Simple devices, like fly-ball governors, were some of the earliest forms of automatic control systems. Today, examples of cybernetics can be found in virtually every automated system in all areas of science, industry, and domestic life. The one domain in which there are few examples of cybernetics is management. Part of the problem is perception: we tend to think of "management" as a creative or intuitive process that does not lend itself to automation or self-control. This perception must change if we are to manage more demanding and complex undertakings in the twenty-first century. The other part of the problem is more practical, centering on the issue of communication with team members who are geographically dispersed. The Internet offers a practical solution to this problem, and with the application of cybernetic concepts to its capabilities, it is now possible to develop systems with the power to address tomorrow's projects.

### The Internet and Project Management

The global communications capabilities of the Internet are well known. It enables people to correspond by e-mail, access information from thousands of databases, display and inform through web pages, and even communicate by voice and video. Of particular significance to project management is the development of commercially available software tools that enable project participants to collaborate real-time through the Internet. These developments are significantly enhancing our ability to plan and control complex undertakings.

Currently there are more than two dozen commercially available software tools that provide collaboration capabilities over the Internet. They provide relatively inexpensive ways of using PCs to do real-time multipoint data conferencing. Participants can share applications, review and edit documents, develop and update schedules and spreadsheets, draw diagrams on electronic whiteboards, and communicate by written text, Internet telephone, and even video conferencing.

The potential to develop a cybernetic system for communicating and controlling projects in real-time regardless of where participants are located is the impetus for a twenty-first century, Internet-based project management system, which the authors are currently developing.

## Developing an Internet-Based Project Management System

### Design Philosophy

The authors' strategy for design and implementation of an Internet-based project management (IBPM) system is based on a very pragmatic philosophy. First and foremost, the technology does not have to be leading edge; in fact, the whole approach relies on what the authors term "just good enough technology." Second, the system has to be a practical tool that project participants will actually use to do their jobs; it must be easy to install, easy to learn, easy to use, and inexpensive enough for even small firms to afford. Third, the system must do more things better than existing systems; in other words, there must be a real incentive for users to switch to it. Next, the system should enable users to manage and control complex undertakings faster, at lower cost, with fewer manual interventions. Finally, the system should be a catalyst for innovation and learning. With these parameters as a guide, the authors formulated the following three-phased program.

### Phase I—Design

The IBPM system will evolve through several design iterations. Each iteration will be shaped by actual project experience; however, the fundamental system design objectives are:

- Ubiquitous: The system will be accessible to all project participants at any time and any place in the world. The Internet makes this kind of accessibility possible.
- Intuitive: Accessing information will be simple and will not require mastering complex commands or rules. Commercially available Internet browsers will be used, and computer commands will be activated by point and click actions of the mouse.
- Timely: Information in the system will reflect the actual status and situation as of the date accessed. The in-house detailed status reporting systems of participants will be linked to the project reporting system by way of corporate Intranets.
- Integrated: All information will be linked, down to the lowest task contributing to the project. Project plans and

status reports will be linked to the participants' in-house detailed work plans and reporting systems.

- Vigilant: The system will scan participants' information to detect and red flag approaching out-of-tolerance conditions of agreed upon goals, tasks, schedules, and budgets. The system will automatically generate status reports at predefined intervals.
- Proactive: When unacceptable conditions are not acted on in a specified time, the system will automatically trigger action or penalty routines to force the responsible party to respond. Punitive actions might include delay of progress payments, reduction of incentives, assignment of performance penalty points, issuance of red flag reports to senior management, and cancellation of task assignments, work orders, or contracts.

The IBPM system will be based on commercially available software tools. It will require virtually no programming and only minimal customization of existing applications.

The initial design effort is to provide the foundation to evolve a cybernetic project management system. The system will make it possible to integrate diverse organizations into a cohesive project team and enjoin the team to accomplish specific objectives on time and within budget. The goal is to provide control without having to create an information support bureaucracy. Ultimately, the system will do more than just inform—it will automatically initiate actions to ensure that project commitments are met—no excuses, no exceptions.

### Phase II—Implementation and Proof of Concept

The IBPM system will be implemented on an actual project to test the concept, demonstrate that value is added, and build the foundation for learning and future enhancements. Implementation will be done in several steps to bring participants up to proficiency at an appropriate rate of speed. Data will be collected to prove by actual comparisons how the process saves time and money and enhances effectiveness.

The implementation plan consists of the following six steps:

1. Select a Project: Select a project to demonstrate the viability of the IBPM system. Identify specific project collaborative activities required to plan and control the project. Specify the collaborative Internet tools to be used. Develop the project protocol (project manual) for managing project activities using the Internet.
2. Install the Tools: Provide each project participant with the Internet tools to be used. Ensure that every participant is working from the same baseline.
3. Train the Project Participants: Conduct training and simulations to assure that project participants understand the tools and the process.
4. Operate the Process: Manage specific aspects of the project using the IBPM system. Identify the attributes to be measured to demonstrate the value-added benefits.
5. Measure and Evaluate the Results: Collect data on an ongoing basis, measure results at regular intervals, and, with all participants, evaluate the results. Document and report on tangible, measurable cost and schedule benefits actually realized by the IBPM system.
6. Improve the Process: Capture ideas, suggestions, and lessons learned.

### Phase III—Apply Learning and Enhance Process

The final phase will be to apply the lessons learned to enhance the process in those areas that offer substantial payoff.

## Profile of an Internet-Based Project

### Overview

An Internet-based project management system is currently being developed on an actual project, involving design and construction of a major facility near Philadelphia. Project participants include the owner, project management team, architect, interior designers, civil engineer, contractors, traffic engineer, public relations consultant, legal counsel, suppliers, and vendors. The project is to be completed in three years at a cost of thirty million dollars. Some unique aspects of the project include constructing new facilities around existing structures, moving personnel between facilities during the phases of construction, and minimizing the impact on daily operations. Traffic congestion, township rezoning issues, and public concerns about the project are additional factors, making proactive communications and stakeholder management important elements of the project plan.

### System Components

As noted, the underlying IBPM design philosophy is to use "just good enough" technology, which means keep it cheap, simple, and practical. Practical means that the system is easy to use and does not place additional administrative demands on project participants. In order to get user acceptance quickly, the system must provide value without requiring users to do more than they normally would to support the project. The IBPM system is designed around standard office PCs, the Windows 95/NT 4.0 operating system, and inexpensive Internet software. The Internet software used includes Microsoft's Internet Explorer 3.02 and NetMeeting 2.0, available free of charge at the present time from Microsoft's Web site.

NetMeeting is a standards-based (ITU H.323) video conferencing, telephone, and multipoint data conferencing product for real-time collaboration on the Internet and corporate intranets. It provides a means to communicate and control project efforts in ways not possible before. For example, virtual project meetings can be held with participants at several geographic locations. Using NetMeeting, they can view, edit, update, or paste information in just about any Windows-based application in real-time, including word processing, spreadsheets, presentation graphics, and project management planning and scheduling software. Communications can be further enhanced by using the audio and video capabilities of NetMeeting.

## Utilization of an IBPM System

Internet capabilities such as e-mail are well known and widely used, so little learning or encouragement is needed to get project participants accustomed to this way of doing business. On the other hand, conducting virtual project meetings and collaborating over the Internet requires a change in mind-set and takes an extra effort to show the value of using the technology. Our experience in dealing with this issue will be discussed later. However, in our IBPM system, we envision project management communicating and controlling project activities in three fundamental ways: passive communications, active exchange, and collaboration.

### Passive Communication

Passive communication is one-way communication, wherein information is provided to all participants and stakeholders at the same time. In addition to traditional techniques, such as newsletters, posters, and flyers, Internet Web sites can be used. Interesting and colorful Web pages can be constructed to give an understanding of all aspects of the project. Some more ambitious Web sites may enable the visitor to walk the project by way of three dimensional graphics, allow comments or questions by e-mail, or even encourage downloading of files and graphics of interest. We have found that this form of communications is relatively inexpensive and an effective way to gauge stakeholder interest in the project.

### Active Exchange

Active exchange provides a way for project participants to access and file project information at any time and from any place in the world where there are Internet capabilities. Typically, the project establishes an Internet server and protocols to enable project participants to view, download, or update project files. Obviously, strict file management and security protection schemes must be enforced to protect the project.

On our project, active exchange activities encompass:

- Project Progress Reports: The project manager issues progress reports to the project's Web site. Web pages display the cost, schedules, and technical status of the project, as well as other items of interest. Video clips are used to show site activities and conditions. Schedules show progress to-date, and the CPM identifies task relationships, task owners, and the current critical path. Cost information is given in Excel spreadsheets and budget curves show plan versus actual. Other information is presented in Microsoft Word or visually in Microsoft PowerPoint. Project participants are responsible for reviewing progress reports, taking action in their areas of responsibility, and providing up-to-date information.
- Participant's Weekly Status Reports: Timely reporting is key to spotting emerging problems early enough to deal with them before they become crises; however, most participants view reporting as an administrative burden to be avoided as much as possible. One way to deal with this is to keep the reporting simple and make it a logical product of the participant's own management effort.

Project participants are encouraged to link their internal management systems to provide output directly to project reporting templates. The templates are pre-formatted Word documents, Excel spreadsheets, Microsoft Project schedules, Access databases, and PowerPoint presentations. In many cases, participants can easily provide detailed, timely reports by importing and exporting file information between their internal management systems and the project Internet server-based information system.

### Collaboration

Using the Internet to collaborate is a practical way to significantly reduce one of the major bottlenecks to effective and uniform project planning and control. For the first time, project participants can communicate and share information despite incompatible computer systems, because the Internet puts everyone on the same information platform. Examples of collaboration in our IBPM system are as follows:

#### *Project Planning Meetings*

Team-based project planning is the key to project commitment. Team members forge strong personal bonds when they work together to define project objectives, strategy, scope, schedules, budgets, and risk issues. On many projects, however, geographic separation and cost constraints make it difficult to get everyone involved to contribute to project planning. Now, using the Internet and a IBPM approach, project managers can facilitate planning meetings and have the participants participate effectively at very low cost.

In our project, the project manager develops a project plan outline and e-mails it to all participants, along with the agenda for the project planning meeting. At the appointed time, the team assembles in a virtual project meeting via the Internet and NetMeeting. By sharing Windows-based applications, they proceed to define the project objectives, scope of work,

work breakdown structure, responsibility matrix, summary schedule, budget, and significant assumptions and risk issues. Several virtual planning meetings may be required, but in each session the participants gain a more complete understanding of their responsibilities, as well as of the responsibilities and problems of their fellow team members. The only time team members need to actually meet is for the signing ceremony, where they and the sponsor demonstrated their commitment by signing the project plan.

#### *Document review and approval meetings*

Document review has always been a laborious and time-consuming process, with documents being sent back and forth (by traditional or electronic mail) several times before being finalized. Now, using the collaboration capabilities of NetMeeting, a document can be viewed and edited in real-time to achieve a final version in one or two meetings. The document can then be filed in a project database accessible to all participants. This feature is particularly useful when it is necessary to refer to a contract, specification, or procedure to quickly answer a question or resolve a problem.

#### *Schedule review and update meetings*

Keeping all participants aligned and focused on accomplishing the project goal is a major effort. Project participants must give clear and accurate schedule progress reports, so that the project manager can synthesize their inputs to assess total project progress. More importantly, trends and emerging issues that can negatively impact progress have to be identified and dealt with as soon as possible. By the same token, opportunities for enhancing the project should also be identified and capitalized on quickly.

Our project uses Windows-based project management software to construct the project CPM and to present and update it in virtual schedule review meetings. We have used Microsoft Project and Primavera Project Planner and find that both work well with NetMeeting. By using NetMeeting, participants do not need to have the applications on their computers, and in many cases they do not even need to know how to use the applications. By sharing applications on the project manager's computer, participants can be coached to provide the needed information.

#### *Problem solving meetings*

As experienced project managers know, problems tend to happen at the worst possible time. Typically, problem solving means setting up a meeting and having participants drop other duties to travel to a distant location, with valuable time lost getting there. Team members may arrive tired, not in the best frame of mind to deal with complex issues, and then find that they do not have all the information or expertise needed to solve the problem. This means that more time is lost (and expenses continue to mount) until the necessary information and expertise can be brought to bear. This situation will change dramatically as the IBPM system is used to attack project problems.

Virtual problem solving meetings can be organized so that expertise can be focused on the problem, regardless of where in the world the expertise is located. Information can be assembled and presented to the participants so they can examine and manipulate it in real-time. To facilitate understanding, actual physical conditions can be viewed by video, and data and reports can be viewed in separate windows beside graphic or pictorial images to provide further insight. Simulations can be constructed and tested for all participants to witness at the same time, and iterative solutions can be explored and discussed until consensus is attained and decisions are made.

#### *Telecommuting*

In addition to shortening the time to solve problems, update information, review documents, and develop project plans, collaboration can also save money by significantly reducing travel. Even when travel is required, team members can keep in touch by e-mail, file sharing, and data-conferencing. It is important to emphasize that virtual meetings do not eliminate the need for people to meet face-to-face, and, in fact, in this age of electronic communication the need for human interaction may be more important than ever. Still, virtual meetings can reduce the number of trips required to deal with low value-added activities.

## Change Management Issues

Enhancing project management's ability to manage complex undertakings requires changing the prevailing mind set. This is especially difficult for experienced project managers. Project management is now a recognized profession with a well-developed body of knowledge, a certification process, and a proven track record for getting things done. Hence, project practitioners naturally think and operate within the existing project management paradigm.

Changing the way people work is always difficult especially if it involves using new technology. Getting a project team to plan and manage their project over the Internet requires that participants not only learn a new technology, but also learn how to interact with each other through this new medium. However, our experience shows that this problem is somewhat similar to that of getting people to accept and use answering machines, voice mail, and fax machines. Initially, many people resisted using these new communication tools; people would actually hang up rather than talk to an answering machine. However, as time passed people learned the value of the technology and made it a normal part of their working world. We fully expect that IBPM systems will transition through a similar life cycle.

## Summary

Information technology is transforming organizational structures, work processes, business relationships, and people's responsibilities in a very dramatic way. Organizational structures and alliances are changing frequently in response to global competition. More demands are being placed on employees at every level to assume a broader range of responsibilities, take charge and make decisions about their work, and to be more responsive to changing needs and conditions. Organizations in virtually every arena of endeavor are embracing project-oriented teams to deal with the volatility of the global environment. The key to success in this project-driven world is communication and control systems that enable teams to amalgamate their capabilities quickly, easily, and at relatively low cost. An IBPM system constructed around commercially available software and the Internet can position project management to be a viable force in the twenty-first century.

### References

Wiener, N. 1948. *Cybernetics.* Wiley.

# It's Gonna Be A Jungle Out There Managing Projects in Project Unfriendly Cultures How to Survive and Thrive in the Next Century

F. Douglas DeCarlo, Project Management Consultant & Coach, ICS Group

## We Haven't Seen Anything Yet: The Project Unfriendly Culture

If you think you're stretched thin now, just wait. As we move into the twenty-first century, yes, even greater demands will be placed on project managers to do more, do it faster, and use fewer resources. Fueled by accelerating competitive forces, the pace of globalization of projects will escalate. Compounding these challenges, project teams will become increasingly more dispersed, diverse, and difficult to manage and to gain team member commitment.

## The Impact

- At the business level: projects that are substantially more complex to manage and control resulting in higher risk.
- At the personal level: greater demands on the project manager's well being, family, and quality of life in general.

## To the Rescue: Methodology and Technology?

The school book approach might be to focus our efforts on trying to tame the jungle by energetically adopting new project management methodologies and supporting technologies including the latest advances in groupware, teamware, and PM software.

Yes, mastery of project management technologies and methodologies will facilitate the project manager's safari through the jungle . . .but alone will not provide safe passage.

After all, if the project is a success and our personal, family, and work lives are emotionally bankrupt, what have we gained?

## It's Not the Jungle We'll Have to Tame, It's Ourselves

The next century will put a premium on back to basics . . . challenging us to redirect our energies to focus on those things that are within our power to change. The fact is that we can't change the competitive scene, the course of globalization, or that projects will become increasingly complex.

What can we change? To borrow a concept from Steven Covey's book, *The Seven Habits of Highly Successful People*, the place to start is to clearly understand the difference between one's circle of concern versus one's circle of influence.

### Circle of Concern

Included in my circle of concern are things over which I have little or no ability to change. A few examples are:

- The price of soy beans
- The economy
- The weather
- My organization's culture not being conducive to getting projects done
- What the competition does.

All too often we see project teams bemoaning and dwelling upon those realities that are outside their sphere of influence. When a team starts to act this way, it starts to give up its power to get things done. Why? because unless and until that something outside of the team changes, the team is powerless (literally has less power) to do what has to be done. The focus of the team's energies shifts to things over which it can do little or nothing. Energy is sapped. By taking a reactive approach, the team soon adopts a defeatist attitude as its modus operandi, which becomes a self-fulfilling prophecy. This is called responding with disability, the opposite of taking responsibility (i.e., responding with ability).

And, when all is said and done, one is still expected to get the project completed successfully.

### Circle of Influence

The trick is to not lose sight of one's circle of influence, or those areas over which one can have a direct impact. Examples include:

- My health and wealth
- Personal and team stress
- Gaining commitment and mutual accountability among team members
- My *response* to events over which I have no control
- Project risk.

**Exhibit 1.** The Ten Laws of the Jungle

| CHALLENGES INTENSIFIED IN THE 21st CENTURY | THE 10 LAWS OF THE JUNGLE INVOLVE: | PERSONAL MANDATE | TEAM MANDATE |
|---|---|---|---|
| Focus, clarity of mission, reason for being, commitment | 1 Purpose | Identifying your life's purpose | Developing a solid business case and cogent project mission statement |
| Motivation, sense of common destiny, mutual accountability | 2. Vision | Creating your ideal work/life style | Creating and experiencing success before the project starts |
| Risk minimization, stress, quality of life | 3. Fear | Conquering personal fear | Building a solid foundation for risk management |
| Loss of self esteem, team efficacy, stress, quality of life | 4. Attitude | Ability to survive and prosper under any circumstances | Proactively managing the project nemesis and supporters |
| Project being pulled in multiple directions, maintaining organizational support | 5. Assertiveness | Not committing acts of self-betrayal | Establishing norms for the project sponsor and functional managers |
| Managing diversity, dispersed teams, effective communication | 6. Conflict | Quickly resolving internal and one-on-one conflict | Establishing team operating and meeting norms |
| Managing complexity, dispersed decision-making, speed, gaining mutual accountability | 7. Empowerment | Knowing how to pull your own strings | Unleashing each team member's potential |
| Innovation | 8. Reflection | Opening up the right brain and the no-brain | Conducting continuous project assessment |
| Speed, building momentum, staying on course, changing direction fast | 9. Action | Getting oneself to take needed action | Enabling the team to take constructive action, to win |
| Ability to move on to the next task or project | 10. Acceptance | Not being in an adversarial relationship with oneself | Embracing project failure and success |

In the twenty-first century (and we already are seeing this), the successful team leader will continually focus the team's energies on those areas where the team is power-full (and not power-less). This then, is the proactive approach which expands the team's circle of influence and drives out negative (reactive) energy and improves the likelihood of success.

The Serenity Prayer sums it up nicely: "Grant us the serenity to accept the things we can't change, the courage to change the things we can, and the wisdom to know the difference."

### Expanding One's Circle of Influence Is the Goal

Expanding one's circle of influence means mastering the inner game of project management as embodied in The Three Secrets and Ten Laws of the Jungle. These focus on the mindset, attitudes, and internal qualities that project managers and their teams will need to adopt in order to thrive in the project jungle, while avoiding both project *and* personal quicksand.

## A Template

The author has refined these secrets and laws in his work with project team members, leaders, and sponsors representing over 125 project teams from Beijing, China, to Bethlehem, Pennsylvania. Projects have included software development, information systems design, new product introductions, continuous improvement, reengineering, and construction with budgets ranging in size from $500,000 to $25 million.

The secrets and laws serve as a template for success because they enable the team to move ahead despite external circumstances.

## The First Secret

### *The goal is to flourish (not merely to get out alive)*

Given the complexities of projects and the associated high risk factors, team members can easily feel overwhelmed and over their heads, with no clear path in sight to take them through the jungle. It's easy to succumb to the temptation to adopt a fatality mindset of "I'll be happy to get out of this one alive." A team that starts off feeling half-defeated or is running scared greatly increases the risk of ever getting the project done.

The challenge of the team leader is to communicate to the team that the goal is not mere survival; it is to prosper and to be better off no matter what the outcome of the project, even if the project fails.

### *The ten laws of the jungle*

The laws respond to the challenges that will be intensified as we move toward the twenty-first century when project teams will be faced with accelerated global competition. The successful team leader will walk the talk by applying these laws to both himself and within the team. Each law serves to expand the leader's and team's circle of influence.

## The Second Secret

### *The Outside = The Inside*

One of the big traps in the project jungle is to think that the jungle (the competition, the project unfriendly organization) is at fault for our difficulties. Feeling powerless results in depression.

Faced with unexpected events that bombard the project, the twenty-first century team leader will be continually challenged to avoid the victim syndrome and enable the team to do the same. That means making the critical distinction between an event that happened versus one's *attitude* about the event. The effective team leader will constantly shift the team's mindset from one of seeing the glass half empty to half full. It's still the same vessel with liquid inside, but it's seen in a new light.

Attitudes *can* be changed instantly. The next time you look out the window on a gloomy day, put on a pair of rose colored glasses. Notice how your outlook changes (even though the clouds are still out there.)

A quote from the *Talmud* reminds the team and the team leader that "We see things not the way they are, but the way we are." In other words, the outside equals the inside.

## The Third Secret

### *You don't need permission*

Faced with new challenges, the effective twenty-first century project manager will need to take the time to master the inner game of project management. That means taking steps to start embracing the three secrets and applying the ten laws.

The good news: To put these secrets and laws into action you don't have to wait for anything or anyone outside of you to change. You can start right now, even before you read the next sentence. Or not. Because nobody is coming to the rescue. And that's also good news because you don't have to depend on anybody else to get started. It will be up to each of us to take responsibility, meaning to respond with ability (or disability). It's a choice. Because in the project jungle of the twenty-first century, there will be no victims, only volunteers.

# Leveraging the Internet and the Intranet in the Project Management Process

Michael Grice, Ernst & Young LLP
Mel P. Barracliffe, Ernst & Young LLP
Sandy VanderHulst, Ernst & Young LLP

## Introduction

Our desire to continuously improve the project management process in the hopes of ensuring the success of the projects we manage has prompted us to invent, or utilize, various tools and technologies. The goals in using these tools have been to make the project management process less complex, less error prone, quicker to execute, and repeatable. Taking a historical view we can see as a classic example the invention of the Gantt chart as a graphical means to communicate schedule and its evolution as a sophisticated component of project management tools like Microsoft Project.

The development of technology to support the project management process can be characterized as an evolution. The hand crafting of project plans using various techniques (such as the Gantt chart, estimating heuristics, budget calculations, and resource optimization) gradually gave way to mainframe and mini-computer systems. These systems helped to reduce the labor required of the project manager, but were not readily accessible or simple to use, nor did they contribute significantly to the improvement of the project management process. The advent of personal computers allowed the development of sophisticated project management tools that were simple to use and very project manager centric. This evolution has certainly contributed to the achievement of our goals of reducing complexity, incidence of errors, and time to execute in terms of the techniques a project manager uses, but it is questionable what contribution has been made to the overall project management process.

As we move closer to the turn of the century, project managers will need to deal increasingly with projects that span the geographical continuum from local to global, the financial continuum from thousands of dollars to several hundred million, and the resource continuum from one person to several hundred. Coupled with this wide range of individual project characteristics that must be dealt with is the increasing interconnectedness of projects. In this context many individual project managers are required to act as one. In this paper we will argue that the future of project management will require tools and technology that embrace a process that can be utilized by individual project managers executing discrete components of work through to multiple project managers directing large scale programs of work.

From a process point of view we have *A Guide to the Project Management Body of Knowledge (PMBOK Guide)* definitions (integration, scope, time, cost, quality, human resources, communications, risk, and procurement) that give us the foundations of a project management process. The ubiquitous presence of the Internet, and its younger sibling—the intranet—in the nineties provides an ideal opportunity for project management to adopt a technology that can enable the project management process. This opportunity will be particularly valuable in the future when as project managers we will need to communicate with each other and the members of our project teams across a broad range of temporal and geographical considerations.

In this paper we will present an Internet model that is being adopted by Ernst & Young LLP to implement our project management process using a combination of people, process, and technology enablers.

## Background to Ernst & Young and the Challenges Faced

Ernst & Young is characterized as a "big six" accounting firm. While accounting, audit, and tax services form a large part of Ernst & Young's business, a significant portion belongs to the management consulting arm. Over 10,500 professionals worldwide perform management consulting assignments. The charter of the management consulting practice is to contribute to the long-term success and competitive strength of clients by helping clients to identify solutions that improve performance, by providing assistance to implement those solutions, and by aiding the client in the management of the subsequent change.

The services we provide and the industry segments served are shown in Exhibit 1.

The diversity of services and industry segments suggests that there is a significant challenge in implementing a consistent approach to the work that we perform. Our solution to the challenge is to view each project in terms of an integrated focus; this focus considers the interaction of people, business

**Exhibit 1.** Ernst & Young Services and Industry Segments

| Ernst & Young Management Consulting Services | Industry Segments Served |
|---|---|
| Reengineering<br>Information technology services, including:<br>Systems strategy<br>Systems development & integration<br>Systems planning and delivery<br>Outsourcing<br>Business change implementation, including:<br>Organization change management<br>Organization alignment<br>Knowledge management<br>Planning & improvement portfolio development<br>Performance measurement | Energy<br>Financial Services<br>Health Care<br>Insurance<br>Manufacturing<br>Real Estate & Construction<br>Retail and Consumer Products<br>Technology, Communications & Entertainment |

**Exhibit 2.** The SPARCC Process

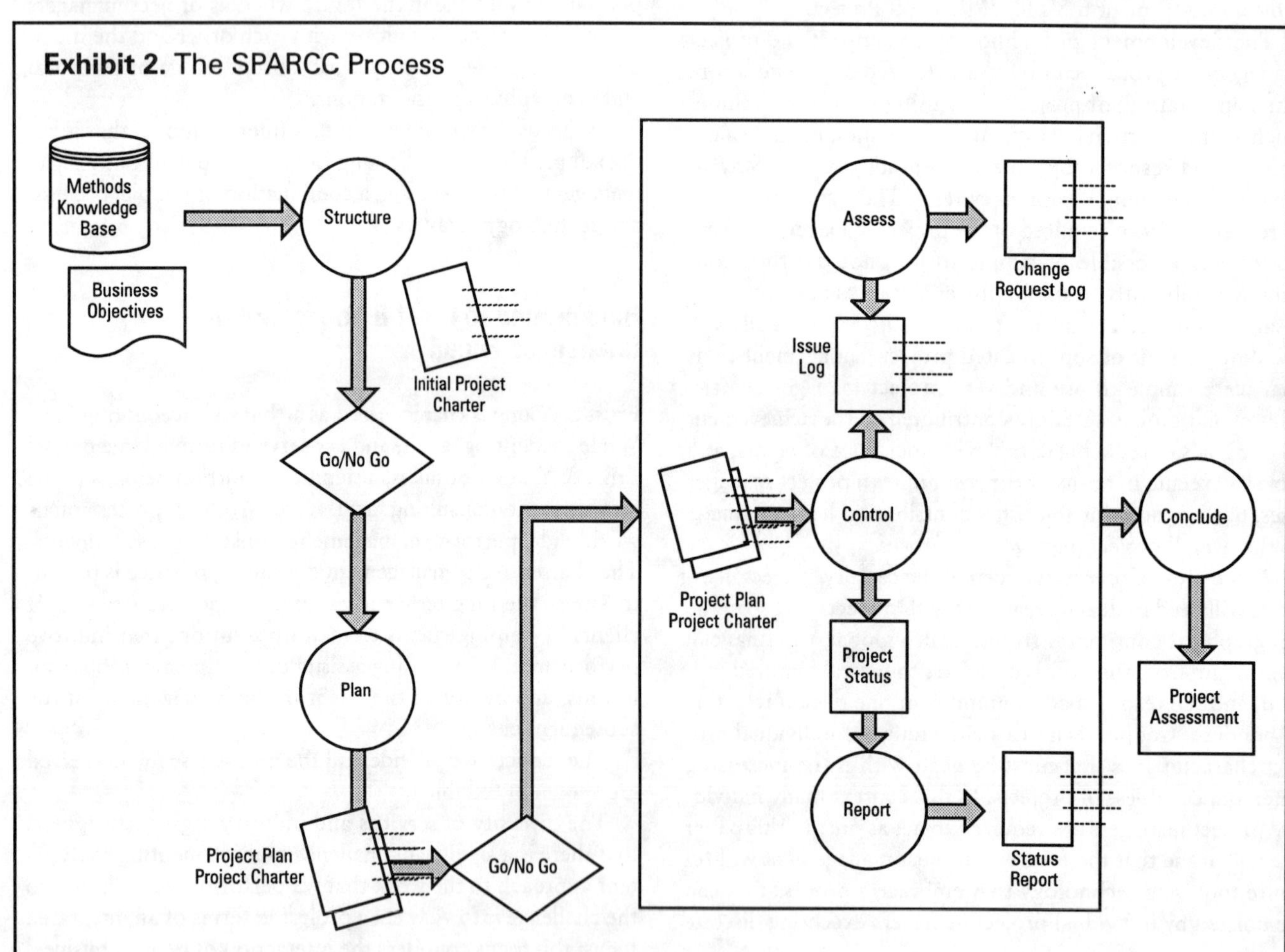

processes, and technology that must be in place to attain the business objectives. Regardless of the type of service provided or the industry segment served, the interaction of people, process, and technology provides a unifying theme across all projects.

The people, process, and technology framework provides a high-level context within which work is performed. To manage the actual work Ernst & Young developed the SPARCC project management process (Exhibit 2). SPARCC encompasses the dimensions within a project of Structuring, Planning, Assessing Change, Reporting, Controlling and Concluding. There is a correlation between the PMBOK process and SPARCC, however this is yet to be formally integrated in our overall method (an issue which we hope to address in the near future). All project managers are trained in the SPARCC process and are expected to manage projects according to its guidelines.

Consultants have access to a rich methodology, which describes the techniques to use when developing collateral in a project. The methodology is organized from both a process and deliverable perspective, which allows the consultant to obtain guidance at different levels of granularity. For example, a consulting team that is reengineering an organization's business processes would use the "business process innovation route map" to determine how the project will be structured and what types of deliverables will be produced. A small team of consultants may be charged with performing a "current state assessment" of the existing business processes. The method provides guidance on how this deliverable is structured and what to do to produce it. The Ernst & Young methodology is known internally as the Fusion Series? and is available commercially as the Navigator Systems Series®.

Clearly, there are several challenges that we face related to the type of work we perform and the support we provide to our project teams. The issues that we have sought to address in the past, and will continue to address in the future, include:

- Evolution and distribution of the methodology
- Knowledge leverage across projects
- Provision of technology frameworks to execute and manage work
- Support for increased globalization of projects
- Providing project management solutions that are scalable.

To address these issues we use the same integration focus employed with our clients—people, process, and technology. To maintain our position as leading provider of consulting services, it is clear that we must invest heavily in our people. This translates to hiring talented individuals that, with appropriate training and experience, will contribute to the diverse skill mix required to deliver value to our clients. Our process as embodied in the methodology is highly regarded. It has taken many man-years of effort and substantial investment for the methodology to reach the level of maturity it exhibits. As the business environment evolves and the needs of our client base change so too must the methodology. Continued investment in the evolution of the methodology is a given. With the commitment to people and process in place, the role of technology as an enabler will be explored.

## The Technology Evolution in the Project Management Process

Although the theme of this paper is to look forward and describe the initiatives we are taking to position our project management process into the twenty-first century, it is worthwhile to briefly describe the journey we have taken thus far. This will serve to illustrate the issues that we hope to address in the next evolution of the project management process.

### Pre-History (circa 1990 and Earlier)

The project management process in this period can be characterized as one with little technology support. Process support existed in the form of handbooks spanning multiple bookshelves. Knowledge reuse between projects was a case of knowing someone who had done it before. Consequently much reinvention of project collateral took place. Tool support was minimal, with possibly some project planning performed with early PC tools. Most projects developed homegrown solutions to assist in the management of the process, using whatever technology was available within the project. Project managers were responsible for maintaining communication within a project and between projects, resulting in much time spent in face-to-face meetings. Projects existed in environments that were isolated from each other.

### The Workstation Era (circa 1992)

It had long been recognized that better tools were needed to support project teams. The development of the automated methods environment (AME) toolkit was the first significant attempt to use technology to enable the project management process and provide better access to methodology. The AME provided automated assistance with project structuring and planning activities. Using the methodology as a knowledge base, project managers could generate workplans and project charters, which they had customized from a generic framework. The methodology itself was available online, allowing team members to access support for the processes and deliverables they were responsible for. A formalized process of knowledge collection began at this time, laying the foundation for greater reuse of collateral between projects.

While this development was a major step forward, some earlier problems were yet to be addressed, and new problems surfaced. Projects continued to operate in isolated environments.

The toolkit provided some elementary workgroup support; however the technical infrastructure required made the implementation prohibitive in most cases. The methodology had previously been restricted to physical handbooks stored in relatively few locations. The electronic version of the methodology was now distributed to almost all consultants. While this increased accessibility to the methodology, the complexity of releasing new versions became several orders of magnitude greater.

### The Workgroup Era (circa 1995 to Now)

The advent of workgroup technology such as Lotus Notes provided the opportunity to address some of the gaps left by the AME. Support for communication between team members had been realized with the introduction of electronic mail. However, the workgroup databases provided a common space for project teams to share collateral and to collaboratively manage the project. In essence the workgroup database provided a repository for project materials and the automation of issue and change management. This shared space maintained a history of the project that was particularly useful when new team members joined a project and for evaluating results at the project's conclusion. The technology itself could scale from one project to many. Individual projects could customize the database to their needs. Access was transparent across geographical boundaries, drawing to a close the isolation of projects characterized in earlier times.

The workgroup databases still required significant technical infrastructure. If the infrastructure were not available at the client site then project teams would have to rely on remote access to databases located within Ernst & Young. Remote access facilities and system response time often caused project teams to abandon this approach, if indeed it was considered at all. When the workgroup solution was applied it proved to be a seductive one, resulting in the proliferation of databases. Consolidating these databases is a formidable problem, particularly when many project teams customized these databases beyond recognition. The methodology access and distribution issues were not resolved; process support was still provided by the AME.

## Looking Forward—The Development of Project Webs

Previous technology implementations of the project management process have yielded reasonable results. However, our goal is to address the issues identified previously and at the same time provide a platform that will accommodate future requirements. Several principles have been identified for the next evolution of technology support for the project management process. They are as follows.

#### *Decentralization*

Projects increasingly operate without a defined center of control. Teams may be split across functional areas and geographical locations. In this context, support for collaboration becomes vital.

#### *Minimal Infrastructure*

Deploying additional technology infrastructure is a logistical problem given the number of consulting staff in the firm. Consultants have to deal with a multitude of tools in performing their work; therefore, the impact to their desktops must be minimized.

#### *Ease of Use*

Project teams should be able to integrate the technology quickly and with minimal training. The technology should not become an excuse for sidestepping the project management process.

#### *Access to Knowledge*

The wealth of knowledge stored in the firm and both methodology and exemplar work products should be integrated with the project management process. The technology that supports the project space should encompass the disparate information sources that project teams need to draw on and provide access to it on a "just in time" basis.

#### *Scalability*

The technology solution must be able to transparently scale across small, medium, and large project teams. The solution should support the growth of projects over time.

Selection of Internet technology as the basis for implementing the next evolution of the project management process came about when we considered the principles of decentralization and minimal infrastructure. Internet capability is rapidly expanding within the firm. Consultant desktops have World Wide Web browsers installed and can connect to the Internet from any office or anywhere that a telephone line is available. Basing the solution on the World Wide Web mitigates the impact on consultant machines and will allow collaboration regardless of where the consultant is located. The ubiquity of the Internet suggests that in many cases we will be able to leverage our solution on top of existing infrastructure at the client sites where work is performed, thus reducing the overhead required to get started.

The development of Internet technology has been watched closely at Ernst & Young. Several internal projects and external products (see for example http: //www.ey.com and http: //ernie.ey.com) have allowed us to build skills in the development of Internet and intranet applications. Our experience has shown that productive solutions can be deployed relatively

**Exhibit 3.** The Project Web

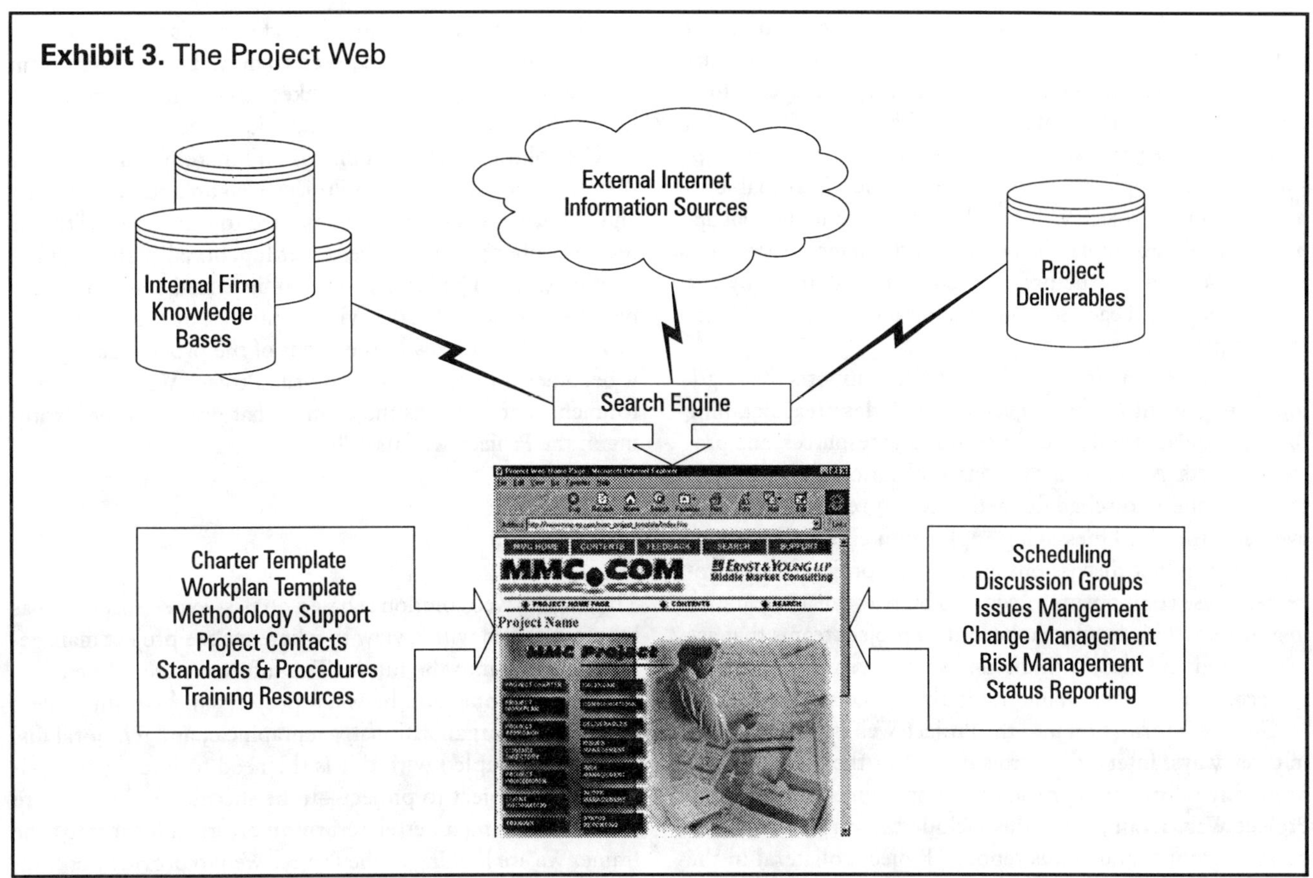


quickly and that these solutions can evolve as the needs of the target audience change. Of particular interest to us is the ability to incrementally evolve solutions. This provides the opportunity to deliver process support and knowledge "just in time." If a section of the method is revised it can be made accessible to the target audience immediately. In the past, revisions would have to be timed to coincide with a static release model that occurred once a quarter.

Internet technology becomes increasingly relevant as more information becomes addressable (through URLs) and desktop products evolve to include web extensions. These developments allow objects related to projects to be easily linked together and for project collateral to be published to the web by desktop tools.

### The Project Web Concept

We have developed a web-based model of project management, which is based on past experience, current Internet capability, and anticipated future developments. This model is aligned to the principles described above and has been realized in the form of a prototype, which will be employed by a number of projects. Exhibit 3 depicts the components that the Project Web encompasses.

The Project Web is based on the notion of a common space for project collaboration that began with the earlier workgroup technology. The key difference is that the Project Web provides a single entry point to project tools and processes that previously were spread among different applications. Search engines built into the Project Web provide the capability to retrieve information from a disparate range of sources. Information stored within the Project Web itself (for example, collateral in the form of deliverables, process support in the form of unstructured text) can be searched. Knowledge objects stored within a variety of databases inside the firm are becoming addressable and may be queried using standard Internet search engines. The external Internet holds a vast array of information, which may be accessed through any of the freely available search services (for example, Yahoo, Alta Vista, Excite, and so on).

The functionality built into the Project Web encompasses all of the components of SPARCC except the conclude process. The structure and plan components are enabled through charter and work-plan templates, which are used to create the specific project charters and work-plans. The assess and control components are enabled through applications that maintain logs of issues, risks, and change requests. The report component is enabled through status reporting applications that allow individual team members to report status and for the project manager to aggregate this information into a project status report. Although the conclude process is not formally implemented, the Project Web itself is an input to the process. All of the SPARCC components are supported through the methodology, which is available to browse on the Project Web or is built into the individual applications. For example, the project charter template steps the user through the structure of a charter as defined by the methodology and each section contains abbreviated guidance for completion.

Other functionality in the Project Web supports the ongoing management of the project and includes areas detailing project standards and procedures, training resources, and project contacts. A common calendar application allows project team members to schedule meetings and record important events. A threaded messaging application allows the project team to conduct discussions around the project. Taken together, these components provide visibility to what is going on in a project. This is of great benefit to project teams that are distributed and also for individuals who are not part of the project team but have an interest in the projects development.

Getting information into the Project Web is accomplished in three ways. Interactive forms that allow the user to create or modify information provide the simplest mechanism in the Project Web. Examples of this include the various logs, discussion groups, and status reports. Project collateral in the form of deliverables (usually documents or applications) can be attached to the Project Web via an electronic submission process. The final method allows the user to publish information to the Project Web directly so that information is accessible as a series of pages. An example of this would be the publication of project standards and procedures. Various publishing tools are available that provide this capability (for example, Microsoft FrontPage), and standard desktop applications are beginning to incorporate extensions that allow publication of material to the web (for example, Microsoft Word). Our goal is to provide tools that make it as easy for the user to publish information to the web as it is for them to produce hardcopy print.

### Supporting reusable and scalable solutions

Providing the Project Web to enable our project management process moves us to the next level in terms of technology support. However, the most significant advantage is the leverage that can be provided by using Project Webs as a means to encourage reusability. The content of a Project Web can be readily packaged as a group of files that is then transportable. Therefore, as more projects are conducted through the Project Web environment, a library can be established that allows successive projects to build on what has gone before. We envisage a web repository that allows individual projects to be searched based on a set of characteristics specified by the user. The infrastructure required to move Project Webs from place to place is minimal and takes advantage of capabilities inherent in the technology already deployed.

The solution has scalability as an inherent characteristic. A single user may operate a Project Web on a standalone machine. A small team may be connected to each other with one team member providing the server functionality through her own machine. The large and often dispersed team may connect to a dedicated server via an intranet or the Internet. A Project Web can grow as the needs of the project team grow; it becomes a matter of hosting the Project Web in an environment that supports the team at that point in time. Nothing in the Project Web itself has to change.

## Conclusions

The Project Web solution is based on past experiences but has been conceived with a view to where we see project management moving into the future. The future we see is one of increased disconnection between projects and within project teams due to organizational, geographical, and temporal distribution. Coupled with this is the need to leverage knowledge from project to project—to be successful in the future means achieving a better return on effort in a shorter time frame. We are looking to the Project Web to provide the common thread that binds disconnected projects and teams together. It is the shared space where all may participate. At the same time, the Project Web will provide "memory" so that others may build on the past and achieve greater success in the future.

# Corporate Pathfinders: The Future of Project Management?

David S. Thompson, Project Management Alliance, LLC

## Introduction

As today's project managers prepare for the next century, perhaps the only real certainty is continued and rapid change, which promises to redefine our professional careers on an ongoing basis. As with explorers of the past, today's project managers find themselves blazing new trails within corporate cultures, facing uncertainties and challenges that require a multitude of skill sets. By the advent of the 21st century, prudent observation would indicate that project management, as we know it today, will have passed through its period of visibility as the latest *popular management approach* to dealing with the business complexities of today and tomorrow. This paper presents the concept of "corporate pathfinders"; a proposed model of how the field of project management will adapt and change to the business conditions of the next century. The model presented herein proposes that businesses will come to the realization that successful management in the 21st Century will be based upon an integrated combination of management skills that draw from a number of traditional academic pursuits.

## Background

The inspiration for this article came from a seminar I attended at last year's PMI Annual Symposium in Boston, MA. This seminar, entitled "MOBP—Managing Organizations By Project: The Cutting Edge of Management," presented by Paul C. Dinsmore, drew my interest based upon Mr. Dinsmore's 1996 *PM Network* articles regarding the concept of MOBP. At this seminar, the audience seemed to be pondering the same questions I was. The general question raised was, *"What's next in the field of Project Management?"* which subsequently stimulated the audience for their visions of the future of project management. No clear answers were derived from the ensuing audience discussions. One comment in particular began my thought process resulting in this paper. The comment raised was that the American Society of Quality Control (ASQC) had enjoyed substantial growth and interest in its membership (Quality Professionals) during the 1880s and has since faded from the forefront of management interest in the 1990s. As we now recognize, management's interest in Quality methods in the 1980s, then considered to be "the cutting edge of management," has gone the way of Management by Objective (MOB) and other popular management theories before it.

This is not to say that these management theories did not provide valuable contributions to the furtherance of management theory. Each, in their own way, left contributions that have withstood the test of time. Consider that objectives, work process definition, performance measurement, teamwork, and worker empowerment (to name a few) are alive and well in the 1990s with no indication that they will leave the realm of current management theory any time soon. These contributions have, for the most part, become internalized within the corporate culture such that their recognition as new and novel management approaches has faded into a standard operating practice. This is good news! As with the free enterprise market system, businesses will ultimately decide the value of various management approaches introduced over time.

The question now becomes "What will history record as the contribution of the field of project management?" Perhaps the concept and methodology of Earned Value, Activity-Based Costing, and effective Cross-Functional Team Management? Time, and corporate internalization of these methods, such that they fade from novelty, will be the deciding factor.

The results of my contemplations over the past year are presented below, with the intent not to fully answer this question, but to offer a perspective based upon what we know today. The model presented herein suggests that more and more businesses will come to the realization that *successful management will be based upon an integrated combination of management skills that draw from a number of traditional academic pursuits including, business, engineering, and the humanities*. At the core of this integrated model are the concepts of: Corporate Pathfinders, Enterprise-wide Planning, Strategic Performance Measurements, and Cross-Functional Teams.

## The More Things Change ...

The old adage that "the more things change, the more they stay the same" seems to hold true. Today, no doubt, we are inundated by change on a revolutionary scale, precipitated by the seemingly endless advance of technological innovation and business globalization. With all of this change happening so fast, we sometimes lose track of those things, which tend

**Exhibit 1.** Things Changing and Not Changing

| Things Changing (much) | Things Not Changing (much) |
|---|---|
| Market Globalization | Business Profitability Objectives |
| Technological Innovation | Business Productivity Objectives |
| Cultural Diversity Tolerance | Business Management Hierarchies |
| Career Stability | Maslow's Hierarchy of Needs |
| Needs for Professional Development | Traditional Academic subjects |

not to fundamentally change over time. Exhibit 1 summarizes "things changing" and "things remaining fairly unchanged."

The point to be made here is that in these times of rapid change, we have a basic set of core "things" on which we can rely for time-tested guidance. Whether the latest cutting-edge management theories and methods are real or perceived is really a matter of marketing. To attain universal recognition as "cutting edge" requires two ingredients: market demand, and effective marketing. Think marketing is not important? Think again. Marketing is the bridge between consumer demand and business opportunity. When marketing is overdone, however, hype ensues, eventually being replaced by consumer burnout.

To place this point into perspective, a general burnout has occurred in today's workforce regarding being inundated with management gurus and "management by best seller." A recent *Fortune* magazine series on management gurus highlights this consumer burnout by discussing the management fads of the past several decades. The article titled "In Search of Suckers" states that "by the 1970s, every ingredient essential to what we now know as 'gurudom' existed, except for the spark to ignite our interest in what the gurus had to say, namely, fear." In the 1970s this spark—fear—was provided by Japan as they began beating the pants off American businesses. The author goes on to say that a new attitude emerged in American businesses, "Somebody, somewhere, knows how to do business—but it isn't us." Ahhh yes, market demand!

The primary drivers behind today's adoption of project management methods are *the increasing rate of technological change; increasing pressures to reduce product/service time-to-market; increasing demands for worker empowerment, cross-functionality, and productivity; work process measurement/improvement; and the increasing trend to outsource non-strategic enterprise work*. All of these drivers call for *new management strategies, systems and skills* that can be integrated into the culture of an enterprise, such that enterprise-wide planning, performance measurement, and control can be achieved in a cost-effective manner.

## At Issue, The Corporate Culture

Recently, several industry-specific terms have been coined to describe a particular industry's approach to modern project management methods. These terms are Enterprise-wide Planning (manufacturing industry), Integrated or Concentric® Project Management (engineering/construction industries), and in a generic sense, "Managing Organizations by Projects" or MOBP, all of which can be summarily defined in the context of their shared theme. The shared theme is: *breaking work down into specifically defined terms of scope, schedule and cost, using advances in technology to better manage business goals and performance objectives.*

Historically (from the time of the Roman Empire), businesses have sought efficiency and productivity gains through refining their organizational hierarchies, often by increasing the segmentation (increasing "niche" expertise) within the enterprise. Over the past three decades, however, led by advances in technology, profound change has continually crept into these traditionally structured business entities at an ever-increasing rate. *The problem is that businesses today are faced with change on a revolutionary scale, which in turn calls for changes in management strategies, methods, and skills that reach beyond current management fads.*

The fact remains that most businesses today operate in a highly structured functional hierarchy with rigid reporting and authority protocols. By their very nature they tend to concentrate on repeatable daily activities (functional operations) in order to increase corporate productivity. As pointed out by Mr. Dinsmore and others, this is changing, at least at the middle to lower management levels within corporate structures as corporations tighten their belts, downsize and outsource. Today, project management methods are being deployed within these functionally based organizations in response to market pressures for increased flexibility and productivity.

This mostly 1990s reemergence is perhaps directly driven by the pressures of reduced product/service time-to-market; increased demands for worker empowerment, cross-functionality, and productivity; continued work process measurement/improvement; and the increased outsourcing of non-strategic enterprise work. These pressures form a natural environment for the use of project management methods. As we know, project management methods deploy a flexible and yet systematic structure of work definition (scope), time (schedule), and resources (people, materials, money) management for today's rapidly changing business environment.

To some businesses, the use of project-based management methods and skills, required to succeed in today's business environment, will be new. Whether new or not, the issue of how to *implement* these methods and skills into their corporate culture, such that they become the normal way to conduct business operations, will prove to be a significant challenge.

Cultural change, on both a personal and professional level, will be required. The need for integrated skill sets and consideration of the potential conflicts of interests between traditional functional management and project management structures and cultures must be addressed and resolved.

## The Vision

With the advent of the Masters in Business Administration (MBA) in the 1940s, contemporary management, as a distinctly recognized profession, was established and has since evolved through various management theories into a mix of fundamental skill sets drawn from the academic areas of business, engineering, and the humanities. This mix of contemporary management skill sets is largely a result of the merging of professional disciplines, driven by the business pressures discussed above. With the emergence of project management methods in the late 1950s and early 1960s, the defense and aerospace industries were among the first to fully grapple with and establish project management methods as a normal way to manage work within their corporate structures. Their challenge was to find a way in which project management methods could effectively coexist within a functionally organized management structure. Their answer was Matrix Management between functional and project managers. The professional field of project management, historically populated by technically trained professionals, has since evolved to what Dr. Kerzner now describes as Modern Project Management. In his 1996 PMI annual symposium article titled "The growth and Maturity of Modern Project Management," Dr. Kerzner points to a shift in project management skill requirements as shown in Exhibit 2.

So, "What are the next evolutionary steps in the field of Project Management?" Based upon the previous points of this discussion I would propose that there will continue to be a demand for the merging of management skills between technical and business management skill sets. The manifestation of this merging is what I have called *"Corporate Pathfinders" (those that discover new routes and explore untraveled regions to mark out new routes for others to follow).* I do not personally subscribe to the thought that businesses will summarily shift their operations to project-based structures. I do, however, believe that project-based methods will continue to find in-roads, and top management support, in the ways businesses conduct their ongoing operations.

For the next 20 years or so, corporations will need to master the evolutionary integration process of Matrix Management. As has been the case for the past several decades, the key to this integration of functional and project based management cultures will lie in addressing both functional and project manager needs in accordance with "Maslow's Hierarchy of Needs." This is to say that corporate scenarios, which pit functional and project managers in a confrontational situation of win/lose, will stop the integration process, cold. Win/win scenarios must be established and backed by equitably distributed reward systems.

**Exhibit 2.** Changing Skill Requirements

| | Technical Skills | Business Skills |
|---|---|---|
| 1960 -1985 | 75% | 25% |
| 1986 - 1993 | 50% | 50% |
| 1994 - 1996 | 10% | 90% |

The cutting-edge management theories of the past several decades have all contributed to the field of management theory and practice. Today's new, broad-based awareness of project management methods and their application to effectively meet business needs will be no different. Corporations will glean the methods and skills that prove to have sustaining value to their operations, and will leave the rest behind. There will always be ongoing business operations that are best managed by functional management structures, theories, and methods. Accordingly, there has been, and always will be, the need for projects within these business operations and hence project management structures, theories and methods. It is not a case of either/or. It is a case of using the right tool for the job.

*What will be new is the emergence of "Corporate Pathfinders," whose job will be to find, establish, and manage new business opportunities for an established business venture.* If the concept of Corporate Pathfinders sounds like the concept of entrepreneurship, you are right. The concept of Corporate Pathfinders, however, contrasts from the definition of entrepreneurs in that *entrepreneurs assume the total business risk for starting and growing business ventures (usually their own) outside of an established corporate business environment.* Professionals who tend toward, and thrive in, a project environment, typically posses most of the skill sets necessary for corporate pathfinding. In fact, analogies have been drawn that highlight the similarities between project managers and entrepreneurs. Project management skills are not in and of themselves enough, however; a keen understanding of business objectives and methods is required.

The challenges facing Corporate Pathfinders is perhaps best met with ongoing professional development training which draws upon, and integrates traditional academic topics, yet establishes a customized and relevant framework to address the changing needs of contemporary corporate managers. In this training, the focus will be on teaching integrated skill sets,

**Exhibit 3.** Corporate Pathfinder Model

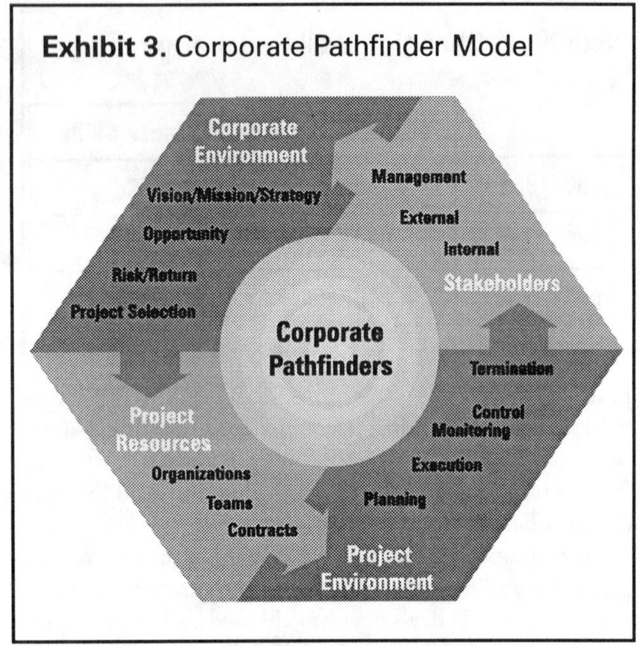


void of organizational position description perspectives, replaced with the concept of Corporate Pathfinders. The focus of such professional development would be on application of these integrated skill sets to the objective of making businesses grow and prosper. These skill sets are summarized in Exhibit 3 and include entrepreneurial spirit, flexibility, innovation, perseverance, leadership, and teamwork.

Business growth and prosperity is perhaps the single link in the corporate objective structure that most directly connects functional and project management goals. The validity of this model is based upon the assumptions that several trends of the last two decades will continue well into the next century. The major trends that this model addresses are technological change, reduced "time-to-market" pressures, ongoing business operations, and work projectization. Exhibit 4 provides a non-time-scaled, yet sequential evolution of project management in the corporate environment.

**Exhibit 4.** Evolution of Project Management

| Functional | Matrix (Weak — Strong) | Corporate Path Finding |
|---|---|---|
| Vertical Functional Expertise and Reporting Structure | Matrixed Expertise and Reporting Structure | Integrated Expertise and Flexible Reporting Structure |
| Vertical Segmentation of Corporate Resources, Responsibility, and Authority | Shared Corporate Resources, Responsibility, and Authority | Integrated Corporate Resources, Responsibility, and Authority on Strategic Business Projects |
| Separate Professional Societies and Organizations (AMA, PMI, ASQC) | Separate Professional Societies and Organizations (AMA, PMI, ASQC) | Integrated Professional Societies and Organizations (AMA, PMI, ASQC) ? |

## Summary

The proposed model of "how project management will adapt and change to the business conditions of the next century" provides a starting point to contemplate the issues of implementation and acceptance, which will ultimately determine the model's validity. The continuing issue for business in the 21st century is "change on a revolutionary scale." This in turn calls for changes in management strategies, methods, and skills that reach beyond periodic management fads. Whether these changes are new or not, the issue of how to implement these methods and skills within a corporate culture, such that they become the normal way of conducting business operations, will continue to be a significant challenge.

### References


In Search of Suckers. 1996. *Fortune* Magazine (October), 119.

Kerzner, H. 1996. "The Growth and Maturity of Modern Project Management." PMI Annual Symposium.

# Project Management 2000: The New Behaviors

Larry A. Smith, Ph.D., Florida International University
Heather Smith, Carnegie Mellon University
Anthony Niederhoffer, Carnegie Mellon University

## Introduction

A new class of managerial talent is evolving to replace the void being created by the reengineered functional manager's role: project managers. The project manager is more agile and adaptable than the functional manager, more likely to succeed by not directing and dictating but by behaving altogether differently.

*Says William Dauphinais, a partner at Price Waterhouse: "Project management is going to be huge in the next decade. The project manager is the linchpin in the horizontal/vertical organizations we're creating."*

*Project management is "the wave of the future," says an in-house newsletter from General Motors' technology and training group, which exhorts, "We need to raise the visibility and clout of this job responsibility!"*

*Says Daniel Cozad, head of PMI's Los Angeles Chapter and a project manager at International Technology Corp., an environmental services outfit: "Project managers are like alcoholics: Only a quarter of them know that's what they are."*

*Says executive VP William Kelvie, Fannie Mae's chief information officer: "Automation and empowerment take away the need to have managers oversee the day-to-day work. Everything has become projects. This is the way Fannie Mae does business today." Managing projects is managing change* (Stewart 1995, 17).

Thomas Kuhn's the *Structure of Scientific Revolutions* is a book about how mental models work. He calls them "paradigms." He defines paradigm as follows: "A constellation of concepts, values, perceptions and practices shared by a community which forms a particular vision of reality that is the basis of the way a community organizes itself." These paradigms, both real and imagined, define the constraints within the community and require new effective behaviors by its members.

The paradigms in business are constantly changing. Rapidly changing value systems, physical environments, educational levels, technology, communication systems, habits and philosophies necessitate new approaches to managing projects. The first step for success in the new paradigms is recognition of these changes. The next essential step is the development of new and effective behaviors for these new cultures. Finally, the discipline to perform these new habits is required to succeed. This paper addresses the behaviors that will be required in the next millennium.

## Recognition of Changes

New communication systems have been introduced in the last 15 years. These include fax machines, e-mail, cellular telephones, pagers and the Internet. These new communication media combined with changing organizational structures have produced a different business environment.

What will managerial careers look like in the 21st century? Managers of several leading-edge companies, as well as members of the International Association of Corporate & Professional Resources, a group of human resource executives and executive recruiters, agreed that future managerial careers will be based on a knowledge-based technical specialty; cross-functional and international experience; competence in collaborative leadership; self-management skills; personal traits of flexibility, integrity, and trustworthiness (Allred 1996).

## The New Behaviors

Project managers of the future will have to change their attitude of entitlement to a behavior of empowerment. They will have to accept new performance measures of continual production. They will have to learn to operate with vague and ill-defined job descriptions. They will no longer be paid for longevity and past successes.

This will require new perception and insights into the new business realities. Commitment and motivation will facilitate a dynamic learning and change process. Greater emotional strength and new analytical skill will be needed to deal with the changing cultural issues that will arise in the future. The new demeanor will consist of a cognizance and ability to influence others to commit and participate in their projects. Managers will have to be willing to share power and control with the rest of the team.

Project managers of the future must recognize several underlying challenges. They must be willing to understand the changing dimensions of the work environment and change accordingly. They must be willing to lead the necessary cultural changes. They must be amenable to using the latest and most effective communication systems to enhance productivity.

The behaviors that will be required to manage projects in the year 2000 and beyond are an extrapolation and elaboration of the behaviors of the '90s. They include: creativity, alignment, cultural understanding, empowerment, time management, teamwork, communication skills, balance, continuous improvement and leadership.

### Creativity: decision making skills to help shape change

To compete effectively in cyberspace, physical assets, so important in bureau space, matter less than intangible intellectual assets. World-class companies need an abundant stock of three resources: concepts—the best and latest ideas and technologies, which means investing in constant innovation; competence—the ability to execute flawlessly to world-quality standards while offering extra services to customers, which means investing in workforce skill and learning; and connections—the best partners to extend the company's reach and leverage its offerings, which means investing in collaboration. These assets rely on human capabilities: creativity and imagination, teaching and learning, trust and respect (Kanter 1996, 247).

The new world of technology, a left-brain environment, requires creative right-brain thinking to develop strategies which could accommodate never before encountered issues and problems.

### Alignment: my goals are your goals are our goals.

Modern project management aligns the three levels of organizational skills portrayed in Exhibit 1.

1. Individual performance: As a leader, you must follow another individual, regardless of hierarchy, if that individual, through experience, skill, and judgment, knows best. That individual's growth demands that you invest more in his or her skill and self-confidence than in your own. Only that individual, not you, has the capacity (the time and opportunity) to "get it done" (Drucker 1996, 205). These new management skills consist of personal goal setting, taking control, prioritizing and doing the right things that produce effective results.
2. Team performance: As a leader, you must follow the team if the team's purpose and performance goals demand it. The team, not you, must develop skills and self-confidence. The team's agreed-upon working approach requires you, like all the others, to do real work (Drucker 1996, 205). Aligning personal goals with project team goals will produce synergistic results.
3. Organizational performance: As a leader, you must follow others, regardless of hierarchy, if the organization's purpose and performance goals demand it. The need for expanding the leadership capacity of others in the organization requires it. Living the vision and values enjoins you to do so (Drucker 1996, 205). It is required that project personnel understand the constraints and consequences of organizational culture. An optimal decision that is not acceptable in a particular culture is a failure in progress.

**Exhibit 1.** Modern project Management

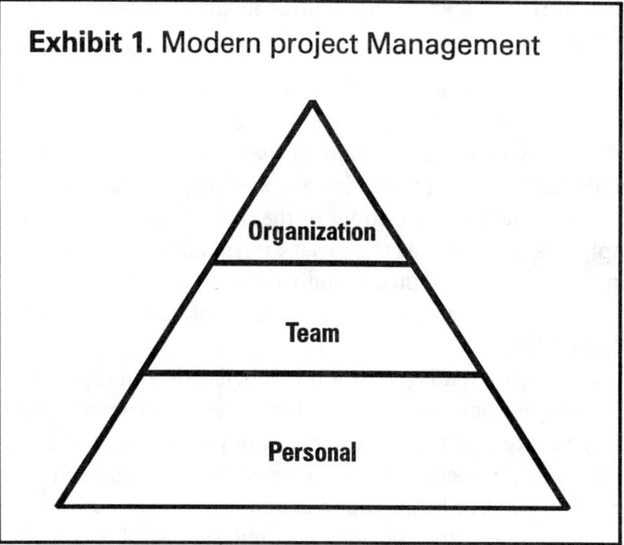


Aligning consists of ensuring that your organizational structure, systems, and operational processes all contribute to achieving your mission and vision of meeting the needs of customers and other stakeholders. They don't interfere with it, they don't compete with it, and they don't dominate it. They're only there for one purpose: to contribute to it. Far and away the greatest leverage of the principle of alignment comes when your people are filled with a true understanding of the needs, when they share a powerful commitment to accomplishing the vision, when they are invited to create and continually improve the structures and systems that will meet the needs. Without these human conditions, you cannot have world-class quality; all you have is brittle programs. Ultimately, we must learn that programs and systems are vital, but that people are the programmers (Drucker 1996).

### Cultural Understanding: think like an anthropologist

Gone are the days when businesses could say, "This is our culture. Conform or leave." Organizations may have been able to afford to exclude talent 25 years ago when the law of supply and demand was on their side. Not today. Competition is heated in attracting the best and the brightest employees—and more work will have to be done to retain them (Capowski 1996, 12).

### Empowerment: seize opportunities as they present themselves

Project managers must get the job done even if they do not have the formal authority to get it done.

People who are just beginning their professional careers should think of an organization as something to create rather than join. Many organizations of the future will serve less as employers and more as tools that individuals can use to advance their careers. Thus, an individual's knowledge of business must increasingly include knowledge of how to organize (Allred 1996).

Tomorrow's managers will try to persuade employees to meet tougher performance standards even as companies severely reduce staff, resources, and motivators (e.g., promotional paths, job security, etc.). To meet this challenge, managers will need to both empower employees with authority and information, and provide them with successful self-management skills.

A manager must use time effectively and to the best advantage of the company. This includes delegating and tracking some tasks or jobs while personally completing others. As a manager, your work needs to be delegated according to its character or immediacy, among the available resources, and based upon capacities or cost (Crooks 1995, 44). This is the next behavior.

### Time Management: understanding what to do with the 24 hours that you have

Doing the important tasks requires that you define your goals and work on the activities that make significant contributions to those goals.

Time turns out to be a confusing commodity. Some people will spend money to save their time, others will spend their time to save money and others will trade money for time at certain periods of their life, preferring to work less for less money. This makes time a contradictory sort of commodity, but one that will become more and more important in our societies (Handy 1994, 31).

Time, therefore, creates the new growth area. Personnel services for the busy, to save time, health, education, travel, and recreation for the affluent, to spend time, equipment and materials for those who want to spend time to save money (Handy 1994, 32).

### Teamwork: recruit people who have the necessary skills and knowledge

In order to create an environment that fosters teamwork, managers must have the following characteristics.

- They must be willing to become more sensitive and understanding with respect to the ethnic, cultural, and gender differences within the workplace and to demonstrate that sensitivity and understanding.
- They must have a vision for the workplace that ultimately results in a significant broadening of the corporate culture and the work place environment.
- They must be willing to craft and implement new and different employment and communication processes to enhance and promote perceptions of fairness and equity.
- They must be willing to bring full and unquestioned commitment to the effective utilization of a diverse workforce.
- They must be the linchpin between their organization and the larger community, to establish the organization as a place where people want to work and be productive and to develop new markets and maintain existing ones.

### Communication: learning to communicate with compassion

Traditionally, managers who lacked communication and planning skills often compensated for these skills through iterative face-to-face discussions, requiring team members to come back to them again and again to clarify performance goals or decision-making authority. To capitalize on the flexibility and speed that are possible through distributed, networked teams, managers and team members will have to form clear, up-front agreements regarding: (a) performance expectations; (b) the team's priorities; (c) how communications are to be carried out among members; and (d) the degree of resource support for telecommuters (e.g., dedicated business lines installed in the home or home-based printers).

Another challenge will be information overload—the kind that occurs when a worker finds 60 e-mail messages waiting. Some people are already finding ways to counter this through the use of "bozo filters"—software programs that automatically screen out the messages of certain e-mail senders. To prevent information overload, communication skills will need to be geared for the virtual organization. An example is the ability to communicate electronically without the subtle, nonverbal cues that we get in face-to- face communications. When these cues are suddenly absent, as they are in e-mail correspondence, the result can be a misunderstanding or misinterpretation of messages that seem extremely blunt or antagonistic (Barner 1996, 14).

Traditionally, if you wanted to communicate with someone in another department, you first had to go up your own chain of command and gradually down the other department's chain of command, then wait for the response to follow the same path back. This "functional silo" pattern is a relic that today's Generation X'ers call "control freakism." Those silo walls are coming down, but the full implications and potential benefits of this rapid change are still unknown. We do know that the demise of functional silos speeds up communications and places a great deal more responsibility and authority in the hands of employees at all levels. As the figurative walls come down, organizations will have to tear down some literal ones as well (Gunn 1996, 19).

### Balance: finding the equilibrium between opposite poles

It is a paradox, one best captured by Jung who said, years ago, that we need others to be truly ourselves. "I" needs "we" to be fully "I." Looking up, however, at the office blocks in every city, those little boxes piled on top of one another up into the sky, one has to wonder how much room there is for "I" amid the filing cabinets and the terminals (Handy 1994, 39).

Similarly, organizations are tight and loose; concerned only about the longer term in some areas but passionate about detail in others (Handy 1994, 48).

We used to think that we knew how to run organizations. Now we know better. More than ever they need to be global and local at the same time, to be small in some ways but big in others, to be centralized some of the time, to be both more autonomous and more of a team, their managers to be more delegating and more controlling. The paradox is neatly summed up in Charles Savage's story, in his book *Fifth Generation Management*, of the manager saying to the new recruit, "The good news is that you have 120,000 people working for you, the bad news is that they don't know it"(Handy 1994, 34).

Understanding, however, is the key. Balancing the opposites, or switching between them, must not be a random or haphazard act. Without a clear rationale for what is happening, the balancing and the switching can be bewildering to those on the receiving end and frustrating for anyone doing the balancing. Without understanding, things do not work out as they should. Living with paradox is like riding a seesaw. If you know how the process works, and if the person at the other end also knows, then the ride can be exhilarating. If, however, the person on the other end does not understand, or willfully upsets the pattern, you can receive a very uncomfortable and unexpected shock (Handy 1994, 48).

### Continuous Improvement: Personal Kaizen

During a business trip to Asia, an educated executive from the Western world visited a wise Zen master. When he arrived, the master asked him what he wanted, and the visitor replied that he wanted to learn how to achieve wisdom. The master nodded, lifted a teapot, and poured its contents into the executive's tiny cup. The cup soon overflowed, and the master kept pouring until the pot was empty. As with any great story, particularly a Zen story, this one has many meanings. One is that you must often unlearn before you can learn more. You have to empty your mind to make room for a new idea (Davis 1994, 41).

Individual traits will always play an important role in professional development. Clearly, the most critical attribute future managers must have is flexibility. The move from bureaucratic to cellular organizations will require managers, among other things, to take the leading role on one project and to fulfill only a specific technical function on another. For individuals who are self-employed professionals, moving from one project to the next may involve changes in industry, employer, and country. Indeed, some career counselors advise managers who have been displaced from traditional organizations to avoid seeking a specific job in a particular industry, but instead learn to be flexible enough to take advantage of whatever opportunities come along. In addition, integrity and trustworthiness will be vital personal attributes in an increasingly collaborative, self-governing workplace. For some traditional managers, the development of such traits will not be easy, as it will require the unlearning of various dysfunctional behaviors (Allred 1996).

### Leadership: motivate people to want to do what you want

Leadership must be learned and can be learned (Drucker 1996, xi).

Leaders of the future will therefore have to have more of the following characteristics (Drucker 1996, 67):

- Extraordinary levels of perception and insight into the realities of the world and into themselves
- Extraordinary levels of motivation to enable them to go through the inevitable pain of learning and change, especially in a world with looser boundaries, in which loyalties become more difficult to define
- The emotional strength to manage their own and others' anxiety as learning and change become more and more a way of life
- New skills in analyzing cultural assumptions, identifying functional and dysfunctional assumptions, and evolving processes that enlarge the culture by building on its strengths and functional elements
- The willingness and ability to involve others and elicit their participation, because tasks will be too complex and information too widely distributed for leaders to solve problems on their own
- The willingness and ability to share power and control according to people's knowledge and skills; that is, to permit and encourage leadership to flourish throughout the organization.

## Summary

With clear objectives in mind, the issue then becomes what a leader will do, how he or she will behave while working with people in pursuit of the end goal.

With the changing work environment, project managers will have to function differently. They will need to discipline themselves to exercise new methods of conduct. "Many of the projects and tasks that you have to do are a lot like running hurdles. You aren't supposed to knock over the hurdles, but there's no bonus for clearing them by an extra margin either. All you really have to do is get over them" (Griessman 1994, 94).

In order to accomplish these goals these new behaviors will be required.

- Creativity: Creativity in decision making to react to changing conditions
- Alignment: Ensuring organizational structures, systems and processes are synchronized to achieve the missions and visions of the company
- Cultural Understanding: Thinking like an anthropologist
- Empowerment: Seizing opportunities as they present themselves
- Time Management: Understanding what to do with the 24 hours that you have
- Team work: Recruiting people who have the necessary skills and knowledge
- Communication: Learning to communicate with compassion
- Balance: Finding the equilibrium between opposite poles
- Continuous Improvement: Realizing the need to grow with the changing environment
- Leadership: Motivating people to want to do what you want
- The development of personal management skills; a passion, dedication and commitment for the work; an understanding and appreciation of individual skills and qualifications; inspiring, visionary, competent decisions made with integrity.

## References


Allred, Brent B; Charles C Snow; Raymond E. Miles. 1996. "Characteristics of Managerial Careers of the 21st Century." *Academy of Management Executive* (November), *10*, 4, 17–27.

Barner, Robert. 1996. 'The New Millennium Workplace: Seven Changes That Will Challenge Managers—And Workers." *The Futurist, 30*, 2.

Capowski, Genevieve. 1996. "Managing Diversity." *Management Review* (June), *85*, 6.

Crooks, John W. 1995. "Are You Ready for the Coming Storm?" *Communications* (January), *32*, 1.

Davis, Stan, and Jim Botkin 1994. *The Monster Under the Bed.* New York : Simon & Schuster Inc.

Drucker, Peter F. 1996. *The Leader pf The Future.* Frances Hesselbein, Marshall Goldsmith, Richard Beckhard.

Griessman, B. Eugene. 1994. *Time Tactics of Very Successful People.* New York: McGraw-Hill, Inc.

Handy, Charles. 1994. *The Age of Paradox.* First published in the United States by the Harvard Business School Press.

Kanter, Rosabeth Moss. 1996. "Can Giants Dance in Cyberspace?" *Forbes, 2* (December).

Ronald A., and Marilyn S. Burroughs. 1996. Work Spaces That Work: Designing High-Performance Offices"; includes related article on team structures and workspace layouts. *The Futurist, 30*, 2.

Stewart, Thomas A. 1995. "The Corporate Jungle Spawns a New Species: The Project Manager." *Fortune, 10* (July).

# Toward a Corporate Project Management Culture: Fast Tracking into the Future

Paul C. Dinsmore, PMP, Dinsmore Associates

What's around the corner for project management as it continues its metamorphous, reinventing itself to take on the demands of an ever-changing world? PM has been affected by the crazy times, the earth-shaking technological breakthroughs, the moods and wants of society, and economies that reel and rock and impose their whims on industry as a whole. What then is likely to peak over the project-management horizon to help meet the challenges of the increasingly wild and woolly times?

The global-change crunch has shoved and shaped general management approaches into different forms over the years. Business professionals have been obliged to come up with new twists for getting things done. Some of these twists have called for 180-degree turnabouts, tossing out old ways and taking a fresh start, or updating valid concepts to meet the needs of a changed setting. Re-labeling of concepts has also been an ongoing thing: reengineering becomes business-process realignment or such, and down-sizing long ago was re-christened right-sizing and, who knows, may evolve into *wonderful-sizing* at some time.

So what has happened to project management over time? And what is likely to come to pass in the future? Has PM been paradigm-shifting its way through the decades, or simply updating itself? Is a re-labeling movement under way, or are significant quantum-leaping developments in the making?

## Here's What Has Happened In the Past

In the sixties and seventies project management emerged as a critical-path based network planning technique for the building of complex vessels and crafts such as submarines and moon-shot vehicles. The planning process was cumbersome and data processing was done on mainframe computers. As a result only major organizations with sophisticated technical staffs were able to apply the critical planning techniques. Updating of plans and schedules was a major problem, due to the complexity of the planning systems.

In the eighties PM software for micro-computers marched into the marketplace. This made computerized project control tools accessible to projects and companies of all sizes. This was a period of "democratization" of project control tools and management techniques, where the primary focus was single-project management.

In the nineties, the concepts of basic project management were communicated to the project public via PMI's *A Guide to the Project Management Body of Knowledge (PMBOK Guide)*. Yet emphasis shifted from single-project management to viewing PM from a broader perspective as the management of projects, or enterprise management, or managing organizations by projects.

The basic name has remained the same. The field is still called project management at this point. So PM has evolved and gone through some moderate metamorphoses, beginning with the mainframe project-control approach to mega-projects, going through the democratization of PM software via microcomputers and finally shifting towards multiple-project management.

## So Where Are We Now?

There are a bunch of views out there about project management: the names are many and they all refer to different pieces of what may indeed be a bigger beast. Here are some of the terms being used in the literature:

- **Project management**, according to *A Guide to the Project Management Body of Knowledge (PMBOK Guide),* is the application of knowledge, skills, tools, and techniques to project activities in order to meet or exceed stakeholder needs and expectations from a project; it balances competing demands among scope, cost, time, and quality. (This implies a focus on managing the tasks, people, and funds of a particular project.)
- **MOBP, managing organizations by projects,** is a *corporate managerial philosophy* based on the principle that company goals are achievable through a web of simultaneous projects, which include corporate strategies, operational improvement, and organizational transformation, as well as traditional development projects.
- **MPM, modern project management is** a term coined in the early nineties suggesting that project management is broadly applicable outside the traditional technical fields, in areas such as marketing, human resources, organization change, and total quality programs.
- **Management of projects** refers to the pluralistic view of project management, with emphasis on applications to multiple projects. Corporate interface and the managing

of project managers are key issues in the management of projects.

- **Enterprise management** suggests a bottom line focus for multiple projects under a common umbrella, with emphasis on the information processing and control side of management.
- **Program management** refers to a series of related projects, or an on-going ever-renewing effort, such as "the space program," commonly used in the United States Department of Defense and aerospace and electronics industries.

Other industry-specific terms are out there, such as *construction management*, preferred in capital construction projects, and *product management*, used in consumer product industries. So, there are different angles from which to see a discipline that has a common core of principles.

## Can Anybody See the Elephant?

Project management can be glimpsed from varying angles; that's why it looks different to different groups. The variances are subtle although substantial; if we assume that everything related to projects is part of one great project-management thing, an analogy can be sketched from the parable about the elephant and the three blind men. The men were urged up to the elephant and asked to divine what it was. The first sided along the flank of the giant beast and said, "This is a wall." The next man fondled the trunk and proclaimed, "This is a pipe." The third one grabbed the tail and cried out, "This is a snake." All made a partial mind picture of something which in fact was much bigger than perceived.

The now-burgeoning field of project management too spans a broader spectrum than most folks perceive. Projects vary from the tiny and multitudinous to the gigantic and singular. Applications range from space shots, systems development, construction, new products, organization change, marketing programs, training events, you name it: anything that starts, develops and ends. This presents a challenge of both language and perception for the broad-stretching profession of project management.

## So What's Around the Corner?

Author Tom Peters has said that no matter how zany his prognostications have been about the "wacky future," reality proved that he had actually been conservative, in spite of the apparent brashness of his initial vision. Things happened at a faster pace and in a more surprising manner than he had originally envisioned. So crystal-balling the future is a challenge even for those who do it for a living.

Peters, who is a mainstream management guru, has been preaching the glories of project management for some time now. He sees project management as a way of getting things done, for jolting companies into a results-based mind set. He cites companies that are project-based or are in the process of making the transformation to projects. Among them are: EDS, CNN, and Imagination. Others are Oticon, Ingersoll-Rand, and Union Pacific Railroad.

Peters pointed as far back as 1992 that project management was the "coming" premier skill. Since five years have gone by, based on Peters' own observations and by what is going on in the industry and at PMI in terms of growth, it's evident that project management is no longer coming but has indeed arrived. Project management is spreading across organizations and is increasingly perceived as a fundamental skill for managing in these times of constant change.

So with Peters' thoughts as a backdrop, let's take a look at what is likely to happen in the field of project management, say, by the year 2010.

### Globalization

The globalization upswing has been going on for years and it has touched business in all corners of the globe. In this vast playing field, world-class players in the best-in-industry category will tend to prosper and perpetuate themselves. Smaller companies have the option of joining international networks and alliances to keep abreast, or being alienated from the global marketplace and trying to survive locally against the tentacles of the world giants.

For major functional organizations, this means having world-class project management in place and contributing to the bottom line. The same is true for projectized organizations like Bechtel, IBM, and ABB, who make their living by delivering successful projects and project-related equipment. Smaller organizations like George Washington University's ESI, which offers training programs, and Primavera, suppliers of PM software, are also under pressure to keep apace of the demand for world-class support and expertise.

Entities like PMI, which will pass the 30,000 member mark in 1997, are working on expanding the formal body of knowledge to insure that all the member-parts of the creature we call "project management" are taken into account. The "Global Forum," a group loosely connected with PMI, which meets before or after most international symposia on project management, is also addressing the cross-cultural issues of managing projects globally. An "ac hoc" Global Project Management Standards Committee, involving standards organizations from around the world, including PMI, is making moves towards global standardization. Project management organizations around the globe will tend to network ever closer to mitigate the challenges of globalization.

## Who Will Be Doing It? And How Will It Be Done?

Project management is changing faces. Based on trends at PMI, more women will practice the art (18 percent of the responses to a survey of PMPs by PMI's certification committee were women). That percentage at the general membership level is certainly on the rise. Mega-trenders have been forecasting the blossoming of females in the marketplace since the early nineties. This trend will continue into the next millennium to the point where women will outnumber men at all levels of responsibility on many project management endeavors.

In 1995, a survey indicated that the typical reader of *PM Network* magazine was a forty-four-year-old male. A major downshift from this age bracket is also going on. A stroll around the hallways at any PMI convention will prove the point, as will a visit to project sites, especially when those projects involve software development or other emerging technologies.

Teams will tend to be more cross-cultural, especially as projects are managed virtually by mullet-disciplined groups scattered about the globe. This means that project personnel will require greater awareness of diversity and more capability in managing intercultural settings.

Project junkies will be increasingly part of the scene. They are like professional football players who loyally play to win for their team, no matter who their team may be at the time. Project junkies will continue to take the "employability" concept to heart, preparing themselves for employment both within the company and outside in the marketplace.

### "Faster Than the Speed of Light"

Since time is ubiquitous, everywhere at the same time, deadlines all around the globe clamor for timely completion, often simultaneously. But that's okay since the race against the calendar's flipping pages and the ticking of the clock set the tone for project work. This start-to-finish characteristic makes projects stand out from other types of operations, as time becomes an important measuring stick for assessing success.

Globalization works in favor of meeting the growing time crunch. Projects can now churn out results twenty-four hours a day, by farming out parts of the work around the globe: design can be done in India, while procurement is handled from Europe, and fabrication takes place in Argentina. Like the old British Empire, the sun need never set on the project work. This trend to take advantage of the twenty-four-hour day will grow.

## Technology

Technology will continue to accelerate the effectiveness of project management. As telecommunications systems become more reliable, particularly worldwide, projects will be managed better and quicker. Quality of images and paperless office capabilities will also keep bureaucracy down and productivity up. Fax machines will be museum pieces, and the Internet will not only provide the highway but will place amazingly powerful software just a few keystrokes away. Stand-alone souped-up microcomputers will be rare, as the Internet will be as reliable as a utility power grid, and up-to-date software will be accessed from the network at any time.

Project management software will continue to become more user-friendly, particularly for the "managing of a single project" variety. More complex software will be available for multiple-project situations and enterprise-wide settings. Although some software packages now propose to control projects on an enterprise-wide basis, the packages of the future will offer easy interface with other company systems and provide an integrated view of multiple projects. These systems will be highly flexible, yet will require considerable customizing upon installation to interface with related on-going company systems.

## Towards a Corporate Project Management Culture

Creating a corporate project management culture requires aligning the company's portfolio of projects so that their contribution to the organization's objectives is maximized. Corporations of the future will formalize interfacing to insure that projects' actions move in arrow-like fashion toward company targets. It requires more than the now-common "grenade over the wall" approach, in which the business planning staff identifies and characterizes the project and then tosses it to an uninformed and uninvolved project management group that is supposed to complete the project.

Once this trend is reverted and full alignment takes place and all parties are on the project-management-culture bandwagon, the term "project management" may come to be seen as an oxymoron. PM applied across the organization will be synonymous with "good management." Since managers will be spending more of their time on projects than on operational-type things, PM might well be considered as a piece of general management!

The surge in project management is following tracks similar to the quality movement of the eighties. Quality control (rejecting the parts that aren't up to snuff) evolved into quality assurance (inspecting the processes as opposed to the individual parts) and finally into various forms of total quality management (managing all the pieces of the organization correctly to get quality results.)

In project management, the initial thrust has been: "How do we manage a project effectively?" (The basic concept of *A Guide to The Project Management Body of Knowledge (PMBOK Guide)*). Lately there is more concern for the management of multiple projects. And the future points toward a more holistic view, something like corporate project management.

While the awakening of major corporations regarding the organizational applications of project management may be perceived as new, it can be argued that the concept has been around for a long time. For instance, "Management by Projects" was the theme of the 10th World Congress on Project Management held in Vienna in 1990. In that congress, topics such as "Flat Flexible Organization Structures" and "Top Management and Project Management" were dealt with in great detail. So even though the management-of-projects concept is just now being "discovered" by many corporations, in professional project management circles the idea has been around for a while. In spite of this fact, it will take a turn of the millennium before most companies jump on the bandwagon.

This means that in the future companies will perceive themselves not as hierarchical, functional organizations, but as fast-tracking entrepreneurial enterprises, made up of a "portfolio of projects"—ever-changing and ever-renewable—all of which need to be done "faster, cheaper, better." Companies thus will embody a project management culture. Project managers will have long replaced middle managers. Company team members at all levels will all be versed in the basics of project management and will naturally apply the concepts both for single projects as well as on an enterprise basis.

Project management will be part of company culture. That culture will be reinforced by some sort of institutional support, perhaps by one of the three classic "homes" for project management:

1. **Project Office (Projoff).** Project offices will still be around. They will support several projects simultaneously, although in some cases they may provide services exclusively to a given project. They will continue to furnish support, tools, and services for planning, scheduling, scope changes, and cost. Project offices will tend to be much more "high tech" since the basic PM concepts will be second nature to company professionals in general.
2. **Center of Excellence (CEPM).** There will be strong tendency toward adoption of the CEPM as the care-keeper of methodologies and for keeping communications channels open between projects and with the outside project management community. The Center of Excellence for Project Management is the gathering point and dissemination point for expertise, but does not assume responsibility for project results. The project office concept will tend to migrate toward the center of excellence.
3. **Program Office, or Project Management Program Office (PMPO).** Organizations that haven't fully adopted a corporate project management culture may have a need to maintain a program office. The PMPO "manages the project managers." The PMPO head might sport titles like: vice-president, or director of projects, or head of project management. In major corporations, the PMPO often concentrates its efforts on prioritized projects. Other projects are managed by departments or units and are given support by the PMPO as needed. As the project management culture becomes ingrained in the organization, the PMPO will also tend to move toward the a more facilitative approach like the center of excellence.

## So What Does It Take to Get the Ball Rolling?

For those organizations who plan to keep up with the times and move toward a project management culture, there is a simple procedure for jump starting companies in that direction. Here are the up-front moves needed to break through natural organization inertia.

1. **Identify allies.** See who believes that boosting project management within the organization is a worthy cause. Pinpoint key stakeholders that need to be on the bandwagon. Initiate informal chats and gather ideas as to how to go about getting others to sign on.
2. **Spread the word.** Use house organs and internal forums to talk up the topic. Use every opportunity to raise the subject. Distribute articles and literature that will raise the awareness level of key stakeholders.
3. **Plan an Executive Session** (half day). Set an objective for the executive session. Something like: "To promote upper management support towards creating a project management culture within the organization." Write two to three pages summarizing the information needed to promote an executive session; include things like background, goals, scope, participants, form of facilitation, and so on. Content should include pre-work, facilitation of the session itself, and post-session debriefings.
4. **Articulate the Executive Session.** Someone needs to orchestrate the executive session. Options are internal facilitators, an experienced change agent from another area of the company, a local university professor, or an outside agent you have worked with and trust. The facilitator should be involved not only in conducting the session itself, but in the pre-work design, development of the event, and the post-session debriefings.
5. **Follow up and keep on pushing.** Once the session has happened, someone needs to keep the ball rolling. Conclusions from the executive session may need to be nurtured and monitored. A follow up visit by the

facilitator may be in order as well to address the question of "what do we do now?"

6. **Follow through with the basics.** A roadmap for putting into place an across-the-board project management culture within an organization was included in the June 1996 column of *PM Network* ("Toward Corporate Project Management: Beefing Up the Bottom Line With MOBP"). That included phases involving a comprehensive survey and needs assessment, design of the steps required for the new PM culture, and implementation requiring training programs including executive briefings, basics seminars, specialty seminars, PMP certification courses (if desired), and on-the job consultation.

Getting people's attention is the first hurdle to leap when the objective is to incorporate a project management culture into an organization. Whether the organization is new to the PM concept or is simply under-utilizing the tools and techniques available, a specific initiative is called for to get things moving in the direction of a project management culture. It takes things like: finding allies, spreading the word, and working out some plans. But it also requires staging an event—a happening of sorts—to shine limelight on the topic and let the idea seep into the pores of the key stakeholders.

## Conclusions

Project management has indeed been affected by the crazy times, the earth-shaking technological breakthroughs, the moods and wants of society, and economies that reel and rock and impose their whims on industry. This is making companies march consciously, or unconsciously, toward a corporate project management culture (to do things faster, cheaper, and better). Major changes will take place in the way organizations perceive PM. Just as simple quality control became big-time total quality management, project management will evolve toward something bigger, seen as an integral part of overall management. It may be called corporate project management, or MOBP—managing organizations by projects—or even total project management. Time will give it a name; what is important is that the corporate project management culture bandwagon is well on the roll, and companies that want to survive and prosper had best be on it.

# A Project Manager Competency Model

Ron Waller, PMP, CEM, Johnson Controls, Inc.

## Introduction

Groups of interested individuals met at Project Management Institute meetings during 1995 and 1996 to discuss the development of a "project managers" Body of Knowledge. The intent was to discuss and identify those additional bodies of knowledge that were not included in PMI's *A Guide to the Project Management Body of Knowledge* (*PMBOK Guide*). It was immediately apparent that a model was required that would describe a range of practice before a revised BOK model could be developed. The initial results of those discussions, with subsequent modifications and expansions by the author, are provided. The results attempt to describe a competency model for project managers that illustrates variations in the range of knowledge and skill required by the continuum of practice and which includes intellectual and moral behaviors consistent with the project manager's *style*. Use of this preliminary model is suitable for a base in an enterprise application.

Competence refers to observable evidence of performance. It includes various practices for selection and recognition of individuals within a labor classification. Competence is presented as a rational basis for making decisions regarding future human performance. Crucial to such judgments is the inference of a minimum future performance from some form of assessment of the individual. This inference requires establishing appropriate evidence. Thus, competence can be defined as having the required behaviors, knowledge, and minimum skill necessary to perform satisfactorily. Preparing to be licensed to drive an auto requires: (1) knowledge—acquired through reading, (2) skill—acquired through practice, and, (3) competence—able to apply. The competence assessment is not graded. Rather, results are in terms of yes/no, competent/not competent, pass/fail, etc. The automobile "driving test" where a minimum level of performance is demonstrated to "pass" is a frequently used competence analogy.

A dictionary definition of competence is "sufficiency of skill, sufficiency of ability." Competence must therefore be measurable, and there must exist some acceptable standard. This requires the setting of standards by some recognized entity. When working to these standards, competence can only be measured on a pass/fail basis. Candidates are either competent or they are not. This is determined by whether the candidate reaches the measurable competence standard.

However, we should not forget about the level of performance. Just passing a competence-based driving test does not mean this level of skill is acceptable for all driving situations. After all, who is comfortable in a complex traffic situation knowing the driver has just been licensed for the first time? Further, passing the driving test (driving competence established) does not mean the individual is ready for a tractor-trailer, off-road, or high-performance vehicle operation. Additional demonstrations of higher levels of performance are necessary before operating these vehicles even though a driving test is all that may be legally required. Christopher Rowe (`995) references the UK Management Charter Initiative (MCI) assessment guidelines which describe the MCI competence approach:

... *collecting sufficient evidence to determine whether an individual is performing competently in their job. It is therefore concerned with the outcome of learning and previous experience as reflected in performance, rather than in learning itself. It is not intended to tell you how well someone can carry out an activity ... as it is not based on a comparative analysis of the achievement of a group ...*

Thus, while competence is like a driving test, assessing the individual's performance against specific fixed standards, behavior inventories focus on how people behave and can be graded. Competence identifies achievement of the minimum level of ability to perform, it does little to measure good performance quality, since the measurement of performance is based in behavior. A model to communicate this need to quantify levels of performance is addressed next.

## Knowledge, Skill, Competence

### The "T" Shaped Manager

Can we model what managers do? Exhibit 1 illustrates the concept of the "T" shaped manager introduced by Turner (1996). This illustration attempts to demonstrate that as management capacity increases, technical capacity decreases. Thus, at lower management levels individuals are likely to have (and need) more technical competency than higher-level managers. While not mutually exclusive, it is very difficult to maintain both a high level management competency as well as high-level technical competency. This model, while accurate, does not include the influence of project topology (characteristics).

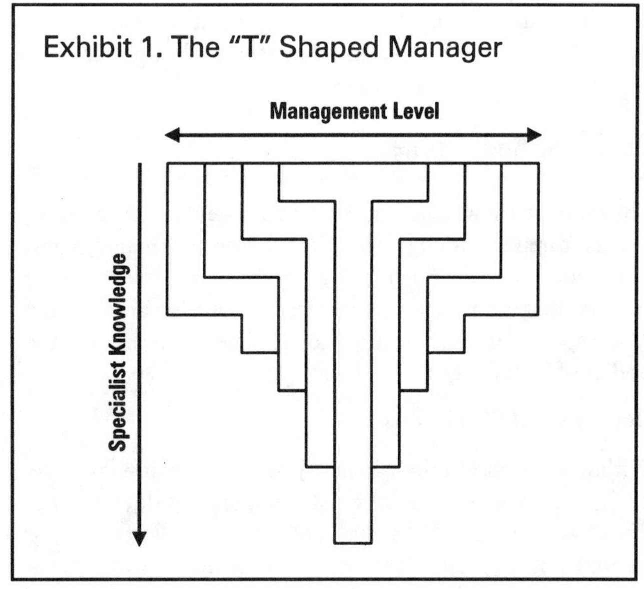


Exhibit 1. The "T" Shaped Manager

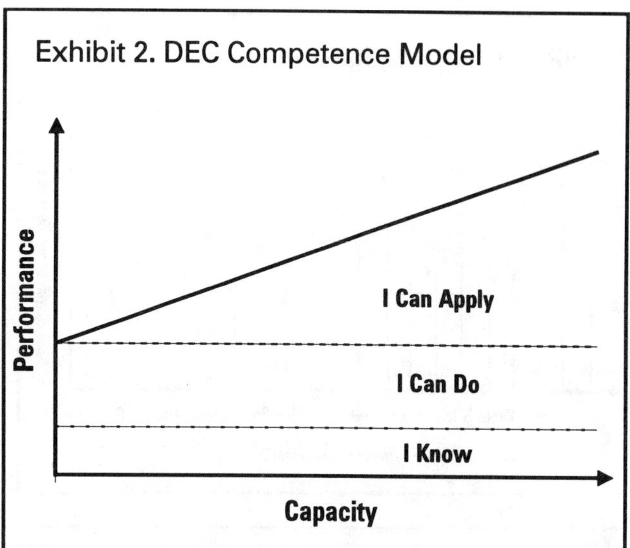


Exhibit 2. DEC Competence Model

## Some Definitions

Rowe (1995) identifies confusion regarding the term *competence* prevalent in the literature. The terms competence, competency, and competencies are frequently used interchangeably within the same context of meaning. Dictionary definitions provide little clarification for the use of the terms when applied to certification of professionals or in individual assessments for organizational purposes.

To reduce confusion, when it is applied to project management certification and enterprise assessments and evaluations, it is suggested that the following use of the terms (after Rowe 1995) be adopted to distinguish between *competence* and *competency*:

*Competence*—A skill and the standard of performance reached (there are no grades in competence evaluation).

*Competency*—The behavior by which *the level of* achievement is measured.

*Note that having achieved competence does not mean that performance is "good."*

The plural of each then gives two different meanings:

*Competences*—The range of skills which are satisfactorily performed.

*Competencies*—The behaviors adopted in competent performance.

It is expected that this adaptation will find favor in HRM as it more easily communicates the performance component desired in evaluating individual skills.

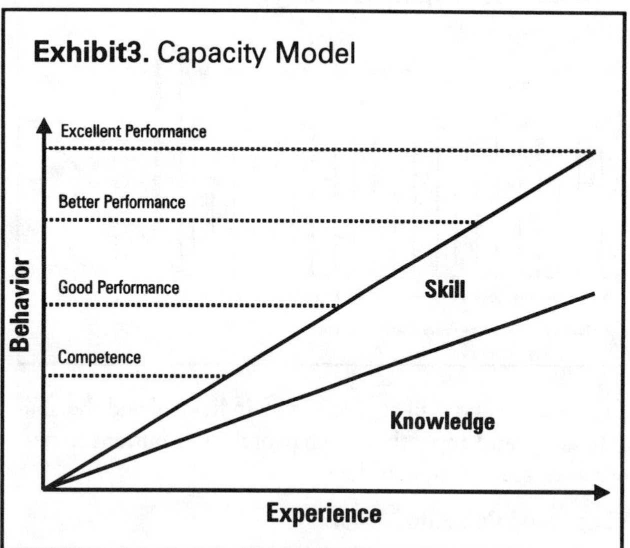


**Exhibit3.** Capacity Model

## Competency Model Elements

### The DEC Competence Model

A summary of the Digital Equipment Company competency model also referenced by Turner (1996) is shown in Exhibit 2. It further explains the competence approach with the three dimensions of competence identified by the descriptions "I know," "I can do," and "I can apply." In my view, these levels actually illustrate the learning process. The learning process starts first with knowledge gathering, followed by skill development, and finally, with sufficient experience, understanding how to adapt and apply the knowledge and skill. Competence might be identified as a single horizontal line set at a predetermined *competence* standard level. In this model, the level of performance is determined *only* by the capacity

**Exhibit 4.** Knowledge and Skill

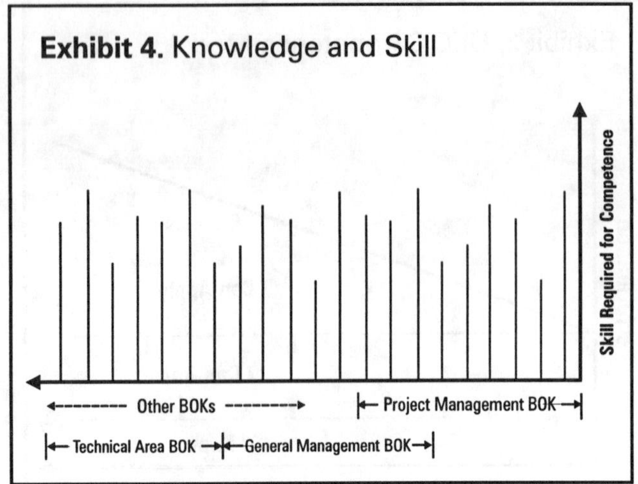


**Exhibit 5.** Project Topology

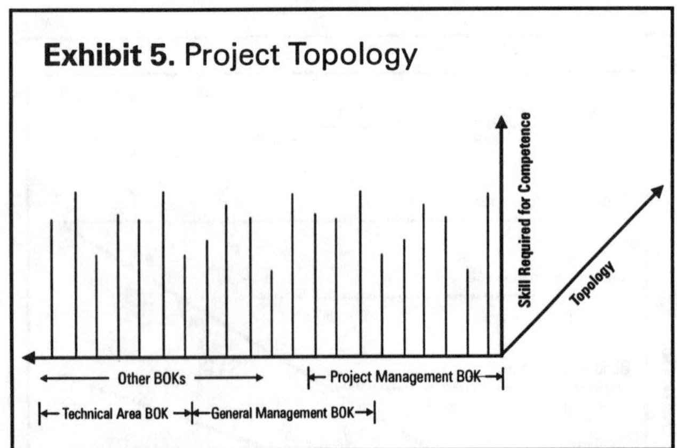


of knowledge and skill attained by an individual and the ability to adapt and apply them. Behavioral contributions to performance are left unidentified.

## A Expanded Capacity Model

For a given group of project characteristics, organizations want to know that performance will be better than that which may be attained at a competence (satisfactory or minimum) level. While competence is defined as attaining a skill standard and is yes/no, competency (performance) is related to behavior and may be graded. Employers and organizations are interested in identifying good performance, not just competence, and assessments should include behaviors, not just knowledge and skill. The relationship between competence and competency is shown in Exhibit 3. While an individual attaining *competence* may be capable of excellent performance, the competence approach does not allow inclusion of a *measure* of this performance. Identifying specific behavior is necessary to suggest that better performance will be attained. An individual with appropriate behavior, learning from education and skill development in conjunction with experience, leads first to competence and then continued improvement. However, project managers with significant knowledge and skill may still not be "good."

## Bodies of Knowledge

The body of knowledge for project managers is comprised of at least three knowledge areas: (1) the project management knowledge area, (2) portions of general management's body of knowledge, and (3) the *technical* knowledge area related to the specific industry of the project. There is overlap in the bodies of knowledge.

### Domains and Skill Levels

Within any organization, industry and culture in which the project is completed there exist a range of influences that would vary the knowledge and skill requirements needed. For example, many project management activities on smaller projects may be done by the project manager, whereas on larger projects staff would be available for many of these. Further, using these same scenarios, the project manager on the smaller project is likely to require a higher skill level in the technical components and focus on these aspects of the project while on the larger project specialized technical resources would be assigned and the project manager might focus on the political requirements. The small-project manager would likely be involved more in task-based activity such as directly using tools/techniques whereas the large-project manager would likely be more involved in managing and directing a larger team. The small-project manager is close to do-it-yourself whereas a very-large-project manager is more like a general manager. Referring to Exhibit 4, for each knowledge area listed on the horizontal axis, skill levels may be indicated by the total length of vertical lines above each knowledge area; the longer the line the higher the skill level. The number of such lines in the knowledge areas would of course vary with the identified skills.

## Project Topology

The project topology (characteristics) are specific to organization, industry and culture within which the project is completed. These characteristics can be relative to size, complexity, uniqueness, client requirements, risk, etc. The characteristics classify projects according to organization standards requirements. The level of skill required in each knowledge area may be different, depending on the particular project. The effect of project characteristics on the required level of skill in each knowledge area is illustrated in Exhibit 5.

### An Analogy

The project topology influences noted above might be analogous to two medical doctors—a general practitioner and a brain surgeon. They are both practitioners, they are both professionals, they both have a medical driving license. However, they each require different levels of skill within the general body of knowledge of the medical profession (PMBOK), their specialty (technical area body of knowledge), and perhaps even within the general management body of knowledge. Regarding performance, the patient in most cases would be interested in the level of skill and expertise each doctor has attained and the "relative performance" of each doctor within the context of their specialty area when compared to other practitioners within the same area. Thus for project managers within the context of the project topology there is a range of various bodies of knowledge with different skill levels required by a project manager within each that is necessary to establish competence. These knowledge/skill modifiers expand the model. For each topology, such as project type or industry, the range of skill in each knowledge area required for competence may be different. These modifiers of knowledge and skill would be illustrated on a third axis labeled "Topology."

## Performance

Up to this point our model includes three axes representing knowledge, skill and topology. However, just as the patient in the analogy above is interested in performance within the context of the application of the skill in a specialty area, so are those who need the services of project managers and project team participants. *Competence* addressees the *what*, but not the *how*. If we are to fully understand the professional development needs of practitioners, then we need to understand the *how* of the profession. This requires a further expansion of our model to include those elements of behavior which were defined previously as *competencies*.

### How Managers Perform

Organizations that use project managers really want to know if a candidate will perform "well." An evaluation of competence provides a starting point. But, further descriptions of a candidate's performance are desired. Such performance measures need to be added to our model in order to describe what attributes of a project manager will likely produce good results in projects.

### A Personal Attribute Inventory (PAI)

The following attributes have been suggested as elements of behavior that can determine how effective we are in performance:

1. Working with information
2. Dealing with tasks
3. Working with people
4. Communicating effectively
5. Problem solving and thinking style
6. Business and commercial awareness.

### The Australian requirements

The PAI listed above are similar to the required Australian (key) competences from the Mayer Report referenced in the AIPM competency standard and which follow:

1. Collecting, analyzing and organizing information
2. Communicating ideas and information
3. Planning and organizing activities
4. Working with others in teams
5. Using mathematical ideas and techniques
6. Solving problems
7. Using technology.

## The MCI "Personal Competence" Model

This model from the MCI tries to capture those aspects of behavior which show *how* managers do their jobs effectively as well as what they do to be effective since competence means "the minimum standard required." With management and project management competencies we want someone to be thoroughly competent in the lay sense of the term.

The MCI model suggests that performance measure distinctions such as being *competent*, as used above, are not based on authority or rank, but rather on personal behavior. The unique combination of talents and qualities that make up each individual and which have been developed since birth and modified by learning and work experience are one form of competencies. These competencies are more tangible, visible, measurable, and exhibit certain forms of behavior. Grading systems are widely used with competency models such as in the personal attribute inventory (PAI) shown above, while competence is merely assessed on a pass/fail basis.

Many project managers could be labeled as having achieved competence who would not be considered "good." What is desired is to identify for an individual a level of ability that is excellent, rather than adequate or that just meets standards. This implies "excellence" that a competency approach would describe, as opposed to "sufficient" in a competence model. To develop this we might assess a mixture of competences (including measurable writing and numerical

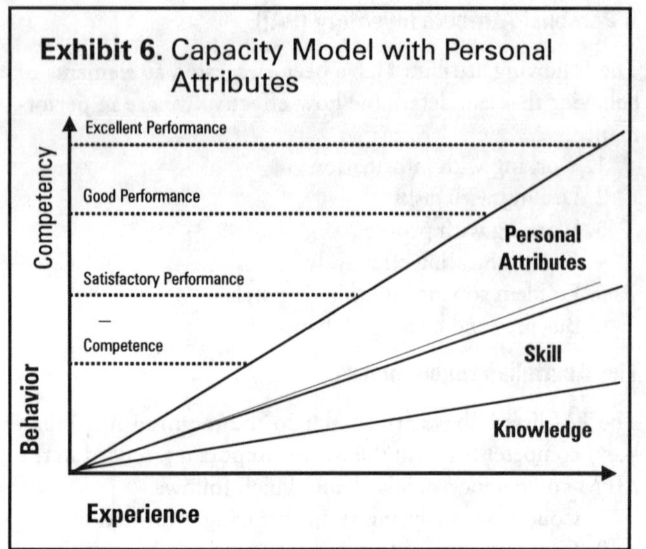


**Exhibit 6.** Capacity Model with Personal Attributes

**Exhibit 7.** Competence and Competency

| Competence | Competency |
|---|---|
| skill based | behavior based |
| standard related | manner of behavior |
| what is measured | how the standard is achieved |

skills) and competencies (required behaviors). But, including behaviors in a competency model is difficult.

## Behaviors and Attributes

Approaches to behavior identification have been variously described as either intellectually based or morally based (head and heart).

Intellectually based behaviors include problem solving, decision making, business awareness, strategic thinking, working with information (many of the tasks of management). Some of these may be learned and many can be evaluated through tests.

Morally based behaviors include integrity, honesty, and individual values. These behaviors are problematic, perhaps impossible, to quantify, and like pornography, are difficult to define, and it is difficult to understand how *courage* could be measured. But, again, like pornography, we usually know it when we see it, and as a judge once observed ... "we nonetheless set standards of decency."

Both of these behavior groups are *attributes*. An attribute is defined as a "quality ascribed to anything or anyone," a "characteristic quality."

*Leadership contains both intellectual and moral aspects of behavior.*

Morally based attributes are difficult to assess with agreed, concrete evidence. Thus they are usually avoided in lieu of intellectually based attributes. Further references in this document to measuring behavior should be ascribed to intellectually based attributes.

Capability is defined as "potential for action, undeveloped ability" (as in competence). Ability is a measure of skill assessment.

When an assessment process does not have elements and indicators (and is thus subjective), it becomes only an assessment of *capability*. There can be no *potentially competent*. You are or you are not.

We must therefore add behaviors, capabilities and (for morally based behaviors) attributes to our vocabulary and to our model.

### Adding Personal Attributes to the Capacity Model

Clearly, the importance of behaviors in assessing individuals relative to future performance cannot be understated. This dimension is then added to the capacity model developed in Exhibit 3, revised and shown in Exhibit 6. This model demonstrates how knowledge, skill and experience work together with behaviors (some learned, others unchangeable) to identify and develop individuals who are capable of outstanding performance.

## A General Competency Model

Rowe (1995) describes a circular model with three components to communicate the relationship of competence and behavior.

- Center—Competences (an identified level of knowledge and skill)
- Middle—Intellectually based behavior (measurable)
- Periphery—Morally based behavior, ethics

In our competency model, the circumference is "soft" (morally based behaviors, i.e. attributes, difficult or impossible to measure) and hardens as you move to the center. The intellectually based behaviors (and capabilities) are in the middle, while the hard center ring contains the measurable *competences*. The relationship of knowledge, skills and behavior relative to competence and competency is shown in Exhibit 7.

The appearance, conduct, tone of voice, verbal demeanor, communication method and body communication content of an individual is an important element of performance. Not all project environments nor clients are the same. Some styles fit better in a project context than others. For example: the *style* of American project managers responsible for lump-sum heavy construction projects can be and usually is different than the *style* of project managers responsible for internally budgeted Information Technology (IT) projects. Not only is the demeanor markedly different, but these attributes that make up the style (and personality) of the project manager are significant factors in dealing (particularly in communicating) with project team members and other project stakeholders. And style certainly varies with culture. Daily interactions with a project manager raised in a Middle ast culture conducting three simultaneous and informal meetings at one time is quite different than the more formal communications approach of the British or Germans. This is not to suggest that any specific project manager cannot be successful on any specific project, they can. But there can be no doubt that some *styles* are better suited than others given the project context, team makeup and client. The attribute referred to here as *style* is meant to convey the notion of this quality as well as the integration of other attributes into the way we act as project managers and individuals in our everyday dealings with and beliefs about people. While some elements of style can be changed at will to some degree, such as our appearance and the words that we speak, others cannot, such as our body language and tone of voice. This attribute, while impossible to measure, is nonetheless more apparent than morally based attributes. The model is expanded to add *style* as a personal attribute of the project manager surrounding the other behaviors, as shown in Exhibit 8 representing the visible outward shell of the individual.

Our enhanced model includes the knowledge-skill identification along with the topology modifiers (the center) replacing the previous word *competence* within the circular model from Rowe (1995) and adding *style* as the outermost circle.

**Exhibit 8.** An Adaptable Model

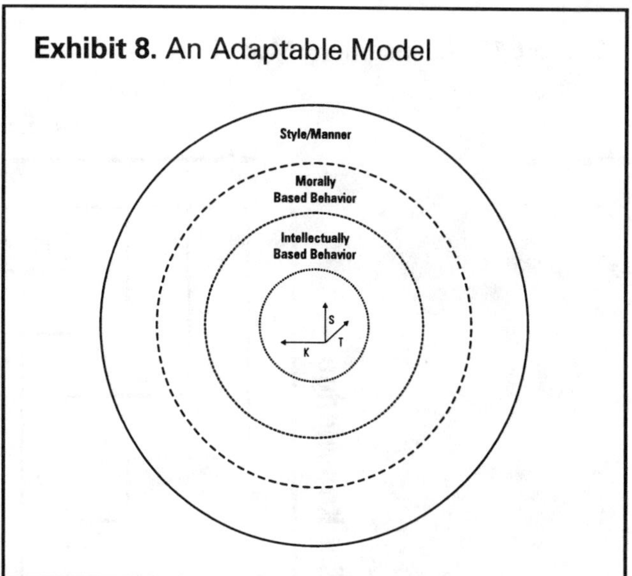


**Exhibit 9.** Enterprise Project Mana Gement

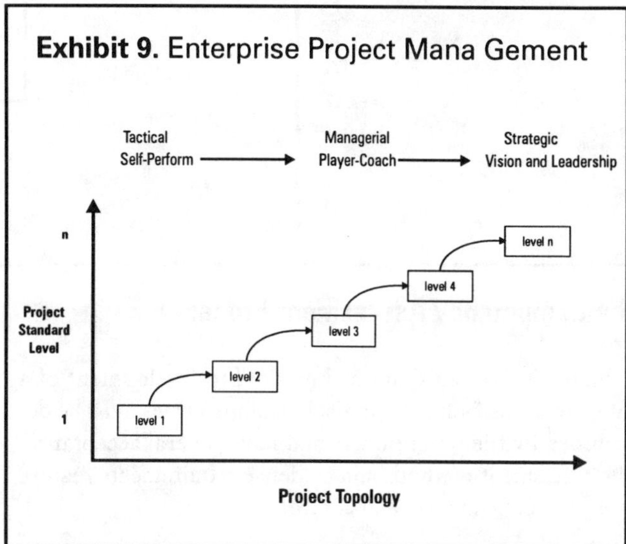


## Enterprise Project Management

So how can this model be used to provide information about candidates and aid in their development? First it is necessary to understand the context of the projects the enterprise in engaged in. There are six primary factors influencing success in managing projects, they are: (1) Culture, (2) Topology, (3) Client, (4) Organization, (5) Team, (6) Project Manager.

In addition to the competency of the project manager, organization and project team competency are necessary to ensure long-term success in projects. First, given the range of project topologies and the enterprise engaged in, various standard levels must be set for accomplishing projects. Within any enterprise, by definition, all projects are not the same. Managing all projects with a fixed set of standards which identify a uniform set of tools, methods and practices will lead to unproductive overly rigorous processes on projects that do not require them and eventually become a burden on the enterprise. The development of enterprise project standard levels is illustrated in Exhibit 9.

For each standard level, a set of competencies may then be determined. These standards would be appropriate for the project topology relative to the processes, methods and practices as well as the tools and techniques to carry them out. At the top of Exhibit 10, three general categories ranging from *tactical* on the left to *strategic* on the right imply the change in focus as the standards of project performance and the desired competencies of the project manager change. Competencies may be assessed for each project standard level and used as an access control technique and to aid development of project managers and team participants.

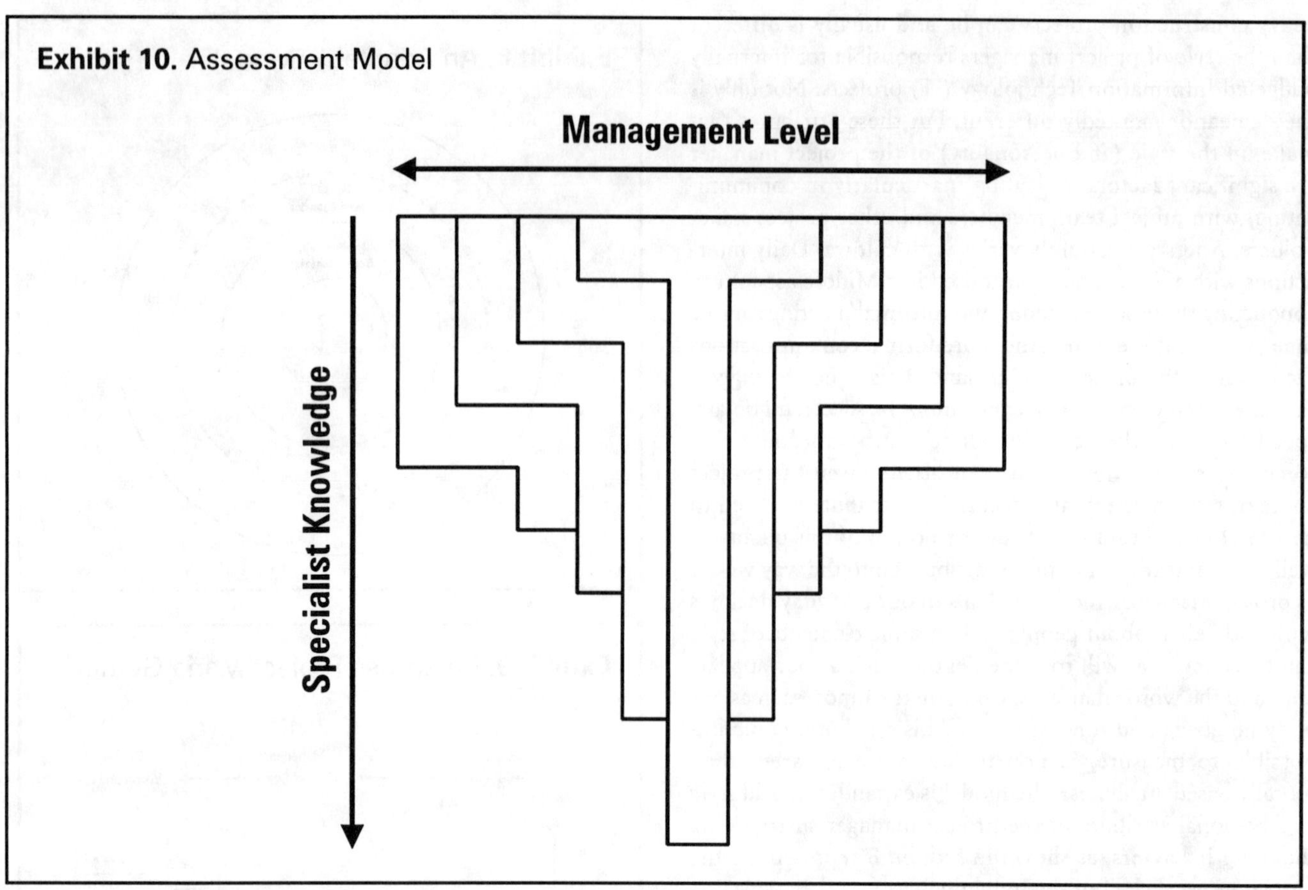

**Exhibit 10.** Assessment Model

## The Competency Assessment Process

Exhibit 10 shows a simplified model for development of a competency assessment approach. Competencies must be determined by the practitioners and have general acceptance. The assessment methods and evidence requirements require careful documentation and control.

## Summary

This model can represent a first step in establishing an enterprise model for competency assessment of project managers. Developing project standards is the first step. Identifying the behaviors of excellent performance is the most difficult and determining the evidence and assessor criteria the most time consuming.

### References

Rowe, Christopher. 1995. "Clarifying the Use of Competence and Competency Models in Recruitment, Assessment and Staff Development." *Industrial and Commercial Training*, 27, 11:12-17.

Turner, Rodney J. 1996. "IPMA Global Qualification, Certification and Accreditation." *International Journal of Project Management*, *14*, 1 (February):1-8.

# Solution Generation: Expanding the View of Project Management

Chris Torkelson, Northwestern Mutual Life Insurance Company
Margaret Combe, Northwestern Mutual Life Insurance Company

## Successful Projects Require Both Effective Solution Generation and Solution Implementation

Projects are successful when the "right things" are "done right." Project management has as much potential to assist in the generation of solutions (right things) as it does to assure the successful implementation of those solutions (things right). The skills, activities and tools required to generate a solution are different than those to implement a solution. In many cases project managers don't just manage the implementation of a solution, they are asked to find the solution and then implement it. Even when asked only to implement the solution project managers must recognize potential risks with proposed solutions. Project managers assigned projects to generate and implement solutions are missing half the equation if the tools in their toolbox focus primarily on managing project implementation. Tools that help project managers to generate creative and innovative solutions are an important part of a robust project management toolbox.

Consider this classic story. A semi-truck driver ignored signs of a low clearance on a back-road highway and sandwiched the trailer of his truck under a concrete bridge spanning the highway. Almost immediately traffic began backing up on both sides of the bridge. A local policeman was soon on the scene and in control of the situation. Being a good project manager, he quickly called the nearest semi tow truck located 30 miles away and requested assistance. This completed, he effectively orchestrated the rerouting of traffic around the blockage. One hour, and many perturbed motorists later, the tow truck arrived. Unfortunately, the truck was so completely lodged under the bridge that the tow truck could not budge it. Unruffled, the patrolman called the rescue squad in a nearby town to bring the "Jaws of Life," a hydraulic metal-cutting machine, to free the truck. The "Jaws" arrived 45 minutes later, but after another hour of work could not free the truck. The patrolman was at a loss, three hours into the blockage and no progress. His quick action to call the tow truck and systematically reroute traffic and then call in the "Jaws of Life," effective implementations of reasonable solutions, had resulted in zero progress. As the police, fire and other rescue personal huddled discussing options, a small boy from a nearby farm tapped one of the policemen on the back and innocently asked, "Why don't you let the air out of the tires?" The semi was freed in 10 minutes.

This story is intended to highlight how effective implementation is not enough to assure a project's success. Effective solution generation, a process that assists with understanding a problem and developing a creative solution, is as important to a successful result as is effective implementation.

The example above had a very simple solution. In real life, problems are seldom this simple. However, the example demonstrates how people tend to jump to solutions. It's human nature to want to solve the problem as fast as possible. The policeman was programmed that when a vehicle is stuck, a tow truck is the answer. If the policeman had taken the time to think about the problem before reacting, would he have identified the solution the boy did? All of us, including project managers, are preprogrammed in one way or another. Providing tools, techniques and best practices geared toward challenging project managers and teams to uncover the root causes of problems, understanding stakeholder issues and generating creative solutions can significantly impact the value of the product delivered.

## A Focus on Solution Generation

The goals of solution generation are different than those of solution implementation. Solution generation focuses on *what*: solving the right problem (not a symptom), and solving the problem optimally (not implementing the first good idea). Solution implementation concerns itself with *how*: solve quickly, cheaply, with expected results.

The processes to effectively complete these activities must also be different. Solution implementation is a structured planning and control process, while solution generation is a structured problem-solving process.

The structured problem-solving process is summarized in Exhibit 1. *Analyzing root causes* entails burrowing below the symptomatic level of the problem to hypothesize what is causing the problem, then using data or expert opinion to validate the analysis of the problem. *Identifying solution objectives* generates agreement on the part of stakeholders as to what a successful solution looks like, and what its most critical elements are. As the problem is analyzed and a picture of

Exhibit 1. Structured Problem Solving Process

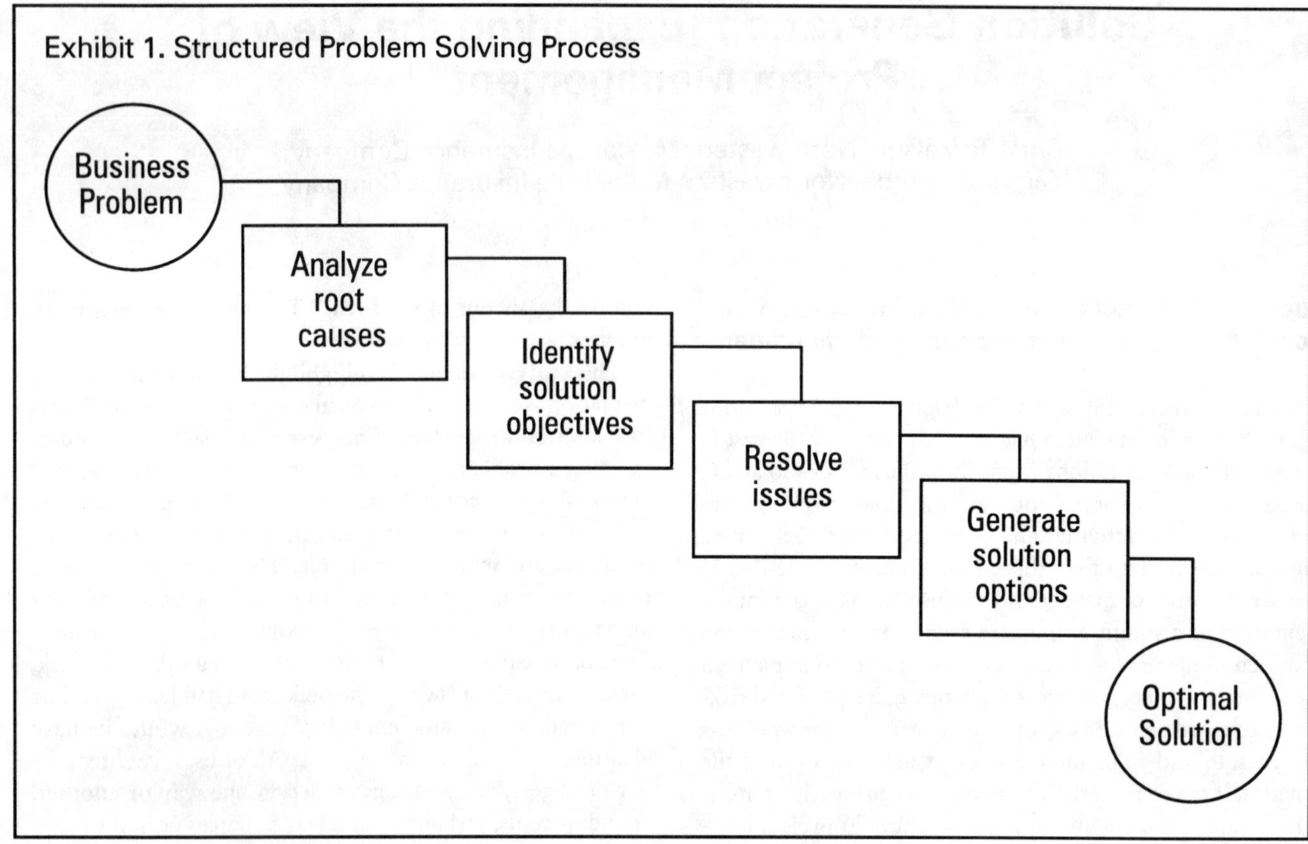


success evolves, issues arise about such things as what cultural changes might be acceptable, how far the solution needs to go in completely solving the problem, and what are the capabilities of the organization to implement solution ideas which might be generated. *Resolving these issues* places boundaries on the range of solutions that will be acceptable. Once the first three steps are accomplished, there is a temptation to gravitate to the most obvious solution, as the local policeman did in the story above. The challenge, in *generating solution options*, is to get beyond the obvious solution, beyond the copycat approach, to identify a solution that is innovative and is optimal for solving the root cause problem.

In solution implementation, controlling and managing tools and activities aid the project manager: work breakdown structures, schedules, budgets. In solution generation, the tools and activities are directed more toward focusing and aligning. Many solution generation tools have their roots in TQM (Total Quality Management) processes; others in creativity research. Many are absurdly simple—a way of organizing thoughts—while others are hypothetical constructs that encourage multidimensional thinking.

In the remainder of this paper, we will visit each of the subprocesses of structured problem solving, identifying the key activities and value-added tools that we've found work to continually hone the focus and alignment of an optimal solution with its root cause business problem.

## Solution Generation Tools and Techniques

As stated above, we break down solution generation techniques into four categories:

- Analyze root causes
- Identify solution objectives
- Identify and resolve issues and
- Generate solution options.

### Step 1. Analyze Root Causes

Examples of tools that fall into this category are *Business Issue Definition Tool,* Stakeholder Analysis, PRIDE, and Why Technique. The *Business Issue Definition Tool* provides an example of a very simple construct a project manager should consider using when first given a project assignment. It is designed to help project managers get a handle on why the project is being requested, who will be impacted and what the impact will be. A portion of the tool as it appears in the Northwestern Mutual Life Insurance Project Manager's Knowledgebase is provided in Exhibit 2. This tool challenges project managers from the start of their projects to define and

**Exhibit 2.** Business Issue Definition Tool

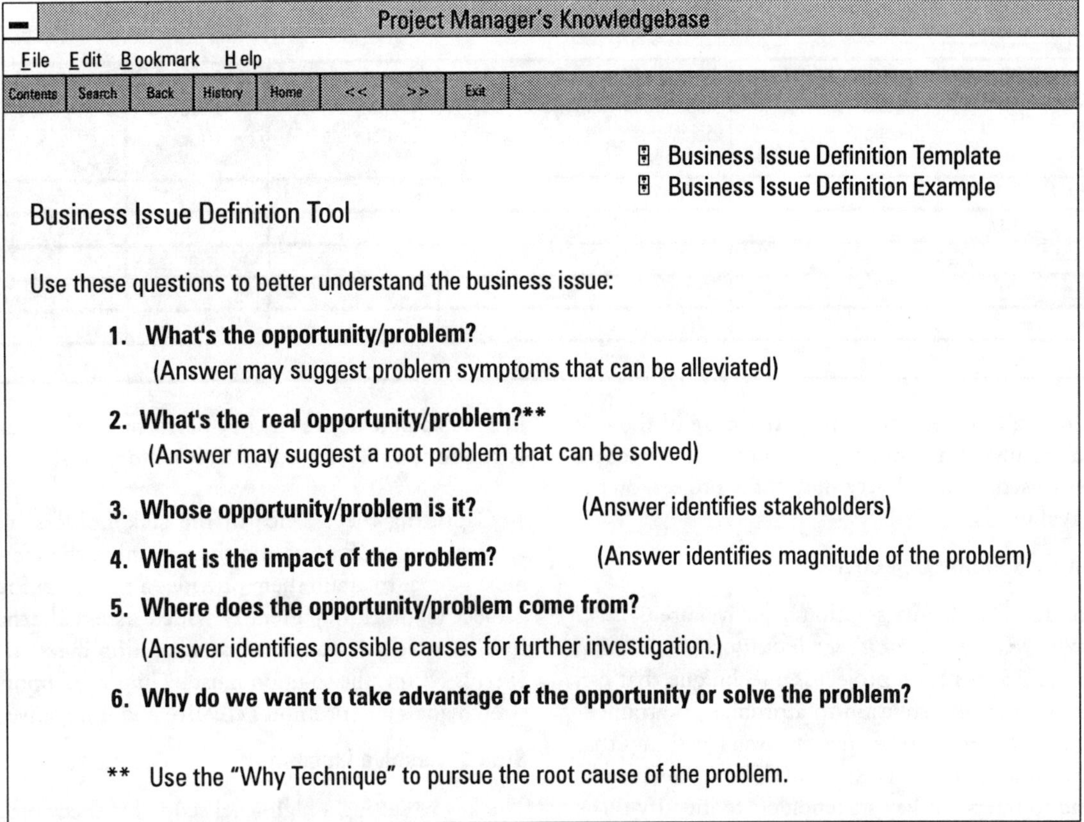

Project Manager's Knowledgebase
File Edit Bookmark Help
Contents Search Back History Home << >> Exit
Business Issue Definition Template
Business Issue Definition Example
Business Issue Definition Tool
Use these questions to better understand the business issue:
1. What's the opportunity/problem?
(Answer may suggest problem symptoms that can be alleviated)
2. What's the real opportunity/problem?**
(Answer may suggest a root problem that can be solved)
3. Whose opportunity/problem is it? (Answer identifies stakeholders)
4. What is the impact of the problem? (Answer identifies magnitude of the problem)
5. Where does the opportunity/problem come from?
(Answer identifies possible causes for further investigation.)
6. Why do we want to take advantage of the opportunity or solve the problem?
** Use the "Why Technique" to pursue the root cause of the problem.

**Exhibit 3.** Critical Success Factors and Key Performance Indicators

| Critical Success Factor | Key Performance Indicator |
|---|---|
| • the customer must be accurately informed of options at first contact | • 98% of customer calls monitored must accurately inform customer of options |
| • generate need based assessment and purchase, if appropriate, within two year time frame | • 85% of individuals contacted must request assessment and 75% of those with identified needs must purchase within two years |

be consciously aware of the reason they are doing the project. This exercise prevents project managers and teams from jumping to solutions before the real issues are understood and forces discussion of end customer needs. In several instances it has caused projects to be cancelled or postponed because the real business issue was deemed not worth addressing at the current time.

The *Why Technique* is another tool that can help get to root causes of problems. Note that it is referenced in the second question in the *Business Issue Definition Tool*. The *Why Technique* is another simple technique that suggests that the project manager ask the question "Why?" until the ultimate reason for doing something becomes clear. "Why is this a problem for this person?" "Why does it have this impact?" This allows the project manager and team to understand the

**Exhibit 4.**

**Issue Resolution Tool**

| ISSUE | Who needs to make the decision? | Issues, obstacles, or dependencies to making decisions | Team Member Responsible | Resolution Date | Date Completed |
|---|---|---|---|---|---|
| | | | | | |
| | | | | | |
| | | | | | |
| | | | | | |
| | | | | | |

reasons for doing a project from the perspective of the end customer and results in the project leader and team members being more focused, from the very start of the project, on the customer's real needs.

## Step 2. Identify Solution Objectives

The key tools to help identify solution objectives are *Critical Success Factors and Key Performance Indicators*. Generating *Critical Success Factors* for a project is a technique that can help assure that the best solution to a problem is attained. *Critical Success Factors* are those five to seven key things that must happen for an effort to be successful. Project managers are prompted to interview key stakeholders to identify those things that are a "must do" or "must have" and then document them, obtain agreement on them and communicate them to the project team. These factors are then kept visible throughout the effort to help the team keep its focus and are eventually used to assess the relative merits of each solution alternative identified.

In the Northwestern Mutual Life Insurance methodology, we define *Critical Success Factors* as "the few key project directives which point the direction for change." They act as a vehicle for focusing the project manager and team on key stakeholder needs, and they are identified by refining the stakeholder expectations. In order to be an effective *Critical Success Factor* a statement must be specific (not "satisfied customers," but "the customer will be accurately informed of options in the first contact"). A *Critical Success Factor* must also identify a direction for change rather than make vague statements about the future (not "this project must allow us to make repeat sales to our customers," but "this project will generate an assessment of existing customers needs and, if a need exists, result in a repeat purchase within a two year time frame").

*Key Performance Indicators* are the actual measures that will be used to determine if the *Critical Success Factor* is met. In the example above the key performance indicators could correspond to the critical success factors as, shown in Exhibit 3.

Capturing the essence of the stakeholders' needs with *Critical Success Factors* and then defining the measures that must be met to attain them provides a necessary focus for the project team as they identify issues, assess alternatives and find creative solutions. Unless a solution meets the *Critical Success Factor*, the solution must be improved upon. This sets stretch goals and promotes creative and innovative solutions.

## Step 3: Resolve Issues

The key to setting a high-level scope for the project is to determine what issues must be dealt with in order to arrive at a suitable solution. For instance, if a key performance indicator, as proposed in Exhibit 3, requires measurement of the percentage of individuals contacted, an issue might be the current lack of data about customer contacts. Another issue in this kind of project might be whether any kind of repeat sale qualifies, or if certain kinds of product sales are the goal.

There are a number of tools that can help focus the efforts to resolve issues. One that our project managers have found particularly valuable is the *Issue Resolution Template*. This tool is available to help a project manager quickly assign responsibilities to resolve issues and to help project team members remain on schedule by systematically answering the issues. The format of the *Issue Resolution Template* is shown in Exhibit 4.

This is another straightforward tool that can significantly impact the focus and quality of decision making. Key things we suggest to project managers using this tool are: always assign responsibility for the issue to a team member, along with a date for bringing back needed information or decisions. To motivate team members to follow through on assignments, we suggest project managers keep this list up to date throughout

**Exhibit 5.** Verb Checklist Example

| Verb | Ideas |
|---|---|
| Magnify | Invite more people occasionally: foreign students, local artists, etc. Increase number of courses in dinner (smaller portions). |
| Minimize | Eat around a smaller table to make it seem more intimate. |
| Rearrange | Have a "picnic" meal on the porch. Have a reverse meal with the dessert first. |
| Substitute | Instead of having TV on during the meal, play music.<br>Instead of always having potatoes, serve something like polenta. |
| Combine | Combine meal and a board game or a puzzle. |
| Adapt | Have everyone in the family prepare one course.<br>Do family menu planning. |
| Modify | Have a catered meal on occasion. |
| Eliminate | Instead of eating dinner, go as a family to serve dinner to the homeless. |
| Put to other uses | Use family meal time to have family conferences about vacations, use of the family car, etc. |

the project, and publish it to the team and sponsors on a periodic basis.

The *Scope Resolution Template* is a method to help a team and stakeholders limit the project's scope to the most important and relevant requirements. The project manager using this tool will ask the person requesting a change in scope to document the following things:

1. A description of what the requestor feels should be added to the scope
2. A summary of the impact on the customers
3. A financial and sales impact of including this request.

Using this as the consistent means by which scope change issues are addressed has several advantages. First, it can limit requests for scope enlargement, because it requires a good amount of analysis and time to write up a request. Second, this will help the requester and the team to discuss and agree upon the impact of the change because the change is documented in writing. Third, because everyone is on the same page when it comes to making the decision on inclusion or exclusion of the request, the time required to make the decision is reduced.

## Step 4. Generation of Optimal Solutions

*Pattern Breaking Tools* are one set of constructs that assist in the generation of the optimal solution.

*Pattern Breaking Tools* are a compilation of numerous techniques designed to assist in generating solution ideas that go beyond the obvious. Along with generating ideas, they can also make the more obvious solution ideas better.

It's useful to first get out as many ideas as possible using brainstorming, then apply one or more of the *Pattern Breaking Tools* to develop additional ideas.

Examples of the use of the tools are provided below.

### *Tool 1: Verb Checklist*

This tool is especially useful for enhancing solution ideas. Take any of the solution ideas developed in brainstorming, and, using the verbs listed, generate ideas to improve the solution idea:

Example: Original problem definition is related to quality of family life. One solution idea is to make mealtime together more stimulating.

### *Tool 2: Metaphoric Thinking*

This tool works especially well in generating broad areas of ideas to enhance processes. It helps to make sure you"ve thought of all areas in which you might be able to affect the process. It consists of trying to draw parallels between your opportunity and a well-known system. First you select a "system" (e.g., a garden, a beehive, a playground, a zoo), and brainstorm all of the elements of that system. Then you identify parallel elements in your own opportunity. Some of the relationships will come quickly and obviously. The elements which do not have the most obvious parallels in your process will, however, generate the most fruitful new ideas.

Example: The opportunity you have identified is to improve your telephone-provided customer service. The "system" you'll use to parallel is a garden.

The attempt in this section was to provide a sample of the types of tools that can assist with solution generation. We focused on the more simplistic tools and examples for the sake of comprehension. More sophisticated tools exist, but require hands-on training and examples to make them useful.

**Exhibit 6.** Metephoric Thinking Example

| Garden elements | Customer phone service elements |
|---|---|
| Seeds | Questions, requests from customers |
| Weeds | Complaints |
| Soil | Knowledge base of service representatives |
| Water | Auxiliary expertise from other areas |
| Sun | Attitude of the service representative |
| Scarecrow | Means of preventing calls by being proactive |

**Exhibit 7.** Project Knowledgebase Main Screen

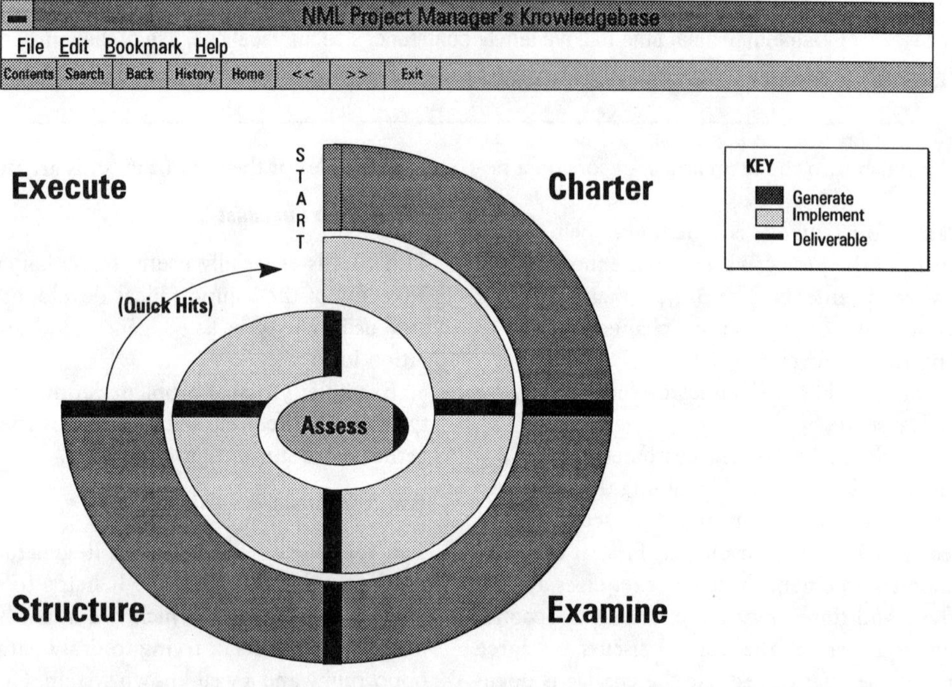


As stated before, the tools you use to support solution generation need to be tailored to your organization's needs. Some tools have wide applicability, while others may be specific to an organization's culture. When considering your organization's needs, examine the project management environment in your organization. If you expect project managers to both generate and implement solutions, consider providing tools, techniques and best practices like those discussed above to help them generate focused and innovative solutions that truly address root causes of problems.

## Integrating Solution Generation With Solution Implementation

Identifying and documenting tools to assist with solution generation is not enough to create an effective Solution Generation process. Once that is accomplished, it is important to integrate these tools with your organization's existing project management methodology. Northwestern Mutual Life did this by developing what we call our "Project Manager's Knowledgebase." The "Project Manager's Knowledgebase" is an online project management methodology that is available on all project managers' desktops in the organization.

Exhibit 7 shows the home screen in the "Project Manager's Knowledgebase" that provides access to all tools, techniques and best practices for our company's project management. The two spirals represent two different levels of analysis. The outer spiral contains tools, techniques and best practices that assist project managers generate the solution. The inner circle contains the more traditional project management practices that are found in the PMBOK and contain the information to assist project managers implement the solution. The spiral design was chosen because it supports the concept that the generation of the solution flows into the implementation of the solution. The concept of iteration is also supported by the spiral design. There are four main phases at both the generation and implementation levels: Charter, Examine, Structure, Execute. Whether developing or implementing a solution, these four major phases need to be followed.

An issue we surfaced and needed to resolve was the lack of trained staff to make updates to any kind of online vehicle ("easily enhanced" was another critical success factor). We were thus prompted to find a programming tool that was simple and direct, allowing us to program changes as easily as to prepare Word documents. The tool allowed two of us to develop content and implement the knowledgebase within six months. Entire sections of the knowledgebase have been rewritten since its introduction a year ago, based on feedback from project managers and advancements in tools and best practices.

Because another issue was a lack of tolerance for extended training, we made the methodology, via the knowledgebase, self-directing. The knowledgebase has supported the training of over 250 project managers in a year's time frame. A three-hour introduction to the knowledgebase is sufficient to get project managers comfortable using the methodology.

## Conclusion

The structuring of a methodology for generating solutions has helped our organization to improve the speed and quality of overall project delivery. Project teams report that they get stuck less frequently, and when they do, the tools of solution generation help to restart the stalled project. Focusing on the formation of an appropriate solution to a business issue has prevented project results that have had to be redone, due to an incorrect assessment of the project's real purpose. And, at times, the solution generation methodology has caused project sponsors and stakeholders to reconsider the need for a project, freeing resources for more important efforts. Even though this portion of the methodology does not concern itself primarily with cost and time, it is clear that these kinds of results aid time to completion, and reduce (even eliminate) costs of the project.

# The Mythical Critical Path: Managing for Project Failure with CPM

William E. Skimin, Integrated Management Systems, Inc.
Elliot Chocron, Integrated Management Systems, Inc

Author Note: This paper is presented to provide a situation that can be used as the basis for a discussion of issues in project management. The company and people described below are fictional.

"So," Ted Winslow said, wrapping up his half-hour presentation, "with everyone's commitment to the plan, we will bring the project in on time, meeting all of Wycoff Manufacturing's requirements."

"Great job, Ted," said Lisa Stevens, general manager of the Control Systems Division. "But the project is just getting started. Give me an update in a month and let me know if we're on track."

Ted took down his charts and headed back to his office. His project timing presentation had been the culmination of six months of hard work. Ted had been put in charge of improving CSD's project performance. A long-time leader in the manufacturing control systems industry, CSD had recently lost several contracts, many going to competitors that had come from the data processing and communications industries, where rapid change and agile product development were a way of life. Moreover, continuing pressure from customers to reduce delivery lead time while demanding "smarter" systems had reduced profit margins, even leading to losses on some contracts. Lisa Stevens had been brought into CSD nine months ago, with two years to either turn it around or clean it up so that it could be sold.

## Implementing Project Management at CSD

Ted, an enthusiastic PM software user, dove right into his new assignment. First, he spent several weeks reviewing CSD's performance on a number of past projects. In the end, he had a list of project problems, the top three of which were:

- Late project changes from the client
- Delays caused by late subcontractor deliveries
- Delays in completing designs caused by conflicts with other jobs that had higher priorities.

In talking to various managers, engineers and other project participants, Ted also found that there was a great deal of variation in the way that projects were managed. Overall, most of the people that Ted spoke with felt that there was very poor communication of the project plan or of their specific responsibilities on a project.

Based on his analysis, Ted developed project templates that would serve as a starting point for any new project plan. He also reviewed published surveys and selected a project management software package. He developed a one-day training class for the engineers and other users that included the reports and templates that would be used at CSD. Finally, he made a one-hour presentation to the department managers on project management basics and the benefits to CSD.

Project planning started during bid preparation. An initial project plan was developed as a part of the bid package using a template selected based on the project scope and budget.

After CSD was awarded the contract, a planning team consisting of the project manager and managers from each of the departments responsible for executing the project would be assembled. They would review the initial project plan, making any changes needed to meet the contract scope and schedule requirements. These changes had to fit into the timing "footprint" established by the template; the critical path defined by the template had to be preserved. If necessary, the planning team could increase the work done in parallel or reduce activity duration, as long as the overall project length did not increase. This review would be accomplished at an intensive three-day "planning workshop," at the end of which each manager would formally commit their departments to the plan by signing a project contract. At that point the project baseline would be set as the basis for future control actions.

Priority was placed on managing activities on the baseline critical path so that problems and issues could be evaluated based on their potential impact on project completion. The assumption was that if the critical path could be maintained all of the other work would fall into place. By focusing attention on the critical path, everyone would work on the tasks that were most important in executing the project plan. Managers had the flexibility to let noncritical tasks slip as needed within the float that was available. Communication would be improved by providing a clear set of requirements and priorities.

## The Wycoff Project

Wycoff Manufacturing issued a Request for Proposals to supply an integrated manufacturing control system for a new plant being built in South America. With an estimated budget of $15 million, it attracted bids from all of the leading control system suppliers, including CSD.

CSD's bid was aggressive, promising delivery in 18 months, at least six months faster than they had been able to deliver similar systems in the past. It was, however, comparable to the lead times quoted by their competitors. Based on his analysis, Ted felt confident that CSD would be able to deliver the Wycoff project on time.

CSD was awarded the contract, based in large part on their final presentation that included an overview of their project control process by Ted.

### The Wycoff Project Planning Workshop

The planning workshop had been completed two days prior to Ted's briefing for Lisa Stevens. After reviewing the workshop objectives and process, Ted began a detailed presentation of the project plan, explaining how they would be able to complete the project in 25 percent less time than before, using critical path management. The project plan, based on a template that Ted had developed by analyzing past projects, had nearly 500 tasks. He had not gotten very far when Bernie Porta, manager of the Electrical Design Group, interrupted him.

"Ted, you've only given me 12 weeks for the wiring harness layout drawings," he said. "I need 16, minimum, plus an extra six, at least, for changes once Wycoff sends the mechanical layouts. That's at nearly twice as long as your plan shows."

"Not only that," said Ben Mertz, the senior buyer for control units. "If I understand your plan correctly, you've only got eight weeks lead time for delivery of N/C control blocks. The market's tight right now and vendors are getting at least 12 weeks, sometimes more."

That set off a crescendo of complaints, until the room became filled with a roar of voices, with each participant pointing out "obvious" problems with the plan. After about five minutes, Ted began to shout over the din, trying to regain control.

"Okay, okay," he said, trying to make himself heard. "I know that you've got a lot of questions and concerns about how we're going to pull this off."

He then went into a detailed explanation of project planning and the critical path method.

"See, Bernie," he said. "Your harness layouts aren't on the critical path, which goes through initial client specifications, mainline control design and chassis construction, and then installation, programming and test at the client site. Your harness design has 10 weeks of float, so you should be all right. It's the same with your N/C control blocks, Ben; you've got eight weeks of float before they're needed."

Ted took the rest of the day leading the group through the complex web of logic that tied all of the tasks together. By 4:30 that afternoon, everyone at least understood how the plan had been put together. Over the next two days, the group added detail, rearranged logic, and documented any issues that still needed to be resolved. The critical path, however, remained inviolate as the group built the plan around it. Despite their lingering skepticism, everyone signed the project contract at the end of the workshop. Two days later, as Ted presented a summary of the plan to Lisa, he was confident that CSD had turned the corner and was ready to deliver the project.

### One Month Later ...

The Wycoff project had been under way for only three weeks and Ted was already seeing trouble. Less than a week after providing the initial specifications package, Wycoff issued a notice stating that a manufacturing process change was being evaluated that would require a revision in the control system layout. It would not change the project scope, but it did mean that several activities, including harness design, would be delayed at least four weeks.

As Ted reviewed the updated plan preparing for his briefing with Lisa, he was shocked to see that initial delivery of control panels to Wycoff had slipped by three weeks and was now on the critical path. Working back through the project logic, it appeared that this had been caused by a combination of noncritical activity delays and earlier-than-expected starts of several critical path tasks. More importantly, the project end date had slipped two weeks against the baseline.

"Let me see if I understand this, Ted," Lisa said, as Ted explained the situation. "We actually started some of the critical tasks earlier than planned and that made us late? Why didn't we see what was going to happen? Did those other tasks slip on their own without our noticing, or did we make a decision to delay them? What can we do to get back on track?"

"We need to stick closer to the plan," Ted replied. I'm going to start collecting updates every week and will ask for reports on every task slippage so that we can analyze its impact on the critical path to prevent further slippage. As far as recovering the two weeks that we've lost, I'm going to authorize limited overtime on the mainline design to pick up the time. It's a small hit on the budget short-term, but I think that we'll pick that up by reducing the amount of rework and wasted overtime later."

"Okay, Ted," Lisa said. "I'm looking forward to your next update in a month."

When he got back to his office, Ted issued a project memo announcing the new update cycle and review procedures. He also signed the overtime authorization for the mainline design team. Picking up his voice-mail, he heard a message from Bernie Porta; the revised process specifications had been delayed another two weeks.

### Another Month Later ...

Over the next four weeks, Ted worked 12-hour days trying to keep up with the flood of project data coming into his office. The situation was aggravated by the fact that he had added several dozen activities to the plan in an attempt to provide better visibility of emerging problems. He brought in Cathy Wallace, an engineer from his old department, on a temporary assignment to help him plow through the data. Both of them spent at least half of their time in department and project meetings, making presentations, explaining which tasks had to start or finish that week, and collecting status reports.

One problem that had been especially vexing concerned the wiring harness layouts. The revised process specifications had finally been delivered. Although they were not complete, they were sufficient to begin the initial designs. Last week, however, Bernie had received a rush job to make revisions to a system that was being installed for another client, tying up two senior designers for at least two weeks. That meant starting the Wycoff job with a less experienced team, adding at least a week to the task. With the earlier delays, that left harness layouts with only two weeks of float against the baseline. With additional changes expected as the specifications were completed, the situation could only get worse.

Overall, the project had lost another two weeks and was now forecast to finish four weeks late.

As he spent hours and days pouring over the project plans, however, Ted began to understand how the initial problems had developed. He had not appreciated how sensitive the project network would be to change as task progress data was added. The critical path had changed so much that the initial baseline plan was now obsolete.

"But, if you can't set a baseline plan to manage against, how will you know when you're in trouble?" Cathy asked, while she and Ted were preparing for the review meeting with Lisa the next morning.

"I don't know," Ted replied. "We had a good plan when we started, then things began to change. Anyway, we'll have to think more about that later; right now we've got to get ready for our meeting with Lisa tomorrow."

### A Critical Realization

"Well, Ted," Lisa said, after Ted had completed his project report. "Things seem to have gotten worse. If we keep slipping at this rate we'll finish nine months late. One thing that confuses me is how much the critical path has changed. I thought that we had identified the most important activities. If they were the critical activities at the start, why aren't they now?"

Ted explained how the critical path is calculated and how, based on his analysis, it had changed over the past two months.

"So, when you talk about 'critical' tasks, you're not really saying that they are the most important, only that they are on the longest path through the project network?" asked Lisa, after he had finished.

"That's right," Ted agreed. "Any slips in any one of those tasks will cause the project to be late."

"So, they're only critical from a timing standpoint," Lisa said. "If you were to analyze the project plan from another point of view, say cost, there might be another 'critical path,' based on the most expensive path through the project. You could have all kinds of ways to identify 'critical' activities, such as resources, quality, risk, profitability, and so forth. Let's say that you have a project where time isn't important, but there is some scarce resource; how would CPM deal with that?"

"Well," responded Ted. "You can add resources to tasks, and some programs let you determine how long a task will take based on the resources assigned to it. You can also assign priorities to tasks and have the program select which ones are to be done if there are overloads. But, the basic analysis will still be based on finding the critical, that is, the longest, path through the network."

"Maybe that's what's happening here, Ted," said Lisa. "Our project is being driven by some other factor or combination of factors. Sure, we have a tight time schedule, but that isn't what's causing the delays. Your original critical path plan showed that the project *could* be done in 18 months, but actually *doing* it requires a different set of measurements and controls, using different techniques."

"Let's meet again next week to talk more about this," she said, with a weary smile. "As far as I can see, this project isn't any different than any other we've done recently; thanks to you, we just have a better picture of the trouble that we're in. Your current situation notwithstanding, I still think that you've got the right idea; maybe the problem lies in the way your going about it."

### Developing a Better Approach

Back in his office, Ted described the meeting to Cathy.

"I don't know a lot about CPM," Cathy said, after he had finished. "But one thing that has struck me is how static it is; you set up the network, analyze it and get the answer. You could re-analyze it a thousand times and the answer wouldn't vary. From what I can tell, and our experience bears this out, there is a lot of potential variation in the plan. Just look at what's happened to the wiring harness design. First, there were delays in receiving Wycoff's specs. Then the duration changed based on the presence of competing work for the same resources. Now there's uncertainty, leading to even more variation, while we wait for the final specs. That one activity alone has several sources of variation, all leading to potential delays, yet none of that is comprehended in the analysis. If I were looking at this project from a manufacturing process control perspective, I'd try to determine where the greatest variation would come from; that would define my 'critical' tasks. Control them and time takes care of itself."

"Here's another type of problem that we couldn't have predicted using CPM," Ted said, handing Cathy a memo from Ben Martz, the senior component buyer. "Our source for N/C control blocks just quoted 20 weeks lead time to fill our order. Ben tells me that if we had gotten our order in just two weeks earlier, we could have gotten them in just eight weeks, but a big order came in just before ours, taking all of their production for the next two months. So, it seems that there is a certain 'lumpiness' in some tasks where capacity comes in lots; miss your window by a week and the delay may be many times that."

As they talked more about the problems afflicting the Wycoff project, Ted and Cathy began to compile a list of sources of delay that were not considered by their critical path plan. A summary of their list is shown in Exhibit 1.

**Exhibit 1.** Potential Sources of Schedure Variation

| Source of Delay |
|---|
| Environmental Factors<br>• Supplier capacity availability<br>• Scarce resource availability |
| Competing Projects<br>• Resource conflicts<br>• Management priorities |
| Changes in Requirements<br>• Technical requirements<br>• Schedule requirements<br>• Resource requirements |
| Other Sources of Variation<br>• Variation of duration estimates<br>• Constraint flexibility<br>• Resource productivity |

### Establishing the ground rules for a successful project control plan

The next morning, Ted had more than a dozen voice-mails detailing problems on specific project tasks. Looking at his calendar, Ted saw that he and Cathy were scheduled to attend five project team meetings that day.

"We've got more data about, but no more control than ever before," Ted mused aloud. Glancing at the list that they had compiled yesterday, he continued. "We're collecting precise measurements of things that vary all over the map. Maybe we should step back to get a better grasp of what's really going on."

"That's just what I've been thinking," said Cathy, walking into Ted's office. "We're buried in details that don't point to the real problem—the most significant sources of variation and project risk."

"Look at our problem list," she continued. "We need to go through the project network and identify which of these apply to each activity and then find the 'critical path' based on potential risk of delay."

"But," Ted protested, "our plan has more than 800 activities. It would take days to evaluate each one. And even then, how would we be able to determine their aggregate impact on the project?"

"I've been thinking about that, too," replied Cathy. "We need to stop looking at the detailed tasks and look at the important outputs that drive the project, things like designs, specifications, purchased components, etc. Once we've identified them and determined when they're needed to keep the project moving forward, then we can look for the 'gotchas' that could make them late."

"Which are the things that we need to control, the sources of variation," said Ted, picking up Cathy's enthusiasm. "We can give responsibility for each of those critical outputs to the manager of the department producing it and ask them to help us identify what could go wrong."

They spent the next three days revising the plan, meeting with each department manager or output owner to identify the most significant sources of risk. They also asked for any outside constraints or factors, like market conditions for key components, that should be reflected in the plan. As they rebuilt the timing network, they grouped tasks into "mini plans," each leading to the completion of one of their key outputs. As the plan grew they noticed that almost every one of the outputs was, in turn, an input to another output. They also saw that the complex logic that had defined their previous plan was mostly gone, replaced by simple relationships that ran through the major outputs, which were now represented by milestone events in the network.

Once the plan was complete, they prepared a control procedure to monitor the status of the critical inputs and outputs. A baseline was established by recording the key input and output event dates. Detailed task status data was still collected weekly, but it was evaluated based on its impact on the associated output. Another procedure was created for developing recovery plans to reduce slippage of inputs and outputs against the plan.

## A Brief Reflection

After they finished putting together the presentation that they would make to Lisa the next morning and Cathy had left for the day, Ted sat back and went through the new plan one last time. Ted was surprised at how simple and intuitive the new plan was. Why hadn't he seen it before? Ted thought back over what had happened over the last three months.

From the beginning, he had taken great care to educate the team on the principles of critical path planning. He had developed standard network templates and reports. He was proud of how the team had pulled together to develop the plan and had bought-off on it. They had identified the critical path and, as a team, had resolved to manage and maintain it.

What had gone wrong? A critical path plan, Ted now understood, is built on assumptions regarding resources, the scope of work, duration estimates, and a well-defined stable process to complete the work. The critical path is just the result of those assumptions. Furthermore, since CPM treats the plan as a closed system, anything that cannot be comprehended in the model is just ignored. Using CPM alone, Ted could not have predicted the N/C control block sourcing problem, where a short delay on a "noncritical" task resulted in a significant delay to the project. CPM cannot identify other "critical paths," based on factors like cost or risk. By relying so heavily on the critical path plan, Ted missed those other important dimensions of the project that ultimately caused the delays.

Ted also realized that, while CPM is a good tool for up-front planning, to determine what is possible, it cannot be the only tool used to manage the work once the project is under way. Ted had been reluctant to let go of his belief that managing the "critical" path was sufficient to execute the program plan. When the project began to deviate from the plan, his first reaction had been that by adding more detail and applying CPM more rigorously he could regain control and direct the project back to its "correct" path. But now he finally understood that the real answer lay elsewhere, that he needed to look at the sources of variation and risk that created delays. By focusing on outputs—on what you have to deliver to keep the project moving forward—you uncover the bottlenecks that will lead to delays. As a project manager, you have to find and fix the bottlenecks that drive the plan. Manage those and the plan that was possible in the beginning becomes achievable.

Satisfied, Ted got up, turned out the light and went home.

"Your new approach makes a lot of sense," said Lisa, after Ted and Cathy completed their presentation. "I know that you haven't found a way to recover the time that we've already lost, but it looks like you're on top of things from here on out. Just one more question, though: what happened to the critical path—your new plan doesn't mention it?"

# Managing Multiple Projects in the Twenty-First Century

Lewis R. Ireland, Ph.D., PMP, Project Technologies Corporation

## Introduction

As organizations search for more efficient and effective means of managing work, project management is selected as the management process of choice. Over the past few decades, project management has evolved to meet the challenges of getting products to market faster and at least cost while meeting customer expectations. These advances in project management are evidenced in the Project Management Institute's initial and revised *Project Management Body of Knowledge* (*PMBOK*) of 1983, 1987, and in *A Guide to the Project Management Body of Knowledge* (*PMBOK Guide*) in 1996.

One result of organizations' searches is managing multiple independent projects by a single project manager. These independent projects are being used to meet the requirements of management for rapid deployment of products and services, but the efficiencies are still being pursued. Grouping projects under a single project manager is the path to achieve more efficiency in the use of resources.

Secondly, organizations divide large projects into smaller projects that "feed" the large project. This large project is viewed as a "program" with supporting projects or a "major project" with subprojects. Division of major projects into subprojects gives better control over expenditures and changing requirements than a large, long-term project. Several deliverable products are identified and defined, with at least one for each subproject.

Grouping projects, either dependent (program or major project with subprojects) or independent (having no relationship between projects), has many advantages during implementation and for planning projects within an organization. Grouping of projects better serves the strategic objectives of an organization and meeting short-term goals for business operations. Tradeoffs between projects and shifting priorities to achieve organization goals is more easily accommodated and accomplished.

## Managing Multiple Projects in the Future

Managing multiple projects by a single project manager is a challenge within many organizations because of current practices that ignore the basics of project priorities, project categories, project standards, and multiple project tool applications. Lack of priorities, categories, standards, and uniform tool applications complicates the startup and initiation of managing multiple projects by project management. Lack of consistency, or an ad hoc approach, to managing projects prevails in existing practices and mitigates against a rapid transition to a multiple project management methodology.

Planning for multiple projects requires a proven project management methodology that includes a project management process, charters, plans, budgets, and schedules. Using a schedule as a project plan is not sufficient for effectively managing multiple projects. Omitting basic tools such as the work breakdown structure further complicates the project manager's ability to effectively manage multiple projects for profit and timeliness.

Organizations using a multiple project management approach must consider new methods of collecting information and reporting that information to the proper individuals. Further, there is a need to establish criteria for the level of management for individual projects and the information requirements from all levels of projects. Reports may be combined or used to single out a project for special review and management. Within the reporting structure, there is also the degree of authority granted the project manager for either reporting or making decisions regarding corrective actions or replanning.

### Program With Subprojects

Exhibit 1 depicts the program, or family of projects, that leads to a single deliverable product or service. Projects within this program all contribute one or more deliverable products to the top-level program. These deliverables are shown in the program's master schedule. All projects have the same priority, i.e., urgency of need, as the program. These projects also are designed to be manageable components of the program.

In a program, the projects are all started based on need within the scope of the program and program start date. The projects are typically one or more projects providing deliverable products to a following project. As depicted in Exhibit 1, product flow is between projects until the last project delivers a product to the program level. The final project could be the assembly of a product, for example.

### Multiple Independent Projects

Exhibit 2 depicts the grouping of unrelated projects, that is to say the projects have no interdependencies. Each project has deliverable products or services that meet specific customer requirements and are closed when that need is met. The priorities of the individual projects relate to urgency of

**Exhibit 1.** Program, A Family of Projects

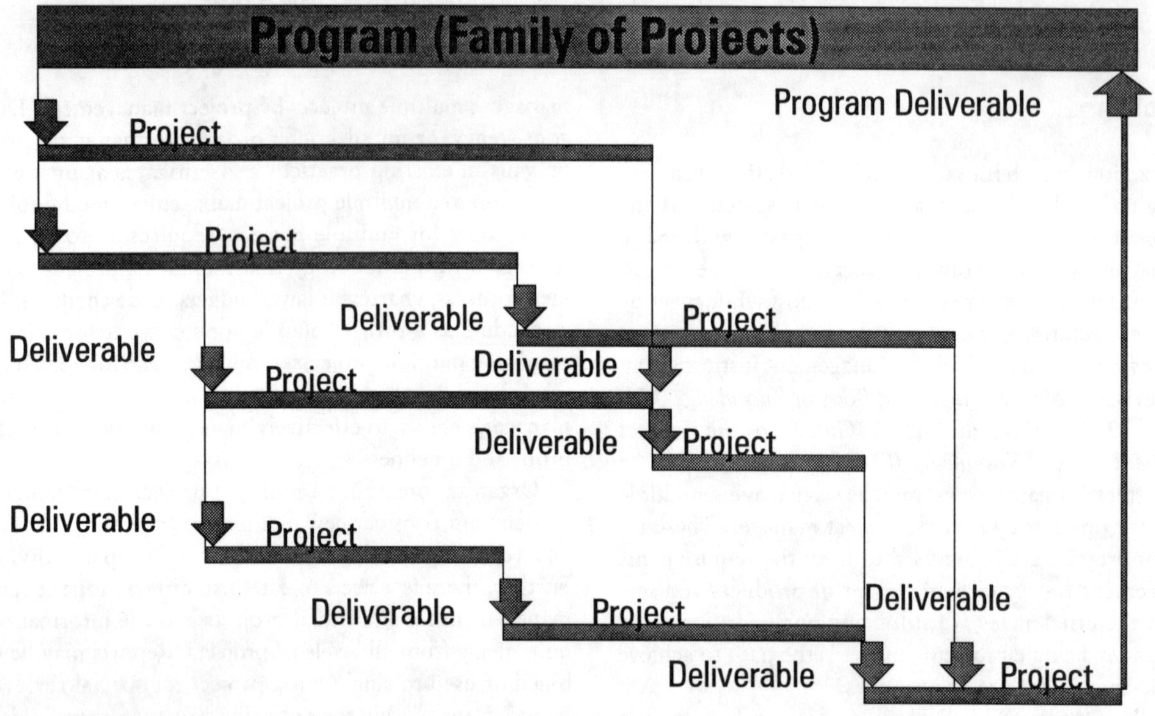

**Exhibit 2.** Grouped Independent Projects

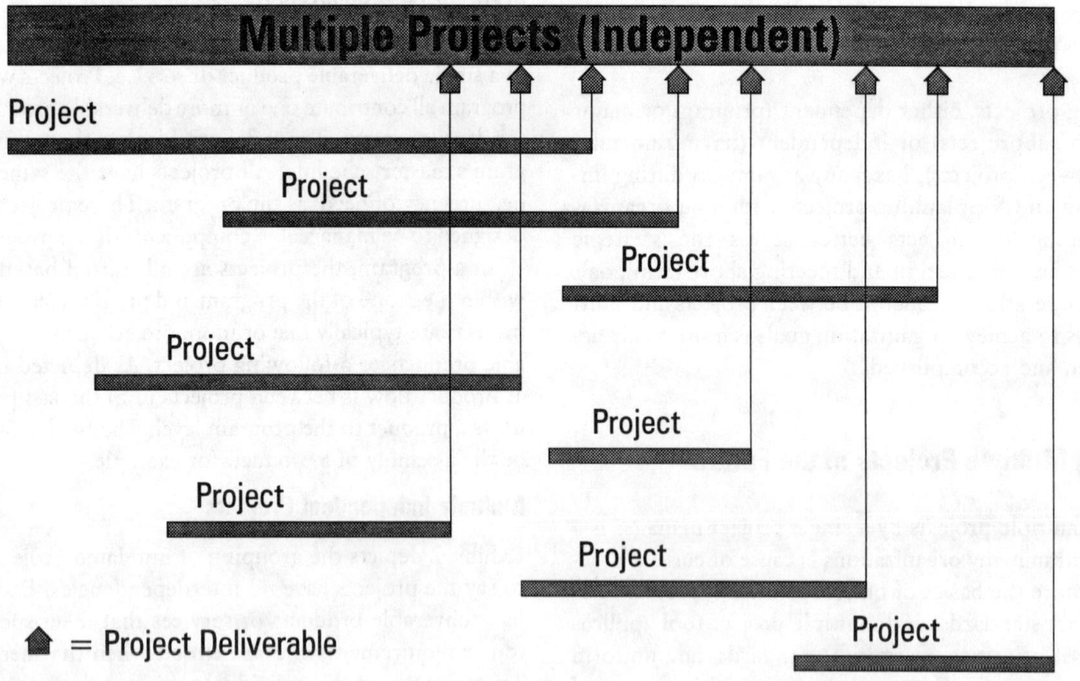

need and there is competition between the projects for resources when one has a higher priority than others.

When grouping projects for better management purposes and greater efficiency, each project has independent start and end dates. The start date is based on the need for the individual project and has no physical relationship to other projects within the group. Relationships for projects are depicted in Exhibit 2 by the arrows for delivery pointing to the capstone area. This delivery also indicates project closure.

### Categories and Priorities

There is often a mistaken belief that project category and project priority are the same. Category relates to the size, dollar value, duration, and overall contribution to the organization's financial health. Priority, on the other hand, is the urgency of need and relates to time of delivery and criticality of delivery date. The two may be related, but should always be treated separately. Sample schemes for project category and project priority are shown below in Exhibits 3 and 4.

Note: This is a sample range in Exhibit 3. Organizations should review project values and determine the range of feasible project values. Typically, Category A would be an exception and perhaps less than 3 percent of the total number of projects. The distribution of project categories is a function of the type of business and the business strategy for projects.

The size and duration of the project is usually determined by dollar value of a project. The greater the dollar value, the greater the contribution to the organization's business base. Categories of projects give an organization the basis for the level of detail required in planning and the selection criteria for the project manager for any given size project. Larger projects would receive more planning and a greater amount of investment in managing the work to successful completion than small projects. Larger projects would also have the more experienced project managers.

The category for the project should be assigned at the beginning of the concept phase based on the parameters known at that time. Subsequent changes to the project's value may cause the project to be reclassified and assigned a different category for subsequent management and execution. Also, the category may be held the same if there is no reason to change. For example, a project with additional work may escalate the project into the next higher category by a few dollars, but nothing will change in either management or execution of the project. Thus, there is no reason to change the category.

Priority, or urgency of need, for a project is typically ranked in three to five levels. The lowest number is the first in order of urgency. Exhibit 4 shows a sample ranking of project priorities with the associated criteria.

Note: This is a sample range for priorities. One should develop a range of three to five levels to differentiate between

**Exhibit 3.** Category of Project or Program (Sample)

| Category | Criteria (Project/Program Value |
|---|---|
| A | Greater than $20M |
| B | $10M to < $20M |
| C | $3M to < $10M |
| D | $1M to > $3M |
| E | Less than $1m |

urgency of need. Discrete numbers should be used rather than a subdivision to indicate finer granularity.

Current trend in industry is to assign all projects Priority 1. When this happens, there is no priority system or guidance as to which project has the greater urgency of need for resources to deliver early. It places all projects in an equally competitive arena for limited resources. The will of management is not exercised as to which is more important in the timing of delivery to customers.

Contrasting the two areas, category and priority, one should not confuse the reasons for using these concepts to establish the basis for decisions during planning and execution. Contribution to the organization's financial health can be attributed to satisfying customers and the amount of revenue generated by projects. Several small, urgent projects may make a greater revenue contribution than a single, large project that is a sustaining business base. Category is assigned to a project based on objective criteria that relates to the dollar value of the work. It is managed based on that criteria. Priority is assigned based on the delivery date for the product or service. The shorter the time available to execute the project, the higher the priority.

### Managing Multiple Projects

Managers of programs need to consider the project life cycle. Each program has a life cycle (e.g., concept, planning, execution, and close-out phases) and the supporting projects typically have only planning and execution phases. Much of the conceptual and planning work is done at the program level with some detail planning accomplished at the project level. Execution is the primary focus of projects in a program while the program manager and staff exercise control functions.

"Category" for a program will typically be in the upper range (i.e., A or B) because of its size and complexity. Priority, however, is based on urgency of need and will also be the

**Exhibit 4.** Priority of Projects (Sample)

| Priority | Criteria |
|---|---|
| 1 | Urgently needed product or service that contributes to the overall strategy or business plan for customer satisfaction. |
| 2 | Urgently needed product or service that meets a commitment to a customer and is less urgent than 1. |
| 3 | Needed product or service that must be delivered within resource limitations and less urgent than 1 or 2. |
| 4 | Needed product or service, to be delivered, contributes to the business, but is less urgent than 1,2, or 3. |
| 5 | Needed product or service that may have a deferred delivery and has little impact on the business. |

same for the program's projects. The assigned priority of the program places it in competition with other projects and programs within the organization for critical resources. The size of the program may also dictate that a project manager be assigned for each project.

Multiple independent projects each have a complete life cycle, e.g., concept, planning, execution, and close-out. Exhibit 2 reflects different start and finish times for individual projects. This places individual projects in different phases for the project manager to plan and execute at the same time. A project manager may experience some difficulty in trying to maintain a balance between the projects because of different phases of the life cycle being pursued at the same time. This situation is compounded by projects having different priorities.

Unlike the program, multiple grouped projects each have a category and priority. Because these projects are small enough to be grouped, it can be assumed that these projects are in the lower dollar categories, i.e., D and E (see Exhibit 3). Priority, however, may be different for each project and could lead to the less urgent projects slipping behind schedule when a resource constraint is imposed. Higher-priority projects would receive first consideration for initial and subsequent resource assignments. The hazard is that low-priority projects may never be completed.

Considerations for assigning individual projects to multiple project management are:

- Projects should be similar in size and low in complexity.
- Projects should be of relatively short duration and require few unique resources.
- Projects should be of similar priorities to permit balancing requirements without completely omitting some projects in resource assignments.
- Projects should be in similar disciplines or technologies.

### Projects Within Multiple Projects

One should evaluate projects prior to making a decision that they will be managed within a multiple project management context. Some criteria for selecting projects to include in a multiple project grouping are:

- Project duration—duration should be relatively short or comparable with other projects. An unusually long project may require special attention or it may be an interrupted work flow project, i.e., one that does not require continuous work such as research project.
- Product or service—the deliverable for the project is either a product or service. Product development should not conflict with providing services or vice versa.
- Interfaces—project interfaces should be relatively simple or interfaces for a group of projects should be with the same participants. It may be better to manage a project with complex interfaces as a separate project.
- Dollar value of project—dollar value of projects should be comparable, if possible. High-dollar-value projects in a multiple project context may not receive the attention required to achieve individual efficiency.
- Resources for implementation—multiple projects typically share human resources to obtain efficiencies in labor usage. When resources are not to be shared, one should question whether the project logically belongs in a grouping of managed projects.
- Priority—multiple projects should have similar priorities for resources within a grouping. When one or more projects are significantly higher in priority, the lower-level projects may never be successfully completed.
- Location—multiple projects *usually* should be in close proximity to a central location to ensure effective management. Widely dispersed projects may be centrally managed if they have a common purpose that dictates the grouping under a program context.
- Logical fit—projects should be a logical fit for the product, technology of the product being produced, and commonality of resource requirements. Grouping projects in any fashion may result in conflicting objectives among the human resources.
- Project life cycle—all projects managed in a multiple project context should have a similar life cycle. (See prior discussion of project life cycle.) For example, software projects have a different life cycle than most hardware

projects. Different life cycles may create more problems than efficiencies gained from grouping projects.

- Customer(s)—projects with the same customer (e.g., buyer, sponsor, end user) can be grouped because there should be better relations with the customer when one project manager serves that customer's needs. This should reduce conflicts in customer priorities and ensure better customer satisfaction.
- Other—there are many other considerations for grouping or not grouping projects for managing in a multiple project context. One should review the facts of each project and be watchful of personality influence in grouping projects.

## Start-Up for Multiple Projects Management

When an organization makes a decision to manage projects in groups, it is often the case that many of the projects are currently ongoing. Planning, at various levels of detail, has been accomplished and schedules have been developed. Work on the planning and direction that a particular project is taking is typically unique from any other project.

An organization may have as many as 250 uniquely planned, ongoing projects at any time. For example, a midwest company in 1994 had more than 160 uniquely planned and implemented projects ongoing at one time. Each project had some similar characteristics, but no one project followed a specific methodology or model. The company recognized the situation and established a professional project management system with exceptional results. Senior management was able to obtain greater visibility into projects through the project management system as well as achieve efficiencies that resulted in a 10–15 percent annual savings (i.e., approximately $7M a year). This savings was reinvested into the company for better facilities.

A second example is from a major international company that was upgrading the Information Technology capability. A dozen different organizational elements were involved in the upgrade; however, there was no central control or coordination. Many small projects were initiated based on the perceived needs of each organizational element, which resulted in a disjointed overall effort to bring about the new Information Technology capability.

Schedules were reviewed as the start point and combined into a single program Each project contributed to the common goal, but not in a coordinated manner. Schedules were in various levels of detail and in different formats. No schedule identified or included interfaces with another project. Time sequencing of activities between project schedules was not considered. Deliverable products were not tied to specific customer requirements.

A 30-day intensive effort gave visibility to the program and laid the groundwork for a coordinated effort. Schedules were keyed into a single system and interface points established for all internal to program and external to facilities items. This initial work gave senior management the information with which to make funding decisions, determine resource allocation priorities, and add missing program components. The missing program components were typically the interfaces and unidentified work between planned projects.

**Exhibit 5.** WBS Coding Scheme for multiple Projects

| WBS Coding Scheme | | |
|---|---|---|
| **Level** | **Typical Project** | **Multiple Project** |
| 1 | 1 | xxx.1 |
| 2 | 1.1 | xxx.1.1 |
| 3 | 1.1.1 | xxx.1.1.1 |
| 2 | 1.2 | xxx.1.2 |
| 3 | 1.2.1 | xxx.1.2.1 |
| 3 | 1.2.2 | xxx.1.2.2 |
| 4 | 1.2.2.1 | xxx.1.2.2.1 |
| etc. | etc. | etc. |

Challenges in bringing together a variety of schedules and work efforts were increased by the geographic separation of the organizational elements. Overseas elements were operating on different calendars for holidays and the different time zones gave rise to the need for extra effort in establishing interface points in time. The different scheduling systems ranged from high-end, fully capable project scheduling software to word processing systems to electronic spreadsheets. The level of granularity between the systems created difficulty in identifying the appropriate level for the interface point being placed in a schedule.

Special rules were required to establish standards for scheduling and to improve the level of detail in individual project schedules. A couple of the schedules contained excessive detail while the majority did not have detail below level 2 of a work breakdown structure. One rule was that the delivering project was responsible for coordinating any changes to the delivery interface point with the receiving project. Another was that each project was to develop a work breakdown structure to level 3, as a minimum, to ensure the level of detail was visible for managing the project.

## Work Breakdown Structure (WBS) for Multiple Projects and Programs

WBS Definition. A product-oriented family tree of project components, which organizes and defines the total scope of the project. Each descending level represents an increasingly detailed definition of a project component. Project components may be products or services.

The strengths of the WBS are:

- Provides a means for defining the total scope of work.
- Ensures that work elements will be defined related to only one specific work effort so that tasks are not omitted or duplicated.
- Used as a basis for cost, time, and quality performance assessments.
- Provides a consistent form for relating elements across cost, time, and quality functions.

The WBS is decomposed to many different levels, based on the need for definition of the project's product and the project's functions. One type of product decomposition to different levels is as follows: (1) System, (2) Subsystem, (3) Assembly, (4) Component. (5) Part, and (6) Piece.

Exhibit 5 shows a commonly used coding scheme for projects and a suggested coding scheme for multiple projects. The objective is to obtain consistent numbering between projects for comparison purposes when assessing cost, time, and quality efficiencies.

The standard coding style shown in the middle column is often automatically generated by scheduling software. However, there is a need to differentiate between the projects while keeping the consistency for comparing elements between projects. The right column provides the basis for doing this by identifying the project through the "xxx" designation. Some organizations use a combination of the calendar year in which the project was started and a serial number. For example, 701 could replace the "xxx" to indicate the first project in 1997 while the "01" would indicate the first in the series of projects. Other coding schemes that meet business requirements may be used when consistency and tracking can be met.

## Managing Multiple Projects

Multiple projects are managed similarly to single projects: one task at a time. The major differences in managing multiple projects are listed below:

- Projects' priorities and rankings are managed by one person in multiple projects to more effectively use resources and meet projects' objectives.
- Multiple projects are managed with the same tool to automatically identify potential conflicts and potential interface points between projects.
- Conflict management between projects is managed by one person in multiple project management.
- Resources within multiple projects are managed by one person for the optimum allocation.
- Dissimilar project life cycles and methodologies are more difficult to manage under multiple project management.
- Project managers may require a broader range of technical knowledge to effectively manage multiple projects.

## Scheduling Multiple Projects

Multiple projects are developed in a manner similar to single projects using a WBS and automated tools to produce a resource-loaded schedule. The individual project schedule is developed to uniform standards, regardless of size, and informally coordinated with other participants as a schedule that meets that project's objectives. While developing the schedule, one must also identify the external interfaces for the project.

Interfaces are important in multiple project management and provide a considerable advantage over stand-alone schedules when properly identified. Several categories of interfaces must be considered:

- Interfaces with other projects within the multiple project program.
- Interfaces with intra-organization activities (except for resources).
- Interfaces external to the organization facilities (e.g., site for installation of product).
- Interfaces with vendors, contractors, or approval agencies.
- Interfaces with customer(s) such as the buyer or owner.

Interfaces may be placed in the schedule as milestones and labeled as "interface." For example, the interface with the customer (buyer) is typically labeled as a delivery date and may be labeled "Interface: Deliver Product A to Customer Z." On the receiving project in a program, the interface may be labeled "Interface: Receipt of Product A from ABC Project." These two interface points on different projects are fixed in time unless mutually agreed to move by the two project managers (project leads).

## Resource Management Under Multiple Projects

Managing human resources under multiple projects may be accomplished by two methods. For large projects or diverse projects managed under a program umbrella, such as the foregoing example, resources are assigned directly to the projects. These resources typically do not cross projects, but stay with a specific project or their functional organization. Diverse projects with different skill requirements cannot make use of the economies of scale.

Projects with similar skill requirements can use human resources across different individual projects and should make the optimum use through scheduling on a continuous work flow basis. Automated scheduling systems support this through a master resource library, which lists every resource to be used on all projects. This single listing of resources permits identifying work profiles for every individual to determine whether they are "scheduled to work" more or less than a normal work day, week, or month.

One of the major contributions of the automated scheduling system is that changes to any project activity, with the applied or allocated resources, will be instantaneously recorded in the computer. Changes that reflect conflict in resource assignments will be recognized for corrective action. The dynamic nature of an automated scheduling system eases the process of efficiently managing resources.

### Multiple Project Reporting

Reporting on multiple projects is similar to reporting on a single project. The requirements for information by customers, senior managers, and other stakeholders do not vary significantly between single projects and multiple projects. Basic questions are:

- Is the project on schedule?
- Are there any problems that affect working to the plan?
- What action is being taken to correct any undesirable situations?
- When will the project be completed?

Rather than reporting individually for each project within the multiple projects, some reports may be consolidated. Others may be done by exception. When a single customer is the owner of multiple projects, reports and reviews may be consolidated.

For example, the master schedule or combined project schedule will serve to report time progress for all projects at one time. This consolidated schedule may be collapsed for some projects while giving all details for one or more projects. Histograms of planned resource utilization gives instant pictures of all or any resource in the resource library.

## Summary and Conclusions

Managing multiple projects can have a dramatic positive effect on the productivity of an organization. Organizations will, however, experience challenges when attempting to consolidate projects under a single project manager if the fundamental practices of project management are not in place. Consistent standards, practices, and methodologies need to be implemented and proven prior to making the consolidation. Proven project management principles must be used to achieve the productivity gains.

Managing multiple projects requires improving the capabilities of the organization in at least two areas. Selecting and training fewer project managers in all functions of project management as well as consistent, uniform procedures can reduce the costs of managing projects in a multiple project environment. Tools capable of linking inter-project interfaces and managing resources in an efficient manner across multiple projects are needed to support organization goals for projects.

Managing programs as a series of small projects provides a greater degree of control over the work. The work is managed and controlled, usually by a project manager, at a lower level than would a large project without subordinate projects. This management approach allows one person, the program manager, to allocate resources across project boundaries and enhance productivity while converging on the program's goals. Project managers focus on meeting the intermediate goals of the program, or the intermediate deliveries of products and services.

It is anticipated that the trend will continue for organizations to adopt the practice of grouping projects under a single project manager and to divide programs into more manageable subordinate projects to enhance productivity levels. Using the principles and processes outlined in PMI's *PMBOK Guide* will give those organizations leverage to meet consistent standards and practices while achieving a more competitive position within their respective industries. New processes, standards, and practices for managing multiple projects are expected to bring forth desktop computer-hosted scheduling tools that are supportive of the multiple project environment.

### References


Project Management Institute. 1983. *Project Management Body of Knowledge (PMBOK)*.

Project Management Institute. 1987. *Project Management Body of Knowledge (PMBOK)*.

Project Management Institute. 1996. *A Guide to the Project Management Body of Knowledge (PMBOK Guide)*.

Lew Ireland. May 1996. Project Management Course: Managing Multiple Projects by Project Management.

Lew Ireland. 1994. Consulting Engagement: Major energy provider upgrading the Project Management System.

Lew Ireland. 1995. Consulting Engagement: International business consolidating the Information Technology projects into a master project.

Lew Ireland. 1995. Consulting Engagement: International business upgrading the Office Automation functions.

Lew Ireland. 1995. Consulting Engagement: Major telecommunications provider.

# Lessons Learned in the Twenty-First Century: Haven't We Been Here Before?

Carl L. Pritchard, PMP, ESI-International

Organizations fail on lessons learned. Despite ongoing international attention to quality and the need to grow as organizations, we continually put our organizational reputations on the line by making the same mistakes time and time and time again. It is a model of futility, as customers, end-users, and organizational participants see history repeat itself. The challenge is *not* entirely in the documentation of lessons learned. Surprisingly, many organizations, which are mature in project management, now do an effective job of tracking and writing down the core elements of their lessons learned. Unfortunately, they do little or nothing to capture the data over the long term. Lessons-learned exercises become valuable for the participants who know and understand the project, but as they depart from the organization, that valuable element of corporate memory is lost forever. In most organizations, it's a nice exercise to remind everyone of the positives and the negatives. In many cases, however, participants don't know *why* they are doing them, and they don't know how to document them, store them, and access them.

## Why Lessons Learned?

Lessons learned represent the history of an organization and the organization's capability to remember what has transpired. Virtually every methodology and every project management text pays at least minor homage to lessons learned, although most analyses recognize that these lessons represent a challenge to the organization in terms of implementation and application.

Lessons learned are valuable from a variety of perspectives. They are valuable for:

- organizational memory,
- quality customer service, and
- employee improvement.

Each of these elements is a hallmark of a viable long-term organization. Organizations that are in for a short-term return will not (and should not) be as concerned about the long-term viability of these critical corporate assets. Organizations that plan on a sustained pattern of growth and reinvestment cannot afford to miss on these issues.

### Organizational Memory

Many organizations, particularly those in the midst of meteoric growth, encounter the challenge of potentially losing organizational memory. In this era of downsizing and "rightsizing," some organizations have seen their most seasoned talent walk out the door. They don't have the capacity to regenerate it. Vast memory can no longer be captured.

A handful of organizations, however, are trying to keep their organizational memories intact. One notable organization is Eastman Chemical, where lessons learned are not only retained in a corporate database but are also reviewed as each new project is implemented. It is no small wonder that Eastman has been recognized for quality with a Malcolm Balridge award. Many of the other pioneers in establishing lessons learned as a mandatory area of study, are within various governmental agencies. The United States Department of Labor's (USDOL's) Unemployment Information Technology Support Center (ITSC) is a joint project between the USDOL, Employment and Training Administration, Unemployment Insurance Service, and various state Departments of Labor to establish a center to support the needs of the fifty-three State Employment Security Agencies (SESAs). Within that program, Maryland's Unemployment Insurance division has done an outstanding job of not only documenting its lessons learned and best practices, but those of other organizations as well, and making them available through the Internet (http://www.itsc.state.md.us) (http://www.itsc.state.md.us/prog_info/bestpract/bestmn.htm). Many organizations are turning to their internal intranets to achieve the same goals. Even as organizations build their databases and make the information available, it remains rare that they incorporate some of the best insights in the best fashion possible. To do this, they need to take a more comprehensive approach to lessons learned, and it must be driven from the upper echelons of management, as will be discussed later in this paper.

### Quality Customer Service

Organizations have a tendency to fluctuate in terms of their levels of customer service. Organizations will hire the staff necessary for quality customer service . . . for a while. Unfortunately, organizations later battle the cost issues and ultimately reduce customer service. It is an unfortunate cycle that only a handful of organizations have avoided.

Much has been written (Treacy and Wiersema 1995) about the value discipline of customer focus. The authors recognize that organizations must focus on a single strength, or lose their market altogether. Some organizations have done that well and remained true to the customer service discipline. In a slightly dated text on 101 companies that profit from customer care (Zemke and Schaaf 1989), the authors point to a plethora of organizations that had the customer as their only focus. Interestingly, only a handful of the organizations cited there would no longer be perceived as having the same level of service today. The companies cited in the text for customer service (Wal-Mart, L.L. Bean, American Express, USAA, and myriad others) all still have relatively high recognition for quality customer service.

In most organizations that achieve such long-term customer-service recognition, it stems in part from lessons learned. They learn lessons not only with the broad base of customers but with the individual customers as well. They can tell you what you have bought through the years, whether or not you have expressed concerns in the past, and how those concerns have manifested themselves. Project managers need do no less. With customers buying products and services a thousand times as expensive, customers should be recognized and acknowledged for their importance to the organization. Sweden's ABB has learned this lesson well. Within its organization, project managers often work the same project for as long as a decade. It's not uncommon for a project manager to oversee only two or three projects in an entire career. As such, project managers have a very narrow focus on their particular customer(s). But the PMs also have great depth in terms of their understanding of those customers. Project managers have subordinates who are regularly briefed on all of the information regarding the project. Project managers regularly draft reports on the information garnered from the customer to their superiors. Information flows well and flows frequently. Thus, if a project manager must be taken away from a customer, there are alternatives. Customers are impressed with the organization's ability to switch managers without dramatic impact. That's a major achievement.

Imagine an organization that invites you to be its customer. It wines you and dines you. It pays close attention to your every need. What has it done? It has set your expectations. These expectations need to now manifest themselves in lessons learned, as the next manager to handle you must treat you exactly the same way. Each customer directed to the organization from you must also be handled the same way. The level of customer service must be maintained.

A classic war story from one of my students came from a woman in a telecommunications organization. She had treated her customer just as described above. She walked the customer through the installation, ensuring every action was handled with utmost care. She and the customer become close allies, working together on business opportunities—learning lessons about how each other should be treated. Specifically, the one thing the customer could not tolerate was unreturned phone calls. Even if the answer was "wait," the customer wanted acknowledgment that the message had been received. When a new PM replaced my student, she did not document this customer curiosity in her lessons learned. The relationship between the two organizations decayed rapidly, and neither side could identify the problem. The systems were installed just as fast, using the same personnel, and the implementation was relatively smooth. Nonetheless, the problems escalated to the point when even minor issues were escalated to upper management.

The problem was not with the projects, the customer, or the project manager. It was a classic case of organizational amnesia. The organization forgot how to interact with the customer. The only cure was a healthy transfusion of lessons learned information from one project manager to the next.

## Employee Improvement

The employee who suffered the brunt of the controversy in that project paid the price for not knowing the lessons learned by the other project manager. He paid the price with a poor corporate image. Employees who have access to lessons learned have the potential to better themselves both internally and externally. Without the support of the organization's historic knowledge, improvement is nigh impossible.

In many organizations, employees are reluctant to share lessons learned. Some team members perceive lessons learned as a hidden way for the organization to find out what went wrong so retribution can be exacted. If that's the case, those organizations are finished. They will never succeed at implementing lessons learned. The only way to improve employees (and the organization as a whole) is to allow them to make mistakes, and learn from them.

In situations where the lessons learned are positive—a function of a new trick, talent, or capability—employees are also reluctant to share the information. They often fear that someone else will use the information more effectively than they have and that they will not get credit for their achievements. As such, the achievements are sometimes lost to history, as they fail to become part of the organizational database.

In any situation, the information is lost because of fear. Fear of peer ostracism or organizational retribution drive project managers and their team members away from generating lessons learned. While organizations put out forms and tell senior managers to encourage the contribution of lessons learned, all of the organization's actions with the team members instead push them away from the exercise.

Such actions can be overcome, but only with support of upper management over an extended period of time. I offer counsel to senior managers and executives, suggesting to them that the lesson learned will become a key tool of the twenty-first century organization. Organizations that effectively build and deploy their lessons-learned databases will effectively vanquish any competition by virtue of superior organizational intellect. I offer approaches and structures and have heard even the most senior organizational executives say, "We'll try it for a few months and see how it works."

I immediately inform them that it won't. Lessons learned are not built in months or even a year. Instead, they are developed by the energies of large numbers of personnel over a period of *years.* Failure to recognize the time-frames dooms the process from the start. For those organizations who determine lessons learned add value, they will eventually recognize that the value stems not from a single "trick of the trade" that was preserved from a project or from a customer risk. Instead, improvements come in day-to-day operations. Team members recognize familiar patterns and avoid them as a matter of course, rather than as a specific risk workaround.

### The Process

The process for infusing a lessons-learned approach into the organizational project management culture incorporates four steps:

- Collection
- Storage
- Update
- Retrieval.

We'll examine each of these in the course of this discussion.

Note that lessons-learned documentation is being treated as a process here, rather than as a single activity or task. That's because lessons learned must be generated on an ongoing basis and must be maintained and updated to ensure their validity. Use of outdated lessons learned can be, in some ways, even more detrimental than deploying them.

## Lessons Learned—Collection

Lessons learned must be collected in a coherent consistent approach. In most twentieth century organizations, the lessons learned are collected in an *ad hoc* fashion, with no organizational design or support. One team member will describe a lesson learned in epic style, while another simply scribbles "Keep good documentation." Without consistency, organizations garner only a small portion of the information they might otherwise collect. Before determining the forms and formats for lessons learned, it is important to identify the qualities of the best lessons.

### What Makes a Great Lesson Learned?

I've talked with hundreds of project managers about this and discovered a series of common themes. The lessons learned that are most valuable are those that are relevant. This means that they pertain to the day-to-day of business, rather than the bizarre anomalies that occasionally arise. Lessons learned that are relevant are those in which a project manager reviewing them can take full advantage and see himself in the story. In addition, the lesson learned must be timely. As the days and weeks following a customer experience or a product experience pass, the lessons are tempered. A vehement personality clash with a customer rep. becomes a "difference of opinion." A debacle involving frustrating delays because of a sub-contractor becomes a "discussion point." The edge is gone. The bloom (in its crimson glory) is off the rose. By documenting lessons learned in a timely fashion, it's possible to capture not only the essence of the experience, but the spirit as well. The classic "keep good documentation" lesson may stem not from a lost shred of paper, but from a customer experience that ended in a flurry of verbal punches. The details of that sordid incident, documented while they are fresh in the minds of the participants, will provide a far more memorable and in-depth lesson than the simple three-word phrase that becomes its fruit. It becomes ingrained as an experience that others will ardently strive to avoid. Toward that end, the lesson learned must be specific. When and where possible and practical (without committing political suicide), names are vital. Specific names within specific organizations become essential fodder for the mill. One contracting officer may spell opportunity within a customer organization, while another may presage dispute. Under such conditions, names become vital. They allow the project manager to take preemptive action to improve relationships or to minimize historic challenges and difficulties. Finally, they must also be in-depth. "Keep good documentation" shows only the thinnest edge of the experience. If the lesson learned stems from a wonderful experience when the organization was saved thousands of dollars by a clear audit trail, regale the reviewer with the full story. Without the history, the environment, and the personalities involved, lessons learned can become a series of stories that some feel don't reflect the realities of their organization.

### How Are They Collected?

In an ideal organization, lessons learned are collected on an ongoing basis by all of the participants in the process. In reality, they will often be shared only by those individuals that have enough history and status within the organization to ensure that their position is not threatened by any insight they might provide. Lessons learned *cannot* be collected anonymously, as

**Exhibit 1.**

| | |
|---|---|
| Establish Key Values & Keywords | Affirm Perf. Rvw. Approach |
| Review Plan with PMs | Set Up Database with Administrator |
| Coach PMs & Teams on LL Retrieval | Coach PMs & Teams on LL Collection |

supplemental information is often required. Thus, lessons learned (particularly in organizations that are not mature in the practice) will not be readily offered by novices but will only be developed well by those trained in the practice.

To train team members and managers in the process of collecting lessons learned, an established practice must be in place. The components of that practice need to be embedded either in a methodology or in a standard operating procedure for the organization. A prototype for such an approach will be outlined later in this paper.

## Lessons Learned—Storage

Lessons learned in most environments become the province of the pack rat or the grail seeker. They are only available to those who preserve everything or those who can find anything. Without either of those two individuals in an organization, the data becomes lore which eventually becomes legend. The lessons are lost, but legends of better times and creative solutions abound.

Some organizations begin the journey toward lessons learned by mandating their development at the end of a project and their storage in the project records. Unfortunately, many project records languish in the project manager's office until some years later, when they can be lost to retirement or a cleaning frenzy. In any case, the lessons learned are valuable only to those who participated in their original development, rather than to the entire organization. As those individuals age and the stories are forgotten, the data is invariably lost.

With the advent of corporate LANs, WANs and databases, there is now a clear glimmer of hope. Some organizations now develop basic lessons-learned storage in simple databases. Keywords are consistent and may include virtually any variety of components. It's vital in a storage system, however, to keep it simple. Too many search areas and too many search terms may render the database nonviable. Stick to the basics of the organization's values and disciplines. Some potential keyword search areas are provided in Exhibit 1.

As you peruse the exhibit, remember that the key to any effective process or system is its simplicity. Do not feel compelled that "more is better." That axiom does not apply here. In this instance, the best systems are those that are simple and well-designed. Fewer search terms will lead to careful review of those terms. The search terms need to be those which most accurately reflect the organization's greatest concerns. For example, a telecommunications organization in the United States would be best served by a lessons-learned database that refers to the specific Federal Communications Commission tariffs applicable to the project in question. A telecommunications organization overseas might do better to include a keyword search on specific international telecom protocols.

The keywords are ultimately one of the determinants of success in utilizing lessons learned.

In an organization that effectively develops lessons learned, a project manager shares the story that he reviewed a stack of lessons learned relating to a particular customer and thought he had learned nothing. The only documentation he found related to a five-year-old project that was conducted by another organization. He jotted down a few notes about that experience and left the stack of paper behind. When he met with the customer for the first time, he mentioned the dated project in passing. "The Acme System?" asked the customer. "That was one of yours?" The project manager replied in the affirmative, pointing out that the last documentation he saw on the project indicated extensive customer satisfaction and a good rapport as the system was closed out. "We're still beating that dead horse," laughed the customer. "It's old, but it still works."

The relationship between the customer and the new project manager was sealed from the start. It was a positive relationship based on an understanding of customer history. Time and again, the project manager listened as the customer marveled at the PM's awareness of the project from years past.

As storage systems are devised, the organization should ensure that there will be broad-band access, with limited interference. The advent of organizational intranets opens a host of possibilities. Team members may review and search information from remote locations around the world.

## Lessons Learned—Update

Even as the information is stored, it is aging. It must be prepared for update or deletion. Some information is virtually timeless. As the information is stored, team members should identify when the information is likely to be rendered invalid and when it will need review. In the nascent stages of lessons-learned database development, such information is not critical. In the long term, however, the information will determine the ultimate success or failure of the system. Without a systematic approach to updates, the information in such a database will ultimately fall victim to its own weight. Rather than suffering from a dearth of data, the organization will suffer from the inundation, drowning in a sea of information, unable to discern what's a lifeboat and what's flotsam.

As the review dates begin to occur, it will become evident to the parent organization that periodic database administration is required. As such, this point has the potential to spell the end of the lessons-learned experience for the organization. This is when lessons learned incur their first notable expense. Someone must invest a significant amount of time to administer the database and ensure information integrity. Many organizations stress that while the database is nice to have, it isn't worth the investment of full-time or part-time personnel.

These organizations will lose the race for the customer. Organizations who wish to build corporate memory need to recognize the need for a librarian. If noone nurtures the data, the data will ultimately become invalid. If the data is maintained, it becomes a marvel, not just for the customer who is surprised at an organization's ability to track relationship histories, but for new staff who have the opportunity to build a knowledge base about their upcoming projects through a consistent, methodical approach.

## Lessons Learned—Retrieval

Getting the lessons learned out of the database is actually one of the largest challenges. There are clear approaches and tactics for getting information *into* such a database. Getting it out is a greater challenge. To get there, the project organization must have more than one champion in the upper echelons of management. That champion must recognize that she is responsible for creating a climate in which failure to examine lessons learned is unacceptable. Repeated mistakes with the same product, the same service, the same customer, or the same tariff are unacceptable. Failure to use new tactics, new approaches, or recently generated information is equally unacceptable. The worst failures in the organization can no longer be measured exclusively in terms of schedule or budget. The worst failures are those of quality. And the worst quality failures are those that had a modicum of predictability, if the lessons learned database had been accessed.

Lessons learned review and retrieval should be tied into performance evaluations. Project managers who fail to achieve time and budget expectations will always come under scrutiny. Those who repeat past errors and fail to take advantage of the advances of their peers are the ones who can ultimately jeopardize an organization. As project managers are evaluated, the question should not be: *How well did you do?* Instead, the question should be: *How did you do in comparison to other projects which incorporate the keywords we value most highly?*

This step alone will not be sufficient. The reviews must also take into account the depth of new lessons learned derived from the experience. It must encourage thorough documentation of all of the issues, new approaches, and insights derived from the project. By rewarding that behavior as well, a lessons learned methodology will flourish. Project managers will be anxious to document every lesson learned they and their team can think of. They will also be anxious to ensure they don't make the mistakes of the past. The organization matures. The lesson is learned.

## Bringing It All Together

How does an organization get started? Most try to grow lessons learned from the ground up. Organizations seeking immediate results will need to encourage the change from the top down. Upper management will initiate the change. Bottom-up approaches will only work if there are measurable results early in the process. Unfortunately, lessons learned do not lend themselves to quick turnaround. They are measured by the organization's ability to serve as an accomplished provider, with the greatest hallmark of all—they don't make the same mistakes twice.

When you can review the checklist below and answer in the affirmative to all of the questions, the journey toward excellence, courtesy of your own organizational memory, has begun.

Did you . . .

- Review the plan to use lessons learned as a key component of project management with the project managers and their teams?
- Establish key values and keywords for the organization, and are they in keeping with organizational strategies and goals?
- Affirm a performance review approach that rewards comprehensive lessons learned and withholds rewards for failure to make use of applicable lessons?
- Set up a database with an administrator, incorporating a system for scheduled updates?
- Coach project managers and team members on the basic practices of lessons learned collection?
- Coach project managers and team members on the basic practices of lessons learned retrieval (as manifested through *your* organization's keywords and *your* organization's database)?
- Implement these processes for using lessons learned across an entire division or organization?
- Set up a means to reevaluate the components of this system to ensure it continues to embody the organization's vision?

### References


Treacy, Michael, and Fred Wiersema. 1995. *The Discipline of Market Leaders*. Reading, MA: Addison-Wesley.

Zemke, Ron, and Dick Schaaf. 1989. *The Service Edge*. New York, NY: New American Library.

# A Message for the Project Manager of the Next Millennium: Don't Burn All Your Bridges to the Past

David H. Hamburger, Management Consultant, Inc., New City, New York

## Introduction

As we approach the next millennium there is much talk about changing the role of the project manager and the tools and techniques that will be used to perform this critical managerial function. Increased product and system technical sophistication, the demand for rapid response, and the need for cost effective performances necessitate the search for change. This change will significantly improve the processes, tools, and techniques used by the project manager. Yet there are many effective project management principles and practices in use today that should not be abandoned simply for the sake of change. As a result, project managers should not automatically burn all of their bridges to the past as the profession prepares for the move into the twenty-first century.

Starting over with a clean slate is not only impractical, but may be foolish. There are many commonsense project management principles and practices employed today that have withstood the test of time. Tools and techniques that have worked well in the past should continue to be applied in the future. Commonsense is timeless and any sound managerial practice that is based on this simple principle will retain its effectiveness in the future.

This paper discusses eight key project management principles that have worked well in the past. Principles that the writer believes should not be abandoned, but should be brought forward into the next millennium. To most readers these principles represent time-tested, established ideas. However, others may see them as new and unique concepts. To the reader who has employed these concepts in the past, it is requested that they not be abandoned simply for the sake of effecting change. To the reader who believes that they reflect novel and innovative ideas, it is suggested that they accept them as new project management concepts for use in the twenty-first century.

## Discussion

Eight commonsense project management principles and practices that have withstood the test of time are covered herein. They are ideas that the writer believes should be reinforced and applied in the project management processes to be employed as the profession enters the twenty-first century. They specifically include the following.

### The Entrepreneurial Project Manager

Project failures, to some extent, can be attributed to behavior patterns and practices that are instituted to suit someone's personal needs or performance standards. The needs of the individual are often met at the expense of the organization's goals. Such personally motivated managerial philosophies are usually counterproductive in the management of a project. To overcome this problem, modern project managers must set aside inappropriate behavior patterns and practices and approach their assignments with an entrepreneurial perspective, making project-related decisions as if they were being made for their own business. By addressing an assigned project in this manner, the best interests of the project will be served, which will ultimately serve the organization's best interests.

An entrepreneurial project manager is a business-oriented, independent thinking person who views each assigned project as a distinct business endeavor, addressing the project's needs as if they represented the needs of a personal business venture. He is goal-oriented, placing the needs of the project above existing personal goals. One assumes that personal goals can best be achieved by successfully executing each assigned project. The lack of an explicitly defined authority statement is of no concern, as the entrepreneurial project manager believes that the authority required to efficiently execute a project is implicit in the assigned responsibility. He also realizes that real authority will only exist when acknowledged by the people with whom the project manager must work. To this end, the entrepreneurial project manager is diligent in his effort to gain the acceptance and respect of the project team and other project stakeholders.

Successful financial performance and fiscal responsibility are important considerations. Projects must be profitable, budgets are to be managed effectively, and cash flow must be controlled. The entrepreneurial project manager does not treat the budget as money that must be spent before the project is completed, but strives to meet the client's requirements in the most cost efficient manner possible. He believes that every dollar saved in the execution of a project is a dollar that can be put to good use.

## Client Satisfaction

The project manager should be her organization's primary client contact over the life of the project, replacing the person who sold the project or negotiated the contract at kick-off, and transferring responsibility to a service or support person or organization on close-out. Project implementation not only focuses on meeting the client's defined requirement, but should also consider the client's stated or unstated expectations. To this end, close working and personal relationships are established with the client to facilitate discovery of any expectations that may exist. Once identified, the client's expectations are addressed. If a desire is unrealistic or unreasonable, the client must be convinced of its inadvisability. If the expectation makes sense and is reasonable, a concerted effort should be made to satisfy the added or modified requirement.

## Negotiating Support

Inherent in a team, cross functional, or matrix approach to project execution is a natural conflict of views between the project and functional entities. Often it is naively assumed that the project participants will identify with the defined goals and work together in harmony. In reality, each group is likely to have a unique perception of its roles and responsibilities, and the manner by which they can best serve the organization. Independent agendas result, as the various groups pursue and defend their ideas of what is best for the organization. These diverse and divergent viewpoints often result in conflicts between the functional groups, and these disagreements, if allowed to fester, frequently become personalized.

The effective project manager should be sensitive to these conflicts, realizing that they are healthy conflicts of principles and not divisive personality clashes. He should see the benefits that may be derived from an organization that has a diversity of viewpoints and takes advantage of these naturally conflicting ideas and principles. In this framework the disagreeing parties are expected to defend their respective points of view within reasonable limits, mindful of the need for a negotiated settlement that will provide a synergistic compromise that reflects the best of both positions. The role of the project manager in this environment is specifically structured to use these conflicts of principle to the benefit of the project. In a team, cross functional, or matrix approach the traditional managerial responsibilities are shared by the project and functional managers. The project manager assumes responsibility for the business issues, while the functional managers retain responsibility for the technical issues.

The project manager addresses the following business issues:

- What is required?
- When do they want it?
- How much money is available?

The functional managers focus on the following technical issues:

- How will the results be accomplished?
- Who will perform the work?
- How much money will be needed?

Gaining functional support and resolving the conflicts between the business and technical needs of the project are achieved through a negotiation process, a process intended to derive a synergistic compromise. Negotiating conflict resolutions will result in unbiased decisions that ultimately serve the best interests of the project and the organization.

Negotiation is a give and take process. To gain functional participant support, the project manager must give something that they may want or need. This is not as simple as it sounds, as the project manager has little to offer the functional participants other than work or a charge number. If a functional group is in need of work, there is rarely a problem in soliciting their support. However, in today's era of downsized organizations, complex requirements, sophisticated techniques, and stringent constraints, the project manager must offer the functional project participants more to gain "buy-in." She must also address the personal needs of the prospective project participant.

The following simple suggestions are offered as "things" that a project manager can give the functional managers to gain support:

- Treat the functional participants with respect. Remember, the project manager needs functional support more than the functional staff needs the project manager and the project.
- Develop the project plan based on functional participant input.
- Provide exposure, recognition, and rewards, when possible.
- Establish interesting and challenging work packages.
- Create opportunities for the development of the functional organization and staff by:
  necessitating advanced technical training
  justifying additional resources
  acquiring new tools and software
  providing on-the-job training for less experienced people, and enhancing the groups technological base.
- Share schedule slack or float for use in leveling the functional group's work load.
- Provide early warning when delays that will affect the functional effort become apparent.
- Take the fear of failure out of the commitment process by acknowledging the fact that a commitment is not a guarantee, but represents a promise of best efforts.
- Use project contingencies to support the functional groups when a budget or schedule commitment can not be met.

- "Give the credit" when things go well and "take the heat" when a problem arises.

### Addressing An Incomplete Statement Of Work

At the beginning of a project it is not uncommon for the project manager to be given a less than complete project definition package, the information needed for organizing the project team and establishing an effective project plan that can be used to control execution. Although this critical data may be incomplete, many project managers find it necessary to start the planning, organizing, and execution processes using the limited data. They assume that the information that may be lacking will eventually surface and expect to incorporate the new data in the plan at that time. Regrettably, the longer one waits for this missing information, the more difficult the related processes become. It is not uncommon for several necessary activities to surface at the "eleventh hour." When these tasks are ultimately identified, they are usually executed:

- in great haste,
- at excessive cost,
- with a good chance that the result will be unacceptable, and likely to displease the client.

Given an incomplete project definition package, the effective project manager may find it necessary to base the planning, organizing, and execution processes on the limited data. However, she should not wait for the missing information to arise in due course. Aware of the deleterious impact of last minute changes; the effective project manager will perform a comprehensive review of the furnished information before the planning process begins. She should immediately identify all missing information, open issues, loose ends, and items in need of clarification. This list of questions should then be presented to the client or other information sources at the earliest possible time. Once the questions have been raised, aggressive pursuit of the necessary answers should follow to ensure earliest possible availability of all information needed to complete a comprehensive plan. This aggressive, proactive approach should also be applied to scope changes and other issues that surface during the course of the project. This way the problems that can result from last minute additions or changes to a project's definition package will be minimized.

### The Importance of the Work Package to Detailed Planning

As previously noted, the planning process is often started with an incomplete project definition. This becomes an issue when the quality of the data is ignored and demands for comprehensive plans based on vague or incomplete information are made. The project manager may respond by creating an elaborate set of colorful documents that may impress management and the client, but the product of this effort will not provide a realistic representation of the project. The resulting plans may look impressive, but they will serve no useful function. Such unrealistic documents are unusable as the basis for controlling the project, as they do not properly define the work to be performed.

The effective project manager is aware of the futility of attempting to develop a realistic, in-depth project plan before the specific elements of work (work packages) have been completely defined. Any plan that fails to consider all of the necessary work will obviously have shortcomings, as a complete delineation of the necessary work packages is the basis for developing all detailed project plans. Planning is seen as a two-stage effort. The first stage, top down planning, starts with a statement of the project's objective and ends with a complete enumeration of the necessary work packages. Once the work packages have been identified, the second stage, bottom up planning, is implemented to develop the necessary detailed plans. Detailed planning is accomplished by first assessing the requirements of each individual work package (e.g., durations, skills, man-days, cost, risk, and so on); and then aggregating these parameters to arrive at the project's total requirements.

Defining the necessary work packages is accomplished by developing a detailed work breakdown structure (WBS). This requires a complete and comprehensive understanding of the following specific criteria usually found in the project's statement of work (SOW):

- A project objective statement
- Definition of the project's performance requirements
- Delineation of all applicable specifications
- Selection of a strategic approach to project execution.

If this information is not available or complete, the project manager should not attempt to develop a detailed plan. He should establish a preliminary or high-level plan as a starting point. The high-level plan may serve as an overview of the project effort, but it should not be used as a working control tool. Missing information should be identified and then actively pursued so that the necessary detailed plans can be developed as early as possible. If the available information is not complete and a realistic detailed plan cannot be developed, contingencies should be included in the plan to compensate for the project's uncertainties and the missing information. The extent of these contingencies will directly relate to the degree of uncertainty and the amount of information that is lacking. The effective manager recognizes the limits of a high-level plan and never presumes that it is sufficient for controlling the work. As a result, obtaining the necessary information becomes his primary concern at the beginning of the project. The project manager should be relentless in the search for this data and should not abandon the effort until the necessary work packages have been identified and the required detailed plans have been developed.

## Planning for Project Uncertainty

Contingency plans are needed to compensate for the inherent weaknesses in the budget, schedule, and specification (risk) areas of a project plan. Each contingency type is assessed and managed differently, as discussed below.

The budget contingency is a supplemental allocation to an estimate to account for errors, omissions, and other uncertainties that affect its accuracy. It represents funds that we are certain will be spent over the life of the project, but the specific applications, timing, and exact amounts are unknown when the estimate is prepared. It should be treated as a standalone element of the estimate and not buried or hidden in the individual line items as a pad. Budget contingencies are needed to address a number of distinct project execution issues:

- *Estimate quality* and the errors that may be made during project execution
- *Adjustments* to the product or system that are required during start-up or commissioning
- *Price protection* in an inflationary period when vendor quotes expire before purchase orders can be placed
- *Escalation* of suggested supplier prices when firm quotations are not attainable
- *Risk mitigation* when risks and specific mitigation strategies can not be defined during estimate preparation.

Each area is assessed separately and the estimated amounts are combined in a central fund, controlled by the project manager. These funds are then used on the problems that actually arise, as the assumed issues may not occur.

Since extra time is rarely given a project, a schedule contingency will only exist when project completion is expected earlier than the required completion date. A schedule contingency will exist when positive slack can be found on the critical path. This contingency is established by initially laying out a schedule that disregards the required completion date. The critical path is then compressed to a point where the expected completion date (earliest finish) is earlier than the required completion (latest finish). Critical path compression can be accomplished in two fundamental ways: reducing activity durations and altering precedence relationships. Reducing activity durations can be accomplished by adding resources, using overtime, or by taking shortcuts. Altering precedence relationships (performing tasks in parallel or overlapping them) can be accomplished by eliminating environmental constraints or by taking prudent risks. Schedule contingency should be maintained as a block of time at the end of the schedule, available to any prior task that is delayed. It is controlled by the project manager who allots the time to those late tasks that are expected to impact project completion.

A specification (risk) contingency plan is needed to prepare the project manager for addressing the potential undesired result when a specific risk is taken. It should be prepared prior to making the risk decision for a number of reasons. The reasons include:

- To provide an estimate of the remedial cost—information needed for risk analysis and determination of a management reserve contribution
- To define, and prepare for, an alternate course of action should the desired result not be achieved
- To convince management of the project manager's preparedness for managing the uncertain situation
- To enhance the project manager's potential for either avoiding the risk or mitigating the possible liability
- To identify small initial investments that can significantly reduce the cost of the potential remedy and/or the fiscal impact of a consequential event.

## Proactively Controlling the Project

Over time, the straightforward concept of cost control has evolved into an illogical, ineffective process because of the misguided approach that is often employed. Some project managers assume that cost control is a reactive process, taking no corrective action until a problem occurs and the overrun is reported. Others erroneously assume that cost control is in the purview of the "bean counters" (accountants) and take no action at all. When it finally becomes apparent that the accountants do not control project cost but merely report expenditures, corrective measures are hastily, and sometimes irrationally, attempted. Waiting for an overrun report limits recovery to the remaining work. This makes no sense, as the overrun usually increases as the budget is expended while the potential source of overrun recovery—the uncommitted portion of the budget—diminishes. By the time an overrun is identified, little remains to be spent, making recovery a virtual impossibility. One cannot fully recover a budget overrun when the amount to be recovered exceeds the total value of the potential recovery source. Faced with this imposing task, some project managers will disregard their budgets, abandon their cost control responsibility, and spend indiscriminately.

The effective project manager recognizes the flaws in the aforementioned reactive methods and approaches project cost control proactively. She firmly believes that one can only control a budget before the money is spent. Control starts with a complete work breakdown structure (WBS) that delineates every necessary work package. Allocating the project budget to the defined work packages results in individual line item budgets. A contingency budget that addresses the issue of project uncertainty is also established as a line item. This budget is used to compensate for the errors, omissions, and other uncertainties that are likely to arise during project execution. Once the work begins, budget overruns are controlled proactively. Each work package expenditure is evaluated before the funds are committed to determine budget sufficiency. If the budget adequately supports the task, the work proceeds. If the budget is insufficient, the project manager considers alternate spending choices. If the potential overrun can not be resolved, the contingency budget is used. This proactive approach will limit or prevent possible overruns and will thereby negate the need for reactive recovery attempts.

Implementing this approach requires the support of the accounting department and the functional organization. Accounting's natural reluctance to open the large number of necessary work package accounts, and their unwillingness to collect and report individual charges, must be overcome. The functional organization must be willing to honor their accepted budgets, avoid mischarges, and proactively commit their allocated funds.

The common approach to schedule control makes no better sense. Projects often start using an exceedingly optimistic, or erroneously structured, schedule as a baseline, and acknowledgment of a delay does not occur until a significant portion of the work has been completed. Once schedule slippage is identified, recovery of the delay can only be achieved by shortening the limited remaining effort. As in the flawed budget control process, delays that increase as the project progresses are accompanied by a decrease in the source of recovery—the uncompleted project effort. Recovering a schedule delay when few activities remain becomes a complex issue. Compressing the remaining project tasks is generally more difficult and costly than taking similar steps at the beginning of a project. The urgency that accompanies last minute recovery often results in panic and a frantic search for solutions. The frequently used approach of "throwing resources" at a delayed activity is not the answer.

The techniques employed to proactively control the schedule are similar to the methods used to control the budget. Each potential compression opportunity is evaluated before the work is started and the most effective steps are taken. Proactively compressing the schedule to create positive slack on the critical path establishes a schedule contingency. Performing this function before the work is started will maximize the desired schedule contingency at minimum cost and minimum risk. This contingency, established in advance, can then be used to absorb the anticipated schedule slippage. This eliminates the panic and stress that frequently occur when delay recovery is implemented near the end of a project and avoids the cost and risk of crashing recovery.

### Budgeting for Risk Mitigation and Remediation

The effective project manager should maintain a formal risk philosophy that he shares with the entire project team. This philosophy should address two distinct risk related issues—risk mitigation and risk taking. Since avoiding and taking a risk represents different approaches, budgeting for these distinct issues will differ.

The risks inherent in most projects must be defined and evaluated; when necessary, mitigation strategies must be developed and applied. Since we are certain to implement these strategies, the probability of spending this money is 100 percent. Therefore, the cost of risk mitigation should be included in the project budget. As a result, risk assessment and mitigation strategy development should be accomplished before the project estimate is completed. If these issues are addressed after the budget has been established, finding the funds will be extremely difficult. If the project definition is not clear, and the potential risks are not easily recognizable prior to estimate preparation, a risk mitigation element should be included in the contingency estimate.

The project manager's risk philosophy should also address the need for taking certain risks to gain specific rewards. This philosophy should:

- provide benefit and remedy estimating guidelines,
- define available assessment tools,
- establish a liability policy, and
- include risk taking decision rules.

One should recognize the possibility that any risk taken to achieve a reward may not turn out as planned, in which case remediation will be necessary. In this situation the probability of effecting remediation is relatively low, as one would not take a risk if the chance of success was not relatively high. Therefore the potential remedial expense should not be included in the project manager's budget. Instead, a management reserve, funded by relatively small contributions from the projects on which such risks will be taken, should be established. This will serve as a self insurance policy for the organization's aggregate, or portfolio, risk. For each risk to be taken, the potential remedial cost and the probability that the money will be spent should be assessed. Once it is decided that the risk will be taken, the product of these values is added to a management reserve that is maintained apart from the project budget. In this manner, the total value of the reserve will theoretically equal the amount of money that the organizations must provide the projects that include risks and ultimately prove unsuccessful. Funding for this reserve account should come from an increased profit margin or projects that are sold, or should be included in the estimated cost of projects that are internally financed.

## Conclusion

The eight commonsense project management principles and practices, discussed herein, represent proven approaches that have withstood the test of time. They represent ideas that the writer believes should not be abandoned simply for the sake of change. Instead, they should be reinforced and applied as the project management profession enters the twenty-first century. The aforementioned concepts are by no means the only usable ideas that should be saved as we move into the next millennium. As you prepare for the twenty-first century "don't burn all your bridges to the past." Each project manager should consider these, and the numerous other, commonsense methods that have worked in the past and should determine which ones will still work in the future. With these proven, workable, methods as a baseline, an effective project management strategy for the next century can be developed.

# Natural Networks—A Different Approach to Planning

E. D. Marion, PM*Pharos Inc.
E. W. Remine, Lucent Technologies Inc.

## Background

Project planning has for decades involved developing schedule networks. These scheduling networks are actually representations or models of the work to be executed on the project, usually broken down into small elements of work called tasks.

The notation most commonly used describes these tasks in terms of a nominal duration and an identification of all the required predecessor or successor tasks. These relationships to other tasks are called dependencies or links and are characterized in one of four standard ways: (1) finish-to-start, (2) finish-to-finish, (3) start-to-start, and (4) start-to-finish. These are illustrated Gantt chart fashion in Exhibit 1.

### Simple Links Are Not Enough

To allow controlling overlap between tasks, a timing offset called lag is added to the link description. Lag can be positive or negative, and so any amount of task overlap or offset can be produced with any of the above standard link types. An example of this linking, called "standard notation," is shown in Exhibit 2.

### Standard Notation Drawbacks

While these relationships provide all the flexibility needed to schedule projects, they suffer from several drawbacks. These are particularly bothersome when planning involves individuals who are functional managers or subject matter experts as opposed to schedulers. Managers have a tendency to think of tasks in terms of the physical work they represent rather than view them as building blocks in a schedule network.

#### *Multiple Links*

First there may actually be multiple physical hand-offs between any pair of real tasks. This means that the physical links must be compared to one another to determine which link controls the relative timing of the two tasks. This link is the one that must be represented as a dependency in the network. Even when this is done, the identification of the controlling link can depend on the durations of the two tasks. This means that the identification of the controlling link should be redone each time the task durations are updated.

#### *Link Type And Lag Selection*

Secondly, the link selected must then be evaluated to determine which of the four link types is most appropriate, and the value of lag that produces the right relative timing must be determined. Notice that in some cases this lag value can depend on either or both task durations, so this too must be reevaluated if task durations are subsequently adjusted.

#### *Correlation To Physical Links*

Lastly, the correlation between the link representation and the actual physical dependencies can be relatively obscure. In the lower sketch in Exhibit 2, for example, the task overlap might actually be gated by (a) an output half-way through task A that allows task B to start, or (b) an output at the *end* of task A that is needed to continue the work previously started in task B. Only the timing results are visible, not the actual physical link relationship.

#### *A Tendency for Too Many Details*

These problems frequently drive planners to decompose projects into smaller and smaller tasks, so that the resulting network more cleanly represents the physical relationships and more accurately models the right overall schedule behavior. The price for this approach is large and complex schedule databases, leading to reports and graphical displays that overwhelm the planners with their voluminous data.

**Exhibit 1.** Standard Relationships

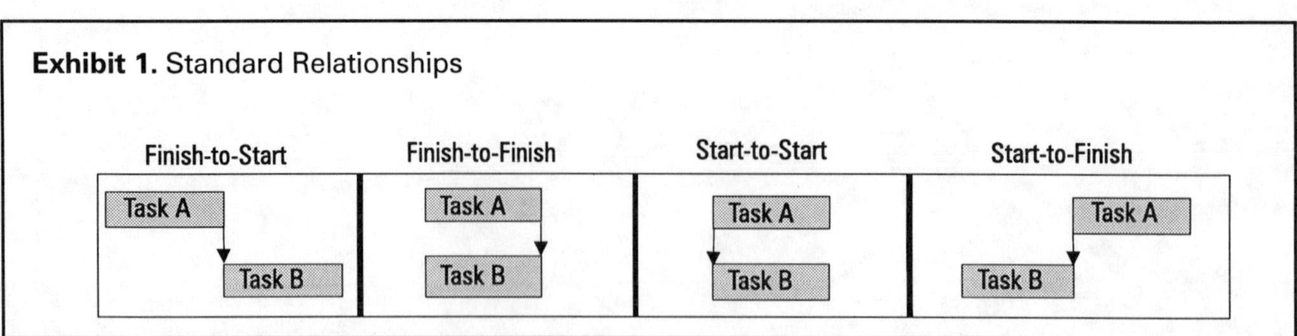

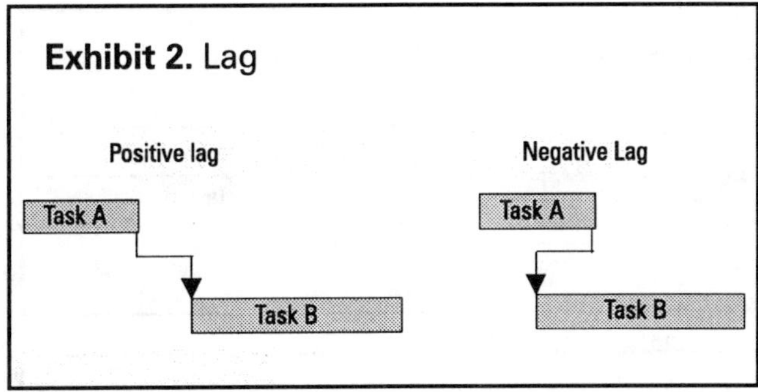


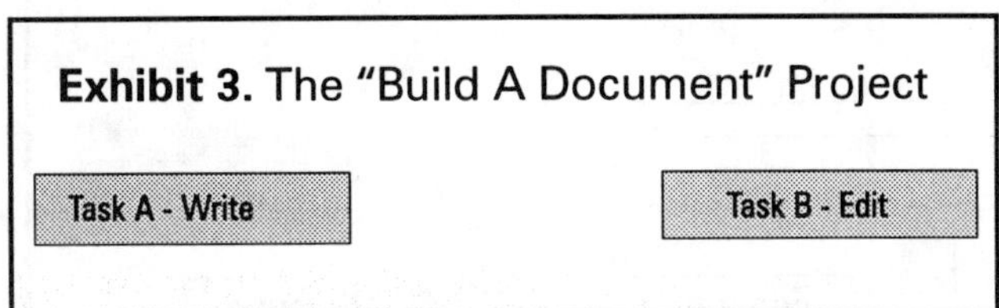


The concept of natural networks was developed to deal with these problems.

## The Natural Network

The fundamental difference between normal scheduling networks and natural networks is the way planners are allowed to define the relationships between tasks. Another term that has been used for natural networks is "unconstrained networks".

### Removing Constraints

For natural networks there are no constraints on the number of links that can be identified between two tasks. Further links can be defined that originate at any point along the time span of a precursor task and can terminate at any point along the time-span of a successor task. As a result planners can directly represent the actual physical links, hand-offs, or dependencies in a way that is comfortable and almost instinctive.

### An Example

In the example shown in Exhibit 3, imagine that a project is being described where a number of authors are contributing to a joint document, and the final editing and assembly of the document is being handled by a group of editors. There are two tasks: (A) authors prepare material and (B) editors assemble the document.

#### *The First Link*

In order for the editors to start, all we need from the authors is the titles of their respective sections, an estimated page count, and a rough bullet topic outline. With this information the editors can start preparing a table of contents, an index, designing the tabs between sections, and finding printers who

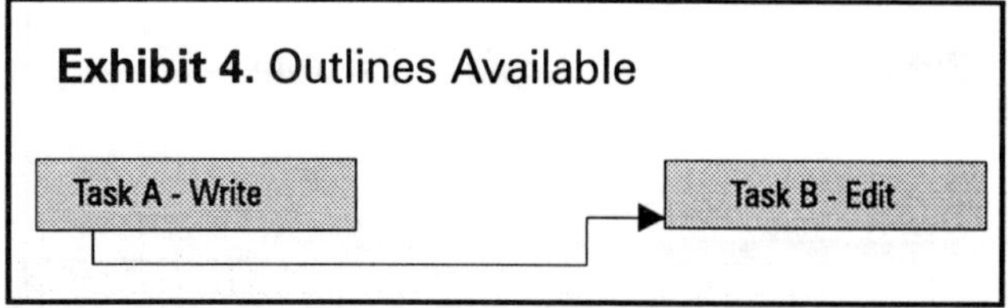


can print the document. The authors indicate that they could all generate the requested material about one tenth of the way through the writing task. This is illustrated in Exhibit 4. The notation for drawing links here uses the distance along the bottom edge of the task box to indicate the fraction of the total task time span that is needed to generate a given output.

#### *The Second Link*

This initial effort won't keep the editors busy for long. They say that about 20 percent of the way through their jobs, they will begin to need some actual chapter material to work on. The authors say that the first draft of anyone's write-up won't be available until about three-quarters of the way through the writing job. This would appear as shown on Exhibit 5. Similarly here, the link notation uses the distance along the *top* edge of the task box to indicate the fraction of the task time span that can elapse before a given input is needed.

#### *The Last Link*

Finally, the editors say they will need the last 10 percent of their job for final cleanup and printing after the last piece of text has been submitted for editing. This would appear as shown on Exhibit 6.

This natural network representation of this small project requires two tasks and three links. Each line representing a link correlates to a physical hand-off or gating event:

- Link 1: Outlines Complete
- Link 2: First Text Draft Available
- Link 3: Last Text Draft Available

When a schedule analysis using this network has been completed, an expected date will be calculated for each of the above events. This means that they can also be used as milestones for status tracking if desired.

Functional/technical managers seem to feel fairly comfortable with this network representation. Experience has shown that it takes less than ten minutes to explain to inexperienced planners how the network notation works and how to use it to lay out their tasks. Both experienced and novice planners adapt smoothly and quickly to this approach to describing the project plan network.

#### *A Standard Network Representation*

To get some sense of how this network representation compares with a typical scheduling network, compare Exhibit 6

**Exhibit 5.** first Text Drafts Available

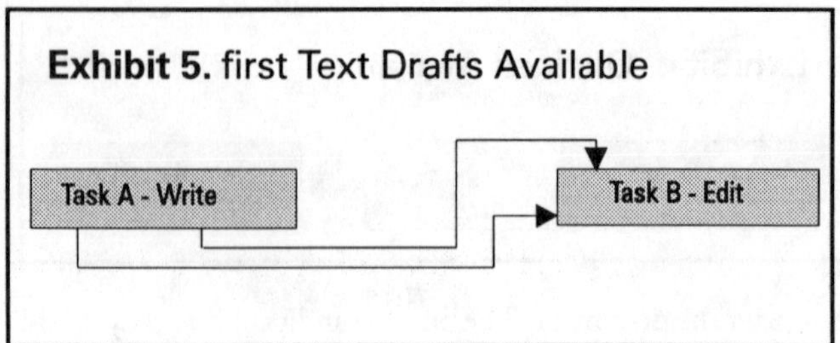


**Exhibit 6.** Last Text Draft Submitted

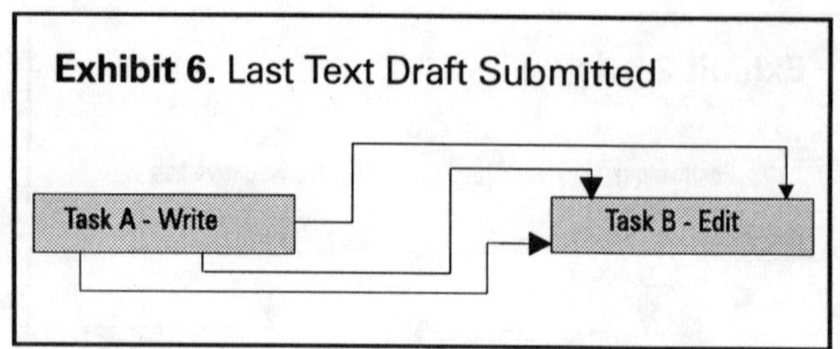


**Exhibit 7.** Standard Network Representation

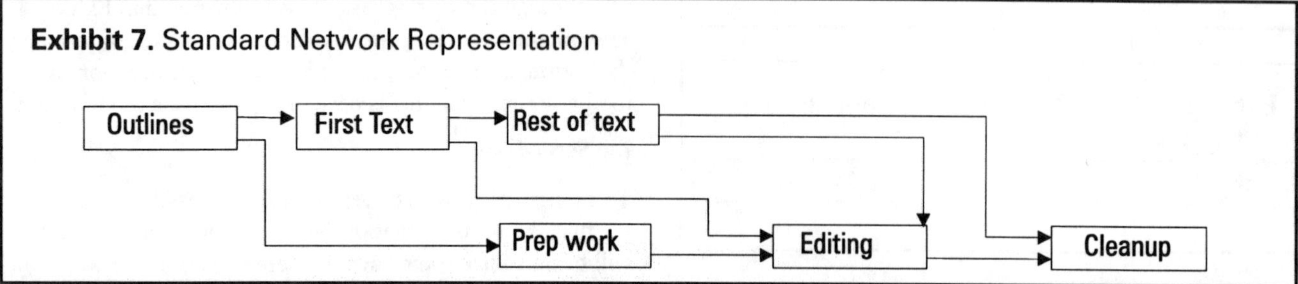


with Exhibit 7. In this figure a roughly equivalent network has been prepared that contains all of the linkages shown on Exhibit 6 but is constrained to one link between pairs of tasks and uses the standard link notation shown in Exhibit 1.

This network representation has six tasks and eight links. It will exhibit the same overall schedule behavior in the sense that as different durations are entered for each of the six elements, the overall project duration will be calculated the same as for the natural network.

Comparisons between end-to-end networks and natural networks for real projects has shown that natural networks tend to be smaller by about a factor of two as measured by the total number of tasks and links that have to be considered by the planner. The simple two-task example used here seems to be reasonable for illustrating many of the comparisons between the two approaches, so it will be the basis for much of the following discussion.

## Why Use Natural Networks As A Basis For Project Plans

There are several reasons why natural networks make a better basis for project planning than end-to-end networks. Some have already been alluded to in the discussions above. In the section below, these reasons have been summarized and augmented with other observations to form a rationale for using natural networks.

### Simpler Networks

The example clearly illustrates how the networks are generally simpler with natural networks. These networks are also easier to develop during the planning process because they allow a cleaner, more direct expression of the planners' intent and understanding. Because they are simpler, less information needs to be recorded to capture the plan, and less information needs to be reviewed by the planners when trying to ensure the correctness of a planning database. Because it is not necessary to subdivide a task in order to capture the schedule effects of intermediate links, natural networks tend to not get fragmented into fine details the way end-to-end networks often do.

### More Meaningful Task Definitions

The tasks that are scheduled in natural networks are defined based on the nature of the work and how the tasks are to be managed. It is not necessary to create a detailed task structure in order to get realistic schedule behavior.

The potential impact of this effect is shown in the example. Even though the standard version of the plan is nominally equivalent, the behavior of individual activities may not be what the planner desires. For instance, the network in Exhibit 7 will allow gaps between the completion of "document prep" and "text editing," and similarly between "text editing" and "final cleanup".

The results could be a start-stop start-stop editing effort. This may be an acceptable work mode for editing, but it is clearly inefficient and may require that effort be charged to the project during the gaps, even when no useful work is being done, in order to ensure that editors are available when needed.

In the natural network, the "editing" job is defined as a single uninterrupted task and will be scheduled that way. If, on the other hand, the editing job can actually be planned as three separate efforts, then the plan can be structured that way, even as a natural network. In fact *any* end-to-end

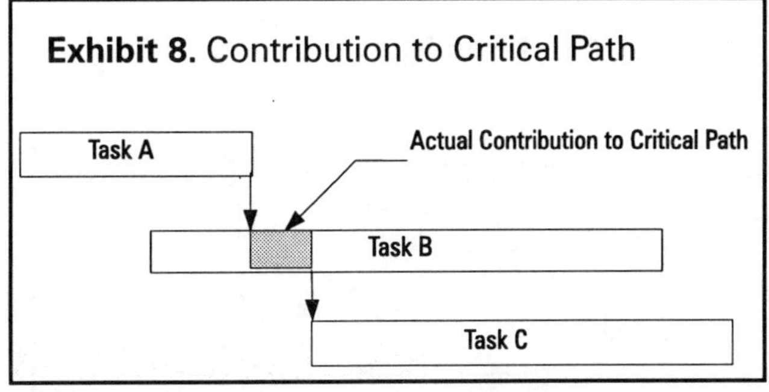

**Exhibit 8.** Contribution to Critical Path

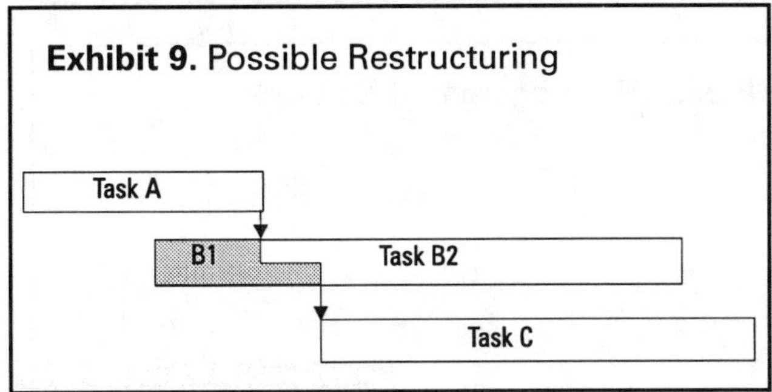

**Exhibit 9.** Possible Restructuring

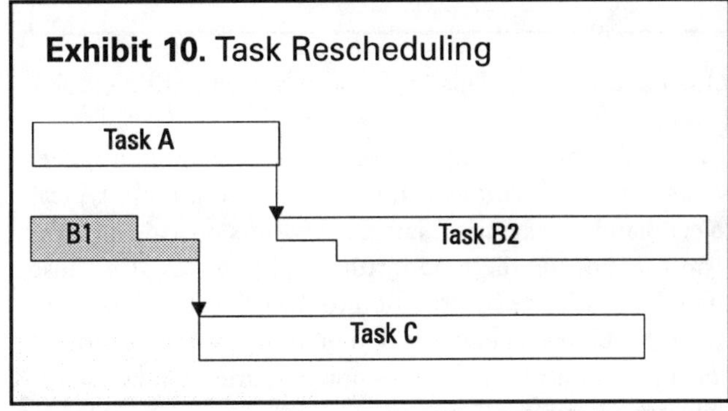

**Exhibit 10.** Task Rescheduling

planning structure can be duplicated as a natural network, but the reverse is not true.

### Links Have Physical Interpretation

In the natural network, all links correspond to physical hand-offs or gating events. In cases where there may be multiple hand-offs, each can be included in the network without having to determine which is currently crucial to the timing of downstream activities. This means that planners can focus on representing the actual process, and let the schedule analysis reflect the link impact.

If judgments or input information changes, causing a reestimate of the durations of individual tasks, the correct link effects will automatically be reflected during the analysis.

A side benefit of having all real hand-offs reflected as links is that each link then also becomes a trackable milestone to be used for statusing during project execution. The hand-off for each link can be identified by name, and the expected date can be determined from the schedule analysis. Thus, all links, even the ones that don't control the timing of subsequent tasks, become useful as metrics of task progress.

### Contribution to Critical Path

Both natural and standard networks allow the determination of which tasks are on the critical path. When tasks of long duration are on the critical path, one attractive possible approach to compressing the overall project schedule is to add resources to these long tasks, and to shorten the project duration by executing these tasks faster.

However, simply knowing that a task is on the critical path is not enough. Situations frequently exist where a task's actual contribution to the extent of the critical path is *smaller* than its duration. This is shown in Exhibit 8.

Here, the final results of Task A are needed to continue work that was started previously in task B. A short time after this hand-off is received by task B, an output is generated by task B that allows task C to start. The assumption is that the project either ends with task C or continues on from the end of task C. Under these circumstances, all three tasks are "on the critical path."

In looking at the dependencies, however, the only portion of task B that must be executed to move the critical path effort forward is the shaded area. This is of special interest when trying to compress the schedule for two reasons.

First, the shaded portion of task C is considerably shorter that the total duration of task C. If one possibility is to add resources to task C and so reduce the interval, then the only portion that needs to be compressed is the shaded portion, not the whole task. Or stated from a different point of view, if task C is accelerated by x percent by adding resources, the project duration will get shorter only by x percent of the shaded duration, not x percent of the total duration of the task.

Second, when the contribution to critical path is smaller than the total task duration, then a possibility exists that a restructuring of the task could result in significant schedule savings. If task B could be structured as two separate activities, an effort that produces the output needed by task C and a separate one that uses the input from task A, then Exhibit 8 can be redrawn as Exhibit 9.

This leads in turn to the possibility that more appropriate scheduling of these efforts that would shorten the schedule would look like Exhibit 10, *if* it is reasonable to break task B into two tasks with a gap between.

If such a restructuring is not possible, then this schedule improvement cannot be realized. The circumstances where the contribution to critical path is significantly smaller than the critical path simply suggests an opportunity that might be worth a second look during project planning.

Whatever the viewpoint, the actual contribution to the critical path for each task is an important item of information

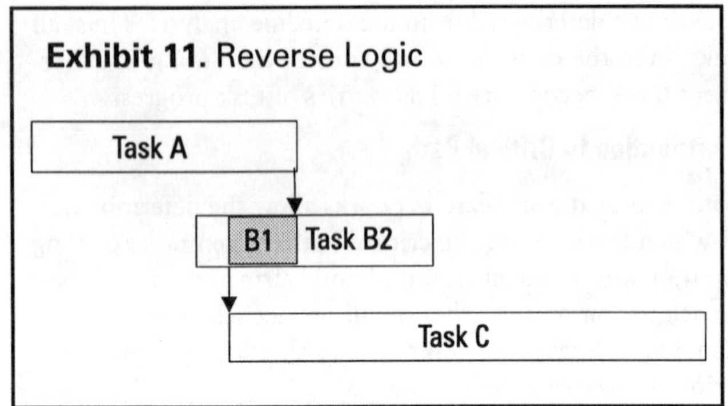

Exhibit 11. Reverse Logic

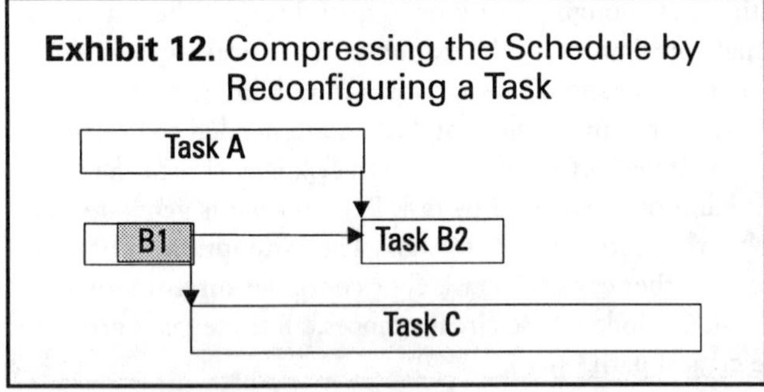

Exhibit 12. Compressing the Schedule by Reconfiguring a Task

when trying to compress a project schedule, or when trying to decide when a task should be watched closely.

Standard network linkages do not allow the determination of the contribution to critical path because only the timing effects of a link are captured in the link data, not the position of a physical hand-off.

### Allows Reverse Logic Detection

It is possible, in constructing scheduling networks, to inadvertently wind up with a circumstance where the longer a particular task takes, the shorter the overall project duration becomes. This can happen with both standard and natural networks. The situation is illustrated in Exhibit 11.

Here the project begins with task A, and the output generated at the end of task A determines when task B can start. If task B were re-estimated to take twice as long, then all parts of task B would expand in duration. But because of the hand-off from task A, the time point at the end of the shaded portion of task B is fixed. The result is that the end of task C moves to an earlier time point. The signature of this situation in a natural network analysis is that it produces a negative contribution to the critical path. The results are of course silly, and are caused by an error in the task structure.

What this really points to is an opportunity to compress the schedule by breaking task B up into two tasks. What the planners should do is start the first part of task B at the earliest opportunity, and continue working until the activity in the shaded portion of the task is complete, then stop. At a later time when the output from task A permits, restart the task

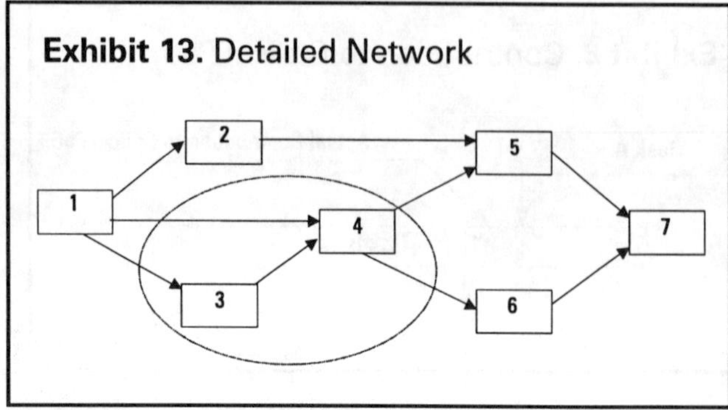

Exhibit 13. Detailed Network

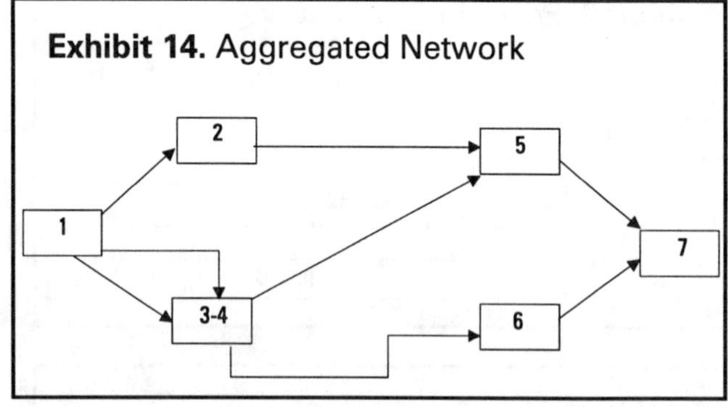

Exhibit 14. Aggregated Network

B effort and finish it. This can be seen by comparing Exhibit 11 to Exhibit 12.

While this may seem like a rather unusual circumstance, several of these situations will normally crop up in a typical project planning exercise. Natural networks provide a mechanism for spotting these opportunities by looking for those situations where the contribution to the critical path is negative. Since standard networks do not allow the calculation of critical path contribution, these opportunities will be harder to identify in standard networks.

### Scalability

The term, "scalability," means that a valid network can be constructed at any level of detail. If the network model is scaleable, then network schedules can be constructed from the top down; that is, an aggregate view of the project can be modeled, and then those portions of the project that need to be planned more carefully, based on the aggregate analysis results, can be expanded in detail. It also means that any subnetwork or group of tasks can be replaced with a different or more detailed set of tasks, without changing the remaining task structure.

A network is scaleable if any arbitrary subset of tasks can be grouped into a single task without changing the remaining network structure. The resulting aggregate network must produce consistent results even if the durations of the remaining task are modified. Consider the network in Exhibit 13.

As before, the network notation used here indicates intermediate exit and entry points by connecting the link lines part-way along the top and bottom edges of the boxes. A simple test of scalability here would be to see if tasks 3 and 4, in the dashed oval, can be replaced with a single aggregate task. This produces the network shown in Exhibit 14.

This aggregated network is equivalent to the detailed network, as long as the planners are willing to treat task 3-4 as a single task. The link from 1 to the midpoint of 3-4 has to be positioned along the time span of the task so that it corresponds to the start time for task 4 in the detailed network. The exit point for the link to task 6 has to be established relative to the longer duration of the combined task. Once these parameters are set, the network will behave the same as the detailed network, even when task durations are modified.

Notice that the original detailed network had only one link between task pairs, but the aggregated network requires two links between task 1 and the new task 3-4. The ability to form valid aggregate networks depends on the capability to define multiple links between task pairs.

The ability to link into the partial-completion points helps to allow graceful aggregation, but this feature can be approximated by using lag with end-to-end links. The reason why it can only be approximated can be seen by examining the link from 1 to the midpoint of 3-4. The lag that would be associated with this link will depend on the duration of task 3-4. If this duration is adjusted, the schedule behavior of an end-to-end link will not be the same as the schedule behavior of the natural network.

The bottom line is that natural networks allow graceful scaling of a planning network, either aggregating portions of the network for a more simplified view, or adding more detail to one portion of the network.

### More robust in face of updates

The working or operating version of the plan is seldom stable. If it is to be useful for tracking progress and predicting the impact of changes, it must be constantly adjusted with new duration estimates to stay current. Here natural networks provide several advantages.

First the inputs needed to update the plan are easier to obtain and are likely to be more accurate. This is because the plan elements map more cleanly to the physical elements of the job. Tasks are defined mostly from the nature of the work and the way the job is to be managed. Job status requests make more physical sense to the manager responsible. Links are hand-offs or events that have direct physical correlates. Asking if they happened, or when are they going to happen, are questions that usually have simple straightforward answers,

Second, since multiple links are captured with percent connect points, changes in controlling links are automatically reflected in the analytical results. There is no need to adjust lag values or redefine a link.

Lastly, in standard networks, where tasks may have been fragmented into several activities to get a more accurate dependency behavior, reflecting a new estimate of task duration may involve finding and updating all of the component activities. In natural networks, where fragmentation is less necessary, the task usually retains its original identity, and only one duration update is necessary.

## Summary

The use of this network notation offers enough advantages over standard network notation that existing tool suppliers should consider converting to this notation in future enhancements of their products. Lucent is currently evaluating a prototype tool from PM*Pharos that allows planning with natural networks as a front end to MS Project and Primavera. . Experience on actual projects with the notation, the process, and the tool have been very favorable. Initial plan generation times were reduced, and project schedule performance compared to previous practices has improved.

# Financial and Organizational Impacts of Project Management

C. William Ibbs, Professor, University of California
Young-Hoon Kwak, Ph.D., University of California

## Introduction

The previous research on the benefits of PM is limited. Most of the study results were presented in qualitative and anecdotal fashion. Such benefits include improving organizational effectiveness, meeting quality standards, and fulfilling customer satisfaction (Al-Sedairy 1994; Boznak 1988; Bu-Bushait 1989; CII 1990; Deutsch 1991; Gross 1990; Ziomek 1984). This research was, however, very general and largely unsubstantiated. In other words, it was not very supportive to managers trying to answer fundamental and challenging questions regarding PM needs, advantages, and particularly *quantitative* benefits.

The goal of this research is to investigate the financial and organizational benefits to organizations that result from the implementation of PM tools, practices, and processes. This study will enable managers to determine when and how to apply PM by analyzing the quantitative relationships and benefits of PM processes. Such information and analysis will help managers better understand and respond to queries from top managers about the cost effectiveness of PM.

## Research Steps

The following are the research steps that are used for this study.

1. Examine past and current study related to PM and find potential areas for in-depth research.
2. Develop a five-level PM Process Maturity (PM)2 Model to position and compare an organization's current PM level.
3. Develop a comprehensive PM maturity benchmarking methodology to evaluate an organization's current PM level and actual project performance.
4. Select target organizations/industries to benchmark.

**Exhibit 1.** Five-Level Project Management Process Maturity $(PM)^2$ Model

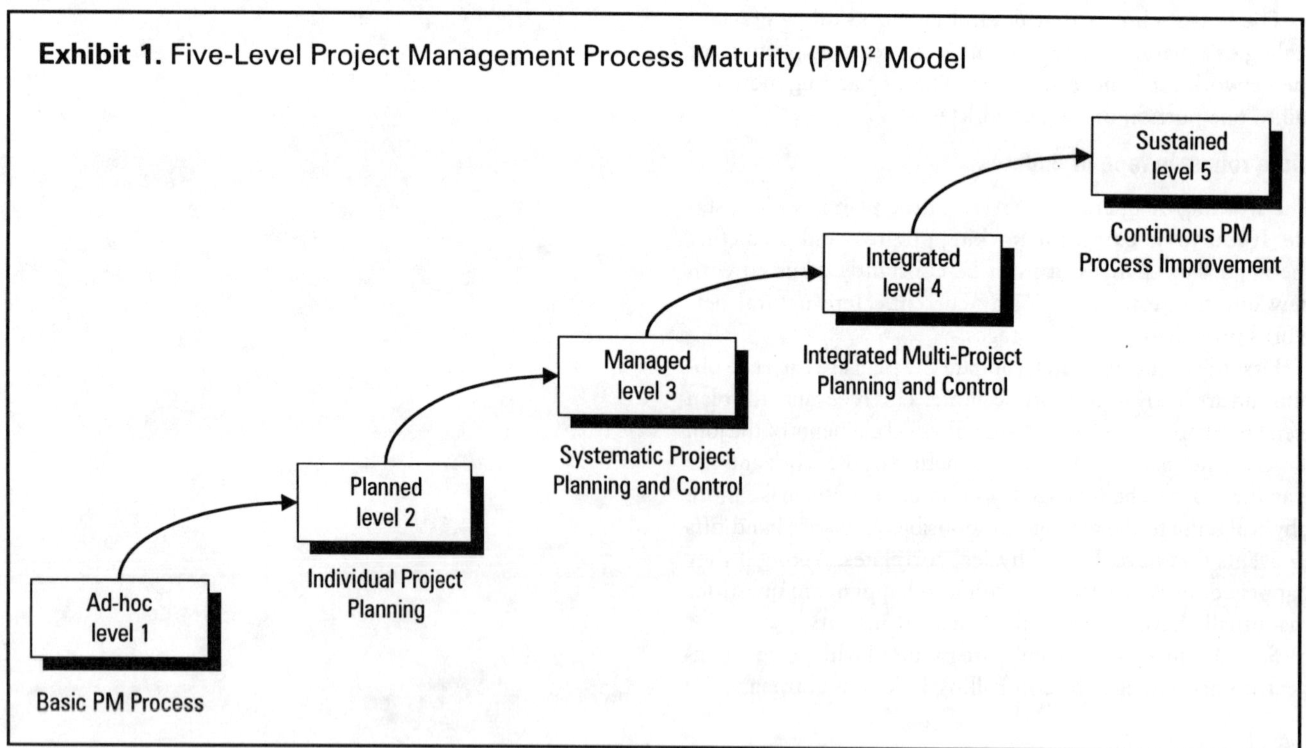

**Exhibit 2.** Overall PM Maturity

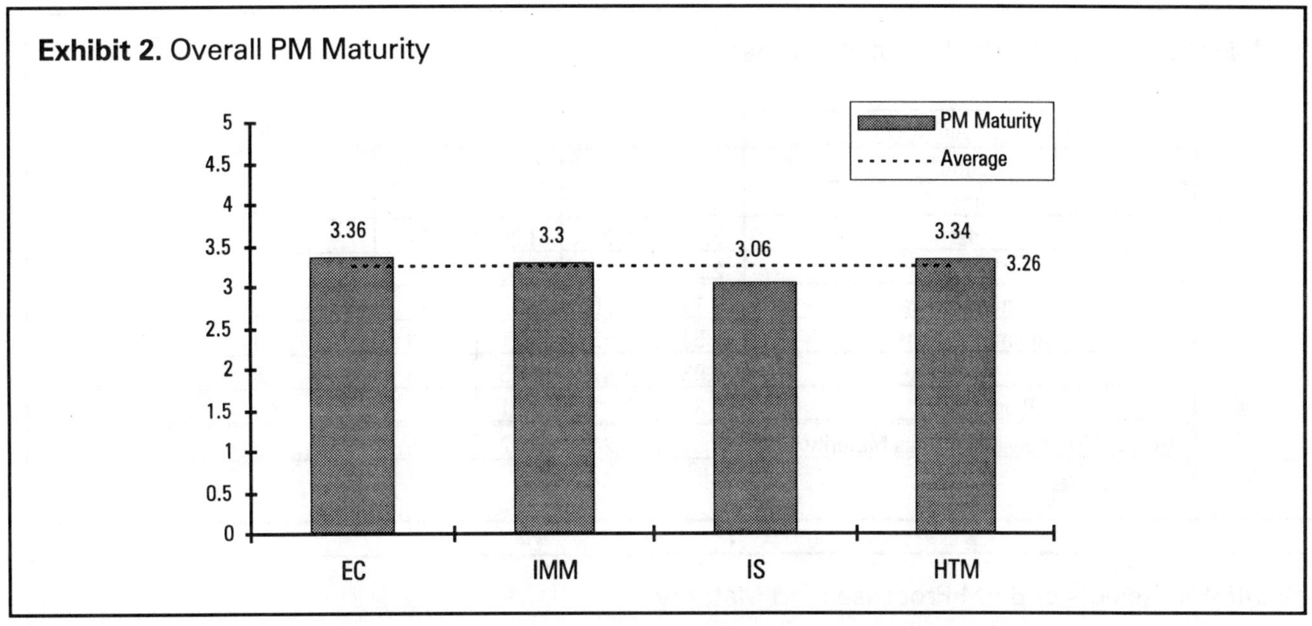


5. Measure an organization's PM maturity level and actual project performance with three-part (PM)2 benchmarking questionnaire.
6. Break down collected information to evaluate and benchmark an organization's PM processes and practices level using specific criteria.
7. Identify an organization's strengths and weaknesses of PM practices and processes.
8. Find the relationship by correlating an organization's PM level and actual project cost and schedule performance.
9. Provide suggestions and recommendations for PM maturity improvement.

## Five-Level Project Management Process Maturity (PM)2 Model

The five-level PM Process Maturity (PM)2 Model is developed by adapting Crosby's maturity model (Crosby 1979), SEI's capability maturity model (SEI 1993), McCauley's organizational maturity model (McCauley 1993), and Microframe's PM maturity model (Microframe 1997) as basic references. Exhibit 1 presents the conceptual model of five-level PM Process Maturity (PM)2 Model.

This five-level (PM)2 model illustrates a series of steps to help an organization incrementally improve the organization's overall PM effectiveness. The objective is to use this model as a basis to locate and position an organization's current PM maturity level. This model also motivates organizations and people to accomplish higher and more sophisticated PM maturity by a systematic and incremental approach.

## Organization's General Information Related to PM Practices

### Organizational Demographics

Thirty-eight companies from four different industries and application areas have participated in this study: fifteen companies from engineering and construction (EC), ten companies from information management and movement (IMM, a.k.a. telecommunications), ten companies from information systems (IS, a.k.a. software development), and three companies from hi-tech manufacturing (HTM). Both private sectors and public sectors were examined.

### Number of Years in PM Practices

Number of years in PM practices answers ranged from one to fifty years, with averages of 15.4 years for EC, 10.7 years for HTM, eight years for IS, and 6.8 years for IMM. The average was 10.7 years. Sixty-one percent of the organizations had less than tem years of experience with PM.

### Annual Cost of PM Services

Annual cost of PM services were computed as a percentage of a company's or department's revenues or sales if that organization was entirely projectized. The average cost of PM services as a percentage of PM spending was 6 percent. Eighty percent of the companies answered that they spend less than 10 percent of total project cost on project management.

**Exhibit 3.** Results of 8 PM Knowledge areas PM Maturity

| PM Knowledge Areas | EC | IMM | IS | HTM | All 38 Companies |
|---|---|---|---|---|---|
| Scope | 3.52 | 3.45 | 3.25 | 3.37 | 3.42 |
| Time | 3.55 | 3.41 | 3.03 | 3.50 | 3.37 |
| Cost | 3.74 | 3.22 | 3.20 | 3.97 | 3.48 |
| Quality | 2.91 | 3.22 | 2.88 | 3.26 | 3.06 |
| Human Resources | 3.18 | 3.20 | 2.93 | 3.18 | 3.12 |
| Communications | 3.53 | 3.53 | 3.21 | 3.48 | 3.44 |
| Risk | 2.93 | 2.87 | 2.75 | 2.76 | 2.85 |
| Procurement | 3.33 | 3.01 | 2.91 | 3.33 | 3.14 |
| Overall PM Knowledge Areas Maturity | 3.34 | 3.24 | 3.02 | 3.36 | 3.24 |

**Exhibit 4.** Resluts of 6 PM Processes PM Maturity

| PM Processes | E-C | IMM | IS | HTM | All 38 Companies |
|---|---|---|---|---|---|
| Initiating Maturity | 3.25 | 3.34 | 3.57 | 3.60 | 3.39 |
| Planning Maturity | 3.61 | 3.49 | 3.43 | 3.55 | 3.53 |
| Executing Maturity | 3.31 | 3.27 | 2.90 | 3.32 | 3.19 |
| Controlling Maturity | 3.55 | 3.31 | 2.98 | 3.25 | 3.31 |
| Closing Maturity | 3.28 | 3.43 | 2.90 | 3.05 | 3.2 |
| Project-driven Org. Environment Maturity | 3.14 | 2.99 | 2.73 | 3.25 | 3.00 |
| Overall PM Processes Maturity | 3.36 | 3.31 | 3.09 | 3.34 | 3.28 |

## PM Maturity Assessment Results

### Overall PM Maturity

The overall PM maturity of the thirty-eight organizations ranged from a low of 3.06 for IS to a high of 3.36 for EC. The average overall PM maturity was 3.26. Since the rating scale ranged from one (lowest) to five (highest), there is still a substantial opportunity for improvement of PM practices for all four industries and application areas. Exhibit 2 compares overall PM maturity of four different industries and application areas.

## PM Knowledge Areas PM Maturity

In accordance with *A Guide to the Project Management Body of Knowledge (PMBOK Guide)* from PMI (PMI 1996), we studied eight PM knowledge areas: scope, time, cost, quality, human resource, risk, communications, and procurement.

Exhibit 3 shows the benchmarking results for these PM knowledge areas. The result shows that all four industries are very concerned about cost management. Also, all organizations were weak on risk management area.

### PM Processes Maturity

The study team proposes a generic PM lifecycle process to measure, compare, and benchmark different PM lifecycle phases accurately. In this study, PM processes are broken down into six different processes: initiating, planning, executing, controlling, closing, and project-driven organization environment. The area of project-driven organization environment was added to investigate the integration aspects and organizational issues of the other five PM processes.

Exhibit 4 shows the benchmarking results of six project lifecycle phases. IS had the lowest PM maturity rating, and EC and HTM had the highest.

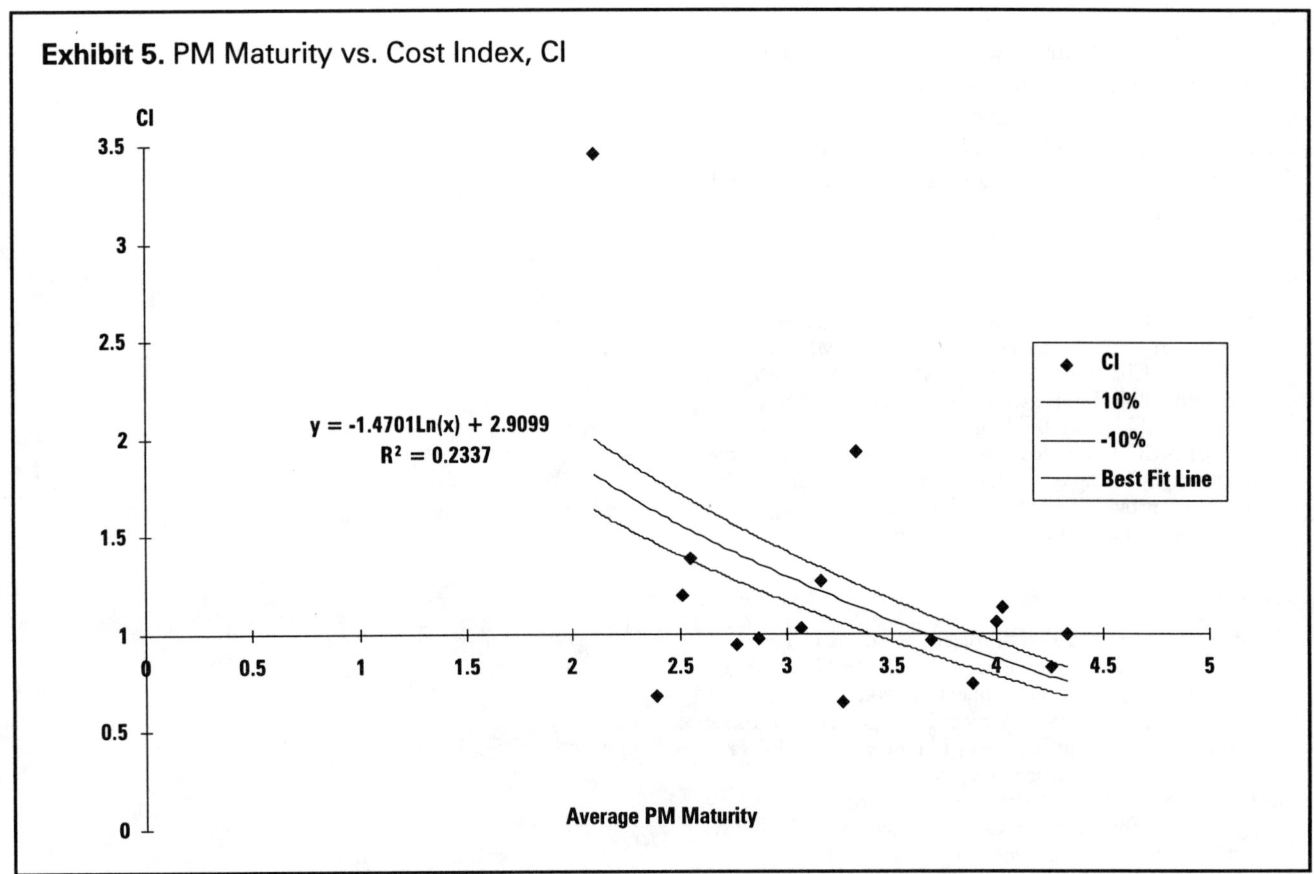


## Relationship between PM Maturity and Actual Project Performance

This paper also analyzes the relationship between organizations' PM process maturity and actual project performance. Project performance is measured by the cost or schedule of the project. To evaluate an organization's project performance, a cost index (CI) and a schedule index (SI) were developed as below. It is assumed that the estimation of CI and SI are accurate. Note that CI and SI are different from the *PMBOK Guide's* cost performance index (CPI) and schedule performance index (SPI). In other words, the smaller the CI and SI, the better the project performance.

*Cost Index, CI=* $\dfrac{\textit{Actual Project Cost}}{\textit{Original Budget}}$

*Schedule Index, SI=* $\dfrac{\textit{Actual Project Duration}}{\textit{Original Project Duration}}$

Exhibit 5 portrays one example of the statistical relationship between overall PM maturity and the cost index. In this analysis, PM maturity is an independent variable and CI is the dependent variable. The heavier line is the best-fit regression equation, and the two lighter-colored lines are the +/- 10 percent control limits. The slope of the curve indicates that higher levels of PM maturity are associated with better cost performance of the project, even considering the small sample size.

## Conclusions

This research provides solid, comparative studies on PM processes and practices across industries and within an industry. The developed benchmarking tools assess organizations' current level of PM strengths and weaknesses to further improve PM effectiveness. This benchmarking procedure quantitatively examines and benchmarks current PM processes and practices of thirty-eight different companies and government agencies in four different industries. This technique can be used for an indefinite period of time for continuous improvement of an organization's PM maturity.

The results of the study show that even the best companies and industries have substantial room for improvement. Also, this analysis has shown that organizational PM maturity level and actual project performance were positively associated. This finding could be interpreted to encourage managers to pursue PM more actively.

This paper is a progress report for benchmarking an organization's PM maturity and for developing an assessment methodology to determine an organization's return on PM investment (PM/ROI). Future research will continue to report on quantitative results and findings by applying this research methodology This benchmarking methodology and the resulting quantitative analyses will aid managers in making better PM investment decisions. Other articles in the future will continue this line of inquiry.

## Acknowledgments

We appreciate the support of the Project Management Institute (PMI) Educational Foundation and PMI/Northern California Chapter. We especially thank Dan Ono, Jim McFarlin, Bob Thompson, Ahmet Taspinar, Mike McCauley, Paul Nelson, Bill Ruggles, Cathy Tonne, and other PMI/NCC Study Team members. We also thank the thirty-eught companies that have participated in this study and provided much valuable information regarding project management practices and processes.

## References

Al-Sedairy, Salman T. 1994. "Project Management Practices in Public Sector Construction: Saudi Arabia." *Project Management Journa* (December): 37–44.

Boznak, Rudolph G. 1988. "Project Management—Today's Solution For Complex Project Engineering." *IEEE Proceedings on Engineering Management.*

Bu-Bushait, K. A. 1989. "The Application of Project Management Techniques To Construction and R&D Projects." *Project Management Journal* (June): 17–22.

CII. 1990. "Assessment of Owner Project Management Practices and Performance." *Special CII Publication* (April).

Crosby, Philip. 1979. *Quality is Free.* New York: McGraw-Hill.

Deutsch, Michael S. 1991. "An Exploratory Analysis Relating the Software Project Management Process to Project Success." *IEEE Transactions on Engineering Management* 38:4 (November).

Gross, Robert L., and David Price. 1990. "Common Project Management Problems and How They Can be Avoided Through The Use of Self Managing Teams." *IEEE International Engineering Management Conference.*

McCauley, Mike. 1993. "Developing a Project-Driven Organization." *PM Network* (September): 26–30.

Microframe. 1997. "Using a Maturity Model to Focus Project Management Improvement Efforts." Microframe's internal publication.

Paulk, Mark C., Charles V. Weber, Suzanne M. Garcia, Mary Beth Chrissis, and Marilyn Bush. 1993. "Key Practices of the Capability Maturity Model, Version 1.1." *Software Engineering Institute*, Technical Report, SEI-93-TR-025.

Project Management Institute, Standards Committee. 1996. *A Guide to the Project Management Body of Knowledge (PMBOK Guide).*

Ziomek, N. L., and G.R. Meneghin. 1984. "Training—A Key Element In Implementing Project Management." *Project Management Journal* (August): 76–83.

# Simultaneous Management: The Paradigm for the New Era of Project Management

Alexander Laufer, University of Maryland at College Park
Gregory A. Howell, University of Mexico

## Introduction

Since today's world is more dynamic and projects must respond to a more compressed schedule, uncertainty has become one of the major factors that influence a project's performance and ultimate success. This is true for all projects—technical, organizational, public, and private—and that is the reason why master project managers are now turning to "simultaneous management" (SM) to solve the intricacies of project management. It's the one dynamic model that has proven successful in effectively compressing project schedule without sacrificing cost or quality (Laufer 1996).

The SM model is composed of nine principles that are a result of ten years of research that included intensive interaction in the field with such corporate leaders as AT&T, Bechtel, DuPont, Exxon, Fluor-Daniel, IBM, J.A. Jones, Morrison & Knudson, Motorola, and Proctor & Gamble. The principles were found to be applicable to a wide spectrum of technological, business, and social projects.

## Evolution of Project Management Models

A better understanding of the SM model may be gained by briefly retracing the evolution of the various models that dominated project management thinking over the last decades. It seems that one can establish four distinct generations of models, each incorporating the principles of the preceding one: scheduling (control), teamwork (integration), reducing uncertainty (flexibility), and simultaneous management (dynamism). Each later model has a greater ability to cope with more situations, from the simple and certain project to the complex, uncertain, and quick one (see Exhibit 1).

The first period noted as scheduling can be traced to the birth of the modern notion of project management during the fifties and early sixties when CPM and PERT techniques emerged on defense and construction projects. The model concentrates on coordination of sequential and parallel activities and control of performance.

A different approach evolved in the seventies when organizations realized the need for managing complex projects, projects consisting of many dissimilar, highly interdependent components mastered by different disciplines. The challenge

**Exhibit 1.** Evolution of Models of Project Management

| Central Concept | Era of Model | Dominant Project Characteristics | Main Thrust |
|---|---|---|---|
| **Scheduling (Control)** | 1960s | Simple, Certain | Coordinating activities |
| **Teamwork (Integration)** | 1970s | Complex, Certain | Cooperation between participants |
| **Reducing Uncertainty (Flexibility)** | 1980s | Complex, Uncertain | Making stable decisions |
| **Simultaneity (Dynamism)** | 1990s | Complex, Uncertain, Quick | Orchestrating contending demands |



PROJECT MANAGEMENT INSTITUTE 28th Annual Seminars & Symposium
Chicago, Illinois: Papers Presented September 29 to October 1, 1997

here was to ensure integration and teamwork between the different participants and to make the team perform as a unified entity.

The above two models fit squarely into a world of certainty. But what we discovered was that the decisive majority of projects in most industries suffer until far into their lives from rapidly changing goals (Howell et al. 1993). The third style for project management, which sprouted during the eighties, aims, therefore, at reducing uncertainty to manageable size. The main challenge of the reducing uncertainty model is to make stable decisions that will stand the test of time.

In the nineties, however, as time to market becomes the driving factor in many industrial companies, we find a new style dominating—simultaneity. Simultaneous managers do subscribe to the old mindset of rational, scientific management and engage their teams in systematic planning. But at the same time, they also adopt a new mindset and spend a great deal of their time scanning and influencing the project's external environment. They start planning very early, but at the same time they also postpone planning. They create a flexible plan by deliberately and carefully combining selected redundancies with an otherwise efficient plan. They do not expect goals and means to be resolved sequentially and separately but rather simultaneously and interactively.

Simultaneous managers do not choose "either-or," but do choose "one and the other at the same time." They are able to see that many "pictures" in our world do not contain just one object. In the picture below, for example, they don't see either a vase or faces, but both.

**Vase or Faces? Or Both?**

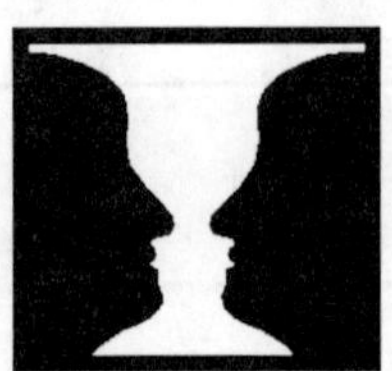

What do we really mean by simultaneity? We all agree that "you are no place at all when you try to be in two places at once." All managers face extremes, e.g., short- and long-term horizons, large issues and small details. Ordinary managers can and often do get stuck at one extreme. However, *simultaneous project managers orchestrate by constantly swinging back and forth to respond to rapidly changing and contending demands.* This act of orchestration is termed simultaneous management.

## Orchestrating Contending Demands

In today's era of uncertainty and accelerated speed, the effective management of *permanent* organizations is achieved by managing contending demands. Our research shows that in managing *temporary* organizations, the constant management of contending demands is even more critical. In other words, orchestrating contending demands *is* project management. Some of the more typical contending demands orchestrated by successful project leaders are the following.

### *Reflection Versus Action*

Successful project leaders adopt the rule, "Objectives first, means later." Yet sometimes they must first explore the means. They also adhere to the rule, "Take the time to do it right the first time." Yet at times they have no choice but to conduct small, quick experiments, knowing that in some they will fail.

### *Divergence Versus Convergence*

To compete in an era where stable information is scarce but competition is fierce, successful project leaders allow enough time to find the right questions and to generate diverging views to expand the range of possibilities. At the same time, to compete in an era where accelerated speed is a dominant factor, they ensure timely convergence, and often, only very selective divergence.

### *Formal Versus Informal*

When possible, successful project leaders employ formal planning and communication means. However, when sufficient time and information are not available, they carry out informal planning, mainly during project meetings, and communicate through informal plan formats, sometimes by simple checklists.

### *Football Versus Basketball*

When uncertainty is high and team size small, successful project leaders establish a team structure and working style similar to that of a basketball game—a fairly loose definition of roles which promotes creative and spontaneous interaction and high adaptability. However, when uncertainty is low and team size large, they adopt a team working style similar to football—they place the players in fixed positions and demand adherence to early plans. But frequently, changing circumstances require quick switch-overs between these two styles, as well as the adoption of other team structures.

### *Conformity Versus Freedom*

Successful project leaders willingly conform to upper management rules and guidelines. They understand the need of their parent company to maintain internal stability and they

**Exhibit 2.** Simultaneous Management Principles

### Planning

***1.Systematic and Integrative Planning***

Start planning as early as possible. Set project objectives and employ a diverging/converging multiphase process. At each phase, prepare all functional plans simultaneously and interdependently.

***2. Timely Decisions Adjusted to Uncertainty***

Adjust the timing of decisions and their degree of detail to the completeness and stability of information. Plan for multiple time horizons and selectively accelerate implementation to obtain fast feedback for further planning.

***3. Isolation and Absorption***

Isolate tasks plagued by very high uncertainty and loosen connections between uncertain tasks. In both cases you absorb uncertainty by selectively employing redundant resources. Divide large projects into independent subprojects and group tasks within projects according to uncertainty.

### Leadership and Integration

***4. Inward and Outward Leadership***

Lead the project throughout while assuming both internal and external leadership roles. Manage decision-making, scan and influence the external environment, keep the momentum, and be ready to intervene swiftly.

***5. Teamwork***

Build multifunctional and multi-organizational teams composed of a small number of individuals with complementary skills. Develop mutual accountability for project results and foster collaboration and enthusiasm by engaging their minds and souls. Sustain teamwork throughout.

***6. Overlapping of Phases***

Involve representatives of downstream phases in project planning as early as possible. To accelerate project speed, overlap project phases. To ensure that schedule is compressed without sacrificing cost or quality, take essential steps related to the other eight principles of simultaneous management.

### Systems

***7. Simple Procedures***

Develop standard and ad hoc procedures, which are simple, easily implemented, and allow a degree of flexibility. Document and share success stories, which promote great flexibility. Employ optimization strategies selectively.

***8. Intensive Communication***

Design and promote an extensive communication system capable of frequently and quickly sharing a large volume of information between a great number of people. Employ multiple mediums, in particular, extensive face-to-face communication, and modern information technology.

***9. Systematic Monitoring***

Systematically monitor project performance as well as the changes in the critical planning assumptions. To understand what's going on, you should both move about and review formal reports.

expect to benefit from accumulated experience. At the same time, however, they often have no choice but to exercise flexibility in implementing these rules, and even to challenge upper management guidelines in order to deliver highly ambitious projects in fast changing environments.

This list may continue to include many other contradictions such as: inward versus outward and micro versus macro attention, enabling versus intervening leadership, efficiency versus redundancy, and so on. This partial list of contending demands is sufficient for our purpose here to illustrate the central role of orchestrating contending demands in today's project management.

## The Principles of Simultaneous Management

The nine principles are divided into three groups—planning, leadership and integration, and systems (see Exhibit 2). The nine principles served the project managers as a checklist and guide for action. These principles are not independent of each other. Quite the opposite. To understand and use them correctly, all nine must be understood and used interdependently.

While the principles are formulated in actionable language, they do not prescribe a deterministic approach. That is, they do not recommend "one best way"; on the contrary, they prescribe that "context is the key." The hallmark of a

**Exhibit 3.** Mind-Set Shifts

| | From: Old Mindset | To: Simultaneous Management Mindset |
|---|---|---|
| **Project Management** | Performing according to plan, with minimal changes, is the essence of project management | Meeting customer needs, while coping successfully with unavoidable changes, is the essence of project management |
| **Objectives** | Objectives are always resolved before means are specified | Objectives and means are often resolved gradually and almost simultaneously |
| **Uncertainty** | Early in the project, analysis of risk by a staff specialist; later in the project, operate under the assumption that uncertainty is negligible | Continuous management of uncertainty by entire team |
| **Optimization** | Efficiency, e.g., all tasks are tightly coupled | Efficiency mixed with essential redundancy, e.g., uncertain tasks are loosely coupled |
| **Leadership** | Inward attention | Outward and inward attention |
| **Integration** | Multifunctional teams; contracting emphasizes risk allocation | Multifunctional and multi-organizational teams; contracting emphasizes cooperation |
| **Speed** | Overlapping of phases | Fast reduction of uncertainty followed by overlapping of phases |
| **Systems** | Systems are the key | People using systems-- and sometimes challenging them-- are the key |
| **Communication** | High tech, emphasis on completeness and accuracy of information | High touch and high tech, emphasis on timeliness of information |
| **Control** | Measurement of project performance -- feedback-based control | Monitoring of environment changes and project performance -- anticipation and feedback-based control |

simultaneous manager is his ability to fit the principle to the project context (project size, complexity, speed, uncertainty, contract type, and so on), by exercising a great deal of discrimination and judgment. The most important quality of the simultaneous management principles is their *adaptability* to different contexts. This renders them useful for coping with uncertainty and change and also makes them applicable to a wide variety of project settings in every industry.

Applying the principles will help the project team to migrate from the old mindset, fraught with overruns and failure, to the new mindset of SM that gives the project team the principles and tools for success (see Exhibit 3). In our age of continuous and fast changes, you should not expect any management concept to be permanent, only the "current best." By conducting your practice according to the SM principles and becoming a reflective practitioner, you will be more prepared for ever-changing managerial styles. You will become your own most reliable "applied researcher" who can identify the right timing for the next shift in mindset.

## References


Howell, G., A. Laufer, and G. Ballard. 1993. "Uncertainty and Project Objectives." *The Project Appraisal* 8: 37–43.

Laufer, A. 1996. "Simultaneous Management: Managing Projects in a Dynamic Environment." *AMACOM.* American Management Association.

# Institutionalizing Project Management: A Necessity for Project Management to Provide Value and Thrive in the Coming Century

William J. Swanston, PMP, Robbins-Gioia, Inc.
William C. Carney, PMP, Robbins-Gioia, Inc.

Although institutionalizing project management within an organization can be an agonizing and time-consuming process, the authors believe it is an absolute necessity for the future viability of project management in the coming century. For our purposes, project management is institutionalized when an organization applies it consistently on all its projects and uses its output to make business decisions. Thus, when seen in this light, institutionalization is the mechanism by which project management will be able to add value within ever changing business environments. In spite of the current trend of managing organizations by projects, it is our belief that unless the project management function adds this type of value within an organization, it will come to be seen as a waste of time, money, and resources, which may ultimately result in its diminished use within organizations.

There are two steps in the institutionalization process. The first step consists of the development of a structured methodology that can be replicated consistently on all company projects. The second step, which is the "critical success step," consists of effectively implementing the methodology. Unfortunately, there are no short cuts when it comes to implementing a project management program. However, without effective implementation, project management will be viewed as a "flavor of the month program that will eventually go away."

## Project Management Methodology Development

The project management methodology for an organization consists of the detailed steps by which it plans and manages its projects. Although the same foundational project management principles make up every sound methodology, the manner in which these principles are employed will be different in each organization. For example, every sound project management methodology must require the development of a scope of work for each project. However, the specific steps, scope

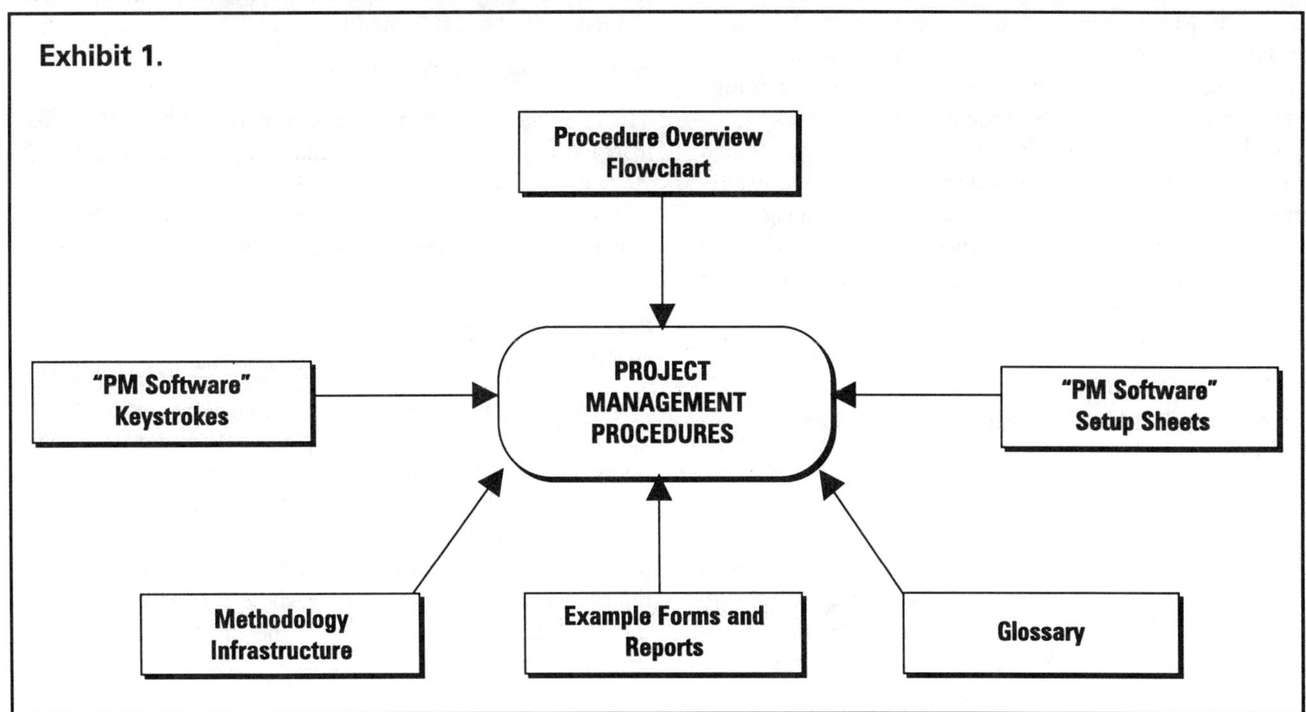

Exhibit 2.

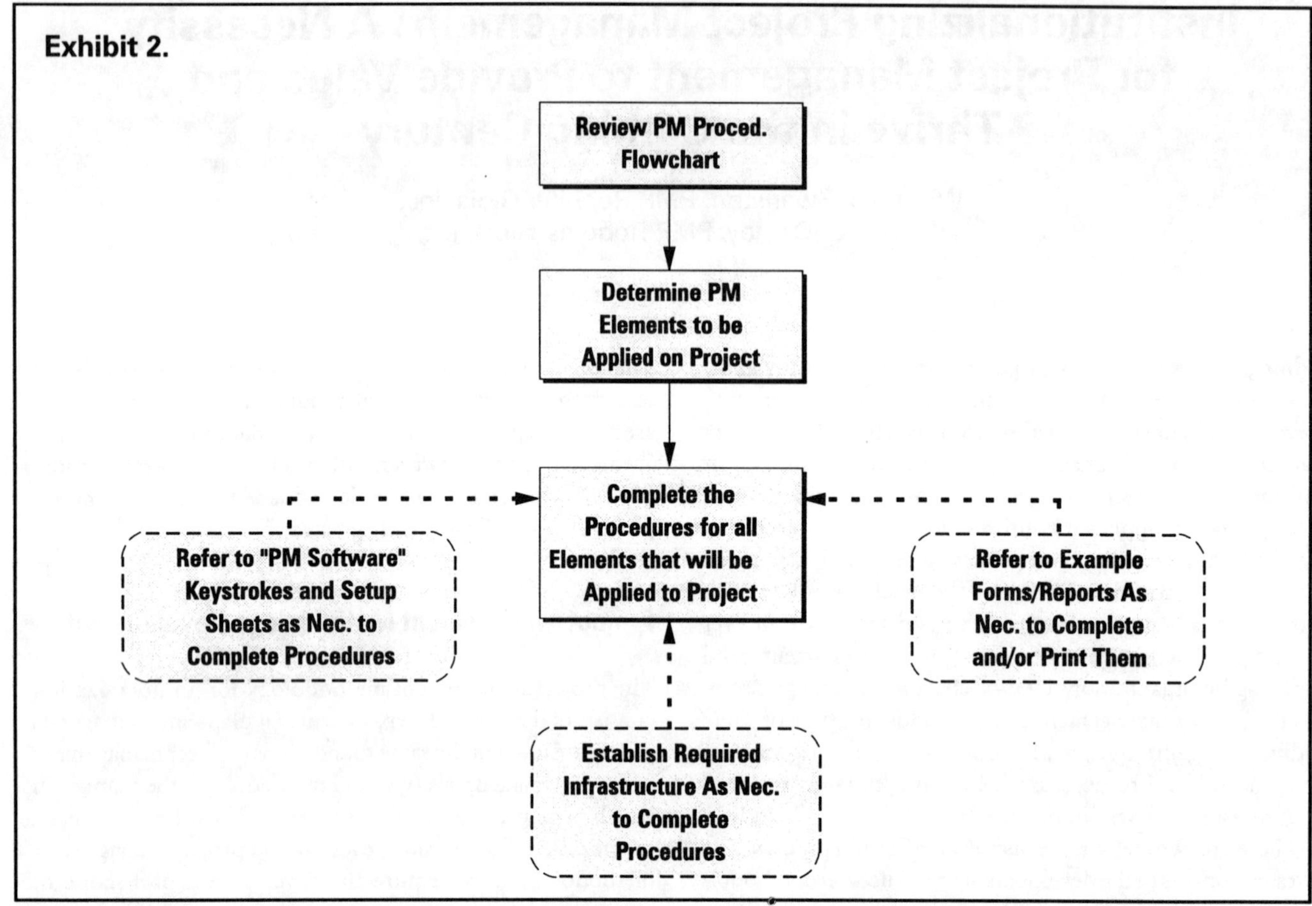


forms, and development process will vary organization by organization. Many organizations expedite the methodology development process by starting with a "canned" or "off the shelf" methodology, and then customize that methodology to reflect the manner in which the organization works.

As the methodology is being developed, it is documented in a project management instruction manual (sometimes referred to as a procedures manual). The project management instruction manual provides the structure necessary to be able to repeat the organization's methodology consistently across all projects. Although there is no one correct way to structure an instruction manual, the following structure has proven to be quite successful.

## Proposed Project Management Instruction Manual Structure

### *Procedures Overview Flowchart*

The procedures overview flowchart provides an overview of the steps required to complete the organization's project management methodology. Each element contained in the process is displayed, along with the specific instruction manual procedures needed to complete the element. The elements that must be applied on all projects (as opposed to the optional elements) can be highlighted in yellow.

### *Project Management Procedures*

The project management procedures are the "heart" of the instruction manual. These procedures provide the detailed steps necessary to successfully plan and manage a project within the organization. All the remaining sections in the instruction manual support the accomplishment of these procedures.

### *PM (Project Management) Software Keystrokes (Determined by PM Software Being Used in the Organization)*

This section provides the project management software keystrokes required to perform the project management procedures. The "PM Software Keystrokes" section is organized to correspond with the "Project Management Procedures" section numbering structure. For example, if the completion of project management procedure 2.3.1.1 requires keystrokes in the project management software, these "keystrokes" will be found under number 2.3.1.1 in the "PM Software Keystrokes" section.

**Exhibit 3.**

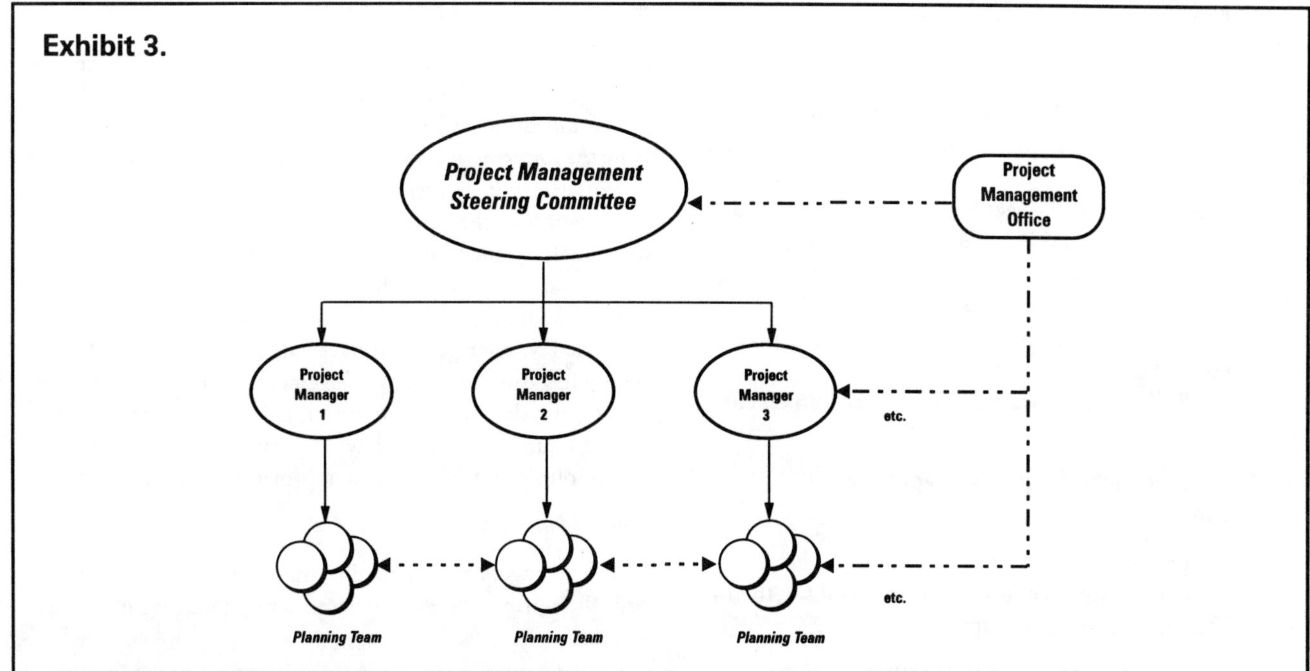


### PM (Project Management) Software Setup Sheets

The PM software setup sheets provide the information needed to create each view, table, and filter called for in the "PM Software Keystrokes" section of the manual. If a required view, table, or filter is not available, refer to the corresponding number in the setup sheets section for the parameters needed to create it. As with the "PM Software Keystrokes" section, the setup sheets numbering structure is organized to correspond with the "Project Management Procedures" section numbering structure.

### Methodology Infrastructure

The infrastructure section defines the project management infrastructure that will be needed to implement the organization's project management methodology. For example, the infrastructure section provides the information necessary to set up the organization's calendar, resource library, or the information needed to send project data via E-mail.

### Example Forms and Reports

This section contains an example of each form and report contained in the project management methodology. Included with each *form* are instructions for locating it on the computer system and printing it out. The back of each *report* contains instructions for printing it out, as well as the instruction manual procedure reference (both the procedure number and page number) which describes how to read and interpret the report.

### Glossary

The glossary defines the terms used in the instruction manual that may be unfamiliar to the user.

## B. Project Management Instruction Manual Utilization

- Step 1. Review the *"Procedures Overview Flowchart."* Also, if necessary, read through the glossary to become familiar with the terms contained in the instruction manual.
- Step 2. Determine the procedures (from the "Process Overview Flowchart") that will be applied on the project. All elements highlighted in yellow are required for each project within the organization. The remaining elements are optional, and are applied as deemed necessary or appropriate.
- Step 3. Complete all procedures required for the project (as determined under step 2) as set forth in the instruction manual.
- Step 4. As the required procedures are completed for the project, use the "PM Software Keystrokes," "PM Software Setup Sheets," and "Infrastructure" sections as necessary to complete the procedures. When you need to access a form, or print out a report, use the "Example Forms/Reports" section to ensure that you are using the proper forms, as well as to ensure that each report is formatted properly.

## Project Management Methodology Implementation

The organization's methodology implementation process employs a phased approach, consisting of the following five phases:

- Phase 1—Establish the Project Management Organization
- Phase 2—Establish A Project Management Culture
- Phase 3—Develop and Deliver Training
- Phase 4—Develop Project Templates
- Phase 5—Pilot Test Methodology (Use a Single Representative Project)
- Phase 6—Roll-Out Full Scale Methodology Implementation

### Phase 1—Establish the Project Management Organization

The following project management structure has been used successfully by the authors and is recommended for the institutionalization of project management.

#### *Project Management Steering Committee (PMSC)*

The PMSC oversees the project management implementation effort. The ultimate responsibility of the PMSC is to provide the project management program with enough "corporate clout" to ensure it is implemented and practiced throughout the organization. The implementation of a project management program must be managed, coordinated, and controlled.

Specific tasks of the PMSC include:

- Conveying the company vision for project management.
- Developing the project management mission statement, along with its goals and objectives.
- Communicating the need for the project management program to the entire organization.
- Releasing project management supporting documentation (i.e., project management program directives).
- Providing support to the project management office (PMO) as needed to drive the organization's implementation efforts (i.e., to keep the implementation moving).
- Resolving implementation problems that cannot be handled at lower levels.
- Providing rewards and recognition to project managers/team members who successfully implement the project management program.
- Measuring the success/progress of the project management implementation effort.

#### *Project Management Office (PMO)*

The project management manager runs the PMO. The size (staffing-wise) of the PMO should correspond to the size of the organization. ***The project management manager must drive the implementation of project management throughout the organization, and serve as the eyes and ears for the PMSC.*** Because of this, the project management manager must be an individual, from within the organization, that is high enough to have the power and authority to do what needs to be done to implement project management methodology/program. Finally, the PM manager must have a detailed understanding of the organization's project management methodology, so that he can provide guidance to individual project managers and project teams when they have difficulty implementing the methodology on their individual projects.

#### *Project Managers*

Project managers are assigned to individual projects and perform the normal duties associated with managing individual projects.

#### *Planning Teams*

Planning teams are interdisciplinary teams that are assembled on a project by project basis to assist in the development of the detailed plans needed to effectively manage the project. Each planning team is made up of the actual individuals who will be performing the work, plus any subject matter experts deemed necessary.

### Phase 2—Establish a Project Management Culture

Implementation of the project management methodology will not be successful without an environment conducive to the discipline of project management. The following elements will help to establish a project management culture.

- The project management function must report to an executive or an executive committee whose authority extends across the organization.
- Defined career paths for project managers and project teams, along with established job descriptions.
- Established pay and incentive structures for project personnel, (e.g., bonuses for project managers, educational opportunities, team-based performance pay, and so on).

If the necessary project management culture does not exist, the existing organizational culture must be assessed, and the barriers that are preventing the existence of a project management culture must be identified. Once these barriers are identified, changes must be instituted in the organizational structure to better support a project management environment.

## Phase 3—Develop and Deliver Training

There are three types of training that should be developed and delivered: pre-implementation training, methodology-based training, and general project management theory training.

### *Pre-Implementation Training*

Pre-implementation training focuses primarily on the "soft/non-technical" skills required by a project manager or project personnel. Specific training may include:

1. Project Team Management: Provides training on the start up and development of project teams, the problems associated with forming a cohesive team, as well as how to "jump start" a team so it becomes effective quickly.
2. "Power Gap" Management: Provides training on how to effectively manage with less than adequate authority. This training would include the use of networking skills to establish power and influence, as well as methods to obtain the "informal" project information that does not show up in status reports, but is essential to the successful management and completion of project.
3. "Functional Boss" Management: Provides training on how to influence the "functional bosses" to get the resources and assistance needed to successfully complete a company project. The ability to do this begins by building open, high trust, two-way relationships with these "functional bosses."

### *Methodology-Based Training*

Methodology-based training focuses specifically on the project management methodology developed for the organization. Included in this training would be:

- Specific training on the use of the project management instruction manual.
- Methodology procedures training.
- Training on the forms and reports contained in the system.

### *General Project Management Theory Training*

Single point lessons are recommended for training on general project management theory. More and more, people in project-oriented companies are resistant to sitting through project management theory workshops. Most people in these companies have been through some type of project management theory class. What they are more interested in, at this point, is how the theory relates specifically to their work situation. For example, say your methodology requires project teams to update their projects using network diagrams. Single point lessons on network updating provide a very effective method for disseminating the required information. Each single point lesson provides the necessary training—as the team needs it. In other words, team members are "spoon fed" the training information as they need it (i.e., J-I-T training).

## Phase 4—Develop Project Templates

If the projects undertaken within the organization are similar in nature, project templates should be developed.

The challenge is to develop the templates to an appropriate level of detail. If the templates are not detailed enough, consistent control across projects will not be possible. If the templates are too detailed, project teams will not be able to develop plans that reflect the way they accomplish their work. In other words, they will not be able to use the plans to manage the project.

## Phase 5—Pilot Test Methodology (Single Representative Project)

Before the project management methodology is rolled out on a full-scale basis, it must be pilot tested. The purpose of pilot testing is to prove-out the project management process (i.e., procedures, templates, and so on) to verify that it works. There is nothing more frustrating than being required to use a process that does not work. The project management methodology should be pilot tested on one or two projects that are representative of the type of projects undertaken within the organization. There are two options that can be used to pilot test the methodology.

- Method 1—Completely develop the methodology before testing it.
- Method 2—Test the methodology (piecemeal) as it is being developed.

Obviously, it is much quicker to test the methodology as it is being developed, but you have to weigh the time factor against the loss of "cradle-to-grave" continuity that is provided by completely developing the methodology before testing it.

## Phase 6—Roll Out Full-Scale Methodology Implementation

Full-scale methodology implementation is rolled out with a project management implementation schedule and project management implementation tracking sheet. The implementation schedule is a detailed time-phased plan for putting in place the project management program for the organization. The project management implementation tracking sheet is a progress report for management (i.e., the PMSC) to keep them informed of implementation progress. Management can use the tracking sheet to determine when higher level pressure needs to exerted on the implementation process.

## Project Management Institutionalization Critical Success Factors

There are several factors that are critical to the successful institutionalization of project management within an organization.

1. Understand what you're up against. You are a change agent! Institutionalizing project management usually requires a new way of looking at the way people do their jobs. Most people will not make this adjustment quickly and/or willingly. Thus, the change process will be a slow process. Determine to be satisfied with first learning to crawl before walking or running.
2. Project management institutionalization requires more than support from management; it requires a genuine commitment for the "long haul." Project management institutionalization can take anywhere from two to five years. It does not happen overnight, and it most certainly will not happen if it is attempted with only "lip service" support from management. The people within the organization that are being called upon to make the "change" will see through "lip service" type support in no time. When they do, the institutionalization process is more than likely doomed.
3. Resolve to work hard to make the institutionalization process work.
4. Determine yourself to settle in for the long haul. This will help provide you with the patience that will be needed.
5. Work to develop relationships with the individuals that you are asking to adopt the new process.
6. Initially, be willing to compromise with regard to project management methodology compliance. In other words, don't demand 100 percent compliance initially. Determine what level of compliance you can live with, and work to achieve that level. Over time, as you develop relationships, you can work with people to bridge the "compliance" gap.
7. Expect resistance, and develop a glass half-full mentality so that you can deal with this resistance in a positive manner.
8. Work to develop WIFM's ("What's In It For Me") for the people you are asking to be a part of the institutionalization process. Find ways to make their jobs easier within the context of the new project management process.
9. Do not develop the project management methodology in a vacuum. If possible, take the time to develop the methodology based on input from the people who will be required to use the process. This may be the only way you will get buy in from them. For example, every project must develop a scope of work. To develop the process for the scope of work, you would talk about the concept with the people in the organization who are responsible for performing this function, and then develop a procedure based on what they tell you. In addition, you could also observe a project in action.
10. Identify and nurture senior officers in the organization who are "champions" of project management.
11. Do not roll out the project management methodology prematurely. If you roll out a program that is not yet fully developed, and does not work, you will only frustrate the people you are asking to make the change. When this happens, successful implementation is seriously jeopardized.

## Summary

Institutionalization of project management requires a dedicated long-term commitment by both the organization's management and its project management community. However, once project management is institutionalized within an organization, its value to the organization can have far-reaching implications. For example, once institutionalized, project management can be used as a key component for the successful implementation of an organization's business process reengineering program by providing the BPR function with the processes, procedures, and tools that will position it to accomplish its mission.

# Leading Into the Next Century

Scott C. Brown MS, MBA, PMP, Submarine Systems International

"We trained hard—but it seemed that every time we were beginning to form into teams, we would be reorganized. I was to learn later in life we tend to meet any new situation by reorganizing, and a wonderful method it can be for creating the illusion of progress while producing confusion, inefficiency, and demoralization" (Petronius 66 A.D.). As we approach the new millennium, change continues to pervade industry at the most fundamental levels. Sweeping environmental changes have forced businesses to redefine the standard *modus-operandi,* removing layers of management, creating a proliferation of teams, and subsequently recasting the role of leadership in industry today. To many involved it may seem chaotic.

Drucker notes that teams have become the work unit as opposed to individuals (1994, 68). Katzenbach and Smith found that there is a basic discipline that makes teams work and that teams and good performance are inseparable (1993). However, the term 'team' is used liberally in society today. A collection of representatives forms a committee, but does not necessarily make a team nor guarantee performance. "Performance" and "committee" are generally mutually exclusive terms based largely on the political nature of organizations. The goals of the team must not be in conflict with the needs of the functional organizations represented. Effective leaders will recognize individual motivations and seek ways to align these with the group goals and develop teams from committees.

Since virtually everyone has equal access to tools and information, in order to gain a competitive advantage, businesses must develop that advantage by maximizing the return on their greatest asset—people. The future of project management depends on our ability to *develop teams from committees* so that we achieve a collective output greater than the sum of the individual contributions. *The key ingredient in efforts to differentiate a business from its competitors is the leadership that empowers the people responsible for executing the processes to perform at a synergistic level.* Dynamic and effective project leadership is how we can achieve this goal.

This paper discusses leadership. It also challenges some conventional wisdom and identifies some of our own predispositions that negatively impact our effectiveness. Our predispostions for managing conflict and the manner in which we deploy specific strengths impact our effectiveness as leaders. What may be an asset in one area, may be a detriment in another. Unfortunately, much of our training has created a substantial inertial mass in our thinking that must be overcome in order to succeed. That blockage is attributed to the left side of the project manager's brain that is used so efficiently in developing plans, making certain that all the right questions have been asked and answered, ensuring that the right resources and funding are in place, and that the right risk mitigation plans have been identified. *This analytically based and emotionally detached behavior that is so critical in the definition phases of a project, can sub-optimize your leadership effectiveness as you implement your projects.* That analytical strength can impede effective execution, the harmony that transcends separateness, as project teams transition through implementation.

Tomorrow's environment will continue to create new and challenging leadership opportunities (and frustrations) not encountered in the traditional hierarchical organizational structures of old. Hersey and Blanchard's situational leadership model is helpful in addressing the appropriateness of different leadership styles given a variety of circumstances. Leaders must adapt their leadership style appropriately to effectively manage conflict throughout the developmental phases to realize the interdependence required for synergistic performance. Pursuing graduate research, the author gathered behavioral data from a group of sixty-six first- and second-level managers participating in a project leadership and management skills training course offered by the Educational Services Institute in partnership with the AT&T School of Business and George Washington University. The following behavioral analysis tools were administered and assessed certain behavioral tendencies applicable to leadership, its effectiveness, what strengths comprise it, and how the behavior is modified in conflict:

1. Porter's Strength Deployment Inventory
2. Schutz's FIROB
3. Thomas-Kilmann's Conflict Mode Instrument
4. Blanchard et al's Leader Behavior Analysis II (LBAII).

Responses from each instrument were analyzed to determine the relationships and correlations that exist between the different behaviors and what impact, if any, each has on leader effectiveness as measured by the LBAII instrument. Several statistical tools were utilized to assess the relationships between a variety of behavioral tendencies, strengths, conflict handling predispositions, and the resultant influence a particular variable has on effectiveness *as defined by the LBAII instrument.* The findings are briefly summarized below:



PROJECT MANAGEMENT INSTITUTE 28th Annual Seminars & Symposium
Chicago, Illinois: Papers Presented September 29 to October 1, 1997

1. The use of constructive modes of handling conflict—collaboration and compromise—indirectly support greater leader effectiveness.
2. The aggregate combination of strength deployment in a situation free of conflict influences leader effectiveness.
   - The deployment of analytical-autonomizing strength in a situation free of conflict correlates negatively with effectiveness.
   - The deployment of the assertive-directing and altruistic-nurturing strengths correlate positively with effectiveness.
3. No inferences on effectiveness can be drawn based on initiative and a desire for interpersonal interaction.
4. No inferences on effectiveness can be drawn based on the migration of strength deployment from a situation free of conflict to a conflict situation.

## Conclusions

### The use of constructive modes of handling conflict—collaboration and compromise—indirectly support greater leader effectiveness.

The results from the analyses performed in this investigation challenge some conventional wisdom. First and foremost, and most surprising, is the absence of a direct correlation between an individual's predisposition for handling conflict and leader effectiveness. Both correlation analysis and analysis of variance indicate that no relationships exist. Logic would argue that a collaborative posture in handling conflict would tend to produce better results, and hence be more effective, than an accommodating or avoidance posture. Research has shown that conflict resolution is critical to generating the interdependence that can produce synergy among team members. Since neither accommodating and avoidance modes for handling conflict lead to constructive resolution of conflict and the subsequent effectiveness that can be demonstrated from high-performing teams, why is this logic not captured in the data? Further investigation into the specific correlations among the conflict handling modes provides some explanation. Moderate negative correlations exist between the competing, collaborating, and compromising conflict modes and the avoidance and accommodating modes. The only significant positive correlation that exists is between the avoidance and accommodating modes. Since an individual that employs avoidance frequently will also tend to utilize an accommodating mode often, the use of other conflict handling modes that tend to support resolution will be lower; one might argue that effectiveness, based in part on conflict resolution, should be higher with lower utilization of avoidance and accommodation modes of handling conflict. Curiously, the data does not directly support this. Indirect support is realized through the canonical analysis on strength deployment and the conflict handling modes.

Roughly 33 percent of the variation in conflict handling modes can be attributed to the linear composite of individual strength deployments. The impact of the deployment of the analytical-autonomizing strength on effectiveness is significant, and the correlation is negative. As project managers, we would be wise not to intermingle the rational analytical planning role with the inspirational leadership function required to develop the synergistic performance through the many changes tomorrow.

Further review of the correlations between deployment of the analytical-autonomizing strength and the conflict handling modes reveals positive correlations with competing, avoidance, and accommodation modes of handling conflict and negative correlations with collaboration and compromising modes of handling conflict. Extrapolating from these correlations, a lower deployment of the analytical-autonomizing strength correlates with higher effectiveness and higher use of the collaborating and compromising modes of handling conflict which actively seek constructive resolution to conflict (the competing mode is a win-lose posturing that does not support constructive resolution). *The consequent indirect inference is that higher use of modes of handling conflict that support constructive resolution increases effectiveness.* As project managers we are all generally aware of this phenomenon, but the absence of a direct correlation is surprising.

A possible explanation for the absence of a direct correlation between the conflict handling modes and effectiveness may be found in the data. The standard deviation in the distribution of effectiveness scores is small. Further development of a survey with higher resolution may prove beneficial as actual differences in effectiveness become more pronounced in the data. This area in particular warrants additional research as conclusive results may help identify predispositions for handling conflict that support greater leader effectiveness.

### No inferences on effectiveness can be drawn based on initiative and a desire for interpersonal interaction.

Similar traditional wisdom may hold that an individual who does not prefer to take initiative may be less effective than someone more prone to act. Courage and persistence to act upon their vision and a desire to accept greater responsibility are two key elements of leadership (Hawks). If an individual is not prone to take initiative, then how can the individual act and accept greater responsibility? However, the data indicates the leader effectiveness and a desire to initiate are independent. Further investigation reveals that an individual's desire to take initiative correlates positively with the use of the competing mode in handling conflict. Inferences from this data are limited without a direct correlation between the competing mode and effectiveness.

Interestingly, the analysis of the impact an individual's desire for interpersonal interaction has on the individual's predisposition for handling conflict showed no relationship. It may be postulated that an individual desiring personal interaction may be less prone to utilize non-constructive modes of conflict resolution which would indirectly and negatively impact leader effectiveness. Further detailed investigation into the specific FIROB responses, in the areas of inclusion, control, and affection, might provide valuable insight into the specific expressed and wanted behaviors of effective leaders.

### The aggregate combination of strength deployment in a situation free of conflict influences leader effectiveness.

The analyses involving responses from the strength deployment inventory yield additional insight into specific behavioral patterns and their impact on effectiveness. The three strength deployments are: altruistic-nurturing; assertive-directing; and analytic-autonomizing. A canonical analysis indicates that the aggregate combination of an individual's strength deployment in a situation free of conflict impacts leader effectiveness. Although the impact is small—roughly 10 percent of the variation in leader effectiveness can be explained by the individual strength deployments in a situation free of conflict. Interestingly, the correlations between strengths and effectiveness provide some insight into what strengths support effectiveness. Both the altruistic-nurturing and assertive-eirecting strengths are positively correlated with effectiveness. However, the correlation between the analytical-autonomizing strength and effectiveness is negative. An over-simplified inference might be that effective leaders rely less upon independent reasoning and more on warm-hearted initiative. As project managers, we must be cognizant of the situation and deploy our strengths in such a manner as to optimize our effectiveness. We cannot afford to be detached and overly analytical when the situation calls for caring direction.

### No inferences on effectiveness can be drawn based on the migration of strength deployment from a situation free of conflict to a conflict situation.

Logic may support that constructive conflict resolution is critical to interdependence, synergy, and, consequently, effectiveness. However, a similar canonical analysis on strength deployment in a conflict situation revealed no relationship with effectiveness. The strength deployment inventory captures individual strength deployments in situations free of conflict and conflict situations. How individuals change their strength deployment to deal with conflict may provide interesting insight into leader effectiveness. Surprisingly, both the analysis of variance and a canonical correlation analysis found that no relationship exists between the *change in strength deployment* and effectiveness. In an effort to understand the absence of a relationship, further review of the individual strength deployments is necessary.

The mean response from the strength deployment inventory indicates a reduction in the altruistic-nurturing strength deployment and consequent and equitable increases in both the assertive-directing and analytical-autonomizing strength deployments as an individual moves from a situation free of conflict to one characterized by conflict. However, there is a moderate negative correlation between the deployment of analytical-autonomizing strength in a situation free of conflict and effectiveness. Since the mean migration includes an increase in the deployment of the analytical-autonomizing strength, the consequent impact might reduce effectiveness. Upon reviewing the individual correlations, the expected negative correlations between each strength exist for both situations free of conflict and conflict situations, and both the assertive-directing and altruistic-nurturing strengths have significant correlations *across the conflict situations*, but particularly absent is the correlation of the analytical-autonomizing strength with any other strength, including the same, *across the situational barrier (no conflict versus conflict).* Since the analytical-autonomizing strength deployment in a situation free of conflict is the only direct correlation with effectiveness, and since nothing can be said about the rest of the strength deployments in a conflict mode based on this, *any inferences on migration of strength deployment and effectiveness require further investigation.*

## Summary and Recommendations

When investigating behavioral tendencies of human subjects, what may be appear logical to the educated mind, may be difficult to support with data. Philosophers and researches will continue the quest to define the quintessential leader (e.g., Odysseus) and the associated behavior that moves individuals to act. Given the sample population, a similar study of high-level executives, with demonstrated leadership abilities, may provide valuable insights into those behavioral tendencies critical to effective leadership. Recommendations for further research based on results of this investigation are as follows:

1. Develop a measure of leader effectiveness with a higher degree of resolution so that differences are more pronounced and more obvious in the data-making relationships with the other behaviors, in particular the conflict handling modes.
2. Perform more extensive analysis on the specific areas of inclusion, control, and affection from the FIROB instrument and investigate individual influence on effectiveness.

3. Investigate further the absence of a correlation between the analytical-autonomizing strength and any strength, including same, from a situation free of conflict and one characterized by conflict.

Daniel Goleman published *Emotional Intelligence* in 1995 which postulates that EQ, a measure of emotional intelligence, may be a greater determinant of success than IQ, the intelligence quotient, because it focuses on the human aspects required for success. If we infer that in every measure of success there is an implied effectiveness, an investigation into EQ's relationship with various behavioral tendencies and leader effectiveness may prove valuable and potentially contentious given the social ramifications. However, as of this publishing, there is no scientifically based measure of EQ available.

It may be postulated that strengths that are conducive to constructive conflict modes, which correlate positively with leader effectiveness, are desirable in agents of change. *By simply understanding our own predispositions for handling conflict and strength deployments, we may be able to modify our behavior in any number of ways to increase our effectiveness.*

As part of the continuing evolution of project management into the next century, we need to break out of our traditional boxes in order to handle the exponential growth in rates of change. Leadership is a constant in the evolution of project management discipline; but it becomes more critical as the rate of change accelerates. Corporations are immersed in an extremely dynamic and competitive environment that warrants continued vigilance. Reengineering their business processes will help maintain or develop competitive advantage. However, these efforts, and subsequent change management efforts will be sub-optimized without effective leadership. The harmonious integration of leadership at the project level and project management discipline will be essential to creating appropriately focused synergistic performance among implementing teams facing the dynamic changes of tomorrow. Corporations must identify and nurture the leaders of tomorrow without a recipe for guaranteed success. Resistance to change and fear will create conflicts that need to be managed constructively in order for teams to transition to the high-performing synergistic work unit that will maximize a corporation's return on its greatest asset—each and every one of us.

### Literature Cited

Drucker, Peter F. 1994. "The Age of Social Transformation." *The Atlantic.* (Nov.): 53–80.

Goleman, Daniel. 1995. *Emotional Intelligence*. New York: Bantam.

Hawks, Val D. "Teaching Leadership." Course Handout. Brigham Young University.

Katzenbach, Jon R., and Douglas K. Smith. 1993. "The Discipline of Teams." *Harvard Business Review* (Mar.–Apr.): 111–120.

## Appendix

## Analysis and Results

### Analysis

**Analysis of variance** was used to investigate the following:

1. The impact that an individual's desire to take initiative has on an individual's predisposition for handling conflict.
2. The impact that an individual's desire for interpersonal interaction has on an individual's predisposition for handling conflict.
3. The impact that an individual's predisposition for handling conflict has on leader effectiveness.
4. The impact of the migration of an individual's strength deployment from a situation free of conflict to a conflict situation has on leader effectiveness.

**Correlation analyses** were performed to determine the correlations between the following:

1. The degree of preference for interpersonal interaction and effectiveness.
2. The degree of preference to take initiative and effectiveness.
3. Effectiveness and degree of analytic-autonomizing strength deployed in a situation free of conflict.
4. Relationship between the conflict handling modes and effectiveness.

**Canonical correlation analyses** were conducted to determine the aggregate correlations that exist between the linear combination of sets of variables in the following:

1. Strength deployment in a situation free of conflict and an individual's predisposition for handling conflict.
2. Strength deployment in a conflict situation and an individual's predisposition for handling conflict.
3. Strength deployment in a situation free of conflict and effectiveness.
4. Strength deployment in a conflict situation and effectiveness.
5. The migration in strength deployment from a situation free of conflict to a conflict situation and effectiveness.

A review of the simple statistics may be beneficial before reviewing the results. An analysis of these simple statistics follows in Exhibit 1.

**Exhibit 1.** Summary of Simple Statistics for Each Instrument

| Variable | N | Mean | Std Dev | Sum | Minimum | Maximum |
|---|---|---|---|---|---|---|
| **Effectiveness** | 65 | 51.8962 | 7.9918 | 3373 | 20 | 70 |
| **Strength Deployment (Free of Conflict)** | | | | | | |
| Altruistic-Nurturing | 66 | 39.3636 | 11.7874 | 2598 | 10.0000 | 66.0000 |
| Assertive-Directing | 66 | 28.5606 | 13.0019 | 1885 | 8.0000 | 57.0000 |
| Analytic-Autonomizing | 66 | 32.0758 | 11.2678 | 2117 | 12.0000 | 71.0000 |
| **Strength Deployment (Conflict Situation)** | | | | | | |
| Altruistic-Nurturing | 66 | 29.9697 | 11.4596 | 1978 | 5.0000 | 56.0000 |
| Assertive-Directing | 66 | 33.0606 | 12.5611 | 2182 | 10.0000 | 67.0000 |
| Analytic-Autonomizing | 66 | 36.9242 | 10.2151 | 2437 | 21.0000 | 63.0000 |
| **FIROB SUM (Interaction)** | 66 | 22.4545 | 10.1059 | 1482 | 4 | 43 |
| **FIROB Dif (Initiative)** | 66 | -0.9091 | 5.0982 | -60 | -17 | 10 |
| **Conflict Handling Modes** | | | | | | |
| Competing | 66 | 5.0455 | 2.8899 | 333 | 0 | 12 |
| Collaboration | 66 | 5.9091 | 2.292 | 390 | 1 | 10 |
| Compromising | 66 | 6.6364 | 2.3247 | 438 | 1 | 11 |
| Avoidance | 66 | 6.7576 | 2.5058 | 446 | 2 | 12 |
| Accommodation | 66 | 5.5758 | 2.1631 | 368 | 1 | 12 |

**Exhibit 2.** Simple Statistics for Effectiveness

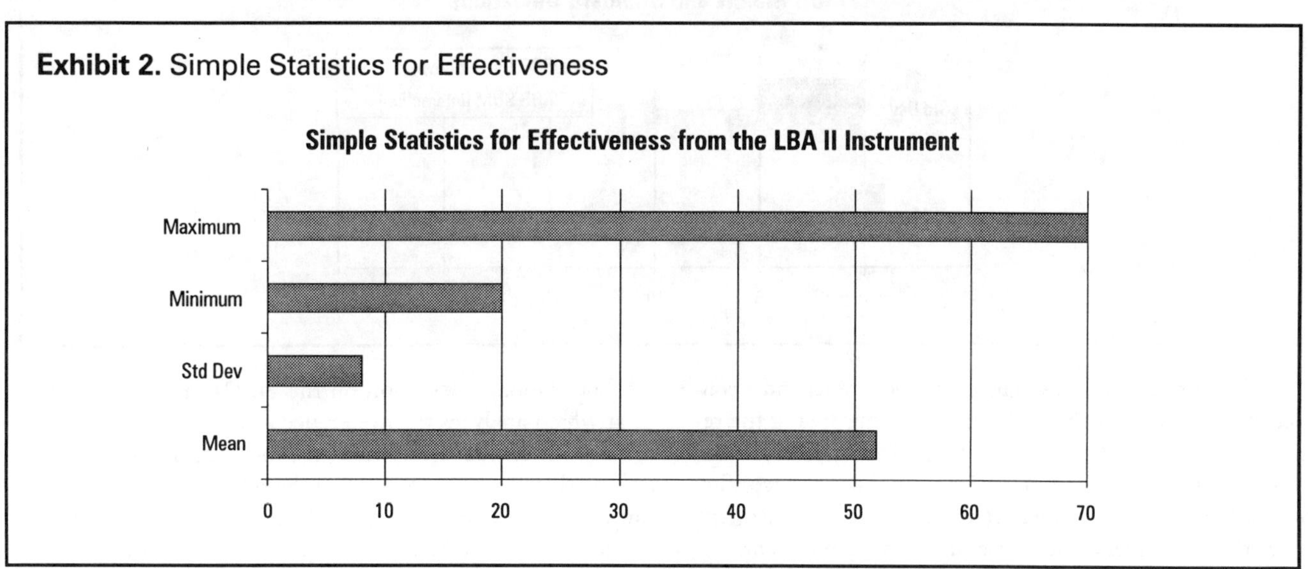


The LBAII instrument defines effectiveness as having a high level of style flexibility and choosing the most appropriate leadership style for the each situation presented. Exhibit 2 captures the simple statistics of the responses to the effectiveness survey.

The mean effectiveness score is fifty-two, which is solidly in the middle of the spectrum for effectiveness scores. Interestingly, the standard deviation is only eight points, which is surprisingly small. The alignment of the means from this investigation within the response spectrum for the LBAII instrument support the validity of the survey of the sample population—the responses from the sample population are valid. Refer to the LBAII instrument for further information.

The simple statistics from the strength deployment inventory yield interesting insight into individual behavior. Exhibit 3 captures the mean responses in both conflict situations.

**Exhibit 3.** Strength Deployment Mean Scores

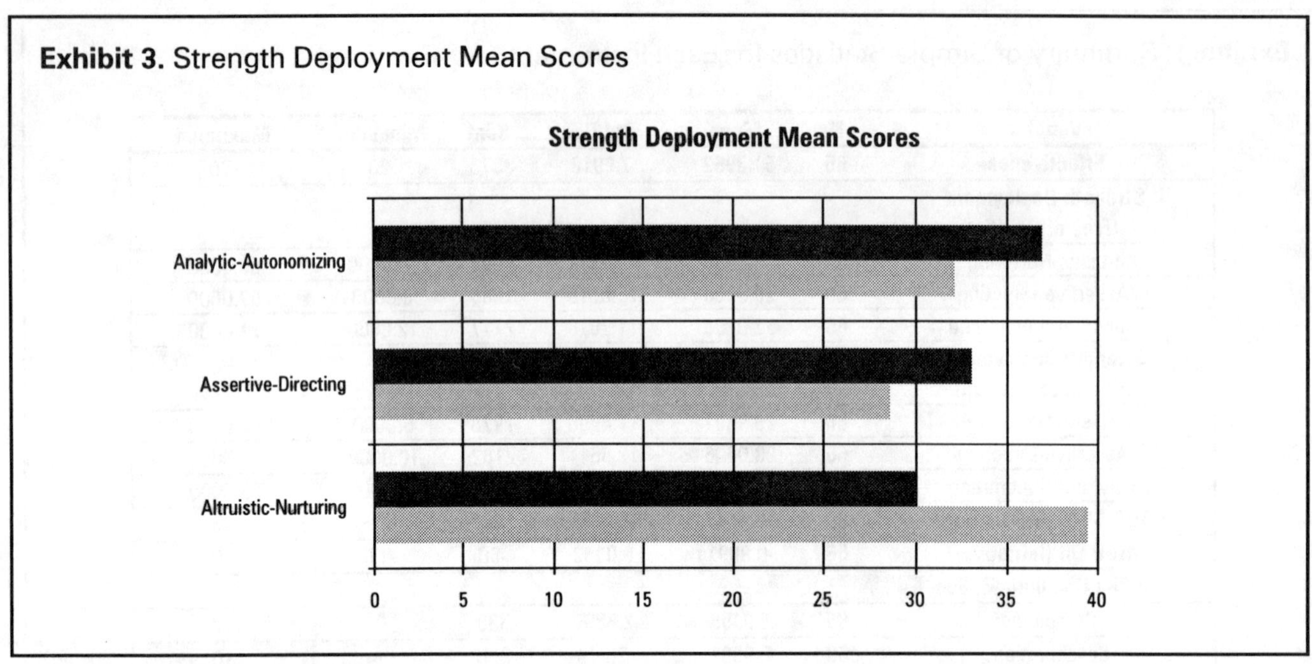


**Exhibit 4.** FIROB Means and Standard Deviations

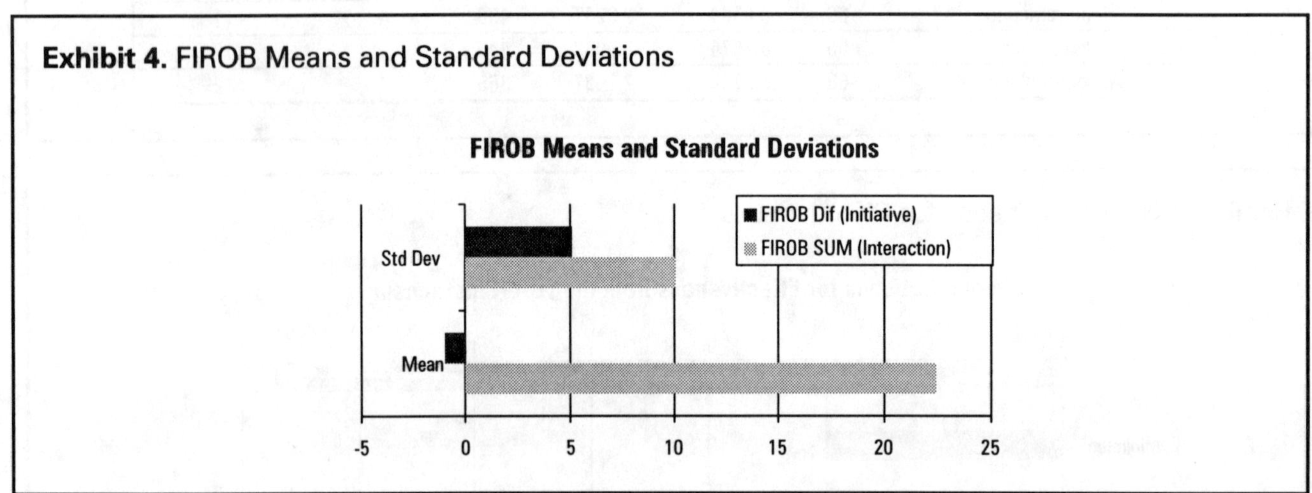


Both mean scores, in a situation free of conflict and a conflict situation, appear in the flexible-cohering area of the response spectrum. However, the migration of strength deployment from a situation free of conflict to a conflict situation involves a reduction in the altruistic-nurturing strength deployment and subsequent and comparable increase in both the assertive-directing and analytical-autonomizing deployments. Individuals tend to become more assertive and analytical in their strength deployment when faced with conflict.

The mean results from the FIROB analysis are also in the middle of the response spectrum. Exhibit 4 captures the means and standard deviations in the responses from the FIROB instrument.

The standard deviation on the FIROB difference score, that which analyzes the preference to take initiative, is very tight—one standard deviation on either side of the mean still falls within the medium band of the response spectrum. The mean FIROB sum score, that which indicates the degree of preference for interaction with people, was on the low side in the medium band, but the standard deviation was twice that of the difference score indicating that individual desire for interaction varies more than individual preference to take initiative.

An analysis of the means from responses to the conflict mode instrument indicates rough equity in the predispositions for handling conflict. Exhibit 5 depicts the mean score of the responses to the conflict mode instrument.

**Exhibit 5.** Conflict Mode Mean Scores

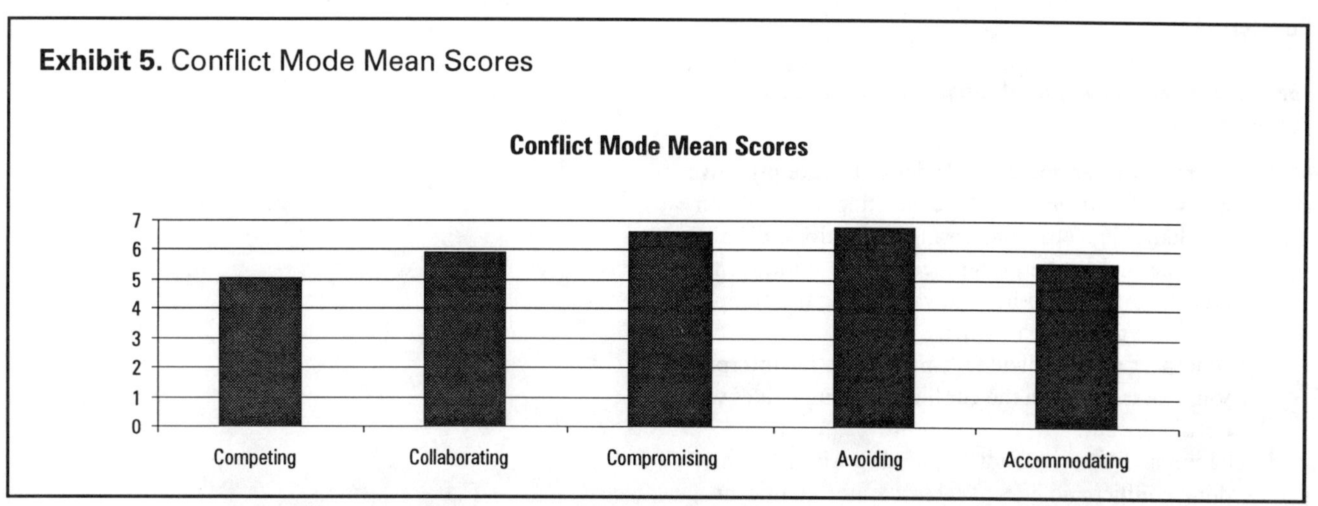


**Exhibit 6.** Color-Coded Behavioral Relationship Matrix

| INSTRUMENT MEASURES | *Leader Effectiveness* SES | *FIROB* E+I Sum | E–I Dif | *Strength Deployment Inventory* All is Well Blue | Red | Green | In Conflict Blue | Red | Green | *Thomas-Kilman Conflict Mode Instrument* Conflict Handling Modes Compe | Collab | Compro | Avoid | Accom |
|---|---|---|---|---|---|---|---|---|---|---|---|---|---|---|
| Effectiveness (**SES**) | 1 | | | + | + | – | | | | | | | | |
| Desire for Interaction (**Sum**) | | 1 | | | | | | | | | | | | |
| Initiative (**Dif**) | | | 1 | | | | | | | | | | | |
| *Strength Deployment (Free of Conflict)* | | | | | | | | | | | | | | |
| Altruistic-Nurturing (**Blue**) | + | | | 1 | | | | | | – | | | | |
| Assertive-Directing (**Red**) | + | | | | 1 | | | | | | | – | – | – |
| Analytic-Autonomizing (**Green**) | – | | | | | 1 | | | | | – | – | | |
| *Strength Deployment (Conflict Situation)* | | | | | | | | | | | | | | |
| Altruistic-Nurturing (**Blue**) | | | | | | | 1 | | | – | – | – | | |
| Assertive-Directing (**Red**) | | | | | | | | 1 | | | – | – | – | – |
| Analytic-Autonomizing (**Green**) | | | | | | | | | 1 | – | | | | – |
| *Conflict Handling Modes* | | | | | | | | | | | | | | |
| Competing (**Compe**) | | | | See Note 1. | | | | | | 1 | | | | |
| Collaboration (**Collab**) | | | | | | | | | | | 1 | | | |
| Compromising (**Compro**) | | | | | | | | | | | | 1 | | |
| Avoidance (**Avoid**) | | | | | | | | | | | | | 1 | |
| Accommodation (**Accom**) | | | | | | | | | | | | | | 1 |

Identity
Significant relationships captured by the data analysis
No significant relationship captured by the data analysis
Both Correlation and Canonical Correlation identified relationships as significant

The lowest mean score, 5.0455, was for the competing mode. Surprisingly, the highest mean, 6.7575, was for the avoidance mode. Although there are appropriate reasons to exercise each of the various conflict modes, the author finds the distribution somewhat surprising. A predisposition to use avoiding or accommodating to handle conflict, as opposed to collaboration (a win-win posturing), may sub-optimize effectiveness.

## Results

***The results from the analysis of variance investigation are defined below.***

1. The impact of an individual's desire to take initiative was *significant* only on the competing mode of conflict handling. The relationship is positive indicating that the higher the preference to take initiative the higher the predisposition towards using the competing mode to handle conflict.
2. The impact of an individual's preference for interpersonal interaction on the conflict handling modes was not significant.
3. The impact of an individual's predisposition for handling conflict and effectiveness was not significant.

***The results of the correlation analyses are defined below:***

1. No correlations were found between the desire to take initiative, the desire for interpersonal interaction, and effectiveness.
2. No correlation between any conflict handling mode and effectiveness was evident.
3. *A moderate negative correlation was found to exist between effectiveness and the application of analytic-autonomizing strength deployment.*

***The results of the canonical analyses are defined below:***

1. The linear combination between strength deployment and conflict handling modes *is significant*.
2. There is a *moderate canonical correlation* between strength deployment in a situation free of conflict and effectiveness.
3. No correlation exists between strength deployment in a conflict situation and effectiveness.
4. No correlation exists between the migration in strength deployment from a situation free of conflict to a conflict situation and effectiveness.

The interrelationships investigated between the various behavioral tendencies and the results are captured in Exhibit 6. Significant positive and negative correlations are identified where evident.

Note 1: Canonical correlation captured the significance between the conflict handling modes and strength deployment. The directions of the correlations are captured in the strength deployment rows.

# The Strategic Pathway of Project Management

Dr. David I. Cleland, University of Pittsburgh, Pennsylvania

"The future ain't what it used to be."
Yogi Berra

The practice of project management has been with us for a long time. Its evolution as a profession is found in the management literature. Today, project management has reached a maturity that entitles it to a rightful place in the practice and the literature of its field. The application of project management has spread to many "nontraditional" uses as it continues to be the principal means by which operational and strategic changes are managed in the enterprise.

In this paper some of the major changes in the management field will be presented, along with a summary of the key contributions that have been made by project management in recent times. From that summary, a few predictions will be made concerning the likely strategic pathway of project management in its future.

## Past Influences

In considering the future of project management, an examination of some of the major forces in the field of the management discipline in the past should be considered. In the last ten to twenty years there have been major forces that have impacted the theory and practice of management. A summary of these forces follow.

### *Competition*

Global competition has become the "name of the game" for contemporary enterprises to follow. Innovation in products and services is coming from places around the world. Product and service life cycles are becoming shorter, and earlier commercialization has become a major consideration in developing and producing successful products and services in the global marketplace.

### *Technology Changes*

Engineering and other technologies appear to be doubling every few years, with innovations in such technologies arising from many places in the global environment. Computer and telecommunications technology have made remarkable progress in the use and management of information and has helped to increase enterprise productivity. Enterprise managers have become aware of the need to advance the technology in organizational processes, when product and service technological changes are made.

### *Management Changes*

Alternative teams are being used more and more to deal with both operational and strategic change. The integration of cross-functional and cross-organizational activities through teams has become a way of life in contemporary enterprises. Downsizing and restructuring have improved organizational efficiency and effectiveness but have caused personal anxiety for people who have been replaced as the result of reengineering initiatives. The management of the enterprise as if its future mattered has become the hallmark of strategic management philosophies. Even the traditional roles of managers has come under question, with contemporary changes reflected in new roles that present-day managers play as counselors, teachers, mentors, facilitators—a radical departure from traditional practices of being the "boss" in charge of other people.

### *New Managerial Skills*

The changing roles of traditional managers, from carrying out traditional management processes to functioning as a facilitator, mentor, teacher, and so forth, is calling more than ever on their interpersonal abilities. The growing use of alternative teams has opened management career fields to people that heretofore had limited opportunity to advance to management and leadership positions. Enterprise managers today realize more than ever that the person doing the job has the most knowledge on how their jobs should be performed. By getting these people to serve on alternative teams organizational productivity can be enhanced.

### *Stakeholder Involvement*

People and entities traditionally outside of the organization have now become recognized as key claimants or stakeholders of those things of value being created by the enterprise. Union leaders and members are becoming contributing members of alternative teams. Customers and suppliers are taking active roles on alternative teams as well to the point of service on new product, service, and organizational design and development teams. The presence of these stakeholders has created a greater awareness on the part of executives to manage the enterprise as if its future mattered—and ensuring that the claims of growing and vocal interest groups are given due recognition.

Given the foregoing influences on the theory and practice of management, what might be the future of project management?

## The Future of Project Management

In considering the future of project management it will be first necessary to review some of the expected changes in our society that will, in some manner, influence the theory and practice of project management. As changes in the political, social, economic, competitive, legal, and technological systems occur, project management will likely be impacted since it provides the principal means by which such change is managed in today's organizations. For example, the promise of an improved or new technology in a planned product or service requires the use of concurrent engineering teams to simultaneously develop the new product, service, and supporting organizational processes. A strategic plan that calls for the expansion of an enterprise's manufacturing capacity will require the appointment of a project team to conceptualize, design, construct, and start up a new manufacturing facility. An enterprise that faces a downturn in the demand for its products and services, and must consider cutting back its expenses, will require a reengineering team to examine its operation to include an assessment of how well its organizational processes are being carried out, an evaluation of the basic design of the organizational structure, and other means for improving its overall efficiency and effectiveness.

Other related project management changes will likely be as follows.

### *Political Changes*

Political changes foster the development and application of project management strategies. The sweeping political changes in the Eastern Europe bloc fostered the abandonment of many of the autocratic social and management philosophies of the communist dominated countries in this bloc. Major changes in the infrastructure of the former communist countries, the need to design and develop competitive business strategies, updating plant and equipment, and improving the managerial and professional skills of employees became critical.

### *Social Considerations*

Social initiatives in a country call for the use of project management to act as a focal point for bringing about major social changes. The Affirmative Action Program in the United States motivated executives to develop proactive programs in their organizations to support equality in the management of personnel in their companies. Equality standards in U.S. colleges and universities prompted the need to develop projects and programs to ensure that such standards were carried out in the hiring of faculty and in undergraduate and graduate study programs.

### *Competitive Alterations*

Competitive changes have fostered increased interest on the part of companies in the use of teams. In some cases, the benchmarking of their competitors has disclosed the use of teams in the product and service strategies, sometimes as they have benchmarked the "best in the industry" performance and found that teams have been used as key elements in the strategy of these best performers. Finding out that a competitor is outperforming a company in the marketplace will motivate the executives to find out why the competitors have been able to do so much better. For example, when the Xerox company found out that Japanese companies were selling their copiers for what it cost Xerox to manufacture their copiers, an immediate investigation was conducted by Xerox to determine the reason. Xerox found that the use of concurrent engineering processes and techniques accounted for the difference. Xerox then initiated concurrent engineering to reduce the time that it took for them to develop their copiers—and be able to compete with the Japanese competitors.

### *Modification of Project Management Practices*

Project management as we know it today will likely change in the future. Advances in communication through computer technology, the integrated voice data and imaging techniques, and the Internet will provide higher levels of communication effectiveness. The growing ability to exchange information on a global basis will help to foster a new world for project management. The ability to use technology for gathering, analyzing, and interpreting data should provide more opportunity for the improvement of the processes and techniques involved in managing projects. With the help of such technologies the typical project manager should have more time to deal with the human element in the management of projects—for this asset will even become more valuable in the future world.

### *Nontraditional Projects*

In the last ten years project management has moved rapidly out of its traditional redoubts and is moving from a speciality strategy into a central task of management for the process of managing product, service, and organizational process change. Project management's original application was principally in construction and Department of Defense projects. As it demonstrated its ability to provide a process and techniques for pulling together cross-functional and cross-organizational activities, organizations began experimenting with the use of teams to deal with other applications. As these applications grew in importance and use, project management and its predisposition to use teams as the basic organizational design extended the use of project management activities to other uses in the enterprise such as:

1. Reengineering applications—These teams are used to bring about a fundamental rethinking and radical redesign of business processes to achieve extraordinary improvements in organizational performance.
2. Concurrent engineering applications—Concurrent product, service, and organizational process development teams to develop, produce, and market products and services earlier, of a higher quality, and at a lower cost.
3. Benchmarking initiatives—Using teams to measure organizational products, services, and processes against the most formidable competitors and industry leaders to use as performance standards for the enterprise.
4. Development of new business development opportunities using teams to explore, design, develop, and execute new ventures for the enterprise.
5. Total quality management initiatives accomplished through the use of teams that utilize cross-functional organizational designs to integrate enterprise quality improvement strategies.
6. Improved quality and productivity in manufacturing and production operations through the use of self-managed production teams.

## Management Philosophy Modifications

One of the major contributions of project management, and alternative team management during the eighties and nineties, has been modifications to the management discipline. These modifications have changed management philosophies, processes, techniques, and the performance standards by which an enterprise's efficacy can be judged. These modifications and their likely continuation include:

1. Acceptance and virtual institutionalization of the matrix organizational design. In such acceptance, the use of project teams overlaid on the traditional organizational structure has become simply "the way we do things around here" in the project and team-driven enterprise entity. This acceptance will continue in the future, with the potential of leading to the gradual disappearance of the matrix organizational design as a distinct entity as it is further amalgamated into the culture of enterprises.
2. Acceptance of the importance of project planning as a means for determining the resources required and how these resources will be used during the life cycle of the project.
3. New organizational design initiatives will be assessed as a means for enhancing the use of a focal point for product, service, and organizational process change. Growing use of the virtual organization to deal with a more active participation of project stakeholders, and the means for the extemporaneous emergence of formal and informal teams in the organization to deal with the pressures of change coming from competitive and environmental sources.
4. Organizational members have found that the opportunities for their growing participation in both the operational and strategic initiatives of the enterprise has heightened their role in decision-making in the enterprise, enhanced their feelings of belonging and contributing to the organization, and through growing opportunities for participation in the affairs of the enterprise, has had a significant influence on their motivation and sharing in the results and rewards of the enterprise.
5. In the late eighties and the early nineties, the growing use of teams has opened broadened opportunities for workers to perform managerial and leadership functions as they work on operational and strategic teams in the enterprise. As workers have participated on these teams, their appreciation of the challenges facing organizational managers and leaders has increased, leading to greater support of such managers and leaders—and a growing desire of workers to become more proactive in the opportunities for them to carry out managerial and leadership activities in their spheres of work. In the future these trends will continue, with a growing base of people in the enterprise who can perform managerial and leadership roles.
6. Managerial control systems in the eighties and nineties have grown in importance in their sophistication. As individuals have served on the various teams available to the enterprise, there has been a growing recognition on the part of these individuals that "self-control" is important and is a major and effective way of insuring that the planned use of resources is "on track" and in line with organizational goals and objectives.
7. The growing use of teams in the eighties and the nineties has brought the management of stakeholders into greater play than was done in the past. A philosophy has developed in contemporary managers and leaders that "everything is related to everything else." Accordingly, the making and execution of decisions is being done more and more with an awareness of the likely systems reverberations of the use of resources

in both the operational and the strategic sense, to include an assessment of the growing influence of stakeholders. This trend will continue in the future, and will likely stimulate the emergence of models and paradigms on how such "systems" considerations can be melded into the design and execution of decisions by future project managers.

8. In recent years there have been new applications of project management, reflecting its use in a wide variety of different industries and organizations. Today, industrial, educational, military, social, governmental, and ecclesiastical organizations use project management to varying degrees of usage. This trend will continue in the future, as the recognition that project management is an effective means of dealing with change becomes recognized by more managers, as leaders, commanders, administrators, and ministry and lay people recognize project management for what it is: a means for dealing with operational and strategic change in the enterprise.
9. The concept and process of strategic management of the enterprise gained acceptance in the late eighties and early nineties. An important part of strategic management is the process of strategic planning when the objective is to develop a sense of direction and acceleration for the enterprise in its future. The growing use of a philosophy of strategic management of the enterprise has been accompanied by the growing use of project management and alternative team management as a means for dealing with environmental and competitive change which faces all organizational entities today. Strategic planning teams have been used successfully by modern enterprises to facilitate the strategic planning process. This trend will likely continue.

Other project management changes include:

1. Continuing the influence that it has had in the past, project management will continue to contribute to the further modification of traditional management approaches and vertical hierarchies in the organizations of the future.
2. Experience and competency in team management and leadership will become major considerations in the selection and promotion of senior managers in the future. The opportunity to gain experience in the management and leadership of teams will continue to grow as teams increase in use in the organizations of the future.
3. The strategic and operational management of technology through projects will become a key pacing factor in the enterprise's ability to offer new and improved products and services, supported by innovative organizational processes.
4. New products and services will be created at unprecedented rates in the future through project management, with the ability to develop such products and services in effective and efficient ways as a key competitive factor. New enterprises will come forth as the relentless changes foster the need for new products and services for the global marketplace.
5. As the use of project management and alternative team management grows, the need for training in the concepts and processes of team management will also accelerate. Universities and colleges will continue to recognize the need for undergraduate and graduate courses and research to advance the state-of-the-art in the theory and practice of project and team management. The developing nations of the world will be particularly anxious to learn more about project management as a way to deal with the awesome changes that are facing such nations.
6. Professional organizations representing the project management community will likely continue to grow in membership, and alternative professional organizations in the field of project management will likely emerge.
7. There will be a growing, closer link of project planning and strategic planning in the enterprise, as it becomes increasingly clear that project results are the pathway to the organization's future.
8. There will be limits to innovative changes in project cost and schedule techniques. The greatest opportunities for the improvement of project management will deal with human and organizational issues. Project monitoring, evaluation, and control will be assumed more by the members of the project team than by formal review and reporting procedures.
9. International political issues over scarce resources will likely not be reduced. The risk of armed conflict over the use of scarce resources such as petroleum, food, water, and critical minerals will be present, with a likelihood that military projects will be undertaken by the stronger nations of the world to contain these conflicts, and work towards settlements that will have some reasonable compromise in the allocation of the world's scarce resources.

## A Turning Point

We are just a few years from turning the corner on a new century which invites speculation about what our future will be like. Will the theory and practice of project management undergo as much change as we have seen in the last forty years in this discipline? Will the future of project management be another time of unprecedented fulfillment, or will it be "business as usual" in this remarkable discipline that is still undergoing change in its theoretical foundations, in its practice, and in its application? Or, will project management become a new game, with new concepts, processes, techniques, and applications?

Project management—and its likely changes—has to be considered from the perspective of the major changes that have impacted our society in the past and in the present. We are in the middle of major transactions cutting across our society, and the outcomes of these transactions are far from certain. Political, economic, social, and technological changes are causing dislocations, and even today—Heraclitus' thoughts that "all is flux, nothing stays still, nothing endures but change" have relevancy.

Project management—and the use of alternative teams—has influenced, and has been influenced, by the forces of change in today's world of management. The interdependency of these forces and the use of teams as elements of operational and strategic change in today's organization will likely continue into the future. Traditional organizational structures are likely to undergo continued modification as the use of teams and higher degrees of employee participation are likely to be found in the organizations of the future. Those authors who write the history of management for the late twentieth century and the first couple of decades after the turn of the century are likely to see that project management was one of the principal forces that influenced the theory and practice of management. Yet the fundamental question remains: What will be the strategic pathway of project management in the future? This paper has hinted at some of the future changes likely to come in project management.

Perhaps the best summarized prediction about the future of project management was given by Stewart who wrote: "Project management is the wave of the future" (Stewart 1997).

## References

1. Stewart, Tom. 1997. "The Corporate Jungle Spans A New Species: The Project Manager." *Fortune* (July 10): 179–180.

# Achieving Agility with Large Programs of Change

Ruta R. Kulbis, Andersen Consulting LLP

## The Climate of the Future

The project management climate of the future will be characterized by larger, longer, and more complex projects. Today's projects involve multiple teams and span multiple geographic areas. The result is a tremendous increase in risks of budget and time overruns. There is also the risk that users and sponsors will be dissatisfied with what is delivered. This is because it is difficult to change one's commitment to the scope, schedule, and budget of a project once it is launched, even if it becomes apparent that the benefits will not be as great as anticipated. Considering the uncertainties associated with large programs of change, it will be critical for success to have the agility needed to react, adapt, and modify.

How should we manage these complexities? We manage this by building agility and flexibility into our management disciplines. One must recognize that all of the facts may not be known on day one of a three to five year project, and management needs to be able to be able to adjust course as it goes forth. Management needs to be able to react not only to changing market conditions, but also to external and internal risks. Management achieves agility by restructuring its efforts into journeys, programs, and small projects.

## Journeys, Programs, and Projects

We need to redefine the terminology for "project management" to distinguish three management disciplines that are implemented at the executive, program, project, and work team levels.

### Journey

The journey being managed is typically a long-term endeavor over the span of three to five years. The journey is not defined along a fixed path and is subject to course corrections. The organization's journey is the general course plotted out at the level of milestones and key outcomes and capabilities. The journey definition is especially applicable to initiatives involving a lot of change. Substantial change is difficult to plan and predict, making early and frequent feedback on the achievement of business results the best way to maintain a managed and controlled course of action.

Organizations constantly move through events that mark changes. Sometimes these changes are clearly expressed with defined milestones and known beginnings or endings. At other times, the changes may be unconsciously combined with events which do not have explicit milestones, and their significance may not be recognized. Journey management therefore must consider the organization's unique history, the realities of past successes and failures as well as perceptions about them, key elements of context, and the key personalities involved.

### Journey Management

Every journey should have a plan for how to get from the current situation to the achievement of its vision. Journey management is the process of guiding successful change. It aims to make change more predictable by managing the uncertainties. Journey management focuses on the alignment of content, context, and course of action to deliver sustainable business value. It focuses efforts at the chief executive officer and board of directors level within an organization. Effort focuses on achieving business results. It communicates business results in terms that executive management uses, e.g., business objectives, financial results, and earnings per share. Journey management continually assesses the benefits that an organization realizes from the outcomes delivered by the program(s). Journey management ensures that business value is created on a permanent basis by continually monitoring progress and context, i.e., the "non-rational" aspects—feelings, behaviors, values, and beliefs of individuals and groups—and the "rational" aspects—strategies, projects, and programs.

When outsiders participate in the definition and navigation of a journey, they offer guidance, advice, consultation, and experience, but they can only influence the business results and outcomes in an indirect way. The organization's leadership ultimately determines the destination; advisors can only help the organization get there.

### Program

From the journey, one or more programs are derived. Programs are large undertakings of six months to three years in duration, that consist of a series of related endeavors. They are typically multi-disciplinary and complex. Programs are initiated to deliver business capability (or releases of business capability) which help achieve business results in terms of the journey. A new business capability is a change in the organization's ability

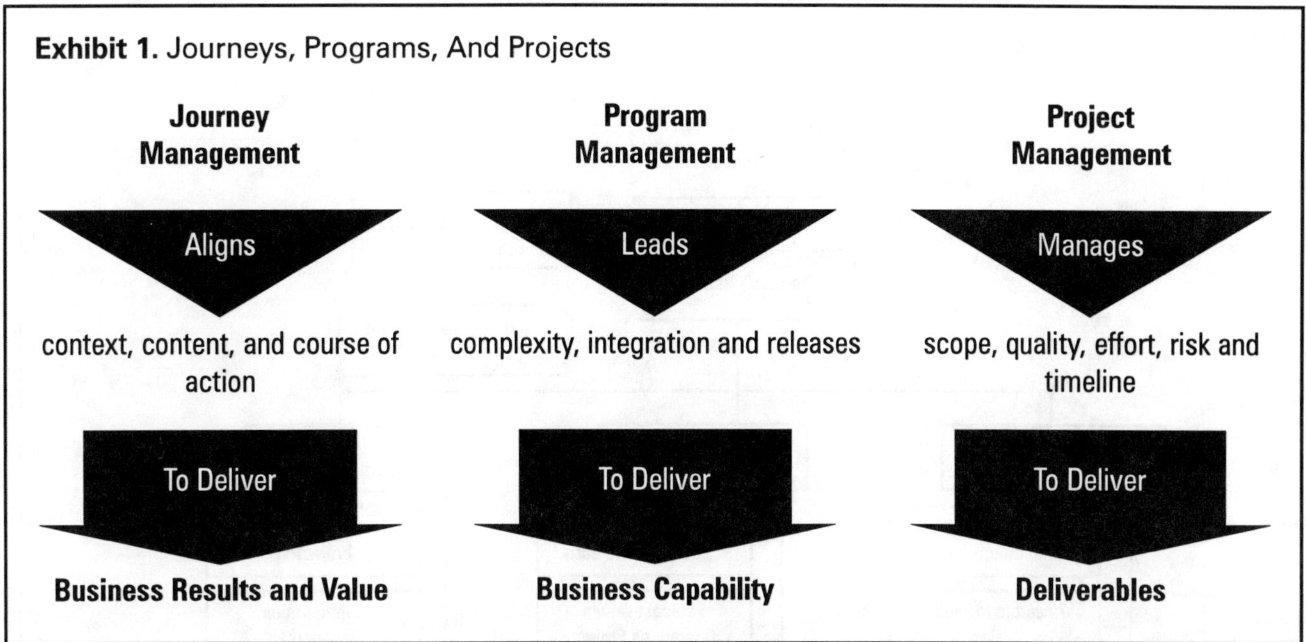


that allows it to perform a certain activity more effectively, taking into account all things that make up that change—for example, a fully deployed computer system with trained users and new processes. The program is reflected by the plan detailing the final solution deliverable and the program plan. The program plan addresses the scope, quality, effort, risk, schedule, resources, and cost/benefit considerations. Based on this information, program management enhances the high-level business case that journey management has developed into a more detailed business case.

### Program Management

Program management focuses on building business capability through the creation, and alignment of project deliverables. Program management authorizes, supports, and monitors projects and ultimately approves project deliverables. Program management is not, however, summarized project management. while both program management and project management deal with common management areas, program management focuses on additional areas that project management does not, as well as dealing at a higher level of detail.

Journey management continually monitors the business context to see whether the targeted business results continue to be valid. If journey management determines that another outcome should be targeted, program management clarifies the implications for effort, quality, risks, and so on. Change may also result from new information from the projects. Program management provides an orderly way for dealing with these changes. By constantly monitoring configuration changes, risks, quality, timeline, and other variables, program management permits changes to take place in a well-controlled manner. Changes are made with proper authorization and knowledge of the impact of proposed or suggested changes.

Key benefits of program management include the following:

- effective alignment of effort, activities, and deliverables with broader missions and strategies
- increased visibility of management goals and objectives
- quantification and qualification of achievements
- quantification of risk
- highlighted dependencies among initiatives
- management of the networks within matrix organizations
- communication with all program team members and stakeholders in terms they understand.

### Project Management

Project management focuses on providing specific deliverables such as computer applications, training materials, and process flows. Projects are typically three to six months in duration, with project teams typically formed with nine to twelve people. The primary emphasis of project management is directed toward creating deliverables through the balancing of scope, quality, effort, risk, and time.

Projects operated in a program management environment find clearer direction of project expectations, support in gaining resources and resource commitments, clear avenues for managing risks, and well defined acceptance criteria for project deliverables.

The three management disciplines are interdependent; in other words, a successful change program depends on the use of all three. And although they are hierarchical in

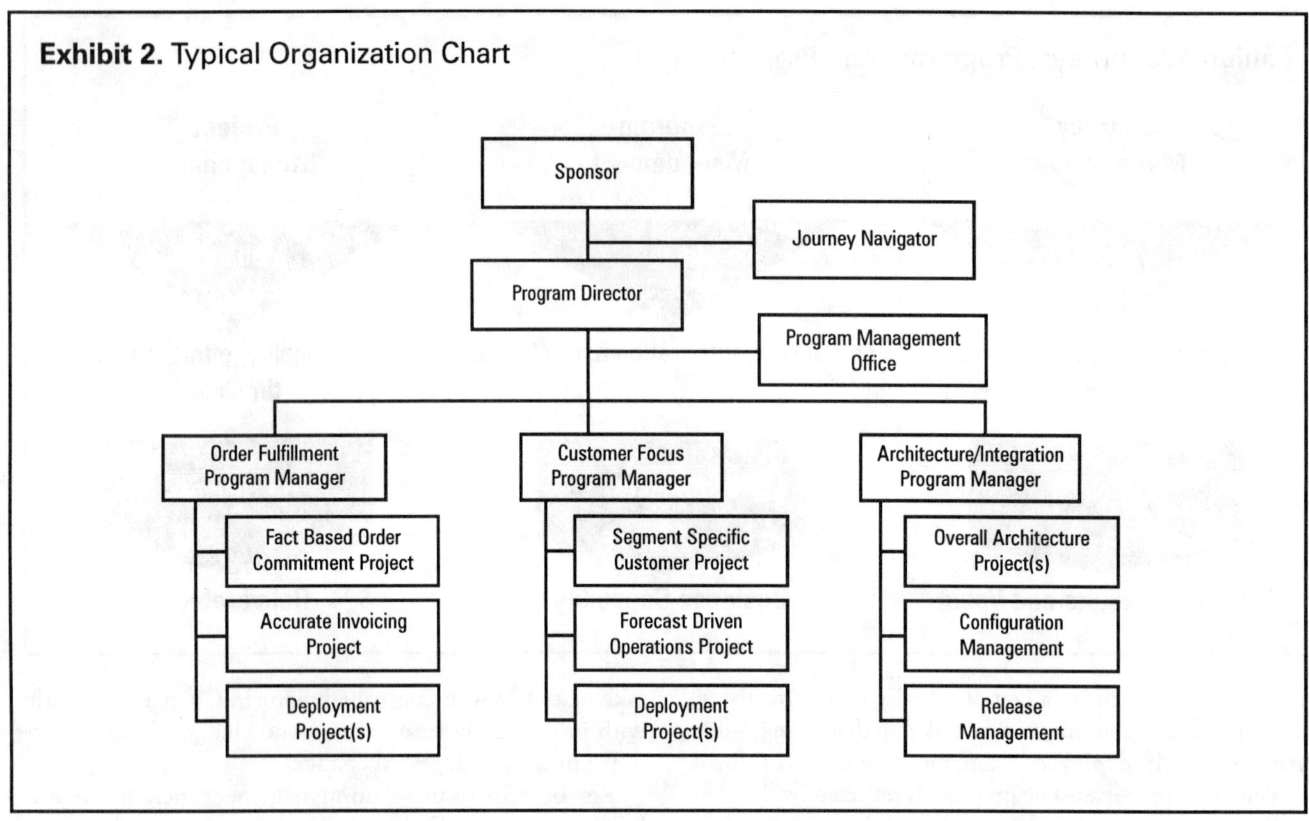

**Exhibit 2.** Typical Organization Chart

nature, it is important to note that they are NOT levels of work. All three management disciplines are applied in varying levels of rigor, to the breakdown of the work effort.

## Program and Project Management Structure

The sample organization chart shows a series of small projects, each of which is designed to create a deliverable as part of a business capability.

In addition, there is an overall architecture and integration function. This is designed to keep all the various projects aligned, so that the total effect of the project deliverables is to create a true change that provides business value.

## Roles and Responsibilities

The journey navigator, program director, program manager, and project manager all have distinct roles and responsibilities within this structure.

### Journey Navigator

The key responsibilities of the journey navigator role are coaching, assessing progress, and suggesting how the organization can do better. The journey navigator shapes the journey with executive management, leads assessments, and develops the journey strategy, including the definition of critical performance measures.

The process of "shaping" the journey is a process of high-level planning—assessing—re-planning performed "shoulder to shoulder" with executive management. This is in contrast to "interviewing" the executive, going back to the office to do the planning, and finally presenting the plan to management. Journey management has a lot to do with setting, influencing, and managing the expectations of executive management.

Journey navigation activities take place at an organization-wide level as well as across one or more business units. The journey navigator works with the program director to define the change program, the objectives, and business capabilities needed to ensure a successful journey. The journey navigator further coordinates with the program director who develops the program plans (including the business case). They work together to ensure that the program plans are meeting the objectives.

### Program Director

The program director leads the creation of the program deliverables. She is directly accountable to the program sponsor and works closely with the program sponsor and journey navigator to make broad directions operational. The program director is responsive to the requirements of the program, the organization, and all its stakeholders.

The program director ensures a feasible plan to get the capabilities delivered as planned. If the direction shifts, this may result in agreed changes in program scope. Very drastic shifts may cause the program director to close programs or launch new programs.

The roles of journey navigator and program director are played by two different people. If there is no one filling the journey navigator role, completing a successful journey is more difficult for the program director.

### Program Manager

The program manager is typically responsible for a significant program deliverable or capability release. Program management involves leadership, coordination, and management of several related projects. In execution of these assignments, a program manager is directly accountable to the program director. The program manager provides periodic reports to the program director and to the executive steering committee on the status of the program.

### Project Manager

The project manager is empowered and authorized by the program. The project manager is responsible for the creation of a deliverable or interim deliverables. The project manager assures that the deliverables created by the project team provide quality, add value, and contribute to the client's success. A project manager in a program environment is able to completely focus on the work required to produce a high quality deliverable or interim deliverable.

## Project Mobilization Process

By the time the program has completed its solution and program planning, the work breakdown structure (WBS), organization breakdown structure (OBS), and responsibility assignment matrix (RAM) have been defined. The program plan has been created, and the individual projects have been identified. The program must now authorize the project's work and deploy resources. The program manager formally authorizes work via a work authorization and commits the resources needed to perform the work. The work authorization is a summary description of a specific project, prepared by program management. It covers scope, project objectives, project development approach, deliverables, level of effort, quality, and risk, and so on. It also specifies the earliest start and latest finish dates for the project. The work authorization is part of the project initiation package.

The program manager prepares a project initiation package to orient the project manager to the project objectives and constraints. It also provides the information he needs to confirm the project baselines, upon which the project's performance will be measured. The baselines include definitions of scope (deliverables and work definition), quality, effort (cost), risk, and time (schedule). The documents that typically make up the project initiation package are listed below:

- Program Orientation and Training Materials
- Work Authorization
- Cost Account(s) and Control Account
- Program Milestones
- Work Breakdown Structure
- Work Breakdown Structure Element (only selected items pertaining to the project)
- Acceptance Criteria (only selected items pertaining to the project)
- Solution Deliverable Specifications (only selected items pertaining to the project)
- Organization Breakdown Structure
- Organization Breakdown Structure Element (only selected items pertaining to the project)
- Program Quality Plan (only selected sections)
- Program Risk Management Plan (only selected sections)
- Program Policies and Standards (only selected items pertaining to the project)
- Responsibility, Accountability, and Authority Profiles (only selected items pertaining to the project).

To launch a project, the program manager and project manager meet together and discuss the detail plans in the project initiation package. The project manager confirms that the project baselines are acceptable.

Once these baselines are jointly agreed to by the program and project manager, the program manager updates, signs, and issues the work authorization. The work authorization triggers the opening of the project cost account(s) and authorizes the project to proceed.

## Case Study

One very successful example of a large program that benefited from this structure is a transformation of the revenue collection systems of one of the largest telecommunications providers in Europe. The program was able to react to changing internal priorities and market conditions. At the same time, it provided significant business value and finished on time, on budget, and with high quality results.

This company is one of the largest telecommunications providers in Europe. It has 230,000 employees and forty million access lines and fifteen million broadband cables to homes. In the advent of deregulation of the European telecommunications market in 1996 and 1998, the company wanted to improve its competitive position through more sophisticated system support. It's challenge was to become a global competitor and transform from a government organization to a publicly held company. Its obstacles included high costs per line, low revenues per employee, and multiple regulators. Its objectives were to become the world's most advanced network within three years. It planned to reduce its workforce by 25 percent, provide improved customer orientation and customer service, and offer state of the art services in multi-media and data transmission.

The specific program under study was created to enhance the telecommunications provider's billing capabilities. The total days of work equaled 50,000 man hours and involved 150 team members. A production system was delivered on schedule, within fifteen months of the start date. One of the keys to the program success was the strict application of the disciplines described here.

The technical environment consisted of a system that was batch oriented, with some on-line extensions. It was designed for an IBM ES9000 mainframe system running under MVS/ESA, CICS. All information was stored in a DB2 database. The solution consisted of two parts. The first part performed the calculation of billing terms and discounts, and the second one was responsible for formatting and outputting billing statements in various forms and at different levels of aggregation(e.g., division, company, and so on). Almost all of the calculations performed were table-driven to ease modification of pricing algorithms and introduction of new products.

Master planning focused on the WBS/OBS and resource plan. The responsibility assignment matrix and WBS elements were used to form small projects that lasted no longer than one quarter (three months). This segmentation of work into small teams finalized the scope of the projects. It also provided detailed estimates for each WBS element of work that needed to be completed and created complete work plans.

Program management served as a mentor and an expert resource to the project managers. Some of the key ways the program manager did this were by:

- Sharing prior experience about what worked well and what didn't
- Providing insight about the ripple effect of proposed changes on other projects and the overall program
- Assisting with, or facilitating, coordination with other projects and functions
- Providing information about stakeholders' working styles and interests
- Providing warning of potential pitfalls
- Providing insight on current program priorities and issues that should be considered when making project/function tradeoff decisions
- Intervening to remove obstacles outside the project manager's control.

The program manager met biweekly with the project manager to discuss project performance, status, and issues. These meetings involved reviews of project status and performance reports. It focused on: (1) progress against project baselines, (2) variances between actual and baselines, and (3) other pertinent issues, including quality and risk. Specifically, the items typically addressed during these meetings included:

- Cost and schedule variances that exceeded specified thresholds
- Cost and schedule performance indices that exceeded thresholds
- Estimate at completion versus budget at completion
- Actual versus planned accomplishment of project milestones
- Actual versus planned resource availability
- Progress in addressing project risks
- Progress in achieving quality measures (i.e., acceptance criteria and quality performance criteria)
- Issues raised by project managers
- Suggested process improvements.

The crucial ingredient in these review meetings was assessment of issues. The process focused on identifying and evaluating alternative corrective actions. The decision results formed the basis for determining when future corrective actions should be taken.

The program manager's program-wide perspective was necessary to understand the larger implications of project-level issues and changes. The program manager was able to assess any tradeoffs needed. For example, using less experienced personnel improved the skills of those individuals, but it also lead to effort or schedule overruns or, in some cases, adversely affected the quality of deliverables.

Program manager monitoring activities also included reviews of key deliverables for acceptability. Usually, such deliverables had been previously reviewed by others. Examples of reviewers included the configuration manager, quality manager, and/or program technology, architecture, or integration experts. A key deliverable warranted a program management review depending on:

The criticality of the deliverable

Any unique competencies the program manager possesses

Problems encountered.

Project performance assessments by program management included the following matters (in addition to the usual reviews of actual versus planned effort and schedule performance):

- Issues of all types raised by the project manager, accompanied by:
  - Descriptions of corrective actions already taken
  - Project change requests covering proposed actions that change the project baselines, and that therefore require the approval of the program manager.
- Satisfactory user involvement and working relationships
- Project team empowerment
- Effective integration with interfacing projects
- Conformance with architecture, configuration, and release management requirements
- Achievement of quality measures, including acceptance criteria
- Progress in reducing risks, including:
  - Effectiveness of any mitigation strategies already adopted
  - Occurrence of risks
  - Identification of additional risks
  - Need to develop and/or implement additional risk mitigation actions.

Based on the project performance monitoring, the program manager judged the effectiveness and efficiency of the project effort. The program manager evaluated progress and determined if different or additional corrective action was needed. Based on this assessment, the program manager provided guidance to the project manager on how best to proceed.

Note that project managers were empowered to implement all corrective actions that did not require changes to the project baselines and did not affect other projects. Some of these changes were addressed immediately by the project managers. Others required project replanning effort prior to being addressed.

## Conclusion

Business results stem from more than the individual components of a solution. Typically, they result from the synergy of various solution components (for example, a strategy to be more differentiated, new plants, a new R&D organization, and executive sponsorship). If one or more solution components do not materialize, the business results of the whole will not fully materialize. The whole is more than the sum of the parts. In large initiatives, the organization cannot wait until the end of the journey for the business results to materialize. Initiatives need to embed flexibility and the ability to adapt into their program and project management structure. Applying the journey, program, and project management disciplines will achieve the agility needed for large programs of change to succeed.

# Monitoring and Rewarding Multiple Projects Using a Weighted Performance Index in a Performance-Based Contract

Noreen Matsuura
Ned Hutchins
Mary Grace Yonts
Robert A. Grow

## Introduction

This paper is a report of a method developed and used to reward multiple projects of varying dollar value, duration, and type over a one-year period. This paper will follow the four steps of project management as emphasized in *A Guide to the Project Management Body of Knowledge (PMBOK Guide)*. The four steps are concept, development/planning, execution/implementation, and termination /closeout.

## Concept

In 1994 the Department of Energy issued a report calling for contract reform. The purpose of contract reform was to expedite cleanup on obsolete and unused parts of the Department of Energy complex through contract reform. The inherent assumption behind contract reform was saving taxpayer dollars. Existing Department of Energy contracts were maintenance and operations and cost plus award fee. In July of 1995 the Department of Energy issued a cost plus incentive fee contract to Kaiser-Hill (K-H), a limited liability corporation formed by ICF Kaiser and CH2M Hill.

In the past, the award fee portion of the contract was qualitatively determined and awarded in a somewhat subjective manner. The intent of the incentive fee was to quantitatively award fees in a more objective manner to expedite cleanup.

The incentive fee portion of the annual budget was supposed to be initiated at the beginning of each federal fiscal year (October) by modification of several incentive fee performance measures into the K-H contract. For fiscal year 1996 the Rocky Flats Field Office set aside over $16 million for Kaiser-Hill incentive fee performance measures.

## Development/Planning

Of the approximately $16 million to be awarded in FY1996, only 3 percent of the total FY 1996 incentive fee or $500,000 was tied to meeting an objective within a budgeted amount. The 1996 fiscal year Rocky Flats budget was in the neighborhood of $600 million. The total budgeted cost of work scheduled (BCWS) of all projects for FY1996 was $85 million for fifty projects. The fifty projects had individual BCWS ranging from $12,000 to $11,154,000. History told us that the number of active projects would change during the year; some projects would be canceled or put on hold while new projects would be initiated. Projects at RFFO are extended over multiple years with FY 1996 being an arbitrary slice in the project. Some projects were inactive, meaning no work would occur during 1996. The concept of a weighted performance index (WPI) was dreamed up by Ned Hutchins with his twenty plus years of project management experience at Occidental Petroleum and other businesses. The WPI for capital and expense projects was developed jointly by K-H and Rocky Flats Field Office (RFFO) project management staff. The goal of the development phase was to write and modify into the contract an incentive fee performance measure for approximately $85 million of project work scheduled to take place between October 1, 1995, through September 30, 1996. The incentive fee performance measure we had in mind consisted of two parts, the weighted performance measure and a performance reward curve. Additionally we needed to include in the contract modification a list of active projects; sources of BCWS, BCWP, and ACWP; a milestone list; a definition of milestone acceptance; and approved sources of changes to BCWS, BCWP, ACWP, active projects, and milestones. Changes to BCWS, ACWP, active projects, and milestone due dates were deemed acceptable if approved by the configuration management organization. The Site Change Control Board (SCCB) is the configuration management organization at Rocky Flats. Changes to project management variables are made by processing a baseline change proposal (BCP) through the Site Change Control Board.

### The Weighted Performance Index

$$WPI = x\,(MPI) + y\,(SPI) + z\,(CPI)$$

### WPI = Weighted Performance Index.

WPI is a combination of three parameters: cost, scope, and schedule. When WPI= 1.0 the performance milestone has been met, the activity is neither over or under budget, and the schedule variance is neither ahead or behind the due date. A WPI of 1.0 is considered to be "getting" what you paid for or adequate performance. A WPI < 1.0 is considered unsatisfactory performance and one of the following or a combination of factors has occurred: the activity is overbudget (CPI < 1.0) or behind schedule (SPI <1.0), or the performance target/milestone was not met. A WPI > 1.0 is indicative of superior performance: the work was accomplished for less than expected (CPI > 1.0) and/or work was completed ahead of schedule (SPI > 1.0).

### MPI = Milestone Performance Index.

$$\frac{\text{Milestones Completed}}{\text{Milestones Scheduled}}$$

The MPI defines and quantifies scope and due dates or milestone and is generally an integer unless partial completion is quantified. For example, suppose the milestone was to drain six tanks in Building 771 by June 30, 1996, and empty had been defined as "operationally empty." If the six tanks had been emptied the MPI would be 1.0. If three of the six tanks were emptied to the standard, MPI would be 0.5, unless partial completion was otherwise defined. Another milestone might be to receive "beneficial occupancy" for a vault in Building 371 by August 31, 1996. The MPI in this case would be 1.0 if RFFO received beneficial occupancy on or before August 31, 1996, and zero if beneficial occupancy was received after August 31, 1996. In the case of a beneficial occupancy milestone, there is no partial credit.

### SPI = Schedule Performance Index.

$$\frac{\text{BCWP (Budgeted Cost of Work Performed)}}{\text{BCWS (Budgeted Cost of Work Scheduled)}}$$

### CPI = Cost Performance Index.

$$\frac{\text{BCWP (Budgeted Cost of Work Performed)}}{\text{ACWP (Actual Cost of Work Performed)}}$$

BCWP, BCWS, and ACWP were available in cost account documents (CADs), work-packages and projects in spending variance reports, project summary sheets, cost performance reports, and other financial reports that are usually released monthly within a week after the end of each month. I'm not sure why, but the contractor changes the names of the reports every fiscal year. The same data is available but may not be in the same report as the previous year. The sources of BCWP, BCWS, and ACWP need to be specified in the performance measure which was modified into the contract; "x,y,z" are decimal weighting factors for the relative importance of the three performance factors.

### x + y + z = 1.0.

For the previous fiscal year and all fiscal year 1996 performance measures, except the project management performance measure (FY 96 C3.07), the incentive fee performance measures had only a milestone performance variable. In some cases the incentive fee was earned if the milestone missed the due date, but was completed before the end of the fiscal year. The WPI = 1.0 (MPI) + 0 (CPI) + 0(SPI). MPI = milestones completed during fiscal year. During fiscal year 1995 and for most of fiscal year 1996 incentive fee performance measures, cost was no object and schedule performance and milestone due dates were defined by the end of the fiscal year.

The decimal weighting factors can be varied a number of ways. One method is to make the decimal factors for all fifty projects to the same fractions. The second method is to change the decimal weighting factors depending on the emphasis for a particular project. Suppose out of fifty projects there are ten building projects, ten software projects, ten environmental projects, ten security projects, and ten HVAC projects. Because the software projects are tying up a significant quantity of company capital but have the potential to return money sooner, management wants the software projects to be completed as soon as possible. The decimal weighting factors in front of the schedule performance index and the milestone performance index could be set at a higher proportion than the factor for the cost performance index. Another method is to multiply the WPI for the ten software projects when ranking performance with the other forty projects.

### Additional Degrees of Flexibility

There are three additional degrees of flexibility which can be used to custom-tailor this fee-bearing performance method. First, for time periods shorter than a year, a percent fee available can be specified to reward project performance quarterly rather than annually. If the total incentive fee available for a year is $1,000,000, the WPI could be measured and awarded both quarterly and annually. For example, for quarters one through four, 10 percent of the available fee could be awarded each quarter, and 60 percent could be awarded for annual performance. Awarding performance more frequently takes into consideration two characteristics of human nature. The two characteristics are attention span and the sunshine disinfectant rule. A parent does not reasonably expect a small child to have an attention span longer than five to ten minutes. In the same way an astute parent entices a child to focus on a desired activity for longer than five to ten minutes, a five-year project will likely benefit from quarterly incentive awards. The sunshine disinfectant rule simply states that which is illuminated is sanitized, or behavior which is illuminated is mostly likely to be self policed or sanitized. Publishing quarterly scores and incentive awards to project managers in an open forum is likely to gain both competitive and self-policing benefits. Second, a fourth factor for safety or quality could be added to the WPI equation. For example, if $500,000 was earned with a WPI score of 1.02 at the end of quarter one but three occupational safety violations were incurred during quarter one, three times one percent of the fee earned for the first quarter could be subtracted. In this case, the contractor would receive $485,000 instead of $500,000. Addition of factors should be limited because the equation becomes cumbersome and complex quickly. The third degree of flexibility is in the reward curve. The reward curve can be a simple straight line, or a step function, or a variety of curves.

### The Shape of the Reward Curve

The reward curve's two axes are the WPI, which ranges from somewhere around .80 to 1.8, and the y-axis, which is the fee awarded in either dollars or percent fee in dollars. In designing a reward curve we identified two places in the curves where some informal behaviorial analysis was useful. The first point is where WPI = 1.0 When WPI = 1.0 project performance is considered to be standard or baseline; the customer is getting what she paid for and when she wanted it. Since incentive fee was designed to reward exceptional performance, some in management think that no incentive fee should be given for WPIs less than 1.0. We discussed several types of reward curves, ranging from step functions to linear functions, and a couple types of curves. Two sample curves were proposed during this period. Both curves awarded some money when WPI = 1.0. One curve awarded 17 percent of the available fee when WPI = 1.0; the other, 40 percent. The psychology behind awarding some money for project performance when WPI = 1.0 is partial positive reinforcement, one of the most powerful motivational tools known. The project manager who achieves a WPI = 1.0 and gets $51,000 but knows $249,000 was left on the table has a powerful incentive to improve performance for the next time period.

The second point is the upper limit on the reward curve. The temptation to inflate cost estimates or pad extra days with an extended due date is mitigated by capitation. Realistic superior performance on government-funded projects as opposed to commercial capital becomes suspect when WPI is greater than 1.10. Historically we knew that an experienced project manager would be hard pressed not to game the system by overestimating, and DOE had a history of having large amounts of unobligated project carryover from year to year. We decided to cap the amount of reward at WPI = 1.06 and 100 percent of the incentive fee available.

The inherent assumption made in the design of this performance measure is that the contractor has 90 percent confidence in a project's cost and schedule, which is usually true in the commercial world.

## Implementation/Execution

### Incentive Fee Performance Measure Contract Modification

A brief discussion of the incentive performance measure, which was modified into the KH contract in August 1996, follows. The maximum available incentive fee was set at $500,000. The title of the performance measure was "FY 96 C3.07 Construction Project Management." The weighted cost, schedule, and Level 1 milestone performance for all active construction projects will be in the range from $\geq$ 0.96 percent to $\leq$ 1.06 percent during FY 1996. Originally we had proposed 20 percent of the fee for each of four quarters and 20 percent for cumulative year end performance. Since the contract modification was not completed until August after three of the FY 1996 quarters were over, the percent fee for total FY 1996 project performance was 40 percent for fourth quarter and 60 percent for year end cumulative performance. As of March 31, 1996, there were fifty active construction projects and forty Level 1 milestones. There was a list of Level 1 milestones and the milestone commitment date. There was also a list of fifty active projects and the BCWS for each project as of March 31, 1996, was part of the contract modification. The WPI decimal fractions were set at: WPI =0.1 (MPI) + 0.5(SPI) +0.4(CPI). For this performance measure there were forty Level 1 milestones as of March 31, 1996, of which twenty-six are identified as "construction is substantially complete." These twenty-six milestones will be met when the following events occur: a "certification document" signed by an authorized official on behalf of Kaiser-Hill, RMRS, SSOC, or DynCorp stating that as of this date, ____________, 1996, the following facility, item, task, or activity, __________, work package ____________, is available for its intended use, and it is, therefore, substantially complete. Accompanying the "certification," as applicable, must be a punch-list or a control list of the remaining items of work to be completed. The date that Kaiser-Hill Vice President Of Construction And Project Management Services B.L. Evans, or his designee, concurs and accepts, on behalf of Kaiser-Hill, that said facility, item, task, or activity is available for its intended use and that the punchlist, and its associated schedule, reasonably and accurately represents the remaining work to be done is the date that this Level 1 milestone will be considered to have been met.

### Completion Report Validation

K-H submitted a completion report with an earnings calculation asking for $200,000 of incentive fee for fourth quarter and $300,000 for cumulative yearend project performance in October 1996. RFFO staff validated or field verified each of the WPI factors and milestone completions. At the end of the year, the list of active projects had been reduced to forty-one or forty-two from the original fifty, depending on how projects which were either combined or divided into one or more projects were counted. After a few weeks of investigation RFFO discovered a number of problems. First, four active projects were not included in the active project list. Second, there were four or five lists of milestone due dates. Third, some milestones scheduled for completion in FY 1997 had been completed in FY 1996, and there was no way to give credit for early completion. Fourth, some milestones were completed after their scheduled due date but within the fiscal year performance period. The corollary occurred when project milestones missed due dates and were not completed during the FY 1996 performance period. There was no penalty method established for either case. Fifth, some milestones were completed ahead of their due dates, and there was no method established to give credit for early completion. Sixth, the Site Change Control Board and the BCP process was operated in loose fashion for FY 1996 with wholesale changes to BCWS, and milestone due dates without RFFO program/project managers being informed of the changes. Seventh, RFFO project and program management organizations were dissolved. Eighth, there was no documentation for returning funds to management reserve where ACWP< BCWS.

The first issue of missing four active projects was the easiest to solve. The second issue of multiple milestone lists was resolved by the attorneys, who determined that the list of milestone commitment dates—which was incorporated into the contract as part of the performance measure—was the one that counted. The sixth issue of passive change control or configuration management we had to accept because there was no alternative, and all changes to BCWS and milestones were signed by RFFO management. The seventh issue of no project or program monitoring during the year was resolved with intensive field work and documentation search to reproduce annual project history and completion. The eighth issue was dropped because there was no mention in the performance measure requiring funds be returned to management reserve when ACWP < BCWS.

RFFO agreed that the intent of the project performance measure was to reward the contractor for good project performance. Good project performance included doing additional work scope and completing milestones early. What we needed was one method which rewarded early finishes and penalized late completion with about the same magnitude. Every project has a graph. The project graph has three lines for BCWS, BCWP, and ACWP with an x-axis of time and a y-axis of dollars. When a project is ahead of schedule, with an early finish, the BCWP earned value line is expected to be on top of the BCWS line. Conversely, when a project is behind schedule, with a late finish, the BCWP earned value line is lower than the BCWS line. What we found by examining all active project graphs was projects with early finishes did not necessarily have BCWP lines above their BCWS lines. We agreed that to reward an early finish we would subtract the absolute value of the difference between BCWS and BCWP from BCWS in the SPI (BCWP/BCWS) for that project. The effect of subtracting an amount from the BCWS increases the WPI score by increasing the SPI. To penalize a late finish we would add the absolute value of the difference between BCWS and BCWP to BCWS in the SPI (BCWP/BCWS). The overall effect is to decrease the WPI by decreasing the SPI. For projects finished early, we took the difference on the day the milestone was completed. For projects finished late, we took the difference on the day the milestone was due. What effect did an early or late milestone finish have on the MPI? In the case where a 1997 milestone was completed in 1996 we added one to the milestones completed, which in effect double credited for 1997 work completed in 1996 by increasing both MPI and SPI. In the cases where a milestone was missed on its due date, but was completed before the end of the fiscal year we decided not to add one to milestones completed.

### Results

By application of the methods discussed above the contractor was awarded approximately $260,000 for FY 1996 project management performance.

## Closeout/Termination

Millions of years ago independent one-celled organisms picked a plasmid engine or a mitochondrial engine. Cells having plasmid engines organized into millions of varieties of plants. Cells that picked mitochodrial engines were able to specialize and organize into thousands of different new animal life forms. Although liver, kidney, skin, and endocrine cells do very different activities, and play different roles in our bodies, what they all have in common is a mitochondrial engine, which processes energy the same way in a liver, kidney, skin, and endocrine cell. What mining, construction, software, and pharmaceutical projects have in common is money fuel in a project management engine. None but the simplest activities can be undertaken without money. The discipline of project management because of its dynamic basis in combination with financial management enterprise systems, such as SAP R3, are mitochondrial engines for business units, which will allow us to organize in different ways unknown today. The weighted performance index (WPI) is a simple performance measure that is capable of comparing on a timely and dynamic schedule different types of projects on a common basis. The Project Management Performance Measure FY96 C3.07 is the first performance measure in a DOE government contract that tied cost, schedule, and scope together in one performance measure to reward above average performance for different activities, which we believe was the intent of contract reform.

## Lessons Learned

It's obvious that the MPI was too simple to accommodate early and late milestone completion. If we were to design another performance measure we would change the MPI to one or more MPI curves. What is a milestone completed three days early worth? What does a milestone completed three days late cost? What is the relative benefit between a milestone completed three days early compared to one completed three months early? A smart customer knows what an early completion is worth and what a late completion costs and could make the MPI curve reflect that dollar amount. By the time the PMI conference rolls around we should have some suggested MPI curves developed.

Like many other initiatives taken by both contractor and government staff, the ideas and concepts embodied in the weighted performance index have disappeared unnoticed in FY1997 incentive fee performance measures. Contract reform initiatives to save taxpayer dollars by using cost plus incentive fee contracts instead of cost plus award fee contracts have gone unreviewed. The incentive fee portion of the KH contract for FY 1996 was set at approximately $16 million. The question no one is asking is what was the total fee KH received for FY 1996?

# Project Management in the Next Century: Engage!

Ken Whiting, PMP, The Knowledge Webb and The University of Phoenix

## Introduction

In the futuristic television series *Star Trek: The Next Generation*, Captain Picard uses "Engage" as the trigger for action to take place. As cited by Roberts and Ross (1995, 42–43), it meant the following:

"Apathy, laziness, distraction, and interference can all lead to a self-inflicted workplace crisis created by the failure to do what needs to be done within acceptable time limits or according to established standards. Panic . . . usually follows. Aboard the Enterprise, important responsibilities were undertaken with a sense of urgency marked by confident resolve and purposeful action. . . . Competently led, [they] were people of enthusiastic spirit who had a keen sense of what was urgent and what could wait. . . . Whether a new course was set or a new priority identified, the only proper response was—'Engage!'"

As identified, numerous negative things can happen when time limits or established standards are violated. What does it take to successfully engage? It takes competent leadership plus confident, enthusiastic people who understand the priorities and are willing and able to take purposeful action around urgent needs.

So what does this have to do with project management in the next century? First, we have to consider the nature of the work to be done.

## The Business Environment

The current business environment is characterized by demands for increased speed in response and execution, widespread globalization of markets, more demanding customers, and disruption in the relationship between employees and employers. Concurrently, the strategic planning process has fallen and risen in favor as leaders seek tools to respond to their environment. All of this occurs in a rapidly changing world.

An ongoing trend has been the need for organizations to quickly produce high-quality, cost-effective products and services while generating a steady stream of new products and services in a global marketplace. Success will only come to those who can respond quickly and appropriately to new information, suggesting that rigid strategic plans are no longer appropriate. While some people categorize recent business programs as fads, the fact remains that factors such as quality are the price of entry to the game. The winners will be those who can compete on speed. Intel is an example of a company that initially attempted to protect its products through legal action against companies that appeared to infringe on its designs. This defensive action was meant to keep competitors from using Intel's research and development to generate "me-too" chips. Intel's leadership, however, had the insight to develop a strategy of advancing the technology so quickly that Intel essentially competes against itself. A company that wants to copy Intel's technology will be left in the dust.

Globalization of markets has expanded. America is characterized as a services-oriented marketplace due to the loss of manufacturing to overseas plants. Now even services are perceived to be global in nature. Widespread telecommunications capabilities make it as easy to reach out and touch someone overseas as it is locally. Twenty-four-hour work days are possible if the knowledge work can shift around the world throughout the course of the day; e.g., systems design and development in India coordinated with work elsewhere. This trend will clearly accelerate with technological advances.

The "good old days" of selling whatever you produced are over. Customers learned that they have choices, and exercise this right frequently. They not only expect high quality products, they also expect to be treated well throughout the buying experience. Each year the bar rises a little bit more. More and more elements of products and services, such as a minimum quality level, will become the price of admission.

Employees are clearly being affected. The unwritten contract between employees and employer that resulted in job security in exchange for loyalty no longer exists. Reengineering was a euphemism for downsizing, supposedly resulting in employees working smarter, not harder. Even the vocabulary of a reengineering guru made business sound like a war zone. In reality, reengineering has a relatively low success rate, and the impact is to kill the "enthusiastic spirit" of employees.

Formerly paternalistic employers now want resilient employees who are more willing to change and capable of quickly bouncing back when change happens. They emphasize employability versus employment: employment does not mean guaranteed employment for life, while the real issue should be the employeeÕs ability to gain the knowledge and skills necessary to remain viable in the market place (employability). As a footnote, however, our company has observed that employers are much happier when they get to make retention decisions versus the employees. Talented and



PROJECT MANAGEMENT INSTITUTE 28th Annual Seminars & Symposium
Chicago, Illinois: Papers Presented September 29 to October 1, 1997

**Exhibit 1.** The Organization of the Past vs. the Future

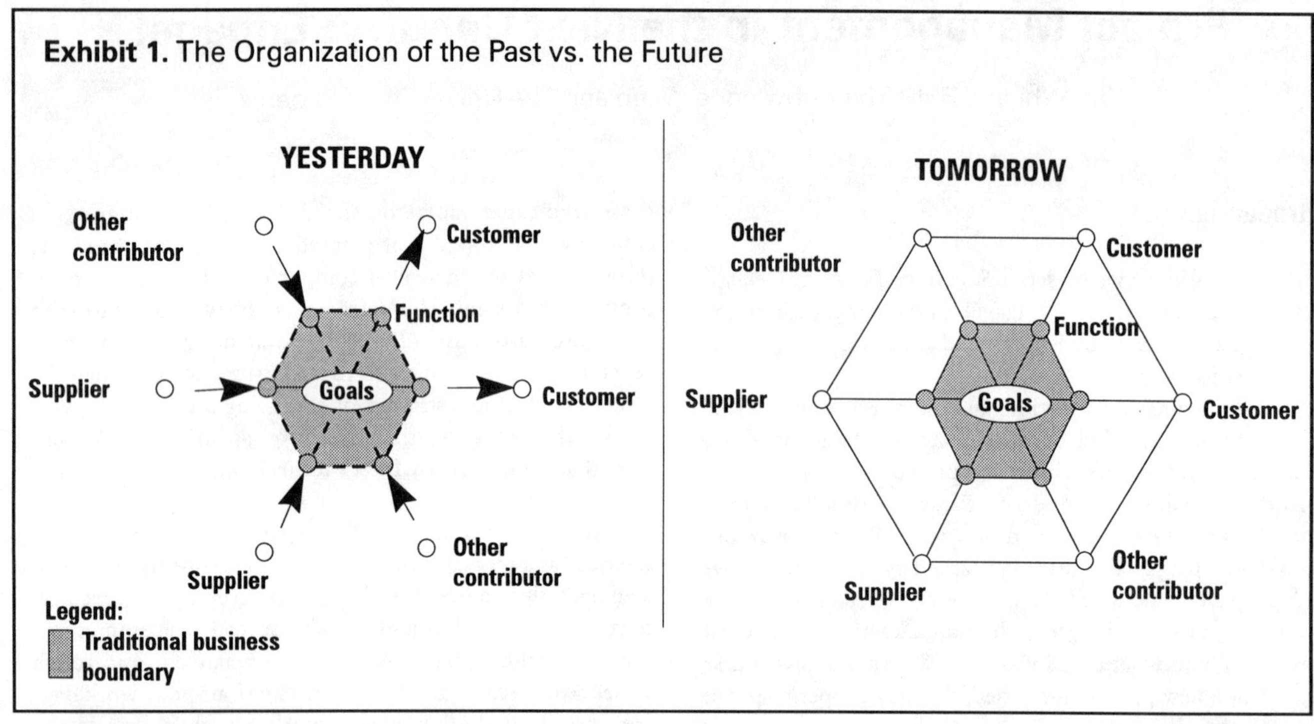


capable employees who act on the employability principle frequently find that their employers did not really want them to execute their rights.

Today, downsizing and the shift from employment to employability seems to be more traumatic for employees than employers. We believe that within a few years, however, employees will espouse employability, and that employers will regret some of their current actions. The business of the future will find itself competing not just to acquire talented people at all levels, but also having to compete at retaining them. This will have significant implications for human resource systems.

Michael Hammer (1996) suggests that there have been three major stages of strategic planning. The first he calls portfolio management, and the major question was how to allocate capital to competing proposals. The second was the era of competitive strategy as triggered by Michael Porter's book of the same name. The third stage has been a focus on core competencies as triggered by the work of Gary Hamel and C. K. Prahalad. Hammer suggests that today a new era is beginning, characterized by an organization focusing on its most capable and flexible processes. Some recent work by Porter (1996) supports that same idea, although he talks of activities rather than a process.

In summary, the overall business environment will be characterized by the need for flexibility to build capability for fast response to customer needs in an increasingly global marketplace. The relationship between employers and employees remains to be seen, but it seems clear that relatively smaller head counts will exist, and turnover ratios will be higher than employers currently expect. The strategic planning process will need to support the new environment.

Our conclusion is that organizations will increasingly identify and work to maintain their core competencies while shedding work that is inconsistent with those competencies. Each company will link its set of core competencies with complementary core competencies of other companies to form a single value chain to meet and exceed customer requirements. These linked businesses, a virtual organization, will share common goals that are driven by customer needs and known to all members of the organization.

Not only will cross-functional cooperation be standard, so also will cross-company cooperation around processes. The processes will be monitored across all companies with corrective action taken as needed to ensure customer satisfaction. New processes will be developed to meet changing customer needs by the virtual organization. However, any specific company may be involved in numerous cross-company processes, sharing its unique competencies across a variety of products and services. Companies may be both cooperating and competing, depending on the process. We see this today, and the trend will accelerate. For example, two competing companies in one market work cooperatively in another market; e.g., U S WEST and TCI compete domestically and partner in the United Kingdom. Adding to the complexity, the life cycle of these products and services will continue to shorten, meaning that these cross-company processes are continually forming and disbanding.

Exhibit 1 graphically demonstrates what is described above. Compare the independent nature of business in the past to the interdependent, networked organization that will exist tomorrow. Yesterday, even if the goals of the firm were known, they were addressed on a functional basis with limited cross-functional work. Suppliers were held at armÕs length, and just to make sure they stayed on their toes, they were periodically threatened with replacement. They did not share knowledge of their customer's goals, so operated completely on a transaction basis. Customers were given what the seller thought was good for them. The overall system was static.

Tomorrow's organization looks different in that communication and relationship links are strong both within the business and between all members of the virtual organization. A shared vision becomes the cornerstone to successful implementation. All members of the virtual organization focus on the shared vision, align the necessary resources around the task, and then follow through collectively to successfully meet the customer's needs. While difficult to show in two dimensions, this environment will be dynamic. The system as a whole will be advancing, and individual components will come and go as needed.

## Implications for Businesses

Another popular phrase from *Star Trek: The Next Generation* was "Make It So." The clear need for this directive to be executed is that "it" needs to be known. This paper started with the definition of engage, and key components included "competent leadership" and knowing "a new course or priority." The virtual organization challenges our current sense of leadership; we debate what leadership is today, who exhibits it, and why. The new environment will be more complex. It will require cross-company leadership agreement on a common vision for the virtual organization. All members of the organization will have to understand the impact to their business and commit to align resources to this priority. Only then will it be possible to "Make It So."

In their daily work, just as on Star Trek, people will have to know what is urgent and what is not. The overall framework needs to be provided by the cross-company leadership focusing on the critical few priorities. Mechanisms must be in place to follow through to ensure that implementation happens as expected and results are achieved in a timely manner.

Time has already been discussed as a competitive advantage. Significant research exists that time is a more critical element in new product development than any other factor. An unfavorable time variance has far greater impact on revenues and market share than does an unfavorable budget variance; some findings indicate that a budget overrun of 50 percent may be financially justified in order to meet the needed time commitment. This trend will certainly continue in the future.

The short life of a product or service, coupled with what is known today about the importance of time-to-market in new product development, will mean that cross-company project teams will need to be able to quickly come together, agree on a shared vision, then plan and execute the project. New members will need to be linked as processes are created, or will break away as processes are abandoned.

The global environment will make some emotional issues of today, such as diversity, irrelevant. Companies that are not diverse in their thoughts and actions will simply not be able to compete. The issue will become competency: the core competencies of the business and the competencies of the people it employees. Virtual organizations will seek complementary competencies wherever they exist, and the test for alliance will be based on the potential impact to each member.

We are already seeing the trend of companies choosing to deal with a smaller number of customers with whom they can develop a mutually beneficial long-term relationship. That trend will increase as virtual organizations focus on the end user of the product or service, rather than focusing on an intermediate customer. Customers are certainly not lowering their standards nor their expectations for improvements, so identifying current and correctly anticipating future customer needs will be critical for the viability of the organization.

As has already been suggested, a relatively small number of core employees will exist within a specific business unit. They will be selected for their competencies, and other needed competencies will be sourced outside as needed. These employees will tend to be more mobile in response to the changing employment agreement today.

Our conclusion is that there will be a high demand for people who can "engage." Short life cycles of products, services, and even processes will mean volumes of new problems that can best be addressed by someone with the skills and expertise of today's project manager who understands *A Guide to the Project Management Body of Knowledge (PMBOK Guide)*.

## Implications for Project Management

Project management as a profession has a relatively short history. Early project management discipline was applied in construction, the defense industry, and data systems. It has been only recently that companies have recognized that there are quite a few major activities that look like projects and require discipline to successfully complete. As Kerzner has pointed out on numerous occasions, any project can be driven to successful completion through executive meddling. He states that it is a sign of project management maturity when a steady stream of successful projects can be delivered. The

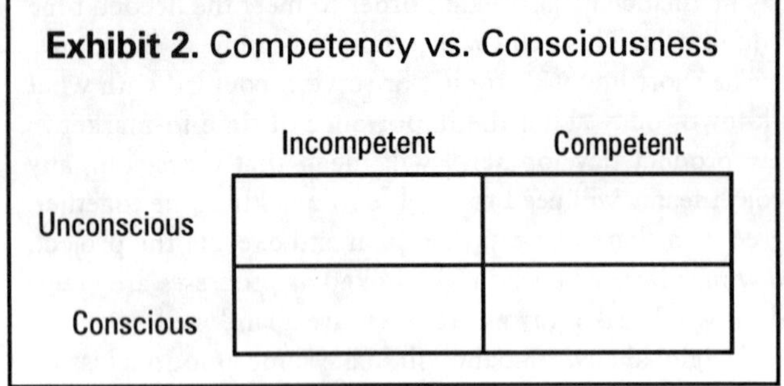


rapid growth of PMI and the popularity of the project management professional certification is itself a testimony to this trend.

As a foundation for the remaining discussion, refer to the model shown in Exhibit 2 involving dimensions of competency and consciousness. There are four quadrants in this model. "Unconsciously incompetent" occurs when a person doesn't know that he doesn't know; he lacks the skills to perform a task. A person like this would fail to plan for a project, fail to deliver the project, and not know that another approach was possible. The "unconsciously competent" person can deliver projects successfully time and again, but does not know what she knows that makes her successful. The "consciously incompetent" person knows that she does not know. An ideal state is "consciously competent;" this person knows that he knows, and can regularly successfully deliver projects by utilizing reliable methods. In this quadrant, personal and organizational learning can occur. The person recognizes new techniques that are reliable, and can explain to others how success is achieved.

Potential project managers can move from unconsciously incompetent to consciously incompetent through reading, training and education. In our experience, it is very difficult to move from incompetence to competence without some sort of supporting infrastructure, such as mentors, formal or informal coaches, and so on, who reinforce the theoretical concepts while the person works on an actual project. PMPs are logical candidates to fill this coaching role.

While everyone would agree that a form of project management has been used for years, it was frequently referred to as "planning" and was successfully done by those who were often "unconsciously competent." The organization of the future cannot afford to rely on such people; time pressures will require corporate knowledge of who are the consciously competent employees who can quickly "engage."

Basics of the knowledge found in the *PMBOK Guide* will be an expected skill set of any employee. The challenge will be to integrate these concepts as necessary in corporate and college curriculums in a practical way.

The *PMBOK Guide* will evolve to encompass the challenges of cross-company and cross-cultural projects. There will be a tendency for organizations to rally around a single global framework, such as the *PMBOK Guide*, in order to gain consistency of common terms, concepts, and so on in their cross-company, cross-cultural projects.

Enlightened companies are moving away from reliance on legal contracts to enforce compliance, and moving towards an environment where any legal action would be the last resort. Rather than voluminous documents aimed at addressing any contingency, members will cooperate based on the expectation of maintaining long-term relationships. The auto industry already provides us models of the expected behavior. Personnel will need both the project management skills to successfully engage and the sensitivity to maintain the relationship among the virtual organization's members. Relationship-based outcomes will be as rigorous as contractual-based outcome, and there will be additional benefit due to contribution toward the best solution from both customer and supplier.

Because of the volume of personnel required and the ongoing nature of these projects, the project manager may not be someone who has sought project management as a career. Instead, his support will be provided by PMPs who are available as needed. Consistent with the focusing around core competencies, organizations may choose to hire this expertise, or if it is considered a core competency, develop and maintain the skill internally.

Concepts from the learning organization certainly apply here. Not only does the individual want to learn from her experience, but the business and the entire virtual organization will need this insight. Organizations cannot afford to repeat mistakes, and the expected churn of employees will mean that the organization cannot afford to let the knowledge reside within a single person. The Deming cycle of plan-do-check-act currently applied to processes will be applied across process and organizational boundaries to support the improvement of all projects and processes.

## Barriers and Enablers to Success

A big barrier to success today is the need to work cross-functionally. Many organizations recognize the need, but struggle in the execution of cross-functional cooperation. Projects fail entirely or in part because of these problems. In the future, the problem will be exacerbated by the need to work cross-company and cross-culturally. Common problems today include issues of turf, politics, desire to build larger empires, and failure to realign reward systems to drive cross-functional behavior. Imagine these same problems extended to the cross-company, cross-cultural organization. Obviously, there will be a need for techniques that enable cross-company cooperation, and in an ever more global environment, cross-cultural cooperation. Current elements of successful teams, according to research, include a clear vision or goal, open communications, and so on. These models will have to be modified to provide understanding of key success factors in a global environment.

Another common barrier today is the ability to plan but inability to execute. Based on Kerzner's definition of project management maturity, many companies have not achieved it. Worse yet, these projects are either completely internal or involve traditional contractor relationships; we should have the knowledge by now to manage them successfully. Implementation fails for a number of reasons, even when senior executives say "make it so." Whether the failure is due to lack of resources, unwillingness to actually take the risk of implementing, fear of loss of power or prestige, or competition among priorities for attention, the result is the same: failure. Tomorrow's environment will be significantly different and more complex. Increasing competitive pressure will tend to weed out those companies that cannot or will not execute, and certainly no virtual organization will want to align with a company that cannot execute.

The lack of change management plans coupled with the tangible project plans will also keep projects from succeeding. The basic change management building blocks of training and education, involvement, revised measurements, reward and recognition, communication, and organizational structure must be considered whenever a significant project launches. In the more complex environment of the future, successful methodologies will be needed to overcome reluctance to change.

A major enabler of success in cross-company processes is that it will become the prerequisite to succeed in the market. It will not be a matter of choice about whether to participate or not. Frequent failure will create its own reward.

Another enabler is the growing recognition of the value of project managers. Kerzner has said that recessions are the best time for project managers, because organizations have to maximize their returns on investment. Therefore, they want to manage the work more professionally to increase the likelihood of success. As companies shrink toward a focus on their core competencies, these should become very good times for project management. Certainly the increase in membership in PMI and certified PMP supports this trend.

## So What Can We Do Today?

We have to begin by looking for examples of the desired behavior in today's environment. The auto industry gives us a model of companies that developed long-term relationships where former adversarial customer/supplier relationships existed. The success of these cross-company processes is critical to all members of the virtual organization, since a failure at any point puts the entire process at risk. Regardless of where a problem exists, all members to the process aid in determining corrective action. While significant problems still exist in that industry, such as ensuring that all members enjoy a reasonable rate of return, it does serve as a starting point.

We can also find companies orienting around processes and abandoning their functional view. The network portion of AT&T years ago abandoned its stovepipe mentality focused around functional skills, interests, and reward systems, and oriented around a business objective of maintaining network reliability. The important fact is that all relevant support systems were modified to support the change. Network reliability information was distributed each business day, and the focus of functional efforts was to keep the network up. The reward system was modified to encourage the same focus.

Businesses need to begin improving their implementation success rate today. There is growing awareness that project management is needed for projects other than construction, data systems, or traditional industries such as defense. What is needed is more learning organization activities that enable the overall success rate to improve. Best practices should be spread throughout the organization. Pitfalls should not trap a competent project leader twice. The result will be more project managers who have confident resolve and take purposeful actions to get the job done.

Proactive development of a project management curriculum in businesses, and the careful development of project managers up a ladder of experience will also increase the likelihood of success. The necessary support infrastructure must be in place to reinforce educational and training efforts.

Integration of project management principles into the broader college curriculum would result in more graduates having basic skill sets when they enter the business world. As Dr. Robert Graham points out, the "accidental project manager" is frequently found trying to manage a project for perhaps the first time. Providing a foundation within the context of other course work would reinforce the ability to manage a project when appointed.

Finally, companies need to begin now to migrate from their traditional transaction-based relationships to more all-encompassing relationships. This is an excellent time to learn as other organizations are trying to do the same. Identify key suppliers and implement a different type of relationship that is built on mutual benefit, trust, and the commitment to improve the overall process. This will test the degree of commitment of each firm; it is not an easy task.

## Summary

The business environment of the future will be significantly different from the current environment, although we have explored themes that can give a sense of direction. The current emphasis on downsizing will result in companies more organized around their core competencies. Increasing global competition will continue to place a premium on the ability of companies to reduce their time-to-market, contain costs, and maintain high quality standards. Individual companies will link with complementary organizations to create cross-company processes that deliver products and services meeting customers' needs. Cross-company cooperation will be necessary to agree on the desired course or priority.

As a result, there will be numerous projects formed around the need to design, develop, coordinate, and implement cross-company processes. They will be so common that management and technical personnel will be expected to have some level of project management skills as a basic competency. To ensure a steady stream of successful projects, these personnel will be supported by professional project managers who are able to mentor and coach as needed. All of these personnel will need to operate "within acceptable time limits and according to established standards." They will undertake these "important responsibilities with a sense of urgency marked by confident resolve and purposeful action." In other words, they will exhibit the only proper response—"Engage!"

### References

Hammer, Michael. 1996. *Beyond Reengineering*. New York: HarperCollins Publishing, Inc.

Porter, Michael. 1996. "What Is Strategy?" *Harvard Business Review* 74:6 (November-December): 61–78.

Roberts, Wess, and Bill Ross. 1995. *Leadership Lessons from Star Trek, The Next Generation*. New York: Pocket Books.

# The Consultative Role of the Project Manager "The Age of Project Mentoring"

Joan Knutson, Project Mentors

The cover story of the September 19, 1994, issue of a *Fortune* magazine article was titled, "The End of the Job." It was reporting a conclusion which has been reached by many employees of large organizations—that jobs as we know them will disappear. Instead of becoming a job holder, a person will become "a package of capabilities, drawn upon variously different project-based situations." Such packages will coalesce into teams around an emerging issue, deal with the issue, then regroup in other team configurations around other issues.

May I contend the following: the role of the project manager is different; the name itself is no longer accurate. Furthermore, the competencies required in this "package of capabilities" has changed.

Let's look at each of these contentions in more detail.

## The Role

Today the role of the project manager is to organize, coordinate, and mentor an enterprise within the larger context of her company or agency. The enterprise to which I refer is a project. This project has a discrete end and a discrete deliverable. The deliverable produced out of that enterprise provides a benefit to the organization either in the form of revenue, savings, or some productivity to the process.

The role of the person who coordinates a project enterprise is that of an "intrapreneur." No. I didn't say an entrepreneur. You read it correctly—an intrapreneur. An intrapreneur is the internal person who will take accountability to see that her enterprise (this project which is a microcosm of the organization) meets the expectations of the business. These expectations might be timely completion and/or highest quality, competitive product and/or produced at the most cost efficient rate. Whatever the expectations, the intrapreneur must coordinate the resources at her disposal in order to meet the stated business objective.

## The Name

If you noticed in the section above, I conscientiously avoided using the term "manage" or "control" because these terms are no longer valid as they relate to the intrapreneur who is accountable to the enterprise. He does not manage resources. The reason? In order to manage resources, a person needs to have authority over those resources, and in most project-related scenarios, the "project manager" does not have this authority.

Therefore, I intentionally used the terms organize, coordinate, and mentor. And if the role has changed, should not the name also change? The old name of project manager or project leader indicated the job of guiding and directing resources, inferring material as well as human resources. The material resources have become easier to organize and coordinate; the key success criteria is the coordination of the human resources. These human resources are the project sponsor, the customer, clients of the project, and the project team members—in other words, any stakeholders who have vested interest in the enterprise.

May I suggest that if the more appropriate role of the project intrapreneur is the coordination of the efforts of the project stakeholders, the new title should be project mentor and that the role is that of project mentoring. Mentoring, by definition, is not fishing for the people but teaching them how to fish. It is providing the guidance necessary for people to accomplish their roles within the project enterprise; it is not doing their jobs for them. It is passing on knowledge and skills so that each group of people who contribute to the enterprise are more capable, more competent, and more successful.

Therefore, if the role has changed, and if we are willing to change the name to be more correct, we must also realize the focus of the project mentor has shifted from being a "manager" to being a "mentor" or "consultant." It is now your job to mentor all your project stakeholders and clients in building in-house project processes and expertise. This ensures you, your project, and your organization the greatest opportunity for success in your project efforts.

In your consultative role, you should take applicable approaches from the project management discipline and the organizational sciences and apply proven techniques to improve project and team behaviors, processes, and methodologies. In short, your consultative efforts are structured to maximize the success of projects within your organization and need to focus both on the "project" and the "organization."

It is your job to consistently deliver measurable improvements while equipping your project stakeholders with the tools and techniques to achieve change and manage practical project management processes themselves. It is your mission to transfer expert knowledge and skills to members of the project community within your sphere of influence and control.

Your management wants, first and foremost, implementation and tangible results. Instead of just a project planner and status report producer, your management is looking for a person with consultative skills who can integrate project management into the everyday fabric of the organization. Companies are looking for help in managing growth, change, and performance. This translates to the client's need for comprehensive implementation assistance.

It is helpful for you to visualize the needs that the consultative efforts that you provide can help identify and the benefits that it will deliver. Deliverables in your consultative role, unlike products such as status reports, are nonetheless entities which can be described and evaluated. There are two major categories within the consultative model, they are the project specific efforts and the enterprise-wide efforts. The enterprise-wide efforts can be further broken down into cultural and process-related efforts. Let's look at each of these in more detail.

## The Project Specific Role

The tasks performed in your project-specific role are similar to what you are currently performing, but with a different mind set. The mind set changes from one of execution and control to one of being a catalyst. Let's break this role into smaller components comprised of the project launch, team building, project midstream audit, and specific problem intervention

### Project Launch

The focus of the mentor is one of facilitation versus doing. So instead of creating the project definition and plan, you will be guiding the intact team through the project planning process, producing a project mission statement, map of the project relationships, a team communication strategy, work breakdown structure, task responsibility matrix, project network, schedule, and contingency plans to name a few of the possible deliverables out of the effort. At the end of the series of work sessions, you aid the team in making a game plan to address the monitoring, tracking, and controlling of the project once it gets under way.

### Team Building

As an internal consultant, you work with your project client and individual contributors to build a strong foundation for effective interpersonal communication—the necessary ingredients for a team. This is a highly customized effort. You will need to do some homework before moving into this consultative endeavor by either talking to your human resource training staff or reading some excellent books which contain exercises on team building.

The goal is to increase team effectiveness and cohesiveness so that project goals can be met with a minimum of conflict, organizational disruption, and hands on "management." As a "mentor" your objective is to provide the means for the team to perform without your day to day involvement.

### Midstream Audit

Several months into a major project, team leads and team members may begin to lose interest or focus, which can have a devastating impact on project results. The "mentor" approaches the project as if she is looking at it for the first time, i.e., looking at the "forest" versus the "trees." Key problems, issues, and roadblocks are identified and analyzed to determine cause and impacts. The team, facilitated by you in your role of consultant, then creates action plans, revised project plans, and/or contingency plans for making changes, solving problems, and removing barriers for progress.

### Problem Intervention

If the project appears in trouble, your role as a consultant is to identify the cause of the problem and identify appropriate action. Your role is not to make the decision, but to facilitate the team in the identification of and corrective activities necessary to get the project back on track.

### Post-Project Evaluation

Everyone working on a project learns and benefits somehow from the experience. But does the organization benefit from what is learned by individual project participants? Often not. This process ensures that team members assimilate project learning's and that the information will be put in a form which can benefit others as well.

## The Enterprise Role

The enterprise role of the project mentor can be divided into two major sub-components: culture and process. Cultural issues address areas where not only the project management process must change, but processes that underlie the entire organization may need to change. Processes address the need for consistency across projects rather then within a project. Both of these roles require an enterprise-wide perspective rather then a project specific perspective.

## Enterprise-Wide Culture

### Performance Development

People need to keep developing and growing, learning more about technical and interpersonal roles in project management. This can be accomplished in several ways, including classroom training, self study, or on-the-job coaching. In the project mentoring role it is your job to make recommendations and to institute (where you can) mechanisms for personal development for the project team members. But what assures that the learning comes back to the job and is cultivated and encouraged until it becomes reality and habit? The project mentor performs this job by working within or helping to create an organizational performance development process.

### Organizational Analysis

An effective project management strategy requires the appropriate organization to support it and an environment conducive to supporting the discipline of project management. You, as a project mentor, may need to analyze and recommend organizational structures that best support a project management environment relevant to your project and your organization and to offer suggestions to remove the barriers that are negatively impacting project management within the enterprise. You can help ensure the strategies are reflected in your company's project organizational structures and in how the discipline is communicated effectively throughout the organization.

### Human Resource Planning and Development

In your role as a project mentor it is your job to not only run your project but to prepare people to run projects. You can assist in this process by identifying skills and designing selection criteria for project managers. You can also effect change by working with the organization to develop a performance review process that is specifically designed to hold people accountable and reward them for their performance on the project team.

## Enterprise-Wide: Process

### Prioritization Process

Establishment of project prioritization criteria is a difficult process. It must be addressed at the highest possible level within the organization. As a project mentor, it is your responsibility to assist the organization in developing a process that reflects and supports the project management process, one for example that supports the resource allocation process. The factors addressed in the prioritization process need to be applied consistently to all projects, so the organization can compare the value of vastly different projects.

### Software

Today's project management software, as a tool used in exercising the project management discipline, has the inherent power to transform data into action plans—and much more. Your ability to take on the role of a consultant can be the bridge that provides a logical connection between project management methodologies, the learning process, and the integration of the tools in the day-to-day work environment. Tactically, you can aid in the customization of your tool to create templates, charts, and reports which are specific to your needs and standardized for the organization. Strategically, you can help evaluate, choose, and implement companion products to enhance the functionality of your chosen tool.

### Methodology

Few companies have escaped the need to rethink their project management strategies and to see that these processes and procedures are correctly documented and disseminated to all the people who engage in project work. You can work with existent off-the-shelf methodologies or build your own to clarify and position the processes, procedures, and methods by which project management work will be done.

## Summary

If the premise behind the *Fortune* article is correct—that a person is not a job holder, but a package of capabilities—and we can also agree that the role of a project manager in this environment is more like a "consultant" then a manager, then we can conclude that the project manager spends less time "directing" and more time "suggesting"; i.e., they have moved from being a manager to being a mentor.

Being a project mentor rather then a project manager requires a mind set that is holistic rather then specific. As a project manager, your focus has been on the project you were assigned. Whereas a project mentor not only accomplishes the project objectives, but also develops her people and organization-wide processes and procedures.

This new role requires new skills. It is your challenge to acquire the necessary consultative and facilitation skills to perform this new role of project mentor. It then becomes your job to change mindset; you are not just a tactical problem solver, you are a strategic enabler to your organization, your project, and yourself.

You'll know you have transitioned to this new role when you've become a designer and implementer of meaningful changes to your project organization's way of doing business.

# Project Horizons: A Perspective for Project Management in the Twenty-First Century

Steven M. Price, S.T. GERANN, Inc.
Dr. Rene-Marc Mangin, Mangin Associates

## Introduction

Project Management is emerging as the predominant strategy to manage key business initiatives and multidisciplinary teams within today's complex business environment. This is largely due to the flexible, responsive, and adaptive nature of project management as a methodology and as a business approach. As business enterprises undergo transformation from a mechanistic to holistic orientation, project management is positioned to address the new business realities and become the vehicle for widening the influence of system thinking. This paper addresses the changing business landscape and its impact upon project management and how project management must adapt to meet challenges in the twenty-first century.

## The Changing Business Landscape

There is a large body of commentary and research that describes the changes occurring within business. These changes have been largely precipitated by global competition, information technology, changing workforce dynamics, rapid and discontinuous change, and complex paradigm shifts. To this end, the business landscape is gradually being transformed from a mechanistic paradigm towards a holistic paradigm, from isolation to integration, and from contention to collaboration. Within this context, managers are searching for a navigable common ground among people, process, systems, and relationships. Project management as a methodology and organizational framework exemplifies the common ground through its process underpinnings and integrative nature—a premise that suggests business and project management are inextricably linked as both move toward the twenty-first century. The changing business landscape is illustrated through the following points.

### *Global Competition*

Competition has increased dramatically at the global, regional, and intra-industry levels and has become a palpable impetus for innovation, cost reduction, process improvement, and multiple initiatives to gain competitive advantage. Globally, new strategies built upon configuring activities through a geographically dispersed area are becoming seamless with improvements in information technology, transportation, and favorable economic and regulatory policy. Seamless boundaries are changing the way competitors compete for their market share and forging a new array of alliances focused upon collaboration, not contention

### *Information Technology*

Technology and more importantly information are now accessible to a larger contingent of the workforce. The ability to transform information into knowledge to gain competitive advantage has spawned what Peter Drucker calls the "Knowledge Society," where knowledge becomes the key currency of exchange. Within this "information economy," organizations compete on the basis of their ability to identify, acquire, evaluate, package, and distribute information effectively and on how they develop and maintain their information infrastructure.

### *Changing Workforce Dynamics*

The Information Age has changed the nature of work just as the Industrial Revolution changed work in the nineteenth century. Work content is now predominantly higher-level cognitive skills focused on collaborative problem solving. The changes in work content have created a new working environment that Olav Alverson calls "systems of persuasion," which focuses on developing and delivering products and services that are differentiated between standardized products (repetitive) and high value added problem solving (customized).

### *Compression*

Product life cycles have been compressed from a pre-WWII average of 12.5 years for new product introduction to approximately two years or less and has created a voracious environment for product development projects to plan, manage, and deploy well-differentiated projects with superb features and benefits.

### *Rapid and Discontinuous Change*

Changes occurring in today's world are rapid, often unpredictable, and discontinuous and are aptly classified as either radical or incremental. Total quality management is a form of incremental change that strives to make quality and vale-added changes over time. Radical change involves quantum



PROJECT MANAGEMENT INSTITUTE 28th Annual Seminars & Symposium
Chicago, Illinois: Papers Presented September 29 to October 1, 1997

leaps to rethink situations where the outcome is discontinuous thinking where the problem is reconfigured and the solution becomes an abrupt departure from the traditional courses of action.

### Complex Paradigm Shifts

Business is operating with multiple paradigms, each of which is changing in response to complex environmental stimuli. The net result has been dramatic shifts in how organizations are structured, managed, operated, and marketed. Organizations have been awakened over the past decade from comfortable market positions, larger organizational structures, and technological malaise, only to face the harsh realities of global competition, cost reduction initiatives, and technological shifts. Many of the paradigm shifts are precipitated by an organization's ability to connect immense amounts of information and define relationships that are critical to planning and positioning strategies.

### The Shift from Mechanistic Thinking

The concept of the "world as a machine" has faded in application and concept. As the dominant paradigm of the twentieth century, the Newtonian mechanical universe has limited our ability to define the problems that we are confronting, constraining our range of responses to problems. Conceptualizing organizations as machines, i.e., an assemblage of parts performing predetermined functions, limits the inclusion of people, and therefore cannot address psychological issues. The significance of our adherence to the machine paradigm is inestimable. Fortunately there is a shift away from mechanism and its inherent flaws concerning linearity and simplified cause-effect relationships. Systems thinking is replacing mechanistic limitations with a holistic perspective and new generation of tools and techniques.

### Systems Thinking

Systems science is a holistic perspective—a combination of analysis and synthesis formulating an integral view of patterns of interaction and connectivity that transcends mechanistic limitations. In a linear world, the whole is the sum of the parts. By analyzing the component parts and connecting then together, the whole is understood. Simple machines can be understood in a mechanistic way, but complex systems cannot. The real world is not always linear, there are multiple goals, and the parts do not always add up to the whole. Human activity systems (e.g., business) rarely pursue a single goal because competing goals and sub-goals are often present. These goals must be collaboratively prioritized or balanced through some form of systematic and systemic problem solving. Complex systems require strategies that accommodate their non-linearity.

### Collaborative Advantage

The era of collaboration is bringing new ways for organizations to create value together rather than merely exchanging ideas and products. Rosabeth Moss-Kanter believes that active collaboration will provide organizations with a competitive edge in the future and that five levels of integration define successful collaborative efforts. These levels include (1) strategic integration with leaders at top levels, (2) tactical integration with middle managers and professionals, (3) operational integration at the day-to-day level, (4) interpersonal integration for creating a vision of future value, and (5) cultural integration to understand and bridge differences (1994).

### Communication

Information Age technology has revolutionized mass communications which reach larger, well-informed audiences with a thirst for current information. Communication is fundamental for all project management applications, yet its importance is highly underestimated. Effective written, oral, and electronic communication is essential for effective project management. Communication is the means by which people involved in the project detect changes in environmental factors and respond to the new conditions in a coordinated manner. The coordination of multidisciplinary teams engaged in multiple activities and operating within a dynamic environment is challenging, and failure to appreciate project complexity by neglecting the inter-relatedness of activities and their timing can be devastating.

### Chaos

The concept of an orderly world, moving in linear, deterministic ways, is being replaced by a larger creative role of disorder and irregularity. The world is actually a "world of systems moving in self organizing ways with emergent and unpredictable outcomes." Although there are still deterministic natural laws, their true effect is a circular phenomenon in which order leads to disorder, and disorder leads to order. The concept of self-organizing systems is replacing old paradigms of determinism and predictability.

### Consciousness

Einstein is often quoted as having said, "No problem can be solved form the same consciousness that created it." Maynard and Mehrtens have isolated seven trends that are affecting our world: (1) shifts in consciousness—people are seen as the creators of their own realities; (2) disenchantment with scientism—the tendency to reduce all reality and experience to mathematical descriptions and physical phenomena; (3) inner sources of authority and power—a new appreciation of "authority from within"; (4) re-spiritualization of society—responses to the lack of balance and purpose; (5) decline in materialism—shifts from competition to cooperation; (6) political and economic democratization—responsibility and accountability for the larger view of humankind; and (7) beyond nationality—the evolution of a world-wide bioregionalism (1993).

#### *Culture*

Edgar Schein believed that "Culture is patterned, potent, and deeply embedded in people's thoughts, perceptions, and feelings. It provides an integrated perspective and meaning to situations; it gives group members a historical perspective and a view of their identity. The major consequence of culture is that it stabilizes things for group members." The "dynamics of culture—how it originates, evolves, and stabilizes in the life of an organization." Schein has identified four kinds of culture traps that are facing organizations: (1) failure to understand the dynamic consequences of cultural phenomena; (2) overemphasis on the process of cultural learning (socialization) and insufficient emphasis on the content of what is actually learned (the actual culture); (3) confusing parts of culture with the whole; and (4) confusing surface manifestations of a culture with the underlying pattern, or what we might think of as the essences or core of the culture (1985).

## The Impact on Project Management—A Business Connection

The linkage between project management and business has been emerging as business strives to manage unique endeavors within an environment that demands flexibility, responsiveness, and adaptability for an ever-changing world. The impact on project management is a multi-faceted challenge. Initially the challenge was to realize the value of project management to plan, manage, and control unique endeavors, i.e., those outside the pure process orientation. However, the general acceptance of project management by business managers has spawned new insights and challenges beyond the traditional project management focus of time, cost, quality, and scope. Now the project management community is facing a distinct mandate to extend the traditional boundaries and infiltrate the inner core of business.

Project management has traditionally been the domain of larger, complex projects requiring an effective methodology to plan, manage, and control resources within strict project constraints. Typically the management of time, cost, quality, and scope have sufficed as a paradigm to optimize and allocate individual skills towards an organizational end. However, the new business realties are transforming traditional paradigms from a command and control function to a response and integration function. Empirical observations suggest that the new business realities are impacting project management in a variety of ways including the following.

#### *Multidisciplinary Problems*

"Real World Problems" are multidisciplinary and do not neatly fit into a single discipline. They possess complex characteristics and are driven by a multitude of inter-disciplinary perspectives and experience levels. As Russell Ackoff observes, "managers are not confronted with separate problems but with situations that consist of complex systems of strongly interacting problems. The effect of categorizing problems by disciplines is that they then tend to be attacked by people in that discipline."

#### *Managing teams in a networked environment*

Networked organizations are "Information Age" organizations designed to adapt quickly, efficiently, and effectively to rapid and discontinuous change. They are characterized by teams forming and disbanding at relatively rapid rates of speed, coalescing around opportunities and key issues, and disbanding when issues are resolved. Knowledge workers are particularly well suited to networked environments because they are self-managed and have direct access to information required for their work. Information technology is critical to their members' ability to interpret information and make decisions without exhaustive analysis.

#### *Project environments are complex*

The project environment is a set of conditions existing within the larger organizational context. These conditions are rarely perceived and interpreted the same way by members of the organization. Project planning must reflect an understanding of the project environment and demonstrate a degree of sensitivity and finesse to ensure goals and objectives are met within the larger organizational context. It is often not the plan that limits its utility, but how the plan fits into the planning environment.

#### *Collaborative Problem Solving*

Collaborative problem solving is about addressing problems and managing relationships. Collaborative power comes from network members' ability to focus attention quickly and effectively to define and analyze problems by tapping the resources and knowledge of the entire network. Effective teams share information, negotiate with a focus on the goal, and work to invent options for mutual gain. Multidisciplinary problems are a collaborative exercise, which forces people to work together. Information exchange is critical to success, but is often complicated by differences in professional paradigms, interests, and values.

### *The New Organization*

Functional, divisional, and matrix organizations have not effectively addressed changes in business realities. Their inflexibility and command and control mentality have led to a new management revolution searching for process improvement and connectivity. Conversely, process organizations have demonstrated improved efficiency because they are more capable of adapting to discontinuous change. The new organization is a flat, disaggregated structure, composed of complex webs of relationships (networks), purpose-driven, team-based, and information technology dependent. Managers in such organizations exist to facilitate the group orientation toward a common purpose and to provide support. Relationships, either temporary or fixed, are central to organizational effectiveness and not process. The boss-subordinate relationship is no longer dominant. It is supplanted by relationships based on the mutual exchange of products, services, and information to ensure attainment of the organizational goals and objectives.

## Project Management Education—Bridging the Gap From Today to Tomorrow

The education debate among project management academics and practitioners continues between fundamentals and application. There may be no clear resolution to the controversy of how best to educate project managers, but a review of the current education systems reveals that a holistic perspective may be problematic.

### *A history of partitioning knowledge*

Partitioning education is the norm at the collegiate level. A review of education statistics reveals that there are thirty prominent fields of study, each with multiple subspecialties. Only one of the thirty fields is labeled as multidisciplinary. The statistics for multidisciplinary education are remarkable. Between 1992 and 1994, approximately 2 percent of the 2.3 million bachelors' degrees awarded were multidisciplinary. At the master's and doctoral level, the percentages decrease to 0.66 percent and 0.50 percent, respectively. During the same period, only 758 degrees in systems science were awarded at all levels. Multidisciplinary or interdisciplinary education has not garnered enough support to become a viable movement. Between 1980 and 1994, approximately one half of one percent of all master's and doctorates awarded were multidisciplinary. Our current educational systems are violating a fundamental precept of design: form follows function. Business is no longer about assembling simple machines; it is about synthesizing information and innovation. Teaching methods and curricula that improve a student's ability to integrate and transfer knowledge from one field to another are clearly becoming the prerequisites for success in the future

### *The Knowledge Society*

Technology and, more importantly, information are now accessible to a larger contingent of the workforce. As Drucker argues, the educated person in the Knowledge Society will need the ability to "understand the various knowledges" (1993). This reinforces the argument that not only knowledge and specialty expertise will be our future currency of exchange, but also knowledge of multiple disciplines that support, influence, control, and interact with process.

### A Guide to the Project Management Body of Knowledge (PMBOK Guide)

The *PMBOK Guide* is an outline of key topic areas relevant to managing projects. But as stated in the preface to the 1996 edition, "clearly, one document will never content the entire PMBOK." The Project Management Institute has made notable gains in representing a uniform body of information relative to project planning, management, and control. Their 1996 *A Guide to the Project Management Body of Knowledge (PMBOK Guide)* outlines nine subject areas relevant to project management, whereby three sections are particularly useful for developing the foundation of systems thinking—integration management, communications management, and human resources management. Although the topic content for any one of these sections is, at best, an outline, the movement toward attempting to understand the whole and its parts is promising.

### *Training, Seminars, and Symposia*

There are an abundance of organizations, both private and professional, that offer subject matter expertise in various formats. Each offering has merit for the target audience, yet few organizations have developed an integrative approach built upon the use of multidisciplinary methodology. In essence, the "education circuit" continues to partition knowledge, thereby propagating the same methodology and thinking found in college settings.

## The Project Management Platform—A Vehicle for Systematic Change

Project management is positioned to address the new business realities through continuing education and by providing methodology, tools, and organizational structure. As business moves toward the twenty-first century, project management will become the predominant strategy and approach to manage unique endeavors and become a vehicle for systematic change. The key factors that constitute systematic change include the following.

#### *Managing Multidisciplinary Teams*

Multidisciplinary teams are required to define and address the complex business problems of today and those that bring about future challenges. Project managers will be required to mange these teams and foster cooperation among subject matter experts and coordinate their efforts and deliverables. An understanding of complex problem situations, technical nuances, and the dynamics of psychology, culture, and differing worldviews will be required.

#### *Facilitating Collaboration*

Collaboration among diverse groups must be balanced against creative energy and innovation to mitigate contention and political leverage. The ability to forge creative alliances in the pursuit of organizational effectiveness and developing unique products and services will be the mandate for future excellence.

#### *Infusing a Holistic Perspective*

Our world is in a dynamic flux of linear and non-linear interactions, a world of complexity and relationships. Adopting a holistic perspective is imperative for visualizing the larger whole and understanding the component parts. An exploration of holistic issues reveals a landscape of subtle connections and uncovers the drivers for integrating knowledge and experience, rather than partitioning and isolating their value.

#### *Aligning organizational goals with unique products/services*

Projects are unique endeavors to align core competencies with the larger organizational mission. Project managers will be the custodians of organizational effectiveness as they create and manage value, satisfy stakeholders and stockholders alike, understanding organizational context, and realizing projects are part of a larger organizational mission.

#### *Fostering cooperation among knowledge workers*

Knowledge workers are the new breed of professionals that derive their intrinsic value by manipulating information and technology to solve complex problems and establish meaningful relationships between seemingly disparate information sources and types. Project managers must appreciate the shift from an industrial, mechanistic mindset to a post-industrial, holistic, Information Age. The context, rules, and interrelationships are changing and project managers must adapt their perspectives to meet the changing currents of how work is accomplished and the empowerment of the knowledge worker.

#### *Facilitating Continuous Improvement*

The world, and in general, most business processes are in flux. Static approached and solutions to a dynamic set of complex problem situations will no longer work. Continuous improvement is the recognition of the strengths and weaknesses of process, people, and systems. The ability to incorporate "best practices" relative to these entities is an on-going effort.

#### *Creating a platform for the learning organization*

The future organization is the learning organization, one that strives to leverage knowledge assets and core competencies into competitive advantage. Project managers must be the architects of the learning organization through their innovative management practices, methodology, and worldview.

#### *Integrating Information technology*

The Information Age has spawned a plethora of communication and computer tools to enhance project management functions. The ability to leverage information technology is essential as both a process tool and enabler of the project management approach.

#### *Understanding the divergence of project management*

Project management is diverging into two orientations—one can be classified as "soft systems," the other as "hard systems" project management. Soft systems project management has a strong conceptual focus where problem situations are ill defined or involve highly complex project environments. Projects of this genre are exemplified by software development, environmental remediation, or projects where "wild or unbounded" problem situations dominate. Hard systems project management exemplifies the traditional project environments such as construction, manufacturing, or projects where definitive goals and objectives can be planned, managed, and controlled.

## Conclusion

The future platform for project management education will include an expanded version of the *PMBOK Guide* with additional topic areas that address a broader perspective of project management applicability and methodology. Future project managers will be better prepared for the complex, dynamic, and turbulent business environments and be equipped with a strong grasp of fundamentals and multidisciplinary tools. The authors view project management as a complex set of skills, capable and focused upon achieving measurable results in a multidisciplinary, team-based environment. The challenges facing project management, and more specifically project management education, have been defined. All that remains is to fulfill the mandate established by the business community and continue to build project management into the preeminent methodology for managing projects and business.

## References


Ackoff, Russell L. 1981. *Creating the Corporate Future*. New York: John Wiley & Sons.

———. 1994. *Systems Thinking and Thinking Systems*. Systems Dynamics Review 10:2–3 (Summer–Fall): 175–188.

Checkland, Peter B. 1981. *Systems Thinking, Systems Practice*. New York: John Wiley & Sons.

Drucker, Peter F. 1993. *Post-Capitalist Society*. New York: Harper Business.

Koskco, Bart. 1993. *Fuzzy Thinking*. New York: Hyperion.

Maynard, Herman Bryant, and Susan E. Mehrtens. 1993. *The Fourth Wave: Business in the 21st Century*. California: Berrett-Koehler.

Metaskill Consulting Group.1994. *Managing in a Network Organization*.

Moss-Kanter, Rosabeth.1994. *Collaborative Advantage: The Art of Alliances. Harvard Business Review* (July–August).

PMI Standards Committee. 1996. A *Guide to the Project Management Body of Knowledge (PMBOK Guide)*.

Price, Steven M. 1997. "Time to Market: The Challenge for Project-Based Management." *IERC Proceedings:* 403–408.

Price, Steven M., and Rene-Marc Mangin. 1997. *Developing a Holistic Perspective for Project Management Education*. Submitted for publication (February).

Schein, Edgar H. 1985. *Organizational Culture and Leadership*. San Francisco: Jossey-Bass.

*The Digest of Education Statistics*. 1996. Tables 208, 209, and 244.

Wheatley, Margaret J. 1994. *Leadership and the New Science: Learning About Organizations from an Orderly Universe*. California: Berrett-Koehler.

# Active Hierarchical Systems: PM Tools for the Future

Vladimir Voropaev , Prof., Sergei Ljubkin, Ph.D.,
Russian Project Management Association/Sovnet-Moscow

## Introduction

The development of methods and tools today is significantly delayed because of the increasing complexity of projects, the condition of economy integration, and other requirements of modern business. The necessity of creating a new type of system is causing the delayed development of PM methods and techniques according to the modern understanding of PM and requirements of its practice. Traditional PM methods and techniques are oriented, generally, just for specific project teams and management of lower levels. They are rooted in a basic (detailed) network of project activities. For middle and higher levels the group of unlinked information models is used as sets of target events (milestones) and consolidated Gantt charts, defined by the network model. Tracking, reporting, and decision-making for all WBS levels are realized by calculations for a detailed network, then the results are transferred to an information model with considerable levels. In the case of complex projects with many participants, these PM systems have the following drawbacks:

- large amount of informational and computation procedures;
- loss of time and, as a result, slow decision-making due to long periods of information transfer and multiple filtration and aggregation;
- loss of accuracy and quality of information;
- low reactivity.

This all reduces the means of well-timed reactivity of project participants on all levels of current changes and demands large costs for management projects. However, potential means of PM are not used enough.

In our opinion, the development of management methods and techniques (according to a modern understanding and trends of PM) has to carry out in the direction of creating a system without lacks, as mentioned above. Attempts to create a PM system for all levels on the basis of the traditional network are not successful because the PM modeling theory does not allow one to perform correct aggregation of project activities, providing approval of adopted solutions for all levels.

We need to start developing appropriate PM systems for PM of the next century. In this paper, the authors suggest the creation of an *active hierarchical system for complex projects* (**AHSPM**), which would provide a base for creation of PM methods and techniques for the next generation.

## Description of AHSPM

To create a PM system, according to modern understanding, new background and development of management methods and techniques, such as the following, are needed:

- the development of modeling (of project activities) theory, allowing correct aggregation of project activities and information;
- the development of formal methods of decomposition of building projects and creating structure models needed for PM;
- construction of the hierarchical system of models with demanded properties as per the requirements of the subjects of the project (investors, ordered-client, contractors, subcontractors, project managers, and so on) and different levels of management;
- the development of methods for correct aggregation of network, methods of analysis, and design;
- the development of methods to perform multilevel calendar plans of activities and to control the process of project realization;
- the organization of effective operation of the hierarchical PM system.

In our opinion, one of the ways to create the new type of PM system is the development of the hierarchical PM system (based on the new PM modeling theory), as well as the development of suitable information technology and methodology for creation and functioning of such a system.

*AHSPM differs from today's PM systems in the following ways:*

- increases activity and efficiency in the work of managers and project teams;
- increases activity and influence of project stockholders by supporting every management level and all participants of project by providing needed information; methods and techniques for coordinated decision-making limited their competence and responsibility;
- reduces stages and volumes of information handling for decision-making;
- reduces expenditures for project management.

At the base of suggested approaches for creation of the AHSPM are scientific results and developments by the authors and their colleagues during the last twenty years, which are approved for investment and construction projects in Russia. The main requirements are:

- Improvement in activity and efficiency of managers' work;
- Submission of managers on each level; project participants with required and sufficient information, methods, and facilities for operative and coordinated decision-making within the limits of their competence, with complete responsibility;
- Improvement in operation of tracking and decision-making due to reducing the number of steps in the information handling and distance of the information internal transfer;
- Minimization of cost for the information-computation procedure of the required quality by the fixed set of PM functions and tasks.

A hierarchical approach for a PM system for complex projects that is based on scientific results and the developments by authors and their colleges is proposed.

### Generalized Network Models

It is proposed to adopt generalized network models(GNM) as a modeling theory of a hierarchical PM system. Theory and methodology of GNM are developed and progressed in works, such as Adelson-Velskiy, Voropaev and Kalinovskaia 1971; Voropaev, Sheinberg et al. 1974; Voropaev 1974; Voropaev, Lebed and Orel 1989; Voropaev, Lebed, Orel et al. 1990; Voropaev and Ljubkin 1989. The main difference between GNM and known types of network models (CPM, PERT, GERT, VERT, and so on) is that it allows circles with unpositive durations ("feedback" links). Also, for the points of project activities, links and time limits at any point of activities are used; both can be sensed as "not early" and "not later."

Described properties of GNM allow one to perform accurate aggregation and equivalent conversion of models that are necessary for creating. Also, there is the possibility that GNM adequately allows different conditions and links, which aren't allowed for other models. They have strict mathematical definition and an advanced theory of methods and algorithms for their analysis and design .

### Project Breakdown Structure

For realization of the hierarchical approach in creating the PM system developed by the authors, composition procedures of presentation and analysis of project information is used. These procedures permit performance of project breakdown structure by different decomposition attributes (structural-spatial, cost, resources, organizational, and so on):

- composition of different breakdown structures with fixed properties;
- decision-making of optimization tasks for creating hierarchical network with fixed properties;
- choosing complete ranges of structure models and cutout fitted to an entire set of project activities meeting the requirements of management levels;
- choosing non-complete ranges fitted to activities set with fixed properties (attributes: executors for every type of job, types and moments of payments, necessary resources, and so on);
- forming of a hierarchical GNM system after chosen graph sections on breakdown structure.

Each GNM belongs with its management level and project participants. Full project GNMs are simulated because they include schedules with same milestone dates.

### Aggregation of Network

The simulation of networks in a hierarchical PM system is provided by using methods of aggregation, which are developed by the authors (Voropaev and Ljubkin 1989; Ljubkin 1991).

Sense of approach: From the basic(detailed), lower level GNM, an aggregation model is formed for the next level. Each activity of the aggregation model is a superposition of a number of the detailed model's activities; input and output relationships, coordinates, and parameters of links and limits are defined by algorithms of aggregation with the purpose of simulating networks according to the one described above.

### Methods of calendar planning and monitoring on hierarchy network

Due to the fact that the hierarchical PM system has properties of equivalence, each management level and participant of a project can use his model for control and planning. Also, he can choose from the hierarchical system of networks a model that (in the best degree) is suited for solving the task of the moment.

In the process of project realization, current changes and adopted solutions appear, which demand correcting the models and recalculation of plans. In this case solutions are agreed upon with top levels and applied simultaneously to all system models.

## Hierarchical Approach to Management of Complex Projects

For the hierarchical PM system we used the above mentioned elements of background to form the PM system; the next main steps are as follows:

1. Creating the project WBS with fixed structure elements parameters;
2. Creating the project structure models and their compositions according to requirements of the PM system;
3. Creating the project OBS in accordance with project composition models (s. B);
4. Fixation of requirements to works detailing and setting activities and information lists in GNM (s. B. C.);

5. Creating GNM in accordance with both s. s. B. C. and s. D;
6. Creating hierarchical GNM by using s. E. and aggregation algorithms;
7. Testing of equivalence and choosing of basic schedules in hierarchical GNM analyses and scheduling;
8. Organizing of current and operative planning, controls, and reporting on the hierarchical GNM in accordance with s. C.;
9. Making design on results of monitoring for elimination of non-desired deviations from planned progress of project.

Elements of methodology and technology for organization and functioning of hierarchical PM systems, which are specific and new compared with traditional systems, are given above.

## Applications

Developments summarized for the given work have been forming for investors' interests and for large irrigation management, melioration water maintenance, and building projects. In the authors' opinions, these developments could be useful for management of large investigation and innovation projects and programs, as in techniques for both social and economic spheres. For the convenience of the next century these developments may be linked with:

- conversion of the defense industry;
- progress of the oil-gas industry and energy system;
- aerocosmic and telecommunication systems;
- privatization and reform of state enterprises;
- system for supporting social defense, foods, dwelling, and health;
- system for using nature's resources and for environment defense;
- and so on.

Application of the hierarchical PM system will give:
fuller realization of trends in PM development;
increasing PM efficiency;

- better use in PM of the potential of top management levels and main project participants;
- significant reduction in cost for PM.

Problems are common for many countries. Solutions of problems, in our opinion, are necessary for following progress of PM methods and tools and for actively using them. Solutions to those problems can obtain international collaboration within the political aspect by specialists in the PM branch.

## Conclusion

Results are concerned with:

- conception of the creation of AHSPM systems;
- formalized methods and techniques of structural decomposition of project management information;
- formalized methods of creating new information structures and aggregates for decision-making in a hierarchical management system;
- new simulation methods of process for the complex project realization; use of (suggested by the authors) the general network model (GNM), which reflects the links of project activities most adequately; analysis of models, including their optimization and calculation;
- creation of the hierarchical system of equivalent models based on GNM and the aggregation-decomposition of models;
- methods of the multilevel scheduling and decision-making in a hierarchical management system;
- organized and functioning AHSPM as a condition of developing information technology.

The proposed hierarchical PM system has a good developed background, as can be seen in works by Adelson-Velskiy, Voropaev, Kalinovskaia, Sheinberg, Lebed, Orel, and Ljubkin. The bigger part of algorithms is realized on a PC and approved in few projects. However, complex program realization and approbation of systems at practice is needed. The authors invite collaboration from anyone who is interested in this problem. The report will discuss the state of developments for AHSPM, and recommendations are given for multidimensional international cooperation of experts in the area of project management systems for the new generation.

### References


Adelson-Velskiy, V.I.Voropaev, and S.E.Kalinovskaia. 1971. "Generalized Network in the Construction Industry. Methods of Designing for Generalized Network." *At Russia Construction*. Moscow: N 4,5.

Ljubkin, S.M. 1991. "Aggregation on Generalized Network of Construction Object. Management and Information Problems in Information Sphere." Moscow, CNIIEUS.

Voropaev, V.I.. 1974. *Models and Methods of Scheduling in Information Management System*. Moscow.

Voropaev, V.I., B.JA.Lebed, and T.JA.Orel. 1989. "Generalized Network in Tasks of the Scheduling Theory." Moscow, CNIIEUS.

Voropaev, V.I., B.JA.Lebed, T.JA.Orel, et al. 1990. "Methodic Guidelines for Using of Composition Methods of Presentation of Information in Construction Management System." Moscow, CNIIEUS.

Voropaev, V.I., and S.M.Ljubkin. 1989. "Hierarchical System of Generalized Networks for Melioration Objects. Improving of Management and Organization Systems for Melioration Constructions." USSR, KRASNOIARSK, SIBNIIGIM.

Voropaev, V.I., M.V.Sheinberg, et al. 1974. "Generalized Network. Methodical Instructions." Moscow, CNIIPIAS.

# Visualizing Project Management and System Engineering as an Integrated Process

Harold Mooz and Kevin Forsberg, Co-Principals
Center for Systems Management

**Exhibit 1.** Optimum Solution Results from Dynamic Tension

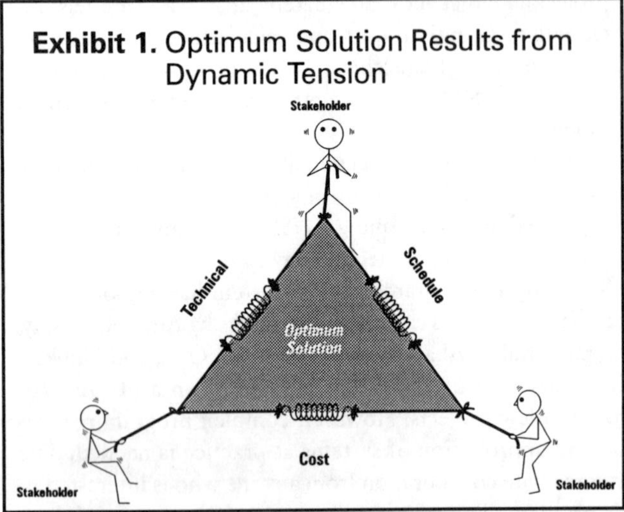


## Introduction

In many project environments project management and system engineering are managed separately. This situation is aggravated by the segregation of these disciplines in university curricula and by the separateness of the corresponding professional organizations. The Project Management Institute (PMI) and International Council on System Engineering (INCOSE) operate independently and usually don't participate in each other's conferences. PMI members are usually not members of INCOSE and vice versa. Analysis reveals that project management and system engineering tools are rarely integrated. Project management—the integration of business management and technical management into systems management—requires discipline and informed implementation. The process model explained here and detailed in our recent book, *Visualizing Project Management* (Wiley & Sons), is a significant step toward visualizing and applying these inseparable processes.

## Background

PMI and INCOSE promote processes that do not share a common vocabulary and are not integrated. Analysis of the technical papers of both organization's national conferences confirms that PMI papers do not address the management of the technical content of the project, and INCOSE papers rarely address the achievement of cost and schedule objectives. Examination of the vendor offerings at annual conferences further reinforces this conclusion: PMI tools and consultants focus on cost and schedule management, and INCOSE tools and consultants focus on technical solution management including requirements management, solution simulation, and decision analysis. Our experience in training thousands of project managers in project intensive organizations confirms this discipline isolation. Yet project managers cannot be successful without orchestrating technical, cost, and schedule factors as an integrated set. To do this effectively they must understand and manage a common process (see Exhibit 1).

Professionals in both disciplines are still attempting to codify their preferred approaches. The 1997 PMI national conference is focused on the future of *A Guide to the Project Management Body of Knowledge (PMBOK Guide)* because in its current state of a collection of individual subjects, it does not depict the project management process. The *PMBOK Guide* must progress to include the management of the technical aspect of the project since that is what normally consumes the cost and schedule that project managers are held responsible for controlling. INCOSE on the other hand is working on a capability maturity model (CMM) fashioned after the Software Engineering Institute approach. This too will be inadequate unless it includes the application of project management as a factor in technical solution achievement.

Project management is a management process that requires discipline and informed application. It is the integration and orchestration of business management and technical management into systems management. It embodies hundreds of terms, dozens of methods and techniques, and the ever growing assortment of supporting tools to help implement the techniques. Project teams must be skilled in the integrated processes of project management and system engineering and to understand when and how to apply the tools. The process model explained here and detailed in our recent book, *Visualizing Project Management,* is a major step toward visualizing and understanding how these two inseparable processes should be co-managed (see Exhibit 2).

## The Situation

Project management and system engineering reference books, handbooks, and bodies of knowledge are typically incorrectly presented as non-connected specialty disciplines rather than as interrelated sequences, processes, and sub-processes. For instance, contracting is treated separately from configuration management even though both are control techniques. Scheduling is usually treated separately from network development, ignoring the fact that scheduling is derived from the network and both are part of tactical planning. Risk management tutorials almost always ignore opportunity management even though they are interdependent. Sections on project control typically deal with data gathering, plotting, and performance measurement (actually project status) none of which is project control. Planning is shown as a phase with a start and end, when in reality planning and re-planning are continual to adjust to the daily reality of the project. Requirements development and management are usually absent or inadequately addressed.

These are just a few samples of the blurred understandings that exist about project management and system engineering. Unfortunately, project managers are usually not trained in system engineering and system engineers are usually not trained in project management. (This is surprising since the critical path, schedule, and cost are typically driven by the system engineering approach.) In enlightened companies project managers must have a system engineering background.

**Exhibit 2.** Project Management Responsibilities

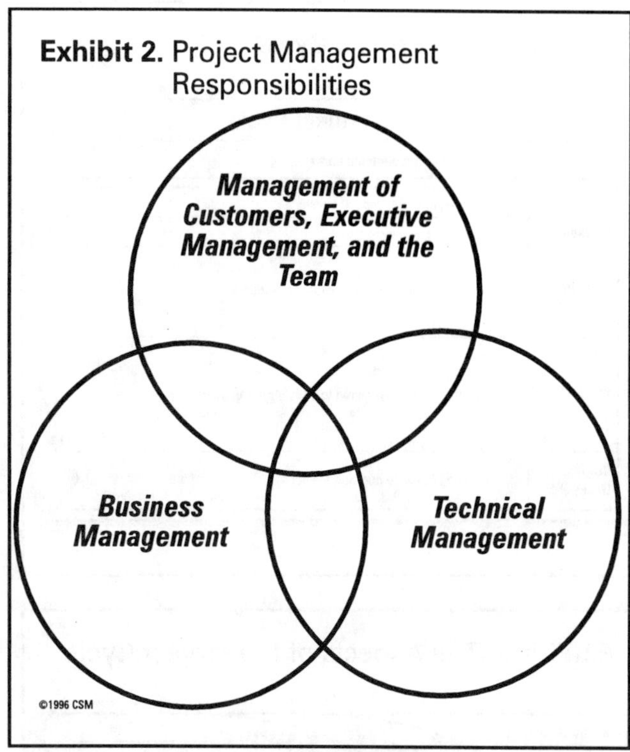
Management of Customers, Executive Management, and the Team
Business Management
Technical Management
©1996 CSM

What has been missing is an easily understood model that illustrates the way projects are best processed: a model that combines the orchestration responsibilities of the project manager with the system engineering and technical development approach of the solution providers; a model that also

**Exhibit 3.** The Four Essentials of Project Management

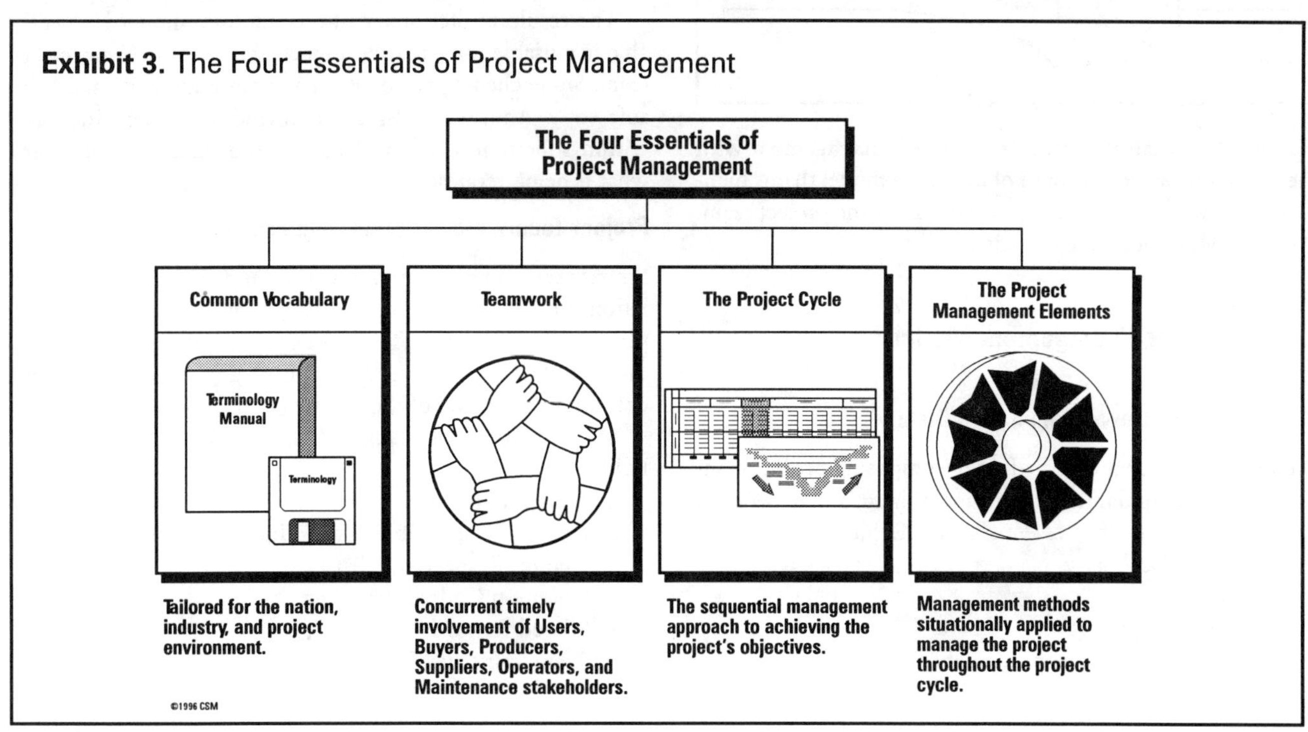
The Four Essentials of Project Management
Common Vocabulary
Teamwork
The Project Cycle
The Project Management Elements
Terminology Manual
Terminology
Tailored for the nation, industry, and project environment.
Concurrent timely involvement of Users, Buyers, Producers, Suppliers, Operators, and Maintenance stakeholders.
The sequential management approach to achieving the project's objectives.
Management methods situationally applied to manage the project throughout the project cycle.
©1996 CSM

**Exhibit 4.** The Project Cycle

| The Project Cycle | |
|---|---|
| Budget | Activities to secure the funding |
| Periods | The objective of groups of phases |
| Phases | Incremental achievement |
| Activities | What must be done to produce the products |
| Products | Tangible evidence required to satisfy control gates |
| Control Gates | Evolving baseline decision events |

©1997 CSM

**Exhibit 5.** The Aspects of the Project Cycle

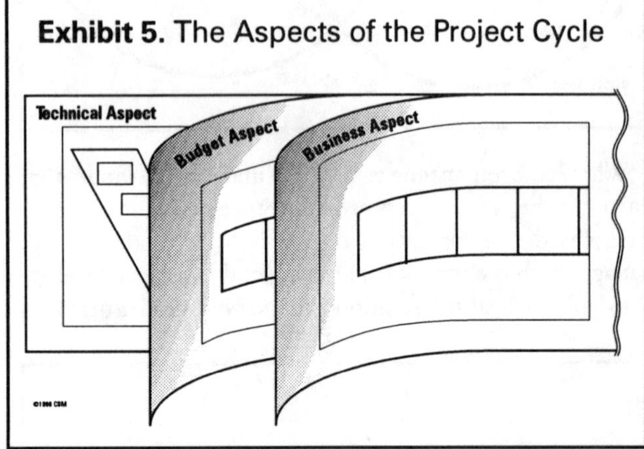


marries the situational aspects of project management with the sequential achievement of objectives; a model that is highly illustrative and intuitive for ease of use by the project team. We have developed such a model.

## Csm's Project Management Model

### Developed Top-Down from a Zero Base

We developed our model by first decomposing project management into fundamental and unambiguous components, which we call the "four essentials" (see Exhibit 3):

- Common Vocabulary
- Teamwork
- The Project Cycle
- The Project Management Elements.

We then visualized the structure of each essential and the relationships among them. Vocabulary and teamwork are perpetual properties of a project, while the project cycle and management elements embody the sequential and situational properties in a dynamic, orthogonal juxtaposition.

We identified additional sub-components: the (sequential) project cycle with three aspects (business, budget, and technical), and ten (situational) project management elements.

In the case of the management elements, we listed and categorized the techniques and tools of project management and system engineering according to how they are used. For instance, user requirements, context of implementation, concept trades, concept of operations, and requirements traceability were grouped into the requirements element. The work breakdown structure, WBS dictionary, network diagrams, critical path analysis, scheduling, estimating, and others naturally fit into the project planning element. Similarly, the techniques of measuring overrun, under-run, earned value, schedule position, and technical performance measurement fit within the project status element. We iterated this process to find that all techniques and tools fit naturally into ten homogeneous groups: the ten project management elements.

## The Four Essentials of Project Management

### Project Vocabulary—The First Essential

A defined project vocabulary should contain the business and technical terminology essential to conducting the project.

The resultant dictionary of terminology should be available in a usable form that best meets the needs of the project team. Some clients provide it on a server and/or in hard and soft copy. Another CSM client includes her terminology within solicitation bid packages to reduce confusion over what is being requested.

### Project Teamwork—The Second Essential

Projects sometimes fail or are inefficient due to adversarial relationships. Adversarial relationships can be avoided by implementing teamwork. Teamwork is often defined as working together to achieve a common goal. However, this definition falls short of the full scope of project teamwork.

Our essentials for teamwork among the project's stakeholders are:

1. A Common Goal
2. Defined Responsibilities and Interrelationships Founded on Respect and Trust
3. Common Code of Conduct
4. Shared Reward
5. Team Spirit and Energy.

Many projects fail to adequately address these teamwork factors between the technical and business personnel resulting in team members operating out of sequence or performing incorrect work.

## The Project Cycle—The Third Essential

Professional project management organizations often have a standard or template project cycle that is based on their preferred management approach (see Exhibit 4).

This cycle is tailored to the uniqueness of the project at hand. Project cycles usually contain periods (such as study, implementation, and operations), and phases within the periods (such as the concept definition phase and the verification phase). They also include activities such as "trade-off candidate concepts," products such as "system concept document," and control gates such as "system concept review." The project cycle is usually composed of three aspects that can be envisioned as layers (see Exhibit 5).

The first is the business aspect, which illustrates the activities and events associated with justifying the project and with running the project as a business. These include such activities as business case development, contracting, and subcontracting. The second is the budget aspect that illustrates the activities leading to the acquiring and allocating of project funds. The third, the technical aspect (system engineering sequence), identifies the activities and events required to provide the optimum technical solution in the most efficient manner. This aspect includes the sequences for incremental or evolutionary development. Included are system or product decomposition, definition, integration, and verification and is best portrayed in a "vee" format to illustrate progressing from system solutions down to detailed content and then upward consistent with integration of the content into the completed system or product (see Figure 6).

Also depicted are off-vee core activities associated with verification planning, risk and opportunity management, and user involvement. The technical aspect is typically the driver of both the critical path and the ultimate cost of the project (see Exhibit 7).

Once a project cycle is determined, all three aspects must be managed situationally by the skilled application of appropriate techniques and tools of the project management elements.

## The Project Management Elements—The Fourth Essential

Project management techniques and tools are grouped into ten application categories, to be employed by the team to manage the project through the project cycle (see Exhibit 8). The ten project management elements are the team's technique and tool box and should contain the best and most effective methods in each category.

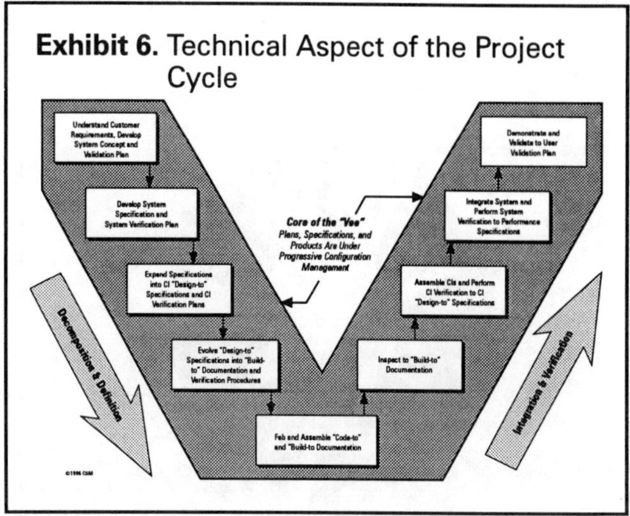


**Exhibit 6.** Technical Aspect of the Project Cycle

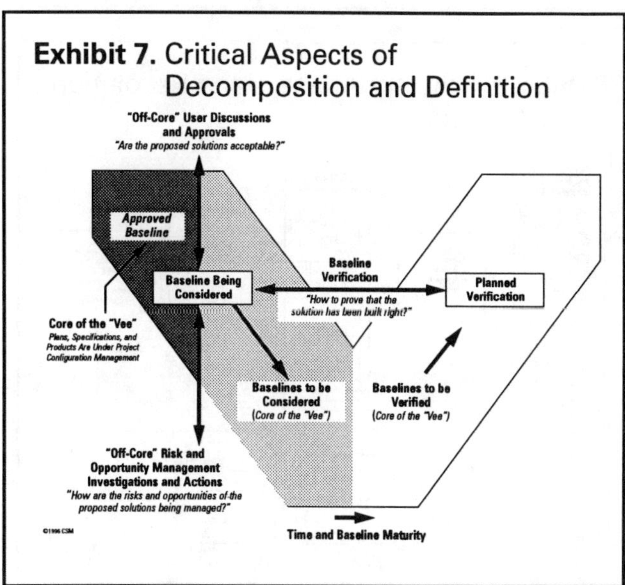


**Exhibit 7.** Critical Aspects of Decomposition and Definition

The team must be skilled in the application of all of the techniques and tools—which is often not the case. Projects do fail by misapplication of excellent techniques.

## The Ten Project Management Elements

The **project requirements element** covers both the creation and management of requirements. It includes requirement identification, substantiation, documentation, concept selection, specification, decomposition, definition, integration, verification, and validation. Techniques and tools include problem analysis and resolution, requirements traceability, accountability, modeling, and others. This element is situational rather than sequential since new requirements are apt to be introduced at almost any point in the project to be

**Exhibit 8.** The Project Management Elements Model

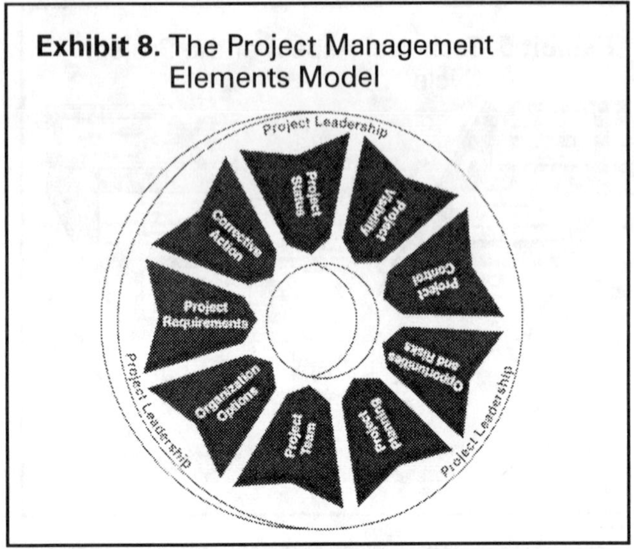


**Exhibit 9.** Problem Analysis and Resolution Process

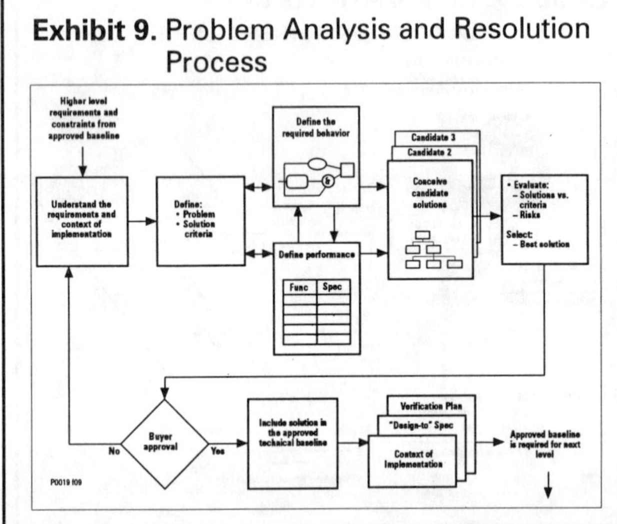


managed concurrently with the existing requirements already being satisfied at lower levels of solution decomposition. Exhibit 9 illustrates the problem analysis and resolution process, and Exhibit 10 illustrates this same process as applied to the technical aspect of the project cycle.

The **organization options element** focuses attention on the strengths and deficiencies of various project structures. There is no single "best" organization, and it is common for several forms to be operative concurrently. Options include functional, project, matrix, integrated product teams, and integrated project teams—even "skunk works." This element provides the basis for adjusting the structure as the project progresses.

The **project team element** provides the techniques and tools for staffing the project. Selection criteria includes character traits, qualifications, and the specific skills required by each project phase. Competency models based on attributes and qualifications form the basis of selection for key positions such as the project manager, business manager, system engineer, planner, and the subcontractor manager.

The **project planning element** provides for the team's conversion of project requirements into task authorizations that include delivery schedules and resource allocations and re-planning to respond to new information and actual events. The planning element includes both manual and computer tools which support and foster efficient team planning.

The **opportunities and risks element** is part of the planning process but is uniquely different and it is often ignored. This element encompasses the identification and evaluation of opportunities with the associated risks and the techniques for mitigating the risks and enhancing the opportunities. Opportunities and risks should be identified and managed throughout the project cycle, so the techniques and tools of this element must be applied continuously.

The **project control element** is required to ensure that planned events happen as planned and unplanned events don't happen. In our model, project control is both proactive and reactive process control. Every function that needs to be controlled must have a standard to be controlled to, a control authority, a control mechanism, and a variance detection system. Using schedule control as an example, the standard is the master schedule, the authority is the business manager, the mechanism is the change board, and the variance detection is the status review.

The **project visibility element** contains the techniques used to ensure that the project team communicates effectively and is informed as necessary about relevant project activity. It includes manual techniques like MBWA (management by walking around) and project information centers, as well as electronic techniques such as E-mail, video conferencing, and fax. The visibility system and associated techniques must be adjusted to fit the active project phase, the organizational structure configuration, organization deployment, and obligations.

The **project status element** is comprehensive measurements of performance against the plan to detect unacceptable variances and to determine the need for corrective action. Status should encompass schedule, cost, technical, and business progress. The evaluation and measurement should also include the rate of change of the variance if not corrected. Earned value and other performance measurement systems are included in this technique and tool group.

The **corrective action element** is the culmination of variance management and reactive project control. Corrective actions are reactive actions designed to return the project to plan. The techniques may include overtime, added work-shifts, an alternate technical approach, new leadership, and so on.

The tenth and most important element, the **project leadership element**, is based on the leader's credibility. Leadership inspires and motivates the team to its personal and collective best. Leadership includes handling different personality traits, supervision maturity levels, and rewards. Most importantly, it includes making sure the team is doing the right things, before making sure that things are being done right.

## Visualizing and Applying the Model

Project vocabulary and teamwork are universal and are essential to successful project management and system engineering. Therefore, they form the base of our project management model and support the project cycle that is developed by the team using both the project vocabulary and teamwork.

The project cycle depicts the sequential management approach and must be tailored to the circumstances of the project. The cycle has three aspects, and the technical aspect is represented by the vee of decomposition and integration. The overall composite project cycle is represented by a cylinder embodying all three aspects.

The techniques and tools of the project management elements are applied situationally to manage the project through the project cycle. In our model, the elements are shown as containers within a disk encircling the cycle so that the techniques and tools within each element can be applied to the phase and aspects of the cycle requiring management attention. Leadership is the element (the glue), that keeps the other nine elements properly applied to the cycle. The element wheel is free to move to the right as the project progresses through the cycle and is also free to rotate to apply the right tools to the management of the project phases (see Exhibit 11).

The power of our model is in its accuracy and simplicity and its uniqueness of combining the technical aspects of project management with the business aspect. The structure portrays how we as project management practitioners actually manage. We implant the vocabulary, foster stakeholder teamwork, create the project cycle, and then orchestrate the techniques and tools of the elements to achieve the desired results.

**Exhibit 10.** Problem Analysis and Resolution Process as Applied to the Technical Aspect of the Project Cycle

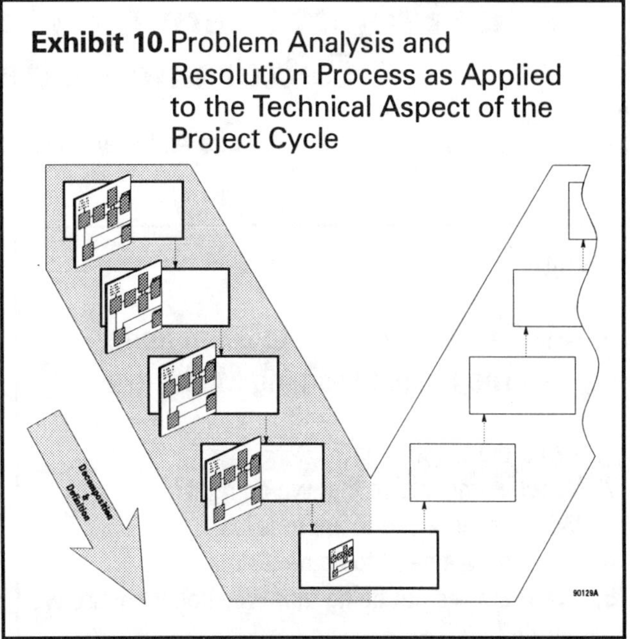


**Exhibit 11.** The CSM Project Management Process Model

## Summary

Almost every undertaking can benefit from a project management approach. Companies of all types are beginning to appreciate the important contribution project management can make to market share and bottom line results.

A highly successful project culture that combines technical management with business management represents the most significant competitive edge a firm can wield in this technology-driven, time-compressed era. Whereas technology is surprisingly easy to clone, a well-integrated, high-performance project methodology is a valuable proprietary asset.

### References


Project Management Institute Body of Knowledge. 1996. *A Guide to the Project Management Body of Knowledge (PMBOK Guide).*

SEI-CMM. Software Engineering Institute Capability Maturity Model. Carnegie Mellon.

Forsberg, Mooz, and Cotterman. *Visualizing Project Management.* Wiley & Sons.

# Make Project Learning a Learning Project: The Way to Better and Better Project Success

Lee A. Peters, M.S.C.E., P.E., Peters & Co.

Exhibit 1.

**Six Simple Questions to Learn from:**
**— The Project Learning Model —**

1. What did we do right?
2. What is imperative that we do right?
3. What do we need to improve?
4. What do we need to do next time?
5. What are we not doing that we should ensure we not do?
6. What new or different thing should we do next time?

Tremendous learning takes place on every project. Research demonstrates that projects are the key learning events in executive development. Our project leaders' developmental training led to the discovery of both a model and a process for making learning intentional.

The model uses six simple questions: What did we do right; what is imperative that we do right; what do we need to improve; what do we need to do next time; what are we not doing that we should ensure we not do; and what new or different thing should we do next time?

The key is the intentional use of these questions as a reflection, an after-action at the end of a phase or at the end of a project. The structure of the debrief will change the learning.

These questions are built into matrices with every aspect of the project system (input, process, resources, metrics, leadership, and results). (See Exhibit 2) We have learned in conducting debriefs after our simulations that we can alter the learning by the questions we ask. Learning is malleable. We believe that a rigorous checklist will squeeze out as much learning as possible.

These checklists can be used at any point in the project process to identify and define what is learned and what needs to be learned.

These questions derived from work facilitating a change of leadership in organizations. These questions elicit much information. The new leader learns about the people and the organization at warp speed.

## Learning Can Be Viewed from Two Dimensions

The first dimension is that individuals, teams, and organizations learn to accomplish projects. (See Exhibit 5) Each project skill set is different. Because a single individual knows project management skills does not mean a project team can function, nor does it mean an organization can effectively cultivate a project environment.

One organization placed such an emphasis on making progress on projects that project teams dived into projects and began working without one iota of planning.

Other organizations structured their project management process from such a functional perspective that the project accountants never learned to be project managers.

The second learning dimension is that of projects. (See Exhibit 6)

If debriefs are structured, a library of learning can be maintained to teach, to improve project processes, and to change organizational approaches.

Project pre-planning can be used to build teams and to develop the "soft" side of projects. The "soft" side is everything that is not part of the project scope.

People and teams will develop their own mechanisms to quickly become productive without ignoring the required "storming" of a newly formed team.

If learning, testing, and growing are emphasized, a project team may "practice" or test themselves and their systems on a part of the project. One paper mill construction team did this by first building a warehouse and then the rest of the paper mill.

If physical constraints prohibit a similar project, then a simulation may be used to test the team. This simulation can take many forms. No matter what form of simulation, the team can learn to work as a team and to manage a huge number of problems.

We are now experimenting with a "learning coach (LC)" in our training programs. The concept of a coach is the intentional contracting for learning and improvement by individuals and by teams with a person who is not consumed by the project fire fighting. This person provides the discipline to make learning intentional.

The learning model may be used as a "self" and "other" evaluation mode to locate learning opportunities.

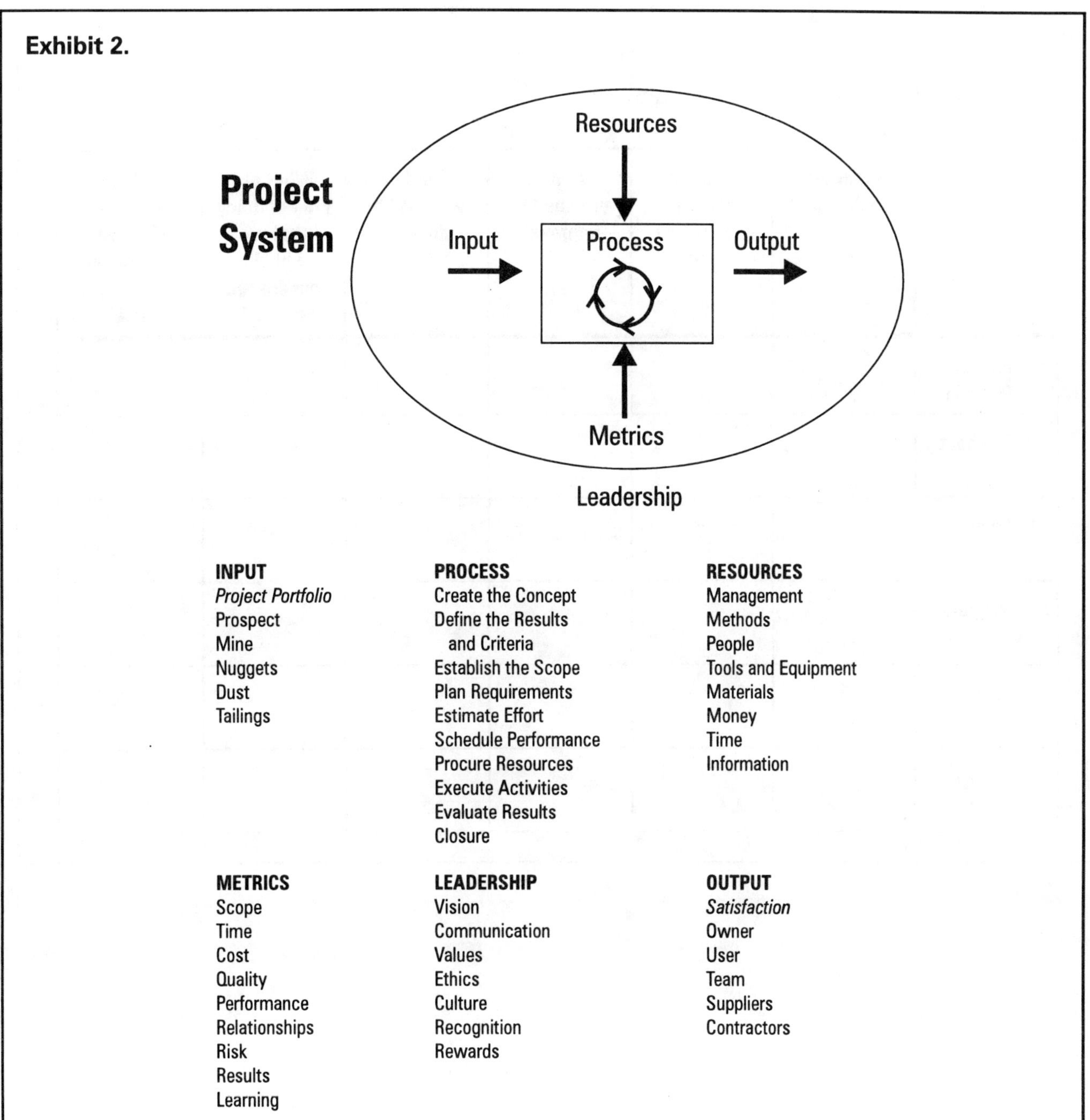


At each phase of the project, the learning coach uses the model to establish new learning contracts for each individual and for the team. The LC then debriefs the previous learning and learning contracts.

The learning process with the discipline and the new role (the learning coach) will deliver tremendous returns. Learning on that project will accelerate. Teams and individuals will learn a broader spectrum of skills because the model addresses the entire project system. Learning will be internalized by the team because it is intentional rather than random. Quality of project completion will increase across the spectrum of projects.

Learning becomes a team activity. Learning is focused on the project process and the team process rather than on just the project alone. Project learning means success on a generation of projects not on just a single project

**Exhibit 3.**

**LEARN FROM A COMPLETED PROJECT— INPUT**

| | What did we do right? | What is imperative that we do right? | What do we need to improve? | What do we need to do next time? | What are we not doing that we should ensure we not do? | What new or different thing should we do next time? |
|---|---|---|---|---|---|---|
| Project Portfolio | | | | | | |
| Prospect | | | | | | |
| Mine | | | | | | |
| Nuggets | | | | | | |
| Dust | | | | | | |
| Tailings | | | | | | |

**Exhibit 4.**

**LEARN FROM A COMPLETED PROJECT – PROCESSES**

| | What do we do right? | What is imperative that we do right? | What do we need to improve? | What do we need to do next time? | What are we not doing that we should ensure we not do? | What new or different thing should we do next time? |
|---|---|---|---|---|---|---|
| Create the Concept | | | | | | |
| Define the Results and Criteria | | | | | | |
| Establish the Scope | | | | | | |
| Plan Requirements | | | | | | |
| Estimate Effort | | | | | | |
| Schedule Performance | | | | | | |
| Procure Resources | | | | | | |
| Execute Activities | | | | | | |
| Evaluate Results | | | | | | |
| Closure | | | | | | |

Exhibit 5.

## Project Learning

**Individual** The skill set to accomplish a project as an individual and as a team member.

**Team** The commitment to excellence and the skills of a team required to cooperate, to communicate, and to achieve project excellence.

**Organization** The environment, leadership, and processes theat nurture ever-improving project success.

Exhibit 7.

## Teams

Responsibility chart
Team Participation
- Roles
- Behaviors

Team Effectiveness
Team Development
Pinch Model
Conflict Resolution
Project Life Cycle
- Stages of Group Development
- Stages of Individual Issues
- Stages of Team Actions

Stages in Pojects

Exhibit 6.

### Learning About a Project

**Project Results:** The benefits the project will deliver

**Project Scope:** The nature and size of the project

**Project Work Performance:** The tasks that are to be completed to complete the project

**Project Process:** The evolution of the project

**Project Management Work:** The tasks that are required to control the project

**Project Management Process:** The flow, the change, the river of project management phases (which are different from the project phases)

**Project Management Scope:** The level of complexity required to control this specific project

**Project Team Work:** The tasks of a team required in order for the team to do both the project work and the project management work

**Project Team Process:** Team processes required to nurture and equip a team to do work as a team

**Project Team:** The assembledge of humans for the purpose of accomplishing a project

**Organizational Project Work:** How an organization conceives, conserves, assigns, reviews, and closes projects

**Organizational Project Process:** How the organization says projects are to be accomplished

**Organizational Project Norms/Culture:** The organizational tradition for accomplishing a project

**Exhibit 8.**

**TEAM DEVELOPMENT**

| | **Behaviors** (observed) | **Actions to Change and Reinforce Behavior** |
|---|---|---|
| **Forming** | | |
| **Storming** | | |
| **Norming** | | |
| **Performing** | | |
| **Adjourning** | | |

**Exhibit 9.**

## Levels of Rehearsals

### Level 1 — Talk Through

A briefing by senior manager(s) on all aspects of the venue.

### Level 2 — Key People

A briefing by the functional area managers on all aspects of their operations.

**Level 3 — Manager's Exercise**

A simulation by functional managers resolving issues similar to those that could be expected to arise.

**Level 4 — All Hands**

A simulation at the actual venue site with the management cadre staffing that venus being confronted with exception-type problems while managers attempt to conduct routine business.

# Project Entrepreneurs for Project-Based Enterprises: Extension or Complement to Project Management Competencies?

Robert J. DeFillippi, Ph.D., Associate Professor and Director, Masters of Science in Entrepreneurial Studies, Suffolk University Sawyer School of Management
Stephen E. Spring, MBA, Director of Marketing, Duncan and Nevison

## Introduction

Project management in the next century will be increasingly performed within temporary project organizations that utilize networks of independently employed project specialists and project subcontractors. We refer to such temporary project organizations as project-based enterprises. Industries that utilize project-based enterprises include film-making, book publishing, software development, construction, business services, and consulting.

According to UCLA management professor William Ouchi, 4,500 multimedia companies in Los Angeles act as a network of overlapping projects in which people and ideas move from node to node. Moreover, the growing number of strategic alliances among firms in many other industries is also fostering the use of project-based enterprises.

Although considerable literature exists on the roles and skills of project managers, there is relativity little written about the roles and skills required for project-based enterprises. Several recent papers at PMI have described the virtual project manager (Ellis 1996; Ono 1996) and have suggested some of the roles, skills, and tools for managing project-based enterprises. However, almost no attention has been given to the project entrepreneurs' role and their contributions to project-based enterprises.

In film-making the project entrepreneur is often the producer, and some observers believe that the skills of the independent film producer are widely applicable to a variety of project-based enterprises and virtual projects (Jones and DeFillippi 1996). The independent producer of films, plays, books, software, or any project-based product or service is an entrepreneur who is both a visionary, resource producer, and controller of quality and budget (Gorman 1996).

Our perspective is that project entrepreneurship entails competencies that both complement and extend the role requirements described elsewhere for virtual and traditional project managers. It is the project entrepreneur who articulates the vision for the project, staffs the project team, creates a project organization, and sustains the project enterprise's commitment and project vision over time. Some have suggested that the economy of the future will provide the greatest rewards to those who can initiate and sustain projects that create value for their stakeholders (Peters 1992).

## Project Entrepreneurial Competencies

### *Visioning*

Visioning is the ability to perceive an entrepreneurial opportunity and articulate a project vision that is technically sound, market focused, and inspirational.

Opportunity recognition is an essential competence for visioning. Project entrepreneurs see opportunities where others see problems or threats to the status quo. Project entrepreneurs are thus alert to subtle informational cues signaling discontinuities in current technology, product or service, business design, or market trends. The ability to perceive and anticipate discontinuous change creates a first mover advantage for the project entrepreneur to create a project vision that capitalizes on the perceived opportunity.

Translating the perceived opportunity into a project vision is a competence integrating conceptual and communicative skill component. Conceptual skills include the ability to imagine a set of project outcomes that create value in the market place and leverage identifiable skills and resources. Hence, project visioning must link available project resource capabilities with market opportunities

Additionally, project visioning cannot be conceived in a vacuum. Successful project entrepreneurs within established business enterprises are often required to develop project visions that support the achievement of either current or prospective business-level missions and strategies. Project visions intended for project-based enterprises face the additional challenge of not interfering with and hopefully complementing the missions and strategies of participating members of the project-based enterprise

Communicative skills include the ability to articulate a rationale for the proposed project that captures the imagination and commitment of prospective resource providers. Hence, the project vision must be both technically sound and inspirational. The most successful project entrepreneurs often display both technical competence and charisma, although not necessarily in equal proportions. Steven Jobs was viewed within Apple as a reasonably competent computer technologist and a world class project guru. By contrast, Bill Gates has always been viewed as a world class software programmer and someone who inspired others by the sheer force of his technical genius and competitive drive.

### *Resourcing*

**Resourcing is** the ability to identify critical resource requirements, evaluate available internal and external sources, and negotiate the commitment (buy in) of resource suppliers and project participants to the project vision.

Effective project entrepreneurs are skilled in estimating the critical resource requirements for translating their project vision into a set of deliverable project outcomes. These skills draw upon the traditional project management tool kit for project planning and include creating a scope statement, a work breakdown structure, activity definition and sequencing, scheduling resource estimating, and budgeting. These are the tools needed to identify what resources are identified and when.

Project-based enterprises bring together participants who presumably supply complementary resources that combine to satisfy the resource requirements for the project vision. Evaluating prospective participants for their resource capabilities is an additional task for the project entrepreneur. The track record of prospective participants in working competently and cooperatively is conveyed both through their portfolio of completed projects and through word of mouth referral networks. Consequently, the successful project entrepreneur needs to be richly connected to the referral network of other project entrepreneurs and project managers.

Often, the project entrepreneur's own reputation becomes the magnet for attracting highly qualified personnel to a project. Project entrepreneurs who have successfully completed significant, cutting edge projects within their industry will themselves have an industry reputation that facilitates attracting high caliber talent. Alternatively, a project entrepreneur without an extensive track record may need to borrow on the reputation of project sponsors in order to recruit the best talent from throughout the industry.

Once having identified suitable resource suppliers, the project entrepreneur is next required to persuade the prospective partners to commit to the project vision (buy in) and to the terms and conditions for participating in the project. During these negotiations, the project entrepreneur may be asked to modify the project vision to accommodate specific agendas or professional perspective of key partners. Managing these negotiations is highly delicate. The entrepreneur runs the dual risk of either rigidly adhering to a personal project vision and hence losing valuable inputs or passively accepting each major partner's vision input, resulting in a compromise vision that is more politically correct than market focused. Hence, the skills with which the project entrepreneur negotiates with project supporters and participants is an essential requirement for resourcing a project.

### *Organizing*

Organizing is the ability to create a structure and culture that effectively organizes and utilizes available talent and mediates conflicts among project participants.

The creation of task boundaries and role and performance expectations for each project participant is an essential activity that the project entrepreneur must exercise at the onset of the project organizing process. Once participant roles are clearly defined it is possible for the project entrepreneur to utilize standard project management tools for tracking costs activity and milestone performance. These control activities are an essential component of project organizing. However, their implementation may be delegated by the project entrepreneur to other project managers.

Team building is an essential role for the project entrepreneur. Project participants must be made to feel that they are part of something more than their prescribed roles and defined tasks. The project entrepreneur should communicate to all project participants that they are significant contributors to a mission worthy of their talent and energies. Moreover, the project entrepreneur should create occasions to reinforce project members' emotional commitment to the project vision. In his study of great project teams, Warren Bennis (1997) found that all great groups believe that they are on a mission from God.

Even the most successful team building efforts will not prevent project participants from periodically engaging in heated disputes over project priorities and methods of addressing project requirements. Indeed, commitment to the project mission may exacerbate conflict among project participants who disagree over mission critical priorities. During these conflicts the project entrepreneur may be required to exercise mediating skills in dispute resolution. Quite often the disputes among project participants reflect principled differences among people with heterogeneous technical qualifications and roles in the project. In such circumstances, the project entrepreneur can assume a judicial perspective that is not partisan to the functional or technical specialties of the disputing parties and provide an impartial authoritative resolution of the conflict.

### *Sustaining*

Sustaining is the ability to sustain project participants' commitments and efforts toward the realization of the project entrepreneur's vision and to transfer the lessons of experience to future projects.

Sustaining the project entrepreneur's vision throughout the ebb and flow of each stage of project management is a critical role for the project entrepreneur. The project entrepreneur must keep all project participants focused on the prize and intervene whenever project setbacks or technical changes tempt project participants to compromise the vision. However, rigid adherence to a vision is a liability that the project entrepreneur must also avoid. Technical and market experience gained during the project should be incorporated into periodic reviews that may include a modification of the project's original vision. However, it is the responsibility of the project entrepreneur to insure that the vision is not compromised for the sake of political expediency.

An additional means of sustaining a project's original vision is to utilize the lessons learned from the project experience to inform the design and execution of a derivative project. This project may well exceed where the original project failed. Perhaps the classic example of this derivative project success was Apple company's technical and commercial market disappointment with the project to design the Lisa computer, which provided the foundations for the spectacular technical commercial success of the project that designed the MacIntosh computer. Hence, the project entrepreneur must be both a student of his project's success and failure and a teacher of the lessons learned to participants in subsequent projects that derive from the initial project.

The project entrepreneur has the opportunity to recruit all or some portion of the original project staff to work on derivative projects that extend the capabilities or market penetration of the original platform project. Some project teams have developed such competencies in working together on a particular type of project that experience curve considerations alone dictate using the same teams on derivative projects. In other cases, however, the stress of working together on a mission-critical project dictates the recruitment of fresh minds and bodies to rejuvenate the project team.

A continuing human resource role for the project entrepreneur is to assess the personal growth of key personnel on a project and to recommend the level of project responsibility and type of project challenge best suited to the person's skills and temperament. Hence the final role for the project entrepreneur is that of talent broker and employment referral agent for previous project partners. This type of employment referral thus contributes to the referral market upon which all project entrepreneurs utilize for staffing their projects with key project personnel.

## Career Implications of Project Entrepreneurship

The preceding summary of the project entrepreneur's role and skill requirements is premised on the belief that organizations will be facing increasing uncertainty regarding future paths to success. Those who can anticipate new opportunities for creating value, and who can transform perceived opportunity into an actionable project vision, will be the primary beneficiaries of what is becoming a project-based entrepreneurial economy.

However, project entrepreneurs also expose themselves to greater risk, which must be weighed against the prospective returns from project entrepreneurship. These risks arise from the requirement that project entrepreneurs challenge the established order. It is possible that the project entrepreneur's vision may imply the creative destruction or cannibalization of a current product, service, or business process. Under these circumstances, the project entrepreneur must anticipate resistance from colleagues who perceive their work priorities jeopardized by the proposed project vision. Should the project entrepreneur fail to create value, those who have resisted the change initiative may be in a position to block the entrepreneur's future opportunities for project initiatives.

As a result, the project entrepreneur's career is likely to resemble the self-employed consultant who moves from work setting to work setting in search of the next great opportunity. Career success is reflected in the portfolio of projects one has successfully competed rather than in tenure or rank within a single employment setting. Instead, the career challenge is to participate in projects of greater scope, innovativeness, and significance for the client organization. Her portfolio of past project contributions and the relations forged during those projects become the experience and network resources to be leveraged in securing new project opportunities. Moreover, her choice of projects reflects a conscious choice of paths for deepening or widening an accumulating set of project entrepreneurial and technical skills.

Project entrepreneurs are also likely to be the biggest beneficiaries of what Frank and Cook (1995) describe as a winner-take-all society in which economic and career rewards will be disproportionately skewed toward those who are the absolute best-in-class in their chosen specialties. Those project management practitioners who can envision and initiate value-creating projects will likely be the most desirable and best compensated members of the project management profession.

So how does one become a project entrepreneur? Based on previous research with project entrepreneurs in the film industry (Jones and DeFillippi 1996) the following six diagnostic questions can help in assessing whether you are directing your career towards becoming a project entrepreneur.

1. How am I developing my skill set within my current project assignments so as to qualify me for more entrepreneurial project opportunities? Am I creating a unique set of skills which might qualify me for initiating a project?

Technical skills in performing assigned project tasks will need to be complemented by the demonstration of project entrepreneurial skills. These skills must be utilized to contribute to one's current project responsibilities while signaling to project supervisors and external observers one's qualifications and aptitude for project entrepreneurship. Each project assignment thus becomes an opportunity to develop and demonstrate project entrepreneurial skills to project clients, superiors, and coworkers.

2. What industry trends do I foresee that might provide an opportunity to utilize my distinctive skill set as a project entrepreneur?

Continuous monitoring of industry trends is essential for identifying project opportunities for which you are most qualified to serve as project entrepreneur. The ebb and flow of demand for different types of project work must be synchronized with your availability to participate in these opportunities. Project entrepreneurs are always looking ahead to the next project opportunity. Moreover, project entrepreneurs view their current project as a platform for building skills and résumé experience that qualifies them for projects valuing such skills and experience.

3. Where can I obtain the opportunity to demonstrate entrepreneurial initiative on project assignments?

Seeking out project assignments that are somewhat ill-structured and leave room for creativity and initiative are most often the target of project entrepreneurs. A highly structured project assignment may provide an opportunity to demonstrate reliability and cost efficiency, but not necessarily the creative skills and leadership qualities of project entrepreneurship. Also, project assignments that entail high levels of market and technical challenge and uncertainty are more likely to provide opportunities for demonstrating project entrepreneurship. These projects also have the highest risks of project failure.

4. Who can I enlist into a support network to advise, mentor, and sponsor my project entrepreneurial career?

Every project assignment provides an opportunity for creating or deepening work relations with coworkers, superiors, and clients. Those relations which prove most durable and mutually respectful are the best candidates for being recruited into your personal career support system. No one person is likely to provide all your career-relevant support needs. Moreover, it is risky to depend upon a single individual for career support, no matter how highly placed or sympathetic he is to your career aspirations. Reputations are built by developing an expanding and diverse circle of project work acquaintances who can assist you in different facets of your project entrepreneurial work.

5. When should I should I say yes to project opportunities and when should I say no to project opportunities based on their advancing my project entrepreneurial career? Can I avoid the career trap of staying fully employed within a technical comfort zone that provides no opportunity for project entrepreneurship?

A project entrepreneurial career is likely to involve a series of transitions through different stages of project responsibility. A continuing career challenge is your determination of when you have sufficiently mastered a particular level of project responsibility in order to seek a project assignment of greater challenge and opportunity. People in all careers are stuck in comfort zones and get typecast by their coworkers and superiors as fitting into a particular role and level of responsibility. Each advance in your project entrepreneurial career requires you to leave the comfort zone of mastery and to become a novice in one or more facets of your new project assignment. Presumably every project assignment significantly utilizes those skills you have mastered so that you may selectively learn new skills without jeopardizing the overall success of the project. One cost of seeking more challenging project assignments is the possibility of being unemployed for longer periods between project assignments than would be the case if you stayed within your comfort zone of project roles and responsibilities.

6. Why do I want to be a project entrepreneur? Do I have the desire to be independent and self-directed in my project career? Am I willing to accept the career risks and uncertainty associated with such a career path? Are my family and closest friends supportive of my career goals?

Project entrepreneurship is not a career choice of convenience. All entrepreneurs face considerable uncertainties and risks in their careers. These risks include much greater reputation risk due to the greater visibility of their contributions to a project's success or failure. Additionally, project entrepreneurs face greater financial risks should an unsuccessful project outcome result in a period of unemployment or should the project entrepreneur voluntarily hold out for projects that provide greater opportunity. Even when fully employed, the project entrepreneur is likely to be so driven and consumed by her project responsibilities that family and loved ones may suffer neglect. Hence, the choice of a project entrepreneurial career is a lifestyle choice that must be fully understood and supported by one's significant others so that the natural tensions and uncertainties of project entrepreneurship can be anticipated.

In summary, the project entrepreneurial role is more than an extension of the body of knowledge of the project manager (Project Management Institute 1996). The primary defining characteristic of the project entrepreneurial role is the entrepreneurial career orientation that underlies the skill set that project entrepreneurs exercise. Although it is possible for project managers to learn the skills of the project entrepreneur, it is necessary for project managers to discover and cultivate the values and aspirations that define an entrepreneurial role within project-based enterprise and an entrepreneurial career within the project-management profession.

## References


Bennis, Warren. 1997. *Organizing Genius: The Secrets of Creative Collaboration*. Reading, MA: Addison-Wesley.

Ellis, Phillip D. 1996. "The Virtual Project Manager Project." Management Institute 27th Annual Seminar/Symposium. Boston, MA.

Frank, Robert H., and Philip J. Cook. 1995. *The Winner-Take-All Society*. New York: The Free Press.

Gorman, Tom. 1996. *Multipreneuring*. New York: Fireside.

Jones, Candace, and Robert J. DeFillippi. 1996. "Back to the Future in Film: Combining Industry and Self-Knowledge to meet the Career Challenges of the 21st Century." *Academy of Management Executive* 10 (41): 89–103.

Ono, Dan. 1996. "The Project Manager in the Virtual Work Place of the Future Project." Project Management Institute 27th Annual Seminar/Symposium. Boston, MA.

Peters, Tom. 1992. *Liberation Management*. New York: Ballantine Books.

Project Management Institute. 1996. *A Guide to the Project Management Body of Knowledge (PMBOK Guide)*. Upper Darby PA: Project Management Institute.

# Integrated Project Delivery and Management for the Next Century

Mark W. Kiker, Holmes & Narver Inc.

Project management, document control, and communication in the next century will be quite different from the tools you use today.

Using tools developed for the Internet and the World Wide Web, we have created Intranet Program Management. Intranet Program Management is a system that uses "off the shelf" programs such as Microsoft Internet Explorer or Netscape Navigator to create a program management system that is:

- FAST—because it is based on Internet technology. Speed is of utmost importance in delivering on-line information such as CADD drawings, schedules, O&M manuals, project correspondence, cost estimates, specifications, building permits, and other documents to the desktop (see Exhibit 1).
- FRIENDLY—Using WEB browsers makes IPM the most user-friendly interface developed.
- FLEXIBLE—IPM can be tailored to fit any program, project, or methodology. It fits the way you work; you are not forced to follow someone's preconceived idea of how to manage your program.
- FREE—(almost) to the end user. Most browsers are very low cost or free. Most of the needed plug-ins can be downloaded and run for free.
- FUTURE Oriented—Since IPM is based on Internet technology, as the WEB advances, so does IPM. You will no longer be outdated by progress in the computer industry. We put all that technology to work for you.

## Features of IPM

- Web-based information access
- Utilizes industry standard Web browsers
    - Netscape Navigator
    - Microsoft Internet Explorer
- Rapid information retrieval
- Read and print electronic documents produced by any standard software
- Limited hardware requirements

**Exhibit 1.**

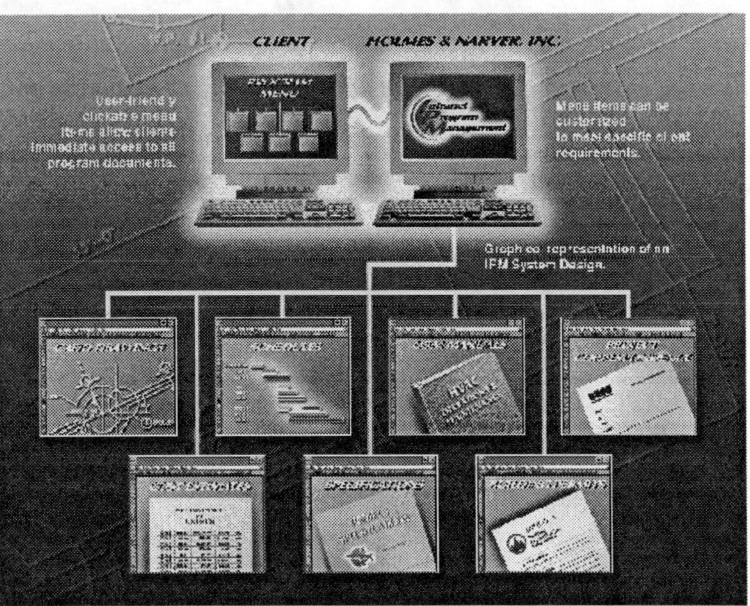

**Exhibit 2.**

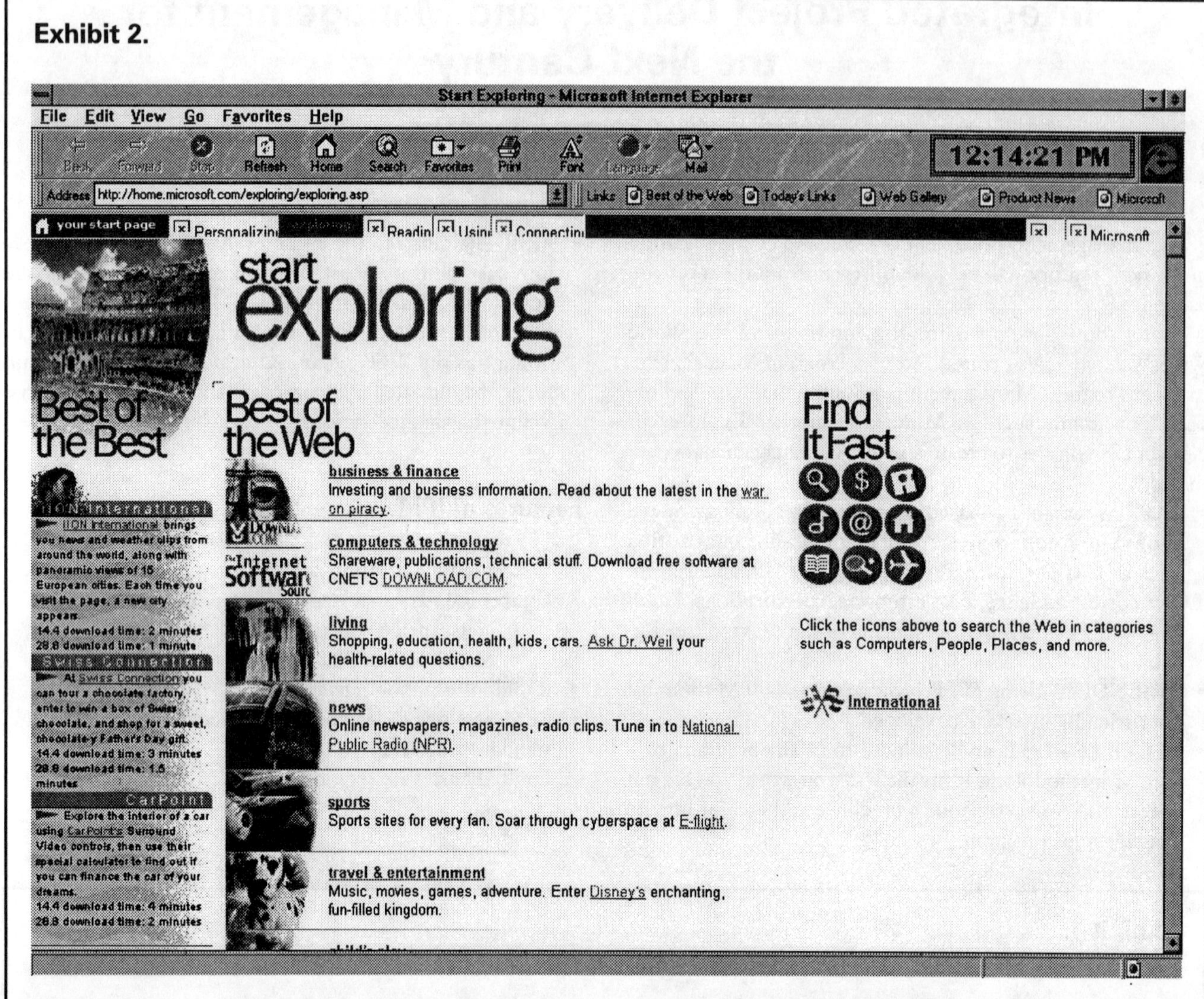


## What is IPM?

Intranet Program Management (IPM) provides Web search engine capabilities to locate specific data across the complete business information landscape, regardless of hardware or software platform.

- Wide and local area networks (WAN/LAN)
- Web browsers
- Graphic viewers
- E-mail connectivity
- Databases
- Applications
- Documents
- Archives

## What Can Be Tracked with IPM? (See Exhibit 3)

1. **Strategic management**
   - Corporate mission
   - Future business trends
   - Future occupancy trends
   - Corporate goals and objectives
   - Corporate strategy
2. **Design**
   - CADD drawings
     - AutoCAD—WHIP Driver
     - Microstation—CGM or ModelServer Publisher
   - Specifications
   - Correspondence
   - Review and approvals
   - Bid process management
   - Cost estimating

**Exhibit 3.**

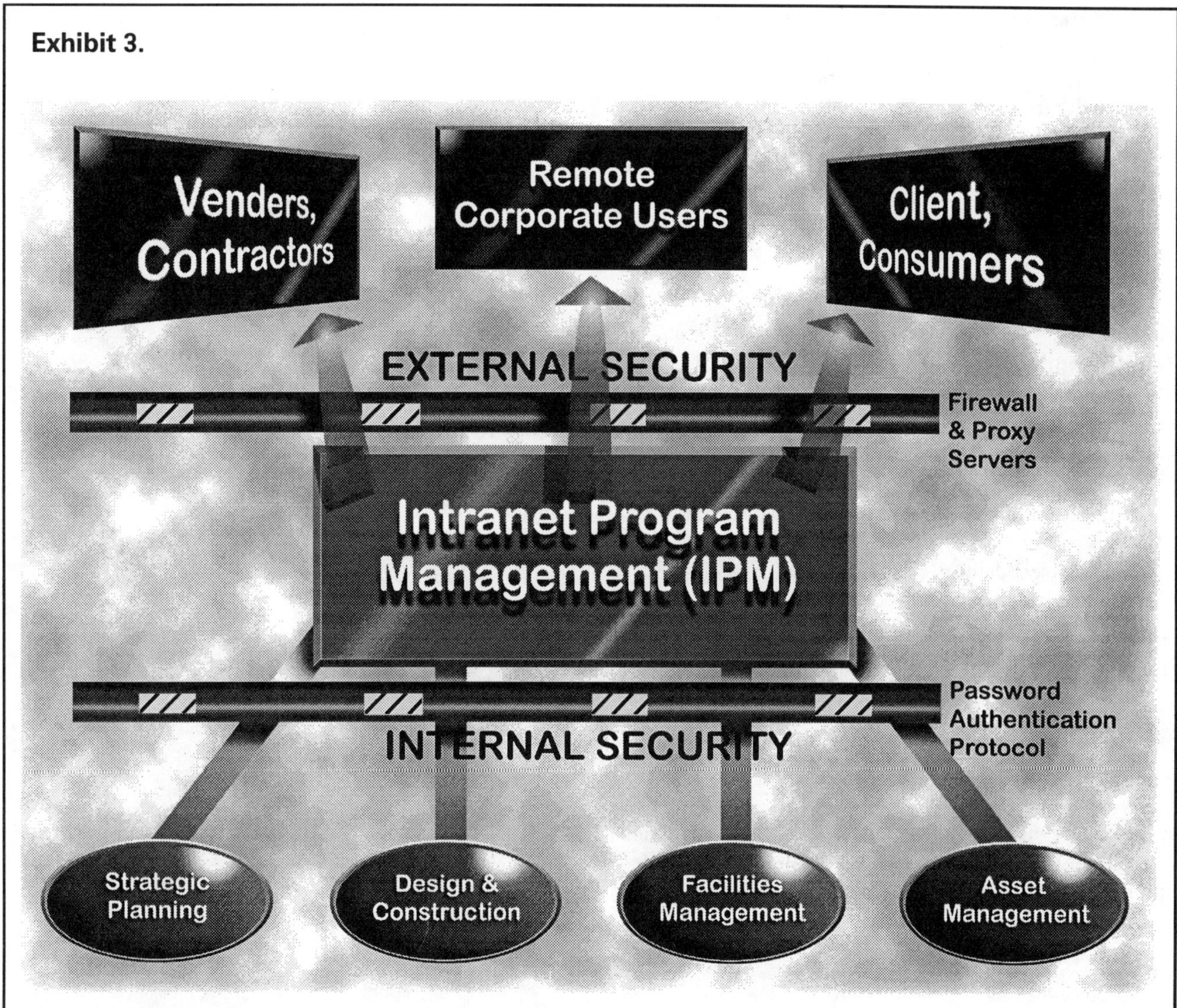


- Contract documents
- Construction site management
- Digital photos—GIF, JPEG
- Schedules—PDFs

3. **Facilities Management**
   - Furniture, fixtures, and equipment (FF&E) inventory control
   - Maintenance, preventative maintenance activity
   - Trouble call response
   - Building standards
   - Churn management
   - Building and systems management
4. **Internal Administration**
   - Scope of work
   - Basis of design
   - Forms
   - Job opportunities
   - Time sheets

## Why Use IPM?

- Universal access to data unimpeded by:
  - Document variety
  - Application variety
  - Operating systems and hardware differences between computers
- Remote access needs
- Documents can be viewed and printed, but not modified

## IPM Implementation Considerations

1. Determine client hardware configuration
2. Standardize user access via one browser
3. Identify desired features
4. Decide on data access methods (search, query, and index)
5. Outline database functionality
6. Select Web presentation quality and graphic interface
7. Determine user community and access
8. Define levels of security

## Benefits and Advantages

- Uniform ease of access to data
- Platform independence
- Rapid, content-centered information retrieval
- On-line document review and approvals save time and money
- Reduce project delivery cycle time
- Simplified start-up
- Reduce software licensing costs
- Customize data access and storage by geography, project type, organizational function

## Archival Issues

At the end of the project you can press all the information onto CD-ROM. No more room full of file cabinets stuffed with hard-copy documents. You can then browse the CD just as you would browse the Internet.

# Being a Project Leader: Knowing When to Lead, When to Manage, and When to Fold—A Model for Creating Excellence in Projects

Lee A. Peters, M.S.C.E., P.E., Peters & Co.

Leadership is the critical success factor for project excellence. The temporal nature of projects creates a challenging environment for project leaders. Leading requires knowing what is leadership and what is not. High performance project managers and project teams must move in multiple dimensions; only one is leadership, much like time travelers. These travel dimensions are: technical (the knowledge), organizational (the team), management (the resources), and leadership (the soul). The astute teams know what skill set is required by the issue at hand.

Project teams who are leaders will add value to a project in a thousand ways. To add value and have impact, these leaders need to know what and how to influence the project and the issues at hand. A leadership model was developed to understand and teach project leadership. It teaches what it is and what it is not!

The leadership model is based on an earlier achievement model (see Exhibit 1).

Exhibit 1.

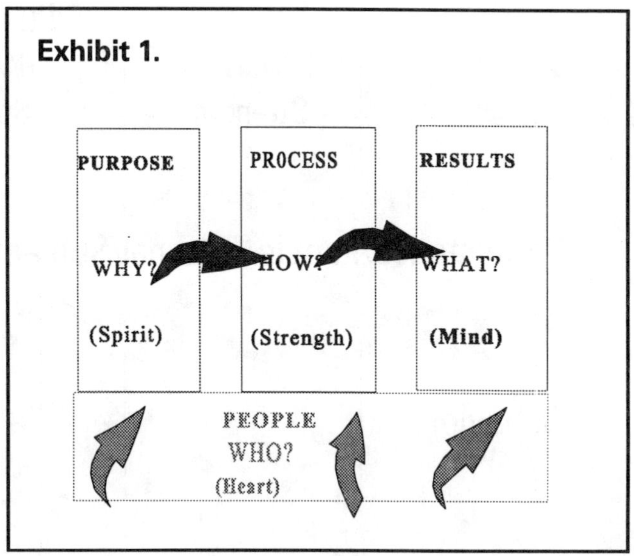


This converts to a one dimensional leadership model (see Exhibit 2).

Exhibit 2.

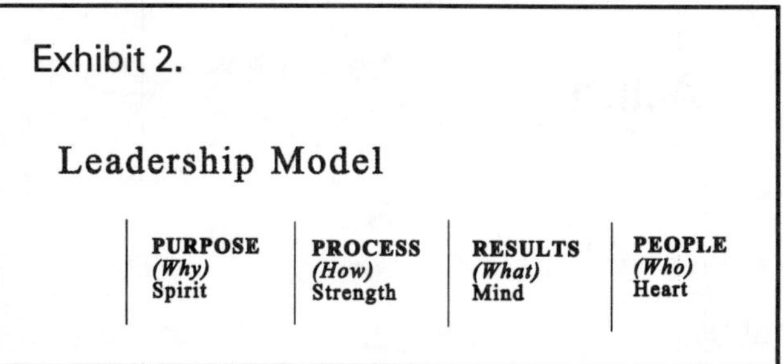


The model is centered on actions with external and internal behaviors that generate more action with the key areas for mission evolved (see Exhibit 3).

The model suggests that eight behaviors comprise the skill set for each dimension (technical, management, organization, and leadership): four internal/objective/personal and four external/subjective/people actions. The two-by-four grid can be quickly edited and discussed by project teams to aid in planning the project plan, to build powerful project processes, and to diagnose project problems (see Exhibit 4).

The same model must be placed on each of the other dimensions (technical, organizational, and management) to build the insight for when and when not to lead (see Exhibits 5, 6, and 7).

One fallacy of our thought pattern is that leadership is singular. Leadership does not reside in a single individual on a project team. The team can use this model to both plan for leadership action and for self (meaning the team) evaluation.

The model makes leadership teachable. In simulations, each person can be hatted with a specific leadership role. As they experience that role, they learn ways to lead. The players will demonstrate both internal and external actions. We also use a learning coach, who gives feedback, in the simulations. Each role is played over four to six hours during three different simulations.

Using this model, leadership can be compared and contrasted to the other dimensions. It can clearly be differentiated from management, which many people believe to be leadership. Leadership for a project can then be planned, implemented, and measured.

Project leaders can use the model to identify and define the issues of project execution; analyze and develop solutions; then implement quality improvements in the project processes, systems, and metrics. Leadership skills will lift the project teams to the level of project shamans—the project mystics who know when to take the proper action.

exhibit 3.

## Leadership Model

| | Process (How) Strength | Purpose (Why) Spirit | Results (What) Mind | People (Who) Heart |
|---|---|---|---|---|
| **Participative/People/External/Subjective** | | | | |
| Behavior | | | | |
| Action | | | | |
| Behavior | | | | |
| **Analytical/Task/Internal/Objective** | | | | |

**Exhibit 4.**

## Leading—The Way*

| | Process *(How)* Strength | Purpose *(Why)* Spirit | Results *(What)* Mind | People *(Who)* Heart |
|---|---|---|---|---|

**Participative/People/External/Subjective**

| | | | | |
|---|---|---|---|---|
| Behavior | Paint the Picture | Search for Limits | Challenge the Process | Celebrate Victory |
| Action | Imprint the Vision | Enable Teams to Act | Ever Improve Success | Instill Courage |
| Behavior | See the Possible | Risk Action | Value Learning | Be the Model |

**Analytical/Task/Internal/Objective**

* Adapted from Kouzes, James M.; Posner, Barry Z.; The Leadership Challenge; Jossey-Bass Publisher; 1987

**Exhibit 5.**

# Managing—The Systems

| Process *(How)* Soul | Purpose *(Why)* Strength | Results *(What)* Mind | People *(Who)* Heart |
|---|---|---|---|
| Describe the Achievable Outcomes | Plan • Methods • Materials • Tools • Equipment • Information | Negotiate Resources | Identify Required • Knowledge • Skill • Attitude |
| Transform the Concept into Achievable Outcomes | Build Methods | Operate Methods | Build Technical/ Administrative Skills |
| See How to Produce the Result | Measure Methods | Resolve Problems | Know Future Needs for Tools, Skills, Attitudes |

Peter & Company 1996

**Exhibit 6.**

## Organizing—The Team

| Process *(How)* Soul | Purpose *(Why)* Strength | Results *(What)* Mind | People *(Who)* Heart |
|---|---|---|---|
| Negotiate Permission Power Protection Positions | Plan Structure and Team Processes | Empower Team with Authority and Responsibility | Relate to Stakeholders |
| Charter the Team | Build the Team Process | Operate the Team Process | Build Relationships |
| See the Team Possiblities | Measure the Team Process | Resolve Conflict | Anticipate Evolving Relationships |

**Exhibit 7.**

## Managing—The Systems

| Process *(How)* Soul | Purpose *(Why)* Strength | Results *(What)* Mind | People *(Who)* Heart |
|---|---|---|---|

Participative/People/External/Subjective

| | | | |
|---|---|---|---|
| Negotiate Scope, Boundaries, Authority | Plan the Means and Management | Resolve Resources | Know the Customer |
| Establish the Mission | Build the Project Process | Operate the Project Management Process | Satisfy the Customer |
| See the Project Possiblities | Measure the Project Process | Review the Risk | Know Future Needs |

Analytical/Task/Internal/Objective

**Exhibit 8.**

## A project team will ask . . .

1. What is the vision?
2. How do we communicate that vision?
3. When will we know the vision is imprinted on all players?
4. What limits our action?
5. How do we remove the restrictive limits/
6. What do we need—Knowledge, skill, attitudes, processes, tools—to act?
7. What is possible in success? Just how good can it be?
8. How do we improve processes to stretch the envelope of success?
9. What do we need to learn . . .
   - individually, as a team, organizationally?
   - to stretch the envelope of success?
10. What courage do all of the players need? What will instill that courage?
11. How do we model bravery?
12. In what ways will we celebrate, recognize, and reward victory?

# The Project Team of Tomorrow

Jeffery Blanton, Chiron Vision

## Introduction

As business heads into the new millennium, both company and employee needs are going to change. For business, the need for managing the rapid rate of change is only going to increase. John P. Kotter sums it up in his book, *Leading Change*: "A globalized economy is creating both more hazards and more opportunities for everyone, forcing firms to make dramatic improvements not only to compete and prosper but also merely to survive. Globalization, in turn, is being driven by a broad and powerful set of forces associated with technological change, international economic integration, domestic market maturation within the more developed countries, and the collapse of worldwide communism" (1996). From the employees' perspective, people will be looking for more of a sense of purpose. Herman Miller asked the question in Peter Senge's *The Fifth Discipline*: "Why can't work be one of those wonderful things in life? Why can't we cherish and praise it, versus seeing work as a necessity? Why can't it be a cornerstone in people's life-long process of developing ethics, values, and in expressing the humanities and the arts" (1990)?

The win-win answer to this dilemma will be the "high performance team" (HPT). The HPT can create the environment to take the worker's effort beyond just doing the job to a very powerful life changing experience. The results for the business will be beyond anyone's expectations. So the combination of personal desire and business necessity will make the HPT the norm rather then the rarity for the companies that survive in the new millennium.

Today, the HPT is more of an aberration that happens by chance versus a planned event. Why has the HPT been so elusive, and what do we now know today about teams to help facilitate HPT in the future? This paper will explore some of the work that can be done by management and the project leader to help facilitate a HPT.

## Definition

First, we need to understand the difference between a performing and a high performing team. John Katezenbach in his book, "*The Wisdom of Teams*," describes a performing team as "a small number of people with complementary skills who are equally committed to a common purpose, goals, and working approach for which they hold themselves mutually accountable" (1993). In today's environment, business is overjoyed when this level of performance can be obtained. Actual true work is being done against the plan. On rare occasions, something magical occurs resulting in a high performing team. The difference, as described by Katzenback, is that *"members are deeply committed to another's personal growth and success.* That commitment usually transcends the team. The HPT significantly outperforms all other like teams, and outperforms all reasonable expectations given its membership." For the team members, the project has become personal.

Teams go through four distinct phases. HPT represents the fourth phase in the team development. These four phases must be done in succession. Teams will find a million ways to remain trapped in a phase or to digress back into earlier phases. Although achieving HPT is clearly more luck or art today then science, many things can be done in earlier phases to promote HPT.

## The Phases

The first phase is "the floundering phase." Team members are concerned about their individual situations rather than the goals of the team. The individual wants to know how this project will effect them. Is the nature of the work going to be of personal interest to them? Based on past experience, is the current make up of the team consisting of members they like and have worked well with in the past? Does this project appear to allow career growth, or will it be career limiting? How does this project fit with their personal goals? Do they really have time to participate on this team, relative to all the other current projects on their plate? For each team member, these and many more questions must be internalized and answered to move successfully forward into the next phase.

To successfully create a HPT, management must realize these concerns will occur and they must be dealt with. Today, management recognizes only one of the two critical criteria in selecting team members. What are the correct technical skills and who matches these requirements? A well defined job description, by position, can be matched to the proper technical skills, relative to academic and professional experience. The second, and much more difficult, is matching the position to the potential team member whose personal desires will be met by the project. Peter Senge's book, *The Fifth Discipline*, describes the need for individuals to develop a personal vision. This personal vision creates the connection between work and the true aspirations of the employee. The company, if necessary, must help to facilitate the development of this vision. Based on the understanding of this vision by management, prospective team members can be identified for their personal desires, as well as their technical skills. In addition, this understanding will allow the team leader, or company management, to help sell the preliminary project vision, relative to the prospective team member's personal vision. This can help to expedite the entire process of working through this floundering phase achieving stronger commitment quicker. The team will not progress to Phase II until the majority of the team members have reached this personal acceptance towards the project. In some cases, even one team member can keep the whole team from moving forward or can cause the team to fall back a phase.

The second phase is the "conflict phase." Team members have individually committed to the project based on personal reasons, but a common vision for the team must be developed. In project management terms, the end result would be a very clearly defined scope statement and project plan. To create the foundation for HPT, the process must become personal. The personal visions must become a shared vision for the team. In *The Fifth Discipline*, Senge discusses the power of a shared vision "in a corporation, as shared vision changes people's relationship with the company. It is no longer 'Their company;' it becomes 'our company.' A shared vision is the first step in allowing people who mistrust each other to begin to work together. It creates a common identity. In fact, an organization's shared sense of purpose, vision, and operating values establish the most basic level of commonality. In exceptional teams, the task is no longer separate from the self... but rather he identified with the task so strongly that you couldn't define his real self without including that task."

Developing the common vision certainly will vary greatly based on team make-up and the magnitude of the project. For a very experienced team, with team members who are very familiar with each other and have achieved high performance on prior teams, the scope and planning process can start almost immediately. For a team with many new members, members from teams coming from challenged teams, or high profile critical projects to the business, considerable time and effort should be taken to develop the shared vision.

The shared vision development process goes well beyond the average half-day kick-off meeting. In many cases, highly trained professionals need to be employed to help facilitate this process. A very dynamic interactive environment must be created requiring the team members to depend on each other for group success while individually being put into a position of vulnerability. If facilitated properly, the team will come away with a very strong common bond. In sports, this environment is often seen in the early preseason practices with grueling physical, two-a-day practices in sweltering heat for the betterment of the team. Professionally, I was involved with a four-day wilderness experience that was used for a challenged team prior to the last phase of the project. Even though this team had been together for a long time and met socially, this experience created a bond and an energy that directly resulted in converting a challenged team to a HPT.

Regardless of the exercise, the goal is to reach the personal level among the team members. The normal scope and the planning process will follow conventional methods, but the dynamics of the team should allow for much more creative thinking and an ironclad team commitment.

The team is now ready for phase three, "the productive team." The plan has been established and the project is being executed. Actual work and progress is being made against the project objectives. This is clearly the goal of all project teams.

With all the preparation work done in the first two phases, will the team move from phase three, productive, to phase four, high performing? There are several additional actions management can take based on past experience to help the team. Collocation of members is critical. This will help to maintain the bond and force the interaction between the team members. It will also help to facilitate communication. The Japanese office style—no offices—can also be used to help enhance impromptu communication. The size of the team or the core team is also important. Membership should be around five to ten, with an ideal size of about seven. For larger teams, the focus should be on creating a HPT for the full-time members. For real large teams, the management should try and create pockets of HPT on the sub-teams. Even if the top level team is a performing team, HPTs can exist throughout the team. Ideally, the HPT effort would be on critical path efforts.

One of the most critical issues for all phases, and even more important during the productive and HPT phase, will be the internal and external leadership. Management must allow the team to determine its own direction and hold the team accountable for its results. The power that responsibility and accountability creates will only work to reinforce the team's internal bonds as the team's success can only be achieved by the success of each of its individual members.

The initial scope will provide a well-defined target and destination for the team, but the team also will need very clear ongoing measurements. These measurement feedback loops must be as real time as possible to give immediate feedback of failures and success to allow for ongoing course adjustments. It is also important to recognize the ongoing successes. Wins produce confidence and provide motivation to the team. This will be very important for teams truly being held accountable for their actions. The confidence generated will also promote bolder and more creative steps by the team, which is the trademark of HPT.

## Conclusion

For any individual who has been lucky enough to participate on a high performing team sometime in her career, you will see the immediate excitement generated in her voice and actions when she talks about the experience. She will describe the fun she had, the amazing challenges she undertook, and how she created deep personal relationships with other team members that will last a lifetime. After having this experience, all other teams pale by comparison, and there will always be the constant search for this level of performance in future teams. As individuals continue to progress from the mundane machine-type mentality of work, they will demand this level of excitement and personal satisfaction from their jobs. The companies that are able to create this environment will attract the best employees and will be rewarded with the results that will make them leaders in their industry. The opportunity and results that high performing teams can generate is unlimited and will take business to heights in the new millennium that cannot even be imagined today.

### References


Kotter, John. 1996. *Leading Change*. United States: Harvard Business School Press.

Senge, Peter. 1990. *The Fifth Discipline*. New York: Currency Doubleday.

Katzenbach, Jon. 1993. *The Wisdom Of Teams*. New York: McKinsey & Company.

# Bellcore's Project Management Center of Excellence:How to Successfully Implement Project Management Within a Company

Carol Rauh, Ph.D., PMP, Bellcore

## Introduction

Business forecasters are predicting a business environment in the twenty-first century that will demand project management for companies to survive. Some characteristics of the twenty-first century environment that make project management essential are:

- Increased competition: It will be critical for companies to be lean and efficient to stay competitive.
- Compression of time: Tasks will have to be accomplished in a much shorter amount of time.
- Risk management: The volatile business climate will require sophisticated risk management skills.
- New organizational structures: Organizations will be flat, small teams will be spread around the world, and performance will be measured based on the results of the team.
- Learning organizations: Companies will need a complete understanding of the complexity of systems. More time will be spent on internal communication to obtain necessary buy-in. Project managers will need to know, globally, who their stakeholders are, and communications management will increase in complexity.
- Networked organizations: Companies will function through outsourcing, strategic alliances, and close interactions with customers and suppliers. For integrated project solutions to succeed, project plans must cover third parties, and an overall project manager with responsibility for the entire solution must be named.
- Information technology based: Companies' IT products and networks will be integrated with those of their partners and customers.

Each of these challenges can be directly addressed by the various methods of the project management discipline. Keeping a company lean and mean to meet increased competition requires that resource utilization be optimized using resource management and leveling techniques. With less time available for task performance, project scheduling techniques, along with sound resource management, will become essential. Sophisticated risk management techniques have been available through the project management discipline for years and will increase in use to minimize company's risk exposure and increase profitability. Increased teaming, particularly with teams that are distributed globally, will mandate exceptional project communications as well as planning, monitoring, and control. With distributed teams and the increased need for communication, more time will be required for identifying stakeholders and obtaining their buy-in. The "soft" skills of project management (leadership, influence, negotiation, and political savvy) will continue to increase in their importance to project success. Networked organizations will introduce complexity in that not only must internal production be managed, but also the work of external organizations as well. This climate demands rigorous use of a wide variety of project management methods to ensure that the project is well integrated across all involved parties and that deliverables are completed on time, within budget, and with quality.

The project management discipline had been looked at by various local organizations within Bellcore (Bell Communications Research, Inc.) since the late eighties. In 1994, Bellcore initiated a corporate-wide effort to look at what was needed corporately to meet the challenges approaching with the twenty-first century. One recommendation was to implement a more rigorous approach to project management throughout the company. Project management certification training was instituted. Recognizing that training alone would not suffice, because students would return to work environments which might not have yet embraced the project management methods, Bellcore established the Project Management Center of Excellence (PMCOE) to operationalize use of these state-of-the-art methods consistently throughout the company.

This paper describes how the PMCOE has implemented project management and will present recommendations. These recommendations are based on our real-life experiences over the last three years, incorporating many of our lessons learned.

## Organizational Structure

Bellcore was created in 1983 during divestiture, when long-distance telecommunications services were split from local telecommunications services in the breakup of AT&T. Bellcore has been the provider of software, consulting, engineering, and research to the seven regional telephone companies (Bell Atlantic, US WEST, Ameritech, and so on) since that time and, in the last several years, has grown its customer base to over 800 customers in various markets.

Bellcore is organized into three strategic business units (SBUs) and Customer Solutions, which is the customer-facing organization (sales, marketing, customer services). The three SBUs are Software Systems, which develops large, complex software solutions to support customer operations; Professional Services, which provides telephone network consulting, engineering, integration, and learning support services; and Applied Research, which conducts leading-edge technology research to support the evolution of the network and the software that supports it.

The PMCOE was put in place to work with project managers and SBUs to embed the use of the project management discipline into the business. It is currently staffed by a director, three project management consultants, and an administrative assistant. The certification training is provided through Bellcore's education, training, and development (ET&D) organization.

## Project Management Certification and Training

Project management certification training was set up in fall 1994 and the first class of students—the advanced class—completed a one-week accelerated program in December and took the PMI exam in June 1995. Our standard certification training began in January 1995 and consisted of twenty-one training days with a three- or five-day course held about every other month. Over time, the number of training days was compressed by condensing the courses, and, to reduce in-classroom time even further, two courses were migrated to CD-ROM, to be taken at a student's convenience. Our current pass rate on the exam is 75 percent.

## Process And Tools

The first thing the PMCOE did was to create a project management methodology for the company. The process was defined by taking materials from *A Guide to the Project Management Body of Knowledge (PMBOK Guide)* as being taught in the certification training and folding them into other corporate processes, such as the sales process and Software Systems' quality method of operation (QMO). This gave project managers and others a resource for understanding where in the existing processes the project management methods should be used. To support the methodology, a series of templates and tools were developed. They are as follows.

### The Project Plan Template and Job Aid

These are "ready to use" formats that can be pulled down from our server onto a project manager's work station to serve as a first iteration of her project plan. Each section within the template and job aid contains "memory joggers" for the project manager to consider in preparing their plan. For example, under the scope section, project managers are prompted to consider the limits or boundaries of the project; what we will and will not do; what the customer will do or provide; and any known timeframes that the customer or third parties need to meet. Project managers, particularly those new on the job, have found this focuses their thinking, facilitates planning with their teams, and reduces overall time spent on their planning effort.

### The Quantitative Risk Assessment and Mitigation Tool

The risk tool guides project managers to identify the business, project/contract, technical, cost, and schedule risks, quantify their impact and probability, plan and cost a mitigation strategy, and calculate management (hard and soft) reserves. Like the project plan tools, the risk tool is stored on the server and can be copied onto a project manager's workstation to provide the first iteration. Again, "memory joggers" are provided (e.g., what risk events could occur due to: use of new or leading-edge technology? ambiguous specifications? changing customer needs? changing market conditions?). This tool has evolved over time from one that initially introduced more structure into the risk management process into the quantitative tool that is being implemented today. Use of the tool—both in its original and current format—has substantially increased awareness of the importance of risk management, broadened risk management from a technical exercise to one which considers the full project context, and reduces the overall effort spent on risk management.

### Guidelines for Determining Level of Project Management Support

The guidelines assist in determining what job classification level a project manager should be, the percent of time the project manager should be assigned, and, for large projects, the size of the project office. Using a matrix, the project manager rates the project based on factors that influence the level of project management needed on the project, such as:

- Strategic importance of the project to the customer
- Strategic importance to Bellcore
- Contract value
- Project complexity.

The score calculated from the factor ratings determines the job classification level. The size and complexity of the project determine the percent of time (a qualitative judgement). To size the project office, these factors are considered in addition to the customer's expectations of the project manager and the type of relationship building required. Like the project plan and risk tools, the guidelines are available on our server.

### Standard Microsoft Project Templates

Since the process of managing and building software releases is fairly consistent across our product lines and from release to release, standard work breakdown structures were created and entered into Microsoft Project, which has been our historic software tool. This enables project managers to have a standard to work from, while permitting modifications based on local practices. The templates are based on the Software Systems' SBU's quality method of operation (QMO), our method for building software projects which has earned us ISO 9000 and SEI/CMM Level 3 certifications. Standard templates were developed for a number of functions; for example, for:

- Project management
- Systems development
- Product deployment
- Learning services
- Documentation.

### Tutorials

Several tutorials were developed and have been used in a variety of ways. The tutorials are Microsoft PowerPoint presentations with full notes. They are used as "canned" presentations, which can be given in full or modified to fit a shorter time slot. Although not originally intended to be used this way, people have also used them as self-study "courses." Our current tutorials are:

- Project management tools and techniques
- Project management overview
- Risk management at Bellcore
- How to build a resource loaded network.

In addition to the benefits for project managers, a benefit to the PMCOE is that the material is "ready to go" so that extensive preparation is not required each time a tutorial is given. As we continue with project management implementation, additional tutorials will be prepared. The tutorials are also located on our server.

### Roles and Responsibilities Matrix

Another guide we prepared early on was a roles and responsibilities matrix. Because initially there were questions about how the project manager function fit with other functions, particularly the line manager, the roles and responsibilities for project managers and other functions that interface with them were defined and communicated. This matrix has resulted in a clearer division of labor between functional organizations, with the benefit of avoiding duplication of effort, avoiding gaps, and saving resources that had been spent negotiating who does what.

## PMCOE Approach to Implementation

Senior management support is critical to project management implementation, and we were fortunate to have the support of our CEO and officers. When the project management effort was announced in late 1994, several live company-wide video broadcasts were held. The CEO and officers discussed the importance of the effort to the business plans for moving forward. This was followed by the PMCOE director meeting with each senior manager individually to discuss the effort and identify their concerns. The next series of meetings were one-on-one meetings with middle managers in whose organizations project managers resided, as well as by interactive meetings with members of their departments.

A team structure was used to rollout the methodology and tools. Teams were formed in both Software Systems and Professional Services In Applied Research, a much smaller organization, and we worked through a single point of contact. The teams consisted of a representative from each business unit (BU) within the SBU. Two PMCOE consultants were assigned to work one-on-one with sets of BUs within Software Systems. One PMCOE consultant was assigned to the Professional Services team (reflecting that Professional Services adopted a centralized approach to implementation). Each consultant provided full-range support based on the needs of the SBU/BU.

The PMCOE offered and continues to provide consulting services on how organizations can embed project management into their business operations, definition of implementation strategies, and plans. These were conducted through customized workshops, small group mentoring (one-on-one mentoring was offered early on, but was not resource effective), and assistance with resolving implementation issues.

Implementation activities typically began with a team meeting discussing the importance of project management, identifying team members' organizational needs and concerns, and describing the services that PMCOE could provide. In many cases, the initial PMCOE service requested was to define, develop, and facilitate a planning workshop based on a specific project for which the BU needed a project plan. Workshops were generally limited to about twenty-five to thirty people to allow for breakout groups and readouts. Where an organization wanted a shorter workshop, materials were designed to require extensive interaction with participants. When time did not permit a workshop, "walk throughs" were done, taking a small group of participants through a flow chart of the project management process and providing an understanding of the tools. We found this to be a shorter, yet effective, substitute. Once knowledge about the process and tools was imparted, we worked with the organization to define and carry out the next steps for ensuring that project management would take hold.

Many times, it was evident that existing processes and cultural issues had to be addressed because they were preventing project managers from doing project management. Organizations had their own ways of operating that had served them well in the past and did not understand why they should do things differently, particularly when, they perceived, it would cost them more money to do so. For example, one primary challenge was the need to bring on board more project managers, because often project managers were carrying a heavy project load and had no time to use the tools. To address this issue, each BU was asked to identify how many additional project managers were needed based on using the tools. On an ongoing basis, the right amount of project manager costs is being put into our cost estimates for new proposals (using our guidelines for determining the level of project management support). Organizations are also continuing to find creative ways to add more project manager resources to existing work, when and where needed, while not impacting overall costs.

Other types of sessions that we have found to be very effective are regular meetings with project managers within specific BUs to discuss the tools and delineate roles and responsibilities. For example, since Software Systems' QMO requires that both a release plan and project plan be written, there were many questions about why both are needed, and which is needed when. We worked with teams of project managers and release managers to define guidelines specifying which projects require both and which require just a release plan.

We also hold periodic user groups, forums, and special events. Our Microsoft Project user group met bimonthly, and our quarterly project managers forums featured topics such as enhancing customer focus, capturing lessons learned, and the latest policy changes impacting project management. We have also brought in guest speakers like Dr. Harold Kerzner.

## Implementation Challenges

Organizational change is never easy because it is hard to give up the old way of doing things. We encountered a number of implementation challenges, of which the following is a brief snapshot.

There was a great deal of resistance to changing current practices. To navigate the resistance, we benchmarked the project management practices of peer and competitor companies and communicated this information widely. This was very effective, particularly when presented in terms of how customers would view our practices compared to key competitors when selecting vendors. Extracting data from internal win/loss reviews relative to project management was also useful (e.g., the project was won because of strong project management or lost for lack thereof).

Frequently, we were asked for quantitative data on the impact of project management to the bottom line. Since there is little by way of published data on this topic, it is strongly recommended that any company seeking to begin a project management implementation effort conduct a cost benefit analysis early on.

Struggles over authority between line managers and project managers also occurred. For example, what is the project manager's role in supervising project team members in relation to the line manager's role? Other roles required clarification also: product manager, release manager, and contract manager. Stepping people through our roles and responsibilities matrix helped them to define these roles within their organizations.

Culture change issues also needed to be addressed to help people move out of their comfort zones and take on new practices, particularly since Bellcore had been commercializing and undergoing tremendous change since the project management effort began. There had been several change efforts over the last several years—was this a flavor du jour? People were particularly cautious about applying new approaches because of fear of doing poorly during performance review. Use of the new approaches needed to be incorporated into organizations' business practices (e.g., the QMO in Software Systems) and performance review process to enable the project management methods to take hold. We also review use of the project management methods as part of our internal audits.

## Impact PMCOE Has Had

Because of PMCOE, there is greater use of the project management methods and templates and greater awareness of their need. They have become a way of life in many organizations and are quickly becoming so in others. The services we provide to our project managers has reduced their learning time and accelerated application of the methods to their jobs. A greater number of projects are being delivered on time and within budget, and customer satisfaction with both deliverables and how the projects are managed has increased.

## Recommendations

In summary, we recommend the following steps, which have worked for us:

- Obtain visible upper management support at the outset
- Secure visible middle management support
- Obtain benchmarked data on how successful companies do project management and quantitative data; use it to persuade non-believers
- Define corporate and, if applicable, local project management practices
- Prepare easy to use templates and tools
- Make them available electronically
- Train and support project managers on using the methods, templates, and tools
- Be persistent in getting people to use the methods, templates, and tools
- Establish user groups where project managers can learn from each other
- Conduct audits to ensure compliance with new business practices
- Be a vocal and visible advocate of project management.

## Conclusion

PMCOE has been instrumental in bringing project management into Bellcore, and, based on our experience, we recommend this approach for companies wishing to meet the business challenges of the next century.

### References


Frank, Howard. 1993. "What Corporate Evolution Means for Managers." *Network Management* (April).

Urban, Glen L. 1995. "Business and Economic Outlook: How Will the Century Close?" *The Conference Board*: 31.

# Global Project Management

# The Pyramids and Implementing Project Management Processes.

Dr. Alaa A. Zeitoun, PMP, International Institute for Learning, Inc.,
Dr. Ahdy W. Helmy, M.D., Indiana University

## Introduction

The superior construction, scale, and accessibility to Cairo of the Gizeh Pyramids have made them the most famous of the Seven Wonders of the World. The pyramids were simply tombs for the Pharaohs. The Great Pyramid in its original state rose 481 feet and is estimated to have contained 2,300,000 blocks of stone. Napoleon estimated that the blocks of stone from the three Gizeh pyramids would have been sufficient to build a wall ten feet high and one foot thick around the whole country of France.

This paper addresses the building of the pyramids and the concepts behind this great project. The intent of the paper is to conduct an analogy between what happened 2600 B.C. and the current principles and processes of project management as outlined in the 1996 *Guide to the Project Management Body of Knowledge* (*PMBOK Guide*), by the Project Management Institute (PMI).

This analogy covers some of the key project management processes: initiation, scope planning, scope definition, activity definition, activity sequencing, activity duration estimation, organizational planning, resource planning, staff acquisition, as well as risk, quality, and communications aspects. The goal is to compare the management of this major construction project that involved about 4,000 construction workers at any given time to what we believe are today's acceptable project management techniques and principles.

Lessons learned from that major effort and how we can improve today's practice of project management are also addressed in this paper.

## Project Charter

The project charting team was composed of the chief architect (project manager), who directed a team of architects. The architects gave their instructions to surveyors. The surveyors in return marked out the site and laid out a thirteen-acre site at Gizeh. The Pyramid's base was designed to form a perfect square. After this layout was done, the architects directed sculpture workers who were to chip rough gutters or slots in quarry walls. Workers then fitted the wooden wedges into the slots, soaked then with water, and the wood expanded and split off chunks of rock. The massive stone chunks were then hammered into rough blocks. A true delegation of authority at all levels.

The blocks were painted with a variety of quarry marks. Some of the marks indicated the block's destination; others cautioned, "this side up." Others gave the name of the quarry gang, such as "the vigorous gang." The responsibilities were divided among groups of workers and every group was held accountable for the destination and the section they were responsible for in this project. Special dolerite hammers were used to chip the stone. Some of the stone blocks were granite, but the most were limestone.

The team was getting the direct sponsorship of the king due to the strategic importance of this project to the kingdom and to the king's immortality.

## Scope Planning

The statement of work's key deliverable was a structural monument meant to preserve the king's body for resurrection based on the ancient Egyptians' strong belief that, in the afterlife, he would use same body, which therefore needed to be protected.

## Scope Definition

The structure was selected to be a pyramidal architectural structure based on a theory projected by the first pyramid engineer, Imhotep, who designed the step pyramids in the Third Dynasty. The structure was meant to be solid enough to defy wear and tear over centuries until the time that the bodies were ready for the other life. The original plan was established to place the monumental structure in a certain spot, which was planned precisely, though not all the details are available to us at the present time. Recently it was discovered that the arrangement of the three pyramidal structures matches a triad of stars in the constellation Orion. The structures were meant to be close to the river Nile, the main route for transportation in Egypt at that time. The project plan was to use the Nile to transport the pink granite stones from quarries in Upper Egypt down the Nile to Gizeh.

## Activity Duration Estimation

Despite the magnitude of the project, the plan was to complete the structure within the Pharaoh's reign. This schedule was actually met and the Great Pyramid was built within the Pharaoh's twenty- three year reign in about 2600 B.C. by men working with the simplest implements, without draft animals, without even the wheel, which was not known at that time.

## Activity Sequencing / Staffing Issues

This project used 100,000 workers divided into groups with about 4,000 construction workers working at any given time. Workers were divided into shifts to maintain work continuously around the clock. They were free citizens drafted for public work. Laborers worked in gangs of eighteen to twenty men, hauling stone blocks up ramps and setting them in place.

Workers at Aswan chipped off the blocks of stone and eased the stones onto log rollers. Whichever surface of the granite block was to be moved face down was finished beforehand so it would slide smoothly onto the ramp. At the ramp's end, workmen loaded granite blocks onto a wooden sledge. By using rollers, ramps, and sledges, work gangs were able to haul blocks weighing up to fifteen tons from the quarry to barges waiting along the Nile hundreds of yards away. At the same time at the pyramid site ramps were built in tiers along the four sides of the pyramid, three to go up and one to go down, each ramp began at one corner and all ended at the topmost level of the construction.

The laborers hauled the heavy stone blocks up the ramps sitting them in place. Finally from the 481-foot apex, the masons cut down the blocks to form the smooth sloping sides of the pyramid.

In essence, some of the activities overlapped and others were in sequence, indicating the old Egyptians' ability to understand different logical sequencing alternatives.

## Team Issues

Despite the great labor, gangs were pleased to work for the Pharaoh, who was God's figure on earth. As a later foreman said, they toiled "without a single man getting exhausted, without a man thirsting," and at last "came home in good spirits, sated with bread, drunk with beer, as if it were a beautiful festival of a God."

The Egyptians demonstrated outstanding engineering skill in designing this outward size pyramid that was called one of the Seven Wonders of the ancient world. King Khufu had planned a somewhat smaller pyramid with his burial chamber sunk deep into bedrock below the base. But as his aspirations grew, he twice enlarged the tomb's plan and each time ordered the burial chamber to be raised higher up, a scope change that was well handled by the project team, which was dedicated to pleasing the customer.

The workers who were drafted for public work were doing so at the time when the flood was covering their own land so their time was used intelligently. The workers were self-motivated with a strong belief that they were worshiping through this work devoted to the Pharaoh who was the godly figure on earth. The gangs were self-selected to work in harmony and they were actually competing with other gangs for a better job to satisfy the God whose spirit they felt was dwelling upon them.

A major lesson for us here is the issue of being "self-motivated." There's nothing stronger than a team's belief in the mission of the project, the value of individual contributions to the team, and how this ties to the bigger picture of the organization's effort.

## Cost Management

Despite the magnitude of the project, expenses were amazingly very low. The entire project was established from natural resources in the form of granite and limestone blocks carved from the mountains of stone in Upper Egypt. The labor was derived from Egypt's own people, who were paid not with money, but with pure satisfaction from doing a job for worship. They received only food and drink during their working hours. The transportation was cost-free using the stream of the river Nile, carrying the wooden barges from its upper level to its lower level in the Delta via water energy. The architects competed at no charge, showing off their expertise to gain the satisfaction of the worshipped Pharaoh. The structure itself was one of the most cost-effective projects known to mankind and one which has defied time and nature. With the expenses as little as described, the Pyramids are still a source of income to Egypt through tourism over centuries past and still to come.

Since the expenses were planned to be as shown above, there was no true need for setting a budget and or exercising cost control measures as we know them today in the world of Earned Value Analysis. This was such an enormous strategic project that meant a great deal to the monarch of Egypt, who is also the godly figure, that the project was an open budget to every expense that it would take to ensure the glorification of the Pharaoh it represented.

## Risk Management

The major risk in the project was the risk of the project failing to protect the body of the King and to ensure the safety of his tomb. Every precaution was taken to misguide and trap all intruders. False burial chambers were set to misguide grave robbers. The final chamber was reached through a grand gallery that was ventilated by two narrow shafts; the ascending corridor was sealed from within by stone plugs. The king's chamber was roofed with enormous granite slabs that formed five stress-relieving compartments. Now, though many slabs have cracked, the roofing remains firm. This gives us an idea of how meticulously the safety of the king's tomb was thought out. Once the ascending corridor was sealed, the workmen blocked other passages including the tomb's entrance with stone slabs. These extraordinary measures fooled even the most ingenious tomb robbers for at least 400 years.

In summary, the major risks were identified, assessed, and a risk handling strategy was carefully followed.

## Quality Management

The quality of the project structure was very well thought out. They chose granite as the building material, the most challenging and strongest stone known to man. Though the Egyptians had no good timber, they imported most of what they used from Lebanon and Syria. Their achievement in woodworking was noteworthy and it has survived because of the country's dry climate. Nationally made goods were given by the people to their Pharaoh to show their gratitude. Egyptian cabinetmakers mastered the making of chariots, coffins, cosmetics boxes, and ornaments found in the tombs attesting to the remarkable skill of the Egyptian craftsman at joinery and veneering.

The architects directed the workers to cut step-like terraces into the irregular sides of the hill where the pyramid was to be erected. These terraces which would serve as the foundation on which all the stone blocks were laid, had to be absolutely levelled if the entire structure was not to be askew.

To assure this level foundation, the pyramid builders erected an extensive system of water-filled trenches about its base. Then, using the water level as a standard they were able to lay out the 13-acre site so evenly that experts using modern instruments have found that the southeast corner of the pyramid stands only 1/2 inch higher than the northwest corner.

To ensure the leveling of the stone blocks, a string was stretched between two sticks of equal length held touching the water connected in water trenches. The ground was then leveled until measuring rods showed the floor was parallel to the string.

The Pyramids of Gizeh were proven recently to be in the exact center of the world's habitable landmasses. This is believed to be attributable to the skills of old Egyptians in astronomy and mathematics.

## Procurement Management

The magnitude of the project dictated the inclusion of different craftsmen with unique skills. This included Egyptian sculptors with skills in dealing with granite, basalt, and leather, Egyptian painters skilled in painting on plaster, and carvers. The paint they used was a mixture of pigment and water with wax or glue as a binder. The pigments were minerals, which is why many of the colors remain remarkably fresh. Carbon was used for black; ocher (iron ore) for brown, red, and yellow; powdered malachite (copper ore) for green; and chalk or gypsum for white.

The tomb of the king contained hundreds of vases and bowls, made from limestone, alabaster, flint, and quartz. The skill of the Egyptians acquired with small stone articles was the basis for their later mastery of gigantic stone blocks.

## Communications Management

There was total harmony between teams of workers involved in the Aswan quarries cutting stones and loading barges and their counterparts on the bank of the Nile. At Gizeh, barges were unloaded and messengers carried messages on the homecoming boats to request more blocks as the establishment in Gizeh was shaping up. There was never a time when the work at Gizeh had to stop because of shortage of stone blocks. As soon as the outer design was being set up, other groups of workers were carrying out their task within the inner design of the pyramid. Every group carried on from where the previous one stopped. Teams functioned without getting in the way of one another. A beautifully orchestrated project plan.

The proof of this harmony in planning the building of the Pyramid was quite obvious in completing such wonder within twenty-three years with this big numbers of workers, at least 4,000 of them working at any given time without any chaos.

Communications were planned for, no barriers to communication existed, and information distribution and close out were easy and clear. Workers had no computers, e-mail, pagers, or answering machines, and yet communication was flawless.

## Conclusions

Nothing about the Pyramids was accidental. Their original heights, their angles of slope, their perimeters, and many other aspects were purposefully laid out according to a specific plan. As an example of the the high precision followed in this major project: if we require a wall that is straight within 1 arc minute per 100 meters and directed exactly due north, then we are going to need a laser theodolite, an accurate survey map, and a qualified professional team. Yet this is the precision that was achieved by the builders of the Great Pyramid more than 4,500 years ago.

Another example is the Pyramid's base. The variation between the longest and shortest sides is less than eight inches, about one-tenth of 1 percent, which is an amazing fact considering that this is measured over a distance of more than 9,000 inches. In addition the corners were set at almost perfect right angles, the kind of accuracy involved in building a Rolls Royce.

The builders of the Pyramids must have had a powerful motive to create what is truly a miracle of surveyor's art. It is this conclusion that drives us to go back to basics in project management and to have the open eyes and mind to learn from other global projects and project managers.

## Lessons Learned

Meticulous choice of the materials used to build the structure ensured the strength of a structure that was able to challenge time and weather changes over centuries. Extreme precision in leveling the foundation protected the establishment of the structure.

The dedication of the crews involved in their tasks allowed them to work in harmony, in one unity, for one goal, to establish a monument that could survive eternity. The most valuable lesson to learn is "whenever there is a will there is a way" in managing any project even one of this magnitude.

The realization that planning needs to be driven by what the key deliverables are, and that the belief of the team in the value of the pursuit is very important. Even the Pharaohs knew the value of emphasizing the conceptual phase, the significance of project managers negotiating for deliverables, and how they must lead and motivate team members. Quality of the work came about smoothly since it was planned for and prevention money was spent up-front so that the errors were kept to a minimum.

Project management processes, as laid out in the *PMBOK Guide*, were used thousands of years ago in this major project. The newly agreed upon and developed terminology in the *PMBOK Guide* should help our organizations communicate and handle present and future project challenges hopefully at least as well as the Pharaohs did.

### References

Casson, Lionel. 1974. *Ancient Egypt*. New York:Time-Life Books.

Hancock, Graham and Robert Bauval. 1996. *The Message of the Sphinx.* Three Rivers Press.

Putnam, James. 1990. *Egyptology.* Shooting Star Press.

# Global Status of the Project Management Profession: Where Are We Now?

David L. Pells, PMP, Mathie, Pells & Associates, Dallas, TX. USA

## Introduction

The modern project management (MPM) profession has been developing now for over thirty years. Since the founding of the International Project Management Association (IPMA, formerly INTERNET) in Europe in 1967 and the Project Management Institute (PMI) in the USA in 1969, over fifty project management professional associations and nonprofit organizations have been formed around the world. In recent years modern project management has increasingly been embraced by industry leaders and professionals around the world, with a resulting explosion in the growth of PMI membership, numbers of PMI chapters around the world, and startup and growth of national project management associations.

In 1995 the first Global Project Management Forum was successfully held in New Orleans, Louisiana, in conjunction with the PMI'95 Seminar/Symposium. All project management associations around the world were invited to come together for the first time, to discuss status of the project management profession in various countries and issues of common global interest. Based on surveys of participating organizations in that first Global Forum in New Orleans, PMI published a book , *The Global Status of the Project Management Profession* in 1996. Subsequently, Global Project Management Forums were held in Paris in June, 1996, hosted by IPMA, and in Boston in October, 1996, again hosted by PMI. At the Boston Global Forum, approximately forty countries were represented, reflecting the continued growth in interest and activity in the project management profession globally. For the Boston Global Forum, various project management associations around the world were again asked to submit "country reports" which summarized status of the project management profession in their respective countries, in response to a set of questions presented in a common format to all project management associations around the world.

This paper summarizes the status of the project management profession as reported in the country reports submitted by various project management associations for the Global Forums in New Orleans in 1995 and Boston in 1996. Status information includes identification of countries in various regions of the world with established project management associations or PMI chapters, industries that are main users of MPM in those countries, and greatest needs and opportunities for growth. Some reflection on the maturity of the profession and experience with MPM within specific industries is also provided. This paper provides a current summarized status of the project management profession around the world, in countries outside the former Soviet Union. The paper should be useful to students and executives in Russia who need to know how other industries and countries are adapting and applying project management.

## The Americas

The project management profession in the Americas is dominated by PMI, based in the United States, which has chapters throughout North America and chapters now being formed in major cities throughout Latin America as well. Established in 1969 by project management experts from the construction, defense and pharmaceutical industries, PMI is now the world's largest project management professional association with approximately 27,000 members in over 100 countries. as A nonprofit professional organization, PMI is based in Philadelphia. Although PMI is an international society, nearly 90 percent of PMI's members are located in North America. A new national project managementassociation, PMI Canada, has recently been established by PMI members and chapters in Canada. No other national project management association currently exists in North or South America.

In the United States and Canada, the project management profession is reaching a mature stage, as PMI has begun establishing close relations with government agencies and is now entering into discussions related to setting national standards and qualifications for project management on government programs and projects. In other American nations, the project management profession is just getting started, as PMI chapters have recently been chartered or are in the formation stages in Argentina, Brazil, Chile, Columbia, Ecuador, Mexico, Peru and Venezuela.

In North America MPM is well established in such industries as aerospace, architecture, construction, defense, energy, engineering, oil and gas, petrochemicals, pharmaceuticals, transportation and several others, where project management concepts and methods have generally been in use for many years. In those industries MPM has been long established in large dominant corporations, many of which have become multinational or global organizations, and which have taken their project management systems and procedures to other countries. During the past ten years, MPM has been increasingly adopted by industries such as information systems and technology, telecommunications, software, health, environmental, entertainment, financial services and manufacturing organizations.

In smaller Latin American countries, MPM has been used to some extent in the dominant industries, where large organizations have international industrial ties to North America, Europe or Japan. For instance, in Argentina, oil, construction and hydroelectric industries are currently the main users of project management. In Ecuador, Peru and Venezuela, it is oil, mining and construction. In Mexico and Brazil, usage and trends for project management are widespread, and reflect the earlier history and trends in Canada and the United States, with leadership in the profession now being undertaken by leading technical universities which have close ties to both local government and industry.

## Africa

The modern project management profession in Africa is most mature in South Africa, where it has been used for over 25 years. A chapter of PMI was established in Johannesburg in 1981; in 1996 a new national project management association was established for the Republic of South Africa (PMI-SA). Also in 1996, the Association of Project Management Zimbabwe (APMZ) was formally launched in Harare, with plans to establish SIGs as chapters of both PMI and APM (U.K.).

In South Africa, organizations in some industries such as architecture, engineering and construction have historically followed British professional practices and standards. Major projects in the petrochemical and minerals industries followed American models. Today, applications and trends are merging, reflecting those in North America, Europe and elsewhere, but adapted to local needs, customs and laws. Newly emerging industries such as information technologies and telecommunications are adopting MPM and the profession itself is growing rapidly, and reflecting global concepts and influences in the process.

A PMI chapter is now being formed in Nigeria, where project management has been supported on World Bank-funded projects, and where project management is used in industries such as oil, gas, construction and infrastructure development. Other African countries are expected to follow this process, as strong local industries emerge and as they enter the global economy.

## The Middle East

In Egypt and Saudi Arabia, MPM has been in widespread use on "hard projects" in the engineering, construction, oil and gas, petrochemicals and utilities industries since the 1970s. Professional project management has also been important on infrastructure projects related to water and wastewater for many years.

An Arabian Gulf chapter of PMI was formed in 1993 in Saudi Arabia, to organize and serve the project management profession for those in both local and multinational organizations working throughout the region. The Gulf Chapter of PMI has members in Bahrain, Kuwait, Oman, Saudi Arabia, UAE and several other countries. In Egypt, the project management profession is represented by a small national organization connected to the Egyptian engineering profession and aligned with the International Project Management Association (IPMA) in Europe.

A PMI chapter was officially chartered in Israel in July, 1996, sponsored by the Management of Technology Department in the School of Business Administration at Tel Aviv University. Main industry users of MPM in Israel include construction, high technology, military and utilities organizations. Project management courses are now being taught at all major Israeli universities.

## Asia Pacific

Countries considered in the Asia Pacific region include Australia, New Zealand, Japan, Korea, Indonesia, Malaysia and the Philippines. Countries which have not yet been surveyed, and which have not yet participated in Global Project Management Forums, are not included, such as China, Thailand, Vietnam, etc.

The MPM profession is most mature in Australia, where the Australian Institute of Project Management (AIPM) was established in 1991, based on an older association called the Project Managers Forum which had been founded in 1976. AIPM now has chapters in all major Australian cities, has close relations with the Australian government and has members from all major Australian industries. AIPM may actually be the world's most advanced project management association at a national level, as it has been working closely with the Australian government for over five years to establish "competency standards" for project managers in Australia. Industry applications and trends in Australia parallel those in North America and Western Europe. In 1996, a PMI chapter was also chartered in Melbourne, reflecting Australia's diverse professional community and ties to the rest of the world, with a second PMI chapter chartered in Sydney in early 1997. Due to Australian geography, an independent Western Australian

Project Management Association (WAPMA) was founded in Perth in 1992, to organize and coordinate the project management profession in Western Australia. WAPMA has 230 members and formal cooperation agreements with both PMI and AIPM. WAPMA plans to merge with AIPM in 1997 or 1998.

A PMI chapter was chartered in New Zealand in 1994, where the project management profession has been growing dramatically in the information technologies and construction industries. Historically, MPM professional skills were imported into New Zealand with foreign-based companies, and used primarily on major projects such as hydroelectric dams, power plants and oil refineries. Now PMI-NZ is working with the New Zealand Qualifications Authority to influence the teaching of project management in NZ universities.

In Japan, the project management profession is represented by the Project Management Committee within the Engineering Advancement Association (ENAA) of Japan, which was established in 1978. ENAA is sponsored by 46 major Japanese engineering, construction and manufacturing companies, and directly supported by the Ministry of International Trade and Industry of the Japanese Government. The usage of MPM in Japan is quite mature in engineering and construction industries, while still growing in general construction. MPM is considered newly introduced and now growing rapidly in manufacturing, high technology and information services industries.

This is generally true for Korea as well. In both Japan and Korea, MPM is still badly needed in Public Services and utilities-related industries where major investments are budgeted. In Korea, the project management profession is represented by the Korean Institute of Project Management and Technology (PROMAT), based in Seoul, which consists of individual professionals, students and corporate members. PROMAT was founded in 1991 to promote MPM in Korea and to foster international exchanges and collaboration. A major organizational member of PROMAT is CERIK, a research and educational organization established by the Korean construction industry to bring leading-edge global practices to Korea.

The Project management profession in Indonesia, Malaysia and the Philippines is represented by PMI chapters founded in those countries in 1995 and 1996. In all three countries, which have large populations and booming economies, interest in MPM is growing rapidly. In Indonesia, the interest in project management and PMI is driven by economic growth and the presence of many North American mining, construction, oil and engineering companies engaged in major projects. As the Indonesian economy has been largely based on natural resources, MPM has been implemented in construction, mining, pulp and paper, petrochemical and agribusiness industries and organizations. Further developments are needed in processing, manufacturing, services and infrastructure-related industries.

In Malaysia, where MPM is relatively newly introduced in many industries, great interest is due to the broad push to modernize the country and economy by the year 2020. While long practiced in some form on many projects, project management is being formally adapted to accomplish several megaprojects, including the new Kuala Lumpur International Airport, the new Kuala Lumpur City Centre and the Bakun Hydroelectric Dam. MPM usage is expanding rapidly within TELEKOM Malaysia, PETRONAS and other major industrial organizations. In smaller companies, however, professional project management is not well known or used.

The Philippines is undergoing a major investment and construction boom, so MPM is most visible in the building industries, architecture and engineering. MPM is also promoted by the World Bank and the Asian Development Bank (ADB), based in Manila. Some companies are starting to obtain project management training, but MPM is not widely used or appreciated due to lack of project management education and information. The new PMI chapter is struggling to improve this situation.

## India, Pakistan and Turkey

Modern project management has been used in India and Pakistan for many years on large projects financed by the World Bank, Asian Development Bank and other international funding agencies. This is especially true of large projects involving international contractors or investors. Because of the mixed nature of the Indian and Pakistani economies, which range from heavily agricultural in some areas to heavy industry and high technology in others, the range of project management experience and implementation is also great. General MPM is visible in large industrial organizations, but not in medium or small companies.

The project management profession in India is currently led by the Project Management Associates (PMA), founded in 1993 in New Delhi. PMA has strong links to Indian government agencies and major industries, and sponsors a Global Symposium on Project Management each December in New Delhi. It also offers various seminars and workshops during the year throughout India. PMA is planning three new chapters in various regions of India in 1997-98. PMA has formal relations with AIPM, ENAA, IPMA, PROMAT, PMI and other international project management organizations.

In Pakistan, principal users of MPM are large industrial organizations and multinational companies working on major projects, especially power, ports, airports, housing, heavy industry and defense projects. Usage of MPM is promoted by the World Bank, ADB and CIDA, but is newly introduced in most non-construction industries. A new Chapter of PMI is in formation stages in Karachi, to provide a focal point for project management profession in Pakistan. No national project management society yet exists in Pakistan.

MPM has been employed in Turkey for many years, especially in the construction, energy and military industries, and on projects involving foreign companies. No national project management association currently exists in Turkey, although chapters of PMI are in the formation stages in both Ankara and Istanbul. Many opportunities exist in Turkey for further development of the project management profession, based on Turkey's large population and economy, strategic location between Europe and Asia, and expanding economic and political ties to Europe, North America and neighboring countries. In addition, several mega projects are planned in Turkey, related to oil and gas pipelines and transportation infrastructure.

## Western Europe

MPM has been in widespread use in many industries and countries in Western Europe for many years, essentially paralleling the usage and history of project management in North America. Professional project management associations exist in nearly all Western European countries, with the largest and most active being the Association of Project Management (APM) in the United Kingdom. Based near London, APM has approximately 5,000 members, sections in all major cities in the United Kingdom, and members in most industries.

The next largest national project management association in Europe is GPM, based in Munich, with approximately 3,000 members. National project management associations also exist in Austria, Denmark, Finland, France, Greece, Ireland, Netherlands, Norway, Portugal, Spain, Sweden and Switzerland. Project management in Italy has previously been represented by the Project Management Committee within the Italian National Engineering Association (ANIMP), but this appears to no longer be active. Every national project management association conducts regular meetings and seminars, and issues a newsletter, all in their local languages.

In 1967, an International Project Management Association (IPMA, formerly INTERNET) was founded in Paris by project management experts from France and Germany, with experts from the UK also immediately joining. IPMA is now a federation of national project management associations as well as individual members worldwide. IPMA publishes books and a monthly journal, and sponsors seminars, workshops and conferences, including a bi-annual World Congress on Project Management. IPMA member associations send representatives to periodic Council of Delegates meetings, who elect an executive board and a president, who lead the association. IPMA is administered by a small staff based in the Uunited Kingdom.

Chapters of the U.S.-based Project Management Institute (PMI) have recently been chartered in England, France, Germany and Italy, with other PMI chapters in the formation stages in Belgium, Ireland, Italy and Spain. Interest in modern professional project management in Europe continues to grow, especially in large industrial organizations involved in international projects and those being forced to become more efficient based on global competition and competition within an integrated European economy.

## Central and Eastern Europe

Countries in Central and Eastern Europe include Albania, Bulgaria, the Czech Republic, Hungary, Poland, Slovakia, Slovenia and the former Yugoslavia. Most of these countries were formerly under the direct control and influence of the Soviet Union prior to 1990. Therefore industrial organizations, educational institutions and professionals were more closely tied to Russian practices and organizations until the late 1980s, with little practical use of modern project management as defined in Western Europe and North America. Now, however, as various economies in this region have been opened up to outside investment and influence, interest in both project management practices and the project management profession have increased. Better project management is needed in all industries and locations in the region, and especially in newly privatized enterprises.

In the Czech Republic, a national project management society, SPPR, was formed in Prague in 1990 by several individuals who had learned about and interacted with IPMA in Western Europe. SPPR has approximately 100 individual members and 8 corporate members, with 25 percent of the participants associated with educational institutions. SPPR is closely aligned with IPMA, is working with government, and sponsors seminars and conferences. Formation of a PMI chapter, aligned with PMI in the USA, was begun in 1996, also in Prague.

The Magyar Gazdasagi Kamara (MGK), Hungarian Project Management Society, was founded in 1991. Based in Budapest, MGK has seen its membership fall in recent years to approximately 30, due to economic problems and members leaving previous positions and professions. MGK conducts approximately three project management seminars each year, issues a regular "Information Letter," and is closely aligned with IPMA in Western Europe.

A chapter of PMI has been in the formation stages in Krakow, Poland, since May, 1994, but little is yet known about project management practices and activities in Poland. A new project management association has been formed in

Slovenia, which will host IPMA's World Congress on Project Management in June, 1998. Several project management professionals in Slovakia are in the early stages of forming an association there. No other professional project management organizations are activities have been started in other countries in the region. Many of these countries are undergoing dramatic economic, political and social changes, which suggests that modern project management is badly needed in the area but will be difficult to organize and promote.

## Baltic States, Russia, Ukraine & Former Soviet Union

The status of MPM in the Baltic States of Estonia, Latvia and Lithuania parallels the status and experience in Central European nations. While no formal project management professional associations have yet been established, a number of project management experts teach and live in this region, with past experience and knowledge gained during Soviet times on Soviet projects and from Universities in Moscow and St. Petersburg. Usage of MPM in this region is similar to that in Poland and the Czech Republic, primarily on projects involving foreign investors and contractors, in newly privatized industrial organizations, and on projects funded by the World Bank or European Bank for Reconstruction & Development.

In Russia, where scientific project management techniques and methods have been taught in universities and technical institutes for many years, modern project management has been poorly implemented in practice, as organizations have struggled to overcome the functional separation of organizations promoted previously in the planned economic system of the Soviet Union. As elsewhere in Eastern Europe, modern project management practices have been implemented on major projects involving Western contractors and organizations ( major oil and gas, infrastructure, buildings projects) and on projects sponsored by the World Bank or other international agencies. Since industrial privatization has been widespread and successful in Russia, many Russian organizations are obtaining project management training and are implementing modern project management in order to enhance productivity and competitive advantages within the new Russian market-based economy.

A Russian Project Management Association (SOVNET) was established in 1990 in Moscow, with the broad support and involvement of major Russian industrial and government organizations. SOVNET, which includes both individual and organizational members, has sponsored international project management conferences in Moscow (1991, 1993, 1997) and St. Petersburg (1995), and conducts local and regional meetings, seminars and workshops. SOVNET is the only project management association in Russia, is an association member of IPMA in Europe, and has formal cooperative relations with other major project management associations worldwide (including APM, PMI, PROMAT, PMA , etc.) Professor Vladimir Voropajev, SOVNET President, participates regularly in international project management conferences and meetings, represents SOVNET at Global Project Management Forums, and is an elected international officer of IPMA.

The World Bank launched a major Project Management Training of Trainers program for Russia in 1993, which continued through 1995 and which was implemented via the Moscow State Construction Institute in Moscow and its associated universities around Russia. Approximately 80 professors of construction management received approximately 100 hours of classroom and software training, with the program designed for these "instructors" to then set up project management education programs throughout the country. Since this program was almost entirely focused on construction projects, benefits to other industries and organizations in Russia have been minor. A similar project management training program was launched by the World Bank for Ukraine during 1995 and 1996.

The Ukrainian Project Management Associations (UPMA) was officially founded in Kiev, Ukraine, in 1995 by Dr. Sergey Bushuyev who has worked closely with the World Bank on their Project Management Training program for Ukraine. UPMA now has approximately 50 members, with ties to universities and industrial organizations in major cities around Ukraine. UPMA has close relations with the Ministries of Privatization, Construction and Industry, as well as with Kiev State University and other academic institutions. Usage of modern project management in Ukrainian industry, however, is occurring at a slow pace, primarily because of the slow pace of privatization and outside investment in the country. The rate of positive economic change has accelerated slightly in 1996 and 1997.

Implementation and usage of modern project management in other countries of the former Soviet Union have occurred in sporadic fashion, primarily associated with foreign investment, major projects involving foreign contractors (Tenghiz Oil Field Development in Kazakhstan, seaport projects in Georgia and Uzbekistan, office buildings in Belarus, etc.). The World Bank has initiated project management training programs for participants from these countries, primarily to support World Bank loans and economic development policies. No professional associations for project management have been established in any of the Newly Independent States; however, outside of Russia and Ukraine, nor have any representatives of these countries yet participated in any Global Project Management Forums.

## Summary

The maturity and status of the project management profession varies widely around the world. It is generally mature in Australia, North America and Western Europe. In many countries MPM is quite mature in certain industries, such as construction or petrochemical, while newly introduced in other industries such as manufacturing, services and utilities. In most countries, better project management is needed by government agencies on public-sector projects.

This paper provides only very cursory information for the regions of the world, such as North America and Western Europe, where the project management profession is relatively mature and MPM practice is widespread. More information is provided for Latin America, the Asia Pacific and other regions where MPM has been more recently introduced to local industries, where the project management profession is young, and for which information on the status of project management activities has only recently been presented to the rest of the world

While not a comprehensive or detailed study of project management in all industries or all countries, this paper has presented a picture of current status of the project management profession globally. It is clear that much progress is needed in many industries and many areas of the world. Based on increased global cooperation within the project management profession, however, we can more clearly understand where we stand today and what is needed for progress in the future.

### References.


Project Management Institute. 1997. *Global Status of the Project Management Profession, Report from the Global Project Management Forum in New Orleans, LA. USA, October, 1995.* Upper Darby, PA.

Project Management Institute. 1997. *Global Status of the Project Management Profession: Report from the Global Project Management Forum in Boston, MA. USA, October, 1996.* Upper Darby, PA.

# Project Management as Key Item for the Successfuls Implementation of Foreign Direct Investments

Dipl.-Ing. Petra Kring, University of Siegen

## Introduction

Since in the course of globalization of markets, international cooperation and worldwide trade are becoming more and more vital and obviously will gain in significance during the decades to come, Western companies are increasingly forced to work internationally. The successful handling of international business will prove to be essential for the survival of the majority of companies.

One way of meeting these future challenges is to go through a process of internationalization, which means to directly invest in countries all over the world. But a great number of problems or, what is more, complete failures of those activities indicate that internationalization obviously cannot be done offhand. Even experienced business managers often find their international ventures far less successful than expected. Consequently, careful preparation, precise and accurate planning, powerful execution and thorough monitoring are more than ever required and thus almost call for the use of project management techniques and methods. This is emphasized by the fact that the conditions under which an internationalization has to be effected show all the traits that define it as a project:

- The internationalization must finally be realized subject to fixed targets concerning time, cost and resources.
- The internationalization process of a company is realized only once and therefore is unique.
- The internationalization in its entirety is a highly complex object that needs to be subdivided in smaller units to make it manageable at all.

In the following, the phenomenon of internationalization will be briefly defined and described. Critical issues will be shown. Subsequently, important items referring mainly to the critical issues of internationalization processes will be discussed with the objective of supplying managers in charge of internationalization with some decisive strategic concepts that will help them carry out their international business ventures successfully.

## The Internationalization of a Company

### From export to foreign direct investment: steps on the way to an international company

Different attempts to explain the general process of internationalization of a company have been developed (Kulhavy 1975; Dittmar 1979). According to Meissner and Gerber (1980) the first international activity of a company normally is the export business; afterwards sales companies are installed to directly serve the various markets. Then international work is done building up cooperations without directly investing abroad. This can be effected through job-order production, franchising and/or licensing activities, contract management, etc. The last step, which according to the definition used in the present text, has to be seen as the genuine internationalization and will be looked at in detail in the following, is the transfer and investment of capital in foreign countries.

Those foreign direct investments can be either implemented by a company independently or they can be realized in cooperation with a (local) partner. In both cases the foundation and erection of totally new companies as well as the merger or acquisition (complete or partial) of existing companies is possible and both may serve either for expansion or substitution purposes. As the final structure of an internationalized company a system of nearly independent firms, a highly integrated network of companies, and combinations of these can be imagined. For each individual foreign direct investment, whether they build only a pure production facility or a subsidiary that disposes of all functions necessary for creating, designing, producing, and selling a complete product, depends on the philosophy and strategy of the company.

### Reasons for Internationalization

The question why companies start international activities has been discussed extensively during the last decades (useful surveys of literature dealing with internationalization theories are provided by Dülfer (1992) and Jordan (1992). To summarize, three main reasons and thus strategies for internationalization can be distinguished (combinations of which can often found):

- Reason 1: A question of costs, leading to a cost-related strategy aiming at cheaper procurement, cheaper production, cheaper R and D, higher economies of scale, etc.

- Reason 2: Market requirements, leading to a market-related strategy initiated by the necessity to evade trade barriers, by the requirement of being close to the client, by the search for new markets or market segments, by a growing competition on the home market, by a competitor who internationalizes ("me too" strategy), etc.
- Reason 3: Taxes or other financial aspects, leading to a strategy aiming at the amelioration of the internal administration of costs (transaction costs), at taking advantage of governmental support (subsidies), at the reduction of the general economic risk, etc.

These reasons and their related strategies are of significant importance for the design of the internationalization process.

## The Internationalization Process - Consequences and Critical Issues

At first glance, the process of internationalization may appear to be nothing but a more or less loose framework for a subsequent series of single projects that do not differ very much from other highly complex projects (turn-key process plants) carried out in an international environment. But taking a look at the company that wants to spread its activities by directly investing abroad it becomes obvious that the said company is going to undergo important changes because non-stationary processes take place. Finding itself in the initial state A at the beginning of the process the company develops and changes during the course of the process and finds itself in a final state B (different from state A) afterwards (see Exhibit 1).

The internationalization has to take place under consideration of fixed and variable external preconditions like markets, infrastructures and country-related specifications (social, economic, political and legal environment) as well as in compliance with internal restrictions given by the aimed international structure of the company itself or its available resources. Since the internationalization process normally consists of several single sub-projects each of which stands for one company facility newly implemented, the goals for the process as a whole as well as for the different projects have to be defined. A design process must be initiated to shape the companies of the future international network according to the objectives to be reached. All this influences the existing company (which may at that time be either still national or already internationalized to a certain degree) significantly by defining new basic conditions and thus requires action leading to stability again.

An exploration study carried out by the University of Siegen (Adlbrecht and Kring 1996) showed that especially the farsighted, competent and adequate handling and design of the following items must be seen as an essential factor for the success of internationalization and therefore as the indispensable basis for a successful transition from the above-mentioned state A to state B:

1. The company's (international and national) strategy
2. The organizational structure concerning both coordination and configuration
3. The communication and information system
4. The selection, qualification and training of personnel
5. The transfer of the company culture
6. Processes (especially the handling and execution of an order).

The named items are all influenced by country-specific features. They are interdependent and therefore must be handled in an all-embracing approach (see Exhibit 2). Whenever one item is neglected the success of the whole project is endangered.

## Project Management Approach

Taking into account the extremely high complexity emerging from the described interactions between cross-sectional functions that express themselves as critical issues it becomes obvious that besides the "conventional" or "classic" approaches to handling international projects (project planning, scheduling, resource planning, cost planning, quality management, contract management, risk and claim management, documentation management, project controlling, etc.) special attention must be paid to the items influencing the structure and concept of the international company as a whole.

## "Classic" Approaches to Handling International Projects

Setting up a Gantt chart for an internationalization project (see Exhibit 3) it becomes apparent that 'classic' project management tools and techniques which shall not be discussed here find their justification in this context, too. Nevertheless they must be applied taking special care of typical difficulties that are likely to appear in the international context, e.g.:

- The handling of local rules and regulations
- A lack of sufficient infrastructure
- Unknown labor markets
- The political climate
- Special market characteristics (see Adlbrecht and Thamhain 1996).

## Additional Approaches Focusing on the Critical Issues of Internationalization

As outlined before, a successful internationalization can only be achieved by an integral concept that helps to realize and communicate a global vision. The handling of the interdependent critical issues plays an important role in this context.

### *Strategy*

Right at the beginning of the internationalization the goals to be reached must be defined and translated into a corresponding strategy. In the course of the process slight changes or revisions might become necessary because of the highly dynamic international environment but in general the objectives should be permanently communicated and kept. It must be realized that existing national goals might be affected by future international ones. In this case priorities should be defined which normally should favor the international goals according to the importance of the new global vision of the company.

Besides that, it's necessary to make sure that all people in touch with the international business are behind the idea and push it. Mutual mistrust, feelings of superiority (towards other nationalities, for example), doubts and criticism or internal competition are out of place. Only the complete support of the staff within all units of the company can guarantee a functioning international cooperation.

### *Organizational Structure*

The general organizational structure of the international company must be fixed. The company has to decide whether it wants to create a basically centralized, decentralized or network structure concerning decision and concerning action. It must be laid down which departments and tasks are to be settled in which country, which tasks must not be separated at all and who takes the responsibility for which activities.

While network structures support a constant and common development of the international company as a whole,

**Exhibit 2.** Critical issues within internationalization

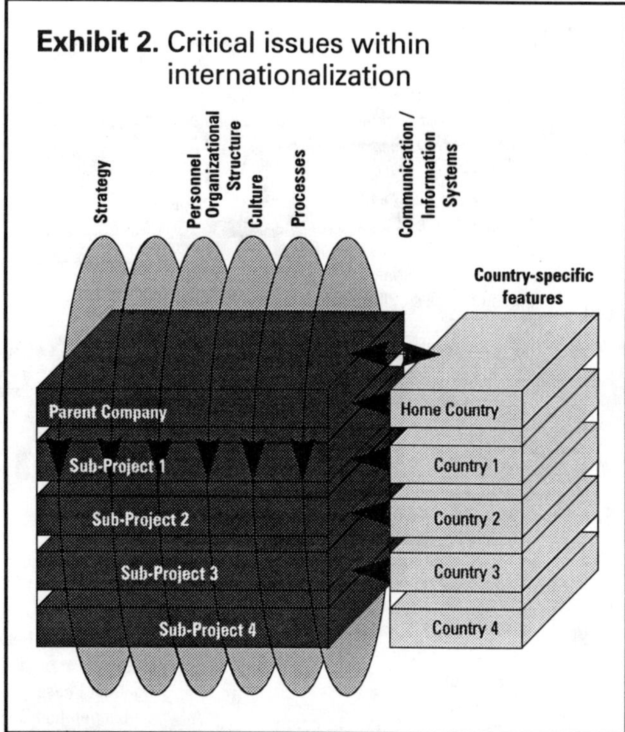


decentralized structures favor flexibility, for instance concerning market requirements. In an international environment centralized structures hardly seem to be favorable because the international potential will not be used as well as possible, the characteristics of the different markets cannot be sufficiently considered without high efforts and thus internationalization may lose its original sense.

The organizational structure as a basic factor must be designed regarding the product and considering the available resources of the company. In general every type of structure can be realized but chances as well as risks differ significantly and a good balance between aspired profit and necessary efforts be must be found.

### *Communication and Information Systems*

The design of communication and information systems depends in the first place on the organizational structure. Decentralized structures require a functioning information system within the single units whereas network structures require highly compatible hard- and software within the international company as a whole. A common language plays an important role in this context as well as common units for calculation, compatible accounting systems, common measuring units, etc.

**Exhibit 3.** Skeleton diagram of a gantt-chart for internationalization

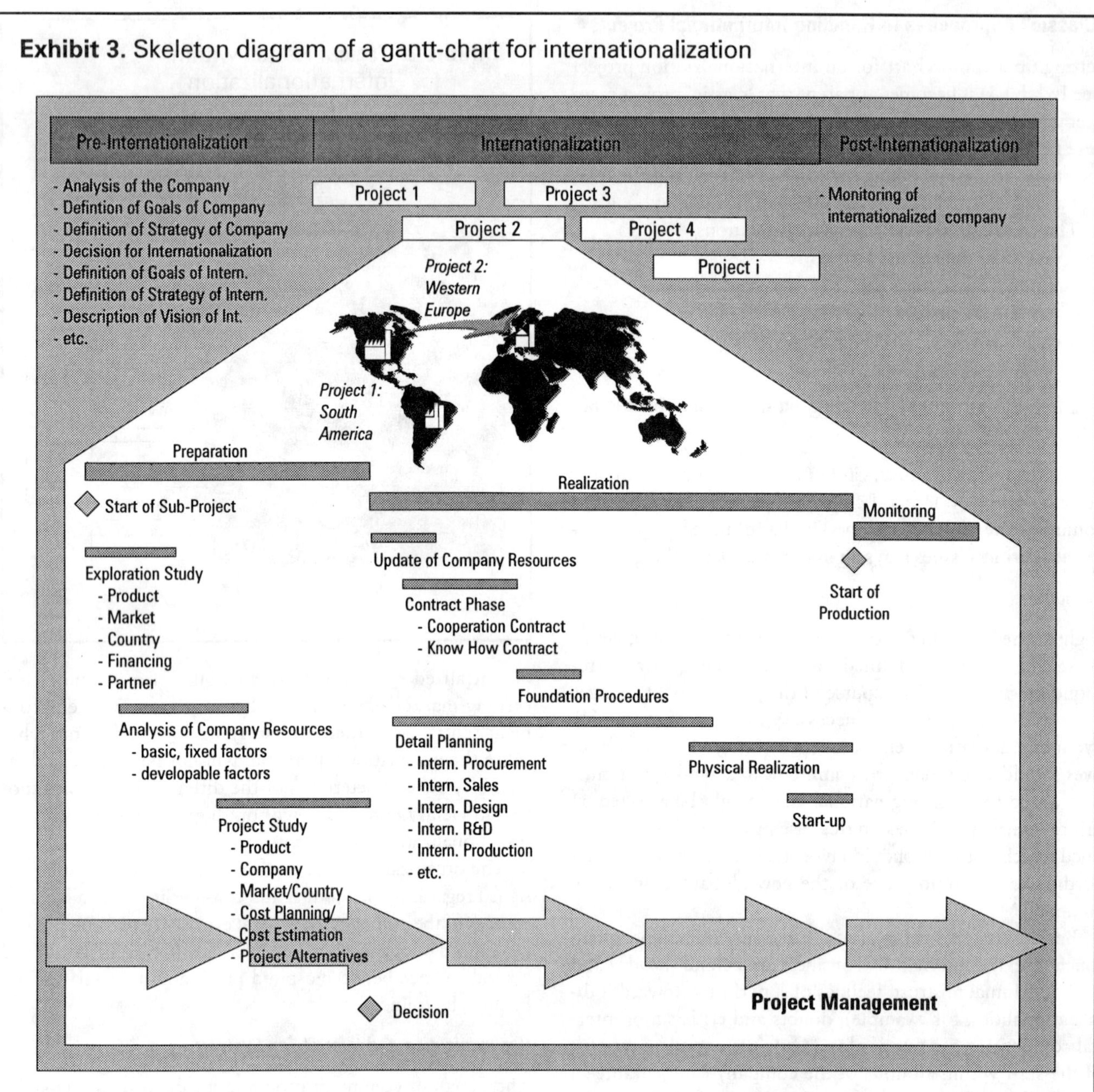


***Qualification, Selection and Training of Personnel***

The personnel of an international company must dispose of additional qualifications compared to the personnel in nationally-oriented companies. Besides professional and social competences the international staff must show language abilities, mobility, flexibility, intercultural understanding and skills as well as know-how concerning country-specific features and their consequences. It must be extroverted, open-minded and free of prejudices.

People that are hired during or after the internationalization must be carefully selected under consideration of the mentioned capabilities. The qualification of those already employed must be checked and if necessary extensive training measures must be introduced. This can be done through courses and guided training on the job on the one hand and by international exchange programs within the company on the other hand.

***Transfer of the company culture***

The international venture needs a homogeneous company culture. The superior goals as well as the way the employees see themselves and the company must be the same throughout all units. The common objectives must be recognized and acknowledged. Different attitudes towards important items like work, deadlines to be kept, motivation, the binding forces of agreements and contracts, quality may lead to serious problems because international clients will show a certain anticipation concerning, for example, the quality of products and performances no matter whether these come from Europe, Asia, America, Africa or elsewhere. In addition annoyance within the international company may be caused because one party probably will feel patronized by the other party that gets the impression that work is not taken seriously enough.

***Processes***

All processes within the international company must be carefully designed and thoroughly controlled. Competences and interfaces must be fixed free of doubt. This is valid for information flows but also for the physical flow of material and products and is of major significance for the handling and execution of orders.

## Conclusion

The common practice of starting internationalization by implementing one or two foreign direct investments at a time when this is required or seems advantageous, then letting things take their course and only reacting to single, external impulses without actively taking care of the internationalization process as a whole must lead to completely unsatisfactory results; the need for important structural changes within the company as a whole either is overlooked or ignored, which finally leads to irreparable difficulties, or the fundamental changes that become necessary with every new step finally reveal themselves to be unaffordable.

To guarantee the successful implementation of the international company network it therefore proves extremely favorable to make use of project management for it allows realization of a far-sighted and integrative approach. It should be applied:

1. To handle the internationalization process as a whole as well as the single sub-projects
2. To take permanent care of the critical issues which must be designed taking into consideration their reciprocal interdependencies and the goals of the internationalization process.

## References


Adlbrecht, Gerald and Petra Kring. 1996. Forschungsprojekt Internationalisierung von Produktionsunternehmen. Ergebnisse einer Vorstudie. Study yet unpublished, carried out by the chair "Management of International Projects" at the University of Siegen in cooperation with an internationally working company of heavy engineering,

Adlbrecht, Gerald and Hans Thamhain. 1996. Setting Up Multinational Operations: Applying Project Management Techniques. In: *Revolutions, Evolutions, Project Solutions. Proceedings to the 1996 PMI Symposium.* Upper Darby, PA: Project Management Institute.

Dittmar, Wolf-Georg. 1979. Internationale Expansionsplanung und -durchführung. In: Dittmar, Wolf-Georg; Meyer, Carl W.; Hoyer, Wolfgang: *Die internationale Expansion planen und durchführen: Management, Marketing, Finanzierung, Besteuerung.* München, Germany: Verlag Moderne Industrie.

Dülfer, Eberhard. 1992. Internationales Management in unterschiedlichen Kulturbereichen. 2., überarbeitete Auflage. Oldenbourg Verlag GmbH. München.

Jordan, Thomas: 1992. *Flows of Pumps. Structure and change in the international division of labour.* Gothenburg

Kulhavy, Ernest. 1975. Multinationale Unternehmung. In: *Grochla, Erwin; Wittmann, Waldemar (eds.): Handwörterbuch der Betriebswirtschaft.* Band 2, 4., vollständig neu gestaltete Auflage. Stuttgart .

Meissner, Hans Günther and Stephan Gerber. 1980. Die Auslandsinvestition als Entscheidungsproblem. In: *Betriebswirtschaftliche Forschung und Praxis.* 32. Jg., p. 217 - 228.

# Project Team Effectiveness Evaluation at Early Project Life Cycle Stage by Example of Target Programs in Russia

Dr. Nikolai I. Ilin, Moscow State University of Civil Engineering
Dr. Olga N. Ilina, Moscow State University of Civil Engineering

## Introduction

The next century is supposed to be a time of disappearing borders among countries and the execution of large-scale international projects. Countries of Central and East Europe are becoming open to international markets, and a lot of business connections and joint enterprises with Western partners have been established.

A large number of target programs have been developed and are now being executed in Russia. Programs of this type can be proposed by different state or private companies and, if approved by the Russian government, are sponsored from the state budget. Target programs suppose a broad foreign participation. These target programs are, practically speaking, large-scale projects with strongly defined goals and tasks and with constraints in time and resources, aimed at solving social and economic problems in Russia (Ilin and Lukmanova 1995).

The Russian government is interested in development of target programs because they stimulate the restructuring of ethe conomy, allow them to solve a wide range of social and economic problems, and assist in the development of new management approaches in Russia.

The next century is also supposed to be the time of global networking, when project team members working on the same task can be located in different parts of the world but communicate effectively via the Internet. The "Internet boom" has already begun and is expected to continue during next five to ten years in Russia as well as in other Central and East European countries.

But, in spite of all the wonders of this hi-tech century, human beings have not changed very much, and interpersonal relations in project team are still extremely important for project success. Project team composition continues to be one of the most critical factors in project management. In our paper we consider the characteristics of target programs in Russia and suggest an approach for evaluation of project team effectiveness that can be executed at early stage of project life cycle.

## Target Programs Development

A target program is aimed at obtaining positive economic, social and other results, and welcomes the participation of a wide range of state organizations and private enterprises, both Russian and foreign.

Currently several hundred target programs from the following branches of economy have been developed and realized:

- Fuel and energy
- Food industry
- Transportation and infrastructure
- Housing
- Chemical industry
- Education, mass media
- Ecology, and others.

A significant number of programs are executed in the fields of biotechnologies, conversion of military defense industries, renovation of civil aviation, development of modern seaports, airports and other transportation centers, housing and reconstruction of water supply systems, telecommunication systems.

These programs can be classified according to their duration as short-term (less than two years), midterm (two to five years), and long-term (more than five years) and according to functional orientation (production, social, ecological, innovation, economic and scientific programs).

According to Russian government decision, a target program should include the following parts:

1. *The scope of program and necessity of its realization.* Criteria for selection of program are: importance for the country, novelty and high effectiveness; necessity of governmental support; interdependence of program activities.
2. *Main goal and objectives of the program.* Hierarchy of program goals and tasks should be developed to provide a systems approach to problem solving.
3. *Program activities.* Program activities provide problem solving at each stage of life cycle: research and technology development; production and connections with cooperators; construction; cooperation with foreign participants; social results; ecology; law.



PROJECT MANAGEMENT INSTITUTE 28th Annual Seminars & Symposium
Chicago, Illinois: Papers Presented September 29 to October 1, 1997

4. *Resources for the program.* There are four categories of resources: financial; equipment and materials, including fuel and raw materials; labor; and information. Financial resources may include not only state budget, but also foreign investments.
5. *Economic mechanism of program realization.* Target programs are allowed to use reduced taxes, state orders, reduced import/export duties and other privileges.
6. *Program management and control.* Program management includes following steps: preparing of development task; program project draft, detailed for next one to two years; business plan and feasibility study; expertise; budget application; concordance with interested departments and organizations; program approval; execution; adjustments; termination.
7. *Social and economic results.* Program results are defined as benefits and costs ratio and include economic, social, ecological, science and other effects.
8. *Program pass.* Program pass is a document keeping data on program duration, steps, financial volume and resources, program developers and executors, main program indexes.

## Project Team Evaluation Model

Target programs are executed by project teams that comprise fifteen to twenty-five members. Project team members are representatives of different organizations and sometimes they are meeting each other for the first time in their lives. But efficiency of project realization depends upon project team efficiency (PMI 1996). An extremely important question is, do the project team members have the capability to work together from the very beginning to the end of project life cycle and to achieve the project goal. That is why it is necessary to develop a project team evaluation model at early project stage.

According to theory about group development stages there are four stages:

- Forming
- Storming
- Norming
- Performing (Carew and Parisi-Carew 1985).

Socioemotional tone is relatively high in the beginning and usually takes a sudden dip in the storming stage (see Exhibit 1)

The question is: how is it possible to determine in which direction a certain project team will develop? Will it overcome dissatisfaction and difficulties or will it disintegrate and be unable to work?

**Exhibit 1.** Socio-emotional tone in group development stages

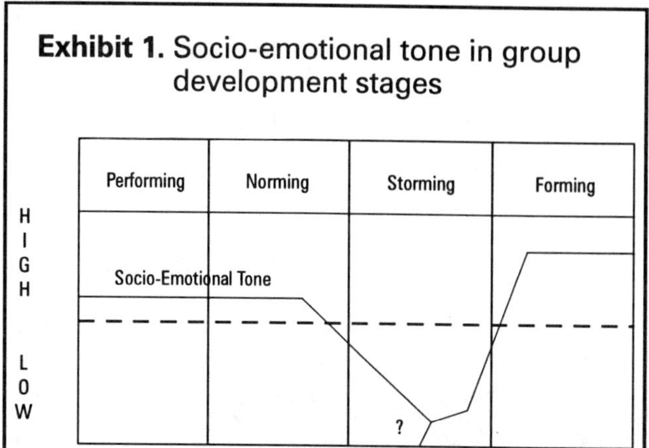


It is possible to answer this with the help of the proposed Project Team Evaluation Model (PTEM). Three indexes are combined in the model:

1. Sociometric index, which characterizes project team members solidarity and their individual positive and negative rankings;
2. Aspiration level, demonstrating achievement motivation of team members; and
3. Orientation of team members on project success, not on relationships or on themselves.

These particular indexes were selected according to three levels of human communication in groups by P.Petrovsky. In the beginning of communication, individuals' perception of colleagues is rather emotional; they simply like or don't like each other, but their emotions don't have serious ground. Further, when the working process starts, team members face their first problems and hence, capability to solve problems, achieve goals and obtain results. And finally, the deepest reason why individuals can be joined or disunited lies in their attachment to common values such as in the Rokeach value survey.

Indexes of values are determined from special tests of each team member. These tests are the sociometric test (both business and leisure-oriented), the Schwarzlander test (determination of aspiration level through goal digression), and the orientation test by Bernard Bass. The Bass test chosen because its approach makes it possible to divide values into three main fields: project success, good relationships, personal success. Indexes have different "weights" (maximum—values orientation and minimum—sociometric index) according to the significance of their contribution to the whole evaluation. (See Exhibit 2.) The efficiency of the project team (Ept) is determined as proximity of the "real" and "ideal" teams triangles, according to the graphical model.

**Exhibit 2.** Project team evaluation model

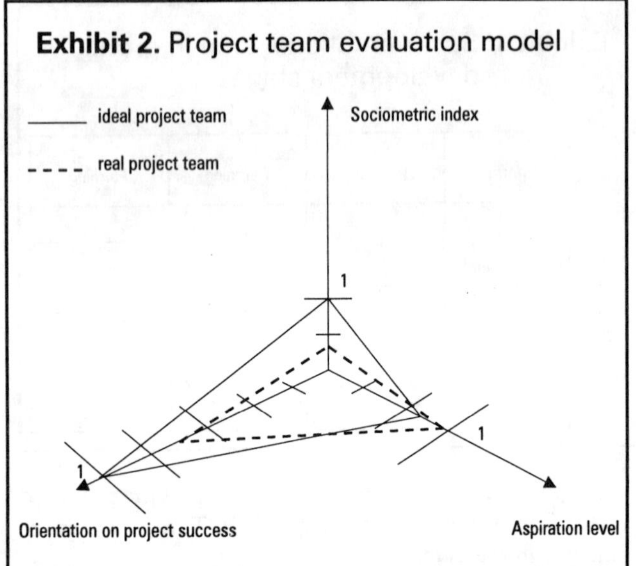


## Project team Evaluation Steps

The tests used in the model allow testing to be done very quickly. As practice testings showed, it takes about three minutes to do the sociometric test, five minutes for the Schwarzlander test, and about ten minutes for the B.Bass test. So, the total testing time is no more than 20 minutes.

Psychological tests were chosen taking into account the possibility of easy results handling with the help of computer software. The developed model is realized in worksheets with graphical interface that makes results representation more vivid.The procedure for project team efficiency evaluation includes the following steps:

- Step 1. Psychological testing of project team members
- Step 2. Input results of tests into software
- Step 3. Computing and graphical representation
- Step 4. Determination of project team efficiency index.

A negative result does not mean that a project team won't be able to work on this project. Evaluation is done at the earliest stage of the project life cycle. Therefore, if a negative result is obtained, it means only that a detailed psychological analysis of project team should be done, and some corrections in team staff can be made or special training with team members provided.

## Conclusion

Target programs (essentially large-scale projects) are very important for restructuring the economy and development of new management approaches in Russia. Foreign companies can participate in target programs as investors or executors. Consideration of all factors influencing project success has to be done carefully, including the human aspects.

Project team evaluation model allows us to analyze the opportunities for further effective work of a project team, and to do it in the beginning of the project. Results of such analysis can be interesting for potential project investors and project managers, and also for psychologists engaged in training and improving project teamwork.

## References

Carew D., Parisi-Carew E., Blanchard K. 1985. Group Development and Situational Leadership: A Model for Managing Groups. *Training and Development Journal.*

Ilin, N., and I. Lukmanova. 1995. *Project Management*. Russia: Dva-Tri.

Project Management Institute Standards Committee. 1996. *A Guide to the Project Management Body of Knowledge*. Upper Darby, PA: Project Management Institute.

# Project Management: Anytime, Anywhere (Using Groupware to Manage and Distribute Project Management Data)

Victoria Spender, The Constell Group
Robert Helminski, PMP, The Constell Group

## The Current Project Management Environment

The project management environment is on the move! Members of a project management team are no longer in the same office, the same building, or even in the same country. Team members cross organizational boundaries and need to be fluent in all functional aspects of the project. That means information about the project needs to be accessible to people at their desks, in their hotel rooms, at client or vendor sites, even in the air. The project management environment is extending beyond just the virtual office—it now includes the entire globe.

Project information now comes in through a variety of sources as well: personal computers, Macintosh PCs, mainframe systems, client/server systems, the Internet and intranets. In addition to the variety of platforms listed above, the data itself no longer appears in a traditional structured format. We can now receive information via e-mail, voice messages, faxes, scanned documents, handwritten notes, word-processed documents, spreadsheets, mainframe databases—the list goes on! This incoming data needs to be reconciled in a way that is useful to *everyone*. In addition to that, the way we *receive* the information needs to be faster and more efficient.

### Where do current project management tools fail?

While current project management software tools are great for charting resources and deadlines, used alone they fail to meet the new and growing needs of today's project team. One of the most critical is the need for a central storage point where users, regardless of time or location, can access the information they require. A second drawback to just using project management software is that the data must be translated into the traditional chart and spreadsheet type format. However, the information people are using today falls into many different forms: contracts, meeting minutes, pictures, graphics, voice messages, etc. What is needed is some type of *container* that can house all these different data types. A third obstacle to the project management software only approach is the expertise level required to use the programs effectively. While the project manager may know his or her way around the MS Project menu system, the program may prove too intimidating for the project team member and too detail-oriented for the director. What is needed is a simple user interface that provides project stakeholders the specific information they need to do their jobs when and where they need it.

All in all, project management tools have been great at automating traditional operational processes, not more complex strategic business processes. Operational systems include the processes for capturing and analyzing data associated with business *transactions*. For example, recording the time and money spent bringing a new product to market. Strategic systems, on the other hand, involve processes that help people work together better to accomplish business goals and usually encompass all parts of the business function. Using the same new product example, a strategic system would examine *how* we bring the new product to market. How can we do it better and faster? In today's highly competitive markets, it is the companies that are focusing on improving their strategic processes, rather than perfecting their operational processes, who will gain the edge. But in order to begin automating strategic systems, something is needed that will enable companies to maximize the knowledge capital of their project team members.

## What is Groupware and How Can it Help?

*Groupware* is software that allows geographically dispersed teams to work together. One of the essential characteristics of groupware is its ability to share information among all members of a workgroup, regardless of time or location. This means information can be exchanged across the country, across the street, or across the hall.

Though this papers deals generally with groupware, it specifically cites and demonstrates the groupware product Lotus Notes™.

### Tapping into Knowledge

Companies rarely distinguish themselves by how good their Gantt charts are. Running a complex project involves more than executing operational systems. It involves business processes—teams of people involved in the ongoing activity of coordinating, collaborating and negotiating, often with groups of employees, outside vendors, suppliers, and customers. As we have seen, companies stand out from the competition not by how well their employees fill out a time sheet, but how quickly they can bring a new product or service to market.

Giving teams the opportunity to brainstorm no matter where they are means we can begin to tap into the company's *knowledgebase* of information. Notes uses discussion databases (essentially electronic bulletin boards) to provide a forum for the project team to exchange information, ideas, comments and suggestions. This information can ultimately develop into a "corporate memory"—an electronic journal that allows individuals to review the activities and findings of previous projects and ultimately reduce the turnaround time for the next project, thereby leading to continuous improvement.

### Speeding Workflow

Efficient workflow is a necessary component of any successful project. However, most off-the-shelf project management software tools do not have the ability to remind team members of upcoming tasks or to flag management of missed deadlines. Nor can they automatically pass documents and forms through various approval levels and notify the appropriate parties if something is sitting unread too long in someone's mailbox. Notes can route forms to supervisors for their electronic signatures, notify a project manager when there is activity with a particular vendor, e-mail weekly assignments to individual team members, and send up the red flag when important milestones are coming up or are seriously delayed. The workflow features of Notes, combined with the monitoring capabilities of project management software, helps project managers not only see what is getting done, but enables them to get it done.

### Creating the total project knowledgebase

Project reports are comprised not just of Gantt and PERT charts, but the same hodgepodge of information found in any complex business process: contracts, policies and procedures, methodologies, performance evaluations, etc. And as indicated earlier, the information itself can appear in a variety of formats—not just text, but graphics, scanned documents, Web pages, downloads from the legacy system, video and sound, embedded objects, links to other documents—any of the variety of ways we communicate in our everyday work. Because Notes documents can contain both structured and unstructured content, they essentially become *object containers* that can store all types of information. That, in turn, means Notes database management becomes more robust than the typical relational or transactional system. A powerful search engine enables the user to easily index and query all the data, no matter what its format. Looking for a phrase inside an embedded Microsoft Word document? Notes will find it. In addition, Notes Versioning Control provides document versioning capabilities in order to track multiple changes made to a single document by different users— a vital component to the change control process.

### Meeting the needs of all users

Not all team members are proficient in the use of project management software tools. Notes provides users with an interface that can recreate a familiar environment, that is, paper forms they are used to filling out. In addition, many of the routines can be automated with macro buttons and routing agents.

Notes, with its integrated e-mail and replication functions, provides the mechanism for users to communicate whenever they want, from wherever they want, and however they want. The key to the power of Lotus Notes in today's heterogeneous corporate systems environments is its extensive multiple platform support. All Notes users can access all servers, exchange information, send and receive e-mail, independent of operating systems and protocols.

Notes provides the project team with a comprehensive toolset. The central repository of information becomes the Total Project Database that can provide the customized views and specialized reporting requirements specific to senior management, who rely on high-level rolled-up summary information, and the detailed action items and tasks for individual team members.

### Security

Companies are making more and more information available not only internally, but outside their corporate walls too. Data security then becomes an issue that takes on even greater importance. Notes offers four levels of security: authentication, access control, encryption and digital signatures.

## The Need for Participation

### (Uncommon) Common Understanding

Project managers are faced with the challenge of integrating the diverse skills and perspectives of sometimes sizable teams of contributors. For all team members to be 100 percemt clear on the project's and each other's issues during a staff meeting would make for interminably long meetings. The pressure is on today to reduce the number and the duration of the meetings we conduct. To make sure that complete understanding has been achieved between team members, sometimes a period of "info-gestion" must take place after a meeting followed by an opportunity for participants to clarify each other's meaning.

Discussion databases provide for all team members to participate or audit on-going clarification discussions. Thank goodness this can be accomplished during times that team members have the opportunity to update themselves on the discussions when their busy schedules allow, and not while they are in the middle of making good progress on their tasks. This can be while taking a break or waiting for another team member's deliverable (finish-to-start dependencies).

Timely communications often means different times for different people. For some it means early in the morning before things get too hectic. For others, it means at home after work. And for others, it means while they take their lunch at their desks. For each of us, the *right* time to communicate and clarify meaning or to get additional information means *different* times. Groupware makes it possible for meaningful conversation to continue when it makes the most sense to the individual participants.

### Planning

Once a common understanding of the project issues has been achieved, project resources can often be the best source of detailed planning information available. They understand the tasks that must be done to deliver what they are accountable for, how their work depends on other tasks, how much work is represented by their task assignments, and how much time they really have available to your project.

There are several groupware applications that facilitate and capture distributed planning information. They all allow for discussion databases to be populated with levels of work breakdown information. For example, a project manager could

1. Create/setup a database for a project plan
2. E-mail the team with the location of the database
3. Notify them of the deadline for their task entries
4. Allow for the breakdown of phases (your phase breakdown) into activities, tasks and milestones. These levels of breakdown correspond to the more familiar discussion topics, responses, and responses to responses.
5. Each form in the database should have fields for:
   - Deliverables
   - Dependencies on other tasks
   - Necessary resources and work estimates.

Human resources have fixed productive output capacities. There are so many factors surrounding a person's true availability to your project, that it is almost impossible for a resource management system to accurately model this constantly changing tug-of-war. A better solution is to ask for a team members own best guess about how many hours per day or per week they can actually provide to your project. If the amount is insufficient, groupware allows for the give and take negotiations between the team member, other project managers, and the resource manager.

### Tracking

One of groupware's greatest contributions is the distribution of the right information to the right people at the right time. In a project environment, all the information at once would be overwhelming. When a project resource needs to see what work needs to be done by them this week, Groupware can provide just the tasks to be accomplished this week by that individual, and it can be done in an e-mail message.

When it comes time to capture actual progress, this e-mail message acts as a turnaround document for the team member to use to enter time spent, time remaining, and notes to the project manager.

## Who Are the Participants and What Do They Need?

Project Stakeholders that have a need to participate in the creation of or have the need to be kept up to date with project related information are listed below:

### The Project Sponsor

Project sponsors are interested in how the budget that they approved for your project is being invested. They want to know that the promised return on investment was not just a good sales job, but is truly what will come out the other end of this endeavor. Therefore, a Gantt chart is not going to satisfy a sponsor's need for information.

Sponsors are looking for a one-line status report that gives them a health indicator of how the project is progressing. Although earned value reporting techniques are not in widespread use in most business environments, the CPI (cost performance index), CV (cost variance), SV (schedule variance) and SPI (schedule performance index) are good ways to briefly report on project health.

### Manager of Project Managers

Managers of project managers need to know that the match between project manager and project assignment is a good one. A mismatch between the challenges of the project and the capabilities of the project manager is a problem at either end of the spectrum. If a project manager is underskilled for the current project load, the manager will find himself assisting much more than he had anticipated. If the project manager feels underutilized because the project is not challenging enough, the manager runs the risk of boredom and poor project performance, or a project manager searching for greener pastures.

Groupware solutions can provide a window into either of these circumstances via the audit of project team discussions, timely documentation of project proceedings, and changes that are being visibly managed, not the obvious lack of communication. Managers of project managers should look for consistently applied management measures, not bursts of activity followed by long quiet spells. Projects go bad one day at a time. Prolonged periods of no news rarely means good news.

### Project Team Members

In an earlier section, we discussed how to best keep project team members in the loop via involvement in planning and tracking activities. It is also important to keep them active in communicating changes, risks, and upcoming challenges in the project execution. Discussion databases are uniquely capable of capturing the issues, proposing solutions, and providing resolution to all the things that go wrong during a project. As soon as a participant makes a change suggestion, it should be logged in the change section of the project database. Responses to the change request should be sought to best understand impact on existing work, and problems or benefits of the suggested change. Changes, risks, and issues should be tracked so that open issues stand apart from closed, accepted changes stand apart from rejected, and mitigated risks stand apart from present dangers.

### Other Project Managers

Managers of other projects need to know when key deliverables will be produced from your project. Many low-end scheduling tools do not allow for dependencies across separate projects. Therefore, having a groupware database with all projects represented makes for an easy access location for key dates and milestones to be stored and accessed.

Managers of other projects also need to know when key resources will become available when finished with your project. Certain groupware applications allow for the consolidation of multiple project information so that resource loading time can be analyzed across all projects. When a new project comes along, a quick assessment can be made of what timeframe is best to try to take it on.

### End-Users or Project Recipients

Every project has customers—users of the product or service that is being created by your project. If they are not kept informed about what is happening on the project ( "When am I going to get it?" or "When do I get to play with it?"), you may get some unwarranted bad press. Another downside of not keeping the customers in the loop is that their phone calls place a heavy burden on your customer support personnel (Don't think so? Just ask 'em.). The lion's share of these questions could be automatically answered by publishing just a small amount of the information discussed here. Most groupware is Internet-ready and can publish this information on the Internet or on your company's intranet.

## What Other Tools Are Out There?

Groupware allows for easy transferability of information regarding your projects. There are other tools that can help with groupware to further provide project information and management. The most common type of tool is referred to as a consolidator product. Consolidators gather information on multiple projects and can add various project information.

### Consolidator Products

Consolidators are software systems that allow for the management and strategic planning of multiple projects. There are a multitude of consolidator products available. They will work in conjunction with project management software tools such as Microsoft Project or Project Scheduler to create and roll-up multiple projects on a much larger scale than the individual tools will. This aids in providing up-to-date tracking and project management. Consolidators enable users to distribute, import and export project information. Some only will work with one software tool such as Microsoft Project while others are more flexible as far as the different applications they will work with. There are some consolidators that in reality are just third -arty software add-ins to existing project management software while others are much larger database systems.

Some examples are ChangePoint's "Remind," Innate's "Multi-Project," Marin Research's "Project Gateway," MicroFrame's "Business Engine," and Moss Micro's "Project Exchange."

- Software Made Easy's "Project Control"

These consolidators can be either large repositories or some are a suite of products that help the Project Manager manage a variety of projects and resources. They also will aid in strategic project planning by allowing access to all information.

### General Overview of Consolidator Projects

The consolidators on the market today have a variety of different features or customization options. A summary of some of the standard features of consolidator project software are :

- Extend project management software
- Maintain standard templates and allow for creation of new projects based on templates
- Consolidate projects
- Summarize projects in different areas
- Schedulers for resources
- Multi-project management
- Time tracking capabilities

- Provide a variety of reports
- Custom project graphics and charts.

### Strengths

The consolidators are large databases of project information. The strengths of the consolidator vary depending on which consolidator is being used and the system it is running on. The consolidator in combination with groupware makes it possible to incorporate standard project management tools and use groupware to document and communicate project information. Many consolidators use Lotus Notes technology to share its information. Other consolidators use standard e-mail systems like Ms Mail or Exchange to communicate project information. Many consolidators have built in reports and can expand the reporting capabilities of groupware.. Some of the advantages of using a consolidator in addition to groupware, such as Lotus Notes, are that it allows for substantial multi project analysis and can enhance the strengths of the existing groupware. The database actively creates and summarizes information providing insight into problems and possible solutions. In addition to tracking multiple projects from many project managers it can alert these managers to any scheduling conflicts that may arise. Some of the consolidators even have a warning system to actively alert project managers if there is a problem. Often they either have a timesheet capability or work in conjunction with a time tracking application and make for easy resource management.

### Weaknesses

The consolidator programs do have weaknesses or perhaps are lacking in some areas.. They do not always interface well with SQL systems or networks already in place. There can be some instability with the software in these situations. It is important to realize, also, that the consolidators are tools and are not the solution to good project management. They still require frequent monitoring by project managers.

## Conclusions

Software has not replaced the project manager (nor will it), but it has made it easier (for the information) to be in all places at all times. When implemented correctly, groupware can make the daunting challenge of project communications management much easier. All levels of a project partnership can be supported by an information strategy that provides WYSIWYN (What You See Is What You Need!)

# Global Project Management: Balancing Product and Profession

Ronald P. C. Waller, PMP, CEM - Johnson Controls, Inc.

## Introduction

Global interest in project management is increasing exponentially and, like national political entities, this interest is driven from multiple sources. Some of these sources are: business (those globally positioned), professional organizations, government, consulting/training/research organizations and of course individuals. Each of these groups has a different set of desired outcomes and not all of the outcomes correlate positively.

In the project management profession, the primary actors may be generally separated into two groups: 1) those in the business of project management (profession developers); and 2) those in the business of managing projects (practitioners). To those in the business of project management, project management may be considered a "product or service." To those in the business of managing projects, project management is a "discipline and profession." Clearly, these groups are necessary for the success of the profession, but a balance must be achieved in the dialogue and direction of global efforts in the continued development of the project management profession.

To justify and clarify this premise requires an inspection of project management practice and use of the term professional. Is managing projects a unique profession, or just the application of a subset of general management profession processes? Is project management just a management methodology subset we use when we are managing unique combinations of activities (projects) rather than repetitive activities (operations) or, as was suggested by one CEO, just a management style? Is it similar to the difference between a medical doctor and a doctor of osteopathy? And, what is a professional? Does having participated as a project team member or having managed a project or projects for others at some point in a persons working life qualify that person as a practitioner in the business of managing projects and thus a professional in the managing projects profession? Or is continuous practice at managing projects for others required to maintain this status?

## The Profession

Larson (1977) suggests that occupations that are considered professions and which are thus endowed with special powers and prestige have three attributes. First a *cognitive* dimension—that which centers on a body of knowledge and techniques which the professionals apply in their work, accompanied by the training necessary to master such knowledge and skills. Second, the *normative* dimension—that which deals with the service orientation of professionals and their distinctive ethics justifying the privilege of self regulation granted by societies. And third, the *evaluative* dimension—that which includes peer review and implicitly compares professions to other occupations and professions. This latter dimension underscores the profession's singular characteristics, autonomy, and prestige, and conformance separates occupations and professions from each other.

While the distinctiveness of professions tends to be founded on a combination of these general dimensions, the cognitive dimension (application and theory) is the primary differentiator of a profession. Members of the profession become communities and share a relatively *permanent affiliation, an identity, personal commitment, specific interests, and general loyalties*.

There is a body of knowledge continuum of project management. First there are unique knowledge areas such as project integration scope and time (level 1); followed by unique combinations of elements of other bodies of knowledge such as earned value (level 2); followed by unique applications of elements of other bodies of knowledge such as cost and risk (level 3); and lastly by heavy use of related body of knowledge elements such as human resources, contracting/procurement, quality and communications (level 4).

Not many would disagree with the distinction of a project management profession, but can one be a 'professional' in multiple professions at the same time? The *Webster's Dictionary* definition of a professional is: "one that engages in a pursuit or activity professionally (conforming to the technical or ethical standards of a profession). " Perhaps a better indication comes from the origins of the word "profession:" *To profess*— "the act of taking the vows of a religious community," or "the act of openly declaring or publicly claiming a belief, faith, or opinion." This origin suggests that

**Exhibit 1.** Professional Progression Pyramid

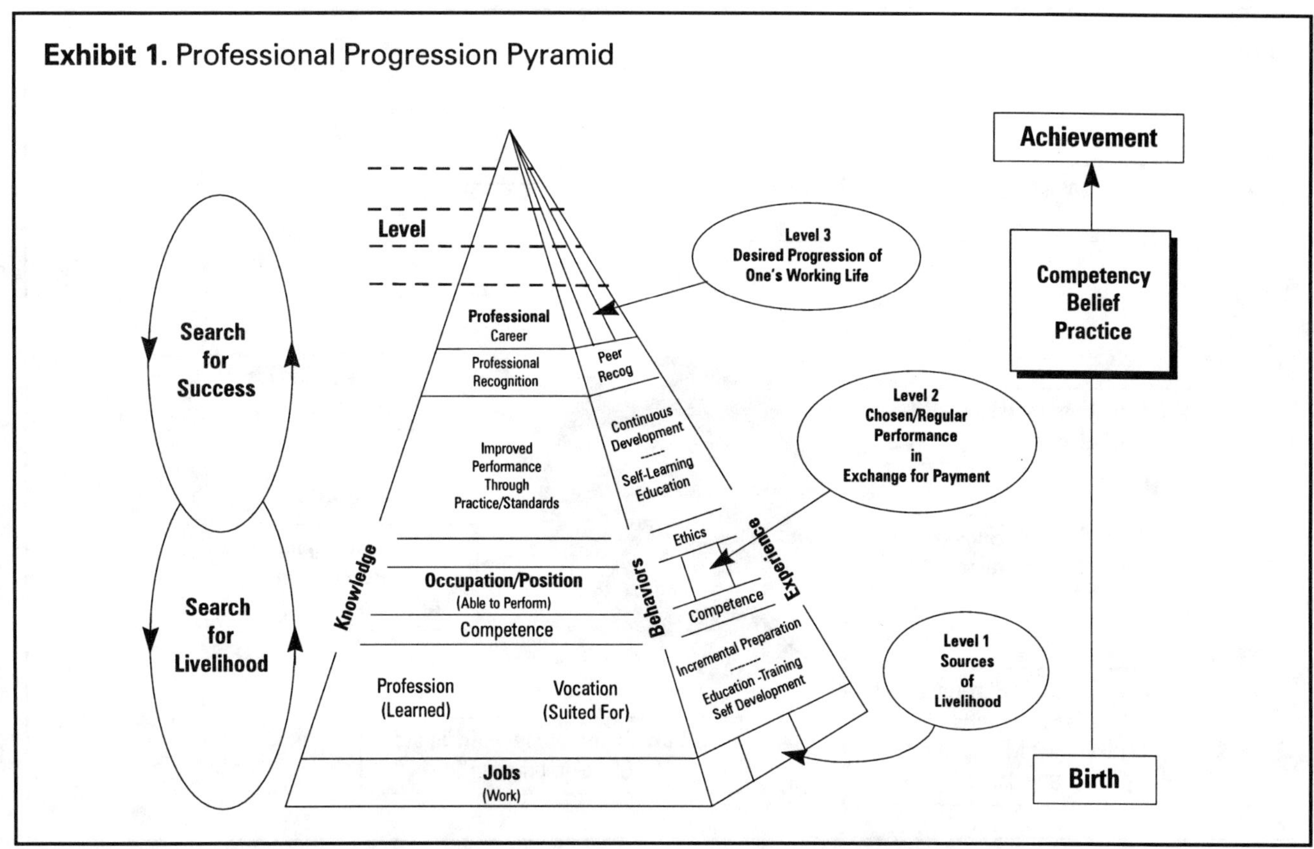


a professional holds a commitment to the profession that is stronger than just being competent or able to perform. It suggests that a professional espouse a dedication to the profession that becomes a distinctive part of everyday life. Webster also defines practitioner as "one who practices the profession."

Exhibit 1. illustrates a progression through life to attain ones desired working profession. Initially, we work at jobs available to support our needs. As we learn and develop skills we may perform services or work in several professions. We may work at many professions over time, and some would argue that they have worked these simultaneously. However, at some point we make a individual decision to identify ourselves as a 'professional' in a profession. This may or may not require peer recognition. Generally, professionals do not answer the question "What is your profession?" with a multiple response unless they are not currently working in their chosen profession by circumstance. This is not to suggest that a person could not be skilled in several disciplines. In fact, many if not most project managers are educated in another profession before becoming a project manager. Many engineers, doctors, and accountants are project managers, and many scientists manage projects. A professional earns a livelihood from the profession as a practitioner, practices it on a daily basis "takes the vows of a community," acts to achieve the professions individual recognition, and "acts openly, declaring and publicly proclaiming the belief, faith, and opinion" of the profession. Professions are much like religion, while you may believe, understand, be knowledgeable of, and even be competent in several, you only practice one at a time and you don't change it on a daily basis.

Is the project management profession comprised of: 1) just project managers; 2) project managers and other project team members who may be professionals in another profession such as cost engineering; and, 3) does this profession include, for example scheduling software engineers and publishers? Just where does the profession begin and end? These distinctions are much more difficult to identify than the difference between profession developers and practitioners mentioned previously although it appears that it would depend primarily on the commitment of the individual to the community of practitioners. If a project management consultant or educator chooses to be identified with the practitioners in the project management community, does that make them a professional in the project management profession even if their standard of work and practice is defined by the consulting or teaching bodies of knowledge and professional communities? Does the title "project management consultant" imply a commitment to the project management or consulting profession? Can it be to both?

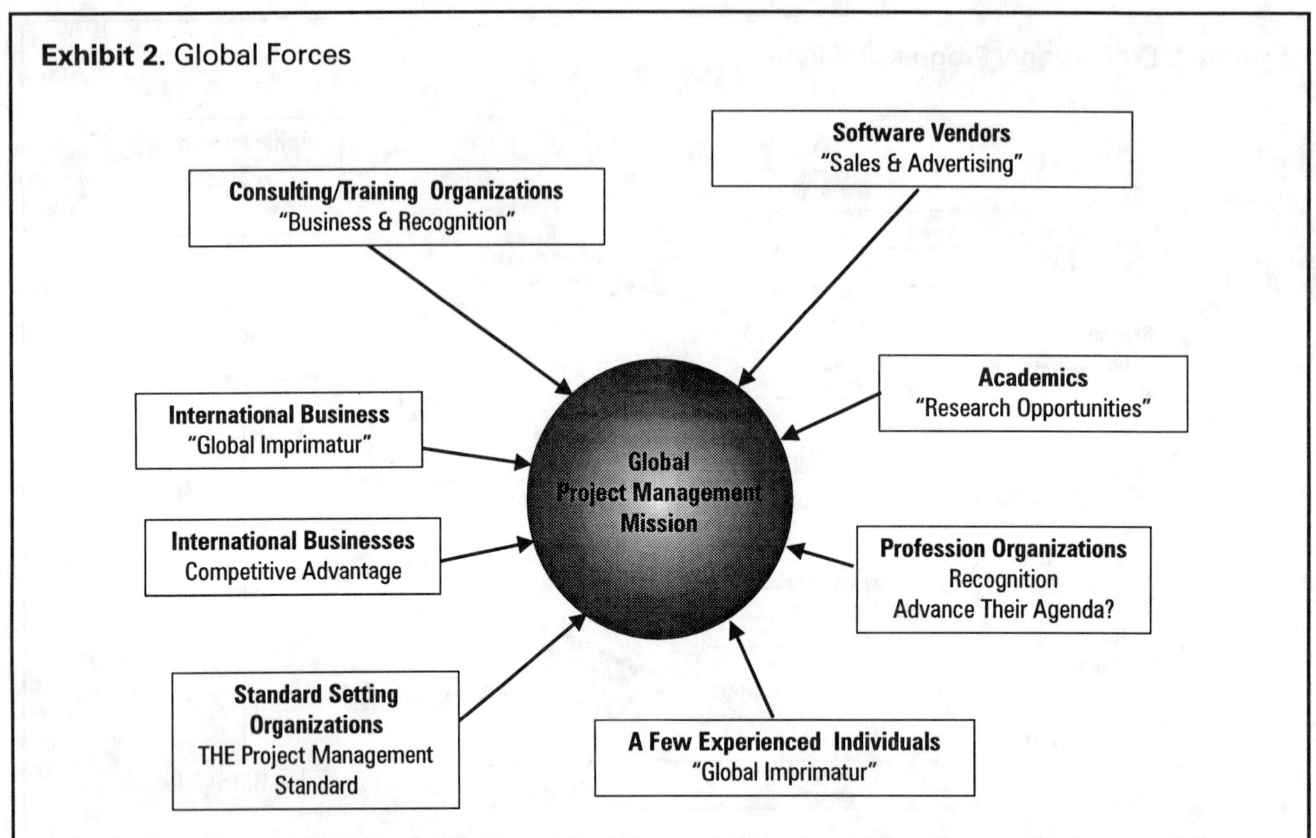


If the premise regarding the nature of professionals involved in the project management profession is valid, who speaks for and determines the direction and development of the project management profession. Is it the professional project practitioners or professionals from other (related) professions? Clearly both groups will continue to develop the profession. It is important to understand the motivations of speakers in a forum that does not identify the practitioners or the profession that is being represented when views and positions are advanced in the global arena.

## The Profession as a Business Driver?

As one inspects the development of the global profession it appears that several national project management "professional organizations" serve as a basis for directly supporting commerce and business! Perhaps these appearances grew out of legitimate support requirements or developed from such relationships. These "back" businesses are generally consulting, training, education or research organizations, or, software/project management journal publishers. Money that is earned from the relationship goes into individual pockets as well as (or instead of) the profession's.

What appears out of step is balance between what we desire as individuals in business and organizations and what may be best for the profession. Certainly the motivation of these professional organization representatives is suspect when the representatives advance positions that first tend to directly or indirectly support the business. One only needs to look at the global activity shown in Exhibit 2 to see the various forces at play in the 'global' project management profession. When individual, business and government needs are being addressed and supported, in addition to supporting the accomplishment of projects, then the creation of business opportunities will coincide with the expansion of the profession. Creating opportunity must be balanced with the needs of the profession. And the needs of the profession should be considered first, not last. For the profession to grow we will need the substantial participation of all parties.

## Global PM Standards and Certification

Interestingly, project management standards and certification are the issues raised in the global project management forum instead of education or communication. While standards such as a body of knowledge represent the basis for a profession, recognition of individual competency is a key component.

The standards most often cited as candidates for a global document are:

- Project Management Institute (PMI) - *Guide to the Project Management Body of Knowledge (PMBOK Guide)*
- Association of Project Managers (APM), U.K. - Body of Knowledge
- British Government Information Technology (IT) Project Management Standard - PRojects IN a Controlled Environment (PRINCE2)
- British Standards Institute (BSI) - Guide to Project Management BS-6079
- International Standards Institute (ISO) - DIS-10006, Quality in Project Management
- Australian Institute of Project Management (AIPM) Competency Standards.

Certification programs advanced as models are:

- PMI Project Management Professional (PMP)
- International Project Management Association (IPMA) Certificated Project Manager (CPM)
- The yet-to-be developed AIPM Registered Project Manager (Reg PM)
- The recently developed APM, APM Professional (APMP).

There is pressure to agree on a global body of knowledge (BOK) with substantial positioning regarding global certification from several professional organization representatives, but are these goals realistic? If they are, what is the process and what is their eventual role in the development of the profession? What is more important, developing a global profession or developing the profession globally?

A body of knowledge defines the profession and practice and changes over time. The PMI BOK first outlined in 1976 is now in its third published version. It represents global development and generally accepted practices for managing projects. It identifies itself in the 1996 version as a *guide* to the project management body of knowledge. The document is organized around nine processes contained in five life cycle steps.

The APM issued their BOK in 1992, with the current version dated July 1993. This document lists 41 "definitions" with low, medium and high knowledge and experience classifications and numerous references for each. It is targeted to support the APM "Certificated project manager" program by providing a document to support the interview assessment process. Several Wstern Europe national member organizations of IPMA have developed or are in process of developing separate national BOK's to support similar certification programs.

PRINCE was originally issued in 1990 by the British Central Computer and Telecommunications Agency (CCTA), a government support organization responsible for providing best practice advice to its government. PRINCE was originally intended to guide the management of public sector IT projects. Some advertise the second release, PRINCE2, as the de facto British standard for project management, noting widespread use in both public and private sectors. In 1996 the British Standards Institute issued BS-6079, ostensibly as the de facto ISO project management standard.

**Exhibit 3.** Standards Evolution

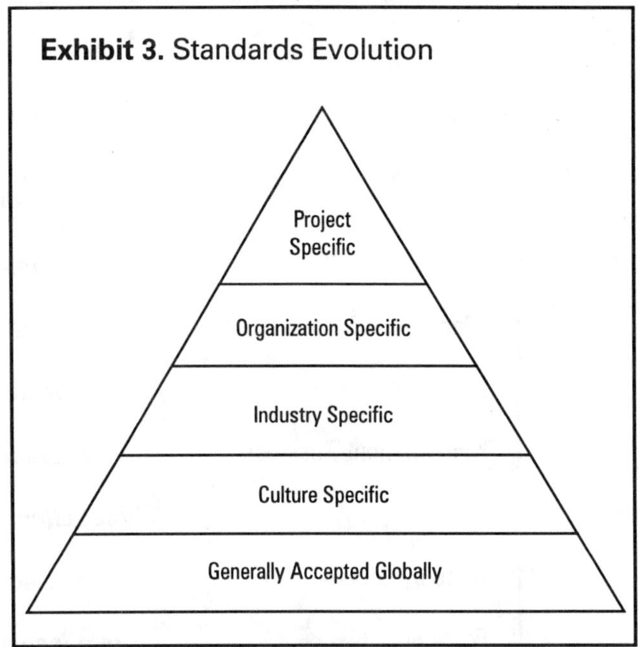


Also in 1996, the AIPM issued its competency standards based on PMI's *PMBOK Guide* and on the APM standards which are intended to support the future development of a registered project manager program in Australia.

There are several other existing western European national standards with yet others in development. PMI is working to have the *PMBOK Guide* accredited by the American National Standards Institute (ANSI) and has offered the document as an Institute of Electrical and Electronic Engineers (IEEE) and ISO project management standard. The British government recognizes its own PRINCE2 and BS-6079, and AIPM has received guarded sponsorship of its competency standard by the Australian Finance and Administration Industry Training and Advisory Body (FAITB) after abandoning a National Office of Overseas Skill Recognition (NOOSR) model.

The substantial majority of project management standards activity originates from English-speaking countries. Is the practice of non-English speaking members of the profession represented fairly in current issues of these documents?

The most widely known project management competency credentials are: 1) The PMI Project Management Professional (PMP) program initiated in 1984 and continuously upgraded. This program is pursuing accreditation by the National Organization for Certifying Agencies (NOCA), a recognized body for accrediting association certification programs. No grandfathering is allowed and approximately

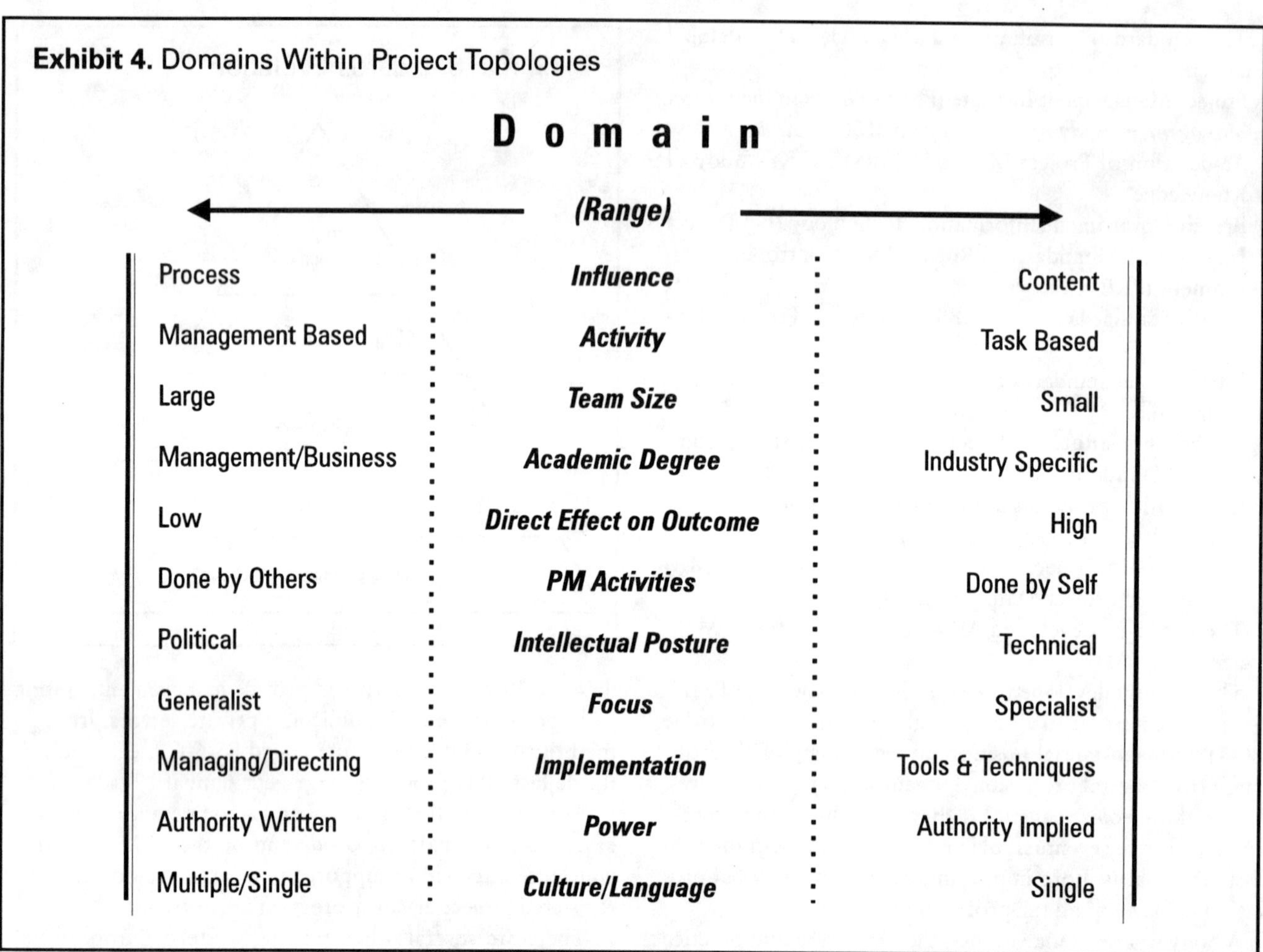


6,500 candidates have been certified. 2) The APM Certificated Project Manager (CPM) launched in 1993. This program allowed grandfathering the first year. It has an age requirement and has certificated approximately 140 candidates to-date. It is the basis for the IPMA national certification program. 3) The APM Professional (APMP) was developed late in 1996 and certified 37 candidates in February 1997. The new APMP credential requires a demonstration of experience and knowledge based on APM's *Book of Knowledge* and BS-6079. 4) The British Institute of Software Engineers (ISEB) certifies project managers in IT. 5) The AIPM intends to launch its RegPM (Registered Project Manager) program late in 1997. The PMI BOK and PMP are cornerstones in this credential.

Exhibit 4. Domains Within Project Topologies
Domain
(Range)
Process
Influence
Content
Management Based
Activity
Task Based
Large
Team Size
Small
Management/Business
Academic Degree
Industry Specific
Low
Direct Effect on Outcome
High
Done by Others
PM Activities
Done by Self
Political
Intellectual Posture
Technical
Generalist
Focus
Specialist
Managing/Directing
Implementation
Tools & Techniques
Authority Written
Power
Authority Implied
Multiple/Single
Culture/Language
Single

## Global Community Needs

It is important to remember that most projects are small and the majority of project managers manage small projects. Equally as important to note are six primary project success factors: 1) the nature of the project delivery environment, 2) the project architecture or topology, 3) the competency and posture of the customer/owner/client, 4) the competency of the organization, 5) the competency of the project team, and finally, 6) the competency of the project manager.

While much of project management is common to almost all projects, variations in process, sometimes substantial, occur from culture (the language, customs and practice of the delivery environment), the industry, the organization, and finally the project topology (the characteristics of project groups). A hierarchy of standards development is shown in Exhibit 3. At each juncture, language, practice or process changes are likely to occur. Since the use of process standards occur at the project level, any global standard would need to be compatible with many variations. Even generally accepted standards are unsuitable if different is what is required.

In addition to these elements, there are other effects (domains) within each project topology group that create differences in project manager knowledge and skill requirements. Some of these domains are illustrated in Exhibit 4.

In contrast to this apparent substantial variance in the nature and delivery of projects, mature, globally organized project-driven organizations desire uniform if not singular processes for all of their projects wherever they occur. These processes however may not be compatible with other industries and businesses. A single project management standard in support of some form of global project manager registration/certification would contain only those processes and practices agreed as acceptable for all global users. This would be required for a certification based on a single standard. A credential based on this global standard is likely to be reduced to such a low common denominator as to become almost useless. As stated by Davidson "... you can't write global standards with a 'one-size fits all' label —it simply cannot be done" (1997).

Variations in domains and process standards appears to make creation of a truly global project manager credential extremely difficult to develop if it is done properly. Agreement on elements such as ethics, age requirements, career stage, education and service may be difficult. More importantly, *recognition, credential standards and assessment processes need practitioner verification and acceptance. They are not appropriately created by groups representing business, industry or academe working separate from regular practitioner scrutiny.* Further, bias, validity and reliability testing, ensuring authenticity, and updating such a credential would consume substantial resources if it could be created, not to mention the difficulty of translating such a credential into multiple languages. As a further example of this difficulty, Stretton declared "It should be noted that the American concept of professionalism and the Australian perception (inherited from the British) are very different. The stringent and high entry-level standards which membership in a professional association implies in Australia appear to be irrelevant in the USA. Therefore, the PMP designation does not qualify as a professional qualification in Australia" (1994).

While a global project manager credential may be difficult or even impossible to create, development of regional credentials (perhaps by culture or continental groupings) could be a likely first step. If regional credentials are successful, then work to merge these regional credentials into a global credential would be appropriate.

## What Can We Accomplish?

Project management is capable of helping all societies since it represents effective methodologies and processes for accomplishing things. From discussions with global business representatives and practitioners, it appears that what is desired by those involved in the day-to-day practice of 'managing projects' is to better understand how to successfully manage projects. This involves better understanding of: 1) project success factors; 2) the ART of project management 3) project management processes; 4) understanding the uniqueness of project processes in industry and cultures and the differences between project managers needed to manage projects; 5) standards which can be used as a starting point in the development of culturally focused documents; 6) identification of what constitutes effective practice (behaviors which create excellent performance) and; 7) continuous knowledge building and knowledge sharing.

While a single glossary or definition list is out of the question given the variance in culture, custom and language we need a correlated project lexicon so that we can better communicate between languages and cultures. We need to share practical standards, methods, and best practices which can guide us in better management of projects and which can be used as a basis for further refinement and expansion.

But, at this point in the development of the profession, the greatest benefit to both the global community as well as the profession is education and communication. Specifically, demonstrating the benefits of project management and how it can help in the successful delivery of projects while identifying practical and successful processes recommended to initiate a project management program in an organization. These are the areas where global efforts should be focused.

## Summary and Conclusion

It appears that much of the present "global project management" dialogue is being driven by "project management business" issues and not advancement of the project management profession or professionalism in managing projects. The dialogue and emphasis must now shift to a new plateau and the interests of those in the business of project management should be balanced with those in the business of managing projects. The dialogue and action steps could consist of:

- Avoid (and declare) conflicts of interest, either real or perceived
- Continue developing knowledge-sharing and knowledge-building networks
- Make all project management standards available pro-bono or contribute them to the public domain; develop a correlated project lexicon
- Initiate discussions about the profession and its boundaries; identify the elements that are common and elements that are different
- Identify basic project management processes and practices that are effective (and specify when they should be used)
- Recognize successful project management practice and identify the behaviors which lead to successful practice; develop theory from practice vs. practice from theory

- Clarify the context of individual, business, government, and public need.

## References


Davidson, Angus. 1997. *Project Manager Today* (April).

Larson, D.L. 1977. *The Rise of Professionalism.*

Stretton, Allan. 1994. A short history of modern project management, part 3. *The Australian Project Manager* 14 (October).

# China - An Eastern Twist for the Project Manager

Jon A. Del Vecchio, Eastman Kodak Company

It becomes second nature. A project concept is presented and the project manager immediately begins to think of the scope, the sequence of activities, the schedule and all the other process functions that make for successful project outcomes. The savvy project manager wouldn't proceed without conscious attention to the details of the project sponsor's expectations around time, cost and quality performance, agreements with suppliers, contractors and the end users, project team formation and organization, risk assessment and any issues that may be unique to the specific project. To knowingly deviate from good project managementpractices is to flirt with disaster.

Yet in China, deviation from Western, generally accepted, good practices is common. Poor scope development and communication, lack of planning, poor contracting practices and lack of risk assessment are among the most common. The knowledgeable project manager would naturally wonder how projects can be completed with any kind of predictable results. The simple answer is that many projects are not completed in a timely and quality fashion. At least not the first time. Western project sponsors and end users would not tolerate this, but many Chinese "customers" not only accept these methods, they expect the delays and performance shortcomings. The only reason for this appears to be an ingredient we won't find in the *PMBOK Guide* ... the Chinese culture.

At first, these crude methods appear to be a stone-age throwback. In many ways, they are. But a second look and a little pondering brings one to the realization that China has come a very long way. It is unprecedented to have a communist political state and a free economy coexist, yet that is exactly what the Chinese are accomplishing. Keeping up with the explosive growth is a monumental task. The public services and transportation infrastructure are constantly being strained and expanded. One might ask how they are able to sustain and maintain this growth if good project managementpractices are not that well known or followed. The answer might lie in a simple concept. We all know physically challenged people who are successful, they just don't allow their handicap to be a barrier. In China, what is lacking in planning and quality is overcome with speed. What is lacking in scope development is overcome with teamwork. What turns out to be unexpected results is overcome with enthusiasm and interpersonal relationships.

This presents a challenge to Western project teams. How does the team take known good practices and meld them with the speed, teamwork and relationships displayed by the Chinese, or any cultural environment it happens to be working in? There is no question that many of the Western methods are superior, but they could likely be enhanced by adopting the cultural aspects, at least in China.

## Background

The writer's experience in China began innocently enough. Due to varied assignments in the past, I was asked to look over a translated lease for a factory in Shanghai, People's Republic of China (PRC). After spending a short time with the future general manager, we quickly determined that much more than a lease review was required. Technical and construction project management support seemed necessary in order to convert a rented concrete shell into a factory to produce high quality, competitively priced circuit boards within six months in a foreign country where we had no experience. Fortunately, the general manager was familiar with project management techniques and had developed a work breakdown and timeline as part of the business case. A common project management understanding created the basis of leadership for the project team.

A leasehold improvement plan was developed which included obtaining a business license and the signing of the lease. The business license and lease negotiations were among the first exposures to Chinese bureaucracy and the difficulties of translation. Knowing we had to take some time with these negotiations, we began to investigate the contracting of technical and skilled labor resources in the Shanghai area in parallel with the licensing and leasing activities. Translation became even more protracted with the introduction of technical terms and construction methods. Photographs of the existing shell and drawings of how the factory layout was to look in its final configuration proved invaluable. We quickly discovered that we had to share a long-range vision of what the factory layout would be, even if it were not to be implemented. Omissions and blank spaces caused confusion and distraction.

The long-range business plan was to start this and future factories with expatriates from the U.S., then train Chinese management people to take over in a three- to five-year period. We approached the building improvements with the same vision. We were to develop a Chinese team of design and construction contractors who could be developed to implement the future factories. This first factory was for we foreigners to gain a working knowledge of implementing facilities projects in China and to bring our Chinese counterparts up the learning curve for working with Westerners.

Investigating building design firms and skilled trade contractors was some of the most interesting work. The culture of doing business and construction was vastly different from the western world. Design firms were commonly tied to contracting firms and were in a minority position within the firms. On one occasion we discovered that the same design people were supposedly employees of two independent construction firms. There were different business charters for construction firms as well. Some were state-owned, some were private and some were tied in to certain development zones either by licensing or interpersonal relationships with the zone or government officials.

Skilled trades continue to be in a constant state of development. For the first factory, it was impossible to explain what copper pipe was and how it was to be installed. By the time we reached the second factory, copper piping materials were available but assembly methods were poor.

Understanding project management techniques remains a challenge for the Chinese. For instance, we regularly plan and/or implement parallel project activities. The Chinese tend to have a series mentality. For example, asking them to begin design without a fully completed plan layout is difficult. They fixate on the missing parts. They may seemingly be convinced to start a parallel task, only to find later that they really did not start.

This leads to another factor in the Chinese culture, and apparently in the Japanese culture as well. They do not know how to say no. They feel that they will disrespect others or lose face if they declare that they cannot accomplish a task on time or that they do not possess the skills to meet a request. This is frustrating to the westerner. There appears to be agreement yet when it comes time to produce, the task is undone. Probing into the reasons for the failure leads to drawn out translations, eventual acceptance of the failure and another commitment. One is never sure about the real reason for failure to meet commitments. These can range from earnest attempts to having no idea of how to perform the task. What has to be preserved in the long run is the personal relationship. Though this is frustrating, the Westerner is still the foreigner and we must flex to be successful in their culture.

## The Circuit Board Assembly Factory

The project team consisted of the expatriate general manager and a project/technical advisor (the writer), both from the United States, who would be on site for two weeks each month, a Chinese project manager, and a Chinese construction company with integrated design. The organization of the project team was that the general manager produced a vision of how the factory was to look in its final configuration. Along with the project advisor, a floor plan layout, an equipment characteristic spreadsheet and an architectural finishes spreadsheet were developed and communicated to the project manager, designers and construction people. After completion and approval, the design was implemented. The factory began operations six months after conceptual design and after one year had ramped up to 700 employees and 75 percent of its planned capacity.

This first factory was a rich learning experience. Having a fairly complete scope, solid project leadership and regular communications minimized the effect of the difficulties regarding translation, contracting in a foreign country, and materials limitations. Teamwork and close communications helped to overcome some significant problems like the performance failure, and subsequent firing of the architectural and plumbing contractor, and the overcoming the bureaucracy of the local government. By the end of the construction activity, a fairly strong project team and set of relationships were formed.

## The Camera Factory

Having developed some confidence around the ability of the Chinese team members from the circuit board factory experience, the camera factory project was to take a similar approach and utilize the Chinese team created by the circuit board factory. This gave the advantage of a quicker start, a reasonable expectation of the resulting quality, and the requirement for as early as possible plant startup. The group of expatriates and U.S. associates were quite different. Some had experience in China and Mexico as well as in the United States. The group was much larger and more diverse. This led to more dispersion of leadership among those who would reside in China and their U.S. counterparts. The Chinese team we had developed from the circuit board factory was not accepted. There was a consensus for more competitive bidding, and separation of design and construction. Since time was to be spent evaluating design companies and construction companies, it was decided that the camera operation would start in part of the circuit board factory space and move to the new factory ahead of the circuit board production ramp up that would occupy the space. That turned out to be a very good decision, since it covered for some of the unanticipated delays.

In the case of the camera factory, a larger team was assembled. The team included a Chinese vice general manager with ten years experience in another U.S. company who acted in the role of project manager. Three Chinese technical support people were hired temporarily to advise on facility type issues. The same Chinese project manager used for the previous project was contracted. Three to five U.S. people were involved on the team as representatives of the manufacturing groups and the writer as project/technical advisor who would be on site for two weeks each month.

The team initially started to interview and evaluate design and construction firms for the purposes of competitive bidding. The environment for doing this was no better than for the first factory. A different design group was chosen to produce the facilities design from similar layout and spreadsheet documentation. This arrangement proved to be more difficult. Since there was no firm decision on the construction company and the design team had no business relationship with a construction company, the design had to be presented and modified many more times delaying design completion. The delays, though frustrating, did not have any significant effect on the completion schedule. A significant power upgrade managed by the local power bureau proved to be the critical path. The construction company that built the circuit board facility was eventually chosen to build the camera factory. The construction was more extensive and despite the design delays, the improvements were completed in six months. After five months, this operation had outgrown its space and over 400 employees were producing molded plastic parts and assembled cameras.

The camera factory was also a fertile experience for learning. The dispersion of leadership reduced the effectiveness of this team. The Chinese were confused while trying to please all parties. The leadership void was eventually filled by the Chinese vice-general manager acting in his originally assigned role as project manager His personal skill and experience, coupled with others being distracted by manufacturing matters, helped to guide the design and construction teams. On the first factory, an assessment of risk led to the decision to adopt the integrated, contracted team structure. Though there was less assurance of competitive pricing, the advantage of the business relationships among the Chinese parties proved valuable. The contracting approach taken by this team was more cumbersome and yielded no savings in cost. The regular visits by the writer as advisor were much less effective due to a rather low level of communication and increased amount of scope change activity. Teamwork was also at a lower level due to the forming of new relationships among the large team. Overall, the project came to a successful close but it could have been smoother if more of the learnings from the first factory had been applied.

## The MiniLab Factory

The third factory was very different from the others. It was purchased as an ongoing business with an operating factory whereas the others were started from a concrete shell. The leased factory housing the manufacturing operation was antiquated and the infrastructure was unsafe and unhealthy from a Western perspective. The goal in this factory was to make safety, health and operational improvements. The challenges were quite different as well. The Chinese employees saw little, if any, problem with the conditions as they were. But visitors from our multinational company were shocked by the conditions. The initial project team was loosely formed and unlike the camera factory, was understaffed. The team members all had multiple responsibilities and were reassigned regularly. This was largely due to the many personnel changes that occurred for the six-month period immediately following takeover. Predictably, improvement work was sporadic and lacked control. Scope and planning was minimal. A more stable project team was assembled around a newly hired facilities manager who would act as the project manager. A project plan for the improvements was developed and was just starting when it was discovered that some of the factory buildings would be demolished by a government resettlement action. At this writing the project team is forming and will resemble the circuit board factory project. There will be an onsite Chinese project manager and a Chinese general manager who will represent the manufacturing group, both employees. The writer will again act in the role as project/technical advisor and will be on site in the early stages and communicate weekly via teleconference. Contracted design and construction services will form the remainder of the team.

Though not completed, the previous attempts at forming a project team have yielded some interesting perspectives. The employees of this factory differ from the other plants in that they have been running the factory with the former owners. A significant number of people are so set in their ways that they cannot accept the changes that we, the new owners, want to implement. Some work has proceeded without proper scoping and planning resulting in quality, safety and rework problems. The experience at this plant challenged the project management process and stimulated analysis of the dynamics of renovation projects.

## The Chinese Twist

Knowledge of the project management process, as we know it, is minimal in China. Yet one has only to observe the enormous growth to see that major projects are being completed.

Seemingly, the Chinese sponsors and end users are satisfied. As project advisor, much of the work the writer did was to expose the Chinese project managers to effective project management practices. Though there was understanding, application of these practices was unfamiliar. Even between the project advisor's regular visits, work would proceed without regard to good practices. Contractors would be engaged and work would be completed with only verbal scope and pricing. Disruption to operations was common. Onsite interface for contractors would change often. Rework was widespread. Though this was chaotic, the Chinese seemed to take it in stride. The result was that work did get done and many were pleased with the progress. The result was that work did get done and many were pleased with the progress. The project advisor's role seemed like "damage control."

Despite the chaos, one had to admire the speed at which things happened. We have heard our customers complain about the slowness of project management process. We also know that if we begin implementation before settling on a defined scope and plan, the results will be less effective. The challenge is to improve the speed of processes and activities by a factor of ten. This sounds impossible at first, like being able to run a mile in twenty-four seconds when the record hovers around 240 seconds. But is possible when processes are mapped, long durations are analyzed and series activities are scrutinized. The skilled project manager can apply this concept while preserving the quality of the results.

Teamwork is yet another area of challenge for the project manager. From the first day, the Chinese talked in terms of teams, even through translations. After two years of working with them, the writer has seen many examples of this. One is the way they handle communications. The Chinese do not hesitate to call their team members immediately when questions arise affecting those members. This at first is rather annoying. Meetings are often interrupted by a pager or cellular phone, but it demonstrates fine teamwork and strong relationships. Another example is typically Chinese: They will quickly add human resources in order to meet requirements. When a concrete floor had to be replaced quickly, a cadre of demolition people and masons arrived within an hour and performed the task overnight, largely by hand. They are so used to doing things in hords that they have a way of avoiding stepping on each others feet. The skilled project manager is already aware of the power of teamwork. What can be reinforced is the importance of reliance on your fellow team members and the need to constantly focus, motivate and reward the team as a whole.

Another factor to consider is cultural norm awareness, and this is not applicable only to China. Fist, we must keep in mind and respect that we are the foreigners working in someone else's country. Trying to force Western norms on the Chinese causes stress and misunderstanding on both sides. It is important to gain understanding of the culture and apply it to the interactions. The face issue is a big one in Eastern Culture. It is better to work through failures to meet commitments than to destroy a personal relationship. Preserving the relationship will be recognized by the Chinese and it will be a motivating force that will pay dividends. Knowing and respecting culture is an initial step. Applying the culture to everyday interactions is "world class."

Enthusiasm is yet another concept to be applied from Chinese experience. Living under Communist rule, one might think that the people would be reliant on the state and might lack motivation. Nothing could be further from the truth. The Chinese are intensely proud of their country and eager to learn. They are enjoying the growth and recognize that it is the foreign investment that is fueling the technology and opportunity. They approach their work with enthusiasm and they focus on pleasing their customers or management. This is a refreshing environment to work in . It is easy to be caught up in the enthusiasm and if the project manager can add this ingredient into her/his project environment, team performance would be enhanced.

## Project Management Process Hybrid

The Chinese deserve to be respected, even applauded, for their progress but there is no denying the formidable abilities of the United States. As U.S. companies establish presence in China, they bring technical and management know-how. After observing methods and skills in China, there is no question that the U.S. can contribute to China's progress and share in the expanding Chinese market.

In project management, while the speed, teamwork and enthusiasm can be threaded into projects, the PMBOK and associated practices can be taught to the Chinese. They need to learn about scoping, planning, scheduling, and quality and formal project management process in general. The result will be that both cultures will be affected in a positive way. The project management process melded into the Chinese culture will create a hybrid for effective project management in China and add another facet to managing projects around the world.

It is no secret that the next century will be global. As business and project managers, we can be assured that we will be working in foreign environments. The lessons learned from the Chinese experience appear to be globally applicable: respect local customs and cultures, expect behaviors and ethics to be different, give the host citizens a chance to know you and yourself a chance to know them, keep an open mind, and go for the "win-win" solution.

# Win the No-Win Situation: Systems Thinking to Improve Project Management

Lou Russell, Russell Martin & Associates

*"Never doubt that a small group of thoughtful, committed people can change the world. Indeed, it is the only thing that can." — Margaret Mead*

Peter Senge's *The Fifth Discipline* demands that organizations adjust, grow and evolve to ensure their survival. Senge says the key is to become a "Learning Organization"—and that's exactly the goal of systems thinking.

## Systems Thinking

Systems thinking (ST) analyzes and models the causes and effects of complex problems, separating them into manageable pieces so we can better understand and fix them. ST is best used on the type of issues that keep rearing their ugly heads despite everyone's best efforts, such as:

- Why are our project skills always lacking?
- Why can't we keep projects on schedule?
- Why is project management training often ineffective?

### Practical example

The best way to see how systems thinking can help you learn more about your self and your problem situation is to look at an example. To better understand the concept, we'll examine the last question above. Don't let Exhibit 1 overwhelm you; it's just a series of small loops. This causal loop diagram is telling the story about "Why is project management training often ineffective?" Remember, this reflects the story of the group of people involved in creating this loop, not necessarily *your* story. One of the strongest benefits of ST is that it reveals the mental models (or assumptions) of the participants.

**Exhibit 1.**

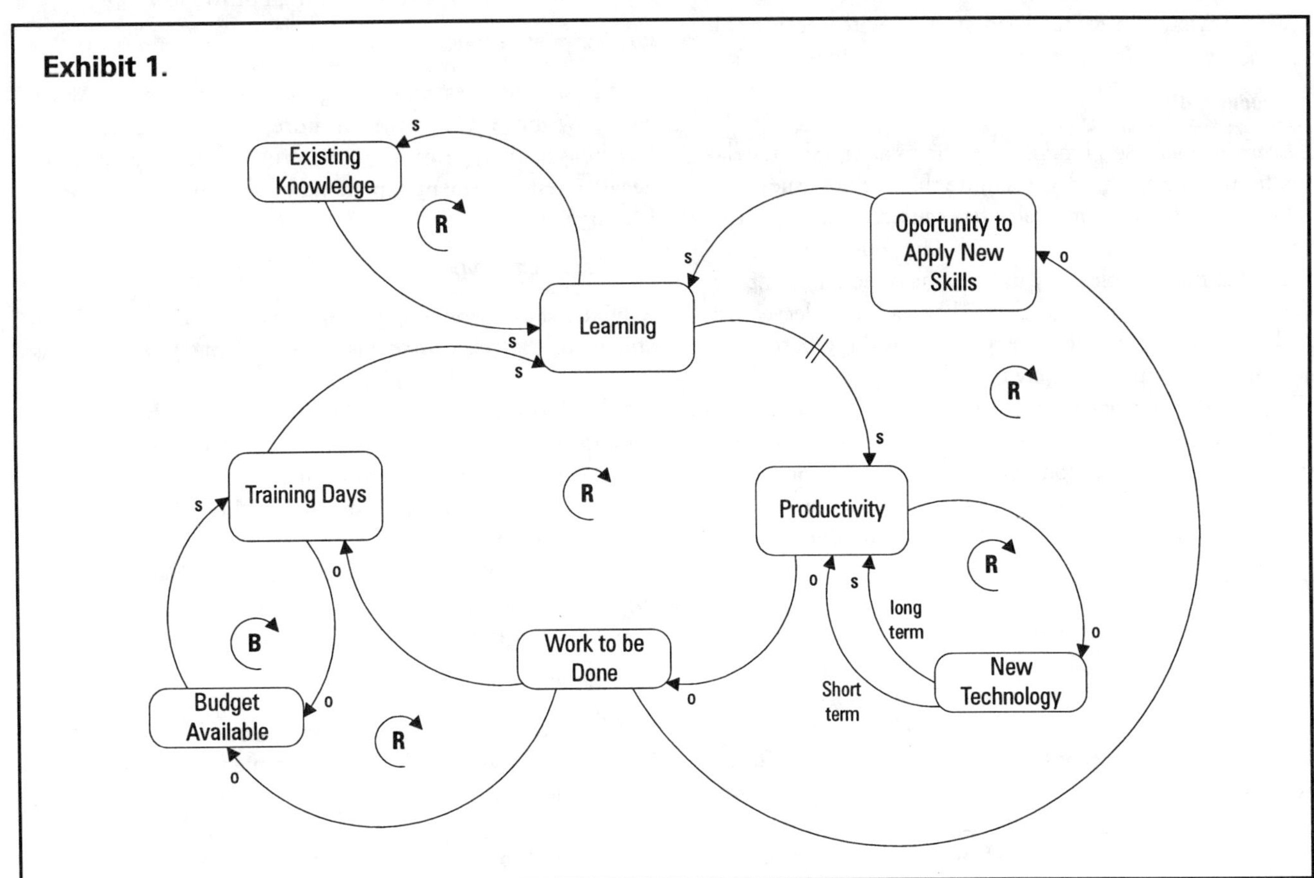

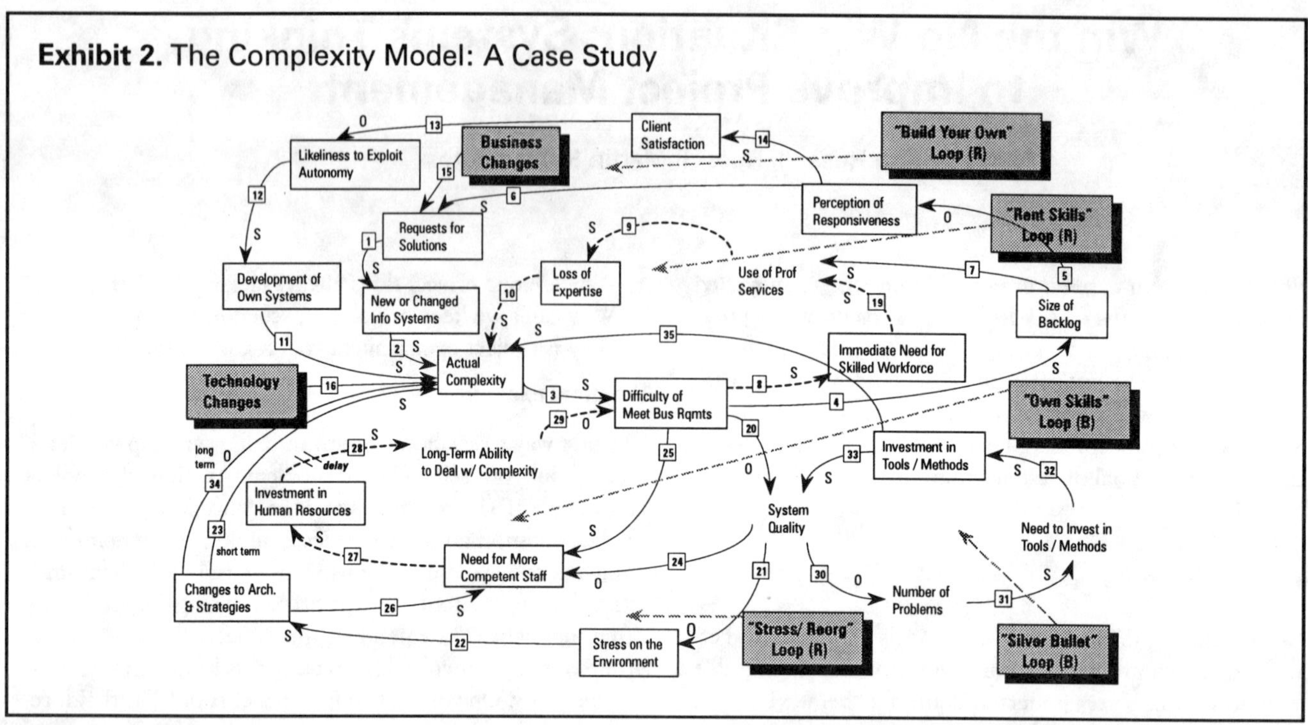


**Exhibit 2.** The Complexity Model: A Case Study

In fact, the value of ST is in the analysis and creation of the model, not in the model itself.

We'll review the center loop starting with the variable *Training Days*. As *Training Days* increases, so does *Learning*.

### Continuous path

As *Learning* increases, *Productivity* climbs after a slight delay (the double lines). This delay is more than a time issue; it actually means that the time delay has caused us to forget that *Productivity* was a direct result of *Learning*. The small *S* means that the variables vary in the same direction: as *Learning* goes up, *Productivity* goes up. That leads to a decrease in *Work to be done*, because everyone is working better and smarter, which, in turn, increases time on *Training*. This is called a *reinforcing loop* — one that will continue up or down if left on its own. Notice that this loop can actually be read sensibly from both directions. Practice reading the loop again, this time seeing what happens if *Learning* decreases. A reinforcing loop spirals up or down depending on the variables.

### Like a thermostat

You are probably thinking that our reinforcing loop is affected by other loops and, although it likely would spiral, something is preventing it from doing that completely right now. For example, as *Training Days* increase, *Budget Available* drops. The small O means that the variables vary in different directions: as *Training Days* go up, *Budget Available* goes down. Then, as *Budget Available* goes down, *Training Days* drops, too. This balancing loop functions like a thermostat, moderating *Training Days*. Like a thermostat, it won't let the other reinforcing loop spiral too high or too low.

### Another reinforcement

When *Learning* goes up, *Existing Knowledge* increases. When we know more, we can learn more, so this also increases *Learning*. This type of loop can provide either positive or negative reinforcement depending on the initial direction of *Learning*.

### Easy fixes don't work

Exhibit 1 shows why simply adding *Training Days*, *New Technology*, or *Budget Available* is not sufficient. Just increasing *Training Days*, for example, will grow the first loop a little, but that loop will ultimately be shut down by the loop that contains *Budget Available*. Typical fixes to this problem that have been tried unsuccessfully in the past become clearly flawed when they are walked through this model. Multiple interventions must be made at different points along the loop; for example, CD-ROM training (more *New Technology*) might be done in concert with better appraisal rewards (more *Opportunity to Apply New Skills*).

## Why do our projects fail?

After attending a systems thinking workshop, some of the Information Systems staff at 3M continued to meet and model what they still believe is a burning question... Why can't IS meet its project goals? The outcome of this self-initiated work was a causal loop diagram that revealed the essence of the problem in their opinion: complexity. Multiple factors and influences contributed to the increasing complexity of the IS projects (Exhibit 2).

The model showed why the solutions that had been tried in the past had failed. With this fascinating but worrisome model, the participants went to management and shared their observations. At this time, decisions were made to grow a systems thinking workshop internally, manage the outsourced work a different way, and control the adoption of "silver bullet technology."

Just as exciting was the personal intervention that many of the participants committed to independent of the management's commitment. One individual committed to ensuring that whenever she works with an outside contractor, she makes sure knowledge transfer occurs. Systems thinking, to them, was creating real and lasting growth and improvement at a personal and corporate level.

## How do you start?

Systems Thinking starts with a team that has a vested interest in a complex problem. The diversity of this team is critical to the quality of the results of the analysis. Unfortunately, the diversity is also directly proportional to the amount of conflict in the analysis process, but this conflict is necessary to move past the obvious and reveal carefully hidden mental models. In practice, although students are strongly warned that systems thinking and modeling should never be done alone, many participants prefer to work alone initially within the team and then share as their thoughts have been clarified (see Howard Gardner's work on intelligence, specifically interpersonal vs. intrapersonal). Teams must be coached to honor the different processing styles and values as they move towards a final story.

### The WHY Question

The groups start by discovering the question that the team wants to answer. The participants are asked to create a "Why" question since using "What" and "How" severely limits their openness to the dynamics of the system. They are strongly encouraged to keep cause and effect out of the question. Some examples are:

- " Why can't I get through the day without caffeine?"
- " Why don't our sales grow more steadily?"
- " Why do I have to constantly cut price?"

### Change the Question

Teams discover the power of the initial question time and time again and often remark that they struggle if they skip or minimize this step. Often the questions evolve as the analysis evolves. It is very rare that a team ends up with the same question at the end that they started with. In fact, one of the benefits of systems thinking is that it often provokes you to ask questions you hadn't thought to ask.

### Top Down Analysis

The top-down approach involves collectively brainstorming (with Post-its) what all the variables might be. The participants are coached by telling them that the variables should be nouns, that they should be as neutral as possible (for example, avoid adjectives in the negative like 'bad projects'), and they should be things that could be measured to check on the progress.

### Measurable vs. Quantifiable

Time is spent talking about the difference between measurable and quantifiable, and that variables do not have to have a quantifiable or numeric measurement. Variables need to be clearly understood and defined nouns that will increase and decrease.

### Get Loopy

When the brainstorming starts to slow down, models are built using reinforcing and balancing loops, hooking these Post-its( together on large white paper. By using this method, teams generally come up with a scope that is too wide and variables that are outside the scope, so the "Why?" question is an important thing to keep revisiting to avoid this confusion. In fact, most teams end up writing the question boldly on a large piece of paper so they can't forget about it.

### Bottom-Up Analysis

The bottom up approach involves starting with one or two variables, generally the most obvious measurements of success in a system (for example, *Successful Projects* might be something you start with to answer the question "Why are our projects failing?"). From these variables the teams move forward and backward and tell the story, discovering new variables as they go. Eventually they try to complete a loop, counting the 'Os' to see whether they have a reinforcing or balancing loop (an even number of 'Os' indicates a reinforcing loop).

### "It's Acting Like That"

The type of loop is validated against the observed behavior of the system, often throwing them back to the drawing board. If teams get stuck and can't move forward, they are encouraged to move backwards instead. As in the previous method, the "Why?" question keeps the team from venturing too far from the issue.

### The Story is the Thing

In all practice, the importance of the storytelling is emphasized. When teams get stuck, they are coached by the facilitators to tell the story again.

### *Learn From Experience*

With practice, teams learn:

- The importance of starting with a shared vision by creating a good "Why?" question (example, Why is it so difficult to keep our skills up to date?)
- How to recognize reinforcing and balancing loops and validate them against the behavior they observe
- How to document delays that cause misdiagnosis and poor intervention
- How to document at least one mental model for each influence
- How to use brainstorming intervention, even on the simplest models, and thinking through why traditional interventions in these specific systems fail

### Learning Surprises!

As practitioners, we were surprised by more than a few things. One of these was the issue of Archetype use. Archetypes are nine common loops (published by Pegasus Communications in Cambridge, Mass.) found in many business situations. These reusable patterns can be used to jumpstart a problem analysis. Although teams are tempted to fit their problem to an archetype when the archetypes are first introduced (to the extent that we noticed that teams actually used the archetype on the wall of the room they were closest to!), they soon settled into a paranoid resistance. Most learned quickly the danger of starting with the answer.

### *Analysis Paralysis*

We also learned that it is easy to fall into analysis paralysis with Systems Thinking, just like any other type of analysis. The analysis process is difficult and draining, and when a model is completely, it is tempting to just hang it up and move on. We recommend that teams return to the model after a break of a week or two to talk about intervention. Since it took years to create the causes and effects of many of these problems, it is unlikely (but not impossible!) that a great intervention can be designed in a few minutes. Intervention is the pay back for Systems Thinking, and without it there is no point in spending the time.

### *Evangelism*

The final learning point was the wonder at the evangelism that this type of thinking creates. As was often discussed, once you start looking at things this way you can't stop. It also hinders your ability to communicate with others who do not think this way. Each team creates groups of individuals who take their final models and use them to change the way their world spins. I have never been part of an approach that generated this much innovative thinking so quickly.

### Facilitator's dream

Systems thinking allows many people to share their unique perspectives and work together to fix the underlying problems. The workshops we have held have already resulted in dramatic, tangible change.

*"All we are given is possibilities—to make ourselves one thing or another."—Jose Ortega Y Gasset*

## The Complexity Story

1 Each Request treated independently, as in a vacuum
2 More systems always lead to More Complexity; Integration better than Interfacing
3 Unintended Consequences; Difficult to Forecast; Interference with Others; Needs of diverse groups must be met with one system; "I didn't have any trouble 15 years ago" (I); Developers always have an excuse
4 Takes longer to get things done; No added staff to cope with added Complexity
5 IT getting slower, doesn't really care (D); IT doesn't understand our problems (U); You can't please everybody (I)
6 We've got to find another way
7 If we just get caught up, we'll be okay
8 We have to respond right now
9 There's no way to make them leave something useful behind, when they go, the knowledge goes
10 They built it and left it for us to maintain, but didn't participate enough and we just don't understand why they did it that way
11 Worry about that later
12 Somebody's got to do it, we can't wait
13 We've got to find another way
14 It's Us and Them
15 Anything that the Client wants is a valid request
16 Let's see: Windows NT, Windows 95, DCE, OO, GUI, RAD, Spiral, Client/Server — to be competitive we have to be current, we can't use obsolete technology
17 [No link numbered 17]
18 [No link numbered 18]
19 Not time to train; Staff too old; Must get the Project done NOW; Maintenance is not my job; Cutting corners is okay; Training is Discretionary; It's easier to get Prof Svcs dollars than a staff requisition
20 IT Projects value only assessment by the Direct User (not Bus. Mgmt) (P); IT measures Quality with an internal focus (I); IT measures Quality with a 'project' focus (I); System is good if it makes my life easier (D); System is good if it helps solve my business problems

(U); IT pushes out technology and is not interested in my problem (U)

21 Firefighting is not detrimental; Keep the Train Running (KTTR); Firefighting is good, and comes with the territory
22 A re-org will help deal with the problem
23 Change = Replacement (but stuff actually does not go away in the short run)
24 It's really a 'people' problem; see also 19
25 See also 19
26 When we change the strategy or architecture, we need to re-orient the staff — again.
27 We must have a curriculum (not a complete solution); This is part of Career Development
28 Need to own these skills for the long haul
29 Collective understanding, retained history
30 Measure Quality by simply number of problems
31 We just need a new technology — that will solve the problems
32 If we need a new technique, let's just get it somehow
33 Once we get new methods, quality will certainly go up
34 We undertake change to reduce complexity — but it works only in the long run
35 Adding more tools and methods actually confuses things even more

**(I) IT Mgmt — (P) Proj Team — (D) Direct Users — (U) User Mgmt**



## Bibliography

BP Exploration Operating Co. *The Tale of Windfall Abbey.*

Chawla, Sarite, ed. *Learning Organizations.**

Kauffman, Draper L., Jr. *Systems 1 and 2, an Intro to Systems Thinking.*

Kim, Daniel H. *Systems Archetypes I.* Cambridge, MA: Pegasus Communications, Inc.

Kim, Daniel H. *Systems Archetypes II.* Cambridge, MA: Pegasus Communications, Inc.

Kim, Daniel H. *Systems Thinking Tools.* Cambridge, MA: Pegasus Communications, Inc.

Kim, Daniel H. and Colleen Lannon. *Applying Systems Archetypes.* Cambridge, MA: Pegasus Communications, Inc.**

Morecroft, John D.W., ed. *Modeling for Learning Organizations.*

Senge, Peter , et al. 1994. *The Fifth Discipline Fieldbook.* New York: Doubleday.

Senge, Peter. *The Fifth Discipline.* (Systems thinking is one of the five disciplines.)

*Learning Organization Web Site: http://world.std.com/~lo
*Pegasus Communications, Inc. (800) 272-0945; (800) 701-7083 (fax).

# The Silent Language of Project Management

By Dragan Z. Milosevic, Portland State University, Pinnell Busch, Inc.

Despite a decade or more of business internationalization and the growing cultural diversity of the U.S. work force, many project managers are unprepared for the multicultural project environment. The common methods for boosting performance in multicultural projects are cross-cultural training programs. They have not yielded the improvements companies desire because such programs' purpose is to increase cultural diversity awareness and lubricate project management processes.

But lubricating the processes cannot address their fundamental performance deficiencies. Many of the processes such as goal setting, scheduling, and organizational structuring came of age in a different environment and before the cultural impact on management became an issue. They are geared toward an unicultural world where one project management approach fits all cultures. Yet the catchwords of the new century are multicultural projects, multicultural teams, and multicultural project management.

The time has arrived to get past the cosmetic changes that cross-cultural programs bring to unicultural project management (UPM). Instead, we should concentrate on discarding the old belief of project management practices being universally applicable around the globe and replace the belief with a new paradigm that project management is culture-bound. That means that project participants from different cultures differently interpret project management practices. It is these different and unspoken interpretations that we have termed "the silent language of project management." The existence of the language engenders a need to obliterate the prevailing teachings of UPM and develop tools to match the project task with the team members' silent language in order to generate enhancements in terms of project schedule, cost, and quality. In so doing, project managers are not without any help. Practitioners and researchers have made some advancements, which, although not the last word on the subject, offer some rules of thumb for others.

## Horror Stories and the Bottom Line

Some companies prove every day that significantly better levels of project management performance in multicultural projects are possible (Solomon 1995, p. 56). But other project managers experience horror stories like those described below as commonplace.

A corporation in the continental United States forms a quality improvement team composed of engineers - three from the United States and two from a Western European country. When the team delves in developing a Work Breakdown Structure, the Americans favor constructing a tentative WBS with several work packages. They believe that the less detailed and precise the WBS is, the less restrictive its implementation would be.

In contrast, the Western Europeans advocate a very detailed WBS. Their need is for more precise and structured WBS planning, with many work packages, which—they believe—enables a machine-like implementation. Soon the planning workshop comes to a gridlock with both groups insisting that their approach is more appropriate.

A fundamental part of any multicultural project's reality is well depicted by this real-life example: project management practices—in this case WBS—vary across cultures.

In another instance, Peter, a Western project manager, walks into the office of a project manager in Africa. They are to negotiate a licensing agreement, a project which hopefully would enable Peter's company to get a foot in the local market. After the exchange of courtesy statements, Peter stresses that his company gave him seven days to finalize the negotiations. He reaches into his briefcase and hands his host the schedule. The host, who holds a management degree from a Western university, lays Peter's schedule on the table without looking at it. Then, he explains that scheduling is about looking into the future; and, as a local adage goes, those who look into the future are either insane or not religious enough; because, he adds, God only knows what the future bears, and worrying about a schedule won't change the future. Having said this, he cheerfully announces that it's time for lunch, where they will discuss which belly dance show to watch that evening.

To Peter, being insensitive to his host's schedule priority may be as dangerous as playing his own schedule priority game. In both scenarios, he would be walking on thin ice with a good chance for the negotiations to collapse even before they began, and the opportunity to crack the local market (the project goal) to be missed.

Most project managers recognize risks posed by practices used by their counterparts from a different culture. The bottom line is obvious: there is an extraordinary risk for misunderstanding project management practices and project failures. Less obvious is what underlies the practices. To successfully resolve the issue, you have to examine the very heart of it—cultural values. This article will examine the influence of cultural values on project management, interpret the silent language, and show how to use the language for successful project management.

## Cultural Software

The story of cross-cultural differences and why they exist draws a striking resemblance to computer software. Read this software plot as a cultural allegory.

Paul Simon, an experienced project manager, negotiates a multimillion-dollar change order on the overseas project site into the wee hours. One hour later he is on the pLane and DiStefano carrying him home. The next day he is in his office, preparing the report.

He logs in the computer only to discover that the software he has been using for years is not available on the computer. From a secretary he learns that "his" software has recently been replaced with another one. "No problem," he thinks to himself. He jumps into the new software and hastily hits the keys. Ten minutes later and half a page through, he decides to format the page. Intuitively, Paul uses the instructions from "his" software, but despite his numerous attempts, the computer responds with a concert of beeps. Another ten minutes of fruitless playing around go by before he nervously calls the secretary for help. She quickly formats the page. As he painstakingly moves through his report processing, so does the "try - beep - call - secretary" torture repeat itself.

Culture, like software, is a program. In particular, culture is the collective mental program of the people in an environment and encompasses a number of instructions. The instructions permeate our behavior and everything that we do. They tell us what we should and should not do. Consequently, every atom of our project management practices is guided by cultural instructions.

Culture, like software, has to be learned through different activities. We begin to learn the cultural instructions through our upbringing, then through education and life experience. Other members of our environment— be it a group, a tribe, a nation—also learn and share with us the same cultural program that is different from other groups, tribes, nations. Being a collective mental program, culture is often difficult and slow to change. The cultural instructions are also embodied in: our family structures, companies, laws, project management, etc. It is this amount of effort needed to change these cultural embodiments that makes the culture change appear so tantalizing (Lane and DiStefano 1992).

Like with software, switching from one to another culture may be a painful experience. For their distinction, cultures contain different instructions. The more distinctive they are, the more different are the instructions. And the more different the instructions, the larger the cross-cultural differences. When substantial cross-cultural differences are present, an unprepared project manager may feel at a loss. To survive, she needs a frame of reference that would help understand (like the secretary in Paul's case) what is happening and the imperatives of surviving. The next section provides such a frame of reference.

## Cultural Variables

Are there variables that permeate all cultures and help understand the root causes of cultural differences in project management practices? The Kluckhohn-Strodtbeck framework provides such variables (1961):

1. Relationship to the environment
2. Time orientation
3. Nature of people
4. Activity orientation
5. Focus on responsibility

**Exhibit 1.** Variations in relationship to the environment and examples of their impact on project management practices

| Cultural Variable | Culture Types | | |
|---|---|---|---|
| Relation To The Environment | Subjugation | Harmony | Mastery |
| **Project Mgmt Practice** | **Managerial Impact** | | |
| Scope Management | Implicit, Ambiguous, Unwilling | Tentative, Gradual, Patient | Explicit, Precise, Ambitious |
| Cost Management | Unfruitful, Fatalistic | Exercise, "Actuals" Count | Factual, Essential, Fruitful |

**Exhibit 2.** Variations in time orientation and examples of their impact on project management practices

| Cultural Variable | Culture Types | | |
|---|---|---|---|
| Time Orientation | Past | Present | Future |
| **Project Mgmt Practice** | **Managerial Impact** | | |
| Scheduling | God Willing | Rolling Wave | Marathon Race |
| Quality Management | Pass Down, After the Fact | Current Impact, Ain't Broke, Don't Fix Corrective | Desired Impact, Continuous Improvement Preventive |

6. Orientation to space.

First, we will explain the variables. Next, possible variations of the variables will be identified. How the variations forge different avenues for exercising project management practices—which is the silent language—will also be illuminated. One assumption will be made here. There is no pure culture employing only one avenue in addressing a certain variable. Rather, many avenues are present. However, some of these avenues are perceived by the members of a culture as being more appropriate than others. We call such avenues the most dominant ones, although others may matter to a lesser extent.

## The Essence Of The Silent Language

### Relationship to the environment

Cultures can be classified according to their relationship to nature or the environment - subjugation to nature, harmony with nature, and domination over nature (Exhibit 1). In some Near Eastern countries, people view life as essentially preordained —everything happens by God's will and, consequently, people are subjugated to nature. In contrast, Americans strive to harness nature's forces and change them as they need. Their belief is that man has the ability to dominate nature. In between these extreme views lies the third way, one seeking harmony with nature. To a Far Easterner, this may mean designing a golf course in concert with the physical environment (Lane and DiStefano 1992).

These different perspectives are certain to impact project management practices such as goal setting and WBS. In a subjugation culture, project managers tend to define both in an implicit, unwilling, and ambiguous way. After all, why bother—everything is preordained and they can't do much about accomplishing goals and WBS. In a domination culture, project managers are expected to define SMART (Specific, Measurable, Attainable, Relevant, and Timely) project goals. A harmony with nature project manager would rely on tentative goals and WBS, recognizing appropriate contingencies for environmental parameters.

The hidden workings of culture may also be demonstrated in project budgeting practice. Project managers from a harmony culture are likely to consider budgeting as an elegant practice that prepares a project for the future but does not really count; it is only actual costs that count. In a subjugation culture, budgeting might be an unfruitful act, going against fatalistic, predetermined outcomes. In contrast, project managers from a domination background look at budgeting as a factual, essential, and fruitful practice that empowers them to keep project cost in check.

### Time Orientation

Cultures differ in how they value time (Exhibit 2). Some cultures emphasize a focus on the past and traditions. When faced with new challenges, they tend to learn how others have dealt with that kind of challenge in the past (Southern Mediterraneans, for example). Americans, primarily focusing on the immediate effects of an action, are present-time oriented, which can be seen in Wall Street's immense emphasis on the quarterly earnings of corporations. In contrast, Japanese are future-time oriented often with the performance goal (known as strategic intent) spanning 20+ years in the future.

Knowledge of time orientation helps one understand practices related to scheduling and quality systems. Present-oriented schedulers are likely to develop a precise schedule for near-future activities, while the longer-term activities will be detailed as more information becomes available—the rolling wave approach. Preserving the deadlines is crucial. Contrary to this, the importance of deadlines would be low in the past-oriented projects, schedules are of a "God Willing" nature, with a summary level of detail, and based on past projects. To the future-oriented schedulers the project is a marathon race, where the start, finishing line, and milestones are known, but the terrain between them is unknown. Schedules will be of a not-so-detailed level and deadlines will likely be treated as tentative.

**Exhibit 3.** Variations in nature of people and examples of their impact on project management practices

| Cultural Variable | Culture Types | | |
|---|---|---|---|
| Nature Of People | Evil | Mixed | Good |
| **Project Mgmt Practice** | **Managerial Impact** | | |
| Project Control | Strict, Inspection-Oriented | Moderate, Situation-Oriented | Loose, Policy-Oriented |
| Procurement Management | Adversarial, Contractual, Win-Lose | Moderate Supervision, Contingency-Based | Partnering, Informal, Win-Win |

What impact do quality systems have on projects? To future-oriented project managers, the impact is profound. It is possible to accomplish the desired quality through *kaizen*—continuous quality improvement, combined with a focus on preventing quality problems. In present-oriented cultures, if a quality problem does not have an immediate impact, the prevailing logic is "If it ain't broke, don't fix it"—apparently a corrective approach. The impact that similar quality problems had in the past projects and a corrective approach are what occupies the minds of past-oriented project managers.

## Nature of People

Does a culture perceive people as good, evil, or mixed (Exhibit 3)? In many African cultures, people view themselves as being essentially sincere, truthful, and honorable. In contrast, some Mediterranean cultures believe the character of the human species is inherently evil. The third way, followed by Americans, is taken by those who see human nature as essentially good, but are cautious so as not to be taken advantage of (Robbins 1993).

You can readily see the impact of human nature on project control and procurement. A strict, inspection-based project control grounded in an underlying suspicion of people is likely to dominate in cultures that focus on the evil nature of humans. Loose, policy-based project control should prevail in cultures that underscore honesty and integrity of people. In mixed cultures, project control is likely to be moderate and based on the specifics of the situation.

Procurement may be in tune with how cultures view the nature of humans. At one end is the evil orientation that accentuates adversarial contractual relationships and a win-lose game. At the other end are cultures that believe in people's goodness and exercise procurement rooted in partnering, informality, and a win-win situation. The mixed orientation's ideal is likely to be procurement relying on moderate supervision of the supplier, with modifications based on contingencies such as a project manager's experience with the suppliers involved.

## Activity Orientation

The activity orientation is how people focus on their activity (Exhibit 4). Some cultures stress doing or action, as Americans do. Hard work and relentless pursuit of accomplishments are crucial to their existence. In return, they expect good pay and promotions as well as other recognitions. What matters to other cultures is being or living for the moment. Greeks, Russians, and Serbs are being-oriented. Their credo is to experience life and pursue immediate fulfillment of desires (Robbins 1993). In between the being and doing positions are cultures with a focus on controlling. They strive for a balance of feeling and thought, mind and body.

This cultural variable has implications for risk management. Risk management in doing-oriented cultures emphasizes risk taking and few rules. They believe that risks can be quantified and managed. In being-oriented cultures, risk aversion is likely to be of primary importance. Project managers will tend to set many rules in order to avoid risks, and when faced with risks, they will act spontaneously. Where a controlling orientation is dominant, project mangers exhibit high risk avoidance and many rules like their counterparts in the being cultures, but their focus will be on risk reduction rather then spontaneity.

## Focus On Responsibility

What responsibility does one have for the welfare of others? If your answer is that one should take care of oneself, then you belong to the individualistic cultures (Exhibit 5). Americans, predominantly of this cultural background, value a person's independence and rugged individualism. Malaysia and Israel are examples of the group cultures. Their emphasis is more on group harmony, unity, and loyalty. Group members have clearly defined rights and responsibilities. The British and French nurture a hierarchical focus (Robbins 1993). They also rely on groups, but the groups are hierarchically

**Exhibit 4.** Variations in activity orientation and examples of their impact on project management practices

| Cultural Variable | Culture Types | | |
|---|---|---|---|
| Activity Orientation | Being | Controlling | Doing |
| **Project Mgmt Practice** | **Managerial Impact** | | |
| Risk Management | Risk-Averse, Many Rules, Spontaneous | High Risk Avoidance Many Rules Reduce Risk | Risk-Prone, Few Rules, Quantifiable, Management Risk |

**Exhibit 5.** Variations in focus on responsibility and examples of their impact on project management practices

| Cultural Variable | Culture Types | | |
|---|---|---|---|
| Focus on Responsibility | Hierarchical | Group | Individualistic |
| **Project Mgmt Practice** | **Managerial Impact** | | |
| Teamwork | Orderly, Formal | Normal Condition, Routine | Instrument, Informal |

ranked and their position is stable over time. This is typical of aristocratic and caste cultures.

An understanding of a culture's focus on responsibility can provide you with insights into teamwork. Teamwork in hierarchical cultures tends to be orderly and formal. Project managers exercise a firm control over the team process, activities, meetings, and information. In contrast, American project managers, with their individualistic culture, treat teams as an instrument and deal with other team members, meetings, and processes only if there is a strong need for it. An informal and volunteer tone is typically prevalent. Teamwork in a group culture is the normal state of affairs, executed as a routine, where despite a strong sense of hierarchy within the group, decisions are typically developed through a group process.

### Orientation To Space

This cultural variable is concerned with how one is oriented towards the surrounding space, especially the sense of the ownership of space relative to others (Lane and DiStefano 1992). Some cultures, American, for example, place a strong emphasis on keeping things private (Exhibit 6). In contrast, other cultures, like Italian, favor doing business in public. Still, others mix the two and take the middle ground.

This cultural variable has implications for project communications. Project managers from the private cultures are likely to engage in one-to-one communications, closed to other individuals. Where the public orientation cultures prevail, you can expect project managers to get involved in multiple interactions with an open style. In cultures with mixed orientation, typical communications tend to be selective in nature and semiclosed to the public.

## Turning Silent Language Into Action

The silent language may trigger serious problems in project management. Scoping, scheduling, budgeting, organizational structuring—anything associated with the project—must be refashioned in an integrated way. In other words, learning the silent language and using it to you advantage is a substantial effort that mandates change in many areas of the project.

Once you have mastered the essence of the silent language, you can apply it in anticipation of the problems in your multicultural project and plan to avoid them. Or, you can wait until you encounter actual problems and use the language to resolve them. Whatever your approach is, these problems may appear between project team members, or they may plague project-level issues such as project performance measurements. In either case, your strategy should focus on four actions:

- Understand your own culture and silent language
- Understand culture and silent language of your team members
- Identify cultural and language gaps
- Avoid problems or resolve the gaps.

**Exhibit 6.** Variations in orientation to space and examples of their impact on project management practices

| Cultural Variable | Culture Types | | |
|---|---|---|---|
| Orientation to Space | Private | Mixed | Public |
| **Project Mgmt Practice** | **Managerial Impact** | | |
| Project Communications | One-To-One, Closed | Selective, Semiclosed | Multiple, Open |

**Exhibit 7.** Cultural interpreter of the silent language of project management

| Cultural Variable | Culture Types | | |
|---|---|---|---|
| Environment | Subjugation | Harmony | Mastery |
| Time Orientation | Past | Present | Future |
| Nature of People | Evil | Mixed | Good |
| Activity Orientation | Being | Controlling | Doing |
| Focus of Responsibility | Hierarchical | Group | Individualistic |
| Orientation To Space | Private | Mixed | Public |

●——● Cultural Profile, Typical American   ×– – –× Cultural Profile of a non-American Team Member   □- - - - -□ Mixed Cultural Profile

*Understand Your Own Culture And Silent Language.* Begin by making a copy of Exhibits 1 to 6, aligning them vertically, and drawing a line connecting the cells that name your own dominant cultural values and project management practices. To demonstrate this, we will use Exhibit 7 in which, for the sake of simplicity, project management practices are left out. Assuming that you are an American, we drew the solid line to identify where you fall along cultural variables.

*Understand culture and silent language of your team members.* Then, draw a line for each team member designating the dominant values of their cultures and corresponding project management practices. Again, for the sake of simplicity, we drew only one dashed line for one of your non-American team members.

*Identify cultural and language gaps.* Now, it is easy to see the gaps between the lines. The gaps are the areas where you, the project manager, might encounter personal problems with other team members or in regard with project-level issues.

*Avoid problems or resolve the gaps.* Once the gaps are identified, you have to select an approach to either avoid the problems before they appear or resolve them if they are present. Your first option is to decide which culturally defined project management practices will be followed. That is called the dominance approach. For example, your decision may be to go with your line in Exhibit 2 and apply American project management practices. Another approach offers the mixed strategy where you would blend the project management practices of all team members. In Exhibit 7, that approach is depicted by the dotted line, meaning that some practices would come from your line and some from your team members' lines. You can also use a synergistic approach that recognizes and transcends the individual elements of the cultures involved (Adler 1991). As you ponder the approach, note that in some project situations you may need to select a single strategy, while in others you may use all of them.

## Implications For Managers And Conclusions

Considering the cultural insensitivity of UPM, the strain of learning the silent language and translating it into action can hardly be overestimated. But by the same token, it is hard to overestimate the benefits for companies whose way of life involves multicultural projects. The projects are not doomed to suffer because project managers do not speak the silent language, but they are burdened with cultural ignorance. Attacking the ignorance by means of generic cross-cultural awareness will not be good enough.

Project managers have the tools to do what they need to do. It is the imagination that must guide their decisions about the silent language, not the other way around. The language may be applied as an aid to modern project management, not as a simplistic cure-all. It is not to be used to stereotype other cultures. And, its mechanistic application won't produce prudent outcomes. Quite to the contrary, only an organic approach supported by the masterly knowledge of both the silent language and the respective cultures will lead to continuous growth of project management. This is not an unrealistic goal. To multicultural project managers who have vision, the silent language will provide a way.

## References


Adler, Nancy J. 1991. *International dimensions of organizational behavior*. Boston, MA: PWS-Kent.

Kluckhohn, F.R. and Strodtbeck, F.L. 1961. *Variations in value orientations*. New York, NY: Row, Peterson & Co.

Lane, Henry W and DiStefano, Joseph J. 1992. *International management behavior*. Boston, MA: PWS-Kent.

Robbins, Stephen P. 1993. *Organizational behavior*. Englewood Ciffs, NJ: Prentice Hall.

Solomon, Charlene Marmer. 1995. Global teams: the ultimate collaboration. *Personnel Journal* (September): 49-58.

# PROJECT MANAGEMENT: THE NEXT CENTURY

# Government

# Project Surprises—Expecting the Unexpected

Alexander Laufer, University of Maryland at College Park
Jody Kusek, US Department of the Interior

## Introduction

Whether projects are technical or organizational, public or private, uncertainty is one of the major factors that influence a project's performance and ultimate success. We present in this article, a new tool—the Critical Assumptions Matrix—to help the project team significantly reduce the negative impact of changes and surprises so frequently encountered in projects suffering from high uncertainty.

## Sources of Uncertainty

It is widely recognized that the unprecedented growth of uncertainty in projects, is the result of the significant transformation that the world has undergone in the last few decades. Its all-pervasive presence is, among others, a consequence of the increasing demands in project speed. Project planning is carried out hastily due to time pressure. But increasing uncertainty is also a consequence of increased environmental awareness, greater community impact on decisions affecting quality of life, and simply by the complexities of today. In addition to the uncertainties faced by businesses, government agencies must contend with their unique constraints, so characteristic of the political system. For example:

- *Shifts in a project's leadership and objectives*—The executive branch of the U.S. government fills senior positions with political appointees who are replaced, approximately every two years. New people coming into an agency, even under the same administration, may not have the same interest in a given project as their predecessors. Also, as a result of usual turnover at the top of the organization, career project managers may be asked to temporarily fill vacancies, or take on other responsibilities, besides managing an ongoing project.
- *Access to and retention of human resources*—If a government project manager needs additional or special resources to complete the project, he or she cannot simply put an advertisement in the newspaper and hire. Strict federal civil service statutes require adherence to special personnel rules such as: position listing, and competitive hiring. Often, highly marketable candidates will not wait for the lengthy government hiring process, and seek employment elsewhere. The ability of a project manager to rapidly deploy needed human resources in a project environment may be impacted by federal civil service laws, when new hires are needed from outside the federal government.
- *Approval of a project's budget*—Federal budgets are appropriated on a one-year basis. While multiyear contracts may carry over funds from one year to the next, available project funds are determined by the total sum of the agency's budget that Congress approves each year. Even the most diligent project manager might end up missing key milestones if faced with a budget far less than needed to accomplish required tasks. Reducing the deficit and balancing the federal budget means less money for discretionary programs and a more intensive scrutiny over each and every project request within an agency's budget.

## Impact of Uncertainty

In today's fast changing world, a project must contend with many unexpected surprises (Laufer 1991, Laufer and Howell 1993). Project plans that do not take into account changes and surprises are bound to fail, as indicated by the conclusions of Morris and Hough (1987). Summarizing all the reports publicly available on project overruns, they concluded: "There are hardly any reports showing underruns ... In all the other cases, representing some three thousand and five hundred projects drawn from all over the world in several different industries, overruns are the norm, being typically between forty and two hundred percent."

A successful project team focuses on maintaining the project plan's stability by actively coping with the adverse impact of uncertainty. More importantly, the team's ability to identify and cope with uncertainty is crucial to the good management and success of the project.

In the new approach adopted by successful project managers, *management of uncertainty* is an essential component of project planning (Laufer 1996). Since people tend to ignore uncertainty, adopting a mindset that focuses on the management of uncertainty requires the systematic use of a tool (March 1994).

The Critical Assumptions Matrix (CAM) is a tool designed to assist with the mindset shift. It increases the project team's ability to identify and cope with uncertainty and can assist them in the preparation of plans before the project's initiation and in monitoring the project during execution. The tool



PROJECT MANAGEMENT INSTITUTE 28th Annual Seminars & Symposium
Chicago, Illinois: Papers Presented September 29 to October 1, 1997

has been successfully applied by companies in the private sector (e.g., Proctor & Gamble) and in the public sector (e.g., Israel Electric Company). The authors are convinced that this tool is essential for dealing with the uncertainty prevalent in government projects as well.

## Monitoring Critical Planning Assumptions

Project objectives and plans are always based on various planning assumptions, such as:

- Next year's approved budget will continue to meet the project's needs.
- There will be sufficient skilled human resources for the next phase of the project.
- No major process technology breakthrough will be needed.

In an era of uncertainty, many of these planning assumptions are not constant for the duration of the project. When an assumption becomes invalid, it often requires an adjustment to the plan or even to the objectives. Successful project teams are aware of the instability of planning assumptions. With the CAM, they articulate the assumptions and are able to identify changes in the assumptions early—before these changes influence subsequent decisions and actions (Mason and Mitroff 1981, Smith et al. 1980, Youker 1992).

The following is an example of using the CAM and a discussion of its advantages, the procedure for using the tool is presented.

## Spoiling Surprises

I was very skeptical of the Critical Assumptions Matrix's usefulness when it was first introduced to me. Several times in the past, as part of risk analysis, I took great pains to identify all the risk factors at the beginning of a project, and often identified more than one hundred factors. Yet I never referred to these lists again later in the course of the project; the analysis was just too complicated and time-consuming. My skepticism, however, was quickly proven to be absolutely baseless. I found that while this technique of articulating and monitoring the critical assumptions demanded only little effort, it resulted in remarkably positive results.

For example, when the manager of my department announced that he was leaving in three months, it didn't occur to me, or to any member of my project team, that this might have a direct impact on our project. Only two weeks later, during the next project meeting, when we reviewed the CAM and encountered the assumption: "We can maintain strong support of management," we suddenly made the connection. We realized that two uncommon decisions we made—the project contracting strategy and the decision to rely on the existing equipment—survived only due to the strong support of our department manager. We didn't want to jeopardize valuable project time by waiting until the new manager took over. Allowing him enough time to form an opinion, and only then learning that he might want us to change these major decisions, would have entailed extensive rework.

Therefore, with the consent of the present manager, I immediately involved the new manager in the project. This turned out to be a crucial move, since the new manager did indeed introduce several significant modifications. By identifying them early in the project life, these changes were easily handled as part of the natural evolution of the scope definition. If these changes had been introduced later, they would have caused considerable damage to our schedule, budget, and work morale. However, we would have accepted them as typical unavoidable project surprises.

Throughout the project, we checked our assumptions regularly, verifying their validity and revising them when necessary. We minimized the amount of rework, by identifying the changes in the assumptions early, in order to adjust the plan before the changes influenced too many future decisions or actions. Since that project, I have used the Critical Assumptions Matrix in all my projects with great success. I learned that by using this anticipatory monitoring device, I can spoil most project surprises. I have also learned that while I can't eliminate all surprises, I can still anticipate many of them before they occur, leaving sufficient time to attenuate and often deaden their impact on the project.

## Advantages of the Critical Assumptions Matrix

### Reminds the project team of the vulnerability of planning assumptions

The CAM constantly reminds the project team: "You are operating under uncertain conditions. Your decisions are based on shaky assumptions—not on solid facts." People working under a tight timetable tend to develop tunnel vision. They are so intent on making progress through action that they ignore changes in the project's external environment and the impact of those changes on the project. Under these circumstances, periodic review of the CAM reminds project participants: "The ground you are standing on is not firm—it is constantly shifting."

Plans are composed of many connected decisions. The further you get from the time of planning, the more difficult it becomes to remember those connections. Therefore, during project execution, you often fail to make timely connections between changes in the planning assumptions and the plan itself. Articulating these assumptions during planning, and monitoring them systematically during execution, ensure early recognition of the connections.

### Enables and encourages a more proactive approach for coping with uncertainty

The story, "Spoiling Surprises," illustrates one way the CAM can be applied—waiting passively for an assumption to change and only then taking an action to minimize its impact. Often, however, the CAM enables and encourages a more proactive approach for coping with uncertainty. Following are three examples of different types of the proactive approach:

*Timely Relocation*—In an office relocation project, one of the critical assumptions was: "We can win employees' support for the move." As the project progressed, the project manager monitoring the CAM, became worried that resistance to the relocation—the second in several years—might not be easily overcome, and might even jeopardize the viability of the entire project. Realizing that he must immediately resolve this uncertainty, he decided to adopt the "small-wins" tactic. He identified the department that would benefit the most from the move, and whose employees did not resist it. By changing the project plan, accelerating a small portion of the project, and relocating this department first, he obtained essential feedback. He was then able to build a positive attitude toward the relocation throughout the company, but only after extending project duration. In this case, the CAM was instrumental in rescuing the project by adjusting both its plan and its objectives.

*Interface*—In a small maintenance project, the project manager formulated the assumption: "The two suppliers will effectively coordinate their work." After the second review of his CAM, he decided that the only way he could contain the uncertainty of coordinating these two suppliers was for he, himself, to manage the interface between them.

*Decoupling*—Early in a research project, primarily through the use of a brief list of assumptions, the researcher recognized that the strong connection between two uncertain tasks—the development of both the hardware and the software—was bound to cause a delay in her research. She identified this problem early enough to be able to decouple these two tasks by making major changes in the research design.

### Enhances open communication

The CAM is also helpful in developing uncertainty awareness not only within the project team but also in discussions with upper management. Periodic review of the matrix invariably draws the attention of everyone to current uncertainties. Following the introduction of the CAM, uncertainty previously neglected (whether intentionally or unintentionally) is brought up for review with management in an atmosphere of extraordinary receptiveness and relevance.

## Implementing the Critical Assumptions Matrix

One of the main advantages of the CAM tool is its user-friendly simplicity. Once the concept of critical planning assumptions is understood by team members, preparing the tool and its use for monitoring the project, will easily become part of the team's second nature. Generating the initial Critical Assumptions Matrix (CAM) shouldn't take more than a few hours, even for complex projects.

The main steps to be followed for implementing the CAM are summarized below.

The project team generates the initial list of critical assumptions at the beginning of the project. The most suitable time is after the main objectives and constraints are well understood, but before they have been articulated and distributed as a formal, binding document.

The list should be updated when major changes occur, and at least at the beginning of every major project phase.

One useful way to generate the initial list of critical assumptions is by brainstorming. The entire project team, meeting together, generates assumptions classified by categories. This facilitates articulation, monitoring, and review of the matrix. Exhibit 1 presents an example in which assumptions are classified in two ways. First, by area, listed as: business and economics, technical and physical, and organizational and human resources. Second, by the ability of the project team to exert an influence over the assumptions, listed as: controlled by the project team, influenceable, and controlled externally. Simple projects, however, may not require more than one category.

Formulating the assumptions is sometimes preceded by identifying all the factors (stakeholders) that lie outside the project but must be taken into account. Thus, for example, the "construction labor" factor is identified, and only then is the assumption articulated: "There will be sufficient skilled construction labor throughout next summer." Less-experienced teams may find that generic checklists of typical factors (e.g., risk factors) facilitate the identification of the specific factors of their project.

The initial list of assumptions is then reduced to include only those that are critical. A critical assumption is both important to the success of the project (i.e., project objectives and major decisions are strongly dependent on the validity of each critical assumption) and judged by the team to suffer

**Exhibit 1.** Critical Assumptions Matrix (CAM)

| Extent of Control | Area | | |
|---|---|---|---|
| | **Business and Economic** | **Technical and Physical** | **Organizational and Human Resources** |
| **Controlled by Project Team** | We can identify acceptable infrastructure options which cost no more than the allowance in the March estimate. (BR) | We can finish the technical feasibility study of the auxiliary equipment by the end of October. (FR)<br><br>Facility layout will be consistent with the existing master plan. (FR) | We will be able to recruit an experienced control engineer before the beginning of project definition. (HD) |
| **Influenceable** | We will receive capital in quantities and on schedule as laid out in March. (HD) | Process changes to each line can be accommodated with minimal changes to infrastructure. (JH)<br><br>Warm water toxicity impact on river water return is not a problem. (SR)<br><br>We will be able to afford and obtain environmental and building permits. (MW, CG) | We can maintain strong support of department and plant management. (HD)<br><br>Engineering services will be provided by ABC. (CR)<br><br>Plant staffing will be available to support the project. (CR) |
| **Externally Controlled** | Sales growth will match the forecast. (HD) | No major process technology breakthrough will be needed. (RR) | There will be sufficient skilled construction labor throughout next summer. (BL) |

from a considerable degree of uncertainty (assumptions that are most prone to fluctuation). The judgment of criticality—degree of dependence and uncertainty—is purely subjective. A typical CAM may contain 10–25 assumptions.

The team then assigns ownership to each assumption—the person responsible for its monitoring. His or her initials, within parentheses, are indicated in the matrix adjacent to each assumption.

The team periodically reviews the matrix, to verify the validity of the assumptions, revising or deleting them when necessary, and to decide whether adjustments to project execution, plan, or objectives are required.

## Summary

In today's fast-changing world, whether in the private or public sector, effective management of project uncertainty is central to project success. Uncertainty permeates all aspects and phases of a project's life. The project team's awareness of the possible effects of uncertainty on their project and their ability to identify uncertainty early, influences the effectiveness of the project's planning and control. Successful teams are not only aware of the instability of planning assumptions but they are also aware of their ability to intervene and search for the remedies to cope with uncertainty.

*Developing awareness* of uncertainty and *acting* to remedy its effects should become part of the project team's natural behavior. The Critical Assumptions Matrix (CAM) was designed for that purpose. Its main contributions are its ability to: (1) remind the project team of the vulnerability of planning assumptions; (2) enable and encourage a more proactive approach for coping with uncertainty; and (3) enhance open communication.

## References


Laufer, A. 1991. Coping with uncertainty in project planning: A diagnostic approach. *The Project Manager*, 7:11–15.

Laufer, A. 1996. *Simultaneous management: Managing projects in a dynamic environment*. AMACOM, American Management Association.

Laufer, A., and Howell, G.A. 1993. Construction planning: Revising the paradigm. *Project Management Journal*, 24:23–33.

March, J.G. 1994. *A primer on decision-making*. Free Press.

Mason, R.O., and I.I. Mitroff. 1981. *Challenging strategic planning assumptions*. Wiley.

Morris, P.W.G., and G.H. Hough. 1987. *The anatomy of major projects*. Wiley.

Smith, W.E., B.A. Toolen, and F.J. Lethem. 1980. The design of organizations for rural development projects—A progress report. *Staff Working Paper No. 375*, The World Bank.

Youker, R. 1992. Managing the international project environment. *International Journal of Project Management*, 10:219–226.

# Local Government - The Next Frontier in Project Management

Margaret S. Goldstein, GMS Consulting, Inc.

## Introduction

Whether you live in a small town or a large city, you've probably read or listened to at least one news story in the last month which covered some aspect of your local government at work. Often the stories cover police investigations, a daring rescue by the fire department, or plans for new public works, like stadiums, roads, or libraries. More often than not, the news is negative: political infighting, employees caught loafing on the job, the occasional graft. Over the years, you develop a picture of the sort of people who work in government, based on the news you hear, and your personal experiences interacting with city and county employees. That being the case, how likely is it that you would agree strongly to the following propositions?

- Local governments do a great job of implementing projects.
- Local government bureaucrats make great project managers.

Not too likely? "project manager" and "government bureaucrat" might even be considered incompatible terms by some people. Being able to lead a project well is not how we generally think of the people to whom we send our local tax dollars. Unfortunately, it's true that local governments and their employees have frequently confirmed our stereotyped opinions of them. In fact, the notion of a "project", outside of traditional public works undertakings like building bridges, roads or airports, is itself a relatively new concept. But the fact is, local governments are not the same as businesses, charities, or private households. Some would argue that these factors make it almost impossible for projects in local government to be concluded on time, on budget, and with high quality. In fact, local government employees must deal with pressures that make this environment unique, and which can have direct and critical impact on the project manager's ability to execute projects successfully. By understanding what these pressures are and how government employees react to and deal with them, the Project Manager can utilize the PMBOK principles and shepherd projects to satisfactory, even exemplary, conclusions.

So what is it about local government that makes it so special, and what do these factors have to say about projects in government? My experience points towards seven key issues that directly or indirectly impact local government's ability to handle projects successfully.

### 1. Management is structured around semi-autonomous fiefdoms.

Local governments are frequently structured in a manner that reflects the extreme diversity of government tasks, and department heads are often given broad latitude in how their specific goals are accomplished. The Police Department is concerned with crime control, the Fire Department with putting out fires, the Water Department with providing clean water, the Finance Department with acquiring funding and paying the bills, etc. While it is true that "Service to Citizens" might be construed as a common goal, on a day to day basis the operations of each department are distinct, and there is often very little overlap. Besides, Service to Citizens is not quantifiable, like net profit after taxes or return on investment, which can be used as yardsticks to measure an entire for-profit enterprise, regardless of its component parts, and which can be used to help justify which projects are funded and what resources are allocated. Service to Citizens can itself only be quantified in terms of the operations of the individual government departmental operations, i.e. the number of 911 Calls for Service handled, fires put out, or bills paid in a timely manner. This results in the head of each department striving to meet or exceed the individual departmental management goals - and often to resent what is perceived to be "meddling" by Budget Directors or MIS executives who are required to take a broader city-wide perspective, and who might have something to say about the distribution of scarce project resources. In fact, it is possible to end up with duplicate projects, especially in common process areas like records management, facility maintenance, or computer network installation and management, as each department head strives to implement solutions that will first and foremost enhance its own operational goals.

### 2. Annual budget cycles lead to uncertainty.

Many local governments have hesitated in initiating any project with a longer than twelve month life cycle, because of fear of committing funding past the current budget year. This has frequently resulted in project proponents skipping over the critical project justification and planning stages (cost/benefit analysis, risk analysis, etc.) in a misguided effort to "just



PROJECT MANAGEMENT INSTITUTE 28th Annual Seminars & Symposium
Chicago, Illinois: Papers Presented September 29 to October 1, 1997

get going on this thing" and get it done before the end of the fiscal year. Unfortunately, this can have just the opposite of the effect intended. If the project flounders or is stalled, perhaps for some perfectly good reasons, it may find itself abruptly killed by those who wield the budget ax. After all, without documentation as to the project's justification, the project is extremely vulnerable to termination. The good news here is that local governments are more frequently seeking project funding through bond issues or other financial instruments which insulate the project schedule from an arbitrary annual budget cycle. This is increasingly relieving project managers from having to struggle to justify, initiate, and implement projects within a time frame dictated solely by a budget process.

### 3. Campaign cycles lead to even more uncertainty.

Politicians need to claim the voters' attention on topics that result in votes. This is a project justification criteria not generally considered vital in the private sector. It often means that the politicians are more focused on service operations rather than project undertakings. Providing reliable garbage pick-up, paving potholes, or planting trees can appear to have a more reliable vote-gathering "payback" than starting a project to overhaul the purchasing process or to provide direct deposit for city employees. On the other hand, an upcoming election can put a fire under a popular project to assure completion in time to generate good campaign publicity, just as an election could temporarily halt or even kill a project suddenly deemed too controversial. And, of course, a change in leadership at the top of the organization can lead to a review of all ongoing or planned projects. A new mayor may not be interested in either starting or completing his predecessor's pet projects. While it is true that all organizations' projects may suffer this fate when a new management team takes over, it is only in government that the possibility of a new agenda may be arriving with the regularity of the local elections.

### 4. The environment is heavily unionized.

Local (and federal) government now has the highest percentage of unionized white collar office workers of any industry. In addition, many local governments also employ large numbers of unionized laborers (construction workers, sanitation workers, etc.) and tradespeople (electricians, carpenters, etc.). While many industries are heavily unionized in some particular employee sector, (like factory workers in the automobile industry, or drivers in the trucking industry), local government (especially large local government) is unique in the diversity of its organized component, which often extends to health care workers (nurses and technicians) as well as the public safety employees (fire and police). While having unionized employees by no means precludes the possibility of executing successful projects, it is certainly a factor to be taken into consideration. After all, projects are about change. And unions are not oriented towards change, since change almost by definition implies insecurity - not what most unions are about. While hardly a project show stopper, a good project manager will include the possibility of a collective bargaining agreement impact in putting together any Project Plan in which unions and their membership are in anyway stake holders in a project.

### 5. The media is watching every move.

Local government is a favorite and reliable source of stories for newspapers, radio, and television. This is a two edged sword for the politician or bureaucrat considering projects to be undertaken. On the one hand, media and public outcry can act as change catalysts, supporting a project that might be meeting internal resistance. On the other hand, the media love reporting on problems, and are less enamored of reporting on projects going well, i.e. staying on budget, coming in on time, and accomplishing project objectives. After all, even efficient and conscientious project managers occasionally make mistakes. And while it is tough acknowledging your mistakes to your Project Team and your bosses, it can be devastating having the same mistakes aired (and often distorted) on the five o'clock news. This is a type of risk that most private sector project managers never have to consider, except in the most extreme circumstances.

### 6. Legal restrictions constrain project activities.

Certain laws limit the government project manager's ability to carry out the project in ways which the private sector project managers are not affected. The most common restriction is in the acquisition process: many products and services must be bid, or acquired through a formal Request for Proposal. The project manager may also have to require vendors to abide by specific contract language, such as payment terms which are standardized for the entire government entity, or include a local ordinance which states that the vendor has no outstanding taxes unpaid, or that the vendor's employees have no outstanding child support payments. These limitations may inhibit the government project manager from the range of choice available to the private sector employee, but such limited flexibility should be acknowledged and handled up front as part of the Project Plan.

### 7. The top priorities are public safety and health.

For the foreseeable future, in any urban environment the bulk of local funds will go towards the ongoing operations of the police, fire, health, and sanitation (water, sewer, and waste disposal) departments. This is true whether or not the function has been privatized or is being carried out by government employees. Any projects, in these domains or any other, will continue to compete with ongoing operations in these critical areas for both funding and staffing. It is not possible for governments to curtail these services in any significant way, just because a related project is being implemented. And any direct and significant negative impact on basic services would bring immediate bad publicity, the wrath of the executive (political) sponsor, and, no doubt, the downfall of the unfortunate project manager.

## The Typical City Project

The factors described above conspire to mold projects in local government along certain lines, in response to those pressures. The typical city or county project will exhibit most of the following traits:

- The project scope is self contained (within one department only) and is generally discussed only within the sponsoring department. This is a reflection of the autonomous nature of many city and county bureaucracies.
- A department staff person will be assigned by upper departmental management as the Project Liaison. This staff person will generally retain all or part of his or her normal non-project duties, stemming from the need to continue support of operational requirements.
- The vendor for the system or service will be responsible for project management. This arises both from the "just get it done" project mentality, as well as a real lack of project management expertise within the ranks of local government employees. It means there may be a potential conflict of interest between the client's goals for the project and the project manager's position as a vendor employee.
- The project schedule is constrained by the annual budget cycle and the periodic election cycles. Project staffing and priority will be secondary to the preparation of the annual budget as well as the political concerns of the sponsoring executive.
- The project is sensitive to external pressures. All concerned with the project will be constantly evaluating how any project concerns (or successes) would appear if the media spotlight were suddenly turned in their direction.
- The project is vulnerable to "scope creep." This can arise from the fact that the initial planning stages were omitted or skimped on, meaning that key requirements were overlooked, or because one of those "external pressures" suddenly forces the project to shift in an unanticipated direction.

## Impact on Projects in the Past

These typical project "traits" have had significant impact on past projects. Projects exhibiting these traits are frequently subject to a loss in continuity in sponsorship, funding, and staff. This can be demoralizing to the Project Team as well as causing an immediate slow down in meeting project milestones. It's hard to stay on schedule if key staff are suddenly removed from a project, or if funds for required materials or equipment are unexpectedly held up for several months. It is also hard to communicate effectively to the sponsor and other project stakeholders when all communications must pass through a single individual who has many other duties to continue to fulfill, may not be a particularly skillful communicator, and who may in fact resent the liaison role he or she has been asked to take on. Any resistance to change already existing in the department is often fueled by a feeling that upper management is trying to force something new on them without explanation. Instead of freely sharing information about the project, information is generally hoarded, and there is often suspicion of the motivations behind the project's goals and objectives. Lastly, the limited ability of a Project Manager to choose specific staff from within the department for projects means that the optimum resources are sometimes not available. It is these traits and their negative impact on project outcomes that have helped to undermine the public's confidence in the ability of local government to run projects capably and use their tax dollars wisely.

## Why Are the Project Winds Shifting?

Local government, especially in large urban centers, has not been especially conducive to established project management techniques precisely *because* these techniques stress time and cost management, encourage the free flow of information, and demand planning, tracking, and evaluation throughout the project life cycle. However, in the last decade, there has been a sea change in outlook towards projects in the local government sector, driven to a great extent by three factors:

1. Citizens and business leaders of these communities are increasingly intolerant of unbridled growth in government costs and the taxes that pay the bills. Government is expected to increase the productivity of its labor, just like the private sector. This forces management to consider costs in deciding which projects to carry out, and to plan more carefully to control costs during the project implementation.
2. There is a higher degree of cooperation between local government and private sector businesses in the community. This results in a cross-fertilization of good ideas between the two groups, through meetings,

joint task forces, and private sector professionals entering local government as high level management staff. Government managers are coming into contact with new staff who consider using formal project management to be the *only* way that a project should be carried out, and who are amazed to learn that in the past (or present), a "project" in local government would often be assigned to someone who has no project management experience or expertise and be funded at taxpayers' expense without the planning, human resources, or tools that could allow it to succeed.

3. The last factor is the astonishing impact of technology on the way local government does business. In many areas, the services performed by local governments are data driven. Without information systems, local governments would be unable to perform these services, or could only perform them in a very inefficient and costly manner. The introduction of a new information system itself is often a major project, and good vendors and consultants bring with them good project management techniques which serve as examples to government employees.

These three factors above have led managers in local government to think in a more formal manner about what a project is and how it should be carried out. However, the introduction of project management techniques must be tempered with an acknowledgment of an organization's culture and structure. Such is especially the case when the organization is large local government. The combination of traditions, law, election cycles and all the other factors previously described can conspire to dismantle the best laid plans. The project manager directing a public sector project must be especially attuned to the organizational culture and competing interests to be successful.

## The Chicago Automated Time and Attendance Project: A Case Study

Starting in the spring of 1994, the city of Chicago undertook to automate the time and attendance procedures for its 41,000 employees. In some respects this was not the typical local government project. The most significant difference is the fact that it stretches across all departmental boundaries. The other key difference is that the project manager is not being provided by the lead vendor on the project, but is an independent consultant directly under contract to the City of Chicago. However, in many other respects, the project was suffering from significant problems that threatened its success before it could even be officially said to be underway. The project reality in 1993 can be summarized as follows:

### *Scope*

This was enormous, ungainly and ill-defined. At the time, all aspects of payroll processing, human resource management systems, and time and attendance tracking were potentially part of the project mix. No cost/benefit studies had been performed to attempt to identify project priorities.

### *Contracts*

None were signed, and key issues of responsibility and expectations were unresolved.

### *Risk*

These were defined only as potential vendor contract obligations or as political considerations.

### *Human Resources*

There was a good project structure (Steering Committee and Project Team), but no formal project management experience or training by any participants.

### *Quality*

Issues of quality were being addressed solely as vendor contractual obligations. There was no discussion of what quality the project would like to deliver to its internal clients.

### *Cost*

There were major vendor compensation estimates only; no total project budget estimates had been developed.

### *Time*

The only schedule had been developed by a potential vendor, and this included, for the most part, only the vendor's own tasks. There was no total project schedule.

### *Communications*

All communications were funneled through two individuals, one of whom was a project champion and who was acting as the City's focal point for the project. There were many meetings, documentation was being handled mostly by a prospective vendor, and a perception that little progress was being made despite many man hours being consumed.

## An Evolution Towards the PMBOK Principles

The City engaged a project manager/consultant in October of 1993. The first significant task by the Consultant was to perform a cost/benefit study covering the major project components of payroll, human resources (personnel) systems, and automated time and attendance. When it became clear that automating time attendance had by far the biggest payback, the Steering Committee decided to trim back the project scope significantly. This also made sense considering the enormity of just this undertaking. With over 41,000 employees, forty separate City departments, close to fifty different unions, many with complicated work rules, and well over 500 work sites throughout the City, automating paper based time and attendance procedures would in itself be an enormous project. The second significant task, which is actually an ongoing process, is to continually introduce and use the PMBOK principles in the execution of the project.

In the three years since the Chicago Automated Time and Attendance (CATA) Project was officially kicked off, much progress has been made, and, while not an unqualified success, the project is well on track towards completion. An entire small data center was built and outfitted with the requisite computer systems. Base time and attendance software was heavily customized to meet the requirements of the numerous bargaining unit contracts as well as general City personnel related ordinances and policies. A three person Help Desk staff handles queries and maintains an "excellent" rating by the system users. Approximately 730 (of 800) total time keeping devices have been installed in 550 City facilities. Thirty five of the City's forty departments have some or all of their employees using the system on a daily basis. While only about 7800 of the City's 41,000 are currently keeping time using the system every day, several thousands more are scheduled to start keeping automated time by the end of the year.

Getting to this point has not been easy. The seven factors first enumerated have all come into play more than once over the course of three years. The most challenging issue for the Project Manager has been to keep the project moving ahead despite having very little real authority in the City government management structure. The following techniques for "herding cats", i.e. influencing without authority, have particular resonance in the local government culture, but they can be applied to some degree in almost any project situation:

### Share information

Information is the coin of the realm in government, where prestige is as much what you know as how much you make. Sharing project information, rather than hoarding it just for a few select executives, promotes project buy-in. It also encourages project participants to share their own information, which can be crucial in avoiding costly blunders. However, you should be sensitive to the management structure when sharing information. This means not embarrassing your sponsors and making sure they are the first to review key project data.

### Be fair

Don't be seen to promote one department's agenda over another. While it may annoy some people some of the time not to receive preferential treatment, it will serve the project goals best in the long run.

### Value every helping hand

Use public praise and training. Since it is difficult to reward government employees financially, you should be generous with public praise when it is deserved and training resources where it makes sense to do so. Use newsletter articles, user group meetings, or letters to the project participant's managers to show your appreciation for a job well done. Provide training for project staff as well as other project participants whenever possible. It shows you're willing to spend project resources on them, will enhance their stature and value (and potential earning power) within their own departments, and will gain you enthusiastic project proponents.

### Publish all policy decisions

This is a specific (and the most important) example of sharing project information. It will keep you out of trouble when you are challenged on specific implementation tasks down the line.

### Provide a "fait accompli" whenever possible

This technique should be used judiciously when you are having difficulty getting a decision made by others, and it threatens to impede the project progress. Make a reasonable decision (after appropriate consultations, of course), document the decision back to those who are concerned, and let them know that the decision will stand if you do not hear back after a certain amount of time. You don't want to hold up the project just because someone else (over whom you have no authority) is giving your project a low priority.

Use the sponsor's "big stick" when all else fails. This should also be used sparingly. No project manager should have to resort to invoking the project sponsor in order to get project tasks accomplished. Save it for really critical instances of non-cooperation when the non-cooperating party is at a high level in the organization.

Use face to face communication as much as possible. While it is imperative to document project tasks, problems, and policies, that communication is unidirectional. You will only really find out what issues your project participants are concerned with if you talk to them. Besides, it's almost impossible to maintain support for a project if the project sponsors and participants feel they're being left in the dark. You may have to devote much more time to communications on a local government project than would be required in other organizations.

Always give your sponsor the "bad news" yourself - and without delay. This is especially important if the bad news is something the media might consider to be of interest. Local government executives really hate to be surprised by questions coming from the Channel 5 news room.

Constantly test the perceptions that are held about the project. Negative perceptions about your project can nullify the positive progress of months of work. Government offices, where people have worked for years, and have friends and colleagues across multiple departments, will loose little time in spreading project information around. Address and rectify misperceptions as quickly as possible. If the problem is serious enough, this is an appropriate use of your executive sponsor support.

PROJECT MANAGEMENT SUCCESS IN LOCAL GOVERNMENT is not an oxymoron—it's simply a new frontier for project management and all it has to offer. Local government employees can learn project management techniques and local governments can benefit by using project management principles. Applied with sensitivity, the PMBOK will guide the project manager to success even in this unique environment.

# Scaling The Bureaucracy: Project Management of The Bureau of Reclamation Enterprise Maintenance Management System

John J. Lambert, US Bureau of Reclamation
Mark Boyle, US Bureau of Reclamation
Allan Mills, PSDI

So you are a functional manager in a large corporation or bureaucracy and your legacy systems are antiquated and dysfunctional. Your business systems are fragmented and much data and user interaction are redundant. Organization boundaries are walled with little or no interaction and cooperation, each with their own stand-alone system. How do you initiate a plan that will bring all the functional groups to the table to integrate the systems? How do you scale the bureaucracy? The Bureau of Reclamation has recently achieved success in integrating five business systems with their Reclamation Enterprise Maintenance Management System (REMMS).

The Bureau of Reclamation manages water-related resources west of the Mississippi River. Besides being the largest wholesale supplier of water in the United States, the agency is the sixth largest generator of hydroelectric power. Reclamation projects include three hundred and forty three storage dams and reservoirs (three hundred and eight of these sites offer a variety of recreation activities), fifty-eight hydroelectric power plants, and fifty-four thousand, five hundred and fifty miles of water conveyance and distribution facilities. Revenues from the sale of power are presently worth $800 million annually. Managing water in the west includes: water supply, power production, water conservation, environmental enhancement, recreation, water treatment, and water quality.

The Reclamation Enterprise Maintenance Management System, or REMMS is a group of commercial and in-house developed computer software systems organized to manage the operation and maintenance of the Reclamation's water and power facilities. REMMS is centered around a computerized maintenance management system called MAXIMO by Project Software and Development Inc. (PSDI) of Cambridge, Ma. The REMMS system integrates five functional administrative groups and their associated automated business practices requirements.

These five functional groups are as follows:

- Facilities operations and maintenance: A work order based planning, scheduling, and coordination system. Cost tracking and facilities maintenance history.
- Inventory management: parts and supplies and warehousing. Parts and supplies are issued by work order.
- Motor Vehicle fleet management: operations and maintenance data are tracked using a work order system.
- Payroll entry system: a single point of entry of labor by work order. The corporate payroll system and the MAXIMO work management system share identical labor hours data for work effort and cost tracking.
- Corporate data warehouse: Access to agency corporate data.

The REMMS project incorporated the installation of twenty client server databases and thirty-seven Windows-based LAN systems in Reclamation area offices across seventeen western states. The REMMS development and implementation project was an extremely fast paced, rapid development effort. The system was fully developed in one year, February 1995 to February 1996, and fully implemented by May 1997.

This paper will discuss how standard project management principals were used to complete the REMMS project on time and meeting all major objectives. The paper is broken down into two major sections:

1. Rapid System Development: Scaling the Bureaucracy: Project stakeholder Management.
2. Rapid System Deployment: Scaling the Bureaucracy: Organizing for Success.

## Rapid System Development: Scaling the Bureaucracy: Project Stakeholder Management

The REMMS project used the principles of project stakeholder management to get high level commitment to the success of the project. "An important part of the management of the project systems environment is an organized process for identifying and managing probable stakeholder in that environment" (Cleland, 1990). The REMMS project has been successful because of the following factors:

- A crisis created an opportunity,
- A clear declaration of the sponsor, and stakeholders,
- A Project Advisory Group (PAG) made up of primary stakeholders was put in place early and maintained throughout the life of the project,

- A Project Concept Document in place signed by sponsors and PAG,
- A thorough project investigation was accomplished as defined and budgeted by the Project Concept Document,
- A Project Initiation Document (PID) in place signed by sponsors and PAG ,
- Software developed using small self managed teams detached from the mainstream organizations,
- Staffing located in one large room with adequate support equipment, fixtures, and space,
- Flexible staffing using staff detail assignments and highly specialized contractor consultants, and
- Detailed budget management and progressive procurement strategies.

## A crisis created an opportunity

The REMMS project, as are many projects, was born out of crisis. The crisis was simple. In the early to late seventies, the Bureau of Reclamation built a huge mainframe computer system to handle all of it administrative and engineering computer applications. In 1994, the largest of these applications was moved to a new platform, leaving only small applications to cover the cost. A decision was made to remove the antiquated mainframe, thus requiring that all remaining applications be replaced, replatformed, or discontinued with in one year. Hence the crisis (self imposed though it was).

## Clear declaration of a project sponsor

One of the key principles to getting complete commitment to the project is to establish a project sponsor or sponsors. The higher in the organization that the sponsor is, the better. In the case of the REMMS project, the sponsor was the Washington Office, director of operations who is the second highest ranking official in the Bureau of Reclamation, second only to the Commissioner. Much effort was required at the beginning of the project to garner the support from this individual as the project sponsor. Once this relationship was secured, it was made official in the form of a memo of record.

## Stakeholders Project Advisory Group (PAG)

Once the official sponsor was established each of our five regional offices was requested to provide a representative to a permanent stakeholders group. The group was named the Project Advisory Group or the PAG for short. The membership of this group grew and changed as the scope was better defined, the group was maintained intact throughout the duration of the project. The PAG held meetings as needed that was usually every two or three months. All project issues involving scope, budget, or interdepartment controversies were presented to the PAG for guidance and direction. Since the primary mission for the REMMS project was to serve the maintenance community, each region supplied one maintenance line manager as a representative. As the project took on new requirements such as the addition of inventory management, and fleet management, new PAG positions were established representation for these stakeholder groups. Also included were representative from the information technologies (IT), property management, and human resource functional areas.

## The project concept document (11/93)

A project concept document was written by the project team and the PAG that defined the following: history of the legacy systems; a general scope; project principles, project objectives; a general description of technical requirements (not the detail requirements); definition of the investigation team (manager and staff); assignment of staff to the Project Advisory Group; the investigation schedule; the investigation budget; the status reporting requirements; and the investigation's deliverables. The project Concept Document was signed by the project sponsors, and the PAG with technical concurrence from the functional line managers (managers of staff assigned to the project). The Project Concept Document was amended one time during the investigation period to extend the schedule, add staff, and adjust the budget. This was done in advance of missing any schedule date.

## Project investigation (11/93–02/95)

The project investigation was guided by two principles born out of a recent failure to produce in-house developed software. They were: (1) To identify the core maintenance management business practices to be automated, and (2) To establish whether or not these requirements could be met using commercial off the shelf software (COTS). The deliverable from the project investigations was as follows: Deliver to the sponsor and PAG, a report detailing the core O&M management business practices used within the Bureau of Reclamation; a description of basic automation requirements to support the core business practices (if any), several alternative software options that fulfill the basic requirements, and a recommendation as to the most appropriate option given cost and time constraints. The project investigation team and the PAG established a requirements matrix that was used to measure all proposed solutions. The team issued a Request For Information (RFI) in Commerce Business Daily stipulating the requirements. The team selected twenty-five software packages from a field of more than one hundred and twenty-five candidates. Each package was evaluated using the requirement matrix. Of the twenty-five, five were selected for review. Of the five, three were beta tested. The investigation recommended that the software MAXIMO, by PSDI be selected. MAXIMO was not the least cost option.

#### Project initiation document (02/03/95)

The finding and recommendations from the project investigation were presented in report form in a document titled: Reclamation Enterprise Maintenance Management System: Project Initiation Document or the "PID" for short. The PID included definitions of the following project elements: assignment of the sponsors, project manager and the project advisory group; the summary of the investigation, the addition of property management functions, the recommended COTS software; the recommendations to develop in-house a customized time and attendance system (pay-role reporting system) to interface with the COTS software; project goals, project objectives; broad definition of the technical requirements; definition of project organization and facilities; statement of assumptions; statements of risks; quality measures; security policy; reporting policy; project schedule; and project budget. The PID was amended two times. Both were amended in advance of missing schedule or budget tolerances. Both were well enough in advance to give the sponsors and stakeholders ample opportunity to influence the project direction, key decisions, and additional funding.

#### Organization, teams and staffing

A decision was made early, to house the REMMS development team in a separate facility office away from the mainstream functional organizations. The REMMS office was set up in an old auditorium. Offices were established using low partitions with ample computer and office equipment and staging areas. This set up proved time and again to be one of the strongest attributes of the REMMS team. The ability to quickly bring staff in and out, to set up mini-training facilities or test environments without excess coordination and advanced scheduling greatly enhanced the team's ability to adapt to solve the problem and move on to the next hurtle. Teams were made up of functional specialists from all part of the Reclamation organization. Each staff member, with a few exceptions, was formally detailed to the REMMS office for periods ranging from one week to one year in duration. Contracts and purchase orders work acquired for expert technical consultant services when needed. Functional teams were created geared to task accomplishment such as maintenance business practices, property management, RITA development, and REMMS data warehouse development.

#### Budget management and progressive procurement strategies

A budget tracking system, tailored to the specific needs of the project was developed early and used throughout the project. One problem was the retrieval of timely cost information commensurate with the speed of the project deployment. Much of the project involved the management of contractors and consultants and yet timely cost information on invoicing was very slow. The solution was to track consultant costs using timesheets and local spreadsheets and retrieve government labor, travel and materials through the corporate accounting system. In this was the accounting system that built to be capable of keeping up with the rapid pace of the project. Cost status reports generated every month or as needed. Burn rate estimates were calculated and used with the schedule to project cost versus an accomplishment scenario. On several occasions the key direction and decisions were made based on the projections.

### Rapid System Deployment: Scaling the Bureaucracy: Organizing for Success

#### REMMS Beta Test—Glen Canyon Dam

As development neared completion, beta testing was conducted by implementation team members and the Glen Canyon staff with assistance and support from the regional office between March 18 and May 31, 1996. During the test, many lessons were learned especially in the area configuration of PCs, printers, drivers, LAN and WAN. Resolution of these issues was much the result of trial and error until such time as the problem was solved and the solution documented. This documentation became essential information as we began our deployment of REMMS. This was also the first opportunity to evaluate our training manuals and implement our train the trainer program. This program utilizes regional staff as trainers for all sites within their region. The PAG and all functional sponsors were invited to Glen Canyon to witness the successful development of REMMS and to be briefed on our implementation strategy. This proved to be very valuable in maintaining Director's continued support for the project.

Getting Focused for Implementation and Rapid Fire Deployment. The project manager, in conjunction with team leaders, conducted an assessment of the following items to ensure that the process that served us well throughout development should be continued.

#### Process

Continuing to meet regularly with team leaders to update progress, identify critical activities/issues; identify the person(s) responsible for completing; establish the schedule and necessary budget to complete the task(s); identify internal and external coordination required. As implementation progressed in the field, weekly conference calls with each site began approximately two months prior to implementation and continued for approximately one month following going live to ensure the system was stable and the users were taking ownership of their system. The role of the project manager was to maintain the focus on teamwork, communication and accountability. It was determined that the organization structure of the implementation team would remain essentially the same as development consisting of a project manager, site specific implementation coordinator, and team leaders for the principle functional areas: maintenance, property, RITA (time and attendance/payroll), IRM, and training.

### Staff Resources

Team leaders reviewed the lessons learned from the beta test and assessed the ability of their team to meet the needs of the sites to be implemented. Close coordination with regional and area offices helped us secure additional staff and make necessary adjustments to target their involvement. The decision was made to continue the consolidation of the teams from dispersed organizations in a central REMMS office in Denver. This was essential in promoting coordination, accountability, and avoided the potential for staff to be diverted to other tasks.

### Consultant Support

With a strategy of multiple site deployment, it was determined that two additional consultants (total of four) were necessary to provide the support to the sites. The principle lead consultant was located in the REMMS office in Denver and the three remaining consultants were on the road and working on sites.

### Budget

As the deployment strategy and schedule evolved, adjustments to the budget became necessary. Additional requirements were identified to ensure the organization and strategy was cost effective. An amendment to the PID was presented to the director's and financial officers of the agency for approval and additional money secured.

### Management Support

To facilitate the exchange of information and create a forum for decision making among the functional sponsors on major issues, the project manager established a Management Advisory Group (MAG). This group met biweekly to be briefed on progress and issues. This proved to be a very valuable tool in promoting harmony between the teams and the business owners of the system.

### Site Sequencing

Sites were strategically chosen for success and scheduled for implementation based on: the interest, enthusiasm, and eagerness of the area manager to be up and running; ability of on-site staff and regional office support staff to complete the necessary advance preparation work.

### Implementation strategy of a typical site

The entire series of sequenced events outlined below took approximately three months per site:

1. Server Installation; Client Installation; Software Installation; Training Database Installation.
2. Train super-users with formal MAXIMO training; initial inventory data conversion.
3. Hands on maintenance data conversion; workshop and primary business practice decisions led by business practice team and consultant.
4. Maintenance data conversion and continued business practice decisions by site personnel and consultant.
5. Review and course correction on maintenance data conversion and additional business practices.
6. Finalize maintenance data and revise business practices by site personnel and consultant.
7. MAXIMO training for remaining site personnel; final inventory data conversion.
8. Parallel operation and revise business practices as necessary.
9. Live Operation.

### Maintaining Sponsor's Support

The importance of this cannot be over emphasized. It is critical that support of the functional sponsors and the Director's be maintained at all times. An opportunity to reinforce this support came at the area manager's conference about halfway through implementation. A hands on presentation of the REMMS system on Grand Coulee's live database was given to all area managers, directors and the commissioner. This provided the opportunity to demonstrate our success and ensure the continued support by senior management.

### Home week—1996

Key staff assembled in Denver during December for three days to assess progress and make the necessary mid-course corrections. Team leaders conducted break out sessions to focus on specific action items and coordinate adjustments to the schedule and resource requirements.

### REMMS Implementation Complete

As of May 31, 1997, the first phase of REMMS was declared complete with all twenty sites in the original plan fully implemented. The REMMS team is currently in the transition phase to long term support. In addition the team is evaluating the requirements, scope, and impacts associated with version upgrades and enhancements.

### Benefits

The benefits that can be identified (Tapscott and Caston 1993) from the project management and alignment of resources of the REMMS project as employed during project development, implementation, and long-term support are as follows:

- Retains the project lead within the area of responsibility of the original principle functional sponsor.
- Places the responsibility on the owners of the system.
- Enables a logical and consistent approach to operation and support.
- Enables rapid development and deployment of version upgrades.
- Promotes harmony between team members and the business owners of the system.
- Enables tailored, single point service to clients (area and regional offices).
- Is cost effective.
- Allows the enterprise nature of our business practices to be consistent.
- Enables a clear division of labor and responsibility.
- Optimizes participation from actual users in the process.
- Facilitates the development and actual usage of the software by end-users. Focuses on object driven development and operation and support.
- Promotes the opportunity to achieve a strategic synergy across Reclamation.

## Conclusions

In less than two and one-half years, Reclamation has completed what many said could not be done. We developed and implemented a fully integrated system of maintenance management, property management, and time and attendance software to conduct operation and maintenance business at Reclamation facilities throughout the western states. Reclamation is improving business practices at all levels to improve efficiency, meet the demand for accurate accounting of expenditures, and formulate more accurate budgets. This combined effort re-images Reclamation as a progressive federal agency with the focus on doing business consistent with agency goals and objectives that include "a government that works better and costs less."

### References

Cleland, David I. 1990. *Project management: Strategic design and development.* Blue Ridge Summit, PA: Tab Books.

Tapscott, Don and Art Caston. 1993. *Paradigm shift: The new promise of information technology.* McGraw-Hill Inc.

# The Mine Environment Neutral Drainage (MEND) Program—A Model of Cooperative Research for Technology Development

C.J. Weatherell, Natural Resources Canada
D.G. Feasby, G. Tremblay, Natural Resources Canada

Acidic drainage is recognized to be one of the largest environmental liabilities facing the mining industry and to a lesser extent the public through abandoned mines. Base metal mine wastes oxidize, produce acid and solubilize metals generating acidic effluents that potentially affect receiving waters. An estimate of the collective liability due to this acid mine drainage from mines is between $2 to $5 billion in Canada alone.

In 1989, the Canadian mining industry, provincial governments and the government of Canada established a partnership to develop technology to predict, prevent and control acidic drainage. This $18.5 million program of research and development is called the Mine Environment Neutral Drainage program (MEND). The three partners each contribute $6 million, expertise and work-in-kind at field sites and research laboratories. The MEND program comprises three full-time program managers, numerous voluntary program and project managers, approximately two hundred volunteers, and about two hundred projects across Canada.

Over the last eight years, the consortium has been very successful in developing acceptable new technology that reduces the liability associated with acidic drainage. An estimated saving of $1 billion in environmental liability is directly attributed to the MEND program. New mines are now able to open without long-term concern about acidic drainage at closure.

MEND has been described as a model for governments and industry to co-operate in technology development. The MEND consortium approach symbolizes the co-operative style of technology development that is gaining momentum and will drive the economy in the next century. The MEND framework, program and project management and methods of transferring developed technology are described.

## Introduction

One of the most significant environmental issues facing the global mining industry today is acidic drainage that affects all sectors of the mining industry including coal, precious metals (gold, silver), base metals (copper, nickel, zinc) and uranium. Acidic drainage is the result of a natural oxidation process whereby sulfur bearing minerals oxidize upon exposure to oxygen and water. The net result is the generation of metal laden effluents of low, acidic pH, that can potentially cause damage to ecosystems in the downstream environment. Acidic drainage is not only caused by mining activities but also civil works. Remedial measures are currently in place at an international airport in Canada after construction of a runway exposed sulphides that resulted in acidic drainage. Acidic drainage also has a positive side. Prospectors use the telltale red streams caused by acidic drainage to locate metal ore deposits. The Voisey's Bay deposit in Eastern Canada and the Red Dog deposit in Alaska are examples.

Although the issue of acidic drainage is not new and has an extensive history spanning decades, and even centuries in Europe, it is not fully understood. In the past ten years, changes in socioeconomic expectations and heightened environmental awareness have made the management of waste a relatively new concept in the mining industry (Price 1995). This coupled with the potential impacts to the environment from mining operations have made the mining industry one of the most intensively regulated and scrutinized industries in the world. As a result of these and other factors, extensive liabilities have been generated in countries such as Canada, United States, Australia, Sweden and Germany by the inability to adequately deal with acidic drainage issues. This liability is essentially the cost incurred by the property owner/manager during or after the life of the mine to ensure that the impact to the environment is minimized and adheres to regional environmental regulations. Costs typically include: the collection, and treatment of acidic drainage; construction of engineered structures to contain mine wastes; relocation of mine wastes to containment areas; or rehabilitating the mine, mill and containment areas after operations have ceased. Major acidic drainage liabilities in North America are typically related to the control of offsite impacts (i.e., before discharging to the environment).

## Scope of the Problem

In the United States approximately twenty thousand kilometers of streams and rivers are impacted by acidic drainage, 85–90% of which receive acidic drainage from abandoned mines (Skousen 1995). Although there are no published estimates of total U.S. liability related to acidic drainage, examples are presented to put a dimension to the problem. The Summitville Mine in Colorado has been declared a Superfund site by the Environmental Protection Agency (EPA) who estimated the total rehabilitation cost at approximately $100 million (U.S.). This figure includes approximately $50,000/day alone for containment and treatment. The Leadville site, also in Colorado, also a Superfund site has an estimated liability of $290 million (U.S.) due to the effects of acidic drainage over the one hundred-year life of the mine. At an operating mine in Utah, U.S. regulators estimate liability at $500–$1,200 million (U.S.) (Murray 1995). Liability estimates for Australia in 1997 and Sweden in 1994 are $900 million and $300 million (U.S.) respectively (Harries 1997, Gustafsson 1997). A recent study has estimated the total Canadian liability between $2 and $5 billion (CDN) (Feasby 1994). Considering the above data, the number of new mining projects currently under development and mining projects in other countries not mentioned above (e.g., South America, South Africa), one can anticipate the total worldwide liability to be in excess of $10 billion (U.S.).

## Response to the Problem

For some time, the Canadian mining industry and the government of Canada had conducted research into methods of establishing sustainable vegetative growth on tailings and waste rock. It was believed that this technology would alleviate acidic drainage problems from these sites, thus allowing mining companies to abandon these sites without future liability. Very successful vegetation methods were developed, and many sites were vegetated. However after several years, the quality of water draining from vegetated sites had not significantly improved, and mining companies were faced with the prospect of continued treatment and future liability. In response to the need to conduct research on acidic drainage, the Canadian mining industry formed a task force in 1986 consisting of a steering committee and a technical working group, with representatives from the mining industry, five provincial governments and two federal government departments. This group was named RATS (Reactive Acid Tailings Stabilization) task force. Its recommendations were published July, 1988 (RATS 1988), and were implemented by a tripartite consortium called the Mine Environment Neutral Drainage (MEND) program. A similar program, the National Uranium Tailings Program (NUTP) was formed in 1983 and focussed on developing predictive models to develop technology to reduce the liability for uranium mine tailings. The program was a federal government initiative that had a fixed budget of $9.5 million, was managed by a group of specialists, and had an advisory board from government and industry. Although some useful and innovative modeling methods were developed, no significant new disposal or management technology resulted. Also, in terms of liability and environmental impact, acid generation from residual sulphides was clearly identified as the priority issue for tailings in uranium mining operations. The NUT Program served as a useful model from which the MEND program was built and demonstrated that to be successful, stakeholder buy-in would be necessary in all stages for any future program. A research plan to spend $12.5 million over five years on acidic drainage projects was produced by the RATS taskforce. Two important objectives were established:

1. To provide a comprehensive, scientific, technical and economic basis for the mining industry and government agencies to predict with confidence the long term management requirements for reactive tailings and waste rock; and
2. To establish techniques that will enable the operation and closure of acid generating tailings and waste rock disposal areas in a predictable, affordable, timely and environmentally acceptable manner.

It should be emphasized that the MEND program is focussed entirely on technology development to reduce the liability associated with acidic drainage.

## Organization

The MEND consortium includes representatives from the mining industry in Canada and abroad (U.S., Australia, Sweden, Norway), provincial governments and the federal government. Representatives from the U.S. government (e.g., former U.S. Bureau of Mines, U.S. Department of Energy, U.S. Bureau of Land Management) were also at the table. The MEND organizational structure was established to include a Board, a Management committee and six technical committees as shown in Exhibit 1.

In 1995, the MEND organization was streamlined by amalgamating the Prediction and Monitoring committees and transferring the function of the International Liaison committee to the Manager of the Secretariat. Roles of the committees are simple. The Board of Directors provides vision and approval of yearly plans and budgets; the Management committee provides 'hands-on' management of the program; and the technical committees address technological solutions. The Secretariat is essentially the 'hub'

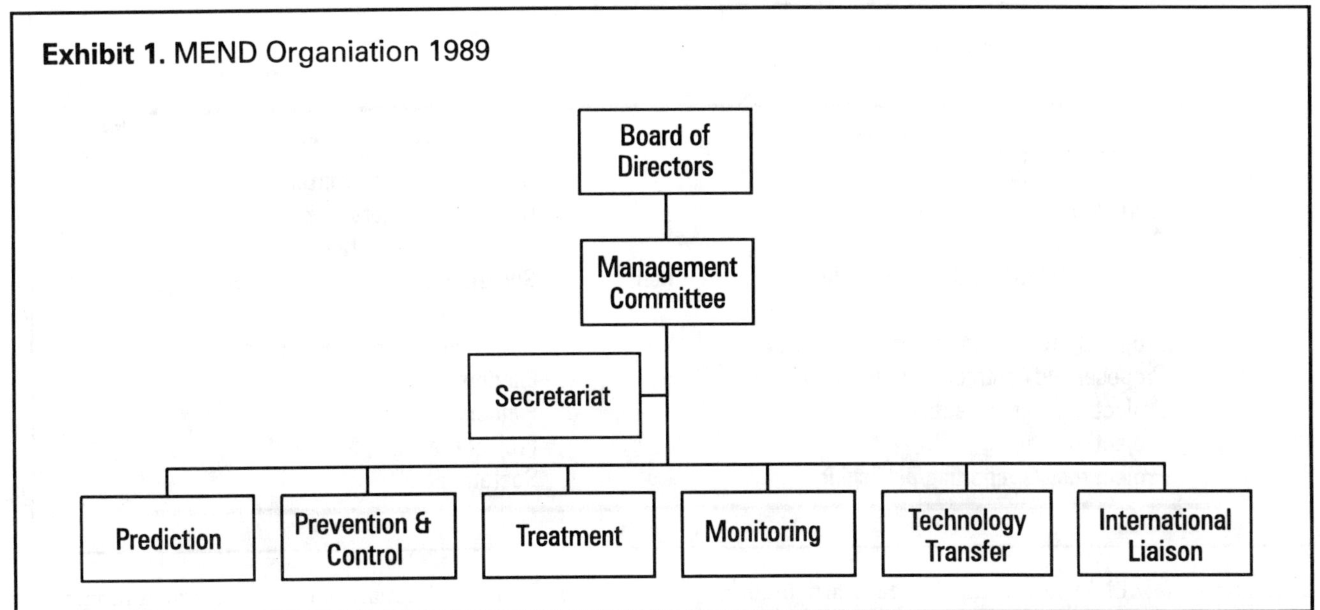


of the organization that ensures coordination of the elements within, and external to MEND. The most important role of the Secretariat is to provide program and project management to the organization. It is apparent that the above organization could be rewritten to resemble any company, real or virtual. The distinctions that make MEND unique are discussed below.

## Operation

Each committee is composed entirely of volunteers from companies across Canada with technical advisors from the U.S., Australia and Sweden. Originally academics and consultants were not included in the technical committees but were relied upon to provide specific technical advice. Over the last three years, this has changed and several consultants and academics are actively involved in MEND. Approximately two hundred volunteers are currently active in MEND. Each committee is chaired by an industry representative or highly placed government official who is typically an expert in the technical field of that committee. Technical committees and the Management committee typically meet twice per year and the Board annually. Research is performed by solicitation from the technical committees (RFPs), unsolicited proposals from industry, consultants and academia or through the contribution of in-kind work credits by the industry. Project managers are assigned from the technical committees although Secretariat personnel accounts for a large proportion of the project managers.

In 1989, it was estimated that expenditures of $12.5 million over five years (RATS 1988) would be required to reduce the liability associated with acidic drainage by 10%. This estimate was revised in 1992 with a Revised Research Plan (MEND 1992) to $18.5 million and the time line expanded to nine years. The program also shifted from an "in kind" project base to having a much larger proportion of the program produced as a result of proposals solicited on a competitive basis. Contractors were drawn from universities, consulting and engineering companies, and research organizations. The adopted procedures are shown in Exhibit 2.

The funding for MEND was divided equally among the three major partners; the mining industry, the federal government and five provincial governments. Written financial commitments totaling $4.25 million were received from the mining industry. To date Canada has contributed 37% of the funding, the provinces 24%, and the industry 39%. Project scopes and budgets are approved by the management committee and funding is secured on a project-by-project basis, as there is no established "pot" of money.

## Project Management

In a project management context, MEND developed from a typical needs/requirements life cycle in which three phases can be readily identified (Frame 1995). Firstly, recognition that acidic drainage issues could not be adequately dealt with corresponded to the 'needs emergence' phase. Next came the 'needs recognition' phase. Here the mining community in Canada, and indeed globally, realized that new technologies had to be developed to address this problem. The result was

**Exhibit 2.** Process and Procedures

| Element | Responsibility |
|---|---|
| Annual plan and budget | Management committee |
| Review/approve annual plan | Board of Directors |
| Scope for projects | Technical committees |
| Scope to MEND participants for funding commitment | Secretariat |
| Request for proposal | Secretariat |
| Proposal review/contractor recommendation | Technical committees, Secretariat |
| Proposal and contractor acceptance | Funders |
| Project manager selection | Funders |
| Project monitoring | Project manager, Secretariat |
| Project results reporting/publishing | Secretariat |

the creation of MEND in the third, 'needs articulation,' phase. The challenges associated with such an organization are many and overcoming these challenges often times difficult. Applying the definition of a virtual project by Adams (1997) to MEND indicates that MEND is indeed a virtual organization. The major challenges encountered in MEND originate from its virtual nature where members of various committees are distributed across Canada in numerous corporate affiliations and have rarely worked together before or have even met face-to-face. The major benefit of MEND also stems from this nature, primarily a collection of readily available, multidisciplinary experts gathered for creative problem solving.

In order to retain focus across the organization several steps were taken. The structure of the MEND organization, the mandates and budgets of the individual committees were clearly defined at the outset (RATS 1988) to avoid any future confusion over roles or responsibilities. Extensive planning throughout the entire organization and annual reviews of the plan helped to maintain the focus for MEND at all levels. Extensive peer review processes of technical scopes both inside and outside of MEND ensured that all aspects of proposed or completed technical projects were addressed. This also reduced the potential for the development of nongeneric or site specific technologies or the 'reinventing the wheel' syndrome. The amount of information brought to the table by participants was often extensive.

Technical meetings and teleconferences held on a regular basis to discuss technical objectives, achievements and future direction imparted a sense of teamwork and group belonging to technical committees. Subgroups of the main technical committees were often employed to focus on a specific technical problem. Task forces were also commonly employed at the management level when required. Approximately fourteen workshops on a variety of technical subjects have been held across Canada. This form of communication was used primarily as a vehicle for the transfer of technology. However, it also served to make non-MEND participants aware of the wealth of information available on the subject and the response by industry to address the issues related to acidic drainage.

Despite all of this, the major criticism of MEND is project management (Young and Wiltshire 1996) as the majority of MEND projects were delivered within scope and budget but often behind schedule. Project control was shifting away from a narrow focus of budget and schedule to include a broader, balanced approach focussed on creative problem solving (Thamhain 1996). As such, tradeoffs were required to achieve an accepted level of creativity and quality. This conundrum is faced on a daily basis in MEND as schedule, scope and quality are constantly weighed against each other to achieve the optimal result. As mentioned, schedule is often sacrificed to achieve a desired level of quality resulting in extended timelines that are a typical criteria employed by external reviewers of the organization.

## Technology Transfer

In 1992, it was agreed that the intellectual property (IP) resulting from MEND sponsored work should be readily available to stakeholders, consultants, academia or the public in general. To ensure this, all IP developed under MEND is assigned to the government of Canada for the benefit of MEND stakeholders. Thus, computer code or developed technology is accessible and cannot be copyrighted, patented

**Exhibit 3.** Technology Transfer Initiatives

| Initiative | Distribution | Number |
|---|---|---|
| Report Publications | Worldwide | 94 |
| Newsletters | Worldwide | 4 |
| Workshops | Canada | 14 |
| Conferences | Canada, U.S., Norway | 8 |
| Annual Reports | Worldwide | 6 (1991-1996) |
| Internet | Worldwide | **Error! Bookmark not defined.** |
| Videos | Worldwide | 2 (4 languages) |

or otherwise used by the contractors for financial gain. Transfer of this technology was given to a separate committee. Tools employed include: newsletters, workshops and conferences, report publications, annual reports, videos and the Internet. Technology transfer initiatives are summarized in Exhibit 3.

With the exception of publications and conferences, access to each of the above initiatives was without charge. Attendance at workshops averaged around eight-five for one- or two-day sessions. Workshop speakers usually donated their time and in some instances were given an honorarium to cover travel costs. The latest MEND conference, Vancouver June 1997, attracted four hundred and sixty-nine delegates from twenty-three countries. Published reports are available for a nominal fee and range from $15–$75 CDN, while conference proceedings are typically $150 CDN. MEND reports are currently being put into a common electronic format (Portable Document Format, PDF) for publication on the Internet. Access to the information will be either via a single report or through a fully indexed, searchable, electronic catalogue.

## Technical Results

The technology being developed includes work in approximately two hundred projects. Although MEND does not have a monopoly on all new technology being developed in Canada, several promising new techniques or refinements of old technologies are being followed. A synopsis of some of the technical results and observations to date include:

- One of the most important results of field observations and the research was the realization that once sulphide minerals started to react, and produce contaminated runoff, it was very difficult, if not impossible, to stop. Also, at some mine sites acidic drainage was observed many years after the pile had been established.
- Chemical test procedures for rock and tailings samples have been refined and considerable progress has been made in developing predictive models and methods for tailings ponds and waste rock piles.
- Models that will predict the performance of dry and wet covers on stacked tailings and rock piles are also being developed and evaluated.
- The use of water covers and underwater disposal are being confirmed as the best prevention technology for unoxidized sulphide-containing wastes.
- Results-to-date on uranium tailings show that oxidation is effectively stopped and techniques are being developed to minimize water contamination so that treatment plants can be shut down in few years.
- Innovative "dry" cover research is indicating that several materials, including waste materials from other industries, provide excellent potential at lower cost for generating moisture retaining, oxygen-reducing surface barriers.
- Several other disposal technologies that will reduce acid generation being investigated including permafrost in northern environments and waste organics from cities (crude compost) as oxygen-consuming covers for mine tailings

As mentioned above, no dramatic technological breakthroughs have been achieved by MEND, but industry reports that a significant reduction in liability has been realized. For one major mining company, using the results of MEND and planning ahead, a reduction in apparent liability of nearly $500 million has been achieved (Natural Resources Canada 1994). Prevention has been determined to be the best strategy, but with many old mine sites, there may be no "walkaway" solutions.

## Other Results

Aside from the huge technical successes, MEND itself represents an innovative method of partnering for technological research and development. A number of reasons can be cited for the success of MEND, the majority of which have been documented previously (Tan 1996, Yeack 1996). A few essential points are summarized below.

1. The high return on the investment financially in terms of knowledge gained and environmental and technical awareness of the scope of the problem and credible scientific solutions.
2. The partnership that has developed between the two levels of government and the mining industry in the search for solutions to a major environmental problem. This partnership has developed in large part because the volunteers participate "at the table" wearing a "MEND hat" rather than their sponsoring organization hat. All partners have an interest in finding lower cost technology that is widely applicable.
3. Engaging a small group of expert coordinators to manage the accounting, extensive reporting and technology transfer. Without the MEND Secretariat, the program would not have been sustainable over the last six years.
4. The extensive peer review process that is both formal and informal, results in enhanced credibility of the information base.
5. A comprehensive system of transferring the knowledge gained during MEND.

As a result of MEND, although by no means exclusively, it is believed that new sulphide deposits can be mined and processed without long term concerns about acidic drainage. This will have a major impact on new mine financing and development. New mines are able to acquire operating permits faster and more efficiently than before since there are now accepted acidic drainage prevention techniques. The new BHP diamond project in northern Canada and the Voisey's Bay base metal project in eastern Canada are examples. The Louvicourt mine in northern Québec adopted MEND disposal technology and has been able to go from the exploration phase to an operating mine within five years with a reduced liability of approximately $10 million. Similar impacts also exist for existing sites in the process of decommissioning. MEND has also fostered working relationships with environmental groups ensuring they are part of the process discussing solutions. Thus, there is reduced resistance to new mining projects in Canada. In contrast, there is general public resistance to mining projects in the United States (e.g., Crown Butte, Montana; Crandon Mine, Wisconsin). Also, confrontation between the industry, regulators and the public is common in the United States.

## Future—Unfinished Business

MEND as it now exists will terminate officially December 31, 1997. The MEND partners have concluded that a new program should be established in 1998 to develop major breakthroughs in reducing the remaining acidic drainage liability and to put in place an international network of technology transfer to validate already developed methods. From a Canadian perspective, not enough international liaison was included in MEND on acidic drainage. Although the climates and local conditions are varied across the world, the challenges have been in many ways similar, in particular the search for cheaper, more reliable and "walkaway" technology, and methods of dealing with waste rock. Among the realities to be dealt with in a new acidic drainage-focussed program are: the shortage of government research funds, shortage of volunteer time in government and industry, and the other issues to be dealt with concerning mining and the environment. The financial and environmental liabilities remain unacceptably high, and abandoned sites belonging to the crown (federal and provincial) are frequently left generating untreated acidic and metal-containing effluents because of the high cost of remediation. Breakthrough technologies are needed for a major reduction in liability; at the very least significant improvements in existing technology for waste rock are needed. The industry-government partnership should be maintained; acceptance of technology is as important as development and implementation. In addition, the monitoring of remediated sites and application of preventive technologies is also required to validate predictions and improve upon field practice. Even today, there exists a large inventory of information that needs to be analyzed and disseminated.

## Conclusions

Although no dramatic technological breakthroughs have been achieved in Canada or worldwide, Canadian industry reports that a significant reduction in liability has been achieved. An evaluation of MEND was conducted in 1996 (Young and Wiltshire 1996) and concluded that the liability had been reduced by $340 million for five mine sites only. It is acknowledged that the reduction in liability is significantly higher than the quoted value with a minimum of $1 billion commonly accepted. The same study also concluded:

- There has been much greater common understanding of issues and solutions;

the research has led to less environmental impact;

- There is increased diligence by regulators, industry and the public;
- MEND has been recognized as a model for industry-government cooperation;
- The work should continue with strong international connections; and
- Future work should include expert practitioners.

It has been suggested that there are too many barriers preventing partnerships (Larson 1997). MEND is a primary example of a successful, multi-stakeholder approach. MEND is a model for cooperation between industry and various levels of government. The Government of Canada, with mining industry and the provincial governments have been pleased to provide a national focus and develop solutions for this environmental problem facing the mining industry.

## References


Feasby, Grant, Robert Jones. 1994. Report of results of a workshop on mine reclamation. Toronto, March 10–11.

Frame, J. Davidson. 1995. *Managing projects in organizations*, Joessy-Bass Publishers, San Francisco: 111.

Gustafsson, Hans. 1997. *Proceedings of the fourth international conference on acid rock drainage*. Vancouver May 31–June 6.

Harries, John. 1997. *Proceedings of the fourth international conference on acid rock drainage*. Vancouver May 31–June 6.

Larson, Erik and John Drexler. 1997. Barriers to project partnering: Report from the firing line. *Project Management Journal*. 28:46-52.

MEND. 1992. Revised Research Plan.

Murray, Gavin, Keith Ferguson, and Henry Brehaut. 1995. *Proceedings of second Australian acid mine drainage workshop*. N.J. Grundon, L.C. Bell Eds. 165:28–31.

Natural Resources Canada. 1994. An investment in Canada, achieving economic growth and sustainable development (November).

Price, B. 1995. *Proceedings of the second Australian acid mine drainage workshop*. N.J. Grundon, L.C. Bell Eds. 17:28–31.

Reactive Acid Tailings Stabilization Program (RATS). 1988. Research Plan, CANMET Special Publication SP88-3, 1988.

Skousen, Jeff and Paul Ziemkiewicz. 1995. *Acid mine drainage control and treatment*. West Virginia University: 13.

Tan, Raykun. 1996. Success criteria and success factors for external technology transfer projects. *Project Management Journal*, 2:45–55.

Thamhain, Hans. 1996. Best practices for controlling technology based projects. *Project Management Journal*, 4:37.

Yeack, William, and Leonard Sayles. 1996. Virtual and real organizations: Optimal pairing. *PM Network*, 8:29–32.

Young and Wiltshire. 1996. Evaluation study of the mine environment neutral drainage program. October.

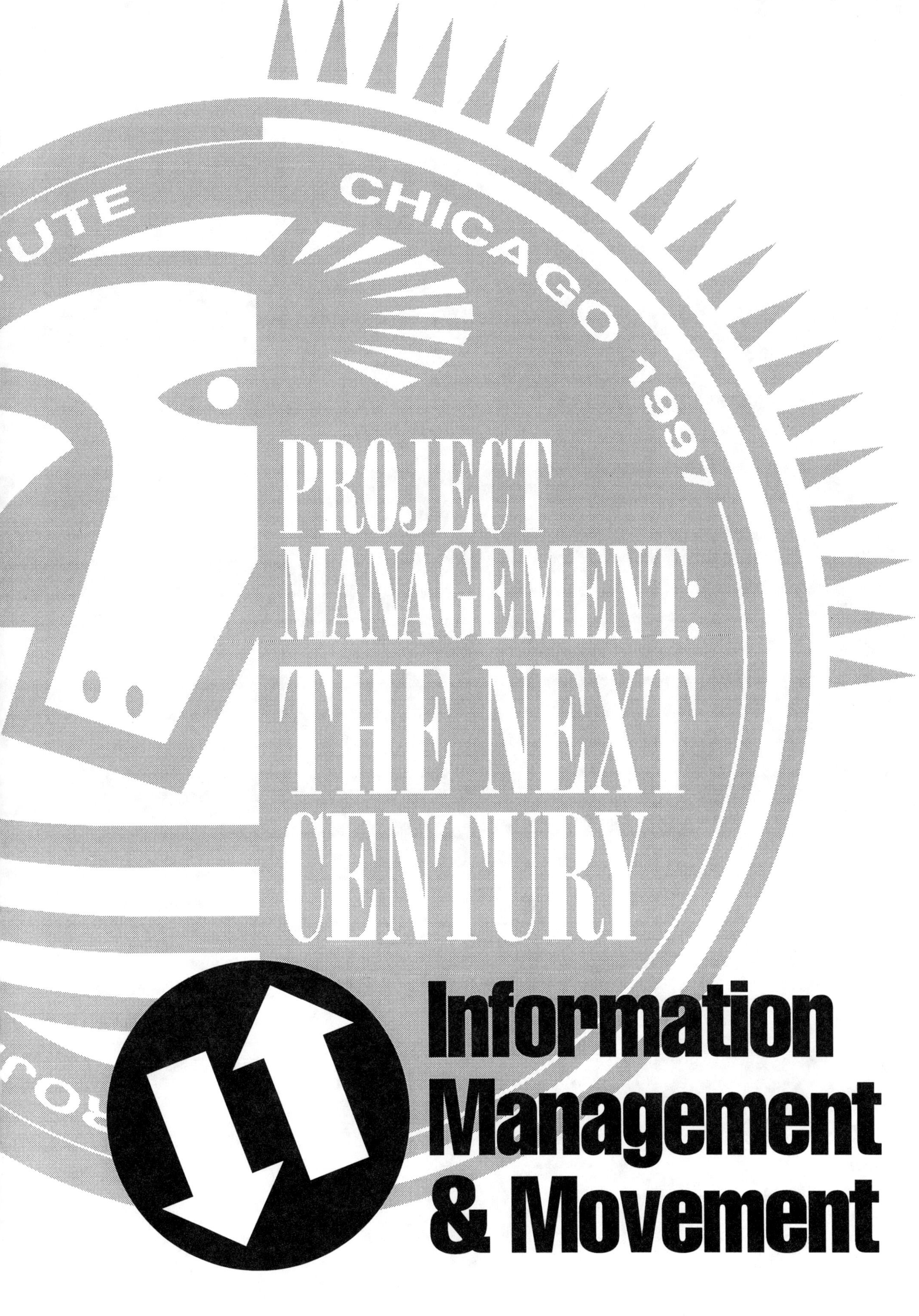


# Information Management & Movement

# A New Era of Program Management Steering Systems Integration Solutions with Next Generation Management

Brian M. Zaas, PMP, Bellcore
Martha M. Geaney, Bellcore

## Introduction

With the growing pace of changes in the telecommunications industry, traditional program management is an inefficient approach for managing the large, complex systems and integration efforts centered around corporate mergers, company reengineering, and technology integration projects.

Today we are in the midst of a telecommunications business revolution accelerated by the Telecom Reform Act of 1996. The marketplace is exploding. New players are emerging. Global competition, new and unfamiliar markets, convergence, portability, network unbundling, internet telephony, and electronic commerce, just to name a few, present challenges that impact:

- revenue generation
- cost reduction
- customer acquisition and retention
- competitive positioning.

Information technology and applications systems departments are building and deploying software and systems on a scale and at a pace rarely attempted before. Your organization may be undergoing reengineering efforts that have resulted in a "just-in-time" workforce, or it may be entering into a new competitive market segment.

Successful programs meet an organization's expectations. Many unsuccessful programs are the result of using technology for technology's sake , applying little or no program management, or implementing program management processes that fail to integrate all of the pieces of the business.

## Did You Know that 84 Percent of New Programs Fail?

Programs fail because technology gets out in front of the people, organizational, and process changes required to deploy technology successfully. Most researchers view failed programs as those that demonstrate cost overruns, schedule overruns, and feature/functionality deficiency. In many cases, these programs represent significant financial and resource impacts as a result of expanded scope and project restarts.

Recent studies indicate that there are patterns for program failures:

- Executive sponsorship and support are minimal
- Little risk planning and management regarding how the technology fulfills the business strategy
- Critical people and process changes required to support the technology are not considered
- Human performance improvement is not planned and managed in line with the project efforts
- Technological architectures and platforms are chosen for the sake of technology and not for achieving business objectives.

Research by the Standish Group shows that a staggering 31 percent of projects will be canceled before they ever get completed. (Standish 1995) Could this cancellation rate be due to our information technology (IT) organizations' inability to define programs in terms of an integrated approach to addressing the business needs?

## Adopting an Integrated Program Management Framework

To be one of the 16 percent of programs that are successful, organizations must adopt an integrated program management framework towards program management. This means that IT organizations must consider the people and process changes in tandem with technology-focused change. People and process change management are at the core of technology realization; this means a new era of program management in which the business drivers are harnessing the power of IT. Clearly defined business objectives provide the road map to drive technology realization. These business objectives guide the next generation of enabling technologies. The business objectives become the focus for core competency development in areas where the company can create competitive advantage.

In the new era of program management, the technology must not get out in front of the people and processes. IT must take the lead to integrate all the pieces of the business to deploy and realize programs that integrate the "whole" aspect of

**Exhibit 1.** Integrated Program Management Framework

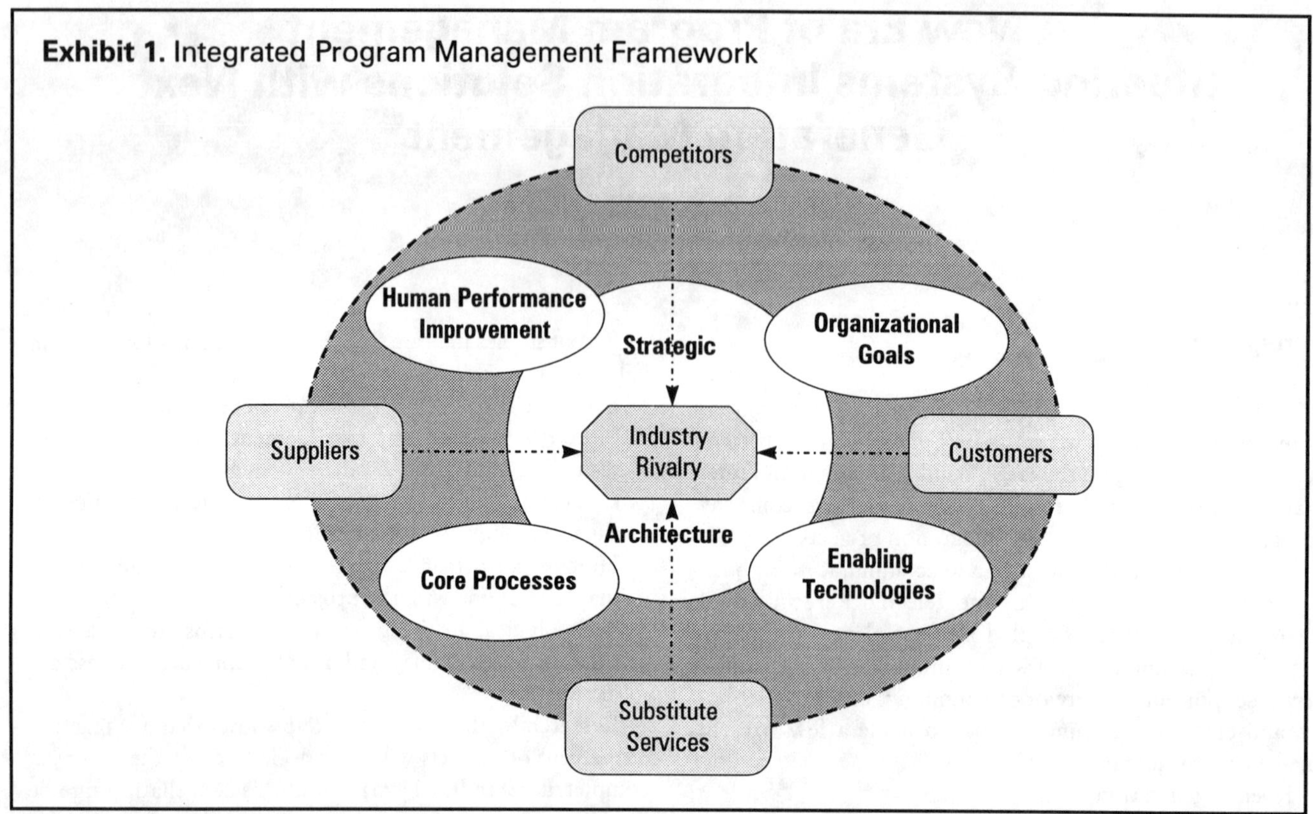


**Exhibit 2.** Components of Integrated Program Management Framework

| Primary Internal Drivers | External Competitive Forces |
|---|---|
| Human Performance Improvement | Competitors |
| Organizational Goals | Customers |
| Enabling Technologies | Suppliers |
| Core Processes | Substitute Services |
| Strategic Architecture | Rivalry among firms |

the business driver. Key areas where today's IT managers need to focus are:

- moving the workforce to the new technology environment meaning more education and training
- building systems for a changed enterprise and redefined jobs, meaning "people" change management

relying on outside vendors to complete critical projects
managing the growing complexity of vendor management
meeting customer and competition-driven timelines.

The purpose of this paper is to set the table for a new era of program management that takes a systems thinking view of business and technology realization. This paper:

- defines "integrated program management"
- describes its attributes
- provides a case study framework
- sets forth measurements for successful program management
- provides an action plan for moving towards a new program management model in an IT organization.

## What Is the Integrated Program Management Framework?

In today's telecommunications environment, companies are focusing more and more on creating a competitive advantage. The information technologies (IT) divisions of these companies are becoming a major focal point for driving competitive advantage. For IT divisions, a program management office focused on monitoring and reporting earned value across its portfolio of projects is no longer sufficient. The integrated program management framework incorporates the primary internal drivers (Miller 1996) and the external competitive forces (Porter 1990) impacting the success of IT organizations. This framework creates a holistic view of program management to guide the IT organization through the continually changing circumstances of the telecommunications industry.

### Primary Internal Drivers

The providers of today's communication technologies are diversified corporations. These diversified corporations function much like the living system of a large tree. The trunk and major limbs are the core products and services; the smaller branches are the primary business units; the leaves, flowers, and fruit are the end products. The root system that provides the nourishment, sustenance, and stability is the core competence of the company (Prahalad 1990, p.67).

In the world of communications, core competence is driven by the efforts of the IT organization. Program managers need to focus on feeding the internal root system of their corporations to outgrow their competition. The primary internal drivers required to gain competitive advantage are:

#### *Human Performance Improvement*

- Does your approach to business-driven program management include preparing your organization's culture for responding to today's competitive, risk-taking environment?
- Does the program include moving the workforce into the new technological environment?

Today's program management approach is one in which business change and breakthrough ideas are driven by leadership. Leadership comes from within the organization's workforce. Eighty percent of the products that companies offer are similar; it's the other 20 percent that makes the competitive difference and that difference is people.

In the new era of program management, human performance improvements occur as a result of leadership-driven change and training that is customized to the individual and specific departmental needs in IT organizations. Training courses include leadership training, problem solving, and personal and team accountability.

#### *Organizational Goals*

- Does your approach to program management include choosing technological architectures and platforms for the sake of technology?
- Does the program address the organizational gaps created by entering into a new competitive market?

In the new era of program management, customer-driven business goals drive IT strategy versus being driven by a technology strategy. A systems thinking feedback loop exists that constantly communicates business goal changes and their impact on the project plan portfolio. As a result, IT determines the risk of changing the portfolio priorities and informs the business units. Consequently, IT reprioritizes the project plan portfolio. The process becomes a dynamic business thinking framework that responds to business changes immediately.

#### *Enabling Technologies*

- Does your approach to program management focus on building core competencies that differentiate you from your competitors and provide long-term strategic focus?
- Does your program management focus take a portfolio view of your project efforts to focus on core skills and capabilities?

An enabling technology (Koen 1997) is a skill or capability critical to enabling the development of an end product or service that is used in your company. The recognition and development of these technologies needs to be driven from within the IT program management organization. Enabling technologies are the result of collective learning in the organization. Critical actions for IT include coordinating diverse software development skills and integrating multiple streams of technologies throughout the IT organization. For example, in the telecommunications industry there is a convergence of technologies in the areas' legacy systems and next generation solutions for the purpose of remaining competitive.

#### *Core Processes*

- Does your approach to program management enable your organization to achieve continuous process improvement?
- Does your program management encourage and enable operating across organizational boundaries for the delivery of product value?

The core processes are those involved with harmonizing the streams of technology throughout the IT organization. These processes focus on the organization of work and the delivery of value in the creation of core end products. Core competence development is a direct result of the communication, involvement, and deep commitment to working across organizational boundaries. Program managers need to better understand the impact of core competence on driving the future of IT initiatives. Program management needs to drive core competency development from within the program initiatives.

#### *Strategic Architecture*

- Does your approach to program management consider the best fit for managing the project portfolio in terms of the organizational structure and culture?
- Does your program management infrastructure position you to accomplish strategic business objectives?

The organizational structure and culture can best be defined in terms of a strategic architecture. The strategic architecture is a road map for the future that identifies which core competencies to build and the constituent technologies to develop. Developing a corporate-wide strategic architecture establishes the objectives for competency building. The task of creating a strategic architecture forces the organization to identify and commit to technical and development linkages across strategic business units (SBUs) that will provide a distinct competitive advantage.

Through a program management focus, today's IT divisions can lead the way in the development and management of the strategic architecture. The consistency of resource allocation and the development of organizational infrastructure appropriate to manage those resources will breathe life into a strategic architecture. A successful strategic architecture will:

- create the managerial culture
- develop a teamwork environment
- institute the capacity to change
- extend the willingness to develop critical resources in way that protects proprietary skills
- drive commitment to long-term goals.

### External Competitive Forces

A new focus for today's program managers is on driving competitive advantage. By competitive advantage, we mean achieving customer-perceived value for the company's products and services that exceeds the costs to the company for creating that value. Program managers today need to be aware that the technology decisions of the IT division are clear competitive differentiators for most telecommunications companies. To be effective, IT strategies must be integrated with the overall corporate strategy, customer-focused marketing strategies, and system development strategies. Senior managers and program managers must understand the competitive forces that determine their companies' profitability.

Michael E. Porter provides an excellent framework for understanding how competitive forces shape strategy. We will utilize the components of this model to define the external competitive forces of the system framework for guiding today's IT efforts. These external forces take the program manager well beyond "earned value" drivers for managing the IT portfolio. Evaluation of these forces provides new insights into the skills program managers need to develop to effectively manage decisions in today's IT divisions. By using a system-focused framework, we better understand the power of IT technology strategy to alter the relationship of competitive forces to favor our companies.

#### *Competitors*

- Have you focused on program management as a core competency to create barriers to entry for the competition?

New competitors bring new capacity, resources, and desire to gain market share to the industry. Effective program management within IT can create barriers to entry for new competitors entering the telecommunications marketplace.

The barriers to entry include:

- driving economies of scale in the development infrastructure
- developing proprietary technology
- building core competencies
- reducing development costs
- improving cycle time.

By understanding your IT organization's capabilities in relation to your competitor's IT capabilities, you can begin to develop skills and resources within the IT project portfolio to meet competitors head on in new technology areas.

#### *Customers*

- Have you considered the impact and benefits to be gained for customers from providing effective program management?

Customers in today's IT environment can fall anywhere in the value chain of the corporation. Customers drive competition within an industry by forcing prices down, bargaining for increased services, and playing one competitor against another. Program managers need to understand the customer value chain in today's market place. The decisions you make managing your IT portfolio will impact the value chain all the way to the end customer of your company's services. By focusing IT program management on driving differentiation and increasing quality, customers become a valuable asset in maintaining competitive advantage over the long term.

#### *Suppliers*

- Are you considering the impact of vendor management and development of supplier relations in terms of program management infrastructure?

With today's focus on outsourcing within the IT arena, supplier management has become critical to the success of program management. Suppliers can reduce company profitability by raising prices or reducing the quality of purchased goods and services. Outsourcing decisions we make in managing the IT portfolio can directly impact our ability to compete effectively. Program managers need to understand the supplier environment and the power of these suppliers on impacting the IT project portfolio. Suppliers can be used effectively to allow IT to focus on its core competencies. Without understanding your areas of competitive differentiation, IT can negatively impact efforts for achieving competitive advantage by allowing suppliers to achieve a powerful position in determining your effectiveness in addressing end customer concerns.

#### *Substitute Services*

- Does your program management infrastructure allow you to identify changing customer requirements and react quickly to competitive challenges?

**Exhibit 3.** Team Performance Assessment (TPA)

*Tools for Continuous Measurement*

| *TEAM PERFORMANCE ASSESSMENT* | | | | | |
|---|---|---|---|---|---|
| 1. To what degree do you understand your team's vision, mission and goals? | | | | | |
| 2. Team goals | 1 | 2 | 3 | 4 | 5 |
| 3. To what degree do you understand your individual goals? | | | | | |
| 4. Individual goals | 1 | 2 | 3 | 4 | 5 |
| 5. To what degree do you understand how your individual goals fit into your team's goals? | | | | | |
| 6. Goals fit | 1 | 2 | 3 | 4 | 5 |
| 7. To what degree do you understand your customer's needs, whether you have direct customer contact or not? | | | | | |
| 8. Customer needs | 1 | 2 | 3 | 4 | 5 |
| 9. How effective is the communication on your team? | | | | | |
| 10. Team comm. | 1 | 2 | 3 | 4 | 5 |
| 11. To what degree do you have input concerning the important decisions made by your team? | | | | | |
| 12. Input | 1 | 2 | 3 | 4 | 5 |
| 13. What degree of risk-taking is the norm for your team? | | | | | |
| 14. Risk taking | 1 | 2 | 3 | 4 | 5 |
| 15. What degree of feedback do you receive concerning job performance? | | | | | |
| 16. Feedback | 1 | 2 | 3 | 4 | 5 |
| 17. What degree of recognition does your team receive? | | | | | |
| 18. Recognition | 1 | 2 | 3 | 4 | 5 |
| 19. To what degree does your team work well together? (Do team members cooperate with and support one | | | | | |
| 20. Works well | 1 | 2 | 3 | 4 | 5 |
| 21. To what degree do you have the power to do your job (such as make commitments, set schedules, etc.)? | | | | | |
| 22. Empowered | 1 | 2 | 3 | 4 | 5 |
| 23. To what degree is your team held accountable for results? | | | | | |
| 24. Accountable | 1 | 2 | 3 | 4 | 5 |
| 25. How satisfied are you that your leaders remove obstacles that get in the way of being customer focused? | | | | | |
| 26. Obstacles | 1 | 2 | 3 | 4 | 5 |
| 27. To what degree do you feel part of the larger team? | | | | | |
| 28. Larger team | 1 | 2 | 3 | 4 | 5 |
| 29. To what degree do you and your team members look for ways to improve quality, productivity, costs and | | | | | |
| 30. Improvements | 1 | 2 | 3 | 4 | 5 |
| 31. What suggestions do you have for improvements internal or external to the team? | | | | | |

Substitute services are the direct result of technology advances, which significantly improve the value to the end customer. As we manage the IT portfolios, we need to understand how they fit into the larger business context. With advancing technologies, program management infrastructure needs to include processes which continually scan the competitive environment to know how competitor's customers are reacting to new products and services. Although we cannot always predict the rise of new technologies and IT capabilities to impact our competitive position, program managers need to enhance our ability to recognize when competitors are creating substitute services for our existing offerings and provide the feedback loop to the business drivers. For example, overnight letter delivery has been replaced by e-mail and internet services.

#### *Rivalry Among Firms*

- Are you focusing on program management as an effective tool in redefining the way in which you compete in today's changing environment?

Management of the IT portfolio is a major component in determining the degree of rivalry among telecommunications companies. The degree of rivalry is impacted by the balance among competitors, level of industry growth, degree of product differentiation, and level of exit barriers. Information technology program managers directly impact the ability of their companies to be price competitive, to bring new products to market, and to develop perceived quality among its customers through their efforts managing the IT portfolio.

**Exhibit 4.** Corporate Quality Survey

**CORPORATE QUALITY SURVEY**

We value your input on its work in order to improve the quality of its service offerings. Please help us by responding to the questions below.

**Please rate our company on** 1-Missed 2-Nearly Met 3- Met 4-Exceeded 5-N/A

*Please check rating which most closely matches your opinion*

| | | 1 | 2 | 3 | 4 | 5 |
|---|---|---|---|---|---|---|
| ***1. BUSINESS RELATIONSHIP*** | | | | | | |
| | ....Your standards for quality | | | | | |
| a. | Understanding your company's business needs | ☐ | ☐ | ☐ | ☐ | O |
| b. | Understanding your competitive position | ☐ | ☐ | ☐ | ☐ | O |
| c. | Providing information about our company and its capabilities | ☐ | ☐ | ☐ | ☐ | O |
| d. | Being accessible when you need them | ☐ | ☐ | ☐ | ☐ | O |
| e. | Responsiveness to your requests | ☐ | ☐ | ☐ | ☐ | O |
| f. | Keeping you informed | ☐ | ☐ | ☐ | ☐ | O |
| g. | Helpfulness of the our company people who worked with you | ☐ | ☐ | ☐ | ☐ | O |
| h. | Effectiveness in solving problems | ☐ | ☐ | ☐ | ☐ | O |
| i. | Respecting the confidentiality of your proprietary information | ☐ | ☐ | ☐ | ☐ | O |
| ***2. EFFECTIVENESS*** | | | | | | |
| a. | Technical skills of the our company staff with whom you had contact | ☐ | ☐ | ☐ | ☐ | O |
| b. | Knowledge of industry needs and technology trends | ☐ | ☐ | ☐ | ☐ | O |
| c. | Quality of presentations/meetings | ☐ | ☐ | ☐ | ☐ | O |
| d. | Maintaining a productive working relationship with you | ☐ | ☐ | ☐ | ☐ | O |
| e. | Producing documents which meet your needs | ☐ | ☐ | ☐ | ☐ | O |
| ***3. BUSINESS MANAGEMENT*** | | | | | | |
| a. | Making it easy to do business with our company | ☐ | ☐ | ☐ | ☐ | O |
| b. | The contract process | ☐ | ☐ | ☐ | ☐ | O |
| c. | Effective project management of this work | ☐ | ☐ | ☐ | ☐ | O |
| d. | Effective internal communications at our company | ☐ | ☐ | ☐ | ☐ | O |
| e. | Setting schedules to meet your needs | ☐ | ☐ | ☐ | ☐ | O |
| f. | Meeting commitments on schedules | ☐ | ☐ | ☐ | ☐ | O |
| g. | Meeting commitments on content of work | ☐ | ☐ | ☐ | ☐ | O |
| h. | Meeting your needs on billing | ☐ | ☐ | ☐ | ☐ | O |
| ***4. VALUE*** | | | | | | |
| a. | Cost-effectiveness of this work | ☐ | ☐ | ☐ | ☐ | O |
| b. | Meeting the business needs of your company | ☐ | ☐ | ☐ | ☐ | O |
| ***5. OVERALL QUALITY*** | | ☐ | ☐ | ☐ | ☐ | O |

Understand the adage "smaller fish get swallowed." Today's successful telecommunication companies need to focus on software development and IT capabilities as core competencies.

## Key Lessons Learned—Driving Program Management

### Business-Driven Technology Focus

- Are you quickly able to implement technological solutions affecting your time to market?
- Are the technological innovations driven by your business process flows, and are they designed in tandem?

The program office must be able to harness the power of IT's innovations so that they are driving the business and are in step with the changes that must occur in the other parts of the enterprise. This can be accomplished through a program management process that evaluates technological innovation on the basis of how it affects the business drivers, the cost, and the impact of the people and process changes necessary to realize the new technology.

**Exhibit 5.** Quality Functional Deployment

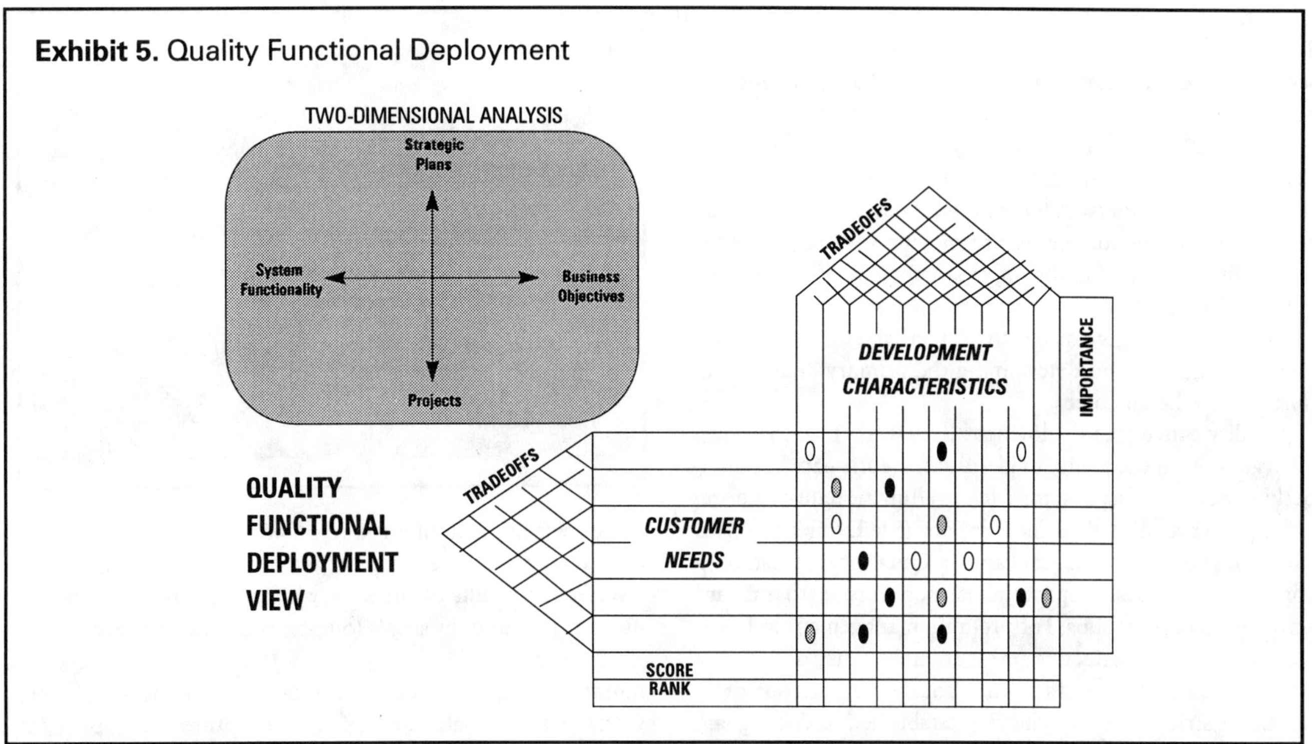


## Process Management Focus

- Does the program management office introduce breakthrough new ways to do business and achieve those breakthroughs for the organization?

In today's environment the program office is designed as a collection agency reporting on budget and schedule. In tomorrow's environment, the program office must drive organizational change. One way to realize this potential is for the program office to be aligned with the organization's business units. Build the program management office into the business's strategic architecture.

Most program office organizations are structured to collect earn value measurement and report on budget and schedule. In the new era of change, a program office will have three fundamental responsibilities:

- **Cross Check**: Collect information from several gauges such as the business unit leaders, the customers, the program portfolio, the project portfolio, the project managers, and the team members.
- **Interpret**: Draw hypotheses, recommendations, and findings from the information that has been gathered.
- **Performance**: This is the program office's opportunity to become the driver of organizational change. The program office will use information to drive the business portfolio and make changes to IT so that IT is effective and competitive. The program office becomes an integral part of the business decision framework with an ability to respond to competitive market challenges.

## What Gets Measured Gets Done

### Metrics to consider to determine success

Most program management organizations fail to achieve competitive advantage for their corporations because they continue to be reactive in nature. Program managers focus solely on the measurement of earned value in determining the success or failure of their project portfolios. In today's competitive environment, the program management function must lead organizational change. While earned value is still an important indicator, it is an end result, not a driver of organizational success. The program management office must look beyond earned value metrics and measure:

- the effectiveness of in-process activities in terms of quality improvement
- the satisfaction of customers in having their expectations met
- the ability of the organization to satisfy the critical success criteria from established business drivers.

Beginning a measurements program can be as simple as using existing assessments, surveys, and off-the-shelf tools.

The focus of team assessment (see Exhibit 3—Team Performance Assessment) on both efficiency and effectiveness is important throughout the life-cycle of each of the projects. Through the use of tools such as the team performance assessment, program managers can measure the effectiveness of in-process activities in terms of quality improvement.

The foundation for successful IT program management is determined by establishing a repeatable method of operations that focuses on understanding customer requirements and expectations. Many companies are moving towards tools for measuring the satisfaction of customers in meeting their needs. (See Exhibit 4—Corporate Quality Survey). These tools provide effective means for driving the direction of future IT programs and determining the primary areas of importance to the customer.

Quality functional deployment (QFD) is a tool that gives an organization the ability to identify tradeoffs between competing critical success factors, feature/functionality requirements, and established business drivers. (See Exhibit 5—QFD Matrix). Program managers can use QFD tools to establish continuous process improvement mechanisms to manage across project portfolios. For program management in IT organizations to be effective, measurement must occur on a continual basis. We need to continuously measure our organization's strides toward achieving established business goals.

## Tools for Continuous Measurement

Today's IT organizations rely on team efforts to accomplish new product development efforts. The team performance assessment (TPA) tool provides a clear measurement of how effectively these teams are operating. The TPA needs to evaluate group composition, group structure, resource availability, organizational structure, group process, situational context, and group task impacts on group effectiveness. Program managers can better understand how effective team-based management is operating within their IT divisions by evaluating data from various performance measurements, including TPAs.

Today's IT successes are built upon team-based management. To be effective, members of IT teams need to feel as though their efforts are considered important by their management. TPAs provide an effective means for determining the level of commitment by a company or business unit to use empowered work teams as the primary organizational structure for production or delivery of services. Further, TPAs provide an effective mechanism for continuously improving the use of teams to accomplish the program goals and objectives.

The Corporate Quality Survey provides significant insight in determining the program efforts that are most important to our customers in judging our work. Customer satisfaction is a primary driver for repeat purchase of services and products. In order for the quality survey to be an effective measurement tool for your IT organization, the survey must be directly tied to the rewards of IT management and IT personnel. By including the results of the customer satisfaction survey as a measure of performance for bonus plan awards, the results of the survey efforts will be a leading indicator of your company's long-term health and success.

**Exhibit 6.**

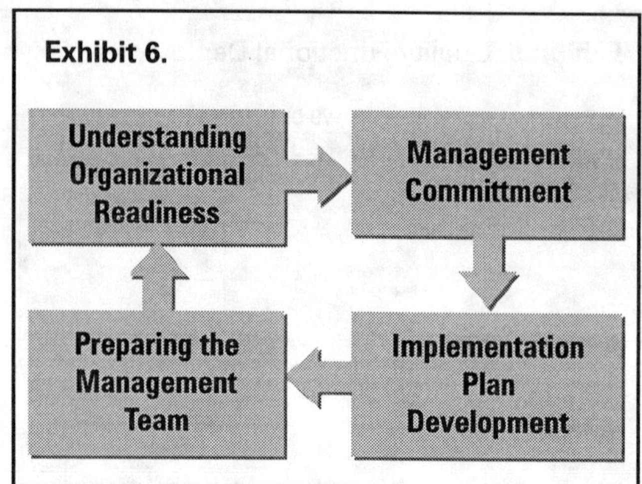


Quality functional deployment (QFD) has been used by hundreds of companies to develop new products (and services) that thoroughly and efficiently capture and implement the true voice of the customer. Quality functional deployment is a method of "mapping" the elements, event,s and activities that are necessary throughout the development process to achieve customer satisfaction. It is a technique-oriented approach using surveys, reviews, relationship matrices, and robust design all centered on the theme of translating the "voice of the customer" into items that are measurable, actionable, and potentially capable of improvement (Schubert 1989).

Quality functional deployment is a systematic approach for identifying and prioritizing customer needs, translating those needs into product/service specifications, and tracking those customer needs throughout the product/service realization process. Quality functional deployment is based on the concurrent engineering philosophy, which has been widely used in manufacturing and aerospace industries. It helps in soliciting input from many stakeholders, facilitates teamwork and communication, and enables user acceptance through early participation. The key to QFDs' competitive advantage is its structured application of the following strategic concepts (Brown 1991).

Preservation of the voice of the customer ensures that customers' needs won't be translated or distorted in the development process. This greatly increases a product's chances of success. A cross-functional team provides input to product realization from all areas of business. Thus the concern of marketing, design, deployment, and support organizations are brought to the surface and dealt with early in the process. Core QFD team members, as well as others called in to help the team, gain profound knowledge of customer wants and the functional perspectives of the other team members. This spreads team building awareness throughout the organization.

## Jump Starting Your Integrated Program Management Framework

Programs fail because technology and process changes are not in lockstep. Program offices fail when they are not building the links among the component parts of the integrated program management framework. In this new era of program management, the program office needs to continuously evaluate its organizational fit. It needs to clearly understand its ability to focus on the primary business drivers and further develop the IT organizations' core competencies. The challenge for implementing an integrated program management framework into your IT division centers around understanding organizational readiness, gaining management commitment, developing an effective implementation plan, and preparing the management team.

Following are key steps to consider in building an integrated program management program office:

### *Understanding Organizational Readiness*

- Do you know the business drivers?
- Have you gathered the information that describes the opportunity?
- Have you sold the problem so that you can begin discussion of a path forward?
- Have you created a vision of the future so that the future is tangible?
- Have you developed a ground swell of interest in the idea before taking action?
- Have you drafted an action plan so that the transition is easier to manage?

### *Getting Management Commitment at Senior and Line Levels*

- Have you worked through the management team so that you can exercise its authority?
- Have you documented its commitment so that everyone understands the resource, time, and budget impacts?
- Are you gathering evidence of success so that you can illustrate the benefits of the new framework?
- Are you celebrating the achievements so that you can maintain the new framework?
- Is the management team exercising new behaviors so that the change is leadership-driven?

### *Developing an Effective Implementation Plan*

- Are you following the implementation plan so that progress is being made and can be measured?
- Have you factored the human response to the new framework into the plan and the budget?
- Have you built the capability to identify and develop core competencies into the implementation plan?

### *Training for Management Team*

- Are you coaching the management team in their new behaviors?
- Does management know how to reward everybody involved so that everyone supports the new framework?
- Is the training focused on developing business vision and communicating change?
- Does the management team know how to access management reports, structure specific requests, and communicate the value of the program office?

## References


Brown, P.G. 1991. "QFD: Echoing The Voice Of The Customer." *AT&T Technical Journal* (March/April).

Koen, Peter. The term "enabling technologies" was taken from course materials presented by Dr. Peter Koen as part of Stevens Institute of Technology, Master's of Technology Management Program. Other readings in the technology management area tend to discuss this concept as "core technologies."

Miller, Gerald. *Managing Change: A Systems Thinking, Holistic Approach.* Contributions to the components of the internal framework are taken from Dr. Gerald Miller's concept of Systems Thinking Framework.

Prahalad, C.K., and Gary Hamet. 1990. *The Core Competence of the Corporation.* Reprinted—Strategic Management of Technology and Innovation. 2nd Edition. 1996.

Porter, Michael E. 1979. "How Competitive Forces Shape Strategy." Reprinted *Harvard Business Review* (March-April).

Schubert, M.A. 1989. "Quality Function Deployment: A Comprehensive Tool for Planning and Development." *IEEE Proceedings of the National Aerospace and Electronics Conference* v. 4.

The Standish Group. 1995. "CHAOS." Available from internet web site @ http://www.standishgroup.com/chaos.hmtl..

Team Assessment survey developed by Bellcore's Change Management Services consultants Jenny Flowers, Beth Nave, and Pete Pawelko.



Special thanks to Dr. Gerald Miller, Dr. Peter Koen, and Patricia Miller for their review and contributions to this paper.

# The Making of a Professional Project Management Organization

James J. Schneidmuller, PMP, AT&T

## Background

In 1990–91, the internal IM&M organization of AT&T found itself where many organizations find themselves today. It was a fairly large organization with a "smokestack" structure that was not meeting the needs of its clients. It had a large number of complex product/service offerings that it made available to its internal client set. The "smokestack" structure made an interrelated implementation of these offerings extremely difficult. Overall accountability was nonexistent since associates were only responsible for their "piece." Technological integration of the service offerings into a solution for the client required an inordinate amount of coordination and effort. Clients were forced into having multiple interface points when a single point of contact was what they desired. Projects were splintered with less than desirable results. The leaders recognized these problems and sought to create a centralized project management group as a part of a planned restructure.

The project managers were to be held accountable for each project under a "the buck stops here" scenario. They would be held accountable for the successful integration of all of the services involved in the project and their implementation. The client would now be presented a single point of contact with a view of the project that matched his own—an undertaking with a specific start and a desired end date with a set of products and/or services successfully integrated and implemented—not a project in piece parts.

## Human Resources

The overall strategy that was employed to create this project management group embodied several different areas of focus. The first area concentrated on the human resource perspective. The organization's sponsor described his vision for the group as "a small group of highly skilled, highly trained professionals." Which associates were available to perform this function of project management? Did those available possess the right skill-set and experience? Did they have a desire to be professional project managers? Would they be comfortable working in a "buck stops here" environment? Where should they be located? The initial approach involved the review of IM&M associates who were performing a project management-like function in the pre-reorganization environment. The resumes were reviewed, and interviews were conducted where necessary. Most were found to have some experience but were lacking in formal project management training and the application of a project management process. The associates' locations aligned, for the most part, with the regional structure of the new organization. Selections were made to arrive at the initial set of project managers.

At the same time, associates external to the IM&M group, with project management experience, were sought. A number of project managers was obtained from another unit. These associates had more project management experience. Many had managed projects in the commercial contract arena. Almost all had already obtained their master's certificate in commercial project management from George Washington University. A large number were already certified project management professionals (PMP). These associates were acquired to seed the IM&M group with seasoned project managers and to provide a mentoring capability. The objective was to successfully merge the groups and create a new group that would fulfill the sponsor's vision.

In summarizing the human resource perspective the following "lessons-learned" are presented:

1. Be sure to understand the sponsor's vision. It will help determine the desired size, skill-set capability, and overall strategy for the group.
2. Assess the capabilities and desire of the project manager candidates—if capability is lacking, emphasis should be placed on the desire, else your investment in training and education will be wasted.
3. Try to "seed" the group with some number of seasoned, experienced project managers. The mentoring opportunity this presents is invaluable! (Actually, each group mentors the other, one about the technology of the projects and the client set, the other about project management.) Coaches or supervisors who are experienced are also invaluable!
4. Some "storming" between the groups occurred. Time must be spent early on focused on team building.

## Process

The next area of focus was a process that the project managers would follow in the management of their projects. Since the experienced project managers brought a process with them, a decision to use it as is, modify it, or create a new one had to be made. A review team was commissioned and charged with the task of making the process decision. This team had both associates that had worked with the process in the other unit and those that had formerly worked within the IM&M unit. Forming the team in this way accomplished several things: (1) it provided an open view of the process for the new environment by those that had utilized the process and by those who were new to the process; (2) it began the teaming that would be necessary between the groups and; (3) it began the sharing and learning between the groups. The team's recommendation was to use the process with some modifications.

An overall process was developed to receive, assign, manage, and close out projects. The process is initialized by the receipt of a project request worksheet (PRW). This form, electronically completed and forwarded, provides the framework of information required for project manager assignment. The scope of the project as well as the target completion date, business case/funding approval, locations, and client information are requested. After discussion with the requester, an assignment is made and notification is returned. The next part of the process was designed to launch the project. This part, the project kickoff process, involves a set of three meetings aimed at getting the project off to a good start. These meetings—the planning session, the internal meeting, and the external meeting—if successfully executed, provide the required up-front planning to insure project success. All of the newer project managers received training in the project kickoff workshop. The next part of the overall process, the implementation phase, was designed to address the standard project management responsibilities of controlling, planning, organizing, scheduling, budgeting, and execution. A jeopardy identification and resolution process was developed as a part of this phase to provide attention to, and resolution of, project jeopardies. The final part of the process, the close out, takes into account items such as the closing out of all work orders, initiation of billing processes, notification/declaration of project completion, internal and external reviews to determine satisfaction and derive lessons learned, release of team members, and a client satisfaction determination. This determination of client satisfaction is based on the project scope and schedule (as agreed to) and the overall effectiveness of the project manager.

Another item created was a supporting process that provided positive reinforcement of project management skills and use of the standardized tools and process, as well as other industry standards. This process, the project evaluation review process (PERP), was developed to provide the project manager and the project team with a proactive, supportive, and professional evaluation of the project to measure the success, or potential success, through interviews, review of project documentation, and expected process deliverables. The use and application of the PERP was especially helpful during the early stages of group formation since it provided on-the-spot, proactive assistance to the new project managers to help with "real" project expectations and issues. Experienced project managers conducted the reviews and provided immediate support to the project, as required.

With respect to the process effort, the lessons learned are:

1. Where practical, involve the project managers in the process development effort. This will more quickly gain their acceptance of the process and will yield a better product. The knowledge they possess related to the work they perform provides invaluable input for this effort.
2. Don't "reinvent the wheel"—there is a lot of project management process information available that can be tailored to fit your needs.
3. Training on the process is important! The project managers need to understand the process from start to finish. They need to also understand the deliverables and your expectations.
4. Think about a review process—not in a threatening sense, but a supportive one. You want to insure project success and provide coaching.
5. You will need to define your own "hot spots" of your process—those process steps that are of particular importance to you and your leaders.

## Education and Training—"The Path to Professionalism"

In order to provide a baseline of education and training for all associates, a broad-based training curriculum was developed. The initial view grouped the desired training into modules of project management, technology, management skills, personal development, PC and software, and quality. Courses in these modules were internally offered and were denoted as core or elective. Each associate's training history was reviewed against this curriculum and an individual development/training plan created. As more of the basic training requirements were met, a focus on an external university master's certificate program evolved. The project managers were strongly encouraged to enroll in the program, as specific budgets would allow. Completing the program and obtaining the master's certificate was furthered encouraged as well as built into the career path (see below).

In addition to the master's certificate focus, the organization encouraged the attainment of project management professional (PMP) status. This was also built into the career path for the project managers (see below). A belief that one important characteristic of the professional project manager was the attainment of PMP permeated the organization.

Lastly, since we also established a standard with respect to project management software (see Standards below), we provided training, through the software company and in-house specialized training, to the associates as well.

Lessons learned associated with this facet of development are:

1. You will need to assess a concentration on a broad-based training curriculum versus a university's master's certificate program. There is some redundancy. We found a "bigger bang for the dollar" with the latter.
2. The associates may have different training needs (e.g., some may need more PC and software knowledge)—be sure to allow for this in your training plans.
3. We found that tying the education/training planning to the career path activity drove the behavior we were seeking—the project managers received the training they needed, they had the ability to be promoted, and we increased the overall credentials and skill level of the group.

## Standards

To support the process and its use by the project managers, another item was developed. A multi-volume set of project management guidelines (PMG) providing standardized models, methods, and procedures was created. The project managers used these as a guide in the management of their projects. Blank forms, completed samples, and detailed descriptions supporting each phase of the process are contained in these volumes.

A standard was established for the project management software package that would be utilized by the project managers. Our thinking in this area was that if we didn't standardize on a specific package we would have a difficult time handling project reports, schedules, variances, and other information generated through this mechanism. Guided by trade publications, software comparison reports, and individual experience, we formed a team to review some seven to ten packages, meet/talk with the vendors (as needed), and provide a recommendation to the leadership team. While this was a challenging and often conflict-generating activity, the team was able to provide a recommendation, which was accepted by my team. Over time, we have broadened our perspective relating to software. Today, given the organization's maturity and the project managers' increased experience, we have the ability to support the use of several commercially available packages.

A standard hardware/software platform was created for the organization. Most of the project managers were equipped with laptop technology to accommodate their travel requirements. An electronic mail package, along with a word processing and spreadsheet package, was obtained.

The last area of standardization was focused on the administrative area. Every company has its own administrative requirements and, certainly, we had those imposed on us! We did have other requirements that we viewed as administrative for which we created a set of standards. In fact, two separate binders were created by two teams of associates. The first, aptly named our Administrative Binder, had attendance tracking, equipment inventory, security, service anniversary recognition, time reporting, and tracking, vacation, vouchers, and corporate credit card information contained within it. The other binder, named most fittingly, our Standards Binder, held organization charts/contact lists, the hardware/software platform configuration, and training and certification information, in addition to several, specific project manager items (budgeting, minutes, success measurements, and so on). The intent of this was to document key standards or requirements defined as "policy" and to provide a tool for sharing information frequently used by all members of the organization.

Lessons learned were:

1. The PMGs were well accepted by the project managers. They were widely used as a reference tool.
2. The decision relating to the selection of the project management software package was not easily obtained. Leadership must provide active involvement and interaction in these kinds of decisions. Once a clear set of needs was established by the leadership team, a fairly quick closure occurred.
3. Make sure you have the necessary funding and support for all acquisitions (hardware, software, and so forth)! If full funding cannot be immediately obtained, a plan for partial deployment must be created.
4. We found that the associates very much appreciated a single source for key administrative responsibilities. Other organizations within the IM&M group used our administrative binder as a model for their own.
5. The standards binder was also well received by the project managers. It provided clear expectations and direction.

## Career Path

With an eye toward the future, the leadership team defined a career path that would *attract, retain, and develop* people who either already were, or who had the capability to be, professional project managers. They did not want the investment in the current population to be for naught. They acknowledged the current corporate culture of changing jobs every eighteen to twenty-four months, this being especially true when a promotional opportunity is sought. The team was operating under the philosophy that project managers improve their skills and capabilities with each project they manage. Each project, based upon its unique characteristics and its different set of functional team members, provides its own lessons for the project manager. It is only through this cycle of learn, manage another project; learn, manage another project; and so on that the individual project manager begins to maximize his capabilities. This repetitive process not only further develops and strengthens the associate's strengths, but also identifies areas of needed improvement solutions, which can be attempted on the next project.

The team reviewed several alternatives that were readily available internal programs and other, external options. The organization's sponsor also provided direction and guidance in this area. An internal plan, referred to as the professional career plan (now called the technical career plan), was selected with sponsor concurrence. This plan encompasses the following areas:

- personnel data (current and proposed level, total years of experience, performance appraisal ratings, and so forth)
- professional orientation—a direct reflection of the project manager's ability to execute the required technical skills (a numeric score arrived at via a skills matrix including software understanding and use, resource utilization, industry standards for project execution, monitoring and control, financial management, and documentation)
- education/experience (a numeric score based upon the defined training and education program and the role of the project manager in her projects as well as the level of performance demonstrated). This is where the master's certificate program and PMI certification were tied into the career path. Certain levels required attainment of the certificate, while other, higher levels required PMP certification.
- interpersonal skills (based on the internal/external demonstration of skills)
- technical coaching (with respect to the project management process and the ability to provide guidance to others)
- business acumen (a knowledge of the client's needs and an overall understanding of the corporation)
- customer focus (the ability to provide complete management of the client needs throughout the project life cycle)
- technical complexity (the ability to manage highly complex and integrated projects; the ability to provide leadership that allows all involved to understand, develop plans, and implement complex projects)
- complexity of projects managed
- nature of work environment (the ability to manage uncertainty of project activities while maintaining full compliance with the triple constraint).

The process supporting this plan involves the project manager's coach/supervisor, the leadership team, and a review panel. This review panel is comprised of other managers from within the IM&M organization, in addition to other TCP associates. One of the project management coaches was a member of this panel. The panel receives and reviews all promotions within the TCP plan. The coach assesses the individual project manager against the TCP criteria as a part of creating the individual's development plan. If determined to be qualified for the next level, the coach completes the required paperwork. This paperwork is reviewed by the project management leadership team, and, if agreed upon, is endorsed and forwarded to the review panel. These promotional packages are reviewed by the review panel at regularly scheduled meetings held approximately every two months. The review panel has the ultimate responsibility of either accepting or denying the promotion.

Lessons learned for this area include:

1. You must identify a career path for the project managers that desire to remain in the profession, but also desire the increase in stature, the recognition, and increased salary that promotions carry with them. If the organization is committed to having a cadre of professional project managers, then it must support the establishment of a plan to maintain the group and grow its skills and capabilities while at the same time rewarding the individual associates. Your ability to attract, retain, and develop project managers will be greatly impacted by this career plan.
2. We were very accepting of the review panel concept. This "external" view provided additional grounding for our promotional recommendations. We rarely had conflicts with the panel or their findings.
3. The criteria we defined in the career plan fit our world. Other criteria or areas of assessment can be defined to match other environments. Be sure to apply whatever criteria you define consistently across the associate universe.
4. Be sure to explain the plan to the project managers. We did this through local coach team meetings, individual one-on-one sessions, and a total organization meeting. This provided the opportunity to insure associate understanding, answer their questions, and obtain their feedback.

5. We found that the plan naturally created a career structure for us in that an entry level and career level position were identified.

## Measurements

Our project manager *measures of success* focused on the industry-standard concept of the triple constraint. Since the projects managed are for internal organizations, there is no contract or formal specifications defined. Instead, the scope evolves as the project begins to mature. We defined these measures to focus on the successful delivery of the project's scope of work (as documented and agreed to by the project manager and client), meeting the project's schedule (ditto previous comments), and the project costs. (Some new thinking submits that there may actually be a "quadruple constraint" to project management taking into account the *politics* of the environment within which the project is being managed.) The IM&M organization had an additional focus on being *easy to do business with* which we also measured. This measure has since evolved to *overall effectiveness*.

The assessment of performance versus scope and schedule has two important defining criteria. The first of these is the client. We created a "scorecard" to obtain the client's feedback for each project. This one-page scorecard asks three questions: "Was the agreed upon scope delivered?" "Was the agreed upon schedule met?" "How would you rate the project manager's overall effectiveness?" In addition to the questions, space is provided for other pertinent comments relating to the project delivery and general IM&M support. The overall effectiveness item is broken into providing proactive status and appropriate documentation, issue identification and resolution, and administering a change management plan. The coach is responsible for obtaining the client's feedback for each completed project.

The other assessment defining criteria is provided by the project manager's coach. This is created in the normal supervisor/subordinate sense. The coach assesses scope and schedule performance based upon what he has learned and observed through interactions with the project manager, the client, and functional team members. Her review of project documentation is also key to making the assessment. Based upon a predetermined weighting between the client and coach input, an overall assessment is made for each project. The company's policy is that each associate receives quarterly feedback relating to performance as well as a final, annual assessment of performance.

Another organizational measure that was adopted in the early stages of group formation was focused on the timeliness of project manager assignment. This was aimed at insuring a timely response to the request for a project manager from within the IM&M organization. This measure has since been abandoned.

What we learned in this area:

1. The leadership team first created a "straw proposal" for annual objectives. This was based on organizational and other input. We would then review them with the associates to gain their input. Final review of the objectives by the leadership team would then be undertaken with a final "rollout" of the objectives occurring in the early spring at a face-to-face total group meeting. Each objective was reviewed and explained. The associate input step is an extremely important one! The overall, final review is equally important since it establishes the final measures and expectations of performance.
2. We never abandoned the triple constraint measures. We don't know how this could be done by professional project managers.
3. We looked to provide a relative balance between client and coach input to the assessment process. Having a slant in either direction can provide an inaccurate assessment.
4. The project managers thrive on feedback. They very much appreciate the quarterly review sessions. There should never be any surprises!
5. We continually fine-tuned the objectives year over year, without totally rewriting them, based upon associate feedback as well as organizational input. Keep asking yourself "what am I looking to measure" and follow the S.M.A.R.T. principle.

## Today

The group today manages large numbers of projects with short, medium, and long durations. These projects generally fall into two categories, infrastructure and business operating unit. The infrastructure projects are initiated from within the IM&M organization and typically involve an optimization and maximization focus. The business operating unit projects are typically initiated by the AT&T units, external to the IM&M organization, and have a more narrowly focused objective. These projects typically create, improve, or adjust a capability for the individual AT&T unit that will ultimately benefit AT&T's customer.

In 1996, the organization was involved in many of the projects undertaken to restructure AT&T. Projects to separate premise and data center assets, establish new human resource and financial systems, and separate the network were managed.

The group's involvement with the Project Management Institute, has been, and continues to be, significant. The project managers demonstrate their commitment and dedication to the profession through their tireless support of PMI. Two new PMI chapters were begun by project managers from the group. The membership in these chapters has steadily increased since these chapters were founded. The group contained three chapter presidents. Those project managers that do not hold an officer position are current members in good standing. Project managers have worked with several universities to begin student chapters. Most of the group belongs to the IM&M SIG (specific interest group). One of the coaches was SIG chair during 1996 and is the IM&M track chair for the 1997 symposium. Almost 100 percent of the project managers have attended at least one PMI annual symposium. Many have presented papers and seminars that have met with rave reviews. Today's organization has 96 percent of its members with master's certificates and 85 percent PMI certified.

Two members of the leadership team were instrumental in starting a project management council within AT&T. This organization is comprised of representatives from most of the AT&T units. It seeks to provide leadership that will help AT&T establish a common and consistent professional project management culture.

Given today's level of success, the following are offered as areas of focus:

1. You **MUST** position the successes of your project managers to heighten the awareness of their talent and importance! Look to involve upper-level leaders in recognizing their efforts. Publish results to these levels to insure their understanding of the value of the group.

Maintain linkage with the Project Management Institute.

2. It provides significant opportunities for networking. It is extremely useful for sharing, benchmarking, and obtaining industry information.

## Challenges for Tomorrow

Surely, any organization is faced with challenges. This group sees these as tomorrow's challenges:

- Cost management—the determination of project costs with the accountability and authority to successfully administer true budget control, tracking, and reporting.
- Organizational sizing—obtaining required data to determine the appropriate number of project managers.
- Scope determinations—obtaining an initial scope definition.
- Technology knowledge—focus on technological training.
- Remote project management—limited budgets and the use of teleconference and other alternatives.
- Re-certification—understand its requirements; gather the appropriate documentation.

# Blood, Sweat, and Cheers: Leading an AT&T Organization to International Organization for Standardization Certification

Melba W. Watts, PMP, AT&T
Marie J. Van Haeren, ISO 9001 Project Manager, AT&T

## Introduction

As we advance toward the millennium, the AT&T Operations Technology Center (OTC) recognizes the critical need to define processes that deliver quality products and services in a timely manner. In line with our goal to foster an environment where continuous improvement is an on-going activity, the OTC process management teams (PMTs) documented the software development process. As part of Network Services, a division of AT&T, the OTC was required to comply with the ISO 9000 Standard. The International Organization for Standardization (ISO), formed in 1946, represents more than 110 national standards bodies. This consortium, covering virtually every industrialized nation in the world, created the ISO 9000 quality system standard series. The ISO 9001 Standard, which covers both design and development of a product, defines twenty quality system requirements and is the most comprehensive of the standards. It was selected because the OTC designs and develops computer software systems. Certification to ISO 9001 demonstrates a commitment to process quality and the desire for continuous improvement. The steps to achieve ISO certification include:

- The creation of a total quality system description which documents compliance to the twenty ISO elements
- Selection of an independent, certified ISO registrar
- A definition of the design and development process
- Procedures for implementing the process
- Evidence of adherence to the process in the form of controlled documents and quality records
- A certification audit to verify compliance to the standard and effective implementation of the quality system
- Recommendation for certification by the ISO registrar
- Periodic surveillance audits; re-certification every three years.

The key to enforcement is auditing with follow-up and closure of all non-conformity findings. Once a registrar is selected, an optional pre-assessment is often used to assess preparedness for certification. The OTC uses Det Norske Veritas (DNV), a Norwegian company with a United States presence.

Underestimating the complexity and scope of our objective, we underwent an ISO 9001 pre-assessment audit in early January 1996. The results of this audit indicated that our organization was far from ready for certification. With crushed egos we set out to decipher what we had to do to comply.

## Our Challenge

The OTC is an organization of over seventeen hundred people, located in six states. Projects span locations and utilize different software development technologies. The quality system and system development process and procedures had to work for all OTC projects. They had to conform to the ISO 9001 Standard, be specific enough to be useful, and be generic enough to apply to all OTC systems, always with a view to minimizing impact to the business and deliverables as well as ensuring that process implementation activities are transparent to the customer.

The system development process is one of six sub-processes within the network technology development (NTD) process, and as such, must comply with the NTD procedures for document control, training, corrective and preventive action, and so on defined in the NTD quality system.

## "The BLOOD"—Developing the Road Map

Based on a review of the feedback from DNV and recognition of our challenge, a decision was made to break the ISO certification effort into more manageable chunks so that we could contain the risk to customer deliverables and devote adequate resources to preparation. Our strategy was to prepare for and obtain certification for a single chunk and continue to expand the scope in successive audits. Two model projects from our Cincinnati location were selected initially. Each model project was required to develop its own project plan using the standard OTC project plan template. The project plan is the heart of the OTC quality system because it provides flexibility by allowing critical decisions to be made and documented at the project level. These plans served as the road map for the project team by identifying the who, what, where, when, and why for the project.

The ISO registration effort was handled as another OTC project with a nine-month duration, so a project plan and schedule were created and served as our road map. We outlined the tasks and defined the criteria for a successful registration. Key components included:

- Revisions to both the quality system and the process documentation
- Definition of local procedures to augment NTD procedures
- Process training
- Establishment of the document library
- Schedules for audits
- Plans for addressing audit findings
- Techniques for closure of corrective actions

## "The SWEAT"—Document, Train, and Audit, Audit, Audit

### Document

The ISO project manager set up shop in Cincinnati and formed a core ISO team that proceeded to execute the project plan. Once the quality system and system development process descriptions were completed, process training was developed and delivered to model project team members. Project tasks were divided among the ISO team members who worked with the model project teams to document local procedures and create and control process output documentation. Quality records and training records were created and stored as evidence of process implementation.

Key documentation must be placed under change control according to the requirements of element 4.5 of the ISO 9001 Standard. The NTD document and data and quality record procedure defined the change control methods and the librarian function that was to be used. Librarian tasks include:

- Acceptance of the document and associated quality records submitted to the library
- Entry into the NTD master list (an electronic catalogue of controlled document information)
- Copying, labeling, and distribution of paper copies of the document
- Maintaining the paper library file

A librarian had been assigned, and the beginnings of a paper library were in place prior to the January 1996 pre-assessment; however, evaluation of the labor-intensive aspect of the library prompted the ISO team to create an electronic paper-less environment. By obtaining a dedicated server and designing an organized directory structure, the team was able to accommodate the varied document types used by both model projects and eliminate most of the paper distribution and filing done by the librarian. Authors were advised to create and store all their controlled documents in electronic format.

A home page was designed and developed for the model projects. The core of the page was a table with the columns identifying the projects and the rows listing documents required by the process. The documents were hyper-linked to the page so that all documentation for a project was available by clicking on the appropriate icon in the table. This proved to be a very valuable tool for organizing project information. Above the table were additional links to related locations such as the NTD master list, process documentation, and so forth.

### Train

Training sessions were held for all associates. Powerpoint presentations were prepared and used for these sessions. The training was required and attendance documented. As the process became fine-tuned, updated versions of the quality system description and system development process were issued. Major changes were communicated via training sessions. Associates' roles in the process and their qualifications to perform them were documented in training plans, which were approved by management.

### Audit, Audit, Audit

Audits were held at numerous times throughout the project. They served dual purposes of learning and monitoring of process conformance. Mock audits were "unofficial" audits conducted by ISO team members and management. They were brief desktop audits, which served primarily as tools to help associates learn the process. Another type of mock audit was held a few days before "official" audits in which model project team members were prepared for the audit. During these two-hour group sessions, a combination of practice auditing and coaching was used.

Documented, "official" audits include pre-assessments, internal audits, the certification audit, and periodic post-certification surveillance audits. The internal audits are required and are conducted by trained auditors from an AT&T auditing group. The other audits are conducted by the registrar, in our case, DNV. In May 1996, we invited DNV to return for a pre-assessment of our rewritten quality system and process. The results of this audit were markedly different from the January 1996 pre-assessment. DNV found our documented quality system description in conformance with the ISO 9001 Standard and our system development process well defined. While imperfections in the process and in our compliance to it were identified, this was to be expected. The "findings" issued by DNV were minimal, and the lead auditor reported that the difference in our audit results since January was dramatic and impressive.

Documenting, training, and auditing are iterative processes. After an audit, findings are entered into the corrective action system. They are assigned to the appropriate owners, who have a prescribed amount of time to respond to the finding. Root cause analysis, corrective, and preventative action plans are required. Once the plans are implemented, evidence is presented to the corrective action coordinator who reviews and approves the closing of the finding. Internal auditors review and provide a final sign-off. We began with binders filled with the findings and related evidence and correspondence and, as with the library, soon moved to electronic documentation. Implementing corrective and preventative action plans often involves improving process documentation, and changes need to be communicated to everyone affected. The document/train/audit/improve cycle occurred several times. An internal audit was held October 1996 and helped to prepare us for a final, brief DNV pre-assessment in November 1996.

The number of pre-assessments was higher than most organizations generally have because we started over after the initial disappointing pre-assessment and because we were determined to be successful, and the pre-assessments helped us reach that goal.

The certification audit was held in December 1996. It took three days. The bulk of the time was spent auditing the project teams. Each model project was audited separately, but the audit was conducted in a modified group format. This was an innovation created during an earlier pre-assessment that worked so well that DNV used it later at other sites. The traditional audit is one person/one auditor (and perhaps a note-taker and internal auditor sitting in). Often the line of audit questioning would turn to responsibilities of someone other than the person being audited. Time was spent running (we actually had "runners" on duty!) to locate the other person so the auditor could get the answer needed. We suggested having the development project manager present for the entire audit because this role was active throughout the process, and many questions were directed there. As the audit progressed through our process, people who interacted in the process were scheduled to be in the room. They left when their portions were completed. For example, we began with development project manager, system architects, and system engineers. As the system architects and system engineers finished their portion of the audit, they left and people working in later parts of the process joined, such as system developers and system testers. This saved a lot of time and frustration and made the audit run very smoothly. It also gave moral support to the people being audited. This approach is highly recommended for team work environments. It requires the concurrence of the registrar.

In addition to the model projects, DNV audited the management representative who is responsible for the quality system. The corrective action coordinator, internal audit coordinator, librarian (including a full library audit), and senior management were audited as well. These individuals were audited separately in their offices.

*The result of the December 1996 certification audit was a recommendation by DNV for certification! We were the first software development process in the new AT&T to earn ISO 9001 certification.* The audit results were an extraordinary leap from our humble initial pre-assessment. We received only a few minor findings, which is almost unheard of. The library received special recognition for its quality.

## Critical Components

A number of critical components contributed to the success of this ISO 9001 certification project. Management support is essential, from the top down. Dedicated resources are an absolute necessity as is buy-in from the organization. Both can be a challenge to obtain without management support. As you gain buy-in, behavioral cues are obvious: people ask questions, show up for prep sessions, and cooperate to implement the process. *Everyone must be involved!* Developing a realistic estimate of time and effort is necessary. The time involved in the reiterative activities of documenting, training, auditing, and improving needs to be adequate. It is not feasible to do these things once: continuous improvement to achieve readiness for certification takes rework.

Many people were instrumental in supporting the certification effort. A management representative, a role defined in the quality system description, was appointed. Two ISO coordinators were dedicated between half and full time to the project. ISO team members assisted in the preparation. The core team consisted of the ISO project manager, internal auditors and ISO consultants, and the Cincinnati ISO coordinators. Constant gentle (and often not so gentle) pressure was applied. The librarian and corrective action coordinator roles were critical to the preparation as well.

The use of technology was tremendously helpful. Our home pages were used during audits. When the auditor wanted to see a document, we just clicked on it. It was much easier than manipulating piles of paper documents. Anything an auditor was expected to need access to was linked to the home page. We projected onto a large screen, which provided excellent visibility for everyone in the audit.

A "war room" was set up for the certification audit. A room was obtained for the three days of the audit and set up with tables, chairs, white boards, phone, computer, and printer connections as well as office supplies. A schedule of ISO team members was established so that people were covering the whole audit period. The room was designed to serve as a central point to organize any critical efforts needed to obtain information and people, address potential findings, and serve as a communications base. The audit went so smoothly we did not need to use the room. It was part of our risk management plan, and we consider it a success that it was unused. We highly recommend this type of preparation.

**Reality gets in the way (pitfalls to avoid)**

When something is new it takes longer. Integrating a new process into the work takes time and initially lengthens the delivery schedule of the product. The danger of missed deadlines and software development project jeopardies was very real. Previously made customer commitments didn't just go away. Startup costs time and money and needs to be built into schedules. When integrating into a schedule previously committed to, something has to give. One of our model projects had tight commitments and inadequate slack in the schedule. Conflict between the pressure of meeting the software delivery schedule and the ISO certification schedule was a significant challenge. "I don't have time" and "I can't" were often heard. The core ISO team provided support and help with document creation and control as well as training, coaching, and auditing. These efforts helped reduce the pressure on the model projects. In an ideal world, the ISO certification effort would be built into a project schedule before commitment.

Management commitment was split between the success of the ISO project and the other project deadlines. Management support grew as the ISO project progressed. It is important to establish at the beginning that adequate management support exists for the certification effort.

## "The CHEERS"—Spreading ISO Fever and Celebrating Success!

In addition to helping the model projects to prepare, imaginative techniques were employed to overcome resistance to the certification effort due to work pressures and lack of knowledge of the process. ISO events such as quizzes, speakers, and short learning sessions were held. We sprang for soft drinks and varied snacks. *Food works!* Attendance increases when people are fed! We awarded ISO bucks (with our vice president's picture on the front) for demonstrating efforts to implement and follow the process and for supporting the ISO effort in general. The bucks were used as entries in monthly prize drawings; food and door prizes were provided too.

All of the audits required planning and preparation. The certification audit was a major effort and was planned beginning two months in advance. The closing meeting at the end of the audit was when the audit results and DNV's decision on whether to recommend us for certification would be announced. AT&T senior management was invited to the meeting, photography and videotaping were arranged, gifts for key project contributors were ordered, and food (of course) was ordered. Two hundred balloons were ready for release. We were determined to be successful so that the decision would be to recommend. The primary thing we did was to prepare thoroughly for the audit. We did have a backup plan in the event we were not recommended.

Immediately *after* the announcement, a team of people released the balloons, tacked up posters, and uncovered food (*let's not forget about the food!*). We even gave out New Year's type noisemakers so that the announcement was greeted by cheers, noisemakers, and balloons. Every single activity was carefully planned, and the event went off smoothly. Everyone who worked on this effort was subsequently given a proud badge of accomplishment: a jacket tastefully (no food pun intended) embroidered with AT&T, the project names, and ISO certification date!

In summary, a successful ISO certification effort takes careful planning, meticulous attention to detail, more time than you originally expect, and the support of the entire organization. It is the type of project that clearly thrives on good project management and one that is rewarding to manage.

# Project Management—the Next Century
# The Age of Empowerment

Roger A. Powell, P.E., M2J, Inc.
Keith R. Pierce, Ph.D., St. Paul Companies

As the year 2000 approaches, there is a growing desire within project management to selectively decentralize some decision-making from the central project level to the local or task level. This follows from the success of team building and empowerment techniques implemented in other areas of management throughout this decade. These techniques have stimulated innovative problem-solving and significant efficiency gains. These techniques have shown that team leaders and team members will internalize the goals of the task if they have a role in controlling the method of the work. Similarly, the importance of the functional manager's involvement and commitment in task performance continues to be recognized. Frequently, the functional manager will be the task leader. For the purpose of this paper, these terms can be used interchangeably. The functional manager has the experience necessary to understand the local constraints and opportunities in order to get a task accomplished in record time. This understanding leads to better decisions in utilizing resources under difficult conditions. Empowering the functional managers to make these decisions utilizes this hard-won experience.

As decision-making is moved to the local level, there will be a reduction in the amount of time management analysis and resource management analysis that must be performed at the project level. This reduces the records keeping and the analysis burden on the project staff. Also, the communication traffic will be reduced. There will be less chance that important information will be lost in a sea of more trivial information. With the functional managers performing triage on the information, only the important and urgent decisions will rise to the project manager level, allowing the project manager to become more of a macro-manager. The project manager can concentrate on the important and critical decisions without becoming overwhelmed by constantly analyzing a flood of data. This allows the project manager to look forward in time. To implement this change some reengineering will be required in *A Guide to the Project Management Body of Knowledge (PMBOK)* area of time management with secondary effects in the areas of communication management, cost management, and integration management.

## Time Management Information—The Current State of the Art

Time management is subject to significant changes and uncertainty throughout the project. Typically, a functional manager is presented with a range of dates from earliest start to latest start and earliest finish to latest finish, and these are subject to frequent changes as other paths are expedited or delayed. This changing set of dates impairs the credibility of the requirements. Understandably, the functional manager typically views the requirements as being externally imposed and somewhat arbitrary. This is counterproductive to the desired personal internal involvement of the functional manager.

For a functional manager with several overlapping tasks from the same or different projects competing for his resources, meeting his time requirements becomes his most challenging problem. Hence, the most frequently asked question by functional managers is: "When do you REALLY need it completed?"

The question is well taken. Has his original requirement date been "padded" by the project manager with contingency time? Are there delays in other paths which will cause him to "hurry up only to wait later?" Is he expending additional funds needlessly to meet his requirement date when there will be no impact on the final completion date? Or, conversely, is the rest of the project running two weeks ahead of schedule and capable of earning a bonus for early completion?

Ideally, project managers will provide functional managers with credible up-to-the-minute time management requirements for each task and the tools necessary to optimally allocate his resources. This is a necessity for implementing the decentralization and empowerment transition.

## Existing Time Management Tools

The first step in the transition is the recognition that our present time management network analysis tools are inherently centralized. They require the central and sequential processing of all time management information using software universally based on the critical path method(CPM). These existing tools do not allow task teams to easily locally evaluate the impact of new developments or to locally allocate resources.

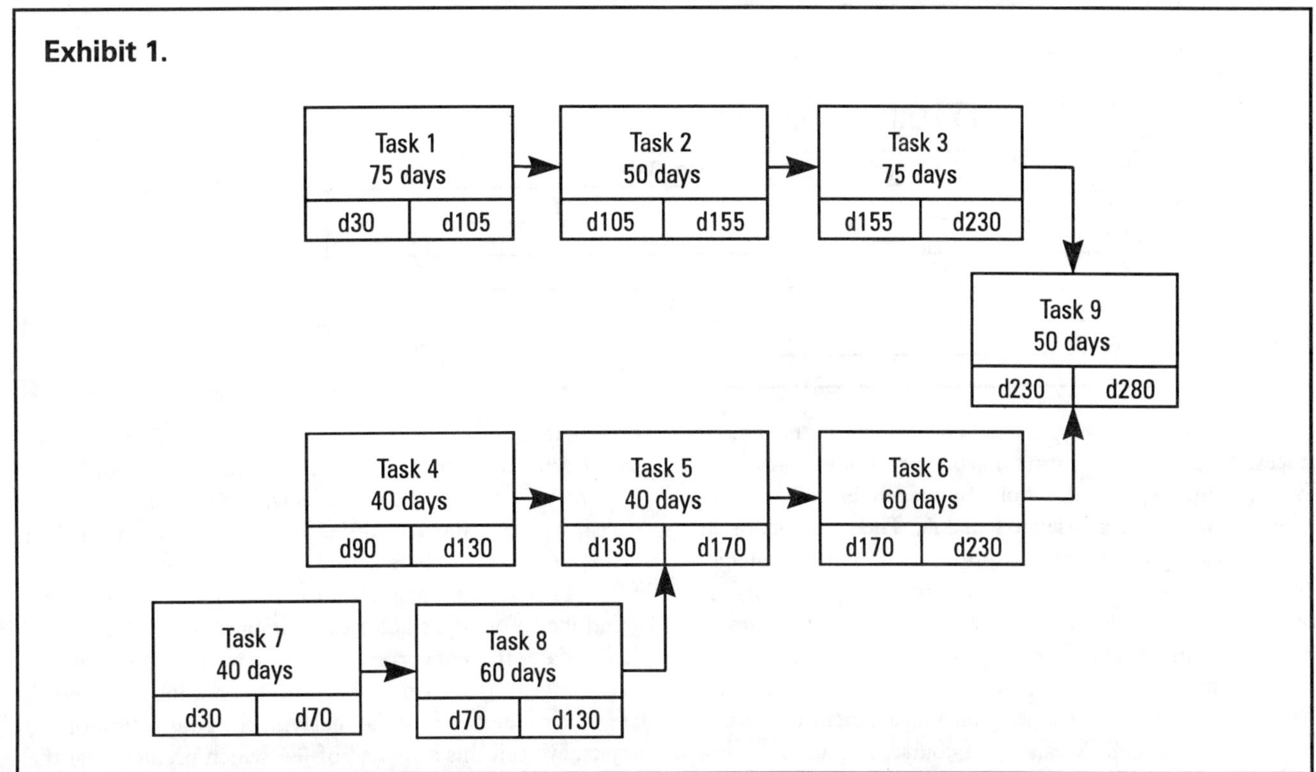


The task group must communicate any and all new information to the project level central analysis center where it is entered into the network model and evaluated. These changes are typically evaluated individually as a "what if" exercise. The potential impact and new directions from the project manager are then communicated back to the task team for action. For example, we have seen many recent demonstrations of new CPM-based resource allocation software tools that tell Sally to work "three hours on Friday and four hours on Saturday on Project C" to maintain the schedule. What an excellent example of micro-management and disempowerment of the functional manager. The problem is not created by the software; it is inherent in the underlying CPM analysis method. It is due to the fact that there is no direct relationship between a change within the network and its impact on the completion date because there is an unknown amount of embedded float time between the two events. The only direct method of determining the impact of a change is to enter the change and rerun the CPM network "what if" analysis at the project level central location. Admittedly, there are some experienced CPM schedulers using more sophisticated software products that can shortcut this analysis. But, these capabilities are found in a small minority of projects. And, nevertheless, the analysis still occurs at the central project level, disempowering the functional managers.

## Resource Allocation Benchmark

Consider how a benchmark resource allocation example would be addressed with today's systems. Assume a functional manager supervises a machining center that can process one work piece at a time. The machine is idle when four work pieces from four different projects arrive simultaneously. What is the optimal order of the work pieces in the queue? Theoretically, to achieve an optimal result, the effect of each combination must be communicated back to the central analysis center for each project and analyzed as "what if" scenarios. The results from each combination must then be resolved by the respective project managers and communicated back to the functional manager. This is a very cumbersome and time-consuming methodology. It would certainly be much more efficient and empowering to present sufficient information to the functional manager to allow him to find the solution locally in real time and act upon it.

## New Time Management Tools

The second step in the transition is to search for and develop the time management tools that will allow all project team members to assess potential impacts immediately and locally. Let's put aside our existing CPM-based systems for a moment and consider our normal process and try to define a system

**Exhibit 2.**

| EXTERNAL ELEMENT INFORMATION FOR TASK 3 | | | | |
|---|---|---|---|---|
| Element | For Task.. | Req. Date | Avail. Date | Delta |
| E1 | 3 | 155 | 151 | -4 |
| E2 | 3 | 155 | 145 | -10 |
| E3 | 3 | 155 | 140 | -15 |
| E4 | 3 | 155 | 145 | -10 |
| E5 | 3 | 155 | 150 | -5 |

that would directly support it. The project management process begins with creating a work breakdown structure (WBS), estimating task durations and dependencies, and creating a network and a baseline schedule. The schedule, or, at least, the completion date is approved by higher management. Components, resources, and so on flow from many locations into the network. The savvy project manager tries to maintain as much contingency time as possible to act as a buffer for unexpected occurrences. As the project progresses, the continual question from higher management is: "Is the project on schedule?" Meaning, of course, is it ahead or behind the approved baseline schedule? Actually, many higher managers don't retain the schedule dates and only rely on the fact that the original baseline schedule plan was approved. They track the health of the project based on deviations to the original baseline plan.

## The Critical Element Method™ (CEM™)

We have constructed a new network analysis system that follows our existing process. We call it the Critical Element Method™(CEM™). First, the project manager begins in the normal manner, creating a network of tasks and their durations as shown in Exhibit 1.

For reasons that will become clear later, the network does not have to include all of the components and resources (which we call elements) required for the project, only the sequence of time-consuming tasks. Second, the project manager selects a desired completion date, which in this example is day 280(d280), entered in the lower right box in the last task(Task 9). Third, the project manager calculates baseline schedule dates backward from the desired completion date through the network to produce a Just-In-Time (JIT) schedule. The left and right lower boxes of each task contain the start and finish baseline schedule dates, respectively. For simplicity in this example, the scheduling calendar is numerically increasing consecutive work days starting at day 1. By its construction, there is no embedded slack (or float) time in the JIT schedule. This is the baseline reference schedule.

Predicted and actual deviations will be measured with respect to this baseline schedule. These deviations are called "delta" values. Since there is no embedded slack or float time in this JIT schedule, each deviation to this schedule will be a direct(one-to-one) predictor of its impact on the final completion date. If an occurrence is going to delay the completion of a task by four days beyond its baseline completion date, this predicts a four-day delay in the completion of the project. We call this a "delta" of +4 which predicts that the actual project completion date will be equal to the original baseline date "plus four" days. Conversely, a negative delta value predicts that the actual completion date will be early by the numerical number of days indicated. This is powerful property. There is a direct connection between a change in the network and the impact on the project completion date. This means that any task team member with the ability to locally calculate a delta value has a direct measure of the predicted impact on the project completion date. Team leaders don't have to keep communicating with the central analysis tool to evaluate each real or imagined change. Each team member can see the impact of the late completion of a task and how it is directly related to the project completion. Also, it creates a simple common language variable for communication between the local task team and the project manager.

Fourth, the project manager supplies each task leader with the baseline schedule dates for the start and the finish of his task.

Fifth, the task leader is responsible for defining the elements(components and resources) necessary to begin his task and determine their availability. Before their entry into the network, these elements are called external elements. These may range from bolts and nuts to carpenters to 110-ton cranes. A sample list of elements for Task 3 is shown in Exhibit 2.

The JIT requirement date for each element comes from the JIT baseline schedule and the supplier of each element predicts its availability date. A delta value for each element is calculated by the following:

**Exhbit 3.**

| PREDICTED TASK COMPLETION DUE TO EXTERNAL ELEMENTS | | | | |
|---|---|---|---|---|
| TASK | DURATION | REQ.COMP. | PRED. COMP. | DELTA |
| 1 | 75 | 105 | 100 | -5 |
| 2 | 50 | 155 | 140 | -15 |
| 3 | 75 | 230 | 226 | -4 |
| 4 | 40 | 130 | 110 | -20 |
| 5 | 40 | 170 | 153 | -17 |
| 6 | 60 | 230 | 211 | -19 |
| 7 | 40 | 70 | 54 | -16 |
| 8 | 60 | 130 | 125 | -5 |
| 9 | 50 | 280 | 260 | -20 |

External Element Delta = Predicted Availability Date - JIT Requirement Date

Since day numbers in this example increase with time, an external element such as E1 with a predicted availability date of day 151 and a requirement date of day 155 will have a delta value of: 151 - 155 = -4. This indicates that the element will be available four days early with respect to the JIT schedule. This element predicts an early project completion of four days. Conversely, a positive delta value indicates that the element will be that number of days late. The simple spreadsheet listing shown in Exhibit 2 can be expanded indefinitely, allowing a very large number of external elements to be monitored and controlled. The start of Task 3 will be dominated by the element with the latest delta value. The task leader can easily see the latest and most critical element is E1 with a delta of -4. This element will constrain the start of Task 3 to no more than four days earlier than the baseline schedule and predicts that the completion of the project will be no more than four days early. The next constraining element is E5 with a delta of -5. If the availability date of E1 is improved to produce a delta of -6 or less, the start of Task 3 will then be determined by then-dominant E5 with a delta of -5. This early start offers the potential for an early project completion and/or contingency time to overcome unexpected occurrences. The task leader is charged with maximizing this contingency time within his task. The elements with more negative delta values (E2, E3, and E4) will be available earlier and will be forced to wait for the element E1 with its greater and dominant delta value. The functional manager can use these earlier elements as potential donors of resources to be redirected to elements with greater delta values. Also, the functional manager can perform some micro-scheduling within his task to reduce the effect of the critical element E1. After the functional manager has exhausted his opportunities to maximize the contingency time in his task completion date, he transmits this information to the project manager in the form of his greatest delta value. In this example, he would transmit: "Task 3 delta = -4."

Sixth, the task predictions would be accumulated by the project manager and listed in a simple spread sheet format as shown in Exhibit 3.

Since the delta values are all taken with respect to the same JIT baseline schedule, they may be evaluated in parallel. The latest (largest positive delta value) task will dominate the other tasks and will have the controlling impact on the completion date: i.e., it will overshadow all other tasks that are less late (indicated by smaller delta values). This is the critical task. By scanning Exhibit 3, the project manager can quickly find the most critical task, Task 3 with a delta of -4. This is a direct predictor that the project completion date can be no more than -4 days or four days early. Further, he can see that the next most critical tasks are Task 1 and Task 8, both with deltas of -5. The project manager can contact the functional manager for Task 3 to determine the external element that is determining his completion, which we saw was E1 in Exhibit 2. It is clear that a major portion of the analysis and improvement effort has moved to the local level without the involvement of the project manager. Further, the communication between the local level and the project manager has been filtered so that only the critical information is presented to the project manager. And, the analysis and communication have used a simple and universal language of delta values.

Assume that after investigation with the functional managers responsible for the critical and near critical tasks, the project manager determines that it is cost effective to expend additional resources to improve the availability of the critical element E4 in Task 3 to a resulting delta of -5 and to do nothing to improve Tasks 1 and Task 8, with delta values of -5. He is accepting a predicted early completion of no more than five days, or five days of contingency time. The project manager has determined a current project status of a delta value of -5. The project manager can transmit this value to his functional managers and his higher management to indicate the current estimate of project completion. The functional managers can use this value as a decision point for their own actions and a threshold filter for urgent communication with the project manager. As long as their predicted task completion is less than the current project status delta of -5, they are not consuming contingency time or jeopardizing the potential of early completion. If, in this example, the functional manager for Task 2 with a delta value of -15 should receive new information on an element's availability that increases its delta to -10, he will instantly know that there is no impact on the predicted schedule since his new delta of -10 is still less than the current status delta of -5. Therefore, no resources are expended unnecessarily to maintain the earlier value. Should an occurrence arise to threaten the current project status delta value, the functional managers are charged with reporting it immediately. As the project is accomplished, the internal tasks may consume some of the contingency time. The project manager can recognize this by updating his current project status delta value.

The CEM provides the functional manager and the project manager with quantitative information directly usable to insure that optimal resources are allocated precisely to elements that will impact the project completion date and that additional resources are not wasted on elements that will have no impact. We believe that the CEM baseline schedule information and the current status delta value provide sufficient information to the functional manager to locally determine an optimal solution to the benchmark resource allocation example presented earlier.

The impact of each element and each task on the project completion date is given by its delta value. The CEM provides a very simple and universally compatible language and information system between the functional manager, the project manager, and higher management. The project manager's task is to control and balance the delta values, which are a direct measure of the impacts on the project completion date.

Since the CEM operates on the same information entered into the existing CPM-based systems, it can be added to existing systems, either internally or externally. Efforts to this end are under way. The Critical Element Method and CEM are trademarks, and the method is patent protected.

## Summary

To maximize the contribution of the functional manager or task leader, they must be empowered to locally manage their tasks through decentralized decision-making. This requires providing them with real time project impact information upon which they base their decisions. The existing time management tools based on the critical path method are inherently centralized and counterproductive to the decentralization and empowerment goal. A new approach called the Critical Element Method is proposed to facilitate this transition.

Using the CEM, we have created a minimal reference network with a JIT schedule (without imbedded slack or float time) and measured predicted deviations (or delta values) from that reference, defining lateness as being positive. These deviations are independent of one another and can be parallel processed. Each deviation is a direct predictor of the impact on the final completion date on a day-for-day basis. We then recognized the concept of dominance, in that the largest delta value will determine the final impact on the project completion date. This provides great power in this method, allowing the individual impacts of a change in the network to be instantly recognized by any project team member without accessing the central analysis system. Further, the use of delta values to measure and communicate schedule impacts creates a simple and universally compatible language that is easily understood within and across projects.

The CEM allows functional managers to monitor every element required for a task independently and in parallel, by the use of delta values. All of the elements may be monitored in parallel by a simple listing that is separate from the network. Therefore, the master network can be simple and contain only the major activities. Critical and near-critical elements are those with the greatest delta values and can be easily identified by the functional manager. The functional manager controls the elements required by his task and reports only status and exceptions to the project manager. This creates a filter that reduces communication traffic significantly to information that has an impact on the project completion date. As the project progresses, the actual status of each event is monitored using a current status delta value, which serves as a threshold for the functional manager. Further, the local task manager has sufficient information from all projects to optimize his resources across projects.

The project manager monitors his project through the functional managers and manages-by-exception only the critical and near critical elements. The project manager becomes much more of a macro-manager.

# The Nature and Source of Disputes in Information Technology Projects

Dr. George F. Jergeas, The University of Calgary
Robert J. Beekhuizen, Shell Canada Resources
V. Lynne Herzog, Public Works and Government Services Canada

## Abstract

This paper examines the nature and source of contractual disputes in information technology (IT) projects. The topic is attracting notice due to the high rate of failure and contract cancellation in the IT Industry. Current approaches to sponsoring, managing, and the completion of IT projects seem fraught with uncertainty, poor communications, a lack of consensus, and ultimately failure. A study of large technology projects in the United States undertaken in 1994 states, "only 9 percent of all such projects are ever completed on time and within their budget, while nearly a third are canceled before completion"(McKenna 1996). An *Information Week* article agreed, stating "half of all client/server development projects are not completed, and many data warehousing projects will meet a similar fate" (Shaku 1996).

The IT industry lags behind other industries in project management experience. It is a relatively young market, with most capital investment projects having occurred in the past ten years. Companies engaged in IT businesses have little historical project data available for reference when planning jobs and preparing bids. Also, there are constantly new players entering the business. The result is that project management expertise has not matured across the IT sector (Vanderluis 1996).

Problems in the industry do not just reside with contractors. Often, owners are unclear on essential requirements for the product they are buying and for its performance. A detailed scope assessment is difficult to achieve; therefore, contracts are signed and executed, and changes and extras creep into the jobs. This leads to substantial increases in cost. Not surprisingly, claims and disputes occur frequently. Typical disputes relate to poor performance, underbidding, mismanagement, and improper application of technology and resources. Claims, disputes, and litigation frequently occur. The results are multimillion dollars of economic impact on governments, taxpayers, and private sector companies. Damages to the reputations of parties involved and the entire IT industry, are another consequence.

An industry survey and literature review is the basis of this paper. The paper lists and discusses causes leading to IT projects' disputes, many of which could be avoided with the effective use of project management tools. These avoidance measures are also discussed.

## Introduction

### What is Information Technology

"Information Technology, or IT as some are calling it, has its roots in Computer Science. However, in today's world, Information Technology encompasses the wide ranging areas of computer connectivity, media and graphics, technology transfer, telecommunications, electronic imaging, information storage and organization, computer - human interaction, microcomputers, and computer programming" (Infostudio.com 1996). Therefore, there is a wide spectrum of products within the industry.

To understand the industry, one must understand that "information technology does not focus on computing, but rather, on the distribution of systems, linking a variety of hardware and software into a single network. The fundamental basis is the communication network and utilization of its services—not exclusively the computer" (InfoStudio.com 1996). The computer can be a tool for effective communication. Software is one of its processes that drives its effective use. IT consists of many devices, including perhaps a manual, to enable a user to do work.

Added to this environment is the inherent changing nature of the IT industry. The industry derives profits based on continuous change. "The IT Industry bases its delivery on a value added basis. Emphasis is on continuing relationships based on customer's ever changing software requirements" (Cooke 1996). With a view to continuing client relationships on their changing and future needs, companies supplying information technology services would appear to have their futures secure providing ongoing and additional project work.

However, the change factor in the IT industry is two-edged. Annually, IT projects are faced with significant and rapid technological change. Because leading-edge technology is frequently involved, there are often performance problems with IT products. These problems stem from limited use and a short-lived product history. Commonly, IT projects are



PROJECT MANAGEMENT INSTITUTE 28th Annual Seminars & Symposium
Chicago, Illinois: Papers Presented September 29 to October 1, 1997

sidetracked because the systems' bugs have not been discovered. Furthermore, the IT sector is "fraught with problems: Insecurities caused by . . . new technologies that render recent acquisitions obsolete" (Lewin 1996). Industry practitioners interviewed also highlighted the dilemma of selecting and applying the right technology, in view of its becoming obsolete within a short time. This is especially true for large-scale IT projects if extended over several years.

To counter the risk of a short product life and early obsolescence, the common temptation is to make changes and adopt new market technologies. The intent is to improve end-product performance, extend its usable life, and add value to the investment. However, what often results from this course of action is a project's scope, schedule, and budget are pushed beyond their limits. Project management and control in the IT sector are not usually well in hand. Consequently, if a project is budget constrained, contract cancellations can and do occur.

Due to the relatively new marketplace, most capital investment in projects has occurred over the past ten years. The IT industry, as a result, lacks depth in project management experience. Many IT managers, with considerable industry experience, have not been exposed to project management principles. Having risen to senior management level without it, they do not see the need to endorse project management in their companies (Vandersluis 1996).

### Research

Research for this paper was limited to interviews with industry professionals, literature research, and lecture material. We limited ourselves to a short period to collect, collate, and interpret the data. The information was reviewed for consistency of opinion on claims and disputes in the IT industry. Our work for this paper included the following:

*Literature Review:* Availability of books on the topic was limited. Three were found, with one dating back to 1982. Most of the literature regarding IT industry claims and disputes was recent computer-based journalistic material. Two items were from the Internet.

*Interviews and Lectures:* Six individuals were interviewed from various spectrums of the IT industry. Four of the individuals were private sector IT providers, while two were owner representatives. Each interview was allotted approximately one hour. However, some lasted much longer because of additional questions generated during the interview. Several days prior to the interview, the authors prepared those being queried by sending them a list of questions for review.

In addition, legal professionals and claims consultants, who lecture the Law for Project Management Course at the University of Calgary, added valuable input into legal precedence concerning the IT industry. Their answers and information were combined with the literature review and interviews to develop our paper.

*Limitation of the Data:* There are two main areas of limitation with the information gathered. The first limitation is the small sample of industry professionals interviewed, and the limited number of companies they represented. The questionnaire results are not statistically valid and are only exploratory in nature. They should not be construed as a definite description of how the IT industry manages itself.

The second limiting factor is the researchers' limited understanding of the IT business and, in particular, the software business. None are from the IT industry, having only peripheral scope of knowledge in the project management practices of that industry. However, we feel there is consistency in the literature, interviews, and lectures to identify relevant factors affecting claims and disputes in the IT industry. We examine these factors and recommend project management tools the industry might use to reduce the number of claims and disputes it currently has.

## The Nature and Sources of it Disputes

The nature of the contract disputes in the IT industry are not unfamiliar to those observed in other industries. The claims are normally for compensation of damages linked to contracts, and not usually cases of tort infringement. Typical disputes are related to poor performance, underbidding of job, changes, poor scope of work, mismanagement, improper application of the technology and resources to use, and/or dissatisfaction with the finished product. Distinguishing IT from other industries is the high rate occurrence. Major areas of dispute are detailed further:

### Scope of Work

Scope of work is a concern of both the owners and the IT industry contractors. Owners complain that contractors underestimate the scope of work in their bids and think that IT contractors use low bids to receive a contract offer. On the other side, IT contractors find owners do not know exactly what they require before engaging a contractor. Inevitably, as the project progresses and the scope details become better understood by the contractors, they claim for extras and changes. The difference of opinion between the owner and the IT contractor to what should be considered a legitimate extra or change results in claims and litigation.

Problems in the IT industry reside with both the owners and the contractors. In addition, owners are unclear on essential final product requirements and how it should perform. They often use IT as a solution to personnel and organizational problems and frequently do not understand their own needs or those of the personnel resources they are buying for.

As a result, owner management frequently does not have a clear scope of work and a clear vision of the product they require. Owners often have a static idea of what they think a software product will do for them. However, IT is not a static industry. The result is funds are put toward a project on a one-time basis, with the IT service delivered in a "Big Bang" creation ( Fox 1982). There is often no follow-up relationship to ongoing client needs. Similar to architecture and engineering (A&E) design contracts, custom software is designed and programmed under time and budgetary constraints that do not allow for front-end planning or final detail design for "getting the bugs out" (Badi 1996). With these factors affecting owner purchase of IT products, a detailed scope assessment can be difficult to achieve. Contracts (or purchase orders) are agreed to, and proceed to execution with biases and preferences that lead to substantial extras. An Industry consultant (Badi 1996) highlighted the case of an Alberta IT project, contracted for thirty thousand dollars that grew during execution to become a one million dollar job.

To develop a better understanding of IT projects' scope of work, industry research and interviews show additional time, effort, and money should be spent on front-end planning (Cooke, Fensury, Rumple 1996; Takach 1989). A construction industry analyst (Maidment 1996) discussed 'S' curve data for that industry. Front-end planning traditionally takes 50 percent of the time, and is allotted only 5 percent of the funding. Similarly, IT industry 'S' curve data shows not only is less money spent on the front-end project planning, but also much less time is put toward it (Fox 1982).

Resolving disputes over IT projects' scope is difficult because the scope is frequently vague and poorly defined. System House Limited contracted with the Bank of Canada for a multimillion dollar project. They eventually walked away from the contract after the two parties could not agree on extras. A senior System House VP cited a key learning: "If there is a lesson, it might be: try to be clear on specifications when you start. And if you realize that you have a difference of opinion, deal with it really quickly rather than let it drag on"(McKenna 1996).

Even if good PM practices are implemented for a project, the IT sector remains inherently risky, particularly concerning large projects. These have a high probability of cost and schedule overruns, even a possibility of cancellation. Large project scope is often too nebulous with too many unknowns outstanding at the time of contract award. A long period of project execution, often over several years, compounds problems in a market of rapid technological change. After several years, neither the owner, or the contractor, properly knows what they have contracted for. Continuing the project makes cost and schedule overruns inevitable. Funds at risk for banks, taxpayers, and the businesses involved are immense. Strategic management of these risks is required. A solution is "to break contracts into manageable chunks and aim at doing things in a small series of successes" (Hubbard 1995).

### Customer satisfaction with the final product

The customer (owner) of IT projects commonly feels the product delivered is not what was wanted, and that the investment was not worth the product delivered. This may be due to poorly defined scope of work by both parties, but is often a consequence of the changing nature of the industry. Products are often obsolete prior to delivery.

Buying IT products based on a static idea of what the product will be results in projects that are developed as "Big Bang" creations, without follow up or testing (Fox 1982). Like many construction contracts, owners place pressure on the IT industry to keep development costs low. When looking to cut corners, testing of the technology is often the first factor cut. The resulting products cannot be used without a great deal of further investment. Finished products do not meet the owner's business process, and product acceptance is disputed based on failed functionality. One industry interview pointed out "people often skip testing" (Shaku 1996). When shortcomings go undetected until the time of the customer acceptance/hand-over, the implications of corrective work usually signifies failure. Additional time/cost requirements, at a late stage in the project, violates the schedule/ budget targets. Claims and disputes arise by trying to salvage something from failures (e.g., by the owner for indemnification, and by the contractor for compensation due to scope ambiguities and/or omissions). This is particularly true of custom work, where the IT product design and programming are under time constraints that do not allow for final detail, and getting the bugs out.

Lack of consideration for testing's importance, and/or perhaps an unwillingness to pay the additional contract costs, is gambling on success. System testing is worth the time and effort. "You really do have to test all parts of the system—client network, middleware, and server—at various levels of use. You need a full-fledged test program and automated testing tools" (Shaku 1996).

Owners and managers who purchase IT products expect them to solve all their personnel problems. They also expect that giving IT tools to their staff will help resource productivity. IT is not free of errors, and cannot resolve staff productivity and resource problems. High expectations by owners lead to the IT product being blamed for causing problems, to which it has not been a party(Fox, 1982).

### Customer Supplier Relationships

Being a relatively new industry, and one customer/server based, traditional contract agreements are not always implemented or signed. Many IT services are provided based on a handshake. Although a handshake can form a legal contract

(Westerlund 1996), this type of agreement runs all the risks involved from poor communications. For an industry relying on change for its ongoing business relationships, claims and litigation among the parties would be reduced if many IT suppliers and their customers were to "Put the whole deal in writing" (Takach 1989).

Not uncommonly, project disputes result from a lack of trust between the parties. Due to poorly defined scope and poor communication, the owner is suspicious of the contractor's profit motives and/or lack of job performance (for which he is unwilling to pay more). Similarly, contractors are suspicious of owners who do not know what they want or need. Owners attempt to gain additional work at no extra cost, while placing the risk and liability on the contractor.

### Project Monitoring

Typically, owner and contractor attention to monitoring project progress is lacking, with no regular communications between the parties of the contract to address project issues occurring. Project management research conducted verifies regular contractor-client consultation is a key critical success factor associated with a project's performance (Pinto and Sleving 1989).

Mismanagement also underlies the source of contract disputes, claims, cancellations, and project failure. Historically, attention has been directed toward technical design and problem solving, and not enough on project management and control. Changes are not recognized and creep into projects undetected. Frequently, formalized change control mechanism and project documentation processes are absent or lacking. Because there is seldom a champion for project management (especially at the management level), attempts are made to reconcile scope differences, cost overruns, and extras after the fact, instead of before they occur.

### The Contracts

Disputes arise despite contracts being formal or casual. The casual handshake contract is one factor, but many IT project contracts are also based on the industry manufacturer's standard purchase agreement (Tackach 1989). This type of contract is not much better than a handshake. They suffice for minor purchase items, but do not set out contractual procedures regarding change and risk allocation. More formal contracts also have their problems.

Many IT services use fixed price contracts as the basis of product delivery. Fixed price contracts work well when the scope of the work is clearly defined. However, unlike the construction industry, which uses a variety of payment options for project delivery, the IT industry does not seem to take advantage of a variety of contracting options. For example, a unit price or cost plus payment schedule may be more appropriate to the delivery of some services than fixed price. One interviewee went as far as to express that "A partnership approach could be used so proper terms of reference are developed" (Rumple 1996). An example is the Alberta Government Motor Vehicles Branch and Systems House arrangement. The IT supplier develops, purchases, supports, and updates the government computer system at its own cost. In return, it receives a percentage of every transaction at Motor Vehicles and Licensing Operations Branches.

McKenna (1996) outlines costly claims and litigation resulting from Canadian Government Contract regulations. Unlike other research for this paper, the article identifies strict regulatory requirements "set in stone" in the Canadian Government Contracts as a factor resulting in claims and litigation. Unlike other agreements entered into by IT industry contractors, government contracts over-regulate change. They have penalty clauses intended to manage and minimize the effects of change in the construction industry. These clauses when applied directly to the IT industry are punitive given the industry's changing nature. By penalizing the IT industry for its inherent change, contracts are entered into that are too restrictive to deliver IT projects. The degree and severity of IT industry claims and litigation is then increased over those of the construction industry for which the contract clauses were originally written. Indemnification clauses for delay and other risk factors are included, which are clearly unfair in apportioning risk and fault.

Many IT contracts do not have clauses to address project quality, effectiveness, testing, or product warranty. In a poorly detailed contract that resulted in litigation of an intellectual property matter, the owner had legitimate concerns about quality. "We know that there was virtually no reference to the quality of the product to be provided by Prism, (Prism Hospital Software Inc.) no warranties or representations about its effectiveness, and most importantly, no provisions for the testing and acceptance of the software. These are fundamental provisions that should appear in every system acquisition agreement" (Potter 1995). Minimizing effects of change is a concern in all contract work. Because the IT industry bases its profits on its technological change, it is difficult to control the resulting costs of the change.

### Intellectual Property

Copyright problems often result in problems of the user being able to modify their software. Agreements to get around these problems are not often written in the delivery packages. When the issue is addressed, there is a poor understanding (ignorance?) concerning the rights to intellectual property and licensing agreements. A postmortem analysis (Potter 1995), in the case of Prism Hospital Software Inc. vs. Hospital Medical Records Inst., indicated that when the contract went sour due to poor product quality, the owner (Prism) modified the vendor's software to meet his needs. He was held liable for license infringements and damages after copying and distributing the modified software to other hospital users. The issues of copyright and intellectual property have to be addressed more fully in IT contracts.

These factors lead to the question of how to avoid, mitigate, and resolve disputes from project inception to before they get out of hand and hamper project delivery, the financial positions, and the reputations of the parties involved, including that of the IT industry in general.

## Recommendation for Avoidance, Mitigation, and Resolution

### A Plan for Success

The first step to avoid problems and disputes is to plan for success from the beginning. Yogi Schultz, president of Corvelle Consulting, lists ten steps toward achieving a successful IT project (Schulz 1995).

1. Build a clear statement of the project goal
2. Appoint a project sponsor (e.g., a manager from the business area who has the most to gain from the project
3. Appoint an IT professional with a track record of managing projects successfully
4. Understand the project benefits and tradeoffs
5. Insist that a project manager create a detailed plan (CPM), and report progress against this plan
6. Insist that the project manager create a budget derived from the plan
7. Create an organization with defined roles and responsibilities
8. Staff the project with full-time individuals
9. Establish a project steering committee (excellent forum to address changes, productivity, quality issues)
10. Stay and select with a set of project technologies (avoid revisiting technology selection as new products hit the market).

### Ensure the contract is clear and sound

The contractual agreement should be clear, sound and fair to both parties. It should:

*Have a well defined scope of work based on project deliverables.* Owners should consider separate contracts for up-front planning and development of project parameters, if project deliverables are not well defined. The project could be broken into one contract for concept planning, and another contract for detailed project design and delivery. These stages are similar to consultant contracts for design of A&E projects. Project implementation would follow under a separate contract, similar to the construction phase of an A&E project (Takach 1989).

*Identify areas of uncertainty and risk.* It is important to consider risk areas. Assess risks against contract performance clauses to determine the impact and who carries the burden. Strategies should follow from the assessments. Negotiate contracts accordingly and assign adequate cost, schedule, and payment contingencies to cover risk areas (e.g., for vagueness or uncertainties in scope.) Large projects are particularly prone to claims and litigation. Consider breaking them into manageable chunks to minimize risk factors (Hubbard 1996.). To reduce the risk of project non-acceptance by clients, ensure the project program addresses money and time requirements for project testing and client satisfaction. Additionally, quality assurance measures and warranty requirements of the project should be clearly identified.

*A well-defined project plan and schedule (CPM-based) are critical to successful project delivery.* Project manager training may be required as cited by McKenna (1996). Being a relatively new industry (Rumple1996), computer contracting is at least ten years behind current construction contracting practices. Takach (1989) supports this when recommending project control checklists be implemented in IT development contracts.

*A formalized change mechanism, which includes impact to the cost schedule, and productivity should be implemented.* Both contracting parties should communicate and document the impact change has on them. Although change is the nature of the IT industry, develop formal contracts with change clauses to apportion the risk of change fairly. This would help address claims and litigation due to changing owner requirements. Eliminating unnecessary delay clauses, which place unfair risk on contractual parties, would also serve to reduce claims and litigation. A defined, formal, and well-documented process for the approval and control of change should be outlined to ensure contracting parties are aware of project change (Kenny 1996). The impact of clauses relating to liquidated damages could be reduced by writing contract clauses, which fairly share risks of these damages among parties to the contract.

*Contracts must define roles and responsibilities.* This requires well-defined interfaces, reporting lines (e.g., manager to manager) and accompanying levels of authorization. Unlike most government contracts, which overstate the authority of the engineer, many IT development contracts do not identify lines of authority, roles, and responsibilities. Clear definition at the outset of the contract would help the parties have a clear line of communication (Cooke 1996). By clearly and fairly apportioning indemnification, many claim and litigation problems surrounding changes, delays, copyright, and patent laws could be overcome. Parties entering contracts for customized software should have a clear understanding of their contract responsibilities to the other party concerning the Copyright and Patent Law. Contracts that do not address indemnification in the IT industry are at increased risk of legal liability and claims (Takach 1992).

*Payment schedules and methods must be clearly identified, with a clear means of monitoring and reporting progress linked to them.* If possible, owners should consider using contract means other than fixed price. Discontinue the use of supplier-generated purchasing contracts (Takach 1989) in favour of ones that apportion risks equally to all parties. The IT industry does not document its agreements and processes well. Write contracts to ensure documentation, notification, and communication processes are in place, which are clearly tied to payment and change processes.

*A well defined dispute resolution process is needed.* Ideally all contractual parties want to avoid claim and dispute situations. However, if a difference of opinion between the owner and contractor regarding compensation arises, an effective means to resolve such matters should be in place. The process must be fair and equitable. Contracts should include proper processes for notification and documentation. The aim is to avoid litigation because of its damaging time, cost, and demotivational factors. "The onset of litigation almost always signals the end of, or at least a painful interruption in, a relationship, whereas the strategic goal of parties who contract with each other in industry is to strengthen a relationship" (Potter 1993). Learning from the PRISM case, Potter goes on to say that "a computer system agreement is par excellence the type of contract which cries out for ADR (alternative dispute resolution), whether it be simply a detailed schedule of quick progressive execution meeting to take place when difficulties arise, or a scheme of mediation or arbitration, or some combination of these other ADR elements." Therefore, make effort up front, when negotiating the terms of IT contracts, to define an ADR mechanism. Resort to ADR rather than stepping immediately into litigation. The process may be negotiation, mediation, fact-finding, or the use of an independent party (e.g., a steering committee). Another alternative is the traditional construction industry one of appointing an owner's representative (e.g., an engineering consultant), acting independently, to judge performance, progress, and scope matters. Do not rely solely on arbitration. When used alone, arbitration has too many of the undesirable features of litigation, features which flow from the confrontational and adversarial nature of arbitration" (Potter 1993).

## Conclusions

The IT industry derives its profits based on continuous change due to technology and industry growth. This differs from the construction industry where delivery of a final project with minimal change is the focus. The IT industry focuses itself on continued customer relationships by satisfying changing customer requirements and adding value to client/server relationships.

The IT industry, being dependent on change for profits, must ensure at the outset that business relationships are cemented in clear communications and clear project scope. Despite the IT industry's lack of knowledge about contracting, the Laws Contracts apply equally to the IT industry as they do to construction contracts. The use of traditional contractual methods, in their fairest and most equitable forms, would serve to minimize IT industry risks and disputes. Appropriate steps regarding IT industry relationships should be taken to strategically address the issues in the project planning, contract, control methods, and training of IT project management personnel.

### References


Cooke, Vern. 1996. Solutions Architect, Digital Equipment of Canada Limited, Interview.

Badi, Syed. 1996. Network Consultant, Digital Equipment of Canada Limited, Interview.

Fensury, Herb. 1996. Project Engineer, Computing Devices Canada Limited, Interview.

Fox, Joseph M. 1982. *Software and Its Development*. Englewood Cliffs, N.J.: Prentice Hall.

Goodbrand Alan. 1996. Independent Computer Consultant, Interview.

Holmes, Allan. 1996. "Winstar Ruling Could Be Bonanza for IT Firms. *Federal Computer Week* 10 (July).

Hubbard, Craig. 1996. "Taking the Risk Out of Business" *Computing Canada* 21:7: 7.

1996. http://www. infostudio. com/IT Programs/BSIT/it.html.

1996. http://www.infostudio.com/IT Programs/BSIT/itcs.html.

Insight Press. 1991. "Business Transactions Involving Intellectual Property." *Insight Press* (September).

Kenny, William. 1996. Cooke Duke Cox Barristers and Solicitors, Lecture.

Lewin, Marsha. 1996. "Transformation Through Proactive Systems: A Case Study." Information Strategy: The Executive's Journal (Spring).

Maidment, Peter E. 1996. Senior Consultant, Revay and Associates Limited, Lecture.

McKenna, Barrie. 1996. "Canceled Contracts Cost Ottawa Millions." *Globe and Mail* (September 4) Front Page.

Pinto, J. K., and D. P. Slevin. 1989. "Critical Success Factors Across the Project Life Cycle." *Project Management Journal* 19: 67–92.

Potter, Richard B. 1993. "Resolving Disputes in the Computer/IT Industry: The courts, ADR, or What?" *International Journal of Law and Information Technology* 107.

Potter, Richard B.QC. 1995. "Reflections Through a PRISM (Case Comment (Prism Software Inc. Vs. Hospital Medical Records Inst.)). *Business Law Reports 2d* 18.

Rumple, Don. 1996. Regional Manager Information Management Policy, Planning & Corporate Services, Canadian Heritage, Interview.

Shaku, Atre. 1996. "Avoiding the Show-killers; How to Stop Projects from Failing Before They Take Center Stage." *Information Week* (February ): 94.

Schultz, Yogi. 1996. "Ten Easy Steps to a Successful IT Project." *Computing Canada* (August 15).

Srajer, Peter J. 1996. Systems Coordinator, City of Calgary.

Takach, George S. 1989. *Contracting for Computers, A Practical Guide to Negotiating Effective Contracts for the Acquisition of Computer Systems and Related Services.* Toronto: McGraw Hill Ryerson.

———. 1992. *The Software Business.* Toronto: McGraw Hill Ryerson.

Vanderluis, Chris. 1996. "Sell PM Internally Toughest Sale of All." *Computing Canada* (March 14): 23.

Westersund, Lowell A. 1996. Milner Fenerty Barristers and Solicitors, Lecture.

# The Science of Making Little Problems out of Big Ones

Eric Spanitz, Project Mentors

Every project manager must defend his project, or negotiate on behalf of the project at some point (and sometimes, daily). By correctly using standard project management techniques, and a little diplomacy, project managers can reduce the size of most problems, reduce their own stress, and appear more professional.

When negotiating with the sponsor or client for a project necessity, too often the project managers go directly to the "dog and pony show" approach. Their preparation for the meeting deals with trying to get the psychological edge and attempting to have the greatest interpersonal impact in order to state their case. Sponsors and clients tend to react to those efforts. The long-term effect on the relationship is that it becomes one of emotion rather than one of professionalism.

Machiavelli said, "among other evils which being enarmed brings you, it causes you to be despised." In order to negotiate successfully, a project manager must have at least one of the three negotiating armaments:

1. Power: which can be described as either a bigger title or corporate position, or as having more money than the opposition. You can use power to "buy out" your needed position.
2. Time: meaning the stronger position is to have more time. To not be in a hurry gives an edge to your position and places the party with the greatest need for speed at a weaker position.
3. Information: as the negotiator, to be more knowledgeable provides a stronger foundation from which to present and defend your position.

Seldom do project managers have sufficient power within an organization to demand attention. It is also rare for time to be spendable currency. That leaves only information acquired about the project to use professionally during any negotiating session.

## Break Down

So a big problem appears. What do you do? What follows is an organized approach to encounter the beast.

### *Step 1. Don't just do something. Stand there!*

Whenever disaster threatens, we have what appears to be a reflexive move toward action. In fact, this response is not so much reflexive as it is learned. Our culture teaches us to be supremely impatient with the status quo, rewards us for heroic solutions, and characterizes the contemplative approach as "slow," "irresolute," "cowardly," "indecisive," and "wishy-washy." The problem is that taking the wrong action usually "breaks what ain't broke," leaves the true problem unattended, and creates further dysfunction that requires considerably more time and effort to mop up. A well-known story relates the situation of the young resident surgeon whose scalpel slips during a delicate operation and cuts a major artery. Observing from the side, his seasoned mentor comments, "If you take your time, the patient will live."

The lesson here is to avoid the temptation to hyper-react by seizing the first available cause. Take the time to carefully analyze the nature of the problem, its chain of effects, your best calculation of "best case" and "worst case" scenarios if the problem is left unattended, and your team's assessment of all the possible causes of the problem, if those causes are not directly obvious. Knowing the problem includes knowing its probable causes, as well as its current and future effects on the situation.

### *Step 2. Divide, Sub-Divide, and Conquer*

Some problems stem from multiple causes and have multiple effects. This is a great time to apply a skills inventory to the situation. Just as you have assembled a team of people based on the skills required to produce detail task deliverables (and presumably have assigned the appropriately skilled people to the individual tasks),

so have you assigned people to detail problems. Just as in creating a WBS for a project, use your team's subject matter expertise to create the problem WBS, and use them to identify "deliverables" for each of the detail elements. Deliverables could take the form of specific action plans that produce quantifiable results.

### *Step 3. Sort the problems on a two-dimensional skills-authority matrix*

Once you've built the problem WBS, blot the items on a two-dimensional matrix that rate each problem on your and your team's technical ability to solve the problem. Conducting this analysis will very quickly identify a set of problems you can handle with a set requiring elevation to a higher authority. The attempt here is to pull as many of the problem details within your hegemony.

The placement of this step as a successor to Step 2 may seem inappropriate. In fact, you cannot conduct this step until after you have assigned the problem details to subject matter experts. They are the ones who need to study the details first and then determine where the gaps in skill sets lie.

Once you conduct this analysis, you acquire a significantly more powerful negotiating position. You have isolated what you need to elevate, have demonstrated that you and your team have the chops to fix significant portions of the problem, and reduce the size and scope of the problem that requires intervention from a higher authority. Your attempt is to make it easy and logical for the higher authority to embrace your plan and to act according to your design.

#### *Step 4. Strap on your euphemisms*

Now the negotiating process begins. This will take courage, will, stamina, openness to creativity, a high pain threshold, and a clear understanding of your bottom line. As in all negotiating sessions, look for ways you and your counterpart can agree on the nature of the problem, on your common interests in solving it, and on win-win solutions. In this situation, you run the risk of appearing to sell out the team in your attempt to pacify the higher authority, so you need to work clearly and resolutely with your team to position your negotiating role. Your ability to communicate this role and to secure your team's understanding and support will determine your success at reaching a solution. If you fail to do this piece of the work carefully, your brilliantly negotiated solution at best will be received coolly and, at worst, will consciously or unconsciously be sabotaged by team members who feel sold out.

#### *Step 5. Commit Yourself*

Once you have negotiated what you need to solve the overall problem, commit yourself to it and ride that horse to the finish line. This does not mean that you should close your mind to new information; it means that you commit yourself to executing the plan that emerges from your negotiating session. Do what you can to bolster approvals you have secured, insist on signatures, and be willing to trot out this documentation if the higher authority starts displaying selective memory. Lead and be quietly visible. Arrive early and stay late. Insist on success.

Ultimately, events may well spiral out of your control. Whatever the situation, keep in mind a story related by Carlos Casteneda, a young anthropology student who spent years in the Arizona desert studying with a Yaqui Indian shaman whom he called Don Juan. One day, Carlos and Don Juan were walking through a narrow canyon when Carlos noticed that his shoe was untied. He bent down to tie it and just at that moment, a rock tumbled down from the canyon rim and narrowly missed Carlos. Don Juan said, "Carlos, the next time you are walking through a canyon and you stop to tie your shoe, a rock will fall from the top of the canyon and wipe you out. Therefore, your only act of freedom is to tie your shoe impeccably."

# Information Management and Movement: Key to Project Success

Frank P. Saladis, PMP, AT&T Information Technology Services

## Introduction

Defining an information management and movement project is an activity open to the imagination. Rapid changes in technology, hardware, software, new service offerings, virtual offices, and international projects all present new challenges. Each of these create more complex project problems and *increase* the number of possible solutions to a client's needs. The term, information management and movement, replaced "telecommunications" as a descriptor because telecommunications appeared too limiting considering the types of technology found in many of today's complex communications projects. But the *movement* of information is *critical* to any project. Project managers are required, for example, to communicate with many different groups to update status, investigate problems, understand risks, resolve conflicts, negotiate for resources, find alternatives, and much more.

## Objectives of This Paper

Since practical information is what most project managers want (something they can use on the job), the information in this paper will be presented in the form of checklists, questions, and suggestions, all of which will hopefully facilitate future project planning efforts.

With the above factors in mind we may approach the subject of information management and movement (IM&M) from two perspectives:

1. Provide examples of typical projects that would be considered as IM&M
2. Provide examples of how information can be distributed to the stakeholders involved.

The information provided here may be of use to the practicing IM&M project manager as well as team members and other stakeholders. With so many projects that could be considered as IM&M, the question that must be investigated is: What information would be useful? To determine these factors several projects were reviewed to identify elements that were common to each. Identifying the major issues and the solutions applied to resolve the obstacles associated with the project would also provide helpful information to project managers in the IM&M field. Discussions with many project managers during PMI meetings or in project management classes also revealed something that project managers want: tools and information that will help them successfully complete their projects. They want lessons learned, techniques, and innovative ideas that will reduce risk, improve schedule and cost performance, keep the customer happy, and at the same time continuously motivate their project teams.

## Types of IM&M Projects

Any project that involves a telephone, a modem, and a computer can be considered an IM&M project. Its the complexity of the project, the technologies involved, and the resources required to execute the project plan that challenge the project manager and the team and set the stage for innovation and learning. Utilizing information from actual projects adds some validity to the ideas and suggested plans proposed in this paper. A few of the projects researched include a variety of technologies such as the following:

The installation of a communications system for a Wall Street trading company: The project involved the construction of four new trading floors; two data centers; redundant voice, data, and network systems; state of the art telephone equipment; coordination with local telephone service providers; rerouting of hundreds of private line circuits; multiple appearances of telephone numbers and lines; weekend and out of hours cutovers to reduce down time; and extensive quality checks to ensure reliable service at opening of business.

Replacement of a twenty-five-year old centrex with an onsite digital PBX for a campus environment of four buildings, 8500 employees, new fiber backbones, and a combination of new and reused horizontal and vertical wire: This project required the installation of a completely new system that was 100 percent functional and tested prior to the actual cutover of desk top equipment and the network.

Relocation of twenty-four business units from one central headquarters location to eighteen different sites, including installation of new PBXs and the replication of existing LANs and WANs at each new site.

Coordinate the upgrade or replacement of voice premises equipment at four hundred locations nationwide to prepare for changes in the national dialing plan.

Split up assets and replicate services in preparation for a major organizational change; splitting one company into three separate companies; coordinate relocation of entire departments, build new networks, create a brand new billing system, share of services, and manage inter-company teams.

Consolidation of an organization from multiple locations to a centralized campus environment: The project includes the relocation of 7300+ employees, construction of new buildings, and the refurbishing of an existing building, a new voice system, a new wire and cable infrastructure, fiber backbone, installation of high capacity facilities, and the coordinated disconnect and reconnect of hundreds of office operations that demand minimal down time.

These are only a few examples of IM&M projects, but they do provide a good background for gathering information that would be useful on many types of projects. Each project had its share of challenges, jeopardies, and conflicts. But each project produced plans, contingencies, teamwork, and new opportunities. They also produced something very important to project managers: lessons learned.

Using information from plans that were developed to manage each of the above projects, a "generic" IM&M project plan could be created. The generic plan would include elements or *Practical Project Techniques* (PPT for short) typical of IM&M projects and that may be useful tools for planning future projects. PPTs that are not applicable to one project may be utilized an another.

## Project Start Up

In order to get things started the project manager should understand the environment in which she will be working. Assuming that a solution has been developed by a sales or account team, the project manager should become familiar with the customer or customer's business and business environment. What is the scope of work? Has a scope been developed? Many IM&M projects start out with a very loose scope of work that requires a fair amount of backtracking and investigation. Find out who is involved in the project from the customer's side. Who owns the project? Who will you, the project manager, meet with and provide information to? As an example, during a project meeting , the purpose of which was to inform the clients about plans to move their organizations to a new facility, the project manager told the clients what they planned to do. After the meeting a client approached the project manager about a separate issue but remarked, "It would be a good idea if the project team would take some time to understand the *mission* of our organization before they started making plans." Some organizations worked with very complex systems, twenty-four-hour-a-day operations, services critical to the business. These things should be understood before plans are developed. Approaching the customer to make sure that her business needs are understood up front can help form better relationships and start the project off on a positive note. The project manager and project team will also benefit from some initial education about the client by understanding the sensitivities the customer is dealing with. This could reduce the number of conflicts that may be encountered during the project.

In consideration of the input from the customer, the first PPT in the IM&M Generic Project Plan is:

**PPT #1—Understand the customer and the environment he works in. Make sure you know his "mission" and hot spots. Obtain his input. Make sure your plan is his plan.**

The next step is to fully understand the scope of your project and its relationship to other projects or sub-projects. Your project may actually be a sub-project of a much larger undertaking. An example would be a relocation where new facilities are being constructed. There may be demolition followed by construction of new offices, technical centers, and office space. A large portion of the project budget is consumed by materials, furniture, and environmental items. The telecommunications component, except for wire and cable, which must be coordinated during the construction, is usually the last component of the project to be completed mainly because you need walls, desks, furniture, conduit, and outlets before the IM&M equipment can be installed. It is essential to make sure that every detail is covered. Every telephone, desktop PC, router, hub, and Lan/Wan connection in every office, technical center, data center, or laboratory must be operational. A comprehensive plan for obtaining customer requirements will help reduce the risk of missing an important circuit or piece or equipment. The next PPT for the IM&M Generic Project Plan is:

**PPT#2—A plan for obtaining customer requirements. A check list or questionnaire that will help the customer understand what is needed for the operation to succeed in the new environment.**

In order to gather requirements it may be helpful to determine what the customer has in the existing environment. An inventory of equipment and services will identify essential items as well as those that may no longer be needed. It will also help identify areas where existing technology is no longer sufficient due to technology advances and new business requirements. Some services that are in place may require very long lead times to order or to be customized. In some cases an organization may not have the flexibility to shut down at one location, disconnect equipment, reconnect at the new location, and then start up again. It may be necessary to completely replicate an office. This would have a major impact on the project budget, especially if this type of work was not included in the scope. (*Remember: understand the customer's mission.*)

1. Here is a suggested requirements gathering plan:
2. A introduction explaining the purpose of the plan
3. Specific contacts and telephone numbers of stakeholders or the key decision makers
4. Background information about the organizations that will be providing the service and/or support
5. A form that is user friendly, possibly in electronic format ( word document or Excel spreadsheet).
6. Organization information: Customer contact names, locations, telephone numbers, email address, fax, and alternate contacts
7. Description of voice system requirements: digital line, analog lines, off-premise extensions, fax machines, voice mail boxes
8. Private line services and point to point connections
9. Circuits to be disconnected
10. Data network requirements
11. Server information
12. Identify all LANs
13. Identify the LAN administrator(s).

Customers need to be kept informed about the activities of major projects, especially since the project will affect her operation permanently or temporarily. They are interested in schedules and status. They want someone whom to whom complain. They want someone to address their questions and focus anxiety towards. The next PPT in the IM&M generic project plan is:

**PPT#3—A plan for providing the customers (the actual end-users and organizations affected by the project) with information, status, and assistance.**

Regular formal presentations especially at the very beginning of the project will help reduce stress, anxiety, and the resistance that many projects face. Information movement is absolutely key to a project's success. We all know the importance of project meetings and project documentation. Project teams communicate to each other but in many cases, the people who will ultimately work in the new environment or with the new technology are left guessing until the last minute.

Here is a suggested communications plan:

1. After the project kick off meeting, schedule information sessions for the community that will be affected by the project. These would be high-level sessions designed to provide an overview of what will happen as the project progresses. These meetings will reduce anxiety and the usual resistance to a new project by demonstrating that the interests of the affected groups are being addressed.
2. Distribute occasional desk drops, one- or two-page project updates that provide information about schedules and other useful information. Another approach would be to create a simple project newsletter.
3. Set up a home page for project information to share plans, schedules, status, and jeopardies.
4. Set up a method for receiving and responding to questions. For large projects a working committee or group of representatives from the organizations affected can be formed. Their purpose would be to disseminate information to their respective teams.
5. During some projects a voice mail broadcast was prepared to remind employees of an activity that was scheduled to take place within a few days.
6. Schedule project information conference calls or "town hall meetings" to provide updates.
7. Don't hide bad news. Make sure the information is reliable, accurate, and straightforward.
8. Designate coordinators from customer organizations to keep their associates informed.

## Project Scope

The project work breakdown structure of many IM&M projects probably includes items such as:

- Construction
- Project Management
- Wire and Cable system ( Backbone, fiber, infrastructure)
- Cable management: Managing the moves and changes, disconnects, repairs, and defective connections
- System Security
- Facility Security
- Internet Access
- Operations and Administration Plan (The operating plan that will take affect when the project is completed)
- Acceptance Testing
- Network—Voice and Data (LAN and WAN)
- Voice System Installation
- Cutover Plans
- Help Desk
- Post Project Reviews

## Project Monitoring and Control

The project manager's challenge, for just about any project , is obtaining information, assessing it, determining the project's health, and taking the appropriate action to keep things on track. Most IM&M projects include multiple technologies, cross organizational teams, external contractors, and a long list of issues that can have a major impact on the project. The project work breakdown structure will probably include items such as:

- Construction
- Project Management
- Wire and Cable system (Backbone, fiber, infrastructure)
- Cable Management: Managing the moves and changes, disconnects, repairs, and defective connections
- System Security
- Facility Security
- Internet Access
- Operations and Administration Plan (The day-to-day operating plan effective at project completion)
- Customer Acceptance
- Network—Voice and Data
- Voice System
- Cutover Plans
- Help Desk
- Post Project Reviews

### PPT4—A plan for monitoring the project, assessing progress, controlling all aspects of the project. and distributing information to the stakeholders.

Any project, regardless of industry and project type, requires a method for monitoring and control. In the early stages of a project it would be beneficial to meet with the project team, stakeholders, and customers, to review the project scope and begin to understand the details and complexity associated with the project by listing the issues that must be resolved. The project kickoff meeting will generate much of the information to get the project started but the *real details* start to come out when the project team begins their regular meetings. The work breakdown structure developed during the planning sessions and the kick-off meeting is scrutinized, reviewed, changed, and added to. The team starts asking questions such as: Where will we get the resources for this? Is this work included in the project budget? Who will authorize the purchase of equipment? And many more questions. An issues list will add more structure to project meetings; it generates questions and possible solutions. It has also been observed that if you keep asking for issues to be identified you *will continue* to receive them, usually with no resolution or owner. One method of stemming the tide of issues is to institute a rule at project start-up that if an issue is raised for which an owner has not been identified, it becomes the responsibility of the person who identified it. This has a dramatic effect in issue reduction. We do not want to discourage input, and we do want project team members to be actively involved in the project, but if some filtering of issues is not practiced the project team will spend much of its time talking about issues instead of resolving them. As the project progresses any items that may have an impact on the project will generally be identified.

## Project Meetings

Once the issues list has been developed it can become part of the regular project meeting agenda. This list is not necessarily an action item list, but it will generate action items that can be clearly understood and will have an identified owner. Controlling project meetings, optimizing the project team's time, and getting the information out quickly should be the main priorities of the project manager. Project meetings should always have a clear objective: Is it a status meeting, a problem-solving meeting, or an information session? Set the agenda to meet the purpose of the meeting. As an example, a status meeting agenda may include the following:

**Meeting Location, Date, and Time:** Include a conference bridge number and access information.

**Meeting Purpose:** Example—Status meeting for the ABC Systems Transfer Project.

**Project Schedule:** A two-week forward and backward look at the project. This will help keep focus on what tasks are coming up as well as tasks that should have been completed. This approach allows the project team to see the impact of a delayed task and also gives them a "heads up" regarding who will be involved and what activities and tasks are on the horizon. It will also assist the team in planning for contingencies.

**Discussion Items:** List the items to be discussed, the owner or person who will be required to address the issue, and a time frame. During status meetings five or ten minutes per item should be sufficient.

**Review of Action Items:** Action items should be numbered and tracked.

**Other Related Issues:** This can be an open discussion to review items that may not have a direct impact on the project but are important and should be considered.

**Next Meeting Date, Location, Time, and Agenda:** Provides an opportunity to prepare for the next meeting.

**Meeting Critique:** Build in some time to obtain feedback from the participants. Comments from the participants will assist in improving meeting effectiveness and give them an opportunity to provide input and enhance the position on the team. It may also have a positive impact when trying to motivate a team that appears to be losing interest.

Project meeting minutes should be prepared immediately after the meeting and certainly within twenty-four hours. Project status changes rapidly so information should always be "fresh." When distributing information the project manager must consider who will receive it. The project team would receive the minutes from the meeting, but the customer or upper management may require a higher level form of status. Sharing internal meeting minutes with a client may result in some surprising actions. Make sure the information you send is accurate and is formatted (edited) for the receiving audience.

**Exhibit 1.**

| REPORT MONTH: | | CURRENT DATE: | |
|---|---|---|---|
| PROJECT NUMBER: PROJECT IDENTIFIER | | NAME: | (Project Name) |
| PROJECT MANAGER : | | PROJECT OWNER: | |
| PM PHONE | | CLIENT CONTACT: | |
| START DATE: | | CLIENT PHONE: | |
| COMPLETION DATE: | | CLIENT ORGANIZATION: | |
| PROJECT HEALTH: | Green = On Schedule<br>Yellow = Some Problems<br>Red = Serious Jeopardy | PROJECT SCHEDULE | ON/OFF |
| DESCRIPTION: Brief project scope | Objective of the project, estimated cost, technical overview, complexity, high level overview. | | |
| STATUS: | Current status of the project- milestones met, critical issues, description of the a jeopardy. Accomplishments, cost data, scheduled events. Customer satisfaction information. | | |

## Managing Information

Many project managers believe that too much information is better than too little. Both can result in problems. Many project managers are guilty of information overload. Sending numerous memos, pages of detailed minutes, long status reports, and copying everyone as either an "FYI" or a "CYA." Project managers should be aware of "infoglut." We use email, fax, internet, online services, voice mail, memos, minutes, status reports, and we copy the world. Do we really need to do this? Information overload can cause a project manager and a project team some serious problems. People tend to disregard what they receive or scan it lightly missing an important issue. If we fill up an email in-box with memos, are we really getting things done or are we just creating more work for the project team? There are alternatives, such as a standard electronic report designed to provide high-level information about a project. This report includes a brief description of the project scope, contact information about the project manager and project owner, and the current status of the project (restricted to a certain number of characters). This report can be posted on an organization's web page. Project files, issues lists, project team contact information, and other useful information can be posted on a web page or in shared folders. When sending e-mail messages verify your distribution list and send only to those who really need the information. Label high priority memos. I would always recommend sending more information than not enough, but considering that many project managers work on multiple projects, project team members are usually assigned to several other teams, project owners own more than one project, and so on. We need to make sure we deliver the appropriate information to the right people at the right time. Project managers need to think in terms of less volume and higher quality. Keeping information "informative" will decrease the amount of time our recipients spend filtering the information.

Sample status report format shown in Exhibit 1.

## Staying Connected

Many project managers are on the move and out of the office. If it isn't a meeting, it's a crisis. How do you stay connected?

The objective is to remain mobile yet have the flexibility to make things happen in a variety of environments and to maintain constant communication with a number of operations, project team members, and remote locations. Constant motion is part of the game of project management (not that project management is a game). You can't always take your support staff with you (if you have one), and you will probably be in the project office for only short periods of time. So your Laptop and your cell phone become your seven-pound support team ready to work for you at a moment's notice (provided your batteries are good, you're within a cell site, and you have access to PC access to the network).

The most critical task of project-related activities these days is doing everything fast and getting the information out faster. Project managers must leverage the technology that are available. Use of email, pagers, cell phones, fax, and voice mail offer some "connectivity" to key contacts, but the project manager needs to go further. Set up a data base with the "vital statistics" of key personnel: names, telephone numbers, addresses, email id, fax number, and cell phone. Other factors to consider are time differences and other people's travel schedules. Inform your project team about your schedule, when you can be reached, and emergency telephone numbers or procedures. Make sure that you have an escalation process in place and a designated back-up to handle situations they may come up in your absence.

## Summary

The IM&M project manager has a unique job. She must understand the technologies involved, the nature of the customer's business, coordinate with multiple organizations and contractors, and report information to an assortment of stakeholders. While managing the project, the information about the project must also be managed. It is important to deliver the right information to the right people as quickly and accurately as possible while avoiding information overload or "infoglut." IM&M projects present many challenges but a well thought out plan for controlling and delivering information will assist in a successful implementation.

### References


AT&T PMO. 1993. AT&T Project Management Guidelines.
AT&T PMO. 1997. Project Files.

# Implementing Project Management: Success Into the Next Century Utilizing Change Management Strategies

Sarah A. Wagner, Electronic Data Systems, Corp.
Maria Mercer, Electronic Data Systems, Corp.

## Introduction

### Context Setting

What's wrong with statements like these: "Top Ten Reasons Project Management Fails" and "Why Project Management Failed?" In short, they are misleading. In most cases when project management is not successfully implemented in an organization, it is not project management that failed. It is the *change* that failed. Focusing only on providing automated tools, best in class methodology, and world-class training may result in short-term benefits. But a successful project management implementation with long-term benefits requires managing transformational change in the organization. The only way project management efforts will be successful into the next century is to first recognize that implementing project management is synonymous with implementing complex change, and second, recognize the importance of incorporating change management strategies into your implementation plan.

This paper, utilizing a real-life case study, will outline some of the root causes for poor project management implementations and give guidance in the form of change management strategies to cure these root causes.

Some of the most common reasons given for the failure of a project management implementation effort are:

- lack of a clearly defined and documented purpose
- lack of ownership and commitment
- lack of established and communicated priorities
- lack of adequate reinforcement to sustain desired behavior
- lack of metrics or the "right" type of metrics to help indicate progress.

These "common reasons for failure" are all obstacles the organization in the case study had to address. Existing project management deliverables and tasks (e.g., scope statements, risk assessments, leadership, and customer reviews) partially address some of the above issues. Unfortunately, unless they are part of a larger change management strategy, they fall woefully short of resolving the issues. The root causes of these issues lie not within project management but in a broader, slightly different methodology called change management.

### Change Drivers

The only thing that is constant is change. Organizations today are faced with an ever-increasing number of changes that tend to be coming at them at an accelerated rate of speed and increasing complexity. Some examples of the drivers behind all this change are rapid developments of new technologies, redefinition of business direction, and, expansion into global markets. Change drivers are forces that cause us to question the way things are today, or the status quo. Change drivers bring into focus, sometimes painfully so, problems with the way things are done both from an individual and organizational standpoint. They can also bring to light opportunities for an individual or organization that have previously gone unnoticed. Either way, the drivers serve as catalysts that motivate us to change ourselves and our organizations. In this case study, the primary change driver was the redefinition of business direction, which was brought about by a strategic business planning effort.

## The Change Process

### The Change Model

Although it seems chaotic, each change moves through a common process that involves moving from current reality to a new, different reality.

What's happening right now in an organization or the status quo is considered the *present state*. The *desired state* describes the way things will look after the change has been implemented. Both the present state and the desired state are made up of components that comprise the organizational system. These components are:

- People: the people's beliefs, skills, and behavior
- Structure: the organizational processes, procedures, and systems that provide structure for the organization
- Culture: the cultural norms, or the collective beliefs, values, and assumptions that implicitly govern the way things are done.

Each component of the system influences and affects every other component within the system. Focusing attention on only one component of the organizational system will sub-optimize the whole and cause the change to fail.

Between the present state and the desired state exists a turbulent time known as the *transition period.* It is while the organization is going through the transition period that the integration of change management and project management strategies to address all components of the organizational system is most critical.

### Transition Period

Why is the transition period so turbulent? Mainly because it involves dealing with the human side of change. The transition period will be unique for every organization. The level of resistance experienced while in the transition period will vary from organization to organization. Some resistance will be extremely overt, with individuals blatantly refusing to adopt the change. Other organizations, such as the one illustrated in the case study, experience a passive type of resistance. This type of resistance tends to manifest itself in more subtle ways, such as giving verbal support but not modeling or reinforcing the new way of doing things. The saying, "people don't resist change, they resist being changed," carries a significant message. Strategies must be developed to address the human factors that will always come into play. These strategies need to be incorporated into the project plan and should revolve around how to minimize resistance and move people smoothly through the transition period.

## Case Study Overview

### Envisioning Change

The theory and models mentioned above came to life as an organization within Electronic Data Systems Corporation (EDS) when it began the task of implementing an organization-wide project management environment. Technical development, the subject of the case study, provides training and development products and services worldwide to EDS employees. The organization's four hundred employees are geographically dispersed with a majority located in three states in the United States and a portion in Europe, Canada, South America, and Asia Pacific.

The primary driver behind the decision to implement a project management environment was the redefinition of the organization's business direction. Specifically, the group had invested six months to develop a five-year strategic business plan. The plan outlined the need to redefine the organization's value delivery cycle by reengineering existing core business processes, as well as adding and developing new core business processes. The initiative to implement a project management environment was significant because it would provide the structure and discipline necessary to manage the projects associated with reaching our new business direction.

### Present State

Before technical development (TD) approved the project management initiative, there had been a few isolated attempts to apply project management methods and tools. Although a project scheduling tool was accessible on the desktop, and corporate project management methodology training was available, the efforts were short-lived. Within a matter of months, efforts to utilize a disciplined approach to manage projects succumbed to turnover in team members and managers, ever-changing priorities, or loss of interest.

In 1995, there were over one hundred projects of various sizes under way in the organization. Very few of these had documented schedules, and none had complete project plans. Project progress and changes were not tracked. Accomplishments, plans, and issues were not communicated consistently, timely, or at the appropriate levels. As a result, there was a perception that projects floundered for extended periods of time and seldom reached completion.

After the project management initiative was identified, a coordinator was assigned to lead the implementation activities. The coordinator was part of a team tasked with implementing the various initiatives that resulted from the redefinition of the organization's business direction.

### Desired State

The technical development director, who was the initiative sponsor, envisioned an environment where applying project management methods and tools would be status quo for the way work was managed in the organization. Specifically, a successful project management implementation meant:

- establishing the ability to manage the organization as a whole and not as a collection of silos
- developing employees who could go anywhere in the company and successfully manage projects to meet business and customer requirements.

Achieving these goals meant enhancing decision support processes, creating a learning environment, and integrating project management methods with existing and new business processes.

## Implementation Approach

### Assumptions

The implementation plan was initially designed as a three-year phased approach. Two significant assumptions guided the plan. First, it was assumed that people believed managing projects using a proven methodology made common sense,

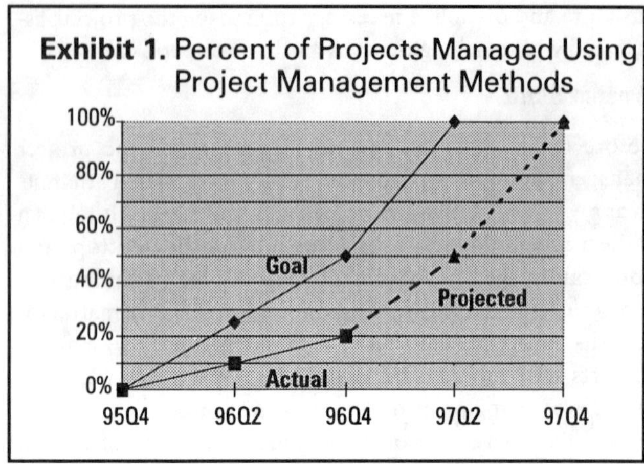


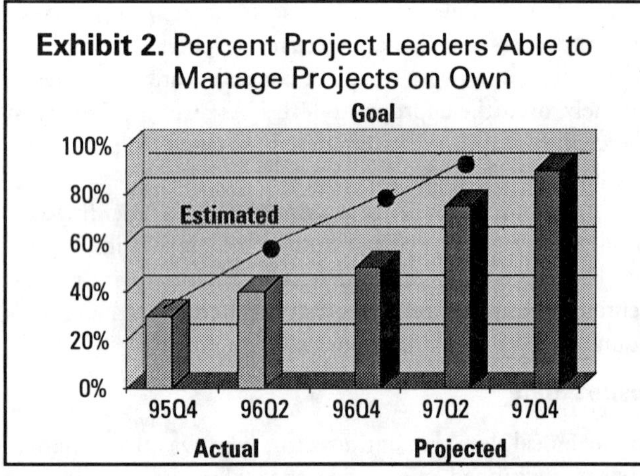


and if they were provided more information about the methods they would embrace and apply them in their day-to-day activities. The second assumption was that it would be possible to increase the level of project management skills and knowledge evenly across the organization.

### First Phase: Activities

In the first year of implementation, activities focused on assisting project leaders and team members to apply the project management methodology. The processes and deliverables were tailored, based on an assessment of the organization's knowledge of project management methods and tools. As a result, a minimum set of deliverables was required for every project. Over one hundred employees participated in hands-on work sessions and Internet relay chats to learn about and share experiences performing project management activities and creating deliverables. An intranet web site was established to make procedures, templates, and guidelines accessible to anyone, anywhere, anytime. Reports were provided to TD leaders on a regular basis to support the project review, approval, and funding processes.

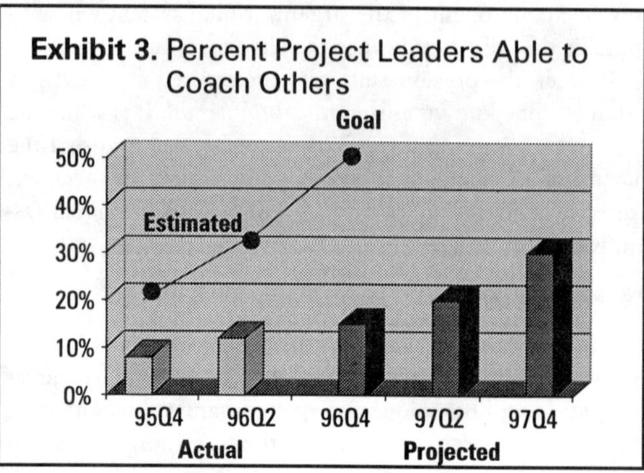


### First Phase: Progress

A metrics plan was executed throughout the first phase of the implementation. One measurement was the number of projects managed by project leaders applying the methodology. As mentioned above, prior to the start of the implementation, the methodology was not applied. At the end of the first year, only 20 percent of the projects met the minimum project management deliverable requirements, compared to the estimate of 50 percent. At that time, progress in reaching the goals was approximately six months behind schedule.

Another set of metrics was the number of project leaders and team members who could perform and ultimately coach others on project management activities. The goal was to develop project management skills and knowledge so that nine out of ten project leaders would be able to perform project management activities on their own. In addition, 50 percent of project leaders would be able to coach others on project management activities. Responses after one year indicated that between 50 to 75 percent of project leaders felt they needed assistance performing project management activities (Exhibit 2), and less than one in ten project leaders believed they could explain project management activities to others (Exhibit 3).

### First Phase: Symptoms of Underlying Problems

Almost 50 percent of the organization actively participated in one or more implementation activities. Information about the implementation efforts was regularly communicated to the entire organization through the intranet, presentations, and e-mail messages. However, the initial metrics indicated that progress was being made more slowly than anticipated. Other symptoms included:

- Data from project reports was not included in decision-making processes at the highest leadership level
- Managers were not requesting or reviewing project reports or deliverables on a regular basis

- The project leaders of several very visible and complex projects did not participate in implementation activities
- The organization's leadership chose not to integrate project and financial processes and data.

## Realizations

Viewed from a project management perspective, the implementation was going according to plan and served as an example of how to apply the methodology to manage a project. The implementation activities received high satisfaction ratings and positive feedback in surveys. Like other successful organizations that experienced a lot of change, there was little initial resistance to the implementation efforts in technical development (Wesley and Whitefeather 1996). So why weren't the goals being reached and why did these troubling symptoms exist?

Upon examining the symptoms, the root causes appeared to be lack of ownership, commitment, and adequate reinforcement of desired project management behavior. It became apparent that no matter how accurate or complete the project management deliverables like effort estimates or work breakdown structures were, they didn't fully address implementing significant changes in people's behaviors, an organization's culture, and work processes. This led to the stunning realization that implementing project management was truly a complex change and required more than just the application of a project management methodology to be successful.

At that point, the project management coordinator sought subject matter experts in change management methods. Together, they reviewed the corporate change management methodology. The methodology provides a framework to assess and implement activities that address the human factors related to change. The change management methodology describes eight transition strategies that can guide an implementation effort successfully through the transition period. The project management coordinator and change management coaches rated how well (excellent, good, fair, or poor) the current implementation activities addressed the transition strategies. Ratings were based on results from an implementation activities survey and additional participant feedback.

1. Team Structure: Fair
   - tailored work force profiles describing the roles, responsibilities, skills, and competencies for project leaders and project coordinators
2. Leadership/Sponsorship: Fair
   - held regular meetings with initiative sponsor
   - met with leadership to understand expectations and requirements of project management for their decision support activities
   - conducted two overview sessions for managers
3. Education and Training: Excellent
   - conducted two fourteen-week modularized, hands-on work sessions for more than one hundred participants
4. Measurement: Fair
   - conducted two project management skills and knowledge assessments
   - conducted an implementation activities satisfaction survey
5. Communication: Excellent
   - established project management intranet web site
   - conducted monthly Internet relay chat sessions
   - communicated events, success stories, and plans in organization-wide presentations and e-mails
6. Relationship Management: Good
   - invited and received participation from internal business partners in implementation activities
7. Performance Management: Poor
8. Business and Technology Integration: Excellent
   - tailored and implemented project management processes, deliverables, and guidelines
   - integrated project management with the project review, approval and funding processes, human resource planning, and new core processes

## Managing the Implementation as a Complex Change

The result of this assessment was the realignment of current and planned implementation activities with the transition strategies. It was decided that current activities addressing strategies that were rated highly would be maintained but would not be enhanced as was previously planned. Strategies rated as "fair" or "poor," like Performance Management and Leadership/Sponsorship, required more and immediate attention. For these strategies, new activities were identified. They included:

### *Team Structure*

Delegating responsibility for conducting the work sessions to others in the organization who wanted opportunities to broaden their project management skills by coaching others.

### *Measurement*

Implementing an ongoing survey to rate how well the implementation activities address the eight transition strategies.

### *Leadership/Sponsorship*

Conducting one-on-one coaching sessions with leadership team to help integrate project data in decision support processes and facilitating working sessions with managers to review the value and use of project management deliverables in team meetings and project reviews.

#### *Performance Management*

Adding project management-specific objectives for performance reviews and guidelines for salary write-ups.

## Results

### Successes

In the twenty-five months of implementing project management, significant and lasting changes occurred in the organization and for team members. Although the implementation had reached obstacles after one year, the timely and seamless integration of project management and change management methods enabled the implementation effort to continue successfully.

- After the implementation of the new Team Structure activities, projected assessments of project management skill and knowledge levels increased by an average of 25 percent.
- Over 50 percent of the organization actively participated in the project management implementation activities.
- More than 25 percent of the organization attended hands-on work sessions to learn more about project management methods and tools.
- Project management data was integrated with the leadership's project review, approval, and funding processes.
- Several team members achieved project management professional certification.

### Lessons Learned

There were several aspects of the implementation effort that were not managed as well as they could be and contributed to the resistance that built up about applying project management methods and tools:

- Implementation activities in the first phase were not selected based on how well they would address resistance from the organization's people, cultural, or structural systems. They were selected due to several misleading factors like incorrect assumptions and previous experiences.
- The influence of multiple levels of sponsors beyond technical development was not recognized. While it's increasingly difficult to control or exert influence over ever-widening spans of control, there were missed opportunities to develop those leaders as sponsors of the project management initiative. Ultimately, the decision to reassign the project management implementation resources was made by management, at one and two levels above the initiative sponsor.
- There were multiple complex changes under way competing for time, resources, budget, and energy in technical development as a result of the strategic business planning efforts. As a result, the change initiatives sub-optimized and weakened the whole effort. Leaders resisted prioritizing or making choices between the change initiatives.
- It is necessary to clearly state the benefits of a project management implementation for each affected role in the organization. Because it was assumed that applying project management methods made common sense, too little time was spent communicating to the individual what the value, or WIIFMs (What's In It For Me), of project management were.

### Recommendations

The implementation of project management must be approached and managed as a complex change that will impact the people, structures, and culture of an organization. As a result, the strategies, plans, schedules, and people accountable for ensuring the change is successful must address the human side of such a complex change.

1. Organize and integrate project management implementation activities around transition strategies:
   - Team Structure: Build a team, or a series of teams, who can help plan, implement, and sustain the project management implementation. Participants should include executive and sustaining sponsors, project manager, subject matter experts, and representatives from different stakeholder groups.
   - Leadership: Establish a sponsorship development program that provides the sponsors with specific activities that establish a shared vision of the implementation and help them express, model, and reinforce support for the project management implementation effort.
   - Education and Training: Establish training and education that will provide stakeholders with the knowledge and skills of methods, tools, and processes integral to the success of the project management implementation effort.
   - Measures: Establish the business value and readiness measures that should be tracked and monitored to enable learning and measure progress as well as results.
   - Communications: Establish communications about the project management effort at all levels of the organization. Establish a formal communication plan that clearly identifies the different levels of audiences and the WIIFM messages.
   - Relationship Management: Determine how the change will impact a customer or supplier and establish

a win-win business relationship for working together. If feasible, include the supplier and customer as part of the planning team.

- Performance Management: Identify desired behaviors and performance results for the project management implementation effort. Establish the reinforcement mechanisms for each behavior (positive and negative) to institutionalize the change.
- Business and Technology Integration: Determine what business processes and practices need to be in place, or redesigned, to support the project management implementation effort. Determine what technology is needed to support the implementation. Design how business processes, practices, and technology will be integrated to support the implementation.

2. Understand the role of a change agent, the person who will be leading the implementation effort. Look for more than just an expert in project management. A change agent requires a different set of skills, such as knowledge of change management concepts, leadership, flexibility, courage, patience, and strong personal ethics.
3. Strive for optimum pace of change. Throughout the implementation the pace changes—listen to the organization's responses and adjust the pace accordingly. "In the end, your organization will change only as fast as it can change" (Wesley and Whitefeather 1996).

## Conclusion

Implementing project management is synonymous with implementing complex change. In order for project management implementation efforts to be successful, the plan must include the people and structural and cultural issues not addressed solely by project management methodologies. Creating a plan that utilizes change management transition strategies will enable project management implementation to be successful into the next century.

### References

Blumstein, Gershon, and Robert Cook. 1996. "Why Project Management Fails And What To Do About It." *Proceedings*. Upper Darby, PA.

The Standish Group. 1995. *Chaos*. Available from Internet site @ <http://www.standishgroup.com/chaos.htm>

Electronic Data Systems, Corp. (EDS). 1993. *Implementing Change Methodology*. Plano, TX.

Wesley, Doug, and Kaye Whitefeather. 1996. *Making a Positive Difference When Your Company is Changing*. Available from Internet site @ <http://www.changecraft.com/Ccbk-3.htm>

# Breaking Up is Hard to Do: Project Managing the AT&T/Lucent Separation

Paul E. Moulder, PMP, AT&T Solutions

## Overview

When AT&T announced on September 20, 1995, that it would split into two new companies, Wall Street analysts responded with glowing reports about the future of AT&T and Lucent Technologies Inc. Speculation was rampant that the benefits of deregulation in the telecommunications industry and the increasing global competition for customers would greatly benefit shareholders moving into the next century. What was not immediately apparent was that in a single stroke, AT&T had created one of the most complex information systems and process projects in United States corporate history. AT&T has one of the world's largest information technology infrastructures comprised of over five hundred information systems that are heavily inter-linked to provide for the operational, financial, and decision support to the corporation. In order to allow for the Oct. 1, 1996, spin-off of Lucent Technologies Inc. as a separate company, this infrastructure would need to be either isolated between or duplicated (cloned ) for both companies without any negative operational, financial, or decision support impacts. It was of particular importance that all the corporate financial results systems and processes be able to continue to collect and report on the corporation's finances during this process due to regulatory oversight and the need for government approval for the separation. Imagine building a new jetliner while in flight in another, and the intricacy becomes easier to understand. There was no margin for error, as the impact on shareholders and customers would be enormous and potentially defeat the venture entirely.

Project managing the isolation and duplication of this infrastructure while maintaining performance and data integrity was possible only by embracing organization-wide project management to quickly integrate the planning and subsequent implementation of hundreds of individual projects into a focused corporate-wide effort to achieve success. There was no previous model or example to study. This was truly a unique, one-time effort with a known start and end date, but without a clear scope. The project management challenges created with the separation announcement were clear from the onset. The determination of scope(s) would be difficult. Resources would be unstable and potentially shrinking as a result of moving to the new company structures. There would be shifting and uncertain accountability for work over time. A continuous high-risk environment would exist, threatening the achievement of aggressive intermediate milestones and the successful separation of the two companies in a compressed time-frame of less than one year. This paper will describe the program and project management techniques utilized in the separation of the AT&T and Lucent Technologies Inc. primary financial systems and processes.

## Shifting the Paradigm

As with any breakup, the emotional consequences persist for a long time but the need to get on with life is immediate. All the more so in this case with the fate of thousands of employees and millions of shareholders and customers in the balance; there was no time for an extended period of mourning.

There were two immediate results of the separation announcement. The first result was a sense of shock, denial, and resistance to the announcement on the part of employees across the company. The impact of the announcement would take months to be fully assessed. The second immediate result was a sense of complete bewilderment on how to proceed with the mission. There was no experienced leadership in this area. There were only some general, high- level objectives, which were extremely aggressive in time-frame and ambiguous in scope. It was clear that current workflow processes would not accomplish the mission within the pre-determined schedule.

Traditional concepts of project life-cycles with concept and planning phases of reasonable duration wouldn't work here. In short the traditional project life-cycle approach to developing cost, schedule, and scope by themselves were a risk factor. It was necessary to approach the program and project management needs in a new way. To develop a hybrid concept of project planning, monitoring, and control. It was clear that "macro" management was in and "micro" management was out. To do this effectively required thinking out of the box and letting go of the traditional approach to planning and control. Trying to develop plans to a comfortable level was impossible, so traditional planning needed to be replaced with strategic direction setting and communications. Traditional monitoring and control were replaced with risk management and quality assurance. While these are elements of good traditional project planning, they are often not given the emphasis they deserve. In the case of this project management problem, they would turn out to be the most important tools available to the project team.

## Creating a New Paradigm

Along with the pure project management issues involved with the separation, organizational issues were also extensive and in many cases ambiguous and under constant revision. Creating an organizational environment that would support the program and project management of the separation was essential.

The solution was to create a virtual organization with representation from all areas of the company, which had responsibility for the development, operation of, and accounting responsibility for the AT&T financial applications, systems, and processes. This virtual organization was called the AT&T Financial Systems and Processes Transition Team. The transition team would remain in existence throughout the life-cycle of the separation and would be responsible for the successful completion of the separation in the systems and processes areas. It provided the managerial foundation and glue from which specific programs and projects were identified, resourced, planned for, and implemented. The most noteworthy aspect of this model was the creation of an "Office of the Project" that was to provide the transition team with the program and project management support during transition. In most respects this project office functioned much as it does in many companies, providing project management skills and tools support as well as progress reporting. In this case, special emphasis was placed on four critical items:

1. Strategic Approach
2. Communications
3. Risk Management
4. Quality Assurance.

As it would be impossible to integrate the hundreds of projects into a single program or project management system for tracking detailed progress in such a short time-frame, these focus areas took on special significance. This would have required the use of trained personnel and resources, which simply did not exist. Such an effort would take, minimally, several months to accomplish and in itself jeopardize the successful completion of the transition process. The need for creating a new paradigm for program and project managing this mammoth undertaking was evident. Where organizations were still struggling to comprehend the impacts, it became clear that the transition team, supported by the project office, would need to take a leadership position in the planning and execution of the individual projects.

The project office focus would need to find ways to accomplish the more traditional detailed plan development, interdependency identification, and close monitoring and control without the resources or tools typically used. Skilled project management resources were also at a premium so creative thinking was required.

The analogy to a military shipping convoy emerged. In the navy convoy concept, all the ships must arrive at the destination safely at the same time. This is the mission. (Stragglers are torpedoed by hostile forces.) Only the lead or flag ship of the convoy has a general course and schedule for the convoy plotted (strategic approach). Typically, the individual ships do not have detailed plans when leaving but are part of a formation that changes direction and speed according to a number of factors. These factors include:

- Weather conditions (organizational, political forces)
- Speed of the slowest ship in the fleet (longest time to complete the journey, i.e.: critical path)
- Intelligence information about hostile forces (risk identification)
- Relationship of ships' positions to one another in the formation (inter-dependence)
- Protection of the convoy by the navy (risk management).

With this concept for managing the systems and processes' projects in place, it was possible to get comfortable with the idea that we did not have to have a detailed road map (course) in advance to get to the pre-determined result. What was necessary was a flexible system of leading the planning for projects at a high level (flag ship) and making sure that all the individual projects (convoy ships) were aware of the risk, organization factors, and direction of the convoy in real time (communications). The individual projects were under general constraints to remain in formation with the convoy or risk failure (interdependence). They would be assisted by the patrolling navy vessels (risk management) to get back into formation or be protected as much as possible (quality assurance). All projects were to share in the latest intelligence information and be on the lookout for anything jeopardizing their progress (risk identification).

With this paradigm in place, action plans were developed to provide support to the transition project teams in each of these four key areas. This allowed the individual teams be accountable for the more traditional project management planning at their level.

## From Paradigm to Practice

The first step was to understand the intermediate milestones and utilize them as high-level scope statements in and of themselves. There were three main intermediate milestones from September 20, 1995, to October 1, 1996. Each of these

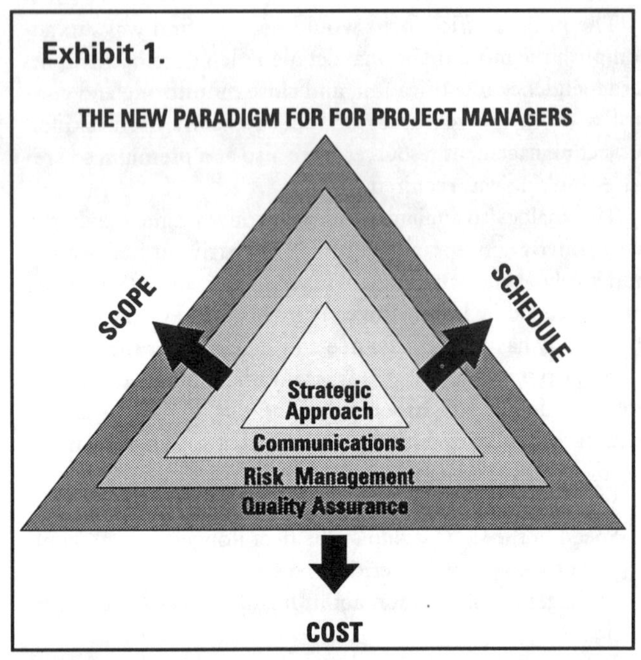
Exhibit 1.
THE NEW PARADIGM FOR FOR PROJECT MANAGERS
SCOPE
SCHEDULE
Strategic Approach
Communications
Risk Management
Quality Assurance
COST

milestones represented significant work to support the Initial Public Offering (IPO) of Lucent stock in the first quarter of 1996. They were also established to satisfy the regulatory, SEC, and IRS stipulations for the separation, to minimize shareholder financial exposure.

The transition work was organized into two major phases:

- Phase 1. All work to be completed in support of the IPO of Lucent Technologies Stock. February 1, 1996.
- Phase 2. All work post-February 1, 1996, in support of the final October 1, 1996 separation of the AT&T and Lucent.

As the February 1, 1996, milestone was a "logical" separation of AT&T and Lucent financial results, there were minimal systems and process impacts. The February 1 milestone work was principally an accounting infrastructure project. While this in no way minimizes the difficulty of achieving this milestone, it was not until after February 1 that the primary work of separating the AT&T financial systems and process applications and infrastructure became of paramount importance.

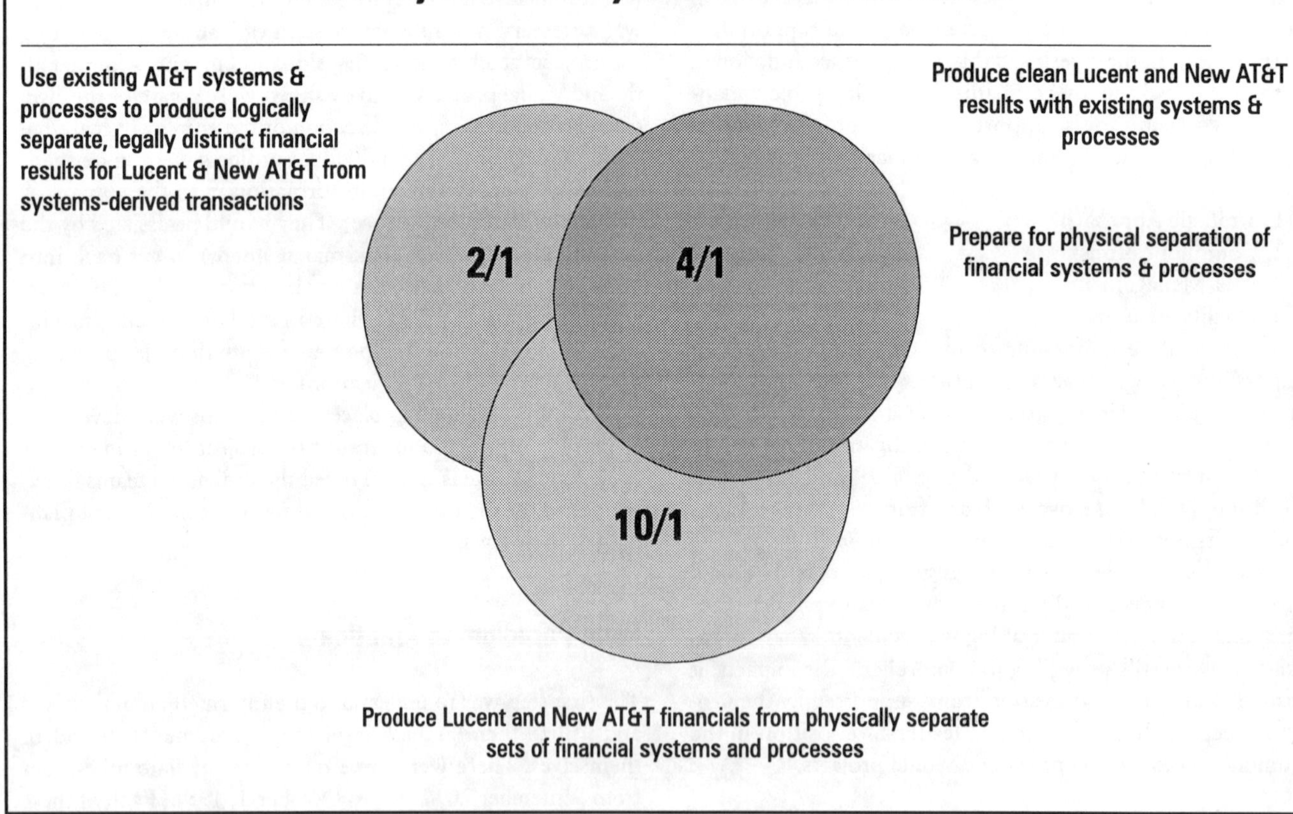
Exhibit 2.
AT&T / Lucent Separation
Three Major Financial Systems & Process Milestones
Use existing AT&T systems & processes to produce logically separate, legally distinct financial results for Lucent & New AT&T from systems-derived transactions
Produce clean Lucent and New AT&T results with existing systems & processes
Prepare for physical separation of financial systems & processes
2/1
4/1
10/1
Produce Lucent and New AT&T financials from physically separate sets of financial systems and processes

A special project team named the "Clone and Go" team was created. This team had total responsibility for the separation of all the corporate financial systems and infrastructure. The short interval from Feb. 1, 1996, to Oct. 1, 1996, meant that a lot of shortcuts were needed to move as quickly as possible from planning to implementation and completion of the systems and infrastructure work. A program level team was formed and work began to develop the project and team management infrastructure in the four critical focus areas.

1. Strategic Approach. A team project management infrastructure was developed to assure the following:
   - Project team roles and responsibilities clearly defined (captains)
   - Overall project plan development and integration (strategy, general course)
   - System interdependency matrix for impact assessments (convoy formation)
   - Change management process (course and speed changes)
   - Progress reporting processes (critical path management)
   - Issues management and tracking (weather conditions monitoring).
2. Communications. Plans were developed to keep all organizations abreast of critical information. Communications tools were developed to include the following:
   - Conducting regular team face to face meetings and conference calls (briefings, communiqués)
   - Employee web-site for project team information, plans, and status (convoy status)
   - Employee e-mail broadcast codes
   - Articles in employee publications
   - Hotline for trouble reporting (warning signals).
3. Risk Management. The process for identifying critical risks and mitigation and contingency planning was established. The risk management process included the following:
   - Implementation of a risk management support center (flag ship C.I.C. war room)
   - Development of an overall risk management process (navy escort patrols)
   - Identification of a risk management support team
   - Integration of the risk management process and project management (convoy management).
4. Quality Assurance. A quality assurance team was established to support the movement of the current AT&T applications into the new AT&T and Lucent structure by:
   - Providing guidelines in the development of system and infrastructure isolation and cloning test plans
   - Providing oversight of major milestones within the project. (quality gates)
   - Assure that all systems are addressed (scope assurance)
   - Aid in issue resolution (formation keeping, May Day support)
   - Develop system completion sign-off process (arrival confirmation).

As these plans were being formed it was also necessary to begin communicating with all affected organizations as quickly as possible. This was made extremely difficult due to the large number of systems (200plus) and the geographic disbursement of the teams.

The project team had a tiered structure with a program level team based in New Jersey and primary sub-team project managers positioned on-site with the applications and operational infrastructure support teams. This set-up permitted a constant project management presence both at a program and project team level. It also permitted the program level team to be mobile and establish a face-to-face presence with each sub-team as needed. In effect there was a virtual program office that could operate from any location with a high degree of effectiveness. This structure was a key success factor for the project. It fostered and facilitated communications both vertically and horizontally across the sub-projects and the program itself. It permitted the primary sub-teams, where the real work was taking place, to remain in-place and not lose time or efficiency. It was set up consciously to place the burdens of travel and efficiency on the project team leadership and not the sub-team project managers or members.

## Applying the New Paradigm

Now that the new project management model was in place, it was time to make it work in support of the stated mission. Would it really work? There would be no opportunity to test this process in advance. This approach would either succeed or fail completely. The team then moved to develop the project planning and monitoring specifics in each of the focus areas.

### Strategic Approach

The strategic approach to the project was determined at the start after it became clear that traditional system development methods would take too long. The approach centered on the concept of either cloning a system for Lucent Technologies or isolating it to one of the companies. This also resulted in a standard testing process as well as identification of the quality gates to measure progress. The goals of this approach were:

- Minimize the required people and IT resources

- Ensure that all applications are in place to support the Oct. 1, 1996, Lucent spin-off
- Allow each system and process owner to create her own schedule, identifying any critical interdependencies
- Standardize requirements for system production migration
- Standardize a certification process for data functionality.

In order to reduce the project life-cycle(s) the project team leadership defined the key planning elements for the overall project plans, and communicated the general planning and integration layout. This was done by having a small team of SME's that could represent the key planning and implementation elements required for any of the systems. It was the development of these standards that shortened planning times significantly for all the system teams and still provided the team(s) with a reasonable level of detail from a project monitoring and control perspective. These standards were project planning templates in both project scheduling software and spreadsheets. The individual project managers were free to use either template but there was a requirement that one be chosen. Project managers were expected to manage their plans and provide progress reporting on a weekly basis.

### Communications

A full spectrum of communications vehicles was utilized. The over-arching philosophy was to communicate everything as filtering might impair the individual projects. Proactive efforts were made to continuously identify any gaps in communication processes and quickly correct them. A cross-checking system was developed to identify what was being communicated and to whom.

### Risk Management

Risk management was handled in an entirely different manner than traditional methods. It was clear that there would be significant risks involved with this project as well as all the other post-Feb. 1, 1996, project work. A transition team risk management war room was established with representation from all the major projects to work issues. This risk management team reported directly to AT&T and Lucent senior management using a predefined process. If a project team issue was deemed to be a high-risk event, it was immediately placed on the overall risk management plan. Here it had the attention of senior management without the need for traditional escalation and jeopardy management processes. This integrated senior management support and decision-making with a daily view of the current risk landscape. a risk management support team composed of SME's in all the project areas and skilled in identifying potential risks was established. The end result was an environment where risk identification was effectively managed and supported. Items were placed into two general categories at any time—critical risk items and key watch items—and given a green/yellow/red status. All critical risk items required a mitigation/contingency plan and key watch items required a mitigation plan. All risk items had a senior management owner.

### Quality Assurance

Project quality assurance was focused on two principal areas:

1. Planning/implementation quality gates and standards
2. Testing validation, certification, and sign-off process.

A quality assurance team was formed as an independent functional team within the project team infrastructure. The program level team members were responsible to the QA team for the submission and review of all project and test plans. The QA team was responsible for reviewing all plans against the pre-determined standards of content and quality and to identify deficiencies. Program and project managers were responsible for correcting deficiencies or for brokering compromises. Program and project managers provided progress status to the QA team that consolidated overall QA program status reporting to senior management. The testing validation and certification process required the identification, in advance of the appropriate levels of management, who would certify that each quality gate was successfully completed. There were dual (AT&T/Lucent) pre-determined management levels/individuals identified for each system and infrastructure component. A sign-off process (forms) with signatures was required. These certification forms were legal documents holding both parties legally responsible for the validation and acceptance of the system or component. It must be noted that the goal was to complete a physical and legal separation of the systems and infrastructure between AT&T and Lucent Tech. Beyond Oct. 1, 1996, both companies were to be independent corporations. These processes were designed to protect both companies from regulatory or shareholder liability after separation.

## Paradigm for the Millennium

As we approach the next century and the new millennium, it is clear that project management professionals will be brought under increasing pressure to perform within more rigorous schedule, cost, and scope constraints. The pace of business is on an upward trend, and the resulting business decisions both small and large will need to be planned for and implemented within shorter time-frames. This increased pace will result in greater project uncertainty (risk) and severe consequences to business for failure to execute on projects effectively.

The project management paradigms for the next century will have their roots in the traditional methods but will more effectively integrate the use of strategic planning, communications, risk management, and quality assurance methods and tools. There will be an increased awareness that the project managers of tomorrow will need to possess even stronger leadership skills to effectively manage teams. The ability to manage in an environment of high stress and uncertainty will be a required skill set, along with a disposition to embrace and harness change as a positive force.

As we approach the next millennium and look back, we are seeing a parallel between the mature manufacturing technologies of the sixties and seventies and project management in the eighties and nineties. Just as the steel and automobile industries had to reinvent themselves and dismantle old paradigms to remain in business, we must look to embrace new ideas and build new paradigms for project management beyond the year 2000.

The breakup of AT&T and Lucent Technologies Inc. provided an example for the project environments of the future. New approaches and tools will be needed to manage in these environments. More and more frequently project managers will be asked to manage projects within fixed and aggressive schedules and with fewer resources and tools at their disposal. On large complex programs and projects, the luxuries of planning optimum resource balanced schedules and budgets will be diminished. In this type of project environment, the project manager will need to rely increasingly on the four focus areas presented in this model to achieve success. Planning and implementation will become concurrent activities in real time, requiring increased emphasis on communications and risk and quality management tools and techniques. The project management technologies of today will need to be developed to keep up with this pace of change, or risk being left behind as a quaint anachronism—anosther failed corporate trend of the eighties and nineties representing how things used to be done. The foundations as we know them today will still exist; however, project managers will have expanded their focus, range, and depth to include these new paradigms for success.

# A Matrix Approval Process for Labor Actuals

Chris Vandersluis, HMS Software

## Introduction

What is it that has otherwise well-organized companies implement two, three, or even more timekeeping systems at the same time? What would prompt otherwise rational people to support multiple entry of such a tedious chore?

Particularly in projectized organizations, the issue of time collection is a hot one. There have been many popular management structures over the years. Recently the notion of "matrix" organizations has been very popular. In a matrix organization, there are people who are responsible for work elements. These people call upon people who manage groups of resources. These resource managers are responsible for the appropriate availability level and skills of their group. Once work has been completed, resources are returned to the resource pool for reassignment or retraining.

Several years ago, the emphasis in most organizations was toward giving power to the resource managers. With a tighter economy and more focus on producing results, many organizations are now giving more power to those who manage the particular projects. The degree to which control is left with the work element managers is the degree to which we could say an organization is "projectized."

There is a movement throughout the world toward more project-oriented organizations, and the more project-oriented a company is, the more this timesheet issue seems to be a problem.

There is little disagreement about the basic layout of a timesheet: some kind of descriptive element along the left, the days listed across the top, hours entered in the cells below. Sounds simple. So why would anyone take issue with this kind of application?

There is an inherent conflict in implementing any timesheet system in a projectized environment, which is not immediately obvious. Over the next few pages, we'll reveal this conflict and propose a potential resolution to it.

## Getting Back to Basics

Why bother with a timesheet system at all? There are several good reasons to automate timekeeping:

- Eliminate errors.
  With manual timekeeping systems, the opportunity to introduce inaccurate data is enormous. Users can easily mistype information or simply not look up correct codes or not have the timesheet add up properly or simply enter work as "miscellaneous." All of this increases work downstream in the timekeeping process and adds work and heartache to everyone.
- Be fast.
  With data entered directly into an automated system, turning data into useful reports or transactional files for moving into other organizational systems becomes much easier and much faster. One of the biggest attractions of automating the timekeeping environment for project managers is access to labor actuals in a more timely fashion.
- Reduce workload.
  With an automated system, controls could conceivably be created to trap typographical errors and other inaccuracies in the timesheet while it is being completed. Also, there is no need to reenter manual time sheets into a computerized system. Finally, calculations, reports, and other time-consuming irritants.
- Ensure that all billing is done accurately and that hours are not lost.
  In any manual timekeeping system, it is difficult if not impossible to establish checks and balances to ensure that billing information is done completely and accurately. An automated system can provide reports that compare expected billings with actual billings and identify any unbilled hours for scrutiny by the billing department.
- Provide the "actual" element of variance reporting. Project-oriented systems often provide some type of variance report. This kind of report shows the actual progress to date against the original plan. While the planned progress is usually maintained in the project system, the actuals must come from somewhere. Automating the timekeeping environment provides the project system with the progressed element of the budget versus actual report.

## Matrix Organizations and the Problems They Bring

Needs of Project Managers: get the data in a timely fashion. It's not ok to wait until labor actuals have gone through the entire financial cycle. Data would return to the project control environment as much as six weeks late. By that time any value from variance reporting will be lost.

A matrix organization is set up in two dimensions. On one axis there is the organizational structure. This structure is

**Exhibit 1.** Organizational Approval

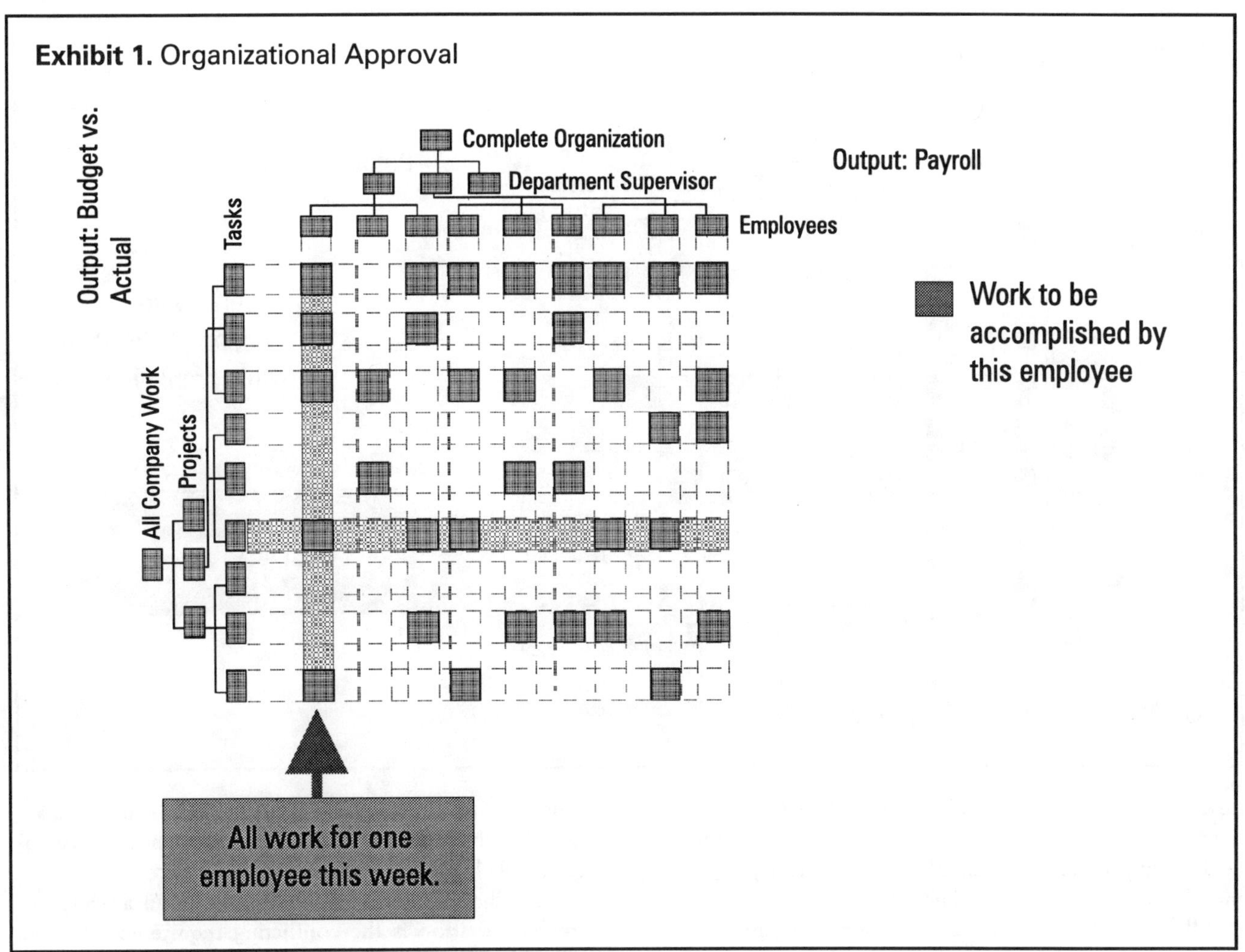


sometimes the traditional hierarchical structure of an organization with supervisors reporting to department heads who report to a more centralized authority. At other times it is a more autonomous resource manager structure where someone is responsible for the training and availability of a certain category of resource.

On the second axis is the work breakdown structure. This can be imagined as the top level being all work the organization does; the second level being perhaps a project level with one entry per project; and a third level being the tasks within that project. Obviously for more complicated projects, additional levels could be generated. This work will be managed by project managers who report to a more central authority and are responsible for the results of the project.

The matrix occurs when the project managers make requests of the resource managers for the resources required to accomplish the project. The project manager must contend with resources, which come from a variety of sources. The resource manager must contend with their resources being used (sometime simultaneously) on a variety of projects.

The problem with this environment is that the hierarchical or organization breakdown structure typically collects time for reasons of "time and attendance" for payroll purposes and sometimes for purposes of "time and billing" for either internal and/or external invoicing. The requirement for such a system is generally payroll-oriented. The requirements are usually quite simple. For salaried staff the only thing the payroll system requires is the number of days worked. If there was time not worked, the payroll system might also track such items as holidays, vacations, and paid or unpaid sick leave. For staff who are paid hourly, there is a further requirement for the number of hours worked and the rate at which work was performed, such as standard or overtime.

For better or worse, most timesheet systems in use today have been established by the finance department for time and attendance purposes.

If billing is also automated, then there is an additional requirement put on the timesheet environment. In this case the timesheet system may also be required to provide more

**Exhibit 2.** Project-Oriented Approval

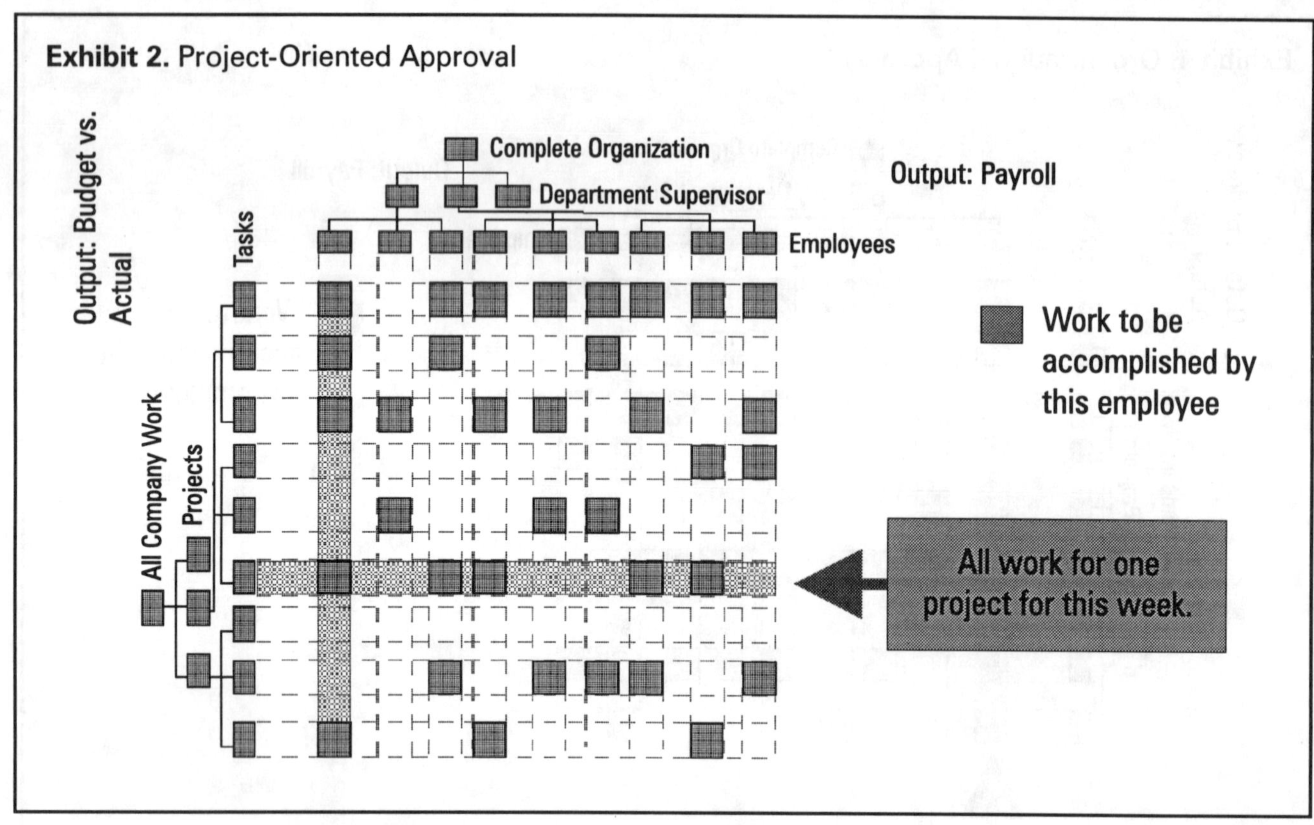


description to the invoice such as the project name being worked on and perhaps the category of work being done. Such billing is often done monthly and is often a part of the month-ending process by Finance.

All of these finance-oriented functions are generally historical in perspective. The furthest forward a financial system will look is the status date of currently collected data.

The authorization process for this level of functionality is from the employee to her supervisor, from there to the department level, then on to the payroll department.

Unfortunately for the project managers of the organization, their requirements for time collection are quite different. A project manager needs to know what hours have been spent on which tasks. This will enable them to produce a budget versus actual analysis and forms the basis of forward forecasting. The project manager also needs to know what progress has been made on a particular task or, more exactly, what the Estimate to Complete is.

The project manager has virtually no interest in which employee actually did the work, or how many hours a particular employee may have worked in the past week.

Unlike Finance, Project Management is future-oriented. The project manager's job is to consistently look for what is left to do. While the project is in progress, the oldest data of interest to the project manager is the current reporting period (e.g. the past week or past month).

The authorization for project data is done by task and aggregated to the project level. Each project manager must approve of all charges against the project for each period.

Yet another issue to further complicate an already unworkable situation is the conflicting requirement for the timeliness of the data.

Payroll must have the timekeeping data quickly in order to produce paycheques. Yet, returning timesheet data to other systems usually has to wait until the current financial cycle is complete. This often means that project managers often cannot see the timesheet data for as long as six weeks after it is spent. Why? For example: If an employee enters his timesheet on the first day of the month, it will not be summarized by Finance for redistribution to other systems until month's end. By the time the month is "closed," it could easily be the middle of the month following.

This is, of course absolutely unacceptable to Project Management. By the time this data can deliver a useful variance report, whatever opportunity existed to make an impact on the project has been lost. Most project managers need to know the actual labor costs within a few days of when they were spent, not a few weeks.

Exhibit 3. The Matrix Approval Process

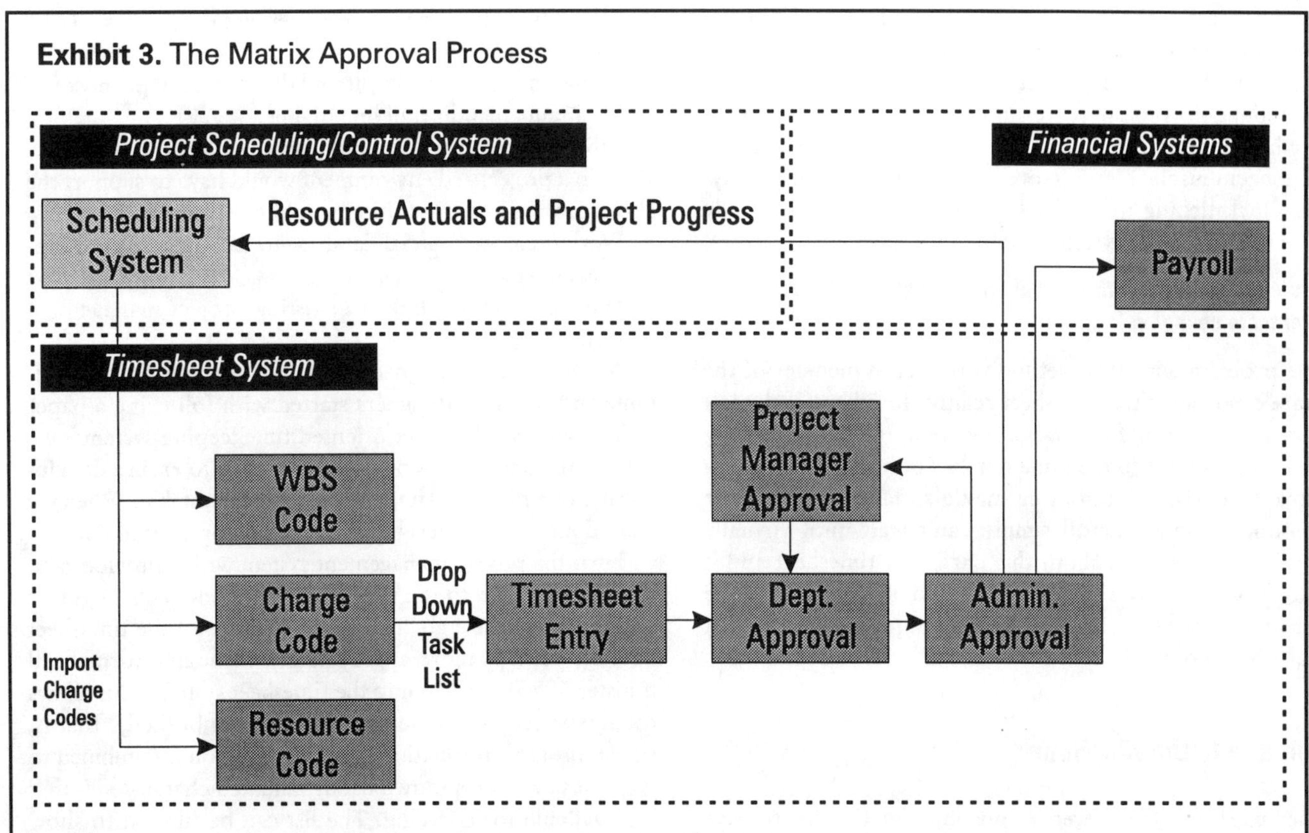


## How Organizations Try to Solve the Timekeeping Dilemma

So, how do matrix organizations deal with the inherent conflict in timesheet requirements? There are a number of approaches taken by different organizations; each has its difficulties.

### Create multiple timesheet systems

The most common response to handling the conflict is to have multiple timekeeping systems. This is never done by design but rather by desperation. Finance usually starts its own system first. Its system is well established by the time Project Management tries to make use of it. Obviously, with its own needs a priority, the Finance timekeeping system either does not have the functionality or does not have the timeliness required or both.

Project Management then creates a completely new timesheet system to "intercept" timesheet data before it is sent to Finance. This results in at least two completely detached timesheet systems. Worse, the systems are almost guaranteed not to reconcile. IF the project management organization is not fully integrated then it is entirely possible that more than one timesheet system will be created to service each project.

### Don't have a timesheet system

Some organizations handle the problem by simply giving up. It's too complicated a problem to solve and for some organizations, if they don't have an explainable solution, they simply won't implement any. Payroll has other methods of taking care of paycheques, particularly if most employees are salaried. Project managers simply do without budget versus actual reporting and variance reporting.

### Don't do activity-based-costing (It's too hard)

Another method of giving up is simply to abandon activity-based-costing as part of the organizational structure. Payroll continues with its own system but management of costs on projects is simply not done. A surprising number of project management environments simply do not include cost management. When asked, project managers say they want to do cost management but cannot get access to actual costs in a format or in time to make the useful.

### Create a customized time-sheet system which either:

#### *Bursts the timesheet into line-by-line approvals*

This solution sounds very elegant. Certainly as an automated feature, it is not complicated to program. Each line item on the timesheet probably lives as an individual record anyway. The problem with this method is that once it is burst apart and sent off to each project manager, the chances of re-assembling the timesheet are almost nil. Each project manager who deletes a line or changes a code means that the entire timesheet must be resent to everyone involved. With the payroll clock ticking in the background, users will ultimately have to by-pass the system simply to get paid.

#### *Routes the timesheet through everyone who might have an interest in changing It*

The problem with this method is that each member of the route can change the timesheet relative to others. If the last person on the route removes a line item, the timesheet may no longer add up to the same number of hours that the employee worked. This routing may also take an inordinate amount of time. Payroll simply can't wait until virtually everyone has agreed about this particular timesheet and it frankly doesn't care about the resolution of 90 percent of the debate. All they want to know is: Has the person worked that many hours or not?

## The Key to the Kingdom

They used to say that every impossible situation has to have a hidden solution somewhere, and happily, there is one here.

What allows us an escape from the matrix organization dilemma is that once the number of hours has been determined for payroll purposes, it is extremely rare that changes in the actual task performed is of interest to them!

This is by no means insignificant. If this is so, then we can break the authorization process into two steps. The first, and it seems the easiest, is to determine the number of hours worked by a particular employee and possibly the rate at which they were worked. Once this data is established and approved, the second phase would begin, allowing the project managers to change the descriptive elements of the timesheet while preventing them from changing the total number of hours worked.

While it seems simple, most automated timekeeping systems do not allow such a process. Because the distinction has never been made between the different requirements of the different parts of the organization, most timesheet systems simply allow that a timesheet is approved or not.

## Escaping the Matrix Trap

A process which escapes the "matrix trap" will have to do the following:

- Get data to the payroll department fast
- Allow project managers to alter data elements of the timesheet without altering totals and perhaps rates
- Maintain the originally entered data for audit purposes
- Maintain an audit trail line-by-line.

Any automated timekeeping system that would have to work in a projectized environment would have to support the above process and in addition would have to:

- Work on a commercial database to facilitate links to pre-existing systems
- Have pre-defined links to existing project management systems.

At HMS we've designed just such a process. Our consultants and software designers started with following a paper trail in successful project-oriented timekeeping systems. We kept to the basic tenets of systems analysis to ensure data integrity; one piece of data, one person accountable. When we were done, we had developed the following flow of data.

First, the project management system would provide valid charge code data to the timekeeping system. This might be accomplished through "real-time" lookups of the timesheet data or, perhaps more appropriately, through a formalized transfer of activity data into the timesheet system. This allows the timesheet data to be updated with "published," that is, stable, project information. This information is combined to create a simple drop-down list of validated charge codes that are available for charging. The list can be filtered to show only the charges that fit particular criteria for that employee, thus reducing further the possibility of invalid data.

Next, the timesheet information is entered by the employee or someone responsible for that employee's time.

Next, the employee releases that information to the person responsible for that employee's attendance. The first path of approvals for the timesheet is designed solely towards the financial system. This typically implies the organizational or departmental structure. Once the attendance has been approved, the timesheet data can now be "posted" to the financial systems. At this point, the number of hours worked in that week by each employee are frozen. This is the opportunity for the timekeeping administrator to ensure that no timesheets are missing and that all timesheets have been approved from the perspective of attendance.

Thus far, this is not much different than many financially oriented structures. What makes the HMS proposal different, however, is the next "loop" in the structure.

Once the data has been posted, it is now made available for reporting back to the project managers. Project managers are given a report by project and task for hours worked the week previous. Project managers are given a grace period during which they can institute changes if required. Should they find a charge to be altered, the project manager creates a debit/credit against any timesheet in existence. Like any debit/credit in a financial system, the debit/credit must equal a zero balance of hours. This functionality allows the project managers to remove hours from one charge code and put it onto a different charge code without altering the original timesheet. Debits and credits are added to the original timesheet while maintaining a complete audit of who entered what. The approvals for the debit/credit can follow any path required, even the original path of the timesheet if desired.

The payroll is unaffected as it has no interest anyway in which charge codes are used. If a billing system is in use, it can get the updated data at the same time as the project management system.

The project management system gets its information as soon as the organization wishes. The variable in such an environment is the amount of "grace period" allowed to the project managers to institute changes before data is posted to the project management environment.

One of the advantages of this kind of environment is its forgiving nature. If a project manager isn't ready or doesn't enter her changes, they can simply be entered after the fact. The data will then self-correct in the next project management update period.

## Alternative Methodologies

One of the counterpoints to this structure often comes from administrators who propose a sequential path of authorization or a burst-apart method. Let's take a moment to consider these alternatives.

### Sequential Authorization

Some administrators believe that if timesheets are sent in sequence from one project manager to another until all the project managers referenced on the timesheet have seen the data, this will allow for the timesheet to be approved and to end up in authorized format ready for both the finance and project groups. The problem with this plan is that each time the timesheet is altered, it must be returned to all project managers yet again for approval. Organizations that have attempted to implement this strategy find themselves with timesheets that are in a perpetual state of approval and never end up being posted to either system. Also, a project manager looking at such data in sequence will be tempted to simply delete charges which seem inappropriate regardless of what effect this may have on the total number of hours worked for the employee.

### Burst-Apart Authorization

With software technology being what it is, it is quite possible to create a software system where each line item of the timesheet is sent separately to the individual project manager responsible so he can authorize the charge. This at first glance seems quite attractive until it is put into practice. The software carefully "bursts-apart" the timesheet (similar to how old multi-page forms burst into sections) and sends it through electronic means for approval. Unfortunately, with the project managers all working independently, the timesheet never reassembles in recognizable format. Employees might suddenly find themselves having worked zero hours. For any employee working on more than one project at a time (as one would in a matrix environment), the chances of reassembling the timesheet to be consistent both with the attendance records and the project managers is close to nil.

## Conclusion

Times are tighter. In today's economy virtually every aspect of an organization must be as effective as possible.

There is no room anymore for duplicate effort in mission critical systems.

For anyone in a project-oriented organization looking to automate timekeeping, she'll need to consider the process of the data and the timeliness with which it arrives at the parties who require it.

Any project-oriented timekeeping process must deliver:

- Timely results to the people who need them
- A structure for approving the labor actuals in two directions:
  1. Organization oriented
  2. Project Oriented
- An ability for project managers to enter changes to the charge definitions without affecting the total number of hours worked by an employee
- An audit trail of entries and changes
- An ability to reconstruct or display originally entered data by the employee
- An ability to return the results to the systems that require them
- For software systems, this results in requirements for systems:
  1. to be based on a commercial database
  2. to have multiple levels of interface allowing for appropriate levels of interface for different types of users
  3. to allow valid charge codes to be pulled directly from a project management system
  4. to allow approvals for attendance to be distinct from approvals for valid charge codes.

# Kick-Starting Project Management for a $1.7B Transformation Program in Bell Canada

Catherine Daw, SPMgroup Ltd.
Suzanne Sills, Bell Canada

## Introduction

How do you take a large organization with a massive transformation program made up of over five hundred projects and keep them on track and lead them towards a successful conclusion? That was the challenge at Bell Canada, where after the first year and a half of a three-year business transformation program, it became clear that some projects were at risk in meeting their deliverables within the time and budget constraints established in 1995. This paper will cover the background leading up to the process of kick-starting the use of a more formal project management process, the unique solution selected, and why and how it was implemented. We will also cover the lessons learned throughout the assignment and where Bell Canada is heading with project management in the future.

## Background

The three-year business transformation (BT) program established at Bell has been one of the most ambitious programs of its kind in the telecommunications industry in terms of the scope and the narrow time-frame. It involved an investment of $1.7 billion dollars over the three years, with part of the investment to realize a net reduction of ten thousand employees out of approximately 45,000 in Bell's telecom operations.

By late 1994, there were very clear signs that Bell Canada had no choice but to change—radically and rapidly—in order to survive and thrive in the coming years. The triple whammy of technology surge, globalization, and consumer choice redrew the telecommunications business in Canada. Three years was the maximum time available to reposition the company within the marketplace.

A meeting of the Bell Canada Board of Directors took place March 27, 1995. This became the focal point for the announcement of the three-year transition plan to employees and the public. This announcement would be one of the most important in Bell's history. Here is how part of that day unfolded.

It began at 8 A.M. with a videoconference briefing from the CEO to executives in three cities—Montreal, Ottawa, and Toronto. During the morning, a call also went out to the CRTC (the Canadian telecommunications regulator) in Ottawa.

At noon, the board meeting began with the CEO and the four members of the senior executive team.

At 4 P.M. the four senior executives conducted teleconference calls to brief their middle management on what the CEO was going to tell employees in the next half hour.

At 4:30 P.M. the unions were formally informed of the news, shortly before the CEO went on the air live to all employees.

At 5 P.M., after the employees had been informed, a news release was issued to the media.

At 5:15 P.M. press conferences took place in Montreal, Ottawa, and Toronto via video conference.

Over the next few months the business transformation structure and governance were put in place. The first phase of "full potential diagnostics" identified eleven major processes for change, with 170 initiatives (programs) and over five hundred individual projects. The majority of projects were reengineering within a process and had high information technology (IT) content. High IT content meant high risk! This started to become painfully evident in 1996 as many projects passed to the development phase. Capers Jones' statement that "the first six factors associated with software disasters are specific failure in the project management domain" was about to be proven at Bell Canada.

The project managers assigned to the BT projects were competent telecommunications professionals, very knowledgeable in their business process. Most had previous experience managing projects within their area of knowledge. Program leaders and project managers were provided training in the Bell Project management methodology but with minimal or no training in project management skills. They were assigned to lead multi-million dollar projects. Bell had in effect asked their project teams to perform as a symphony orchestra when most of them were still learning the scale.

Once it was realized that there was a huge competency gap in project management, nailing down the solution was easy. Bell *did not* have time to develop the skills internally. They *did not* want to demoralize a lot of people who were working very hard by parachuting in contract project managers. They *did* want to leave a legacy of project



PROJECT MANAGEMENT INSTITUTE 28th Annual Seminars & Symposium
Chicago, Illinois: Papers Presented September 29 to October 1, 1997

management expertise behind when BT finished. They also recognized that internal core project management competency and expertise would be critical to their ongoing success. Two solutions resulted: short term—contract coaching and facilitation by seasoned project management professionals, and long term—build core competencies internally.

## Solution

For the short term, (BT) senior project management facilitator/coaches were provided through two "broker firms." Bell was looking for a unique set of skills: extensive experience in facilitation, team building, risk management, negotiation, communications, quality management, coaching, overall project management process support, *and* information system development experience.

Bell had two methodologies that the BT project teams were expected to follow. The first one, integrated project management process (IPMP), documented the methods for managing projects including project phases, gates, and governance. The second, information systems development guide (ISDG), documented the systems activities and deliverables required for each IPMP phase. The shortcomings that surfaced during BT with these methodologies were predominantly in two areas: *adherence* and *thoroughness*. Teams were not adhering to the requirements specified in IPMP and ISDG. This was as a result of tight time-frames and because the rigour that should have been applied at "gate reviews" was not enforced. The thoroughness that was lacking was in areas of project controls, monitoring, risk management, tools, and communications.

A pool of twenty facilitators/coaches was selected through the two "broker firms" using a two-step screening process. Project administrators were also selected with proficiency in MS Project to provide support during the project planning process as well as assist new Bell project administrators as they were assigned to a project. Orientation sessions were held with all consultants to prepare them for the Bell environment, the short-term processes that were being established, and the facilitation/coaching role.

Most of the projects had team members in five key regional areas: Toronto, Ottawa, London, Montreal, and Quebec City. This in itself provided unique challenges in planning and managing projects. Suzanne was responsible for the overall project management team and also for all projects originating in Ontario. She also recruited an internal resource in Montreal who had some project management experience and was fluent in French. This person was responsible for supporting and providing facilitators to projects originating in the Quebec region.

## Implementation

There was an urgency to getting these projects back in alignment as quickly as possible. Many of the projects had large project teams and budgets that were potentially in jeopardy. Time was of the essence. There was a need for these projects to complete by the end of 1997 in order to realize the benefits (estimated at $1.7 billion) and meet their workforce reduction targets. With that in mind, an assessment process was developed and executed to identify "at risk" projects. Teams were not "forced" into using the project management assistance—the potential for counterproductive resistance was too high. Instead, the teams were "sold" on the positive outcomes for their project. The intensity of the "sales" effort decreased proportionately to the degree of difficulty with which the project was faced. Soon assistance was actively sought rather than sold as early successes of other projects became known.

For each candidate project, a more formal assessment and preliminary review was conducted by the assigned PM facilitator with the Bell PM prior to beginning the facilitated planning sessions with the project team. This involved a review of existing project plans, identifying key team members to be involved in the planning, and determining major issues and concerns to be addressed. (Many typical issues involved scope management, project ownership, and team building.) They also developed an overall planning approach that would work for the particular team and project. The focus was very much on working as a coach to the project manager and not taking over the management of either the project or the process. Commitment and buy-in to the process were identified as critical success factors.

Planning sessions were organized with key members of the project team as identified by the Bell project manager. Usually, a limited time of three to four days was set up because these projects were under way at the same time that the planning sessions were being conducted. There was a certain amount of sensitivity to being taken away from the critical activities of "doing the work" rather than "planning the work." Although many of the project teams were only meeting on a part-time basis, the planning period generally spanned three to six weeks in duration.

The initial planning session was introduced by the lead consultant (one of the senior facilitators was selected to oversee the process and provide support and guidance to all of the facilitators), using standard presentation material. During the session the project team was walked through the process and set the stage for the planning exercise. The facilitator needed to maintain high energy and the focus of the team. Well-organized agendas, planning components, and use of templates made the sessions very effective. Suzanne's team, with facilitator input, had established a work breakdown structure (WBS) template based on the IPMP and ISDG. The template provided a base while allowing for change to accommodate the uniqueness of each particular project. A wide range of approaches and techniques to completing the planning were employed. These included short duration sessions spread over time; long, intense sessions over a short-time span; and dividing the planning into work teams and having them work in their own work environments and reconvene as the full team for reviews. The use of external project administrators allowed the planning team to see the results of its plans immediately. Plotting of project work plans was run overnight and put up on the wall for the team to view the next day. Facilitators were to ensure process while the project team focused on content. Project plans ranged in size from five hundred to over three thousand activities for a total project life of six to eighteen months. At the height of the assistance being provided, twenty-one projects were receiving facilitation and coaching support.

We learned a lot as projects were brought into the planning and coaching process. From our first five project teams we learned the following facts, and these facts held true for all of the subsequent teams:

- Dates and milestones were established to meet financial realities before the full extent of the work was known.
- Project plans were built working backward from the dates making it impossible for the teams to know what was a realistic date.
- Project plans were mostly just task lists. The critical path (if there was one) was forced.
- Task durations were generally too long (one to three months).
- No one was actually "working the plan."
- There was no agreement on scope well into the project
- The business people put unreasonable pressure on the systems people to reduce time/costs without fully understanding the consequences.

In summary, the project teams felt constrained by the dates, which made it difficult for them to identify other options. The planning process became even more important in ensuring project and overall BT success.

As projects went through the planning process and back out to the field for implementation, word spread about the use of professional PM facilitators and its benefits. We gained momentum and support throughout the organization not only in the lower ranks but up through to senior executives.

## Case Study of One Project

Catherine was assigned in mid-September to one of the large mission critical projects that was to provide a replacement to a legacy system for a foundation database to the full Bell Canada network. The project had over 120 people assigned full time, consisted of five major sub-releases to be introduced over a one year period, and had a budget over $25 million. The team was made up predominantly of members from Bell Sygma (Bell Canada's internal provider of technology services and development). The project manager recognized the need for a fully integrated plan that would include both Bell Canada's and Bell Sygma's work. The scope of the project had never been clearly defined or fully approved. Two initial releases had been implemented with unstable software to meet a shortened implementation date and had not been signed off by the business owners of the product. In addition, implementation of major components of the product was constrained by an overall release management process under control of another group.

The team had project fatigue, and there was a great deal of reluctance by many team members (and their functional managers) to participate in the planning process. The project manager, however, had struggled to manage the project with separate plans and task lists that were not getting the job done. He recognized that they had to do something different and it had to be drastic. He enthusiastically embraced the support offered to provide a project management facilitator and a structured planning process.

The initial three days of planning were spent on establishing the project scope, constraints, and project objectives and determining assumptions and project organization. Project organization and structure proved to be not only one of the most contentious issues but the major and ongoing stumbling block during the planning exercise and its subsequent implementation. Exhibit 1 shows the organizational structure as it existed and the proposed project structure. There were many issues at play in terms of roles that various people saw for themselves. This resulted in confused project objectives and insufficient management support for the formal project management planning and its benefits to a project at risk. Slowly over time this changed as the project manager and team extolled the benefits of the project planning and the focus it provided to the team for getting the job done. It also became a learning experience for senior management to have a detailed plan put before them in which it was difficult to poke holes.

After the first two weeks of planning, a "plan for the plan" charter and schedule were established to complete the project planning for three sub-releases. This was presented

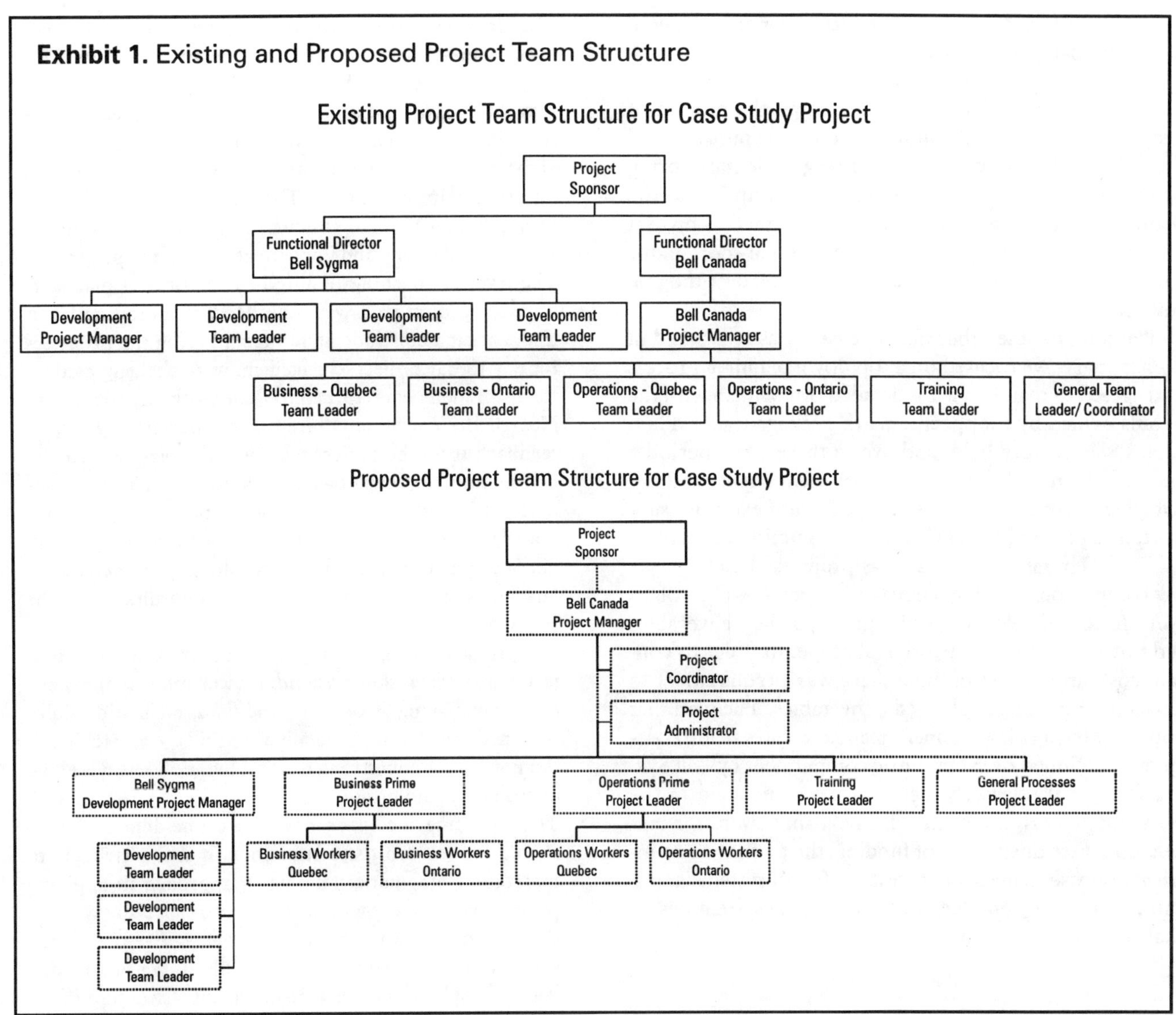

**Exhibit 1.** Existing and Proposed Project Team Structure

to senior management from both Bell and Bell Sygma to gain support and approval. Although it received support, in reality the approval was not adhered to by all the participants. After six weeks we agreed to take a hiatus from planning and begin the implementation process using the plan as far as it had been completed. This also allowed the Bell Sygma team members to work on completing a major deliverable that was date sensitive.

The six-week period had provided time for the team to work on a part-time basis on planning while they also continued with their current task responsibilities. There was a great deal of stress on the team due to existing project dates and severe resource shortages. We learned that the best process was short, effective planning sessions with specific team members to minimize time away from the actual "doing." Over the initial six weeks we accomplished the following:

- a project charter and scoping document
- a WBS based on the standard template with modifications for the project; it was release-focused and deliverable-driven
- two sub-releases merged into one release due to the high number of dependencies and sharing of resources; an initial high-level plan for this combined release
- use of a high-level plan (based on top down planning) allowing key project leaders to plan and manage the detail for their responsibility areas
- a project plan for existing sub-releases, which had already been implemented. These sub-releases were in a constant "fix" mode due to poor implementation and deliverable management. This strategy allowed these fixes to existing production software to be treated as an actual project with

its own plan with clear deliverables, acceptance criteria, and formal quality management.

The project plan for already implemented releases was kicked off in early November and began the process of project monitoring and controls. An outside project coordinator was hired by the Bell PM to get the monitoring process quickly in place with minimal disruption to the team. An internal team member was assigned as project coordinator and was coached by the external coordinator for a period of three months before she took over the role full time.

Planning for the other major release was reinitiated in mid-January. We focused on a top down planning process and agreed to maintain a less detailed overall plan with the details owned by the specific work package leader. Planning sessions were held, and over a three-week period a fully integrated plan with all major components and deliverables were created. This received senior executive support, and plan implementation began in mid-February.

Since February the project has progressed and is nearing completion of the two outstanding releases. The plans were followed relatively well, although the deliverables did not always match the original scope. In order to contain costs and deliver on time there was a requirement to de-scope some of the planned deliverables. The plan that had included a risk assessment made the dates realistic despite a continued over-optimistic commitment by Bell Sygma. The final release, which was never included in the planning process, was canceled. The main reasons for cancellation were due to lack of funding, the tie-in with an intricate release management strategy for all systems applications, and the complexity of the original system design that required streamlining.

## Lessons Learned

As more projects were brought into the process, numerous lessons emerged in terms of the planning and subsequent coaching of plan implementation. Lessons, issues, and process for planning were shared amongst the facilitators as a continuous improvement process. This was done both through status reporting to Suzanne's team and regular bi-weekly conference calls (after all we were working for a telecommunications company) with the facilitators wherever we were. Key lessons included:

- Managing the team's expectations of the planning process was crucial. Team members needed to understand that frustration, "surprises," and recycling were a normal part of planning. Planning is hard work, and more effort spent in planning would improve their success factor.
- The teams were often structured along traditional, functional lines rather than from a project perspective. This made reporting and identifying roles and responsibilities very difficult for the project manager. Project team structure was also challenged by the geography, cross functional members, and two organizations (Bell Canada and Bell Sygma) playing equal roles. The understanding and use of project organizational structure played a key role in the successful planning and implementation of the projects.
- The level of coaching required by the project managers once the project plan was complete was more significant than anticipated. Understanding and using the processes for day-to-day project management were challenging once the team members returned to their work environments.
- Not all the consultants hired were successful. Initially, feedback from the project team was the biggest factor in determining the consultant's effectiveness. This was a mistake. The team was too dependent on the consultant's knowledge and could not judge or even question the value. Subsequently, the senior consultant or a member of Suzanne's team accompanied all new consultants for the first few days.
- The primary hiring criteria for consultants were *first,* project management skills; *second,* proven and recent experience in managing IT projects; and *third,* facilitation skills. It turned out that if the facilitation skills were lacking, it did not matter how strong the first two skill sets were; the consultant could not succeed.
- There is a fine line between what *must* be done and what *should* be done in these situations. It was a struggle to maintain a pragmatic, minimalist approach in applying project management with novice teams especially without the supporting infrastructure in place. Even with the short-term process that was established, we had to pull back on some of the initial requirements (structure of the WBS, post-planning review, and uninterrupted planning). In many areas the consultants' desire to "do it right" often had to give way to "getting it done."
- Some of the BT projects would not have been approved had there been the proper project planning in the first phase of the project. Knowing the true cost of development and implementation could have resulted in a non-viable business case from a financial perspective.

## Where We Are Today

The good news . . . the business transformation initiative has been the major contributor to Bell's turnaround. It has helped to improve Bell's cost structure and restore the company's financial strength. Bell Canada today is a much more competitive company and is much better positioned for the new global marketplace. Of the original 170 initiatives, most are complete. By the end of 1997, the company expects to achieve a minimum of $1.3 billion in total BT benefits. It is very pleased with steady improvement that has been seen in its corporate performance as it moves through this unprecedented transformation. An additional and real benefit of BT is the major role it has played in forcing the cultural change within Bell Canada.

In terms of project management, Bell has initiated the long-term solution to embrace the need for professional project management. There is a project currently under way to establish PM standards corporate-wide, identify and develop core competencies, implement a standard tool set, and augment existing methodology.

Bell Canada has also become a corporate member of PMI and encourages employees to join and participate in the certification program, all positive steps to not only kick-starting such an ambitious program of change, but for future endeavours as they continue to meet the challenges and forces of the new telecommunications marketplace.

# Communications and Information Technology as a Competitive Weapon in Project Management

José Angelo Santos do Valle, PROMON Eng. Ltd

## Summary

The development of communications and information technology (C-IT) tools establishes a very important link among business strategies, project management, product-engineering, and systems architecture. This paper presents the C-IT tools that really increase the effectiveness of project management processes, a history of their evolution, future trends, and the related groupware procedures for fully integrated planning as a key of success for project management professionals.

## Introduction

The globalization of the economy brings to the market new partners and competitors with new concepts, methods, technologies, and products. Architects and engineers design buildings, industry facilities, and infra-structure using the latest techniques, energy-saving conservation processes, safety, and electronic gadgets to make sure their projects attain their client's objectives. Managers must use the same approach when delivering new technology solutions to generate competitive advantage in project management.

The market is rapidly changing and demands that companies reduce prices, accelerate operations, and increase quality. The response of the companies comes by reducing the number of hierarchical levels and lateral expansion of responsibilities with the professionals executing tasks, not functions. In a constant review of strategies, tactics, and operational processes, the development of communications and information technology (C-IT) establishes a very important link among business strategies, project management processes, product-engineering, and systems architecture. It is essential to build C-IT systems, tailored according to business objectives, in order to support the continuously changing landscape of the project management processes.

The impact of the fantastic evolution of communications in the decision-making process can be easily observed and will grow faster. The project manager can make a decision in minutes by joining several experts, consultants, and engineers, miles and miles away, through a video-conference meeting. The collaborative work and the on-line sharing of management and technical documents is allowed by the new functions of the computer in a C-IT architecture/network. The computer is not only a machine to perform calculations and text/data editing. It is a real machine of communication and collaborative work.

The goal of this paper is to present the C-IT tools, which really increase the effectiveness of project management processes related with the role of the project management company (PMC) in adding value to the chain of suppliers, designers, contractors, and partners in general. The information is a fundamental support for the humanity, such as energy and matter, according to Fritz Machlup, an Austrian economist who wrote in 1962 that the generation, processing, delivery, and updating of information is a factor of production. The information systems add value to the management processes. As an example, the database can be so valuable that it becomes sometimes a product of the company.

The main C-IT tools for project management, described in this paper, are:

- Electronic Mail (voice mail)/Video Conference
- Document Sharing/Workflow
- EDMS (Enterprise Document Management System)
- Client/Server corporate networks: Intranet—Internet
- Corporate Information System
- EIS (Executive Information System).

## Evolution of C-IT Methods

The evolution of the technical documents, from paper to digital, replaced the concept of the original/copy since all printouts are originals. The use of the MODEM/FAX board of personal computers to deliver digital files to the partner/client in order to receive comments or approval, rather than in paper or in floppy disks, is more productive, since all partners can edit the text or spreadsheet and send it back to the other partner. The electronic mail technology through the Internet makes this process easier because the digital files can be delivered as attachments to the electronic messages. Now, for security purposes, FTP (file transfer protocol) servers are used for this delivery. The people in charge of the document deal with the electronic file and not with printouts that become obsolete in minutes. However, inside the companies, the delivery of printed texts/spreadsheet, and even the delivery of digital files, is replaced by the sharing of this digital file in a client/server architecture network, accessed by people involved in the preparation, comments, and approval of the documents. Now, modern technologies for document management and control monitor the workflow in the company and partners. The different methods for delivering of information have been replaced by no delivery, but sharing the information.

The evolution of the meeting processes is clear. The invitation and agreement is faster through the e-mail. The displacement of the persons is significantly reduced through videoconference. Now, the decision-making process is faster and more effective because the manager can join more consultants or additional partners who can deliver more information to make better and faster decisions. Two years ago, the Internet was considered a tool used only to search information. Now, it is recognized as a technology to improve productivity, and the combination of Internet and intranet is changing the way companies deal with suppliers and partners.

## Groupware

The management activities consist basically of dealing with human resources. The processes related to these activities need the integration of many C-IT tools. This is named groupware. The main groupware functions are document sharing, electronic mail, video-conference, workflow, and so on. The environment of these functions are corporate networks LAN-WAN, intranet, Internet, and so forth. Today, the concept of *software* and *hardware* is fully consolidated. It may be difficult to state immediately a definition of these two words, but almost everyone knows what they mean. Nevertheless, we should develop the concept of *groupware*. Groupware is the appropriate use of a set of C-IT tools, related to the sharing of information among people. Professionals work in teams. The core of project management activities is to manage human resources arranged in teams, which need to communicate, share, and transfer documents. The exact definition is not important. The use of other names, such as teamwork, workgroup, peopleware, CSCW (computer-supported collaborative work), and CE (concurrent engineering), is not important but the concept and the use of groupware is a key to obtaining success in project management activities.

### Document Sharing

The collaborative work requires interactive analysis and knowledge sharing. A report requested by a client is valuable when it was shared in its preparation with other users to gain their insight and ideas. The recipients should be able to continue the analysis initiated by the original author. In this way, the analysis process becomes an interactive exchange. Many users can pursue different analysis paths from a common starting point. To meet the challenge of providing interactive analysis, users must have access and be able to change the logic used to create the report. On this level, a server-based file management system is required to support user collaboration. Rather than send a text or a spreadsheet, the people involved in its preparation can share it, along with all the phases such as preparation, comments, approval, and issue.

### Electronic Mail

The e-mail is a combination of telephone, telex, fax, and mail functions, yet more convenient and faster. Some benefits of the e-mail are financial because of the reductions of cost due to international phone calls. The project manager can enlarge his network, worldwide, more effectively and less costly. Most times, the immediate interaction with the recipient, such as in phone calls, is not necessary; it involves just requiring or sending information. In these cases, the time reduction is relevant by avoiding the failure of the telephone calls. Other important features are the possibility to send digital files as attachments to the message, send the message to groups of people, reply and forward functions, and keep track of messaging such as the written statement of a phone contact. The possibility to interchange text data to mail through cut and paste increases the productivity. The e-mail text editing style is more convenient and less formal than old letters.

The e-mail is considered the most used function in the intranet/Internet. One of the common complaints about e-mail and even voice-mail is that the mail box fills up faster than a user has time to isolate and address the really important issues. Research institutions are developing intelligent agents to help the users deal with hundreds of mail messages and information daily. These agents will act as electronic personal assistants that can change the priority or forwar automatically the message to others, based on the subject, or delete some messages from specific people, temporarily. In the future, messages will comprise multimedia features, such as data, voice, and images combined through objects by applications named applets. The recipient can open and see texts and spreadsheets attached to messages without the computer application program that was used to generate the text or spreadsheet.

### Video-Conference

The video-conference associated with some telephone link or hands-free functions to support meetings and other electronic gadgets, such as data-show, allow the project manager to join partners and experts everywhere with a relevant reduction in cost due to travel and time. An important feature of video-conferences is the possibility to show papers, photos, or drawings through a specific camera with zoom capabilities. The discussion is more effective by switching the cameras showing people and papers with visual information.

### Workflow

The information is in the core of the communication. The enterprise communication of information is based on documents, digital (electronic) or paper. The workflow is the appropriate, planned, and controlled flow of electronic documents in different phases, such as preparation, review, approval, and issuing. The document flow is related to a document planning that was never done in the companies. All the paths of each document are foreseen. This technique is related to the technology EDMS hereinafter described and comprises the digitalization of documents produced in paper, with cost reduction in storage, more effective document retrieval, more productive access and view of documents, and finally, more quality. In the traditional methods, the documents were sent from one person to another in paper with some delays in some destinies. When the document is digital, it gains the capability of being distributed instantaneously as well as being shared among teams, through corporate networks, and intranet/Internet herein described.

### EDMS—Enterprise Document Management System

The EDMS technology comprises the complete control of digital documents in the paperless-storage company, digitalization of documents received in paper through a scanner, and definition of the workflow. The plot/printouts are used only to view the documents. Bigger computer screens allow more windows open at the same time with less printouts. The main groupware function, related to this technology, is the sharing of texts, spreadsheets, and schedule data by the professionals involved in design, manufacturing, constructions, tests, and so on. The EDMS is related to the new enterprise retrieval, access, and distribution process. For instance, it outgrows the traditional manual and microfilm techniques for storing and retrieving documents. Major documents are already produced in digital files. The ones produced in paper are digitized by the scanner. Similarly, the creation, updating, and delivery of maintenance manuals, for instance, is easier with the proper workflow associated with EDMS. The major characteristic is the sharing of the document among the professionals in charge of the preparation, comments, approval, and issuing.

The "red-line" function allows comments on documents. Specific software is combined to complete the production cycle with relevant gains in time, quality, and generating track information for project managers. Personally, it makes it easy to deal with financial records, business correspondence, business files, schedules, specifications, budgets, and meeting notes through file management functions, with cabinets and folders arranged as directories and sub-directories. In the highly complex world of large-scale projects, quick and ease access to key documents is fundamental. Complex projects have thousands of documents. Document management is a challenge for a worldwide project management company, hereinafter mentioned as PMC. A key element of successfully performing projects is the timely and accurate management of documents.

All project correspondence is also coordinated through a proper workflow. A PMC will implement this activity involving clients, the PMC itself, and all other partners. Design changes and other project changes are top priority requirements for identification, transmission, and notification to all the involved contractors and suppliers. Because it is crucial to quickly transmit changes to the project groups involved, a PMC uses both document management system and electronic data interfaces (EDI—Electronic Data Interchange) to effectively link these groups. EDI is a computer-to-computer exchange of inter-company business documents in a public standard format. It bridges the gap between different project locations with different computers. EDI combines translation, storage, and transmission services, providing paperless transactions between different companies.

### Networks—Intranet/Internet

In the world connected through networks, the information is available anywhere at the precise moment it is needed. People can share updated information wherever they are. They do not need to leave the office to look around at clients or competitors, to search new market patterns, and to get comments about their action plans. The concept of network is clear to the professionals as the way they are joined into teams. It is associated with hardware and software, important features of C-IT tools described here. It is observed in the fusion of functions in corporate networks with intranet and Internet, named extranet. They are viewed here, in the perspective of the project manager.

#### Client-Server Corporate Networks

The main support for groupware functions is the client/server network architecture. It allows more effective integrated planning with single data entry and on-line and real-time information about the project activities and documents stored in a corporate database in single data entry mode, avoiding repetition and mistakes. In this architecture, the servers are computers of big capacity to store and deliver information, such as fax servers, internet servers, data servers, and so on, joined with other smaller computers, the clients, and where the people deal with the information. The gain in productivity and quality is obtained by entering information just once and by only one person, reducing effort, errors, and data superposition.

In this environment, the computer programs, which run in multi-user mode, deliver more productivity gains in the management processes. The multi-user management programs by CPM networks allow the people involved in project management, technical supervisors and engineers, to update information and perform resource leveling, progress control, financial analysis, and what-if scenarios, with more integration. The information is collected, stored, processed, summarized, and viewed by the professionals in different levels of summarization, according to profile and criteria of access previously defined with productivity and quality gains, by avoiding printed reports, which become obsolete a few minutes after they are printed. For instance, the travel expenses report is filled and approved on-line with the appropriate codes, which generate information automatically for the accounting department and payment orders to travel agencies.

## Intranet

The intranet is a network inside a company that links the company's people and information, so that makes people more productive, information more accessible, and navigation possible through all the resources and applications, such as databased research and product development, sales and marketing, human resources, and financial transactions. The main services provided by the intranet are information sharing, workflow management, directories of people and things, groupware, e-mail, communication and collaboration, navigation, full-text indexing/searching, database/application access, and real-time audio/video communication. Some applications flow out of the intranet's services, others are custom developed by each enterprise, and still others are provided by commercial software vendors.

The wide range of applications address business needs, such as the following:

- The sales force needs up-to-date information about the products and services, and it needs a system that allows orders to be taken and tracked from the road.
- Members of a project team, which may be distributed across territories and time zones, need a way to communicate and share information so they can work together more efficiently.
- Information sharing across project teams avoids overlap and incongruities.
- The technical support staff needs a way to track customers and their problems, ensuring successful resolution of each reported problem and providing a way for customers to "help themselves" resolve basic problems.
- New employees need a way to find information on company procedures, organization, and benefits as soon as they come on board.
- The marketing staff needs a way to access, through a consistent interface from any desktop, all the customer and market research databases the company maintains.

The intranet is more likely to be a newspaper than a book. The information in the server is updated at faster rates and less costly, rather than revisions in the old paper corporate manuals. The main benefit of the intranet is that enterprise programs, technical, and/or management programs can be immediately accessed by users anywhere on the intranet. The development and implementation are much faster and the cost savings over the old desktop-centric models are significant. Further, users do not need extensive training. The applications run in familiar interface with known rules: just point and click the mouse.

## Internet

Web technology is the most significant technological advance in human communication since the printing press. Customizable news is one of the fastest growing services available on the Internet. The World Wide Web (WWW) will reduce our dependence on mechanical output devices such as plotters, microfilm printers, and physical document delivery services. Here are the main economic benefits of web technology:

- It enables data to be kept current. Printed documents and microfilms go out of date. Web sites can be updated each time a product or component is revised without destroying a costly inventory of printed documents or films.
- Workers can retrieve information as they need it, automatically, without asking other workers to send a document or answer a question. This automation saves time—no waiting for people to call back—and it saves labor.
- Web technology also reduces costs associated with making and distributing physical documents. However, part of this savings is offset if people make copies of these documents on local printers to read, mark up, or carry to the factory floor.
- Web technology gives workers a common tool for retrieving data from a variety of computer types.

It lets engineers retrieve product information, software updates, and background data on suppliers. It also lets workers download engineering software updates, bug-fixes, libraries, drivers, and so on.

- Web sites are a low-cost way to distribute product information to potential customers.
- A web site can enable suppliers to download the product data they need for making components and subsystems such as three-D CAD models, equipment data, and specifications.

The world wide web is based on the Internet, a collection of private and government data communications networks connected to each other. The Internet relies on the same TCP/IP (Transmission Control Protocol/Internet Protocol) used in most local-area networks (LANs). Hence, electronic messages can be transmitted to any part of the worldwide Internet with the same software used on LANs. What differentiates the World Wide Web from ordinary electronic mail is the "hypertext transfer protocol" (http). This protocol enables text and graphics to be transmitted between different brands of computers using a common language, the "hypertext markup language" (HTML). Like other markup languages, HTML consists of ASCII characters combined with codes that define type sizes and properties of the text on the screen.

### Intranet Combined with Internet (Extranet)

Intranets can be used in combination with Internet, allowing a number of ways to improve communications and reduce manufacturing errors. These might include:

- Setting up a site for all engineering drawings. Such a site will enable manufacturing people to look at the latest revision of a drawing without a trip to the print crib or a microfilm file.
- Building data sites for each product-development project. The sites can include project specifications, drawings for review, screen shots of product concepts, results of structural analyses, and three-D CAD models available for downloading, viewing, and redlining.
- Distributing approved CAD models, workers can then download models for modification or to use as the basis for new designs.
- Distributing mechanical component libraries. Approved valves, fasteners, bearings, controllers, tools, work-holding fixtures, and much more can be made available on the site.

## Corporate Informantion System/EIS (Executive Information System)

The information management and control performed through server-based corporate information systems have a vital role to play in the decision-making processes when related to administration, engineering, financial, and marketing characters. These systems run on local area networks (LAN), or intranets, the most integrated as possible, with information like:

- Internal address list (human resources information)
- Clients/partners/suppliers information
- Internal electronic mail
- Purchasing orders and product information
- Tickets/hotel reservation/reporting
- Personal/corporate digital files/workflow
- Internal/external news
- Internal/external standards/patterns/rules
- Operational guidelines
- Automatic forms submittal/approval
- Database information
- Shared decisions
- Financial management and control.

Intensive administration, engineering, management, and marketing programs are more effective if supported by database tools. The selection of valuable information in huge databases is named datamining. These databases are called datawarehouses and they are part of an important function of research in millions of data. This represents a greater knowledge about the business environment.

The Internet may help the data acquisition through well-defined corporate home pages, with the following features:

- Market researches
- Purchase orders
- External e-mail
- Information to public
- Information from public
- Corporate image.

The intranet, extended to clients, partners, and suppliers, through remote access to the corporate network, allows more features:

- Delivery track
- After-sell assistance
- Support to clients
- Guidelines to partners
- Specification to suppliers
- Financial transactions.

### Datawarehouses

The datawarehouse is a big database, part of the decision support systems. The competitive challenges of today´s business atmosphere is driving many IT shops to deliver scaleable decision support systems that can support growing user bases, as well as an increasing amount of warehoused data. Proper datawarehouse design is important to the success of the enterprise business decision support system. If users are unable to easily access and analyze accurate and consistent data in an acceptable period of time, the value of the corresponding application will be minimal. In order to maximize the organization's effort, on-line analytical processing (OLAP) must be linked with the business strategies in a client/server architecture. One of the most valuable assets of the enterprise is the operational data used in managing day-to-day business activities. The numeric data provides frequent measures of performance. By developing a datawarehouse, corporations are organizing the data in a way that makes the data useful to decision- makers, through charts and graphs.

## Integrated Planning

Companies are avoiding past excesses, using C-IT tools to manage inventories better and boost workers' productivity. These technologies are the basis to the global teams, formed by mobile professionals, in the globalization environment. The companies need more efficiency and competitiveness, and the keyword for success is *integration*. The information of different areas such as financial, distribution, and shop floor must be in a unique database where are also stored all the administration and marketing information. The integration allows faster and better decisions through a global control of corporate processes. Another important issue is the use of on-line information real-time updated. The C-IT technologies described in this paper will be a competitive weapon, as far as they can be fully integrated, resulting in an increase of the effectiveness of the project management processes. The market demands the companies to reconfigure faster and faster. This means that the professionals must reconfigure themselves. They need to learn, practice, and keep track of these technologies and their evolution. Electronic mail, video-conference, Internet, and intranet are technologies of communication that are related to the information systems previously mentioned, in order to provide the enhancement of productivity and effectiveness of the integrated planning. The fully integrated planning is a goal of the project management professionals.

## Future Trends

The computers will not look much like today's machines, and we will not work with them exactly as we do today. But fifteen years from now, personal computers by whatever name, in whatever size, will still be the main tools for corporate business and project management. By 2012, voice input will be so widespread that man will speak normally with the words captured by a noise canceling high-sensitive microphone. The computer will be our full-time wireless telephone with deep integration between computer and telephone functions. The PC will be full-time on-line, will always be turned on, and will play back our messages, having auto-answered many of them through the intelligent agents, our virtual assistant who will communicate to us all his decisions and actions as well as our agenda. The intelligent agents such as electronic wizards and personal assistants will help us to learn faster the use of applications and perform repetitive tasks. So, the project managers are allowed to spend their time with the core business activities. Sophisticated electronic agents can learn on their own by following our example. They can watch us browsing or clicking and confirm with us what it learned, or we teach it directly such as telling him to throw away all messages from xyz-person.

The use of keywords will be widespread since it allows faster access of text/data. In the Internet, it allows customized news. As the agent is set up, it will search for keywords in its database and retrieved articles, newsletters, and so on, sorting the results by frequency and using some rules or statements to filter unwanted stuff. The PC will become an appliance, not making nearly the same demands on our time as today's PCs. We can expect more reliability from the whole infrastructure of the Internet and private networks. When both are reliable and all the security and performance enhancements are made, major companies will shut down their private wide-area networks and move their traffic onto the Internet. One of these enhancements comprise the use of EDI (electronic data interchange), which allows transfer of big masses of data, including financial statements such as payment orders, improving business relationships. In the nineties, the 80/20 was a major principle in corporate communications. That rule said that 80 percent of corporate voice and data traffic stayed inside the company, and 20 percent went outside. In the first decade of next century, the rule will be much more like 50/50. Voice recognition will open computing to most people who are non-participants today.

### Wireless Connectivity

Connectivity will be a major key to do business, derived from partnership. The computers will be connected full-time to intranet/ Internet. The term for this wander-anywhere/stay-connected approach is "ubiquitous computing." It is generally accepted that all communications are headed for a wireless future. Today that move is still not yet feasible: band-width limitations, technical problems, and the capital costs of the yet-to-be-built wireless infrastructure stand in the way. But it's coming, as sure as tomorrow. And it's going to change how we think about communications. For PC users, universal, continuous, wireless connectivity will also change how we work and how we envision the role of PCs in our work lives because of the convenience and productivity of having the network resources available all the time. Wireless will introduce cultural change and attitude change with new habits such as reading and answering e-mail during a meeting. Actually, matters will probably reach a point in companies, as wireless networking spreads, where reading and answering e-mail during slow moments in meetings isn't seen as bad manners, but as making the most of our time.

## Conclusions

All primary sources of competitive advantage such as knowledge, partnership, and so on are related with the technologies described in this paper. For example, partnership is related with connectivity. The people/computer is the key interface to project management processes. The companies must define a plan for data and its migration, addressing issues like security, ownership, replication, and access. They shall consider the role of the corporate networks with planning information, such as activities data, contract data, document control, and workflow (EDMS), external data suppliers, datawarehouse, Internet, intranet, video-conference, and other tools. The companies shall consider some groupware/people features when developing their architecture designed to gain competitive advantage. The project management processes are changing and growing worldwide, outside the offices and factories, bypassing many traditional boundaries of countries, partners, and competitors. Project management professionals need continuous technology update and a long term C-IT blueprint to truly obtain the key for success. It is difficult to live in a structure during construction or permanent reform. Handling the transition to a new C-IT architecture is just as crucial as the initial systems design.

Major advances in C-IT have been the most exciting and far-reaching developments in science and technology in the late twentieth century. Personal computers, networks, Internet, multimedia, electronic banking, and satellite television are just a few innovations. That have became an intrinsic part of the day-to-day life of the organizations, allowing virtual teams and a new way to do business. The rapid pace of C-IT innovations and diffusion will be maintained in the next century as computing, telecommunications, broadcast, and multimedia continue to converge on common digital-based techniques. Management theorists, since the fifties, have linked C-IT tools to power shift in organizations, such as growing influence of companies with expertise in these technologies. This technical revolution has generated more effectiveness and productivity gains for the companies, which are recognized as a competitive advantage.

Information is a powerful advantage for decision-makers. They can collaborate as a team, sharing ideas and knowledge, as well as information. The competitive advantage in project management is related to the proactively decision-making process. A timely, knowledge-based decision reflects the organization's advantage providing business solutions through user collaborative work and proactive discovery. The increasing convergence of technologies and growing access to high-speed networks getting more information is leading to a big shift in the capacity for decision-making of project managers. As the world economies become more interconnected and more competitive, there is an increasing need for organizations to join design and manufacturing teams that collaborate for the life of a project and then disperse. This is a challenge for project managers who need integrated use of these technologies.

Recent researches indicate that the cultural aspects are the main barrier to the implementation of these technologies in the companies. A top down commitment for troubleshooting is needed, as well as investments in the acquisition and training people in these technologies. More important is the implementation phase, when all the team must be involved with simple objectives, such as the creation of an island of success, which motivates the others to implement the new technologies associated with the change in their processes. Professionals who love getting the information at their finger tips must provide data, load the information into databases, and admit to change the way they work, regarding further benefits. The solution to the cultural resistance of some professionals is the implementation of a simple, realistic, user-driven, and well-defined communications and information program for project management with top down commitment, reviewing the corporate processes, the key for success.

## References


Drucker, P. 1994. "The Theory of Business." *Harvard Business Review.*

Machlup, F. 1962. "The Production and Distribution of Knowledge." Princeton, NJ: Princeton University Press.

Project Management Institute. 1996. *A Guide to the Project Management Body of Knowledge (PMBOK Guide).* Project Management Institute.

Quinn, J. 1992. "Intelligent Enterprises." *Sloan Management Review.*

# The Twenty First Century: How You Will Automatically Control the Schedule, Cost, and Status of Dozens of Projects

John Rakos, John J. Rakos & Associates Consultants Ltd.

## Introduction

The system was developed for a large telecommunications and informatics services group in one of the departments of the Canadian federal government. This group has over one hundred systems projects being developed for dozens of internal clients. The projects range from small, three to six month efforts, to major Crown projects involving hundreds of millions of dollars, produced internally as well as by outside contractors. Most of the projects are small enough to be stand alone, but some of the larger projects, called programs, consist of several smaller components, called projects. These component projects have many interdependencies that have to be accounted for in a consolidated schedule.

Upper levels of management as well as all the project stakeholders need to know the schedule progress of all these

Exhibit 1.

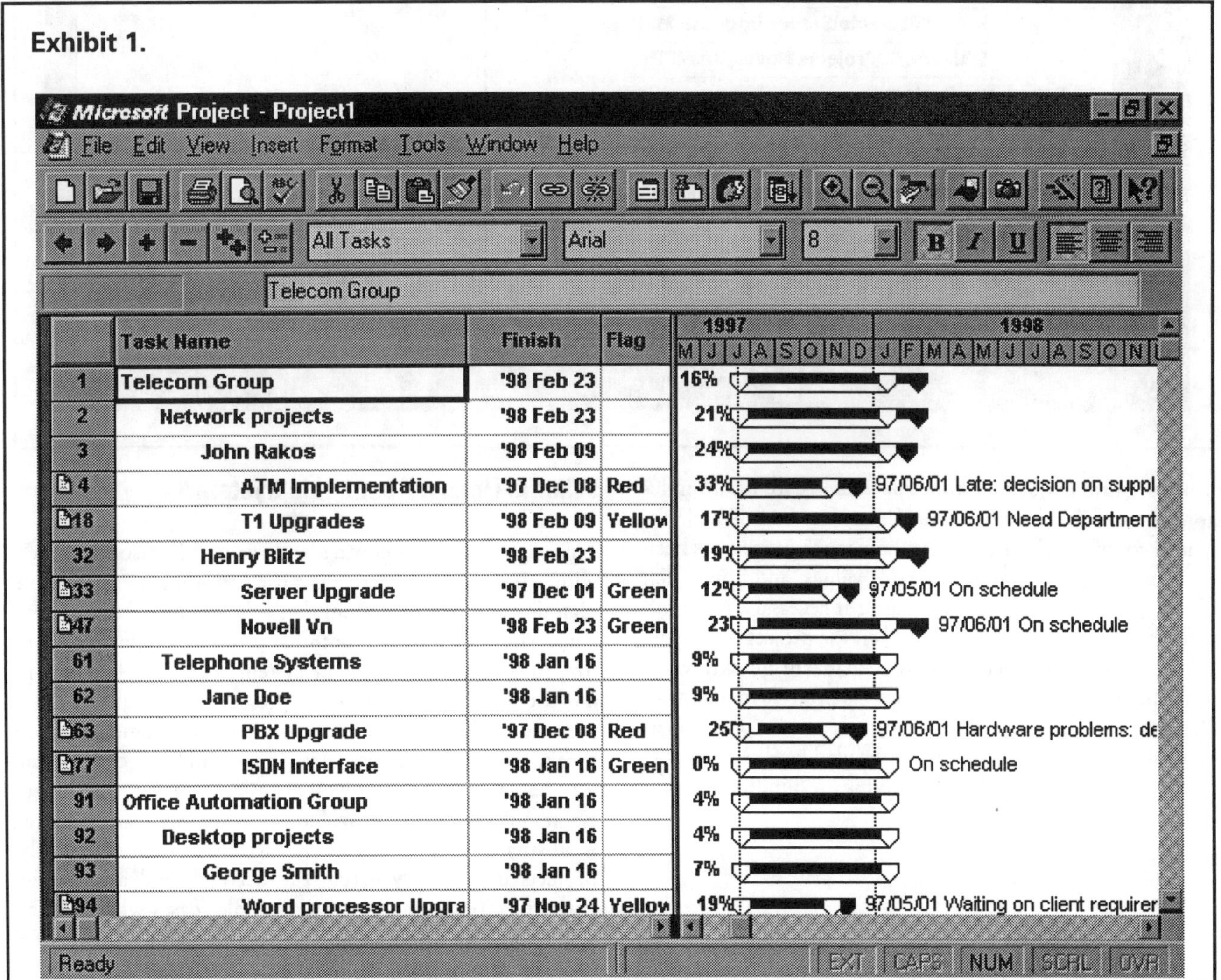

**Exhibit 2.**

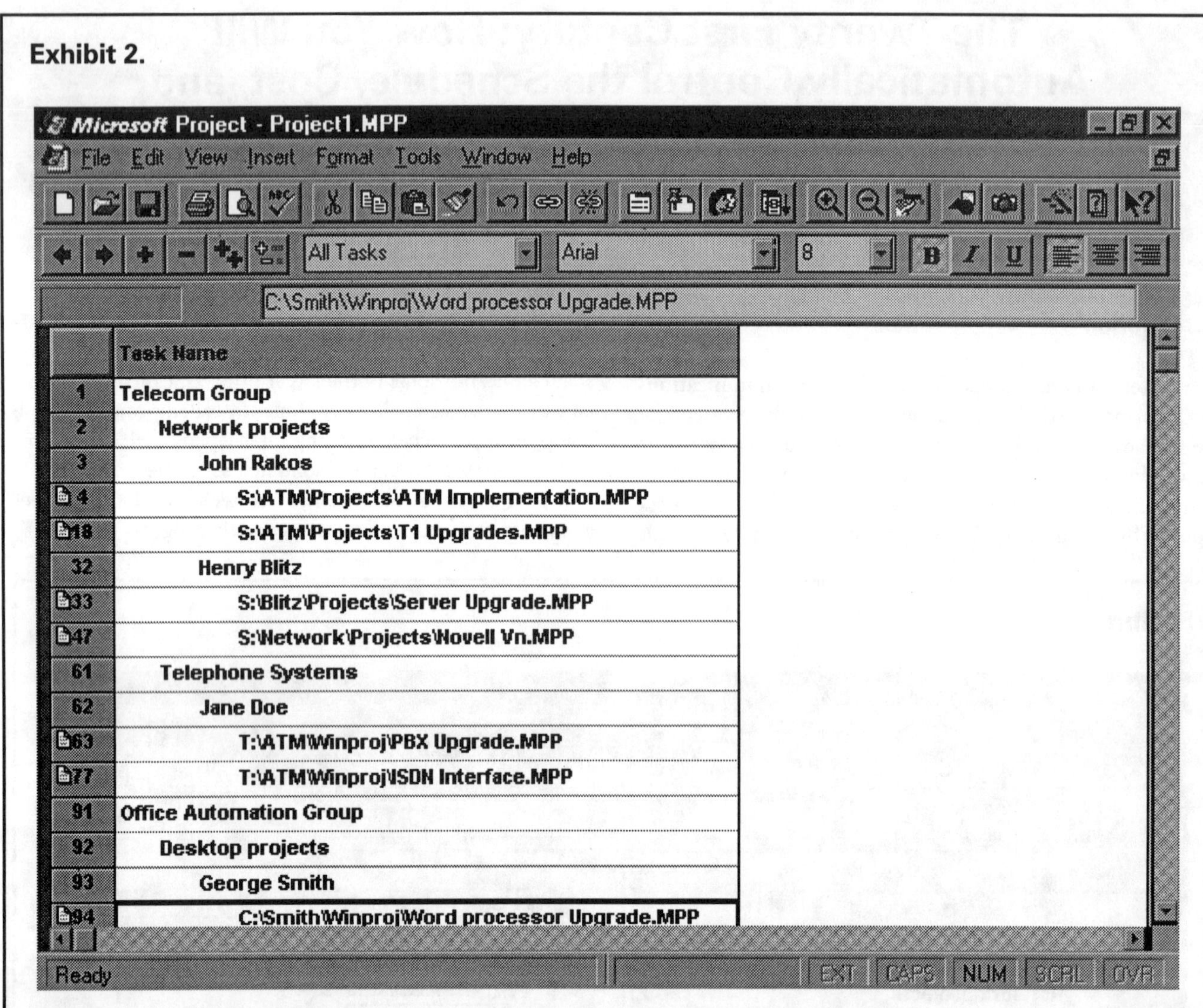


projects: Have major milestones been met? Are future milestones rescheduled? When will the project be finished? Financial control is also important: how much money has been spent, what are the projects' earned values, and how much will be spent by fiscal year and quarter if necessary. Most important, management needs to know if the project needs special attention. They need a system that will quickly warn them about any issues that can cause the projects to go astray. They need to see a summary picture of all the projects, as well as be able to drill down to the detailed level. As you may imagine, it is very difficult to do all this for hundreds of projects.

## What Is Unique About This System?

This paper will show how a system using Microsoft Project™ with a few custom macros was used to implement a simple planning and control system that solves many of these problems. The system is used both for project planning and control. At the planning stage the system helps to define and input a plan for all the group's projects. We found that 90 percent of the projects fit into one of five standard Word breakdown structure templates. These templates contain major phases, milestones as well as tasks at detail level. Financial templates are also provided to ensure that fiscal planning is adequate. At the controlling stage the system rolls all the projects up monthly across the network and summarizes them for reporting. The roll up handles cases where several 'sub' schedules comprise an integrated schedule, and it even handles inter-project dependencies.

**Exhibit 3.**

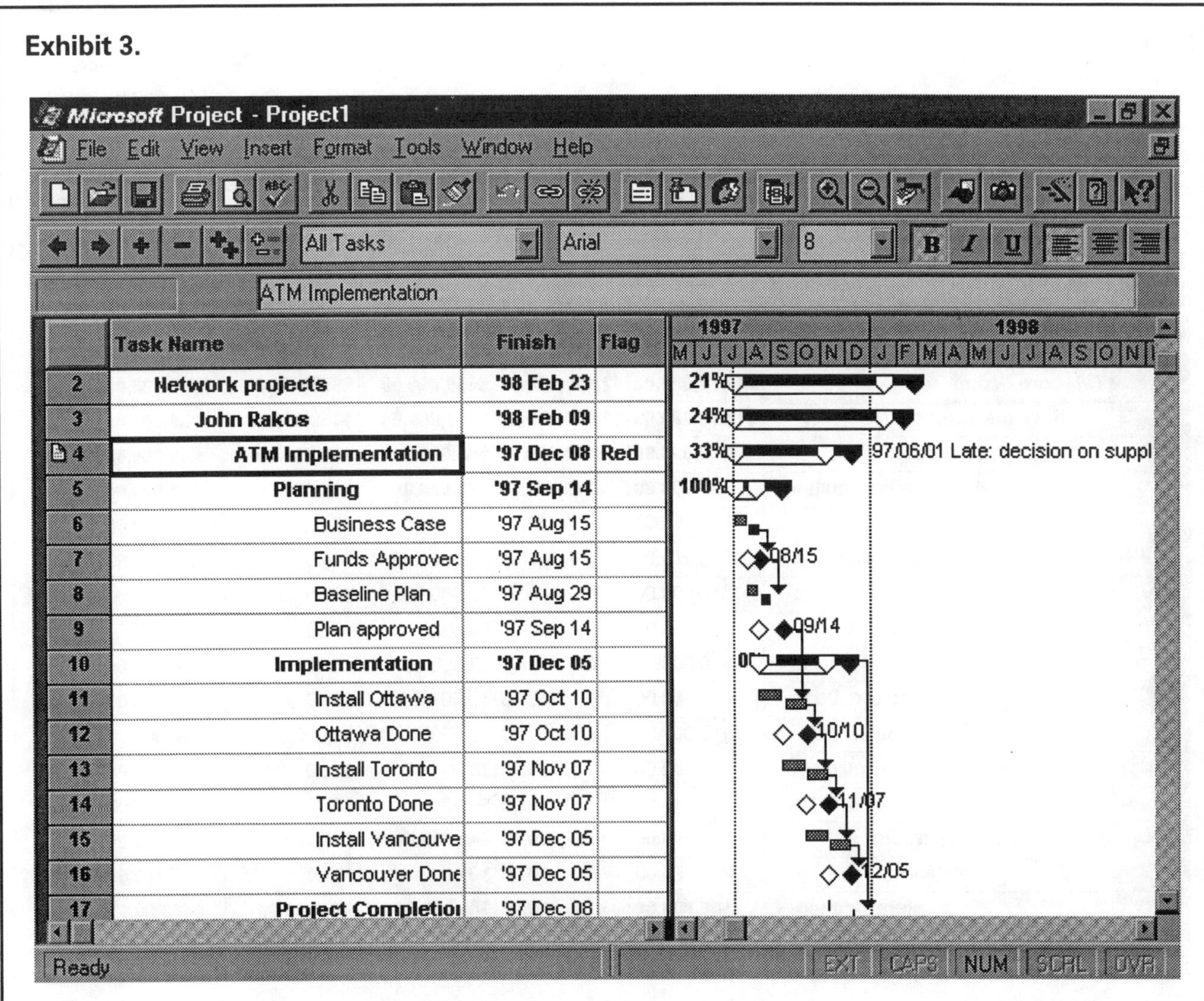


Once the roll up is done, reports are printed that show schedule progress for each project, financial performance, and highlight any problems. The project files even contain a status report for each project. The reports can be displayed at any outline level. Critical milestones and deliverables are identified and reports showing only these items can be produced. Most importantly, the reports flag any issues that need fast reaction from management.

## The Results

Exhibit 1 shows one of the most useful outputs. This report is the first page of the summary of dozens of projects. This view is a double Gantt showing the progress of projects versus the baseline plan. Each detail line on the Gantt represents one project. Note that the "Task Name" column contains a meaningful hierarchy of how the projects are organized. Roll up into this hierarchy was accomplished using a macro written in Visual Basic. The user simply creates a structure project file such as Exhibit 2. Note that the detail lines are simply (network) directory path names. The macro rolls up the referenced projects into the hierarchy.

We find that one of the most useful items is the "flag" field. To highlight any issues that need attention, the flag is set to "Red," "Yellow," or "Green." If "Red" appears in the field, the project needs immediate action from management. If "Yellow," the project needs action soon from management. If "Green," the project needs no action, but there may be some issues that management needs to be aware of. Each project title bar is annotated with a phrase that summarizes the status of the project. For a project labeled "Red," the text is the action item that management needs to take immediately. For a project labeled "Yellow," the text is the action item that

**Exhibit 4.**

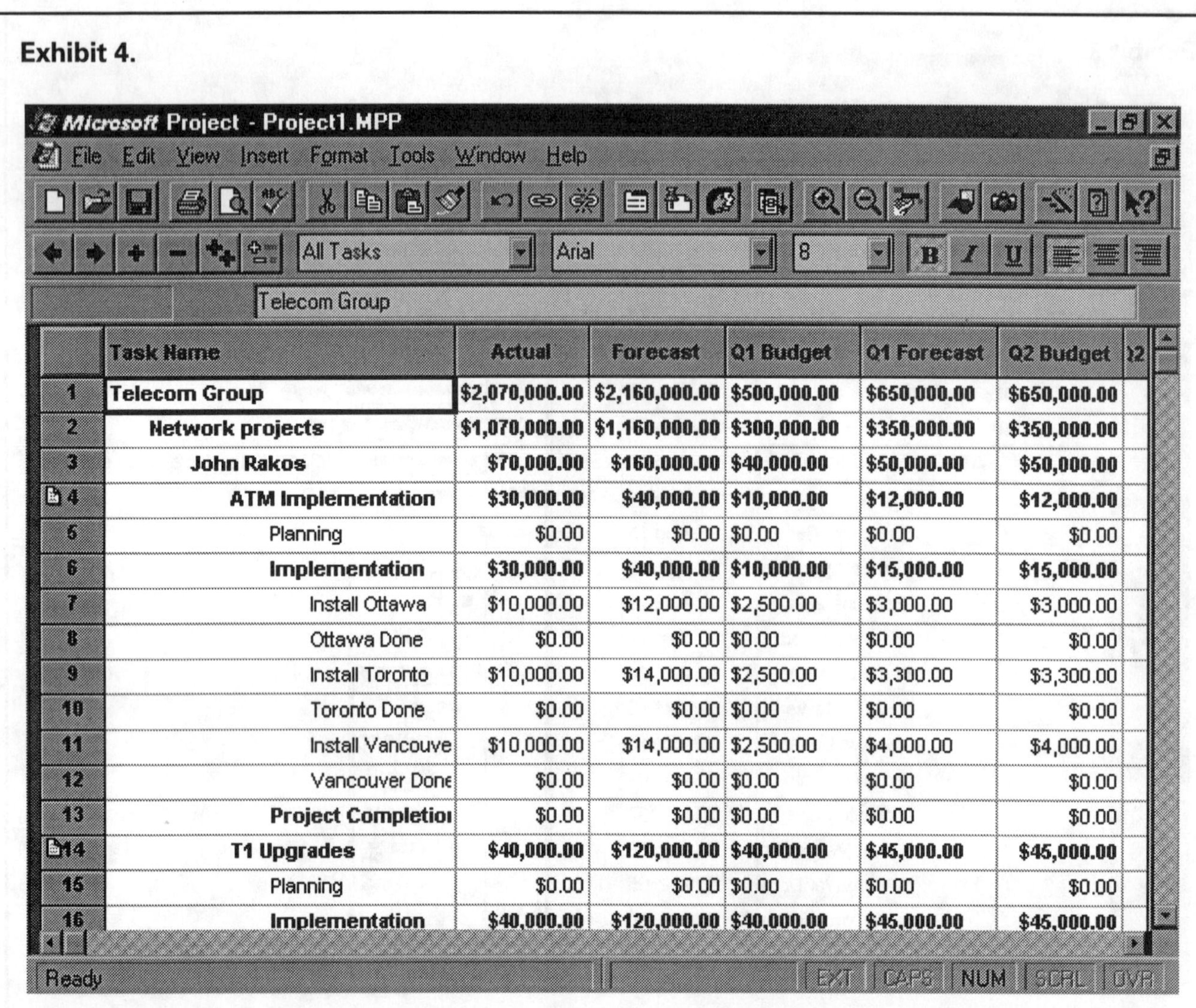

| | Task Name | Actual | Forecast | Q1 Budget | Q1 Forecast | Q2 Budget |
|---|---|---|---|---|---|---|
| 1 | **Telecom Group** | **$2,070,000.00** | **$2,160,000.00** | **$500,000.00** | **$650,000.00** | **$650,000.00** |
| 2 | **Network projects** | **$1,070,000.00** | **$1,160,000.00** | **$300,000.00** | **$350,000.00** | **$350,000.00** |
| 3 | **John Rakos** | **$70,000.00** | **$160,000.00** | **$40,000.00** | **$50,000.00** | **$50,000.00** |
| 4 | **ATM Implementation** | **$30,000.00** | **$40,000.00** | **$10,000.00** | **$12,000.00** | **$12,000.00** |
| 5 | Planning | $0.00 | $0.00 | $0.00 | $0.00 | $0.00 |
| 6 | **Implementation** | **$30,000.00** | **$40,000.00** | **$10,000.00** | **$15,000.00** | **$15,000.00** |
| 7 | Install Ottawa | $10,000.00 | $12,000.00 | $2,500.00 | $3,000.00 | $3,000.00 |
| 8 | Ottawa Done | $0.00 | $0.00 | $0.00 | $0.00 | $0.00 |
| 9 | Install Toronto | $10,000.00 | $14,000.00 | $2,500.00 | $3,300.00 | $3,300.00 |
| 10 | Toronto Done | $0.00 | $0.00 | $0.00 | $0.00 | $0.00 |
| 11 | Install Vancouve | $10,000.00 | $14,000.00 | $2,500.00 | $4,000.00 | $4,000.00 |
| 12 | Vancouver Done | $0.00 | $0.00 | $0.00 | $0.00 | $0.00 |
| 13 | **Project Completio** | $0.00 | $0.00 | $0.00 | $0.00 | $0.00 |
| 14 | **T1 Upgrades** | **$40,000.00** | **$120,000.00** | **$40,000.00** | **$45,000.00** | **$45,000.00** |
| 15 | Planning | $0.00 | $0.00 | $0.00 | $0.00 | $0.00 |
| 16 | **Implementation** | **$40,000.00** | **$120,000.00** | **$40,000.00** | **$45,000.00** | **$45,000.00** |

management needs to take soon. For a project labeled "Green," there need not be text attached, but project managers may use it to apprise management of some issue.

Most of the project plans are simple: ten to at most fifty line items per project. Usually the major phases, milestones, and deliverables are sufficient. Since the projects are rolled up completely, the user can drill down to more detailed information simply using the outlining features of MSProject. Exhibit 3 shows such a drill down. This level of detail is usually not necessary for management reporting.

## Financial Data

Exhibit 4 shows a view in which financial data can be controlled. This financial "spreadsheet" is incorporated right into MSProject, and is simply presented as a table. This was accomplished using a macro written in Visual Basic. The macro basically adds eighteen additional cost columns to the existing MSProject provided ones. The macro also allows basic arithmetic operations among the columns so that totals, variances, and other data can be calculated and displayed. The data for the summary tasks is the sum of the detail ones, so that total group and individual budgets are automatically calculated.

## Project Update

Monthly each project manager updates his project file with actual data for past tasks and any revisions for future tasks. To show financial performance, actual dollars spent and estimated forecast dollars are entered into the appropriate columns. If there are any problems with the project,

**Exhibit 5.**

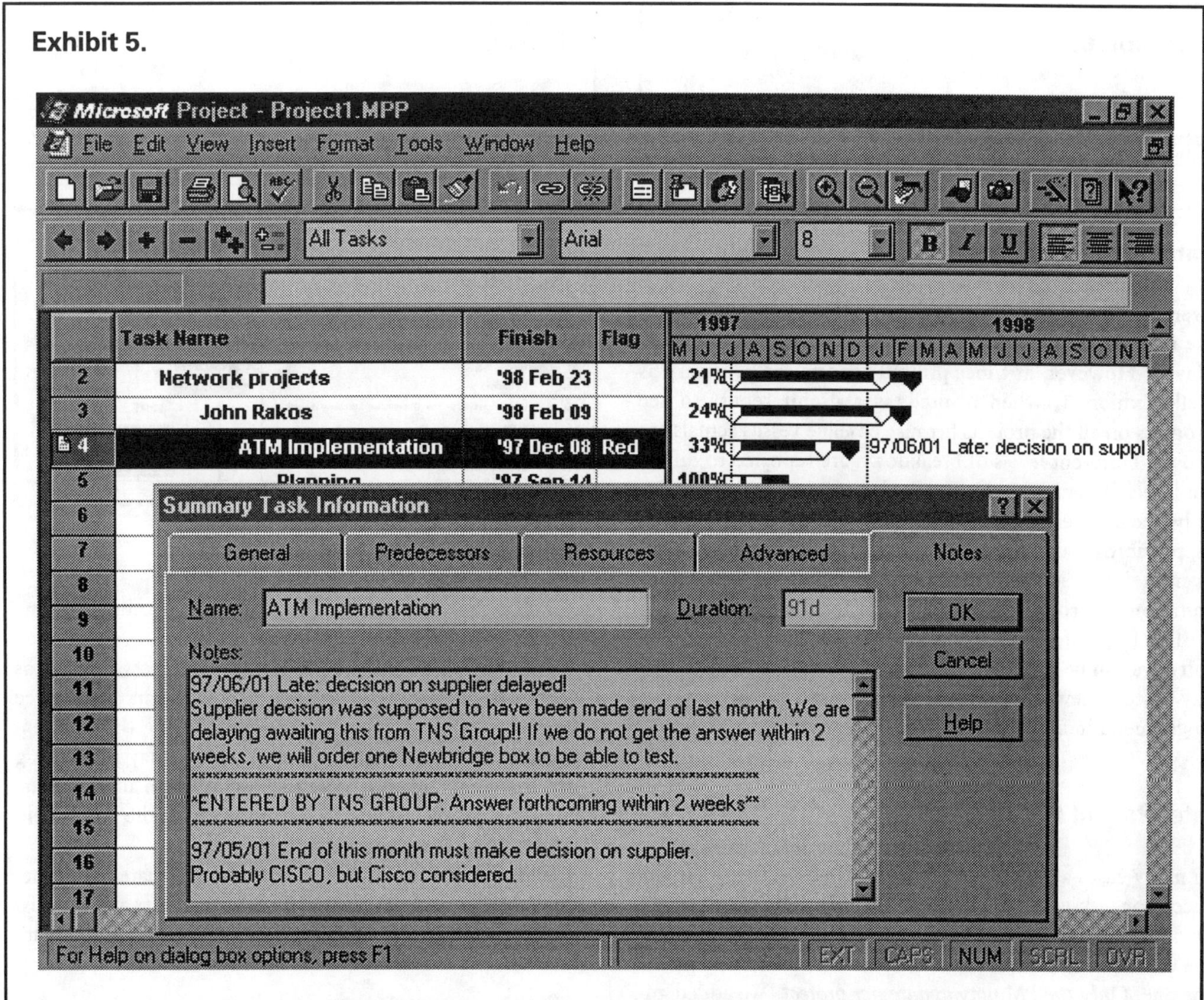


the issues are detailed in the "Notes" field of the appropriate task. (See Status Reporting). Once per month each project is rolled up from the disk file of the appropriate project manager, who may be anywhere on the network. The reports go to several levels of management. These managers need to be aware of any problems and react using the usual project management methods.

## Status Reporting

The software tool allows a long text field to be attached to each line item. This is called the "Notes" field. The software also allows the first line of the Notes field to be displayed as annotations on the Gantt chart. The Notes for the project title line is used as a concise status report (Exhibit 5). The Notes of any item may contain any detailed information that the project manager wishes to impart to the manager (or whoever is displaying the field). The Notes of the project title line can be used for a summary of the problem and a date. This line will be displayed on the Gantt.

As seen in Exhibit 5, the Notes item can be used as a historical journal of the issues associated with the project. As the issues get resolved, a solution statement and date can be added at the top of the problem list, thus keeping a chronological list of the issues and resolutions.

If read-write access is allowed to the project file, the Notes can be used as a groupware documentation interchange. Anyone who has write access to the file can insert a reply or comment into the Notes. These changes must be explicitly stored back on the originator's file.

**Exhibit 6.**

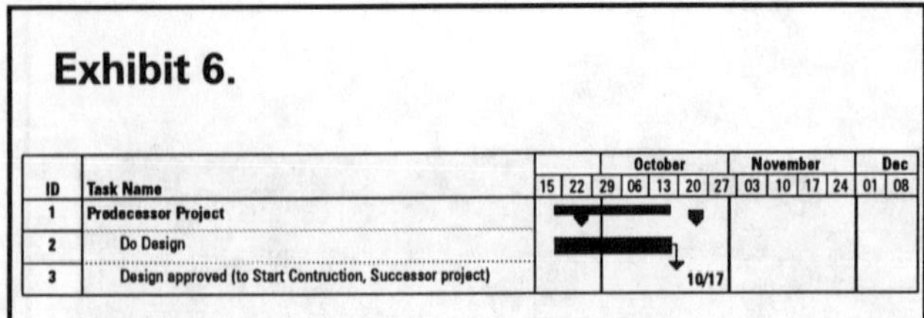


**Exhibit 7.**

| ID | Task Name |
|---|---|
| 1 | Successor Project |
| 2 | Design Approved (from Predecessor Project) |
| 3 | Do construction |

September | October | November: 08 15 22 29 06 13 20 27 03 10 17 24 01 — 09/20

## Hard Copy Reporting

Everyone is encouraged to look at the roll up on-line. Since the roll ups are dynamic, the latest information will be displayed. However, at times printed reports are necessary as well. Exhibit 1, when printed, is a useful report to see progress on all the projects because baseline versus actuals are shown. Different levels of breakdown are reported to different levels of management. Top level management may receive only one line per project. The next level receives major phases, possibly meaningful milestones. The next may receive deliverables and so forth. Exhibit 4 (printed) shows another common report used by management for financial control.

The full suite of the usual reports built into the normal software can be produced. Macros have been written so that any custom view or report can be produced by clicking on a single menu item or toolbar icon.

## Inter-Project Dependencies

In many cases a predecessor task is in one project while the successor task is in a separate project file. MSProject allows Dynamic Data Exchange links, but this is dangerous because the predecessor project can automatically update the successor one. *Only the PM may update her project.* We added another level of control using Visual Basic macros.

Exhibit 6 and 7 show two project plans. Figure 6 is the Predecessor Project containing the predecessor task *Do Design.* For clarity it contains a milestone *Design Approved.* This milestone is the predecessor to Successor Project *Do Construction* (Exhibit 7). We repeated the *Design Approved* milestone in the successor project only to warn the PM that the project has an external dependency, and we set special codes to link the *Design Approved* milestone in the predecessor project to the *Design Approved* milestone in the successor project. The files are rolled up (using a macro), then another macro is run to find the interdependencies and establish the links.

Exhibit 8 shows the results of the macro. The projects are rolled together and the predecessor and successor items are linked.

- Identify risky project activities that should be closely monitored during the removal action.

**Exhibit 8.**

| ID | Task Name |
|---|---|
| 1 | Predecessor Project |
| 2 | Do Design |
| 3 | Design Approved (to Start Construction, Successor Project) |
| 4 | Successor Project |
| 5 | Design Approved (from Predecessor Project) |
| 6 | Do construction |

mber | October | November | Dec: 15 22 29 06 13 20 27 03 10 17 24 01 08 — 10/17, 10/17

## Problem Determination

Several custom searches or "filters" are used to help anyone pinpoint any issues that may require attention. A "Search by Flag" filter can be used to show only projects flagged as "Red" (or "Yellow" or "Green"). The user can quickly see these projects, drill down to the issue causing the problem and assess the indicated action request. He may react using other available tools (for example, e-mail or an actual phone call), and perhaps respond to the originator in the Notes field of the issue.

Similar filters can be used to see issues associated with specific clients, projects, areas, and project managers and even list those items that are dependent on tasks in another project plan.

## Conclusions

The system has worked out very well—mainly because management indicated from the start that it wishes to see the project roll ups monthly. Those managers that are using it find that it is giving them the exact information that they require to keep abreast of the projects in their areas. The system has also been well received by the participants. It adds very little extra work: about thirty minutes per project per reporting period. The client is considering implementing it for the rest of the department.

For further information please phone or fax the author at (613) 727-1626.

# An Innovative Approach to Sharing Lessons Learned Across a Telecommunications Company

Stacy Miltiades, PMP, Bellcore
Michael J. Ahern, PMP, Bellcore
Alicia Esposito, Bellcore
Patricia Matson, Project Manager, Bellcore

## Introduction

One of the management challenges of the twenty first century will be the "compression of time." More tasks will have to be accomplished in a reduced timeframe while meeting and exceeding customer expectations. This challenge has driven Bellcore to focus its project-management efforts on "continuous improvement" to be poised for the twenty first century. The need to learn from past mistakes and to perform the project management tasks "right" in the shortest amount of time has motivated Bellcore to embrace and use modern computing technology to share "lessons learned" company-wide.

This paper describes the real-life experience of creating a process and an on-line database for lessons learned. It also describes how the process and database were deployed across a geographically dispersed telecommunications company.

The goal of this paper is to give other project managers practical ideas to foster the communication and sharing of lessons learned from past projects and to integrate those lessons learned into present and future projects.

## Background

Historically Bellcore has collected and analyzed data from lessons-learned sessions. Typically, these lessons learned had been limited to the project itself or occasionally collected and shared within smaller organizations. Additionally, data collection was frequently done only at the conclusion of the project, sometimes resulting in the loss of important lessons observed in the earlier stages of the project's lifecycle. A third historical aspect of lessons learned at Bellcore is that the focus tended to be on the technical aspects of the project without always including the more business-oriented lessons. By

**Exhibit1.**

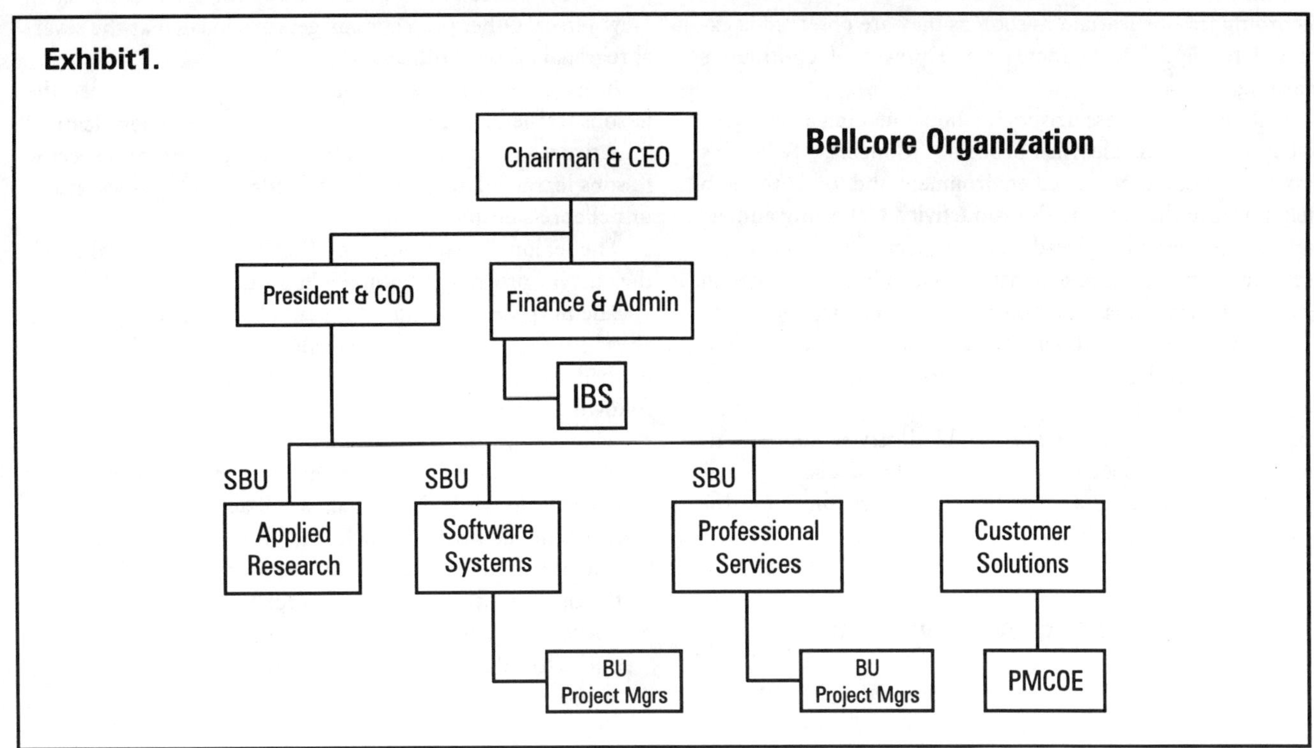

Exhibit 2.

*Process for Lessons Learned*

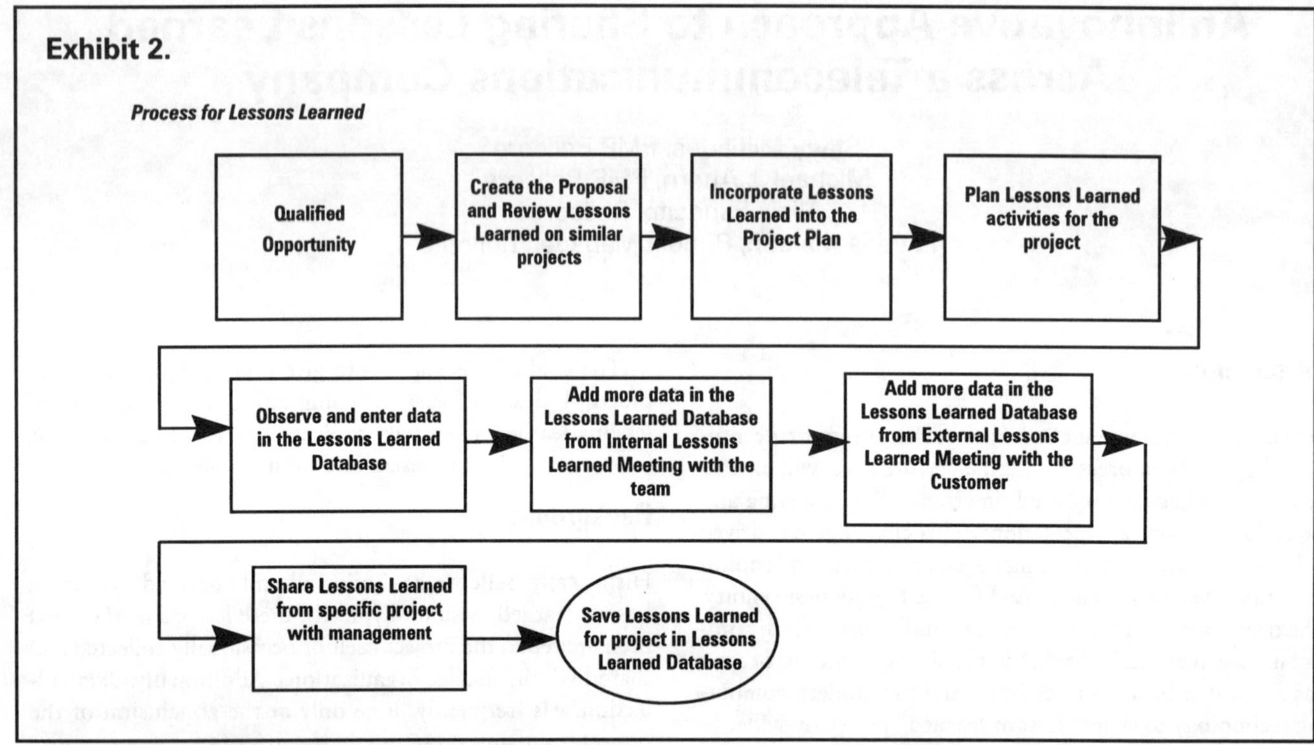


adopting a corporate-wide and continual process for sharing lessons learned across projects and focusing on both the technical and the business aspects of the project, Bellcore hopes to increase its competitive edge. Learning from the successes and failures of projects across an entire corporation and recording lessons learned as soon as they are observed is expected to significantly increase the power of continuous learning.

One of the business drivers for implementing a systematic corporate lessons learned process is to increase Bellcore's growth in a commercialized environment and to continue to help improve the company's productivity. Collecting and using lessons learned is already a key aspect of Bellcore's project management process. Sharing lessons learned across an entire organization is a key component of certification at level five of the Software Engineering Institute's (SEI) capability/maturity model (CMM) for software development. The recognition of a strong project management process, emphasized by past client experiences, and industry-standard certifications, such as CMM and ISO 9000, can be a strong competitive differentiator and perhaps even a requirement for entry into certain markets.

## Research and Planning for Lessons Learned

The lessons learned strategy was initiated in the Project Management Center of Excellence (PMCOE) organization in Bellcore. This organization is responsible for providing consultation, training, and support on the Bellcore project management process to the project managers in the three Bellcore strategic business units (SBUs). The majority of the project managers are located in three different counties in New Jersey. Other project managers are located at the several regional account offices.

A project management consultant from PMCOE led the lessons learned initiative. The objective of the lessons learned initiative was to create a lessons learned process and specific lessons learned data categories to address the business needs of Bellcore's business units.

The lessons learned strategy first consisted of evaluating the current process and doing a literature search.

The purpose of the literature search was to investigate the "best in class" project management methods for lessons learned. Overall, the "best in class" methods consisted of the following findings/recommendations:

- Observe lessons learned during all of the phases of the project's life-cycle. This technique enables mid-project corrections while the project is still active.
- Schedule the final lessons learned meeting soon after project closure to ensure project members' participation and the quick recall of information relating to the project.
- Focus lessons learned on a pre-prepared list of data categories to help the project team concentrate on the priority areas.

- Motivate the project managers to use the lessons learned process. Some project managers are reluctant to associate their names with lessons learned from a mistake they made. The impact of not sharing those types of lessons is that other project managers could potentially end up repeating the same mistakes.

## Implementation of the Lessons Learned Solution

Based on the "best in class" findings, the following plan was developed. First, the PMCOE project management consultant proposed a lessons learned process and data categories. This proposal was shared with the project managers from the business units. A prototype of the database was then developed and trialed by the project managers. This approach facilitated the buy-in from the project managers and also added a reality check.

Thus, the objective of the lessons learned solution was to create a lessons learned process and lessons learned data categories that could be used consistently by the project managers across Bellcore. The steps involved in the actual implementation of the lessons learned solution included:

- Creation and review of the lessons learned process
- Creation and review of the lessons earned data categories
- Developing the lessons learned prototype
- Testing the lessons learned prototype.

### Creation of the lessons learned process

The PMCOE project management consultant proposed the lessons learned process. This process consisted of actions that the project manager and the project team would take in the "planning," "implementation," and "close-out" phases of the Bellcore project management process. Figure 2 shows the flow of the lessons learned process.

The proposed process was reviewed with the project managers from the business units, and their feedback was incorporated for improving the process description. A description of the lessons learned process is described below.

#### *Planning Phase*

1. The project manager searches the lessons-learned database for lessons learned on similar projects.
2. The project manager incorporates the relevant lessons he learned from previous projects into the project plan for the specific project.
3. The project manager plans/schedules the lessons learned activities including:
   - Timeframes for collecting lessons learned
   - Dates for lessons learned meetings with the project team and the customer.

#### *Implementation Phase*

The project manager and the project team implement project activities and observe and enter their lessons learned in the Lessons Learned Database.

#### *Close-Out Phase*

1. The project manager and the project team review their project's lessons learned available in the database and reach agreement on the final content. The final agreement is also captured on-line.
2. The project manager and the key project team members meet with the customer and discuss lessons learned from the customer's perspective for the project.
3. The project manager enters the customer's lessons learned in the Lessons Learned Database.
4. The project manager informs management that the lessons learned are finalized for the specific project and can be viewed in the Lessons Learned Database.

### Creation of the lessons learned data categories

The "best in class" literature search and Bellcore's project management experiences supported the need for capturing both the business aspects of managing a project as well as the technical aspects. A draft list of lessons learned data categories was put together and reviewed with the project managers from the business units. The project managers suggested that some areas be changed and other data categories be added. The lessons learned data categories that are included in the database are listed below.

- **Overall Project**
  (chance to start over, schedule, profitability, quality, customer satisfaction)
- **Project Planning**
  (project plan)
- **Risk Management**
  (identifying risks, managing mitigation strategies)
- **Scope/Requirements Changes**
  (initial requirements, requirements reviews, scope creep)
- **Project Manager/Project Team**
  (communications, integration, consistency of personnel, experience of personnel)
- **Customer Interaction**
  (communications, relationship, managing expectations)
- **Contract Compliance**
  (managing contract changes, negotiating contract changes)
- **Strategic Business Unit Specific**
  (lessons specific to that strategic business unit).

For each of these lessons learned data categories, multiple questions are asked, such as: "What went right?" "What went wrong? "What can be improved?"

## Developing the Lessons Learned Prototype

The PM consultant from PMCOE provided the final lessons learned process and data categories to the internal business systems (IBS) consultant for the development of the prototype. The IBS organization is responsible for developing internal business systems for Bellcore. From the lessons learned process and data categories, the IBS consultant developed the functional requirements for the Lessons Learned Database. Once the lessons learned requirements were reviewed and baselined with the PMCOE project management consultant, IBS developed the lessons learned prototype.

IBS used Bellcore's existing Lotus Notes infrastructure as a platform for the database. Many of the project managers in Bellcore were already familiar with the infrastructure, thus decreasing the learning curve associated with training on the new database. This design also increased the project managers and project team's productivity by making information available to anyone, anytime, anyplace.

## Testing the Lessons Learned Prototype

The PMCOE project management consultant, the IBS consultant, and two experienced project managers from two different business units partnered and developed a project plan for the trial of the lessons learned prototype. This project plan defined the goals for the prototype, identified the participants for the trial, clarified the expectations from the participants, and specified the timeframe for the trial.

The goals for testing the prototype were to:

- Validate the lessons learned functional requirements designed to address the project management needs of Bellcore's business units
- Test the capability of accessing the lessons learned prototype from the corporate locations of the business units
- Test the capability of displaying lessons learned in a useful way to enable the easy retrieval of information by the business units.

Sixteen participants were selected from the three strategic business units. For continuity, eight of these participants were the same project managers who helped finalize the "proposed" lessons learned process and data categories. Additionally, other key stakeholders with a critical role on an actual project team were also selected to participate in the trial. These key stakeholders included a quality methods operations consultant, a product manager (responsible for the strategy for a specific software product), a release manager (responsible for managing the day-to-day activities of a software release), a solutions manager (responsible for integrating features from multiple software products into one solution), and a supervisor responsible for managing project managers and solutions managers.

During the trial, the expectations from the participants were to:

- Test the lessons learned prototype to ensure that it would meet the functional requirements. Specifically, the participants were to create lessons learned and test the ways that data was displayed for retrieval and reuse.
- Provide feedback on their testing experience by completing a written questionnaire.

The initial estimate was two to three hours to collect lessons learned and enter those lessons into the database, and about one and a half hours to retrieve and reuse lessons learned from other projects. The trial was structured over a two-week period. During the first week, the participants were asked to enter lessons learned for their projects and then complete Part 1 of the usability questionnaire, which focused on data entry features. During the second week, the participants were asked to retrieve and reuse the lessons learned already in the database, and complete Part 2 of the usability questionnaire, which focused on the reuse of information. The estimated two weeks of testing extended to two and a half weeks to accommodate the participants.

To set the stage for the trial, the participants were invited to attend a meeting, which included a review of the lessons learned functional requirements, the process, and the data areas. At that meeting, the features and capabilities of the lessons learned prototype were also demonstrated.

Participants liked the structure of the trial, which enabled them to test the lessons learned prototype at their convenience from their own personal computers. This flexibility also enabled them to socialize the lessons learned prototype with their coworkers and provide consolidated feedback.

## Observations from Testing the Lessons Learned Prototype

The following summarizes observations from testing the lessons learned prototype:

- Allow sufficient time for testing the prototype. The estimated two weeks for testing the prototype needed to be extended to two and a half weeks. Some participants were hard pressed to complete the prototype testing activities based on the original estimate.
- Stay in frequent contact with the participants to encourage their completion of the testing of the lessons learned prototype. Stress the benefits to be derived from sharing lessons learned with others.
- Test the installation of the lessons learned prototype to work out bugs prior to launching the full-scale testing of the prototype. Some difficulties were encountered due to the improper installation of the lessons learned software. Even during the trial, the installation and performance of

the Lessons Learned Database needs to be easy to encourage its use.

- Choose prototype technology that helps to minimize training or start-up time. The lessons learned prototype was easy for the participants to use. As previously mentioned, it was built using Lotus Notes, which is very familiar to most Bellcore employees, since it is the corporate standard used for email.
- Secure management support to ensure that the roll-out is successful. Project managers said that they needed support from the management team to implement the process and use the database. Additionally, making project managers and project teams aware of the lessons learned process and database, as well as motivating them to use them, were viewed as the keys to a successful implementation.

## Roll-out Strategy for the Lessons Learned Database

We plan to deploy the lessons learned process and database across Bellcore in June 1997. The deployment will be kicked off with a letter from Bellcore's president citing his strong commitment to continuous process improvement and the importance of the lessons learned process in helping to reach this corporate goal.

Further, the lessons learned process will be incorporated into the Bellcore project management process and communicated to all Bellcore employees. In addition to the built-in online help provided in the Lessons Learned Database, training sessions will be offered to anyone using the database.

A staggered roll-out plan will be recommended to the business units, including the following suggestions:

- From the 1996 lessons learned paper documents, select at least five key projects of critical importance to the business unit and populate the Lessons Learned Database with this historical information.
- From the 1997 projects, select five to ten projects of strategic importance to the business unit's profit and loss and start observing and capturing lessons learned.

The roll-out plan also includes an incentive to encourage the use of the process and database. The people who will be entering lessons learned will receive a "recognition note" from both their immediate supervisors and their general managers thanking them for taking the time to share their lessons learned and contributing to our corporate goal of continuous process improvement.

To ensure continuous improvement, the deployment and use of the lessons learned process and database will be monitored and upgraded as necessary. A user group will be formed to provide a continuous feedback loop to the design team. Bimonthly conference calls with the user group will become the forum for the discussion, agreement, and prioritization of improvements to the lessons learned process and database.

## Recommendations

Based on this real-life experience, the following lessons learned recommendations are offered:

1. Ensure that your lessons learned observers include representation from the key project functional areas (e.g. requirements, design, development).
2. The lessons learned observers should have strong knowledge of the processes involved in the project. These representatives should offer breadth and depth of perception.
3. As the project manager, be open and receptive to having your decisions reviewed in retrospect.
4. Include the lessons learned activities in the project's schedule; otherwise they will not get recorded.
5. Emphasize to each lessons learned participant that "You know something valuable and if you share this knowledge, it could help others prevent problems; they will do the same for you."

### Acknowledgments

The authors would like to thank the project managers within Bellcore who contributed their knowledge to the completion of the lessons learned requirements, to those who contributed to the lessons learned prototype effort, and to everyone who is using the lessons learned process.

### References

Kerzner, Harold. 1995. "Project Management." Van Nostrand Reinhold: 504.

Project Management Institute. 1996. *A Guide to the Project Management Body of Knowledge (PMBOK Guide)*: 46.

Urban, Glen L. 1995. *Business and Economic Outlook: The Conference Board.* The 21st Century Corporation: 31.

Weiss, Joseph W., and Robert K. Wysocki. 1992. "5-Phase Project Management." *Closing the Project.* Addison-Wesley: 103.

Whitten, Neal. 1995. "Managing Software Development Projects." John Wiley & Sons, Inc.: 130.

# Information Systems

# The Corporate Intranet for Project Management

John J. Lucas, Work Management Solutions, Inc.

Intranets and the Web technologies that define them could be the most important paradigm shift in the corporate enterprise since the introduction of the PC's in early '80s. Nearly 70 percent of the Fortune 1000 companies are intranet-ready now. The impact of global access, low infrastructure cost, and a very fast rate of return on investment have moved the corporate enterprises to adopt and implement this technology rapidly.

This paper will investigate the growth, the business case for the technology, and the reasons why it has the potential for great acceptance and success. We will explore the impact of the intranet on the use of project and work management processes in the coming years and how this may forever change how these project management techniques are used.

The chart in Exhibit 1 represents how easily work can be integrated using an intranet.

## The Evolution of Technology

Since the first use of computer technology in the '50s to develop project plans and logic using computer algorithms, project management has adapted to the technology and computer environment available to take advantage of the advancing technology. From the PERT techniques of the '50s to the arrow diagramming methodology of the '60s to the precedence diagramming methodology of the '70s, project managers have used the fast pace of computer technology to make project planning more usable, more realistic, and friendly to the end user. The early computer models feature coding sheets, computer rooms, and big expensive plotting devices with users waiting anxiously for the results to flow back to them from the secure processing rooms. The process was slow but the results proved to be useful.

The advent of the mini-computer allowed projects of sufficient size to buy their own mini-computers and their own project management systems. This advance brought the computer to the same location as the project staff and gave greater control over the use and access to the project

**Exhibit 1.**

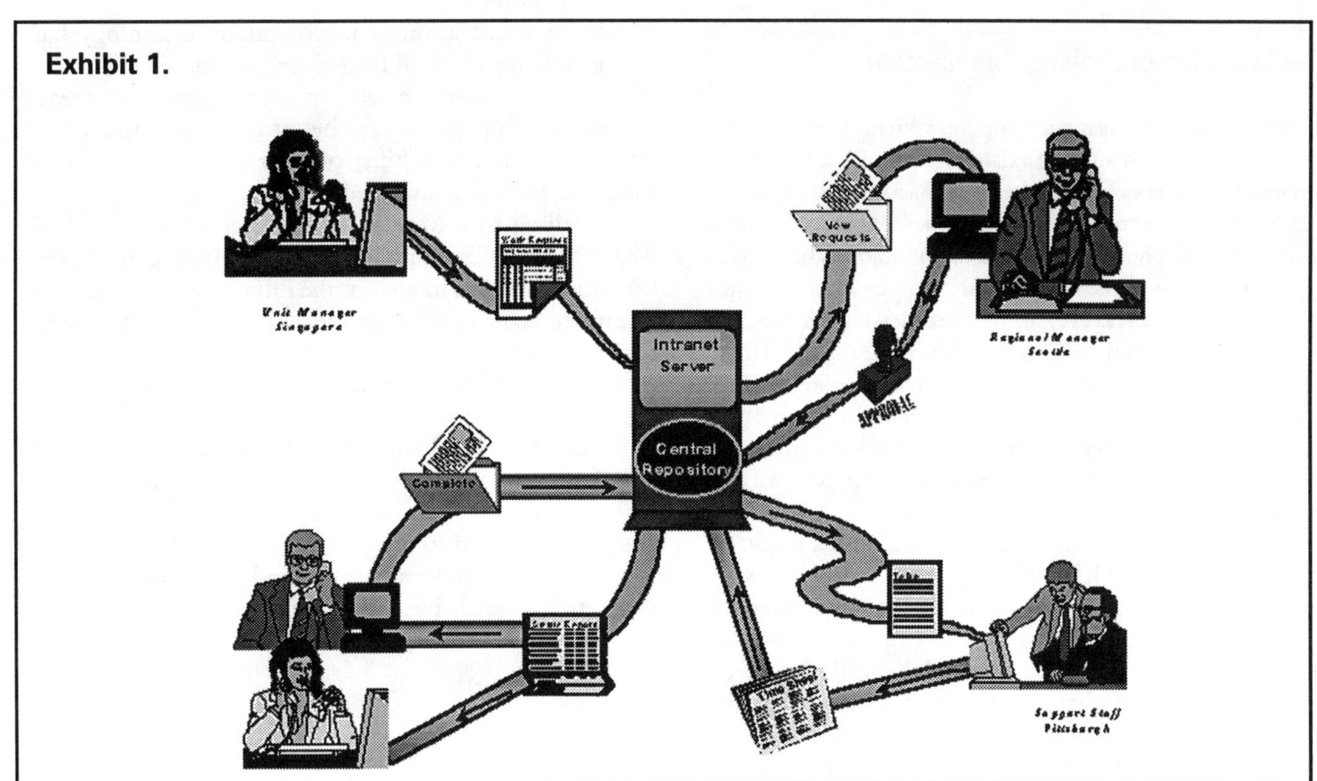

management staff. Could it get any better than this? Project management systems were becoming more user friendly, reducing processing turnaround time, and increasing in functionality.

The late 1980's brought the PCs to the desktop and the advent of PC-based project management systems. Although sufficiently limited in functionality and features, the early versions of PC software gave greater control to the individual project planner and expanded the use and market for more corporate users to begin to use project management software for other purposes. Being able to plan and schedule work at your desktop proved intriguing and valuable. However, the difficulty of properly integrating project work and corporate resources across the entire enterprise proved to be a significant limitation to centralized planning.

With the introduction of the client/server environment, everything could be stored on a central repository and the local client workstations could do their own project planning. However, the approach of client server underestimated the time and investment necessary to implement the infrastructure. Many of the tools and procedures that corporate information services managers took for granted on the mainframe computer were non-existent in the client/server world. It has taken several years for this environment to mature to state where it can be successfully managed and implemented, still at a significant cost.

## The Evolution of Project Management

Project management is not a computer system. The principles of project management have existed for centuries. It is an approach to the successful achievement of accomplishing a goal within a budget and time frame to a defined set of specifications and/or criteria. The principles and methodologies have made significant strides in the documentation of the specific project management processes over the past decades. Only in the 20th century have we had the technology to advance the use of these principles, expand their limits, and advance the rate at which project management can be applied to plan and manage projects and work of all sizes and complexity. Much of this has been the result of the Project Management Institute's impact as a professional development center for our ideas.

We began by managing single projects with a single resource pool (the old "build a pyramid" model). As resources needed to be borrowed, loaned, or contracted for from other sources, it became more necessary to be able perform multi-project management of the work and the resources. This approach was a start but had significant limitations in its usefulness. Enterprises needed to manage all the work that was done by its staff including non-project work. Other tools may have been helpful but limited the ability to centralize the data. Time reporting as a means to collect time to understand the nature of the work became an increasingly important tool for overall work management in the enterprise. Work initiation and tracking software combined with time reporting began to create the central data repository needed by business managers. The use of computer technology enabled these uses to advance rapidly. However, we had many groups within the enterprise using different tools and approaches to solve their unique problems.

## The Enterprise's Needs

The corporate enterprise has evolved from the project repository to the personal repository to need for a corporate repository of information. The nature and content of the information needs to be defined and understood how it relates to all the work management processes that go on within an organization. Based upon our years of experience within this area, we have found that enterprises are interested in knowing about all the work that is being done in all locations to obtain a collective view while allowing for local action and management. The time value of information is important as well as access from anywhere. The interest in utilizing the infrastructure that is in place is common theme. Bottom line results are important.

An important advance in computer technology has emerged. Using much of the existing computer infrastructure, the internet and the easy to use browsers have created a unique opportunity for better communication, collaboration, and accessibility of information to corporate users wherever they may be located.

According to a May 5, 1997 article in *Information Week* entitled "Corporate Internet/Planning Guide", the new organizational model for the intranet age will have an integrated team-based structure with a small management gap, and learning, experimenting and creativity will be essential and will be nurtured by the organization. The focus of the enterprise will be the customer and it will need to be able to act and adapt quickly. In successful companies, technology people should become more involved with the business and marketing people, and the business people are advised to be more involved with technology. The difference between business and technology will become indistinguishable.

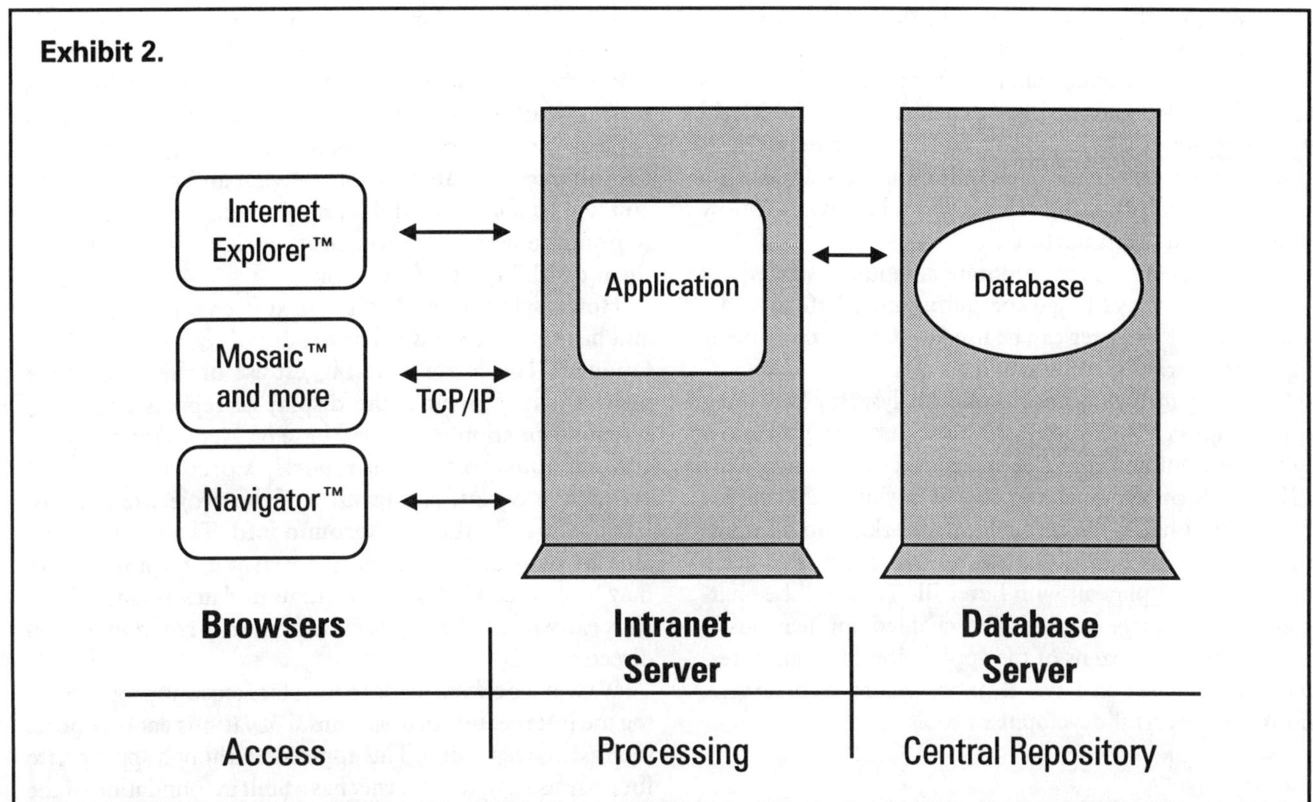


## The Internet and the Intranet

Hambrecht and Quest, in a recent publication, made the following statements, "We believe that the internet is arguably the most significant phenomenon impacting commerce and culture for the remainder of the 20th century. We expect that Internet-based content and activities will expand from less than $100 million (in 1996) to over $10 billion by the end of the decade."

The history of the Internet dates back to the late '60s. It was further developed in the '70s using the TCP/IP networking protocol and became the "network of networks" in the '80s for e-mail and file transfers, primarily in government and university environments. The 1990's saw the coming of age of the Internet with creation of user-friendly browsers, search engines for the masses, and the introduction of support languages like Java.

Before we go further, it is useful to define the Internet and the intranet. The Internet is the global connection of servers linked to share information and communicate either on a personal level or company basis. The intranet is a corporate environment set up to facilitate the sharing, communication, and use of applications within the corporate community with access to the Internet.

Hambrecht and Quest go on to say they believe that the intranet is now entering the mainstream of corporate life and will increase dramatically in its use through 1999. The use of the intranet has obvious value as a core communication and information system. However, it is expected that there will be unprecedented proliferation of applications for business use in this timeframe. All of our customer sources confirm this intent.

It is easy to see this as a reality when one considers that over 35 million corporate desktops are already wired for the intranet (IDC). The Forrester Research Group says that over 80 percent of the Fortune 1000 companies already have the necessary TCP/IP networks installed and that over 60 percent have or have initiated intranet projects in the last year.

Almost every market research firm has their forecast. Zona Research, Inc. of California expects corporate Web server shipments destined for intranet use to expand from some three million installed now to more than 500 million by the end of 1999. The Gartner Group of Stamford, CT says that 75 percent of all Fortune 1000 organizations will be running intranets by the next year.

What is the appeal of the intranet to the enterprise? This results from a number of key and important needs that are being fulfilled. They include; instant access, instant update, low infrastructure cost to implement, interoperability, interconnection to other information sources (Hot Links), and the ease of software distribution. All of these value statements are related to the technology. The impact of this on the future of computing for intranet application centers around standards based technology. This means that information-sharing capabilities of the World Wide Web now exist across any TCP/IP based network. It allows users to navigate quickly for shared information across the enterprise and with today's browsers, it now has a common user interface.

This represents a new corporate computing strategy of a shift back to server-based computing and platform independence. The Browser can be used on fat and thin clients and most operating systems and computers.

According to the Gartner Group Analyst Ray Laracuenta, most applications today are static publishing or moving content online. This is classified as Level I usage. Level II centers on the enabling day to day applications for Web use and using the intranet as a workgroup-computing platform. By 1999, Gartner Group expects to see a "best of breed" plateau with Level III. They will be characterized by a large base of Web-enabled applications, a consolidation of dozens of the application program interfaces (API) we see in Level II, more secure Web servers, and more powerful development tools.

## Project Management and the Intranet

We have already seen the importance of the intranet by the sheer numbers and interest which exists in the enterprise of today. The intranet will, at a minimum, improve communication and collaboration among the project participants. We will now look at how it will impact the overall processes and tools of project management in the next year or so and then beyond.

Many of today's software tools have begun the process by web-enabling their applications by allowing users access to their systems through the internet for report viewing or accessing static information. This approach allows existing software tools to provide the Level I usage as defined by the Gartner Group. It doesn't do much to change the project management processes. These are the most direct and easiest approach to adapting legacy host and client server technology to the Web.

Level II is the first step where technology will begin to change the way project management systems and processes will be defined over the next several years. Here we are talking about ways to use technology to change the workflow, improve user access and communication, and to create a dynamic Web-based business application system. New products will be built specifically for the intranet. These systems will create project and work management systems that require an active dialog between the browser and the database. Applications will be built to be easily "personalized" by workgroup within the enterprise while maintaining the integrity of the application. The intranet project/work management system will access the server database and be able to immediately have access to other data sources for information viewing and even retrieval. You will be able to send data to other data sources directly from the browser. Authorization rights will only limit the accessibility of information.

How might this work in the next five years? Experience and history have shown that the use of technology is evolutionary. The current and biggest use of the intranet for project management is the display of reports and other static information to a broad base of users. One can get a current update of status reports, stored business and schedule progress, and profiles of the project team, project goals, and other background info. The users will be able to send messages, receive personal responses, and may be included for frequent status updates as authorized. This early form of usage will be primarily communication directed.

We will see efforts made to interface existing products using the Internet for form submittal of various data elements such as time reporting. This approach although appropriate for early users of the Internet has a built in foundation of the existing technology environment. The Internet well is bound by the limits of the current technology.

Technology has seen the greatest advances where project management visionaries will look at the intranet and determine how this approach will be able to benefit them. Let's dream a little.

- If all users could access project data regardless of the size of their computer?
- If the project data needed could be readily requested ... and received ... from anywhere ... any time?
- If project data could be accessed, received, input, and used while working online?
- If each work group within an enterprise could customize the way they work while maintaining data integrity?
- If the entire workflow and processes could be modeled in such a way to have access to all required supporting information?
- If the power of the desktop tools could be integrated into the working model of the Intranet?

The intranet will help you manage the work processes from initiation, to authorization, during performance and through closure of your projects.

The intranet will allow each project manager, executive, or user to have a key input on how they will use and interact with the project data. An executive may have a need to review all projects and their status weekly in both tabular and graphic views. He/she may want to send an immediate message to get more direct information from one of the staff or may want to query the database for additional drill down information on different levels of the work structure. More detailed product specifications or progress reports may be required or a quick look at the client's organization or current business activity. A quarterly review of how all the work effort is going against the plan and accomplishment of company goals may be another need.

The project manager will want to make sure that status data and reports are received in a timely manner. The project manager may want to question status, forward messages, or seek more detail. The future work management system for use by project and resource managers might have the following characteristics:

### Infrastructure Setup

- Work Structures
  - Projects, Administration, Ad hoc, and other work
- Resource Structures
  - Organization
  - Skills
  - Other groupings
- Attributes
  - Flexibility in categorizing data

### Initiate Work

- Initiate new work
  - Content
  - Scope and estimates
  - Date requirements
- Authorize work request/SOW
- Assign work to performing department
- Initiate Change Orders

### Authorize Work

- Define Work Category (Form Types)
  - Tasks (time reporting levels)
  - Budget by level of detail desired
- Define Authorized Resources
  - By individual or higher level groupings
- Authorization Date Range
  - Open or close account for time charging

### Perform the Work

- Time Reporting via Intranet
- Approval by Authorized Persons
- Feedback
  - Estimates to Complete
  - Comments and Work Notes
- Review and Status

### Complete the Work

- Accept Closure of SOW
- Close Out the Charge Number
  - By person
  - By department
  - Total account closure

### Document-based Hot Links (Examples)

- Human Resource Systems
  - Employee Manual
  - Resource Resumes
- Statement of Work
- Systems and Procedures
- Custom Built Links

The use of the intranet will allow for both the standalone application of Web-based applications and the integration of other technologies such as client/server with the Web to extend and expand to meet the requirements of all work managers.

## Closure

The intranet offers a way global organizations will communicate, collaborate, and distribute information. It offers a low cost worldwide access to information associated with the work management process. We can be sure that project managers and the technology professionals will be working to take advantage of this opportunity and to advance the state-of-the-art in project management.

# Project Management in the Client/Server Environment

Steven M. Barger, Greenbrier & Russel, Inc.

## Introduction

As most of us already know, Information Technology has a fairly dismal track record when it comes to delivering projects on time and within budget. Many sources (Gartner Group, *Software* magazine, etc.) provide survey after survey showing systems projects that achieve the miraculous on time, within budget and actually meeting the real needs of the users as falling in the 3 to 10 percent range. In any other profession (including the government), a success rate of 10 percent would put most industries out of business. How did we get to such a precarious position? Myopic focus on the technology is how. Our concern should be for the future in that the technology is only going to change at an ever increasing rate. Client/server, distributed systems and N-tier architectures are more complex than our traditional systems were by an order of magnitude.

## Why Our Projects Fail

When we use traditional IT methods to manage these complex technologies, we only set ourselves up for failure. There are several key areas why these projects fail (Booch 1996). Often we fail to properly manage or understand the risks. We end up building the wrong thing. We become blindsided by technology by choosing a wrong piece of the puzzle or by misunderstanding the limitations of the current technology

Since the risks for these new technologies are significantly greater than those that we faced just five or ten years ago, it is up to the project manager and his/her key leaders to first understand then to properly manage the risks. At the least, the project manager should understand the technology being considered and should build his/her team with experts in the particular technology.

By building the wrong thing, we often look to the new technology to solve the wrong problem. An example of this is a customer that built a state of the art distribution system to reduce shipment time from vendor to customer to less than ten days. Meanwhile, a competitor, who chose a less aggressive technology, and focused purely on speed and efficiency, was able to build a system that would allow shipment times from vendor to customer in less than three days.

We become blindsided by technology when we forget how unstable the new tools can be. There are many cases of shops that selected or installed new development tools, new LAN configurations, or new database components during their construction or implementation phases and lived to regret the unplanned outages.

## Change in Delivering Systems

The new technologies of client/server, distributed systems, n-tier, etc. are really changing the way IT manages systems development. What makes these technologies different are the raised user expectations, the lack of architectural vision (due to the inexperience in the specific technologies), the relative complexity compared to the previous generation of systems, the extensive use of external resources, and the use of independent development teams.

We simply must be aware that users are reading PC Week and might even be able to code Visual Basic and we should use this skill as a benefit to the project. As a project manager, choosing your lead technical people with the skills in the appropriate technology they can assist you in getting over the humps. Since these new systems are often much more complex in terms of technology and often in terms of their scope (cross-functional vs. departmental), we should always perform a Technical Risk Assessment early on in the life cycle. These risk assessments can include what ifs and contingency plans to allow for cases where individual or groups of components fail. By relying on outside resources, you should simply be aware and manage their motivation and their expectations. Many project managers have run into trouble by working with vendors who agreed to help if they could get a big(ger) piece of the puzzle.

## Accidental Project Manager

One factor that has not changed is the way our project managers are assigned to most of the systems projects. Most project managers become project managers by accident. They often came from a technical background and may even know one piece of the current technical puzzle. Often, they are picked because they have a strong technical background, are a hard-nosed manager, have experience in the industry, or my favorite, someone who is currently available. These are not the wrong reasons; they are just not the right reasons. The best project manager is the one who can get the job done, and will likely need a different set of skills for each project. This means that you should not be afraid to switch project managers if the circumstances surrounding the project change

## Importance of PM and Architects

What many shops eventually realize is that the project manager and team of architects are critical to the success of the project. The term "architects" refers to a one or more folks responsible for the overall development strategy and architecture of the system. Often there is a lead architect referred to as the Systems Architect. Reporting to him or her may be an Application Architect, who is responsible for every part of the application that is visible to the user; a Technical Architect, who is responsible for the technical platform, development environment and any of the infrastructure pieces; and a Data Architect, who is responsible for the data including any conversions or interfaces.

We find that the project manager for client/server systems is a unique and imperative discipline and requires that the project manager (minimally) has the following skills: credibility, sensitivity and leadership. There are many demands placed upon the project manager specific to new technologies in IT. Acquiring adequate resources in today's job market is very difficult and expensive. Motivating personnel can be challenging when the technical hurdles seem insurmountable. Helping others overcome those hurdles and staying on track can be a full time effort. Making the hard trade-offs is perilous in an environment that is extremely slanted towards increased functionality and scope creep. Plan for failure by allowing the architects and developers to try new ideas early on, utilizing unbelievable communications skills so that everyone knows what they need to know.

The team of architects faces demands as well. In addition to some of the same demands that the project manager faces (such as dealing with obstacles, planning for failures, and lots of communication), they face a new set of demands. They must have experience in some facet of the new technology that they are attempting to assemble a system from. And, they must have an architectural vision that allows them to see past the technology hype to determine what is really best for the user, not what is fun for the technologists. They should assist the project manager in planning for failures by identifying the critical areas and the areas with the most risk.

### PM as Integrator

The project manager often serves as an integrator of the C/S system. They must be especially attuned to the risks that a high-technology project faces. They must be aware and understand the relative immaturity of the components that are used to construct a client/server, etc. system. They must be able to integrate a project team with experience in client/server architecture, business analysis, GUI design, multi-vendor databases, middleware, client operating systems, middleware operating systems, server operating systems, and object oriented technology. The project team must be brought in at the right time and must be able to quickly assimilate into the team regardless of physical location or prior experience with the team.

### Architect as Integrator

The architects also serve as integrators of a client/server system. They must have detailed knowledge of the various components that make up the system. They must be ready to investigate and replace components in the event that a particular component does not work as expected or is no longer available. They must know how to coordinate the development of components by separate teams, then assist in the assembly of those components into the system desired by the user.

## Critical Success Factors

I have identified several factors that are critical to the successful delivery of a client/server system. The rest of this paper focuses on these seven factors.

### Assessment of Project Manager potential

The first critical success factor is the assessment of the project manager's potential. There are many ways to do this, but the minimum is to check the project manager for core competencies in the areas of Project Integration Management, Project Scope Management, Project Time Management, Project Cost Management, Project Quality Management, Project Human Resource Management, Project Communications Management, Project Risk Management, and Project Procurement Management (Project Management Institute 1996).

### Training Curriculum

Second, invest in a training curriculum for the project manager and the architects. Too often, the concentration is on specific technical components. An emphasis on the skills required for the project manager (listed above) will assist him or her when the going gets tough. The architects require more broad training including some understanding of the difficulties faced by the project manager, in addition to constant updates on the emerging technology.

### Responsibility Matrix

A third success factor is the use of a simple tool commonly known as a Responsibility Matrix. Complete understanding of who is responsible for which tasks will make a big difference. Spending a little time up front by getting each person to agree to and understand their involvement (ranging from final approval to may be notified) really helps each person take charge of their area of responsibility.

## Development Methodology

A fourth critical success factor is the correct use of a development methodology. There are many methodologies out there, and I am not about to recommend a specific one, but there are several points regarding a methodology for guiding the process of a client/server development effort. Above all, the methodology must be iterative. It must allow for short cycles of analysis, design, development and integration, with the ability to refine in each cycle. Also, don't be afraid to customize specific portions of your current methodology as the target technology changes. Minor additions to cover new key technology areas, can make an "old" methodology work with the new technology.

## Clear Charter, Business Commitment, and the Right People

The remaining three critical success factors you already know, but sometimes a little reminder that they still apply to the project that feels like a quantum leap in technology. A clear charter is especially important to remind the technologists that the primary purpose of the system may not be to try out all of the latest tools listed in *Software* magazine. Business commitment is especially important because client/server projects often require a considerable investment for creation of the infrastructure. Finally, the project team is critical. Getting the right people at the right time and making sure that they are communicating is key to overcoming the unavoidable hurdles.

## References

Booch, Grady. 1996. *Object Solutions.*

Project Management Institute. 1996. *A Guide to the Project Management Body of Knowledge.* Upper Darby, PA: Project Management Institute.

# Project Management Meets the Year 2000 Challenge

Vicki Shapiro, United Services Automobile Association
Nancy Shutt, United Services Automobile Association

## Introduction

As the millennium approaches, everyone who uses a computer is realizing that their current systems may not work correctly with a year 2000 date. United Services Automobile Association (USAA) is tackling this issue. In 1995, USAA created a Change of Century (CofC) Program Management Office (PMO) and hired four project managers. All of USAA's computer systems are to be tested and certified as "century compliant." "Century compliant" means a system works correctly with dates from 1999 and beyond.

The business risk of successfully processing through the millennium has many facets. Most companies begin their year 2000 efforts by focusing on their older mainframe systems. Many legacy mainframe systems built in the 1970's are requiring programming modifications to become "century compliant." However, the risk is just as great with personal computing (PC) products and external business interfaces. Companies are buying and leasing both hardware and software today that is not designed to work after the year 2000. These products may either be replaced or fade into obsolescence depending on the vendor's response. Project planning identifies all of the year 2000 processing risks and prepares a company to initiate proactive projects.

The creation of project manager positions within the PMO offered an opportunity for USAA to use graduates from its project management curriculum. USAA based its curriculum on PMI's *PMBOK Guide* (1996), and many of its graduates have passed the Project Management Professional (PMP) exam. This paper addresses how the new project managers defined a consistent CofC project management process and then applied it to USAA's applications. This paper focuses on the process implemented in two Property and Casualty (P&C) Insurance system application areas: Auto/Property Underwriting and Claims Processing. Year 2000 considerations are given throughout the paper.

## Applying the Four-Phase Project Life Cycle

With the aid of a project management mentor familiar with the *PMBOK Guide*, the new project managers first developed a management plan to define a CofC project management process as their first project. The CofC Program Officer approved the

**Exhibit 1.**

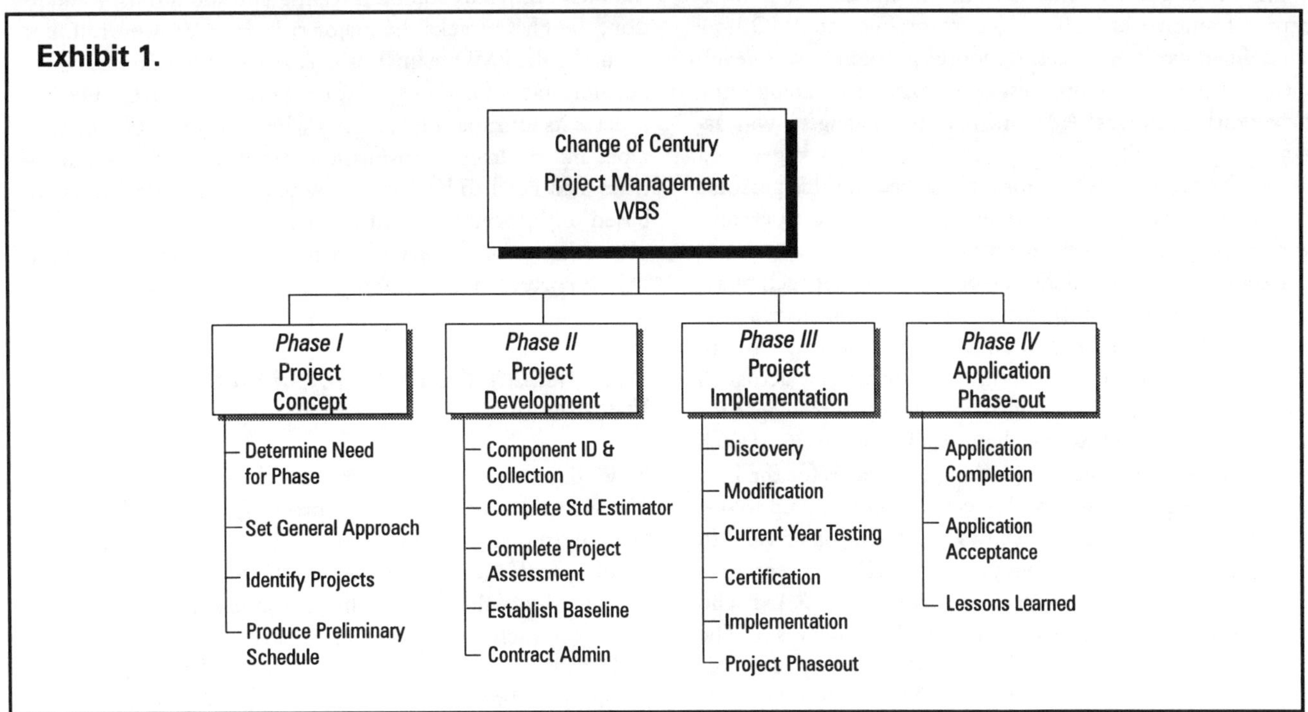

**Exhibit 2.**

Phase I - Project Concept
**Responsibility Accountability Matrix** (RAM)

| **Work Packages** | Responsibility Area | | | | | |
|---|---|---|---|---|---|---|
| | Work Package Mgr | Applic. Mgr | Applic. Exec | CofC PM | CofC Exec | CofC PMO |
| Determine Need for Phase | P D T | R | A | F | | S |
| Set General Approach | P D T | R | A | F | | S |
| Identify Projects | P D T | R | A | F | | S |
| Produce Preliminary Schedule | P D T | R | A | F | C | |

*Legend:*
A - Approval / Final Approval
D - Documentation
P - Perform the Work
S - Support
C - Change Control Board Authority
F - Facilitation
R - Review
T - Track Progress & Reporting

management plan and the project managers proceeded to define their Project Charter and Framework for their roles within the CofC program. The Framework applied the *PMBOK Guide* Project Life Cycle approach to the company's CofC methodology. For each phase in the Project Life Cycle, the project managers defined a work breakdown structure(WBS), a responsibility accountability matrix (RAM), reporting criteria, major deliverables and completion percentages.

The PMO gained benefits from the creation of a documented framework. CofC project teams and the PMO now had defined work packages. A reporting structure was developed that tracked the progress of a project team completing these work packages. A "work package manager" was assigned responsibility for completing the work packages for a phase. The work packages for a phase became this person's projects to lead based on the principle that "one person's work package is another person's project."

Exhibit 1 shows the defined work packages for each phase in the CofC project management process. Documentation defines the completion criteria for each work package. To ensure consistency of status reporting and forecasting across all CofC projects, the PMO defined completion percentages for each work package towards the overall completion of each phase. For example, the completion percentages for the four work packages in Phase One, Project Concept, add up to one hundred percent. Exhibit 2 shows the RAM for Phase 1 in the CofC project management process. PMO representatives and application area management agree via the RAM who performs the work, reviews it, and finally approves it. The RAM shows that the application area is ultimately responsible for completing the work, and the PMO exists to facilitate the application area's efforts. Identifying these relationships early helped manage the expectations of everyone associated with the project. Using the RAM set the expectation that the PMO existed to provide year 2000 expertise and to manage the overall USAA effort.

When project teams were planning in the Project Concept phase, the PMO helped identify risk areas and potential projects. As project teams progress to the implementation phase, the PMO provides common testing considerations. In addition, the PMO tracks the major risks for USAA overall. For example, the PMO maintains a database of the external business interfaces for USAA. Not only does a company need to process its information correctly when the year 2000 arrives, tapes and electronic transmissions received from external entities also need to be correct. When business decisions are based on information sent from other companies, it is another change of century effort to confirm that information will be correct in the future!

## Implementing the CofC Project Management Process

Now that the project managers had clearly defined a project management process for CofC projects, they faced the challenge of implementing it in application areas that were not familiar with PMI or the *PMBOK Guide*. Without diluting the integrity of the process, the project managers adapted the process to each of their assignments.

First, the project managers reinforced the importance of planning and preparing for the year 2000 risk. Through a

**Exhibit 3.**

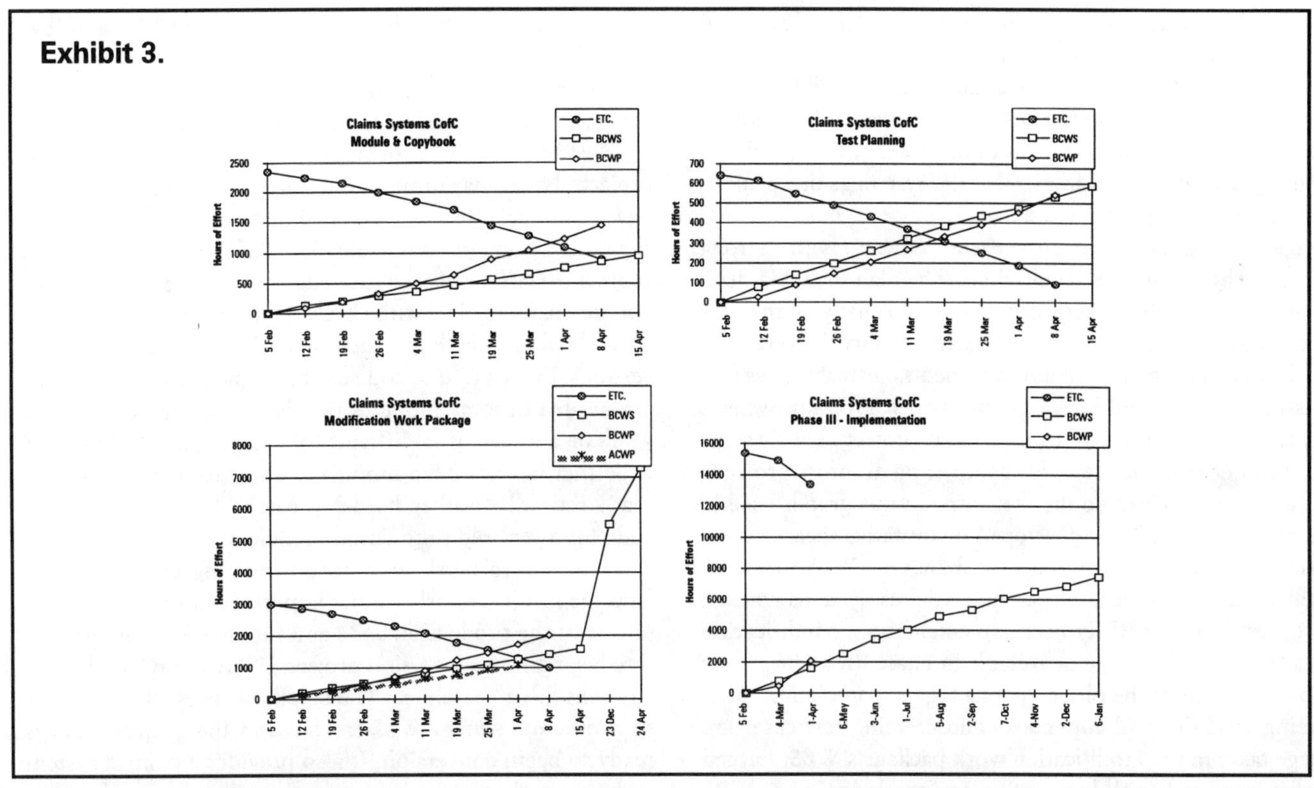


rigorous planning effort in Phase 1, all of the projects were planned and scheduled, which helped the business community see the CofC impact in both monetary and personnel costs. The overall CofC effort needed the business community's support because these projects took resources away from other strategic business-oriented projects. Most business communities have benefited from their information systems department buffering them from many mainframe changes, such as operating system upgrades. Many CofC conversions were designed to be operationally transparent to the business community, yet the CofC effort required business sponsors to supply some of their information systems resources for the CofC projects.

Identifying the PC products at risk played an even larger role in getting the business sponsor's support. The advent of the PC has allowed business people to work directly with vendors in obtaining hardware and software packages. Departments have created their own PC applications and have purchased or leased turn-key packages to automate many of their practices. Implementing the Phase 1 planning made the year 2000 risk more visible to the business community.

In some cases, there is a more direct impact to the business community if one of its PC or LAN packages will not work in the year 2000. Much of the impact to the business depends on how the vendor plans to respond to his product not working in 2000. A vendor may do one of the following: fix the product in a later release or version; replace the old product with a brand new product; or discontinue selling and supporting the old product. The business community may not have anticipated or budgeted for the necessary response to the vendor's action. For example, a replacement product could have different features that would require additional training. If a vendor will no longer support its product, the business community will need to find a new product on the market to meet its needs. Involving the business community in the planning effort with PC products helps gain sponsor support for the mainframe conversion projects as well. The business community's support is also critical when negotiating with vendors and other external interfacing companies.

After gaining support for Change of Century projects, it was time to implement the plans. The Auto/Property Underwriting Systems and Claims Systems projects provide an excellent contrast of how the project management process maintained consistency in projects with different technical approaches and project organizations. The findings are centered around a phased versus big bang conversion approach, different resourcing approaches, and different project organizational structures.

### Phased vs. Big Bang

The P&C Underwriting project teams, specifically Property Systems' team, identified separate projects for its different kinds of policy processing. They could convert their personal articles floater policies separate from their flood policies or their homeowner policies. Each project was planned and consolidated into an overall Property plan.

The Claims Systems' project team planned one large project to convert its system because of the system's interrelationships. Their approach was to maintain two parallel systems and then test and implement the system as one project. At first this approach created some concern, but the CofC project manager and the project team came up with a strong plan to show how they could do it. The plan included decision points so the project's direction could change if the project team did not meet its schedule and quality deliverables.

Both project teams employed earned value techniques successfully to track and forecast performance. Property Systems tracked the progress of an individual project as well as its overall performance towards completing all of its projects. Claims Systems created the first earned value graphs used in the CofC effort. They developed quantitative measures for large tasks within a work package manager's WBS for phase deliverables. Exhibit 3 shows how Claims Systems tracked progress in Phase III, Project Implementation. Modification is a large work package deliverable in Phase III, and it makes up 40 percent of the phase's percentage of completion. Analyzing modules and copybooks and creating test cases are large tasks in the modification work package's WBS. Earned value was used at all levels of project tracking: lower WBS tasks (Modules and copybooks, test planning), work package phase deliverables (modification), and the CofC project management process life cycle phase (Phase III).

The CofC project managers were continually educating the work package managers about the principles of earned value tracking and forecasting. While information systems personnel were familiar with estimating work and recording actual hours, the concept of tracking work package completion based on "earned" hours versus "actual" hours was new. At first, project teams wanted more credit towards the completion of a task when their actual hours exceeded the earned hours!

Regardless of the CofC approach, every application has some specific processing that has already encountered a 2000 or later date. USAA calls these specific 2000 date requirements "drop dead dates," and project teams identified these risks during their Phase 1 planning efforts. The CofC project manager and the project team monitor these "drop dead dates," and the team makes system changes as warranted to prevent problems from occurring. Managing these specific "drop dead dates" is crucial when working on year 2000 conversion projects.

### Resourcing: Outsource, Addsource, In-house

Because a lot of year 2000 work requires repetitive changes to date fields in program logic, CofC projects appeared suitable candidates for outsourcing. USAA's preference was to contract with a company to outsource the conversion work using a fixed-price contract. This kept more USAA employees available to work on strategic business changes that would require their business knowledge. By having a fixed-price contract, the contractor assumed a lot of the conversion risk.

The PMO contracted outsourcers for ninety day conversion projects. Ninety day project cycles allowed conversion work to have a minimal effect on other coding projects which touched the same system or subsystem. The PMO expected the outsourcer to staff the project as needed to meet the date or to negotiate a new end date with USAA before signing the contract.

The risks can be high when preparing for year 2000 conversions. Every piece of code has to be analyzed, and changes are needed in some modules that have not been touched in years or decades. It is difficult to find people familiar with code that has not been modified. The author may have already retired! Another hardship can be finding the source code for a very old production module or copylib.

Preparing to work with an outsourcing contractor did help the PMO see early on the importance of creating a duplicate of the production code and running parallel tests before beginning a conversion project. USAA's CofC methodology calls this a "baseline." The baseline proves all the correct source components are assembled and the project team is ready to begin conversion. It also provides a control system and expected results to use when parallel testing the converted code. (Change of century conversions do not change functionality.)

Working with an outsourcer for code conversion was foreign to most USAA P&C systems personnel. USAA personnel were accustomed to making their own coding changes and occasionally hiring a contract programmer on a time and material basis. Eliciting the cultural change needed to supply a complete work package to an outsourcer was a challenge. Completeness at the handoff was critical because the outsourcer was working on a fixed-price contract, and USAA personnel were not accustomed to building a "baseline" before making modifications to a project.

Another outsourcing challenge was supplying all of the system statistics required by outsourcing firms during the contract negotiations. Supplying the statistics took a lot of the project team's time, and the numbers were asked for in many different combinations. Application programmers ended up writing ad hoc programs to gather the statistics the outsourcer wanted to support his estimating. Supplying this information during the contract negotiations was definitely new to USAA's programming culture where most maintenance projects are estimated and done in-house with USAA personnel running the project.

Other alternatives to outsourcing are doing all of the work in-house or doing the work in-house with the aid of contract programmers. Using contractors on a time and material basis to fill project resource requirements is called addsourcing in this paper. In-house staffing with some addsourcing has worked well at USAA for those project teams that want a more hands-on approach to their conversions. Many teams want to make the changes themselves, but need some extra manpower for easily defined repeatable tasks.

Property Systems chose the outsourcing approach since it was able to break up its conversion into manageable pieces. In fact, Property Systems supported the pilot projects for both outsourcing contractors USAA has used for CofC conversions. Reporting earned value on the Personal Articles Floater (PAF) project was challenging for several reasons. Because this was a fixed-price contract, the outsourcer definitely would not share his actual time or costs with USAA. The USAA project manager and the outsourcing project manager agreed to define the percentage of value each milestone contributed to the project. The outsourcer provided a Gantt chart giving specific target dates for each milestone. When the project met these milestones, a cumulative percentage was calculated from each milestone's percentage of importance. After the lessons learned session, the project would be 100 percent complete. The USAA project manager was able to graph the progress of the project by placing the cumulative percentage complete on the y-axis and the elapsed days on the x-axis.

When working with outsourcers, USAA found many of the outsourcers' project managers did not understand the earned value concept. Some could recite earned value jargon, but USAA's outsourcers could not develop an applicable chart to track the project. It took the aid of USAA's contracted project management mentor to develop the PAF earned value graph with the USAA project manager. Exhibit 4 shows the earned value graph.

**Exhibit 4.**

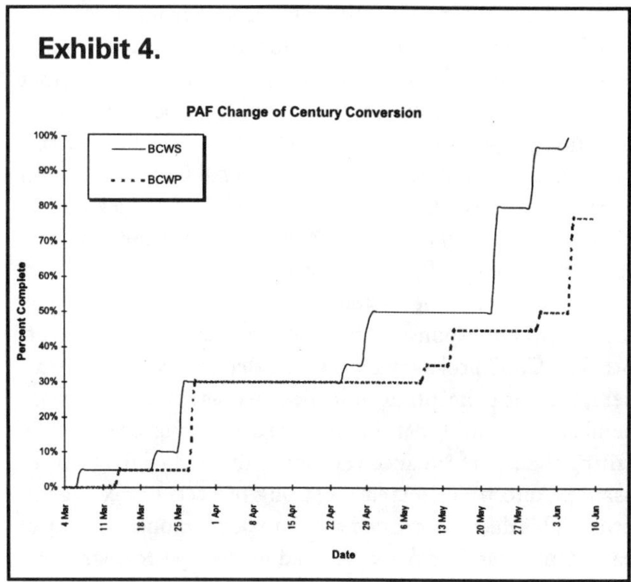


The PAF project's progress was interesting to watch. It was scheduled to be a 94-calendar-day project. However, on elapsed Day 68, the USAA project manager forecasted the project would take 100 days while the outsourcing project manager strongly denied it. One week later the outsourcing project manager was asking for an extension! The overall project time for the outsourcer was 112 days. Exhibit 4 shows the project was only 77 percent complete as of June 10 when it should have been completed.

One last point on earned value reporting. The PAF outsourcing project manager had a tracking spreadsheet that listed every module in a testing work package. The team diligently recorded its progress and the project manager gave USAA a chart of actual progress each week. However, it took USAA several weeks and the aid of the Program Officer to persuade the outsourcing project manager to include the estimate of when he planned to complete testing modules in his chart. The outsourcing project manager did not see that he had to have a plan of when he would complete testing modules to be able to track and forecast his progress. One could conclude from USAA's outsourcing experience that there is a lot of room for improvement in the application of project management principles to software projects.

The Claims Systems project had much better success than Property's PAF project in regards to applying project management. The team had created a detailed work breakdown structure with bottom-up estimating to create its project plan. The team eagerly tracked its progress using measures like modules, copylibs, and test cases completed. Their morale increased as they saw their efforts result in a schedule performance index (SPI) greater than one. From an outsider's viewpoint, it appeared that the team had thought through their project and were working their plan piece by piece.

## Project Organizational Structure

Application area management chose varied ways to organize their CofC project teams. Both Auto Underwriting Systems and Claims Systems were business critical systems that warranted the attention of a project manager from the CofC PMO. CofC project managers only had referential authority from the USAA officer running the CofC PMO. None of the project managers had been managers in the traditional line management structure, so the application area executive's support was crucial.

Both Auto and Claims line management created dedicated project teams. While the team members still participated in regular on-call maintenance duties, they were not assigned to any other project work. The application areas differed regarding to whom they assigned responsibility and accountability for their CofC projects.

Claims Systems assigned a strong line manager to be in charge of its overall CofC effort. He was directly involved with the detailed project planning and initial implementation efforts. After buying into the CofC project manager's ideas, the Claims line manager provided formal authority to implement the ideas with the project team. This is not to say that implementing new project management concepts was easy for the CofC project manager. Only that other Claims Systems line managers had a peer in their functional line organization associated with the CofC effort. Also, a line manager was familiar with each team member's work when it came time to write individual performance reviews.

Auto Underwriting Systems designated the CofC project manager to be responsible and accountable for its overall effort. The CofC project manager attended the executive's staff meetings with the other auto line managers. Project team members were told that the CofC project manager would be writing their performance reviews at the end of the year. In essence, Auto tried to create a strong project matrix organization. This decision created some anxiety among the project team. Only true line managers had written performance reviews in the past, and team members were concerned that management would not really know what they had done during the year if a line manager was not involved. Also, the team felt excluded from the Auto Systems organization at times because they were organized different than their peers in Auto Systems. Most of the team members were uncomfortable with all of the change they were experiencing. They were learning and applying new project management principles, dealing with outsourcing companies, and prototyping a new organizational structure.

In hindsight, some Auto tasks were more difficult because a line manager was not involved. Requesting additional Auto personnel was always a formal process, because the line managers controlled all of the resources. When it came time to do performance reviews, the line managers balked at having the CofC project manager participate in their meetings. The CofC project manager ended up writing the performance reviews, but the line managers controlled the salary and bonus determinations, and they conducted the performance review sessions with individual team members.

## Conclusion

The USAA CofC PMO is successfully applying a consistent project management process as well as educating company personnel about *PMBOK Guide* concepts. It is rewarding to see the CofC project managers' initial planning efforts now implemented in the CofC project teams. Each team maintains a project plan, and the PMO reports the scheduled performance index at various organizational levels biweekly.

Other USAA projects have used the CofC PMO as an example of how to apply *PMBOK Guide* principles. Since the documentation of the CofC project management process, USAA has initiated much larger efforts to facilitate the use of project management techniques. In addition to the increasing number of training programs, all of the information systems executive management have attended special courses at the encouragement of the chief information officer. USAA now has a dedicated team which is responsible for facilitating the roll out of project management practices throughout USAA.

Whatever approach a team selects to ensure its systems will work in the year 2000, thorough project management practices help teams keep track of the multiple risks and projects. With proper planning and definition, a program management office can apply a consistent project management process to projects with varying details.

### References

Project Management Institute Standards Committee. 1996. *A Guide to the Project Management Body of Knowledge.* Upper Darby, PA: PMI.

# How to Consider the Fuzziness of Planning Knowledge In Project Management Software Using the Theory of Fuzzy Sets

Jens Federhen, University of Siegen, Germany

## Introduction

In project management, expressions like "we are *a bit late* with our detail design" or "the new drilling center will be delivered *at the beginning of April*" or "it will be *quite expensive*" are very common. Such terms do not cause any problems for the communication among human beings (on the contrary: they make our communication very effective!) but problems arise when we are forced to specify them in more detail. For instance, if we had to update the project network plan on our computer, we would have to enter an exact new finish date for the detail design works, thus we would have to explain exactly what we mean by "a bit late," that is, we would have to state how many extra days (or hours or weeks) we need because our EDP tool will only accept one figure and a time unit. As everyone knows that planning knowledge can never be exact, the confidence in such plans is often low. However, plans that are not generally accepted are in great danger of not being kept.

The theory of fuzzy sets is known to be a means for handling vague data. It was developed by L. A. Zadeh in 1965 (Zadeh 1965). Since then, there have been numerous successful applications especially in controlling technical processes that are difficult to model with traditional techniques. Concentrating on project scheduling we will see in this paper that the principles of the fuzzy set theory are also applicable to project management problems.

## A Short Overview of the Theory of Fuzzy Sets

In order to understand how the theory of fuzzy sets can be applied to project management, we need to know some of its fundamentals.

### Basic approach

The motivation to develop this theory at all was that the natural language we use for written and especially for oral communication often proves to be a more powerful "tool" for describing situations in our daily life than those tools we use when modeling such situations for calculation and decision purposes (Zimmermann 1985). The theory of fuzzy sets provides us with a kind of "interface" to depict natural language expressions in computer models. To illustrate the basic approach of this theory, let us consider a very general example before concentrating on project management. We say "the water is hot", a computer needs to know "the water temperature is $x$°C" where $x$ is a real number, e.g. 35 or 95.8. The question is now, what temperatures can be called "hot." Of course, we can say that all temperatures between 80°C and 97.3°C are "hot." But then, 78°C or 97.4°C could not be called "hot" any more. Such a strict interpretation often does not make sense.

The theory of fuzzy sets can solve this problem by interpreting the problem as a problem of sets. There is a universe $T$ of all possible temperatures $T1$, $T2$, ... , $Tn$. The mathematicians write:

$T = \{T1, T2, \dots, Tn\}$.

Then, there is a sub-set $H$ of those temperatures in $T$ which can be called "hot." For each of the $Ti$ in $T$ we can now say, whether it belongs to $H$ or not. The difference between a normal "crisp" set and a fuzzy set is that if $H$ is a crisp set, the $Ti$ can either belong to $H$ or not. If $H$ is a fuzzy set, intermediate states are allowed, too, that is, the $Ti$ can belong *partly* to $H$. Therefore, a new quantity is introduced: the degree of membership (or simply "membership") $\mu H$ which is assigned to every $Ti$ in $T$ and which tells in how far $Ti$ belongs to $H$. The expression $\mu H(Ti) = 0.8$ means that $Ti$ belongs to $H$ for 80% or is an 80%-member of $H$. A fuzzy set thus is a set of pairs:

$H = \{ (T1,\mu H(T1)), (T2,\mu H(T2)), \dots, (Tn,\mu H(Tn)) \}$.

Now, let us have another look at the universe $T$. Until now, it has been assumed to consist of $n$ elements, where $n$ is a natural number 1, 2, 3, ... With respect to temperatures, however, we will normally not have to consider individual temperature values but the whole temperature axis, so $T$ contains an infinite number of elements. To match the above definition, we must assign a degree of membership to each point on the temperature axis. Therefore, we establish a so-called membership function:

$\mu H = f(T)$.

### Properties of Fuzzy Sets

In order to describe and to compare fuzzy sets, some properties have been defined (Zimmermann 1985; Rabetge



PROJECT MANAGEMENT INSTITUTE 28th Annual Seminars & Symposium
Chicago, Illinois: Papers Presented September 29 to October 1, 1997

**Exhibit 1.** Height and Alpha-Level-Set of A Fuzzy Set

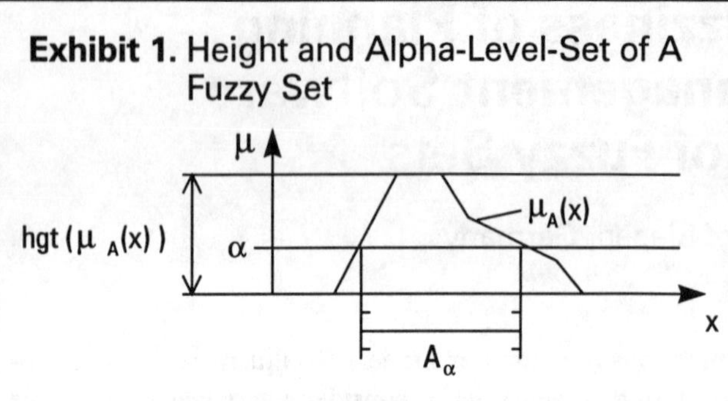


**Exhibit 2.** Union and Intersection of Crisp and Fuzzy Sets

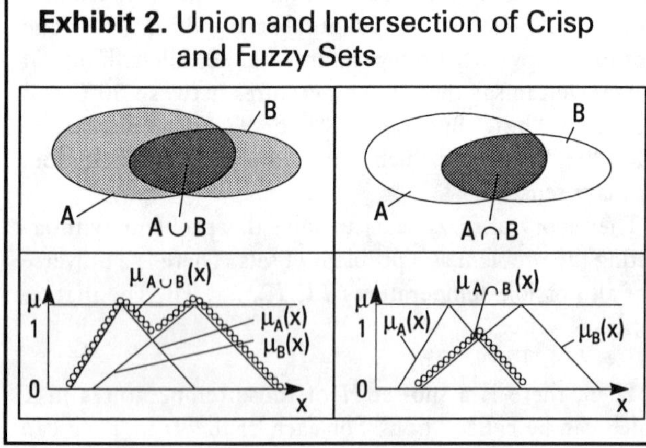


1990). In this paper we need to know the terms "alpha-level-set" and "height."

The alpha-level-set (or "α-cut") $A\alpha$ of a fuzzy set $A$ is the (crisp) set of elements which belong to the fuzzy set at least to the degree α. (Remark: The alpha-level-set for α ( 0 is called "support" of the fuzzy set and the alpha-level-set for α = 1 is called the "core" of the fuzzy set.)

The height hgt($A$) of a fuzzy set $A$ is the greatest membership degree in $A$. If the height of a fuzzy set is one, we say that the fuzzy set is "normalized."

Exhibit 1 shows the height and one alpha-level-set of a fuzzy set. Instead of the temperature we have chosen the more general variable $x$.

## Mathematical Operations with Fuzzy Sets

We will now see some examples which show that it is possible to calculate with membership functions. The results of mathematical operations with fuzzy sets will again be fuzzy sets. As fuzzy sets are characterized by their membership function, fuzzy mathematical operations use membership functions as arguments and the results they deliver will be membership functions as well.

Let us first have a look at the union and intersection of two fuzzy sets (Zadeh 1965; Zimmermann 1985; Rommelfanger 1988). The membership function of the union of

**Exhibit 3.** Approximation of Membership Functions Via Alpha-Level-Sets

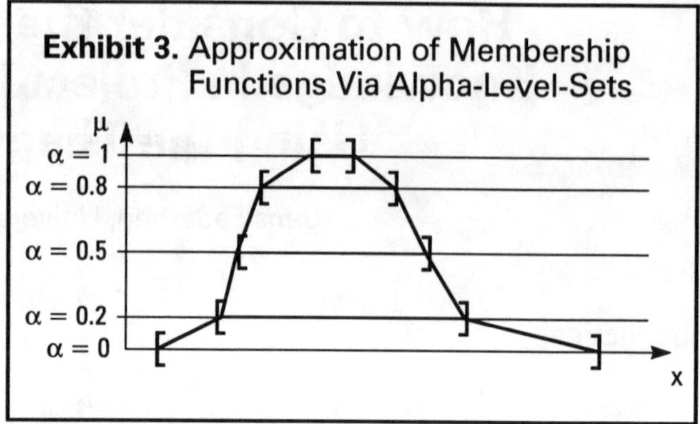


two fuzzy sets $A$ and $B$ can be determined as the maximum of the two arguments. This is shown in Exhibit 2 together with the intersection which uses the minimum instead of the maximum.

$\mu A{\cup}B(x) = \max(\mu A(x), \mu B(x))$

$\mu A{\cap}B(x) = \min(\mu A(x), \mu B(x))$

**Exhibit 1: Height and Alpha-Level-Set of A Fuzzy Set**

Apart from pure set operations, membership functions can also be used for arithmetic operations (Zimmermann 1985, Rommelfanger 1988, Kaufmann and Gupta 1991). Like before, the operations known in classic arithmetic are transformed in such a way that they use membership functions as arguments and deliver membership functions as results. (These membership functions are often called "fuzzy numbers" because they can model expressions like "about six," "not quite 7" etc.)

In this paper, we do not want to deduct step by step the formulas to apply but only show the principle. To do so, let us recall that the alpha-level-set of a fuzzy set is an interval $[a, b]$ of real numbers. (Remark: The term $[a, b]$ symbolizes the set of all real numbers between $a$ and $b$.) If one knows several alpha-level-sets and draws them into a $\mu$-$x$-diagram, the limits of the alpha-level-sets can be linked such that at least an approximated version of the membership function is available. We could be sure to get the exact membership function only if we knew an infinite number of different alpha-level-sets. (Remark: There are other methods of fuzzy arithmetic which do not have this inconvenience but which have other ones. Anyway, for scheduling with fuzzy data it is not really necessary to have exact membership functions.)

Now, calculation with membership functions can be reduced to calculation with intervals. The result of the addition of two intervals $[a1\ b1]$ and $[a2, b2]$ is again an interval the limits of which are determined summing up the lower limits and the upper limits of the argument intervals:

$[a1, b1] + [a2, b2] = [\,(a1+a2), (b1+b2)\,]$.

To determine the maximum of two intervals $[a1\ b1]$ and $[a2, b2]$ we simply have to find the maximum of the two lower and the two upper limits:

max ( [$a$1, $b$1], [$a$2, $b$2] ) = [ max ($a$1, $a$2), max ($b$1, $b$2) ].

Exhibit 4 shows the fuzzy versions of the minimum and maximum operation. Note that the maximum of two triangular membership functions is not necessarily a triangular membership function again.

## Application of the Fuzzy Set Theory to Project Planning

In the third part of the paper we will see how to apply the fuzzy set theory to project management. Our main example will be project scheduling but it is also possible to use this approach for other project management dimensions.

Project schedules are usually based on network plans. To make use of the principles of the fuzzy set theory in network planning, we will proceed in two major steps. The first step is to "fuzzify" the temporal quantities contained in network plans and use fuzzy arithmetic for the forward and backward pass. The second step is to consider the fuzziness of the network logic as well.

### Membership Functions tor Temporal Quantities

A project schedule can contain activities, events and relationships. In general, the planner will only have a fuzzy imagination of activity durations and event times, so these quantities can be treated as fuzzy quantities and characterized by membership functions. Exhibit 5 shows two examples. The first one shows an estimate of a duration. To express this estimate in words we could say that the activity will take "about three to four weeks." The second example shows a fuzzy date of an event that will take place "at the end of September or the beginning of October."

### Network Planning With Fuzzy Temporal Quantities

We have seen how to model the vagueness of event dates and activity durations using membership functions. We have also seen how to perform arithmetic operations with membership functions. Now, it is easily imaginable that we can use membership functions and fuzzy arithmetic when calculating the network plan (Dubois and Prade 1978; Rabetge 1990).

It is interesting to recognize that in fuzzy project scheduling there are earliest and latest dates calculated already in the forward pass because the use of membership functions implies that we are working with intervals rather than with single figures. Another change is that we have to use a minimum and a maximum duration while in classic network planning there is only one duration.

The results of the fuzzy forward and backward pass can be presented in a fuzzy Gantt chart (Federhen 1995, 1996, 1997a). To give an example of such a diagram, exhibit 6 shows a screen shot of a software prototype for fuzzy project scheduling. On the left, the chart contains a column for the membership functions of the activity durations. On the right, the membership functions of the start and finish dates are presented. A person who is familiar with fuzzy arithmetic can retrace the forward and backward pass from this diagram.

**Exhibit 4.** Fuzzy Addition and Fuzzy Maximum as Examples of Fuzzy Arithmetic

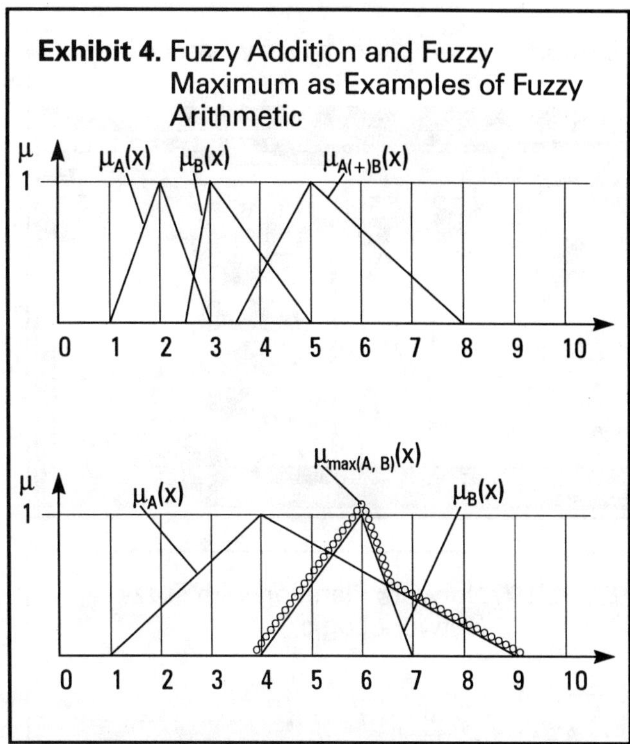


**Exhibit 5.** Two Examples of Membership Functions for Temporal Quantities

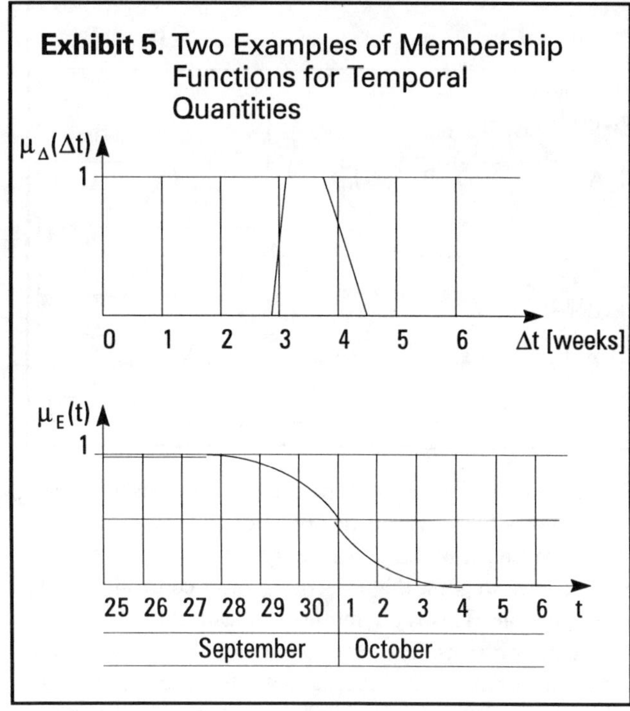

**Exhibit 6.** Example of a Fuzzy Gantt Chart

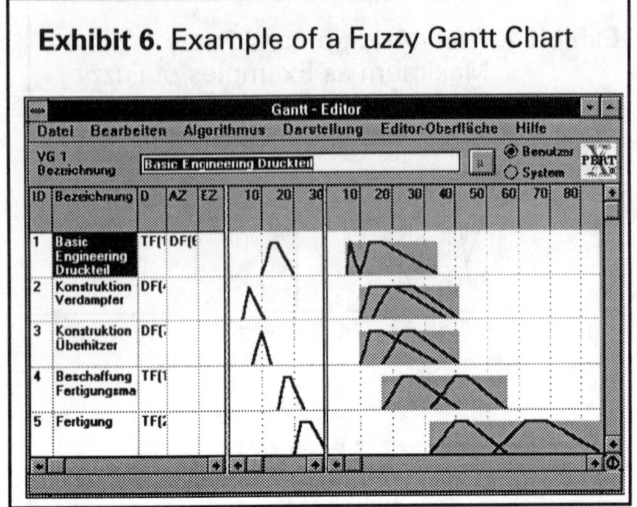


**Exhibit 7.** Network Planning with Fuzzy Network Logic

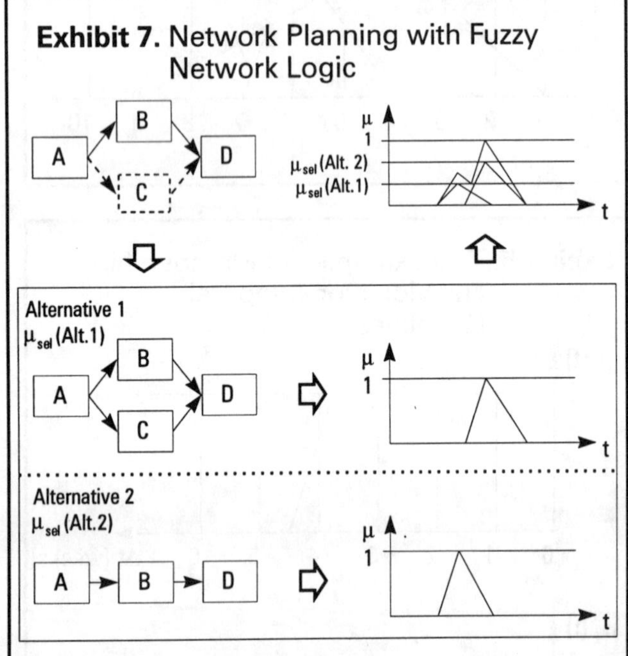


Note that the fuzziness of the events is obviously increasing with every fuzzy arithmetic operation. In a large network, this can cause problems if the interval of the project finish date becomes so great that effective project controlling is no longer possible. This is an impressive illustration of the project's temporal risks. The natural reaction of a project manager to these risks is to fix target dates for important events within the project (the so-called "milestones"). The verbal formulation of such target dates is very often fuzzy (e.g. "the foundations shall be ready by the *beginning of April*"). We have seen that this can be modeled using membership functions. These membership functions then work as a kind of filter for those calculated by the system bringing down the fuzziness to a reasonable level again. Target dates are thus of special significance in fuzzy project scheduling, and it is interesting to see that they play exactly the same role in a fuzzy network plan as they do in the imagination of the planner (Federhen 1995, 1996, 1997a).

## Considering Fuzziness in the Network Logic

Until now, only the temporal quantities of a network have been regarded as fuzzy quantities. The sequence of activities (the "logic" of the network) was assumed to be well-defined and always the same. In general, however, the planner's imagination of the project's logic is vague, too. Uncertainties in the logic of a network may even have a much greater impact on the total project than those in duration and event time estimates.

To have only a fuzzy imagination of a network logic means that one is unable to say exactly how that network will look like, that is, which activities and which relationships it will contain. Thus, in principle several different network plans can be set up, each one representing one alternative logic of the project (Federhen 1997b).

Each of these networks can be calculated as described above so that in the end for each start and finish event there are as many membership functions as there are alternative network logics. To consider the uncertainties in the network logic in one membership function, we have to aggregate the membership functions resulting from the different alternatives. This aggregation can be performed in different ways. The easiest way is the union of all alternatives as described earlier.

Another approach can be found by the following reflection (Federhen 1997b): We have set up several networks, each one describing one alternative logic of the project. As a rule, the different alternatives will be more or less close to the course of the project we will observe in reality. We do not know in advance which alternative will be the closest to reality, but an experienced planner will have a feeling which alternatives have better chances and which ones have less good chances. This can be expressed by a degree of membership called "selection certainty $\mu sel$." The set of alternative network logics is thus considered as a fuzzy set. Multiplying the alternative membership functions of the events by their selection certainty before the aggregation, we get a result that considers the different relevance of the network logic alternatives. We only have to make sure that the result is normalized because the multiplication by the selection certainty has changed the height of the alternative membership functions. Exhibit 7 illustrates how different network logics can be deducted if the sets of activities and relationships are considered as fuzzy sets. It also shows the different membership functions of the project finish event and the aggregated membership function.

There is still one important problem to be solved with setting up the alternative network logics. We cannot expect the planner to formulate all network logics to be considered. This would not only mean an intolerable amount of work, it would also force the planner to specify his planning knowledge in such a detailed way that it could probably no longer be called "fuzzy."

To solve this problem we need a kind of "incomplete" description of the alternatives in the network logic. One way to do so is the use of plus-/minus-networks (Federhen 1997c). We formulate one basic network. Then, we set up plus-/minus-networks to consider alternatives. In a plus-/minus-network, all elements that are part of the basic network but shall no longer be considered in the actual alternative are listed up as "minus-elements" and those elements which have to be added to the basic network in order to describe the actual alternative are listed up as "plus-elements." This procedure has already been successfully applied to keep data on variants in parts lists. If the plus-/minus-networks only refer to a small part of the fundamental network they can be combined so that the number of alternative networks is greater than the number of plus-/minus-networks.

**Exhibit 8.** $\mu$-Editor in X-Pert

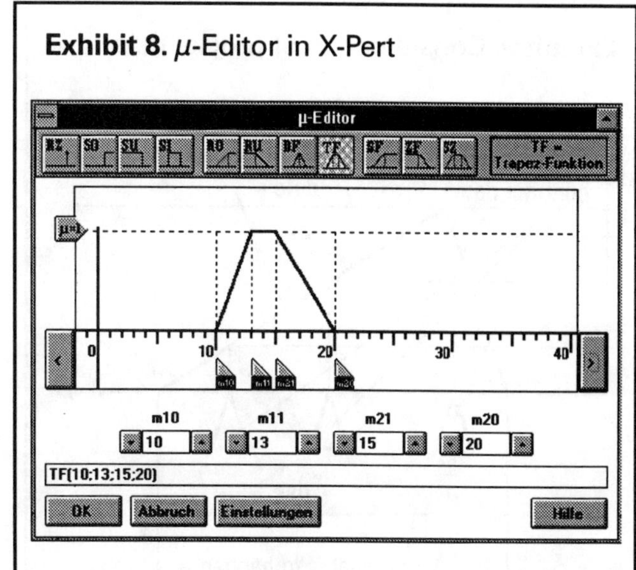


## Software Systems for Project Management with Fuzzy Data

At the moment, there are no commercial software systems for project management known to the author that explicitly work according to the principles of the fuzzy set theory and there will probably be a lot of additional research work to be done before these methods become more widespread. It is therefore difficult to make remarks how to implement project management software capable of dealing with fuzzy data.

In exhibit 6, an example of a software prototype called "X-PERT" (Federhen 1995) is shown. This stands for "eXtended PERT" and wants to indicate the fuzzy extension of the classic PERT method.

X-PERT is based on a relational database management system. In order to facilitate data entry, two graphic editors are used. The Gantt-Editor shown in Exhibit 6 contains two tabular screen elements for the activity and relationship data (in Exhibit 6, the relationship table is hidden). A further screen element is used for depicting the fuzzy Gantt chart. The surface of the Gantt-editor is intentionally made to resemble that of traditional project management software systems. For the entry of user-defined membership functions, the $\mu$-editor (Exhibit 8) is used.

## Conclusion

We have seen that the theory of fuzzy sets is a means to handle vague data in project plans. On the basis of the fuzzy network logic, even more powerful tools are within reach. Knowing about alternative ways to continue the project by fuzzifying the network logic the project manager can be supported in serious situations (e.g. the system can make proposals how to change the schedule when an important delivery is postponed). Furthermore, it seems to be worth while to consider fuzziness not only in project scheduling but also in other project management dimensions such as resources and costs.

Compared to classic models, the consideration of the fuzziness means additional efforts with respect to entering and processing data, but the results will contain much useful and important information, too (Rabetge 1990; Federhen 1995, 1996).

First, planning data is always more or less vague because we cannot know exactly what will happen in the future. Expressing planning knowledge in bare figures thus means a severe loss of information which can lead to serious misinterpretation.

Second, we should recall that we use project plans in order to make sure that the project's goals (e.g. target date and budget) are met. There is always the risk that we will fail to do so. Our plans should consider this risk and compare what *can* happen (e.g. the interval of possible finish dates) to what *is to* happen (e.g. the target date prescribed by top management or the customer). As shown in Exhibit 9, in traditional methods the information about how exact the results are gets lost whereas in those methods based on the fuzzy set theory this information is systematically collected and processed.

This not only shows the project manager where his action is needed. The decision about how to handle project risks is left with him as well, and it is not delegated to the computer system that is not capable of taking that decision (Dörfel and Schöpke 1993). This is probably the most important improvement of the fuzzy approach, apart from the fact that

**Exhibit 9.** Consideration of project risks

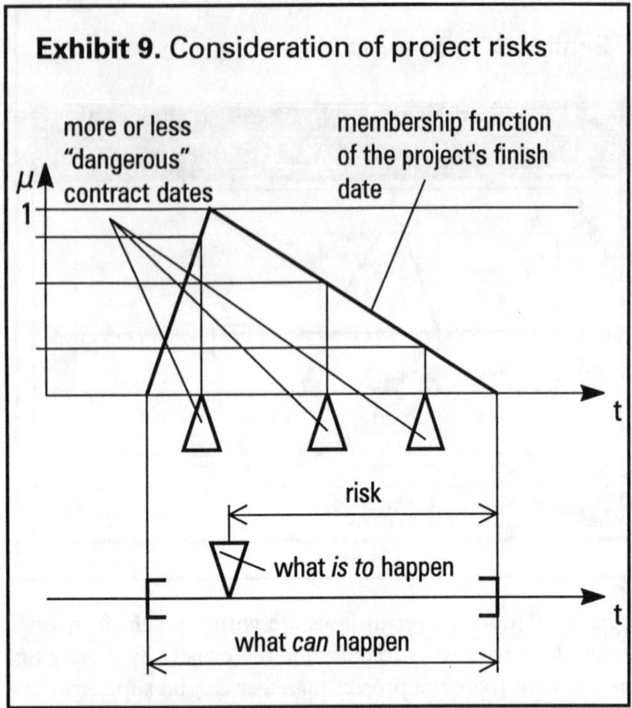


fuzzy models are more correct (or more "humane") representations of the imagination a planner has of a project.

## References


Dörfel, Frank and Giesela Schöpke. 1993. *Schädliche Schärfe: Ideen zu einem Fuzzy Projektmanagement.* GPM-Formum der GPM Gesellschaft für Projektmanagement; Weimar, 22–25 September.

Dubois, Didier and Henri Prade. 1978. Algorithmes de plus courts chemins pour traiter des données floues. In: *R.A.I.R.O Recherche Opérationelle / Operations Research* 12, No. 2 (Mai): pp. 213–227)

Federhen, Jens. 1995. *Entwicklung eines Programmsystems für die Netzplantechnik unter Berücksichtigung der Unschärfe von Informationen.* Final Diploma Thesis, University of Siegen (Tutor: Prof. Dr. Gerald Adlbrecht): November.

Federhen, Jens. 1996. Development and Implementation of a Fuzzy Network Algorithm. In: Aliev, R. A.; Bonfig, K. W.; Aliev, F.; Wieland, F. (editors): *Proceedings of the Second International Conference on Application of Fuzzy Systems and Soft Computing, ICAFS '96, Siegen, June 25 - 27, 1996:* pp. 525–533.

Federhen, Jens. 1997a. Netzplantechnik mit unscharfen Zeitangaben. In: Biethahn, Jörg, Hönerloh, Albrecht, Kuhl, Jochen and Nissen, Volker (Eds.): *Fuzzy Set-Theorie in betriebswirtschaftlichen Anwendungen.* Munich: Verlag Franz Vahlen.

Federhen, Jens. 1997b. Considering the Fuzziness in the Imagination of the Logic of Network Plans. In: *Proceedings of the Second European Workshop on Fuzzy Decision Analysis and Neural Networks for Management, Planning and Optimization (EFDAN'97). Dortmund, Germany, June 10 - 11, 1997*

Federhen, Jens. 1997c. *Netzplantechnik mit unscharfer Ablaufstruktur.* Draft (to appear); University of Siegen

Kaufmann, Arnold and Madan M. Gupta. 1991. *Introduction to Fuzzy Arithmetic: Theory and Applications.* New York: Van Nostrand Reinhold.

Rabetge, Christian. 1990. *Fuzzy Sets in der Netzplantechnik.* Diss. Göttingen, zugl. Wiesbaden: Dt. Univ.-Verl.

Rommelfanger, Heinrich. 1988. *Entscheiden bei Unschärfe: Fuzzy Decision Support-Systeme.* Berlin, Heidelberg, New York: Springer-Verl.

Zadeh, Lotfi Asker. 1965. Fuzzy Sets. In: *Information and Control* 8:, pp. 338 - 344.

Zimmermann, Hans-Jürgen. 1985. *Fuzzy Set Theory and Its Applications.* Boston, Dordrecht, Lancaster: Kluwer-Nijhoff Publishing.

# Vendor Partnering: Systems Development Sourcing in the Next Century

Vicki Wong, Nissan Motor Corporation
Janet Mentzer, Ralphs Grocery Company

## The Concept

### Background

Like most companies, Nissan Motor Corporation turned to outsourcing when the systems development capacity of its Information Technology Management (ITM) department fell short of demand. After receiving less than desired results on several multimillion dollar projects, ITM management began looking for ways to ensure more consistently successful outcomes. In May 1996, Nissan began implementation of a *vendor partnering* program to address some of these concerns. This paper will discuss vendor partnering as a viable alternative to traditional outsourced development, and analyze the lessons learned from Nissan's experience with its implementation.

### Definition

At its most simplistic level, vendor partnering is a streamlined approach to procurement which eliminates the solicitation steps, and replaces them with a pre-qualified set of prime contractors (see Exhibit 1). During procurement planning, the vendor partners are reviewed to determine which has the strengths required for the project. The project charter is developed in conjunction with this vendor. The solicitation planning process, the solicitation process, and the source selection process are not required as the vendor has already been selected and the contract awarded. No RFP (request for proposal) or RFQ (request for quote) is required from the performing organization (ITM), and no proposals are received for review from prospective sellers in the vendor partnering approach. Fees would be based on actual hours and expenses incurred towards production of a fixed set of deliverables.

### Benefits

Anticipated benefits of this approach include:

- Enables projects to begin more quickly by reducing procurement lead time.
- Removes adversarial relationships created by competitive bid and fixed price arrangements. By eliminating the need to continually 'sell' their services, vendor partners could function more effectively as extensions of internal staff rather than promoting their allegiance (i.e., "leave your business cards at the door").
- Reduced costs through use of a fee structure which encourages risk sharing between the performing organization and its vendor partners. The assumption is that some of the hidden contingency built into fixed price arrangements to account for uncertainty would be eliminated.
- Reduced potential liability and risks from employing contractors for long, continuous periods of time. All programmer-analyst contractors would be subcontracted as necessary by the vendor partner, based on project staffing requirements.

## Implementation

ITM management selected three firms to be its vendor partners from the set of system integrators who had performed work previously at Nissan. System development projects

**Exhibit 1.** Modified Procurement Process Using Vendor Partners

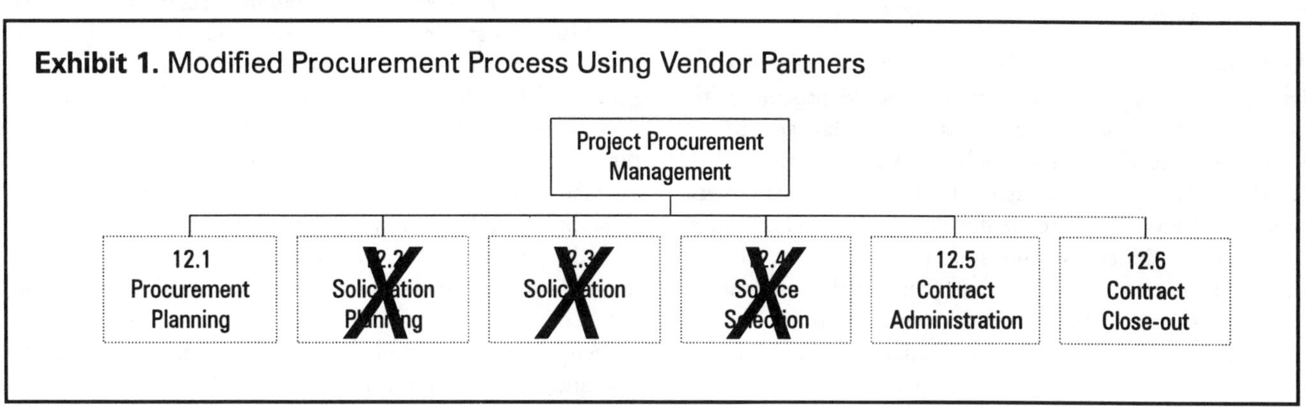

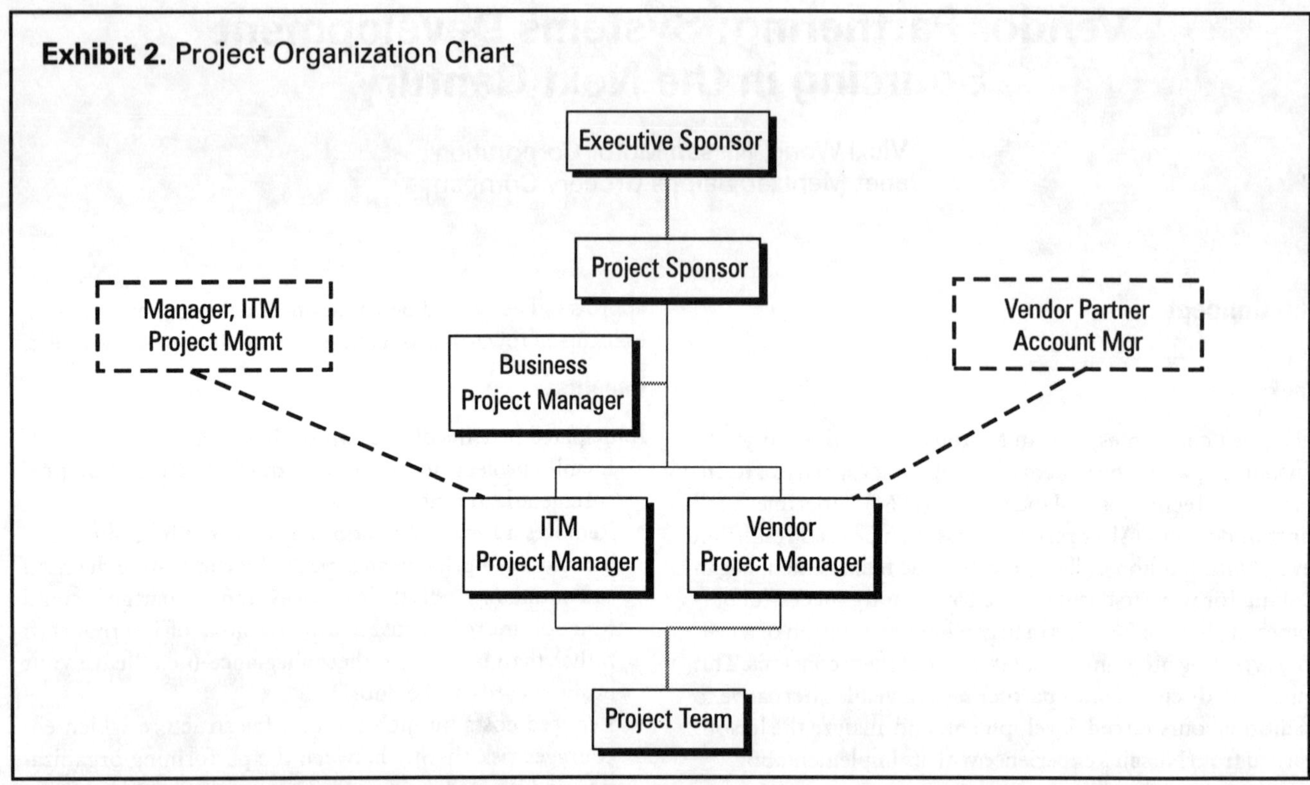

**Exhibit 2.** Project Organization Chart

were awarded to a vendor partner based on Nissan's assessment of each vendor's strengths. "Fixed deliverables" were identified from Nissan's SDLC (systems development life cycle) methodology and published project management practices. All proposed vendor staff were pre-screened, to ensure that their qualifications were appropriate for the project (i.e., demonstration that they had done similar work before in terms of project role, technology, life cycle phase, etc.). Estimating guidelines were set which included project management not to exceed 15 percent of total effort (based on a 1-to-7 expected leverage model), an additional 3 percent allocation for managing issues and change requests, expenses not to exceed 15 percent of total cost, and contingency of 5–15 percent (depending on type of project).

### Project Organization

As defined in Nissan's *Guide to ITM Project Management Processes*, each project would have a Project Management Office (PMO) consisting of a Business Project Manager (BPM) who would typically be from the business area sponsoring the effort, an ITM Project Manager (IPM), and a Vendor Project Manager (VPM) from the Vendor Partner firm. The Project Management Office is responsible for guiding the project through its life cycle; each member shares in the responsibility for the success of the project as a whole. In order to clarify roles, only one of these Project Managers has primary responsibility for any given project manager task, activity, or deliverable; the others could function as participants, contributors, or reviewers. Exhibit 3 is an example of how Nissan defined the roles of BPM, IPM, and VPM for one area of project management responsibilities.

### Results

In the first year since its launch, two-thirds of the ninety-six projects were performed using vendor partners. This marked a substantial increase in capacity over what could have been accomplished by internal resources alone, with an average of seven projects per ITM project manager. (As a point of reference, Nissan's guidelines for what constitutes a project adhered to the principle of "that which can be accurately estimated"; project duration is typically between two to nine months.) The non-vendor partnered projects tended to be either feasibility studies or implementation projects where internal systems knowledge was readily available (e.g., conversion to COBOL II, simple enhancements to existing systems). Both types of projects had successes which were delivered on time and on budget, as well as failures where clients were dissatisfied with the results. Common reasons for failure include those one would normally attribute to a project: greater risks with the larger projects, lack of client participation, change in sponsorship, unclear requirements resulting in scope creep, etc.

Vendor partnering allowed Nissan to eliminate the effort and lead time for competitive bidding on work to be

**Exhibit 3.** Project Control Responsibilities, excerpt from Guide to ITM Project Management Processes

| Activity/Deliverable | BPM | IPM | VPM |
|---|---|---|---|
| Control all fiscal aspects of the project | | Responsible | Contribute |
| Submit weekly budget updates (Project Summary Workbooks) to the Manager, ITM Operations | | Responsible | Contribute |
| Monitor and track the project budget | Review | Responsible | Contribute |
| Collect and enter actual project hours in Project Workbench for all team members including part-time members such as QA staff | | Monitor | Responsible |
| Analyze project actuals and variances in Project Workbench against the Project Plan | Review | Review | Responsible |
| Document and assess Change Requests and Issues; escalate unresolved Change Requests and Issues | Contribute | Monitor | Responsible |
| Resolve Issues and Change Requests in a timely manner | Participate | Monitor | Responsible |
| Create Weekly and Monthly Project Status Reports, and after approval, distribute them | Review | Review | Responsible |
| For Project Status Reports, review, approve, or both. (Approve by signing paper copy for Project Control File.) | Review | Approve | |
| Update the weekly ISD Project Flash Report with accurate status indicators | | Review | Responsible |
| Maintain project status reports and all other required project documents in the Project Control File (paper) and the Project Knowledge Base (electronic) | | Monitor | Responsible |
| Create the Project Checkpoint Review Document (at the end of each phase) | Contribute | Review | Responsible |
| Conduct Project Checkpoint Review Meetings (at the end of each phase) | Participate | Participate | Responsible |
| Attend all meetings with Project Sponsor and Executive Sponsor | | Participate | Responsible |
| Ensure project team adherence to ITM project management and development standards (including ASG turnover and data modeling requirements) | | Monitor | Responsible |

done, resulting in faster project startup of as much as two to three months. It also saved internal staff time for acquisition of technical resources and simplified procurement administration (i.e., vendor partner acting as the prime contractor means fewer Purchase Orders need to be created for contract labor). The vendor partners were able to bring industry or application specific talent to projects, that would not have been accessible through other sourcing options. Screening of vendor partner personnel gave Nissan greater control over project staffing decisions than would have been possible in a traditional outsourced project.

## Lessons Learned

**Determine When It Is Appropriate to Use Vendor Partners.** Recognize that "one size does NOT fit all," and that vendor partnering may not be the best solution for delivery of systems development services in all cases. Nissan found that vendor partnering reduced its flexibility for quick client response on small programming/coding projects. Instances where it does make sense to use a vendor partner may be when you have:

- No internal expertise on new technology
- Large projects (e.g., eighteen or more months from conception through implementation, project team of ten or more)
- "One time shot" (e.g., Year 2000 or a major technology upgrade) that does not need to be repeated
- Heavy business analysis component (and internal resources lack depth in business analysis skills)
- High-risk projects (employment of broader expertise as a risk mitigation strategy).

**Be Prepared for Staff Resistance.** Nissan encountered extreme staff resentment to the use of consultants and vendor partners. What level of commitment is necessary to make vendor partnering a success in your organization? Many employees mistakenly presume that the hourly rates paid for consultants have a direct correlation to their take home salary, as would be expected in a contractor situation. In addition, resentment can come from a number of other sources ranging from bruised egos ("we could have built that system ourselves, we didn't need any help"), to loss of career opportunities ("the consultants get to do all the new development, while I'm stuck doing maintenance work") and fear for job security ("this is just the beginning; soon the entire department will be outsourced"). Address the issue with internal staff straight on; clear communication on what is happening and why vendor partners are being used may reduce some of this resistance. Be prepared and anticipate their questions.

**Partnership Requires Coordination.** In order for the vendor project manager and internal project manager to function effectively as a single face to the clients, coordinate beforehand! (e.g., Know what the other is going to say to the clients, get consensus on what your respective roles will be in the meeting, coordinate who's presenting which agenda items, decide what the project management team's position is on open and anticipated issues.) Remember the axiom of "agree in public, disagree in private": communications must be coordinated between the vendor project manager and the internal project manager to reflect an agreed upon status of the project to senior management and all project stakeholders. If the desired behavior is still not achieved, you may need to coach and counsel vendor partner staff (including your vendor project manager) just like any other project resource.

**Project Management Emphasis Changes with Vendor Partnering.** The skills that are required to manage a vendor partnered project differ considerably from managing a 'normal project' using internal resources. With vendor partnering, the focus of the ITM or internal project manager shifts to contract administration, and away from traditional time and cost management. This may require training your project managers in a new set of skills. Key responsibilities under contract administration include:

- *Quality control*— verifying that the deliverables meet your company's standards for development and meet the business client's requirements. Recognize that the timing will be different than what you may be used to; quality control in a vendor partnered project will be intermittent (e.g., at the completion of a work product or deliverable), rather than ongoing as in the situation when one has sole control over managing the project team. Nissan found it necessary to have internal staff who could review the deliverables to ensure adherence to standards. Don't overlook tool usage; remember to ensure that any deliverables which are going to be your property are produced in tools which your company uses (including word processing, diagramming, data modeling, etc.). Request copies of work products; regression test scripts developed by the vendor partner are particularly useful and will enable you to better support the system once it's in production.
- *Performance reporting* —monitoring the hours spent on time and materials contracts or the deliverable status on fixed price contracts. Monitoring the project schedule, cost, and the technical performance of the vendor was new for most Nissan project managers. Project managers were also faced with a management perception of price gouging by some vendor partners; monitoring the work was critical to ensure extra work was not being done in order to drive up fees in a time and materials situation. This takes effort and requires experience of what is a reasonable effort to

expect for the completion of tasks, work products, or deliverables.

- *Approving vendor payments* —monitoring the payment to the vendor and approve payments based on the progress of the vendor on the project. Payments can be based on deliverables or hourly progress, depending on the contract agreement for the project. Nissan decided on a policy of issuing progress payments based on completion and approval of work products (i.e., small, discrete increments of deliverables), since it was felt that hours worked did not guarantee work product quality or level of completeness. This was a new skill for most of the project managers at Nissan and also required adapting our project management practices to include managing progress payments on fixed price contracts.
- *Managing warranty issues*— ideally, you would like to have clients exercise all system functionality within the warranty period. Sometimes issues arise because of inaccurate assumptions made by the vendor partner that an internal resource, with better knowledge of the systems, would not have made. Hopefully most of these assumptions would have been caught in your quality control review, but there still may be some which remain (e.g., assumptions about the "cleanliness" or volume of data on system performance if system test did not include volume testing using production data).

**Control Expenses by Using Local Talent.** Insist that vendor partners staff the project using local talent. There may be good reason to bring in one or two project team members from out of town (e.g., industry or package-specific expertise), but generally if you're located in one of the major metropolitan areas, local help should be available. Business practices of some system integrators may not support your objective of keeping expense costs down (e.g. "revenue flows to the office who staffs the project"). Having an understanding of your vendor partner's revenue and cost structure will help you create a mutually beneficial partnership.

**Resolve the Leverage Issue Up Front with the Vendor Partner.** The profit model and rate structure of many systems integrators are often based on assumed utilization levels which vary by job title and responsibilities. Those with the highest rates have lower targets for utilization. In a typical Big Six Consulting example, junior consultants are generally expected to be "billable" at nearly 100 percent of their available hours, managers and senior managers at 70–80 percent, whereas a partner might only be required to bill 40–60 percent of their time to client work (since a major responsibility is also to sell new work). Fixed price cost structures typically assume participation levels which allow the vendor to meet these utilization targets. On a time and materials arrangement, agree beforehand what role senior members (e.g., senior managers, partners) from the vendor organization should play on the project, and include this participation in the project plans. Separate the role they play from that of the vendor project manager; they should not be considered part of the project management overhead unless they are the ones actually performing the project management responsibilities of managing issues, change requests, capturing actual hours, writing status reports, etc. In addition to limiting project management effort to 15 percent of the total project effort, Nissan found it necessary to require vendor partners separate quality assurance/subject matter expertise from account management activities. The former may add value to the process, but the latter is strictly a vendor internal issue and would not be paid for.

**Decide on What's a 'Fair' Profit and Share the Risks.** Remember that your vendors are in the service business to make money, and that you generally get what you pay for. It is your job to control the profit margin to a mutually satisfactory level. A common fallacy is that you get more with fixed fee arrangements; the reality is that at best, you get exactly and only what you asked for, which may be far less than what you intended. It may make sense to vary the fee structure by phase within your systems development life cycle. For example, have fixed price contracts for the Definition phase, which are often time-boxed and limited in duration since their purpose is to answer the question "what do I need to know in order to charter the next piece of work" and move into a time and materials arrangement in later phases which have more unknowns (e.g., Analysis and Design, Construction, Implementation). For time and materials contracts, consider negotiating rate discounts based on either: a stair-step structure (i.e., different levels of volume discounts based on the total amount of work awarded to a vendor partner in a given period), or individual project variables such as project size, duration, and utilization (i.e., "the greater the leverage the greater the discount").

Both parties should be able to benefit and share the financial risks in a vendor partnering arrangement. Financial risk sharing could include incentives for early delivery that meets your standards for quality and acceptance, and on the flip side, penalties for late delivery. Work with your legal and procurement departments to develop contractual language that includes elements of risk sharing and fairly protects both parties.

You may need to manage client expectations on the use of vendor partners. Nissan found some clients who responded negatively to the higher cost structure, compared to the cost structure of internal delivery. From their perspective, they got "less bang for the buck." This is another reason for establishing in advance the criteria for vendor

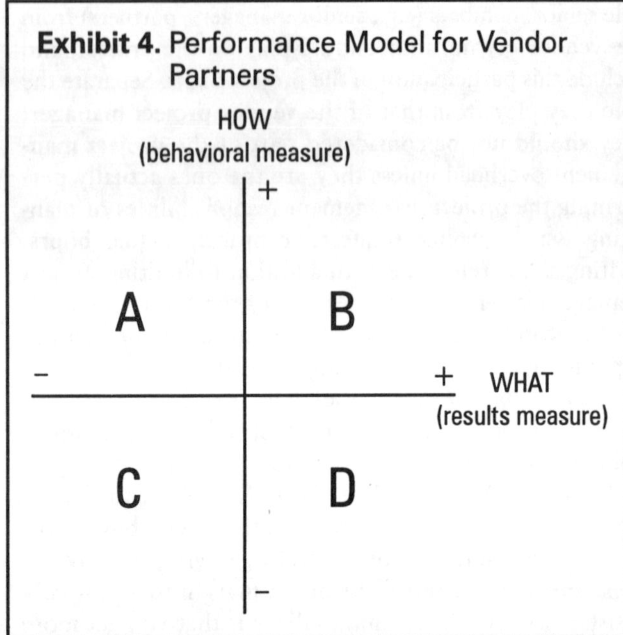

**Exhibit 4.** Performance Model for Vendor Partners

partnered projects, and communicating this to your client community at the start of the budgeting process for systems work. Vendor partnering that is sold to clients as a cost-savings measure will ultimately fail to meet their expectations.

**Manage Warranty Time.** How do you get effective use out of the remaining staff that you and your vendor partner keep around during the warranty period if nothing breaks? Warranty is typically not an issue with internally staffed projects; although your project has been completed, the individuals have either transitioned into a systems maintenance capacity, or have moved on to another project but are still available to resolve any operational problems that surface. The same principle can be applied to warranty work; transition the vendor partner staff to other project work. If no project work is immediately available, identify some non-critical "filler" tasks such as simple screen or report modifications that can be assigned to the warranty support staff and completed well within the warranty timeframe.

**Adapt Your Methodology to Manage Vendor Performance.** Be as specific as possible when it comes to setting expectations on performance. Provide the vendor partner with copies of your methodology, tool set standards, sample deliverables, project manager templates, financial spreadsheets, etc. in advance of project startup. Make sure the vendor partner is aware that conformance is mandatory and non-negotiable! This message must be consistently reinforced at all levels, from the internal project manager through your management and executive management. Be prepared for process improvements as new issues are encountered and your experience with vendor partners matures. Some of the nuances that required modification of Nissan's published project management practices include: clarifying the roles of IPM (ITM project manager) and VPM (vendor project manager), describing the documentation necessary to substantiate time and material invoices, clarifying the authorization for work documents, and determining the method for calculating progress payments. Our ability to adapt as our sophistication grew would not have been possible without a full-time methodologist with appropriate experience to support the ongoing refinement of our practices.

**Include Behavioral Measures in Performance Evaluations to Address Attitudinal Issues.** The tradeoff to the revised procurement process with vendor partnering is an expected shift in attitude and behavior by the vendor that may be foreign to some of the more aggressive marketers. Nissan still experienced instances of "big guys trying to keep out the little guys" as vendors still tried to sell instead of acting as extensions of Nissan staff. Trust and partnership between the ITM project manager and vendor project manager did not always occur (e.g., there were instances where vendor staff changed documents after they had been reviewed by ITM project manager without the ITM project manager's knowledge). Some ITM project managers also experienced push back by the vendor project managers on using Nissan's established project management processes.

How can you address issues with vendor attitudes? Nissan Motor Corporation recently created an employee performance model that gives equal emphasis to behavioral aspects ("How" you work with others) as well as outcomes (results or "What" you get done). That same corporate philosophy can be applied towards vendor partners. The graphical charting of behavior and outcomes creates four quadrants (see Exhibit 4). Quadrant B represents the attitude and performance most desired in a vendor partner, who can be described as: calm, focused on business, listens to other ideas and opinions, builds consensus that leads to decisions, gives credit and takes responsibility, communicative, honest, team-oriented, self-starter, guides others, action-oriented, inclusive, creative, expert, efficient, thorough, resourceful, logical, and timely. With Nissan's payment policy of paying for results, vendor partners who fall into Quadrant A are likely to self-correct. The majority of Nissan's issues were with vendor partners who failed to embody a partnership spirit (D Quadrant behavior). In our experience, if top people at vendor partner firm did not act in partnership spirit, it was unlikely that their staff would. Have an understanding of whether the top person (e.g., the account manager in the vendor organization) is primarily there to serve, or are they just "in it for the bucks." Those that are in it for a long-term relationship seemed to approach vendor partnering with the desired teaming attitude.

**Hold the vendor partner accountable by employing the 4 C's.** The vendor partner needs to be held *accountable* as well as responsible for successful project outcomes. Knutson (1997) defines responsibility as "the ethical commitment to accomplish the work on time, within budget, of the quality promised, within a positive team environment" whereas accountability is "the consequence or reward for meeting a commitment." Vendor partners can be managed as a resource, using many of the same techniques that you would use on anyone assigned to your project:

- Coaching—Provide feedback to vendor staff and vendor project managers as needed on an immediate basis for mid-course corrections in performance.
- Counseling—Conduct formal assessments of vendor staff, as well as overall vendor performance at the conclusion of the project. Enter these assessments into a vendor database which can be used to determine awarding of subsequent work.
- Consequences—Consider both short and long term measures, financial and otherwise. Financial consequences could include incentives and penalties held in an escrow account, and paid out when the accumulative performance merits. "Make an example" of the consequences of disobedient behavior by promptly removing vendor staff who are not performing up to expectations.
- Consistency—Provide a level playing field for all vendor partners (e.g., master agreements should be the same for all vendor partners, they're easier and more efficient to manage and enforce). Communication to vendor partners about performance deviations should be consistent, from internal project manager through all levels of management. Nissan experienced problems with this when some individuals would "make exceptions" and "cut deals" with vendors on issues of performance.

**Be Clear on Who Plays "Bad Cop."** When push comes to shove, and all the coaching and counseling has not resulted in the desired improvements to performance or behavior, who is going to deliver the tough message? Is your management willing and politically able to play "bad cop" and show the vendor the door if necessary? The internal project manager is the one person who should *not* play this role; it places a strain on open communication and the atmosphere of teamwork with the vendor project manager. Make sure your internal project manager does not confuse quality control with a 'bad cop' role; the purpose of quality control is ensuring the product meets with your company's needs, while the latter is for administering punishment which are the consequences of undesired performance.

## Sourcing For The Next Century

Due to the enormity of risks and unknowns with Year 2000 projects, the trend is increasing towards time and materials rather than traditional fixed price arrangements. As we've seen at Nissan, this type of fee arrangement has its disadvantages, but ones which can be managed. Keep in mind two simple rules: 1) external sourcing does not mean an abdication of management responsibilities, and 2) caveat emptor ("let the buyer beware"). Vendor partnering may be your best bet for future success!

### References


Bailey, Rodney PMP. 1996. Approving Systems Projects: Eight Questions an Executive Should Ask. *PM Network* (May): 21-24.

Cavendish, Penny and Martin D. Martin, Ph.D. 1987. *Negotiating and Contracting for Project Management*: 32-38.

Ernst & Young LLP U.S. 1994. *Organizational Change Management Training Guide* (Level 1 v.4).

Knutson, Joan. 1997. How to be a Mentor: 10 Discussion Topics. *PM Network* (February): 13-15.

Larson, Erik and John A. Drexler, Jr. 1997. Barriers to Project Partnering: Report from the Firing Line. *Project Management Journal* (March): 46-52.

Nissan Motor Corporation. 1997. *Culture Change: A Plan for Performance.*

Nissan Motor Corporation. 1997. *Guide to ITM Project Management Processes* (4 April).

Project Management Institute Standards Committee. 1996. *Guide to the Project Management Body of Knowledge.* Upper Darby, PA: pp. 123-133.

# The Project Office - Why More Companies Are Adopting It To Help Manage IT Projects

Thomas R. Block, PMP

## Introduction

The emergence of project offices on the Information Technology (IT) landscape has been driven by a desire to improve the success rate of projects that continually become more complex and the need to relieve the project manager of the administrative chores associated with managing a project. To better understand the impact of this emergence, let's examine where organizations are today and how they got there.

## Where Are Organizations Today?

First, let's review the evolution of hardware and software and its impact on projects. In 1981, the only system support for a project was on a mainframe computer using Artemis. It cost the project at least $25,000 per month for that service. Few project managers were convinced that the value of the information from Artemis was worth that kind of money. The subsequent continuing capability increases of the personal computer in the workplace and the explosion of project management software have changed the minds of many project managers. It is no longer a cost issue. Today, most projects use project management software on a powerful personal computer for planning and control. Large organizations are linking project data repositories that feed "Executive Dashboards" for senior management. Since better tools are used, the natural tendency is to expect better results. The expectations of senior management and the customer have increased in the last decade, yet the success rate of projects has not. The Standish Group (1994) surveyed 8,380 projects in 1994 and found that only 16.2 percent were completed within the triple constraints, namely; on-time, within budget, and with all the features and functions initially specified. Another alarming fact from the study is that for every 100 projects started, 94 were restarted. A subsequent study, in 1996, by the Standish Group of the same companies indicated that some improvement was being made as user fight failures with better management. One of the better management practices cited was the use of the project office (King 1997).

When senior management spends money on tools to improve project results and the projects don't improve, they conclude that project management tools are of little value and should not be used. They revert to their own past experiences and decide that the solution is to assign more systems engineers and possibly an expert to help a struggling project. This expert often knows something about project management and the use of the tools. The expert assists the project in planning and control and transfers project management knowledge to the project team. The project manager, seeing the value of someone overseeing the day-to-day project details, decides to designate a person with that responsibility. Thus we see the emergence of a one-person project office. The project manager normally praises the work of the expert who then emerges as a "folklore hero" in the organization. Probably this person will be asked to help save other struggling projects. The demands for their time increases to a point where additional staff is needed. Thus, we see the emergence of an internal project management consulting function. Subsequently, this group is referred to as a project office. This normally is the scenario that takes place in most organizations. The functions of a project office and the numbers of professionals assigned to the project office evolve over time as the need arises.

## What Is a Project Office?

A project office is in the eye of the beholder. Research has shown that it can be anything an organization wants it to be. In the past, the project office meant a program to maintain and train best practices and be keepers of the project management discipline. It was recognized widely as a static repository of project management information controlled by the training organization. Lately, the concept has been redefined, out of necessity, to assume an operational support role for the project manager. In this context, the project office can be defined as an organizational entity that assists the project manager achieve the goals of the project by providing assistance in planning, estimating, scheduling, monitoring and controlling the project. The project office concept is similar to the military concept of an operations office (S3/G3) that supports a battalion or higher commander. The operations office is composed of staff officers and enlisted persons that assist the unit commander in accomplishing the mission of the organization. The military trains both commanders and staff officers in the same manner. Likewise, the goal of a project-driven organization is to train everyone in project management fundamentals and to tailor advanced project management training for those individuals who will be promoted into those management positions. Like the operations office (S3/G3), the project office can be located at several levels in the organization, from project to business unit, and staffed with varying numbers of professionals. The professionals who staff the project office should be experienced and trained in advanced management and leadership skills because they will continually interface with senior project personnel, senior management and the customer. Many of the project office personnel should be certified project management professionals (PMPs). The need for the project office and its importance to increase the probability of completing successful projects is examined next.

## The Need for a Project Office

Certainly the poor track record of projects, described in the Standish Group study, has caused more interest in helping project managers. Secondly, the complexity of projects increases as technology increases. A desktop roll out of a client/server solution is a lot more complex than hooking dumb terminals to a mainframe. The many details of this roll out have to be coordinated, planned and scheduled. The project office assists the project manager in this important function lest the project manager get mired in the weeds of detail. For example,

*A recent Request for Proposal (RFP) from a Federal agency required the contractor to provide 1,900 local area networks (LAN) and 48,000 work stations at over 100 locations of varying size in two years. To add to the complexity, the agency requires that work be done only on weekends and that equipment cannot be staged on site.*

The project manager needs help from the project office in handling this type of detail planning otherwise his other important duties will go unattended. Thirdly, the project manager must accomplish a number of duties throughout the life cycle of a project. The most important duty is to make things happen and influence others. The project manager does not have the time to enter, manipulate and schedule data in the latest project management software. This is the responsibility of the project office. The project manager must be knowledgeable of the tool and conscious of project performance, but he must not become mired in the data entry. The entire project may be lost if the project manger doesn't delegate the detailed scheduling, status and variance reporting duties to the project office. If this happens, the project manager is foregoing the important leading, negotiating, and customer relationship duties. Fourthly, there is renewed heightened awareness of project management due to the increasing number of professionals trained in project management, the increasing number of certified PMPs, the increasing number of universities offering advanced degrees in project management, the increasing use of project management software, and corporate downsizing. Many solicitation requests require a project management response. The days of "Trust Me" are over. The customer wants to see detailed project plans and schedules. The customer also expects the contractor to manage according to the plans submitted in the proposal. These factors have created an additional burden on the project manager. The detailed planning, scheduling, resource loading and status and variance reporting has to be done, but not solely by the project manager. The project office is responsible for assisting the project manager in these duties. Fifthly, more organizations are concerned with reducing cycle times and getting products to market sooner. There is more emphasis on re-use of data and products and more pressure to stop reinventing the wheel. These organizations also want to matrix their highly skilled but scarce professionals on multiple projects and they want project data consolidated and simplified on an "Executive Dashboard" display. The project office is best suited to accomplish these new demands. Earlier, it was mentioned that most project offices evolved in organizations based on necessity. It's important to review these project office types to better understand their broad range of services.

## Types of Project Offices

I have established five broad categories of project offices based on my research. The categories are training, methodology, consulting, project support and project managers. I will also indicate where they are generally found in organizations and the staffing profiles of the personnel by using project management experience and salary as the parameters. As mentioned earlier, project office is in the eye of the beholder. The first type of project office has a training orientation.

### Training

This project office develops and delivers project management courses either with their staff or a contracted vendor. The courses are designed to cover project management basics and are offered to anyone in the organization without much regard to job need. The content of the courses will likely follow the guidance in the *Guide to the Project Management Body of Knowledge* (PMI 1996). This type of project office is usually part of a larger training organization and the staff normally has very little practical project management experience. The cost of this staff could be classified as low to medium, $25K–$45K.

### Methodology

This project office develops project management process, promotes best practices, maintains a repository of lessons learned, and evaluates project management software. This organization, with its limited functions, has been traditionally called "The Project Office"; however, this perception is changing rapidly because of an increasing demand to provide more services. Usually, this project office is part of a larger training or technology organization and the staff has some practical project management experience. The cost of this staff could be classified as medium, $45K–$70K.

### Consulting

This project office provides proposal support by writing the project management plans or reviewing the plans before submission. They also provide project start-up and recovery assistance and limited project support. Project support is limited because of the high consultant cost. The consultant's purpose is to transfer project management knowledge to the team, not administer the project system. This project office is usually part of a larger consulting or technology organization and the staff normally has a great deal of practical project management experience. The cost of this staff could be classified as high, $70K–$110K.

### Project Support

This project office provides the direct project services and the number of professionals varies, from one to as many as five depending on the size and complexity of the project. The services include task scheduling, reports consolidation and distribution, operation of the project management software, visibility room maintenance, and maintenance of the project workbook or repository. This type of project office is usually part of the project organization and the staff normally has some practical project management experience. The cost of this staff could be classified as low to medium, $25K–$45K.

### Project Managers

This project office provides the project managers for the projects. It is their home cost center. The manger of this project office is responsible for establishing a progressive project management job code family and career development for the project managers. Encouraging the project managers to become certified by the Project Management Institute is also the manager's responsibility. This project office is usually part of a technology organization or in an industry business unit. Normally, the staff has a great deal of practical project management experience. The cost of this staff could be classified as very high, $70K–$180K.

## Vision of the Future

I have shown that there are a wide variety of project offices. Probably as many as there are companies. The ideal project office should contain all the functions that increase the probability of successful projects. Note that I did not say "ensure project success". Even with all the functions operating in a project office, there is no guarantee of success. Project success is a journey, not a destination. The project manager and the team have to work toward project success one day at a time. There are too many variables that have to be juggled by the project manager. To reduce the variables, the ideal project office should be the project management center of excellence and be perceived as a "full service" provider of project management knowledge, processes, training, tools and techniques. Most importantly, the project office must be perceived as a provider of highly skilled and dedicated professionals that can get the job done. The project office of the future should provide the following functions and capabilities to be considered a full service provider.

- Project Management Methods and Standards
- Project Management Training
- Project Management Consulting
- Project Support
- Project Managers.

The full-service project office can be located at any level of the organization; however, to be most effective there has to be a project office presence at the project. The level of services provided by the project office varies by level in the organization. At project level, the primary function of the project office is project support. At business unit level, the project office functions may also include consulting, standards and a stable of project managers. The project support function at business unit level involves roll up of project information and the "executive dashboard." The project office at corporate level should be considered the "Project Management Knowledge Leader" with responsibility for overall project management policy, technology refreshment, the project management training curriculum, project managers development program and coordination of methods and standards and data repositories. For example, Perot Systems Corporation hired a project management thought leader recently to implement project management throughout their organization. The communication linkage between the project offices at each level is important to maintain the integrity and discipline of the standards and reports. The staffing at each level should be based on the size of the project. At project level, the project offices could have one to four or more persons. Hal O'Rourke, at FIRSTAR Bank in Milwaukee, ran a highly successful one-person project office while Bill Arnoult manages a seven-person project office for an EDS Federal account. The project office at business unit level should have the most staff if the consulting function and the project managers are at that level. The corporate level project office should have the fewest professionals since the mission at corporate level is one of policy development, enforcement and coordination. Having project offices at multiple levels in the organization allows for career growth in the project management field. The full range of staffing levels allows the organization to develop their own project management professionals and project managers. Many organizations are faced with a shortage of competent project managers. They can choose to develop their own project managers or hire from outside their organization at considerable risk and cost. Most organizations want to develop their own but lack the resolve to begin before the need is upon them.

## Possible Functions of a Project Office

Let's take a look at some of the possible functions of the full service or mature project office. The project office is the stalwart of project management methods and standards.

### *Methods and Standards*

The processes are developed, used and refined as best practices by the project office. From these processes, metrics are developed to measure project performance and improvement. These best practices and lessons learned are stored in a repository for use on subsequent projects. Many large organizations are effectively using their intranet and the Web as repositories of best practices. The project office also is involved in internal benchmarking of projects as well as project evaluation. A mature project office will eventually get involved with external benchmarking to further try to improve project performance.

### *Training*

The project office is concerned with training consistency. A project office in a small company may have to develop and deliver the project management training or broker it to a vendor. In large organizations, the training is normally developed and delivered by a corporate training organization. Here the project office is concerned primarily with the integrity of the curriculum. In either case, the project office should provide a full range of project management training to develop project mangers and their teams. A full range of training should be progressive. A basic course followed by computer based project simulations would be available to project managers and team members alike. Management Worlds Inc., in Summit New Jersey has an excellent curriculum of progressive project management simulators that can be tailored to the organization's needs. The advanced project management subjects would be offered to potential project managers. Risk management, earned value analysis and return on investment are just a few examples of advanced training. The advanced training should be preceded by competency diagnostics for all potential project managers. Tailored development plans are then developed using the results of the diagnostic. Project Management Institute certification examination preparation courses should also be offered to the project managers.

### *Project Support*

In most organizations, project management means scheduling. In addition to scheduling, the project office is also involved with project planning, resource estimating, project control, reporting, variance analysis, and administrative support. The administrative support can be significant especially if the Federal government is involved. For example, a study conducted in 1990 by Captain Patrick O'Connell of the U.S. Navy found that 70 percent of the action items pursed on a major weapons systems program involved administrative actions rather than directly productive activities (Frame 1994). The office maintains the issue tracking and change control processes. The visibility room or "war room" is established and maintained by the project office and they maintain or feed an enterprise-wide project management system.

### *Project Consulting*

This function, if executed properly, can do more to sell the organization and the customer than all the rhetoric imaginable. The project office gets involved with project start-up assistance and project recovery assistance. It can gain an inseparable relationship with the project manager. The reputation of the project office is enhanced by continued responsiveness to the project management needs of the organization. The consulting function also includes proposal support either as writers or reviewers. This is an excellent way to write project support into the project proposal and share the cost with the customer.

### *Project Managers*

The project mangers are assigned to the project office for administrative reasons and to monitor their career development, job assignments and job performance. The project managers are subsequently assigned projects of varying duration and complexity based on availability and experience.

## Progressive Benefits of a Project Office

The longer the project office exists the greater the benefits. The real benefit is implementing project management throughout an organization through the project office. Listed below are the benefits.

***Predictable, Reusable Project Management Tools and Techniques***

The consistent application and self evaluation of project management methodologies by the project office eventually will produce positive results. Templates can be reused on subsequent projects and estimates and schedules will be more reliable and predictable. Project reporting should be less subjective and senior management will have fewer surprises.

***Staff Professionalism in Project Management***

The discipline to consistently use project management reinforces the project management training received by the staff. Staff professionalism is increased by continual use of the prescribed tools and techniques on-the-job. It is an enormous waste of money to train professionals and not require them to practice what they learned in their training. Corporations spend millions on project management training yet get little return on their investment because the management chain doesn't endorse the corporate-wide implementation of project management.

***Culture Shift to Project Management***

Eventually, the consistent application of project management will produce a culture change toward project management. With more organizations downsizing and right sizing, some have capsized. By default these organizations have become organized by project but have not begun to manage by projects. However, the consistent use of project management by the project office will produce a project driven organization.

***Productive Project Teams***

Project teams are more productive when the staff is trained in the same project management methodology, tools and techniques. The project office adds the discipline within the organization that allows the project staff to practice what they have been train to accomplish. The use of a common management language reduces misunderstandings that lead to costly errors and enables the use of matrix resources. The combination of all these elements increases productivity.

***Organizational Improvement***

When the productivity of the projects increase, the productivity of the entire organization should also increase. Normally, this is true unless there is one project that is so bad that it negates the improvements of all the other projects. I have always maintained that the ultimate goal of project management is organizational improvement and profitability.

***Profitability Improvement***

There is intense interest by senior management to improve the profitability of the organization. Since projects have greater visibility through technology refreshments, senior management is looking harder at the project mangers to produce profitable outcomes. The project office is positioned well to aid the project manager and to enforce the project management discipline to increase the probability of successful, profitable projects.

***Global Recognition***

Most large organizations want to be recognized as global competitors. The ISO 9000 standards have caused organizations to review their internal management practices. These reviews have often indicated a haphazard approach with little or no consistency. The quick answer was more training but there was still no improvement. Training without management commitment to a process is meaningless and costly. The project office indicates management commitment to a project management process that in time will improve projects and the organization. Eventually, through the continual enforcement of project management by the project office, the organization can be recognized for its "world class" delivery of successful projects.

## Implementing a Project Office

The value of a project office was discussed in the above paragraphs. This section addresses the actions necessary to establish project management in an organization by implementing a project office. I will present a methodology that can be refined and reused each time another project office is established. I will also discuss the issues that normally should be considered and a recommended way to approach selling the project office concept to senior management. These steps should be followed to implement the project office in an organization.

***Assess Your Organization***

You have to find out what's happening in the entire organization. You must determine which business units are using project management and which are not. It doesn't matter whether it's a small organization or a large one. People take pride in whatever they have developed and find useful. Often each business unit is doing project management differently. The assessment allows you to uncover these differences and choose the best practice and try to improve it. Focus groups are useful to get all business unit representatives to cooperate in improving the best practice and adopting it for their business unit's use. During the assessment many issues will surface regarding the implementation of a project office. Below are issues that are common to most organizations.

- The project office value to the organization
- The cost hit to the bottom line

- The project office value to the customer
- Whether to include the project office cost in the bid
- Kill the "good cop-bad cop" syndrome
- Who identifies and develops the project managers
- The value of internal consulting and mentoring.

These issues should not be set aside to be addressed later. They should be frankly addressed in the comprehensive roll-out plan.

#### *Prepare a comprehensive roll-out plan and budget*

The comprehensive roll-out plan should be developed jointly with all business unit representatives to breakdown the resistance to change barriers, to obtain buy-in from the representatives and ultimately their senior managers, and to gain commitment to implement the plan. A "Gap Analysis Chart" is useful to organize your thoughts as to where you are and where you want to be with the project office. This chart puts the entire plan in perspective and allows for a progressive roll out that can be budgeted appropriately. Throughout this planning process, every effort must be made to dispel the perception of "empire building." Nothing will kill this effort sooner than senior management's belief that this is a costly endeavor with no bottom-line benefit.

#### *Identify a senior management champion*

This could be the most important task in attempting to roll-out a project office and to mitigate the perception of "empire building." A project champion at the senior level is an absolute necessity if the roll-out is to succeed. The higher the level in the organization the better the chance of success. The axiom that "When the body moves, the head tends to follow" isn't always true in organizations that have tried to implement project management. Often there is strong project management use and support at the lower organizational levels, yet very little project management acceptance at the top. If this situation exists in an organization, it is not managing by project and cannot be considered a project-driven organization.

#### *Obtain funding*

Often the process of obtaining funding can be a humbling experience; however, it doesn't have to be. It should go smoothly if you have buy-in from the business unit representatives and the budget is progressive. A progressive budget portrays a smooth increase in cost throughout the year. It conveys the impression that staff will be increased only as the need arises and therefore the overhead costs will not be uncontrolled. The keys to success are a the well thought out, comprehensive roll-out plan and the champion. The champion can help gain support throughout the organization for the roll-out plan and budget with a few telephone calls.

#### *Prepare a comprehensive communication plan*

A communication plan is often overlooked in a project office roll-out. It is vital to the subsequent success of the project office. The organization must be bombarded with information about the capabilities of the project office and its willingness to help the business units. Keep in mind that the ultimate goal of the communication plan is to gain awareness and customers for the project office. The plan should address the project office roll-out and how to mitigate any organizational issues. Various media should be used, and the plan should include the message announcement frequency. Many organizations do a good job of communicating a roll-out but fail to consistently advertise the capabilities of the project office. A consistent message is very important in a growth organization that is hiring new employees or procuring new organizations. In a few months, there will be hundreds of employees that weren't in the organization during the roll-out and are unaware of the project office announcements and its capabilities. The communication plan has to include the delivery of consistent and frequent project office messages.

#### *Proceed intelligently and slowly*

If an organization hasn't used project management consistently, they probably don't need it overnight. The concept of implementing project management throughout an organization through the services of the project office often is not readily apparent. This concept will require a continual sell in the organization so it's better to proceed intelligently and slowly based on immediate need. Capitalize on success but continue to grow the capability slowly into a mature project office, a project office that provides a full service.

#### *Selling the concept*

This is the most important step that you have to take to implement a project office. Your success or failure hangs in the balance so this cannot be taken lightly. Here are the steps that must be taken.

- Execute the comprehensive communication plan
- Identify champions at all levels in the organization
- Brief your champions continually using all media
- Conduct a pilot with a supportive organization
- Broadcast the results of the pilot
- Keep communicating regularly.

## Evolution of Services of the Project Office

The key to the project office success is continual growth in the project management services provided. Never give the allusion that you are an empire builder. Always be short of staff to the requirements and never, never sacrifice quality performance.

A small project office can gain an excellent reputation quickly through responsive, quality service. Conversely, the reputation can also be tarnished quickly with one mediocre consulting engagement.

## Summary

The project office is just emerging as a vital ingredient to increase the probability of project success. In the future, projects will continue to rise in complexity placing greater strain on the project team. The project office assumes the role of assisting the project manager in managing the successful project. As a project office matures to a full service provider of project management, organizations will begin to reap the full benefits of a project office—the implementation of project management throughout the entire organization through the project office.

References


Frame, J.D. 1994. *The New Project Management*. San Francisco: Jossey-Bass.

King, Julia. 1997. IS Reins In Runaway Projects. *Computerworld* (February): pp. 1,16.

Project Management Institute Standards Committee. 1996. *A Guide to the Project Management Body of Knowledge*. Upper Darby, PA: PMI.

The Standish Group International. 1994. Charting the Seas of Information Technology. *Chaos Re*port.

# Just Do It Won't Do: Minimal Project Management for IT Professionals

Lou Russell, President, Learning Facilitator, Russell Martin & Associates

"The project manager is the linchpin in the horizontal/vertical organizations we're creating." — William Dauphinais, Price Waterhouse

Imagine you are in a room with 100 people. Take a moment and think about how you would, with a team of four other people, gather as many signatures as possible (one per person max) on a single sheet of paper in two minutes. This exercise would demonstrate some basic truths of why project management is so difficult—the requirements would prove to be unclear (can we tear the paper in pieces, must we stay in this room, are initials sufficient ... ?) and the constraints daunting (not enough time, not enough resources, too much to cover, competition, conflict ... ). Consider taking this same competitive room of people and changing their focus: their new goal is to try to get them all to get as many signatures as possible together. As a project manager of this new task, this adds to the problems inherent in project management. Not only are you faced with the original challenges but now you are faced with managing multiple small projects within a single goal. At any time, any team could decide their goals are more important than the team goal. This is project management in the Information Technology arena.

In this paper, I will share with you some of the ways you can stack the cards in your favor on a information technology project. These are not magical techniques and most of them are not new. They are not difficult, either.All it takes is discipline and diligence. What matters most is that someone is actually doing project management. Within that context, I will share specific techniques for quantifying risk, estimating unknowns, transferring knowledge and managing development options.

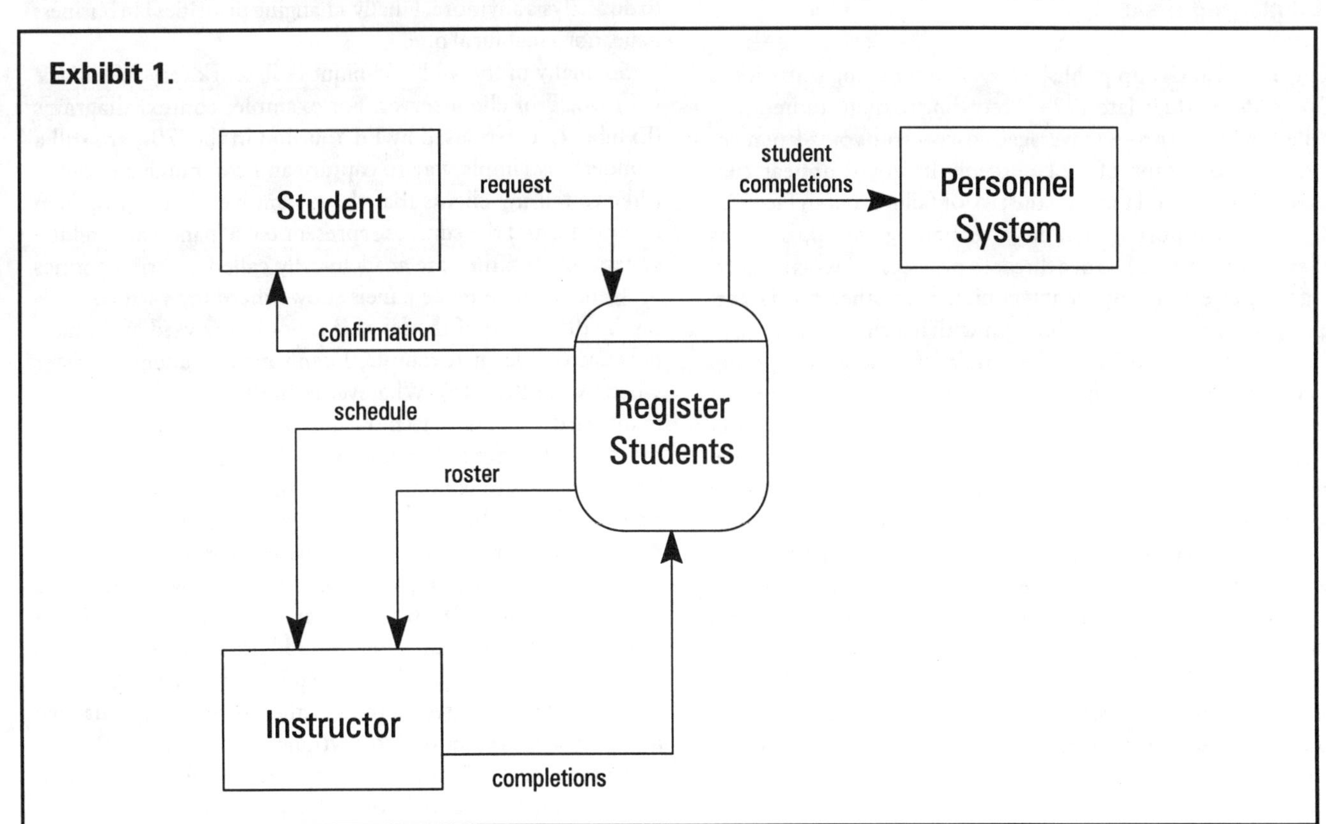

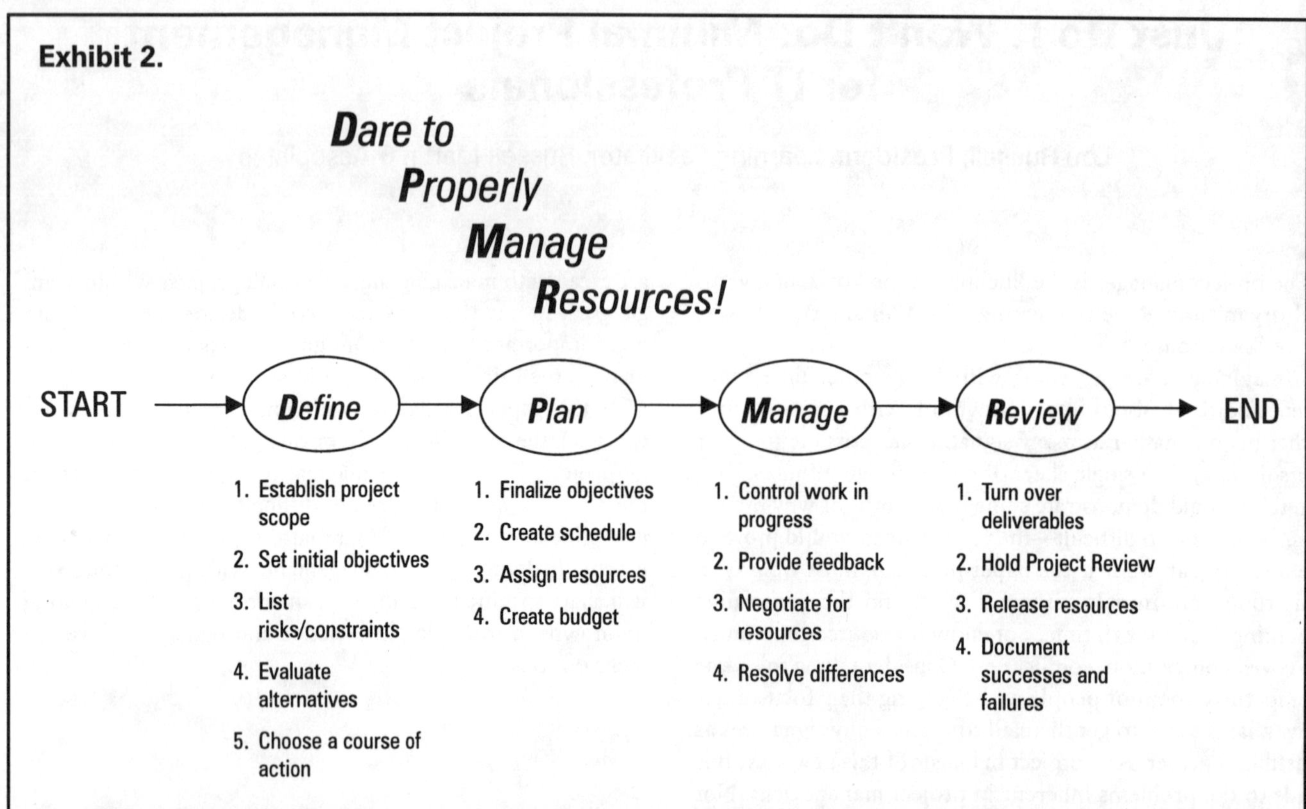
Exhibit 2.
Dare to
Properly
Manage
Resources!
START
Define
Plan
Manage
Review
END
1. Establish project scope
2. Set initial objectives
3. List risks/constraints
4. Evaluate alternatives
5. Choose a course of action
1. Finalize objectives
2. Create schedule
3. Assign resources
4. Create budget
1. Control work in progress
2. Provide feedback
3. Negotiate for resources
4. Resolve differences
1. Turn over deliverables
2. Hold Project Review
3. Release resources
4. Document successes and failures

## Quantifying Risks

The Standish Group published some interesting statistics in *Computerworld* in late 1994. According to their studies, cancelled and failed projects averaged cost overruns of 189 percent and time overruns of 222 percent. It would appear that client/server would increase the risk of failure, but in fact, Capers Jones reported that new technology itself, such as client/server, posed less of a threat to project success as neglecting the project management techniques. In other words, certainly the new technology brought with it a challenging learning curve, but even this could be handled if someone stepped up to managing the project. Look at the following list of risks: creeping scope, unrealistic expectations, inadequate requirements and changing priorities. All of these are present in client/server projects, but it is also interesting to note that they were present in the mainframe projects as well; in fact, they are present in any project. Client/server may encourage creeping scope just by its ability to be flexible (it was sometimes nice to be able to say during a mainframe project "we can't do that with this computer"). I have noticed that some people actually believe all the ads they've read about client/server, and this does lead to unrealistic expectations (lower cost, lower development time). Inadequate requirements seem to be a symptom of client/server due to the faulty conclusion that there is no need to do analysis anymore. Finally, changing priorities is a business issue, not a technical one.

So, many of the 'old' techniques still work very well in the wild world of client/server. For example, context diagrams (Exhibit 1) as espoused by Ed Yourdon in the '70s, are still a wonderfully simple way to capture and communicate scope. I like to tell my clients that the system we are creating is in the middle and the squares represent fence panels around the system (in fact, they are academically called external entities or agents). These fence panels show where my yard is: if it's on the other side of the fence it is not in my yard and I have no control over it (example, I can't make students register when I want them to). Whatever is on this side of the fence is in my yard, and I have to mow it, so to speak. The purpose of this diagram is not to freeze scope—that would just be denial. The purpose is to communicate on an ongoing basis with the customers what the scope is. If the scope changes, as it always does, the diagram is added to (maybe another input or output, or maybe a new fence panel) and everyone agrees that the scope has changed. With this agreement comes the inevitable discussion of what to do about it—add time, add money or do a really bad job at the additional requirements. Troubles occur when everyone disagrees about whether the scope has changed and estimates are not tied to anything concrete.

Unrealistic expectations occur when people are not honest up front. Most people on failed projects would admit to

**Exhibit 3.**

## Overall Project Risk

Average:

***Size*** - How "big" is this system or how long will it take relative to others you have done?

Rated 1(small) - 10(large)

***Structure*** - How stable are the requirements?

Rated 1(fixed) - 10(undefined)

***Technology*** - How understood is the technology?

Rated 1(old) - 10(new)

An item >5 is best NOT treated informally!

you in private that they knew they were in big trouble at the very beginning. Why hide this? Exhibit 2 shows a simple checklist of the things that should be documented before a project begins, better yet, before it is approved. Any missing answer is a very bad sign and a significant risk. For example, I know of one large project that has no executive sponsor. This is not a problem that will go away.

As I said, client/server seems to be an excuse to return to the days of "hurry up and code." An old joke in *The Psychology of Computer Programming* by Gerald Weinberg is still true today: a project manager rushes into the room and says, "Great news! We got the project approved. Okay, you folks start coding and I'll go find out what they want." Instead of coding now, people are playing with visual development tools. It is not the fault of the tools; it is the fault of our eternal quest to find the easy way out. There are a couple of flaws with this "hurry up and GUI" approach. First, at least 20 percent of the processing of a system will not have inputs or outputs. These engine processes are often forgotten about and coded haphazardly at the last minute. If the engine is faulty, it really doesn't matter what the outside of the car is like. Second, prototyping death spirals can only be controlled by a prioritization of the requirements (the WHAT) mapped to the business objectives (the WHY). No requirements, no mapping, no control.

There are three manageables on any project: time, cost and quality. People may say they want all three, but in reality, only one can be No. 1 priority, one No. 2, and one neglected. Generally, behavior speaks louder than words. For example, if your project seems to be running out of time, are you more likely to get additional resources (more cost) or are you more likely to be encouraged to work more hours free (less quality)? Sitting everyone down with this simple model in the beginning of a client/server project is a great way to see what the hidden agendas are. Ask them to individually rate the priorities in their opinion, then share. Remember, many people believe that client/server technology guarantees either faster or cheaper projects, or both. It is best to discover these misconceptions in the very beginning. Also, you may find out that two departments have different priorities which will inevitably cause conflict and have to be resolved. If one department needs the project because of a regulatory time constraint but the other feels it needs to be done very inexpensively, there will be no pleasing anybody. In fact, it will alleviate the stress of the development team as a whole to know the reality of the situation going in. Since most people initially behave as if

**Exhibit 4.**

## Detailed Project Risk

| Risk Factors | Likelihood | Impact | Action |
|---|---|---|---|
| Production platform changes during project | M | M | Add time for training on new technology |
| Project Manager gets transferred | L | H | Plan meetings for backup to PM |
| People resources not available | M | H | Prioritize activities to cut if insufficient resources |

H = High M = Medium L = Low

quality is the number one goal, it does cause a great deal of stress if that is truely not the case. Keep this initial worksheet around—project constraints tend to change as projects hit milestones or management changes. This chart helps everyone balance the ramifications of changing course. Towards the end of this article, I will share what to do when you are falling behind in one of this categories.

But how do we quantify these risks? How can we force ourselves to confront our organizational optimism, our corporate denial? Here are three techniques, from simple to more complex.

The first, and simplest technique I like to call "Quick n' Dirty" Risk Assessment. Again, as a group with your clients if possible, ask everyone to rate the following three criteria from one to ten (risky):size (number of components, time to develop), structure (stability of the business requirements) and technology. This rating should be completely dependent on the team of people that will be doing the project. For example, technology might be new for a team although old for the company. Exhibit 3 shows an example of a client/server project replacing financial systems. After the rating is completed, ask each person to average their results. A risk of greater than five is best not treated informally. Simply put, the higher the risk, the more project management controls are necessary. The higher the risk, the more milestones to check progress.

A slightly more complex approach to risk is to brainstorm scenarios about surprises that could occur on your project. Exhibit 4 shows a table for summarizing these. To get started on your list, consider surprises that have hit projects you've been on in the past or projects you've heard of. Brainstorm across the following topics: people, process, organization, technology, time, cost and quality. Notice the column on "Likelihood." I now believe that it is useless to fill this column out— you don't know, or you're probably wrong. However, the 'Impact' column does help you prioritize how seriously you want to build contingency plans. The "Action" column does not have to be detailed unless you want it to be. Based on work described by Peter Senge in *The Fifth Discipline*, scenario planning can be done more rigorously by combining these surprises into scenarios. Dealing with these stories helps project teams discover faulty mental models that they have. I have found one other value emerges from this type of work: when you brainstorm scenarios, either using the simpler or more complex approach, you have already slightly experienced the shock of these things really happening so when they do happen, as one or two will, you will see it coming quicker, you will not be as surprised and you will be able to move more quickly.

### Estimating Unknowns

AT&T had (pre-divestiture) a wonderful process for estimating that was developed by Bell Labs in the early '70s. Although this calculation is based on an initial guess (and adding or multiplying anything against a guess just makes a bigger guess … ), this formula helps project managers justify the estimates that they make. In client/server, the impact of some of these factors is daunting.

First, come up with a base work effort duration, assuming that the task will be done by an average person with average abilities. Next, determine the skill level of the actual person that will be doing the task and their understanding of the business. These two factors have the most effect on the estimate.Multiply by the following amounts for:

Skill level: Multiply base by .75 to 4.0

Business knowledge: Multiply new base by .5 to 1.5

This may seem extreme, but think about it. Isn't it likely that a person who has no skill at a task will take at least four times longer to do it than the average person?

Next, build in a factor for project administrative activities like training, walkthroughs, status meetings and reviews. In this step, add another 10–20 percent of the cumulative amount. Finally, build in a factor for non-project time like illness, vacation, e-mail, corporate meetings, phone tag and special assignments. Depending on your corporate culture, this adds another 25–30 percent to the cumulative amount. It would be incredibly time-consuming to make these three adjustments to every project activity. In fact, you may use your project management software to show that your resources are only available 70 percent (to cover the non-project time) or you may build in single dummy tasks to hold the time. The first factor, the people factor, is the only one that must be applied individually to each activity.

Now comes the hard part: you have to take this figure in to the powers-that-be and tell them that your four-day task will actually take twelve. You may feel like you just can't do that. Project management requires a great deal of honesty. By looking at the factors above, you know rationally that it will take twelve days, so you either fess up to it now, or plan to work the additional eight hours from 5 p.m.– 1 a.m. in addition to your usual 8 a.m.–5 p.m..

## Transferring Knowledge

Many managers mistakenly believe that you can hire external client/server consulting, place them on a project and your internal people will learn through some magical osmosis. Time and time again this has proven to be completely untrue and valuable business knowledge has left with the consultant. The flaw in this theory comes down to the principle of serving two masters—you can't do it. Consultants are there to complete a project successfully. Sure, in the beginning they can take the time to carefully duplicate all their efforts and nurture the internal staff but when the going gets tough, as it always does, the first thing that will be abandoned is the non-essential knowledge transfer. The external consultants are not rewarded for that, so if you want knowledge transfer to occur, you must measure that it occurs (we value what we measure) and build that into the reward structure. For example, allocate project activities and build time into the schedule. Again, this is simply a choice between time and quality—in this case, knowledge transfer.

## Managing Development Options

Client/server does require a little different way of doing development and RAD is an approach that fits nicely in this highly volatile world of technology. As mentioned before, there is still process analysis to do on non-interface processes, yet even more critical, in my opinion, is the data model. Without well managed data analysis, no prototyping in the world will save you. The performance problems that are inevitable in client/server (multiple vendors, incompatible products, networking constraints, haphazard queries) can be minimized with flexible, maintainable relational data base designs. Don't skip the data modelling—it will get you. Notice that this model is not linear; it iteratively can throw you back and forth. Project management in this iterative environment becomes a juggling act where multiple priorities are managed on a macro level. If you do not have a project manager who has the ability to stay out of the micro-level, a client/server project is doomed to failure. If you have a project manager who was promoted for being a brilliant technician, you are taking the chance that when the going gets tough, that person will dive again into what he or she does best (the technology) and no one will be watching the barn door, as we say in the heartlands.

## What to Do If You're Behind (or It's Your Behind)

Up to this point, I have spent a lot of time on preparation and project planning. Once the project gets going, the project managers add to their plate of responsibilities. Not only are they planning the next milestone in detail, but they are also organizing and controlling the phase that the project is currently in. The most critical activity while controlling is troubleshooting. What happens when things start to slip? First of all, in any project if the project manager sees a big problem on a task estimate (for example, it takes four times longer to do than planned), it isn't rationalized away ("Oh, they were just tired that day …"). There is every reason to believe that all future tasks will take four times as long as well. This is supported by the sage advice offered by Fredrick Brooks in his classic book *The Mythical Man Month*: "… how does a project get behind? One day at a time."

Suppose you are running out of time. You have these options: add resources (which may actually increase your duration—not generally a good strategy), add overtime (cost), sacrifice quality (generally the default if no one decides to react), or cut scope. Cutting scope and phasing in the project are generally the most rational choices. If you are budget constrained, you can add time, sacrifice quality or cut scope. Finally, if your quality is slipping, you can add dollars (buy help, buy better tools, buy consulting), add time, or cut scope. Sometimes none of these are comfortable choices but you will always choose something, even if it is only by default. For example, if you choose to force your people to work tons of free overtime to maintain budget or rescue the schedule, your quality will slip. No. 3 priorities generally do not slip because of intent; they slip because of neglect.

## Summary

"For the new middle manager, power flows from sources other than position. One is expertise in project management itself."—Tom Stewart, *Fortune* (July 10, 1995)

In summary, client/server projects are not that different from traditional mainframe projects, but they do tend to magnify the project management weaknesses that have always been present, including creeping scope, unrealistic expectations, inadequate requirements and changing priorities. By documenting the scope and constraints, answering the tough questions at the start of a project, completing some type of risk analysis, creating a realistic schedule through more rational estimates and troubleshooting, project managers can succeed with client/server. An analogy will illustrate the true role that a project manager plays on a client/server project:

Once upon a time, there was a land that was inhabited by pigs. These pigs had a problem because they were quickly running out of food. After discussing their plight, they decided to take their last remaining food and build a boat. With this boat they would sail across the sea—none of them had ever been across the sea and none of them really knew whether there would be food on the other side, but it was their only hope. They built the boat and set sail.

This is just like your role as a project manager of a client/server project. Your job is not to have the idea to build the boat; your job is not to build the boat; in fact, your most important job is not even directing the boat. You must keep the pigs from eating the boat.

# Electrifying Software Development

David Irving, Synergy International Limited

## Introduction

The New Zealand Government started deregulating the electricity industry in 1990. The final phase was announced in June 1995; the Wholesale Electricity Market was to begin trading on 1 October 1996. The market rules took a year to develop, being finalised in June 1996.

The development of computer systems to enable the new market to operate, was based on best guesses. There were some significant changes in the final rules revisions which impacted the systems developments just weeks before their scheduled completion. Also, the systems were developed on three continents, making the integration of designs and systems more difficult than usual.

This paper examines many of the problems encountered, and their resolution. It also explores some of the lessons learned and the benefits of doing a two-year development in less than six months.

## Background

Prior to 1990, the Electricity Corporation of New Zealand (ECNZ) had a virtual monopoly of generation and distribution, and over sixty local power companies operated local networks supplying retail customers. These power companies were restricted to their own geographical areas.

About 80 percent of New Zealand's generation is hydro-electric, the balance being thermal (17 percent) and geothermal (3 percent). Because of geography most generation capacity (70 percent) is in the South Island whereas, due to demography, most consumption (70 percent) is in the North Island. A High Voltage Direct Current (HVDC) link, which has a capacity of 1200MW, provides the only connection between the two islands.

### Significant Events

- July 1994: Trans Power New Zealand (TPNZ) was split from ECNZ to form a State-Owned Enterprise (SOE).
- June 1995: The government announced a restructuring of the electricity industry, including the creation of the Wholesale Electricity Market (WEM). The Electricity Market Company (EMCO) was established and, together with TPNZ, was given responsibility for the development and operation of the WEM.
- June 1996: The rules for the operation of New Zealand's WEM are agreed by the industry.
- 30 September 1996: The first bids and offers are received for the start of the WEM at midnight.

### The Way Things Used To Be

Prior to February 1996 ECNZ generated 95 percent of New Zealand's electricity. It provided costs of generation at each power station to TPNZ on a weekly basis for scheduling purposes. TPNZ created a demand forecast based on previous demand levels, time of day, day of week and weather forecasts. Scheduling was a relatively simple "load fill," where the cheapest generators were scheduled first allowing for some complexities such as the HVDC capacity of 1200MW constraining transfer of power between the North and South Islands. TPNZ published a daily schedule to ECNZ detailing the expected generation requirements of each station. TPNZ also performed the function of Dispatch; the process of notifying each station of the exact generation requirements on a real-time basis.

The old system would deal with approximately seventy station costs and a forecast of demand. Most effort was put into optimising water flows as they progressed down a river chain. For example, ECNZ has twelve hydro-electric stations on the Waikato River, so accounting for the elapsed time for water flow, dam lake levels and the capacity of each station facilitated very efficient water use.

### Rules For The New Wholesale Electricity Market

The WEM rules were defined by a series of Working Groups involving selected market participants. Most major players in the electricity industry registered as market participants, but the market is optional and several organisations operate as non-market participants. The market is operated by EMCO using a pool concept, where the pool buys and sells electricity at spot prices based on marginal prices, i.e. the price is set by the most expensive individual generation in any trading period.

By 1 p.m. each day, all market participants are required to submit bids and offers to the Scheduler via EMCO for each of the forty-eight half-hour trading periods in the next day. Generation offers may contain up to five price bands and purchase bids may contain up to ten bands per half-hour trading period. EMCO publishes a forecast spot price for each location for each half hour in the schedule. Each market participant can amend their bid or offer up to four hours



PROJECT MANAGEMENT INSTITUTE 28th Annual Seminars & Symposium
Chicago, Illinois: Papers Presented September 29 to October 1, 1997

before the event, after which changes without a bona fide reason will be penalised.

EMCO passes all Bids and Offers to the Scheduler (TPNZ) which also receives non-market participants' bids and offers for quantities of electricity exceeding 5MW. Therefore, the scheduler has a complete picture of availability and demand. It must produce and distribute a schedule at least every two hours. This process matches quantities and prices, bid and offered, taking into account line constraints and locations of both capacity and demand. This differs from the previous optimisation in that it attempts to find the lowest cost to the purchaser, rather than the lowest cost of generation. As events occur that may affect the schedule, parties inform TPNZ via EMCO and the schedule is revised. This is done as many times as required up to real-time dispatch.

The schedule gives the quantity cleared at each location for each market and non-market participant. The pre-market systems used approximately seventy costs and locations for generation, and eighteen regions for demand, giving approximately 1,260 permutations. The combinations of banded offer quantities and prices with location can now create up to 16,800 offer transactions. Similarly, with the greater number of banded bids from fifty purchasers, and the 500 or so demand locations, the daily number of bid transactions could exceed 5,000,000. Because of this increase in complexity a linear programming technique is used to create the schedule.

Market participants access their own scheduled quantities via EMCO's Trading system (COMIT). EMCO, in its capacity as Clearing and Settlement Manager, publishes various prices at various stages. Forecast prices are issued with each schedule. Provisional prices are published at 9 a.m. on the day after actual consumption, and are more accurate than the forecast prices because they are based on actual metered quantities rather than estimated values. At the end of each month the final metered values are used to determine final prices. In most cases the metered values will not change from the provisional to the final price calculation but, due to the flows of electricity around the network, any change in a metered value can affect prices for other locations. Practise shows that differences between provisional and final prices are minor.

TPNZ, in its capacity as Dispatcher, issues instructions for actual generation quantities directly to generators.

### Metering and Reconciliation

TPNZ meters all Grid Exit Points (GXPs). Unless any other party is actively selling electricity at the same GXP, the incumbent power company is assumed to have consumed the metered amount. If another party is active at a GXP, it must meter its own supply and submit the information to the National Reconciliation Manager (NRM). The NRM subtracts any metered usage, or adds any metered embedded generation, to derive the incumbent power company's use.

From its own and other parties' metering information the NRM reconciles quantities of electricity supplied to in the Retail Electricity Market. All remaining quantities are passed to EMCO where the WEM is reconciled either to long term contracts or from the spot market. EMCO also performs a settlement function where the value of supply is transferred from the purchaser to the generator.

## Creation of the WEM

In February 1996 a new SOE, Contact Electricity, was established and 35 percent of generation capacity transferred to it, to create competition in generation. This left ECNZ with 60 percent of generation capacity and a small number of independent generators held the remaining 5 percent.

An Interim WEM was established in early 1996 to allow both ECNZ and Contact Electricity to establish their new business practices. Since ECNZ had long term contracts with the Power Companies, true competition during this early stage was limited, and Contact effectively operated as a subcontractor to ECNZ.

The full WEM began on 1 October 1996. Only at this point would there be true competition between generators. Although there was the potential to receive enormous numbers of bid and offer transactions, in practise the market tends to involve approximately 30,000 transactions in any one day's trading.

## Wholesale Market Systems

The most notable change in the new Wholesale Market is the competitive nature of bidding and offering for electricity.

### Systems Overview

In order to facilitate bidding and offering, EMCO built a new market system called COMIT. It also displays schedules to the relevant parties. COMIT encompasses a range of other information provision facilities such as E-mail, Internet Web pages and Reuters news facilities.

TPNZ developed a new optimisation algorithm to calculate the least cost supply of electricity. From a scheduler's perspective it is based purely on the bids and offers received and does not account for hydrological flows. From a Dispatcher's perspective, it schedules to the real-time demand as monitored by TPNZ's Electricity Management System (EMS).

TPNZ also developed an information warehouse known as the TPNZ Information Exchange (TPIX), which gathers

**Exhibit 1.** Wholesale Electricity Market Systems

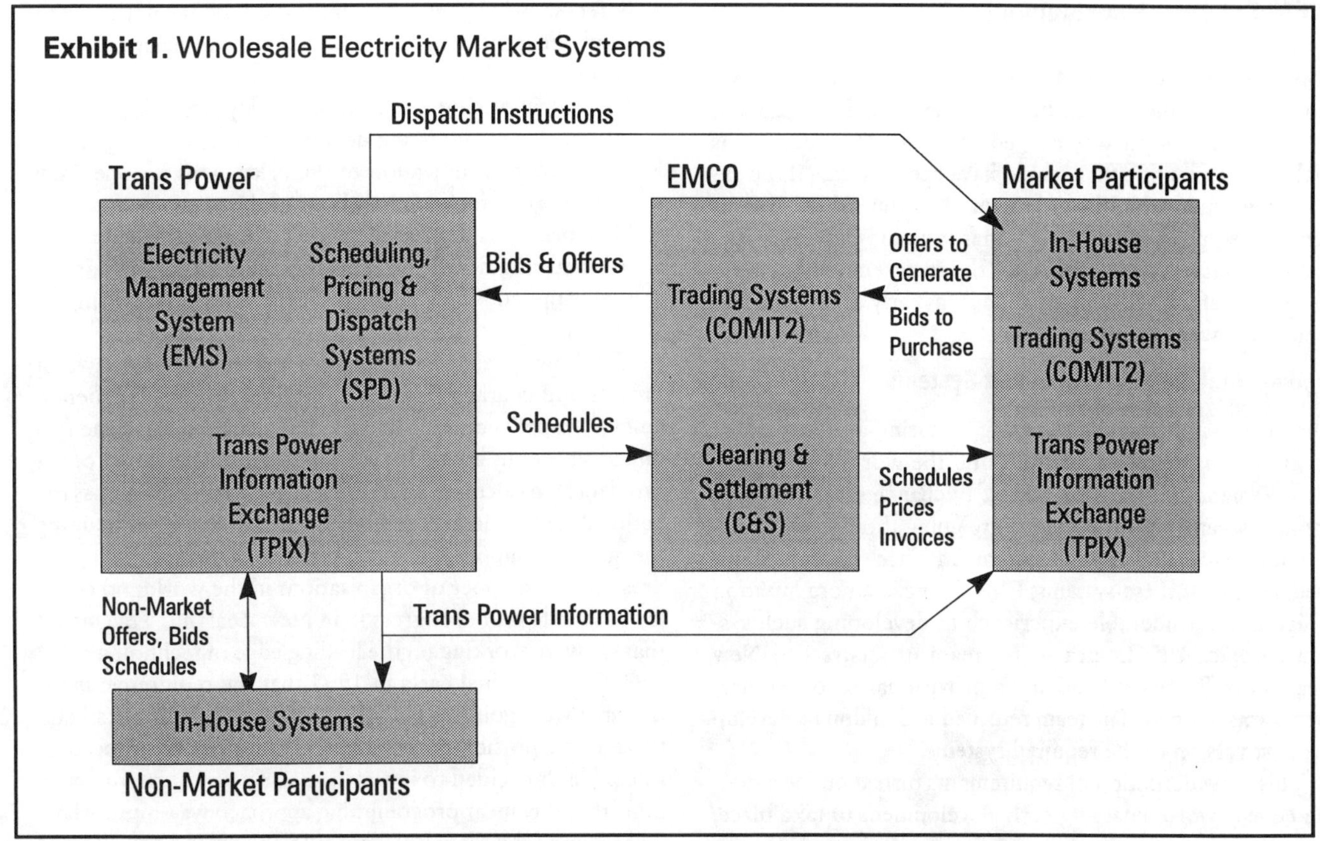


information from a variety of existing TPNZ information systems and makes it available to the outside world. TPIX is available through EMCO's COMIT terminals and to non-market participants.

The new market systems were developed within the rules of the wholesale market, which have some requirements in terms of information provision to specified parties and the timing of delivery. The systems must be very robust, and must have an appropriate level of support to allow these deadlines to be met. Similarly, the location of each system must facilitate the requirements of the market rules. For example: TPNZ's operational systems are located at its control centres in Hamilton and Christchurch, EMCO's systems are located in its head office in Wellington. Suitable communications links must allow the deadlines imposed by the rules to be met.

### Hardware, Software and Developers Chosen

EMCO required trading and financial systems, choosing Logica UK to develop the main COMIT application, and Logica New Zealand to develop the Clearing and Settlement system using Borland Delphi.

TPNZ needed Scheduling, Pricing and Dispatch (SPD) systems, choosing Cegelec ESCA in Seattle, Washington, U.S.A. ESCA used a product called AIMMS, supported from Holland, to develop the linear programming optimisation routine which, in turn, used CPLEX as the solver. The initial Graphical User Interface was developed using Microsoft Access. The Information Exchange system was seen as a corporate warehouse of information and SAS New Zealand was chosen to develop TPIX using its SAS programming language.

The hardware selected by each party was different. EMCO chose to use a Sun Unix environment while TPNZ chose a mixture of Digital Unix in Wellington for TPIX and Digital Open VMS in Hamilton for SPD. The AIMMS model required a PC environment for which the Hewlett Packard Pentium Pro was chosen.

Oracle was selected by all parties as the preferred database environment, but the variety of hardware and development environments required several different versions.

So, we had a variety of environments being developed by several organisations residing on three different continents. This, compounded by the absolutely fixed timeframe, gave the project that "Mission Impossible" feel. Both EMCO and TPNZ had to develop software in a timeframe which would not have been considered possible under normal circumstances. However, the 1 October date had been fixed by the government and, as there was a General Election fixed for 12 October, it was etched in tablets of stone. Not only was there an election due, but New Zealand was changing its electoral method, moving to a form of proportional representation.

## WEM Systems Development

Both organisations selected developers based on a set of "potential" requirements. Selection criteria were drawn up and a formal evaluation was carried out, but the process was slightly less scientific than would have been the case if the exact requirements had been known. The timetable for confirming requirements was such that it would have been impossible to select developers after the requirements had been fixed. Therefore, selecting developers as early as possible was seen as a lower risk option.

### Trading, Clearing and Settlement Systems

The business of providing Trading, Clearing and Settlement functions has many parallels around the world and even in New Zealand, for example: Stock Exchange systems. There are also several countries which are going through deregulation and have their trading systems in place. Having examined several of these systems, EMCO chose an organisation which has considerable experience in developing such systems: Logica UK. Logica sent a team of analysts to New Zealand in February 1996 and a provisional set of requirements was defined. The team returned to London to develop the first version of the required systems.

This early definition of requirements turned out be a double-edged sword, enabling early development to take place, but impacting the development process with subsequent change requirements. The geographical separation of EMCO and the developers made the change management process more difficult to control. One additional problem was a lack of user requirements. The system was designed from scratch and the eventual users had no experience in using the type of systems needed to operate a market.

The electricity industry in New Zealand transacts several million dollars each day. Systems which deal with these transactions must be accurate, auditable and reliable. It is a less than ideal situation to have to develop such systems under the high pressures of a short timeframe and changing requirements.

### Scheduling, Pricing and Dispatch Systems

Although this appears to be three different systems, the nature of the problem is really the same. The scheduling and dispatch aspects attempt to predict the use of electricity at each location and determine the best pattern of generation, taking into account the cost and location of the generators, to meet the demand.

The scheduling process matches the generators' offers to the power companies' demand bids for up to 35 hours in the future. The dispatch process matches the same offers to real time demand measured at this precise moment, up to four hours into the future.

Pricing is done in three different ways:

- Forecast pricing gives an indication of what the price would be if the demand was as bid and the generation pattern was as scheduled.
- Provisional pricing is done immediately after the event using provisional metering details for the demand, giving a more accurate indication of the price. This is done daily to give prices for each half hour of the previous day.
- Final pricing is done at the end of the month when the final metering details have been gathered and any corrections applied. The market is cleared and settled using final prices.

The flow of electricity is governed only by the laws of physics and characteristics such as line capacity, frequency, voltage, impedance, etc., and can be calculated using the formulae most of us learned in school physics. The nature of the problem is to calculate how the electricity will flow across the national grid, allowing for all the factors, but still maintaining the quality of supply. While this problem is currently being addressed by a number of organisations in the world, no country has made more progress than New Zealand. This meant that we were working on the leading edge of technology.

TPNZ identified early in 1995 that the requirements for this area were going to be difficult to determine in detail and there was a possibility that some calculations could become infeasible. It decided to invest in an early prototype to determine that the linear programming approach was appropriate, what type of the requirements could be met and the effect of various calculations on run times. With hindsight this turned out to be one of the most important decisions of the entire market development.

## Risk Assessment

This section examines some of the areas which could be considered extreme risks.

### Timeframe

There were several aspects to this area of risk: constant pressure, things going wrong left no time to recover, and there were very few options for "Plan B.". As with any project with an absolutely fixed end date, we simply managed the scope, cost and quality of the project.

The scope was aggressively pruned to leave only those items which were required by the rules. Any other items were deferred until a later date. Some areas were addressed in a very basic way and have since been, or are still planned to be, improved.

The cost was controlled by examining design options and selecting the most cost effective. There were one or two items where cost was simply "whatever it takes" but these were limited to absolutely core requirements and were managed very carefully.

### Interface Design

We identified the boundaries between each project and identified the interfaces required to enable the overall application architecture to work. Discussions on this topic necessitated international travel or conference telephone calls. Agreement often took far longer than would have been the case if all parties had been in the same location. We managed to design one or two reasonably elegant interfaces but we were left with having to design and build conversion processes to transfer data from one system to another.

### Leading Edge or Bleeding Edge

Much of what was required for the scheduling, pricing and dispatch application had never been done in a commercial environment before. Some work had been carried out in the academic world, but translating this into a robust working application required significant effort. This was seen as the most critical area of the development.

The early development of a prototype enabled options to be explored and many valuable lessons to be learned. It confirmed the approach, timing and quality of the results. With hindsight, if we had not developed the prototype, the final SPD application could not have been developed in time.

### Critical Resource Allocation

The most knowledgeable people are one of the greatest assets of such a project. Introducing new members to the team can often reduce productivity in the short term We found it was often more productive to support the existing team members, by removing all the trivial day-to-day hassles and allowing them to achieve a higher rate of productivity, than it is to introduce an extra person into the team.

## Project Team Structure

### Team Effort

We determined quite early in the planning that the only possibility of meeting the deadline was to build an excellent team of people. As with the New Zealand America's Cup campaign, a good team can achieve a true synergy and produce far more than the sum of the individuals' efforts.

We worked very hard to create a team culture. While we allocated tasks and held individuals accountable for their progress, we encouraged people to ask for help when they needed it, and when an issue was identified we worked on a strategy for the team to resolve it.

### Eradication of Egos

At one of the first project meetings we put a cardboard box near the door with a message that read "If you brought your ego to this meeting with you, please place it in this box and collect it on the way out." This created a team culture in which issues were discussed from a dispassionate viewpoint. Although one or two people operated on the fringe of the team, the vast majority were wholeheartedly team players.

We created an atmosphere where everyone was prepared to do any job within the team, so long as they had the skills to do it. Therefore, some of the more senior members of the team wrote test data for the junior members, and checked test results by ticking off from two lists of numbers or data items.

### Culture

The setting of a deadline by the government was seen as a constraint imposed by someone from outside of the project. To an extent, we all had a common "enemy" and this helped create the desired culture. It was everyone versus the system. We had established the "War Room" mentality.

It also helped that this culture permeated the wider project team including EMCO, TPNZ and all the development teams. If a problem was identified, we got the relevant people round a table or a conference call and discussed it until resolved.

## Management Techniques

### Focus

From day one we concentrated on the "must haves". If we identified an optional task, we shelved it until someone started to scream for it to be put back into the scope. We never threw anything away, we simply scheduled items for after the October deadline. Having identified the critical tasks we prioritised them so that the super-critical were tackled first. This ensured that, if a delay occurred it impacted one of the 'not quite so critical tasks'.

### Scope

As soon as an area of the project was clearly defined its scope was frozen and formal change management was applied. This ensured that changes were considered and not applied without good reason. This was particularly important as any change could affect a part of the project being developed overseas.

The usual technique of managing scope, time, quality and costs became one of manipulating scope, quality and cost. Even within the constraints of cost and scope there was a limit on the cost so we were left juggling the scope and the quality. Some aspects needed to be of the highest quality and were developed as such. Others could have a lesser quality solution put in on day one, with the better solution delivered later. These were carefully managed and agreement reached with other areas of the project and with the project sponsor.

### Communication

We tried to keep all the relevant people up to date with events. This was not a case of "tell everything to everyone" otherwise we would have suffered from information overload. Where possible, we tried to deliver information on a need to know basis. We didn't always get it right; some instances of people not being told what they should have created a few problems. Also, people ignoring what they thought was not relevant to them caused similar problems.

The most important aspect of communications was that between the geographically separated parts of the team. Keeping the overseas people up to date and getting their agreement on changes presented its own problems. Moving people around the world is time consuming and removes them from their part of the team, but telephone conversations are not as productive as sitting round a table or using a whiteboard. We did our best to achieve the right balance.

### Honesty

When you have established a co-operative team environment, one of the easiest ways of undermining all your good work is to conceal problems. We managed to achieve a level of honesty among the various parties which is unusual in such a major project. We managed to avoid the "us and them" attitude and reaped the benefits of concentrating on the task rather than the politics.

The environment encouraged people to raise issues and, once raised, there was an "all hands to the pumps" atmosphere until the issue was resolved. In many cases an issue was resolved by people from outside of the organisations directly responsible for the issue. Throughout the project the one phrase that was totally absent was "not our problem."

## Conclusion

The real benefits of the project were in the achievement of its objective. There was a single aim: to implement a Wholesale Electricity Market by 1 October 1996. This date was set politically, before the true scope and complexity was known. The fact that a team was created which could implement the systems required, regardless of the complexity uncovered, was remarkable. The integration of systems which were developed by parties with a wide geographical separation, with very different development and operational environments was also remarkable. Few people will ever know just what effort went into creating the Wholesale Electricity Market in New Zealand.

In learning from this project, I would propose the following approach to other, less time-critical projects:

- Focus very clearly on what must be achieved to satisfy the core requirements. Even in a low pressure project it is beneficial to deliver a core system which satisfies the main requirements as early as possible. This gives users a chance to learn about the system and changes can be made before final system delivery. In a high pressure project it is essential to begin delivery as early as possible.
- Set very clear deadlines and do whatever it takes to achieve them. A project which develops a culture of not missing deadlines will achieve most of them. A project in which deadlines are regularly missed will develop a culture where it doesn't matter if something is late. It always matters.
- True synergy works. A team can achieve much more than a bunch of individual experts. Never underestimate the power of the team culture. If done well, it is a team culture, if done badly it is simply office politics. Some people are experts in their field but simply cannot survive in a team environment. These people should be kept outside the team and used for specific tasks only, otherwise they can severely disrupt the team culture.
- Keep people informed. This is a difficult judgement call between burying people with information and not letting the right people know what they need to know. It is usually worth starting with spreading a little too much information and trim it down as people tell you they don't want certain things.
- If you can create a project environment where "Honesty is the best policy" you have a much better chance of achieving your objectives. When a problem is identified and openly discussed it is more likely to be solved, than if someone keeps it secret hoping to solve it before anyone finds out.

In an average career in IT project management you would be fortunate to be involved in a successful implementation of a high pressure project such as this one. If you can participate in more than one project of this nature, then you are very privileged indeed. I consider myself very privileged, and would like to thank everyone involved in this project.

# Approaches Towards Effective Project Management

Larry Goldsmith PMP, c.w. Costello & Associates

Information Technology departments are being faced with new challenges resulting from continued corporate downsizing. Undermanned IT shops are left to address ever-increasing information demands. Companies are combating traditional inadequacies, historically poor project success ratios (number of project successes to overall projects attempted), and the new reality (delivering systems in shorter time frames, with higher quality, and less resources) in two significant ways—implementing a project management discipline, as defined by the Project Management Institute (PMI), and improving quality measures through process improvement techniques espoused by the Capability Maturity Model "CMM" from the Software Engineering Institute (SEI). This paper investigates the complementary nature of the two approaches by tackling the topic of qualified vs. effective project managers and how the two approaches can be leveraged to reduce the journey toward Effective project management.

## Project Management

Let's begin by examining some definitions related to the topic at hand. PMI defines project management as "The application of knowledge, skills, tools, and techniques to project activities in order to meet or exceed stakeholder needs and expectations from a project. Meeting or exceeding stakeholder needs and expectations invariably involves balancing competing demands among Scope, Time, Cost, and Quality" (PMI 1996).

The following definition is provided by the United States Office of Personnel Management:

**Project Manager/Director - Occupation Code: 189.177-030.** Plans, directs, and coordinates activities of designated project to ensure that goals or objectives of project are accomplished within prescribed time frame and funding parameters: Reviews project proposal or plan to determine time frame, funding limitations, procedures for accomplishing project, staffing requirements, and allotment of available resources to various phases of project. Establishes work plan and staffing for each phase of project, and arranges for recruitment or assignment of project personnel and modifies schedules or plans as required. Prepares project reports for management, client, or others. Confers with project personnel to provide technical advice and to resolve problems. May coordinate project activities with activities of government regulatory or other governmental agencies.

## What Makes a Qualified Project Manager?

Research leads us to believe that poor project management skills are a major contributor to the overwhelming number of systems delivery failures and dismal record of on-time, in budget, useable applications. As companies look for ways to improve their information technology success ratio, they are turning to PMI for guidance, direction, and ultimately, certification. PMI's *A Guide to the Project Management Body of Knowledge* (*PMBOK Guide*) provides the basics for those interested in the discipline of project management. The *PMBOK Guide* provides an introductory view of the knowledge and practices most prevalent in projects. It is not fully detailed nor is it extensively exhaustive. It provides a guideline and direction for understanding and employing the constructs of project management.

The knowledge found in the *PMBOK Guide* also forms the basis for evaluating a person's level of understanding. It is a vehicle for appreciating the structure surrounding project management, the manner and environment common to projects, and a flavor for the intricacies of how the many project management processes integrate. This structure is rooted in nine process areas which include:

- Project Integration Management
- Project Human Resource Management
- Project Scope Management
- Project Risk Management
- Project Time Management
- Project Procurement Management
- Project Cost Management
- Project Communications Management
- Project Quality Management

Successfully passing a test covering the process areas represents one piece of the puzzle leading to attainment of the Project Management Professional (PMP) designation. The remaining piece consists of accumulating a minimum point count spread across the following three categories:

### *Education and Training*

This area addresses the level of formal education the applicant has received (e.g. Bachelor's or Master's degree) along with any specialized project management training received.

#### Experience

This area investigates the lengths and levels of work experience directly attributable to projects, project management, and general management (e.g. supervisor, director, etc.)

#### Service

This area recognizes the contributions the applicant has made to the project management discipline.

Becoming a certified project manager might address the question of *"What Makes a Qualified Project Manager?"* but it just scratches the surface of this topic. Once certification is achieved, the learning for a project manager does not end. Quite the contrary, ongoing education, training, and practice are required to keep skills sharp. This discussion thus leads us to the following question.

## What Makes an Effective Project Manager?

We have just spent a considerable amount of time defining a "qualified" project manager. This begs us to ask:

Does QUALIFIED = EFFECTIVE?

The obvious answer to this equation is NO! To better explain this answer, we must begin by examining the different types of categories and projects we will encounter.

### Technical

*Stable*: This project type is characterized by familiar technology, well-defined requirements, a known and consistent management environment, flexible cost and schedule constraints, and minimal need for innovation. An example of this project type could be an enhancement project for an existing system.

*Volatile:* Volatile projects usually include technology unfamiliar to the company, poorly defined requirements, an uncertain management environment, rigid or tight cost and schedule constraints, and the challenge of significant innovation. This project type is prevalent today in the form of data warehousing/data mining systems.

*Mixed:* Mixed projects will contain some stable elements and some volatile elements. An example of this project type might be a re-hosting effort where we are taking a mainframe application with known functionality and porting it to a Unix client/server environment.

### Economic

*High Leverage:* This type of project adds revenue, market share, or produces a competitive advantage for the company to leverage into increased profitability. An automation project (order entry or electronic data interchange, aimed at increasing throughput) is an example.

*Low Leverage:* This type of project is targeted at the cost side of the corporation. An automation project being implemented in support of a business process re-engineering effort would be a low-leverage project; for example, a project replacing multiple general ledger systems, supporting individual business units, with a single enterprise general ledger system.

*No Leverage:* This type of project is usually driven by technology needs but does nothing to increase revenue or reduce costs. An example of this is the replacement of an old package application or old hardware which is no longer supported by the original manufacturer.

All projects you will ever manage can be characterized as a combination of one technical and one economic type. It is because of this fact that answering the question of effectiveness is so difficult. So let's explore some additional criteria which we'll call project management competencies. We must evaluate a project manager through the context of project management competencies in conjunction with project categories to determine effectiveness.

## Project Management Competencies

1. Business Achievement
   - Business Awareness
   - Commitment To Quality
   - Knows The Competition
   - Eye On Cost.
2. Problem Solving
   - Initiative
   - Information Gathering
   - Analytical Thinking
   - Conceptual Thinking.
3. Influencing/Negotiating
   - Interpersonal Awareness
   - Organizational Awareness
   - Anticipation Of Impact – Risk
   - Resourceful Use Of Influence.
4. People Management
   - Motivating Others
   - Communication Skills
   - Developing Others— Empowering
   - Active Listening And Delegating.
5. Self-Management
   - Self-Confidence
   - Stress Management
   - Concern for Credibility
   - Part of Solution Not Problem.

The competencies can be split into two major categories, Technical and Influence. The technical grouping encompasses categories 1 and 2, and the influence grouping includes categories 3, 4, and 5. Effective project managers strive to place as many of these competencies in their tool kit as possible. This allows them to exhibit the appropriate skill set as dictated by the project. For example, what competencies would be most appropriate for a volatile, high-leverage project?

A quick recap shows that "Volatile" projects include technology new to the company, incomplete requirements, tight cost and schedule constraints, and the need for innovation. This scenario dictates having a project manager with:

- Strong problem-solving skills to best handle the chaotic environment exemplified by volatility and the pressures of a high-leverage project
- Influencing/negotiating skills are equally important as change/scope management will run rampant throughout this project with the increased level of uncertainty from new technology coupled with incomplete requirements
- People management skills to best handle the personnel in this very demanding high-pressure project.

The above competencies are not an all inclusive list of what is needed to successfully bring this project to fruition, but they do stand out as highly critical to increase the probability of success.

We always hear that experience is the best teacher. This is supported by the fact that certification requires demonstrating one's long term commitment to the project management discipline. We have presented some ideas directed at defining a "qualified" or "effective" project manager and experience plays a role here too. Our experience is then leveraged on our next project. What works and doesn't work within that next project is then internally measured against our baseline—project management knowledge/experience. Our experience therefore represents our individual process which is only repeatable by us individually.

This raises the question: Can managing the project management process help to create "Qualified or Effective" project managers faster or more efficiently? The answer to this question leads us into a discussion of the Capability Maturity Model and the foundations of process management. As with our project management discussion, we will begin again with some basic definitions.

## Process Management

Webster defines *Process* as "A system of operations in producing something ... a series of actions, changes, or functions that achieve an end or result." We then take the next step and see that SEI defines *Software Process as* "A set of activities, methods, practices, and transformations that people use to develop and maintain software and the associated products (e.g. project plans, design documents, program code, test cases, and user manuals)."

**Exhibit 1.** The Five Levels of Software Process Maturity

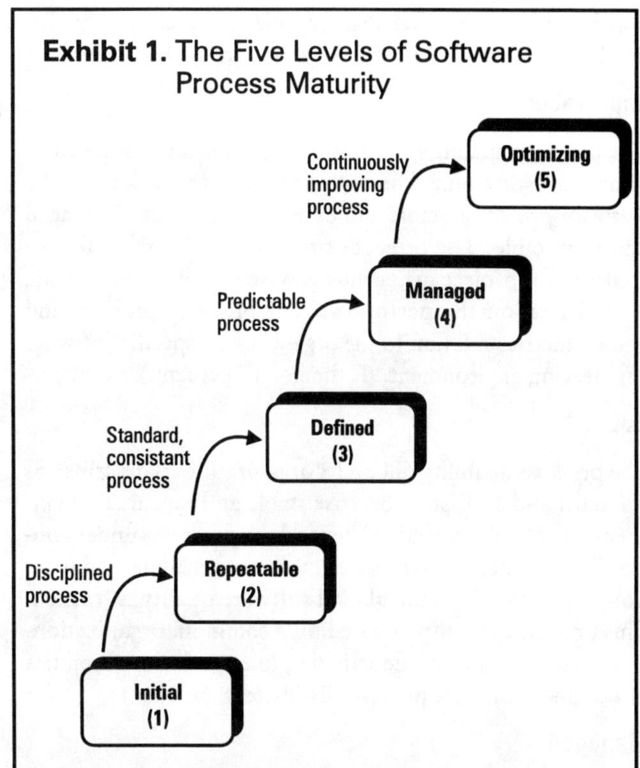


Finally, we offer the following definition of *Process Management:* A discipline which encompasses the definition, management and improvement of complex business processes thereby making the projects based on those processes more effective.

The numbers of "qualified or effective" project managers are not sufficient to support the total global demand for the project management discipline. The SEI was formed and the CMM was created in part to assist with overcoming the deficiency in staffing demands. The CMM is separated into two major parts, the levels of maturity and the definition of key process areas to assist in achieving those maturity levels. The maturity levels are displayed in Exhibit 1 below and followed by a brief definition of each.

### Initial

The process capability of Level 1 organizations is unpredictable because the process is constantly altered as the work progresses (i.e., the process is ad hoc). Schedules, budgets, functionality, and product quality related to projects are unpredictable. Performance is highly dependent on the capabilities of specific individuals and varies with their experience, skills, knowledge, and motivations. There are few stable processes in evidence, and project success can be predicted only by individual rather than organizational capability. (Estimate: 76 percent of all U.S. IT shops are at this level.)

### Repeatable

The process capability of Level 2 organizations can be characterized as disciplined because planning and tracking of the software project is stable and earlier successes are leveraged and repeatable. The project's process is under the effective control of a project management system, following realistic plans based on the performance of previous projects and known metrics relevant to the organizations specific software engineering environment. (Estimate: 15 percent.)

### Defined

The process capability of Level 3 organizations is described as standard and consistent because stable and repeatable management activities are added beyond the processes under control. Within established product lines, cost, schedule, and functionality are under control, and software quality is tracked. This process capability is based on a common, organization-wide understanding of the activities, roles, and responsibilities in a defined software process. (Estimate: 8 percent.)

### Managed

The process capability of Level 4 organizations is extremely reliable and predictable because the process is measured and operates within objective quantifiable limits. This level of maturity allows an organization to predict trends in process and product quality within the quantitative bounds of these limits. When these limits are exceeded, action is taken to correct the situation. Software products are of high quality. (Estimate: <1 percent.)

### Optimizing

The process capability of Level 5 organizations can be characterized as continuously improving because Level 5 organizations are focused on increasing the range of their process capability, thereby improving the process performance of their projects. Improvement occurs both by incremental advancements in the existing process and by innovations using new technologies and methods. (Estimate: <1 percent.)

## How Can the CMM Help?

The CMM cannot accelerate the timeline toward becoming a *qualified* project manager, it can, however, reduce the learning curve and mitigate risk associated with developing an *effective* project manager. Let's explore the Key Process Areas (KPA) associated with each level and comprehend how they can support the aforementioned competencies.

### Level 2 - Repeatable

The identification of successful processes and practices is the first step in developing *effective* project managers. We need the technical competencies to develop our requirements and plans. For example, we rely heavily on business achievement and problem-solving skills to assist in the formulation of interview guides for capturing requirements, and logical groupings of activities focused on implementation. We need the Influence competencies to track and manage the project from inception to completion. For example, influencing/negotiating skills are necessary when developing the Statement of Work in the areas of risk management, change management, and roles/responsibilities.

- *Requirements Management*: Requirements management involves establishing and maintaining an agreement with the customer on the requirements for the software project.
- *Software Project Planning*: Software project planning involves developing estimates for the work to be performed, establishing the necessary commitments, and defining the plan to perform the work.
- *Software Project Tracking and Oversight*: Software project tracking and oversight involves tracking and reviewing the software accomplishments and results against documented estimates, commitments, and plans, and adjusting these plans based on the actual accomplishments and results.
- *Software Subcontract Management*: Software subcontract management involves selecting a software subcontractor, establishing commitments with the subcontractor, and tracking and reviewing the subcontractor's performance and results.
- *Software Quality Assurance*: Software quality assurance involves reviewing and auditing the software products and activities to verify that they comply with the applicable procedures and standards and providing the software project and other appropriate managers with the results of these reviews and audits.
- *Software Configuration Management*: Software configuration management involves identifying the configuration of the software (i.e., selected software work products and their descriptions) at given points in time, systematically controlling changes to the configuration, and maintaining the integrity and history of the configuration throughout the software life cycle.

### Level 3 - Defined

Making the Level 2 knowledge available and accessible to the entire organization is the next step in developing *effective* project managers. We need the technical competencies to document our processes and practices. For example, developing a reuse strategy, designing the support infrastructure, and populating the repository require projects based on best practice. We need the influence competencies to ensure the they are utilized effectively. For example, influencing/negotiating skills are necessary for demonstrating the value-add, mentoring and training new and existing project managers, and institutionalizing the processes and practices.

- *Organization Process Focus*: Organization process focus involves developing and maintaining an understanding of the organization's and projects' software processes and coordinating the activities to assess, develop, maintain, and improve these processes.
- *Organization Process Definition*: Organization process definition involves developing and maintaining the organization's standard software process, along with related process assets, such as descriptions of software life cycles, process tailoring guidelines and criteria, the organization's software process database, and a library of software process-related documentation.
- *Training Program*: Training program involves first identifying the training needed by the organization, projects, and individuals, then developing or procuring training to address the identified needs.
- *Integrated Software Management*: Integrated software management involves developing the project's defined software process and managing the software project using this defined software process.
- *Software Product Engineering*: Software product engineering involves performing the engineering tasks to build and maintain the software using the project's defined software process (described in the Integrated Software Management key process area) and appropriate methods and tools.
- *Intergroup Coordination*: Intergroup coordination involves the software engineering group's participation with other project engineering groups to address system-level requirements, objectives, and issues.
- *Peer Reviews*: Peer reviews involve a methodical examination of software work products by the producers' peers to identify defects and areas where changes are needed.

### Level 4 - Managed

At this level, *effective* project managers have well defined metrics to assist them with managing their projects.. We utilize the technical competencies to capture and formulate appropriate metrics. For example, identifying how to measure the processes and developing mechanisms for capturing metrics. We need the influence competencies to ensure the they are utilized effectively. For example, influencing/negotiating skills are necessary for supporting the metrics use, mentoring and training new and existing project managers, and institutionalizing the measurements.

- *Quantitative Process Management*: Quantitative process management involves establishing goals for the performance of the project's defined software process, which is described in the Integrated Software Management key process area, taking measurements of the process performance, analyzing these measurements, and making adjustments to maintain process performance within acceptable limits.
- *Software Quality Management*: Software quality management involves defining quality goals for the software products, establishing plans to achieve these goals, and monitoring and adjusting the software plans, software work products, activities, and quality goals to satisfy the needs and desires of the customer and end user for high quality products.

### Level 5 - Optimized

We are furthering our efforts at his level by using the technical competencies to evaluate performance and effectiveness, and the influence competencies to gain consensus on the appropriate enhancements to our processes and procedures to achieve our goals and objectives.

- *Defect Prevention*: Defect prevention involves analyzing defects that were encountered in the past and taking specific actions to prevent the occurrence of those types of defects in the future.
- *Technology Change Management*: Technology change management involves identifying, selecting, and evaluating new technologies, and incorporating effective technologies into the organization. The objective is to improve software quality, increase productivity, and decrease the cycle time for product development.
- *Process Change Management*: Process change management involves defining process improvement goals and, with senior management sponsorship, proactively and systematically identifying, evaluating, and implementing improvements to the organization's standard software process and the projects' defined software processes on a continuous basis.

## Conclusion

This paper has attempted to answer three prevalent project management issues through an examination of the offerings of two highly influential organizations, PMI and SEI. Those issues are outlined and summarized below:

1. How do I define a *qualified* project manager?
2. How do I define an *effective* project manager?
3. How can I accelerate the development of an *effective* project manager?

We recognize the Project Management Institute as the governing body with respect to the project management discipline with North America. It is therefore by PMI standards that we take our criteria for qualification. The criteria was extracted from their certification process documentation. This represents a comprehensive understanding of what is involved in managing projects and serves as our guide. Belief in this rigid position then requires the attainment of the PMP designation to be recognized as qualified. This position is being reinforced by the increasing number of PMI corporate memberships, those corporations subsequent institutionalization of a formalized project management position and advancement track for personnel, and the corporations requirement that project managers be certified.

Effectiveness on the other hand is not as clear cut. It is subjective in nature and extremely situational in practice. The contention of this paper is that project managers need to be more than planners and monitors to be effective. The criteria put forward for effectiveness suggests that the influence categories of project management competencies are what make a project manager effective and must be framed in the context of the type of project being managed. This is meant to verify that the project manager has the appropriate skills for the assigned project.

And finally, the paper suggests that by leveraging the experience of our current project managers, within the guidelines of the Capability Maturity Model, we can accelerate the learning and produce *effective* project managers more rapidly, efficiently, and with reduced organizational risk. The benefits of this are too numerous to list here but the end target should be a significant increase in successful projects.

It is therefore recommended that any organizational attempt to improve the delivery of information technology dependent business solutions include input from both the *PMBOK Guide* and the Capability Maturity Model.

# Linking Corporate Strategy to the Selection of IT Projects

Bruce Miller, PMP, Project Management Services, Origin Technology In Business

As organizations prepare for the 21st century, being able to identify, justify, and prioritize your selection of Information Technology (IT) projects will become more critical. By clearly understanding your organization's strategic direction and corporate bottom-line, you can begin to formulate a direct relationship between the IT projects you choose and these objectives.

The approach highlighted within this paper has been successfully implemented within Fortune 500 companies and the Federal government. By using this structured, portfolio management approach, you will be able to identify and invest in only those projects that have high success potential based upon organizational strategies, objectives, and core competencies.

## Background

Most organizations select and fund IT projects based on only a few, if any, criteria. IT projects are often funded solely on their perceived merits or their project owner's political clout. Once the top IT projects have been prioritized, projects are funded until the IT budget has been completely allocated. Little rigor is included in the prioritization and the overall ranking is purely subjective. In addition, important criteria that may directly impact a project's success are not taken into consideration. In most cases, corporate strategic factors are rarely considered or are deemed irrelevant to the IT project selection process.

As organizations continue to consolidate their business processes and closely monitor resources, IT projects will compete directly for the same funds being allocated to traditional investments such as new product development or research and development efforts. In order for IT projects to compete with more traditional corporate initiatives, they must be subjected to the same rigor and business justification as these other investments. The IT project's strategic value and alignment with corporate objectives must be clearly recognized or the project will not be adequately sponsored or funded.

The following process describes a systematic, rational approach for selecting and prioritizing IT projects based upon corporate strategic and tactical objectives. This process considers may criteria that may be overlooked in a less structured environment and provides an ongoing methodology for assessing the introduction of new IT projects or re-evaluating existing projects due to budget changes. In addition, the process creates up-front agreement and organizational buy-in because the key decision makers create the judgment criteria. Lastly, this approach establishes the business case for your investment and allows for a complete audit trail of the decision process.

## Getting Started—Review Strategic Objectives

In order to begin this process, you must carefully review the strategic objectives of your organization. For most organizations, this can be achieved by reviewing existing information, such as the strategic plan. Review the key drivers within your company or organization. Most organizations are driven by financial or cost measures, such as Profit, Sales, Earned Value, Net Present Value (NPV), Internal Rate of Return (IRR), or Economic Value Added (EVA). Although financial metrics are extremely important and directly impact the bottom line, other key criteria should be included that are often not easily measured. Customer Need, Process Improvement, and Employee Satisfaction may be key components within your corporate strategy, but have been difficult to consider or overlooked within your current IT project selection decision-making process. Cost is a factor that should be considered in any IT project selection process, but will only be indirectly included within the decision-making criteria. Cost is addressed when analyzing the IT project's Benefit to Cost ratio results. Carefully focus on identifying the most critical success factors for your company or organization, as they will establish the foundation of your project selection criteria.

## Create an IT Project Selection Model

Once the key strategic criteria have been identified, work closely with individuals within your organization to discuss any additional criteria that should be taken into consideration. These discussions can most effectively be organized through structured meetings or facilitated workshops, allowing participants to focus on brainstorming, dialogue, and group decision-making. These discussions will result in more specific criteria that should be considered when selecting IT

**Exhibit 1.** IT Project Selection Model

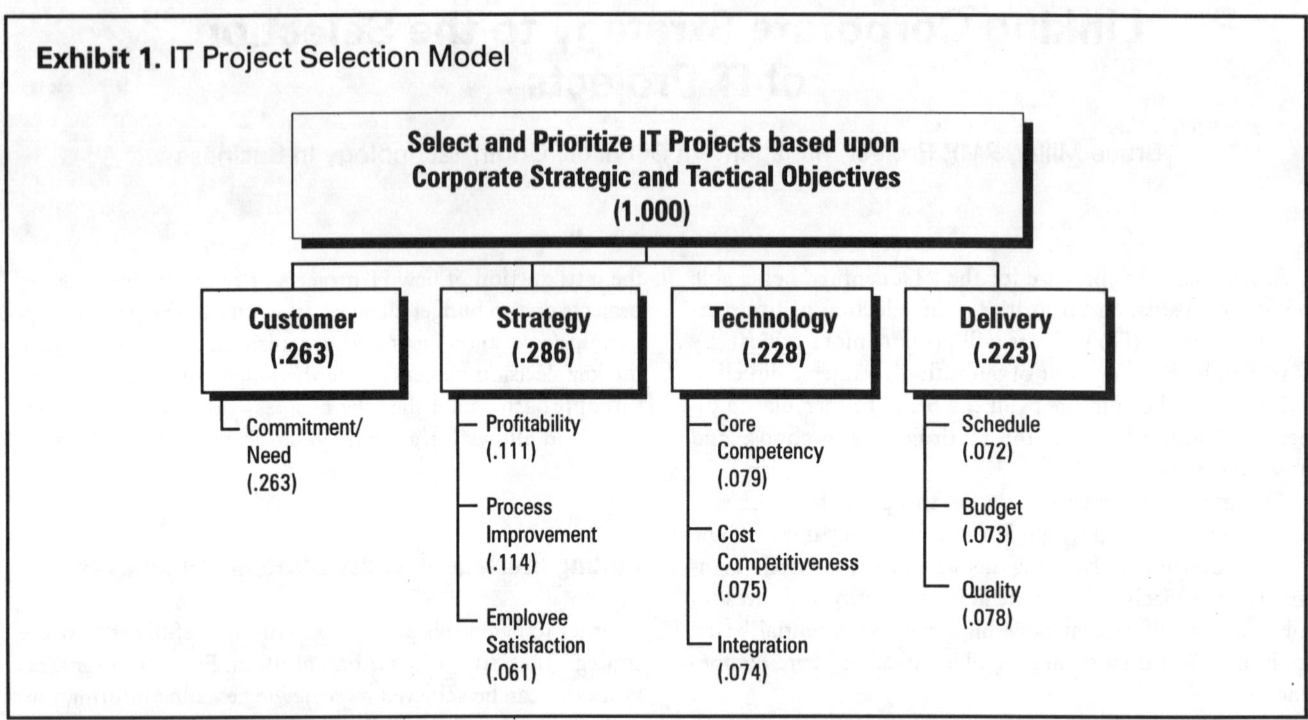


**Exhibit 2.** Criteria Definitions

| Criterion | Definition |
|---|---|
| **Customer** | **Measures customer commitment to the IT Project in terms of need.** |
| **Strategy** | **Measures IT Project alignment with company goals & objectives.** |
| – Profitability | Measures IT Project profitability impact in terms of cost savings. |
| – Process Improvement | Measures the ability of the Project to improve business processes (time). |
| – Employee Satisfaction | Measures professional satisfaction of employees working the project. |
| **Technology** | **Measures organizational ability to meet Project technical requirements.** |
| – Core Competency | Measures organizational technical core competency to perform project. |
| – Cost Competitiveness | Measures organizational ability to provide cost competitive solution. |
| – Integration | Measures IT Project's ability to integrate with existing technology. |
| **Delivery** | **Measures the company's ability to successfully deliver the project.** |
| – Schedule | Measures IT organization's ability to complete the project on schedule. |
| – Budget | Measures IT organization's ability to complete the project within budget. |
| – Quality | Measures IT organization's ability to deliver functional quality solution. |

**Exhibit 3.** Distribution of Top Level Criteria

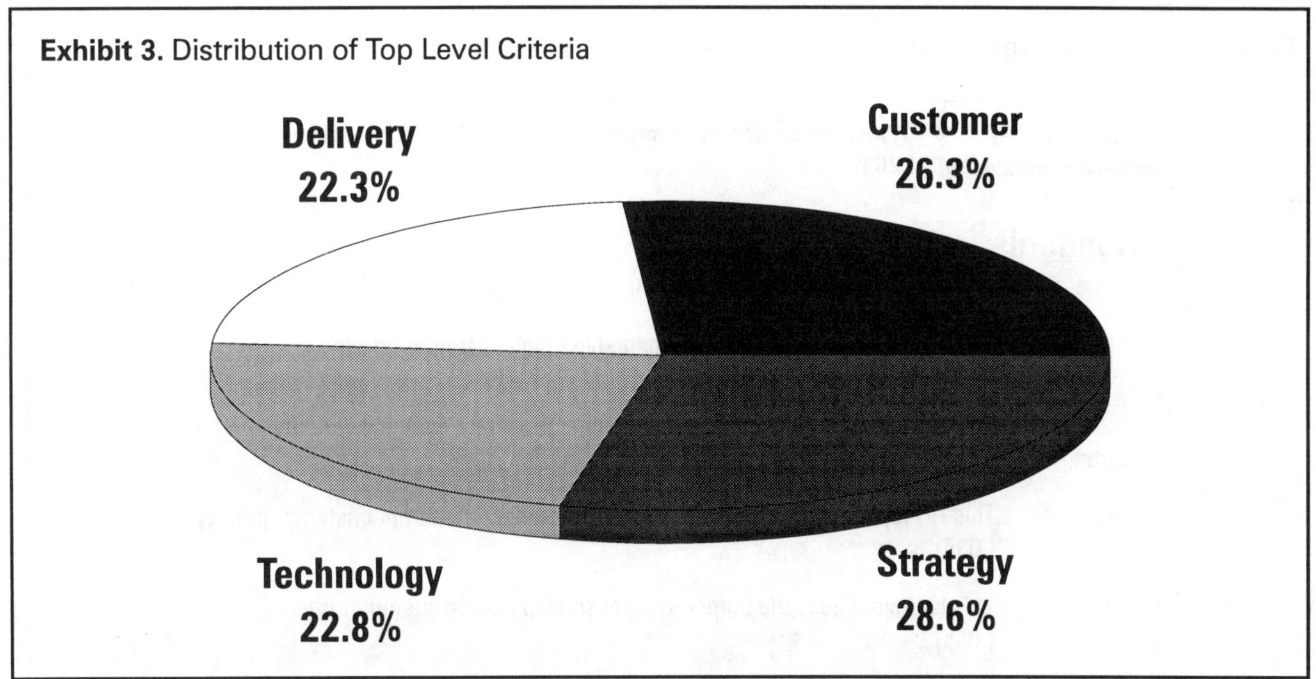


projects *in addition* to the overall objectives of the organization. The business need, the ability to successfully staff and execute the project, and your organization's or an outsourced organization's technical ability to deliver the solution are examples of additional criteria that have been previously applied at the Information Technology organizational level for consideration within the model.

After the criteria have been identified, organize the ideas by group or category. Duplicate or redundant criteria should be eliminated and all criteria should be closely reviewed for final inclusion in the IT project selection model. Twelve to fifteen criteria are the maximum required to appropriately model your IT project selection decision-making process. Refine the criteria and establish a draft IT selection model for your team's review. Exhibit 1 is a model based upon key selection criteria from a number of corporate and federal organizations.

In addition to finalizing the IT project selection model, the stakeholders must formulate clear definitions for each of the criterion within the model. The criteria definitions must be articulated in enough detail so that all the stakeholders understand the true meaning and intent of each criterion. For example, Profitability can be described as "the measure of the Information Technology project's profitability impact in terms of cost savings." Clear definitions are also extremely important when assigning appropriate importance or weightings to all criteria. Exhibit 2 contains the definition of each criterion within the IT project selection model.

## Determine the Importance of Each Selection Criterion

After developing the draft IT project selection model, work closely with key decision-makers directly involved with the project selection process to assign relative importance or weightings to each criterion. This also can be accomplished within a workshop setting. Eight to twelve key decision-makers are suggested for workshop participation. By bringing together the stakeholders, the ability to share ideas and achieve consensus dramatically increases. The key criteria established can be prioritized using a simple spreadsheet or a more sophisticated technique such as the Analytical Hierarchy Process (AHP) or Multi-Attribute Utility Theory (MAUT).

The Analytic Hierarchy Process (AHP) is the methodology used for the remaining examples. AHP is a decision modeling method developed at the Wharton School of Business at the University of Pennsylvania by Dr. Thomas L. Saaty. AHP provides a structured framework that allows for the comparison of both qualitative and quantitative criteria to derive weights and establish priorities of alternatives used within the decision-making process. Regardless of the technique selected, these models will allow you to assign importance or weights to the IT project selection criteria.

The relative importance of all the IT project selection criteria can be generated through the technique of pairwise comparisons. This technique provides the decision-makers with the ability to focus solely on the two decision criteria being evaluated in isolation, without the distraction or confounding impact of all the other criteria. Within the model

**Exhibit 4.** Standard Descriptions for Customer

**Customer** — **Measures customer commitment to the IT Project in terms of need. (.263)**

**Standards**

- Strong — This IT Project has corporate sponsorship / high customer priority. (.263)
- Moderate-Strong — This IT Project has corporate sponsorship / moderate customer priority. (.122)
- Moderate — This IT Project has limited corporate sponsorship / moderate customer priority. (.085)
- Low — This IT Project has little corporate sponsorship / some customer priority. (.055)
- None — This IT Project has no corporate sponsorship / little customer priority. (.031)

**Exhibit 5.** IT Project Selection Results

| IT Project Name | Dependency | Score | Cost ($000) | * Benefit/Cost |
|---|---|---|---|---|
| Marketing and Sales - 2.2 Enhancement | 1 | 0.739 | 400 | 18.48 |
| Intranet 1.0 - Buy | 2 | 0.652 | 450 | 14.49 |
| Marketing and Sales - 2.2 Buy Module | 1 | 0.722 | 600 | 12.03 |
| Resource Management 3.0 - Build | 3 | 0.672 | 600 | 11.20 |
| Resource Management 3.0 - Buy | 3 | 0.604 | 650 | 9.29 |
| Intranet 1.0 - Build | 2 | 0.554 | 600 | 9.23 |
| Human Resources 4.0 - Buy | 4 | 0.590 | 775 | 7.61 |
| Accounting 3.3 - Enhancement | 5 | 0.600 | 800 | 7.50 |
| Human Resources 4.0 - Build | 4 | 0.572 | 900 | 6.36 |
| Accounting 4.0 - Replace (Buy) | 5 | 0.620 | 1,200 | 5.17 |
| Accounting 4.0 - Replace (Build) | 5 | 0.579 | 1,400 | 4.14 |

*Selected Projects are shaded; Dependency shows correspondence to other project alternatives*

** Benefit/Cost Ratio results multiplied by 10,000; Overall Budget for this example is $3.5 Million*

framework, a "top-down" approach is recommended, starting with the major and most significant criteria, then working down through the subcriteria. Relative importance for individual criterion and overall weightings for the entire model are determined using this technique. The highest possible score for a project as measured against the model will equal one, with the overall percentage value being distributed across all IT project decision criteria. Exhibit 3 shows the overall distribution of top level criteria weights for our example.

## Establish Standards to Measure IT Project Alignment with the Model

After refining the IT project selection model and reviewing and discussing the assigned weightings, the next step is to establish standards by which to measure the ability of each IT project to meet the objectives of the model. The standards are defined in terms of intensities and allow the decision team to rate all IT projects against the same standards. Standards must be defined to clearly differentiate each IT project's ability to meet the objectives of each decision criterion. Standard weightings can be assigned using the same pairwise comparison technique used to generate the criteria importance values. Exhibit 4 contains an example set of standards for the customer criterion.

## Test a Sub-set of Previous Projects

Once the IT project selection model has been established, test the model against a pre-existing baseline, such as IT projects that were evaluated the previous year. Each IT project should be evaluated independently against the model, one at a time. The IT projects will be scored between zero and one, with the higher scores identifying which projects are most aligned with the goals and objectives of the model. The testing process will allow the decision team the ability to view, discuss, and refine the IT project selection model based upon the test results. The model should be refined as appropriate and finalized before full-scale implementation.

## Implement This Process

Most IT projects are owned by a variety of sponsors. When implementing the IT project selection decision process, allow the project sponsors and project managers to evaluate their projects against the model. As the projects are being evaluated, the project managers should also provide the business justification. A group workshop or meeting provides an excellent opportunity to discuss the outcome of each IT project's rating against the model. Institute peer reviews to monitor and verify judgments. Once all IT projects have been evaluated, allow the sponsors to discuss their overall rating of the projects with a team of representative stakeholders and make any final adjustments as appropriate. IT project alternatives, such as a buy or build decision, can also be considered and selected within the model. IT projects with a high rating against the model will be considered for selection. Projects that do not fare well against the model will not be selected. Both the IT project rating and the project cost should be considered when assessing the results. The final selection of IT projects should be based on the analysis of the model results *in addition to* on-going stakeholder discussion and final judgment. Exhibit 5 displays the IT project selection results for five IT projects and subsequent alternatives.

## Conclusion

By formulating a direct relationship between the IT projects you implement with the strategic objectives of your organization, you will be able to identify, justify, and invest in only those projects that have high success potential and impact the bottom line. This approach facilitates faster, better, more cost-competitive decisions by implementing a systematic, rational, proven approach. By considering both strategic and tactical criteria within your IT project selection process, you will develop a logical, well-justified business case for your IT investment decisions.

### References

Saaty, Thomas L. 1990. *The Analytic Hierarchy Process*. Pittsburgh, PA: RWS Publications.

# Just In Time Project Management for System Development

Shari G. Stern, PMP, AT&T
MaryGrace Allenchey, PMP, AT&T

## Introduction

Just In Time (JIT) Project Management is not an oxymoron. JIT project management connotes a reactionary, undisciplined and crisis management approach but the project management professional discipline requires rigorous planning.

This JIT approach actually required meticulous and continuous planning to minimize cost, meet schedule commitments, optimize use of human and material resources, effectively implement project activities, and successfully deploy project deliverables.

The AT&T Team deployed a JIT project management strategy to implement a major system infrastructure and platform change.

## Scope

This project encompassed changes in system infrastructure and platform. It included the migration from multiple stand alone application systems in a Sun ® Microsystems Workstation based client/server architecture, to a PC-based three-tier (Data, Process and Presentation layer) architecture. The project used Object-Oriented methodology. The human resources were not trained in the new development methodology and inexperienced in the new platform technologies.

This project was implemented in a nine month period including six weeks of training per resource. It was comprised of two teams each lead by a project manager. The application team had six members and the data team had seven members. A Subject Matter Expert (SME) was shared by the teams.

## Technological Change

Changes in the technology illustrated in Exhibit 1, included the following:

- Tools
- Language
- Methodology
- Platform.

## Human Resource Management

Once the project objectives, scope and deliverables were finalized, the project management tam faced the difficult but not uncommon challenge of procuring the appropriate human and material resources.

Procurement of skilled, experienced human resources was constrained by the requirement to use existing, in-house system development professionals. The in-house professionals were equipped with business process knowledge, and were experienced developers in structured system development methodologies. Analysts were steeped in functional analysis techniques, using entity relationship diagrams for data analysis and producing Function Logic and Logical Design Specifications. Technical leaders had migrated from IMS/COBOL applications to expertise in the UNIX/C system environment; and Human Factors Engineers (HFE) produced screen interfaces for Unix/C applications. Developers were experienced Unix/C programmers and testers built their test plans and test cases for the traditional, structured test environment.

This project required technical professionals with skills and experience in Object Oriented Analysis and Design methodology and C++ programming, as well as the three-tier architecture. The project deliverables included a PC-based desktop environment and separate Data, Presentation and Process layers, three- tier system architecture.

A JIT strategy was developed and deployed to address this challenging project management opportunity to simultaneously retool the technical staff and meet project objectives and deliverables.

There were three primary goals of this JIT approach to resource management:

- Optimize team members' existing knowledge, skill, and experience
- Train the technical staff in new system development methodology and technologies
- Minimize the impact of the team members' inexperience and lack of knowledge and skills in the new development environment, on the project cost, schedule and deliverables.

To optimize individual contributions, team members were assigned the role of SME in their area of system development professional expertise. Each SME team member was responsible for the successful delivery of their specific

**Exhibit 1.** Technology Changes

| Environment | Pre Project Platform | Post Project Platform |
|---|---|---|
| Hardware | HP™, SUN® Microsystems, PC | HP™, SUN® Microsystems, PC |
| Operating System | SUN® Microsystems /OS | HPUX™, MS™ Windows |
| Application Software | UNIX/C X-Toolkit | UNIX/C++, Visual C++™, Visual Basic™ |
| Database | Sybase™, Flat Files | Sybase™ |
| Development Tools | Devguide, XEN, CounterPoint | Visual C++™, PowerBuilder™ |
| Development Methodology | Structured Analysis/Design | OMT (OO Rumbaugh) |
| Applications | FD-Snapshot, CSGR, MIDUS, Route T3, SNAP, T3 Analysis, XRIN | CPIE-PPI |

system development output products from Data Analysis, Object Oriented Analysis, Object Oriented Design, Human Factors Engineering and Testing. The SME's identified the required activities and were completely empowered to make decisions and execute them for there successful implementation.

In addition, an Object-Oriented expert was added to the project team as the technical lead in the new O-O methodology and three-tier system architecture.

Retooling the technical staff required schedule, and cost control and risk analysis. The approach required a comprehensive and common understanding, as well as immediate application, of the new development methodologies and technologies. The training must be accomplished efficiently and effectively to support the project schedule requirements and the new skills must also be appropriately applied to ensure the quality of project deliverables.

The following JIT strategy provided the required cost and schedule controls as well as the risk mitigation plan.

All team members attended the training sessions as a group to ensure a common understanding, as well as provide on-going peer support, in the new methodologies and technologies.

Training sessions were conducted in phases to optimize immediate application of new skills. Immediately following Object Oriented Analysis training, the team performed the initial OO Analysis activities; immediately following Object Oriented Design training, the team performed the initial OO Design activities; and immediately following the C++ training, the team commenced coding.

Specialized training was also provided immediately before it was to be used. HFEs attended Visual C++™ classes for the new Presentation Layer requirements. Analysts received Paradyme Plus™ training for Object Oriented documentation. Developers attended Sybase™ training for Inter-Process Communications (IPC) programming requirements.

The Object Oriented technical expert guided the application and implementation of the new skills of the team members. This support was applied throughout all phases of the project to optimize human resource skills and knowledge as well as meet project time, cost and quality objectives.

Courses suitcased by the instructor to conduct classes at the project team's work location were scheduled whenever possible. The on-premises training minimized the cost of training, optimized the training schedule and enabled customizing the curriculum to support specific project requirements and emphasis. This JIT training approach eliminated travel and lodging costs, and non productive travel time. It also maximized the number of team members trained simultaneously. The curriculum was enhanced to demonstrate application of the new methodologies and technologies to the CPIE-PPI project.

This JIT project management strategy proved to be an effective human resource management approach to meet the project's human resource objectives. It optimized team members' expertise, retrained the technical staff, and minimized the learning curve. This approach enabled the project management team to secure and deploy the required technical resources JIT to staff and perform required project activities.

## Hardware and Software Management

The program management strategy for the hardware and software procurement was to obtain the products as needed, and control costs. These products included the developers desktop hardware and software, ordering and installation of

PCs, Paradyme Plus™, Visual Basic™ and Visual C++™. The software products to support the transition to a three-tier architecture were also ordered and installed on a JIT basis. In addition the desk top hardware for the User Community was procured during the development testing phase and deployed in time for Customer Acceptance testing and product deployment.

The project had a major dependency upon the Architecture organization whose responsibilities included the evaluation, selection, ordering, and installation of all hardware and software products. When the project manager confirmed there was no Architecture transition plan for both hardware and software selection, or ordering and installation, a comprehensive JIT risk mitigation plan was implemented. Included in the risk mitigation strategy was a teaming effort with the Architecture organization to control costs and meet schedule constraints. This was accomplished with the implementation of a schedule with the following critical activities:

Prioritize software selection to coincide with the development schedule

Order and track the delivery of the products

- Test the delivered products
- Install the tested products.

Migration to the new infrastructure frequently required the purchase of initial releases of vendor software which significantly contributed to the following problems:

- Software sold as a networked product only worked as a stand-alone
- Different versions of client and server software were shipped
- Undocumented bugs in the software.

When it became apparent that new products required a product certification plan, the team's JIT approach included early identification of the problem, and rapid deployment of expert resources for its resolution. For example, when the GUI development effort experienced difficulties an AT&T SME was brought from New Jersey to Atlanta, Ga. for an onsite resolution.

The JIT project management approach to this complex change provided the advantages of cost and schedule control, and effective implementation of a new hardware and software infrastructure.

## Lessons Learned

The JIT project management approach proved to be an effective risk mitigation strategy for this project. Acknowledging that all processes and approaches can be improved, there were significant lessons learned from this project. These should be considered in the project plans for system development projects embracing new Information Systems methodologies and technologies.

### Expect the unexpected.

#### *First*

Plan for a steep learning curve for the new hardware and software technologies as well as new development methodology with significant increases in activity duration.

In creating the plan, the project manager researched other Object Oriented development efforts to gain an understanding of the methodology and the technology. The implementation strategy employing the JIT approach to training and the development effort was an outgrowth of that research. The training and learning curve was planned for OOA, OOD and C++.

The additional training and learning curves were not fully understood. The GUI development effort was significant.

Another area impacting the project were bugs in vendor software. The project used new versions of the vendor software and discovered bugs which had not been found prior to the release. This added significant time to the effort while the team worked with the vendor's technical team for resolution.

#### *Second*

Plan for the new infrastructure/platform deployment in a phased approached to minimize multiple simultaneous changes.

Illustrated in Exhibit 1, the entire environment changed with one project. This not only created technical complexities but also compounded the normal resistance to change and significantly increased the levels of frustration of the team. For example: When a problem arose, it was difficult to isolate the source (design, software, code, hardware, data, etc.). A major memory leak problem was eventually traced to a combination of: a vendor software bug, GUI design, and hardware size. With a phased approach to Infrastructure/platform change, some of the elements would have been more stable.

#### *Third*

Include testing of vendor provided hardware and software in the project plan to identify and fix defects and incompatibilities.

As a result of a separate Architecture organization responsibilities were not defined and a number of invalid assumptions were made. There was a disconnect in the two teams schedules and priorities. The service agreements between the teams did not include the testing of the purchased vendor hardware and software by the Architecture organization. As a result, multiple problems were uncovered during development instead of in a pre-deployment hardware and software testing environment.

### *Fourth*

Select a SME with a track record for successful implementation and deployment of the technology and proven teaching and mentoring techniques.

The SME, Technical Leader, should have a history of successful project deployment using the methodology and software. The SME role needs to be understood by all team members. For example, the SME approached the team with the idea the team members should attempt the effort (analysis, design or code) and learn by their mistakes. The team members were frustrated by this method and frequently felt they had no idea how to begin the work effort. Coupled with development time constraints, this teaching methodology created increased tension and the potential undermining of the team effort.

### *Finally*

Hire SMEs for each area of the development effort, i.e. Presentation, Inter-Process Communication, and Object Oriented Methodology.

JIT project management and cost containment can be achieved when a SME for a development area is brought on board for the design effort and is retained to jump start the work. In this project, with the completion of the analysis and design phases, the entire team was deployed to concurrent development efforts. For example, the Data Objects, IPC and Presentation Objects were developed concurrently.

The need for specialized SMEs became particularly apparent during the testing phase. Multiple problems in the presentation layer development could have been avoided if an experienced GUI SME had been leading the GUI design team.

## Conclusion

The JIT approach supported the Risk Management, Resource Management, Procurement Management, Communications Management, Time and Cost Management, as well as Quality Management requirements for successful attainment of the project goals and objectives. The technical staff was trained in new development methodologies, the hardware and software was upgraded to the client/server platform and the end-users received enhanced application functionality.

The JIT project management strategy coupled with the lessons learned and deployed in a phased approach, is an effective Information Systems project management strategy for the transition and implementation of a new system development and architecture infrastructure.

### Glossary

CPIE - Capacity Planning Integrated Environment ( GUI Layer & Application Layer)
CSGR - Cross Section Grooming Report (Application)
FD-Snapshot - Data
HFE - Human Factors Engineer
HPUX - Hewlett Packard UNIX
IPC - Inter-Process Communications
JIT - Just in Time
MIDUS - Multi-level Interactive Digital Utilization System (Application)
OOA - Object Oriented Analysis
OOD - Object Oriented Design
OMT - Object Modeling Technique
PPI - Planning Provisioning Interface (Data Layer)
PC - Personal Computer
Route T3 - Routing Tool (Application)
SME - Subject Matter Expert
SNAP - Sub Network Analysis and Planning (Application)
T3 Analysis - Analysis Tool (Application)
XRIN - Express RIN Grooming Report (Application)

### References

Rumbaugh, James, et al. 1991. *Object-Oriented Modeling and Design*. Englewood Cliffs, N.J.: Prentice Hall.

# A Project Managers Survival Guide to Object-Oriented Methodologies

Edward M. Copenhaver, Daugherty Systems

## Introduction

Today, many companies are looking for a silver bullet to solve "technically challenged" programs or organizations. When doing so, companies occasionally look for new "leading edge" ways to deliver products to market faster, cheaper and more effectively. When searching for ways to deliver such a silver bullet, many organizations look at Object-Oriented (O-O) methodologies to deliver such promises.

While I am an advocate of the use of O-O methodologies, I can assure you that it is *not* a silver bullet. Many project managers put their entire trust in the *method*, but forget the *process* and common project management Principles. No methodology will ever replace a necessary process for delivering software or any other product. A methodology can provide a mechanism for delivering software faster, cheaper and more effectively, but only when coupled with a rigorous process to drive the methodology.

When many organizations move to O-O methodology they tend to credit any successes on the fact that they moved to O-O. The simple fact is that any move to a formal methodology is generally a reason for success. In discussing this topic with several O-O industry experts, the general consensus is the same: "Having helped many companies transition to O-O methodology, generally the consensus is that O-O has long term cost and productivity benefits. Many companies experience successes simply because they have moved from "seat-of-the-pants" programming to a structured way of analyzing and solving the problem domain."

## Object-Oriented Methodologies

### Why use object-oriented methodologies?

According to a July 26, 1996 *Information Week* article, "Objects will penetrate 80-90% of all US companies by 1998." According to Marc Andreessen, cofounder of Netscape, "Instead of being content providers, people will be object developers. The object marketplace will start up pretty quickly. This is going to have a dramatic change on the way people produce applications."

Both are very powerful and bold statements. Why will U.S. companies be interested in Object Technology? Object Technology is the next evolution of software development that is available to provide cost effective, robust systems in shorter times to market.

When addressing cost effectiveness, It is important to understand that it can only be achieved through serious long term commitment to Object-Oriented Technology.

In Exhibit 1, below, the dashed line B is the cost of Structured Information Engineering practices over time. In any organization, the cost of building a system today is not much different that is was a year ago or what it will be a year from now (exception for market rate changes, inflation, etc.). The use of Object-Oriented methods can vary over time. As organizations begin the use of Object-Oriented methods, note how the cost is reflected in lines A and C as being more costly to the organization than that of Structured Information Engineering. However, over time, line C drops significantly below the cost of Structured Information Engineering where line A remains above. The difference between lines A and C is the commitment that an organization has to the long-term use of Object-Oriented Technology. Where there is a strong commitment to re-use, libraries, and standards, the long-term costs can be significantly decreased. If management is only paying lip service to the commitment to Object-Oriented Technology, the costs will continue to remain above those of Structured Information Engineering Practices.

Note that many organizations, committed or not, lose faith and give up before they see the benefits of their labor. Object-Oriented analysis and design can take substantially more time. Additionally, the resources needed to be successful in building Object-Oriented systems are more costly. These two factors make management nervous. When they see an analysis and design phase taking longer and costing more, it can become very uncomfortable. It then becomes easy to abandon Object-Oriented technologies and go back to what they know and is comfortable.

### Deciding when to use object-oriented methodologies

Many organizations have been faced with the decisions of "if" and "when" to use Object-Oriented techniques. I believe that all companies, all programs, all organizations can benefit from the use of objects. There are some factors that should be considered before leaping head first into O-O.

***Commitment***

This is the most important factor in deciding if an Object-Oriented approach is to be used. All levels of an organization must understand what they are agreeing to and be committed to supporting the decision to the end.

Senior management will want to know why those first projects are taking so long. Upper management will not immediately recognize the need for restructuring parts of an their organization to better support future O-O projects. Middle management will begin to have doubts when they see their budgets increase and nothing appears to be turning out. The project manager must work with all levels of the organization to set those expectations and ensure that the continued commitment to O-O is still there.

***Changing requirements***

Ill-defined projects and those that will suffer from constantly changing requirements *may* benefit from an O-O implementation. O-O requires that the project be defined by modeling the problem. Ill-defined projects become well defined as the analysis model is created. Projects that will have consistently changing requirements will benefit by the modular design that will be created with O-O. This is not to be confused with the execution of a change management plan or change control board, obviously these functions will still need to be in place. In O-O, change can come easier through the analysis, design and early construction.

***Payback period***

Some organizations focus on the fact that much of the payback of using O-O comes from lower long term maintenance costs. They feel that O-O may not be right for them since their products have short, one to two year, life spans and then is thrown away to be replaced by a new product. Their logic is that without long term maintenance there will not be a long term maintenance cost, thus no need for O-O. If their products do have a short life span it is not because the business problem, or need for a program goes away, but because it is constantly being replaced with newer technology programs that service the same business problem. If an organization wants to be able to successfully reduce its time to market for these replacement programs, then O-O may hold the key to their success. A good object design will be as simple as is possible and will reflect the business domain by modeling true to life objects. When done properly, the designs will have many reusable components. These components, like building blocks, can be used in the designs of the replacement program. Obviously, some of the components may need to be upgraded, however think how much further ahead the next release can be if the model of the business is already even 50 percent complete.

**Exhibit 1.** Structured IE vs. Object-Oriented Methods

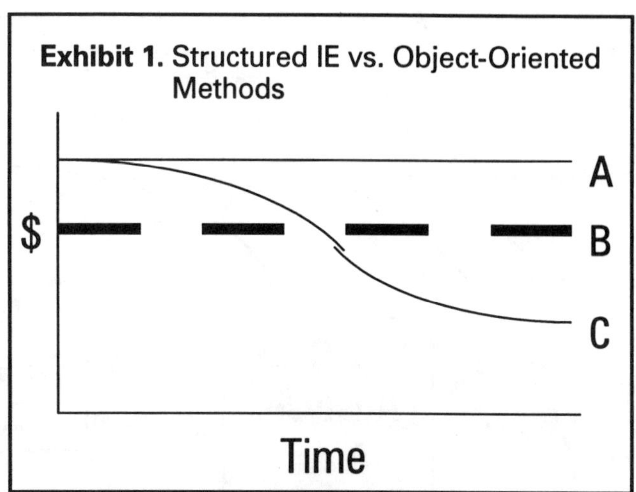


**First Project: What it should consist of**

So at this point we have decided that we are ready to tackle our first O-O project. We think that it can add value to our organization. All levels of management agree that they will support it and they have an understanding of the budget, time and resource constraints. But now how do we chose to start and what is the best project? The first O-O project is the most important as its success will fuel future projects, or its failure will drown hopes of continuing to develop O-O systems.

The first project should be a small project that has value. In a structured environment, it should be something that is estimated to be achievable in three to six months. It must be a project that is considered of value to the organization. While this project should not be a mission-critical application, it should be substantial enough that it gets the proper support to see it through.

Since we are discussing first projects, it's not likely that the organization has many (or any) O-O resources sitting around waiting for that first project. How do you build a dedicated team that will be successful? I suggest that, when looking within the organization, there is emphasis placed on adaptability. Generally speaking, people who have been developing systems by the seat of their pants or utilizing structured information engineering systems for long periods of time may not adapt easily to O-O. Structured information engineering focuses on the processes and data elements. O-O focuses heavily on behavior. Many people find this a difficult transition. When people are identified and show a significant interest in being a "company guinea pig," I suggest sending them to an Object-Oriented overview class. Many reputable firms offer three- to seven-day classes on Object-Oriented Analysis and Design. Sending them to a class such as this does two things: first it gives the student a sense of the type of abstract work that is ahead of them if they decide to join the

**Exhibit 2.** Focus Teams Working Thhrough Object-Oriented Analysis and Design

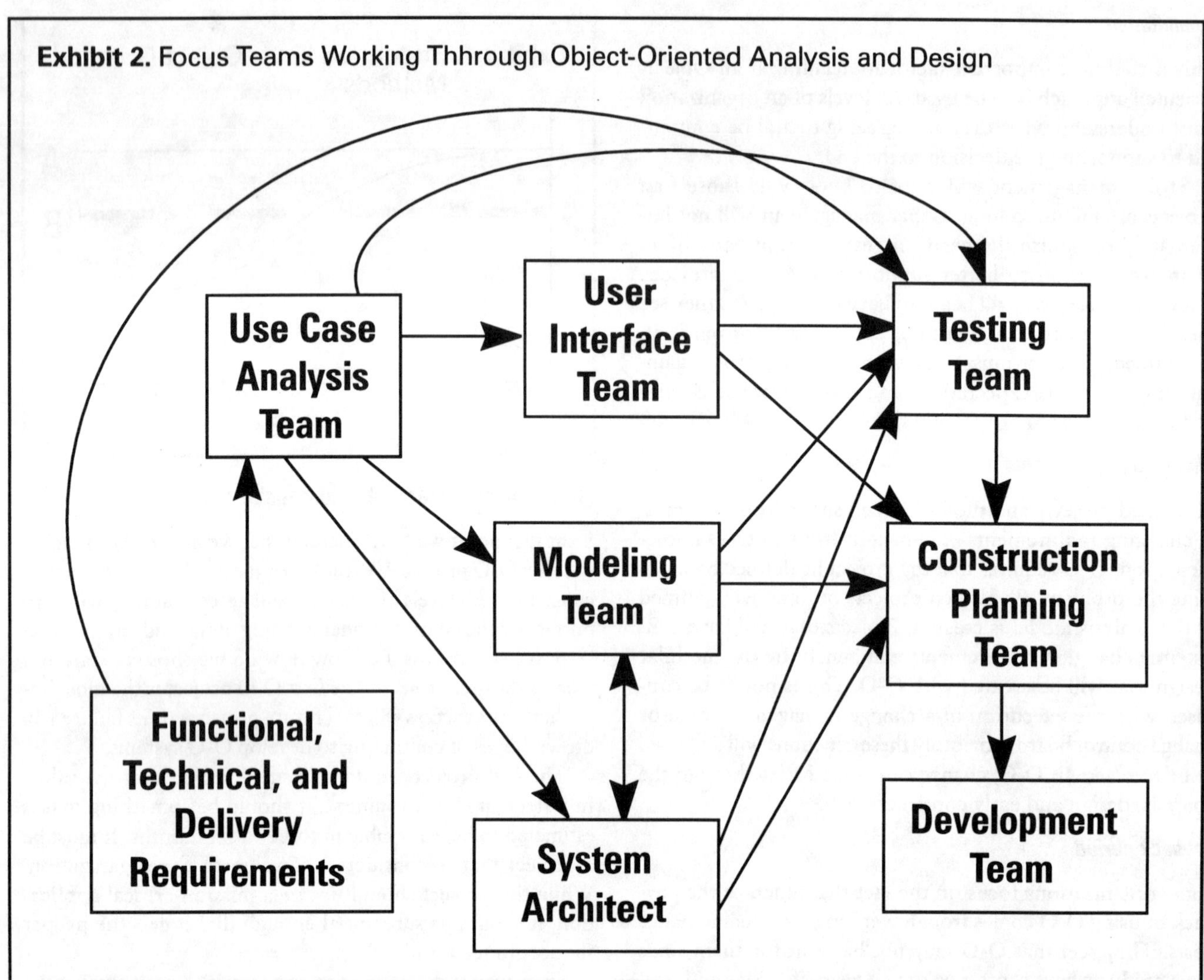


team, and secondly it can provide feedback to the project manager if the student is able to comprehend the techniques.

The next item on the shopping list should be a mentoring program. This is an entirely different way to build systems. There are many companies out there who offer varying degrees of mentoring and project technical leadership to help organizations successfully implement O-O projects. Look for those specializing in assisting companies move into O-O by providing coaching, classroom activities, and mentoring. The team should be staffed with sufficient mentoring resources that each employee has someone to turn to for help. Set expectations up front with the firm that progression of the employees knowledge in O-O will be measured and their success will be measured on their ability to help implement the project and the ability to transfer knowledge to the team.

Hiring new resources into a company in another option. There are two things to keep in mind when doing this. If you have capable resources in your company, they need to be utilized first. There will be a lot of hurt feelings if "the new guy gets the good assignment and I am pigeonholed into a go-nowhere position." Secondly, there are many different schools of O-O. Different people subscribe to different "mentors." While UML (Unified Modeling Language) promises to close this gap, it is important that the organization has worked with the mentoring firm to determine the best set of standards for the organization. Once this has been completed, then interviewing candidates becomes easier since it will be easy to determine if they subscribe to the standard set for your organization.

## Organizing for Object-Oriented Projects

### Focus Team Approach

Nothing new here—all team members need to understand where they fit in the organization. The way the market is trending, is that object-oriented programmers and modelers can, for the most part right their own tickets. If they do not feel that they are contributing to an organization in a significant manner they may abandon the project in search for more interesting work. To combat this behavior, I suggest the following team approach to O-O projects.

#### *The Requirements Team*

I always find it interesting that so many O-O methodologies forget how difficult it can be to capture a good set of requirements. So many methodologies start by telling you to start with the problem statement and then write Use Cases. Who wrote the problem statement? Is it significant enough to understand the functional, technical and delivery requirements? It may be necessary to begin the project with a team to first build the requirements. This requirements team should work separately from the development team. The initial project requirements should be gathered up front—not while the development team is trying to analyze and design the system. I believe that the requirements phase to the Analysis phase should be waterfall. As further releases are to be defined, the requirements phase can be reopened and those new requirements should be treated as a new projects done in succession behind the initial project. Note: I further believe that the beginning of an Analysis phase of a project has its own mini-requirement's phase also. The requirements team should consist of domain experts (some from the user community), technical experts and should report to the project Technical Lead. The team size will vary from two to six, depending significantly on the size of the effort. Their deliverable is a set of functional, technical, and delivery requirements that is agreed upon by the user community, the project team and the project manager, is considered to be testable by the Quality Assurance Manager, and is achievable in approximately nine months. Their deliverable is shared with the user community, the Use Case Analysis Team, and the Test Team.

#### *The Use Case Analysis Team*

The Use Case Analysis Team takes its directions straight from the Requirements Specification. The Use Case Analysis Team should consist of some domain and technical experts, some of which may have come from the Requirements Team. Working with the user community, this team will take the requirements to another level by writing Scenarios and Use Cases to further understand the requirements and how people and processes will interact with the new system. An important thing to look our for here is to be careful to fully understand the interactions a new system will have with existing systems. A stovepipe system that does not integrate well with existing system can be considered a failure. This team should also consist of representation from the user community, and be lead by the Technical Lead. The team size will vary from two to five, depending upon the size of the effort. Once a Use Case is agreed upon it is shared with the Test Team, the User Interface Team, the Modeling Team and the Architecture team.

#### *The User Interface Team*

The User Interface Team will take input of the Use Cases and begin working with the user community to identify to format of all screens and reports. Prototypes should be used and depending on the nature of the application, Human Factors engineers may be necessary to ensure the ergonomics of the system. This team is generally smaller, two to three engineers building and documenting the interface. If Human Factors Engineers is used, they would be in addition to the two to three engineers. This team will work closely with the user community and will be lead by the Lead Developer

#### *The Modeling Team*

The Modeling Team is responsible for building the analysis, functional and dynamic models necessary to fully exploit the system. Taking input from the Use Cases, the Modeling Team will not interact very much with the user community, but will have their work verified by domain experts to ensure that they have captured the problem correctly. Again, depending on the size of the effort, the modeling team will consist of two to three people and will report to the System Architect.

#### *The System Architect*

The System Architect, with the Modeling Team reporting to him/her, will be responsible for the logical and physical models of the system. In addition, the System Architect may have to take responsibility for networks, hardware and necessary infrastructure that may be required when building a distributed system. The Architect will have to work closely with any existing infrastructure teams to ensure that the proposed system can be supported when completed.

#### *The Testing Team*

The Testing Team will begin working as a single person during the requirements gathering phase to verify that all requirements are in fact testable. As the project progresses into an "assembly line," the Use Case Team, the User Interface Team, The Modeling Team and the System Architect will pass their deliverables to the testing team. This team will build the test plans and the test scripts necessary to verify that the system meets requirements. This team will report to the Quality

**Exhibit 3.** Recommended Team Layout

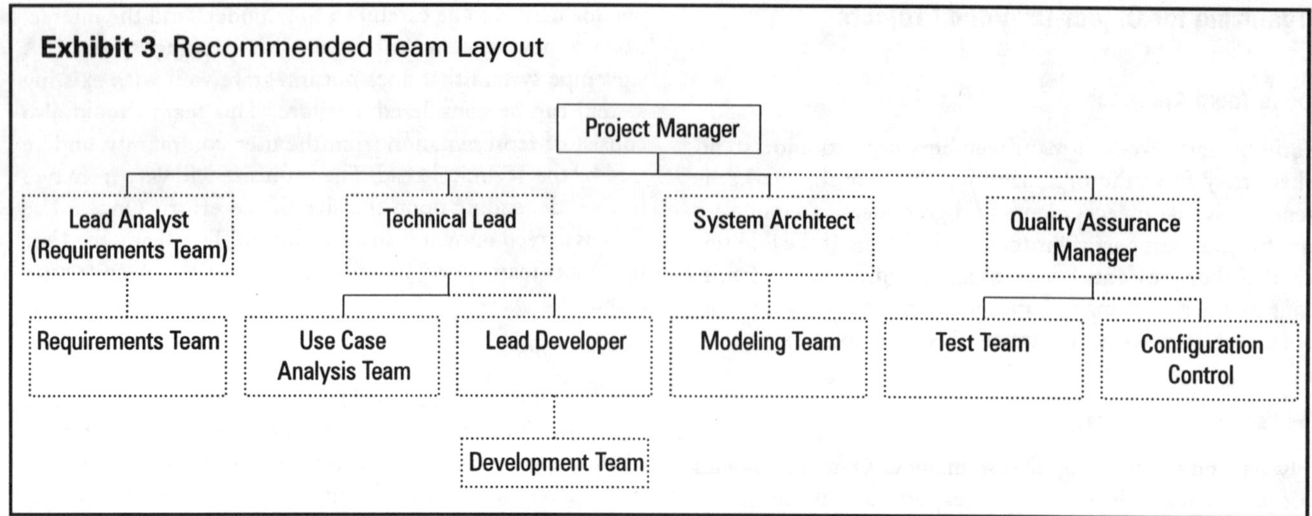


Assurance Manager and again will be sized according to the size of the effort. On average, the testing team will be two to six people.

### The Construction Planning Team

The Construction Planning Team is the project manager, the Technical Lead, the System Architect, the Quality Assurance Manager, and the Lead Developer. The purpose of this team is to take the outputs from the various teams mentioned above and ensure that the deliverables are sufficiently detailed to turn it over to the development team to begin coding. The Construction Planning Team will be responsible to review progress and update schedules and task assignments on a weekly basis. Their output is an updated project plan and a task list to the development team every week.

### The Development Team

The Development Team will take the work plans created from the Construction Planning Team forward and build the appropriate software. Once unit-tested, the Development Team will work with the Testing Team to complete the testing of the software components.

Organizationally, I recommend a team layout as is depicted in Exhibit 3.

## Staffing Issues

If the wave of O-O has not yet hit your city, when it does, get ready for quite a ride. In many cities there is substantially more O-O work than there are people. Therefore, if your project is not considered exciting, or begins to bog down you will have trouble getting and keeping resources. I am not talking specifically about permanent resources, but more especially contract resources.

If your company or organization is new to O-O, you will need assistance from seasoned veterans who are familiar with building OO software. If you are considering the use of sub-contractors, know and understand the differences in the expectations of two general types of sub-contractors.

### General Labor Contractors

General labor contractors are those types that take the marching orders and build as requested. Know their limitations. Remember, as general labor, you are absorbing their risk. This type of labor is generally a little cheaper then OO consultants. They sometimes will offer mentoring and knowledge transfer, however, if you are using an OO Consulting firm for the knowledge transfer and to assist you in leading this effort, I recommend discouraging mentoring by general labor contractors. O-O seems to be more of an art than a science to me today. Many people attack the same problem in very different ways. Not necessarily wrong, but different ways. This can threaten the O-O consulting firm if they think that a general contractor has yours or some amount of your team's ear. In fact, this could be a breach of contract if you are holding the O-O consulting firm contractually responsible for knowledge transfer.

General labor contractors are always looking for a great opportunity to learn and build their skills. If you treat them the same as you treat any full-time employee, and give them opportunities to grow as your project does, they will stick with your project if it hits a short rocky period.

### O-O Consulting Firms

If O-O is new to your company or organization, you may need someone to help you make the transition, help lead the teams, and to help with mentoring and knowledge transfer. As stated above, many companies are doing this today, but few are considered successful in knowledge transfer, so get references. As stated with general labor contractors, even with O-O consultants, know their limitations. Remember, everyone cannot be an expert on everything. Make sure that the project is being staffed by the O-O consulting firm with the appropriate resources at the appropriate time. Further, utilize the services of one firm to lead the effort of your transition and knowledge transfer. Too often, companies try shopping for cheaper resources and building a conglomerate of several opinions from several companies arguing over who is right and who is the leader. If you chose one firm to assist you in your transformation, they should have a common approach that will lead to less confusion and more productivity.

Put these people in lead roles. Have them lead your team, not go off in the corner and do the work themselves. Be sure that the project plan has sufficient time built in to allow for proper mentoring, and be sure that there is a measurable means to hold the O-O consulting firm accountable to ensure that the mentoring occurs. Since this team will be in a lead role, be sure that there is significant risk on the part of the O-O consulting firm to ensure that there is a timely delivery and that expensive last-minute experts don't have to be called in the save the day. And as always, treat these contractors the same as regular full-time employees.

# Taking Charge for the Next Century: Selling Project Management to a Reluctant Organization

Jeff Nielsen, Northwest Airlines Inc.
Ann McGuire, First Data Corporation

Information System (IS) departments came of age in functional organizations centered around the needs of mainframe processing. Today, new architectures, increased sophistication of applications and off-the-shelf solutions require a different organization and facilitation by project managers to implement successful IS projects. The challenge often comes in selling this approach to people entrenched in processes of the past.

## THE PROBLEM

Early IS environments were equipment-intensive. Hardware was expensive, and architectures were constrained by the limitations of the systems available. In order to operate mainframe systems successfully, rigid rules were required to avoid compromising the integrity of the system. From an organizational standpoint, this led to a high-level of departmentalization. There was little flexibility and control of system changes was held by a select few.

The demands of today's marketplace have forced changes to this approach. IS customers want solutions faster, with more flexibility to meet their unique needs. They are technically literate and want more input into the computing solutions provided. This has led to the distilling of the IS function throughout the organization. Client/server architectures are responding to these needs by putting more computing power and software flexibility in the hands of the end users. However, these distributed IS groups often share resources such as a centralized database or common sub-routines to provide cost savings or to ensure consistency in the information provided.

These trends in the computing industry have led to an enhanced need for communication and control in order to provide standard interfaces, control scope and eliminate redundant efforts. At the same time, the flattening of organizations to get closer to the customer and reduce costs has limited the middle-management staff that could facilitate this communication. Enter the project manager whose role it is to integrate the efforts across the organization in delivering a product on time and within budget.

Project management is the key to success in the changing, fast-paced scenario we see today. However, many IS organizations are slow to evolve from the old way of doing business. Project managers may face obstacles in implementing true project management in this environment. Obstacles to successful implementation of project management include lack of upper management support, turf wars and lack of the benefits of a disciplined approach.

Upper management trained in the old school of IS thought often do not fully grasp the benefits of true project management. Their reactive mode of management is results-oriented and has little patience for long-term planning. In keeping with the old way of thinking, managers tend to hold tightly to the authority needed for a project manager to be truly effective.

Middle managers scarred by constant force reductions are threatened by loss of control over their territory. Empire building is seen as the way to management success as opposed to solutions based on teamwork. They share upper management's short-range view and are resistant to give up resources to long-term goals as long as there are fire-fighting opportunities in the offing.

This reactive mode of management leaves little time for documentation and the subsequent identification and correction of underlying problems. The result is a repetition of the same problems. In this environment, people are rewarded for fixing problems instead of being rewarded for preventing them.

## The Solution

Within the environment described, it is often up to the project managers within the existing structure to initiate the move to more effective project management.

### Informal Network

Overcoming these obstacles as a functional organization migrates to a matrix organization requires a ground swell support by project managers throughout the organization. Specifically, this can be accomplished by developing a network of project managers within the company to share best practices and lessons learned. This effort starts with a select few meeting, knowing that things could be better, and wanting to do something. To expand the group listing of all employees with the Project Manager title can usually be obtained from the Human Resources department. Using this list to distribute information about the group meetings and the group's desire to support each other will bring more interested parties into the network.

### Formal Group

From the informal project management network, a more formal structure can evolve. The group begins to meet on a regular basis, select a leader, build support for a standard process for project management, and gain support for their viewpoint by sharing the benefits of their experience through training and mentoring other employees. The transition from an informal to a formal group is a necessary but difficult step. Formality brings with it the bureaucracy that can stagnate enthusiasm. Getting bogged down in the development of a charter and formal leadership can alienate those that were earlier committed. Selecting a strong leader who is dedicated to making the group work, supports good processes and practices, and is willing to provide mentoring of those less skilled is of paramount importance.

Initially, avoid making the group's goals too broad or too specific in order to cater to a larger audience. It is important to have similarities within the group's roles and processes to build on. Publishing the results (minutes) of the meeting to your list of project managers will show those not yet attending that there is a benefit in attending the meetings. At this point all support to the group is on their "own" time, so it must be shown to be a benefit to them before they start making time in their schedules to attend. A well-run group that meets regularly to discuss project management topics and support mentoring will be ready for the next step in gaining organizational acceptance.

## Project Management Champion

Once the project manager network has become a formal group within the organization, a champion must be sought. The individual preferably is at an executive level or is highly respected by executives throughout the company. The champion also needs to be well rounded in project management principles and practices. With the assistance of the project management champion, the group can go about the business of getting top-down buy-in for project management. This is the most difficult step in the process. It requires a well-thought-out and designed sales pitch. PMI has helped by providing a presentation that can be tailored to the needs of the organization. The local chapter has a copy or one can be provided by PMI's executive office.

Identification of the division that is most likely to "buy" the sales pitch should be scheduled first. Getting their support will help in selling to the other divisions. Ultimately the goal at this point is to legitimize the support for the group by obtaining commitments of money and people's time to help the group continue to function.

## Executive Support

After generating enthusiasm within the upper levels of management, carefully selected projects can be used as prototypes to demonstrate the effectiveness of project management processes and tools. There is normally a pocket of strong project management commitment that has been using project management processes and can show how that commitment has benefited their projects. In order to quantify the benefits, a baseline must be established and a key project selected that will showcase the project management benefits. Ensure that this project is successful! Documentation of lessons learned can provide the information needed to share with the rest of the organization in the benefits of project management. Executives exposed to the kind of information and control provided by proven project management techniques soon become avid advocates. A movement from a functional organization to a matrixed one begins by project managers consolidating into teams. Executives will then begin helping to sell it to middle management.

## Organization-wide Acceptance

When executives have expressed their support for project management and demonstrated their commitment, middle-level managers then view this as another vehicle for advancement. Instead of the empire building path to the top, they now have a means of using teamwork to their benefit as well as the companies benefit. They are more receptive to the changes needed to make project management effective. Successful projects continue to reinforce and expand the use of project management principles as defined in the *PMBOK Guide*.

## Documentation

Throughout the process, it is important to gather good metrics to support the position that good project management techniques result in improved and less costly software development. Without documenting the lessons learned to help others avoid repeating the same mistakes, processes will not be improved. Also, reactive solutions will continue to get rewarded rather than proper planning.

## Conclusion

Selling project management to people mired in processes of the past is a long and difficult task. The movement from informal groups of mutual support to a formal group with a strong leader and finally to executive sponsorship within an accepted project management organization takes determination and hard work. The payoffs for both the project managers in terms of networked support and formal career progression, and the organization in terms of more successful projects, are worth the effort.

# Managing Multiple Projects in Large IS Organizations

Steve Yager, Artemis Management Systems , Inc.

It is useful to briefly review the history of project management in the IS field before proceeding with a discussion of the issues involved with multi-project management. Contrary to what seems to be the commonly held belief, project management is not a new undertaking for the IS industry. In truth, IS was one of the first to attempt to implement the project management discipline and project management software in the late 1960s and early 1970s. The concept of identifying "projects" and tracking the status of project tasks and the effort expended on them has been in place in most IS organizations since then. Compared with the sophisticated application of project management techniques in other industries such as utilities, petrochemicals, and aerospace however, IS has not been in the vanguard. IS project management for the most has been considered a budgeting exercise in the planning phase, and a time keeping effort in the tracking stage. IS did not embrace the critical path concept as quickly as did their counterparts in other industries. One fundamental reason for this was that the early project management software systems were particularly oriented to managing large, complex, single projects for the most part. IS very often did not even participate in the selection of project management software for other departments, even though this software was going to operate on IS maintained computers, predominately mainframes. The evolution of project management software to today's client/server systems has finally produced tools which can be readily applied to large IS organizations with hundreds of projects running simultaneously.

## The IS Multi-Project Environment

There are some fundamental differences between the so-called traditional project management applications and today's IS application. These are:

1. IS applications are fundamentally multi-project.
2. Both project and non-project (maintenance) work must be planned and tracked.
3. The major emphasis is on resource utilization, rather than task and project completion.
4. Many IS projects are abandoned before completion.
5. There are many repetitive type of projects.
6. Project work is budgeted, usually on an annual basis.

The fact that the very nature of a large IS organization is that it handles many projects simultaneously is why there is so much potential for payoff in implementing project management techniques properly. On major complex projects such as in the aerospace industry, external factors most often are the ones that affect project timetables. Managers do not have as much opportunity to control project priorities. In the IS field managers can actually utilize the project management data they receive to make adjustments to priorities and assignments to accomplish their business objectives. But the most critical concept to grasp in managing multiple projects for IS is that rather than assigning resources to tasks, IS managers assign tasks to resources. This is the reverse of the traditional project management technique, where more emphasis is placed on the project/task than the resource/task. IS multi-project management is actually "resource utilization" management. This difference perhaps accounts for the lack of ready adoption of the critical path method and earlier implementation of project management software based on CPM.

There are three critical questions which IS managers have to answer in the multi-project environment:

1. Are resources assigned to the highest priority work?
2. Are my resources utilized fully?
3. Are my resources completing their assignments on time and within budget?

The emphasis is on "resources" because, unlike their counterparts in other industries, IS managers don't have the luxury of being able to add twenty programmers or analysts for two months to complete a critical project. The main goal of the IS manager in a multi-project environment is to adjust his resource assignments to accomplish the most critical tasks, in a situation where estimates are not always accurate, external factors do come into play (such as project cancellations), and there is a sizable amount of "non-project" work to accomplish. Proper implementation of project management techniques and software can greatly improve the manager's and organization's efficiency in such an environment.

## Implementing Project Management

One of the first steps which should be taken is an assessment of project management maturity of the IS group. Much has been written about the fact that somewhere in excess of 80 percent of software development organizations are classified at the lowest (Level 1) on the Software Engineering Institute's Capability Maturity Model. But it is the author's opinion that

**Exhibit 1.**

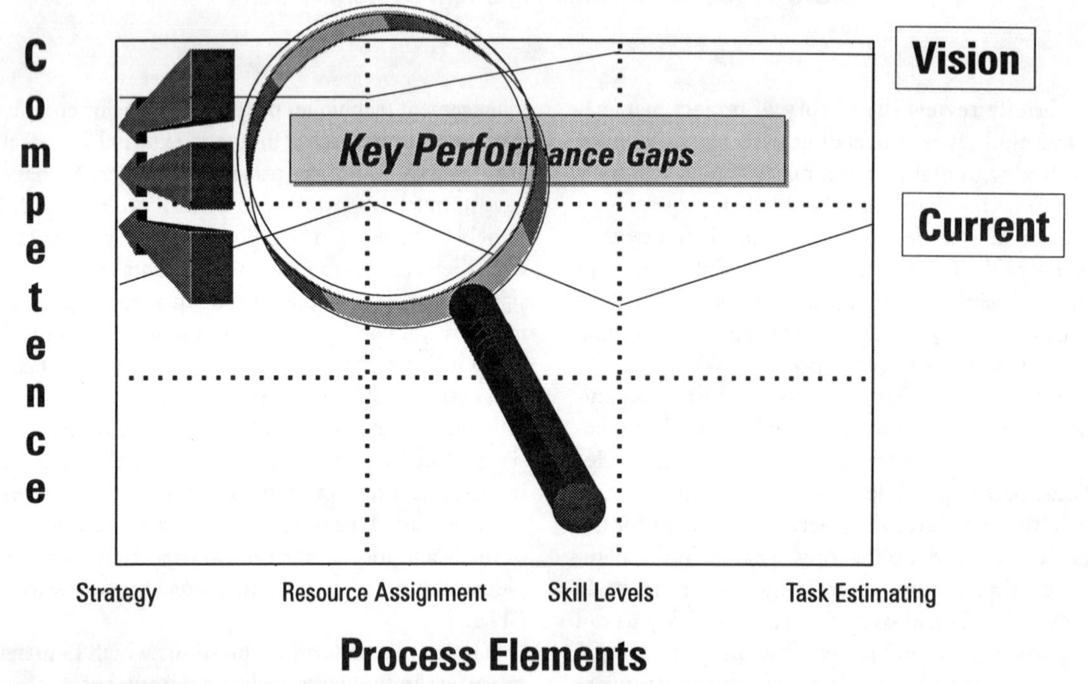

Competence

Key Performance Gaps

Vision

Current

Strategy Resource Assignment Skill Levels Task Estimating

Process Elements

**Exhibit 2.**

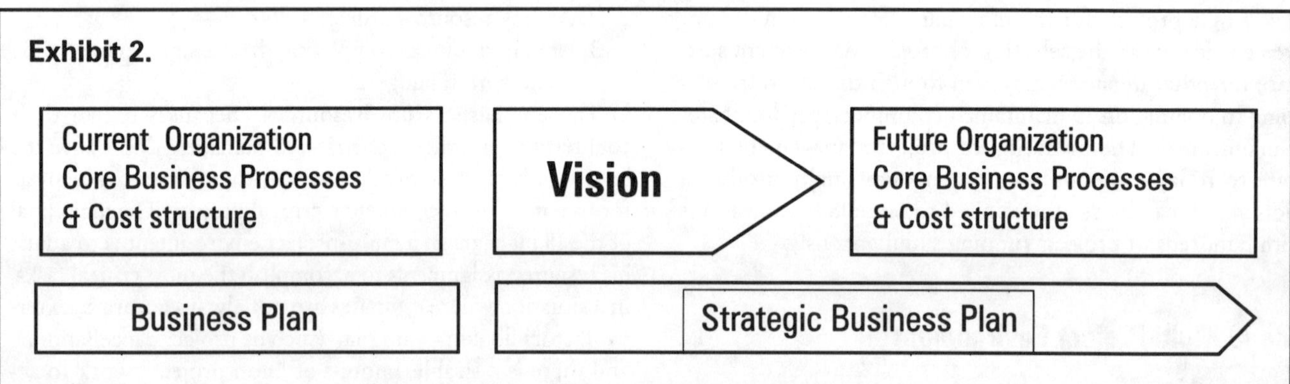


the real goals of assessing an organization's project management maturity should be:

So that the organization knows what its current capabilities are before attempting to implement a formalized multi-project management approach.

As a measuring guideline to check on future progress. Are we really making progress in managing our project?

It is recommended that this assessment be formal and that it be done before implementing a project management software system. This is critical because project management software does not cure process-related problems. The implementation of formal project management techniques is part of managing a fundamental change in the business processes of an organization. Investment in high technology hardware, software and systems alone is inadequate. Meaningful changes occur only when people are committed to and capable of performing new roles in a new business environment.

The formal assessment should consist of three parts:

1. Structured interviews
2. Individual self assessment
3. A workshop with the team leading the project management implementation and operational staff to obtain consensus.

What this assessment does is measure the organization's project management competence at a given point in time.

Some of the key competence issues to be measured and questions to be asked might be:

### Skill Levels

- Is there a formalized skill assessment process?
- Is there a program to develop new skills?
- Is there a clear understanding of the types of skills required for particular tasks?

### Resource Assignment Competence

- Do managers have awareness of available capacity once project plans are approved?
- At what point are specific resource/task assignments made?
- What is the review/approval process for resource assignment?

Exhibit 1 is a simple diagram showing the results of such an assessment.

One of the key items on which consensus should be reached is the "vision" or "where would we like to be"? Properly done, the project management competence assessment will show many areas for potential improvement. But just as all projects can't be handled at once, improving an organization's project management maturity in all key areas can't be done at once. So it is important that the entire organization have a plan which is understood by all concerning what will be the key focus areas for the future. It is recommended that this assessment process be repeated at regular intervals so that management has a clear picture of where the organization stands relative to the "vision". Another clear benefit of the assessment process is that it will show progress being made as a formal project management process is implemented.

## The Process Control Group

One question which can be raised is who should lead the project management maturity assessment. It is the author's recommendation that this effort be run by a Process Control Group. The inherent multi-project, repetitive types of projects, project/non-project environment of a large IS organization makes the establishment of a Process Control Group almost essential to successfully implementing project management. This responsibility can be combined with others in a project or program support office if desired, but the critical factor is to recognize that project management implementation is about managing changes in business "processes."

In addition to conducting an initial and regular assessments of project management maturity, this group charter should include:

1. Standardizing the procedures for scheduling, statusing, and reporting both project and non-project work.
2. Piloting new processes prior to general implementation.

## Multi-project and Program-based

As has been noted earlier, IS organizations are inherently multi-project. And in today's business process re-engineering climate, they are also inherently "program-based". Exhibit 2 illustrates this.

A *Program* is a collection of related projects which facilitate the realization of corporate strategic business objectives. *Program Management* is that set of management activities and processes which facilitates the translation, conversion, prioritization, balancing and integration of new strategic initiatives within the context of the current organization and planned time and cost constraints, thereby minimizing risk and maximizing benefit to the organization.

Large IS organizations support the program management activities of the corporation with their multiple project operations.

## The Technology

A successful project management implementation in a large IS department will require installation and operation of project/resource management software. What are some of the key requirements of such software for this particular environment?

1. Usability
2. Standardized, open database
3. Multi-project and multi-user capability
4. Security functions
5. Resource management orientation
6. Template capability
7. Simplified statusing mechanism.

Usability is probably the most critical factor to a successful implementation of project management software. Every single member of the IS group will be a user of the system. The system should be adaptable to the organization's way of doing business, not the reverse. One of the principal reasons that IS did not embrace earlier project management software was that is was cumbersome to use and not oriented to the inherent multi-project, resource-focused needs of IS managers. An important point to emphasize is that there are many different roles performed by members of the IS organization; the same user interface doesn't have to be utilized by all. In fact, a project management system that offers a role-based or customizable user interface has many advantages regarding acceptance by the user community. Usability can best be judged, not by how flashy the GUI is, but how oriented the interface is to the particular user's responsibility. Not every user will be producing barchart graphics from the system, so not every user should be exposed to a fundamental barchart interface. The second requirement is the use of a standard, open database as the project management repository. Since most IS organization's have chosen a commercially available database management system for other corporate applications, there is no reason not to use the same database for project management information. One of the latest trends resulting from the business process re-engineering impact on corporate culture is a move to "managing by projects" as a core business philosophy. This concepts treats project management information as a strategic corporate resource, just like financial and human resource data. The general availability of enterprise-wide project management systems based on standard, open database architectures provides a convenient mechanism to corporations moving to the "management by projects" philosophy.

The ability to handle multiple projects and multiple users is also key to IS. There should be no practical limits on the number of projects which the project management system can handle. It should be recognized that there will be performance differences when running queries or report against hundreds of projects ( which should be extremely fast), versus a complex resource analysis of the same number of projects. And it should also be understood that few team members need to perform such analysis, while many may need to run reports. Another factor which should be evaluated before choosing a system is the flexibility of the identification system for projects, tasks, resources, and codes. This is a key area where the project management system can adapt to the IS ways of doing business rather than vice-versa. An IS organization needs an enterprise-wide project management system, which means a true capability of handling multiple users. A purely desktop-based system could never be implemented for this reason. Users need accurate and timely project/resource data, and can't wait for another user to free up a locked project on his desktop. It in the area of handling multiple users that today's project management software system offer differing approaches. Some restrict project access to a single user at a time, just as the pure desktop approach. Others allow unlimited access with the consequent potential for lack of change control. And some offer a flexible middle ground, with access control for certain functions and open reporting access.

This brings us to the next key requirement, namely security. As noted above there many project management roles in the IS environment. Consequently there should be functionality that allows an administrator to control who has access to what data, and the type of access they have. In the project management field, this situation is more complex than simply read/write privileges at a file or record level. Consider that both a resource working on a project and the project manager both need write access to update certain status data on tasks. But the project manager, by the simple act of changing the relationship between two tasks, with the resultant downstream effect on all other in-progress and planned tasks on the project, affects much more data. What is needed for this environment is a combination of data-level security and functional security, which can be specified by individual user. The data-level security controls what projects and resources a user has access to (including whether or not the user even knows of the project's existence), while the functional security controls what functions (analysis, mass updating, task progressing, etc. ) the user can perform on the particular project/resource. The administrative effort that is required to implement such a security mechanism should not be underestimated; but this effort will result in smooth operation of the project management system.

Since there are many repetitive types of projects in IS work, it makes sense to utilize a template approach to project planning. And to implement project management software which supports the template concept. Ideally, once the major project templates have been established a project manager should be able to construct his detail project plans in short order. The template functionality should have a mass updating/editing capability to enable this. Consideration should also be given to assigning the initial creation of the project templates to the Process Control Group mentioned earlier.

Resource orientation is probably the next most important requirement (after usability) when implementing a project management system in IS. The fundamental philosophy for IS managers is to maximize utilization of their limited resources. So the project management software must approach the problem in this way also. Tasks are assigned to resources and therefore data entry should be structured in this fashion. As a manager, I need to know:

- Who hasn't reported project effort (timesheets)?
- Where and when is my available capacity?
- What is the effect of a transfer of one of my resources?
- Can I substitute resources with similar skills?

It should be possible to obtain this information in a timely way, and ideally without running reports. Most IS managers would prefer to see answers in an on-line query rather than a report. Most would also prefer exception-based reporting, being notified perhaps by a programmable "agent" when a deviation to plan or budget occurs within some limits they can establish and control. Another important "resource oriented" consideration is the resource analysis results presented by the project management software. The IS multiple project environment is one of constant change and managers should recognize that the resource analysis results obtained from today's project management software give guidance to a manager for planning his resource assignments. None gives a 100 percent perfectly optimized answer. Adjustments can be and should be made by the responsible manager. One of the best approaches to this problem is the "rolling wave concept." Since the most critical projects and tasks are those that are either underway or in the near term, detailed resource assignment planning for those should be the focus. As work progresses, the analysis timeframe can be moved along.

The final key requirement which should be considered when implementing project management software is a simplified method of statusing resource effort and task progress. Since the analysis produced by any project management system depends on the timeliness and accuracy of the progress data, it must be easy for the users to enter this data. They must see the system as an aid to them, not a burden! The preferred status mechanism is moving to automated time tracking systems which tie to the project management database. This is a natural occurrence since most IS organizations already have some form of timesheet system implemented for chargeback purposes. As part of the implementation process, consideration should be given to either enhancing the current timesheet system to allow task status data to be entered, or implementing a new time tracking system. The commercially available systems do offer many advantages including automatic filling in of project and task data based on planned work, multiple approval levels, chargeback interfaces, and web-enabled timesheets.

One common question raised by those attempting to implement multi-project management in an IS organization is that there may not be any detailed project plans that can be used as templates. In other words, no formal project management history exists. In this case, consideration should be given to implementing a data collection effort first by utilizing and new or enhanced timesheet system. After several months of operation in this manner, sufficient data will be available to begin pilot project planning system operation.

## Conclusion

Large-scale IS organizations present one of the best opportunities for implementing project management techniques which can show real results. But due to the fact that every staff member is a project management system user, the project environment has so many projects, and the fact that changes occur so frequently, the implementation requires careful planning. Serious consideration should be given to the aforementioned Process Control Group concept, and most importantly the pilot project roll-out approach. It is unrealistic to think that an enterprise-wide implementation will be accomplished in two months.

# New Product Development

# TRIZ: Tools for Accelerating New Product Development

Karen Tate, PMP, The Griffin Tate Group, Inc., Cincinnati, Ohio
Ellen Domb, Ph.D., The PQR Group, Upland, California

## Can Innovation Be Learned?

Traditional views of creativity in the new product development process assume that the innovation process is one of chance and that really good ideas come from those people who are either born creative or are outsiders to the process or product in question. People who do not see themselves as creative (most of us) are discouraged by these beliefs and their attempts to innovate are stifled, limiting their creativity potential. When this situation is combined with the economic and organizational pressures on new product development teams for meeting aggressive schedules with low risk and high performance, breakthrough ideas are inhibited. In today's competitive environment and downsized workforces, New Product Development Teams need to "innovate on demand". TRIZ, the Russian acronym for, *Theory of Solution of Inventive Problems*, is a unique and powerful method that teams can use to predict technical trends, develop product design features, and to find innovative solutions to tough design problems.

## What is TRIZ?

TRIZ is relatively new to the United States. It is a knowledge-based system derived from the analysis worldwide patents by Russian G.S. Altshuller and his associates. They found three general rules for creative solutions to technical problems:

- Problems and solutions were repeated across sciences and industries
- Patterns of technical evolution were repeated across industries and sciences
- Innovations used scientific effects outside the field where they were developed

TRIZ provides the problem solver with systematic and structured methods for analyzing the situation and developing new ideas for solutions that better satisfy customers and specifications. TRIZ converts your problem (see Exhibit 1) into a TRIZ general form so TRIZ general solutions can be evaluated for applicability to your problem.

### Where can TRIZ be applied?

TRIZ has usefulness in the following:

- New product development
- New process development

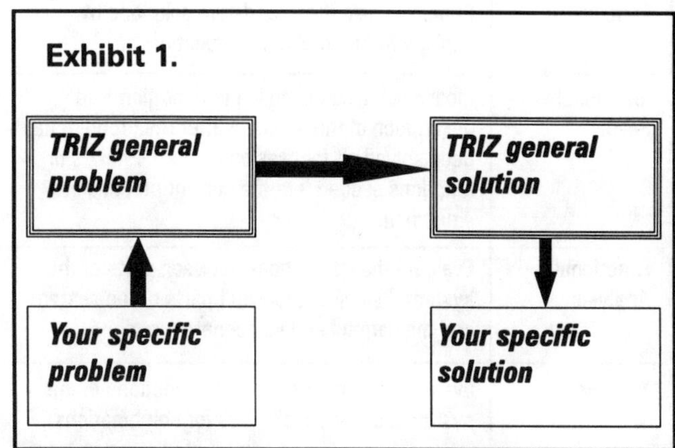


- Manufacturing quality or productivity problems
- Technical problems where no apparent solution exists
- Research & Development

And anytime it is stated or believed that the desired solution is not possible. In addition to providing conceptual ideas for solutions, a major benefit of TRIZ is the ability to open the mind of the problem solver to new ideas.

## What Are the Benefits of TRIZ?

- Reduced time to market for new products & processes.
- Fewer iterations of "Trial & Error"
- Rapid, focused, promising concepts for solutions to tough problems
- Increased creativity & innovation of the people who use & practice TRIZ
- Structured, repeatable process for problem analysis & developing innovation

## What Are the Components of TRIZ?

TRIZ consists of a collection of techniques that are used together or alone as needed depending on the type of problem and the amount of information available about the problem. The major components are:

**Exhibit 2.**

| TRIZ Component | Description | Problem Solved |
|---|---|---|
| Principles | Principles help the user derive solutions by analogy for the problem in question | Eliminate trade-offs and compromises in technical systems by eliminating contradictions |
| Ideal Final Result | Ideal Final Result is an implementation-free description of the situation after the problem has been solved. It focuses on customer needs or functions needed, not the current process or equipment. | Defines the boundaries of the problem and opens the mind of the problem solver to "impossible solutions" |
| Functional Analysis | Evaluate the interactions between parts of the system. Pinpoints the exact parts of the system and the harmful and inadequate functions. | Analyzes all of the functions, both beneficial and harmful performed by the system and by each of the components of the system. |
| Trimming | Evaluates the necessity of the functions in the system and the possibilities for combinations | Streamlines the system, eliminates unnecessary components and functions. Consider how the beneficial functions could be improved and the harmful functions removed by simplifying the system, "trimming" subsystems or components. |
| Technology Forecasting | Predicting the future developments in technical systems and each of the components of the system. All systems evolve towards the ideal final result by increasing ideality, defined as: Ideality = S Benefits / (S Costs + S Harm) | Defines the direction in which the system should evolve to deliver more value either by offering more benefits with no increase in cost or harm, or the same benefits for less cost, or with less harm. |

## Principles

A basic principle of TRIZ is that a technical problem is defined by contradictions. That is, if there are no contradictions, there are no problems. This radical-sounding statement forms the basis for the TRIZ problem solving methods that are fastest and easiest to learn, Principles. Principles solve contradictions, which are the classical engineering "trade-offs." The desired state can't be reached because something else in the system prevents it. In other words, when something gets better, something else gets worse. Classical examples include:

- The product gets stronger (good) but the weight increases (bad)
- The bandwidth increases (good) but requires more power (bad)

The vehicle has higher horsepower, but uses more fuel

The ability to overcome this dilemma is dependent on the problem solver's knowledge base. The solution to the problem of a stronger and lightweight vehicle requires prior knowledge of materials or design techniques. If the problem solver does not possess this experience, or knowledge, the problem will seem impossible to solve. By using TRIZ, the problem solver can draw upon the experience of the world's most successful inventors: Edison, DaVinci, etc. by studying and applying Principles to the problem at hand for new ideas to satisfy the requirements.

TRIZ expands the possible solution space for the team beyond their collective experience and breaks "paradigm paralysis" so that breakthrough ideas can be developed and implemented. See exmaples of selected Principles in Appendix A.

## Appendix A: Excerpts from the 40 Inventive Principles With Examples

### 1. Segmentation

***A. Divide an object into independent parts.***

- Replace mainframe computer by personal computers.
- Replace a large truck by a truck and trailer.
- Use a work breakdown structure for a large project.

***B. Make an object easy to disassemble.***

- Modular furniture
- Quick disconnect joints in plumbing

***C. Increase the degree of fragmentation or segmentation.***

- Replace solid shades with Venetian blinds.
- Use powdered welding metal instead of foil or rod to get better penetration of the joint.

### 2. Taking out

***A. Separate an interfering part or property from an object, or single out the only necessary part (or property) of an object.***

- Locate a noisy compressor outside the building where compressed air is used.
- Use fiber optics or a light pipe to separate the hot light source from the location where light is needed.
- Use the sound of a barking dog, without the dog, as a burglar alarm.

### 3. Local quality

***A. Change an object's structure from uniform to non-uniform, change an external environment (or external influence) from uniform to non-uniform.***

- Use a temperature, density, or pressure gradient instead of constant temperature, density or pressure.

***B. Make each part of an object function in conditions most suitable for its operation.***

- Lunchbox with special compartments for hot and cold solid foods and for liquids

***C. Make each part of an object fulfill a different and useful function.***

- Pencil with eraser
- Hammer with nail puller
- Multi-function tool that scales fish, acts as a pliers, a wire stripper, a flat-blade screwdriver, a Phillips screwdriver, manicure set, etc.

### 4. Asymmetry

***A. Change the shape of an object from symmetrical to asymmetrical.***

- Asymmetrical mixing vessels or asymmetrical vanes in symmetrical vessels improve mixing (cement trucks, cake mixers, blenders).
- Put a flat spot on a cylindrical shaft to attach a knob securely.

***B. If an object is asymmetrical, increase its degree of asymmetry.***

- Change from circular O-rings to oval cross-section to specialized shapes to improve sealing.
- Use astigmatic optics to merge colors.

### 7. "Nested doll"

***A. Place one object inside another; place each object, in turn, inside the other.***

- Measuring cups or spoons
- Russian dolls
- Portable audio system (microphone fits inside transmitter, which fits inside amplifier case)

***B. Make one part pass through a cavity in the other.***

- Extending radio antenna
- Extending pointer
- Zoom lens
- Seat belt retraction mechanism
- Retractable aircraft landing gear stow inside the fuselage (also demonstrates Principle 15, Dynamism).

### 8. Anti-weight

***A. To compensate for the weight of an object, merge it with other objects that provide lift.***

- Inject foaming agent into a bundle of logs, to make it float better.
- Use helium balloon to support advertising signs.

***B. To compensate for the weight of an object, make it interact with the environment (e.g. use aerodynamic, hydrodynamic, buoyancy and other forces).***

- Aircraft wing shape reduces air density above the wing, increases density below wing, to create lift. (This also demonstrates Principle 4, Asymmetry.)
- Vortex strips improve lift of aircraft wings.
- Hydrofoils lift ship out of the water to reduce drag.

### 13. 'The other way round'

***A. Invert the action(s) used to solve the problem (e.g. instead of cooling an object, heat it).***

- To loosen stuck parts, cool the inner part instead of heating the outer part.
- Bring the mountain to Mohammed, instead of bringing Mohammed to the mountain.

***B. Make movable parts (or the external environment) fixed, and fixed parts movable).***

- Rotate the part instead of the tool.
- Moving sidewalk with standing people
- Treadmill (for walking or running in place)

***C. Turn the object (or process) 'upside down'.***

- Turn an assembly upside down to insert fasteners (especially screws).
- Empty grain from containers (ship or railroad) by inverting them.

### 14. Spheroidality - Curvature

***A. Instead of using rectilinear parts, surfaces, or forms, use curvilinear ones; move from flat surfaces to spherical ones; from parts shaped as a cube (parallelepiped) to ball-shaped structures.***

- Use arches and domes for strength in architecture.

***B. Use rollers, balls, spirals, domes.***

- Spiral gear (Nautilus) produces continuous resistance for weight lifting.
- Ball point and roller point pens for smooth ink distribution

***C. Go from linear to rotary motion, use centrifugal forces.***

- Produce linear motion of the cursor on the computer screen using a mouse or a trackball.
- Replace wringing clothes to remove water with spinning clothes in a washing machine.
- Use spherical casters instead of cylindrical wheels to move furniture.

### 19. Periodic action

***A. Instead of continuous action, use periodic or pulsating actions.***

- Hitting something repeatedly with a hammer
- Replace a continuous siren with a pulsed sound.

***B. If an action is already periodic, change the periodic magnitude or frequency.***

- Use Frequency Modulation to convey information, instead of Morse code.
- Replace a continuous siren with sound that changes amplitude and frequency.

***C. Use pauses between impulses to perform a different action.***

- In cardio-pulmonary respiration (CPR) breathe after every five chest compressions.

### 22. "Blessing in disguise" or "Turn Lemons into Lemonade"

***A. Use harmful factors (particularly, harmful effects of the environment or surroundings) to achieve a positive effect.***

- Use waste heat to generate electric power.
- Recycle waste (scrap) material from one process as raw materials for another.

***B. Eliminate the primary harmful action by adding it to another harmful action to resolve the problem.***

- Add a buffering material to a corrosive solution.
- Use a helium-oxygen mix for diving, to eliminate both nitrogen narcosis and oxygen poisoning from air and other nitrox mixes.

***C. Amplify a harmful factor to such a degree that it is no longer harmful.***

- Use a backfire to eliminate the fuel from a forest fire.

### 27. Cheap short-living objects

***A. Replace an expensive object with a multiple of inexpensive objects, comprising certain qualities (such as service life, for instance).***

- Use disposable paper objects to avoid the cost of cleaning and storing durable objects. Plastic cups in motels, disposable diapers, many kinds of medical supplies.

### 28. Mechanics substitution

***A. Replace a mechanical means with a sensory (optical, acoustic, taste or smell) means.***

- Replace a physical fence to confine a dog or cat with an acoustic "fence" (signal audible to the animal).
- Use a bad smelling compound in natural gas to alert users to leakage, instead of a mechanical or electrical sensor.

***B. Use electric, magnetic and electromagnetic fields to interact with the object.***

- To mix two powders, electrostatically charge one positive and the other negative. Either use fields to direct them, or mix them mechanically and let their acquired fields cause the grains of powder to pair up.

***C. Change from static to movable fields, from unstructured fields to those having structure.***

- Early communications used omnidirectional broadcasting. We now use antennas with very detailed structure of the pattern of radiation.

***D. Use fields in conjunction with field-activated (e.g. ferromagnetic) particles.***

- Heat a substance containing ferromagnetic material by using varying magnetic field. When the temperature exceeds the Curie point, the material becomes paramagnetic, and no longer absorbs heat.

### 32. Color changes

***A. Change the color of an object or its external environment.***

- Use safe lights in a photographic darkroom.

***B. Change the transparency of an object or its external environment.***

- Use photolithography to change transparent material to a solid mask for semiconductor processing. Similarly, change mask material from transparent to opaque for silk screen processing.

### 40. Composite materials

***A. Change from uniform to composite (multiple) materials.***

- Composite epoxy resin/carbon fiber golf club shafts are lighter, stronger, and more flexible than metal. Same for airplane parts.
- Fiberglass surfboards are lighter and more controllable and easier to form into a variety of shapes than wooden ones.

## Appendix : TRIZ References

### Technical articles and tutorials

http://www.triz-journal.com

### Books


Breakthrough Press 916-974-7755 or BRKTHRU@bytheway-books.com

*Creativity as an Exact Science* (text) by G. Altshuller

*And Suddenly the Inventor Appeared* (stories) by G. Altshuller,

translated by Lev Shulyak

Collections of papers by James Kowalick and Ellen Domb

GOAL/QPC 800-643-4316 or Service @ GOAL.COM

TRIZ: An approach to Systematic Innovation (report)

Victor Fey and Eugene Rivin: *The Science of Innovation: A Managerial Overview of the TRIZ Methodology.* The TRIZ Group 810-433-3075. TRIZGR@aol.com

John Terninko, Alla Zusman, and Boris Zlotin*: Step-by-step TRIZ: Creative Solutions to Innovative Problems.* Responsible Management (603) 659-5186. john@terninko.com


### Conference Proceedings


Total Product Development 1995, 1996. American Supplier Institute, (800)462-4500 or ASI@amsup.com

Quality Function Deployment Symposium 1996, 1997 and Quality Function Deployment Symposium Tutorials 1995, 1996, 1997. Quality Function Deployment Institute, (313) 995-0847 or QFDI@quality.org


### Software

The Invention Machine

800-595-5500 or http://www.invention-machine.com

# Using the Principles of QFD to Prioritize Projects

Robert F. Hales - ProAction Development, Inc.

## Abstract

Quality function deployment (QFD) is well established in many companies as an effective tool of product development. In product development, QFD is used to identify which product attributes are most important to the customer. It is then used to identify critical predictive design metrics which the product development team can monitor in order to ensure that the resulting product has the correct attributes. The process clarifies issues by helping a team realize where they need to focus their attention. It also helps eliminate the influence of corporate politics by forcing explicit decisions. Typical results include:

- Better, more successful products in the marketplace because the development team develops an intense understanding of what the customers want
- Faster product development because the perspectives of the major functional disciplines are considered and resolved concurrently early in the project
- Reduced product life cycle costs because manufacturing, support, and retirement issues are considered as part of the design

However, few companies which rely on QFD in product development are using the same principles to help them do a better job of selecting projects. This is unfortunate because many of the same principles apply. For example, both products and projects must satisfy their customers. Products which do the best job of understanding customer needs will tend to be more successful in the market. Projects which will best help the organization accomplish its objectives will tend to be more successfully performed by the organization.

This paper will present a practical process for prioritizing projects. The process uses the principles of QFD to ensure that the projects undertaken by an organization will make optimal strategic use of the organization's resources. The paper will include a description about how to identify the customers of an organization's projects. It will then indicate how representatives of each of these customer groups can be brought together to jointly prioritize potential projects. A method for quickly identifying the objectives of the organization will be described. It will also be shown how these objectives can be translated into selection criteria. The use of selection criteria to prioritize the proposed projects will be established. Finally, the impact of project cost, level of effort, and a variety of risks will be demonstrated.

## Introduction

Product development organizations have long been under pressure to reduce their development cycle time. They have also been forced to improve the quality of the products they produce by focusing their effort on those parts of a product which deliver the most value to a customer. The combination of the need for speed and the need for better products led many Product Development organizations to learn and apply the principles of QFD.

QFD is a process through which customer outcomes (needs and wants) are rigorously translated into a product definition. In the approach the author uses most often, this involves answering the following questions:

- Which customers are most critical to the success of the product?
- Specifically, what outcomes are those customers seeking when they purchase a product?
- Which of those outcomes is most critical?
- How do those customers recognize a product capable of delivering the outcomes they are seeking?
- Which of those recognition metrics are most critical to get right for the product to succeed?
- How well do we have to perform against these different recognition metrics in order to succeed?
- What are some alternative paths we could take in order to achieve the required level of performance?
- Which of these design paths would be the most efficient and cost-effective for us to implement?

Now, organizations as a whole are being put under the same pressures. They need to get more done. They need to produce higher quality results. And, they need to do so with fewer resources than were previously available. Organizations need to prioritize and focus. The author believes that the principles of QFD can be an effective tool to help organizations do this. This paper will present a practical QFD-based process for prioritizing projects that demonstrates this thesis.

## The Process

Over the last ten years the author has discovered that one of the keys to success with QFD is to use the process to answer the questions the team using the process needs to answer. This applies when being used to prioritize projects as when

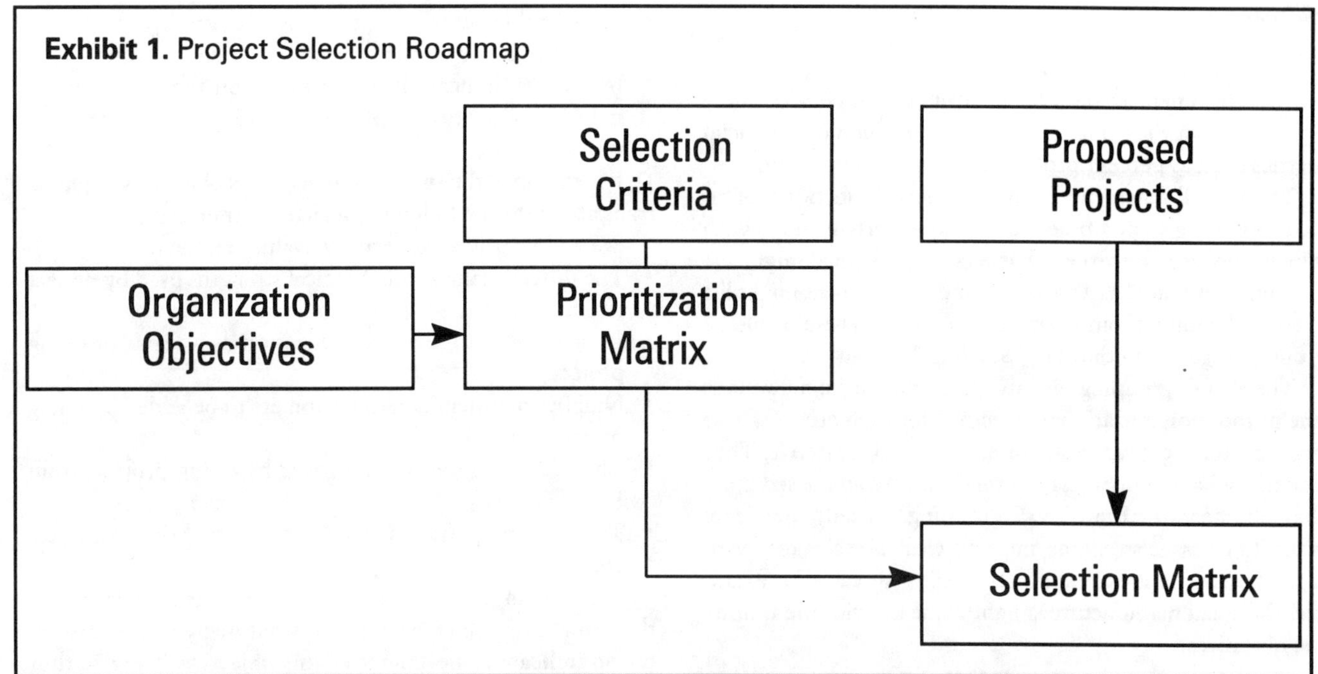


**Exhibit 1.** Project Selection Roadmap

being used to develop products. When prioritizing projects, a team would probably want to answer:

- Who needs to buy-in to the prioritization of projects?
- What do each of those stakeholders want the organization to accomplish with the projects it undertakes?
- Which of these objectives is most critical for the organization to accomplish?
- How can the stakeholders consistently judge whether a project will help them accomplish their objectives?
- Which of these selection criteria are most important to the overall success of the organization?
- How well does each proposed project help the organization accomplish its objectives?
- What are the relative costs associated with each proposed project?
- Which projects deliver the most value to the organization?
- Which projects would we focus on?

These questions are answered through the process illustrated in Exhibit 1. First, a planning team goes through a detailed situation analysis to identify the organization's objectives. These objectives are prioritized to reflect the organization's strategy. The prioritized objectives are then translated into measurable selection criteria using the prioritization matrix. The resulting prioritized selection criteria are used as the basis for comparing proposed projects. Each proposed project is rated relative to how well it would help the organization improve its performance against the prioritized selection criteria. They are also rated for cost and risk. We will now look at each of these steps in more detail.

## Define and Prioritize Objectives

There are probably many good ways to identify the objectives of the organization. The author uses a process which includes an in-depth Strength, Weaknesses, Opportunities, and Threats (SWOT) analysis. The team, after meeting with current and potential customers lists all of the strengths, weaknesses, opportunities, and threats of which they are made aware. The author likes to have each functional area go through this exercise prior to meeting with the team. This ensures that the SWOT analysis encompasses as many different perspectives as is reasonable.

Throughout this paper, a small manufacturing company (a combination of several real companies) will be used as an example. For the sake of this example, the following SWOT statements were identified:

***Strengths:***

- Strong technical know-how
- Strong customer knowledge.

***Weaknesses:***

- Aging facilities
- Aging work force.

***Opportunities:***

- International expansion
- Transfer technology into related or similar markets.

***Threats:***

- Seasonal nature of business
- Two customers account for majority of business.

In addition they might identify some common financial metrics such as percent profit and required investment.

The SWOT statements from the different functional organizations are grouped based upon the underlying issue with which they are concerned. For example, finance might list "seasonal revenues" as a weakness and management might list "Seasonal nature of our business" as a threat. These would be grouped together with other "Seasonal" statements.

The SWOT groupings are analyzed and the team develops one or more organizational objectives for each group. These organizational objectives are directional and subjective. They describe what the organization might want to do based upon the statements in the SWOT grouping. Usually, the team wants to leverage strengths, improve weak areas, take advantage of opportunities, and protect against threats. For example, the small manufacturer might come up with the following objectives:

We want to work on projects that ...

- Leverage our knowledge of the technology
- Make us less seasonal
- Increases our base of customers
- Helps us attract new talent
- Helps us move into foreign markets
- etc.

The resulting list of objectives is then prioritized by the team. The author generally uses a nine point scale. Nine indicates the most important objective on the list and one indicates the least important objective. All of the other objectives are rated relative to these anchoring limits. With discipline, the team is able to quickly determine which are the critical objectives and which objectives can be safely ignored.

The final prioritized list reflects the true strategy of the organization. The high priority organizational objectives are those on which the organization should focus.

## Translate Organizational Objectives Into Selection Criteria

Perhaps the most difficult part of the whole process is the translation of the organizational objectives into selection criteria. Here the team answers the question "How can we consistently judge whether a project will help us accomplish our objectives?" for each of the important objectives. This is not a trivial exercise and, in general, is greatly aided by a facilitator experienced in the process.

In order to be useful in this process, selection criteria should:

- Be estimable before the project is underway
- Be applicable to all the projects under consideration
- Include an indication of the direction the value should move in order to comply more closely to the organization's strategy.

For example, the small manufacturer's objectives might be translated into the following selection criteria:

We will prioritize projects by evaluating the ...

- The differentiating technological strengths used by project (from List)
- Improvement to seasonal utilization as a result of doing project
- Number of potential new customers to be added by doing project
- The recruiting metrics improved by doing project (from List)
- Total size of international markets project helps us address
- etc.

Each cell in the Prioritization Matrix is then evaluated by the team asking the question "To what degree does this criterion indicate achievement of this objective?" The author uses a nine point scale to indicate this degree. Nine shows strong indication while a one implies minimal indication. A zero or a blank implies that the value of the criterion does not indicate achievement of the objective. It should be noted that this matrix should be evaluated on a row by row basis so that the relative impact of each of the selection criteria can be determined for a given organizational objective.

After the cells have all been evaluated, the final prioritization of the selection criteria is calculated. This is done by calculating a weighted sum of all the ratings in a given column. Each of the ratings is multiplied by the importance of the Organizational Objective to which it is related. All of the resulting weighted ratings are then summed on a column by column basis. Usually these sums are then reduced to percentages so that they might be more easily compared.

The final prioritization of the Selection Criteria shows how well each Criterion will indicate that a project will help achieve the Organization's Objectives. The larger the number, the more critical the Selection Criterion.

## Selecting the Projects

The Selection Matrix is now used to prioritize the Proposed Projects based upon how each Proposed Project will affect the values of the Selection Criteria. The Selection Criteria are made the rows of this matrix and the Projects being considered are made the columns.

Each cell in the Selection Matrix is evaluated using the decision tree shown in Exhibit 2. If the Proposed Project will improve the organization's performance against the Selection

**Exhibit 2.** Selection Matrix Decision Tree

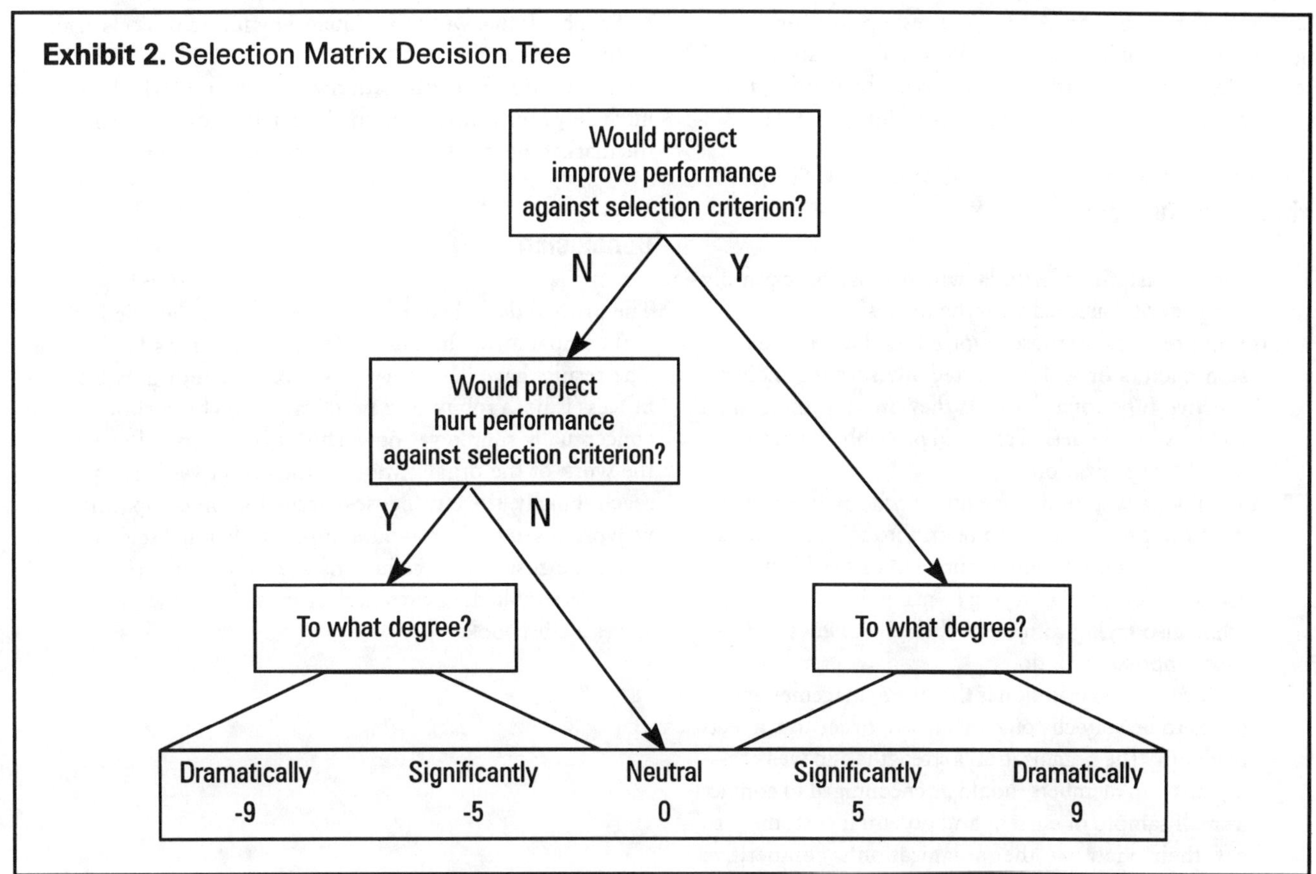


Criterion, it receives a positive rating. The strength of the rating indicates the degree to which the Project will improve the organization's performance. On the other hand, if the Project will actually hurt the organization's performance against the Criterion, it will receive a negative rating. Again, the strength of the rating indicates the degree to which the Project will hurt the organization's performance.

Again, a weighted sum of the project ratings is calculated. All the ratings in a given column are multiplied by the importance of the appropriate selection criteria. These weighted ratings are then summed for each project. This sum indicates the relative benefit being delivered by a particular project. A positive sum indicates that the project will do something to help you strategically. On the other hand, a negative rating indicates that the project will actually take the organization away from where it wants to go strategically. Obviously, projects with negative ratings should be avoided and those with very positive ratings should be promoted.

The relative cost and risk of each project should also be explored. Generally, the author encourages the management team to evaluate the relative investment and labor costs. The risk of incurring additional cost due to use of new technologies, or new applications of technology, are also identified. The benefit rating is divided by these "cost" factors. The result is a benefit/cost ratio for each proposed project.

Care should be taken to not place too much emphasis on the numbers. They are relative indications of which projects are best at addressing the issues. They are not extremely precise. Small differences in the calculated importance are probably not significant. However, large differences indicate that one project is clearly better than another. Obviously, the team needs to examine the resulting priorities to determine that they really do make sense. Adjustments in the ratings can easily be made. However, it is critical that the team not start manipulating the ratings in order to bring favorite projects to the head of the list.

When it has been determined that the relative ratings are accurate, the team needs to make the actual selection. Generally, the team will start with the projects delivering the best benefit/cost ratio and allocate the required resource. If the organization has the ability to take on additional new projects, the projects are considered in order of the benefit/cost ratio until the organization no longer has sufficient resource available.

This process should be part of the organization's regular planning process. As new projects are proposed, the organization can quickly gauge how well they will fit into the overall plans of the organization. Also, those responsible for updating the organization's objectives will be able to save a lot of the time by using the existing materials as the starting place for their work. Long term consistency is thus promoted.

## Criteria for Success

There are at least three criteria which must be carefully watched in order to succeed with the process.

1. It is important that those involved on the team be decision makers or well respected advisors for their respective functional areas. If they are not, the results will be second guessed and will probably not really affect the organization.
2. It usually pays to have a facilitator who is experienced with the process lead the team through the process. Having the boss facilitate puts him or her in the very awkward position of trying to make the process work while also trying to present their own views. It is almost impossible to do.
3. The third success criterion is that the management team needs to be very customer aware. In order to correctly identify the organization's strengths and weaknesses, the team members should be encouraged to contact a small sample of current and potential customers to get their view of the organization's competitive strengths and weaknesses. The sample should probably include representatives from those who are not currently very satisfied with the organization. This will add a great deal of realism to the list of weaknesses.

## Project Costs and Benefits

This process does not come for free. The organization will likely incur some expense in collecting the data for the situation analysis. However, the biggest expense by far is the cost of taking critical managers out of their normal jobs for a period of two to three days. There isn't much that can be done to avoid this cost and still obtain the benefits sought by the organization.

However, to put things in perspective, assuming that some up front work has been done to get customer input, two or three days dedicated to the process will enable the organization to:

- Agree on an organizational strategy,
- Define exactly how the organization will judge the goodness of projects,
- Prioritize any proposed projects based upon how they will help the organization accomplish its objectives, and
- Set up a frame work to evaluate any future projects against the same criteria.

In addition, the organization will have a tool which can immediately reprioritize projects should drastic changes occur in the market place. That is a very powerful two or three days.

## Conclusion

The process described in this paper has been applied at several companies with, and without, the author's facilitation. The results have been very positive. This indicates that the process is both robust and practical. It has been shown to be conceptually simple yet powerful. It is a practical way to tie the work of the organization to the objectives it is trying to reach. Finally, since it focuses discussion on comparing how well proposed projects would impact individual selection criteria, the resulting conclusions are easier to arrive at and more defensible than current decisions. Truly, the process deserves a close look.

# Earned Value—The Next Generation—A Practical Application for Commercial Projects

Jim Sumara, Harris Corporation
John Goodpasture, Lanier Worldwide, A Harris Company

## 1.0 Introduction

Earned Value systems are one of the most useful and meaningful tools used to status, report, and analyze project cost, schedule, and performance. Unfortunately, their important benefits have too often been lost because earned value systems are thought to be too complex and costly to implement for many commercial projects. In part, this has occurred because earned value systems were originally invented to solve very real project measurement problems in complex cost-reimbursable programs. Thus, they have traditionally been *cost-centric*, reflecting the high priority that cost assumes in cost-reimbursable contract environments. But in many projects, *time* is the highest priority resource. Indeed, so important is time that it has become one of the most important elements of quality in modern business practice.

This paper describes an earned value system that is a simple and practical program management tool to influence programmatic behavior when applied to *time-centric or time-constrained* projects. The essence of the technique is to "earn" task starts and finishes. Thus, task leaders are measured on the "earned value" of "starts and finishes" of project tasks; and, the project manager's measurement focus is directed toward *accomplishment of tasks* necessary to achieve results in the *time allowed* for achieving the scope of the project. But, the principal benefit obtained and *compelling reason to employ this tool is that the application of earned va lue stimulates project improvement* to the betterment of the project objective.

## 2.0 Traditional Earned Value Measurements

The purpose of earned value is to *measure accomplishment* of the project's scope and objective, and *predict outcome* at completion, using units of measure which are at the core of the value system of the project. Traditionally, the core value has been money, and the focus has been cost. When used to measure project progress with cost metrics, the typical measurements are given in *A Guide to the Project Management Body of Knowledge* in Chapter 10.

But, there are many reasons why it is difficult, essentially impractical, to apply these conventional earned value measurements in commercial projects. They include: no time card or time accounting system, poor timecard compliance even when it exists, no job numbers, no overhead calculation

**Exhibit 1.** Earning Rules

| Rule | Definition or Application |
|---|---|
| A Finish is: | Valued as 1 or 0. The task has completed its scope; the scheduled successors to this task can begin work as planned in the schedule network. |
| A Start is: | Valued as 1 or 0. The first task under the work element summary task is started; generally this means that the predecessor tasks are completed, task is properly staffed, resources are in place, and effort has begun to be applied in a meaningful manner; incidental activity is not credited as a start. |
| Partial credit | A task is either started or it is not started; it is finished or it is not; there is no partial credit for progress toward finish; incidental starting activity is not "counted"; all WBS deliverables are completed. |
| Un-weighted Credit | For the simplest system, all tasks are weighted equally, 1 or 0 for the start and for the finish |
| Weighted Credit | For a more complex system, there are multiple methods for applying weight. For instance, weight heavily the tasks that are on the critical path. Lesser weight could be given to tasks that are not critical, but have little slack, and thus are candidates to become critical [thus they are "near critical" from a risk perspective]. Or, effort can be evaluated in advance and planned into the schedule, so that tasks are weighted according to effort [not duration] |



PROJECT MANAGEMENT INSTITUTE 28th Annual Seminars & Symposium
Chicago, Illinois: Papers Presented September 29 to October 1, 1997

**Exhibit 2.** Process Steps for Time-Centric Earned Value

| Steps | Step Deliverable | Who Does It? |
|---|---|---|
| 1. Construct WBS of Product Nouns | Hierarchical WBS | Project Manager & WBS element managers |
| 2. Write Tasks for actions necessary to produce nouns | Verb-led statement of work for the WBS element | WBS element managers with work element team members |
| 3. Schedule and network tasks with definitive start and end dates; add resource constraints; conduct risk analysis with Monte Carlo techniques, and establish risk weighted dates. Determine critical and near critical paths | CPM Network of tasks with risk evaluation and resource plan | Project Manager & WBS element managers |
| 4. Establish Earning Rules | List of Rules with definitions in a Rules Dictionary [if necessary] | Project Manager |
| 5. Claim earnings of starts and finishes periodically as appropriate | List of claimed starts and finishes | WBS element manager |
| 6. Validate Claims; Analyze data for trends, predict completion | Validation reconciliation & Analysis | Project Manager or administrator |
| 7. Create report of Variances and analysis | Report | Project Manager or administrator |

or cost allocation system, no ledger for associating cost with projects, and many other reasons. So, in spite of recognized benefit, the redesign of the business to overcome these "deficiencies" is often impractical.

For many commercial projects, cost, at least product or service development and launch cost, has a much lower priority than time or performance, the other two elements of the triple constraint. A prominent example of a higher priority element is time-to-market for a new product or service (Shiba, Graham, Walden 1993, 10). Therefore, there is a need to focus earned value management technique on the core value of time.

## 3.0 Earned Start-Finish System

The Earned Start-Finish system is time-centric. In a time-centric system, the purpose is to "earn" the time elements of the project plan, specifically answering the two questions: are tasks starting on time; are they finishing on time? This "start-finish" time-centric system retains the most important features of the cost-centric approach: that is, a focus on accomplishment; measurement of performance against plan; and a predictive outlook on completion.

### 3.1 Time-Centric System Structure and Components

The time-centric earned value system is a simple one of measuring, analyzing, and reporting on task starts and finishes. Like the cost-centric system, the time-centric system depends on the information contained in the WBS [nouns, deliverables], the project tasks [verbs], and project schedule [tasks ordered by time, linked by relationships]. Each task within the project schedule is aligned with a deliverable of the WBS, and measured by its success of delivering a "deliverable" of the WBS. So, in order to be able to claim success a task must start and must finish. But, how are claims to be measured? Successful project teams define *both* the *rules of measurement* and the *metrics or measurement systems that go with the rules.* The recommended "accounting" rules are given in Exhibit 1.

### 3.2 Process Steps for Time-Centric Earned Value

Process steps necessary to implement a time-centric "start-finish" earned value system are given in Exhibit 2.

### 3.3 Graphical portrayal of the system

An example project is outlined in Exhibit 3 and shows the planned, unweighted, project starts and finishes. Exhibit 4 shows this same data as cumulative *planned* starts and finishes, and includes the cumulative *actual* starts and finishes for this example. Using two information elements, the slope of

Exhibit 3. Planned Tasks, Example Project

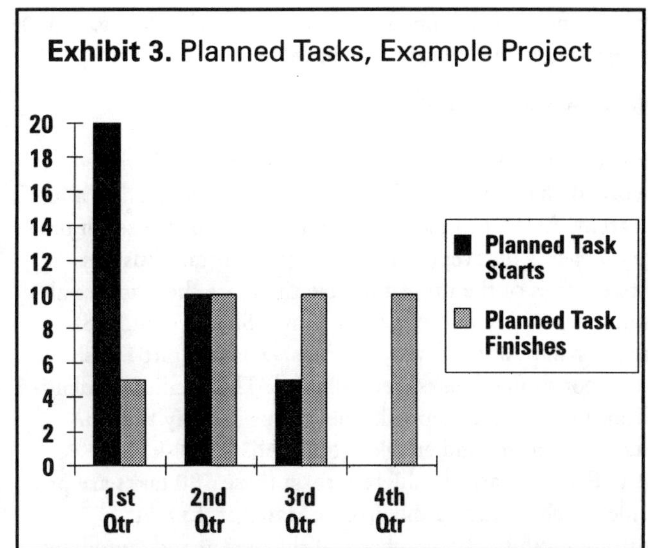


Exhibit 4. Example Actuals vs. Planned Performance

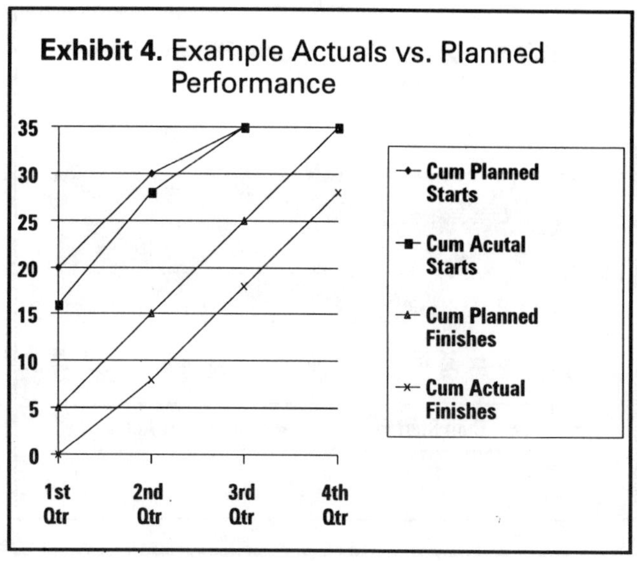


Exhibit 5. P2000 Project Planned and Actual Starts

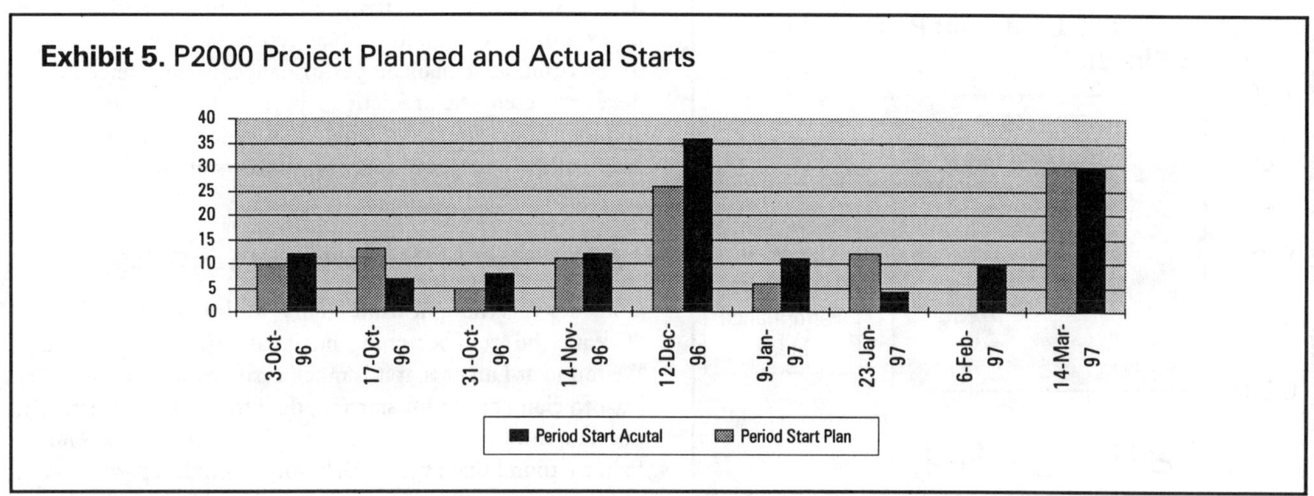


the cumulative curve, and the remaining starts and finishes, actual start and finish dates can be *predicted.*

For instance, from Exhibit 4, the following is data is available: At the beginning of the first quarter, there is a variance of (four) task starts, sixteen actual vs twenty planned. Four starts were not earned. However, after the end of the first quarter, twenty-eight task starts are claimed, and credited. The *slope of activity in the first quarter is greater than planned* as shown by the steeper curve. In fact, ten starts were planned in the period, and twelve were claimed, for a total of 16+12=28 starts claimed at the end of the second quarter. Within the resolution of the graph, for the third quarter, with only seven tasks remaining to start, and a productivity of 12/quarter, it is *predictable* that the project will "complete" all of the starts on plan. A similar analysis comes from the slope of the actual finishes. The actual curve is consistently seven tasks behind. The project is *predicted* to finish near the end of the next quarter.

The earned start-finish system is more limited as a management tool for prediction than the cost-centric system. Limitations arise because cost is not included in the earned value equation, and so not all of the information potentially available in a project is used. *But, this limitation can be mitigated by having a high degree of granularity in the project scheduling, thereby reducing the predictive errors in estimating the future from past performance.* Predicting the project outcome is also a component of analyzing the project risk. In fact, risk analysis of schedule-limited projects is many times a risk analysis on cost or performance risk (Hulett 1997, 53), even these risk elements may not be directly measured.

Predictive behavior assumes that performance index of any given task is related through the project work package environment and summary tasks to the performance index of other tasks. If all tasks are independent, then, of course, the completion of one task does not predict the completion of another task. But, this limitation is common to the predictive

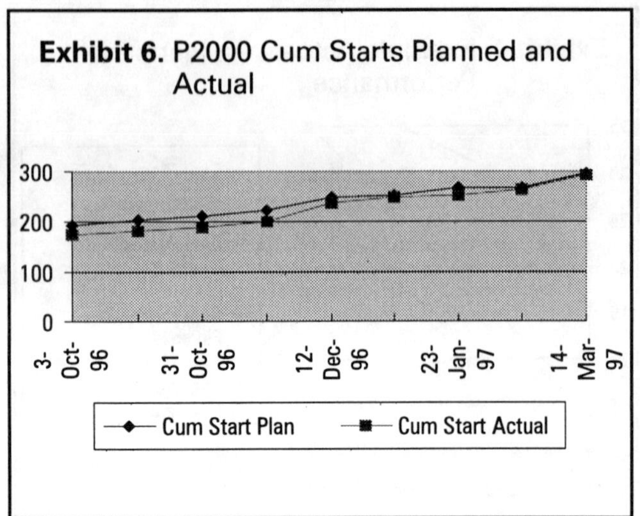


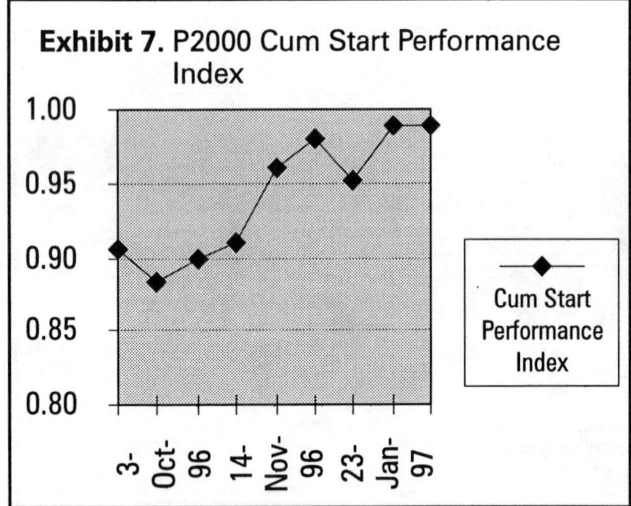


aspects of all earned value systems. As with all predictions, the extrapolation assumes that recent behavior in the past will be repeated in the near future.

*Thus, the best use of all earned value systems is stimulate project improvement activity.*

## 4.0 Applying the System

Process-2000 is a project on-going within Lanier Worldwide, an office products-and-services sales and distribution company within the Harris Corporation. Elaborate labor-hour cost accounting systems for internal operations is not justified by its business model. However, Process-2000 is a complex project to be managed, involving the activities of over fifty dedicated staff members, and the insertion of numerous technology and process improvements within Lanier in a time-constrained framework. Therefore, the Process-2000 project uses time-centric earned value reporting.

### 4.1 Process 2000 project results

Process-2000 is controlled at the summary level with a networked chart of approximately 500 tasks arranged in a hierarchy. At the top of the hierarchy are a limited set of *program events* that represent the most important business imperatives of the project. Below them are the traditional summary and detail schedules. Finish-Start and Start-Start relationships are allowed; no Finish-Finish, Start-Finish, or time-constrained tasks were allowed. This facilitates identification of project dependencies, helps identify the true start and finish, and enables good statistical risk analysis. An "Earned Start-Finish" report on these 500 tasks are provided each month to the Project Manager. Exhibit 5 through Exhibit 10 are charts of the period and cumulative data of six months of activity. Included are the performance indexes of the cumulative actual performance normalized to the cumulative planned performance. Performance indexes represent the predictive aspects of this methodology and they approximately model the schedule performance index of the cost-centric earned value system of BCWP/BCWS

### 4.2 Conclusions and lessons learned from P2000

Consider this thought from Henry Wadsworth Longfellow: "Great is the art of beginning, but greater the art of finishing". We found at Lanier that it is much easier to start a task, or at least to claim credit for starting, than to finish. Consistently, our data shows starts more close to plan than finishes. And, in fact, we found that as John Galsworthy, English novelist said, "beginnings are always messy". That is, it is relatively easy to claim a start based on a meeting or a phone call, but has the task really started? So, it is important, as part of the rules, to establish when task activity has really started. Finishes are better behaved because the deliverable is often tangible.

We found that a constant and consistent focus on getting started and getting finished did indeed stimulate project improvement. Many tasks were reconsidered more carefully in the network of the project plan as the metric became better understood. The predictive nature of the curves did indeed stimulate project improvements to overcome missed milestones. Happily, these improvements invalidated predictions based upon past performance extrapolation.

The maintenance effort to keep the data current is much less than in cost centric system simply because there is less of it. However, the debates between Project Manager and Work Element Manager over "claims" were similar to those experienced with cost-centric systems.

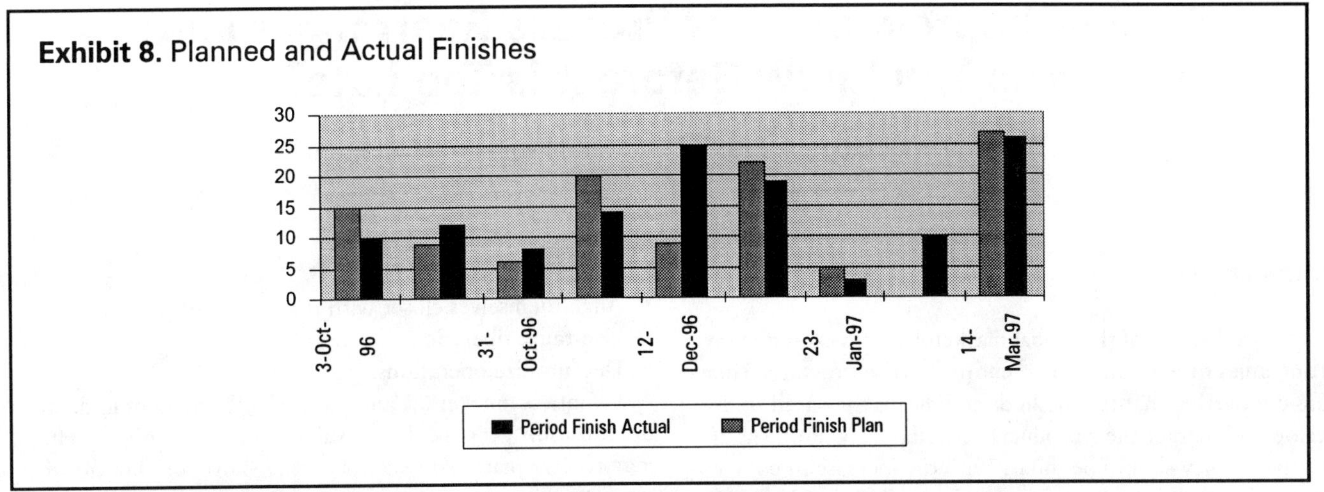


**Exhibit 8.** Planned and Actual Finishes

We developed this methodology because we were looking for an approach that kept the entire project team focused on key milestones and at the same time, provided estimate at completion (EAC) visibility to the project management team. Since our projects are time critical, we needed a way to obtain project status as painlessly as possible. The "earned value" system described in this paper helped us achieve these goals. Collecting data on task "starts & finishes" proved to be a straight forward way to status projects and maintain milestone focus. This methodology also provides the measure of predictive outlook based upon past performance we require. Since predictions do stimulate management alternatives, this information is used to improve project performance. The success of the system so far is that Lanier will continue to apply the principles in future projects.

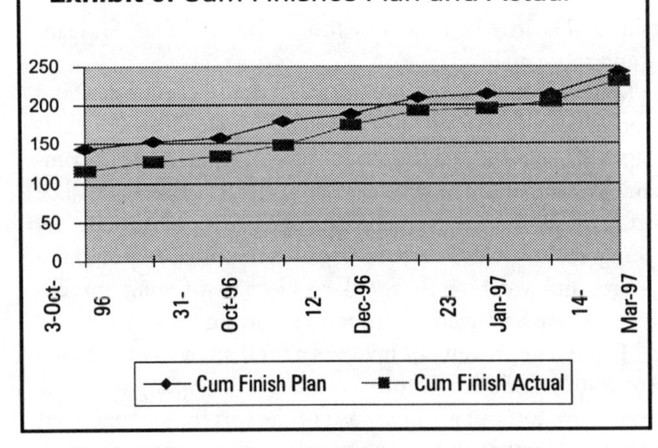


**Exhibit 9.** Cum Finishes Plan and Actual

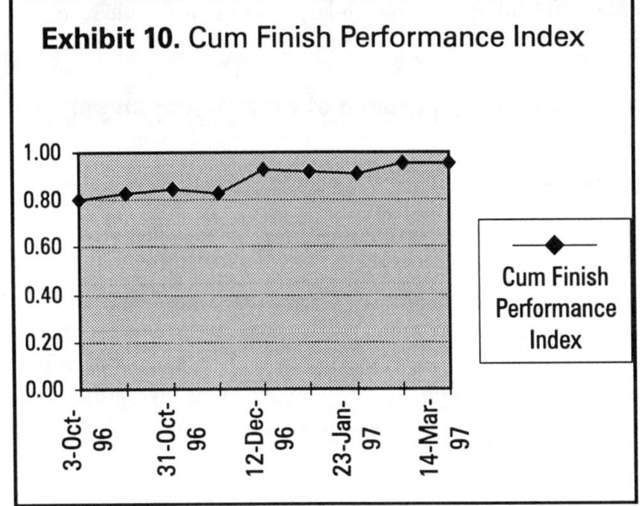


**Exhibit 10.** Cum Finish Performance Index


## Article

Hulett, David T. 1997 Revisiting "What is a Project" From the Risk Analysis Perspective. *Program Management Journal* Vol 28, Number 1 (March): 53-54.

## Book

Shiba, S., Graham, A., Walden, D. 1993 *A New American TQM, Four Practical Revolutions in Management.* Cambridge, Ma: Center for Quality Management

# Process Improvement or Process Rearrangement: Will You Know Before It Is Too Late?

Douglas B. Boebinger, P.M.P., Integrated Process Developers

## Introduction

The introduction of the global marketplace has caused many companies to re-evaluate their entire business structure. They are discovering that the methods and means they used to develop and market their products yesterday may not be as effective as they should be today. With the increase in competition as a result of such influences as the GATT and NAFTA treaties as well as overwhelming growth of the Internet, companies that stand still in their product and process development will swiftly be passed by those who are hungrier, leaner and more agile.

Many companies are looking towards re-organization and process re-engineering in order to meet the these new challenges. The problem is, how will these companies, your company, know that the re-organization and re-engineering will be a true process improvement as opposed to a process "re-arrangement"? Corporate re-organization is simply shaking the tree and watching the monkeys move to different branches. Process re-arrangement is simply changing the way you "do it." Process improvement involves a total analysis of the current state and desired future state of the company from the ground up. It is not a white wash of the current company but a re-development of it. True process improvement is much more difficult but yields much larger, more profitable results!

## The Traditional Approach of Process Improvement

### Re-Organization:

During the last recession companies realized that they had become too large and cumbersome to efficiently perform in the new global marketplace. These companies believed that their re-organization would be the silver bullet to solve these problems. These re-organizations were characterized by what has been called "right sizing," a nice way of saying that the company was reducing its workforce, including "white collar" workers.

Besides meeting new global marketplace challenges, company re-organizations were performed to do one, or more, of the following:

- Increase operational efficiency
- Minimize operation costs
- Maximize corporate profits
- Align themselves closer with their customers
- Centralize operations
- Decentralize operations.

Countless time, effort and money has been spent in the re-organization process. The results are usually mixed. They may receive marginal benefits, in the short run, but not the substantial outcomes they anticipated.

This is substantially due to the fact that most re-organizations are done in the following order:

1. Re-organize by selecting the type of organizational structure desired and fitting the company into it..
2. Each area of the company defines what and how their respective aspect of the company will function.
3. Develop processes to support each area's work responsibilities.
4. Discover that the organization cannot support the process properly and efficiently.
5. Re-re-organize to support the process thus expending additional time, money and resources.

This process continues down to the lowest level of the company. The result, more often than not, leads to sub-optimization of each aspect of the company rather than an optimization of the company as a whole. This type of "optimization of the parts" yields corporate disconnects and duplication of functions which cause the new organizational structure to function less effectively than originally intended. This results in less realized benefit than desired. Slowly the company fattens up on people and procedures to put "bandaid" solutions on major problems. Soon the organization is bogged down again in excessive overhead, procedures and their resulting costs. Correcting these problems may itself lead to yet another re-organization. This wastes precious corporate assets (both people and money) as well as the most precious of resources, time.

### Re-Engineering:

Once the company has re-organized, they then turn to the next business at hand—saving money. In other words, how to do the work cheaper. Process re-engineering is also becoming a major focus of companies who want to run leaner while maintaining, or increasing, their current workloads. It is a simple rule of math. Productivity is defined as the following:



PROJECT MANAGEMENT INSTITUTE 28th Annual Seminars & Symposium
Chicago, Illinois: Papers Presented September 29 to October 1, 1997

Productivity = (Work Throughput) / (Number of Work Hours Performed)

Given this definition, in order to maintain the same productivity level while decreasing the number of work hours performed, the company will need to decrease the work throughput. This, however, is unacceptable. The company wants to increase, or at least maintain, work throughput while reducing the number of work hours performed ("right sizing"). The only way to do this is to increase work throughput. There are two options available to accomplish this increased throughput.

- Work Harder—i.e. Just Do It *Faster*
- Work Smarter—i.e. Just Do It More *Efficiently.*

As the office joke goes "Beatings will continue until morale improves." Although there may be room to improve throughput by working harder, the company will not receive substantial gains over a long period of time. Working harder by increasing the number of workdays, the number of work hours, etc. will only lead to a disgruntled, unmotivated workforce which is not the type of environment that will lead to substantial improvements in efficiencies.

The only true way to increase productivity for the long term is to work smarter. Working smarter means determining the minimum work required to be performed with the minimum of effort yielding the maximum benefit. This may yield some hard facts to accept. Old ways of doing business may no longer be appropriate. Administrative process requirements may prove to be more of a hindrance than a help.

To obtain this work smarter advantage, many companies are re-inventing their processes. Great efforts have been undertaken to re-develop how to do business in the future under the new organizational structure. After all, how can we do the same old thing with fewer people?

Again, a great effort is expended to re-invent the process. Again, each area of a business develops how they will do their work. Again, each area will optimize their own work. Statements are made such as "If we could get more complete information earlier we could yield better results" or "If we had the proper amount of time to do our work, we could produce better information for others." Corporate initiatives may be developed to highlight, and thus resolve, major business problems. Whereas corporate initiatives typically are well intended, they may not actually result in a net benefit to the company. If their total impact on the company isn't evaluated, the results of the actions may yield further problems which may, in reality, be worse than the initial one targeted.

## A New Way of Process Improvement

The problem with re-organizing and re-engineering is not that they, themselves, are bad. It is the how, and when, they are accomplished which is bad. If re-organization and re-engineering don't yield the desired results, then what will? To answer this we need to look at the basic laws of business. Just as their are undeniable laws of physics, there are undeniable laws of business which, if broken, yield catastrophic results.

**Exhibit 1.** Undeniable Laws of Process Re-Engineering

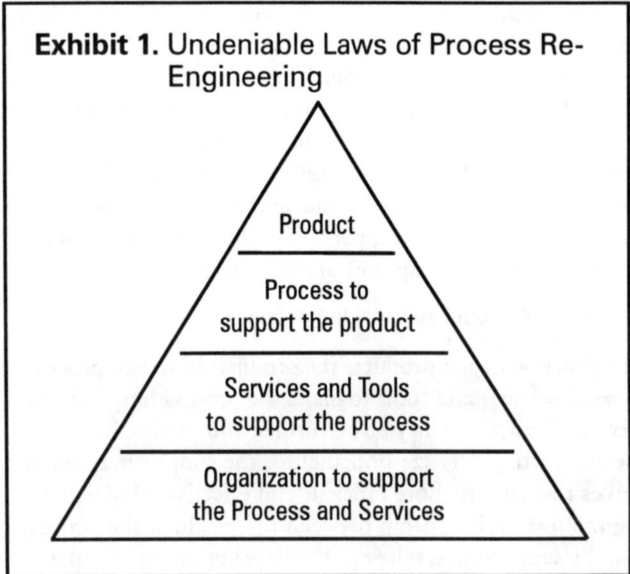


Re-inventing a company is a four step operation. The steps must be followed in the proper order or the results will be less than desired as discussed previously. The four steps are:

1. Determine the *Product* the company should produce.
2. Determine the *Process* which will efficiently produce the product.
3. Determine the *Services and tools* which will effectively support the process.
4. Determine the *Organizational structure* which will efficiently support the process, services & tools.

### What products should I produce that the customer will buy?

When entrepreneurs begin to think about starting a new business, the first thing they think of is not "what organizational structure should I use." The first thing they think of is "what product (or service) will I produce that the customer will buy?"

The product must have a perceived value greater than the competition's product. This requires a customer driven analysis of the marketplace, the competition, the economic conditions, etc. Be forewarned, do not skip over this step. Otherwise, the company will not know what to focus their process on.

### The processproduces the product

After the product is determined the entrepreneur focuses on how to consistently, reliably, and profitably produce the product. In other words, what process will assure that the time to market will be faster than the competition. The ability to be the low cost producer, first to market and with the best product will yield a substantial competitive advantage. The question is "How do you develop the optimal process to produce the product?" After all, it is the process that produces the product.

Practicing what is preached, the means utilized to develop the re-engineered process is, itself, a process with the re-engineered process as the desired end product to be "purchased"/used by the company. The steps to develop the process is the main emphasis of this article.

### Services and tools support the process

The process is what produces the product; however, processes need services and tools to make the process function efficiently. The activity may be performed without the benefit of the supporting service; nonetheless, the supporting service makes the activity more efficient and effective. Understanding the inter-relationship between the product, the process and the supporting services and tools is important in order to develop efficiencies and to understand the optimal organization to support it.

### The organization supports the process

Only after all of all this information has been developed will the entrepreneur determine what organizational structure will best support the process. Many in business fail to make this realization. The organization supports the process, not the other way around.

Therefore, based on these basic business premises, if the company is going to "re-invent" itself successfully the company needs to follow these same rules.

## Developing the Process, Supporting Services and Tools, and Organization

The steps required to re-engineer the process are:

1. Identify the current process
2. Assess the strengths and weaknesses of the current process
3. Determine the optimal product partitioning
4. Envision the new process
5. Create the new process
6. Determine what supporting services and tools are required
7. Develop the new organization
8. Implement the new process, supporting services and organization
9. Continuous process improvement.

### Identify the current process

It is extremely difficult to plan out the new process if the company is not first knowledgeable of its current process. To understand and document the current process the company will need to go through roughly the same methodology outlined in the "Developing the New Process" section below, except instead of inventing the process the company is documenting the current process. It may seem unnecessary to perform this step; however, the results of doing this effort will be three fold:

1. Identification of disconnects and inefficiencies which will need to be addressed in the new process
2. Strengthen the resolve of the company that a new process should be properly developed due to the frustration of the documenting current, poorly defined process.
3. Development of a baseline to use in comparing and analyzing the new process for true process improvements.

### Assess the strengths and weaknesses of the current process

Based on the determination that the company wants to be customer driven, it will need to evaluate the current process based on the customer. Questions that should be asked:

1. How satisfied are our customers with our current product/service?
2. What enhancements would the customer desire in the future?
3. How satisfied are our competitor's customers with the competitor's products?
4. What would it take to convince a competitor's customer to purchase our product/service?
5. What elements of the current process support customer requirements?
6. What elements of the current process hinder/don't support customer requirements?
7. What re-occurring problems exist in the current process?
8. What aspects of the current process allow the organization to function efficiently?
9. What "short-cuts" to the current process have people developed to get the product/service to market?
10. How well do our suppliers interact with the current process?

The customer information (questions 1-4) can be determined through face-to-face discussions, focus groups, surveys (mailings or by telephone), or any of the other means available. The process information (questions 5 -10) can be determined by interviewing a sampling of people from your organization and your supplier's organizations. This sampling should be representative of the various levels of personnel, from the Chairman of the Board to the newly hired employee. They should also be representative of all functional areas.

(i.e. planning, accounting, engineering, purchasing, manufacturing, customer support, sales).

From this information the company will be able to identify opportunities for improvement. These opportunities may come in the form of :

- improved customer satisfaction
- lower cost
- increased quality
- improved time to market.

### Determine the optimal product partitioning

As stated previously, the process must support the product. Therefore, an understanding of the product must precede the development of the new process. In order of the product to be of the highest quality, it must function as "one unit." It is the tendency of the traditional design process to make each component of the product as "perfect" as possible. In other words, to optimize each component with respect to cost, quality and function. After all, it is not the components that the consumer is purchasing, it is the end product, the whole system, that the consumer is purchasing. Therefore, the company must focus on optimizing the product as a whole, not its parts, to truly satisfy the customer.

The discipline of systems engineering is a vital tool in the understanding of how to efficiently and effectively optimize the whole system, both functionally as well as its attributes. Determining the best way to partition a system into its various subsystem and components together with how to cascade this information to the various subsystems and components is key to accomplishing a quality product. The system engineering "V" shows how the products functions and attributes are cascaded down on the left side of the "V" from system to subsystem to component during the design portion of the process. The functions and attributes are then are validated up the right side of the "V" from component to subsystem to system to assure the product meets its intended functionality and attribute goals.

### Envision the new process

It is time to dream! In this stage the company should develop the high level concept of the new process. Objective, measurable goals should be set concerning the new process. Just as the opportunities determined in the previous step were categorized along customer satisfaction, time, cost, and quality lines, the goals can also be put into these classifications.

- Customer Satisfaction
- Time
- Cost
- Quality

The goals must be customer driven as the customers are the ones creating sales revenue by buying the product. Goals must also be set without influence from current constraints.

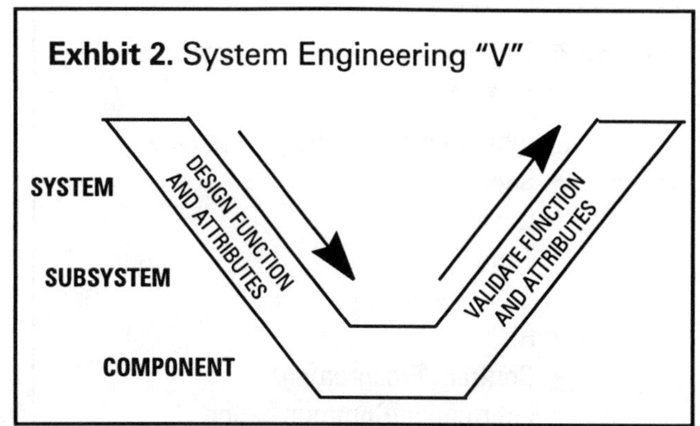


**Exhibit 3.** Five Phases of a Process (PMVOK, 1996)

The five phases of the process are:

- Initiating Processes
- Planning Processes
- Executing Processes
- Closing Processes
- Controlling Processes

Developing the goals based on pre-determined constraints will restrict the creativity desired in developing the new process. Thus, paradigm shifts will need to be made, traditional aspects of the business (process, organizations, functional, etc.) must be abandoned. Simply put, there must be no "sacred cows" or the company will limit the amount of improvement realized.

These goals must be objective, not subjective. They must be measurable in order to determine if the company truly has process improvement as opposed to process re-arrangement.

### Create the new process

In order to meet the goals just outlined, a new process must be developed. This is typically the most difficult segment to perform. It will require substantial original thinking, analysis and interactions to achieve the required end result. Two scenarios typically occur during the process development effort.

1. The team developing the process will take a broad brush approach and develop a process at such a macro level that it cannot be implemented at the working person's level, or
2. The team will get so bogged down into detail that they lose focus of the overall goals, i.e. they are so focused on the bark pattern of the various trees in the forest, they forget the purpose of being in the forest.

In order to prevent these two scenarios from occurring, a clear process development philosophy and methodology

**Exhibit 4.** Eight Functions of a Process (PMVOK, 1996)

The eight functions of the process are:

- Scope
- Quality
- Time
- Cost
- Risk
- Contract/Procurement
- Information/Communication
- Human Resources

**Exhibit 5.** Support Services and Tools

Typical Support Services and Tools:

- Project Management
- System Engineering
- Program Reviews
- Computer Aided Design
- Supplier/Vender Evaluation
- Quality, Reliability and Serviceability
- Accounting

must be utilized. A philosophy of a single, common core process to be practiced by all product development teams will allow for later process improvement efforts to be successful. This will also maximize the use of shared resources, as these resources will not need to learn a new product development process for each project they are involved on.

A methodology of focusing on one of the five typical phases of the process at a time (as shown in Exhibit 3), defining it to a pre-determined level of detail and then proceeding to the next phase of the process will yield a structure approach to the development of the process.

The level of detail with which each phase of the process are developed should start at a macro level and work down to the details. At each level of detail the eight functions of the process, (as shown in Exhibit 4) must be developed. Utilization of the Work Breakdown Structure method of project plan development is quite useful for this work. This allows for focused work which will result in a better understanding of the intricacies of the new, integrated process.

This may seem like a lot of work, and you are correct. In the actual application of the product to the process, the product development team will deal with all of these stages and functions. Thus, it is better to do it right the first time then to do it wrong for each project that goes through the flawed process. You may also think that the company can streamline this process by going straight to the detail level; however, experience has proven that this will actually take longer. This is due to the problem that the development team is not grounded in a basic understanding of philosophy of the new process.

### Determine what supporting services and tools are required

A product development process can be developed and implemented, but may not be as efficient as it could be. For example, there are many ways to develop an article. You could use a #2 pencil and line paper, make corrections manually, type set the document and print it on a hand press. Or you could use modern desktop publishing techniques to write, edit and publish the paper. Both have the ability to yield a quality article; however, the first method will take longer to do. Supporting services and tools are any instrument, etc. which is applied in the performance of a task/activity (i.e. process step). The task may be performed without the benefit of the supporting service; however, the supporting service makes the activity more efficient and effective.

In order to achieve the best utilization of the supporting services and tools, the company may have as one of its process development philosophies that all product development teams use common supporting services and tools. This will also allow for later process improvement efforts to be successful.

### The Integrated Process Matrix

With product partitioning determined, the new process developed and the supporting services and tool requirements understood the company is able to understand the inherent inter-relationships between these three facets of an integrated process. A three dimensional "Integrated Process Matrix" made from these three items will graphically show:

- which portions of the product partitioning perform which processes
- which processes use which supporting services and tools to make them efficient
- which portions of the product use which supporting services and tools.

This type of information is very useful when implementing the new product partitioning, process and supporting services and tools. In order to truly achieve a common, integrated product development process the company must have a firm understanding of all the inter-dependencies. The "Integrated Process Matrix" will be invaluable for continuous process improvement, discussed later in this paper.

### Create the new organization

As was discussed earlier, after the product has been determined and the optimal partitioning developed, the process has been developed to produce the product and the supporting services & tools identified then, and only then, it is time to investigate the type of organization desired. Remember, "The Organization Supports the Process and Services."

One of the eight functions of the process is "cost." This function includes the determination of all of the resources required to execute the process and services. These resources are the facility requirements, equipment and tool requirements, supplier/vendor requirements, and personnel requirements. As important as it is to identify all the resources, it is equally important to understand how they all need to work, and communicate, together. This information has also been developed during the creation of the process as part of the "Information / Communication" function of the process.

There are numerous organizational structures which the company may use and the selection of the type of organizational structure is not as important as developing a culture within the new organization which will allow for open communication and working relationships. As discussed previously, the "Integrated Process Matrix" demonstrates which product partitions, process tasks and services relate with each other. This is very beneficial in determining natural work groups and teams which need to be put in place to perform the process and services.

### Implement the new process, supporting services and organization

With the new process and organization developed it is time to implement them. Much has been written about implementing change within an organization; therefore, it will not be revisited here. Remember, communication and honesty are required to minimize the fear and insecurity which can result from the implementation of the new process and organization.

### Continuous Process Improvement

Continuous process improvement will keep the company on the leading edge of its industry. It will also reduce the need for total process and organizational revisions. One reason companies make such drastic changes is because the company has become inefficient. As was discussed at the beginning, companies will fall behind simply by standing still. It is easier to make small course corrections along the way than major course revisions all at once.

Continuous process improvement, as its name implies, must be continuous, an ongoing effort, and an improvement, not just re-arrangement. In order to accomplish this a methodology must be put into place to assure these two items occur. Since the process re-engineering was performed and the "Integrated Process Matrix" was developed along three major areas (product partitioning, process and support services and tools), it makes sense to continue this into the process improvement arena. Therefore, three teams, working in conjunction with each other, should be developed to oversee the continuous process improvement effort. The three teams, and their respective responsibilities, would be as follows:

**Exhibit 6.** Three Dimensional Integrated Process Matrix

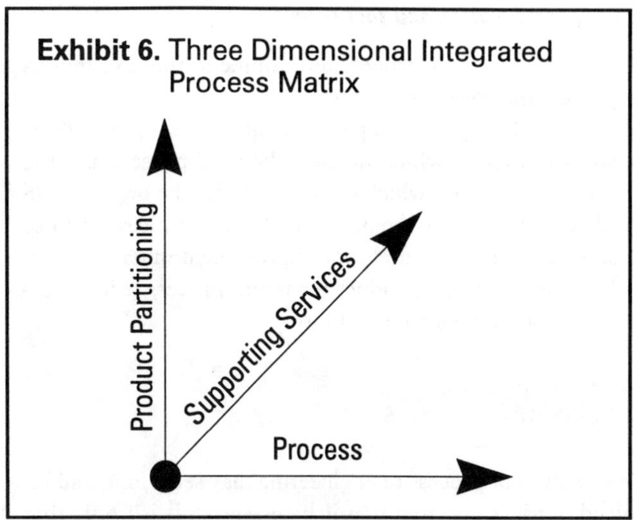


#### *The Product Team*

- Support the total process development and continuous process improvement effort
- Identify, develop and implement specific processes, based on the total process and the supporting services & tools created, across the organization
- Identify and notify the process team and supporting services and tool team of product improvement initiatives
- Interface with the process team and supporting services and tool team to assure total process compatibility

#### *The Process Team*

- Lead the total process development and continuous process improvement effort
- Identify, develop and implement process improvements, based on the product partitioning and the supporting services and tools created, across the organization to assure commonality of process
- Identify and notify the product team and supporting services and tool team of product improvement initiatives
- Interface with the process team and supporting services and tool team to assure total process compatibility
- Initiate "process improvement teams" either along the "product," "process," or "supporting service and tool" line, depending on the type of improvement identified

***The Support Services and Tool Team***

- Support the total process development and continuous process improvement effort
- Identify, develop and implement common supporting services and tools, which nurture the total process and the product partitions which use them, across the organization
- Identify and notify the product team and process team of supporting services and tool improvement initiatives
- Interface with the product team and process team to assure total process compatibility

## Conclusion

This method of process re-engineering may seem long and involved but it is essential that it be essential. It is ironic that people and companies never have the time, money or resources to do it right the first time but seem to have these resources to do it over when their backs are against the wall. Clearly, this is not the most efficient way to resolve the problem. It is easier, less expensive and less time consuming to do fire prevention than fire fighting. Doing proper process re-engineering and continuous process improvement is fire prevention. Doing traditional re-organization and process re-arrangement is fire fighting. A properly developed, well integrated product development process which produces the products customers want with an organization that supports the process will assure the company that they have truly achieved process improvement and not just accomplished process re-arrangement.

### References

Project Management Institute (PMI). 1996. *A Guide to the Project Management Body of Knowledge*. Upper Darby, PA: PMI.

# Integrating Project Management and New Product Development

Aaron J. Shenhar, Stevens Institute of Technology
Alexander Laufer, Technion, Israel Institute of Technology

## Abstract

The discipline of project management has been used extensively for several decades in the construction and defense industries. Today, however, it is increasingly used in a variety of industries and in all kinds of efforts, including new product development. Yet, many technical managers in the new product development organization find it difficult to capture the complexities involved in their projects and integrate the skills and experience gained in the project management field to their product development efforts. Furthermore, from a conceptual viewpoint, both project management and product management are still in their early stages and still suffer from a scanty theoretical basis. This paper suggests a comprehensive model for integrating the two disciplines together and capturing the interactions between them. We use a modern, three dimensional conceptual model for a joint analysis of product development and project management. This model classifies projects according to their levels of uncertainty, complexity and pace, and it represents the dynamic tension and risk found in projects of various types.

## Introduction

Project management has become a central activity in most industrial organizations and across many industries (Kerzner 1994). Traditionally, project management has been used extensively in the construction industry on one hand, and in the defense and space industries on the other hand. In both arenas large contracts between public sector customers and profit oriented contractors perpetuated the development of project management techniques and tools for planning, budgeting monitoring etc., as well as legal, organizational, and control mechanisms. Typical examples are *A Guide to the Project Management Body of Knowledge* (*PMBOK Guide*) developed by the Project Management Institute (PMI 1996) or the military standards developed by the DoD and NASA for managing large system development efforts. Today, however, projects are used in a myriad of industries and as a way of achieving a variety of additional outcomes—new product development, product improvement, process design, process improvement, software development, theory and technology development, and many more. Many of these areas still lack much of the knowledge and experience needed for effective management of projects, and much too often they rely on intuition, common sense and simple trial and error. The result is that most projects today suffer from time and budget overruns, and even when completed many do not meet customers' and/or contractors' expectations.

The purpose of this paper is to discuss a new conceptual framework for the analysis and understanding of projects. In particular, we combine the disciplines of project management and new product development. The paper suggests a context-free framework that will help capture the complexities involved in today's projects across many industries and technologies. The proposition is based on a contingent, project-specific approach, implying that project management style must be adapted to the project type. The result is a detailed classification model that will help managers classify their project and elicit its major managerial implications.

## Historical and Conceptual Perspectives

Management historians usually point to the 1950s as the era in which the current approach to project management was born and to several large defense programs executed at that time (Synder 1987). Given the comprehensive nature of projects today, it is surprising to find that research and theory development on the management of projects has been slow to adapt to the relatively fast growth of project activity in organizations and that it did not contribute sufficiently to a better understanding of the complex nature of projects. Since the inception of the project concept, several major trends have directed project management thinking, each encompassing the previous one. During the 1950s and 1960s, the concept of PERT was established, becoming almost synonymous with project management. In the 1970s the notion of teamwork became central to project management thinking. During these years research attempted to understand the intricate between team management, team communication patterns and project success (Allen 1977; Thamhain and Wilemon 1986). The 1980s could later on be marked by the era of investigating project organizations, project uncertainties and project risks e.g. (Tushman and Nadler 1986). However,



PROJECT MANAGEMENT INSTITUTE 28th Annual Seminars & Symposium
Chicago, Illinois: Papers Presented September 29 to October 1, 1997

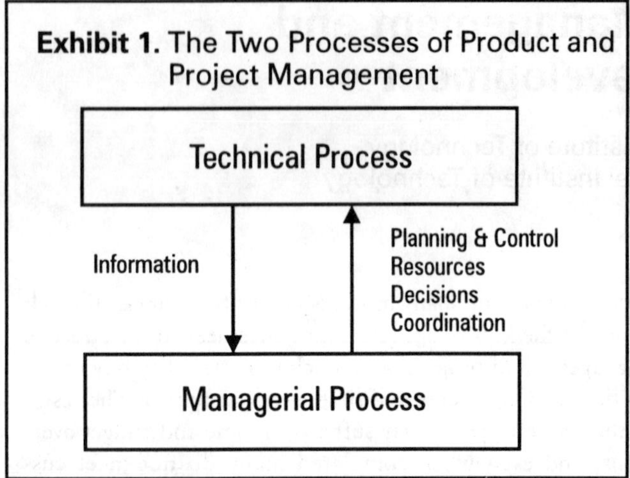


**Exhibit 1.** The Two Processes of Product and Project Management

as the 1990s evolve, many realize that managing a project means more than managing a sequence of risky activities and integrating teamwork. Today, the pace of new products developed and introduced is constantly increasing, time to market is more critical, product life cycle is getting shorter, and development resources are more scarce. Additional insights into the management of projects are forcefully needed as will be shown in the coming discussion.

Project managers frequently emphasize the uniqueness of their project and often find literature to be too general for product planning or project decision making (Pinto and Covin 1989). Consider, for example, the construction of a new hotel as compared to the development of a new spacecraft. Or the building of the English Channel Tunnel [8] to the development of a new home appliance. All such efforts are called projects, and all are managed by a project management team; yet they are so much different (Shenhar 1993). Although some distinctions between projects have been demonstrated previously by several authors (Cash, McFarln and McKenney 1988; Ahituv and Neumann 1984; Whellwright and Clark 1992), the conceptual differences among projects are more ample than usually reflected by the literature.

## Toward Integration of Project Management and Product Development

Any project execution involves linking two different, though not disjoint, processes along the various phases of the project's lifecycle. The first process consists of technical activities that lead to the assembling of external and/or internal pieces of technological knowledge to create and shape the characteristics of the project's outcome. The second process involves the managerial activities that are performed to allocate, utilize, and monitor the project's resources; coordinate the parties involved; manage the communication and information flow; and support the technical process via decision making and data management (see Exhibit 1).

The technical process in projects includes, among other things, the selection of the product's concept and configuration, the engineering design of various units, and the building and testing activities that lead to the actual construction of the final product. In some projects the completion of the engineering design requires more than one cycle (or design cycle) of designing, building and testing, followed by additional designing (or redesigning), rebuilding, and more testing (Wheelwright and Clark 1992). Design cycles are usually taken on until the preferred configuration, specifications, and design are frozen (called the moment of design freeze). Typically, the technical process is characterized by an initial period in which multiple changes may take place, up to the moment of design freeze, followed by a second period in which almost no changes are made, until the final product is build and tested.

The managerial process in project execution involves planning, scheduling, budgeting, contracting, organizing, staffing, and controlling activities, as well as information gathering and sharing, decision making, negotiation, and other coordination activities. Project planning is usually described as a process of activities that start by breaking the project's work into a "work breakdown structure" in a tree-like form that separates the work into the product's subunits and additional support activities (Lavold 1988). Each activity is then assigned to the organizational unit or team responsible for its execution, it is budgeted, and its projected length is estimated. This process results in a project schedule, intermediate milestones, and a project budget that are set in advance as constraints for project management (Laufer and Howell 1993).

Usually, different industries and different projects emphasize only one of these processes. Construction projects, for example, are mostly concerned with managerial issues. They are judged by how well they meet time and budget constraints, while the technical problems have usually been solved long ago, and even prior to the project initiation. In contrast, product development projects are often focused on the technical and design issues, leaving the managerial problems unattended. This approach leads often to considerable waste of time and resources. How to integrate these two views and capture the complexities of both processes in one framework? This question is addressed next.

## The UCP Model for Project Analysis

One may see each project along three distinct dimensions: uncertainty, complexity and pace (Laufer, Denker, and Shenhar 1995) (see Exhibit 2):

Generally, uncertainty has been defined as an inability to predict future outcomes or as the difference between the amount of information required to complete a task and the amount of information already possessed (Galbraith 1977). Various types of uncertainty in projects may be noted, technological, environmental, geographical, financial, political, etc. Complexities in projects can, again be attributed to different factors such as project scope, variety, quantity, and inter dependability of components. Finally, pace (or time frame) of the project, may depend on the urgency of the project and how strict are its schedule requirements.

It is clear that as one moves further out on each dimension, the risk involved in the project increases. The most risky projects are the most uncertain, complex and fast. How can this concept be used as a managerial framework for a better understanding of the nature of projects? And how can it be applied for adapting a proper management style? What one needs is to break the three dimensions into specific practical categories of projects in which distinct styles can be identified and adapted. The following chapter presents some possible categorization based on our studies in recent years.

**Exhibit 2.** Project Analysis: The UCP Model

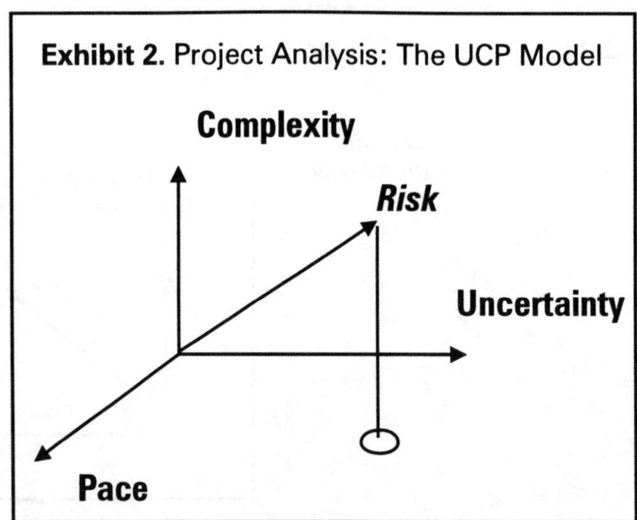


## The Classification of Projects

The first two dimensions of uncertainty and complexity were recently addressed in a study where a two-fold framework for project classification was suggested and studied (Shenhar 1993; Shenhar and Dvir 1996). Within this framework, projects and products were classified into four types, according to their technological uncertainty at the moment of the project's initiation. They were also classified into three levels of system complexity (or scope), according to their location on a hierarchical ladder of systems and subsystems.

### The Technological Uncertainty Dimension

Type A—Low-Tech Projects are those projects that rely on existing and well established technologies. Examples are construction, road building "build to print" projects, where a contractor is required to rebuild an existing product .

Type B—Medium-Tech Projects rest mainly on existing base technologies but incorporate some new technology or feature. This is the first type of product development projects. Examples include many industrial projects of incremental innovation, as well as improvements and modifications of existing products.

Type C—High-Tech Projects are defined as projects in which most of the technologies employed are new, but existent, having been developed prior to the project's initiation. Examples are developments of new computers or many defense developments.

Type D—Super High-Tech Projects are based primarily on new, not entirely extant technologies. This type of projects is relatively rare, and is usually carried out by only a few and probably large organizations or government agencies.

### The System Complexity (Scope) Dimension

The system complexity dimension is divided into three levels, and in most cases a typical element in one level may be considered as a subsystem of the level above it.

1—An Assembly is a collection of components and modules combined into a single unit. A radar receiver, a missile's guidance and control unit, or a computer's hard disc or printer are common examples of assemblies (subsystems) within larger systems; CD players, radios, coffee machines and other home appliances can also be considered as assemblies.

2—A System is a complex collection of interactive elements and subsystems within a single product, jointly performing a wide range of independent functions to meet a specific operational mission or need. Radar, computers, missiles, cars, and aircraft, are typical examples of systems performing independent tasks.

3—An Array is a large, widely dispersed collection of different systems that function together to achieve a common purpose. A nation's air defense system, or a public transportation network of a large city are typical arrays.

Here, too, one may think of other ways to categorize complexity. It may come from the number of elements, their variety, or interconnectedness.

**Exhibit 3.** Project Management Contingencies

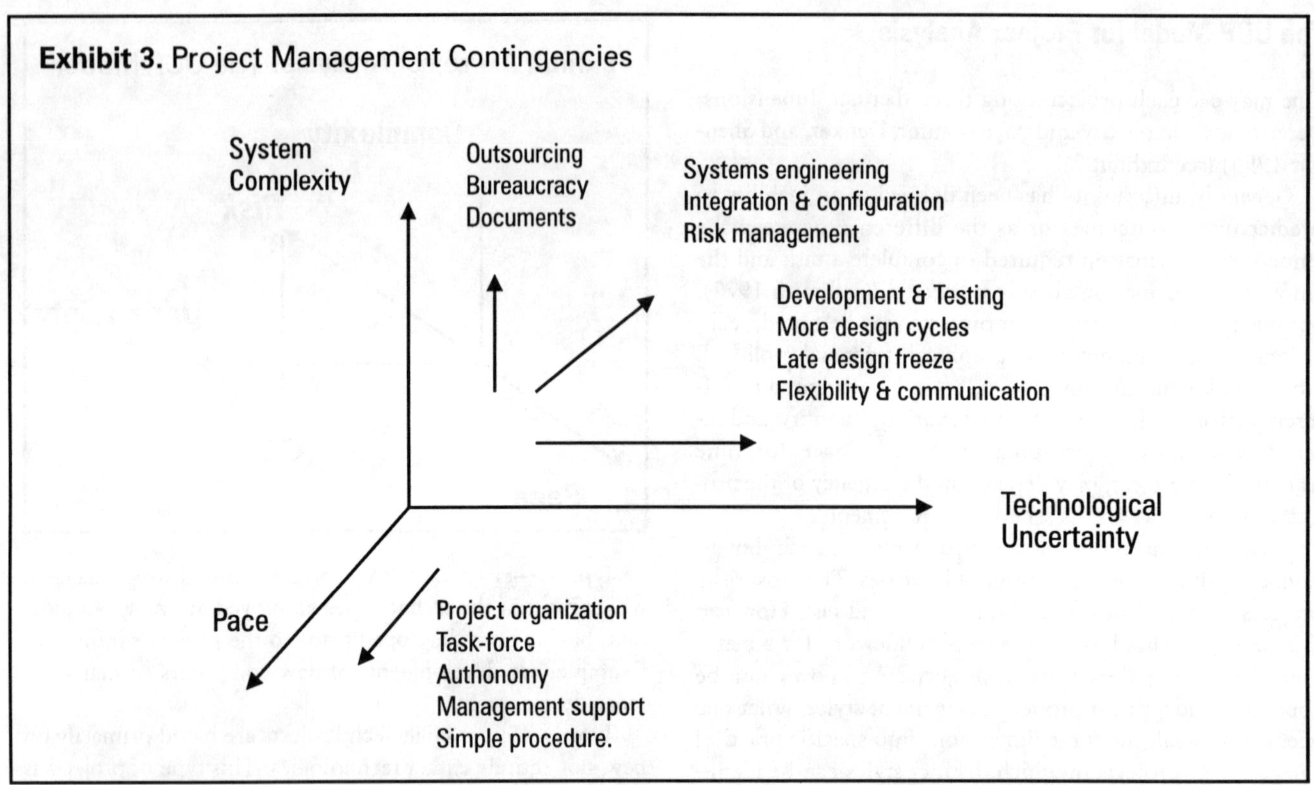


### The Pace Dimension

Project pace expresses the time-frame available for project completion. Some projects may have shorter periods than others, and they need therefore to be managed in a quicker pace. A possible typology for project pace can be divided into two types:

1. Regular Pace—are usual industrial, government or private sector endeavors. Although such projects are characterized by a firm time-frame and a contracted commitment between the parties, including liability payments in case of project overruns, a delay in project completion is often tolerated and even compensated for.
2. Fast Pace—are the most urgent, most time-critical projects. Meeting the project schedule is critical to success. Any delay in this type of project means project failure. Typical examples may be industrial projects set up to achieve a fast, competitive edge or to leapfrog competition, or specific military projects that must address a timely mission during war-time. Another example may be space exploration missions designed to launch a satellite to intercept a comet on a particular date.

## Product and Project Contingencies

Using these typologies one can identify contingencies in project management styles along the three dimensions. These contingencies seemed consistent as each variable is changed and they even describe increasing trends as can be seen in Exhibit 3 and as summarized by the following discussion.

When moving from lower to higher technology projects while keeping the complexity of the project unchanged, project managers' concerns are moving progressively toward additional technical and engineering issues—more design, redesign, simulation and testing, and longer periods of flexibility in specifications. These are characterized by an increased number of design cycles and by a later moment of design freeze. Similarly, project communication—either formal or informal—tends to intensify with technological uncertainty. Type A projects do not require any development work. They should be designed, planned and executed as designed. The main concern in the execution of such projects is the managerial process—sticking to plan and make it work within budget and schedule. Higher level of uncertainty, however, require development work. The technical process in these projects becomes more and more complicated as the level of uncertainty increases. Projects are associated with increased risk, extensive periods of development and even overruns due to unexpected technological differences.

Contingent trends along the system complexity dimension are also consistent, albeit different. In general, increased complexity with constant uncertainty, results in larger projects, and in additional concerns for formal administrative issues, i.e., more planning, tighter control, more subcontracting, and increased bureaucracy. As such one can see the managerial process becomes more intense and more formal as project complexity increases.

When moving from regular to fast pace projects, the picture changes again. The time criticality in fast projects requires specific organizational forms. Such projects are usually executed in pure project type structures and the establishment of task forces. If the company is structured in matrix or functional forms, this requires breaking away from the usual structure, and often causing much confusion in other areas.

An additional interesting trend can be seen upon a combined move along the dimensions of uncertainty and scope. Managing the execution of high and super high-tech system projects require more than just detailed planning tools and sufficient technical and engineering skills. Many of these projects find it necessary to incorporate the tools of System Engineering to optimally harmonize an ensemble of subsystems and components. Another problem is system integration, which gets more complex in system level projects of high levels of uncertainty. Similarly, configuration management seems also to be a major problem in high complexity high-tech and super-high-tech projects. Special software is needed in such projects to keep track of all the decisions and changes, and to identify the potential interactions that would occur with each change. Finally, there is risk management. Although all projects involve a certain level of risk, higher complexity, higher tech projects are more sensitive to the problems of risk management and to the need for systematic risk analysis.

## Conclusion

It is clear that projects manifest a wide range of variations, and that not all projects are alike, namely, "a project is *not* a project is *not* a project." It appears that the typical characteristics of projects are less common than has been reflected in the literature and that the traditional notion of seeing all projects as fundamentally similar should be modified by adapting a more project-specific theoretical approach. Product development efforts must be seen both in their technical and managerial aspects. The proper emphasis and blend between these two process depends upon the project type and should be determined prior to the projects initiation.

Our three dimensional model may be seen as a basis for managerial attention to better manage their projects. Management and organizations at large should deliberately adopt a more project-specific approach to the management of projects. An explicit, clear identification of the project type prior to execution, should provide a basis for a suitable adaptation of managerial attitudes and management style, for the proper selection of project managers and project team members, for establishing the proper project organization, and for a better choice of managerial tools.

### References


Ahituv, Niv, and Seev Neumann. 1984. "A flexible approach to information system development." *MIS Quarterly*, June: 69-78.

Allen, Thomas J. 1977. Managing the Flow of Technology. Cambridge, MA: MIT Press.

Cash, James I. Jr., Warren F. McFarlan, and James L. McKenney. 1988. *Corporate Information Systems Management.* Homewood, Ill: Irwin.

Galbraith, Jay R. 1977. *Organization Design.* Reading, MA: Addison-Wesley.

Kerzner Harold. 1994. *Project Management: A Systems Approach to Planning, Scheduling, and Controlling, 5th edition.* New York: Van Nostrand Reinhold.

Laufer, Alexander. and G. A. Howell. 1993. "Construction Planning Revisiting the Paradigm." *Project Management Journal,* 24, 3, September, pp. 23-33.

Laufer Alexander, Gordon Denker, and Aaron J. Shenhar, 1995. "Simultaneous Management: The Key to Excellence in Capital Projects." *International Journal of Project Management,* 14, 1, pp. 189-199.

Lavold, Garry D.,1988. "Developing and Using the Work Breakdown Structure." In Cleland, D. I., and King, W. R. *Project Management Handbook,* 2nd ed. New York: Van Nostrand Reinhold: 302-323.

Lemley, Jack K. 1992. "The channel tunnel: Creating a modern wonder of the world." *PM Network,* July: 14-22.

Pinto, Jeffrey K. and Jeffrey G. Covin. 1989. "Critical factors in project implementation: a comparison of construction and R&D projects." *Technovation,* 9: 49-62.

PMI. 1996. *A Guide to the Project Management Body of Knowledge.* Upper Darby PA: Project Management Institute (PMI).

Shenhar, Aaron J. 1993. "From low to high-tech project management." *R&D Management*, 23, 3: 199-214.

Shenhar, Aaron J., and Dov Dvir. 1996. "Toward a Typological Theory of Project Management." *Research Policy,* 25, pp. 607-632.

Snyder, James R. 1987. "Modern project management: How did we get here—where do we go?" *Project Management Journal,* 28, 1: 28-29.

Thamhain Hans J. and David L. Wilemon. 1987. "Building high performing project teams." *IEEE Transactions on Engineering Management,* 34, 2: 130-142.

Tushman, Michael L., and D. Nadler. 1986. "Organizing for innovation." *California Management Review,* 28, 3: 74-93.

Wheelwright, Steven C., and Kim B. Clark. 1992. "Creating project plans to focus product development." *Harvard Business Review,* March-April: 70-82.

Wheelwright, Steven C., and Kim B. Clark. 1992. Revolutionizing Product Development. New York, NY: *The Free Press.*

# Integrating A Metrics Framework Into An Integrated Circuits Development Process

Shailesh U. Hegde, Texas Instruments (India) Limited, Bangalore, India
Indradeb P. Pal, Hewlett-Packard International Software Operations, Bangalore, India
Kasa Srinivasa Rao, Texas Instruments (India) Limited, Bangalore, India

## 1.0 Introduction

Integrated Circuit (IC) product development is a multi-functional activity involving participation from marketing, planning, design, manufacturing, assembly/test and qualification organizations. With the ever-increasing demand for quality, on-time delivery, and demands for larger number of products to be developed to capture design wins, enhanced emphasis is on development processes with well-defined metrics (Armstrong 1995, Stehlin 1995, and Lynch and Cross 1995). This paper describes comprehensive metrics and analysis methods for IC product development.

A typical IC product development flow spans the complete spectrum of product development starting from customer requirements and going up to volume production. There are specific milestones with a list of activities to be completed while progressing from one milestone to the next. There are metrics at each milestone to give quantitative information.

This paper is organized as follows. Section 2 describes a typical IC product development flow. Section 3 discusses a metrics framework in the context of the typical IC product development flow. Section 4 deals with the deployment and implementation aspects. Section 5 discusses the analysis methodology. Finally, Section 6 has conclusions. An application of the metrics framework, described in this paper, to memory products can be found in a related paper by the authors (Hegde et al 1997).

## 2.0 IC Product Development Flow

A typical IC product development flow starts with a set of customer requirements and ends with a product shipped to the customer. The "voice of the customer" is translated into a tangible product via intermediate milestones of *prescreen*, *business plan*, *product plan*, *design*, *prototype*, and *final production*. Each milestone corresponds to a major set of completed activities. A project "flows" through these milestones, and there is a project review at each milestone to assess the progress. The first milestone is the *prescreen* with activities such as product conceptualization, market analysis, competitive analysis, risk assessment, and generation of preliminary specifications. These activities are normally done by planning and marketing organizations. The second milestone is the *business plan generation*. This involves a detailed cost analysis, return-on-investment analysis, resource identification and generation of a preliminary project plan. This activity is best done by a cross-functional team consisting of representatives from planning, marketing, design, manufacturing and quality assurance. The third milestone of *product plan* involves various planning activities, including generation of a detailed project plan, simulation plan, test plan, qualification plan, and an in-depth risk assessment. The next milestone of *design* is the main design activity coupled with extensive simulations and audits. The fifth milestone of *prototyping* involves fabrication, testing, manufacturability assessment and customer feedback. If there are any problems identified during prototype verification, redevelopment activity is initiated. The last milestone *of volume production* is the culmination of all design, prototyping and verification activities leading to final product and its ramp-up.

It is to be noted that each milestone completion requires appropriate approvals (from management, design leader, fabrication manager, quality and reliability manager, etc.). It is possible a project may feedback to a completed milestone depending on its status, e.g., a problem found on prototype silicon may initiate a redesign activity. It is also possible that a project may get canceled during any milestone review due to business reasons.

## 3.0 Metrics Framework

There are several stakeholders focused on different aspects of product development, and hence interested in different types of metrics. Based on this, two broad categories of metrics can be defined : *global metrics* and *micro metrics*. Company executives are interested in global metrics such as revenue, product quality, market share, development cycle time and yield ramp-up. Project managers and design engineers are interested in global metrics and also in micro metrics such as design reuse, planning index, detailed schedules, adherence to recommended flows, level of automation and team skill development. Internal/external customers are interested in

**Exhibit 1.** Metrics Stakeholders

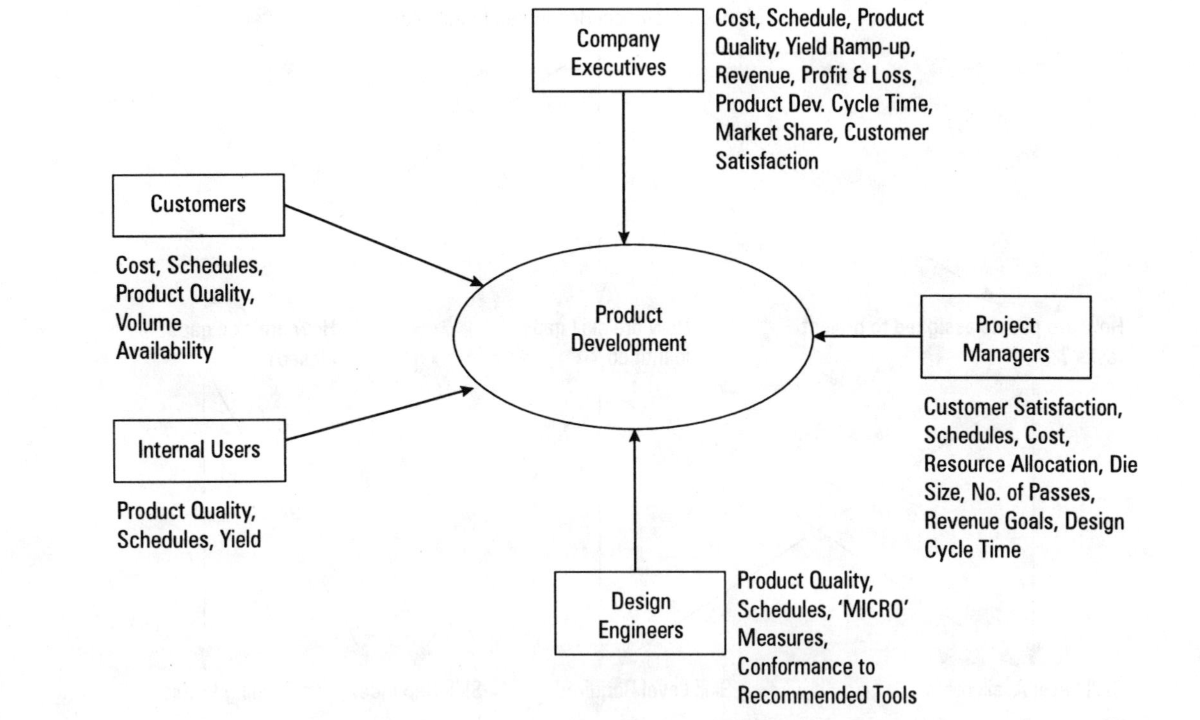

Company Executives
Cost, Schedule, Product Quality, Yield Ramp-up, Revenue, Profit & Loss, Product Dev. Cycle Time, Market Share, Customer Satisfaction

Customers
Cost, Schedules, Product Quality, Volume Availability

Product Development

Project Managers
Customer Satisfaction, Schedules, Cost, Resource Allocation, Die Size, No. of Passes, Revenue Goals, Design Cycle Time

Internal Users
Product Quality, Schedules, Yield

Design Engineers
Product Quality, Schedules, 'MICRO' Measures, Conformance to Recommended Tools

**Exhibit 2.** Goal-Question-Metric Paradigm

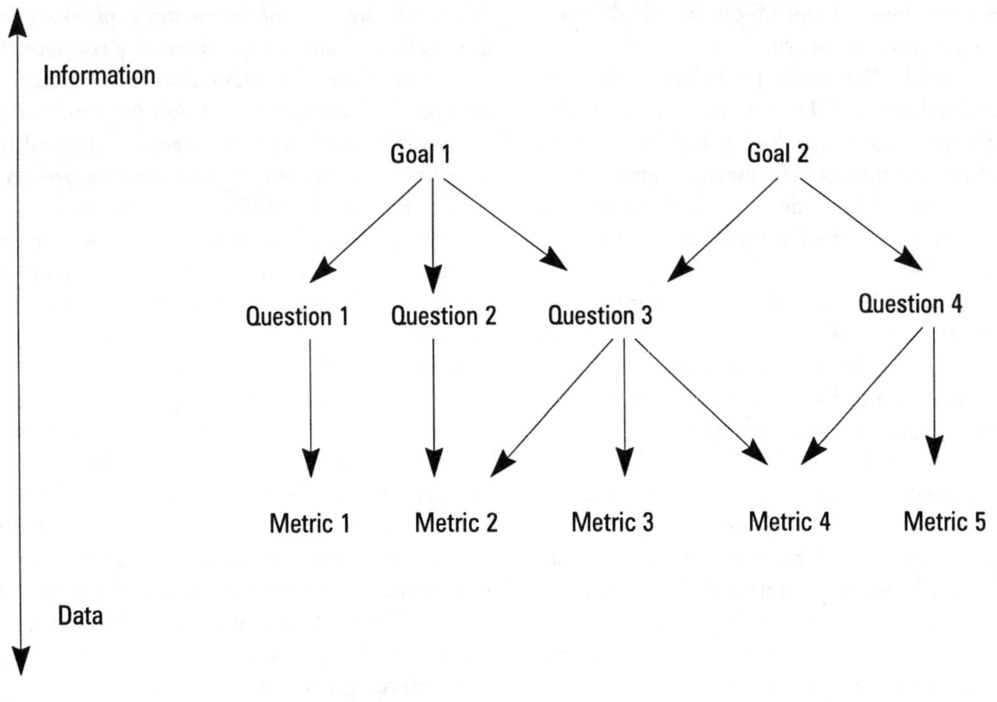

Information

Goal 1 Goal 2

Question 1 Question 2 Question 3 Question 4

Metric 1 Metric 2 Metric 3 Metric 4 Metric 5

Data

**Exhibit 3.** GQM Example

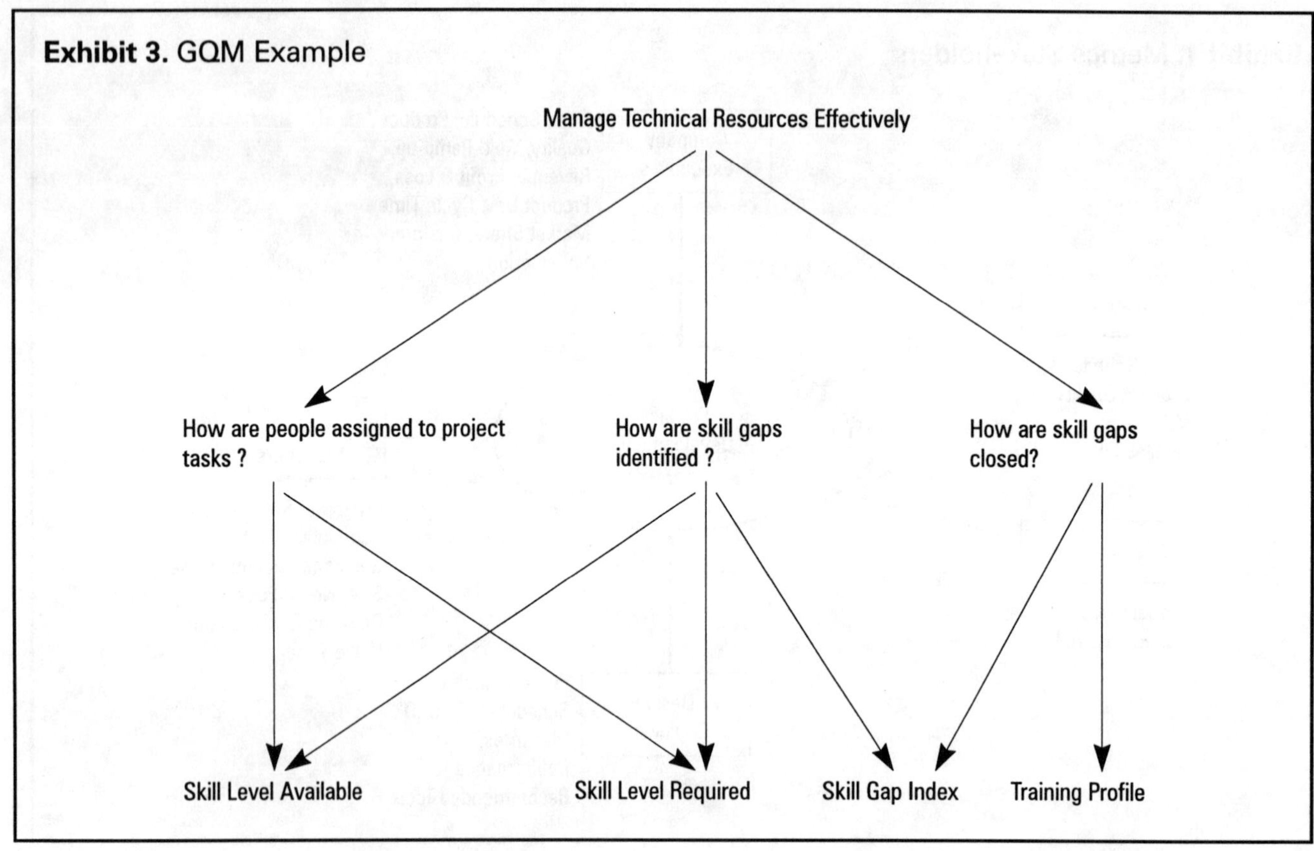


metrics such as cost, schedules, product quality and volume availability. This multiplicity of metrics requirements by different stakeholders, as shown in Exhibit 1, makes it impossible to describe product development simply by a single number and calls for a metrics framework.

A metrics framework that caters to different views of stakeholders has been developed. Detailed information is collected at the beginning of a project and at regular intervals during the execution of a project. The metrics framework is captured as a spreadsheet. Micro metrics and global metrics "bubble up" as different views of the collected data from spreadsheet calculations.

The metrics framework has been designed to capture different factors affecting the IC product development. A spreadsheet captures this in the form of a template. The metrics template is independent of any specific IC product development process details. However, the typical IC product development flow described in Section 2.0 and the generic steps involved in it are considered in designing the template. The reason for the metrics to be independent of the process details is because they are derived from the goals of the stakeholders using the Goal-Question-Metric (GQM) approach (Silverthorn 1995). The general concept of GQM is illustrated in Exhibit 2, and an example of applying GQM to a specific stakeholder issue is shown in Exhibit 3.

Currently, the global metrics include *time to market*, *design effort*, *on-time delivery*, *design quality index* and *designer productivity*. The micro metrics include *break-up of time to market*, *break-up of design effort*, *planning index*, *reuse index*, *CAD software index*, *hardware configuration*, *flow automation index*, *documentation index*, *lessons learned*, *reasons for multiple passes* and *skill information*. Although this categorization of metrics is based on typical IC design projects, it can be customized to suit other types of IC products.

The first sheet of the metrics spreadsheet gives a summary of the product. It has information about the product name, primary contact person, product team members, customers, product applications, manufacturing technology, salient design aspects and components, intellectual property generated and the design flow.

The second sheet captures quantitative data related to project execution. Major activities of product development are identified, following the milestones described in Section 2.0, as specification development, design, fabrication, silicon characterization and design assessment, assembly/test, qualification, redevelopment, customer qualification and release-to-production. A distinction is made between the activities related to the first pass of product development, and all the other activities (of passes 1.1, 1.2, 2.0, etc.) are classified under redevelopment. Against each of these major activities,

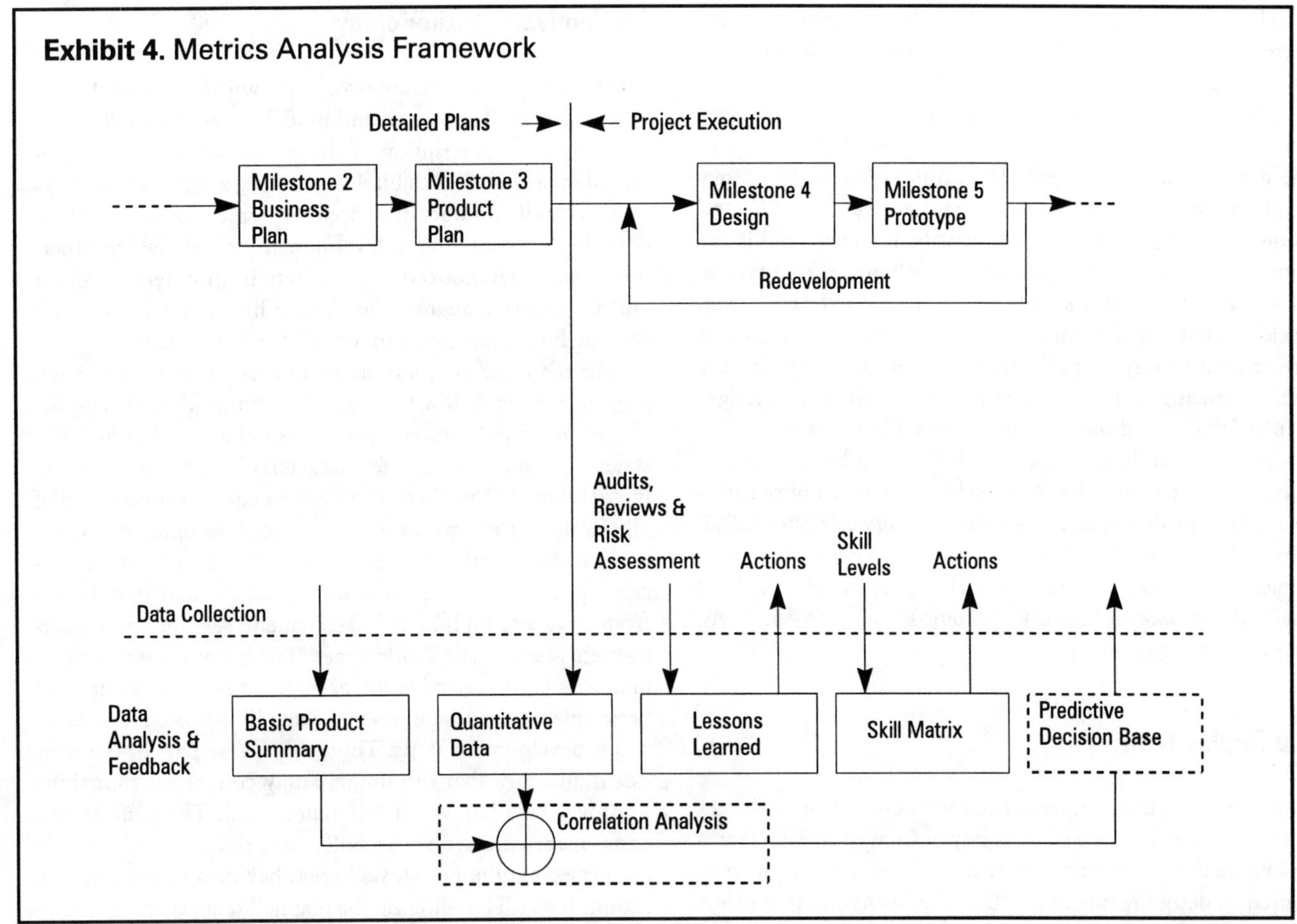


planned and actual staff months of effort by designers is collected. Finally, all the effort is added up to obtain the global metric of *design effort*. For different activities and for the complete project, *planning index* is calculated as (100 * Planned staff months / Actual staff months). It is to be noted that design effort data can be collected periodically during the execution of a project and can be synchronized with the milestone reviews. *On-time delivery*, a global metric, is defined as (100 * Customer required calendar months / Actual calendar months). Planned and actual calendar months for different activities are also collected as break-up of time to market information. The information on the minimum number of masks required, number of masks planned and actual number of masks released is collected. *Design quality index* is defined as (Minimum number of masks required / Number of masks released). All the masks released after the first pass are counted under the redevelopment activity. *Designer productivity* is defined as (Total number of transistors / Design effort). While counting the number of transistors, highly repetitive structures such as memory cores, are not included. *Reuse index* is calculated as the average of reuse of design tools, library cells, design modules and process/technology files. This is captured for design and redesign activities.

Computer Aided Design (CAD) tools and hardware resources play an important role during IC product development. For each CAD tool, time spent in learning, getting customization done and in fixing bugs is compared against the actual use time. An average over all the CAD tools gives the *CAD software index*. If a new tool is introduced and a lot of time is spent on getting it to work, then this number will be high. Similarly, if a tool crashes often and requires extensive support, again this number will be high. As part of the *hardware configuration*, information on total computing power, available memory/disk space and network efficiency is captured.

Different steps of a typical IC design flow (such as architecture definition, logic design, simulation, placement and routing, etc.) are rated on a five-point scale measuring the level of automation. A low rating on this scale indicates that a step is being done manually and vice versa. *Flow automation index* is calculated as the average of automation levels of individual design steps. Against each design step, fraction of the total design effort spent on that step is also recorded.

The third sheet of the metrics spreadsheet captures *lessons learned* in a free format. It also lists reasons for multiple passes and suggestions for avoiding them.

The last sheet contains the *skill matrix*. It is a form of capturing the skills required to execute a project and of the people working on that project. The ratings of skill proficiency levels range from an *entrant* to a *master*. *Generic skills* and *domain specific skills* are first identified. Generic skills are those skills which are required for development of a typical product (e.g., design, simulation, parasitic extraction and back annotation). Domain specific skills are those skills that are related to target application domains and very specific manufacturing technologies (e.g., sigma-delta filter design, 256M DRAM technology, etc.). The skill matrix is filled in for generic and domain specific skills at the beginning of a project to determine the skill level requirements of the project. The spreadsheet calculates the *skill required vector (SRV)*. Then, the skill level of each member of the project team assigned to the project is filled in. The spreadsheet calculates the *skill available vector (SAV)*. A comparison of *SRV* and *SAV* gives the *skill gap*.

## 4.0 Deployment

With the definition of metrics and the design of spreadsheet complete, the next step is to get buy in from the design teams to initiate data collection. The metrics framework can be presented to design teams to get their alignment and to address their concerns.

It is preferable to entrust the task of collecting metrics to a design support team that interfaces regularly with all the design projects so that the collection and interpretation of various metrics remain the same across projects. This is also important to ensure that the data collected over a period of time has predictive value. The design support person can meet a project leader at the beginning of the project and gather initial set of data related to product information, planning, skills required and skills available. Thereafter, at regular intervals of four to six weeks, the person collects data pertaining to CAD tools and hardware environment related issues from the project leader. At the end of the project, complete product information, such as number of modules, library cells, break up of design effort and lessons learned can be documented.

The data collection can be automated partially using workflow management tools, such as InConcert (Xsoft 1995).

## 5.0 Analysis Methodology

The metrics analysis framework, shown in Exhibit 4, provides the overall approach and model for analyzing the metrics. The basic description of the components has been presented in Section 3. Exhibit 4 shows only a subset of the tasks of a typical IC product development. A metrics methodology provides "visibility" to a development process which otherwise could go unnoticed (e.g., if there is no system to collect bull's eye charts, quantitative data of how many projects are on schedule at any given time is difficult to obtain).

The metrics analysis framework recognizes six key components (shown below the dotted line in Exhibit 4). The *Basic Product Summary* component is determined at an early stage and comprehends the characteristic of the product being developed. The *Quantitative Data* component consists of all the data from various steps of the development process that can be quantified. It corresponds to the global and micro metrics. The *Lessons Learned* component is obtained from reviews, audits, risk assessment sessions and postmortem sessions at all milestones. The lessons learned information is key to effective risk assessment sessions resulting in better planning, design, and in general improvements to all major development steps. Thus, this is one part of the metrics framework that can immediately contribute to making improvements happen at a detailed level. The *Skill Matrix* component consists of the skills required and available for project execution. For all skill areas having a significant gap, actions for skill building can be planned (e.g., training in specific areas). The skill matrix can be filled in at the end of a project to determine the skill improvements and as input to subsequent project planning.

The quantitative data, such as on-time delivery indicated by bull's eye charts, can help in initiating recovery plans in case of delays. However, the significant use of this data should be to look for trends and correlation when design effort, productivity and design quality are analyzed in relation to reuse, flow automation and information contained in the basic product summary. This is to provide a model of predictive value which is especially useful in project planning activities. The two components, *Correlation Analysis* and *Predictive Decision Base*, are drawn in dotted lines to indicate that systematic investigation is required before meaningful conclusions can be drawn to feed improvements into the development process. The long term analysis of quantitative data necessarily involves analysis of data across products. Hence, it is important to stratify this data set by product categories. If a trend is observed over a small number of products, technical reasons for that trend need to be explained to generalize it. However, if a trend is observed over a large number of products (e.g., more than ten), it immediately acquires a predictive value and should be considered as an input during planning.

The data can be analyzed for trends over multiple years. The deployment of a metrics framework facilitates data collection on a periodic basis which in turn can highlight trends over time. These trends provide the management a view of the impact of the development process and help focus attention on areas requiring improvements.

The data can also be used to benchmark product development activities against competitors' processes.

## Conclusions

This paper has described a comprehensive metrics framework for IC product development . This can be considered as the beginning of "IC engineering" analogous to software engineering. The paper has also addressed the deployment and data analysis.

The metrics collection should not be a significant overhead to product development. With the help of workflow management tools and advanced CAD flows, it should be possible to automate data collection. This results in accurate data and also in making data collection a part of the process.


### Acknowledgments

The authors wish to acknowledge the support received from the Texas Instruments Memory Methodology Metrics working group, the TI India IC Design Core Competency team, the TI Semiconductor Product Development Process Methods team, and the TI Corporate Metrics team.


### References


Armstrong G. 1995. Improving the semiconductor group product development process. Texas Instruments Technical Journal 12 (March-April) .

Stehlin B. 1995. The product development process based on the SC business process. Texas Instruments Technical Journal 12 (March-April).

Lynch R. and Cross K. 1995. *Measure Up!* Cambridge, MA: Blackwell Publishers.

Hegde S., Pal I. and Rao S. 1997. A product development flow with metrics for memory designs. IEEE International Workshop on Memory Technology, Design and Testing, San Jose, CA (August).

Silverthorn M. 1995. Sustaining software engineering process improvement: you get what you measure. International Conference on Software Engineering Practices, New Delhi, India (February).

*InConcert Education*. 1995. Cambridge, MA: Xsoft Advanced Information Technology.

# A Framework for Innovation

J. Levene, K. R. H. Goffin, Cranfield School of Management

## Introduction

It is widely acknowledged that companies need to be more innovative—they need to introduce products, services and new or improved processes on a regular basis. However, the management of innovation is a complex area, involving issues that span the organization, business strategy and its implementation.

It is an area that poses many questions for organizations. For example:

- How good are they at creating a pool of ideas for new products/services which match market needs?
- How good are they at choosing the right products and services to develop?
- How often do they typically introduce new products and how long does it typically take them?

These were the background questions that form the focus of this paper.

The time required to develop and introduce a new product, variously referred to as *time-to-market* or *cycle time,* is a key performance measure which is often targeted by companies for improvement. This is because "time to market is widely viewed as a key source of competitive advantage, particularly in fast-cycle industries" (Datar et al. 1997). But cycle-time is not the only aspect of innovation that needs improvement and this paper has a broad focus that considers innovation as a total process.

Without introducing new products frequently, companies can quickly lose competitiveness and market share—"if you do not innovate, old products will be overtaken by new technology" (Gourlay 1996). A recent survey of European manufacturing managers identified the ability to introduce new products as one of the key challenges now facing European companies (De Meyer and Pycke 1996). Several major companies who have recognized this have launched innovation initiatives. For example, an executive from the German company Siemens recently stated, "Any intelligent corporate strategy must have innovation at its very heart" (Houlder 1996a). Other companies which are also launching projects to promote more innovation include Renault, Philips, Ericson, British Telecom and BASF (Houlder 1996b).

## The Need for Innovation—Drivers

The factors that drive change and combine to create the need for companies to innovate have been examined by Sheth and Ram (1987). They have summarized the drivers of innovation as:

- The changing needs of the customer
- The changing business environment
- Competitors and competition
- Technological pressures

Innovation carries some risks and many new products either fail to get to market effectively or never reach their promised potential in the marketplace. Both of these situations point to a poor innovation process. The first, poor management of the product development process, the second poor choice of product. The effect on the company and its financial performance is much greater from the latter. The way to avoid these situations is to have a total product development process which is driven by an organization whose culture understands, encourages, rewards and lives innovation.

Comprehensive innovation encompasses not only improving product and service delivery but optimizes the underlying way in which an organization develops the right products, processes and services. New products and services are essential sources of revenue and profit in all markets; companies that fail to introduce them on a continual basis risk being overtaken by their competitors.

Research by Cranfield School of Management (Goffin et al. 1997) has shown that the leading companies in any industrial sector typically introduce ten times as many new products to the market as average companies. Becoming more innovative; more effective at successfully developing new products, processes and services and bringing them to market, is a difficult task but one which should not be left entirely to a specialist part of the organization. If innovation is seen as just the prerogative of just one department—typically the research and development department then the organization is cutting off valuable input and idea generation from those areas closer to the customer. In leading organizations, research and development is not a department but a state of mind—an obligation of each and every part of an organization.

In order to understand the complex process of innovation, a framework is an essential tool for management—to support and stimulate the process. Innovation can be viewed as a discrete process or a set of processes that start with creative input and finish with products or services delivered successfully to market. Input to the innovation process should come from all parts of the organization and ownership or at least responsibility for the overall process should be put in place so that it takes account of business strategies and policies. Regular checks and audits of the process should ensure that all parts of the organization continue to contribute.

## Innovation

The Oxford English dictionary defines "innovation" as "*Introducing something new*". From a business perspective this definition needs to be put into a more specific context, as restricting the interpretation of innovation to just new products is akin to limiting project management to critical path methods. Innovation in an organization can also be applied to product and service improvement and there is no reason not to widen the area of application even further to encompass business processes. So there are very few limits to the scope of innovation; potentially its application can lead to valuable increases in shareholder (or stakeholder) value.

### What innovation means in a business sense

Managing innovation is difficult and the question has even been asked "to what extent can product innovation be planned?" (Johne and Snelson 1988). A key problem is the wide range of factors which influence the success or failure of new products, including the generation of ideas, allocation of resources, the skill of key staff and the organization of development teams (ibid.). Gobeli and Brown (1993) identified the typical problems that companies face with managing product innovation. Problems exist at every stage of product innovation; from the creation of ideas, to the choice of the best ideas, to product development, to the introduction of products onto the market. Therefore, companies face a difficult task in trying to stimulate more efficient innovation.

One widely publicized approach by the 3M company has been the use of tough financial measures to highlight the importance of product innovation and stimulate the development of more new products. One goal used by 3M is that 30% of revenues must be generated by products less than four years old (The Economist 1995). However, managing innovation is difficult because it is not necessarily a logically structured process and despite the constant stream of publications on innovation, it is far from clear how best companies can become more innovative.

Data on companies' innovation rates is rarely published. Although companies such as Hewlett-Packard and 3M publish the amount of revenue which has been generated by new products in their annual reports, few other direct indications are available.

### The traditional "narrow" view of product-to-market

Much has been published on the need for companies to develop new products faster and therefore much emphasis has been placed on reducing cycle time (Datar et al. 1997). Fast New Product Development (NPD) is one of the key themes of Time Based Competition, which was largely promoted through the work of Stalk and Hout (1990) and has been a key focus in manufacturing industry since the end of the 1980s.

Fast cycle time is given credit in the business press with two main advantages. If the product which is introduced is a totally new concept, then being first-to-market enables a company to define key market requirements and establish itself before competitors enter the market. In established markets, introducing new products faster gives real competitive advantage, because products which reach the market sooner are credited with increased profit and market share (ibid.).

Although some researchers have found that faster cycle time affects market share positively, provided the lead over competitors was above a minimum *threshold* level (Datar et al. 1997), regrettably, the advantages of short cycle times are not backed by clear, unequivocal evidence in the wider business literature. For example, in a comprehensive study of the chemicals industry, Cooper and Kleinschmidt (1993) found that the link between fast cycle time and profitability was weak. Similarly, Ellis and Curtis (1995) showed that fast research and development in isolation does not lead to effective innovation and assert that "it is futile to expect large profit gains from shortening cycle time".

The focus in the literature on cycle time and its reduction implicitly assumes that the right products are being delivered and these fit the marketing and delivery strategies of the organization. By inference, for innovation to be a major influence on competitive advantage it must cover the upstream activities that link strategy to product (or service) delivery and therefore the view of innovation has to widened both in breadth and depth. The breadth of innovation should cover the subject areas not only of new products but also improvements to existing products, such as release of new models, version releases in software development or the use of new materials or formulations. The depth of innovation should cover both upstream and downstream activities i.e. the complete lifecycle of innovation from idea to customer delivery.

## Framing and Managing Innovation

How can innovation be managed effectively? The key issues in promoting innovation in an organization are:

1. Creating a common understanding of innovation and the need for every department (and not just primarily

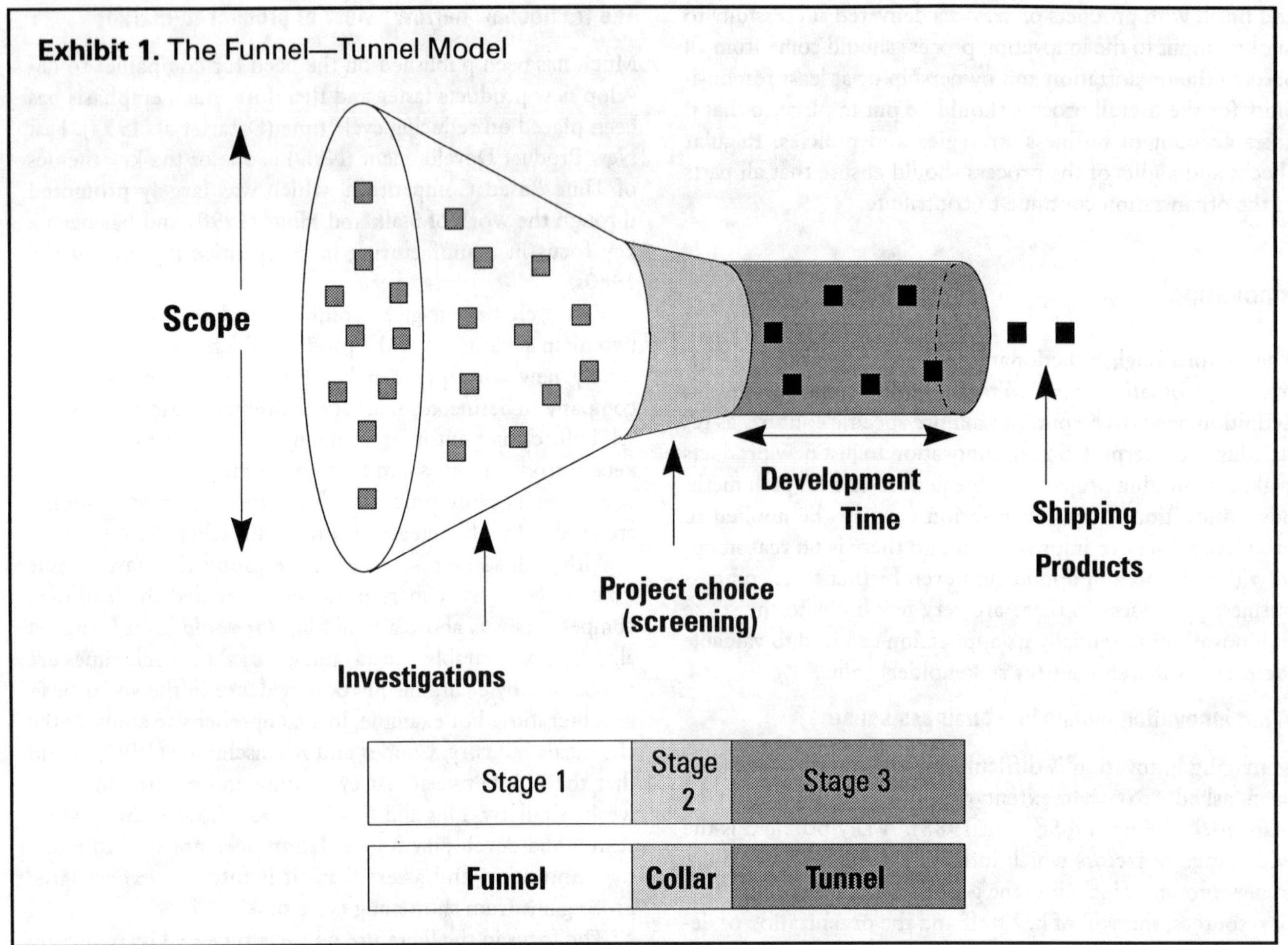


research and development) to actively contribute ideas on new products, processes and services.

2. Adopting measures which make innovation more quantifiable and therefore tend to stimulate a company's capacity for innovation. The combination of this and the previous point will effectively "institutionalize" innovation in the organization.
3. Ensuring that there is a recognized and effective process for choosing the best ideas for further development ("screening")
4. Developing the chosen products, processes and / or services in the quickest and most efficient way with the support of every department (project management).

Innovation and new product development should not be separated. This close integration is illustrated in Exhibit 1. The model which represents the three stages of the generic innovation process has been adapted from the ideas of Wheelwright and Clark (1995)

**Stage 1—"The Funnel"**

Innovation within a company should be an efficient process by which new ideas are first generated, collated and assessed (the "funnel"). The size of the funnel ("scope") should be set by the business strategy, which defines the areas and markets in which a company chooses to compete. Within the chosen scope, a wide range of ideas from a variety of sources are essential. In order to generate a wide range of high-quality ideas, it is essential that the full potential of an organization is realized and that all employees understand the nature of innovation and actively contribute to it. Creativity can play a key role in the generation of ideas and some leading companies have found that investments in training their staff in creativity techniques have paid dividends (Majaro 1988).

But creativity should not be limited to an occasional brainstorming session amongst a select few but should be encouraged by proactive communication between all levels of people in the organization, customers and suppliers. Such communication can take the form of "organized" creative initiatives using techniques such as Think Tanks and suggestion schemes (ibid.) or it can also be achieved by more casual methods of walk-about and "pizza" lunches.

Market research is often used to collect information on customer needs and therefore generate ideas for innovation. However, it should be noted that customers may not always be able to articulate all of their requirements. Therefore, there is opportunity for innovations which satisfy previously unknown needs and creates new markets. The *Walkman* personal stereo is a good example; it was developed without market research and demonstrates Sony's philosophy of using innovation to create new opportunities. As Morita, Sony's Chairman, puts it "We don't believe in doing market research for a new product unknown to the public. So we never do any. We are the experts"(Gill 1992).

Throughout this stage of idea generation and sorting many ideas will be discarded; they may be too difficult technically, they may require scarce skills or resources and there will also be many organization specific reasons for their rejection. The ideas may have potential for subsequent development and could warrant re-cycling at a later time, so recording and cataloguing of their details and reasons for rejection is a valuable source of future ideas.

### Stage 2—"The Collar"

Resources are nearly always limited and so it is essential not to squander them on the wrong projects. In Stage 2, (the "collar") the ideas need to be screened by management, with the best ones selected for in-depth analysis of their technical and commercial feasibility. Analysis of the reasons why projects have failed has identified five critical dimensions on which to evaluate projects. Screening projects against these dimensions will identify any potential problems, improve the project selection process and reduce risk. The dimensions that should be used as screening criteria for projects are:

- Fit with company goals and culture
- Technological feasibility
- Market value
- Regulatory issues
- Environmental issues

The techniques of financial evaluation of projects are well known and applied widely. Taking account of the various dimensions is more difficult and applying techniques such as, multi-choice decision making (Kepner and Tregoe 1965) or a "balanced scorecard" approach (Kaplan and Norton 1992) are more suitable at this stage.

Management needs to clarify the reasons for project selection or rejection and feed these back to the organization to improve the quality of future ideas. The final stage of screening leads to a number of ideas that are chosen to be developed (in the "tunnel") into new products, services or processes.

**Exhbit 2.** Narrow Creativity

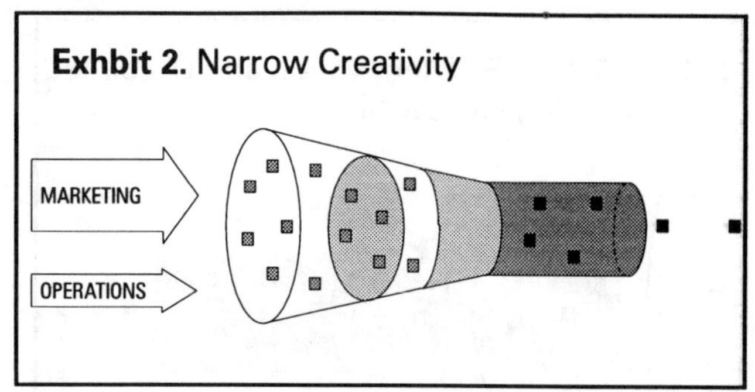


### Stage 3—"The Tunnel"

Project management has been the main support of the traditional development of new products or services to enable it to be quick and efficient. At many companies this stage has not been sufficiently integrated with the funnel. This can lead to products or services being developed without the whole organization being clear on how and why these projects were selected. The problems this can cause with project scope definition are enormous and, no doubt, has contributed to the failure or some product development. This, in turn, leads to problems of realization, implementation within the organization and how to deliver them to customers.

After faster NPD became recognized at the end of the 1980s as a pertinent goal for companies, there followed a wave of prescriptive articles on the ways in which it could be achieved (see, for example; Toepfer 1995). Many of these were based on anecdotal evidence from specific development projects which have questionable external validity. The widespread acceptance of anecdotal evidence allowed claims to be made that certain techniques would reduce cycle time significantly.

For example, one technique which was hailed as a major advance in reducing cycle time was Quality Function Deployment (QFD—a Japanese method for ensuring that customer requirements are accurately captured. Griffin (1992) has clearly shown this belief to be flawed. Another technique which has been prescribed as the way to accelerate new product development is concurrent engineering (CE), in which all functional areas commence work on NPD simultaneously. However without effective project management, CE can be difficult to apply.

## Application of the Model

Wheelwright and Clark (1995) report using their model several times as a basis for discussing innovation. Although it is a very simple approach, we have also found that presenting managers with the model allows them to articulate problems with innovation at their companies. Three examples of the results of these type of discussions are given below.

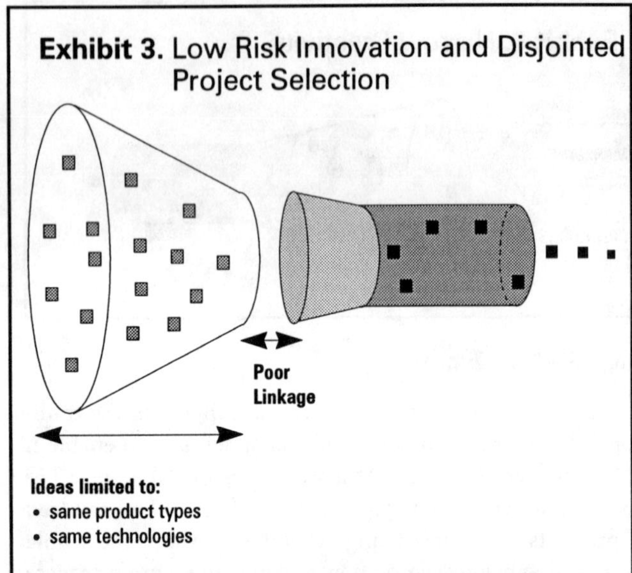


**Exhibit 3.** Low Risk Innovation and Disjointed Project Selection

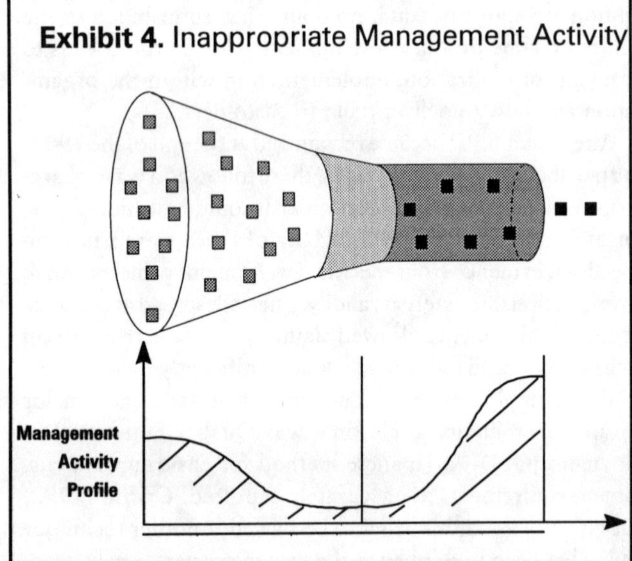


**Exhibit 4.** Inappropriate Management Activity

### a) International Airline

An operations manager was concerned that his company, an international airline, was less innovative than a major competitor—one which constantly developed new products (services). The Funnel & Tunnel was explained to the manager and he was asked to explain how it applied to his company. On his analysis of the funnel for collecting creative ideas for new products and services, he identified:

- The main source of ideas was a suggestion scheme which was inefficient and bureaucratic.
- Many employees probably do not understand what innovation means in the context of a service industry. Consequently they did not contribute ideas.
- Ideas for innovation were often developed by one part of the organization in isolation—cross-functional teams were not used for innovation management (see Exhibit 2).
- Following the discussions, the manager felt in a stronger position to improve innovation management and corresponding changes have been made to stimulate more innovation by bringing different parts of the organization together to work on new ideas.

### b) Automotive Parts Supplier

This company is the European market leader for specific car components. Management were aware that they were not as innovative as their main competitor—a company that had entered the market only a few years before but had since introduced new products on a regular basis. Management identified problems in both their Funnel & Tunnel.

Ideas collected in the funnel were always limited to low risk—same type of products, same technologies—options. Their whole product portfolio was, viewed critically, in their own words a set of good product line extensions but nothing more.

This led to a number of problems:

- The management of the Tunnel was poor with very wide variations in time-to-market between projects.
- The link ("collar") between the projects selected and the market knowledge was low, resulting in a relatively high rate of failures.

As a consequence of the Funnel & Tunnel discussions, the company has introduced a tighter NPD process and now includes a risk analysis in its portfolio management. Risk is now viewed as a necessity on a portion of the product portfolio.

### c) Household Goods

This company is a UK-based market leader for household goods. They have a reputation for technology and have a charismatic managing director with an engineering background. The Funnel & Tunnel model showed that the management team did not spend sufficient management time working on reviewing projects at the "collar" stage. The managing director liked to be involved in stimulating innovative ideas (many of which had in the past come from him directly), his continuing involvement resulted in:

Fire-fighting the delays on new product introductions.

Little time devoted to project selection.

This became patently clear to the management team when they were asked to draw the "Management Activity Profile" (amount of time they spent on projects over the innovation cycle).

The above diagram (Exhibit 4) shows that they were active at the ideas stage and the time leading up to market launches. However, too little time was spent on project selection—project selection was (literally) the last item (number six) of the six monthly management meeting agenda. Consequently, projects were reviewed in a rush at the end of the meetings. This meant that too little analysis was done and research and development received no clear feedback on why certain projects were selected whilst others were rejected.

The project selection process is now a separate management meeting where a whole day is devoted to close discussions with research and development leading to project selection.

## Conclusions

Faster NPD cannot be achieved simply by applying project management techniques to the downstream activities of innovation. Broader organizational aspects also need to be considered. In addition the skills and motivation of the people working on innovation is crucial, as is their commitment to fast cycle time.

However, this is an under-researched area. Many questions remain to be answered and they should be addressed by empirical research. The case studies illustrate some of the lessons that companies can learn by "stepping back" and analyzing their innovation process.

In conclusion, it can be said that there is a wide range of techniques for faster NPD that contribute to the framing of innovation, but that the use of any of these will not, in itself, guarantee reduced cycle times. Bringing the right products to market faster is the responsibility of everyone involved in innovation and it is essential to engender the right attitudes, encouragement and commitment throughout the organization.

The Funnel and Tunnel Model offers a framework for further understanding the intricacies and relationships of the process of innovation.

### References


Datar, S., Jordan, C.C., Kekre, S., Rajiv, S. and Srinivasan, K. Advantages of Time-Based New Product Development in a Fast-Cycle Industry. *J. of Marketing Research*, Vol. XXXIV, No. 1, February 1997, pp36-49.

Gourlay, R. Innovation Roulette—How do you Launch a New Product while ensuring the Old Model keeps earning. *Financial Times*, 23rd January, 1996, p147

De Meyer, A. and Pycke, B. Falling Behind in Innovation: The 1996 Report on the European Manufacturing Futures Survey. *INSEAD Working Paper Series*, No. 96/95/TM, 1996.

Houlder, V. Management: Innovation under the Spotlight. *Financial Times*, 22nd January 1996, p131.

Houlder, V. Technology: Quiet Revolution. *Financial Times*, 26th March 1996, p143.

Goffin, K., Szwejczewski, M. and New, C. Innovation Levels in UK Manufacturing Industry: An Exploratory Study. *4th International Product Development Conference, Stockholm*, 26-27th May, 1997

Sheth, J.N. and Ram, S. *Bringing Innovation to Market: How to break Corporate and Customer Barriers.* Wiley (1987)

Johne, F.A. and Snelson, P.A. Success Factors in Product Innovation: Selective Review of the Literature. *J. Prod. Innov. Manag.*, Vol. 5, No. 2, June 1988, pp114-128.

Gobelli, D.H. and Brown, D.J. Improving the Process of Product Innovation. *Research Technology Management*, Vol. 36, No. 2, 1993, pp38-44.

Anonymous. Unthinking Shrinking. *The Economist*, Vol. 337, No. 7941, 9th September, 1995, p46.

Stalk, G. Jr. And Hout, T.M. *Competing Against Time* Free Press 1990

Cooper, R.G. and Kleinschmidt, E.J. Major New Products: What Distinguishes the Winners in the Chemical Industry? *J. Prod. Innov. Manag.*, Vol. 10, No. 2, March 1993, pp90-111.

Ellis, L.E. and Curtis, C.C. Speedy R&D: How Beneficial? *Research Technology Management*, Vol. 38, No. 4, July-August 1995, pp42-51.

Wheelwright, S.C, and Clark, K.R. *Product Development Challenge: Competing through Speed, Quality and Creativity* Harvard Business Review 1995

Majaro, S. *The Creative Gap: Managing Ideas for Profit* Longman 1988

Gill, G.K. Sony Corporation; Workstation Division. *HBR Case Study* 9-960-031 (1992)

Kepner, C.H. and Tregoe, B.B. *The Rational Manager—a Systematic Approach to Problem Solving and Decision Making* Macmillan 1965

Kaplan, R.S. and Norton, D.P. The Balanced Scorecard—Measures that Drive Performance *Harvard Business Review* Vol. 70 Iss. 1 Jan./Feb. 1992 pp71-79

Toepfer, A. New Products—Cutting the Time to Market. *Long Range Planning*, Vol. 28, No. 2, 1995, pp61-78.

Griffin, A. Evaluating QFD's Use in US Firms as a Process for Developing Products. *J. Prod. Innov. Manag.*, Vol. 9, No. 2, June 1992, pp171-187.

# Schedule Control for High-Technology Product Development: Challenges and Solutions

Amjad S. Hanif, Intel Corporation
Bret Nobley, Intel Corporation

## 1. Introduction

Intel Chairman Andy Grove best described the state of the electronics industry with the title of his recent book, *Only the Paranoid Survive*. With the rapid shift of computing paradigms and explosive growth in demand, achieving great success in a market segment has proven to be a difficult task. Mainstays like IBM, Intel, and Hewlett-Packard are constantly at risk of falling behind the competition. As recent events indicate, the primary guarantors of success are innovation and time-to-market, causing project performance to be more critical than ever.

The aggressive nature of today's business environment has led to an emphasis on schedule control practices for the purpose of improving project performance. While casual approaches to scheduling may have sufficed in a previous era, upstarts and stalwarts agree that a formal project controls methodology is now indispensable. This paper draws upon the recent experience of large-scale microprocessor design programs at Intel Corporation in identifying the challenges which confront schedule control. After examining issues ranging from the nature of design work to the growing size of engineering teams, the focus turns to the methodology that has been developed to meet these challenges.

## 2. Challenges to Schedule Control

Several factors complicate the job of schedule control with regard to high-technology projects. The causes range from the industry's relatively recent adoption of PM practices to other factors unique to integrated circuit design.

### Nature of Product Design

Estimating durations for project tasks is inherently difficult for cutting-edge products. Unlike projects in other industries, this type frequently sets out to explore uncharted waters. The technical goals are usually based on the development of enabling technologies over the course of the project. Because these goals are ambitious, the breakthrough dependency introduces a high degree of uncertainty, which manifests itself in schedules that continually slip beyond baseline and spiral over budget.

For most projects, historical data is an adequate estimating tool. However, in the case of microprocessor design, the relevant technology changes so rapidly that past performance does not correlate directly with the scope of future programs. The challenge lies with the controller to develop methods for building schedules that take into account the uncertainty inherent in experimental design.

### Focus on Speed

Time-to-market is so crucial today that the division between success and failure for projects can be measured in weeks. At Intel, first-line technical managers are responsible for each of their team's schedules. Because of the competitive need to complete the design quickly, milestone dates receive particular attention from management. The technical managers are placed under intense pressure to build schedules that agree with the project commit dates and, not surprisingly, the schedules which they develop are often prone to slippage. Furthermore, the top-down developed plans do not always reflect the reality of conditions at the front-lines. The challenge for project controllers is to develop methods to overcome the tendency toward optimistic schedules and ensure that realistic plans are being developed.

Because time is so important, the control methodology must also be designed so that it is flexible and capable of keeping up with the rapid pace of the project. In most instances, frequent updates to the schedule are necessary, perhaps on a weekly basis. The absence of frequent updates can relegate the schedule to a mechanism for project reporting rather than control.

### Growth in Team Sizes

For the earliest microprocessors, design teams larger than fifteen engineers were extremely rare. Currently, the industry has seen a dramatic rise in the number of designers required for each generation of a product, due primarily to the growing size and complexity of integrated circuits. Barring major productivity breakthroughs, the trend toward larger teams will continue into the next century. The greater complexity leads to an increase in resources and deliverables, and complicates the process of schedule management. These factors test the limits of current software tools and project control methods. Furthermore, as teams grow in size, some companies have resorted to spreading them over several corporate sites. This geographical dispersion of teams impacts communication and coordination between project sites, and has a direct influence on the ability to manage a project.

### Manager Resistance

While not necessarily a factor in every organization, manager resistance can become a major barrier to effective project control. In the past, some technical managers have demonstrated an aversion toward formalized scheduling practices. Engineering managers are often uncomfortable revealing schedules to their counterparts because they fear criticism of their schedules and possibly exposing lower productivity. Also, a lack of training in project management practices causes engineering managers to be reluctant about relinquishing control to a process they do not readily understand and often leads to complaints about the time required for "unproductive" planning work. Furthermore, in the absence of centralized project control, managers have complete autonomy over reporting their progress. Self-reporting often prompts a simple, yet inadequate "we're on schedule" response. While this may be said with the best of intentions, experience has shown that without formal training, managers are ill-equipped to plan beyond the current horizon. A formal control methodology can supply data to chart everyone's performance and judge the quality of their plans.

## 3. Building the Schedule

Taken together, the previously mentioned barriers create a formidable challenge for any project controls team. Over the course of recent design programs at Intel, a process has been developed to manage these schedule issues from startup to close.

The project team begins by building the initial work breakdown structure (WBS). The internal Project Controls Group (PCG) facilitates a meeting with senior technical managers to determine how the standard design flow should be adapted for use on the project. Manager involvement at this level is imperative for the purpose of building an accurate baseline and gaining commitment to the process. During this step, key milestones are identified and defined by the managers. The PCG utilizes the WBS to build a sample network diagram of the design flow, which in turn forms the basis of a critical path model created with commercial software. Projects are typically divided into several design teams; subteams within each team follow the standard flow to complete their responsibilities. All sub-team managers are given the schedule template to model their team's design duties. The files are then integrated into a master schedule, with each manager owning their team's schedule.

**Exhibit 1.** Weekly Update Cycle

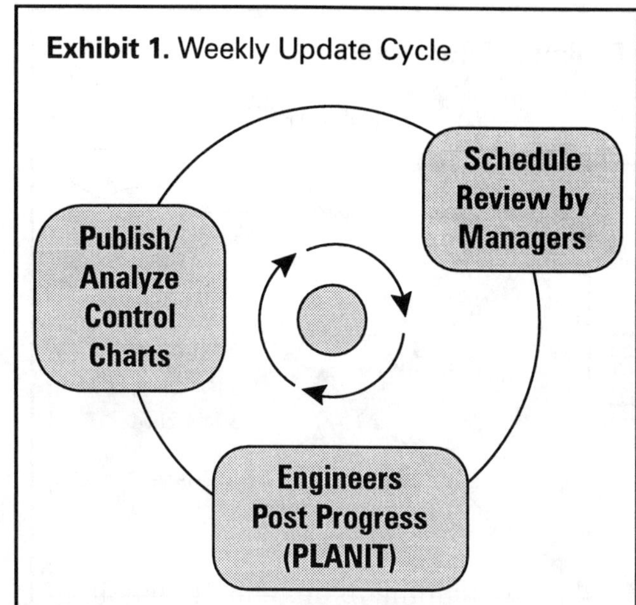


The large size of the teams and the focus on speed dictate the use of a schedule with a high degree of accountability. As a result, the project schedules are designed as entirely resource-driven models. This requires the manager to assign each task in the schedule to a specific individual. The manager also determines the number of days of pure work required (Effort) and the rate at which the person will work (Work-Rate); the duration of the activity is calculated as Effort divided by Work Rate. Most scheduling packages allow tasks to be modeled in this fashion.

To improve accountability, each resource on the team is also assigned a standard set of tasks which represent their non-design responsibilities. The set includes activities such as training, unplanned work (Work-Rate); the duration of the activity is calculated as Effort divided by Work Rate. Most scheduling packages allow tasks to be modeled in this fashion.

To improve accountability, each resource on the team is also assigned a standard set of tasks which represent their non-design responsibilities. The set includes activities such as training, unplanned work, and attending meetings. The ultimate goal of this kind of detail is to assess productivity at the project level and to use the data in identifying obstacles to progress. This information is also used to revise future plans.

## 4. Updating the Schedule

The next step in the process is to create a system for updating the schedule on a consistent basis. As noted above, the unwieldy nature of design work and the focus on speed mandate a frequently updated schedule. Based on these needs, a

**Exhibit 2.** Effort Trend

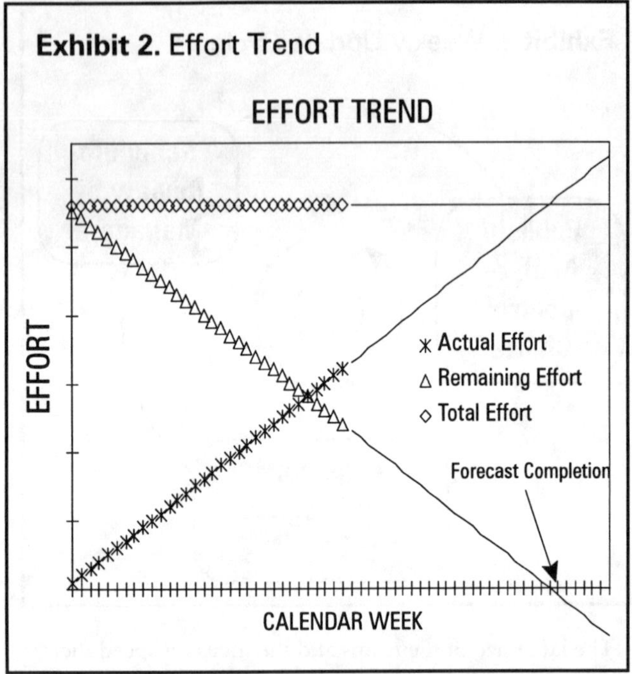


cycle of weekly updates, reviews, and analyses is used on the project.

### Manager's Review

The first step of the cycle shown in Exhibit 1 calls for managers to review their schedules. The managers, in cooperation with a member of the PCG, follow a checklist of steps. First, they review key milestone dates and look for any that have slipped or contracted since the previous week. After understanding the reasons behind any changes, they are assisted with a review of the team's critical path. In addressing this issue, managers make adjustments to the task's remaining Effort and Work-Rate as necessary. Finally, each resource's loading profiles are reviewed and the workload is adjusted as needed. During the weekly review period, managers are also expected to resolve any schedule issues that are raised in previous staff meetings.

### Posting Progress

At the cycle's second step, the schedule is updated based upon the work performed during the previous week. Experience has shown that top-down schedules from managers fail to capture the true scope of work involved. Since the best estimates come from those actually engaged in the work, any update routine must incorporate bottom-up feedback. Such feedback serves as a "sanity check" to ensure that realistic plans are being published and counteracts the tendency of managers to build optimistic schedules. On a large microprocessor design program, gathering responses from every participant on a consistent basis requires a massive logistical undertaking.

In order to accomplish this task, a software application was developed internally to run under UNIX. The tool, called PLANIT, is similar to commercially available time sheet applications. Once launched, PLANIT automatically identifies the user and shows a list of changes which their manager has made to the schedule since the previous week. The user then has the option to accept or deny the changes. If declined, the changes will be reversed in the schedule file and the manager notified via email of their refusal. In the next step, the posting screen displays all of the design and non-design tasks assigned to the engineer in the master schedule. In a corresponding cell, the user records the time spent working on each task during the previous week. The software subtracts the posted effort from the remaining effort. Engineers also have the option to manually increase or decrease the remaining effort on a task, giving them the power to modify their manager's schedules. Users can also re-open previously closed tasks and create new ones within the schedule. Hence, PLANIT is a tool which tracks the performance of a team and brings control of the schedule down to the people responsible for the day-to-day work.

The posting period lasts 36 hours and the names of people who have not posted are subsequently reported to their managers. At the cutoff time, the updates are imported into the schedule so that a report may be generated and sent to each team manager. The report shows the amount of time posted to every activity by each resource and any adjustments in the remaining effort which result in a duration change.

### Published Control Charts and Analyses

The initial steps of the weekly cycle ensure that the schedule is consistently updated by the users and managers. The final phase involves publishing the revised charts and analyses based on the fresh schedule. The suite of charts is specifically designed to audit the quality of schedules and status the team on their progress. These published reports are used in weekly staff meetings to identify critical issues and areas of improvement.

## 5. Selected Control Charts

### Effort Trend

The effort chart tracks each team's performance on a weekly basis through the life of the project. The y-axis represents Effort in person-days, while the x-axis portrays the calendar weeks spanning the course of the project. Three points are plotted for each week: "Actual Effort" (AE), "Remaining Effort" (RE), and "Total Effort" (TE). The RE line on the chart is a summation of the remaining effort on all design tasks in a team's schedule. Similarly, the AE line is the running total of the effort that has been posted against all tasks in the schedule. The TE is the weekly sum of the remaining and actual effort.

Several observations can be made regarding this chart. First, the RE line should correspond to the headcount available to the team. For example, if a team has 5 people assigned to it for four weeks, the remaining effort should be no more or less than 20 workdays x 5 people, or 100 person-days. A larger number indicates that resources are overloaded and that work is unlikely to be completed on-time without corrective action. A number less than headcount might suggest that some of their responsibilities are not being modeled by the manager, or that the team has a surplus of resources.

The Remaining Effort line should also trend down each week at a rate equal to the team's headcount. As the engineers post their time, that number is subtracted from the remaining effort on each task. Continuing the previous example, the 5 person team should have remaining effort decline by 5 engineers x 5 days/week, or by 25 person-days per week. Time that is posted to non-design activities does not reduce the remaining effort on design tasks, and hence, the above example is a best-case scenario which assumes 100 percent productivity. The difference in slope between actual effort and remaining effort trends indicates how much work is not contributing directly to the design goals. The form of the line is also a key indicator of project status. Periods of time where the remaining effort trend has a near zero slope exemplify cases in which specific issues may be hampering progress.

**Exhibit 3.** Effort Distribution

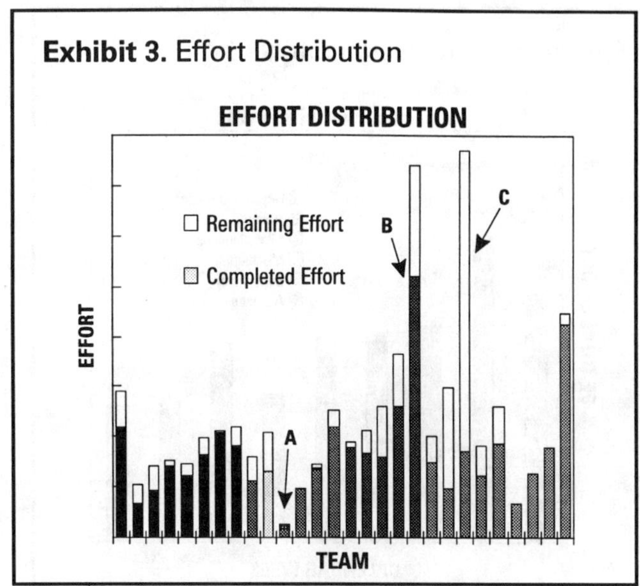


The Remaining Effort line is also used to predict when each team will likely finish based upon their recent performance. This is accomplished by drawing a best-fit line over a range of data points, usually the previous five to thirteen weeks. The line is projected until it intersects the x-axis, at which point, remaining effort equals zero. The x-intercept indicates the forecast completion date. An important measure of the schedule quality is the difference between the date pre-

**Exhibit 4.** Early Finish Profile

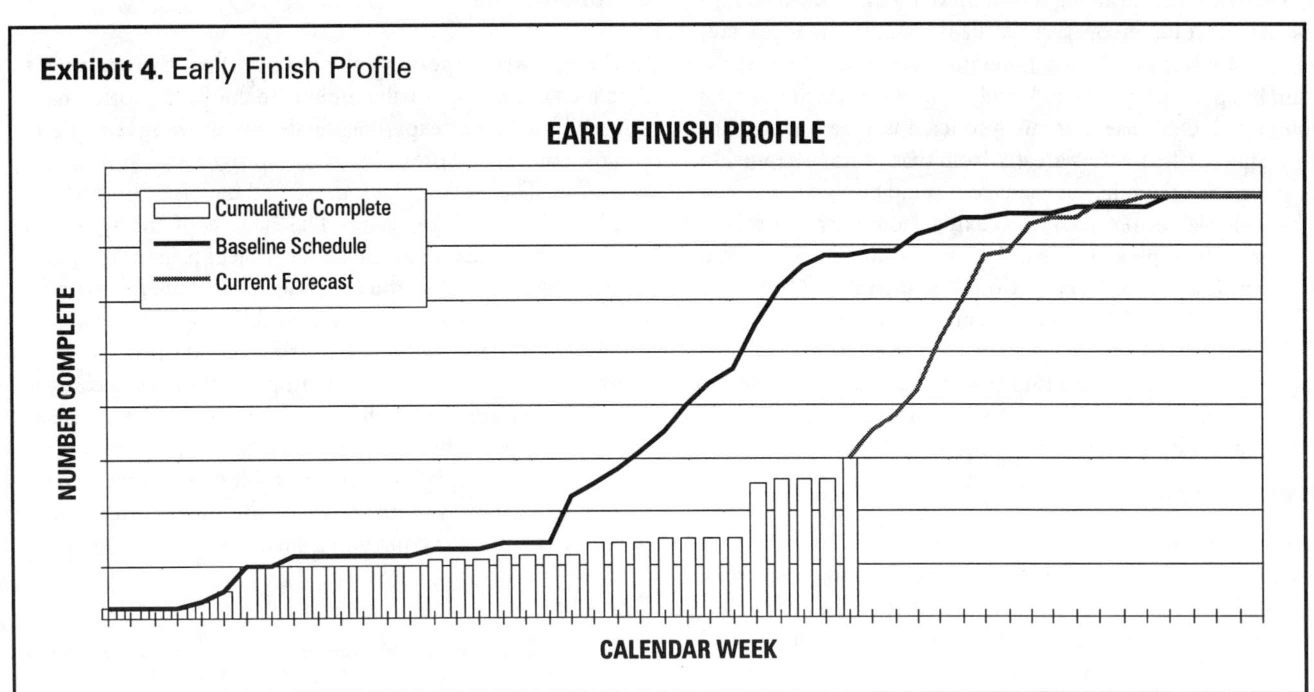

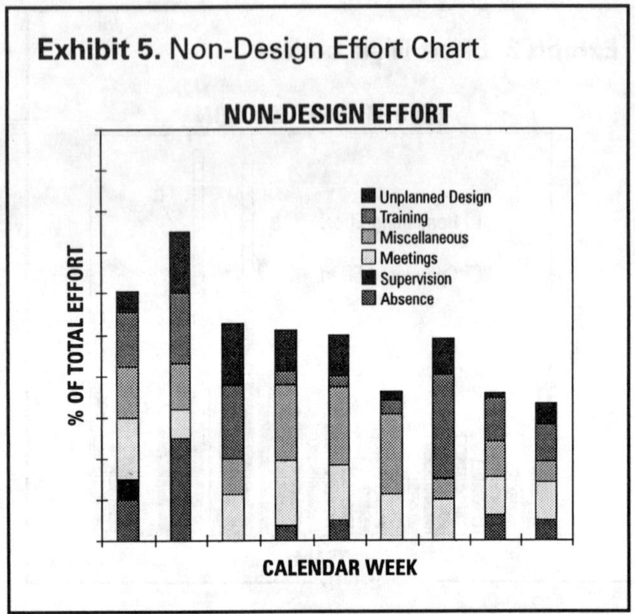

Exhibit 5. Non-Design Effort Chart

dicted by the effort trend and the date indicated by their critical path model.

The Total Effort line is the combination of the actual and remaining points. A slope of zero is preferred, indicating that the overall effort estimate has not changed. The most dangerous case in such projects is a line which steadily creeps upward.

### Effort Distribution

Another key chart, Effort Distribution (Exhibit 3) is used to compare effort estimations between teams on the same design activity (i.e., drawing schematics). Again, the y-axis represents effort in person-years while the x-axis provides a column for each team. Each column portrays the total effort the team has planned for the task and the portion which has been completed. One case that raises concern is a team whose total planned effort varies greatly from that of other teams. In auditing the schedule, the manager should be able to explain why their plan differs to such an extent from the other teams.

Three examples are described in Exhibit 3: A) a team which has estimated far less effort than the others; B) a team which has planned for much greater effort; and C) a team which has completed a proportionally lower amount of their total effort. Using the chart in this manner can be a basis for not only improving plans, but resource balancing between teams to ensure everyone can complete on-time.

### Early Finish Profile

Based on a summary of the early finish dates for a particular task, a profile can be created to show the ramp to completion. The design of this chart identifies progress at the project level. The y-axis indicates the number of teams to reach the milestone and the x-axis represents calendar weeks. The baseline profile comes from the initial schedule and shows the cumulative number of teams planning to reach the milestones each week during the life of the project. As data is collected each week, the actual number of teams to reach the milestone is plotted as a column. A line is drawn from the current week onward to show the profile based on the most current schedule. By drawing attention to overall slips, the chart can identify cases where project-wide factors may be impeding progress.

### Non-Design Effort

The wealth of data generated by the weekly cycle also lends itself to tracking an often overlooked, yet significant component of projects. During the posting process, each engineer also posts to non-design categories. The chart shows, on a weekly basis, how much time was posted to each category as a percentage of their total effort. This enables managers to be aware of the non-design factors that affect employee productivity.

### Specific Research

Aside from the standard suite of charts, the methodology also allows very specific research to be done. From the project database, detailed information can be extracted regarding performance against schedule. In diagnosing schedule slips, managers frequently request data about their team from previous weeks. Using the data generated in the posting cycle, a very detailed analysis can be done to show exactly where engineers have been posting their time. Such an analysis lends itself to identifying barriers to improved productivity.

## 6. Conclusions

As the industry forges into the next century, the challenges described in this paper will continue to confront project managers. The nature of experimental design, growing team sizes, and the competitive pressures, show no signs of abating in the near term. The methodology presented here is a comprehensive response to these issues. The success of the system is based on the inclusion of the entire project team in the planning process, and a rigorous analysis of the schedule data by the project controls group. The weekly cycle serves as the backbone of the system. The posting required of the engineers each week facilitates bottom-up feedback and helps ensure that they agree with the plans their managers are making. The data from the updates is used by the project controls team to audit the quality of plans and identify areas of concern. This iterative process provides the timely information which is essential for controlling such fast-paced projects.

## Reference

Archibald, Russell D. 1992. *Managing High-Technology Programs and Projects*. New York: John Wiley & Sons, Inc.

# Resource Allocation Information System for the Next Century

J. Reddy Nukalapati, MS, PMP, Lucent Technologies

## Introduction

Resource allocation is a strategic activity for all organizations, large or small, since there are always more opportunities than available resources. This paper describes a way of managing scarce resources through a resource allocation process. This is accomplished by focusing more on customers and less on traditional product lines.

Lucent Technologies designs, develops, manufactures, and markets communications systems and technologies ranging from microchips to entire networks. Business Communications Systems (BCS) is one of the four main divisions at Lucent Technologies. BCS develops and supports communications systems for business enterprises around the globe. Our customers range in size from small businesses with two or three telephones to larger corporations with voice and data networks stretching throughout the world.

The key function I will describe to you is strategic portfolio management. Resource allocation decisions have a significant impact on the availability of new product and service platforms and underlying technologies. Delivering high quality products and services to the market at the right time is critical to business success. To develop those offers, platforms and core technologies building blocks must be available in advance. BCS continues to emphasize reducing the cycle time. Project management skills are critical to the achievement of this objective.

Prior to 1996, BCS was organized by product lines with a general manager responsible for revenue and profit and loss for each product line. Resources were assigned to each product line. Movement of resources between product lines was very slow. Because of the extended time it took to move resources between product lines, it was very difficult to shift resources to respond to new opportunities in the market place in a timely way.

In addition, there was no systematic information available on projects across platforms. It was therefore difficult to measure the performance of the division on all projects. There was a high degree of concern at the senior management level that resource utilization was not optimized.

## New Approach to Resource Allocation

The senior management team decided on a new approach to resource allocation. Rather than managing resources solely by product lines, a senior leadership forum was established, to make investment decisions based on the relative merits of all projects. The forum could identify low performance projects and reassign resources to projects with higher performance potential.

At the same time, the senior team wanted to move the investment portfolio in strategic directions. They also wanted to reinforce product development processes to reduce time-to-market.

### Implementation for Resource Allocation

A standard electronic form was established to collect the necessary information from users. We have established a user group, which is a small subset of users, to review customer feedback. The electronic profile form covered the following major areas:

- Project name, description, contact, group name
- Primary focus, priority
- Product market focus, customer segmentation
- Business case/ financial information
- Key decision gates
- Costs for all support organizations

Exhibit 1 illustrates a section of the profile form covering customer segmentation and associated business screens.

## Information System

One of the major challenges was collecting information from 100+ users in multiple locations. In order to test the concept, a subset of key data was collected in an Excel Spreadsheet for quick analysis. Later, a database was established in Microsoft Access, with a Word template as an input document. This allowed one person, the database administrator, to collect data and upload it into one pc. Summary reports were then distributed to users, since users did not have direct access to the database. The common complaint was that the user could not see all the information since it was maintained in a database split in multiple tables on a pc. In addition, updates become a

Exhibit 1.

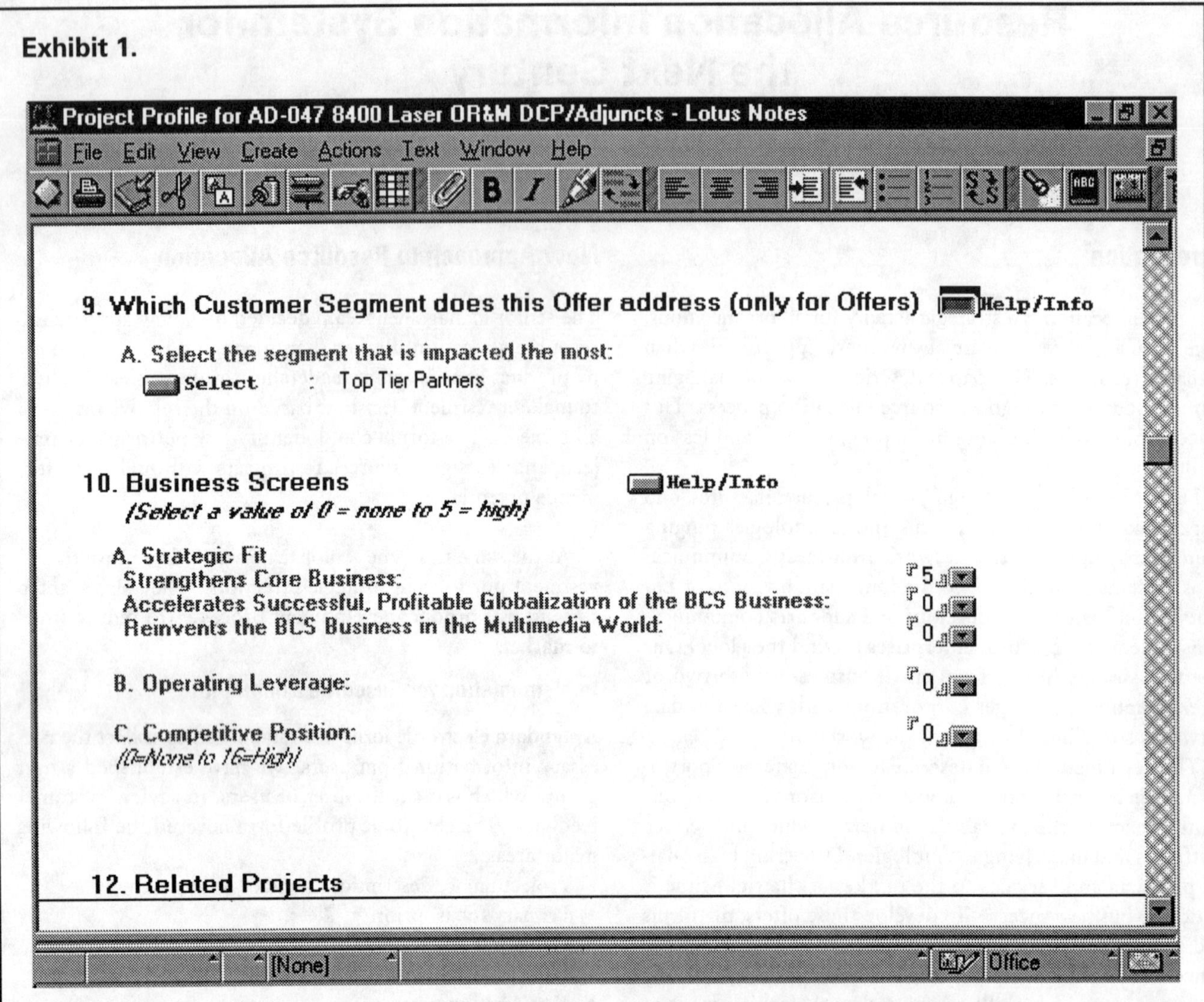


major event and could not be accomplished by the user on timely basis. Collecting project updates even twice a year proved to be a major task.

To improve the user interface, Lotus Notes was selected as the system to maintain all profile information on-line. With the Lotus Notes implementation, all project information was visible to the user as a document. The user can read, update and print the information at any time and in any place, provided network access is available. The system also provides quick on-line help for the user. This greatly reduced the significant problems associated with providing instructions and documentation to all users.

## Criteria for Ranking Projects

The set of criteria shown in Exhibit 2 were used to help rank projects. Each criterion had a score of 1 to 5. The project score was then calculated based on the score for each criterion. These criteria are described below:

- *Product-Market Newness:* this is a score based on whether the project involves a new or current product, and whether it is being offered to new or current markets.
- *Discounted Revenue:* It is revenue discounted by the weighted cost of capital
- *Percent ROS:* It is the ratio of Operating Income to Revenue
- *Net Present Value* (NPV) *Payout:* This is the ratio of Net Present Value to the development expenses required for the project; Includes R&D, Marketing, and Advertising;

**Exhibit 2.**

| Score | Product / Market Newness (1) | Financial | | Attractiveness Criteria | | | |
|---|---|---|---|---|---|---|---|
| | | Disc Revenue | % ROS | NPV Payout | Risk Adj. Factor | Strategic Thrust Score | Time To Market (days) |
| 1 | C/C = 1 | < 9 | < 17% | < 1 | < .4 | < 1.5 | 460 > |
| 2 | N/C = 2 | 9 - 45 | 17% - 27% | 1 - 2 | .4 - .58 | 1.5 - 2.5 | 210 - 460 |
| 3 | C/N = 3 | 45 - 85 | 27% - 38% | 2 - 4 | .58 - .67 | 2.5 - 3.5 | 140 - 210 |
| 4 | N/N = 4 | 85 - 145 | 38% - 50% | 4 - 7 | .67 - .8 | 3.5 - 4.5 | 30 - 140 |
| 5 | | 145 > | 50% > | 7 > | .8 > | 4.5 > | < 30 |

(1) C/C = Current Product / Current Market
N/C = New Product / Current Market
C/N = Current Product / New Market
N/N = New Product / New Market

| Overall | Score |
|---|---|
| H | > 18 |
| M | 14 - 17 |
| L | < 13 |

**Exhibit 3.**

| Project | Project Analytical Overview | | | Project Reference Points | | |
|---|---|---|---|---|---|---|
| | Mkt Entry & Expansion | Financial | Business Screens | Revenue ( $ in Millions ) | R & D ( $ in Millions ) | Ship Date |
| **High Attractiveness Projects** | | | | | | |
| A | High | High | Medium | 231.2 | 0.7 | 4/16/97 |
| **Medium Attractiveness Projects** | | | | | | |
| B | Low | High | Medium | 163.6 | 1.8 | 9/30/96 |
| **Low Attractiveness Projects** | | | | | | |
| C | Medium | Low | Low | 8.5 | 0.9 | 10/1/96 |

In the future, all support organization expenses such as training, material logistics, etc., will be included.

- *Risk Adjustment Factor:* This is an indication of the implied risk of attaining the financial objectives. During the first cycle, we asked each manager to subjectively assess the project risk. However, using this method, the variation of risk between projects could not be easily explained. Currently, it is based on four factors: development stage of the project, percentage of non-US revenue, product market newness and project break-even year. The overall risk adjustment factor is automatically calculated based on the assigned values for each factor.
- *Strategic Thrust:* This is a measure of the project(s) alignment with the BCS strategy.
- *Time to Market:* This is the interval in calendar days between project start and ship dates.

**Exhibit 4.**

| Product / Market | | Current | New to BCS | New to Industry |
|---|---|---|---|---|
| Radical | R&D | 0% | 7% | 5% |
| | Revenue | 0% | 0% | 6% |
| Next Generation | R&D | 11% | 19% | 0% |
| | Revenue | 6% | 13% | 0% |
| Derivative | R&D | 5% | 2% | 1% |
| | Revenue | 3% | 6% | 1% |
| Current | R&D | 49% | 1% | - |
| | Revenue | 61% | 4% | - |

**Exhibit 5.**

| | % Non-US Revenue | | |
|---|---|---|---|
| | Low 0% - 20% | Medium 20%-70% | High 70%-100% |
| R & D | 77% | 19% | 4% |
| Revenue | 74% | 24% | 2% |

## Portfolio Management

The senior leadership forum was presented with overall project attractiveness summaries and an overall BCS portfolio (Exhibit 3). The forum studied the current portfolio. Project decisions were based on how the portfolio is being impacted.

- *Market/Product Newness:* The objective is to not only maintain the installed base but also to invest and grow by targeting new opportunities (Exhibit 4).
- *Globalization:* Globalization is a strategic thrust, and investment decisions are made to nurture international opportunities (Exhibit 5).
- *Risk Payback matrix:* This measures a project's assessed risk relative to its NPV Payout Ratio. It is presented as a Low, Medium or High attribute (Exhibit 6).
- *Stage of Development /Process:* The product realization process has been segmented into planning, development and realization. By tracking the opportunities at the planning level, for example, BCS knows the future revenue potential from projects at the planning stage (Exhibit 7). It can answer questions like "Can the product development funnel at the early stage support the BCS goals two to five years down the road? If not, how can the business stimulate new ideas and find new opportunities?"
- *Time to Market:* Even though time to market is not directly influenced by the resource allocation process, the Senior Leadership Forum constantly reviews the status of the development interval. The interval was about eighteen months, and process and management teams are working towards a target of 9 months (Exhibit 8)

A note of caution: Organizations, in their zeal to address all opportunities, may try to do too many projects in parallel. This prolongs the product development time for all projects since the limited resources are spread over more projects. This phenomenon was clearly articulated in the book "Developing Products in Half the Time".

## Alignment with Support Organizations

During the first cycle of resource allocation, we tackled only expenses within the marketing organizations. However, the feedback from process teams stated emphatically that projects often experienced delays because funding was not available for new projects in the support organizations. This happens when budgets are set annually based on historical spending and expense-to-revenue ratios. Given a pool of money at the beginning of the budget period, resources were often assigned to on-going programs while some new projects were shorted. The executive team had to intervene to resolve bottlenecks in three of eleven organizations. In addition, a new discipline has been introduced in the functional organizations that they will work only on approved projects.

## Role of Project Manager

It would have been extremely difficult to accomplish this activity without a project manager controlling the program. Several functions described in *A Guide to the Project Management Body of Knowledge* (PMI 1996) were used. For example, after finishing one cycle, 176 changes have been made to the Profile Form and to the database. During the next cycle, the change control procedure recorded 219 changes.

Also, risk identification and management were critical activities. For example, when the ACCESS database was being developed, a contingency plan to provide critical information in another system was established. In addition, the project procurement management issues had to be clearly understood when contracting a segment of work.

**Exhibit 6.**

| RISK ADJUSTMENT / PAY BACK | | Low >=0.7 | Med 0.4 - 0.7 | High <=0.4 |
|---|---|---|---|---|
| High ( >= 7.0 ) | R&D | 0% | 4% | 2% |
| | Rev | 0% | 11% | 8% |
| | P | 8.7 | 8.1 | 15.3 |
| Med( 1.0 - 7.0 ) | R&D | 10% | 23% | 14% |
| | Rev | 15% | 18% | 29% |
| | P | 2.3 | 3.2 | 3.3 |
| Low ( <= 1.0 ) | R&D | 19% | 20% | 7% |
| | Rev | 8% | 9% | 3% |
| | P | 0.3 | 0.4 | 0.2 |

**Exhibit 7.**

| | Planning | Development | Realization |
|---|---|---|---|
| R&D | 29% | 45% | 26% |
| Revenue | 14% | 23% | 63% |

**Exhibit 8.**

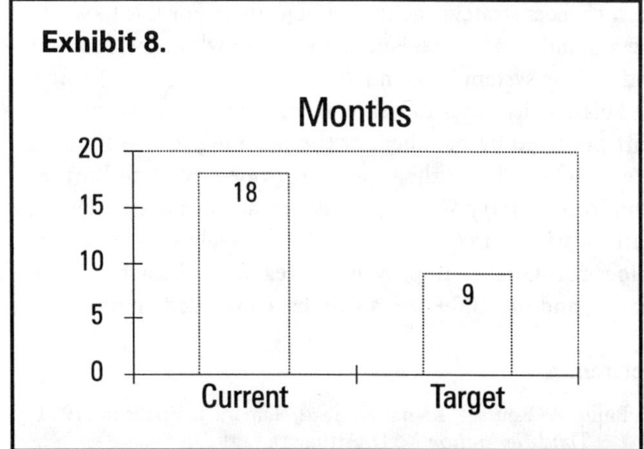


## Lessons Learned

- High-level strategic direction shortens planning intervals: During the first cycle of implementing the system, it took more than two months, and several meetings, to come to agreement on priorities and the relative importance of various platform groups. For the second round, senior leadership set a strategic direction, which provided the basis for developing group plans within a range of 10 percent.
- Care must be used in estimating System Access requirements: The initial plan was to provide access to one or two members in each team. Ultimate usage was about ten times more than anticipated. This has important implications regarding training and administration.
- Non-standard software platforms create problems: Anticipating the complexity of implementation, we have selected only Lotus Notes 3 version of software rather than Notes 4, which did have additional functionality and was available at that time. Even this level of standardization created significant problems since some users had prior dot releases. These had to be upgraded to the minimum level. In addition, the Notes software required more RAM, since this application is much more complex than the usual applications, i.e., e-mail or reading stored documents.
- Additional Human Factors improvement is required: The system was changed from a centralized control, with one person in charge of the Microsoft ACCESS relational database, to a user input and output system. We tested it with a small set of users and created on-line Help in the form itself, for each question, and an electronic user documentation. This reduced the distribution interval by a week and improved the user interface by a factor of 10. However, it can be improved further. Additional on-line help capability can be provided when the system is migrated to Notes 4.1.
- Project cost accounting must be standardized: All supporting organizations did not use the same cost structure in analyzing and inputting project costs. In some organizations, overheads are kept separate from project costs. This is being addressed with a comprehensive program of financial policy standardization and user training
- Quality standards and training are needed: Users must fully understand the purpose and value of what they are being asked to do. There is a tendency in some to simply input some data and complete the form, rather than provide the relevant information since they do not see a value yet. We expect better quality of inputs over time, as planners see management using the information in making decisions.
- Make it a mainstream activity: As long as the users feel that it is just an additional form to be filled out, and continue to use their other traditional ways of doing business, it becomes a burden. To be successful, a system has to be brought to the main stream of an operation. The ultimate challenge of a system is that it should help them do their jobs more effectively (value added).
- Linkage to strategy is critical: Without this linkage, decision making is inconsistent, time consuming and off the mark.

## Conclusions

In this article, I have described a process that a division of a multi-billion dollar company is developing to manage its resource allocation activity to maximize the satisfaction of customer needs as well as shareholder expectations. These are evolving concepts within the organization. This is not a mechanical model that allows managers to plug in some variables and achieve the results.

Resource allocation systems must be tailored to the business, to meet strategic goals and objectives. For this to work, the alignment of management and those who provide input and use the system is essential.

This activity requires vision, team work and on-going support provided by members of the planning teams. I would like to acknowledge the support provided by Herb Burton, Tom Jordan, Terry Warner, Frank Pecca, Dana Becker Dunn, Carl Pavarini, Dan Carroll, the Solution Realization/Resource Allocation Quality Improvement Team, the User Feedback Group, and the 200+ users who have provided inputs.

## References

Philip A. Roussel, Kamal N. Saad, Tamara J. Erickson, 1991, *Third Generation R&D,* Arthur D. Little, Inc

Project Management Institute (PMI). 1996. *A Guide to the Project Management Body of Knowledge.* Upper Darby, PA: PMI.

Preston G. Smith, Donald G. Reinertsen, *Developing Products in Half the Time,* New Product Dynamics

# The Roadrunner Project: Toward World-Class Practices In the Next Century

Dr. Roger D. Beatty, PMP, AT&T, Herndon, VA

## Context

The ideas that resulted in the Roadrunner Project were born on New Jersey back roads in the winter of 1987-1988. Those of you who have ever lived in or visited central New Jersey are certainly aware that back road driving is both a necessity and an art form. I turned to self-improvement programs in order to ameliorate the travails of my two-hour daily round trip. The asphalt highway proved to be fertile ground. I focused my self-training on a single question: how do the most successful people explain their success? Is there a common thread? Do they cite any guidelines or principles? Ideas and creative thoughts ricocheted inside my car like a roadrunner in the California brush. I pondered Dr. Wayne Dyer's advice on how to be a no-limit person. I listened to two people who started mega-businesses (BFI and Mary Kay Cosmetics) with only $500.00. I studied Mike Vance, a creative engineer for Walt Disney, and his program on creative thinking. I adopted his working definition of creativity, "Creativity is the making of the new and the rearranging the old in a new way." Creative thinking, he reasoned, is an ability inherent to each one of us. Creativity not only molds the life of individual, but it is also the motive force in civilizations. After careful study I internalized one of his credos, "Remember, you can't learn anything from experiences you're not having!" This thought was but one of the many pieces of wisdom that influenced the Roadrunner Project.

The revelation that was the most intriguing to me was from Lee Iacocca, the famous automobile executive. He recalled his personal experience with the Ford Mustang prototype. This was his personal moment of truth, a watershed event in his career. It was the initial executive assessment of the clay model. With the fate of the legendary motor vehicle hanging in the balance, Mr. Iacocca's first glance seared like lightning! It was an incredible and outstanding discovery that he made that day. The Ford Mustang radiated with an alluring illusion, "It looked like it was moving, even when it was standing still!" This concept of illusory motivity struck me with its simplicity and its utility. Lee Iacocca's observation of his automotive icon affected my design of the Roadrunner Project. In point of fact, the structural framework of Roadrunner was created and formed to promote the illusion of speed in every aspect of the project.

Three key principles became evident to me as a result of my study of successful people. These were the three common themes in their own explanations of their success:

- Define focused goals and objectives
- Develop a detailed action plan
- Review plan and revise it during execution.

There are two implicit considerations that glue these principles together. First, the goals and objectives must be translated into an overall action plan that includes a business plan with detailed financial assumptions. It is essential that all possible financial aspects be examined in detail. Second, successful people have no word for failure. They may modify their plan daily, or make major revisions, but the word is not in their lexicon, and failure is never considered to be a viable option. They do not accept the possibility of failure.

## Opportunity

The first significant opportunity to integrate these principles of innovation into new product development (NPD) came in 1993. During this time, an executive leadership team was planning for a new multi-million dollar product line. This product line focused on technology services that used software applications distributed over computer networks. As planning for this new product line commenced, the leadership team issued many directives. The paramount edict was the expectation to "improve the speed of our progress and accelerate the implementation to drive improved results." In answer to the call, the Roadrunner Project began in 1993 as an entrepreneurial venture by a single manager in a very large business unit in a very large telecommunications company. Roadrunner is the result of a dedicated attempt to develop methods, processes and tools to prototype a new approach to complex technical project integration management.

These new services were vital to the corporate business plan. They consisted of state-of-the-art software applications that facilitate the use of client/server and network computing architectures. It is vital that these services be delivered to customers within target market windows. These services act as enabling agents to deliver world-class customer service in such vital areas as billing and customer care.

The philosophical framework was constructed to adapt project integration practices to new product development in a creative, innovative and successful manner. The vision for the Roadrunner Project is defined by four key words:

- Breakthrough
- Optimization
- Accountability
- Alignment.

These four key words represent the vital underpinnings of the philosophy that guided the development of Roadrunner. The goal of Roadrunner is the same as virtually every project: deliver a quality product or service faster, reduce costs, reduce staffing requirements and enhance training of personnel. This is simply the triple constraint, the management of time, quality and cost. (Faster! Better! Cheaper!) The Roadrunner Project was developed to address this standard problem in a creative and innovative, yet effective way.

## Methodology

Roadrunner methodology is typical for a software development organization. It consists of several discrete steps. The first and most important step is to define the project in terms of an organizational business need that has a high priority. The project definition is then evaluated by the product team which functions much like a project office. After approval from the product team, a project champion is selected. The role of project champion is essential to the success of the project. The skill levels of the project champion serve as an index to the probability of a project's successful outcome. The project champion next assembles a very small, but effective team. The team, working in the context of the larger organization, is responsible to establish and follow project principles that facilitate the completion of project outputs in very short time frames. These principles should emphasize speed and also focus on high quality deliverables.

The work is conducted in a distributed environment which enables the assignment of work packages to the lowest possible staff level. A distributed environment implies that the project integration management is also distributed. This approach requires as a prerequisite that the organization's processes are designed to function in the distributed environment. A process management team is generally considered to be mandatory because distributed processes do not work well without nourishment. Quality gates are inherent to all processes. They should be well-defined and they should require enough documentation to ascertain that all quality gate conditions have been met. At a minimum, a quality gate should consist of a checklist and a signature page. The purpose of the quality gate is to document the examination and approval of all outputs by team members and stakeholders.

In the case of the Roadrunner Project, project management tools were essential to its success and its purpose. The priority was to develop manual tools as needed. Next the methods and tools were trialed as a prototype. Incremental improvements were added via the testing process. The final step was to champion the use of the method and tools by both project team members and the organization's management team.

These multiple steps in the methodology are designed to achieve a significant reduction in new product development costs during the software design and development stages.

## Principles

Form follows function in the Roadrunner Project. As with Lee Iacocca's Ford Mustang, the Roadrunner Project was designed in every detail to promote the illusion of speed. Each and every project principle was subjected to a rigid specification – does this principle connote acceleration of movement? If it is true that each person is a prisoner of their own perceptions, then these principles are a conspiracy to subvert those paradigms that tend to decelerate. Imagine a coagulum, such as a coagulated mass or rock, in which each piece is inextricably melded into the aggregate. Each component, distinct yet integral, substantiates the cognition of a hard and strong substance. From the project's apex, the dictionary definition of roadrunner as a "largely terrestrial bird of the cuckoo family that is a speedy runner and range from California to Mexico and eastward to Texas," to the final iota, Roadrunner is a homogenate created by the compression of illusory principles into the overall structural component.

Twelve conventional project principles were replaced by twelve Roadrunner principles:

| **Traditional Project Principles** | ***replaced with*** | **Roadrunner Principles** |
|---|---|---|
| standard terminology | *replaced with* | terminology that emphasizes speed |
| large team size | *replaced with* | MicroTeam |
| team leader | *replaced with* | project champion |
| formal meetings | *replaced with* | TimeSlices |
| meeting minutes | *replaced with* | BriefNotes |
| centralized project | *replaced with* | distributed project |
| formal meetings | *replaced with* | focused, intense work sessions |
| bureaucratic style | *replaced with* | find a way to succeed |

| complex documents | *replaced with* | short, accurate strawperson documents |
|---|---|---|
| long review periods | *replaced with* | brief, structured reviews and signoffs |
| slow implementation | *replaced with* | immediate implementation |
| lack of communication | *replaced with* | frequent short status communications |

This catena is carefully crafted to continuously suggest acceleration of work packages. The Roadrunner principles represent a major divergence from standard approaches to project integration management. All traditional principles that did not convey the illusion of speed were tossed. This approach must be internalized by the Project Champion in order to instill the Roadrunner Project principles into the MicroTeam, the SMEs and the support teams. In essence, Roadrunner consists of twelve key methods that are reinforced by twelve key principles. The principles serve as the disciples to the methods.

Some of the Roadrunner principles are typical of contemporary project integration management approaches and are discussed in *A Guide to the Project Management Body of Knowledge*. For example, the concept of a project champion is familiar to all. Frequent status reports are viewed as essential to the knowledge area known as Project Communications Management. Also, the concept of small project teams is widely discussed in literature cited by Project Management Institute (PMI) reference books and study guides. Many sources exist in which principles similar to Roadrunner principles are espoused. The primary point of divergence is due to the fact that these other principles are often couched within a standard project management approach.

The unique quality of the Roadrunner Project is the coalescence of customized criteria. There are three anchor points in the spectrum of speed: the MicroTeam, TimeSlices and BriefNotes. These three compound words metaphorically serve to constantly reinforce the over-arching need to accomplish work in an accelerated mode.

The MicroTeam is the absolute key to the equation. The working Roadrunner team must be as small as possible in order to keep the project focus narrow. The recommendation is that the MicroTeam consist of three (3.00) equivalent headcount (EHC) or less. These three EHC should be composed of not more than seven staff members. Each staff member is nominated to the team on the basis of specific skill sets. Each member of the MicroTeam is a part-time contributor. This supports the dual concepts of distributed project management and distributed process management. The nature of the part-time contribution further stimulates the need to carefully define the project skill requirements, the project roles and the impact on the resource pool. It further serves to promote cross-training and cross-project communications, both of which can contribute to the development of common services or tools. In the actual Roadrunner Project, the Roadrunner MicroTeam consisted five staff people with a total of 1.55 EHC, including the project champion (.75 EHC), three SMEs (.25 EHC each) and engineering support (.05 EHC).

The MicroTeam evolved into a highly focused and highly productive entity in the organization, saving hundreds of thousands of dollars in the design and development phases. It is also important to note that the MicroTeam consistently presented itself to the balance of the organization as a "MicroTeam" to conspicuously and redundantly communicate and maintain its unique identity.

The concept of a TimeSlice is extremely important in the Roadrunner context. The contemporary software development work environment is one in which each work group must be able to thrive on chaos. If you can count on one thing for constancy, it is the fact that new product development often feels totally chaotic. Formal meetings do not work well in this environment. While formal meetings may serve well for code inspections or quality gates, they tend to encourage the staff to work with longer slack times. In general, we do not wish to slow down the completion of any task. In accelerated mode, the need for instant information, clarification or communication is frequent. Some of these needs may be met by electronic mail or voice mail, but many require a brief meeting of the team. A TimeSlice is a very brief meeting in which information is exchanged quickly and efficiently to all team members. A TimeSlice may be scheduled or unscheduled. Its most important characteristic is that it is highly focused and facilitated by a PAL (Purpose, Agenda, Time Limit) format. It has been found that asking for a brief

TimeSlice sends a positive subliminal message to participants. It is very effective during the negotiation step in which staff members are asked to allocate their time to a meeting. TimeSlice is probably the most powerful of all the compound terms in the Roadrunner vocabulary

The concept of BriefNotes was born out of necessity. Most people are not attracted to the role of official note-taker in a formal meeting. The documentation of meeting minutes is a time-consuming task. It places a great burden on a single individual to capture the essence of the meeting. The more detailed the meeting minutes, the more difficult this role. As a note-taker, have you ever felt panicked because you could not keep up with the dialogue? Or have you felt the pang on anxiety when a senior manager rendered an observation that you did not quite understand but were too intimidated to seek clarification? The development and distribution of formal meeting minutes can substantially drain a note-taker's time. The purpose of BriefNotes is to deliver the less formal, but highly focused and effective notes recorded during TimeSlices. It is yet another method to support the triple constraint: quality notes in minimal time with reduced costs.

Given the three anchor concepts, MicroTeam, TimeSlice, and BriefNotes, it is a simple step for the project champion to implement the other Roadrunner Project principles. The productivity engine in Roadrunner is focused and intense work sessions in order to develop and deliver outputs. Two examples come to mind. The members of the MicroTeam were distributed between Florida and New Jersey. In Florida, 1.25 EHC of the team met in order to define the Work Breakdown Structure (WBS). A private work area was prepared and the work continued almost non-stop until the complete WBS was developed along with a list of open issues. Later in New Jersey, the same team members met to develop the WBS into a PC-based project management tool. A conference room was re-arranged to accommodate a production line of laptop computers (relatively new at the time) and the team worked late into the night in order to complete the set of hierarchical project schedules with its roll up reporting capability.

All Roadrunner documentation was clear but concise. Viewgraphs from a standard presentation package were used instead of complex documents. If complex documents were required, then references to them would be made. If the process required a complex document, then the viewgraph package would be created in parallel and delivered with the final package. There are obvious examples of complex documents that must be developed, e.g., engineering drawings and detailed design documents, but all other documentation would be completed in the most minimal form according to the process definition. It has been learned that the process of documentation, especially formalized examples, can significantly lengthen the completion of tasks. It is recommended that the overall information flow and each document be subjected to a quality review. This aspect is too critical too overlook. The time to develop mature documents takes many times the effort that is needed to develop the working outline. The potential for savings in this area is worth the time to investigate.

It is assumed in a Roadrunner Project that the MicroTeam will find a way to succeed no matter how difficult the situation. Within the scope of its objectives, the team is empowered to get the job done. As long as the business requirement is valid, the team is expected to complete its assignment in an aggressive time frame. It is expected that the project sponsor will establish clear boundaries and expectations in writing. The purpose of the Roadrunner Project is to develop all outputs consistent with the accelerated process for new product development.

Consistent and clear communication is essential to the success of the project. The project champion must be an exceptional communicator. A role of the project champion is to coach the members of the MicroTeam to ensure that information is properly shared in both directions. Communication is inherent in every project task. Clarification may be required by a task owner. Validation may be required from a supplier, a partner or the customer. While it is essential to promptly report the completion of each task, it is just as important to communicate the precise status of work in progress. The more automated the technology, the more effective the communications and overall project control.

Finally, quality gates and project reviews must be executed with precision. Careful planning is required in order to schedule and execute an effective review event. It was observed that an uncoordinated review process could take many weeks as the review document meandered its way through a large, distributed organization. The reviewing organization temporarily assumes control for the document or deliverable. At this point, the output is really out of the control of the authoring team. The reviewing organization distributes the document to its own staff members, most of whom are not essential to the outcome. Then this organization has to schedule its own internal review, compile the results and determine how to proceed. Does this sound familiar to you? If not, consider yourself very fortunate. It has been learned that even complex review processes can be reduced to one or two day intervals with advance planning and communication. In other words, one day to review the material after delivery and one day to conduct the actual review meeting or quality gate.

## Implementation

The implementation of the Roadrunner Project was accomplished by means of an off-the-shelf project management tool for personal computers. While Roadrunner can be executed via manual processes, it was developed using a standard tool in order to provide a common approach to new product development within the organization. This tool is scaleable and may be shared. The defined tasks are based on the standard development process. Given that it provides support for a single process and that it uses a standard project management tool, the implementation offers the capability for rapid organizational alignment. It is repetitive and therefore can benefit from incremental improvements from a quality point of view. The tool requires minimal training and a shallow learning curve. In these days of LAN-based servers, it can be easily shared within a software development organization. Since the tool is standardized, the various project implementations can be rolled up into informative management reports. When the Roadrunner Project was tested in 1993, project management tools had less features. Advanced feature sets and tight coupling of project management software with electronic mail communications have provided exciting capabilities that may be used to further automate the Roadrunner Project principles. The goal of Roadrunner was to embed the principles in a simple, elegant and repeatable technology, and the project management software for personal computers really filled the bill.

Roadrunner was implemented in two distinct models. The first was the Resource Management Model (RMM) and the second was the Documentation Management Model (DMM). These two models exist both at a detail level and a roll-up summary level. Due to space limitations, only the RMM will be considered here.

The RMM consists of two pieces of technology. The standard project management tool which has links to a standard electronic spreadsheet. The project management tool codifies the process into discrete tasks which may be presented in text form as well as a Gantt chart. The spreadsheet component of the RMM is replete with project control information that is innovative in concept. The spreadsheet may be executed in manual format or computerized format, but the latter carries with it more flexibility in terms of automated analysis.

The RMM contains three major spreadsheet sections: the Process Section, the Core Section and the Expansion Section. The Process Section is simply the column in which the process steps are enumerated in sequential order. Each task is listed in turn. Ideally, these tasks will correlate with the organization's standard process for new product development. This technique is excellent for ensuring conformity to the standard process and enforcing alignment of all work groups. In addition, when implemented on a LAN-based server, it is an excellent method for access to current information by the management team and peer groups. The Process Section, then, is a straight-forward display of the NPD process. It can be extended to include a functional description of the task as well as the work group which is responsible to complete it.

The Core Section is the most innovative and powerful component in the RMM. The Core Section defines the most important categories of manageable resources. In the Roadrunner Project, the five most important resources for each task were defined to be: Cost, Time, Staff Headcount, Days of Training and Quality Metric. Each manageable resource is measured in terms of a target estimate of the resource required to complete the task, the actual quantity of resource expended to complete the task and the delta or variance between the target and the actual amounts. In its fullest form, this structure is data-intensive. However, since it is scaleable, the requirement for data may be adapted from one project to the next within the boundaries set by the management team.

The Expansion Section is supplementary in nature. It is used to include additional data, mostly in text form, such as notes, document codes or references and lessons learned. This section may be used as a repository for expert knowledge that could be developed into an artificial intelligence tool. It is a text section, but it is very valuable for capturing qualitative information that has many uses throughout the organization. Its use as a training aid can be quite significant. For example, it can include helpful hints and short-cuts which make it a valuable job aid.

The RMM is designed in terms of multiple objectives. It provides a summary view of each task, role and responsibility plus the data to be managed. It can be used to optimize the use of parallel processes in the new product development process. It emphasizes the use of data as the basis of decision making for the allocation of resources. It can improve the planning, use and management of resources. Perhaps most importantly, it offers a simple technique to focus reengineering work on a manageable set of priority problem functions.

The RMM resulted in the creation of five innovative concepts. It provides a "holistic view" of a project. This view may be achieved at a summary level or at a detailed level. Roadrunner teams tried both approaches and they worked equally well. It enables teams to "maximize parallel processes." This is nothing new to Project Management Professionals, but it may be to others. It simulates the accounting technique of variance analysis by "managing the deltas." In other words, for each process task, you check the variances and highlight the largest ones. This leads to the concept of "focused reengineering." Do not attempt to reengineer an entire process. Focus on the areas indicated by your data. Reengineer only those tasks with the highest impact. Finally, it allows "trickle-down empowerment," the responsibility for the task flows down to the work package level with clearly established bounds of empowerment.

## Conclusion

The Roadrunner Project resulted in the delivery of new technology services in record time for the organization. This new technique slashed all existing records for new product development. The organization closed new contracts and delivered its new services to the line operations groups. The Roadrunner Project "resulted in clearly successful projects and will serve as the benchmark for future platform leadership efforts." Clearly, the Roadrunner Project, and other projects like it, have much to contribute toward the refinement of world class practices in the next century, perhaps even in the next millennium! Let's hope for that.

# Case Study: Reducing An Organization's New Product Development (NPD) Introduction Timelines

Kenneth D. Delcol, PMP, PEng, PE-SCIEX
Co-author: Pierre Burnier, PE-SCIEX

Many organizations are under great pressure to reduce their NPD introduction timelines. This paper discusses how PE-SCIEX was able to reduce its NPD timeline from five years to between one and two years. The reduction was achieved in under two years during which the pharmaceutical instrument market was under going dramatic changes forcing manufacturer's development time down from years to months. This paper addresses four critical areas of change:

- Organizational changes
- NPD philosophy
- Gating introduction
- Professional project management introduction.

## Company Background

PE-SCIEX is an organization that was born out of the need to analyze material on the NASA Martian expedition project and has grown from a research organization to a world leader in the research, the design and the manufacturing of mass spectrometers. The instruments are used to detect very low levels of substances in the pharmaceutical, environmental and clinical industries.

The inability of the organization to handle rapid product development programs became obvious by 1992. The NPD timeline during this time period stretched over five years. The long NPD timeline was beginning to hurt the organization's competitive position since the products developed by PE-SCIEX were now beginning to move from the early adopters in research institutions into the hands of the early majority in the main stream market. The paradigm shift created by PE-SCIEX's technology was finally successful in crossing the market place chasm between the early adopters and the main stream market(Moore 1991). As a result of this successful crossing a new set of expectations from the market were introduced into the product with a corresponding reduction in the time to respond to those expectations. In addition larger and more aggressive competitors are now becoming more interested in the market since there was a discontinuity in the technology that lowered some of the market entry barriers.

## Organizational Changes

The old organizational structure was product based starting from research and development through product development and manufacturing. This structure created a competitive environment between the product lines that ignored commonality and promoted the 'not invented here' syndrome. To over come this problem senior executives switched the organizational structure to a functional organization. The emphasis of research and development was changed to purely scientific research with short, medium, and long term goals. Research no longer supports product development and manufacturing activities. The refocusing of research away from engineering research back into fundamental scientific research has created renewed excitement within this group and has rapidly increased the organization's scientific knowledge base.

A senior executive with time to market experience was hired to head the product development organization. The new director of product development promptly switched the engineering organizational structure to a project driven functional structure and created a new concept group and project management group. The new concept group works closely with research and smoothes the transition from hand crafted fragile research breadboards to engineering concepts. The concept group is responsible for performing fundamental system and engineering analysis with the goal of reducing the product's technical risk. The engineering analysis looks to gain an understanding of the critical factors in the design of the product to ensure the company's ability to reliably manufacture the product. This is accomplished by building engineering breadboards using existing and new technology to duplicate the results found in research. The concept group is also actively involved in looking at new ways to solve old problems that are not directly related to a given NPD project.

The engineering emphasis in product development was switched from a 'feasibility test as you go' approach that produced difficult to manufacture products to basic hard core engineering using top down design, based on specifications, and standards. The days of tinkering engineering were put to an end and replaced with a professional high-tech industry approach, that emphasizes up front planning and designs that work first on paper. Switching to the functional organization provided the necessary support to create a professional environment within each of the engineering disciplines.

Earlier product introductions indicated the transition from product development into Manufacturing was not very smooth i.e. the products were not well designed for manufacturing and a number of manufacturing issues were not considered. To address this problem a new manufacturing group called Manufacturing Process Engineering [MPE] was created. The goals of the group include working with product development in all aspects of the product design phase to address manufacturing problems up-front and taking responsibility for the introduction of the new product into manufacturing. This group addresses all aspects of manufacturing including design for assembly, manufacturing procedures, purchasing, and vendor capabilities.

Once the new organization was in place a professional project manager was recruited to build a project management organization within product development. This person was hired into a senior position within product development. The project management function combines both traditional project management and project engineering functions. This removes the need for planning personnel and allows the project manager to obtain greater project ownership since they plan, execute and oversee all aspects of the project. PE-SCIEX has made use of advances in both computer hardware and software technology to allow the combining of the two functions. Standardization of the product development and planning processes has significantly simplified the mechanical portions of project startup activities.

The product line organization made use of the 'overall the wall' approach to product development. The product based organizational structure failed to provide the necessary focus for NPD projects since the structure did not adequately address the problems of conflicting priorities and goals faced by functional groups. To overcome the focusing problems project management and NPD project teams consisting of dedicated core members from the different functional groups within product development, marketing and manufacturing were introduced. Dedicated core members maintain primary responsibility with the project until completion. The use of dedicated NPD teams and the physical movement of team members to common areas further enhanced the project management function.

The previous organizational structure did not include critical vendors that supplied either components and/or design services in the development of products. To further complicate the situation an adversarial approach was taken with all vendors, including ones that were providing design functionality. With the creation of NPD project teams critical vendors were invited to become active members of the NPD project team. This new relationship with critical vendors has resulted in reduced costs, improved vendor relationships and

**Exhibit 1.** Big Bang vs. Incremental Approach

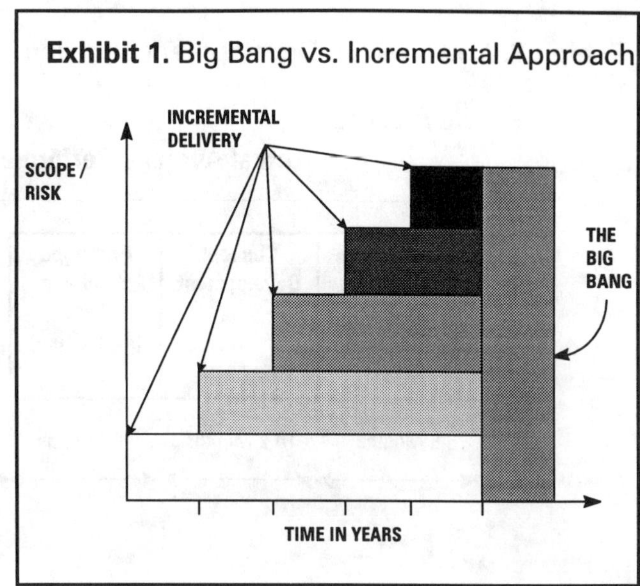


greater vendor commitment to the different product lines. Vendors actively participate in the product design phase by providing input on suggested design solutions, manufacturing capability, new methods, testing, and tooling trade-offs. Temporary seat assignments are available for both vendors and temporary project staff in the project's common work area.

## NPD Philosophy Change

The Big Bang approach was used to develop products prior to the introduction of project management. This approach consisted of parallel research and product development that involved significantly changing all of the product's major systems and their associated interfaces at the same time including the science/technology behind the systems. The lines between engineering and research were blurred as well as the lines within engineering. The shear magnitude of the number of changes quickly overwhelmed the organization's ability to manage them.

To overcome this problem an incremental development approach was taken to minimize the number of product changes that a given project had to cope with and to ensure the science behind the changes was well understood, see Exhibit 1. This approach has resulted in better up-front product definition, reducing the need to deal with ambiguous product definitions. Marketing is now able to prioritize their requirements based on features that are well understood and have a high chance of successful delivery to the market. To further support the limiting of project scope a maximum project duration of two years is set with a target duration of one year.

In addition significant effort was placed into controlling and minimizing the number of changes at a given system

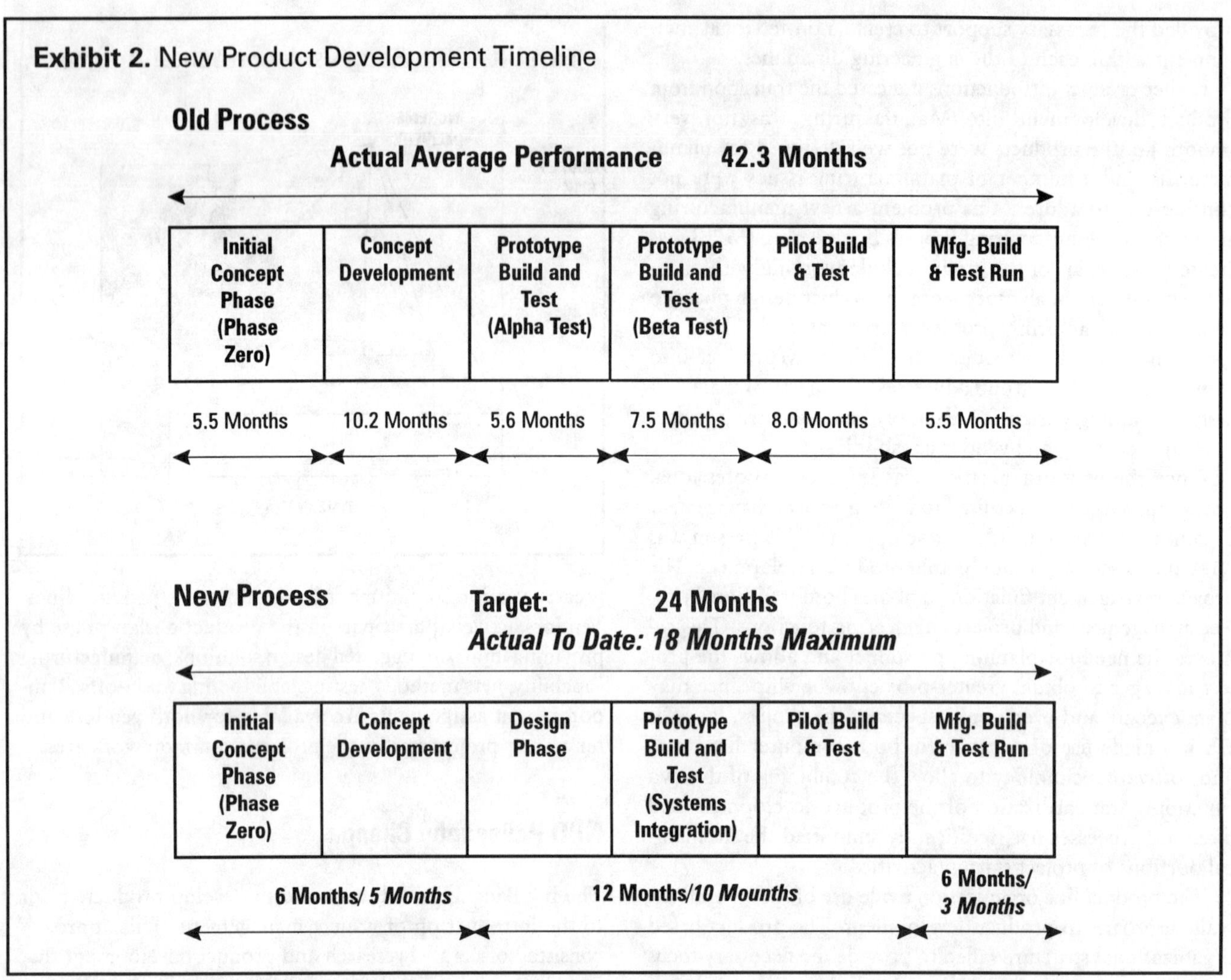

**Exhibit 2.** New Product Development Timeline

boundary. Project plans were modified to emphasis the creation of system interface documents for all engineering disciplines early in the development process. Limiting the number of changes improved the focus of the NPD teams and up-front clarification of system interfaces allowed more independent work while at the same reducing both risk and time to market. Standardization of hardware and software components along with design guidelines were introduced to help simplify the impact of changes on a given system boundary i.e. if a change had to occur, attempts were made to make use of standard components to help manage the impact of the change.

The incremental approach to product development supports the evolution of the product by addressing changing customer needs and advancements in technology. The evolution product development path is very well suited to the total quality management philosophy of constant improvement over time. To avoid the possibility of being caught by a discontinuity in technology and/or science, the PE-SCIEX product development approach supports a parallel revolutionary/breakthrough path which is the sole responsibility of Research. In this area Research is involved in developing new science and using pre-released technology in an attempt to develop out-of-the-box thinking in solving new and existing business problems.

Experience to date is very successful with three products being introduced in under 18 months and four more products well along in the development process, see Exhibit 2. A hidden benefit of the incremental approach is an increase in market presence of PE-SCIEX as a result of enhancements to the current product lines being introduced at an accelerated rate, thus allowing customers to address business problems faster than expected.

## NPD Gating Introduction

At PE-SCIEX projects are viewed as the delivery tools for products and that a company's success is built on its products, thus projects must create the conditions for product success. To prevent projects from running out of control a detail product/project gating procedure was developed. The gating procedure is used to identify weaknesses in product concepts and their associated projects before the organization commits significant resources in the development of the product. The fundamental procedure is based on the work of Dr. R. Cooper [1] with minor modifications from Coopers and Lybrand Consulting. The fundamental procedure does not provide any guidance with respect to gauging the health of the project that is responsible for the delivery of the product. Using the Project Management Body of Knowledge [PMBOK] a number of project related checks aimed at determining the condition of the delivery project were added to the basic gating procedure. These checks ensure fundamental project management activities are occurring in a quality fashion in the appropriate project phases.

Executive management, product development, and Marketing buy-in was obtained through the use of training courses which used both the products of PE-SCIEX and its competitors to facilitate the discussion as to why products fail and succeed. Further commitment was obtained by allowing the people who would use the gating procedure to help in its development and maintenance. All NPD projects use the same procedure with the same set of questions to ensure consistency across projects. The NPD process was modified to make the gating procedure its central component where the deliveries of the different product development phases feed the information requirements of the gating procedure. The organization's NPD documentation was modified to reflect this new reality.

Prior to its introduction into the NPD process a trial run was done on a completed project to obtain a feel on how to use the procedure. The trial run help uncover a number of potential problems and confirmed known problems on the completed project. The introduction of the new procedure into the organization consisted of having all in-progress NPD projects start using the procedure when the project was to enter into its next project phase and having all new NPD projects start using the procedure from the beginning of the development process.

Refinement of the gating procedure is occurring over time as more experience is gained in its use i.e. questions are modified, added and removed. Presently each question is weighted the same, since the organization felt that insufficient experience exists to date to intelligently assign weights to different questions: this will not occur until more data is collected to determine if the procedure warrants such complexity.

The benefits of the gating procedure identified to date include:

- Greater organizational commitment to a gating decision [proceed, killed, recycled, conditional, and hold] associated with a project since stakeholders now have a frame of reference from which to gain an understanding of the decision.
- Significant improvements in the quality of the information generated by the NPD team has occurred since they now understand the need for and the use of the information.
- Better guidance for the NPD team, project manager, stakeholders, and ISO Auditors as to the type of information required at a review meeting to assess if the product/project is fundamentally sound.
- Removal of any differentiation between hardware and software products i.e. the procedure applies equally to both types of products.

## Professional Project Management Introduction

Establishing the fundamental project management building blocks was considered critical for improving the organization's NPD timelines. The first step was to establish the project management organizational structure, relationships and responsibilities. To ensure the organizational commitment to project management the following items were put in place:

- reporting of the project management function directly to the senior executive champion, the director of product development,
- defining and obtaining senior executive commitment to the roles and the responsibilities of project managers in the NPD process,
- establishing the rules governing which projects professional project managers will work on,
- creating dedicated project teams under the control of a project manager who draws staff from all of the functional organizations,
- creating a senior executive project review process for all projects, and
- linking project management as the primary driver of the strategic initiative of time to market and a major contributor to the total quality management initiative.

Project Managers were made responsible for all aspects of the NPD process starting from the concept phase all the way to the launch phase. Functional managers outside of the product development structure e.g. manufacturing and marketing support the project management process due to its direct linkage to a strategic organizational initiative. Senior executives receive NPD status reports from a single source i.e. the project managers and not the functional managers. The manager of project management uses NPD projects to support initiatives in other functional organizations to help gain support of the appropriate functional managers e.g. all new NPD projects must perform tolerance stack-up calculations in support of the new mechanical engineering initiative, the newest NPD project carried out the manufacturing initiative of restructuring the bill of materials for a given product to support external vendors. The action of supporting other functional initiatives in NPD projects has allowed project management to gain influence in a number of areas where direct hierarchical support does not exist.

Linking project management as the key driver of the time to market initiative was of primary importance. Project managers sit on the front lines in the NPD process and can quickly identify bottlenecks. Their firsthand knowledge of problems and work-arounds are key in helping to create the environment for long term change aimed at reducing NPD timelines. Project managers successes to date include:

- identifying and helping to justify additional personnel in critical functional groups that support the NPD process,
- establishing and supporting the roles of vendors in the NPD process,
- implementing and modifying existing business systems to support the project environment e.g. integrating project software with time sheets, postmortem review, and project warehouses,
- improving and standardizing project documentation by using the Project Management Body of Knowledge to identify missing context and templates to provide structure; this now allows Project Managers to concentrate on the content of the project's documentation rather than the organization of the documentation.

The final step associated with the introduction of project management was the standardization of project management techniques such as: work breakdown structure, issues handling, change control, detailed planning and status reporting, charter of accounts, and financial analysis. Planning templates were created to help facilitate NPD projects.

## Results

With all of the changes in place to improve the NPD timelines, four products have completed the development process and four other products are in various development states using the process. Of the four completed projects the longest delivery time from initial concept was 18 months, with the shortest being eight months; in addition one project was killed. The ability to reduce the timelines below the target of twenty-four months is the result of the following:

- Changing the product definition process from a Swiss Army knife approach i.e. the product must solve all problems at the same time, to products that address specific business needs. This change lead to better up front product definition which prevented the tendency of taking on too much.
- Providing good organizational focus and support. Project management was key in this area by preventing project members from being drawn into non-project related activities and ensuring all parts of the organization had the same priorities to ensure project success.
- Building good project teams. In one instance the product development group took longer to design the product than expected; however the manufacturing group was able to cut the build times in half by working with the product development group; both groups working together were able to reduce the product introduction time by two months.
- Generating higher than expected enthusiasm from vendors in the design and prototype phases of a NPD project. This resulted in identification of up front design flaws, different manufacturing techniques, better than expected turn around times on prototype parts and reduced cost of production parts; in addition some vendors have requested earlier involvement in the NPD process.
- Reducing the amount of politics involved in making decisions around the fate of a project i.e. the gating procedure has brought a structured approach using tangible evidence to an area that previously used an unstructure approach based on intangibles.
- Using conservative estimates as to the impacts of the organizational changes on the NPD timelines. Minimal NPD timeline impacts were expected from both the concept and the MPE groups. However both of these groups were able to address technical risks and manufacturing concerns sooner than expected in the development cycle thus avoiding costly redesign work and delays in the later phases of the cycle.
- Using conservative estimates as to the impact of the changes in the engineering design philosophy. The shift in engineering emphasis from feasibility to top down design using basic engineering principles drastically improved the quality of the engineering design and the reduce the amount of rework required in later phases of the development cycle. The introduction of system interface boundaries and the need for up front definition of these boundaries help to clarify and solidified the design effort much earlier than expected. Engineers were made to think of the ripple impact of interface changes early in the design and address the impacts up front rather than settle for a compromise solution later in the design.

With the successful reduction in the timelines of the NPD process, a new area of opportunity was created i.e. portfolio management of both products and projects. The need to do this is the direct result of an incremental NPD philosophy that emphasizes market focus and flexibility with timely delivery. The two areas of portfolio management are interrelated; however each area has its own specific concerns that are independent of the other e.g. product portfolio management looks at the timing of features for different markets without regard to resource availability of project staff and the ability of vendors to supply the necessary technology. Portfolio management must addresses both product and project requirements at the same time to ensure an organized and consistent roll-out of product features to meet the market needs in a timely fashion. PE-SCIEX is in the process of implementing tools and techniques to help in managing these areas.

The gating procedure is a critical tool in helping to improve NPD timelines since its very effective at identifying weak projects and giving senior executives opportunities to intervene before proceeding forward. Greater emphasis and support of up-front product definition, technical/market analysis, and project planning was obtained from senior executives as a result of the gating procedure consistently identifying the same weak areas in NPD projects. As result of doing the additional up front work fewer surprises are occurring in subsequent NPD development phases. The gating procedure was also instrumental in helping to generate support for expanding the role of project management and its associated techniques within the organization

## Conclusion

PE-SCIEX is now capable of rapidly moving a well defined product from the planning phase through the remaining NPD life cycle phases. The next biggest area of opportunity lies in improving the transfer of ideas through research into concept development. The dramatic reduction in the NPD timelines experienced by PE-SCIEX was not the result of a single action but the result of a combination of deliberate actions aimed at specific areas in the NPD life cycle. Each new action built on the direction of the previous initiatives and helped lay the ground work for a new set of possible directions. The combined set of actions create an environment in which NPD projects flourish. Concentrating on the middle to latter portions of the NPD life cycle processes allows an organization to obtain immediate NPD timeline improvements; however further improvements in the timeline will only come from addressing the weaknesses found in the up-front NPD life cycle processes. A long term strategy aimed at reducing an organization's NPD timeline is critical for ensuring success.

### Book


Cooper, Robert. 1993. *Winning at New Products Accelerating the Process from Idea to Launch*. Addison Wesley

Moore, A. Geoffrey, 1991. *Crossing The Chasm*. Harper Business.

# Integrating Across Functional Interfaces Panel Discussion

Gregory D. Githens, PMP MaxiComm Project Services, Inc.
Kimberly A. Johnson, 3M Corporation
Alexander Walton, PMP, Harris Corporation

The panelists will describe issues, experiences, insights, and strategies for improving project integration performance in new product development. The audience is encouraged to participate and learn from the panelists and from each other.

## Integration Affects Project and Enterprise Performance

Integration of functional work is a frequent and significant new product development challenge (Griffin and Hauser, 1996). Many organizations have downsized and claim they have empowered their people, but do not know nor apply the basics of an environment for project success. Poor integration is characterized by disjointed development efforts, conflict, and confusion. Products are boring and low-value because developers avoid difficult choices and "do what is easy." The traditional paradigm of specialization, fragmentation, and control are barriers to performance.

For example, an important problem is the separation of "project control" by having functions maintain budgets and project managers handle time schedules. The product vision gets lost as functional and project members battle over metrics, resources, and symbols.

World-class organizations differ from average organizations in their application of cross-functional project integration. Excellent project integration fosters winning products, satisfied customers, and high personal satisfaction.

Exhibit 1 presents a model of NPD integration that identifies several important concerns in project integration

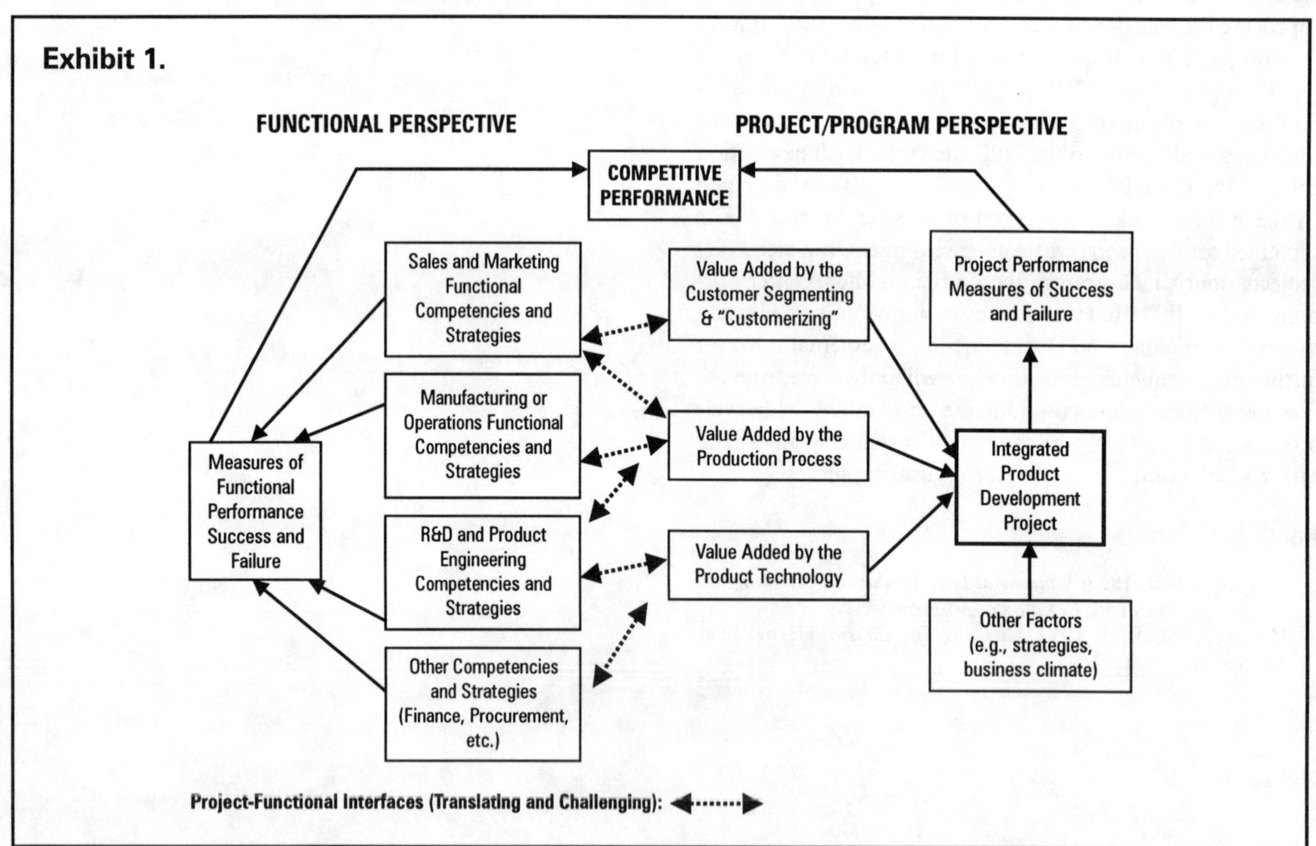

**Exhibit 2.** Several Strategics for Integrating Project and Functional Department Efforts

***Co-Location and physical infrastructure***

Excellent project managers know that frequent and rich communication is essential to good integration. They carefully consider the advantages and disadvantages of co-location and arrangement of the workspace.

***Technology infrastructure***

Tools and technology are potentially important enablers for cross-functional performance. Excellent project managers realize that tools are helpful, but project team members should not become slaves to their tools.

***Personnel selection, transfer, and cross training***

As individuals spend more time in other functional areas they improve knowledge of how the other groups accomplish work. Excellent project managers are careful in how they chose and develop their team members.

***Culture and socialization***

This may be the most important area to effective integration across functional interfaces. Excellent project managers understand that informal networks, common mental models, and conflict avoidance/management are both barriers as well as facilitators of functional work.

***Organizational structure***

Organizational structure influences integration. Excellent project managers understand the strengths and weaknesses of various project organizations such as matrix organizations, stand-alone project teams and project coordinators and learn to make their projects operate effectively.

***Incentives and rewards***

Excellent project managers understand the issues of individual versus team compensation and recognition and functional rewards versus cross-functional rewards are important components of motivation. They develop project integration strategies that work for the norms of their organizations.

***Formal management processes***

Companies increasingly develop and use processes to discipline and synchronize their product innovation efforts. Excellent project managers know how to work this process well.

management. The left hand groups of elements are the functional areas of traditional organizations: marketing, sales, production, research, and so forth. The project/program group describes the unique and temporary work that develops and delivers product innovations.

The model also points out common interfaces between the goals of functional work and of project work. These interfaces are the points where conflict is most visible.

Typically, conflict arises from different perspectives of work, different rewards and incentives, and different cultures. Failing to address conflict leads to polarization and loss of long-term organizational competitiveness. Integration skills help organizations to separate and synthesize the views of the organization hierarchy and NPD process flows.

The interface is also the point where the functions and the project add the value that makes the product competitive. Project management leverages and facilitates the value-creating process by making the competencies and limitations of the contributors more visible. The project skills used to mediate conflicts, and to measure and create value are essential to success.

There are a number of important elements necessary for long-term organizational performance. In poorly-performing organizations, the value propositions, competencies, and strategies are isolated and weakly integrated. In better-performing organizations, there are defined strategies and visible effort applied to integration. The main area for attention should be on the facilitators of cross-functional cooperation such as evaluation criteria, reward structures and management expectations (Song, Montoya-Weiss, and Schmidt 1997).

## Interfaces and Integration

The double-headed arrows in Exhibit 1 indicate the interfaces. These are the points is where integration is essential to effective development.

Concurrent techniques and process have great potential for improving product development performance. Management techniques such as Quality Function Deployment help integrate the "voice of the customer" with the "voice of the technology." The skills and characteristics of the project team and the supporting organization are important precursors to adopting tools and techniques that fostering effective project integration. These skills include personal leadership and group discipline. Project integration management is an **applied** strategy and differentiates between successful and unsuccessful innovators.

Organizations have differing cultures, traditions, and value-creating propositions in their business functions. These differences create conflict. However, the process of working through the various issues is central to creativity in all forms of product innovation.

## Integration Strategies, Behaviors, and Roles

The project manager is the person who sets the tone for integration of functional work. Excellent project managers are those who achieve excellent business results without diminishing the contributions of functional contributors. Mediocre project managers approach project development as task masters and schedule coordinators.

Exhibit 2 lists several project integration strategies, which a project manager can select and use. Since there is no one best way to manage, a test of project management expertise is the way that the project manager uses the principles to improve cross-functional integration.

The project manager plays two roles (Githens, 1996) in projects: as translator and challenger of policy. Project managers perform their challenger and translator role *at the interface*. For example, the project manager is often the individual who must facilitate the process of developing project requirements for verbalized customer wants. This is the translator role. If the requirement is not feasible, then the project manager is the person who confronts the problem and works out alternative strategies. This is the challenger role. Excellent project managers perform both roles well, and these roles largely account for the success of project integration.

The role of functional managers changes in two ways. First, is functional managers increasingly are also project managers and measured for their project performance. Second, is that functional manager-executives learn new roles as project sponsors and lead the organization in prioritizing projects, establishing priorities among various functional strategies, and "groom the track" through setting direction, architecting the product line, managing the product portfolio, and supporting the enabling processes (Wheelwright and Clark, 1995).

## Future Prospects

Project management must adapt and change with the business conditions of the next century. The increasing use of new rapid communications technologies, virtual teams, and international/global markets will offer both promises and problems for the NPD Project Management practitioner. Project integration is a subtle, complex, and interdependent practice. NPD success is largely driven by the effectiveness of project management, in particularly the development, selection, and implementation of NPD strategies, techniques and tools for improving integration of functional interfaces.

## References


Griffin, Abbie and John R. Hauser. 1996, Integrating R&D and Marketing: A Review and Analysis of the Literature, *Journal of Product Innovation Management,* 13-3 (May) 191-215

Song, X. Michael, Mitzi M. Montoya-Weiss, and Jeffrey B. Schmidt 1997 Antecedents and Consequences of Cross-Functional Cooperation: A Comparison of R&D, Manufacturing, and Marketing Perspectives, *Journal of Product Innovation Management,* 14-1 (January) 35-47

Githens, Gregory D. 1996 Creating Value in Product Innovation: Project Management Capability is Strategic, *PMNetwork* 3 (March) 13-16

Wheelwright, Steven C. and Kim B. Clark, 1995 *Leading Product Development,* New York: The Free Press

# Building on the Stage/Gate: An Enterprise-wide Architecture for New Product Development

Beebe Nelson, Ed.D., Product Development Partners, Inc.
Bob Gill, Product Development Partners, Inc.
Steve Spring, Duncan-Nevison

## I. The Stage/Gate Process: A Foundation.

The foundation for managing and executing individual product development projects in today's corporation is the stage/gate process. This important process was first defined as a repeatable corporate process about ten years ago (Cooper 1993). Before that, new products were developed chiefly in an "over the wall" way, with each function handing its work on to the next. Increased competition and more demanding customers pushed companies to find ways to reduce cycle time and new product failure rate. They identified the sequence of activities required to develop products and defined these as a process – usually called the *stage/gate* or *phase/review* process – which was carried out by a team comprised of members of the key functional organizations, and which was reviewed by management at specified intervals.

The focus in the stage/gate process is on the execution of individual projects or programs. By specifying clear stage-by-stage deliverables and clear check points – gates, or management reviews — the use of stage/gate processes brought product development activities and decision making under closer scrutiny and better control. As they clarified the process, companies were able to introduce good project management techniques and concurrent engineering practices, and many were able also to achieve cycle time reduction. They also improved their ability to manage risk by making key project parameters more certain, thus allowing them to weed out less promising programs earlier in the development process.

## II. From Stage/Gate to Aggregate Product Planning

The stage/gate process, however, leaves some important issues unaddressed. It focuses on individual projects, and can become bureaucratic if applied in a "one size fits all" way. More important, decisions on which programs to continue are made at the review gates in the context of a single program with no clear way to compare benefits from program to program. When limited resources have to be deployed, the stage/gate decision making process does not provide reviewers with the information they need to make decisions across programs. And perhaps most important, there is no clear way to decide what programs will be included in the development portfolio. It is this last stage/gate shortcoming that this paper addresses.

Choosing the best portfolio of programs for development, and managing that portfolio over time, requires that management consider the *aggregate* of possible development programs in the context of its business strategies and objectives, and also in the context of the other corporate processes involved in product development (Crawford 1996; Souder and Mandakovic 1986). Several things become clear as we "chunk up" to the aggregate or portfolio level of new product decision making.

First, we get a very different view of the role of strategy in product development decision making. In stage/gate decision making fit with strategy is an important criterion for moving a program through the gates. However, if we are looking at one project at a time there is no way of telling whether the aggregate of projects fulfills the strategy. When we ask the question of strategic fit about the portfolio of programs, we can begin to select a combination of programs which together forward the strategy, and we can look for portfolio balance around such issues as risk/return, markets addressed, and technology leverage.

Second, we are better equipped to consider individual new products in the context of enhancing technology capabilities, platforms, product lines, and product families (McGrath 1995). This allows for better long range product planning, including the intentional development of line extensions and derivatives from initial products, as well as planned platform regeneration and replacement. For example, this way of thinking can show that it is desirable to resource a program with low initial ROI because it provides downstream advantages as part of a product family.

Third, we can begin to address the all-important issue of technology management as we see the portfolio of programs drawing on and developing different aspects of the corporation's technology capability (Roussel *et al* 1991). An understanding of the product portfolio in relation to the technology of the corporation permits management to make decisions based on broad business objectives. This in turn enables management to address the question of what they are getting for their research and development investment.

Fourth, by thinking of the programs in aggregate, we can identify and act on opportunities with greater flexibility, and can link product lines and technologies to meet customer needs and competitor threats. Real innovation does not come in neat boxes: corporations whose development efforts are driven by customer needs are often pushed to develop products outside their traditional offerings, which in turn can lead to whole new platforms or product lines. But when development teams are held to thinking in terms of a single product, they are not in a position to act on a deep understanding of customer needs.

Finally, when the portfolio of programs is managed in the aggregate, corporations are better able to manage resources across programs, better able to avoid having programs compete for finite resources in the development pipeline.

As Kent Crawford has pointed out (Crawford 1996, 1), "effective product development necessitates a much broader view of organization management. Product development processes must encompass the entire business planning, administering, directing, and controlling functions, in addition to the traditional areas of project management. A holistic approach to project management is required where organizations have a need to more effectively manage multiple product development efforts."

In Exhibit 1, we see *project management* as the ground level set of practices for product development; the *stage/gate* process requires good project management practices for successful implementation. Moving up a level, the practices and disciplines of *portfolio* or *aggregate* project management allow the product development effort to respond to the complexities of managing multiple projects over time; this multiple and complex view, finally, provides the discipline needed to link product development to the organization's processes and strategies. Reading down, the top of the pyramid provides direction for aggregate product management; the stage/gate

**Exhibit 1.** The Management Pyramid

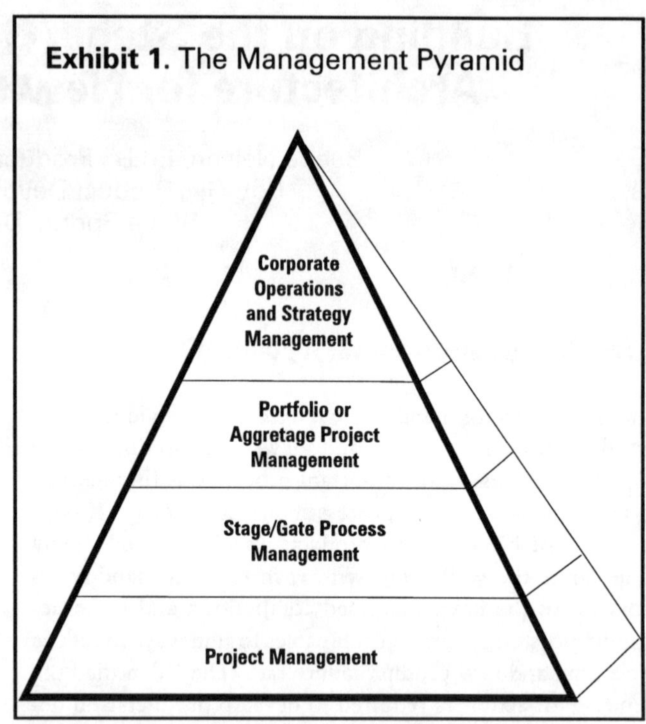


**Exhibit 2.** The Expanded Product Development Process

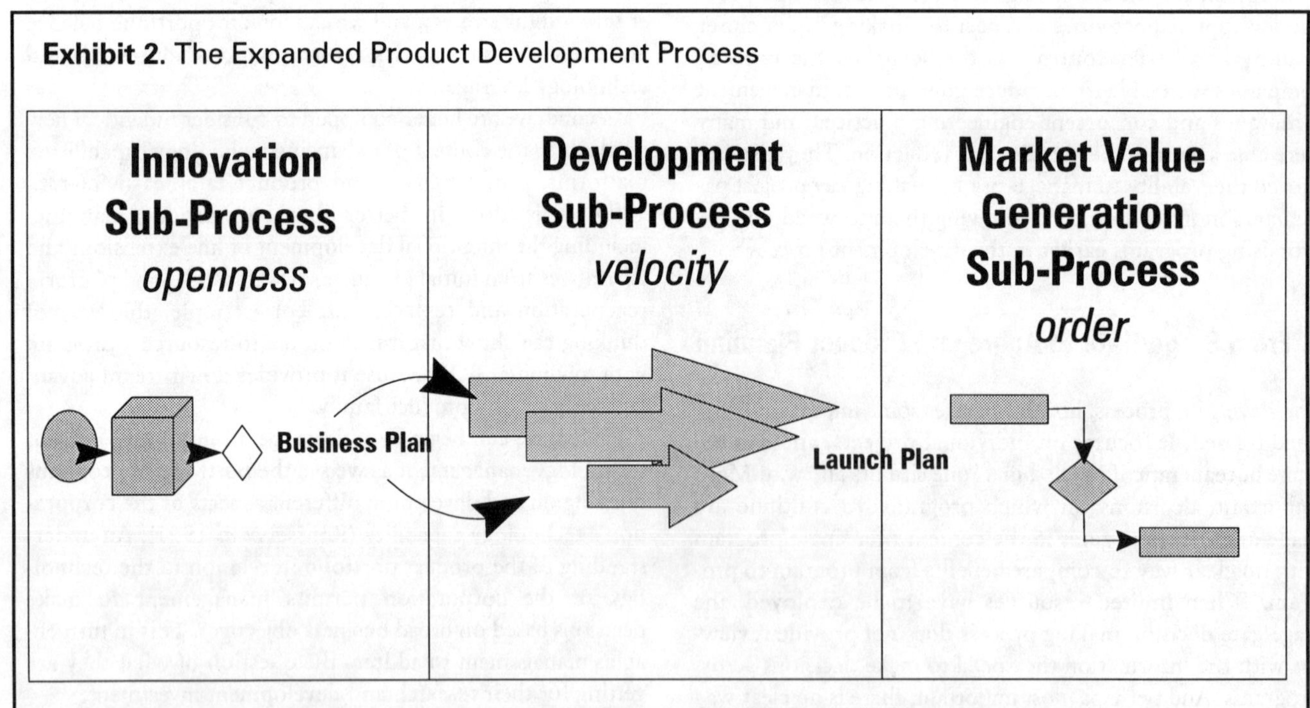

process provides the discipline for translating the strategic objectives of the corporation into manageable projects; and project management provides the discipline for successful stage/gate implementation.

To achieve holistic, integrated new product management, we have been working with companies who are beginning to think in terms of an *Expanded Product Development Process*. The expanded process begins not with an identifiable program or product concept but in the broader arena of strategic goal setting and opportunity identification, and it ends not with a successful product launch but with successful integration of new products into the ongoing business. This expanded product development process includes three subprocesses.

- the Innovation Subprocess, sometimes called the "Fuzzy Front End," is characterized by openness and the nurturing of new ideas and opportunities. Project boundaries may be fluid, and screens and filters have low thresholds to encourage experimentation and exploration.
- the Development Subprocess is characterized by velocity of execution and speed to market. It is in this subprocess that a corporation can achieve cycle time reduction and process repeatability, particularly when clear customer requirements, clear product definition, and clear link to strategy are achieved in the upstream process.
- the Market Value Generation Subprocess is characterized by order and integration of new products into the existing product line. It includes post launch reviews and the planning of product ramp up and decline (product life cycle planning).

These three subprocesses are tied together by systematic reviews and metrics.

1. Strategic portfolio management reviews make decisions about the selection and resourcing of the portfolio of products. These reviews are held in the context of the corporation's overall planning calendar.
2. Operational reviews support ongoing decision making about projects in the development pipeline. These reviews are held regularly by the functions responsible for this aspect of the development process.
3. Stage/gate reviews are focused on individual programs, and are held as appropriate in terms of the program's timetable and milestones.

Distinguishing between these different kinds of reviews allows product development decision makers to address issues dealing with both individual programs (risk/return, strategic fit, competitive advantage) and with the portfolio of programs (portfolio balance, resourcing). This clarification of reviews and decision making encourages senior management to focus on strategic decision making, and encourages teams to focus on speedy implementation.

## Managing the Product Development Process Enterprise Wide

An understanding of the expanded product development process leads us to ask how product development links to the key business processes enterprise wide. Hammer and Champy (1993) propose that to understand the enterprise as *process* rather than *function* amounts to a revolution. Unfortunately, the work of transforming the modern corporation from a functional organization to a process organization produced, in many cases, only downsizing. Functionally organized corporations simply did more with less and called it reengineering.

Nonetheless, an understanding of the corporation as composed of a small number of key processes (usually about seven) can help us identify the connections that must be managed in order for product development to be successful. Exhibit 4 shows a typical process map, to which the supporting processes of Human Relations, Finance, and Information Management are often added. In this map, Product Development is shown as one of six processes. The process detail indicates the steps that a corporation might include, both at the management level (*identify opportunity, charter product development team*) and at the team level (*understand customer needs, develop product concept, define and develop product*), in specifying its product development process. The other business process, however, include activities and areas of concern that are key to successful product development. At Polaroid Corporation, for instance, the *Product Development Process (PDP)*, which is their stage/gate process, is differentiated from *New Product Delivery (NPD)*. PDP outlines deliverables, activities, gates, and metrics for teams and reviewers. NPD, which has never been as fully articulated, expresses the understanding of the corporation that to be successful PDP must be linked to many other business processes.

In working with clients we follow seven steps which provide a roadmap for managing the enterprise wide product delivery process (Gill, Nelson, Spring 1996). These seven steps begin with *setting new product targets*, a function of the Strategy Development and Management Process. Without clear targets and the allocation of resources to meet those targets, the product development effort will lack support from upper management. The next steps in the enterprise wide product delivery process comprise the activities under the Product Line Management Process. The corporation must *gather and understand market information* (steps 2 and 3), including customer and competition, and this information must be integrated with an understanding of the technology and process capabilities of the corporation. It is at this point that the Market Management Process and the Technology Development Process will be integrated into the product delivery process. In fact, we have found that it is often the people responsible for

**Exhibit 3.** Enterprise-Wide Product Development

Market Management
Strategy Development and Management
• generate company vision/mission
• set new product targets
• allocate resources
Product Line Management
• gather and understand market information
• develop strategic criteria for product portfolio selection
• generate product line plans
• select and manage product portfolio
Product Development
• identify opportunity
• charter product development team
• understand customer needs
• develop product concept(s)
• define and develop product
Demand Fulfillment
• receive orders
• make and stock product
• fill and ship order
• bill customer and collect payment
Technology Development

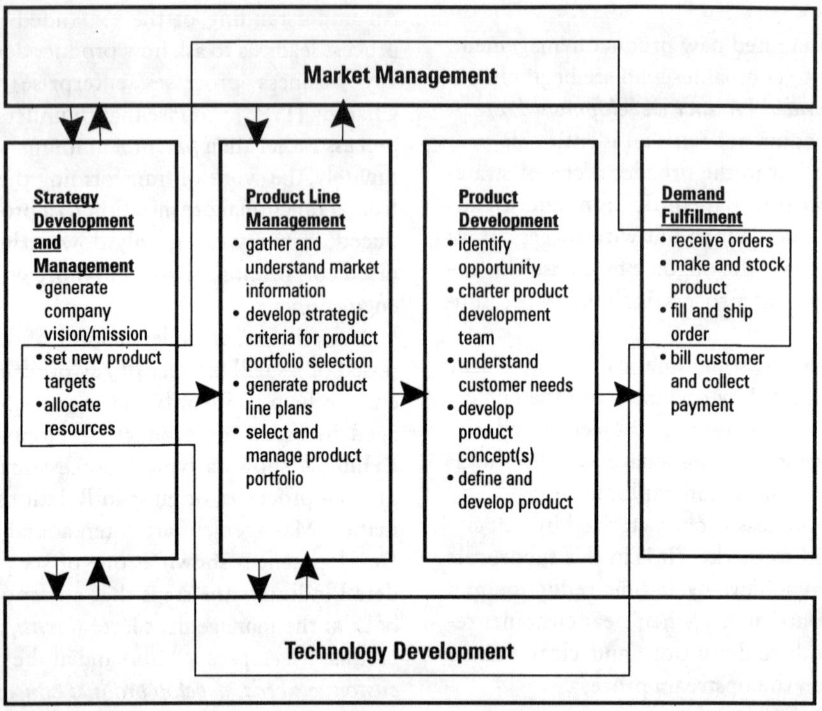

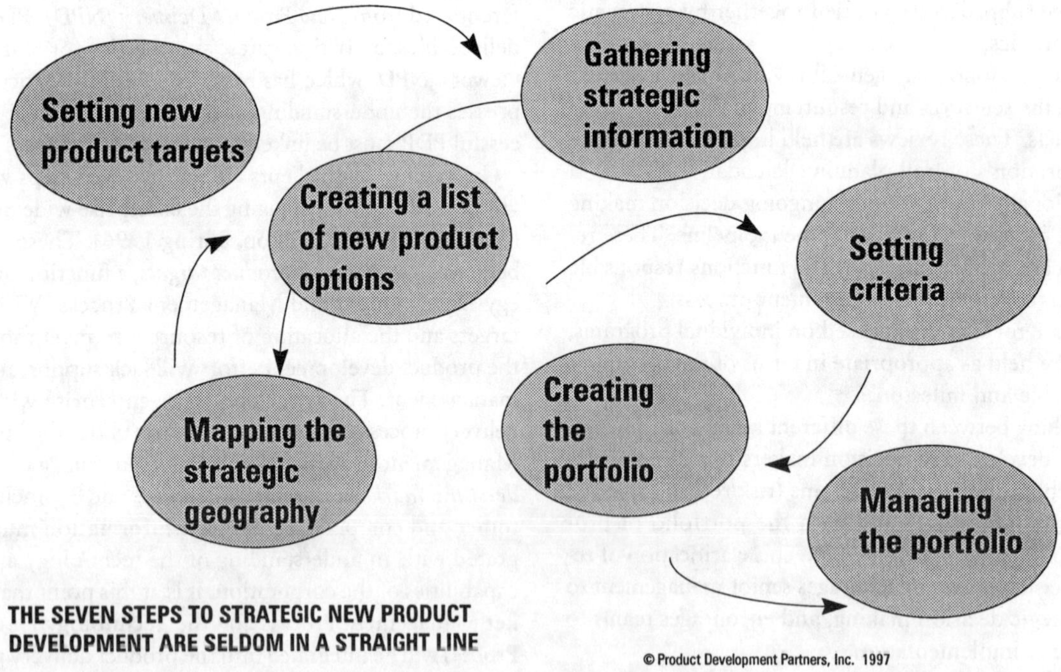

**Exhibit 4.** Seven Steps: Linking Product Development And Strategy

Setting new product targets
Gathering strategic information
Creating a list of new product options
Setting criteria
Mapping the strategic geography
Creating the portfolio
Managing the portfolio
THE SEVEN STEPS TO STRATEGIC NEW PRODUCT DEVELOPMENT ARE SELDOM IN A STRAIGHT LINE
© Product Development Partners, Inc. 1997

the Technology Development Process who push the corporations to articulate product/technology/customer linkages through the use of product/technology roadmaps (Willyard and McClees 1987) and variations on QFD (Quality Function Deployment; Griffin 1992) so that technology resources can be deployed effectively.

Step 4 is simply to list all of the product and opportunity options that are available to the product delivery process. Often this information is scattered throughout the corporation: Market Management is in close contact with the customer, Technology Development is working on numbers of technology advances, and others in the company have good ideas which they are either working on or have shelved because they can't get resources. Before any selection of a product portfolio can be undertaken, the corporation needs to have a way of gathering together all these sources of possible products and listing them in comparable form. This deceptively simple step can be a difficult one to accomplish because of the territorial boundaries it needs to cross.

*Developing strategic criteria for product portfolio selection* is step 5 in the process. Although this step is the responsibility of the Product Line Management Process, it calls upon the work of the Strategy Development and Management Process to articulate a strategy for the corporation from which new product strategy can be understood. A constant failure of product development is the shifting of strategic priorities, which keeps teams from being able to move quickly from identified opportunity to product. Unless the product delivery process is thought of as enterprise wide, executives are prone to involve themselves during the Product Development Process itself, where their influence is historically more distracting than helpful (Wheelwright and Clark 1992).

*Selecting the product portfolio* depends on the accomplishment of the earlier steps. We have found that many companies still use a linear planning process which compares product to product and results in a prioritized list. The processes which result in good portfolio planning involve iterative multidimentional (matrixed) displays of information which move decision making from linear to strategic, from implicit to explicit, and from individual to collaborative (Gill, Nelson, Spring 1996). This kind of decision making requires supporting tools to help management compare and contrast a lot of different information while engaging in discussions that result in collaborative decision making. We have found that displaying information in "bubble charts," which allow for up to seven or eight variables to be displayed in one frame, provides an excellent and flexible methodology to promote portfolio decision making. Commercially available software analysis tools provide databases that can keep track of product information and display it against comparable and strategically relevant criteria, thus generating multiple scenarios which display the portfolio candidates against different criteria. Such tools enable the corporation to keep ongoing track of its product options and to support decision making by generating portfolio scenarios for use at reviews.

Step 7 is managing the portfolio. In most product development stage/gate processes, individual projects are managed as they move through the pipeline. In making our view enterprise wide, we see that what must be managed is the aggregate product portfolio as it promises collectively to deliver on strategic goals and as it collectively draws on the corporation's finite resources (Harris and McKay 1996). This seventh step also links the product delivery process to the Demand Fulfillment Process. Too often, product development fails to make a clear connection with the supply side of the corporation. New products are seen by that process as competing with existing products, and lack of planning and integration means that even a potentially successful product is under-marketed or poorly distributed, and so fails to meet its potential. Further, the product lifecycle is often not managed, and so existing product information is not fed back to Product Line Management for optimal planning.

These steps are seldom if ever followed linearly: rather, the corporation will find itself moving from one step to another iteratively, developing information as best it can in one step, returning to that step when the information can be more fully developed. The steps enable the corporation to act out of an understanding of its enterprise wide product delivery process. When the corporation takes on the practices of the Seven Steps, linking its product development efforts to corporate strategy and thus making optimal use of its product development resources, it is able to make portfolio decisions that create balance and synergy through involving the cooperative participation of management

The expanded view of product development, and the recognition of its fit within the key business processes of the corporation, will allow corporations to bring discipline to the management of product development and aggregate product planning. The management of the new product portfolio will be to the next decade of new product program management what the stage/gate was to the decade of themid 1980's to the mid 1990's. Managing across programs increases the complexity of program management, and it requires new project management tools and new ways of thinking.

## References

Cooper, Robert G. Winning at New Products: Accelerating the Process from Idea to Launch. 2nd ed. Reading, MA: Addison-Wesley, 1993.

Crawford, J. Kent. "Effective Product Development Through Holistic Project Management." Project Management Institute 27th Annual Seminar/Symposium. Boston, 1996.

Gill, Bob, Beebe Nelson, and Steve Spring. "Seven Steps to Strategic New Product Development." The PDMA Handbook of New Product Development. New York: Wiley, 1996.

Griffin, Abbie. "Evaluating QFD's Use in U.S. Firms as a Process for Developing Products." Journal of Product Innovation Management. 9:171-187 (March 1992)

Hammer, Michael, and James Champy. Reengineering the Corporation. A Manifesto for Business Revolution. New York: HarperCollins, 1993.

Harris, John R, and Jonathan C. McKay. ""Optimizing Product Development Through Pipeline Management." The PDMA Handbook of New Product Development. New York: Wiley, 1996.

McGrath, Michael E. Product Strategy for High-Technology Companies: How to Achieve Growth, Competitive Advantage, and Increased Profits. New York: Irwin. 1995.

Roussel, Philip A., Kamal N. Saad, and Tamara J. Erickson. Third Generation R&D: Managing the Link to Corporate Strategy. Boston: Harvard Business School Press, 1991.

Souder, W. E., and T. Mandakovic. "R&D Project Selection Models." Research Management. 1986.

Wheelwright, S. C. and K. B. Clark. Revolutionizing Product Development: Quantum Leaps in Speed, Efficiency, and Quality. New York: Free Press, 1992.

Willyard, C. W., and C. W. McClees. "Motorola's Technology Roadmap Process." Harvard Business Review. 1987.

# Distributed Project Management—Managing the Process of Managing Projects

Brian K. Ferrilla, CEO, System Solvers, Ltd.

## Introduction

Process management is a particularly effective way to reduce the resource congestion that plagues organizations which undertake many projects across shared staff resources. The traditional project management approach with its focus on the project manager monitoring and maintaining the project's progress, however, may obscure the overall process. A more effective means of managing a project is through "distributed project management" (DPM) techniques—a term coined by System Solvers, Ltd. to describe the transfer of the project management process to the actual team members themselves. This paper discusses the opportunity for the distributed project management concept in an organization as well as an introduction to the tools available for its facilitation.

## Project Process Workflow

To better understand the concepts of distributed project management (DPM), one should focus attention on the fundamental building blocks of how a team-oriented project is executed: the process workflow. The workflow for a particular project outlines the milestones as well as the description and sequence of tasks to be completed to support the attainment of each milestone.

Though the workflow describes the work breakdown structure for the project as well as the estimated time to completion of each task, the assignment of these tasks to the various team members is an important step in defining the success of the project.

Traditionally, a project kickoff meeting would facilitate the initial interaction of the team members to obtain an

**Exhibit 1.** Dpm At Work

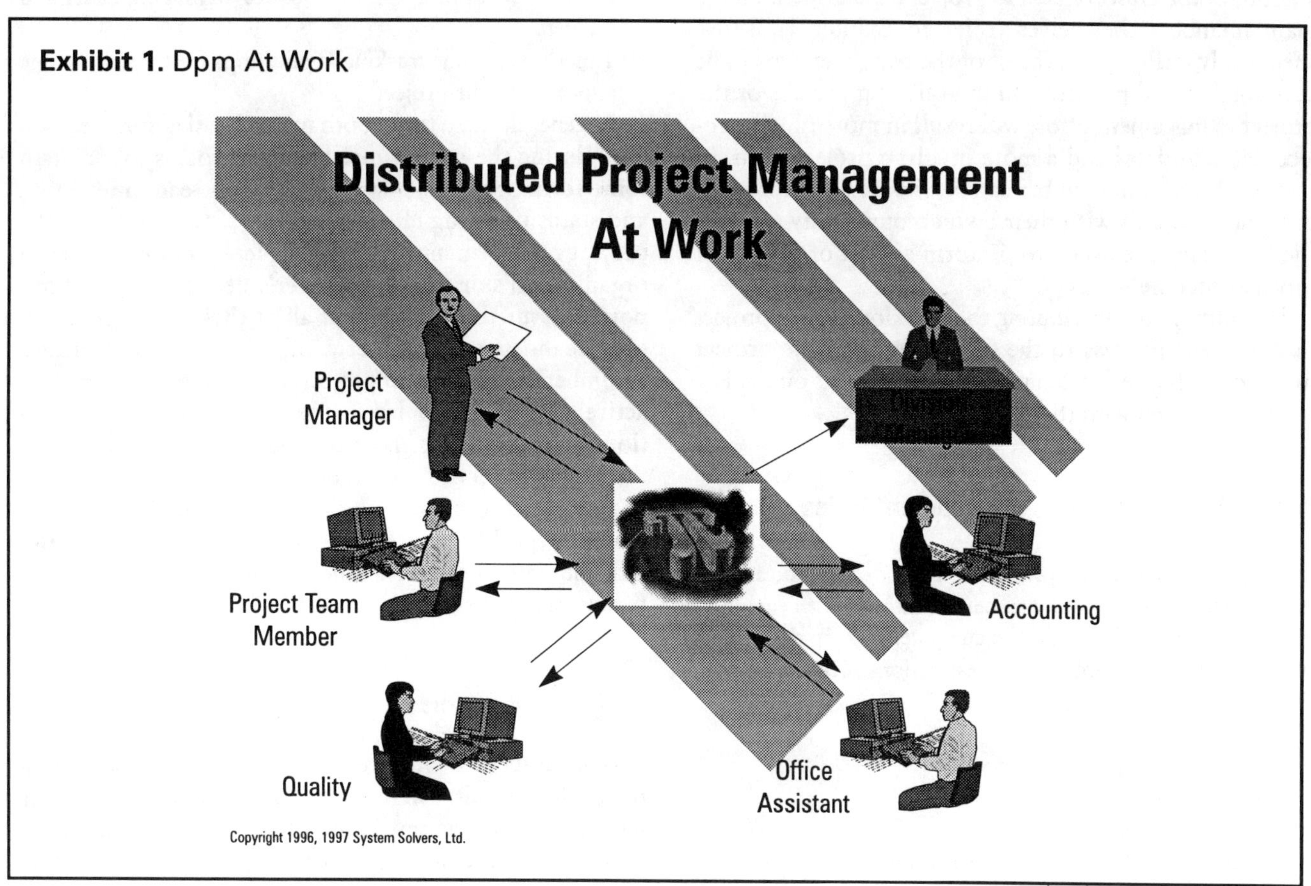

understanding of the project approach and the tasks that will be assigned to them as well as anticipated completion dates. The progress associated with each team member's tasks is typically monitored by the project manager via routine (possibly weekly) team meetings or on an individual basis. Thus, the project manager has the responsibility of "management by walking around" to always have a current pulse on the overall project.

In reality, the pulse of the project is typically outdated by anywhere from one day to several weeks depending on the frequency of interaction that the project manager demands with the team members. In fact, by the time the project manager compiles all of the information for the status update, which he would use to update the project timeline, the status has likely changed many times over. This constant catch-up process can be viewed as a reactive approach to project management since issues which arise may not effectively be able to be dealt with until after they have come to light. In this traditional scenario, the project manager is expending a significant amount of time interacting with team members simply to maintain the project's current status.

The goal of distributed project management is to invert the process of managing the project and place a significant amount of the effort related to project management on the team members themselves (refer to Exhibit 1). More specifically, the empowerment of the team members to be accountable and proactive in the ongoing process of the project management effort will result in more timely project status updates and a more involved project team. In essence, each team member can be viewed as an independent business unit with their own accountability towards the tasks they are asked to perform as part of the larger project outcome.

In addition, by distributing the workload of the project management process to the team members, the project manager will have more time available to focus on the key issues associated with the project.

## Team Member Process Involvement Roles

During the course of any project, a number of routine actions are performed by all team members to interact with each other, the project manager, and the customer to keep the project moving forward. Examples of these actions include:

- Task delegation
- Task feedback
- Reviewing team member's work
- Enforcing quality and accountability
- Open issue management
- Project chronological narrative logging
- Status meetings
- Creating and reviewing deliverables
- Customer relationship management
- Key event management
- Monitoring project metrics

These actions must be performed as part of the project process workflow that has been laid out by the project manager. Traditionally, companies have documented their project management standards, process workflow, and procedures in hard copy binders for use as reference material. The project manager's familiarity with these offline libraries of procedures and their ability to enforce them becomes the critical cog in the project process management effort.

In the traditional project management approach, these actions are facilitated with a number of productivity tools which serve special purposes to accomplish a specific job. These tools may include:

- Interoffice memos, intercoms, telephone conversations, voice mail, mail, and email for status communications
- Spreadsheets for task management and status
- Scheduling/progress reporting tool (e.g. MS Project) for calculating and reporting resource utilization
- Sticky notes for reminders of upcoming actions
- Project accounting applications for managing costs and budgets
- Timesheet or time tracking applications for managing time allocated to the project

In general, these tools, both manual and automated, are used during the project management process to maintain some form of consistency in the project team interaction and status updating efforts. The use of these tools in the project management process is typically tailored to each organization's or project manager's desire. The most important issue to notice is that all of these tools generally operate independently of each other! In essence, there are a number of "islands" of project management information actively being manipulated at any given time. This situation obviously lends itself to potential chaos and additional project coordination efforts to keep all parties focused on a current, accurate pool of project data. It is the job of the project manager to control this chaos with a significant amount of effort which in itself is not the most efficient use of their time.

## Use of Technology

Recent advances in software, hardware and networking technology have resulted in the creation of a number of building blocks to aid in the revolution of the project management process. The concept of distributed project management relies

**Exhibit 2.** DPM Technology Components

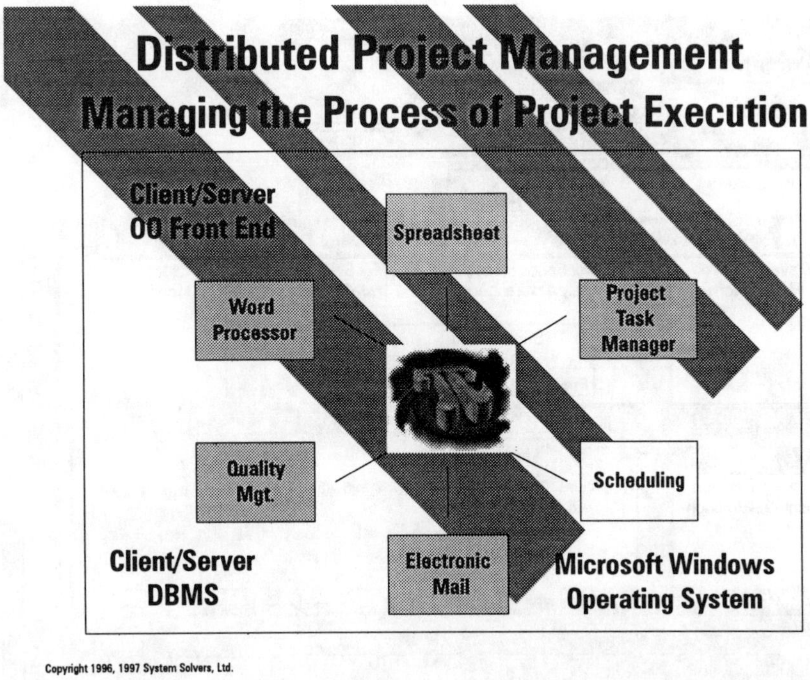
Distributed Project Management
Managing the Process of Project Execution
Client/Server
OO Front End
Spreadsheet
Word Processor
Project Task Manager
Quality Mgt.
Scheduling
Client/Server DBMS
Electronic Mail
Microsoft Windows Operating System
Copyright 1996, 1997 System Solvers, Ltd.

**Exhibit 3.** DPM Internet Integration

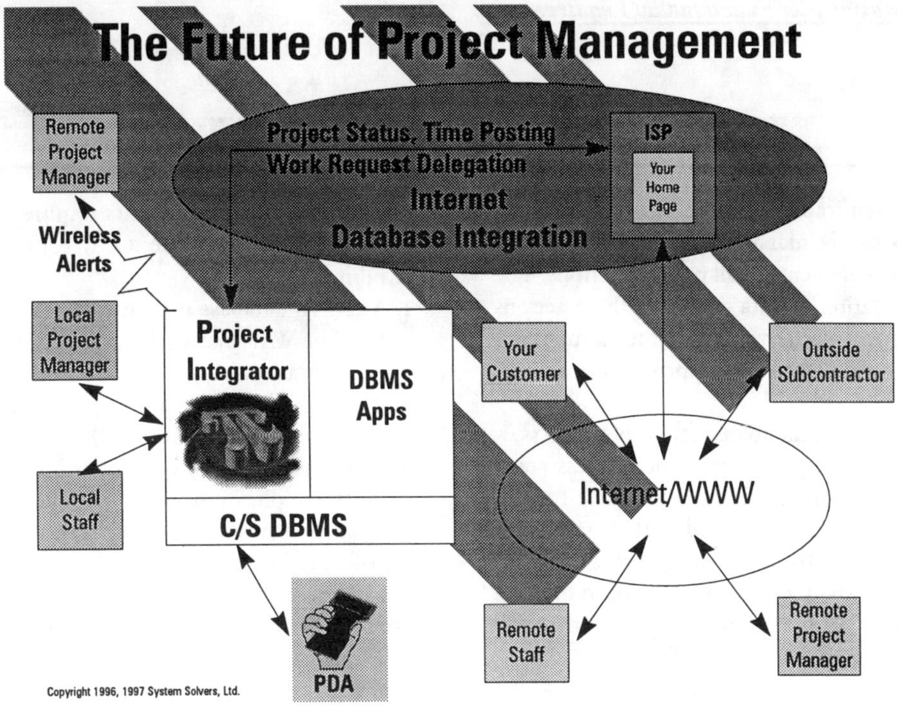
The Future of Project Management
Remote Project Manager
Project Status, Time Posting
Work Request Delegation
Internet
Database Integration
ISP
Your Home Page
Wireless Alerts
Local Project Manager
Project Integrator
DBMS Apps
C/S DBMS
Your Customer
Outside Subcontractor
Local Staff
Internet/WWW
PDA
Remote Staff
Remote Project Manager
Copyright 1996, 1997 System Solvers, Ltd.

**Exhibit 4.** On-Line Project Process Flow

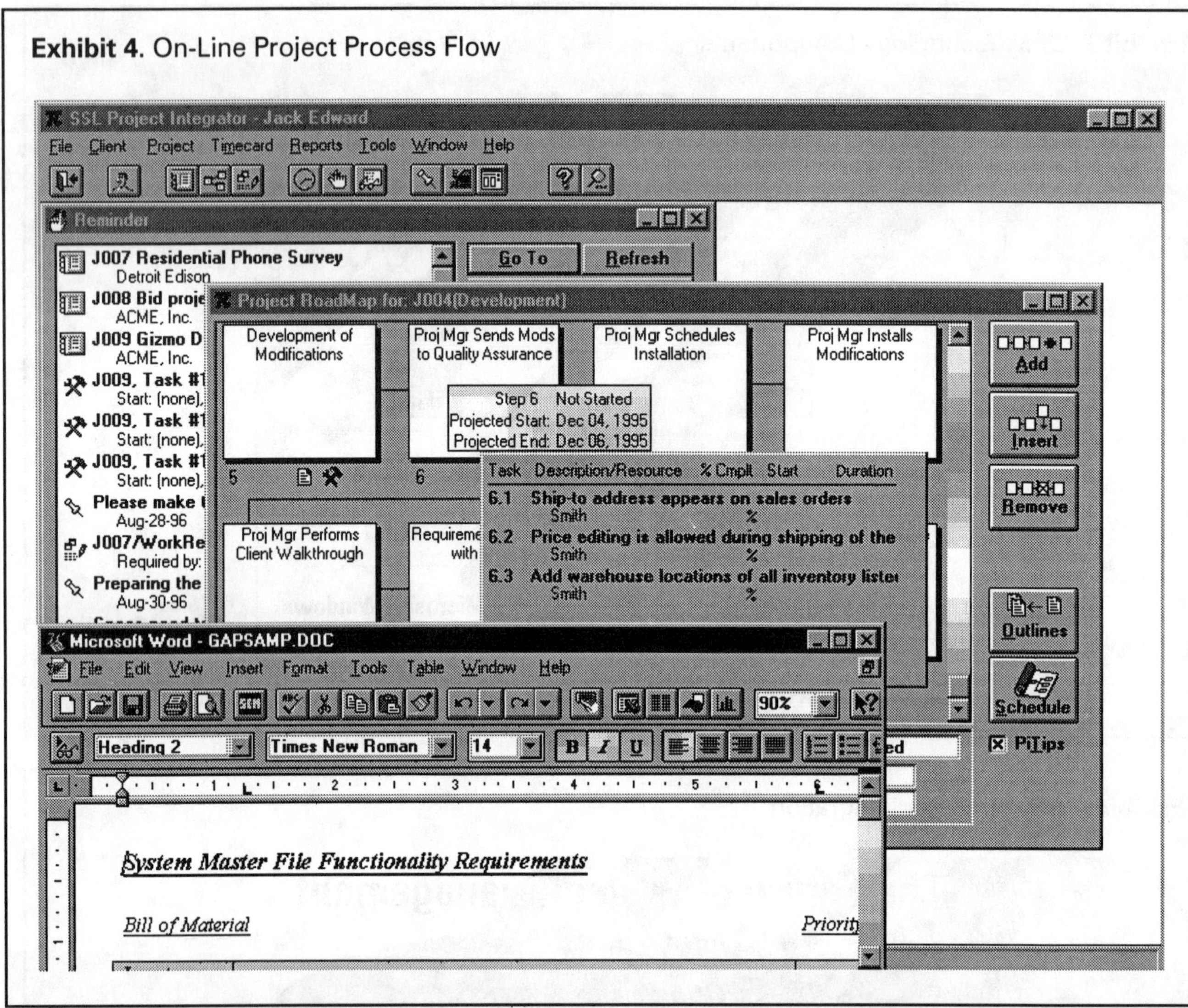


on the tightly interwoven framework of a project team's actions. This framework can be managed within a central database containing the data elements of all possible actions. The vehicle for the manipulation of data related to these actions is the network of computer workstations that team members utilize to communicate the creation and progress of the actions.

With today's client/server database technology, it is possible to take existing project management process standards and maintain them on-line in an interactive forum. The network of users that are involved with a particular project can then interact with the on-line process, via execution of the actions embedded in the process, to provide continuous feedback as each member progresses through their assigned efforts.

The technology components required to support a distributed project management environment include (refer to Exhibit 2):

1. A central database management system (DBMS)
2. LAN or WAN network connectivity of team member workstations
3. A process management and project execution tool (e.g. SSL Project IntegratorTM)
4. Project productivity tools (wordprocessor, spreadsheet, CAD application, etc.)
5. Project resource scheduling tool

An optional technology component would be the use of the Internet or a corporate Intranet. This technology offers benefits that are only now starting to be realized. The Internet infrastructure facilitates on-line transaction processing (i.e. execution of project actions) from truly distributed resources: in the next cubical or from a desk somewhere else on the globe (refer to Exhibit 3). Though this capability is only in its infancy, the future will see the opportunity to leverage this technology fully for the logging of project actions by "virtual" project team members located anywhere in the world.

An understated opportunity for the utilization of the Internet/Intranet infrastructure is the unique ability to bridge all team members regardless of their desktop workstation technology, e.g. CAD station, UNIX, Macintosh, IBM PC, palmtop, etc. This is a truly remarkable vision since there has been no successful mechanism to date which offers the level of real-time project team member communication independent of their physical location and desired desktop environment.

## Facilitating the Project Management Process

The technology components above can be used to support the distributed project management process. The tight integration of a central database management system with an integrated process management and project execution tool provides very powerful DPM capabilities. An example of a real-life implementation of such a tool would be System Solvers, Ltd.'s Project IntegratorTM, an innovative client/server project execution tool which integrates with today's leading DBMS including Oracle, Sybase, and MS SQL Server.

Examination of each aspect of the project management process yields an understanding of the application of these technology components.

### *Workflow*

On-line storage and retrieval of the general steps to completion of a project (milestones) as well as a detailed identification of the tasks to be performed and the type of resource to be assigned within each step. If projects can be categorized, it is feasible to store a "template" of the workflow for use as a foundation process for any new project of the type required. This on-line workflow concept has an added benefit of being used to capture and enforce an ISO certified project process.

A graphical representation of this information, as exemplified in the Project RoadmapTM technology within the SSL Project IntegratorTM tool, provides an interactive view of the process (refer to Exhibit 4). All data supporting the steps and tasks are maintained in a central database.

### *Task delegation*

Utilizing a central team member database, tasks can be defined within a project and then delegated electronically to team members as database transactions. Team members are notified electronically of incoming tasks and priorities.

### *Task feedback*

Utilizing central timecard and worklog databases, team members can provide real-time status updates at the task level as well as a detailed justification of the time expended to complete a task. Such feedback data would include effort expended on a task, percent completed, effort remaining on the task, etc. This feedback instantly provides the project manager or other team members with an understanding as to the impact this status update has on the project as a whole.

### *Reviewing team member's work*

Utilizing the central timecard and worklog databases described above, project managers can electronically review team members' task feedback to determine the accuracy and verify justification of work performed. In essence, the project manager becomes the "gatekeeper" to review, question, or enhance, the feedback provided. The importance of this activity is heightened when accurate project billing data needs to be produced.

### *Enforcing quality and accountability*

Use of an on-line quality assurance mechanism at the task level allows project managers to enforce desired quality checks on tasks upon their completion by the team members. Tasks can't be flagged complete by the team member until they have completed an on-line quality checklist related to the task as initially outlined by the project type template or by the project manager himself.

### *Open issue management*

Unforeseen uses of resources virtually always occur on any team project of magnitude. A central database for logging open issues as they arise, delegating them to appropriate team members, and managing their ultimate resolution should be performed on-line as an extension to team members' on-line feedback. In addition, monitoring the use of resources on open issues can be managed via the task feedback mechanism.

### *Project chronological note logging*

The ongoing documentation of all customer-level, project-level, and task-level notes by team members serves as a central chronological narrative history of the day-to-day events surrounding a project. This information serves as an audit trail as well as a point of reference for future projects which may justify a change to the project workflow on the next project of a similar type.

### *Status meetings*

Status meetings as defined in the traditional project management model have an altered agenda under the distributed project management concept. In the traditional model, for example, the weekly status meeting includes a go-around to all team members to report on their progress since the last status meeting — a very *reactive approach* to the project management process. In the DPM model, the status meeting becomes a *strategy* meeting since all project status data is already known by team members and project managers *before* the meeting due to the central task feedback mechanism. This results in a *proactive approach* to the project management process

### *Creating and reviewing deliverables*

Project deliverables take on many forms — documents, spreadsheets, drawings, videos, sound clips, photos, etc. — all of which must be interwoven with the project's execution process. The process of how a project is executed has embedded within it the type of deliverable to be created at the step and task level. A proven project process, or Project RoadmapTM as expressed by SSL's Project IntegratorTM technology, will have the required deliverables to be created actually embedded within the database supporting the roadmap (refer to Exhibit 4.). This concept allows for the use of template standard deliverables to be used as a foundation within a specific project's execution. Also, this embedding of the deliverables to the Project RoadmapTM adds to the scope of the project's central data repository. The use of MS Windows based applications allows for the maintenance of a secure, normalized, and integrated set of deliverable "objects" created in those applications.

### *Customer relationship management*

Involving the customer in the project status process is critical to the project's success. Utilizing the central database of task feedback maintained by the team members, updated project timelines and project status reports can be instantly produced to communicate with the customer. In addition, extending the database itself to the customer via remote access techniques or utilizing the Internet, customers can interact with their project information themselves at their convenience. This on-line customer service concept offers a proactive approach to managing projects by involving the customer in the distributed project management process.

Managing the details outlining the characteristics of a customer's organization may also become important if multiple project team members may be interacting with the customer organization. A central database of these characteristics, contacts, and past project work must be available as an aid for troubleshooting open issues or for managing the current project's expectations.

### *Key event management*

Proactive project management can only be accomplished by a project manager constantly dedicating their efforts to simultaneously monitoring every delegated task across all projects and applying various decision-making business rules to maintain progress. In reality, this is not physically possible due to the logistics of person-to-person communication as can be seen in the reactive nature of the traditional weekly status meeting approach. However, maintaining a central database of "event alerts" which have been configured by project managers or team members based on the desire to be informed when a particular condition occurs can provide management by exception focus of the project team. The occurrence of a pre-defined event leads to a trigger in the database which results in the immediate creation of an Internet Email, a page, or a fax to be sent to the team member requesting the feedback.

### *Monitoring project metrics*

The distributed project management concept of allowing team members to provide feedback at the task level on a real-time basis into a central database facilitates the instant analysis of project metrics across a number of dimensions of projects. The fundamental data required to perform productivity and profitability analysis is provided by the team members as transactions at the task timecard and worklog level. The inherent capabilities of the database allows for the grouping and sorting of data across a number of typical dimensions including resource, customer, project, department, project type, dates, and project status as examples.

## Management by Exception

Taking the concept of distributed project management a step further, with the assumption that the routine project management activities are essentially managed by the team members themselves on a pseudo real-time basis (i.e. hourly, daily, etc.) and posted to a central repository of project information, then the information that supports the project status would be available for the project manager to scrutinize on-demand. More specifically, with the appropriate tools, this scrutiny can be performed on an exception basis, i.e. what are the key issues now and what is required to resolve them?

With the client/server database technology discussed earlier, the selective retrieval of these issues yields a powerful management by exception environment. Tasks that have not been completed, tasks completed late, open issues remaining open over some time frame, rate of manpower expended on a task exceeding that anticipated, unbilled hours — these are all examples of exceptions that require project management action. DPM can facilitate the identification of the exceptions and provide the project manager with time to address them.

## DPM Implementation Issues

The implementation success of a distributed project management environment is driven based on a number of key factors:

- Implementation of a Management-By-Project Philosophy
- Organization Culture
- Availability of a Proven Project Management Process
- Planned Investment

### Implementation of a Management-By-Project Philosophy

The concept of managing-by-project has been recently looked upon in a serious light by many of the world's top organizations for application internally, even though they may not be a provider of project-oriented services to their customers.

The reasons are simple. Project management principles can be applied to any form of effort which requires the planning and execution of a sequence of defined tasks performed by resources to reach a desired goal for a particular customer (internal or external). Also, the routine measurement of the progress of these tasks provides a true business gauge as to the ongoing ability for the team resources to meet their targets for the project scope outlined.

Examples of the application of this concept in the more traditional operational aspects of an organization would include:

- Sales—pre-sales efforts, lead follow-up
- Marketing—trade shows, seminars, newsletter development, marketing campaigns
- Finance—period end, annual reports, tax filing
- Engineering—design, new product development

In each case, it is possible to create a project management process workflow, associate project deliverables, and define tasks to be performed by team members.

### Organization Culture

An important corollary to the implementation of the MBP philosophy and the distributed project management concept is that there must be a corporate culture that is willing to support it. This culture must start at the top and be woven down through all levels of project team interaction via corporate policy. Depending on the breadth of the roll-out of the MBP concept, team members could include everyone from professional project managers and technical resources down to secretaries, assistants, and department supervisors.

One of the potential dangers with enforcing this commitment is the feeling on the part of the team members that they are now being held accountable for all work they perform on any project and will be closely scrutinized. This may lead to a sense of an "over-the-shoulder" management style potentially resulting in counterproductivity and dissension if not properly presented to the staff. The team members must see the benefits of DPM and want to contribute.

### Availability of a Proven Project Management Process

A prerequisite for the implementation of DPM in an organization is a well thought out project process workflow. Based on the type of project, this workflow must consider the applicable steps (milestones), the tasks required to support each steps' completion, and the deliverable objects that must be produced. The granularity of the tasks defined should be created such that they can be delegated on a team member by member basis. In most transitions from a traditional project management approach to a DPM approach, there is a need to review and enhance the processes and procedures currently in place to ensure their congruency with the DPM project execution system.

### Planned Investment

The investment associated with the implementation of a distributed project management environment is very much based on the technology required to facilitate the real-time electronic interaction among project team members. From a technology standpoint, the key components are restated below:

- A central database management system (e.g. Oracle, Microsoft SQL Server, Sybase)
- Team member PC workstations capable of supporting the MS Windows or Web Browser environment
- Database server hardware and operating system (e.g. Novell Netware or Microsoft NT)
- LAN or WAN network connectivity (e.g. Token Ring, Ethernet, 10BaseT)
- A process management and project execution tool (e.g. SSL's Project IntegratorTM)
- Project productivity tools (e.g. MS Word, MS Excel, etc.)
- Project resource scheduling tool (e.g. MS Project, Primavera, etc.)

It is estimated that the implementation of the technology components above would require an investment of $3,000-$5,000 per team member. For organizations that may already have a comparable technology infrastructure, a respective investment estimate would be in the $1,000-$2,000 range per team member.

Additional soft investments need to be considered for a DPM implementation:

- Training of project managers and team members

- Installation and implementation assistance from outside vendors
- Annual maintenance costs related to the technology tools
- Internal project management process review and potential restructuring
- Internal resources assigned to manage the DPM implementation project itself
- Opportunity costs related to the roll-out of the technology

# Industrial Cooperation in a Competitive Environment—The Story of the Advanced Photo System

Chris S. Adams, PMP, Eastman Kodak Company

## Introduction

On April 22, 1996, consumers from around the world began buying and using products and services from an entirely new photographic system offered by forty different companies. The simultaneous introduction worldwide by these companies was a historic moment in the photo industry. However, that's just part of the story.

The products and services of the Advanced Photo System evolved from an unprecedented collaborative process involving Eastman Kodak and its top competitor, Fuji, as well as three leading camera companies: Canon, Minolta, and Nikon. The film, cameras, and photofinishing services were based on several key new technologies and a set of detailed specifications, developed jointly by the five System Developing Companies (SDC). Licenses were then offered to other photographic companies, so that they could also make products or offer services for the Advanced Photo System. This collaboration was done in accordance with laws governing antitrust behavior.

This paper addresses 4 topics:

1. Why was cooperation necessary and desired?
2. What methods were employed to ensure that the SDC would make progress and achieve the ultimate goal?
3. What factors were critical to the success of the effort?
4. What did Kodak learn from the experience?

This project, named "Orion" within Kodak, was among the most ambitious projects ever for the photographic industry leader. Initial brainstorming of concepts began in the mid 1980's, shortly after the introduction of the Disc system. Searches for partners lasted from the late 1980's to the early 1990's. By November, 1991, a 5-party, 82-page agreement had been reached just on how we would work together, not on matters specific to the actual system, which had yet to be developed. There were several major setbacks in technology and in reaching consensus on how the new system would look but everyone was ready in April, 1996, a date agreed upon two years earlier.

The risks were high. What would the consumers want in a new system? Would they be pleased with the offering? Would the new technologies work? Could we launch within an acceptable window of time, before competing products made the Advanced Photo System obsolete? Could the SDC reach agreement on specs while each party protected its own interests? Could Kodak realize an acceptable rate of return from such a huge investment? It was within this context that the SDC both collaborated and competed.

## The Need for Cooperation

In order to understand why cooperation was necessary, you must first examine the nature of the photographic industry and its condition in the late 1980's. There are just a handful of companies who drive major innovation; among them are the five who became known as the SDC for the Advanced Photo System. There are dozens of other companies who also supply products and services to the industry, which had sales of $65-70 billion in 1995.

Companies in the photo industry want people to capture, process, store, and use images. Anything offered that increases picture taking and usage benefits the industry. Some fifteen billion exposures are taken annually worldwide. Growth in the business has traditionally been driven by innovation in the form of new and easier to use products. For example, the 126 format was introduced in the late 1960's, followed by the 110 system in the 1970's, Disc in the early 1980's, and point and shoot 35mm cameras in the mid-1980's. There has always been an *evolutionary* trend upward in exposures taken, driven by population growth, amount of discretionary income, and product cost. However, each major product innovation caused an additional spike upward to a new level in photo activity—a *revolutionary* gain.

In the late 1980's, Pete Palermo was the General Manager of Kodak's Consumer Imaging business unit, the one that focuses on products for the average snapshooter. There were strong opinions among some people that traditional silver halide photography was mature and warranted no further investment. Instead, as the reasoning went, put all emphasis on driving manufacturing costs and prices down. Spend research dollars on digital imaging which was still in its infancy, but was expected to explode in popularity. Palermo had a different vision. While manufacturing costs and the digital arena deserved attention, he also recognized that there was still room for innovation in silver halide products. Customer data and research studies indicated that 35mm cameras, even though described as "point and shoot," still required a film loading operation that intimidated some people. In addition, technologies were under development at Kodak that offered the promise of additional features like multiple print sizes from the same roll of film. Palermo and others saw the possibility of a new system that removed some barriers and added new attractions at the same time. This system could cause the next spike upward to a new level in picture taking.

It was decided that we would look at all aspects of the picture taking process and drive innovation wherever it made sense, based on the identified needs of our customers. These customers included the final consumer and the operators of photofinishing equipment. The new system would be based on the needs of our customers. It would not be a technology "push" from the innovator. Palermo felt that success would depend on a collaboration among industry innovators and he initiated steps that led to the formation of the SDC.

From Kodak's perspective, the benefits of cooperation outweighed the risks of losing competitive advantage. First, a unified support of the new system by industry leaders would virtually guarantee a broad-based acceptance of any new standards. The VHS/Beta conflict in the early days of video technology demonstrated convincingly how a single company with a proprietary system has a difficult challenge in gaining worldwide acceptance. Apple Computer's troubles in recent years provide another example.

A second benefit of cooperation was that the expertise of the SDC members would complement one another. The theory, validated later in the project, was that more and better ideas would surface in the concept and development stages. This would result in a more appealing and more robust product. Later in this paper we'll discuss examples of the synergy within SDC in more detail. A third benefit of cooperation was that the cost and resource burden of development could be shared among more parties.

A fourth benefit of cooperation was the potential to reduce the product development cycle time. The theory is that development work could be shared by companies working in parallel. The topic of cycle time had several interesting facets in this project. There *were* cases in which work was shared to save time. However, the nature of the SDC relationship caused delays as well. Basically, each of the five members had veto power on any technology and design issue of significance. Gaining agreement often required lengthy reviews of data, hundreds of pages of faxes, and hours of personal debate. Ultimately, each of the companies launched products on the agreed upon date of April 22, 1996. Each member realized the importance of the new Advanced Photo System and the potential rewards for participation. The collaboration on development of the system led each company to have complete confidence that the others would be ready on time. This peer pressure had a significant positive affect on the project success as measured from a schedule perspective.

A fifth and last major benefit of the SDC cooperation would be the consistent advertising push on a worldwide basis. Each company, of course, would be calling attention to the benefits of its own products, but all would be emphasizing the benefits of the Advanced Photo System in general. Consumers would be expected to hear a similar message from different companies. This would help Kodak and other companies achieve a goal of a stepwise increase in industry photo activity.

## Advanced Photo System Description

It is not the intent of this paper to dwell on the features or technology of the new photo system, but a brief description will help the reader understand some of the challenges we faced as well as the excitement felt by team members. The Advanced Photo System film uses traditional silver halide chemistry, but the plastic support onto which the chemicals are coated is entirely new and represents only the second time the support has been changed for consumer film in Kodak's 117 year history. The support needed to change to accommodate the new film cassette, which is all recyclable plastic and has no film leader showing. The consumer simply drops the cassette into the camera (it will only fit one way) and closes the lid. For each frame in the roll, the consumer may choose one of three sizes: classic (like a standard 35mm print), group (slightly wider print) or panoramic. The camera easily fits in a shirt pocket or purse. Its small size is a benefit of the smaller film size, about 60 percent of the area of a 35mm negative, but 6 times larger than a Disc negative. Advances in chemistry have allowed film manufacturers to maintain the quality one would see in a 35mm print.

Prints are returned in an envelope along with an index print (contains a miniature image of each picture on the roll) and the original cassette, which contains the processed negatives. While the prints may go in photo albums, the cassette and index prints may be neatly stored in specially designed containers for easy future reference—no more shoeboxes! Ordering of re-prints is easy because each index print has an identification number that matches one found on the cassette. You simply select your frame numbers and quantities and give the cassette back to the retailer. This eliminates the need to look at and handle negatives. A key technology that makes much of this possible is a new magnetic layer on the film, which allows communication among the consumer, camera, and photofinisher.

Every component of the photo system changed: the film (chemistry, support, and magnetic layer), the cassette, the camera, and the photofinishing equipment.

## Methods Used in the Cooperative Effort

### The First Steps

The SDC members were—and are—intense competitors. When Kodak initially approached the others, a great deal of suspicion had to be overcome by all involved. In the end, all five companies realized that cooperation was necessary to achieve the goal of industry growth. In short, the other companies became convinced of the same benefits to cooperation discussed earlier. A lengthy agreement was signed to ensure that the companies would work together in good faith and to minimize risk if the SDC collapsed before products were commercialized. Royalty and patent ownership understandings were also reached. When the SDC was originally formed, the members had only the most general notion of what might be created. We knew we wanted something revolutionary and had information on barriers to consumer usage, but the specifics were yet to be determined. This was a challenge in itself as we sought to define project requirements.

Product features were driven by consumer research. More than 22,000 people were surveyed in a series of studies conducted worldwide by Kodak to determine the features of most importance to them in an ideal picture-taking system. This market research is a Kodak strength. While some information was kept internally for competitive reasons (e.g., camera styling and film packaging graphics), other results were shared with SDC members to support a list of basic system features like drop-in film loading and three print sizes.

Another early activity in the project for SDC was to define and agree upon a set of standards. This became the "backbone" which would be referenced by all product manufacturers. The standards covered the basic elements of the system: the camera, the film cassette, equipment for processing and printing the film images, and how digital information would be encoded and read. Definitions and agreements were not easily reached and required much negotiation. One reason was the language and culture barrier. The Japanese required Kodak to define and explain the differences between "targets," "goals," and "objectives." We sometimes used these words interchangeably. Another reason for the difficulty in reaching agreements was the need for each company to protect its own interests. A third reason for difficulty is that the SDC members may have had different priorities. An important matter to one was not necessarily a "front burner" issue for another company.

The standard-setting process, while often painful, focused the SDC members on the ultimate goal: a reliable product which would delight the customer. The standards were made available to licensees beginning in April, 1994. Educational forums were held for licensees so that they would understand and comply with the standards. Participating companies still had two years to design products that met Advanced Photo System specifications with their own innovations included for reasons of differentiation. The SDC agreed upon the April, 1996 introduction date early in 1994, after estimating when the technology that SDC was developing would be mature and how much time licensees would need to understand the system and develop their own products.

### Organization

They say a camel is a horse designed by committee. The word "committee" is seldom used in business anymore because of negative connotations: inactivity, non-productive activity, long cycle times, etc. Well, the SDC formed a series of committees. It *did* take a long time to reach agreement for the reasons cited earlier. At times, the negotiations resembled a government bureaucracy. However, progress was made and the goals were achieved. The system of interlocking committees fostered communication of the right topics at the right levels. Detailed work could be "pushed down" to teams and people with the appropriate skills and knowledge.

The *Steering Committee* was at the top and included key business and technical leaders from the five companies. It was responsible for overall strategic direction and decision making. The Steering Committee agreed upon the introduction date and resolved disagreements at lower levels. The *Working Committee* was composed of technical leaders from SDC. It managed the evaluation of system features and technologies developed for the Advanced Photo System. One of its key roles was to recommend which features and technologies should be incorporated. The Steering Committee ultimately decided to accept or reject the suggestions.

The problem of having different priorities and interests was mentioned earlier. One example of this surfaced within the Working Committee. The camera companies (Nikon, Canon, Minolta) proposed a film cassette design early in the project that was made of metal and had about twenty parts that would require hand assembly. Keep in mind that a company like Kodak would be making millions of these each year. Such a product would have had a unit cost of ten times the design actually used. The proposed design would have made camera design simpler, but was totally inconsistent with Kodak and Fuji goals and impractical from a manufacturing point of view.

The *Specifications Subcommittee* reported to the Working Committee and developed the system specification document. This document defined the selected technologies (new or existing) required to meet the customer feature requirements. It also defined the dimensions and standards for the film, film cassette, camera, and photofinishing equipment. This document is what was given to licensees for a fee, so that they could develop their own products that would be compatible with the new system. While the Working Committee developed and tested designs, selecting the best for the new system, the Specifications Subcommittee documented the selections in a way that would minimize misinterpretation by a third party.

The *Patent Committee* determined which of the patent claims owned by the SDC should be licensed. Various categories of patents were established by this team, and patents were sorted and royalty fees established. To give an idea of the work of this team and the project complexity, over 2700 patent applications were filed that related to the Advanced Photo System. Kodak generated roughly 60 percent of the critical patents issued to date. The *Licensing Committee* was responsible for the SDC agreements and for transferring the system technologies and specifications to the photographic industry. A help desk was established to aid licensees and document updates are distributed as needed. Today, over fifty companies have purchased a license for the Advanced Photo System.

### Communication

The Kodak development team in Rochester, N.Y. was thousands of miles away from the SDC members in Japan. Cultural and language differences were also barriers. Effective, continuous, and relevant communication was critical to success. An excellent policy was implemented early: all key communication would be done by fax. In addition to the value of a written record, errors in translation were lessened. It should be noted that the Japanese were gracious in that all of their fax communication was in English. During peak times of SDC activity, the fax traffic reached 200 pages per day received at the Kodak site. Internally, the Kodak team put another success factor in place: all SDC communication went to one fax machine. It was sorted for review and distribution by the project manager and chief technical leader. Outbound communication went through the same one fax machine. This control mechanism ensured that the Kodak team was unanimous in its position on a given topic and spoke with one voice.

In spite of the distance challenge, face to face meetings were necessary and occurred approximately every 2-3 months, with the location alternating between the U.S. and Japan. Translators were used, requiring twice as much time as a meeting might take where all parties shared the same native language. All SDC members seemed thoroughly prepared for meetings, thanks to the detailed attention given to agendas prior to the meetings and the quality of each company's team. Kodak ensured that it understood its position on each issue, had the data ready to support it, and developed contingency plans based on most likely reactions of other SDC members. Good preparation did not guarantee brief meetings—they were just shorter than they would have been otherwise. Skillful negotiations by all parties with the underlying shared vision of an exciting new photo system facilitated progress and success. A tele-video conference was used at one point. While the participants saw the potential value in certain situations, the face to face meetings were perceived to be more effective, possibly due to the complexity and importance of the issues.

## Key Success Factors

A number of factors contributed to the success of the project. The most important was that all five members of the SDC were committed to the effort. For all but one (Canon), silver halide imaging is the core of their business. The SDC shared the same vision of launching a new system to benefit the consumer and the industry. There were several serious disagreements throughout the project about key requirements and specifications. While in the middle of these intense negotiations, there were doubts that the issues would be resolved. However, the shared vision and the realization that no company individually was likely to succeed with the new system gave the SDC determination to work through the problems.

All SDC members had a sense of urgency about the project. Together, they knew that there was a window of opportunity that wouldn't be open forever. Most analysts predict that digital capture, storage, and display of images is the future, but the technology is not yet here to give the desired quality at an affordable price. Silver halide imaging yields extraordinary value. Technology does not stand still; it will improve over time. The Advanced Photo System both provides new benefits to traditional photography and serves as a bridge to the digital future.

Within Kodak, there was also a sense of urgency. Once agreement was reached on key requirements, the Kodak team felt that the other SDC members would be ready on the agreed upon launch date with products. The Kodak team wanted to also be ready—with the best product offering. Even though the SDC collaborated to design the system, they never lost sight of the fact that they were intense competitors in the marketplace.

The Kodak team that interfaced with the SDC was intentionally kept small. There were three key individuals: the Kodak project manager, the project chief technical leader, and the project commercial affairs leader (he was the lawyer who drafted the SDC agreements and provided counsel on all matters related to the relationships among the SDC companies and between SDC and licensees). These three gentlemen worked as a team for over five years, through launch of the new system. It was a sign of their own commitment to success. The continuity was important for three reasons. One was the stable leadership internally, for the benefit of the Kodak team. The second reason was the building and maintaining of relationships within SDC. It is disconcerting for any company to see the faces of their negotiating partner change. The stability allowed professional and personal relationships to develop and created a climate that nurtured trust. The third reason for the importance of continuity was related to the complexity of the technology and SDC relationships. The learning curve for a new addition to the team would have been too steep.

Another success factor was meeting preparation, which was extensive. Setting the agendas for SDC meetings was an effort in itself, with much fax traffic back and forth. For each meeting, the Kodak team discussed the issues, formed a position, anticipated reactions from other SDC members, prepared contingencies, and documented key points in advanced (proposals, experimental data, etc.). It was obvious from the meetings that the Japanese companies were equally prepared. The teams did not allow the time pressure of the meetings to alter their positions. In other words, even though the project itself felt time pressure, the negotiating teams did not feel a need to come back from a meeting with agreement on an issue if it meant compromising their position. However, there *were* some meetings that went well on into the night, to take advantage of the time together to make progress.

The two film companies complemented each other's skills. Kodak and Fuji had different design approaches that allowed each to look at problems from a different perspective. Fuji was very good with technical details and managed action item lists thoroughly. Kodak took a broader systems view. Kodak introduced; Fuji followed up. Kodak introduced more revolutionary ideas; Fuji's mindset was more evolutionary. Kodak excelled at statistical analysis, tolerances, and dimensioning. Fuji tested everything and helped to uncover some issues. The companies found a way to effectively blend these skills so that a more robust product could be introduced.

Kodak senior management was resolute in its support of the process. They stepped in when needed to keep the project moving forward, but otherwise allowed the project team to work at its own pace and style within the SDC. The Kodak team had direct access to the President of Consumer Imaging and to the CEO. Key decisions in the negotiating process were not slowed by the bureaucracy often associated with large companies.

## Lessons Learned

A multi-company effort to develop specifications for a new product requires one to choose partners carefully. Each company will have their own rationale for participating. Is there a shared vision that will lead to success? Is there enough flexibility that each partner will be able to accomplish their own individual goals while supporting the collaboration effort? The strategy for collaboration must be well defined and agreed to by all parties. What are the boundaries for discussion and effort? As with any type of effort, the complexity increases with the number of partners. It is doubtful that the Advanced Photo System project could have been successful with any more SDC members than the five we had.

Project success is often attributed to having the "right" people on your team. Kodak had the right people in leadership positions. They were aggressive, persistent, and committed to success. They were experienced negotiators and had excellent communication skills. They were open minded to new ideas. They shared a common vision for the future of Kodak and the industry. A sponsor or manager who is initiating a new project must think about the key roles and attributes (like those mentioned) required for success in those roles. Then the candidates with the best combination of attributes should be selected.

Negotiating teams for the companies must communicate with one another promptly and often. Although the fax traffic for SDC was heavy and overwhelming at times, it was effective. The single contact point within Kodak served us well. Meeting preparation and follow-up must be thorough. Internal analysis after a meeting of what went well and what went wrong leads to suggestions for improvement in the next meeting. The project team within a company must also communicate well. In addition to documenting agreements, decisions, and action items, the effective team will stay focused on its strategy (revising when appropriate).

Finally, as with all projects, there must be strong and visible sponsorship. The project team has a duty to update the sponsors regularly on progress and issues. The sponsors have an obligation to help when needed. There were times in the Advanced Photo System project when the senior management of each company was required to resolve a disagreement among the SDC negotiators. This was an effective and necessary use of the time and talents of the managers. They stayed out of the way of the project team otherwise and allowed them to do their job.

## Conclusion

The System Developing Companies and licensees successfully launched the Advanced Photo System on schedule worldwide in early 1996. Features were delivered to consumers that they wanted in a new system. The response has been tremendous. Post-launch research of owners of the Kodak version of the cameras revealed some of the most positive feelings ever about a new product. Four out of five were more satisfied with their new camera than the one they typically used. Four out of five were taking better pictures and making fewer mistakes. Over 95 percent said they would recommend the new photo system to others.

The launch brought elation—and a huge sigh of relief—from the companies involved. There were times when we wondered if we could deliver the products on time. There were times when we thought the entire collaboration would fall apart. We often wondered if the effort was worth the personal sacrifice. We overcame all of the obstacles to deliver a breakthrough product for genuine growth in the photographic industry and we now have a wealth of experience to apply to similar efforts in the future.

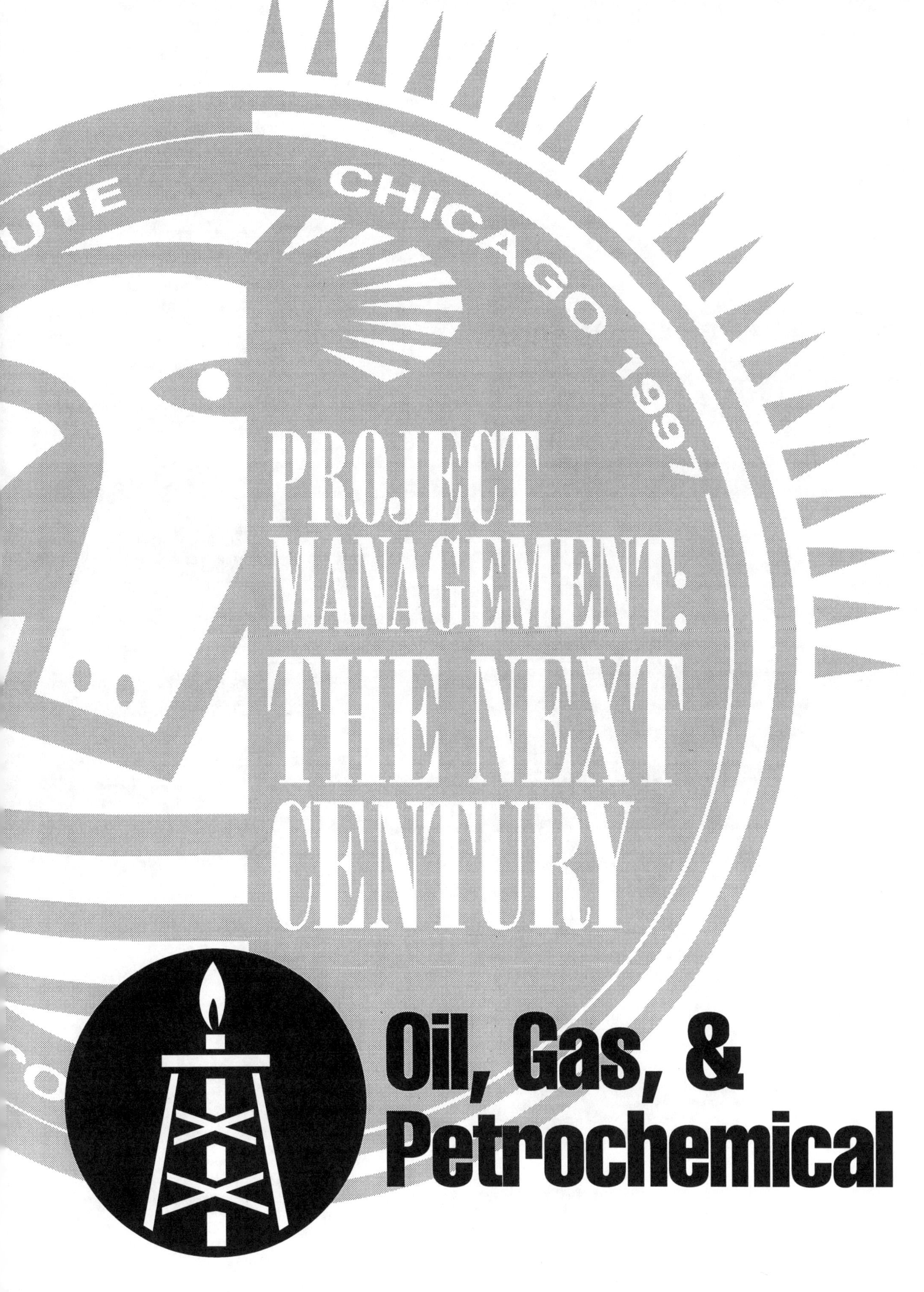
UTE
CHICAGO 1997
PROJECT MANAGEMENT: THE NEXT CENTURY
Oil, Gas, &
Petrochemical

# Value Added Project Management: Doing the Project Right is Not Enough

Dennis J. Cohen, Ph.D., Strategic Management Group, Inc. (SMG)
Judd Kuehn, Project Resources, Chevron U.S.A. Inc.

How many times have you heard a project manager lament, "I did everything right but the business people screwed it up!"? One would have to wonder how something like that could happen, especially when the project manager followed PMBOK down to the letter. Maybe the business died not because the project went wrong, but because it was the wrong project to begin with. While it is extremely important that a project be done right, the future of project management requires that it be the right project in the first place. As businesses incorporate PMBOK into their project management processes more frequently, the realization that implementation techniques are not always enough to make a project successful has come to the foreground. The emphasis in project management is shifting from planning, executing and controlling, to initiating and closing. As time will tell, the latter are the most crucial areas for the project management process of the future.

This paper will review the circumstances under which Chevron Corporation developed the Chevron Project Development and Execution Process, (CPDEP). CPDEP emphasizes initiating and closing from a business perspective. We will then go on to discuss some of the important underlying principles associated with the process. In closing, we will discuss how these principles might help to improve projects in general, especially information systems projects.

## The Development of CPDEP

When you think of a successful project, how would you describe it? What would you say? "It was on time and under budget?" "The stakeholders said it was a success?" Or, "It provided a significant business return to the company?" Classically in the world of project management, we have used the first phrase to define our project success. The second statement has also often been used to describe a "good" project. But today, we are hearing the third statement more frequently, as the focus of project management shifts to initiating and closing.

This change reflects the changing role and environment in which project managers work today. Traditionally, project managers have been handed a project and told to go and build it within a given budget and timeframe. In some cases, the project manager has been asked to determine the budget, schedule the project, and develop a project plan accordingly. And though customers and/or stakeholders needed to be satisfied with the outcome, it was sometimes true that what drove customers and stakeholders, provided only a short-term fix. The project went from being successful to being unsuccessful as time moved forward.

Today, we project managers are frequently being asked to manage the company's assets. This forces us to look beyond the area of project management, (because it puts the responsibility to look out for the company's best interest on us) even if it means that we do not satisfy all of our stakeholders or customers. Sometimes, this can even result in our having to kill our own projects. But why is this change occurring? Let's say you manage your project so it's on schedule and under budget and you even make some of your key stakeholders happy with the results (i.e., operations is happy because your project didn't upset current operations). Does this ensure a business success for the company? Not necessarily. Like many large corporations, we have had our share of projects that were on time and under budget, yet were not the best business decision for the company overall.

Here are a few experiences that we at Chevron have had:

At one point, we operated a large plant constructed in the mid-western United States. At the time the project was conceived, the product we wanted to produce was in high demand and commanded a premium price. Based on this, a plant was designed, funded and constructed by our project professionals.

The plant was actually completed ahead of schedule and under the approved budget. Our project team considered it a great success. But the plant was mothballed and closed shortly after it was commissioned. The project was a success, but the business died!

Another example was a project to acquire and develop some very promising exploration acreage. Based on sound research technology and good project management, we spent significant money to drill wells. We drilled the wells and discovered oil and gas. Although the potential identified here was significant, there was no supporting

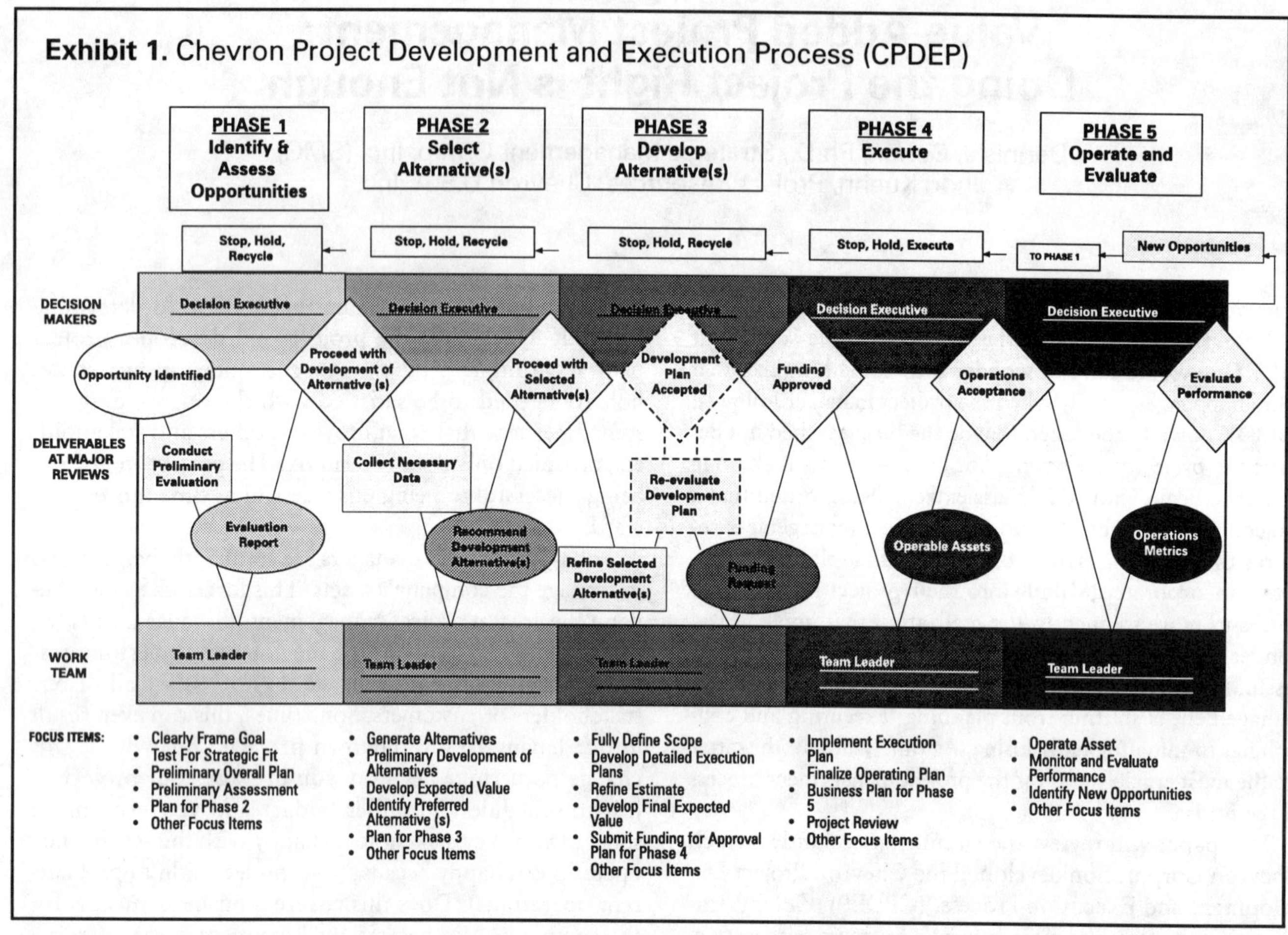

**Exhibit 1.** Chevron Project Development and Execution Process (CPDEP)

infrastructure or economically feasible way to move the products to market and so the acreage sits idle to this day.

So what went wrong with these opportunities? In the first case, we didn't fully understand the dynamics of the market. When the market changed, we were left out in the cold. Had we recognized that the market might change, we might have opted not to build the plant, (or at least to have modified the plan). In the second case, we didn't look far enough ahead or get input from other technical disciplines to fully understand the scope of the project. The project team had a myopic view of the world based on the technology of discovering oil and gas. They never considered the costs and difficulties of moving materials to market because they did not define the project in a strategic business framework. From their narrow technical point of view, they did their job; they found oil and gas. From a broader business perspective, though, they did not produce an asset with an adequate return on investment and did not add value for shareholders. The business contribution was nil. In fact, in the end, these projects actually subtracted value from the business.

## Lessons Learned and Underlying Principles

The lessons that can be learned from the above situations are these:

- Make sure any business opportunity is clearly defined, the market understood, and that stakeholders are defined and understood.
- Even after a project has begun, the business environment and the project's alignment with that environment must continually be tested.
- Look at the "whole" project and understand all of the steps of the business chain.
- Executing a project well doesn't guarantee success.

To help better accomplish our business goals, Chevron has made a change to the way we look at projects. As a result, we've created and introduced CPDEP.

CPEDP is a 5-Phase process that provides a formalized, disciplined method of managing projects and other asset development techniques. With its structured process of making decisions and analyzing risk, CPDEP has improved how Chevron approaches such varied tasks as negotiating

**Exhibit 2.**

High
Random Success
•Good Projects
•Average Execution
Consistent Success
•Good Projects
•Good Execution
Ability to Make Right Decisions
Mid
Success Unlikely
•Poor Projects
•Poor Execution
Random Success
•Poor Projects
•Good Execution
Low
Mid
High
Ability to Implement Decisions in Best Way Possible

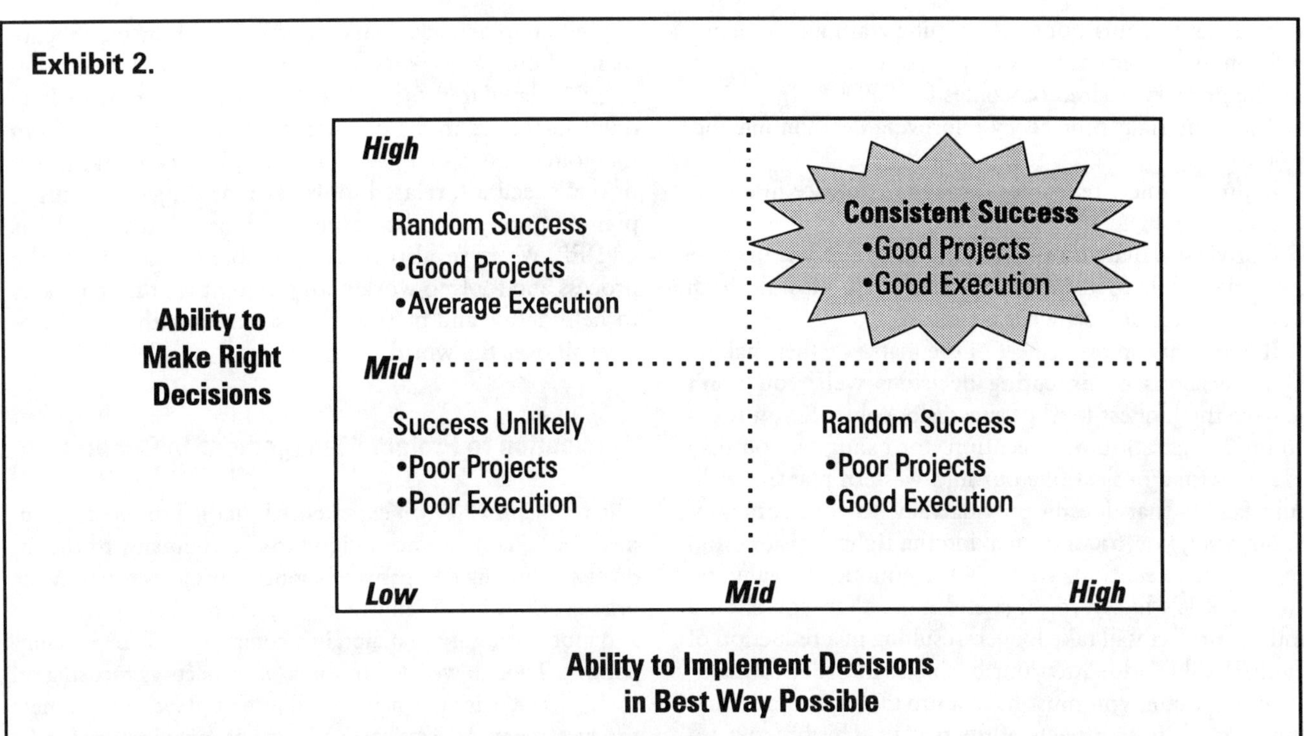

**Exhibit 3.** CPDEP Impact on Asset/Project Value

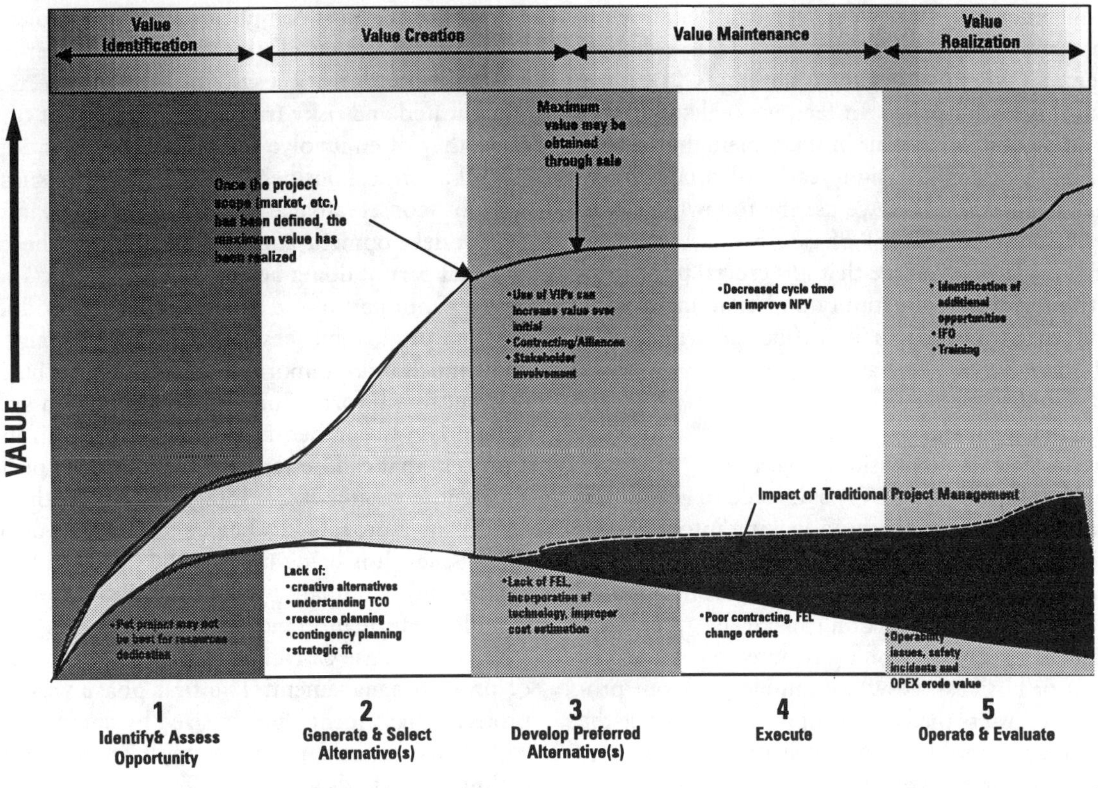

Value Identification
Value Creation
Value Maintenance
Value Realization
VALUE
Once the project scope (market, etc.) has been defined, the maximum value has been realized
Maximum value may be obtained through sale
•Use of VIPs can increase value over initial
•Contracting/Alliances
•Stakeholder involvement
•Decreased cycle time can improve NPV
•Identification of additional opportunities
•IFO
•Training
Impact of Traditional Project Management
•Pet project may not be best for resources dedication
Lack of:
•creative alternatives
•understanding TCO
•resource planning
•contingency planning
•strategic fit
•Lack of FEL, incorporation of technology, improper cost estimation
•Poor contracting, FEL change orders
•Operability issues, safety incidents and OPEX erode value
1
Identify& Assess Opportunity
2
Generate & Select Alternative(s)
3
Develop Preferred Alternative(s)
4
Execute
5
Operate & Evaluate

mergers and acquisitions, developing training curricula, and conducting environmental assessments.

The primary desired outcomes for CPDEP are:

- Select the right projects by improving decision making, and
- Improve project outcomes through excellence in execution.

Our view is that you simply can not ignore one of these outcomes while focusing on the other. You must do both well. Echibit 2 depicts what we mean.

If you focus on one aspect of the matrix, either making right decisions or executing decisions well, you don't achieve the highest level of success possible. If you focus on implementation or execution, for example, you may end up with a project like our mid-western plant; a well-built facility that doesn't provide value to your company. If, however, you focus on making the right decisions and neglect the execution, you may leave money or value on the table. It's likely you'll spend more than you should and the project will take longer, resulting in a reduction of the true value added to your business. In order to maximize this value, you must have a broader focus, one that encompasses both aspects of the matrix. This broader focus will increase your ability to achieve consistent project success time and again.

Early on, Chevron's focus was to improve project execution. This was brought about primarily as a response to industry benchmarking data. We quickly realized, however, that improving project execution only addresses half of the problem, so when we began to develop CPDEP, we tried to address both aspects. In fact, we realized that if you don't do a good job in your business planning and decision making, you can lose significant potential for creating value. To illustrate this, we use the following curve, that shows value versus CPDEP Phase.

From this curve you can see that it is crucial to properly frame the business opportunity and examine a wide range of alternatives. We actually define the primary objectives of Phase 1 of CPDEP as:

- Identify opportunities,
- Clearly frame goal, and
- Test for Strategic fit with business objectives.

Notice that Phase 2 of CPDEP is devoted to generating and selecting alternatives to avoid locking into a choice prematurely. It is not until Phase 3 that the team focuses on the preferred alternative and develops it conceptually.

We've learned that if you don't make the right decisions, excellent execution won't guarantee the success of your project or business. Now, we routinely ask our project managers to assess the business opportunity, define the customers and stakeholders, and explicitly define success in business terms prior to embarking on a project plan.

This approach has even carried over to how we execute many of our projects. Now when we approach major decisions related to project execution, we frequently include our contractors in the decision making process and form integrated teams that use CPDEP to plan the work. Many of our execution related tools, such as project execution planning, rely on the same team based principals as CPDEP. We have also recently embarked on using the process and tools to work with our joint venture partners, to help define and plan work associated with major projects all over the world.

## Application to Project Management In General

The problems Chevron experienced that led to the development of CPDEP are not unique to the company, to the industry, or to any company engaging in projects today. Most organizations are finding that projects are becoming more and more necessary to maintain a company and keep it competitive. Though we used to think of projects as focusing on things like creating a new building or a developing a new product, today, projects cover all sorts of organizational shifts as business environments constantly change. Companies must engage in change projects to remain competitive. Reorganizations, process improvement, and reengineering are a few examples.

Perhaps the most complicated types of projects are the development and installation of new computer-based processing and information systems. These projects are quite complicated and risky from a technical point of view, because they often involve convoluted organizational issues as well as critical business and competitive issues. Even in the most conservative and stable companies, information system development and improvement are becoming an essential part of doing business. These projects were once only a minor part of the business, because production was the core of most businesses. Now these systems have become much more important in determining business success because information and computerized systems are tantamount to competitive advantage. Organizations need a process that can better help them control project management, keeping it an integral part of the business. CPDEP as a process has been successful in dealing with these issues. It is being used by the Chevron Information Technology Company, which handles Chevron's most complex information management projects.

That's because CPDEP is an example of the third phase of project management. The first phase was traditional project management characterized by command and control structures and processes with an over reliance on technical methods such as PERT and CPM. The second phase that has a very strong influence on project management today, is the project leadership approach with more emphasis on organizational, interpersonal, and team issues, and more sophisticated technical tools in broader areas of project management (Graham 1989).

This second approach is well supported by PMBOK, because CPDEP represents a new emphasis on project management as a business process (PMI 1994). And it's not as if this area has been ignored in the past; Hewlett Packard has long emphasized the economics of project returns (HBR; Return Map: Tracking Product Teams 1991). The time has come, however, for a greater emphasis on project management as a business process for all kinds of projects, not just new product development and new facility creation. This is especially true for information technology projects if my (DJC) recent experiences in a few client companies represent general trends, as I suspect they do.

In two of the companies I've interacted with recently, information processing is the business of the organization. In another, it is a major part of the business. In all three cases, the use of a process like CPDEP would probably help solve some of the major problems presently plaguing them; problems that stem from a split between technical and business approaches to the project portfolio in general and toward each project in particular.

The project portfolio should represent a selection process that is driven by strategic considerations (Graham and Englund 1997). Ideally this should begin with upper management establishing criteria for project selection and developing a process for determining which projects should be pursued and which should be put on hold until resources are available. CPDEP allows for this process by requiring an extensive review of options during the first two phases. This review forces project personnel and upper management to work through these important business issues before projects are begun. It is also used to classify projects to get a better picture of the project portfolio as a pipeline; something especially important in a company like Chevron, where any given project can take a very long time.

In one of the client companies I visited recently, there was almost no strategic consideration of the project portfolio. Upper management was just beginning to communicate a strategic direction vaguely making a connection to the many projects in force. In another organization I visited, there was some strategic thinking about projects going on in the upper echelons, but not much understanding or discussion of strategy at the project level. In yet another firm, a selection process was in place at high levels of the organization, but was not pushed down to more tactical levels. None of the companies have a process like CPDEP that forces an ongoing dialogue between the project team and various levels of upper management about strategic issues as integral parts of the first two phases of any project.

Ideally each project in a company should be "owned" by business management rather than by technical function management. Real ownership includes the ownership of problems as well as successes. In one company, I was told that business management claimed to be owners of the project, but the minute there was a problem, they pointed their finger at the technical managers. This situation created a heavy burden for the technical information systems managers. They were blamed for the failure of major projects, and took on the responsibility for fixing the problems. In the end, however, one major factor was out of their control; the full participation and cooperation of business management.

Until project teams are fully integrated with the project manager taking on the role of general manager rather than technical manager, projects will fail. Technical managers and professionals will not be able to do the business planning aspect of the project themselves, nor will they be able to manage projects in a larger business context. This will result in the wrong project being executed well technically, or in poor execution, because the technical process is executed well, but without proper input on the business side. One major software development company with whom I'm familiar, uses a business generalist as project manager. That person is backed up by a project engineer for technical support so both the business and technical focuses of the project are represented (Graham and Englund 1997).

CPDEP starts off from the very beginning asking hard business questions about the problem that the project is supposed to solve, and requires that the team generate a wide variety of alternatives from both a technical and business perspective. Upper business management becomes engaged from the beginning in a dialogue about important business issues. Even the most technical of project managers is forced to deal with the broader business perspective, and to rely on team members with business backgrounds.

In fact, one of the most impressive aspects of CPDEP is that it structures such a strong business framework that everyone uses business terms to frame their projects. Thinking of projects as the development of assets with a specific return to the company over time is second nature to Chevron project managers. They think about shareholder value, especially for their large upstream projects. This is in contrast to a large information systems company in which I've worked, where they have a lot of trouble connecting the results of their projects to any business result at all, even though these projects are specifically targeting at upgrading services for the company's customers. Part of the problem is that the nature of the products and services of an information services company seem somehow disconnected from traditional products and services, but the bigger part of the problem lies in the fact that this company is not developing a process like CPDEP, which forces business analysis from the very beginning.

Finally, CPDEP has added a new dimension to the post-project appraisal process. We have known for a long time that post project reviews have helped to keep projects on track and improve the process over the long run (Gulliver 1987). CPDEP Phase 5 is a continuous assessment of the business success of the project; a phase that must be completed over the course of a long period of time. All kinds of projects can benefit from this process, but complex information processing projects should benefit most as CPDEP will help business managing these kinds of projects to help determine their business value added.

PMBOK helps us to execute projects well, but it is not enough to guarantee business success. Project managers must have the technical skills to execute their projects and the leadership skills to support their teams and manage stakeholders. And while these are very important, it's also true that the project manager of today and tomorrow needs general management skills in order to understand how their projects fit into the larger strategic picture of the company, and how to get the most value added for shareholders.

## References


Graham, Robert. 1989. *Project management, as if people mattered.* Bala Cynwyd, PA: Primavera Press.

Graham, Robert and Randal Englund. 1997. *Creating an environment for successful projects.* Prepublication manuscript, Chapter 2.

Gulliver, F.R. 1987. *Post-project appraisals pay.* Harvard Business Review. (March).

Harvard Business Review. 1991. *Return map: Tracking product teams.* (January).

Project Management Institute. 1994. *A guide to the project management body of knowledge (PMBOK).* Upper Darby, PA: Project Management Institute.

# Competition Drives Change in Organizational Structure—Functional to Project Matrix

William V. Leban, Keller Graduate School of Management

## Background

### Industry & Position

Natural Gas Pipeline Company (Natural) owns and operates almost thirteen thousand miles of interstate pipeline. Its natural gas transmission system has two major subsystems, the Amarillo and Gulf Coast Systems, interconnected by the A/G Line. Both systems terminate in the Chicago area. In addition, Natural owns various gas storage fields in Iowa, Illinois, and Texas and leases storage capacity in Oklahoma.

Natural maintains approximately 8% of the U.S. natural gas transmission industry market share. Prior to recent changes in regulation, Natural had provided natural gas sales, storage, and transportation services to gas distribution companies, as well as to producers, marketers, power plants and other pipelines.

### Regulation & Change

Previously, the interstate pipeline operations were subject to extensive regulation by the Federal Energy Regulatory Commission (FERC). The FERC regulated, among other things, rates and charges for the resale and transportation of gas in interstate commerce, the construction and operation of interstate pipeline facilities, and the accounts and records of interstate pipelines.

FERC issued Order 636. This mandated a role change for natural gas transmission companies. Their traditional merchant function to buy and resell natural gas was changed to one of natural gas transporter. Natural's throughput, sales plus transportation, is approximately one thousand, five hundred and fifty BCF per year. Sales dropped from 70% of throughput in 1984, to zero in 1994. Consequently, transportation increased from 30% of throughput in 1984 to 100% in 1994.

Natural gas procurement has become the responsibility of local utilities and other customers, with pipelines transporting and storing natural gas. While the gas transmission industry has existed for many years (the initial parts of Natural's system were constructed in the thirties), the introduction of competition with reduced regulation has occurred over the last several years.

### Competition

Natural's transportation competitors consist of interstate pipelines that own facilities in the vicinity of the Chicago metropolitan area. Competition for gas transportation and storage may be provided by one or more other pipelines, depending on how each pipeline markets its services to meet customer needs. For example, Natural has the lowest priced one hundred-day storage service, fifty versus sixty cents per MMBtu charged by its competitor, American Natural Resources (ANR). However, Natural's average firm transportation rate from the mid-continent gas supply region to Chicago is higher, sixty-one versus fifty-three cents per MMBtu when compared to ANR.

Transportation rates, adequate pipeline capacity, and the availability of storage services are key factors in determining Natural's ability to compete for particular transportation business. By upgrading pipeline facilities to reduce operating costs and adjusting flow patterns on Natural's system to better utilize spare capacity, Natural enhances its competitive position.

## Business Situation

Natural follows traditional business lines with the following vice-presidential areas: marketing, accounting, transmission, rates and engineering. The transmission area is responsible for operating the interstate natural gas transmission system, with all other areas performing support functions. Engineering plays a major role in deciding how facilities are used and determines what new facilities should be installed to meet customer needs.

With changes introduced by the FERC, Natural moved from a monopolistic market with geographic boundaries to one of price sensitive, competitive services. Therefore, Natural's engineering area redefined its role. Previously, Natural was more reactive in responding to well-developed, long-term customer needs in a captive market, with a high probability of cost recovery. The new competitive environment requires a more proactive role in recognizing and reducing pipeline system operating inefficiencies (to reduce cost) and developing more individualized customer-based strategies (to make gas transportation and storage services more attractive to the customer).

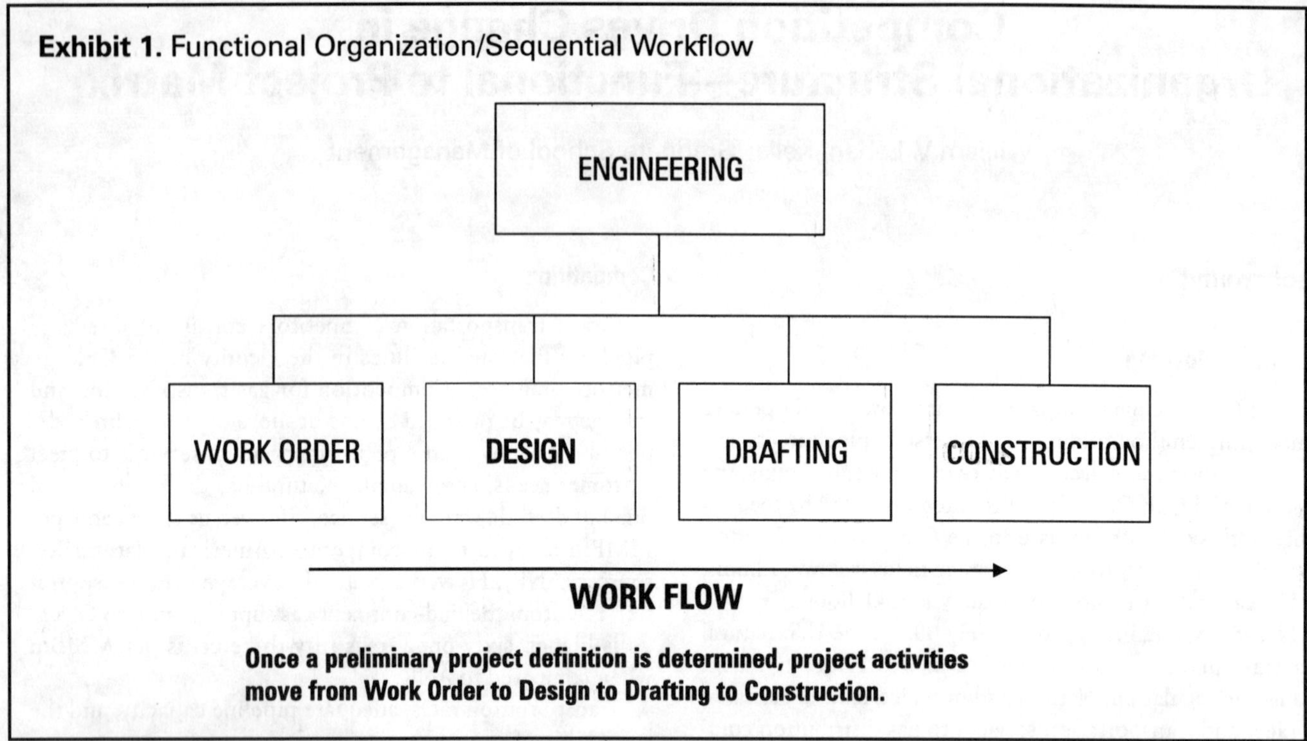


**Exhibit 1.** Functional Organization/Sequential Workflow

**Once a preliminary project definition is determined, project activities move from Work Order to Design to Drafting to Construction.**

### Engineering Responsibilities

Natural's Engineering area (approximately one hundred and forty staff with an annual $100 million capital expenditure budget) performs three main functions in supporting project activities: design, drafting and construction administration. These had traditionally been accomplished under a functional organization structure. Activities include engineering, specification, procurement and construction of replacement, upgrade, or new facilities. Specific projects vary in scope, from designing a gas dehydration tower to developing a major gas storage facility.

### Previous Functional Organization Structure

Under the prior functional organization structure, four distinct departments had well-defined project responsibility when given a preliminary project definition. These departments, their responsibilities, and the sequence of the tasks they performed are described below:

| Department | Sequence | Functional Responsibility / Tasks |
|---|---|---|
| Work Order | 1. | Estimate cost based on project definition. |
| Work Order | 2. | Receive authorization for expenditure. |
| Design | 3. | Detailed engineering design. |
| Design | 4. | Specify required materials. |
| Drafting | 5. | Determine drawing requirements. |
| Drafting | 6. | Prepare design and construction drawings. |
| Construction | 7. | Prepare request for proposal. |
| Construction | 8. | Make bid selection. |
| Construction | 9. | Administer construction contract. |

As described above, each department performed specific technical and administrative-type tasks in support of project activities. Departments were broken down into tasks, with each group of tasks dependent on completion by the previous group. Projects had a sequential line of development, meaning tasks were handled one at a time, with each one completed before moving on to the next. Groups such as environmental, land, corrosion, metallurgy, etc., maintained a support role.

### Historic human resource background

Engineers in the departments, had company experience that could be classified in one of the two types shown in Exhibit 2. Type 1 engineers are routinely assigned to construction with Type 2 engineers placed in design. Some engineers in the engineering area are considered experts based on their years of field experience working on pipeline or station facilities. Other engineers have technical experience in such specialized

**Exhibit 2.** Engineering Experience Types

**Historically, engineers in Natural's Engineering area can be included in one of the following experience types:**

**TYPE 1 Pipeline field operating and facility construction, or**

**TYPE 2 Engineering equipment design, cost estimating, drafting, and procurement**

areas as electric power design, gas processing, structural engineering, controls, and automation programming.

## Focus of Change

As a result of the change in business environment, Natural's engineering area determined that it must address the following issues:

*Issue 1. Focal Point of Responsibility and Accountability.*

The planning and implementation of project activities require a focal point of responsibility. A stronger tie to customers (internal/transmission area or external/marketing services) to provide better project definition and continuity.

*Issue 2. Match Company Resources to Customer Needs.*

Projects are evaluated, selected, and planned based on their contribution to meeting company and customer objectives. Establishing project priorities and schedules should be based on matching company resources to customer needs.

## Alternatives for Change

To increase the effectiveness of work flow, the following alternatives were developed to address the stated focus of change:

*Alternative 1. Maintain existing functional organization and categorize projects.*

Categorize projects so that tasks are distributed and processed based on established criteria. Field personnel or central office design engineers would be assigned to projects based on the categories shown in Exhibit 3. Personnel would receive assignments based on their experience and skills.

The design engineer, for Category II and III projects, would prepare the job scope and required material specifications. A Work order would prepare the necessary cost estimates to support the project approval process. A sequential work flow would continue, as information would next be sent to drafting and then on to construction for implementation. In addition, projects would be prioritized within each department.

*Alternative 2. Establish a Project Management Concept for all Projects.*

Establish project teams to plan, organize, monitor, and control all aspects of project activities. Teams would be assigned projects based on the project categories stated in Alternative 1. A project team, headed by a project manager who is assigned project engineers, would be responsible for all aspects of a project: design, cost estimation, drawings, material procurement and contract administration. Projects would evolve with parallel lines of development, meaning that several tasks, addressing different functional areas, could be handled simultaneously. Project activities could be accomplished by the engineer and support personnel in the following manner:

| Work Flow | | Tasks | Previous Functional |
|---|---|---|---|
| A | 1. | Estimate cost / receive approval | Work Order |
| | 3. | Detailed engineering design | Design |
| | 5. | Determine drawing requirements | Drafting |
| B | 2. | Receive authorization for revised activities | Work Order |
| | 4. | Specify required materials | Design |
| | 6. | Prepare design and construction drawings | Drafting |
| C | 7. | Prepare request for proposal | Construction |
| | 8. | Make bid selection | Construction |
| | 9. | Administer construction contract | Construction |

Project engineers would be a catalyst in coordinating project tasks. Decisions would be made based on their impact on all facets of the project. Team members would work together in a group to assist each other based on their experience.

*Alternative 3. Field Extension, Engineering Services Group and Project Teams in a Project Matrix Organizational Structure.*

Use field personnel to plan and implement Category I projects. Establish an engineering services group (ESG) for Category II projects. Use project teams for all Category III projects. See Exhibit 4 for the organizational structure of Alternative 3. The ESG would include specialists with field experience, who could answer questions and address problems on the operation and maintenance of existing facilities. If technical specialists (electrical or gas processing, for example) were required, they would be available from the functional support group.

**Exhibit 3.** Categories of Capital Expenditure Activities

Listed below are categories of the capital expenditure activities performed in Natural's Engineering area:

| | |
|---|---|
| CATEGORY I | <u>Field Recognition & Implementation</u> |
| | (30% of the number of projects/approximately $2.5 million/year) |
| | No safety system involved |
| | No design required |
| | No environmental considerations |
| | Under $25,000 |
| Example: | Install cathodic protection devices along with the pipeline |
| Basis: | Well-defined guidelines |

| | |
|---|---|
| CATEGORY II | <u>Design & Operating Experience Required</u> |
| | (10% of the number of projects/approximately $3.5 million/year) |
| | Design required. Sketches and material specifications |
| | No drawings required |
| | No enviornmental considerations |
| | Under $100,000 |
| Examples: | Install air compressor, liquid pump or drip tank |
| Basis: | Experienced designer approves activities |

| | |
|---|---|
| CATEGORY III | <u>Detailed Design & Formal Contracts</u> |
| | (60% of the number of projects/approximately $94 million/year) |
| | Design and drawings required |
| | Environmental permits, etc. required |
| | Engineering to prepare all Bill of Materials |
| | Formal contract |
| | Unlimited expenditure |
| Examples: | Install pipeline loop or gas compressor units |
| Basis: | Applicable standards and company procedures must be followed |

## Basis for Selection

Management determined that the best alternative would be a structure in which:

- Engineering can focus on internal customer (pipeline operating) needs by using field personnel and the engineering services group.
- Project teams, addressing external customer needs, would handle activities that require a broader, less defined role of coordinator over project activities and thereby act as a focal point.
- Technical specialist directly support project team activities.

Alternative 3, field extension, engineering services group and project teams in a project matrix organizational structure, met these criteria and was implemented in Natural's engineering area. A comparison of the sequential versus simultaneous work flow (Exhibit 5), relates the broader focus on project activities.

## Impact on Stated Issues

The selection of Alternative 3, field extension, engineering services group and project teams, has the following impact on the engineering area's focus of change:

*Impact on Issue 1. Focal Point of Responsibility and Accountability.*

By placing the experience experts in the engineering services group, internal customers, such as transmission, have direct access to individuals who can most likely satisfy their

**Exhibit 4.** Project Matrix Organization/Simultaneous Wokflow

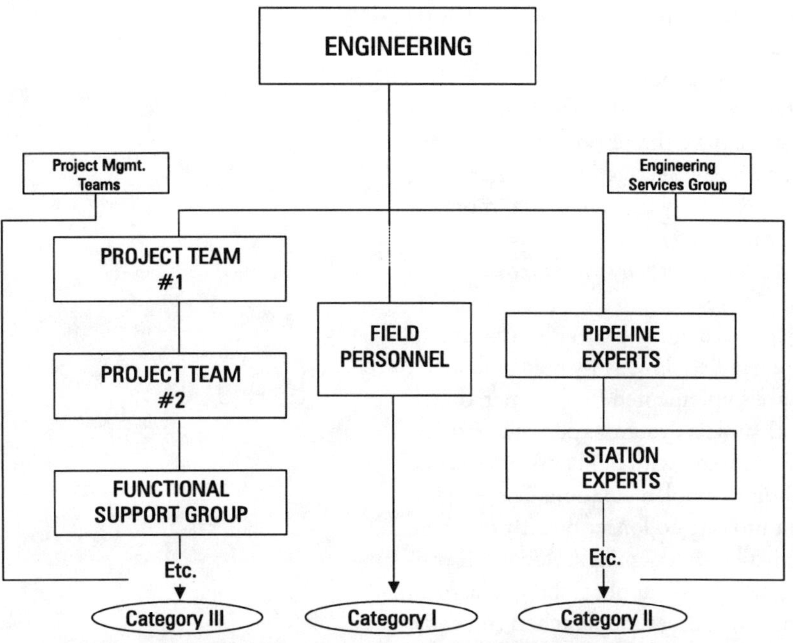


Project engineers, field personnel, and functional or experience experts are focal point to handle project activities. Design, Cost, Drafting, etc., considerations are made simultaneously. Project category responsibiliites are identified.

**Exhibit 5.** Work Flow

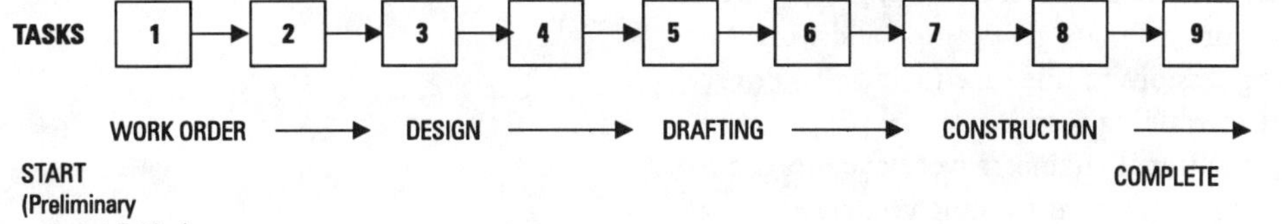


**Simultaneous Work Flow - Project Matrix Organization**

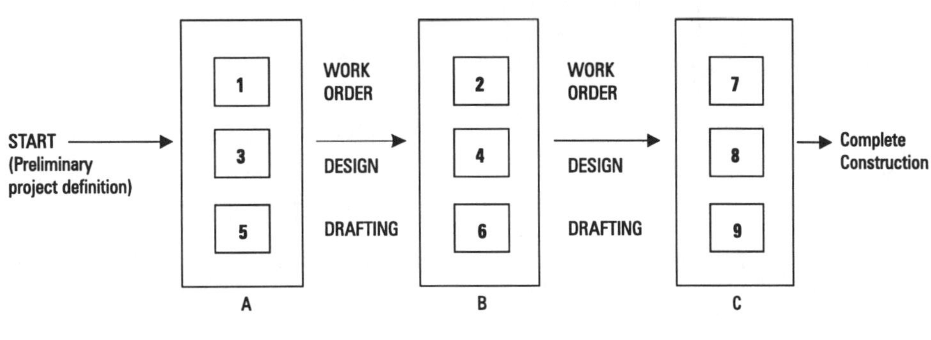

needs. By forming project teams, engineers can work directly with marketing to analyze and develop the best project alternative for external customers.

By maintaining a functional support group, which reports to project managers, technical experts focus on specific engineering disciplines to address problems. In addition, this group provides consistent responses. Project managers, as leaders of the project teams, have the responsibility and authority to make decisions on project activities. Therefore, they have the primary responsibility to plan, direct, monitor, and control project activities.

*Impact on Issue 2. Match Company Resources to Customer Needs.*

By categorizing projects, Category I activities that maintain pipeline integrity are handled directly by field personnel. Engineering standards are implemented by field personnel. By assigning Category II projects to an experience expert, projects gain an advocate to work with field personnel to assist in development and direct implementation. These maintenance and replacement projects no longer directly compete with the larger dollar activities. By assigning Category III projects to a team that has technical support, there is a focal point of coordination and resources are matched to needs. Project cost, scheduling, and performance goals are the focus of the team.

## Implementation

Placement to a project team or within an engineering services or functional support group was made based on an engineer's experience, knowledge, and abilities. Some engineers were promoted to the new project manager position and were sent to leadership training sessions to fine-tune their skills. Project engineers were sent to training sessions on the project management concepts; functional engineers were encouraged to upgrade their skills with technical training courses. Job experience and training has enabled engineers to develop into a valuable resource for the company. Focus groups met on a regular basis (once every two weeks) to address problems with procedures, communications, etc. A continuous review of how the new organization operated has revealed an upgrading of services and a better utilization of human resources.

## Conclusion

Competitive forces dictate the need for proactive project coordination in meeting the demands of Natural's internal and external customers. Alternative 3, field extension, engineering services group, and project teams in a project matrix has provided an organizational design and the proper allocation of human resources necessary to meet engineering's focus of change.

# Project Evaluation by Fuzzy Lift-Slab Model

Luba Ebert, P.Eng., MPR Extensys

## Introduction

Project evaluation is usually done at the end of the project based on client's satisfaction. Unfortunately, at times, not much attention is paid to evaluating a project during its life cycle. In such a case the project manager misses the opportunity to make improvements to the project organization based on feedback from the project team.

The Lift-Slab Model (LSM) (Robinson 1981 and 1988) encourages a periodic evaluation during the duration of a project. It provides a framework for improving the project organization. The LSM consists of four elements presented as vertical columns: characteristics of the *external environment* (EE); *task technology* (TT) or work process; *structure and administrative* system (SA); characteristics of the *people-culture* (PC). The organization is represented by a plate (organization plate) attached to the columns at the points E, T, S and P (see Exhibit 1). A plate at high level represents a healthy and successful organization.

The *Environment* (EE) dimension varies from certain, stable, and predictable market conditions, technology, competition, etc., to uncertain, unstable, and unpredictable; the regulatory agencies involvement varies from noninvolvement to involvement. The *Task* (TT) dimension reflects the relationship between tasks (no relationship at the bottom and high at the top), training required, interrelationship between people, etc. The *Structure* (SA) column concerns decision making and management style (autocratic at the bottom, shared at the top), planning, organization structure (rigid at the bottom versus flexible at the top), etc. The *Culture* (PC) dimension includes factors such as satisfaction with the work group and with self on the job (dissatisfaction at the bottom, satisfaction at the top), trust of peers and managers (no trust versus high trust), motivation (work for pay versus interest in the project), conflict (solved by management versus dealt with openly).

The plate regardless of its height, must be level in order to indicate a smoothly working organization. Otherwise factors in any of the columns that cause the plate to shift may require attention; this is an indication of stress. The process of evaluation, directed by the project manager, involves the project team, clients, senior management and others. The date collected by survey questionnaires, individual interviews, and small meetings will help to establish the plate's shift at a certain time.

**Exhibit 1.** The Lift-Slab Organizational Model

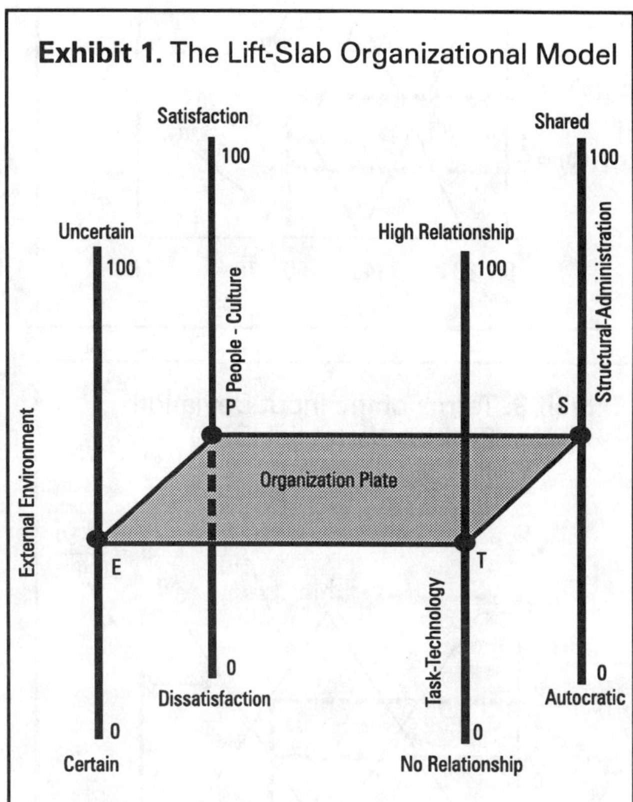


Making use of my experience as a project manager of a gas compressor installation project in this paper, I generalize the LSM using fuzzy logic (Bojadziev and Bojadziev 1995 and 1997). The generalized model will be referred to as Fuzzy Lift-Slab Model (FLSM). The rationale to introduce FLSM is that complex projects involve various types of internal and external uncertainties and subjectivity due to human participation. Fuzzy logic employs fuzzy sets and numbers to handle and describe imprecise data. It is a facilitator for common-sense reasoning and could serve as a tool for project managers.

## Fuzzy Lift-Slab Model (FLSM)

The project manager must recognize a shift of the organization plate called plate deviation. For that purpose the project

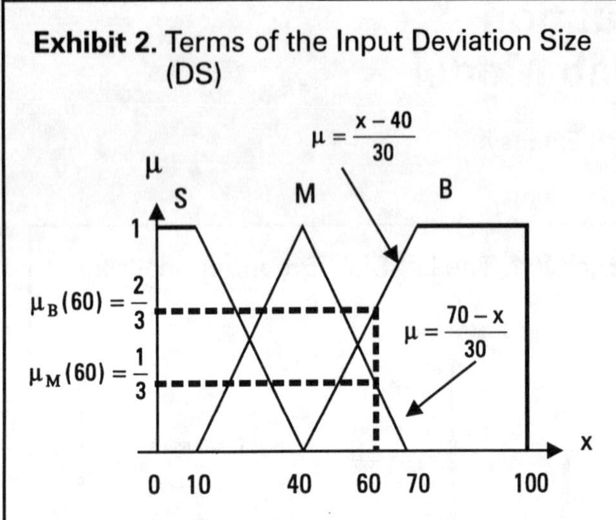

**Exhibit 2.** Terms of the Input Deviation Size (DS)

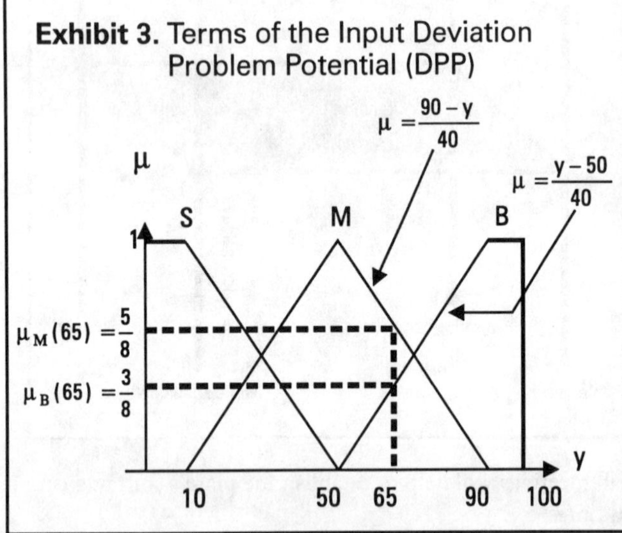

**Exhibit 3.** Terms of the Input Deviation Problem Potential (DPP)

manager observes and assesses the project situation. The observations which are subjective and depend on his or her knowledge and experience are expressed as numbers on scales from 0 to 100 attached to the four columns (Exhibit 1). This allows the project manager to get a sense for the problems the deviation could cause. A small plate deviation and a small plate deviation problem potential are permissible within certain limits. Otherwise the manager has to take action according to the priority of the deviation. The project manager has to address three important questions:

1. What is the deviation size?
2. What is the deviation problem potential?
3. What is the priority of the deviation?

The contribution of this paper is that the dealing with the above questions is based on fuzzy logic control (FLC).

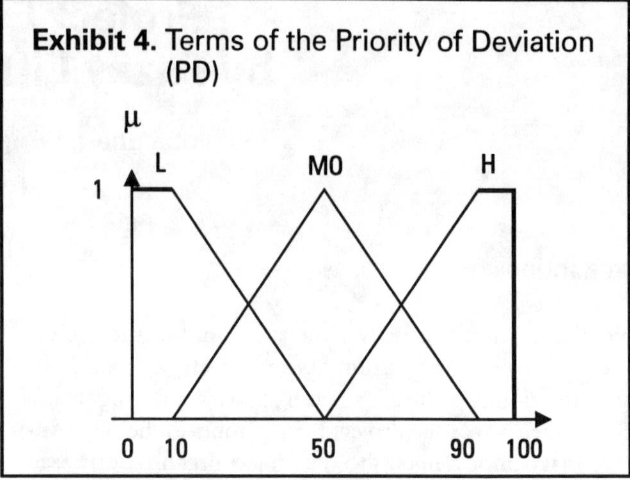

**Exhibit 4.** Terms of the Priority of Deviation (PD)

Deviation size and deviation problem potential are the inputs of the FLSM; priority of the deviation is the output. Following the fuzzy logic control methodology (Bojadziev and Bojadziev 1997) we introduce a proper number of if ... then rules. The application of the rules produces the required result in the form of membership function of a fuzzy set. The defuzzification procedure gives a crisp value according to which the project manager will take action.

## Modeling the Control Variables

The inputs *deviation size* (DS) and *deviation problem potential* (DPP), and the output *priority of deviation* (PD) considered as linguistic variables are modeled here as follows:

DS = { S (small), M (medium), B (big)},
DPP = { S (small), M (medium), B (big)},
PD = { L (low), MO (moderate), H (high)},

where S, M, B, L, MO, H are called terms of the corresponding linguistic variables. They are fuzzy numbers whose shapes and locations are carefully selected on Exhibits 2–4. Equations of segments to be used later are indicated in the Exhibits.

At a certain time to selected by the project manager, the *characteristics Environment, Task, Structure* and *Culture* are estimated on a scale between 0 and 100. The estimated values called readings are denoted by x1, x2, x3, x4 correspondingly. They give the heights of the supporting columns of the plate (state of organization) in Exhibit 1. The deviation size measured on the scale x, called also base variable x, labeled (DS)x (Exhibit 2) is defined as the largest difference (xi-xj(, i.e.,

(DS)x = max{( xi-xj(}, i, j = 1, ... , 4. (1)

The reading for the deviation problem potential measured on the scale y, or base variable y, labeled (DPP)y (Exhibit 3) is defined as

$$(DPP)y = 100 - ((x1+ x2+ x3+ x4), \quad (2)$$

where ((x1+ x2+ x3+ x4) is interpreted as average plate level. The justification of definition (2) is that a higher average plate level means small potential problems and vice versa.

The values (DS)x and (DPP)y on the axis x and y, according to the FLC methodology have to be matched against appropriate terms in Exhibits 2 and 3. This will be illustrated later.

### If ... then Rules and Decision Table

The number of the *if ... then* rules (called also production rules) is nine, the product of the number of terms in each input DS and DPP. The rules designed by the manager to suite a Gas Compressor Installation Project considered in this paper are presented in Exhibit 5.

The terms L, MO, H in the nine cells belong to the output *priority of deviation* (PD). The rules read:

Rule 1: If DS is S and DPP is S then PD is L,
Rule 2: If DS is S and DPP is M then PD is MO,
Rule 3: If DS is S and DPP is B then PD is MO,
Rule 4: If DS is M and DPP is S then PD is L,
Rules 5: If DS is M and DPP is M then PD is MO,
Rule 6: If DS is M and DPP is B then PD is H,
Rule 7: If DS is B and DPP is S then PD is MO,
Rule 8: If DS is B and DPP is M then PD is MO,
Rule 9: If DS is B and DPP is B then PD is H.

The application of control rules is called *firing*. While there are nine rules in our case, only four will be fired. That depends on the values (DS)x and (DPP)y in a particular situation.

### Aggregation and Defuzzification

*Aggregation* or *conflict resolution* is the methodology that is used in deciding what control action should be taken as a result of the firing of several rules. It is presented in final form as the membership function (agg of a fuzzy set consisting of parts of some terms of the output priority of deviation.

*Defuzzification* is an operation that produces a nonfuzzy control action, a simple value, that adequately represents the membership function of an aggregated control action.

## Gas Compressor Installation Project

### Project Description

The aim of the project was to relocate a 8300 hp Reciprocating Compressor Unit from an existing facility to a Gas Plant approximately X km North, at a cost of $23 Million. The unit was required to provide spare horsepower in order to allow two of the existing units at the Plant to be shut down for maintenance. In addition, for the first two years of operation, the Reciprocating Compressor Unit was required on the outlet of the Plant due to increased contract gas sales. The project was to start at the beginning of January 1995 with an in-service date of November 1, 1995. An external engineering contractor was hired.

**Exhibit 5.** Decision Table for If...Then Rules

| | | Deviation problem potential | | |
|---|---|---|---|---|
| | | S | M | B |
| Deviation Size | S | L | MO | MO |
| | M | L | MO | H |
| | B | MO | MO | H |

Three months into the project (January–March) the Planing Group advised that the Reciprocating Compressor Unit could not be relocated since it was required for a proposed expansion at the existing facility. A similar unit from another facility would be used that lead to changing the in-service date to April 1, 1996.

Since the contract for additional gas by November 1, 1995 had already been signed, a temporary compression needed to be found to cover the period from November 1, 1995 to April 1, 1996. The next two months (April, May) were spent trying to locate compressor units. Two units were available, one of which had to be in operation by Nov. 1, 1995. The work was challenging, having to compress a process usually taking twelve to eighteen months into six months. The project had an extremely fast track schedule for the design, procurement and installation. At that time (five months from the beginning of the project), being the project manager, I decided to evaluate the project.

### Evaluation of the vertical columns

*External Environment (EE):* For the first five months of the project the market conditions were unstable and unpredictable. The producers constantly changed their gas requirements and the location of the delivery points that resulted in problems of Compressor relocation. In addition, we had competition from other companies. Construction could not start until the project was approved by the National Energy Board (NEB). In order to minimize the cost to the organization in the event the project was not approved by the

NEB, engineering was kept to a minimum. During this period committing resources to the project was difficult. The reading given to EE was x1=75, which is close to the top of the column EE in Exhibit 1.

*Task-Technology (TT):* The normal working environment was process oriented concerning the drawings execution and approvals. There was little interaction and good relationship between the different Disciplines, Construction and Operations. The reading given to TT was x2=15.

*Structure-Administration (SA):* The project planning was done for the team, the scope was defined and scheduled and the budget imposed. The lack of input from the team presented a lot of problems with commitment and buy-in. The schedule was agreed to, but the budget was not entirely accepted by all involved, especially Operations Department. In addition operations personnel were unhappy with the choice of the Reciprocating Compressor Unit and this lead to friction. The reading assigned to SA was x3=15.

*People-Culture (PC):* For the first five months all involved parties cooperated little to moderately. The fact that the project had been assigned to an external engineering contractor caused some dissatisfaction among drafting and engineering personnel. The project manager also was dissatisfied since the planning and marketing groups were making decisions without enough consultations. Finally, the interest in the project was moderate. The reading evaluated for PC was x4=35.

## Application of Fuzzy Logic Technique

Substituting the column readings x1=75, x2=15, x3=15, and x4=35 into formulas (1) and (2) gives (DS)x=60 and (DPP)y=65. The matching of these values against the appropriate terms of DS (M and B) and DPP (M and B) presented in Exhibits 2 and 3, correspondingly, produces the fuzzy input readings

(M(60)=(,    (B(60)=(,    (M(65)=(,    (B(65)=(.

The strength of the rules (or levels of firing) expressing the "and" parts of the rules to be fired are

min ((, () = (,  min ((, () = (,  min ((, () = (,  min ((, () = (,

where min (a, b) =a if a<b or min (a, b) =b if a>b. The fuzzy input readings that belong to the terms M and B (DS) in Exhibit 2 and M and B (DPP) in Exhibit 3 involve only the PD terms in the shaded cells in Exhibit 5 (intersection of rows and columns). This leads to firing of rules 5, 6, 8, and 9.

Control output (CO) of each rule is defined by operation min applied on its strength and conclusion (the "then" part of the rule) as follows:

- CO Rule 5: min ((, MO),
- CO Rule 6: min ((, H),
- CO Rule 8: min ((, MO),
- CO Rule 9: min ((, H).

Noting that the output of rule 5 is included into rule 8, and the output of rule 6 into rule 9, the aggregation of the control outputs of rules 8 and 9 produces

(agg(z) = max{min ((, (MO(z)), min ((,(H(z))}.

This is the union of the fuzzy numbers MO and H, the second and third terms of the control output PD (Exhibit 4), sliced correspondingly with the straight lines (=( and (=( paralleled to the axis z. The result is shown in Exhibit 6.

For defuzification of (agg(z) we apply the height defuzzification method (HDM): the weighted average of the midpoints of segments m1m2 and h1h2 with weights the heights of the segments (see Exhibit 6). For the crisp value zc we get

zc = [(((35+65)/2+((65+100)/2)]/((+() = 62.19 ( 62.

The crisp value 62 represents the priority of deviation on a scale from 0 to 100. The interpretation in terms of control action is that a serious measure has to be taken by the project manger to stabilize the organizational plate at a higher level. Hence the attachment points at the four columns EE, TT, SA, and PC, correspondingly at heights 75, 15, 15, and 35, have to be raised and leveled. That requires special attention first to the components *Task* (TT), *Structure* (SA) and second to *Culture* (PC) and *Environment* (EE).

## Control Action

Here the control action taken by the project manager after the first evaluation (crisp value 62) is explained.

### *External Environment (EE) Action*

The project manager froze the scope of the project and obtained senior management approval. The recommendation, in mid-June, was to install one permanent 7,000 hp gas turbine and a temporary 5,000 hp gas turbine unit. A preliminary schedule indicated an in-service date of January 2, 1996. Senior management mandated that the 7,000 hp unit be in-service by November 1, 1995. The funding was in place and material and human resources were assigned to the project.

### *Task Technology (TT) Action*

In order to complete the design and issue drawings for construction in a month and a half, the project manager requested the authority to bypass the normal procedures. The drawing package was divided into subsystems. The majority of the construction work was prefabricated off site, a process not previously undertaken by the company's construction department. Construction started as soon as the design and drawings were completed for a particular subsystem. This too was unprecedented and required much coordination throughout all levels of the project.

### *Structure Administration (SA) Action*

Due to the fast track nature of the project the project manager ensured that effected disciplines engaged in brainstorming and problem solving. The project manager demanded that an operations person be assigned to the team to express field personnel's views and requirements. In order to expedite decisions with regard to the design changes, an engineer was sent to the site to work closely with construction inspector and contractor. The project manager negotiated with different departments in order to bypass the existing procedures. Hence, allowing the team to focus on getting the facility complete and not be concerned about rules and regulations.

### *People-Culture (PC) Action*

The project manager had lobbied to pull the project back inhouse. As a result the members of the team wanted to prove that they could complete the project for less time and money with a team of one third the size proposed by the consulting group. The project manager encouraged people to make decisions, be flexible, and cooperative.

### *Outcome of the control action*

The control action taken by the project manager based on the FLSM successfully raised the level of the plate representing the state of the organization while decreasing the plate deviation.

### *Repetition of the evaluation process*

The evaluation technique can be applied more than once during a project. This is especially so when the project is a lengthy one, or the action taken by the manager after the first evaluation is unsatisfactory.

## Conclusion

Traditionally, the company's projects were low on all columns: *Structure* (SA)—highly structured and autocratic organization; *Tasks(TT)*—process oriented tasks; *Culture* (PC)—survival based culture; *Environment* (EE)—highly regulated, non competitive environment. With the onslaught of deregulation, a quick response to a changing market was needed—the *Environment* column rose drastically. Consequently, the organization plate was far from being leveled and this caused significant strain in the organization. This project was successful because it deviated from the established company structure, standards and procedures. It was one of the first in this mode. Senior management was entirely committed to the project and provided the project manager with the authority to bypass some rules and regulations. The proper use of FLSM raised and leveled the organizational plate.

**Exhibit 6.** Aggregated Output $F_{agg}(z)$; Crisp Value $z_c=62$

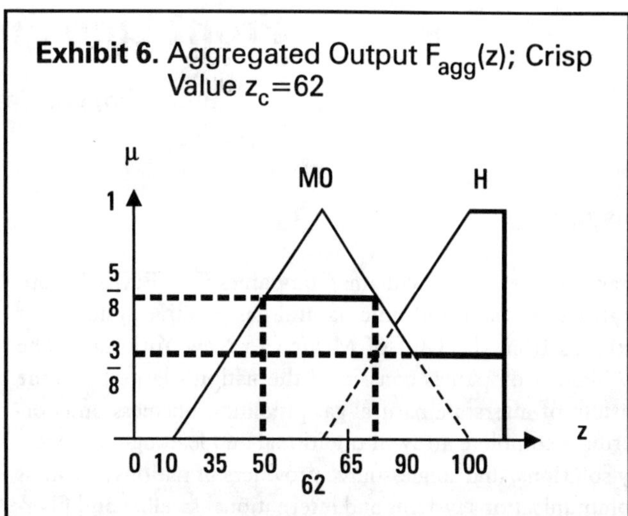


Fuzzy Logic Control provided the project manager with a measure for the priority of action needed to improve a certain situation. The action to be taken depended entirely on the knowledge and experience of the manager in charge. Ultimately, there was a general satisfaction with the results. The project was a success.

## Acknowledgment

The author tanks G. Robinson for providing his thesis and G. Bojadziev and M. Bojadziev for permission to use their second book in draft.

## References

Bojadziev, G. and M. Bojadziev. 1995. *Fuzzy sets, fuzzy logic, applications.* World Scientific, Singapore.

Bojadziev, G. and M. Bojadziev. 1997. *Fuzzy logic for business, finance, and management.* World Scientific, Singapore.

Robinson, Gary. 1981. *The effects of mid-management training on an engineering company branch office.* Unpublished Master's Research Project, Pepperdine University, Los Angeles.

Robinson, Gary. 1988. Project Management Critique: A process to increase project management effectiveness. Project Management Institute. Seminar/Symposium, San Francisco, California (September 17–21): 85–90.

# Front Line Project Tracking

Bruce Orr, Williams Company on Orr

## History

Transco, one of The Williams Companies (NYSE:WMB), operates a ten thousand-mile natural gas pipeline system that extends from the Gulf of Mexico to New York City. The Williams Companies consists of the nation's largest-volume system of interstate natural gas pipelines; business units offering a complete array of traditional and leading-edge energy solutions; and single-source providers of national business communications systems and international satellite and fiber-optic video services. Transco information is available on the World Wide Web at www.tgpl.com. It is within this network of pipelines that the as-built alignment sheet program was born. The work to as-built our alignment sheet included thirteen states and two thousand right-of-way miles.

An alignment sheet is a 24" x 36" sheet of paper that shows our pipelines in relation to a an aerial photography of the area. Upon this sheet, we have also placed information about our pipeline characteristics, such as, pipe sizes, test stations for cathodic protection, property owners, and stationing of geographic features that cross our right-of-way.

As our pipeline grew and changed, information of its changes was in several documents in our organization. These document included survey field notes, construction reports, foreign line crossings, and other internal documents. Information from these documents, was then manually placed on an alignment sheet drawing, for use by the organization. Computer Aided Drafting began to change this paper document into electronic files. It is from these changes, where the project begins.

## Needs Assessment

The beginning of the alignment sheet program started with the objective of completing the updates of all the alignment sheets with four operators, a part time coordinator/operator and a checker, in four years. Upon analyses, of our objective, it became clear that we would need to develop a schedule, a means for tracking this schedule and develop a plan to achieve our goals.

## Schedule

A formal written breakdown of the work associated with the alignment sheet program was not available at the beginning of the project. This information in the past was given to be in and around a number by previous project recall. The program needed this basic information to develop a scheduled for the alignment sheet program. We constructed an alignment sheet from the beginning and recorded the various steps involved with this process. Our analysis of the process identified the following steps:

- *ALG*. An ASCII text file was created using field note information and saved using the extension .alg, hence the step ALG. This is the first step because it puts all the twists and turns of the pipeline and its associated geographic features into a data file that can be read into a CAD file. The computer program was developed in-house by our computer analyst staff as an enhancement to the CAD system. Most of this step had been completed under another program that used the same twists and turns of the pipeline to develop drawings used in Department of Transportation (DOT) compliance.
- *Graphic*. The graphic portion of the process was the actual manipulation of the line and text that comprises the meat of the drawing. The CAD operator or mapper takes property, geographic and pipe information and determines its place on the drawing. This is a tedious process that involves the most time. Several internal documents are read and analyzed to determine if there is a geographic relation to other features on the sheet. The main tool used for this step is the CAD software program.
- *Photo*. The aerial photograph of the pipeline is outsourced to an aerial company that specializes in this field. The flight line is determined in-house and given to the contractor to be flown in fall or early spring when the foliage is at a minimum. One part of the system is flown every year so we had a backlog of photos of various vintages to choose from. The photo is scanned and placed in the CAD file as a Raster image to provide a background for the area.
- *Revision*. Verifying and offering a second opinion on the interpretation of the data is the work of the checker. The sheets are marked with corrections and returned back to the mapper for revisions. During the revision, the corrections of checker are made on the sheet. Any last minute

**Exhibit 1.**

| | Task Name | Duration | Start | Finish | Predecessors |
|---|---|---|---|---|---|
| 1 | ...Leidy Lateral 25-1000 | 289.88d | Mon 9/27/99 | Fri 10/6/00 | |
| 2 | P-4-1 | 3.13d | Mon 9/27/99 | Thu 9/30/99 | |
| 3 | ALG | 4h | Mon 9/27/99 | Mon 9/27/99 | |
| 4 | CREATE GRAPHICS | 21h | Mon 9/27/99 | Thu 9/30/99 | 3 |
| 5 | ADD PHOTO | 1h | Mon 5/22/00 | Mon 5/22/00 | 10 |
| 6 | REVISIONS | 5h | Fri 9/29/00 | Fri 9/29/00 | 14 |
| 7 | FINAL LAYOUT | 5h | Tue 10/3/00 | Tue 10/3/00 | 12 |
| 8 | P 4 71 | 3.13d | Thu 9/30/99 | Tue 10/5/99 | |
| 9 | ALG | 4h | Thu 9/30/99 | Thu 9/30/99 | 4 |
| 10 | CREATE GRAPHICS | 21h | Thu 9/30/99 | Tue 10/5/99 | 9 |
| 11 | ADD PHOTO | 1h | Mon 5/22/00 | Mon 5/22/00 | 5 |
| 12 | REVISIONS | 5h | Mon [illegible] | Mon [illegible] | 6 |
| 13 | FINAL LAYOUT | 5h | Fri 10/6/00 | Fri 10/6/00 | 7 |
| 14 | ..Checking | 744h | Mon 5/22/00 | Thu 9/28/00 | 11 |
| 15 | | | | | |
| 16 | | | | | |

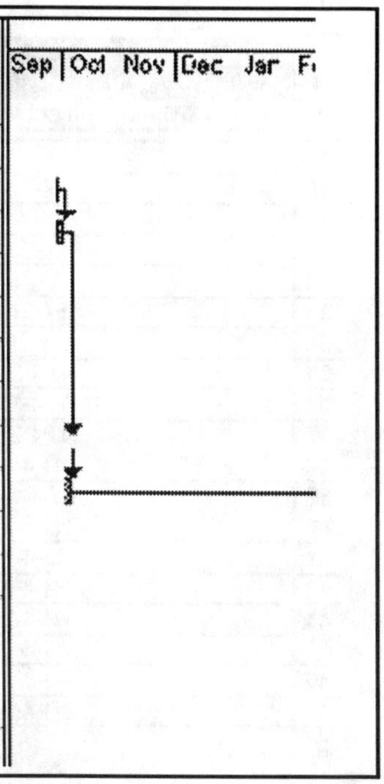

Sep | Oct | Nov | Dec | Jan | F

data is placed in the drawing and resubmitted back to the checker for a final check before the final layout.

- *Final Layout*. Final layout as the name implies is the last step of turning the sheet into an approved document in the organization. The drawings are plotted and signed.

With the identification of the steps determined, we next move our attention toward the quantity of work involved. Lists of existing drawings gathered and checked against all the existing alignments in our drawing vault. With the new lists complied, we began to construct the schedule.

The software used to do the project schedule was Microsoft Project. The name field was populated by the state indented to the drawing number for the first two tasks to be completed. With the completion of the first two steps or WBS, the photo is attached and the drawing is sent to the checker. The WBS as defined by the PMBOK guide as "*A deliverable-oriented grouping of project elements which organizes and defines the total scope of the project. Each descending level represents an increasingly detailed definition of a project component. Project components may be products or service.*" Leaving the checker task, the final two WBS are completed, namely revision and final layout (see Exhibit 1).

## Tracking

The scheduling software we used did not work well when we began tracking. Our intent was to track individual CAD operator hours for each WBS and provide management, with an earned value graph, Microsoft Project did not meet that requirement. The conclusion was that we needed another tool to provide us with an earned value graph. Through hours of trial and error, we came to the conclusion that our tracking would be better done under Excel. Linking the schedule to a spreadsheet using the process of, linking a document, works well with the Microsoft software packages.

The time operators spent on each WBS is accumulated in a worksheet that is e-mailed to the part-time coordinator for inclusion into the accumulated weekly time workbook. The time is not directly linked, but a lot of duplicate typing is avoided. The operator, alignment sheet identification, date and WBS code are the data recorded on the time sheet.

A workbook that accumulates the weekly times was created to record the time as stated above (see Exhibit 2).

The sheets of the workbook were set up so each operator's time was accumulated separately. The time spent for each task on a drawing was totaled by the month and inserted into earned value workbook (see Exhibit 3).

The earned value workbook was divided into two sheets. One sheet contained the graph and the other, accumulated the time. The sheet that accumulated the time linked a schedule

**Exhibit 2.**

| | B | C | D | E | CT | CU | CV | CW | CX | CY |
|---|---|---|---|---|---|---|---|---|---|---|
| 3 | [illegible] | [illegible] | [illegible] | TOTAL HOURS | MONTHLY TOTAL | TUESDAY | WEDNESDAY | THURSDAY | FRIDAY | SATURDAY |
| 4 | Group & Gunn | Sheet No. | Type of Work | | MARCH | 4/1/97 | 4.2/97 | 4/3/97 | 4/4/97 | 4/5/97 |
| 28 | | | REVISION | 0.5 | 0.0 | | | | 0.5 | |
| 29 | | I-4-22 | photo | 4.5 | 0.0 | | | | | |
| 30 | | | REVISION | 3.5 | 0.0 | | 1.0 | 2.0 (?) | 0.5 | |
| 31 | | I-4-23 | photo | 6.5 | 0.0 | | | | | |
| 32 | | | REVISION | 3.5 | 0.0 | | 3.0 | | 0.5 | |
| 33 | | I-4-24 | photo | 3.5 | 0.0 | | 4.0 | | | |
| 34 | | | REVISION | 4.5 | 0.0 | | 4.0 | | 0.5 | |
| 35 | 24-1988 (?) | NJ-4-31 | GRAPHIC | 5.5 | 2.0 | | | | | |
| 36 | | NJ-4-32 (?) | GRAPHIC | 5.0 | 2.0 | | | | | |
| 37 | | NJ-4-33 | GRAPHIC | 7.0 | 2.0 | | | | | |
| 38 | 24-1972 | NJ-4-1 | GRAPHIC | 8.0 | 2.0 | | | | | |
| 39 | | NJ-4-1A | GRAPHIC | 4.5 | 2.0 | | | | | |
| 40 | | NJ-4-2 | GRAPHIC | 5.0 | 2.0 | | | | | |
| 41 | | NJ-4-3 | GRAPHIC | 5.5 | 2.0 | | | | | |
| 42 | | NJ-4-4 | GRAPHIC | 8.0 (?) | 2.0 | | | | | |
| 43 | | NJ-4-5 | GRAPHIC | 5.0 | 2.0 | | | | | |
| 44 | | NJ-4-6 (?) | GRAPHIC | 7.0 | 2.0 | | | | | |
| 45 | | NJ-4-7 | GRAPHIC | 8.0 | 2.0 | | | | | |
| 46 | | NJ-4-8 (?) | GRAPHIC | 7.0 | 2.0 | | | | | |

**Exhibit 3.**

| | A | B | C | D | E | F | G |
|---|---|---|---|---|---|---|---|
| 1 | **Drawing Earned Value Analysis** | | | | | | |
| 2 | | | | | | | |
| 3 | | Baseline | Baseline | Baseline | Actual | Baseline | EARNED |
| 4 | Description | Start | Finish | Hours | Hours | Hours(earned) | VALUE |
| 5 | | DATE | DATE | | 6/96 | 6/96 | 6/96 |
| 6 | **...Main Line Alignment 26-0100** | 6/3/96 | 11/25/97 | | | | |
| 7 | NC-4-1 | 6/3/96 | 6/5/96 | | | | |
| 8 | *CREATE GRAPHICS* | 6/3/96 | 6/5/96 | 21 | 34 | 21 | |
| 9 | *ADD PHOTO* | 1/1/97 | 1/1/97 | 1 | | | |
| 10 | *REVISIONS* | 8/13/97 | 8/13/97 | 5 | | | |
| 11 | *FINAL LAYOUT* | 8/13/97 | 8/14/97 | 5 | | | |
| 12 | NC-4-2 | 6/5/96 | 6/10/96 | | | | |
| 13 | *CREATE GRAPHICS* | 6/5/96 | 6/10/96 | 21 | 32 | 21 | |
| 14 | *ADD PHOTO* | 1/1/97 | 1/1/97 | 1 | | | |
| 15 | *REVISIONS* | 8/14/97 | 8/14/97 | 5 | | | |
| 16 | *FINAL LAYOUT* | 8/14/97 | 8/15/97 | 5 | | | |
| 17 | NC-4-3 | 6/10/96 | 6/12/96 | | | | |
| 18 | *CREATE GRAPHICS* | 6/10/96 | 6/12/96 | 21 | 32 | 21 | |
| 19 | *ADD PHOTO* | 1/1/97 | 1/1/97 | 1 | | | |
| 20 | *REVISIONS* | 8/15/97 | 8/18/97 | 5 | | | |
| 21 | *FINAL LAYOUT* | 8/18/97 | 8/18/97 | 5 | | | |
| 22 | NC-4-4 | 6/12/96 | 6/17/96 | | | | |

with a modified table. This table showed the Task, Baseline Start, the Baseline Finish and the Baseline Hours. We used the existing data from the schedule and linked it to the spreadsheet. The procedure for linking a schedule to a spreadsheet is outlined as follows:

- Open both applications.

**Exhibit 4.**

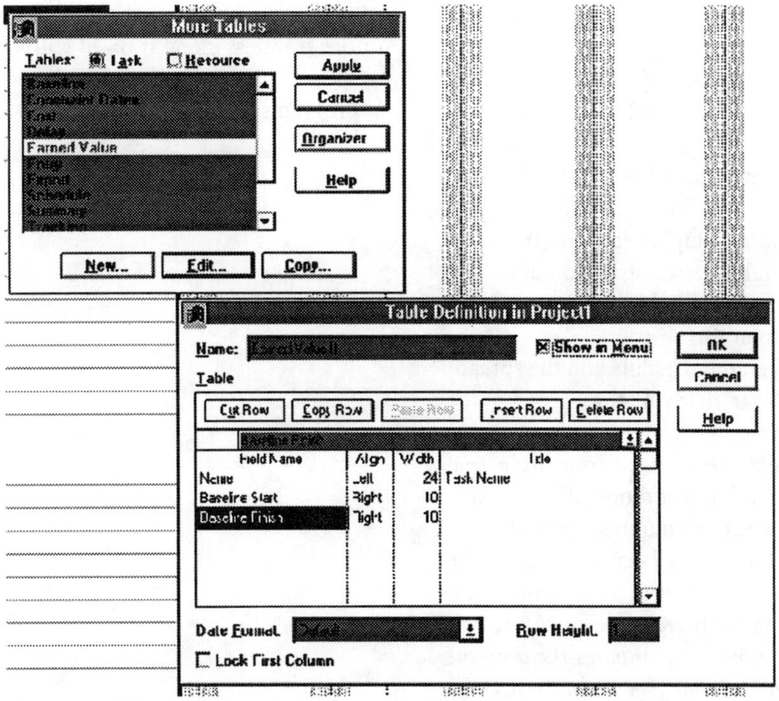

**Exhibit 5.**

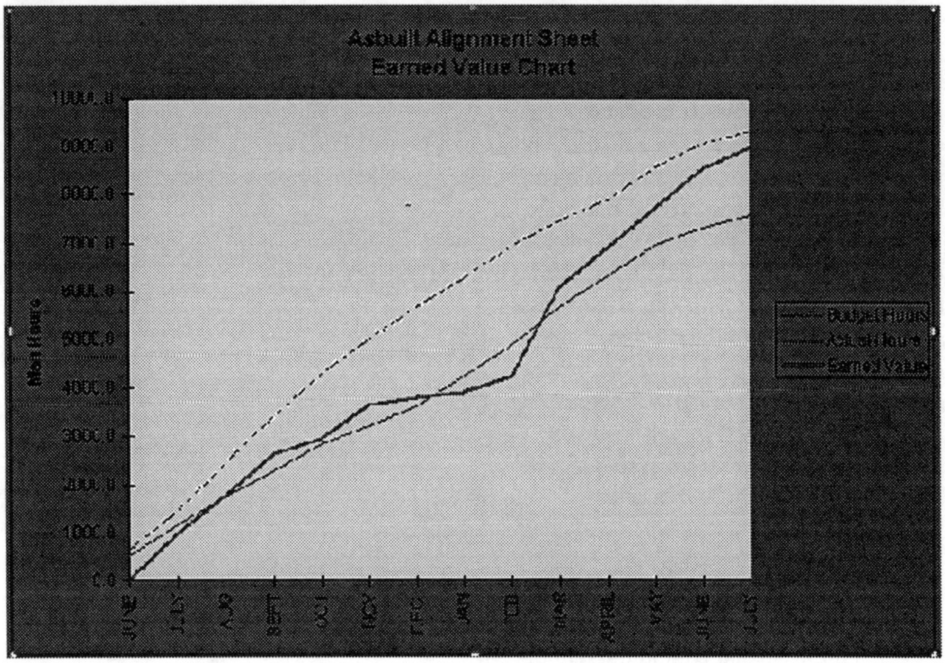

- Go to the MSproject program, highlight the data and execute the copy command under the Edit menu,
- Switch to the file running under Excel,
- Select the upper left-hand corner where the data is to be placed,
- Under Edit select paste command, and
- In the dialog that appears, select Paste Link and Text options.

We made a custom table that included only the task, baseline start, baseline finish and baseline hours fields in the scheduling program. This was accomplished using the View => Table:Entry=> More Tables...=> Earned value => Copy command, we deleted all the fields and inserted the four that we needed (see Exhibit 4).

The link established between the schedule and the spreadsheet, then create the first four fields of the earned value workbook. The actual hours that are totaled in the accumulated weekly times worksheet are inserted into the actual hours columns of the Earned value workbook. The Baseline hours are placed in their respective columns. Earned value hours are awarded after the work has been verified by the part-time coordinator and recorded in their columns. The earned value as defined by the PMBOK guide as "*A method for measuring project performance. It compares the amount of work that was planned with what was actually accomplished to determine if cost and schedule performance is as planned.* ... The spreadsheet is ready to produce a plot (see Exhibit 5).

## Plan

As the project proceeded, different work methods were tried and evaluated. The act of tracking hours was sufficient to identify processes that were not working as planned and also, areas where it was working well. For example, constructing an alignment sheet had each sheet being completed by one operator start to finish. Junior mappers now do all the CAD intensive work and the senior mappers compare field book information and other internal documents with the alignments sheets and make changes before going to the checker. Time is not wasted by a junior mapper on the analytic effort, where experience plays a major role, but is encourage to find the best process inputting information in CAD. The continuation of the project will undoubtedly identify other areas that can be improved upon and ways where cost can be reduced.

## Conclusion

The earned value concept and the current computer technology allow real-time information on schedules associated with the alignment sheet program. Senior management can be supplied information using the earned value concept such as what is being done, how much progress is being completed, and where the project is within a certain degree of accuracy. A more seamless integration of software would be helpful in further use of this concept in other front line project tracking programs.

# How Do We Manage What We Cannot Find?

Ray Piper, Union Carbide Corporation

Technology is doubling every two years. Technology and employees' needs are accelerating faster than ITS groups can deal with implementation. This paper will be out of date by the time you read it, but unless you implement it now you will never be where you should have been!

## Introduction

Most successful organizations have a powerful communication infrastructure. A company's ability to communicate fast and effectively is essential to business success. It is natural, therefore, that we would be attracted to the Information Superhighway. Although we mostly refer to the Internet when we refer to online services, the full-range of information services has caught the interest of many companies within the United States. However, there is some homework to be done before we take the step of embroiling our companies in Cyberspace. As we move towards paper-less organizations, there is a desperate need for an accelerated ability to find data that is available within our systems. Internal browsers and intranets may be the low-cost answer. They are now being installed by as many as 55% of large U.S. companies. The reasons are obvious;

1. More than 80% of the information in a typical office resides in unstructured documents.
2. Personal productivity is hampered by employees unknowingly reinventing documents that already exist within the system.
3. Indications are, as much as 30% of employee time may be spent looking for data, highlighting the need for browsers and intranets.
4. There is a more urgent need to find our way through the data to reach what is wanted when we want it—need for browsers and intranets.
5. Installation costs for browsers and intranets can be as little as hundreds of dollars depending on existing company hardware and software, which needs to be compatible and networked.

## How Does All This Affect the Oil, Gas and Petrochemical Industry?

Current forecasts from the petrochemical industry indicate that there will be an increase in project work executed overseas. Overseas access to home-based data will be critical.

The ability to use electronic mail has made the earth a smaller place and has made the notion of global project teams possible. The wonder of e-mail is that it is not constrained by geography, by time-zone or by the availability of the addressee. Also, not only text but any file attachments can now also be transmitted with this media. Project plans, drawings, reports, programs and digitized audio and video clips can be attached to any message. The cost of a message is not at all affected by distance and the cost per message has become insignificant. All this data flying through Cyberspace has to settle somewhere. The question is; "When it settles will I ever find it again?" I believe intranets and browsers are the answer.

New technology certainly destroys millions of jobs but it also creates millions of jobs. New technology has always caused industry shifts such as from blacksmiths and buggy whip manufacturer's to car and airplane industries. Where technology is impacting the population dramatically is in the shift to more technologically skilled needs as more manual related jobs are being replaced by smart systems. There are, and will continue to be, many shifts within our industry and most will be necessary just for survival.

1. Rapid development of ITS has put an urgent burden on industry to dramatically increase training in all sectors.
2. The movement of conceptual costs into a higher percentage of total enterprise costs, earlier expenditures related to ITS systems in project execution.
3. It will be easier to shift low-tech work abroad to leverage low cost of engineering and construction.
4. With technology changing every two years, a project that takes three to four years to build, is two generations out of date, extinct, before it is online. This is not tolerable. We have to compress projects or defer technology improvements. Neither is a practical proposition.

**Exhibit 1.**

**Exhibit 3.**

*Electronic Manuals*

- **Project Requirements Manual (PRM)**
- **HS&E Project Review Requirements**
- **Project Metrics Requirements Manual**
- **Value Engineering Workshop**

***Single Click Selection:***

**Exhibit 2.**

## What Can Browsers and Intranets Do For Me?

Browsers can locate and launch electronic files or applications and can be operated as a multiuser application from any networked location. The proceedings of many organizations like the PMI are now issued exclusively in Adobe format on CD's that have Adobe's Acrobat Reader preinstalled. Intranets allow easy access and sharing of huge libraries of best practices and industry experience. Web servers are the machines that store the intranet programs. Browsers take a minimum time to develop and can operate with minimal maintenance while using freely distributed software. One of the key advantages of intranets is this short development cycle required to roll out the application. While some applications often require weeks or months of development, intranets take days and sometimes hours.

Benefits accrue mainly through improvements in people and work process efficiency and in the use of lessons learned ultimately translating into scope, schedule and cost reduction. With ready access to work process documentation, procedures, guidelines, forms and training, there will be:

- Less time spent looking for information,
- More consistent and immediate application of best practices resulting in reduced life cycle cost,
- Reduction in duplicated effort in terms of developing forms, procedures and instructions, and
- Templates will be used for maximum efficiency, less training and consistent formats.

Once an intranet is installed and a browser is identified or developed, much of the technical work can be handled by employees without advanced degrees in computer science. This helps keep support focused on getting out the business message and not tinkering with the underlying technology.

Look at Exhibits 1 and 2. Which looks the most user friendly? Exhibit 1 is what we have become accustomed to within the Windows 95 environment.

This can be a nightmare and does not lend itself to efficiency in searching for valuable information. The most important point is that even with this image on your screen, you may not know that the information you need is on another server in another location. The next step after searching unsuccessfully, within the areas you are familiar with, is to develop the information yourself. This could be the nineteenth time this information has been replicated within the corporation. This is not adding value.

In Exhibits 2 and 3, one can move efficiently from option to option without knowing where documents are stored or even which software is required. Copies can be made of the read only files, they can be saved under a different name or simply browsed for reference purposes.

**Exhibit 4.**

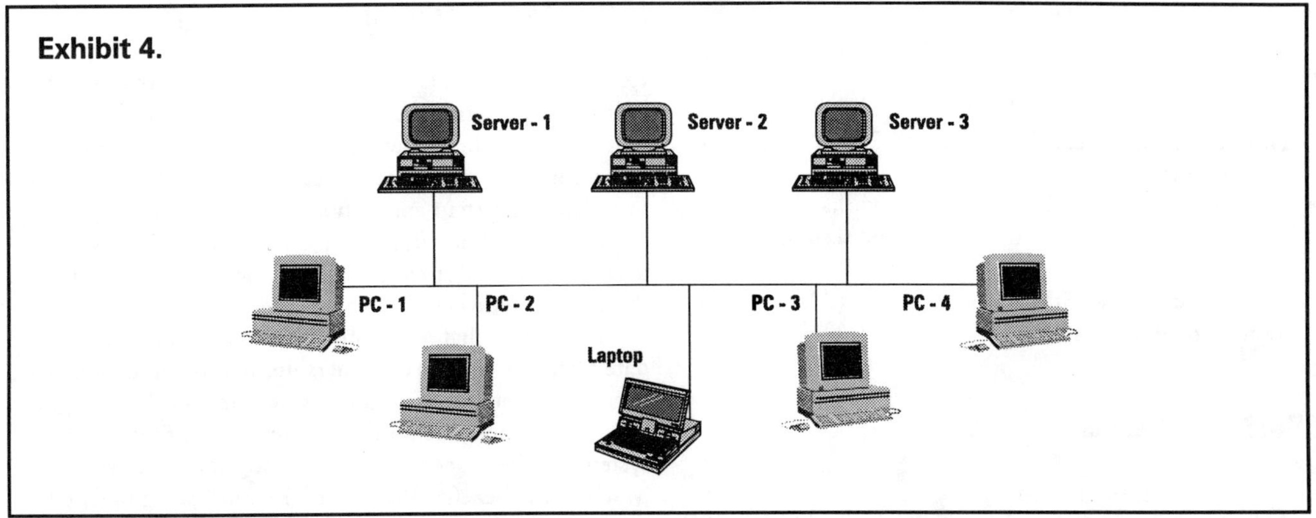


1. Intranets work marvels for text and graphical information. It's a great place to create an online employee handbook, post rules and procedures.
2. An intranet is a company information system that in most cases operates as an electronic version of a bulletin board and newsletter.
3. Browsers are designed to provide the engineering organization and its project partners in the business, R&D, operations and procurement, easy and effective access to electronic project work processes and project management documentation and tools, via the intranet.

## Do We Have Any Facts to Consider?

It is essential that companies that have desktop PCs loaded with individual copies of word processing, spreadsheet and communications software, promoting activity and not productivity, move to providing software residing on servers. Not only does this dramatically reduce the time needed to update software, but it also ensures compatible software is available to all employees and improves rapid and consistent communication. Other facts to consider are as follows;

- Intranets are expanding five times faster than Internet's.
- Reports say that Douglas Aircraft is to replace four million pages of documentation yearly.
- Browsers can reduce inefficiency of dealing with individual requests for human resource data.
- Office and phone directories, HR information, etc., costs between $50 to $100 per employee.
- They have lowered staff/costs by help desks going online. Employees help themselves.
- Study by U.S. Computer indicates web technologies reduce internal networking costs by as much as $11 million over four years on large networks.
- Reduces cost—less time spent searching for information improving personal productivity.
- Enables Work Process consistency.
- Computer-based training is placed at employees' fingertips.
- Institutionalizes forms, procedures and processes.
- Can support photographs, audio, 3D rendered animation and video.
- User friendly—don't have to know data location.
- Security—both view and change available.
- Reduces the paper chase, green and lower cost.
- No programming involved—uses hyperlinks.
- Owners can maintain documents evergreen.
- Reader/browser software is most often free.
- Automates employee and department surveys.
- Improves communications—instant and free.
- Allows access to outside resources—CII, PMI, conferences, etc.
- Can be managed by clerical employee or technician.
- Deploys proven Internet technology but totally inside the organization and within appropriate commercial security.
- Means a reduction of paper and the cost of paper handling.
- Hugely reduces computer storage requirements.
- Reduces problems with e-mail overload with easier access to data.
- Increases accuracy and timeliness of information.
- One consistent interface for employees to learn and use.
- Available information is clearly visible.
- Drastically reduces information search time.
- Enables sharing and reuse of tools and information, greatly improving productivity and communication.

- Reduces redundant page creation and maintenance, templates for all documents are at employees' fingertips.
- One-time archive and development cost.
- Enables sharing of reduced resources and skills.
- Has been used to hear the company CEO talk about the corporate vision.
- Immediate access via Local Area Networks (LAN's) or Wide Area Networks (WAN's), as can be seen in Exhibit 4.
- Not duplicated by EDMS (Electronic Data Management System) or Windows 95.

## EDMS vs. Intranets

- Documents vs. Information.
- Indexing vs. Association (hyperlinks). Indexing can get quite complex and is not always user friendly.
- Centralized vs. Distributed with owners.
- Drawings, equipment files, vendor data vs. Policies, procedures, Human Resource data, phone directories, location maps, newsletters communication.
- Requires training vs. Intuition.

There is a case for both EDMS and intranets. Neither replaces the other but they can, and should, function together.

## Do We Have a Competency Crisis That Will Prevent Us Implementing?

Cheryl Currid of Currid and Co. in Houston, Texas, has written extensively on the competency crisis. Intranets can reduce the effect of the competency crisis because they are so easy and intuitive. A competency crisis can strike anytime technology is introduced or changes radically. It renders previously productive people unable to do their jobs. When technology is introduced it often rocks processes and day-to-day activity so much that some people become functionally incompetent.

Productivity drops even for those who welcome new technology. The problem is not technology, it is people. People often wallow in the productivity pits and the situation doesn't get any better on its own. It takes months and sometimes years of work to get people to relearn their jobs. The cure? Giving employees extensive training courses? It doesn't solve the problem. It takes an extensive program, customized for each work discipline. The problem still does not go away, it lies dormant until the next major technological opportunity arrives. With intranets, training is accessible to all employees on the screen.

## Is This An Extension of Reengineering?

Reengineering has succeeded in enabling the development of uniform engineering work processes, procedures, tools and best practices. These new work processes have demonstrated that significant capital savings can be achieved through rigorous and consistent application. A barrier, however, has always been the limited ability to share and maintain up-to-date electronic information with all the various users across the corporation.

Project data that is accessible on servers is often not updated because of lack of ownership. Before an intranet has been implemented, work process owners must be identified and made responsible for the maintenance of files within the system and be responsible for keeping the data evergreen. Much of the benefit relies on information being updated in real time. This requires that 'owners' must be identified for each group of data.

## How Can Employees Be More Effective?

We can be more effective by providing real time access to data, forms, procedures, work process maps and training materials. Employees should be able to share project management information from external associations and societies, as well as lessons learned or project metrics data that would allow continuous improvement in work processes and performance. Interacting and networking across locations lacking either an electronic bulletin board or forum can enable the team concept to bridge distance in an environment where international communication will be essential.

Some few employees may play games on their PC or search without need and therefore reduce personal productivity. However, this is not an employee problem, this is a management problem. If employees really are abusing the tools made available, they should be dealt with through the management process. We should not take the tools away, we should manage people properly. Intranets are a productivity tool and should be implemented to add value. Employees must be made aware that the long term goal is to improve personal productivity so that more time is available for meaningful value added activities.

## What Are the Challenges for Us as Individuals?

As employees, we must take responsibility for our own destiny. It's okay to blame the boss, ITS and even the computer, but in the final analysis, we are the ones who have to overcome competency problems or we may find our replacement doing it for us. The growth of intranets mirrors the trend toward greater employee responsibility for managing our own destiny. We must endeavor to get rid of hard copies of files, books and manuals and challenge ourselves to find information faster.

Digital photography becomes a powerful tool with the introduction of intranets. Engineering can assist construction work in that data can be photographed, downloaded and transmitted to the home office or around the world for information and design needs. These progress photographs can also be stored for reporting purposes and for estimating without sending people to job sites. This application, through the intranet, can reduce paper consumption, travel costs and bring the location to the home office in seconds.

When our peers resist change it forces the retention of two systems. Mentor those who are reluctant to change and help in promoting new technology. Managers should walk about more and see how employees are using new technology. Audit the groups and encourage efficiency improvement throughout the department. Encourage employees to share their successful techniques in team meetings.

## Where To From Here?

We want our team members to share information efficiently and to avoid items dropping through the cracks, to hear news quickly and to easily find key documents and other crucial information.

All that is needed is space on a server somewhere. The more relevance to the material you are putting on the server, the more employees will use it. Make it look nice by adding some graphics on the 'home page.'

Mark Gibbs, a writer for PC World says, "One of my clients was planning to build a corporate intranet. I suggested he look to see how many already existed within his company. He replied that there were none, this would be the first. After being persuaded to check, he found there were already seven servers out there. It was because the ITS department was too slow and it was easy for these departments to solve the issue themselves."

The push to move towards intranets comes not from popularity but from the need for a manageable infrastructure. Systems management is the number one ITS problem. It will remain a major problem for a very long time and intranets will take many years to emerge, unless the concept is pushed up from the roots.

The intranet presumes that it doesn't matter where the data is located. It assumes the end-user has a standard interface with which to access it and a broadband network over which to move it.

## What's Happening in Other Industries?

A Business Research Group survey of one hundred and sixty nine companies found that 23% already have an intranet and 30% are studying the technology. The same group says that the amount of mid-size and large companies introducing some kind of intranet has increased from 11% in 1995 to 55% in 1996, and will reach 70% in 1997.

MCI has more than twelve thousand employees using their intranet to follow its motto of "Collaborate, don't duplicate." Intranets can be used as an electronic repository of a company's knowledge. Where better to store best practices with easy immediate access by all employees. William Rich, senior VP of Mitre Tek in Va., says, "We wanted a way for every employee to know everything the company knows."

The beauty of intranets is that they work over the existing systems. If you have LAN's and WAN's, you don't have to put in any extra wires or new protocol. Almost all companies, regardless of size, are saying that this is an expenditure of less than $10,000. In some cases this cost can be less than Lotus Notes or Microsoft Exchange. Whether it is BMW AG in Munich, Fujitsu Ltd. in Tokyo, Credit Lyonnias in Paris, or Boeing in Seattle, managers in charge of intranets have difficulties identifying disadvantages of the technology.

Robert Tharp of NASA's Internet division says that they can have engineers working together worldwide, in different time zones and countries. He adds that project managers keep all the information on a server and different scientists and engineers are allowed access to different parts of that information.

There are greatly reduced security issues because intranets are fenced off from the outside by 'firewalls' that allow employees to look out, but keep others from looking in.

## Conclusion

Investment in computer technology should yield between twenty and fifty percent productivity improvement. If it isn't, either the computers aren't working or the employees aren't on board. Most often it's not the computers. Intranets can surely help realize and improve these personal productivity exhibits.

Some people wrongly believe that intranets and browsers will replace existing systems. Instead, they are complementary. Their payback can be felt mostly through the removal of administrative roadblocks, providing a self-service smorgasbord of information in an environment never experienced before.

There is a hidden cost, the cost of not deploying intranets at all. It can take a while for companies to exhibit out how to exploit a new technology. But once they do, the returns can be dramatic for the early implementers, companies that beat their competition. One day we will look around and find that intranets are running the company and users will be relying on them like they do the ATM.

We have empowered people through more compatible hardware and software. The next step is to empower employees by making information easily retrievable. The information exists but the searchers have no idea where to look because current ITS systems cannot guide them to it. PCs and servers have become the culprits in that they have become convenient pools into which reams of valuable information pour and expeditiously disappear. We cannot compete with overseas salaries. Our technology is our advantage and we must use it fully to improve personal productivity. This is our competitive advantage.

Today, all this is possible. In fact, companies already have much of what they need to do the job. The technology and computing power is there and employees are eager to become tomorrow's knowledge workers. The missing element is the intranet to bring it all together. Bill Gates says, "And what that really means ... is they're empowered to make decisions. When that happens, productivity soars."

## References

Currid, Cheryl. President of Currid and Co. Houston

Lucas, John J. 1995. *Work management: Why can't information managers manage*. PMI Conference.

Piper, Ray G. 1995. *Reengineering implementation for project management*. PMI Conference 1995

SunWorld Online 1996/1997

Aiello, Carlo. 1996. *Intranets vs. EDMS*. Union Carbide White Paper.

# Risky Business—Developing a Standardized WBS to Mitigate Risk on Refinery Turnarounds

Ben E. Voivedich Jr., PMP

The ability to successfully manage a turnaround hinges on the project manager's ability to control the scope of work. Rigorously control the scope and the ever-present risk of cost and schedule overruns are substantially reduced. While methods such as work order cutoff dates and capital project submission milestones help to curtail "scope creep," the single most effective method would be for turnaround managers to adopt the use of work breakdown structures (WBS). By establishing that the WBS must represent all work and all costs of the turnaround, serve an integrative function of tying costs and schedules together, reconcile to the business accounting systems, and act as a communication tool for the turnaround, the risk of things such as undefined scope "appearing" late in the project are significantly reduced.

For the benefit of those who are not yet familiar with the PMI project management terminology including the use of the WBS acronym, a brief description is in order. A work breakdown structure is a component or task oriented breakdown of the turnaround scope. Others have described it as a "flexible industrial language for describing, planning, and managing" work (Luby, Peel, and Swahl 1995). Using a "tree" structure, the WBS defines all the work to be done on the turnaround by levels of increasing detail identified as WBS elements or "buckets." It often serves the function of integrating cost and schedule. Exhibit 1 shows a WBS for a turnaround involving two units broken down to level two buckets. Note that the bucketed costs of the Level two elements add up to the total cost of the level one element. This is a core principle of WBS development that I call the "unity" principle. The total costs of each level of the WBS are always equal. If the level one WBS element defined as "Spring '98 Turnaround" has a cost of $25 million, then the summarized cost of all buckets at level two must equal $25 million. At level three, the total cost of all elements must still equal $25 million and so on down to whatever level of detail is required to adequately manage the turnaround.

This "unity" principle can also be applied to scheduled activities for the turnaround. Every activity described on any schedule developed for use on the turnaround must be coded so that it is represented by one and only one of the WBS buckets. By making sure that all costs and schedules are "unified" for the turnaround, you end up with an integrated cost and schedule system that fully describes the turnaround scope.

Once you attain "unity," the second step involves standardization of the WBS. An important component of standardization of the WBS is tying it to the business accounting structure. For most plants, the two main documents that describe turnaround costs are the work order and the purchase order. Usually all plant personnel and the "evergreen" contractors charge their labor on timecards. The timecards usually allocate time by work order. For other services, the plant usually issues a purchase order with a fixed price or a "not to exceed" price tied to a prenegotiated set of rates. Every timesheet charge by work order and every purchase order line item must be tied to one and only one of the WBS elements.

What should the structure of a turnaround WBS look like? In an excellent *PM Network* article, Robert Youker states that a "WBS is an artistic blend of process, product, and organization" (Yorker 1991). Level one of the WBS should normally represent the total budget for the turnaround including associated overhead costs. But when you get to level two and lower, the WBS must be reflective of not only what work is to be done but be cognizant of the phase issues involved in managing a turnaround project and how the work is to be performed and by whom.

But being cognizant of resources applied to the work can lead to confusion in the development of the WBS. A WBS describes a component of the work; it does not represent who will do the work. Exhibit 2 shows how a WBS should not be done. The resources used to perform the scope of work are

**Exhibit 1.** Simple WBS at Level 2

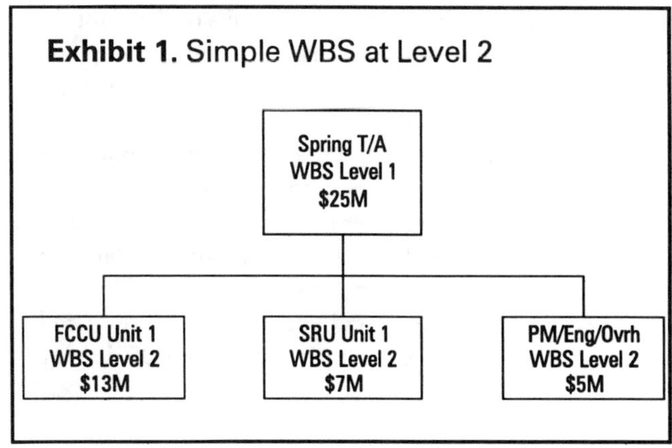

**Exhibit 2.** A WBS Does Not Describe the "Who", it Describes the "What"

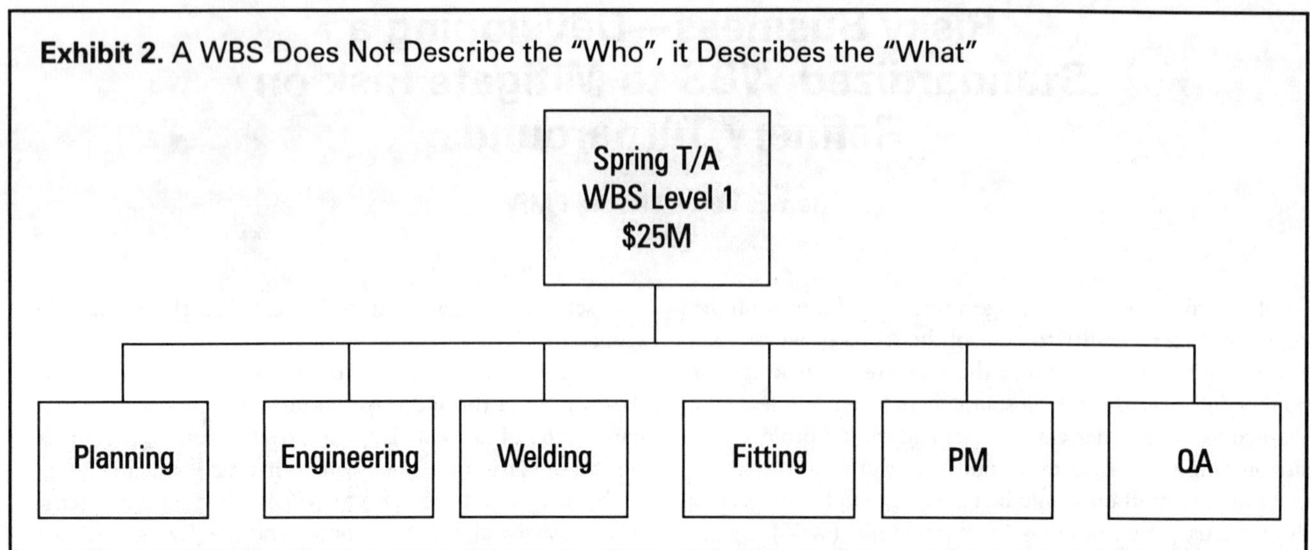


described through a related but separate structure called an organization breakdown structure (OBS). Often the OBS elements are the "functional" departments and major subcontractors that perform the turnaround (i.e., maintenance planning, maintenance electricians, engineering subcontractor, major T/A contractor's welders, etc.). As an example, a work order on a turnaround may require the "engineering to reroute pipe to the exchanger." This work may be performed by the plant engineer or subcontracted to an engineering firm described in the OBS.

A tougher issue often encountered in determining level two elements of the WBS involves phases. A common method of describing the phase of a turnaround is by engineering, procurement, and construction. The problem with using phase to describe level two is shown in Exhibit 3. First of all, at level three there are redundant WBS elements for the FCCU #1. Using this WBS, we cannot roll up all the budget, actual costs, and current performance information for the FCCU Unit 1. Secondly, we are treating "engineering" as a component of the work instead of the FCCU Unit. I believe that this is the wrong approach to WBS development. Level two of the WBS should describe major units of the plant that will be worked on during the turnaround. (For larger plants, level two may identify complexes or areas of the plant with units detailed at level three.)

Please note that rollups of work based on the phase can still be achieved by coding activities using the applicable phase. Most modern computer software for cost and scheduling allows the coding of activities so that sorts or rollups by phase, responsibility, area, etc., can be done. I could not envision performing a turnaround without the ability to code activities. However, while coding is related to WBS development, it can not replace it.

At the third level of the turnaround WBS, the element of work described is normally the equipment class. As noted on Exhibit 4, the classes of work include exchangers, piping, electrical, pumps, etc. If you do not have a level two element for project management/engineering/overheads, you can create an "equipment class" for these items to capture budget, actual costs, and performance at level three.

At level 4 of the WBS, we would have the specific pieces of equipment related to the level three element. Again, Exhibit 3 notes examples of these as they relate to their level three elements.

Once we have described the WBS down to the equipment level, we have established a common communications tool that can be used by all participants on the turnaround. (While most active participants on the turnaround may use the work order number for communication, this is not a practical method for communicating progress to plant management.) As any PMP can tell you, one of the best ways to reduce risk is through better communication. Others have written that the WBS helps "describe a complicated, technical, state of the art project to team members (and stakeholders) from different backgrounds" (Harell 1994). The tree-like structure of the WBS lends itself to easy communication. Printed out down to level three or four, it can be used at pre-turnaround meetings with both large and small contractors to discuss what is to be done. Critical path schedules rolled up and summarized at level two or three of the WBS are easy for management and operations personnel to comprehend.

A byproduct of the adoption of a common WBS is the benefits of standardization. If all plant turnarounds are described using a common WBS, over time the plant departments and contractors should be able to assemble better cost estimates and schedules. At a nuclear facility for which my company performs turnaround (outage) assistance, the adoption of a

**Exhibit 3.** Using this WBS Creates Redundant Components

Spring T/A
WBS Level 1
$25M
Engineering
WBS Level 2
$2.5M
Procurement
WBS Level 2
$12.5M
Construction
WBS Level 2
$10M
FCCU 1Unit
Level 3
SRU Unit
Level 3
FCCU 1Unit
Level 3
SRU Unit
Level 3
FCCU 1Unit
Level 3
SRU Unit
Level 3


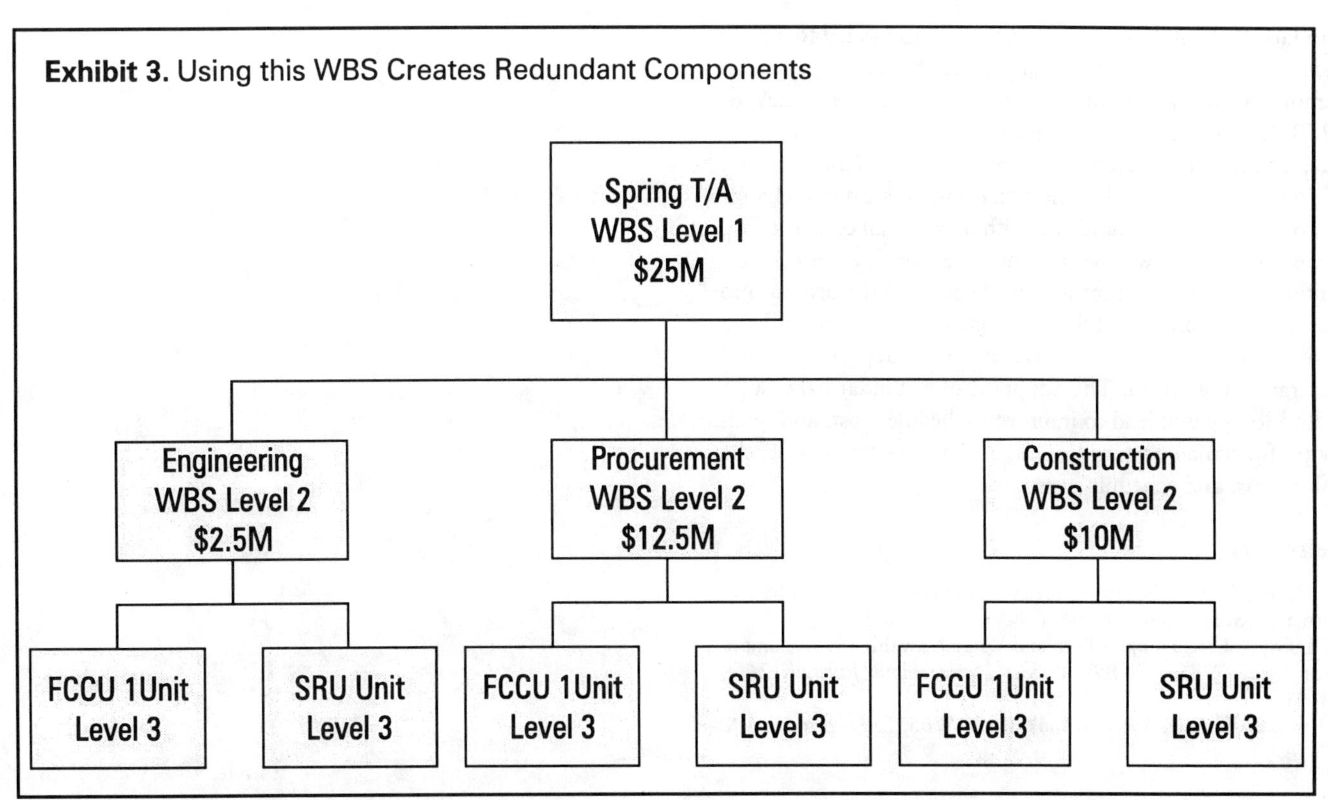

**Exhibit 4.** Segment of a Turnaround WBS Down to Level 4

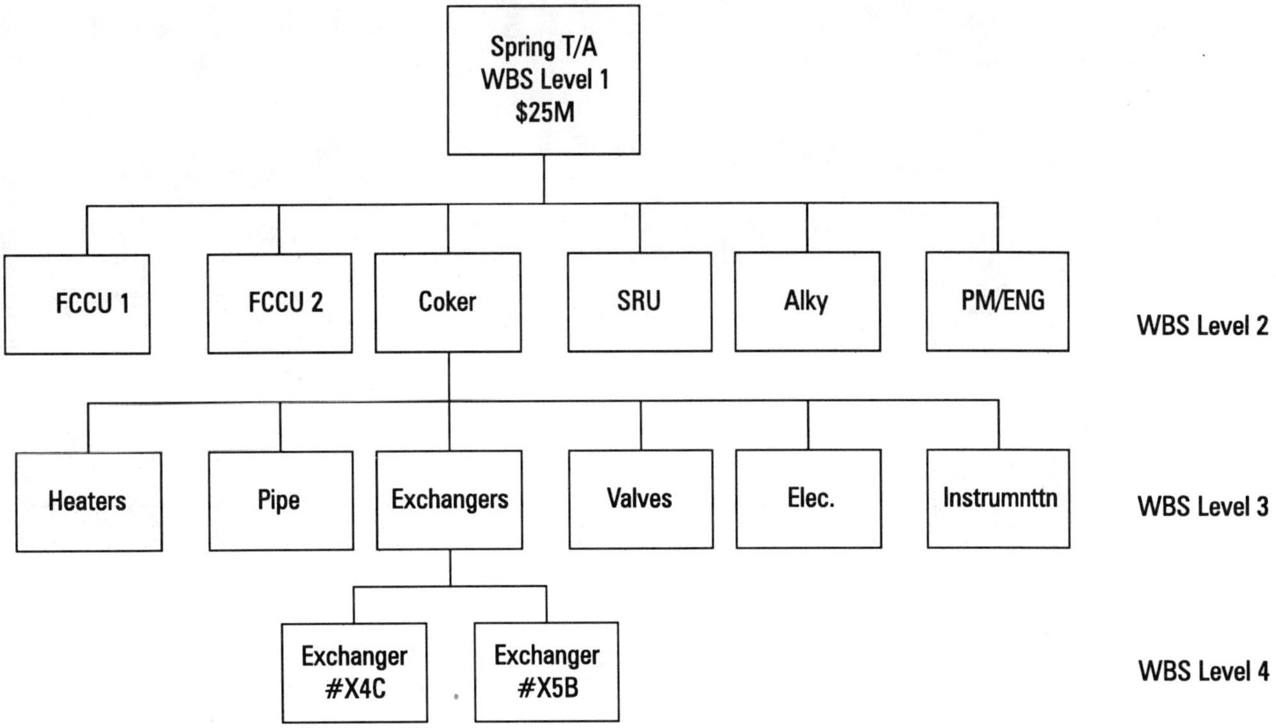

Spring T/A
WBS Level 1
$25M
FCCU 1
FCCU 2
Coker
SRU
Alky
PM/ENG
WBS Level 2
Heaters
Pipe
Exchangers
Valves
Elec.
Instrumnttn
WBS Level 3
Exchanger
#X4C
Exchanger
#X5B
WBS Level 4

standard WBS and other management tools has led to a 31% reduction in the time needed to perform the turnaround. Assuming a thirty-day turnaround and plant revenues of $250,000 per day, the savings amount to $2.5 million dollars; a sum sure to catch the attention of any plant manager.

In conclusion, whether the turnaround is a catalyst change out or a major plant shutdown with new capital construction, the use of a WBS will help to mitigate risk. It serves the essential function of integrating the elements of the project into a cohesive whole. It is relatively easy to implement and can easily be understood by the various plant departments and contractors involved. The adoption of a standardized WBS methodology will lead to improved schedule, cost, and quality performance on turnarounds and as a result reduces the risk of cost and schedule overruns.

## References


Harell, Clayton W. 1994. Breaking the communication barrier with a WBS. *PM Network*, 8:8, 6–8.

Luby, Robert, Douglas Peel, and William Swahl. 1995. Component based WBS (CWBS). *Project Management Journal*, 26:4, 38–43.

Youker, Robert. 1991. A look at the WBS. *PM Network*, 5:8, 33–36.

# Who Will Change the Diapers?

Francis Hartman, PEng PhD, The University of Calgary, Canada
Adrian Ilincuta, MSc, Quantel VECO Engineering, Canada
Ernie Vindevoghel, PEng, Quantel VECO Engineering, Canada

## Introduction

We live in a complex, rapidly changing world. Changes are broad and profound and can take many forms. Changes impact our life, our business and the way we think. Can we afford to ignore them? Are we ready, flexible and intuitive enough to anticipate changes and plan accordingly?

While thinking about the next century, it becomes evident that the pace of change will escalate. Regarding these future changes, we must deal with the following questions:

- What are the best ways to change?
- What will upcoming alternatives look like?
- What role will project management play in what we will do in the future?

This paper provides some possible answers to these questions in the context of the petrochemical industry, based on the following material:

- Results of a research study conducted at The University of Calgary to find the best practices of the construction and petrochemical industries as well as seven other industry sectors.
- A case study of a performance/success measurement program designed and currently under implementation at Quantel VECO Engineering Ltd.

The two subjects presented above are future oriented and are based on a long-time collaboration between The University of Calgary and Quantel. The measurement program initiated by Quantel is based on research from The University of Calgary, and the whole program for process improvement is being applied organizationwide.

We will present:

- The survey results,
- How we can use the results (translate them into practice),
- The design and development of the measurement instrument,
- Implementation of the measurement program,
- Expected benefits (and problems encountered), and
- Conclusions

## Background

The University of Calgary was given a specific mandate by the industry for project management research. This mandate was prepared by a group of industry representatives, including members from over thirty-five sponsoring companies, one of which is Quantel VECO. The mandate included taking a look at best practices to develop a better approach to project management. The challenge being to accommodate all that had changed in the business and commercial world and that was not reflected in standard project management practices and publications such as PMBOK and the many books on project management that crowd the shelves.

The detailed results of this study were presented in a paper at the PMI symposium in Boston in 1996 (Hartman and Ashrafi 1996). Development of this work into S.M.A.R.T. project management is being presented in another paper at this symposium in Chicago, 1997 (Hartman 1997). This material has led to field testing of a new approach to project management that has saved significant costs and time while improving the quality of the end product. This paper covers the following topics:

- What led to this change?
- What can others learn from us?
- How can projects be better managed in the future?
- What can we learn from other industries?

## What Led to this Change?

Simply put, there is a significant latent opportunity for process improvement in the way many petrochemical projects are developed. These opportunities exist at every stage in the development and implementation of a capital project. They start with the selection of the correct projects to develop based on correct and appropriate information with which to make the decision to invest.

Once the decision to invest has been made, the definition of the project can be improved through the involvement of the right people at the right time in this part of the project. Operations, as well as development and project personnel, should be involved in the project definition process. Wherever possible, the EPC contractor and major suppliers, especially the process licenser should be involved in definition of the project.

As the work is contracted out, appropriate contracting strategies need to be employed if we are to align the stakeholders sufficiently well to achieve the best balance of everyone's needs. Common objectives need to be defined (typically the completed facility), and differences need to be identified, managed and respected.

Specifications also offer opportunities to improve performance. For a long time, owners have been giving EPC contractors solutions to solve rather than sharing the real problems and using the expertise and breadth of experience of their contractor to help save them both time and money. Similarly, EPC contractors have been telling manufacturers and suppliers how to build their products, as well as insisting on their own construction processes being used by local contractors. All of this has led to higher costs and delays, to say nothing of the associated frustration and mistrust. Use of performance specifications are clearly the way of the future.

## What Can Others Learn From Us?

There are many useful things that are done in the oil and gas/petrochemical industry that other industrial sectors can learn from. Here are a few examples:

- Single-source for design and construction leads to better integration of design and implementation.
- Use of plastic models or, more recently, 3D CAD to visualize the final product before it is built helps not only in the construction process but allows operators to view the end product while design changes are relatively cost effective, to incorporate changes that facilitate operation after the facility is built.
- Effective data collection on past performance and research on areas for improvement (e.g., through CII).
- Accepted processes for engineering, procurement and construction that are generally fairly standard to the industry, enabling people to move between projects more effectively.

These and other advantages can be transferred to other industries where these practices do not exist.

## How Can Projects Be Better Managed in the Future?

Following the innovations in this industry that are occurring in the North Sea through the CRINE and NORSOK initiatives, as well as the new ideas and areas of focus under study by the Construction Industry Institute (CII) or in practice on some of the larger projects on the east coast of Canada helps us identify opportunities for process improvement that have already been identified by others as well as being studied at The University of Calgary and other institutions. Some of these are summarized below.

- Improved alignment of all stakeholders on projects.
- Use of effective risk-sharing agreements based on life cycle costs and involving owner, EPC contractor and key suppliers.
- Use of alliances on large projects and for ongoing series of smaller projects.
- More effective use of risk analysis and proactive risk management tools.
- Use of performance specifications instead of company standard, detailed specifications.
- Greater and more effective use of value engineering and constructability.
- Awareness of communication as a key element in project success.

Beyond these elements, already in the process of being implemented in the petrochemical industry for capital projects, there are other opportunities to bring the cost of construction as well as operating costs down while improving quality and reducing time to market. Further, there are other areas to be considered, such as selection and scoping of projects so that they provide the right return on investment. To find these opportunities, we need to turn to other industries to see what they do that can be translated to the petrochemical business to its advantage.

### *Guaranteed on time project delivery [the live entertainment industry]*

Here is one industry that would shock us if they were late with a project. Imagine the opening ceremonies of the Olympics: the torch bearer runs into the arena and the public address system blares out "zip round the block again, we are not quite ready"! How has the live entertainment industry maintained its tradition of timely opening of new shows? Partly this has been done by allowing some contingency—but we all do that, and it is not always possible to do so. In the live entertainment industry, consciously or not, the team's focus is directed from artistic creativity to creativity in ensuring timely delivery. The key point is that creativity is not turned off—as we do when we "freeze" designs (arguably a myth)—but creativity is actively sustained but redirected. There are other elements to their success, but taking this one and applying it to the petrochemical business, we could encourage the team working on design to coordinate its deliverables more carefully with procurement and construction. The construction and procurement personnel could focus on solving schedule delays and developing creative work-around solutions for them, even before they occur.

### *The right project at the right price [the investment industry]*

Selection of one project over another is often a combination of who has presented the best proposal before Approval For Expenditure (AFE), corporate politics and expediency. Real rates of return are often lower than expected or projected at AFE time. A study by Ashore (1993) suggests that this difference is an average of 3%. In other words, if the AFE proposal suggests that the return was to be 12%, the real return was likely to be just 9%. There is strong evidence to suggest that this figure is low!

When investing in stocks, bonds or other options, two factors are considered: the return on investment and the risk. When selecting projects, we normally do so based on single-point estimates with the bland assumption that this is a real and accurate projection of what will happen. In a pilot study in Canada that included some U.S.-based companies, none of them used a risked forecast of revenues opex and capex. Adding this dimension—as one company has since done—significantly changes the decision making process and the results. We think it does so for the better!

### *Absorbing the Right Technologies [Dentists]*

One of the few industries where new technologies, treatments and materials seem to appear and be used on a regular basis is in dentistry. Most practicing dentists will stay abreast of new technology that will give them greater reliability, better use of their time and improved quality. This is their competitive advantage.

In our business, we are reluctant to change or try new technologies before someone else has been a guinea-pig with them (and survived). Even the experiences in the North Sea have left companies cautious in adopting proven better ways to manage projects. Dentists are not in the business of inventing, so the "not invented here" syndrome is generally not present. Dentists assess the clinical trial results and are supported by an infrastructure designed to protect the public. There is no such infrastructure for the petrochemical business, other than voluntary ones. Dentists take time out to keep up with new techniques and technologies. They often need to stay registered practitioners. This is not a requirement in our business (although this is changing in North America). What we can do becomes obvious: Higher fees for engineering services will allow the engineering contractors to train personnel and stay current with relevant technologies. Collaboration in noncompetitive research and in testing new technologies will reduce individual company risks while maintaining appropriate competitive edges.

### *Planning Effectively [Geomatics and Brain Surgery]*

In surveying, we locate a point by triangulation. This means taking two views of the same point. Before brain surgery is undertaken, careful studies are made to preclude the worst outcomes and to maximize the potential for success. In managing our projects, we rarely have time to plan properly, let alone do so twice!

Yet in field trials, planning well and doing so twice (once, then again in a different way to validate the plan) has repeatedly led to better, lower cost and faster project delivery.

These are just a few areas to consider for further improvement of the project delivery process. There are many more. Knowing where to start is the biggest challenge. This was one of the challenges that Quantel VECO faced.

## The Challenge

Some of the questions asked by Quantel VECO included the following: Can we improve in what we do? Can we apply the research results as a fix to our "real" problems? What to change if we have to change something? Are we sure that we are making the right decision? The yet unknown answers to the above questions prompted the development and the implementation of the performance/success measurement program at Quantel VECO Engineering.

Lately, Quantel VECO Engineering (QVE) has experienced tremendous business changes partly as a result of a takeover. In our case, all the above questions were unanswered. At the same time, QVE was aware of the impact resulting from globalization, and of the changes in today's business environment compared to only a few years ago. Knowing that being ready for the future entails being flexible, being able to adapt and respond, finding new ways to do things, QVE decided to go ahead with a performance/success measurement program.

We all know that today, in order to compete and be on the leading edge, we must seek and attain high performance and success. It seems that the future is indeed "change" and the best way to stay in synch with the future is to keep the quest for change alive. On the one hand, we have the results from a recent research study conducted by The University of Calgary showing us some of the best practices within different industries. On the other hand, we have the dilemma of what to implement from all these results. In order to answer this dilemma, we measured our own performance/success to find opportunities for improvement and then to implement the findings from research.

It is known that many companies' business rely on constantly measuring client satisfaction using internal and external opinion surveys. For an engineering company in the consulting business, this is definitely not an easy task. QVE's approach was to capture four different perspectives for the projects we wanted to measure in order to get more information on what is important for each project's participant.

## The Measurement Instrument Development

QVE obtained the ISO 9001 certification a few years ago. We generally keep performance data information regarding our completed projects as part of the follow-up procedure. Although in the past, we measured time, cost, quality and safety as indicators for our performance, we actually found that many times for two similar projects with equal performance indicators, client satisfaction was totally different. As a result, we decided to make the following distinction:

- Performance is reality measured, and
- Success is how clients perceive our performance.

We found that measuring only hard aspects of our performance did not provide enough information to explain the success or the nonsuccess of the projects. To solve the puzzle, we developed a more detailed measurement instrument that included hard and soft aspects that may impact on success.

The measurement instrument came out of a major brainstorming session involving most of QVE's project managers and some of our clients. After getting their feedback, we tried to accommodate all the ideas and created a flexible measurement instrument. In any of our projects, there are several groups involved who we will call project stakeholders:

- QVE project managers,
- Client,
- Client operation, and
- QVE team.

Ultimately, the success of the project is determined by how all the stakeholders perceive the project performance. Knowing that each stakeholder has different expectations, we considered that it is very important to capture their different perspectives in order to have a better understanding of what is ultimately important for success.

The measurement instrument contains four forms. One form is to be completed by QVE's project managers after project completion. There are two distinct forms based on the size of the project. This sheet captures mainly performance data and a few aspects about the team involved with the project.

The next form is to be completed by client representative and is mainly focused on soft aspects related with the success of the project such as effectiveness of communication, attitudes, team work, new ideas, etc.

The third form is to be completed by the operation people, people from the field who actually build the project.

The last sheet is to be completed by the QVE team, people who were involved with the project (project engineers, different disciplines, procurement etc.).

The expectation is that by putting together the results from a number of completed projects and analyzing the results we will be able to determine opportunities for improvement.

## Implementation

The performance/success measurement program is under implementation within QVE organization. A number of necessary small steps were taken in order to get commitment from the people involved:

- Upper level of management,
- Project managers, and
- Clients.

The actual implementation of the measurement program involves a lot of effort that is internally directed and there is no immediate benefit for the project or the people involved.

We went through a series of presentations and we included the measurement program in our manual but we are still at the very beginning of the implementation so concrete results are not available at this time. We are into the process of gathering data for a number of projects and to start the analysis.

As we mentioned before this is just the first step. After we analyze the results and find opportunities for improvement, the hardest part is still to come, namely to implement the changes. We as a company see the whole changing cycle as:

- Measure,
- Find opportunities,
- Implement changes, and
- Measure again.

This is an ongoing cycle with no start or end point if we want to be successful. Some of the expected benefits of the measurement program are presented below:

- **Benefits for QVE:**
  assess own activity,
  provide legitimacy and credibility for future decisions,
  measure progress on productivity, and
  use the results for benchmarking and marketing studies.
- **Benefits for the client:**
  increased credibility and trust for working with a particular engineering organization,
  increased likelihood to have a successful project, and
  opportunities for getting the best service.
- **Benefits for the project managers:**
  improved personal recognition,
  improvement on learning curve, and
  provide reliable database for further decisions.

The measurement program implemented at QVE is future oriented. It was designed to accommodate future changes. We have developed a database system to keep all the information, a database that can be also used for business development purposes. For analysis of the results, we use the S-plus statistical software package, to run multiple regression analysis. Also visual representations of the results are available for understanding the general trends in our performance/success.

When trying to determine what roll project management will play in what we will do in the future, we see a transition from micro to macro level. Regardless of the nature of the business of any organization, the project manager/project management role will be to see the opportunities of implementing practices from different industries that are not yet the norm for the industry. Again, project managers will be seen as people who can bring on the future by pursuing ideas to success. The mentality of doing things in a certain way, because this is the norm for industry, is not going to work anymore. The message is clear: there will always be some winners and some losers in the game. From both parts we can learn about what to do and what not to do.

## Conclusions

What does this all mean? This paper provides some possible answers to the questions presented at the beginning of the paper. There is no silver bullet solution for all the problems the future will bring. Each organization should follow its own path. We presented only our experience and some selected results from a recent research study.

Change in technology, work environment, the economy, politics and more will continue to affect how we manage projects. As we move forward, we can no longer afford to be reactive to situations, as others will be ahead of us. What is needed is an open mind to how we may address the next generation of problems and opportunities. Using the best practices of other industries is not a bad start, as we are really importing "proven" methods and tricks, simply adapting them to our own set of circumstances.

### References

Hartman F.T. 1997. *Trends and improvements: Looking beyond modern project management.* Project Management Institute, Annual Symposium and Seminar, Chicago.

Hartman, F.T. and Ashrafi, R. 1996. *Failed successes and successful failures.* Project Management Institute Annual Symposium and Seminar, Boston. 907–911.

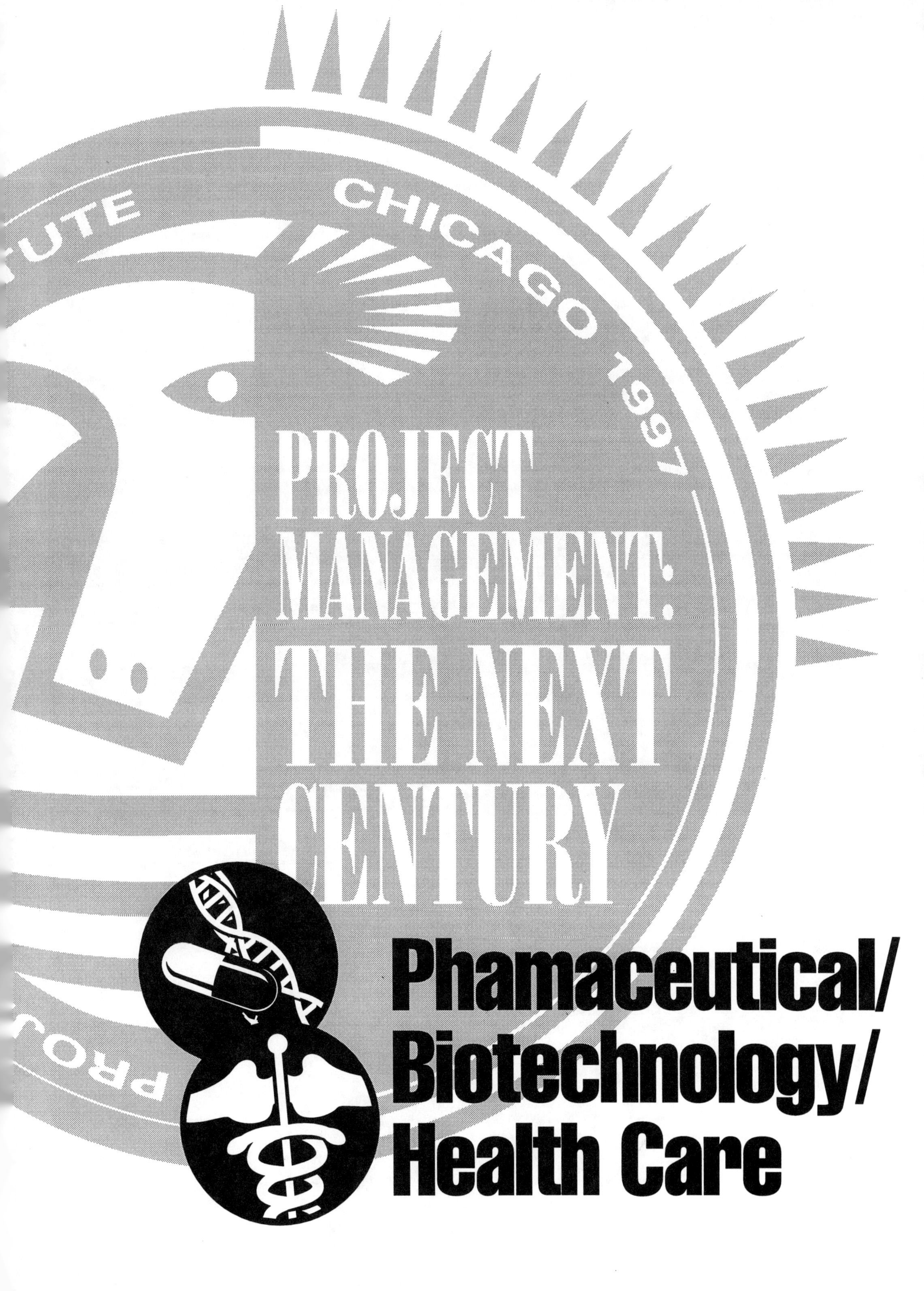

CHICAGO 1997
PROJECT MANAGEMENT: THE NEXT CENTURY
Phamaceutical/
Biotechnology/
Health Care

# Integrated Planning: Project Management Striving to Create a Highly Efficient Business Environment

Jacqueline Donahue, Zeneca Pharmaceuticals
Graham Fawcett, Zeneca Pharmaceuticals

To gain critical business advantage in the pharmaceutical market place, new and innovative approaches to project management have become a top priority. Reorganization, project focused organizational structures, and process improvement techniques have all been adopted to speed-up and stream-line the drug development process. Within the context of these changes a variety of tools to aid in this new approach have been developed and implemented.

This paper will examine Integrated Planning (IP), which is a new project management and planning environment that has been developed and implemented throughout Zeneca Pharmaceuticals International. IP was developed and adopted and is utilized to create a new and more interactive environment for projects and departments. The following information examines IP's implementation in the International Drug Regulatory Affairs Department and how it operates alongside the rest of the business. The paper will cover:

- A definition and introduction of the system,
- Core elements for success,
- Benefits of the system,
- How the Regulatory departmental plans tie into each of the other departmental plans across the entire future business,
- Future of Integrated Planning, and
- Summary.

## What is Integrated Planning?

The objective of Integrated planning is to deliver consistent and current planning information to worldwide businesses by consolidating all planning information for all departments into a centralized repository, with immediate visibility provided to project teams and/or departments as required. The environment to support this objective, called Integrated Planning (IP), uses a relational database system, front loaded with "off the shelf" project management software. The relational database was chosen because it can accommodate and ma-

**Exhibit 1.** Individual Departmental Planning Systems

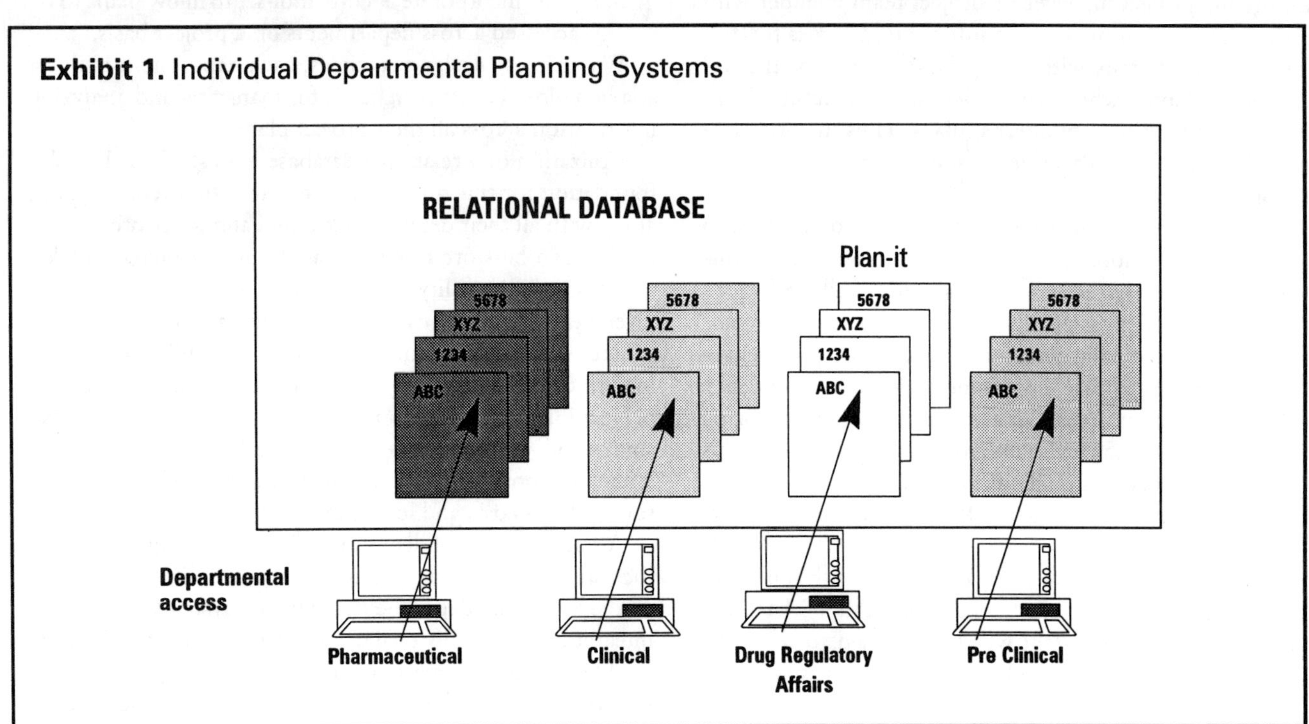




PROJECT MANAGEMENT INSTITUTE 28th Annual Seminars & Symposium
Chicago, Illinois: Papers Presented September 29 to October 1, 1997

**Exhibit 2.** Cross-Demartmental Planning System (Integrated Planning)

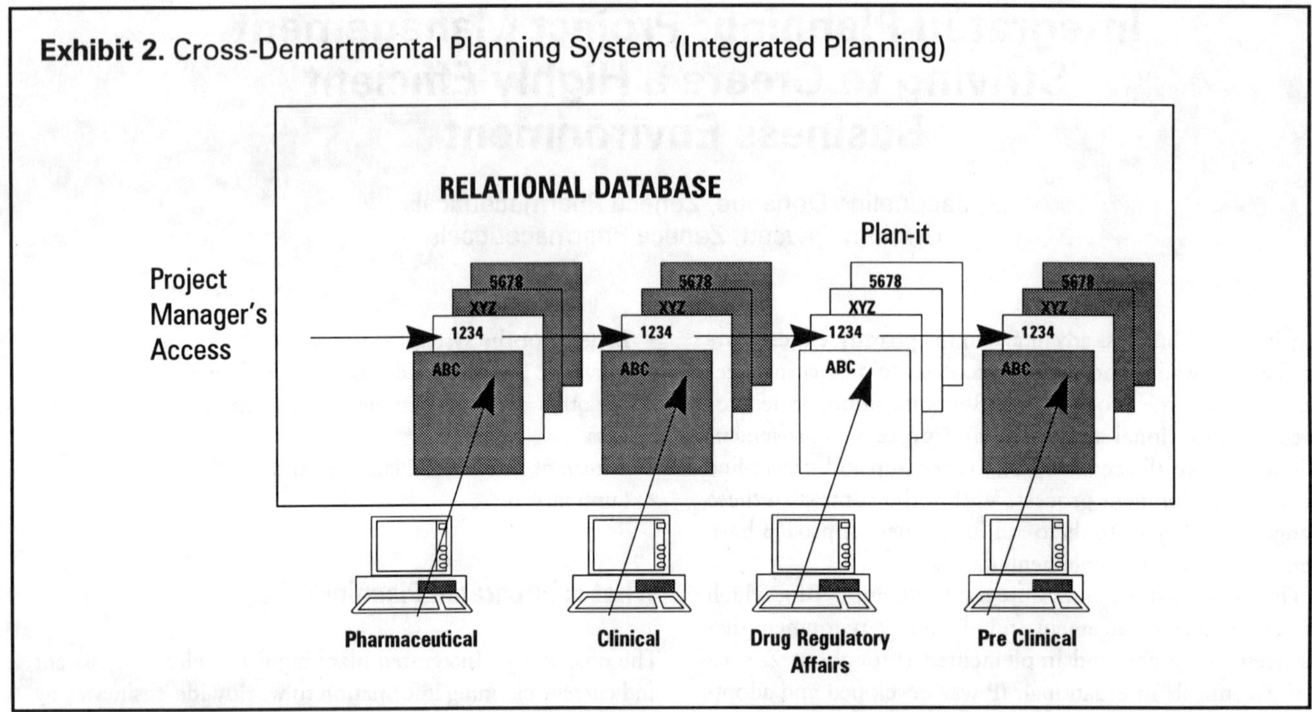


nipulate huge amounts of information, and the front-end software chosen is user-friendly and familiar to many users throughout the business.

IP is a single environment, comprised of individual departmental planning systems, all operating off a common database of plans (refer to Exhibit 1). This environment can support the project manager or project team member who needs to access and manipulate information across the full range of departments within a specific project, or the departmental planner who needs to determine resource allocation across a multitude of internal plans. Thus the organizational 'matrix' of both projects and departments can be supported.

In addition to providing appropriate and tailored access to planning information, appropriate tools to use against this common database have also been designed for all the various users. Customized cross-project reporting and modeling tools have been created to accommodate individual preferences and needs. This inclusive environment allows a dependency network to be built across departmental boundaries, for all plans supporting a particular drug development project. This aspect of integration throughout the business environment is novel and the use of such a network will be described in more detail later.

The first step to implementing IP is to establish sound departmental planning systems (refer to Exhibit 1). Each departmental planning system will be designed to meet the planning needs of that particular department. In establishing a departmental system, a few basic rules need to be adhered to if this system is to fit within the IP environment.

1. It must operate off the common planning database and store its plans in this database.
2. It must be built within a standard technology set, to allow departmental systems to fit together.
3. It must incorporate a 'core' tool-set to allow plans to be accessed across departments on a project basis.

Within these design principles, each department builds a system tailored to its own needs for managing and analyzing information across all their project plans.

Utilization of a relational database has established a solid foundation for this robust environment. Hundreds of plans, along with all their detailed milestones and descriptive information can be stored, manipulated, and extracted quickly and easily. This ability to look across multiple projects has given versatility and insight into the impact of time and resources within a department. Resource scheduling and workload tracking can be easily mapped out. This pool of current project information gives management the tools to plan resource and manpower effectively and efficiently. Accurate assessments about work commitments can be made, and this in turn reduces costs and lost opportunities.

A stable individual departmental system is required before the integrated component can be activated, linking together all the individual departmental planning systems. To support integration, each individual departmental system will be compatible with the IP environment and equally important, each department should be well trained and comfortable utilizing their own system. If these individual planning systems are not established well then integration will be much more difficult. Once the individual departmental planning systems are established, the access across departments can be turned on. This gives the departmental project representative the ability to view all the plans for that project across the entire business (refer to Exhibit 2).

In the regulatory department we implemented such a planning system. Our system is called PLAN-IT and uses the common IP relational database, front-loaded with an "off the shelf" planning software package. This departmental planning system has created a central pool of information within the regulatory department that all department members can access. Reports can be generated to monitor the cross-project flow of documentation into the department and manpower can be allocated according to the demand. Information about annual events, such as annual progress reports for the IND, for all projects within the department can be consolidated and reported on by anyone at any given time (refer to Exhibit 3). Making this information accessible to all, with immediate visibility eliminates duplication of effort and increases the accuracy of information. Since each project manager is responsible for reviewing and updating their own project information, that information is accurate and current.

Along with a robust and stable system it is important to establish a strong and interactive system and process support group, both within the individual department and cross-departmental. With every new system there is a learning curve, and support to the users is critical for its success. We have established user support at both the individual department level and on a cross-departmental project level. This ensures that the needs of all user types are addressed. Innovative systems are powerful tools, but if the user is afraid or frustrated and will not use them, then they are not very valuable.

## Core Elements

There are certain core elements that must be agreed upon across all the functions to ensure proper integration and success for a computer-based planning system. The basic elements are as follows:

- Use of common terms for shared milestones or activities,
- Agreement on common activity dependencies (links), from department to department,
- Use of standardized development plans (templates) for consistency and ease,
- Routine maintenance of information by keeping dates and activities current, and
- Plans to be made visible across departmental boundaries.

These basic core elements help ensure that all departments are working from a common platform, communication is

**Exhibit 3.** Relational Database Departmental Planning System

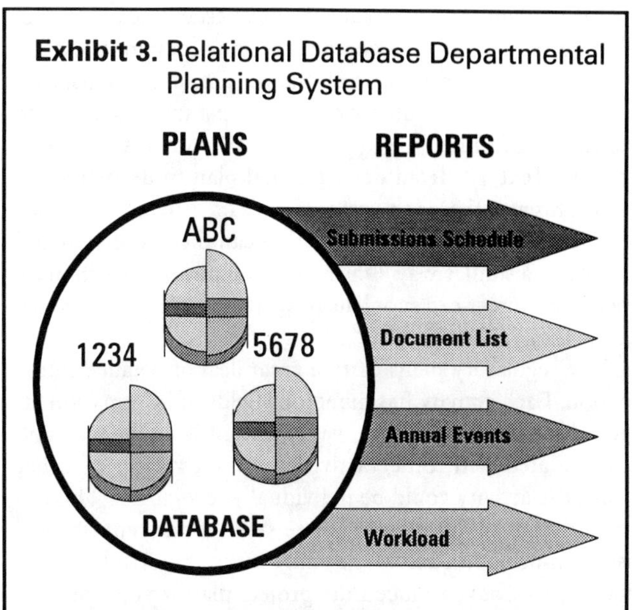


open, and terms are defined and agreed. To ensure this was established a cross-departmental team was formed in the initial phases of the IP project. This team discussed and negotiated common shared pharmaceutical developmental milestones and agreed upon common terminology that all departments would use to describe these activities. A list of these mapped milestones was distributed to all the departmental groups to incorporate into their own departmental templates and plans.

Once these plans are created and made live onto the system cross-departmental access will be turned on. This access will provide read-only access across a departmental boundary. However, tools to link project plans across department boundaries are also provided. It then becomes possible to build a project dependency network across the entire business to support the drug development process. To build this network, the individual departmental representatives meet and agree upon which milestone and activities need to be linked. Once these links have been identified, they are stored as key information in the common database. This linking is used to ensure that these dates are keep consistent from department to department. A more detailed description of creating links will be covered a little later.

Within the IP environment, individual departments create and maintain a variety of standardized plans for the various stages of drug development. These standardized plans are called templates, and carry a generic version of all the necessary activities, resources, time-scales and dependencies for each department. Each department has the flexibility to create and format their own standardized plan according to the custom needs of their own department. There are only two components that need to be consistent throughout all the department plans. The mapped milestones established in the beginning (along with the common terminology for these activities) must be carried on all the departmental plans. Secondly, several attributes or specific parameters need to consistently be identified, (e.g., Study ID numbers should always be Text 10) from departmental plan to departmental plan. This way there is a common core or structure on which all plans are based. The information can then be shared and viewed in a similar way. Once these components are in place each department can supplement with as much or as little detail as they find necessary.

The regulatory plans carry a great deal of detailed information. Each activity has numerous fields of information attached so that if an activity was extracted from the plan and consolidated with other activities from a variety of other plans, the activity could be individually recognized. This approach enables the user to create stand-alone reports with useful information across the entire business portfolio. Templated plans have reduced the project plan set-up time significantly. The structure and timeframes are already incorporated, so the time can be spent on individualizing the plan to that specific project by modifying and deleting various details. This approach also promotes scenario creation. The user can modify various components of the plans and can see the effect on resource allocation or the completion of the project. The more user friendly the system and the plans are to work with, the more compliant the user will be.

Using the system and keeping the information current is one of the most important components to the success of Integrated Planning. Immediate visibility and consistency of worldwide planning information illustrates how IP can be a very powerful and extremely useful tool for the businesses of the future. But, the downside to this is; if these elements are not embraced by all, then IP will not function optimally and the tool's strength weakens.

## Benefits

The major benefits of IP are as follows:

- Immediate visibility of plans across the business,
- Increase in communication and team environment across the business,
- Increase in accountability and ownership of dates of the various departments,
- Decrease in duplication of effort,
- Rapid access to information and reports,
- Consistent project planning across the business,
- Better quality information within a department, and
- Ability to do scenarios easily.

The immediate visibility of project plans promotes communication between the various departments and resources working on a single project that creates the environment to drive projects forward. The vision and goals are viewed, debated and then ultimately shared by the team. This visibility also will lead to accountability for a specific activity or the delivery of a document. The viewing and sharing of plans can decrease duplication of effort. Items that may have been carried on all project plans can now be carried on the owner's plan and then linked to the other applicable plans. The creation of these links then ensures that consistency of dates throughout the business is maintained. The system can also consolidate information, within a department, into one place. This decreases the multitude of individual spreadsheets and files maintained by numerous resources within the department. The flexibility of the system and the built-in custom features allows information to be consolidated, filtered and sorted. Each individual has immediate access to this information and can generate valuable reports to follow a specific project, or workload across many projects.

## Creation of Links or Dependencies

The creation of links or dependencies from one departmental plan to another needs to be an open, but structured, interactive communication among project team members. Links need to be carefully established. Setting up too many links can cause a monitoring and maintaining nightmare, too few can cause miscalculations of commitments. The project manager does not want to be constantly amending their plan, but it is important that key dates that may be driving critical activities be linked. The IP environment is designed to compare two different departmental plans at a time. The two plans are shown side-by-side on the screen. Once the linked activity is agreed upon, it is as simple as clicking on the activity on the one plan and then clicking on the corresponding activity on the other plan, then choose the type of dependency desired (e.g., Start-Start, Finish-Start). This would be repeated for all the activities that need to be linked on that departmental plan. This entire exercise would have to be carried out for each plan and its corresponding departmental relationships. Initially this will be a time consuming process, but once the links are set, monitoring these activities becomes extremely quick and easy. A report is generated that lists all the linked activities whose dates differ. This report can then be used to negotiate these date changes at a team meeting, or to amend a user's own departmental plan with the update. It is important to note that cross-departmental links are only used to generate these reports as a tool to highlight inconsistencies across linked plans. The links are not used to automatically reschedule activities in a department that is impacted by changes of another department's plan. It is much more important for departmental project representatives to be notified of conflicts, and for these conflicts to be resolved after appropriate negotiation.

## Future of Integrated Planning

Integrated Planning is designed to expand and adapt to the future of the business needs. The flexibility of the system and the formation of user groups creates a dynamic environment of mobility and expansion; changing regulations, new functions and/or countries, modified developmental timing, can all be incorporated and amended to keep the system current. As the users work on the system, improvements and enhancements like new time-saving functionality, along with streamlining the templates to reflect new business practices can easily be added or incorporated. This is all possible with this system because of its robust nature and the ease of programming within the software.

The next phase of IP will incorporate further resource modeling that can expand the business' ability to monitor and optimize the use of resources to an even more efficient level. Project forecasting will be a consolidation of actual data, and not just best guess estimates. Project managers will be able to back up the need for increase headcount with data.

We are expanding the use of IP to more and more units of the business; reaching out to deliver this system worldwide. Think of the competitive edge businesses will obtain by having immediate, current access worldwide to project status. The creative adaptability and growth potential of this system is almost unlimited.

## Summary

Integrated Planning is a new planning environment that incorporates the capacity of a database with the ease and flexibility of end-user friendly planning software. The major role of IP is to enable consistent project planning across businesses. The immediate visibility promotes communication across the business and creates a platform to facilitate the move to a project-led organization that will carry the business well into the 21st century. This move to a project-led organization will afford opportunities to optimize resources and time that will lead to a potential reduction in development time, and result in a highly efficient business.

# Project Management: The Change from Project Management to Project Leadership in the Pharmaceutical Industry

Roger G. Harrison, Ph.D., Eli Lilly and Company,

## Introduction

By most standards the pharmaceutical industry, as we see it represented by today's companies, has been very successful. Several diseases have been eradicated and many others controlled so that they are no longer the major causes of morbidity and mortality that they were even as recently as in the fifties in the developed world. Major innovations have been made in genomics and the understanding of diseases at a molecular level, and it seems that we are at the dawn of new opportunities as we move forward into the next millennium. Profitability has also been relatively high and major companies have continued to invest heavily in continued exploration of new opportunities. However, within this encouraging picture there are several unsettling concerns. These include the undue pressure on the industry to reduce prices for its products, the erosion of market opportunity by the rapid introduction of generic entities post-patent expiration, the increasing burden of regulations, and the frighteningly high cost and increasing length of time associated with drug development. Additionally competitive pressures in the industry have increased owing to consolidations and with the impact that "fast followers" can have within the same therapeutic area. Within this framework, it has been suggested that the industry must make deep changes or face slow death. While this is perhaps an exaggeration, the industry has uniformly asked itself how to get faster at bringing drugs to the market, reduce costs, and maintain quality. Several technological approaches are supporting initiatives to speed the research and development process. These include the use of combinatorial chemistry, high volume screening, computational chemistry, and the opportunities represented by the emerging field of genomics. In the efforts to reduce costs, there has been a focus on reengineering business processes, outsourcing noncore businesses, and mergers or acquisitions. Quality has been addressed in several ways including a stronger focus on customer requirements and greater emphasis on staff training. However, this paper will suggest that one of the changes that can have the greatest impact on speed to market and cost management will be the transition from traditional project management to true project leadership.

## Project Management in the Pharmaceutical Industry

The development process for a new pharmaceutical product is often described as "complex," sometimes being compared in cost and complexity to the design and development of a major new aircraft. However, while the risks are high (typically only one in ten thousand of compounds tested become drugs), and with failures occurring at even late stages of development after huge investments have been made, it could be erroneous to describe the development process as highly complex. Complexity may be manifested in particular tasks, or be caused by the duration of projects and number of tasks. The former complexity requires high skill levels in order to be effective, while the latter requires robust business processes and methodology that ensures learning is shared. The development process in the pharmaceutical industry is rendered complex by the duration and number of tasks, but this apparent complexity can be dramatically lessened where robust business processes are in place, and where experienced staff understand the cross functional linkages necessary to bring a product through all the necessary stages of development.

At Eli Lilly and Company, project management has evolved over several years. It has long been recognized that in order to be successful in the development process, a team of cross functional individuals need to take responsibility for managing the tasks associated with product development. In the seventies, the leadership of such teams often fell to the scientist who had been involved in the discovery of the new chemical entity. The positive aspect of this was that it built in the high level of commitment often felt by this lead scientist, but also carried with it the inexperience that these individuals often had as team leaders and their poor awareness of all the tasks that had to be performed in developing the potential drug. Additionally this model had a significant opportunity cost owing to the lessening of such a key scientist's role in the continuing discovery process. As a consequence of this, project management groups were established within the company in the eighties. Experienced scientists were asked to take on the role of full time project managers. Individuals taking on these roles were often from a research background and were provided with limited guidance on the expectations from a project manager. Consequently the role tended towards one of coordination and communication. Power and decision making authority was still vested in the functions and the project management staff had limited capability in influencing key decisions. Additionally, since part of the role was seen as bringing together people that had an involvement in the project, team meetings tended to become large and cumbersome. This led inevitably to project team meetings being largely for information sharing, and not strategy and decision making. Timelines continued to move to the right with little accountability felt for delivery of the project on time and budget. To address the size of these team meetings the next stage in evolution was to create core teams made up from individuals charged with representing a functionality or groups of linked functions. Such groups were made up of eight to ten people and were better suited, at least in size, to truly debate strategy and develop plans that would be translated, operationally, by subteams representing the functions. Project management skills had continued to evolve and the business processes were beginning to be documented and refined. However, timelines continued to drift and, while progress undoubtedly was being made in reducing the overall time of development, there was still a disappointing lack of correlation between planned milestones and actual events. Challenges of resource allocation, decision making authority, focus, accountability, and communication needed to be addressed. As part of this, it was perhaps important to redefine what a team really is, and as a working definition the following seems reasonable:

"A team is a small number of people with complementary skill sets who are committed to a common purpose, performance goals, and approaches for which they hold themselves mutually accountable." Key words in this definition are associated with commitment and accountability. Both of these need to be addressed in order to build successful teams. However, it is also be necessary to address additional barriers to success that include poor planning, poor communication, staff inexperience, inconsistent business processes, and the inability to balance resource allocation over time and across projects, that is, portfolio management. In the nineties a major step in addressing the above issues was made through the establishment of Product Teams during the commercial phase of development of a potential drug candidate. These teams are made up of individuals representing various functional groups and led by a senior member of management, often an individual with deep experience in the therapeutic area for which the drug was being developed. Unlike previous project teams, the members of this team report directly to the team leader not to the functional area, and are collocated together. All members of this "core team" are fully dedicated to the project, immediately giving an absolute sense of focus and ownership. Typically this core team would have eight to ten members and would be responsible for strategy, policy, and financial planning for the product. Membership of the core team typically includes an operations manager, a clinical process leader, a chemistry, manufacturing and control manager, an information manager, a therapeutic area physician, a marketing manager, a global expert, and representation from legal and financial areas. A larger operational team, also of fully dedicated people, is made up of key technical staff supporting the project, and, unless requiring laboratory resources, are also collocated and report to members of the core team. In this new model the functions have become responsible for providing qualified staff to the teams and for ensuring that their remaining capabilities are aligned with team needs as defined in the development plans. In order for this model to be effective, planning skills had to be improved and then resource allocations made according to the ability of the organization to support these plans. The first part of this, planning, has been addressed by the product teams developing a vision, mission, and strategic goals from which a series of overarching plans are evolved. These are translated into detailed operational plans and married with resource requirements. The composite of these plans, including all the stages necessary to reach the market and those for successful commercialization, are represented into a contract of deliverables that is approved (or otherwise) by a senior executive group of the company (the Portfolio Management Committee). Once approved, the team and the functional areas are responsible and accountable for delivery of the product on time and on budget. The organization is responsible for ensuring resources are provided as defined in the contract. Members of the portfolio management committee require detailed knowledge of the business and need to be decisive in balancing the resources requested across all of the concurrent operating product teams. One possible downside of the totally focused team model is that the teams do, and should, define a wide area of value adding opportunities that could be pursued for their projects, it then requiring an oversight group to balance resource allocation with the most attractive opportunities. Having made these decisions and empowered the teams to deliver, it is important, unless there are manifestly obvious reasons, not to change the resource allocation and support for the team.

## Leadership

Obviously defining someone as a leader does not necessarily confer the person with leadership skills, and it can be further suggested that these leadership skills are not necessarily the same as those defined in the *Project Management Book of Knowledge* (PMBOK) for a project manager. In this book, a project manager is defined as being skilled in integration management, and management of scope, time, cost, quality, human resources, communications, risk, and procurement. In the product team model, these are the skills expected in the operations manager, effectively the COO of the self-sustaining business that has been created. On the other hand the leader has a different role. He or she must lead the team in creation of the development plans and create an environment, throughout the organization, of total commitment to the execution of these plans. To achieve this there must be a well articulated vision based on the "end in mind," this often being the claims that it is anticipated will be made in the product label as well as a positioning in the future marketplace, and is the driver for the discussion of options that could lead to the desired result. The leader must also ensure that metrics are in place and that everyone understands their roles in reaching the end goals (a responsibility matrix for example), and above all, that everyone has a sense of accountability. Very importantly, this should not be accountability in a draconian sense but should be that created from an inherent believe in the value of what is being done, which in turn leads to a strong sense of commitment. Ideally, accountability should not be seen as having a strong connection with reward or punishment, and any failure should be used an opportunity to learn and improve. While fostering understanding of individual accountability and responsibility will help a team there are still many other skills that a leader must demonstrate in order to be successful. At the heart of these is credibility, which can be earned through experience and knowledge of the business, not necessarily having all the answers, but sufficient experience to facilitate discussions in which others can reach the best conclusions for themselves. Additionally, building and maintaining trust will be a critical element for the successful team leader. Undoubtedly a project manager can also be a good team leader, but a good team leader does not always make a good project manager. However, in the race to move projects forward rapidly and effectively to the market there is little doubt that the greatest asset that a team can have is effective leadership.

## Teams

There are several general principles that a team should address together. These include the focusing on essential processes, not structures or boundaries. This means endeavoring to avoid territorial issues and dealing with what has to be done and who has the capability to do it. The team leader should also help the team in establishing aggressive (possibly outrageous) performance targets. The initial reactions to such challenges may be that they cannot be achieved, but reflection often causes a team to reexamine existing practices and suggest alternate solutions sometimes with dramatic time or cost saving benefits. The team must also ensure that it is not taking on such challenges without the commitment of the larger organization, and building the awareness, and support from, the others involved in the project is critical. Business-wide communication is a key part of the core team's responsibilities and is an essential part of ensuring success in meeting goals.

While the team leader's role on the core team is important, each member of the team has their own leadership roles within a function. For example the chemistry, manufacturing, and control (CM&C) representative leads a team made up of representatives from process chemistry, analytical chemistry, formulation sciences, quality control and assurance, regulatory affairs, environmental, and facilities planning. Consequently, while the breadth of responsibility is smaller, exactly the same leadership skills are required from the individual leading this group as from the core team leader. However, unlike the core team leader, this person usually does not have direct reporting responsibility for the team members since these are mainly laboratory functions. This lack of authority requires a true partnership to be established between the CM&C leader and the functional area management in such a way that the functions understand the project requirements and align their staff accordingly. It is also important that the functions change their mindset to recognize that their primary role is to support the teams' in the achievement of their goals, and that this requires them to keep in mind the commitments made as represented in the product timeline. Functional management must focus on the development of staff in their areas of responsibility, to equip them for the roles that they take on teams, and ensure that their business processes are consistent with the best possible practices. The team leader also has key role in staff development and must work with direct line supervision to identify development opportunities and performance objectives for members of the team.

## Learning

Every team will make decisions, which with the benefit of hindsight, they will wish they had not made in exactly that way. They will also make some that work out extraordinarily well. In each case, these are opportunities for learning and passing that experience to other teams. It is very important that periodically a team pause, capture learning, document it, and share it widely in the organization. Such behaviors lead to continued advancement of an organizational capability and allow future teams always to build on what has gone before. A team leader's role in making this happen is again another critical facet of the responsibility. Ideally this learning will be captured in a way that allows each team, as it enters a new phase of activity, to access and evaluate the experiences of previous teams. It is important that such data bases also give reference to where more detail can be found and to the individual who can further help in more detailed discussions. Part of the reward for teams should be based on their willingness to document and share learning in this way, since without such an environment the team experience becomes one of isolated internally focused islands. Such behavior, while potentially enabling a team to meet its time and cost goals, will not enable the organization to be ultimately successful in continually streamlining business practices. Learning can also be shared on a daily basis through informal gatherings of those representing the same functions on core teams. Thus, the CM&C leaders, for example, can periodically meet as a group and discuss business processes, specific team experiences, and continued development of project management skills and capabilities. Functional line management is an important catalyst for ensuring that these discussion opportunities are created.

Collocation and dedication of resources are critical themes of the product team model established at Eli Lilly and Company. This may not represent the most efficient use of resources as, in a well-managed organization, multitasking can be accomplished where several projects can be worked on by a single individual. However, such multitasking leads to conflicting priorities and in order to be effective has to assume that all tasks will be completed according to the schedule. In the real world, timeline shifts do occur, owing to unanticipated outcomes of experiments or studies, and then, in a domino effect, several timelines are affected. In the dedicated staffing model, there are the advantages associated with fully understanding project goals, completely being integrated with other work dependencies, and having a higher level of commitment associated with knowing the importance of their specific contribution. Such an environment can create a level of dedication to common purpose not always seen in a large company and is greatly facilitated by the informal interactions that occur in a shared area. It is, however, important to avoid the possibility of forming an inner circle group, because of their collocation, and pay less attention to the equally critical staff who are unable to collocate because of laboratory or management functions. Effective communication to this wider group as well as involving them in key decisions is an important role of the core team and its leader.

## Conclusions

While the above model is a result of an ongoing evolution in the leadership of teams in one company in the pharmaceutical industry, it would be wrong to suggest that this is the only effective model. Teams will be critical to any business that has a multiplicity of functions contributing over time to a common goal, but, as long as the teams clearly understand the expected deliverables, have individual and joint accountability, are adequately resourced, have skilled people at all levels, and have strong leadership, then any model of team organization can probably work. However, to address the challenges of increasing cost and duration of the drug development process it may be necessary to establish new models that attempt to dramatically impact the time and cost of development. This is the route chosen at Eli Lilly and Company. Time will tell whether it has been effective.

# Panel Discussion
# How to Terminate Projects and Live to Tell the Tale!

Dr. William Dunn, Eli Lilly and Company

## Description of Panel Discussion

One of the more difficult challenges for project managers in the pharmaceutical industry is to deal with the fact that the majority of the projects are unsuccessful. Some reasons for project termination include excessive cost of development, lack of market opportunity, safety issues, lack of efficacy, changing corporate priorities, and lack of management support.

Although it is well documented that most projects are terminated, it is also understood that successful projects usually have overcome significant obstacles to reach their goals. Sometimes those projects have been "killed" and resurrected based on the "never say die" attitude of key people on the team. These success stories become part of the folklore of companies. Therefore, the recommendation to terminate a project is very difficult to reach and the ultimate decision is usually open to "second guessing."

A significant responsibility of the project manager in the pharmaceutical industry is to lead the team toward a termination recommendation as quickly and effectively as possible for the majority of projects (pre Phase III). This can often be a somewhat thankless task as management, researchers, marketing and others pose the inevitable question, "Can't we just do one more study before we make a decision?" An additional challenge is that now many projects involve collaborations with other companies so the decision to terminate a project may not be made unilaterally.

Experienced project managers have learned that the process is most effective when objective success criteria are agreed upon by management and the team during the development of the project plan. Then the information generated is measured against those criteria. If the data do not meet these criteria then the recommendation is to terminate the project.

In addition, project managers need to understand and effectively work with not only the project team but also the management groups to ensure that appropriate interaction and communication is occurring throughout the process of the development of the success criteria, the analysis of information, and the ultimate termination recommendation and decision.

During this interactive session, experiences on project termination will be shared and discussed by meeting participants. Considerable emphasis will be placed on establishing success criteria, getting approval of those criteria, measuring results against the criteria, and working through the development of a termination recommendation and final decision. Finally, we will discuss under what circumstances a terminated project should be resurrected.

# Use of Computer Simulation in the 21st Century by the Work Teams

Jeffrey S. Brown, P.E. Eli Lilly and Company

## Introduction

*"Revolutions are not made; they come."* Wendell Phillips

In 1854 a self-taught English mathematician, George Boole, published "An Investigation of the Laws of Thought, on Which Are Founded the Mathematical Theories of Logic and Probabilities." In this work, he introduced Boolean algebra that is central to the study of pure mathematics and is the basis of computer technology. Despite his lack of any degree, George Boole's work revolutionized mathematics. In the future, members of work teams that do not have a formal academic degree will find themselves revolutionizing their work environment using computer simulation programs just as George Boole revolutionized mathematics.

This paper is about the use of such a model, the manner in which it is being introduced to members of a work team, and how they are using it to test their own improvement ideas. Just like George Boole, individuals like these team members using computer simulation tools will exert a powerful influence on how we improve our business in the future.

## The Driver

*"Changing conditions demand changing methods, and to hold to outgrown methods because of a loyalty to an irrelevancy destroys our integrity and encourages the lie."* Gerald Hamilton Kennedy

The incredible upsurge of global competition beginning in the early nineties is the driver that encouraged the business unit I am in at Eli Lilly and Company, Bulk Pharmaceutical Manufacturing, to develop a new operational philosophy that allows a quicker response to market changes. The basis of the philosophy traces its roots to what is called the "7-S framework" (Waterman, Peters, Phillips, 1980). The 7-S framework is a mental model, which illustrates the notion that to effectively change an organization, one must take into account the relationships between "structure," "strategy," "systems," "style," "skills," and the "shared values" of the organization.

The outcome of this effort is not the subject of this paper, but the operational "style" as illustrated by the model entitled "The Map" shown in Figure 1 is important to the subject. The new style called on individual work teams and their members to participate directly in the improvement process. The concept of incremental improvements, or KAIZEN as it is described in Japan, is illustrated in the section identified as "Primary Loop." Also included in the Primary Loop activities are the manipulation of the built in system variables. System improvements developed off-line are illustrated in the areas of the diagram called "Improvement" and "Breakthrough."

It is important to understand the process illustrated by "The Map" is not only for improvements but also to operate the process right the first time. This is an important concept as it would be a mistake to view this model as just an improvement system instead of one that gets at improvements and running the system effectively. To develop and implement improvements, work teams must have the will, the skills, and the tools. Until the nineties, work teams did not have all the tools available necessary to conduct the analysis necessary to identify where changes could be made in their process. Prior to this, the analysis was done by engineers and management. Computerization has changed that and now work teams have the ability to review operational data, conduct their own analysis, and determine if their process is in control and capable. This has inevitably lead to the work team taking the next step of developing and implementing operational improvements based on what they have learned from the data. The revolution has begun. Work teams, primarily made up of nondegreed personnel, are now in a fundamental position to improve the process in areas previously reserved to the technical and managerial support staff.

## Types of Models

"The software industry has offered up many different kinds of models in its first fifty years of existence, so there is no shortage of ideas to draw on when it comes to business modeling. In fact, the problem with modeling is not a shortage of models but an abundance of models that have almost no capability for productive interaction." – Dave A. Taylor

The term model or modeling has many different associations and it is important to discuss some of them to clarify the differences. The current use of modeling in business can be characterized by, but not limited to, one of the following:

- System models—7-S framework discussed previously is a good example of this type of model.



PROJECT MANAGEMENT INSTITUTE 28th Annual Seminars & Symposium
Chicago, Illinois: Papers Presented September 29 to October 1, 1997

Exhibit 1. The Map

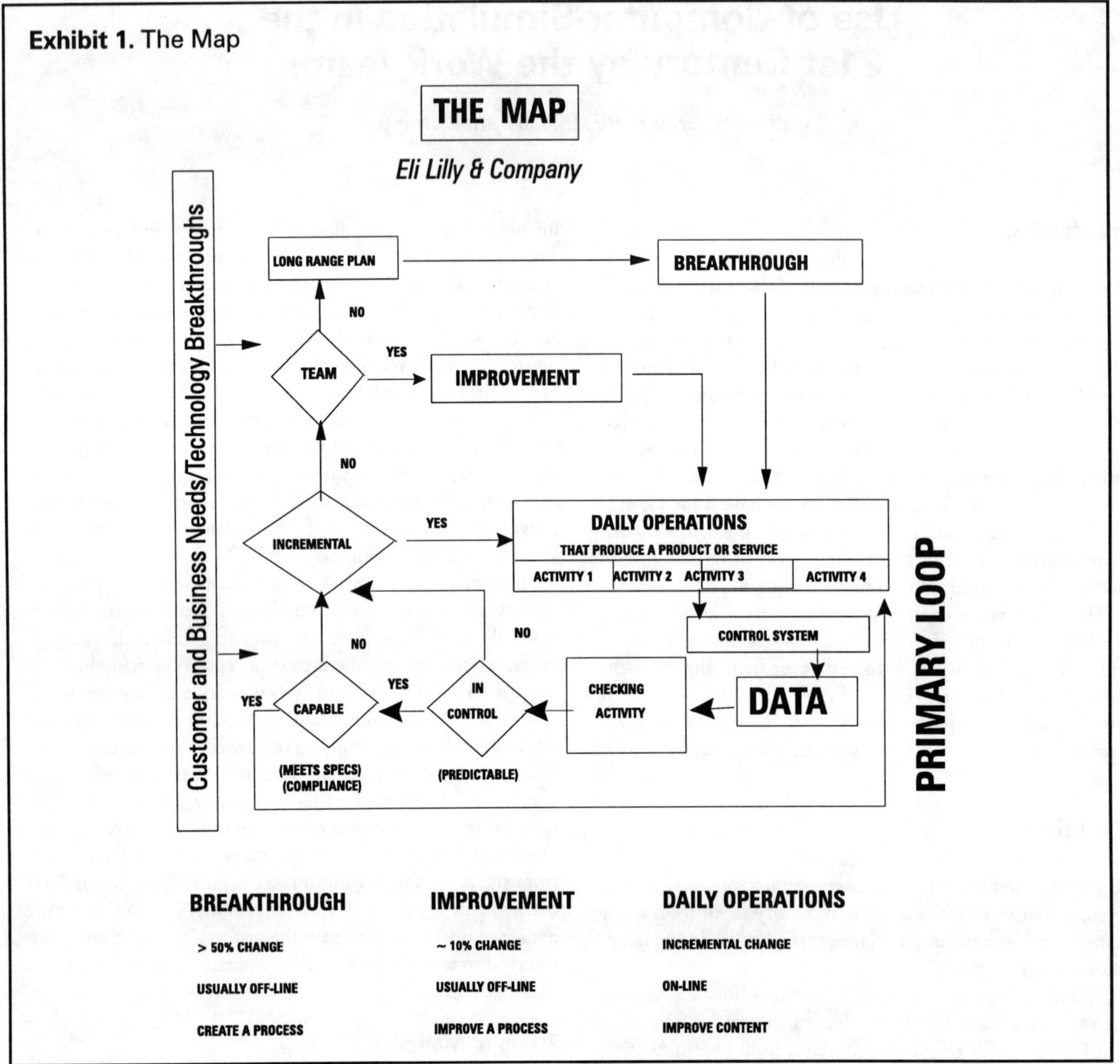


- Mind Maps—used to show relationships often drawn on paper.
- Decision models—used to identify possible outcomes of an activity.
- Financial models—programs use for financial management.
- Data models—programs used to collect and manipulate data to determine patterns or relationships.
- Workflow models—flow charts or software that display how specific operations are performed.
- Process models—programs used to determine process output based on inputted data.
- Simulation models—programs used to imitate a process or system in sufficient detail that the model can be used test different "what if" questions—similar to process models except they are so detailed that all the activities, entities (what is being processed), and resources of a system or process are represented.

## Why Use Simulation Modeling?

*"Take calculated risks. That is quite different from being rash."* George S. Patton in a letter to Cadet George Patton, Jr., June 6, 1944

With simulation models you can test new ideas or simulate extreme conditions to understand the dynamics of your system without putting it at risk. If a simulation model of the most critical process was performed by any company and then never used to improve the process it would have been worth the effort. Why? It would be worth the effort because in the development of the model, the company would have been required to define the control system for the process. The basic elements of a control system include customer identification, understanding the valid requirements, establishment of the work flow and accountability, and the measures used to determine if the process was successful (process predictors and quality outcome indicators). Once the control system has been defined and validated, the company will have a foundation for understanding the dynamics of the process when a change takes place.

At the work team level, the team can use a simulation model to help them determine how staffing requirements will be affected under various scenarios (illness, emergency events, vacations, production requirements, etc.). Teams also use simulation models to perform analysis of bottlenecks, cycle time reduction, production scheduling, cost reduction, and a host of other activities associated with the operation. The information developed by the model is critical in developing projects to make improvements to the system and respond to customers changing requirements.

## The Tools

*"There are times when one would like to hang the whole human race."* Mark Twain

There are a lot of software models out there that are used for model simulation. In one search on the Internet over one hundred vendors were identified as meeting the search criteria. The vast selection of models available on the market is overwhelming and most are too complex for a work team to develop their own models. Our engineers have used *Crystal Ball* by Decision Engineering and *Stella II* by High Performance Systems. *Crystal Ball* is a forecasting and risk analysis program for spreadsheets and *Stella II* is a full-blown simulation model. While I have seen excellent results from both models, both are used best by technical types in the development phase. Neither fit the criteria of having the simplicity needed for interfacing with the work team member who does not have a degree or special technical training in the development phase. The tool my process team is working with is *Process Model* by Process Model Corporation. What makes this model different is the use of flow charts to design the model. The vast majority of work team members know how to produce a flow chart and those who do not can be quickly taught.

The selection of simulation software is not straightforward or easy. The development of Object Models, Object Technology, and Object-Oriented Software is taking off and that means there will be more selections to choose from in the future. If program is going to be used in the development phase by those who do not have strong technical background you will want to look for a product that has a simple and user-friendly front end.

## The Obstacles

*"If there is no price to be paid, it is also not of value."* Albert Einstein

Employee job paradigms are mental models of how the employee views their relationship to their job and these often produce some of the strongest obstacles to the implementation of anything new. This has proven to be particularly true with members of the work team that have jobs that have not changed over time. Often the project manager in charge of introducing the new system will hear comments from work team members like, "I hired on to operate this process. I've done that for fifteen years and I didn't hire on to do statistics or run computer programs." Creating a new vision, a new paradigm successfully requires skill, forethought, and strong support from the management team.

Education and skill levels of work team members are of utmost importance. The work age between twenty and sixty-four years draws from a population pool described below (from the U.S. Census Bureau, 1990).

| Age Group | Millions | % |
|---|---|---|
| 20-24 years old | 19.4 | 13% |
| 25-29 years old | 20.8 | 14% |
| 30-34 years old | 22.2 | 15% |
| 35-39 years old | 20.6 | 14% |
| 40-44 years old | 18.8 | 13% |
| 45-49 years old | 14.1 | 9% |
| 50-54 years old | 11.6 | 8% |
| 55-59 years old | 10.4 | 7% |
| 60-64 years old | 10.6 | 7% |
| **Total** | **148.5** | |

The total percentage of schools that had computers used by students in 1984 was 27.3% and the total used at home was 11%. In 1993, the total percentage of schools using computers was: college—55%, high school—58%, grades 1–8—69% and the total percentage used at home was: college—33%, high school—29%, grades 1–8—25%. The data is from

Exhibit 2.

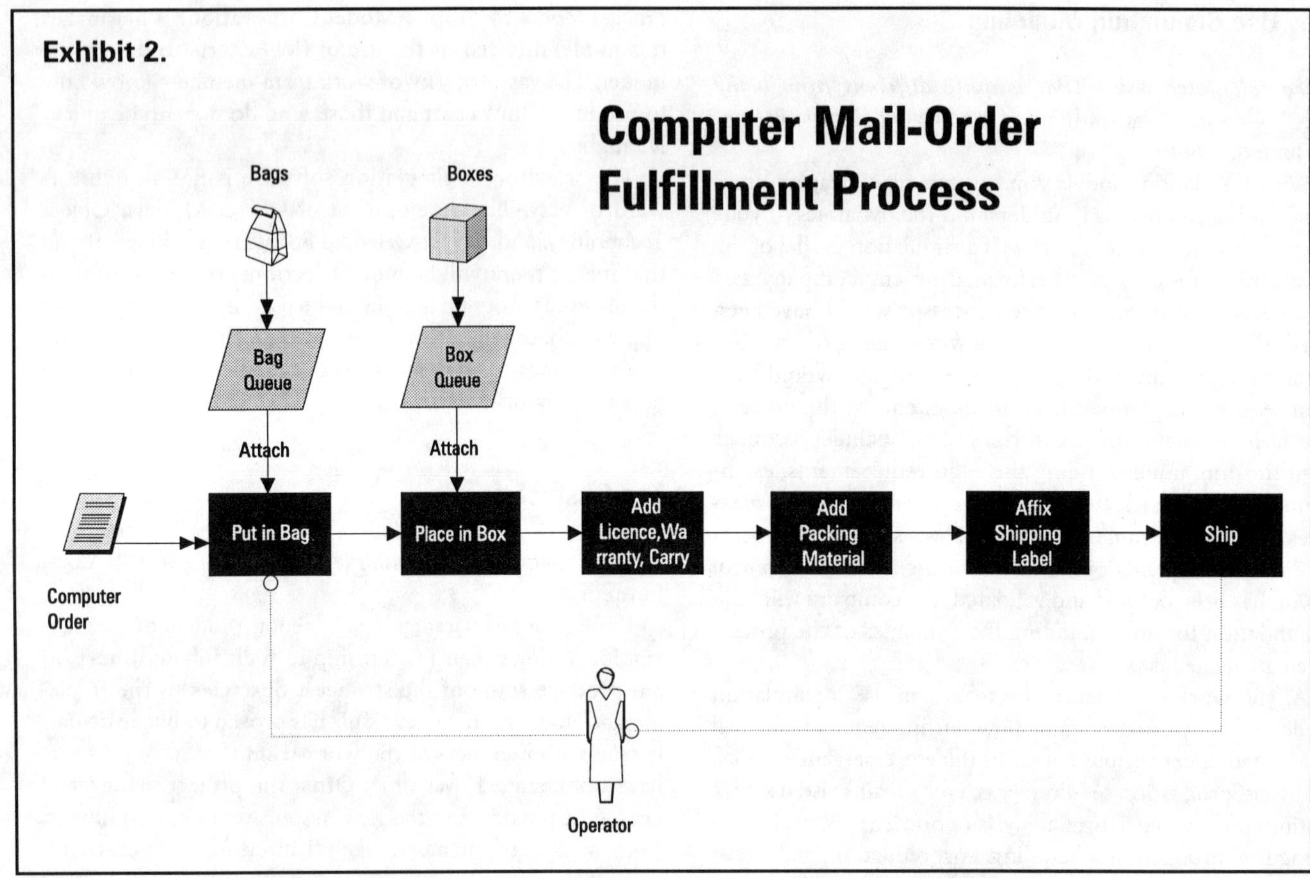


the National Center for Educational Statistics. It can be said that the majority of the 1997 workforce is made up of individuals who have never used a computer in school. This data shows us that most work team members with only a high school education will need special training in order to effectively use computers. It also suggests that most of our college graduates in the workforce may not have had adequate computer training. It is obvious that anyone wanting to have members of work teams utilize the computer in creative ways will need to consider the lack of computer skills and how to meet that challenge if they are to be successful.

There is hope for computer literacy in the future. In fact, systems analysts and computer scientists are the second fastest growing occupation in the U.S. and the number of students exposed to computer training today is higher than in 1993. Computer technology is growing at an exponential rate and the improvements will increase the ability to use the computer by more people in the future with less training. An example of this was announced by IBM in April, 1997, when they told the public that we can expect voice-actuated hand-held computers that will be much more powerful than the 1997 desktop computer in the 21st Century.

## Implementation Strategy

*"Before beginning, prepare carefully."* Cicero

"Management by Project" is an effective way to initiate changes in work teams. This might be challenged as an inappropriate description because the changes are being made to manufacturing system. As noted in the *Project Management Body of Knowledge* (PMBOK), "Operations and projects differ primarily in that operations are ongoing and repetitive while projects are temporary and unique. A project can thus be defined in terms of its distinctive characteristics — a project is a temporary endeavor undertaken to create a unique product or service." It is valid to define the product of the project as the implementation of a new and "unique" operational style, such as that illustrated by "The Map." It has a definite beginning and end as does the introduction and use of a new tool to a work team. A good reference for this approach is *Project Management in Manufacturing and High Technology Operations – Second Edition* written by Adedeji Bodunde Badiru and published by John Wiley & Sons.

Assuming the change to the operational style illustrated by "The Map" is complete then the addition of a new tool to the work team in the form of a simulation model would be viewed as a new project. The Scope of the project is to provide a simulation model that can be used by members of the work team to model their operations for understanding and to test improvement ideas. The project must provide a means to overcome any adverse paradigms and educational needs the work team members have that would provide an obstacle to the full implementation and use of the new tool. The project is complete when the work team successfully designs/runs its first model and is able to analyze the results in a report to management concerning an operation or improvement opportunity they choose.

The strategy called for the introduction of two programs with user-friendly front ends for team members to use in their daily work. Each of these programs put the team member in control of the development portion of the program. The two programs used were *Project KickStart for Windows* by Experience Software and *DecideRight* by Avantos. The first program is used to develop and schedule project tasks and resources and the second is used to assist in decision making. The work team has several "Key Result Areas" around which they develop "Objectives" each year to improve or fix problems. Using the *KickStart* program to develop project plans addressing their Objectives and the *DecideRight* program to help the team in their decisions. Both programs have standard reports the team then used to communicate their project information or how they made their decisions.

Use of these programs allowed the team to build their confidence in using the computer as a tool and this made the introduction of the simulation program, *Process Model* by PROMODEL Corporation fairly easy. This program uses *ABC FlowCharter* by Micrografx, Inc. as the interface to the simulation model. To use the model, the work team develops a flow chart (process flow) of the activity they are interested in modeling. Exhibit 2 is an example of a simple flow chart used as a demo to train team members how to use the program.

They then add resources and determine the probability distribution they want to use to represent that activity. The distribution used most often is the triangular that contains the most likely limit, the lower limit, and the higher limit for the activity in question.

As with every new endeavor, there are those on the team that can be described as early adapters. They are the members who readily try new things. These early adapters were targeted for being the first to use the new program. As they gain experience and comfort with it, the others on the team will begin to use the program. The verdict is still out, but the team members working with the program are excited about the ability to model their resource requirements and the improvement ideas they have for parts of the process they control.

## A Look at the Future

*"My interest in the future is because I am going to spend the rest of my life there."* Charles Kettering

*"We stand today at the edge of a new frontier. The new frontier of which I speak is not a set of promises, it is a set of challenges."* John F. Kennedy

In the future we will see business engineered along with the software that will not only do those daily tasks required by our business activities, but will be able to simulate various scenarios off-line to test 'what if' analysis. With the advent of Object Technology and continuing advancement in computer technology, the software and the business will be completely integrated. The application that tracks an explicit portion of the process workflow will be part of the same application the CEO uses to determine the global state of the business. David Taylor does an excellent job explaining this in his book *Business Engineering With Object Technology* published by Wiley & Sons.

He has called the integration the tasks of Data, Process, Workflow, Financial, and Simulation models "Convergent Engineering." We are already beginning to see this occur with young businesses such as the Japan owned *7-Eleven* chain where the owners have implemented convergent engineering and are reaping a 40% profit.

The future is where we are going to live and it is not a promise of great things for us so much as a fact that we will be challenged beyond our wildest imagination. The paradigms some have concerning the limitations of the work teams to effect change through the use of computer simulation programs will be shattered and those on the work teams are going to suffer a form of culture shock as they adopt these changes. Like waves endlessly crashing ashore, the challenges will come one after another and those living in the 21st Century will be as shocked when a change does not come along as the small town is when the Toyota Plant chooses their site today.

It is for these reasons that work teams will play a most important role in the business world of the 21st Century. Those companies who prepare for it will be the winners in their respective industries tomorrow. Those who do not embrace the changes taking place at the grass roots level will not reap the rewards, but will be the boat people of the future—adrift at sea.

# Globalization of Project Planning in a Pharmaceutical R&D Environment

Dennis W. Engers, Sanofi Research, a Division of Sanofi Pharmaceuticals, Inc.
Philippe Cremades, Sanofi Research

## Sanofi History

Sanofi Research is a company born from the amalgamation of several pharmaceutical firms. In the last two decades, through progressive acquisition of several international pharmaceutical companies, Sanofi has secured a prominent position in the pharmaceutical world. Sanofi is a majority owned subsidiary of ELF Aquitaine and ranks in the top thirty largest pharmaceutical groups and top ten producers of luxury perfumes and beauty products. Sanofi's talent for discovering original compounds and the capacity for developing these compounds are fundamental prerequisites for success within the pharmaceutical group. Sanofi Research has a strong team among the two thousand five hundred R&D employees at the nine centers, located in six countries around the world. While each R&D center has preserved its own individuality, there is plenty of opportunity for exchange of ideas, personal contact and a good sense of competition. Sanofi has centers located in Great Valley, Pennsylvania, United States; Montpellier, Toulouse, Labège, Gentilly, France; Alnwick, United Kingdom; Budapest, Hungary; Riells, Spain and Milan, Italy.

The majority of R&D activities are directed toward four major therapeutic areas including: thrombosis, cardiovascular, central nervous system disorders and oncology. Sanofi has opted for a strategy aimed at developing leading products in each of these areas. During 1996, Sanofi reached several decisive milestones and confirmed the fundamental role that R&D plays in the company's growth strategy into the 21st century. Achievements that were applauded throughout the year by both the scientific and financial community, place Sanofi among the most promising R&D organizations in today's pharmaceutical industry. Sanofi has seven compounds in preclinical investigation, four in phase I clinical trials, twelve in phase II clinical trials, four in late stage phase III clinical trials and three major products currently being filed throughout the world.

## Why Global Planning at Sanofi?

During 1994, Sanofi completed a comprehensive external audit of their information platform and organizational workflow. Sanofi decided to rework four programs including: electronic document management environment (GED), management of clinical trial supplies sourcing (CTS), planning/scheduling information system and laboratory information management system (LIMS). To ensure consistency between the information systems, a Department for Information Systems Users (DCUSI) was created. A user project leader and programmer project leader were appointed to lead each project. This organization was new for Sanofi where programmers were involved in the project from start to finish, attended user meetings and participated in defining needs. The old customer/supplier relationship was replaced by a new programmer/user partnership.

With regard to planning/scheduling, Sanofi elected to take a bold, innovative step to deploy a unique planning system that would directly link their major research centers involved with all R&D product development. This global initiative has exceeded industry best practice for design and implementation speed. Sanofi is the first major pharmaceutical firm that has successfully instituted a global R&D planning, scheduling and resource management system.

## Strategy for Selection

Sanofi set out with a simple strategy for selection of a new planning tool. Planning is useful only when the information is relevant to the customer. Constraints for the new planning system became evident, that is, to develop a single unique system (one project = one plan) and to decentralize the system for entering information at the source and to assess precise workload for the departments. The Global Planning Team was organized as a partnership between Information Systems (I/S) and the user groups. Project managers for I/S and the users were appointed. All global scientific functions (Clinical, Preclinical, Regulatory), industrial, project direction and finance appointed representatives to the Global Planning Team.

The first phase was to reengineer the process, leading those involved to agree on a way to work and summarize, in writing, the global requirements. A key goal was to keep the planning process from interfering with the progression of compounds entering early development.

The second phase consisted of software package characteristic identification. Specification setting and protocol selection for the system characteristics (RFP) was completed by the user group. The Request For Purchase was sent to several vendors (4–6) with demonstrations scheduled with the three leading vendors, based on the vendor response. A second trip was scheduled with our Unix systems engineer to confirm technical and financial aspects of their proposals. After careful study, the users recommended OPX2, the project management software from SYSECA, a subsidiary of the Thomson group.

## Why OPX2?

Prior to 1994, SYSECA developed numerous programs specific to project planning and management for major sectors of businesses in the aerospace, energy, defense and engineering industries. Since 1994, SYSECA has offered OPX2 as a commercial product. SYSECA created a new group called PLANISWARE, with Thomson CSF as the main stakeholder.

OPX2 was developed to meet primary characteristics that included: the ability to manage plans within a matrix organization; the ability to enlist multiusers in updating data online; the ability to work in multilanguage environments; the abili-

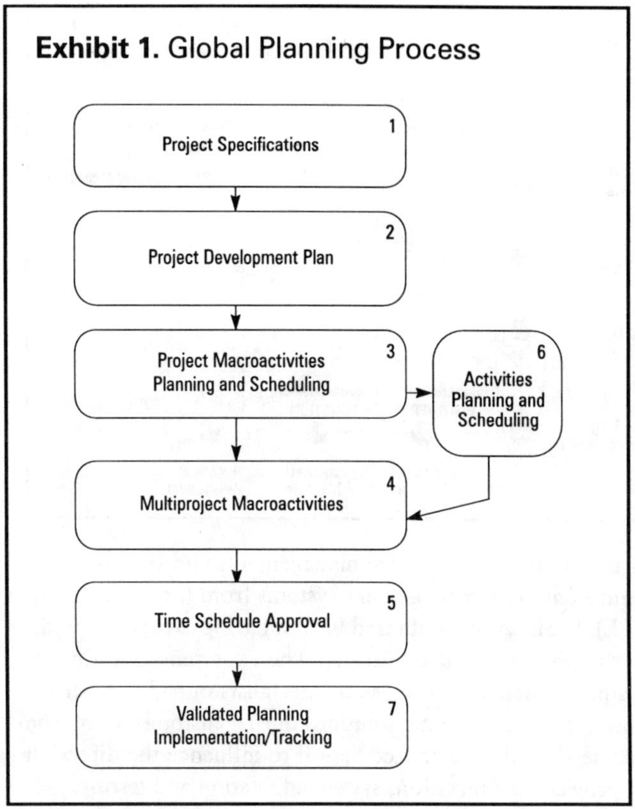


**Exhibit 1.** Global Planning Process

**Exhibit 2.** Information Systems Architecture

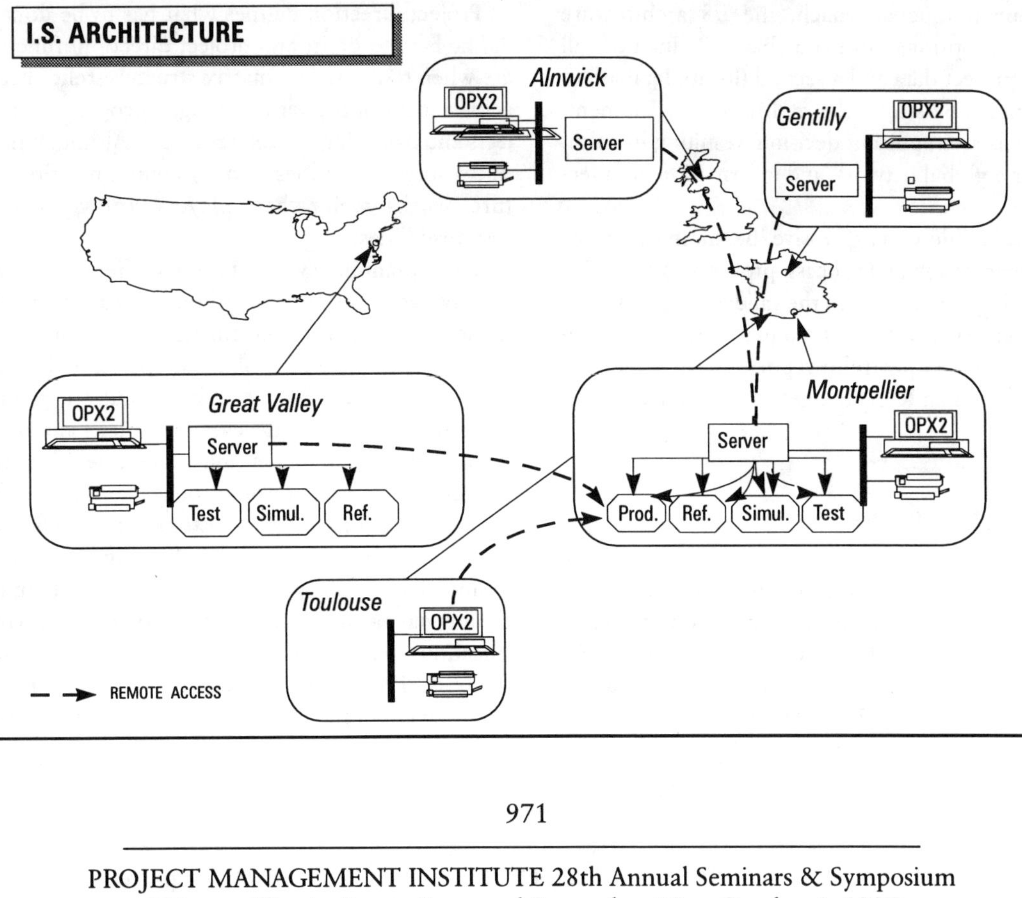

I.S. ARCHITECTURE

Alnwick: OPX2, Server
Gentilly: OPX2, Server
Great Valley: OPX2, Server, Test, Simul., Ref.
Montpellier: OPX2, Server, Prod., Ref., Simul., Test
Toulouse: OPX2

REMOTE ACCESS

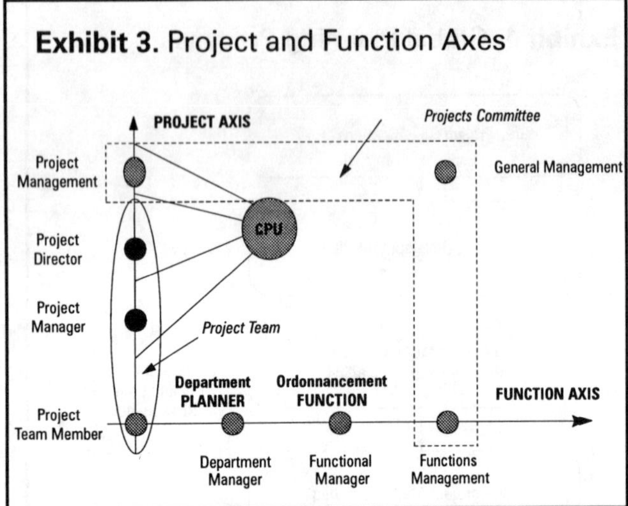


**Exhibit 3.** Project and Function Axes

ty to incorporate resource management; and the ability to utilize database management systems from the shelf (ORACLE). SYSECA was criticized for not having experience within the pharmaceutical industry. The experience within our team, coupled with the use of specialists outside of our industry, provided unique solutions during customization. The partnership also permitted Sanofi to influence the direction of project customization, system adaptation and testing.

OPX2 operates on a Unix system, with the database server located on the Montpellier server. Application servers are located at each site. In order to improve access time, a reference database is maintained and updated monthly at each site. Due to our unique approach, the I/S architecture mapped out two options: one database to include all Macroplans for project data and a second (local) database to include departments by site in the multilevel environment. This approach was an important decision, resulting in an increased need for a global network and information architecture.

The project schedule was aggressive, beginning with the evaluation of organization and process, progressing to OPX2 tool selection and culminating with the validation of planning templates. The team verified study templates based on global experiences, designed portfolio reports for management review and developed an R&D budget with effective project forecasting.

## A Vision Turned into Reality

Sanofi faced heavy pressure to succeed from the competitive pharmaceutical environment. Many of these constraints required adaptability and flexibility to resolve. Since 1982, Sanofi maintained a highly centralized planning unit that utilized a single methodology (PERT). Departments felt little involvement in the planning process (ownership) and seldom used the project plans for decisions and/or resource evaluation. Only the project managers used the project plans for reference.

The Global Planning Team was charged with several key objectives including: the planning must be decentralized into the scientific departments; the Central Planning Unit (CPU) will continue to provide portfolio and strategic analysis; the planning system must be global, with real time, online access from the research centers; the planning system must maintain logic and dates for all projects and provide data for portfolio management (time, duration, resources); and the planning system must provide capabilities for multidepartment and multiproject analyses.

The primary goal was to provide Sanofi with the means to ensure the best possible management of our R&D project portfolio and to optimize time management through the best possible use of our resources. Expected outcomes include: shortened development cycles, enhanced decision making, improved quality of information, better use of resources (people, funds) and access to global project information.

For project management to be successful, effective planning, scheduling and resource workload must be realized. The Global Planning Team recommended several, distinct roles for the relevant planning groups ( i.e., Central Planning Unit, Project Direction, Functional Ordonnancement and Department/Services). Project management routinely functions within a matrix structure that crosses two axes; namely, Function and Project.

Project direction defines what has to be done; functions define how to do it; and project direction/ functions negotiate when to do it. The matrix structure relies heavily on the achievement of proper planning, a proper vision of the projects and balancing limited resources. Although the matrix induces some difficulties (mostly communications), the structure works well when players know their roles and responsibilities.

For a planning system to work effectively, a proper balance between the project and function axes must be well understood. General management is responsible for strategic management of the portfolio and operational management of the projects, including conflict resolution, priority setting, validation of strategic development plans and determination of project measurements (milestones, decision points). Project direction is responsible for achieving the stated objectives, ensuring that key milestones are reached in terms of time, quality and cost. Central planning is responsible for the maintenance of the portfolio database, working closely with senior management and the functional ordonnancement on questions related to multiproject workload and portfolio analysis. Project team members are responsible for the achievement of the project objectives within their department and providing scientific expertise within the team. Team members work with their department planners on questions related to timing and resources for the department to meet short-term objectives. Each plan is managed according to three horizons: Contractual (0–3 months), Firm (3–12 months) and Budgetary (6–18 months). This approach permits confidence intervals to be aligned with short and long term project goals. The functional ordonnancement (Clinical, Preclinical, Regulatory) are responsible for all development projects for the departments they represent in terms of time and workload, globally. An integrated planning system must account for the different levels of detail specific to each area of responsibility.

## Stages of Deployment

Successful global deployment of any new application requires careful examination of the existing work environment. Prior to the technical installation of OPX2, Sanofi provided broad employee (250) access to basic training in planning and scheduling. Training sessions were conducted at all research centers (in three different languages) against a common syllabus, providing a basic understanding of planning techniques.

Once the technical aspects of the new planning system were well understood, the major functions (Clinical, Preclinical, Regulatory) began designing their study templates. Specific to each department, templates were assembled for every major batch of work (i.e., studies) normally included in a development project. Each template was built within the context of a standard work breakdown structure (WBS) and a resource breakdown structure (RBS). Another key success factor was securing ownership from Departmental Management for their templates (leader group). Templates were designed in close collaboration with the function ordonnancement, department planners and department management. Templates addressed uniform task definition, time, schedule, as well as resource, manpower and external contractors.

Sanofi exceeded industry best practice deployment timeframe as compared to the pharmaceutical industry and other industries (e.g., telecommunications/automotive) for identification, selection and installation. Sanofi completed this global planning initiative in less than one year, as compared to an industry average of 3–5 years or 4–6 years for other industries. Currently, Sanofi's R&D budget is based on the OPX2 project forecasting and scheduling process.

**Exhibit 4.** Planning Levels

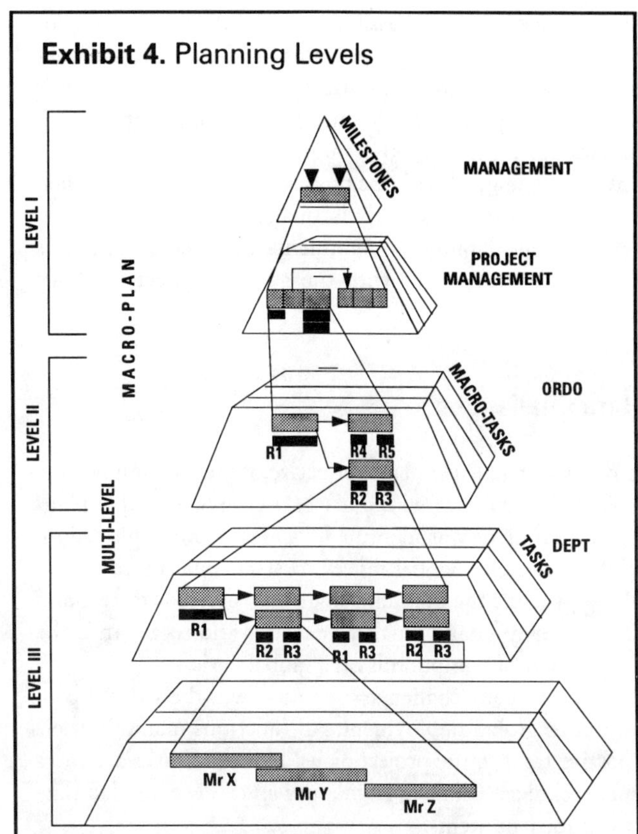


## Sanofi Planning Environment

Successful OPX2 deployment within Sanofi required a clear understanding of process and quality control. The project strategy is defined by project direction and validated by Sanofi management. Once the project strategy is agreed upon, the work plan becomes a contract between project direction and scientific departments. Each month, project review meetings are conducted with representatives of the functions (Ordos), central planning and project direction to review the project status. Deviations from the original plan are identified and the plan is confirmed (or amended). As a result, a reference plan is issued (globally) as part of the regular update process. Special attention is given to studies on the critical path, key decision points, go/no go decisions and/or regulatory milestones. Deviations are documented within the OPX2 Notepad to ensure timely, global communications to all users.

A planning tool is useful only if the recorded data is relevant. The planning system cannot be an isolated tool, but must be adapted to the work environment. Our experience demonstrates that planning tends to standardize process and assist with quality assurance in the departments. Clear benefits for the scientific department now include full integration across site and function. Multiproject analysis of resources and workload are now possible and directly assist with project forecasting and budget preparation. Direct involvement by the departments in the preparation of generic templates is critical. Participation by site and international department planners during the initial planning session ensure that the plans remain aligned with the project strategy and work plan. Through detailed work analysis, quality decisions are driven by resource availability. Commitments are based on rationale that must be consistent with the agreed project strategic plans.

## Future Challenges

For research to be useful and effective, it must be innovative. In order to keep pace with our R&D efforts, a unique planning environment was identified, validated and deployed on a global basis. As Sanofi moves to streamline the decision making process, the planning environment needs to respond in a manner to enable quality decisions and to advance the full portfolio of compounds on a global basis.

The first major challenge for Sanofi was the natural progression to global deployment. All functions maintain their respective tasks in the project plans. However, tasks/activities from Preclinical, Clinical, Regulatory and CPU exceeded thirty-five thousand items.

A major initiative to reduce the number of activities (by 50%) and to simplify the templates began in early 1997. The Global Planning Team recommended that the OPX2 database be stratified into three levels that are customer specific. Level I is the Strategic/CPU level for management that includes key milestones, decision points and global resources. Level II is the ordo/project direction level that captures studies (batch of work) for each project on a site/project/department basis. Level III is the department level (multilevel) that allows detailed activities to be managed locally, according to the need of each department. Implementation of multilevel planning will be completed 3-4Q97.

The second major challenge was to address poor user response times by upgrading the global network and servers at all research centers. Currently, Sanofi has over one hundred and twenty accounts with read/write access. Two factors impact the response time for the local user. First, the local server and network must be optimized. Second, remote access to the MacroPlan database (located in Montpellier, France) must be significantly improved. The local network was audited at each major research center. Improvements for the intersite network are scheduled for 3Q97. Server capacity Great Valley, Montpellier, Toulouse, Gentilly and Alnwick will have significant upgrades to their memory and processors. The target for improving response time on a global basis is mid-97. Other query tools for the occasional user have been identified to decrease the demand on the system. Business Objects, an ORACLE query tool, was installed mid-year to provide read access.

The third major challenge for globalization of project planning is adapting to multicultural differences within Sanofi. Planning has been a reflection of the success (or failure) of the harmonization and integration that has occurred within Sanofi. Study templates were built to reflect industry best practice for all aspects of Clinical, Preclinical and Regulatory work to support global registration. However, differences in work practices are frequently uncovered as a consequence to effective project planning. For global planning to be fully functional, ownership and reliance on the project plans must be a measure of our ultimate success.

During 1996, OPX2 was used to build the global project plans supporting the budget preparation for Preclinical Development. Goals for the 1998 budget preparation are to expand the application into the Clinical Development and Regulatory Affairs groups. Our long term success for effective global project/portfolio management will include validated plans, well understood project objectives with linked, strategic plans.

Successful planning for Sanofi is a direct result of a global team effort. As thousands of tasks are performed everyday in R&D product development, it is essential to ensure that an efficient way of working (through effective planning) is well understood. Thanks to everyone's efforts, the OPX2 tool is operational in record time. Senior management and the Global Planning Team have played a key role to ensure that the OPX2 tool as well as the planning environment is a success. We must always remember that "planning is only useful when the information is relevant to the users."

# Program Management: A Key for Integrated Healthcare Delivery Systems

Ken Jones, Ernst & Young LLP
Jolene Weiskittel, Health Alliance of Greater Cincinnati

*"I was myself last night, but I fell asleep on the mountain, and they've changed my gun, and every thing's changed, and I'm changed, and I can't tell what's my name, or who I am!"*
Rip Van Winkle, by Washington Irving

Change is rocking the healthcare industry. Much like Rip Van Winkle's experience, it seems sudden, confusing, and sometimes even frightening. The market forces for change are demanding high quality care at reduced cost. In virtually every major metropolitan market, hospitals are consolidating while new competitors enter markets. Competition, market share, quality, and cost reduction are the focus on healthcare delivery system today. The driver of this change is managed care.

This paper presents the experience of The Health Alliance of Cincinnati and Ernst & Young LLP in establishing a program management office to manage a large portfolio of information technology projects. It describes the business drivers behind The Health Alliance, the need for significant new information technology investments and explores how program management has been implemented and its impact on the organization. Finally, lessons learned during the first year in operating the program management office are summarized.

## The Drivers of Change

In January 1995, The Health Alliance of Greater Cincinnati, a network of hospitals in the greater Cincinnati/ northern Kentucky region, was formed. The Alliance began with Christ and University Hospitals, and later incorporated St. Luke Hospitals (mid '95) and Jewish Hospitals (January 1996). The Alliance was created to position the member hospitals and physician organizations to compete under managed care as it evolves in the United States. Under managed care, insurance companies set the rates doctors, pharmacies, and hospitals can charge for services. This is a significant change in the economics of health care delivery and is forcing institutions to get much bigger to leverage economies of scale and drive down costs.

The formation of The Health Alliance was a first step in developing an Integrated Healthcare Delivery Network (IHDN) in Greater Cincinnati. As managed care takes over as the dominant method of healthcare financing in the United States, the IHDN will become the dominant form of healthcare delivery. IHDN's like The Health Alliance will compete aggressively for market share and because of this market competition offer the promise of:

- increased quality of services rendered,
- reduced costs,
- improved access to services,
- stronger physician support and training,
- improved operational efficiency, and
- delivery of service by the system far beyond what any hospital could do individually.

The key strategy for achieving these outcomes is to shift quickly and significantly to investments in information technology. Information systems are the critical component to enabling new organizational structures and care delivery processes. The objectives of these investments are to:

- provide integrated care delivery systems,
- move patient information seamlessly between Alliance members,
- maintain a high level of patient confidentiality,
- consolidate financial management systems,
- consolidate system operations,
- implement enterprisewide networks, and
- and establish electronic data interchange with key suppliers and payers.

Common systems and easy information exchange for care management and financial processes are central to the ability of The Health Alliance to reduce costs while maintaining high-quality and patient satisfaction.

As if the imperative for market change were not sufficient, The Health Alliance, like most organizations, faces significant Year 2000 issues. These issues mandate a large number of system replacements or significant new investment in antiquated systems. Most of the Year 2000 corrective actions must be in place by the summer of 1999 in order to assure minimal interruption of services. The world that Rip Van Winkel faced when he woke up on the mountain is truly the world of healthcare today.

**Exhibit 1.** Project Portfolio Management

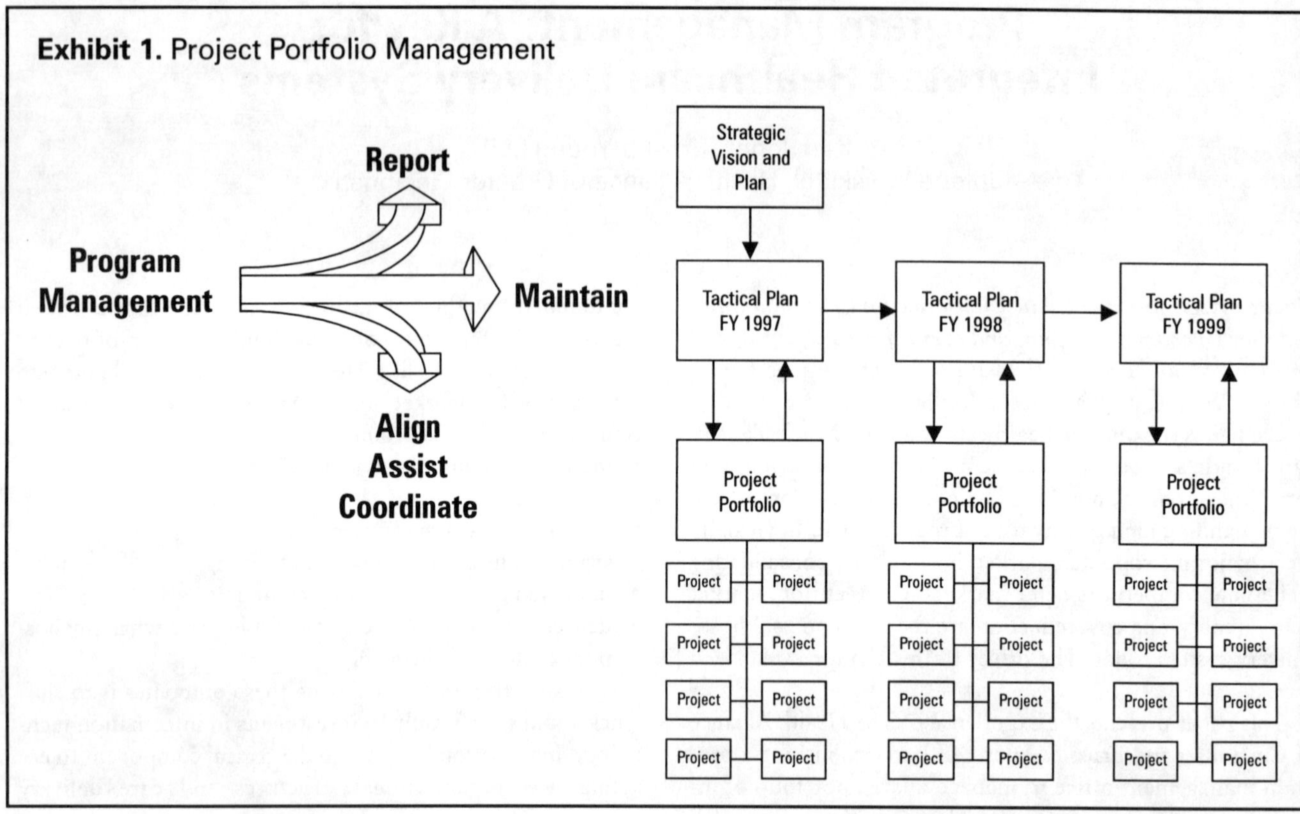


## Positioning for Change

To meet the challenges of managed care, executive management concluded that significant new information systems investment was required. New systems were needed to support:

- Patient Care Systems (registration, utilization analysis, documentation, results/order entry, etc.),
- Alliance-wide Ambulatory Care,
- Managed Care Systems,
- Financial Accounting, HR/Payroll, Materials Management and Fixed Assets,
- Patient Accounting,
- Pharmacy Management,
- Infrastructure,
- Decision Support, and
- Enterprise Master Patient Index.

Once the scope of the change was understood, a three-year IT tactical implementation plan was developed and aligned with the strategic plan. For each year in the tactical plan, a portfolio of projects was identified, prioritized, and scheduled. As it became apparent that a large number of projects would be needed over the three-year period, the issue of overall coordination and alignment became critical to achieving a successful outcome. One analysis of the situation indicated that under the status quo for managing projects, The Health Alliance could experience cost increases of 12 to 15% above planned capital outlays annually due to poor project performance and lower business benefits. To mitigate these risks, the Alliance embraced program management as a key component of its implementation strategy and created a Program Management Office (PMO) in the summer of 1996.

The PMO was chartered as a project with responsibilities to:

- Ensure project consistency through the establishment of planning, reporting, and knowledge capture standards,
- Monitor compliance with established program standards and recommended corrective actions as needed,
- Coordinate the program's projects with other related initiatives in the areas of knowledge sharing, issues resolution, and workplan synchronization,
- Provide overall control and coordination of program progress, quality, and performance, and
- Promote efficiencies by providing shared administrative services.

Procedurally, the PMO is responsible for providing the following services to the project teams and executive management:

- Portfolio risk and performance analysis with recommendations,
- Financial Tracking and Reporting,
- Integrated Planning and Support,
- Knowledge Coordination,

**Exhibit 2.** Synchronizing Threads of Project Execution

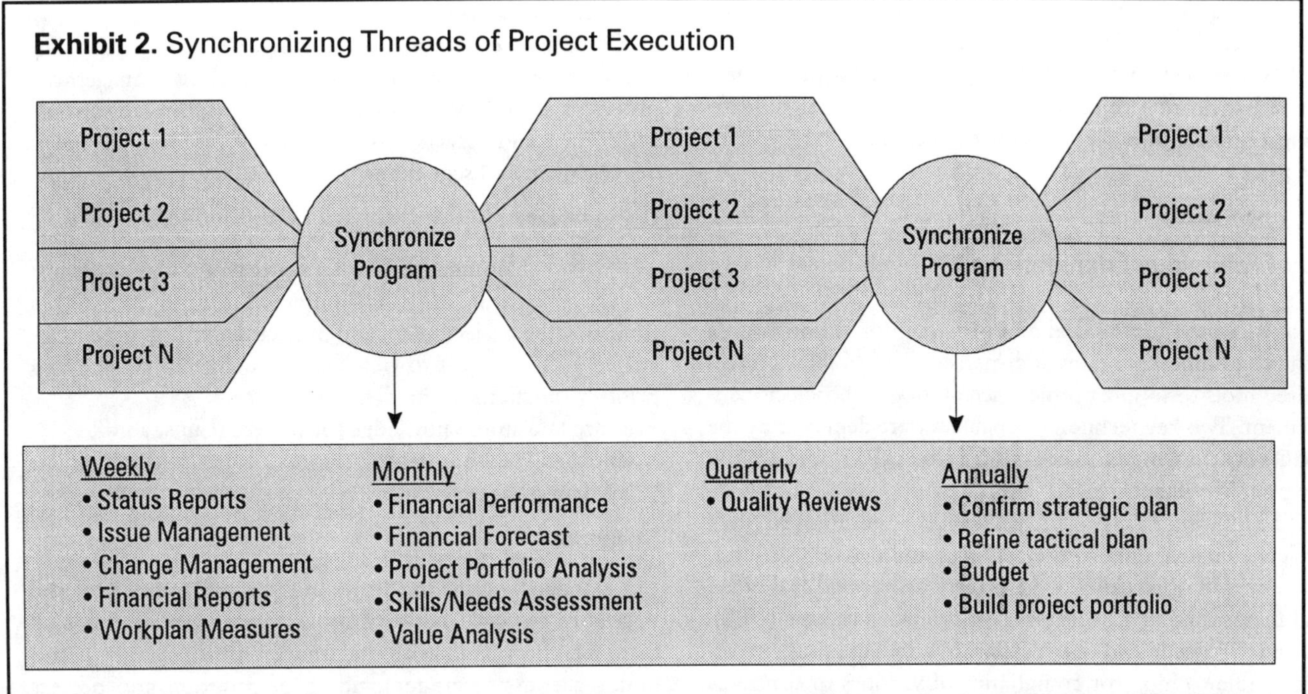


- Project Management Process Training,
- Risk and Quality Management, and
- Technology enablers for project control and project accounting.

As it has evolved at The Health Alliance, program management reports how the overall program is performing to the strategic plan, maintains the alignment of the tactical plan to the strategic plan, and aligns, assists, and coordinates the actions of the project team to function within a portfolio of projects.

Overall, the PMO acts both as the role of coach and "cop." The PMO is the group of individuals whose goal is to make projects as successful as possible. This is accomplished by eliminating redundant tasks, providing a common technical infrastructure for project management, and assisting in all phases of plan development, performance, and conclusion. However, the PMO is also charged with enforcing the standards of the program. In this capacity, the PMO reports project performance that falls outside of expected norms and is proactive in working with project managers to clarify and correct deviations.

## Coordinating Multiple Project Threads

With time to market and Year 2000 as critical drivers, projects have been sequenced in parallel threads of execution as much as possible. While parallel execution reduces elapsed project execution time, it also increases the risk of poor project performance through reduced knowledge reuse, poor coordination, poor communication, inefficient deployment of resources, and duplication of effort. To keep the multiple parallel threads tied together as a coordinated group moving toward common objectives, the PMO acts as the agent to assure overall synchronization.

Program synchronization occurs on a periodic basis designed to detect problems early and provide a constant flow of information for executive decisioning. Each week, all projects report a balanced scorecard of project performance data including: project scope (financial, temporal, and deliverable) and project management process performance (issue management, change management, workplan management). The individual project reports are combined into a program dashboard report that uses colored indicators (red, yellow, green) to report project performance to executive management.

Monthly, the PMO, reports overall project portfolio performance to an IT Governance Board that reviews the program's financial performance and progress toward tactical goals. Issues that cannot be resolved at the project or program level are elevated to the Governance Board.

Quarterly, projects conduct process quality reviews. Each project receives a quality rating that measures eighteen different aspects of the project's performance as well as the effectiveness of project sponsorship. The quality review provides an opportunity for the project manager to gain perspectives from independent third parties. The review also gives the program manager the opportunity to identify systemic problems that may impact other projects.

A rolling three-year tactical plan is updated annually. The process requires realignment of the tactical plan to the strategic business plan, tactical adjustments based on actual project performance and project reprioritization, and finally identifying a new set of project objectives in the new third year of the plan.

## Key Technology Enablers

Coordinating the financial and project information from a number of different teams at dispersed physical locations required tools to support project accounting and project management. Two key technology enablers were deployed by the PMO: (1) the Project Accounting System (PAS) and (2) the Program Workbench.

The PAS is a Microsoft Access based application to track project financial data to the resource and deliverable level. The key unit of tracking is the project deliverable as defined and maintained in a deliverable breakdown structure (DBS). Using a DBS code and resource information, the program office is able to monitor compliance of vendors to contracts (timing and dollars), manage budget to actual performance, track commitments to projects separate from expenses incurred by projects, and report, on a near real-time basis, the financial performance of the project portfolio.

The Program Workbench is an application developed by Ernst & Young to support large project/program team environments. At the core of the Program Workbench is a set of Lotus Domino databases with Internet browsers (Netscape, Microsoft Internet Explorer, etc.) and the Lotus Notes client supported on the desktop. Program Workbench is designed to provide an integrated workgroup environment that supports virtually all aspects of the project management control, reporting, and knowledge sharing processes. The key components of Program Workbench are:

### Projects and People Management

This part of the application provides access to information concerning all initiatives, projects, and personnel working on projects at The Health Alliance. The initiative and project documents contain specific information such as goals, objectives, value propositions and organization. The personnel forms allow users to enter, update, and manage information about themselves and their teams.

### Project Control

On a day-to-day basis, this is the most widely used portion of the application. Project control includes:

- Weekly Status Reporting (individual and project),
- Issue Management,
- Change Management,
- Workplan Actuals Reporting, and
- Consolidated Resource Forecasting.

All forms to support these key project management processes are created, stored, and communicated electronically. The tool interacts with Microsoft Project for workplan development and scheduling.

### Deliverables

The deliverables management repository provides centralize storage and sharing of project outputs. The repository allows sponsors, the project team, and project teams not directly involved with a project to view and use deliverables. The two primary functions of the database are to:

- share and store knowledge for project teams, and
- allow all Health Alliance personnel access to the completed deliverables.

### Standards

The standards define the "rules of the road" for all projects. A readily available body of program standards helps new team members familiarize themselves with the program and builds a common understanding of program and project management processes. Some examples are:

- Frequency of status reports,
- Quality assurance measures and processes,
- Issue management guidelines, and
- Issue escalation procedures.

## Impact of Program Management

Looking back on our experience since July 1996, program management has made a number of impacts on the organization.

1. The Program Management Office was able to quickly implement a project accounting system that provides project financial performance data on a weekly basis. The project accounting information leads the general ledger by as much as one hundred and twenty days and supports a level of detail tracking and analysis that is not currently available in the Alliance financial management systems. Timely and detailed project financial information is critical to effective decision making.
2. Use of automated tools for project control (status reporting, issues management, change management, deliverable management, workplan management) went from almost 0 to 65 active users. The key success factors in gaining system acceptance and utilization were:
    - Commitment by project managers and executive sponsors to use the tools,

- Support for HTML (Netscape) clients,
- Application training, and
- Project management awareness and skill building training.

3. Program management became recognized as having a positive impact on IT project performance and is beginning to have an impact at the executive leadership level outside of IT. Success in program management for IT is generating interest in the same kind of approach in other change efforts.
4. Executive decisions (as they are impacted by IT projects) are now more likely to be based on data rather than individual perceptions. Prior to having detailed project data, project decisions were based largely on subjective criteria. Now, managers look at project management performance, project financial performance, resource deployments, and the project queue when making decisions.
5. A portfolio approach has provided an understanding of where individual project performance stands in relationship to the larger view. Many of the projects are important, but some are more important. Project priorities can shift depending upon technical, organizational, or environmental factors. The portfolio approach allows management to "see the forest" and exert more effective management control.
6. As the program matures, new sets of issues start to arise. Now that a number of project have been completed, the task of organizing the project outputs into knowledge objectives becomes more critical. The teams are comfortable using a workgroup environment and are capable of effectively sharing knowledge. The tools must continue to evolve to support a more sophisticated knowledge management and sharing process.

## Lessons Learned

As we continue to improve our program management processes, we have identified a number of "lessons learned." By incorporating these lessons learned into our ongoing processes, we hope to improve the program's overall performance and mitigate risk. Some of the key lessons learned are:

1. The Alliance was formed from four separate organizations. In many cases, the Alliance was a single organization in name only and not able to move at the pace dictated by the tactical plans. Infrastructure building projects are generally less threatening and less visible politically and are therefore "safer" in the initial execution of the tactical plan. More visible projects that touch core business processes should have added contingency for time and more emphasis and investment in organizational change management.
2. Technology for project accounting and project control is critical to enabling executive decision making and project management processes. There is an overhead to support this technology that tends to be ongoing throughout the life of the program. You must commit resources (human, financial, and technology) to the program technology.
3. Plan on significant and ongoing investment in project management training and skill building. Training needs to be appropriate to the level of the individual. Use just in time and reinforcement training to help teams improve specific areas of performance (status reporting, issue management, scheduling, etc.).
4. Resistance to change was greater than anticipated which resulted in incorrect assumptions on pace of change. People's ability to participate in and support change are larger constraints on project and program performance than is the availability of financial resources.
5. Program management and project management is not only educating IT but also educating the business unit sponsor and the end user. A greater degree of project discipline is required from IT; business users need to learn how to become partners in the process. As partners, they share responsibility for the outcome not just final acceptable or rejection of the end product.
6. Use an implementation team to focus on bringing up the Program Management Office. If possible, the PMO should be started before other projects are launched in order to establish the common process and technology environment. A focused implementation team can work out the logistics of the program office, performing initial training, and establish the initial set of program standards quickly. Projects that launch before the PMO is ready are harder to pull back into the program umbrella.
7. Run the PMO as a project. It should have a project charter, workplan, and required deliverables. As a project, the PMO is subject to all the standards establish for any other project in the program.

## Conclusion

Rip Van Winkel eventually adjusted to his new environment. He embraced the strange new world that he encountered and actually found that world preferable to the one he had left behind. The IT organization at The Health Alliance is significantly different today from where it was a year ago. Project management processes are better understood, a number of projects have been successfully planned and completed, and components of the future state information systems are starting to be deployed and benefit the organization.

In health care today, far-reaching change is upon us. The Health Alliance is aggressively moving to embrace this change. Program management provides the structure, coordination, and information needed to rapidly implement and achieve a functioning, competitive and growing integrated healthcare delivery system that can fully realize the goals of decreased cost and exceptional quality.

# PROJECT MANAGEMENT: THE NEXT CENTURY

# PMBOK Functions

# Why Is Traditional Accounting Failing Managers?

Gary Cokins, CPIM, ABC Technologies, Inc.

## Summary

Critics have claimed that traditional managerial accounting is at best useless and at worst dysfunctional and misleading. Today's general ledger and budgeted spending systems support departmental and "stovepipe" managerial philosophies. In contrast, activity-based costing (ABC) information supports project and process-based thinking.

Cross-functional processes are now recognized as the integrating theme for how work gets done, how outputs are produced, and how customers get served. Only ABC can bring true fact-based measures and visibility to costs, without the dreaded and often distorting cost allocations. Further, ABC both quantifies what all outputs cost, in addition to product costs, and more importantly why things have costs. These insights are gained by identifying and measuring the cause-and-effect related activity cost drivers. Cost drivers provide sound logic, which leads to orders-of-magnitude and better accuracy of the costs of outputs, products, services, and customers.

ABC then serves as the framework to associate these true costs with their value and waste, their strategic importance, their level of performance, and other "attributes" of work. All of this cost and trait data are further translated into which products, customers, or internal company-sustaining people cause and consume all of the resources . . . and in exactly what proportions.

Ultimately cost data is simply a means-to-ends where the ends are the decision-making of the organization. Today an emerging focus is to become a "learning organization." Unlike traditional accounting reports, which managers react to by being happy or sad, ABC data makes them smarter!

ABC is becoming successful because there is a structural problem resulting from deficiencies with the *existing,* traditional financial accounting methods. Traditional accounting relies on the general ledger (G/L), which is a collection of account balances where transactions are recorded. The G/L's focus is not on what is the work and conversion of raw materials into finished products; in contrast, ABC's focus is on the work.

As a solution, ABC acts as a translator for the G/L, not a replacement for it. The G/L's substantial payroll-related amounts give managers virtually no visibility to the *content of work* going on nor the interrelationships between that work and other work or products or customer services. To further weaken the G/L's usefulness, it is organized around separate departments or cost-centers, whereas individuals within these artificial groupings are continuously commingling and multi-tasking within and among the numerous projects and core business processes.

ABC solves the G/L's structural deficiency by translating the G/L into a much differently organized and more flexible database. One key difference is that ABC describes the activities with an "action-verb-adjective-noun" grammar convention, such as "inspect defective products." People relate better to this cost-wording, and it also allows for linear relationships with variable costs and their activity costs rates. This information is essential for cost estimating.

How long will companies want to perpetuate making decisions with their traditional costing systems? How long can they remain competitive with them?

## Why Is Traditional Accounting Failing Managers?

The approach selected to describe this paper is by using an interview of myself, the author:

***Q 1.1: Some organizations would argue that they have gotten along for years without using activity-based costing or ABC. Why then would they need ABC today?***

A 1.1: In the past, organizations were profitable or, if they were in the not-for-profit sector, were well funded. Also, in the past, their organization was simpler relative to today, with less variety and diversity of products, services, and customers. Consequently their overhead costs were lower.

In the past, organizations could make mistakes, and their profitability would mask the impact of their wrong or poor decisions. They could carry unprofitable products and customers because the winners would more than offset the losers.

Back then, organizations could still survive with misleading cost allocations and the lack of visibility from their general ledger cost systems.

Today the margin for error is slimmer. Organizations can't make as many mistakes as they could in the past and remain competitive. Price quotations, capital investment decisions, and make versus buy decisions all require a sharper pencil today. Many of their competitors understand the cause-and-effect



PROJECT MANAGEMENT INSTITUTE 28th Annual Seminars & Symposium
Chicago, Illinois: Papers Presented September 29 to October 1, 1997

connections which drive costs. The resulting price squeeze is making life more difficult relative to the past.

And today, the road is no longer long and straight, but it is windy with bends and hills, which doesn't give much visibility or certainty to the future. Organizations need to be agile and continuously transform their cost structures and work. This is difficult to do when organizations don't understand their cost structures and economics.

***Q 1.2: ABC seems to have a "schizophrenic" reputation. Some people claim that ABC is just a better way to more accurately allocate costs to products or customers. Others suggest that ABC is a better form of cost information used for continuous improvement and to manage business processes. Which is correct? Is ABC an accounting tool or a management tool?***

A 1.2: ABC is schizophrenic because it is both a better process management tool and a cost assignment-to-outputs tool.

Many organizations need the data strictly for *strategic purposes*. Complexity and increased proliferation of products and customers have increased their overhead costs, without an adequate way of tracing to who or what consumes it. Organizations can no longer intuitively guess where and with whom they are making profit. They need ABC to segment the diversities and properly trace the consumption of their resource costs.

Organizations also realize that regardless of the source of their profits, they must manage the process costs and remove waste and unused capacity. Their use of a ABC is for *operational purposes*. Since the structural inadequacies of their existing general ledger systems deny them a process-based view of workflow cost across their organizational boundaries, they need ABC to understand where those costs are, what drives them to occur, and which costs may be low-value-added or potentially impactable near term.

Up-front, these organizations use the ABC data to reengineer by defining the as-is state, which usually introduces some organizational shock since the real truth about costs comes out. They focus on activity management. Post reengineering organizations next link the same ABC data with their continuous improvement, TQM, and process management programs. Many will use ABC data as the inputs for their "balanced scorecard" performance measurements.

The ABC data is simply means to ends. That is why ABC should never be labeled as an improvement program or "fad of the month." ABC data simply makes visible the economics of the organization, which are occurring with or without ABC present.

***Q 1.3: Please describe the key issues and concerns that people and organizations have with activity-based costing, or ABC.***

A 1.3:The issues with ABC depend on where an organization is with regard to ABC, and there are three starting points:

- *Beginners*—the issue is how to get started. They know ABCs' value but not the path.
- *Pilots*—pilots have begun their discovery with ABC. They know there have been some implementation failures. They want to increase the likelihood of success.
- *Advanced and mature users*—these organizations have always been interested in two goals: (1) to institutionalize ABC into a permanent, repeatable, and reliable production system, and (2) to establish the ABC output data to serve as an enabler to their ongoing improvement programs, like TQM, change management, cycle-time compression, core competency, business process reengineering, and so on.

But there are new emerging issues for the *advanced and mature ABC users*:

- integrating the ABC output data with their decision-support systems, like capital investment justification
- integrating the ABC data with cost estimating and predictive planning, including activity-based budgeting (ABB)
- learning the skills and rules for re-sizing, reshaping, re-leveling, and otherwise readjusting the model's structure in response to solving new business problems with the ABC data
- collecting and automatically importing the data into the ABC system.

***Q 1.4: Perhaps you could give us a basic overview of what ABC is. More specifically, could you explain how ABC works, and how is it different from what is done today?***

A 1.4: It's easier to understand ABC if we start with what is done today. If you simply ask a sample of managers how happy they are with their existing financial data to make decisions in order to improve their organization's competitiveness, you can guess the answer. It's thumbs-down. We've already touched on some of the causes that stem from structural deficiencies of the general ledger. They simply can't relate to the data or find it wanting.

Many financial systems are used for command-and-control accounting police purposes when in fact the best uses for financial data is for predictive planning, cost estimating, and decision support. Again the traditional general ledger approaches fall short with rigid two or three step allocation structures, which still result in arbitrary allocations, not traced due to causality. And these cost allocation schemes do not capture the step-variable cost behavior that one gets from the cost assignment logic and cost drivers used in an ABC system.

Most organization's cost allocation schemes are at best useless, and at worst dysfunctional and misleading. There are plenty of "allocation food fights," which disturb people, including transfer-pricing.

ABC resolves and corrects these structural shortcomings of the general ledger by using an advanced cost re-assignment mechanism. ABC flows costs with the understanding that events trigger work to happen. Consequently, the costs, which measure the event's effect, then flow back towards from the event. Most events, called activity cost drivers, start with customers who effectively place the demands on work which then shows up as costs.

ABC does not use general ledger language like "payroll" or "maintenance" but instead uses phrases like "process international invoices." These phrases, which describe the work activities that people and equipment perform, are worded as an "action verb-adjective-noun" grammar convention; employees can relate much better to this language and sense they can favorably impact the work it describes.

Next, these defined activities, which have translated the organization chart into its elements (hence dissolving the chart and leaving it behind), can be directly traced to those suppliers, products, base-services, customers, or outputs that are causing the work to occur and fluctuate. Better yet, this tracing can recognize in what proportions the diversities of the cost receivers uniquely govern the consumption of the work costs.

If work is consumed by other work that is too far removed to recognize the diversity of the final cost receiver, that is fine with ABC. By default that work activity cost can be directly traced to other work that does drive it and which is intermediate to the final products. For example, when personnel spends more time recruiting with a high turnover area, the work of that area is effectively more expensive.

This power of ABC to reassign cost along an arterial flow network without regard to levels or "steps"—and at the element of work, not a department—gives it great accuracy. ABC is far superior to cost allocations computed on "columns-to-rows" spreadsheets, which only the accountants can understand.

To add to the power of ABC, the same activity cost data used to reassign costs to the cost receivers can also be assigned sequentially and additively to see and understand the costs of the end-to-end business processes. Again, the structural deficiency of the vertical cost-center structured general ledger prevents managers from seeing this horizontal view.

Finally, ABC allows "attributes" to be scored and graded against the activities. ABC attributes allow managers to differentiate activities from one another. Multiple activities can be simultaneously tagged with these grades, and of course the dollars trail along at the activity level.

***Q 1.5: You have been involved with ABC since the 1980s—some people refer to you as one of its "pioneers." By looking back on its history, what pet peeves do you have about how ABC has progressed?***

A 1.5: First, I'm not so sure I'm a pioneer as much as an archaeologist. Most managerial improvement methods have been written about and discussed for decades. I was fortunate to get involved when the tools and greater needs for them emerged.

The areas of ABC which have surprised me as the impediments to progress with the ABC movement are: (1) the slow recognition of ABC as a behavioral change management tool, (2) the excess amount of unnecessary detail and precision placed in the pilot ABC models, and (3) poor model designs and architecture of the cost flow assignment logic.

1. ABC project managers have been slow on the up-take to recognize the behavioral change management aspects of the ABC data. ABC is a socio-technical tool, and the emphasis should be on the socio. Many ABC project teams see ABC as simply a better measuring scheme or cost allocator. However, it's real value is introducing undebatable fact-based data, which can be used by employees to build business cases, to quickly recognize business problems or opportunities, and to test hypotheses. The last use is important so that good conclusions can be attained prior to taking actions.

2) Many accountants and engineers presume that "precise inputs equates to accurate outputs." With ABC's reassignment of cost logic, errors are not additive or compounding; they dampen out as the accumulating costs approach their ultimate cost receiver. As a consequence, the ABC flow model can tolerate reasonable input errors and still yield roughly right numbers. In the end, the level of accuracy depends on what decisions are made with the data.

Unfortunately, the ABC teams never start at the end decision and discuss the accuracy requirements of the data, but they presume tremendous levels of detail and precise inputs. This leads to oversized ABC models that are way past the diminishing returns on incremental accuracy. The ABC projects fail under the weight.

3) Poor model designs lead to poor results. It's that simple. Yet most ABC projects are first-time efforts, even if they are lead by very talented people. As a consequence, the models usually have odd shapes and sizes that are inconsistent with the degrees of variety or diversity of the products and customers and with the degree of complexities in the business processes.

***Q1.6: It appears as if the case for ABC data is pretty strong. What do you see as the future for ABC?***

It goes without saying that ABC will become the organization's permanent, repeatable, and reliable production system for managerial accounting. The only issue is how quickly that will happen. And as institutionalization happens, the subsequent issues are: (a) how deep and granular will the levels of detail be for the ABC system, and (b) how frequently will the costs be updated. Today many organizations refresh their ABC data monthly, but with greater computing power coming, we'll head into the shorter time intervals of weekly, daily, and, ultimately, dynamic costing.

The future of ABC is in the areas of (1) tool convergence, (2) data visualization and animation, (3) uses of the data for predictive planning and unused capacity management, and (4) model design validation, industry standardization, and certification.

1) The output of ABC data is frequently the input to another system, such as a customer order quotation system. There will be a convergence as these now somewhat separate tools become part of a tool suite.

2) Someone once said to me, "If you can't draw a picture of it, you can't understand it." Data visualization is coming. With ABC, visualizing is a natural for better viewing the model's shape and assignment logic. Also, for viewing the business processes, ABC's end-to-end view of activities, it will be logical to move beyond racked-and-stacked numbers and move to viewing process flow charts.

3) ABC is not really an "accounting police" tool to punish people for their past behavior. ABC data is business intelligence used to either (a) see and assess things, through the lens of costs and work activities, much of which have never been seen before; or used to (b) estimate the cost consequences of future decision options.

For assessing the organization's behavior, ABC's data will give much more clear and accurate views of the costs of just about anything imaginable to place a cost on. Fact-based decision-making will replace today's reliance on people's intuition and assertions.

The big opportunities for ABC are in predictive planning, cost estimating, and managing unused or unnecessary capacity. Here the ABC model will have captured all the cost rates and traits of the current state. I like to think of it as the "inertia" or speed the organization is currently running at, and burning resource costs at that rate. That data is all calibrated to use for project future costs of various "what-if" scenarios. This is done by estimating new quantities of the cost drivers to "reverse-calculate" the ABC model to solve for the level of resources to be consumed in the "to-be" state.

4) The rash of poor model designs and construction will be resolved as the rules and properties of ABC models are documented and understood. Industry process templates and standard dictionaries, albeit a level or so above where employees uniquely define their work, are inevitable. They will speed an ABC start-up plus introduce consistency, which is sorely needed by the benchmarking industry that suffers from an apples-and-Oreos syndrome.

***Q1.7: You have consistently stated that an impediment that has slowed widespread acceptance of ABC involves the "rate of learning" about ABC. Training courses and books exist on ABC. Why then do you see the ABC movement as slow-going?***

A1.7: There are three factors which seem to apply drag or friction to the ABC movement, which itself is actually picking up steam: (1) costs are outside most people's comfort zones, (2) the degree of organizational resistance to change, including ABC, is grossly underestimated, and (3) for some organizations, there is insufficient cost pressures, but these organizations are becoming a minority.

(1) Costs measure the effect of events much more than their root cause. And costs are not tangible or physical. You cannot go to a store and purchase a couple of costs. What would they look like? Costs really reside in an abstract information space somewhat like a shadow or echo. I like ABC costs to be thought of as a sonar-imaging system; here we "see" the effect of the cost drivers.

(2) Resistance to change is natural to people. They like the status quo. They usually will not try something new or different unless there is some combination of (a) dissatisfaction with their current situation, and (b) a vision of what a better condition looks like. With regard to managerial accounting, most people are unhappy with their current accounting data but cannot articulate why. When they are helped with understanding why, they then see ABC as a rescue line that resolves the structural deficiencies of their general ledger data.

(3) The more that organizations discover they are in a profit margin squeeze, that they are threatened with limited funding, or become anxious that they cannot comfortably gauge the cost consequences of their decisions, then the more they take interest in ABC.

***Q1.8: Traditional information systems are created with planning that emphasizes a substantial amount of up-front "requirements definition." Is this practice effective for designing ABC systems?***

A1.8: The step of requirements definition planning often taken with systems projects may be appropriate for most projects, but not necessarily for ABC. ABC has a tremendous "leveling problem"—it is difficult to determine in advance what levels of detail and where. There are many interdependencies within an ABC model that ultimately govern those levels plus the accuracy of the outputs. Hence, it is better to quickly construct a baseline ABC model and then iteratively make adjustments from that scale model.

A rapid ABC model design simulation also helps accelerate the organizational learning about how ABC really works, not just its concepts and benefits. The initial ABC model built this way is basically a disposable, throwaway model, a place where you can make your mistakes and fix them in the next iteration. The ABC model design remains intact; it is just the data that can be discarded. However, surprising to the participants, the output data already begins to directionally reveal new facts or results counter to the organization's belief system that up until now were part intuition and part legacy.

The alternative to a rapid design followed by iterative adjusting is a potentially large-scale failure. I look at the up-front scale model design as an insurance plan; you pay a little premium, just a few days up-front, to prevent a later disaster, plus assure that everyone's learning about ABC is taking place.

If you teach people to fish, they can fish forever. Quickly learning what ABC is all about and what data is involved can allow fine-tuning via sensitivity analysis based on the initial ABC model.

***Q1.9: We frequently hear about the importance of cost drivers? What is so important about them, and are there any misconceptions about them?***

A 1.9: Cost drivers are the "pump and valve" of the ABC cost reassignment system. They are critical because not only do they segment and flow the costs to reflect the diversity of the products and customers, but they govern the accuracy of the output.

Resource drivers are the first out of the chute. They simply reflect how much various people do various work activities. Here, precision is not as important as simply having plenty of little estimates. Next, the activity cost drivers take over. They reassign the costs toward their target final cost objects. What is nice about these is that they truly have a linearly variable relationship between the activity cost and its driver quantity. A large misconception is that all activity cost drivers must be measurable and imported from a transaction-based data file. In reality, employees have tremendous insights in their brains and can estimate the quantities or proportions of the driver to their cost objects. There is a minor fall-off in accuracy, but at a tremendous cost-savings in data collection.

The largest misconception is that overall accuracy, or the flip-side error, of the final cost outputs (products, base-services, and customers) is governed by the precision and accuracy of the inputs. In reality, since ABC is a reassignment system, error does not snowball, it dampens out. And the assignment logic is really a "direct-costing" architecture. Hence, the real contributing source of accuracy is not the input data, but the cost assignment logic network itself!

***Q 1.10: You have said that ABC's future would be part of a "tool convergence." Can you expand on that?***

A 1.10: Cost data is only part of the equation. As is often mentioned, after senior management has set a vision and defined the strategies, the all important core business processes become the mechanism to deliver the value. Processes are key and time, quality, service, and cost, all "derivatives" of the process that are inextricably braided together. You really cannot measure one in isolation from the others.

Process modeling software tools are becoming important. When operations that are sorely in need of redesign are attempted to be fixed, the big decisions have been made by gut feel. Modeling removes relying on intuition. When process modeling and ABC are combined, you get synergy. By adding simulation software for what-if scenarios, and adding flow-charting software for visualization, and adding on-line analytical processing (OLAP) software tools for instant diagnosis, you develop a suite of tools. These software tools are converging into a suite of tools. A carpenter with only a hammer would be somewhat limited, but not so with a belt full of tools.

Management science can be operationalized out of the textbooks and into practice as the information revolution marries the methodologies revolution.

# A Framework for Applying Various Project Risk Management Methods and Tools

Kalle Kähkönen, VTT, Building Technology, Finland

## Introduction

Project risk management has been an area of active and continuous research and development, particularly within the last three decades. As one main result, numerous manual and computer-based methods and tools have emerged to manage risks when projects are planned and carried out. The theoretical assumptions and mathematics behind these techniques can surprisingly differ from each other. It seems obvious that a single technique has rather limited possibilities to be applicable and provide real benefits. This usefulness is particularly linked to the type of project and experience/knowledge of the project key personnel and organization in question. Thus, a single technique cannot usually provide a satisfying solution; rather one should:

- Know the significant principles of successful project risk management. In general, keep it simple, and make it more complex only when it is useful to do so [Chapman and Ward 1997].
- Master several practical techniques.

A wide variety of different manual and computer-based methods and tools is a somewhat confusing and even frustrating situation for project practitioners who are trying to identify and after that apply the appropriate methods and tools. The objective of this paper is to provide a "road map" for applying various project risk management methods and tools for practical project risk management purposes. First,

**Exhibit 1.** Effectiveness of Various Proactive and Reactive Techniques with Respect to Different Projects and Their Level of Uncertainty

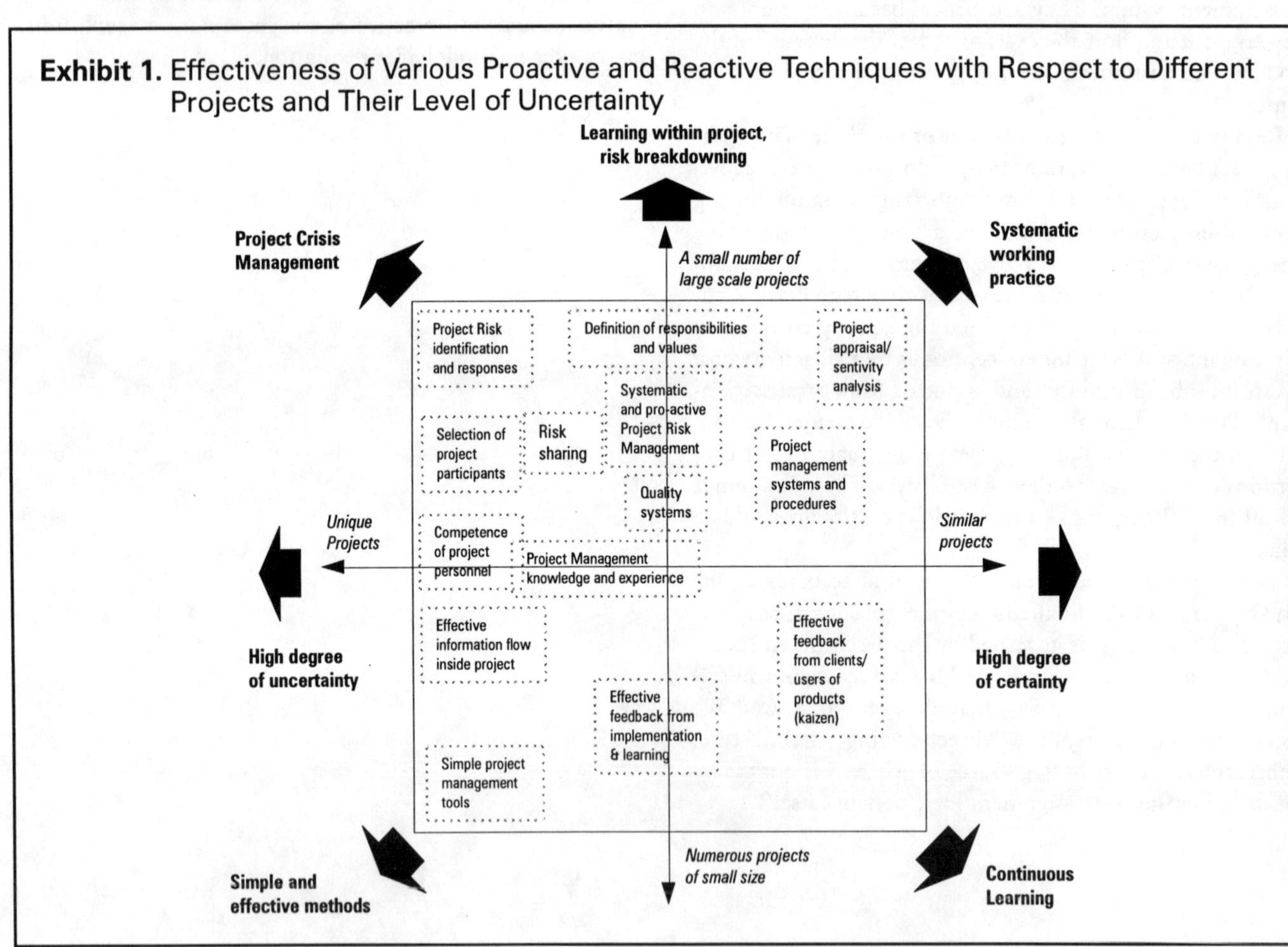

**Exhibit 2.** Proactive Project Risk Management Process Model

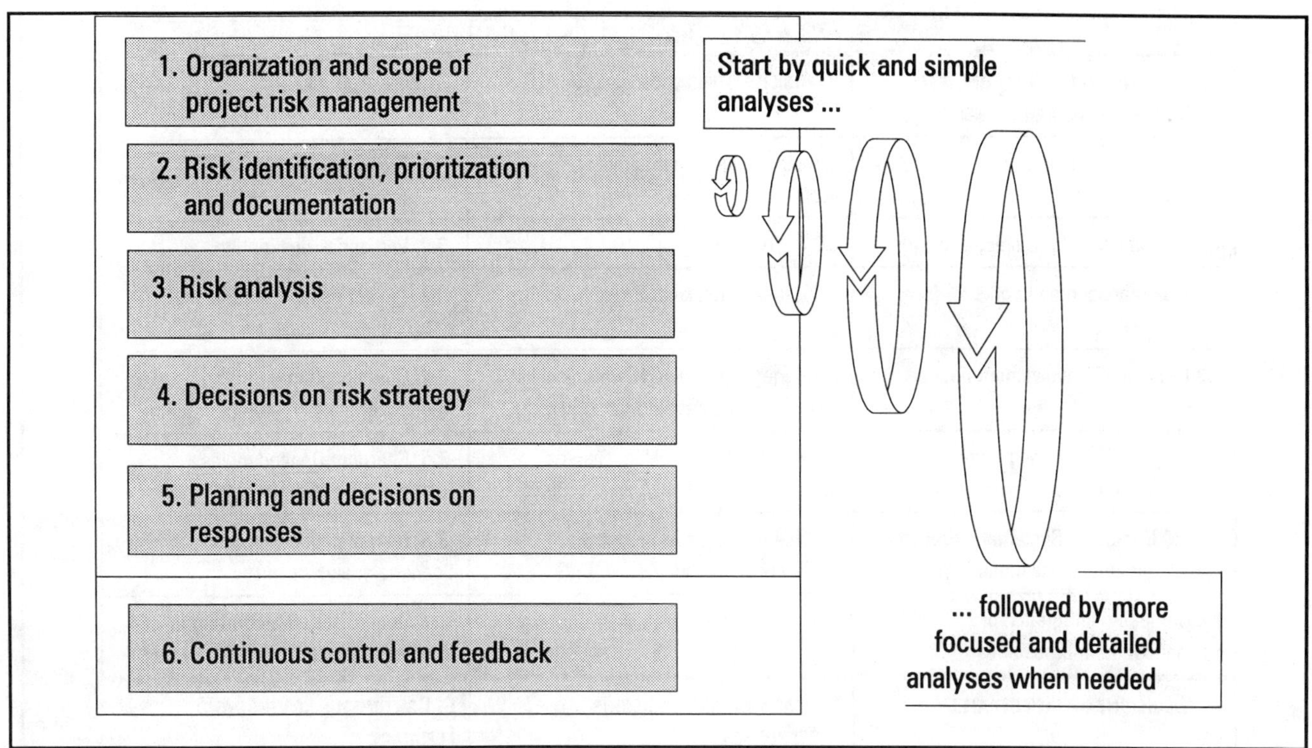


the relevance of reactive and proactive project risk management approaches is analyzed with respect to different projects and their needs. Second, a generic model of project risk management processes is presented together with various approaches/levels to carry out tasks of these processes.

## Project Risk Management Processes

### Proactive and Reactive Risk Management

Definition: Systematic project risk management means advanced preparation and decision-making for minimizing the consequences of possible adverse future events and, on the contrary, to maximize the benefits of positive future events.

According to this definition project risk management is more relating to "planning" rather than "management," which usually refers to on-line control of events. It is widely accepted that project risk management must be seen as a proactive technique to identify potential risks, analyze them, do response planning, and make necessary decisions. However, the usefulness of proactive risk management is strongly dependent upon the characteristics of business and projects in question. Many project management and general management techniques seem to effectively reduce uncertainty under certain conditions. Likewise, proactive project risk management seems to be the most useful approach when the levels of uniqueness and uncertainty of projects is high and the projects are relatively large ones (see Exhibit 1).

### Proactive Risk Management Process

Rather wide agreement exists within the research and development community about the principles of the proactive systematic risk management (for example, see Anon 1996; Chapman 1995; Diekmann et al. 1998; Norris et al. 1988; Raftery 1994; Wideman 1992). Additionally, when we take into account various needs of different projects, the decision-making that produces the required risk management plan and required control/information feedback, we get a representation of the systematic project risk management process, which now includes six sub-processes (see Exhibit 2).

One should notice that the generic model shown in Exhibit 2 has two sub-processes (4 and 5) addressing risk responses and decision-making relating to them. Too often the proactive project risk management efforts put too much emphasis on risk analysis, resulting in a situation where response planning has only a minor role.

**Exhibit 3.** Project Risk Management Road Map: Levels And Strategies

| PROJECT RISK MANAGEMENT ROAD MAP | | |
|---|---|---|
| **1. ORGANIZATION AND SCOPE OF PROJECT RISK MANAGEMENT** | **2. RISK IDENTIFICATION** | **3. RISK ANALYSIS** |
| 1.0 No need to focus on risk management | 2.1 Experience and intuitive awareness | 3.1 Project risk list |
| 1.1 Personal task for project manager | 2.2 Interviewing | 3.2 Verbal risk description |
| 1.2 Risk management workshop(s) | 2.3 Generic checklist: Broad headings | 3.3 Project risk list & additional data: Causes, timing, responsibility |
| 1.3 Facilitator's involvement needed | 2.4 Generic checklist: Hierarchical list including more detailed risk drivers | 3.4 Quantification & charting: Impacts of risks on project outcome |
| 1.4 Project: Systematic procedures for continuous risk management | 2.5 Experiential checklist: Generic headings + problems/earlier projects | 3.5 Charting: Dependencies between individual risks |
| 1.5 Company: Systematic procedures for continuous risk management | 2.6 Use of checklists + decision conferencing technique | 3.6 Quantification & charting : Scenario analysis |
| 1.6 Company: Integration of management procedures | | 3.7 Quantification & charting : Simulation model |
| **4. DECISIONS ON RISK STRATEGY** | **5. PLANNING AND DECISIONS ON RESPONSES** | **6. CONTINUOUS CONTROL AND FEEDBACK** |
| 4.1 Modify project objectives | 5.1 Response list | 6.1 Responsibility control |
| 4.2 Risk avoidance | 5.2 Response list & additional data: costs of responses, timing | 6.2 Advanced reporting practice |
| 4.3 Risk prevention | 5.3 Quantification & charting: Effects of planned responses | 6.3 Regularly updated experiential checklist (hierarchical) |
| 4.4 Risk mitigation | 5.4 Quantification & charting: Trade-off analysis | 6.4 Project risk knowedge base: Problems encountered, close events |
| 4.5 Develop contingency plans | | |
| 4.6 Keep options open | | |
| 4.7 Monitor situation | | |
| 4.8 Accept risk without any actions | | |

## Project Risk Management Road Map

The project risk management model presented in Exhibit 1 can be used to portray a "road map" of various reachable levels and/or strategies of proactive project risk management practice. In Exhibit 3 different levels of each sub-process reflect our current understanding of the different learning and performance stages of the proactive project risk management sub-processes. These levels provide a simple means to explain the spectrum of various possibilities to carry out each sub-process.

Each category in this map presents first the most simple techniques followed by gradually increasing levels of work and complexity. It is important to focus on the added value, which is provided by the subsequent level when one is trying to identify the appropriate level for a particular situation.

**Exhibit 4.** Project Risk Map and Its Graphical Symbols

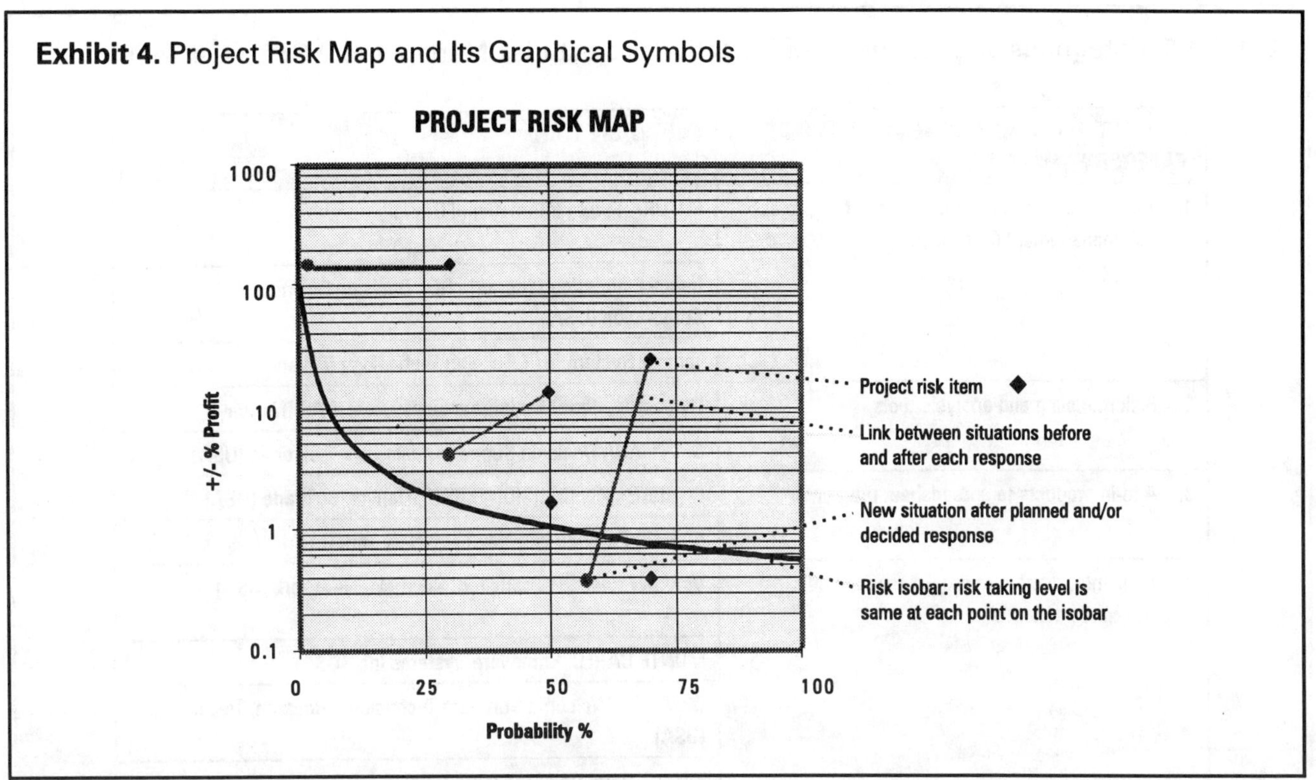


## Levels and Strategies of Proactive Project Risk Management

### Organization and Scope of Project Risk Management

1.0 No need to focus on risk management
1.1 Personal task for project manager
1.2 Risk management workshop(s)
1.3 Facilitator's involvement needed
1.4 Project: systematic procedures for continuous risk management
1.5 Company: systematic procedures for continuous risk management
1.6 Company: integration of various management procedures

Planning has proved to be a crucial task for successful implementation of project risk management. Previous cases of successfully applying project risk management techniques can only be used as a starting point. Usually one needs to tailor the relevant organization and scope carefully to meet the needs of a project in question and capabilities of the project personnel.

### Risk Identification

2.1 Experience and intuitive awareness
2.2 Interviewing
2.3 Generic checklist: broad headings
2.4 Generic checklist: hierarchical list including more detailed risk drivers
2.5 Experiential checklist: generic headings plus problems from earlier projects
2.6 Use of checklists plus decision conferencing technique

Risk identification is in most cases the actual starting point for proactive project risk management. The problem that is too often met during this sub-process is that it feels like paperwork where links to the live project environment are missing. Results from our recently implemented tool (Kähkönen and Huovila 1996) support Niwa's (Niwa 1988) findings that in relatively large-sized projects the function required is a collection of large amounts of regularly updated experience data on risks that actually happened during similar projects in the past. This experience data has proven to add considerable value to the risk identification sub-process and likewise it is decreasing the natural reluctance to carry out new additional tasks.

### Risk Analysis

3.1 Project risk list
3.2 Verbal risk description: characteristics and probability
3.3 Project risk list and additional data: causes, timing of relevance, responsibility
3.4 Quantification and charting: impacts of risks on project outcome
3.5 Charting: dependencies between individual risks

**Exhibit 5.** Categories and Examples of Proactive Project Risk Management Software Tools

| PROJECT RISK MANAGEMENT SOFTWARE CATEGORY | SOFTWARE TOOL |
|---|---|
| 1. Tools supporting systematic pro-active project risk management processes | FUTURA,Futura International Group |
| | Range Estimating Program - REP, Decision Sciences Corporation (USA) |
| | Temper System, VTT Building Technology (Finland) |
| 2. Risk modeling and analysis tools | DynRisk™ , TerraMar Informasjonsystemer AS (Norway) |
| | DPL™, ADA Decision Support Menlo Park, California (USA) |
| 3. Add-in products to spreadsheet programs | Crystal Ball®, DECISIONEERING, Denver, Colorado (USA) |
| | @RISK, Palisade Inc, Newfield, New York (USA) |
| 4. Tools integrated with project management software packages | @RISK Project, Palisade Inc, Newfield, New York (USA) |
| | MONTE CARLO, Primavera Systems Inc. (USA) |
| | OPERA™ , Welcome Software Technology, Houston, Texas (USA) |
| | Risk +, Program Management Solutions Inc. (USA) |

3.6 Quantification and charting : scenario analysis
3.7 Quantification and charting : simulation model

It seems that the risk analysis phase is too often a stumbling block when the systematic project risk analysis is applied. It might happen that the wrong types of analysis methods are applied, resulting in information which is of very little or no use at all. During the analyses of different project risks, one should remember that each step should increase the understanding of those people involved. Further and more detailed analyses should be applied only if they are necessary. A warning signal of selection of the wrong analysis technique is that the team carrying out proactive risk analysis loses touch of the importance and real magnitude of project risks by focusing on fine-tuning numerical values of risk parameters.

## Decisions on Risk Strategy

4.1 Modify project objectives
4.2 Risk avoidance
4.3 Risk prevention
4.4 Risk mitigation
4.5 Develop contingency plans
4.6 Keep options open
4.7 Monitor situation
4.8 Accept risk without any actions

A single project risk can be addressed by one or several responses. The generic responses and risk strategies shown above are based on (Chapman and Ward 1997).

## Planning and Decisions on Responses

5.1 Response list
5.2 Response list and additional data: responsibility
5.3 Quantification and charting: effects of planned responses
5.4 Quantification and charting: trade-off analysis

Generally speaking more attention should be given to response planning and decision-making. Various graphical means—i.e., "charting"—can be very useful for showing the effects of responses and to communicate about them. Exhibit 4 represents a project risk map that is a means to graphically illustrate the overall project risk composed of individual risks, their importance and likelihood, and the effects of planned actions.

## Continuous Control and Feedback

6.1 Responsibility control
6.2 Reporting practice: monthly recorded risk events and updated risk list, standardized risk classification
6.3 Regularly updated experiential checklist (hierarchical)

6.4 Project risk knowledge base: Problems encountered, close events

Continuous control and feedback finally provides a basis for the continuity to proactive project risk management. As mentioned earlier, the experience data about risks, which has took a turn for real problems, has proved to be very useful and can add value to proactive risk management process in a way that encourages project managers to carry on with this task.

## Computer Programs for Proactive Project Risk Management

Current computer programs for project risk management are reflections of our current understanding. The solutions provided by various tools can be surprisingly different. It seems obvious that each software package is providing a limited contribution to the wide spectrum of needs of project risk management. It seems that more holistic tools in terms of overall integration of systematic working method, flexible risk modeling, and analysis capabilities are still missing at present.

Computer programs for project risk management fall generally into four main categories (see also exhibit 5)

1. Tools supporting systematic proactive project risk management processes. These tools are used as guidebooks, checklists or a framework according to which risk identification and analysis process is organized. The tools of this category are simple and easy to use but one must be familiar with the required 'way-of-thinking' and other assumptions when these tools are applied in project practice.
2. Risk modeling and analysis tools. Within these computer programs the attention is on modeling and analysis of risks with the means of probabilistic distributions, Monte Carlo simulation, Latin Hypercube etc. Tools of this type are mathematically oriented.
3. Add-in products to spreadsheet programs. These computer programs are also very much risk analysis oriented tools taking often advantage of the same analysis techniques as in the previous category.
4. Tools integrated with project management software packages. These computer programs are add-inn products to project management software packages. For example, one can model uncertainty with regard to the availability of resources having effects on project schedule. As a result a master schedule showing also effects of identified risks can be obtained.

## Summary and Conclusions

In this paper several cognitive maps of different issues were presented to portray the world of project risk management. These maps were used to explain the scope of project risk management, its sub-processes and levels, relevant strategies, and recent software tools. Particularly the levels and strategies of project risk management can prove to be a means to assess the maturity of the company or its key personnel to carry out proactive project risk management. On the other hand, in many cases it can prove to be irrelevant in trying to reach the most "advanced" levels—for example project risk simulation models.

The "maps" can be used to identify the most appropriate levels of project risk management. These appropriate levels can vary between different companies, business environments, and projects.

### References


Chapman, Chris. 1995. *PRAM Guidelines.* United Kingdom: University of Southampton, Department of Accounting and Management Science: 26.

Chapman, Chris, and Stephen Ward. 1997. *Project Risk Management.* United Kingdom: John Wiley & Sons Ltd.

Diekmann, J.E., E.E. Sewester, and K. Taher. 1988. *Risk Management in Capital Projects.* Construction Industry Institute, Source Document 41, The University of Texas at Austin.

Kähkönen, Kalle, and P. Huovila. 1996. "Systematic Risk Management in Construction Projects." *Proceedings of the Forth Annual Conference of the International Group for Lean Construction.* The University of Birmingham, School of Civil Engineering, August 26–27, Birmingham.

Niwa, K. 1988. "Knowledge-based Risk Management in Engineering: A Case Study in Human-Computer Co-operative Systems." *Wiley Series in Engineering and Technology Management.* John Wiley & Sons, Inc.

Norris, C., J. Perry, and P. Simon. 1992. *Project Risk Analysis and Management.* A guide by APM, The Association of Project Managers, High Wycombe, United Kingdom.

Project Management Institute, Standards Committee. 1996. *A Guide to the Project Management Body of Knowledge (PMBOK Guide).* Upper Darby, PA.

Raftery, John. 1994. *RISK ANALYSIS in Project Management.* London: E & FN Spon.

Wideman, R. Max., ed. 1992. "Project and Program RISK MANAGEMENT." *The PMBOK Handbook Series Volume 6.* Upper Darby, PA.: Project Management Institute.

# A Process-Based Model for Project Planning and Management

William E. Skimin, Integrated Management Systems, Inc.

Imagine that you have been asked to develop two project plans. Each project has a total budget of $200 million and will require the efforts of more than 1,000 people to complete in three years. The first client is a general contractor, and the project is the design and construction of a shopping mall and office complex. The second client is a multinational manufacturing company, and the project is one of several consumer product projects of comparable scope that will be undertaken by the company during that time period. At the first meeting with each client, you will present your recommended planning approach for her project, explaining how your approach will ensure that the project will be completed within the organizational, time, and budget constraints provided. What will you say to each of them?

These projects represent the past and future of project management. Large construction projects fit *A Guide to the Project Management Body of Knowledge (PMBOK Guide)* definition of a project as "a temporary endeavor undertaken to create a unique product or service" (PMI 1996, 4). Note that in this context "past" does not mean obsolete, but rather represents the traditional core from which the project management discipline developed. Recent articles in the business press (for example, Stewart 1995) have described the rapid growth and adoption of project management in non-traditional settings. The list of varied PMI specific interest groups attest to the growing interest in project management by business at large. Ever-shortening product life cycles, simultaneous product development efforts, and downsizing have all placed greater importance on creating organizations that can react quickly to new opportunities. The techniques and practices that comprise project management fit well into this new corporate milieu.

The application of these techniques in new settings, by organizations that have a strong operational focus, represent what the *PMBOK Guide* terms "management by projects."

The term "project management" is sometimes used to describe an organizational approach to the management of ongoing operations. This approach, more properly called management by projects, treats many aspects of ongoing operations as projects in order to apply project management to them (*PMBOK Guide* 1996, 6).

Our second hypothetical project fits into this broader context, whereby the principles of project management are applied to an ongoing, not temporary, endeavor to create a new, but not unique, product.

The approach that you would present to the first client is pretty straightforward; a review of the project planning model presented in the *PMBOK Guide* would be a good starting point. Addressing the needs of the second, however, is quite a bit more challenging; after defining the concept, the *PMBOK Guide* states that "although an understanding of project management is obviously critical to an organization that is managing by projects, a detailed discussion of the approach itself is outside the scope of this document" (*PMBOK Guide* 1996, 6).

## A New Project Planning Methodology

This paper describes a project planning methodology designed for organizations that manage by projects. The approach recognizes that these organizations view projects within the framework of day-to-day operations, not as unique endeavors. Projects are accomplished by organizational units executing defined business processes: development, design, construction, test, validation, and so on. Each unit receives inputs and transforms them into outputs by following a particular process.

In our product development example, for instance, the design department may work on several new product projects simultaneously. As a department, their success will be measured by the quality and timeliness of their output within the department budget constraints. Their performance on a given project will be governed by a combination of the quality and timeliness of the inputs that they receive, and their ability to execute the design process efficiently.

Using the approach described here, planning starts with the identification of the individual business processes that will be required to execute the project. A project plan is built out of those process elements, linked together to represent the flow of work through the project. Managing the project throughout its execution phase focuses on the measurement and communication of process status data, and maintaining stable processes in conformance to the plan. Long-term project management success is based on achieving measurable sustained process improvements.

## Background on Process-Based Planning

In a series of articles originally published in *PMNetwork* and *Project Management Journal,* Kenneth G. Cooper used process simulation models to identify the impact that rework has on project success (Cooper 1993a, 1993b, 1993c, 1994). Observing that "the traditional art/science of complex development project management is a failure," (Cooper 1993a, 5) Cooper concluded that "we need to improve our fundamental understanding of how projects really work" (Cooper 1993c, 21). While his studies raised a number of important issues and demonstrated the truly dynamic nature of projects, most practicing project managers do not have access to the simulation tools utilized by Cooper. Anyone involved in new product development projects, however, would benefit from carefully reading his articles to gain a better understanding of why such projects rarely go according to plan.

A recent *Project Management Journal* article (Giammalvo et al. 1996) described how statistical process control (SPC) techniques had been applied to CPM schedules to identify opportunities for process improvements on a large oil field project. A key element of the approach was the development of process flow charts describing how key portions of the project would be executed. These charts served two important purposes. First, they provided a communications tool, ensuring that all of the project participants had a common understanding of what was to be done and their role in the process. Second, they identified milestone events that could be used to measure the process. Using a combination of CPM and SPC techniques, the authors reported that they were able to shorten the original schedule by nine months, with opportunities for further improvement.

## Key Concepts of the Process Planning Model

The process planning approach suggested here is based on the following underlying concepts:

- Projects are not unique undertakings, but are part of the day-to-day functions of the organization.
- Projects coexist with day-to-day operations, sharing resources and competing for management attention. When faced with a conflict between a project and operations, management will more often than not give priority to the latter, since it generates revenue and ties up capital, while projects are cost centers.
- The primary functions of project management in an organization that manages by projects are to maintain horizontal and vertical project communication and project control.
- Project activities are carried out by non-dedicated organizational groups that are often faced with conflicting priorities and resource shortfalls. Effective communication of requirements is essential in this environment. Horizontal communication refers to communication across units at the same level, generally those that are directly involved with executing project tasks. Vertical communication moves information up the organizational hierarchy, a requirement for effective decision-making. Project control relies on the ability to provide the right information, to the right person or group, at the right time so that problems can be resolved.
- The long-term success of project management in these organizations will be based on achieving sustainable process improvements.
- In an organization where the primary focus is operations, success is measured in operational terms. Each of the project participants is measured in terms of process improvements and efficiency. The project manager will likewise be evaluated on his ability to complete projects efficiently, demonstrating ongoing process improvements (e.g., shorter product development cycles).

## Developing a Process-Based Project Plan

These concepts lead to a very different project planning approach than the "unique undertaking" model. Look, for example, at the process of developing a project activity network. As described in the "Project Time Management" section of the *PMBOK Guide*, the process starts by defining all of the activities that must be performed to complete the project output. Those activities are then sequenced, usually using a CPM-based tool. Duration estimates are applied to the activities, and a project schedule is created.

The procedure for developing a process-based plan is quite different, analogous to planning a factory layout. First, since the activities that will be included in the project plan are a part of the day-to-day operations of the organization, there is no need to undertake an extensive effort to define activities that will be unique for the project. In fact, except in those cases when the organization is implementing a process change (replacing physical model testing with computer-aided analysis, for example), all of the activities should be well defined and documented. Furthermore, the activities will be arranged into "work cells," representing the various processes that will be executed to complete the project. Finally, the plan is completed by linking processes together to represent the flow of work-in-process from one cell to the next.

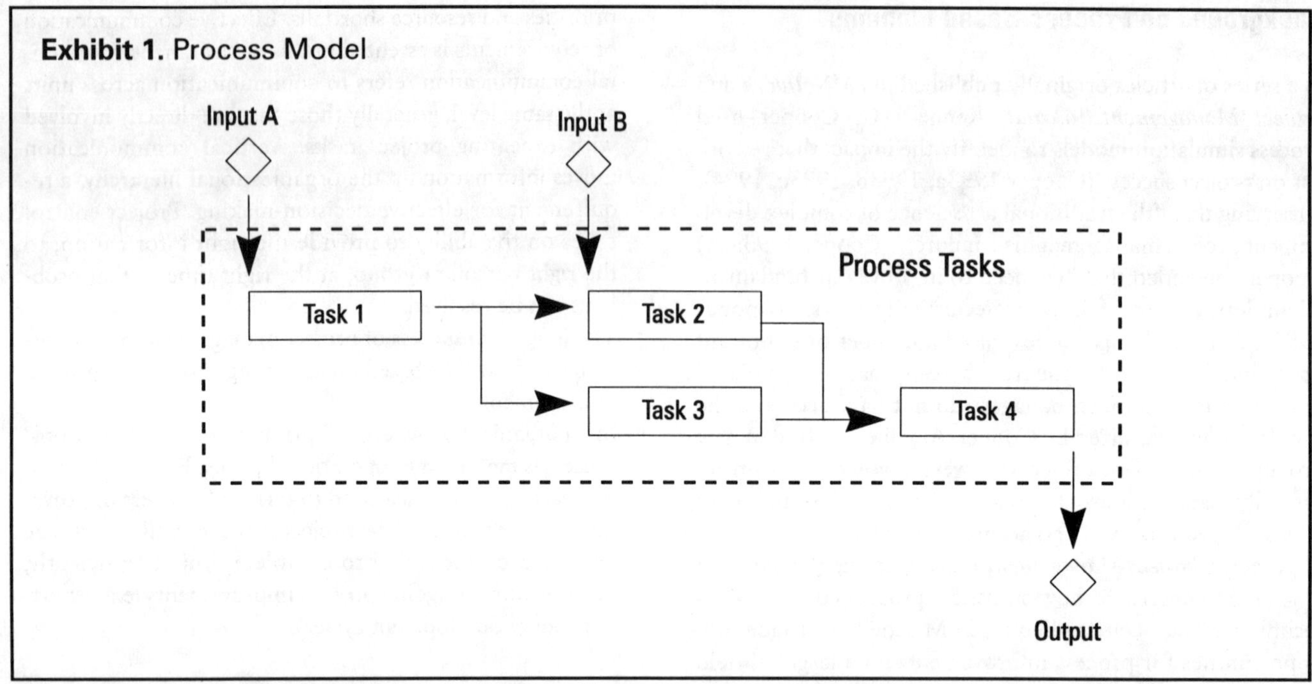

Exhibit 1. Process Model

## Defining Component Processes

Processes are the building blocks of project plans, so it is important that they be correctly identified and defined. In this context, a process is a business function that transforms inputs into outputs that are required by the project. This output may be either the final project deliverable, or an intermediate product that is required by another process participating in the project. There are three elements that must be described for each process:

1. **Inputs**: All processes require one or more inputs before they can be executed. Inputs include information, material, and resources. A process may require that all inputs be available before the process can start, or at various points through the process. For example, the design process requires certain inputs to start, such as product specifications and design resources. Additional inputs in the form of design direction will be needed as the process proceeds. Finally, a design review and approval will be required before the final output can be completed.
2. **Outputs**: Each process produces a specific output. While a process may produce more than one output, there will generally be one principal output that defines the purpose of the process. For example, a market analysis process may produce several detailed studies, but the overall objective is to provide information needed to make a decision on whether or not to proceed with the project.
3. Process Tasks: Each process is defined in terms of the tasks needed to convert inputs into outputs. These tasks may be linked to form self-contained logic networks using standard CPM techniques. Process inputs and outputs should be explicitly identified as milestone events, separate from the tasks representing process work. Resources and costs may be assigned to tasks if required.

Exhibit 1 presents a process model schematic. Note that all of the tasks are contained within the process, and that external relationships are defined solely by the process inputs and outputs.

Creating consistent process definitions, including documenting precise input requirements and output specifications, may be the most difficult and time consuming aspect of implementing this approach; everyone assumes that they understand the processes, but careful scrutiny will reveal many differences in the details. Giammalvo et al., for example, said that this was the most difficult part of their effort, "especially if there are multiple [process] owners or complicated relationships" (Giammalvo et al. 1996, 28). The result, however, is improved understanding and buy-in by the various process participants, both crucial ingredients for long-term success.

## Dependencies in a Process-Based Plan

Dependencies define the sequence in which tasks must be completed. As described in the *PMBOK Guide*, dependencies may be either mandatory or discretionary (i.e., defined by

**Exhibit 2.** Dependencies Between Processes

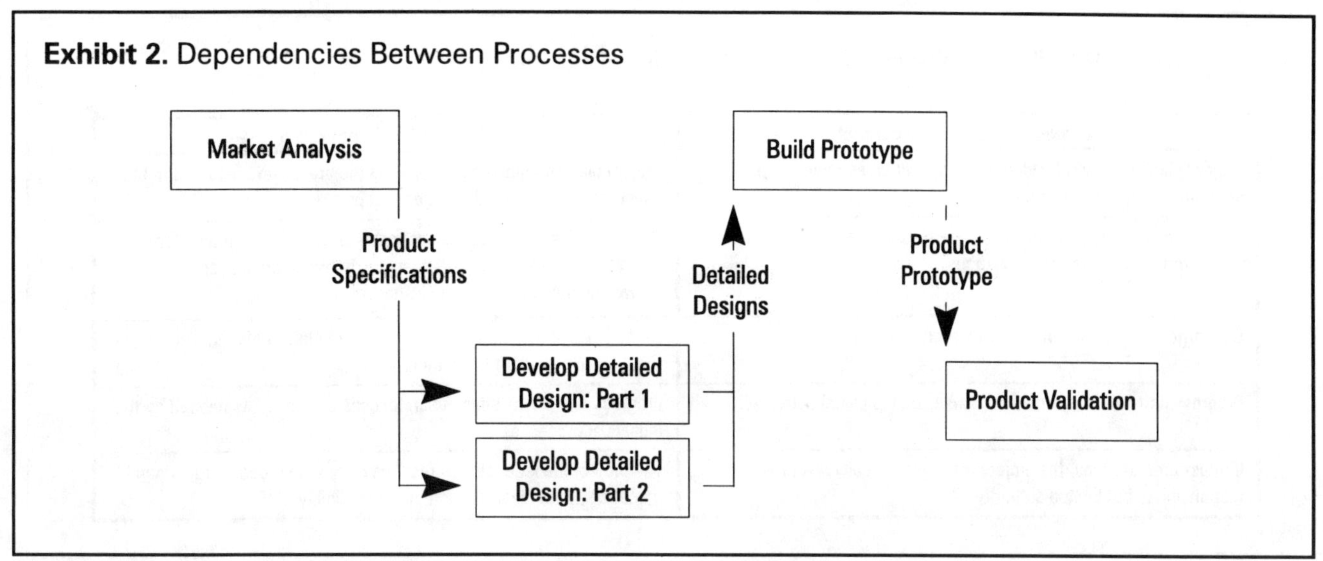


policy, preference or "best practice"). In a process-based plan, dependencies take on a specific meaning depending upon the role that they play in defining the project plan. Dependencies that link tasks *within* a process fall within the broad *PMBOK Guide* definition. The only restriction is that they may not establish a link to a task outside the process.

Dependencies *between* processes are defined strictly in terms of the process inputs and outputs; all dependencies coming into a process must be defined through an input event, while all dependencies out of a process must go through an output. Furthermore, inter-process dependencies must represent the delivery of a specific output from one process to another (an input to the receiving process). These relationships should be well defined and based on specific process requirements.

Dependencies based on external constraints are also tied to process inputs and outputs. For example, a customer-imposed project review date would be represented as a target associated with the outputs that are to be reviewed.

## Building the Project Plan

Two things are required to create a process-based project plan:

- Well defined models, as described above, for each process that is required to execute the project, and;
- An inventory of all of the project outputs, including both the final project deliverables and the intermediate outputs that flow from one process to another.

The list of project outputs defines the scope of the project. This is consistent with the *PMBOK Guide* definition of project scope as "the sum of the products and services to be provided as a project" (PMI 1996, 170). The author provided a more detailed discussion of project scope definition in a process-based planning framework in an earlier article (Skimin et al. 1991).

The process to produce each project output must be identified. For example, if one output is "system durability confirmation," then there must be a process to perform the requisite durability tests. The process model must include a definition of the inputs that are required to perform the tests (e.g., product samples, performance standards, test specifications, test equipment, and technicians) and the specific tasks that must be performed to produce the output. The process model, in effect, defines a plan for that specific project output.

Where there are multiple outputs from a common process, each should be represented individually in the project plan. For example, there may (should!) be a common process model for detailed part design. The inputs to such a process would include detailed technical specifications, product packaging layouts, and product styling data, plus appropriate design and engineering resources. The tasks within the process may include developing an initial design, engineering review, detailing, checking, and release. If there are fifty separate part design drawings required for the project, then the process should be represented fifty times in the project plan. Each instance of the process may be different in terms of the time required to complete each task or the amount of resources required, but the definition of inputs and outputs should be the same for each drawing. It may, for example, take only four weeks to complete the design of a simple bracket assembly, versus sixteen weeks for the control panel, but both need the same inputs and must meet the same design release requirements.

Exhibit 2 shows how inter-process dependencies are used to create a project plan. Each box represents the process to

**Exhibit 3.** Comparison of Two Approaches to Project Planning

| "Unique Undertaking" Approach | Process-based Approach |
|---|---|
| Project planning starts by identifying the activities required to accomplish the project scope. | Project planning starts by identifying the processes that need to be executed to complete the project scope. |
| Dependencies are used to sequence tasks and may represent both mandatory and discretionary linkages. | Dependencies within processes may represent either mandatory or discretionary linkages. Dependencies between processes are based on well defined input/output relationships. |
| One large complex activity network represents the total project plan. | Many small simple networks representing individual processes, linked together to represent the total project |
| Progress and status information focuses on individual activities. | Progress and status information focuses on the inputs needed by the individual processes. |
| In most organizations, the project manager typically has broad responsibility but limited authority. | The project manager shares responsibility with process (functional) managers, with clear division of responsibility. |

create the specific output. The outputs of each process define the links between processes. Note that the multiple instances of the "Develop Detailed Design" process use a common input, "Product Specifications," and that their outputs (Detailed Designs) feed into the "Build Prototype" process.

## Project Organization and Control

The role of the project manager in an organization that manages by projects is different than in a pure project organization. Such organizations generally follow a matrix design, wherein the project manager functions as a coordinator or facilitator. Even in those cases when the project manager has been given broad responsibility for the final outcome of the project, functional managers typically retain control over budgets and resources.

Examined from the process perspective, the division of responsibility between the project and functional managers is clearly defined. Functional managers are responsible for managing individual processes. Their performance is evaluated in operational terms: how efficiently can they convert inputs into outputs? Their attention is therefore focused on improving process efficiency to reduce the cost per unit of output, while meeting quality and schedule requirements. Their major concern is ensuring that they will receive the proper inputs on time to meet their downstream customers' requirements without incurring extra costs. Delays in the receipt of key inputs can lead to the need for extra manpower or overtime to meet output requirements. Nor do they want to have resources sit idle waiting for input to arrive. From a project reporting standpoint, therefore, the functional managers need to know when they will receive inputs so that they can maintain an efficient, low cost process. They also need to be advised about changes in output requirements so that they can react to changing priorities with minimum disruption to ongoing operations. In turn, they need to provide the project manager with process status information.

The project manager is responsible for ensuring that all of the processes are working together to produce the required project outputs. They identify and resolve bottlenecks that cause delays, clarify process requirements, and expedite the flow of inputs and outputs where needed. To do so, they must ensure that the information needed to measure both individual process performance (e.g., the time required to convert inputs to acceptable outputs) and the overall flow of deliverables between processes (e.g., required versus available dates for process inputs) is available. As stated earlier, they must also make sure that the information is communicated between groups and across levels of the organization. Ultimately, they should be able to answer the question, "Where am I in trouble?" for a manager at any level in the organization.

A description of a process-based project control system is provided elsewhere in these proceedings (Chocron and Krolicki 1997).

In large organizations, the process model may require a third dimension in the organizational matrix, the process manager. A description of such a three-dimensional project organization was presented at the 1996 PMI Symposium (Glidewell 1996).

## Summary Comparison Between "Unique Undertaking" and Process-Based Project Planning

As the practice of project management expands, the techniques that comprise the "generally accepted project management knowledge and practices" will be challenged by complex new applications. This paper describes a process-based project planning approach for organizations that manage by projects. Exhibit 3 compares this approach to the "unique undertaking" project planning model described in the *PMBOK Guide*.

### References


Chocron, Elliot, and John Krolicki. 1997. "Deliverables Management: Managing Project Complexity." *Project Management Institute 1997 Proceedings*.

Cooper, Kenneth G. 1993a. "The Rework Cycle: Why Projects Are Mismanaged." *PMNetwork* (February): 5–7.

———. 1993b. "The Rework Cycle: How it Really Works . . . And Reworks. . . . " *PMNetwork* (February): 25–28.

———. 1993c. "The Rework Cycle: Benchmarks For the Project Manager." *Project Management Journal* (March): 17–21.

———. 1994. "The $2,000 Hour: How Managers Influence Project Performance Through the Rework Cycle." *Project Management Journal* (March): 11–24.

Giammalvo, Paul D., Djodi Firman, and Evi Dwiyani. 1996. "Implementation of a Continuous Improvement Program Using Data From CPM Schedules." *Project Management Journal* (June): 24–34.

Glidewell, Don. 1996. "The Three Dimensional Matrix—An Evolution In Project Management." *Project Management Institute 1996 Proceedings*.

Skimin, William E., Darrel E. J. O. Smith, John Krolicki, and Kenneth D. Zenner. 1991. "Scope Management On An Automotive Tooling Project." *Project Management Journal* (September): 22–26.

Stewart, Thomas A. 1995. "The Corporate Jungle Spawns A New Species: The Project Manager." *Fortune* (July).

# The Challenge of Information System "Millennium" Projects: Attracting and Retaining People

Mark Dinman, EDS, St. Louis Resource Center
Cathy Wolanzyk, EDS, Warren, OH Resource Center

**Exhibit 1.** EDS Corporate Values

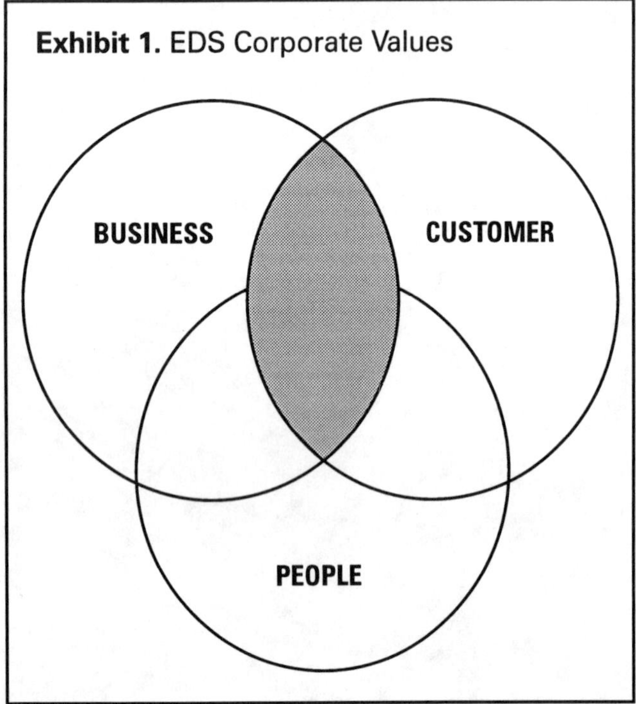


## Introduction

In February 1997, the Information Technology Association of America (ITAA) released a report titled: "Help Wanted: The Information Technology Workforce Gap at the Dawn of a New Century." In testimony before the Senate Committee on Labor and Human Resources on April 24, 1997, Harris Miller, president of the ITAA, described the information technology (IT) workforce shortage as a crisis. Indeed, the IT industry is facing a dramatic human resource crisis. Roughly two-thirds of IT companies view the shortage of skilled IT workers as a barrier to their growth (ITAA 1997). At the time the ITAA study was conducted (December 1996), there were an estimated 190,000 unfilled IT positions—about one vacancy for every ten positions (ITAA 1997). What is driving this industry's growth to create such an acute shortage of skilled human resources?

Information technology now permeates almost every aspect of our daily lives. It is no wonder that the industry has experienced phenomenal growth. More specifically, there are three driving factors to the current IT resource demand. They include:

- Competitive pressures to provide "enterprise-wide" IT solutions
- Explosive growth of the Internet
- Impact of the inevitable century date change (CDC) on information systems
  (Baker, Barrett & Himelstein 1997, p 36).

While the authors find the acute IT industry workforce shortage an extremely interesting and critically important issue to discuss, this paper focuses on project management of CDC projects—particularly with regard to human resources. We will start by giving some background information on EDS corporate values and the challenges IT leaders currently have and will continue to face at the dawn of the next century. Secondly, we will discuss the information systems millennium problem and implications for project management. Next, the authors will share their lessons learned and some final thoughts.

## EDS—Corporate Values System

EDS has over 98,000 employees world-wide providing information technology products and services in forty-five countries. While EDS maintains some products, the bulk of business consists of providing IT services. Recognizing the need to reinforce corporate culture, EDS established a values system, which serves as a reminder to every employee of the importance and interdependence of the three elements: customer, business, and people.

### Our Customer

We are in business to serve our customers' needs. The nature of our work places us in a special kind of partnership with our customers. For us to succeed, the customer must succeed. Therefore, we:

- Provide outstanding customer service
- Achieve results for our customers
- Commit to excellence in everything we do.

### Our Business

The highest standards of conduct and sound business judgment form the cornerstone of the way EDS does business. This enables us to continue to earn the trust of our investors,

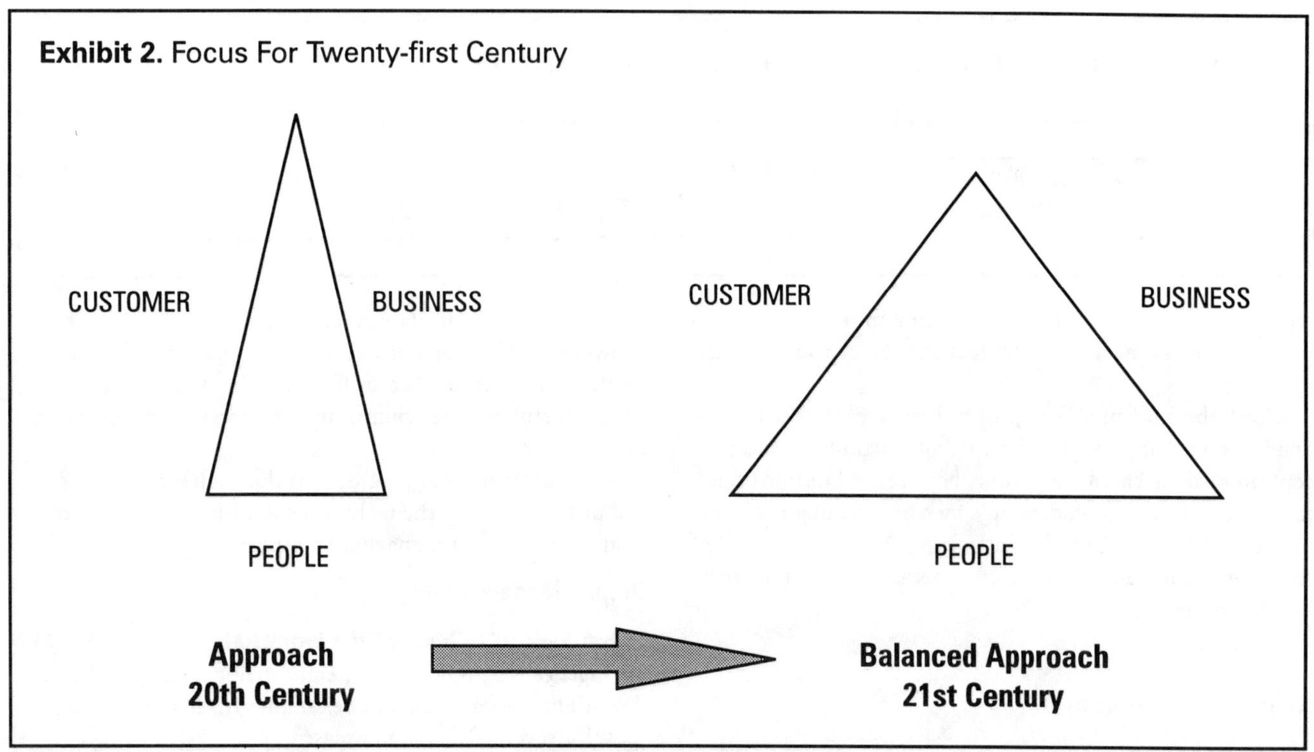


**Exhibit 2.** Focus For Twenty-first Century

customers, and employees. To put these principles into practice, we:

- Maintain the highest standards of ethical behavior
- Work to make a fair profit
- Treat EDS' assets as our own
- Strive for professionalism
- Contribute to the growth of EDS.

### Our People

Our people are our most important resource. We strive to retain the best people by providing an exciting and rewarding place to work. Because we recognize the importance of people, we:

- Value and respect the individual
- Strive to attract, develop, and retain the most outstanding people
- Base rewards on performance, creativity, and contribution
- Promote from within; give the best person the job
- Keep lines of communication open, including access to the open door
- Cooperate and work as a team.

## The Challenge of IT Leadership

The challenge of leadership at EDS is to keep all three aspects of the corporate values in relative balance. In the long run, the success of each value depends on the success of the other two. As a service provider, one cannot run a profitable business if the customer is not satisfied (and successful). Additionally, you cannot meet your customer's needs if you do not have the people with the required skills and mindset.

In the past, EDS and other IT providers did not have the same level of competition that exists in today's marketplace. There were few large service providers. Additionally, the number of differing technologies and their corresponding level of complexity were relatively low compared to today's environment. Consequently, the fewer skills required made it easier to train individuals and have an adequate supply of skilled resources. Organizations such as EDS could rely on IT industry training and the education system to provide an ample supply of IT labor. With an adequate supply of labor and a generally less competitive marketplace, IT service providers focused their efforts on growing their businesses and meeting their customers' needs. If problems were encountered, the inexpensive solution was to utilize more resources. In a less competitive market, profit margins were high enough that expending more resources did not always impact business objectives.

While a strategy focused on customers and business may have worked well for IT services in the twentieth century, this cannot continue into the twenty-first century (Exhibit 2). In today's competitive environment, with the complex technological skill sets required and the shortage of skilled IT workforce, more attention *MUST* be paid to the people aspects. Resource plans must be carefully created to support new business. With lower profit margins in today's competitive

**Exhibit 3.** Annual Cost of One Megabyte of Computer Memory

| | 1963 | 1972 | 1983 | 1996 |
|---|---|---|---|---|
| Actual Dollars | $2,100 | $432 | $14 | $1.08 |
| 1995 Dollars | $10,559 | $1,619 | $22 | $1.08 |

market and higher labor costs, utilizing more resources to meet customers' needs could affect the ability to meet business objectives.

Given the current shortage of skilled IT professionals, individuals not happy with their current assignments and perception of their career directions have several options open to them. This makes leadership's task of retaining individuals more difficult. The task of attracting and retaining skilled resources for millennium projects is perhaps one of the greatest challenges.

## Millennium Projects

### The Problem

Why is there so much hype about the century change? Briefly, for those of you who may not be aware, many information systems represent and process years with just the last two digits (and in a few cases, one digit!). This was originally done to save expensive storage space (Phillips & Farrell 1997) (see Exhibit 3 below). Additionally, as the cost of storage dropped, utilization of two digit years became a standard in some cases. For example, programmers in training at Andersen Consulting were taught to use two digit years as late as 1992 (Phillips & Farrell 1997).

Those systems that are not modified to allow for processing and/or storage of a four-digit year can erroneously interpret "00" as 1900 instead of 2000. Just imagine the possible repercussions of an information system performing incorrect calculations, logical comparisons, and sorts. How many of the Internal Revenue Service's systems are dependent on date calculations? The real problem is NOT systems failing, but appearing to work properly and producing bad data, reports, interfaces, and so on.

The Gartner Group, a respected market research firm in the industry, estimated, as early as 1996, the total cost of addressing the millennium problem to be around $600 billion (*USA Today* 1996). In 1996, Gartner also estimated that only ***one in five*** organizations will have addressed the millennium problem ***by the end of 1997*** and ***only 50 percent*** of the companies in the world will be year-2000-compliant ***by the end of 1999*** (Cassell, Schick, Hall & Phelps 1996). Granted, there are many consultants creating hype about the problem. However, even if you conservatively assume half of these predictions are true, satisfactorily addressing the IT millennium problem still requires significant resources, and that cannot be overlooked.

Industry experts also agree that the challenge of millennium projects is NOT the technical solution, but the coordination and/or project management aspects.

### Project Management

If you look at *A Guide to the Project Management Body of Knowledge (PMBOK Guide)*, eight major areas are affected. The list below has some brief examples from millennium projects for seven of the eight areas:

#### *Scope Management*

- Identification and breakdown of a millennium project into manageable pieces.

#### *Cost Management*

- Cost avoidance used to justify a millennium project when no perceivable value is added.
- Litigation costs if systems fail or operate incorrectly.

#### *Time Management*

- Undeniable and absolute fixed deadline to complete millennium projects.

#### *Communication Management*

- Communicate and establish awareness of the millennium problem.
- Obtain customer and/or executive management buy-in.
- Communicate effectively throughout project .

#### *Quality Management*

- Test massive changes effectively.
- Identify, document, and implement standard work processes.
- Track and retrofit maintenance work.

#### *Risk Management*

- Analysis of alternative approaches (convert, replace, or do nothing).

- Identification of business impact if project is not completed in time.

#### *Procurement Management*

- Compliance of all subcontractors and/or vendors to year 2000.

## Human Resource Management

While the authors agree that all of the project management aspects are critical, the successful completion of a millennium project cannot exist without proactive human resource management. There is no question—if the resources are not treated fairly and proactively managed, they will leave. The costs of losing resources include:

- Recruiting/hiring replacements
- Identifying additional resources to offset lost time resulting from personnel turnover
- Tarnishing company reputation: What will the customer think if they see high turnover rate? What will other employees think?

Most of the articles published thus far on IT millennium projects do not sufficiently address or emphasize the human resource issues. Many articles refer to the technical problem and solution alternatives (including outsourcing). Even if an organization plans to outsource the millennium project, familiarity with that firm's reputation and how it treats its people would be an additional factor in an outsourcing selection. Any organization is vulnerable to the high turnover costs listed above. Outsourcing a millennium project makes the organization's survival in the next century dependent on the firm providing the year 2000 conversion services.

As many IT service providers have discovered in today's labor market, attracting and retaining experienced IT resources on millennium projects is very challenging. While millennium projects provide some good opportunities for less experienced or entry-level individuals, it is still difficult to find the required number of people. Why are resources so difficult to attract and retain?

- Lack of technically challenging work—concern for career growth/development
- "Newer technologies" (client/server, graphical user interface, and so on) are much more attractive
- Fierce competition for few resources
- Little or no training available for mainframe COBOL "legacy" systems
- "Downsizing" and "reengineering" have changed employee attitudes forever—loyalty to one organization no longer exists.

## Millennium Project Experience and Lessons Learned

Amid the doomsday rhetoric there is a glimmer of sunshine for millennium project managers, but the time to act is now. There are many challenges unique to year 2000 projects, such as the immovable deadline and the scope of work. However, the greatest challenge is managing the human resources required to get the job done. For one of EDS' current clients, this challenge began almost three years ago.

This client's year 2000 project was initially estimated at seventy person years based upon a project plan that included the following highlights:

- Planning and Impact Analysis
- Assessment and Estimation
- Developing Deployment Strategy
- Implementation and Verification.

In 1995, due to the lack of interest in the millennium problem, it was nearly impossible to gain executive sponsorship. The first hurdle to overcome was "executive denial." Management simply could not accept the fact that there was indeed a problem. Secondly, educating the management staff on the magnitude of the scope of this project was required. Next, we finalized the human resource requirements (including number of resources and skill sets). Finally, funding issues were addressed.

Most experts would agree that the technical solutions required by this client's millennium project were not complex by design. However, the overall management of this project was incredibly complicated. First and foremost came the decision on how to break the work up into manageable units. Impact packages (sub-projects) were created to focus on completing the client's mission critical systems during the first year. Then the "minimum change" rule was adopted to select the dates that required expansion (instead of blindly changing any date found during analysis). This decision required us to have some senior-level personnel capable of analysis in our resource pool. Choosing an analysis tool was time consuming but turned out to be a beneficial investment. Although utilizing a tool in no way eliminates the need for significant manual effort, once the learning curve was overcome, productivity gains became evident during the initial phases of the project. An additional benefit of using an analysis tool was improved quality of the implementation of impact packages.

Once all parties agreed to the high-level plan, the hunt was on for the dozens of resources required to carry it out. So, how hard could it be to find COBOL mainframe programmers? With all the downsizing happening in corporate America at that time, finding qualified resources should have been simple. It was not. The global shortage of workers, specifically in the IT industry, made this task quite difficult.

**Exhibit 4.** Team Organization

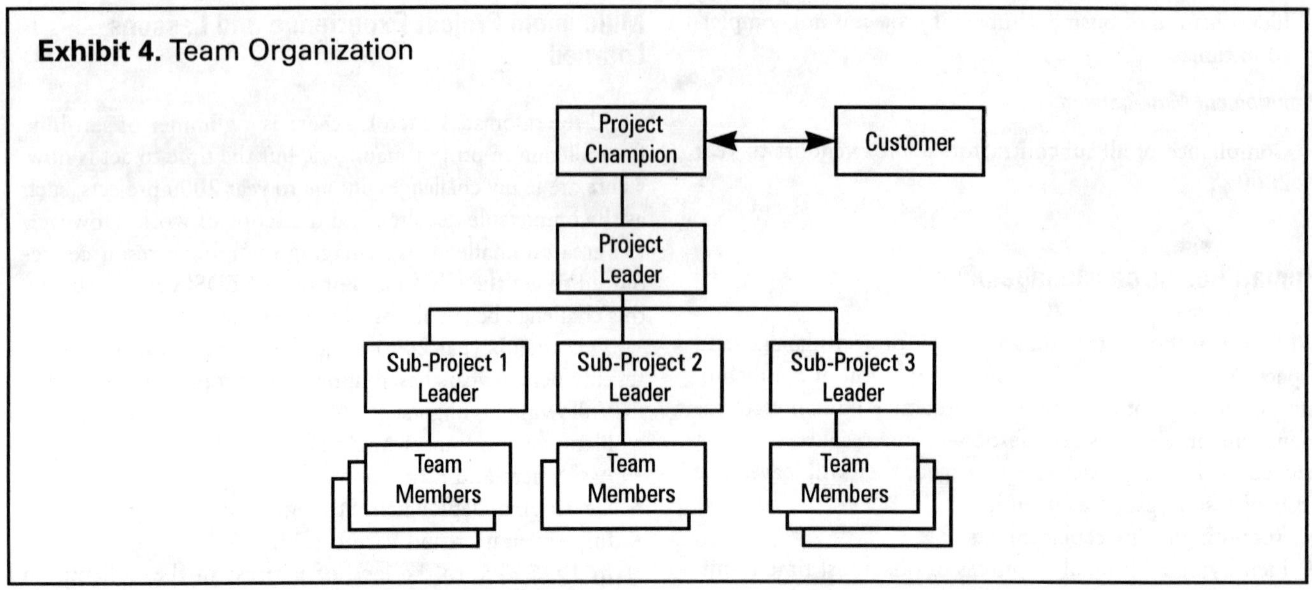


This resource shortage was the driving force behind establishing a global team with technical support groups in Ohio, Missouri, Pennsylvania, North Carolina, and Australia.

By diversifying the team as shown in Exhibit 4, we were successful in obtaining the number of resources to keep the project plan on schedule. Having multiple teams enabled us to schedule concurrent sub-projects (Exhibit 5). However, the level of complexity involved in managing this project increased significantly. This was partially due to communication between remote locations, concurrent sub-projects, and the sheer number of people on the team (close to fifty). Over the past eighteen months, we have learned numerous lessons, but the three key ones are outlined below:

## Permanent People

We quickly and painfully experienced first hand the loss of momentum due to attrition of some of our key people. Then we made the unfortunate mistake of trying to "stop the bleeding" by using temporary resources. The learning curve for processes and procedures was steeper than we realized but essential for project success. We believe it is vital to have a full-time project leader as well as a full-time core team using standard processes and procedures.

## Skilled People

It became evident within the first few months of the project that we needed to find the optimum combination of skill sets. When the team consisted mainly of less experienced employees, they did not have the analytical skills and experience required to be productive. Likewise, when the team consisted predominantly of experienced employees, they were not challenged and sought other opportunities. So we determined that the best mix was one experienced resource to every two or three inexperienced resources. This provided us the means to "grow" one of the subordinate team members into a project leader for the next sub-project.

## Challenged People

While some experts favor a "millennium factory" environment (where systems are upgraded via assembly line style with a subset of people focused on analysis, another subset on construction, and yet another on testing), we decided to break the overall project up by system. Each system was then treated like a mini-standalone project. These standalone projects had a project leader responsible for creating and maintaining a project plan. Each of these project teams experienced the entire life cycle from definition through implementation. This gave everyone on the team exposure to all areas within the project and a feeling of ownership. It also helped to avoid resource stagnation and keep them interested.

With recruiters offering a $10,000 bounty for programmers with the right skills (Wall Street Journal 1996, 1), and labor costs increasing 30 percent over the last twelve months (Information Week 1997, 24), we investigated many alternatives to help retain our resources. Admittedly, we did experience a large amount of turnover in the early days of the project. We evaluated several alternatives and proactively chose a plan to keep our people satisfied and challenged. Some of the alternatives we looked at follow below:

- Monetary incentives earned at pre-determined milestones within the project
- On the spot "signing" bonuses/lump sum payments
- Performance awards for both individuals and teams
- Individual career development:

- Project management opportunities for inexperienced team members
- Executive and/or corporate exposure for experienced team members
- Time limitations: employee commits to year 2000 then company pays to re-skill him
- Time trading: for each hour worked a ratio of time is "banked" for personal use
- Alternative work arrangements: flex hours, flex place
- Team building activities: make work a fun place to be.

In addition to those alternatives listed above, there are hundreds of others. It is the responsibility of the project manager to know her people well enough to proactively keep them interested in their project. If one is not successful in retaining their people in this highly competitive market, the only other alternative available is to "grow your own" resources as the millennium draws near. Unfortunately, over the past few years, university students earning computer science degrees dropped by 43 percent (ITAA 1997), COBOL is no longer offered in many colleges, and time is running out.

## Conclusion

As documented by the ITAA study "Help Wanted," the IT industry is already embroiled in a significant labor supply crunch. As the new century approaches, the impending century date change will put even more pressure on the IT services labor supply. Taking a step back from the IT services industry, it is true that people—their knowledge and skills—makes or breaks the success of *ANY* service provider. Since the primary product a service provider possesses is its skilled people, attention to recruiting, developing, and retaining those people is vital to the service provider's future existence and success.

Although the ITAA study found that 71 percent of firms feel that IT resources are in higher demand than other skilled workers, it is probably true to varying degrees that other industries are also facing a shortage of skilled resources. There is no easy solution. In the case of the IT industry, the ITAA feels that any investment individual firms make in recruiting and training will not be sufficient to solve the labor shortage. In testimony before the Senate Labor and Human Resource Committee, ITAA President Harris Miller advocated a joint effort on the part of private industry, the education system, and all levels of government in order to tackle the problem.

As the new century approaches, the extent to which organizations are successful at attracting, developing, and retaining their employees will determine their future success. In fact, any service provider that gains an edge on attracting, developing, and retaining people will have a distinct competitive advantage entering the twenty-first century.

**Exhibit 5.** Project Timeline

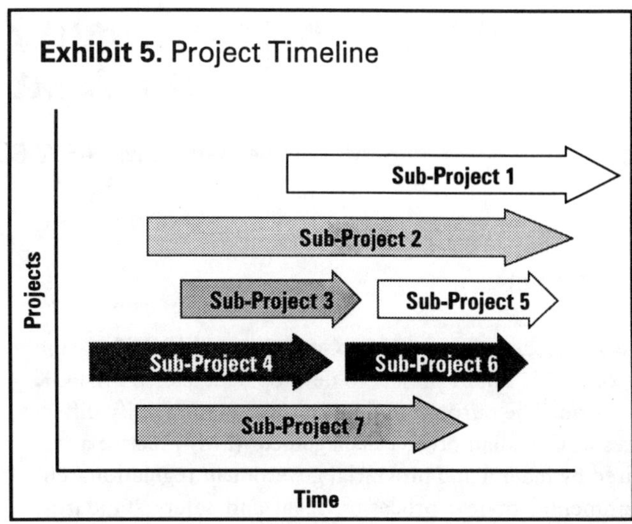


### References


Baker, Barrett, Himelstein. 1997. *Business Week* (March 10).

Cassell, Schick, Hall & Phelps, Gartner Group. 1996. "Time Marches On—Less Than 900 Working Days to January 1, 2000" (June 28). Also available at WEB address: *www.gartner.com/forms/meyr2000.rsp.html*

Information Technology Association of America. 1997. "Help Wanted: The IT Workforce Gap At the Dawn of a New Century" (February).

———. "Testimony of Harris N. Miller." 1997. Available from WEB address: www.itaa.org/testim2.htm (April 24).

*Information Week*. 1997 (April 7): 24.

Phillips & Farrell, Morgan Stanley U.S. Investment Research. 1997. "Y2K Watch:Digital Plague Oozes Across Planet" (March 26). Also available from WEB address: *year2000.com/pdf/y2k_rptP.pdf*

*USA Today*. 1996. "Year 2000 Poses Computer Software Headache" (March 8).

*Wall Street Journal*. 1996 (October 29): 1.

# A Project Management Knowledge Structure for the Next Century

R. Max Wideman, FPMI, AEW Services, Vancouver, BC, Canada

## Introduction

This paper describes a "Next Generation PMBOK" arising out of a PMI Board project to develop a Canadian PMBOK extension. The purpose of the extension is to identify differences in Canadian project management (PM) practice as required by federal and provincial government regulations, environmental review processes, legal and safety standards, cultural differences, and so on. These all impact PM practice as a professional discipline.

However, to capture such issues systematically, we needed an organized checklist as a reference baseline. Otherwise, we would only succeed in generating a random collection of casual observations. Such a checklist must cover both "generic" PM and "areas of PM application" (APMA).

So, the initial focus of the Canadian PMBOK extension project has shifted to establishing a list of discrete PM terms, ideally assembled into some logical structure. We will refer to this as a "Project Management Knowledge Structure" (PMKS), and to its content as "Project Management Knowledge Descriptors" (PMKDs). We hope this exploratory paper will generate useful discussion and pave the way for the future of PM.

## We Are Not Alone in This Endeavor

The need for a PMKS, described above, is not the only one. In fact, the history of similar attempts is instructive and worth recounting briefly.

As early as 1668, the English philosopher John Wilkins presented a universal classification scheme to London's Royal Society. His scheme divided all of reality into forty root categories, including "things; called transcendental," "discourse," and "beasts." Today, Wilkins' system is remembered only as an example of the arbitrariness of attempts to classify knowledge. Though interest peaked in the eighteenth century, attempts have continued. PMI's 1987 *Project Management Body of Knowledge (PMBOK)* was an attempt to capture a specialized area of knowledge in a similar way.

Recently, the moribund fields of knowledge organization have reemerged. The reason is the Internet Web—that powerful mass of distributed and disparate information, if only we knew what to look for. And do not underestimate its value. By 1999, the Web could contain more words than the whole of the Library of Congress!

Some recent attempts to organize that information are startlingly reminiscent of John Wilkin's seventeenth century attempts. But there is a difference. The most popular sites on the Web are those— like the Yahoo! (Internet URL 1997, 1) or AltaVista (Internet URL 1997, 2) search engine sites—that attempt to exert some order on this anarchic collection of information. These powerful search engines provide the tools to extract long lists of data sources, but the results are often overwhelming unless we can narrow the search. Interestingly, after a search, AltaVista provides access to a context-sensitive thesaurus-like hierarchy of words that can be included or excluded for further searching.

Suddenly, the problems of knowledge classification and indexing are of commercial importance! So, a significant use for a PMKS is in tracking down needed information. A consistent grouping of subject matter would also be invaluable to educators and practitioners in their research, education, training, and practice. Identifying a realistic scope of PM for professional purposes would also be a significant step forward.

## But on What Basis?

Surprisingly, library science turns out to be of little help. The most common systems in the United States, the Dewey Decimal System and Library of Congress Classification, were developed during the close of the nineteenth century. Even librarians admit that they are poor at classifying "newly" established fields such as PM. If you want confirmation, just check out project management as a subject area!

Moreover, unlike a physical book or document, a digital document can be placed in several category locations at the cost of only a few bytes. Automated techniques based on keyword indexing for information retrieval from large databases is not much more encouraging. The reason is simple. If humans have a hard time figuring it out, getting a computer to do it is nearly impossible.

There are other issues. What should be included? Certainly, the specific PM practices of particular APMAs, such as information technology, software development, or construction—each with its own particular requirements, techniques, and vocabulary—should be included. A basis for distinguishing

**Exhibit 1.** Simple Concept Map

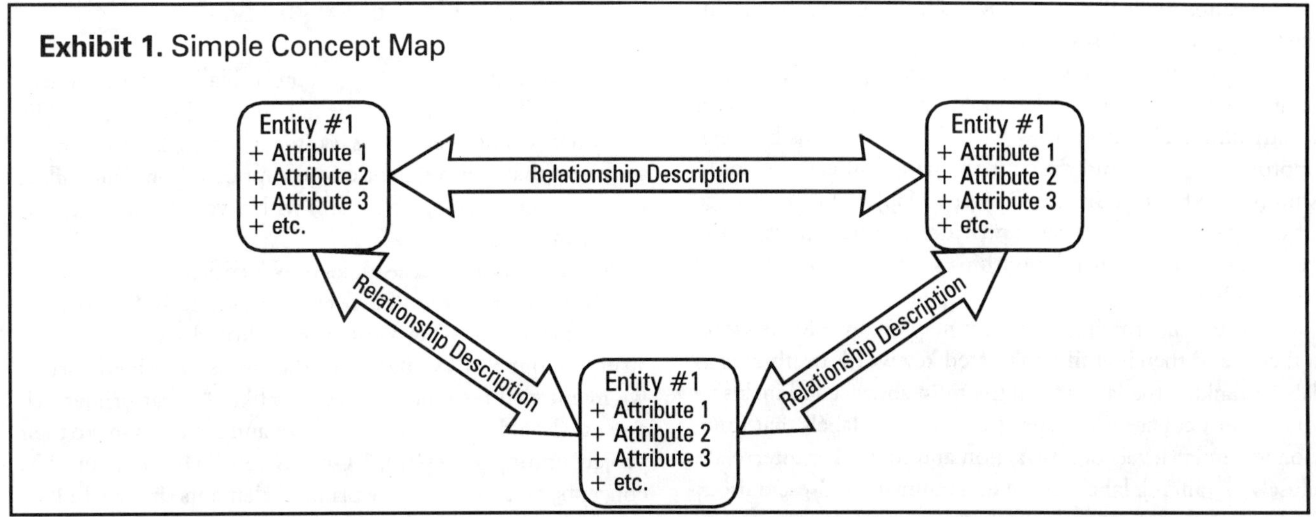


between APMA groupings, by the way, has been described in a recent paper (Shenhar et al. 1997).

But how much knowledge in related general management professions, such as financial management, accounting, ethics and law, should be included? How can the information be presented and in what order? We need guidance.

## Models to the Rescue

Pictorial models help us understand complex relationships. They can broaden and clarify our perspectives by helping us to see the big picture, avoiding confusion in how things work, and expressing rules more simply by clarifying relationships. Who, for instance, would be able to grasp the complexities of nature's DNA structure without the colored 3-D graphics we see on TV?

Project management is also a complex structure, and there have been a number of attempts to capture it through models. Some examples include the early "schedule-cost-performance" model, the "scope of PM" model, the "matrix model," the 1987 *Project Management Body of Knowledge* "star" model, or the "3-D integrative toolbox model (Wideman 1991). Few of these capture the totality of project management.

A very recent model depicts a wheel made up of nine management elements or spokes, held together by a tenth, its rim (Forsberg et al. 1996, 1). The wheel progresses along a three-stranded axle representing the project life cycle. The model appears to be too complex for our purpose, but Forsberg's work is important for several reasons.

In addition to the usual topics of teamwork, project life cycle, and the elements of management control, Forsberg et al. first emphasize the importance of communicating through a common vocabulary for each project—even small ones. They then differentiate between "technical" management and "project" management. Most crucial, they separate the "perpetual" aspects of the project life-cycle imposed by the project environment, the "sequence-driven" aspect imposed by logical performance, and the "situation-driven" aspect imposed by managing. These are facets of PM that are commonly overlooked and a serious weakness of the current *A Guide to Project Management Body of Knowledge (PMBOK Guide)*.

A thoughtful *Project Management Journal* paper on PM descriptors observes that "Information today is produced in such quantities that our efforts may be repeatedly wasted simply because it is not possible to determine what work has already been done or, at a minimum, we spend more time looking *for* documents than looking *at* them" (Abdomerovic 1992). This paper describes research on some two thousand titles from which the author abstracted more than eighteen hundred descriptors and organized them into a structured hierarchy. This structure has two difficulties: the hierarchy gives no indication of the rules or relationships implied by entering a descriptor at any given location, and it has up to eighteen levels—rather more than practical. Nevertheless, the paper provides a valuable resource for our project.

## Concept Mapping, the Preferred Choice

Hitherto an area of interest only to cognitive science, artificial intelligence, and educational technology, "concept mapping" is now considered by researchers and educators to be an excellent way of capturing a knowledge area. It is used, for example, by systems analysts to gain an understanding of systems planned for automating or upgrading. The method forces discovery of basic conceptual units and their relationships, typically by a knowledgeable group in a brainstorming wall-board session.

In a node-link concept map, the nodes represent concepts, entities, or things that are described by labels, each with a set of attributes. The links show both the connections between appropriate nodes and describe the nature of each relationship (see Exhibit 1, Simple Concept Map). A big advantage of the concept map is that it provides a visual image of the components and their relationships so that it can be studied very easily.

Steps to constructing a concept map involve: focusing on a theme and then identifying related key words or phrases as labels; ranking the labels from the most abstract and inclusive to the most concrete and specific; clustering labels that function at similar levels of abstraction and those that interrelate closely; arranging labels into a diagrammatic representation; adding attributes to each label if/as appropriate; and connecting the labels with linking lines and naming each link-line with a relationship description.

Typical relationships include one or more of the following: has part(s); implements; has goal(s); uses; satisfies; has output(s); has example(s); or relates to (undefined generic relationship). A subtlety of the approach is that any attribute or relationship might be converted into an entity if its content is to be further elaborated, or vice versa. Obviously, concept maps can get very complicated depending on the number, type, and level of detail of the relationships exposed.

However, graphical software is now available that greatly facilitates concept mapping. One example is SemNet, short for Semantic Networks (SemNet 1991). This innovative Mac software works like a word processor but can be used to portray any descriptive domain of knowledge. Essentially, SemNet is a hypertext environment that can be elaborated with objects like charts, pictures, sounds, multimedia, and web documents. They can even be merged together. Another for the PC-Windows environment is Visio (Visio 1990). Visio uses "drag and drop" symbols from a selection of drafting templates. Its power is in the automatic attachment of relationship arrow links to the concept nodes, complete with descriptive text of the relationship automatically displayed in the shaft of the arrow.

Bear in mind, however, that the "maps" thus developed represent only the view of the knowledge area according to the perspective selected. Believe it or not, it turns out that the concept map found most useful in teaching and learning is one with which PM people are most familiar—the organization chart. Like the typical organization chart, the more general and inclusive concepts are at the top and the more detailed ones at the bottom. However, the boxes need elaborating with their attributes, and the links must be annotated to show the specific relationships.

## PMKS Theme, View, or Project Goal

The complexity of PM is like the proverbial elephant and two blind men. The man feeling the tail says it is like a rope, while the other feeling the trunk says it is like a snake. In fact, we all know that it is a gigantic oval supported on four pillars (scope, quality, time, and cost?) with a variety of exotic attachments!

Since PM is an overhead, its only justification is to ensure optimum success in both process and output, but particularly the output. So what view of PM should we take in constructing our PMKS? Based on the issues described earlier, we might well respond to questions like: "What primary elements should enterprises recognize and refine to make their projects more successful?" Or: "Given PMI's existing PM concepts, what are the new primary elements that we in PMI should now articulate to our sponsoring enterprises?" Or, more simply, "What view of PM must we convey to be successful into the next century?" No matter the exact wording, the result should be roughly the same.

Successful project management teaches us that we must first be clear on our objectives, and then state our assumptions. After that, the starting point for developing a new PMKS concept model must be the most fundamental things we know about project management.

## Objectives for Structuring the PMKS

For our PMKS objectives we may again borrow from Forsberg's observations on the essentials of a PM model (Forsberg et al. 1996, 3). To create a PMKS that:

1. Is explicitly and operationally defined as to structure, variables, and relationships
2. Is obviously valid and intuitive to all project stakeholders
3. Is generally applicable throughout the project environment in a way that accounts for the complexity and dynamics of the project process
4. Is validated empirically in the real project world.

To this we might add the following practical considerations:

5. Is simple, logical, and understandable, but comprehensive and flexible
6. Keeps the number of hierarchical levels within practical limits
7. Builds on existing PM understanding
8. Uses familiar terms and phrases that facilitate both electronic and non-electronic retrieval of PM-relevant information
9. Identifies and cross-links to hierarchies and word sets that apply to more than one branch of the structure
10. Does not impose any proprietary view of PM.

With reference to item 9, the cross-linking suggested would highlight both overlaps between areas of PM application and the 'fractal' nature of project management. A 'fractal' is defined as a geometric shape having the property that each smaller portion of it can be viewed as a reduced scale replica of the whole—a common feature of the PM process!

## Assumptions

We are assuming that the PMKS will be used to:

- Assemble knowledge and experience encompassed by PM
- Provide a basis for comparing features and practices in different environments, cultures, and areas of application
- Run electronic and non-electronic information searches based on the contained PMKDs
- Establish a reference baseline for education, training, and application endeavors.

As part of the PMKS assumptions, we also need to establish the founding definitions of "project management," "project," "management" and "success." The more convincing and focused that we can make these definitions, the more useful the structure. Given the stated objectives, we propose the following. Note, however, it is not so much the exact wording but the intent that is important.

- Project Management: The art and science of managing a project from inception to closure as evidenced by successful product delivery and transfer.
- Project: A unique process or undertaking designed to create a new product or service.
- Management: The act of planning, organizing, coordinating, commanding, and controlling (Fayol 1984).
- Success (project success): The perception of satisfaction on the part of the stakeholders, firstly with the resulting product or service, and secondly with the process that achieved it.

## Criteria for Exclusion

Our assumptions would not be complete without also including criteria for exclusion. Obviously, the boundary between project management knowledge, information or experience, and general management disciplines is bound to be a fuzzy line resulting from different perceptions and usage. It may also vary with the complexity and technology of the project.

In principle, the essential guidelines are that:

- The PMKS excludes most areas of general and technical management, such as accounting, law, personnel administration, and the theoretical basis for the technology vested in a project and its associated disciplines, which are not immediately relevant to managing a project.
- The PMKS therefore does include sufficient reference to relevant material in other management and technology disciplines to enable the PM practitioner to be effective in understanding and appreciating project requirements and technical management issues.

For example, an understanding of the part of accounting that deals with the collection, identification, and allocation of actual costs is vital knowledge for the PM practitioner.

## The Starting Point

Following the concept mapping methodology described earlier, the fundamental relationships of PM surfaced as follows:

- Universal Practice: An overriding body of common practices has been identified as appropriate for most projects.
- Area of Application: The dominant technology involved in the project has a major influence on how it should be managed.
- Client Environment: This determines how projects are generated and has a major influence on how they are structured.
- Commitment: A project represents a commitment to scope, quality, time, and cost between the project's management and its client or sponsor.
- Project Integration: A project is a short-lived arrangement of people integrated for the purpose.
- Uncertainty: This provides both opportunity for the client and risks to the project.
- Management Processes: These are the major project contribution and responsibility.
- Real Time (Life Cycle): Perpetual, sequential, and situational aspects play a major role in successful project completion.
- Success: The ultimate objective of project management is success in all its aspects.

Note that commitment to scope, quality, time, and cost is the dominant theme of communication across the client/project boundary. This commitment is perhaps the most fundamental PM relationship of all. These entities and their relationships are shown in Exhibit 2, Concept Map of Project Management. The PMKS is shown as an outline in Appendix A.

## Conclusions

This paper provides background and a rational basis for using concept mapping methodology to develop a project management knowledge structure (PMKS). The resulting relationship-based PMKS would greatly facilitate researching, learning, and practicing project management into the next century. The PMKS would consist of an orderly arrangement of project management knowledge descriptors (PMKDs).

The goals and objectives of the PMKS are described as well as the assumptions and criteria for both inclusion and exclusion. The potential for both "universal" and specific "areas of PM application" (APMA) are provided for, together with the rationale for each APMA.

At a later stage, the author intends to work with the author of an earlier 1992 *Project Management Journal* paper to elaborate the PMKS using the PMKDs referenced in that earlier paper. Meantime, it is hoped that this presentation will engender discussion and progress on the vital issues of scope, storage, and efficient retrieval of project management knowledge. Ideally, it should also attract the interest and participation of representatives from other countries.

### References


Abdomerovic, M. 1992. "Project Management Descriptors." *Project Management Journal.* Upper Darby, PA: 42.

Fayol, H. 1984. *General and Industrial Management.* Rev. ed. IEEE Press, NY.

Forsberg et al. 1996: 22.

Forsberg et al. 1996: 18.

Forsberg, K., H. 1996. *Visualizing Project Management.* Mooz & H. Cotterham. NY: John Wiley & Sons.

Internet URL: http://www.yahoo.com

Internet URL: http://altavista.digital.com

Shenhar, A. J., and R. M. Wideman. 1997. "Toward a Fundamental Differentiation between Projects." Paper awaiting presentation. PICMET Conference, Portland.

Wideman, R. M. 1991. "Appendix A: A Historical Perspective." *A Framework for Project and Program Management.* Upper Darby, PA.: Project Management Institute.

SemNet Research Group. 1991. Available from Internet URL: http://apple.sdsu.edu/logan/SemNet.html

Visio Corporation. 1990. Available from Internet URL: http://www.visio.com


## Appendix A

**Project Management Knowledge Structure Developed From Concept Mapping**
**(Existing Pmi Pmbok "Managements" Are Shown Starred: * )**

### Universal (Has as primary concepts . . . )

#### ***Client Environment** (Consists of . . . )*

Culture, attitudes, and other limitations of the type of sponsoring organization, location, and country

#### ***Commitment (Consists of four interactive variables . . . )***

Project scope management* (Has outputs . . . )
- Definition of the project's products and changes thereto

Project quality management* (Has outputs . . . )
- Conforming to requirements

Project time management* (Has outputs . . . )
- Schedules, milestones, forecasting to completion

Project cost management* (Has outputs . . . )
- Estimating, budgeting, cost containment, final cost forecasting

#### ***Project Integration** (Has sub-parts . . . )*

Human resource management* (has outputs . . . )
- Temporary team work, i.e., assembling people, team building, motivating . . .

Managing the work of the project (has outputs . . . )
- Assembling material resources, facilitating production, productivity, scope of work . . .

Communication management* (has outputs . . . )
- Listening, directing, reporting, conducting meetings, fellowship, public relations . . .

Information management (has outputs . . . )
- Data collection, distribution, visibility, storage, and retrieval

#### ***Uncertainty (Has sub-parts . . . )***

Risk management* (has outputs . . . )
- Risk identification, assessment, mitigation

#### ***Management Processes** (Has sub-parts . . . )*

Overviewing and "strategizing" the project (has outputs . . . )
- Visioning, developing goals and objectives, leading, performance standards . . .

Procurement management* (has outputs . . . )
- Formal (external, legal) contracting; Informal (internal) resources negotiation . . .

Control management (has outputs . . . )
- Planning, organizing, directing, coordinating, monitoring, corrective action . . .

#### ***Real Time (Life Cycle)** (Has sub-parts . . . )*

Perpetual (Uses . . . )
- Conditions imposed by the sponsoring organization throughout the project

Sequential (Uses . . . )
- Generic periods (major phases): Concept; development; execution; finishing

Situational or cyclical (Uses . . . )

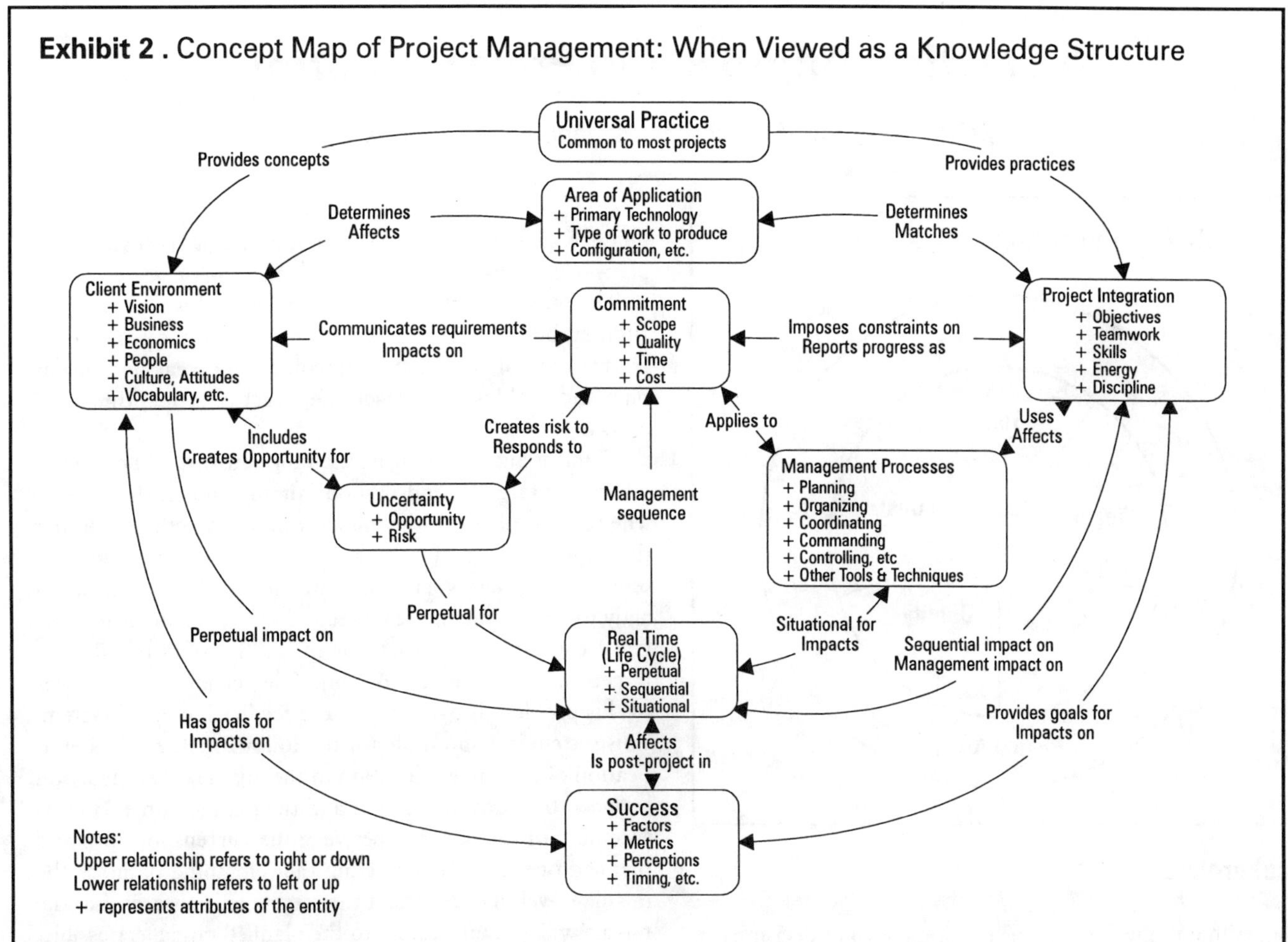


**Exhibit 2 .** Concept Map of Project Management: When Viewed as a Knowledge Structure

***Success (Responds to . . . )***

Factors implicit in the client's organization
Identifying measurable key indicators of project success; Establishing satisfactory "quality grade" . . .

## AREAS OF PROJECT MANAGEMENT APPLICATION (APMA) (Has sub-types . . . )

APMA divisions presume that for a successful outcome, different projects or sub-parts need to be managed differently according to the nature of the WORK required to create the resulting PRODUCT.

***Tangible-Craft (Has as examples . . . )***

Projects whose products are tangible and the result of craft work. Examples include building, engineering works, infrastructure works, and construction, generally.

***Tangible-Intellect (Has as examples . . . )***

The product is tangible, but the main effort is intellectual. Examples include the development of new products in manufacturing.

***Intangible-Craft (Has as examples . . . )***

The main value of the product is intangible, but the effort to accomplish it is effectively routine "craft" work. Examples include plant maintenance shutdown and updating a procedures manual.

***Intangible-Intellect** (Has as examples . . . )*

The main value of the product is intangible and the result of intensive intellectual work. Examples include research work, developing a new theory, writing new software, and writing a book.

# A Practical Approach to Project Control

Mickey Granot, Granot-Striechman Management Consultants LTD

**Exhibit 1.** Control Areas

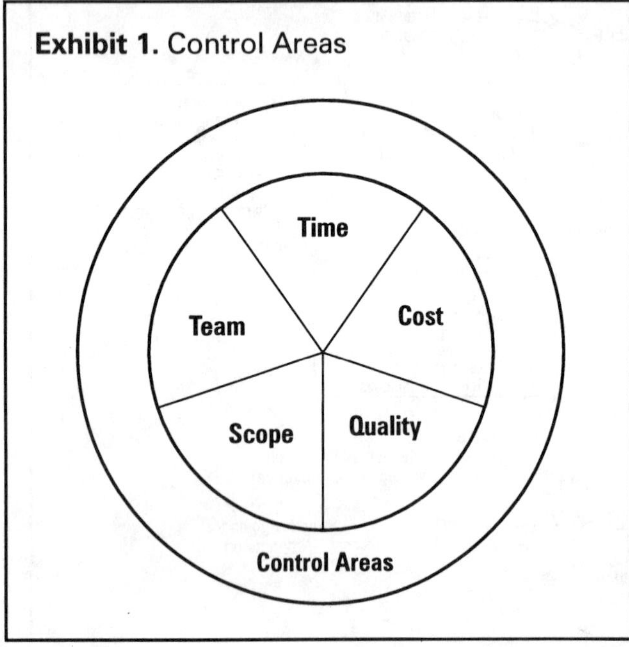


## Background

Controlling the project means making the right decisions at the right time during project execution. In order to make the right decisions, the project manager needs to have the best possible information in the needed time and a sound methodology of decision-making—project control methodology accompanied by effective and easy to use tools.

This paper deals with the most important phase of the project—*project execution*—and with the most difficult management challenge of this phase—*project control*. It also deals with presenting the roles, areas, planning process, and execution of a control system.

## The Roles of the Controlling System

Project management process is roughly split into two phases—*project planning* and *project controlling*. During the planning phase the management effort is focused on generating the best possible plan. This plan, however, is based on previous experience and old data which is, sad to say, irrelevant but the best available during this phase. When the planning phase is over and project plan is approved, the execution phase begins and then we discover the weakness of our plan—*things just won't work the way we planned them.*

The most important thing to understand is that we can't avoid it, but we sure can deal effectively with it using an effective control system that outcomes any weakness of our plan and enables us to reach the target of scope, time, and cost.

Think about launching a long-range missile: you can guess where the target is and without aiming launch the missile. The result is obvious; the missile will hit something, but not the target. You can aim using the most advanced aiming system ensuring that when launching the missile it is aimed exactly to the middle of the target and then . . . launch and forget. I can assure you that this missile is going to miss the target similar to the previous one. The technological answer to this problem is by using a close feedback control system. This system is responsible for the following roles: 1) identification of the current location of the missile; 2) comparison between the current location and the planned one; 3) measurement of the distance between the current location and planned one, and 4) correcting the remaining path for the missile travel in order to hit the target. This ensures that the missile will end up as close to the planned target as possible.

In order to establish an effective control system, we must first understand that similar to the missile control system, the roles of the project control system are:

- Identification: Prompt identification of project progress in each controlling area (see next paragraph).
- Comparison: Compare achieved progress to planned (which makes it clear that the best possible plan is crucially needed).
- Measurement: Measure deviation between actual progress achieved and the planned one.
- Correcting: Make decisions, take actions, and re-plan the rest of the project in order to overcome deviations.

We will use the synonym ICMC for the roles of the control system.

## Control Areas

Effective project control requires controlling the following areas:

Controlling time and cost means making sure that the project is kept on track and time and that cost slippages are identified and dealt with in such a manner that ensures the project is finished within time and cost constraints.



PROJECT MANAGEMENT INSTITUTE 28th Annual Seminars & Symposium
Chicago, Illinois: Papers Presented September 29 to October 1, 1997

**Exhibit 2.** Planning Of Control Areas

| Question | Control Area | | | | |
|---|---|---|---|---|---|
| | Scope | Time | Cost | Quality | Team |
| What is to be controlled? | Scope Changes | Time Slippage | Cost Slippage | Process, Specifications | Moral, Motivation, Understanding of goals, roles and responsibilities |
| When to control it? | Event Driven, Periodic CCB meetings | Periodically | Periodically | Event Driven, Process Driven | Periodically, Event Driven |
| Who is the control task owner? | Assign a task owner to the control tasks | | | | |
| How to perform the control task? | Define a scope management process | Earned Value | | Define quality assurance and control procedures | Interviews, Audits, Team meetings |
| What are the expected and excepted results? | Define expected results and tolerance. It is crucial to determine tolerance every result which is inside the accepted area, even if it is not the expected one should not generate a corrective action. | | | | |
| To whom the control information is to be reported? | Prepare a communication program, specifying Who should get, What information, When and How? | | | | |

Controlling quality means making sure that the quality of the project deliverables is the quality that the project client intended to get.

Controlling scope means managing changed in scope effectively ensuring changes are brought into the project after a thorough investigation and with full awareness of their impact on project time and cost.

Controlling team means making sure that team motivation, enthusiasm, and direction are kept throughout the project.

In each control area the ICMC principles apply, and the aim is to ensure project manageability, which leads us to a successful finish and not being managed by the project.

As previously mentioned we need a sound plan for each control area; without it, controlling the project is impossible. This means that by the end of the project planning phase the project plan must have a schedule, budget, quality program, and scope, team roles, and responsibilities definitions. The plan must also consist of a control plan.

## Planning the Control System

Things you do not plan are things you are not going to do. But this is not the only reason for planning the control system; another important reason is to avoid the danger of too much data driving the decision-making process to be impossible.

Effective project control requires firm control plan. For each of the control fields, the control plan should answer the following questions:

- What is to be controlled?
- When to control it? (Control points should be close enough to each other, but not too close.)
- Who is the control task owner?
- How to perform the control task?
- What are the expected and excepted results?
- To whom is the control information to be reported?

These questions, as related to each control area, are explained in table 1:

The control plan should be an integral part of the project plan and be documented in the project file.

## The Control Process

The control process in each control point and for each control area is as described:

A. Collecting actuals

B. Calculating control indexes

C. Making forecasts

D. Re-planning the rest of the project.

Collecting actuals means getting field information describing the accurate stage of the project. Calculating control indexes is impossible without a baseline plan; having the plan calculating the indexes is based on mathematics, or another algorithm, to compare and measure deviations from plan. Making forecasts is trying to determine what would be the impact of the current situation both in the task level and the project level. Re-planning the rest of the project is going over again through all the original project planning phases, generating a new plan that overcomes deviations, or excepts them due to their low impact.

### Collecting Actuals

Time and cost actuals are: actual deliverable percent complete and actual investment in labor and cost. In order to be as accurate as possible, percent complete should be calculated based on a quantitative measure of deliverable completion; any other form is probably a bad guess, which may lead to a wrong understanding of project status and thus to wrong decisions. Therefore, it is crucial during project planning to determine quantitative measures of finished deliverables for each task.

Quality actuals are measures of qualitym, as defined in the quality plan, that are collected through quality tests.

Scope actuals are collected through scope changes reported according to the change management process, as defined during the planning phase.

Team actuals are collected through personal meetings with team members, group meetings, and audits.

### Calculating Control Indexes

"You can not manage what you can not measure." No good decisions can be made during project execution without quantifiable, or at least verifiable, measures of achievement. In order to be able to calculate measures, a plan is needed. The plan is the base for the calculation of control indexes.

Time and cost indexes are: cost variance (CV)/cost index (CI), and time variance (TV)/time index (TI). Cost variance measures the cost slippage; cost index measures relative cost slippage; time variance and index are measuring the same but in the time field. The calculation are based on the earned value method:

- CV = ACWP (actual cost of work performed) - BCWP (budgeted cost of work performed)
- CI = CV/ACWP
- TV = BCWS (budgeted cost of work scheduled) - BCWP
- TI = TV/BCWS

And the meaning is the same; if the variance indexes are greater then zero then slippage occurred, and the task analyzed is exceeding its planned time and/or cost. If the variance indexes are smaller than zero then the task is ahead of time and/or cost, and if the variance indexes are zero then the task is currently advancing according to its plan. The same logic applies to the indexes only instead of zero use the value one.

Quality indexes are harder to define due to the fact that they are different between one project and another, and one product to another. But, quality should be measured in quantifiable measures of the process and the product; therefore, the need for a quality plan is enhanced.

Scope changes are not measured for themselves but rather by their impact on time, cost, quality, and team morale.

Team measures are based on estimated ranks for different fields and therefore are subject to be biased by the measuring person. To avoid the bias it is important to use more than one measuring mechanism, to be consistent, and to use at least one group mechanism of measuring.

It is very important at this stage to determine if the slippages identified require taking corrective actions or not. This again enhances the importance of determining tolerances during the project planning phase. Without those tolerances determined, a project manager might find that every slippage initiates a reaction, and, as a result, precious time is wasted on events that required no action. Only those slippages that exceed their predetermined tolerance should be dealt with.

### Making Forecasts

To those slippages that exceeded their predetermined tolerance a forecast should be made. The forecast role is to show the project manager what would happen to the project *if no* corrective action is taken. The forecast is basically a quantitative measure of the impact of the current achievements to the rest of the project, assuming no corrective actions are taken.

Time and cost forecasts are made using earned value calculations, and based on the indexes calculated earlier (using variance adds the calculated variance to the original plan and using indexes multiplies the original plan).

Scope, team, and quality forecasts are made regarding their impact on time and cost, according to the measurements and the needed corrective actions.

### Re-Planning the Rest of the Project

One of the main ideas here is the customization of the "dynamic programming" concept, embedded in the forth phase of the control process. The concept is to re-plan the rest of the project, as if it is a new project, starting today with the

**Exhibit 3.** Project Results

| Control Areas | | Projects | | | | |
|---|---|---|---|---|---|---|
| | | A | B | C | D | E |
| Time | P | 30 months | 24 months | 20 months | 18 months | 6 months |
| | A | 31 months | 23 months | 20 months | 17 months | 6 months |
| Cost | P | $2.5 M | $3.3 M | $1.8 M | $2.1 M | $0.9 M |
| | A | $2.8 M | $3.2 M | &1.9 M | $2.3 M | $0.7 M |
| Scope | | 83 Change requests 52 Approved Chanfes | 96 Change requests 70 Approved Chanfes | 73 Change requests 56 Approved Chanfes | 28 Change requests 25 Approved Chanfes | 49 Change requests 38 Approved Chanfes |
| Quality | | Final Tests Pased first Time. Ovaer all customer satisfaction on scale of 1-5: - 4.9 | Final Tests Pased firs Time. Ovaer all customer satisfaction on scale of 1-5: - 4.8 | Final Tests Pased firs Time. Ovaer all customer satisfaction on scale of 1-5: - 4.9 | Final Tests Pased firs Time. Ovaer all customer satisfaction on scale of 1-5: - 4.9 | Final Tests Pased firs Time. Ovaer all customer satisfaction on scale of 1-5: - 4.9 |
| Team | | Team moral at end of project on a scale of 1-5: - 4.8 | Team moral at end of project on a scale of 1-5: - 4.7 | Team moral at end of project on a scale of 1-5: - 4.9 | Team moral at end of project on a scale of 1-5: - 4.7 | Team moral at end of project on a scale of 1-5: - 4.8 |

last updated targets and a new base data for the decision-making process. That does not mean that what happened and causes for the actual performance are of no importance; rather it means that the investigation of the causes should be postponed until the project closure phase.

The deliverable of this phase is an updated project plan, again covering all aspects of the project and including an updated schedule, budget, and quality plan. The new plan also consists of all the corrective actions that are taken in order to overcome slippages and other events, which badly influence the ability to achieve project goals within project constraints.

Experience using this concept shows success and project termination with overall deviations between plan and performance not exceeding predetermined thresholds. For five projects this method was introduced; the project results are detailed in Exhibit 3.

The first three projects were all at the same organization, from the field of hardware and software products development. The forth project is a software development project, and the fifth project is a construction project. All projects were executed between 1994 and 1997.

## Conclusion

A successful project needs a good plan and a control plan, and then a sound consistently executed control system. To effectively control a project one should consider all areas of control and avoid concentrating on the easy, obvious areas. Effective control means controlling the time, cost, quality, scope, and team at the right time and reacting according to measurable, verifiable results based on actual performance and measured against planned performance. Not every deviation requires taking a corrective action; only those deviations exceeding predetermined thresholds should generate corrective actions. The corrective actions should be embedded in a new plan for the remaining work in the project, as if it is a new project that starts at the control point; causes for the actual performance should be investigated at the end of the project during the closure phase, unless no other option for taking a corrective action exists. The lessons learned at project close-out review should be used for improving processes for the next project.

# Case Study: Successfully Introducing Project Management to an Organization

Kenneth D. Delcol, PMP, PEng, PE-SCIEX
Co-author: Pierre Burnier, PE-SCIEX

Many organizations are having great difficulty introducing project management techniques. The future of many small and medium-sized organizations with a global orientation will hinge on their ability to introduce and improve their project management techniques. This paper discusses the successful introduction and continual development of project management techniques into PE-SCIEX, a medium organization, by covering the following topics:

- Introduction Strategy
- Reducing Project Risk
- Building Fundamentals
- Standardized Techniques
- Leveraging
- Education.

## Company Background

PE-SCIEX is an organization that was born out of the need to analyze material on the NASA Martian expedition project and has grown from a research organization to a world leader in the research, the design, and the manufacturing of mass spectrometers. Similar to large organizations, PE-SCIEX must rely heavily on its vendor base to not only supply products but to actively participate in its development efforts. The nature of the product has created the need for a global vendor base.

The inability of the organization to handle rapid product development programs became painfully obvious by 1992. Like many companies with limited resources PE-SCIEX initially attempted to grow its own internal project management practices based on reports from consultants, books, internal people turned project managers, and courses. These actions had little impact on the new product development time line. Failure of the homegrown approach was due to the lack of: project management experience, team focus, techniques and tools, and a systematic approach to managing global development teams.

## Introduction Strategy

Senior management decided to hire a senior executive champion for project management into the organization, due to the initial failure of project management. This person was hired as the director of product development and brought a rich history of engineering and project management experiences from the aerospace industry.

The first course of action was to create an organizational structure within product development that would support project management. This resulted in the following organizational changes within product development:

- switching the structure from product line to functional
- recruiting functional managers who had experience in cross functional project teams and who recognized the importance of project management.

Once the new organization was in place a professional project manager was recruited to build a project management organization within product development. This person was hired into a senior position within product development and was interviewed by the different functional and senior executives to ensure a good fit within the overall organization.

Short- and long-term project management goals were developed keeping in mind the current organizational objectives of ISO certification, time to market, and total quality management. To initially introduce project management techniques into the organization, an obtainable start-up project was selected with the following characteristics: well understood technical risks, a balance in the capabilities of the team members, low market risk, and the organization was familiar with the product. Two additional goals of the project besides the standard project management delivery goals were to:

- refine and test standard project management techniques to meet the specific needs of PE-SCIEX
- identify weakness in the time to market approach used at PE-SCIEX.

## Reducing Project Risk

The Big Bang approach was used to develop products prior to the introduction of project management. This approach consisted of parallel research and product development that involved significantly changing all of the product's major systems and their associated interfaces and at the same time including the science/technology behind the systems. The lines between engineering and research were blurred as well as the lines within engineering. The shear magnitude of the number of changes quickly overwhelmed the organization's ability to manage them.

To overcome this problem an incremental development approach was taken to minimize the number of product changes that a given project had to cope with and to ensure the science behind the changes was well understood (see Exhibit 1). To further support the limiting of project scope a maximum project duration of two years was set, with a target duration of one year.

In addition, significant effort was placed into controlling and minimizing the number of changes at a given system boundary. Project plans were modified to emphasize early in the development process the creation of system interface documents for all engineering disciplines. Limiting the number of changes improved the focus of project teams, and up-front clarification of system interfaces allowed more independent work while at the same reducing both risk and time to market.

The incremental approach to product development supports the evolution of the product by addressing changing customer needs and advancements in technology. To avoid the possibility of being caught by a discontinuity in technology and/or science, the PE-SCIEX product development path supports parallel revolution, which is the sole responsibility of research.

Experience to date is very successful with three products being introduced in under eighteen months and two more products well along in the development process. In addition, research has become more focused during this time period. A hidden benefit of the incremental approach is that PE-SCIEX market presence has increased as a result of enhancements to the current product lines being introduced at an accelerated rate.

**Exhibit 1** Big Bang vs. Incremental Approach

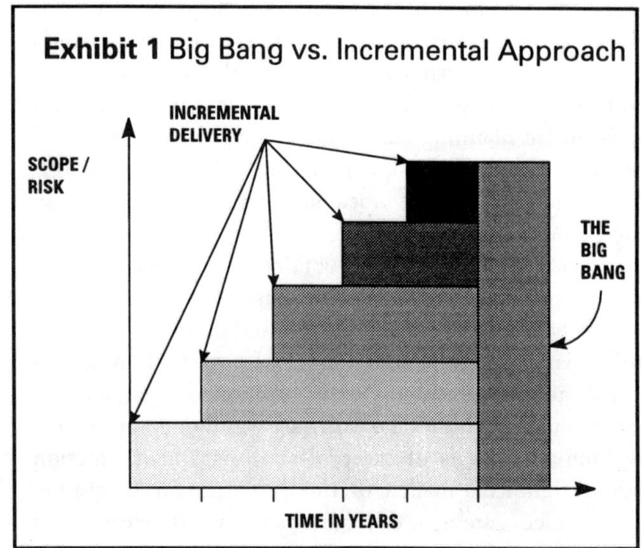


## Fundamental Project Management Building Blocks

Establishing the fundamental project management building blocks was considered critical for the long-term growth of project management practices. The first step was to establish the project management organizational structure, relationships, and responsibilities. To ensure the organizational commitment to project management the following items were put in place:

- reporting of the project management function directly to the senior executive champion, the director of product development
- defining and obtaining senior executive commitment to the roles and the responsibilities of project managers in the product development process
- establishing the rules governing which projects professional project managers will work on
- creating dedicated project teams under the control of a project manager who draws staff from all of the functional organizations
- creating a senior executive project review process for all projects
- linking project management as the primary driver of the strategic initiative of time to market and a major contributor to the total quality management initiative.

A refinement of the existing product development documentation standard was undertaken to address project management specific issues as defined in *A Guide to the Project Management Body of Knowledge (PMBOK Guide*) and to provide standardization across all projects. The PE-SCIEX product development documentation was product-oriented and lacked details with respect to the project responsible for delivering that product. The documentation structure was changed to support the product development cycle through the addition of project management documents, e.g., status reports, stakeholder reports, postmortem, and so on and the addition of project management specific components found in the *PMBOK Guide;* e.g., goals/objectives, stakeholders' analysis, risk analysis, communication plan, and so on, to the internal structure of existing documents. Templates were created for all project documents to ensure consistency across all projects.

The final element of the fundamental project management building blocks was defining the components of a project management information system [PMIS]. The long-term goals of the project management function served as the driving force behind the definition of the system. A holistic approach was taken that would see the integration over time of the PMIS to other business systems, such as payroll, accounting, and product management. In addition to the standard project management planning and control requirements, the PMIS contained requirements for non-standard project management functions such as document control, issues, action items, and so on.

Executive level buy-in was obtained by gaining commitment to the long-term project management goals and the need to begin using advanced tools and building historical project databases now for use on future projects. Novice-level project management software and its associated add-ons were evaluated. This level of software was found not to meet the long-term goals of the project management function without significant manual overhead to maintain the system.

A detailed statement of requirements was developed and supplied to potential vendors. The selected software avoids the need for a large number of add-ons, exceeds the current organizational needs, and provides both the necessary infrastructure and the tools to meet long-term project management goals.

To ensure successful implementation of the new software, a significant amount of up-front effort was placed on configuring the software tools to reflect the characteristics of the PE-SCIEX organization planning structure. In addition, standard displays, reports, planning templates, and filters were created to support the different types of users. Training was provided to all types of users including executives, project managers, and team leaders. With training in place, a project roll plan was used to provide an orderly transition from switching from the old PMIS software to the new PMIS software.

## Standardized Techniques

To further develop project management practices within the organization, a number of standard techniques were introduced into the organization. The techniques are based on industry practices and were tailored to fit the PE-SCIEX organization.

### Work Breakdown Structure [WBS]

To promote standardization across all product lines and their associated derivative products, a common WBS was introduced. For a given product line, certain components of the WBS are not required and are ignored during the project planning phase; however, the common WBS structure allows for easy component analysis and enhances the commonality between the product lines.

The WBS combines both the work breakdown and the product breakdown structure. The final step in this area is the modification of the accounting system to include the WBS code of account as a component in the general ledger account number. This will provide detailed project cost breakdowns to the WBS level for both control and historical analysis. The combining of the breakdown structures and account numbering system avoids future cross-referencing problems.

The WBS is incorporated into the project planning and control section of the PMIS and into the project documentation system. The planning and control software allows the user to view the project based on WBS, and specific planning templates were created for a number of components within the WBS. New projects are making use of the WBS in the early planning phase to identify all work areas in the project. The goal is to make project teams account for all areas of the WBS even if there are no changes in a given area of the product for a specific project.

### Chart of Accounts

To simplify project planning a reduced list of cost accounts are used by the projects. A number of accounts that are directly related to overhead charges was removed since the company no longer supports very large multiple-year [over two years] projects. The planning and control software uses the reduced list of cost accounts. The incorporation of the cost accounts into the planning cycle has helped project teams to look beyond the standard labor and material cost and to start focusing on other aspects of project costs such as tooling, travel, and consulting.

### Reports

Project reporting is split into two major areas: the high-level stakeholders and the project team. Prior to standardization high-level stakeholders received varying content, quality, and frequency of reports from different projects. To avoid "information overload," a two-tiered approach was developed for relaying information to high-level stakeholders. The first tier consists of a monthly detailed report with fixed content. This report was developed in conjunction with project managers and high-level stakeholders. Highlights of the report include: standard project status indication, status justification, identification of change requests, accomplishments, earn value, and open issues that could affect the project's duration, cost, and quality. The report has received a high level of acceptance and has reduced the amount of time and confusion associated with reporting. The earn value reporting is phased in as new projects are added to the PMIS.

The second tier of high-level stakeholder reporting consists of a summary report generated from the detailed reports and a resource head count for the functional groups within product development. This report is used by the company's senior executives in a monthly review process to address projects that are in difficulty and prioritize between product lines and their associated projects. Senior executives are extremely happy with the new reporting method and are inquiring about advanced feature capability within the PMIS sooner than expected.

To address resource loading, cost, and scheduling issues encountered by project teams, a number of standard reports and display layouts were developed in the PMIS using the PE-SCIEX planning structure. Display layouts were also standardized since they could easily be printed and included directly into documents. Standard reports and display layouts were provided to ensure consistency between projects, to reduce the amount of learning and complexity within the PMIS, and to avoid reinventing the wheel.

### Change Control

A project change control methodology was introduced to prevent uncontrolled scope creepage. Scope creepage was the Achilles heal of previous projects at PE-SCIEX due to the long development time. The product development staff had become accustomed to changing scope and its associated changes in requirements, while at the same time owner staff, namely marketing staff, was accustomed to not fully defining the requirements of the product. By limiting the length of projects the opportunity for scope creepage was reduced, and better product definition was obtained by answering the following question: In a given period, what can we accomplish of value to the customer?

Change control was designed to highlight scope creepage to high-level stakeholders after a product concept was defined and to obtain their acceptance of the ramifications of the change request. Introduction of the process required education of high-level stakeholders, product development, and marketing. The key item for high-level stakeholders was showing them the impact of uncontrolled change requests on their projects. Product development and marketing staff were instructed as to the value of the change control process and the ramifications of working on unapproved change requests.

Each change request is reviewed by the project team for its impact on the project with respect to scope, schedule, cost, and time. Stakeholders are informed when change requests are received and are consulted when there is significant impact to the project to determine their preferred course of action. The project manager has the ultimate authority of accepting the change request.

In parallel, the purchasing department established a vendor change control process for projects that protected the vendors from unauthorized change requests while allowing flexibility for the product development groups. Prior to the introduction of vendor change control, parts were modified by engineers without purchasing knowledge, thus resulting in potential overruns, schedule slippage, and quality control rejections.

### Financial Analysis

A standard approach to project costing was developed with the finance department that identifies costs that are included in a project's budget, i.e., types of charges and who can charge. This allows a meaningful, standard approach to the financial analysis of projects based on where the product is within the product development life cycle. Early in the product life cycle a basic product cost structure is developed and, if possible, a comparison is made to existing product costs. An estimated selling price and volume is obtained. A high-level cost estimate of the project is developed based on the estimated cost of the current product/project phase and the development cost of previous projects. A simple break-even analysis is performed based on the above information.

A more detailed net present value analysis is performed when the project enters into the higher cost project/product development phases. This analysis is based on a standard product revenue analysis spreadsheet that contains entries for all development costs, manufacturing costs, volume, and sales drivers over the life of the product. A single scenario is completed by entering in the appropriate information for the scenario. Three basic scenarios are analyzed, i.e., worst case, optimistic, and most likely. The results of the three scenarios establish the worst and best case boundaries of the product.

### Gating

To prevent projects from running out of control, a detailed product/project gating procedure was developed. The gating procedure is used to identify weaknesses in product concepts and their associated projects before the organization commits significant resources in the development of the product. The fundamental procedure is based on the work of Dr. R. Cooper (1993) with minor modifications from Coopers and Lybrand Consulting. Additional enhancements to the fundamental gating procedure were made to address the quality of execution of the project responsible for the delivery of the product. Executive management and marketing buy-in was obtained through the use of training courses, allowing those affected to help in the development and maintenance of the procedure.

The gating system is the central component of the product development procedure. The deliveries of the product development process feed the information requirements of the gating process. The gating process has:

- improved organizational commitment to projects
- enhanced the quality of the information generated by the project
- provided greater clarity to the project manager and ISO auditors as to the type of information required to assess if the product/project is fundamentally sound

- prevented weak projects from proceeding forward and draining resources.

## Leveraging

To help with the rapid introduction of project management a number of existing formal business systems were modified for use with projects. These included the engineering change notification [ECN], corrective action, non-conformance reporting, and warehousing systems. Modifications to the first three systems were made that allowed project personnel to quickly make changes using the basic process structure; i.e., the emphasis is on notification, identification, and resolution and not on formal control and sign off. The advantage to this approach is the project team's familiarity with the existing processes. Integrating the project warehouse with the production warehouse was done to provide a controlled process in which project parts are received, and quality is checked and stored using existing business practices while avoiding duplication of work and reducing the project's resource requirements.

Other groups outside of the project management function were used in assisting with the introduction of project management techniques. Consultants played a major role in the research, evaluation, and implementation of different PMIS components. The vice president of manufacturing, a strong supporter of project management techniques, delivered earned value and planning presentations to the senior executive. This person is still used today along with the project management champion in selling techniques and processes to the senior executive. Positioning the project manager as the single point of contact for a development project has resulted in a strong buy-in from the marketing group into the project management process. Marketing has developed roll out plans for products and is a strong supporter of change control and early up front product/project definition.

## Education

To ensure continual adoption and development of project management into the organization, an education strategy was developed. The basis of this strategy is centered around the following items:

- hiring qualified personnel
- *PMBOK Guide*
- increased organizational awareness
- internal and external courses.

Potential project managers are checked for organizational fit with respect to product development functional managers, physiological profiles, and skills. Given the nature of the product, few people have the appropriate technical background, hence the emphasis lies in the person's capability to learn and adapt. The educational profile used is one that contains a combined business and engineering background in projects. This was purposely done to help jump start the organization and avoid a long learning curve within the project management function.

The *PMBOK Guide*, coupled with the organizational goals and the current state of project management practices within PE-SCIEX, forms the basis from which training objectives and priorities are established. *PMBOK Guide* is used to establish the broad (horizontal) knowledge-based requirements for a project manager, while the organizational goals establish the additional requirements of a specific project management knowledge area within the guide. Educational emphasis during the first two years of project management introduction was in the following *PMBOK Guide* areas: integration, scope, time, and cost management. This is not surprising given the past performance of previous projects. Project quality training was simply an extension of existing ISO 9001 practices. As PE-SCIEX makes greater use of global development teams, future areas of training will include: procurement, communication, team building, and risk management.

With project management practices still in the introductory phase, a significant amount of effort is devoted to raising the awareness of the need for project management and its associated practices. The make up of the people attending introductory courses is changing from managers and team leaders to project team members and from product development staff to personnel from other functional groups within the company. The adoption of project management practices in other areas of the organization is starting to occur.

Project manager training involves the use of an extensive computer-based training library of business-related topics including specific project management topics. Where possible, external training courses are used to obtain the basic skills and knowledge associated with industry recognized topics, while internal training courses focus on company specific issues, procedures, and knowledge. Training associated with new tool introduction does not occur until the tool is customized and ready for roll out. In this situation the vendor will use the customized tool configuration as an example during the training course. Additional training is provided, if necessary, as a result of enhancements to the tool.

## Conclusion

The critical elements to the successful introduction of project management within PE-SCIEX are as follows:

- realizing the organization was not capable of developing its own internal project management skills within the given time frames
- having the support of executive champions in the establishment and ongoing development of the project management process
- using a professional project manager to rapidly establish and develop a successful project management organization
- aligning project management goals with the organizational goals, and positioning the project management function as a key component in obtaining these goals
- organizing the product development process so that projects can succeed by managing a reasonable amount of risk
- selecting and delivering on an attainable start-up project
- taking a longer term approach to project management capabilities, which helped in the early identification of techniques and tools prior to needing them, thus allowing time to develop the techniques and tools
- choosing the right software tools and taking the time to customize them, which addressed a number of standardization problems
- modifying existing business processes to support projects, which reduced the amount of time to create internal project processes and achieves greater buy-in.

The last item to remember is that the introduction of project management into a small- or medium- sized company is normally viewed as an infringement of territory, individuality, and/or creativity. In this situation a reasonable amount of patience is required since the organization's culture is changing. At the same time the implementers require flexibility to take advantage of unexpected situations that will further promote the introductory process. A holistic introductory approach is required; i.e., the introduction is not a linear process but is a parallel process in which the implementers move between different objectives, nudging them forward towards their goals. With the successful introduction of project management within PE-SCIEX completed, the real work of continuing to advance and grow the process to continually meet the future challenges of the organization is only beginning.

## References

Cooper, Robert. 1993. *Winning at New Products Accelerating the Process from Idea to Launch.* Addison Wesley.

# Managing Projects with Technological Changes in the Next Century

Dr. Janet K. Yates, San Jose University, California
Dr. Adel K. Eskander, P.E., U.S. General Services Administration

## Introduction

To survive the transition into the twenty-first century, project managers, owners, architectural and engineering firms, constructors, and their employees must keep pace with the newly developing dynamic and challenging data transmission technologies.

During the past five years there have been major changes in the way that members of the engineering and construction industry (E/C) have been communicating with each other. In the eighties and the early nineties, members of the engineering and construction industry (E/C) and project managers used manual filing systems and conventional methods to send and receive information. Now e-mail, voice mail, and the internet are becoming the preferred methods to distribute, receive, and file information.

In the engineering and construction (E/C) industry, construction companies, owners, and several professional construction organizations are investing large amounts of money in research and development (R&D) to create new construction methods and tools that can reduce labor costs, reduce construction duration, improve productivity, provide real time schedules, improve quality, reduce construction material waste, and improve safety (Georgia Institute of Technology).

In Japan, there is a shortage of laborers, and the Japanese laws do not permit importing laborers; therefore, most of the research and development has been concentrated on automation and robotics. "Japanese universities conduct little research in sharp contrast to institutes of higher learning in the United States, where 60 percent of all basic research is conducted, backed heavily by the Federal Government. The intense R&D activities of the Japan's builders is unmatched in the United States" (Levy 1993). Kajima Corporation is one of the oldest and largest construction companies in Japan, and its members have developed several automated machines to overcome the labor shortage and to increase productivity; examples of these machines are the automatic ceiling board installation and the shield tunneling machines, including one of the world's largest, which is almost forty-six feet in diameter (Levy 1993).

It is obvious that the construction industry is looking for ways to move away from conventional construction methods and techniques where in the past a construction site meant a heavy concentration of laborers, and it is moving in the direction of industrializing construction projects. In the past, if a site condition at a construction site would effect the project cost and schedule, it required that someone from the main office, and the architect/engineer (A/E) firm, be contacted to provide information on how to proceed. This could result in a site visit by the project team to investigate the situation in order to make a decision. Now this type of situation can be transmitted to the main office through the use of digitized cameras at the job site and video conferencing at multiple locations.

Up until the late seventies, engineers, architects, and designers used creativity in detailing drawings and developing specifications for each project. In recent years, the engineering approach to projects has improved by utilizing standard details for drafting and standardized specifications such as the ones produced by the American Institute of Architects (AIA) and the Construction Specification Institute (CSI). These specifications are used as the bases for specifications development; therefore, this new information sharing technology reduces the amount of hours needed to complete the design phase of a project.

Another example of the use of new technology is when the government uses the World Wide Web (WWW) to advertise its contracts. Contractors can submit their bids through the web and awards can also be processed in this manner.

When an examination is performed on how projects were managed in the past and how they are managed now, it becomes obvious that machines and technology are permeating the process. Computers, if used properly, can improve efficiency, but they cannot be used without the information that must be entered by engineers and managers.

## Effect of Future Technology on the Type of Materials and Equipment Used in Construction Projects

In a world where the population is continuously increasing, and its natural resources are continuously decreasing, it is probable that current construction materials will no longer be available in the future, and new versions will replace those materials currently in use. Construction labor force will have to develop new and improved techniques to handle and work with the future types of equipment and materials. Construction materials manufactures will have to upgrade their processing lines to be able to produce the future construction materials. Engineers and architects will have to become knowledgeable with new market technology and new materials in order to be able to compete in the future. Estimators for contractors and designers will have to change and modify their databases to accommodate the future types of materials.

The New York State Center for Advanced Technology (CAT) in Automation and Robotics is researching the areas of intelligent materials processing and process control, autonomous navigation, sensor-based telerobotics, dexterous manipulation, precision assembly, pattern recognition, and machine vision. Application areas include aluminum extrusion, resistance welding, thermal coating, rapid product prototyping, intelligent vehicle highway system, nuclear power plant maintenance and repair, document processing, and remote sensing (CAT).

Materials from outer space are another possibility that is currently being researched by National Aeronautics and Space Administration (NASA); e.g., once humans have reached Mars, bases could rapidly be established to support not only exploration but experimentation to develop the broad range of civil, agricultural, chemical, and industrial engineering techniques required to turn the raw materials of Mars into food, propellant, ceramics, plastics, metals, wires, structures, and so on (Zubrin 1994).

Robotics equipment, automated data management and data generation systems, expert systems, and new generation of construction materials are paving the road to the future of the construction industry, and they can not be avoided. Prefabricated construction elements are being used widely and increasingly due to their economical value in terms of labor cost reduction and the precision in the fabrication process that reduces wasted materials, which in turn reduces construction costs.

## Automating the Management of Project Development

New projects are developed based on social or environmental needs. Private investors or public officials are prompted by these needs to develop capital projects. Some type of economical, risk, financial, and market analysis must be performed in order to spend capital funds. Using today's technological advancements these analyses are performed with the assistance of computer software and data input from individuals who rationalize the results and write the reports.

The environmental consciousness of our society forces the construction industry into developing projects without negatively impacting the environment, preserving the surrounding areas, and being environmentally safe. Addressing environmental issues when developing projects is becoming the norm for all capital projects and some minor projects; therefore, many environmental consultants and engineering and architectural firms are developing data banks that include various site environmental impact conditions. Currently, there are several environmental software packages that contain large environmental databases that are used for site simulations to develop various models for projects or prospective sites.

Urban development projects have a unique feature that adds to its complexity; that is, social impact that can cause major schedule delays and possible scope changes by introducing new elements to the project. Social impact studies are known for their important role in the project development phase; thus, it is important to complete them as soon as possible. In order to develop social impact assessment, there are several generic social science tools that can be applied systematically to the planning process (Delli priscoli 1981; Goodman 1984). Professor Goodman of Polytechnic University has described social forecasts as assumption-based, value driven, and rarely neutral, and they may be normative statements reflecting what forecasters feel the world "ought to be" (Goodman 1984).

Several methods have been developed for evaluating social trends in the past and for forecasting the future social conditions using mathematical methods and computer simulations. With the increasing technological advancement in data collection and data sharing, it is possible that a master plan can be developed that includes social information relating to all communities being built into a national master map format; thereafter, projects information can be entered, and the analysis can be done instantaneously.

There are several simulation programs that can provide reliable economical and risk forecasts and analyses. Providing for current trends of computers and software developments, future project development could be programmed and analyzed with the use of expert systems, also known as artificial intelligent systems (AIS), and minimum human efforts—just project data inputs.

## Automating the Management of Procurement

Methods of contracting vary between public and private sector. There is tremendous pressure on the construction industry to change its methods of communications between the parties involved, from adversary to partnering. This type of pressure has affected the methods used for contracting in the public sector, and consequently several procurement restriction regulations have been relaxed. The competition for automating the construction contracts procurement process began in 1994 when Vice President Al Gore announced the Procurement Reform Act. Many procurement management software programs have been developed and some of them are accessible through the Internet, and these software packages can be used for advertising, announcing, and awarding contracts over the Internet web. Legal concerns have risen from the use of electronic signatures and legal implications, but it they are used and will continue to be used.

Many government agencies, and private corporations, are procuring contracts, processing contracts modifications, and managing contracts files using computer software, and companies and government agencies are using credit cards to award and make payments on small contracts. Electronic signatures have been used on various types of small purchases, and the United States General Services Administration (US GSA) is in the process of adopting a new software called "SACONS" that allows the use of electronic signatures. Private and public sectors are using electronic funds transfer to pay contractors, and contractors are submitting payment requests through electronic mail (e-mail).

Today's technologies allows the procurement processes to become paperless; therefore, the rules and regulations are adapting to the new technologies. The opportunities are unlimited for construction contracts to be advertised on the World Wide Web (WWW), and national and international contractors are invited to bid projects. International Standards has been developed, and many United States companies are adopting the International Organization for Standardization (ISO 9000) standards in order to become more competitive globally (Yates and Anifftos 1996).

## Automating the Management of Design

There has been an ongoing development process for the methods and techniques used in managing design and construction projects. Since ancient times, there have been several successful projects, which were developed, designed, and constructed without the use of modern technologies, such as power construction machinery, robots, computers, testing laboratories for materials and equipment, and standards for buildings and safety codes. Some examples of these projects are the Pyramids, the Eiffel Tower, the Hoover Dam, the Brooklyn Bridge, and so on. The original design of these projects were generated, formulated, and developed by elite groups of individuals, and these individuals were recognized nationally and internationally for their unique accomplishments. In an era of quality management and team work the concept of individuality has diminished and is becoming obsolete; instead, the standardization of several project elements has become the norm.

One suggested method for developing various design ideas and overcoming the foreseeable shortage in the engineering and architects workforce is to perform around the clock design activities, involving engineers and architects from around the world through electronic communication systems (Yates 1993). The management of design requires interfacing with clients and owners, modeling different design schemes, performing design reviews, and performing code compliance reviews, and these types of activities require decision-making authority and judgments. Since construction projects are unique, and each one has its own characteristics, the project design phase can be automated to a certain extent using machines and computers, but the design must be evaluated by project managers and the project team. Future projects in the next century may include project designs in different planet atmospheres, deep water climates, floating cities, and space stations; the thinking process for these designs and projects needs will be originated by engineers, designers, and architects, but the actual design calculations, design development, and generation of the design documents can easily be automated.

## Automating the Management of Construction

"Developed countries like Japan and the United Kingdom have construction industries that are split into about 25: 65: 10 percent civil engineering: building: process, and they are becoming increasingly involved in repair and maintenance work" (Cleland and Gareis 1994, 26-1). Performing the construction work and delivering a completed constructed project is becoming challenging and complicated day after day. The management of a construction site with a lot of robotics equipment performing the work can become more of a scientific operation.

Project managers of the future should be able to deal with the old and the new as many of the existing structures will continue to exist in the next century, and they will require major repairs and modernization projects. Some of the existing vital structures may fail due to natural disasters, and replacement structure(s) will be needed. As the world population continues to increase, the demand for housing will continue to develop, precipitating the need for civil engineering projects to service these houses. There are several other types of projects that should be considered by project managers and construction managers; these projects are specialty projects such as experimental sites, space stations, and laboratories for various experiments.

The intent of automation, and the use of robotics in construction, are to reduce time, improve quality, reduce cost, improve efficiency, and provide precise controls. Many of the repairs and modernization projects will continue to have the extensive demand for manual laborers, while new construction can be fully automated and remotely controlled by the use of computers and robots. In the case of future modernization projects, project managers will still have to have the knowledge of the old methods of project management, where dealing with various trades, unions regulations, and the unexpected existing site conditions are the daily routine, but with using tomorrow's tools and technologies to communicate. In the case of new construction, project managers will have to learn about robotics equipment and site management where more moving vehicles and less laborers are the controlling factors.

## Automating the Management of Documentation

In the near future, manual filing systems, paper files, and archive warehouses will no longer be in existence. Electronic filing has become the accepted method to operate and run an efficient operation in the current era. Methods to input and maintain electronic filing have yet to become standardized, and companies are developing their own individual methods for keeping their records in logical order. Transferring information and data into electronic media is advancing and improving day after day; it initially began with manual typing, then document scanners were introduced to the market and they are continually improving, and computers with voice activation technology and touch screen computers are already developed.

Looking at the current trend of technological advancement in the computer and electronic fields, the next century could have no paper, and electronic devices could be the main method for storing and retrieving information' therefore, capabilities of computers to search and locate documents, files, and information in the future are expected to be far superior to the ones available today.

### Transmission of Information and Ideas

In the early days pigeons were used to deliver and transport messages and information, messengers were used both inland and overseas, and later airmail became the preferred fast method of transmitting information. Recently electronic data transmission has become an acceptable method for transmitting and communicating. The forms of transmitting information and documentation have evolved from paper media to electronic media, and from wire transmission to wireless transmission.

The concept of documentation has emerged from the need to complement human memories; therefore, agreements, contracts, site conditions, designs, and specifications have to be entered in some form of documentation to reduce or negate misunderstanding, disagreements, and/or conflicts between the various individuals and groups involved in a project. The developments of such documentation are usually based on the results of several project meetings, contract reviews, design reviews, changes in agreed to conditions, and so on. In order for these documents to become valid and acceptable to all parties, they have to be transmitted for review and concurrence.

### Access to Information

Today's technology allows information to be accessed from remote locations without the need to be present at a specific site. The use of electronic communications, telephones, faxes, modems, and video conferences allows employees and employers to reconfigure their office space needs, work schedules, and work locations. These types of communications have affected the commercial real estate industry, where many corporations downsized their offices in major cities because of the costly rental rates for commercial office space, and they offered their employees several options, such as early retirement, work at home, work flexible hours, and work part-time at the office and part-time at home, to allow two individuals to share the same office space, and relocate to another location. All these conveniences became available because of the existing methods to access information from remote locations at affordable costs.

Information accessing and retrieving from remote locations has permitted many small engineering and architectural firms to compete with other major firms due to their ability to maintain offices at remote locations at low rent, low overhead, and hiring qualified individuals at less salaries due to lower cost of living.

### Speed of Transmitting and Accessing Information

When personal computers were first introduced in early seventies, they were designed to solve complicated mathematical formulas and equations. At that time their speed was considered to be a technological breakthrough and they saved engineers tremendous amounts of time in solving multidimensional design problems. As the need for increased speed continually grew, there has been a rapid advancement in computer information processing speed and technology.

An important element of decision-making processes is to have access to the most recent projects related information. When decisions are made and communicated quickly to project staff, it helps reduce the costs related to schedule delays; therefore, projects in the next century will probably be on fast tracks, where multiple contracts are in progress concurrently, and decisions are constantly needed in order to proceed with the work. Using the high speed of data transmission technology, decisions can immediately be translated into actual field work, and consequently contractors incur costs, which can be costly if decisions are not given full evaluation and analysis. In contrast, in current project management practice, decisions are not immediately translated into the actual field work.

## Conclusion

In the future, the qualification requirements for project managers will be different from the qualifications in the past and the ones required now. In the future, project managers must be able to obtain accurate information from venders, contractors, and subordinates and see that this information is properly entered and used by computer software programs and other future technology. The foreseeable future technology will automate a majority of everyday functions as they are known to the industry today; therefore, it is foreseeable that current methods for project management will not be the methods used in the future, and project managers will perform as decision-makers, negotiators, and public relation liaisons and will be well-versed in technical and management techniques. Macro-management is expected to be the preferred method and practice for project management. In order to successfully manage projects in the next century, management by objective should be exercised. The importance of management by objective is that it aligns the project goals with the goals of the project team and the goals of the organization. Management by objective helps set performance objectives at the beginning of the project.

The project manager tools for the next century are communication and speed. The expected future methods for communication are electronic technologies, and the rate of communicating accurate information could be a determining factor in the success of future project managers.

In the next century, it is expected that two types of construction projects will continue to dominate the industry; these projects are: building new structures and repairing, restoring, and modernizing existing structures. Each type of these projects will require different management skills and knowledge. New construction projects will depend on full or semi-automated project systems and construction sites, and repair projects will require knowledge of today's management tools plus tomorrow's knowledge of the types of materials, equipments, tools, control systems, and communication.

The construction industry is moving into a broader spectrum, and the existence of the World Wide Web (WWW) has allowed for global competition for design and construction contracts. Many design and construction firms are concerned with their ability to keep qualified employees in this globally competitive market. In Japan, some of the major construction companies provide their employees compensation for housing, and the companies' resorts are made available for employee and their families for vacations (Levy 1993).

The objectives of inventing new technologies are to increase safety for the laborers, employees, and structures; reduce project duration; provide secure structures; and reduce total project cost while maintaining high quality. The engineering and construction industry, as well as the telecommunications industry, are advancing and improving, and they will continue to do so in the next century. Therefore, in order for project managers to manage projects in the future, they must learn and understand the changes in industry goals, values, and objectives.

## Recommendations

To achieve the intended end results, project managers must have the technical knowledge and the ability to learn and quickly adapt and adjust as technology moves forward into the next century. Some of the knowledge that project managers currently possess will become less valuable with the development of new technologies.

In order to address managing projects in the twenty-first century, it is important for project managers to be aware of the type of changes in technology and projects that will be taking place in the next decade, the type of technological innovations that may be implemented in the near future, and their impact on project management practices. Some of these future project-related advancements are the technical attributes of future facilities, technical improvements by contractors and suppliers, innovative technical ideas, and process improvements and how they alter the construction environment and their impact on future project management practices.

Project managers should take advantage of the powerful computer capabilities available for tracking and monitoring projects, product and materials management, equipment management, resource management, and project management software(Lientz and Rea 1995).

With downsizing, and advancements in computer technology, project managers of the future will need several types of communication skills such as typing, technical writing, phone skills, and the ability to manage and communicate multitasks concurrently. The use of expert systems as a mean to access information and reach decisions is another skill that project managers will need to posses.

There should be an approved international training and certification program accepted by members of the engineering and construction industry that requires cyclical training for project managers. The training program should include new management methodologies, as well as advancement in the engineering and construction fields. Companies should institute minimum training requirements for their project managers that provide an overview of new technologies and the companies' view of future project management techniques.

## References


Cleland, David I., and Roland Gareis. 1994. *Global Project Management Handbook.* New York: McGraw-Hill, Inc.: 26-1.

Delli priscoli, Jerry. 1981. "People and Water: Social Impact Assessment Research." *Water Spectrum* (Summer).

Georgia Institute of Technology. *Construction Research: Innovative Construction Technologies.*

Goodman, Alvin S. 1984. *Principles of Water Resources Planning.* Englewood Cliffs, NJ: Prentice Hall, Inc.

Levy, Sidney M.1993. *Japan's Big Six: Inside Japan's Construction Industry.* New York: McGraw-Hill, Inc.

Lientz, Bennet P., and Kathryn P. Rea. 1995. *Project Management for the 21st Century*. Academic Press.

New York State Center for Advanced Technology (CAT) in Automated Robotics.

Yates, Janet K., and Stylianos C. Anifftos. 1996. "International Standards: U.S. Construction Industry Competitiveness." *Cost Engineering Journal* 38 (7): 34.

Yates, Janet K. 1993. "Construction Workforce in the Year 2000." *Cost Engineering Journal* 35 (7): 17.

Zubrin, Robert M. 1994. *The Significance of Martian Frontier.* Ad Astra.


This paper reflects the opinion of the authors and not those of the United States Government or the General Services Administration.

# Project Management Maturity Model

Anita Fincher, U.S. Dept of Agriculture, National Finance Center
Dr. Ginger Levin, GLH, Inc.

## Introduction and Background

The Software Engineering Institute (SEI) developed the capability maturity model (CMM) for software as a way for organizations to improve the way software is built and maintained. The CMM shows how an organization's software engineering practices evolve under various conditions. It was developed as a progressive standard to help an organization continuously improve its software practices.

About the same time that the SEI was developing the CMM, the Project Management Institute (PMI) developed the first *Project Management Body of Knowledge (PMBOK)*. The 1987 document defined the *PMBOK* as the topics, subject areas, and processes required to apply management principles to practices. PMI issued its 1996 edition of the *PMBOK* as *A Guide to the Project Management Body of Knowledge (PMBOK Guide)*. It presents nine project management processes that describe how project management elements interrelate. A total of thirty-seven project management sub-processes are presented, with each sub-process described in terms of its inputs, outputs, and tools and techniques.

The *Project Management Maturity Model (PMMM)* presented herein builds on the nine project management processes in the 1996 *PMBOK Guide* by presenting goals to be used to assess an organization's maturity level in project management, using similar concepts to the CMM. The *PMMM* is based on a comparable framework to that of SEI's CMM in terms of process evolution with five levels, indicators of process maturity, and capability.

Goals in each level are presented as a results statement to describe an observable feature of an organization that has effectively implemented the particular portion of the *PMBOK Guide* knowledge area. The *PMMM*, like the CMM, is based on an evolutionary and systematic process improvement approach. Organizations can use the *PMMM* to determine where specific key interventions are required to assist in improving project management practices and targeting process improvements.

## An Overview of a Level 1 *PMMM* Organization

Specific goals and activities are not described for a Level 1 *PMMM* organization. Similar to the CMM, it is assumed that all organizations are operating at Level 1 before the introduction of any project management processes. In Level 1, projects are managed in an ad hoc fashion, and there is no formal project management methodology used. The organization can still have effective projects, but like Level 1 in the CMM, many projects are accomplished through heroic efforts. People working on projects either struggle with the existing process in place in the organization or tend to invent a process as they work on the project. Characteristics of organizations operating at Level 1 in the *PMMM* are listed below according to each *PMBOK Guide* knowledge area.

### Project Integration Management

Project plans are not prepared in an organized fashion, and generally, a project schedule constitutes a plan. A formal change control process or system does not exist in the organization.

### Project Scope Management

Project scope management is not understood or followed; a project may or may not end up meeting customer needs. There is no formal methodology used to decide when to initiate a project; many projects originate because individuals just decide to do them, and the projects may not be officially sanctioned by management. Other projects begin when dictated by management. Project managers are assigned on an ad hoc basis.

### Project Time Management

Standardized templates for project schedules are not used. Project management software is just beginning to be introduced in the organization and may only be used to list specific tasks to be performed without consideration of network logic or resource requirements. Schedule development may not be realistic as projects are unlikely to be completed when planned.

### Project Cost Management

Costs tend to exceed available budget as poor cost estimating or no cost estimating is performed. Resource planning is ad hoc and not coordinated with cost estimating.

### Project Quality Management

Quality control and quality assurance generally are performed only by external organizations to the performing organization

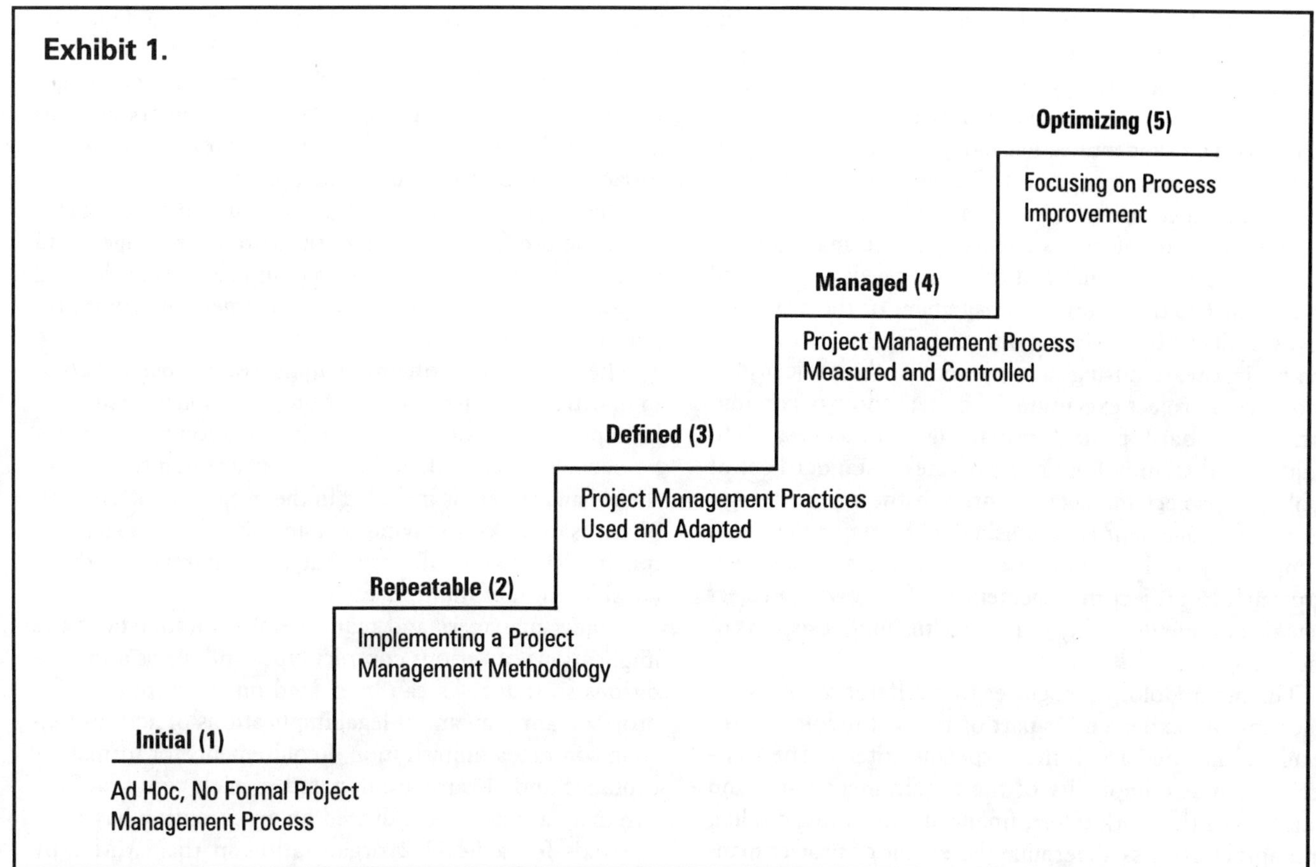


or after the fact by auditors as required by a specific contract. Inspection is the tool used for quality control with a narrow and specific meaning. Project overruns and rework are common and expected.

### Project Human Resource Management

Project managers who are successful are heroes and are rewarded individually. The organization is struggling with the concept of a matrix organization; functional managers are unwilling to share authority with project managers. Most projects are performed under functional organizations or through a weak matrix task force type structure.

### Project Communication Management

Project performance reports are prepared only as needed or requested by senior managers, the contract, or the customer. Performance reporting is limited to status reporting and descriptions of accomplishments. Analysis of variance is not performed.

No regular project reviews are held. Performance reviews are only held if requested by a customer or as a condition of a contract.

Project closeout is not separately planned or managed and is not considered until deliverables have been presented to the customer. Some projects are never closed out.

### Project Risk Management

A risk management plan is not prepared. Risks are identified after the fact.

### Project Procurement Management

A procurement management plan is not prepared. Requirements for formal acceptance and closure are not provided in writing or defined in advance.

## *PMMM* Level 2—Repeatable—Implementing a Project Management Methodology

By the time an organization reaches *PMMM* Level 2, its project management methodology is repeatable and under basic management control. Similar to that of the CMM Level 2, project managers prepare project plans and estimates and control project performance. Best practices are gathered at the project level, and there is a marked difference in the style of work from Level 1 organizations. Members of the organization have participated in project management training programs. This training includes training in the project management methodology, project management software, team building, requirements analysis, analysis of variance and earned value, risk identification and quantification, and project procurement management. Training in requirements analysis and specification also is provided to customers.

The purpose of the standard project management methodology is to ensure that customer needs are met and to standardize the internal management of the organization's projects. It provides a structured approach to guide the project team during development of the project plan and during project execution. The methodology communicates standard project management practices, techniques, and terminology and provides a standard set of tools for project managers. Through the methodology, project management is established as a core professional competency in the organization. It provides a consistent approach to project management while allowing project managers some flexibility to manage the unique aspects of each project.

The methodology recognizes that differences in its application are expected. As part of the methodology, projects are classified according to specific criteria. These criteria, such as complexity of the requirements; size and duration of the work effort; financial and strategic value; and amount of risk determine the extent of project management required. For all projects, plans in some fashion are required, and approval levels are dictated by the classification schema in place. Project reviews also are required at different levels depending on the particular project in the classification. Standard project management software is adopted and made part of the methodology.

Since all projects are based on needs and requirements, the importance of accurate requirements specification is noted. A system to monitor and control changes to requirements is necessary. Standard approaches for project planning, including the development of project and team charters, work breakdown structures (WBS), and activity lists are under review to serve as possible templates for future efforts. The organization is considering standard quantifiable metrics in terms of cost, schedule, and quality; unquantified objectives, such as achieving customer satisfaction, may still be used.

Cost estimates are prepared either through a top-down approach by the project manager or in a bottom-up fashion by project team members. Top-down approaches use analogous estimating as the primary methodology. Schedule and cost control are limited to monitoring performance to detect variances from the plan.

The Level 2 organization is preparing a quality policy. The emphasis in quality management is on the product of the project as quality is considered to be inspected into the project rather than built in. Quality audits are conducted on an exception basis or if required under contract. Quality control consists of inspection so customers are not aware of errors but is evolving toward a prevention approach to keep errors out of the process.

The organization is moving toward use of a strong matrix structure for its project work as project managers and functional managers are working out respective roles and responsibilities. A responsibility assignment matrix is prepared for each project.

The initial requirements analysis assesses needed communications requirements, but project resources still may be expended on communicating information that may not be needed by all stakeholders. Risks are identified, and their management is included in the project plan. The emphasis is on risks involving cost and schedule impact, not quality. Risks generally are analyzed separately without consideration of multiple effects.

Project managers and team members understand the implications of various contract types and terms and conditions so that risks can be passed on to suppliers. The project team is aware of legal implications of actions taken in contract administration. Requirements for formal acceptance and closure are dictated in each contract. Procurement audits are conducted on an exception basis.

Goals for a Level 2 organization in the *PMMM* by *PMBOK Guide* knowledge area are as follows.

#### Project Integration Management

*Goal 1. The organization has implemented a standard methodology for project management.*

*Goal 2. Project plans are prepared and signed-off; management reviews are defined.*

#### Project Scope Management

*Goal 1. Affected groups and individuals agree to commitments related to the project through a formal project initiation process.*

*Goal 2. The project management team, including customers, receive training in requirements specification.*

*Goal 3. A system monitors and controls changes made to requirements.*

*Goal 4. Standard WBS templates are developed and available.*

#### Project Time Management

*Goal 1. People receive training in the standard project management software package which has been selected for use in the organization.*

*Goal 2. The schedule is issued for use in planning and tracking.*

***Project Cost Management***

*Goal 1. Cost estimates are documented for use in planning and tracking.*

***Project Quality Management***

*Goal 1. Noncompliance issues are addressed through quality control inspection and audits if required under a contract.*

***Project Human Resources Management***

*Goal 1. Employees are trained on the organization's standard project management methodology.*

*Goal 2. Responsibility assignment matrices are prepared and reviewed for use on similar projects.*

***Project Communications Management***

*Goal 1. A system of regular performance reports and reviews is implemented.*

***Project Risk Management***

*Goal 1. Project risks are identified and analyzed.*

*Goal 2. Employees receive training in risk analysis techniques.*

***Project Procurement Management***

*Goal 1. Employees receive training in project procurement management.*

*Goal 2. Suppliers agree to commitments.*

*Goal 3. Ongoing communications are maintained with suppliers.*

## *PMMM* Level 3—Defined—Project Management Practices Used and Adapted

The Level 3 *PMMM* organization is one in which its project management practices are used by the organization as a whole. The project management methodology, however, does not restrict projects and is adapted as needed. Best practices are shared.

At this stage, project plans are prepared regularly. The level of detail depends on the specific project classification. All stakeholders contribute to the planning process. Assumptions from project plans are documented and shared across the organization. The purpose of the plans is to facilitate communication among project stakeholders and to provide a baseline for performance measurement and project controls.

Customers and the project team are part of the requirements specification effort, and both sign off, with supplier participation as appropriate, to ensure that requirements are well understood. The project plan and the performance measurement baseline, however, are viewed differently with the project management baseline representing management control that changes only intermittently and in response to approved scope changes. Project plans, though, continually change and are reviewed as more detail is available. Plans include each *PMBOK Guide* knowledge area, either as a standalone document or as part of the overall project plan. A specific change control system for requirements, cost, and schedule is developed for each project, and a work authorization system is in place.

The methodology includes project selection criteria and a formal project initiation process. Project managers generally are assigned before the execution phase and work with others in the project initiation phase. A written scope statement is developed as part of scope planning to establish criteria for project decisions. A scope verification process ensures that there is customer acceptance of project deliverables.

Templates are available and used for planning. The WBS serves as the basis for schedule development, cost estimating, and risk management. In schedule development, other scheduling techniques are used in addition to precedence or arrow diagramming methods. The project schedule is approved according to the project management methodology and base-lined for use to measure and report schedule performance. Crashing and fast tracking techniques are used. Life cycle costing is being introduced and used so that the effect of project decisions on the cost of using the products of projects are known. Resource planning and cost estimating are coordinated. The cost baseline serves as a time-phased budget to measure and monitor project cost performance. Earned value analysis is used for performance measurement and for forecasting.

Project quality management addresses both project management and the specific products. The organization has quality standards in place, and team members recognize that quality is built into the project, not inspected in. Tools and techniques for quality planning are used regularly to help the project team anticipate the occurrence of potential quality problems. Checklists are used and standardized to ensure there is consistency in frequently performed activities; they become part of the project's records. Quality assurance activities are performed routinely, with quality audits providing a structured review to address lessons learned. Trend analysis is used to monitor technical, cost, and schedule performance; unanticipated rework is minimal.

The organization is examining alternative reward and recognition systems that are team-based to support the project environment. Customers and suppliers may be team members. There is more certification of project management professionals in the organization. The organization uses a variety of structures for its projects, and how the project is organized often is influenced by the skills and capabilities of specific team members. The responsibility assignment matrix is prepared at various levels of the project to define responsibilities of organizational units and specific individuals. the organizational breakdown structure complements the WBS. Team building training emphasizes the temporary nature of project management, the dual reporting relationship that exists in the matrix structure, and communications skills; team development occurs throughout the project.

Key management reviews are held regularly. Standard performance reports are prepared. A project management information system is used throughout the life cycle. Metrics are in place for cost, schedule, and quality. Performance reports provide the level of detail required by stakeholders as documented in the project communications plan. Project closeout begins on day one of the project and ends when the final deliverable is presented to the customer, and an indexed series of project records is prepared for archiving with formal documentation of lessons learned.

Risk management is a continuous activity, with risk identification addressing both positive and negative outcomes. Previous projects and commercial databases are reviewed to help identify risks. Contingency planning is an ongoing part of risk management planning and is integrated as required into other parts of the project plan. Specific estimates are made of needed reserves.

If the organization is submitting a proposal, the prospective project manager is part of the proposal development process. If the organization is reviewing proposals from suppliers, the project manager is a member of the evaluation team and works to prepare the evaluation criteria. Throughout, the project manager works in partnership with the procurement department.

Goals for a Level 3 organization in the *PMMM* by *PMBOK Guide* knowledge area are as follows.

**Project Integration Management**

*Goal 1. A standard project management methodology for the organization is developed and maintained.*

*Goal 2. A specific project's defined process for project management is a tailored version of the organization's standard methodology.*

*Goal 3. Information related to the use of the organization's project management methodology by various projects is collected, reviewed, and made available through the use of a project management information system.*

*Goal 4. Affected groups and individuals agree to all project baselines.*

**Project Scope Management**

*Goal 1. Project scope management activities are planned.*

*Goal 2. As part of the project objectives, metrics are used for cost, schedule and quality.*

*Goal 3. A scope verification process ensures customer acceptance of the deliverables of the project.*

*Goal 4. Customers and suppliers participate in the needs-requirements life cycle along with the project team.*

*Goal 5. Changes to baselines are controlled.*

**Project Time Management**

*Goal 1. Project time management activities are planned.*

*Goal 2. A variety of scheduling techniques are considered and used on each project.*

**Project Cost Management**

*Goal 1. Cost management activities are planned.*

*Goal 2. Life cycle costing is used.*

*Goal 3. Resource planning and cost estimating are closely coordinated and outside validation of cost estimates is performed.*

**Project Quality Management**

*Goal 1. A quality policy and specific quality standards are established and agreed to by those affected.*

*Goal 2. Project quality management activities are planned, and tools and techniques for quality planning are used regularly to pinpoint potential problems.*

*Goal 3. Quality assurance activities are conducted.*

*Goal 4. Procedures are in place as part of the overall change control process to handle needed process adjustments.*

**Project Human Resource Management**

*Goal 1. Project human resource management activities are planned.*

*Goal 2. The organization works in a variety of structures for its projects.*

*Goal 3. Resource commitments between groups and organizations are agreed to by those affected.*

*Goal 4. Customers and suppliers often are members of each project team.*

*Goal 5. Training activities are planned so that individuals receive the training needed to perform their roles on projects.*

**Project Communications Management**

*Goal 1. Project communications management activities are planned and tightly linked with organizational planning.*

*Goal 2. Results of planning activities are regularly reviewed and revised as required to ensure continued applicability.*

*Goal 3. Performance reporting emphasizes earned value and analysis of variance.*

*Goal 4. Project records are maintained in an organized fashion for future use and assessment.*

#### Project Risk Management

*Goal 1. Project risk management activities are planned.*

*Goal 2. Project risk management is a continuous activity throughout each project.*

#### Project Procurement Management

*Goal 1. Project procurement management activities are planned.*

*Goal 2. Project managers work in partnership with contracting officers and suppliers.*

### *PMMM* Level 4—Managed—Project Management Process Measured and Controlled

In the Level 4 *PMMM* organization, project management is a natural part of each person's job, practices are well-understood and followed, support exists for the project management process, and project management teams and functional organizations work well together. Projects support and link to the organization's strategic and tactical plan.

Project work is integrated with the ongoing operations of the performing organization with product and project scope integrated. Assumptions from project plans are documented and reviewed to reassess and reengineer the planning process as required. Changes are coordinated across knowledge areas and projects. Management is able to anticipate when a project is in difficulty at an early stage and determine appropriate courses of action to follow. By use of performance measurement techniques, the magnitude of any variations that may occur can be anticipated. Control processes (scope, schedule, quality, and cost) are integrated so that inappropriate responses in one area do not cause problems in other areas. Checklists organized by sources of risks are prepared.

Alternative approaches to project management are encouraged; training includes methods of alternative identification and creative thinking techniques. Templates are reviewed and improved upon. The customer and supplier are regular team members with heavyweight team structures used. Best practices are continually established in all areas. Project management software emphasizes management of multiple projects and links between projects.

A team-based reward structure is in place for the organization. Project costs are used as an element of this system, but controllable and uncontrollable costs are estimated and budgeted separately to ensure rewards reflect actual performance. The project team can measure itself and its performance against the performance expectations of stakeholders. Improvements in individual skills and team capabilities are noted and used to facilitate identifying and developing better ways to do project work. A centralized system is maintained on capabilities/expertise of staff members for use in resource planning.

Communication alternatives are used appropriately so that communications are received in a timely way to support project success. Needed communication systems are reviewed at the onset of the project to ensure they are in place as required. Performance reporting provides information on scope, schedule, cost, quality, risk, and procurement in an integrated fashion, and reports are prepared on a routine and an exception basis. Earned value analysis provides measures as to whether or not work is accomplished as planned and to indicate project success or failure. Risk triggers serve as early warning signals of risk events.

The organization's quality improvement initiatives are designed to improve both the quality of project management and the quality of specific products. This includes taking action to increase the effectiveness and efficiency of projects to provide added benefits to stakeholders. Investment in project quality improvement is borne by the performing organization, not by specific projects. Benchmarking is used as a way to generate ideas for improvement. Experiments are used and applied to project management issues. Metrics are in place, used, and continually refined as operational definitions to describe in specific terms what something is and how it is measured by the quality control process.

It is recognized that the buyer/seller relationship exists at many levels on each project. Procurement audits are conducted routinely as a structured review to identify successes and failures that warrant transfer to other efforts under way.

Goals for a Level 3 organization in the *PMMM* by *PMBOK Guide* knowledge area are as follows.

#### Project Integration Management

*Goal 1. Project work is integrated with the ongoing operations of the performing organization.*

*Goal 2. Project control processes are integrated.*

*Goal 3. Project changes are coordinated across knowledge areas and across the entire project.*

*Goal 4. Management is able to anticipate at an early stage when a project may be in difficulty and determine appropriate courses of action to follow.*

*Goal 5. Best practices are established in various knowledge areas and communicated throughout the organization to become part of the continuously evolving project management methodology.*

*Goal 6. The project management information system is used for management of multiple projects, and managers of project managers receive training.*

*Goal 7. Information related to the use of the organization's standard project management process by various projects is collected, reviewed, and made available.*

#### Project Scope Management

*Goal 1. Product and project scope management are integrated to ensure work of the project results in delivery of the specified product.*

*Goal 2. Projects selected are supportive and link to the organization's strategic plan.*

*Goal 3. The process for scope verification establishes and documents the level and extent of project completion.*

#### Project Time Management

*Goal 1. The organization's practices contribute to commercial duration estimating data bases.*

#### Project Cost Management

*Goal 1. The organization's practices contribute to the development of commercial parametric cost estimating models.*

*Goal 2. Different project cost metrics are available and provided to project stakeholders.*

#### Project Quality Management

*Goal 1. The organization's quality improvement initiatives include both the quality of project management and the quality of the project product.*

*Goal 2. The organization's quality policy is refined so it can be adopted and used by each project.*

*Goal 3. The organization uses benchmarking to generate ideas for improvements.*

*Goal 4. Experiments are used and applied to project management issues.*

*Goal 5. Measurable goals for project quality management and priorities are defined.*

*Goal 6. Actual progress toward achieving project quality management goals is quantified and managed.*

#### Project Human Resources Management

*Goal 1. The organization has adopted a team-based performance incentive system.*

*Goal 2. Metrics are used so the project team can measure itself and its performance against the performance expectations of project stakeholders.*

*Goal 3. Improvements in both individual skills and team capabilities are noted and used to facilitate, identify, and develop better ways to perform project work.*

#### Project Communications Management

*Goal 1. Performance reporting provides information on scope, schedule, cost, risk, procurement, and quality in an integrated fashion.*

*Goal 2. Project communication management is used to predict early in the project whether the project will be successful and to alert management early to any potential problems.*

*Goal 3. A special review at the end of each project is conducted after completing all closeout activities specifically to assess lessons learned and any changes needed to the organization's project management methodology.*

#### Project Risk Management

*Goal 1. The organization contributes to expert judgment in the project risk management field.*

*Goal 2. Checklists organized by sources of risk are prepared and reviewed for use by application area.*

*Goal 3. The organization uses its lessons learned databases as a source of information for needed types of reserves based on project type.*

#### Project Procurement Management

*Goal 1. It is expected and recognized that the buyer/seller relationship exists at many levels on each project.*

*Goal 2. Performance reporting tools are such that success/failure of a supplier can be predicted in most cases in advance.*

*Goal 3. Procurement audits are routinely conducted as a structured review of the procurement process to identify successes and failures that warrant transfer to other efforts under way.*

### Level 5—Optimizing—Focusing on Process Improvement

The Level 5 *PMMM* organization is one in which the project management methodology operates routinely, and projects meet schedule, cost, technical, and quality requirements. Roles and responsibilities in the organization are well understood. Because the process operates routinely, people focus on its systematic improvement. Project work is integrated with ongoing operations, and deliverables from different functional specialities are integrated. The organization regularly participates in and is active in benchmarking forums as a way to continue to generate ideas for improvement and to refine its metrics. The organization's focus is on changing the project management process as required for strategic reasons. It strives to improve its project management processes and further refine them to meet new challenges.

Goals for a Level 5 *PMMM* organization are as follows.

*Goal 1. Continuous project management process improvement is planned.*

*Goal 2. Participation in the organization's project management process improvement activities is organization-wide, and improvement activities are coordinated across the organization.*

*Goal 3. Project work and ongoing operations are integrated, and both are valued contributors to the organization's success.*

*Goal 4. The project management information system interfaces easily with other information systems.*

*Goal 5. Appropriate new technologies for project management are transferred into normal practice across the organization as incorporation of technology changes is planned.*

*Goal 6. Cultural differences are accepted and valued.*

*Goal 7. The organization continues to generate ideas for improvement and to refine its metrics by knowledge area.*

# Project Management in an Era of Increasingly Rapid Change

Jean McWeeney, PMP, Sterling Information Group, Inc.
Leslie Martinich, Compaq Computer Corporation

Fundamental technology changes take place approximately once every eighteen months and that pace of change is increasing. Fundamental change is no longer an unusual circumstance during a project's life; change is a constant. Project managers must learn to factor this into their planning. Additionally, they need to utilize more effectively their general management skills, including leading, communicating, negotiating, problem solving, and influencing the organization, in order to lead their projects through both internal and external changes.

The pace of change today—in technology, in the global marketplace, and in organizational flux—is unprecedented. Successful project managers are the ones who accept this fact of business life and learn how to lead their teams through change. Their greatest tests as well as their greatest accomplishments occur during times of change.

In this presentation, we discuss the effect of change on project teams and how effective project managers extend their skills to guide those teams through change.

## Four Phases of Change

The first step toward effective project management is to understand the four phases of change. See Exhibit 1. A project team and each team member's productivity levels go through predictable cycles during each of these phases. Understanding the phases and recognizing the predictable symptoms enables you, the project manager, to model appropriate behavior and to assist those team members who become stuck in an early phase.

The first phase of change is resistance. Do you remember your first reactions to the announcement that your project was being canceled? It was probably something like "No! That's a ridiculous idea!" Denial is common at this stage. What was your reaction to the news that your organization was merging with another? Very negative, *resistant* reactions are to be expected when people first learn of an impending change. That is what you should expect from the team members on your project. During this resistant phase, productivity drops precipitously.

The second phase of change is characterized by low productivity. During this phase, team members are facing a great deal of anxiety and many unknowns. There is ample opportunity for rumor. What will happen? During this phase team members have not yet bought into whatever the change is; perhaps they do not yet know what their next project will be or how their current project is to change. If they do know the nature of the change, they have not yet accepted it.

The third phase of change is acceptance. At this stage, team members have figured out that the change is really going to happen, and they have figured out how they can fit into the new direction of the project.

The fourth phase of change is the recognition of new opportunities. The project manager is frequently at this phase when the team is still in the first resistance phase. At this point it is important to explain how you went through the same emotions, too. Empathize and validate their feelings. Did the project your team worked so hard on get canceled? Then have a wake, ritual, or ceremony to "celebrate" the end and put some closure to it. Explain to the team the four phases of change and how they are going to feel. Show them the phases of change productivity graph.

Do not expect that because you have explained these phases to the team that things will change overnight. The team or individual may attempt to get out of whatever phase they are stuck in several times before it finally works. Recognition of this will help you deal with your team members more effectively.

## General Management Skills

Resisting change is useless; it's coming whether you like it or not. Therefore, a second step toward effective project management is to expand your general management skills to be attentive to change. These skills include leading, communicating, negotiating, problem solving/decision-making, and influencing.

### Leading

Leading during times of change requires the project manager to be attentive to external issues. You must be one step ahead of technology, legal, and regulatory shifts. You must know how these external issues affect the project. For example, should the platform of choice be client/server or the Internet?

Will your organization be facing deregulation in the near future? Will the project result in a product that is already out of date if it is completed according to schedule and with the current specifications?

Once you become aware of any external issues affecting the project, you need to convey this information to the project team. Let them know of the alternatives. If you feel a change in plan is needed because of external issues, get the team on board.

External issues must also be conveyed up the organization. Consider outlining cost/benefit tradeoffs. Remember, you are an *agent* of change and you must help lead the organization toward appropriate solutions.

Various leadership skills are needed to be an effective change agent. They include good listening skills, the ability to synthesize information from disparate sources, and effective communication and influencing skills.

Besides leading the organization through external issues, internal issues must be attended to. You need to "look up, look down, look all around." That is, be attentive to changes within your own project team, and be attentive to what is happening within other, parallel project teams or organizations. Look for what direction the organization is taking with regard to products or mergers. What does that mean for the future of your project? For example, would a merger with a company with similar projects affect yours? The same leadership skills and attentiveness to change possibilities is needed to deal with these internal issues.

### Communication

In times of change, your skills at communicating will need to expand to recognize that change can be difficult or even threatening for people. You should keep team members well informed on issues of change but focus on the relevant information. If you have a message of change, remember to focus on the clarity of your message. Three things will help organize your message for clarity: first, know what you want to communicate; second, drop what is unimportant; and third, structure it for effectiveness (have a beginning and an end) (Daly 1996).

Use both formal and informal methods of communication. Formal communications allow for a consistent message. Informal communication channels allow for more questions and answers. Remember to be honest, be consistent, and be non-threatening.

Listen attentively. Do you hear signs of an individual getting stuck in one of the four phases? Watch the body language. Clarify what you are hearing to understand the key points of what the other person is saying: "What I hear you saying is . . . " You can reduce anxiety or other negative feelings by reflecting the other's feelings: "My sense is . . . "

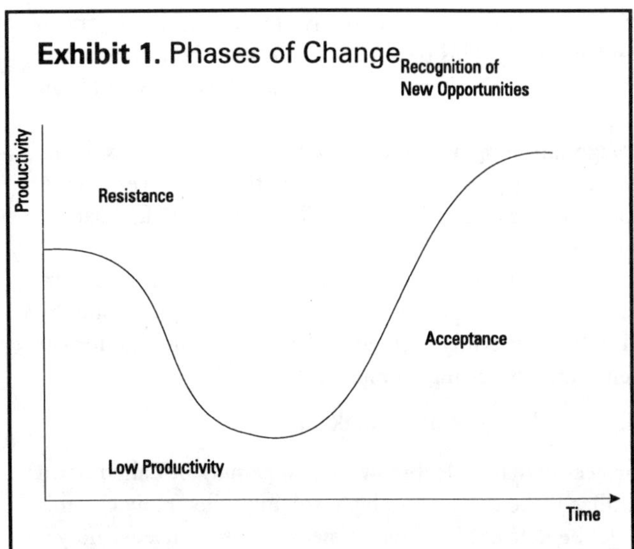


Understand that information will be filtered, possibly inadvertently, and a message of change may become distorted. The rumor mill may heat up. Have you ever experienced a reorganization that resulted in the rumor that a nemesis was getting reassigned? You and your team may jump for joy; you may even feel free to say what you really feel to your nemesis, only to find out that your nemesis has become your new boss. Be prepared for a lot of misinformation as well as surprises during times of change.

### Negotiation

*A Guide to the Project Management Body of Knowledge (PMBOK)* defines negotiation as conferring with others in order to come to terms or reach an agreement. Project management frequently involves constant negotiation, especially in times of rapid change. There are a few methods that you, as the project manager, can use to ensure your negotiations are successful.

First, understand both parties' interests. Do you know why the other party is insisting on something? Will it help get the product out on time? Will it advance her career? Is she concerned about budgetary constraints? And don't forget to understand why what you are asking for is important to you or your project. Is it really that important?

Secondly, you should understand both parties' alternatives when presenting your case. Alternatives help define the lower bounds of negotiation. If time is a constraint, could you buy a product from another company instead of developing it yourself? Is this alternative acceptable to you and the other party? Perhaps just leaving things as status quo is another acceptable alternative. Knowing your alternatives is an important part of successful negotiating.

What do you believe the other party's alternatives are? He may not reveal them directly; you may need to spend some time in data-gathering and creative brainstorming to try to formulate them. This step is critical. If your best offer is less attractive than his alternative, then he will work with his alternative rather than your offer.

Negotiation requires creativity. Learn to think outside the (PM)box. Engage your team and any other resources at your disposal in finding alternatives. This can be the fun part of negotiating!

In times of rapid change, spend up-front time understanding the other parties' interests. Actually you should be doing that constantly; you won't have much time to do that when things are changing rapidly!

### Problem Solving/Decision Making

A project manager dealing with change may be called upon to utilize more creative problem solving skills. How can this project be delivered in time to meet the users' needs and yet be adapted to changing technology? Or, how can a team meet the changing requirements from the customer? *PMBOK Guide* defines problem solving as including problem definition and decision-making. Causes and symptoms of a problem must be distinguished. Decision-making includes identifying potential solutions and making a choice among them.

During times of change, you may have to adopt a different style of decision-making from what you are used to. This is situational; this style is appropriate for that type of situation. Usually this type of decision-making style entails making quick, autonomous decisions. How do you become proficient at this? First, recognize that this style is important, valuable, and sometimes necessary. Slow decision-makers often get left behind at this time. For example, you may decide to delay a product in order to incorporate the latest platform changes. This type of situation has often meant the difference between a product that leads and a straggler that plays catch-up. Another method for becoming more proficient at quick decision-making is to seek a mentor. Try to observe a quick decision-maker in action. Learn from them that it is okay to make the riskier decisions. Oftentimes they are also considered leaders.

This type of decision-making may require a shift in your personality and require you do some stretching. You may begin using less well developed parts of your personality or decision-making styles. But remember that you will gain confidence the more you do this. Practice makes perfect.

Remember that quick decision-making is situational. It does not have to be used under all circumstances.

### Influencing

Why is being able to influence important during times of rapid change? During a time of flux, a lot of issues get reevaluated and decisions get made. Therefore, there are lots of opportunities for the project manager to positively influence the organization's direction.

In order to be successful at influencing you need to recognize who the decision-makers in the organization are and understand how to work with them. There are oftentimes two types of decision-makers within the organization: rational ones and ambitious, deceitful ones. You will need to deal with each in a different manner. A prerequisite for ensuring your success with either is: BE TRUSTWORTHY.

To successfully influence the rational decision-makers, first, understand their goals or agenda. Find out what drives them. How do you accomplish that? You can try the direct approach: ask them. Of course, this is sometimes impossible or the rational decision-makers may have a hard time articulating it. If the decision-makers have a hard time articulating their goals, try the "what-if string" method. Imagine pulling on a string as you ask a series of questions: "If we did this, would that get us closer to . . . ?". Or "What if we tried this approach?" Each question should lead you and the decision-makers closer to an articulation of what their goals are. If neither method is possible, you can derive the decision-maker's goal from the corporate goal.

To get the rational decision-maker to accept your ideas, you must be articulate and enthusiastic. You need to tie your goals to your decision-maker's and provide solutions. Remember to be flexible in adapting your goals to others'.

Unfortunately, there are oftentimes ambitious, deceitful decision-makers within the organization. You will need to learn to recognize who they are for they can oftentimes be saboteurs. Do not attempt to understand their motives or agendas. Their goal is usually personal ambition. To get them to accept your ideas, tie your solution to their success. Again, be flexible. One risk you assume in dealing with this type of decision-maker is being perceived as selling out. You should be willing to assume this risk if it will help you accomplish your goals.

### Success

The above tactics should help you remain successful as a project manager in an era of increasingly rapid change. Oftentimes change allows for growth and the opportunity to stretch your abilities. Remember the four phases of dealing with change and the general management skills outlined above. They should help ensure your success on any given project.

### References

Daly, John. 1996. "Bolstering Your Communication Effectiveness." Presentation. The University of Texas at Austin, The Institute for Managerial Leadership. Austin, Texas.

# Team Development Meets the Performance-Based Culture

G. Alan Hellawell, Jr., PMP, Eastman Kodak Company

## Introduction

In late 1993, the Board of Directors of a struggling Eastman Kodak Company went outside the company for the first time in corporate history and hired Mr. George M. C. Fisher as chairman, president, and CEO. A major reason for this unprecedented move was to dramatically improve corporate performance. One of Mr. Fisher's earliest major initiatives was to introduce expectations for a performance-based culture the object of which was, he said, "to encourage and reward good performance in every aspect of the business, and to take immediate action when performance falls short."

## Performance-Based Culture

Mr. Fisher focused on three aspects of leadership, all of which relate directly or indirectly to this new culture:

Bringing company values to life in all we do.

Creating an exciting and rewarding workplace.

Building a performance-based culture that delivers business results.

He has said he is committed to "rebuilding the corporation on a platform based on five key values." Managers throughout the company are accountable for adherence to them. Values directly related to performance improvement and the performance-based culture include:

- Uncompromising integrity in all that we do—placing the success of the business and its people ahead of personal gain.
- Trust—Giving people the freedom they need to do their job well.
- Credibility—Consistently delivering on commitments.
- Continuous improvement and personal renewal—making sure people have the opportunity to learn and grow.

An exciting and rewarding workplace is, above all, one that brings out the best in people. The performance-based culture involves high standards and clear expectations and measures. Managers are measured and compensated, in part, on each of these via a management performance commitment plan (MPCP) process. Other company employees are measured and compensated, in part, based on a performance commitment plan (PCP) , a similar process, which is described below.

Many would agree that performance-based culture is Mr. Fisher's most important and far-reaching initiative to date. This paper describes two project team development processes that we developed to promote significantly improved performance on the part of Kodak project teams and individuals who staff them, in direct response to the performance-based culture expectation.

The first is a project team development and leadership assessment process to evaluate team function and environment. It facilitates problem solving and progress tracking on key aspects of team function. It also provides information to upper management on their success in creating an environment which promotes project team success.

The second is a project team performance management process, key elements of which include a project performance matrix and the individual performance commitment plan. The former is a matrix of key project deliverables (elements of the work breakdown structure), each scored in proportion to its importance to overall project success. The latter is an individual matrix of "personal deliverables" over which the individual has either influence or control. One or more of the influence deliverables is taken directly from the project performance matrix(es).

## Project Team Development and Leadership Assessment Process

The Kodak Imaging Commercialization Processes Teamwork and Leadership Survey is at the core of the assessment process. The survey was created internally based on categories developed by J. R. Hackman and R. E. Walton at Harvard University. Design and development was carried out by Kodak's Dr. Rick Herbert, who holds engineering and behavioral science degrees. The survey permits Kodak project teams to assess the team function and environment, and to facilitate problem solving and performance tracking and improvement. It has proved useful as a team development tool. As word of its usefulness spread, so did its use to other types of Kodak projects.

Exhibit 1 is a view of how the processes and concepts noted above relate to each other.

The survey consists of two parts. The first is a series of forty-six forced response questions. The second part of the survey is three open-ended questions. The survey is normally administered to the project leader, members of the project team, and (perhaps) to other key stakeholders. It is administered anonymously. The responses may be scored and summarized

**Exhibit 1.** Relationship of Processes and Concepts

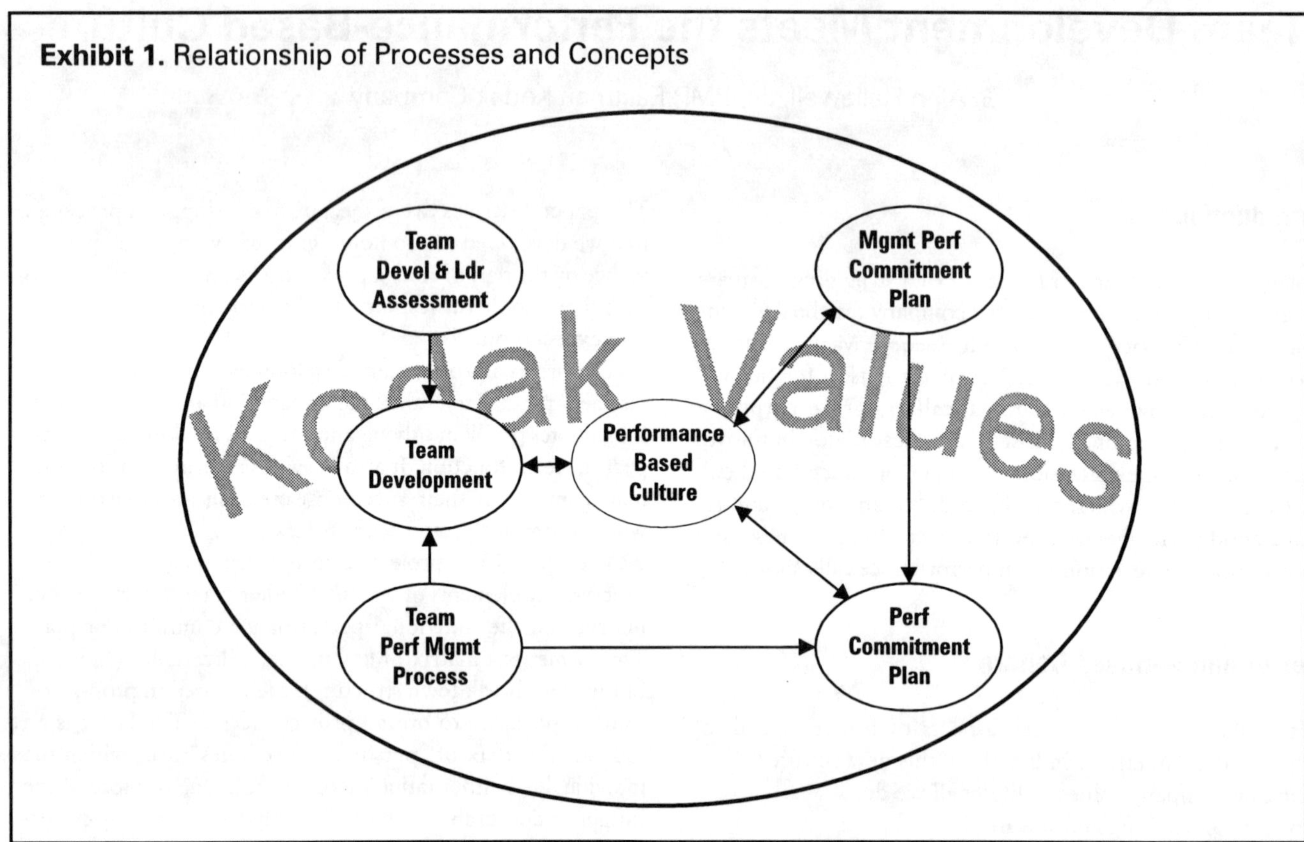


locally, or with assistance of an internal corporate administrative unit. The forced response questions cover six dimensions:

- Clear, Engaging Direction
- Empowerment
- Enabling Structure
- External Environment
- Leader Capability
- Team Capability

The team and leader capability dimensions provide many clear possibilities for team development. Merely going through the assessment process itself has helped members to understand each other's concerns and to use that knowledge to develop new linkages with themselves. The first four dimensions are directed primarily at management development opportunities, though interaction between managers and the project people also presents team development opportunities.

As noted, responses to the forty-six questions may be input to a corporate database, which contains equivalent data from several dozen other Kodak projects. Statistical analysis on a question-by-question basis between a project and the average of all projects is a feature of the report program. Analysis of a given project or organization unit is also possible over time. Questions are worded in a way that promotes action when improvement opportunity is considered significant.

The open-ended questions are of the typical "plus, zero, minus" (+,0,-) genre:

- What went particularly well and should be continued?
- What learning or advice do you have for projects in the future?
- What was difficult, frustrating, or went poorly?

The assessment process has been administered periodically during a project. Early in the project life cycle, it was used to point out opportunities for improving the planning process and for bringing on board a better mix of expert resources, for example. One might contend that information of this nature exists and is easy to obtain without need for an assessment process. Perhaps so, but our experience is that the quantified information coming from those closest to the issues really did capture management attention in a way that drove beneficial change.

The assessment process was also used near the end of an unsuccessful project. The project was to deliver the prototype of a product slated for installations at about a dozen sites around the world. The prototype project team learnings and advice were of paramount importance in this case. The major improvement opportunities related to technical details of the installation and debug phase of the project. The assessment process was administered independently to the management team and to the technical project team. A

**Exhibit 2.** Statistical Analysis Example

| | Your project (n = 17) | Total other projects (n = 689) |
|---|---|---|
| 02. Our goals are challenging, yet realistic. | | |
| Agree | x1% | y1% |
| Neither agree nor disagree | x2% | y2%* |
| Disagree | x3% | y3% |

* Significant at the .15 level.

very interesting aspect of the process was that both groups arrived at very similar conclusions and learnings. For example, they shared the perception that the management team had missed opportunities, which contributed substantially to the failure of the project, by repeatedly denying specific technical project team requests.

The assessment process was used after completion of a project, to develop project critical success factors and learnings on a large, lengthy, and successful product commercialization project. We describe this methodology in detail because it is the most comprehensive of the three assessment processes described above.

## Assessment Methodology

Internal Kodak consultants met with the program manager and a member of his staff to develop a contract for the project assessment, shortly after the product was introduced to the market. Key elements of the single-page contract include:

- Objectives
- Intended Audience
- Benefit/Value (to consultants and client)
- Approach
- Deliverables
- Milestones
- Roles and Responsibilities
- Estimated cost

Four interviewers interviewed well over 100 project stakeholders, a statistically significant sample representative of contributing organizations and organization level. We interviewed about one quarter individually, including most managers—and the remainder in groups of from about eight to twenty people. Two interviewers attended each group interview, one to lead the conversation and the other to document the conversation. Before we started the interviews, we mailed more than 100 overtly coded teamwork and leadership surveys to the second group and received about 35 percent anonymous responses. We used this raw data in the group interviews to promote understanding and to test for consensus. The surveys were coded and the interviews conducted by product subsystem and organization level.

During the interview process interviewers met repeatedly to review interviewee verbatims, synthesize "bullets" from similar verbatims, and develop themes from the bullets. Ultimately, twenty themes emerged at two levels: corporate and program. These included "senior management attention and constancy of purpose" (corporate level) and "use of project management tools and techniques" (program level). We very carefully worded the bullets, based on **repeatedly heard,** similar positive verbatims and repeatedly heard, similar negative verbatims of the theme. We used this information to develop the analysis comments, comparisons, and recommendations. Using the latter theme as an example, we reported:

- A positive bullet: There was good employment of project management (PM) process in "x" area . . . this program went about as well as anyone could hope or expect.
- A negative bullet: Some planning failures in "y" area were clearly due to absence of PM discipline. This increased confusion, cost and work . . . long hours were held in high regard. Absence of good process was rewarded!
- A comment: Formal project management practices were used with more success than on previous major projects.

This section of the report was about fifteen pages, distilled from over 200 pages of notes. We further distilled this into a two-page set of critical success factor bullets. (One related to the PM tools and techniques theme is: "Managers must distinguish between long hours due to the task itself and the same due to failure to plan the task.")

**Exhibit 3.** Key Consultant Learnings

There were some important lessons learned by the interviewers about the process they executed:

- Be crystal clear about the intent of the assessment. Establish the all-contract elements with the sponsor. Address the need for anonymity of survey respondents. Determine the conditions of use of the final product.
- Handle "negative" data with extreme caution. Keep good documentation, recognizing that challenges of the data are likely to be made by someone, somewhere. Place these comments carefully into perspective. Word them in objective, non-accusatory language. Avoid the pitfall of assigning motives. Protect sources.
- Valid perspectives differ. Joy in one place and pain in another cannot be averaged as "OK." Seek to understand the distinction and report it. Managers and the technical community had different experiences, as they should have!
- Carefully determine exact boundaries around the assessment process. What stakeholders and what phase(s) of the project life cycle should be included? Should customers, partners, suppliers, and vendors be included?
- Finally, we guarantee you the process will take longer than you think!

## Project Team Performance Management Process

Traditionally, many Kodak project team members have seen little, if any, linkage between overall project results and their performance evaluation and pay. Project recognition and reward activities were commonly developed and executed by the project team at their discretion and with little, if any involvement, in the overall process by management.

Recently, however, Mr. Fisher's performance-based culture initiative was a key enabler of efforts to orchestrate a unique project team performance management process described below. But first, the scenario.

Managers of a large, important production operation were at the end of the proverbial rope in efforts to sustain improvements directed toward invariance. Consequently, they commissioned a group of technical staff experts from another organizations to answer two questions:

1. Can invariance be achieved through evolutionary changes to the current process? If so, how?
2. If not, what specifications must the redesigned process meet?

The experts were empowered to an unprecedented degree in terms of funding and freedom to experiment with production processes. At the same time, the challenge to them to deliver results was daunting. Many of the experts openly acknowledged the paradigm shift and were clearly energized by it.

## Project Management Intervention

The project management consultant collaborated with the program manager to develop a contract as described above. Key elements of this contract included the following.

The consultant would offer services to each project leader in developing, tracking, and controlling their project plan and would accept, with report to the program manager, a project leader's decision to decline assistance. The program manager announced this possibility to all hands at the outset. Deliverables of these few projects in which they declined support were tracked, reported, and scored nonetheless.

A certain percentage of the performance commitment plan score of the consultant would be taken from the combined performance matrix score of all projects, whether or not the consultant was involved.

Several program assessments employing one or both parts of the Kodak Imaging Commercialization Processes Teamwork And Leadership Survey would be conducted.

## The Performance Commitment Plan

The paradigm shift began for many project teams with a process to develop a personal performance commitment plan (PCP) in collaboration with their supervisor. The PCP is simply a matrix of performance pinpoints, which quantify results and (perhaps) behaviors, to be demonstrated in the forthcoming time period, coupled with a series of performance levels for each pinpoint. The person is at least a part-time project member, so the expectation is that one or more of the PCP pinpoints is tied to project deliverables. This is easy to do because the team created a WBS and associated project schedule that specifies the deliverables it is committed to produce and their timing.

The PCP shown in Exhibit 4 is divided into three sections, one for each of the "publics" that the company and each of its organizations is dedicated to serving. For purposes of this paper, only the second section, "Customer Satisfaction" is addressed. The PM consultant and his supervisor agreed that 45 percent of the total weight of his PCP score would be driven by the scores of a program and one of its component projects. The percentages were also agreed by the program manager. Using this model, the "AOP" (annual operating plan) column defines satisfactory performance, and this corresponds to a matrix score of 100 points. (The consultant also delivers periodic training and students rate his performance

**Exhibit 4.** Performance Commitment Plan

## 1997 Performance Commitment Plan for: I. M. Consultant

| | | | Min (0) | AOP (100) | Max (200) | Result | Weight | Score |
|---|---|---|---|---|---|---|---|---|
| *Employee Satisfaction 10-20%* | Training & Development - EDP | Hrs | <40 | 40 | >40 | | 5% | |
| | Training & Development - Partnering | No. of Contracts | 1 | 2 | 3 | | 10% | |
| *Customer Satisfaction 30-70%* | Program X Overall Project Performance | PM Matrix Score | 300 | 700 | 1000 | | 20% | |
| | Project X1 Project Performance | PM Matrix Score | 300 | 700 | 1000 | | 25% | |
| | "PM 101" Overall Student Satisfaction | Course Eval Score | 5 | 7 | 9 | | 20% | |
| *Shareholder Satisfaction 20-50%* | Unit Revenue | Plan Variance | -2.5% | 0 | +2.5% | | 5% | |
| | Personal Revenue | Plan Variance | -5% | 0 | +5% | | 10% | |
| | Project Value Index | Unit Ratio | 96 Baseline | 1 | 2 | | 5% | |
| | | | | | | | 100% | |

**Date: 97/01/24** **Matrix Score:** 0

**Performer Signature:** **Supervisor Signature:**

on a scale of one to nine.) The program and project matrix scores are described in the following section.

The matrix score is a contributing factor in establishing the consultant's overall performance and thus it is a contributing factor to determining the consultant's pay. Details of these two areas are beyond the scope of this paper.

### The Project Performance Matrix

For mutually agreed WBS tasks and/or summary tasks, the team established with the program manager a number of points to be awarded for production of the deliverable. No deliverable, no points. As the projects unfolded, there were occasional situations which made it clear that subsequent deliverables were no longer viable, and these were renegotiated and the associated points were reallocated to new, remaining deliverables. This situation accounted for less than 10 percent of the total points.

The project performance matrix shown in Exhibit 5 is an extract of one of the Microsoft Project ® software reports used in the program. This report shows some of the tasks of one to which a total of 1000 points were assigned. It also shows the person responsible. Physical progress on tasks was given status and points were totaled normally every two weeks.

The project management consultant who supported this program has over twenty odd years of project experience. He reported he had never seen a program in which people did as good a job of "planning the work, then working the plan."

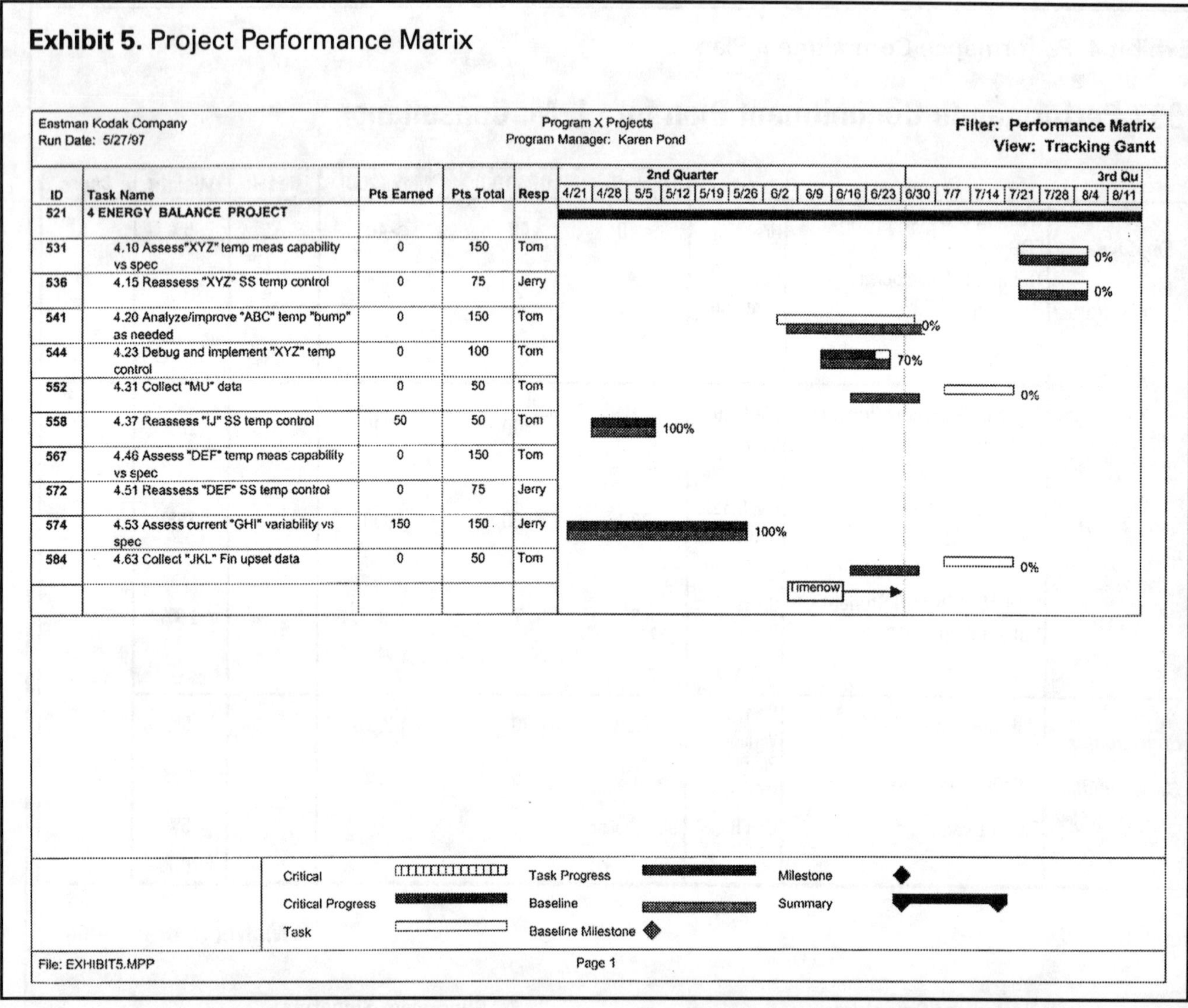

**Exhibit 5.** Project Performance Matrix

Eastman Kodak Company
Run Date: 5/27/97

Program X Projects
Program Manager: Karen Pond

**Filter: Performance Matrix**
**View: Tracking Gantt**

| ID | Task Name | Pts Earned | Pts Total | Resp |
|---|---|---|---|---|
| 521 | 4 ENERGY BALANCE PROJECT | | | |
| 531 | 4.10 Assess"XYZ" temp meas capability vs spec | 0 | 150 | Tom |
| 536 | 4.15 Reassess "XYZ" SS temp control | 0 | 75 | Jerry |
| 541 | 4.20 Analyze/improve "ABC" temp "bump" as needed | 0 | 150 | Tom |
| 544 | 4.23 Debug and implement "XYZ" temp control | 0 | 100 | Tom |
| 552 | 4.31 Collect "MU" data | 0 | 50 | Tom |
| 558 | 4.37 Reassess "IJ" SS temp control | 50 | 50 | Tom |
| 567 | 4.46 Assess "DEF" temp meas capability vs spec | 0 | 150 | Tom |
| 572 | 4.51 Reassess "DEF" SS temp control | 0 | 75 | Jerry |
| 574 | 4.53 Assess current "GHI" variability vs spec | 150 | 150 | Jerry |
| 584 | 4.63 Collect "JKL" Fin upset data | 0 | 50 | Tom |



File: EXHIBIT5.MPP

Page 1

The project management consultant met with each project manager and most teams. The consultant described possible services and the fact that a certain portion of his PCP was based on the success of their project. All understood that his service was offered, not mandated. The consultant expressed conviction that these two facts combined to yield an unprecedented level of mutual support.

Several weeks before a major, yearend milestone, the program manager convened a workshop with project managers and other stakeholders to summarize results to date and develop a path forward. Results of the Kodak Imaging Commercialization Processes Teamwork and Leadership Survey were reviewed, upgraded, and summarized. It was further agreed by consensus that the assessment would be repeated three more times in the implementation phase of the program in the forthcoming year.

Final evidence of the success of the overall program (beyond the fact that the program performance management matrix score was calculated to be just shy of 900 points) was the fact that management was so impressed with program performance that they cloned additional programs in short order.

## Conclusions

Looking back over the projects cited above, we offer the following as the most important and powerful learnings, which we hope may be useful in your practice:

- New paradigms, such as greatly increased freedom to experiment, are more likely to take hold when management demonstrates constancy of purpose and uncompromising integrity (the drive toward invariance, for example).

- Project team members generally responded enthusiastically to the challenge to be measured by the results of their project deliverables. Deliverables were challenging. Performance commitment plans linked to pay worked for a great majority of contributors.
- Project team members generally responded well when they could see alignment of the PCP process they were engaged in with the words and deeds including MPCP's of all levels of management.
- Project teams planned their work, then worked their plans more so than in the past, an important part because of the linkage to their PCP. Again, integrity and constancy of purpose of the program manager was vital.

# Making Change a "Constant": Becoming a "Change Master"

Deborah S. Kezsbom, Ph.D., MRA Management Resources, Inc.

## Introduction

Few business leaders today would deny the essential characteristics for high performance in this competitive environment. Empowered workers, astute cost estimating and participative management techniques, customer focus and responsiveness, partnering and alliances, team leadership strategies, and quality management processes are *each* critical to increasing an organization's **competitiveness** and chances for *survival* within the global economy.

For many organizations, building and maintaining these essential capabilities will require *major change*. Meeting the challenges of change always bears benefits, to the individual and to the organization. Considering the scope and speed of change within our organizations and within the concepts of project management, there will be **priceless** opportunities for those of us who position ourselves and our employees right, and take *personal responsibility* for our organization's and our own future. Not only must project managers and project specialists be conscious of changes that may *affect their immediate circumstances*, but must create change within the organization that shall effect **the organization's future . . . perhaps its very existence.**

This paper presents practical skills and techniques necessary for senior level-management, project managers, line managers, and their specialists to innovate and manage organizational and *individual change*. Emphasis is placed on *proven* techniques in which the manager and/or team leader may further develop the skills as an "innovator," "coach," and "mentor" for the growth of our organization, and our people! *In fact, this paper may, indeed, change the meaning of "change management" as we practice it in project management, and as we define it in* A Guide to the Project Management Book of Knowledge.

## The Era of Change

Change is a topic very much on the minds of managers and professionals today. Most would agree that the pace of change is so great, we are left with less than sufficient time to think about decisions *before* they are made. In the context of organizations, change is "nothing new": It has *always* occurred! Perhaps what makes professionals today believe that their era *is* unique is that much *of modern organizational change is driven by the global economy and the global market competition that accompanies it.*

Global competition requires managers, leaders, and professionals to think of ways to change their organization **continuously** in order to gain the competitive advantage! In fact, in the past decade, managers have led the following changes:

- Leading a workforce has prompted significant changes in their values and needs.
- They have adjusted leadership techniques to meet the needs of this changing and diverse workforce.
- Organizations have restructured and downsized to become leaner, with fewer layers of corporate hierarchy. This required managers to operate more as team leaders, leaders, coaches, and mentors.
- Flexible work systems have enabled many companies to meet the needs of an increasingly professional workforce. This requires the manager to adapt to the knowledge worker and their managerial needs.
- Reengineering within organizations has reduced steps in work processes and has helped organizations to focus on their core competencies. Managers have initiated the adaptation to organizational transformation and unique business processes.
- Quality management has given the workforce more power in the workplace, including involvement in the decision-making, planning, and implementation processes, and in achieving customer satisfaction. Managers have had to increasingly learn to "innovate" as opposed to "operate."
- Information technologies have been implemented to increase worker productivity. Managers have certainly adapted to the need for technological skills and the rapidly changing technologies.

The changes taking place in business and industry can be summarized into four major elements: **(1) globalization of competition; (2) delayering of organizations; (3) growth of computerization and computer networks; and (4) the emergence of the information highway.** As a result of these changes, companies who wish to remain competitive into the twenty-first century will need to adjust in order to survive! New companies shall come into being, and the older—once perceived as "stable"— organizations that do not heed the signs within their environments, shall perish.

## Types of Change

Many types of changes may occur within any firm or organization. "Strategic" types of change include the following:

- **Technology change** pertains to the organization's production process.
- **Product and service changes** refer to new product or services outputs of the organization.
- **Strategy and structure changes** pertain to the administrative areas, including structure, goals, policies, reward and performance measurement systems, labor relations systems, information systems, planning, and accounting.
- **People and culture changes** refer to changes in attitudes, skills, expectations, and behavior of employees.

In project management, our history has taught us to prevent or minimize what we believe to be "unnecessary" changes, especially within the scope of the project (depending, of course, on the types of contracts and industry) and the definition of work. Change control techniques are prevalent in the literature and in practice, and are *essential,* in many ways, to project configuration and scope. However, **change management**, as we define it for purposes of this paper . . . and for the future success of organizations . . . refers to managing innovation, creativity, and unique applications, organizational and system-wise. These are the changes that may affect the *competitiveness and profitability of the organization of the twenty-first century.*

*Organizational change* is the adoption of a new idea or behavior by an organization. The required elements of **any** successful change include: an idea or a new approach to doing things; a perceived need for change; adoption, which occurs when the decision-makers choose to actually go ahead with an idea; implementation, which occurs when targeted employees actually use the new idea, technique, or behavior; and resources, which must be allocated to make things happen and bring about the change. This is an era of "constant change," constant communication, and fast-changing technologies. It is an era in which customers demand quality and value. It is an era of employee empowerment and changing global relationships and structures. Traditional ways of doing business are gone, along with old habits and systems! It is difficult to let go of systems and habits that have been developed over a lifetime; but if companies are to achieve and maintain success they must continue to reinvent themselves, on almost a constant basis.

## Surviving "Transformation"

For organizations to survive continuous transformation or reinvention, there has to be some factor that binds people together. The one critical factor for success, therefore, is a firm's system of drawing its people together toward a **common purpose.** For example, for several firms, changes in the workplace have helped create unifying systems such as continuous improvement that bind their people together. Motorola provides an example of an exceptional company whose success is largely a result of its systematic approach to implementing change. In Motorola's case, the unifying factor lies in the use of a common language to help unify its people.

Since the organization is an open, organic system, it will be affected by both **internal** and **external forces for change.** Internal change forces are pressures that come from a worker, group, or a department. Sometimes the pressure is cost reduction, poor worker morale over some inequity in the reward system, or the quality of work life. Although morale and motivation are not often the impetus for change programs, existing as symptoms rather than problems within the organization, they are almost always tied to the basic problems within the firm, which can lead the effective manager to examine, diagnose, and eventually understand the true factors within the organization which led to these symptoms.

External forces are those outside the organization that can signal that a change is needed. Government regulations, sky rocketing healthcare costs, and the wave of cultural diversity sweeping across our nation are all powerful examples of external forces that necessitate change.

## Implementing Change

In the past, companies have tried to reinvent themselves by becoming better competitors. Their efforts have gone under many "banners": total quality management," "total cost management," "reengineering," "rightsizing," "business transition," " business transformation," and cultural change, are just a few. In almost every case, the goal has been the same: to cope with new more, more challenging markets by changing the way business is conducted. A few of these programs have been quite successful, while others have been utter failures. Most fall, however, somewhere between the two, with a distinct tilt toward the failure end of the scale. But the **lessons learned** from these failures will be relevant to more and more organizations, as the business environment becomes increasingly competitive. One **major lesson** to be taken away is that change involves a variety of techniques and appropriate structures and strategies which, like the project itself, go through numerous phases and require time to complete.

## Effective Change Strategies

One of today's most effective change strategies involves a combination of approaches which are *both* **organic** and

**mechanistic** in nature, especially when we deal with technical changes. *Organic processes* are needed in the initiation phase of change to encourage innovation. *Mechanistic processes* are needed in the implementation stage to ensure that change is completed. To create change using this "twin approach," one should follow some very basic steps outlined below:

- Alternate between structures, using what is referred to as "*switching structures.*" For instance, take a day off from the mechanistic routines and have the change agents brainstorm new ideas. Once this is accomplished, you may change back to the more mechanistic format.
- Create "venture teams" that are empowered to develop new ideas.
- Encourage the development of " champions of ideas" by providing some "slack time" for creative people, which is so characteristic of corporate entrepreneurship.

When attempting to bring about change in new products' design and services, for instance, look to the **horizontal linkages** across the organization. Research, marketing, and production must integrate their perspectives and information into workable innovations for the organization. New product decisions must be made jointly based on these **horizontal linkages** and not on the bases of marketing's desires, technical's desires, nor production's desires alone. Again, with product innovation **synergy prevails!**

## People, Strategy and Structure

Administrative changes may refer to any change or innovation in the design and structure of the organization, including information systems, the hierarchy and chain of authority, and department groupings. These changes may, indeed, be critical to successful program and/or project management. Administrative changes are best accomplished through a more "top-down" process. Naturally, top-down parallels a more "mechanistic structure." *Notice that the more mechanistic approaches that succeed with administrative innovation will fail miserably with more technical changes.*

When it comes to people and change, training is the vehicle generally used to change people's skills, attitudes, and behaviors. New ways of thinking may be instilled by a focused change effort directed at corporate norms and values. This is what is practiced in the **total quality management** approach.

## Resistance to Change: Why Does Something So "Good" Feel So Bad!

Any change, no matter how beneficial it may appear to be to employees and to the organization, will meet with and often be sabotaged by **resistance.** The failure of many recent large-scale efforts at corporate change can be associated *almost directly* to employee resistance. Total quality management (TQM) is an excellent example. Evidence indicates that a large number of firms have attempted to implement TQM within their organizations and have gained little in their competitive position, as a result of their change efforts. *If we examine closely the true failure of these change efforts, implementation and the process of involvement have usually gone awry.*

Within any size organization, or with any individual attempt at change, there exist several valid reasons for the resistance to change that we, as astute business people, must recognize, accept, and overcome. These reasons include, but may not be limited to, the following plausible causes:

- **Self-Interest:** Some people resist change because they have a vested interest in the way things are done. For example, they may enjoy the work flow or their position—and change threatens them.
- **Habit:** Working the same way day after day has certain appeal to some people. For many individuals, life is a set pattern of getting up, going to work, coming home, and going to bed. People naturally become accustomed to "sameness," and get into the habit of doing tasks a certain way. Changes in personnel, work flow, structure, or technology threaten the continuation of a pattern or set of habits.
- **Fear:** Change introduces uncertainty and a degree of fear. People fear having to learn a new way, or becoming accustomed to a new leader or manager and possibly failing. For instance, some employees may be offered an opportunity to relocate in order to take a different, better-paying job in the firm, but may still resist, considering this change "risky." It is the possibility of failure that represents one of the greatest risks of all.
- **Peer Pressure:** It appears that regardless of our age, peers often can apply pressure to resist change! For example, peers may resist the introduction of automation because they assume, and sometimes correctly, that fewer workers will be needed to perform the job. These peers may pressure an individual who may otherwise see the benefits of automation and support its potential to improve productivity.
- **Bureaucratic Inertia:** Large organizations have a built-in resistance to change because of the traditional rules, policies, and procedures. The all too familiar refrain is: "This is the way we have done it for years! Why change?" Inflexible rules, red tape, policy, and traditionally built-in ways of conducting business are difficult to overcome. Quality philosophies, for instance, such as Crosby's "doing things right the first time," were not met initially with

the utmost enthusiasm by managers. The idea, as we now know, met barriers of resistance and stonewalling.

## Minimizing Resistance to Change

Before change in organizations can truly take place, overcoming or reducing the resistance to change and encouraging and building support for changes is needed. W. Edwards Demming believed that all workers have a pride of workmanship, and it is management's responsibility to remove the impediments to pride of workmanship, thereby leaving room for worker empowerment . There are no simple, always perfect solutions for reducing the resistance to change, but some of the following options may prove useful.

**Education and Communication:** Explaining through a variety of mediums of communication why change is needed is *especially helpful when there is resistance to change because of a genuine lack of information.* Open communication allows everyone to prepare for the change. Paving the way, by showing the logic and benefit of the change, helps lower employee resistance.

**Participation and Involvement:** Involving those that are responsible for the implementation of the change into the actual design of the change is likely to increase their commitment.

**Facilitation and Support:** Being supportive is an important management characteristic when change is implemented. Managers must show support by providing training opportunities and helping to facilitate the change.

**Negotiation and Commitment:** Resistance to change can be reduced through negotiation. Discussion and analysis can help managers identify points of agreement, and those that need further negotiation.

## Developing Self Leadership

Resistance to change is almost always a dead-end street. Career opportunities come when you align immediately with the new organization's needs and realities. Organizations want people who *adapt* **fast**—not those who resist or are "psychologically" unplugged! Mobility and not mourning makes you a valuable member of the organization and of any group. In today's world, career success belongs to the committed, to those who invest themselves passionately in their jobs and who *recommit* quickly when change reshapes their environment and their work.

What we are witnessing today are raw survival techniques to help organizations deal with the fierce competition and fleeting opportunities. What we as leaders of self and others must do is emphasize **action**! Make yourself valuable. Help create a high velocity organization. This all suggests that one must learn to create role clarity for yourself. Chase down the information you need. Show initiative in getting your bearings and in aligning your and your followers' efforts with the organization's larger plan. Since uncertainty will be prominent, your ability to tolerate ambiguity and uncertainty will be your most critical skill. Loosen up! Prepare to feel your way along into the future, and, most of all, develop your ability to improvise.

It really does not matter anymore whether you are a mechanic, a teacher, an engineer, or a physicist. You will need specialized knowledge and to know how your field or profession is changing. Concentrating on *outcomes* will also keep you from "falling in love" with a particular methodology. Your organization's (and your own job) security depends on how valuable you are to your customer. Sharpen your insights into your personal "marketplace" and always keep in mind that there are both internal and external customers. Taking our jobs for granted means taking our customers for granted, and that is risky business. Taking customers for granted is just plain stupidity!

Rapid organizational change guarantees us that almost everyone is going to bear some battle scars in the years to come. But what is best for your career? Depersonalize the situation and lead others to do the same. Ideally, you and the people you lead or work with will accept change as an exercise that, though sometimes painful, helps build more organizational (and emotional) muscle.

### Bibliography

Carr, Clay. 1994. "7 Keys to Successful Change." *Training* (February): 55–59.

Kezsbom, D., D. Schilling, and K. Edwards. 1989. *Dynamic Project Management: A Practical Guide for Managers and Engineers*. John Wiley & Sons.

Price Pritchett. 1995. *New Work Habits for a Radically Changing World*. Pritchett & Associates, Inc. Dallas Texas.

# The Influence Tactics Project Managers Use with Their Team Members

David R. Lee, University of Dayton
Patrick J. Sweeney, University of Dayton
George A. Bohlen, University of Dayton

## Introduction

Successful project managers require the proper blend of technical, managerial, and interpersonal skills. While all these skills are important, this paper focuses specifically on the interpersonal skills area. One noteworthy interpersonal skill is the ability to influence other people. For project managers, this is a critical skill. Unfortunately, there is a serious lack of information about the use of influence techniques in the project management setting. This paper is an attempt to expand our knowledge in this area by investigating the influence tactics that project managers use to influence their team members.

The first section of the paper focuses on several elements of the influence process. This is followed by a brief overview of relevant research in the influence area. The main focus of the paper is on reviewing the survey results of project management professionals as they indicate their frequency in using certain influence techniques.

## Influence Process Concepts

Influence can be defined as the process by which people persuade others to follow their advice, accept their suggestions, or comply with their orders. The capability to influence others is an essential factor for managers. However, the influence process is often complex and difficult to predict. The effectiveness of an influence attempt is based on the perceptions held by various individuals and the interaction of multiple variables.

Three main elements of the influence process include the methods employed, the skill of the person in applying these methods, and the perceptions of the target people. The responses of the target individuals are often based upon their assessments of the situation and their estimates regarding the possible consequences associated with their behavior. Many types of conscious behavior are predicated on how the target individuals view the sources of power of the initiators.

In an organizational setting, power is normally associated with one's position in the organization or with certain characteristics of the individual. Legitimate, reward, coercive, and informational powers fall into the positional domain. Conversely, powers stemming from one's expertise, charisma, persuasiveness, or persona are more personal type of powers. The greater the external perceptions of one's power, the greater is the opportunity for this individual to use a variety of different influence methods. Some people prefer to use certain influence methods partly because they have the appropriate skills to employ the methods, or perhaps they are just comfortable using certain approaches. Then again, some people behave in specific ways because of the expectations of other people.

The literature shows that people attempt to "get their way" by using a variety of influence methods. The subjects in Falbo's (1977) study initially used 346 influence strategies. Falbo was able to collapse this number into sixteen major power strategies. Kipnis et. al. (1980) identified the following eight dimensions of influence: assertiveness, ingratiation, rationality, sanctions, exchange, upward appeals, blocking, and coalitions. Others have since proposed changes to this listing, both with respect to the number and title of the influence approaches. Consultation, personal/inspirational appeals, and legitimating strategies often appear on other lists of influence categories (Yukl and Tracey 1992).

In describing influence methods, some researchers use the words *influence strategy* and *influence tactic* interchangeably. For our purposes, the words convey different meanings. The term *strategy* refers to a higher level of generality than a *tactic*. Tactics are specific expressions of a general strategy. As an example, the specific tactic of providing technical information in support of your request is reflective of a rational reasoning type strategy.

The general influence strategies provide a means to categorize or label individual influence tactics. In this exploratory study, attention is focused on how frequently project managers use nineteen specific influence tactics with their team members. Several researchers developed and correlated specific influence tactics with general influence strategies. Where we found multiple references to a specific influence tactic or when a particular influence tactic was suggestive of a different cognitive process, we attempted to incorporate it into our final set of influence tactics. We included several tactics for more complex strategies like assertiveness, which has more interpretative facets to it. Conversely, inspirational appeal or consultation can be adequately covered with one tactic. In this current study we used behavioral statements of twelve

**Exhibit 1.** Influence Strategies

| STRATEGY | STRATEGY DESCRIPTION |
|---|---|
| Assertiveness | The strategy of using forceful approaches, such as demands, harsh language or intimidation to convince the team member to do what you want. |
| Bargaining | The strategy of using approaches based on an exchange of benefits or favors. An example is promising a team member a reward of benefit for doing what you want. |
| Coalition | The strategy of mobilizing or enlisting the support of co-workers or other people in the organization to help you influence the team member. |
| Consultation | The strategy of gaining the support of a team member by seeking his/her participation in the decision making process or in planning specific steps on how to carry out a proposal. |
| Expertise | The strategy of referring to your past experience or special knowledge as a means to influence the team member. |
| Friendliness | The strategy of getting the team member to think favorably of you or to get the member in a good mood before making your request. |
| Higher Management Support | The strategy of seeking the assistance of higher management to directly influence the team member or mentioning that your request already had the approval of higher authorities. |
| Inspirational Appeal | The strategy of using emotional statements that arouse enthusiasm, increase self-confidence, or foster commitment by appealing to a team member's basic values or ideals. |
| Legitimizing | The strategy of explicitly indicating that a request is within your scope of authority or that it is consistent with organizational practices, policies or typical role expectations. |
| Personal Appeal | The strategy of asking the team member to do something out of friendship or loyalty. |
| Rational Reasoning (Rationality) | The strategy of using logical arguments and factual information in support of your requests. |
| Sanctions | The strategy of threatening the team member with a negative outcome or penalty if the member does not comply with your requests. |

primary influence categories or strategies. These general influence strategies are described in Exhibit 1.

Rather than evaluate an exhaustive list of influence tactics, we selected a broad-based but parsimonious list with the expectation that we would get a larger response rate with our survey. Our expectation was fulfilled when we received over 600 responses to our survey. Since there were non-responses for a few tactics by several respondents, the sample size ranged from 611 to 616 for each of the nineteen influence tactics. This is the largest sample size of any known study on influence strategies or tactics.

## Methodology

As a target audience, we selected contemporary project managers who were registered attendees at the 1995 Project Management Institute Conference. In our questionnaire we asked project managers to rate how frequently they used nineteen tactics "to influence a team member to do what you want." Given a Likert five-point scale, their options were: 1) Never, 2) Seldom, 3) Occasional, 4) Frequently, and, 5) Usually. The questionnaire was specifically designed for this study, and completed surveys were returned anonymously through the

**Exhibit 2.** High-Use Influence Tactics

| INFLUENCE TACTIC | INFLUENCE STRATEGY | OVERALL MEAN |
|---|---|---|
| I carefully explain to the team member the reasons for my request. | Rational Reasoning | 4.305 |
| I involve the team member in the planning/decision-making process so that he or she will do what I want. | Consultation | 4.222 |
| I use logic to convince the team member to do what I want. | Rational Reasoning | 3.978 |
| I appeal to the team member's higher values, competitive spirit or organizational loyalty to generate enthusiasm to carry out my request. | Inspirational Appeal | 3.423 |

**Exhibit 3.** Low-Use Influence Tactics

| INFLUENCE TACTIC | INFLUENCE STRATEGY | OVERALL MEAN |
|---|---|---|
| I have a strong face-to-face confrontation with the members. | Assertiveness | 1.978 |
| I simply order the team member to do what was asked. | Assertiveness | 1.792 |
| I express my anger verbally so that the team member will do what I want. | Assertiveness | 1.781 |
| I threaten to give the team member an unsatisfactory performance appraisal unless he or she does what I want. | Sanctions | 1.217 |

mail. The questionnaire also included questions on pertinent demographic, experiential, and employment factors.

## Nature of the Sample

The survey response rate was an impressive 36 percent of the conference attendees or 616 project managers. The gender mix was 77 percent male and 23 percent female. Seventy-three percent of the respondents were born in the United

States of America, but fifty-one other countries were represented. The vast majority of the project managers were working in the United States (79 percent) and Canada (11 percent). The remaining respondents were working in thirty-nine different countries. All but four of the respondents managed more than one project, and 73 percent had managed six or more projects and had more than five years experience as a project manager. Almost 74 percent worked in corporations with over one thousand employees. In the way of a brief summary, the major portion of the respondents were experienced, American male project managers working in medium to large companies in the United States.

## Data Analysis

The focus of our analysis centered on three research questions. The first question deals with the degree of usage of the different influence methods. The second explores potential use differences based on gender. The third considers experience level.

**Research Question No. 1: Do project managers use certain influence tactics more often than other influence tactics?**

In other words, what are the high-use and low-use influence tactics. A visual analysis of the overall frequency use means for each influence tactic suggested a reasonable high-use group and a low-use group. Thc selected cut-off for the high-use was a mean of 3.0 or higher. The low-use group consisted of those tactics with a mean of less than 2.0. These influence tactics along with their means are presented in Exhibits 2 and 3.

Coincidentally, the high- and low-use groups include four influence tactics. Two influence tactics in the high-use group are associated with the rational reasoning influence strategy. The other two are suggestive of the consultation strategy and the inspirational appeal strategy. In the low-use group, three tactics relate to the assertiveness influence strategy and one to the sanctions strategy.

The consultation, inspirational appeal, and the sanctions strategy were each represented by one tactic in the total set of nineteen influence tactics. Rational reasoning was represented by two tactics and assertiveness by four tactics.

One tactic associated with assertiveness in a different influence research study (i.e., "I repeatedly remind the team member of what I want.") had a mean use rate over 2.0, and consequently it was not included in the low-use category. A different analysis of the data suggests that this tactic might actually correlate more closely with a legitimating type strategy.

**Research Question No. 2: Do the high-use and low-use tactics vary by gender?**

With some slight variations, the nineteen influence tactics were evaluated by approximately 136 female and 477 male project managers. The top four high-use tactics and the bottom four low-use tactics did not vary by gender. They are the same as shown in Exhibits 2 and 3 for the total combined survey sample. However, there are some use differences between the genders. On the average, female project managers "carefully explain to the team member the reasons" for their requests more frequently than male project managers. In the low-use category, female project managers, on the average, report that they do not "threaten to give the team member an unsatisfactory performance appraisal" as frequently as male project managers.

One other influence tactic moved slightly about the 3.0 cutoff for female project managers. The mean for this tactic, which related to a higher management support type strategy, was 3.09. A comparative analysis with the male group suggests that female project managers more frequently "obtain the advance support of higher management to backup" their requests.

**Research Question No. 3: Does the use of influence tactics vary according to the experience level of the project manager?**

For this measure we used the number of projects managed as a way to view experience. Project managers were considered to be in the more experienced group if they managed six or more projects. The sample size for the more experienced group was approximately 443 for each influence tactic. The less experienced group consisted of about 162 project managers.

Experience level did not have an effect on the earlier high and low rankings. The results for the experienced and less experienced project managers were the same as noted in Exhibits 2 and 3. However, one significant difference was that the more experienced project manager more frequently involved "the team member in the planning/decision-making process so that" the person would do what the manager wanted.

## Implications for Project Managers

Rational reasoning, consultation, and inspirational appeal are the reported high-use tactics. Influence tactics based on threats, fear, or assertiveness are in the low-use group. However, project managers use many other influence tactics to influence team members. As mentioned earlier, appropriateness and effectiveness depend on a variety of perceptual and situational factors. Conceivably, a single tactic or combination of influence tactics might be the "best fit" for a certain situation. Therefore, project managers should be able to effectively use a broad array of influence tactics. Project managers also need to enhance their abilities to "read" or diagnose different situations and select a suitable influence method. An underlying theme is that there is no one best influence tactic or set of tactics for all situations.

In developing the application skills, it is useful to examine some factors associated with the different influence tactics. Our attention here will focus on just the high- and low-use influence tactics in this study. Rational reasoning, for instance, is fundamentally based on good analysis and presentation. Oftentimes these two items take preparation time. Therefore, one should properly evaluate the facts, interrelationships, and potential outcomes before using the rational reasoning strategy. Actually some of these thoughts apply to all the strategies, but are even more evident for rational reasoning. Economic analysis, sensitivity analysis, risk analysis, along with survey information, and proper evaluation of historical data are very useful in the analysis stage. Network diagrams, Gantt charts, and development of different scenarios often find meaningful application in the presentation stage.

Another high-use influence tactic is consultation. These tactics can be used effectively even in low to moderate power situations; however, success with consultation tactics normally hinges on certain communication skills. An essential skill for consultation is active listening. As opposed to reading, writing, and speaking skills, few of us receive any formal training in the listening area. Listening to understand and withholding judgment stand out as two keys to good listening. Selecting the proper time and environmental setting are two other important success determinants. Good communication feedback skills also facilitate the use of the consultation strategy. Another nice side effect of consultation is that through participation, the team member typically develops more commitment to implementing the agreed upon course of action.

Rational reasoning and consultation are more mental type approaches versus the emotionally based inspirational appeal tactics. Having an inspirational appeal tactic show up in the high-use group merely reaffirms our nature as human beings. Basically we are capable of reasoning, but we also have emotions. Frequently we overly focus our attention on the so called "professional attributes" and overlook other human dimensions of our team members. For inspirational appeal tactics to work, the project manager must articulate a meaningful vision of the future. Focusing on higher- level team outcomes, corporate objectives, or some other superordinate goal often creates inspiring purposes. Inspirational appeal tactics basically are designed to enlist the support of the team member. Thus, it is helpful to be able to incorporate an element of positive reinforcement into the appeal. In a way, inspirational appeal is similar to the expectancy theory of motivation. Essentially, we are suggesting to the team member that certain efforts will lead to some level of performance. This in turn will result in positive outcomes. Inspirational tactics typically appeal to the inner nature of the person to do something of higher level versus a basic quid pro quo exchange tactic.

There are situations where assertiveness and sanctions-type tactics are appropriate. Most likely they are used after other influence tactics fail or where there is some previous record of poor performance by the team member. Generally, these are very low-use tactics in most project management settings. In the case of sanctions tactics, part of the success is based on coercive power of the project manager. Beyond the potential lack of this power, there are definite risks in using sanctions or punitive type methods. One risk is that many other people in the organization may disagree with the negative measures and feel that the project manager is inept or lacks creativity in applying other corrective management approaches. Punitive measures, if incorrectly applied, can adversely affect cohesion of the team and detract from goal accomplishment. Additionally, the use of such measures may come back to haunt the project manager on other projects in the future.

If project managers are going to use sanctions methods, then some guidelines are in order. First, the project manager should obtain all the facts about the performance issue before using these tactics. Secondly, the sanctions threat should be progressive in severity and commensurate with the issue. Thirdly, the issue should be properly documented, and the threat of a punishment should receive higher management support or pre-approval before it is used. Using sanctions-type tactics in moments of heightened emotion normally are quite ineffective and often require future apologies.

Assertiveness-type tactics may not have the same repercussions as the sanctions methods. Nonetheless, most people object to someone using assertive approaches with them. These tactics can again affect team cohesion, reduce open communication, and perhaps even cause defensive behaviors by the target person. If assertiveness tactics are going to be used, the project manager should collect the facts and use a specific tactic appropriate to the situation.

Perhaps a more important issue with sanctions and assertiveness-type influence tactics is in fact that they are low-use methods. When team members or other people see or hear about these tactics being used, they may begin to suspect some type of problems with the project or with the project manager. The reported use means for these tactics ranged from seldom to never. Therefore, using these methods is really quite unusual and may cause negative stress within the team.

It is interesting to note that female project managers carefully explain the reasons for their requests more frequently than men. They also threaten less with unsatisfactory performance reports. Both usage levels seem to be in the right direction, and intuitively these differences seem plausible. Besides these two differences, the level of similarity between the genders is very positive. Therefore, team members can probably expect to encounter similar types of influence behaviors from female and male project managers. A corresponding expectation could apply to experienced and non-experienced project managers. As noted earlier, the influence response means for these two groups showed a high level of commonality.

## Conclusion

This study clearly identifies the high-use and low-use influence tactics that project managers use with their team members. Gender and experience level account for very few differences in the final analysis. In fact, when gender findings and experience level comparisons are factored into the overall equation , the results suggest that we may be seeing something akin to general professional norms emerging within the project management discipline.

### References


Falbo, Toni. 1977. "Multidimensional Scaling of Power Strategies." *Journal of Personality and Social Psychology* 35 (August): 537–547.

Kipnis, David, Stuart M. Schmidt, and Ian Wilkinson. 1980. "Intraorganizational Influence Tactics: Explorations in Getting One's Way." *Journal of Applied Psychology* 65 (January): 440–452.

Sweeny, Patrick J., David R. Lee, and George A. Bohlen. 1996. "Organizational Team Support and Commitment." *Project Management Institute Conference Proceedings* (October): 846–852.

Yukl, Gary, and J. Bruce Tracey. 1992. "Consequences of Influence Tactics Used With Subordinates, Peers, and the Boss." *Journal of Applied Psychology* 77: 525–535.

# A Holistic Framework for Managing Risks in Construction Projects

D.P. Mootanah, Anglia Polytechnic University, United Kingdom

## Introduction

The movement of individual economies towards a more global and more competitive structure is a sign that the next millennium will bring more benefits to those who can seize the opportunity when it arises. Competitive advantage will depend, among other factors, on whether one can assess the ratio of risk to reward effectively. The construction industry is one player on the market, and its vulnerability to risks cannot be underestimated. The risks inherent to the industry not only come from the management of projects but also from many external factors that are often beyond the control of decision-makers within the industry. Holistic risk management brings together different approaches and levels of risk control under one generalized structured framework. This will enable the user of such a framework to benefit from various risk management techniques and tools, and will ensure that the right strategy is adopted for each particular business case or project. Hence maximum benefits can be reaped from using the appropriate level of risk management. However the degree of risk acceptability and control will depend on how effectively the framework is utilized in making risk management decisions for projects.

This paper proposes a holistic framework for identifying, assessing, and managing not only project risks but also other risks peripheral to construction projects. A brief account of the associated procedure linking the different phases of the framework is presented.

## Framework Outline

The holistic framework provides a comprehensive approach to reach realistic solutions for assessing and controlling project risks. The framework will inevitably have to be adapted to the level of risk control required. In effect, whatever level is chosen, it is best practice to conduct group risk study in the form of risk workshops or brainstorming meetings that will involve the relevant people (the project stakeholders) concerned with the project. These risk workshops are facilitated and administrated by a risk coordinator or facilitator who should have the necessary experience in risk analysis and assessment techniques and in risk management systems in general.

The proposed framework is divided into the following phases that successively:

- prepare the necessary logistics for determining the needs for risk control
- identify and capture the uncertainty
- model the uncertainty and specify the associated risks
- assess and analyze the risks according to the level of analysis required
- look at all possible actions that can be taken to mitigate the risks
- prepare and apply a risk management strategy in line with the requirements of the organization
- set up or maintain a data base for recording useful information on risks and carry out periodic risk management reviews.

Exhibit 1 illustrates how the different phases are interlinked within the framework.

## The Preparation Phase

This phase takes place through pre-study meetings between the project manager and the selected risk coordinator. They have to prepare the risk study logistics, which include selecting a venue for the study, the facilities, and other logistics like computers, flip-charts, slides, questionnaires, checklists, databases, and so on. The objectives and scope of the risk study are defined and agreed. The project phases at which risk workshops are to be carried out are established. The risk management study team is selected and will generally consist of the project manager, the risk management coordinator/facilitator, end-user representatives, client representatives, and members of the project team including the architect, engineers, designers, quantity surveyors/cost consultants, estimator, construction manager, environmental specialist/engineer, technicians, and possibly relevant suppliers. Another activity during this phase is to gather the required information on the project such as the business plan; the project brief including the project purpose, objectives, and scope; the funding arrangements made; the program and phasing requirements; life-cycle cost information; any drawings and specifications; the contractual and legal aspects for all phases of the project life-cycle; the design concept; the construction and commissioning aspects of the project; and any external factors that

**Exhibit 1.** The Holistic Risk Management Framework

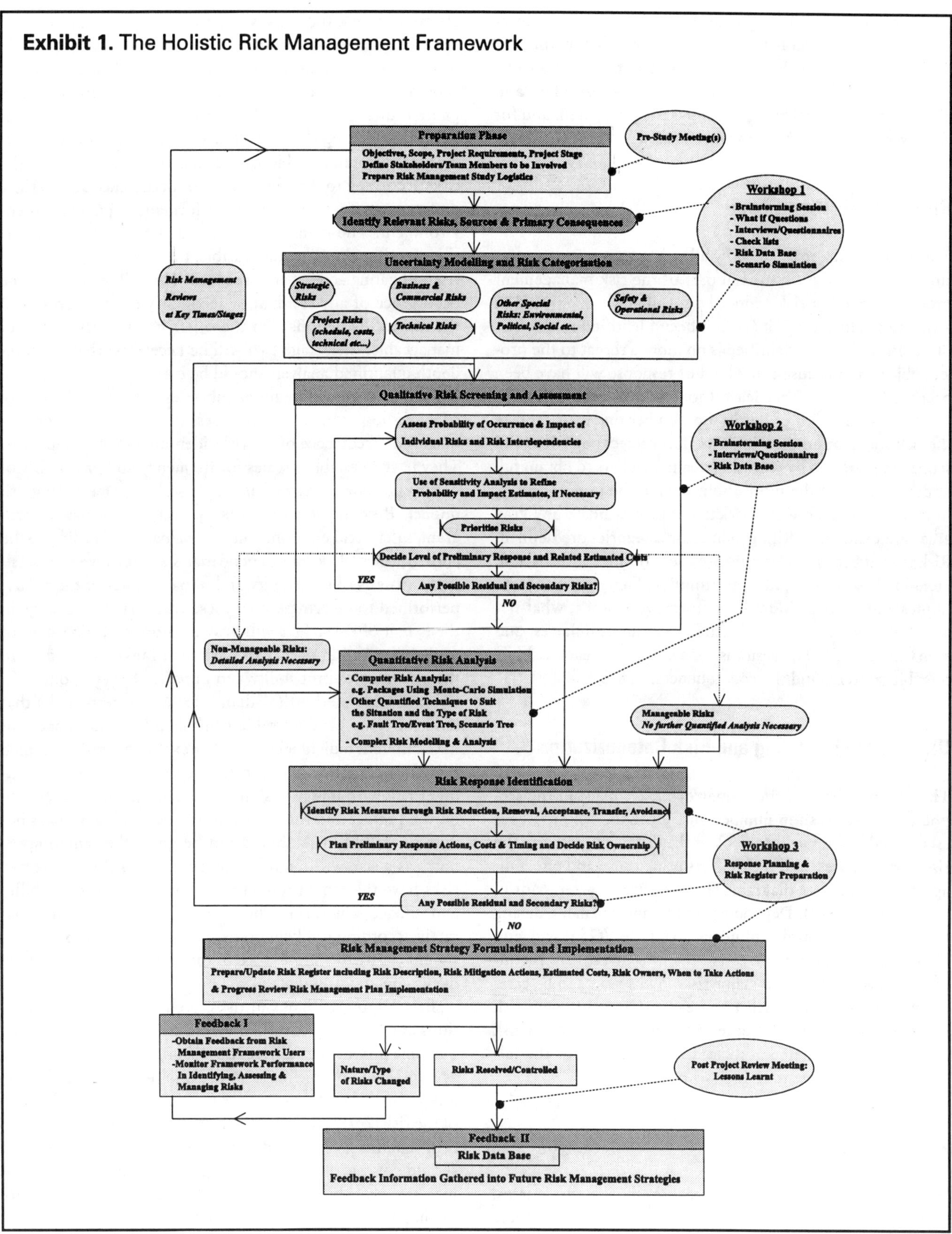

might influence the management of any phase of the project life-cycle. The project manager and risk coordinator will have to define and select the methodology and techniques to be used for the risk management study. A study procedure and program for the particular project has to be prepared, and for each workshop the agenda will be agreed.

## Risk Identification Phase

This phase is acknowledged by all risk management professionals to be the most crucial part of the risk management process. Indeed, a risk cannot be specified or quantified in any way whatsoever if it has not been identified in the first place. In fact, a risk identified is no more a threat to the project objectives because some kind of response will have been prepared, or at the very least, thought of. As shown in Exhibit 1, the first aim of workshop number one is to capture the risk sources and their impacts. The project objectives and scope are reviewed by workshop team members to obtain full understanding of the motivations behind the project and its functions. For each work package or project phase any gray areas are examined. Risk headings or categories are defined. Risk identification techniques are used to find concerns, risk areas, risk sources, and opportunities. Some typical techniques and tools include: brainstorming sessions, what-if?-analysis, risk checklists, risk databases, questionnaires, and scenario analysis. The result is a description of each risk, its possible sources, and the consequences.

## Uncertainty Modeling and Risk Categorization

This second phase of the framework takes place in the second part of workshop number one. Once the list of risks is established, team members look at the difference between the risks, their causes, and their effects using cause and effect diagrams or Ishikawa diagrams (Turner 1993; Carter, Morin, and Robbins 1994). Depending on the time available during the workshop, simple influence diagrams (Goodwin and Wright 1991) can also be constructed to investigate the interrelationships between major risks. Thus risks can be categorized again under each risk heading, and any new risk headings can be added if necessary. The importance of risk impact is not evaluated at this stage. This is left for the following risk assessment or analysis phase.

## Analysis Phase

At this point, we have a list of categorized risks, the sources, and their effects. We now have to assess the impact of these effects and rank the risks, so that the response can be properly planned. All too often, a common problem is to decide when to stop the assessment or what level of assessment should be carried out. To avoid paralysis by analysis, this phase is divided into two distinct stages. The first stage consists of evaluating the importance of those high-order risks that can threaten the objectives of the project and ranking the risks according to their likelihood of occurrence and to their impact on project costs, time, performance, quality, and environment. The manageability of each risk is examined. If risks are thought to be manageable, then possible preliminary risk mitigating actions are prepared. This will make clear the occurrence of any residual or secondary risks as a result of the mitigating actions. On the other hand, if risks are not manageable, then stage two will be necessary; that is, an in-depth quantified analysis should be carried out.

Risk management team members engage in the first stage of workshop number two to assess the importance and frequency of occurrence of the risks identified in workshop one. They have to establish scales for frequency and probability of occurrence of risks as well as simple scales for measuring risk impact. Risk impacts on costs, quality, performance, program, safety, and environment are evaluated according to the chosen scales. Risk interdependencies are reviewed. A sensitivity analysis of probability and impact values of the risks is performed to determine how these will vary with change in the extent of risks. This will provide more realistic values of probability and impact. Risks are then ranked according to their product of probability and impact. However, one limitation of this method (Williams 1996) concerns risks that have the same product value of probability and impact but have different individual values. For example, a risk with high probability and low impact can have the same product as another risk with low probability and high impact. Depending on the project and the nature of the risk, a low impact but high probability risk should not be given the same importance as a risk with high impact and low likelihood. If two risks have the same product value but different probability and impact values, then those risks should be ranked separately according to likelihood and according to impact. This should clarify the importance of those risks independently of likelihood and/or impact.

Based upon the ranks of risks, preliminary mitigation actions and resulting costs can be estimated. For risks having the same product but different probability and impact values, as explained above, the response should be guided by the uniqueness of each case rather than dominated by the rank of the risk. For those risks, the response should be as follows: if probability is high and impact is low, then the response should concentrate on reducing the likelihood. If impact is high and probability is low, then the response should reduce the impact or consequence of the risk if it happens.

The second stage of workshop two involves quantified risk analysis techniques as shown in Exhibit 1. One of the most popular risk analysis techniques used by project risk analysts is probabilistic analysis with Monte-Carlo simulation, which will generally produce quick estimates of the most probable project costs and program. Calculations of possible project cost and duration can be done by hand by considering the three cases of minimum risk effect, maximum risk effect, and the most likely risk effect on each project variable. However, computer software with spreadsheet facilities can generate in no time graphs of probability against cost and time. Most risk analysis software has built-in features that help customize standard probability distributions, such as triangular (maximum/most likely/minimum), uniform, normal, Bernoulli, and many others. For each work package or project activity, the user inputs a series of probable values or simply chooses the statistical profile that best fits the way costs and durations can vary throughout all phases of the project. For each single risk variable, the software will select a random value from the probability distribution and will compute the project cost or duration independently of other variables. The final output is a graph of probability of occurrence against cost or time for the overall project. The use of risk analysis software allows the possibility of modeling risks for large and complex projects, in particular where a great number of risks are suspected. Interdependence between risks can be worked out easily on most risk software that has the capacity to accommodate structural risk models. Other techniques like sensitivity analysis (or spider diagrams), decision analysis, scenario analysis, and event-tree analysis are also currently used in project risk analysis. However, before considering applying quantified risk analysis techniques or adopting a risk analysis software, the following questions should be asked: Has the right choice of technique or computer software been made? Are the requirements clear? To what extent does the project justify the use of specialist techniques? Does the organization have the necessary skilled personnel (risk analysts) to apply these specialist techniques? Has all risk information been assembled to be processed by the software selected? Indeed, one limitation of software is that it is only an aid or an additional tool in the decision process and hence cannot replace the experience of a decision-maker. Moreover, the computer program will give results based on the information that is only fed into it. These results will also depend on the analysis skill of the risk analyst. If irrelevant or insufficient data are input, the results can induce wrong decisions.

## Risk Response Identification

Having assessed or quantified the risks to the project, this section explains how to prepare the appropriate strategy for controlling risk occurrence and for mitigating the consequences of any risks materializing. The third workshop reunites the team members and must produce a risk response strategy that will be implemented by the project manager. The team for this phase may be updated if necessary, although it is preferable to involve the same team members present in the previous phases. For each risk, team members have to identify all possible measures that can be taken to control risk occurrence and their impact. Exhibit 2 exemplifies some possible strategies for managing project risks. The performance of these measures in mitigating risk occurrence and impacts is assessed so as to expose the eventuality of any residual or secondary risks. The potential benefits of implementing risk measures and the related costs of risk action are determined. Hence those measures with the highest benefit to cost ratios are selected for implementation. However, the responsibility for managing each risk remains to be allocated. Deciding on the right time to allocate the risk is quite important in that this should neither happen too early, when the significance of the risk is not fully understood, nor too late when risk control can be difficult. The party best able to control risk occurrence, as well as the party best capable to bear the consequences of the risk, have to be decided before formulating a definite response strategy.

## Risk Management Strategy Formulation and Implementation

The selected risk actions have to be classified and timed according to the rank of the risk, the likelihood of risk occurrence, the impact of the risk on the project objectives, the level of risk acceptability, and the degree of risk manageability. A risk register is prepared to include the necessary information to enable sound decisions to be made and to monitor the performance of risk mitigating measures. A typical risk register will include the risk description, the date when the risk was raised, the current status of the risk, the likelihood of occurrence and impact, the rank and importance of the risk, the risk action and estimated costs, when to take the risk mitigating action, and the risk owner and progress review. This risk register can be updated at risk management reviews of the same project or for future project risk studies. Once a risk register has been set up, it can be used and updated at any phase of the risk management process. Whee the risks are complex, a risk action schedule (New South Wales PWD 1993) should be developed as a series of timed and planned risk measures that are assigned to the relevant risk owners.

**Exhibit 2.** Example of Possible Risk Management Strategies

| Possible course of action | Some possible action examples |
|---|---|
| Except the risk | • Accept the risk and mitigate its consequences |
| Reduce the risk | • Modify methods of construction<br>• Limit the use of novel technology<br>• Wait for more information; e.g., conduct an in-depth investigation<br>• Change the contract strategy |
| Transfer the risk | • Insure the risk<br>• Transfer risk from client to contractor<br>• Transfer risk from contractor to specialist sub-contractor<br>• Transfer risk from contractor to bank in the form of a bond or guarantee |
| Share the risk | • Risk shared between joint-venture partners |
| Avoid the risk | • Review the project objectives<br>• Consider replacing part of the project<br>• Cancel the overall project |

After the third workshop, the risk coordinator prepares a risk management plan using all the information obtained from the previous phases of the risk management process. The plan remains as a risk working document for the project team and stakeholders to control risks throughout the project lifecycle. The relevant contents of a risk management plan include the objectives and scope of the project; the major decisions reached from the risk management study; the list of risks, sources, and consequences; the results from risk assessment/analysis (that is likelihood, impact, and rank of risks); the risk response strategy; and proposals for implementing the strategy devised.

## Feedback Phase

The nature and types of risks keep changing with time. After implementing the risk strategy, the possible occurrence of secondary risks has to be envisaged seriously. Similarly, portions of risks that have been managed can remain. On the other hand, we are also left with risks that have been managed fully and effectively. Therefore, in order to circulate maximum information on risk status, and also on the running of the framework itself, feedback is necessary at different levels. First, newly identified risks and remaining risks have to be returned into the framework again. Second, resolved risks have to be recorded into a risk management database for future projects. Third, feedback is required from the project team on the risk management plan and on the response strategy during the project life-cycle. Finally, the performance of the system in controlling risks has to be periodically appraised by means of risk management reviews. These reviews are held to identify any new risks and necessary mitigation measures, to modify any risk actions, to update the risk register, and to reconsider the general risk management strategy if necessary. The frequency of these risk reviews will depend on the length of the project, on the project complexity, and on the commitment of the project stakeholders to control project risks. It is definitely good practice to hold a post-project review meeting (shortly after project completion) to record all lessons learned from the risk management study into the risk database.

## Proposed Procedure Associated with the Holistic Risk Management Framework

The proposed procedure for the risk study is based on a two-day study duration. A possible indicative format for this procedure is set out in Exhibit 3. The success of the framework depends largely on how effectively the risk coordinator manages the process. Therefore, it is imperative to examine what attributes the risk coordinator should possess to achieve the results expected. It is good practice to choose an external risk coordinator for the following reasons: (1) the fact that he is not a member of the organization involved, impartiality will be guaranteed, hence promoting the free flow of ideas; (2) he will have a different perspective on the organization and will not be committed to any usual way of doing things: this will bring more interest in the risk study and may especially help in the creative process of identifying risks, and (3) he will work full time on the 'project' (i.e., planning, administrating,

**Exhibit 3.** Indicative Risk Management Study Procedure

| | PROJECT: | | | | | |
|---|---|---|---|---|---|---|
| | Proposed Duration | | Agenda/Aimed Activities | Who is involved | Proposed Method/Tools | Expected Deliverables/Output |
| 1. Pre-Study Risk Meeting 1 | 2 hr. | | • Agree on RM study objectives, scope, procedure, & methodology<br>• Identify team members<br>• Prepare information pack<br>• Project objectives at relevant stage | RMSI RMC PM | Consultation | Objectives, scope, procedure, & methodology clearly defined<br>Team members selected<br>Information pack ready |
| | | | **WORKSHOP PHASE** | | | |
| 2. Preliminary Risk Meeting<br>{Time: 9 to 10.30 a.m.} | 1.5 hr. | Day (1) | • RM process overview<br>• Finalize study procedure<br>• Information presented | RMC<br>PM<br>TMs | Presentation<br>Discussion | Team members fully informed about the RM process and agree on RM study procedure |
| 3. Risk Workshop 1: Risk Identification and Categorization<br>{Time: 11 a.m. to 1 p.m.} | 2 hr. | Day (1) | • Identify & define risk areas/headings<br>• Identify & define risks, sources & primary consequences<br>• Categorize risks | RMC<br>PM<br>TMs | Brainstorming<br>Checklists<br>What-If? analysis<br>Questionnaires<br>Influence diagrams<br>Risk scenarios | Risk description<br>Risk list, sources, & consequences |
| 4. Risk Workshop 2: Risk Assessment/Analysis<br>{Time: 2 p.m. to 5 p.m.} | 2-3 hr. | Day (1) | • Agree on probability & impact scales<br>• Assess probability & impact of risks<br>• Calculate risk importance<br>• Rank/prioritize risks | RMC<br>PM<br>TMs<br>{RA} | Brainstorming<br>Questionnaires<br>Sensitivity analysis<br>Probability trees<br>Scenario trees<br>Influence diagrams<br>Decision trees<br>Event trees | Risk assessment table including:<br>Risks, sources, and consequences<br>Probability/impact/importance scores<br>Ranks of risks & risk matrix |
| 5. Computer Risk Analysis (optional)<br>{Time: 9 a.m. to 12 p.m.} | 3 hr. | Day (2) | • Program & cost risk analysis<br>• Other issues: risk interdependencies and sub-risks | RMC<br>PM<br>TMs<br>RA | Probabilistic analysis with Monte-Carlo simulation<br>Other applied computer modeling techniques | Most likely program & costs of project under risk considerations<br>Sub-risks identified and analyzed |
| 6. Risk Workshop 3: Response Planning & Risk Register Preparation<br>{Time: 2 p.m. to 5 p.m.} | 2-3 hr. | Day (2) | • Identify risk mitigation measures<br>• Plan the measures and timing<br>• Assess performance of measures<br>• Identify any residual or secondary risks | RMC<br>PM<br>TMs | Brainstorming<br>Discussion<br>Questionnaires | Risk management Register including risk description, risk Measures, costs, risk owners, implementation dates, & timing |
| 7. Finalize Risk Management Plan | | | • Writing-up of RM plan including:<br>• Project details, risk list, risk assessment/analysis<br>• RM action plan & sets of measures | RMC | Reporting | Risk Management Plan including outcome of RM study<br>Action strategy |
| 8. Feedback from RM Study Participants | | | • Workshop participants to review risk management plan and to comment on it | RMC<br>PM<br>TMs | Consultation | Risk management plan reviewed and agreed<br>Information gathered for risk database |

*RMC: Risk Management Coordinator* *PM: Project Manager* *RA: Risk Analyst*
*RMSI: Risk Management Study Initiator* *TM: Risk Management Team Member*

and facilitating the risk study) and thus will be fully responsible and accountable for the success of the risk study. His primary role is to plan and organize all activities involved for the risk study from the initial risk management phase to the last post-project review meeting. Advised by the project manager, he will gather the required information for the study, prepare the risk management procedure, and select team members. The risk coordinator also has to guide the risk team through the probable risk areas and provide expert advice on the qualification and quantification of risks. He also reports on the risk study and prepares the risk management plan.

The risk coordinator's necessary attributes to ensure success should include reasonable experience in risk assessment, analysis, and management techniques. She must possess a working knowledge of creative thinking techniques like brainstorming. Good communication, presentation, and negotiation skills allied with elementary management skills are the necessary requirements for success. She must maintain a flexible approach to problem solving and demonstrate objectivity and lateral thinking ability in finding the right solutions for the right challenges. Above all, she must be able to motivate the team to achieve its maximum potential throughout the different phases of the risk management process.

## Conclusion

This paper has presented a holistic framework for project risk management in the construction industry. The framework proposed is supported by a clearly stated procedure that can be carried out by a multidisciplinary team in a workshop environment. The risk management workshops produce a risk register and a risk management plan for the project team to control risks during the project life-cycle. An indicative workshop agenda is supplied for the preparation of successful risk workshops. However, the process will have to be adapted to the particular needs of different projects and modified accordingly. Periodic review of the framework will also ensure that maximum benefits are effectively secured. Project teams within the construction industry can tailor this framework to their respective projects and hence improve their overall control on uncertain events that are so typical to construction projects.

### References


Carter B., J.M. Morin, and N. Robbins. 1994. *Introducing RISKMAN—The European Project Risk Management Methodology.* Oxford, England: NCC Blackwell Limited.

Central Unit on Procurement Guidance No. 41. 1993. *Managing Risk and Contingency for Works Projects.* United Kingdom: HM Treasury.

Cooper, D., and C. Chapman. 1987. *Risk Analysis for Large Projects.* John Wiley and Sons Limited.

Edwards, L. 1995. *Practical Risk Management in Construction.* London, United Kingdom: Thomas Telford Publications, Thomas Telford Services Limited.

Flanagan, R., and G. Norman. 1993. *Risk Management and Construction.* United Kingdom: Blackwell Scientific Publications.

Godfrey, P.S. 1995. *Control of Risk: A Guide to the Systematic Management of Risk from Construction.* London, United Kingdom: CIRIA.

Goodwin, P., and G. Wright. 1991. *Decision Analysis for Management Judgment.* Chichester, United Kingdom: John Wiley and Sons.

New South Wales Public Works Department. 1993. *Risk Management Guidelines.* Sydney, Australia: NSW Government.

Ritchie, B., and D. Marshall. 1993. *Business Risk Management.* United Kingdom: Chapman and Hall.

Simister, S.J. 1994. "Usage and Benefits of Project Risk Analysis and Management." *International Journal of Project Management* 12 (1): 5–8.

Turner, J.R. 1993. *The Handbook of Project-Based Management.* The Henley Management Series, McGraw-Hill Book Company Europe.

Williams, T.M. 1994. "Using a Risk Register to Integrate Risk Management in Project Definition." *International Journal of Project Management* 12 (1): 17–22.

———. 1996. "The Two-Dimensionality of Project Risk." *International Journal of Project Management* 14 (3): 185–186.


### Acknowledgments


The author gratefully acknowledges the joint support of the research sponsors: Dearle and Henderson International Construction Consultants and Anglia Polytechnic University, in United Kingdom.

# Another Thirty Years? Using AI Techniques for Resource Constrained Network Scheduling

Francis Hartman, The University of Calgary, Canada
Daji Gong, The University of Calgary, Canada

## Introduction

Computerization has made the heuristic methods of resource constrained network scheduling popular for the last several years. Numerous commercialized software packages with the capacity of resource constrained network scheduling, such as MS Project, Time Line and Premavera, are available in the market place today. However, many criticisms of heuristic methods have risen over the past few years to draw the attention of practitioners and scholars, e.g., Johnson (1992) and Farid and Manoharan (1996). The main focus of the criticisms is the accuracy of the heuristic methods. As a matter of fact, this type of criticism is not new in academic circles. A widely accepted view is that the heuristic methods are problem dependent or not capable of solving a general class of resource constrained network scheduling problems characterized as combinatorial problems.

For the last three decades in an exploration of new solutions, the most promising contributions are recent development of artificial intelligence techniques such as TABU search (Glover 1989 and 1990), simulated annealing (SA), (e.g. Boctor 1995), and genetic algorithm (GA) (e.g., Chan et. al. 1996). These techniques claim the capability of solving a general class of problem with improved accuracy, reaching an optimum or a near optimum solution by, for example, minimization of the project duration. However, the applications of these techniques are not without practical problems. A primary concern is that these techniques are highly dependent on the capacity of computer hardware. They require a large computer memory and high computation speed to perform an intelligent search effectively. Another concern is the randomness of the search results because virtually all these techniques are of a stochastic nature.

Having witnessed the dramatic advance of computer technology for the last ten years, the authors have no doubt that AI techniques should be seriously considered as the twenty-first century's tools for resource constrained network scheduling. However, can industry benefit from the research in this domain step-by-step with its progress? This paper presents a study concerning the "accuracy-process time" trade-off in resource constrained network scheduling. It is intended to inspire the thinking that, "Although AI techniques are not perfect now, do we need another thirty years for real world applications, or can we harness this technology today while the research and improvements are in progress?"

The study uses an AI technique, called seed screening or S-screening, developed by the authors, for a general class of resource constrained network scheduling problems. In their earlier research, the authors (1997) recommended the use of a multiple duration mode in resource constrained network scheduling. This research clearly showed that using S-screening with a multiple duration mode version in resource constrained network scheduling can produce a better result than using it with a single duration mode version. The conclusion was that changing the way an AI technique is used (e.g., using a multiple duration mode version to replace the single duration mode version) can let the users benefit quickly from the AI technique. This can be done today at the current development stage, although its further improvement is of importance.

The study presented in this paper is a further exploration of the same concern. It consists of two parts: 1) accuracy study and, 2) "accuracy-process time" trade-off study. Twenty-eight examples were developed from ten project networks with different levels of resource constraint for the study. In the accuracy study, Time Line 6.0 was used as a benchmark package to represent a class of typical traditional heuristic methods which are called TH method in this paper. Its scheduling results are compared with the results using S-screening. Time Line 6.0 was selected because of its excellent performance in a benchmarking study undertaken by Johnson (1992). In the "accuracy-process time" trade-off study, the relation between the accuracy and computation time of S-screening is examined.

In this study we extracted two results: 1) The results derived using S-screening are, in general, better than or equal to the results derived using the TH method; 2) S-screening is able to deliver a result which is at least the same as the TH method and a better result with a certain probability at an acceptable level of computation time on a personal computer. The study shows that the development of AI techniques has shown some practical value for real world applications at its current stage of development. Industry can benefit from applying these new techniques while adopting a strategy of "accuracy-process time" trade-off as well as other recommended strategies, as outlined later in this paper. AI-based

Exhibit 1. List of Examples

| ID | Source | No of activity | Published duration | 1 | 2 | 3 | 3 |
|---|---|---|---|---|---|---|---|
| 04-01* | Weglarz et al. | 5 | 7 | 5 | 5 | 3 | 3 |
| 05-01* | Meredith et al. | 10 | 15 | 22 | | | |
| 06-01* | Davis et al. | 27 | 64 | 6 | 6 | 6 | 6 |
| 06-02 | | | | 5 | 6 | 6 | 6 |
| 06-03 | | | | 7 | 7 | 7 | 7 |
| 06-04 | | | | 8 | 8 | 8 | 8 |
| 07-01* | Weglarz et al. | 7 | 8 | 5 | | | |
| 07-02* | | | 11 | 4 | | | |
| 08-01* | Johnson | 22 | 20 | 10 | 10 | 10 | 10 |
| 08-02 | | | | 9 | 9 | 9 | 9 |
| 08-03 | | | | 8 | 8 | 8 | 8 |
| 08-04 | | | | 7 | 8 | 8 | 8 |
| 09-01* | Davis | 11 | 20 | 6 | 7 | 6 | 6 |
| 10-01* | Christofides et al. | 10 | 21 | 6 | 6 | 6 | 6 |
| 12-01* | Shanmuganayagam | 11 | 40 | 8 | 1 | 1 | 1 |
| 13-01* | Moder et al. | 43 | | 6 | 6 | 6 | 6 |
| 13-02 | | | | 7 | 7 | 7 | 7 |
| 13-03 | | | | 8 | 8 | 8 | 8 |
| 13-04 | | | 74 | 10 | 10 | 10 | 10 |
| 13-05 | | | | 12 | 12 | 12 | 12 |
| 13-06 | | | | 14 | 14 | 14 | 14 |
| 13-07 | | | | 16 | 16 | 16 | 16 |
| 14-01* | | 73 | 106 | 3 | 7 | | |
| 14-02 | | | 105 | 3 | 9 | | |
| 14-03 | | | 89 | 4 | 7 | | |
| 14-04 | | | 88 | 4 | 8 | | |
| 14-05 | | | 83 | 4 | 9 | | |
| 14-06 | | | 82 | 5 | 7 | | |

* an original example published in an article.

techniques will continue to benefit from further research and development from now into the next century.

## Description of the Study

S-screening is a heuristic rule-based stochastic search algorithm for a general class of resource constrained network scheduling problems. It uses a heuristic rule associated with the efficiency of resource usage in a local objective function. In addition it uses an overall objective function associated with project time to guide the search direction. S-screening applies a two-level search strategy. It generates candidate schedules, screens them to identify seed partial schedules, and then further explores the seed partial schedules in an intensive search. In order to avoid the local optima brought in by the use of the heuristic rule and to make the search more effective, S-screening uses an approach that incorporates a

**Exhibit 2.** Computation Results

| ID | TH method result | S-Screening | | | |
|---|---|---|---|---|---|
| | | best result | worst result | No. of iterations | Computation time |
| 04-01 | 7 | 7 | 7 | 50 | <1 (sec.) |
| 05-01 | 15 | 15 | 15 | 50 | <1 (sec.) |
| 06-01 | 67 | 64 | 64 | 2000 | ≈10.5 (min.) |
| 06-02 | 73 | 70 | 70 | 2000 | ≈10.5 (min.) |
| 06-03 | 60 | 53 | 54 | 2000 | ≈10.5 (min.) |
| 06-04 | 48 | 47 | 47 | 2000 | ≈10.5 (min.) |
| 07-01 | 8 | 8 | 8 | 50 | <1 (sec.) |
| 07-02 | 11 | 11 | 11 | 50 | <1 (sec.) |
| 08-01 | 22 | 20 | 21 | 2000 | ≈ 5 (min.) |
| 08-02 | 25 | 24 | 24 | 2000 | ≈ 5 (min.) |
| 08-03 | 32 | 29 | 29 | 2000 | ≈ 5 (min.) |
| 08-04 | 34 | 31 | 31 | 2000 | ≈ 5 (min.) |
| 09-01 | 20 | 20 | 20 | 50 | <1 (sec.) |
| 10-01 | 21 | 21 | 21 | 50 | <1 (sec.) |
| 12-01 | 40 | 40 | 40 | 50 | ≈1.4 (sec.) |
| 13-01 | 140 | 129 | 130 | 2000 | ≈ 32 (min.) |
| 13-02 | 127 | 116 | 118 | 2000 | ≈ 32 (min.) |
| 13-03 | 106 | 96 | 97 | 2000 | ≈ 32 (min.) |
| 13-04 | 82 | 74 | 77 | 2000 | ≈ 32 (min.) |
| 13-05 | 67 | 63 | 63 | 2000 | ≈ 32 (min.) |
| 13-06 | 57 | 53 | 54 | 2000 | ≈ 32 (min.) |
| 13-07 | 51 | 51 | 51 | 2000 | ≈ 32 (min.) |
| 14-01 | 105 | 96 | 99 | 2000 | ≈ 45 (min.) |
| 14-02 | 96 | 95 | 97(32%*) | 2000 | ≈ 45 (min.) |
| 14-03 | 92 | 85 | 87 | 2000 | ≈ 45 (min.) |
| 14-03 | 92 | 85 | 87 | 2000 | ≈ 45 (min.) |
| 14-04 | 86 | 84 | 85 | 2000 | ≈ 45 (min.) |
| 14-05 | 83 | 82 | 84(4%*) | 2000 | ≈ 45 (min.) |
| 14-06 | 89 | 80 | 82 | 2000 | ≈ 45 (min.) |

* probability of occurrence.

method similar to the cooling temperature approach in the simulated annealing as well as a Tabu list memory structure that keeps the explored partial schedules away for a certain period of time. The details of the algorithm and its features will be introduced in other papers.

Ten project networks, published by several authors in their articles (see Exhibit 1) were used in the study. The resource constraints in each of the networks are further revised as shown in Exhibit 1. By this revision, a total of twenty-eight examples are developed. The twenty-eight examples were used by S-screening as well as the TH method in our studies. Since S-screening is a stochastic procedure, the occurrence of the derived project time has a certain degree of probability. For each case, at least fifty tries were performed, a set of project times

**Exhibit 3.** Percentage Comparisons Between the TH Method and S-screening Results

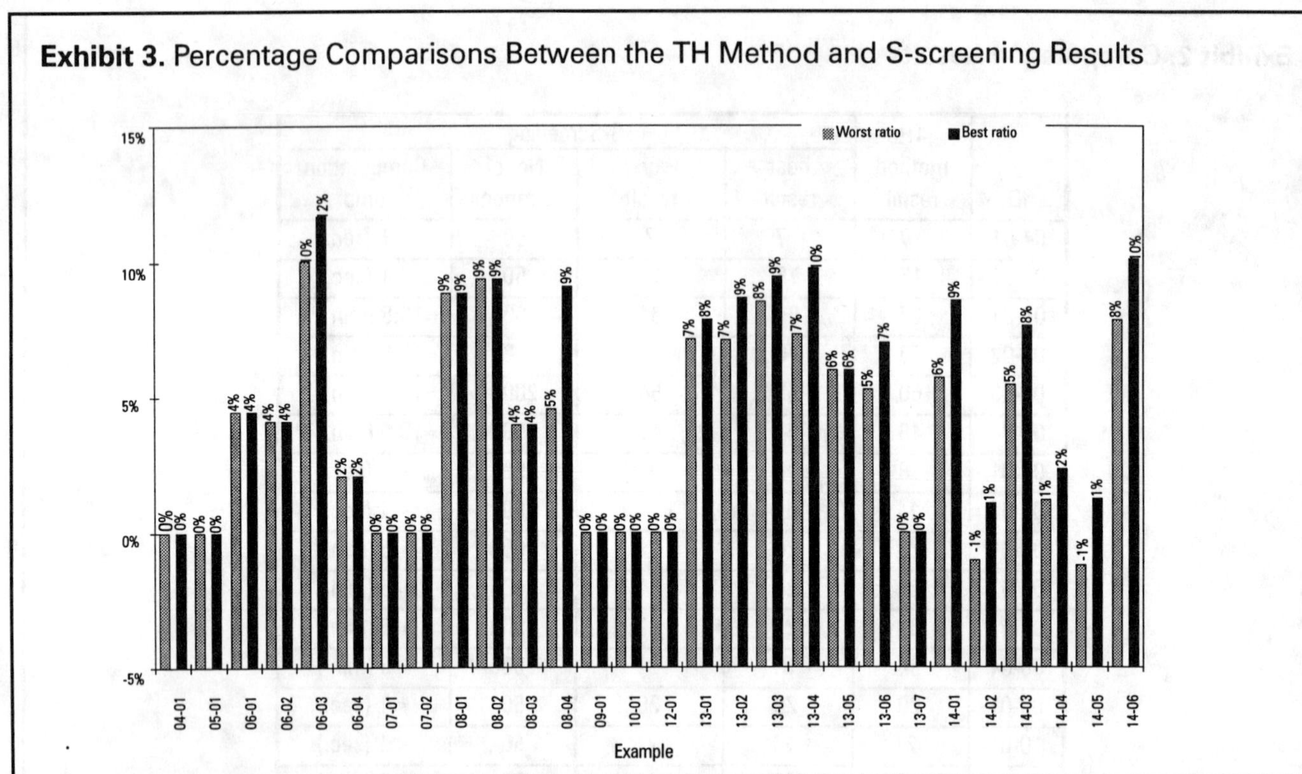


was recorded, and their probabilities of occurrence were calculated. The shortest derived project time is referred to as the best obtained result or the best result, and the longest derived project time is referred to as the worst obtained result or the worst result while using S-screening on each example network.

There are two parts in the study, namely 1) accuracy study; and 2) time-accuracy study. The accuracy study calculates the difference between the best and worst result using S-screening in each example, and compares these to the results derived using the TH method. The time-accuracy study concerns a trade-off between the accuracy and time for performing S-screening. In this study, the derived TH method result is input into S-screening as a threshold value. S-screening performs a search and stops when its derived result is at least equal to or better than the threshold value in each case. The computation times in each case are recorded. The study intends to examine the computation time of S-screening if the required accuracy is the same as for the TH method.

S-screening is programmed in a Windows 95 environment and run on a Dell DIMENSION XPS P133c PC with sixteen MB RAM. It extracts project data from a MS Access database. The user can define the number of tries for a reliability test, the number of iterations in each try, the size of a Tabu list, and a threshold value to let S-screening make a stop/no stop decision during the computation. After the computation, S-screening returns the computation results back to the database for a further analysis.

## Data Analysis, Discussions and Concluding Remarks

The computation results for the accuracy study are listed in Exhibit 2. On average, the difference between the best and worst result is about 1 percent. While compared with the S-screening best results, the TH method has worse results in twenty out of the twenty-eight examples and no one result is better. While compared with the S-screening worst results, the TH method has worse results in eighteen out of the twenty-eight examples. The TH method has better results only in two examples, i.e. Examples 14-02 and 14-05. The probabilities of obtaining the worst results in the two examples are 32 percent and 4 percent, respectively. Exhibit 3 depicts the percentage comparisons between the TH method and S-screening results. The average reduction of total project time is 4.8 percent in the best case scenario and 3.8 percent in the worst case scenario while using S-screening in the twenty-eight examples. However, S-screening is time consuming in its computation for a large network. Exhibit 2 shows the approximate computation time in each case.

The results of the "accuracy-process time" trade-off study are listed in Exhibit 4. The data show that the computation

Exhibit 4. Computation Times

| | Computation time (Sec.) | | Project time | | | Computation time (Sec.) | | Project time | |
|---|---|---|---|---|---|---|---|---|---|
| ID | Mean | Max. value | Max. value* | %** | ID | Mean | Max. value | Max. value* | %** |
| 04-01 | <1 | 1 | 7 | 100 | 12-01 | 1.42 | 15 | 40 | 100* |
| 05-01 | <1 | 1 | 15 | 100 | 13-01 | 4.98 | 14 | 140 | 26 |
| 06-01 | 5.68 | 15 | 67 | 56 | 13-02 | 6.20 | 31 | 127 | 22 |
| 06-02 | 3.92 | 11 | 73 | 76 | 13-03 | 1124 | 35 | 106 | 36 |
| 06-03 | 3.06 | 7 | 60 | 28 | 13-04 | 7.00 | 19 | 82 | 28 |
| 06-04 | 10.82 | 35 | 48 | 54 | 13-05 | 1600 | 41 | 67 | 54 |
| 07-01 | <1 | 1 | 8 | 100 | 13-06 | 4.32 | 12 | 57 | 46 |
| 07-02 | <1 | 1 | 11 | 100 | 13-07 | 1726 | 56 | 51 | 100* |
| 08-01 | 1.40 | 7 | 22 | 34 | 14-01 | 1098 | 30 | 105 | 36 |
| 08-02 | 4.12 | 36 | 25 | 64 | 14-02 | N/A | | | |
| 08-03 | 1.24 | 5 | 32 | 54 | 14-03 | 13.84 | 48 | 92 | |
| 08-04 | 1.54 | 4 | 34 | 12 | 14-04 | 184 | 1164 | 86 | |
| 09-01 | <1 | 1 | 20 | 100 | 14-05 | N/A | | | |
| 10-01 | <1 | 3 | 21 | 100 | 14-06 | 3.86 | 5 | 89 | |

time of using S-screening is less than one minute in most cases with the exceptions of examples 14-02, 14-04, and 14-05. Exhibit 4 also lists the maximum values of the derived project times and their probabilities of occurrence. In most examples, the probability of occurrence of the maximum value is smaller than 100 percent. These smaller probability values indicate that S-screening can deliver even a better result with a certain degree of possibility, that is equal to one minus the tabled probability value, when an imposed threshold value is the same as the project time derived using the TH method.

Undoubtedly, S-screening needs to be further improved in its accuracy, because its outcome cannot always be guaranteed to be the optimum result with an ideal frequency of occurrence of 100 percent. However, the study shows that S-screening can reduce project time effectively under a given availability of resources compared with the TH method. This remark is even generally valid in the "worst scenario," i.e., considering only the worst S-screening results. This reduction in project time does not need extra resources. Rather, this is because S-screening can use the available resources more effectively. Correspondingly, the project cost associated with the need of extra resources and the effective use of available resources can be reduced. Thus S-screening brings values to the users even in its present form.

Apparently S-screening is time inefficient. One can argue that the quality of a scheduling result should be a main concern. However, inefficiency in computation time can be a significant obstacle for a real world application. Some application strategies should be useful, in order to take the advantage of applying an artificial intelligence technique for resource constrained network scheduling at the current development stage:

- Using a powerful computer such as a micro workstation with a high computation speed and a large enough RAM
- Planning a work of resource constrained network scheduling well in advance (at least minutes before it is needed)
- Using the strategy of "accuracy-process time" trade-off when a large computation time is not available, and
- Letting the computer do a thorough search without supervision of the user in a time period after office hours to find an optimum solution and improve the work efficiency of the user.

The two studies demonstrate the advantages of applying an Artificial Intelligence technique, specifically S-screening, for a practical use at the current development stage. Although more studies are needed to further confirm the reliability of using such an Artificial Intelligence technique, the evidence presented in the study shows that the following conclusions may be drawn:

- As a bottom line, an artificial intelligence technique like S-screening is able to deliver a result which is **at least** the same as the TH method and often a better result can be achieved in an acceptable level of computation time such as one minute on a personal computer.
- An artificial intelligence technique like S-screening also brings an opportunity to find a much better result, even an optimum solution, when a large amount of computation time or a powerful computer is available.
- While much research continues in order to further improvement, an artificial intelligence technique like S-screening can bring benefits for a practical use. Another thirty years of waiting for better CPM-like algorithms may not be necessary.

## References


Boctor, F.F. 1995. "Resource Constrained Project Scheduling by Simulated Annealing." *International Journal of Production Research* 34 (8): 2335.

Chan, Weng-Tat, et al. 1996. "Construction Resource Scheduling with Genetic Algorithms." *The Journal of Construction Engineering and Management* 122 (2, June): 125–132.

Christofides, et al. 1987. "Project Scheduling with Resource Constraints: A Branch and Bound Approach." *European J. of Operational Research* 29: 262–273.

Davis, Edward W., and James H. Patterson. 1975. "A Comparison of Heuristic and Optimum Solutions in Resource Constrained Project Scheduling." *Management Science* 21 (8, April): 944–955.

Glover, F. 1989. "Tabu search—Part I." *ORSA Journal on Computing* (No.1): 190–206.

Glover, F. 1990. "Tabu search—Part II." *ORSA Journal on Computing* (No.2): 4–31.

Gong, Daji, and Francis Hartman. 1997. "Resource Constrained Network Scheduling with a Multiple Duration Mode: A Practical Approach." *Proceeding of the 2nd CSCE Construction Specialty Conference.* Sherbrooke, PQ, Canada.

Johnson, Roger V. 1992. "Resource Constrained Scheduling Capabilities of Commercial Project Management Software." *Project Management Journal* XXII (No. 4, Dec.): 39–43.

Meredith, Jack R., and Samuel J. Mantel, Jr. 1985. "Project Management—A Management Approach." 3rd edition. New York: *John Wiley & Sons, Inc.*: 408–410.

Moder, et al. 1983. "Project Management with CPM, PERT, and Precedence Diagramming." 3rd edition. New York: Van Nostrand Reinhold Co.: 220–225.

Shanmuganayagam V. 1989. "Current Float Techniques for Resources Scheduling." *Journal of Construction Engineering and Management* 115 (3): 401–410.

Tabot, F. Brian. 1982. "Resource-Constrained Project Scheduling with Time-Resource Tradeoffs: The Nonpreemptive case." *Management Science* 28 (10): 1197–1210.

Weglarz, et al. 1977. "Algorithm 520, An Automatic Revised Simplex Method for Constrained Resource Network Scheduling." *ACM Transactions on Mathematical Software* 3 (3, Sept.): 295–300.

# A Hitchhiker's Guide to Project Management

Tom Buttle, P.Eng., PMP, Director, Business Transformation, Bell Canada

Wisdom is knowledge plus experience. This project management treatise of hints and tips is intended as a project manager's quick reference guide and, hopefully, also provides an appreciation for development team members.

This is not original work; I definitely did not invent much of this material. But, I have paraphrased and condensed considerable information from books, courses, and, most importantly, experienced project managers. One final caveat, this document does not try to prove or justify facts.

## Introduction—Project Management Overview

Historically, project management likely dates to the Tower of Babel or the Egyptian pyramids; however, modern techniques did not flourish until the Manhattan Project with its resultant atomic bomb. Today, most organizations create new products and services via project teams; the ultimate success of any project will be due to continued focus on customer needs from a scope, quality (a.k.a. performance), time, and cost perspective.

This working paper is organized around the Project Management Institute's (PMI) defined project management areas; namely: integration, scope, quality, time, cost, risk, procurement, human resources, and communications. It is important to realize that a project will likely fail if any of these areas is compromised. As much as possible, I have used values and examples relevant to the telecommunications industry (i.e., my home turf).

Most definitions utilized are courtesy of PMI and appear at the start of each section; the following ones are generic. Project management is the application of knowledge, skills, tools, and techniques to project activities in order to meet or exceed stakeholder needs and expectations from a project. A project is a temporary endeavor undertaken to create a unique product or service, or a problem scheduled for solution (Juran). The project life cycle consists of the following phases: concept, development, implementation, and termination (sub-phases and terminology differences between organizations inevitable); a phase produces verifiable deliverables and acts as a management control point (i.e., gate). An activity is an element of work performed during the course of a project; it normally has an expected duration, an expected cost, and expected resource requirements. Activities are often subdivided into tasks while work packages contain multiple activities creating a deliverable.

## Integration—Directing the Symphony

Integration management ensures that the various elements of a project are properly coordinated.

### Project Plan Development—No Plan Equals No Control

A project plan is a formal, approved document used to guide both project execution and project control. The primary uses of the project plan are to document planning assumptions and decisions, to facilitate communication among stakeholders, and to document approved scope, cost, and schedule baselines. A project plan may be summary or detailed, and accuracy increases over time (i.e., by phase). The baseline is the original plan agreed to by the project sponsor and team, plus any agreed upon changes; set prior to development, it includes detailed elements of the project and product specifications, costs, and time frames, normally within a 10 percent deviation.

Initial planning is the most vital part of a project; do not circumvent. Best results are obtained when a project manager is assigned early in the planning stages, preferably during the concept phase. A project's goals and objectives, without a detailed plan on how to implement them, will ultimately fail. You can't manage what you don't measure; corollary: what gets measured, gets done. Embrace the concept of total quality management (TQM); everything must be planned. After performing a task, check results to plan, then take action to correct or improve.

Assemble the results of all planning areas into a consistent, coherent document. At a minimum, the project plan includes: a project charter (includes scope); work breakdown structure; baselines for schedule and cost; required staff; key risks and issues; interdependencies with other projects; plus references to supporting detail (e.g., business, operations, and technical requirements). Electronic access to all project information, especially the project management portion, is vital for today's distributed teams and stakeholders.

The first rule of planning is "be prepared to re-plan." A project manager plans continually, more so at the start of a project than near its completion. Project planning is "simple"; just answer these questions: what must be done, how should it be done, who will do it, when must it be done, how much will it cost, and how good does it have to be?

Organizations should utilize a common methodology, including formats/templates. Establish project documentation methodology for deliverables, status, and change control. Sponsor agreement to frequency and content is crucial, especially when sponsors change.

Sponsor and team commitment to the project plan, in blood (i.e., signatures), is mandatory; customer alignment is also crucial. All project constraints and assumptions must be clearly identified to stakeholders.

### Project Plan Execution— Measures Baseline To Actual

Project termination (acceptance, review, and turn-over to support) is the goal. Team alignment to project goals is important; everyone must know when we are finished, why we are successful, and who gets to vote.

Manage by walking around; show interest in each team member's work. The project manager should meet everyone working on the project, including contractors' personnel. A project manager spends 80 percent of her time communicating with stakeholders. Short (i.e., one hour), weekly project team reviews are mandatory; focus on project risks, potential changes, and outstanding action items.

A major project management function is to help remove roadblocks for the team so that it can perform its work. Open communications is a key component in addressing the inevitable project issues.

### Change Control— Regulates Baseline Alteration

Prevention of baseline obsolescence is the key goal; a current project plan is the result. An effective change control procedure, with proper authorization, is mandatory to limit scope creep (and leap!). A multi-step process is required: initiation describes the change; evaluation of the impact on scope, schedule and cost; and authorization by the originator and project manager if the cumulative deviation is within specified tolerances (normally 10 percent), else the project sponsor. A change control form includes: description; impacts on scope, cost and schedule; and authorization feedback plus signatures.

Anyone can initiate change requests: the sponsor, customer, project team, and sometimes even externally (e.g., telecommunications commissions (CRTC/FCC) or standards bodies (CSA/UL)). The project sponsor must accept full responsibility for significant scope changes altering a project's direction. Project performance reports highlight budget and schedule variations, creating change.

## Scope—Defines Your Target's Boundaries

Scope is the sum of the products and services to be provided as a project. Scope management controls objectives, including changes, through the project life cycle.

### Charter—Plants The Seed In Fertile Ground

The charter is the 'contract' between the project manager and sponsor and explains why we have a project plus the project manager's mandate. It describes the problem, mission, scope, objectives, benefits, assumptions, and any expectations; typical size is two to three screens. Most importantly, define the right problem; the way it is defined determines the solution possibilities—gather enough data to evaluate alternatives and constraints. The mission provides the end vision to the team and specifies: what to do, for whom, and how it will be done; also specify how success will be measured. Scope defines a project's boundaries; explicitly state what is, and is not, included via an in/out list. Objectives describe the desired end-state, not tasks or solutions, and are SMART (Specific at a high level, Measurable, Attainable, Realistic, and Time-limited), plus each provides a single result (i.e., deliverable). Ensure implementation and support objectives are included. Benefits and strategies show project strengths, weaknesses, opportunities, and threats (SWOT). Assumptions must be explicit, use a list, and emphasize schedule and cost ranges plus any constraints.

The project sponsor must sign the charter and ensure funding. The project team must also fully support and clearly understand the charter. The project charter is frozen—changes are controlled and reflected in the project management plan.

### Scope Definition—Helps You Do Things Right

The work breakdown structure (WBS) is a deliverable-oriented grouping of project elements, which organizes and defines the total project scope. Each descending level represents an increasingly detailed definition of a project component. Project components may be products or services.

Create a WBS with knowledgeable people, preferably the ones doing the work or with similar skills, soon after project kick-off. Two basic styles are available: organization chart and indented; create via Post-it notes or Spread-sheet, respectively (software packages available). Keep breaking activities down until each task takes ten days (five days unloaded) to complete for ±10 percent variance prior to the start of development;

one month for ±50 percent pre-concept. Include all contractor activities in the WBS; if unknown, use milestones. Ensure identified activities include testing, review meetings, rework, status reporting, and any required training.

The project segmentation method is unimportant (phase and function is normal); the key to success is "identify all activities to measurable detail." WBS does not infer sequence or linkages, nor is it scheduling. The WBS levels are: program, project, function, process, activity, task, sub-task, and technique; need more levels? Name your own. Large projects could have up to six or eight levels and paths need not go to the same depth.

Every work package needs a statement of work (SOW) that contains: a name (a complete thought—verb plus object); description (sufficient detail so that a capable person understands); WBS number; deliverable(s); quality criteria (performance requirements—answers the question, "How do I know when I'm done?"); dependencies; and constraints (e.g., special test needs or external events). Plus, each activity needs a name, duration (span, normally in workdays; effort is reflected in costs), full costs (estimated salary, expense, contract, and capital), resource names when assigned (else job title), plus RACI (Responsible, Accountable, Consult, Inform) (a.k.a. linear responsibility chart).

## Quality—Is Defined by Your Customer

Quality management ensures baseline results meet, or exceed, customer and stakeholder expectations. Quality planning identifies which quality standards are relevant and determines how to satisfy them. Quality assurance evaluates overall project performance on a regular basis to provide confidence that the project will satisfy the relevant quality standards. Quality control monitors specific process results to determine compliance to relevant quality standards and identifies ways to eliminate causes of unsatisfactory performance.

### Assurance —Quality as a Way of Life

Product quality outlives both project schedule and cost; don't compromise it. Quality reduces overall costs; typical life cycle costs are 10 percent R&D, 30 percent acquisition, and 60 percent operations, administration, and maintenance (OA&M).

Quality must be built into the company; ISO 9000 defines the components of the quality system, which must be managed to ensure "quality objectives" are met. Prefer ISO compliant (registered) subcontractors; ISO 9000 ensures traceability. Consistency requires effective training, tools, and processes with best-case examples and checklists.

Plan, Do, Check, and Act (PDCA or Shewhart cycle) is the road to continuous improvement. Useful planning tools are: affinity diagrams, interrelationship diagraphs, tree diagrams, prioritization matrices, matrix diagrams, process decision program charts, and activity network diagrams. Plan, Organize, Execute, Track, and Steer (POETS) is the project management equivalent to PDCA.

Process reengineering and TQM introduction require adherence to project management practices; implementing these programs within an operating business is like wiring a house with the power on.

### Control—Delivering an Excellent Product

For an individual, quality is pride of workmanship. Control data is needed by the person doing the work; this feedback enables continuous improvement. A project manager must never accept poor quality work.

Create product metrics while planning; include them in baseline scope. When producing requirements, specify how they will be tested; if one can't be tested, it isn't a requirement. Deliverables require performance specifications; quality is conformance to these requirements.

Quality objectives must be ambitious but also realistic and achievable. Quality characteristics are defined by being producible (with conformity), usable, reliable, maintainable, available, operable, flexible, acceptable (social wise), and affordable.

Market research helps identify end customer needs. Questions (specific areas important) to ask customers are: what do you like, what do you want changed, and what is missing? One must probe for answers.

Team feedback, walk-throughs, reviews, and trials are important ways to build quality into products. Quality control is also team interaction, including meeting structure, discipline, ground rules, action registry mechanism, change control, status reports, check points, and measurement. Audits and reviews improve processes and products, respectively; they must never be witch hunts; the review is a failure if the reviewed learn nothing.

Changes and bug fixing have the greatest impact on quality and cost, in the latter stages of a project. Rule of thumb is: the cost of a change, including fixes, increases tenfold in each succeeding phase; ergo, do it right the first time.

Most projects, due to their short-term nature, do not use statistical concepts (testing is the exception). But it is important to understand in order to deal with subcontractors.

Some "tools" are control charts, Pareto diagrams, cause/effect diagrams, histograms, scatter diagrams, and sampling.

A successful project has satisfied stakeholders; sometimes this means killing projects expediently. Project wrap-up must include a final evaluation; the sponsor approves variances and outstanding issues. Share project experiences, both what worked and what didn't, with other teams. Lessons learned must be told in context, be timely, relatable, and complete.

## Time—20/20 Foresight Is a Myth

Time management plans, estimates, schedules, and controls all activities to ensure timely project completion; use manageable work packages from the WBS as input.

### Sequencing—Ordering the Chaos

Sequence all activities via precedence or arrow diagramming methods (PDM/ADM). Activity relationships include: finish-to-start (common), start-to-start, finish-to-finish, and start-to-finish; all may include lead/lag time and composites are possible. Watch for serial activities that could be done in parallel and dependent activities that could start prior to predecessor completion. Show supplier/customer activities where known; otherwise, use milestones.

### Estimating—Use Knowledgeable People

Estimate too high—lose opportunities; too low—waste money. Resourceful estimators, along with a historical database, are the key to success (versus guess). Use "function point"estimating for large software developments. Project managers estimate their activities and facilitate other areas. Contractors must confirm their activity durations before scheduling commences.

Loading must be aboveboard and be applied to activities. Never apply contingency to specific activities; keep it in reserve, or else it will be spent. Many estimating methods are available; two example methods are outlined below. Breakthrough projects can reduce or remove loadings with team agreement. Estimates exclude uncontrollable delays (e.g., CRTC/FCC); use "best guess" for these activities. Estimate activity duration independently of predecessors and successors. Finally, verify project estimates with an uninvolved expert or mentor.

PERT Estimate = (OE + (4 * TE) + PE) / 6; where: optimistic estimate is the one-in-twenty best case; typical estimate is the most likely time; and pessimistic estimate is the one-in-twenty worst case.

Estimate = UE * (1+EF+PL) * (1+NPL) * (1+PC) / RA, sometimes rounded; where: unloaded estimate is average productive time (person-days) for a dedicated resource to complete activity with no distractions; efficiency factor is 10–15 percent for junior/unknown people; project loss time is 10 percent for discussions, phone calls, and so on; non-project loss is 40 percent, the industry standard (organizations in transition could be 60 percent); phase contingency is normally 50 percent at assessment, 25 percent at proposal, and 10 percent at agreement (all prior to development phase); resource allocation is percentage of time working on activity.

### Scheduling—Applies Time and Resource Constraints

Many systems are available for scheduling; Microsoft Project is common and inexpensive. Don't schedule more activities than you can handle; manage at the work package level on large projects. Initial scheduling assumes unlimited resources; this is a best case solution. Include holidays, vacations, and training in project calendars.

Eliminate multiple critical paths; give extra float or resources to the risky activities. Any critical path activity slippage shifts the project end-date equally. Try to keep fixed-duration activities off the critical path (e.g., CRTC/FCC approval, disclosure).

Shorten activity duration by increasing resources, reducing scope (with sponsor agreement), or changing the process (i.e., efficiency gains); never reduce quality. Remember that planned overtime increases risk; it may be needed later in the project. Resource leveling helps avoid peaks and valleys in their usage but likely delays project completion date.

Here is a simple scheduling approach. Using a Post-it WBS, mark each leaf (not summary tasks) with predecessor(s) indicated in SOW. Create a PERT chart using WBS leaves on a large piece of paper. Fix obvious missing predecessors and successors. Add estimated unloaded duration to each leaf. Enter information into scheduling program. Add company holidays to calendar (unrealistic completion date). Assign resources to all tasks. Resolve all conflicts by adding more resources or deferring tasks; add a dependency to the second task when deferred. Apply efficiency, experience, and learning curve factors, plus vacation and training for each resource. Add loading factors to each task. Apply any external forces (e.g., Nortel schedule, Xmas brown-out). Add the contingency factor to get a realistic schedule.

### Charting—Pictorially Presents Your Project

Use Gantt, critical path method, and resource utilization charts available in MS Project. Gantt charts are the best visual aid but exclude interrelationships; show with an extra column. Columns for accountable and responsible names are also useful. CPM and performance evaluation and review technique are similar, but PERT applies probabilities to all durations (useful when historical data is lacking). Both methods work with activity-on-arrow and activity-on-node (preferred for readability) diagrams.

### Control—Measure Baseline to Actual; React to Variance

If a project falls five days behind schedule, it will likely be late or have poor quality. Get team agreement at kick-off that unsolicited status will be provided by all. Manage by walking around (by phone, if distributed). Focus daily on critical path and risky activities, plus rookies; facilitate alternative solutions to problems. At least weekly, collect activity status: WBS number, percent complete, expected completion date, accomplishments, changes to plan, problems, action plans, and other comments.

## Cost—The Cash Value of All Activities

Cost is an element of the baseline scope, quality, and time; all four variables cannot be specified simultaneously (i.e., at least one must be allowed to vary). Cost management maintains financial control of the project.

### Planning/Estimating—The Profitability Factor

Generally, if its not profitable, don't do it. Typical economic indicators are: net present value (NPV), including probability; discounted payback period; return on investment (ROI); and, in most companies, project scores based on selected governance criteria. Organizations generally have tools to help in these calculations; such as: decision risk analysis (DRA), and economic evaluator (EE is currently mandatory for CRTC filings).

Accurate development costs (generated from the WBS), revenue estimates, and cost savings are crucial; rule of thumb is: proceed if economics are still positive after doubling costs and halving revenues. Ensure full life cycle support costs are used (e.g., installation, spares). Activity based costing (ABC) is justified when indirect business costs are large, and there is a significant variation in resource consumption across projects.

### Budget—Investment Management

The cost baseline allows all project funding forms to be completed (e.g., quarterly forecast, external R&D, contract). The program management office keeps current costs (usually developed by comptrollers) for labor, loadings, and subcontracts. Remember to include funds for language translation and for team celebrations. R&D activities produce tax credits in Canada; documentation must be kept on a calendar basis for seven years.

An integrated cost/schedule system shows the maturity of project-driven companies; if not available, track your own current, detailed status until the typical monthly budget actuals are issued, then reconcile the differences.

### Control—Project Tracking

The project manager authorizes all project expenses (team must remit copy), including people's time via SOWs. Regular input is required from team members and suppliers.

Earned value is the best method to track progress, but it doesn't replace vigilance. The baseline (budgeted cost of work scheduled (BCWS)) plots cumulative effort (percent, hours, or cost) versus time (percent or schedule) for the entire project; the result is an "S" curve ending with the total budget at completion (BAC). Add executive control points (i.e., gates) to the time axis. With frequent monitoring, you can now plot both actual product completed (earned value or budgeted cost of work performed (BCWP)) and actual effort expended (actual cost of work performed (ACWP)) to graphically see current project status. From this data, one can then easily calculate cost variance (CV = BCWP - ACWP) and schedule variance (SV = BCWP - BCWS); a positive number is good.

The critical ratio = cost performance index * scheduled performance index, where CPI = BCWP / BCWS and SPI = BCWP / ACWP. If the value is: <0.6 return money; <1.1 green; <1.3 amber; >1.3 red. The estimate at completion (EAC) = BAC / CPI. The nameless project depicted below is in trouble. Once a project is 15 percent complete, earned value techniques can accurately predict both completion time and costs. To overcome the 90 percent done syndrome, it is usually better to award earned value only to completed activities. Use spreadsheets if no tools standardized.

## Risk—Being Too Cautious Is the Greatest Risk

Risk is the effect of uncertain occurrences affecting project objectives; they can be ignored (and fixed), avoided, or deflected, but not controlled. Risk management identifies, quantifies, and responds to project risks; it includes maximizing the results of positive events and minimizing the consequences of adverse events.

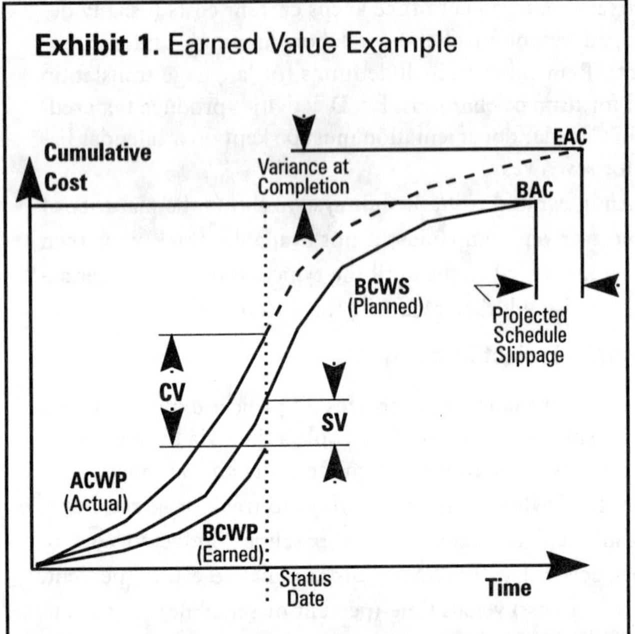


### Identification/Quantification—Knowing Your Enemies

Every organization should create a risk laundry list; teams can then easily select risk items and add additional ones pertinent to their project. Analysis techniques include: brainstorming, sensitivity, probability, Delphi, Monte Carlo, decision tree, and utility/decision theories. Customer interviews plus a WBS analysis provide crucial input. After identifying significant risks, classify via scope, quality, schedule, and cost; reassess within each project phase since risks change over time. Risk elements include: loss frequency and severity, reliability of the available information, and manageability.

The following simple process can help identify and action project risks with the core team. Individually take five minutes to list the risks that are relevant to the project (a complete thought only, not great detail) then create a group list via a round-robin. Spend a few minutes to jointly build on this list and understand everyoneÕs input. Via group consensus, estimate the probability of occurrence and impact (exact numbers not required). Graph the results; assign caretakers to all risks. The caretakers create straw-model mitigation strategies (not necessarily the prime to perform the risk activities generated) and babysit the risk for the projectÕs life.

Risks are highest at project conception and during change; the highest cost impact occurs during widespread implementation. Risks never have a zero percent probability of occurrence. Multi-path convergences in the PDM/ADM increase risk substantially, and subcontracts always increase a project's risk. Something new to the organization or significant R&D (bleeding edge) also increases project risk; use modeling, simulation, prototyping, and trials if possible. Prioritize risks (probability * amount at stake); economic sensitivity analyses, and the DRA's tornado diagram are useful tools.

### Mitigation—Reducing Uncertainty

The goal is to make opportunity out of uncertainty. Each risk must have a mitigation strategy; build these activities into the WBS. Create contingency plans; proactive, versus reactive, alternatives are best. Document results and evaluate, using TQM techniques.

Take risks only when the benefits outweigh the losses, and you can afford to lose. Historical project databases help reduce today's risks; expert system tools build on this knowledge. Use force-field analysis (e.g., organization, not-invented-here, public concern) to strengthen positives, and weaken/skirt negatives. Add float to risky activities (also your best people), and try to remove them from the critical path. Insurance is a risk buffer, as is project contingency.

A fully committed project champion is mandatory, along with stakeholder agreement; a sound business case maintains support. Tackle all "surprises" head-on and review risks often—they change over time. Risks should be discussed at every team meeting. Challenge the accuracy of all numbers prior to making decisions.

## Procurement—More Than a Handshake Required

Procurement management acquires project resources to produce the end product.

### Specification—What You Want

State requirements precisely; accuracy increases delivery success. Each requirement should be accompanied by an acceptance test; if you canÕt test it, it is not a requirement. Specifications include: functional requirements, network and system components, interfaces, OA&M, communications (e.g., access, LAN, WAN), performance (system sizing, response time, capacity, throughput, availability, reliability, and evolution), hardware (preferred platforms, sparing, environmental, physical, electromagnetic emissions, and power), security (network, customer access, and fraud control), documentation (training, maintenance, operation, practices, format, and language), training, and testing/verification (lab, trials, procedures, strategies, test cases, recovery, and backout).

The work package SOW is used to "contract" work internally.

### Acquisition—What You Get

Prepare a potential supplier list in parallel with the specification. For external project resources, one typically issues a request for information, proposal, or quotation (RFI/RFP/RFQ), with an attached specification. It is important to schedule time for supplier meetings and their bid preparation. Crash projects needing knowledgeable people or prototype construction may bypass bidding if a qualified supplier list is maintained; the risk is CRTC/FCC complaints.

Qualify potential suppliers in parallel with their bid preparation; tie evaluation to value and complexity. Qualification evaluates: management, technical, and manufacturing capabilities; quality control; location and financial strength, plus any previous history (successes and disasters). Company visits, plus Dunn & Bradstreet reports or equivalent, provide other essential data.

Bid evaluation, normally accomplished via a point system, selects the best supplier based on cost (including ongoing), risk (via qualification), and, most importantly, compliance to the specification.

Negotiation is more than getting the lowest price, it is establishing a relationship that meets both parties needs; if not, walk away after exploring options. Preparation is mandatory for success. It is important to know what motivates contractors. Once a contract is signed, notify all other bidders.

### Administration—Contracting Requirements

Validation and acceptance of subcontracted work is essential; the project manager is accountable for the entire product. Most organizations have a purchasing support group to assist in project contract management, including those for consultants.

Two principle types of contracts are fixed price and cost based; variations are possible by using incentives and cost plus (percentage or fixed fee) schemes. The objective is to minimize risk while maintaining incentive for efficient supplier performance.

Contracts not only specify the required product but must also include: any development plan (and design reviews), acceptance, installation, maintenance, repair, upgrades, documentation, training, quality, warranty, schedule, and special considerations. Ensure software contracts include source code ownership; right to modify (RTM) is preferred; in escrow is a last resort.

To limit costly court battles, specify an arbitration method. Also, never change a contractor's plans unless they are flawed or too costly. Finally, being a friend of a contractor is dangerous; being friendly is not.

## Human Resources—Make, or Break, the Project

Human resource management makes the most effective use of the people involved in the project.

### Organizational Planning—Processes and Systems

The project manager's authority must be public company knowledge. The project manager is accountable to the sponsor and is normally the assignment manager for team members.

Decide on team structure early in the project life. A team of seven is ideal; with team leaders, a good project manager can manage fifty-six people effectively. Larger projects require a project management team. Collocation nurtures teamwork; distributed teamwork requires excellent communications to succeed.

Each activity needs someone who is accountable and others who are responsible. Use the best people on critical-path and high-risk activities. Key project people should be available for at least six months after product introduction.

### Staff Acquisition—Company Processes and Systems

Utilize the SOW's to canvass and select team members. Also, listen to team members; they are unlikely to recommend lemons. Most organizations have numerous processes and databases to aid in the selection and management of resources; use them diligently.

Resource leveling helps optimize project costs (but likely extends completion date). Get rid of unproductive core team members quickly, and redo the schedule whenever people are reassigned or unavailable. If a person is part time, specify working arrangement up front; effectiveness decreases when working on simultaneous projects (100 percent, 50 percent, 25 percent, 7–12 percent for one, two, three, and four projects, respectively).

### Team Development —The Human Element

A project manager's qualities are typically: team player, experienced (with knowledge), communicator, negotiator, and facilitator; a profit and customer focus is paramount. Versatility is key: bold and audacious at times, caring and nurturing at times, plus sometimes even pushy.

Project managers lead, integrate, make decisions (try to understand the consequences of your actions prior to making decisions), and communicate. A project manager must understand the area they manage (but don't do team's work). Projects succeed via teamwork, and shared leadership is best on multidisciplinary teams; coaches don't boss (but a coach still calls some of the plays). Control activities, not people, based on work done and deal fairly with everyone. Remem-

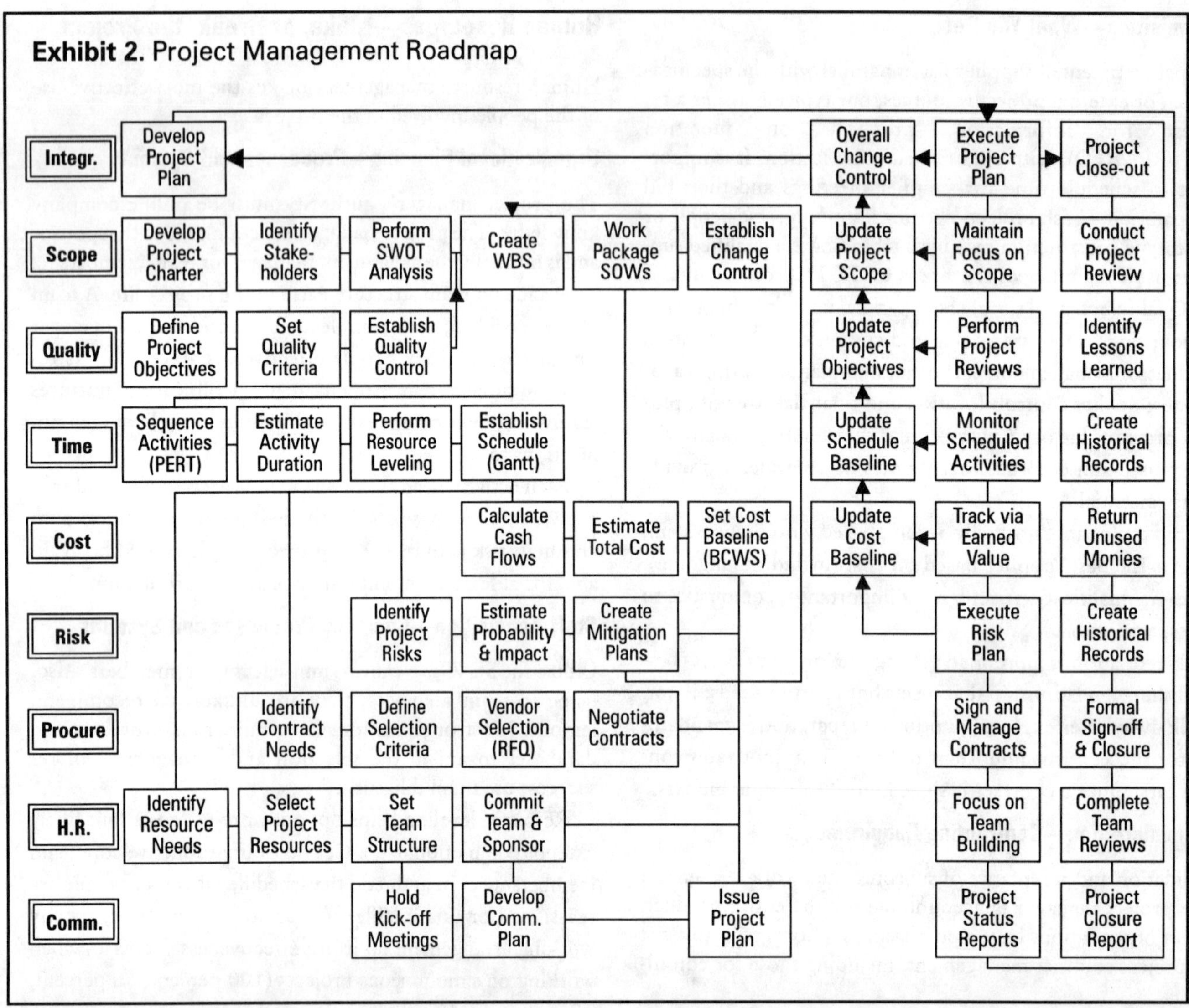


ber, reward success, not just hard work, and never embarrass people in public.

Team building, starting with project kick-off, is crucial for extraordinary results; getting commitment is the key. An early team kick-off meeting is key to ensuring shared knowledge and buy-in to scope and objectives. Team members must know their roles and responsibilities. A team's performance over time is typically: forming, norming, storming, performing; make conflict positive, and become performing quickly. Conflict resolution is crucial; one can confront (problem solve), compromise, force, smooth, or withdraw. Only confrontation has a win-win possibility; find a solution that is not unacceptable to both sides.

Performance reviews are done by the project manager; three hundred and sixty degree feedback is encouraged. Constructive criticism guidelines: think it through before speaking (don't shoot from the lip); criticize in private (praise in public); take only one point at a time, on time; criticize without comparison; and criticize with specificity, not labels.

A project manager must hide nothing from the sponsor or reviewers; never offer excuses, just state facts. Finally, remember to have fun; celebrate both the large and small successes. Even a wake has team healing power. A signed project charter, appropriately packaged or mounted, creates a memorable trophy that means something to the participants.

## Communications—Honesty Is the Only Policy

Communications management organizes and controls all the information to meet project needs. The communications plan establishes how the team communicates and how customers and stakeholders access the team.

The communicator is responsible for communications—not the listener; I don't care if I'm not understood, as long as I'm not misunderstood (Fuller). Active listening is important; until the message is accepted, no communication occurs. LISTEN formula is: Lean forward, use I statements, Stay focused, Take notes, Eye contact, and Nod your head. "Speaking for" and "listening for" commitments are very important for generative teams. Team members' declared commitment is crucial.

Share all information in a timely fashion with the project team and stakeholders (a puzzle is hard to discern when pieces are missing); it is a critical commodity. In general, one can never over-communicate. The medium (oral, written, or visual) is an important aspect of all communications. Public relations (PR) is a specialist function in most organizations; use them for dissemination of information to the general public.

Working meetings can include about six people; larger scale meetings can only be used for information transfer. Remember to ask questions; never assume you know the answers. The most valuable, and least used, word in a project manager's vocabulary is "no."

## Summary—The Big Picture (But Small Print)

## References—Furthering Your Knowledge


Lewis, J.P. 1993. *The Project Manager's Desk Reference.* Probus Publishing.

Kerzner, H. 1995. *Project Management: A Systems Approach to Planning, Scheduling, and Controlling.* Van Nostrand Reinhold; Edition 5.

Meredith, J.R., and S.J. Mantel. 1989. *Project Management, A Managerial Approach.* J. Wiley & Sons; Edition 2.

Project Management Institute (PMI) Standards Committee. 1996. *A Guide to the Project Management Body Of Knowledge (PMBOK Guide).* PMI.

# Methods of Managing Risk for a Major Construction Project

Michael S. Terrell, PE, PMP, Duke Power Company
Anthony W. Brock, PE, PMP, Duke Power Company

**Exhibit 1.** Typical S/G Cavity

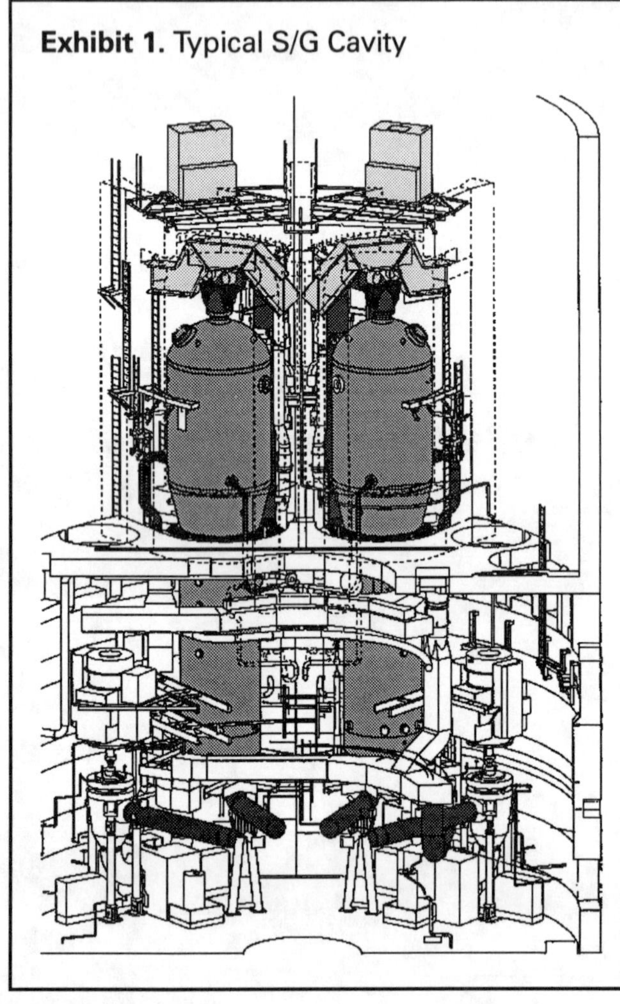

## Introduction

Duke Power Company is replacing the steam generators (S/G) at Catawba Nuclear Station Unit 1 and McGuire Nuclear Station Units 1 and 2 at an estimated cost of $500 million. The scope of the replacement outages involves the removal and replacement of the steam generators, providing necessary special handling equipment, removing or modifying existing plant structures, and rerouting piping and electrical systems connected to the generators. Each outage is estimated to consume approximately 450,000 work hours and involved approximately 3,000 schedule activities. Each generator replacement is scheduled to be implemented during a fifty-five-day window of a ninety-day outage. The replacement of the steam generators at Catawba occurred during the summer of 1996. The McGuire replacement outages are scheduled for the first and fourth quarters of 1997.

A project of this magnitude is replete with opportunities for risk management. Considerable time was spent identifying, quantifying, mitigating, and managing potential risk items. Two examples of how the project team managed risk items are discussed in this paper. These two risk items are internal communications and fit-up of the new steam generators.

## Background

The scope of each replacement outage involves the removal and replacement of the four steam generators, providing necessary special handling equipment, removing or modifying existing plant structures, and rerouting piping and electrical systems connected to the generators. Each outage is estimated to consume approximately 450,000 work hours and involved approximately 3,000 schedule activities implemented during a fifty-five-day window of a ninety-day outage.

The steam generators are housed in the reactor buildings inside reinforced concrete cubicles with removable steel walls and domes. Located above the enclosure domes are air handling units and associated steel platforms. Six piping systems connected to the generators have to be severed before the old steam generators can be unbolted from their support structures. A major portion of the reactor building has to be disassembled to remove the old steam generators, and then reassembled once the new steam generators are installed. Exhibit 1 shows two typical steam generator cavities and associated components.

## Risk Identification

Since this was the first steam generator replacement project for Duke, the project team visited numerous replacement projects under way around the United States, Europe, and Japan. Lessons learned from these projects were factored into the overall project plans. In addition, over 700 lessons learned from the Catawba replacement outage were identified, categorized, reviewed, and factored into the execution plan for the first replacement outage at McGuire.

One of the key concerns of the project team throughout the development of the outage schedule was how accurate and realistic the plan was in relation to what others had been able to accomplish on similar projects around the world. At several key points in the schedule development process, the project team brought in experts that had been involved in other replacement projects to review the plans, resources, assumptions, and other project data. Each of these reviews provided course corrections; however, each of these reviews indicated that the execution plans were fundamentally on target.

During initial development of the project plans it became obvious that we needed to develop contingency plans to address the many areas where we would potentially have to deviate from the base plan. The project team developed a contingency data base for the purpose of defining items that could cause problems, and these items were reviewed and prioritized to determine which would be addressed in the schedule and which ones would be handled through process changes.

## Internal Communications Risk Management

The Steam Generator Replacement Project at Duke was involved with replacing generators at two nuclear stations during an eighteen-month period. Consequently, it was necessary to set up site organizations at both of the stations. The project team determined that internal communications between the various team members of the project represented a significant risk item. The 120-plus member project team was distributed between the two nuclear stations and the corporate office. Additionally, the project had to develop several new processes and interfaces to existing station processes for implementing the necessary changes to plant systems. These new processes and interfaces were also identified as significant communications risk items. Three major subcontractors were utilized during the replacements. Therefore, the communications plans and processes had to facilitate the integration of these entities.

To quantify and mitigate the risks associated with internal communications, we developed and implemented a series of tabletop simulations. These simulations were designed to test and practice various communication interfaces and processes that would be used during the outages. These simulations were conducted several weeks before the start of the first outage using key project players, simulated work packages, and facilities mockups. The sessions identified communication interface problems as well as actual execution problems that were corrected before the first outage began. These sessions also provided input into the project's plan for internal and external communications.

Several methods of internal communications were established to meet the challenges and risks associated with a virtual organization such as the Steam Generator Replacement Project. Daily performance reporting tools were used to keep the project on track. These included several sorts of the schedule data, earned value reports defining schedule performance, work hour expenditures versus expected expenditures, radiation dose reports tracked against a target of expected exposures, milestone comparisons at a high level, and other specific reports generated as needed at critical points in the execution cycle. These tools offered data that helped keep the project support groups focused on the same priorities. The reports were distributed in multiple formats including bulletin boards (traditional and electronic), at status review meetings, and through the corporate intranet. Face-to-face turnovers between craft crew supervisors and project managers were utilized to ensure clear communications of the progress of past shifts as well as plans for the current and upcoming shifts. Throughout each shift, project managers met to discuss interfaces and plans for the week. This combination of written reports and face-to-face communications helped keep focus on critical activities and prevent other activities from being forgotten.

## Steam Generator Fit-Up Risk Management

The major risk item identified for the project was the fit-up of the new steam generators to the existing piping systems and support structures. The replacement generators are approximately sixty-eight feet tall, fifteen feet in diameter, and weigh over 400 tons. Each generator has four fit-up locations and multiple fit-up constraints.

The complexity of the steam generator fit-up necessitated the formation of a sub-project team to quantify the risks, develop contingencies, mitigate the risks, and finally provide risk response control during the outages. The fit-up team developed a matrix that indicated each fit-up constraint's tolerances, contingency associated with each tolerance, associated work hour impact, and probability of occurrence. This information was used to run schedule scenarios to determine the impact to critical path of the various scenarios. Once the critical path impact was known, a decision tree was developed to determine which scenario represented the greatest impact to the schedule. Activities and logic were added to the schedule with zero hour durations (in lieu of separate fragnets), such that if the contingency option was necessary, the appropriate activity duration could quickly be input into the schedule as decisions were made to implement contingencies. This data was used to develop a decision matrix. This allowed the fit-up team to quickly determine the impact of each option during the outage. Exhibit 2 shows the decision tree.

**Exhibit 2.** S/G Fit-up Decision Tree

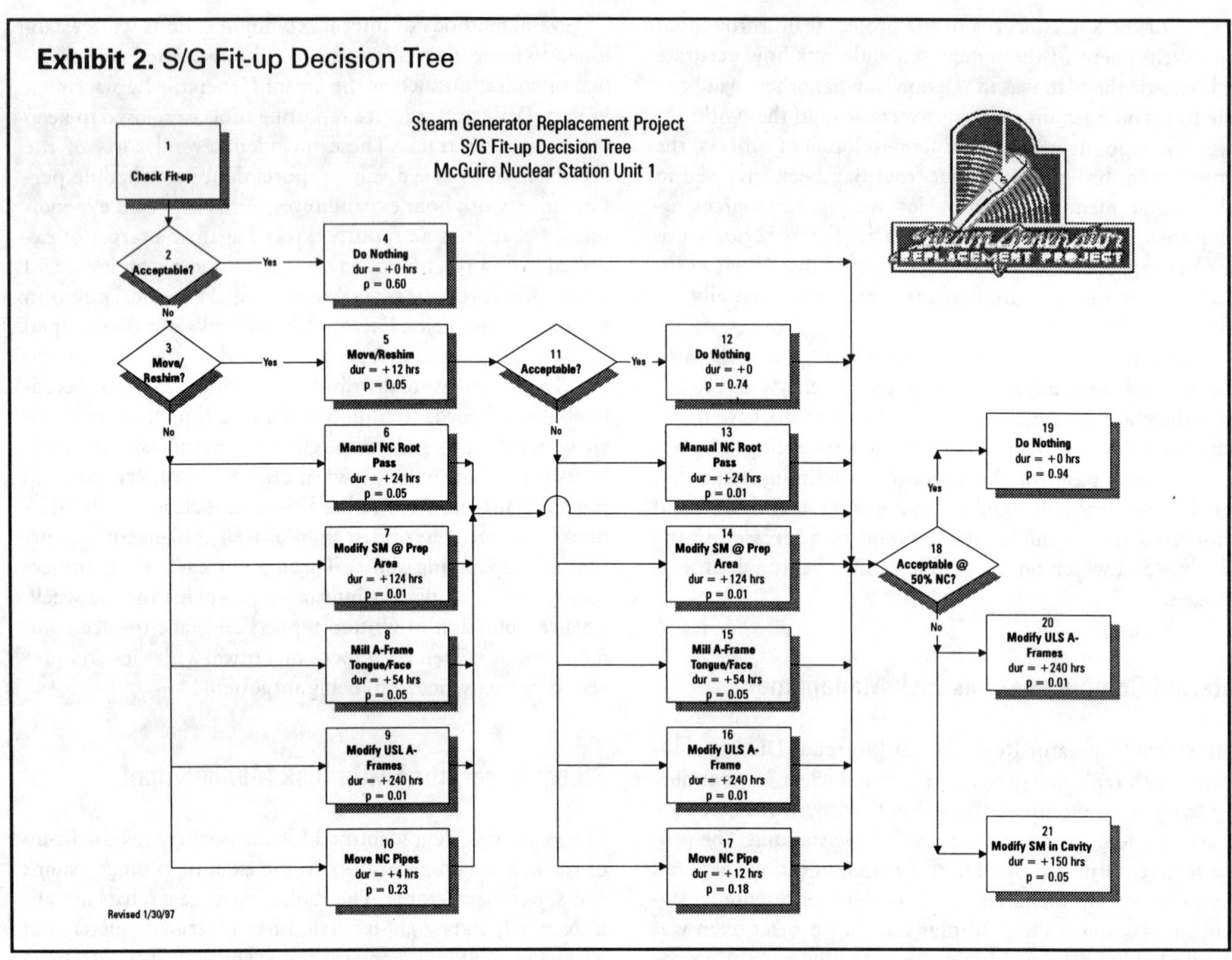


Critical fit-up criteria were defined for the four locations, reactor coolant pipes, main steam pipes, support columns, and upper lateral supports. These criteria were adjustable to only a very narrow tolerance. Deviations from these tolerances would necessitate the implementation of contingency options based on the degree of the deviation. For example, the tolerance on each of the two reactor coolant pipes was -0.000" to +0.040". Failure to meet this criteria could have resulted in rework on the other fit-up interfaces and increased the project critical path by as much as 10 percent. Exhibit 3 shows the four areas associated with fit-up.

The first fit-up constraint involved the reactor coolant pipe connections. The two 31" diameter nozzles of the generator had to be located within a tolerance of 0.00" – 0.040" axial and 0.00" – 0.060" radial. The second fit-up constraint was associated with the setting of the generators on the four support columns. Each column had to carry a specific amount of the generator weight, and each of the six-bolt holes on each support column had to align with the bolt holes on the generator support pads. The third constraint involved the fit-up of the upper lateral support ring (ULS). The ULS had fourteen different fit-up tolerances ranging from -0.25" to +8.0" depending on the location. Finally the main steam nozzle had to align with the existing 32" diameter main steam piping at the top of the generator. Any one of these fit-up constraints provides ample opportunity for risk; however, all four areas had to be fit-up.

To mitigate some of the risk items, Framatome Technologies, Inc., was contracted to take measurements of the existing plant systems, as-built conditions of the new steam generators, machine the reactor coolant piping and nozzles, and to calculate the shim thickness for the support columns. The measurements were used to predict optimum fit-up conditions. The predictions were dependent on prioritizing the various fit-up locations. The relative risk values from the decision tree were used to prioritize the options. Several of the contingency options for the upper laterals represented significant schedule impacts. Based on this evaluation we made the decision to incorporate some of the contingency options in the schedule during a non-critical path time frame. This enabled us to address these high impact items as scheduled work rather than contingency work.

The last step in effectively managing these fit-up risks was controlling and responding to the risk items during the setting of the generators. After the steam generators were set on the support columns, fit-up data was gathered from the four locations. The fit-up team used the data along with the decision matrix to determine which contingencies, if any, would be implemented.

## Fit-Up Results

The generator fit-ups at Catawba went extremely well. The effort expended in identifying, quantifying, mitigating, and developing a risk response plan paid great dividends. On two of the generators, the reactor coolant piping had to be moved slightly to achieve fit-up. On the forth generator, shims were improperly installed and had to be adjusted causing a twelve-hour delay in achieving fit-up. The lessons learned at Catawba were factored into the fit-up team's plan for McGuire. For example a new method of moving the generators into initial fit-up location was developed, and the root cause of the improper shim installation was identified and corrected. The durations of the contingency options and the probabilities of each item were revised for McGuire based on actual data at Catawba.

The generator fit-ups at McGuire Unit 1 were very good. Only one generator required the implementation of a contingency. The third generator had to have the reactor coolant piping moved to achieve fit-up. Because of the work done before the outage started to identify risk management options, we were able to quickly determine the appropriate course of action to achieve fit-up on this generator and avoid delaying the critical path.

## Conclusion

The project minimized communications problems by identifying key stakeholders' communication needs through tabletop simulations. These sessions enabled the project team to understand the risk of poor and inaccurate communications before the first outage. The knowledge gained during these sessions facilitated the project's ability to adjust to changing communications needs during the outage at Catawba. Lessons learned concerning communications were factored into the McGuire 1 outage. One of the major changes implemented at McGuire was the development of detailed craft scheduled and budget planning and status reports for each craft team. These reports enabled the craft supervisors to better understand their contribution to the overall project plan.

**Exhibit 3.** S/G Fit-up Locations

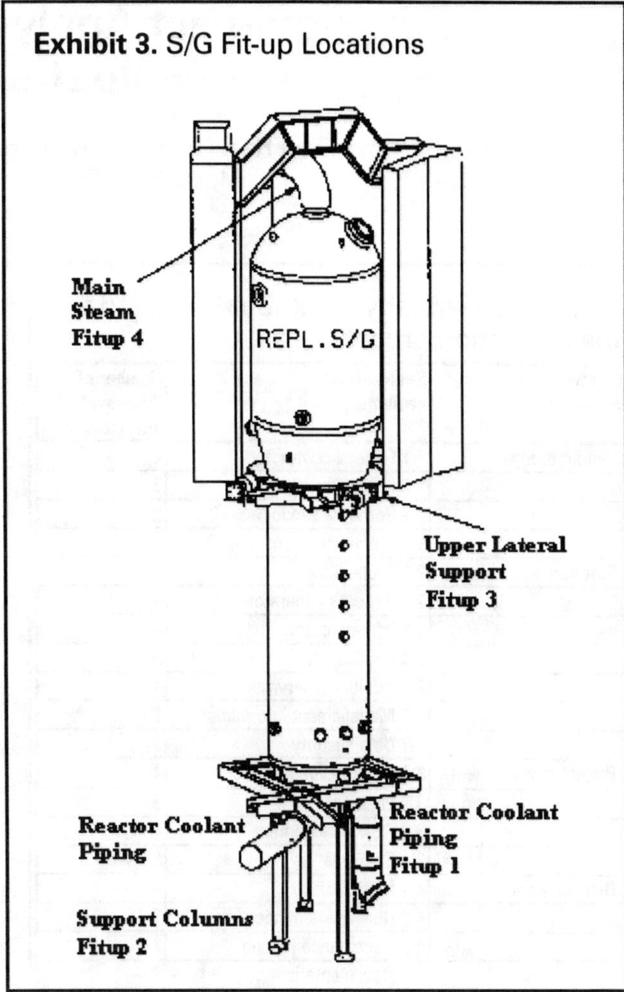


Risk management activities associated with the fit-up of the steam generators enabled both Catawba and McGuire 1 outages to successfully implement the most challenging portion of the replacement outages with no impact to critical path. This is a significant accomplishment since the fit-up of the generators could have caused a 10 percent addition to the critical path.

# After-the-Fact Analysis of the Alternative Evaluation Process

Tzvi Raz, Faculty of Management, Tel Aviv University
Mordechai Shwartz, Leshem-Nituv Inc.

**Exhibit 1.** Hierarchy of attributes applied to the evaluation process

| First-level attributes | Second-level attributes | Number of third-level attributes |
|---|---|---|
| 1. Vendor group | 1.1 General contractor | 4 |
| | 1.2 Hardware vendor | 2 |
| | 1.3 Software vendor | 2 |
| | 1.4 Communications vendor | 1 |
| 2. Software solution | 2.1 Architecture | 3 |
| | 2.2. Process generator | 5 |
| | 2.3 Infrastructure | 4 |
| | 2.4 Application | 5 |
| | 2.5 Additional services | 4 |
| | 2.6 Management information | 2 |
| | 2.7 Data security | 3 |
| 3. Project management | 3.1 Organizational concept | 4 |
| | 3.2 Personnel | 3 |
| | 3.3 Risk management | 4 |
| | 3.4 Schedule | 5 |
| 4. Development | 4.1 Methodology | 4 |
| | 4.2 Quality assurance | 3 |
| | 4.3 Acceptance testing | 3 |
| | 4.4 Documentation | 3 |
| | 4.5 Deployment | 3 |
| 5. Hardware | 5.1 Architecture | 4 |
| | 5.2 Central hardware | 7 |
| | 5.3 Remote-site hardware | 5 |
| | 5.4 Communications | 5 |
| | 5.5 Technology | 4 |
| | 5.6 Operating system | 4 |
| 6. Other services | 6.1 Transition | 3 |
| | 6.2 Training | 3 |
| | 6.4 Hardware maintenance | 3 |
| | 6.5 Software maintenance | 2 |

## Introduction

At several points in the life cycle of a project there is a need to select one out of a number of mutually exclusive alternatives. The most commonly applied alternative selection methodology is based on scoring the various alternatives with respect to a set of attributes, which might have different weights, calculating the weighted sum of scores for each alternative, and choosing the one with the highest total score. The amount of effort invested in identifying the relevant attributes, determining the respective weights, scoring the alternatives, and analyzing the results might vary depending on the importance of the decision and the amounts at stake, ranging from a few hours for trivial situations to several person-months in the selection of the general contractor for a major project. This effort is mainly a function of the number and level of detail of the attributes considered and of the number of evaluators who are asked to score the alternatives. In addition to the actual effort invested in evaluating the alternatives, the process also requires a significant amount of elapsed calendar time to allow for scheduling meetings, gathering data, distribution of documents, and so on.

Although the main purpose of the evaluation process is to lead to the best alternative, it is also important to carry it out efficiently, without unnecessary delays or expenditure of effort. An after-the-fact analysis may help identify the elements of the process that could be improved without affecting the quality of the decision. Specifically, we would like to determine whether the same results could have been obtained with a smaller investment of time and resources.

Of course, in order to reach valid recommendations that are widely applicable, a large sample of alternative selection instances should be studied. However, organizations that face several alternative evaluation situations in the course of the year could benefit from studying the performance of the last cases while preparing for the next one.

## Background

In this paper we present the after-the-fact analysis of the alternative-selection process that was carried out to select the general contractor for a multimillion dollar information technology project. Three companies responded to the request for proposals with complete bids. The evaluation process involved, in addition to cost criteria, over a hundred qualitative attributes organized in a weighted three-level hierarchy, as shown in Exhibit 1.

The set of attributes and their respective weights were determined by a team of four experts through a group-brainstorming process that required an investment of fifty person-hours. The evaluation process was supported by a software tool specifically developed for this purpose. The tool provided data capture and management functions, extensive data security features to prevent mishandling and unauthorized changes to the evaluation data, and some basic statistical analysis capabilities. Development of the tool required an investment of an additional fifty person-hours. Eight evaluators were asked to rate each of the three alternative bids submitted and to score each bid on each of the attributes using a seven-point scale. The group of evaluators included the four experts who defined the attribute hierarchy. Each evaluator required an average of eighty hours to read through the proposal documents and to rate the various attributes. The total effort invested in the evaluation process was estimated at 1,000 person-hours.

## Basic Results

The original analysis of the three bids indicated that in terms of the total score for the qualitative attributes, exclusive of cost, suppliers A and B were very close ( 87.92 percent versus 87.62 percent), with supplier C a distant third with a total score of 78.79 percent. On the cost side of the analysis, the total cost for supplier A was about 40 percent lower than that of supplier B and about 25 percent lower than supplier C. Consequently supplier A was awarded the contract. In the after-the-fact analysis, we would like to investigate whether the same conclusion regarding the ranking of the three suppliers could have been reached with less effort. To this end we will investigate the sensitivity of the conclusions to variations in the number of evaluators, number of attributes, weights, and scoring scheme.

## Evaluators

The eight evaluators were experts on the various aspects of the project and rated the three alternatives on those attributes that they felt confident in evaluating. Exhibit 2 shows the number of third-level attributes evaluated by each of the evaluators.

Overall there were 518 attribute evaluations, for an average of 4.84 evaluators per attribute. Each evaluator required a certain amount of time to go over the material and to arrive at an opinion in order to assign the score. A key question is whether we could have reached the same conclusion with fewer evaluators. Specifically, we looked at the issue of whether the information provided by the evaluators who rated fewer attributes made any difference with respect to the overall score. This analysis is summarized in Exhibit 3, which shows the total scores for the three alternatives, calculated based on various combinations of evaluators, selected according to the extent of attribute coverage they provided.

**Exhibit 2.** Number of attributes evaluated by each evaluator

| Evaluator | Number of attributes evaluated | % attributes evaluated |
|---|---|---|
| 1 | 83 | 77 |
| 2 | 43 | 40 |
| 3 | 43 | 40 |
| 4 | 53 | 49 |
| 5 | 89 | 82 |
| 6 | 58 | 54 |
| 7 | 60 | 56 |
| 8 | 89 | 82 |

From Exhibit 3 we see that basing the decision on the two evaluators who were able to rate the largest numbers of attributes (evaluators 5 and 8, who each rated eighty-nine attributes, although not necessarily the same attributes) would have given us coverage for 101 of the 107 attributes, representing 94 percent of the total weight assigned to the hierarchy of attributes. In this case, alternative B would have been preferred to alternative A, with C a distant third. The other columns in Exhibit 3 were calculated in the same manner. We can see that the relative ranking of A and B varies across the table: alternative B was preferred to alternative A up to the point where the last two evaluators (2 and 3, who rated the smallest number of attributes—forty-three each) were taken into consideration. However, in all the combinations examined, the difference between alternatives A and B was very minor. This analysis suggests that it was not necessary to employ eight evaluators; the same basic conclusion could have been reached by fewer.

## Number of Attributes

Overall there were 107 usable attributes. In many attributes the difference in scores among the alternatives was very small. These attributes did not contribute much to differentiating among the alternatives, raising the question of whether they should be taken into account at all as part of the total scores. To examine this question, we used the coefficient of variation as a normalized measure of attribute variability. For each attribute the standard deviation of the three alternative scores and the average of the three scores were calculated. The coefficient of variation was then calculated as the standard deviation divided by the average.

The attributes were sorted by the value of the coefficient of variation. As shown in Exhibit 4, only sixty-nine attributes had

**Exhibit 3.** Total scores based on different groups of evaluators

| Number of evaluators | 2 | 3 | 4 | 5 | 6 | 8 |
|---|---|---|---|---|---|---|
| Evaluators included | 5,8 | 5,8,1 | 5,8,1,7 | 5,8,1,7, 6 | 5,8,1,7, 6, 4 | All |
| Number of attributes scored | 101 | 104 | 106 | 106 | 107 | 107 |
| % of original weight covered | 94 | 96 | 99 | 99 | 100 | 100 |
| Total score A | 89.20 | 87.64 | 87.94 | 87.86 | 87.87 | 87.92 |
| Total Score B | 90.63 | 89.43 | 89.94 | 89.39 | 88.65 | 87.62 |
| Total score C | 81.69 | 78.80 | 79.01 | 79.35 | 79.17 | 78.79 |

**Exhibit 4.** Total scores based on attributes with the largest variability

| Coefficient of variation cut-off value | Number of attributes included | % of attributes included | Weighted sum of scores A | B | C |
|---|---|---|---|---|---|
| All attributes | 107 | 100% | 87.92 | 87.62 | 78.79 |
| 0.05 | 69 | 64.5% | 86.37 | 85.65 | 73.44 |
| 0.10 | 39 | 36.4% | 85.94 | 85.27 | 67.20 |
| 0.20 | 12 | 11.2% | 84.16 | 85.23 | 57.05 |

a value of the coefficient of variation greater than 0.05, thirty-nine attributes had a value greater than 0.10, and twelve had a value greater than 0.20. The exhibit shows, for each of these cut-off values, the number of attributes included and the total weighted scores.

Exhibit 4 presents an interesting finding: the same basic conclusion (alternatives A and B are close to each other, and alternative C is significantly inferior to both) could have been reached on the basis of a smaller number of the attributes with higher variability. However, as we add more attributes with weaker differentiating power, the difference between the two leading alternatives and the third one becomes less marked: the score of C is lower by twenty-eight points when only the twelve attributes with the largest variability are considered, versus ten points when all the attributes are taken into account. This finding suggests that in order to rule out the weakest alternative we did not need to weight and score all 107 attributes; it would have been sufficient to consider the handful of attributes expected to exhibit the greatest difference among the three alternatives. Further, the inclusion of attributes that do not differentiate among the alternatives has the undesirable result of masking true differences.

## Weights

The weights for the attributes were determined by the four experts who developed the attribute hierarchy. The average weight per attribute was 0.93%, with the range from 0.17% to 2.80%. Here again one may attempt to simplify the alternative-selection process by including only the most important attributes, as measured by their weights. The key question is whether exclusion of low-weight attributes will affect the decision. In order to investigate this issue, we calculated the total scores of the three alternatives calculated, using the most heavily weighted attributes required to obtain 90 percent, 80 percent, and 50 percent of the original total weight. The results are shown in Exhibit 5.

Analysis of Exhibit 5 reveals that just less that one-third of the attributes (thirty-two) accounted for half of the total weight, sixty-seven attributes accounted for 80 percent, and eighty-three attributes accounted for 90 percent. Further, the numerical results obtained with various numbers of attributes are very close, and the basic conclusion (alternatives A and B lead and are close to each other; alternative C is a distant third) is not affected at all. Here again, a possible conclusion would be to focus the evaluation on the most important attributes and to save the effort involved in dealing with the rest. The last three columns in Exhibit 5 show that the scores

**Exhibit 5.** Total scores based on the attributes with the largest weights

| % of original weight | Number of attributes | Weighted sum of scores | | | Unweighted average score | | |
|---|---|---|---|---|---|---|---|
| | | A | B | C | A | B | C |
| 50% | 32 | 86.66 | 85.90 | 76.30 | 86.61 | 85.95 | 76.61 |
| 80% | 67 | 87.37 | 87.43 | 76.57 | 87.65 | 88.25 | 77.13 |
| 90% | 83 | 87.50 | 87.39 | 77.76 | 87.83 | 88.04 | 79.02 |
| 100% | 107 | 87.92 | 87.62 | 78.79 | 88.64 | 88.41 | 81.05 |

**Exhibit 6.** Total scores based on a binary rating scheme

| | Threshold value | | | | | | |
|---|---|---|---|---|---|---|---|
| | 7 | 6.75 | 6.5 | 6.25 | 6 | 5.5 | 5 |
| **Number of attributes above the threshold** | | | | | | | |
| Alternative A | 4 | 10 | 33 | 53 | 76 | 99 | 107 |
| Alternative B | 10 | 16 | 34 | 55 | 72 | 94 | 107 |
| Alternative C | 2 | 5 | 25 | 42 | 51 | 63 | 80 |
| **Total weighted score** | | | | | | | |
| Alternative A | 3.52 | 9.77 | 28.53 | 42.48 | 66.32 | 89.85 | 100.00 |
| Alternative B | 8.93 | 13.81 | 28.69 | 45.08 | 62.79 | 86.64 | 100.00 |
| Alternative C | 1.53 | 4.59 | 20.97 | 34.70 | 40.60 | 52.00 | 67.69 |

obtained when the attributes are given equal weights are very close to the weighted scores. Thus, in this case avoiding altogether the issue of attribute weights would not have affected the selection.

## Scoring Scheme

The final aspect of the evaluation process that we studied was the scoring scheme. Here, the evaluators were asked to apply a seven-point scale. We wished to see whether a coarser scale, with fewer points, and consequently easier to apply, would have yielded similar results. Since we did not want to guess at the mapping between the original scale and other multiple-point scales, we limited our analysis to binary scales based on various thresholds. The thresholds were determined as follows. If the score on a given attribute was greater than or equal to the threshold value, then the alternative was given a '1', otherwise a '0'. The total score of each alternative was calculated as the number of attributes that received a '1'. Exhibit 6 shows the binary scores obtained for various thresholds. The exhibit also shows the weighted scores obtained by adding the weights of the attributes that received a '1'. The threshold values for this part of the analysis ranged from seven down to five. By examining Exhibit 6 we can see that the basic conclusion that alternative C is inferior to the other two alternatives could have been reached, regardless of the threshold value or of whether the attributes were weighted or not. The relative ranking of alternatives A and B changed, depending on the threshold value: for higher threshold values, alternative B appears to be superior, and as the threshold is lowered alternative A closes the gap and then takes over the lead. The conclusion from this analysis is that a more detailed scoring system is helpful to distinguish between close alternatives, but a binary rating scheme is perfectly acceptable to screen out inferior alternatives.

## Concluding Remarks

The after-the-fact analysis of this case shows that we could have reached the same basic conclusion with fewer evaluators, fewer attributes, and a simpler scoring scheme and without bothering about weights. A rough estimate indicates that we could have saved about half of the 1,000 person-hours invested in the evaluation of the three alternatives.

A key characteristic of this case was that one of the alternatives was clearly inferior to the other two. The analysis suggests that we could have identified the inferior alternative with a minimal investment. Thus, a possible approach for future evaluation would be to apply two cycles. The first cycle, which would be aimed at screening out inferior alternatives, could be carried out by a small number of evaluators, using a binary scale to assess a small number of key attributes. Then, more effort could be invested in a second round in order to find significant differences among the remaining alternatives and to highlight the relative advantages and disadvantages.

Of course, these conclusions are based on a single case, and in order to verify their validity and applicability we should compare our results with those of other similar analyses in a variety of situations. One convenient method for doing this would be to institute an after-the-fact process in the organization, to be carried out after each bid. Analysis of the patterns and trends should provide valuable information regarding the amount of effort appropriate for the various types of alternative-selection problems that the organization encounters.

# Do Service Projects Require Enhancement of the PMBOK Guide?

Max Smith, PMP, Digital Equipment Corporation

Before beginning to discuss what service projects do or don't require in relation to the *PMBOK Guide*, we need to review the nature of service projects and how they might differ from more traditional projects.

My earlier experience with projects is based upon managing a set of activities that have defined end objectives, that are more or less ordered, and that have well-defined start and completion dates along with well-defined budget or cost objectives. The *PMBOK Guide* has evolved from projects with similar attributes and supports this experience.

So what's different about service projects? And, what is meant by service projects? Service projects can be thought of as a project class where the client contracts with another for work that is associated with operations rather than an end item. In the past, this has typically been such things as maintenance and cleaning, and more recently computer and mailroom operations. The definition does not include service activities like contracting for a design because these will normally have the standard project attributes of well-defined budgets and ending criteria.

In recent years some of the service projects have become very large. This has occurred when major corporations have examined their core competencies and benchmarked these and others of their operations. A result has been that some of these corporations have seen an advantage for contracting for services to perform operations that were not a core competency and could be better performed by an appropriate contractor. If a transfer of assets is involved, then these have generally been called "outsourcing" projects.

Restructuring in corporations has also created emphasis on service projects. In restructuring, corporations are focusing on their core business and assigning non-core activities to others. Most of these "other" activities are service-related, and the assignment often takes the form of a service project, "outsourcing," or similar arrangement. The nature of the project is to transfer the activities from the corporation to the new entity, the contractor. These projects have many characteristics in common with non-service or "traditional" projects, as found in the aerospace and engineering construction industries and supported by the *PMBOK Guide*. But, service projects also have unique features that are critical for their success, both for the client and the contractor.

A significant amount of these type of service projects are occurring in computer-related activities, where the rapid change in technology places a very large demand on corporate resources just to stay current. As the corporation focuses on its core competencies, it makes sense to outsource networks, personal computers, servers, and similar items, including the physical assets and the related support and maintenance services.

The corporation expects that it will lower its operating costs and attain higher performance because of the service project. The contractor expects to grow its business with appropriate profitability while meeting the corporation's performance expectations. Both sets of expectations are realizable.

The service project has two distinct phases. A transition phase when assets may be transferred and when the service delivery is implemented and brought to the required performance levels, and an operations phase when the performance levels of the service delivery are maintained. The transfer of assets may occur quickly in relation to the achievement of the required service levels. The physical transfer can occur at the time the contract is signed; assets and perhaps personnel go from the corporation to the contractor. *But, it may take years to achieve operating conditions that are satisfactory to both parties.* This is in contrast to non-service projects where the completion is in physical terms (mechanical completion) and a formal acceptance.

How does this correspond with the prevailing PMI definitions of a project? The *PMBOK Guide* distinguishes between operations and projects as follows: *Operations and Projects differ primarily in that operations are ongoing and repetitive while projects are temporary and unique.* Service projects are typified by instances when a set of operations of an organization are transferred and performed by another organization. In the case of outsourcing, these are characterized by the relocation of assets (capital and human) that may happen quickly or over a period of years along with the introduction of new practices and procedures. The first phase of the service project is filled with typical project activity, but as the life cycle matures the activity settles into ongoing and repetitive effort. And if the service project is successful, it is "evergreen."

Project management knowledge, as we know it in the *PMBOK Guide*, provides the foundation for service projects, but this needs to be augmented with the knowledge and tools that are associated with conventional business management

Exhibit 1.

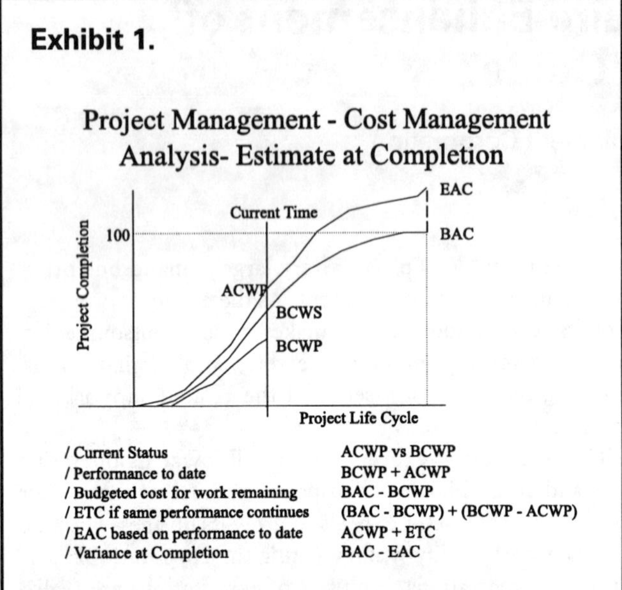


to account for the business needs of service projects. In the following, each of the elements of the *PMBOK Guide* is discussed in relation to service projects with consideration for additional elements or activities that are needed for a successful service project.

## Scope

A clear statement of work (SOW) is essential in service projects just like any other type of project. The SOW defines the work that is to be performed. For service projects, however, it is often necessary to go past the "what" and include some of "how" the work will be performed. This is particularly relevant in situations where the contractor's work processes may impact or interfere with the work processes of the client.

Particular emphasis in the SOW is needed in the definition of roles and responsibilities between the contractor and the client. Recall that a project objective is to move a defined set of operations from the client to the contractor. Much of the client's process and procedures may be poorly documented and buried in the culture. This will lead to oversights in the definition of the requirements and hence in the SOW. It should be expected that the *client would have a continuing role and responsibility to examine the contractor's solutions and evaluate them in terms of prior practice and participate in assimilating the new processes.* This in turn may lead to changes in the contractor's standard service offerings and in the contract. The scope statements must accurately describe the services to be delivered, so that if the new processes conflict with necessary but not well documented client requirements, there is a clear basis for defining changes.

*Change Control is a critical activity for these service projects.* Since there may be many unknowns, and the client's practices and procedures may be poorly documented, the scope statements must be concise and clear and well linked to the WBS to provide the basis for identifying and defining changes. Change control serves to protect the contractor from doing uncompensated work out of scope, but equally important, it serves the client as a vehicle to adjust the new processes to conform with the business needs of his organization.

## Schedule

Schedule performance is as critical on a service project as any other project, but the schedule performance is normally related to individual work packages on the WBS and not the entire project. Even though the contract has a defined term, it is usually the goal of both the contractor and the client that the service agreement continues indefinitely. This is certainly different from usual project schedule concepts and metrics that are linked to project completion with a fixed end date. The metrics of "mechanical completion" and "acceptance test" are augmented or replaced with business metrics, like response time and satisfaction for the client and "cash flow," "margin," and "PBT" for the contractor. As long as the business metrics are satisfactory it should be expected that the service would continue to be provided.

In a ranking of service project objectives, it is often the case that financial and quality objectives have a higher priority than schedule. The project manager may willingly "trade-off" schedule to attain financial or quality objectives. The term or performance period of the service project usually spans multiple years and includes a *transition phase* to re-disposition the assets as well as implement the new practices and procedures. The transition phase will have most of the characteristic project attributes described in the *PMBOK Guide*, but will just have different completion criteria. *Until these quality and financial objectives are met, the transition phase of the project is incomplete, and it may make sense to extend the planned completion date of the transition phase.*

## Cost

Cost management for traditional projects is focused on cost control. These projects have an assigned budget as well as a defined completion date. The *PMBOK Guide* provides an extensive tool set for analyzing the cost of work budgeted and the cost of work performed and estimating the cost of the work remaining. The typical picture that we work with is illustrated in Exhibit 1.

**Exhibit 2.**

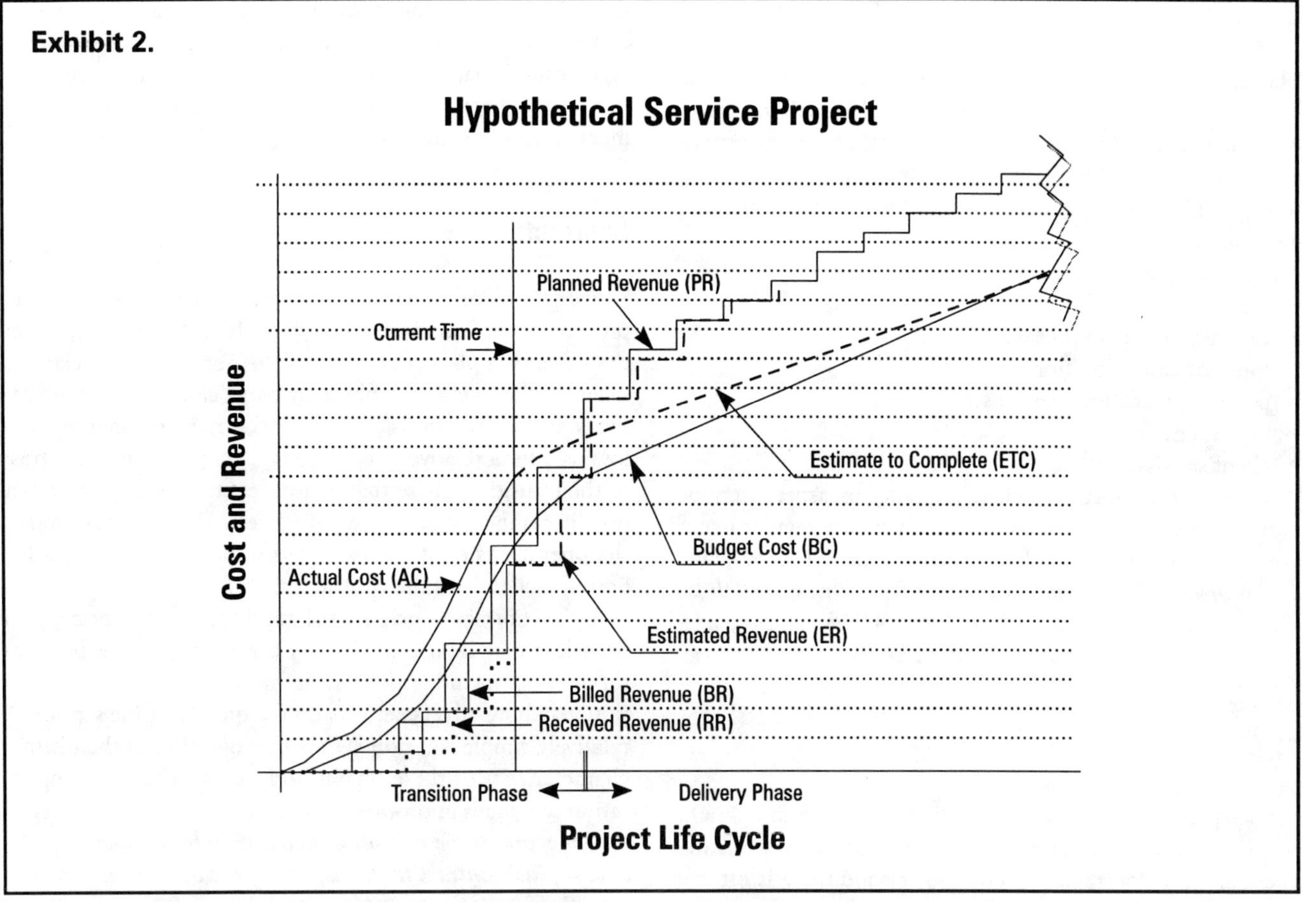


Cost management in service and outsourcing is more a matter of managing the total financial picture. In particular, managing revenue is equal if not more important than managing costs or expenses. The relationship between cost and revenue determines the profitability of the project. This is of paramount importance to the contractor. From the point of view of the client, the contractor's cost is nearly irrelevant, but the contractor's revenue, which is the client's cost, is what is of utmost importance to the client. Revenue is of primary importance to both the client and the contractor.

Financial management should substitute cost management for service projects to account for both revenue management and cost management. The project manager is concerned with his costs (planned versus actual), but he and his company are equally concerned about business metrics like cash flow, margins, PBT, accounts receivable, and so on. The standard cost curves (planned versus actual) should be augmented with similar revenue information, as shown in Exhibit 2.

In this view of the service project, some the business metrics (or indicators) become apparent, cash flow correlates to the difference between the revenue and cost curves, and margin looks like:

- Planned Margin = PR – BC/BC
- Actual Margin = BR – AC/AC
- Forecast Margin = ER –ETC/ETC

An indicator of accounts receivable or the aging of receivables can be obtained by comparing the billed revenue against the planned revenue, and billed revenue to received revenue.

Exhibit 2 is unfortunately indicative of many service projects with respect to cash flow, where the indicator of cash flow is the cumulative difference between revenue and cost. *The cash flow is negative for most of the transition phase.* Clients often expect the contractor to initiate project activities at her own expense, which starts the project with negative cash flow. And, this condition may persist for some time acting as a negative motivator for the entire project team (client and contractor) that affects the quality of the services. *This negative cash flow situation can be remedied by introducing a mobilization period with appropriate lump sum payment at the beginning of the project or major project phase.* This would tend to alleviate a major risk area for the client, and this is appropriate since the ultimate responsibility for identification of risks and their subsequent treatment must rest with the owner or client.

## Quality

The client normally initiates a service project to improve the level of quality as well as reduce costs. The quality metrics will relate directly to the delivered service, and every service has associated quality metrics. In desktop services projects, for example, the services quality metrics typically include items like:

- maintenance response time
- mean time to repair
- call handling response time
- time for call resolution
- percent satisfactory responses
- mean time to install
- client satisfaction.

In-service projects the client's quality measures may be part of the contract. The contractor's primary quality issues are achieved as part of fulfilling the contract requirements. *The project is best served if the quality metrics, like those above, are maintained as control charts, including mean, variance, control limits, and specification limits.*

## Risk

Service projects are a little deceptive with regard to risk. On one hand the services seem to be well known to both the client and the contractor; on the other hand there is often a *semantics difference that can lead to disagreement during implementation*. The magnitude of the impact of the change to the client, when shifting from one set of practices and procedures to another, is not generally well understood by either party. The client often takes a position to preserve practices and procedures, and this may represent a change to the contractor's service offering. Many of the client's practices and procedures are not well documented and are simply buried in the way they do business. Some of these may be associated with critical competitive advantage so there is no recourse but to change the service offering.

Changing (sometimes called tailoring) the service offering can have ruinous effects on the contractor's margin requirements if not well managed since much of the services are already low margin activities. As the contractor adjusts to accommodate these client-induced changes he begins to lose efficiency and productivity that comes with his standard operations. If the contractor is not appropriately compensated for these changes to his standard offerings, then he is forced to reduce costs in other areas in an attempt to maintain margin requirements. This can lead to a general deterioration of service.

Risk management for service projects must include consideration for dealing with these types of unknowns. Client/contractor project reviews should include topics related to actual service delivery versus the client's expectations. Significant deviations would be subject to the change process. It may also be appropriate that the client set up a management reserve for these instances.

## Contracts

Service contracts tend to be multi-year agreements. The "true project" work is completed early in the total engagement in the transition phase but most of the performance period is taken by the operations phase. In most cases, the service delivery in the operations phase is fixed price, low margin, and low risk, for a relatively repetitious activity. This is in contrast to the transition phase that is non-repetitious, high risk, but usually compensated by the same fixed price consideration as the operations phase. This situation presents problems for both the client and the contractor.

If the contractor includes risk funds in his fixed price, then the client may be overpaying for the service. If the contractor does not include risk funds in his prices, then margin erosion may have adverse effects on the quality of the service. A relatively simple solution is in the recognition of the distinct characteristics of these phases and that a different compensation scheme is appropriate for each.

*The work in the transition phase may be compensated by a 'cost plus' contract terms, while service delivery is compensated by fixed price arrangements.*

## Human Resources

There are a number of human resource considerations that require special attention in service projects. Probably the most significant is that the project must migrate a user community from one set of working procedures to another. This could represent a severe disruption in operations if not handled carefully, especially if the migration is accompanied with "downsizing." The HR plan must be a collaborative effort between the client and contractor that is based upon thorough and documented understanding of this user transition and accompanied by a program of communication and support. The objective is to monitor and maintain productivity at a high level and also record the improvement in productivity as a result of the project.

Another human resource consideration is that the distinct difference between the transition and operation phases of service projects tends to require different skill sets of the project manager. The transition phase requires a project manager who can deal with unique situations in a changing environment while controlling scope and driving the schedule.

The delivery phase places an emphasis on maintenance of stability and control. All project managers do not have an equal abundance of skill sets required by the respective phases, and *it often makes sense to plan a change of project managers at the end of the transition phase.* This may be well understood by the contractor, but unless this is communicated and understood by the client, it could be misunderstood and create a problem. And, usually the better the project manager is during transition phase, the more difficult it is for the client to accept a change of project managers

## Communications

Project communications is always a critical element and this is even truer with service projects. The primary reason for this is that the project directly effects the client's user community. Any problems that are felt by this community have a way of quickly escalating to major complaints. Changes that will have a beneficial outcome for the client are often met with complaint until they are understood and integrated into the normal work processes.

The communications plan needs to be jointly developed by the client and the project manager. It should anticipate the user reaction to the change and provide response that allays the user concern. It is necessary that the client play a key role not only in the development of the communications plan, but especially in its delivery.

## Summary

Service projects are a growing segment in the project management endeavor. This growth will continue as long as corporations continue to focus on their core competencies and look to others to provide essential related services that are not core competencies

The major differences between service projects and more 'traditional' projects are:

- The continuing requirement to "manage the business"
- The continued maintenance of good client/contractor relations, including end users, while at the same time maintaining high quality service levels at the agreed prices.

The *PMBOK Guide* provides the basic framework for managing service projects, but a shift of emphasis in some areas is needed. It is necessary to shift the focus from cost management to financial management. Business objectives must be met, and the project manager must manage change and be prepared to 'trade-off' schedule performance to achieve financial and quality objectives. The project manager must establish a change process with the client that can accommodate some alteration to the standard service products. This is often necessary to preserve client processes that involve unique competitive advantage.

The current wave of service projects is in response to corporate strategies to focus on their core competencies and contract with others to obtain necessary support services. This puts stress on those who were providing these services. Generally, they are obliged to change job functions, either within the corporation, or, as is often the case, seek employment elsewhere. Those who remain with the corporation must adjust to a new service provider with new practices and procedures. Sensitivity to the pressures on the client's workforce is essential. The project manager, with the client management, must put communications vehicles in place to keep all aware of progress and attainment of performance standards. This is a difficult adjustment and transition.

This transition contains many unknowns with accompanying risks. The risk in the transition phase is substantially greater than in the operations phase. This suggests contract arrangements in which the risk is shared between the client and the contractor during the transition phase, and fixed prices for the operations phase may be appropriate.

Service projects with their accompanying client/contractor alliance are a major factor in the changing business environment. They represent win-win opportunities, and project management is the key to realization of the opportunity.

## Call to Action

Service projects have a number of attributes that require additional tools for the project manager. Many of the appropriate tools may currently be in use by various individuals; some new tools may have to be created. It is beyond the capability of a single individual to describe a comprehensive tool set. Accordingly, a service and outsourcing specific interest group (SAO SIG) has been created. The mission of the SAO SIG is:

"To promote Professional Project Management performance of Service and Outsourcing Projects through sharing of experience, identification of successful processes, guidelines and standards, and the development of appropriate enhancements of the PMBOK."

The SAO SIG will achieve its mission by compiling the knowledge and experience of its members and through SAO SIG projects. These projects will include surveys and interviews of major organizations that are actively engaged in service projects, either as a contractor or client, to ascertain good and bad practices and procedures. The results of these efforts will provide the basis for improved management of service and outsourcing projects, and appropriate recommendations for enhancement of the *PMBOK Guide*.

# The Gut-Wrenching Profiles of Project Life Cycles

David A. Maynard, ITT

**Exhibit 1** Completion Probability Characteristic

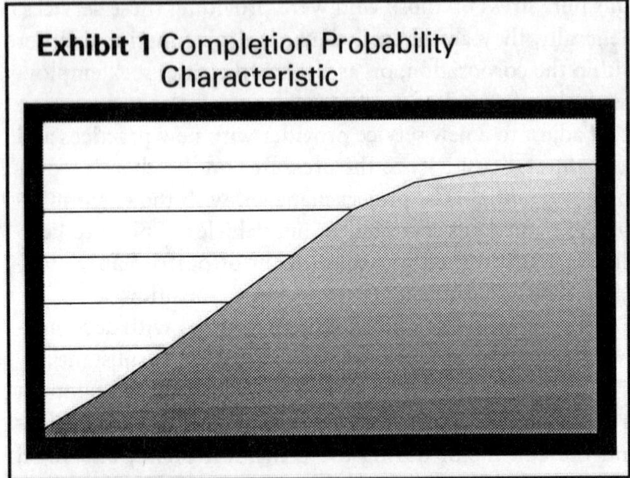

## Introduction

While studying *A Guide to the Project Management Body of Knowledge (PMBOK Guide)* for the PMP exam, the author was struck by the "gut-wrenching" influences of project life cycle characteristics. Taken in combination, the characteristics present an ominous view of a project. Each characteristic described in the *PMBOK Guide's* discussion in "The Project Management Context" seems to be calculated to make a project manager's life difficult!

The *PMBOK Guide* points out three characteristics (cost, completion probability, and influence) and states that project life cycles share a number of common characteristics. Perhaps there are many more than these three which might be described and examined! The collection and examination of data with the intent of identifying more common characteristics would be an interesting study. However, this paper will discuss, in detail, the meaning and implications of the *PMBOK Guide* documented three.

Taken individually, each characteristic seems complacent and harmless. It is when the three characteristics are combined in a dynamic sense that the true distributing trends can be identified. Each seasoned project manager intuitively understands the dynamics of the project life cycle. Hopefully, this paper will help document this intuitive understanding.

## The Three Characteristics

The *PMBOK Guide* identifies three primary life cycle characteristics that all projects share: cost/staffing, completion probability, and influence. Only one of the characteristics is presented in a graphical format—cost and staffing. While the *PMBOK Guide* does attempt to scale the magnitudes or time scales for the cost/staffing graph, few could argue the assumed trend.

It is obvious that the three characteristics would, and most likely do, vary greatly from one project to another. Costs would reach a maximum at one point in a specific project and at quite a different point in another. The *PMBOK Guide* has rightfully presented the characteristics in a general format, and left the more specific nature of their impacts to the reader.

In spite of the illusive nature of specific trends, the "missing" two characteristics can be generally stated and graphed. This addition to the *PMBOK Guide* material offers a background for a very interesting examination of the dynamics of project life cycle characteristics.

## Development of the "Missing" Two Graphics

### Graphic of the Completion Probability Characteristic

Graphics for either the completion probability or influence characteristics are not illustrated in the *PMBOK Guide*. But a "word picture" is supplied. The *PMBOK Guide* states that the completion probability characteristic starts low at the beginning of the project, and progressively gets higher as the project continues. Exhibit 1 is the author's view of the completion probability characteristic. This graphic is in agreement with the *PMBOK Guide's* "word picture." At the start of the project, (left hand side of the X-axis) the project has its lowest probability of completion. As the project continues along its life cycle (to the right along the X-axis), the probability of completion gradually increases. The author chose to show the completion probability approaching maximum asymptotically, rather than in a linear fashion, since completion often seems a "sure thing" long before the project is actually completed.

### Graphic of the Influence Characteristic

Again, the *PMBOK Guide* gives a "word picture of the tendencies of the Influence characteristic." The influence characteristic is described as "highest at the start and gets progressively lower as the project continues." Exhibit 2 is the author's view of the stakeholders' influence characteristic. The author's concept of this characteristic shows maximum influence at the start of the project (left side of the X-axis) decreasing to a low value (but not zero) at the extreme right side of the X-axis. It was felt that influence never actually decreases to zero, while a project is in progress. Notice that the characteristic takes on a decided "isoinfluence" shape similar to the isobar charts used in weather mapping. In support of this assumption, it can be assumed that the project manager has a consistent and reliable desire to influence—within the confines of the chronological stage of the project.

### The Cost and Staffing Graphic

The *PMBOK Guide* does include a graphic of the cost and staffing characteristic. Additionally, the *PMBOK Guide* describes the trend as: " . . . low at the start, higher towards the end and drop rapidly as the project draws to a conclusion." Exhibit 3 is a representation of the *PMBOK Guide*-supplied graphic. Obviously, this graphic shows not the cumulative costs, but rather the project burn rate.

As implied by the title of the characteristic (" . . . and staffing") the *PMBOK Guide* graphic seems to represent a labor-intensive project, with the peak of staffing (thus cost) at about the three-quarter point in the project. Product or hardware intensive projects may have the "bulge" of costs shifted more toward the start of the project since initial procurements must be made to accommodate the various vendors; lead times.

## Dynamics of the Characteristics

In order to examine the interactions of the three *PMBOK Guide* characteristics, a common frame of reference for a project life cycle must be established. Unfortunately, because of the wide variety of project types and objectives, a common set of life cycle milestones (e.g.: concept exploration, demonstration, engineering, production, and operations) are not practical.

In order to form a common framework for discussion, a project can be divided into five chronological phases: start, early, middle, mature, and completion. To aid in the examination of the dynamics of the project life cycle characteristics, Exhibit 4 was created. This exhibit will serve as the method for structuring the discussion of the dynamic influences of project life cycle characteristics. Information to fill in the exhibit was simply taken from the given and derived graphics for each characteristic. Certainly, the interpretations of low, medium, high, and so on are casual and dependent upon the observer.

### Start Phase—Everything Seems Fine

During the start phase, the probability of completion is low. Very little progress has been made toward the end goal. The

**Exhibit 2**

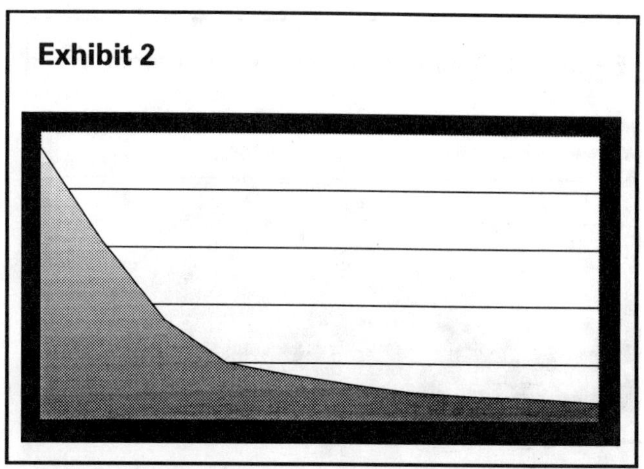

entire effort lays ahead filled with thousands of reasons why the project may never be completed. At this phase, Senior management may not be too reluctant to cancel the project (assuming cancellation is a possibility).

Simultaneously, the degree of influence that may be asserted to affect the outcome of the project is also high. With few staffed on the project, and virtually endless possibilities of direction available, the project manager can isolate and select alternatives nearly at will. The project team is relatively small at the start so direct control and intervention by the project manager is a distinct advantage.

Finally, (assuming a labor-intensive project) the cost (burn rate) of the project is low. Simply put, only a few salaries need to be paid. The project manager can exercise financial control without the attention and burden that comes with a high rate of expenditures. The start phase contains a happy coincidence of characteristic values. Completion, influence, and cost characteristics are all "project management" friendly. No wonder project jokes often call this phase the "honeymoon" phase.

### Early Phase—The Wild Ride Starts

The early phase starts to reveal some of project management's darker influence. The project's burn rate has increased, thus increasing the criticality of decision-making and the cost of mistakes. The project no longer has a small select startup group. It's now on it's way to becoming fully staffed. All those salaries add up astonishingly quickly.

To compound this trend, the amount of influence that the project manager can exert over the direction of the project has diminished. The all-important beginning and planning decisions are made. The course is charted and potential options have been forever eliminated. Also, the increased number of project workers makes it more difficult for the project manager to directly discuss, understand, and interact with the project individual team members.

While things are costing more, and with a decreased ability to control their outcome, the completion of the project appears

**Exhibit 3.** Cost and Staffing Characteristic

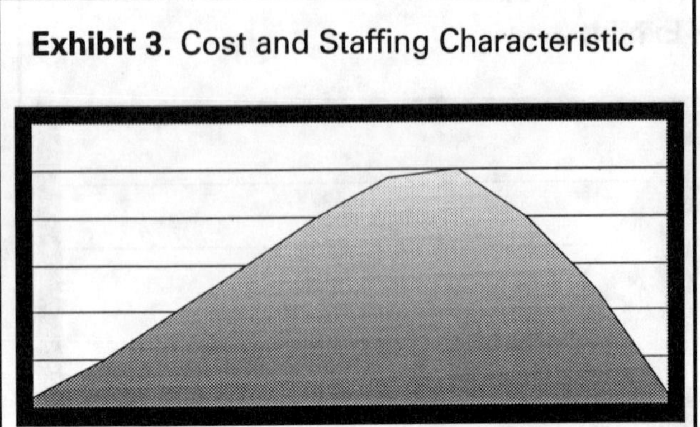

more firm than when first started. Concrete goals and objectives have been set and people are in place to begin achieving them. The mad rush has started! The project has more money, less control, and things seem destined to happen.

This rapid change in dynamics clearly points out the value of proper planning prior to project start! From this point on, the heydays of the start phase, and planning can never be recovered.

### Middle Phase—A Roller Coaster Ride!

During this phase of a project, the "gut-wrenching" characteristics assume a life of their own. The burn rate has peaked. Money will never be spent at a higher rate than during this phase. The number of people assigned to the project has also peaked. Money is being spent "hand over fist." This usually means the project will receive the direct attention of senior management. After all, it is their job to keep track of the "big burners" and insure things are going well. Financial status reporting and schedule achievement are often critically viewed and managed.

Influence has steadily diminished and continues to decline from only "medium" to "low" when this phase is exited. So, the project is spending a great deal of money, and with only limited control available to effect changes! While senior management will often demand that the project manager "regain control" of the project and costs and insure completion, the dynamics of the situation demand the opposite.

Sadly, completion of the project is not a certainty. Even at the peak of expenses, the outcome is not guaranteed. While, some of the project team can sense the probability of completion is on the rise, there still exists the possibility that the project will not complete! In a fashion similar to a roller coaster, the ride is scary (cost and influence), and the end is only a glimmer in the imagination of the people in the lead car.

### Mature Phase—A Sigh of Relief

The turbulence of the middle phase passes and things appear to brighten for the project manager and team. The burn rate has thankfully declined! Persons assigned to the project during the middle phase are no longer needed. They may be either "matrixed out" to another project or assigned to another ongoing activity. Most of the attention attracted to the project during the high burn rates of the middle phase has also declined. No longer is the project the favorite topic of senior management meetings and financial reviews.

Disturbingly, the degree of influence over the course of the project also declined. If the earlier creeping limitations of influence phases were upsetting to the project manager, the mature phase will be even more so. Control of the project "as it was in the beginning" can never be restored.

Happily, the probability of completion has nearly peaked—it's now obvious to many on the project that it will indeed be completed. Enough funds have been spent, enough salaries have been converted to increased project value, and enough of the initial plans have been accomplished to make completion a distinct possibility.

### Completion Phase—The Ride Ends

As the influence of the project manager and stakeholders sinks to its lowest point in the entire life cycle, the completion phase begins. This far into the project plan, tight control over the fate of the project is a thing of the distant past. The project is essentially on "auto-pilot."

Marked by the decline of the burn rate to levels not experienced since the start of the project, financial worries now center on identifying the work remaining and assuring that it can be completed within budget. Many people have been removed from the project and those remaining know exactly what needs to be done.

Completion is now unquestioned by the majority of the project team. It seems that even the most doubtful participant believes that the project will indeed be completed. Very few, if any, project-level guidance decisions remain. Completion is at hand! Hopefully, everyone is congratulating the project manager on the "job well done!"

### Recap

What an experience! What seemed like a nice project at the start, seemed to get out of control quickly. Costs escalated, senior management attention was drawn to the project, and the project manager seemed to lose authority rapidly. More and more people began being assigned to the project, increasing communication complexities and costs. Then, things got better, the burn rate decreased, and the end seemed to be in sight. Suddenly, the project is near completion. Gut wrenching!

**Exhibit 4.** Project Phase vs. Characteristic Value

| | Start | Early | Middle | Mature | Completion |
|---|---|---|---|---|---|
| Completion | Low | Medium | High | Very High | Certain |
| Influence | Very High | High | Medium | Low | Low |
| Cost | Low | Medium | High | Medium | Low |

## Summary

Did the description of the interactions of project characteristics sound like your project? The good news is that it's normal. The bad news is that the gut wrenching seems inevitable. While the actual point of when a characteristic reaches its highs and lows will change, the dynamic interactions will probably lead to a somewhat similar scenario.

Understanding and accepting these trends are not only important to the project manager and the project team, but senior management must also be aware of them. The ride is not as scary if everyone knows what to expect and when it starts. What is pointed out by this examination of characteristic dynamics is the need for proper prior planning. The time spent planning before the start of the project can never be recaptured. Before the wild ride starts, it's critically important to have detailed, well thought-out, and well understood plans. Once it starts, the project quickly becomes committed to spending money—with ever decreasing control!

### References

PMI Standards Committee. 1996. *A Guide to the Project Management Body of Knowledge (PMBOK Guide)*. Upper Darby, PA: Project Management Institute.

# The Window Delay Analysis Technique: The Clear Solution of the Coming Millennium

Anamaria I. Kohler, M.S., E.I.T, Carter & Burgess
Dr. John D. Borcherding, The University of Texas at Austin

## Introduction

Delays in construction schedules are nothing new. Even when the Egyptians built the Great Pyramid of Gizeh around 2500 BC, delays often surfaced, and finger-pointing became a popular pastime of all parties involved in the ancient project. Unfortunately for the Egyptian workers, the blame seemed to consistently land on their shoulders regardless of the true cause of the delay. I assume that the Nile crocodiles were particularly well fed during that century!

As the construction industry enters the twenty first century, are we less naive than the Egyptians? Both owners and contractors have viewed delay analysis techniques as after-the-fact weapons to expediently slaughter one another in courtroom battles. This inefficient application of delay analysis techniques must be tempered in order to propel the construction industry into a new century where legal dramas are simply relics of a claims-conscious past.

The first section of this paper is a review of the most common delay analysis techniques applied in the construction industry. The successive sections deal with the results of a survey designed to discover the most effective delay analysis technique. The survey was given to a Delphi panel of twenty experts whose forte lies in the schedule analysis arena. Both the strengths and the shortcomings of the "ideal" analysis technique are brought into focus.

## Delay Analysis Techniques

Schumacher (1995) stated the following about the evolution of delay techniques:

"At least three techniques have evolved over the last 30 years. They are generically known as "what-if" evaluations (otherwise known as impacted as-planned analysis), "but-for" evaluation, and Contemporaneous Period Analysis (window analysis). Primarily, they differ in the baseline that is used to measure the delays."

### Window Analysis Technique

The window analysis technique (WAT) is the most advantageous of all the as-planned approaches, according to C.Popescu (1991). The most effective as-planned based delay impact analysis utilizes a scenario with a CPM program, which is fully implemented and updated frequently. This brings the greatest benefit to both the owner and contractor and minimizes controversy during dispute resolution.

Using CPM-based networks, the window analysis breaks up the project into smaller time periods defined by major schedule revisions. These smaller time periods are referred to as "windows." Each succeeding window becomes the contemporaneous "baseline" schedule, and previous windows are ignored. Each window is "framed" between two revisions (Galloway 1990). Example: Window number one is framed between the initial as-planned schedule (baseline) and the first schedule revision. There are two schedules for each window—an as-planned and an actual. The actual project completion date is the end of the final window.

In other words, the window technique "relies on the simulation of progressive updates of the as-planned schedule to yield incremental extensions on the contract's milestones as a result of each delay" (Fredlund 1990). The window technique is useful in proving that controlling critical paths change, pinpointing when these changes occur, and indicating what would have happened had the contractor been able to adhere to his as-planned schedule (Fredlund 1990).

### Impacted As-Planned Technique

Zafar (1996) believes "this is one of the simplest ways of doing a delay analysis where the baseline schedule is affected for different delays, one after another." This technique also uses a CPM network to demonstrate delay impacts; however, the original approved as-planned schedule is the only baseline utilized to evaluate individual delays as they occur. This method does not update the schedule using actual as-built information, and there is no comparison of the "impacted" schedule with the actual as-built information (Trauner 1990). Unlike the impacted as-planned technique, the window technique does update the as-planned schedule and uses the new impacted as-planned for comparison with the actual schedule.

Callahan (1992) believes, "Under the as-planned method, the contractor is entitled to a time extension only if the scheduled completion is delayed beyond the extended contract completion date. The as-planned method employs the planned schedule to measure the delay, regardless of whether the actual construction in the field differs from the planned."

In this statement lies the inherent problem with the impacted as-planned technique.

### But-For Technique

The but-for technique is considered to be "less of a CPM technique than a legal standard for evaluating delay claims" (Barba 1994). This technique is commonly used in court to prove specific delay claims due to its visual nature. A contractor may use this technique to claim entitlement for compensation from a date earlier than the required contract completion date. Barba states:

"In determining the merit of such a claim the 'but for' approach compares the actual date of project completion with the point in time at which the work would have been completed but for delays caused by other factors or parties."

The but-for technique essentially "pulls out all owner delays that affected the as-built critical path. The amount of compensable delay is the difference in time between the actual completion date shown on the as-built schedule and the completion date shown on the but-for schedule" (Schumacher 1995).

### Summary of Techniques

It becomes clearly evident by examining Exhibit 1 that the window analysis technique is the most comprehensive of the three analysis techniques described in the preceding paragraphs. WAT is the only technique out of the three that acknowledges the dynamics of the schedule. The critical path is not static. In fact, it may go through dynamic fluctuations upon every update. The windows technique captures these fluctuations.

However, along with this advantage, the window technique does have some drawbacks. It requires an extensive amount of data input to maintain accurate results, and a skilled scheduler is essential to interpret and analyze the updated reports.

Exhibit 1. Characteristics of Delay Analysis Techniques

| Attributes | W | I | B |
|---|---|---|---|
| ■ Based on Critical Path Method | X | X | X |
| ■ Need Skilled Schedule Analyst | X | X | X |
| ■ Based on Dynamic As-Planned Schedule | X | | |
| ■ Distinguishes between Delay Types | X | X | X |
| ■ Accounts for Critical Path Shifts | X | | |
| ■ Recognizes Concurrencey of Delays | X | | X |
| ■ Degree of Data Intensity | H | M | H |
| ■ Forward or Backward Based Analysis | F | F | B |

## Survey Methodology

The main intention of the survey was to determine the most frequently applied delay analysis technique in the construction industry. Data collection was based on the Delphi method. The Delphi method requires the researcher to identify a panel of experts with which to conduct his survey and have an iterative exchange of ideas over a substantial period of time.

The selection criteria for the panel of experts was based on the following:

- Must have ten years or more delay analysis experience
- Must have applied in practice at least one of the techniques on a regular basis
- Must be willing to be included in an iterative process that could last one year
- Must be comfortable sharing ideas with academia.

The initial screening based on these criteria was conducted via telephone interviews. Twenty members were finally selected to become part of the Delphi panel. Sixty percent of the panel participants had roles of project management consultants. Twenty percent were scheduling specialists, and the other 20 percent were attorneys specializing in construction claims.

## Survey Results

Exhibit 2 depicts the original thirteen questions asked in the survey.

### Review of Responses

Thirteen out of the twenty respondents indicated that the window technique is the delay analysis tool they apply in practice. In fact, eleven out of these thirteen people have applied the windows technique for at least five years, and eight people have used it for over ten years.

Eleven out of the thirteen respondents also answered affirmatively to question 6, "Have you used this technique for allocating delays among the GC and subcontractor?" This overwhelming response indicates that the windows technique contains a greater amount of flexibility than the other delay analysis techniques, allowing you to pinpoint delays down to the subcontractor level. This is extremely important on projects where the general contractor plays the role of a broker, allowing the subcontractors to perform all of the project activities.

The way delays are represented in the analysis is extremely important. All thirteen survey participants that implement the window analysis technique stated that delays are represented as separate activities. The impacted activity is broken into two separate activities and the delay activity is

**Exhibit 2.** Summary of Questions

1. What techniques are you familiar with?
2. Check the techniques that you have used or are using as a delay analysis tool.
3. Which one technique do you apply in practice?
4. How long have you been using this technique?
5. Have you ever used this technique for allocating delays among the GC and the owner?
6. Have you ever used this technique for allocating delays among the GC and subcontractor?
7. Why did you chose to apply this technique over the others listed above?
8. Have you in any way modified this technique to suit your needs? If yes, please describe these mods.
9. What do you believe to be the greatest strengths of this technique?
10. What do you believe to be the major limitations of this technique?
11. What do you believe to be the perceived shortcomings of the remainder of the techniques?
12. How do you represent delays?
13. How do you distinguish between owner-caused and contractor caused delays?

**Exhibit 3.** Top 10 Strengths of the Window Analysis Technique

| | |
|---|---|
| **1.** | Great visual impact. |
| **2.** | Court Friendly: most effective on juries |
| **3.** | Most credible delay analysis technique and the most persuasive. |
| **4.** | Considers revisions in logic and critical path: dynamic. |
| **5.** | Looks at delays contemporaneously giving the most accurate picture. |
| **6.** | Analyzes delays caused by all project participants. |
| **7.** | Easier to assign delay responsibility by viewing specific windows. |
| **8.** | Gives contractors a "fresh start" by updating the baseline: eliminates focus on impacts of past changes. |
| **9.** | The project is divided into manageable parts for analysis. |
| **10.** | Recognizes concurrency of delays. |

inserted in-between. By using this method, the delay can be coded so that a report can be easily generated. This report indicates all delays, which activities they affect, and for what duration.

### Top Ten Lists

The top ten strengths of the window analysis technique, as indicated by the survey participants, are listed in Exhibit 3.

The window analysis technique has a very persuasive list of positive attributes that make it the logical choice for a schedule analysis tool. However, the windows technique does have some limitations that should be a caveat to every professional schedule analyst.

## Concluding Remarks

A progressive owner who recognizes the benefits of spending money initially on the preplanning stage of a project, instead of after the fact on lawyers fees, will also embrace the application of the windows analysis technique over all other delay analysis methods. An owner that exhibits these traits will be ready for the future of project management.

### References

Barba, Evans M., and Thomas C. Caruso. 1994. *Approaches to Schedule Delay Analysis*. Session 1012 Ninth Annual Construction Superconference, Barba-Arkhon International Inc.

**Exhibit 4.** Top 10 Limitations of the Window Analysis Technique

| | |
|---|---|
| **1.** | Need accurate and detailed contemporaneous documents to obtain accurate updates. |
| **2.** | Excessive expenditures are incurred to analyze the windows when faced with inadequate support data. |
| **3.** | Schedules are not updated consistently and accurately to implement technique. |
| **4.** | Not as accepted by seasoned construction lawyers. |
| **5.** | The maximum number of Windows must be limited to 5 but no less than 2 for optimum effectiveness. |
| **6.** | The outcome can be manipulated by the selection of the Window cut-off dates. |
| **7.** | A small delay could become a non-issue in later windows; therefore, a time extension granted now could turnout to be a "gift" later. |
| **8.** | The as-planned schedule must be well thought out and detailed in order to be an accurate baseline for the first window. |
| **9.** | The analysis must be done contemporaneously to be fully effective. |
| **10.** | If the contract is not required to follow the guidelines, the technique is almost impossible to apply. |


Callahan, Michael T., Daniel G. Quackenbush, and James E. Rowings. 1992. *Construction Project_Scheduling.* Mc-Graw Hill, New York.

Fredlund, Donald J., and Gui Ponce de Leon. 1990. "Delay Evaluation Using Record Schedules." *1990_AACE Transactions.* R.2.1-R.2.7.

Galloway, Patricia D., and Kris R. Nielsen. 1990. *1990 PMI Seminar/Symposium.* Calgary, Alberta: 412–418.

Popescu, Calin. 1991. "Selecting As-Planned Base in Project Disputes." *1991 AACE Transactions.* C.2.1-C.2.4.

Schumacher,Lee. 1995. "Quantifying and Apportioning Delay on Construction Projects." *Cost_Engineering* (February): 11–13.

Trauner, Theodore J. 1990. *Construction Delays.* R.S Means Company Inc., Kingston, MA.

Zafar, Zartab Q. 1996. "Construction Project Delay Analysis." *Cost Engineering* (March): 23–27.

# PMP Certification: To Succeed You Must Plan, Prepare, Practice, and Perform

Noel Hutson, PMP

The global quest for professional certification in project management by the Project Management Institute is a chain reaction that is gaining asymptotic proportions. Many factors contribute to this academic pursuit, but the main one are PMI's decision to keep the PMP certification process at a high academic caliber, the challenge of practicing project managers to become certified, and the hope of recognition by their current or future employer. The PMP certification process is a demanding one, whether you are an honor student or an experienced practicing project manager. These guidelines are from my many years of involvement with annual PMI symposium/seminar/workshops and the Portland chapter's education program as facilitator, trainer, mentor, and proctor; they are meant to help you prepare and pass the PMP test outright, the first time.

## Modes of Preparation

### Self Study

If you are in a remote area or far from a local PMI chapter, or if you choose to do so, this method of study may be your only choice. The "personal study program" consisting of a PMBOK Q&A and a computer disc is a DOS- based computer training program, which will enhance your preparation for the actual computer testing by Sylvan Technology Center, in the city nearest your home.

### Group Study

Project management colleagues interested in becoming certified sometimes get together and prepare for the test as a team effort, which is the next best way.

### PMP Review Course

This is the ideal way to prepare for the PMP test. Most of the research and hard work is done for you. The advantage of this method of preparation is that you have as your mentors the Chapter Education Committee, whose members are themselves PMPs in touch with PMI regarding the latest changes in the testing procedure—outstanding presenters who are themselves certified or practitioners in their field of expertise and the networking between the students themselves.

## Remote Preparation

**Acquiring the Desire.** The first step in certification is to acquire the desire to become certified. Without a deep inner desire, it will be very difficult to find the motivation necessary to prepare properly.

**Overcoming the Fears.** A reasonable amount of fear about the examination is to be expected and will probably be beneficial. But paralyzing fear must be overcome by talking with those who have taken the examination and/or vocalizing your fears to colleagues you know and trust.

**Gaining the Courage.** Think of the many project managers and executives who fly thirteen hours non-stop from Australia, New Zealand, Asia, and Europe to take the examination in the United States. Think of those project managers that do not use English as their first language but come to the United States with their dictionaries in hand to take the examination. Think of the young students who do not have much experience in actual produce management, who must rely on their intellect and teaching to answer the questions. Only when your courage is greater than your fear will you have the motivation necessary to take the examination and become certified.

**Collecting the Material.** You should have a copy of the full review package, the new *A Guide to the Project Management Body of Knowledge (PMBOK Guide),* and class handouts. In addition you should supplement your reading material with additional books on cost, quality, scheduling, human resources, communications, and contracting. Flash cards are also available, or can be made, to allow you to quickly review many of the types of questions on the examination.

**Knowing the Target Syllabus.** The "themes and concepts" in the sample question booklet or PMBOK Q&A is the summary of the 250 questions in the database for each subject. After adjusting for the recent upgrading of the *PMBOK Guide*, this should be your syllabus. Make sure you cover all the topics in your study.

**Knowing the PMP Framework.** The project management framework booklet contains the basic overview approach to project management. Many ideas can be picked up about the definition, purpose, and method of project management.

**Knowing the PMBOK Guide.** About 50 percent of the questions will be from the new *PMBOK Guide*. It should be the basic supporting document for your study. There will be several questions directly from the glossary terms. Remember, 10 percent of the questions will be general project management knowledge.

**Reading the Resources Material.** Begin to cycle through your reading material by keeping a special notebook for notes about each subject and/or by highlighting the important information. As you cycle through the eight subjects, you will be increasing your breath and depth of project management knowledge. That is why it is important to give yourself plenty of time to read through the resource material and for all your strategic planning.

**Drilling for the Examination.** Allowing for adjustments that the PMP certification question database has been revised to incorporate into the new *PMBOK Guide*, drilling with the sample questions furnished by PMI is a good way to prepare for the examination. The sample questions go side-by side with the actual question. When you can answer the twenty sample questions correctly for each subject in under five minutes, you have the speed and discipline to take the actual examination. The use of flash cards, which forces you to understand the principle of the question rather than just select the correct answer from the multiple choice questions, is an additional drilling tool.

**Decision to Sit for the Examination.** At one extreme are those who want to know it all perfectly, and so they postpone sitting for the test. At the other extreme are those who sit for the test without adequate preparation. It has been accepted that it is a grueling test, but with adequate coaching and preparation, you can sit and pass the test. When you feel you can pass a minimum of six subjects, that is when you should send in your application for PMP testing.

## Proximate Preparation

**Application for PMP Testing.** Your application for the PMP certification should be in the PMP certification manager's office, with the necessary fees, well in advance of the actual date you plan to take the test at the Sylvan Technology Center in the city nearest you.

**Reviewing the Study Material.** By this time you have made several reviews of the new *PMBOK Guide*, flash cards, sample questions, supporting literature, supplementary literature, and handouts. The notes and highlighting you have done will make it easy for you to remember the salient aspects of the material.

**Staying Focused.** Remember to cover all the target syllabus items in the "themes and concepts" for each of the eight subjects in the sample questions booklet. Review the above periodically and keep the breadth and depth of the material alive in your consciousness.

**Critical Last Two Weeks.** The last two weeks before the examination are the critical two weeks of your preparation. If you have not sat for an examination for a few years it may be worth taking time off work to prepare. Whatever you do in these two weeks is going to impact your performance on the examination.

**A Good Night's Sleep.** For most people it is important to sleep well the night before the examination. An extra hour of good sleep will benefit most. Remember, the primacy of quality of sleep over quantity of sleep.

**The Last Review Cycle.** Just before you leave home on the day of the examination, plan on a two-hour "last minute" review cycle of the eight subjects. Strive to keep the content of the highlights of the information alive and focused.

## Taking the Test

**Be Focused.** You have done your best to prepare for the test. Now is the time to be focused and prepare for the day-long very demanding intellectual exercise. The first few minutes of the test will be very grueling as you review the actual test questions for the first time. Do not be intimidated by how others are responding. Your dedicated study and hard work will clear your vision as you settle down to respond to the question

**First Things First.** At the Sylvan Technology Center, you will be at a computer station and answering all the questions on the computer screen via the keyboard. The order of the subjects are fixed by PMI. You may go backwards and forwards to any of the forty questions in a given subject, but once you leave that subject you will not be able to access that subject. It is acceptable to write down the important formulas on PMI-furnished scrap paper for reference later. The drilling exercises you practiced will stand you in good stead, as you conserve seconds on questions you score easily and quickly for answering questions that require more time. Remember you have fifty minutes to answer forty questions for each of the four subjects and that you must answer a total of 160 questions in a total of three hours and twenty minutes for each of the morning and afternoon sessions.

**Known Principle.** If you know the principle of the test question, the correct answer will be obvious to you from among the multiple answers. Check the appropriate number in the answer screen right away. Make sure that other answers do not relate to the principle questioned.

**Unknown Principle.** If you do not know the principle of the test question, eliminate what you consider to be wrong answers, and check the appropriate number for what you consider the correct answer in your answer screen. Be especially careful of questions with "except," "not," and so on, and read the question several times until you correctly understand what is really being asked.

**Extra Attention Questions.** If you draw a blank for a question of if it is outside your intellectual grasp, note the number of the question and put a question mark next to it, on your scrap paper, and proceed to the next question.

**Missed Question.** If you have spare time, guess the answer to the questions you missed (the ones with the question marks), and check the appropriate number in the answer screen

**Checking.** Review each segment for accuracy in marking the answers. Make sure you have answered all forty questions for each subject.

**PMI Comments.** Include your comments regarding the questions and test procedures for PMI and include all scrap paper furnished by PMI to STC. Do not accept or include any scrap paper from the center.

**Lunch Break.** Your spare time and hour lunch break give you adequate time to review certain key parts of the afternoon session, with the insights you have of the morning session of the PMP exam. Use this time wisely, as it may mean the difference between passing and failing your weakest segment.

**Afternoon Session.** Follow the above guidelines, and you will walk away from the test—it is hoped—with a triumphant and joyful confidence for having done your best. The post-test experience is an intellectual and psychological release for a job well done.

## Exam Results

With computerized testing, you will automatically know whether you have passed or failed the test after you have completed all eight subjects. If you have passed the test, the next step is to apply for qualification, and when you are qualified, PMI will send you a PMP certificate and PMP pin. If you have failed two subjects, you will have to sit for the two specific subjects over again. If you pass these two subjects and are qualified you will receive your PMP certificate and pin. If you failed three or more subjects at the first sitting, or failed one subject at the second sitting, you will have to sit for all eight subjects a third or second time, respectively.

## Summary

PMP certification is an important step in demonstrating to yourself, your peers, and your management that you are a highly qualified project manager. The effort before humanity must be done in an organized way with the most modern tools available. The increasing activity regarding certification of project managers speaks loudly of the belief in professional project management certification. To that end, we should thank those who have motivated us to PMP certification and look forward to being a mentor for those who will then look to us for encouragement in the certification process.

# PROJECT MANAGEMENT: THE NEXT CENTURY

# Utilities

# Complex Information System Project Management System View II

Ed Mechler, CCP, Equitable Resources Inc.

## Introduction

The theme of this paper is the twenty first century world view of project managers. The concepts will especially affect project managers in the utility and software industry. After a brief review of the present conditions, a suggested world view, General Systems Theory, will be presented. The implications of the theory upon project managers and software engineers will follow. The paper will end with an example of the integrated effort of a project manager within the utility and software industry.

## Present Conditions

To any one in business there is no doubt the conditions are changing. Within the business environment there is worldwide industries and competition, low cost quality products and services, innovated products and services, etc. For the utility industry, the conditions are further complicated by deregulation. The culture of an organization is downsizing, outsourcing, reorganizing, cost cutting, benchmarking, centralizing, decentralizing, etc. All of which produce enormous amounts of anxiety. The operational loop of a business, i.e., input-transformation-output-feedback, is undergoing reengineering, computerizing, cost cutting, and transforming into virtual offices, etc. This results in a slow down in product/service development instead of the desired faster development.

Many authors list the above conditions to advance a concept or methodology that will help alleviate the adverse effects. However, no author, at least anecdotally, has listed all the various concepts and methodologies that are available and very few have integrated two or more together. The following is a list of some of the aids to lessen the adverse effects. They will be listed by the name I use now but most have been around for while under various aliases.

- Strategic management,
- Management by objectives,
- Project management,
- Just in time inventory,
- Team building,
- Quality control,
- Concurrent engineering, and
- Software engineering.

So far I have listed the obvious changes occurring in business and some concepts and methodologies to help alleviate the adverse effects. We have a set of conditions and methods to handle them. However, we are not getting the desired results. What is missing? The roots to the answer of this questions can be found examining certain disciplines aids and exams plus certain recent authors. As the first example, examine *A Guide to the Project Management Body of Knowledge* (PMBOK) published by Project Management Institute. It integrates planning, objectives, teams, quality, risk, communications, requirements, etc. Another area to examine is ICCPs certification exam for computer professionals. It integrates human and organizational frameworks, system concepts, data and information, system development, technology, financial management, management sciences, etc. An example of an author to examine is Professor Cleland's book "Project Management Strategic Design and Implementation." To paraphrase the fundamental concept of the book it is the integration of strategic management and project management. These examples contain a wholeness or integration of parts. What is missing, is a new world outlook, zeitgeist, value system, or small "p" philosophy that deals with the totality, not individual pieces.

## General Systems Theory

General System Theory (GST) is usually associated with the twentieth century as Peter Senge does in "The Fifth Discipline." However, even with a cursory investigation, one can trace the concepts from the early Greeks, nationalism versus atomism, through the various philosophical schools of thought, to the twentieth century. The theory has never become a driving force for a number of proposed reasons, i.e., the Renaissance transformation from a belief to a scientific (primarily analytic) epoch, the rapid application to a select field of the new practitioners, the high returns from the previous prescribed methodologies, etc. My present hypothesis, in addition to those stated, is that we were never able to quantify the concepts but this may be changing with the advent of fuzzy sets and chaos theory. But, we need GST as a driving force now because the returns of the present philosophy are diminishing. We need a change at this level to continue to grow.

GST is a set of concepts for seeing wholes. The key word is "system" or the wholeness of a phenomenon, culture, organization, information system, object, etc. "General" implies that the concepts can be applied across a wide area of interests, as shown by Gause and Weinberg in their GST masters program. "Theory" is a combination of theoretical and practical. Paraphrasing Ackoff, a system is a whole that cannot be divided into independent parts. Put more formally, a system is a whole that contains two or more parts that satisfy the following five conditions:

1. The whole has one or more defining functions.
2. Each part can affect the behavior or properties of the whole.
3. Subsets of parts are separately necessary but insufficient for carrying out a defining function.
4. No part of a system has an independent effect.
5. No subset of parts has an independent effect.

The primary difference between, with what I will call twentieth century scientific thinking (TCS) and GST, is the parts of the whole are very interrelated to each other and to the whole in GST and independent in TCS. Within GST they can not be isolated, studied, and enhanced independently. The best parts of similar systems can not be removed and placed together to form a super system. The essence of GST is the interrelationship of the parts to themselves and to the whole.

As an example, there is a business organization that has two product lines with a centralized engineering department. To associate costs, it is decided to decentralize the engineering department into each product line. Besides the potential economic increase, more engineers may be needed for the same amount of work, the function of engineering control is lost. Now the objectives of the engineers will be oriented toward production and not the engineering standards. Another example is, a service company marketing department is not doing as good as the industry leader. Under analysis, it is determined the industry leader marketing department uses a special software package that interfaces with the customer. The service company implements the package and it fails. The customer needs of the service company were different than the industry leader. We can not isolate or implement ideal parts without considering the interrelations with other parts and the whole.

Another characteristic of GST that captures its essences is structure. As the parts form, with the interrelationships to each other and the whole, an example of an existing system or a new system emerges. The structure, in a generic form, is shown in Exhibit 1; the system definition is from Laszlo, a collaborator of Bertalanffy, who is credited with revitalization of the theory in the middle of the twentieth century. The system takes on a life and definition of its own. As an example, stop for a moment and determine how you would explain an automobile to an indigenous person from a rain forest. It would be very difficult, for the word "automobile" to us is an all encompassing definition depending on the level of sophistication required. It has its inputs, processes, outputs, environments, etc. All the characteristics come to mind instantly. It would take reams of paper to describe it analytically where systematically one word is enough. It would be extremely difficult to explain it to the rain forest person, as his or her systems would be to us.

An implication of structure is design, purposeful or random. If we partition structures into natural ones in nature and those that are built by humans, we can attribute design functions to both areas. If we further divide human structures into sociological, i.e., government agencies, business organizations, economics, etc., and mechanistic, i.e., computers, automobiles, aircraft, etc., we can say that more design has been applied to the mechanistic than the sociological. We can also say, generally, that more mechanistic structures reach higher levels of success than sociological ones. We need to apply more conscious human thought, system design, to social structures. In addition, structure and design play an important role in the life cycle of each system. Each system could have drastic and dynamic changes during its existence. It is not an understatement to say that the utility industry is experiencing a dramatic change now and in the foreseeable future. This further implies more applied human design through various time periods to ensure continual success.

The fundamental point I have been trying to make is, our world view must change from a independent, analytic point of view to an interrelated, system, design or, General System Theory. We are *not* in the mode of analyzing parts and implementing but in the building of new systems, i.e., organizations, economies, etc.

## Project Management Implications

"Project" has many definitions, most of which are similar. The one I favor is "Projects are resource-consuming activities used to implement organizational strategies, achieve goals, and contribute to the accomplishment of the organizational mission...." Project managers (PMs) usually implement projects, where as occasionally they are involved in requirements development. PMs usually balance system performance, costs and schedule. PMs pull all the parts of implementation and the system together to be successful. The implication is, PMs are already working within the system world view. I think PMs are, but need to increase their understanding of GST. First, acquire the book by Ervin Laszlo "The Systems View of the World" (or visit http://www.amazon.com). Then concentrate on understanding concepts, in addition to the ones in Exhibit 1, such as:

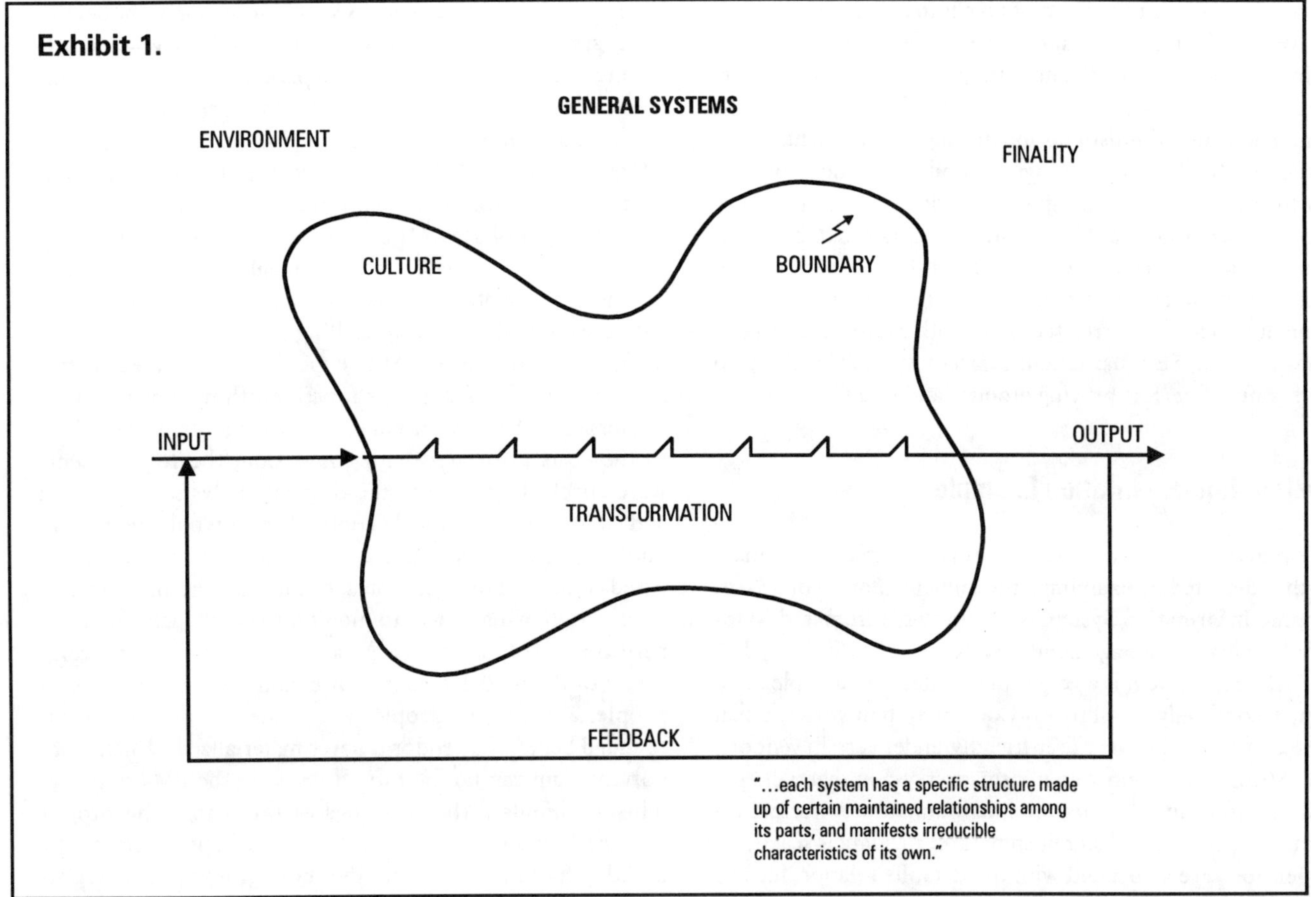


- Isomorphism—viewing as systems permits translation of concepts from one type of system to another.
- Equifinality—there exists many ways to achieve an objective.
- Multifinality—there exists many ends to achieve an objective.
- Imbedded Systems—subsystems within systems and the relationships.
- Dynamic Systems—a nonlinear system that changes over time.
- Chaos Theory—behavior of deterministic, nonlinear dynamical systems.

The implications for the PMs within the utility/energy industry are over whelming. Besides the need to use GST concepts more, they are faced with deregulation. We must face the fact that the road to deregulation doesn't have many road signs. Projects will be implementing executive visions. Projects will be unusual, time constraint, and highly monitored. Above all, the scourge of PMs, projects will be prone to failure and cancellation due to changing conditions. Utility PMs need to be implementing the GST concepts already.

## Software Engineering Implications

It has been reported numerous times that we are in an information society. We have always needed information to make decisions; the more information the better the decision. Economically, there was a cut off of acquiring information because of diminishing returns. If the "information society" means we have greater access to data and information to enhance our decision making then it appears to be a reasonable description. At the heart of the information society is the computer and information systems allowing us to manipulate more data and develop more information, economically. Viewing these concepts from a GST point-of-view, the computer and information systems are tools to most organizations. This is professed by many people but in reality computers and information systems become ends in themselves. GST thinking must take over placing the computer and information system in the proper perspective within other systems.

The implications to the software engineer (SE), a specific (a task force exists to make SE a profession) and generic (all the types of people that work on information systems) term, is the same as the PM but at a higher intensity. The SE is, in most cases, the PM within the software industry. The industry is growing so fast that the SE must take into account along with the systems being organizational tools. The SE must be multidimensional for he or she must translate the needs of the organization into a set of functions to develop a working system. Then the SE must coordinate the development of the system with all the technological conditions, including the hardware, always reviewing with the organization to assure required performance. Finally, the system needs to be maintained and enhanced. Even if a person has no experiences with the software industry it is apparent there are an enormous number of interrelated parts with multiple interrelations that the SE must take into account. GST appears to have found a perfect proving ground, and it has.

## System Implementation Example

The practical application benefits of GST world view can be further depicted by examining the implementation of a Geographic Information System (GIS) and/or Automated Mapping/Facility Management System (AM/FM). The GIS/AM/FM System is a very sophisticated and complex system, second only to a Process Control System with the real time constraint, but very user-friendly under certain vendors. A GIS/AM/FM System is an information system that uses spacial relationships as a common denominator. A normal information system is algebraic in nature; the data is scalar, no dimensions are associated with the data, its relationships or processes. The GIS/AM/FM Systems, though, are geometric; each datum is multidimensional, i.e., each datum has a x,y-point for position and a possible z-point for altitude associated with it and its relationships and processes. In other words, the GIS/AM/FM System locks the data to an existing, physical, real space. In addition, GIS/AM/FM Systems rely on images more so than tables or lists. This system is well suited for the maps used within the utility industry. "Maps" is some what a misnomer; the maps have roads, etc. and utility facilities but also contain facility data, i.e., pipe size, installation date, pole type, etc. As a result of the fit, many utilities are converting to the GIS/AM/FM Systems from the hand drawn paper versions for economic reasons and the additional benefits the system provides, i.e., system analysis, data analysis, integration to other systems, etc.

The GIS/AM/FM project at Equitable Resources, Inc. (ERI) started in 1986 with a beneficial report from an outside engineering firm. For the next four years, the analysis and design phases of the system were completed. The project was coordinated from the engineering department with a team of operational people (end-users), engineers and one information specialist; a number of operational people had some background in computer systems. A model of the transmission and distribution gas systems was developed for the pilot; most GIS/AM/FM vendors supply software to model the utility system but an unique model needs to be developed. After an extensive economic analysis period, the decision to implement was made at the end of 1990 with the selection of a implementation project manager and allocation of funds. To a large and unusual degree, the organizational system took control of the project and delivered the results of the analysis and design phases. Of course, as with any system, there was a predominant dedicated individual.

The implementation phase of the project started in 1991 with the contracting of a consulting company with extensive background in GIS/AM/FM; expertise in this area wasn't readily available. The major function of implementation is conversion of hard paper data into the computer system. Due to the costs associated with conversion, the requirements were checked again with the original analysis/design team and additional operational people, changes would be on hold until conversion was complete. A steering committee was initiated comprised of operational, engineering, accounting, and information management to monitor the costs, schedule, and performance of the project. An attempt to form a team, comprised of the model vendor, conversion vendor, information people, and project people, was made but due to an unfounded belief of a vendor it never materialized. When a important team can not be form it becomes the PMs responsibility to simulate the workings of the team. The project manager's management hierarchy was kept informed by monthly status reports. With the above groups the interrelated organizational parts were captured to voice their input to the project.

A GIS/AM/FM System can be stand alone with some loss of functionality, unless an elaborate process is developed for passing data. The ERI system was on the main frame initiating changes to the physical as well as the procedural functions; the system was not the normal type that further exasperated the information people. Human hardware/software interfaces were develop and implemented. Software interfaces to other systems were developed, i.e., customer information system to acquire data on loading to operate the network analysis system. The process of map and data collection, conversion, checking hard and soft returns was developed, tested, and implemented. The project interrelated parts were captured to assure schedule, cost, and performance.

Within Exhibit 1, there is the inter or operational loop, input, transformation, output, feedback, and the outer or strategic loop, environment, culture, finality. The relationships between these loops is at every level. So far the discussion has emphasized the inner loop, now the outer loop will be discussed. From outside agencies, there has been cautious positive responses, due, in my opinion, to a lack of understanding of the system and the data and processes it replaces. Recently, with various events across the country and retirement of knowledgeable people, accuracy has become an issue. This trend will enhance the system. During the project a major problem developed with the conversion vendor. It was highly recommended to change vendors but was rejected. The rejection was due to the lack of understanding of multiply ways of reaching the objective and caused a year delay in the completion of the project. Finally, the culture of the organization could be equated to dead reckoning flying when the project began and instrument flying now. The culture of a system is the hardest characteristic of an organization to change and without GST much harder. In this case, even though the operational people were involved from the beginning, the change would be horrendous. Various statements were made about the system and all were unfounded. The approach taken was to answer each as they emerged. These interrelated parts are much harder and more time consuming to handle within a project.

## Conclusion

We all understand that conditions and events are changing, especially to a type of system called a business organization. These changes will affect everyone for at least the next ten years, executives, managers, engineers, technicians, project managers, and software engineers. I have suggested a different world view, General System Theory, because the conditions and events are quite different and our present approach is not returning results as good as it has over the last few hundred years. I have shown the affects on project managers and software engineers and an application utilizing the concepts. I hope I have peeked your interest.

### References


Ackoff, Russell L. 1994. The Democratic Corporation. Oxford University Press: NY, 18–21.

Cleland, David I. Project Management Strategic Design and Implementation. Tab Books, Inc.: Blue Ridge Summit, PA, 38.

Gause, Donald C., and Gerald M. Weinberg. 1973. "On General Systems Education." General Systems, 18: 137–146.

Laszlo, Ervin. The Systems View of the World. George Braziller, Inc. 12.

Mechler, Ed. "GIS/AM/FM Project Management System View." The Best of AM/FM/GIS 92–93. AM/FM: International, Aurora, CO, 70, 82.

Senge, Peter M. 1990. The Fifth Discipline The Art & Practice of The Learning Organization, Doubleday/Currency: New York, 68.


### Additional Reading List


Laszlo, Ervin. 1972. "The Systems View of the World." Braziller, New York.

Simon, H.A. 1981. "The Sciences of the Artificial." 2nd. Ed., MIT Press: Cambridge MA.

Churchman, C.W. 1979. "The Systems Approach." Delta Publishing Co. Inc.: New York.

———. 1979. "The Systems Approach and Its Enemies." Basic Books, Inc.: New York.

Weinberg, G.M. 1975. "An Introduction to General Systems Thinking." John Wiley and Sons: New York.

Weinberg, G.M., and D. Weinberg. 1979. "On The Design of Stable Systems." John Wiley and Sons: New York.

Cleland, D.I., and King, W.R., 1972. "Management: A Systems Approach." McGraw-Hill, Inc.: New York.

———. 1975. "System Analysis and Project Management." McGraw-Hill, Inc.: New York.

# An Overview of the Steam Generator Replacement Project at Catawba Nuclear Station

Anthony W. Brock, PE, PMP, Duke Power Company
Michael S. Terrell, PE, PMP, Duke Power Company

## Introduction

The Steam Generator Replacement Project (SGRP) at Catawba Nuclear Station represents one-third of the scope of the Steam Generator Replacement Project being conducted by Duke Power Company. Duke Power is replacing the steam generators (S/G), at McGuire Nuclear Station Units 1 and 2, and at Catawba Nuclear Station Unit 1 at an estimated cost of $500 million. The purpose of this paper is to present the reader with an overview of the key project management elements of the Steam Generator Replacement Outage at Catawba Nuclear Station. This outage took place during the summer of 1996.

## Background

All three units involved in steam generator replacement outages are pressurized water reactor systems (PWR). The key components of PWR systems include a reactor vessel, steam generators, reactor coolant pumps and a pressurizer. Catawba and McGuire are replacing all the steam generators at the three affected units. Degradation of the tubes inside these steam generators has caused the expected life of this equipment to be much less than originally designed. Studies concluded that it was more cost effective to replace the steam generators than to continue the long-term program of plugging tubes that would ultimately result in down rating the generating capacity of the stations.

The decision was made in 1990 to replace steam generators and the first project team members were assigned in 1991. Between 1991 and the first outage, the team concentrated on procurement specifications and engineering for the new units as well as detailed planning for the actual replacement outages. The first replacement outage began in June of 1996 at Catawba. The replacement outages for McGuire Nuclear Station are scheduled for 1997.

## Scope

The Catawba replacement involved the removal and replacement of the steam generators, providing necessary special handling equipment, removing or modifying existing plant structures and rerouting piping and electrical systems connected to the generators. Field work started approximately four months prior to the shutdown of the reactor. The Catawba outage was estimated to consume approximately 355,000 work hours through approximately three thousand schedule activities. The replacement of the steam generators occurred during the refueling outage in the summer of 1996. The reactor was scheduled to be offline for ninety-three days.

Extensive evaluations and design effort were expended by project team members to develop a specification for new steam generators. The new Babcock and Wilcox steam generators are approximately sixty-eight feet tall, fifteen feet in diameter and weigh over four hundred tons. Each generator contains 6,633 tubes that have a total length of approximately one hundred miles (total of all four). The tubes were manufactured by Sumitomo Metals in Japan.

The steam generators are housed inside the reactor buildings inside cubicles with partially removable steel walls and domes. Located above the enclosure domes are air handling units and associated steel platforms. Six piping systems connected to the generators had to be severed before the generators could be unbolted from the support structures holding them in place. While the piping systems were being severed, the air handling units, associated platforms, enclosure domes and walls had to be removed. In fact, a major portion of the reactor building had to be disassembled to remove the steam generators.

To lift and transport the steam generators out of containment, a special temporary lifting device (TLD) was mounted to the station's polar crane inside the reactor building. Once the steam generator was lifted, it had to be laid down and transported out the reactor building equipment hatch. This was accomplished by installing a rail system that spanned from the interior of the reactor building through the equipment hatch.

To complete the transfer of the steam generators from the cavities to the exterior handling hoist, a rail system was constructed that extended to the outside of the reactor building via the equipment hatch. This handling system required us to modify the existing ramp to the equipment hatch and to install a Manitowoc 4100 ringer crane

**Exhibit 1.** SGRP Implementation Interface Model

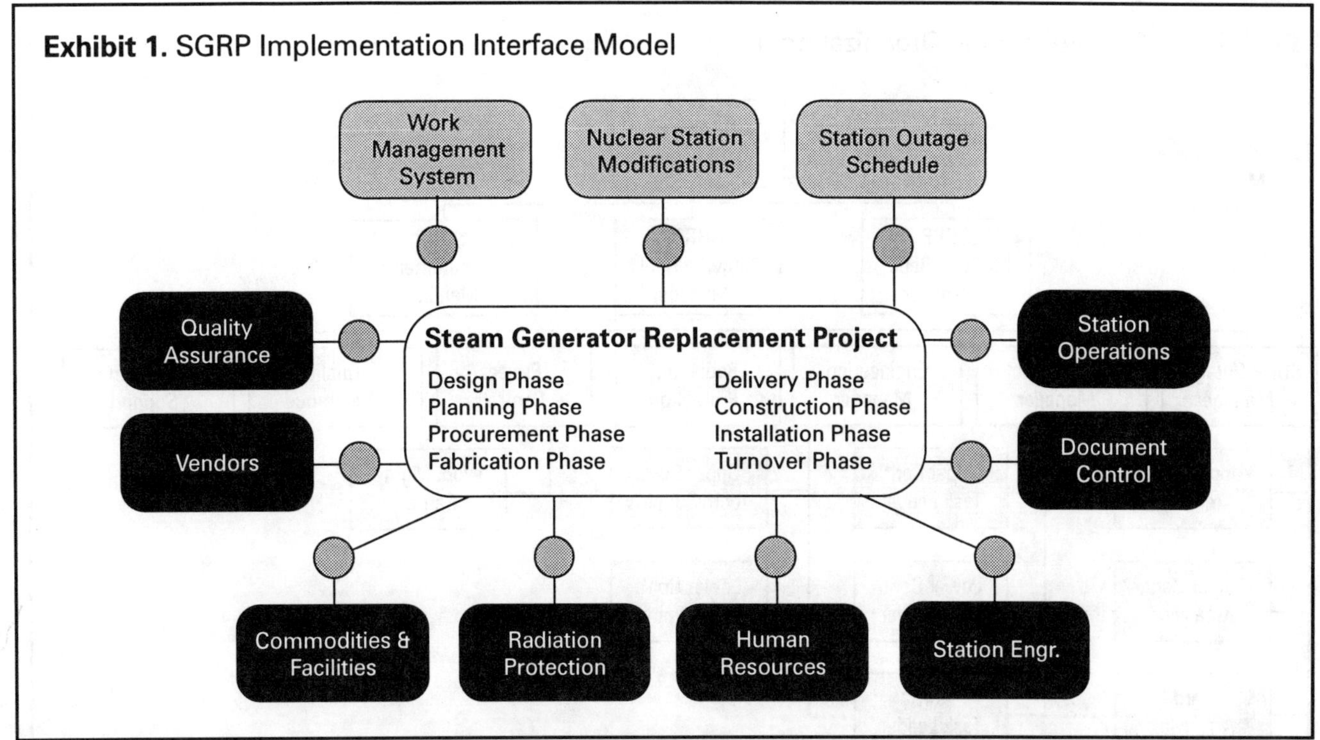


near the base of the ramp to facilitate materials and equipment movement.

Additional activities associated with removing the steam generators included building scaffolds, installing temporary power, lighting and services, installing lead shielding to reduce exposure to radiation and removal/replacement/modification to the different piping systems including feedwater, main steam, blowdown and nuclear sampling.

## Project Integration

The project level plans included a work breakdown structure built around a series of nuclear station modification (NSM) packages. Each of these packages included input from all stakeholders affected by the associated package. An example is the package to install the interior and exterior structural systems used to move the steam generators out of and into the reactor building. This system covered much of the refueling canal inside the building, spanned the equipment hatch and extended outside the reactor building into the yard for handling equipment access. Organizations involved in the installation and operation of this handling system included engineering, radiation protection, security, station maintenance and refueling organizations, and station operations.

Each of these groups had a different set of expectations and needs that had to be integrated into the package scope documents. These scope documents were then translated into individual package schedules and these individual schedules were used to form the overall outage schedule. Prior to integration, each package schedule was resource loaded for the various craft and certain special equipment that would be used to implement the work. The project's outage schedule was then integrated into the overall station outage schedule through a series of summarized project activities that were updated on a daily basis.

After the overall schedule was integrated, the final resources levels were determined by reviewing the various resources individually in relation to the outage sequencing and activity float results. These resource numbers were then broken down into specific skills and qualifications and the resources were requested and scheduled for the project.

In order to ensure continued input by the various stakeholders during the project life cycle, the project team developed Interface Agreements and processes (see Exhibit 1) for the various organizations critical to project success. The Interface Agreements defined the players, expectations, roles and responsibilities of the individuals and deliverables of each of the organizations. Some station processes needed to be modified to meet the particular needs of the project. These process changes were documented and agreed to by both project and station management.

The Interface Agreements and revised processes descriptions were included in the Steam Generator Replacement Project Manual, the controlling document for the project. The Project Manual included sections for:

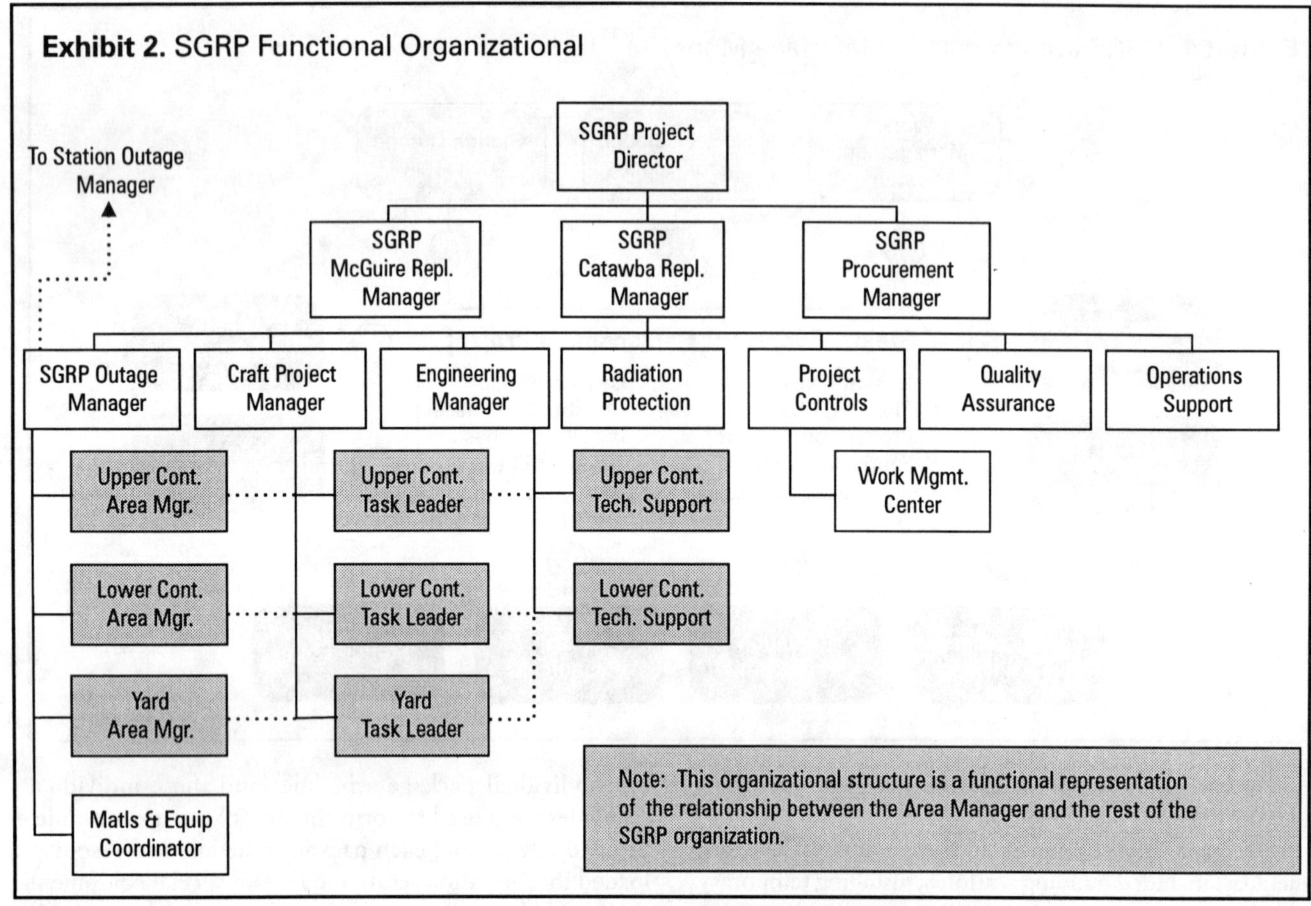


- Interface Agreements,
- Various Project Level Plans,
- Work Place Procedures,
- Work Control Processes,
- Risk Management,
- Modification Scope Documents,
- Tabletop Outage Preparation Sessions,
- Project Licensing Reports,
- Lessons Learned Program,
- Information Bulletins,
- Facilities Implementation Plans, and
- Software and Data Quality Assurance.

The Project Manual was a "living document" in that it underwent changes to reflect the current state of the project from development through implementation and final project close-out.

Documentation of all field work was maintained through Duke Power Company's Work Management System (WMS). WMS is an online system of work orders defining blocks of work and all controlling procedures and documents required for execution, inspection and verifications and close-out. This online system of work orders also allowed the station operations group to define the different plant conditions required for execution of the work. In addition, it allowed the execution craft to document their work, allowed project management to review the current execution status and allowed station work control to review for final documentation.

## Human Resources

Responsibility for project plan development and execution was delegated to a group of area managers assigned responsibilities for upper containment, lower containment and yard. In addition, they were responsible for assuring that each modification package scope was implemented and that each stakeholder's interests were addressed. The area managers were responsible for development of the individual schedules and the overall integrated schedule. Interfaces between these individuals and the station's work control organization rested with a project outage manager. The organizational structure shows the area manager's relationship within the SGRP organization (see Exhibit 2).

The area managers were responsible for the initial development of plans for their areas and for refinement of the plans as the scope matured. From this plan came the craft resources needed for plan execution. Actual craft numbers at peak of implementation came to six hundred and seventy with an additional support organization of around one hundred and fifteen. The majority of these numbers were Duke Power employees and the balance was supplied from various labor vendors.

While these area managers did not have direct reports in the organization, they were responsible for providing priorities for the execution and support teams. The function of the area manager most closely aligns with the project manager's role in the balanced matrix organization as shown in *A Guide to the Project Management Body of Knowledge (PMBOK)*.

## Time Management

The steam generator replacement project team chose Primavera's Finest Hour as the platform for the project schedule. The early phases of the project life cycle included scope development and engineering schedules. These schedules laid out the project planning and engineering activities in units of days. Modification (NSM) scope documents were used to develop the initial work breakdown structure and later to develop details for craft execution. The first phase of the project was the development of the engineering documents and drawings that would eventually be used in the field for craft execution.

The overall station outage duration was managed by the Catawba Nuclear Station Work Control organization. Their typical outage plan has around ten thousand individual activities. The platform of choice for the Catawba Nuclear Station Work Control organization was Artemis Prestige. The station's and SGRP's work control organizations decided that the SGRP project team would maintain a separate network connected to Catawba's network through a series of summary activities. The SGRP network contained approximately three thousand activities that were represented as approximately three hundred summary activities in the station schedule. These activities were updated daily in order to show impacts to either schedule. In addition, critical interface activities were identified in both the SGRP schedule and the station's schedule. Data was transferred between networks using ASCII batch files.

The expected duration of the entire replacement outage was estimated to take approximately ninety-five days. The implementation work schedule was twenty-four hours per day, seven days per week. The schedule was maintained on an hourly basis, updated at 9:00 A.M. each day and work was monitored using both earned value for schedule performance and actual cost values for cost performance.

Resources were defined in the Finest Hour resource library for each of the different craft types. In addition to craft resources, several critical equipment resources were included. Early in the development of the plan, we believed that the polar crane was the limiting resource in the reactor building for the project. Once this was determined, the schedule was leveled on the polar crane resource such that the critical path for the outage ran through activities requiring the polar crane resource. As a side note, two additional knuckleboom cranes were installed in upper containment to relieve the load on the polar crane. Any activity that could be accomplished using these additional hooks were resourced to the knuckleboom cranes thereby shortening the expected duration of the outage.

The critical path for the project was defined as any activity having twenty-four hours or less float. These activities were prioritized each day for execution emphasis. Immediately prior to the first day of the outage, a schedule baseline was established for daily comparison to define earned values.

## Cost Management

The total cost estimate for the Catawba replacement outage, including the cost of the steam generators, labor, materials and consumables was $170 million. The labor required for the outage was estimated at 355,000 hours. This figure was developed by estimating the resources required for each task, generating resource utilization curves from the scheduling tool, and then developing staffing levels to meet the resource demands. The estimates for each task were developed by project personnel and representatives of the craft that would implement the work. The resource utilization curves contained several peaks associated with the start dates for the scheduled activities. By looking at the early and late dates together, a staffing level was selected to optimize each resource type. The staffing solution assumed that work would be scheduled around the clock, seven days per week and that one-third of the resources would be scheduled off at any given time.

Once the staffing curves were available, the percentage difference between the resource estimates and the staffing estimate was calculated. This difference was used to modify the resource estimates for each activity. Next "level of effort" type resources (support activities such as building and maintaining scaffolding) were removed from the schedule. Finally, the resource estimates were reviewed once more and adjusted. This resulted in a budgeted cost of work scheduled (BCWS) figure of 155,364 hours and a total resource estimate of 355,000 hours. Schedule performance was tracked and reported daily while cost performance was reported weekly.

Throughout the various stages of project development and execution, an emphasis on project cost control was maintained. The project developed a cost tool called the Cost Estimate Deviation Report (CEDR) that was used to control both positive and negative changes to overall project costs. Early emphasis on scope control was strictly enforced in order to define the overall project cost for funding purposes. Later, emphasis on labor changes for the execution craft allowed the project team to continue to control scope growth while maintaining appropriate productivity and schedule performance.

## Risk and Lessons Learned

Although the steam generator replacement project was the largest project to be undertaken at Catawba since initial construction, the technology was not new. Other domestic and foreign utilities had already completed or were implementing similar projects. To capitalize on their experiences, the project team visited numerous replacement projects underway around the United States, Europe and Japan.

Lessons learned from these projects were factored into the individual modifications and the overall project plans. As a side note, over seven hundred lessons learned from the Catawba outage have been factored into the McGuire 1 and 2 plans. Conversely to assure ourselves that our plans were realistic from an independent point of view, the project team brought in experts that had been involved in other replacement projects to review the plans, resources, assumptions and other project data. Each of these reviews provided minor course corrections; however, they also indicated that the execution plans were fundamentally on target.

The project team determined that communications and new processes should be addressed as risk items. One solution to address these risks was to implemented a series of tabletop simulations to test and practice various aspects of the outages. Critical communications and process interfaces were simulated. These simulations were conducted several weeks before the start of the outage using key project players, simulated work packages and facilities mockups. These simulation sessions identified communication interface problems as well as actual execution problems that were corrected before the outage began.

An expectation of the project team was to develop a contingency database of risk issues throughout the project. Each item was reviewed and action was taken in accordance with the degree of risk. Some examples of risk mitigation was the purchase of spare equipment and materials, full-scale mockups and proving runs on welding processes and pipe decontamination equipment as well as extra training for key craft activities.

Perhaps the largest risk for the execution of the outage was the fit-up of the new generator to the existing piping system previously cut from the old generators. The process used to address this risk can be found in a separate paper entitled, *Methods of Managing Risk for a Major Construction Project,* by the same authors.

## Communications

The steam generator replacement outage at Catawba was obviously out of the ordinary for the management and work groups at the operating station. Station personnel operated Unit 2 while dealing with this major construction effort on Unit 1. The project's communications plans had to address the needs of a host of groups in the station as well as the Nuclear Regulatory Commission, the Catawba Owners Group, vendors, suppliers, the implementation craft and other companies planning similar projects. One person was dedicated full-time to be the focal point for all outside information requests including on-site visits. This allowed the project team to focus on communications with the execution craft and with the appropriate station groups.

Daily performance reporting tools were used to keep the project on track. These included several sorts of the schedule data, earned value reports defining schedule performance, work hour expenditures versus expected expenditures, radiation dose reports tracked against a target of expected exposures, milestone comparisons at a high level, and other specific reports generated as needed at critical points in the execution cycle. These tools provided data that focused the project execution and support groups on the same priorities.

As discussed in the project integration section of this report, the primary tool for documentation of field work was the Work Management System work orders. Different organizations had to know the real time status of each work orders to enable the station to return to power operations. The project team chose to use the WMS process because this system is the station's normal process for controlling work.

One of the highlights of project's communications plan was the use of an intranet home page. This home page was available to anyone within the company to view the project's organization, project status, progress photos, etc. Through an interactive panel on the home page, anyone could automatically send digital message to any member of the team through their personal pager. (For McGuire the home page has been upgraded with video clips and still photographs from the Catawba outage.)

Another communication tool employed by the project team was the use of a series of video cameras at critical locations within and outside the reactor building and a series of viewing stations around the site. This tool was the direct result of the project's efforts to control radiation dose by allowing viewing of the hands-on work while outside the Radiation Control Area. The axiom "a picture is worth a thousand words" applied to this tool because one could see what was going on in real time without going into the reactor building.

## Quality

One of the Project Manual sections referenced in the integration section of this report defines the project's Quality Assurance (QA) program. Inherent to nuclear power operations are very rigorous quality standards for modifications, maintenance and operations. All procedures have stringent hold points for verifying that these quality standards are met. In addition, critical work has rigorous inspections by quality control inspectors. All aspects of the replacement project are aligned with the approved corporate QA program.

When deviations were identified, the QA program required a detailed problem investigation be done. The purpose of this investigation was to define the root cause and implement actions to keep this problem from happening again. In addition, these root causes were reviewed to see if they apply elsewhere within the station and other company facilities.

Some aspects of the operations and maintenance of the new steam generators required revisions to the licensing documents issued by the Nuclear Regulatory Commission and other regulator agencies. These revisions required many levels of review and approval, both within and outside the company.

## Procurement

The procurement aspect of the Steam Generator Replacement Project included specifying and purchasing the steam generators as well as the selection of equipment, materials, tools, vendor services and contract resources. A single point contact was established between the project and the corporate purchasing department. This individual was responsible for all contract administration for the project.

In addition, the project established a separate commodities and facilities organization to purchase, receive, warehouse and distribute project materials, tools and equipment. This organization functioned separately from, but in close association with the station's organization in order to minimize total cost to the project.

## Conclusion

This paper has been written using the knowledge areas found in PMI's *A Guide to the Project Management Body of Knowledge (PMBOK)*. It is intended only to describe some of the project management tools that the Steam Generator Replacement Project team used to manage the planning and execution of the project at Catawba Nuclear Station. Development of these tools and processes was based on experience of successful project management within and outside of Duke Power.

While the tools provided adequate and timely information for managing the project, technical problems caused delays in installing the secondary systems and subsequent insulation. In support of these delays in lower containment, reassemble of upper containment was delayed. Overall outage duration ended at one hundred and nine days and expended 472,000 craft work hours. The project management tools employed provided indicators along the way that allowed early decisions to be made to support revisions to the plan. These decisions allowed the project team to communicate with the stakeholders so adjustments could be made in their activities. The project team has reviewed all the lessons learned at Catawba and have factored them into the plans for McGuire Units 1 and 2.

# A Soft Landing: Making Information Project Solutions Last

Edwin J. Mantel, ComEd

Many of us probably had the opportunity to see the movie Apollo 13 that was a documentary on the Apollo 13 mission back in 1970. I had a little trouble with the movie to begin with since I had to adjust to Forest Gump playing Captain James Lovell but I worked my way through that after the first twenty or thirty minutes. Here is a phrase that James Lovell said and I think it captures the essence of the movie. It is "Houston, we have a problem here."

These words changed the purpose of that mission. The landing on the moon no longer was the key objective but the landing back on earth, the safe return of the astronauts became the focus of that mission.

The focus of the Apollo 13 mission shifted from the repetitious to the unique. From the moon landing to the earth landing. From the challenges of a lunar mission to the bottom line results of getting the astronauts back. It shifted from the mission as a whole, solely to the return of the crew and the soft landing.

What does Apollo 13 have to do with information management projects? I think, unfortunately, not nearly enough.

Information management projects, whether they be computer real time systems, records systems, or imaging systems, seem to fall into three distinct phases. The first is the design development and technical problem solving. The second is the implementation or actual roll out of the project involving things like collection and reconciliation of previous databases, training and process incorporation. What I mean by process incorporation is that the information system augments a part of the business process. The last part is the managing of the new information from the new tool to help you begin to actually realize the benefits.

The Apollo13 mission after the canister exploded became 100% focused on the results. The new results of getting the astronauts home. By contrast, in most information management projects, focus is placed on phase 1, which is the design and the development and the solution of technical problems. In many cases, phase 2, the training, data resolution and reconciliation and process incorporation, we tend to hope that the users will somehow do that. And when it comes to ROI, I think many of us pray that no one ask about it at all.

However, in business today, particularly in the electric utility industry, competition really is here. Some of us have seen it more than others, but the bottom line is that our oxygen tank has exploded. And with that, like Apollo 13, where the focus of the mission shifted to the end, the focus in information management projects needs to shift to the end of the mission as well. It needs to focus on realizing the ROI as the end results. We need to bring the mission of an information project to a soft landing.

An interesting thing has happened over the past twenty years with information management systems and information technology it is known as the information management conundrum. Conundrum is something that doesn't seem to be logical. For instance, in spending, we have seen almost an exponential increase over the past twenty years but in productivity gains, that slope has not tracked what we have seen in spending. So the conundrum is, the more we spend the less we seem to be gaining. I believe the conundrum exists because early information projects focused on reduction in personnel. You install a new customer information system and you can replace half your clerical staff. A new billing processing system and your reduce your staff in the accounts payable area. A new inventory management system and you are able to significantly reduce your inventory and do better buying. But we have moved out of that range. Now most information management projects focus on things like process improvement, quality improvements, timeliness of information and customer satisfaction.

Realizing these kinds of benefits, requires a sustained focus and a plan as part of the project as the system installation begins to wind down. What I would like to share with you is an overview of a major application that we have installed at Commonwealth Edison over the past few years. I will cover some of the lessons that we learned in trying to develop ways in which we could achieve the soft landing of realizing the return on our investment for this project.

The system is known as EWCS. The Electronic Work Control System. It is installed at six dual unit nuclear sites. It is integrated software and we will talk about integrated in a minute. It's process augmentation and we will talk about that in a little bit as well. This entire project was a twenty-four million dollar investment.

The EWCS program is an electronic work control as stated earlier. It is integrated in all aspects of work control including items such as preparation and scheduling of work, tool control, surveillance, out of service, document control, archiving of records, plant data and plant modifications.

There are several modules in the EWCS program. Six to be specific. The MS module centers around work control, the OS module is for out of service, CD is our controlled documents module that tracks and monitors controlled documents throughout the plant. The engineering design change module or EDCM is responsible for managing engineering work and design changes. RMS is the records module that is our indexing system to our records that are generated during plant operation. And then we have an electronic work items system that basically white collar management time accounting.

It is an integrated environment and by integrated what I mean is that a user can easily navigate from one module to the next so that we begin to integrate the functions of maintenance, out of service, engineering and document control into one common process flow for the plant.

The integration not only comes from the flow through these various process while in the same system, but it comes from the data as well. Basically we have a data structure with one common database in the middle that contains all the plants pedigree information and relevant references to that equipment database, such as work request history, engineering history, and the modules would tap off that same common database as they need to reference the necessary processes that they are augmenting. This common database has been used as a target database for several other systems like labor distribution and time accounting and parts inventories so that we are all running off the same common base of information.

That was a very quick idea of the concept of the system we were installing. My group's challenge was to implement this system at all of our six nuclear sites as quickly as possible. At the time prior to implementation, we had several fragmented computer systems that were standalone and did not work off common databases. In several cases, many of the operations were centered around paper processing and paper routing and were not augmented by computer technology at all. So this would be a significant step forward.

The approach to the project was to do a module phase in type of technique. We would be phasing in the modules in a logical series across all six sites, much similar to the way a subdivision is built. In one case, we would be having foundations laid, on another side of the subdivision, we may be doing the framing for the structure of the house and some place else the roofers are out putting up the roofing. In another section, we will have the electricians doing their work and the plumbers doing their work and they sort of work through this as a series of activities and houses progressively get completed in a subdivision manner. This is the approach that we chose for the installation of the modules. In essence, there were times when we had activity at all six sites. Project team was about seventy-five members sometimes we swelled up to one hundred. We were augmented by site project teams. The installation was about a 2 1/2 year project and a 24 million expenditure.

The project progressed and we began installing the system over this two year period. Not very far into the project, some of the early installation sites senior managers began to ask exactly when, where, and how they would start to realize some of the benefits that this system was suppose to result in.

My first thought was that you are really asking the wrong the guy, I am just the installer of the system. The ROI is not really my responsibility, I am just the installation project manager. My next thought was that they really shouldn't be asking me anyway because the benefit is to the users and the users report to you not me so why don't you go ask them. For instance, if you think the system is going to have some benefit in the work control area, then why not set the challenge for them to reduce the work control staff by 10% over the next year or perhaps you could establish standards for work package quality and measure improvement in quality over the next couple of years and measure and set some standards along those lines. After second thought, I did not think this was the answer they were looking for either.

Anyway, what I said was "let me look into it and I will get back and tell you what I find." I went back and looked at the initial funding request for the system to see what kind of items were listed as benefits that would offset the cost. The benefits seemed to fall into three areas. First, the elimination of work, particularly the elimination of the support of numerous legacy computer systems that were currently operational at the plants. Another large grouping was management opportunities, things like management time accounting that would allow managers to understand what their people were working on and whether they were working on the most important things, seemed to be a benefit. Also, another major benefit was accurate work history that was readily available and process information that would allow you to better manage the processes, making sure you are at optimal performance. That tied into process improvements in general and some specific process improvements had been indicated. For instance, the value of linking of related documents.

Procedures, drawings and modifications could be cross-referenced to the same work request. There should be some decrease in duplicate work requests. If I had a common system where everyone knew what other people were working on, it would seem that we would be able to eliminate parallel path efforts on solving same problems. Some electronic routing of information seemed to be a benefit. The use of models. Models are basically similar backgrounded work requests that could be called up at a later date, minor changes made to it and we would be able to generate newer work requests. The idea here is that everything was not going to be discovery. Equipment conflict checking with another indicated benefit. When doing out of service work, you could easily be able to check on a piece of equipment before clearing out of service to see if there may be another out of service or work request clearing tied to that piece of equipment. Automatic and expended records indexing was another benefit. A list of controlled documents was readily available to an engineer as he prepared a modification. Document revision notification, if a drawing for instance had a change pending to it and it was used in a particular work package, then the foreman would be notified electrically of a pending change to that drawing before he or she went out and actually worked on a package. Consolidation of numerous site databases was an indicated benefit, a process improvement, one common source of accurate information. Validation of retention requirements was a common retention list for documents that would be consistent across all the sites and we would not have to explore or rediscover what retention requirements were for a given document. And finally, online plant configuration information was a key benefit to the engineering departments as we moved towards tighter configuration and control.

The first approach that we used to identify the ROI was to measure the obvious. The question I asked was "what exactly were the savings that we realized from the elimination of the legacy systems?" We were able to track each system targeted for replacement over the course of several years as we were installing this integrated system. We monitored ongoing CPU charges and IS maintenance of those legacy systems that were progressively being shut down as we merged the information into the common integrated system. The big line item here is that total expenditures for legacy system maintenance over the course of the several years of installation dropped from the $450,000 range down to less than the $85,000 range. This has continued to drop to a fix on fail basis with a cost of only a few thousand dollars annually. This a fairly straightforward measurable benefit that totals about $400,000 per year.

Well at $400,00 per year the ROI on this system was just hacked down immediately to a mere one hundred and twenty years. Not exactly the story I wanted to tell senior management. It did not seem like measuring the obvious was going to give me a lot, so we moved to a second approach. This approach was to conduct site assessments using a subset of the project team. We would actually go out and spend a week at a site, interviewing, talking with people and looking at their work process flows to see what benefits they were receiving from the installation of the system. Three plants were assessed within the next two months. At this point we still had three plants to install the system at.

The assessment format was a series of structured interviews of a cross section of the site. We were usually in the forty to fifty range in our interviews and they were about one hour interviews. Additionally, we had in field observation of the site personnel using the system to do daily work. The assessment objectives where straightforward and very detailed. Specifically, they were to determine the present effectiveness of the system, establish a trending baseline, identify advance training needs, determine if management expectations in the use of the system were understood, determine system knowledge level of senior and middle managers, verify the utilization and understanding of any site procedures and guidelines surrounding the use of the system. Identify processes that were not taking full advantage of the system, identify and publish any good practices that we saw, evaluate the effectiveness of the site administrators, and document any process improvement opportunities.

What we found was much more interesting that what we thought we were going to find. We did begin to be able to itemize some specific benefits that the sites were receiving from utilization of the system. I would like to highlight the subtlety that you need to be looking for when you do look for the ROI.

In the maintenance area for instance, we found that we were able to background work requests and create packages at a rate of about four to one in certain types of situations. We also found some reassignment of personnel in the operations department and some reduction of full-time equivalence during outages where these individuals were used to run and route packages.

In engineering, there was a marked reduction in close out time for design change packages. The time had dropped from months to weeks but this was not necessarily man months worth of work versus weeks of work. It was some reduction in time in terms of man-hours gained, but it was mostly chronological time gained. We also saw that there was a better integration of engineering information with maintenance, for instance, the maintenance people were aware of design changes that were underway that would effect their work requests. The idea of one single source of information versus many seemed to have a benefit. And finally, the issuance of affected documents lists or ADLs wound up with better quality packages put together, but again this is very difficult to quantify.

In engineering, we did see some reassignment of individuals. We saw some specific examples of where a system engineer was able to avoid some rework and some missed ordering of parts because he was able to easily review a work request. Again these were subtle items.

We could not quantify everything but we were able to do some quantification of benefits. We saw two to three people reductions. We saw several reassignments of individuals but the payroll was still there. Perhaps there was avoidance of overtime and contractors. Again very difficult to quantify. If we were to extrapolate this out, I was able to now get the ROI down around seventeen years. Still not anywhere close to where we wanted to be.

More importantly, the assessment brought out other issues that were of greater concern than not being able to fully quantify some of the return on investment.

During the course of our interviews and observations, we did target specific areas to get a feel for how the users felt and what they thought of the system in their regular job duties. One area centered around the data. If the users have a high degree of confidence in the data that is in the system, it should expedite their processes and allow them to do work quicker. We reviewed the findings regarding user confidence in the data at three sites. We conducted surveys at three months after installation another five months after installation and another nine months after installation. It would have been nice to see 100% in the usually and always area. And while the percentages did seem to increase with the length of time the system was operational, there was clearly an opportunity to improve the users confidence in the data at all three sites. Better confidence in the data should directly relate to improved ROI.

We also looked at specific areas within the station. Specifically the administrative and central file operation to see whether or not the people who use the system in their daily job were using the enhance features that would allow them to work more productively. Again, the three sites were looked at and unfortunately what we found was that in most cases, especially during early phases of the use of the system, the users were not using the system to its full potential and even in the advance case with Braidwood with nine months past installation, a large majority of the people were still not using the full features of the system. Clearly it looked like we were not getting the best bang for our buck.

Similarly in the engineering department we found the same kind of trend. A gradual use of the full features of the system but significant opportunities to improve.

The maintenance area was tracked the same way. We were beginning to see a common pattern.

We also wanted to get a feel for middle management department head involvement and engagement with the use of the system.' The thought here was that if middle management and the department heads do not understand how to use the system that their people use then it would be difficult for them to manage the work that their department is responsible for. What we found was that the management of the sites, no matter how long after turn on had occurred, never or seldom or only at best occasionally used the system or even understood anything about it. It was clearly a management void here. It was very difficult for management to set expectations in the utilization of a process based system if they do not understand anything about it.

In summary our findings showed us that:

- Not all system features were being used,
- The confidence in the data was weak,
- Little department head or manager knowledge or involvement,
- Site administration was weak,
- There was no ongoing training program that would accommodate personnel turnover,
- The initial training was not processed-focused but rather system functionality focused,
- There were work processes out there that inhibited system use,
- Only required information was being entered into the system not additional information on a work request closeout for instance that would allow you to trend and track why a job had been delayed,
- No management expectations for use of the system had been established,
- It was difficult to extract management reports that would slice and dice the information, and
- Continuing hardware and network problems.

Well this sounded a lot like the call to Houston. We clearly had a problem here. Solving this problem or even being aware that there was a problem out there was not part of our overall project installation mentality or focus or functionality but clearly we were in a series situation with many road blocks prohibiting the site from maximizing their ROI. We were not going to be able to get this system down on the ground and safely back to earth with the maximum return on our investment without these problems being resolved and we had not planned on doing anything along these lines at all.

We reviewed "the rest of the story" as Paul Harvey would say with site management and they wanted to know what *we* were going to about resolving this issues. Clearly if we were going to set up system and mechanisms that were going to solve the issues surrounding the full realization of the return on investment for this project, that effort would be beyond the scope of the implementation plan. We had not really realized that this was going to be our responsibility. But nevertheless, senior management expected it of us.

This brought us to approach three that was to hit this issue of realizing our ROI to its fullest extent on several fronts. In particular, we targeted site administration, training, data, management support and continuous measurement. What I would like to do at this time is go into each of these five areas. Talk specifically about some of the things we tried; review the success factors and some of the barriers that lead to less than success.

We had not anticipated having to set up the administration of the system at the site level, but we were into that. We needed to establish responsibility for the site system sponsor, a site executive steering committee and establish a site system administrator, training coordinator, site coordinator and report coordinator.

The results of the site administration effort was generally successful. A sit sponsor is an individual who would generally take ownership for the system utilization at the site. The site sponsor was a senior manager. He had, at least, access to the top site management. He was a single point of contact for our installation and support group. On the negative side, they generally did not understand the system or its full potential because they were too far removed from the day-to-day use. Additionally, this responsibility at some sites was moved among several individuals and there was a loss of continuity. However, establishing a site sponsor was, all and all, a positive step. The site executive steering committee's purpose was to help set some policy and overall expectations for the utilization of the system at that site. Again it was a positive sense because it engaged some senior managers to a limited degree. Unfortunately, their agendas were generally full and site administrator's and sponsor's management of this group of site senior managers was generally wanting. In that sense, I mean they were not well prepared to set goals and objectives or to bring specific issues to the table for the sites steering committee to deal with. All in all the site steering committees were generally ineffective.

The system administrator role was a success. It was generally filled with a site technical person who had technical knowledge of the system and also solid computer skills. They developed into an answer man for the user base. Additionally, their home base was clear. Most of them were placed in the local site MIS department. The turnaround on the job was low with resulting stability. We tied them in with a help line that would allow users to get quick responsive help relevant not only to their system problems but also to some of the specific process problems within their site. The site coordinator role was also a success but not as much as with the system administrator. It was indeed a full-time position that was recognized and staffed by the sites. It was usually filled by someone who had evolved from the system turn-on group and they generally understood the system and the potential of what it could be used for. Unfortunately, they were generally junior managers. They did not know how to manage upward and set goals and objectives and to gain support of groups such as the executive steering committee. They had little management experience in terms of budgeting skills, presentation skills and project management skills. It was a mixed success on the site coordinator role but generally a positive thing.

Two more roles were identified. One was the site training coordinator and the last one was the site report coordinator. The training coordinator was a recognized position. However, it was often a high rotation spot with significant turnover and the home base for that position, in some cases, in the training department and in other areas it was in the administration department and in other areas it was in the MIS department. Unfortunately, most of the site training coordinators were new hires and had little knowledge of the system. The site training coordinator role, the purpose of which was to support ongoing training efforts, generally failed. The site report coordinator role suffered from much the same problems and the site training coordinator role and never really got off the ground at the sites. So in summary, our efforts with site administration were mixed. We were successful in having positions created and staffed that would help with the ongoing day to day running of the system and that was about it.

Training was another targeted area. We needed to revamp the initial training to be job specific versus system skills training. We needed to work with the sites to attempt to establish and ongoing training program. We decided to develop CBT or computer based training courses for system introduction. We took on the effort of developing a supervisor or department heads manager handbook that focused not on how to do things with the system but rather on the value of doing things with the system and the value of some of the information that is contained within the system. Finally, we developed process-focused system online help.

Training to the process as opposed to the use of the system was a far greater challenge than we had anticipated. In many cases, the processes surrounding the system were not standard. For instance, while we could write and track work requests with the system, one site might be on a twelve-week rolling schedule another site might be on an eight-week rolling schedule. This scheduling process had a significant impact on how we would train the users to use the system within the context of the broader processes. Also, our installation schedule was extremely tight and too difficult for us to change the training format immediately We actually did not catch up with process training until the last turn-on. Process training also only showed the users what he had to know to do work that was initially very positive, unfortunately, without looking at other areas of what the system could do, the user coming out of process training really never understood the capabilities of the system. For instance, an individual in the work control area preparing work requests never really understood how the system interfaced with engineering in preparation of mods. Consequently, he lost that richness of knowing what engineering was doing as he prepared his work package. Nevertheless, training to the process as opposed to the system use was a better approach and got our turn-ons off to a much more solid start by lessening the extent of the turn-on productivity dip.

Establishing ongoing site based training programs was generally a failure. To date, this has not been achieved due to high turnover of site personnel. With that, the knowledge of how to use the system even in spite of having excellent training material available and lesson plans available suffered. Site priorities usually shifted quite a bit based upon outages and classes that were scheduled, ended up being canceled. I think another major issue was that the program was not accredited. In that sense, an accredited program such as license operator training or maintenance or instrumentation training class is accredited by the INPO organization and therefore has certain standards to meet. This warrants a certain degree of attention from the training departments. We did not have that luxury. We were not part of an accredited program and consequently to a great extent training became a secondary item at most sites. Our thoughts are that in 1997, we will expand the central training group to support the six sites.

Developing a CBT course was very successful. The sites actually were so happy with the thought and the concept of it and some of the initial parts of the program that they agreed to pay for it. It did engage managers in the sense that it was easy for them to call up on their computer and work through it at their own pace. It covered some fundamentals of the system and at least could allow them to develop the skill set of logging into the system and viewing information. It did not get to the point of teaching them what all the information meant or more sophisticated navigation but it was a very good introduction to the system and it began to clear away some of the fog. It actually evolved into a key lynch pin for the small successes that we did have with ongoing training in the sense that as an individual would rotate to a new job position or new individuals would report they would be signed up for the CBT course. They would at least gain a fundamental knowledge of the system. Our plans are to expand CBT in the future.

We recognized that a problem existed with getting managers and department heads engaged in the use of the system. If we were going to gain in productivity it was going to be important for them to understand how their reports were using the system to do work and how the information that was gathered during the work process could be utilized and analyzed in cycling back through the work process to improve the work process. For instance, if information regarding the delay of work requests or jobs out in the field was recorded on a daily bases by the supervisors and then analyzed over a period of time, managers could begin to understand why work was delayed. They could look at correlation between the types of delays and the types of work done so that they could use that information to improve the flow of information or flow of the work process and hopefully get more work done in shorter periods of time with better use of resources. The task at hand was to somehow engage the managers in an understanding of the system. This proved to be very difficult. As I had noted earlier, several of the surrounding work processes were inconsistent from one site to the next. We also had difficulty translating the point of view of a manager that should be focused on productivity and cost and efficiency into how the system produced reports, displayed information and collected information. It was difficult to transition to the right point of view. For instance, in order to get useful information from a work management system, it was important to cross correlate many parameters. For instance, as noted earlier, delays of jobs might need to be crossed-correlated to work-groups, to the type of work being done, to the department doing the work, to the time when the work was being done, outage, non-outage related, ore even to exposure levels in the area. This got to be very complex. Also the managers and the department heads have limited attention spans. I say not as viewing them as five-year olds but they have many things on their radar screens and to capture enough of their time to teach them what was out there in terms of tools to help them manage better was a challenge. After several attempts to develop handbooks that were centered around screen displays and some explanations of the fields that were entered into those screens, we finally settled on a handbook that talked about the value of information. For instance, we would take a work request panel display and show where delay codes would be added and have a brief discussion on the value of delay codes and how they could be used to manage work. At this point, we are just beginning to issue this handbook and do not have results as to its effectiveness yet. But we are somewhat comfortable with the fact of trying to focus on value instead of how to do things, since most managers need to understand what the information is telling them.

Online process help was a real winner. The system did not have much online help other than system information. We wanted to work in process help as well. It augmented initial training. It was very well received by the users because it was readily available and relevant. It was easy for us to keep updated as new information or changes were made to the system. It was also there when they needed it. It help reduce processing delays and the impact of inconsistencies in the utilization of the system.

Our next area focused in terms of developing some mechanisms and tools to gain the return on investment of the system and resolve some of the issue problems that were out there centered around data. In this specific case, similar to some of the site administration responsibilities, we did create the position of data steward. It did have a home. It was assigned to the configuration management section of the site engineering departments. Configuration management and data seemed to be one in the same and was an accepted norm. This got us off to a good start in getting the position recognized and supported. We documented all of the sources of the data and the reconciliation process when we merged in the hundreds of databases into one common database. We detailed the loading process and explained it to a lot of people that seemed to take away the mysticism of where numbers came from. We also, in future turn-ons of the system at other sites using different modules, established data teams that were a combination of site personnel and project team personnel working together so that at turn-on there would be a comfort factor with the users regarding the data and information.

The results of these data efforts were highly successful, primarily because they engaged the user early on in the system. They set up some site accountability. They established credibility with users and got out the facts instead of the rumors. It also created a continuous improvement mechanism. For instance, if an individual work analyst would see a piece of information on a screen that seemed to be incorrect, maybe an equipment piece number did not tie to the right equipment or thought something might have a safety related significance but it was not indicated, or there had been a change in the plant that might have effected a piece of information or in some cases there was information that he was aware but it was absent from the screen, an engineering request (ER) could be quickly written using the system, tag the omission or problem and send it off to the data steward who then would reconcile that issue and give notification back of problem resolution. So we set up a continuous improvement mechanism for data quality that actually used the system as the mechanism to do that.

The fourth area that efforts were established to move us toward maximizing a return on investment was the area of management support. This is different than site administration support in the sense that site administration is really concerned with the day-to-day operation and use of the system while management support was really focusing more toward the processes and process improvement efforts using information from the system to help improve those processes. Also, it focused on what was going to happen in terms of system operation from a centralized basis after all the modules were turned on and up and running. This would involve things like continual software change management, module utilization expansion to other processes, documentation of the system and any major enhancements that were necessary. Four initiatives were under taken in management support. These were, create a support team, establish user groups, engage the senior process sponsors and establish site liaisons.

It became clear that as we were passing the half-way point in the project, this is a two year project mind you, that the sites that had been turned on and using the system for a while were in need of different services than the sites that were getting ready to turn-on the system. We ended up seeing a need to create support teams as opposed to just project turn on teams. This required the change-out of people. The people in a project team are not necessarily the right skill set or knowledge level or even in some cases, demeanor as those that are needed for a support team activity. Support is much more of a political job than a technical job because you are moving into the subtleties of the utilization of the system and you are touching on business processes. Many control and management tools were needed. For instance, change procedures for software release processes, some sort of prioritization mechanism for figuring out when we would want to make a change to the system, mechanisms to engage the users and to change process. These were all mechanisms that needed to be put into place that actually did not exist. As noted earlier, it became increasingly apparent that a support team in place at the end of the project to support the users in an ongoing basis was an absolute necessity.

The other area we focused on was the creation of user groups. The user groups fell into several specific areas in particular one was site system administration. This was a user group of system administrators and site coordinators. We talked about these individual roles previously. They would meet on a regular basis and they evolved in terms of their skill set for the management of the system. They resolved common problems and shared common opportunities and tricks, ideas and issues.

We also established system user groups. These were more of the process focused people. The data stewards was a user group, maintenance supervisors, work analyst, work control schedulers, predefine or surveillance coordinators, system engineering, material managers and several others. These were all people that had common process responsibility at the different sites and should share common use and interest and issues regarding the system.

As could be expected, some of the user groups excelled while some drifted and others failed. Our role was to be the catalyst to initially create the user groups, set up initial agendas, chair the initial meetings and set up an environment so that they would begin to stand on their own and resolve their own problems. In that case, some were capable of doing that while others were not.

I think a profile of a successful user group is one where the members actually own the process. For instance, in the surveillance and predefined areas it was the surveillance coordinators that made up the user group and attended the meetings. In the engineering area, which group never really got off the ground the attendee was just a member of tech staff and this rotated around several individuals. There was never any continuity established or specific definition of issues or opportunities. The user groups that had the best chance of success also had the authority to change their collective processes. We usually saw in successful user groups, the emergence of a natural leader. In some cases, several natural leaders. They had courage to take on issues to take over the agendas to begin to set goals and objectives. The successful user groups had mutually agreed on goals, objectives and schedules. These almost always came from the natural leader as we began to phase out our responsibility of kick starting the user groups. They also had shared experiences outside of the user group activities. For instance, and I will go back to one of the best user groups, our predefined surveillance user group, whenever we were doing a site visit for an assessment or an assist visit all of the members of the predefine user group would attend and participate and they would help look at the other site in terms of opportunities or good ideas or issues or concerns. They would share those experiences together outside just their user group activity. They also were recognized for their contribution. Senior managers would recognize a user group and point to them in terms of their achievements. Last of all, most of the members needed to have excellent system knowledge. If you are involved in a situation where you are setting up user groups as a mechanism to maximize your return on investment, these are some things you may want to keep in mind to try to create a situation where most of the elements of success are actually there.

We also tried to engage senior site process sponsors. Our thought was that if we could tie the senior person into the system and he or she could gain a knowledge of it and see some of the management opportunities that were there. Our hope was that this would begin to integrate the system into his business process. Generally, this effort failed. The reasons were that most of senior process sponsors had full agendas. To be successful in this required that the process sponsor actually would have to understand the system. Most of them did not have time to really understand the system. There was also a lack of strong functional managers. For instance, we may have a process sponsor in maintenance at one of our sites but there would be little agreement or interaction between him and his peer at another site. Strong functional managers could initiate that kind of interaction but in many cases our functional managers did not exist. Also, unfortunately, most of the initial difficulties with getting work done were caused by technical problems and that seemed to be the path of least resistance from most process sponsors. The system was blamed for many of the initial problems and that thought process just carried on through even as the system became more and more stable. Most of the latter issued really centered around process problems. For instance, there was an issue where some equipment was inadvertently taken out of service at one of our plants and the out of service module was pointed to as the blame for the system because it did not stop the operator from issuing the out of service tag that had some inconsistencies in it that he would have caught if he would had followed his procedure and crossed checked some drawings. It is a funny thing that you get to a point to where I think some expectations are that more sophisticated computer and information management systems can replace a thought process. They just can't. So there needs to be some realization of the systems limitations and the need for people to still wake up in the morning and put their head on straight when they go to work.

On the bright side, recently there has been numerous changes in management in the last six to nine months. The inconsistencies among the sites have been recognized as a real hindrance to economies of scale and strong functional managers are beginning to become appointed and brought into critical areas such as work control. This is very encouraging. Expectations are being set. The site process sponsors that are being pulled together by the functional managers are beginning to work past the system excuses and actually are starting to look at their work processes.

As I had stated earlier, many of our site administrators were blessed with solid system knowledge and knowledge of their plant operations but were politically and project-wise immature. The thought was to create a series of site liaisons to augment them. Someone from the support or project team was assigned a site to spend about 20% of their time at that site working with the system and site administrators developing improvement plans and establishing goals and objectives. They basically augmented the site coordinators in those areas where they did not have the political or business skill sets. In some cases, the liaison was well received. Particularly if that liaison had previously worked at that site. At other sites they were viewed as outsiders, corporate meddling in their affairs. Since the liaisons were not full-time positions, but rather project team members, they were doing general support and turn-on work. They were just being pulled in too many directions. The bottom line is the idea of the site liaisons was discontinued after six months.

Our fifth area of setting up mechanisms to obtain the ROI was to establish assessments, third party reviews and also create management reports. We decided to continue with our high profile site assessment and assist visits that had uncovered some of the initial issues. These were generally positive in the sense that there were entrances and exits with senior management. We had large teams between twenty to thirty people, most of which were from other sites collectively coming together in a team effort. An opportunity for common sharing and cross site sharing was created. We conducted a series of one hour skills workshops that were now included in the assessments and assist visits. They targeted on key things like navigating through the system, getting reports out and analyzing relationships among data. The one hour skills workshops were nice little shots that we could include in the assessments and help build the overall skill sets of the site. We also issued a formal report that was our mechanism for feedback to the site in terms of what we have served.

On the negative side, the assessment and assist visits were logistic nightmares trying to line up the site to be able to have individuals attend mini-workshops. Also, it was difficult to get the right people and senior management available at the same time for entrances and exits. Obviously, getting a team together from other sites was a challenge given the rotating outage schedules. Probably the last thing that was a problem was, unlike a quality assurance assessment, we did not request corrective action plans from the sites. We did not get into policing types of situation. Also, no corrective actions meant that there was not a documentable commitment about what the site was going to do to solve a problem. All in all, though the annual assessments and assist visits were useful and they are continuing to this date.

We also engaged a third party assessor to do an opportunity assessment. In particular, we contracted with a firm to take a look at similar processes in the engineering area. For instance, they looked at specific areas of a site that were getting ready to turn on the system versus a site that had been using a system for about a year and half, they pinpointed some opportunities where the site was going to turn-on the system and began to realize some productivity gains. This was a useful exercise. It would have been more useful if we would have done it earlier on and more often.

The last area was developing management reports. These centered around system feature utilization reports and process management reports, these are two very distinct items to measure. The utilization reports were produced on a monthly basis. They compared six sites to each other in areas of how the sites were using selected features within the EWCS system. For instance, we were measuring the percent of work request tasks that were generated from backgrounding. As the sites begin to use more of the power of the system they should begin to approach the 100% range in using backgrounded information. As you can see, we were up near the 80% range but there was about a 20% opportunity for us to improve over time. One of the sites in particular, Dresden had just turned on and you can see their increase in the use of the backgrounding feature during February and March with use flattening and then beginning to upswing through June. Budget cuts unfortunately resulted in staff that was supporting these reports being assigned to other areas of the company. Consequently, we can no longer support the generation of these kinds of comparative reports. This was unfortunate, because in the areas where we were beginning to measure some of the sites utilization of the system, the site coordinators and site management were beginning to take an active interest and begin to ask why they were only at 60% versus 80% versus someone else at 90%. This is a useful competition to create and was beginning to be affective however, financial constraints just ended up with us in a central group no longer being able to support this activity. The sites could not collectively get together and pick it up themselves.

We have also, over the past six months developed reports that measure process management. For instance, we developed a report dealing with the process target of having Out of service request routed to operating by the end of the fifth week in our work planning schedule. By establishing a meaningful performance measurement parameter that is a critical measure of the health of a specific process, you can engage in continual process improvement. It is important that the measure be accepted by the process owner, be somewhat tamper-proof and difficult to manipulate. It is also extremely important to create a culture where information such as this is used and accepted in a positive manner. What that means is that management does not use it to beat people up but rather uses it to help people excel!

In summary, our approach number three that was a coordinated hard hitting effort on many fronts to try to set up mechanisms to maximize the return on investment of this system fall into three categories. The winners: process focused training was ultimately a winner in spite of some limitations that I had noted. Computer based training was an absolute winner. Online help was a very good idea, very effective and growing. Data management is continuing to grow and helps users gain confidence in the system. Creating a central support team has been completed. The support team has the expertise and knowledge and recognition by all six sites. Leaving a support team in place and actually planning for it was a success. Finally, the emergence of strong functional process sponsors is beginning to have some benefits and with them come the management reports that allow them to understand what is going on at each of the sites so that they can begin to look at process improvement.

Some ideas with mixed results were system administration and the managers value handbook. The user groups I discussed, had some winners and some losers. Where there were winners they were tremendously successful. Third party assessments needed to be done more often and earlier on. Management reports were good ideas but could not gain support from the sites to sustain it. Assessment and assist visits was another mixed idea but the benefits seemed to outweigh the drawbacks.

The losers are the ideas that never quite got off the ground. Trusting in user support of ongoing training. I think we will be moving to a centralized training group. We could never quite engage the site sponsors. However, recently the functional process managers are supplanting the need to do this. The establishment of the liaison had only limited success.

## Conclusions

Measure early so you can compare later. Engage the process managers up-front. Plan for the project wind down as well as you plan for the project itself. Do assessments or assists visits. Whatever you want to call them, but get out there and find out what is going on in the trenches and write it down.

Set up mechanisms to compare, contrast and in some cases embarrass because it is effective. Plan to develop a management structure and tools for use when the system is completed so that the system can be self sustaining.

## Our Current Status

It has been four years since we turned the system on at the first site. It has been two years since we turned it on at our last site. We have achieved technical stability. Resolved almost all of the data issues. We are struggling with ongoing training. We have finally engaged senior managers in the process improvement process. We are definitely past "the system made me do it" excuse and focusing on process problems. We are beginning to tighten down with management reports.

We have not in any way gotten our full return on our investment, but we are headed in that direction. I believe that we are poised for a "soft landing" of this system. In all honesty, when this project took off and we were focused on installing the system at the six sites, a soft landing for us meant basically turning the system on. It was redefined by our senior management and a soft landing meant much more. It meant setting up the tools and the mechanisms, the organizations and the structures and the personnel that would allow us to maximize to return on our investment. Our initial mission had been changed much as the Apollo 13 mission had been changed to not completing a certain list of tasks and duties but rather like Apollo 13 focusing on the end. With Apollo 13, it was getting three astronauts back home safely, with software installation it was getting the return on our investment so that we could begin to move in the competitive age.

# The Life Cycle for a Large Software Database Application—A Pragmatic Approach

Harvey F. Hoffman, Canberra Industries, Inc.

## Introduction

Several authors have proposed project life cycle models (PMBOK 1996, Pressman 1982). This paper explores a variation of the software life cycle model that focuses on acquiring and deploying a large software database application. This software life cycle plan identifies five major phases for incorporating a large software database project into a facility's operations. The distinct phases that apply to nuclear utility companies and other industrial facilities include the following:

- Phase 1—Problem Identification
- Phase 2—Specification
- Phase 3—Acquisition
- Phase 4—Deployment
- Phase 5—Maintenance

The project manager (PM) assigned to carry this effort to fruition must plan on considering all these phases in an effort to gain support from the communities impacted by the application. Without obtaining the backing of the stakeholders including prospective in-house developers, users, software maintenance personnel, training and other service departments the likelihood of a timely and successful implementation diminishes.

The tasks and the project manager's role associated with each phase are reviewed. Case histories based on a Health Physics Information System database software application used by Nuclear power plants provides illustrative examples. Phases 3 and 4 provide the core of the discussion as we believe that most future major software efforts should involve procurements rather than internal design and development efforts.

## Phase 1—Problem Identification

Frequently, a manager discovers a database-related problem after someone throws up their hands and cries out for help in managing data or perhaps after a government regulatory agency cites a problem with the company's record keeping practices. Following several meetings, operational personnel frequently agree upon a baseline set of concerns and issues, which they convert into software requirements. Thus is born a preliminary specification. After ascertaining that the resolution of the problem would save the company more money than maintaining the status quo or that it corrects the inadequacies identified by the reviewing government agency, management assigns a project manager.

In the case of nuclear power plants, a need exists to maintain and provide vital records required for federal and state regulatory and procedure compliance. These records and controls may include personnel data, internal and external dose data, authorization to perform duties on specific radiation work permits (RWP), authorization to enter specific radiation controlled areas (RCA), scheduling for bioassay tests, training, creating radiation work permits, controlling equipment inventory, survey data, etc. Very often this information exists in several databases managed by different internal customers within the nuclear power plant. The MIS department frequently faces the task of consolidating this information and then placing it onto a modern platform containing a current operating system and database software application program. The health physics organization can then apply the controls and generate the reports required to meet regulatory requirements.

MIS must perform cost and technical analyses to understand the significance and depth of the problem. Before proceeding further, the company must understand the cost of doing business without any changes. This analysis must include any liabilities associated with governmental regulations and procedures. These preliminary calculations provide a budgetary funding estimate for the project investment. Recovering the investment in three to five years after installation represents a typical financial expectation. If the company cannot recoup its costs within that time period, then the plan's proponents should not anticipate any further corporate involvement.

In summary, Phase 1 concludes with the completion of an agreement on the technical and financial need for the application and management decision to go forward.

## Phase 2—Specification

Following the decision to pursue a solution, the stakeholders develop and agree on the system requirements. The output of this effort represents the corporate need or project specification. The project manager must exercise care to include all requirements identified by the corporate community. On the other hand, the PM must ensure that a single dominant stakeholder does not bias the requirement toward a particular internal or external vendor.

The community must arrive at agreement on fundamental usage. For example, single use or concurrent use by multiple individuals. Does the community prefer client/server architecture, where multiple PCs access data from a central server, or host-based, multiuser environment, where multiple people sign on directly to a multiuser host computer? Does the community demand a specific relational database application, or hardware platform, or operating system?

From a technical perspective, the stakeholders must gain insight into the quantity of data, rates, type, and information flow. Most everyone starts with a definition of the required personnel, demographic, and training data. The MIS department in collaboration with the in-house users also examine the interface requirements and the trending and graphics requirements.

The software specification should include the functional requirements needed to meet mandated local, state, regional, federal, and industry requirements. Corporate requirements will include internal record keeping needs, ability to use plant specific setup parameters, data verification methods, report generation (plant specific and governmental), permit creation and processing, special end of year procedures, Help menus, user menus, and default settings. The system should be modifiable to include site specific parameters to allow for future changes in plant design and operation procedures.

If required, the specification should include provisions for unique calculations or algorithms. In the case of nuclear power plants, these algorithms may incorporate features to meet calculations required by stringent NRC safety requirements. Consideration should be given to the need for platform and relational database independence. In a world with dynamic changes in software and hardware platforms, and uncertainties in small software company's continued viability, considerations should be given to the value of software and hardware independence.

Software and hardware equipment interfaces require examination. These interfaces include printers, barcode or magnetic code readers, and network protocol interfaces. Reader interfaces frequently requested by customers include the MGP Instruments models MG 91 and MG 101, Eberline, Alnor and Rados units. Common bioassay interfaces include data import from Abacos, thyroid, and urinalysis equipment. The count systems may require air sample import. Sites working with nuclear materials also frequently require thermoluminescent dosimeter (TLD), electronic dosimeter, and Personnel Access Data System (PADS) interfaces.

As anyone who has used a complex software application recognizes, good documentation is crucial to the maintenance and successful implementation of the application package. A definition of the supplied documentation should be part of the specification. A typical definition of the documentation may be found in IEEE 730 - 1989. The specification may include the requirements for the generation of a Software Quality Assurance Plan (SQAP), a Software Requirements Specification (SRS), Software Design Document (SDD), a Software Verification and Validation Test Plan (SVVP), and a Software Verification and Validation Report (SVVR). In addition to the IEEE specified documents, other useful material includes the software application user guide and training materials.

## Phase 3—Acquisition

The acquisition process requires identifying prospective vendors and/or developers (including internal departments), creating and submitting a bid package to industry, evaluating the responses, and awarding the contract. The bid package consists of the product specification, a statement of work including a top-level schedule, an equitable set of award criteria to assist in the evaluation of the proposal responses, applicable quality assurance standards, and terms and conditions.

### Make Versus Buy

With companies that have a large and aggressive MIS department, the make versus buy decision may rise. The project manager must organize the process leading to a decision on selecting the in-house developer or making an external purchase. The MIS department together with the user departments contribute to the available software trade study, evaluation, and decision.

This task requires control by a strong project manager. Frequently, MIS personnel are current or former programmers. Programmers enjoy challenges and programming. Often the MIS personnel will want to take on the task themselves. Before the project turns into a fait accompli, the project manager must help the participants create a fair evaluation matrix taking into account the true capabilities of the entire in-house staff and the corporate needs. An objective assessment of the true project cost and schedule should be the main determinant.

The reader may detect a note of bias in this analysis. This author is firmly in the camp that believes that you stay in the business you know best. A luncheonette will likely not venture into the dairy farm business just because it uses milk or cream. In the same way, I believe a nuclear power company should stay in the business it knows best and seriously question the idea of entering the software database arena.

In the effort to honestly and openly evaluate corporate capabilities, the project manager must make certain that he or she obtains satisfactory responses to the following questions:

- Does the department have enough people to dedicate to the development effort?
- Does the department have a sufficiently competent staff to engage in a major development effort?
- Is the MIS staff comfortable with the in-house software quality assurance requirements and can they apply these requirements to a development effort?
- Does the MIS department have expertise in the documentation of design and test requirements?
- Does the MIS department have a group that can be dedicated to maintaining the program after initial project completion?
- Does the training department have adequate staff to develop product documentation and other training material?

Project managers want the project to succeed—no matter who does it. Project managers have technical, budget, and schedule responsibilities. Many companies operate in a matrix environment, in which the project managers do not *own* the personnel. The project manager should impartially compare labor, material costs and schedule for internal development and external purchase for the following tasks (at a minimum):

- Specification Preparation,
- Specification Review,
- Software Development and Maintenance Tools,
- Product Documentation (e.g., Software Quality Assurance Plan, Software Requirements Specification, Software Design Document, Software Verification and Validation Plan, Software Verification and Validation Report, Software Performance Report, Software Modification Form, Software Configuration Management Plan, Users Manual, Training Manual),
- Commercial Relational Database Software,
- Database Application & Interface Software Development,
- Database Application & Interface Software Customization,
- Health Physics & Database Software Installation,
- Factory Acceptance Testing,
- Informal Site Testing,
- Formal Software Quality Assurance Testing,
- Data Migration,
- Training Course Development,
- Staff Training, and
- Ongoing Software Maintenance.

The last item, software maintenance, can easily be overlooked. Project managers realize the need for ongoing software maintenance following product installation. Invariably, program usage will identify unforeseen problems resulting in software corrections that must be incorporated into the application. Users will request software modifications to improve the application's ease of use. New internal procedures resulting from corporate or government changes will force program modifications. New federal regulations or interpretations of government rulings mandate changes. Finally, operating system updates, database version changes, language upgrades and platform obsolescence will require continuous application software maintenance. All of this requires a quality dedicated maintenance software team.

Difficulty arises in attempting to ascertain if the in-house costs and schedule are realistic and competitive. If the question persists, then pursue a comparison with independent software suppliers and developers. If the in-house MIS department competes head-on with external companies, eyebrows may be raised and companies will question the efficacy of making the bid investment. External companies may believe that the internal organization benefits from 'insider' knowledge and favoritism. Project or purchasing managers have been known to seek external bids for the sole purpose of providing competition for the in-house team. An objective assessment of the true project cost and implementation schedule should be the main selection determinants. The imposed processes, procedures, and documentation should be identical for both the internal and external bidders.

## Bid Package

The project manager should guide the preparation of a proposal bid package. Typically the package includes a specification, a statement of work that includes a schedule and payment schedule, award criteria, special instructions, and general corporate terms and conditions. A specification compliance matrix represents a major aid in evaluating competing responses and should be requested as part of the proposal instructions. The matrix requires each vendor to comment on each specification paragraph and confirm compliance or noncompliance with each paragraph.

As with any evaluation process the project manager should make certain to identify the decision criteria and their relative importance before the process begins. The project manager should also perform an industry survey to identify prospective vendors, so that qualified vendors receive the proposal bid package. Send the proposal package to qualified vendors with a realistic return due date to permit the vendors to prepare a complete and accurate response.

### Bid Evaluation

If the collective management decision moves a company to request outside vendors to submit quotes, then once again the evaluation process proceeds. As part of the process, contact existing application users and ask about their experience with the product, training and services that the vendor provided. Request a product demonstration from the competing vendors. Ascertain the difference between the features in the fielded product and the features proposed for your application. Understand the amount of customization suggested by the contractor and honestly evaluate the schedule impact of incorporating the new features into the baseline system. Frequently, nonstandard hardware and software interfaces are schedule drivers. Many nonstandard interfaces can only be thoroughly tested at the user's site that may require some dedicated test time.

Evaluate the specification compliance matrix. Be sure that other customer's experience with the product and the product demonstration are part of the evaluation criteria.

The software application price should not be the sole selection determinant. The full service company not only provides the software application, but also the training and service organization that can work with your staff during the crises. Frequently this company also provides annual product updates and an annual users group meeting wherein people can meet other product users and discuss common issues and concerns. Very often the software manufacturer will base product enhancements on the results of these meetings. Cost then enters the matrix. A possible distribution of the evaluation weighting factors follows:

| Evaluation Criteria | Percentage Weighting Factor |
|---|---|
| Compliance Matrix | 30 |
| Product Demonstration | 20 |
| Other User's Experiences | 10 |
| Management Team | 10 |
| Training & Service | 10 |
| Price | 20 |
| Total | 100 |

## Phase 4—Deployment

A database application software deployment involves the steps and timetable shown below:

- Selecting and obtaining the hardware platform: 4–8 weeks
- Modifying the baseline database application software with the unique customizations: 4–50 weeks
- Selecting, obtaining software licenses, and installing supporting application packages such as an operating system or relational database: 2 weeks
- Application software installation: 2–3 weeks
- Data migration: 4–8 weeks
- Training: 4 weeks
- Environment creation (test, training, production): 1 week
- Database tuning: 1 week
- Network Connection configuration: 1–2 weeks
- Interface testing: 1–6 weeks
- Preliminary system test: 3–8 weeks
- Site acceptance test: 1–8 weeks

This process typically requires from three to six calendar months assuming that unique customizations are not required and do not encounter any serious problems. The variability of the tasks depends on system complexity including the number and complexity of the interfaces, the number of clients in a system, the customizations required, and the thoroughness of the site testing. Data migration may require gathering the data residing in older systems, placing the data into ASCII based tables and writing scripts to transfer the data into the new system. Very often during this process, the site MIS personnel find data elements for which a location does not exist in the new software application. This requires a software customization, if the old data is required.

Most sites create a training and production environment. The training environment may use a fictitious database or a version of the production database. Some sites also create a test environment in which a variety of new product and performance tests can be tried without fear of ruining anything of importance. The test environment also represents an ideal area to evaluate new version releases and test logic changes.

The site acceptance test can be as simple as performing a subset of a standard SVVP or completing a thorough evaluation of every system feature and printing out all reports, and evaluating every screen. This effort could take several months.

## Phase 5—Maintenance

Managers sometimes overlook the cost of software maintenance. Project managers familiar with hardware products realize the need for ongoing maintenance following product installation. Software products require the same attention. Invariably, program usage will identify unforeseen problems resulting in software corrections that must be incorporated into the application. Users will request software modifications to improve application's ease of use. New internal procedures resulting from corporate or government changes will force program modifications. New federal regulations or interpretations of government rulings mandate changes. Finally, operating system updates, database version changes, and language upgrades will require continuous application software maintenance. All of this requires a dedicated maintenance team. The software house that provides the application should offer this ongoing support. Products developed by internal corporate MIS groups must recognize that the project continues long after product delivery.

Although engineers tune the database during the installation process, it requires ongoing effort. The following items should be performed periodically by MIS personnel:

1. Monitor Performance
   - Monitor File I/O
   - Monitor tables and Indices
   - Monitor space utilization
2. Database tuning
   - Distribute tablespaces among different disks based upon usage
   - Resize table and index storage parameters based upon statistics
   - Add/remove Indices for faster response to complex queries
   - Adjust System Parameters based on changing needs
3. Database maintenance
   - Defragment tablespaces
   - Cleanup temporary (unused) space
   - Archive unused data
   - Perform Backup and/or Recovery

## Summary

This paper offers project managers insights into the acquisition, installation and maintenance of large database software products based on experiential lessons within the nuclear power industry. As in most cases, project success is based on clearly defining the site's requirements, understanding the capabilities of the internal staff, keeping people informed, thoroughly evaluating existing fielded product solutions, and having reasonable expectations. A major aspect of the software life cycle for a large database product includes the requirement for product upgrades and other maintenance needs which some companies overlook.

### References


Pressman, Roger S. 1982. *Software Engineering: A Practitioner's Approach*. New York: McGraw Hill.

Project Management Institute. 1996. *A Guide to the Project Management Body of Knowledge* (PMBOK). Upper Darby, PA: Project Management Institute.

# There Are Only Three Answers

A. Richard Diederich, Eastern Project Services
Linda E. Cowan, PECO Energy

## Introduction

Many project managers operate in an environment where their project team members, customers and stakeholders are subject to conflicting demands. The matrix situation often arises in utilities, as well as in other large companies, particularly in organizations with a strong functional focus (e.g., sales, production, accounting).

In the current utility environment, developing changes to improve company competitiveness are often assigned to teams with a number of part-time players from these functional organizations. Often the part-time members don't have a clear picture of what their "home" organization expects them to do nor do they know how they are supposed to act in their dealings with teams.

When project managers ask for work or information from someone who in not their organizational line subordinate, there are only three functional answers. By making the use of these answers an accepted and widespread practice, organizations can increase their effectiveness by reducing the energy spent on ambiguous statements and misunderstandings.

## The Three Answers

Within this foggy matrix of teams, change, empowerment, and project managers, three answers emerge, representing all the possible functional responses to requests for work from anyone who is not an organizational supervisor. The completeness and power of the answers are usually accepted intuitively when they are first heard. They will also be placed in behavioral context later in the paper.

### Why Does It Work?

The three answers are effective because they match the behavior that would take place if an organization were well trained in developing empowered organizations and managing organizational change. By working within the framework of the three answers, team members reach the desirable, functional outcomes without extensive training.

The interaction is usually initiated by the project manager who asks such an employee for a work product. A typical request would start, "In order to complete part of this project, I need you to...." After some discussion, clarification and negotiation, the project manager should accept only one of the three answers.

## Answer 1

### I agree...and I'm comfortable committing to it

This positive response can be given when:

- The request has been made to the right organizational unit.
- The work can be done within known time and resource constraints.
- The recipient is empowered to balance priorities and resources in order to accomplish tasks like this.

The wording conveys three distinct messages.

1. "I agree..." The work to be done has been mutually agreed upon. Perhaps some negotiation has taken place, but the outcome is agreed to by both parties. There should be no surprises in what is produced.
2. "...comfortable..." The request is not a strain on the resources or time available. The work is clearly within the boundaries of things I am empowered to do.
3. "...committing..." This is not a vague statement of uncertain future actions. I am giving my word that it will be done.

## Answer 2

### It looks o.k. but I will check with my supervisor.

This answer conveys a positive response, but with some bounds on the commitment to the project. The reasons for reservation might include:

- Uncertainty about the organizational responsibility for tasks like this.
- Inability to commit sufficient resources to the project without higher organizational approvals.
- Concerns about funding or schedule.

Again, the specific wording conveys specific messages:

1. "It looks O.K...." implies agreement on what is to be done. The scope of the task is agreed to.
2. "...I will check..." The individual has accepted responsibility for the next step. A promise of a prompt response

to the PM is implied. As this response can be expected fairly frequently in changing organizations, PM's should assure that this responsibility split is maintained. Otherwise, the PM may get a significant burden of multiple meetings and phone calls to resolve this answer.

3. "...supervisor." The response will have the support of the next level in the organization.

## Answer 3

### I disagree, but it's o.k. for you to check with my supervisor

This answer carefully preserves the opportunity for continued organizational dialog, while clearly expressing disagreement. Less functional responses under the circumstances that lead to answer 3 often include curse words, hand gestures and loud voices. The answer is used when:

- The organizational responsibility for the work is clearly somewhere else.
- Line management channels have not informed the recipient of the request of the need for participation.
- Some cultural or interpersonal issue is interfering with a positive outcome.

Once again, the wording carries meaning.

1. "I disagree..." The reason for disagreement is not explicitly stated, but probably well understood by both parties as a result of the interactions which led to the answer.
2. "... it's O.K. for you..." The possibility of the issue needing more organizational clout to be resolved is accepted. The outcome is not anything personal, but the PM will have to raise it for resolution.
3. "...my supervisor." If anything is to be done, it will take someone else with a higher level of organizational authority to work it out.

## Context: Empowerment And Change

If a deeper understanding of the reasons for the effectiveness of the three answers in needed, it is best understood in the context of empowerment and change management.

### Employee Empowerment

The word "empowerment" implies that power that is owned or controlled by someone or some organization is given to a person who previously was powerless in this area. It is commonly used to describe circumstances where the management of an organization exerts less detailed control over the activities of its employees, thereby allowing the employees to have a larger impact on the effectiveness of their organizations.

As utilities have increasingly felt the pressure of competition and the corresponding need to reduce the cost of their products, reductions in management staffing levels have occurred and employees have become less constrained in what they can do. The increase in decision-making authority, however, is not frequently well defined. In a traditional utility organization, years of interaction taught employees corporate culture, decision styles and authority levels through experience and coaching. The new expectations of employee behavior are poorly defined and need to be learned rapidly as changes occur in the market and in the organization.

If employee behavior stays as it was in the traditional organization, many decisions will be routinely pushed to a manager. Similarly, the previous culture would support the manager accepting the upward delegation with the result being overworked managers and frustrated employees. If the situation were static, the employees would eventually figure out how to make decisions like the manager. But the situation in utilities today is far from static.

The best way to clarify the employees' degree of empowerment is to describe their roles in broad terms and let them do their work, accepting responsibility for tasks which are clearly okay, rejecting those that are clearly out of bounds, and checking with the management for those that are gray. Choosing among the three answers makes the employee define empowerment in just this way.

Empowerment has been defined at one utility as giving employees maximum freedom with boundaries being self-imposed by asking themselves (Topaz 1990):

- Would my supervisor approve?
- Would the Board of Directors approve?
- Would the ratepayers think this is okay?

The three answers build on this philosophy by adding the ability to commit to actions across organizational boundaries.

## Managing Organizational Change

Almost by definition, projects represent change. Their purpose is to create something that didn't exist before. In the case of organizational improvement initiatives, process changes and many information technology system implementations, the changes and impacts are significant.

The organizational change process involves several key roles (Connor 1988). One is that of the *sponsor*, the individual who controls the resources which are needed to make the change. In addition to resource responsibility, the sponsor provides clear direction and communicates the desired outcomes to the organization personnel. Sponsors are usually executives

**Exhibit 1.**

**Company name(s)**

The Three Answers:

1. I agree...and I'm comfortable committing to it.
2. It looks O.K., but I will check with my supervisor
3. I disagree, but it's O.K. for you to check with my supervisor.

*Wallet Cards, shown here approximately full size, were critical in the use of the three answers*

in a utility setting, but also may be customers or clients for a project.

In order to do the work necessary for the change to occur, a *change agent* is needed. Although the agent may not have the direct authority to cause the change to happen, the agent acts with the referred authority and support of the sponsor. Project managers are usually in the role of change agent.

The last role is that of *change target*, the individual(s) who are to change in order to accommodate the new circumstances or situation. The employees that a project manager needs to do project support tasks on a part-time basis are often also targets.

For the project manager of a process improvement initiative in a matrix context, the situation plays out like this: The PM has clear direction from the sponsor about what needs to be done. In order to accomplish this, tasks need to be worked on by targets who are supervised by a third person. The workers and the supervisor (also a target) are concerned about the outcome and not nearly as clear as the PM about what the sponsor is trying to achieve.

The three answers clarify these relationships in day-to-day interactions by providing a structure to interactions that reflects the sponsor-agent-target model of roles in a change environment.

Answer 1 ("I agree...") is well suited to clear situations. Answer 2 ("It looks O.K., but...supervisor") allows a target to gracefully check about whether the requested actions are sponsored within his or her organization. Answer 3 ("I disagree...") questions the sponsorship of the requested action, and allows the issue to be resolved by those who are organizationally closer to the sponsor.

## Implementing the Three Answers

The three answers were first identified during a period of rapid change in PECO Energy's Nuclear Group. The time was characterized by resolution of operating plant licensing problems, reengineering projects, new plant startups and implementation of project management (Tuman 1990). Eventually an executive wrote the answers on a scrap of paper and occasionally refer to them in meetings. There was little effect. The breakthrough came when a division manager had wallet cards printed with the three answers (Exhibit 1). The ability to refer to the cards for the appropriate wording made potential users more confident and the cards created the perception of widespread organizational support. Cards could be given to others during interactions, dispersed to team members as reminders and kept for personal reference. The first printing of one thousand cards was gone within a month.

Some examples of implementation follow:

### The Lone Ranger

Individual project managers were the first to adopt the three answers. Supported by the wallet cards, they worked to achieve their project objectives with individuals in a wide variety of organizations in the matrix environment. They derived power from the answers by giving wallet cards and starting interactions by saying, "I think that these are the only answers that are appropriate and I want us to reach one of them. Is there another answer that you want to add?" By obtaining up front agreement on the form of the answers, discussions were focused and conflict was limited.

### The Outsourcing Contractors

One of the organizational changes that took place was the outsourcing of construction work. Previously, contractor work within power plants was supervised by a utility employee or performed by utility personnel. There was concern about how the contractor engineering, planning and supervisory employees would successfully interact with power plant organizations. The situation was further complicated by having two major contractors at the site in competition for every project. The three answers provided the solution.

A large facilitated meeting was held with the contractors' supervisory personnel, the utility project management/construction management organization and management representatives of the power plant groups with construction interfaces. Introduced by the project management division manager, each contractor and plant organization manager indicated sponsorship of the new arrangement and the use of the three answers in dealings between organizations. As further indication of sponsorship, special wallet cards were printed, headed by the logos of the utility and both contractors. Every contractor supervisory employee left the meeting with a supply.

### The Financial Information Systems Projects

During this general timeframe, other PECO project teams were working to replace the computer based financial information systems that served the entire enterprise. After some false starts, clear sponsorship of the projects, a project organization, an implementation plan and a communication plan were established (Diederich 1995). Because of the widespread impacts of these systems, project personnel were frequently requesting information and task accomplishment from employees throughout the company. The three answers were specifically sponsored by the senior executives of the utility for use in interacting with employees in all organizations.

In addition to providing successful responses to requests by project personnel, the three answers also proved useful in dealing with requests for features or changes from system users. When discussions led to such requests, the project team members' responses were directed by the three answers. This reinforced the use of the answers and led to increased project change control.

## Summary

The three answers have proved to be very effective in helping teams work functionally in a highly matrixed utility environment. The use of wallet cards produces consistency and encourages the use of the answers in day-to-day interactions. Because little training is needed for implementation, even individual efforts can be successful, but higher level sponsorship will help make use of the answers widespread throughout the organization.

### References


Connor, Daryl R., and Jack A. Newman. 1988. "Managing a Successful Organizational Change." *Healthcare Financial Management.* (June): 62–68

Diederich, A. Richard. 1995. Communications for the Software Big Bang. *Proceedings of the Annual Seminars/Symposium.* Project Management Institute: Upper Darby, PA.

Topaz, Lionel. 1990. "Empowerment—Human Resource Management in the 90's." *NRECA Management Quarterly.* (Winter).

Tuman, John, Jr., and Drew B. Fetters. 1989. "Project Management—Agent for Change." *Proceedings of the Annual Seminars/Symposium.* Project Management Institute: Upper Darby, PA.

# Application of PMBOK Principles for RTDBE Project

Richard A. Donica, Newberg/Perini
Raymond Belair, ComEd

ComEd is the owner of the Braidwood Nuclear Power Station located approximately sixty miles southwest of Chicago, Ill. Each of the two units boasts 1175 megawatts electric output via their Westinghouse Pressurized Water Reactor Nuclear Steam Supply System. Monitoring of the nuclear reactor vessel inlet and outlet water temperatures was accomplished through a composite mechanical and electrical assemblage called the RTD Bypass System (RTDBS). A sample of the coolant water is diverted through one and two-inch schedule 160 stainless steel pipes from the reactor outlet (hot leg) and inlet (cold leg). The water sample is then brought into contact with temperature probes called RTDs (Resistance Temperature Detectors). The readings from these thermocouples are then routed to nuclear instrumentation and panels.

The RTDBS has historically posed problems for the plant. The high system pressure (2450 psi) and elevated temperatures (638( F) promote frequent component leakage. Virtually every refueling outage has included plans for repairing coolant leakage from one or more of the system components. This proved to be a constant burden to the plant's operation & maintenance budget. Further, the plant has strict limits on the amount of system leakage that can be tolerated and still remain operational. The RTDBS has been responsible for bringing generating units down for repair. Thus, not only O&M budget, but generation revenues were negatively impacted as well.

The system is also a significant contributor to the radiological dose in the area. The components tend to trap "crud" or insoluble metal residues that are highly radioactive. The RTDBS is traditionally considered to be one of the dose intensive systems in the plant and has resulted in an ever-increasing dose accumulation for plant staff and outage workers. At an estimated cost of $15,000 to $30,000 per REM (quantifiable radiological dose unit, Roentgen Equivalent Man), the system became even a greater burden on the station.

Although obvious why elimination of the RTDBS was desirable, the price tag required significant analysis before approval was forthcoming. The new system eliminates all of the piping assemblies and components. A more sensitive temperature detector is embedded in a thermowell that is placed in the direct coolant stream. Electrical cables carry the resultant signals to cards for processing. The new system effectively eliminates leaking and grossly reduces area dose.

System removal and replacement posed some interesting challenges. One involves the fact that this evolution has been accomplished at several other nuclear stations in the United States. A review of completed projects revealed that the accumulated dose to do the work was decreasing. The industry average for the job was approximately 100 REM per unit. The industry best four loop unit dose was 40.3 REM and dual unit value was 140 REM. The expectations for the work at the Braidwood Stations were to accomplish the work with much better than the industry average marks.

Schedule definition and compliance was essential. Each day the unit is offline represents a revenue loss of $300 to $700 thousand. Lengthening the outage to accommodate to RTD Bypass Elimination (RTDBE) work was not an option. The work would have to be done within the work window provided. The large number of personnel involved in the work, the small work area available and the required harmonious coexistence with many other ongoing activities in the area would complicate this timely completion of the work.

Budgetary compliance was expected. It was a measuring tool used by the utility as one means to determine project team and contractor performance adequacy. Therefore budget compliance was imperative.

## Scope Management

The work scope included the demolition of the existing system and replacement with a new electromechanical thermowell system. The project was budgeted for over four years. Approval to proceed from one life cycle stage to the next was sporadic and unpredictable. Lengthy postponement required a new manpower and dollar estimate that was elevated from the one previously submitted. The project was placed on hold pending new budget approval and preparatory work was tabled. Final authorization was received about five months before scheduled outage work start. The project charter was issued, by management external to the project, in a modification approval letter (MAL), which provided the work authorization and scope.

Benefit/cost analysis for implementing the mod was performed by a separate workgroup and is beyond the scope of this paper.

Major project deliverables included:

1. Demolition of electrical portion of existing RTDBS system,

2. Demolition of mechanical portion of existing RTDBS system,
3. Machining of 3" return stubs, 2" cold leg taps and 1" hot leg taps,
4. Welding of 3" caps and new thermowells,
5. Installation of new conduit, junction boxes, support, cables and splices,
6. Inspection and testing of installation,
7. Completion of required documentation, and
8. Disposal of the resultant scrap material.

Quantifiable project parameters for completing the work included:

| Objective | Metric |
|---|---|
| • Within defined budget | $2.5 million |
| • By a specified end date | No outage impact, ahead of schedule |
| • With minimal rework | No major weld repairs |
| • With no lost time accidents | Zero LTA |
| • Within established radiological dose goal | Bettering the 145 REM best with a 138 REM goal |

The scope was expected to be relatively stable, however much discussion resulted over issues regarding the installation of quick disconnects. The final decision to use the quick disconnects between the RTD pigtail and field cable was not in time for use in unit 1 but was implemented in the unit 2 outage.

A work breakdown structure was created through progressive decomposition of the overall work scope. The planning necessary to achieve the desired duration at the budgeted cost was a challenge. To fit within the defined work window for unit 2, 100% wrench time for the maximum crew size would be required, i.e., a crew needed to be actually working on the job twenty-four hours per day.

## Quality Management

Nuclear plants are notorious for detailed quality assurance programs and laborious inspections. Braidwood Station is no exception. Inspections and tests were planned to meet the program requirements and to provide the necessary assurance that the work would be acceptable when completed. The aggressive schedule did not allow for major rework events. There was adequate time in the schedule to do the job one time. Failure to do so, especially on work activities like welding the 3" stainless pipe caps, would cause the project duration to be exceeded. Considering a daily offline cost of $300,000 to $700,000, efforts to assure that things were done right the first time were deemed prudent expenditures.

Telephone interviews were conducted with representatives of other utilities who had completed the RTDBE. Past problems and successes were recorded and used in the formulation of the project plan. Quality critical issues were captured and risk analyzed to determine the appropriate level of response. One item was of particular concern. Some utilities had experienced weld failure on the schedule 160, 3" stainless pipe, to six thousand-pound cap. This failure was cited at multiple stations. Because of logistics, such a failure could not be detected until very late in the project; yet remedial actions would impact the completion of the project. It became evident that the project would only be successful if it was planned in detail, the plan implemented with a high level of efficiency and emergent challenges resolved with dispatch.

Team buy-in was necessary if the required synergism to achieve world class results were to be possible. Given that the cost of quality is justified by the end result, special steps to assure quality were implemented. A benchmarking trip to the Pacific Gas & Electric's Diablo Canyon Nuclear Station at San Luis Obispo, California was conducted. This one-week excursion had a major impact on the success of the project. PG&E personnel were very open as we watched them implement the RTDBE work on their second unit. They had earlier completed the unit 1 work and had incorporated their lessons learned items into the plan. The degree of planning, sound execution of the work and degree of understanding of the project by the workers was admirable. Being able to observe their implementation established a strong baseline for the Braidwood work.

A key aspect of the Diablo preparation that was significantly amplified at Braidwood was the use of mockups. This was viewed as a mechanism to achieve several objectives:

1. Detect potential problems,
2. Establish mitigating contingencies,
3. Establish and perfect new work methods,
4. Train implementing craft in work execution,
5. Enhance the degree of efficiency of implementation,
6. Practice potential quality problem activities to reduce failure risk, and
7. Enlighten team members in the overall tasks at hand.

Training needs were identified and differentiated into three major areas:

1. High radiation exposure work evolutions,
2. High duration evolutions that could be mitigated with training, and
3. Industry specialized skill shortcoming anticipated due to the high number of nonlocal craftspersons.

Training predominantly took the form of mockups and ad hoc work discussion sessions. A large site warehouse was secured and dedicated to the training of RTDBE workers. Mockups included the following:

1. Machining of the 27.5" to 29" pipe nozzles,
2. Welding of the schedule 160 stainless steel 3" pipe to six thousand-pound class stainless steel cap fitting,

3. Welding of the sacrificial mandrels to the 1" pipe stubs (for subsequent machining operations),
4. Cut off of the existing piping (using portable band and reciprocating saws) while maintaining foreign material exclusion,
5. Transporting high radiation and contaminated piping components (some in excess of 450 pounds),
6. Storing high radiation and contaminated piping (some in excess of 30 REM),
7. Application and removal of specially designed lead shielding,
8. Insertion of thermowells into pipe bosses,
9. Insertion of the RTDs into thermowells,
10. Field to pigtail cable splicing,
11. Penetration to field cable splicing, and
12. Portable band saw blade change (safety and contamination control).

The applicable quality standards were defined. Quality Control personnel were trained on the mockup, and NDE techniques were formalized. Benefit/cost analysis focused on the cost of rework, both from a man-hour and man-rem expenditure as well as the impact of delaying the return-to-service date of the unit. Process flowcharts were created and posted to aid in the presentation of the work sequence logic to the team. Overview and audit was conducted by ComEd Quality Verification personnel with accolades and no adverse findings noted.

Final outage quality results were extremely favorable. The welds, which offered a real potential for duration extension, passed inspection on the first try. Only a very few minor repairs/reworks were necessary.

## Time Management

Time management is of critical importance by the vary nature of an outage. Thousands of activities must be scheduled and implemented to return the unit online. Costs for one of the 1175 MW units being offline vary from $300K to $700K per day. It is therefore essential that each job is completed as scheduled, but also that impact to other jobs is minimized.

Our work breakdown structure was created based on decomposition of the defined work scope. Historical information and fragnets were gleaned from past related projects. The activity list with supporting detail, once baselined, was continually updated, as new data became available. The product description, based on the ComEd costing hierarchy, was initially broken into construction and demolition. Mandatory dependencies were established and then overlaid with discretionary dependencies that resulted from the output of other major sections including risk, cost, etc. External dependencies established the basic time windows that the work had to be completed in. There were several windows of opportunity, some more critical than others. These included the following:

1. Independent pre-outage (no external milestone commitments),
2. Dependent pre-outage,
3. Pre-OOS outage,
4. Outage breach, and
5. Post breach pre-startup

Initially, Primavera's Finest Hour( was used to create the network. A precedence diagram network was created for the project. Many of the stakeholders were interested in reviewing the fragnet and asked that it be transmitted via e-mail. Since this is was not the official ComEd PC-based software for work planning, the stakeholders could not view the file. Thus our fragnet was shifted to Microsoft Project(. This program functioned adequately for the level 1 and 2 scheduling activities.

The project was scheduled in detail to assure the proper coordination and interface of the multiple crafts and departments involved. The extremely limited work area necessitated a choreographed work sequence. As the outage neared, it became necessary to decide whether to enter the entire fragnet for the work into the station's mainframe-based P2( outage schedule or enter a single windowed activity to placehold the project in the overall outage framework. It was decided to break precedence and enter the entire project network diagram into the station outage schedule to allow bilateral interaction between the project fragnet and the station milestones. Failure to make these logical ties would not allow the project and the remainder of the outage to interact. Implementation of the nineteen-foot long schedule was actually rather easy, similar to a conductor directing the tempo and nuances of a new symphony.

Nonlocal craftspersons do not typically arrive well versed in the skills necessary for nuclear plant work. This had to be factored into the project. We upgraded skills using training and mockup activities. Because of this offsetting strategy, efficiency reductions were not factored into the work schedule.

Various work calendars were created. Resource leveling heuristics were employed to reach the best level of personnel. Due to the limited time windows and reduced crew size mandated by workspace limitations, the wrench time of the workers in the containment had to be maximized. Work in the containment results in significant inefficiencies due to access/egress, dress-out and undressing in anticontamination garments and the difficulty experienced through radiation protection imposed controls. Final work hours resulted in the use of four independent twelve-hour shifts. The shifts started at 6:00 A.M., 8:00 A.M., 6:00 P.M., and 8:00 P.M. This achieved continuous wrench time by using hands-on turnover.

Performance measurement and reports were made. Lessons learned were solicited by all outgoing craft from both unit evolutions resulting in the successful implementation of over seventy-five new innovations. The work met and exceeded the established schedule in that the work was completed ahead of schedule and in total support of the outage.

## Cost Management

Based on the WBS, man-hour estimates were made for each activity. A beginning level of resources was applied and the duration of the various work windows calculated. Manpower was then adjusted to allow the work to be accomplished within the confines of the allowed work window. The obvious desired project length was Just-In-Time when compared with the remainder of the outage. Duration compression techniques were used to fit the work in the windows via crashing and fast tracking.

Cost and man-hour estimates were created based on the work breakdown structure and duration/resource planning applied based on historical data relevant to the Braidwood station. The man-hours were multiplied by the established rate to determine overall labor cost estimates.

The man-hours expended were tracked by established cost code items. The cost codes were selected to allow in process and post completion evaluation of the performance efficiency and estimate accuracy of the project. The final analysis of cost data revealed labor expenditures to be under the estimate by approximately one percent.

## Risk Management

Many contingencies were considered based upon a hypothetical set of conditions at the plant. It was necessary to address only those contingencies whose probability and degree of impact warranted consideration. Based upon the premise of "earned monetary value," the probability of a risk item occurring was multiplied by the estimated impact value of the event. Several of these events were addressed by the use of mockups. Allowing the craft to perform the tasks at our mockup facility until an acceptable level of competency was demonstrated mitigated high-risk evolutions and activities highly dependent on craft capability.

Some of the identified major risks and implications included:

1. Failure to complete the job on time resulting in startup delay,
2. Exceeding the appropriated budget,
3. Injuries resulting in lost time and monetary loss,
4. Radiation exposure in excess of established limits,
5. Collateral damage to plant systems, and
6. Failure of the work during the final testing phase.

Since proven technology has less risk than innovations, whenever possible new ideas were mockup tested to determine and resolve potential problems prior to implementation. New innovation, as a rule, turned out to be worth the effort and resulted in reduced dose and time. The project stakeholders were interviewed to compile their perceived risks. Sources of risk included change in requirements (quick disconnects), inaccurate estimates, lack of skilled labor, lack of craftspersons, etc.

## Human Resource Management

Staffing requirements were calculated as a function of work timing, required simultaneous evolutions and the number of personnel that could work in the area at one time. Staffing constraints existed at several levels including:

1. Increased number of nonlocal craftspersons due to the proliferation of other work in the area,
2. Limited physical work area preventing introduction of large quantities of personnel,
3. Required wrench time to meet established time windows, and
4. Anticipated time loss for containment work inefficiencies.

The organization was predominantly a strong matrix with station support members constituting the weak matrix organization. Strong matrix core organizations included the contractor, the owner's construction department, radiation protection, ALARA, work control, quality control and the pipe-machining contractor.

The craft were building trade unions signatory to PHMMA/IA with the exception of Pipefitters, which operate under a local agreement. There is a strong separation of function along the jurisdictional boundaries established at the site. Role and responsibility assignments were defined and assigned before the outage by position, and later by individual when assigned to the project. A staffing management plan was established to control who was added to or removed from the project and when. Personnel were added as late and released as soon as possible to mitigate costs. The key supervisory personnel were brought on board thirty days before the start of the outage both to familiarize them with the upcoming work and to detail the work activities by incorporating the work experience of these team members.

The various crafts participated in the mockup training in such quantities as to provide adequate back up should some personnel not be available due to attrition or other reasons. This also provided a reasonable contingency should personnel receive their maximum allowable dose before work completion. A "team" mindset was essential to achieve the synergy necessary to complete the project in world class fashion. A major attempt was made to educate the team in the overall project requirement and how their particular operations tied into the overall goal.

Extensive discussions with the work groups were held to establish a strong understanding of each group's part in the overall project. Further meetings were held in conjunction with the mockup training to review and discuss the specific tasks of each group. These discussions were predicated on the premise that most personnel will try their best to provide the services requested when they understand exactly what is required.

Personnel were instructed in the expectation for each evolution. The team responded as anticipated and desired. There was a strong sense of ownership shared among the team. The level of cooperation between the subset groups was exemplary. This commonality among the team was a major contributor to the success of the operation.

Team reward and recognition included constant monitoring of our progress against the industry's previous RTDBE projects. The team adopted mindset of beating the industry's best-kept interest high and energies focused to do the best possible job for each facet of the project. Final recognition for the unit one job accomplishments was the distribution of a "ball cap" touting the world class status of the RTDBE effort. The cap became a desired commodity, still worn by various craftspersons many months later.

Based on past experiences at Braidwood and our observations at Diablo Canyon, a war room format was implemented. The second floor of an adjacent field office building was utilized. Craft and supervision briefings were held in this room in addition to required meetings. Personnel assigned to the project from the radiation protection work planning and ALARA departments, along with the pipe-machining contractor, were housed in a common office area. A video monitor of the containment operations was housed in this office for work monitoring. Maintaining the key personnel in a common area to resolve occurring problems was extremely efficient. It helped maintain continuity of the work and maintain schedule.

The team achieved its defined goals and maintained a strong interest in the overall project. The only consequential shortcoming involved the craft union's staggered filling of our request for craftspersons. Because the calls were not filled as requested, training and mockup completion were not accomplished as efficiently as desired. Overall, the efforts of the workers were excellent.

## Contract/Procurement Management

ComEd procured the RTDs and thermowells from Weed Instrument. Contracts for the disposal of radioactive scrap items and piping machining were awarded to Alaron and PCI respectively. Delivery of some items were "Just In Time," although not necessarily by design. Material and service procurement documents were created and submitted with a date required indicated. These lead times were calculated to allow procurement. Upon receipt, palletization, inspection and verification of adequacy would be accomplished before the start of work. Without prior discussion or authorization, purchasing representatives reassigned delivery dates based upon the published work start dates. This was unacceptable. The modified dates were not communicated to the ordering organization and the work start date used did not reflect pre-outage evolutions. Once discovered, great effort was necessary to expedite delivery of items.

Although providing countless hours of concern, all necessary items and services were purchased and delivered on time and in support of the outage.

## Communications Management

Communication was one of the most important components of the project. During the planning and pre-outage stages, open weekly meetings were conducted to facilitate information transfer. Meeting notification, meeting minutes and relevant document distribution was accomplished using e-mail and predefined distribution lists. Information transmittal to the approximately fifty stakeholders was quick and easy.

During the work, each twelve-hour shift began with a general briefing. This was conducted jointly by project management, craft supervision and radiation protection personnel. The workers were informed of the work completed during the last twelve hours, problems or conditions observed, expected evolutions planned for the next twelve hours and any other relevant information. The work crews would break out afterwards and the foremen would conduct job specific briefings to assure that each worker was informed of his or her part in the shift's evolutions. At mid-shift a mini-briefing update was conducted to make any required mid-course adjustments.

formation passed between the RTDBE team and the station work controllers.

Formal acceptance by the client was conducted as a three-part process. Initially, the work packages were reviewed to assure that the work was complete, adequately documented and in compliance with specified regulations, standards and procedures. Next, a joint modification walkdown was conducted to visually assure the work to be in compliance with the established requirements. Finally, detailed testing was implemented to assure the expected functionality of the new system. When all items were satisfied, formal acceptance was granted.

Lessons learned items were captured throughout the outage. A debriefing was conducted with all participating craft to gather perceived problems and recommendations for improvement. The process was well received by the workers and a great volume of suggestions was received. Over one hundred valid items were selected as being potential improvement items, of which seventy-five were implemented for the unit 2 work.

## Summary

The RTDBE project was a great challenge and offered opportunities for implementation of many of the PMBOK principles. The team members met success on all fronts, a result of sound project management principles and dedication.

Scope was defined up front, maintained and controlled. Quality was achieved consistent with the needs of the project and supportive of the established work schedule. The project was completed on time without adversely impacting the outage. The project was completed within budget. Risks were assessed, quantified and adequately mitigated to assure that outage goals were met. Human resources were calculated, procured and allocated to accomplish the work. The team achieved a synergism that involved each player and made each individual an integral part of the project. Required materials and services were obtained as needed. Communications were maintained at a heightened level and players knew where they and each faction stood with regard to project status. Each essential facet of the defined PMBOK was addressed and acceptable results were obtained. Sound project management principles contributed to for the successes of this project.

### References

Project Management Institute. 1996. *A Guide to the Project Management Body of Knowledge*, Project Management Institute: Upper Darby, PA.

# What is Project Management?

Noel Hutson, PMP

In global business organizations, there are three disciplines that interact, namely, general management, project management and technical management. As children we learnt to ride tricycles, and as teenagers we learnt to ride bicycles and as adults we perhaps have learnt to ride the unicycle. And so in modern business organizations, and at the present stage of our evolutionary growth, we need the tricycle of general, project and technical management for balance. This, I presume, is the reason for the growing and increasing global interest in project management, as an emerging new management skill, in our modern world of business organizations. With that as a framework for the future of project management, let us try to simplify and discover, What is meant by project management, in modern business language.

## Project Management

### *A General Purpose Tool*

Project management is not limited to space technology, utilities, engineering, or research. Project management is a general purpose management tool, that can bring projects to successful completion and to the satisfaction of the project stakeholders, given the traditional constraints, of defined scope, desired quality, budgeted cost, and a schedule deadline. Hence, project management is applicable to any organization with the core objectives of scope, quality, schedule and cost. A limited list of organizations using project management are, space technology, utilities such as power, gas, telephone, etc., banks, manufacturing, construction, research, pharmaceutical, etc.

### *An Art*

Project management is a system of principles and methods employed in the performance of a set of activities. Highly motivated project managers have a passion of excellence and these triumphant successes are often celebrated by recognizing the project team for a job well done. After the constraints of scope, cost, schedule and customer satisfaction are met, it is the quality of goods and services that separates one organization from the competitors.

### *A Process*

A process may be defined as a prescribed as a series of actions that bring about an end result. Project management as a process is a system of disciplined, organized activities that result in an outcome of finished goods and services, for the betterment of human welfare.

### *A Philosophy*

Project management is a way of seeing, a viewpoint, and perspective of getting things done. It is a system of motivating concepts and principles, that brings order, vision and clarity to an organization, by aiming people, material and energy, in the same direction of convergence. Due to the project manager's belief in the global philosophy of project management, he or she is able to cohesive the project individuals into a highly motivated project team, towards project success.

### *A Science*

The increasing global interest in the theory and practice of project management is moving project management from a process, a philosophy and an art to a science. The experimental knowledge of global projects has been verified by actual experience which is promoting project management to a science. The qualitative and quantitative belief in project management is gradually migrating project management to experience proven scientific methods, in the integration of energy, systems and interconnection.

### *A step to upper management*

Traditionally function or line management and technical management have been career ladders to upper management. With the demonstrated skills of people leadership and a track record of steady stream of successful projects and customer satisfaction, project management is providing project managers and their career paths, a special step to upper management.

### *Viable Projects*

A good project manager constantly manages the core objectives of scope, quality, schedule and cost management, and the facilitating objectives of contracts, risk, communications and human resources management. This prevents the project manager from unknowingly managing dead-end projects. Dead-end projects are projects that have not been adequately planned, projects that do not have authorized funds, projects that have not been for screened for risk, environmental and regulatory restrictions and other conflicts that can halt the project. A viable project is a project in which the project manager has reasonably done his or her preliminary research on all aspects of the project, before accepting responsibility to lead the project team, from beginning to end, and smoothly sailing to project success.

### *Over-laps with General and Technical Management*

Project management overlaps and interacts with general management and technical management. That is why project managers should take an interest in general management and technical management relative to their organizations. Conversely, general management and technical management should take a general interest in project management

### *Single Person Authority, Responsibility and Accountability*

Just as the conductor of a symphonic orchestra is the sole person who directs his or her many musicians through the movements of the composers symphony, and to the satisfaction of the musical tastes of his audience, so the project manager is the single person authorized to be responsible and accountable for leading his project team through the concept, development, execution and finish stages of the project, and to the satisfaction of the project stakeholders.

### *Communications*

You cannot have synergy without good communications. Communications is the glue that holds people together. To have a super project team we need a super glue, and that super glue of super communications, is aiming our antennas at the same satellite, for clear two-way communications. And successful communications is the art of acting and accepting, together.

### *Teamwork*

Great project success has been accomplished only through teamwork. The power of team work may be obvious, in projects as a space shuttle mission and conquering Mt. Everest, where some impossible goals were realized under very difficult conditions. However, during ordinary projects, where there is motivation and teamwork, project goals are realized with the synergy of teamwork.

### *General Technological Management*

Besides being a people specialist, a good project manager is a generalist in the various technologies of their organization, relative to the projects being managed.

### *People Leadership*

A good technical manager does not automatically become a good project manager. Project management is primarily people leadership. A good project manager knows that people are not managed, but led. Leaders to the right thing right the first time, while managers do things right. An outstanding project manager is a practitioner of people skills such as leadership, motivation, teamwork, communications, and conflict management. An outstanding project manager knows that the difference between being a referee, an umpire, leading with a stick or brute force management and being a coach, leading with a carrot or leading by example with a purpose. A good project manager is an outstanding people person that has a highly motivating influence on their followers' behavior and performance.

### *Transformation of Matter Into Spirit*

Human research into the properties of the world of matter reveal that matter is plurality, energy and system in the analytical direction and unity, quantum and totum in the synthetic direction and that the ultimate human purpose is to transform matter into spirit, by rising upwards together as a species, and thus converting matter into spirit.

## Summary

In summary, modern project management is the third element of organizational management systems that is bringing balance, harmony and success in global organizations. As the world changes, so will project management, as we become more and more clear of the power of project management, along with general management and technical management, in bringing increase to human welfare and the fantastic future awaiting humanity.

# Assigning Priorities That Work

George Wilson, PMP, ComEd

## Introduction

Inevitable! Such are the forces and consequences at the dawning of the next century. The new millennium is rushing toward us and we are incapable of avoiding or evading it. This paper will explore various common practices for assigning priorities to projects. The author suggests a new slant on this difficult task that results in a very defensible assignment of priorities and resources to projects in any organization. Utility companies must adopt such an approach in order to forge a competitive advantage in the deregulated environment of the next century.

## Priority First?

Priority only applies after a decision has been made to attempt a project. This decision should be based in some screening mechanism aligned with the corporate strategy and goals. We can find examples of every conceivable reason for attempting a project. The ABC project was the boss's idea, or implements the latest technology, or should result in increased efficiencies, or is expected to reduce operating or production costs. These all can be valid justifications. However, faced with limited resources, which project has the highest priority? We will explore the issue of priority in a moment. First, we must consider the decision to attempt a project.

Most utilities mix these two steps and have difficulty distinguishing between priority, financial criteria, regulatory criteria, strategic importance or other factors that may be included in their project initiation process. I was able to document three different processes in use at ComEd (Chicago). Multiple project initiation processes may be appropriate depending on the nature of the work involved. The problem is that most companies do not implement such processes consistently because there is no separation of the factors used for determining priority from those used in deciding to attempt the project. Sometimes a project is assigned a high priority, which is then used to justify it's continued existence, even though other minimum criteria are not satisfied. This problem can be avoided if the decision to proceed and the assignment

**Exhibit 1.** Customer Project Management

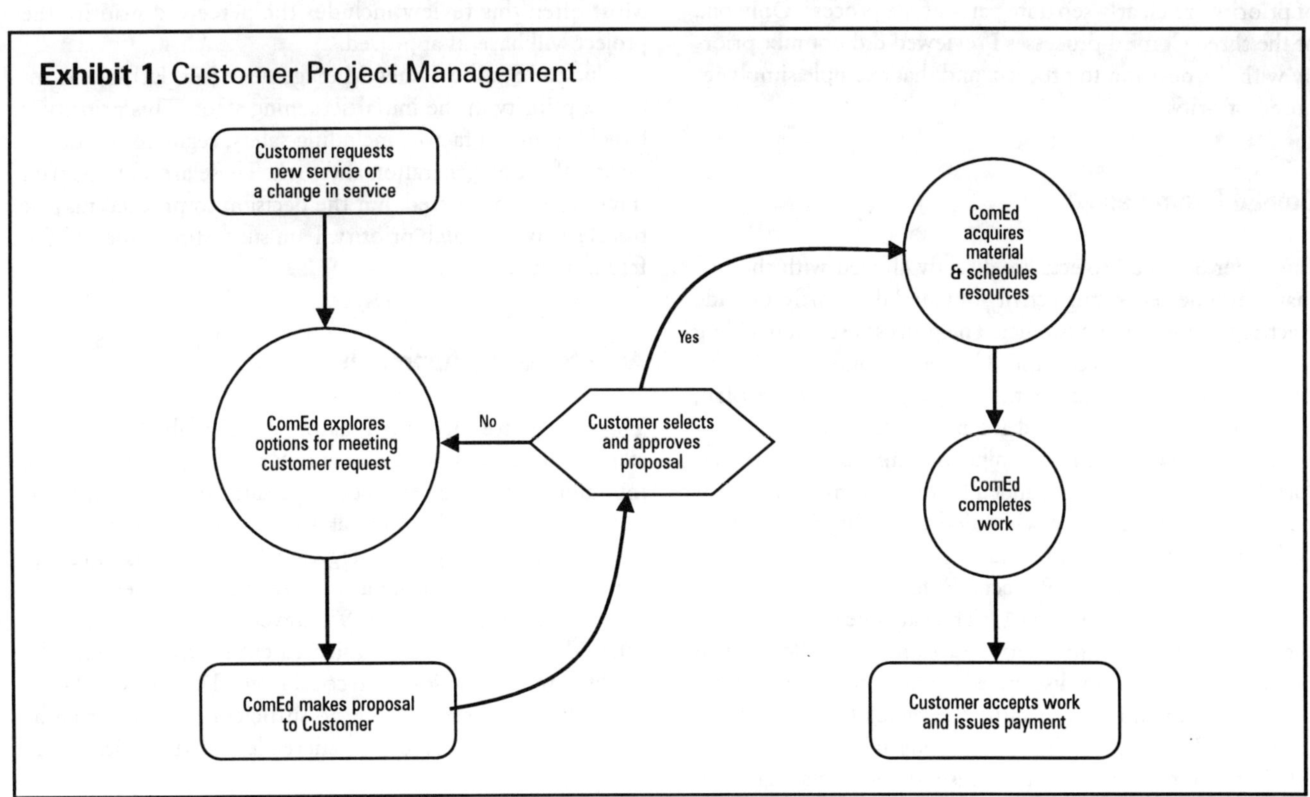

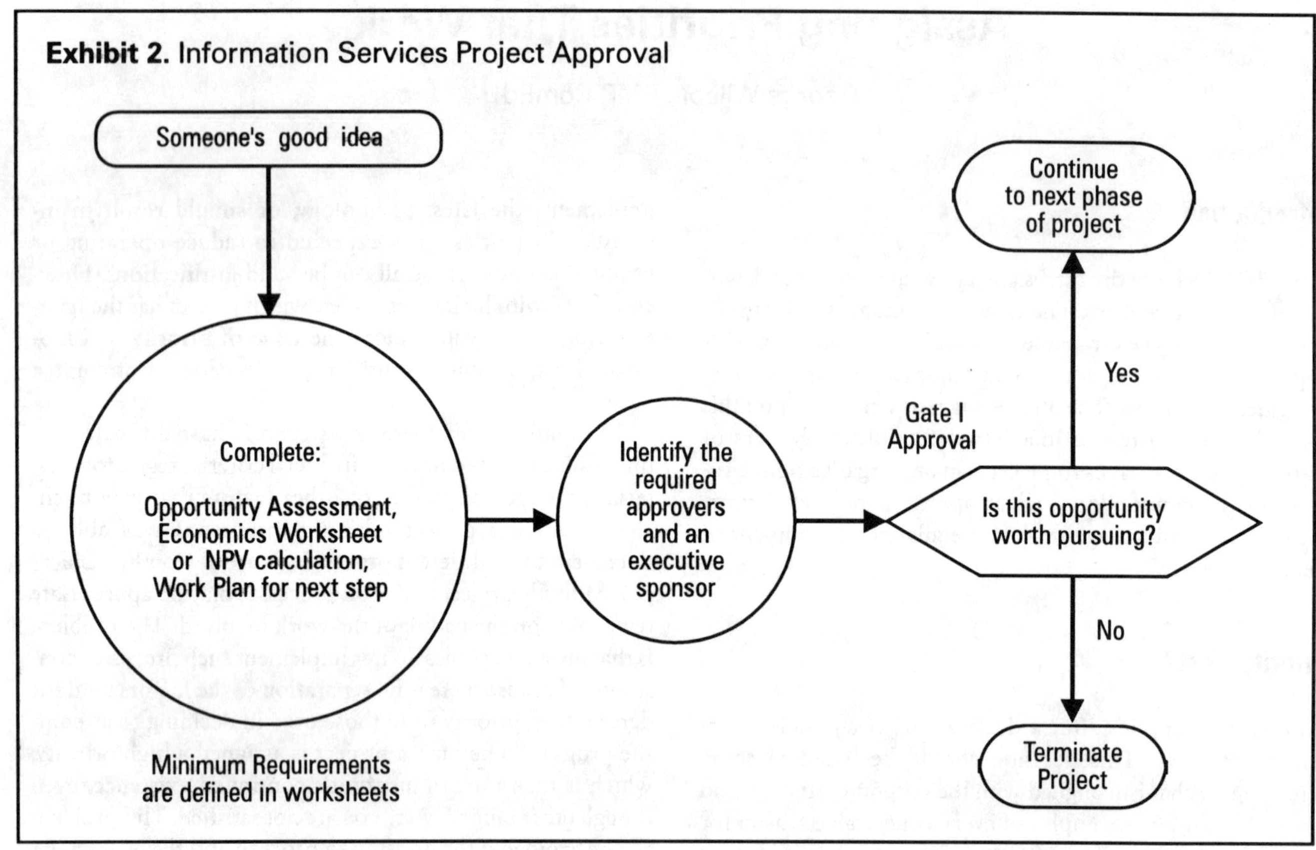
Exhibit 2. Information Services Project Approval
Someone's good idea
Complete:
Opportunity Assessment, Economics Worksheet or NPV calculation, Work Plan for next step
Minimum Requirements are defined in worksheets
Identify the required approvers and an executive sponsor
Gate I Approval
Is this opportunity worth pursuing?
Yes
Continue to next phase of project
No
Terminate Project

of priority are clearly separate parts of the process. Only one of the three ComEd processes I reviewed did not mix priority with the decision to proceed, and that example simply ignored priority.

## ComEd Examples

Customer Service Projects are directly aligned with the primary revenue generating activity of ComEd. Namely, provide electric service to the customer. The process used in deciding to attempt a project is controlled by the customer (see Exhibit 1). The customer requests the project, approves the plan, agrees to fund the effort, and accepts the deliverable. ComEd provides the expertise in planning and implementing the effort. Since all projects are funded by the customer, priority is not an issue. Projects are scheduled according to the availability of resources and materials.

Information Services Projects (Exhibit 2) must survive a gate process called "Method 1." The gate one criteria is simple. Is this opportunity worth pursuing? This decision is based on information discovered while completing several work sheets intended to quantify the value of the project deliverables. This decision is actually made at a review meeting where proponents present their case to senior management. Most often this review includes the perceived priority the project will have, if approved.

Nuclear Station Issues Management (see Exhibit 3) includes priority in the initial screening steps. This priority is based on several factors including safety, regulatory requirements, affect on generation and such. These are all important things to be considered, but the decision to proceed may be based solely on a high priority. I am suggesting a slightly different model.

## An Alternative Approach

This alternative model is illustrated in Exhibit 4. The first step should always be to do enough research to determine if minimum threshold criteria can be satisfied. What criteria? Each organization should establish a set of minimum criteria that are tied directly to strategic goals. If a goal is to reduce costs, a criteria might be a one year pay-back period, or a positive Net Present Value. Whatever threshold criteria are established must be communicated clearly to everyone who might have a good idea to be considered. This threshold must be applied consistently, and be sufficient to ensure that all qualifying projects can be considered legitimate projects to be completed.

**Exhibit 3.** Nuclear Station Issues Management

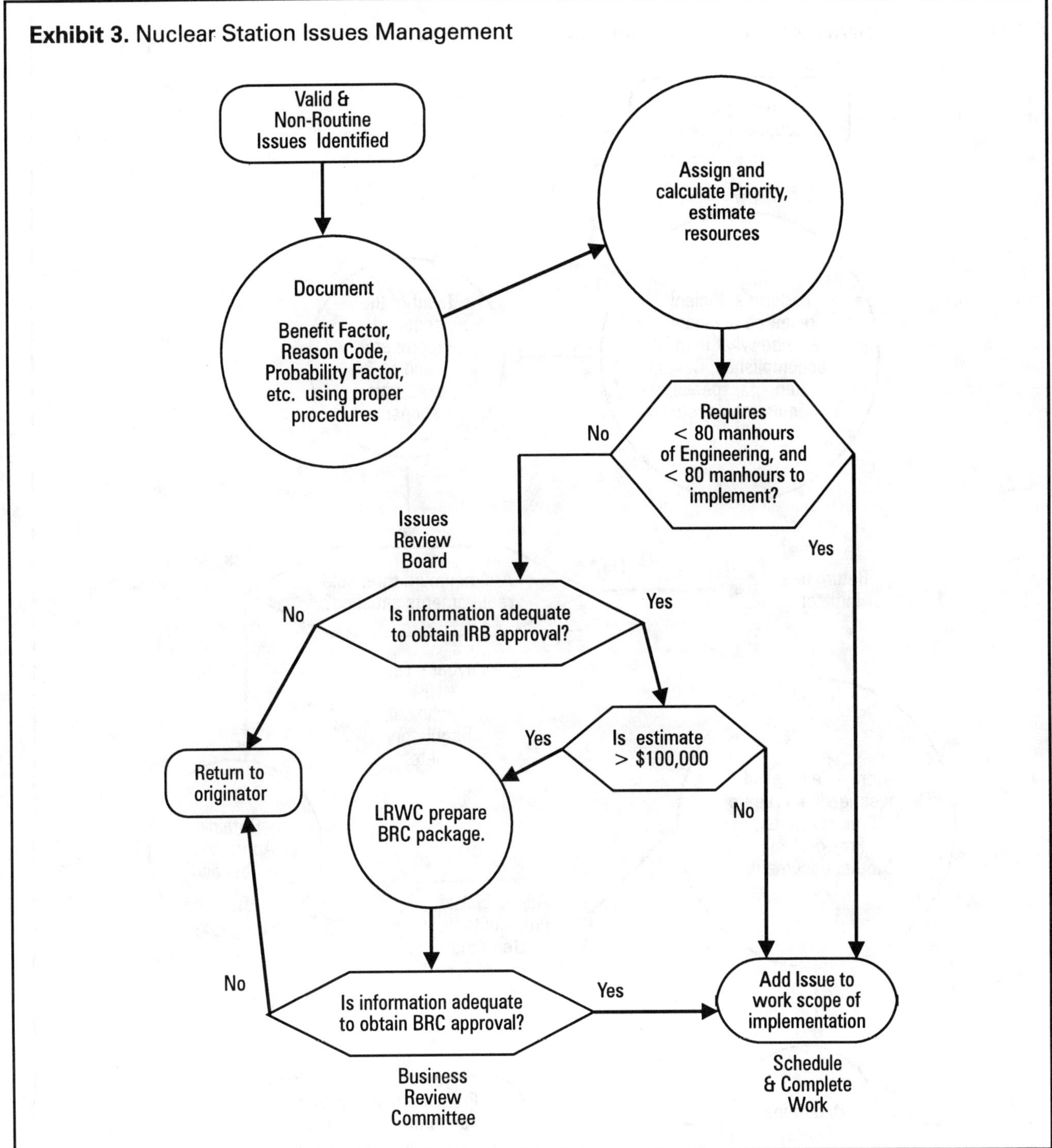


## Now—Priority!

All projects on the table to be completed compete for the same resources. The following set of priorities may be applied to projects in any organization.

A. Required for continued operation.

- lRequired immediately (twenty-four hours to one week),
- Required within ninety days,
- Required within one year, and
- Required date more than one year out.

B. Will provide a direct increase in net income.

**Exhibit 4.** Alternative Model for Project Initiation

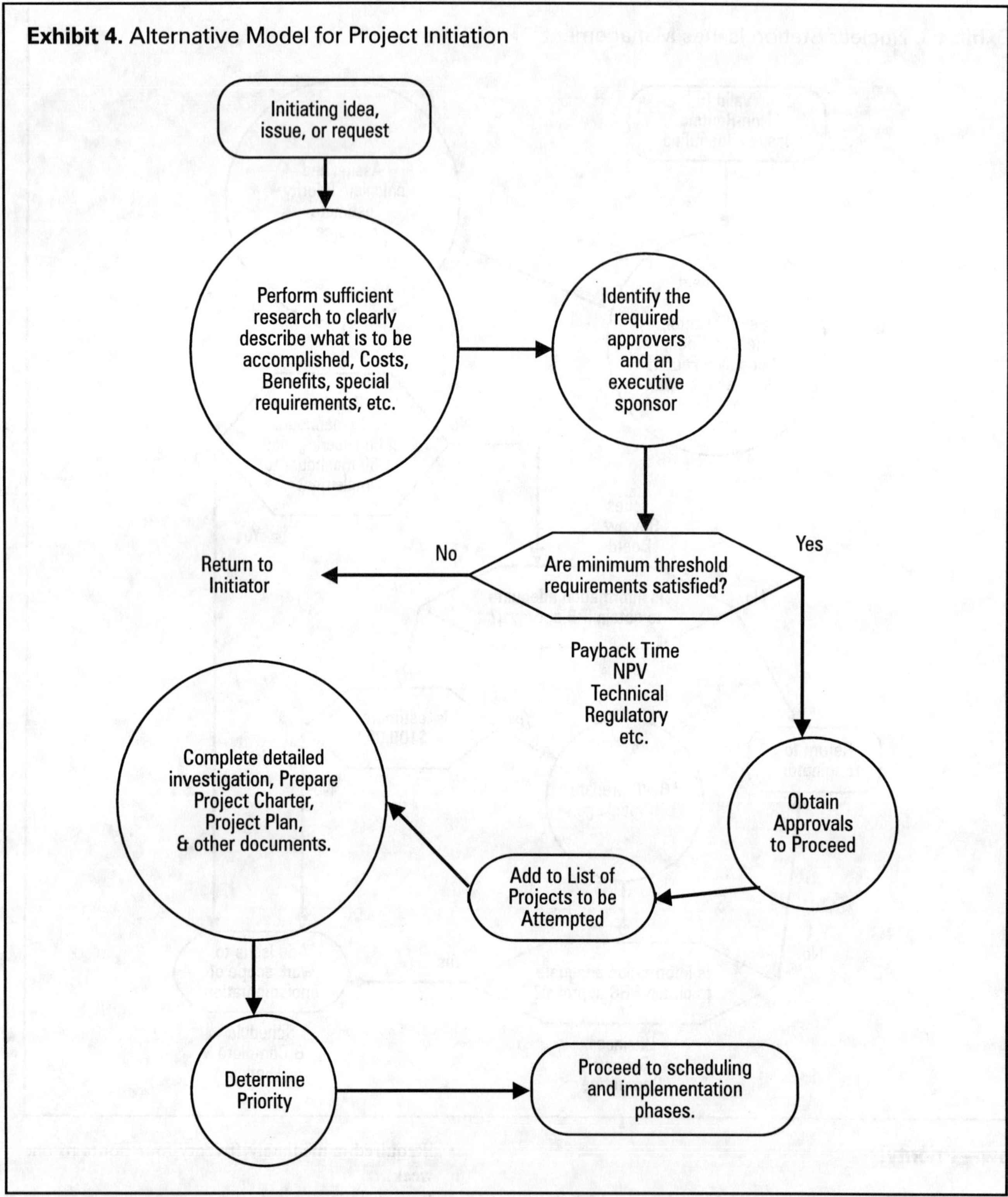


- Lower costs, and
- Increase revenues.

C. May indirectly result in an increase in net income.

- Increase in human efficiency,
- Increase in technological efficiency,
- Increase in human productivity, and

- Increase in technological productivity.

D. Neat to do, no identifiable financial benefit to the organization.

The purpose of any priority system is to provide the manager with a method for evaluating and adjusting the assignment of resources to the backlog of work. Since any single resource can only work on one project or task at any point in time, and each priority may be assigned to any number of projects, we must have some method for assigning relative priority to the A's, B's, etc. When an organization can break down each priority into smaller subcategories, this task becomes easier. The simple approach is to assign a range of work sequence numbers to each priority, assuming that all A's are more important than all B's, and so forth. A real world situation is not usually that simple. For example, a B1 that can be completed within ninety days might be assigned a higher work sequence number than an A4 (or maybe an A3). I am suggesting that a second axis of parameters might affect the mix of priority and work sequence numbers. My example was based on "Time" as that second axis. The priority listing can now be converted into a matrix as illustrated in Exhibit 5.

## Using the Priority Matrix

At this point, I should try to respond to several questions. First, "Why would anyone do a project that has no financial benefit to the organization?" It is possible for a project to have a financially neutral outcome, yet be good for moral or to move to a different technology. There could be many other possibilities, and by including this broad category I have not ruled out the boss's pet project. Second, "How does this matrix make it easier to prioritize and assign resources? It appears that we are getting more complicated." The answer to this is found by a manipulation of the matrix we just created.

You might notice (see Exhibit 5) I have drawn diagonal lines connecting the corners of all the boxes, lower left to upper right. Now tilt the page so that the lower right corner box is at the bottom of the structure. The result will be the table entries realigned on the diagonal. Reading left to right and top to bottom, the order of the priority categories is:

A1, B1-1, A2, B2-1, B1-2, A3, C1-1, B2-2, B1-3, A4, C2-1, C1-2, B2-3 , B1-4, C3-1, C2-2, C1-3, B2-4, C4-1, C3-2, C2-3, C1-4, D1, C4-2, C3-3, C2-4, D2, C4-3, C3-4, D3, C4-4, D4.

## A Defensible Priority

When you consider the realities of typical project requirements, this order of priority makes perfect sense. A project that will result directly in lower costs within one week should be a higher priority than one which is required for continued operation within one year. Some would argue that a consideration for priority should be the absolute size of the financial benefit. I agree, and this is the best way to rank the projects within the priority category. Others might like to see a factor for a minimum return on investment (ROI) or quickness of pay-back. I prefer to use these first as threshold factors, to screen projects for approval. Once a project is approved, the ROI and pay-back time are often not as important as the factors I have used to build the priority matrix. However, once the threshold is satisfied, the relative value of ROI or pay-back time could be used as a secondary ranking within the initial priority categories, and this approach would include the size of the financial benefit.

We can now assign a number range to each of the above priority categories. I might decide that the lower number will be worked first (higher priority), so that the A1 category is 1–99. It follows that B1-1 would be 100–199 and A2 would be 200–299 and so forth. This process results in a list of projects in a priority order that even the most ardent project champion will find hard to dispute. However, we must always be flexible. If anyone can present a solid case why a project should be assigned a higher priority number, I am happy to oblige. Of course, if this results in displacing another project, the case for this action will probably need to be heard by those affected.

## Be Consistent!

The final caution is to maintain consistency in applying these priorities. Every project cannot be an A priority. A certain amount of management discipline is necessary in the use of any management tool. The process I have described sounds deceptively easy to implement. However, the hardest part is to consistently apply a known criteria or rule set to the items within a priority category. Try to avoid a final step that is based on one persons opinion. I have used this methodology very successfully. However, your success will depend on the level of integrity you bring to the process.

## Conclusion

I have provided a set of priorities that can be applied in a very general sense. I have also explained how to construct a priority system that will provide an easily understood assignment of priority numbers to every project on the list for completion. All you need to do is assign resources to those projects at the top of the list.

**Exhibit 5.** Priority Matrix

Can be completed within:

| Week | 90 Days | One Year | > One Year |
|---|---|---|---|
| A1<br>Required for continued operation within one week. | A2<br>Required for continued operation within 90 days. | A3<br>Required for continued operation within one year. | A4<br>Required for continued operation but required date more than one year out. |
| B1-1<br>Will directly result in lower costs. | B1-2<br>Will directly result in lower costs. | B1-3<br>Will directly result in lower costs. | B1-4<br>Will directly result in lower costs. |
| 2-1<br>Will directly result in increased revenues. | B2-2<br>Will directly result in increased revenues. | B2-3<br>Will directly result in increased revenues. | B2-4<br>Will directly result in increased revenues. |
| C1-1<br>Will result in an increase in Human efficiency. | C1-2<br>Will result in an increase in Human efficiency. | C1-3<br>Will result in an increase in Human efficiency. | C1-4<br>Will result in an increase in Human efficiency. |
| C2-1<br>Will result in an increase in technological efficiency. | C2-2<br>Will result in an increase in technological efficiency. | C2-3<br>Will result in an increase in technological efficiency. | C2-4<br>Will result in an increase in technological efficiency. |
| C3-1<br>Will result in an increase in Human productivity. | C3-2<br>Will result in an increase in Human productivity. | C3-3<br>Will result in an increase in Human productivity. | C3-4<br>Will result in an increase in Human productivity. |
| C4-1<br>Will result in an increase in technological productivity. | C4-2<br>Will result in an increase in technological productivity. | C4-3<br>Will result in an increase in technological productivity. | C4-4<br>Will result in an increase in technological productivity. |
| D1<br>No financial benefit, Neat to do. | D2<br>No financial benefit, Neat to do. | D3<br>No financial benefit, Neat to do. | D4<br>No financial benefit, Neat to do. |

# Zero-to-Five Hundred in Four Weeks: Can You Effectively Manage This?

J. Norman Jones, PMP, Project Manager, Newberg/Perini, Division of Perini Corp.
Roger Francoeur, Construction Superintendent, ComEd

## Introduction

Imagine working in the most heavily regulated industry in the United States. The place that you work at is closely scrutinized by the government, the press, and by well-organized citizen groups dead-set against your very existence. It's your assignment to hire, train, and manage five hundred temporary workers over just a few weeks to perform risk-laden work, around-the-clock, in a plant with over eleven thousand procedures.

Envision a workplace where employees must undergo a rigorous background screening and training process just to be admitted into the front door. Think about servicing highly radioactive, sensitive equipment that must protect the lives and property of thousands of people while providing them with a reliable source of electricity. You have zero production workers, so, you hire five hundred—in four weeks! After three or four weeks of stable work, you will be asked to reverse the process and trend downward to zero again. Does this seem short for the implementation phase of a project life cycle? Actually, it is not. Some nuclear refueling outages move even faster.

Now, imagine this same industry struggling to cut its costs sharply as it emerges from one hundred years of regulated protection and enters an exploding free market. All of this while stricter operating requirements multiply to ensure absolute public safety. Welcome to the world of nuclear power plant maintenance support.

## Background

ComEd, a division of Unicom Corporation, is the largest nuclear utility in America. It owns and operates six dual-unit nuclear power stations. One of those six, Braidwood, is located sixty-five miles southwest of Chicago, Ill. Following ten years of construction, both of its reactors were declared commercially operable in 1988, just three months apart. Each reactor core contains 193 nuclear fuel assemblies. Eighty-four of these are changed out at the end of each eighteen month fuel cycle. Braidwood Unit One completed its sixth refueling in the Spring of 1997 while Unit Two is scheduled for its sixth refueling in the Fall of 1997.

Each Braidwood unit contains a 3425 MWt Westinghouse four-loop pressurized water system. Its reactor and steam generators provide the main turbine with a heat source. Borated water, pressurized to over 2200 psi and heated to more than 5000 F, flows from the reactor into tubes within four steam generators. There the water's heat is transferred through the tubes to clean purified water outside them to generate steam. This steam is then piped to a dual-flow high pressure turbine, three dual-flow low pressure turbines, and a hydrogen-cooled 1175 MWe Westinghouse generator.

ComEd contracts for support services when it needs to augment its own in-house maintenance workforce. The GN Venture is a joint venture formed by Newberg/Perini (a division of the Perini Corporation), Phillips, Getschow Co., and J.R. Foster Electric Co. It has provided contract maintenance and modification support services to Braidwood since 1989. A full service firm, the Venture has supported eleven refueling outages so far at Braidwood. All work assigned to the Venture is self performed.

Braidwood does not use contracted craft support during non-outage periods if the work can be performed by ComEd's own site workforce. Likewise, to save money, the station chooses to contract minimal amounts of pre-outage support work. This strategy forces a short hire-in window for outage-support contract labor. It is typically three to five weeks ahead of an outage. We hire between 350 and 550 workers in this time period and integrate them into work crews, quickly and effectively.

## Logistics

ComEd's management personnel decide which work to contract and which work to perform using the station's own maintenance employees. Shop resource loading, required training, work window timing, and radiation levels are but a few of the criteria used to complete the selection. This division of work, known as a work split, is reviewed by senior station management for approval and funding. All work approved to be contracted out is forwarded to the site construction superintendent for assignment.

The construction superintendent sends maintenance, modification, and support work to the Venture's work control department for evaluation. There the work is sorted by craft discipline to begin the human resource planning process. Work activities are coded into the Venture's work tracking system. A copy of each written work request is forwarded to the production department for craft jurisdiction review. This check confirms that accurate inputs will flow from our field walk downs and labor estimates.

Because of the complexity of much of the work, each accessible job is field analyzed through a physical walk down. We estimate the job's duration and identify other special needs such as scaffolding requirements, insulation status, lighting demands, and craft prerequisite skills. The work analysts identify and reserve parts and materials. They also probe a job history database for pertinent facts from past maintenance activities to include in the work package. We use these walkdowns to address all unique issues.

Information collected from the walkdowns and estimates fuels the development of the outage resource plan. Projected labor needs are conveyed to the respective trade unions during a pre-outage meeting. The actual calls for hire are placed to the union halls in the week preceding the scheduled hire date. Each of the unions provides names and social security numbers of their referrals at least two days prior to the scheduled hire date. This allows ComEd just enough time to screen the referrals before their arrival for both unescorted access (security badge) and training requirements. The time required to inprocess each new hire, from date of hire through training and security badging, ranges from one to five days.

Being accepted and hired is simply the beginning of the craft worker's inprocessing. Several more hurdles must be cleared before starting work. Each new worker must provide personal references and a detailed work history listing all employers, supervisors, etc., for the entire previous five years. If the worker has received nuclear security access before, then, just an update since leaving a ComEd site is required. A psychological profile and proof of fitness-for-duty (drug testing) are also requisites.

If a worker has not been at a ComEd site for more than a year, Nuclear General Employee Training (NGET) is required. After completing NGET, a whole (radionuclide) body count is needed. It measures a person's baseline level of internal radioactive contamination. Next is a special class for all nonstation personnel, contractor orientation. A thorough safety class follows. Then, depending on the worker's job classification, work package orientation classes. Fire watch training is there, along with fall protection and rigging training. Everyone must have training in foreign material exclusion and most will have confined space training too.

Finally, a plant tour wraps up the process. After classroom training is complete, the job superintendent explains the Venture's expectations, answers any questions, and work may finally begin. This occurs five hundred times between a dozen different job classifications, all in less than four weeks.

## Scope

The Venture accepts more than two thousand work activities each refueling outage. Over four hundred of these requests come to us in technical, written work packages. We perform most of this work with the mechanical and electrical trades. Several other trades perform less technical but no less important work as a support function; however, this work requires fewer work packages. More than five hundred scaffolds must be built. At least four hundred requests to remove and replace pipe insulation can be expected. Another three hundred requests support snubber testing along with inspections for pipe erosion and corrosion. We install and service the site's considerable temporary power needs. Also, we hang lead blanket shielding (to reduce radiation exposure), do radiation decontamination work, distribute anticontamination clothing, and perform general area clean-up in both clean and contaminated work areas. Mountains of paperwork govern these activities, and workers must be trained to use and understand all of this paper.

## Time

Braidwood typically completes its refuel outages within a fifty to sixty day window. Our work begins a few weeks before reactor shutdown and continues until the plant is back online. By choice, the station schedules several thousand work tasks during each refuel outage. While all of these tasks do not relate to the refueling of the unit, it is often the safest and most convenient time period in which to perform the work. Sometimes we do work during this period to reduce shop backlogs while contract labor is on site.

The number of people needed to perform this work and their skill sets depend upon many variables. The most obvious is the volume of work activities scheduled. While work volume is an important factor, the work windows allotted to perform this work drive the actual numbers and level of skill. All contracted maintenance work and other physical changes and improvements performed at the station are done with Building Trades Union craft labor. Good skill sets are a natural trait of craftspersons who belong to the Building Trades Unions. This is a result of the excellent specialty training provided to them by their respective unions. Hiring workers skilled in their trade is essential to completing work safely and satisfactorily in the time planned by the outage schedulers.

Assigning the Venture modifications of longer duration encourages craft workers with higher skills to accept work at the station. Getting better workers improves our wrench time. Jobs of longer duration also help us to resource level our maintenance support schedule. Better yet, if we can schedule portions of the work online it reduces the slope of our in-processing curve, or the slope of our craft reduction curve. Both are important contributors to efficiency but a reduction in the slope of our hire-in curve is the more significant of the two.

## Cost

While nuclear safety is clearly the station's number one priority, a "firm budget" policy underpins its financial health. Cost is a critical variable requiring continuing, tireless attention. The station's senior managers recognize this and regularly seek ways to lower costs and improve efficiency. They expect no less from their maintenance support contractor. The challenge is never ending. We must reduce costs while improving the margins of both safety and quality.

The first step toward cost control is recognizing its components. This requires a good cost management plan that is different from a good *computerized* cost system. The latter we can purchase retail. But effective cost management involves people and is a vital part of our integrated management plan. A Venture work planner reviews the data compiled from field walkdowns for number of tasks and expected duration. These facts determine whether the job gets a single cost code, or a more detailed cost structure. Some of the cost plan's other components are scope control, schedule monitoring, and resource leveling. We use a computer to track all of these and to analyze their interactions.

Cost authorization is fundamental to our management process. The customer must approve all expenditures prior to their accrual. Other aspects include data collection points, methods of analyzing output, and our cost reporting procedure. We also look at the different types of work that we will track. Small, routine, single-shift maintenance support tasks may only require a level-of-effort estimate taken from our job history files. Large, complex tasks and plant modifications require a work breakdown structure with fully developed estimates. These tasks will also have a specific objective, a detailed scope, and a refined schedule with a focus on bottom line efficiency.

All work requests receive a global cost code used throughout the operation to assign labor charges to the right account. A cost function number provided by ComEd is used for billing. Internal cost codes are assigned that track each work task's contribution to our overall costs. These codes are matrixed back into ComEd's respective cost codes for O&M and investment as well. This system permits job cost accruals that match our estimate breakdowns. It also permits us to roll up the overall cost for each work request. We provide current cost updates each week on authorizations, period costs, accrued costs, our original estimates, and forecast at completion costs.

We believe our employees are an asset to engage. Typically, one states the worth of an asset in terms of its acquisition costs, or its market value. Neither of these are suitable for establishing the worth of a firm's employees. To do this, we measure productivity. We recognize that work can expand to fit the time or dollars available. The work we complete reflects our company's productivity when compared to the hours we use to produce it. We can modify our productivity by changing the number of tasks that we expect to complete in a given time period. Likewise, employee morale can affect the time required to complete the same number of tasks. Our productivity is affected by many variables, some of which are beyond our control. Productivity measures the yield of our product. This becomes critical to judging the effectiveness of five hundred new employees.

The station's productivity is a product of the energy it produces and the time period required to produce it. A nuclear station will typically employ eight to nine hundred people full time. The average loaded payroll cost per hour worked approximates $40.00. These statistics suggest annual savings of $4,000,000 are possible by increasing productivity by one half-hour per person, per day. Another method of achieving these benefits would be to hold productivity firm and to improve revenues by increasing net generation over a like time period.

Both examples of productivity are also examples of costs. These are the pieces of the cost versus revenue equation that we can usually control. Our customers, to some degree, control our revenues; likewise, our managers, to some degree, control our costs. This is a basic principle that we must subscribe to if our companies are to survive in a competitive utility marketplace.

## Quality

We perform all support work under the auspices of ComEd's quality program. This simplifies the exchange of work between departments. The expectations of workers are consistent across all work groups and it allows us to standardize training. It also promotes uniform quality, regardless of whether ComEd does the work or contracts it. All site work activities are audited by the station's Site Quality Verification Department. This is an internal quality assurance group that confirms work to be both procedural and regulatory compliant. Venture personnel are trained to ComEd's quality program at a level commensurate with their assigned tasks.

The Venture supplements the station's quality control (QC) inspection staff. Inspectors are certified to ComEd's quality program and matrixed to the station's QC Supervisor for direction. This sharing of inspectors permits the station to maximize the use of its quality resources. All welders are certified using ComEd's weld program. Nondestructive examinations are performed by the station or by a specialty contractor under the station's direction. This one-station, one-program philosophy improves work quality, efficiency and eliminates duplicate costs.

## Human Resources

The GN Venture is organized as a project. Its mission is to effectively manage work at Braidwood to the customer's satisfaction. To do this, the company draws on the resources of its Venture Partners and operates much like a strong matrix. Partner salaried employees are assigned to the site in management positions on an as-needed basis. Each returns to their respective employer at the end of the outage. Job assignments are filled using the "best athlete" available. Because of the Venture's strong team identity, a visitor to the project would not likely realize that management personnel are actually from different partner companies.

Similarly, ComEd brings additional outage support personnel to the site. Many of them come from elsewhere within the company. They work for a corporate group that supports refuel outages at multiple sites. Each moves to another site upon outage completion. Other transient professionals are hired through ComEd's staff augmentation contractors to supplement its outage staff.

The brief outage work periods hinder staffing. It is hard to break free for short periods the caliber of workers needed. We have developed a pool of reliable, temporary professionals and craftspersons. Most of the time, we are able to hire an adequate number of qualified, available workers from this cadre to support each outage. The short work cycles also encumber team building. We have tried to mitigate this by varying our employee reward and recognition program. Our gratitude awards have covered the spectrum, from candy bars to savings bonds. Our observations tell us that in our environment the greatest payback is from recognition.

Our people work in a common facility. They join together in a "war room" setting to do status reviews, discuss daily plans, and perform high level pre-job briefings. We have also integrated the Venture's office into ComEd's site construction office. This provides an intimacy between the two work groups that would otherwise be unachievable. It bolsters ownership and accountability and it also expands the field of choices when we select individuals to supervise special projects. ComEd has often chosen Venture employees to provide leadership for high profile projects on site. Likewise, the Venture often performs special projects under the leadership of a ComEd employee. Ours is a truly effective matrix.

Projects staffed with transient workers bring human resource issues that differ from those presented by a company's full-time employees. Every outage is unique and so is the blend of people who work on it. The work scope, staffing needs, and specialty skill requirements are always changing. This work setting tends to attract "free spirited" individuals who can accept fast paced change when it is seen as positive in nature. If the change is perceived as having negative impact, the transient worker's response is likely to be more lively than that of a permanent employee. This is but one of the many differences between the two work groups.

Statistics suggest that our workforce will become increasingly diverse as we enter into the 21st century. Tomorrow's project managers will need "soft skills" that far exceed their technical skills. Managers with exceptional people skills will be in great demand. The challenges we face today are difficult, yet they will pale against those we will face in the future. Good human resource skills are mandatory if one is to be a successful project manager.

## Communications

Communication is an important function in any work environment. It becomes even more important when the workers are temporary and the project is of short duration. The exchange of information flows freely on our site. During outages, we begin our morning at the Station's plan of the day meeting. Our supervisors' internal plan of the day meeting is next. This meeting is also attended by the station construction department's field engineers and representatives of radiation protection. Then, we do a collective shift briefing for all Venture craftspersons. All of these activities occur in less than two hours.

Throughout the day, ComEd and Venture supervisors communicate in person, by telephone and by e-mail. A follow-up with station work planning in the early afternoon confirms our next sixteen hour work window. We convey this information to both day shift and afternoon shift supervisors at 3:00 P.M. The afternoon shift then takes over, providing a briefing of scheduled activities to all craft on the incoming shift.

While it may seem from this description that we spend all of our time in meetings, it is not the case. This is a very interactive process from which a lot of information flows. It moves information between work groups quickly and it serves the needs of outage stakeholders.

## Risk

All commitments carry with them a certain degree of risk. Safety represents the most significant risk that we experience on labor intensive projects. Industrial and nuclear safety metrics reflect the success of the project's management team. They may also mirror the team's effort at communications and human relations. *A Guide to the Project Management Body of Knowledge* does not address safety as a unique topic but those of us who manage large, manual-labor workforces know that it stands tall in importance. The negative notoriety that comes with a worker injury is adequate encouragement to identify and eliminate work hazards. To reduce the risk of injury to workers, safety requires a greater commitment from management than any other issue.

Transient workers present the utility with additional risk. One work procedure violation on one critical piece of equipment can easily expose the utility to both public criticism and regulatory censure. These violations, often called "contractor control incidents," bring no less embarrassment to the contracting firm. To lessen this exposure, we must train temporary workers quickly and thoroughly while maintaining strict work controls. If we do not, our customer will likely explore other risk alternatives.

A risk often unrecognized is the inability to establish a firm work scope. It is important to hire the right talent for the assigned tasks. If those tasks change, or new ones emerge, the skills initially requested may no longer suffice. Even if the correct skills remain available, scope changes hinder production and increase the end costs. Future competition among utilities will surely drive a conscious effort to reduce these risks.

## Procurement

ComEd contracts labor support services through the GN Venture. While ComEd retains the right to purchase materials through the Venture, it seldom does. Typically, the station manages all procurement and the receipt inspections of parts and materials. It is the Venture's responsibility to requisition, handle, install, and document the parts and materials that it uses. If quality documentation or parts concerns arise, we work together to correct them.

The maintenance-modification support work at Braidwood is done under a cost reimbursable, fixed-fee contract. This type of contract serves both parties well when the work scope is either difficult to define or changes often. The Venture has encountered both circumstances. Ordinarily, the work we receive is well planned and scheduled. There are occasions though where the scope emerges as the work progresses. The station has made notable progress in its ability to delineate work scope. It puts far more effort into planning and scheduling the work than in the past. If this trend continues, the station will no doubt reevaluate its risk-versus-reward contract policies. Until then, this contractual arrangement permits the station to request services before a work scope is defined.

## Conclusion

Each outage comes to a close for us as quickly as it began. Our personnel reductions are swift. Some days we lay off more than one hundred workers. Work packages are closed out as the reactor moves into its operational mode. Our goals and objectives receive a final review. We probe our successes and identify our weaknesses by conducting lessons learned meetings. Input to this process is solicited from craftspersons, supervisors, and management alike. The results are prioritized by value added and assigned to a specific team member for evaluation and corrective action. Once outage close out is complete and post-outage critiques are assembled, the schedule cycle begins again.

Our present challenge is to complete quality refueling outages, safely, faster and at lower costs. A clear course has been charted. To achieve this, will require continuous improvements and the pursuit of new competencies. The Venture's support services represent roughly 10% of Braidwood's total O&M costs. Reducing the Venture's costs by 20% would reduce Braidwood's O&M costs by just 2%. To ask for innovations that save 20%, while holding the volume and quality of services constant, seems an unrealistic expectation. Yet, a 2% reduction in O&M for the site seems very realistic. Regardless of one's perspective, or the numbers used, O&M costs must be reduced. To achieve these reductions, we must cultivate workers who can imagine the future, then help them identify steps to achieve our common goals of steady employment and reliable, economical electricity. Ultimately, our challenge is to transform resistance to change into momentum for improvement.

Utilities like ComEd will likely need a more cooperative, transient internal workforce to reduce their own costs. It is difficult today to recruit highly qualified craft labor for fifty-day outages by offering eight-hour shifts and five-day work weeks (i.e., no overtime). Yes, the use of overtime to shorten outages can make employment more attractive. A sixty-, seventy-, or eighty-hour work week will entice more people to accept the call. But will those accepting it be highly-qualified and well-trained in the discipline of their trade? Must we provide training or will they come trained for the tasks that we have called them to perform? Refueling outages of less than thirty days will not allow much time for worker task training. Yet refuel outages longer than thirty days will not be competitively economical because it means fewer days online to produce electricity (revenue).

Ready or not, deregulation will mean major changes to utilities like ComEd. All across America, these utilities are scrutinizing every aspect of their operations for improved efficiencies, cost savings, and ways to strengthen their bottom line. Unprecedented consolidations will occur in the next few years as utilities merge or are taken over, the inevitable effect of free-market forces. Companies that do business with these utilities must be prepared to react in a proactive way if they intend to stay in business. As we struggle with ways to improve our ability to hire five hundred nuclear outage support workers quicker so that they can work even shorter outages, we know we have our work cut out for us. But, because we anchor our processes on the fundamentals of proven, effective project management and the fact that the only constant is change, we are prepared for the challenges that lie ahead. Working as partners with a focus on market realities, both utilities and support firms can expect to survive if each is prepared to embrace and adapt to imminent, sweeping change.

# Project Management in the Utility and Infrastructure Industries

Dr. Francis Hartman, The University of Calgary
Dr. Rafi Ashrafi, The University of Calgary

## Introduction

Like many other industries, the utility and infrastructure industries are facing a number of challenges, such as deregulation, pressure for lower costs, higher risks, demands to improve productivity, stringent regulatory and environmental requirements, changing economic conditions, increased open competition, and price control by public utility commissions, to mention just a few. These challenges demand that the utility and infrastructure industries review their project management practices and adapt to changes for the business needs of the next century. This paper presents results of a pilot study based on interviews of fifty-one project owners, contractors and consultants on seventeen recent utility infrastructure projects in Alberta, Canada. The results of the survey indicate that utility and infrastructure industry owners, contractors and consultants have different views of project success factors, priorities and metrics. The utility and infrastructure projects of our sample identified opportunities for process improvement in the following areas:

- Communication between departments within the same company, between project team members, and between all stakeholders,
- Practices in the planning and definition phases of the project, and
- Project team development, career development and training for the individuals in the team.

If these findings can be generalized, it is recommended that utility and infrastructure companies begin to place more emphasis on the definition and planning phases of the projects. This will allow the reduction of resources necessary for the actual project execution. The threat of deregulation means that utility companies must learn to be more effective in their work. The paper describes how this might be achieved using team development and project management processes specifically developed to nurture continuous improvement through learning. Selected cross learnings from other industries' best practices are also reported. By properly understanding, focusing and aligning major stakeholders on critical success factors, metrics and priorities identified in this study, utility and infrastructure industries can help ensure success in their future projects.

## Background and Definitions

In today's society, as many projects run over budget, behind schedule and fail to meet stakeholders' expectations, effective project management becomes of paramount importance. In order to determine what effective project management is, it is necessary to study the management of a variety of projects in a variety of industries. The root causes of both success and the failure need to be evaluated to improve current project management efforts. Each industry, even each company, has its own way of managing projects. The purpose of this study was to investigate the effectiveness of project management practices within the infrastructure and utilities industries. The practice of utility and infrastructure management has evolved over a period of years, from the building of roads, irrigation canals, and the vast system of superhighways across North America. As the projects and working conditions have changed, so have the methods of project management. New technology, complex social, environmental, and economic culture shifts, have added new challenges for modern day projects.

The utility industry enjoyed a boom period in the sixties until the oil embargo of 1973. During the mid-seventies to mid-eighties, in addition to cost, the industry struggled to face the crisis of statutory regulations, environmental constraints, trade union practices, safety, societal and political changes, financial constraints, and changing market conditions. In the mid-eighties to mid-nineties more uncertainties in the project environment were added due to increases in project complexity, advancement in technology, skill shortage, contractual specifications and interest and inflation fluctuation. The industry, however, adapted successfully to the working environments of the mid-eighties to mid-nineties. However, it seems from our sample survey that the industry is somewhat complacent and appears slow to embrace advancements in project management. Developments in the project management during the last two decades have resulted in changes in project management tools, techniques and processes, as well as in the project environment. The utility industry faces the challenges of deregulation, advancement in technology, public awareness, pressure on utilities to compete without monopoly protection, satisfying environmental and other regulations

**Exhibit 1.** Utility Industry: Project Success Factors, Metrics and Priorities In Order of Importance

| Rank Order | Project Success Factors | Metrics | Priorities |
|---|---|---|---|
| 1 | Project mission | Project Scope defined | End user satisfaction |
| 2 | Communication | On time | Performance |
| 3 | Stakeholders satisfaction | Completion defined | Time |
| 4 | Environment & external issues | Responsibilities assigned | Cost |
| 5 | Top management support | Resources supplied | Team development |
| 6 | Business purpose achieved | Within budget | Career development and training |
| 7 | Technology & expertise | Customer satisfaction evaluated | |
| 8 | Owner's consultation | Milestones met | |
| 9 | On time | Deliverables identified | |
| 10 | Completed to specification | Critical success factors identified | |

and providing service on demand at reasonable rates. The utility industry needs to improve its project management practices to address these issues and satisfy its stakeholders.

For clarity, we define below the key terms used in this study.

***Utility***

"Public utility means a system, works, plant, equipment or service for the (1) conveyance of telecommunication, (2) conveyance of travelers or goods over a railway or tramway, (3) production, transmission, delivery or furnishing of water, heat, light or power, either directly or indirectly, to or for the public, and (4) an oil pipeline the proprietor of which is declared by the Energy Resource Conservation Board." (*The Public Utility Board* (PUB) *Act of the Province of Alberta*). The act also identifies the limitation of the profit earning capability of a utility. Utilities are regulated for profit based on the applications periodically made to the PUB. However, at the same time, the utilities are fairly guaranteed a certain rate of return on their investments, as long as overall the projects come within the projected annual budget.

***Infrastructure***

"Subordinate parts of an undertaking, especially permanent installations as basis for operations" (Oxford Dictionary). Today the definition of an infrastructure project is not limited to roads, buildings, water storage, treatment and distribution systems, as it traditionally has, but may include communication systems, power distribution networks, and natural resource processing, transportation and distribution systems.

Utility and infrastructure projects are highly interrelated. The introduction of new technology in the more traditional utility and infrastructure projects is very low compared to other industries, such as in software or telecommunications. As well, funding for many of the new utility and infrastructure projects have shifted away from the traditional publicly funded zero profit margin to privately funded market driven, with significant margins. Off balance that financing has become increasingly important to fiscally stretched governments. At the same time, investment opportunities for new players are emerging. This creates new stresses and challenges for project managers. This study evaluates both publicly and privately funded projects.

## Research Methodology

This paper presents the current state of project management practices in the utility and infrastructure projects and identifies areas for improvement. A survey instrument was developed to obtain information on critical success factors, project metrics, and project priorities. The purpose was to find out three things. What was considered important for project success? What was measured during the various phases of the project? What were the project drivers during various phases of the project? We were also interested in the extent to which project success factors, project metrics and project drivers were in alignment with each other. Another issue we tried to asses was the alignment of the major stakeholders: owner, contractor and consultant on issues such as project success factors, project metrics and project drivers. The data on these aspects were collected through personal interviews. A total of seventeen projects were studied, based on interviews with fifty-one owners, contractors, and suppliers. The overall value of these projects generally ranged from two million to twenty million dollars, with a few larger projects. The projects represent a wide variety, and consisted of three telephone/cable, one electric utility, two water projects, two natural gas, five infrastructure (public sector), and four infrastructure (private sector) projects. Most of the projects were completed during 1994–1996. The average number of years of experience of the interviewees was greater than ten.

## Results

### Utility Industry

Exhibit 1 shows the average project success factors, metrics and priorities in order of importance as identified by the three major stakeholders.

### Project Success Factors

The survey results indicated that perceived project success was not based only on meeting cost, schedule constraints and technical specifications, but also on end-user satisfaction and communication. The top ten critical success factors, in order of importance, as identified by all the three stakeholders, on average, over all the four project phases of definition, planning, execution, and termination, for the utility industry projects as identified by our survey were:

- Project has a clearly defined mission,
- Proper communication channels are established,
- Project satisfies the needs of the sponsor, users and other stakeholders,
- Environmental and external issues are properly addressed,
- Top management provides necessary resources,
- Project achieves the stated business purpose,
- Appropriate technology and expertise are available,
- Owner is consulted at all stages of project development and implementation,
- Project is completed on time, and
- Project is completed to specification.

### Project Metrics

The results of the data analysis show that overall, project metrics are not used consistently in the utility industry. The top ten project metrics were:

- The scope of the project is clearly defined and quantified,
- The project is completed on time or ahead of time,
- Project completion is precisely defined,
- Responsibilities are assigned,
- Resource requirements are identified and supplied as needed,
- The project is completed within a predetermined budget,
- Customer satisfaction is evaluated,
- Milestones are identified and met,
- Deliverables are identified, and
- Project success factors are identified.

The least used performance metric for all three stakeholder group was a quality management program. The general response was that companies have a quality management program, however it is not something they apply to their projects. It is particularly surprising that owners reported this. This response is not surprising with regard to suppliers, as quality is controlled routinely in the manufacturing process. Project managers just get the product off the production line. The sense from our study was that respondents regarded quality as "someone else's" responsibility. For the survey group as a whole, the results suggest that a quality management program is something that gets addressed in response to the initiatives of management or by their outside consultant.

### Project Priorities

The project priorities in order of importance were:

- End user satisfaction,
- Project performance,
- Time,
- Cost,
- Team development, and
- Career development and training.

End-user satisfaction was given more importance in the execution and termination phases as compared to the definition and planning phases. The project team should not wait until the end of projects to determine whether they have produced something that truly fits the needs of their customers; rework at this point could be very expensive.

**Exhibit 2. Infrastructure Industry: Project Success Factors, Metrics, and Priorities In Order of Importance**

| Rank Order | Project Success Factors | Metrics | Priorities |
|---|---|---|---|
| 1 | Project mission | Within budget | End user satisfaction |
| 2 | Stakeholders satisfaction | Critical success factors identified | Cost |
| 3 | Within budget | Milestones met | Performance |
| 4 | Completed to specification | On time | Time |
| 5 | Communication | Deliverables identified | Team development |
| 6 | Business purpose achieved | Project scope defined | Career development and training |
| 7 | Owner approval | Resources supplied | |
| 8 | Owner's consultation | Customer satisfaction evaluated | |
| 9 | Technology & Expertise | Responsibilities assigned | |
| 10 | Top management support | Completion defined | |

Project team development was not a priority for any of these utility projects.

### Observations

There was a lack of alignment of owner, consultant, and contractor/supplier on critical success factors, project metrics and priorities. Some of the observations of the characteristics of the utility industry derived from the survey interviews were:

- Projects in the utility industry are often completed by different departments within the same organization. This results in a discrete, functional approach ("over the wall" style) to project management that can be attributed in part, to the repetitiveness of their projects, and in part to traditional functional organizations as opposed to matrix of cross functional ones. In general, operational costs are accounted for by departments as opposed to the individual projects. This allows them to offset one project's overruns with another project's surplus, within any particular department. This leads to loss of control in projects and may well hide inefficiencies. Such inefficiency is further exacerbated by a poor team atmosphere, where individuals are not particularly challenged nor typically expected to contribute to projects outside the scope of their departments.
- It appears that utility project owners do relatively little up-front planning compared to other industries. This may be because they can afford to mobilize extra resources when a project requirements arises, or it may be because the projects are to some degree repetitive and their development pattern is well understood.
- It was observed in general that consultants and suppliers have very little or no involvement during the definition and planning phases of the project. Arguably this is the primary reason of misalignment between these three major stakeholders. More involvement of suppliers/contractors in the definition and planning phases could improve their understanding of the work, owners needs, the key priorities and the measurement and control systems planned for the project. Equally, this would lead to a better understanding by the owner of their needs. All of this would result in improved alignment and communication, leading to more effective project execution.
- The approach taken by regulated utilities working in a monopoly situation to management of projects is quite

different to those of industries that must compete in an open market.

- Public utilities tend to emphasize cost control at the expense of schedule in project execution. They tend not to look for schedule acceleration or earlier revenues as these are difficult to account for in most public jurisdiction organizations.
- Comprehensive project management procedures and tools are not used in most of the utility projects in this study. This is partly because they cost less and are less complex than large scale energy industry projects where the use of such tools and procedures is more common place. Also, the utility industry generally does not have either the requirement or incentive to fast track projects that the private sector industry "for profit projects" such as petrochemical plants have.
- Companies within the utility industry are generally monopolies and are regulated as to rate of return and services that they must provide. Crudely put, the more you spend on capital projects, the more you charge customers for their use.
- The present trend of deregulation will force a change. Incoming competition will force the need to become more efficient in order to retain a market place.

### Recommendations for the utility industry

It is recommended that the utility industry reexamines its project management practices to ensure that it offers services at truly competitive prices based on open market competition. A substantial increase in upfront planning, in conjunction with proper resource allocation, should also be implemented. Alignment of all the major stakeholders on project success factors, project metrics and the setting of project priorities at the definition phase of projects is of prime importance. To ensure that efficiency is further increased, team building should be implemented right from the definition phase of the project and this should, wherever practical, include consultants, contractors and key suppliers. Also, the involvement of consultants and suppliers during the definition and planning phase will help align stakeholders and their priorities in determining project success factors, metrics and project priorities.

## Infrastructure Industry

The infrastructure industry is well established and has developed many industry standards for project management. Exhibit 2 shows project success factors, metrics and priorities in order of importance as identified by the three major stakeholders.

### Project Success Factors

The average ranking for the top ten project success factors for infrastructure projects were identified as follows:

- The project has a clearly defined mission,
- The project satisfies the needs of the owners/sponsors, end users, and all other key stakeholders,
- The project is completed within budget,
- The project is completed to specification,
- Proper communication channels are established at appropriate levels in the project team,
- The project achieves its business purpose,
- Owner is informed of the project status and his/her approval is obtained at each stage,
- Owner is consulted at all stages of project implementation,
- Appropriate technology and expertise are available, and
- Top management is willing to provide the necessary resources.

### Project Metrics

The top ten project metrics were:

- The project is completed within a predetermined budget,
- Critical success factors are identified,
- Milestones are identified and met,
- The project is completed on time or ahead of schedule,
- Deliverables are identified,
- The scope of the project is clearly defined and quantified,
- Resource requirements are identified and supplied as needed,
- Customer satisfaction is evaluated,
- Responsibilities are assigned, and
- Project completion is precisely defined.

### Project Priorities

The project priorities in order of importance were:

- End-user satisfaction,
- Cost,
- Performance,
- Time,
- Team development, and
- Career development and training.

### Observations

- Time, cost, and quality oriented towards the client satisfaction are all indicators that determine the success of the projects surveyed.
- Project metrics were used for these projects, but project selection factors were not clearly defined. The decision to proceed with a project was usually based upon "operating necessity" or "convenience" rather than on purely economic reasons.

- The degree to which planning tools were used was more dependent on the size of the project as opposed to the success of the project.
- Poorly defined scopes of work were identified as the primary cause of the majority of the problems experienced.
- Communication was identified as a necessary tool for successfully resolving problems as they arise.
- The majority of the infrastructure projects in this study were part of much larger long term plans and therefore gained the support of top management.
- The rate at which new technology is introduced is low compared, for example, to the software industry.
- Infrastructure is considered a mature industry and provides a strong foundation for effective project management.
- The causes for failure or problems in the infrastructure industry include poorly defined scope, breakdown in communications, and insufficient contingencies in the schedule for weather.

### Recommendations for the infrastructure industry

As an industry with a long history, and presumably with performance records stretching back in time, one might rationally expect more predictable results. Better data collection is likely needed to eliminate influences stemming from hidden contingencies and "budget juggling." Better use of historical data as a foundation to forecast project outcomes could be used. Range estimating, the use of target costs and schedules and associated risk and contingency planning would likely reduce schedule overruns.

Effective planning and the use of planning tools should enhance project success, particularly if projects are planned with contingency schedules and delivery methods built in. Planning for other important elements, such as effective communication, stakeholder alignment and rational risk sharing with consultants and contractors would probably enhance project performance. The strategic management of sets of related projects as a program will help set priorities, thus eliminating "operating necessity" and "convenience" as primary project selection drivers.

### Similarities in practices of utility and infrastructure industries

Eight out of ten critical success factors for both industries were the same. There was no difference in the metrics used; however the order of importance was different in both cases. End-user satisfaction was a top priority for both industries. For the utility industry, other priorities, in order of importance, were end-product performance, time and cost, whereas, for the infrastructure industry, the order of importance was cost, performance then time.

### Differences in practices of utility and infrastructure industries

The utility industry works in a regulated environment. These organizations have to satisfy many stakeholders, leaving limited choices for them in terms of how to manage their projects. The utility industry has more public sector funded projects. Most of the projects are of small to medium size, are less complex and tend to be of a repetitive nature. Project management practices seems to be traditional and less effective than other industries. Environmental and external issues are one of the major concerns. Compared to the studied utility projects, those in the infrastructure sector were a little larger and more complex in nature. Their project management practices seem to be more mature, and effective in the infrastructure projects studied compared to those in the utility industry. One possible reason for these differences may be more decision making choices and competition are available in one industry compared to the other. Environmental and external issues are no longer a significant problem for infrastructure projects.

## Conclusions

To face current and future challenges, the utility and infrastructure industries should consider keeping abreast of the developments in project management and nurture continuous improvement through learning from the best practices of other industries such as new product development. Both sectors could benefit from more effective front-end planning, especially getting the major stakeholders and the project team together early on. It is important to establish project success criteria, metrics used, and project priorities effectively. It is critically important to understand project phase dynamics and alignment of all the major stakeholders on project success factors, metrics and priorities.

### References

Hartman, Francis, and Rafi Ashrafi. 1996. "Failed Success and Failures." *Proceedings of Annual Seminar/Symposium*. Boston, MA: 907–911.

Hubbard, Darrel. 1990. "Successful Utility Project Management From Lessons Learned." *Project Management Journal*, 3 (September): 19–23.

Salpatas, J.N., and W.S. Sawle. 1986. "Measuring Success of Utility Projects Past, Present and Future." *Proceedings of Annual Seminar/Symposium*. Montreal, Canada, 67–76.

Wallace, Ronald. 1990. "A History of the Project Management Applications in the Utility Industry." *Project Management Journal*, 3 (September): 5–11.

Wiegand, Francis. 1990. "Managing Multiple Capital Projects in the Electric Utility Industry." *Project Management Journal*, (September): 13–17.

# A Quality Model for the Project Management Process

George K. Wissborn, P.Eng., PMP, Ontario Hydro, Pickering, Canada
William R. Symmons, P. Eng. PMP, Ontario Hydro, Pickering, Canada
Michael Stefanovic, P.Eng., PMP, Procept Associates Ltd, Toronto, Canada

## Introduction

### Overview of Ontario Hydro

Ontario Hydro operates Nuclear, Thermal and Fossil electrical plants in the province of Ontario, Canada. Since the seventies, we have installed approximately 15,000 MWe of Nuclear power at three different sites. The final unit came online in 1993 and at that juncture the Nuclear Division moved from a design & construction oriented organization to an operating and maintenance organization. This has led to a needed change for the project management skills originally developed to build generating stations. The emphasis is now on scaled-down maintenance and modification projects.

Each of the operating plants (Pickering, Bruce, and Darlington Generating Stations) found a need for a project department at each site that could handle many smaller projects simultaneously, up to eighty or ninety projects each, varying from 0.5M$ to 150M$. This required many more project managers and leaders but with varying degrees of skill and capability.

### Current Environment

At the Pickering Station (which has eight units of 540 MWe each) a project management group was formed. We have found the "marriage" of operating station procedures for plant modifications and the discipline of the project process to be difficult. Operating personnel had a need to "get the change over with" so that they could generate power, and the project managers had a need to plan well before they could execute.

This created a number of challenges to be dealt with:

- Requirement to execute needs planning with the station customer,
- Requirement to execute projects in accordance with rigorous station procedures,
- Need to link the project tasks to the station procedures,
- Clear definition of project deliverables,
- Identification of procedural hold points and authorizations, and
- Standardization of the project life cycle across the organization.

### Need for Standardization

To meet the station's needs to (a) ensure that any changes cause minimum impact on production and (b) changes to operating systems do not compromise the regulatory requirements placed on the station, a standardized process was required that, if followed, would ensure that the project meets station requirements and all activities are procedurally compliant. To this end we looked for:

- More emphasis on up front planning,
- Station systems engineers involvement in reviews,
- Commonly accepted project life cycle and project phases, and
- Commonly accepted terminology by all participants.

### Evolution of the Project Management Process Model (PMPM)

In order to meet the need for a guide that project managers could follow, we developed a standardized approach to project management in the form of a Project Management Process Model (PMPM). This model includes the ability to readily guide participants to the applicable procedures. The model was first issued a year ago and placed in trial use during which time feedback on the usefulness and quality of the guide was solicited. The guide is in its sixth issue at this time and is now incorporated into the Division's Project Management Manual.

This paper presents the PMPM, which through a process of continuous feedback from the users remains a "living" document subject to continuous improvement.

## The Model

### Model Layout and Format

The project phases have been arranged to flow from left (Identification Phase) to right (Close-out Phase) that is in line with common convention when presenting chronological events. A thick vertical line separates the definition phase from the execution phase to clearly indicate that point in time when the project is approved and fully funded. Since project control functions are applicable to the entire project life cycle, they are identified at the bottom of the page spanning the entire model. The model is distributed exclusively in its color version. Black and white copies cannot convey the various aspects of the project management process nearly as effectively. However, since we have little control over people making black & white copies, we have augmented the color scheme with other features, recognizable on black & white copies, such as grey shading, the use of italics and underlining.

### The five standardized project phases

During the process of generating "standardized" life cycle phases, a number of sources were consulted, i.e., *A Guide to the Project Management Body of Knowledge* (PMBOK), the Ontario Hydro Nuclear (OHN) Project Management Manual and a number of other publications, which all exhibit numerous variations regarding the breakdown of the project life cycle. We found the following set of project phases to be the most suitable one for our environment:

- Identification Phase,
- Initiation Phase,
- Definition Phase,
- Execution Phase, and
- Close-Out Phase.

Many texts refer to a Development Phase, however, it was felt that, by its nature, any development effort is intrinsic to the definition of a project.

### The five sub-sections of the execution phase

Due to the complexity of the Execution Phase, especially within the environment of a nuclear station, we found the following division into sub-phases advantageous:

- Engineering,
- Installation Preparation,
- Installation,
- Commissioning Preparation, and
- Commissioning.

Two features should be noted here:

First, some overlap does occur between the Sub-phases of the Execution Phase. For example, during the commissioning sub-phase, the Commissioning Reports must be reviewed and accepted by the design authority. Although this activity is an engineering responsibility, it is shown in the commissioning sub-phase and it occurs well after the majority of the design and engineering tasks are completed.

Second, the functional sub-phases "Installation Preparation" and "Commissioning Preparation" are identified separately in order to align the model with the structure of our Change Control Procedure, recognizing that compliance with this procedure is tied to our operating license.

### Procurement and Organizational Project Tasks

Organizational Project Tasks and the Procurement Tasks are generally specific to the execution and close-out phases and, therefore, are shown to span both phases.

### Quality Gates

The concept of "Quality Gates" is not a new one. They are merely hold points that must be satisfied before the project can proceed.1 We felt that:

1. The Model is designed to identify all agreed-to Quality Gates,
2. The term "Quality Gate" perfectly conveys the notion that the project cannot proceed unless it has passed the Quality Gate, and
3. The emphasis on quality is a key component of any project management process.

Quality Gates are identified by framing (for black & white copies of the model) and also by a yellow background (as enhancement for color prints) that appears as a light gray shade on black & white copies.

### Deliverables

For all projects of appreciable size and complexity, a great volume of documentation (software) is being generated. Some of that software exists in the form of stand-alone documentation, properly numbered and signed off. Other software may simply consist of memoranda, e-mail or minutes of meetings. In creating the model, we have attempted to identify those software deliverables that are of critical importance to the execution of a typical project, representing minimum requirements for successful project completion. This set of documents should also be contained in the official project file.

Deliverables are identified in the model by the use of italics (for black & white reproductions) and also by using the color red (as enhancement for color prints). Quality Gates are also Deliverables.

### Events/activities related to safety, quality, and the environment

The management of safety, quality, and environmental issues is of great importance for all projects. Underlining has been added in order to facilitate the identification of activities that are directly or indirectly related to these areas and the color green is used to enhance color reproductions.

### Outage Related Documentation

The Pickering Nuclear Generating Station has eight reactor units and is the world's largest. This translates into four unit outages per year. Considering such an intense outage program, it comes as no surprise that the outage planning group requires certain documentation on a preset date, specifically chosen for each particular generating unit, usually three months prior to the start of a the outage. Such documentation includes work requests entered into the work management system (called DR's), such as installation DR's and Commissioning DR's as well as Work Plans for installation and commissioning activities. Note: A "DR" is a work request entered into an electronic work management system. These documentation requirements are specifically flagged by framing the task and giving it a blue background that on black & white copies shows up as a gray shade, somewhat darker than that of the Quality Gates.

### Identification of applicable procedures

The Model identifies all existing and relevant procedures governing the various activities and events. This feature greatly assists the project teams in their efforts to comply with all procedures in support of our operating license plus those implemented by line management.

### Use of the model as a planning tool

At the beginning of the project life cycle the model is found to be of great help when generating the first draft of the Level 1 project schedule, particularly during the project kick-off meeting. Furthermore, we encourage all project teams, project leaders and clients to use the model as an up-front planning aid for the purpose of recording any agreements concerning software deliverables and all events or activities that would be considered applicable to the particular project at hand (see model legend). In addition, a signed copy, kept on file, serves to record that "understanding" for future reference.

### Simplified documentation for small projects

It has long been recognized that a way has to be found to simplify the preproject approval documentation for small projects or projects with limited complexity. This applies specifically to documents such as the Needs Statement, Project Charter, Project Execution Plan, Release-Quality Cost Estimate and the Business Case Summary. The organization already makes use of an "Internal Work Request" (IWR) form for work of significantly lower value when compared with a typical project. This work generally has a value in the range of $50,000 to $300,000, (no firm range has been established) and/or is of a nature that requires little engineering or involvement by regulatory agencies. For these "small" projects, a standard addendum template has been developed to cover the above-mentioned documents. The model makes reference to this by adding the applicable addendum number in the square box at each of the appropriate activities. Refer to the model's legend for a list of addenda.

## The Guide to the Project Management Process Model

### Description

The guide is meant to be a detailed reference and a supporting document to the Project Management Process Model for managing projects within the Projects and Modifications Department.

The chosen level of detail lies somewhere between the model and the existing procedures. The guide is not meant to be a procedure. It attempts to answer the questions: what (Description), why (Purpose), when (Timing) and who (Responsibility). *For answers to the question* how, *reference is made to the model that lists the applicable existing procedures.*

The organization of the guide closely follows the project life cycle phases of the model. Except for the Introductions each chapter is dedicated to one Project Life Cycle Phase. For each Quality Gate, Deliverable or Task in the model, there is a corresponding heading in the guide. Furthermore, under each heading, side notations such as: Description, Purpose, Timing, Responsibility and Quality Process are inserted so that the reader can easily focus on these issues within each topic.

The guide is currently published in an 8-1/2" x 11" spiral-bound format, however, other versions are anticipated for the future, such as:

- full size three ring binder (office version),
- pocket size (site version),
- diskette, and
- online.

Volume I includes the text of the guide and also includes a color copy of the model in an 11" x 17" format.

Volume II contains the appendices with description of the sample project, and examples of various documents in general or for the sample project.

### Purpose

The guide is designed to complement the *Project Management Process Model*. Its purpose is to provide helpful, step-by-step directions for managing projects within the Pickering Nuclear Division. After a period of application within the Projects & Modifications Department, the guide may be adopted for use outside of the department, or even the division.

The target audience for the model and the guide is very diversified and generally consists of:

- Projects and modifications department section managers,
- Line (functional) managers,
- Project leaders,
- Project team members, and
- Other project stakeholders.

Although the provision of project management training is not a primary objective of the guide, it can be used as a reference in training sessions. However, it is assumed that the users of the guide have fundamental knowledge of project management.

### Timing

Development of the guide was started in July 1996 and was first issued for use in May 1997.

### Responsibility

The guide was prepared by the Projects and Modifications Department of the Pickering Nuclear Division.

### Quality Process

During its development, the guide went through several iterations. The initial version consisted of one, all encompassing volume. However, we found this to detract too much from its intended purpose as a reference guide. Primarily for that reason the guide has been split into two volumes, Volume I being the guide itself and Volume II containing all sample documents (Appendices).

The guide structure was further improved by organizing the information around the categories of: *What, Why, When, Who and How.* This greatly improved the clarity of the text as well as easy retrieval of information. An overall table of contents can be found in the front of the guide and for additional convenience, a table of contents can also be found in front of each individual chapter. Standard side notations further help focus on specific issues within each topic.

The sample project documentation contained in Volume II of the guide (for a project entitled: Transport and Work Equipment Garage) attempts to further support the guide by providing actual examples for deliverable documents identified in the model and the guide. Their selection is focused on the project planning processes.

In order for the guide to be properly introduced within the department, a series of "walk-through" sessions were organized. The users' "buy-in" was achieved by involving the departmental staff in the preparation of the model and the guide.

## Future Steps

This guide, together with the model is a living document and it will be used for managing all divisional projects. Feedback will be gathered on experiences with the guide and it will be revised periodically to include the lessons learned.

One by-product of the development of the model and the guide was a clear identification of areas that currently lack procedures. This has been the catalyst for the start of a program designed to have those missing procedures added.

Initiatives have already been taken outside of the Pickering Nuclear Division, in other areas of the corporation, to develop similar Project Management Process Models and Guides. This is encouraging since standardization of the project management process within the corporation can yield substantial benefits

### References

Piper, Ray. 1995. "Jazzing Up Your Work Processes." *Proceedings of the Project Management Institute Seminar/Symposium*. Upper Darby, PA: Project Management Institute.

**Exhibit 1.**

# Appendix A

## Excerpt from the "Quality Model for the Project Management Process"

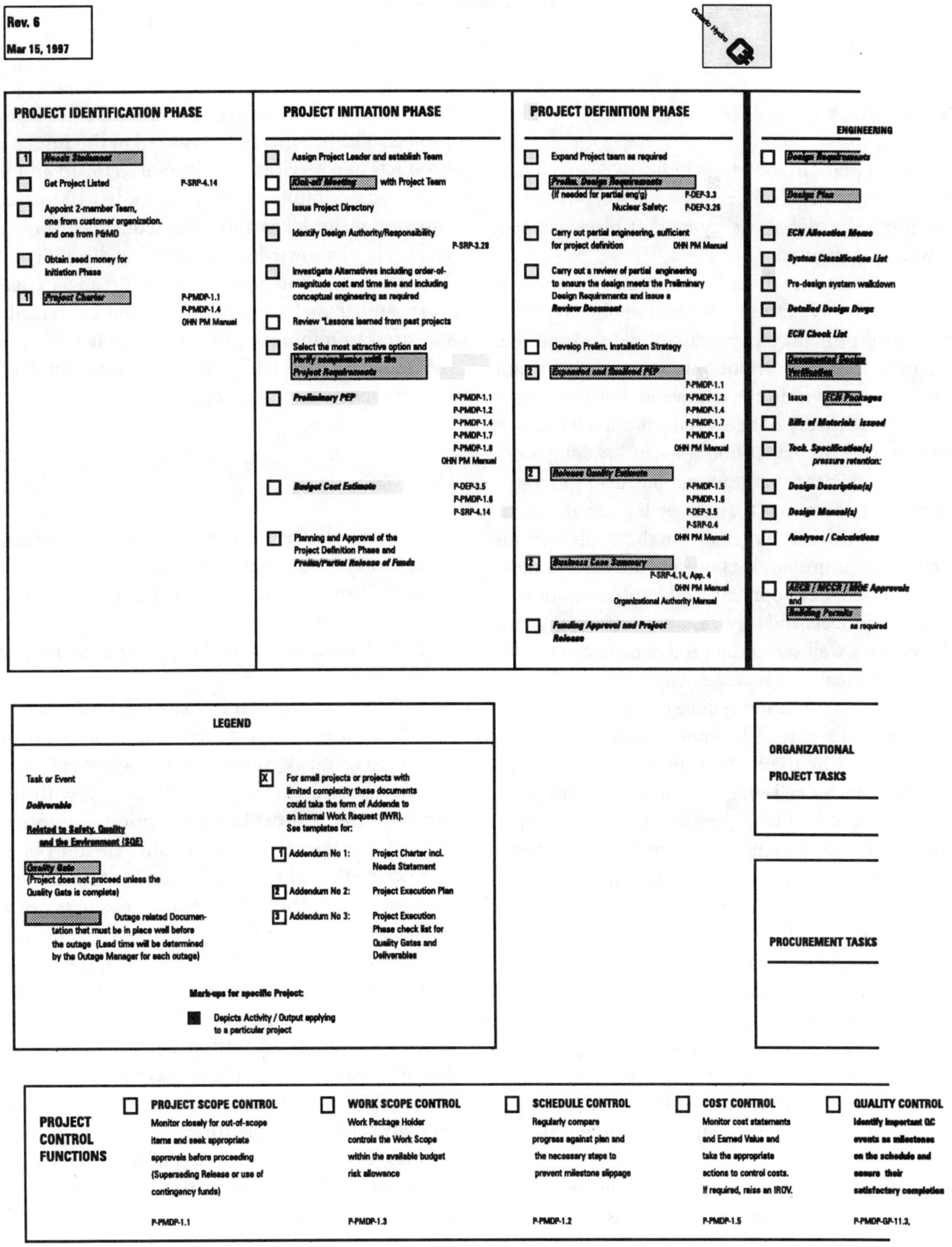

Rev. 6
Mar 15, 1997

Ontario Hydro

### PROJECT IDENTIFICATION PHASE

- [1] ***Needs Statement***
- ☐ Get Project Listed — P-SRP-4.14
- ☐ Appoint 2-member Team, one from customer organization. and one from P&MD
- ☐ Obtain seed money for Initiation Phase
- [1] ***Project Charter*** — P-PMDP-1.1, P-PMDP-1.4, OHN PM Manual

### PROJECT INITIATION PHASE

- ☐ Assign Project Leader and establish Team
- ☐ ***Kick-off Meeting*** with Project Team
- ☐ Issue Project Directory
- ☐ Identify Design Authority/Responsibility — P-SRP-3.28
- ☐ Investigate Alternatives including order-of-magnitude cost and time line and including conceptual engineering as required
- ☐ Review "Lessons learned from past projects
- ☐ Select the most attractive option and ***Verify compliance with the Project Requirements***
- ☐ ***Preliminary PEP*** — P-PMDP-1.1, P-PMDP-1.2, P-PMDP-1.4, P-PMDP-1.7, P-PMDP-1.8, OHN PM Manual
- ☐ ***Budget Cost Estimate*** — P-DEP-3.5, P-PMDP-1.6, P-SRP-4.14
- ☐ Planning and Approval of the Project Definition Phase and ***Prelim/Partial Release of Funds***

### PROJECT DEFINITION PHASE

- ☐ Expand Project team as required
- ☐ ***Prelim. Design Requirements*** (if needed for partial eng'g) — P-DEP-3.3; Nuclear Safety: P-DEP-3.26
- ☐ Carry out partial engineering, sufficient for project definition — OHN PM Manual
- ☐ Carry out a review of partial engineering to ensure the design meets the Preliminary Design Requirements and issue a ***Review Document***
- ☐ Develop Prelim. Installation Strategy
- [2] ***Expanded and Detailed PEP*** — P-PMDP-1.1, P-PMDP-1.2, P-PMDP-1.4, P-PMDP-1.7, P-PMDP-1.8, OHN PM Manual
- [2] ***Release Quality Estimate*** — P-PMDP-1.5, P-PMDP-1.6, P-DEP-3.5, P-SRP-0.4, OHN PM Manual
- [2] ***Business Case Summary*** — P-SRP-4.14, App. 4, OHN PM Manual, Organizational Authority Manual
- ☐ ***Funding Approval and Project Release***

### ENGINEERING

- ☐ ***Design Requirements***
- ☐ ***Design Plan***
- ☐ ***ECN Allocation Memo***
- ☐ ***System Classification List***
- ☐ Pre-design system walkdown
- ☐ ***Detailed Design Dwgs***
- ☐ ***ECN Check List***
- ☐ ***Documented Design Verification***
- ☐ Issue ***ECN Packages***
- ☐ ***Bills of Materials issued***
- ☐ ***Tech. Specification(s)*** *pressure retention:*
- ☐ ***Design Description(s)***
- ☐ ***Design Manual(s)***
- ☐ ***Analyses / Calculations***
- ☐ ***AECB / MCCR / MOE Approvals*** and ***Building Permits*** as required

### LEGEND

Task or Event

***Deliverable***

**Related to Safety, Quality and the Environment (SQE)**

***Quality Gate*** (Project does not proceed unless the Quality Gate is complete)

Outage related Documentation that must be in place well before the outage (Lead time will be determined by the Outage Manager for each outage)

[X] For small projects or projects with limited complexity these documents could take the form of Addenda to an Internal Work Request (IWR). See templates for:

| | |
|---|---|
| [1] Addendum No 1: | Project Charter incl. Needs Statement |
| [2] Addendum No 2: | Project Execution Plan |
| [3] Addendum No 3: | Project Execution Phase check list for Quality Gates and Deliverables |

**Mark-ups for specific Project:**

■ Depicts Activity / Output applying to a particular project

### ORGANIZATIONAL PROJECT TASKS

### PROCUREMENT TASKS

### PROJECT CONTROL FUNCTIONS

- ☐ **PROJECT SCOPE CONTROL** — Monitor closely for out-of-scope items and seek appropriate approvals before proceeding (Superseding Release or use of contingency funds) — P-PMDP-1.1
- ☐ **WORK SCOPE CONTROL** — Work Package Holder controls the Work Scope within the available budget risk allowance — P-PMDP-1.3
- ☐ **SCHEDULE CONTROL** — Regularly compare progress against plan and the necessary steps to prevent milestone slippage — P-PMDP-1.2
- ☐ **COST CONTROL** — Monitor cost statements and Earned Value and take the appropriate actions to control costs. If required, raise an IROV. — P-PMDP-1.5
- ☐ **QUALITY CONTROL** — **Identify important QC events as milestones on the schedule and ensure their satisfactory completion** — P-PMDP-GP-11.3,

# Organizing Around Learning, Reengineering, Revenue Growth, and Project Management: A Case Study

Nicholas Kallas
Gary Murphy
Robert Nowosielski

## Executive Summary

The changes taking place in the utility industry due to federal and state (re)deregulation, and changing market dynamics that are redefining the global energy market place are well known and well documented.

This paper proposes, and describes in terms of an energy delivery case study, that effective orchestration of reengineering principles, project management discipline, and revenue generating growth strategies cannot only generate significant business improvements within the operation, but also create the platform for the delivery of new products and services.

Faced with increasing competition some utility companies are in the process of identifying unique business processes and skills as core competencies that can be leveraged to generate new sources of revenue either within the traditional industry domain or in future markets outside the current utility domain. The design, development, and implementation of revenue oriented products and services imply efforts that are unique and therefore well served by project management.

Second order (radical, not incremental) reengineering efforts are required to significantly reduce energy delivery operating and maintenance costs. The implementations of these efforts are well served by the body of project management knowledge because each one is one of a kind that takes place over several months. When reengineering efforts are organized around a vision consistent with leveraging core competencies, synergies in cost savings through productivity improvements, and revenue generation through exploiting the new business processes can be realized.

This case study walks through the conceptual design, development, and preliminary implementation phases of a combined outage and storm management, and design and mapping capabilities. These two integrated business processes were reengineered using traditional reengineering tools and objectives. The processes were viewed with the end-state goal of leveraging the company's core competencies in infrastructure management.

The project life cycle duration is driven both by new product development and reengineering business events. The reengineering based costs to implement the project scope versus productivity savings need to start showing returns on investment within eighteen to twenty-four months since inception of the project. The benefits to be realized in the future after related products and services have been developed and marketed.

The description of the case study as a project template showing major steps and their sequence, timing, continuity and reuse of knowledge, and teaming dynamics are discussed. The learnings and pinch-points already experienced and those anticipated are highlighted and explained. The methods used to minimize project life cycle time and avoid implementation risks while ensuring successful development of new revenue streams are discussed.

## Interests

The energy delivery business process is organized around three customer defined outcomes:

1. "When I flip the switch, I expect the lights to come on,"
2. "If I do loose power, I expect it to be restored quickly," and
3. "If I decide to start or expand a business in your service territory, I expect the connection to the infrastructure to be quick, simple, and hassle-free."

Internal and external benchmarking with local and nationwide competitors based on quick restoration of service showed that the corporation could benefit by employing best practice methodologies and emerging technology to improve the outage and storm management business process.

Recognizing the value of quick service restoration to the success of the energy delivery business, the organization embarked on a reengineering process to redefine this portion of the business. The operational objectives included reducing costs, improving restoration performance, and improving customer satisfaction. There was the clear recognition that developing breakthrough performance in this area could potentially serve as the platform for revenue generating opportunities. Because of this strategic alignment, senior management sponsorship was very strong and served as a key factor in the success of this effort.

## Vision

The energy delivery physical plant is operated, maintained, and managed by more than one process, system, data, and organization. Therefore, since there is no off-the-shelf technology that can deliver one system to operate all aspects of the physical plant and cannot throw away all of the existing systems, technology from multiple vendors needs integration with the as-is and to-be systems.

The elements of the visioning efforts were to provide end-to-end business solutions where "off the shelf" products and suppliers are moved to think and act outside their particular application box by facilitating integrated thinking (not distributive) among all parties.

It was clear from the start that the Organization, Jobs, Skills, and Values, Beliefs, and Norms (OJSVBN) of the reengineered processes would be redefined in parallel with the exploitation of technology. Visioning sessions took place with key internal and external people who covered the technology and OJSVBN aspects of how will do business in the next five to ten years. Additionally, since these processes are not outsourced they have to align with the vision of the corporate future, and core competencies. Alignment with strategic objectives also enhances the survival and support levels of the efforts.

The vision captures current reactive work management and facilities' design needs as related to the operations, supervisors, and upper management. The marketing and sales perspectives are also invaluable inclusions to the vision statements because early incorporation of these requirements ensures a marketable service at the design phase. Defining the high level business processes through intense, one day focus meetings produced quick and documented common understanding for the core team.

### Business Processes Definition

Since the core team was envisaging a second order change to the current (as-is) processes revision of these was not done in detail and the as-is processes were not used as the starting point of the transition to the future (to-be) processes. The core team decomposed the two to-be processes into a small number of sub-processes that could be described in the procurement cycle. The high level data entities such as equipment, maps, facilities, work initiation, and customer were also documented making sure that all the data necessary to facilitate the processes were accounted. The business system interfaces and integration showing source and sink relationships for each data class were also recognized with the objective to minimize the number of interfaces, data redundancy, and duplication.

Iterations with the business and information services verified, validated, and updated, the three diagrams (process, data, business system interfaces) before communicating to the corporate community and the marketplace.

The process definition stage incorporated the OJSVBN and IT aspects of the reengineering process at the same table, working as one team with common goals and mutual benefits. Sharing and leverage of the business and IT knowledge, predisposition, commitment, resource linkage, and distinct competencies were prevalent throughout these efforts.

## First Steps

The objectives of the first steps are to start the implementation of the vision by maintaining continuum and momentum through the core team members, and minimizing the knowledge transfer effort for incoming resources. The first steps described here are not necessarily sequential or in order. Parallel execution, and intermingling of steps is acceptable as required by situation circumstances.

### Best Practices and Industry Scans

There are many solutions and providers to the business problems encapsulated in the process definitions. In order to assure the team that the correct solution would surface for evaluation best practices and industry scan steps were undertaken.

The industry scans included accessing the Internet, contacting known solution providers, contacting known utility industry consulting firms, reviewing utility trade journals, and scans of nontraditional utility industry trade journals that might have similar business processes such as the telecommunications industry. The scans provided a quick method of surfacing additional information and data regarding our business processes and provided some additional reassurance to the team that the *right* solution would be found. Most of this work was done from the desktop and via phone surveys.

A key requirement of the solution was quick implementation. A key element in assuring the team that a solution would provide quick turn-around with reduced associated risk was to initiate best practices visits. The team visited utilities that faced similar business problems and excelled in solving them. For example, utilities that by the nature of their location needed to excel in outage management because they experienced many storms. The vendors were not included in the visits, just the customers of the solutions. This allowed the utility representatives to be as critical as they wanted about the vendor and the vendor's applications. The best practices team absorbed how well the products, services and suppliers could meet the needs because open sharing of knowledge took place during these visits that included both successes and failures.

The visits were extremely valuable and cannot overemphasize their worth to the project. It allowed the team to experience solutions under operational conditions that were exposed to the business problems being addressed by this effort. The visits also provided assurances that aggressive schedules could be developed and met. The team understood where risk mitigation should be placed in order to increase quality of the benefits. The visits also provided the context by which the solution providers would be evaluated. The visits were intense, tiring and the short time expedited was well worth the expense.

## RFI/RFP Cycle

The best practices visits and the industry scans produced more than a sufficient number of viable solution suppliers to ensure competitive bidding. In order to reduce the number of RFP recipients and to reduce the total effort during the selection process, the team chose a Request for Information (RFI) cycle. The RFI document was centered on the high level business processes previously identified. The recipients were required to address the manner in which their organization and products could support the processes. The document was very thin, less than fifteen pages, and was cycled in two weeks. A few recipients declined to respond and the team quickly assessed the remainders for viability. Within fifteen days of the beginning of the RFI cycle, a list of six RFP recipients remained.

The goal of the Request For Proposal (RFP) team remained on short cycle time to select the correct vendor(s) to meet PECO Energy's needs. Again a thin RFP, less than one hundred pages, was created centered on the business processes with the addition of technical and contractual requirements as well as requirements for data conversion. The RFP required the recipients to describe the manner in which all of the requirements would be met, even though none of the six recipients could provide a complete solution with in-house applications. This forced the vendors to form partnerships, with one of the providers acting as prime contractor. The RFP recipients were required to respond within fifteen days.

Further evaluation of the partnerships showed that the corporation was not achieving the expected business value and reductions in the total costs of systems integration. In this case complete synchronization of suppliers at the business and technology levels did not come to fruition. During the presentations of the end-to-end solutions, it became clear that each vendor could only address the functionality and implementation of their own products very well and proposed customizations for the integration points.

The technical, cost, and business management evaluations of the offered solutions were accomplished in less than twenty days. To perform the application functionality evaluation, a team of thirty-five subject matter experts (SMEs) was selected from all of the affected business areas: distribution engineers, linemen and troublemen, customer call takers, analysts, mappers and drafters, and project team members. Since a short turn-around time was required, and most of the evaluation team members were not involved with the best practices visits, each of the vendor teams was required to make a one day presentation to the evaluation team. The presentations included a business scenario that would demonstrate the manner in which the proposed system solution would address the real-world business problems. This allowed the evaluation team to easily translate the technical language of the RFP into everyday utility business world experience.

The actual evaluation of the application solutions was performed by the evaluation team in three days. A weighted decision process based directly on the RFP and business scenario materials was defined that addressed approximately thirty different functional areas. There was a two day review of the all of the functionality provided by each application facilitated by the team leads. The goals achieved during the pre-evaluation period were a common understanding of the final evaluation process and sharing of knowledge among the SMEs on their focus processes.

In order to reduce the time needed to perform the actual evaluation, a groupware facilitation system was used. This software allowed each user to vote on each of the functional areas at the same time. The software tallied the votes and provided evaluation statistics immediately at both the detail and summary levels. The tendency in most evaluations is to have one SME discussing a point at a time. The utilization of groupware allowed many points being identified, cataloged, and evaluated in parallel. The entire evaluation scoring process took ten hours. The solutions with the highest scores were subsequently evaluated in business and contractual terms and negotiations were initiated to get Letters of Intent (LOIs) signed with the vendors.

The use of groupware was highly successful and is recommended to anyone performing a similar process. It allowed for quick turn-around and provided the correct level of detail. At the end of the evaluation, each member of the team was asked to provide feedback on the process. All said it was a very satisfying experience and each member felt that their views and concerns were heard. Most felt that in using the software the bias of a single individual did not unduly influence the entire team, personalities and status did not sway the voting.

The materials collected during the evaluation process served as direct inputs to the LOIs, and covered agenda and discussion point during LOI and other contract and work negotiations.

## Phase Zero

The LOIs specify a preliminary stage named phase zero where the more definitive work and budget packages are agreed upon. The purpose of this working together exploratory and bonding phase is to establish benchmarks, closely scrutinize the feasibility of the total effort, provide more definite budgets and arrive at second level application and interface design specifications. This relatively short period of the project life cycle (less than 10% of the project implementation cycle), is useful in establishing the working organization of the formal project where the corporation and the suppliers have to pull together resources that can perform as a unit towards common interests by making each other successful. The phase is also clarifying the contract details and is providing a formalized agreement for the corporation and its suppliers to work together. The successful specification of the interfaces will show that suppliers are flexible in working with other suppliers and that their applications can accommodate out of the box changes.

The Business Process Review (BPR) model is the main process during the phase zero cycle. The BPRs are conducted at the project site using the base systems as the starting point for comparison of the "as-is" and the "to-be" states. A list of inter-process gaps is emerging that will enhance the interoperability of the individual products and serve as the future baseline offering. The BPR elements that are corporation specific are taken back to the business to determine their business value. Only those elements that are deemed essential to the business will be developed as part of the initial roll out of the solution. This process asserts both the supplier and corporate interests. An example of new functionality that emerged during the BPR's and will be delivered with the baseline product for outage management is substation modeling. This functionality will allow representation of the entire distribution system from the secondaries through the substations and will enable the call grouping algorithm to correctly assign outage incidents to either the distribution or transmission system.

As with any end-to-end business solution effort, interface development is one of the most challenging areas. Interfaces cross supplier boundaries at the product and organization levels. The solutions to these challenges require out of the box thinking across the project. Innovative solutions have already taken place for the customer system interfaces. Through simple system changes timely and accurate information can be provided to customers for outages. Also, the integration of the Supervisory Control And Data Acquisition (SCADA) with the outage management will enable the corporation to provide both internal and external customers with more accurate outage history.

## Organization

Three guiding principles anchored the organizational dynamics and structure of such a large project. The high level work packages are the obvious guiding factor where the processes and their first level decomposition resulted in direct work package construction. The second principle was the encapsulation of the reengineering components (OJSVBN and IT) into the organization by individuals who have working knowledge of these skills. The third requirement was that the revenue growth component is in the organization represented by marketing and sales contributors so that interests for new products and services business events are aligned with the project timelines. A separate entity in the organization is representing the management systems where measurement of project performance relevant to the cost benefit analysis of the overall effort takes place at regular intervals.

The organization chart clearly reflects the reengineering and revenue growth components working towards the common scope. Social activities peripheral to the work packages strengthen the formal organization to achieve practical bonding among the project team members. A variety of simple reward systems also help by encouraging healthy competition specially within the regulated environment that the project life cycle operates.

### Management of the Knowledge Talent

Upper management embraced, agreed upon, and facilitated the knowledge (information) based style of direction where each member of the core team was recognized and chosen for their distinct and in depth expertise in the areas of concern for the effort. Management clearly communicated to the core team the business goals for the project and challenged the core team honestly, openly, skillfully, and without threat with identifying technology and business discontinuities, orthodoxies, and competencies to achieve the communicated objectives. The knowledge talent understood that team decisions are timely and without question implemented by management. For example, during the supplier selection cycle each member of the knowledge basis and management had one equal vote, and in many evaluation areas management did not vote at all. The knowledge talent decisions were readily accepted and implemented as supplier awards, contract terms and conditions, and information transfer to subsequent steps in the project life cycle.

Management's expectation from the core team was to adopt the "tennis doubles" behavior where members performed outside their typical roles and responsibilities box as required by the weekly deliverables' schedule. This technique rectified resource issues and democratically assured that team members produced to their abilities, willingness, and security around work packages. The second advantage of this approach was the organizational linkage, and sharing of business and technology knowledge as provided by the two organizations around one common working table.

## Communications

Acceptance and support for the project relied heavily on the communications approach that consisted of three tiers. Executive briefings take place conveying the relationship of the business scoreboard of the project to the strategic cost avoidance and revenue growth goals of the enterprise. Presentations and project updates keep middle management informed with brief data on project milestones. Supervisors and operators are frequently and actively involved in business process reviews, and other project phases as needed with the suppliers and/or company project teams. Since there are two main processes tailoring these communications to each recipient group is preferred because it reduces information overload, keeps the momentum and interest high, reduces complexity, and takes less time to complete than one all comprehensive communications package going out to all.

The communication packages are extracts of already existing materials that are updated automatically in the computerized project controls environment. Computerization of the project documentation enables timely, accurate, and uniform communication of messages readily accessible throughout the company locations.

## Core Team Dynamics

Continuity, reuse of materials, sustaining momentum, and accumulation of overall knowledge into a pool were the primary drivers behind the notion of establishing a core team from the inception and visioning pre-project phases, to project concept and close out. The establishment of the core team took place before the formal project kick-off and will carry through to project finish. Additional objectives of the core team are planning ahead, and taking major corrective actions if required, and keeping in sync with the strategic goals of the business.

Full membership to the core team is restricted to company employees who have the option of deploying external resources to accomplish tasks as long as the corporation's competitive intelligence remains intact. Fielding in and out of team members occurs as needed and as permitted by other matrix commitments. Since each member of the team retains a fairly comprehensive knowledge of the whole effort it is possible to interchangeably utilize members' time for decision making. For example, different subsets of the core team participated in the writing, evaluation, negotiations, award, letter of intent, phase zero, and contract for each of the two processes.

The team uses electronic groupware for voting, alternative analysis, brainstorming, and convergent thinking. Utilization of electronic project management, communications, methodology, and collaborative tools is standard operating practice by team members. The team has learned that these tools reduce consensus reaching time, and increase quality and productivity of output.

## References

Drucker, Peter. 1994. Post-Capitalist Society. Harper Collins.

Fisher, Roger and Ury, William. 1991. Getting to YES. Negotiating Agreement Without Giving In. Penguin Books. 2nd ed.

Kerzner, Harold. 1995. Project Management. A Systems Approach to Planning, Scheduling, and Controlling. Van Nostrand Reinhold. 5th ed.

Project Management Institute. 1996. *A Guide to the Project Management Body of Knowledge*. Project Management Institute: Upper Darby, PA.

# Supply Chain Management and Project Management as Partners

Gwenn C. Carr, PECO Energy

## Background

PECO Energy Company is moving into a deregulated energy market without a corporate culture or experience based on operating in such an environment. The utility mindset of customers as ratepayers has been in effect since utilities began providing service, however, to quote a popular commercial, "The rules have changed."

The rules have changed in Pennsylvania. PECO Energy serves 1.5 million residential customers in the state of Pennsylvania. These consumers will soon have the opportunity to select the company that generates their electricity. In 1996, the state legislature passed and Governor Ridge signed the Electric Competition Act. All Pennsylvania consumers will have a choice by January 2001. Beginning this year, the state's electric utilities will begin conducting pilot programs to determine the most effective way to phase in choice.

One of PECO Energy's positioning strategies to prepare itself for the competitive environment is to develop supply chain management into a core competency to enable work process improvements and turn its suppliers into strategic assets.

## Advantages of Supply Chain Management

In Fortune 500 companies, the advantages of managing the supply chain have reaped rewards of up to 30% in total cost savings. Levi Strauss & Co., which generated profits of $700 million in 1995, has completely revamped their entire supply chain. Their change team even created a handbook on change entitled *Individual Readiness for a Changing Environment* (Sheff 1997) as a part of the change initiative. Companies such as Fruit of the Loom, Cargill, Heineken and Microage are redesigning their supply chains so that they will be in a position of market leadership (Mescher 1997).

Books such as *The Connected Corporation* by Jordan Lewis, describe new ways of working with suppliers that are described as "Alliances." This is a different approach to the time honored tradition of keeping suppliers at arms' length in adversarial relationships focused on lowest cost.

As described by the Gartner Group, an information technology analysis service, logistics competence requirements over the next five years will drive many enterprises to collaborate with their trading partners (Mescher 1995). As the logistics process expands beyond enterprise system boundaries, concurrent integrated logistics systems will be needed. An integrated logistics system is an event driven framework of applications to measure, manage, analyze, and optimize a collaborative business process focused on the procuring and supplying of goods and services.

## Scope of this Paper

Supply Chain Management, defined as orchestrating a concert of resources to manage the process of creating and fulfilling the market's demand for goods and services (Mescher 1996), requires rethinking the business process. Changes such as these across enterprises do not occur in quantum leaps overnight. This is where project management techniques can partner with supply chain management to enable the transition to new and different modes of operating that will enable a competitive advantage.

The focus of this paper is on the unique approach that PECO Energy has taken to organize, plan and control the transition from a transaction based purchasing organization to an organization employing supply chain management techniques.

This paper will:

- Describe the strategy to enable the transition,
- List project management techniques used as an enabler for the transition,
- Discuss communications management as a critical success factor,
- Enumerate examples of vehicles used in communications management, and
- Share lessons learned.

## The Strategy for Transition

Supply chain management requires an integration revolution (Mescher 1997). The most striking aspect of the evolution from sharing information within an enterprise to an extended enterprise supply chain logistics systems strategy is its overwhelming heterogeneity. Linking trading partners requires systems to reconcile disparate business models and data context and notion. To accommodate the complexity

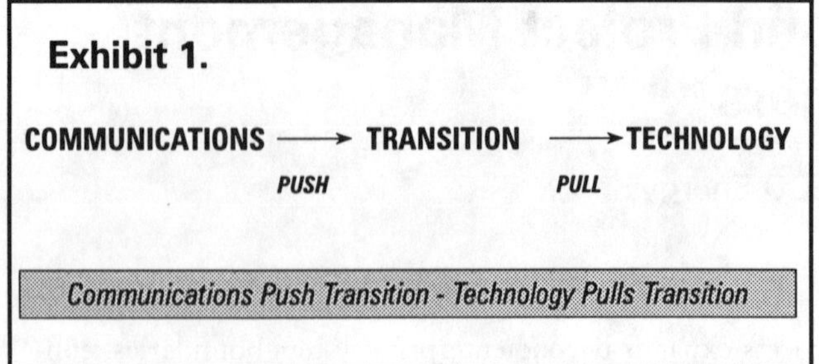


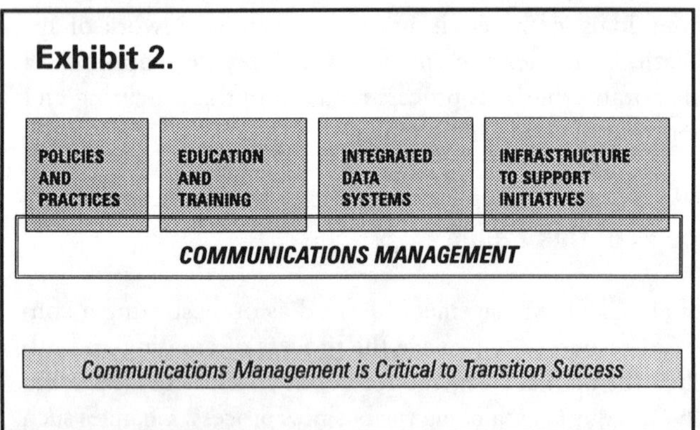


and the quickly changing nature of business, we need to eliminate the seams between stovepipe applications, reuse data and processing logic and create the virtual enterprise by linking applications between enterprises (Mescher 1996).

As the integration revolution takes place, new sources of data become available. These new sources provide an opportunity to work differently and shift old operating paradigms.

The strategy for PECO Energy's transition to supply chain management was to use technology to pull the effort and communications to push the effort (see Exhibit 1).

The use of the word technology did not include only information systems. It included any mechanism deemed appropriate to solve the problem. Wherever possible, standard application packages would be used to share information or to generate queries and reports against established databases. No new applications would be developed.

An enterprisewide work management, supply management and financial management package was also being implemented during the transition. We were able to leverage these implementation efforts to assist us on our journey to achieve competitive advantage and change outdated business practices.

The transition of the transaction based organization to an organization understanding and using supply chain management as a process required developing policies and practices, integrating data systems, delivering educational and training programs, building infrastructure to support various initiatives and communicating about the changes. Communications management was seen as a key link (see Exhibit 2).

## Project Management as an Enabler

According to *A Guide to the Project Management Body of Knowledge* (PMBOK), project management is an integrative endeavor—an action, or failure to take action, in one area will usually affect other areas. the supply management organization at PECO Energy recognized that in the transition to supply chain management, various initiatives would be underway concurrently and that project management techniques were an effective and efficient way to plan, execute and control the transition.

Project management training was provided as the organization was formed so that the basic project management techniques of writing project plans, assigning work packages, defining work breakdown structures, developing schedules and responsibility matrices could be used in team settings. There was an expectation expressed that these techniques would be used and resources were provided to document the results of the above described activities. The documentation resulting from these activities was available on the local area network for information sharing purposes.

A biweekly project meeting was held to review the status of the projects. A common format was developed for project status reports and these reports were e-mailed to members of the supply organization and various business units. When a shared drive became available, this information was placed in the appropriate location and individuals could access it as appropriate.

## Project Communications Management

Project communications management, according to *PMBOK*, includes the processes required to ensure timely and appropriate generation, collection, dissemination, storage, and ultimate disposition of project information. It provides the critical links among people, ideas, and information that are necessary for success.

As in any change effort, communication efforts were seen to be critical. *A Communications Plan for Moving Forward* was developed that included a sharing and a listening component (see Exhibit 3).

Communicating frequently and with various vehicles was seen as important to the success of the transition. With changes in technology, we were able to use several innovative approaches to communication. These techniques included developing a *Communications Support Plan* that was signed by the Supply Leadership Team and a representative of the Corporate and Public Affairs Division. This plan enabled the various teams to draw on corporate resources for communications support in a planned and controlled manner. Other vehicles for communication included the use of audio tapes,

Exhibit 3.

- Company newsletters
- Videotapes
- Presentations
- E-mail notes
- Shared drive access
- Policy guidance

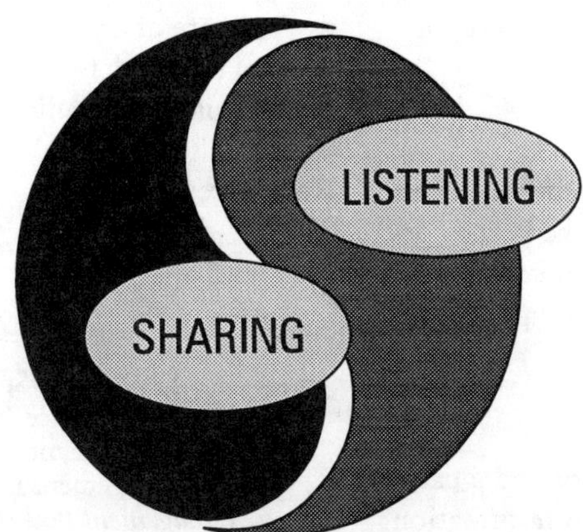


- Employee Commitment Index
- Feedback to
- Supervisors/Managers
- Business Results

*Supporting Changes in Operating Practices*

e-mail, voice mail, videotapes, presentations, project meetings, electronic bulletin boards, facilitated electronic meetings, the Internet and the capabilities of a shared drive. A short description of some of the approaches used follows.

### Audio Tapes

Audio tapes were made of update reports and trip reports. These tapes (about twenty minutes in length) were provided to senior management and others in the organization who were interested in learning about the transition effort.

### E-mail

Prior to the implementation of key systems, training and communication materials in addition to changes in policy were distributed to a wide range of individuals by e-mail. This was an effective method for ensuring that the right individuals had the information necessary to carry out their responsibilities.

A weekly survey to determine the impact of the change effort was also distributed throughout the organization. The results of the survey were used to give feedback to managers on the level of change anxiety in their organization.

### Voice Mail

Messages were broadcast to a large group of employees (both in the supply organization and the businesses) using the voice mail system. These messages included update information about the status of various initiatives. The three minute tapes included high-level descriptions of activities accomplished and provided an opportunity for those who were not a part of the teams to learn about the initiatives. This method of communication provided an opportunity for a different method of contact and a potentially broader audience. As a result of these communications, listeners called project managers to learn more details about the initiatives.

### Videotapes

An initial videotape was made to spread the word about the accomplishments of two of the cross functional teams that had been successful in changing the business process. Individuals on the teams spoke about their experience with the new method of obtaining supplies. This tape was not scripted, but was a series of interviews with team members and was shown to newly formed teams and as a part of management presentations.

A follow-up tape was made to chronicle the success of one of the cross functional teams six months later. This tape was videoed at the production point for the commodity and included comments from field users of the new process.

### Presentations

A number of presentations were provided to all levels of the organization. During Phase 1 of the project senior management was the target, during Phase 2 middle management was the focus. For one forum a free lunch was used as an incentive to draw a sold-out audience.

### Project Meetings

The notes from project meetings were kept electronically as the meeting was held. This correspondence could be sent out at the end of the meeting to the individuals involved, their superiors and the members of the leadership team. This provided an opportunity for the members of the project team to determine the wording of the items as the status was reported as well as the wording of the action items.

### Electronic Bulletin Boards

A folder titled "Supply" was set up in the shared folder area of the corporate mail messaging system. Anyone in the corporation could access the folder. It included the latest information on the transition or topics of interest on supply chain management.

### Electronic Meetings

Electronic meetings were held with a facilitator and a carefully thought out agenda to resolve issues on information needs. During these meetings, a list of prepared questions to be resolved during the session was fed to each participant's lap-top. The results of the sessions could be viewed online immediately (some sections of the meeting on a large screen for all to view). During one of these sessions, suppliers were included to learn from their expertise. The results of the sessions could be sent via e-mail to each of the participants within one hour of the close of the meeting.

### Internet Access

Standard application packages were used over the Internet to collaborate with suppliers. This allowed us to use the expertise of those who could not be located within close proximity geographically.

### Shared Drive Capability

The intent of the shared drive is to provide an information sharing capability with a minimum of administrative restrictions. The ability to share information through this mechanism provides an opportunity to adopt new business practices that enhance our ability to be competitive. As we gain experience with this area and patterns begin to emerge, the guidelines for use may change.

The types of information available included: legal documents, training documentation, meeting schedules, project updates, reports, templates, performance indicator information, current presentations, policies and procedures.

## Lessons Learned

- Communicate early, often and with various vehicles,
- For audiences unfamiliar with project management techniques, explanation may be necessary; especially when assigning ownership of tasks,
- Adhere to the spirit of project management techniques; for some audiences the laws of project management are overwhelming,
- A picture of a vision (during a transition) is more valuable than tightly defined specs, and
- Use win/win techniques.

### References


Mescher, Art. 1995. Integrated Logistics Systems. Research Briefings (May).

———. 1996. Evolution of SCM Strategy. Research Briefings (August).

———. 1997. Case Studies in Supply Chain Management. SCM Conference (April).

———. 1997. Keynote Address. SCM Conference (April).

Project Management Institute. 1996. *A Guide To The Project Management Body Of Knowledge*. Upper Darby, PA: Project Management Institute.

Sheff, David. 1997. Levi's Changes Everything. *New Rules for Business* (July) 27–31.

# Student Paper Award Winner

# Virtual Project Management: Tools and the Trade

Connie L. Guss, PhD. Candidate, Project Management Specialization Programme
The University of Calgary, Calgary Alberta.

## Abstract

This paper investigates the broad subject of project management organizations as they enter a new era of organizational arrangements. Practitioners and academics often refer to these arrangements as globally dispersed or as virtual project enterprises. This paper focuses on four related areas of virtual project organizations and their project teams. First, the paper presents a brief history about approaches to project management theory and practice and defines virtual project organizations. Next, the paper addresses challenges concerning communication and technology for virtual project organizations. Third, the paper summarizes four key organizational structures that form the basis of project-based organizations. This context is necessary in showing why some of the problems in understanding organizational structures are related to how well this information is communicated through models. An evolution of management approaches necessitates a modification in the types of project management models and communication tools. The paper introduces a new model that is capable of educating practitioners about the importance of focusing on people-centered project management tools for virtual project organizations. The final section of the paper examines one strategic and operational planning and communication tool: the round table road mapping method. The tool is simple yet it is important in understanding the level of personal involvement that may be required for successful communication and planning in non-traditional virtual project structures.

## Section I: Theory and Practice

### Introduction

Project management-based organizations understand performance, cutting costs, and reducing product or service time to market as a requirement for survival in an aggressive business environment. As early as the thirties, project-based organizations gauged success using easy-to-quantify factors such as financial performance and scheduling efficiency. The accelerated rate of change in communication technology has punctuated the need to measure areas of business that are difficult to quantify, such as customer satisfaction and organizational communication. (The introduction of the communication technology concept is credited to Edward Demming in the fifties. The term is most often associated with work in the field of manufacturing and operations.) The result may be misaligned goals among projects teams, their organizations, and clients.

Project organizations need to treat their success as an emergent quality measurable by flexible, qualitative, and quantitative indicators. This need is even more clearly seen in virtual project organizations. These organizations are uniquely organic in that their critical business processes may cut across temporal and geographical boundaries with impacts at different points in a project. The road mapping method is a powerful tool that is capable of aligning a project organization, project team members, and their clients. The following section provides the insight necessary to understand the usefulness of people-oriented tools and their role in shaping theory and practice.

### The Backbone of Project Management

Constant transitions are occurring in management styles, organizational structures, and project management techniques. Project management professionals tend to be at different stages of acceptance and willingness to change and adopt planning and communication technology. Therefore, project management professionals are more likely to embrace a multidisciplinary approach to project management practice and study as a means of being responsive to solving real world problems. Problem solving often requires project organizations to validate or challenge common assumptions as well as contribute to the development of theory. However, eliciting and distributing knowledge in project management is difficult because experts share only parts of their terminology and conceptual systems. The key is for project management practitioners to recognize and work around the empirical limitations of a young science while continually moving the project management profession forward.

The relative inexperience of project management as a science creates some difficulty in clearly introducing the phenomenon of virtual project organizations. Although discussion of virtual project organizations and their teams is appearing in the literature with increasing regularity, definition and terminology are considerably different. Therefore, discussion of these differences is a significant stage in the process of eliciting common knowledge.

**Exhibit 1.** Terms Describing Virtual Project Organizations and Their Teams

| Terms | Authors |
|---|---|
| Spider Webs | Reich, 1991 |
| Modulars, Clusters, Learning Networks, Perpetual Matrices, Or Spinouts | Bartlett and Ghoshal, 1989; Miles and Snow, 1986; Quinn, 1992; and Rodal and Wright, 1993 |
| Third Millennium Groups | Kostner, 1994 |
| Virtual Organizations | Handy, 1995 |
| Boundaryless Organizations | Ashkenas , Ulrich, Jick and Kerr, 1995 |
| Postmodern Organization | Duffy, 1994 |
| Alternate Officing | Packard, 1996 |
| Extended Enterprises and Flexible Manufacturing Networks | Landay, 1996; Barnatt, 1995; Chesborough and Teece, 1996; and Yeack and Sayles, 1996 |
| Distributed Global Workteams | Knoll and Jarvenpaa, 1996 |
| Turbo Task Forces, Or Autonomous Work Groups Outside Existing Organizational Structures | Jessup, 1996; Mezias and Glynn, 1993; Knoll and Jarvenpaa, 1996 |
| Virtual Factory | Upton and McAfee, 1996 |

### What are Virtual Project Organizations?

Although a seemingly radical organizational approach, virtual project organizations are touted as the next form in the evolution chain of organizational structures. Jan Hopland initially coined the term *virtual corporation* to describe an organizational web comprised of a small, globally dispersed *ad-hoc* team forming an enterprise (Rodal and Wright 1993). Since then, the rapid growth of electronic networking and communication technologies in many different industries is resulting in a proliferation of terms that attempt to describe the concept. Exhibit 1 lists some of the most common names to describe virtual organizations and virtual teams.

Advances in understanding how organizational structures impact project management depends in part on how experts define the concept behind the problems. Elements of several definitions of virtual teams are from Kostner 1994; Barnatt 1995; Chesborough and Teece 1996; Knoll and Jarvenpaa 1996; and Hartman and Guss 1996. Hartman and Guss pull together the most common concepts in theoretical and empirical research to form the following definition of a virtual project team:

> A temporary group of trained people separated by geographic, temporal or psychological distance, who work across organizational forms, depend on face to face (f+f) and remote communication with the intent of satisfying business requirements of sharing skills and working toward common team and client goals.

A virtual project organization may quickly deploy its resources to form project teams that are capable of responding to emerging project work. Although technologically able, virtual project organizations are still most likely to exist across other more traditional organizations. For example, contract employees may work interactively with home-based organization staff and project team members from other organizations who may employ a hierarchical or matrix structure. These project teams may be composed of customers, suppliers, functional departments, and even competitor companies with a common goal of exploiting brief windows of opportunity on any type of project, anywhere, at anytime, and in any place. Despite inconsistency in defining virtual entities, an important issue is that geographic location is no longer a primary context to define a business opportunity.

## Section II: Technology and Virtual Organizations

Many projects in the mid-nineties employ project team members that have no option to meet f+f. Ultimately, the challenge may lie in developing communication and management systems that work without f+f interaction. However, research is only beginning to challenge the belief that computer-mediated communication reduces personal influence. Walther found that anticipation of future interaction (a team knew if it would work with a client again) accounted for the differences between use of virtual communication and f+f interaction on "the immediacy, similarity, composure and receptivity of group members" (Walter 1996, 12). Researchers are also finding that electronic media can facilitate "hyperpersonal" (better than f+f) communication (Walther 1996; Knoll and Jarvenpaa 1996). Despite empirical and case studies that

**Exhibit 2.** Some Technologies Used by Virtual Project Organizations and Their Teams (Note: This Work Is Similar to Work from Guss 1996.)

| Technology | Description | Common Uses |
|---|---|---|
| **Group Decision Support Systems (GDSS)** | · Software to enable information exchange; information processing and group management. Poole and Holmes (1995) report that teams using GDSS had longer and more effective decision paths, but not better organized paths. Part of the difficulty in accepting GDSS is that professionals often believe that orderliness correlates highly with the quality of decisions. | · Making group decisions<br>· Electronic brainstorming<br>· Newsgroups and bulletin boards to share information |
| **Desktop Videoconferencing** | · Software and small hardware attachment (camera) to the top of a computer monitor. The tool provides interactive, synchronous visual and auditory stimulus. Although Integrated Services Digital Networks are better for videoconferencing, they can only handle a limited number of frames per second, giving lower quality 'freeze frame' communication. Often, user's perception of communication quality is linked to frame rate. | · Personal meetings where synchronous communication is beneficial<br>· Projects where team members are working together<br>· Situations when tough decisions need to be made, and visual cues are important |
| **Electronic Mail (Email).** | · A communication tool useful in exchanging information one-to one (or to many people when using the real-time chat feature), within or outside of the Internet. Email is one of the most widely used and accepted communication channels for low-level information exchange combined with high-involvement attributes (i.e. need for speed). | · Information exchange<br>· Document file transfer<br>· Informal and personal communication<br>· Logistics arrangements for travel and meetings<br>· Issuing memorandums |
| **Internet** | · Software freely obtainable via a computer and modem. The universal language is called Hypertext Markup Language (HTML). This language forms the basis for windows based search engines designed for simple browsing of any Internet site. | · Web-based team building and project management tools<br>· Graphic interface to transmit Computer-Aided Designs<br>· Electronic: meetings, marketing, customer support, Data Interchange<br>· Email and Internet Relay Chat<br>· Pipeline directly to existing Project Management software |

contradict this finding, the literature generally agrees that some level of f+f contact is desirable.

Exhibit 2 provides a brief review of some common communication technologies employed by virtual project organizations and their teams. The rapid rate of technology availability is one major stimulus working to level the playing field among larger and smaller project-based organizations. Alternately, smaller virtual project organizations may prefer to hire contract experts rather than invest in the human capital necessary to develop internal communication expert systems. Regardless of the path, smaller project organizations can more often afford the technology necessary to be competitive. Therefore, radically new relationships with contractors, suppliers, and clients are no longer the domain or privilege of larger project organizations.

Despite rapid advances in technology, human resistance may be the most significant barrier to communication in virtual project organizations. In some cases, project managers may perceive technology to be unproven or less effective. Project management professionals may also be faced with determining what kind of use communication tools work best within their project teams and between teams and the virtual project organization. One difficulty is that critical information about the culture, communication tools, and management approach

**Exhibit 3.** Relationship among Management Approaches

| | Routine | Novel |
|---|---|---|
| Customer Focus | I<br>Process Management | II<br>Management by Project |
| Systems Focus | III<br>Operations Management | IV<br>Project Management |

Nature of Work

in virtual project organizations may be unavailable or not evident to all project team members. Part of the problem is that management approaches are not always clearly identifiable. The next section introduces the relationships among key management approaches.

## Section III: Management Approaches

Project managers are still facing common difficulties in creating a shared mental model of familiar organizational structures such as project management, management by projects, and program management. A clearer understanding of existing structures is necessary to understand the current and potential arrangement of a virtual project organization. Exhibit 3 presents the theoretical relationship among four key management approaches. These approaches may all play a role in the growth and development of virtual project organizations.

Until the fifties, Quadrant III dominated, resulting in over-the-wall working (Turner, Peymai and Stewart 1995). The goal consisted of maximizing efficiency of routine tasks in each organizational cell. The resulting lack of customer focus prompted the use of a management by project approach (Quadrant II). For example, the management by project approach adapts well to a flatter power structure and a flexible organization whose project procedures are essentially reinvented for each project (Turner, Peymai and Stewart 1995). In the late fifties, the Cold War and rapid economic development sparked the popularity of a project management approach (Quadrant IV). The major drawback in the foundation of traditional project management is that it is rooted in a command and control approach similar to a functional hierarchy. Therefore, the actual internal system of management rather than the external or a customer focus (Quadrant I) may essentially drive a project (Turner, Peymai and Stewart 1995). There may be many practitioners who disagree with this table because it suggests that project management is not customer-focused. In practice, each approach is not mutually exclusive. The real value of the table is to show the breadth of management approaches that a virtual project organization may be working across. An appealing feature of the project management approach is that it is more capable of allowing an organization to learn from its mistakes while providing a platform for cross-functional communication in novel project environments. Alternately, process management (Quadrant I) is a very customer-focused approach born from the need to maximize operating efficiency on less complex projects that may have core characteristics.

Project organizations may not even be aware of these theoretical distinctions because real-world project management is complex and requires the use of a combination of management approaches. The project management literature is more apt to agree that a major part of managing successful projects involves delivering value to customers (Ilnicutta and Hartman 1996; Mills and Turner 1995; Turner, Peymai and Stewart 1995). This finding has led practitioners to question the effectiveness of traditional or lag indicators such as delivery on time, cost, and quality specifications even though these indicators are the established cornerstones of project management. The combination of more complex and uncertain projects and a business climate that demands a strong customer focus may continue to blur the lines between Quadrant II and IV (Exhibit 3). More certain is that a strong customer focus in project management will help practitioners understand the risk, uncertainty, and complexity inherent in projects undertaken by virtual project entities.

Because of the heightened role of the customer in project management, the communication of information about management structure through models requires discussion (Ilincutta and Hartman 1996; Thamhain 1996; Reich and Benbasat 1996). Models need to expose practitioners to new ways of thinking about concepts as an essential part of the success of project management in new and unfamiliar organizational arrangements. Models should provide information to practitioners about the necessity of asking *why* and *how* to align business and project goals in environments where physical distance separates the major project players. Exhibit 4 presents a schematic of two different cognitive processes (A and B) necessary to understand project alignment (Process B is considered the dominate mode in traditional project management.)

Reich and Benbasat (1996) note that although linkage or alignment is a key concern in most organizational approaches, there is no consensus about how to achieve alignment. Alignment is more central to information systems research than project management research. However, inconsistency in its definition and study are also a problem. For example,

**Exhibit 4.** (A And B): Alignment in Project Management

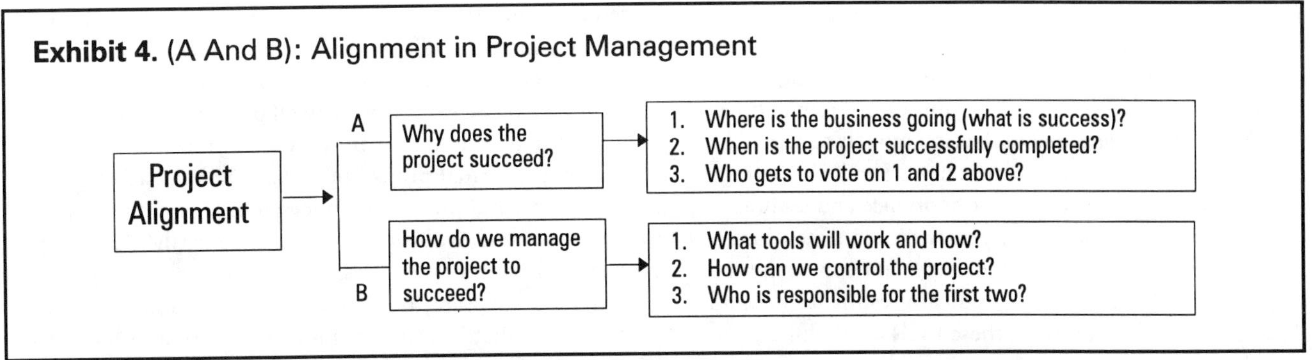
Project Alignment
A
Why does the project succeed?
1. Where is the business going (what is success)?
2. When is the project successfully completed?
3. Who gets to vote on 1 and 2 above?
B
How do we manage the project to succeed?
1. What tools will work and how?
2. How can we control the project?
3. Who is responsible for the first two?

**Exhibit 5.** The SMART Project Model

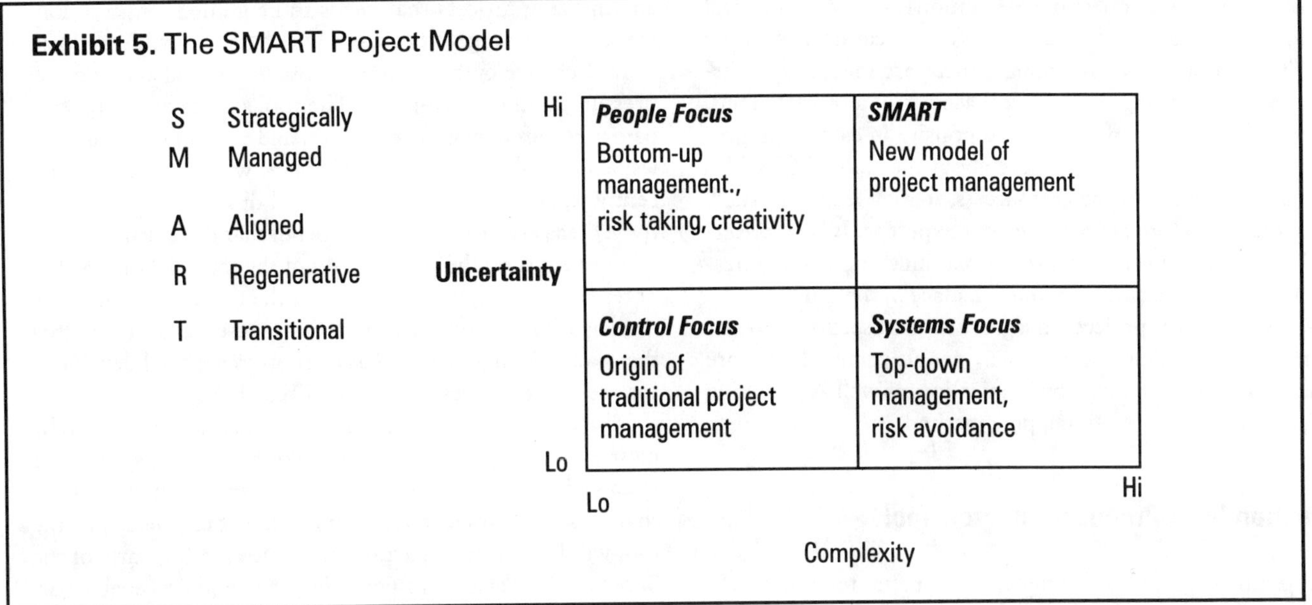
S Strategically
M Managed
A Aligned
R Regenerative
T Transitional
Uncertainty
Hi
Lo
People Focus
Bottom-up management., risk taking, creativity
SMART
New model of project management
Control Focus
Origin of traditional project management
Systems Focus
Top-down management, risk avoidance
Lo
Hi
Complexity

the term *linkage* is also reported as *alignment* (Galliers 1987; Henderson and Sifonis 1992); *coordination* in Venkatraman (1989); and *fit* in Lederer and Mendelow (1989). Conversely, traditional project management is more consistent in its discussion and use of the term *alignment*. Traditional project management most often approaches the question of success as a problem of balancing technical, process, and people-oriented tools and techniques (Exhibit 4-B). However, recent studies in project management are showing the value of investigating what works well and finding out why a project is successful (Exhibit 4-A). The focus in this process (Exhibit 4-B) is on *generative* learning, in which an organization examines radical possibilities beyond present boundaries imposed by problem solving (Barrett 1995). Hartman's (1996) SMART (strategically, managed, aligned, regenerative, and transitional) model effectively communicates the information presented in Exhibit 4 (A and B). The SMART model's (Exhibit 5) uniqueness lay in its goal of initially examining why projects succeed. Thus, project success is a case of aligning customer user functionality needs with business and project-organization objectives and vise versa.

The SMART model answers three simple questions (Exhibit 4-A) as a first step in figuring why projects succeed. The model suggests that in highly complex and uncertain project characteristics of virtual environments, the customer may have limited foresight, such as their needs are unarticulated and remain unmet by a traditional closed problem solving approach.

Strategically managed projects are projects that build short-term project plans to complement an organization's long-term business plan. The model suggests that planning should include analysis of how each project will contribute to realizing the organization's long-term business direction. Thus, alignment refers to the fit between each project and the overall organizational business goals of the sponsor organization, the project team, and the client. To achieve alignment, the project organization, as well as their project teams, need to engage in regenerative behavior. Regenerative behavior refers to the processes and practices that build trust and commitment and encourage open debate while minimizing destructive conflict. This concept is most similar to Barrett (1995), whose definition of *organizational* requires organizations to examine their underlying organizational foundations.

The SMART model is one of the first models to articulate customer focus as its central component. Similarly, perceptions are slow to change about the importance and usefulness of people-oriented project management tools. Practitioners trained in the traditional project management approach tend to rely on tools that produce lag indicator estimates (i.e., on budget, on schedule). Although these tools are definitely important in project management, their usefulness in estimating project success is questionable. Empirical and theoretical findings indicate that lead or "soft" indicators concerned with communication and management are inherently intertwined in managing the technical aspects of a project. Thus, lead indicators are often more responsive in estimating project success. Time will tell more about the ability of lead indicators in estimating project success, sharing lessons learned, and increasing project management expertise. It is more certain that people-centered project planning and communication tools will occupy a prominent space in the tool-belt of a successful virtual project manager. The next section provides a more in-depth discussion of why people centered tools are important in facilitating communication, as well as providing an example of the road mapping method.

## Section IV: A Process-Centered Tool

Project managers must continually seek better tools and techniques to overcome limitations and inefficiencies in projects. Communication inefficiencies may be even more evident in virtual organizations because of reduced access and reliance on non-verbal communication cues. Communication may even be considered as the connective tissue of a virtual project. The difficulty is in tapping into what is essentially the transmission of communication energy needed to facilitate the transfer of knowledge among project team members, their organizations, and clients. An organic metaphor of a nerve impulse shows areas of potential bottlenecks in the sender, receiver, and audience relationship (Exhibit 6).

One of the most difficult tasks of a virtual project organization may be in training project team members how to communicate intended or tacit knowledge (on the job knowhow). A parallel problem exists to initially train a nerve to develop a "memory" to recognize and respond to patterns of impulses, avoid blocks, and elicit a desired response. The entire project team (or the whole body), in the case of the nerve, experiences a shift in energy required to send and receive a communication. Similarly, in virtual project organizations, recruitment of a critical number of team members may be required for effective communication. This, in turn, may result in a natural shift in the power base so it is shared among project team members. Essentially, the value of communication may be experienced by all project team members, not only the project manager and the organization's senior management. Virtual project organizations may actually facilitate the natural process in understanding communication as organizational evolution and not necessarily a problem with individual team members.

The road mapping process is one communication and planning tool that is well suited for use in virtual project organizations. The tool treats communication and planning as an emerging process that needs to be guided and not controlled. An emergent process is one that is flexible and can shift or change over time in response to internal and external pressures and opportunities. The tool's roots are in participatory research including: cultural and anthropological studies; aboriginal healing circles; medicine wheels; and, more recently, in law through mediation and dispute resolution. All these areas are grounded in the belief that the essential focus of a project is on the people and not the tools. Masur (1993) notes that the origin is unclear, but the common theme is in participation and self-direction. Other researchers claim that the road mapping method has its roots in a model developed for use by executives (Veltrop and Yost 1988).

The road mapping method is participatory and *adhoc* by nature so that participants can take full responsibility for strategy formulation. The project organization must allow for shared power (or clear access and support to power), or the tool will have little impact on the value creating parts of the organization. Personal responsibility is essential to enable participants to 'buy in" at the start of the process. However, if top management is not committed, team members' risk taking behavior may be unsupported (MacArthur 1993).

Despite their merits, participatory tools are less often sought because they require continual learning and innovative thinking by the whole project organization. This tool requires a non-traditional focus on problem solving. Rather than fixing problems, the method examines the underlying framework that is generating the problems. Srivastva and Cooperrider (1996) speak of this approach as "Appreciate Inquiry." Appreciative inquiry is a form of generative learning capable of leveraging key aspects of an organization's culture and communication systems. This level of inquiry is accessible through the road mapping tool. The resultant product is a solid framework of an organization's underlying framework that may explain why some problems tend to persist even when they have been "fixed." This framework should be examined by studying what works well within an organization, what drives its success, and what shared mental model or vision is needed for success.

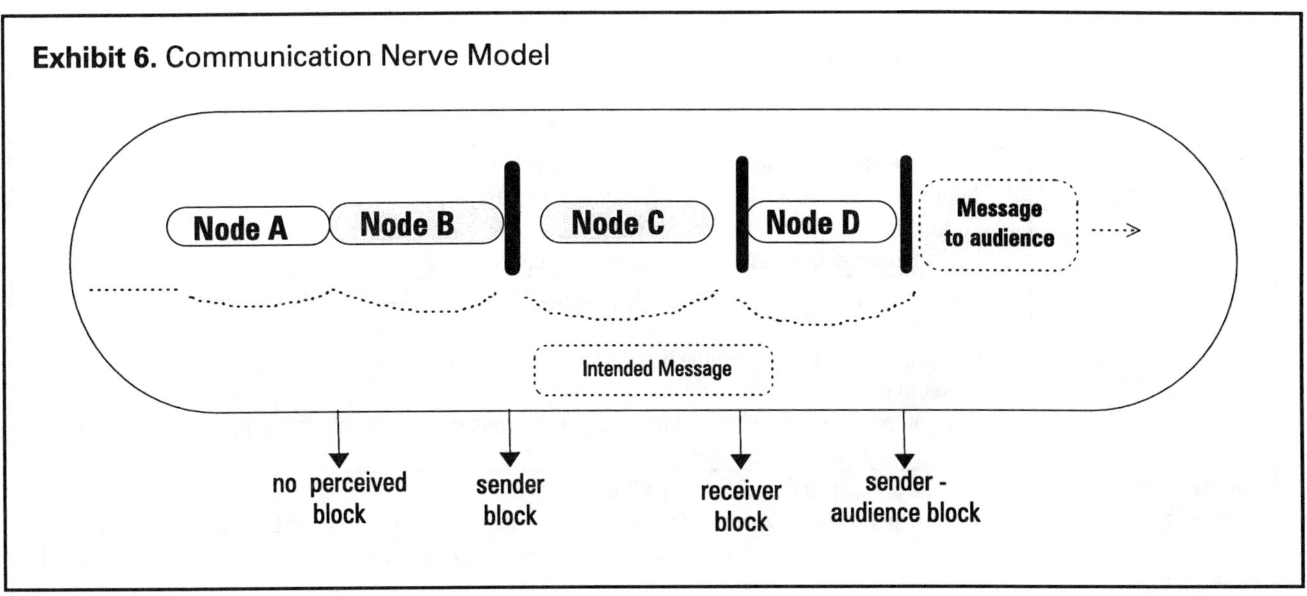


**Exhibit 6.** Communication Nerve Model

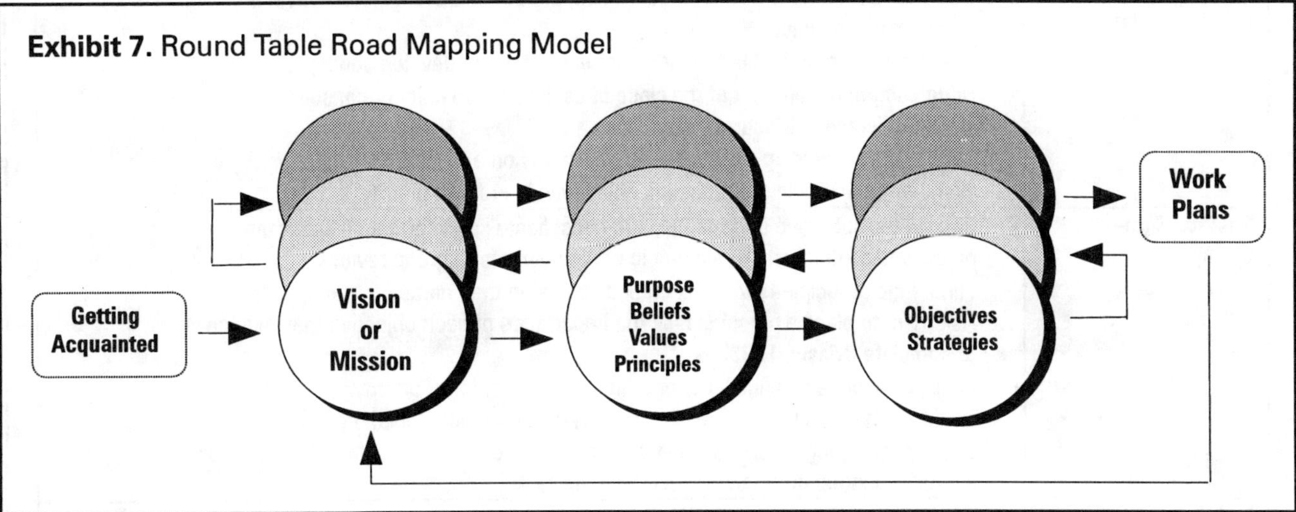


**Exhibit 7.** Round Table Road Mapping Model

The original road mapping model shown in Exhibit 7 originally includes seven steps: vision, purpose, beliefs, values, principles, objectives, and strategies.

Participants engage in a one—to-two-day workshop, guided by their choice of facilitators. The number of participants, time available, readiness of the participants, and skill of the facilitator play a key role in determining the length of a participatory planning process (Coyne 1992). The road mapping method may be conducted using computer groupWare, or f+f, or a combination of both. Exhibit 8 outlines the steps developed by the author to conduct a road mapping session.

Copies of the draft road map should be made available immediately after the meeting closes to signal the initial completion of the initial process. The whole process may take one to two days depending on the size of the group. Subsequent review sessions should also be established before the close of the meeting. The key is to ensure that participants are responsible for follow-up on each issue.

## Summary

All indications are that the phenomenon of the virtual project organizations is here to stay. Project management is necessarily problem-driven, so that lessons are often *adhoc*, and communication mistakes may be repeated. As a young science, project management is constantly reexamining its foundations and building on its understanding of how to manage a successful project. The key issue is for project managers to ask the right questions. Project managers must understand why people-centered communication tools are important and how to select and use the most appropriate technology. Often,

**Exhibit 8.** Steps in the Road Mapping Method

| Steps | Instructions |
|---|---|
| **Getting Acquainted (1)** | · Exchange personal, informal information, and define skill sets. Introductions are simple and focused away from roles and work titles.<br>· Break the larger group into smaller subgroups of 3-6 people who should not be well acquainted and allow time for some personal discussion. |
| **Vision (2)** | · Request subgroups to discuss elements of the organization (or team) vision statement.<br>· Bring subgroups together in the first round by recording their words on flipcarts or electronic whiteboards.<br>· Pull common themes and words from each round and synthesize information into a collective vision statement. |
| **Purposes (3) , Beliefs (4) and Values (5), and Principles (6)** | · Use the process in Step 2 for Steps 3 to 6.<br>· Ask subgroups to discuss beliefs, values and principles, and purposes in turn for each round (often participants have up to five rounds per concept). |
| **Identify Objectives (7)** | · Ask each subgroup to list the organization, project and client's qualitative or quantitative objectives.<br>· Use the same round table format as previous steps to develop concepts.<br>· Bring subgroups together at the close of each round to unify or consolidate similar objectives (Masur, 1993).<br>· Conclude by recording the agreed on objectives on a flipchart or whiteboard.<br>· Work with the whole group to rank objectives in order of priority. |
| **Review-Sign-On (8)** | · Review the subgroup information, and consolidate key information about the objectives on flipcharts or electronic whiteboards for a group review.<br>· Encourage participants to 'walk around', and sign their names to the objectives. Ask them to place a personal rank the importance of each objective they sign on to complete (Masur, 1993).<br>· Record objectives on flipcharts or whiteboards in order of priority.<br>· Decide as a group how to handle objectives that are not signed off by anyone. Suggest revisiting these issues at a later date, or drop them. Alternately, ask for a small volunteer group to take on the extra tasks. |
| **Link Objectives to Strategies (9)** | · Work with each subgroup to link objectives and strategies.<br>· Form subgroups on the basis of names signed to objectives and begin developing a framework of strategies for each objective ( *how* should the objective be accomplished).<br>· Use the same round table format as previous steps.<br>· Post the collection of strategies for a group review. |
| **Prepare for a Work Plan (9) and Closure (10)** | · Slow down the pace before the final product is handed out, and verbalize what the group is thinking What do I do now? . Masur cites this step as crtical in keeping the process on track (Masur, pers. comm., 1995).<br>· Explain why the Road Map is just a guiding framework for the development of specific workplans in future planning sessions. |

these decision are made with little previous knowledge or experience with virtual project organizations or their project teams. However, there is no question that the tools and the trade of project management will continually work to shape each other and rise to the challenge of managing virtual projects.

## References

### Books

Quinn, J. B. 1992. *Intelligent Enterprise*. New York: Free Press.

Reich, R.R. 1991. *The Work of Nations*. New York: Vintage Books.

Srivastva, Suresh, and David Cooperrider. 1996. *Appreciative Management and Leadership: The Power of Positive Thought and Action in Organizations*.

### Internet (Electronic Documents)

Ashkenas, R., D. Ulrich, T. Jick, and S. Kerr. 1995. *The Boundaryless Organization*. Available from Internet: http://www.mgmt.utoronto.ca/~wensle/reviews/bprev1b .html

Bartlett, C., and S. Ghoshal. 1996. *Beyond the M-Form: Toward a Management Theory of the Firm*. Available from Internet: http://www.gsia.cmu.edu/bosch/bart.html

Jessup, Leonard M., ed. 1996. *Pushing the GSS Envelope: Distributed Collaboration for Virtual Teams on the World Wide Web*. Available from Internet: http://ezinfo.ucs.indiana.edu /~ljessup/gw cent3.html

Knoll, Kathleen, and Sirkka L. Jarvenpaa. 1996. Learning to Work in Distributed Global Teams. Available from Internet: http://uts.cc.utexas.edu/~bgac313/hicss.html.

Landay, William. 1996. Extended Enterprises Spell Success. Available from Internet: http://www.reengineering.com/articles/may96/extenter.htm

### Journal Articles

Barrett, Frank J. 1995. "Creating Appreciative Learning Cultures." *Organizational Dynamics* (Autumn).

Barnatt, Christopher. 1995. "Office Space, Cyberspace and Virtual Organization." *Journal of General Management* 20(4, Summer): 78–91.

Chesbourough, Henery, and David J. Teece. 1996. "When is Virtual Virtuous? Organizing for Innovation." *Harvard Business Review* (Jan.–Feb.): 64–73.

Cohen, Lance. 1995. "Teaching with Technology." *Business Quarterly* 58(2).

Duffy, Margaret. 1994. "Ten Prescription for Surviving and Thriving in the Virtual Organization." *Public Relations Quarterly* 39.

Guss, Connie L. 1996. *Virtual Teams, Project Management Processes and the Construction Industry*. Conference Proceedings from CIBA, Bled, Slovania.

Handy, Charles. 1995. "Trust and the Virtual Organization." *Harvard Business Review* 40-50.

Henderson, J.C, and J. Sifonis. 1992. "Strategic Alignment: A Model for Organizational Transformation through Information Technology." In *Transforming Organizations*, edited by T.A. Kocham and M. Useem. New York: Oxford University Press.

Kostner, Jaclyn. 1994. "Teams Without Walls: Third Millennium Groups." *PM NetWork* (February): 39–41.

Lederer, A., and A. Mendelow. 1989. "The Coordination of Information Systems Plans with Business Plans." *Journal of Information Management Systems* 6(2): 5–19.

MacArthur, Andrew A. 1993. "Community Partnership—A Formula for Neighborhood Regeneration in the 1990s?" Community Development Journal 28 (4): 305–315.

Mezias, S.J., and M. A. Glynn. 1993. "The Three Faces of Corporate Renewal: Institution, Revolution, Evolution." *Strategic Management Journal* 14.

Miles, R.E., and C.C. Snow. 1986. "Organizations: New Concepts for New Forms." *California Management Review:* 28.

Packard, Susan. 1996. "Productivity Could be Lost in the Virtual Office." *Boston Business Journal* 16.

Poole, Marshall Scott, and Michael Holmes. 1995. "Decision Development in Computer-Assisted Group Decision Making." *Human Communication Research* 22.

Reich, Horner, and Izak Benbasat. 1996. "Measuring the Linkage Between Business and information Technology Objectives." *MIS Quarterly* (March): 55–81.

Rodal, Alti, and David Wright. 1993. "A Dossier on Partnerships." *The OPTIMUM: Journal of Public Sector Management* 24 (3).

Thamhain, Hans, J. 1996. "Best Practices for Controlling Technology-Based Projects." *Project Management Journal* (December): 37–47.

Turner, Rodney, Reza Peymai, and Kyle Stewart. 1995. "Process Management: The Versatile Approach to Achieving Quality in Project Based Organizations." *Journal of General Management* 21(1): 47–61.

Upton, David M., and Andrew McAfee. 1996. "The Real Virtual Factory." *Harvard Business Review* (July–August): 123–133.

Venkatraman, N. 1989. "The Concept of Fit in Strategy Research: Toward Verbal and Statistical Correspondence." *Academy of Management Review* 14(3): 423–444.

Walther, Joseph B. 1996. "Computer-Mediated Communication: Impersonal, Interpersonal and Hyperpersonal Interaction." *Communication Research* 23 (1).

Yeack, William, and Leonard Sayles. 1996. "Virtual and Real Organizations: Optimal Pairing." *PM NetWork* (August): 29–32.

## Papers, Manuals, and Reports

Coyne, Kathleen. 1992. *Popular Planning For Community Based Development*. Masters Degree Project, Faculty of Environmental Design. Calgary, Alberta: The University of Calgary.

Galliers, R.D. 1987. *Information System Planning in Britain and Australia in the mid-1980s: Key Success_Factors*. PhD Dissertation. London: University of London.

Hartman, Francis, and Connie L. Guss. 1996. "Virtual Teams: Constrained by Technology or Culture?" Proceedings from the International Conference on Engineering and Technology (IEMC). (1996). *Managing Virtual_Enterprises: A Convergence of Communications, Computing and Energy Technologies*. Conference Proceedings. Vancouver BC, Canada.

Ilincutta, Adrian, and Francis Hartman. 1996. *Risk Management and Success for Software Industry*. Presentation Summary. The University of Calgary, Calgary, Alberta.

Masur, L.C. 1993. *Roadmaps and Round Tables: Strategic Planning for Small to Mid Sized Non-governmental_Organizations*. Camrose, Alberta: Canadian Centre for Quality Improvement.

Mills, R.W., and Turner, J.R. 1995. "Projects for Shareholder Value." *The Commercial Project Manager.* McGraw-Hill.

Veltrop, W., and B. Yost. 1988. *The Roadmap Model*. Unpublished.

## Contacts

Hartman, Francis. 1996. Informal Meeting Notes. The University of Calgary, Calgary. Alberta. Phone: 403-220-7178.

Masur, Pers. Comm. (February, 1995). Email: cmasur@acs.ucalgary.ca. Calgary, Alberta

## Technical Program Author Contact Listing:

Mr. Wayne F. Abba
Office of the Secretary of Defense
OUSD (A+T) API/PM
3020 Defense Pentagon- 3E1025
Washington, DC 20301-3020
703-695-5166

Mr. Chris Adams
Eastman Kodak Company
F-8 / B-12 / Kodak Park
Rochester, NY 14652-4417
716-722-6804

Mr. Artem V. Aleshin
Bremen University
Institute of Project
Management & Information
B. Perejslavska Str. 15, apt. 83
Moscow 129041
Russia
007095-280-56-24

Mr. Hashem Al-Tabtabai
Kuwait University
Civil Engineering Department
College of Engg. and Petroleum
PO Box 5969
Safat 13060
Kuwait

Ms. Colleen Andreoli
USAA,,9800 Fredericksburg Rd.
AB-2-W
San Antonio, TX 78288
210-498-3581

Dr. John Audi
Edwards and Kelcey, Inc.
529 Main Street, Suite 203
Boston, MA 02129
617-242-9222

Mr. Steven M. Barger
Greenbrier & Russel, Inc.
1450 E. American Lane, Suite 1700
Schaumburg, IL 60173
847-330-4287

Mr. Michael J. Barlow
ACS,,1103 Avenue B
Arnold A.F.B., TN 37389-1500
615-454-3610

Dr. Roger D. Beatty, PMP
AT&T
2355 Dulles Corner Blvd., Suite 400
Herndon, VA 20171
703-713-5482

Dr. Paul B. Blacker
Lockheed Martin Idaho Technologies
Company
PO Box 1625
Idaho Falls, ID 83415-3710
208-526-0660

Mr. Jeffery Blanton
Chiron Vision
555 West Arrow Hwy
Claremont, CA 91711
909-399-1508

Mr. Tom Block
PerotSystems,,4430 Altura Ct.
Fairfax, VA 22030
703-591-3083

Mr. Kenneth G. Bobis
Western International University
15273 S. 31st Street
Phoenix, AZ 85048
602-943-2311 x.625

Mr. Douglas Boebinger, PMP
Integrated Process Developers
313 Buckingham
Canton, MI 48188
313-317-4686

Ms. Laurie K. Bosley, PMP
Solbourne
4464 Marengo Place
Las Vegas, NV 89117
702-365-8457

Mr. Anthony Brock, PE, PMP
Duke Power Company
1413 Longbrook Drive
Charlotte, NC 28270
704-875-4371

Mr. Scott C. Brown, PMP
AT & T Submarine Systems
Room 3J-420
101 Crawfords Corner Rd.
Holmdel, NJ 07733
908-949-9658

Mr. Jeffrey S. Brown
Eli Lilly and Company
PO Box 99
Clinton, IN 47842
317-832-4330

Mr. Tom Buttle, PMP
Bell Canada
Director – Business Transformation
F6B - 33 City Center Dr.
Mississauga, ON L5B 2N5
Canada
905-949-7177

Ms. Gwenn C. Carr
PECO Energy
965 Chesterbrook Blvd.
Wayne, PA 19087
610-640-6925

Mr. Elliot Chocran
Integrated Management Systems, Inc
3135 S. State Suite 104
Ann Arbor, MI 48106
810-492-2208

Mr. Roger Clawson
State of Oregon
361 SW 4th St.
Gresham, OR 97080
503-373-1044 x. 266

Dr. David I. Cleland
University of Pittsburgh
School of Engineering
Industrial Eng. Dept.
1035 Benedum Hall
Pittsburgh, PA 15261
412-624-9833

Dr. Dennis J. Cohen
Strategic Management Group
3624 Market Street – UCSC, 3rd Floor
Philadelphia, PA 19104
215-387-4000 ext. 295

Mr. Gary Cokins
ABC Technologies
30495 Oakview Way
Bingham Farms, MI 48025-4631
810-642-1296

Mr. Edward M. Copenhaver
Daugherty Systems
85 Weldon Way #B
Newnan, GA 30263-1862
770-254-9500

Ms. Lynn Crawford
Univ. of Technology, Sydney (UTS)
Faculty of Design,
Architecture & Building
PO Box 123
Broadway, NSW 2007
Australia
61-2-9514-8730

Mr. Carl W. Crosswhite, Jr.
Boeing Defense and Space Group
PO Box 3999, MS 3A-FC
Seattle, WA 98124-2499
206-773-7094

Ms. Catherine Daw
SPMgroup, Ltd.
3266 Yonge St., Suite 2022
Toronto, ON M4N 3P6
Canada
416-485-1584

Mr. F. Douglas DeCarlo
ICS Group
40 Richards Avenue
Norwalk, CT 06854
203-838-1150

Dr. Robert J. DeFillippi
Suffolk University
Frank Sawyer School of Management
8 Ashburton Place
Boston, MA 02108-2770
617-573-8243

Mr. John A. Del Vecchio
Eastman Kodak Company
14 Stillmeadow Dr.
Rochester, NY 14624
716-726-5944

Mr. Kenneth Delcol
PE – SCIEX
71 Four Valley Drive
Concord, OT L4K 4V8
Canada
905-660-9005 ext. 355

Mr. A. Richard Diederich
Eastern Project Services
615 Fernfield Cir.
Wayne, PA 19087
610-687-5080

Mr. Lucio Jose Diniz
LD&M Consultores Associados S/C
Alameda da Serra, 420 - CJ. 510-511
Nova Lima, MG
34.000.000, Brazil
031-286-3405

Mr. Mark A. Dinman
EDS,,13736 Riverport Drive, DC 1020
Maryland Heights, MO 63043
314-344-5482

Mr. Paul C. Dinsmore, PMP
Dinsmore & Associates
Rlia Primeiro De Marco 21/12
Rio De Janario, Brazil
5521-221-7622

Ms. Jacqueline Y. Donahue
Zeneca Pharmaceuticals
1800 Concord Pike
PO Box 15437
Wilmington, DE 19850-5437
302-886-4814

Mr. Richard Donica
Newberg/Perini
651 Washington Boulevard
Chicago, IL 60661-2123
815-458-2801 x.2390

Dr. William J. Dunn
Eli Lilly & Co
Lilly Corporate Center
Indianapolis, IN 46285
317-276-6267

Rear Admiral Joseph Dyer
Naval Air Station at Patuxent River
22347 Cedar Point Rd
Patuxent River, MD 20670-1161

Dr. David Eager
University of Technology - Sydney
PO Box 123
Broadway 2007
Australia
61-2-9514-2687

Ms. Luba Ebert
4037 Ruby Ave
North Vancouver, BC V7R 4B4
Canada
604-984-7918

Mr. Dennis W. Engers
Sanofi Research
9 Great Valley Parkway
Malvern, PA 19355
610-889-8630

Mr. Roger L. Erickson
W.J. Schafer Associates, Inc.
3309 Panorama Dr., SE
Huntsville, AL 35801
205-533-4244

Mr. W. David Featherman
Project Performance Corporation
209 Wachusett Street #1
Jamaica Plain, MA 02130
617-524-3196

Mr. Jens Federhen
University of Siegen
Paul-Bonatz-Str. 9-11
Siegen 57068 Germany
49-271-740-2631

Mr. Brian Ferrilla
System Solvers, Ltd.
30685 Barrington Ave. #100
Madison Hts., MI 48071
810-588-7400

Ms. Anita Fincher, PMP
US Dept. of Agriculture / National
Finance Ctr. PO Box 60000
New Orleans, LA 70160
504-255-6402

Dr. Owen C. Gadeken
Defense Systems Management College
9820 Belvoir Rd., Suite G38, FD-ED
Fort Belvoir, VA 22060-5565
703-805-5425

Mr. David M. Gallegos
Robbins-Gioia, Inc.
11 Canal Center Plaza, Suite 200
Alexandria, VA 20109
703-706-9086

Mr. Brian J. Gegan
KPMG Peat Marwick LLP
400 Capitol Mall, Suite 800
Sacramento, CA 95814-4407
916-554-1754

Mr. Gregory D. Githens, PMP
MaxiComm Project Services
2429 South Main St.
Findlay, OH 45840
419-424-1164

Dr. Shlomo Globerson
Tel Aviv University
School of Business Administration
Ramat Aviv, Tel Aviv 69978
Israel
972-3-6408515

Mr. Larry Goldsmith
C.W. Costello & Associates
8430 Bryn Mawr Avenue, STE 685
Chicago, IL 60631
773-693-8000

Ms. Margaret S. Goldstein
GMS Consulting, Inc.
935 E. 49th St.
Chicago, IL 60615
773-924-9191

Mr. Rick Goltz
United Space Alliance
8703 Hibiscus Ct.
Cape Canaveral, FL 32920
407-861-4471

Mr. Mickey Granot
Granot-Striechman
Management Consultants LTD
17 Weisborg St.
Tel Aviv, 69358
Israel

Mr. Stephen P. Gress
Management Technologies Inc.
3331 W. Big Beaver Rd., Suite 105
Troy, MI 48084
810-643-1915

Mr. Michael Grice
Ernst & Young LLP
104 Decker Court
Irving, TX 75062
214-665-5828

Mr. Andrew F. Griffith
Independent Project Analysis, Inc.
3022 Regents tower St., #346
Fairfax, VA 22031
703-273-8715

Mr. Robert F. Hales
Proaction Development, Inc.
1680 Grey Fox Trail
Milford, OH 45150
513-248-0680

Mr. David Hamburger
David Hamburger Mgt. Consultants, Inc.
19 Zabela Drive
New City, NY 10956-7149
914-352-1564

Mr. Amjad S. Hanif
INTEL Corporation
MPI-112
2200 Mission College Blvd.
Santa Clara, CA 95052
408-765-5718

Dr. Roger G. Harrison
Eli Lilly & Company
Lilly Corporate Center
Indianapolis, IN 46285-1010
317-276-4155

Mr. John D. Harrison, PMP,REM,CCM,EIT
Metcalf Eddy, Inc.
3838 N. Sam Houston Pky E., Suite 440
Houston, TX 77032
281-590-8830 x.107

Dr. Francis Hartman
University of Calgary
Department of Civil Engineering
2500 University Drive N.W.
Calgary, AB T2N 1N4
Canada
403-220-7178

Mr. Shailesh Hegde
Texas Instruments (India)
Wind Tunnel Rd.
Bangalore, Karnataka
580 017
India
91-80-526-9451

Mr. G. Alan Hellawell, Jr.
Eastman Kodak Co.
145 Willow Bend Dr.
Penfield, NY 14526-1138
716-722-7279

Dr. Edward J. Hoffman
NASA Headquarters
Office of Training and Development
NASA HQ Code FT
Washington, DC 20546-0001
202-358-2182

Mr. Harvey Hoffman
Canberra Industries, Inc.
800 Research Parkway
Meriden, CT 06450
203-639-2211

Mr. John L. Homer
BMW Constructors, Inc.
1740 West Michigan Street
Indianapolis, IN 46222
317-267-0400

Mr. Colin Huddy
Clear Communications Ltd.
Private Bag 92143
Auckland, New Zeland
64-9-912-4360

Mr. Noel Hutson, PMP
820 NE 160th Avenue
Portland, OR 97230
503-230-3756

Dr. Bill Ibbs
University of California Berkeley
Dept. of Civil Engineering
213 McLaughlin Hall
Berkeley, CA 94720
510-643-8067

Dr. Nikolai I. Ilin
Moscow State University of Civil Engineering
1 st. Tverskaya-Yamskaya str., 26, apt. 38
Moscow 125047
Russia
423-553-7306

Mr. Lewis R. Ireland
Project Technologies Corporation
20290 Doewood Dr.
Monument, CO 80132-8050
719-481-9628

Mr. David Irving
Synergy International Limited
PO Box 11-545
Wellington, New Zealand
64-4-499-0333

Dr. George F. Jergeas, PE
The University of Calgary
Department of Civil Engineering
2500 University Drive N.W.
Calgary, Alberta T2N 1N4
Canada
403-220-8135

Mr. Ken Jones
Ernst & Young LLP
One Indiana Square, Suite 3400
Indianapolis, IN 46204
317-681-7740

Mr. J. Norman Jones, PMP
Newberg/Perini Corp.
651 W. Washington Boulevard
Chicago, IL 60661-2123
815-458-2801 ext. 2397

Mr. M. Dale Jordan
General Motors Truck Group
1999 Centerpoint Parkway
MC 483 550 351
Pontiac, MI 48341
810-753-7444

Mr. Clinton Jullens
Lockheed Martin Skunk Works
18653 Ventura Blvd. #173
Tarzana, CA 91356
805-572-6392

Mr. Youngsoo Jung
Ssangyongsoo Engineering and Construction Co., Ltd.
CIC Planning Dept.
87 Samsung-dong, Kanguam-gu
Seoul 135-090 Korea
82-2-513-7932

Dr. Kalle Kahkonen
VTT Building Technology
PO Box 1801
02044-VTT Finland
358-9-456-4560

Dr. Nicholas Kallas
PECO Energy
2301 Market Street, N3-2
Philadelphia, PA 19101-8699
215-841-6976

Mr. Bruce Kay
Electronic Data Systems
10824 Lasalle
Huntington Woods, MI 48070
810-753-0277

Dr. Deborah S. Kezbom
Management Resources Inc.
420 East 72 St.
New York, NY 10021
212-794-6527

Mr. Mark Kiker
Holmes & Narver, Inc.
999 Town & Country Rd
Orange, CA 92868
303-799-6075

Ms. Joan Knutson
Project Mentors
211 Sutter Street, 5th Floor
San Francisco, CA 94108
415-955-5777

Mr. Paul E. Konkel
Konkel and Associates,
26581 Royale Dr.
San Juan Capistrano, CA 92675
714-364-3932

Mr. Waldemar H. Koscinski, PMP
Department of the Navy
2531 Jefferson Davis Hwy
Arlington, VA 22242
703-602-3476 x. 377

Ms. Petra Kring, Dipl. Ing
The University of Siegen
Paul-Bonatz-Strass 9-11
Fachbereich 11
Management Int. Projekte
57068 Siegen, Germany
49-271/740-2631

Mr. Ramakrishnan Krishnan
Ford Motor Company
FPDS Project Mgt. PDC Bldg.
MD#122, GC-F58
PO Box 2053
Dearborn, MI 48121-2053
313-390-4276

Ms. Ruta R. Kulbis
Andersen Consulting LLP
3773 Willow Rd.
Northbrook, IL 60062
847-714-2242

Mr. John J. Lambert
U.S. Bureau of Reclamation
PO Box 25007, Att: D-5501
Denver, CO 80225-0007
303-236-3386 x. 201

Mr. Carl C. Lang
The Boeing Company
PO Box 3999, MS 8769
Seattle, WA 98124-2499
206-773-3413

Dr. Alexander Laufer
Technion National Building Research Station
Vice Dean, Civil Engineering
Technion, Haifa 32000 Israel
972-4-8292364

Mr. William V. Leban
Keller Graduate School of Management
Suite 1000
One Tower Brook Lane
Oakbrook Terrace, IL 60181
630-571-2358

Dr. David R. Lee
University of Dayton
300 College Park
Dayton, OH 45469-2235
513-229-3443

Dr. R.J. Levene
Cranfield School of Management
Cranfield University
Cranfield, Bedford MK43 0AL
England
44(1234)751122 x. 4410

Mr. John J. Lucas
Work Management Solutions, Inc.
75 Wells Avenue
Newton, MA 02159
617-964-1633

Mr. Joseph A. Lukas
Eastman Kodak Company
1 Bellflower Circle
Fairport, NY 14450
716-722-5804

Mr. Scott Mairs, PMP
CITICORP
4 Campus Circle
Westlake, TX 76262
817-491-7464

Mr. Edwin J. Mantel
ComEd
1400 Opus Place
Downer's Grove, IL 60515
630-663-2999

Mr. Edwin D. Marion
PM Pharos, Inc.
137 Cambridge Dr.
Berkeley Hights, NJ 07927
908-508-9294

Ms. Noreen Matsuura
U.S Department of Energy
Rocky Flats, PO Box 928
Golden, CO 80928
303-966-2926

Mr. Richard D. May
ABB Environmental Services, Inc.
2590 Executive Center Circle East
Tallahassee, FL 32301
904-656-1293

Mr. David A. Maynard
ITT
5519 River Run Trail
Fort Wayne, IN 46825
219-487-6795

Mr. Bryan R. McConachy, PE, PMP
Bramcon Project Consultants Ltd.
1400-1500 West Georgia St.
Vancouver, BC V6G 2Z6
Canada
604-684-7114

Ms. Jean M. McWeeney, PMP
Sterling Information Group Inc.
1717 West 6th Street, Suite 340
Austin, TX 78703-4778
512-344-1045

Mr. Ed Melcher, CCP
Equitable Resource Inc.,,420 Blvd. Of the Allies, 8th Floor
Pittsburgh, PA 15219
412-553-6144

Mr. Vladimir N. Mikheeve
Project Management Centre (Moscow)
Room 1303, 29 Vernadsky Dr.
Moscow 117943
Russia
7-095-131-1436

Mr. Bruce Miller, PMP
Origin Technology in Business
8044 Montgomery Rd., Suite 200 W
Cincinnati, OH 45236-2929
513-985-1402

Dr. Donald J. Miller
Experian
5601 E. LaPalma Ave.
Anaheim, CA 92807
714-385-7320

Mr. Don Miller
Wyeth-Ayerst Research
PO Box 8299
Philadelphia, PA 19101
215-688-4400

Dr. Dragan Milosevic
Pinnell/Busch, Inc.
16190 SW Theresa Court
Beaverton, OR 97007
503-293-6280

Ms. Stacy Miltiades
Bellcore
444 Hoes Lane, Room 4A-832
Piscataway, NJ 08854-4182
908-699-220

Mr. Das P. Mootanah
Anglia Polytechnic University
88 West Avenue
Chelmsford, Essex CM1 2DF
United Kingdom
0-1245-252-272 c.0044

Mr. Harold Mooz
Center for Systems Management
19046 Pruneridge Avenue
Cupertino, CA 95014
408-255-8090

Mr. Paul E. Moulder
AT&T Solutions
140 Sprague Ave.
S. Plainfield, NJ 07080
201-443-3748

Mr. Gary Neights
RWD Technologies, Inc.
10480 Little Patuxent Parkway
RWD Bldg. Suite 1200
Columbia, MD 21044-3530
410-730-4377 x. 7474

Dr. Beebe Nelson
Product Development Partners Inc.
49 Temple Street
Newton, MA 02165
617-928-3413

Dr. Andras Nemeslaki
Weatherhead School of Management
Dept. of MIDS
10900 Euclio Avenue
Cleveland, OH 44106-7235
216-386-2144

Mr. Robert C. Newbold
Creative Technology Labs
37 Grieb Trail
Wallingford, CT 06492
203-265-7590

Mr. Jeff Nielsen
First Data Corporation
10826 Farnam Dr. Stop U-41
Omaha, NE 68154
402-222-8881

Mr. Brian Nofzinger
3020 James Avenue South
Minneapolis, MN 55408

Mr. J. Reddy Nukalapati
Lucent Technologies
211 Mount Airy Rd., Room 2C210
Basking Rodge, NJ 07920
908-953-8578

Mr. Edward A. O'Connor
Bausch & Lomb, Inc.
1400 No. Goodman St.
PO Box 450
Rochester, NY 14609
716-338-5575

Mr. Tsuneyoshi Oguri
JGC Corporation
14-1, Bessho 1-chome, Minami-ku
Yokohama, 232
Japan
81-45-721-7644

Mr. Gerard P. O'Keefe
Resolution Management Consultants
Inc.
PO Box 1006
Mt. Pleasant, SC 29465
803-849-8003

Mr. Bruce Orr
Transcontinental Gas Pipeline Corp.
341 Aragon
Los Alamos, NM 87544
505-672-9340

Mr. Steven Pascale
Digital Equipment Corporation
1770 Wedgewood Commons
Concord, MA 01742
508-493-8633

Mr. David Pells, PMP
Mathie, Pells & Associates
PO Box 542226
Dallas, TX 75354
214-526-8981

Mr. Lee A. Peters
Peters & Company
70 N. Main Street
Zionsville, IN 46077
317-873-0086

Mr. Raymond G. Piper
Union Carbide
PO Box 471
Texas City, TX 77592-0471
409-948-5242

Ms. Anamaria Popescu-Kohler
Carter & Burgess
1101 Leah Ave, #1014
San Marcos, TX 78666
512-385-4881

Mr. Roger A. Powell, PE
M2J, Inc.
1740 Hollins Rd.
Bensalem, PA 19020
215-244-4106

Mr. Steven M. Price
S.T. Gerann
PO Box 1374
Princeton, NJ 08542-1374
609-252-1676

Mr. Carl L. Pritchard
Educational Services Institute
517 Wilson Place
Frederick, MD 21702
703-558-3133

Mr. John Rakos
John J. Rakos & Associates
14 Palsen St.
Nepean, ON K2G 2V8
Canada
613-727-1626

Ms. Carol Rauh
Bellcore RRC4A833
444 Hoes Lane
Piscataway, NJ 08854
908-699-8822

Dr. Tzvi Raz
Tel Aviv University
Faculty of Management
Ramat Aviv, Tel Aviv 69978
Israel
972-3-640-8230

Ms. Lou Russell
Russell Martin & Associates
6326 Rucker Rd., Suite E
Indianapolis, IN 46220
317-475-9311

Ms. Rose Russett
General Motors Powertrain Group
850 Joslyn Rd
Pontiac, MI 48340
810-857-4637

Mr. Richard E. Ryder
Plan-Tech Inc.
22000 Spring Brook
Farmington Hills, MI 48338
810-615-0333

Mr. Hiromitsu Sakamoto
Takenaka Corporation
21-1, 8-chome, Ginza, Chou-ku
Tokyo, 104 Japan
81-3-3542-7100 (Ext: 3413)

Mr. Frank P. Saladis
AT&T
97 Mountain View Ave.
Staten Island, NJ 10314
212-387-5325

Mr. Jose Angelo Santos do Valle
PROMON Eng. Ltd.
Praia do Flamengo,
154 - 9 andar - Flamengo
Rio de Janeiro, RJ
22207-900
Brazil
55-21-555-2768

Mr. Jhan Schmitz
International Bechtel Inc.
New Airport Projects Coordination Office
8/F Shui On Centre, 8 Harbor Rd
Wanchai, Hong Kong
852-2829-6734

Mr. James J. Schneidmuller
AT & T
2 Gatehall Drive, Rm 1B119
Parsippany, NJ 07054
201-682-3430

Ms. Vicki Shapiro
United States Automobile Association
9800 Fredericksburg Rd.
San Antonio, TX 78288
210-496-5159

Dr. Aaron J. Shenhar
Stevens Institute of Technology
Hoboken, NJ 07030
201-216-8024

Mr. Bill Shepherd, PMP
Decision Dynamics
4600 East West Hwy.
Bethesda, MD 20814
301-657-8500

Mr. William E. Skimin
Integrated Management Systems, Inc.
3135 S. State Suite 104
Ann Arbor, MI 48106
810-492-2226

Mr. Max B. Smith
Digital Equipment Corp.
5555 Windward Parkway West
Alpharetta, GA 30201
770-343-1343

Dr. Larry A. Smith
Florida International University
9611 Conchshell Manor
Plantation, FL 33324
954-370-7507

Mr. Stephen M. Somermeyer
Eli Lilly & Company
Lilly Corporate Center
Indianapolis, IN 46285
317-276-4569

Mr. Eric Spanitz
Project Mentors
211 Sutter Street, 5th Floor
San Francisco, CA 94108
415-955-5777

Ms. Victoria Spender
The Constell Group
619 River Drive, Bldg. 1
Elmwood Park, NJ 07407-1360
201-703-8300

Mr. Matthew Steigerwald
Integration Management Systems, Inc.
3135 S. State St., Suite 104
Ann Arbor, MI 48108
313-996-0500

Ms. Shari Stern
AT&T
1200 Peachtree St. (6n27)
Atlanta, GA 30309
404-810-8524

Mr. Lawrence Stern
People Places LLC
2220 Glendaloch Rd
Ann Arbor, MI 48104
313-668-6828

Mr. James R. Sumara
Harris Corporation
1025 W. Nash Blvd. MS - 300
Melbourne, FL 32919
407-724-3289

Mr. William J. Swanston
29165 Grove
Livonia, MI 48154
313-513-5816

Ms. Karen Tate
The Griffin Tate Group
3604 Carpenter's Green Lane
Cincinnati, OH 45241-3219
513-984-8150

Mr. Michael Terrell, PE, PMP
Duke Power Company
4631 Chuckwood Drive
Charlotte, NC 28227
704-875-4000 x. 2784

Mr. David Thompson
Project Management Allience, LLC
1821 Lefthand Circle, B-2
Longmont, CO 80501-6740
303-774-1906

Mr. Chris Torkelson
Northwestern Mutual Life Insurance
720 E. Wisconsin Ave.
Milwaukee, WI 53202
414-299-3138

Dr. Shigehisa Tsuchiya
Chiba Institute of Technology
2-17-1 Tsudanuma
Narashino-shi,,275
Japan
81-474-78-0348

Mr. John Tuman, Jr., PE, PMP
Management Technologies Group, Inc.
PO Box 160
Morgantown, PA 19543
610-286-2178

Mr. Tom Vanderheiden
Project Management &
Control Consultants, Inc.
1451 E. Northcrest Dr. / PO Box 4093
Highlands Ranch, CO 80126
303-791-3121

Mr. Chris Vandersluis
HMS Software
9900 Cavendish #305
St. Laurent, QC H4M 2V2
Canada
514-333-0718

Mr. Ben E. Voivedich, Jr., PMP
PMCC, Inc.
1373 Corporate Square Blvd.
Slidell, LA 70458
504-641-0477

Prof. Vladimir Voropaev
Russian Project Management Assoc.
Room 1303, 29 Vernadsky Prospect
Moscow 117943
Russia
7-095-133-26-11

Ms. Sarah A. Wagner
Electronic Data Systems Corp.
ED-04-204
5236 Tennyson Parkway
Plano, TX 75042
800-325-0576 xt. 64449

Mr. Ron Waller, PMP
Johnson Controls, Inc.
1701 W. Civic Dr., PO Box 591/ A-3
Milwaukee, WI 53201-0591
414-228-3808

Mr. Richard Watson
Fidelity Investments
41 Belle Vista
Boston, MA 02146
617-563-9273

Ms. Melba Watts
AT&T
Room 717-3, 221 E. Fourth St.
Cincinnati, OH 45202
513-629-5623

Mr. Carl Weatherell, M.Sc., C.Chem
Natural Resources Canada
555 Booth St.
Ottawa, ON K1A 0G1
Canada
613-995-3097

Mr. Kenneth Whiting
The Knowledge Web
6901 S. Yosemite, Suite 207
Englewood, CO 80112
303-793-9900

Mr. R. Max Wideman
AEW Services
2216 west 21st Avenue
Vancouver, BC V6L 1J5
Canada
604-736-7025

Mr. Tammo T. Wilkens, PE, PMP
LA County MTA
3112 Amigos Dr.
Burbank, CA 91504
213-922-1464

Mr. Charles J. Williams
Black & Veatch Infrastructure
10604 West 148th St.
Overland Park, KS 66221
913-458-3206

Mr. George A. Wilson
COM ED
2720 Asbury Dr.
Aurora, IL 60504
630-820-0835

Dr. Itzak Wirth
St. John's University
College of Business Administration
8000 Utopia Parkway
Jamaica, NY 11439
718-990-6476

Mr. George K. Wissborn, PE, PMP
Ontario Hydro
Box 160, Brock Rd. S. P24
Pickering, ON L1V 2R8
Canada
905-839-1151

Ms. Vicki Wong
Nissan Motor Corporation
18501 S. Figueroa St.
Gardena, CA 90248-4500
310-771-5070

Mr. Steve Yager
CSC Artemis,,6260 Lookout Rd.
Boulder, CO 80301
303-581-3120

Dr. Janet K. Yates
San Jose State University
Civil Engineering Department
One Washington Square
San Jose, CA 95192-0083
408-924-3853

Mr. Bruce D. Yost
Lockeed Martin Engineering & Science Co.
Mail Stop: 240A-4
Moffett Fielf, CA 94035-0168
415-604-6839

Mr. Robert J. Yourzak, P.E.
Robert Yourzak & Associates, Inc.
7320 Gallagher Dr., Suite 325
Minneapolis, MN 55435
612-831-2235

Mr. Brian Zaas
Bellcore
Systems Integration Services
331 Newman Springs Rd.
Red Bank, NJ 07701-5699
908-758-2111

Dr. Alaa A. Zeitoun, PMP
International Institute for Learning, Inc.
723 Charter Woods Dr.
Indianapolis, IN 46224
317-247-6005

# Tides of Change
# PMI '98 Long Beach

9-15 October, 1998, Long Beach, California, USA

## CALL FOR PAPERS
### ABSTRACT SUBMISSION KIT

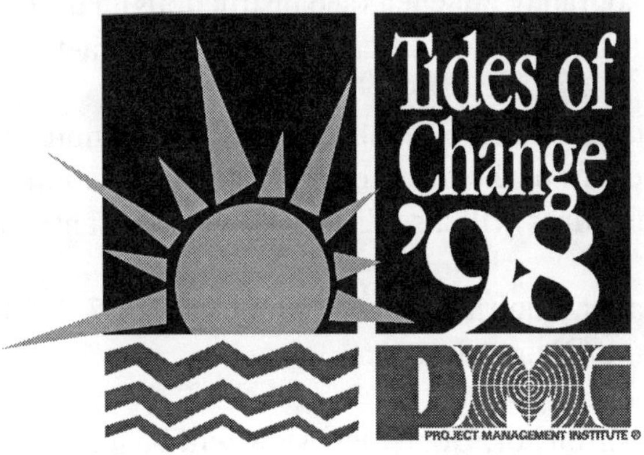


Date: Must be submitted by January 15, 1998

To: **Mr. Quentin Fleming**
PMI '98 Technical Program Chairman
C/O PMI Publications
40 Colonial Square
Sylva, NC 28779 USA

E-mail: bookauth@pmi.org

**To:** All Prospective Authors/Presenters for PMI '98 Long Beach

Thank you for your interest in preparing an abstract for consideration in PMI's 29th Annual Seminars & Symposium Technical Program. Please use the attached guidelines in preparing your submission. All abstracts should be responsive to the theme "Tides of Change". The ideal paper would deal with how project management is changing or will change in the coming years.

Competition for Technical Program slots has grown tremendously over the past few years. Since there is only a limited number of presentation slots available, be sure to get your abstract in on time.

Enclosed you will find all the information needed for submitting your abstract. Please fill out and return, with you abstract, the signed **Abstract Information Form** with a short abstract and biography attached (see instructions). Failure to return all the required information will result in disqualification of your abstract.

Remember that all presentations must be supported by a professional paper for the *Proceedings* and for the benefit of the membership. Failure to submit a paper in accordance with PMI's guidelines will also disqualify your presentation.

If you should have any further inquiries, please call me at 714-731-0304. I can also be reached by e-mail at quentinf@ix.netcom.com.

The Technical Program Coordinator, Bobby Hensley, will be handling the abstracts and receiving the final papers. He can be reached at: 704-586-3715 or bookauth@pmi.org.

Hope to see you in Long Beach!

Sincerely,

Quentin Fleming
PMI '98 Technical Program Chairman

# PMI '98, Long Beach
# TECHNICAL PROGRAM ABSTRACT GUIDELINES

The Symposium theme is **"Tides of Change"**. The PMI '98 Team invites you to share your project management experiences in adapting PMBOK principles to a world of change about to enter the 21st century. Papers must be identified by one of the following Tracks:

- Aerospace / Defense
- Automotive
- Design Procurement & Construction
- Education & Training
- Environmental Management
- Financial Services
- Future of Project Management
- Global Project Management
- Government
- Information Management & Movement
- Information Systems & Software
- Manufacturing
- New Product Development
- Oil, Gas, & Petrochemical
- Pharmaceutical / Health Care
- PMBOK Education
- Project Management Tools & Techniques
- Professional Development
- Service & Outsourcing Projects
- Utilities
- Women in Project Management
- Project Management Poster Session (general topics) *

*** This year we will be offering a PM Poster Session for authors who wish to present in this format. The session will also be an option for authors whose papers were selected as alternates and not for regular presentation. Alternate authors may submit a paper for publication in the Proceedings as well as participate in the Poster Session. Poster Sessions may be conducted in a language other than English to accommodate non-English speaking participants. However, all publishable material for the Proceedings must be in English only. More information will be made available to those who are interested.**

A highly interactive program is desired. Papers should elicit participation from the audience and serve as a springboard for further discussion. Papers should reflect applicability of project management principles and should provide inspiration to those who are looking for ways to better manage their own "unique" projects.

A complete **Presenter's Guide** will be furnished to accepted authors. The guide will include detailed instructions on preparing and submitting Final papers.

PMI policy requires all paper presenters to register for the Seminars & Symposium at their own expense.

Authors of accepted papers are subject to PMI's Standard Conditions and Copyright Agreement. Paper selection decisions by the PMI '98 Technical Program Committee are final. All papers accepted for presentation are subject to editing for clarity and space considerations. PMI and the '98 Technical Program Committee reserves the right to withdraw papers that do not meet official guidelines and schedules from further consideration.

**FORMAT:**

- Abstracts should be at least **500** words, and should present the essential features of the forthcoming paper.
- Abstracts should list the title of the paper, the author(s), their company affiliation, and the abstract.
- The length of the final paper should be approximately **4200** words. The complete manuscript should be from five to seven pages, including all attachments and graphics.
- Final papers should be submitted in accordance with the Presenter's Guidelines provided to selected authors.

**THE PREFERRED PAPER WOULD:**

- Be original in concept or approach. **(MUST NOT HAVE BEEN PREVIOUSLY PRESENTED)**
- Contribute to the Project Management Body of Knowledge (PMBOK).
- Focus on "Tides of Change" issues within the Tracks.
- Apply to "real life" situations.
- Be free of commercial sales content.

**SPECIAL NOTE:**

Since there are only a limited number of slots available, the PMI '98 Technical Committee requires that all abstracts be submitted **by the deadline** in order to be considered for inclusion in the program. Late submissions will not be accepted. The **Abstract Information Form** must be completed, signed, and returned with the abstracts and Biographies in order to be considered.

**Process:**

**Mail Abstracts, Information sheet and short biography To:**

PMI '97 Technical Program Chairman
C/O PMI Communications
40 Colonial Square
Sylva, NC 28779 USA

- The deadline for abstracts is **January 15, 1998.**
- Selected authors will be notified by **March 6, 1998.**
- **Completed** papers will be due **no later than June 2, 1998.**

**Failure to meet applicable deadlines can result in the disqualification of your paper**

## PMI '98 Long Beach
## Abstract Information Form

Note: Each paper must list one author as the "lead" author. This individual will be the primary contact for all correspondence. Please type or print clearly.

Lead Author's Name:_______________________________ PMI Member [ ]
Job Title:_______________________________
Company or Affliation:_______________________________
Address:_______________________________
City/State/Zip:_______________________________
Country: _______________ Phone: _______________
Fax:_______________ E-mail: _______________

**Correspondence is sent via regular U.S. Mail. For authors outside the U.S. please list fax number and e-mail address to ensure timely notification of important information.**

**Track:** _______________________________
(Please select the most appropriate track)

**Alternate track if space is unavailable in your first choice:** _______________
**Would you consider doing a poster session if your paper is not selected?** Yes [ ] No [ ]

**Title of Paper:** _______________________________

_______________________________

Please attach the following to this form when submitting:

1. **The 500 word abstract.**

2. **A short abstract for promotional purposes, no longer than 60 words**. This will appear in the Registration Brochure and the Final Program Booklet. Use this description to explain why attendees should come to your session.

3. **A 100-word-or-less biography of each author**. PLEASE DO NOT SEND RESUMES OR VITAE. This biography (in paragraph form) will be used as an introduction to accepted presenters at the symposium. Include current and other important positions held, professional experience, education, affiliations, etc.

_______________________________ _______________
Lead Author's Signature Date

*Office use only*
Control No: _______________ Forwarded to Track:_______________